The Broadview Anthology of

BRITISH LITERATURE

Concise Edition

Volume B
Second Edition

The Broadview Anthology of British Literature: Concise Edition

The Age of Romanticism
The Victorian Era
The Twentieth Century and Beyond

The Broadview Anthology of

BRITISH LITERATURE

Concise Edition

Volume B
Second Edition

GENERAL EDITORS

Joseph Black, University of Massachusetts, Amherst
Leonard Conolly, Trent University
Kate Flint, University of Southern California
Isobel Grundy, University of Alberta
Don LePan, Broadview Press
Roy Liuzza, University of Tennessee
Jerome J. McGann, University of Virginia
Anne Lake Prescott, Barnard College
Barry V. Qualls, Rutgers University
Claire Waters, University of California, Davis

broadview press

BROADVIEW PRESS — www.broadviewpress.com
Peterborough, Ontario, Canada

Founded in 1985, Broadview Press remains a wholly independent publishing house. Broadview's focus is on academic publishing; our titles are accessible to university and college students as well as scholars and general readers. With over 600 titles in print, Broadview has become a leading international publisher in the humanities, with world-wide distribution. Broadview is committed to environmentally responsible publishing and fair business practices.

© 2013 Broadview Press
Reprinted with corrections 2017

LIBRARY AND ARCHIVES CANADA CATALOGUING IN PUBLICATION

  The Broadview anthology of British literature / general editors, Joseph Black ... [et al]. — Concise ed., 2nd ed.

Includes bibliographical references and index.
Contents: v. B. The age of romanticism. The Victorian era. The Twentieth century and beyond.
ISBN 978-1-55481-133-5 (v. B)

1. English literature. I. Black, Joseph Laurence, 1962– II. Title: British literature.

PR1109.B773 2011   820.8   C2011-902318-0

Broadview Press handles its own distribution in North America
PO Box 1243, Peterborough, Ontario K9J 7H5, Canada
555 Riverwalk Parkway, Tonawanda, NY 14150, USA
Tel: (705) 743-8990; Fax: (705) 743-8353
email: customerservice@broadviewpress.com

Distribution is handled by Eurospan Group in the UK, Europe, Central Asia, Middle East, Africa, India, Southeast Asia, Central America, South America, and the Caribbean. Distribution is handled by Footprint Books in Australia and New Zealand.

Broadview Press acknowledges the financial support of the Government of Canada through the Canada Book Fund for our publishing activities.

Typeset by Kathryn Brownsey
Cover design by Lisa Brawn

PRINTED IN CANADA

Contributing Editors and Writers

Managing Editor	Don LePan
Assistant Managing Editor	Laura Buzzard
Developmental Editors	Laura Buzzard, Jennifer McCue
Editorial Coordinator	Jennifer McCue
General Academic and Textual Editors	Laura Cardiff, Colleen Franklin, Morgan Rooney
Design Coordinator	Kathryn Brownsey

Contributing Editors

Katherine O. Acheson
Suzy Anger
Phanuel Antwi
Melissa Bachynski
Robert Barrett
Gisele Baxter
Donald Beecher
Sandra Bell
Emily Bernhard Jackson
Joseph Black
Carol Blessing
Robert Boenig
Sarika Bose
Matthieu Boyd
Benjamin Bruch
Laura Buzzard
Michael Calabrese
Laura Cardiff
Lisa Celovsky
Noel Chevalier
Mita Choudhury
Youngjin Chung
Massimo Ciavolella
Anna Clark
Elisha Cohn
Thomas J. Collins
Leonard Conolly
Darryl Domingo
Annmarie Drury
Dianne Dugaw
Siân Echard
Rose Eckert-Jantzie
Warren Edminster
Rachel Eisendrath
Garrett Epp
Michael Faletra
Emily Farrell
Christina Fawcett
Christina Fitzgerald

Adrienne Fitzpatrick
Andrew Fleck
Melissa Free
Maura Giles Watson
Stephen Glosecki
Amanda Goldrick-Jones
Katie Gramich
Erik Gray
John Greenwood
Isobel Grundy
Stephen Guy-Bray
Douglas Hayes
Peter C. Herman
Heather Hill-Vasquez
John Holmes
Diane Jakacki
Eleanor Johnson
Ian Johnston
Susan Kattwinkel
Michael Keefer
Amy King
David Klausner
Scott Kleinman
Chris Koenig-Woodyard
Gary Kuchar
Roger P. Kuin
Lydia K. Lake
Wendy Lee
Don LePan
Ruth Lexton
Roy Liuzza
Kirsten Lodge
Marie Loughlin
D.L. Macdonald
Hugh Magennis
Anne McWhir
Tobias Menely
Britt Mize
Alexander Mueller

Ian Munro
Sarah Neville
Meghan Nieman
David Oakleaf
Maureen Okun
Philip S. Palmer
Virginia Philipson
Jude Polsky
Anne Lake Prescott
Joyce Rappaport
Joseph Rezek
Shelby Richardson
Terry Robinson
Herbert Rosengarten
Jason Rudy
Janice Schroeder
Chester Scoville
John T. Sebastian
Kelly Stage
Emily Steiner
Ashley Streeter
Martha Stoddard-Holmes
Julie Sutherland
David Swain
Carol Symes
Andrew Taylor
Peggy Thompson
Jane Tolmie
Rebecca Totaro
David Townsend
Yevgeniya Traps
Melissa Valiska Gregory
Martine van Elk
Fred Waage
Andrea Walkden
Craig Walker
Claire Waters
David Watt
William Weaver

Vivienne Westbrook   Adrienne Williams Boyarin
David Williams   James Winny

CONTRIBUTING WRITERS

Laura Cardiff	Jane Grove	Andrew Reszitnyk
Jude Polsky	Camille Isaacs	Dave Ross
Victoria Abboud	Erik Isford	Nora Ruddock
Jane Beal	John Geddert	Jason Rudy
Jennifer Beauvais	Shoshannah Jones Square	Anne Salo
Rachel Bennett	Stephanie King	Janice Schroeder
Emily Bernhard Jackson	Chris Koenig-Woodyard	Carrie Shanafelt
Rebecca Blasco	Gabrielle L'Archeveque	Nicole Shukin
Jess Boland	Philip Laven	Helena Snopek
Matthieu Boyd	Jessica Legacy	James Soderholm
Julie Brennan	Don LePan	Anne Sorbie
Andrew Bretz	Anna Lepine	Martha Stoddard-Holmes
Laura Buzzard	Kelly Loewen	Jenna Stook
Paul Johnson Byrne	John McIntyre	Ashley Streeter
Emily Cargan	Brett McLenithan	Alexandria Stuart
Darryl Domingo	Carrie Nartkler	Candace Taylor
Victoria Duncan	Byron Nelson	Kaitlyn Till
Adrienne Eastwood	Robin Norris	Yevgeniya Traps
Wendy Eberle-Sinatra	Kenna Olsen	David Van Belle
Zachary Edwards	Kendra O'Neal Smith	Deirdra Wadden
Peter Enman	Laura Pellerine	Shari Watling
Emily Farrell	Tiffany Percival	Matthew Williams
Christina Fawcett	Virginia Philipson	Bj Wray
Joanne Findon	Allison Pitcher	Nicole Zylstra

LAYOUT AND TYPESETTING

Kathryn Brownsey   Susan Chamberlain

ILLUSTRATION FORMATTING AND ASSISTANCE

Cheryl Baldwin	Lisa Brawn	Eileen Eckert

PRODUCTION COORDINATORS

Tara Lowes   Tara Trueman

PERMISSIONS COORDINATORS

Merilee Atos	Emily Cargan	Jennifer Elsayed
Chris Griffin	Amy Nimegeer	

PROOFREADERS

	Joe Davies	
Jennifer Bingham	Martin Boyne	Lucy Conolly
Judith Earnshaw	Rose Eckert-Jantzie	Lynn Fraser
Anne Hodgetts	Amy Neufeld	Lynn Neufeld

Editorial Advisors

Rachel Ablow, University at Buffalo, SUNY
Phanuel Antwi, University of British Columbia
Dabney Bankert, James Madison University
Stephen C. Behrendt, University of Nebraska
Sumangala Bhattacharya, Pitzer College
Kim Blank, University of Victoria
Rita Bode, Trent University
Andrew Bretz, Wilfred Laurier University
David Brewer, Ohio State University
Susan Brown, University of Guelph
Catherine Burroughs, Wells College
Elizabeth Campbell, Oregon State University
William Christmas, San Francisco State University
Nancy Cirillo, University of Illinois, Chicago
Joanne Cordón, University of Connecticut
David Cowart, University of South Carolina
Alex Dick, University of British Columbia
Len Diepeveen, Dalhousie University
Daniel Fischlin, University of Guelph
Robert Forman, St. John's University
Peter Francev, Victor Valley College
Mark Fulk, Buffalo State College, SUNY
Julia Garrett, University of Wisconsin
Barbara Gates, University of Delaware
Dawn Goode, James Madison University
Chris Gordon-Craig, University of Alberta
Bruce Graver, Providence College
Natalie Grinnell, Wofford College
Stephen Guy-Bray, University of British Columbia
Tassie Gwilliam, University of Miami
Elizabeth Hodgson, University of British Columbia
John Holmes, University of Reading

Romana Huk, University of Notre Dame
Michael Keefer, University of Guelph
Gordon Kipling, University of California,
    Los Angeles
Emily Kugler, University of California, San Diego
Sarah Landreth, University of Ottawa
William Liston, Ball State University
Paula Loscocco, Lehman College
Kathleen Lundeen, Western Washington
    University
Peter Mallios, University of Maryland
Carl G. Martin, Norwich University
Martin McKinsey, University of New Hampshire
Rod Michell, Thompson Rivers University
Byron Nelson, West Virginia University
Robin Norris, Carleton College
Michael North, University of California,
    Los Angeles
Lesley Peterson, University of North Alabama
John Pollock, San Jose State University
Joseph Rezek, Boston University
Jason Rudy, University of Maryland
Andrew Scheil, University of Minnesota
Carol Senf, Georgia Tech
Ken Simpson, Thompson Rivers University
Sharon Smulders, Mount Royal University
Goran Stanivukovic, St. Mary's University
Marni Stanley, Vancouver Island University
Tim Stretton, St. Mary's University
Nicholas Watson, Harvard University
Kevin Whetter, Acadia University
Julian Yates, University of Delaware

CONTENTS

THE VICTORIAN ERA

THE TWENTIETH CENTURY AND BEYOND

[Note to Instructors in Canada, UK, and Australia: *Mrs. Dalloway* is among over 300 available editions from Broadview, any one of which may be packaged together with the anthology volume at no extra cost to the student. (For copyright reasons, Broadview is unable to make its edition of *Mrs. Dalloway* available for sale in the United States until 2021.)]

PREFACE

Each of the two volumes of the Concise Edition of *The Broadview Anthology of British Literature* has now become more popular than any of the six volumes of the full anthology. More and more frequently we hear academics saying that they are reluctant to choose a full anthology—whether the Broadview, the Longman, or the Norton—for a British Literature survey course, but that they want a concise anthology that offers more than do competitors such as Norton's Major Authors edition or Longman's *Masters of British Literature*. The two-volume Concise Edition of *The Broadview Anthology* is certainly less comprehensive than the full six volumes—but it nevertheless offers tremendous breadth as well as real depth of coverage. That was true of the first edition of this volume, and we believe it to be even more the case with this second edition.

When we asked academics for advice as we began to prepare a second edition, we received a great many helpful suggestions. In many cases we've been able to adopt those suggestions. Charles Darwin, Sir Arthur Conan Doyle, Sylvia Townsend Warner, J.M. Coetzee, and Zadie Smith are among those given full author entries for the first time. We've also added new selections by a number of authors who were already included in the anthology—among them William Wordsworth, Seamus Heaney, and Carol Ann Duffy. We've added new contextual materials as well—including material on "The Natural, the Supernatural, and the Sublime" in the *Age of Romanticism* section, and material on "The New Art of Photography" in *The Victorian Era*. Throughout the anthology there are additions of a more modest sort.

Most academics we consulted were also of the view that we should not make what was already a very wide-ranging and comprehensive "concise" edition any larger than it already was; the consensus was that any additions should be balanced by cuts. One way to decrease the size of an anthology is of course through excerpting—but excerpting is in many ways an unsatisfactory compro-

mise, and for the most part we have resisted any impulse to take that approach with greater frequency. Indeed, excerpts from three major works that were included in the first edition of this volume (selections from De Quincey's *Confessions of an English Opium Eater*, material from Carlyle's *Sartor Resartus*, and the Nausicaa chapter from Joyce's *Ulysses*) have been cut from the new edition. (We should hasten to add for those who like to teach these works, however, that nearly everything cut from the bound book anthology remains very much available on the companion website to the volume.)

We are also making an increasing number of works from the full six-volume anthology (or from its website component) available in stand-alone *Broadview Anthology of British Literature* editions. Tennyson's *In Memoriam*, for example, which was previously included in these pages, will now be available *both* as part of a stand-alone *Broadview Anthology of British Literature* edition of Tennyson's selected poetry *and* as part of the website component of the anthology's Concise Edition.

As with the stand-alone volumes in the Broadview Editions series, stand-alone "BABL editions" may readily be combined with one or more volumes of the anthology in a shrink-wrapped specially priced package. The options include Shelley's *Frankenstein*, all of Austen's novels, six of Dickens's novels (as well as a short volume of his performance fictions), Stevenson's *Dr. Jekyll and Mr. Hyde*, Conrad's *Heart of Darkness*—and literally hundreds more. (In most cases there is no additional cost whatsoever to the student when one of these volumes is packaged together with an anthology volume; in others there may be a nominal additional charge.)

That, then, is how we have tried to "square the circle" of including more material in the new edition without making it any larger; we hope you will like the result.

As with the first edition, we have been pleased that a substantial majority of those we consulted have shared our own feeling that it would be a shame to take an entirely "major authors" approach to a concise edition—to include *only* those authors and works already established as canonical. Obviously, the emphasis in any concise anthology will inevitably be more on the canonical than is the case with a more comprehensive anthology. But we have wanted to provide some alternatives for those instructors who prefer, even within the restricted compass of a two-term British literature survey, to teach one or two lesser-known works alongside a good selection of the "greatest hits." Readers will thus find in these pages John Wilmot and Aemelia Lanyer as well as William Shakespeare and Christopher Marlowe; Eliza Haywood and Anne Finch as well as Jonathan Swift and Alexander Pope; Augusta Webster and Algernon Charles Swinburne as well as Alfred, Lord Tennyson and Matthew Arnold; Katherine Mansfield as well as T.S. Eliot and Virginia Woolf.

Much as we have valued the wealth of advice we have received, we should also confess that in a few cases we have *not* followed the consensus that emerged from our editorial research. The initial research we conducted, for example, suggested very clearly that we should omit any selection of Hardy's prose fiction from the anthology. While we acknowledge the view that Hardy's fiction can only be taught adequately through a reading of his novels, we feel a strong case can be made that the outstanding qualities of his fiction may also be found in compressed form in some of his short stories—"The Son's Veto" being an outstanding example. And, had we relied only on the results of our editorial research, we would also not have included Carol Ann Duffy in the concise edition. That research, however, was conducted primarily among academics in North America; in this case, our departure from the course of action suggested by the research was driven by our sense that Duffy is increasingly acknowledged within Britain itself as a poet of central importance.

A particularly well-received feature in the full anthology has been the inclusion of a wealth of contextual materials. Inevitably, many of these have been dropped in the concise edition, but we have resisted any impulse to cut all the "contexts" to make way for the texts themselves; even within the confines of the shorter version of the anthology, we felt it important to offer a selection of materials to help illuminate some of the historical and cultural background.

The central principles of the full anthology are of course retained in this concise edition. The introductory materials and the annotations are unchanged, as are the supplementary materials.

A FRESH APPROACH

To those with some awareness of the abundance of fresh material and lively debate in the field of English Studies in recent generations, it may seem surprising that this abundance has not been more fully reflected in the number of available anthologies. Thirty-five years ago there were two comprehensive anthologies designed for courses surveying British Literature: *The Norton Anthology of English Literature* and one alternative. In the years before the 2006 publication of *The Broadview Anthology* there were still two choices available—the *Norton* and one alternative. Over that time span *The Longman Anthology of British Literature* had replaced *The Oxford Anthology of English Literature* in the role of "alternative," but there had been no expansion in range of available choices to match the expansion of content and of approach that had come to characterize the discipline itself. The number of available handbooks and guides to writing had multiplied steadily (to the point where there are literally hundreds of available choices), while the number of comprehensive anthologies of British literature had remained at two.

For those of us who have been working over the past decade and more on *The Broadview Anthology of British Literature*, it is not difficult to understand why. The very expansion of the discipline makes the task of assembling and editing an anthology that fully and vibrantly reflects the ways in which the British literary tradition is studied and taught an extraordinarily daunting one. The sheer amount of work involved is enormous, but so too is the amount of expertise that needs to be called on. With that background very much in mind, we charted a new course when it came to the preparation of *The Broadview Anthology of British Literature*. Rather than dividing up the work among a relatively small number of academics, and asking each of them to handle on their own the work of choosing, annotating, and preparing introductions to texts in their own areas of specialization, we involved a large number of contributors in the process (as the pages following the title page to this volume attest), and encouraged a high degree of collaboration at every level. First and foremost were (and are) the distinguished academics who serve as our General Editors for the project, but in all there were literally hundreds of people involved at various stages in researching, drafting headnotes or annotations, reviewing material, editing material, and carrying out the work of designing and typesetting the texts and other materials. That approach allowed us to draw on a diverse range of talent, and to prepare a large anthology with unusual speed. It also facilitated the maintenance of a high degree of consistency. Material was reviewed and revised in-house at Broadview, by outside editors (chief among them Colleen Franklin, an academic with a wide-ranging background and also a superb copy editor), by a variety of academics with an extraordinarily diverse range of backgrounds and academic specialities, and by our team of General Editors for the project as a whole. The aim was not only to ensure accuracy but also to make sure that the same standards were applied throughout the anthology to matters such as extent and coverage in author introductions, level of annotation, tone of writing, and student accessibility.

We have followed those same principles in the preparation of this second edition. Our General Editors have throughout taken the lead in the process of making selections. Along the way we have been guided by several core principles. We have endeavored to provide a selection that is broadly representative, while also being mindful of the importance of choosing texts that have the capacity to engage readers' interest today. Where inexpensive editions of works are available in our series of paperback Broadview Editions, we have often decided to omit them here, on the grounds that those wishing to teach one or more such works may easily order them in a combination package with the anthology; on these grounds we have decided against including *Frankenstein*, *Pride and Prejudice*, or *Heart of Darkness*. (However, we have included selections from *The Last Man* to represent Shelley and the first four chapters of *Pride and Prejudice* to represent Austen.)

Any discussion of what is distinctive about *The Broadview Anthology of British Literature* must focus above all on the contents. In every section of the anthology there is material that is distinctive and fresh—including not only selections by lesser-known writers but also less familiar selections from canonical writers. The anthology takes a fresh approach also to a great many canonical texts. Perhaps most notably, the Medieval section of the anthology includes not only Roy Liuzza's translation of *Beowulf* (widely acclaimed as the most engaging and reliable translation available), but also new translations by Liuzza of many other works of Old English poetry and prose. Also included in the Medieval section is a new translation by Claire Waters of Marie de France's *Lanval*.

In a number of these cases the distinctive form of the anthology facilitates the presentation of content in an engaging and practical fashion. Notably, the adoption of a two-column format allows for some translations (the Waters translation of Marie de France's *Lanval*, the James Winny translation of *Sir Gawain and the Green Knight*) to be presented in parallel column format alongside the original texts, enabling readers to experience something of the flavor of the original while providing convenient access to an accessible translation. Similarly, passages from four translations of the Bible are laid out parallel to one another for ready comparison.

The large trim size and two-column format also allow for greater flexibility in the presentation of visual materials. Throughout we have aimed to make this an anthology that is fully alive to the connections between literary and visual culture, from the discussion of the CHI-RHO page of the Lindisfarne Gospels in the Medieval section of the anthology (and the accompanying color illustration) to the inclusion in the twentieth-century section of several skits from "Monty Python's Flying Circus" that may be discussed in connection with film or television versions. Along the way appear several full-page illustrations from the Ellesmere manuscript of Chaucer's *Canterbury Tales* and illustrations to a wide variety of other works, such as *Robinson Crusoe*, *Gulliver's Travels*, and paintings by the Rossettis.

CONTEXTUAL MATERIALS

Illustrations are also an important part of the background materials that form a significant component of the anthology. These materials are presented in two ways. Several "Contexts" sections on particular topics or themes appear in each volume of the anthology. Presented independent of any particular text or author, these include broadly based groupings of material on such topics as "Religion and Spiritual Life," "Print Culture, Stage Culture," "The New Art of Photography," "The Abolition of Slavery," "Work and Poverty in Victorian England," and "The Place of Women in Society." The groups of "In Context" materials each relate to a particular text or author. They range from the genealogical tables provided as a supplement to *Beowulf*; to materials on "The Eighteenth-Century Sexual Imagination" (presented in conjunction with Haywood's *Fantomina*); to an examination of "T.S. Eliot and Anti-Semitism," which accompanies Eliot's work. For the most part these contextual materials are, as the word suggests, included with a view to setting texts in their broader literary, historical, and cultural contexts; in some cases, however, the materials included in "Contexts" sections are themselves literary works of a high order. The autobiographical account by Eliza M. of nineteenth-century life in Cape Town, for example (included in the section in Volume 5 on "Race and Empire"), is as remarkable for its literary qualities as it is for the light it sheds on the realities of colonial life. In the inclusion of texts such as these, as well as in other ways, the anthology aims to encourage readers to explore the boundaries of the literary and the non-literary, and the issue of what constitutes a "literary text."

WOMEN'S PLACE

A central element of the broadening of the canon of British literature in recent generations has of course been a great increase in the attention paid to texts by women writers. As one might expect from a publisher that has played an important role in making neglected works by women writers widely available, this anthology reflects the broadening of the canon quantitatively, by including a substantially larger number of women writers than have earlier anthologies of British literature. But it also reflects this broadening in other ways. In many anthologies of literature (anthologies of British literature, to be sure, but also anthologies of literature of a variety of other sorts) women writers are set somewhat apart, referenced in introductions and headnotes only in relation to issues of gender, and treated as important only for the fact of their being women writers. *The Broadview Anthology* strenuously resists such segregation; while women writers are of course discussed in relation to gender issues, their texts are also presented and discussed alongside those by men in a wide variety of other contexts, including seventeenth-century religious and political controversies, the abolitionist movement, and World War I pacifism. Texts by women writers are front and center in the discussion of the development of realism in nineteenth-century fiction.

"BRITISH," "ENGLISH," "IRISH," "SCOTTISH," "WELSH," "OTHER"

The broadening of English Studies, in conjunction with the expansion and subsequent contraction of British power and influence around the world, has considerably complicated the issue of exactly how inclusive anthologies should be. In several respects this anthology (like its two main competitors) is significantly more inclusive than its title suggests, including a number of non-British writers whose works connect in important ways with the traditions of British literature. We have endeavored first of all to portray the fluid and multilingual reality of the medieval period through the inclusion not only of works in Old and Middle English but also, where other cultures interacted with the nascent "English" language and "British" culture, works in Latin, in French, and in Welsh. In later periods the word "British" becomes deeply problematic in different respects, but on balance we have preferred it to the only obvious alternative, "English." There are several objections to the latter in this context. Perhaps most obviously, "English" excludes authors or texts not only from Ireland but also from Scotland and from Wales, both of which retain to this day cultures quite distinct from that of the English. "English literature," of course, may also be taken to mean "literature written in English," but since the anthology does not cover *all* literature written in English (most obviously in excluding American literature), the ambiguity would not in this case be helpful.

The inclusion of Irish writers presents a related but even more tangled set of issues. Through most of the seventeenth, eighteenth, and nineteenth centuries almost the whole of Ireland was under British control—but for the most part unwillingly. In the last of the six periods covered by the anthology, Ireland was partitioned, with Northern Ireland becoming a part of the United Kingdom and the Republic of Ireland declared independent of Britain on 6 December 1921. Less than two months earlier, James Joyce had completed *Ulysses*, which was first published as a complete work the following year (in Paris, not in Britain). It would be obviously absurd to regard Joyce as a British writer up to just before the publication of *Ulysses* and an Irish writer thereafter. And arguably he and other Irish writers should never be regarded as British, whatever the politics of the day. If on no other grounds than their overwhelming influence on and connection to the body of literature written in the British Isles, however, we have included Irish writers—among them Swift, Wilde, Shaw, Beckett, and Heaney as well as Joyce—in this anthology. We have also endeavored to give a real sense in the six period introductions of the anthology, in the headnotes to individual authors, and in the annotations to the texts themselves, of the ways in which the histories and the cultures of England, Ireland, Scotland, and Wales, much as they interact with one another, are also distinct.

Also included in this anthology are texts by writers from areas that are far removed geographically from the British Isles but that are or have been British possessions. Writers such as Olaudah Equiano and Mary Prince are included, as they spent all or most of their lives living in what were then British colonial possessions. Writers who came of age in an independent United States, on the other hand, are not included, unless (like T.S. Eliot) they subsequently put down roots in Britain and became important British literary figures. Substantial grey areas, of course, surround such issues. One might well argue, for example, that Henry James merits inclusion in an anthology of British literature, or that W.H. Auden is more an American

poet than a British one. But the chosen subject matter of James's work has traditionally been considered to mark him as having remained an American writer, despite having spent almost two-thirds of his life in England. And Auden so clearly made a mark in Britain before crossing the Atlantic that it would seem odd to exclude him from these pages on the grounds of his having lived the greater part of his adult life in America. One of our competitors includes Sylvia Plath in their anthology of British literature; Plath lived in England for only five of her thirty years, though, and her poetry is generally agreed to have more in common with the traditions of Lowell, Merwin, and Sexton than with the currents of British poetry in the 1950s and '60s.

As a broad principle, we have been open to the inclusion of twentieth- and twenty-first-century work in English not only by writers from the British Isles but also by writers from British possessions overseas, and by writers from countries that were once British possessions and have remained a part of the British Commonwealth. In such cases, we have often chosen selections that relate in one way or another to the tradition of British literature and the British colonial legacy. For example, the Chinua Achebe story in the anthology concerns the divide between British colonial culture and traditional Nigerian culture.

THE HISTORY OF LANGUAGE, AND OF PRINT CULTURE

Among the liveliest discussions at meetings of our General Editors were those concerning the issue of whether or not to bring spelling and punctuation into accord with present-day practice. We finally decided that, in the interests of making the anthology accessible to the introductory student, we should *in most cases* bring spelling and punctuation in line with present-day practice. An important exception has been made for works in which modernizing spelling and punctuation would alter the meaning or the aural and metrical qualities. In practice this means that works before the late sixteenth century tend to be presented either in their original form or in translation, whereas later texts tend to have spelling and punctuation modernized. But where spelling and punctuation choices in later texts are known (or believed on reliable authority) to represent conscious choice on the part of the author rather than simply the common practice of the time, we have in those cases, too, made an exception and retained the original spelling and punctuation. (Among these are texts by Edmund Spenser, William Cowper, Samuel Taylor Coleridge, William Blake, Emily Brontë, and Bernard Shaw.)

Beyond this, we all agreed that we should provide for readers a real sense of the development of the language and of print culture. To that end we have included in each volume examples of texts in their original form—in some cases through the use of pages shown in facsimile, in others by providing short passages in which spelling and punctuation have not been modernized. A list of these appears near the beginning of each volume of the anthology.

We have also included a section on the history of the language as part of the introduction to each period. And throughout the anthology we include materials—visual as well as textual—relating to the history of print culture.

A DYNAMIC AND FLEXIBLE ANTHOLOGY

We at Broadview recognize that, although time constraints make the concise anthology a practical and economical text choice for many instructors, some may nevertheless want to teach a number of non-canonical works—not all of which may be included in our concise edition. For this reason, we offer those instructors the possibility of choosing some additional texts that are included in the full, six-volume *Broadview Anthology of British Literature* but not in the concise edition. Simply visit our website, peruse the full anthology's table of contents, and provide the publisher with a list of desired selections; Broadview will then make available to students through their university bookstore a custom-made coursepack with precisely those materials included.

The two volumes of the anthology may be shrink-wrapped together at a special price, and each volume may also be combined in a special-price shrink-wrapped package with one or more of the over 350 volumes in the Broadview Editions series.

THE BROADVIEW LIST

One of the reasons we were able to bring a project of this sort to fruition in such a relatively short time is that we were able to draw on the resources of the full Broadview list: the many titles in the Broadview Editions series, and also the considerable range of other Broadview anthologies. As the contributors' pages and the permissions acknowledgments pages indicate, a number of Broadview authors have acted as contributing editors to this volume, providing material from other volumes that has been adapted to suit the needs of the present anthology; we gratefully acknowledge their contribution.

As it has turned out, the number of cases where we have been able to draw on the resources of the Broadview list in the full sense, using in these pages texts and annotations in very much the same form in which they appear elsewhere, has been relatively small; whether because of an issue such as the level of textual modernization or one of style of annotation, we have more often than not ended up deciding that the requirements of this anthology were such that we could not use material from another Broadview source as-is. But even in these cases we often owe a debt of gratitude to the many academics who have edited outstanding editions and anthologies for Broadview. For even where we have not drawn directly from them, we have often been inspired by them—inspired to think of a wider range of texts as possibilities than we might otherwise have done, inspired to think of contextual materials in places where we might otherwise not have looked, inspired by the freshness of approach that so many of these titles exemplify.

EDITORIAL PROCEDURES AND CONVENTIONS

APPARATUS: The in-house set of editorial guidelines for *The Broadview Anthology of British Literature* now runs to over 40 pages, covering everything from conventions for the spacing of marginal notes, to the use of small caps for the abbreviations CE and BCE, to the approach we have adopted to references in author headnotes to name changes. Perhaps the most important core principle in the introductions to the various volumes, in the headnotes for each author, in the introductions to

"Contexts" sections, and in annotations throughout the anthology, is to endeavor to provide a sufficient amount of information to enable students to read and interpret these texts, without making evaluative judgments or imposing particular interpretations. In practice that is all a good deal more challenging than it sounds; it is often extremely difficult to describe why a particular author is considered to be important without using language that verges on the interpretive or the evaluative. But it is a fine line that we have all agreed is worth trying to walk; we hope that readers will find that the anthology achieves an appropriate balance.

ANNOTATION: It is also often difficult to make judgments as to where it is appropriate to provide an explanatory annotation for a word or phrase. Our policy has been to annotate where we feel that most first- or second-year students are likely to have difficulty understanding the denotative meaning. (We have made it a practice not to provide notes discussing connotative meanings.) But in practice the vocabularies and levels of verbal facility of first- and second-year students may vary enormously, both from institution to institution and within any given college or university class. On the whole, we provide somewhat more annotation than our competitors, and somewhat less interpretation. Again, we hope that readers will find that the anthology has struck an appropriate balance.

THE ETHICS AND POLITICS OF ANNOTATION: On one issue regarding annotation we have felt that principles are involved that go beyond the pedagogical. Most anthologies of British literature allow many words or phrases of a racist, sexist, anti-Semitic, or homophobic nature either to pass entirely without comment, or to be glossed with apologist comments that leave the impression that such comments were excusable in the past, and may even be unobjectionable in the present. Where derogatory comments about Jewish people and money-lending are concerned, for example, anthologies often leave the impression that money-lending was a pretty unsavory practice that Jewish people entered by choice; it has been all too rare to provide readers with any sense of the degree to which English society consistently discriminated against Jews, expelling them entirely for several centuries, requiring them to wear physical marks identifying their Jewish status, prohibiting them from entering most professions, and so on. *The Broadview Anthology* endeavors in such cases, first of all, not to allow such words and phrases to pass without comment; and second, to gloss without glossing over.

DATES: We make it a practice to include the date when a work was first made public, whether publication in print or, in the case of dramatic works, made public through the first performance of the play. Where that date is known to differ substantially from the date of composition, a note to this effect is included in parentheses. With medieval works, where there is no equivalent to the "publication" of later eras, where texts often vary greatly from one manuscript copy to another, and where knowledge as to date of original composition is usually imprecise, the date that appears at the end of each work is an estimate of the date of the work's origin in the written form included in the anthology. Earlier oral or written versions are of course in some cases real possibilities.

TEXTS: Where translations appear in this anthology, a note at the bottom of the first page indicates what translation is being used. Similar notes also address overall textual issues where choice of copy text is particularly significant. Reliable editions of all works are listed in the bibliographies for each period, which are included on *The Broadview Anthology of British Literature* website (http://sites.broadviewpress.com/bablonline/) to facilitate ready revision. (In addition to information as to reliable editions, the bibliographies provide for each author and for each of the six periods a select list of important or useful historical and critical works.) Information on which editions have been drawn on in preparing texts for these pages is also included with the bibliographies. Copyright information for texts not in the public domain, however, is provided within the books in a section listing Permissions Acknowledgments.

INTRODUCTIONS: In addition to the introductory headnotes for each author included in the anthology, each "Contexts" section includes a substantial introduction, and each period includes an introduction to the era as a whole. These period introductions provide a sense not only of the broad sweep of literary developments in the period, but also of the historical, social, and political background, and of the cultural climate. Readers should be cautioned that, while there is inevitably some overlap between information presented here and information presented in the author headnotes, an effort has been made to avoid such repetition as much as possible; the general introduction to each period should thus be read in conjunction with the author headnotes. The general introductions aim not only to provide an overview of ways in which texts and authors included in these pages may connect with one another, but also to give readers a sense of connection with a range of other writers and texts of the period.

READING POETRY: For much of the glossary and for the "Reading Poetry" section that appears as part of the appendices to each volume, we have drawn on the superb material prepared by Herbert Rosengarten and Amanda Goldrick-Jones for *The Broadview Anthology of Poetry*; this section provides a concise but comprehensive introduction to the study of poetry. It includes discussions of diction, imagery, poetic figures, and various poetic forms, as well as offering an introduction to prosody.

MAPS: Also appearing within the books are maps especially prepared for this anthology, including, for each period, a map of Britain showing towns and features of relevance. Each volume also includes a map showing the counties of Britain and of Ireland, maps of both the London area and the inner city, and world maps indicating the locations of some of the significant places referenced in the anthology—and, for the second volume, showing the extent of Britain's overseas territories.

GLOSSARY: Some other anthologies of British literature include both glossaries of terms and essays introducing students to various political and religious categories in British history. Similar information is included in *The Broadview Anthology of British Literature*, but we have adopted a more integrated approach, including political and religious terms along with literary ones in a convenient general glossary. While we recognize that "googling" for information of this sort is often the student's first resort (and we acknowledge too the value of searching the web for the wealth of background reference information available there), we also recognize that information culled from the Internet is often far from reliable; it is our intent, through this glossary, through our introductions and headnotes, and through the wealth of accessible annotation in the anthology, to provide as part of the anthology a reliable core of information in the most convenient and accessible form possible.

OTHER MATERIALS: A chart of monarchs and prime ministers is also provided within these pages. A range of other adjunct materials may be accessed through *The Broadview Anthology of British Literature* website. "Texts and Contexts" charts for each volume provide a convenient parallel reference guide to the dates of literary texts and historical developments. "British Money" provides a thumbnail sketch of the world of pounds, shillings, and pence, together with a handy guide to estimating the current equivalents of monetary values from earlier eras.

ACKNOWLEDGMENTS

The names of those on the Editorial Board that shaped this anthology appear on the title page, and those of the many who contributed directly to the writing, editing, and production of the project on the following two pages. Special acknowledgment for this new edition should go to Developmental Editor Jennifer McCue, who has been instrumental in tying together all the vast threads of this project and in making it a reality; to Senior Editor Laura Buzzard, who has led the way in drafting introductory materials and annotations for the new material, and done so with great skill and unfailing grace; to Kathryn Brownsey, who has been responsible for design and typesetting, and has continued to do a superb job and to maintain her good spirits even when faced with near-impossible demands; to Joe Davies, for the range of his general knowledge as well as for his keen eye as our primary proofreader for the entire project; to Merilee Atos, who has done superb work on the vast job of clearing permissions for the anthology; and to Leslie Dema, Nora Ruddock, and Christine Handley, who have ably and enthusiastically taken the lead with marketing matters.

The academic general editors and all of us in-house at Broadview owe an enormous debt of gratitude to the hundreds of academics who have offered assistance at various stages of this project. In particular we would like to express our appreciation and our thanks to the following:

Rachel Ablow, University of Rochester
Katherine Acheson, University of Waterloo
Kenet Adamson, Southwestern Community College
Bryan Alexander, Middlebury College
Sharon Alker, Whitman College
James Allard, Brock University
Ella Allen, St. Thomas University
Rosemary Allen, Georgetown College
Laurel Amtower, San Diego State University
Robert Anderson, Oakland University
Christopher Armitage, University of North Carolina, Chapel Hill
Clinton Atchley, Henderson State University
Gerry Baillargeon, University of Victoria
John Baird, University of Toronto
William Baker, Northern Illinois University
Karen Bamford, Mount Allison University
John Batchelor, University of Newcastle
Lynn Batten, University of California, Los Angeles
Stephen Behrendt, University of Nebraska
Alexandra Bennett, Northern Illinois University
John Beynon, California State University, Fresno
Daniel Bivona, Arizona State University
Robert E. Bjork, Arizona State University
John Black, Moravian College
Scott Black, Villanova University
Rita Bode, Trent University
Robert Boenig, Texas A & M University
Matthew Borushko, Stonehill College
Rick Bowers, University of Alberta
Patricia Brace, Columbus State University
David Brewer, Ohio State University
William Brewer, Appalachian State University
Susan Brown, University of Guelph
Sylvia Brown, University of Alberta
Sheila Burgar, University of Victoria
Catherine Burroughs, Wells College
Rebecca Bushnell, University of Pennsylvania
Michael Calabrese, California State University
Elizabeth Campbell, Oregon State University
Gregory Castle, Arizona State University
Cynthia Caywood, University of San Diego

Jane Chance, Rice University
Ranita Chatterjee, California State University, Northridge
William Christmas, San Francisco State University
Nancy Cirillo, University of Illinois, Chicago
Eric Clarke, University of Pittsburgh
Jeanne Clegg, University of Aquila, Italy
Thomas J. Collins, University of Western Ontario
Thomas L. Cooksey, Armstrong Atlantic State University
Kevin Cope, Louisiana State University
David Cowart, University of South Carolina
Catherine Craft-Fairchild, University of St. Thomas
Roger Davis, Red Deer College
Carol Davison, University of Windsor
Alexander Dick, University of British Columbia
Len Diepeveen, Dalhousie University
Mary Dockray-Miller, Lesley College
James Doelman, Brescia University College, University of Western Ontario
Frank Donoghue, Ohio State University
Chris Downs, Saint James School
Alfred Drake, Chapman University
Ian Duncan, University of California, Berkeley
Julie Early, University of Alabama, Huntsville
Roxanne Eberle, University of Georgia
Siân Echard, University of British Columbia
Garrett Epp, University of Alberta
Joshua Eyler, Columbus State University
Ruth Feingold, St. Mary's College, Maryland
Dino Franco Felluga, Perdue University
Joanne Findon, Trent University
Larry Fink, Hardin Simmons University
Daniel Fischlin, University of Guelph
Christina Fitzgerald, University of Toledo
Verlyn Flieger, University of Maryland
Robert Forman, St. John's University
Allyson Foster, Hunter College
Lorcan Fox, University of British Columbia
Roberta Frank, Yale University
Jeff Franklin, University of Colorado, Denver
Maria Frawley, George Washington University
Mark Fulk, Buffalo State College
Constance Fulmer, Pepperdine University
Christine Gallant, Georgia State University

Andrew Galloway, Cornell University
Michael Gamer, University of Pennsylvania
Barbara Gates, University of Delaware
Jonathan C. Glance, Mercer University
Susan Patterson Glover, Laurentian University
Daniel Gonzalez, University of New Orleans
Jan Gorak, University of Denver
Chris Gordon-Craig, University of Alberta
Ann-Barbara Graff, Georgia Tech University
Bruce Graver, Providence College
Mary Griffin, Kwantlen University College
Michael Griffin, formerly of Southern Illinois University
George C. Grinnell, University of British Columbia, Okanagan
Elisabeth Gruner, University of Richmond
Bonnie Gunzenhauser, Roosevelt University
Kevin Gustafson, University of Texas at Arlington
Stephen Guy-Bray, University of British Columbia
Ruth Haber, Worcester State College
Dorothy Hadfield, University of Guelph
Margaret Hadley, University of Calgary
Robert Hampson, Royal Holloway University of London
Carol Hanes, Howard College
Michael Hanly, Washington State University
Lila Harper, Central Washington State University
Joseph Harris, Harvard University
Katherine Harris, San Jose State University
Anthony Harrison, North Carolina State University
John Hart, Motlow State Community College
Douglas Hayes, Lakehead University
Jennifer Hellwarth, Allegheny University
David Herman, Ohio State University
Peter Herman, San Diego State University
Kathy Hickock, Iowa State University
John Hill, US Naval Academy
Thomas Hill, Cornell University
Elizabeth Hodgson, University of British Columbia
Jim Hood, Guilford College
Joseph Hornsby, University of Alabama
Scott Howard, University of Denver
Jennifer Hughes, Averett University
Sylvia Hunt, Georgian College
Tara Hyland-Russell, St. Mary's College
Catherine Innes-Parker, University of Prince Edward Island

Jacqueline Jenkins, University of Calgary
John Johansen, University of Alberta
Gordon Johnston, Trent University
Richard Juang, Susquehanna University
Michael Keefer, University of Guelph
Sarah Keefer, Trent University
Lloyd Kermode, California State University,
    Long Beach
Brandon Kershner, University of Florida
Jon Kertzer, University of Calgary
Waqas Khwaja, Agnes State College
Helen Killoran, Ohio University
Gordon Kipling, University of California, Los Angeles
Anne Klinck, University of New Brunswick
Elizabeth Kraft, University of Georgia
Mary Kramer, University of Massachusetts, Lowell
Wai-Leung Kwok, San Francisco State University
Marilyn Lantz, East Mississippi Community College
Kate Lawson, University of Waterloo
Linda Leeds, Bellevue Community College
Mary Elizabeth Leighton, University of Victoria
Eric Lindstrom, University of Vermont
William Liston, Ball State University
Sharon Locy, Loyola Marymount University
Ross MacKay, Malaspina University-College
Peter Mallios, University of Maryland
Arnold Markley, Penn State University
Louis Markos, Houston Baptist University
Nick Mason, Brigham Young University
Pamela McCallum, University of Calgary
Patricia McCormack, Itawamba Community College
Kristen McDermott, Central Michigan University
John McGowan, University of North Carolina
Brian McHale, Ohio State University
Jim McKeown, McLennan Community College
Thomas McLean, University of Otago, New Zealand
Susan McNeill-Bindon, University of Alberta
Jodie Medd, Carleton University
Rod Michell, Thompson Rivers University
David Miller, Mississippi College
Kitty Millett, San Francisco State University
Britt Mize, Texas A&M University
Richard Moll, University of Western Ontario
Amy L. Montz, Texas A&M University
Monique Morgan, McGill University

John Morillo, North Carolina State University
Lucy Morrison, Salisbury University
Lorri Nandrea, University of Wisconsin-Steven's Point
Mara Narain, Texas Christian University
Byron Nelson, West Virginia University
Carolyn Nelson, West Virginia University
Claudia Nelson, Southwest Texas State University
Holly Faith Nelson, Trinity Western University
John Niles, University of Wisconsin, Madison
Michael North, University of California, Los Angeles
Mary Anne Nunn, Central Connecticut State University
David Oakleaf, University of Calgary
Tamara O'Callaghan, Northern Kentucky University
Karen Odden, Assistant Editor for *Victorian Literature
    and Culture* (formerly of University of Wisconsin,
    Milwaukee)
Erika Olbricht, Pepperdine University
Patrick O'Malley, Georgetown University
Patricia O'Neill, Hamilton College
Delilah Orr, Fort Lewis College
John Pagano, Barnard College
Kirsten Parkinson, Hiram College
Diana Patterson, Mount Royal College
Cynthia Patton, Emporia State University
Russell Perkin, St. Mary's University
Marjorie G. Perloff, Stanford University
Jim Persoon, Grand Valley State University
John Peters, University of North Texas
Todd Pettigrew, Cape Breton University
Alexander Pettit, University of North Texas
Jennifer Phegley, The University of Missouri,
    Kansas City
John Pollock, San Jose State University
Mary Poovey, New York University
Gautam Premnath, University of Massachusetts, Boston
Regina Psaki, University of Oregon
Laura Quinney, Brandeis University
Katherine Quinsey, University of Windsor
Tilottama Rajan, University of Western Ontario
Geoff Rector, University of Ottawa
Margaret Reeves, Atkinson College, York University
Cedric Reverand, University of Wyoming
Gerry Richman, Suffolk University
John Rickard, Bucknell University
Michelle Risdon, Lake Tahoe Community College

David Robinson, University of Arizona
Solveig C. Robinson, Pacific Lutheran University
Laura Rotunno, Pennsylvania State University, Altoona
Brian Rourke, New Mexico State University
Christopher Rovee, Louisiana State University
Nicholas Ruddick, University of Regina
Jason Rudy, University of Maryland
Donelle Ruwe, Northern Arizona University
Michelle Sauer, Minot State University
SueAnn Schatz, Lock Haven University of Pennsylvania
Dan Schierenbeck, Central Missouri State University
Norbert Schürer, California State University,
    Long Beach
Debora B. Schwartz, California Polytechnic University
Janelle A. Schwartz, Loyola University
John T. Sebastian, Loyola University
David Seed, University of Liverpool
Karen Selesky, University College of the Fraser Valley
Carol Senf, Georgia Tech University
Sharon Setzer, North Carolina State University
Lynn Shakinovsky, Wilfred Laurier University
John Sider, Westmont College
Judith Slagle, East Tennessee State University
Johanna Smith, University of Texas at Arlington
Sharon Smulders, Mount Royal College
Jason Snart, College of DuPage
Malinda Snow, Georgia State University
Goran Stanivukovic, St. Mary's University
Thomas Steffler, Carleton University
Richard Stein, University of Oregon
Eric Sterling, Auburn University Montgomery
James Stokes, University of Wisconsin, Stevens Point
Mary-Ann Stouck, Simon Fraser University
Nathaniel Strout, Hamilton College
Brad Sullivan, Western New England College
Lisa Surridge, University of Victoria
Joyce A. Sutphen, Gustavus Adolphus College
Beth Sutton-Ramspeck, Ohio State University
Nanora Sweet, University of Missouri, St. Louis

Dana Symons, Simon Fraser University
Andrew Taylor, University of Ottawa
Elizabeth Teare, University of Dayton
Doug Thorpe, University of Saskatchewan
Jane Toswell, University of Western Ontario
Kim Trainor, University of British Columbia
Herbert Tucker, University of Virginia
John Tucker, University of Victoria
Mark Turner, King's College, University of London
Eleanor Ty, Wilfrid Laurier University
Deborah Tyler-Bennett, Loughborough University
Kirsten Uszkalo, University of Alberta
Lisa Vargo, University of Saskatchewan
Gina Luria Walker, The New School, New York City
Kim Walker, Victoria University of Wellington
Miriam Wallace, New College of Florida
Orrin Wang, University of Maryland
Hayden Ward, West Virginia State University
David Watt, University of Manitoba
Ruth Wehlau, Queen's University
Lynn Wells, University of Regina
Dan White, University of Toronto at Mississauga
Patricia Whiting, Carleton University
Thomas Willard, University of Arizona
Tara Williams, Oregon State University
Chris Willis, Birkbeck University of London
Lisa Wilson, SUNY College at Potsdam
Ed Wiltse, Nazareth College
Anne Windholz, Augustana College
Susan Wolfson, Princeton University
Kenneth Womack, Pennsylvania State University
Gillen Wood, University of Illinois,
    Urbana-Champaign
Carolyn Woodward, University of New Mexico
Julia Wright, Wilfrid Laurier University
Julian Yates, University of Delaware
Arlene Young, University of Manitoba
Lisa Zeitz, University of Western Ontario

THE AGE OF ROMANTICISM

Perhaps the spirit and ethos of the Romantic era and its creative output are nowhere better captured than in the evolution of clothing during the period. When the artistic, literary, and political changes that are usually associated with Romanticism began in the 1780s, the heavy and elaborate costumes of the eighteenth century still prevailed, constricting their wearers into a rigid formality and mirroring contemporaneous social and aesthetic structures. In the heady years surrounding the French Revolution, when the possibility of greater freedom seemed within reach, these stiff garments gave way to loose, flowing dresses for women, clothes cut from muslins and patterned cottons that had been rendered relatively inexpensive by increasing British imperial control in the East and by technological advances in

weaving in Britain itself. During the same period, local militiamen, sporting magnificent military uniforms, demonstrated Britain's growing national pride, all the while masking persistent fear of French invasion. By the time the Romantic period drew to a close in the mid-1830s, these looser fashions and glittering uniforms had themselves been superseded by the tightly laced corsets, salt-and-pepper trousers, and bell skirts heavily supported by hoops and petticoats that are now inextricably associated with English Victorianism.

Morning dress, c. 1800.

Ball dress, c. 1800.

Richard Dighton, *George "Beau" Brummell*, 1805. Brummell, the leading "dandy" of the age, brought into fashion a new style of dress coat, pantaloons, and black evening dress for men. Brummell was fastidious about cleanliness as well as clothing, but denounced perfume for men and any form of showy display.

As the combination of freedom and militarism expressed by Romantic fashions suggests, the fifty years between the French Revolution and the reign of Queen Victoria were neither historically simple nor culturally straightforward. Despite its seeming cohesiveness and unity, the Romantic period was a complex nexus of revolution and conservatism, of bold iconoclasm and hidebound conventionality. Revolutions played a central role in shaping the Romantic period—and continue to shape our perceptions of it. The form and structure of the British Romantic era, as well as the very concept of "Romanticism," have changed radically in recent decades. What in the mid-twentieth century was seen as a literary period centered on five or six major poets—all male—and a select number of prose writers—also all male—has gradually come to be seen as an era made up of writers and thinkers of different genders, beliefs, and social backgrounds. Whereas familiarity with British Romantic poetry once meant having read only William Blake, William Wordsworth, Samuel Taylor Coleridge, Lord Byron, Percy Bysshe Shelley, and John Keats (collectively known as "The Big Six"), today, the voices of Mary Robinson, Anna Laetitia Barbauld, Felicia Hemans, and Letitia Landon—all respected and popular in their day but largely unstudied until recently—are seen as integral to a proper understanding of the period's verse. So too with Romantic non-fiction, which was once seen as consisting of the prose of Coleridge, Charles Lamb, and William Hazlitt, but now encompasses the proto-feminist writing of Mary Wollstonecraft, the didactic prose of Hannah More and Maria Edgeworth, and the natural sketches and observations of Dorothy Wordsworth. The prose fiction of the period (aside from a nod or two acknowledging Jane Austen and Sir Walter Scott) was once given short shrift; the drama was, generally, neglected. At this moment, Mary Shelley's novels—particularly *Frankenstein* (1818) and *The Last Man* (1826)—receive at least as much critical attention as do the works of her husband Percy Shelley, with *Frankenstein* probably being read more widely than any other single work of the Romantic period; Austen's works are now seen to hold a central position in the history of the novel; and the work of other writers of fiction—from William Godwin to Mary Hays, Amelia Opie, Mary Robinson, and Charlotte Smith—has been much more fully and more favorably assessed. In the study of drama, a similar, if less marked, shift has occurred, with the importance of the work of Hannah Cowley, Elizabeth Inchbald, and Joanna Baillie, as well as that of Percy Shelley and of Byron, being newly recognized.

If recent decades have brought a substantial shift in the emphasis placed on various authors in the study of the Romantic period, they have also brought a shift in the way the period as a whole is perceived. Whereas Romantic literature in English was once discussed far more with reference to nature and to the imagination than it was with reference to politics or to ideology, a broader perspective is now almost universally acknowledged as essential to a more comprehensive sense of the period.

Not everything has changed however; it is still almost universally accepted that the Romantic mind-set and the literary works it produced were shaped, above all, by the French Revolution and the Industrial Revolution.

For Romanticism, the French Revolution was epoch-making. When the Bastille fell on 14 July 1789 and the French National Assembly issued its demo-cratic, anti-monarchical *Declaration of the Rights of Man and Citizen* on August 27 of the same year, it seemed to the people of Great Britain, a mere 12 miles across the Channel, that a new dawn was on the horizon. For liberals and for many authors, artists, and intellectuals this dawn was a rosy one, promising not only greater equality and better government in France itself, but also the beginning of a thoroughgoing transformation of the world. Mary Robinson's "Ainsi Va Le Monde" (1791) provides a vivid sense of the degree to which a fervent faith in and enthusiasm for freedom knew no bounds in the breasts of many writers of the time:

Hark! "Freedom" echoes thro' the vaulted skies.
The goddess speaks! O mark the blest decree,—
Tyrants Shall Fall—Triumphant Man Be Free!

Wordsworth, present in France during the early days of the Revolution, famously wrote of it later, "Bliss was it in that dawn to be alive!" while his friend and fellow poet Robert Southey recalled that "a visionary world seemed to open ... [N]othing was dreamt of but regen-eration of the human race." Mary Wollstonecraft, who had recently published *A Vindication of the Rights of Woman*, moved to Paris in 1792, inspired by revolution-ary idealism. The Revolution became a central Roman-tic metaphor, as well as a central psychological influence on the first generation of Romantic writers.

The younger generation too, particularly Byron and Shelley, were stirred by revolutionary fervor. What these poets hoped for, however, was a continuation of the *spirit* of the French Revolution. For, in actuality, Words-worth's new dawn soon darkened into a terrible thun-derstorm and a rain of blood. In August of 1792, the leaders of the Revolution overthrew the French monar-chy, and, a month later, a Parisian mob massacred more than a thousand prisoners whom they believed to be Royalist conspirators. Extremist Jacobins[1] now prevailed over more moderate Girondins,[2] and the Revolution turned into the Reign of Terror (1793–94). In January 1793, King Louis XVI went to the guillotine; Marie Antoinette followed him in October. France declared war on Britain in 1793, and Britain quickly reciprocated the declaration. As the terror progressed under the guidance of Maximilien Robespierre, thousands of aristocrats, clergy, and alleged opponents of the Revolu-tion were guillotined including, eventually, Robespierre himself. In 1794, France offered to support any and all revolutions abroad, proceeding to invade its neighbors. In 1799, Napoleon had himself named First Consul for life, and, in 1804, he crowned himself Emperor. When he invaded the Iberian Peninsula in 1807, Britain intervened to aid the Spanish and Portuguese. The Napoleonic Wars, as these military conflicts came to be known, did not end until Napoleon was thoroughly routed at the Battle of Waterloo in 1815.

What had begun as a movement for democracy, then, had become a military dictatorship. Looking back from a distance of 24 years, Byron wrote, in *Childe Harold's Pilgrimage* (1812–18), that the French made themselves a fearful monument:

The wreck of old opinions ...
... the veil they rent
And what behind it lay all earth shall view.
But good with ill they also overthrew,
Leaving but ruins, wherewith to rebuild
Upon the same foundation, and renew
Dungeons and thrones ...   (*Childe Harold* 3.82)

---

[1] *Jacobins* The term was used throughout the Romantic period to denote those in sympathy with the radical, revolutionary ideals associated with the French Revolution. Those opposing the Revolu-tion were termed "anti-Jacobins." The ideological differences between the radical Jacobins and the conservative anti-Jacobins were often played out in the novels of the late eighteenth and early nineteenth century.

[2] *Girondins* A loosely affiliated coalition of moderate republicans, the Girondins controlled the French Legislative Assembly from late 1791 to late 1792, when they were ousted by more radical politi-cians. Many Girondin leaders were summarily executed during the Reign of Terror.

William Heath, *The Battle of Waterloo* (detail), 1815. British infantrymen to the right are firing into the ranks of the French cavalry. The full battle involved approximately 75,000 French troops under Napoleon; the Duke of Wellington commanded an allied force of well over 100,000. The casualties totaled over 50,000—60 per cent of them French.

The Revolution's promise of freedom died in a frenzy of oppression, destruction, violence, and imperialism, and many of Britain's intellectuals watched in horror, gradually turning from bold liberalism to a cautious conservatism they saw as both pragmatic and necessary. To use the political terminology that first developed out of the seating arrangements in the French National Constituent Assembly in 1789, they moved from the left of center to the right of center; Wordsworth, Coleridge, and Southey, all radical thinkers in their youth, were firm conservatives by the end of their lives. Others—such as Barbauld—remained politically on the left but became disillusioned, both by the course that revolution had taken in France and by the failure of the British to embrace the principles of freedom. Barbauld surveyed what seemed to her a decadent and oppressive England in "Eighteen Hundred and Eleven" (1812)— "The worm is in thy core, thy glories pass away"—and Shelley despaired in "England in 1819" (composed in 1819, but not published until 1839) at "Rulers who

neither see nor feel nor know, / But leechlike to their fainting country cling."

The British government's response to the developments in France had been swift and repressive. In 1794, the right of habeas corpus—which required the state to show legitimate cause for imprisonment and to carry out trials in a timely manner—was suspended. As a result, those accused of crimes could be held for an indefinite period. In 1795, Parliament passed the Treasonable Practices Act, which made criticism of the government a crime; in the same year, it passed an act that limited the size of public meetings and the places in which they could be held. The Combination Acts of 1799 and 1800 forbade workers to associate for the purposes of collective bargaining. To enforce all these restrictive measures, the government set loose a herd of spies, many of whom acted as *agents provocateurs*, infiltrating liberal and radical groups and prompting them to commit criminal acts they otherwise might not have committed. In at least one important case, that of the Cato Street Conspiracy of

1820—a scheme to murder cabinet ministers and stage a government *coup*—these government agents first urged on and then exposed conspirators who were punished with hanging or with transportation to Australia. In Scotland and Ireland, authoritarianism could be even more severe, particularly since rebellion there required no instigating. In 1798, the United Irishmen, led by Theobald Wolfe Tone and Lord Edward Fitzgerald and assisted by French forces, attempted a country-wide uprising to achieve complete Irish independence. The rebellion ended in failure, and the oppression of the Irish under British rule became more strongly entrenched than ever.

If the French Revolution and the 22 years of war with France that followed produced ruinous government authoritarianism, they also acted to create for the first time a widespread and shared sense among British citizens that England, Wales, Scotland, and, to a lesser extent, Ireland, formed one cohesive nation: Great Britain. Scotland had been linked to England by the Union of 1707, while union with Ireland, which had been firmly under English control since the time of Cromwell, was made official with the Act of Union in 1800. The wars with France allowed the English people to see themselves as leading a larger body defending liberty and freedom (even if that liberty and freedom were now, ironically, defined by a conservative authoritarian mind-set). At the same time, the wars raised very real threats of invasion—there were scares in 1778, 1796–98, and 1803, and Wales was actually invaded in 1797. The threats from without acted to foster cohesion within. Foreign travel was out of the question for all but the very rich or the very brave, and this forced the British to turn inward and discover their own country instead. Sir Walter Scott's collection of folksongs and ballads, *Minstrelsy of the Scottish Border* (1802–03), Thomas Moore's *Irish Melodies* (1807–34), and Felicia Hemans's *Welsh Melodies* (1822) gave their readers a sense of the nation's rich past, celebrating the blend of cultures that went into making up Great Britain. Regional poets, such as Robert Burns and John Clare, gave proud voice to those cultures, so that the individual nations which made up the one great nation were simultaneously celebrated for their respective traditions and recognized as within the British fold. Long poetical works such as John Thelwall's *The Hope of Albion; or Edwin of Northumbria* (1801) expanded the sense of an epic British

mythology, while collections such as Hemans's *Tales and Historic Scenes* (1819), a celebration of military valor, fostered a sense of pride in present-day accomplishments.

T.W. Huffram, *Theobald Wolfe Tone*, date unknown. Tone is shown in French uniform.

James Gillray, *United Irishmen in Training*, 1798. The famous English caricaturist here portrays the Irish as cruel buffoons; they are assaulting a British uniform stuffed with straw.

Thomas Girtin, *Westminster from Lambeth*, c. 1800. Girtin's watercolor was one of a series of sketches for a panorama of London (now lost).

The sense of a larger Britain served as further confirmation of the English belief that their country was particularly, even divinely, favored. Such notions were perhaps given their most memorable, if also most ambivalent, expression in the opening to William Blake's "Preface" to *Milton* (1804), in which ancient England is linked with Christ:

And did those feet in ancient time
Walk upon England's mountain's green?
And was the Holy Lamb of God
On England's pleasant pastures seen?
And did the countenance divine
Shine forth upon our clouded hills?[1]

Although Blake leaves it up to his reader to determine whether the answers to these rhetorical questions are yes or no, the stanza that follows explicitly figures England as a land worthy of being the new Jerusalem (if only sometime in the future):

I will not cease from mental fight,
Nor shall my sword sleep in my hand,
Till we have built Jerusalem
In England's green and pleasant land.

Between these invocations of the divine in Britain, however, Blake inserts an insidious question, one that began to plague English writers and citizens more and more as the Romantic period progressed: "was Jerusalem builded here / Among these dark Satanic mills?" The phrase "dark Satanic mills" has become the most famous description of the force at the center of the Industrial Revolution. Even as the French Revolution changed the consciousness of the British people, this other revolution in their own country had as much impact on them as did any conflagration abroad.

---

[1] *And did those feet ... clouded hills* The opening two stanzas (a total of 16 lines) were set to music by Charles H.H. Parry in 1916; under the title "Jerusalem," these verses have become an unofficial national anthem for the English.

TREVITHICKS,
PORTABLE STEAM ENGINE.

Catch me who can .

Mechanical Power Subduing
Animal Speed .

Illustration of an early locomotive engine, 1808.

In the sixteenth and seventeenth centuries, the British Isles, and England in particular, had begun undergoing extensive changes in economic structure. The pace of change increased dramatically as the eighteenth century progressed. From being a largely rural nation with a largely agricultural economy, Britain became an urban nation with an economy based in manufacturing. James Watt's refinement of the steam engine and James Hargreaves's invention of the Spinning Jenny (a machine that allowed cotton to be spun on several spindles simultaneously) were only the most famous of a host of changes that produced a boom in industrialization. Factories sprang up in what had once been countryside, and the populations of towns and cities, particularly those associated with manufacture, swelled. At the beginning of the 1770s, about a quarter of England's population lived in urban centers, but by 1801 that proportion had risen to one-third, and by the 1840s half of the English population resided in cities. In 1750, the total English population was roughly 5.5

million; by the time of the first census in 1800, it had grown to 8 million, while the population of Scotland and Ireland totaled more than 6.5 million. By 1831, the total population of Great Britain was thus approximately 14 million. This increase fueled the Industrial Revolution from both ends, supplying more consumers eager to acquire goods and more able bodies to work in factories that produced those goods.

Industrialization also contributed to an important shift in the country's social structure. The paradigm of classes and ranks that placed the nobility at the top with everyone else keeping to their places beneath had begun to change as early as the seventeenth century, with those involved in business and commerce growing wealthy enough to exert power of their own. The process was greatly accelerated in the late eighteenth and early nineteenth centuries as more and more factory owners and other men of business—and they were exclusively male—amassed larger and larger fortunes. Still, the road that led from newly acquired wealth to social acceptance remained a long and circuitous one. An inherited fortune stemming from longstanding ownership of large amounts of land—and the rents thereby produced—remained the most respectable form of wealth. To possess a good deal of money as a result not of belonging to the "landed gentry" but rather of having amassed it through commercial activity was considered more than faintly disreputable. It might take two or three generations before the taint of anyone in the family having been "in trade" (a term applied to industrialists as much as to tradesmen) was removed, and the source of the family fortune forgotten. The social nuances involved in such transitions were vividly captured in the novels of Jane Austen; here, for example, is her description of the Bingley sisters in *Pride and Prejudice* (1813):

> They were rather handsome, had been educated in one of the first private seminaries in town, had a fortune of twenty thousand pounds, were in the habit of spending more than they ought, and of associating with people of rank; and were therefore in every respect entitled to think well of themselves, and meanly of others. They were of a respectable family in the north of England; a circumstance more deeply impressed on their memories than that their brother's fortune and their own had been acquired by trade.

George and I.R. Cruikshank, *Sporting a Toe at Almacks*, 1821. Many clubs were restricted to men; Almack's was an exclusive London club controlled by a group of society women. During "the season" a fashionable ball was held at Almack's every week.

Fine gradations of respectability were attached to every occupation, with social position often at odds with financial circumstances. Members of the clergy and their families, for instance, though sometimes impecunious, were generally respected; whether members of the gentry or born into the working class, they often moved in elevated social circles. Physicians, defined as those medical men who had a degree from a university, could sometimes move in the "best circles" in a community, although apothecaries and surgeons, who gained their knowledge through apprenticeship, could not.

The Romantic literary world reflected the increased social mobility possible during the period. John Keats, for example, was the son of a stable keeper who had increased his financial standing by marrying the daughter of the stable owner. Keats trained as a surgeon-apothecary (a job that combined the duties of a present-day pharmacist, general practitioner, and surgeon), but,

at the age of 18, he came into an inheritance and was able to devote himself entirely to literature. He wrote to a friend that he thought he would "be among the English poets" after his death, and, as it turned out, no social barriers could prevent that from occurring. Similarly, Samuel Taylor Coleridge, a parson's son who attended a London charity school as a child, ended his life lauded and respected as "The Sage of Highgate."

The Industrial Revolution may have increased social mobility; it certainly allowed goods to be produced more efficiently. But it also devastated large portions of England's underclasses, the agricultural laborers and peasants who had benefited, however slightly, from the land-based economy that was passing away. In Wordsworth's "Tintern Abbey" (1798), the reference to "vagrant dwellers in the houseless woods" describes a very real phenomenon. In the late eighteenth and early nineteenth centuries, a series of Enclosure Acts resulted in the continued conversion of formerly common land into large, privately held estates.[1] To be fair, enclosures did often result in an increase in agricultural production, but they also often spelled ruin for thousands of small farmers. Large landholders benefited from their enlarged acreage, but many of those who had heretofore been able to eke out a living from a tiny patch of land and sell their modest surpluses now lost all ability to support themselves. These smallholders and their families were forced either to labor for others for meager wages, to migrate to the city and enter the manufacturing workforce, or to turn to begging or thievery. Poor harvests in 1794–95, 1799–1800, and 1810–11 worsened the plight of the rural poor even further. The proliferation of vandals, vagrants, and beggars in the writing of this era thus reflected a growing social reality.

The leading literary figures of the day were, for the most part, sympathetic to the plight of the poor in a time of growing inequity, but, beyond that, they held widely divergent attitudes concerning these developments, and concerning the commoners themselves. Anna Laetitia Barbauld was one writer who sought to ameliorate the inequities that had become so characteristic of English life; she condemned the power relations involved, harshly criticizing the privileged, and took a view of commoners that saw them as prey to vice as a result of the circumstances in which they had been placed through economic hardship and lack of education. As she wrote in *Thoughts on the Inequality of Conditions* (1800),

> Power enables the indolent and the useless not only to retain, but to add to their possessions, by taking from the industrious the natural reward of their labour, and applying it to their own use … It is not sufficiently considered how many virtues depend upon comfort, and cleanliness, and decent apparel. Destroy dirt and misery, and you will destroy at once a great many vices.

It is the approach of William Wordsworth, however, that has more often been taken to characterize British Romanticism. That approach posits nature as central to human experience—nature in its simpler or wilder forms, not distorted by human artifice. Wordsworth was interested not only in "the beautiful and permanent forms of nature" but also in the ways in which human passions are excited by these forms; he describes "the mind" (rather than nature) as "My haunt, and the main region of my song." He was vitally interested, too, in the minds of those whom he saw as most closely connected to the natural world. If Barbauld's focus was very largely on the struggle to ameliorate conditions for the poor, Wordsworth's was more on the worth inherent in the hearts and minds of rural common folk—and on the associated poetic value. In the same year as Barbauld wrote her *Thoughts on the Inequality of Conditions*, Wordsworth expressed his ideals in the 1800 "Preface" to *Lyrical Ballads*:

> The principal object, then, proposed in these Poems was to choose incidents and situations from common life … Humble and rustic life was generally chosen, because, in that condition, the essential passions of the heart find a better soil in which they can attain their maturity, are less under restraint, and speak a plainer and more emphatic language; because in that condition of life our elementary feelings coexist in a state of greater simplicity, and, consequently, may be more accurately contemplated, and more forcibly communicated; because the manners of rural life germinate from those elementary feelings, and, from the necessary character of rural occupations, are more easily comprehended, and are more durable; and, lastly, because in that condition the passions of men are incorporated with the beautiful and permanent forms of nature.

Poems in *Lyrical Ballads*, such as "Michael," "The Ruined Cottage," "Idiot Boy," and "Resolution and Independence," represent Wordsworth's attempt to put those ideals into practice. In "Resolution and Independence," the poet encounters an old, poor, itinerant leech-gatherer, ending the poem by admiring "In that decrepit Man so firm a mind." Whereas Barbauld regarded theft as a justifiable response to the oppression of extreme poverty in an iniquitous social system, Wordsworth pays homage to the old leech-gatherer for earning an "honest maintenance" despite the "many hardships" he must endure.

---

[1] *Enclosure Acts … privately held estates* The process of enclosure was not new; it had been occurring since the late Middle Ages, in response to population pressures and as Britain was transformed first into a largely mercantile economy and then into an industrial society.

If the rural working-poor fared badly during these years, life for the workers in the cities and the unemployed-poor was just as bad. In 1815, at the instigation of large land holders, who stood to benefit from high prices for grain, the government passed the Corn Laws to institute a substantial tariff on imports of grain from foreign countries, making such imports much more expensive.[1] The tariff was effective in protecting British grain producers; at the same time, it inflated the price of bread and other foodstuffs for the consumer. The poor in the cities suffered particularly, and, from 1815 until the Corn Laws were finally repealed in 1845, they remained a lightning rod for political dissent.

Had conditions for the urban poor been better in other respects, the Corn Laws might have had less impact. The British government, however, assured by Adam Smith's highly influential work of economic philosophy, *The Wealth of Nations* (1777), that the best way to encourage national economic success was to leave businesses free to grow without hindrance, for the most part adopted a laissez-faire[2] approach to regulating treatment of employees and working conditions during this period. In practice, "laissez-faire" ultimately meant shifts of as much as 15 hours at a stretch, often for very young children. Wages were kept as low as manufacturers could manage and injuries were common; children were the preferred workers for clearing jams in mechanized looms, for example, and the frequent result was the loss of the tiny fingers and hands that made them ideal for the job. Workers' health was often ruined by unsanitary working and living conditions—employers often owned not only the factories, but the slums in which their workers lived—and by unfettered pollution.

It is often assumed that the worst extremes of the Industrial Revolution in Britain occurred during the Victorian era, but, by the time Victoria came to the throne, Parliament had already been pressed to take a succession of measures to restrict the abuse of children: the largely ineffectual Health and Morals of Apprentices Act (1802), the Regulation of Cotton Mills and Factories Act (1819), and the Act to Regulate the Labour of

Children and Young Persons in the Mills and Factories of the United Kingdom (1833). Even after the passage of this last, children as young as nine could be forced to work nine-hour days, and thirteen-year-olds to work twelve-hour days; still, this represented a degree of improvement from the late eighteenth and early nineteenth centuries. Robert Blincoe, for example, an orphan raised in a London workhouse and transported in 1799, at the age of seven, to work in the Lowdham Mill near Nottingham, described his life at the mill to John Brown in 1829:

A

MEMOIR

OF

ROBERT BLINCOE,

An Orphan Boy;

SENT FROM THE WORKHOUSE OF ST. PANCRAS, LONDON,

AT SEVEN YEARS OF AGE,

TO ENDURE

THE HORRORS OF A COTTON-MILL,

THROUGH HIS INFANCY AND YOUTH.

WITH A MINUTE DETAIL OF HIS SUFFERINGS.

BEING

THE FIRST MEMOIR OF THE KIND PUBLISHED.

BY JOHN BROWN.

London:
PRINTED AND PUBLISHED BY RICHARD CARLILE,
62, FLEET STREET.

Price One Shilling.

Title page, *A Memoir of Robert Blincoe*, first published in 1828, re-issued in 1832. Demonstrations in 1832 and 1833 for factory reform frequently cited the evidence of factory conditions that he had provided, and Blincoe testified before the Royal Commission that investigated the issue of child labor in 1833.

---

[1] *grain ... expensive* In Britain, "corn" denotes grain, most commonly wheat; what North Americans call "corn" is referred to in Britain as "maize."

[2] *laissez-faire* "Let do" (French).

Blincoe heard the burring sound [of the machinery] before he reached the portals and smelt the fumes of the oil with which the axles of twenty-thousand wheels and spindles were bathed the moment he entered the doors. The noise appalled him, and the stench seemed intolerable. It was the custom at Lowdham Mills, as it is in most water mills, to make the apprentices work up lost time [i.e., time when the machines had been unable to run during regular working hours], by working over hours ... When children of seven years of age had to work fourteen hours every day in the week, Sundays excepted, any addition was severely felt ... Almost from the first hour [Blincoe] entered the Mill, till he arrived at a state of manhood, it was one continual round of cruel and arbitrary punishment.... I asked him if he could state the average number of times in which he might safely say he had suffered corporal punishment in a week. His answer invariably was, that his punishments were so various and so frequent, it was impossible to state with anything approaching to accuracy.... Supper consisted of milk-porridge, of a very blue complexion [together with] bread partly made of rye—very black, and so soft they could scarcely swallow it, as it stuck like bird-lime to their teeth.

If the government addressed such outrages only with reluctance—sometimes Parliamentary committees looking into allegations would not hear any direct testimony from the workers—many citizens found them harder to ignore. Demonstrations of popular dissatisfaction were frequent and took various forms. Luddites, followers of the imaginary "General Ned Ludd," attacked and broke machinery during the years 1811–16, sometimes to force concessions from their employers but sometimes simply to express their dissatisfaction with creeping mechanization. After the bad harvests and the passage of the Corn Laws in 1815, food riots occurred across the country. Coercion Acts were passed in 1817 to try to stifle dissent, but they provoked strong antagonism, and both in London and in parts of Scotland some republican groups advocated revolution. Throughout the 1820s, farm workers staged violent protests, culminating in mass barn-burnings in 1830. Perhaps the most famous popular uprising was the 1819 gathering of roughly 80,000 mill workers at St. Peter's Field, near Manchester. A peaceful demonstration that ended with an address to the crowd by Henry Hunt,[1] this gathering so alarmed the local gentry that they sent drunken, armed militiamen to break it up and arrest Hunt. The militiamen attacked the crowd with their sabers when it jeered them, and the ensuing melee left 11 dead—including one trampled child—and more than 400 injured, many from saber wounds.

"Peterloo," as it came to be dubbed by the radical press, in reference to the British victory at Waterloo four years earlier, was a seminal event in nineteenth-century politics and economics. Parliament did nothing to relieve the sufferings of these poor or the hundreds of thousands like them, instead strengthening its repressive powers by passing the Six Acts at the end of 1819. These Acts made it a crime to demonstrate; gave magistrates the power to enter private homes to search for weapons; outlawed meetings of more than 50 people unless all those attending a meeting were residents of the parish in which the meeting was held, thus effectively curtailing any kind of large gatherings; tightened the guidelines on what could be considered blasphemous or treasonous libel; and raised the newspaper tax, thereby cutting the circulation of formerly inexpensive radical newspapers.[2]

POLITICAL PARTIES AND ROYAL ALLEGIANCES

For most of this period, the upheavals among the lower classes found little reflection in the English government, where the Tories held sway from 1783 to 1830, with only one short interruption. The Tories were the conservative party: they saw themselves as upholders of law and tradition, determined to preserve the prevailing political and social order. From 1793 to 1801, and again from 1804 to 1806, the Tories—and the country—were led by Prime Minister William Pitt, whose fiscal restraint and willingness to suppress political protest (sometimes with open brutality) made him a hero to some and a villain to many others. After Pitt died in

---

[1] *Henry Hunt* Known as the "Orator," Hunt (1773–1835) was a radical speaker and agitator, renowned for his advocacy of Parliamentary reform and the abolition of the Corn Laws.

[2] *Six Acts ... newspapers* The Six Acts ultimately proved repugnant to certain members of the liberal Whig party—who subsequently became politically powerful—and led to the liberal Reform Act of 1832. Thus, the eventual result of the massacre was a measure of relief from the extraordinarily repressive measures it had spawned.

office in 1806, certainly of overwork and probably of alcoholism—his last words were either, "Oh, my country! how I leave my country!" or "I think I could eat one of Bellamy's veal pies," depending on the source—the Tories continued in power, on their own or in coalition, until 1830.

The Whigs, who remained the party of opposition during this time, presented themselves against the Tories as advocates of greater civil and religious liberty. In reality, neither party would have been called "Liberals" or "Democrats" by today's standards, but the Whigs did advocate the abolition of the slave trade, Catholic emancipation (which would allow greater political participation to Catholics, heretofore barred from a role in government), and Parliamentary reform. From 1782 to 1806, the leader of the Whigs was the charismatic Charles James Fox, gambler, gourmand, and political colossus, whose political machinations made him as many enemies as friends. Not until 1806, a year after Fox's death, would the Whigs participate in government—and then for only a relatively short period, as part of a coalition. They would not gain power in their own right until 1830. They were then at last able to pass the Reform Act of 1832 (also known as the Great Reform Act), which extended voting rights to a broader spectrum of propertied males,[1] redistributed Parliamentary seats, and brought significantly fairer political representation.

While the politicians plotted and schemed, the British royal family suffered its own difficulties. George III, who had ascended the throne in 1760, embodied Toryism both politically and personally; traditionalist, ponderous, and domestic, he produced a large family, embraced conservative politics, and allegedly liked to wander the countryside incognito, chatting with farmers. In 1788, however, he suffered a bout of mental illness that lasted until early 1789. This illness, now believed to be the result of the hereditary blood disease porphyria, reappeared in 1810, leaving him permanently insane. In 1811, when it became apparent that the King would not recover, his eldest son was declared Regent.

Monarchs of the House of Hanover traditionally clashed with their eldest sons, and George III and the Prince, who would become George IV, were no differ-

Sir Thomas Lawrence, *The Prince Regent in Profile*, c. 1814. The Prince knighted Lawrence, the leading English portraitist of the day, in 1815, saying that he was "proud in conferring a mark of favor on one who had raised the character of British art in the estimation of all Europe."

ent. Bred to wait for his father to die, growing ever fatter (at the end of his life he weighed more than 300 pounds), the Regent was a stark contrast to his thrifty father. In 1787, when he was 25, his debts totaled more than £160,000 (equivalent to about £8,000,000 today). He lived with a Roman Catholic mistress whom he later married, secretly and unconstitutionally, before abandoning her for a series of other mistresses. Later, to secure relief from debts, he married his cousin Caroline of Brunswick, a woman he found so instantly and completely loathsome that his first words upon seeing her were, "I am not well; pray get me a glass of brandy." Although they did manage to produce one daughter, Charlotte, who later died in childbirth, the Prince and his wife never lived together, and his attempt to divorce her after his accession in 1820 was one of the great scandals of the period.

---

[1] *Reform Act … propertied males* The changes are estimated to have altered the composition of the electorate to approximately one in seven males from fewer than one in ten.

Sir Thomas Lawrence, *Caroline Amelia
Elizabeth of Brunswick*, 1804 (detail).

George IV was not without redeeming virtues; notably, he was a keen patron of the arts, particularly architecture. In addition to a magnificent pavilion in Brighton, he and his architects built Trafalgar Square, modified and improved Buckingham House into Buckingham Palace, and created parks, streets, and crescents throughout London. He was an enthusiastic reader and promoter of literature, as well as a generous patron of the sciences, establishing several fellowships and prizes. Nonetheless, the Prince became a figure of increasing public contempt. Leigh Hunt described him as "a libertine head over heels in debt and disgrace, a despiser of domestic ties"; Percy Shelley called him, in prose, an "overgrown bantling [infant]," and, in poetry, "the dregs of [his] dull race." When he died in 1830, *The Times* wrote, "There never was an individual less regretted by his fellow creatures than this dead King."

IMPERIAL EXPANSION

Even as Britain was experiencing its own internal power struggles and upheavals, the nation was expanding its presence around the globe. Throughout the first half of the nineteenth century, Britain was well on its way to forging the Empire that would reach full flower in the Victorian period. The East India Company, founded by a group of London merchants in 1600, controlled most of eastern India by 1765, and thereafter continued to extend their administrative and governmental control over the sub-continent. British interest in China began in the late eighteenth century, when Britain began to import the tea that would soon become a staple of the British table, and rose throughout the 1800s. Increased contact with—and domination of—various parts of the Far East led to increased fascination with its cultures, a fascination widely reflected in literature. "Eastern" influence pervades the prose and poetry of this period, from William Beckford's novel *The History of the Caliph Vathek* (1786), to Byron's *Eastern Tales* (1813–14), to Percy Shelley's *Alastor* (1816), where the protagonist makes his way

> through Arabie
> And Persia, and the wild Carmanian waste,
> And o'er the aerial mountains which pour down
> Indus and Oxus from their icy caves,
> In joy and exultation [he] held his icy way,
> Till in the vale of Cashmire …
> he stretched
> His languid limbs.

Wearing her India cotton frock, sipping her tea from Canton, coffee from Yemen, or chocolate from Mexico, the English consumer of the Romantic period felt the influence of imperial expansion everywhere, from the commodities she purchased to the pages she turned.

But if the British Empire brought rewards to the nation's citizens, it all too often entailed exploitation and horror in the colonies themselves. Chief amongst these was the slavery that fueled the economy of the British West Indies. The mass of sugar required to

James Gillray, *Fashionable Contrasts, or the Duchess' Little Shoe Yielding to the Magnitude of the Duke's Foot*, 1792. At the time, the press had been fawning over Princess Frederica Charlotte Ulrica Catherina, who had just married Frederick Augustus, Duke of York; the daintiness of her feet had been particularly praised.

James Gillray, *The Plum Pudding in Danger*, 1805. Napoleon and British Prime Minister William Pitt are shown carving up the globe, with Napoleon skewering Europe and Pitt helping himself to the ocean. (1805 saw both the Battle of Trafalgar, at which the British under Lord Nelson established dominance at sea, and the Battle of Austerlitz, at which Napoleon defeated Russian and Austrian armies to cement his control of the Continent.)

Sir Charles D'Oyly, *The Emporium of Taylor & Co. in Calcutta*, c. 1825–28.

sweeten Britain's tea, coffee, and chocolate was cultivated, cut, and processed on these islands by slaves who worked under inhuman conditions until they literally wore out—at which point their white masters simply purchased fresh replacements. Over the course of the eighteenth century, British slavers transported some three million slaves to the West Indies and other agricultural colonies; the economic success of the port towns Bristol and Liverpool was based in large part on the important part they played in the English slave trade—and the trade in sugar from plantations that relied on slave labor.[1]

Arguably the strongest resistance to slavery in the West Indies came from the slaves themselves. The British invaded the formerly French island of Saint-

Dominique in 1793 in order to aid in the suppression of a slave uprising led by Toussaint L'Ouverture but withdrew five years later, having sent more troops to the West Indies over that period than they had sent to America during the War of Independence. When a subsequent effort by Napoleon also failed and the former slaves founded the Republic of Haiti in 1804, the message that emancipation was inevitable had registered widely in Britain.

Emancipation was also spurred by a widespread and effective protest movement within Britain. Between 1787, when protests first began, and 1791, abolitionists gathered 500 petitions against slavery from across Britain. In all some 400,000 signatures were collected; this was Britain's first large-scale petition campaign. The abolitionist movement attracted support from Evangelicals, from Whig politicians, and from radicals, and has been described as the first British political movement in

---

[1] *trade in sugar ... slave labor* At the start of the American Revolution, British imports from the largest sugar plantation center, Jamaica, were worth five times more than British imports from the Thirteen Colonies.

the modern sense. The leading figures in the movement were abolitionists Thomas Clarkson, Granville Sharp, and William Wilberforce, but it also drew considerable support from the poets of the day, among them William Cowper, Hannah More, William Blake, Mary Robinson, Anna Laetitia Barbauld, and Ann Yearsley (whose *A Poem on the Inhumanity of the Slave Trade* [1788] inveighed against the very business that supported her home town of Bristol).

Central to the literature of the abolitionist movement were books written by former slaves, such as Olaudah Equiano and Mary Prince, which laid out plainly the horrors of a slave's life and openly sought sympathy and fellow-feeling from readers. In his autobiography, *The Interesting Narrative of the Life of Olaudah Equiano* (1786), Equiano described conditions both in the West Indies and in America. As he observed with telling effect, the system bred degradation for "free negroes" as well as for slaves:

> I have often seen slaves, particularly those who were meagre, in different islands, put into scales and weighed; and then sold from three pence to six pence to nine pence a pound. My master, however, whose humanity was shocked at this mode, used to sell by the lump. And at or after a sale it was not uncommon to see negroes taken from their wives, wives taken from their husbands, and children from their parents, and sent off to other islands, and wherever else their merciless lords chose, and probably never more during life to see each other! ...
>
> [Free negroes] live in constant alarm for their liberty; and even this is but nominal, for they are universally insulted and plundered without the possibility of redress; for such is the equity of West Indian laws, that no free negro's evidence will be admitted in their courts of justice.

Such accounts, coupled with a determined and prolonged campaign and with the effects of the growth of the Asian sugar trade, led to the abolition of the slave trade in 1806–07, and (following another uprising, this time in Jamaica in 1831–32) to an act in 1833 that provided for the full abolition of slavery. The persecution of blacks by whites, however, continued both in the West Indies and throughout the British Empire.

Several of the leading names of English Romantic poetry are noticeably absent from the list of writers who wrote frequently and explicitly in favor of abolition. Wordsworth,[1] Coleridge, Byron, Shelley, and Keats were in general all sympathetic to the aims of the abolitionist movement, and Coleridge in particular spoke out strongly both against slavery itself and against the maintenance of the slave trade, memorably writing that "a slave is a person perverted into a thing," and slavery not so much "a deviation from justice as an absolute subversion of all morality." (Coleridge's views regarding slavery became significantly more conservative, however, later in his life.) It has been plausibly suggested that some major works of Romantic poetry (notably Coleridge's "The Rime of the Ancient Mariner" [1798] and Keats's "Lamia" [1819]) may usefully be read in relation to the slave trade. But directly pressing for the abolition of slavery through verse in the manner of Cowper, Robinson, and Yearsley was never a significant part of these poets' agendas.

THE ROMANTIC MIND AND ITS LITERARY PRODUCTIONS

It is not surprising that in a world overwhelmingly concerned with change, revolution, and freedom the makers of literature should be similarly preoccupied; as has already been discussed, the French Revolution and its aftermath lent vital force to the Romantic impulse. That force, though, was not exerted on all the literary minds in the Romantic era with equal force or in quite the same direction. For several of the leading figures of English Romanticism, the freedom that animated the poetic imagination was only tangentially related to the collectivist enterprise that the revolution in France had represented. Instead, it was very much an *individual* freedom; the freeing of the individual mind and the individual soul took pride of place. Subjective experience and the role that it played in the individual's response to and experience of reality are dominant themes in the works of the Romantics. Wordsworth's "Ode: Intimations of Immortality" (1807) surveys what becomes of the "heaven-born freedom" with which every individual who enters the world is born. Percy Shelley's

---

[1] *Wordsworth* In *The Prelude*, Wordsworth admits that in the 1790s "this particular strife had wanted power / To rivet my affections." He did write two sonnets (one to Clarkson, one to Toussaint L'Ouverture) in 1807, the year in which abolition of the slave trade was accomplished.

Mont Blanc (1817) is an extended exploration of power and creativity, and Keats's various Odes continually express their author's fascination with the connection between physical experience and the individual human imagination. In Byron's work, subjectivity, creativity, and epistemological questing all find expression in a series of heroes for whom the power of the will is a central concern. The question of what it means to be an individual looms large in the works of all these authors.

Nature became a fulcrum in the balancing of subjective and objective in the Romantic construction of reality, and most of the period's leading writers were particularly preoccupied with the relationship between the natural world and the individual mind. Percy Shelley appealed to the wind, "Make me thy lyre, even as the forest is," and, in "Tintern Abbey," Wordsworth recognized nature as

> The anchor of my purest thoughts, the nurse,
> The guide, the guardian of my heart, and soul
> Of all my moral being.

This commingling of self and nature was, at least in part, an expression of the late eighteenth- and early nineteenth-century tendency to see the natural world in opposition to the human world. In the same poem, for example, Wordsworth describes himself as coming to nature

>   more like a man
> Flying from something that he dreads than one
> Who sought the thing he loved.

Less frequently did poets of the Romantic period comment on the relationship between humans and nature as an objective reality. The focus was much more often on what non-human nature had to offer to the individual human soul than on how humans in aggregate were reshaping the natural world. Barbauld was unusual in observing and commenting on the latter clearly; in her grim survey of England in "Eighteen Hundred and Eleven," she described how

> Science and Art urge on the useful toil,
> New mould a climate and create the soil, …
> On yielding Nature urge their new demands,
> And ask not gifts but tribute at her hands.

Such clear-eyed observations of human manipulation of nature were few and far between.

The importance of the subjective sense of reality to the Romantic imagination also comes out clearly in the widespread fascination with the visions experienced in dreams, in nightmares, and other altered states. The question Keats poses at the end of "Ode to a Nightingale" (1819)—"Was it a vision, or a waking dream?"—is of a sort that occurs frequently in the literature of Romanticism. Among the many works of the period that touch on this theme are Coleridge's fragment "Kubla Khan" (which he claimed came to him during a drug-induced sleep); Keats's visionary *The Fall of Hyperion: A Dream*; Mary Shelley's *Frankenstein* (the story of which came to her in a dream, and in which Victor Frankenstein acquires the habit of taking "every night a small quantity of laudanum" in order to "gain the rest necessary for the preservation of life"); and De Quincey's *Confessions of an English Opium-Eater*.

In the work of female writers of the period, interest in the individual and the mind often took different forms from those that engaged the interest of male writers. Many were concerned with education: Hannah More produced a series of Cheap Repository Tracts designed to enlighten the poor, while Maria Edgeworth gained fame as a children's writer and educationalist. Mary Wollstonecraft authored not only her famous *Vindication of the Rights of Woman*, but also *Thoughts on the Education of Daughters* (1787) and *The Female Reader* (1772). The Romantic period abounded in outspoken female writers who engaged with the issues of their day and sought to make a difference in their world. In their own time, however, such authors were often derided as "Bluestockings," unnatural women who revealed their prudishness through their interest in intellectual pursuits. In their own day, the writings of these authors made little, if any, difference to the social, legal, and economic position of women, who remained little more than property in the eyes of the law for many more years. But over the longer term their impact was considerable; Wollstonecraft and the Bluestockings laid the intellectual foundations for the social and political progress of women that would slowly be achieved over the next 200 years and more.

It would be a mistake to think of the female writers of the Romantic period as solely concerned with women's rights and with the stereotypical "female

J.M.W. Turner, *Melrose Abbey*, 1822. The lines in the lower left corner are (slightly misquoted) from Canto 2 of Sir Walter Scott's long poem *The Lay of the Last Minstrel* (1805): "If thou would'st view fair Melrose aright, / Go visit it by the pale moonlight."

arenas" of education and religion, however. Much of the writing by women in this period is as rich, strong, and plaintive as anything produced by their male counterparts. Mary Robinson, for example—famous first as an actress and mistress of the Prince of Wales, then as a successful poet and novelist—earned the admiration of both Wordsworth and Coleridge (who called her "an undoubted genius") and preceded them in the writing of poetry concerned with the poor and disenfranchised. In her *Elegiac Sonnets* (1784), Charlotte Smith displayed all the power, control, and skill at incisive self-examination that has come to be associated with the male Romantics. Poet Felicia Hemans rivaled (indeed, perhaps surpassed) Byron in popularity. Playwright Joanna Baillie, famous for producing works that, as she put it, "delineate the progress of the higher passions in the human breast," was considered by Walter Scott to be "the best dramatic writer since the days of Shakespeare."

One area of common ground for almost all Romantic writers, male and female, was a strong interest in the "Imagination," the creative power by which an individual took the raw material of the physical world and transformed it into art. Although "Imagination" was recognized as being distinct from religious inspiration, descriptions of imaginative or poetic power often took on strong religious overtones, as in Blake's assertion that "One Power alone makes a Poet: Imagination, the Divine Vision." Coleridge, Blake, and Wordsworth were all deeply invested in the notion of the poet as *vates*, or prophet. And the imagination was seen as invested with moral as well as prophetic power. Like earlier ages (though unlike our own), the Romantics saw the realms of the aesthetic and the moral as being closely bound up with each other. But whereas earlier ages had tended to see literature as expressing truths emanating from elsewhere and the ethical element of literature as inhering in its ability to illustrate virtues and vices and point out moral lessons, the leading Romantics tended to locate the moral element, not only of literature but of life itself, in the imagination and tended to see the imagination as embodying truth as well as morality. "The great instrument of moral good," wrote Shelley in his *Defence of Poetry* (1821), "is the imagination," while Keats proclaimed that "what the imagination seizes as

beauty must be the truth."[1] More broadly, a belief took root among poets—the great male Romantic poets in particular—that the aesthetic and imaginative truths of poetry were possessed of a transcendent status, a status that placed such insights above the historical or scientific truths of the ordinary world.

Another opposition that animates the literature of the Romantic period is that between sense and sensibility—a tension with parallels to that between reason and emotion in the intellectual landscape of any age, but also one possessing elements particular to the late eighteenth and early nineteenth centuries. In this era, the terms "sentiment," "sentimentality," "sentimentalism," and "sensibility" were all widely used (and to some extent overlapped in meaning), but none more so than "sensibility." The concept of "sensibility" entailed strong emotional responsiveness, with life and literary work animated by powerful feeling. Indeed, "sensibility" was frequently associated with emotional excess: when Jane Austen describes Marianne's "excess of sensibility" in *Sense and Sensibility* (1811), she is using the notion of sensibility in ways that would have been familiar to any late eighteenth- or early nineteenth-century reader:

> She was sensible and clever; but eager in every thing;
> her sorrows, her joys, could have no moderation.
> She was generous, amiable, interesting: she was every
> thing but prudent. The resemblance between her
> and her mother was strikingly great. Elinor saw,
> with concern, the excess of her sister's sensibility;
> but by Mrs. Dashwood it was valued and cherished.

It may well be that most educated Britons of the period privileged sense over sensibility in very much the way that Austen appears to do. But it is also true that the feelings associated with the Romantic sensibility—above all, as they were expressed in poetry—became the defining passions of the age. And the poetry of sensibility carried intellectual as well as aesthetic force; for a considerable period it stood in the vanguard of the movement for social and political change.

---

[1] *what the imagination ... truth* Keats's notion of the value of "negative capability—that is, when a man is capable of being in uncertainties, mysteries, doubts, without any irritable reaching after fact and reason"—destabilizes in interesting ways the connections that he and other Romantics drew between morality and the imagination and between the imagination and truth.

That is not to say that the distinction separating poets of sensibility from the rest was entirely clear; far from it. Rather in the way that competing factions today will sometimes each accuse the other of being controlled by their emotions rather than their reason, many in the late eighteenth century tried to situate sensibility in a natural alliance with political views they opposed. Anti-Jacobins suggested there was a natural affinity between the supposed excesses of sensibility and those of political radicalism, while radicals often portrayed sensibility as associated with reactionary political views. In truth, the language of sensibility was used by both sides.

Also among the oppositions that occur throughout the literature of the Romantic period are the natural and the artificial, and the original and the imitative. If "artificial" is taken simply to mean "human-made," of course, the distinction between the natural and the artificial is purely a matter of physical process. But "artificial" and "natural" as matters of taste and of style have more fluid meanings. As the culture of sentiment and of sensibility grew over the course of the eighteenth century, "artificial" came to be used less and less frequently to mean "displaying special art or skill" and more and more frequently to mean "contrived, shaped in a way not spontaneous or natural," or even "not expressive of reality." The divide between natural and artificial was felt to connect with that between "novelty" of thought and expression—"originality," as we would call it—and the "servility" of the stale or overly imitative. Whereas the Neoclassical poets had proudly imitated classical models, often devoting themselves to translations of Classical works into English poetry, Romantic writers—and the leading Romantic poets in particular—had little interest in seeing the work of earlier eras as models to be imitated. They might admire the poets of earlier eras, they might be inspired by them (by Shakespeare and by Milton above all), they might aspire to similar glory, but they had no interest in taking the same path to glory. If not entirely for the first time, then certainly to an unprecedented degree, originality came in the Romantic period to be seen as a criterion of poetic achievement. Even at the beginning of the period we find judgments on poetic worth being made largely on the grounds of the originality the verse displays. A 1791 assessment of a volume of Robinson's poetry, for example, sets up an opposition between the original and

the natural—two qualities often assumed to normally accompany each other:

> The attempt at originality is in all pursuits laudable. Invention is a noble attribute of the mind. But the danger is, lest, by pursuing it too intensely, we deviate so far from ease and nature, that the real object of Poetry, that of touching the heart, be lost.

A more familiar set of oppositions involving the natural and the artificial, the "original" and the imitative, is put forward by William Hazlitt in his *The Spirit of the Age* (1825), as he assesses at the end of the Romantic period the place of Wordsworth in the poetry and the intellectual life of the age:

> His popular, inartificial style gets rid (at a blow) of all the trappings of verse, of all the high places of poetry: "the cloud-capt towers, the solemn temples, the gorgeous palaces," are swept to the ground. ... All the traditions of learning, all the superstitions of age, are obliterated and effaced. We begin *de novo* on a *tabula rasa* of poetry ... He chooses to have his subject a foil to his invention, to owe nothing but to himself. ... Taught by political opinions to say to the vain pomp and glory of the world, "I hate ye," seeing the path of classical and artificial poetry blocked up by the cumbrous ornaments of style and turgid common-places, so that nothing more could be achieved in that direction but by the most ridiculous bombast or the tamest servility, he has ... struck into the sequestered vale of humble life, sought out the muse among sheep-cotes and hamlets, and the peasant's mountain-haunts, has discarded all the tinsel pageantry of verse, and endeavored (not in vain) to ... add the charm of novelty to the familiar.

In passages such as this one, we may see the paradigms according to which the literature of the Romantic period is still largely seen being articulated even before the period had ended. On the one side are the natural, the spontaneous, the original, fresh and new; on the other, the artificial, the studied, the imitative, the tired, and traditional. On the one side, imagination and sensibility; on the other, excessive rationalism. On the one side, a passion for freedom, especially, aesthetic freedom and freedom of the spirit; on the other, restraint, reaction,

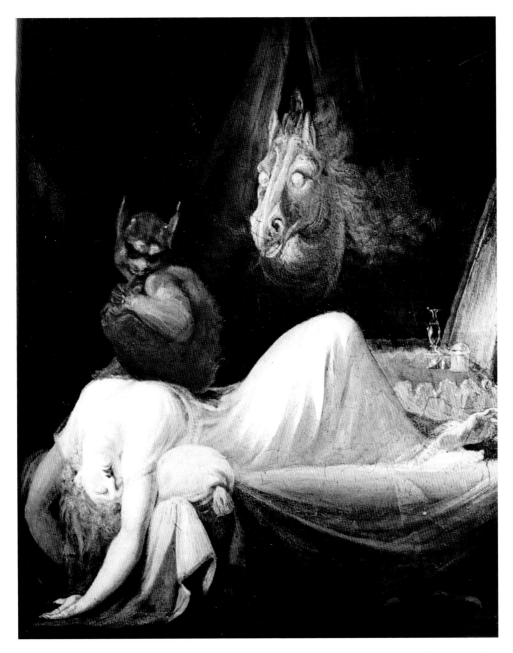

Henry Fuseli, *The Nightmare*, 1790–91. The Swiss-born artist Fuseli (1741–1825) moved to England in 1779, and soon became one of the leading artistic figures of the day. Beginning in 1781, Fuseli painted several different versions of *The Nightmare*, for which he became famous; it remains an iconic image of the Gothic sensibility, and of Romantic interest in what we now term "the unconscious."

Fuseli moved in London's artistic and intellectual circles through the 1790s, and was briefly involved romantically with Mary Wollstonecraft before her marriage to William Godwin.

Jacques-Louis David, *Bonaparte*, 1798.

Artist unknown, *A Stoppage to a Stride over the Globe*, 1803.

William Blake, "The Sun Standing at His Eastern Gate," illustration to John Milton's "L'Allegro," c. 1816–20.

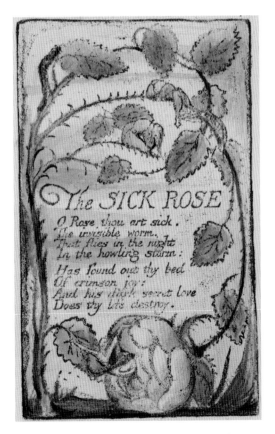

THE SICK ROSE

O Rose thou art sick.
The invisible worm.
That flies in the night
In the howling storm:

Has found out thy bed
Of crimson joy:
And his dark secret love
Does thy life destroy.

William Blake, "The Sick Rose," from *Songs of Experience*, 1794.

Philip James de Loutherbourg, *Coalbrookdale by Night*, 1801. The small Shropshire town of Coalbrookdale has been sometimes described as the birthplace of the Industrial Revolution. Located in a gorge on the River Severn, it was the site of the first ironworks that used the modern method of smelting with coke rather than charcoal (an innovation of Joseph Darby in 1709). Together with the adjacent towns of Madeley, Ironbridge, Jackfield, and Coalport, Coalbrookdale was part of an early industrial powerhouse; at the end of the eighteenth century it had a greater concentration of furnaces and forges than anywhere else in the world. Darby's son Abraham also constructed the world's first iron bridge nearby in 1779; the bridge and much of the old ironworks remain today, and the Ironbridge Gorge has been declared a World Heritage Site.

Thomas Phillips, *George Gordon, Lord Byron*, 1813. Byron is wearing clothing of a sort native to the region of Epirus (then part of Albania, now part of northern Greece); he had bought this outfit while traveling through the area in 1809.

Elizabeth Leveson-Gower, *Mountain Landscape*, c. 1830. Leveson-Gower published two volumes based on her watercolor images of Scottish landscapes, the first a collection of etchings, *Views of Orkney and the North-Eastern Coast of Scotland* (1807), and the second a volume of twenty aquatints, *Views on the Northern and Western Coasts of Sutherland* (1833). The artist intended that various of the wide Sutherland images be joined together to form 360 degree scenic panoramas.

J.M.W. Turner, *The Burning of the Houses of Parliament*, 1835. In the 1830s it became Turner's practice to send unfinished work (often with only rough underpainting completed) to the Royal Academy in advance of its annual exhibition. During the period devoted (in the case of other artists) to the varnishing of already-completed work, Turner would complete the painting itself, often watched by a sizeable crowd. An eyewitness, E.V. Rippingille, described Turner completing *The Burning of the Houses of Parliament* in 1835:

> For [the] three hours I was there ... he never ceased to work, or even once looked or turned from the wall in which his picture was hung. A small box of colors, a few very small brushes, and a vial or two, were at his feet ... In one part of the mysterious proceedings Turner, who worked almost entirely with his palette knife, was observed to be rolling and spreading a half-transparent stuff over his picture, the size of a finger in length and thickness. As Callcott was looking on I ventured to say ... "What is that he is plastering his picture with?" to which enquiry it was replied, "should be sorry to be the man to ask him" ... Presently the work was finished: Turner gathered his tools together, put them into and shut the box, and then with his face still turned to the wall, and at the same distance from it, went sidelong off, without speaking a word to anybody ... Maclise, who stood near, remarked, "There, that's masterly, he does not stop to look at his work; he knows it is done, and he is off!"

J.M.W. Turner, *Slavers Throwing Overboard the Dead and Dying—Typhoon Coming On*, 1840. Turner's painting depicts a 1781 incident in which Captain Luke Collingwood of the slave ship *Zong*, with his ship running short of water and other supplies when it had been blown off-course during a severe storm, ordered that all sick and dying slaves be thrown overboard; 133 were killed as a result. Insurance was a factor in Collingwood's decision; compensation could be claimed for property lost or jettisoned in storms, but not for slaves killed by disease or other natural causes. The incident became widely publicized and spurred support for the abolitionist movement. In the ensuing legal case the court upheld the insurance company's financial liability; no criminal charges were brought against the captain. In the twentieth century the incident became the basis for several literary works, including a long poem by David Dabydeen and a novel by Fred D'Aguiar.

oppression. On the one side, in short, the Romantic; on the other, the classical, the neoclassical, the conservative.

If these sets of oppositions often bear some correspondence to reality, it is important to recognize that the correspondences are just as often loose and unreliable. Romantic literature—the Romantic period itself— is filled with unexpected parallels, with surprising evolutions, with unexpected paradoxes, with outright contradictions. The Della Cruscans[1] and their followers, for example, have often been taken to task for the supposed artificiality of their verse. Wordsworth, usually seen as the great poet of a natural world set apart from the oppressive workings of the human-made world of cities and factories, wrote, in 1833, that "Steamboats, Viaducts, and Railways … Nature doth embrace / Her lawful offspring in Man's art." Coleridge, who in the early 1790s felt strongly the attractions of sensibility and planned to establish a community in Pennsylvania founded on revolutionary democratic ideals, became in later life as dismissive of sensibility as he was of revolutionary fervor. Byron, the paradigmatic Romantic figure, professed to reject many of the impulses at the core of the Romantic movement; in "To Romance" (1807), he vows to leave the realms of romance "for those of truth":

> Romance! disgusted with deceit,
> Far from thy motley court I fly,
> Where Affectation holds her seat,
> And sickly Sensibility …

Keats, for his part, is perhaps at his most enthusiastic when he exclaims not over nature or freedom but over the experience of classical literature ("On First Looking into Chapman's Homer" [1816]) and classical art ("On Seeing the Elgin Marbles" [1817], "Ode on a Grecian Urn" [1819]). The distinctions made in the attempt to define the essence of the Romantic, in short, often become elusive or indistinct when it comes to particulars; indeed, such divisions can be downright misleading. Throughout most of the nineteenth and twentieth centuries, literary critics and theorists tended to accept

very much at face value the Romantics' self-representations of the nature and importance of their work; more recently, these self-representations have been frequently problematized and widely challenged.

There have been few challenges, however, to the view that this was a period of revolutionary developments—or to the notion that at the center of those developments (so far as English literature is concerned) was an extraordinary body of verse. Looking back, in 1832, Letitia Landon was among those who identified poetry as a particular locus of change:

> Already there is a wide gulf between the last century and the present. In religion, in philosophy, in politics, in manners, there has passed a great change; but in none has been worked a greater change than in poetry, whether as regards the art itself, or the general feeling towards it.

Poetic ambition was in itself central to the spirit of Romanticism. When they spoke of the confident outpouring of Romantic verse, Romantic poets did not hesitate to compare their own work to that of the great poets of the past—and to feel themselves capable of such greatness. "I would sooner fail than not be among the greatest," wrote Keats.

The tendencies of our own age, when poetry is usually taken in small doses and the lyric mode predominates, sometimes lead modern readers to place far less emphasis than did the Romantics themselves on their longer works. The shorter poems of the Romantic canon (among them Blake's "The Tyger" [1794], Wordsworth's "Ode: Intimations of Immortality" [1807], Coleridge's "Dejection: An Ode" [1802], Byron's "She Walks in Beauty" [1814], Shelley's "To a Skylark" [1820], and Keats's odes and sonnets) are justly celebrated, and Wordsworth and Coleridge's *Lyrical Ballads* is rightly seen as the era's most significant single volume of literature. But even as these works retain pride of place, it is important to give full notice too to the vast range of the ambitions of the Romantic poets— ambitions that found their fullest expression in extended poetic work. Blake's long prophetic poems charted new territory for English verse, both in the poetry itself and in his unique marriage of the verbal and the visual. Robinson's more substantial works include the long sonnet sequence *Sappho and Phaon* (1796) and the series

---

[1] *Della Cruscans* The Della Cruscans were poets of sensibility, who, in the late 1780s and early 1790s, took the lead in exuberantly embracing revolutionary freedom in the wake of the French Revolution.

of longer poems on related themes that were eventually published as the sequence *The Progress of Liberty* (1806). Over the course of some 50 years, Wordsworth re-worked his poetic autobiography, *The Prelude*, into an 8,000-line epic. Coleridge's narrative poems "The Rime of the Ancient Mariner" and "Christabel" (1800) are works of modest extent by comparison with these—but still long by modern standards. Byron gave extraordinary new life to the epic romance with *Childe Harold*, broke new ground poetically with what he termed the "epic satire" of *Don Juan* (1824), and wrote seven full-length poetic dramas. Shelley's long works encompass not only the complex allegorical drama *Prometheus Unbound* (1820) but also the poems "The Mask of Anarchy" (1819) and "Adonais"[1] (1821) and the poetic drama *The Cenci* (1819). Keats's *Endymion* (1818) is another memorable work of epic proportions. And, though Keats abandoned both the original epic-length version of his *Hyperion* (1819) and the later *The Fall of Hyperion: A Dream* (1821), what remains of both also constitutes a very substantial poetic achievement. Charlotte Smith's monumental poem of history, nature, and the self, "Beachy Head" (1807), is a landmark in early nineteenth-century poetry, while George Crabbe's *The Borough* (1810) memorialized village life in meticulous detail. Felicia Hemans remains best known for her short poems "Casabianca" (1826) and "The Homes of England" (1827), but her most significant works are the poetic drama *The Siege of Valencia* (1823) and the 19 poems that together comprise *Records of Woman* (1828).

The ambitions of the Romantic poets extended, too, to poetic theory and criticism; to a heretofore unprecedented degree, the leading poets of the time were also the leading critics and theorists. Wordsworth's "Preface" to *Lyrical Ballads*, in its various versions, Shelley's *A Defence of Poetry*, Coleridge's scattered but enormously influential body of literary theory and criticism, and the critical insights of Keats's letters, have all long been regarded as central documents in the literature of Romanticism. But other leading writers too wrote perceptively and extensively about literature—among them Barbauld, Landon, and Elizabeth Inchbald.

The novel, dramatic writing, and the essay all

flourished alongside poetry in the Romantic period, even if these genres were not accorded the same degree of respect as poetry. Barbauld commented wryly on the situation of the novel in 1810:

> A collection of novels has a better chance of giving pleasure than of commanding respect. Books of this description are condemned to the grave and despised by the fastidious; but their leaves are seldom found unopened, and they occupy the parlour and the dressing-room while productions of higher name are often gathering dust upon the shelf.

Though such laments reflected the perception of the novel fairly accurately, the novel nonetheless became increasingly popular, and the changes and innovations to the form arising during the Romantic period continue to reverberate and resonate to this very day.

The Romantic era saw the decline of that mainstay of eighteenth-century prose, the epistolary novel, and the development and proliferation of other forms of fiction. James Hogg produced one of the great masterpieces of psychological literature, *The Private Memoirs and Confessions of a Justified Sinner* (1824). Historical novels—especially those celebrating nationhood—became increasingly popular, among them Maria Edgeworth's *Castle Rackrent* (1800), Sydney Owenson's *The Wild Irish Girl* (1806), and Jane Porter's *The Scottish Chiefs* (1810). It was Sir Walter Scott, however, who took the genre of the historical novel and made it his own. Perhaps the most influential fiction writer of the Romantic period, Scott single-handedly reshaped notions not just of "the historical novel" but of the novel itself. After beginning his career as a highly successful poet, he switched to long fiction in 1814 and produced a succession of extraordinarily popular novels, including *Waverley* (1814), *Rob Roy* (1817), and *Ivanhoe* (1819), the first modern bestsellers. Using his works to explore the ongoing political struggles of the time—the clash between traditionalism and progress, the tempting attractions of an idealized past that is really a cover for abuse and exploitation, the struggles and missteps that characterize the creation of a just society—Scott at the same time created vivid, entirely engrossing characters. Indeed, one hallmark of his writing is his ability to use these fully realized individuals to give human expression to broad social and political issues.

---

[1] *Adonais* Subtitled "An Elegy on the Death of John Keats," the poem is a pastoral elegy, written by Shelley upon hearing of Keats's death.

Scott produced more than 25 full length novels, as well as a number of other works. His use of dialect and his decision to set his works almost exclusively in Scotland validated the language and folklore of regional and marginalized people at a time when "British" was increasingly equated with "English." His use of editorial personae, interlocutors, mediated (sometimes twice-mediated) story presentation, and complexly constructed authorial selves raise questions about the natures of authority and authorship, the difficulty of interpretation, and the concept of truth itself. Scott not only largely created the now well-known version of "Scotland" as a land of kilts and clans, with fierce rivalries fought out against a backdrop of misty mountains and purple heather, filled with eccentric but kind-hearted peasants, he also anticipated or pioneered many of the devices associated with modern and post-modern literature.

Many novels of the period, including Scott's, had roots in an earlier form of long prose fiction, the romance. Whereas "romance novel" today denotes a form of pulp fiction focused on romantic love as wish-fulfillment, the tradition of romance literature has its roots in medieval tales of the supernatural, of chivalry, and of courtly love, in which a sense of the extraordinary or the fantastic continually colors the narrative. The genre of romance made its influence felt in several different sorts of literary work in the Romantic era, but none more so than the Gothic. Gothic novels of the late eighteenth and early nineteenth centuries typically investigate human responses to supernatural occurrences, or those things known to be "impossible," thanks to the advances of science and natural history. These novels tend to feature stereotypical characters and to take place in worlds temporally or geographically distant from England. The surrounding landscape is often highly symbolic, reflecting the psychological world of the characters, and the heroine's plight—and the protagonist was almost without fail a heroine—is usually rendered in often highly expressive rhetoric, full of rhapsodic feeling. The structure of the Gothic novel frequently corresponds to the political and social tensions that result from the integration of long-ago, remotely historical time—preserved in ancient castles or abbeys—into an otherwise modern world. The Gothic setting of Charlotte Smith's *Emmeline, the Orphan of the Castle* (1788), for example, allows for the exploration of social concerns such as English laws of primogeniture[1] and women's social status and identity within the frame of a courtship novel. Her novel illustrates the ways in which the frightening, distorted world of the Gothic could also serve as a forum for social commentary—as it also does in William Godwin's *Caleb Williams* (1794) and in Eliza Fenwick's *Secresy* (1795). Gothic novels such as Matthew Lewis's *The Monk* (1796), Charlotte Dacre's *Zofloya, or The Moor* (1806), Charles Maturin's *Melmoth the Wanderer* (1820), and Anne Radcliffe's series of highly successful Gothic novels, including *The Romance of the Forest* (1791) and *The Mysteries of Udolpho* (1794), welcomed their readers into a world marked by sexual perversity, threatened female virtue, and grotesque sights and experiences. Concerned with revealing what lay repressed or hidden behind the mask of middle-class conformity, the Gothic also often veered into savagery and melodrama, tendencies captured perfectly in the following exchange from *The Vampyre* (1819), by John Polidori, in which a mysterious villain extracts a promise from his traveling companion:

> "Swear!" cried the dying man raising himself with exultant violence. "Swear by all your soul reveres, by all your nature fears, swear that for a year and a day you will not impart your knowledge of my crimes or death to any living being in any way, whatever may happen, or whatever you may see."—His eyes seemed bursting from their sockets; "I swear!" said Aubrey; he sunk laughing upon his pillow, and breathed no more.

If the heightened atmosphere of the Gothic novel often veers toward imaginative excess, it can also foster literary art of the highest order—as *Frankenstein*, Mary Shelley's famous first novel, amply demonstrates. The story of a "monster" who turns against his creator Victor Frankenstein, *Frankenstein* is, on one level, a gripping tale of adventure, written with apparent simplicity. But it is also a text that brings together virtually all the great themes of the era: freedom and oppression; science and nature; society and the individual; knowledge and power; gender and sexuality; dream and reality; creation

---

[1] *primogeniture* The common-law right of the first-born son to inherit the entire estate, to the exclusion of younger siblings.

and destruction; self-deception and self-discovery; death and life; God and the universe.

If one strand of the tradition of romance literature runs through the evolution of the Gothic novel, a very different strand runs through the development of the courtship novel in the Romantic period. From Frances Burney's *Camilla* (1796) to Elizabeth Susan Ferrier's *The Inheritance* (1824), the pages of Romantic fiction are filled with young people who are misguided, thwarted, and, ultimately, united in love. It seems no exaggeration to say that no author of the period was as successful with the courtship genre as was Jane Austen. Between 1811 and 1817, her six major novels were published, all of them warmly engaging yet sharply observant and often satirical, telling of courtship, social class, and domestic life. Much as her novels do not engage directly or obviously with the large issues of her age, Austen reveals a shrewd awareness of both politics and economics, particularly as they concern women; her novels emphasize the limited possibilities open to women during the period in which she wrote. But within this limited frame, Austen provides a vividly three-dimensional picture of the shaping of female character, of the inner world of the emotions as much as the outer world of social behavior. Austen's heroines are preoccupied with wooing, marriage, and the minutiae of income, entailment,[1] and other details of domestic and marital economy, precisely because these dominated and defined the lives of women of the period, while her concentration on "3 or 4 Families in a country village" (as she famously remarked to her niece) draws attention to the geographical and physical constraints imposed on middle- and upper-class women during this time. Even the happy endings that have delighted generations of Austenites are undercut by the obvious and acknowledged fictionality of the novels—emphasized through authorial asides, direct appeals to the reader, and other devices—by means of which Austen suggests that all happy endings may be mere fictions.

Austen was a skilled stylist, as well as a keen-eyed social critic, bringing to her novels an unprecedented range of novelistic technique. With *Lady Susan* (an early novella, written around 1794, but not published until

1871), she proved herself adept at epistolary narrative; with *Sense and Sensibility*, *Pride and Prejudice*, and *Emma* (1815), she brought new flexibility to the use of the third-person narrative voice, demonstrating perfect pitch in a variety of ironic tones, and pioneering the technique now known as free indirect discourse. In this mode of narration, the apparently independent third-person narrative voice temporarily assumes the viewpoint of one or more of the characters—or indeed of an entire social class, as is the case with the famous opening to *Pride and Prejudice*: "It is a truth universally acknowledged, that a single man in possession of a good fortune, must be in want of a wife." In her tone, Austen is at a great remove from the leading poets of the Romantic period, but in the importance she places on the exercise of moral imagination—both by her characters and through her own narrative style—she is very much at one with the age.

Other Romantic novels sought to reflect the social and political concerns of the world around them in fiction more fully and more directly than did either most Gothic novels or most courtship novels; a number of writers used the novel as a means of challenging prevailing beliefs and mores. Maria Edgeworth's series of Irish novels—*Castle Rackrent* (1800), *Ennui* (1809), *The Absentee* (1812), and *Ormond* (1817)—explored the colonial relationship between England and Ireland. William Godwin's *Caleb Williams* (1794) sought to reveal, in the author's words, the "perfidiousness exercised by the powerful members of the community against those who are more privileged than themselves." Hogg's *Private Memoirs* was a powerful indictment of the smug superiority that could be engendered by religious zeal. And Mary Hays's *The Victim of Prejudice* (1799), a passionate tale of a young woman who dares to resist the pressure put upon her to marry the man who has raped her, was among those novels that spoke powerfully of injustice in a male-dominated society. Conservative voices also spoke out loudly through the medium of prose fiction; important anti-Jacobin novels of the period include Jane West's *A Tale of the Times* (1799), Elizabeth Hamilton's *Memoirs of Modern Philosophers* (1800), and Charles Lucas's *The Infernal Quixote* (1801). And a number of novelists used the novel as a means of making politically pointed connections with other parts of the world, whether to cast a

---

[1] *entailment* Legal provisions specifying that a property may not be sold or otherwise disposed of by the owner, as it must pass to the owner's (male) heirs upon his death.

critical eye on the course of European imperialism—as in Sydney Owenson's *The Missionary* (1811)—or to criticize aspects of British society by presenting them through the view of an outsider—as in Hamilton's *Translations of the Letters of a Hindoo Rajah* (1796).

While the novel prospered and evolved, so too did the genre of non-fictional prose. With the rise of the periodical (see "The Business of Literature" section below) came the rise of first critical and then more general essays, designed to engage, enlighten, and entertain the reader. William Hazlitt, originally intended for the Church and later an aspiring painter and philosopher, turned his hand to writing and became the most trenchant cultural critic of his time. His works include dramatic, literary, and art criticism, as well as political journalism, general essays, and his famous collection of pieces on important figures of the eighteenth century and the Romantic period, *The Spirit of the Age* (1824). His friend Charles Lamb rivaled Hazlitt's renown as an essayist, although his style was very different. Where Hazlitt used plain language and popular modes of construction to express his points cleanly and carefully, Lamb cultivated a more genteel style, rich in allusions and puns, with the resulting prose emerging as both thoughtful and rhetorically complex. Together, the two played a central role in the development of the essay during the Romantic period, but they were far from the only practitioners of the art. From Francis Jeffrey, whose pieces in the *Edinburgh Review* made literary criticism an exercise in stylish perspicacity, to Thomas De Quincey, whose psychological probing anticipates Freud, Romantic essay writers came in all shapes and sizes.

In the field of drama, the Romantic period is traditionally seen as an era of great "closet dramas."[1] And, given that the period produced both Byron's powerful verse drama, *Manfred* (1816–17), his iconoclastic meditation on sin and damnation, *Cain* (1822), and Shelley's mythographic masterpiece, *Prometheus Unbound*, its reputation as a breeding ground for rich, multi-layered private theatricals may fairly be said to be well deserved. Other serious plays failed on the stage but were widely read and highly praised as literature. Chief among these was Joanna Baillie's series of tragedies,

collectively entitled *Plays on the Passions* (1798–1812); depicting the passions "in their rise and progress in the heart" was Baillie's intent, and she believed that such drama could have a moral purpose, though she made no transcendent claims for the moral value of the imagination. Drama, in her view, "improves us by the knowledge we acquire of our own minds, from the natural desire we have to look into the thoughts, and observe the behavior of others." Baillie's explorations in psychology harked back to Enlightenment concepts, but her plays also engaged powerfully with the issues of her own day, primarily the question of women's rights.

In Byron's view, the distaste many serious writers felt for the public theater in this period was entirely justified:

> When I first entered upon theatrical affairs, I had some idea of writing for the [play]house myself, but soon became a convert to Pope's opinion of that subject. Who would condescend to the drudgery of the stage, and enslave himself to the humours, the caprices, the taste or tastelessness, of the age? Besides, one must write for particular actors, have them continually in one's eye, sacrifice character to the personating of it, cringe to some favorite of the public, neither give him too many nor too few lines to spout ...

Baillie was rather more charitable, attributing the low tolerance of audiences for serious drama to an escapism born of a desire to find refuge from the "commercial hurricane" of the age—and locating a good deal of the problem in the poor acoustics and lighting of the theaters of the day:

> The Public have now to choose between what we shall suppose are well-written and well-acted plays, the words of which are not heard, or heard but imperfectly by two-thirds of the audience, while the finer and more pleasing traits of the acting are by a still greater proportion lost altogether; and splendid pantomime, or pieces whose chief object is to produce striking scenic effect, which can be seen and comprehended by the whole.

---

[1] *closet dramas* Plays written not for the stage but for private performance—in a private room or "closet"—or to be read.

As both Byron's and Baillie's comments indicate, the theater in this period was, in some sense at least, thriving. People thronged to the theaters, where they saw plays by such popular and prolific playwrights as Hannah Cowley and Elizabeth Inchbald, as well as successful dramas such as Samuel Taylor Coleridge's *Remorse* (1812) and Charles Maturin's *Bertram* (1816). The Stage Licensing Act of 1737 meant that, in London, only two theaters, Covent Garden and Drury Lane (and, in the summer, the Haymarket) were permitted to present "legitimate" drama, but this in no way limited theatrical production. Stage entertainments of all sorts were held in venues from pubs to tents. In cities and provinces outside London, theaters sprang up to meet the demands of an increasing audience: a survey completed in 1804 counted 280 playhouses throughout the nation. The Licensing Act also required the texts of plays to be submitted to the Lord Chamberlain for censorship before performance. As a result, many works intended for the stage were forced into the closet; perhaps the most famous example is Shelley's *The Cenci*, which features not only father-daughter incest but also parricide. Many, however, were not, and a roll call of drama produced between 1780 and 1834 features everything from light comedy to melodramatic tragedy and from pantomimes to operas, as well as spectacles that featured impressive special effects.

THE BUSINESS OF LITERATURE

The thriving literary scene of the period is intimately tied to developments in the worlds of book publishing, bookselling, and book marketing. The most influential of these was the rise of the periodical. By the 1760s, there were more than 30 periodicals in London alone, including monthly journals, quarterly magazines, collections of reviews and essays, all designed to inform and stimulate their readers. This boom in the periodical press meant increased employment for those who sought to become men and women of letters; the demand for articles often outweighed the supply. For readers and publishers, it meant an ever-growing number of publications in which reviews of the latest books might appear. Published books were expensive—a three-volume novel could cost a total of nine shillings,

roughly $40 today—but reviews often printed long extracts, and thus readers could experience the book through the review. Such extracts were also, of course, excellent advertisements for the books under review.

At the same time as the number of periodicals increased, so did ways of obtaining books. Between 1740 and 1790, the number of outlets nearly doubled. Most obviously, books could be bought: well-established bookshops flourished in cities all over the nation. In provincial towns and villages, where bookselling was not profitable on its own, literature was often sold side by side with stationery, patent medicines, and even groceries. Because the cost of books put them outside the means of many readers, however, some booksellers began to lend volumes to customers for a small fee, thus initiating the circulating library. A patron would pay a yearly fee, enabling him to borrow books as he pleased.

Although both circulating and subscription libraries offered a good value, they still lay outside the financial resources of those below the lower middle classes. For these readers, there were other alternatives. Pedlars and hawkers sold street literature that included ballads, sermons, and tracts. Those who could not afford library subscriptions but who wished to read something more than broadsheet ballads or pamphlets often formed book clubs in which a number of people contributed money to buy a single book, which they would then share. After all had read the book, it might well be sold to a local bookseller, with the proceeds put toward the price of a new one. Slightly more formally, in numerous towns and villages, the local male elite came together to select and discuss books and pamphlets, usually on a controversial topic of the day. This literature, too, was sold on, often by means of an auction among members at the end of the year.

Perhaps as a result of these efforts in group reading, or perhaps simply because people enjoyed it, reading aloud remained a feature of the Romantic era. The fiction and the non-fiction of the period abounds in scenes of communal reading, and the visions that come down to us range from Countess Granville's admission that when her husband read *Don Juan* to her "I roared till I could neither hear nor see" to Henry Austen's description of his sister Jane as one who "read aloud with very great taste and effect. Her own works, probably, were never heard to such advantage as from her own

Thomas Rowlandson, *Dr. Syntax and a Bookseller*, 1812.

J. Bluck, after Augustus Charles Pugin, *Ackermann's Art Library* (detail), c. 1812–15. Rudolf Ackermann (1764–1834) moved to London from his native Germany and opened a print shop in London on the Strand in 1795, selling books and artist supplies as well as prints, and exhibiting paintings. He later also began to publish color-plate books, the most notable of which was *The Microcosm of London*, a three-volume set with 104 hand-colored aquatint plates by various artists (including Thomas Rowlandson and Augustus Pugin), published between 1808 and 1811.

mouth." Writers of the Romantic period were not very far removed from a time when illiteracy was more common than literacy, a time when literature was still an oral art. It is worth bearing in mind that many of them wrote texts intended to be read aloud, and many of their works gain luster from being heard.

"ROMANTIC"

Of the six periods into which the history of British literature has long been conventionally divided, the era of Romanticism is by far the briefest, extending over less than 40 years. Arguably it is also the most intense, particularly during the years 1789–1815: the era not only of the French Revolution and the Napoleonic Wars but also of the era's most tumultuous literary developments—and most lasting literary achievements.

This was unquestionably an age of contradiction. It was a period in which political consciousness spread through society in unprecedented ways, with a great growth in collective awareness not only among those whose hearts resonated with revolutionary developments on the continent but also amongst workers, the disenfranchised poor, women, and anti-slavery activists. It was also a time of unprecedented growth in awareness of humans as individuals, of a rights-based political individualism, and of the Romantic individualism of the soul.

Applying a broad title to any literary or historical period is always risky. As much as any group of authors and thinkers may at first appear to have in common, deeper examination tends to reveal complexities and complications. Literature, like history, does not occur in isolation. One idea bleeds into another: revolutions are often old ideas returning under new names; factions develop, and their members deny that they are in any way related to the members of other factions. In its own time, Romanticism—a label never used by any of its writers, but rather first applied by the Victorians looking back on the period—was very frequently a house divided. "Lakers"[1] like Wordsworth and Southey de-

nounced the "Satanic School"[2] of Shelley and Byron, who in turn produced vicious satires of these elders. "The Cockney School"[3] of Londoners Leigh Hunt and John Keats was derided by critics of the day, while writers now long ignored, such as Felicia Hemans, Samuel Rogers, and Thomas Moore, were lauded for their skill and rewarded with tremendous popularity. The Romantic era gains richness and interest if we view it not as a perfect stream but rather more accurately as a thick murmuring torrent of powerful voices that chorused and clashed, that simultaneously sought and struggled. These mingled tones together make up the voice of a movement that changed English literature.

A CHANGING LANGUAGE

Of all the places in which the political clashes of the Romantic period made themselves felt, perhaps the most surprising was in the arena of linguistics. Concern with questions of nationalism and political loyalties reached into the very language of Britain. From 1750 onward, the book market was flooded with pronunciation guides, a deluge inspired by the belief that standardized pronunciation would foster a sense of national unity. In this case, "standard" pronunciation meant the speech of educated urban dwellers. Even as many adhered to the essentially Tory belief that this supposedly standard speech was superior, there grew up a precisely opposite point of view, largely expressed by radical publishers and writers, that in the everyday speech of the common people one might find all that was best and most true about England: honesty, frankness, and English liberty given verbal form. In his *Classical Dictionary of the Vulgar Tongue* (1785), Francis Grose transcribed and celebrated the speech of commoners in their many regional variations, and, in 1818, the radical William Cobbett published his *Grammar of the English Language*, a book which explicitly treated language as a political

---

[1] *Lakers*   The Lake Poets were so known because they resided in the Lake District of northwest England; the three most famous Lake Poets were Wordsworth, Coleridge, and Southey. The name "the Lake School of Poetry" was first used—derisively—in the *Edinburgh Review*.

[2] *Satanic School*   The name was first used by Southey in *A Vision of Judgment* (1821), as a condemnation of writers, Byron and Shelley foremost among them, whose literary output was "characterized by a Satanic spirit of pride and audacious impiety."

[3] *Cockney School*   The term first appeared in negative reviews of Hunt's poetry in *Blackwood's Magazine* in 1817. John Scott, the editor of *The Statesman*, a literary journal founded by Hunt, died in a duel fought over the contemptuous "Cockney" designation.

matter. Cobbett took issue with the "false grammar" that he saw as having been put forward by eighteenth-century "authorities" such as Samuel Johnson, and attacked the grammatical slips as well as the privileged position of kings and nobles in a chapter entitled "Errors and Nonsense in a King's Speech." He addressed his work to the less privileged classes, who he believed should be enabled to participate in political discussions—"to assert with effect the rights and liberties of [their] country." As Cobbett saw it, "tyranny has no enemy so formidable as the pen."

Evidence of the Romantic celebration of "common language" can be found throughout the literature of the period. It accounts in part for the huge popularity of Robert Burns—a poet whose greatest effects come from his mixing of standard English with his native Scots dialect. But it finds its most famous expression in the "Preface" to the 1800 edition of *Lyrical Ballads*. There, Wordsworth writes that

> "men" in "low and rustic life" hourly communicate with the best objects from which the best part of language is originally derived; and because, from their rank in society and the sameness and narrow circle of intercourse, being less under the influence of social vanity they convey their feelings and notions in simple and unelaborated expressions. Accordingly, such language, rising out of repeated experience and regular feelings, is a more permanent, and far more philosophical language …

Still, it is important to note that Wordsworth's opinions on this point represented a minority view, and the Romantic belief in the "philosophical language" of "low and rustic life" was altogether short-lived, becoming less and less widely held. Fifteen years later, one finds Wordsworth's collaborator on *Lyrical Ballads*, Coleridge, writing that

> The best part of human language, properly so called, is derived from reflection on the acts of the mind itself. It is formed by a voluntary appropriation of fixed symbols to internal acts, to processes and results of imagination, the greater part of which have no place in the consciousness of the uneducated man …

As the Romantic period slid into the Victorian and the vogue for rustic or uneducated authors passed away, so the point of view represented in Coleridge's remark came to dominate, and "standard" educated English became more and more widely accepted as an ideal to which all should aspire. However, even as the varieties of English were to some extent dissolving into the forms of standard English over the course of this period, many regional variations persisted, and the forms of standard English itself were far from unchanging.

In pronunciation, the most significant change in "standard British English" was the disappearance of the /r/ sound before many consonants, and before a pause, so that in words such as "harm" or "person," for example, the "r" has since the late eighteenth century been flattened into the smooth "hahm" or "pehson" associated with modern "standard English" pronunciation. Interesting geographical variations have developed over this change, however. In Scotland and in Ireland, as in Canada and most of the United States, the "r" has continued to be sounded in such contexts; these varieties of English are referred to by linguists as "rhotic." In Australia, New Zealand, and South Africa, on the other hand, as well as in some parts of the United States, for instance in Massachusetts and some other parts of New England, non-rhotic forms have come to predominate in much the same way as they have in England.

As the rhymes of English poetry reveal, there were also changes in the sounding of some vowels in the late eighteenth century. In the early eighteenth century, for example, Alexander Pope rhymed "tea" with "obey"; other rhymes suggest that "sea" was pronounced in a manner closer to "say" than to "see." By 1797, however, Coleridge could rhyme "sea" with "free"; and by the end of the Romantic period the older pronunciations of such words had almost certainly died out.

Eighteenth-century habits of capitalization and punctuation were also largely abandoned during this period. Capitalization and typography had generally been considered the business of the compositor rather than that of the author, and the tendency in the early and mid-eighteenth century had been to capitalize (or sometimes italicize) a wide range of nouns. By the end of the century, patterns of usage were coming to approximate the conventions of modern English.

Paragraphing remained less strongly conventionalized than it is now—many writers tended to start new paragraphs very infrequently—and the conventions for writing direct speech were still unstable, with the practice of using double quotation marks surrounding the exact words spoken starting to become common at the end of the eighteenth century. The practice of using single rather than double quotation marks did not become common in Britain until later in the nineteenth century and did not become entirely standardized as British usage until the twentieth century.

History of the Language

and of Print Culture

In an effort to provide for readers a direct sense of the development of the language and of print culture, examples of texts in their original form (and of illustrations) have been provided for each period. A list of these within the Age of Romanticism appears below. Overviews of "the business of literature" and of developments in the history of language during this period appear on pp. 26–30, and a "Contexts" section on various aspects of "Reading, Writing, Publishing" appears on pp. 211–26.

Robert Burns, all poems (1785–99) in original spelling and punctuation, pp. 131–35.

William Blake, all poems (1789–94) in original spelling and punctuation, pp. 63–84.

William Blake, *Songs of Innocence and of Experience*, 1789–94, title page for the full work, p. 63; "The Little Black Boy," p. 64; title page for *Songs of Experience*, p. 67; frontispiece, *Songs of Experience*, p. 67; "The Tyger," p. 69. See also the color insert pages.

William Blake, *The Marriage of Heaven and Hell*, 1793, illustrated plates, pp. 79–83.

Samuel Taylor Coleridge, all poems (1795–1836) in original spelling and punctuation, pp. 279–318.

William Blake, illustrations for John Stedman, *Narrative of Five Years' Expedition against the Revolted Negroes of Surinam*, 1796, pp. 356–57.

William Wordsworth, all poems (1798–1850) in original spelling and punctuation, pp. 139–210.

William Wordsworth, "I wandered lonely as a Cloud," 1807, facsimile of page from *Poems in Two Volumes* with manuscript additions, pp. 170–71.

Thomas Rowlandson, *Dr. Syntax and a Bookseller*, 1812, p. 27.

J. Bluck, *Ackermann's Art Library*, c.1812–15, p. 27.

Felicia Hemans, all poems (1812–29) in original spelling and punctuation, pp. 423–31.

George Gordon, Lord Byron, all poems (1814–23) in original spelling and punctuation, pp. 363–82.

John Keats, all poems (1816–20) in original spelling and punctuation, pp. 434–56.

John Brown, *A Memoir of Robert Blincoe*, title page, 1832, p. 10.

Anna Laetitia Barbauld

_1743 – 1825_

William Blake admired Anna Laetitia Barbauld's poetry, as did Samuel Taylor Coleridge, who walked forty miles to meet her, and William Wordsworth, who said about the Barbauld poem "Life": "I am not in the habit of grudging people their good things, but I wish I had written those [final] lines." Although born in the provinces, Barbauld became in her own day a leading figure in London literary life. She composed innovative and influential poetry, hymns, children's literature, political pamphlets, essays, and works of literary criticism. She also established herself as a leading educator and political and social activist. By the time of her death, however, her literary reputation had begun to fade, and she was largely forgotten until recent critical work renewed interest in this talented and versatile professional writer.

Anna Laetitia Aikin was born in Leicestershire to Jane Jennings and John Aikin, a nonconformist Presbyterian minister and schoolteacher at the Warrington Dissenting Academy in Yorkshire. Schooled by her father, she was a precocious child who studied the classics early in life. In her late teens she became acquainted with the influential educator and scientist Joseph Priestley and developed a lasting friendship with him and his wife. Barbauld was inspired by Priestley's poetry, and he was impressed by hers; he eventually encouraged her to publish her first volume, _Poems_ (1773). This collection of lyrics, hymns, epistles, and mock-heroic poems, published under her birth name, went through five editions in four years and received considerable critical acclaim, _The Monthly Review_ calling it a "great accession to the literary world." That same year Barbauld printed _Miscellaneous Pieces in Prose_ with her brother, John Aikin (later the editor of a radical journal, _Monthly Magazine_).

Living at her father's school prepared Barbauld to run her own boys' boarding school, which she started with her husband, the dissenting clergyman Rochemont Barbauld, whom she married in 1774. During this period she wrote her popular and influential _Lessons for Children_ (1787–88) and _Hymns in Prose for Children_ (1787), designed for the very young. Both went through many printings and continued to be read in the United States and England until the close of the century. During the school breaks Barbauld and her husband often stayed in London; she became acquainted with important writers such as Joanna Baillie, Hannah More, and, in later years, Walter Scott, William Wordsworth, and Maria Edgeworth (who was briefly her pupil, and who became a friend). Barbauld associated with a variety of religious dissenters and was herself, broadly speaking, Unitarian in her views, though she seems to have been more concerned with the influence of religion on human sympathies than she was with theological issues (such as the Unitarian doctrine that God should be regarded as a unity rather than as a trinity of father, son, and holy spirit).

By 1785 her husband's mental instability required them to close the school (he eventually became violent and later committed suicide), and from this point on, Barbauld committed herself solely to literary work. In her political pamphlets and essays of the 1790s, Barbauld addressed ethics, education, and political economy, and argued for freedom of religion and conscience—a cause dear to the hearts of Dissenters. She also argued strongly for the abolition of slavery (at a moment when the movement had suffered a setback) in her verse *Epistle to William Wilberforce* (1791); and in the essay *Sins of Government, Sins of Nation* (1793) she derided the British government for its involvement in the war against France. Barbauld then turned to editorial work, producing the first collection of *The Correspondence of Samuel Richardson* (1804), which includes her biography of the author. She also published *The British Novelists* (1810), a fifty-volume collection featuring the work of 28 novelists, both male and female, along with Barbauld's biographical and critical prefaces. In her general introduction to *On the Origin and Progress of Novel-Writing*, she argued for the value of novels for both education and enjoyment. This was pioneering in its recognition of the novel as a serious genre.

In 1812 Barbauld published her final work, the prophetic poem *Eighteen Hundred and Eleven*. Written in a pessimistic tone, the poem traces the cyclical rise and fall of national empires, indicts Britain for its involvement in the war with France, and predicts the fall of the British Empire. At the end of the poem, "Genius" leaves for America, the nation Barbauld suggests will replace Britain as the new empire. The poem elicited widespread criticism for what was deemed its "anti-patriotism." John Wilson Croker's abusive attack in the *Quarterly Review* used to be credited with effectively ending Barbauld's publishing career, but this is not accurate: she continued writing into the 1820s. After her death in 1825 her niece published two collections of her works.

⌘ ⌘ ⌘

Washing Day

> … and their voice,
> Turning again towards childish treble, pipes
> And whistles in its sound.[1]

The Muses[2] are turned gossips; they have lost
The buskined step,[3] and clear high-sounding phrase,
Language of gods. Come, then, domestic Muse,
In slipshod measure loosely prattling on
5 Of farm or orchard, pleasant curds and cream,
Or drowning flies, or shoe lost in the mire
By little whimpering boy, with rueful face;
Come, Muse, and sing the dreaded Washing-Day.
Ye who beneath the yoke of wedlock bend,
10 With bowed soul, full well ye ken° the day   *know*
Which week, smooth sliding after week, brings on
Too soon; for to that day nor peace belongs
Nor comfort; ere the first grey streak of dawn,

The red-armed washers come and chase repose.
15 Nor pleasant smile, nor quaint device of mirth,
E'er visited that day; the very cat,
From the wet kitchen scared, and reeking hearth,
Visits the parlour, an unwonted° guest.   *infrequent*
The silent breakfast meal is soon dispatched
20 Uninterrupted, save by anxious looks
Cast at the lowering sky, if sky should lower.
From that last evil, O preserve us, heavens!
For should the skies pour down, adieu to all
Remains of quiet; then expect to hear
25 Of sad disasters—dirt and gravel stains
Hard to efface, and loaded lines at once
Snapped short—and linen-horse° by dog   *clotheshorse*
    thrown down,
And all the petty miseries of life.
Saints have been calm while stretched upon the rack,
30 And Guatimozin[4] smiled on burning coals;
But never yet did housewife notable
Greet with a smile a rainy washing-day.
But grant the welkin° fair, require not thou   *sky*
Who call'st thyself perchance the master there,
35 Or study swept, or nicely dusted coat,

---

[1] *and their voice … sound* Cf. Shakespeare's *As You Like It* 2.7.161–63: "and his big manly voice, / Turning again toward childish treble, pipes / And whistles in his sound."

[2] *Muses* In classical mythology, nine goddesses who presided over learning and the arts.

[3] *buskined step* I.e., tragic mode. Actors in Athenian tragedy wore buskins, or high, thick-soled boots.

[4] *Guatimozin* Cuauhtémoc, the last Aztec emperor (c. 1495–1522), was captured and tortured by Cortés's Spanish conquistadors when they invaded the Aztec capital (now Mexico City).

Or usual 'tendance; ask not, indiscreet,
Thy stockings mended, though the yawning rents
Gape wide as Erebus,[1] nor hope to find
Some snug recess impervious; should'st thou try
40 The 'customed garden walks, thine eye shall rue
The budding fragrance of thy tender shrubs,
Myrtle or rose, all crushed beneath the weight
Of coarse checked apron, with impatient hand
Twitched off when showers impend: or crossing lines
45 Shall mar thy musings, as the wet cold sheet
Flaps in thy face abrupt. Woe to the friend
Whose evil stars have urged him forth to claim
On such a day the hospitable rites;
Looks, blank at best, and stinted courtesy,
50 Shall he receive. Vainly he feeds his hopes
With dinner of roast chicken, savoury pie,
Or tart or pudding:—pudding he nor tart
That day shall eat; nor, though the husband try,
Mending what can't be helped, to kindle mirth
55 From cheer deficient, shall his consort's brow
Clear up propitious; the unlucky guest
In silence dines, and early slinks away.
I well remember, when a child, the awe
This day struck into me; for then the maids,
60 I scarce knew why, looked cross, and drove me from
    them;
Nor soft caress could I obtain, nor hope
Usual indulgencies; jelly or creams,
Relic of costly suppers, and set by
For me their petted one; or buttered toast,
65 When butter was forbid; or thrilling tale
Of ghost, or witch, or murder—so I went
And sheltered me beside the parlour fire:
There my dear grandmother, eldest of forms,
Tended the little ones, and watched from harm,
70 Anxiously fond, though oft her spectacles
With elfin cunning hid, and oft the pins
Drawn from her ravelled stocking, might have soured
One less indulgent.—
At intervals my mother's voice was heard,
75 Urging dispatch; briskly the work went on,
All hands employed to wash, to rinse, to wring,

To fold, and starch, and clap, and iron, and plait.[2]
Then would I sit me down, and ponder much
Why washings were. Sometimes through hollow
    bole°   bowl
80 Of pipe amused we blew, and sent aloft
The floating bubbles, little dreaming then
To see, Mongolfier,[3] thy silken ball
Ride buoyant through the clouds—so near approach
The sports of children and the toils of men.
85 Earth, air, and sky, and ocean, hath its bubbles,[4]
And verse is one of them—this most of all.
—1797

Eighteen Hundred and Eleven,[5] A Poem

Still the loud death drum, thundering from afar,
O'er the vext nations pours the storm of war:
To the stern call still Britain bends her ear,
Feeds the fierce strife, the alternate hope and fear;
5 Bravely, though vainly, dares to strive with fate,
And seeks by turns to prop each sinking state.
Colossal Power[6] with overwhelming force
Bears down each fort of freedom in its course;
Prostrate she lies beneath the despot's sway,
10 While the hushed nations curse him—and obey.
    Bounteous in vain, with frantic man at strife,
Glad Nature pours the means—the joys of life;
In vain with orange blossoms scents the gale,
The hills with olives clothes, with corn the vale;
15 Man calls to Famine,[7] nor invokes in vain,

---

[1] *Erebus* In Greek mythology, a place below the earth that the dead pass through on their way to Hades, or the underworld.

[2] *clap* Smooth; *plait* Fold.

[3] *Mongolfier* Montgolfier brothers, from Annonay, France, who invented and launched the first hot-air balloon in 1783.

[4] *Earth … bubbles* Cf. Shakespeare's *Macbeth* 1.3.83: "The earth hath bubbles, as the water has."

[5] *Eighteen Hundred and Eleven* Britain's war with France, begun in 1793, would not end until the Battle of Waterloo in 1815. By 1811, Russia, Austria, and Spain, Britain's allies, had already capitulated to the strength of Napoleon's army; Britain was in financial distress; and King George III had been declared insane.

[6] *Colossal Power* Napoleon Bonaparte (1769–1821), emperor of France.

[7] *Famine* In 1811 there was widespread hunger in Britain and much of Europe due to crop failures in the preceding years, as well as the necessity of providing food for soldiers.

Disease and Rapine° follow in her train;   *plunder*
The tramp of marching hosts disturbs the plough,
The sword, not sickle, reaps the harvest now,[1]
And where the soldier gleans the scant supply,
20 The helpless peasant but retires to die;
No laws his hut from licensed outrage shield,
And war's least horror is the
            ensanguined° field.   *blood-stained*
        Fruitful in vain, the matron counts with pride
The blooming youths that grace her honoured side;
25 No son returns to press her widowed hand,
Her fallen blossoms strew a foreign strand.
—Fruitful in vain, she boasts her virgin race,
Whom cultured arts adorn and gentlest grace;
Defrauded of its homage, Beauty mourns,
30 And the rose withers on its virgin thorns.
Frequent, some stream obscure, some uncouth name
By deeds of blood is lifted into fame;
Oft o'er the daily page some soft one bends
To learn the fate of husband, brothers, friends,
35 Or the spread map with anxious eye explores,
Its dotted boundaries and penciled shores,
Asks where the spot that wrecked her bliss is found,
And learns its name but to detest the sound.
        And think'st thou, Britain, still to sit at ease,
40 An island queen amidst thy subject seas,
While the vext billows, in their distant roar,
But soothe thy slumbers, and but kiss thy shore?
To sport in wars, while danger keeps aloof,
Thy grassy turf unbruised by hostile hoof?
45 So sing thy flatterers; but, Britain, know,
Thou who hast shared the guilt must share the woe.
Nor distant is the hour; low murmurs spread,
And whispered fears, creating what they dread;
Ruin, as with an earthquake shock, is here,
50 There, the heart-witherings of unuttered fear,
And that sad death, whence most affection bleeds,
Which sickness, only of the soul, precedes.
Thy baseless wealth dissolves in air away,[2]

Like mists that melt before the morning ray:
55 No more on crowded mart or busy street
Friends, meeting friends, with cheerful hurry greet;
Sad, on the ground thy princely merchants bend
Their altered looks, and evil days portend,
And fold their arms, and watch with anxious breast
60 The tempest blackening in the distant West.[3]
        Yes, thou must droop; thy Midas dream is o'er;
The golden tide of Commerce leaves thy shore,
Leaves thee to prove the alternate ills that haunt
Enfeebling Luxury and ghastly Want;
65 Leaves thee, perhaps, to visit distant lands,
And deal the gifts of Heaven with equal hands.
        Yet, O my country, name beloved, revered,
By every tie that binds the soul endeared,
Whose image to my infant senses came
70 Mixt with Religion's light and Freedom's holy flame!
If prayers may not avert, if 'tis thy fate
To rank amongst the names that once were great,
Not like the dim cold crescent[4] shalt thou fade,
Thy debt to Science and the Muse unpaid;
75 Thine are the laws surrounding states revere,
Thine the full harvest of the mental year,
Thine the bright stars in Glory's sky that shine,
And arts that make it life to live are thine.
If westward streams the light that leaves thy shores,
80 Still from thy lamp the streaming radiance pours.
Wide spreads thy race from Ganges[5] to the pole,
O'er half the western world thy accents roll:
Nations beyond the Appalachian hills[6]
Thy hand has planted and thy spirit fills:
85 Soon as their gradual progress shall impart
The finer sense of morals and of art,
Thy stores of knowledge the new states shall know,
And think thy thoughts, and with thy fancy glow;

---

1 *The sword ... now* Napoleon sent his soldiers out unencumbered with baggage; consequently, most of them were starving and were forced to steal food.

2 *Thy baseless wealth ... away* 1810 saw the failure of many British businesses, and in 1811, the country itself was threatened with financial collapse.

3 *The tempest ... West* Relations had been strained between England and the United States since the French Revolution; Barbauld here foresees the beginning of the War of 1812.

4 *crescent* Symbol of the Ottoman Empire, which had been in decline throughout the eighteenth and into the nineteenth century.

5 *Ganges* Sacred river of India.

6 *Appalachian hills* Mountain range in the eastern United States.

Thy Lockes, thy Paleys[1] shall instruct their youth,
90   Thy leading star direct their search for truth;
Beneath the spreading platan's[2] tent-like shade,
Or by Missouri's rushing waters laid,
"Old father Thames" shall be the poet's theme,
Of Hagley's woods[3] the enamoured virgin dream,
95   And Milton's tones the raptured ear enthrall,
Mixt with the roar of Niagara's fall;
In Thomson's glass[4] the ingenuous youth shall learn
A fairer face of Nature to discern;
Nor of the bards that swept the British lyre
100   Shall fade one laurel, or one note expire.
Then, loved Joanna,[5] to admiring eyes
Thy storied groups in scenic pomp shall rise;
Their high souled strains and Shakespeare's noble rage
Shall with alternate passion shake the stage.
105   Some youthful Basil[6] from thy moral lay
With stricter hand his fond desires shall sway;
Some Ethwald,[7] as the fleeting shadows pass,
Start at his likeness in the mystic glass;
The tragic Muse resume her just control,
110   With pity and with terror purge the soul,
While wide o'er transatlantic realms thy name
Shall live in light, and gather all its fame.
     Where wanders Fancy down the lapse of years
Shedding o'er imaged woes untimely tears?
115   Fond moody Power! as hopes—as fears prevail,
She longs, or dreads, to lift the awful veil,
On visions of delight now loves to dwell,
Now hears the shriek of woe or Freedom's knell:
Perhaps, she says, long ages past away,
120   And set in western waves our closing day,

Night, Gothic night, again may shade the plains
Where Power is seated, and where Science reigns;
England, the seat of arts, be only known
By the gray ruin and the mouldering stone;
125   That time may tear the garland from her brow,
And Europe sit in dust, as Asia now.
     Yet then the ingenuous youth whom Fancy fires
With pictured glories of illustrious sires,
With duteous zeal their pilgrimage shall take
130   From the Blue Mountains,° or Ontario's lake,   *in Pennsylvania*
With fond adoring steps to press the sod
By statesmen, sages, poets, heroes trod;
On Isis' banks[8] to draw inspiring air,
From Runnymede[9] to send the patriot's prayer;
135   In pensive thought, where Cam's slow waters[10] wind,
To meet those shades that ruled the realms of mind;
In silent halls to sculptured marbles bow,
And hang fresh wreaths round Newton's[11] awful brow.
Oft shall they seek some peasant's homely shed,
140   Who toils, unconscious of the mighty dead,
To ask where Avon's[12] winding waters stray,
And thence a knot of wild flowers bear away;
Anxious enquire where Clarkson,[13] friend of man,
Or all-accomplished Jones[14] his race began;
145   If of the modest mansion aught remains
Where Heaven and Nature prompted Cowper's[15] strains;
Where Roscoe, to whose patriot breast belong
The Roman virtue and the Tuscan song,
Led Ceres to the black and barren moor

---

[1] *Lockes … Paleys* Men as eminent as John Locke and William Paley. John Locke (1632–1704), English philosopher who wrote about political, intellectual, and religious freedom and William Paley (1743–1805), English theologian and moral philosopher, who defended Christianity in many of his texts.

[2] *platan* Plane tree.

[3] *Hagley's woods* Cf. *The Seasons*, "Spring," in which James Thomson writes about Lord Lyttleton's lush estate in Worcestershire.

[4] *glass* Mirror; i.e., nature as reflected in Thomson's *The Seasons*.

[5] *Joanna* Scottish playwright Joanna Baillie (1762–1851), who was often compared with Shakespeare.

[6] *Basil* Character in Baillie's tragedy *Count Basil* (1798).

[7] *Ethwald* Character in Baillie's tragedy *Ethwald* (1802).

[8] *Isis' banks* Bank of the River Thames at Oxford, known as the Isis.

[9] *Runnymede* Site where King John signed the Magna Carta (1215).

[10] *Cam's slow waters* River at Cambridge.

[11] *Newton* Sir Isaac Newton (1642–1727), mathematician, physicist, and professor at Cambridge University.

[12] *Avon* River that runs through Stratford, where Shakespeare was born.

[13] *Clarkson* Thomas Clarkson (1760–1846), abolitionist, whose work helped to end the British slave trade in 1807.

[14] *Jones* Sir William Jones (1746–94), judge and scholar, who promoted Asian and Sanskrit studies.

[15] *Cowper* William Cowper (1731–1800), English poet.

150 Where Ceres never gained a wreath before:[1]
With curious search their pilgrim steps shall rove
By many a ruined tower and proud alcove,
Shall listen for those strains that soothed of yore
Thy rock, stern Skiddaw, and thy fall, Lodore;[2]
155 Feast with Dun Edin's° classic brow their sight,   *Edinburgh's*
And visit "Melrose by the pale moonlight."[3]
        But who their mingled feelings shall pursue
When London's faded glories rise to view?
The mighty city, which by every road,
160 In floods of people poured itself abroad;
Ungirt by walls, irregularly great,
No jealous drawbridge, and no closing gate;
Whose merchants (such the state which commerce brings)
Sent forth their mandates to dependant kings;
165 Streets, where the turbaned Moslem, bearded Jew,
And woolly Afric, met the brown Hindu;
Where through each vein spontaneous plenty flowed,
Where Wealth enjoyed, and Charity bestowed.
Pensive and thoughtful shall the wanderers greet
170 Each splendid square, and still, untrodden street;
Or of some crumbling turret, mined by time,
The broken stairs with perilous step shall climb,
Thence stretch their view the wide horizon round,
By scattered hamlets trace its ancient bound,
175 And, choked no more with fleets, fair Thames survey
Through reeds and sedge pursue his idle way.
        With throbbing bosoms shall the wanderers tread
The hallowed mansions of the silent dead,
Shall enter the long isle and vaulted dome
180 Where Genius and where Valour find a home;[4]
Awestruck, midst chill sepulchral marbles breathe,
Where all above is still, as all beneath;
Bend at each antique shrine, and frequent turn

To clasp with fond delight some sculptured urn,
185 The ponderous mass of Johnson's[5] form to greet,
Or breathe the prayer at Howard's[6] sainted feet.
        Perhaps some Briton, in whose musing mind
Those ages live which Time has cast behind,
To every spot shall lead his wondering guests
190 On whose known site the beam of glory rests:
Here Chatham's eloquence in thunder broke,
Here Fox persuaded, or here Garrick[7] spoke;
Shall boast how Nelson, fame and death in view,
To wonted victory led his ardent crew,
195 In England's name enforced, with loftiest tone,
Their duty—and too well fulfilled his own:[8]
How gallant Moore,[9] as ebbing life dissolved,
But hoped his country had his fame absolved.[10]
Or call up sages whose capacious mind
200 Left in its course a track of light behind;
Point where mute crowds on Davy's[11] lips reposed,
And Nature's coyest secrets were disclosed;
Join with their Franklin, Priestley's[12] injured name,
Whom, then, each continent shall proudly claim.
205   Oft shall the strangers turn their eager feet

---

[1] *Roscoe ... before* William Roscoe (1753–1831), historian and MP, who promoted the use of the moors for agriculture; *Ceres* Roman goddess of agriculture.

[2] *Skiddaw ... Lodore* Mountain and waterfall in the Lake District, England.

[3] *Melrose ... moonlight* Site of the beautiful Melrose Abbey ruins in the Scottish Borderlands; cf. Sir Walter Scott's *The Lay of the Last Minstrel* 2.1: "If thou woud'st view fair Melrose aright, / Go visit it by the pale moonlight." See also p. 18 in the Introduction to the Age of Romanticism.

[4] *vaulted dome ... home* St. Paul's Cathedral, home to statues of eminent British men and women.

[5] *Johnson* Samuel Johnson (1709–84), scholar and author of *The Dictionary of the English Language*.

[6] *Howard* John Howard (1726–90), prison reformer and philanthropist.

[7] *Chatham* William Pitt, 1st Earl of Chatham (1708–78), prime minister and famous patriot and orator; *Fox* Charles James Fox (1749–1806), parliamentarian and orator; *Garrick* David Garrick (1717–79), famous English actor and dramatist.

[8] *Nelson ... his own* Admiral Horatio Nelson, English war hero, spoke these famous words before he died at the Battle of Trafalgar in 1805: "England expects that every man will do his duty."

[9] *Moore* Sir John Moore (1761–1809), general who led a retreat during the Napoleonic Wars; he saved his troops, but died in the process.

[10] [Barbauld's note] "I hope England will be satisfied," were the last words of General Moore.

[11] *Davy* Sir Humphrey Davy (1778–1829), physicist and chemist, whose lectures were renowned.

[12] *Franklin* Benjamin Franklin (1706–90), American scientist, inventor, and statesman; *Priestley* Joseph Priestley (1733–1804), English scientist and theologian, whose correspondence with Franklin led to Priestley's experimentation with and discoveries regarding electricity; Priestley was persecuted for his support of the French and American Revolutions, which led to his emigration from England to America.

The rich remains of ancient art to greet,
The pictured walls with critic eye explore,
And Reynolds be what Raphael[1] was before.
On spoils from every clime their eyes shall gaze,
210 Egyptian granites and the Etruscan vase;
And when midst fallen London, they survey
The stone where Alexander's ashes lay,[2]
Shall own with humbled pride the lesson just
By Time's slow finger written in the dust.
215   There walks a Spirit o'er the peopled earth,
Secret his progress is, unknown his birth;
Moody and viewless° as the changing wind,   *invisible*
No force arrests his foot, no chains can bind;
Where'er he turns, the human brute awakes,
220 And, roused to better life, his sordid hut forsakes:
He thinks, he reasons, glows with purer fires,
Feels finer wants, and burns with new desires:
Obedient Nature follows where he leads;
The steaming marsh is changed to fruitful meads;
225 The beasts retire from man's asserted reign,
And prove his kingdom was not given in vain.
Then from its bed is drawn the ponderous ore,
Then Commerce pours her gifts on every shore.
Then Babel's towers[3] and terraced gardens rise,
230 And pointed obelisks invade the skies;
The prince commands, in Tyrian purple drest,
And Egypt's virgins weave the linen vest.
Then spans the graceful arch the roaring tide,
And stricter bounds the cultured fields divide.
235 Then kindles Fancy, then expands the heart,
Then blow° the flowers of Genius and of Art;   *blossom*
Saints, Heroes, Sages, who the land adorn,
Seem rather to descend than to be born;
Whilst History, midst the rolls consigned to fame,
240 With pen of adamant inscribes their name.
     The Genius now forsakes the favoured shore,
And hates, capricious, what he loved before;

Then empires fall to dust, then arts decay,
And wasted realms enfeebled despots sway;
245 Even Nature's changed; without his fostering smile
Ophir[4] no gold, no plenty yields the Nile;
The thirsty sand absorbs the useless rill,°   *stream*
And spotted plagues from putrid fens distill.
In desert solitudes then Tadmor[5] sleeps,
250 Stern Marius then o'er fallen Carthage weeps;[6]
Then with enthusiast love the pilgrim roves
To seek his footsteps in forsaken groves,
Explores the fractured arch, the ruined tower,
Those limbs disjointed of gigantic power;
255 Still at each step he dreads the adder's sting,
The Arab's javelin, or the tiger's spring;
With doubtful caution treads the echoing ground,
And asks where Troy or Babylon[7] is found.
     And now the vagrant Power no more detains
260 The vale of Tempe, or Ausonian plains;[8]
Northward he throws the animating ray,
O'er Celtic nations bursts the mental day:
And, as some playful child the mirror turns,
Now here now there the moving lustre burns;
265 Now o'er his changeful fancy more prevail
Batavia's dykes than Arno's[9] purple vale,
And stinted suns, and rivers bound with frost,
Than Enna's plains or Baia's[10] viny coast;
Venice the Adriatic weds in vain,
270 And Death sits brooding o'er Campania's[11] plain;

---

[1] *Reynolds … Raphael* Sir Joshua Reynolds (1723–92), eminent English portrait artist, and Raphael (1483–1520), famous Italian Renaissance painter and architect.

[2] *stone … lay* The British Museum mistakenly believed it had purchased the tomb of Alexander the Great.

[3] *Babel's towers* Cf. Genesis 11.3–9. The Babylonians attempted to create a tower that would reach heaven; God punished them by giving them different languages and scattering them around the earth.

[4] *Ophir* Cf. 1 Kings 9.28: "And they came to Ophir, and fetched from thence gold."

[5] *Tadmor* Biblical land in ancient Syria.

[6] *Marius … weeps* Gaius Marius (157–86 BCE), Roman Consul and general who was once called the "savior of Rome"; upon aging and falling from power, he was said to have wept among the ruins of Carthage.

[7] *Troy* Ancient city in Asia Minor, subject of the Trojan War in Homer's *Iliad*; *Babylon* Ancient Mesopotamian city known for its wealth and beauty, destroyed in 689 BCE.

[8] *vale of Tempe* Valley in Greece celebrated by ancient poets for its beauty; *Ausonian plains* Virgil called Italy "Ausonia."

[9] *Batavia* Republic, now the Netherlands; *Arno* River in Italy.

[10] *Enna* Sicilian valley; *Baia* Italian village on the Bay of Naples, celebrated for its spas in Roman times.

[11] *Campania* Italian province whose plains were marshy and malarial.

O'er Baltic shores and through Hercynian groves,[1]
Stirring the soul, the mighty impulse moves;
Art plies his tools, and Commerce spreads her sail,
And wealth is wafted in each shifting gale.
275 The sons of Odin[2] tread on Persian looms,
And Odin's daughters breathe distilled perfumes;
Loud minstrel bards, in Gothic halls, rehearse
The Runic rhyme, and "build the lofty verse:"[3]
The Muse, whose liquid notes were wont to swell
280 To the soft breathings of the Aeolian shell,[4]
Submits, reluctant, to the harsher tone,
And scarce believes the altered voice her own.
And now, where Caesar saw with proud disdain
The wattled hut and skin of azure stain,[5]
285 Corinthian columns rear their graceful forms,
And light verandas brave the wintry storms,
While British tongues the fading fame prolong
Of Tully's eloquence and Maro's[6] song.
Where once Bonduca whirled the scythed car,
290 And the fierce matrons raised the shriek of war,[7]
Light forms beneath transparent muslins float,
And tutored voices swell the artful note.
Light-leaved acacias and the shady plane
And spreading cedar grace the woodland reign;
295 While crystal walls the tenderer plants confine,
The fragrant orange and the nectared pine;
The Syrian grape there hangs her rich festoons,
Nor asks for purer air, or brighter noons:
Science and Art urge on the useful toil,
300 New mold a climate and create the soil,

Subdue the rigour of the northern Bear,[8]
O'er polar climes shed aromatic air,
On yielding Nature urge their new demands,
And ask not gifts but tribute at her hands.
305   London exults:—on London Art bestows
Her summer ices and her winter rose;
Gems of the East her mural crown adorn,
And Plenty at her feet pours forth her horn;[9]
While even the exiles her just laws disclaim,
310 People a continent, and build a name:
August she sits, and with extended hands
Holds forth the book of life to distant lands.
    But fairest flowers expand but to decay;
The worm is in thy core, thy glories pass away;
315 Arts, arms and wealth destroy the fruits they bring;
Commerce, like beauty, knows no second spring.
Crime walks thy streets, Fraud earns her unblest bread,
O'er want and woe thy gorgeous robe is spread,
And angel charities in vain oppose:
320 With grandeur's growth the mass of misery grows.
For see,—to other climes the Genius soars,
He turns from Europe's desolated shores;
And lo, even now, midst mountains wrapt in storm,
On Andes' heights he shrouds his awful form;
325 On Chimborazo's[10] summits treads sublime,
Measuring in lofty thought the march of Time;
Sudden he calls:—"'Tis now the hour!" he cries,
Spreads his broad hand, and bids the nations rise.
La Plata[11] hears amidst her torrents' roar,
330 Potosi[12] hears it, as she digs the ore:
Ardent, the Genius fans the noble strife,
And pours through feeble souls a higher life,
Shouts to the mingled tribes from sea to sea,
And swears—Thy world, Columbus, shall be free.
—1812

[1] *Hercynian groves*   Black Forest in Germany.

[2] *Odin*   Supreme Norse god.

[3] *build the lofty verse*   From Milton's *Lycidas* (10–11): "He knew /
Himself to sing, and build the lofty rhyme."

[4] *Aeolian shell*   Aeolian harp, a musical instrument that produces
sound when the wind passes through its strings.

[5] *Caesar … stain*   Cf. Julius Caesar's *The Gallic Wars* 5.14: "All the
Britains, indeed, dye themselves with wood, which occasions a bluish
color, and thereby have a more terrible appearance in fight."

[6] *Tully*   Marcus Tullius Cicero (106–43 BCE), Roman orator,
philosopher, and politician; *Maro*   Publius Vergilius Maro, or
Virgil (70–19 BCE), Roman poet, author of the *Aeneid*.

[7] *Bonduca … war*   Queen of the ancient Iceni Celts, Boadicea
(sometimes written as "Bonduca" or "Boudicca") led a massive
rebellion against the Romans in about 60 CE; she committed suicide
upon the failure of the mission.

[8] *northern Bear*   Ursa Minor, a constellation that includes the
North Star.

[9] *horn*   Horn of plenty, or cornucopia, contains an abundance of
the essentials and luxuries of life.

[10] *Chimborazo*   Volcanic mountain in Ecuador.

[11] *La Plata*   City in Argentina.

[12] *Potosi*   City in Bolivia. All three countries were home to movements resistant to colonial rule. The region was famous for its gold
deposits.

On the Death of the Princess Charlotte[1]

Yes, Britain mourns, as with electric touch
For youth, for love, for happiness destroyed,
Her universal population melts
In grief spontaneous, and hard hearts are moved,
5 And rough unpolished natures learn to feel
For those they envied, leveled in the dust
By Fate's impartial stroke; and pulpits sound
With vanity and woe to earthly goods,
And urge and dry the tear. Yet one there is
10 Who midst this general burst of grief remains
In strange tranquility;[2] whom not the stir
And long drawn murmurs of the gathering crowd,
That by his very windows trail the pomp
Of hearse,[3] and blazoned arms, and long array
15 Of sad funereal rites, nor the loud groans
And deep-felt anguish of a husband's[4] heart,
Can move to mingle with this flood one tear.
In careless apathy, perhaps in mirth
He wears the day. Yet is he near in blood,
20 The very stem on which this blossom grew,
And at his knees she fondled, in the charm
And grace spontaneous which alone belongs
To untaught infancy. Yet oh forbear!
Nor deem him hard of heart; for awful, struck
25 By heaven's severest visitation, sad,
Like a scathed oak amidst the forest trees,
Lonely he stands—leaves bud, and shoot, and fall;
He holds no sympathy with living nature
Or time's incessant change. Then, in this hour,
30 While pensive thought is busy with the woes
And restless cares of poor humanity,
Think then, oh think of him, and breathe one prayer,
From the full tide of sorrow spare one tear
For him who does not weep!
—1819

The Rights of Woman[5]

Yes, injured Woman! rise, assert thy right!
Woman! too long degraded, scorned, opprest;
O born to rule in partial° Law's despite,   biased
Resume thy native empire o'er the breast!

5 Go forth arrayed in panoply[6] divine;
That angel pureness which admits no stain;
Go, bid proud Man his boasted rule resign,
And kiss the golden sceptre of thy reign.

Go, gird thyself with grace; collect thy store
10 Of bright artillery glancing from afar;
Soft melting tones thy thundering cannon's roar,
Blushes and fears thy magazine° of war.   storehouse

Thy rights are empire: urge no meaner claim,—
Felt, not defined, and if debated, lost;
15 Like sacred mysteries, which withheld from fame,
Shunning discussion, are revered the most.

Try all that wit and art suggest to bend
Of thy imperial foe the stubborn knee;
Make treacherous Man thy subject, not thy friend;
20 Thou mayst command, but never canst be free.

Awe the licentious, and restrain the rude;
Soften the sullen, clear the cloudy brow:
Be, more than princes' gifts, thy favours sued;—
She hazards all, who will the least allow.

25 But hope not, courted idol of mankind,
On this proud eminence secure to stay;
Subduing and subdued, thou soon shalt find
Thy coldness soften, and thy pride give way.

---

[1] *Death ... Charlotte* The popular Princess Charlotte Augusta (1796–1817), daughter of the Prince of Wales, the future King George IV, died at the age of 21 of complications from childbirth.

[2] *one there is ... tranquility* Charlotte's father is said to have openly expressed his disdain of his daughter, linked, no doubt, to his feud with her mother.

[3] *by his very windows ... hearse* The Prince of Wales did not attend his daughter's funeral.

[4] *husband* Leopold of Saxe-Coburg, whom Charlotte married in 1816.

---

[5] *The Rights of Woman* Cf. Mary Wollstonecraft's *A Vindication of the Rights of Woman* (1792).

[6] *panoply* Lavish ceremonial attire.

30 Then, then, abandon each ambitious thought,
Conquest or rule thy heart shall feebly move,
In Nature's school, by her soft maxims taught,
That separate rights are lost in mutual love.
—1825

The Baby-House

Dear Agatha,[1] I give you joy,
And much admire your pretty toy,
A mansion in itself complete
And fitted to give guests a treat;
5 With couch and table, chest and chair,
The bed or supper to prepare;
We almost wish to change ourselves
To fairy forms of tripping elves,
To press the velvet couch and eat
10 From tiny cups the sugared meat.
    I much suspect that many a sprite
Inhabits it at dead of night;
That, as they dance, the listening ear
The pat of fairy feet might hear;
15 That, just as you have said your prayers,
They hurry-scurry down the stairs:
And you'll do well to try to find
Tester[2] or ring they've left behind.
    But think not, Agatha, you own
20 That toy, a Baby-house, alone;
For many a sumptuous one is found
To press an ampler space of ground.
The broad-based Pyramid that stands
Casting its shade in distant lands,
25 Which asked some mighty nation's toil
With mountain-weight to press the soil,
And there has raised its head sublime
Through eras of uncounted time—
Its use if asked, 'tis only said,
30 A Baby-house to lodge the dead.
Nor less beneath more genial skies
The domes of pomp and folly rise,
Whose sun through diamond windows streams,

While gems and gold reflect his beams;
35 Where tapestry clothes the storied wall,
And fountains spout and waters fall;
The peasant faints beneath his load,
Nor tastes the grain his hand have sowed,
While scarce a nation's wealth avails
40 To raise thy Baby-house, Versailles.[3]
And Baby-houses oft appear
On British ground, of prince or peer;
Awhile their stately heads they raise,
The admiring traveller stops to gaze;
45 He looks again—where are they now?
Gone to the hammer[4] or the plough:
Then trees, the pride of ages, fall,
And naked stands the pictured wall;
And treasured coins from distant lands
50 Must feel the touch of sordid hands;
And gems, of classic stores the boast,
Fall to the cry of—Who bids most?
Then do not, Agatha, repine
That cheaper Baby-house is thine.
—1825

The Caterpillar

No, helpless thing, I cannot harm thee now;
Depart in peace, thy little life is safe,
For I have scanned thy form with curious eye,
Noted the silver line that streaks thy back,
5 The azure and the orange that divide
Thy velvet sides; thee, houseless wanderer,
My garment has enfolded, and my arm
Felt the light pressure of thy hairy feet;
Thou hast curled round my finger; from its tip,
10 Precipitous descent! with stretched out neck,
Bending thy head in airy vacancy,
This way and that, inquiring, thou hast seemed
To ask protection; now, I cannot kill thee.
Yet I have sworn perdition to thy race,
15 And recent from the slaughter am I come
Of tribes and embryo nations: I have sought

---

[1] *Agatha* Though Agatha has not been definitively identified, she is believed to have been the daughter of a friend of Barbauld's.

[2] *Tester* Sixpence coin.

[3] *Versailles* The famously self-indulgent palace of the French king Louis XIV (1638–1715).

[4] *the hammer* Auctioneer's gavel; that is, auctioned for sale.

With sharpened eye and persecuting zeal,
Where, folded in their silken webs they lay
Thriving and happy; swept them from the tree
20 And crushed whole families beneath my foot;
Or, sudden, poured on their devoted heads
The vials of destruction.[1]—This I've done,
Nor felt the touch of pity: but when thou—
A single wretch, escaped the general doom,
25 Making me feel and clearly recognise
Thine individual existence, life,
And fellowship of sense with all that breathes—
Present'st thyself before me, I relent,
And cannot hurt thy weakness.—So the storm
30 Of horrid war, o'erwhelming cities, fields,

And peaceful villages, rolls dreadful on:
The victor shouts triumphant; he enjoys
The roar of cannon and the clang of arms,
And urges, by no soft relentings stopped,
35 The work of death and carnage. Yet should one,
A single sufferer from the field escaped,
Panting and pale, and bleeding at his feet,
Lift his imploring eyes—the hero weeps;
He is grown human, and capricious Pity,
40 Which would not stir for thousands, melts for one
With sympathy spontaneous: 'Tis not Virtue,
Yet 'tis the weakness of a virtuous mind.
—1825

---

[1] *vials of destruction* I.e., pesticides.

CHARLOTTE SMITH
1749 — 1806

As was the case with many early women writers, Charlotte Smith became a published author largely as a result of pressing financial circumstances. She succeeded in providing for herself and her family first through poetry and then through fiction—and became one of the shaping forces of English Romanticism through her writing. Her work enjoyed enormous popularity in her own day; as the nineteenth century advanced, her sentimental style fell out of fashion and her reputation, like that of so many other sentimental writers, waned.

Smith (née Turner) was born into the landed gentry in 1749 in London; her father was a country gentleman in Sussex, to which county Smith remained devoted throughout her life. Charlotte was the second of three children and her mother died giving birth to her brother when she was three years old. Her education was typical for someone of her gender and social class; she attended a fashionable boarding school between the ages of eight and twelve, at which point she left school and entered "society." Her father remarried in 1764 and it was arranged that Charlotte would marry the following year, at the age of 15. Her husband, Benjamin Smith, was the son of a West Indian merchant and was living beyond his means. Her father-in-law died in 1776, leaving a will that attempted to prevent his legacy from being wasted by his wayward son. The document was so complicated, however, that Smith was to spend the rest of her life going to the courts to fight for her children's inheritance. (Her case became well known in London, and it is probably the basis for the law case in Dickens's *Bleak House*.) Benjamin Smith continued his spendthrift ways and was imprisoned for debt in 1783. For a time, Smith and their growing family lived with him in prison.

In 1784, when Smith first turned to writing professionally, she was 35 years old and had nine living children. Desperate for money while her husband was still in prison, she composed *Elegiac Sonnets*. These remarkable sonnets, famous for their melancholy, pessimism, and pathos, represent an important stylistic achievement in their ability to convey a highly personal effect through an understated and impersonal style. This volume was extremely popular, and she later repeatedly rearranged and enlarged the collection. Among the additions were many poems supposedly written by characters in the novels she wrote later. By 1851 her sonnets had gone through 11 editions. Both Wordsworth and Coleridge learned from her, admiring her more in their youth than they were later willing to admit. Both used Smith's work as a model for working out their new style of Romantic self-expression.

More money troubles were to follow for Smith. When her husband was released from prison in 1785, he fled to France to escape his creditors and Smith followed with the family. While in France she discovered Antoine-François Prevost's controversial *Manon Lescaut* and translated it into English.

In 1785 Smith returned to England with her children; she separated from her husband one year later. From this point onward, she was the sole supporter of her family, a position made more difficult by the fact that at this date everything earned by a wife legally belonged to her husband. In 1788 her first novel, *Emmeline*, was published; from then on she published almost a novel a year. Smith drew on the circumstances of her own life for her fiction: she often portrayed women married to cruel or dissolute husbands, and still more often grasping or incompetent lawyers, while scenes from her stay in debtor's prison appear both in *Ethelinde* and in *Marchmont*. If her own life figured frequently in her work, however, so did many of the great public issues of the day; her fiction is sharply critical of empire, the slave trade, the class system, and marriage laws. She was a strong early supporter of the French Revolution, but was also sensitive to the plight of French emigrés in England after the Terror; in 1793 she published the 800-line blank-verse poem *The Emigrants*.

Although she was known primarily as a novelist and, in the later part of her life, as a children's author, she continued to write poetry. In her last years she suffered from arthritis, which made writing difficult. *Beachy Head*, one of her finest poems, was published the year after her death, in 1807. Wordsworth wrote that she was "a lady to whom English verse is under greater obligations than are likely to be either acknowledged or remembered."

⌘⌘⌘

from *Elegiac Sonnets*

I

The partial Muse,[1] has from my earliest hours
    Smil'd on the rugged path I'm doom'd to tread,
And still with sportive° hand has snatch'd   playful
        wild flowers,
    To weave fantastic garlands for my head:
5   But far, far happier is the lot of those
    Who never learn'd her dear delusive art,
Which while it decks the head with many a rose,
    Reserves the thorn, to fester in the heart.
For still she bids° soft Pity's melting eye   commands
10   Stream o'er the ills she knows not to remove,
Points° every pang, and deepens every sigh   sharpens
    Of mourning friendship, or unhappy love.
Ah! then, how dear° the Muse's favors cost,   expensive
    If those paint sorrow best—who feel it most![2]

2
Written at the Close of Spring

The garlands fade that Spring so lately wove,
    Each simple flower which she had nursed in
        dew,
    Anemonies,[3] that spangled every grove,
    The primrose wan, and hare-bell[4] mildly blue.
5 No more shall violets linger in the dell,°   wooded valley
    Or purple orchis variegate[5] the plain,
Till Spring again shall call forth every bell,°   flowering plant
    And dress° with humid hands her   prepare
        wreaths again.—
    Ah! poor Humanity! so frail, so fair,
10   Are the fond visions of thy early day,
    Till tyrant Passion,° and corrosive Care,   suffering
    Bid° all thy fairy colours fade away! Another   orders
        May new buds and flowers shall bring;
    Ah! why has happiness—no second Spring?

---

[1] *partial* Favorable, prejudiced; *Muse* Goddess of poetic inspiration, the invocation of which is a tradition going back to Classical antiquity.

[2] [Smith's note] "The well-sung woes shall soothe my pensive ghost; / He best can paint them who shall feel them most." Pope's "Eloisa to Abelard." 366th line.

[3] [Smith's note] Anemonies. *Anemony Nemeroso.* The wood Anemony. [Flowering plant having brilliant blossoms, common to Great Britain.]

[4] *primrose* Wild flowering plant noted for its yellow blossoms; *hare-bell* Wild hyacinth, blue-bell.

[5] *orchis* Orchids; *variegate* Make varied.

11
To Sleep

Come, balmy Sleep! tired Nature's soft resort!¹
On these sad temples all thy poppies² shed;
And bid gay dreams, from Morpheus'³ airy court,
    Float in light vision round my aching head!⁴
5 Secure of all thy blessings, partial° Power!   *favorable, prejudiced*
    On his hard bed the peasant throws him down;
    And the poor sea-boy, in the rudest° hour,   *most harsh*
    Enjoys thee more than he who wears a crown.⁵
Clasp'd in her faithful shepherd's guardian arms,
10   Well may the village-girl sweet slumbers prove;
And they, O gentle Sleep! still taste thy charms,
    Who wake to labour, liberty, and love.
But still thy opiate aid dost thou deny
To calm the anxious breast, to close the streaming eye.

39
To Night

I love thee, mournful, sober-suited°   *darkly clothed*
    Night!
  When the faint moon, yet lingering in her wane,
And veil'd in clouds, with pale uncertain light
    Hangs o'er the waters of the restless main.°   *sea*
5 In deep depression sunk, the enfeebled mind
    Will to the deaf cold elements complain,
    And tell the embosom'd grief, however vain,
To sullen⁶ surges and the viewless wind.
Tho' no repose on thy dark breast I find,
10   I still enjoy thee—cheerless as thou art;
    For in thy quiet gloom the exhausted heart

---

¹ *balmy* Soothing; *resort* Escape.

² *poppies* Opium, which induces sleep, is made from poppies.

³ *Morpheus* God of sleep and dreams.

⁴ [Smith's note] "Float in light vision round the poet's head." Mason. [Cf. line 12 of William Mason's "Elegy V. On the Death of a Lady," (1760).]

⁵ [Smith's note] "Wilt thou upon the high and giddy mast / Seal up the ship boy's eyes, and rock his brains / In cradle of the rude impetuous surge?" Shakespeare's *Henry IV*. [Cf. *II Henry IV*, 3.1.18–20. Smith here substitutes "impetuous," for the original "imperious."]

⁶ *sullen* Make sluggish or slow.

Is calm, tho' wretched; hopeless, yet resign'd.
While to the winds and waves its sorrows given,
May reach—tho' lost on earth—the ear of Heaven!

44
Written in the Church-yard at Middleton in Sussex

Press'd by the Moon, mute arbitress° of   *female judge*
    tides,
  While the loud equinox⁷ its power combines,
    The sea no more its swelling surge confines,
But o'er the shrinking land sublimely rides.
5 The wild blast, rising from the Western cave,
    Drives the huge billows from their heaving bed;
    Tears from their grassy tombs the village dead,⁸
And breaks the silent sabbath of the grave!
With shells and sea-weed mingled, on the shore
10 Lo! their bones whiten in the frequent wave;
    But vain to them the winds and waters rave;
They hear the warring elements no more:
While I am doom'd—by life's long storm opprest,
To gaze with envy, on their gloomy rest.

59
Written September 1791, during a remarkable thunder storm, in which the moon was perfectly clear, while the tempest gathered in various directions near the earth

What awful pageants° crowd the   *majestic displays*
    evening sky!
  The low horizon gathering vapours shroud;
    Sudden, from many a deep-embattled cloud
Terrific thunders burst, and lightnings fly—
5 While in serenest azure,° beaming high,   *intense blue*
    Night's regent,° of her calm pavilion proud,   *moon*

---

⁷ *equinox* Time of year at which the sun crosses the equator, rendering day and night of equal length.

⁸ [Smith's note] Middleton is a village on the margin of the sea, in Sussex, containing only two or three houses. There were formerly several acres of ground between its small church and the sea, which now, by its continual encroachments, approaches within a few feet of this half-ruined and humble edifice. The wall, which once surrounded the church-yard, is entirely swept away, many of the graves broken up, and the remains of bodies interred washed into the sea; whence human bones are found among the sand and shingles on the shore.

Gilds the dark shadows that beneath her lie,
   Unvex'd by all their conflicts fierce and loud.
—So, in unsullied dignity elate,
10   A spirit conscious of superior worth,
In placid elevation firmly great,
   Scorns the vain cares that give Contention birth;
And blest with peace above the shocks of Fate,
   Smiles at the tumult of the troubled earth.

70
On being cautioned against walking on an headland overlooking the sea, because it was frequented by a lunatic

Is there a solitary wretch who hies°   hastens
   To the tall cliff, with starting° pace or slow,   fitful
And, measuring, views with wild and hollow eyes
   Its distance from the waves that chide° below;   scold
5 Who, as the sea-born gale with frequent sighs
   Chills his cold bed upon the mountain turf,
With hoarse, half-utter'd lamentation, lies
   Murmuring responses to the dashing surf?
In moody sadness, on the giddy° brink,   dizzying
10   I see him more with envy than with fear;
He has no nice felicities° that shrink[1]   good fortunes
   From giant horrors; wildly wandering here,
He seems (uncursed with reason) not to know
The depth or the duration of his woe.

74
The Winter Night

"Sleep, that knits up the ravell'd sleeve of care,"[2]
   Forsakes me, while the chill and sullen blast,
   As my sad soul recalls its sorrows past,
Seems like a summons, bidding me prepare

5 For the last sleep of death.—Murmuring I hear
   The hollow wind around the ancient towers,[3]
While night and silence reign; and cold and drear
   The darkest gloom of Middle Winter lours;°   scowls
But wherefore° fear existence such as mine,   why
10   To change for long and undisturb'd repose?
Ah! when this suffering being I resign,
   And o'er my miseries the tomb shall close,
By her,[4] whose loss in anguish I deplore,
   I shall be laid, and feel that loss no more!

84
To the Muse[5]

Wilt thou forsake me who in life's bright May
   Lent warmer lustre to the radiant morn;
   And even o'er Summer scenes by tempests torn,
Shed with illusive light the dewy ray
5 Of pensive pleasure?—Wilt thou, while the day
   Of saddening Autumn closes, as I mourn
In languid, hopeless sorrow, far away
   Bend° thy soft step, and never more return?—   aim
Crush'd to the earth, by bitterest anguish pressed,
10   From my faint eyes thy graceful form recedes;
   Thou canst not heal an heart like mine that bleeds;
But, when in quiet earth that heart shall rest,
   Haply° may'st thou one sorrowing vigil keep,   by chance
   Where Pity and Remembrance bend° and weep![6] kneel
—1784–97

---

[1] [Smith's note] "'This delicate felicity that shrinks / When rocking winds are loud.' Walpole. [Horace Walpole (1717–97); these lines are untraced.]

[2] [Smith's note]   Shakespeare. [Cf. Macbeth 2.2.36.]

[3] [Smith's note]   These lines were written in a residence among ancient public buildings.

[4] her Smith's daughter, Anna Augusta (d. 1795). Cf. Smith's "Sonnet 65," not included in this anthology.

[5] Muse Goddess of poetic inspiration, the invocation of whom is a tradition going back to Classical antiquity.

[6] [Smith's note]   "Where melancholy friendship bends and weeps." Thomas Gray. [Cf. "Epitaph on Sir William Williams," line 12, by Thomas Gray (1716–71).]

THE FRENCH REVOLUTION
CONTEXTS

Debate about the French Revolution, which was to open English eyes to the possibility of political change in their own country, began shortly after the 14 July 1789 storming of the Bastille (during which a Parisian crowd swarmed the prison in search of ammunition, freeing seven prisoners and killing the governor in the process). The revolution forced English men and women to re-examine their most basic societal tenets: their system of government and their handling of issues such as individual civil rights and liberties, rights of inheritance, and sufferance. Discussion of the Revolution triggered a massive increase in the production of written materials. On the pages of novels, periodicals, sermons, chapbooks, handbills, song sheets, and poetry, English writers debated their new relationship with France and its implications for issues of social and political reform at home.

On 4 November 1789, moral philosopher, mathematician, and dissenting preacher Richard Price delivered a sermon venerating the French Revolution and equating it with England's Glorious Revolution of 1688–89, the bloodless revolution in which James II was replaced by William III and Mary II (a key moment in the evolution of constitutional monarchy in Britain). "Struggle no longer against increasing light and liberality," he warned. "Restore to mankind their rights; and consent to the correction of abuses, before they and you are destroyed together." Such views became more and more widespread over the course of the next few months. On 14 July 1790, Parisians gathered near the ruins of the Bastille to celebrate the Revolution's first anniversary, and there was celebrating in Britain too; according to the London *Times*, the anniversary gathering represented "a magnificent association of FREE MEN, emancipated from the shackles of despotism within so short a space of time." The newspaper declared the revolution "a Phenomenon on which surrounding empires look with admiration." Such feelings ran counter to age-old habit; since 1688, the English had tended to think of themselves as progressive guardians of liberty, and had thought of the French as intolerant and slavish in their Catholicism. To many in Britain, however, English attitudes did not seem to have changed. Rather, the French revolution merely represented their long-overdue and much-needed Glorious Revolution.

To be sure, English support for the ideals of the French Revolution was far from being universal. The most important expression of early opposition to those ideals was that of politician and writer Edmund Burke, whose *Reflections on the Revolution in France* was published on 1 November 1790. Burke had strongly supported the American revolution fifteen years earlier as representing an ordered and constitutionally-based response to tyranny, and he surprised many with his vigorous condemnation of the French revolution as undermining the foundations of constitutional monarchy. In Burke's view, the suggestion of Price and others that a monarch owes his lawful authority solely "to the choice of the people" was either "nonsense, and therefore neither true nor false, or it affirms a most unfounded, dangerous, illegal and unconstitutional position."

Burke's long essay came to be regarded as a classic statement of conservative principles, and one of the works written in answer to it, Thomas Paine's *Rights of Man*, as a classic expression of Enlightenment principles of human liberty. The voice of Paine, an expatriate Englishman who had moved to America in 1774, was joined in Britain by voices such as those of William Godwin, Mary Wollstonecraft, and other prominent reformers who were later labeled "Jacobins." Condemning Burke's allegiance to "canonized forefathers," Wollstonecraft accused him of clinging to an ideology of inherited rights: "any personal present convenience should prevent a struggle for the most estimable advantages. This is sound reasoning," she quipped, "in the mouth of the rich and short-sighted."

In 1792, a Republic was declared in France, and the Revolution's violence escalated. In May, the English government, fearing rebellion on its own soil, vowed to eradicate "wicked and seditious writings"; shortly thereafter, it banned Paine's *Rights of Man (Part II)*. In August, Louis XVI and Marie Antoinette were marched out of the Palace of the Tuileries and placed under house arrest—and an increasing number of English began to feel alienated from their French neighbors. Within the conservative English imagination, the French were becoming savages, choosing anarchy over liberty. Even some reformers began to reconsider their view of the Revolution, although they continued to lobby in England for expanded suffrage, electoral reform, and the natural rights of citizens.

In late 1792, Maximilien Robespierre and his Committee for Public Safety took control of Paris and brutally demonstrated their intolerance for any enemy of the republic. The Committee put Louis XVI on trial, and the King and Queen soon joined the list of beheaded aristocrats, clergy, and counter-revolutionary suspects. The English anti-Jacobin movement gathered momentum as citizens expressed horror at these "un-English" acts. By this time other European nations had been considering intervention in France for more than two years. In April 1792, France declared war on Austria; after the execution of the King in early 1793, other countries (Britain included) joined to form the "First Coalition" against France. Over the next several years, the French government remained in a state of turmoil, but French forces held their own against their various enemies, with a young general named Napoleon Bonaparte playing an increasingly important military role. In 1799, Bonaparte seized power, and, for the next fifteen years, the powerfully enigmatic Corsican dominated the European stage.

For some in England, the French by that time had lost their way. In William Wordsworth's view, the oppressed had, in a few short years, "become Oppressors in their turn," and had "changed a war of self-defence / For one of conquest, losing sight of all / Which they had struggled for." Yet, as Godwin noted, all "the great points embraced by the revolution remain entire: hereditary government is gone; hereditary nobility is extinguished; the hierarchy of the Gallican church is no more; the feudal rights, the oppressive immunities of a mighty aristocracy, are banished never to return."

⌘ ⌘ ⌘

from Richard Price, *A Discourse on the Love of Our Country, Delivered on Nov. 4, 1789, at the Meeting-House in the Old Jewry, to the Society for Commemorating the Revolution in Great Britain*

Richard Price (1723–91) was a well-known Dissenting preacher, mathematician, and political thinker. This sermon initiated England's debate about the French Revolution by likening it to England's Glorious Revolution of 1688.

The love of our country has in all times been a subject of warm commendations; and it is certainly a noble passion; but, like all other passions, it requires regulation and direction. There are mistakes and preju-dices by which, in this instance, we are in particular danger of being misled. I will briefly mention some of these to you, and observe,

First, That by our country is meant, in this case, not the soil or the spot of earth on which we happen to have been born; not the forests and fields, but that community of which we are members; or that body of companions and friends and kindred who are associated with us under the same constitution of government, protected by the same laws, and bound together by the same civil polity.

Secondly, It is proper to observe, that even in this sense of our country, that love of it which is our duty, does not imply any conviction of the superior value of it to other countries, or any particular preference of its laws and constitution of government. ... All our attachments should be accompanied, as far as possible, with right opinions.—We are too apt to confine wisdom and virtue within the circle of our own acquaintance and party. Our friends, our country, and in short every thing related to us, we are disposed to overvalue. A wise man will guard himself against this delusion. He will study to think of all things as they are, and not suffer any partial affections to blind his understanding....

Thirdly, It is proper I should desire you particularly to distinguish between the love of our country and that spirit of rivalship and ambition which has been common among nations.—What has the love of their country hitherto been among mankind? What has it been but a love of domination; a desire of conquest, and a thirst for grandeur and glory, by extending territory, and enslaving surrounding countries? What has it been but a blind and narrow principle, producing in every country a contempt of other countries, and forming men into combinations and factions against their common rights and liberties? ... As most of the evils which have taken place in private life, and among individuals, have been occasioned by the desire of private interest overcoming the public affections; so most of the evils which have taken place among bodies of men have been occasioned by the desire of their own interest overcoming the principle of universal benevolence: and leading them to attack one another's territories, to encroach on one another's rights, and to endeavour to build their own advancement on the degradation of all within the reach of their power....

... I have just observed, that there is a submission due to the executive officers of government, which is our duty; but you must not forget what I have also observed, that it must not be a blind and slavish submission.... [T]he tendency of every government is to despotism; and in this the best constituted governments must end, if the people are not vigilant, ready to take alarms, and determined to resist abuses as soon as they begin.... This vigilance, therefore, it is our duty to maintain. Whenever it is withdrawn, and a people cease to reason about their rights and to be awake to encroachments, they are in danger of being enslaved, and their *servants* will soon become their *masters*.

... We have, therefore, on this occasion, peculiar reasons for thanksgiving—But let us remember that we ought not to satisfy ourselves with thanksgivings.... Let us, in particular, take care not to forget the principles of the Revolution.[1]...

First; The right to liberty of conscience in religious matters.

Secondly; The right to resist power when abused. And,

Thirdly; The right to choose our own governors; to cashier them for misconduct; and to frame a government for ourselves....

I would farther direct you to remember, that though the Revolution was a great work, it was by no means a perfect work; and that all was not then gained which was necessary to put the kingdom in the secure and complete possession of the blessings of liberty....

But the most important instance of the imperfect state in which the Revolution left our constitution, is the INEQUALITY OF OUR REPRESENTATION.... When the representation is partial, a kingdom possesses liberty only partially ... but if not only extremely partial, but corruptly chosen, and under corrupt influence after being chosen, it becomes a *nuisance,* and produces the worst of all forms of government—a government by corruption.... We are, at present, I hope, at a great distance from it. But it cannot be pretended that there are no advances towards it, or that there is no reason for apprehension and alarm.

The inadequateness of our representation has long been a subject of complaint. But all attention to it seems now lost, and the probability is, that this inattention will continue, and that nothing will be done towards gaining for us this essential blessing, till some great calamity again alarms our fears, or till some great abuse of power again provokes our resentment; or, perhaps, till the acquisition of a pure and equal representation by other countries ... kindles our shame....

What an eventful period is this! I am thankful that I have lived to it.... I have lived to see a diffusion of knowledge, which has undermined superstition and error—I have lived to see the rights of men better

---

[1] *Revolution* England's Glorious Revolution of 1688, which ended the reign of King James II and limited the monarch's power under a constitutional monarchy.

understood than ever; and nations panting for liberty, which seemed to have lost the idea of it. I have lived to see THIRTY MILLIONS of people, indignant and resolute, spurning at slavery, and demanding liberty with an irresistible voice; their king led in triumph, and an arbitrary monarch surrendering himself to his subjects. —After sharing in the benefits of one Revolution, I have been spared to be a witness to two other Revolutions, both glorious.[1]—And now, methinks, I see the ardour for liberty catching and spreading; a general amendment beginning in human affairs; the dominion of kings changed for the dominion of laws, and the dominion of priests giving way to the dominion of reason and conscience.

Be encouraged, all ye friends of freedom, and writers in its defence!… Behold kingdoms, admonished by you, starting from sleep, breaking their fetters, and claiming justice from their oppressors! Behold, the light you have struck out, after setting AMERICA free, reflected to FRANCE, and there kindled into a blaze that lays despotism in ashes, and warms and illuminates EUROPE!

Tremble all ye oppressors of the world! Take warning all ye supporters of slavish governments, and slavish hierarchies! Call no more (absurdly and wickedly) REFORMATION, innovation. You cannot now hold the world in darkness. Struggle no longer against increasing light and liberality. Restore to mankind their rights; and consent to the correction of abuses, before they and you are destroyed together.

from Edmund Burke, *Reflections on the Revolution in France* (1790)

A political writer and politician, Edmund Burke (1730–97) wrote the *Reflections* as a rebuttal to Price's *Discourse on the Love of Our Country*. Burke's conservative critique of the revolution was published two years before Louis XVI was executed, and it set the tone for the loyalist side of England's revolution debate.

You will observe, that from Magna Charta to the Declaration of Right,[2] it has been the uniform policy of our constitution to claim and assert our liberties, as an *entailed inheritance* derived to us from our forefathers, and to be transmitted to our posterity; as an estate specially belonging to the people of this kingdom, without any reference whatever to any other more general or prior right. By this means our constitution preserves a unity in so great a diversity of its parts. We have an inheritable crown; an inheritable peerage[3]; and a House of Commons[4] and a people inheriting privileges, franchises, and liberties, from a long line of ancestors.

This policy appears to me to be the result of profound reflection; or rather the happy effect of following nature, which is wisdom without reflection, and above it. A spirit of innovation is generally the result of a selfish temper, and confined views. People will not look forward to posterity, who never look backward to their ancestors. Besides, the people of England well know that the idea of inheritance furnishes a sure principle of conservation, and a sure principle of transmission; without at all excluding a principle of improvement. It leaves acquisition free; but it secures what it acquires. Whatever advantages are obtained by a state proceeding on these maxims, are locked fast as in a sort of family settlement; grasped as in a kind of mortmain[5] for ever. By a constitutional policy, working after the pattern of nature, we receive, we hold, we transmit our government and our privileges, in the same manner in which we enjoy and transmit our property and our lives. The institutions of policy, the goods of fortune, the gifts of providence, are handed down to us, and from us, in the same course and order. Our political system is placed in a just correspondence and symmetry with the order of

---

[1] *After sharing … both glorious* Price refers first to the Glorious Revolution, then to the American and French revolutions.

[2] *Magna Charta* England's Great Charter of 1215 was a precedent-setting document that limited the power of King John; *Declaration of Right* Brought about by the Glorious Revolution, this bill increased the power of Parliament and is fundamental to English constitutional law.

[3] *peerage* Nobility.

[4] *House of Commons* Lower house of Parliament, to which representatives from various districts are elected.

[5] *mortmain* Legal term for the perpetual tenure of land by a corporation (often ecclesiastical).

the world, and with the mode of existence decreed to a permanent body composed of transitory parts; wherein, by the disposition of a stupendous wisdom, moulding together the great mysterious incorporation of the human race, the whole, at one time, is never old, or middle-aged, or young, but, in a condition of unchangeable constancy, moves on through the varied tenor of perpetual decay, fall, renovation, and progression. Thus, by preserving the method of nature in the conduct of the state, in what we improve, we are never wholly new; in what we retain, we are never wholly obsolete. By adhering in this manner and on those principles to our forefathers, we are guided not by the superstition of antiquarians, but by the spirit of philosophic analogy. In this choice of inheritance we have given to our frame of polity the image of a relation in blood; binding up the constitution of our country with our dearest domestic ties; adopting our fundamental laws into the bosom of our family affections; keeping inseparable, and cherishing with the warmth of all their combined and mutually reflected charities, our state, our hearths, our sepulchres, and our altars.

Through the same plan of a conformity to nature in our artificial institutions, and by calling in the aid of her unerring and powerful instincts, to fortify the fallible and feeble contrivances of our reason, we have derived several other, and those no small benefits, from considering our liberties in the light of an inheritance. Always acting as if in the presence of canonized forefathers, the spirit of freedom, leading in itself to misrule and excess, is tempered with an awful gravity. This idea of a liberal descent inspires us with a sense of habitual native dignity, which prevents that upstart insolence almost inevitably adhering to and disgracing those who are the first acquirers of any distinction. By this means our liberty becomes a noble freedom. It carries an imposing and majestic aspect. It has a pedigree and illustrating ancestors. It has its bearings and its ensigns armorial. It has its gallery of portraits; its monumental inscriptions; its records, evidences, and titles. We procure reverence to our civil institutions on the principle upon which nature teaches us to revere individual men; on account of their age, and on account of those from whom they are descended. All your sophisters cannot produce anything better adapted to preserve a rational and manly

freedom than the course that we have pursued, who have chosen our nature rather than our speculations, our breasts rather than our inventions, for the great conservatories and magazines of our rights and privileges....

History will record, that on the morning of the 6th of October, 1789, the King and Queen of France, after a day of confusion, alarm, dismay, and slaughter, lay down, under the pledged security of public faith, to indulge nature in a few hours of respite, and troubled, melancholy repose. From this sleep the Queen was first startled by the voice of the sentinel at her door, who cried out to her to save herself by flight—that this was the last proof of fidelity he could give—that they were upon him, and he was dead. Instantly he was cut down. A band of cruel ruffians and assassins, reeking with his blood, rushed into the chamber of the Queen, and pierced with a hundred strokes of bayonets and poniards the bed, from whence this persecuted woman had but just time to fly almost naked, and, through ways unknown to the murderers, had escaped to seek refuge at the feet of a king and husband, not secure of his own life for a moment.

This King, to say no more of him, and this Queen, and their infant children (who once would have been the pride and hope of a great and generous people), were then forced to abandon the sanctuary of the most splendid palace in the world, which they left swimming in blood, polluted by massacre, and strewed with scattered limbs and mutilated carcases. Thence they were conducted into the capital of their kingdom. Two had been selected from the unprovoked, unresisted, promiscuous slaughter, which was made of the gentlemen of birth and family who composed the King's body guard. These two gentlemen, with all the parade of an execution of justice, were cruelly and publicly dragged to the block, and beheaded in the great court of the palace. Their heads were stuck upon spears, and led the procession; whilst the royal captives who followed in the train were slowly moved along, amidst the horrid yells, and shrilling screams, and frantic dances, and infamous contumelies, and all the unutterable abominations of the furies of hell, in the abused shape of the vilest of women. After they had been made to taste, drop by drop, more than the bitterness of death, in the slow torture of a journey of twelve miles, protracted to six hours, they were, under a guard, composed of those very soldiers who had thus conducted them through this famous triumph, lodged in one of the old palaces of Paris, now converted into a bastile for kings.

Is this a triumph to be consecrated at altars? to be commemorated with grateful thanksgiving? to be offered to the divine humanity with fervent prayer and enthusiastic ejaculation?…

We are but too apt to consider things in the state in which we find them, without sufficiently adverting to the causes by which they have been produced, and possibly may be upheld. Nothing is more certain, than that our manners, our civilization, and all the good things which are connected with manners and with civilization, have, in this European world of ours, depended for ages upon two principles; and were indeed the result of both combined; I mean the spirit of a gentleman, and the spirit of religion. The nobility and the clergy, the one by profession, the other by patronage, kept learning in existence, even in the midst of arms and confusions, and whilst governments were rather in their causes, than formed. Learning paid back what it received to nobility and to priesthood; and paid it with usury,[1] by enlarging their ideas, and by furnishing their minds. Happy if they had all continued to know their indissoluble union, and their proper place! Happy if learning, not debauched by ambition, had been satisfied to continue the instructor, and not aspired to be the master! Along with its natural protectors and guardians, learning will be cast into the mire, and trodden down under the hoofs of a swinish multitude.[2] …

from Thomas Paine, *Rights of Man* (1791 and 1792)

Thomas Paine (1737–1809) was indicted for treason because of his unflinching reformist reply to Burke's *Reflections on the Revolution in France*. After fleeing to France, he was imprisoned for not supporting

---

[1] *usury* Interest, especially at an exorbitantly high rate.

[2] *swinish multitude* This became one of Burke's most infamous and frequently-cited comments. Though Burke is probably here referring to a particular faction of extremists, and not to average citizens, many reformers took this comment as proof of arrogance among the conservatives.

Louis XVI's execution. He was spared the guillotine, and spent the rest of his years in America.

"*THE RIGHTS OF MAN;—or—TOMMY PAINE, the little American Taylor, taking the Measure of the CROWN, for a new Pair of Revolution-Breeches.*" *Humbly dedicated to the Jacobine Clubs of France & England!!! by Common Sense* (1791). This anti-Jacobin caricature suggests that Thomas Paine, who was once a tailor, is no match for the enormous legacy of the English monarchy.

There is scarcely an epithet of abuse to be found in the English language, with which Mr. Burke has not loaded the French Nation and the National Assembly. Every thing which rancour, prejudice, ignorance, or knowledge, could suggest, are poured forth in the copious fury of near four hundred pages. In the strain, and on the plan Mr. Burke was writing, he might have written on to as many thousands. When the tongue or the pen is let loose in a frenzy of passion, it is the man, and not the subject, that becomes exhausted....

As Mr. Burke occasionally applies the poison drawn from his horrid principles, not only to the English nation, but to the French Revolution and the National Assembly, and charges that august, illuminated and illuminating body of men with the epithet of *usurpers,* I shall, *sans ceremonie,* place another system of principles in opposition to his.

The English Parliament of 1688 did a certain thing, which, for themselves and their constituents, they had a right to do, and which it appeared right should be done: But, in addition to this right, which they possessed by delegation, *they set up another right by assumption,* that of binding and controlling posterity to the end of time. The case, therefore, divides itself into two parts; the right which they possessed by delegation, and the right which they set up by assumption. The first is admitted; but, with respect to the second, I reply—

There never did, there never will, and there never can exist a parliament, or any description of men, or any generation of men, in any country, possessed of the right or the power of binding and controlling posterity to the "*end of time,*" or of commanding forever how the world shall be governed, or who shall govern it; and therefore, all such clauses, acts, or declarations, by which the makers of them attempt to do what they have neither the right nor the power to do, nor the power to execute, are in themselves null and void. Every age and generation must be as free to act for itself, *in all cases*, as the ages and generations which preceded it. The vanity and presumption of governing beyond the grave, is the most ridiculous and insolent of all tyrannies.... It is the living, and not the dead, that are to be accommodated. When man ceases to be, his power and his wants cease with him; and having no longer any participation in the concerns of this world, he has no longer any authority in directing who shall be its governors, or how its government shall be organized, or how administered....

While I am writing this, there are accidentally before me some proposals for a declaration of rights by the Marquis de la Fayette[1] (I ask his pardon for using his former address, and do it only for distinction's sake) to the National Assembly, on the 11th of July 1789, three days before the taking of the Bastile; and I cannot but remark with astonishment how opposite the sources are from which that Gentleman and Mr. Burke draw their principles. Instead of referring to musty records and mouldy parchments to prove that the rights of the living are lost, "renounced and abdicated forever," by those who are now no more, as Mr. Burke has done, M. de la Fayette applies to the living world, and emphatically says, "Call to mind the sentiments which Nature has engraved in the heart of every citizen, and which take a new force when they are solemnly recognized by all:—For a nation to love liberty, it is sufficient that she knows it; and to be free, it is sufficient that she wills it."...

It was not against Louis the XVIth, but against the despotic principles of the government, that the nation revolted. These principles had not their origin in him, but in the original establishment, many centuries back ... Perhaps no man, bred up in the stile of an absolute King, ever possessed a heart so little disposed to the exercise of that species of power as the present King of France. But the principles of the government itself still remained the same. The Monarch and the Monarchy were distinct and separate things; and it was against the established despotism of the latter, and not against the person or principles of the former, that the revolt commenced, and the revolution has been carried.

... When despotism has established itself for ages in a country, as in France, it is not in the person of the King only that it resides. It has the appearance of being so in show, and in nominal authority; but it is not so in practice, and in fact. It has its standard every-where. Every office and department has its despotism, founded upon custom and usage. Every place has its Bastile, and every Bastile its despot. The original hereditary despotism, resident in the person of the King, divides and subdivides itself into a thousand shapes and forms, till at last the whole of it is acted by deputation. This was the case in France; and against this species of despotism, proceeding on through an endless labyrinth of office, till the source of it is scarcely perceptible, there is no mode of redress. It strengthens itself by assuming the appearance of duty, and tyrannises under the pretense of obeying....

---

[1] *Marquis de la Fayette* Vice president of the National Assembly. La Fayette composed the initial draft of the *Declaration of the Rights of Man and of the Citizen.*

THE CONTRAST
1792

BRITISH LIBERTY

FRENCH LIBERTY

RELIGION.   MORALITY.
LOYALTY OBEDIENCE TO THE LAWS
INDEPENDANCE PERSONAL SECURITY
JUSTICE INHERITANCE PROTECTION
PROPERTY. INDUSTRY. NATIONAL PROSPERITY
HAPPINESS

ATHEISM   PERJURY
REBELLION TREASON ANARCHY MURDER
EQUALITY MADNESS. CRUELTY. INJUSTICE
TREACHERY INGRATITUDE IDLENESS
FAMINE NATIONAL & PRIVATE RUIN
MISERY

WHICH IS BEST

Thomas Rowlandson, after a drawing by Lord George Murray, *The Contrast*, 1792.

The Contrast, by Thomas Rowlandson, after a drawing by Lord George Murray (1792).

As to the tragic paintings, by which Mr. Burke has outraged his own imagination, and seeks to work upon that of his readers, they are very well calculated for theatrical representation, where facts are manufactured for the sake of show, and accommodated to produce, through the weakness of sympathy, a weeping effect. But Mr. Burke should recollect that he is writing history, and not *plays*; and that his readers will expect truth, and not the spouting rant of high-toned exclamation....

Not one glance of compassion, not one commiserating reflection, that I can find throughout his whole book, has he bestowed on those who lingered out the most wretched of lives, a life without hope, in the most miserable of prisons. ... His hero or his heroine must be a tragedy-victim expiring in show, and not the real prisoner of misery, sliding into death in the silence of a dungeon.

As Mr. Burke has passed over the whole transaction of the Bastile (and his silence is nothing in his favour), and has entertained his readers with reflections on supposed facts distorted into real falsehoods, I will give, since he has not, some account of the circumstances which preceded that transaction. They will serve to show, that less mischief could scarcely have accompanied such an event, when considered with the treacherous and hostile aggravations of the enemies of the Revolution....

The mind can hardly picture to itself a more tremendous scene than what the city of Paris exhibited at the time of taking the Bastile, and for two days before and after, nor conceive the possibility of its quieting so soon. At a distance, this transaction has appeared only as an act of heroism, standing on itself; and the close political connection it had with the Revolution is lost in the brilliancy of the achievement. But we are to consider it as the strength of the parties, brought man to man, and contending for the issue. The Bastile was to be either the prize or the prison of the assailants. The downfall of it included the idea of the downfall of Despotism....

That the Bastile was attacked with an enthusiasm of heroism, such only as the highest animation of liberty could inspire, and carried in the space of a few hours, is an event which the world is fully possessed of. I am not undertaking a detail of the attack; but bringing into view the conspiracy against the nation which provoked it, and which fell with the Bastile. The prison to which the new ministry were dooming the National Assembly, in addition to its being the high altar and castle of despotism, became the proper object to begin with. This enterprise broke up the new ministry, who began now to fly from the ruin they had prepared for others....

During the latter part of the time in which this confusion was acting, the King and Queen were in public at the balcony, and neither of them concealed for safety's sake, as Mr. Burke insinuates. Matters being thus appeased, and tranquillity restored, a general acclamation broke forth, of *Le Roi à Paris—Le Roi à Paris*—The King to Paris. It was the shout of peace, and immediately accepted on the part of the King. By this measure, the King and his family reached Paris in the evening, and were congratulated on their arrival by Mr. Bailley, the Mayor of Paris, in the name of the citizens....

The French constitution says, *There shall be no titles*; and, of consequence, all that class of equivocal generation, which in some countries is called "*aristocracy*" and in others "*nobility*" is done away, and the *peer*[1] is exalted into MAN....

It is, properly, from the elevated mind of France that the folly of titles has fallen. It has outgrown the baby-clothes of *Count* and *Duke*, and breeched itself in manhood. France has not levelled; it has exalted. It has put down the dwarf, to set up the man. The puny-ism of a senseless word like *Duke*, or *Count*, or *Earl*, has ceased to please. Even those who possessed them have disowned the gibberish; and, as they outgrew the rickets, have despised the rattle. The genuine mind of man, thirsting for its native home, society, contemns the gewgaws[2] that separate him from it. Titles are like circles drawn by the magician's wand, to contract the sphere of man's felicity. He lived immured within the Bastile of a word, and surveys at a distance the envied life of man....

The patriots of France have discovered, in good time, that rank and dignity in society must take a new ground. The old one has fallen through. It must now take the substantial ground of character, instead of the chimerical ground of titles; and they have brought their titles to the altar, and made of them a burnt-offering to Reason.

If no mischief had annexed itself to the folly of titles, they would not have been worth a serious and formal destruction, such as the National Assembly have decreed them; and this makes it necessary to enquire farther into the nature and character of aristocracy....

Nothing can appear more contradictory, than the principle on which the old governments began, and the condition to which society, civilization, and commerce, are capable of carrying mankind. Government, on the old system, is an assumption of power, for the aggrandisement of itself; on the new, a delegation of power, for the common benefit of society. The former supports itself by keeping up a system of war; the latter promotes a system of peace, as the true means of enriching a nation. The one encourages national prejudices; the other promotes universal society, as the means of universal commerce. The one measures its prosperity, by the quantity of revenue it extorts; the other proves its excellence, by the small quantity of taxes it requires....

Never did so great an opportunity offer itself to England, and to all Europe, as is produced by the two Revolutions of America and France. By the former, freedom has a national champion in the Western world; and by the latter, in Europe. When another nation shall join France, despotism and bad government will scarcely dare to appear. To use a trite expression, the iron is becoming hot all over Europe. The insulted German and the enslaved Spaniard, the Russ and the Pole, are beginning to think. The present age will hereafter merit to be called the Age of Reason, and the present generation will appear to the future as the Adam of a new world.

---

[1] *peer* Member of the hereditary nobility.

[2] *gewgaws* Gaudy baubles.

Samuel Taylor Coleridge, Letter to Charles Heath (1794)

> Romantic poets Robert Southey (1774–1843) and
> Samuel Taylor Coleridge (1772–1834), inspired by
> the social and political idealism manifested across
> the channel, planned an English utopian settlement
> (or "Pantisocracy," as they called it) in Pennsylvania
> in 1794—a plan that Coleridge outlines below in his
> letter to Charles Heath. The following poems by
> Coleridge and Southey demonstrate the profound
> sense of hope and optimism typical of English
> radicals in the 1790s. This hope was to fade as both
> men became disillusioned with the revolution later
> in their lives.

Jesus College, Cambridge. 29th August, 1794

Sir,

Your brother has introduced my name to you; I shall
therefore offer no apology for this letter. A small but
liberalized party have formed a scheme of emigration on
the principles of an abolition of individual property. Of
their political creed, and the arguments by which they
support and elucidate it, they are preparing a few
copies—not as meaning to publish them, but for private
distribution. In this work they will have endeavoured to
prove the exclusive justice of the system and its practicability; nor will they have omitted to sketch out the code
of contracts necessary for the internal regulation of the
society; all of which will of course be submitted to the
improvements and approbation of each component
member. As soon as the work is printed, one or more
copies shall be transmitted to you. Of the characters of
the individuals who compose the party, I find it embar-
rassing to speak; yet, vanity apart, I may assert with
truth, that they have each a sufficient strength of head
to make the virtues of the heart respectable; and that
they are all highly charged with that enthusiasm which
results from strong perceptions of moral rectitude, called
into life and action by ardent feelings. With regard to
pecuniary matters it is found necessary, if twelve men
with their families emigrate on this system, that 2000£
should be the aggregate of their contributions; but infer
not from hence that each man's quota is to be settled
with the littleness of arithmetical accuracy. No; *all* will
strain *every* nerve, and then I trust the surplus money of
some will supply the deficiencies of others. The minutiae of topographical information we are daily endeavouring to acquire; at present our plan is, to settle at a
distance, but at a convenient distance, from Cooper's
Town on the banks of the Susquehannah. This, however, will be the object of future investigation. For the
time of emigration we have fixed on next March. In the
course of the winter those of us whose bodies, from
habits of sedentary study or academic indolence, have
not acquired their full tone and strength, intend to learn
the theory and practice of agriculture and carpentry,
according as situation and circumstances make one or
the other convenient.

Your fellow Citizen,
S.T. Coleridge

Samuel Taylor Coleridge, "Pantisocracy" (1794)

No more my visionary soul shall dwell
On joys that were; no more endure to weigh
The shame and anguish of the evil day,
Wisely forgetful! O'er the ocean swell
Sublime of Hope, I seek the cottag'd dell
Where Virtue calm with careless step may stray,
And dancing to the moonlight roundelay,
The wizard Passions weave an holy spell.
Eyes that have ach'd with Sorrow! Ye shall weep
Tears of doubt-mingled joy, like theirs who start
From Precipices of distemper'd sleep,
On which the fierce-eyed Fiends their revels keep,
And see the rising Sun, and feel it dart
New rays of pleasance trembling to the heart.

Robert Southey, "On the Prospect of Establishing a Pantisocracy in America" (1794)

Whilst pale Anxiety, corrosive Care,
The tear of Woe, the gloom of sad Despair,
And deepen'd Anguish generous bosoms rend;—
Whilst patriot souls their country's fate lament;
Whilst mad with rage demoniac, foul intent,
Embattled legions Despots vainly send

To arrest the immortal mind's expanding ray
Of, everlasting Truth;—I other climes
Where dawns, with hope serene, a brighter day
Than e'er saw Albion° in her happiest times,   *England*
With mental eye exulting now explore,
And soon with kindred minds shall haste to enjoy
(Free from the ills which here our peace destroy)
Content and Bliss on Transatlantic shore.

10

from Samuel Taylor Coleridge, "Once a Jacobin Always a Jacobin" (1802)

> Samuel Taylor Coleridge's recantation of revolutionary ideals was one of the most dramatic of any Romantic poets. As more and more people were executed, the euphoric tone of Coleridge's *Destruction of the Bastille* gave way to a blunt statement of disavowal: "We were never, at any period of our life, converts to the system of French politics," he claimed. "Once a Jacobin Always a Jacobin" was published in London's *Morning Post*.

This charitable adage was at one time fashionable in the ministerial circles; and Mr. Pitt[1] himself, in one of his most powerful speeches, gave it every advantage that is derivable from stately diction. What he thus condescended to decorate, it were well if he had attempted to prove. But no! he found it a blank assertion, and a blank assertion he suffered it to remain. What *is* a Jacobin? Perhaps the best answer to this question would be, that it is a term of abuse, the convenient watchword of a faction. . . .

But though we should find it difficult to determine what a Jacobin *is*, we may however easily conjecture what the different sects of Anti-Jacobins have meant by the word. The base and venal creatures, and the blind and furious bigots, of the late ministry, comprehended under that word all who from whatever cause opposed the late war, and the late ministry, and whom they hate for this opposition with such mortal hatred, as is usual with bigots alarmed, and detected culprits. "*Once a Jacobin always a Jacobin,*" signifies no more in the minds

of these men, than "*such a one is a man, whom I shall never cease to hate.*" With other men, honest and less violent Anti-Jacobins, the word implies a man, whose affections have been warmly and deeply interested in the cause of general freedom, who has hoped all good and honourable things both *of*, and *for*, mankind. In this sense of the word Jacobin, the adage would affirm that no man can ever become altogether an apostate to liberty, who has at any time been sincerely and fervently attached to it. His hopes will burn like the Greek fire, hard to be extinguished, and easily rekindling. Even when he despairs of the cause, he will yet *wish* that it had been successful. And even when private interests have warped his public character, his convictions will remain, and his wishes often rise up in rebellion against his outward actions and public avowals. Thus interpreted, the assertion, "*Once a Jacobin always a Jacobin,*" is so favourable a representation of human nature, that we are willing, too willing perhaps, to admit it even without proof. There is yet a third class of Anti-Jacobins, and of this class we profess ourselves to be, who use the word *Jacobin* as they use the word, *Whig*, and both words only for want of better; who confess that Jacobin is too often a word of vague abuse, but believe, that there are certain definite ideas, hitherto not expressed in any single word, which may be attached to this word; and who in consequence uniformly use the word, Jacobin, with certain definite ideas attached to it, those ideas, and no other. A Jacobin, in *our* sense of the term, is one who believes, and is disposed to act on the belief, that all, or the greater part of, the happiness or misery, virtue or vice, of mankind, depends on forms of government; who admits no form of government as either good or rightful, which does not flow directly and formally from the persons governed; who,—considering life, health, moral and intellectual improvement, and liberty both of person and conscience, as blessings which governments are bound as far as possible to increase and secure to every inhabitant, whether he has or has not any fixed property, and moreover as blessings of infinitely greater value to each individual than the preservation of property can be to any individual,—does consequently and consistently hold that every inhabitant who has attained that age of reason, has a natural and inalienable right to an *equal* share of power in the choice of the

---

[1] *Mr. Pitt* Tory prime minister William Pitt, who governed from 1783 until 1801.

governors. In other words, the Jacobins affirm that no legislature can be rightful or good, which did not proceed from universal suffrage. In the power, and under the control, of a legislature so chosen, he places all and every thing, with the exception of the natural rights of man, and the means appointed for the preservation and exercise of these rights, by a direct vote of the nation itself—that is to say, by a constitution. Finally, the Jacobin deems it both justifiable and expedient to effect these requisite changes in faulty governments, by absolute revolutions, and considers no violences as properly rebellious or criminal, which are the *means* of giving to a nation the power of declaring and enforcing its sovereign will. In brief, therefore, a Jacobin's creed is this: 1. A government is the organ, by which form and publicity are given to the sovereign will of the people; and by which that will is enforced and exercised. 2. A government is likewise the instrument and means of purifying and regulating the national will by its public discussions, and by direct institutions for the comforts and instruction of the people. 3. Every native of a country has an equal right to that quantity of property, which is necessary for the sustenance of his life and health. 4. All property beyond this, not being itself a right, can confer no right. Superior wisdom, with superior virtue, would indeed confer a right of superior power; but who is to decide on the possession? Not the person himself, who makes the claim: and if the people, then the right is given, and not inherent. Votes, therefore, *cannot* be *weighed* in this way, and they *must not* be weighed in any other way. Nothing therefore remains possible, but that they must be *numbered*. No form of electing representatives is rightful, but that of universal suffrage. Every individual has a right to elect, and a capability of being elected. 5. The legislature has an absolute power over all other property, but that of article 3: unless the people shall have declared otherwise in the constitution. 6. All governments not constituted on these principles are unjust governments. 7. The people have a right to overturn them, in whatever way it is possible, and any means necessary to this end become, *ipso facto*,[1] right means. 8. It is the right and duty of each individual, living under that government, as far as in him lies, to impel and enable the people to exercise these rights.—The man who subscribes to *all* these articles is a complete Jacobin; to many, but not to all of them, a Semi-Jacobin, and the man who subscribes to any one article (excepting the second, which the Jacobin professes only in common with every other political sect not directly an advocate of despotism), may be fairly said to have a *shade* of Jacobinism in his character. If we are not greatly deceived we could point out more than one or two celebrated Anti-Jacobins, who are not slightly infected with some of the worst symptoms of the madness against which they are raving; and one or two acts of parliament which are justifiable only upon Jacobin principles. These are the ideas which we attach to the word Jacobin; and no other single word expresses them. Not republican; Milton[2] was a pure republican, and yet his notions of government were highly aristocratic; Brutus was a republican, but he perished in consequence of having killed the Jacobin, Caesar. Neither does Demagogue express that which we have detailed; not yet Democrat. The former word implies simply a mode of conduct, and has no reference to principles; and the latter does of *necessity* convey no more than that a man prefers in any country a form of government, without monarchy or aristocracy, which in any country he *may* do, and yet be no Jacobin, and which in some countries he can do without any impeachment of good sense or honesty: for instance, in the purely pastoral and agricultural districts of Switzerland, where there is no other property but that of land and cattle, and that property very nearly equalized. Whoever builds a government on personal and natural rights is so far a Jacobin. Whoever builds on social rights, that is, hereditary rank, property, and long prescription, is an Anti-Jacobin, even though he should nevertheless be a republican, or even a democrat....

---

[1] *ipso facto* Latin: by that very fact.

[2] *Milton* English poet John Milton (1608–74), who wrote several pamphlets in support of Oliver Cromwell's Commonwealth government.

Thomas Spence, "The Rights of Man for Me: A Song" (1795)

Thomas Spence (1750–1814) wrote the following song while confined in Newgate prison on charges of high treason. This song, like many of its day, served to express the radical ideology of English Jacobins. Often sung in pubs during reform meetings, Spence's verses articulated defiance toward the political status quo and advocated natural rights for all British males. (Even among the radicals, it was relatively rare to find an advocate of full rights for women.) "The Rights of Man for Me" appeared in Thomas Spence's weekly publication, *Pig's Meat*. The title of the one-penny weekly captures the central conflict of Jacobins and loyalists with an ironic nod to conservative Edmund Burke's reference to "a swinish multitude" in his *Reflections on the Revolution in France*.

(Tune: *Maid of the Mill*)

There are twenty fine schemes held up by the great,
    To deceive silly souls, d'ye see?
And render them passive for pure conscience sake,
    And mould them to fell tyranny;
5 Yet for all their fine arts with their priests in their aid,
    Their threats and their deep policy,
I'll laugh them to scorn, while loudly I sing,
    The Rights of Man boys for me.

This world for the poor they say never was made,
10   Their portion in the heav'ns be,

And say that they envy them their happy lot,
    So certain's their felicity;[1]
But thank them for naught, if the heav'ns they could let,
    Few joys here the poor would e'er see,
15 For *rents* they must toil and for *taxes* to boot,
    The Rights of Man then for me.

Then cheer up all you who have long been oppressed,
    Aspire unto sweet liberty;
No fetters were formed for a nation to bind,
20   That had the brave wish to be free:
To Gallia° then look and blush at your chains,   *France*
    And shake off all vile slavery,
And let each man sing, till loud echoes ring,
    The Rights of Man boys for me.

25 As for me though in prison I oft' have been cast,
    Because I would dare to be free,
And though in black Newgate I now pen this song,
    My theme I've not altered you see;
In jail or abroad whatever betide,
30   My struggles for freedom shall be,
Whate'er fate bring, I will think, speak and sing,
    The Rights of Man boys for me!

---

[1] *And say ... felicity* William Paley (1743–1805), theologian and moralist, notoriously made this rather disingenuous argument in his *Reasons for Contentment* (1792).

WILLIAM BLAKE
1757 – 1827

"I labor upwards into futurity," etched William Blake onto the back of one of the copper plates which constituted the "tablets" of his visionary art. A poet and artist whose work was sorely undervalued during his own lifetime, Blake recognized that his was a genius before its time. The mysterious and powerful poetry that he crafted to convey his vision would eventually be recognized as having revolutionary significance; for the past century or more Blake has been widely considered to be a great poet of the Romantic era.

Blake was born one November evening in 1757 above his parents' hosiery shop in the Soho district of London. James and Catherine Blake, religious Dissenters whose non-compromising beliefs were those of a growing number of tradespeople, allowed their son to pursue a program of self study that saved him from being schooled under the institutional authorities he instinctively abhorred. Although his parents were generally indulgent, there are hints that Blake balked even under their natural expressions of authority. He received a thrashing for declaring he had seen the face of God, and was accused of lying when he reported passing a tree bespangled with angels. Since his family could not afford the expense of artistic training, he was apprenticed at fourteen to a highly respected engraver, with whom he lived for seven years while learning the trade which would thereafter earn him his living.

During the period of his apprenticeship, Blake began writing the poems that were eventually collected in *Poetical Sketches* (1783)—the only volume of his verse originally printed by letterpress rather than by the "illuminated" methods he later originated. Of his parents and three siblings, Blake retained lasting affection only for his younger brother, Robert. Blake claimed to communicate daily with the spirit of Robert after his early death from tuberculosis. Indeed, the unique style of relief etching or "Illuminated Printing" which Blake later devised was imparted, he claimed, by Robert in a visitation. Etching words backwards into copper plates so that they would reverse to normal upon printing, Blake in 1788 produced his first illuminated texts with "All Religions Are One" and "There is No Natural Religion." It was a defining moment for him, one in which words and images converged into an indivisible and prophetic expression. He soon applied his new method of printing to a larger project, the poetic and pictorial depiction of a young soul descending into the realm of matter, recounted in *The Book of Thel*.

Blake's words and designs "interanimate each other," in the words of one critic; a master of color, he, at times, achieved unearthly effects in his hand-tinted books, of which no two copies were exactly the same. Rather than reflecting the tones of the natural world, Blake's color—and indeed the vividness of his verse—aim towards the supernatural. Similarly, what separates his poetry from that of contemporaries, such as Wordsworth and Coleridge is his lack of interest in "painting Nature." For Blake, the true aim of art was to tune the senses and the imaginative faculties to the higher pitch of a spiritual reality, not to the natural world. For this reason, Blake detested what he called the "muddy" colors, nuanced shade work, and secular sensibilities of an artist such as Rembrandt, while revering the determined outlines, bright colors, and unequivocal contrasts of light and dark achieved by High Renaissance painters such as Michelangelo and Raphael.

The bold, declarative, and (to some modern eyes) exaggerated style which Blake admired in painting is paralleled in many of his literary preferences. His work has close associations with the declamatory traditions of prophecy, of the aphorism, of the political pamphlet, and of the proverb. *The Marriage of Heaven and Hell* (1790) contains some of his most chiseled epigrams: "The cut worm forgives the plow" and "The tigers of wrath are wiser than the horses of instruction." The Bible was a tremendous imaginative reserve upon which he drew all of his life. He admired Dante, Milton, Spenser, and Shakespeare, supplied commissioned designs for editions of Milton's *L'Allegro*, *Il Penseroso*, *Paradise Lost*, and *Paradise Regained*, and left behind an unfinished series of watercolors illustrating Dante's work. He was also influenced by the architecture and sepulchral art of Westminster Abbey and by the literary gothic of Edward Young's *Night Thoughts* and Robert Blair's *The Grave*, versions of which he illustrated. If he was in many respects an outsider to his own culture, Blake was fully a man of the times in his love of the popular "forgeries" of James Macpherson (author of the "Ossian" poems) and Thomas Chatterton, as well as in his enjoyment of works of Gothic fiction such as Ann Radcliffe's *The Mysteries of Udolpho* (1794).

On at least two occasions Blake struck out to earn a reputation as an artist in his own right. The first occasion came at the end of his apprenticeship, when he submitted a portfolio to the Royal Academy of Arts (under the presidency of Sir Joshua Reynolds) and was accepted into the Academy. Yet he failed to emerge out of obscurity, and was forced to set up an engraver's shop. For twenty years Blake would resign himself to the grueling schedule of a copy engraver, recognized only by a few of his friends as a formidably original artist, and almost wholly overlooked as a poet. In 1809, energized by a gallery showing of works by Dürer, Michelangelo, Giulio Romano, and others, Blake renewed his association with the Royal Academy to launch a solo exhibition of his own work. With the exception of a caustic review or two, the public remained unmoved by—possibly unready for—the idiosyncratic light Blake cast upon subjects such as "The Body of Abel found by Adam and Eve."

Blake found his soul mate in Catherine Boucher, the illiterate daughter of a market gardener. He taught her to read and trained her in the preparation of copper plates, the hand coloring of prints, and the stitching of pages into bound copies. Catherine was evidently a submissive, devoted wife, and some have denigrated Blake's traditional and even misogynist approach to marriage, citing his pronouncement that "the female ... lives from the light of the male." At the same time, however, Blake approved of the arguments for sexual equality made by Mary Wollstonecraft in *A Vindication of the Rights of Woman* (1793). Blake radically proposed that carnal pleasure was a portal to the divine. In *Visions of the Daughters of Albion* (1793), Blake abjures sexual domination and celebrates "the moment of desire!" in a manner highly unconventional at the time. Visitors to the Blake home reported coming across the couple reading naked in a garden house in their back yard, enjoying the innocence of their private Eden and rejecting the narratives of shame and the Fall.

The rewriting of the Biblical drama of the Creation and Fall that underlies nearly all of Blake's work was influenced by radical Dissenters who celebrated nudity as a symbol of unfallen humanity. Blake was also influenced by the mystical systems of Emanuel Swedenborg and Jacob Boehme, and tapped into veins of esoteric knowledge related to the cabbalistic teachings of the Freemasons, the Rosicrucians, and Paracelsus. He also had associations with decidedly non-mystical political movements that were bravely calling for democratic reforms at a time when the English monarchy was intent on quashing sympathizers with the American War of Independence and the French Revolution.

Blake never fully participated in an organized movement of any kind, be it religious or political. His was "a voice crying in the wilderness," an unsystematizable voice urging men and women to realize their "human form divine." Unwilling to conform to any system not of his own creation, Blake's language grew increasingly esoteric and opaque in later major prophecies such as *The Four Zoas*, *Milton* (1804), and *Jerusalem* (1804–20).

One vision that Blake explores over and over again is that of an earthly Eden triumphing over forces of repression. This is the common theme of *The French Revolution* (1791), *America: A Prophecy* (1793), *Europe: A Prophecy* (1794), and *The Book of Urizen* (1794). When Blake summons Albion, figure of the human form divine in *Jerusalem*, to "Awake!" he is calling for a spiritual revolution in which humanity awakens to the knowledge that the republic of heaven is immanent.

Blake imagined the spiritual dimensions of the geography of London in particularly vivid detail. That the material double of his holy city was corrupt lends a sharp edge to Blake's vision. As one Blake biographer writes, "it was a time when mobs and rioters often controlled large areas of the city; there were riots by sailors, silk-weavers, coal-heavers, hatters, glass-grinders ... and bloody demonstrations over the price of bread." The biting simplicity of "The Chimney Sweeper" and "The Little Black Boy" in Blake's *Songs of Innocence and of Experience* (1789–94) are testimony to his acute sensitivity to the realities of poverty and exploitation that accompanied the "dark satanic mills" of the industrial revolution.

In this London, Blake admitted to living in fear that his artistic vision and eccentric tendency to converse with angels and ghosts would land him in trouble with the authorities—a fear horribly realized in 1803. The Blakes had been generously invited by William Hayley, an eminent poet and wealthy patron of the arts, to live in a country cottage at Felpham. One day a drunken private in the Royal Dragoons, John Scofield, fell into a heated argument with Blake at his garden gate. Blake physically evicted the abusive soldier from the premises. Scofield subsequently accused Blake of making seditious remarks against the Crown, an offense punishable by death. Hayley generously paid for his friend's bail and his defense, and Blake was eventually acquitted, to the thunderous approval of the court. However, the incident stamped itself upon his sensitive mind; he raised it to mythological proportions in the convoluted poetic symbology of *Jerusalem*, where the Law is figured as the nauseous region of "Bowlahoola," while Scofield and his cohorts appear as "ministers of evil."

As the culture around him placed increasing faith in the physical laws of natural science, Blake's insistence on the incorruptible coordinates of imaginative truth cast him as an increasing oddity. Many of Blake's contemporaries considered him insane. London was shifting to a secular orientation under the rise of industrial culture. Against the grain of the times, Blake continued producing labor-intensive printings of illuminated books, none of which proved to be a commercial success. Only twenty-eight copies of *Songs of Innocence and of Experience* are known to exist, sixteen of *The Book of Thel*, nine of *The Marriage of Heaven and Hell*, and five of *Jerusalem*.

In his last years, just as he had reconciled himself to poverty and obscurity, Blake attracted the first following he had ever enjoyed, a small group of painters called "the Ancients." Charles Lamb and a few other writers of the period also expressed admiration, but the glimmerings of a full-fledged "Blake industry" did not appear until years after his death, when his art and poetry were discovered by Dante Gabriel Rossetti and the Pre-Raphaelites. Rossetti and, later, William Butler Yeats edited volumes of Blake's poems, and appreciation grew of his powerful poetic as well as painterly achievements. By the middle of the twentieth century, academics around the world were devoting themselves to the scholarly study of Blake's work, which was also exerting a profound influence on the literary and popular culture of the time. Blake was an inspiration to the generation of Beat poets clustered around Allen Ginsberg and to many in the 'sixties counterculture who took up his call to open the "doors of perception" (words straight from *The Marriage of Heaven and Hell*), trying everything from the hallucinogenic drugs proposed by Aldous Huxley, to communal living and free love to approximate his visionary universe. The future had finally caught up with William Blake.

⌘ ⌘ ⌘

from *Songs of Innocence and of Experience*
Showing the Two Contrary States of the
Human Soul

Title page, *Songs of Innocence and of Experience*.

from *Songs of Innocence*

Introduction

Piping down the valleys wild
Piping songs of pleasant glee
On a cloud I saw a child.
And he laughing said to me.

5 'Pipe a song about a Lamb:'
So I piped with merry chear.[1]

---

[1] *chear* The usual practice of this anthology regarding modernization of spelling and punctuation has not been followed in the case
of Blake; his idiosyncrasies have been retained.

'Piper pipe that song again'
So I piped, he wept to hear.

'Drop thy pipe thy happy pipe
10 Sing thy songs of happy chear.'
So I sung the same again,
While he wept with joy to hear

'Piper sit thee down and write
In a book that all may read—'
15 So he vanish'd from my sight
And I pluck'd a hollow reed

And I made a rural pen,
And I stain'd the water clear,
And I wrote my happy songs
20 Every child may joy to hear
—1789

The Ecchoing Green

The Sun does arise,
And make happy the skies.
The merry bells ring
To welcome the Spring.
5 The sky-lark and thrush,
The birds of the bush,
Sing louder around,
To the bells chearful sound.
While our sports shall be seen
10 On the Ecchoing Green.
Old John with white hair
Does laugh away care,
Sitting under the oak,
Among the old folk.
15 They laugh at our play,
And soon they all say.
'Such such were the joys.
When we all girls & boys,
In our youth-time were seen.
20 On the Ecchoing Green.'

Till the little ones weary
No more can be merry
The sun does descend,
And our sports have an end:
25 Round the laps of their mothers.
Many sisters and brothers,
Like birds in their nest,
Are ready for rest:
And sport no more seen,
30 On the darkening Green.
—1789

The Lamb

Little Lamb who made thee
      Dost thou know who made thee
Gave thee life & bid thee feed.
By the stream & o'er the mead;
5 Gave thee clothing of delight,
Softest clothing wooly bright;
Gave thee such a tender voice,
Making all the vales rejoice;
      Little Lamb who made thee
10   Dost thou know who made thee

      Little Lamb I'll tell thee,
      Little Lamb I'll tell thee:
He is called by thy name,
For he calls himself a Lamb:
15 He is meek & he is mild,[1]
He became a little child:
I a child & thou a lamb,
We are called by his name.
      Little Lamb God bless thee
20   Little Lamb God bless thee.
—1789

"The Little Black Boy"

The Little Black Boy

My mother bore me in the southern wild,
      And I am black, but O! my soul is white.
White as an angel is the English child:
But I am black as if bereav'd of light.

5 My mother taught me underneath a tree
And sitting down before the heat of day.
She took me on her lap and kissed me.
And pointing to the east began to say.

'Look on the rising sun! there God does live
10 And gives his light. and gives his heat away.
And flowers and trees and beasts and men receive
Comfort in morning joy in the noon day.

'And we are put on earth a little space.
That we may learn to bear the beams of love.
15 And these black bodies and this sun-burnt face
Is but a cloud, and like a shady grove.

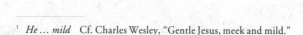

[1] *He ... mild* Cf. Charles Wesley, "Gentle Jesus, meek and mild."

'For when our souls have learn'd the heat to bear
The cloud will vanish we shall hear his voice.
Saying: "come out from the grove my love & care,
20   And round my golden tent like lambs rejoice."'

Thus did my mother say and kissed me.
And thus I say to little English boy.
When I from black and he from white cloud free,
And round the tent of God like lambs we joy:

25   Ill shade him from the heat till he can bear.
To lean in joy upon our fathers knee
And then Ill stand and stroke his silver hair.
And be like him and he will then love me.
—1789

The Chimney Sweeper [1]

When my mother died I was very young,
And my father sold me while yet my tongue,
Could scarcely cry 'weep weep weep weep.'[2]
So your chimneys I sweep & in soot I sleep.[3]

5   Theres little Tom Dacre who cried when his head
That curl'd like a lambs back, was shav'd. so I said.
'Hush Tom never mind it, for when your head's bare.
You know that the soot cannot spoil your white hair.'

And so he was quiet, & that very night.
10   As Tom was a sleeping he had such a sight,
That thousands of sweepers Dick, Joe Ned & Jack
Were all of them lock'd up in coffins of black,

And by came an Angel who had a bright key,
And he open'd the coffins & set them all free.

15   Then down a green plain leaping laughing they run
And wash in a river and shine in the Sun.[4]

Then naked & white, all their bags left behind.
They rise upon clouds, and sport in the wind.
And the Angel told Tom if he'd be a good boy.
20   He'd have God for his father & never want joy.

And so Tom awoke and we rose in the dark
And got with our bags & our brushes to work.
Tho' the morning was cold, Tom was happy & warm.
So if all do their duty, they need not fear harm.
—1789

The Divine Image

To Mercy Pity Peace and Love,
All pray in their distress:
And to these virtues of delight
Return their thankfulness.

5   For Mercy Pity Peace and Love.
Is God our father dear:
And Mercy Pity Peace and Love.
Is Man his child and care.

For Mercy has a human heart
10   Pity a human face:
And Love, the human form divine.
And Peace, the human dress.

Then every man of every clime,
That prays in his distress,
15   Prays to the human form divine
Love Mercy Pity Peace.

And all must love the human form,
In heathen, turk or jew.[5]

---

[1] *The Chimney Sweeper* Children were often forced to climb up chimneys to clean them—a filthy, dangerous, and unhealthy job. A law ameliorating their working conditions was passed in 1788, but it was rarely enforced.

[2] *weep … weep* The child is attempting to say "sweep," the chimney-sweeper's street cry. The act of 1788 should have prevented the apprenticing of children younger than eight.

[3] *in soot I sleep* The sweeps used their bags of soot as blankets.

[4] *And wash … Sun* The act of 1788 called for weekly washings for sweeps.

[5] *heathen … jew* Cf. Isaac Watts, "Praise for the Gospel": "Lord, I ascribe it to thy Grace / And not to Chance, as others do, / That I was born of *Christian* Race, / And not a *Heathen*, or a *Jew*." Whereas Watt's emphasis had been on the theological underpinnings for a hierarchy of birth that took for granted the inferiority of other races and religions, Blake's emphasis is on loving even those whom his society despises.

Where Mercy, Love & Pity dwell,
20 There God is dwelling too.
—1789

Holy Thursday [1]

'Twas on a Holy Thursday their innocent faces clean
The children walking two & two in red & blue
    & green[2]
Grey headed beadles[3] walkd before with wands as
    white as snow
Till into the high dome of Pauls they like Thames
    waters flow

5   O what a multitude they seemd these flowers of
        London town
Seated in companies they sit with radiance all their own
The hum of multitudes was there but multitudes of
    lambs
Thousands of little boys & girls raising their innocent
    hands

Now like a mighty wind they raise to heaven the voice
    of song
10 Or like harmonious thunderings the seats of heaven
        among
Beneath them sit the aged men wise guardians of the poor
Then cherish pity, lest you drive an angel from your
    door[4]
—1789

---

[1] *Holy Thursday* Each year since 1782, the 6,000 children in
London's charity schools had been brought to St. Paul's Cathedral
for an annual service of thanks-giving. Though "Holy Thursday" is
the name given to Ascension Day, these services always occurred on
a Thursday, usually in May, but never on Ascension Day.

[2] *in ... green* The school uniforms.

[3] *beadles* Officials.

[4] *cherish ... door* Cf. Hebrews 13.2, "Be not forgetful to entertain
strangers; for thereby some have entertained angels unawares."

Infant Joy

I have no name,
    I am but two days old.
What shall I call thee?
I happy am
5   Joy is my name.
Sweet joy befall thee!

Pretty joy!
Sweet joy but two days old,
Sweet joy I call thee;
10 Thou dost smile.
I sing the while
Sweet joy befall thee.
—1789

Nurse's Song

When the voices of children are heard on the green
    And laughing is heard on the hill,
My heart is at rest within my breast
And every thing else is still

5   'Then come home my children, the sun is gone down
And the dews of night arise
Come come leave off play. and let us away
Till the morning appears in the skies.'

'No no let us play, for it is yet day
10 And we cannot go to sleep
Besides in the sky, the little birds fly
And the hills are all coverd with sheep'

'Well well go & play till the light fades away
And then go home to bed'
15 The little ones leaped & shouted & laugh'd
And all the hills ecchoed.
—1789

Title page, *Songs of Experience.*

Frontispiece, *Songs of Experience.*

from *Songs of Experience*

Introduction

Hear the voice of the Bard!
Who Present, Past, & Future sees
Whose ears have heard,
The Holy Word,
5 That walk'd among the ancient trees.[1]
Calling[2] the lapsed Soul
And weeping in the evening dew:
That[3] might controll
The starry pole;
10 And fallen fallen light renew!

---

[1] *Holy Word … trees* Cf. Genesis 3.8: "And they heard the voice of the Lord God walking in the garden in the cool of the day: and Adam and his wife hid themselves from the presence of the Lord God amongst the trees of the garden."

[2] *Calling* The subject here is ambiguous, and could either be the bard or the Holy Word.

[3] *That* Most likely the referent here is the lapsed soul, but it may also be the Holy Word.

O Earth, O Earth return!
Arise from out the dewy grass;
Night is worn,
And the morn
15   Rises from the slumberous mass.

'Turn away no more:
Why wilt thou turn away
The starry floor[1]
The watry shore
20   Is giv'n thee till the break of day.'
—1794

The Clod & the Pebble

'Love seeketh not Itself to please.
Nor for itself hath any care;
But for another gives its ease.
And builds a Heaven in Hells despair.'

5   So sang a little Clod of Clay.
Trodden with the cattles feet:
But a Pebble of the brook.
Warbled out these metres meet.

'Love seeketh only Self to please,
10   To bind another to Its delight;
Joys in anothers loss of ease,
And builds a Hell in Heavens despite.'[2]
—1794

Holy Thursday

Is this a holy thing to see.
In a rich and fruitful land,
Babes reducd to misery.
Fed with cold and usurous hand?[3]

5   Is that trembling cry a song?
Can it be a song of joy?
And so many children poor?
It is a land of poverty!

And their sun does never shine.
10   And their fields are bleak & bare.
And their ways are fill'd with thorns
It is eternal winter there.

For where-e'er the sun does shine.
And where-e'er the rain does fall:
15   Babe can never hunger there,
Nor poverty the mind appall.
—1794

The Chimney Sweeper

A little black thing among the snow:
Crying 'weep, weep,' in notes of woe!
'Where are thy father & mother? say?'
'They are both gone up to the church to pray.

5   'Because I was happy upon the heath.
And smil'd among the winters snow:
They clothed me in the clothes of death.
And taught me to sing the notes of woe.

'And because I am happy & dance & sing.
10   They think they have done me no injury:
And are gone to praise God & his Priest & King
Who make up a heaven of our misery.'
—1794

The Sick Rose

O Rose thou art sick.
The invisible worm.
That flies in the night
In the howling storm:

5   Has found out thy bed
Of crimson joy:

---

[1] *starry floor*   The sky, the floor of heaven.

[2] *builds ... despite*   In Milton's *Paradise Lost* (1.254–55), Satan declares, "The mind is its own place, and in itself / Can make a Heaven of Hell, a Hell of Heaven."

[3] *usurous hand*   I.e., the hand of someone engaged in lending money at interest.

And his dark secret love
Does thy life destroy.
—1794

The Fly

Little Fly
Thy summers play.
My thoughtless hand
Has brush'd away.

5 Am not I
A fly like thee?[1]
Or art not thou
A man like me?

For I dance
10 And drink & sing:
Till some blind hand
Shall brush my wing.

If thought is life
And strength & breath:
15 And the want
Of thought is death;[2]

Then am I
A happy fly,
If I live,
20 Or if I die.
—1794

The Tyger

Tyger Tyger, burning bright,
In the forests of the night;
What immortal hand or eye.
Could frame thy fearful symmetry?

5 In what distant deeps or skies.
Burnt the fire of thine eyes?

On what wings dare he aspire?[3]
What the hand. dare seize the fire?[4]

And what shoulder, & what art,
10 Could twist the sinews of thy heart?
And when thy heart began to beat,
What dread hand? & what dread feet?

What the hammer? what the chain,
In what furnace was thy brain?
15 What the anvil? what dread grasp.
Dare its deadly terrors clasp!

When the stars threw down the spears[5]
And water'd heaven with their tears:

---

1 *Am ... thee* Cf. Shakespeare, *King Lear* 4.1.36–37: "As flies to wanton boys, are we to the gods, / They kill us for their sport."

2 *If thought ... death* Cf. René Descartes's statement "Cogito, ergo sum" ("I think, therefore I am").

3 *what ... aspire* In Greek mythology, Icarus fashioned wings of wax and feathers; these melted when he attempted to fly too close to the sun.

4 *What ... fire* Prometheus stole fire from heaven to give to humans.

5 *threw down the spears* Either in surrender or as an act of rebellion —it is uncertain which.

Did he smile his work to see?
20 Did he who made the Lamb make thee?[1]

Tyger Tyger burning bright,
In the forests of the night:
What immortal hand or eye.
Dare frame thy fearful symmetry?
—1794

Ah! Sun-Flower

Ah Sun-flower! weary of time,
  Who countest the steps of the Sun:
Seeking after that sweet golden clime
Where the travellers journey is done.

5 Where the Youth pined away with desire,
And the pale Virgin shrouded in snow:
Arise from their graves and aspire.
Where my Sun-flower wishes to go.
—1794

The Garden of Love

I went to the Garden of Love.
  And saw what I never had seen:
A Chapel was built in the midst,
Where I used to play on the green.[2]

5 And the gates of this Chapel were shut,
And 'Thou shalt not'[3] writ over the door;
So I turn'd to the Garden of Love,
That so many sweet flowers bore.

And I saw it was filled with graves,
10 And tomb-stones where flowers should be:
And Priests in black gowns, were walking their
    rounds,

---

[1] *Did he ... thee*   Tigers are not mentioned in the Bible.

[2] *A Chapel ... green*   Possibly a reference to the erection of a chapel on South Lambeth Green in 1793.

[3] *Thou shalt not*   The phrase that introduces most of the Ten Commandments (Exodus 20.3–17).

And binding with briars,[4] my joys & desires.
—1794

London

I wander thro' each charter'd[5] street,
  Near where the charter'd Thames does flow,
And mark in every face I meet
Marks of weakness, marks of woe.

5 In every cry of every Man,
In every Infants cry of fear.
In every voice; in every ban.
The mind-forg'd manacles I hear

How the Chimney-sweepers cry
10 Every blackning Church appalls.
And the hapless Soldiers sigh
Runs in blood down Palace walls

But most thro' midnight streets I hear
How the youthful Harlots curse[6]
15 Blasts the new born Infants tear[7]
And blights with plagues the Marriage hearse.
—1794

The Human Abstract

Pity would be no more.
  If we did not make somebody Poor:
And Mercy no more could be.
If all were as happy as we;

5 And mutual fear brings peace;
Till the selfish loves increase.

---

[4] *binding with briars*   Prior to the nineteenth century, binding graves with briars was a common practice.

[5] *charter'd*   Privileged, licensed. While charters grant freedoms, they often do so for a select minority (such as merchants) and thereby simultaneously oppress the majority.

[6] *Harlots curse*   Referring both to the oaths she utters and the venereal diseases she spreads.

[7] *Blasts ... tear*   A reference to the blindness caused in infants if they contract certain venereal diseases (such as gonorrhea) from the mother.

Then Cruelty knits a snare,
And spreads his baits with care.

He sits down with holy fears,
10   And waters the ground with tears;
Then Humility takes its root
Underneath his foot.

Soon spreads the dismal shade
Of Mystery over his head;
15   And the Catterpiller and Fly.
Feed on the Mystery.

And it bears the fruit of Deceit.
Ruddy and sweet to eat;
And the Raven his nest has made
20   In its thickest shade.

The Gods of the earth and sea.
Sought thro' Nature to find this Tree
But their search was all in vain:
There grows one in the Human Brain
—1794

Infant Sorrow

My mother groand! my father wept.
Into the dangerous world I leapt:
Helpless, naked. piping loud;
    Like a fiend hid in a cloud.

5   Struggling in my fathers hands:
Striving against my swadling bands:
Bound and weary I thought best
To sulk upon my mothers breast.
—1794

A Poison Tree[1]

I was angry with my friend;
    I told my wrath, my wrath did end.
I was angry with my foe:
    I told it not, my wrath did grow.

5   And I waterd it in fears,
Night & morning with my tears:
And I sunned it with smiles,
And with soft deceitful wiles.

And it grew both day and night.
10   Till it bore an apple bright.
And my foe beheld it shine,
And he knew that it was mine.

And into my garden stole.
When the night had veild the pole;
15   In the morning glad I see.
My foe outstretchd beneath the tree.
—1794

——————

[Plate 1][2]

The Marriage of Heaven and Hell[3]

[Plate 2]

The Argument[4]

Rintrah[5] roars & shakes his fires in the burdend air;
Hungry clouds swag[6] on the deep

Once meek, and in a perilous path,
The just man kept his course along
5   The vale of death.
Roses are planted where thorns grow,
And on the barren heath
Sing the honey bees.

Then the perilous path was planted:
10   And a river, and a spring

---

[1] *A Poison Tree* A manuscript version of this poem is entitled "Christian Forbearance."

[2] *[Plate 1]* The illustrated plates are reproduced below on pp. 79–83.

[3] *The Marriage ... Hell* Blake combines the titles of two works by the Swedish visionary Emanuel Swedenborg (1688–1772), *A Treatise Concerning Heaven and Hell, and of the Wonderful Things Therein, as Heard and Seen by Emanuel Swedenborg* (1758, trans. 1784) and *Conjugial Love* (1768, trans. 1790).

[4] *The Argument* For the imagery of "The Argument," Cf. Isaiah 5.1–7, 7.23–25, 35.1–10.

[5] *Rintrah* The character of Rintrah, a prophet and herald, reappears in Blake's *Europe a Prophecy* (1794) as well as in his *Milton*.

[6] *swag* Sag, hang heavily.

On every cliff and tomb;
And on the bleached bones[1]
Red clay[2] brought forth.

Till the villain left the paths of ease,
15   To walk in perilous paths, and drive
The just man into barren climes.

Now the sneaking serpent walks
In mild humility.
And the just man rages in the wilds
20   Where lions roam.

Rintrah roars & shakes his fires in the burdend air;
Hungry clouds swag on the deep.

[Plate 3]

As a new heaven is begun, and it is now thirty-three
years since its advent: the Eternal Hell revives.[3] And lo!
Swedenborg is the Angel sitting at the tomb; his writings are the linen clothes folded up. Now is the dominion of Edom,[4] & the return of Adam into Paradise; see
Isaiah XXXIV & XXXV[5] chap.

Without Contraries is no progression. Attraction
and Repulsion, Reason and Energy, Love and Hate, are
necessary to Human existence.

From these contraries spring what the religious call
Good & Evil. Good is the passive that obeys Reason
Evil is the active springing from Energy.

Good is Heaven. Evil is Hell.

[Plate 4]

The Voice of the Devil

All Bibles or sacred codes have been the causes of the
following errors.
1. That Man has two real existing principles Viz: a Body
& a Soul.
2. That Energy. calld Evil. is alone from the Body. &
that Reason. calld Good. is alone from the soul.
3. That God will torment Man in Eternity for following
his Energies.
But the following Contraries to these are True
1. Man has no Body distinct from his soul for that calld
Body is a portion of soul discernd by the five Senses, the
chief inlets of Soul in this age
2. Energy is the only life and is from the Body and
Reason is the bound or outward circumference of
Energy.
3. Energy is Eternal Delight

[Plate 5]

Those who restrain desire, do so because theirs is
weak enough to be restrained; and the restrainer or
reason usurps its place & governs the unwilling.

And being restrained it by degrees becomes passive
till it is only the shadow of desire.

The history of this is written in *Paradise Lost*.[6] & the
Governor or Reason is call'd Messiah.

And the original Archangel or possessor of the
command of the heavenly host, is calld the Devil or
Satan and his children are call'd Sin & Death[7]

But in the Book of Job Miltons Messiah is call'd
Satan.

For this history has been adopted by both parties

It indeed appear'd to Reason as if Desire was cast
out, but the Devils account is, that the Messiah [Plate 6]
fell. & formed a heaven of what he stole from the Abyss[8]

---

[1] *bleached bones* Cf. Ezekiel 37.1–11, in which Ezekiel sees life resurrected from a valley of bones.

[2] *Red clay* Since God created Adam from "the dust of the ground" (Genesis 2.8), "Adam" is sometimes said to mean "red clay" in Hebrew.

[3] *As a ... revives* Swedenborg had predicted that the Last Judgment would occur in 1757, coincidentally the year of Blake's birth. In 1790, the "now" of the poem, Blake is 33, Christ's age when He was crucified and rose again.

[4] *Edom* Cf. Genesis 27.40, in which "Edom" is another name for "Esau," whose brother Jacob stole his inheritance. Like "Adam," "Edom" suggests redness.

[5] *Isaiah XXXIV & XXXV* Prophecies of divine vengeance and restoration, respectively.

[6] *Paradise Lost* The rest of this section contains Blake's own reading of Milton's epic.

[7] *Sin & Death* Cf. *Paradise Lost* 2.746–814, in which the birth of Satan's daughter, Sin, and the son of their incestuous union, Death, are described.

[8] *It ... Abyss Paradise Lost* 6.824ff. describes God's defeat of Satan, originally the Archangel Lucifer, and Satan's expulsion from heaven, along with his rebel faction.

This is shewn in the Gospel, where he prays to the Father to send the comforter[1] or Desire that Reason may have Ideas to build on, the Jehovah of the Bible being no other than he who dwells in flaming fire Know that after Christs death, he became Jehovah.

But in Milton; the Father is Destiny, the Son, a Ratio[2] of the five senses. & the Holy Ghost, Vacuum!

Note. The reason Milton wrote in fetters when he wrote of Angels & God, and at liberty when of Devils & Hell, is because he was a true Poet and of the Devils party without knowing it.

A Memorable Fancy[3]

As I was walking among the fires of hell, delighted with the enjoyments of Genius; which to Angels look like torment and insanity. I collected some of their Proverbs: thinking that as the sayings used in a nation. mark its character, so the Proverbs of Hell, shew the nature of Infernal wisdom better than any description of buildings or garments

When I came home; on the abyss of the five senses. where a flat sided steep frowns over the present world. I saw a mighty Devil folded in black clouds, hovering on the sides of the rock, with corroding [Plate 7] fires[4] he wrote the following sentence now percieved by the minds of men, & read by them on earth.

How do you know but ev'ry Bird that cuts the airy way,
Is an immense world of delight, clos'd by your
senses five?[5]

Proverbs of Hell[6]

In seed time learn, in harvest teach, in winter enjoy.
Drive your cart and your plow over the bones of the
    dead.
The road of excess leads to the palace of wisdom.
Prudence is a rich ugly old maid courted by Incapacity.
5 He who desires but acts not, breeds pestilence.
The cut worm forgives the plow.
Dip him in the river who loves water.
A fool sees not the same tree that a wise man sees.
He whose face gives no light, shall never become a star.
10 Eternity is in love with the productions of time.
The busy bee has no time for sorrow.
The hours of folly are measur'd by the clock, but of
    wisdom: no clock can measure.
All wholsom food is caught without a net or a trap.
Bring out number weight, & measure in a year of dearth
15 No bird soars too high. if he soars with his own wings.
A dead body. revenges not injuries.
The most sublime act is to set another before you.
If the fool would persist in his folly he would become
    wise
Folly is the cloke of knavery.
20 Shame is Prides cloke.

[Plate 8]

Prisons are built with stones of Law, Brothels with
    bricks of Religion.
The pride of the peacock is the glory of God.
The lust of the goat is the bounty of God.
The wrath of the lion is the wisdom of God.
5 The nakedness of woman is the work of God.
Excess of sorrow laughs. Excess of joy weeps.
The roaring of lions, the howling of wolves, the raging
    of the stormy sea, and the destructive sword. are
    portions of eternity too great for the eye of man.
The fox condemns the trap, not himself.
Joys impregnate. Sorrows bring forth.
10 Let man wear the fell of the lion. woman the fleece of
    the sheep.
The bird a nest. the spider a web. man friendship.

---

[1] *he prays … comforter* In John 14.16–17, Christ says He will pray to the Father to give mankind another comforter, the Holy Ghost.

[2] *Ratio* Sum.

[3] *Memorable Fancy* Blake's "Memorable Fancies" are modeled on the "Memorable Relations" in which Swedenborg recounts his visionary experiences.

[4] *corroding fires* A reference to Blake's use of acids to etch the copper plates from which he printed his poems. More extended accounts of the printing process occur on plates 14 and 15.

[5] *How do … five* Cf. Thomas Chatterton, *Bristowe Tragedie, or the Dethe of Syr Charles Bawdin* (1768): "How dydd I know that ev'ry darte / That cutte the airie waie / Myghte nott find passage toe my harte / And close myne eyes for aie?" (133–36).

[6] *Proverbs of Hell* A diabolical version of the Old Testament's Book of Proverbs.

The selfish smiling fool & the sullen frowning fool.
    shall be both thought wise. that they may be a rod.
What is now proved was once only imagin'd.
The rat, the mouse, the fox, the rabbet; watch the roots,
    the lion. the tyger. the horse. the elephant. watch
    the fruits.
15   The cistern contains: the fountain overflows
One thought. fills immensity.
Always be ready to speak your mind, and a base man
    will avoid you.
Every thing possible to be believ'd is an image of truth.
The eagle never lost so much time as when he
    submitted to learn of the crow.

[Plate 9]

The fox provides for himself. but God provides for the
    lion.
Think in the morning. Act in the noon, Eat in the
    evening, Sleep in the night,
He who has sufferd you to impose on him knows you.
As the plow follows words, so God rewards prayers.
5   Thy tygers of wrath are wiser than the horses of
    instruction
Expect poison. from the standing water.
You never know what is enough unless you know what
    is more than enough.
Listen to the fools reproach! it is a kingly title!
The eyes of fire, the nostrils of air, the mouth of water,
    the beard of earth.
10   The weak in courage is strong in cunning.
The apple tree never asks the beech how he shall grow,
    nor the lion the horse, how he shall take his prey.
The thankful reciever bears a plentiful harvest.
If others had not been foolish, we should be so.
The soul of sweet delight, can never be defil'd,
15   When thou seest an Eagle. thou seest a portion of
    Genius. lift up thy head!
As the caterpiller chooses the fairest leaves to lay her
    eggs on. so the priest lays his curse on the fairest
    joys.
To create a little flower is the labour of ages.
Damn. braces. Bless relaxes.
The best wine is the oldest. the best water the newest.

20   Prayers plow not! Praises reap not!
Joys laugh not! Sorrows weep not!

[Plate 10]

The head Sublime, the heart Pathos, the genitals
    Beauty. the hands & feet Proportion.
As the air to a bird or the sea to a fish, so is contempt to
    the contemptible.
The crow wish'd every thing was black, the owl, that
    every thing was white.
Exuberance is Beauty.
5   If the lion was advised by the fox. he would be cunning.
Improvent makes strait roads, but the crooked roads
    without Improvement. are roads of Genius.
Sooner murder an infant in its cradle than nurse
    unacted desires
Where man is not nature is barren.
Truth can never be told so as to be understood. and not
    be believ'd.
10   Enough! or Too much

[Plate 11]

The ancient Poets animated all sensible objects with
Gods or Geniuses, calling them by the names and
adorning them with the properties of woods, rivers,
mountains, lakes, cities, nations, and whatever their
enlarged & numerous senses could perceive.

And particularly they studied the genius of each city
& country. placing it under its mental deity.

Till a system was formed, which some took advantage of & enslav'd the vulgar by attempting to realize or
abstract the mental deities from their objects: thus began
Priesthood.

Choosing forms of worship from poetic tales.

And at length they pronounced that the Gods had
ordered such things.

Thus men forgot that All deities reside in the human
breast.

[Plate 12]

A Memorable Fancy

The Prophets Isaiah and Ezekiel dined with me, and I asked them how they dared so roundly to assert. that God spoke to them; and whether they did not think at the time, that they would be misunderstood, & so be the cause of imposition.

Isaiah answer'd. 'I saw no God. nor heard any, in a finite organical perception; but my senses discover'd the infinite in every thing, and as I was then perswaded. & remain confirm'd; that the voice of honest indignation is the voice of God, I cared not for consequences but wrote'

Then I asked: 'does a firm perswasion that a thing is so, make it so?'

He replied, 'All poets believe that it does. & in ages of imagination this firm perswasion removed mountains; but many are not capable of a firm perswasion of any thing'

Then Ezekiel said. The philosophy of the east taught the first principles of human perception some nations held one principle for the origin & some another, we of Israel taught that the Poetic Genius (as you now call it) was the first principle and all the others merely derivative, which was the cause of our despising the Priests & Philosophers of other countries, and prophecying that all Gods [Plate 13] would at last be proved to originate in ours & to be the tributaries of the Poetic Genius, it was this. that our great poet King David desired so fervently & invokes so patheticly, saying by this he conquers enemies & governs kingdoms; and we so loved our God. that we cursed in his name all the deities of surrounding nations, and asserted that they had rebelled; from these opinions the vulgar came to think that all nations would at last be subject to the jews.

'This' said he, 'like all firm perswasions, is come to pass, for all nations believe the jews code and worship the jews god, and what greater subjection can be'

I heard this with some wonder, & must confess my own conviction. After dinner I ask'd Isaiah to favour the world with his lost works, he said none of equal value was lost. Ezekiel said the same of his.

I also asked Isaiah what made him go naked and barefoot three years? he answered, 'the same that made our friend Diogenes the Grecian.'[1]

I then asked Ezekiel. why he eat dung, & lay so long on his right & left side?[2] he answered. 'the desire of raising other men into a perception of the infinite this the North American tribes practise, & is he honest who resists his genius or conscience. only for the sake of present ease or gratification?'

[Plate 14]

The ancient tradition that the world will be consumed in fire at the end of six thousand years[3] is true. as I have heard from Hell.

For the cherub with his flaming sword is hereby commanded to leave his guard at tree of life, and when he does, the whole creation will be consumed, and appear infinite. and holy whereas it now appears finite & corrupt.

This will come to pass by an improvement of sensual enjoyment.

But first the notion that man has a body distinct from his soul, is to be expunged; this I shall do, by printing in the infernal method, by corrosives, which in Hell are salutary and medicinal, melting apparent surfaces away, and displaying the infinite which was hid.[4]

If the doors of perception were cleansed every thing would appear to man as it is, infinite.

For man has closed himself up, till he sees all things thro' narrow chinks of his cavern.[5]

---

[1] *Diogenes the Grecian* Founder of the Cynic school of philosophers, who advocated and practiced a lifestyle of extreme simplicity. In Isaiah 20.2–3, Isaiah is commanded by the Lord to walk "naked and barefoot" for three years.

[2] *why … side* As he was instructed by the Lord in Ezekiel 4.4–6.

[3] *The ancient … years* In Genesis 8.21, just after the Flood, God promises not to destroy the world again. The New Testament, however, contains several prophecies that it will be destroyed, this time by fire (Luke 12.49, 2 Peter 3.5–7). The traditional figure of six thousand years seems to have been obtained by combining the six days it took to make the world (Genesis 1) and the idea "that one day is with the Lord as a thousand years" (2 Peter 3.8).

[4] *this I … hid* In conventional etching, only the lines of the design are burned away by the acid, the rest of the plate being protected by an acid-proof substance such as wax. In Blake's relief etching process, however, almost the whole surface of the plate is burned away, leaving the lines in relief.

[5] *chinks … cavern* Cf. the allegory of the cave in Plato, *Republic*, and the image of the camera obscura in John Locke (1632–1704), *An Essay Concerning Human Understanding*.

[Plate 15]

A Memorable Fancy

I was in a Printing House in Hell & saw the method in which knowledge is transmitted from generation to generation

In the first chamber was a Dragon-Man. clearing away the rubbish from a caves mouth; within, a number of Dragons were hollowing the cave,

In the second chamber was a Viper folding round the rock & the cave, and others adorning it with gold silver and precious stones

In the third chamber was an Eagle with wings and feathers of air, he caused the inside of the cave to be infinite, around were numbers of Eagle like men, who built palaces in the immense cliffs.

In the fourth chamber were Lions of flaming fire raging around & melting the metals into living fluids.

In the fifth chamber were Unnam'd forms, which cast the metals into the expanse.

There they were reciev'd by Men who occupied the sixth chamber, and took the forms of books & were arranged in libraries.

[Plate 16]

The Giants who formed this world into its sensual existence and now seem to live in it in chains, are in truth. the causes of its life & the sources of all activity, but the chains are, the cunning of weak and tame minds. which have power to resist energy. according to the proverb, the weak in courage is strong in cunning.

Thus one portion of being, is the Prolific. the other, the Devouring; to the devourer it seems as if the producer was in his chains, but it is not so, he only takes portions of existence and fancies that the whole.

But the Prolific would cease to be Prolific unless the Devourer as a sea received the excess of his delights.

Some will say, 'Is not God alone the Prolific?' I answer, 'God only Acts & Is. in existing beings or Men.'

These two classes of men are always upon earth. & they should be enemies; whoever tries [Plate 17] to reconcile them seeks to destroy existence.

Religion is an endeavour to reconcile the two.

Note. Jesus Christ did not wish to unite but to seperate them, as in the Parable of sheep and goats![1] & he says 'I came not to send Peace but a Sword.'[2]

Messiah or Satan or Tempter was formerly thought to be one of the Antediluvians[3] who are our Energies.

A Memorable Fancy

An Angel came to me and said. 'O pitiable foolish young man! O horrible! O dreadful state! consider the hot burning dungeon thou art preparing for thyself to all eternity, to which thou art going in such career.'

I said. 'perhaps you will be willing to shew me my eternal lot & we will contemplate together upon it and see whether your lot or mine is most desirable.'

So he took me thro' a stable & thro a church & down into the church vault at the end of which was a mill; thro' the mill; we went. and came to a cave. down the winding cavern we groped our tedious way till a void boundless as a nether sky appeard beneath us & we held by the roots of trees and hung over this immensity, but I said, 'if you please we will commit ourselves to this void, and see whether providence is here also, if you will not I will?' but he answerd. 'do not presume O young-man but as we here remain behold thy lot which will soon appear when the darkness passes away.'

So I remaind with him sitting in the twisted [Plate 18] root of an oak. he was suspended in a fungus which hung with the head downward into the deep;

By degrees we beheld the infinite Abyss, fiery as the smoke of a burning city; beneath us at an immense distance was the sun, black but shining round it were fiery tracks on which revolv'd vast spiders. crawling after their prey; which flew or rather swum in the infinite deep, in the most terrific shapes of animals sprung from corruption. & the air was full of them, & seemd composed of them; these are Devils. and are called Powers of the air, I now asked my companion which was my eternal lot? he said, 'between the black & white spiders'

---

[1]   *Parable ... goats* Cf. Matthew 25.32–46. God divides the nations "as a shepherd divideth his sheep from his goats," placing the sheep, who are to be saved, on his right hand, and the goats, who are damned, on his left.

[2]   *I ... Sword* From Matthew 10.34.

[3]   *Antediluvians* Those who existed before the Flood.

But now, from between the black & white spiders a cloud and fire burst and rolled thro' the deep blackning all beneath, so that the nether deep grew black as a sea & rolled with a terrible noise: beneath us was nothing now to be seen but a black tempest, till looking east between the clouds & the waves. we saw a cataract of blood mixed with fire and not many stones throw from us appeard and sunk again the scaly fold of a monstrous serpent at last to the east, distant about three degrees[1] appeard a fiery crest above the waves slowly it reared like a ridge of golden rocks till we discoverd two globes of crimson fire. from which the sea fled away in clouds of smoke, and now we saw, it was the head of Leviathan,[2] his forehead was divided into streaks of green & purple like those on a tygers forehead: soon we saw his mouth & red gills hang just above the raging foam tinging the black deep with beams of blood, advancing toward [Plate 19] us with all the fury of a spiritual existence.

My friend the Angel climb'd up from his station into the mill; I remain'd alone, & then this appearance was no more, but I found myself sitting on a pleasant bank beside a river by moon light hearing a harper who sung to the harp. & his theme was, 'The man who never alters his opinion is like standing water, & breeds reptiles of the mind.'

But I arose. and sought for the mill, & there I found my Angel, who surprised asked me, how I escaped?

I answered. 'All that we saw was owing to your metaphysics: for when you ran away, I found myself on a bank by moonlight hearing a harper, But now we have seen my eternal lot, shall I shew you yours?' he laughd at my proposal; but I by force suddenly caught him in my arms, & flew westerly thro' the night, till we were elevated above the earths shadow: then I flung myself with him directly into the body of the sun, here I clothed myself in white,[3] & taking in my hand Sweden-borgs volumes sunk from the glorious clime, and passed all the planets till we came to saturn, here I staid to rest & then leap'd into the void. between saturn & the fixed stars.[4]

'Here' said I! 'is your lot, in this space, if space it may be calld,' Soon we saw the stable and the church, & I took him to the altar and open'd the Bible, and lo! it was a deep pit, into which I descended driving the Angel before me, soon we saw seven houses of brick,[5] one we entred; in it were a [Plate 20] number of monkeys. baboons, & all of that species chaind by the middle, grinning and snatching at one another. but witheld by the shortness of their chains; however I saw that they sometimes grew numerous, and then the weak were caught by the strong and with a grinning aspect, first coupled with & then devourd, by plucking off first one limb and then another till the body was left a helpless trunk. this after grinning & kissing it with seeming fondness they devourd too; and here & there I saw one savourily picking the flesh off his own tail; as the stench terribly annoyd us both we went into the mill, & I in my hand brought the skeleton of a body, which in the mill was Aristotles Analytics.[6]

So the Angel said: 'thy phantasy has imposed upon me & thou oughtest to be ashamed.'

I answerd: 'we impose on one another, & it is but lost time to converse with you whose works are only Analytics.'

Opposition is True Friendship

[Plate 21]

I have always found that Angels have the vanity to speak of themselves as the only wise; this they do with a confident insolence sprouting from systematic reasoning;

Thus Swedenborg boasts that what he writes is new; tho' it is only the Contents or Index of already publish'd books

---

[1] *three degrees* Paris is three degrees east of London.

[2] *Leviathan* The beast Leviathan is described in Job 4.1; Psalms 104.26; Isaiah 27.1; Revelation 11.7, 12.9, 13.2, 20.1–3. Blake may also be thinking of Thomas Hobbes's *Leviathan; or, The Matter, Form, and Power of a Commonwealth, Ecclesiastical and Civil.*

[3] *clothed … white* Cf. Revelation 7.9, in which those who have been redeemed are clothed in white when they appear before Christ's throne.

[4] *void … stars* In the Ptolemaic world system, Saturn was the outermost planet, and bordered on the sphere of the fixed stars.

[5] *seven … brick* John addresses the book of Revelation to the "seven churches which are in Asia" (Revelation 1.4).

[6] *Analytics* Aristotle's two treatises on logic.

A man carried a monkey about for a shew. & because he was a little wiser than the monkey, grew vain. and conceiv'd himself as much wiser than seven men. It is so with Swedenborg; he shews the folly of churches & exposes hypocrites, till he imagines that all are religious. & himself the single   [Plate 22] one on earth that ever broke a net.

Now hear a plain fact: Swedenborg has not written one new truth: Now hear another: he has written all the old falshoods.

And now hear the reason. He conversed with Angels who are all religious. & conversed not with Devils who all hate religion, for he was incapable thro' his conceited notions.

Thus Swedenborgs writings are a recapitulation of all superficial opinions, and an analysis of the more sublime. but no further.

Have now another plain fact: Any man of mechanical talents may from the writings of Paracelsus or Jacob Behmen,[1] produce ten thousand volumes of equal value with Swedenborg's. and from those of Dante or Shakespear. an infinite number.

But when he has done this, let him not say that he knows better than his master, for he only holds a candle in sunshine.

A Memorable Fancy

Once I saw a Devil in a flame of fire. who arose before an Angel that sat on a cloud. and the Devil uttered these words.

'The worship of God is. Honouring his gifts in other men, each according to his genius. and loving the [Plate 23] greatest men best, those who envy or calumniate great men hate God, for there is no other God.'

The Angel hearing this became almost blue but mastering himself he grew yellow, & at last white pink & smiling, and then replied,

'Thou Idolater, is not God One? & is not he visible in Jesus Christ? and has not Jesus Christ given his sanction to the law of ten commandments and are not all other men fools. sinners, & nothings?'

The Devil answer'd; 'bray a fool in a morter with wheat. yet shall not his folly be beaten out of him:[2] if Jesus Christ is the greatest man. you ought to love him in the greatest degree; now hear how he has given his sanction to the law of ten commandments: did he not mock at the sabbath,[3] and so mock the sabbaths God? murder those who were murderd because of him?[4] turn away the law from the woman taken in adultery?[5] steal the labor of others to support him?[6] bear false witness when he omitted making a defence before Pilate?[7] covet when he pray'd for his disciples, and when he bid them shake off the dust of their feet against such as refused to lodge them?[8] I tell you, no virtue can exist without breaking these ten commandments: Jesus was all virtue, and acted from impulse.[Plate 24] not from rules.'

When he had so spoken: I beheld the Angel who stretched out his arms embracing the flame of fire & he was consumed and arose as Elijah.[9]

Note. This Angel, who is now become a Devil, is my particular friend: we often read the Bible together in its infernal or diabolical sense which the world shall have if they behave well

I have also: The Bible of Hell:[10] which the world shall have whether they will or no.

One Law for the Lion & Ox is Oppression
—1793

___

[1] *Paracelsus* Philippus Aureolus, Theophrastus Bombastus von Hohenheim (1493–1541), Swiss physician and alchemist; *Behmen* Jakob Boehme (1575–1624), German mystic.

[2] *bray ... him* Proverbs 27.22. This devil can quote scripture to his purpose; *bray* Crush.

[3] *mock ... sabbath* In Exodus 20.8–11; Matthew 12.8–12; Mark 2.27, 3.2–4; Luke 14.3–5; John 5.16.

[4] *murder ... him* In Exodus 20.13; see the martyrdom of Stephen (Acts 7.58–60).

[5] *turn ... adultery* In Exodus 20.14; John 8.3–11.

[6] *steal ... him* Cf. Exodus 20.15; Matthew 26.6–13.

[7] *bear ... Pilate* Cf. Exodus 20.16; Matthew 27.11–14; Mark 15.2–5.

[8] *covet ... them* Cf. Exodus 20.17; Matthew 10.14; Luke 9.5.

[9] *who ... Elijah* Cf. 2 Kings 2.11: "There appeared a chariot of fire, and ... Elijah went up by a whirlwind into heaven."

[10] *Bible of Hell* A reference to Blake's own work. In addition to the Proverbs of Hell (plates 7–10), this bible is sometimes said to include such later works as *The [First] Book of Urizen*, *The Book of Ahania*, and *The Book of Los* (1794–95).

1

2

3

4

5

6

Plate 7

roding fires he wrote the following sentence now percieved by the minds of men, & read by them on earth.

How do you know but ev'ry Bird that cuts the airy way,
Is an immense world of delight, clos'd by your senses five?

Proverbs of Hell

In seed time learn, in harvest teach, in winter enjoy.
Drive your cart and your plow over the bones of the dead.
The road of excess leads to the palace of wisdom
Prudence is a rich ugly old maid courted by Incapacity.
He who desires but acts not, breeds pestilence.
The cut worm forgives the plow.
Dip him in the river who loves water.
A fool sees not the same tree that a wise man sees.
He whose face gives no light, shall never become a star.
Eternity is in love with the productions of time.
The busy bee has no time for sorrow.
The hours of folly are measur'd by the clock, but of wis-
dom: no clock can measure.
All wholsom food is caught without a net or a trap.
Bring out number weight & measure in a year of dearth.
No bird soars too high, if he soars with his own wings.
A dead body revenges not injuries.
The most sublime act is to set another before you.
If the fool would persist in his folly he would become
wise
Folly is the cloke of knavery.
Shame is Prides cloke.

7

Plate 8

Proverbs of Hell

Prisons are built with stones of Law, Brothels with
bricks of Religion.
The pride of the peacock is the glory of God.
The lust of the goat is the bounty of God.
The wrath of the lion is the wisdom of God.
The nakedness of woman is the work of God.
Excess of sorrow laughs. Excess of joy weeps.
The roaring of lions, the howling of wolves, the raging
of the stormy sea, and the destructive sword, are
portions of eternity too great for the eye of man.
The fox condemns the trap, not himself.
Joys impregnate. Sorrows bring forth.
Let man wear the fell of the lion, woman the fleece of
the sheep.
The bird a nest, the spider a web, man friendship.
The selfish smiling fool, & the sullen frowning fool, shall
be both thought wise, that they may be a rod.
What is now proved was once, only imagin'd.
The rat, the mouse, the fox, the rabbet; watch the roots;
the lion, the tyger, the horse, the elephant, watch
the fruits.
The cistern contains: the fountain overflows.
One thought fills immensity.
Always be ready to speak your mind, and a base man
will avoid you.
Every thing possible to be believ'd is an image of truth.
The eagle never lost so much time, as when he submit-
ted to learn of the crow.   The

8

Plate 9

Proverbs of Hell

The fox provides for himself, but God provides for the lion.
Think in the morning. Act in the noon. Eat in the even-
ing. Sleep in the night.
He who has suffer'd you to impose on him, knows you.
As the plow follows words, so God rewards prayers.
The tygers of wrath are wiser than the horses of in-
struction.
Expect poison from the standing water.
You never know what is enough unless you know what is
more than enough.
Listen to the fools reproach! it is a kingly title!
The eyes of fire, the nostrils of air, the mouth of water,
the beard of earth.
The weak in courage is strong in cunning.
The apple tree never asks the beech how he shall grow,
nor the lion, the horse; how he shall take his prey.
The thankful reciever bears a plentiful harvest.
If others had not been foolish, we should be so.
The soul of sweet delight, can never be defil'd.
When thou seest an Eagle, thou seest a portion of Ge-
nius. lift up thy head!
As the caterpiller chooses the fairest leaves to lay
her eggs on, so the priest lays his curse on
the fairest joys.
To create a little flower is the labour of ages.
Damn, braces: Bless relaxes.
The best wine is the oldest, the best water the newest.
Prayers plow not! Praises reap not!
Joys laugh not! Sorrows weep not!

9

Plate 10

Proverbs of Hell

The head Sublime, the heart Pathos, the genitals Beauty,
the hands & feet Proportion.
As the air to a bird or the sea to a fish, so is contempt
to the contemptible.
The crow wish'd every thing was black, the owl, that eve-
ry thing was white.
Exuberance is Beauty.
If the lion was advised by the fox, he would be cunning.
Improvent makes strait roads, but the crooked roads
without Improvement, are roads of Genius.
Sooner murder an infant in its cradle than nurse unact-
ed desires.
Where man is not nature is barren.
Truth can never be told so as to be understood, and
not be believ'd.
Enough! or Too much.

10

Plate 11

The ancient Poets animated all sensible objects
with Gods or Geniuses, calling them by the names and
adorning them with the properties of woods, rivers,
mountains, lakes, cities, nations, and whatever their
enlarged & numerous senses could percieve.
And particularly they studied the genius of each
city & country, placing it under its mental deity.
Till a system was formed, which some took advantage of & enslav'd the vulgar by attempting to
realize or abstract the mental deities from their
objects: thus began Priesthood.
Choosing forms of worship from poetic tales.
And at length they pronounced that the Gods
had orderd such things.
Thus men forgot that All deities reside
in the human breast.

11

Plate 12

A Memorable Fancy

The Prophets Isaiah and Ezekiel dined with
me, and I asked them how they dared so roundly to
assert, that God spoke to them; and whether they
did not think at the time, that they would be misunderstood, & so be the cause of imposition.
Isaiah answer'd. I saw no God, nor heard
any, in a finite organical perception; but my senses discover'd the infinite in every thing, and as I
was then perswaded, & remain confirm'd; that the
voice of honest indignation is the voice of God, I
cared not for consequences but wrote.
Then I asked: does a firm perswasion that a
thing is so, make it so?
He replied. All poets believe that it does, &
in ages of imagination this firm perswasion removed mountains; but many are not capable of a
firm perswasion of any thing.
Then Ezekiel said. The philosophy of the east
taught the first principles of human perception
some nations held one principle for the origin &
some another, we of Israel taught that the Poetic
Genius (as you now call it) was the first principle
and all the others merely derivative, which was the
cause of our despising the Priests & Philosophers
of other countries, and prophecying that all Gods
would

12

would at last be proved to originate in ours & to be the tributaries of the Poetic Genius, it was this that our great poet King David desired so fervently & invokes so pathetically, saying by this he conquers enemies & governs kingdoms; and we so loved our God, that we cursed in his name all the deities of surrounding nations, and asserted that they had rebelled; from these opinions the vulgar came to think that all nations would at last be subject to the jews.

This said he, like all firm perswasions, is come to pass, for all nations believe the jews code and worship the jews god, and what greater subjection can be

I heard this with some wonder, & must confess my own conviction. After dinner I ask'd Isaiah to favour the world with his lost works, he said none of equal value was lost. Ezekiel said the same of his.

I also asked Isaiah what made him go naked and barefoot three years? he answerd, the same that made our friend Diogenes the Grecian.

I then asked Ezekiel, why he eat dung, & lay so long on his right & left side? he answerd, the desire of raising other men into a perception of the infinite this the North American tribes practise, & is he honest who resists his genius or conscience, only for the sake of present ease or gratification?

13

The ancient tradition that the world will be consumed in fire at the end of six thousand years is true, as I have heard from Hell.

For the cherub with his flaming sword is hereby commanded to leave his guard at tree of life, and when he does, the whole creation will be consumed and appear infinite and holy whereas it now appears finite & corrupt.

This will come to pass by an improvement of sensual enjoyment.

But first the notion that man has a body distinct from his soul, is to be expunged; this I shall do, by printing in the infernal method, by corrosives, which in Hell are salutary and medicinal, melting apparent surfaces away, and displaying the infinite which was hid.

If the doors of perception were cleansed every thing would appear to man as it is: Infinite.

For man has closed himself up, till he sees all things thro' narrow chinks of his cavern.

14

A Memorable Fancy

I was in a Printing house in Hell & saw the method in which knowledge is transmitted from generation to generation.

In the first chamber was a Dragon-Man, clearing away the rubbish from a caves mouth; within, a number of Dragons were hollowing the cave.

In the second chamber was a Viper folding round the rock & the cave, and others adorning it with gold silver and precious stones.

In the third chamber was an Eagle with wings and feathers of air, he caused the inside of the cave to be infinite, around were numbers of Eagle like men, who built palaces in the immense cliffs.

In the fourth chamber were Lions of flaming fire raging around & melting the metals into living fluids.

In the fifth chamber were Unnam'd forms, which cast the metals into the expanse.

There they were received by Men who occupied the sixth chamber, and took the forms of books & were arranged in libraries.

15

The Giants who formed this world into its sensual existence and now seem to live in it in chains; are in truth, the causes of its life & the sources of all activity, but the chains are, the cunning of weak and tame minds, which have power to resist energy, according to the proverb, the weak in courage is strong in cunning.

Thus one portion of being, is the Prolific, the other, the Devouring: to the devourer it seems as if the producer was in his chains, but it is not so, he only takes portions of existence and fancies that the whole.

But the Prolific would cease to be Prolific unless the Devourer as a sea received the excess of his delights.

Some will say, Is not God alone the Prolific? I answer, God only Acts & Is, in existing beings or Men.

These two classes of men are always upon earth, & they should be enemies; whoever tries to

16

to reconcile them seeks to destroy existence.

Religion is an endeavour to reconcile the two.

Note. Jesus Christ did not wish to unite but to separate them, as in the Parable of sheep and goats! & he says I came not to send Peace but a Sword.

Messiah or Satan or Tempter was formerly thought to be one of the Antediluvians who are our Energies.

A Memorable Fancy

An Angel came to me and said O pitiable foolish young man! O horrible! O dreadful state! consider the hot burning dungeon thou art preparing for thyself to all eternity, to which thou art going in such career.

I said, perhaps you will be willing to shew me my eternal lot & we will contemplate together upon it and see whether your lot or mine is most desirable.

So he took me thro' a stable & thro' a church & down into the church vault at the end of which was a mill: thro' the mill we went, and came to a cave, down the winding cavern we groped our tedious way till a void boundless as a nether sky appeard beneath us & we held by the roots of trees and hung over this immensity; but I said, if you please, we will commit ourselves to this void, and see whether providence is here also, if you will not I will? but he answerd, do not presume O young-man but as we here remain behold thy lot which will soon appear when the darkness passes away.

So I remaind with him sitting in the twisted

17

root of an oak, he was suspended in a fungus which hung with the head downward into the deep:

By degrees we beheld the infinite Abyss, fiery as the smoke of a burning city; beneath us at an immense distance was the sun, black but shining round it were fiery tracks on which revolved vast spiders, crawling after their prey; which flew or rather swum in the infinite deep, in the most terrific shapes of animals sprung from corruption. & the air was full of them, & seemd composed of them; these are Devils, and are called Powers of the air, I now asked my companion which was my eternal lot? he said, between the black & white spiders

But now, from between the black & white spiders a cloud and fire burst and rolled thro' the deep blackning all beneath, so that the nether deep grew black as a sea & rolled with a terrible noise: beneath us was nothing now to be seen but a black tempest, till looking east between the clouds & the waves, we saw a cataract of blood mixed with fire and not many stones throw from us appeard and sunk again the scaly fold of a monstrous serpent; at last to the east, distant about three degrees appeard a fiery crest above the waves slowly it reared like a ridge of golden rocks till we discoverd two globes of crimson fire, from which the sea fled away in clouds of smoke, and now we saw, it was the head of Leviathan, his forehead was divided into streaks of green & purple like those on a tygers forehead; soon we saw his mouth & red gills hang just above the raging foam tinging the black deep with beams of blood, advancing toward us

18

us with all the forc... [faded]

My friend the Angel climb'd up from his station into the mill; I remain'd alone, & then this appearance was no more, but I found myself sitting on a pleasant bank beside a river by moonlight hearing a harper who sung to the harp. & his theme was, The man who never alters his opinion is like standing water, & breeds reptiles of the mind.

But I arose, and sought for the mill & there I found my Angel, who surprised asked me how I escaped?

I answerd, All that we saw was owing to your metaphysics; for when you ran away, I found myself on a bank by moonlight hearing a harper. But now we have seen my eternal lot, shall I shew you yours? he laughd at my proposal; but I by force suddenly caught him in my arms, & flew westerly thro' the night, till we were elevated above the earths shadow; then I flung myself with him directly into the body of the sun, here I clothed myself in white, & taking in my hand Swedenborgs volumes sunk from the glorious clime, and passed all the planets till we came to saturn, here I staid to rest & then leap'd into the void, between saturn & the fixed stars.

Here said I! is your lot, in this space, if space it may be call'd, Soon we saw the stable and the church, & I took him to the altar and open'd the Bible, and lo! it was a deep pit, into which I descended driving the Angel before me, soon we came to seven houses of brick, one we enterd; in it were a num

19

number of monkeys, baboons, & all of that species chaind by the middle, grinning and snatching at one another, but witheld by the shortness of their chains; however I saw that they sometimes grew numerous, and then the weak were caught by the strong and with a grinning aspect, first coupled with & then devour'd by plucking off first one limb and then another till the body was left a helpless trunk. this after grinning & kissing it with seeming fondness they devourd too; and here & there I saw one savourily picking the flesh off of his own tail; as the stench terribly annoyd us both we went into the mill, & I in my hand brought the skeleton of a body, which in the mill was Aristotles Analytics.

So the Angel said: thy phantasy has imposed upon me & thou oughtest to be ashamed.

I answerd: we impose on one another, & it is but lost time to converse with you whose works are only Analytics.

20

I have always found that Angels have the vanity to speak of themselves as the only wise; this they do with a confident insolence sprouting from systematic reasoning.

Thus Swedenborg boasts that what he writes is new; tho' it is only the Contents or Index of already published books.

A man carried a monkey about for a shew, & because he was a little wiser than the monkey, grew vain, and concievd himself as much wiser than seven men. It is so with Swedenborg; he shews the folly of churches & exposes hypocrites, till he imagines that all are religious, & himself the single one

21

one on earth that ever broke a net.

Now hear a plain fact: Swedenborg has not written one new truth: Now hear another: he has written all the old falshoods.

And now hear the reason. He conversed with Angels who are all religious, & conversed not with Devils who all hate religion, for he was incapable thro' his conceited notions.

Thus Swedenborgs writings are a recapitulation of all superficial opinions, and an analysis of the more sublime, but no further.

Have now another plain fact: Any man of mechanical talents may from the writings of Paracelsus or Jacob Behmen, produce ten thousand volumes of equal value with Swedenborgs, and from those of Dante or Shakespear, an infinite number.

But when he has done this, let him not say that he knows better than his master, for he only holds a candle in sunshine.

A Memorable Fancy

Once I saw a Devil in a flame of fire, who arose before an Angel that sat on a cloud, and the Devil utterd these words.

The worship of God is. Honouring his gifts in other men each according to his genius. and loving the great

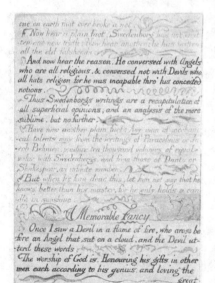

22

greatest men best, those who envy or calumniate great men hate God, for there is no other God.

The Angel hearing this became almost blue but mastering himself he grew yellow, & at last white pink & smiling, and then replied.

Thou Idolater, is not God One? & is not he visible in Jesus Christ? and has not Jesus Christ given his sanction to the law of ten commandments and are not all other men fools, sinners, & nothings?

The Devil answer'd; bray a fool in a morter with wheat, yet shall not his folly be beaten out of him; if Jesus Christ is the greatest man, you ought to love him in the greatest degree; now hear how he has given his sanction to the law of ten commandments: did he not mock at the sabbath, and so mock the sabbaths God? murder those who were murderd because of him? turn away the law from the woman taken in adultery? steal the labor of others to support him? bear false witness when he omitted making a defence before Pilate? covet when he prayd for his disciples, and when he bid them shake off the dust of their feet against such as refused to lodge them? I tell you, no virtue can exist without breaking these ten commandments: Jesus was all virtue, and acted from im-

-pulse

23

pulse: not from rules.

When he had so spoken: I beheld the Angel who stretched out his arms embracing the flame of fire & he was consumed and arose as Elijah.

Note. This Angel, who is now become a Devil, is my particular friend: we often read the Bible together in its infernal or diabolical sense which the world shall have if they behave well.

I have also: The Bible of Hell: which the world shall have whether they will or no.

One Law for the Lion & Ox is Oppression.

24

Engraved circa 1792 and appended as the conclusion (Plates 25, 26, and 27) to *The Marriage of Heaven and Hell* (1790–93), "A Song of Liberty" is an important part of Blake's canon. The poem reiterates and anticipates a number of themes significant to the artist; perhaps most prominent among these are the myth of revolution announced in the cry of "Empire is no more!"—and the prophetic belief in salvation through religious faith. The song can be seen as a key founding document of British Romanticism in its celebration of freedom, its rejection of reason as the focus of human existence, and its insistence on equality. Blake's engravings of vegetative motifs—looped vines, various leaves, branches, flame-like foliage—and two soaring birds to accompany the textual manuscript further contribute to the Romantic vision of the text.

Although the "Song" invariably appears as the last verse in all extant manuscript copies of *The Marriage of Heaven and Hell*, recent criticism suggests that the poem may not have been intended originally to serve as part of the longer work; some scholars have noted the sometimes striking differences in style and content between "A Song of Liberty" and the preceding plates, while others have suggested that the "Song" was to have been published as a separate pamphlet.

⌘ ⌘ ⌘

A Song of Liberty[1]

1. The Eternal Female[2] groand! it was heard over all the Earth:

[1] *A Song of Liberty*   The poem appears as the last three plates (25–27) of *The Marriage of Heaven and Hell* (1790–93), Blake's long prophetic poem, composed in the period following the French Revolution.

[2] *Eternal Female*   The Eternal Female appears in a variety of guises in Blake's poetry; cf. "Earth" and "Earth's Answer" in the opening poems of the *Songs of Experience* (1789), and the "nameless shadowy female" in the Preludium to *Europe* (1794). Here, it seems to birth the revolutionary spirit itself.

2. Albions[3] coast is sick silent; the American meadows faint!

3. Shadows of Prophecy shiver along by the lakes and the rivers and mutter across the ocean? France rend down thy dungeon

4. Golden Spain burst the barriers of old Rome;[4]

5. Cast thy keys O Rome into the deep down falling, even to eternity down falling,

[3] *Albion*   Oldest known name for the island of Great Britain. Albion is also the primeval man, son of the Greek god Poseidon, who founded a country on the island that was then named after him, and who is central to the mythology of Blake's poetic vision.

[4] *old Rome*   The center of religious authority for Catholics.

6. And weep[1]
7. In her trembling hands she took the new born terror howling:
8. On those infinite mountains of light now barr'd out by the atlantic sea, the new born fire stood before the starry king!
9. Flag'd with grey browd snows and thunderous visages the jealous wings wav'd over the deep.
10. The speary hand burned aloft, unbuckled was the shield, forth went the hand of jealousy among the flaming hair. and[2] hurl'd the new born wonder thro' the starry night.
11. The fire, the fire, is falling!
12. Look up! look up! O citizen of London enlarge thy countenance; O Jew, leave counting gold![3] return to thy oil and wine; O African! black African! (go, winged thought, widen his forehead.)
13. The fiery limbs, the flaming hair, shot like the sinking sun into the western sea.
14. Wak'd from his eternal sleep, the hoary element roaring fled away;
15. Down rushd beating his wings in vain the jealous king; his grey brow'd councellors, thunderous warriors, curl'd veterans, among helms, and shields, and chariots, horses, elephants: banners, castles, slings, and rocks,
16. Falling, rushing, ruining! buried in the ruins, on Urthona's[4] dens;

17. All night beneath the ruins, then their sullen flames faded emerge round the gloomy king.
18. With thunder and fire: leading his starry hosts thro' the waste wilderness[5] he promulgates his ten commands,[6] glancing his beamy eyelids over the deep in dark dismay,
19. Where the son of fire in his eastern cloud, while the morning plumes her golden breast.
20. Spurning the clouds written with curses. stamps the stony law to dust. loosing the eternal horses from the dens of night, crying Empire is no more! and now the lion & wolf shall cease.[7]

Chorus

Let the Priests of the Raven[8] of dawn. no longer in deadly black, with hoarse note curse the sons of joy. Nor his accepted brethren whom tyrant, he calls free: lay the bound or build the roof: Nor pale religions letchery call that virginity that wishes but acts not!
For everything that lives is Holy[9]
—1792–93

---

[1] *weep* "and bow thy reverend locks!" was deleted from the copper plate following "weep." These five words are absent in all extant manuscript copies except Copy L (now in the collection of Robert N. Essick) and Copy M (in the collection of E.B. Bentley and G.E. Bentley, Jr.); these two manuscripts consist of plates 25–27 only, with plate 25 in its first state.

[2] *and* This marks the end of Plate 25 in manuscripts of *The Marriage of Heaven and Hell.*

[3] *Jew … counting gold* Since the middle ages European Christian society has condemned Jews for the practice of money-lending, which was in most European countries one of the few professions that Jews were allowed to follow. Blake's anti-Semitic image reflects a stereotypical association, commonly held in England at the time, of Jews with greed.

[4] *Urthona* Cf. Blake's *Book of Thel* (1789). Urthona is one of the four "Zoas," divisions that result from the fall of the primeval man, Albion; he is linked to the imagination, inspiration, and creativity. Urthona's female counterpart is "Enitharmon," and his fallen form is "Los," usually depicted as a blacksmith. The three other Zoas are

"Urizen" (incarnation of law and reason), "Tharmas" (nature, instinct, and unity), and "Luvah" (passion and love).

[5] *wilderness* This marks the end of Plate 26.

[6] *ten commands* Blake repeatedly rejects the Ten Commandments throughout *The Marriage of Heaven and Hell*, a stance consistent with his antinomian position, which discards social law and morality in favor of individual faith, associated for Blake with energy and joy.

[7] *Empire is no more! … shall cease* Cf. Plate 6 of Blake's *America* (1793): "For Empire is no more, and now the Lion & Wolf shall cease" (15).

[8] *Priests of the Raven* The Raven represents the fear of death; in its association here with the "priests," the Raven is connected to orthodoxy and its emphasis on such fear.

[9] *For everything that lives is Holy* Cf. Plate 8 of Blake's *America*: "For every thing that lives is holy, life delights in life" (13).

Mary Wollstonecraft
1759 – 1797

When Mary Wollstonecraft died in 1797 she was a literary celebrity. The most recognized female political writer of her day, Wollstonecraft tackled issues such as women and education, human rights, the "unnatural distinctions" of class, and the relationship between the sexes. Her prominent public profile was, however, severely diminished five months after her death when William Godwin published his *Memoirs of the Author of a Vindication of the Rights of Woman*. Godwin, who was Wollstonecraft's husband and intellectual companion, included controversial details of her sexual and emotional history in his book, which shocked many of her

admirers. Her reputation was restored to some extent by the women's rights movement in the second half of the nineteenth century, and the women's movement of the 1970s elevated her to the status of a feminist icon. Even those who do not associate themselves with feminism now acknowledge Wollstonecraft as an important writer and thinker of the late eighteenth century—and *A Vindication of the Rights of Woman* as a core text in the Western tradition.

Wollstonecraft was born in London on 27 April 1759 to Elizabeth Dixon and Edward Wollstonecraft; she was the eldest daughter among seven children. The Wollstonecrafts were a middle-class, modestly prosperous family whose fortunes went into a gradual decline. Edward attempted to transform himself into a gentleman farmer, moving the family to Epping, Barking, and finally to Beverley in Yorkshire. These moves exacerbated the family's financial difficulties. As well, Wollstonecraft's father was a violent man. As a child, Wollstonecraft frequently intervened in her father's outbursts in order to try to protect her mother. For solace and respite, she turned to her close friend, Jane Arden. Arden's father, John, was a teacher and philosopher who encouraged Wollstonecraft's self-education and provided her with access to his library.

When Mary was 15 the Wollstonecrafts moved to Hoxton, on the outskirts of London. Here, Wollstonecraft was befriended by her next-door neighbors, the Reverend and Mrs. Clare. They became her surrogate family and were responsible for introducing her to Fanny Blood, with whom she would develop an intensely passionate and possibly romantic friendship. Years later, Wollstonecraft described her connection to Blood as "a friendship so fervent, as for years to have constituted the ruling passion of my mind." Blood became the model for Ann in Wollstonecraft's autobiographical novel, *Mary, A Fiction*.

In 1778, Wollstonecraft made the decision to leave home and earn her own living. Now 19, she took a job as a paid companion to a Mrs. Dawson, a widow in Bath. When her mother became ill in 1781, however, Mary returned to London to nurse her. After months of pain, Elizabeth Wollstonecraft died and Mary took up residence with the Bloods. Shortly afterwards Wollstonecraft's sister Eliza married Meredith Bishop, a well-to-do shipwright. After Eliza gave birth to a daughter in 1783, she fell into a deep postpartum depression that Wollstonecraft attributed to Bishop's cruelty. Wanting to rescue her sister, Wollstonecraft convinced Eliza to run away from her husband and child. (At the time, children legally belonged to the father.) Bishop eventually gave up his attempts to bring his wife back, and their daughter died just days before her first birthday.

Wollstonecraft soon realized that she and Eliza would need to find their own source of financial support. In 1784, together with Fanny Blood, they opened a school at Newington Green, north of London. Here, Wollstonecraft met Richard Price, a preacher and a leader of the Dissenters. His congregation was a Unitarian-like group whose political positions on freedom and equality influenced Wollstonecraft's developing ideas. In 1785, Fanny Blood left Newington Green to marry her long-time suitor, Hugh Skeys, in Lisbon. Wollstonecraft joined them several months later when she heard that Fanny was having trouble with her first pregnancy, but despite her efforts both Fanny and her child died a few days after the birth. Wollstonecraft returned to London where her school's financial problems had worsened during her absence. To raise money, she wrote her first book, *Thoughts on the Education of Daughters*. Joseph Johnson, a leading radical bookseller (that is, publisher) and a fellow Dissenter, published the book in 1787. The book's modest success was not enough to save the school, but it did establish Wollstonecraft in the debate on women's education.

Following the collapse of the school, Wollstonecraft became a governess to the Kingsborough family in Ireland, but it was not a happy development; she was doubtless drawing on experience when she later wrote that governesses "are not always treated in a manner calculated to render them respectable in the eyes of their pupils." She did, however, exert an apparently life-long influence on one of her pupils, who grew up to be a public champion of women's rights. Wollstonecraft soon fell into a depression that was diagnosed as nervous fever. She continued writing, though, beginning work on *Mary: A Fiction*. When she was dismissed from her position as governess, still within the year 1787, she returned to London and convinced Johnson to publish *Mary*. He also hired her as a reviewer for the *Analytical Review*, a monthly progressive periodical. Through her reviews she became an influential voice in the decade of ferment that was coming. Through Johnson, Wollstonecraft met Henry Fuseli, an artist and self-described genius. Although Fuseli was married, Wollstonecraft felt he was her soulmate and they soon began an affair.

Wollstonecraft embraced the start of the French Revolution with excitement. When Edmund Burke published his *Reflections on the Revolution in France* (1790), a treatise that attacked revolutionary ideas, Johnson urged Wollstonecraft to write a reply. She quickly crafted *A Vindication of the Rights of Men*, published anonymously less than a month after the appearance of Burke's book. A few weeks later, a second edition was published under her name, and this solidified her reputation as a radical. In early 1792, she became famous throughout Europe when her new book, *A Vindication of the Rights of Woman*, was published. Written in only six weeks, *A Vindication* presented the case for universal rights, social equality, and women's economic independence. As Wollstonecraft pointed out, the refusal of those who had espoused revolutionary principles of equality to extend rights to women represented a betrayal of those supposedly universal principles.

Eager to obtain first-hand knowledge about the Revolution, and just as eager to escape her deteriorating affair with Fuseli, Wollstonecraft traveled to France in December 1792. There she met Gilbert Imlay, an American and a fellow radical whose lover she soon became. When she discovered she was pregnant, Imlay registered her at the American Embassy as his wife, even though they were not married, so that she could claim the protection of American citizenship. In May 1794, she gave birth to a daughter whom she called Fanny, and two months later Imlay returned to England, leaving mother and child alone. Wollstonecraft's *An Historical and Moral View of the French Revolution* was published in London later that year.

Wollstonecraft's relationship with Imlay was strained, and when she returned to London in April 1795 she discovered he had been unfaithful. Distraught, she attempted suicide but was prevented by him. As a way of distancing himself from her, as well as tracking some bothersome financial losses, Imlay sent her (with Fanny) to Scandinavia on a business trip. She returned to England in September to find him living with another woman. Outraged and increasingly depressed, Wollstonecraft attempted suicide a second time by jumping off Putney Bridge into the Thames. This time, fishers pulled her out of the water.

In January 1796, Wollstonecraft published *Letters Written during a Short Residence in Sweden, Norway, and Denmark*. The book was highly successful, and the praise she received on its publication helped to restore her sense of purpose and mental health. In March, she met Imlay for the final time, and in April she began to write her next novel, *Maria, or The Wrongs of Woman*. In that month she also began a relationship with William Godwin, a leading radical writer and political philosopher to whom she had been introduced by Johnson a few years earlier. They planned a serious mutual commitment without the form of a marriage service, but when Wollstonecraft became pregnant they decided to marry for the sake of the baby. Their marriage on 29 March 1797 caused something of a scandal when it was revealed that Wollstonecraft had never been formally married to Imlay. On 30 August 1797, she gave birth to a daughter, Mary, later to become the wife of Percy Shelley and the author of *Frankenstein*. Only 38 years old, Wollstonecraft died on 10 September from complications resulting from the childbirth. Godwin was left with her manuscripts, and in 1798 published her *Posthumous Works* (which he naively expected to cement her fame) along with his controversial biography.

⌘ ⌘ ⌘

from *A Vindication of the Rights of Woman*

INTRODUCTION

After considering the historic page, and viewing the living world with anxious solicitude,[1] the most melancholy emotions of sorrowful indignation have depressed my spirits, and I have sighed when obliged to confess that either nature has made a great difference between man and man, or that the civilization which has hitherto taken place in the world has been very partial.[2] I have turned over various books written on the subject of education, and patiently observed the conduct of parents and the management of schools; but what has been the result? A profound conviction that the neglected education of my fellow-creatures is the grand source of the misery I deplore; and that women, in particular, are rendered weak and wretched by a variety of concurring[3] causes, originating from one hasty conclusion. The conduct and manners of women, in fact, evidently prove that their minds are not in a healthy state; for, like the flowers which are planted in too rich a soil, strength and usefulness are sacrificed to beauty; and the flaunting leaves, after having pleased a fastidious eye, fade, disregarded on the stalk, long before the season when they ought to have arrived at maturity. One cause of this barren blooming I attribute to a false system of education, gathered from the books written on this subject by men who, considering females rather as women than human creatures, have been more anxious to make them alluring mistresses than affectionate wives and rational mothers; and the understanding of the sex has been so bubbled[4] by this specious[5] homage that the civilized women of the present century, with a few exceptions, are only anxious to inspire love, when they ought to cherish a nobler ambition, and by their abilities and virtues exact respect.

In a treatise, therefore, on female rights and manners, the works which have been particularly written for their improvement must not be overlooked; especially when it is asserted, in direct terms, that the minds of women are enfeebled by false refinement; that the books of instruction, written by men of genius, have had the same tendency as more frivolous productions; and that,

---

[1] *solicitude* Concern.

[2] *partial* Biased.

[3] *concurring* Occurring together.

[4] *bubbled* Deluded, fooled.

[5] *specious* Superficially plausible yet misleading.

in the true style of Mahometanism,[1] they are treated as a kind of subordinate beings, and not as a part of the human species, when improvable reason is allowed to be the dignified distinction which raises men above the brute creation, and puts a natural sceptre in a feeble hand.

Yet, because I am a woman, I would not lead my readers to suppose that I mean violently to agitate the contested question respecting the equality or inferiority of the sex; but as the subject lies in my way, and I cannot pass it over without subjecting the main tendency of my reasoning to misconstruction, I shall stop a moment to deliver, in a few words, my opinion. In the government of the physical world it is observable that the female in point of strength is, in general, inferior to the male. This is the law of nature; and it does not appear to be suspended or abrogated[2] in favour of woman. A degree of physical superiority cannot, therefore, be denied—and it is a noble prerogative! But not content with this natural pre-eminence, men endeavour to sink us still lower, merely to render us alluring objects for a moment; and women, intoxicated by the adoration which men, under the influence of their senses, pay them, do not seek to obtain a durable interest in their hearts, or to become the friends of the fellow creatures who find amusement in their society.

I am aware of an obvious inference—from every quarter have I heard exclamations against masculine women; but where are they to be found? If by this appellation men mean to inveigh[3] against their ardour in hunting, shooting, and gaming,[4] I shall most cordially join in the cry; but if it be against the imitation of manly virtues, or, more properly speaking, the attainment of those talents and virtues, the exercise of which ennobles the human character, and which raise females in the scale of animal being when they are comprehensively termed mankind—all those who view them with a philosophic eye must, I should think, wish with me that they may every day grow more and more masculine.

This discussion naturally divides the subject. I shall first consider women in the grand light of human creatures who, in common with men, are placed on this earth to unfold their faculties; and afterwards I shall more particularly point out their peculiar designation.

I wish also to steer clear of an error which many respectable writers have fallen into; for the instruction which has hitherto been addressed to women has rather been applicable to ladies, if the little indirect advice that is scattered through Sandford and Merton[5] be excepted; but, addressing my sex in a firmer tone, I pay particular attention to those in the middle class because they appear to be in the most natural state. Perhaps the seeds of false-refinement, immorality, and vanity have ever been shed by the great. Weak, artificial beings, raised above the common wants and affections of their race in a premature unnatural manner, undermine the very foundation of virtue, and spread corruption through the whole mass of society! As a class of mankind they have the strongest claim to pity; the education of the rich tends to render them vain and helpless, and the unfolding mind is not strengthened by the practice of those duties that dignify the human character. They only live to amuse themselves, and by the same law that in nature invariably produces certain effects, they soon only afford barren amusement.

But as I purpose taking a separate view of the different ranks of society, and of the moral character of women in each, this hint is, for the present, sufficient; and I have only alluded to the subject because it appears to me to be the very essence of an introduction to give a cursory account of the contents of the work it introduces.

My own sex, I hope, will excuse me if I treat them like rational creatures, instead of flattering their fascinating graces and viewing them as if they were in a state of perpetual childhood, unable to stand alone. I earnestly wish to point out in what true dignity and human

---

[1] *Mahometanism*   Archaic term for Islam.

[2] *abrogated*   Repealed, abolished.

[3] *inveigh*   Denounce.

[4] *gaming*   Gambling.

[5] *Sandford and Merton*   Thomas Day (1748–89), English poet, philanthropist, political essayist, and author of *The History of Sandford and Merton* (1783), a children's novel that gives expression to Day's educational theories, which are based on the work of Jean-Jacques Rousseau. Highly didactic, the novel contrasts the corrupt, conventional education of spoiled Tommy Merton, son of a Jamaican plantation owner, with the natural education of virtuous Harry Sandford, son of an honest farmer.

happiness consists: I wish to persuade women to endeavour to acquire strength, both of mind and body, and to convince them that the soft phrases, susceptibility of heart, delicacy of sentiment, and refinement of taste are almost synonymous with epithets of weakness, and that those beings who are only the objects of pity and that kind of love, which has been termed its sister, will soon become objects of contempt.

Dismissing then those pretty feminine phrases, which the men condescendingly use to soften our slavish dependence, and despising that weak elegancy of mind, exquisite sensibility, and sweet docility of manners supposed to be the sexual characteristics of the weaker vessel, I wish to show that elegance is inferior to virtue; that the first object of laudable ambition is to obtain a character as a human being, regardless of the distinction of sex; and that secondary views should be brought to this simple touchstone.

This is a rough sketch of my plan; and should I express my conviction with the energetic emotions that I feel whenever I think of the subject, the dictates of experience and reflection will be felt by some of my readers. Animated by this important object, I shall disdain to cull[1] my phrases or polish my style: I aim at being useful, and sincerity will render me unaffected; for, wishing rather to persuade by the force of my arguments than dazzle by the elegance of my language, I shall not waste my time in rounding periods,[2] or in fabricating the turgid bombast of artificial feelings, which, coming from the head, never reach the heart. I shall be employed about things, not words—and, anxious to render my sex more respectable members of society, I shall try to avoid that flowery diction which has slid from essays into novels, and from novels into familiar letters and conversation.

These pretty superlatives, dropping glibly from the tongue, vitiate[3] the taste and create a kind of sickly delicacy that turns away from simple unadorned truth; and a deluge of false sentiments and over-stretched feelings, stifling the natural emotions of the heart, render the domestic pleasures insipid that ought to sweeten the exercise of those severe duties that educate a rational and immortal being for a nobler field of action.

The education of women has, of late, been more attended to than formerly; yet they are still reckoned a frivolous sex, and ridiculed or pitied by the writers who endeavour by satire or instruction to improve them. It is acknowledged that they spend many of the first years of their lives in acquiring a smattering of accomplishments; meanwhile strength of body and mind are sacrificed to libertine[4] notions of beauty, to the desire of establishing themselves—the only way women can rise in the world—by marriage. And this desire making mere animals of them, when they marry they act as such children may be expected to act: they dress, they paint,[5] and nickname God's creatures.[6] Surely these weak beings are only fit for a seraglio![7] Can they be expected to govern a family with judgment, or take care of the poor babes whom they bring into the world?

If then it can be fairly deduced from the present conduct of the sex, from the prevalent fondness for pleasure—which takes place of ambition and those nobler passions that open and enlarge the soul—that the instruction which women have hitherto received has only tended, with the constitution of civil society, to render them insignificant objects of desire—mere propagators of fools! If it can be proved that in aiming to accomplish them without cultivating their understandings they are taken out of their sphere of duties, and made ridiculous and useless when the short-lived bloom of beauty is over,[8] I presume that rational men will excuse me for endeavouring to persuade them to become more masculine and respectable.

---

[1] *cull* Choose carefully.

[2] *rounding periods* Crafting graceful sentences.

[3] *vitiate* Render impure, corrupt.

[4] *libertine* Licentious.

[5] *paint* I.e., wear make-up.

[6] *they dress ... God's creatures* From Shakespeare's *Hamlet* 3.1.142–46: "I have heard of your paintings, well enough. God hath given you one face, and you make yourselves another. You jig and amble, and you lisp, you nickname God's creatures and make your wantonness your ignorance."

[7] *seraglio* Harem.

[8] [Wollstonecraft's note] A lively writer, I cannot recollect his name, asks what business women turned of forty have to do in the world? [Wollstonecraft is perhaps referring to a remark made by a libertine character in Frances Burney's *Evelina*, Lord Merton.]

Indeed the word masculine is only a bugbear:[1] there is little reason to fear that women will acquire too much courage or fortitude, for their apparent inferiority with respect to bodily strength must render them, in some degree, dependent on men in the various relations of life; but why should it be increased by prejudices that give a sex to virtue and confound simple truths with sensual reveries?

Women are, in fact, so much degraded by mistaken notions of female excellence that I do not mean to add a paradox when I assert that this artificial weakness produces a propensity to tyrannize, and gives birth to cunning, the natural opponent of strength, which leads them to play off those contemptible infantine airs that undermine esteem even whilst they excite desire. Let men become more chaste and modest, and if women do not grow wiser in the same ratio, it will be clear that they have weaker understandings. It seems scarcely necessary to say that I now speak of the sex in general. Many individuals have more sense than their male relatives; and as nothing preponderates[2] where there is a constant struggle for an equilibrium without[3] it has naturally more gravity, some women govern their husbands without degrading themselves because intellect will always govern.

CHAPTER 2

The Prevailing Opinion of a Sexual Character Discussed

To account for, and excuse, the tyranny of man, many ingenious arguments have been brought forward to prove that the two sexes, in the acquirement of virtue, ought to aim at attaining a very different character: or, to speak explicitly, women are not allowed to have sufficient strength of mind to acquire what really deserves the name of virtue. Yet it should seem, allowing them to have souls, that there is but one way appointed by Providence to lead mankind to either virtue or happiness.

If then women are not a swarm of ephemeron[4] triflers, why should they be kept in ignorance under the specious name of innocence? Men complain, and with reason, of the follies and caprices[5] of our sex, when they do not keenly satirize our headstrong passions and grovelling vices. Behold, I should answer, the natural effect of ignorance! The mind will ever be unstable that has only prejudices to rest on, and the current will run with destructive fury when there are no barriers to break its force. Women are told from their infancy, and taught by the example of their mothers, that a little knowledge of human weakness, justly termed cunning, softness of temper, outward obedience, and a scrupulous attention to a puerile kind of propriety, will obtain for them the protection of man; and should they be beautiful, every thing else is needless for, at least, twenty years of their lives.

Thus Milton describes our first frail mother; though when he tells us that women are formed for softness and sweet attractive grace,[6] I cannot comprehend his meaning; unless, in the true Mahometan strain, he meant to deprive us of souls and insinuate that we were beings only designed by sweet attractive grace, and docile blind obedience, to gratify the senses of man when he can no longer soar on the wing of contemplation.

How grossly do they insult us who thus advise us only to render ourselves gentle, domestic brutes! For instance, the winning softness so warmly, and frequently, recommended that governs by obeying. What childish expressions, and how insignificant is the being—can it be an immortal one?—who will condescend to govern by such sinister methods! "Certainly," says Lord Bacon, "man is of kin to the beasts by his body; and if he be not of kin to God by his spirit, he is a base and ignoble creature!"[7] Men, indeed, appear to me to act in a very unphilosophical manner when they

---

[1] *bugbear* Imaginary creature invoked to cause fear.

[2] *preponderates* Weighs more, predominates.

[3] *without* Unless.

[4] *ephemeron* Short-lived.

[5] *caprices* Whims, fancies.

[6] *Milton ... grace* John Milton contrasts Adam and Eve, the first man and woman, in *Paradise Lost* (1667): "For contemplation he and valour formed, / For softness she and sweet attractive grace" (4.297–98).

[7] *Certainly ... creature* Francis Bacon (1561–1626), English philosopher and statesman, author of *Essays or Counsels Civil and Moral* (1625). The quotation is from Essay 16, "Of Atheism."

try to secure the good conduct of women by attempting to keep them always in a state of childhood. Rousseau[1] was more consistent when he wished to stop the progress of reason in both sexes, for if men eat of the tree of knowledge,[2] women will come in for a taste; but, from the imperfect cultivation which their understandings now receive, they only attain a knowledge of evil.

Children, I grant, should be innocent; but when the epithet is applied to men, or women, it is but a civil term for weakness. For if it be allowed that women were destined by Providence to acquire human virtues and, by the exercise of their understandings, that stability of character which is the firmest ground to rest our future hopes upon, they must be permitted to turn to the fountain of light, and not forced to shape their course by the twinkling of a mere satellite.[3] Milton, I grant, was of a very different opinion; for he only bends to the indefeasible[4] right of beauty, though it would be difficult to render two passages, which I now mean to contrast, consistent. But into similar inconsistencies are great men often led by their senses.

To whom thus Eve with *perfect beauty* adorn'd.
My Author and Disposer, what thou bidst
Unargued I obey; so God ordains;
God *is thy law, thou mine*: to know no more
Is Woman's *happiest* knowledge and her *praise*.[5]

These are exactly the arguments that I have used to children; but I have added, "Your reason is now gaining strength, and, until it arrives at some degree of maturity, you must look up to me for advice—then you ought to think and only rely on God."

Yet in the following lines Milton seems to coincide with me when he makes Adam thus expostulate[6] with his Maker.

Hast thou not made me here thy substitute,
And these inferior far beneath me set?
Among *unequals* what society
Can sort, what harmony or true delight?
Which must be mutual, in proportion due
Giv'n and receiv'd; but in *disparity*
The one intense, the other still remiss
Cannot well suit with either, but soon prove
Tedious alike: of *fellowship* I speak
Such as I seek, fit to participate
All rational delight—[7]

In treating, therefore, of the manners of women, let us, disregarding sensual arguments, trace what we should endeavour to make them in order to co-operate, if the expression be not too bold, with the supreme Being.

By individual education, I mean—for the sense of the word is not precisely defined—such an attention to a child as will slowly sharpen the senses, form the temper, regulate the passions as they begin to ferment, and set the understanding to work before the body arrives at maturity; so that the man may only have to proceed, not to begin, the important task of learning to think and reason.

To prevent any misconstruction, I must add that I do not believe that a private education can work the wonders which some sanguine[8] writers have attributed to it. Men and women must be educated, in a great degree, by the opinions and manners of the society they live in. In every age there has been a stream of popular opinion that has carried all before it, and given a family character, as it were, to the century. It may then fairly be inferred that until society be differently constituted, much cannot be expected from education. It is, however, sufficient for my present purpose to assert that whatever effect circumstances have on the abilities, every being may become virtuous by the exercise of its own reason; for if but one being was created with vicious inclinations that is positively bad, what can save us from atheism? Or, if we worship a God, is not that God a devil?

---

[1] *Rousseau* Jean-Jacques Rousseau (1712–78), Geneva born philosopher, composer, and essayist.

[2] *tree of knowledge* In Genesis 2.17, God forbids Adam and Eve to eat of the tree of the knowledge of good and evil; tempted by the serpent, Eve disobeys and Adam follows suit.

[3] *satellite* Subordinate, secondary planet orbiting round a larger one.

[4] *indefeasible* Incapable of being defeated.

[5] *To whom ... praise* Milton, *Paradise Lost*, 4.634–38. [Wollstonecraft's italics.]

[6] *expostulate* Remonstrate, argue.

[7] *Hast ... delight* Milton, *Paradise Lost*, 8.381–91. [Wollstonecraft's italics.]

[8] *sanguine* Cheerfully optimistic.

Consequently, the most perfect education, in my opinion, is such an exercise of the understanding as is best calculated to strengthen the body and form the heart. Or, in other words, to enable the individual to attain such habits of virtue as will render it independent. In fact, it is a farce to call any being virtuous whose virtues do not result from the exercise of its own reason. This was Rousseau's opinion respecting men:[1] I extend it to women, and confidently assert that they have been drawn out of their sphere by false refinement and not by an endeavour to acquire masculine qualities. Still the regal homage which they receive is so intoxicating that until the manners of the times are changed and formed on more reasonable principles, it may be impossible to convince them that the illegitimate power, which they obtain by degrading themselves, is a curse, and that they must return to nature and equality if they wish to secure the placid satisfaction that unsophisticated affections impart. But for this epoch we must wait—wait, perhaps, until kings and nobles, enlightened by reason, and preferring the real dignity of man to childish state, throw off their gaudy hereditary trappings: and if then women do not resign the arbitrary power of beauty, they will prove that they have less mind than man.

I may be accused of arrogance; still I must declare what I firmly believe: that all the writers who have written on the subject of female education and manners from Rousseau to Dr. Gregory[2] have contributed to render women more artificial, weak characters than they would otherwise have been; and, consequently, more useless members of society. I might have expressed this conviction in a lower key, but I am afraid it would have been the whine of affectation and not the faithful expression of my feelings, of the clear result which experience and reflection have led me to draw. When I come to that division of the subject, I shall advert[3] to the passages that I more particularly disapprove of in the works of the authors I have just alluded to; but it is first necessary to observe that my objection extends to the whole purport[4] of those books, which tend, in my opinion, to degrade one half of the human species and render women pleasing at the expense of every solid virtue.

Though, to reason on Rousseau's ground, if man did attain a degree of perfection of mind when his body arrived at maturity, it might be proper, in order to make a man and his wife one, that she should rely entirely on his understanding; and the graceful ivy, clasping the oak that supported it, would form a whole in which strength and beauty would be equally conspicuous. But, alas! Husbands, as well as their helpmates, are often only overgrown children; nay, thanks to early debauchery, scarcely men in their outward form—and if the blind lead the blind,[5] one need not come from heaven to tell us the consequence.

Many are the causes that, in the present corrupt state of society, contribute to enslave women by cramping their understandings and sharpening their senses. One, perhaps, that silently does more mischief than all the rest is their disregard of order.

To do every thing in an orderly manner is a most important precept which women, who generally speaking receive only a disorderly kind of education, seldom attend to with that degree of exactness that men, who from their infancy are broken into method, observe. This negligent kind of guess-work—for what other epithet can be used to point out the random exertions of a sort of instinctive common sense, never brought to the test of reason?—prevents their generalizing matters of fact: so they do today what they did yesterday, merely because they did it yesterday.

This contempt of the understanding in early life has more baneful[6] consequences than is commonly supposed; for the little knowledge which women of strong minds attain is, from various circumstances, of a more desultory[7] kind than the knowledge of men, and it is acquired more by sheer observations on real life than from comparing what has been individually observed with the results of experience generalized by speculation.

---

[1]   *Rousseau's … men*   Jean-Jacques Rousseau, *Émile* (1762), Book One.

[2]   *Dr. Gregory*   John Gregory (1724–73), Scottish physician, author of *A Father's Legacy to His Daughters* (1774), an influential conduct book for young women.

[3]   *advert*   Take notice.

[4]   *purport*   Intention.

[5]   *blind lead the blind*   Matthew 15:14: "And if the blind lead the blind, both shall fall into the ditch."

[6]   *baneful*   Destructive, poisonous.

[7]   *desultory*   Irregular, unmethodical.

Led by their dependent situation and domestic employments more into society, what they learn is rather by snatches; and as learning is with them, in general, only a secondary thing, they do not pursue any one branch with that persevering ardour necessary to give vigour to the faculties and clearness to the judgment. In the present state of society, a little learning is required to support the character of a gentleman; and boys are obliged to submit to a few years of discipline. But in the education of women, the cultivation of the understanding is always subordinate to the acquirement of some corporeal accomplishment; even while enervated[1] by confinement and false notions of modesty, the body is prevented from attaining that grace and beauty which relaxed half-formed limbs never exhibit. Besides, in youth their faculties are not brought forward by emulation; and having no serious scientific study, if they have natural sagacity it is turned too soon on life and manners. They dwell on effects, and modifications, without tracing them back to causes; and complicated rules to adjust behaviour are a weak substitute for simple principles.

As a proof that education gives this appearance of weakness to females, we may instance the example of military men who are, like them, sent into the world before their minds have been stored with knowledge or fortified by principles. The consequences are similar; soldiers acquire a little superficial knowledge, snatched from the muddy current of conversation, and, from continually mixing with society, they gain what is termed a knowledge of the world; and this acquaintance with manners and customs has frequently been confounded[2] with a knowledge of the human heart. But can the crude fruit of casual observation, never brought to the test of judgment, formed by comparing speculation and experience, deserve such a distinction? Soldiers, as well as women, practice the minor virtues with punctilious[3] politeness. Where is then the sexual difference when the education has been the same? All the difference that I can discern arises from the superior advantage of liberty, which enables the former to see more of life.

It is wandering from my present subject, perhaps, to make a political remark; but, as it was produced naturally by the train of my reflections, I shall not pass it silently over.

Standing armies can never consist of resolute, robust men; they may be well-disciplined machines, but they will seldom contain men under the influence of strong passions or with very vigorous faculties. And as for any depth of understanding, I will venture to affirm that it is as rarely to be found in the army as amongst women; and the cause, I maintain, is the same. It may be further observed that officers are also particularly attentive to their persons, fond of dancing, crowded rooms, adventures, and ridicule.[4] Like the fair sex, the business of their lives is gallantry. They were taught to please, and they only live to please. Yet they do not lose their rank in the distinction of sexes, for they are still reckoned superior to women, though in what their superiority consists, beyond what I have just mentioned, it is difficult to discover.

The great misfortune is this: that they both acquire manners before morals, and a knowledge of life before they have, from reflection, any acquaintance with the grand ideal outline of human nature. The consequence is natural; satisfied with common nature, they become a prey to prejudices, and taking all their opinions on credit, they blindly submit to authority. So that, if they have any sense, it is a kind of instinctive glance that catches proportions and decides with respect to manners, but fails when arguments are to be pursued below the surface, or opinions analyzed.

May not the same remark be applied to women? Nay, the argument may be carried still further, for they are both thrown out of a useful station by the unnatural distinctions established in civilized life. Riches and hereditary honours have made ciphers[5] of women to give consequence to the numerical figure; and idleness has produced a mixture of gallantry and despotism into

---

[1] *enervated* Mentally weakened.

[2] *confounded* Disordered, confused.

[3] *punctilious* Carefully polite.

[4] [Wollstonecraft's note] Why should women be censured with petulant acrimony, because they seem to have a passion for a scarlet coat? Has not education placed them more on a level with soldiers than any other class of men? [See Jonathan Swift's "The Furniture of a Woman's Mind."]

[5] *ciphers* Neutral symbols which can change the value of other numbers depending on their position.

society which leads the very men who are the slaves of their mistresses to tyrannize over their sisters, wives, and daughters. This is only keeping them in rank and file, it is true. Strengthen the female mind by enlarging it and there will be an end to blind obedience; but, as blind obedience is ever sought for by power, tyrants and sensualists are in the right when they endeavour to keep women in the dark, because the former only want slaves, and the latter a play-thing. The sensualist, indeed, has been the most dangerous of tyrants, and women have been duped by their lovers, as princes by their ministers, whilst dreaming that they reigned over them.

I now principally allude to Rousseau, for his character of Sophia[1] is, undoubtedly, a captivating one, though it appears to me grossly unnatural; however, it is not the superstructure but the foundation of her character, the principles on which her education was built, that I mean to attack; nay, warmly as I admire the genius of that able writer, whose opinions I shall often have occasion to cite, indignation always takes place of admiration, and the rigid frown of insulted virtue effaces the smile of complacency, which his eloquent periods are wont to raise when I read his voluptuous reveries. Is this the man who, in his ardour for virtue, would banish all the soft arts of peace and almost carry us back to Spartan discipline?[2] Is this the man who delights to paint the useful struggles of passion, the triumphs of good dispositions, and the heroic flights which carry the glowing soul out of itself? How are these mighty sentiments lowered when he describes the pretty foot and enticing airs of his little favourite! But, for the present, I wave the subject, and, instead of severely reprehending[3] the transient effusions of overweening[4] sensibility, I shall only observe that whoever has cast a benevolent eye on society must often have been gratified by the sight of humble mutual love, not dignified by sentiment, or strengthened by a union in intellectual pursuits. The domestic trifles of the day have afforded matters for cheerful converse, and

innocent caresses have softened toils which did not require great exercise of mind or stretch of thought: yet, has not the sight of this moderate felicity excited more tenderness than respect? An emotion similar to what we feel when children are playing, or animals sporting,[5] whilst the contemplation of the noble struggles of suffering merit has raised admiration and carried our thoughts to that world where sensation will give place to reason.

Women are, therefore, to be considered either as moral beings, or so weak that they must be entirely subjected to the superior faculties of men.

Let us examine this question. Rousseau declares that a woman should never, for a moment, feel herself independent, that she should be governed by fear to exercise her natural cunning, and made a coquettish slave in order to render her a more alluring object of desire, a sweeter companion to man whenever he chooses to relax himself.[6] He carries the arguments, which he pretends to draw from the indications of nature, still further and insinuates that truth and fortitude, the corner stones of all human virtue, should be cultivated with certain restrictions, because, with respect to the female character, obedience is the grand lesson which ought to be impressed with unrelenting rigour.

What nonsense! When will a great man arise with sufficient strength of mind to puff away the fumes which pride and sensuality have thus spread over the subject! If women are by nature inferior to men, their virtues must be the same in quality, if not in degree, or virtue is a relative idea; consequently, their conduct should be founded on the same principles and have the same aim.

---

[1]   *Sophia*   Character in Jean-Jacques Rousseau, *Émile*, Book Five.

[2]   *Spartan discipline*   The militaristic Greek city-state of Sparta was infamous for its harsh laws, outlined in Plutarch's account of Lycurgus (*Lives*), which controlled nearly every aspect of the lives of its citizens.

[3]   *reprehending*   Finding fault with.

[4]   *overweening*   Arrogant.

[5]   [Wollstonecraft's note]   Similar feelings has Milton's pleasing picture of paradisiacal happiness ever raised in my mind; yet, instead of envying the lovely pair, I have, with conscious dignity, or Satanic pride, turned to hell for sublimer objects. In the same style, when viewing some noble monument of human art, I have traced the emanation of the Deity in the order I admired, till, descending from that giddy height, I have caught myself contemplating the grandest of all human sights;—for fancy quickly placed, in some solitary recess, an outcast of fortune, rising superior to passion and discontent.

[6]   *Rousseau ... himself*   See Jean-Jacques Rousseau, *Émile*, Book Five.

Connected with man as daughters, wives, and mothers, their moral character may be estimated by their manner of fulfilling those simple duties; but the end, the grand end of their exertions should be to unfold their own faculties and acquire the dignity of conscious virtue. They may try to render their road pleasant, but ought never to forget, in common with man, that life yields not the felicity which can satisfy an immortal soul. I do not mean to insinuate that either sex should be so lost in abstract reflections or distant views as to forget the affections and duties that lie before them, and are, in truth, the means appointed to produce the fruit of life; on the contrary, I would warmly recommend them, even while I assert that they afford most satisfaction when they are considered in their true, sober light.

Probably the prevailing opinion, that woman was created for man,[1] may have taken its rise from Moses's poetical story;[2] yet, as very few, it is presumed, who have bestowed any serious thought on the subject ever supposed that Eve was, literally speaking, one of Adam's ribs,[3] the deduction must be allowed to fall to the ground; or, only be so far admitted as it proves that man, from the remotest antiquity, found it convenient to exert his strength to subjugate his companion, and his invention to show that she ought to have her neck bent under the yoke because the whole creation was only created for his convenience or pleasure.

Let it not be concluded that I wish to invert the order of things; I have already granted that, from the constitution of their bodies, men seem to be designed by Providence to attain a greater degree of virtue. I speak collectively of the whole sex; but I see not the shadow of a reason to conclude that their virtues should differ in respect to their nature. In fact, how can they, if virtue has only one eternal standard? I must, therefore, if I

reason consequentially, as strenuously maintain that they have the same simple direction as that there is a God.

It follows then that cunning should not be opposed to wisdom, little cares to great exertions, or insipid softness, varnished over with the name of gentleness, to that fortitude which grand views alone can inspire.

I shall be told that woman would then lose many of her peculiar graces, and the opinion of a well-known poet might be quoted to refute my unqualified assertion. For Pope[4] has said, in the name of the whole male sex:

Yet ne'er so sure our passion to create,
As when she touch'd the brink of all we hate.[5]

In what light this sally[6] places men and women, I shall leave to the judicious to determine; meanwhile I shall content myself with observing that I cannot discover why, unless they are mortal, females should always be degraded by being made subservient to love or lust.

To speak disrespectfully of love is, I know, high treason against sentiment and fine feelings; but I wish to speak the simple language of truth, and rather to address the head than the heart. To endeavour to reason love out of the world would be to out Quixote Cervantes[7] and equally offend against common sense; but an endeavour to restrain this tumultuous passion, and to prove that it should not be allowed to dethrone superior powers, or to usurp the sceptre which the understanding should ever coolly wield, appears less wild.

Youth is the season for love in both sexes; but in those days of thoughtless enjoyment, provision should be made for the more important years of life when reflection takes place of sensation. But Rousseau, and most of the male writers who have followed his steps,

---

[1] *woman ... man* "And the Lord God said, It is not good that the man should be alone; I will make him an helpmeet for him" (Genesis 2.18–25).

[2] *Moses's ... story* I.e., Genesis. Moses was believed to be the author of the Pentateuch, the first five books of the Bible: Genesis, Exodus, Leviticus, Numbers, and Deuteronomy.

[3] *Adam's ribs* "And the Lord God caused a deep sleep to fall upon Adam, and he slept: and he took one of his ribs, and closed up the flesh instead thereof; And the rib, which the Lord God had taken from man, made he a woman, and brought her unto the man" (Genesis 2.22–23).

[4] *Pope* Alexander Pope (1688–1744), English poet and satirist.

[5] *Yet ... hate* Alexander Pope, "Epistle II: To a Lady (Of the Characters of Women)," from "Epistles to Several Persons," *Works*, 51–52 (1735).

[6] *sally* Sudden attack on an enemy.

[7] *out Quixote Cervantes* I.e., even more than the hero of Cervantes's picaresque novel, *Don Quixote*, be determined to carry out a lofty albeit impossible goal.

have warmly inculcated[1] that the whole tendency of female education ought to be directed to one point: to render them pleasing.

Let me reason with the supporters of this opinion who have any knowledge of human nature: do they imagine that marriage can eradicate the habitude of life? The woman who has only been taught to please will soon find that her charms are oblique sunbeams, and that they cannot have much effect on her husband's heart when they are seen every day, when the summer is passed and gone. Will she then have sufficient native energy to look into herself for comfort and cultivate her dormant faculties? Or, is it not more rational to expect that she will try to please other men; and, in the emotions raised by the expectation of new conquests, endeavour to forget the mortification her love or pride has received? When the husband ceases to be a lover— and the time will inevitably come—her desire of pleasing will then grow languid, or become a spring of bitterness; and love, perhaps, the most evanescent of all passions, gives place to jealousy or vanity.

I now speak of women who are restrained by principle or prejudice; such women, though they would shrink from an intrigue with real abhorrence, yet, nevertheless, wish to be convinced by the homage of gallantry that they are cruelly neglected by their husbands; or, days and weeks are spent in dreaming of the happiness enjoyed by congenial souls until their health is undermined and their spirits broken by discontent. How then can the great art of pleasing be such a necessary study? It is only useful to a mistress; the chaste wife, and serious mother, should only consider her power to please as the polish of her virtues, and the affection of her husband as one of the comforts that render her task less difficult and her life happier. But, whether she be loved or neglected, her first wish should be to make herself respectable, and not to rely for all her happiness on a being subject to like infirmities with herself.

The worthy Dr. Gregory fell into a similar error. I respect his heart, but entirely disapprove of his celebrated *Legacy to his Daughters*.

He advises them to cultivate a fondness for dress,[2] because a fondness for dress, he asserts, is natural to them. I am unable to comprehend what either he or Rousseau mean when they frequently use this indefinite term. If they told us that in a pre-existent state the soul was fond of dress, and brought this inclination with it into a new body, I should listen to them with a half smile, as I often do when I hear a rant about innate elegance. But if he only meant to say that the exercise of the faculties will produce this fondness—I deny it. It is not natural; but arises, like false ambition in men, from a love of power.

Dr. Gregory goes much further; he actually recommends dissimulation,[3] and advises an innocent girl to give the lie to her feelings, and not dance with spirit, when gaiety of heart would make her feel eloquent without making her gestures immodest. In the name of truth and common sense, why should not one woman acknowledge that she can take more exercise than another? Or, in other words, that she has a sound constitution; and why, to damp innocent vivacity, is she darkly to be told that men will draw conclusions which she little thinks of? Let the libertine draw what inference he pleases; but I hope that no sensible mother will restrain the natural frankness of youth by instilling such indecent cautions. Out of the abundance of the heart the mouth speaketh;[4] and a wiser than Solomon[5] hath said that the heart should be made clean, and not trivial ceremonies observed,[6] which it is not very difficult to fulfil with scrupulous exactness when vice reigns in the heart.

Women ought to endeavour to purify their heart; but can they do so when their uncultivated understandings make them entirely dependent on their senses for

---

[2] *fondness for dress* Gregory, *A Father's Legacy to His Daughters*, 55–57.

[3] *dissimulation* Concealment, feigning; Gregory, *A Father's Legacy to His Daughters*, 57–58.

[4] *Out of … speaketh* Matthew 12.34: "O generation of vipers, how can ye, being evil, speak good things? For out of the abundance of the heart the mouth speaketh."

[5] *a wiser than Solomon* I.e., Jesus; see Luke 11.31.

[6] *the heart … observed* Matthew 23.25: "Woe unto you, scribes and Pharisees, hypocrites! For ye make clean the outside of the cup and of the platter, but within they are full of extortion and excess."

---

[1] *inculcated* Taught through force or persistence.

employment and amusement, when no noble pursuit sets them above the little vanities of the day, or enables them to curb the wild emotions that agitate a reed over which every passing breeze has power? To gain the affections of a virtuous man is affectation necessary? Nature has given woman a weaker frame than man; but, to ensure her husband's affections, must a wife—who, by the exercise of her mind and body whilst she was discharging the duties of a daughter, wife, and mother, has allowed her constitution to retain its natural strength, and her nerves a healthy tone—is she, I say, to condescend to use art and feign a sickly delicacy in order to secure her husband's affection? Weakness may excite tenderness and gratify the arrogant pride of man; but the lordly caresses of a protector will not gratify a noble mind that pants for and deserves to be respected. Fondness is a poor substitute for friendship!

In a seraglio, I grant that all these arts are necessary; the epicure[1] must have his palate tickled or he will sink into apathy; but have women so little ambition as to be satisfied with such a condition? Can they supinely[2] dream life away in the lap of pleasure, or the languor of weariness, rather than assert their claim to pursue reasonable pleasures and render themselves conspicuous by practising the virtues which dignify mankind? Surely she has not an immortal soul who can loiter life away, merely employed to adorn her person, that she may amuse the languid hours, and soften the cares of a fellow-creature who is willing to be enlivened by her smiles and tricks when the serious business of life is over.

Besides, the woman who strengthens her body and exercises her mind will, by managing her family and practising various virtues, become the friend and not the humble dependent of her husband; and if she, by possessing such substantial qualities, merit his regard, she will not find it necessary to conceal her affection, nor to pretend to an unnatural coldness of constitution to excite her husband's passions. In fact, if we revert to history, we shall find that the women who have distinguished themselves have neither been the most beautiful nor the most gentle of their sex.

Nature, or, to speak with strict propriety, God, has made all things right; but man has sought him out many

inventions to mar the work. I now allude to that part of Dr. Gregory's treatise where he advises a wife never to let her husband know the extent of her sensibility or affection.[3] Voluptuous precaution, and as ineffectual as absurd. Love, from its very nature, must be transitory. To seek for a secret that would render it constant would be as wild a search as for the philosopher's stone, or the grand panacea:[4] and the discovery would be equally useless, or rather pernicious, to mankind. The most holy band of society is friendship. It has been well said, by a shrewd satirist, "that rare as true love is, true friendship is still rarer."[5]

This is an obvious truth, and the cause, not lying deep, will not elude a slight glance of inquiry.

Love, the common passion in which chance and sensation take place of choice and reason, is, in some degree, felt by the mass of mankind; for it is not necessary to speak, at present, of the emotions that rise above or sink below love. This passion, naturally increased by suspense and difficulties, draws the mind out of its accustomed state and exalts the affections; but the security of marriage, allowing the fever of love to subside, a healthy temperature is thought insipid only by those who have not sufficient intellect to substitute the calm tenderness of friendship, the confidence of respect, instead of blind admiration and the sensual emotions of fondness.

This is, must be, the course of nature—friendship or indifference inevitably succeeds love—and this constitution seems perfectly to harmonize with the system of government which prevails in the moral world. Passions are spurs to action and open the mind; but they sink into mere appetites, become a personal and momentary gratification, when the object is gained and the satisfied mind rests in enjoyment. The man who had some virtue whilst he was struggling for a crown often becomes a voluptuous tyrant when it graces his brow; and, when

[3] *never to let ... affection* Gregory, *A Father's Legacy to His Daughters*, 87–88.

[4] *wild a search ... panacea* Alchemists believed in the existence of a philosopher's stone, a substance which could turn base metals into gold, as well as a grand panacea, a medicine that could cure all illnesses.

[5] *that rare ... rarer* François de La Rochefoucauld (1613–80), French essayist, author of *Réflexions; ou Sentences et maximes morales* (1665).

[1] *epicure* One devoted to physical pleasures.

[2] *supinely* Indolently, literally on one's back.

the lover is not lost in the husband, the dotard,[1] a prey to childish caprices and fond jealousies, neglects the serious duties of life, and the caresses which should excite confidence in his children are lavished on the overgrown child, his wife.

In order to fulfil the duties of life, and to be able to pursue with vigour the various employments which form the moral character, a master and mistress of a family ought not to continue to love each other with passion. I mean to say that they ought not to indulge those emotions which disturb the order of society and engross the thoughts that should be otherwise employed. The mind that has never been engrossed by one object wants vigour—if it can long be so, it is weak.

A mistaken education, a narrow, uncultivated mind, and many sexual prejudices tend to make women more constant than men; but, for the present, I shall not touch on this branch of the subject. I will go still further and advance, without dreaming of a paradox, that an unhappy marriage is often very advantageous to a family, and that the neglected wife is, in general, the best mother. And this would almost always be the consequence if the female mind were more enlarged: for it seems to be the common dispensation[2] of Providence that what we gain in present enjoyment should be deducted from the treasure of life—experience; and that when we are gathering the flowers of the day and revelling in pleasure, the solid fruit of toil and wisdom should not be caught at the same time. The way lies before us, we must turn to the right or left; and he who will pass life away in bounding from one pleasure to another must not complain if he acquire neither wisdom nor respectability of character.

Supposing, for a moment, that the soul is not immortal, and that man was only created for the present scene; I think we should have reason to complain that love, infantine fondness, ever grew insipid and palled upon the sense. Let us eat, drink, and love, for to-morrow we die,[3] would be, in fact, the language of reason, the morality of life; and who but a fool would part with a reality for a fleeting shadow? But, if awed by observing the improbable powers of the mind, we

disdain to confine our wishes or thoughts to such a comparatively mean field of action that only appears grand and important, as it is connected with a boundless prospect and sublime hopes, what necessity is there for falsehood in conduct, and why must the sacred majesty of truth be violated to detain a deceitful good that saps the very foundation of virtue? Why must the female mind be tainted by coquettish arts to gratify the sensualist and prevent love from subsiding into friendship, or compassionate tenderness, when there are not qualities on which friendship can be built? Let the honest heart show itself, and reason teach passion to submit to necessity; or, let the dignified pursuit of virtue and knowledge raise the mind above those emotions which rather embitter than sweeten the cup of life when they are not restrained within due bounds.

I do not mean to allude to the romantic passion which is the concomitant[4] of genius. Who can clip its wing? But that grand passion not proportioned to the puny enjoyments of life is only true to the sentiment and feeds on itself. The passions which have been celebrated for their durability have always been unfortunate. They have acquired strength by absence and constitutional melancholy—the fancy has hovered round a form of beauty dimly seen—but familiarity might have turned admiration into disgust; or, at least, into indifference, and allowed the imagination leisure to start fresh game. With perfect propriety, according to this view of things, does Rousseau make the mistress of his soul, Eloisa, love St. Preux[5] when life was fading before her; but this is no proof of the immortality of the passion.

Of the same complexion is Dr. Gregory's advice respecting delicacy of sentiment,[6] which he advises a woman not to acquire if she have determined to marry. This determination, however, perfectly consistent with his former advice, he calls indelicate, and earnestly

---

[1] *dotard* Senile person.

[2] *dispensation* Divine ordering of the world.

[3] *Let us ... die* Isaiah 22.13.

[4] *concomitant* Accompaniment.

[5] *Eloisa ... St. Preux* Eloisa/Julie is the heroine of Rousseau's epistolary novel *Julie, ou, La Nouvelle Héloïse* (1761). Julie falls in love with her tutor, St. Preux, but is forced to marry her father's friend, Wolmar. St. Preux and Julie meet again many years later, and Julie ultimately admits on her deathbed that she has never stopped loving him.

[6] *advice ... sentiment* Gregory, *A Father's Legacy to His Daughters*, 116–19.

persuades his daughters to conceal it, though it may govern their conduct—as if it were indelicate to have the common appetites of human nature.

Noble morality!, and consistent with the cautious prudence of a little soul that cannot extend its views beyond the present minute division of existence. If all the faculties of woman's mind are only to be cultivated as they respect her dependence on man; if, when a husband be obtained, she have arrived at her goal and, meanly proud, rests satisfied with such a paltry crown, let her grovel contentedly, scarcely raised by her employments above the animal kingdom; but if, struggling for the prize of her high calling, she look beyond the present scene, let her cultivate her understanding without stopping to consider what character the husband may have whom she is destined to marry. Let her only determine, without being too anxious about present happiness, to acquire the qualities that ennoble a rational being, and a rough inelegant husband may shock her taste without destroying her peace of mind. She will not model her soul to suit the frailties of her companion, but to bear with them: his character may be a trial, but not an impediment to virtue.

If Dr. Gregory confined his remark to romantic expectations of constant love and congenial feelings, he should have recollected that experience will banish what advice can never make us cease to wish for, when the imagination is kept alive at the expense of reason.

I own it frequently happens that women who have fostered a romantic, unnatural delicacy of feeling waste their lives in imagining how happy they should have been with a husband who could love them with a fervid increasing affection every day, and all day. But they might as well pine married as single—and would not be a jot more unhappy with a bad husband than longing for a good one. That a proper education or, to speak with more precision, a well stored mind would enable a woman to support a single life with dignity, I grant; but that she should avoid cultivating her taste lest her husband should occasionally shock it, is quitting a substance for a shadow. To say the truth, I do not know of what use is an improved taste if the individual be not rendered more independent of the casualties of life; if new sources of enjoyment, only dependent on the solitary operations of the mind, are not opened. People

of taste, married or single, without distinction, will ever be disgusted by various things that touch not less observing minds. On this conclusion the argument must not be allowed to hinge; but in the whole sum of enjoyment is taste to be denominated a blessing?

The question is whether it procures most pain or pleasure? The answer will decide the propriety of Dr. Gregory's advice, and show how absurd and tyrannical it is thus to lay down a system of slavery; or to attempt to educate moral beings by any other rules than those deduced from pure reason, which apply to the whole species.

Gentleness of manners, forbearance, and long-suffering[1] are such amiable Godlike qualities that in sublime poetic strains the Deity has been invested with them; and, perhaps, no representation of his goodness so strongly fastens on the human affections as those that represent him abundant in mercy and willing to pardon.[2] Gentleness, considered in this point of view, bears on its front all the characteristics of grandeur combined with the winning graces of condescension;[3] but what a different aspect it assumes when it is the submissive demeanour of dependence, the support of weakness that loves, because it wants protection, and is forbearing, because it must silently endure injuries, smiling under the lash at which it dare not snarl. Abject as this picture appears, it is the portrait of an accomplished woman, according to the received opinion of female excellence, separated by specious reasoners from human excellence. Or, they kindly restore the rib and make one moral being of a man and woman—not forgetting to give her all the "submissive charms."

How women are to exist in that state where there is to be neither marrying nor giving in marriage,[4] we are not told. For though moralists have agreed that the

---

[1] *Gentleness ... long-suffering* "But the fruit of the Spirit is love, joy, peace, longsuffering, gentleness, goodness, faith, meekness, temperance: against such there is no law" (Galatians 5.22–23).

[2] *abundant ... pardon* "Let the wicked forsake his way, and the unrighteous man his thoughts: and let him return unto the Lord, and he will have mercy upon him; and to our God, for he will abundantly pardon" (Isaiah 55.7).

[3] *condescension* Gracious behavior shown to a social inferior.

[4] *neither ... marriage* "For in the resurrection they neither marry, nor are given in marriage, but are as the angels of God in heaven" (Matthew 22.30).

tenor[1] of life seems to prove that man is prepared by various circumstances for a future state, they constantly concur in advising woman only to provide for the present. Gentleness, docility, and a spaniel-like affection are, on this ground, consistently recommended as the cardinal virtues of the sex; and, disregarding the arbitrary economy of nature, one writer has declared that it is masculine for a woman to be melancholy. She was created to be the toy of man, his rattle, and it must jingle in his ears whenever, dismissing reason, he chooses to be amused.

To recommend gentleness, indeed, on a broad basis is strictly philosophical. A frail being should labour to be gentle. But when forbearance confounds right and wrong, it ceases to be a virtue; and, however convenient it may be found in a companion, that companion will ever be considered as an inferior and only inspire a vapid tenderness, which easily degenerates into contempt. Still, if advice could really make a being gentle, whose natural disposition admitted not of such a fine polish, something towards the advancement of order would be attained; but if, as might quickly be demonstrated, only affectation be produced by this indiscriminate counsel, which throws a stumbling-block in the way of gradual improvement and true melioration[2] of temper, the sex is not much benefited by sacrificing solid virtues to the attainment of superficial graces, though for a few years they may procure the individuals regal sway.

As a philosopher, I read with indignation the plausible epithets which men use to soften their insults; and, as a moralist, I ask what is meant by such heterogeneous associations as fair defects, amiable weaknesses, &c.? If there be but one criterion of morals, but one archetype for man, women appear to be suspended by destiny, according to the vulgar tale of Mahomet's coffin;[3] they have neither the unerring instinct of brutes, nor are allowed to fix the eye of reason on a perfect model. They were made to be loved, and must not aim at respect, lest they should be hunted out of society as masculine.

But to view the subject in another point of view. Do passive, indolent women make the best wives? Confining our discussion to the present moment of existence, let us see how such weak creatures perform their part. Do the women who, by the attainment of a few superficial accomplishments, have strengthened the prevailing prejudice merely contribute to the happiness of their husbands? Do they display their charms merely to amuse them? And have women, who have early imbibed notions of passive obedience, sufficient character to manage a family or educate children? So far from it that, after surveying the history of woman, I cannot help agreeing with the severest satirist, considering the sex as the weakest as well as the most oppressed half of the species. What does history disclose but marks of inferiority, and how few women have emancipated themselves from the galling yoke of sovereign man? So few that the exceptions remind me of an ingenious conjecture respecting Newton: that he was probably a being of a superior order accidentally caged in a human body.[4] Following the same train of thinking, I have been led to imagine that the few extraordinary women who have rushed in eccentrical directions out of the orbit prescribed to their sex were male spirits, confined by mistake in female frames. But if it be not philosophical to think of sex when the soul is mentioned, the inferiority must depend on the organs; or the heavenly fire, which is to ferment the clay, is not given in equal portions.

But avoiding, as I have hitherto done, any direct comparison of the two sexes collectively, or frankly acknowledging the inferiority of woman, according to the present appearance of things, I shall only insist that men have increased that inferiority until women are almost sunk below the standard of rational creatures. Let their faculties have room to unfold, and their virtues to gain strength, and then determine where the whole sex must stand in the intellectual scale. Yet let it be remembered that for a small number of distinguished women I do not ask a place.

---

1   *tenor* Continuous meaning.

2   *melioration* Betterment.

3   *Mahomet's coffin* It was believed that Mohammed's coffin was suspended in mid-air at his tomb in Medina, Saudi Arabia.

4   *Newton ... body* Newton and his scientific discoveries were held in extremely high regard during the eighteenth century; consider, for example, Pope's *Epitaph. Intended for Sir Isaac Newton, in Westminster-Abbey* (1730): "Nature and nature's laws lay hid in night; / God said 'Let Newton be' and all was light."

It is difficult for us purblind[1] mortals to say to what height human discoveries and improvements may arrive when the gloom of despotism subsides, which makes us stumble at every step; but, when morality shall be settled on a more solid basis, then, without being gifted with a prophetic spirit, I will venture to predict that woman will be either the friend or slave of man. We shall not, as at present, doubt whether she is a moral agent or the link which unites man with brutes. But, should it then appear that, like the brutes, they were principally created for the use of man, he will let them patiently bite the bridle and not mock them with empty praise; or, should their rationality be proved, he will not impede their improvement merely to gratify his sensual appetites. He will not, with all the graces of rhetoric, advise them to submit implicitly their understanding to the guidance of man. He will not, when he treats of[2] the education of women, assert that they ought never to have the free use of reason, nor would he recommend cunning and dissimulation to beings who are acquiring, in like manner as himself, the virtues of humanity.

Surely there can be but one rule of right, if morality has an eternal foundation; and whoever sacrifices virtue, strictly so called, to present convenience, or whose duty it is to act in such a manner,[3] lives only for the passing day and cannot be an accountable creature.

The poet then should have dropped his sneer when he says:

If weak women go astray,
The stars are more in fault than they.[4]

For that they are bound by the adamantine[5] chain of destiny is most certain, if it be proved that they are never to exercise their own reason, never to be independent, never to rise above opinion, or to feel the dignity of a rational will that only bows to God—and often forgets that the universe contains any being but itself and the model of perfection to which its ardent gaze is turned—to adore attributes that, softened into

virtues, may be imitated in kind, though the degree overwhelms the enraptured mind.

If, I say, for I would not impress by declamation when Reason offers her sober light, if they be really capable of acting like rational creatures, let them not be treated like slaves, or like the brutes who are dependent on the reason of man when they associate with him; but cultivate their minds, give them the salutary, sublime curb of principle, and let them attain conscious dignity by feeling themselves only dependent on God. Teach them, in common with man, to submit to necessity, instead of giving, to render them more pleasing, a sex to morals.

Further, should experience prove that they cannot attain the same degree of strength of mind, perseverance, and fortitude, let their virtues be the same in kind, though they may vainly struggle for the same degree; and the superiority of man will be equally clear, if not clearer; and truth, as it is a simple principle, which admits of no modification, would be common to both. Nay, the order of society as it is at present regulated would not be inverted, for woman would then only have the rank that reason assigned her, and arts could not be practised to bring the balance even, much less to turn it.

These may be termed Utopian dreams—thanks to that Being who impressed them on my soul and gave me sufficient strength of mind to dare to exert my own reason until, becoming dependent only on him for the support of my virtue, I view, with indignation, the mistaken notions that enslave my sex.

I love man as my fellow; but his sceptre, real or usurped, extends not to me, unless the reason of an individual demands my homage; and even then the submission is to reason, and not to man. In fact, the conduct of an accountable being must be regulated by the operations of its own reason, or on what foundation rests the throne of God?

It appears to me necessary to dwell on these obvious truths because females have been insulated, as it were; and, while they have been stripped of the virtues that should clothe humanity, they have been decked with artificial graces that enable them to exercise a short-lived tyranny. Love, in their bosoms, takes the place of every nobler passion; their sole ambition is to be fair, to raise emotion instead of inspiring respect; and this ignoble desire, like the servility in absolute monarchies, destroys

---

[1] *purblind* Imperfectly sighted.

[2] *treats of* Discourses on.

[3] *to act in such a manner* I.e., to sacrifice duty to convenience.

[4] *If weak ... they* "Hans Carvel" (1700) by Matthew Prior.

[5] *adamantine* Unbreakable.

all strength of character. Liberty is the mother of virtue, and if women be, by their very constitution, slaves, and not allowed to breathe the sharp invigorating air of freedom, they must ever languish like exotics, and be reckoned beautiful flaws in nature.

As to the argument respecting the subjection in which the sex has ever been held, it retorts on[1] man. The many have always been enthralled by the few; and monsters, who scarcely have shown any discernment of human excellence, have tyrannized over thousands of their fellow-creatures. Why have men of superior endowments submitted to such degradation? For is it not universally acknowledged that kings, viewed collectively, have ever been inferior, in abilities and virtue, to the same number of men taken from the common mass of mankind—yet have they not, and are they not still treated with a degree of reverence that is an insult to reason? China is not the only country where a living man has been made a God.[2] Men have submitted to superior strength to enjoy with impunity[3] the pleasure of the moment; women have only done the same, and therefore until it is proved that the courtier, who servilely resigns the birthright of a man, is not a moral agent, it cannot be demonstrated that woman is essentially inferior to man because she has always been subjugated.

Brutal force has hitherto governed the world; and that the science of politics is in its infancy is evident from philosophers scrupling to give the knowledge most useful to man that determinate distinction.

I shall not pursue this argument any further than to establish an obvious inference: that as sound politics diffuse liberty, mankind, including woman, will become more wise and virtuous.

from CHAPTER 3

The Same Subject Continued

… I wish to sum up what I have said in a few words, for I here throw down my gauntlet and deny the existence

of sexual virtues, not excepting modesty. For man and woman, truth—if I understand the meaning of the word—must be the same; yet for the fanciful female character, so prettily drawn by poets and novelists demanding the sacrifice of truth and sincerity, virtue becomes a relative idea, having no other foundation than utility, and of that utility men pretend arbitrarily to judge, shaping it to their own convenience.

Women, I allow, may have different duties to fulfil; but they are human duties, and the principles that should regulate the discharge of them, I sturdily maintain, must be the same.

To become respectable, the exercise of their understanding is necessary; there is no other foundation for independence of character. I mean explicitly to say that they must only bow to the authority of reason instead of being the modest slaves of opinion.

In the superior ranks of life how seldom do we meet with a man of superior abilities, or even common acquirements? The reason appears to me clear: the state they are born in was an unnatural one. The human character has ever been formed by the employments that the individual, or class, pursues; and if the faculties are not sharpened by necessity, they must remain obtuse. The argument may fairly be extended to women; for, seldom occupied by serious business, the pursuit of pleasure gives that insignificancy to their character which renders the society of the great so insipid. The same want of firmness, produced by a similar cause, forces them both to fly from themselves to noisy pleasures, and artificial passions, until vanity takes place of every social affection, and the characteristics of humanity can scarcely be discerned. Such are the blessings of civil governments, as they are at present organized, that wealth and female softness equally tend to debase mankind and are produced by the same cause; but allowing women to be rational creatures, they should be incited to acquire virtues which they may call their own, for how can a rational being be ennobled by any thing that is not obtained by its own exertions?

—1792

---

[1] *retorts on*   Answers back.

[2] *China … God*   See *A Discourse on the Love of Our Country* (1789) by Richard Price (1723–91), English philosopher and writer.

[3] *impunity*   Safety from punishment.

IN CONTEXT

Contemporary Reviews of *A Vindication of the Rights of Woman*

Early reviews of *The Vindication of the Rights of Woman* divided largely along party lines. Reviewers from *The Analytical Review* and *The Monthly Review*, for example, praised the work while more conservative papers such as *The Critical Review*, *The General Magazine*, and *The Gentleman's Magazine* attacked it. Excerpts from *The Analytical Review* and *The Critical Review* are reprinted below.

from *The Analytical Review* 12 (1792)

... It is with some reluctance that for the present we take our leave of this singular, and, on the whole, excellent production. The subjects which it investigates, are of the utmost importance to human nature, and we should be wanting in our engagements, and in our duty, if we passed it over too slightly. This circumstance makes it necessary to defer the further analysis to a future Review, when we shall proceed to the remaining topics of this volume.

It might have been supposed that Mrs. W. had taken advantage of the popular topic of the "Rights of Man" in calling her work "A Vindication of the Rights of Woman," had she not already published a work, one of the first answers that appeared to Mr. Burke, under the title of "A Vindication of the Rights of Man." But in reality the present work is an elaborate *treatise* of *female education*. The lesser wits will probably affect to make themselves merry at the title and apparent object of this publication; but we have no doubt if even her contemporaries should fail to do her justice, posterity will compensate the defect; and have no hesitation in declaring, that if the bulk of the great truths which this publication contains were reduced to practice, the nation would be better, wiser and happier, than it is upon the wretched, trifling, useless and absurd system of education which is now prevalent.

from *The Critical Review* 4 (1792)

One of the strictest proofs in mathematical demonstrations, is the reducing the questions to an absurdity; by allowing, for instance, that the proposition is not true, and then showing that this would lead to the most obvious inconsistencies. Miss Wollstonecraft has converted this method of proceeding with the same success: reasoning on the boasted principles of the Rights of Man, she finds they lead very clearly to the object of her work, a Vindication of the Rights of Woman; and, by the absurdity of many of her conclusions, shows, while we admit the reasoning, that the premises must be, in some respects, fallacious.

Dismissing then those pretty feminine phrases, which the men condescendingly use to soften our slavish dependence, and despising that weak elegancy of mind, exquisite sensibility, and sweet docility of manners, supposed to be the sexual characteristics of the weaker vessel, I wish to shew that elegance is inferior to virtue, that the first object of laudable ambition is to obtain a character as a human being, regardless of the distinction of sex; and that secondary views should be brought to this simple touchstone.

This is the outline of her plan; but before she proceeds to show that this change would be suitable, useful, advantageous, it will be first necessary to prove that there is no sexual distinction of character; that the female mind is equally fitted for the more arduous mental operations; that women are equally able to pursue the toilsome road of minute, laborious, investigation; that their judgments are equally sound, their resolution equally strong. After this is done, the benefit derived must be considered; and, when all are strong, to whom must the weaker operations belong? The female Plato will find it unsuitable to "the dignity of her virtue" to dress the child, and descend to the disgusting offices of a nurse: the new Archimedes will measure the shirts by means of the altitude taken by a quadrant; and the young lady, instead of studying the softer and more amiable arts of pleasing, must contend with her lover for superiority of mind, for greater dignity of virtue; and before she condescends to become his wife, must prove herself his equal or superior.—It may be fancy, prejudice, or obstinacy, we contend not for a name, but we are infinitely better pleased with the present system; and, in truth, dear young lady, for by the appellation sometimes prefixed to your name we must suppose you to be young, endeavour to attain "the weak elegancy of mind," the "sweet docility of manners," "the exquisite sensibility," the former ornaments of your sex; we are certain you will be more pleasing, and we dare pronounce that you will be infinitely happier. Mental superiority is not an object worth contending for, if happiness be the aim. But, as this is the first female combatant in the new field of the Rights of Woman, if we smile only, we shall be accused of wishing to decline the contest; if we content ourselves with paying a compliment to her talents, it will be styled inconsistent with "true dignity," and as showing that we want to continue the "slavish dependence."—We must contend then with this new Atalanta; and who knows whether, in this modern instance, we may not gain two victories by the contest? There is more than one bachelor in our corps; and, if we should succeed, Miss Wollstonecraft may take her choice.

This work is dedicated to M. Talleyrand-Perigord, late bishop of Autun, who, in his treatise on National Education, does not seem to be perfectly convinced that the rights of man extend to woman; yet in France the diffusion of knowledge, our author asserts, is greater than in any other European nation, on account of the more unreserved communication between the sexes, though what the ladies have gained in knowledge they seem confessedly to have lost in delicacy. The following passage we must transcribe, for we confess we do not fully understand it.

Contending for the rights of woman, my main argument is built on this simple principle, that if she be not prepared by education to become the companion of man, she will stop the progress of knowledge, for truth must be common to all, or it will be inefficacious with respect to its influence on general practice. And how can woman be expected to co-operate unless she know why she ought to be virtuous! unless freedom strengthen her reason till she comprehend her duty, and see in what manner it is connected with her real good? If children are to be educated to understand the true principle of patriotism, their mother must be a patriot; and the love of mankind, from which an orderly train of virtues spring, can only be produced by considering the moral and civil interest of mankind; but the education and situation of woman, at present, shuts her out from such investigations.

In this work I have produced many arguments, which to me were conclusive, to prove that the prevailing notion respecting a sexual character was subversive of morality, and I have contended, that to render the human body and mind more perfect, chastity must more universally prevail, and that chastity will never be respected in the male world till the person of a woman is not, as it were, idolized, when little virtue or sense embellish it with the grand traces of mental beauty, or the interesting simplicity of affection.

The first sentence is erroneous in fact and in reasoning: it is contradicted by the experience of ages, the practice of different nations. The second sentence is a curious one—How can she be supposed to co-operate (we *suppose* in the progress of knowledge) unless she know why she ought to be *virtuous?* Virtuous! Here must be some mistake: what has virtue to do with the progress of knowledge? As to freedom, strengthening the reason, &c. we see no occasion for metaphysical investigation on this subject: that virtue is connected with prosperity and happiness, and vice with misfortune and misery, she might learn, not from Locke, but the New Testament. The concluding sentence of the first paragraph is still more strange. Patriotism may be very properly instilled by a *father,* and we must beg leave to differ in opinion from this lady in another point: we are confident, from frequent and extensive observation, no arguments can confute the opinion that we have formed, and we must still persist in thinking, that the education and situation of women, *at present,* really and effectually *inspire* the *love* of *mankind.* We do believe with Miss Wollstonecraft, that chastity will be respected more, when the person of a woman ceases to be idolized, and the grand traces of mental beauty are principally conspicuous. ...

from *Maria; or The Wrongs of Woman*

CHAPTER 5

"My Father," said Jemima, "seduced my mother, a pretty girl, with whom he lived fellow-servant; and she no sooner perceived the natural, the dreaded consequence, than the terrible conviction flashed on her—that she was ruined. Honesty, and a regard for her reputation, had been the only principles inculcated by her mother; and they had been so forcibly impressed that she feared shame more than the poverty to which it would lead. Her incessant importunities[1] to prevail upon my father to screen her from reproach by marrying her, as he had promised in the fervour of seduction, estranged him from her so completely that her very person became distasteful to him; and he began to hate, as well as despise me, before I was born.

"My mother, grieved to the soul by his neglect, and unkind treatment, actually resolved to famish herself and injured her health by the attempt; though she had not sufficient resolution to adhere to her project, or renounce it entirely. Death came not at her call; yet sorrow, and the methods she adopted to conceal her condition, still doing the work of a house-maid, had such an effect on her constitution that she died in the wretched garret where her virtuous mistress had forced

her to take refuge in the very pangs of labour; though my father, after a slight reproof,[2] was allowed to remain in his place—allowed by the mother of six children who, scarcely permitting a footstep to be heard during her month's indulgence,[3] felt no sympathy for the poor wretch denied every comfort required by her situation.

"The day my mother died, the ninth after my birth, I was consigned to the care of the cheapest nurse my father could find; who suckled her own child at the same time, and lodged as many more as she could get in two cellar-like apartments.

"Poverty, and the habit of seeing children die off her hands, had so hardened her heart that the office of a mother did not awaken the tenderness of a woman; nor were the feminine caresses which seem a part of the rearing of a child ever bestowed on me. The chicken has a wing to shelter under; but I had no bosom to nestle in, no kindred warmth to foster me. Left in dirt, to cry with cold and hunger till I was weary, and sleep without ever being prepared by exercise, or lulled by kindness to rest, could I be expected to become any thing but a weak and rickety babe? Still, in spite of neglect, I continued to exist, to learn to curse existence, [her countenance grew ferocious as she spoke,] and the treatment that rendered me miserable seemed to sharpen my wits. Confined then in a damp hovel, to rock the cradle of the succeed-

---

[1]   *importunities* Attempts to get attention.

[2]   *reproof* Rebuke.

[3]   *during her month's indulgence* I.e., during the period when she herself had been recovering after childbirth.

ing tribe, I looked like a little old woman, or a hag shriveling into nothing. The furrows of reflection and care contracted the youthful cheek, and gave a sort of supernatural wildness to the ever-watchful eye. During this period, my father had married another fellow-servant, who loved him less and knew better how to manage his passion than my mother. She likewise proving with child, they agreed to keep a shop: my stepmother—if, being an illegitimate offspring, I may venture thus to characterize her—having obtained a sum of a rich relation for that purpose.

"Soon after her lying-in,[1] she prevailed on my father to take me home, to save the expense of maintaining me, and of hiring a girl to assist her in the care of the child. I was young, it was true, but appeared a knowing little thing and might be made handy. Accordingly I was brought to her house; but not to a home—for a home I never knew. Of this child, a daughter, she was extravagantly fond; and it was a part of my employment to assist to spoil her, by humouring all her whims and bearing all her caprices. Feeling her own consequence before she could speak, she had learned the art of tormenting me, and if I ever dared to resist, I received blows, laid on with no compunctious hand,[2] or was sent to bed dinnerless, as well as supperless. I said that it was a part of my daily labour to attend this child with the servility of a slave; still it was but a part. I was sent out in all seasons, and from place to place, to carry burdens far above my strength, without being allowed to draw near the fire, or ever being cheered by encouragement or kindness. No wonder then, treated like a creature of another species, that I began to envy, and at length to hate, the darling of the house. Yet, I perfectly remember that it was the caresses, and kind expressions of my step-mother, which first excited my jealous discontent. Once, I cannot forget it, when she was calling in vain her wayward child to kiss her, I ran to her, saying, 'I will kiss you, ma'am!'; and how did my heart, which was in my mouth, sink, what was my debasement of soul, when pushed away with—'I do not want you, pert thing!' Another day, when a new gown had excited the highest good humour, and she uttered the appropriate

dear, addressed unexpectedly to me, I thought I could never do enough to please her; I was all alacrity,[3] and rose proportionably in my own estimation.

"As her daughter grew up, she was pampered with cakes and fruit, while I was, literally speaking, fed with the refuse of the table, with her leavings. A liquorish tooth[4] is, I believe, common to children, and I used to steal any thing sweet that I could catch up with a chance of concealment. When detected, she was not content to chastise me herself at the moment, but, on my father's return in the evening (he was a shopman), the principal discourse was to recount my faults, and attribute them to the wicked disposition which I had brought into the world with me, inherited from my mother. He did not fail to leave the marks of his resentment on my body, and then solaced himself by playing with my sister. I could have murdered her at those moments. To save myself from these unmerciful corrections, I resorted to falsehood, and the untruths which I sturdily maintained were brought in judgment against me, to support my tyrant's inhuman charge of my natural propensity to vice. Seeing me treated with contempt, and always being fed and dressed better, my sister conceived a contemptuous opinion of me that proved an obstacle to all affection; and my father, hearing continually of my faults, began to consider me as a curse entailed[5] on him for his sins: he was therefore easily prevailed on to bind me apprentice to one of my step-mother's friends, who kept a slop shop[6] in Wapping.[7] I was represented (as it was said) in my true colours; but she 'warranted,'[8] snapping her fingers, 'that she should break my spirit or heart.'

"My mother replied, with a whine, 'that if any body could make me better, it was such a clever woman as herself; though, for her own part, she had tried in vain, but good nature was her fault.'

"I shudder with horror when I recollect the treatment I had now to endure. Not only under the lash of my task-mistress, but the drudge of the maid, appren-

---

[1]   *lying-in*   Period of rest following childbirth.

[2]   *compunctious hand*   I.e., Jemima was beaten without pity, or indeed any concern.

[3]   *alacrity*   Readiness.

[4]   *liquorish tooth*   Sweet tooth, i.e., fondness for sweets.

[5]   *entailed*   Irrevocably attached.

[6]   *slop shop*   Shop that sold inexpensive, ready-made clothing.

[7]   *Wapping*   District of East London.

[8]   *warranted*   Guaranteed.

tices, and children, I never had a taste of human kind-ness to soften the rigour of perpetual labour. I had been introduced as an object of abhorrence into the family; as a creature of whom my step-mother, though she had been kind enough to let me live in the house with her own child, could make nothing. I was described as a wretch whose nose must be kept to the grinding stone—and it was held there with an iron grasp. It seemed indeed the privilege of their superior nature to kick me about like the dog or cat. If I were attentive, I was called fawning, if refractory,[1] an obstinate mule, and like a mule I received their censure on my loaded back. Often has my mistress, for some instance of forgetful-ness, thrown me from one side of the kitchen to the other, knocked my head against the wall, spit in my face, with various refinements on barbarity that I forbear to enumerate, though they were all acted over again by the servant, with additional insults, to which the appel-lation of *bastard* was commonly added with taunts or sneers. But I will not attempt to give you an adequate idea of my situation, lest you, who probably have never been drenched with the dregs of human misery, should think I exaggerate.

"I stole now—from absolute necessity—bread; yet whatever else was taken, which I had it not in my power to take, was ascribed to me. I was the filching cat, the ravenous dog, the dumb brute who must bear all; for if I endeavoured to exculpate[2] myself, I was silenced without any enquiries being made, with 'Hold your tongue, you never tell truth.' Even the very air I breathed was tainted with scorn; for I was sent to the neighbouring shops with Glutton, Liar, or Thief written on my forehead. This was, at first, the most bitter punishment; but sullen pride, or a kind of stupid desperation, made me, at length, almost regardless of the contempt which had wrung from me so many solitary tears at the only moments when I was allowed to rest.

"Thus was I the mark of cruelty till my sixteenth year; and then I have only to point out a change of misery, for a period I never knew. Allow me first to make one observation. Now I look back, I cannot help attributing the greater part of my misery to the misfor-tune of having been thrown into the world without the grand support of life—a mother's affection. I had no one to love me, or to make me respected, to enable me to acquire respect. I was an egg dropped on the sand; a pauper by nature, hunted from family to family, who belonged to nobody—and nobody cared for me. I was despised from my birth, and denied the chance of obtaining a footing for myself in society. Yes; I had not even the chance of being considered as a fellow-creature—yet all the people with whom I lived, brutal-ized as they were by the low cunning of trade, and the despicable shifts of poverty, were not without bowels,[3] though they never yearned for me. I was, in fact, born a slave, and chained by infamy[4] to slavery during the whole of existence, without having any companions to alleviate it by sympathy, or teach me how to rise above it by their example....

"At sixteen, I suddenly grew tall, and something like comeliness[5] appeared on a Sunday, when I had time to wash my face and put on clean clothes. My master had once or twice caught hold of me in the passage; but I instinctively avoided his disgusting caresses. One day however, when the family were at a Methodist meeting, he contrived to be alone in the house with me, and by blows—yes, blows and menaces—compelled me to submit to his ferocious desire; and, to avoid my mis-tress's fury, I was obliged in future to comply, and skulk to my loft at his command, in spite of increasing loath-ing.

"The anguish which was now pent up in my bosom seemed to open a new world to me: I began to extend my thoughts beyond myself and grieve for human misery, until I discovered, with horror—ah! what horror!—that I was with child. I know not why I felt a mixed sensation of despair and tenderness, excepting that, ever called a bastard, a bastard appeared to me an object of the greatest compassion in creation.

"I communicated this dreadful circumstance to my master, who was almost equally alarmed at the intelli-gence; for he feared his wife and public censure at the meeting. After some weeks of deliberation had elapsed, I in continual fear that my altered shape would be

---

[1] *refractory* Stubborn, non-compliant.

[2] *exculpate* Clear oneself from blame.

[3] *bowels* Heart, compassion.

[4] *infamy* Scandalous reputation.

[5] *comeliness* Beauty.

noticed, my master gave me a medicine in a phial which he desired me to take, telling me, without any circumlocution,[1] for what purpose it was designed. I burst into tears, I thought it was killing myself—yet was such a self as I worth preserving? He cursed me for a fool, and left me to my own reflections. I could not resolve to take this infernal potion; but I wrapped it up in an old gown, and hid it in a corner of my box.

"Nobody yet suspected me, because they had been accustomed to view me as a creature of another species. But the threatening storm at last broke over my devoted head—never shall I forget it! One Sunday evening when I was left, as usual, to take care of the house, my master came home intoxicated, and I became the prey of his brutal appetite. His extreme intoxication made him forget his customary caution, and my mistress entered and found us in a situation that could not have been more hateful to her than me. Her husband was 'pot-valiant,'[2] he feared her not at the moment, nor had he then much reason, for she instantly turned the whole force of her anger another way. She tore off my cap, scratched, kicked, and buffeted me until she had exhausted her strength, declaring, as she rested her arm, 'that I had wheedled[3] her husband from her. But, could any thing better be expected from a wretch whom she had taken into her house out of pure charity?' What a torrent of abuse rushed out, until, almost breathless, she concluded with saying, 'that I was born a strumpet;[4] it ran in my blood, and nothing good could come to those who harboured me.'

"My situation was, of course, discovered, and she declared that I should not stay another night under the same roof with an honest family. I was therefore pushed out of doors, and my trumpery[5] thrown after me, when it had been contemptuously examined in the passage lest I should have stolen any thing.

"Behold me then in the street, utterly destitute! Whither could I creep for shelter? To my father's roof I

had no claim when not pursued by shame—now I shrunk back as from death from my mother's cruel reproaches, my father's execrations.[6] I could not endure to hear him curse the day I was born, though life had been a curse to me. Of death I thought, but with a confused emotion of terror, as I stood leaning my head on a post and starting at every footstep, lest it should be my mistress coming to tear my heart out. One of the boys of the shop passing by heard my tale, and immediately repaired to his master to give him a description of my situation; and he touched the right key—the scandal it would give rise to if I were left to repeat my tale to every enquirer. This plea came home to his reason, who had been sobered by his wife's rage, the fury of which fell on him when I was out of her reach, and he sent the boy to me with half-a-guinea,[7] desiring him to conduct me to a house where beggars, and other wretches, the refuse of society, nightly lodged.

"This night was spent in a state of stupefaction, or desperation. I detested mankind, and abhorred myself.

"In the morning I ventured out, to throw myself in my master's way, at his usual hour of going abroad. I approached him, he 'damned me for a b——, declared I had disturbed the peace of the family, and that he had sworn to his wife never to take any more notice of me.' He left me; but, instantly returning, he told me that he should speak to his friend, a parish-officer,[8] to get a nurse for the brat I laid to him; and advised me, if I wished to keep out of the house of correction, not to make free with his name.

"I hurried back to my hole, and, rage giving place to despair, sought for the potion that was to procure abortion and swallowed it, with a wish that it might destroy me at the same time that it stopped the sensations of new-born life, which I felt with indescribable emotion. My head turned round, my heart grew sick, and in the horrors of approaching dissolution,[9] mental

---

[1] *circumlocution* Indirect speaking.

[2] *pot-valiant* Courageous due to the affects of alcohol.

[3] *wheedled* Seduced by flattery or gentle coaxing.

[4] *strumpet* Derogatory term for a woman who has a number of sexual partners.

[5] *trumpery* Worthless clothing goods.

[6] *execrations* Expressions of intense loathing.

[7] *half-a-guinea* Gold coin.

[8] *parish-officer* General term for person holding any one of several elected positions within a parish, including churchwarden, surveyor, overseer of the poor, constable, etc.; overseers of the poor set and collected poor rates, as well as administering benefits to those in need.

[9] *dissolution* Death.

anguish was swallowed up. The effect of the medicine was violent, and I was confined to my bed several days; but, youth and a strong constitution prevailing, I once more crawled out to ask myself the cruel question, 'Whither I should go?' I had but two shillings[1] left in my pocket, the rest had been expended, by a poor woman who slept in the same room, to pay for my lodging and purchase the necessaries of which she partook.

"With this wretch I went into the neighbouring streets to beg, and my disconsolate appearance drew a few pence from the idle, enabling me still to command a bed; until, recovering from my illness, and taught to put on my rags to the best advantage, I was accosted from different motives, and yielded to the desire of the brutes I met with the same detestation that I had felt for my still more brutal master. I have since read in novels of the blandishments[2] of seduction, but I had not even the pleasure of being enticed into vice.

"I shall not," interrupted Jemima, "lead your imagination into all the scenes of wretchedness and depravity which I was condemned to view, or mark the different stages of my debasing misery. Fate dragged me through the very kennels[3] of society: I was still a slave, a bastard, a common property. Become familiar with vice, for I wish to conceal nothing from you, I picked the pockets of the drunkards who abused me; and proved by my conduct that I deserved the epithets with which they loaded me at moments when distrust ought to cease.

"Detesting my nightly occupation, though valuing, if I may so use the word, my independence, which only consisted in choosing the street in which I should wander, or the roof, when I had money, in which I should hide my head, I was some time before I could prevail on myself to accept of a place in a house of ill fame[4] to which a girl, with whom I had accidentally conversed in the street, had recommended me. I had been hunted almost into a fever by the watchmen[5] of the quarter of the town I frequented; one, whom I had unwittingly offended, giving the word to the whole pack. You can scarcely conceive the tyranny exercised by these wretches: considering themselves as the instruments of the very laws they violate, the pretext which steels their conscience hardens their heart. Not content with receiving from us, outlaws of society (let other women talk of favours), a brutal gratification gratuitously as a privilege of office, they extort a tithe[6] of prostitution, and harass with threats the poor creatures whose occupation affords not the means to silence the growl of avarice. To escape from this persecution, I once more entered into servitude.

"A life of comparative regularity restored my health; and—do not start[7]—my manners were improved in a situation where vice sought to render itself alluring, and taste was cultivated to fashion the person, if not to refine the mind. Besides, the common civility of speech, contrasted with the gross vulgarity to which I had been accustomed, was something like the polish of civilization. I was not shut out from all intercourse[8] of humanity. Still I was galled[9] by the yoke of service, and my mistress often flying into violent fits of passion made me dread a sudden dismission, which I understood was always the case. I was therefore prevailed on, though I felt a horror of men, to accept the offer of a gentleman, rather in the decline of years, to keep his house, pleasantly situated in a little village near Hampstead.[10]

"He was a man of great talents, and of brilliant wit; but, a worn-out votary of voluptuousness,[11] his desires became fastidious in proportion as they grew weak, and the native tenderness of his heart was undermined by a vitiated[12] imagination. A thoughtless career of libertinism[13] and social enjoyment had injured his health to such a degree that, whatever pleasure his conversation afforded me (and my esteem was ensured by proofs of

---

[1] *shillings* Coins of small value.

[2] *blandishments* Flattering words.

[3] *kennels* Gutters.

[4] *house of ill fame* Brothel.

[5] *watchmen* Before the Police Act of 1839, men were formally appointed to guard city and town streets from sunset to sunrise.

[6] *tithe* Tenth of one's earnings.

[7] *do not start* I.e., do not be startled, shocked.

[8] *intercourse* Social interaction or communication.

[9] *galled* Irritated, chafed.

[10] *Hampstead* North London suburb.

[11] *votary of voluptuousness* Person devoted to sensuality.

[12] *vitiated* Rendered impure, soiled.

[13] *libertinism* Unrestrained, licentious conduct.

the generous humanity of his disposition), the being his mistress was purchasing it at a very dear rate. With such a keen perception of the delicacies of sentiment, with an imagination invigorated by the exercise of genius, how could he sink into the grossness of sensuality!

"But, to pass over a subject which I recollect with pain, I must remark to you, as an answer to your often-repeated question—'Why my sentiments and language were superior to my station?'—that I now began to read, to beguile[1] the tediousness of solitude, and to gratify an inquisitive, active mind. I had often, in my childhood, followed a ballad-singer to hear the sequel of a dismal story, though sure of being severely punished for delaying to return with whatever I was sent to purchase. I could just spell and put a sentence together, and I listened to the various arguments, though often mingled with obscenity, which occurred at the table where I was allowed to preside: for a literary friend or two frequently came home with my master to dine and pass the night. Having lost the privileged respect of my sex, my presence, instead of restraining, perhaps gave the reins to their tongues; still I had the advantage of hearing discussions from which, in the common course of life, women are excluded.

"You may easily imagine that it was only by degrees that I could comprehend some of the subjects they investigated, or acquire from their reasoning what might be termed a moral sense. But my fondness of reading increasing, and my master occasionally shutting himself up in this retreat for weeks together to write, I had many opportunities of improvement. At first, considering money (I was right!" exclaimed Jemima, altering her tone of voice) "as the only means, after my loss of reputation, of obtaining respect, or even the toleration of humanity, I had not the least scruple to secrete a part of the sums entrusted to me, and to screen myself from detection by a system of falsehood. But, acquiring new principles, I began to have the ambition of returning to the respectable part of society, and was weak enough to suppose it possible. The attention of my unassuming instructor, who, without being ignorant of his own powers, possessed great simplicity of manners, strengthened the illusion. Having sometimes caught up hints for

thought from my untutored remarks, he often led me to discuss the subjects he was treating, and would read to me his productions, previous to their publication, wishing to profit by the criticism of unsophisticated feeling. The aim of his writings was to touch the simple springs of the heart; for he despised the would-be oracles, the self-elected philosophers, who fright away fancy while sifting each grain of thought to prove that slowness of comprehension is wisdom.

"I should have distinguished this as a moment of sunshine, a happy period in my life, had not the repugnance the disgusting libertinism of my protector inspired daily become more painful. And, indeed, I soon did recollect it as such with agony, when his sudden death (for he had recourse to the most exhilarating cordials to keep up the convivial tone of his spirits) again threw me into the desert of human society. Had he had any time for reflection, I am certain he would have left the little property in his power to me: but, attacked by the fatal apoplexy[2] in town, his heir, a man of rigid morals, brought his wife with him to take possession of the house and effects before I was even informed of his death—'to prevent,' as she took care indirectly to tell me, 'such a creature as she supposed me to be from purloining[3] any of them, had I been apprized of the event in time.'

"The grief I felt at the sudden shock the information gave me, which at first had nothing selfish in it, was treated with contempt, and I was ordered to pack up my clothes; and a few trinkets and books, given me by the generous deceased, were contested, while they piously hoped, with a reprobating[4] shake of the head, 'that God would have mercy on his sinful soul!' With some difficulty, I obtained my arrears of wages; but asking—such is the spirit-grinding consequence of poverty and infamy—for a character[5] for honesty and economy, which God knows I merited, I was told by this—why must I call her woman?—'that it would go against her conscience to recommend a kept mistress.' Tears started in my eyes, burning tears; for there are situations in

----
1 *beguile* Charm away.

2 *apoplexy* Stroke.
3 *purloining* Stealing.
4 *reprobating* Condemning.
5 *character* I.e., formal reference from an employer.

which a wretch is humbled by the contempt they are conscious they do not deserve.

"I returned to the metropolis; but the solitude of a poor lodging was inconceivably dreary after the society I had enjoyed. To be cut off from human converse, now I had been taught to relish it, was to wander a ghost among the living. Besides, I foresaw, to aggravate the severity of my fate, that my little pittance would soon melt away. I endeavoured to obtain needlework; but, not having been taught early, and my hands being rendered clumsy by hard work, I did not sufficiently excel to be employed by the ready-made linen shops when so many women, better qualified, were suing[1] for it. The want of a character prevented my getting a place; for, irksome as servitude would have been to me, I should have made another trial had it been feasible. Not that I disliked employment, but the inequality of condition to which I must have submitted. I had acquired a taste for literature during the five years I had lived with a literary man, occasionally conversing with men of the first abilities of the age; and now to descend to the lowest vulgarity was a degree of wretchedness not to be imagined unfelt. I had not, it is true, tasted the charms of affection, but I had been familiar with the graces of humanity.

"One of the gentlemen, whom I had frequently dined in company with while I was treated like a companion, met me in the street and enquired after my health. I seized the occasion, and began to describe my situation; but he was in haste to join, at dinner, a select party of choice spirits; therefore, without waiting to hear me, he impatiently put a guinea into my hand, saying, 'It was a pity such a sensible woman should be in distress—he wished me well from his soul.'

"To another I wrote, stating my case and requesting advice. He was an advocate for unequivocal sincerity; and had often, in my presence, descanted[2] on the evils which arise in society from the despotism of rank and riches.

"In reply, I received a long essay on the energy of the human mind with continual allusions to his own force of character. He added, 'That the woman who could write such a letter as I had sent him could never be in

want of resources, were she to look into herself and exert her powers; misery was the consequence of indolence, and, as to my being shut out from society, it was the lot of man to submit to certain privations.'[3]

"How often have I heard," said Jemima, interrupting her narrative, "in conversation, and read in books, that every person willing to work may find employment? It is the vague assertion, I believe, of insensible[4] indolence when it relates to men; but, with respect to women, I am sure of its fallacy, unless they will submit to the most menial bodily labour; and even to be employed at hard labour is out of the reach of many whose reputation misfortune or folly has tainted.

"How writers, professing to be friends to freedom and the improvement of morals, can assert that poverty is no evil, I cannot imagine."

"No more can I," interrupted Maria, "yet they even expatiate[5] on the peculiar happiness of indigence,[6] though in what it can consist, excepting in brutal rest, when a man can barely earn a subsistence, I cannot imagine. The mind is necessarily imprisoned in its own little tenement; and, fully occupied by keeping it in repair, has not time to rove abroad for improvement. The book of knowledge is closely clasped against those who must fulfill their daily task of severe manual labour or die; and curiosity, rarely excited by thought or information, seldom moves on the stagnate lake of ignorance."

"As far as I have been able to observe," replied Jemima, "prejudices, caught up by chance, are obstinately maintained by the poor to the exclusion of improvement; they have not time to reason or reflect to any extent, or minds sufficiently exercised to adopt the principles of action, which form perhaps the only basis of contentment in every station."

"And independence," said Darnford, "they are necessarily strangers to, even the independence of despising their persecutors. If the poor are happy, or can be happy, *things are very well as they are*. And I cannot conceive on what principle those writers contend for a

---

[1] *suing* Asking, applying.

[2] *descanted* Commented on.

[3] *privations* Absence of comforts.

[4] *insensible* Incapable of feeling.

[5] *expatiate* Write or speak copiously on a subject.

[6] *indigence* Poverty.

change of system who support this opinion. The authors on the other side of the question are much more consistent who grant the fact; yet, insisting that it is the lot of the majority to be oppressed in this life, kindly turn them over to another, to rectify the false weights and measures of this, as the only way to justify the dispensations of Providence.[1] I have not," continued Darnford, "an opinion more firmly fixed by observation in my mind than that, though riches may fail to produce proportionate happiness, poverty most commonly excludes it by shutting up all the avenues to improvement."

"And as for the affections," added Maria, with a sigh, "how gross,[2] and even tormenting do they become, unless regulated by an improving mind! The culture of the heart ever, I believe, keeps pace with that of the mind. But pray go on," addressing Jemima, "though your narrative gives rise to the most painful reflections on the present state of society."

"Not to trouble you," continued she, "with a detailed description of all the painful feelings of unavailing[3] exertion, I have only to tell you that at last I got recommended to wash in a few families, who did me the favour to admit me into their houses without the most strict enquiry, to wash from one in the morning till eight at night for eighteen or twenty-pence a day. On the happiness to be enjoyed over a washing-tub I need not comment; yet you will allow me to observe that this was a wretchedness of situation peculiar to my sex. A man with half my industry, and, I may say, abilities, could have procured a decent livelihood and discharged some of the duties which knit mankind together; whilst I, who had acquired a taste for the rational—nay, in honest pride let me assert it, the virtuous enjoyments of life—was cast aside as the filth of society. Condemned to labour, like a machine, only to earn bread, and scarcely that, I became melancholy and desperate.

"I have now to mention a circumstance which fills me with remorse, and fear it will entirely deprive me of your esteem. A tradesman became attached to me, and

visited me frequently, and I at last obtained such a power over him that he offered to take me home to his house. Consider, dear madam, I was famishing: wonder not that I became a wolf! The only reason for not taking me home immediately was the having a girl in the house with child by him; and this girl, I advised him—yes, I did! Would I could forget it!—to turn out of doors: and one night he determined to follow my advice. Poor wretch! She fell upon her knees, reminded him that he had promised to marry her, that her parents were honest! What did it avail? She was turned out.

"She approached her father's door in the skirts of London, listened at the shutters, but could not knock. A watchman had observed her go and return several times—Poor wretch! (The remorse Jemima spoke of seemed to be stinging her to the soul, as she proceeded.)

"She left it, and, approaching a tub where horses were watered, she sat down in it, and, with desperate resolution, remained in that attitude[4]—till resolution was no longer necessary!

"I happened that morning to be going out to wash, anticipating the moment when I should escape from such hard labour. I passed by, just as some men, going to work, drew out the stiff, cold corpse—let me not recall the horrid moment! I recognized her pale visage; I listened to the tale told by the spectators, and my heart did not burst. I thought of my own state, and wondered how I could be such a monster! I worked hard; and, returning home, I was attacked by a fever. I suffered both in body and mind. I determined not to live with the wretch. But he did not try[5] me; he left the neighbourhood. I once more returned to the wash tub.

"Still this state, miserable as it was, admitted of aggravation. Lifting one day a heavy load, a tub fell against my shin and gave me great pain. I did not pay much attention to the hurt until it became a serious wound, being obliged to work as usual or starve. But, finding myself at length unable to stand for any time, I thought of getting into an hospital. Hospitals, it should seem (for they are comfortless abodes for the sick), were expressly endowed for the reception of the friendless; yet I, who had on that plea a right to assistance, wanted the recommendation of the rich and respectable, and was

---

[1] *dispensations of Providence* Providential management of the world.

[2] *gross* Unrefined, lacking sensitivity.

[3] *unavailing* Of no avail, no use or hope.

[4] *attitude* Posture, bodily position.

[5] *try* Put to the test.

several weeks languishing for admittance; fees were demanded on entering; and, what was still more unreasonable, security for burying me—that expense not coming into the letter of the charity. A guinea was the stipulated sum—I could as soon have raised a million; and I was afraid to apply to the parish for an order, lest they should have passed me I knew not whither.[1] The poor woman at whose house I lodged, compassionating[2] my state, got me into the hospital; and the family where I received the hurt sent me five shillings, three and sixpence of which I gave at my admittance—I know not for what.

"My leg grew quickly better; but I was dismissed before my cure was completed because I could not afford to have my linen washed to appear decently, as the virago[3] of a nurse said, when the gentlemen (the surgeons) came. I cannot give you an adequate idea of the wretchedness of an hospital; everything is left to the care of people intent on gain. The attendants seem to have lost all feeling of compassion in the bustling discharge of their offices; death is so familiar to them that they are not anxious to ward it off. Everything appeared to be conducted for the accommodation of the medical men and their pupils, who came to make experiments on the poor for the benefit of the rich. One of the physicians, I must not forget to mention, gave me half-a-crown, and ordered me some wine, when I was at the lowest ebb. I thought of making my case known to the lady-like matron;[4] but her forbidding countenance prevented me. She condescended to look on the patients, and make general enquiries, two or three times a week; but the nurses knew the hour when the visit of ceremony would commence, and every thing was as it should be.

"After my dismission, I was more at a loss than ever for a subsistence, and, not to weary you with a repetition of the same unavailing attempts, unable to stand at the washing-tub, I began to consider the rich and poor as natural enemies, and became a thief from principle. I could not now cease to reason, but I hated mankind. I despised myself, yet I justified my conduct. I was taken, tried, and condemned to six months' imprisonment in a house of correction. My soul recoils with horror from the remembrance of the insults I had to endure until, branded with shame, I was turned loose in the street, penniless. I wandered from street to street until, exhausted by hunger and fatigue, I sunk down senseless at a door where I had vainly demanded a morsel of bread. I was sent by the inhabitant to the work-house, to which he had surlily bid me go, saying, he 'paid enough in conscience to the poor' when, with parched tongue, I implored his charity. If those well-meaning people who exclaim against beggars were acquainted with the treatment the poor receive in many of these wretched asylums, they would not stifle so easily involuntary sympathy by saying that they have all parishes to go to, or wonder that the poor dread to enter the gloomy walls. What are the common run of workhouses but prisons, in which many respectable old people, worn out by immoderate labour, sink into the grave in sorrow to which they are carried like dogs!"

Alarmed by some indistinct noise, Jemima rose hastily to listen, and Maria, turning to Darnford, said, "I have indeed been shocked beyond expression when I have met a pauper's funeral. A coffin carried on the shoulders of three or four ill-looking wretches, whom the imagination might easily convert into a band of assassins hastening to conceal the corpse and quarrelling about the prey on their way. I know it is of little consequence how we are consigned to the earth;[5] but I am led by this brutal insensibility, to what even the animal creation appears forcibly to feel, to advert to[6] the wretched, deserted manner in which they died."

"True," rejoined Darnford, "and until the rich will give more than a part of their wealth, until they will give time and attention to the wants of the distressed, never let them boast of charity. Let them open their hearts,

---

[1] *I was afraid … whither* One applied for poor relief from the parish in which one was last legally settled; terms of legal settlement included being born into a parish, renting property of a certain value, working for over a year and a day, serving an apprenticeship of seven years or more, marrying into the parish, etc. If one applied for poor relief without meeting the settlement requirements, one would be sent back to a parish in which one did.

[2] *compassionating* Having compassion for.

[3] *virago* Bold woman, scold.

[4] *matron* Woman in charge of the nurses.

[5] *how we are consigned to the earth* I.e., how we are buried.

[6] *advert to* Pay attention to.

and not their purses, and employ their minds in the service if they are really actuated by humanity; or charitable institutions will always be the prey of the lowest order of knaves."

Jemima returning, seemed in haste to finish her tale. "The overseer farmed[1] the poor of different parishes, and out of the bowels of poverty was wrung the money with which he purchased this dwelling, as a private receptacle for madness. He had been a keeper at a house of the same description, and conceived that he could make money much more readily in his old occupation. He is a shrewd—shall I say it?—villain. He observed something resolute in my manner, and offered to take me with him and instruct me how to treat the disturbed minds he meant to entrust to my care. The offer of forty pounds a year, and to quit a workhouse, was not to be despised, though the condition of shutting my eyes and hardening my heart was annexed[2] to it.

"I agreed to accompany him; and four years have I been attendant on many wretches, and"—she lowered her voice—"the witness of many enormities.[3] In solitude my mind seemed to recover its force, and many of the sentiments which I imbibed in the only tolerable period of my life returned with their full force. Still, what should induce me to be the champion for suffering humanity? Who ever risked any thing for me? Who ever acknowledged me to be a fellow-creature?"

Maria took her hand, and Jemima, more overcome by kindness than she had ever been by cruelty, hastened out of the room to conceal her emotions.

Darnford soon after heard his summons, and, taking leave of him, Maria promised to gratify his curiosity, with respect to herself, at the first opportunity.
—1798

---

[1] *farmed* Contracted out care or maintenance for a fee.
[2] *annexed* Included as a condition.
[3] *enormities* Gross breaches of law or morals.

WOMEN AND SOCIETY

CONTEXTS

In the later eighteenth century, women's education and social status became a topic of heated debate among philanthropists, political and educational theorists, and many middle- and upper-class parents. As the first excerpt in this section, from William Blackstone's *Commentaries on the Laws of England*, shows, women's identity in marriage was subsumed under that of their husbands—as it was subsumed under that of their fathers before marriage. Women could not conduct business, own property (unless widowed), reject their fathers' choice of husbands for them, or choose to divorce their husbands. Without legal status they had no representation in Parliament; the idea of female suffrage was one entertained by only the most radical thinkers.

A common concern voiced by educational theorists at the time was that the fashion of educating women in "accomplishments" would help them to attract a husband but would not equip them to fulfill their roles as capable wives or mothers. Instead, many began to stress moral, religious, and domestic training. While more radical feminists, such as Mary Wollstonecraft, insisted that changes in gender roles and assumptions about female nature were essential to improving the status of women, these ideas were not generally accepted. Nevertheless, many of those who supported traditional notions of female roles and behavior advocated education reform along similar lines—insisting that practical education for women would benefit society as a whole. The excerpts printed here from Catharine Macaulay's *Letters on Education*, a series of letters to a fictional friend, Hortensia, criticize the idea that women's education "should be of an opposite kind to that of males." The weaknesses that were typically considered natural in women were a result of education and situation only, she argues, and women should not accept this assumption of inferiority. She proposes one standard of rational conduct by which both sexes should be judged and attacks traditional gender ideologies and the often-praised female art of "coquetry," by which women attempt to manipulate men. These ideas align Macaulay with Wollstonecraft, who was deeply influenced by the work, and later praised Macaulay in her *Vindication of the Rights of Woman* (1792). Others were less sympathetic, however; upon publication, Macaulay's *Letters* made her the subject of many personal attacks. In general, the work was more influential in France than in England.

The next excerpt is taken from French novelist and playwright Olympe de Gouges's *The Rights of Woman*, a piece with many similarities to Wollstonecraft's work of the following year. De Gouges's pamphlet also emphasizes the importance of female education and professional opportunities to the betterment of society and compares women's situation with that of slaves, demonstrating the corrupting effect on men of such arbitrary power over both groups. De Gouges's political agitation extended far beyond women's rights, and during the French Revolution she published writings that criticized the violent actions of the revolutionaries and were viewed as sympathetic towards the monarchy. When her expression of these opinions led to her arrest and execution, the newspaper of the Committee of Public Safety declared, "She wanted to be a statesman, and it seems the law has punished this conspiratress for having forgotten the virtues befitting her sex."

A more conservative approach to female education is exemplified in novelist Maria Edgeworth and her father Richard Lovell Edgeworth's *Practical Education*, excerpted here, which emphasizes moral education (as opposed to the acquisition of accomplishments). Conservative thinkers such as the Edgeworths tended to advocate women's training in "traditional female virtues" of modesty, piety, and obedience; such an education consisted of instruction in domestic duties and Christian principles. Quaker philanthropist Priscilla Wakefield's *Reflections on the Present Condition of the Female Sex* proceeds along similar lines, positing that women will be better able to fulfill their roles as wives and mothers if given opportunities for education and professional advancement. She also helps to bring to public attention the plight of many genteel women faced with social and economic difficulties while lacking the skills or opportunities that would enable them to help themselves.

Reverend Richard Polwhele's poem "The Unsexed Females" was part of the backlash against thinkers such as Macaulay and Wollstonecraft that occurred at the turn of the century, following a decade of debate initiated by those two women's works. While Polwhele's poem celebrates women he sees as modestly virtuous, it depicts Wollstonecraft and her followers as unnatural, anti-Christian women driven by a godless "Reason." His poem contains numerous footnotes (most of which are included here) that extend and amplify his arguments.

Hannah More's *Strictures on the Modern System of Female Education*, excerpted here, advocates separate spheres for men and women and emphasizes the education of young women in Christian virtue, morality, and rational education in practical matters. Like most conservative thinkers, More believed that social divisions of class and gender were ordained by God and should not be challenged. Though her ideas for the education of women are, practically speaking, similar to Wollstonecraft's, More insisted on female subordination to men.

The final piece excerpted here, William Thompson and Anna Wheeler's *Appeal of One Half of the Human Race*, challenges those utilitarians who overlooked women in their search for universal happiness, as did many of Thompson and Wheeler's fellow reformers. It also argues for female suffrage and takes issue with the misogynist belief that women's interests are best represented by those of their husbands. Written primarily by Thompson but with key passages by Wheeler, the *Appeal* extends many of the ideas developed by Wollstonecraft in her *Vindications of the Rights of Woman*. It examines the faults in the economic system that help to create the social iniquities Wollstonecraft examines, and extends Wollstonecraft's comparison of women to slaves, comparing the status of plantation laborers in the New World and of Turkish harem-slaves with that of Englishwomen.

⌘⌘⌘

from William Blackstone, *Commentaries on the Laws of England* (1765)

from BOOK 1, CHAPTER 15: OF HUSBAND AND WIFE

By marriage, the husband and wife are one person in law: that is, the very being or legal existence of the woman is suspended during the marriage, or at least is incorporated and consolidated into that of the husband, under whose wing, protection, and *cover* she performs everything; and is therefore called in our law-French[1] a *feme-covert*; is said to be a *covert-baron*, or under the protection and influence of her husband, her *baron*, or

lord; and her condition during her marriage is called her *coverture*. Upon this principle, of a union of person in husband and wife, depend almost all the legal rights, duties, and disabilities that either of them acquire by the marriage. I speak not at present of the rights of property, but of such as are merely *personal*. For this reason, a man cannot grant anything to his wife, or enter into covenant with her; for the grant would be to suppose her separate existence, and to covenant with her would be only to covenant with himself. And therefore it is also generally true that all compacts made between husband and wife when single are voided by the intermarriage. A woman indeed may be attorney for her husband; for that implies no separation from, but is rather a representation of, her lord. And a husband may also bequeath

---

[1] *law-French* Corrupt dialect of Norman French used in English law books until the reign of Edward III (1327–77).

anything to his wife by will; for that cannot take effect till the coverture is determined[1] by his death. The husband is bound to provide his wife with necessaries by law, as much as himself; and if he contracts debts for them, he is obliged to pay them: but for anything besides necessaries he is not chargeable. Also, if a wife elopes, and lives with another man, the husband is not chargeable even for necessaries—at least if the person who furnishes them is sufficiently apprized of her elopement. If the wife be indebted before marriage, the husband is bound afterwards to pay the debt; for he has adopted her and her circumstances together. If the wife be injured in her person or her property, she can bring no action for redress without her husband's concurrence, and in his name as well as her own; neither can she be sued without making the husband a defendant.…

These are the chief legal effects of marriage during the coverture, upon which we may observe that even the disabilities which the wife lies under are for the most part intended for her protection and benefit. So great a favourite is the female sex of the laws of England.[2]

from Catharine Macaulay, *Letters on Education* (1790)

from LETTER 21:
MORALS MUST BE TAUGHT ON IMMUTABLE PRINCIPLES

… In order to take from public sentiment a reproach which leaves a deep stain on the human character, and to correct many irregularities, and even enormities, which arise from incorrect systems of ethics, it ought to be the first care of education to teach virtue on immutable principles, and to avoid that confusion which must arise from confounding the laws and customs of society with those obligations which are founded on correct

principles of equity. But as you have had patience to go through my whole plan of education, from infancy to manhood, it is but fair that I should attend to your objections, and examine whether my plan is founded on error, or on the principles of reason and truth. Know then, good Hortensia, that I have given similar rules for male and female education, on the following grounds of reasoning.

First, That there is but one rule of right for the conduct of all rational beings; consequently that true virtue in one sex must be equally so in the other, whenever a proper opportunity calls for its exertion, and, *vice versa*, what is vice in one sex cannot have a different property when found in the other.

Secondly, that true wisdom, which is never found at variance with rectitude, is as useful to women as to men, because it is necessary to the highest degree of happiness, which can never exist with ignorance.

Lastly, that as on our first entrance into another world our state of happiness may possibly depend on the degree of perfection we have attained in this, we cannot justly lessen, in one sex or the other, the means by which perfection, that is another word for wisdom, is acquired.

It would be paying you a bad compliment, Hortensia, were I to answer all the frivolous objections which prejudice has framed against the giving a learned education to women; for I know of no learning worth having that does not tend to free the mind from error and enlarge our stock of useful knowledge. Thus much it may be proper to observe, that those hours which are spent in studious retirement by learned women will not in all probability intrude so much on the time for useful avocation as the wild and spreading dissipations of the present day; that levity and ignorance will always be found in opposition to what is useful and graceful in life; and that the contrary may be expected from a truly enlightened understanding. However, Hortensia, to throw some illustration on what I have advanced on this subject, it may be necessary to show you that all those vices and imperfections which have been generally regarded as inseparable from the female character do not in any manner proceed from sexual causes, but are entirely the effects of situation and education. But these observations must be left to further discussion.

---

[1] *determined* Terminated.

[2] *So great … England* Not until 1870, with the Married Woman's Property Act, did women gain the right to retain their earnings. In 1882, amendments to this Act allowed them to keep personal property that they brought to or acquired during a marriage. They also finally gained a legal identity separate from their husbands', and could then enter into legal contracts and seek restitution in courts.

from LETTER 22:
NO CHARACTERISTIC DIFFERENCE IN SEX

... It must be confessed that the virtues of the males among the human species, though mixed and blended with a variety of vices and errors, have displayed a bolder and a more consistent picture of excellence than female nature has hitherto done. It is on these reasons that when we compliment the appearance of a more than ordinary energy in the female mind, we call it masculine; and hence it is that Pope has elegantly said "a perfect woman's but a softer man."[1] And if we take in the consideration that there can be but one rule of moral excellence for beings made of the same materials, organized after the same manner, and subjected to similar laws of nature, we must either agree with Mr. Pope, or we must reverse the proposition, and say that "a perfect man is a woman formed after a coarser mold." The difference that actually does subsist between the sexes is too flattering for men to be willingly imputed to accident; for what accident occasions, wisdom might correct, and it is better, says Pride, to give up the advantages we might derive from the perfection of our fellow associates than to own that nature has been just in the equal distribution of her favours. These are the sentiments of the men; but mark how readily they are yielded to by the women—not from humility, I assure you, but merely to preserve with character those fond vanities on which they set their hearts. No; suffer them to idolize their persons, to throw away their life in the pursuit of trifles, and to indulge in the gratification of the meaner passions, and they will heartily join in the sentence of their degradation.

Among the most strenuous asserters of a sexual difference in character, Rousseau[2] is the most conspicuous, both on account of that warmth of sentiment which distinguishes all his writings, and the eloquence of his compositions: but never did enthusiasm and the love of paradox, those enemies to philosophical disquisi-

tion, appear in more strong opposition to plain sense than in Rousseau's definition of this difference. He sets out with a supposition that Nature intended the subjection of the one sex to the other; that consequently there must be an inferiority of intellect in the subjected party; but as man is a very imperfect being, and apt to play the capricious tyrant, Nature, to bring things nearer to an equality, bestowed on the woman such attractive graces, and such an insinuating address, as to turn the balance on the other scale. Thus Nature, in a giddy mood, recedes from her purposes, and subjects prerogative to an influence which must produce confusion and disorder in the system of human affairs. Rousseau saw this objection, and in order to obviate it he has made up a moral person of the union of the two sexes, which, for contradiction and absurdity, outdoes every metaphysical riddle that was ever formed in the schools. In short, it is not reason, it is not wit; it is pride and sensuality that speak in Rousseau, and, in this instance, has lowered the man of genius to the licentious pedant.

But whatever might be the wise purpose intended by Providence in such a disposition of things, certain it is that some degree of inferiority, in point of corporal strength, seems always to have existed between the two sexes; and this advantage, in the barbarous ages of mankind, was abused to such a degree as to destroy all the natural rights of the female species and reduce them to a state of abject slavery. What accidents have contributed in Europe to better their condition would not be to my purpose to relate, for I do not intend to give you a history of women; I mean only to trace the sources of their peculiar foibles and vices, and these I firmly believe to originate in situation and education only: for so little did a wise and just Providence intend to make the condition of slavery an unalterable law of female nature, that in the same proportion as the male sex have consulted the interest of their own happiness, they have relaxed in their tyranny over women; and such is their use in the system of mundane creation, and such their natural influence over the male mind, that were these advantages properly exerted, they might carry every point of any importance to their honour and happiness. However, till that period arrives in which women will act wisely, we will amuse ourselves in talking of their follies.

---

[1]　*a perfect ... man*　Reference to Alexander Pope, "Epistle 2: To a Lady, on the Characters of Women" (1735), lines 271–72: "Heaven, when it strives to polish all it can / Its last best work, but forms a softer man."

[2]　*Rousseau*　In his *Émile* (1762), French philosopher Jean-Jacques Rousseau argues that female children should be educated, but should be taught to remain subordinate and submissive to men.

The situation and education of women, Hortensia, is precisely that which must necessarily tend to corrupt and debilitate both the powers of mind and body. From a false notion of beauty and delicacy, their system of nerves is depraved before they come out of their nursery; and this kind of depravity has more influence over the mind, and consequently over morals, than is commonly apprehended. But it would be well if such causes only acted towards the debasement of the sex; their moral education is, if possible, more absurd than their physical. The principles and nature of virtue, which is never properly explained to boys, is kept quite a mystery to girls. They are told, indeed, that they must abstain from those vices which are contrary to their personal happiness, or they will be regarded as criminals, both by God and man; but all the higher parts of rectitude, everything that ennobles our being, and that renders us both innoxious and useful, is either not taught, or is taught in such a manner as to leave no proper impression on the mind. This is so obvious a truth that the defects of female education have ever been a fruitful topic of declamation for the moralist; but not one of this class of writers have laid down any judicious rules for amendment. Whilst we still retain the absurd notion of a sexual excellence, it will militate against the perfecting a plan of education for either sex. The judicious Addison animadverts on the absurdity of bringing a young lady up with no higher idea of the end of education than to make her agreeable to a husband, and confining the necessary excellence for this happy acquisition to the mere graces of person.[1]

Every parent and tutor may not express himself in the same manner as is marked out by Addison; yet certain it is that the admiration of the other sex is held out to women as the highest honour they can attain; and whilst this is considered as their *summum bonum*,[2] and the beauty of their persons the chief *desideratum*[3] of men, Vanity and its companion Envy must taint, in their characters, every native and every acquired excellence. Nor can you, Hortensia, deny that these qualities, when united to ignorance, are fully equal to the engendering and rivetting all those vices and foibles which are peculiar to the female sex—vices and foibles which have caused them to be considered, in ancient times, as beneath cultivation, and in modern days have subjected them to the censure and ridicule of writers of all descriptions, from the deep thinking philosopher to the man of ton and gallantry, who, by the by,[4] sometimes distinguishes himself by qualities which are not greatly superior to those he despises in women. ...

from Olympe de Gouges, *The Rights of Woman*[5] (1791)

Man, are you able to be just? It is a woman who asks you the question; you will not take that right, at least, away from her. Tell me: what has given you the sovereign power to oppress my sex? your strength? your talents? Observe the Creator in His wisdom; survey nature in all its grandeur, to which you seem to want to compare yourself, and give me, if you dare, an example of this tyrannical power. Go back to the animals, consult the elements, study the vegetables, cast a glance, finally, over all the modifications of organized matter; and submit to the evidence when I give you the means to; search, excavate, and distinguish the sexes, if you can, in the government of nature. Everywhere you will find them mingled, everywhere they cooperate as a harmonious consort in this immortal masterpiece.

Man alone has dressed up this exception as a principle. Bizarre, blind, bloated with sciences and degenerated, in this age of enlightenment and wisdom, into the crassest ignorance, he wants to rule like a despot over a sex which has received all the intellectual faculties; he pretends to rejoice in the revolution, and to claim his rights to equality, in order to say no more about it.

---

[1] *judicious Addison ... person* Reference to an article in *Spectator* No. 66 (16 May 1711) actually written by Richard Steele; *animadverts* Comments critically.

[2] *summum bonum* Latin: greatest good.

[3] *desideratum* Latin: thing desired.

[4] *by the by* Incidentally; as a side issue.

[5] *The Rights of Woman* Translated from the French by D.L. Macdonald.

DECLARATION OF THE RIGHTS OF WOMAN
AND OF THE FEMALE CITIZEN

To be decreed by the National Assembly in its last sessions or in that of the next legislature.

PREAMBLE

The mothers, daughters, sisters, representatives of the nation, demand to be formed into a national assembly. Considering that ignorance, neglect, or contempt of the rights of woman are the sole causes of public misfortunes and the corruption of governments, have resolved to set forth in a solemn declaration the natural, inalienable, and sacred rights of woman, that this declaration, being constantly present to all the members of the body social, may ever remind them of their rights and their duties; that the acts of the power of women, and those of the power of men, being capable of being every moment compared with the end of all political institutions, may be more respected; that the claims of the female citizens, founded hereafter on simple and incontestable principles, may always tend to the maintenance of the constitution and of good morals, and to the general happiness.

Accordingly, the sex that is as superior in beauty as in courage, in the sufferings of maternity, recognizes and declares, in the presence and under the auspices of the Supreme Being, the following Rights of Woman and of the Female Citizen.

FIRST ARTICLE

Woman is born free and remains equal to man in rights. Social distinctions can only be founded on common utility.

2

The end of all political association is the preservation of the natural and imprescriptible[1] rights of woman and of man: these rights are liberty, property, security, and above all resistance to oppression.

3

The principle of all sovereignty resides essentially in the Nation, which is nothing more than the union of woman and man: no body, no individual, can exercise an authority which does not emanate expressly from it.

4

Liberty and justice consist in rendering to others all that belongs to them; thus the exercise of the natural rights of woman has no other limits than the perpetual tyranny that man opposes to it; these limits should be reformed by the laws of nature and of reason.

5

The laws of nature and of reason prohibit all actions hurtful to society: nothing that is not prohibited by these laws, wise and divine, may be hindered, nor may anyone be compelled to do what they do not enjoin.

6

The law should be the expression of the general will; all the female and male citizens should concur personally, or by their representatives, in its formation; it should be the same for all: all the female and all the male citizens, being equal in its eyes, should be equally admissible to all honours, positions, and public employments, according to their capacities, and without any other distinctions than those of their virtues and their talents.

7

No woman is exempt; she is accused, arrested, and detained in cases determined by the law. Women, like men, obey this rigorous law.

8

The law should impose only those penalties which are strictly and evidently necessary, and no one can be punished except by virtue of a law established and promulgated previously to the offense and legally applied to women.

9

Whenever a woman is declared guilty, all rigour is exercised by the law.

---

[1] *imprescriptible* That cannot legally be taken away.

10

No one should be molested for their opinions, even fundamental ones; woman has the right to mount the scaffold; she should equally have the right to mount the tribune,[1] provided that her actions do not disturb the public order established by the law.

11

The free communication of thoughts and opinions is one of the most precious rights of woman, since this liberty ensures that fathers acknowledge their children. Every female citizen may therefore say freely, I am the mother of a child who belongs to you, without a barbarous prejudice to force her to conceal the truth, provided she is held responsible for the abuse of this liberty in the cases determined by the law.

12

The good of the majority is necessary in order to secure the rights of woman and the female citizen; this security should be instituted for the advantage of all, and not for the particular good of those women to whom it is entrusted.

13

For the maintenance of the public force, and for the expenses of government, the contributions of woman and man are equal; she takes part in all the drudgery, in all the laborious tasks; she should therefore take the same part in the distribution of positions, of employments, of commissions, of honours, and of business.

14

The female and male citizens have the right to determine, by themselves or by their representatives, the necessity of public contributions. The female citizens cannot enjoy this right except by being allowed an equal share, not only in wealth, but also in public administration, and by being allowed to determine the amount, the basis, the collection, and the duration of taxation.

15

The mass of women, united for the purposes of taxation with that of men, has the right to demand of all its public agents an account of their administration.

---

[1] *tribune* Raised platform or dais for addressing an assembly.

16

Every society in which the security of rights is not assured, and the separation of powers is not determined, has no constitution; the constitution is null and void if the majority of the individuals who make up the nation has not cooperated in drawing it up.

17

Property belongs to both sexes, individually or collectively; it is everyone's inviolable and sacred right; as it is a true patrimony of nature, no one may be deprived of it, except when public necessity, legally ascertained, evidently demands it, and on condition of a previously established and just indemnity.

from Maria Edgeworth and Richard Lovell Edgeworth, *Practical Education* (1798)

PRUDENCE AND ECONOMY

In the education of girls we must teach them much more caution than is necessary to boys: their prudence must be more the result of reasoning than of experiment; they *must* trust to the experience of others; they cannot always have recourse to what *ought to be*, they must adapt themselves to what is. They cannot rectify the material mistakes in their conduct. Timidity, a certain tardiness of decision, and reluctance to act in public situations are not considered as defects in a woman's character; her pausing prudence does not to a man of discernment denote imbecility, but appears to him the graceful auspicious characteristic of female virtue. There is always more probability that women should endanger their own happiness by precipitation than by forbearance.

Promptitude of choice is seldom expected from the female sex; they should avail themselves of the leisure that is permitted to them for reflection. "Begin nothing of which you have not well considered the end," was the piece of advice for which the Eastern Sultan paid a purse of gold, the price set upon it by a sage. The monarch did not repent of his purchase. This maxim should be engraved upon the memory of our female pupils by the repeated lessons of education. We should even in trifles avoid every circumstance which can tend to make girls venturesome, which can encourage them to trust to their good fortune, instead of relying on their own prudence....

In the choice of friends, and on all matters of taste, young women should be excited to reason about their own feelings. "There is no reasoning about taste," is a pernicious maxim; if there was more reasoning, there would be disputation upon this subject. If women questioned their own minds, or allowed their friends to question them concerning the reasons of their "preferences and aversions," there would not probably be so many love matches, and so few love marriages. It is in vain to expect that young women should begin to reason miraculously, at the very moment that reason is wanted in the guidance of their conduct. We should also observe that women are called upon for the exertion of their prudence at an age when young men are scarcely supposed to possess that virtue; therefore women should be more early, and more carefully educated for the purpose. The important decisions of a woman's life are often made before she is twenty; a man does not come upon the theatre of public life, where most of his prudence is shown, till he is much older.

from Priscilla Wakefield, *Reflections on the Present Condition of the Female Sex; With Suggestions for Its Improvement* (1798)

from CHAPTER 3
THE NECESSITY OF WOMEN BEING EDUCATED FOR THE EXERCISE OF LUCRATIVE EMPLOYMENTS SHOWN, AND THE ABSURDITY OF A WOMAN HONOURABLY EARNING A SUPPORT BEING EXCLUDED FROM SOCIETY, EXPOSED

In the education of females, the same view actuates every rank: an advantageous settlement on marriage is the universal prize, for which parents of all classes enter their daughters upon the lists; and partiality or self-complacency assures to every competitor the most flattering prospect of success. To this one point tends the principal part of female instruction; for the promotion of this design, their best years for improvement are sacrificed to the attainment of attractive qualities, showy superficial accomplishments, polished manners, and, in

one word, the whole science of pleasing, which is cultivated with unceasing assiduity as an object of the most essential importance.

The end is laudable, and deserving of every effort that can be exerted to secure it; a happy marriage may be estimated among the rarest felicities of human life, but it may be doubted whether the means used to accomplish it are adequate to the purpose, as the making a first impression is by no means effectual to determine the preference of a wise man. It is not then sufficient that a girl be qualified to excite admiration; her own happiness, and that of the man to whom she devotes the remainder of her days, depend upon her possession of those virtues, which alone can preserve lasting esteem and confidence.

The offices of a wife are very different from those of the mere pageant of a ballroom; and as their nature is more exalted, the talents they require are of a more noble kind: something far beyond the elegant trifler is wanted in a companion for life. A young woman is very ill-adapted to enter into the most solemn of social contracts who is not prepared, by her education, to become the participator of her husband's cares, the consoler of his sorrows, his stimulator to every praiseworthy undertaking, his partner in the labours and vicissitudes of life, the faithful and economical manager of his affairs, the judicious superintendant of his family, the wife and affectionate mother of his children, the preserver of his honour, his chief counsellor, and, to sum up all, the chosen friend of his bosom. If a modern female education be not calculated to produce these effects, as few surely will judge it to be, who reflect upon its tendency, it is incompetent to that very purpose, which is confessedly its main object, and must therefore be deemed imperfect, and require reformation....

from CHAPTER 6
LUCRATIVE EMPLOYMENTS FOR THE FIRST AND SECOND CLASSES SUGGESTED ... WITH STRICTURES ON A THEATRICAL LIFE

Transitions in private life from affluence to poverty, like the sable pageantry of death, from their frequency produce no lasting impressions on the beholders. Unexpected misfortunes befall an acquaintance who has been caressed in the days of prosperity: the change is lamented, and she is consoled by the visits of her friends, in the first moments of affliction; she sinks gradually into wretchedness; she becomes obscure, and is forgotten. ... A few remarks upon the nature of those employments which are best adapted to the higher classes of the sex, when reduced to necessitous circumstances, may, perhaps, afford useful hints to those who are languishing under the pressure of misfortune, and induce abler pens to treat a subject hitherto greatly neglected.

Numerous difficulties arise in the choice of occupations for the purpose. They must be such as are neither laborious nor servile, and they must of course be productive, without requiring a capital.

For these reasons, pursuits which require the exercise of intellectual rather than bodily powers are generally the most eligible.

Literature affords a respectable and pleasing employment for those who possess talents and an adequate degree of mental cultivation. For although the emolument is precarious, and seldom equal to a maintenance, yet if the attempt be tolerably successful, it may yield a comfortable assistance in narrow circumstances and beguile many hours, which might otherwise be passed in solitude or unavailing regret. The fine arts offer a mode of subsistence congenial to the delicacy of the most refined minds, and they are peculiarly adapted, by their elegance, to the gratification of taste. The perfection of every species of painting is attainable by women, from the representation of historic facts to the minute execution of the miniature portrait, if they will bestow sufficient time and application for the acquisition of the principles of the art, in the study of those models which have been the means of transmitting the names and character of so many men to the admiration of posterity. The successful exercise of this imitative art requires invention, taste, and judgment: in the two first, the sex are allowed to excel, and the last may be obtained by a perseverance in examining, comparing, and reflecting upon the works of those masters who have copied nature in her most graceful forms. ...

The stage is a profession to which many women of refined manners and a literary turn of mind have had

recourse. Since it has been customary for females to assume dramatic characters, there appears to have been full as great a proportion of women who have attained celebrity among those who have devoted themselves to a theatrical life, as of the other sex—a fact which argues that there is no inequality of genius in the sexes for the imitative arts. The observation may operate as a stimulant to women to those pursuits which are less objectionable than the stage, which is not mentioned for the purpose of recommending it, but of proving that the abilities of the female sex are equal to nobler labours than are usually undertaken by women. The profession of an actress is indeed most unsuitable to the sex in every point of view, whether it be considered with respect to the courage requisite to face an audience, or the variety of situations incident to it, which expose moral virtue to the most severe trials. Let the daughters of a happier destiny, whilst they lament the evils to which some of their sex are exposed, remember those unpropitious circumstances that have cast them into a line of life in which it is scarcely possible to preserve that purity of sentiment and conduct which characterizes female excellence. When their errors are discussed, let the harsh voice of censure be restrained by the reflection that she who has made the greatest advances towards perfection might have fallen, had she been surrounded by the same influences.

That species of agriculture which depends upon skill in the management of the nursery ground, in rearing the various kinds of shrubs and flowers for the supply of gentlemen's gardens and pleasure grounds, would supply an elegant means of support to those women who are able to raise a capital for carrying on a work of that magnitude. Ornamental gardening, and the laying out of pleasure grounds and parks with the improvement of natural landscape, one of the refinements of modern times, may likewise afford an eligible maintenance to some of those females who, in the days of their prosperity, displayed their taste in the embellishment of their own domains.

The presiding over seminaries for female education is likewise a suitable employment for those whose minds have been enlarged by liberal cultivation, whilst the under parts of that profession may be more suitably

The most renowned actress of the day was Sarah Siddons (1755–1831), born into the theatrical family of Roger Kemble. Siddons's most famous role was that of Lady Macbeth, which she first played in 1785. Above left is a detail from a painting (c. 1790) of her playing the role opposite her brother; at right is George Henry Harlow's *Sarah Siddons in the Scene of Lady Macbeth Sleepwalking* (1814). Siddons's farewell stage performance had been as Lady Macbeth in 1812.

filled by persons whose early views have been contracted within narrower limits. After all that can be suggested by general remarks, the different circumstances of individuals must decide the profession most convenient to them. But it is a consolatory reflection that amidst the daily vicissitudes of human life, from which no rank is exempt, there are resources from which aid may be drawn, without derogating from the true dignity of a rational being.

from Richard Polwhele, "The Unsexed Females: A Poem, Addressed to the Author of *The Pursuits of Literature*"[1] (1798)

Survey with me, what ne'er our fathers saw,
A female band despising Nature's law,[2]
As "proud defiance"[3] flashes from their arms,
And vengeance smothers all their softer charms.
5   I shudder at the new unpictured scene,
Where unsexed woman vaunts the imperious
     mien;°   *bearing*
Where girls, affecting to dismiss the heart,
Invoke the Proteus of petrific art;[4]

With equal ease, in body or in mind,
10 To Gallic freaks or Gallic faith resigned,
The crane-like neck, as Fashion bids, lay bare,
Or frizzle,[5] bold in front, their borrowed hair;
Scarce by a gossamery film carest,
Sport,[6] in full view, the meretricious° breast;[7]   *whorish*
15 Loose the chaste cincture,[8] where the graces shone,
And languished all the Loves, the ambrosial zone;
As lordly domes inspire dramatic rage,
Court prurient Fancy to the private stage;
With bliss botanic[9] as their bosoms heave,
20 Still pluck forbidden fruit, with mother Eve,
For puberty in sighing florets pant,
Or point the prostitution of a plant;
Dissect[10] its organ of unhallowed lust,

---

[1] *the Author ... Literature* Thomas James Mathias, whose extremely popular satirical poem *The Pursuits of Literature* (1794–97) reacted against radical politics, particularly against feminists such as Mary Wollstonecraft. Polwhele draws on Mathias's comment in the poem's preface that "our *unsexed* female writers now instruct, or confuse, us and themselves, in the labyrinth of politics, or turn us wild with Gallic frenzy" (i.e., ideas inspired by the French Revolution).

[2] [Polwhele's note] Nature is the grand basis of all laws human and divine: and the woman who has no regard to nature, either in decoration of her person or the culture of her mind, will soon "walk after the flesh in the lust of uncleanness, and despise government." [Polwhele quotes from 2 Peter 2.10.]

[3] [From Polwhele's note] "A troop came next, who crowns and armour wore / And proud defiance in their looks they bore" Pope. The Amazonian band—the female Quixotes of the new philosophy are here too justly characterised. ... [Polwhele quotes Alexander Pope's "The Temple of Fame" (1711), lines 342–43. *Amazons* Members of a legendary race of warrior women from Scythia; *Quixotes* Idealists, dreamers. "Female Quixotes" refers more specifically to Charlotte Lennox's famous novel of 1752, *The Female Quixote*.]

[4] *Proteus* God who could change shape at will; *petrific* Able to turn to stone, or to turn something else to stone.

[5] *frizzle* Curl in small curls.

[6] [From Polwhele's note] To "sport a face" is a cant phrase in one of our universities, by which is meant an impudent obtrusion of a man's person in company. It is not applicable, perhaps, to the open bosom—a fashion which we have never invited or sanctioned.

[7] [Polwhele's note] The fashions of France, which have been always imitated by the English, were, heretofore, unexceptionable in a moral point of view; since, however ridiculous or absurd, they were innocent. But they have now their source among prostitutes—among women of the most abandoned character. ...

[8] *cincture* Girdle for the waist, sometimes surrounding the breasts as well.

[9] [Polwhele's note] Botany has lately become a fashionable amusement with the ladies. But how the study of the sexual system can accord with female modesty, I am not able to comprehend. I had at first, written, "More eager for illicit knowledge pant, / With lustful boys anatomise a plant; / The virtues of its dust prolific speak, / Or point its pistil with unblushing cheek." I have, several times, seen boys and girls botanizing together.

[10] [Polwhele's note] Miss Wollstonecraft does not blush to say, in an introduction to a book designed for the use of young ladies, that, "in order to lay the axe at the root of corruption, it would be proper to familiarize the sexes to an unreserved discussion of those topics which are generally avoided in conversation from a principle of false delicacy; and that it would be right to speak of the organs of generation as freely as we mention our eyes or our hands." To such language our botanizing girls are doubtless familiarized; and they are in a fair way of becoming worthy disciples of Miss W. If they do not take heed to their ways, they will soon exchange the blush of modesty for the bronze of impudence. [Polwhele refers to Mary Wollstonecraft's "Introductory Address to Parents," from her *Elements of Morality, for the Use of Children* (1792), but he misrepresents her argument, which is that children can be discouraged from masturbating by being taught about the sexual organs and by having

And fondly gaze the titillating dust;
25   With liberty's sublimer views expand,
And o'er the wreck of kingdoms[1] sternly stand;
And, frantic, midst the democratic storm,
Pursue, Philosophy! thy phantom-form.[2]
    Far other is the female shape and mind,
30   By modest luxury heightened and refined;
Those limbs, that figure, though by Fashion[3] graced,
By Beauty polished, and adorned by Taste;
That soul, whose harmony perennial flows,
In Music trembles, and in Color glows;
35   Which bids sweet Poesy reclaim the praise
With faery light to gild fastidious days,
From sullen clouds relieve domestic care,
And melt in smiles the withering frown of war.
Ah! once the female Muse,[4] to *Nature* true,
40   The unvalued store from *Fancy*, *Feeling* drew;
Won, from the grasp of woe, the roseate hours,
Cheered life's dim vale, and strewed the grave with
    flowers.
But lo! where, pale amidst the wild,[5] she draws

Each precept cold from sceptic Reason's[6] vase;
45   Pours with rash arm the turbid stream along,
And in the foaming torrent whelms the throng.[7] …
See Wollstonecraft, whom no decorum checks,
Arise, the intrepid champion of her sex;
O'er humbled man assert the sovereign claim,
50   And slight the timid blush[8] of virgin fame.

from Hannah More, *Strictures on the Modern System of Female Education, With a View of the Principles and Conduct Prevalent among Women of Rank and Fortune* (1799)

from VOLUME 1, CHAPTER 4:
COMPARISON OF THE MODE OF FEMALE EDUCATION IN THE LAST AGE WITH THE PRESENT AGE

A young lady may excel in speaking French and Italian, may repeat a few passages from a volume of extracts; play like a professor, and sing like a siren;[9] have her dressing-room decorated with her own drawings, tables, stands, screens, and cabinets; nay, she may dance like Sempronia[10] herself, and yet may have been very

---

explained to them "the noble use which they were designed for." In her *Vindication of the Rights of Woman* (1792) she also argues that the study of botany can be consistent with female modesty.]

[1]   [Polwhele's note]   The female advocates of democracy in this country, though they have had no opportunity of imitating the French ladies in their acts of atrocious cruelty, have yet assumed a stern serenity in the contemplation of those savage excesses. "To express their abhorrence of royalty, they (the French ladies) threw away the character of their sex, and bit the amputated limbs of their murdered countrymen. I say this on the authority of a young gentleman who saw it. I am sorry to add that the relation, accompanied with looks of horror and disgust, only provoked a contemptuous smile from an illuminated British fair-one." See Robison—p.219. [John Robison's *Proofs of a Conspiracy Against All the Religions and Governments of Europe* (1797).]

[2]   [From Polwhele's note]   Philosophism, the false image of philosophy. …

[3]   [Polwhele's note]   I admit that we are quickly reconciled to the fashion of the day, and often consider it as graceful, if it offends not against delicacy.

[4]   *Muse*   One of nine daughters of Zeus and Mnemosyne, each of whom presided over and provided inspiration for an aspect of arts and sciences.

[5]   [Polwhele's note]   "A wild, where flowers and weeds promiscuous shoot; / A garden tempting with forbidden fruit" Pope. [From Alexander Pope's *Essay on Man* (1733) 1.7–8.]

[6]   [Polwhele's note]   A troubled stream only can proceed from the vase of skepticism; if it be not "the broken cistern that will hold no water" [from Jeremiah 2.13].

[7]   [Polwhele's note]   "Raging waves, foaming out their own shame"—St. Jude. Such were those infamous publications of Paine and others, which, like the torrents of December, threatened to sweep all before them—to overwhelm the multitude. [Polwhele quotes from Jude 1.13 and refers to Thomas Paine's *The Rights of Man* (1791–92), his reply to an attack on the French Revolutionaries by Edmund Burke.]

[8]   [Polwhele's note]   That Miss Wollstonecraft was a sworn enemy to the blushes, I need not remark. But many of my readers, perhaps, will be astonished to hear that at several of our boarding schools for young ladies, a blush incurs a penalty.

[9]   *siren*   Mythical creature, part woman and part bird, whose enchanted songs were said to lure sailors to their destruction.

[10]   *Sempronia*   Infamous woman of ancient Rome, known for her loose morals, who was said to have taken part in Cataline's conspiracy to overthrow the government in 63 BCE. According to Roman historian Sallust, Sempronia "had greater skill in lyre playing and dancing than there is any need for a respectable woman to acquire. There was nothing that she set a smaller value on than seemliness and chastity."

badly educated. I am far from meaning to set no value whatever on any or all of these qualifications; they are all of them elegant, and many of them properly tend to the perfecting of a polite education. These things, in their measure and degree, may be done, but there are others which should not be left undone. Many things are becoming, but "one thing is needful." Besides, as the world seems to be fully apprized of the value of whatever tends to embellish life, there is less occasion here to insist on its importance.

But, though a well bred young lady may lawfully learn most of the fashionable arts, yet it does not seem to be the true end of education to make women of fashion dancers, singers, players, painters, actresses, sculptors, gilders, varnishers, engravers, and embroiderers. Most men are commonly destined to some profession, and their minds are consequently turned each to its respective object. Would it not be strange if they were called out to exercise their profession, or to set up their trade, with only a little general knowledge of the trades of all other men, and without any previous definite application to their own peculiar calling? The profession of ladies, to which the bent of their instruction should be turned, is that of daughters, wives, mothers, and mistresses of families. They should be therefore trained with a view to these several conditions, and be furnished with a stock of ideas and principles, and qualifications ready to be applied and appropriated, as occasion may demand, to each of these respective situations: for though the arts which merely embellish life must claim admiration, yet when a man of sense comes to marry, it is a companion whom he wants, and not an artist. It is not merely a creature who can paint, and play, and dress, and dance; it is a being who can comfort and counsel him; one who can reason and reflect, and feel, and judge, and discourse, and discriminate; one who can assist him in his affairs, lighten his cares, soothe his sorrows, strengthen his principles, and educate his children.

from VOLUME 1, CHAPTER 6: ON THE EARLY FORMING OF HABITS. ON THE NECESSITY OF FORMING THE JUDGMENT TO DIRECT THOSE HABITS

An early habitual restraint is peculiarly important to the future character and happiness of women. They should when very young be inured to contradiction. Instead of hearing their bon-mots[1] treasured up and repeated to the guests till they begin to think it dull when they themselves are not the little heroine of the theme, they should be accustomed to receive but little praise for their vivacity or their wit, though they should receive just commendation for their patience, their industry, their humility, and other qualities which have more worth than splendour. They should be led to distrust their own judgment; they should learn not to murmur at expostulation, but should be accustomed to expect and to endure opposition. It is a lesson with which the world will not fail to furnish them, and they will not practice it the worse for having learnt it the sooner. It is of the last importance to their happiness in life that they should early acquire a submissive temper and a forbearing spirit. They must even endure to be thought wrong sometimes when they cannot but feel they are right. And while they should be anxiously aspiring to do well, they must not expect always to obtain the praise of having done so. But while a gentle demeanor is inculcated, let them not be instructed to practise gentleness merely on the low ground of its being decorous and feminine, and pleasing, and calculated to attract human favour; but let them be carefully taught to cultivate it on the high principle of obedience to Christ.

1 bon-mots French: witticisms.

from William Thompson and Anna Wheeler, *Appeal of One Half the Human Race, Women, Against the Pretensions of the Other Half, Men, to Retain Them in Political, and Thence in Civil and Domestic Slavery* (1825)

from INTRODUCTORY LETTER TO MRS. WHEELER

With you I would equally elevate both sexes. Really enlightened women, disdaining equally the submissive tricks of the slave and the caprices of the despot, breathing freely only in the air of the esteem of equals, and of mutual, *unbought, uncommanded* affection, would find it difficult to meet with associates worthy of them in men as now formed, full of ignorance and vanity, priding themselves on a *sexual* superiority, entirely independent of any merit, any superior qualities, or pretensions to them, claiming respect from the strength of their arm and the lordly faculty of producing beards attached by nature to their chins! No: unworthy of, as incapable of appreciating, the delight of the society of such women, are the great majority of the existing race of men. The pleasures of mere animal appetite, the pleasures of commanding (the prettier and more helpless the slave, the greater these pleasures of the brute) are the only pleasures which the majority of men seek for from women, are the only pleasures which their education and the hypocritical system of morals with which they have been necessarily imbued, permit them to expect....

Even under the present arrangements of society, founded as they all are on the basis of individual competition, nothing could be more easy than to put the *rights* of women, political and civil, on a perfect equality with those of men. It is only to abolish all prohibitory and exclusive laws—statute or what are called "common"— the remnants of the barbarous customs of our ignorant ancestors; particularly the horrible and odious inequality and indissolubility of that disgrace of civilization, the present marriage code. Women then might exert in a free career with men their faculties of mind and body, to whatever degree developed, in pursuit of happiness by means of exertion, as men do. But this would not raise women to an equality of happiness with men: their rights might be equal, but not their happiness, because

unequal powers under free competition must produce unequal effects.

In truth, the system of the most enlightened of the school of those reformers called political economists is still founded on exclusions. Its basis is too narrow for human happiness. A more comprehensive system, founded on equal benevolence, on the true development of the principle of Utility,[1] is wanting. Let the *competitive* political economists be satisfied with the praise of causing the removal of some of the rubbish of ignorant restrictions, under the name of laws, impeding the development of human exertion in the production of wealth. To build up a new fabric of social happiness, comprehending equally the interests of all existing human beings, has never been contemplated by them, and is altogether beyond the scope of their little theories; aiming at the utmost at increasing the number of what they style the happy middling orders, but leaving the great bulk of human beings to eternal ignorance and toil, requited by the mere means of prolonging from day to day an unhealthy and precarious existence. To a new science, the *social science*, or the science of promoting human happiness, that of political economy, or the mere science of producing wealth by individual competition, must give way.

from PART 2

As soon as adult daughters become wives, their civil rights disappear; they fall back again, and remain all their lives—should their owners and directors live so long—into the state of children or idiots, the passive property of their owners; protected by the law in some few respects only, like other slaves, from the excessive abuse of despotic power.

Woman is then compelled, in marriage, by the possession of superior strength on the part of men, by the want of knowledge, skill, and wealth, by the positive, cruel, partial, and cowardly enactments of law, by the terrors of superstition, by the mockery of a pretended vow of obedience, and to crown all, and as the result of all, by the force of an unrelenting, unreasoning, unfeeling public opinion, to be the literal unequivocal

---

[1] *principle of Utility*   Central principle of utilitarianism, an ethical theory developed by Jeremy Bentham and others.

slave of the man who may be styled her husband. I say emphatically the slave; for a slave is a person whose actions and earnings, instead of being under his own control, liable only to equal laws, to public opinion, and to his own calculations, under these, of his own interest, are under the arbitrary control of any other human being, by whatever name called. This is the essence of slavery, and what distinguishes it from freedom. A domestic, a civil, a political slave, in the plain unsophisticated sense of the word—in no metaphorical sense—is every married woman. No matter with what wealth she may be surrounded, with what dainties she may be fed, with what splendor of trappings adorned, with what voluptuousness her corporeal, mental, or moral sweets may be gathered; that high prerogative of human nature, the faculty of self-government, the basis of intellectual development, without which no moral conduct can exist, is to her wanting.... Till laws afford married women the same protection against the restraints and violence of the men to whom they are married, that they affect to afford them against all other individuals; till they afford them the same protection against the restraints and violence of their husbands, that their husbands enjoy against their caprices and violence, the social condition of the civilized wife will remain more completely slavish than that of the female slave of the West Indies....

Be consistent, men! Ye stronger half of the race, be at length rational! Three or four thousand years have worn threadbare your vile cloak of hypocrisy. Even women, your poor, weak, contented slaves, at whose impotence of penetration, the result of your vile exclusions, you have been accustomed to laugh, begin to see through it and to shudder at the loathsomeness beneath. Cast aside this tattered cloak before it leaves you naked and exposed. Clothe yourselves with the new garments of sincerity. Be rational human beings, not mere male sexual creatures. Cast aside the ferocious brute of your nature: give up the pleasures of the brute, those of mere lust and command, for the pleasures of the rational being. So shall you enjoy the love of your *equals*, enlightened, benevolent, graceful, like yourselves, founded on an appreciation of your real merits: so shall you be happy. For the intercourse of the *bought* prostitute, or of the *commanded* household slave, you shall have full and equal participation in the compounded and associated pleasures of sense, intellect, and benevolence. To the highest enjoyments of which your nature is susceptible, there is no shorter road than the simple road of equal justice....

Women of England! women, in whatever country ye breathe—wherever ye breathe, degraded—awake! Awake to the contemplation of the happiness that awaits you when all your faculties of mind and body shall be fully cultivated and developed; when every path in which ye can exercise those improved faculties shall be laid open and rendered delightful to you, even as to them who now ignorantly enslave and degrade you....

ROBERT BURNS
1759 – 1796

There is a riddle among certain linguists: "What is the difference between a language and a dialect?" Answer: "A language is a dialect that has an army and a navy." The point is well taken and the widespread use of the English language across the planet no doubt is connected to the huge successes of the British navy in the last two and a half centuries. But when we sing Robert Burns's "Auld Lang Syne" on New Year's Eve we repeat a dialect piece that made good without the backing of an army or a navy. No doubt the distinctive resonance of Burns's Ayrshire dialect has helped to make the words of "Auld Lang Syne" memorable, but its popularity also rests on the degree to which it speaks the language of the heart, conveying a strong sense of mortality and of the blessings of memory itself.

Burns was born in Ayrshire, a county in southwestern Scotland, and spent his early years laboring with his father, a tenant-farmer who died in 1784. Intending to accept a position on a plantation in Jamaica, Burns gave up on this scheme when his first volume of poems, *Poems, Chiefly in the Scottish Dialect* (1786), brought him instant acclaim and the means to a more comfortable life. The Scottish dialect in which he wrote was descended from the Northumbrian dialect of Old English and had been known originally as "Inglis." In the eighteenth century it came to be called "Scots." Mostly gathered in Edinburgh, the champions of the Scottish Enlightenment attempted to be equally fluent in Scots and English. Burns owes his reputation as "Heaven-taught plowman" to his ear for his Scots dialect, but he also knew how to write using English diction.

In some of his best poems, broad Scots and formal English alternate—indeed, nearly overlap. Burns's most famous narrative poem, the mock-heroic "Tam o'Shanter," is one in which we may see and hear the double-fluency of the poet, his broad Scots dialect giving way to "pure English." Many readers, both in Burns's time and in our own, have felt some relief when the poetry gives us a brief shower of "pure English." But by not forsaking the richness of his dialect, Burns was helping to ensure his future status as Scotland's national poet—and dealing a blow to the class prejudice against him that was always present, despite the Edinburgh aristocracy's celebration of him when *Poems* first appeared.

Burns's *Poems* became known as the "Kilmarnock edition," after the place in which the book was published. Already at twenty-seven, Burns had written his most famous poems, and he spent much of the rest of his short life helping to formalize an oral tradition in Scotland, contributing many of the works collected in James Johnson's *The Scots Musical Museum* and in George Thomson's *Select Collection of Original Scottish Airs*. Although never a wealthy man, Burns refused any money for his contribution to this work.

Burns's reputation as a lover for a time rivaled his fame as a poet. Having fathered several illegitimate children, he finally settled down in 1788 with a former lover, Jean Armour, in the town of Dumfries, where he received a commission as an excise (tax) officer. Thereafter he seems to have become a good family man and to have enjoyed relative prosperity in the last years of his life. Burns's love songs often express both his love of women and his feeling for his craft, as in "Green grow the rashes": "Auld nature swears, the lovely dears / Her noblest work she classes, O: / Her prentice han' she tries on man, / An' then she made the lasses, O." Burns also collected all the bawdy songs he inherited and invented in *The Merry Muses of Caledonia*, published shortly after his death (and subjected to expurgation and suppression ever since).

A rebel in religion (he chafed against his strict Calvinist upbringing, although he attended church his entire life) and a sympathizer with the revolutions in America and France, Burns often wrote politically charged poems. In "Robert Bruce's March to Bannockburn" (popularly known as "Scots, wha hae"), for example, we hear a war-cry for emancipation: "Lay the proud usurpers low! / Tyrants fall in every foe! / Liberty's in every blow! / Let us do, or die!" Burns could also see the world from the lowliest, humblest places, even to the point of reckoning the mischief and malice of plowing up a field mouse from its home and seeing the calamity from the mouse's point of view ("To a Mouse").

Burns drew heavily on oral tradition, using the ballad form to produce what many consider his masterpiece: "Love and Liberty: A Cantata," commonly known as "The Jolly Beggars" (published posthumously in 1799). The cantata is a series of songs sung by a group of vagabonds, who recall past events in their lives. Burns was strongly influenced by his literary predecessors—perhaps most notably the Scottish Chaucerians of the fifteenth and sixteenth centuries (Gavin Douglas, William Dunbar), and the eighteenth-century Scottish poets Allan Ramsay and Robert Fergusson, whose work supplied him with materials and forms for his comprehensive refashioning of the lyric tradition in Scotland.

Burns was only thirty-seven when he died from an attack of rheumatic fever in 1796, on the day that his wife gave birth to the couple's ninth child. He was buried in St. Michael's Churchyard, Dumfries, Scotland, but his remains were later moved to a mausoleum. Scottish people around the world continue to celebrate Burns's birthday each year on 25 January.

⌘ ⌘ ⌘

To a Mouse, On Turning Her Up in Her Nest with the Plough

Wee, sleekit, cowrin, tim'rous beastie,
⠀⠀O, what a panic's in thy breastie!
Thou need na start awa sae hasty,
⠀⠀⠀⠀Wi' bickerin' brattle![1]
5⠀I wad be laith° to rin an' chase thee,⠀⠀⠀⠀⠀⠀⠀⠀*loath*
⠀⠀⠀⠀Wi' murd'ring pattle!°⠀⠀⠀⠀⠀⠀⠀⠀⠀⠀⠀*plough spade*

I'm truly sorry man's dominion
Has broken nature's social union,
An' justifies that ill opinion,
10⠀⠀⠀⠀Which makes thee startle,
At me, thy poor, earth-born companion,
⠀⠀⠀⠀An' fellow mortal!

I doubt na, whyles,° but thou may thieve;⠀⠀*at times*
What then? poor beastie, thou maun° live!⠀⠀*must*
15⠀A daimen icker in a thrave[2]
⠀⠀⠀⠀'S a sma' request;
I'll get a blessin wi' the lave,°⠀⠀⠀⠀⠀⠀⠀⠀⠀⠀*rest*
⠀⠀⠀⠀An' never miss't!

Thy wee-bit housie, too, in ruin!
20⠀It's silly wa's° the win's are strewin!⠀⠀⠀⠀⠀*walls*
An' naething, now, to big° a new ane,⠀⠀⠀⠀⠀*build*
⠀⠀⠀⠀O' foggage° green!⠀⠀⠀⠀⠀⠀⠀⠀⠀⠀⠀⠀⠀*moss*
An' bleak December's winds ensuin,
⠀⠀⠀⠀Baith snell° an' keen!⠀⠀⠀⠀⠀⠀⠀⠀⠀⠀⠀*bitter*

25⠀Thou saw the fields laid bare an' waste,
An's weary winter comin fast,
An' cozie here, beneath the blast,
⠀⠀⠀⠀Thou thought to dwell,

---

1 *bickerin' brattle* Hurrying scurry.

2 *A daimen icker in a thrave* The odd ear in 24 sheaves of corn.

Till crash! the cruel coulter° past   *plow blade*
30   Out thro' thy cell.

That wee-bit heap o' leaves an' stibble,
Has cost thee monie a weary nibble!
Now thou's turn'd out, for a' thy trouble,
    But° house or hald,°   *without / belongings*
35 To thole° the winter's sleety dribble,   *bear*
    An' cranreuch° cauld!   *hoar frost*

But, Mousie, thou art no thy lane,[1]
In proving foresight may be vain:
The best-laid schemes o' mice an' men
40   Gang aft agley,[2]
An' lea'e us nought but grief an' pain,
    For promis'd joy!

Still thou art blest, compar'd wi' me!
The present only toucheth thee:
45 But, Och! I backward cast my e'e
    On prospects drear!
An' forward, tho' I canna see,
    I guess an' fear!
—1785

The Fornicator

Ye jovial boys who love the joys,
    The blissful joys of lovers;
Yet dare avow with dauntless brow,
    When th'bony lass discovers;
5 I pray draw near and lend an ear,
    And welcome in a frater,°   *brother*
For I've lately been on quarantine,
    A proven Fornicator.

Before the congregation wide
10   I pass'd the muster fairly,
My handsome Betsey by my side,
    We gat our ditty° rarely;   *sermon*
But my downcast eye by chance did spy

What made my lips to water,
15 Those limbs so clean where I, between
    Commenc'd a Fornicator.

With rueful face and signs of grace
    I pay'd the buttock-hire,[3]
The night was dark and thro the park
20   I could not but convoy her;
A parting kiss, what could I less,
    My vows began to scatter,
My Betsey fell—lal de dal lal lal,
    I am a Fornicator.

25 But for her sake this vow I make,
    And solemnly I swear it,
That while I own a single crown,
    She's welcome for to share it;
And my roguish boy his mother's joy,
30   And the darling of his pater,°   *father*
For him I boast my pains and cost,
    Although a Fornicator.

Ye wenching blades whose hireling jades°   *prostitutes*
    Have tipt ye off blue-joram,[4]
35 I tell ye plain, I do disdain
    To rank ye in the quorum;
But a bony lass upon the grass
    To teach her esse mater,[5]
And no reward but for regard,
40   O that's a Fornicator.

Your warlike kings and heroes bold,
    Great captains and commanders;
Your mighty Caesars fam'd of old,
    And conquering Alexanders;
45 In fields they fought and laurels[6] bought
    And bulwarks strong did batter,
But still they grac'd our noble list
    And ranked Fornicator!!!
—1785

---

1 *no thy lane* Not alone.

2 *Gang aft agley* Go oft awry.

3 *buttock-hire* Church fine charged to fornicators.

4 *tipt ye off blue-joram* Given you the pox.

5 *esse mater* Latin: to be a mother.

6 *laurels* Leaves of the bay laurel tree were once a symbol of victory in battle.

Flow gently, sweet Afton[1]

Flow gently, sweet Afton, among thy green
   braes!°   *banks*
Flow gently, I'll sing thee a song in thy praise!
My Mary's asleep by thy murmuring stream—
Flow gently, sweet Afton, disturb not her dream!

5   Thou stock-dove whose echo resounds thro' the glen,
Ye wild whistling blackbirds in yon thorny den,
Thou green-crested lapwing, thy screaming forbear—
I charge you, disturb not my slumbering fair!

How lofty, sweet Afton, thy neighbouring hills,
10   Far mark'd with the courses of clear, winding rills!° *brooks*
There daily I wander, as noon rises high,
My flocks and my Mary's sweet cot° in my eye.   *cottage*

How pleasant thy banks and green valleys below,
Where wild in the woodlands the primroses blow;
15   There oft, as mild ev'ning weeps over the lea,
The sweet-scented birk° shades my Mary and me.   *birch*

Thy crystal stream, Afton, how lovely it glides,
And winds by the cot where my Mary resides!
How wanton thy waters her snowy feet lave,°   *wash*
20   As, gathering sweet flowerets, she stems thy clear wave.

Flow gently, sweet Afton, among thy green braes!
Flow gently, sweet river, the theme of my lays!°   *song*
My Mary's asleep by thy murmuring stream—
Flow gently, sweet Afton, disturb not her dream!
—1792

Ae Fond Kiss[2]

Ae° fond kiss, and then we sever;   *one*
   Ae fareweel, alas, forever!
Deep in heart-wrung tears I'll pledge thee,

Warring sighs and groans I'll wage thee.
5   Who shall say that Fortune grieves him,
While the star of hope she leaves him?
Me, nae cheerful twinkle lights me;
Dark despair around benights me.

I'll ne'er blame my partial fancy,
10   Naething could resist my Nancy:
But to see her was to love her;
Love but her, and love forever.
Had we never lov'd sae kindly,
Had we never lov'd sae blindly,
15   Never met—or never parted,
We had ne'er been brokenhearted.

Fare-thee-weel, thou first and fairest!
Fare-thee-weel, thou best and dearest!
Thine be ilka° joy and treasure,   *every*
20   Peace, Enjoyment, Love and Pleasure!
Ae fond kiss, and then we sever!
Ae fareweel, alas, forever!
Deep in heart-wrung tears I'll pledge thee,
Warring sighs and groans I'll wage thee.
—1792

Robert Bruce's March to Bannockburn[3]

Scots, wha hae° wi' Wallace[4] bled,   *who have*
  Scots, wham° Bruce has aften led,   *whom*
Welcome to your gory bed,
      Or to victorie!

5   Now's the day, and now's the hour;
See the front o' battle lour;°   *threaten*
See approach proud Edward's power—
      Chains and slaverie!

Wha will be a traitor knave?
10   Wha can fill a coward's grave?

---

1 *Afton* River that runs through southwestern Scotland.

2 *Ae Fond Kiss* Burns wrote this love song for Nancy McLehose (the two called each other "Sylvander" and "Clarinda"), when she left England to reunite with her husband in Jamaica.

3 *Robert Bruce … Bannockburn* In 1314, Robert the Bruce, King of Scots, fought successfully for a free Scotland in a battle against the English under Edward I at Bannockburn.

4 *Wallace* Sir William Wallace led numerous battles against the English under King Edward I.

Wha sae base as be a slave?
　　Let him turn and flee!

Wha, for Scotland's King and Law,
Freedom's sword will strongly draw,
15　Free-man stand, or Free-man fa',
　　Let him on wi' me!

By Oppression's woes and pains!
By your Sons in servile chains!
We will drain our dearest veins,
20　　But they shall be free!

Lay the proud usurpers low!
Tyrants fall in every foe!
Liberty's in every blow!—
　　Let us Do or Die!
　　　　　—1795

A Man's a Man for A' That

Is there for honest poverty
　　That hings° his head, an' a'° that;　　　*hangs / all*
The coward slave—we pass him by,
　　We dare be poor for a' that!
5　For a' that, an' a' that.
　　　Our toils obscure an' a' that,
　　The rank is but the guinea's stamp,
　　　The Man's the gowd° for a' that.　　　*gold*

What though on hamely° fare we dine,　　　*simple*
10　　Wear hoddin grey,[1] an' a that;
Gie° fools their silks, and knaves their wine;　　*give*
　　A Man's a Man for a' that:
For a' that, and a' that,
　　Their tinsel show, an' a' that;
15　The honest man, tho' e'er sae° poor,　　　*so*
　　Is king o' men for a' that.

Ye see yon birkie,[2] ca'd° "a lord,"　　　*called*
　　Wha struts, an' stares, an' a' that;

---

[1] *hoddin grey* Coarse, woolen peasant cloth.

[2] *birkie* Conceited, swaggering fellow.

Tho' hundreds worship at his word,
20　　He's but a coof° for a' that:　　　*fool*
For a' that, an' a' that,
　　His ribband,° star,[3] an' a' that:　　　*ribbon*
The man o' independent mind
　　He looks an' laughs at a' that.

25　A prince can mak a belted knight,
　　A marquis, duke, an' a' that;
But an honest man's aboon° his might,　　　*above*
　　Gude faith, he mauna fa' that![4]
For a' that, an' a' that,
30　　Their dignities an' a' that;
The pith° o' sense, an' pride o' worth,　　　*importance*
　　Are higher rank than a' that.

Then let us pray that come it may,
　　As come it will for a' that,
35　That sense and worth, o'er a' the earth,
　　Shall bear the gree,[5] an' a' that.
For a' that, an' a' that,
　　It's coming yet for a' that,
That Man to Man, the world o'er,
40　　Shall brithers be for a' that.
　　　　　—1795

Comin' thro' the Rye

CHORUS

O, Jenny's a' weet,[6] poor body,
　　Jenny's seldom dry;
She draigl't[7] a' her petticoatie
　　Comin thro' the rye!

5　Comin thro' the rye, poor body,
　　Comin thro' the rye,
She draigl't a' her petticoatie,
　　Comin thro' the rye!

---

[3] *ribband, star* Emblems of nobility.

[4] *mauna fa' that* Mustn't have that befall him.

[5] *bear the gree* Have the victory.

[6] *a' weet* All wet.

[7] *draigl't* Draggled; dragged through the mud.

Gin° a body meet a body
    Comin thro' the rye,   *suppose*
10 Gin a body kiss a body,
    Need a body cry?

Gin a body meet a body
    Comin thro' the glen,
15 Gin a body kiss a body,
    Need the warld ken?°   *know*

Chorus

O, Jenny's a' weet, poor body,
    Jenny's seldom dry;
She draigl't a' her petticoatie
20   Comin thro' the rye!

  —1796

A Red, Red Rose

O, my luve's like a red, red rose,
  That's newly sprung in June;
O, my luve's like the melodie,
    That's sweetly play'd in tune.

5 As fair art thou, my bonie lass,
    So deep in luve am I;
And I will luve thee still, my dear,
    Till a' the seas gang° dry.   *go*

Till a' the seas gang dry, my dear,
10   And the rocks melt wi' the sun;
And I will luve thee still, my dear,
    While the sands o' life shall run.

And fare thee weel, my only luve!
    And fare thee weel, a while!
15 And I will come again, my luve,
    Tho' 'twere ten thousand mile!

  —1796

Auld Lang Syne[1]

Should auld acquaintance be forgot,
  And never brought to mind?
Should auld acquaintance be forgot,
    And auld lang syne!

Chorus

5 For auld lang syne, my dear,
    For auld lang syne.
We'll tak a cup o' kindness yet,
    For auld lang syne.

And surely ye'll be° your pint stowp![2]   *raise*
10   And surely I'll be mine!
And we'll tak a cup o' kindness yet,
    For auld lang syne.

Chorus

We twa° hae run about the braes,°   *two / hills*
    And pou'd° the gowans° fine;   *pulled / daisies*
15 But we've wander'd mony a weary fit,°   *foot*
    Sin'° auld lang syne.   *since*

Chorus

We twa hae paidl'd in the burn,°   *stream*
    Frae morning sun till dine;
But seas between us braid° hae roar'd   *broad*
20   Sin' auld lang syne.

Chorus

And there's a hand, my trusty fiere!°   *friend*
    And gie's° a hand o' thine!   *give us*
And we'll tak a right gude willie-waught,[3]
    For auld lang syne.

Chorus

  —1796

---

[1] *Auld Lang Syne* Times long since passed.

[2] *stowp* Drinking glass.

[3] *gude willie-waught* Hearty glass of draught beer.

WILLIAM WORDSWORTH
1770 – 1850

Since about 1815, William Wordsworth has been acknowledged as a central figure in the English Romantic Movement. *Lyrical Ballads*, produced in conjunction with Samuel Taylor Coleridge though largely Wordsworth's project, marks a decisive break with the formalism and neo-classicism of eighteenth-century literature. It became the touchstone of a new literary sensibility that gave its faith to the benevolence of feeling, and of the vehicle it associated most with feeling: a poetry of sincerity. And it established the idea of Nature as the measure by which to judge whether a poem's expression of feeling was genuine or not.

Wordworth's poems respond powerfully to the major developments of his day—including the French Revolution, war, and industrialization. That response, however, was marked by many tensions and contradictions. It is the play of those contradictions that give such weight and continued authority to Wordsworth's work.

Wordsworth was born in the Lake District of England, in West Cumberland, and spent his boyhood absorbing the natural beauty around him. The death of his mother when he was eight, and of his father only five years later, unsettled the lives of William and his four siblings. Their situation was worsened by the fact that the only substantial legacy their father left was a sum owed to him by his employer, Lord Lonsdale, who withheld the money until his death in 1802. Along with his three brothers, William was sent to school at Hawkshead. His sister Dorothy—later his confidante, secretary, and source of inspiration—found herself shifting among various relatives.

At Hawkshead Wordsworth and his brothers boarded at the home of Ann Tyson, who became a surrogate mother to Wordsworth, encouraging his love of nature and tolerating his habit of roaming the countryside. Wordsworth paid close attention to and frequently conversed with the town's working people. His observations would inform the representation of many of the humble rural characters who appear in his poetry. Leaving the Lake District for the first time in 1787, he entered St. John's College, Cambridge. During this period he made two walking tours with his friend Robert Jones, first through France and the Alps during a crucial period of the French Revolution, and later through Wales (excursions described in Books Six and Fourteen respectively of the 1850 *Prelude*).

These adventures quickened Wordsworth's belief in the healing powers of nature and of his own responsive imagination, and they also awakened radical sentiments. While traveling in France in 1791–92 he was swept up in the heady excitement that followed the French Revolution (1789). Young Wordsworth also fell in love with Annette Vallon, whose politics (Royalist) and religion (Catholic) he did not share, and they produced a daughter, Caroline, out of wedlock. Too poor to remain in France, which was now at war with England, Wordsworth returned to his country a divided man, his disillusionment growing as France fell into the Reign of Terror.

Financial concerns fed Wordsworth's doubts about his political convictions and his choice of vocation. In 1795, however, Wordsworth received a legacy of £900 from a friend, Raisley Calvert, whom he had nursed through his final illness. With this sum, and a rent-free cottage in Alfoxden provided by other friends, Wordsworth was able to set up housekeeping with his sister Dorothy, with his friend Coleridge not far away at Nether Stowey. (Describing his relationship with Coleridge in an 1832 letter to a friend, Wordsworth declared, "He and my beloved sister are the two beings to whom my intellect is most indebted.") Long walks and talks with Coleridge resulted in an extraordinary literary collaboration, *Lyrical Ballads, with a few other poems* (1798), a slender, anonymously-published volume that opens with Coleridge's literary ballad "The Rime of the Ancient Mariner" and closes with Wordsworth's blank-verse meditation, "Lines, Composed a Few Miles Above Tintern Abbey." The volume sought to combat what the authors saw as the increasingly marginal position of the poet in society, and the overly artificial language on which poetry relied.

As Coleridge and Wordsworth had expected, critics attacked the tone and subject matter of the volume. In the Preface to the Second Edition (1800)—perhaps the most famous poetic manifesto in the language—Wordsworth explained and defended the decision he made "to choose incidents and situations from common life, and to relate or describe them, throughout, as far as was possible, in a selection of language really used by men." In poems such as "Michael" and "The Brothers" (added to the 1800 edition of *Lyrical Ballads*), Wordsworth shows the strength and dignity with which the Lake District's inhabitants endure hardship, living in harmony with the natural world, removed from the taint of urban superficiality. Wordsworth was thus in an important sense what he is often taken to be, a "poet of nature." But his main object was not to depict directly "the beautiful and permanent forms of nature" but rather to explore how "the passions of men are incorporated with" such forms, and to depict the "ennobling interchange" between the natural world and the mental world. It is the mind, ultimately, that was Wordsworth's "haunt, and the main region of my song."

After a brief, inhospitable stay in Germany in 1798–99, during which Wordsworth wrote the "Lucy" poems (the identity of "Lucy" is unknown) and Coleridge assimilated German philosophy, Wordsworth and his sister returned to England and took up residence at Dove Cottage in Grasmere. Here Dorothy kept journals that have since become famous in their own right, and Wordsworth composed some of his finest lyrics, including "Resolution and Independence," "The Solitary Reaper" (a memorial of his walking tour through Scotland), and *Ode: Intimations of Immortality from Recollections of Early Childhood*, all of which were later published in his *Poems, in Two Volumes* (1807).

In 1802, Wordsworth married a childhood friend, Mary Hutchinson, and began a period of relative tranquility and poetic fruitfulness, although these years were not without grief and disappointment. By 1812, two of his five children were dead, his brother John had been lost at sea, his friendship with Coleridge (whose health was deteriorating as his opium addiction deepened) had become strained, and *Poems, in Two Volumes* had suffered damaging reviews.

Then in 1814 Wordsworth published *The Excursion*, a long blank-verse meditation that was a forecast and first installment of his planned epic, *The Recluse*. The book was poorly reviewed, even ridiculed. Nevertheless, Wordsworth by this time had gained a growing audience of devoted admirers, and his reputation from this low point began to establish itself firmly.

Like *The Excursion*, *The Prelude*, which Wordsworth had begun in 1799, was intended as a subsidiary piece that would be incorporated into *The Recluse*. He completed a two-book version of *The Prelude* in 1799 and a much expanded thirteen-book poem in 1805. He then continued to revise the poem for the rest of his life. This epic in blank verse—which Coleridge, upon hearing it, declared a "prophetic Lay"—describes the growth of the poet's mind from earliest memories to adulthood. By the end of his journey in the poem, Wordsworth reaffirms both providential design and the revolutionary potential of the imagination. *The Prelude* is a great, long lesson showing "how the mind of Man becomes / A thousand times more beautiful than the earth / On which he dwells."

In 1813, the Wordsworth household left Grasmere for the more expansive environs of Rydal Mount. There the poet, his beloved sister, and his wife lived out their days. The move was made possible by Wordsworth's improved financial situation, the result of a literary patronage granted by Lord Lonsdale and a position as Stamp Distributor for Westmorland. In the eyes of the younger generation (including Percy Shelley, Lord Byron, and Robert Browning), the patronage and the government position seemed to transform the once radical poet into a hypocritical and complacent hireling. As they saw it, Wordsworth had abandoned his early commitment to be the voice of the disenfranchised and the poor. Increasingly skeptical of external revolutions and political agitation, Wordsworth saw himself not as having abandoned his ideals but rather as having internalized—or spiritualized—his commitment to truth and liberty.

During his middle and old age Wordsworth wrote numerous sonnets, including *Ecclesiastical Sketches* (1822), which takes England's religious history as a primary subject. Having begun as a poetic and political revolutionary, he ended his life an iconic figure of the early Victorian era. Queen Victoria crowned him her Poet Laureate in 1843, and admirers flocked to the Lake District to seek him out in his home. The influence of his poetic style remained strong until well into the twentieth century, and Victorian writers of prose and poetry alike—including Tennyson, Charles Dickens, George Eliot, and Elizabeth Gaskell—acknowledged their debt to the life he had breathed into ways of thinking about nature, poetic feeling, and the human imagination.

⌘ ⌘ ⌘

from *Lyrical Ballads, 1798*

ADVERTISEMENT

It is the honourable characteristic of Poetry that its materials are to be found in every subject which can interest the human mind. The evidence of this fact is to be sought, not in the writings of Critics, but in those of Poets themselves.

The majority of the following poems are to be considered as experiments. They were written chiefly with a view to ascertain how far the language of conversation in the middle and lower classes of society is adapted to the purposes of poetic pleasure. Readers accustomed to the gaudiness and inane phraseology of many modern writers, if they persist in reading this book to its conclusion, will perhaps frequently have to struggle with feelings of strangeness and awkwardness: they will look round for poetry, and will be induced to enquire by what species of courtesy these attempts can be permitted to assume that title. It is desirable that such readers, for their own sakes, should not suffer the solitary word Poetry, a word of very disputed meaning, to stand in the way of their gratification; but that, while they are perusing this book, they should ask themselves if it contains a natural delineation of human passions,

human characters, and human incidents; and if the answer be favourable to the author's wishes, that they should consent to be pleased in spite of that most dreadful enemy to our pleasures, our own pre-established codes of decision.

Readers of superior judgment may disapprove of the style in which many of these pieces are executed. It must be expected that many lines and phrases will not exactly suit their taste. It will perhaps appear to them that, wishing to avoid the prevalent fault of the day, the author has sometimes descended too low, and that many of his expressions are too familiar, and not of sufficient dignity. It is apprehended that the more conversant the reader is with our elder writers, and with those in modern times who have been the most successful in painting manners and passions, the fewer complaints of this kind will he have to make.

An accurate taste in poetry, and in all the other arts, Sir Joshua Reynolds[1] has observed, is an acquired talent, which can only be produced by severe thought, and a long continued intercourse with the best models of composition. This is mentioned not with so ridiculous a purpose as to prevent the most inexperienced reader from judging for himself; but merely to temper the

---

[1] *Sir Joshua Reynolds* Renowned portrait and history painter, and first President of the Royal Academy (1723–92).

rashness of decision, and to suggest that if poetry be a subject on which much time has not been bestowed, the judgment may be erroneous, and that in many cases it necessarily will be so.

The tale of Goody Blake and Harry Gill is founded on a well-authenticated fact which happened in Warwickshire. Of the other poems in the collection, it may be proper to say that they are either absolute inventions of the author, or facts which took place within his personal observation or that of his friends. The poem of the Thorn, as the reader will soon discover, is not supposed to be spoken in the author's own person: the character of the loquacious narrator will sufficiently show itself in the course of the story. The Rime of the Ancyent Marinere was professedly written in imitation of the style, as well as of the spirit of the elder poets; but with a few exceptions, the Author believes that the language adopted in it has been equally intelligible for these three last centuries. The lines entitled Expostulation and Reply, and those which follow, arose out of conversation with a friend who was somewhat unreasonably attached to modern books of moral philosophy.

We Are Seven

A simple child, dear brother Jim,
  That lightly draws its breath,
And feels its life in every limb,
What should it know of death?

5 I met a little cottage girl,
She was eight years old, she said;
Her hair was thick with many a curl
That cluster'd round her head.

She had a rustic, woodland air,
10 And she was wildly clad;
Her eyes were fair, and very fair
—Her beauty made me glad.

"Sisters and brothers, little maid,
How many may you be?"

15 "How many? seven in all," she said,
And wondering looked at me.

"And where are they, I pray you tell?"
She answered, "Seven are we,
And two of us at Conway[1] dwell,
20 And two are gone to sea.

"Two of us in the church-yard lie,
My sister and my brother,
And in the church-yard cottage, I
Dwell near them with my mother."

25 "You say that two at Conway dwell,
And two are gone to sea,
Yet you are seven; I pray you tell
Sweet Maid, how this may be?"

Then did the little Maid reply,
30 "Seven boys and girls are we;
Two of us in the church-yard lie,
Beneath the church-yard tree."

"You run about, my little maid,
Your limbs they are alive;
35 If two are in the church-yard laid,
Then ye are only five."

"Their graves are green, they may be seen,"
The little Maid replied,
"Twelve steps or more from my mother's door,
40 And they are side by side.

"My stockings there I often knit,
My 'kerchief there I hem;
And there upon the ground I sit—
I sit and sing to them.

45 "And often after sunset, Sir,
When it is light and fair,
I take my little porringer,[2]
And eat my supper there.

[1] Conway Seaport of southern Wales.

[2] porringer Small metal or earthenware basin from which broth or porridge is eaten.

"The first that died was little Jane;
50   In bed she moaning lay,
Till God released her of her pain,
And then she went away.

"So in the church-yard she was laid,
And all the summer dry,
55   Together round her grave we played,
My brother John and I.

"And when the ground was white with snow,
And I could run and slide,
My brother John was forced to go,
60   And he lies by her side."

"How many are you then," said I,
"If they two are in Heaven?"
The little Maiden did reply,
"O Master! we are seven."

65   "But they are dead; those two are dead!
Their spirits are in heaven!"
'Twas throwing words away; for still
The little Maid would have her will,
And said, "Nay, we are seven!"
—1798

Lines Written in Early Spring

I heard a thousand blended notes,
While in a grove I sat reclined,
In that sweet mood when pleasant thoughts
Bring sad thoughts to the mind.

5   To her fair works did nature link
The human soul that through me ran;
And much it griev'd my heart to think
What man has made of man.

Through primrose-tufts, in that sweet bower,
10   The periwinkle trail'd its wreathes;
And 'tis my faith that every flower
Enjoys the air it breathes.

The birds around me hopp'd and play'd:
Their thoughts I cannot measure,
15   But the least motion which they made,
It seem'd a thrill of pleasure.

The budding twigs spread out their fan,
To catch the breezy air;
And I must think, do all I can,
20   That there was pleasure there.

If I these thoughts may not prevent,
If such be of my creed the plan,
Have I not reason to lament
What man has made of man?
—1798

The Thorn[1]

1

There is a thorn;° it looks so old,   *thorn bush*
In truth you'd find it hard to say,
How it could ever have been young,
It looks so old and grey.
5   Not higher than a two-years' child,
It stands erect this aged thorn;
No leaves it has, no thorny points;
It is a mass of knotted joints,
A wretched thing forlorn.
10   It stands erect, and like a stone
With lichens it is overgrown.

2

Like rock or stone, it is o'ergrown
With lichens to the very top,
And hung with heavy tufts of moss,
15   A melancholy crop:
Up from the earth these mosses creep,
And this poor thorn they clasp it round

[1] [Wordsworth's note]   Arose from my observing, on the ridge of Quantock Hill, on a stormy day a thorn which I had often passed in calm and bright weather without noticing it. I said to myself, "Cannot I by some invention do as much to make this Thorn permanently an impressive object as the storm has made it to my eyes at this moment?"

So close, you'd say that they were bent
With plain and manifest intent,
20   To drag it to the ground;
And all had joined in one endeavour
To bury this poor thorn for ever.

3

High on a mountain's highest ridge,
Where oft the stormy winter gale
25   Cuts like a scythe, while through the clouds
It sweeps from vale to vale;
Not five yards from the mountain-path,
This thorn you on your left espy;
And to the left, three yards beyond,
30   You see a little muddy pond
Of water, never dry;
I've measured it from side to side:
'Tis three feet long, and two feet wide.

4

And close beside this aged thorn,
35   There is a fresh and lovely sight,
A beauteous heap, a hill of moss,
Just half a foot in height.
All lovely colours there you see,
All colours that were ever seen,
40   And mossy network too is there,
As if by hand of lady fair
The work had woven been,
And cups,° the darlings of the eye,   blossoms
So deep is their vermilion° dye.   red

5

45   Ah me! what lovely tints are there!
Of olive-green and scarlet bright,
In spikes, in branches, and in stars,
Green, red, and pearly white.
This heap of earth o'ergrown with moss,
50   Which close beside the thorn you see,
So fresh in all its beauteous dyes,
Is like an infant's grave in size
As like as like can be:
But never, never any where,
55   An infant's grave was half so fair.

6

Now would you see this aged thorn,
This pond and beauteous hill of moss,
You must take care and choose your time
The mountain when to cross.
60   For oft there sits, between the heap
That's like an infant's grave in size,
And that same pond of which I spoke,
A woman in a scarlet cloak,
And to herself she cries,
65   "Oh misery! oh misery!
Oh woe is me! oh misery!"

7

At all times of the day and night
This wretched woman thither goes,
And she is known to every star,
70   And every wind that blows;
And there beside the thorn she sits
When the blue day-light's in the skies,
And when the whirlwind's on the hill,
Or frosty air is keen and still,
75   And to herself she cries,
"Oh misery! oh misery!
Oh woe is me! oh misery!"

8

"Now wherefore thus, by day and night,
In rain, in tempest, and in snow,
80   Thus to the dreary mountain-top
Does this poor woman go?
And why sits she beside the thorn
When the blue day-light's in the sky,
Or when the whirlwind's on the hill,
85   Or frosty air is keen and still,
And wherefore does she cry?
Oh wherefore? wherefore? tell me why
Does she repeat that doleful cry?"

9

I cannot tell; I wish I could;
90   For the true reason no one knows,
But if you'd gladly view the spot,
The spot to which she goes;
The heap that's like an infant's grave,

The pond—and thorn, so old and grey;
95   Pass by her door—'tis seldom shut—
And if you see her in her hut,
Then to the spot away!
I never heard of such as dare
Approach the spot when she is there.

10

100   "But wherefore to the mountain-top
Can this unhappy woman go,
Whatever star is in the skies,
Whatever wind may blow?"
Nay rack your brain—'tis all in vain,
105   I'll tell you every thing I know;
But to the thorn, and to the pond
Which is a little step beyond,
I wish that you would go:
Perhaps when you are at the place
110   You something of her tale may trace.

11

I'll give you the best help I can:
Before you up the mountain go,
Up to the dreary mountain-top,
I'll tell you all I know.
115   'Tis now some two and twenty years,
Since she (her name is Martha Ray)
Gave with a maiden's true good will
Her company to Stephen Hill;
And she was blithe and gay,
120   And she was happy, happy still
Whene'er she thought of Stephen Hill.

12

And they had fix'd the wedding-day,
The morning that must wed them both;
But Stephen to another maid
125   Had sworn another oath;
And with this other maid to church
Unthinking Stephen went—
Poor Martha! on that woeful day
A cruel, cruel fire, they say,
130   Into her bones was sent:

It dried her body like a cinder,
And almost turn'd her brain to tinder.[1]

13

They say, full six months after this,
While yet the summer leaves were green,
135   She to the mountain-top would go,
And there was often seen.
'Tis said, a child was in her womb,
As now to any eye was plain;
She was with child, and she was mad,
140   Yet often she was sober sad
From her exceeding pain.
Oh me! ten thousand times I'd rather
That he had died, that cruel father!

14

Sad case for such a brain to hold
145   Communion with a stirring child!
Sad case, as you may think, for one
Who had a brain so wild!
Last Christmas when we talked of this,
Old Farmer Simpson did maintain,
150   That in her womb the infant wrought
About its mother's heart, and brought
Her senses back again:
And when at last her time drew near,
Her looks were calm, her senses clear.

15

155   No more I know, I wish I did,
And I would tell it all to you;
For what became of this poor child
There's none that ever knew:
And if a child was born or no,
160   There's no one that could ever tell;
And if 'twas born alive or dead,
There's no one knows, as I have said,
But some remember well,
That Martha Ray about this time
165   Would up the mountain often climb.

---

[1]   *tinder* Dry, flammable substance that will take fire from a spark.

16

And all that winter, when at night
The wind blew from the mountain-peak,
'Twas worth your while, though in the dark,
The church-yard path to seek:
170 For many a time and oft were heard
Cries coming from the mountain-head,
Some plainly living voices were,
And others, I've heard many swear,
Were voices of the dead:
175 I cannot think, whate'er they say,
They had to do with Martha Ray.

17

But that she goes to this old thorn,
The thorn which I've described to you,
And there sits in a scarlet cloak,
180 I will be sworn is true.
For one day with my telescope,
To view the ocean wide and bright,
When to this country first I came,
Ere I had heard of Martha's name,
185 I climbed the mountain's height:
A storm came on, and I could see
No object higher than my knee.

18

'Twas mist and rain, and storm and rain,
No screen, no fence could I discover,
190 And then the wind! in faith, it was
A wind full ten times over.
I looked around, I thought I saw
A jutting crag, and off I ran,
Head-foremost, through the driving rain,
195 The shelter of the crag to gain,
And, as I am a man,
Instead of jutting crag, I found
A woman seated on the ground.

19

I did not speak—I saw her face,
200 Her face it was enough for me;
I turned about and heard her cry,
"O misery! O misery!"
And there she sits, until the moon
Through half the clear blue sky will go,
205 And when the little breezes make
The waters of the pond to shake,
As all the country know,
She shudders and you hear her cry,
"Oh misery! oh misery!"

20

210 "But what's the thorn? and what's the pond?
And what's the hill of moss to her?
And what's the creeping breeze that comes
The little pond to stir?"
I cannot tell; but some will say
215 She hanged her baby on the tree,
Some say she drowned it in the pond,
Which is a little step beyond,
But all and each agree,
The little babe was buried there,
220 Beneath that hill of moss so fair.

21

I've heard the scarlet moss is red
With drops of that poor infant's blood;
But kill a new-born infant thus!
I do not think she could.
225 Some say, if to the pond you go,
And fix on it a steady view,
The shadow of a babe you trace,
A baby and a baby's face,
And that it looks at you;
230 Whene'er you look on it, 'tis plain
The baby looks at you again.

22

And some had sworn an oath that she
Should be to public justice brought;
And for the little infant's bones
235 With spades they would have sought.
But then the beauteous hill of moss
Before their eyes began to stir;
And for full fifty yards around,
The grass it shook upon the ground;
240 But all do still aver
The little babe is buried there,
Beneath that hill of moss so fair.

23

I cannot tell how this may be,
But plain it is, the thorn is bound
245　With heavy tufts of moss, that strive
To drag it to the ground.
And this I know, full many a time,
When she was on the mountain high,
By day, and in the silent night,
250　When all the stars shone clear and bright,
That I have heard her cry,
"Oh misery! oh misery!
Oh woe is me! oh misery!"
　　—1798

Expostulation and Reply[1]

"Why William, on that old grey stone,
　　Thus for the length of half a day,
Why William, sit you thus alone,
And dream your time away?

5　"Where are your books? that light bequeath'd
To beings else forlorn and blind!
Up! Up! and drink the spirit breath'd
From dead men to their kind.

"You look round on your mother earth,
10　As if she for no purpose bore you;
As if you were her first-born birth,
And none had lived before you!"

One morning thus, by Esthwaite lake,[2]
When life was sweet I knew not why,
15　To me my good friend Matthew spake,
And thus I made reply.

"The eye it cannot choose but see,
We cannot bid the ear be still;

Our bodies feel, where'er they be,
20　Against, or with our will.

"Nor less I deem that there are powers,
Which of themselves our minds impress,
That we can feed this mind of ours,
In a wise passiveness.

25　"Think you, mid all this mighty sum
Of things for ever speaking,
That nothing of itself will come,
But we must still be seeking?

"—Then ask not wherefore, here, alone,
30　Conversing as I may,
I sit upon this old grey stone,
And dream my time away."
　　—1798

The Tables Turned
An Evening Scene on the Same Subject

Up! up! my friend, and clear your looks,
　　Why all this toil and trouble?
Up! up! my friend, and quit your books,
Or surely you'll grow double.[3]

5　The sun above the mountain's head,
A freshening lustre mellow,
Through all the long green fields has spread,
His first sweet evening yellow.

Books! 'tis a dull and endless strife,
10　Come, hear the woodland linnet,
How sweet his music; on my life
There's more of wisdom in it.

And hark! how blithe the throstle° sings!　　*thrush*
And he is no mean preacher;
15　Come forth into the light of things,
Let Nature be your teacher.

---

[1]　*Expostulation and Reply*　As Wordsworth suggests in the advertisement to *Lyrical Ballads*, this poem is based on a conversation he had with the writer and critic William Hazlitt (1778–1830).

[2]　*Esthwaite lake*　Located at Hawkshead (in England's Lake District), where Wordsworth attended grammar school. The real conversation that inspired this poem took place not at Hawkshead but at Alfoxden.

---

[3]　*double*　Doubled over.

She has a world of ready wealth,
Our minds and hearts to bless—
Spontaneous wisdom breathed by health,
20   Truth breathed by cheerfulness.

One impulse from a vernal wood
May teach you more of man;
Of moral evil and of good,
Than all the sages can.

25   Sweet is the lore which nature brings;
Our meddling intellect
Mishapes the beauteous forms of things
—We murder to dissect.

Enough of science and of art;
30   Close up these barren leaves;
Come forth, and bring with you a heart
That watches and receives.
    —1798

Lines Written a Few Miles above
Tintern Abbey

*On Revisiting the Banks of the Wye during a Tour,
July 13, 1798*[1]

F ive years have passed; five summers, with the length
    Of five long winters! and again I hear
These waters, rolling from their mountain-springs
With a sweet inland murmur.[2] Once again
5   Do I behold these steep and lofty cliffs,
Which on a wild secluded scene impress
Thoughts of more deep seclusion; and connect
The landscape with the quiet of the sky.
The day is come when I again repose
10   Here, under this dark sycamore, and view

---

[1]   *Lines ... 1798* In a later commentary on this poem, Wordsworth
writes that "No poem of mine was composed under circumstances
more pleasant for me to remember than this. I began it upon leaving
Tintern, after crossing the Wye, and concluded it just as I was
entering Bristol in the evening, after a ramble of 4 or 5 days, with
my sister. Not a line of it was altered, and not any part of it was
written down till I reached Bristol."

[2]   [Wordsworth's note]   The river is not affected by the tides a few
miles above Tintern.

These plots of cottage-ground, these orchard-tufts,
Which, at this season, with their unripe fruits,
Among the woods and copses lose themselves,
Nor, with their green and simple hue, disturb
15   The wild green landscape. Once again I see
These hedge-rows, hardly hedge-rows, little lines
Of sportive wood run wild; these pastoral farms
Green to the very door; and wreaths of smoke
Sent up, in silence, from among the trees,
20   With some uncertain notice, as might seem,
Of vagrant dwellers in the houseless woods,
Or of some hermit's cave, where by his fire
The hermit sits alone.

                    Though absent long,
These forms of beauty have not been to me,
25   As is a landscape to a blind man's eye:
But oft, in lonely rooms, and 'mid the din
Of towns and cities, I have owed to them,
In hours of weariness, sensations sweet,
Felt in the blood, and felt along the heart,
30   And passing even into my purer mind
With tranquil restoration—feelings too
Of unremembered pleasure; such, perhaps,
As may have had no trivial influence
On that best portion of a good man's life;
35   His little, nameless, unremembered acts
Of kindness and of love. Nor less, I trust,
To them I may have owed another gift,
Of aspect more sublime; that blessed mood,
In which the burthen of the mystery,
40   In which the heavy and the weary weight
Of all this unintelligible world
Is lighten'd—that serene and blessed mood,
In which the affections gently lead us on,
Until, the breath of this corporeal frame,
45   And even the motion of our human blood
Almost suspended, we are laid asleep
In body, and become a living soul:
While with an eye made quiet by the power
Of harmony, and the deep power of joy,
50   We see into the life of things.

                    If this
Be but a vain belief, yet, oh! how oft,
In darkness, and amid the many shapes

Of joyless day-light; when the fretful stir
Unprofitable, and the fever of the world,
55 Have hung upon the beatings of my heart,
How oft, in spirit, have I turned to thee
O sylvan Wye! Thou wanderer through the woods,
How often has my spirit turned to thee!

And now, with gleams of half-extinguish'd thought,
60 With many recognitions dim and faint,
And somewhat of a sad perplexity,
The picture of the mind revives again:
While here I stand, not only with the sense
Of present pleasure, but with pleasing thoughts
65 That in this moment there is life and food
For future years. And so I dare to hope
Though changed, no doubt, from what I was, when first
I came among these hills; when like a roe°   deer
I bounded o'er the mountains, by the sides
70 Of the deep rivers, and the lonely streams,
Wherever nature led; more like a man
Flying from something that he dreads, than one
Who sought the thing he loved. For nature then
(The coarser pleasures of my boyish days,
75 And their glad animal movements all gone by)
To me was all in all. I cannot paint
What then I was. The sounding cataract
Haunted me like a passion: the tall rock,
The mountain, and the deep and gloomy wood,
80 Their colours and their forms, were then to me
An appetite: a feeling and a love,
That had no need of a remoter charm,
By thought supplied, or any interest
Unborrowed from the eye. That time is past,
85 And all its aching joys are now no more,
And all its dizzy raptures. Not for this
Faint[1] I, nor mourn nor murmur: other gifts
Have followed, for such loss, I would believe,
Abundant recompence. For I have learned
90 To look on nature, not as in the hour
Of thoughtless youth, but hearing oftentimes
The still, sad music of humanity,
Not harsh nor grating, though of ample power
To chasten and subdue. And I have felt
95 A presence that disturbs me with the joy

Of elevated thoughts; a sense sublime
Of something far more deeply interfused,
Whose dwelling is the light of setting suns,
And the round ocean, and the living air,
100 And the blue sky, and in the mind of man,
A motion and a spirit, that impels
All thinking things, all objects of all thought,
And rolls through all things. Therefore am I still
A lover of the meadows and the woods,
105 And mountains; and of all that we behold
From this green earth; of all the mighty world
Of eye and ear, both what they half create,
And what perceive; well pleased to recognize
In nature and the language of the sense,
110 The anchor of my purest thoughts, the nurse,
The guide, the guardian of my heart, and soul
Of all my moral being.

                    Nor, perchance,
If I were not thus taught, should I the more
Suffer my genial° spirits to decay: creative
115 For thou art with me, here, upon the banks
Of this fair river; thou, my dearest Friend,[2]
My dear, dear Friend, and in thy voice I catch
The language of my former heart, and read
My former pleasures in the shooting lights
120 Of thy wild eyes. Oh! yet a little while
May I behold in thee what I was once,
My dear, dear Sister! And this prayer I make,
Knowing that Nature never did betray
The heart that loved her; 'tis her privilege,
125 Through all the years of this our life, to lead
From joy to joy: for she can so inform
The mind that is within us, so impress
With quietness and beauty, and so feed
With lofty thoughts, that neither evil tongues,
130 Rash judgments, nor the sneers of selfish men,
Nor greetings where no kindness is, nor all
The dreary intercourse of daily life,
Shall e'er prevail against us, or disturb
Our cheerful faith that all which we behold
135 Is full of blessings. Therefore let the moon
Shine on thee in thy solitary walk;

---

[1] *Faint* Lose heart; grow weak.

[2] *my dearest Friend* I.e., Dorothy Wordsworth, Wordsworth's sister.

And let the misty mountain winds be free
To blow against thee: and in after years,
When these wild ecstasies shall be matured
140 Into a sober pleasure, when thy mind
Shall be a mansion for all lovely forms,
Thy memory be as a dwelling-place
For all sweet sounds and harmonies; Oh! then,
If solitude, or fear, or pain, or grief,
145 Should be thy portion, with what healing thoughts
Of tender joy wilt thou remember me,
And these my exhortations! Nor, perchance,
If I should be, where I no more can hear
Thy voice, nor catch from thy wild eyes these gleams
150 Of past existence, wilt thou then forget
That on the banks of this delightful stream
We stood together; and that I, so long
A worshipper of Nature, hither came,
Unwearied in that service: rather say
155 With warmer love, oh! with far deeper zeal
Of holier love. Nor wilt thou then forget,
That after many wanderings, many years
Of absence, these steep woods and lofty cliffs,
And this green pastoral landscape, were to me
160 More dear, both for themselves, and for thy sake.
—1798

from *Lyrical Ballads, 1800, 1802*

PREFACE[1]

The first Volume of these Poems has already been submitted to general perusal. It was published as an experiment, which, I hoped, might be of some use to ascertain how far, by fitting to metrical arrangement a selection of the real language of men in a state of vivid sensation, that sort of pleasure and that quantity of pleasure may be imparted, which a Poet may rationally endeavour to impart.

I had formed no very inaccurate estimate of the probable effect of those Poems: I flattered myself that they who should be pleased with them would read them with more than common pleasure: and, on the other hand, I was well aware that by those who should dislike them they would be read with more than common dislike. The result has differed from my expectation in this only, that I have pleased a greater number than I ventured to hope I should please.

For the sake of variety, and from a consciousness of my own weakness, I was induced to request the assistance of a Friend,[2] who furnished me with the Poems of the *Ancient Mariner*, the *Foster-Mother's Tale*, the *Nightingale*, and the Poem entitled *Love*. I should not, however, have requested this assistance, had I not believed that the Poems of my Friend would in a great measure have the same tendency as my own, and that, though there would be found a difference, there would be found no discordance in the colours of our style; as our opinions on the subject of poetry do almost entirely coincide.

Several of my Friends are anxious for the success of these Poems from a belief that, if the views with which they were composed were indeed realized, a class of Poetry would be produced, well adapted to interest mankind permanently, and not unimportant in the multiplicity, and in the quality of its moral relations: and on this account they have advised me to prefix a systematic defence of the theory upon which the poems were written. But I was unwilling to undertake the task, because I knew that on this occasion the Reader would look coldly upon my arguments, since I might be suspected of having been principally influenced by the selfish and foolish hope of *reasoning* him into an approbation of these particular Poems: and I was still more unwilling to undertake the task, because, adequately to display my opinions, and fully to enforce my arguments, would require a space wholly disproportionate to the nature of a preface. For to treat the subject with the clearness and coherence of which I believe it susceptible, it would be necessary to give a full account of the present state of the public taste in this country, and to determine how far this taste is healthy or depraved; which, again, could not be determined without pointing out in what manner language and the human mind act and re-act on each other, and without retracing the revolutions, not of literature alone, but likewise of society itself. I have therefore altogether declined to

---

[1] *Preface* This preface first appeared in the 1800 edition of *Lyrical Ballads*, and was revised for the 1802 edition.

[2] *Friend* Samuel Taylor Coleridge (1772–1834). Coleridge gives his account of their plan in his *Biographia Literaria*, chapter 14.

enter regularly upon this defence; yet I am sensible that there would be some impropriety in abruptly obtruding upon the Public, without a few words of introduction, Poems so materially different from those upon which general approbation is at present bestowed.

It is supposed, that by the act of writing in verse an Author makes a formal engagement that he will gratify certain known habits of association; that he not only thus apprizes the Reader that certain classes of ideas and expressions will be found in his book, but that others will be carefully excluded. This exponent or symbol held forth by metrical language must in different areas of literature have excited very different expectations: for example, in the age of Catullus, Terence, and Lucretius and that of Statius or Claudian;[1] and in our own country, in the age of Shakespeare and Beaumont and Fletcher, and that of Donne and Cowley, or Dryden, or Pope.[2] I will not take upon me to determine the exact import of the promise which by the act of writing in verse an Author, in the present day, makes to his Reader; but, I am certain, it will appear to many persons that I have not fulfilled the terms of an engagement thus voluntarily contracted. They who have been accustomed to the gaudiness and inane phraseology of many modern writers, if they persist in reading this book to its conclusion, will, no doubt, frequently have to struggle with feelings of strangeness and awkwardness: they will look round for poetry, and will be induced to inquire by what species of courtesy these attempts can be permitted to assume that title. I hope therefore the Reader will not censure me if I attempt to state what I have proposed to myself to perform; and also (as far as the limits of a preface will permit) to explain some of the chief reasons which have determined me in the choice of my purpose: that at least he may be spared any unpleasant feeling of disappointment, and that I myself may be protected from the most dishonorable accusation which can be brought against an Author, namely, that of an indolence which prevents him from endeavouring to ascertain what is his duty, or, when his duty is ascertained, prevents him from performing it.

The principal object, then, which I proposed to myself in these Poems was to choose incidents and situations from common life, and to relate or describe them, throughout, as far as was possible, in a selection of language really used by men; and, at the same time, to throw over them a certain colouring of imagination, whereby ordinary things should be presented to the mind in an unusual way; and, further, and above all, to make these incidents and situations interesting by tracing in them, truly though not ostentatiously, the primary laws of our nature: chiefly as far as regards the manner in which we associate ideas in a state of excitement. Low and rustic life was generally chosen because, in that condition, the essential passions of the heart find a better soil in which they can attain their maturity, are less under restraint, and speak a plainer and more emphatic language; because in that condition of life our elementary feelings co-exist in a state of greater simplicity, and, consequently, may be more accurately contemplated, and more forcibly communicated; because the manners of rural life germinate from those elementary feelings; and, from the necessary character of rural occupations, are more easily comprehended, and are more durable; and lastly, because in that condition the passions of men are incorporated with the beautiful and permanent forms of nature. The language, too, of these men is adopted (purified indeed from what appear to be its real defects, from all lasting and rational causes of dislike or disgust) because such men hourly communicate with the best objects from which the best part of language is originally derived; and because, from their rank in society and the sameness and narrow circle of their intercourse, being less under the influence of social vanity they convey their feelings and notions in simple and unelaborated expressions. Accordingly, such a language, arising out of repeated experience and regular feelings, is a more permanent, and a far more philosophical language, than that which is frequently substituted for it by Poets, who think that they are conferring honour upon themselves and their art, in proportion as they separate themselves from the sympathies of men,

---

[1] *Catullus, Terence, and Lucretius* Roman poets of the first and second centuries BCE; *Statius or Claudian* Roman epic poets of the first and fourth centuries CE, respectively.

[2] *Shakespeare and Beaumont and Fletcher* The age of Renaissance drama, during which Shakespeare, Francis Beaumont, and John Fletcher wrote; *Donne and Cowley* John Donne and Abraham Cowley, poets of the seventeenth century; *Dryden* John Dryden, Poet Laureate from 1668 to 1688; *Pope* Alexander Pope, a major poet of the eighteenth century.

and indulge in arbitrary and capricious habits of expression, in order to furnish food for fickle tastes, and fickle appetites, of their own creation.[1]

I cannot, however, be insensible of the present outcry against the triviality and meanness both of thought and language, which some of my contemporaries have occasionally introduced into their metrical compositions; and I acknowledge that this defect, where it exists, is more dishonorable to the Writer's own character than false refinement or arbitrary innovation, though I should contend at the same time that it is far less pernicious in the sum of its consequences. From such verses the Poems in these volumes will be found distinguished at least by one mark of difference, that each of them has a worthy *purpose*. Not that I mean to say that I always began to write with a distinct purpose formally conceived; but I believe that my habits of meditation have so formed my feelings, as that my descriptions of such objects as strongly excite those feelings will be found to carry along with them a *purpose*. If in this opinion I am mistaken, I can have little right to the name of a Poet. For all good poetry is the spontaneous overflow of powerful feelings: but though this be true, Poems to which any value can be attached, were never produced on any variety of subjects but by a man who, being possessed of more than usual organic sensibility, had also thought long and deeply. For our continued influxes of feeling are modified and directed by our thoughts, which are indeed the representatives of all our past feelings; and, as by contemplating the relation of these general representatives to each other we discover what is really important to men, so, by the repetition and continuance of this act, our feelings will be connected with important subjects, till at length, if we be originally possessed of much sensibility, such habits of mind will be produced, that, by obeying blindly and mechanically the impulses of those habits, we shall describe objects, and utter sentiments, of such a nature and in such connection with each other, that the understanding of the being to whom we address ourselves, if he be in a healthful state of association, must necessarily be in some degree enlightened, and his affections ameliorated.

I have said that each of these poems has a purpose. I have also informed my Reader what this purpose will be found principally to be: namely to illustrate the manner in which our feelings and ideas are associated in a state of excitement. But, speaking in language somewhat more appropriate, it is to follow the fluxes and refluxes of the mind when agitated by the great and simple affections of our nature. This object I have endeavoured in these short essays to attain by various means; by tracing the maternal passion through many of its more subtle windings, as in the poems of the *Idiot Boy* and the *Mad Mother*; by accompanying the last struggles of a human being, at the approach of death, cleaving in solitude to life and society, as in the Poem of the *Forsaken Indian*; by showing, as in the Stanzas entitled *We Are Seven*, the perplexity and obscurity which in childhood attend our notion of death, or rather our utter inability to admit that notion; or by displaying the strength of fraternal, or to speak more philosophically, of moral attachment when early associated with the great and beautiful objects of nature, as in *The Brothers*; or, as in the *Incident of Simon Lee*, by placing my Reader in the way of receiving from ordinary moral sensations another and more salutary impression than we are accustomed to receive from them. It has also been part of my general purpose to attempt to sketch characters under the influence of less impassioned feelings, as in the *Two April Mornings*, *The Fountain*, *The Old Man Travelling*, *The Two Thieves*, &c., characters of which the elements are simple, belonging rather to nature than to manners, such as exist now, and will probably always exist, and which from their constitution may be distinctly and profitably contemplated. I will not abuse the indulgence of my Reader by dwelling longer upon this subject; but it is proper that I should mention one other circumstance which distinguishes these Poems from the popular Poetry of the day; it is this, that the feeling therein developed gives importance to the action and situation, and not the action and situation to the feeling. My meaning will be rendered perfectly intelligible by referring my Reader to the Poems entitled *Poor Susan* and the *Childless Father*, particularly to the last Stanza of the latter Poem.

---

[1] [Wordsworth's note]   It is worth while here to observe that the affecting parts of Chaucer are almost always expressed in language pure and universally intelligible even to this day.

I will not suffer a sense of false modesty to prevent me from asserting that I point my Reader's attention to this mark of distinction, far less for the sake of these particular Poems than from the general importance of the subject. The subject is indeed important! For the human mind is capable of being excited without the application of gross and violent stimulants; and he must have a very faint perception of its beauty and dignity who does not know this, and who does not further know that one being is elevated above another, in proportion as he possesses this capability. It has therefore appeared to me that to endeavour to produce or enlarge this capability is one of the best services in which, at any period, a Writer can be engaged; but this service, excellent at all times, is especially so at the present day. For a multitude of causes, unknown to former times, are now acting with a combined force to blunt the discriminating powers of the mind, and unfitting it for all voluntary exertion to reduce it to a state of almost savage torpor. The most effective of these causes are the great national events which are daily taking place,[1] and the increasing accumulation of men in cities, where the uniformity of their occupations produces a craving for extraordinary incident, which the rapid communication of intelligence hourly gratifies. To this tendency of life and manners the literature and theatrical exhibitions of the country have conformed themselves. The invaluable works of our elder writers, I had almost said the works of Shakespeare and Milton, are driven into neglect by frantic novels, sickly and stupid German Tragedies, and deluges of idle and extravagant stories in verse.[2] When I think upon this degrading thirst after outrageous stimulation, I am almost ashamed to have spoken of the feeble effort with which I have endeavoured to counteract it; and, reflecting upon the magnitude of the general evil, I should be oppressed with no dishonorable melancholy, had I not a deep impression of certain inherent and indestructible qualities of the human mind, and likewise of certain

powers in the great and permanent objects that act upon it which are equally inherent and indestructible; and did I not further add to this impression a belief that the time is approaching when the evil will be systematically opposed, by men of greater powers, and with far more distinguished success.

Having dwelt thus long on the subjects and aim of these Poems, I shall request the Reader's permission to apprize him of a few circumstances relating to their *style*, in order, among other reasons, that I may not be censured for not having performed what I never attempted. The Reader will find that personifications of abstract ideas rarely occur in these volumes; and, I hope, are utterly rejected as an ordinary device to elevate the style, and raise it above prose. I have proposed to myself to imitate, and, as far as is possible, to adopt, the very language of men; and assuredly such personifications do not make any natural or regular part of that language. They are, indeed, a figure of speech occasionally prompted by passion, and I have made use of them as such; but I have endeavoured utterly to reject them as a mechanical device of style, or as a family language which Writers in metre seem to lay claim to by prescription. I have wished to keep my Reader in the company of flesh and blood, persuaded that by so doing I shall interest him. I am, however, well aware that others who pursue a different track may interest him likewise; I do not interfere with their claim, I only wish to prefer a different claim of my own. There will also be found in these volumes little of what is usually called poetic diction; I have taken as much pains to avoid it as others ordinarily take to produce it; this I have done for the reason already alleged, to bring my language near to the language of men, and further, because the pleasure which I have proposed to myself to impart is of a kind very different from that which is supposed by many persons to be the proper object of poetry. I do not know how without being culpably particular I can give my Reader a more exact notion of the style in which I wished these poems to be written than by informing him that I have at all times endeavoured to look steadily at my subject; consequently, I hope that there is in these Poems little falsehood of description, and that my ideas are expressed in language fitted to their respective importance. Something I must have gained by this practice, as it is friendly

[1] *great national ... place* I.e., the wars against France and the Irish rebellion.

[2] *frantic novels ... verse* References to popular Gothic novels of the time, such as Matthew Gregory Lewis's *The Monk* (1796) and the novels of Ann Radcliffe, and to the German sentimental melodramas translated and staged during the 1780s.

to one property of all good poetry, namely, good sense; but it has necessarily cut me off from a large portion of phrases and figures of speech which from father to son have long been regarded as the common inheritance of Poets. I have also thought it expedient to restrict myself still further, having abstained from the use of many expressions, in themselves proper and beautiful, but which have been foolishly repeated by bad Poets, till such feelings of disgust are connected with them as it is scarcely possible by any art of association to overpower.

If in a Poem there should be found a series of lines, or even a single line, in which the language, though naturally arranged and according to the strict laws of metre, does not differ from that of prose, there is a numerous class of critics, who, when they stumble upon these prosaisms, as they call them, imagine that they have made a notable discovery, and exult over the Poet as over a man ignorant of his own profession. Now these men would establish a canon of criticism which the Reader will conclude he must utterly reject, if he wishes to be pleased with these volumes. And it would be a most easy task to prove to him that not only the language of a large portion of every good poem, even of the most elevated character, must necessarily, except with reference to the metre, in no respect differ from that of good prose, but likewise that some of the most interesting parts of the best poems will be found to be strictly the language of prose, when prose is well written. The truth of this assertion might be demonstrated by innumerable passages from almost all the poetical writings, even of Milton himself. I have not space for much quotation; but, to illustrate the subject in a general manner, I will here adduce a short composition of Gray,[1] who was at the head of those who by their reasonings have attempted to widen the space of separation betwixt Prose and Metrical composition, and was more than any other man curiously elaborate in the structure of his own poetic diction.

In vain to me the smiling mornings shine,
    And reddening Phoebus[2] lifts his golden fire:
        The birds in vain their amorous descant join,

Or cheerful fields resume their green attire:
These ears alas! for other notes repine;
A different object do these eyes require;
My lonely anguish melts no heart but mine;
And in my breast the imperfect joys expire;
Yet Morning smiles the busy race to cheer,
And new-born pleasure brings to happier men;
The fields to all their wonted tribute bear;
To warm their little loves the birds complain.
I fruitless mourn to him that cannot hear
And weep the more because I weep in vain.

It will easily be perceived that the only part of this Sonnet which is of any value is the lines printed in Italics: it is equally obvious that, except in the rhyme, and in the use of the single word "fruitless" for fruitlessly, which is so far a defect, the language of these lines does in no respect differ from that of prose.

By the foregoing quotation I have shown that the language of Prose may yet be well adapted to Poetry; and I have previously asserted that a large portion of the language of every good poem can in no respect differ from that of good Prose. I will go further. I do not doubt that it may be safely affirmed that there neither is, nor can be, any essential difference between the language of prose and metrical composition....

I ask what is meant by the word Poet? What is a Poet? To whom does he address himself? And what language is to be expected from him? He is a man speaking to men: a man, it is true, endued with more lively sensibility, more enthusiasm and tenderness, who has a greater knowledge of human nature, and a more comprehensive soul, than are supposed to be common among mankind; a man pleased with his own passions and volitions, and who rejoices more than other men in the spirit of life that is in him; delighting to contemplate similar volitions and passions as manifested in the goings-on of the Universe, and habitually impelled to create them where he does not find them. To these qualities he has added a disposition to be affected more than other men by absent things as if they were present; an ability of conjuring up in himself passions, which are indeed far from being the same as those produced by real events, yet (especially in those parts of the general sympathy which are pleasing and delightful) do more nearly resemble the passions produced by real events

---

[1] *Gray* Thomas Gray (1716–71). Wordsworth quotes his *Sonnet on the Death of Richard West.*

[2] *Phoebus* Apollo, god of the sun and of poetry.

than any thing which, from the motions of their own minds merely, other men are accustomed to feel in themselves; whence, and from practice, he has acquired a greater readiness and power in expressing what he thinks and feels, and especially those thoughts and feelings which, by his own choice, or from the structure of his own mind, arise in him without immediate external excitement.

But, whatever portion of this faculty we may suppose even the greatest Poet to possess, there cannot be a doubt but that the language which it will suggest to him must, in liveliness and truth, fall far short of that which is uttered by men in real life, under the actual pressure of those passions, certain shadows of which the Poet thus produces, or feels to be produced, in himself. However exalted a notion we would wish to cherish of the character of a Poet, it is obvious that, while he describes and imitates passions, his situation is altogether slavish and mechanical, compared with the freedom and power of real and substantial action and suffering. So that it will be the wish of the Poet to bring his feelings near to those of the persons whose feelings he describes—nay, for short spaces of time, perhaps, to let himself slip into an entire delusion, and even confound and identify his own feelings with theirs; modifying only the language which is thus suggested to him, by a consideration that he describes for a particular purpose, that of giving pleasure. Here, then, he will apply the principle on which I have so much insisted, namely, that of selection; on this he will depend for removing what would otherwise be painful or disgusting in the passion; he will feel that there is no necessity to trick out or to elevate nature: and, the more industriously he applies this principle, the deeper will be his faith that no words which his fancy or imagination can suggest will be to be compared with those which are the emanations of reality and truth. . . .

It is not, then, in the dramatic parts of composition that we look for this distinction of language; but still it may be proper and necessary where the Poet speaks to us in his own person and character. To this I answer by referring my Reader to the description which I have before given of a Poet. Among the qualities which I have enumerated as principally conducting to form a Poet, is implied nothing differing in kind from other men, but

only in degree. The sum of what I have there said is that the Poet is chiefly distinguished from other men by a greater promptness to think and feel without immediate external excitement, and a greater power in expressing such thoughts and feelings as are produced in him in that manner. But these passions and thoughts and feelings are the general passions and thoughts and feelings of men. And with what are they connected? Undoubtedly with our moral sentiments and animal sensations, and with the causes which excite these; with the operations of the elements and the appearances of the visible universe; with storm and sunshine, with the revolutions of the seasons, with cold and heat, with loss of friends and kindred, with injuries and resentments, gratitude and hope, with fear and sorrow. These, and the like, are the sensations and objects which the Poet describes, as they are the sensations of other men, and the objects which interest them. The Poet thinks and feels in the spirit of the passions of men. How, then, can his language differ in any material degree from that of all other men who feel vividly and see clearly? It might be *proved* that it is impossible. But supposing that this were not the case, the Poet might then be allowed to use a peculiar language when expressing his feelings for his own gratification, or that of men like himself. But Poets do not write for Poets alone, but for men. Unless therefore we are advocates for that admiration which depends upon ignorance, and that pleasure which arises from hearing what we do not understand, the Poet must descend from this supposed height, and, in order to excite rational sympathy, he must express himself as other men express themselves. To this it may be added, that while he is only selecting from the real language of men, or, which amounts to the same thing, composing accurately in the spirit of such selection, he is treading upon safe ground, and we know what we are to expect from him. Our feelings are the same with respect to metre; for, as it may be proper to remind the Reader, the distinction of metre is regular and uniform, and not like that which is produced by what is usually called poetic diction, arbitrary, and subject to infinite caprices upon which no calculation whatever can be made. In the one case, the Reader is utterly at the mercy of the Poet respecting what imagery or diction he may choose to connect with the passion, whereas, in the other, the metre obeys certain laws, to which the Poet and Reader both willingly submit because they are certain, and because no interference is made by them with the passion but such as the concurring testimony of ages has shown to heighten and improve the pleasure which co-exists with it.

It will now be proper to answer an obvious question, namely, why, professing these opinions, have I written in verse? To this, in addition to such answer as is included in what I have already said, I reply in the first place, because, however I may have restricted myself, there is still left open to me what confessedly constitutes the most valuable object of all writing whether in prose or verse, the great and universal passions of men, the most general and interesting of their occupations, and the entire world of nature, from which I am at liberty to supply myself with endless combinations of forms and imagery. Now, supposing for a moment that whatever is interesting in these objects may be as vividly described in prose, why am I to be condemned, if to such description I have endeavoured to superadd the charm which, by the consent of all nations, is acknowledged to exist in metrical language? To this, by such as are unconvinced by what I have already said, it may be answered that a very small part of the pleasure given by Poetry depends upon the metre, and that it is injudicious to write in metre, unless it be accompanied with the other artificial distinctions of style with which metre is usually accompanied, and that by such deviation more will be lost from the shock which will be thereby given to the Reader's associations than will be counterbalanced by any pleasure which he can derive from the general power of numbers. In answer to those who still contend for the necessity of accompanying metre with certain appropriate colours of style in order to the accomplishment of its appropriate end, and who also, in my opinion, greatly under-rate the power of metre in itself, it might perhaps, as far as relates to these Poems, have been almost sufficient to observe that poems are extant, written upon more humble subjects, and in a more naked and simple style than I have aimed at, which poems have continued to give pleasure from generation to generation. Now, if nakedness and simplicity be a defect, the fact here mentioned affords a strong presumption that poems somewhat less naked and simple

are capable of affording pleasure at the present day; and, what I wished *chiefly* to attempt, at present, was to justify myself for having written under the impression of this belief.

But I might point out various causes why, when the style is manly, and the subject of some importance, words metrically arranged will long continue to impart such a pleasure to mankind as he who is sensible of the extent of that pleasure will be desirous to impart. The end of Poetry is to produce excitement in co-existence with an overbalance of pleasure. Now, by the supposition, excitement is an unusual and irregular state of the mind; ideas and feelings do not in that state succeed each other in accustomed order. But, if the words by which this excitement is produced are in themselves powerful, or the images and feelings have an undue proportion of pain connected with them, there is some danger that the excitement may be carried beyond its proper bounds. Now the co-presence of something regular, something to which the mind has been accustomed in various moods and in a less excited state, cannot but have great efficacy in tempering and restraining the passion by an intertexture of ordinary feeling, and of feeling not strictly and necessarily connected with the passion. This is unquestionably true, and hence, though the opinion will at first appear paradoxical, from the tendency of metre to divest language in a certain degree of its reality, and thus to throw a sort of half consciousness of unsubstantial existence over the whole composition, there can be little doubt but that more pathetic situations and sentiments—that is, those which have a greater proportion of pain connected with them—may be endured in metrical composition, especially in rhyme, than in prose. The metre of the old Ballads is very artless; yet they contain many passages which would illustrate this opinion, and, I hope, if the following Poems be attentively perused, similar instances will be found in them.....

I have said that Poetry is the spontaneous overflow of powerful feelings: it takes its origin from emotion recollected in tranquillity: the emotion is contemplated till by a species of reaction the tranquillity gradually disappears, and an emotion, kindred to that which was before the subject of contemplation, is gradually produced, and does itself actually exist in the mind. In this mood successful composition generally begins, and in a mood similar to this it is carried on; but the emotion, of whatever kind and in whatever degree, from various causes is qualified by various pleasures, so that in describing any passions whatsoever, which are voluntarily described, the mind will upon the whole be in a state of enjoyment. Now, if Nature be thus cautious in preserving in a state of enjoyment a being thus employed, the Poet ought to profit by the lesson thus held forth to him, and ought especially to take care that whatever passions he communicates to his Reader, those passions, if his Reader's mind be sound and vigorous, should always be accompanied with an overbalance of pleasure. Now the music of harmonious metrical language, the sense of difficulty overcome, and the blind association of pleasure which has been previously received from works of rhyme or metre of the same or similar construction, an indistinct perception perpetually renewed of language closely resembling that of real life, and yet, in the circumstance of metre, differing from it so widely, all these imperceptibly make up a complex feeling of delight, which is of the most important use in tempering the painful feeling which will always be found intermingled with powerful descriptions of the deeper passions. This effect is always produced in pathetic and impassioned poetry; while, in lighter compositions, the ease and gracefulness with which the Poet manages his numbers[1] are themselves confessedly a principal source of the gratification of the Reader. I might perhaps include all which it is *necessary* to say upon this subject by affirming what few persons will deny, that, of two descriptions, either of passions, manners, or characters, each of them equally well executed, the one in prose and the other in verse, the verse will be read a hundred times where the prose is read once. We see that Pope, by the power of verse alone, has contrived to render the plainest common sense interesting, and even frequently to invest it with the appearance of passion....

I know that nothing would have so effectually contributed to further the end which I have in view as to have shown of what kind the pleasure is, and how that pleasure is produced, which is confessedly produced by metrical composition essentially different from that which I have here endeavoured to recommend: for the Reader will say that he has been pleased by such composition; and what can I do more for him? The power of any art is limited; and he will suspect that, if I propose to furnish him with new friends, it is only upon condition of his abandoning his old friends. Besides, as I have said, the Reader is himself conscious of the pleasure which he has received from such composition, composition to which he has peculiarly attached the endearing name of Poetry; and all men feel an habitual gratitude, and something of an honorable bigotry for the objects which have long continued to please them: we not only wish to be pleased, but to be pleased in that particular way in which we have been accustomed to be pleased. There is a host of arguments in these feelings; and I should be the less able to combat them successfully, as I am willing to allow that, in order entirely to enjoy the Poetry which I am recommending, it would be necessary to give up much of what is ordinarily enjoyed. But, would my limits have permitted me to point out how this pleasure is produced, I might have removed many obstacles, and assisted my Reader in perceiving that the powers of language are not so limited as he may suppose; and that it is possible that poetry may give other enjoyments, of a purer, more lasting, and more exquisite nature. This part of my subject I have not altogether neglected; but it has been less my present aim to prove that the interest excited by some other kinds of poetry is less vivid, and less worthy of the nobler powers of the mind, than to offer reasons for presuming that, if the object which I have proposed to myself were adequately attained, a species of poetry would be produced which is genuine poetry; in its nature well adapted to interest mankind permanently, and likewise important in the multiplicity and quality of its moral relations.

From what has been said, and from a perusal of the Poems, the Reader will be able clearly to perceive the object which I have proposed to myself: he will determine how far I have attained this object; and, what is a much more important question, whether it be worth attaining; and upon the decision of these two questions will rest my claim to the approbation of the public.

—1800, 1802

---

[1] *numbers* Meter.

[*There was a Boy*]

There was a Boy, ye knew him well, ye Cliffs
And Islands of Winander![1] many a time,
At evening, when the stars began
To move along the edges of the hills,
5   Rising or setting, would he stand alone,
Beneath the trees, or by the glimmering lake,
And there, with fingers interwoven, both hands
Press'd closely palm to palm and to his mouth
Uplifted, he, as through an instrument,
10 Blew mimic hootings to the silent owls
That they might answer him. And they would shout
Across the wat'ry vale and shout again
Responsive to his call, with quivering peals,
And long halloos, and screams, and echoes loud
15 Redoubled and redoubled, a wild scene
Of mirth and jocund din. And, when it chanced
That pauses of deep silence mock'd his skill,
Then, sometimes, in that silence, while he hung
Listening, a gentle shock of mild surprise
20 Has carried far into his heart the voice
Of mountain torrents, or the visible scene
Would enter unawares into his mind
With all its solemn imagery, its rocks,
Its woods, and that uncertain heaven, receiv'd
25 Into the bosom of the steady lake.
        Fair are the woods, and beauteous is the spot,
The vale where he was born: the Church-yard hangs
Upon a slope above the village school,[2]
And there along that bank when I have pass'd
30 At evening, I believe, that near his grave
A full half-hour together I have stood,
Mute—for he died when he was ten years old.
—1800

[*Strange fits of passion I have known*][3]

Strange fits of passion I have known,
And I will dare to tell,
But in the Lover's ear alone,
What once to me befell.

5   When she I lov'd, was strong and gay
And like a rose in June,
I to her cottage bent my way,
Beneath the evening moon.

Upon the moon I fix'd my eye,
10 All over the wide lea;°   meadow
My horse trudg'd on, and we drew nigh
Those paths so dear to me.

And now we reach'd the orchard plot,
And, as we climb'd the hill,
15 Towards the roof of Lucy's cot°   cottage
The moon descended still.

In one of those sweet dreams I slept,
Kind Nature's gentlest boon!
And, all the while, my eyes I kept
20 On the descending moon.

My horse mov'd on; hoof after hoof
He rais'd and never stopp'd:
When down behind the cottage roof
At once the planet dropp'd.

25 What fond and wayward thoughts will slide
Into a Lover's head—
"O mercy!" to myself I cried,
"If Lucy should be dead!"[4]
—1800

---

[1] *Winander* Windermere, the largest lake in England's Lake District.

[2] *the village school* Hawkshead Grammar School in Esthwaite.

[3] *Strange ... known* This and the following two lyrics are part of a group of five lyrics now commonly called the "Lucy poems," all of which were composed during the winter of 1798–99, when Wordsworth and his sister were in Germany. The identity of Lucy is unknown (if she existed at all); she is not the Lucy of Wordsworth's poem *Lucy Gray* (1800). Some critics believe that in these poems Wordsworth attempts to express his feelings for his sister.

[4] *If ... dead* In an earlier manuscript version, another stanza followed: "I told her this: her laughter light / Is ringing in my ears; / And when I think upon that night / My eyes are dim with tears."

WILLIAM WORDSWORTH

Song [She dwelt among th'untrodden ways]

She dwelt among th'untrodden ways
Beside the springs of Dove,[1]
A Maid whom there were none to praise
    And very few to love.

5 A violet by a mossy stone
    Half-hidden from the Eye!
—Fair, as a star when only one
    Is shining in the sky.

She liv'd unknown, and few could know
10   When Lucy ceas'd to be;
But she is in her Grave, and Oh!
    The difference to me.
—1800

[A slumber did my spirit seal][2]

A slumber did my spirit seal,
    I had no human fears:
She seem'd a thing that could not feel
    The touch of earthly years.

5 No motion has she now, no force
    She neither hears nor sees
Roll'd round in earth's diurnal° course   *daily*
    With rocks and stones and trees!
—1800

Lucy Gray[3]

Oft I had heard of Lucy Gray,
    And when I cross'd the Wild,
I chanc'd to see at break of day
    The solitary child.

5 No Mate, no comrade Lucy knew;
    She dwelt on a wide Moor,
The sweetest Thing that ever grew
    Beside a human door!

You yet may spy the Fawn at play,
10   The Hare upon the Green;
But the sweet face of Lucy Gray
    Will never more be seen.

"To-night will be a stormy night,
    You to the Town must go,
15 And take a lantern, Child, to light
    Your Mother thro' the snow."

"That, Father! will I gladly do;
    'Tis scarcely afternoon—
The Minster°-clock has just struck two,   *church*
20   And yonder is the Moon!"

At this the Father rais'd his hook,
    And snapp'd a faggot-band;[4]
He plied his work, and Lucy took
    The lantern in her hand.

25 Not blither° is the mountain roe,   *more merry*
    With many a wanton° stroke   *frolicsome*

[1] *Dove* Name of numerous rivers in England, one of which is in the Lake District.

[2] *A slumber ... seal* Of this poem, Coleridge wrote to a friend in April 1799: "Some months ago Wordsworth transmitted to me a most sublime epitaph. ... Whether it had any reality, I cannot say. Most probably, in some gloomier moment he had fancied the moment in which his sister might die."

[3] *Lucy Gray* Based on an account of a drowned girl told to Wordsworth by his sister. In his note, Wordsworth says that after the girl had become lost in a snowstorm, "her footsteps were traced by her parents to the middle of the lock of a canal, and no other vestige of her, backward or forward, could be traced. The body, however, was found in the canal. The way in which the incident was treated and the spiritualizing of the character might furnish hints for consulting the imaginative influences which I have endeavoured to throw over common life with Crabbe's matter of fact style of treating subjects of the same kind." (Wordsworth refers to the poet George Crabbe [1754–1832].)

[4] *faggot-band* Cord for binding a bundle of firewood.

Her feet disperse the powd'ry snow,
That rises up like smoke.

The storm came on before its time,
30 She wander'd up and down,
And many a hill did Lucy climb:
But never reach'd the Town.

The wretched Parents all that night
Went shouting far and wide;
35 But there was neither sound nor sight
To serve them for a guide.

At day-break on a hill they stood
That overlook'd the Moor;
And thence they saw the Bridge of Wood,
40 A furlong¹ from their door.

And now they homeward turn'd, and cry'd
"In Heaven we all shall meet!"
When in the snow the Mother spied
The print of Lucy's feet.

45 Then downward from the steep hill's edge
They track'd the footmarks small;
And through the broken hawthorn-hedge,
And by the long stone-wall;

And then an open field they cross'd,
50 The marks were still the same;
They track'd them on, nor ever lost,
And to the Bridge they came.

They follow'd from the snowy bank
Those footmarks, one by one,
55 Into the middle of the plank,
And further there were none.

Yet some maintain that to this day
She is a living Child,
That you may see sweet Lucy Gray
60 Upon the lonesome Wild.

O'er rough and smooth she trips along,
And never looks behind;
And sings a solitary song
That whistles in the wind.
—1800

Nutting

It seems a day,
(I speak of one from many singled out)
One of those heavenly days which cannot die,
When forth I sallied from our cottage-door,
5 And with a wallet° o'er my shoulder slung,   knapsack
A nutting crook² in hand, I turn'd my steps
Towards the distant woods, a Figure quaint,
Trick'd out in proud disguise of Beggar's weeds°   garments
Put on for the occasion, by advice
10 And exhortation of my frugal Dame.³
Motley accoutrements! of power to smile
At thorns, and brakes,° and brambles, and,   thickets
  in truth,
More ragged than need was. Among the woods,
And o'er the pathless rocks, I forc'd my way
15 Until, at length, I came to one dear nook
Unvisited, where not a broken bough
Droop'd with its wither'd leaves, ungracious sign
Of devastation, but the hazels rose
Tall and erect, with milk-white clusters hung,
20 A virgin scene!—A little while I stood,
Breathing with such suppression of the heart
As joy delights in; and with wise restraint
Voluptuous, fearless of a rival, eyed
The banquet, or beneath the trees I sat
25 Among the flowers, and with the flowers I play'd;
A temper known to those, who, after long
And weary expectation, have been bless'd
With sudden happiness beyond all hope.
—Perhaps it was a bower beneath whose leaves
30 The violets of five seasons re-appear
And fade, unseen by any human eye,

¹ *furlong* Measurement equal to 220 yards, or one eighth of a mile.

² *nutting crook* Hooked instrument for gathering nuts.

³ *my frugal Dame* Ann Tyson, at whose house Wordsworth boarded during his school years.

Where fairy water-breaks[1] do murmur on
For ever, and I saw the sparkling foam,
And with my cheek on one of those green stones
35 That, fleec'd with moss, beneath the shady trees,
Lay round me scatter'd like a flock of sheep,
I heard the murmur and the murmuring sound,
In that sweet mood when pleasure loves to pay
Tribute to ease, and, of its joy secure
40 The heart luxuriates with indifferent things,
Wasting its kindliness on stocks° and stones,   *stumps*
And on the vacant air. Then up I rose,
And dragg'd to earth both branch and bough, with crash
And merciless ravage; and the shady nook
45 Of hazels, and the green and mossy bower
Deform'd and sullied, patiently gave up
Their quiet being: and unless I now
Confound my present feelings with the past,
Even then, when from the bower I turn'd away,
50 Exulting, rich beyond the wealth of kings
I felt a sense of pain when I beheld
The silent trees and the intruding sky.

Then, dearest Maiden![2] move along these shades
In gentleness of heart with gentle hand
55 Touch—for there is a Spirit in the woods.
—1800

Michael

Wordsworth said this pastoral poem is founded on two real incidents, one of "the son of an old couple having become dissolute, and run away from his parents" and the other of "an old shepherd having been seven years in building up a sheepfold in a solitary valley." In combining these tales, he said in a letter to Thomas Poole, "I have attempted to give a picture of a man of strong mind and lively sensibility, agitated by two of the most powerful affections of the human heart—parental affection and the love of property, landed property, including the feelings of inheritance, home, and personal and family independence." As in his poem "Brothers," Wordsworth writes "with a view to show that men who do not wear fine clothes can feel deeply" and attempts "to draw a picture of the domestic affections, as I know they exist among a class of men who are now almost confined to the north of England. They are small independent proprietors of land, here called 'states-men,' men of respectable education, who daily labor on their own little properties. The domestic affections will always be strong amongst men who live in a country not crowded with population; if these men are placed above poverty. … Their little tract of land serves as a kind of permanent rallying point for their domestic feelings, as a tablet on which they are written, which makes them objects of memory in a thousand instances, when they would otherwise be forgotten."

Michael
A Pastoral Poem

If from the public way you turn your steps
Up the tumultuous brook of Green-head Gill,[3]
You will suppose that with an upright path
Your feet must struggle; in such bold ascent
5 The pastoral Mountains front you, face to face.
But, courage! for beside that boisterous Brook
The mountains have all open'd out themselves,
And made a hidden valley of their own.
No habitation can be seen; but such
10 As journey thither find themselves alone
With a few sheep, with rocks and stones, and kites[4]
That overhead are sailing in the sky.

It is in truth an utter solitude,
Nor should I have made mention of this Dell
15 But for one object which you might pass by,
Might see and notice not. Beside the brook
There is a straggling heap of unhewn stones!
And to that place a story appertains,

---

[1] *water-breaks* Places where the water flow is broken by underlying rocks.

[2] *Maiden* In a longer manuscript draft of the poem, a passage originally intended to lead up to "Nutting" describes a maiden named Lucy ravaging a bower.

[3] *Gill* Steep, narrow valley with a stream running through it. Green-head Gill is near Wordsworth's cottage at Grasmere.

[4] *kites* Small falcon-like birds of prey.

Which, though it be ungarnish'd with events,
20 Is not unfit, I deem, for the fire-side,
Or for the summer shade. It was the first,
The earliest of those tales that spake to me
Of Shepherds, dwellers in the valleys, men
Whom I already lov'd, not verily
25 For their own sakes, but for the fields and hills
Where was their occupation and abode.
And hence this Tale, while I was yet a boy
Careless of books, yet having felt the power
Of Nature, by the gentle agency
30 Of natural objects led me on to feel
For passions that were not my own, and think
At random and imperfectly indeed
On man; the heart of man and human life.
Therefore, although it be a history
35 Homely and rude, I will relate the same
For the delight of a few natural hearts,
And with yet fonder feeling, for the sake
Of youthful Poets, who among these Hills
Will be my second self when I am gone.

40 Upon the Forest-side in Grasmere Vale
There dwelt a Shepherd, Michael was his name,
An old man, stout of heart, and strong of limb.
His bodily frame had been from youth to age
Of an unusual strength: his mind was keen
45 Intense and frugal, apt for all affairs,
And in his Shepherd's calling he was prompt
And watchful more than ordinary men.
Hence he had learn'd the meaning of all winds,
Of blasts of every tone, and often-times
50 When others heeded not, He heard the South[1]
Make subterraneous music, like the noise
Of Bagpipers on distant Highland hills;
The Shepherd, at such warning, of his flock
Bethought him, and he to himself would say
55 The winds are now devising work for me!
And truly at all times the storm, that drives
The Traveller to a shelter, summon'd him
Up to the mountains: he had been alone
Amid the heart of many thousand mists
60 That came to him and left him on the heights.
So liv'd he till his eightieth year was pass'd.

And grossly that man errs, who should suppose
That the green Valleys, and the Streams and Rocks
Were things indifferent to the Shepherd's thoughts.
65 Fields, where with cheerful spirits he had breath'd
The common air; the hills, which he so oft
Had climb'd with vigorous steps; which had impress'd
So many incidents upon his mind
Of hardship, skill or courage, joy or fear;
70 Which like a book preserv'd the memory
Of the dumb animals, whom he had sav'd,
Had fed or shelter'd, linking to such acts,
So grateful in themselves, the certainty
Of honorable gains; these fields, these hills
75 Which were his living Being, even more
Than his own Blood—what could they less? had laid
Strong hold on his affections, were to him
A pleasurable feeling of blind love,
The pleasure which there is in life itself.

80 He had not passed his days in singleness.
He had a Wife, a comely Matron, old
Though younger than himself full twenty years.
She was a woman of a stirring life
Whose heart was in her house: two wheels she had
85 Of antique form, this large for spinning wool,
That small for flax, and if one wheel had rest,
It was because the other was at work.
The Pair had but one Inmate in their house,
An only Child, who had been born to them
90 When Michael telling° o'er his years began   counting
To deem that he was old, in Shepherd's phrase,
With one foot in the grave. This only son,
With two brave sheep dogs tried in many a storm,
The one of an inestimable worth,
95 Made all their Household. I may truly say,
That they were as a proverb in the vale
For endless industry. When day was gone,
And from their occupations out of doors
The Son and Father were come home, even then
100 Their labour did not cease, unless when all
Turn'd to their cleanly supper-board,[2] and there
Each with a mess of pottage[3] and skimm'd milk,
Sat round their basket pil'd with oaten cakes,

---

[1] *South*   South wind.

[2] *supper-board*   Table.

[3] *pottage*   Stew of vegetables, and sometimes meat, boiled in water.

And their plain home-made cheese. Yet when their meal
105   Was ended, LUKE (for so the Son was nam'd)
And his old Father, both betook themselves
To such convenient work, as might employ
Their hands by the fire-side; perhaps to card[1]
Wool for the House-wife's spindle, or repair
110   Some injury done to sickle, flail,[2] or scythe,
Or other implement of house or field.
Down from the ceiling by the chimney's edge,
Which in our ancient uncouth country style
Did with a huge projection overbrow°   *overhang*
115   Large space beneath, as duly as the light
Of day grew dim, the House-wife hung a lamp;
An aged utensil, which had perform'd
Service beyond all others of its kind.
Early at evening did it burn and late,
120   Surviving Comrade of uncounted Hours
Which going by from year to year had found
And left the Couple neither gay perhaps
Nor cheerful, yet with objects and with hopes
Living a life of eager industry.
125   And now, when LUKE was in his eighteenth year,
There by the light of this old lamp they sat,
Father and Son, while late into the night
The House-wife plied her own peculiar work,
Making the cottage thro' the silent hours
130   Murmur as with the sound of summer flies.
Not with a waste of words, but for the sake
Of pleasure, which I know that I shall give
To many living now, I of this Lamp
Speak thus minutely: for there are no few
135   Whose memories will bear witness to my tale.
The Light was famous in its neighbourhood,
And was a public Symbol of the life,
The thrifty Pair had liv'd. For, as it chanc'd,
Their Cottage on a plot of rising ground
140   Stood single, with large prospect North and South,
High into Easedale, up to Dunmal-Raise,
And Westward to the village near the Lake.
And from this constant light so regular
And so far seen, the House itself by all
145   Who dwelt within the limits of the vale,
Both old and young, was nam'd The Evening Star.

---

[1] *card* Comb out impurities.

[2] *flail* Tool for threshing corn.

Thus living on through such a length of years,
The Shepherd, if he lov'd himself, must needs
Have lov'd his Help-mate; but to Michael's heart
150   This Son of his old age was yet more dear—
Effect which might perhaps have been produc'd
By that instinctive tenderness, the same
Blind Spirit, which is in the blood of all,
Or that a child, more than all other gifts,
155   Brings hope with it, and forward-looking thoughts,
And stirrings of inquietude, when they
By tendency of nature needs must fail.
From such, and other causes, to the thoughts
Of the old Man his only Son was now
160   The dearest object that he knew on earth.
Exceeding was the love he bare to him,
His Heart and his Heart's joy! For oftentimes
Old Michael, while he was a babe in arms,
Had done him female service, not alone
165   For dalliance and delight, as is the use
Of Fathers, but with patient mind enforc'd
To acts of tenderness; and he had rock'd
His cradle with a woman's gentle hand.

And in a later time, ere yet the Boy
170   Had put on Boy's attire, did Michael love,
Albeit of a stern unbending mind,
To have the young one in his sight, when he
Had work by his own door, or when he sat
With sheep before him on his Shepherd's stool,
175   Beneath that large old Oak, which near their door
Stood, and from its enormous breadth of shade
Chosen for the Shearer's covert from the sun,
Thence in our rustic dialect was call'd
The CLIPPING° TREE, a name which yet it bears.   *shearing*
180   There, while they two were sitting in the shade,
With others round them, earnest all and blithe,
Would Michael exercise his heart with looks
Of fond correction and reproof bestow'd
Upon the child, if he disturb'd the sheep
185   By catching at their legs, or with his shouts
Scar'd them, while they lay still beneath the shears.
And when by Heaven's good grace the Boy grew up
A healthy Lad, and carried in his cheek
Two steady roses that were five years old,

190 Then Michael from a winter coppice[1] cut
With his own hand a sapling, which he hoop'd
With iron, making it throughout in all
Due requisites a perfect Shepherd's Staff,
And gave it to the Boy; wherewith equipp'd
195 He as a Watchman oftentimes was plac'd
At gate or gap, to stem or turn the flock,
And to his office prematurely call'd
There stood the urchin, as you will divine,
Something between a hindrance and a help,
200 And for this cause not always, I believe,
Receiving from his Father hire of praise.
Though nought was left undone which staff, or voice,
Or looks, or threatening gestures, could perform.
But soon as Luke, full ten years old, could stand
205 Against the mountain blasts, and to the heights,
Not fearing toil, nor length of weary ways,
He with his Father daily went, and they
Were as companions, why should I relate
That objects which the Shepherd loved before
210 Were dearer now? that from the Boy there came
Feelings and emanations, things which were
Light to the sun and music to the wind;
And that the Old Man's heart seemed born again?
Thus in his Father's sight the Boy grew up:
215 And now when he had reached his eighteenth year,
He was his comfort and his daily hope.

While this good household thus were living on
From day to day, to Michael's ear there came
Distressful tidings. Long before the time
220 Of which I speak, the Shepherd had been bound
In surety for his Brother's Son, a man
Of an industrious life, and ample means,
But unforeseen misfortunes suddenly
Had press'd upon him, and old Michael now
225 Was summon'd to discharge the forfeiture,
A grievous penalty, but little less
Than half his substance. This un-look'd for claim
At the first hearing, for a moment took
More hope out of his life than he supposed
230 That any old man ever could have lost.
As soon as he had gather'd so much strength
That he could look his trouble in the face,

It seem'd that his sole refuge was to sell
A portion of his patrimonial fields.
235 Such was his first resolve; he thought again,
And his heart fail'd him. "Isabel," said he,
Two evenings after he had heard the news,
"I have been toiling more than seventy years,
And in the open sunshine of God's love
240 Have we all liv'd, yet if these fields of ours
Should pass into a Stranger's hand, I think
That I could not lie quiet in my grave.
Our lot is a hard lot; the Sun itself
Has scarcely been more diligent than I,
245 And I have liv'd to be a fool at last
To my own family. An evil Man
That was, and made an evil choice, if he
Were false to us; and if he were not false,
There are ten thousand to whom loss like this
250 Had been no sorrow. I forgive him—but
'Twere better to be dumb than to talk thus.
When I began, my purpose was to speak
Of remedies and of a cheerful hope.
Our Luke shall leave us, Isabel; the land
255 Shall not go from us, and it shall be free,[2]
He shall possess it, free as is the wind
That passes over it. We have, thou knowest,
Another Kinsman, he will be our friend
In this distress. He is a prosperous man,
260 Thriving in trade, and Luke to him shall go,
And with his Kinsman's help and his own thrift,
He quickly will repair this loss, and then
May come again to us. If here he stay,
What can be done? Where every one is poor
265 What can be gain'd?" At this, the old man paus'd,
And Isabel sat silent, for her mind
Was busy, looking back into past times.
There's Richard Bateman, thought she to herself,[3]
He was a parish-boy[4]—at the church-door
270 They made a gathering for him, shillings, pence,
And halfpennies, wherewith the Neighbours bought
A Basket, which they fill'd with Pedlar's wares,

---

[1] *coppice* Thicket of small trees.

[2] *free* I.e., not mortgaged.

[3] [Wordsworth's note] The story alluded to here is well known in the country. The chapel is called Ings Chapel and is on the road leading from Kendal to Ambleside.

[4] *parish-boy* Youth cared for and supported by the parish.

And with this Basket on his arm, the Lad
Went up to London, found a Master there,
275 Who out of many chose the trusty Boy
To go and overlook his merchandise
Beyond the seas, where he grew wond'rous rich,
And left estates and monies to the poor,
And at his birth-place built a Chapel, floor'd
280 With Marble, which he sent from foreign lands.
These thoughts, and many others of like sort,
Pass'd quickly thro' the mind of Isabel,
And her face brighten'd. The Old Man was glad,
And thus resum'd. "Well! Isabel, this scheme
285 These two days has been meat and drink to me.
Far more than we have lost is left us yet.
—We have enough—I wish indeed that I
Were younger, but this hope is a good hope.
—Make ready Luke's best garments, of the best
290 Buy for him more, and let us send him forth
To-morrow, or the next day, or to-night:
—If he could go, the Boy should go to-night."

Here Michael ceas'd, and to the fields went forth
With a light heart. The House-wife for five days
295 Was restless morn and night, and all day long
Wrought on with her best fingers to prepare
Things needful for the journey of her Son.
But Isabel was glad when Sunday came
To stop her in her work; for, when she lay
300 By Michael's side, she for the last two nights
Heard him, how he was troubled in his sleep:
And when they rose at morning she could see
That all his hopes were gone. That day at noon
She said to Luke, while they two by themselves
305 Were sitting at the door, "Thou must not go,
We have no other Child but thee to lose,
None to remember—do not go away,
For if thou leave thy Father he will die."
The Lad made answer with a jocund voice,
310 And Isabel, when she had told her fears,
Recover'd heart. That evening her best fare
Did she bring forth, and all together sat
Like happy people round a Christmas fire.
Next morning Isabel resum'd her work,
315 And all the ensuing week the house appear'd
As cheerful as a grove in Spring: at length

The expected letter from their Kinsman came,
With kind assurances that he would do
His utmost for the welfare of the Boy,
320 To which requests were added that forthwith
He might be sent to him. Ten times or more
The letter was read over; Isabel
Went forth to shew it to the neighbours round:
Nor was there at that time on English land
325 A prouder heart than Luke's. When Isabel
Had to her house return'd, the Old Man said,
"He shall depart to-morrow." To this word
The House-wife answered, talking much of things
Which, if at such short notice he should go,
330 Would surely be forgotten. But at length
She gave consent, and Michael was at ease.

Near the tumultuous brook of Green-head Gill,
In that deep Valley, Michael had design'd
To build a Sheep-fold,[1] and, before he heard
335 The tidings of his melancholy loss,
For this same purpose he had gathered up
A heap of stones, which close to the brook side
Lay thrown together, ready for the work.
With Luke that evening thitherward he walk'd;
340 And soon as they had reach'd the place he stopp'd,
And thus the Old Man spake to him. "My Son,
To-morrow thou wilt leave me; with full heart
I look upon thee, for thou art the same
That wert a promise to me ere thy birth,
345 And all thy life hast been my daily joy.
I will relate to thee some little part
Of our two histories; 'twill do thee good
When thou art from me, even if I should speak
Of things thou canst not know of.——After thou
350 First cam'st into the world, as it befalls
To new-born infants, thou didst sleep away
Two days, and blessings from thy Father's tongue
Then fell upon thee. Day by day pass'd on,
And still I lov'd thee with encreasing love.
355 Never to living ear came sweeter sounds
Than when I heard thee by our own fire-side
First uttering without words a natural tune,
When thou, a feeding babe, didst in thy joy
Sing at thy Mother's breast. Month follow'd month,

---

[1] *Sheep-fold* Stone-walled pen for sheep.

360 And in the open fields my life was pass'd
And in the mountains, else I think that thou
Hadst been brought up upon thy father's knees.
—But we were playmates, Luke; among these hills,
As well thou know'st, in us the old and young
365 Have play'd together, nor with me didst thou
Lack any pleasure which a boy can know."

Luke had a manly heart; but at these words
He sobb'd aloud; the Old Man grasp'd his hand,
And said, "Nay, do not take it so—I see
370 That these are things of which I need not speak.
—Even to the utmost I have been to thee
A kind and a good Father: and herein
I but repay a gift which I myself
Receiv'd at others hands, for, though now old
375 Beyond the common life of man, I still
Remember them who lov'd me in my youth.
Both of them sleep together: here they liv'd
As all their Forefathers had done, and when
At length their time was come, they were not loth
380 To give their bodies to the family mold.
I wish'd that thou should'st live the life they liv'd.
But 'tis a long time to look back, my Son,
And see so little gain from sixty years.
These fields were burthen'd° when they   *mortgaged*
                came to me;
385 'Till I was forty years of age, not more
Than half of my inheritance was mine.
I toil'd and toil'd; God bless'd me in my work,
And 'till these three weeks past the land was free.
—It looks as if it never could endure
390 Another Master. Heaven forgive me, Luke,
If I judge ill for thee, but it seems good
That thou should'st go." At this the Old Man paus'd,
Then, pointing to the Stones near which they stood,
Thus, after a short silence, he resum'd:
395 "This was a work for us; and now, my Son,
It is a work for me. But, lay one Stone—
Here, lay it for me, Luke, with thine own hands.
Nay, Boy, be of good hope: we both may live
To see a better day. At eighty-four
400 I still am strong and stout; do thou thy part,
I will do mine. I will begin again
With many tasks that were resign'd to thee;

Up to the heights, and in among the storms,
Will I without thee go again, and do
405 All works which I was wont to do alone,
Before I knew thy face. Heaven bless thee, Boy!
Thy heart these two weeks has been beating fast
With many hopes—it should be so—yes—yes—
I knew that thou could'st never have a wish
410 To leave me, Luke, thou hast been bound to me
Only by links of love, when thou art gone
What will be left to us! But, I forget
My purposes. Lay now the corner-stone,
As I requested, and hereafter, Luke,
415 When thou art gone away, should evil men
Be thy companions, let this Sheep-fold be
Thy anchor and thy shield; amid all fear
And all temptation, let it be to thee
An emblem of the life thy Fathers liv'd,
420 Who, being innocent, did for that cause
Bestir them in good deeds. Now, fare thee well—
When thou return'st, thou in this place wilt see
A work which is not here, a covenant
'Twill be between us——but whatever fate
425 Befall thee, I shall love thee to the last,
And bear thy memory with me to the grave."

The Shepherd ended here; and Luke stoop'd down,
And as his Father had requested, laid
The first stone of the Sheep-fold; at the sight
430 The Old Man's grief broke from him, to his heart
He press'd his Son, he kissed him and wept;
And to the House together they return'd.
Next morning, as had been resolv'd, the Boy
Began his journey, and when he had reach'd
435 The public Way, he put on a bold face;
And all the Neighbours as he pass'd their doors
Came forth, with wishes and with farewell pray'rs,
That follow'd him 'till he was out of sight.
A good report did from their Kinsman come,
440 Of Luke and his well-doing; and the Boy
Wrote loving letters, full of wond'rous news,
Which, as the House-wife phrased it, were throughout
The prettiest letters that were ever seen.
Both parents read them with rejoicing hearts.
445 So, many months pass'd on: and once again
The Shepherd went about his daily work

With confident and cheerful thoughts; and now
Sometimes when he could find a leisure hour
He to that valley took his way, and there
450 Wrought at the Sheep-fold. Meantime Luke began
To slacken in his duty, and at length
He in the dissolute city gave himself
To evil courses: ignominy and shame
Fell on him, so that he was driven at last
455 To seek a hiding-place beyond the seas.

There is a comfort in the strength of love;
'Twill make a thing endurable, which else
Would break the heart: Old Michael found it so.
I have convers'd with more than one who well
460 Remember the Old Man, and what he was
Years after he had heard this heavy news.
His bodily frame had been from youth to age
Of an unusual strength. Among the rocks
He went, and still look'd up upon the sun,
465 And listen'd to the wind; and as before
Perform'd all kinds of labour for his Sheep,
And for the land his small inheritance.
And to that hollow Dell from time to time
Did he repair, to build the Fold of which
470 His flock had need. 'Tis not forgotten yet
The pity which was then in every heart
For the Old Man—and 'tis believ'd by all
That many and many a day he thither went,
And never lifted up a single stone.

475 There, by the Sheep-fold, sometimes was he seen
Sitting alone, with that his faithful Dog,
Then old, beside him, lying at his feet.
The length of full seven years from time to time
He at the building of this Sheep-fold wrought,
480 And left the work unfinished when he died.

Three years, or little more, did Isabel,
Survive her Husband: at her death the estate
Was sold, and went into a Stranger's hand.
The Cottage which was nam'd The Evening Star
485 Is gone, the ploughshare has been through the ground
On which it stood; great changes have been wrought
In all the neighbourhood, yet the Oak is left
That grew beside their Door; and the remains

Of the unfinished Sheep-fold may be seen
490 Beside the boisterous brook of Green-head Gill.
—1800 (PREFACE REVISED IN 1802)

[*I griev'd for Buonaparté*][1]

I griev'd for Buonaparté, with a vain
And an unthinking grief! the vital blood
Of that Man's mind what can it be? What food
Fed his first hopes? What knowledge could *He* gain?
5 'Tis not in battles that from youth we train
The Governor who must be wise and good,
And temper with the sternness of the brain
Thoughts motherly, and meek as womanhood.
Wisdom doth live with children round her knees:
10 Books, leisure, perfect freedom, and the talk
Man holds with week-day man in the hourly walk
Of the mind's business: these are the degrees
By which true Sway doth mount; this is the stalk
True Power doth grow on; and her rights are these.
—1802

Ode to Duty

Stern Daughter of the Voice of God![2]
O Duty! if that name thou love
Who art a Light to guide, a Rod
To check the erring, and reprove;
5 Thou, who art victory and law
When empty terrors overawe;
From vain temptations dost set free;
From strife and from despair; a glorious ministry.

There are who ask not if thine eye
10 Be on them; who, in love and truth,
Where no misgiving is, rely

---

[1] *I ... Buonaparté* According to Dorothy Wordsworth, this sonnet was composed in 1802, the year that Napoleon Bonaparte declared himself First Consul of France for life.

[2] *Stern ... God* Cf. Milton, *Paradise Lost* 9.652–54: "God so commanded, and left that Command / Sole Daughter of His voice; the rest, we live / Law to ourselves, our Reason is our Law."

Upon the genial° sense° of youth: *natural / vitality*
Glad Hearts! without reproach or blot;
Who do thy work, and know it not:
15 May joy be theirs while life shall last!
And Thou, if they should totter, teach them to stand
    fast!

Serene will be our days and bright,
And happy will our nature be,
When love is an unerring light,
20 And joy its own security.
And bless'd are they who in the main
This faith, even now, do entertain:
Live in the spirit of this creed;
Yet find that other strength, according to their need.

25 I, loving freedom, and untried;
No sport of every random gust,
Yet being to myself a guide,
Too blindly have reposed my trust:
Resolved that nothing e'er should press
30 Upon my present happiness,
I shoved unwelcome tasks away;
But thee I now would serve more strictly, if I may.

Through no disturbance of my soul,
Or strong compunction in me wrought,
35 I supplicate for thy control;
But in the quietness of thought:
Me this uncharter'd freedom tires;
I feel the weight of chance desires:
My hopes no more must change their name,
40 I long for a repose that ever is the same.

Yet not the less would I throughout
Still act according to the voice
Of my own wish; and feel past doubt
That my submissiveness was choice:
45 Not seeking in the school of pride
For "precepts over dignified,"
Denial and restraint I prize
No farther than they breed a second Will more wise.

Stern Lawgiver! yet thou dost wear
50 The Godhead's most benignant grace;

Nor know we anything so fair
As is the smile upon thy face:
Flowers laugh before thee on their beds;
And Fragrance in thy footing treads;
55 Thou dost preserve the Stars from wrong;
And the most ancient Heavens, through Thee are fresh
    and strong.

To humbler functions, awful Power!
I call thee: I myself commend
Unto thy guidance from this hour;
60 Oh! let my weakness have an end!
Give unto me, made lowly wise,
The spirit of self-sacrifice;
The confidence of reason give;
And in the light of truth thy Bondman let me live!
—1807

Resolution and Independence

There was a roaring in the wind all night;
  The rain came heavily and fell in floods;
But now the sun is rising calm and bright;
The birds are singing in the distant woods;
5 Over his own sweet voice the Stock-dove°   *wild pigeon*
    broods;
The Jay makes answer as the Magpie chatters;
And all the air is fill'd with pleasant noise of waters.

All things that love the sun are out of doors;
The sky rejoices in the morning's birth;
10 The grass is bright with rain-drops; on the moors
The Hare is running races in her mirth;
And with her feet she from the plashy[1] earth
Raises a mist; which, glittering in the sun,
Runs with her all the way, wherever she doth run.

15 I was a Traveller then upon the moor;
I saw the Hare that rac'd about with joy;
I heard the woods, and distant waters, roar;
Or heard them not, as happy as a Boy:
The pleasant season did my heart employ:

---

[1] *plashy* Having many puddles or pools of water; wet.

20   My old remembrances went from me wholly;
     And all the ways of men, so vain and melancholy.

     But, as it sometimes chanceth, from the might
     Of joy in minds that can no farther go,
     As high as we have mounted in delight
25   In our dejection do we sink as low,
     To me that morning did it happen so;
     And fears, and fancies, thick upon me came;
     Dim sadness, and blind thoughts I knew not nor could
         name.

     I heard the Sky-lark singing in the sky;
30   And I bethought me of the playful Hare:
     Even such a happy Child of earth am I;
     Even as these blissful Creatures do I fare;
     Far from the world I walk, and from all care;
     But there may come another day to me,
35   Solitude, pain of heart, distress, and poverty.

     My whole life I have liv'd in pleasant thought,
     As if life's business were a summer mood;
     As if all needful things would come unsought
     To genial faith, still rich in genial good;
40   But how can He expect that others should
     Build for him, sow for him, and at his call
     Love him, who for himself will take no heed at all?

     I thought of Chatterton,[1] the marvellous Boy,
     The sleepless Soul that perish'd in its pride;
45   Of Him who walk'd in glory and in joy
     Behind his plough, upon the mountain-side:[2]
     By our own spirits are we deified;
     We Poets in our youth begin in gladness;
     But thereof comes in the end despondency and
         madness.

50   Now, whether it were by peculiar grace,
     A leading from above, a something given,

---

1   *Chatterton* Poet Thomas Chatterton (1752–70), who, after
failing to make a living as a poet in London, poisoned himself at the
age of seventeen.

2   *Him who … mountain-side* Scottish poet Robert Burns (1759–
96), known as "the Ploughman Poet" because of his farming
background.

Yet it befel, that, in this lonely place,
When up and down my fancy thus was driven,
And I with these untoward thoughts had striven,
55   I saw a Man before me unawares:
     The oldest man he seem'd that ever wore grey hairs.

My course I stopped as soon as I espied
The Old Man in that naked wilderness:
Close by a Pond, upon the further side,
60   He stood alone: a minute's space I guess
     I watch'd him, he continuing motionless:
     To the Pool's further margin then I drew;
     He being all the while before me full in view.

As a huge Stone is sometimes seen to lie
65   Couch'd on the bald top of an eminence;
     Wonder to all who do the same espy
     By what means it could thither come, and whence;
     So that it seems a thing endued with sense:
     Like a Sea-beast crawl'd forth, which on a shelf
70   Of rock or sand reposeth, there to sun itself.

Such seem'd this Man, not all alive nor dead,
Nor all asleep; in his extreme old age:
His body was bent double, feet and head
Coming together in their pilgrimage;
75   As if some dire constraint of pain, or rage
     Of sickness felt by him in times long past,
     A more than human weight upon his frame had cast.

Himself he propp'd, his body, limbs, and face,
Upon a long grey Staff of shaven wood:
80   And, still as I drew near with gentle pace,
     Beside the little pond or moorish flood
     Motionless as a Cloud the Old Man stood;
     That heareth not the loud winds when they call;
     And moveth altogether, if it move at all.

85   At length, himself unsettling, he the Pond
     Stirred with his Staff, and fixedly did look
     Upon the muddy water, which he conn'd,°   *studied*
     As if he had been reading in a book:
     And now such freedom as I could I took;
90   And, drawing to his side, to him did say,
     "This morning gives us promise of a glorious day."

A gentle answer did the Old Man make,
In courteous speech which forth he slowly drew:
And him with further words I thus bespake,
95 "What kind of work is that which you pursue?
This is a lonesome place for one like you."
He answer'd me with pleasure and surprise;
And there was, while he spake, a fire about his eyes.

His words came feebly, from a feeble chest,
100 Yet each in solemn order follow'd each,
With something of a lofty utterance drest;
Choice word, and measured phrase; above the reach
Of ordinary men; a stately speech!
Such as grave Livers[1] do in Scotland use,
105 Religious men, who give to God and Man their dues.

He told me that he to this pond had come
To gather Leeches,[2] being old and poor:
Employment hazardous and wearisome!
And he had many hardships to endure:
110 From Pond to Pond he roam'd, from moor to moor,
Housing, with God's good help, by choice or chance:
And in this way he gain'd an honest maintenance.

The old Man still stood talking by my side;
But now his voice to me was like a stream
115 Scarce heard; nor word from word could I divide;
And the whole Body of the man did seem
Like one whom I had met with in a dream;
Or like a Man from some far region sent;
To give me human strength, and strong admonishment.

120 My former thoughts return'd: the fear that kills;
The hope that is unwilling to be fed;
Cold, pain, and labour, and all fleshly ills;
And mighty Poets in their misery dead.
And now, not knowing what the Old Man had said,
125 My question eagerly did I renew,
"How is it that you live, and what is it you do?"

He with a smile did then his words repeat;
And said that, gathering Leeches, far and wide
He travelled; stirring thus about his feet
130 The waters of the Ponds where they abide.
"Once I could meet with them on every side;
But they have dwindled long by slow decay;
Yet still I persevere, and find them where I may."

While he was talking thus, the lonely place,
135 The Old Man's shape, and speech, all troubled me:
In my mind's eye I seem'd to see him pace
About the weary moors continually,
Wandering about alone and silently.
While I these thoughts within myself pursued,
140 He, having made a pause, the same discourse renewed.

And soon with this he other matter blended,
Cheerfully uttered, with demeanour kind,
But stately in the main; and, when he ended,
I could have laugh'd myself to scorn, to find
145 In that decrepit Man so firm a mind.
"God," said I, "be my help and stay° secure;   support
I'll think of the Leech-gatherer on the lonely moor."
—1807

Composed upon Westminster Bridge
Sept. 3, 1803[3]

Earth has not any thing to show more fair:
Dull would he be of soul who could pass by
A sight so touching in its majesty:
This City now doth like a garment wear
5 This beauty of the morning; silent, bare,
Ships, towers, domes, theatres, and temples lie
Open unto the fields, and to the sky;
All bright and glittering in the smokeless air.
Never did sun more beautifully steep
10 In his first splendor valley, rock, or hill;
Ne'er saw I, never felt, a calm so deep!

---

[1] grave Livers I.e., those who live seriously.

[2] Leeches Used at this time by doctors for drawing the blood of patients. A leech gatherer would find leeches by standing in shallow water and allowing them to attach themselves to his legs.

[3] Composed ... 1803 Wordsworth misremembered the date of composition, which was actually (according to Dorothy Wordsworth's Grasmere Journals) 1802, when Wordsworth took a brief trip to France, where his former lover Annette Vallon lived with their daughter, Caroline.

The river glideth at his own sweet will:
Dear God! the very houses seem asleep;
And all that mighty heart is lying still!
—1807

[The world is too much with us]

The world is too much with us; late and soon,
  Getting and spending, we lay waste our powers:
Little we see in nature that is ours;
We have given our hearts away, a sordid boon!
5 The Sea that bares her bosom to the moon;
The Winds that will be howling at all hours
And are up-gathered now like sleeping flowers;
For this, for every thing, we are out of tune;
It moves us not. Great God! I'd rather be
10 A Pagan suckled in a creed outworn;
So might I, standing on this pleasant lea,
Have glimpses that would make me less forlorn;
Have sight of Proteus coming from the sea;
Or hear old Triton blow his wreathed horn.[1]
—1807

[It is a beauteous Evening]

It is a beauteous Evening, calm and free;
  The holy time is quiet as a Nun
Breathless with adoration; the broad sun
Is sinking down in its tranquillity;
5 The gentleness of heaven is on the Sea:
Listen! the mighty Being is awake
And doth with his eternal motion make
A sound like thunder—everlastingly.
Dear Child! dear Girl![2] that walkest with me here,
10 If thou appear'st untouch'd by solemn thought,
Thy nature is not therefore less divine:
Thou liest in Abraham's bosom[3] all the year;

---

[1] Proteus Shape-changing sea god; Triton … horn Sea god with the head and torso of a man and the tail of a fish. He was usually depicted blowing on a conch shell.

[2] Dear … Girl Wordsworth's daughter Caroline.

[3] Abraham's bosom The resting place for souls bound for heaven. See Luke 16.22: "And it came to pass, that the beggar died, and was carried by the angels into Abraham's bosom."

And worshipp'st at the Temple's inner shrine,
God being with thee when we know it not.
—1807

London
1802[4]

Milton! thou should'st be living at this hour:
  England hath need of thee: she is a fen
Of stagnant waters: altar, sword, and pen,
Fireside, the heroic wealth of hall and bower,
5 Have forfeited their ancient English dower
Of inward happiness. We are selfish men;
Oh! raise us up, return to us again;
And give us manners, virtue, freedom, power.
Thy soul was like a Star and dwelt apart:
10 Thou hadst a voice whose sound was like the sea;
Pure as the naked heavens, majestic, free,
So didst thou travel on life's common way,
In cheerful godliness; and yet thy heart
The lowliest duties on itself did lay.
—1807

The Solitary Reaper[5]

Behold her, single in the field,
  Yon solitary Highland Lass!
Reaping and singing by herself;
Stop here, or gently pass!
5 Alone she cuts, and binds the grain,
And sings a melancholy strain;
O listen! for the Vale profound
Is overflowing with the sound.

---

[4] London, 1802 Written immediately after Wordsworth's return from France, when he was struck by the differences between his native country and France after the Revolution. Milton died in 1674.

[5] The Solitary Reaper Suggested by the following passage in Thomas Wilkinson's Tours to the British Mountains (1824): "Passed a female who was reaping alone: she sung in Erse [a Gaelic language] as she bended over her sickle; the sweetest human voice I ever heard: her strains were tenderly melancholy, and felt delicious, long after they were heard no more."

No Nightingale did ever chaunt
10 So sweetly to reposing bands
Of Travellers in some shady haunt,
Among Arabian Sands:
No sweeter voice was ever heard
In spring-time from the Cuckoo-bird,
15 Breaking the silence of the seas
Among the farthest Hebrides.

Will no one tell me what she sings?
Perhaps the plaintive numbers° flow   *verses*
For old, unhappy, far-off things,
20 And battles long ago:
Or is it some more humble lay,
Familiar matter of today?
Some natural sorrow, loss, or pain,
That has been, and may be again!

25 Whate'er the theme, the Maiden sang
As if her song could have no ending;
I saw her singing at her work,

And o'er the sickle bending;
I listen'd till I had my fill:
30 And, as I mounted up the hill,
The music in my heart I bore,
Long after it was heard no more.
—1807

[*My heart leaps up*]

My heart leaps up when I behold
A Rainbow in the sky:
So was it when my life began;
So is it now I am a Man;
5 So be it when I shall grow old,
        Or let me die!
The Child is Father of the Man;
And I could wish my days to be
Bound each to each by natural piety.
—1804

In Context

"I wandered lonely as a Cloud": Stages in the Life of a Poem

The earliest version of this poem was composed in 1804 and first published in 1807. It was evidently inspired by an entry in Dorothy Wordsworth's journal from two years earlier, describing a scene at Glencoyne Bay, Ullswater, observed by Dorothy and William on their way back to Grasmere after a long ramble. Appearing below are the scene as described by Dorothy in the journal; William's first version of the poem; a facsimile copy of the page in the copy of *Poems in Two Volumes* in which William began to compose an additional stanza to the poem; a transcription of his handwritten jottings; and William's revised version, with the added stanza and some other changes (which was not published until 1815).

from Dorothy Wordsworth, *Grasmere Journal* (Thursday, 15 April 1802)

When we were in the woods beyond Gowbarrow park we saw a few daffodils close to the water side. We fancied that the lake had floated the seeds ashore and that the little colony had so sprung up. But as we went along there were more and yet more and at last under the boughs of the trees, we saw that there was a long belt of them along the shore, about the breadth of a country turnpike road. I never saw daffodils so beautiful. They grew among the mossy stones about and about them, some rested their heads upon these stones as on a pillow for weariness and the rest tossed and reeled and danced and seemed as if they verily laughed with the wind that blew upon them over the lake, they looked so gay ever glancing ever changing. This wind blew directly over the lake to them. There was here and there a little knot and a few stragglers a few yards higher up but they were so few as not to disturb the simplicity and unity and life of that one busy highway.

[I wandered lonely as a Cloud]

I wandered lonely as a Cloud
That floats on high o'er Vales and Hills,
When all at once I saw a crowd
A host of dancing Daffodils;
5   Along the Lake, beneath the trees,
Ten thousand dancing in the breeze.

The waves beside them danced, but they
Outdid the sparkling waves in glee—
A Poet could not but be gay
10   In such a laughing company:
I gazed—and gaz'd—but little thought
What wealth the show to me had brought:

For oft when on my couch I lie
In vacant or in pensive mood,
15   They flash upon that inward eye
Which is the bliss of solitude,
And then my heart with pleasure fills,
And dances with the Daffodils.
—1807

I wandered lonely as a cloud[1]

l

A host of golden Daffodi ls
Beside
~~Along~~ *the Lake beneath the trees*
                              vernal
All dancing ~~dancing~~ *in the breeze*
  Continuous

              ⎧ *ed*
~~Close crowd~~⎨*ing, [?like]*
              ⎩
~~As numerous~~ ^*as the stars that shine*
  and twinkle

            on⎫
At midnight, in⎨ *the milky way*
            ⎭

                    a⎫
They stretch'd ⎨*in*⎬ *never ending line*
                    ⎭
Along the margin of a bay
Ten thousand saw I at a glance
Tossing their heads in spritely dance

[I wandered lonely as a Cloud]

I wandered lonely as a cloud
  That floats on high o'er vales and hills,
When all at once I saw a crowd,
A host, of golden daffodils;
5   Beside the lake, beneath the trees,
Fluttering and dancing in the breeze.

Continuous as the stars that shine
And twinkle on the milky way,
They stretched in never-ending line
10   Along the margin of a bay:
Ten thousand saw I at a glance,
Tossing their heads in sprightly dance.

The waves beside them danced, but they
Outdid the sparkling waves in glee:
15   A poet could not but be gay,
In such a jocund company;
I gazed—and gazed—but little thought
What wealth the show to me had brought:

For oft, when on my couch I lie
20   In vacant or in pensive mood,
They flash upon that inward eye
Which is the bliss of solitude;
And then my heart with pleasure fills,
And dances with the daffodils.
—1815

---

[1] *I wandered ... cloud* Transcription of Wordsworth's manuscript
(see previous page for facsimile).

Elegiac Stanzas

Suggested by a Picture of Peele Castle, in a Storm, painted by Sir George Beaumont[1]

I was thy Neighbour once, thou rugged Pile!°   *castle*
   Four summer weeks I dwelt in sight of thee:
I saw thee every day; and all the while
Thy Form was sleeping on a glassy sea.

5 So pure the sky, so quiet was the air!
So like, so very like, was day to day!
Whene'er I look'd, thy Image still was there;
It trembled, but it never pass'd away.

How perfect was the calm! it seem'd no sleep;
10 No mood, which season takes away, or brings:
I could have fancied that the mighty Deep
Was even the gentlest of all gentle Things.

Ah! THEN, if mine had been the Painter's hand,
To express what then I saw; and add the gleam,
15 The light that never was, on sea or land,
The consecration, and the Poet's dream;

I would have planted thee, thou hoary Pile!
Amid a world how different from this!
Beside a sea that could not cease to smile;
20 On tranquil land, beneath a sky of bliss:

Thou shouldst have seem'd a treasure-house, a mine
Of peaceful years; a chronicle of heaven—
Of all the sunbeams that did ever shine
The very sweetest had to thee been given.

25 A Picture had it been of lasting ease,
Elysian[2] quiet, without toil or strife;
No motion but the moving tide, a breeze,
Or merely silent Nature's breathing life.

Such, in the fond delusion of my heart,
30 Such Picture would I at that time have made:
And seen the soul of truth in every part;
A faith, a trust, that could not be betray'd.

So once it would have been—'tis so no more;
I have submitted to a new control:
35 A power is gone, which nothing can restore;
A deep distress hath humaniz'd my Soul.

Not for a moment could I now behold
A smiling sea and be what I have been:
The feeling of my loss will ne'er be old;
40 This, which I know, I speak with mind serene.

Then, Beaumont, Friend! who would have been the
    Friend,
If he had lived, of Him whom I deplore,°   *mourn*
This Work of thine I blame not, but commend;
This sea in anger, and that dismal shore.

45 Oh 'tis a passionate Work!—yet wise and well;
Well chosen is the spirit that is here;
That Hulk which labours in the deadly swell,
This rueful sky, this pageantry of fear!

And this huge Castle, standing here sublime,
50 I love to see the look with which it braves,
Cased in the unfeeling armour of old time,
The light'ning, the fierce wind, and trampling waves.

Farewell, farewell the Heart that lives alone,
Hous'd in a dream, at distance from the Kind![3]
55 Such happiness, wherever it be known,
Is to be pitied; for 'tis surely blind.

---

[1] *Suggested by ... Beaumont* In 1794, Wordsworth spent a month in Rampside, Lancashire, which is located across the Morecambe Bay from the Furness Peninsula, where the ruins of Peele Castle stand. In 1806 he saw the two pictures of this castle that had been painted by Sir George Beaumont, a landscape painter who was Wordsworth's friend and patron. Wordsworth's youngest brother, a captain with the East India Company, drowned when his ship sank off the Bill of Portland in February 1805.

[2] *Elysian* Blissful. Referring to Elysium, where, according to classical mythology, the blessed reside after death.

[3] *Kind* Human race.

But welcome fortitude, and patient cheer,
And frequent sights of what is to be born!
Such sights, or worse, as are before me here.
60 Not without hope we suffer and we mourn.
—1807

Ode
[Intimations of Immortality]

In an 1843 letter to Isabella Fenwick, Wordsworth
explained the experiences from his own life on
which this ode is based, saying, "Nothing was more
difficult for me in childhood than to admit the
notion of death as a state applicable to my own
being.... I used to brood over the stories of Enoch
and Elijah, and almost to persuade myself that,
whatever might become of others, I should be
translated, in something of the same way, to heaven.
With a feeling congenial to this, I was often unable
to think of external things as having external existence, and I communed with all that I saw as something not apart from, but inherent in, my own
immaterial nature. Many times while going to
school have I grasped at a wall or tree to recall
myself from this abyss of idealism to the reality. At
that time I was afraid of such processes. In later
periods of life I have deplored, as we have all reason
to do, a subjugation of an opposite character, and
have rejoiced over the remembrances, as is expressed
in the lines—

> Obstinate questionings
> Of sense and outward things,
> Fallings from us, vanishings; etc."[1]

Wordsworth wrote the first four stanzas of the poem
in 1802, and two years elapsed before he completed
the poem in 1804. In 1815 he changed the title to
"Ode: Intimations of Immortality from Recollections of Early Childhood," its more common title
today. He also replaced the Latin epigram from
Virgil with the last three lines from "My heart leaps

up": "The Child is Father to the Man: / And I could
wish my days to be / Bound each to each by natural
piety."

Ode
[Intimations of Immortality
from Recollections of Early Childhood]

Paulo majora canamus.[2]

There was a time when meadow, grove, and stream,
  The earth, and every common sight,
      To me did seem
      Apparelled in celestial light,
5 The glory and the freshness of a dream.
It is not now as it has been of yore;—
      Turn wheresoe'er I may,
        By night or day,
The things which I have seen I now can see no more.

10   The Rainbow comes and goes,
        And lovely is the Rose,
        The Moon doth with delight
Look round her when the heavens are bare;
        Waters on a starry night
15   Are beautiful and fair;
    The sunshine is a glorious birth;
    But yet I know, where'er I go,
That there hath passed away a glory from the earth.

Now, while the Birds thus sing a joyous song,
20   And while the young Lambs bound
        As to the tabor's[3] sound,
To me alone there came a thought of grief:
A timely utterance gave that thought relief,
        And I again am strong.
25 The Cataracts blow their trumpets from the steep,
No more shall grief of mine the season wrong;
I hear the Echoes through the mountains throng,

---

[1] *Obstinate ... etc.* Lines 141–43.

[2] *Paulo majora canamus* Latin: "Let us sing of loftier things." From
Virgil's Fourth Eclogue.

[3] *tabor* Small drum.

The Winds come to me from the fields of sleep,
    And all the earth is gay,
30   Land and sea
Give themselves up to jollity,
    And with the heart of May
Doth every Beast keep holiday,
    Thou Child of Joy
35 Shout round me, let me hear thy shouts, thou happy
    Shepherd Boy!

Ye blessed Creatures, I have heard the call
    Ye to each other make; I see
The heavens laugh with you in your jubilee;
    My heart is at your festival,
40   My head hath it's coronal,°   *wreath*
The fullness of your bliss, I feel—I feel it all.
    Oh evil day! if I were sullen
    While Earth herself is adorning,
    This sweet May-morning,
45   And the Children are pulling,
        On every side,
    In a thousand valleys far and wide,
    Fresh flowers; while the sun shines warm,
And the Babe leaps up on his mother's arm:—
50   I hear, I hear, with joy I hear!
    —But there's a Tree, of many one,
A single Field which I have looked upon,
Both of them speak of something that is gone:
    The Pansy at my feet
55   Doth the same tale repeat:
Whither is fled the visionary gleam?
Where is it now, the glory and the dream?

Our birth is but a sleep and a forgetting:
The Soul that rises with us, our life's Star,
60   Hath had elsewhere it's setting,
    And cometh from afar:
    Not in entire forgetfulness,
    And not in utter nakedness,
But trailing clouds of glory do we come
65   From God, Who is our home:
Heaven lies about us in our infancy!
Shades of the prison-house begin to close

    Upon the growing Boy,
But he beholds the light, and whence it flows,
70   He sees it in his joy;
The Youth, who daily farther from the East
    Must travel, still is Nature's Priest,
    And by the vision splendid
    Is on his way attended;
75 At length the Man perceives it die away,
And fade into the light of common day.

Earth fills her lap with pleasures of her own;
Yearnings she hath in her own natural kind,
And, even with something of a Mother's mind,
80   And no unworthy aim,
    The homely° Nurse doth all she can   *simple*
To make her Foster-child, her Inmate Man,
    Forget the glories he hath known,
And that imperial palace whence he came.
85 Behold the Child among his new-born blisses,
A four year's Darling of a pigmy size!
See, where 'mid work of his own hand he lies,
Fretted by sallies of his Mother's kisses,
With light upon him from his Father's eyes!
90 See, at his feet, some little plan or chart,
Some fragment from his dream of human life,
Shaped by himself with newly-learned art;
    A wedding or a festival,
    A mourning or a funeral;
95   And this hath now his heart,
    And unto this he frames his song:
    Then will he fit his tongue
To dialogues of business, love, or strife;
    But it will not be long
100   Ere this be thrown aside,
    And with new joy and pride
The little Actor cons another part,
Filling from time to time his "humourous stage"[1]
With all the Persons, down to palsied Age,
105 That Life brings with her in her Equipage;

---

[1] *humourous stage* From Elizabethan poet Samuel Daniel's *Muso-philus* (1599), in reference to the different character types (defined by their dominant temperaments, or "humors") depicted in Renaissance drama.

As if his whole vocation
Were endless imitation.

Thou, whose exterior semblance doth belie
    Thy Soul's immensity;
110 Thou best Philosopher, who yet dost keep
Thy heritage, thou Eye among the blind,
That, deaf and silent, read'st the eternal deep,
Haunted for ever by the eternal mind—
    Mighty Prophet! Seer blest!
115   On whom those truths do rest,
Which we are toiling all our lives to find;
Thou, over whom thy Immortality
Broods like the Day, a Master o'er a Slave,
A Presence which is not to be put by;
120   To whom the grave
Is but a lonely bed without the sense or sight
    Of day or the warm light,
A place of thought where we in waiting lie;
Thou little Child, yet glorious in the might
125 Of untamed pleasures, on thy Being's height,
Why with such earnest pains dost thou provoke
The Years to bring the inevitable yoke,
Thus blindly with thy blessedness at strife?
Full soon thy Soul shall have her earthly freight,
130 And custom lie upon thee with a weight,
Heavy as frost, and deep almost as life!

    O joy! that in our embers
    Is something that doth live,
    That nature yet remembers
135   What was so fugitive!
The thought of our past years in me doth breed
Perpetual benedictions: not indeed
For that which is most worthy to be blest;
Delight and liberty, the simple creed
140 Of Childhood, whether fluttering or at rest,
With new-born hope for ever in his breast:—
    Not for these I raise
    The song of thanks and praise;
    But for those obstinate questionings
145   Of sense and outward things,
    Fallings from us, vanishings;

    Blank misgivings of a Creature
Moving about in worlds not realized,[1]
High instincts, before which our mortal Nature
150 Did tremble like a guilty Thing surprised:
    But for those first affections,
    Those shadowy recollections,
    Which, be they what they may,
Are yet the fountain light of all our day,
155 Are yet a master light of all our seeing;
    Uphold us, cherish us, and make
Our noisy years seem moments in the being
Of the eternal Silence: truths that wake,
    To perish never;
160 Which neither listlessness, nor mad endeavour,
    Nor Man nor Boy,
Nor all that is at enmity with joy,
Can utterly abolish or destroy!
    Hence, in a season of calm weather,
165   Though inland far we be,
Our Souls have sight of that immortal sea
    Which brought us hither,
    Can in a moment travel thither,
And see the Children sport upon the shore,
170 And hear the mighty waters rolling evermore.

Then, sing ye Birds, sing, sing a joyous song!
    And let the young Lambs bound
    As to the tabor's sound!
We in thought will join your throng,
175   Ye that pipe and ye that play,
    Ye that through your hearts to day
    Feel the gladness of the May!
What though the radiance which was once so bright
Be now for ever taken from my sight,
180   Though nothing can bring back the hour
Of splendour in the grass, of glory in the flower;
    We will grieve not, rather find
    Strength in what remains behind,
    In the primal sympathy
185   Which having been must ever be,
    In the soothing thoughts that spring

---

[1] *realized* Seeming real.

Out of human suffering,
    In the faith that looks through death,
In years that bring the philosophic mind.

190 And oh ye Fountains, Meadows, Hills, and Groves,
Think not of any severing of our loves!
Yet in my heart of hearts I feel your might;
I only have relinquished one delight
To live beneath your more habitual sway.
195 I love the Brooks which down their channels fret,
Even more than when I tripped lightly as they;
The innocent brightness of a new-born Day
        Is lovely yet;
The Clouds that gather round the setting sun
200 Do take a sober colouring from an eye
That hath kept watch o'er man's mortality;
Another race hath been, and other palms[1] are won.
Thanks to the human heart by which we live,
Thanks to its tenderness, its joys, and fears,
205 To me the meanest flower that blows can give
Thoughts that do often lie too deep for tears.
        —1807

from *The Excursion*
[*The Ruined Cottage*]

This excerpt is taken from Wordsworth's nine-book epic *The Excursion, Being a Portion of The Recluse, A Poem* (1814). It was intended as the second part of the tripartite *The Recluse*, which was never completed, and *The Excursion* was the only part of the poem published during Wordsworth's lifetime. *The Prelude* was planned as an autobiographical introduction to the project. The portion from *The Excursion* reprinted here is from the end of Book 1, which is titled "The Wanderer," and was originally conceived and written as a poem entitled "The Ruined Cottage."

Of the character of the Wanderer (the principal character of the poem), Wordsworth says, "Had I been born in a class which would have deprived me of what is called a liberal education, it is not unlikely that, being strong in body, I should have taken to a way of life such as that in which my Pedlar passed the greater part of his days. At all events, I am here called upon freely to acknowledge that the character I have represented in his person is chiefly an idea of what I fancied my own character might have become in his circumstances," combined with aspects of several real-life acquaintances.

[*The Ruined Cottage*]

SUPINE the Wanderer lay,
His eyes as if in drowsiness half shut,
The shadows of the breezy elms above
Dappling his face. He had not heard my steps
5   As I approached; and near him did I stand
Unnotic'd in the shade, some minutes' space.
At length I hailed him, seeing that his hat
Was moist with water-drops, as if the brim
Had newly scooped a running stream. He rose,
10 And ere the pleasant greeting that ensued
Was ended, "'Tis," said I, "a burning day;
My lips are parched with thirst, but you, I guess,
Have somewhere found relief." He, at the word,
Pointing towards a sweet-briar, bade me climb
15 The fence hard by, where that aspiring shrub
Looked out upon the road. It was a plot
Of garden-ground run wild, its matted weeds
Marked with the steps of those, whom, as they pass'd
The gooseberry trees that shot in long lank slips,
20 Or currants hanging from their leafless stems
In scanty strings, had tempted to o'erleap
The broken wall. I looked around, and there,
Where two tall hedge-rows of thick alder boughs
Joined in a cold damp nook, espied a Well
25 Shrouded with willow-flowers and plumy fern.
My thirst I slaked, and from the cheerless spot
Withdrawing, straightway to the shade returned

---

[1] *palms* Prizes. (In ancient Greece, palm branches or wreaths were often awarded to the winners of foot races.)

Where sat the Old Man on the Cottage bench;
And, while, beside him, with uncovered head,
30 I yet was standing, freely to respire,
And cool my temples in the fanning air,
Thus did he speak. "I see around me here
Things which you cannot see: we die, my Friend,
Nor we alone, but that which each man loved
35 And prized in his peculiar nook of earth
Dies with him, or is changed; and very soon
Even of the good is no memorial left.
—The Poets, in their elegies and songs
Lamenting the departed, call the groves,
40 They call upon the hills and streams to mourn,
And senseless rocks; nor idly; for they speak,
In these their invocations, with a voice
Obedient to the strong creative power
Of human passion. Sympathies there are
45 More tranquil, yet perhaps of kindred birth,
That steal upon the meditative mind,
And grow with thought. Beside yon Spring I stood,
And eyed its waters till we seemed to feel
One sadness, they and I. For them a bond
50 Of brotherhood is broken: time has been
When, every day, the touch of human hand
Dislodged the natural sleep that binds them up
In mortal stillness; and they minister'd
To human comfort. As I stooped to drink,
55 Upon the slimy foot-stone I espied
The useless fragment of a wooden bowl,
Green with the moss of years; a pensive sight
That moved my heart!—recalling former days
When I could never pass that road but She
60 Who lived within these walls, at my approach,
A Daughter's welcome gave me; and I loved her
As my own child. O Sir! the good die first,
And they whose hearts are dry as summer dust
Burn to the socket. Many a Passenger
65 Hath blessed poor Margaret for her gentle looks,
When she upheld the cool refreshment drawn
From that forsaken Spring; and no one came
But he was welcome; no one went away
But that it seemed she loved him. She is dead,
70 The light extinguished of her lonely Hut,

The Hut itself abandoned to decay,
And She forgotten in the quiet grave!

"I speak," continued he, "of One whose stock
Of virtues bloom'd beneath this lowly roof.
75 She was a Woman of a steady mind,
Tender and deep in her excess of love,
Not speaking much, pleased rather with the joy
Of her own thoughts: by some especial care
Her temper had been framed, as if to make
80 A Being—who by adding love to peace
Might live on earth a life of happiness.
Her wedded Partner lacked not on his side
The humble worth that satisfied her heart:
Frugal, affectionate, sober, and withal
85 Keenly industrious. She with pride would tell
That he was often seated at his loom,
In summer, ere the Mower was abroad
Among the dewy grass—in early spring,
Ere the last Star had vanished. They who passed
90 At evening, from behind the garden fence
Might hear his busy spade, which he would ply,
After his daily work, until the light
Had failed, and every leaf and flower were lost
In the dark hedges. So their days were spent
95 In peace and comfort; and a pretty Boy
Was their best hope—next to the God in Heaven.

"Not twenty years ago, but you I think
Can scarcely bear it now in mind, there came
Two blighting seasons when the fields were left
100 With half a harvest. It pleased heaven to add
A worse affliction in the plague of war;
This happy Land was stricken to the heart!
A Wanderer then among the Cottages
I, with my freight of winter raiment, saw
105 The hardships of that season; many rich
Sank down, as in a dream, among the poor;
And of the poor did many cease to be
And their place knew them not. Meanwhile abridg'd
Of daily comforts, gladly reconciled
110 To numerous self-denials, Margaret

Went struggling on through those calamitous years
With cheerful hope: but ere the second autumn
Her life's true Help-mate on a sick-bed lay,
Smitten with perilous fever. In disease
115 He lingered long; and when his strength return'd,
He found the little he had stored, to meet
The hour of accident or crippling age,
Was all consumed. Two children had they now,
One newly born. As I have said, it was
120 A time of trouble; shoals of Artisans
Were from their daily labour turn'd adrift
To seek their bread from public charity,
They, and their wives and children—happier far
Could they have lived as do the little birds
125 That peck along the hedges, or the Kite[1]
That makes his dwelling on the mountain Rocks!

    "A sad reverse it was for him who long
Had filled with plenty, and possess'd in peace,
This lonely Cottage. At the door he stood,
130 And whistled many a snatch of merry tunes
That had no mirth in them; or with his knife
Carved uncouth figures on the heads of sticks—
Then, not less idly, sought, through every nook
In house or garden, any casual work
135 Of use or ornament; and with a strange,
Amusing, yet uneasy novelty,
He blended, where he might, the various tasks
Of summer, autumn, winter, and of spring.
But this endured not; his good humour soon
140 Became a weight in which no pleasure was:
And poverty brought on a petted° mood   *sulky*
And a sore temper: day by day he drooped,
And he would leave his work—and to the Town,
Without an errand, would direct his steps,
145 Or wander here and there among the fields.
One while he would speak lightly of his Babes,
And with a cruel tongue: at other times
He toss'd them with a false unnatural joy:
And 'twas a rueful thing to see the looks
150 Of the poor innocent children. 'Every smile,'

Said Margaret to me, here beneath these trees,
'Made my heart bleed.'"
                    At this the Wanderer paused;
And, looking up to those enormous Elms,
He said, "'Tis now the hour of deepest noon.—
155 At this still season of repose and peace,
This hour, when all things which are not at rest
Are cheerful; while this multitude of flies
Is filling all the air with melody;
Why should a tear be in an Old Man's eye?
160 Why should we thus, with an untoward mind,
And in the weakness of humanity,
From natural wisdom turn our hearts away,
To natural comfort shut our eyes and ears,
And, feeding on disquiet, thus disturb
165 The calm of nature with our restless thoughts?"

He spake with somewhat of a solemn tone:
But, when he ended, there was in his face
Such easy cheerfulness, a look so mild,
That for a little time it stole away
170 All recollection, and that simple Tale
Passed from my mind like a forgotten sound.
A while on trivial things we held discourse,
To me soon tasteless. In my own despite
I thought of that poor Woman as of one
175 Whom I had known and loved. He had rehearsed
Her homely Tale with such familiar power,
With such an active countenance, an eye
So busy, that the things of which he spake
Seemed present; and, attention now relax'd,
180 There was a heart-felt chillness in my veins.—
I rose; and, turning from the breezy shade,
Went forth into the open air, and stood
To drink the comfort of the warmer sun.
Long time I had not staid, ere, looking round
185 Upon that tranquil Ruin, I return'd,
And begged of the Old Man that, for my sake,
He would resume his story.—
                              He replied,
"It were a wantonness, and would demand
Severe reproof, if we were Men whose hearts
190 Could hold vain dalliance with the misery

---

[1] *Kite* Small bird of prey of the falcon family.

Even of the dead; contented thence to draw
A momentary pleasure, never marked
By reason, barren of all future good.
But we have known that there is often found
195 In mournful thoughts, and always might be found,
A power to virtue friendly; were't not so,
I am a Dreamer among men, indeed
An idle Dreamer! 'Tis a common Tale,
An ordinary sorrow of Man's life,
200 A tale of silent suffering, hardly clothed
In bodily form. But, without further bidding,
I will proceed—
          "While thus it fared with them,
To whom this Cottage, till those hapless years,
Had been a blessed home, it was my chance
205 To travel in a Country far remote.
And glad I was, when, halting by yon gate
That leads from the green lane, once more I saw
These lofty elm-trees. Long I did not rest:
With many pleasant thoughts I cheer'd my way
210 O'er the flat Common. Having reached the door
I knock'd—and, when I entered with the hope
Of usual greeting, Margaret looked at me
A little while; then turn'd her head away
Speechless, and sitting down upon a chair
215 Wept bitterly. I wist° not what to do,   *knew*
Or how to speak to her. Poor Wretch! at last
She rose from off her seat, and then—O Sir!
I cannot *tell* how she pronounced my name.
With fervent love, and with a face of grief
220 Unutterably helpless, and a look
That seemed to cling upon me, she enquired
If I had seen her Husband. As she spake
A strange surprise and fear came to my heart,
Nor had I power to answer ere she told
225 That he had disappear'd—not two months gone.
He left his House: two wretched days had pass'd,
And on the third, as wistfully she rais'd
Her head from off her pillow, to look forth,
Like one in trouble, for returning light,
230 Within her chamber-casement she espied
A folded paper, lying as if placed
To meet her waking eyes. This tremblingly

She open'd—found no writing, but therein
Pieces of money carefully enclosed,
235 Silver and gold. 'I shuddered at the sight,'
Said Margaret, 'for I knew it was his hand
Which placed it there; and ere that day was ended,
That long and anxious day! I learned from One
Sent hither by my Husband to impart
240 The heavy news—that he had joined a Troop
Of Soldiers, going to a distant Land.
—He left me thus—he could not gather heart
To take a farewell of me; for he fear'd
That I should follow with my Babes, and sink
245 Beneath the misery of that wandering Life.'"

   "This Tale did Margaret tell with many tears:
And when she ended I had little power
To give her comfort, and was glad to take
Such words of hope from her own mouth as served
250 To cheer us both—but long we had not talked
Ere we built up a pile of better thoughts,
And with a brighter eye she look'd around
As if she had been shedding tears of joy.
We parted. 'Twas the time of early spring;
255 I left her busy with her garden tools;
And well remember, o'er that fence she looked,
And, while I paced along the foot-way path,
Called out, and sent a blessing after me,
With tender cheerfulness; and with a voice
260 That seem'd the very sound of happy thoughts.

   "I roved o'er many a hill and many a dale,
With my accustomed load; in heat and cold,
Through many a wood, and many an open ground,
In sunshine and in shade, in wet and fair,
265 Drooping, or blithe of heart, as might befall;
My best companions now the driving winds,
And now the 'trotting brooks' and whispering trees,
And now the music of my own sad steps,
With many a short-lived thought that pass'd between,
270 And disappeared. I journey'd back this way
Towards the wane of Summer; when the wheat
Was yellow; and the soft and bladed grass
Springing afresh had o'er the hay-field spread

Its tender verdure. At the door arrived,
275 I found that she was absent. In the shade,
Where now we sit, I waited her return.
Her Cottage, then a cheerful Object, wore
Its customary look—only, I thought,
The honeysuckle, crowding round the porch,
280 Hung down in heavier tufts: and that bright weed,
The yellow stone-crop, suffered to take root
Along the window's edge, profusely grew,
Blinding the lower panes. I turned aside,
And strolled into her garden. It appeared
285 To lag behind the season, and had lost
Its pride of neatness. From the border lines
Composed of daisy and resplendent thrift,[1]
Flowers straggling forth had on those paths encroached
Which they were used to deck: Carnations, once
290 Prized for surpassing beauty, and no less
For the peculiar pains they had required,
Declined their languid heads—without support.
The cumbrous bind-weed, with its wreaths and bells,
Had twined about her two small rows of peas,
295 And dragged them to the earth.—Ere this an hour
Was wasted.—Back I turned my restless steps,
And, as I walked before the door, it chanced
A Stranger passed; and, guessing whom I sought,
He said that she was used to ramble far.
300 The sun was sinking in the west; and now
I sat with sad impatience. From within
Her solitary Infant cried aloud;
Then, like a blast that dies away self-stilled,
The voice was silent. From the bench I rose;
305 But neither could divert nor soothe my thoughts.
The spot, though fair, was very desolate—
The longer I remained more desolate.
And, looking round, I saw the corner stones,
Till then unnotic'd, on either side the door
310 With dull red stains discolour'd, and stuck o'er
With tufts and hairs of wool, as if the Sheep,
That fed upon the Common, thither came
Familiarly; and found a couching-place
Even at her threshold. Deeper shadows fell

315 From these tall elms; the Cottage-clock struck eight;
I turned, and saw her distant a few steps.
Her face was pale and thin, her figure too
Was changed. As she unlocked the door, she said,
'It grieves me you have waited here so long,
320 But, in good truth, I've wandered much of late,
And, sometimes—to my shame I speak—have need
Of my best prayers to bring me back again.'
While on the board she spread our evening meal,
She told me, interrupting not the work
325 Which gave employment to her listless hands,
That she had parted with her elder Child;
To a kind Master on a distant farm
Now happily apprenticed—'I perceive
You look at me, and you have cause; to-day
330 I have been travelling far; and many days
About the fields I wander, knowing this
Only, that what I seek I cannot find.
And so I waste my time: for I am changed;
And to myself,' said she, 'have done much wrong,
335 And to this helpless Infant. I have slept
Weeping, and weeping I have waked; my tears
Have flowed as if my body were not such
As others are; and I could never die.
But I am now in mind and in my heart
340 More easy; and I hope,' said she, 'that heaven
Will give me patience to endure the things
Which I behold at home.' It would have grieved
Your very soul to see her; Sir, I feel
The story linger in my heart: I fear
345 'Tis long and tedious; but my spirit clings
To that poor Woman—so familiarly
Do I perceive her manner, and her look,
And presence, and so deeply do I feel
Her goodness, that, not seldom, in my walks
350 A momentary trance comes over me;
And to myself I seem to muse on One
By sorrow laid asleep; or borne away,
A human being destined to awake
To human life, or something very near
355 To human life, when he shall come again
For whom she suffered. Yes, it would have grieved
Your very soul to see her: evermore

---

[1] *thrift* Common plant that bears pink, white, or purple flowers.

Her eyelids drooped, her eyes were downward cast;
And, when she at her table gave me food,
360 She did not look at me. Her voice was low,
Her body was subdued. In every act
Pertaining to her house affairs, appeared
The careless stillness of a thinking mind
Self-occupied; to which all outward things
365 Are like an idle matter. Still she sighed,
But yet no motion of the breast was seen,
No heaving of the heart. While by the fire
We sate together, sighs came on my ear,
I knew not how, and hardly whence they came.

370   "Ere my departure to her care I gave,
For her Son's use, some tokens of regard,
Which with a look of welcome she received;
And I exhorted her to have her trust
In God's good love, and seek his help by prayer.
375 I took my staff, and, when I kissed her babe
The tears stood in her eyes. I left her then
With the best hope and comfort I could give;
She thanked me for my wish;—but for my hope
Methought she did not thank me.
                                    I returned,
380 And took my rounds along this road again
Ere on its sunny bank the primrose flower
Peeped forth, to give an earnest of the Spring.
I found her sad and drooping; she had learned
No tidings of her Husband; if he lived
385 She knew not that he lived; if he were dead
She knew not he was dead. She seem'd the same
In person and appearance; but her House
Bespake a sleepy hand of negligence.
The floor was neither dry nor neat, the hearth
390 Was comfortless, and her small lot of books,
Which, in the Cottage window, heretofore
Had been piled up against the corner panes
In seemly order, now, with straggling leaves
Lay scattered here and there, open or shut,
395 As they had chanced to fall. Her Infant Babe
Had from its Mother caught the trick of grief,
And sighed among its playthings. Once again
I turned towards the garden gate, and saw,

More plainly still, that poverty and grief
400 Were now come nearer to her: weeds defaced
The harden'd soil, and knots of wither'd grass;
No ridges there appeared of clear black mold,
No winter greenness; of her herbs and flowers,
It seemed the better part were gnawed away
405 Or trampled into earth; a chain of straw,
Which had been twined about the slender stem
Of a young apple-tree, lay at its root;
The bark was nibbled round by truant Sheep.
—Margaret stood near, her Infant in her arms,
410 And, noting that my eye was on the tree,
She said, 'I fear it will be dead and gone
Ere Robert come again.' Towards the House
Together we returned; and she enquired
If I had any hope: but for her Babe
415 And for her little orphan Boy, she said,
She had no wish to live, that she must die
Of sorrow. Yet I saw the idle loom
Still in its place; his Sunday garments hung
Upon the self-same nail; his very staff
420 Stood undisturbed behind the door. And when,
In bleak December, I retraced this way,
She told me that her little Babe was dead,
And she was left alone. She now, released
From her maternal cares, had taken up
425 The employment common through these Wilds,
    and gain'd
By spinning hemp a pittance for herself;
And for this end had hired a neighbour's Boy
To give her needful help. That very time
Most willingly she put her work aside,
430 And walked with me along the miry road
Heedless how far; and, in such piteous sort
That any heart had ached to hear her, begged
That, wheresoe'er I went, I still would ask
For him whom she had lost. We parted then,
435 Our final parting; for from that time forth
Did many seasons pass ere I return'd
Into this tract again.
                        Nine tedious years;
From their first separation, nine long years,
She lingered in unquiet widowhood;

440 A Wife and Widow. Needs must it have been
A sore heart-wasting! I have heard, my Friend,
That in yon arbour oftentimes she sat
Alone, through half the vacant Sabbath-day,
And if a dog passed by she still would quit
445 The shade, and look abroad. On this old Bench
For hours she sate; and evermore her eye
Was busy in the distance, shaping things
That made her heart beat quick. You see that path,
Now faint—the grass has crept o'er its grey line;
450 There, to and fro, she paced through many a day
Of the warm summer, from a belt of hemp
That girt her waist, spinning the long drawn thread
With backward steps. Yet ever as there pass'd
A man whose garments showed the Soldier's red,
455 Or crippled Mendicant in Sailor's garb,
The little Child who sate to turn the wheel
Ceas'd from his task; and she with faltering voice
Made many a fond enquiry; and when they,
Whose presence gave no comfort, were gone by,
460 Her heart was still more sad. And by yon gate,
That bars the Traveller's road, she often stood,
And when a stranger Horseman came, the latch
Would lift, and in his face look wistfully;
Most happy, if, from aught discovered there
465 Of tender feeling, she might dare repeat
The same sad question. Meanwhile her poor Hut
Sank to decay: for he was gone—whose hand,
At the first nipping of October frost,
Closed up each chink, and with fresh bands of straw
470 Chequered the green-grown thatch. And so she lived
Through the long winter, reckless and alone;
Until her House by frost, and thaw, and rain,
Was sapped; and while she slept the nightly damps
Did chill her breast; and in the stormy day
475 Her tattered clothes were ruffled by the wind;
Even at the side of her own fire. Yet still
She loved this wretched spot, nor would for worlds
Have parted hence; and still that length of road,
And this rude bench, one torturing hope endeared,
480 Fast rooted at her heart: and here, my Friend,
In sickness she remained; and here she died,
Last human Tenant of these ruined Walls."

The Old Man ceased: he saw that I was moved;
From that low Bench, rising instinctively
485 I turn'd aside in weakness, nor had power
To thank him for the Tale which he had told.
I stood, and leaning o'er the Garden wall,
Reviewed that Woman's sufferings; and it seemed
To comfort me while with a Brother's love
490 I bless'd her—in the impotence of grief.
At length towards the Cottage I returned
Fondly, and traced with interest more mild,
That secret spirit of humanity
Which, 'mid the calm oblivious tendencies
495 Of Nature, 'mid her plants, and weeds, and flowers,
And silent overgrowings, still survived.
The Old Man, noting this, resumed, and said,
"My Friend! enough to sorrow you have given,
The purposes of wisdom ask no more;
500 Be wise and cheerful; and no longer read
The forms of things with an unworthy eye.
She sleeps in the calm earth, and peace is here.
I well remember that those very plumes,
Those weeds, and the high spear-grass on that wall,
505 By mist and silent rain-drops silver'd o'er,
As once I passed, did to my heart convey
So still an image of tranquillity,
So calm and still, and looked so beautiful
Amid the uneasy thoughts which filled my mind,
510 That what we feel of sorrow and despair
From ruin and from change, and all the grief
The passing shows of Being leave behind,
Appeared an idle dream, that could not live
Where meditation was. I turned away
515 And walked along my road in happiness."

He ceased. Ere long the sun declining shot
A slant and mellow radiance, which began
To fall upon us, while beneath the trees
We sat on that low Bench: and now we felt,
520 Admonished thus, the sweet hour coming on.
A linnet warbled from those lofty elms,
A thrush sang loud, and other melodies,
At distance heard, peopled the milder air.
The Old Man rose, and, with a sprightly mien°   *countenance*

530 Of hopeful preparation, grasped his Staff:
Together casting then a farewell look
Upon those silent walls, we left the Shade;
And, ere the Stars were visible, had reached
A Village Inn—our Evening resting-place.
—1814

Surprised by Joy

Surprised by joy—impatient as the Wind
I turned to share the transport—Oh! with whom
But Thee,[1] deep buried in the silent tomb,
That spot which no vicissitude can find?
5 Love, faithful love, recalled thee to my mind—
But how could I forget thee? Through what power,
Even for the least division of an hour,
Have I been so beguiled as to be blind
To my most grievous loss?—That thought's return
10 Was the worst pang that sorrow ever bore,
Save one, one only, when I stood forlorn,
Knowing my heart's best treasure was no more;
That neither present time, nor years unborn
Could to my sight that heavenly face restore.
—1815

Mutability[2]

From low to high doth dissolution climb,
And sink from high to low, along a scale
Of awful° notes, whose concord shall not fail;   awe-inspiring
A musical but melancholy chime,
5 Which they can hear who meddle not with crime,
Nor avarice, nor over-anxious care.
Truth fails not; but her outward forms that bear
The longest date do melt like frosty rime,
That in the morning whitened hill and plain
10 And is no more; drop like the tower sublime
Of yesterday, which royally did wear
His crown of weeds, but could not even sustain
Some casual shout that broke the silent air,
Or the unimaginable touch of Time.
—1822

Steamboats, Viaducts, and Railways

Motions and Means, on land and sea at war
With old poetic feeling, not for this,
Shall ye, by Poets even, be judged amiss!
Nor shall your presence, howsoe'er it mar
5 The loveliness of Nature, prove a bar
To the Mind's gaining that prophetic sense
Of future change, that point of vision whence
May be discovered what in soul ye are.
In spite of all that beauty may disown
10 In your harsh features, Nature doth embrace
Her lawful offspring in Man's art; and Time,
Pleased with your triumphs o'er his brother Space,
Accepts from your bold hands the proffered crown
Of hope, and smiles on you with cheer sublime.
—1835

---

[1] *Thee* Catherine, the Wordsworths' daughter, who died in June 1812 at the age of three.

[2] *Mutability* From *Ecclesiastical Sonnets*, a sequence of poems dealing with the history of the Church of England.

IN CONTEXT

Visual Depictions of "Man's Art"

While one artistic tradition emphasized the "harsh features" of the products of the industrial revolution, many painters in the first half of the nineteenth century depicted such subjects as viaducts and railways in ways which suggested that, like Wordsworth, they saw these as nature's "lawful offspring."

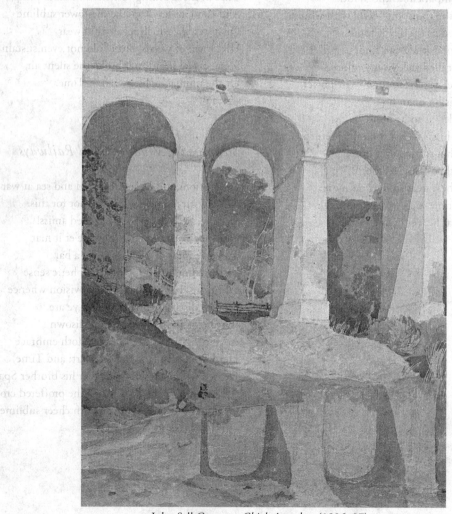

John Sell Cotman, *Chirk Aqueduct* (1806–07).
The aqueduct, built between 1796 and 1801, is 70 feet high.

J.M.W. Turner, *Rain, Steam and Speed* (1844).

The Prelude

Wordsworth first began this blank-verse epic poem—generally regarded as his crowning achievement—in 1798, as a preface to his projected masterpiece, *The Recluse*, a philosophical poem that was never completed. Throughout his life Wordsworth referred to *The Prelude* simply as "the poem on my life," "the poem on the growth of my mind," or "the poem to Coleridge." It was his wife, Mary, who, publishing the piece a few months after his death, gave it the title by which it is now known.

The history of *The Prelude* is a long and complex one, spanning over forty years of revisions that saw several preliminary versions before the final, fourteen-book poem was completed in 1839. Wordsworth began *The Prelude* in 1798, during a lonely, cold winter in Germany, during which he and his sister Dorothy struggled with homesickness. This first part, which deals with Wordsworth's early childhood, and a second part describing his adolescence (composed after Wordsworth's return to England in 1799) formed the two books of the 1799 *Prelude*.

Wordsworth returned to *The Prelude* again in 1804, expanding the piece to five books that covered his life through his residence at Cambridge. After completing this version, Wordsworth began envisioning the project as a poem of epic proportions that would re-examine his life and convictions. In the expanded version of thirteen books, Wordsworth revisits France of the 1790s in his imagination, reliving those painful years and showing how, in the face of disappointment at the failure of the French Revolution and the growth of tyranny in Europe, he was restored through his ties with nature. This version, completed in May of 1805, begins with echoes of Milton's *Paradise Lost* as Wordsworth describes his vision of the fallen world in which he began his quest to develop his poetic imagination. Still spanning Wordsworth's childhood and maturity, the work no longer proceeds chronologically, but instead moves continuously between past and present as the poet recollects events and then examines their effects on his development. By the poem's end, he emerges from these events transformed and with his poetic sensibilities fully developed.

Wordsworth continued to revise *The Prelude* until 1839, when Dora Wordsworth (the poet's daughter) prepared a beautiful copy of the poem in its fourteen-book version. When *The Prelude* was first released in 1850, critics were often puzzled as to how it should be classified. In part, the poem is a familiar verse epistle to Coleridge and a testament to the power of friendship. At the same time, it is a personal narrative of spiritual journey. Yet the prophetic narrator and the deliberate parallels with other epics elevate the work above the merely personal and provide a representative story of a naive English adolescent who, maturing during the aftermath of a failed revolution, learns to celebrate his heritage.

It was not until the twentieth century that the earlier 1798 and 1805 versions of *The Prelude* were discovered. Both of these have since received much independent critical attention and have been seen by some critics as superior to the final version.

The Two-Part Prelude of 1799

FIRST PART

Was it for this
That one, the fairest of all rivers, loved
To blend his murmurs with my Nurse's song,
And from his alder[1] shades, and rocky falls,
5   And from his fords and shallows, sent a voice
That flowed along my dreams? For this didst thou
O Derwent, travelling over the green plains
Near my "sweet birth-place,"[2] didst thou beauteous
    Stream
Make ceaseless music through the night and day,
10   Which with its steady cadence tempering
Our human waywardness, composed my thoughts
To more than infant softness, giving me,

Among the fretful dwellings of mankind,
A knowledge, a dim earnest of the calm
15   Which Nature breathes among the fields and groves?
    Beloved Derwent! fairest of all Streams!
Was it for this that I, a four year's child,
A naked Boy, among thy silent pools
Made one long bathing of a summer's day?
20   Basked in the sun, or plunged into thy streams,
Alternate, all a summer's day, or coursed
Over the sandy fields, and dashed the flowers
Of yellow grunsel,[3] or when crag and hill,
The woods and distant Skiddaw's[4] lofty height
25   Were bronzed with a deep radiance, stood alone,
A naked Savage in the thunder shower?
    And afterwards, 'twas in a later day
Though early, when upon the mountain-slope
The frost and breath of frosty wind had snapped
30   The last autumnal crocus, 'twas my joy

John "Warwick" Smith, *Ulls-water in Paterdale*, 1792–95.

---

1   *alder*   Tree resembling a birch and usually found in wet places.

2   *sweet birth-place*   From Coleridge's *Frost at Midnight* (1798).
Wordsworth's childhood home was in Cockermouth, Cumberland,
through which the Derwent River flows.

3   *grunsel*   Groundsel, a common weed.

4   *Skiddaw*   Mountain in Cumberland.

To wander half the night among the cliffs
And the smooth hollows, where the woodcocks ran
Along the moonlight turf. In thought and wish,
That time, my shoulder all with springes° hung,   *snares*
35   I was a fell destroyer. Gentle Powers!
Who give us happiness and call it peace!
When scudding on from snare to snare I plied
My anxious visitation, hurrying on,
Still hurrying hurrying onward, how my heart
40   Panted; among the scattered yew-trees, and the crags
That looked upon me, how my bosom beat
With expectation. Sometimes strong desire,
Resistless, overpowered me, and the bird
Which was the captive of another's toils[1]
45   Became my prey; and when the deed was done
I heard among the solitary hills
Low breathings coming after me, and sounds
Of undistinguishable motion, steps
Almost as silent as the turf they trod.
50   Nor less, in spring-time, when on southern banks
The shining sun had from his knot of leaves
Decoyed the primrose-flower, and when the vales
And woods were warm, was I a rover then
In the high places, on the lonesome peaks,
55   Among the mountains and the winds. Though mean
And though inglorious were my views, the end°   *result*
Was not ignoble. Oh, when I have hung
Above the raven's nest, by knots of grass,
Or half-inch fissures in the slipp'ry rock,
60   But ill sustained, and almost, as it seemed,
Suspended by the blast which blew amain,°   *violently*
Shouldering the naked crag, oh at that time,
While on the perilous ridge I hung alone,
With what strange utterance did the loud dry wind
65   Blow through my ears! the sky seemed not a sky
Of earth, and with what motion moved the clouds!
        The mind of man is fashioned and built up
Even as a strain of music: I believe
That there are spirits, which, when they would form
70   A favoured being, from his very dawn
Of infancy do open out the clouds

As at the touch of lightning, seeking him
With gentle visitation; quiet Powers!
Retired and seldom recognized, yet kind,
75   And to the very meanest not unknown;
With me, though rarely, in my early days
They communed: others too there are who use,
Yet haply aiming at the self-same end,
Severer interventions, ministry
80   More palpable, and of their school was I.
        They guided me: one evening, led by them,
I went alone into a Shepherd's boat,
A skiff that to a willow-tree was tied
Within a rocky cave, its usual home;
85   The moon was up, the lake was shining clear
Among the hoary mountains: from the shore
I pushed, and struck the oars, and struck again
In cadence, and my little Boat moved on
Just like a man who walks with stately step
90   Though bent on speed. It was an act of stealth
And troubled pleasure; not without the voice
Of mountain-echoes did my boat move on,
Leaving behind her still on either side
Small circles glittering idly in the moon
95   Until they melted all into one track
Of sparkling light. A rocky steep uprose
Above the cavern of the willow tree,
And now, as suited one who proudly rowed
With his best skill, I fixed a steady view
100   Upon the top of that same craggy ridge,
The bound of the horizon, for behind
Was nothing—but the stars and the grey sky.
—She was an elfin pinnace;[2] twenty times
I dipped my oars into the silent lake,
105   And, as I rose upon the stroke, my Boat
Went heaving through the water, like a swan—
When from behind that rocky steep, till then
The bound of the horizon, a huge Cliff,
As if with voluntary power instinct,°   *imbued*
110   Upreared its head: I struck, and struck again,
And, growing still in stature, the huge cliff
Rose up between me and the stars, and still

---

[1]   *toils* Meaning both "snares" and "labor."

[2]   *pinnace* Small boat typically used to service larger vessels.

With measured motion, like a living thing,
Strode after me. With trembling hands I turned,
115 And through the silent water stole my way
Back to the cavern of the willow-tree.
There, in her mooring-place I left my bark,
And through the meadows homeward went with grave
And serious thoughts: and after I had seen
120 That spectacle, for many days my brain
Worked with a dim and undetermined sense
Of unknown modes of being: in my thoughts
There was a darkness, call it solitude
Or blank desertion; no familiar shapes
125 Of hourly objects, images of trees,
Of sea or sky, no colours of green fields:
But huge and mighty forms, that do not live
Like living men, moved slowly through my mind
By day, and were the trouble of my dreams.
130   Ah! not in vain ye Beings of the hills!
And ye that walk the woods and open heaths
By moon or star-light, thus from my first dawn
Of childhood did ye love to intertwine
The passions that build up our human soul,
135 Not with the mean and vulgar° works of man,   *ordinary*
But with high objects, with eternal things,
With life and nature, purifying thus
The elements of feeling and of thought,
And sanctifying by such discipline
140 Both pain and fear, until we recognise
A grandeur in the beatings of the heart.
    Nor was this fellowship vouchsafed to me
With stinted kindness. In November days,
When vapours, rolling down the valleys, made
145 A lonely scene more lonesome, among woods
At noon, and 'mid the calm of summer nights
When by the margin of the trembling lake
Beneath the gloomy hills I homeward went
In solitude, such intercourse was mine.
150   And in the frosty season when the sun
Was set, and, visible for many a mile,
The cottage windows through the twilight blazed,
I heeded not the summons: clear and loud
The village clock tolled six; I wheeled about
155 Proud and exulting like an untired horse

That cares not for its home.—All shod with steel
We hissed along the polished ice, in games
Confederate, imitative of the chase
And woodland pleasures, the resounding horn,
160 The pack loud bellowing, and the hunted hare.
So through the darkness and the cold we flew,
And not a voice was idle: with the din,
Meanwhile, the precipices rang aloud,
The leafless trees and every icy crag
165 Tinkled like iron, while the distant hills
Into the tumult sent an alien sound
Of melancholy not unnoticed while the stars,
Eastward, were sparkling clear, and in the west
The orange sky of evening died away.
170   Not seldom from the uproar I retired
Into a silent bay, or sportively
Glanced sideway leaving the tumultuous throng
To cut across the shadow° of a star   *reflection*
That gleamed upon the ice: and oftentimes
175 When we had given our bodies to the wind
And all the shadowy banks on either side
Came sweeping through the darkness, spinning still
The rapid line of motion, then at once
Have I, reclining back upon my heels,
180 Stopped short; yet still the solitary cliffs
Wheeled by me, even as if the earth had rolled
With visible motion her diurnal° round;   *daily*
Behind me did they stretch in solemn train
Feebler and feebler, and I stood and watched
185 Till all was tranquil as a summer sea.
    Ye Powers of earth! ye Genii of the springs!
And ye that have your voices in the clouds
And ye that are Familiars of the lakes
And of the standing pools, I may not think
190 A vulgar hope was yours when ye employed
Such ministry, when ye through many a year
Thus by the agency of boyish sports
On caves and trees, upon the woods and hills,
Impressed upon all forms the characters°   *signs*
195 Of danger or desire, and thus did make
The surface of the universal earth
With meanings of delight, of hope and fear,
Work° like a sea.   *seethe*

Not uselessly employed
I might pursue this theme through every change
200 Of exercise and sport to which the year
Did summon us in its delightful round.
We were a noisy crew: the sun in heaven
Beheld not vales more beautiful than ours
Nor saw a race in happiness and joy
205 More worthy of the fields where they were sown.
I would record with no reluctant voice
Our home amusements by the warm peat fire
At evening, when with pencil, and with slate
In square divisions parcelled out, and all
210 With crosses and with cyphers scribbled o'er,[1]
We schemed and puzzled, head opposed to head
In strife too humble to be named in verse,
Or round the naked table, snow-white deal,°   pine
Cherry or maple, sat in close array
215 And to the combat—Lu or Whist—led on
A thick-ribbed army,[2] not as in the world
Discarded and ungratefully thrown by
Even for the very service they had wrought,
But husbanded through many a long campaign.
220 Oh with what echoes on the board they fell—
Ironic diamonds, hearts of sable hue,
Queens gleaming through their splendour's last decay,
Knaves wrapt in one assimilating gloom,
And Kings indignant at the shame incurr'd
225 By royal visages. Meanwhile abroad
The heavy rain was falling, or the frost
Raged bitterly with keen and silent tooth,
And interrupting the impassioned game
Oft from the neighbouring lake the splitting ice
230 While it sank down towards the water sent
Among the meadows and the hills its long
And frequent yellings, imitative some
Of wolves that howl along the Bothnic main.[3]
Nor with less willing heart would I rehearse

235 The woods of autumn and their hidden bowers
With milk-white clusters hung; the rod and line,
True symbol of the foolishness of hope,
Which with its strong enchantment led me on
By rocks and pools where never summer-star
240 Impressed its shadow, to forlorn cascades
Among the windings of the mountain-brooks;
The kite, in sultry calms from some high hill
Sent up, ascending thence till it was lost
Among the fleecy clouds, in gusty days
245 Launched from the lower grounds, and suddenly
Dash'd headlong—and rejected by the storm.
All these and more with rival claims demand
Grateful acknowledgement. It were a song
Venial,° and such as if I rightly judge   pardonable
250 I might protract unblamed; but I perceive
That much is overlooked, and we should ill
Attain our object if from delicate fears
Of breaking in upon the unity
Of this my argument I should omit
255 To speak of such effects as cannot here
Be regularly classed, yet tend no less
To the same point, the growth of mental power
And love of Nature's works.
Ere I had seen
Eight summers (and 'twas in the very week
260 When I was first transplanted to thy vale,
Beloved Hawkshead![4] when thy paths, thy shores
And brooks were like a dream of novelty
To my half-infant mind) I chanced to cross
One of those open fields which, shaped like ears,
265 Make green peninsulas on Esthwaite's lake.
Twilight was coming on, yet through the gloom
I saw distinctly on the opposite shore
Beneath a tree and close by the lake side
A heap of garments, as if left by one
270 Who there was bathing: half an hour I watched
And no one owned them: meanwhile the calm lake
Grew dark with all the shadows on its breast,
And now and then a leaping fish disturbed
The breathless stillness. The succeeding day

[1] *With crosses ... o'er* See Milton's *Paradise Lost* 8.83: "With centric and eccentric scribbled o'er." Here Wordsworth uses this heroic diction to describe a game of tick-tack-toe.

[2] *Lu or Whist* Popular card games; *thick-ribbed army* Pack of cards made of thick cardboard.

[3] *Bothnic main* Gulf of Bothnia, between Sweden and Finland.

[4] *Hawkshead* Where Wordsworth attended grammar school.

275 There came a company, and in their boat
Sounded with iron hooks and with long poles.
At length the dead man 'mid that beauteous scene
Of trees, and hills, and water, bolt upright
Rose with his ghastly face.[1] I might advert
280 To numerous accidents in flood or field,
Quarry or moor, or 'mid the winter snows,
Distresses and disasters, tragic facts
Of rural history that impressed my mind
With images, to which in following years
285 Far other feelings were attached, with forms
That yet exist with independent life
And, like their archetypes, know no decay.

There are in our existence spots of time
Which with distinct pre-eminence retain
290 A fructifying virtue,[2] whence, depressed
By trivial occupations and the round
Of ordinary intercourse, our minds
(Especially the imaginative power)
Are nourished, and invisibly repaired.
295 Such moments chiefly seem to have their date
In our first childhood. I remember well
('Tis of an early season that I speak,
The twilight of rememberable life)
While I was yet an urchin, one who scarce
300 Could hold a bridle, with ambitious hopes
I mounted, and we rode towards the hills;
We were a pair of horsemen: honest James[3]
Was with me, my encourager and guide.
We had not travelled long ere some mischance
305 Disjoined me from my comrade, and through fear
Dismounting, down the rough and stony moor
I led my horse and, stumbling on, at length
Came to a bottom where in former times
A man, the murderer of his wife, was hung
310 In irons; mouldered° was the gibbet[4] mast,   decayed

---

[1] *At length ... face* In June 1779, shortly after Wordsworth arrived at Hawkshead, a schoolmaster from a neighboring village drowned while swimming in Esthwaite Water.

[2] *fructifying virtue* I.e., power to make fruitful.

[3] *honest James* Most likely the family's servant.

[4] *gibbet* Structure similar to a gallows from which the bodies of people sentenced to execution are suspended, often inside a metal cage.

The bones were gone, the iron and the wood,
Only a long green ridge of turf remained
Whose shape was like a grave. I left the spot,
And, reascending the bare slope, I saw
315 A naked pool that lay beneath the hills,
The beacon on the summit, and more near
A girl who bore a pitcher on her head
And seemed with difficult steps to force her way
Against the blowing wind. It was in truth
320 An ordinary sight but I should need
Colours and words that are unknown to man
To paint the visionary dreariness
Which, while I looked all round for my lost guide,
Did, at that time, invest the naked pool,
325 The beacon on the lonely eminence,
The woman and her garments vexed and tossed
By the strong wind. Nor less I recollect
(Long after, though my childhood had not ceased)
Another scene which left a kindred power
330 Implanted in my mind.
                    One Christmas time,
The day before the holidays began,
Feverish, and tired and restless, I went forth
Into the fields, impatient for the sight
Of those three horses which should bear us home,
335 My Brothers and myself. There was a crag,
An eminence which from the meeting point
Of two highways ascending overlooked
At least a long half-mile of those two roads,
By each of which the expected steeds might come,
340 The choice uncertain. Thither I repaired
Up to the highest summit; 'twas a day
Stormy, and rough, and wild, and on the grass
I sat, half-sheltered by a naked wall;
Upon my right hand was a single sheep,
345 A whistling hawthorn on my left, and there,
Those two companions at my side, I watched
With eyes intensely straining as the mist
Gave intermitting prospects of the wood
And plain beneath. Ere I to school returned
350 That dreary time, ere I had been ten days

A dweller in my Father's house, he died,[1]
And I and my two Brothers, orphans then,
Followed his body to the grave. The event
With all the sorrow which it brought appeared
355   A chastisement, and when I called to mind
That day so lately passed when from the crag
I looked in such anxiety of hope,
With trite reflections of morality
Yet with the deepest passion I bowed low
360   To God, who thus corrected my desires;
And afterwards the wind, and sleety rain,
And all the business of the elements,
The single sheep, and the one blasted tree,
And the bleak music of that old stone wall,
365   The noise of wood and water, and the mist
Which on the line of each of those two roads
Advanced in such indisputable shapes,
All these were spectacles and sounds to which
I often would repair, and thence would drink
370   As at a fountain, and I do not doubt
That in this later time when storm and rain
Beat on my roof at midnight, or by day
When I am in the woods, unknown to me
The workings of my spirit thence are brought.

375   Nor sedulous° to trace   *diligent*
How Nature by collateral° interest   *indirect*
And by extrinsic passion peopled first
My mind with forms, or beautiful or grand,
And made me love them, may I well forget
380   How other pleasures have been mine, and joys
Of subtler origin, how I have felt
Not seldom, even in that tempestuous time,
Those hallowed and pure motions of the sense
Which seem in their simplicity to own
385   An intellectual charm, that calm delight
Which, if I err not, surely must belong
To those first-born affinities that fit
Our new existence to existing things
And in our dawn of being constitute
390   The bond of union betwixt life and joy.

          Yes, I remember when the changeful earth

And twice five seasons on my mind had stamped
The faces of the moving year, even then,
A Child, I held unconscious intercourse
395   With the eternal Beauty, drinking in
A pure organic pleasure from the lines
Of curling mist or from the level plain
Of waters coloured by the steady clouds.
          The sands of Westmoreland, the creeks and bays
400   Of Cumbria's[2] rocky limits, they can tell
How when the sea threw off his evening shade
And to the Shepherd's hut beneath the crags
Did send sweet notice of the rising moon,
How I have stood to images like these
405   A stranger, linking with the spectacle
No body of associated forms
And bringing with me no peculiar sense
Of quietness or peace, yet I have stood
Even while my eye has moved o'er three long leagues
410   Of shining water, gathering, as it seemed,
Through the wide surface of that field of light
New pleasure, like a bee among the flowers.
          Thus often in those fits of vulgar joy
Which through all seasons on a child's pursuits
415   Are prompt attendants, 'mid that giddy bliss
Which like a tempest works along the blood
And is forgotten, even then I felt
Gleams like the flashing of a shield; the earth
And common face of Nature spake to me
420   Remememberable things: sometimes, 'tis true,
By quaint associations, yet not vain
Nor profitless if haply° they impressed   *by chance*
Collateral[3] objects and appearances,
Albeit lifeless then, and doomed to sleep
425   Until maturer seasons called them forth
To impregnate and to elevate the mind.
——And if the vulgar joy by its own weight
Wearied itself out of the memory,
The scenes which were a witness of that joy
430   Remained, in their substantial lineaments

---

[1] *ere I ... died* Wordsworth's father died on 30 December 1783. His mother had died five years earlier.

[2] *Westmoreland ... Cumbria* Westmoreland and Cumbria (usually called Cumberland) were counties in the Lake District.

[3] *Collateral* I.e., indirect, lying aside from the main interests of the poet.

Depicted on the brain, and to the eye
Were visible, a daily sight: and thus
By the impressive agency of fear,
By pleasure and repeated happiness,
435 So frequently repeated, and by force
Of obscure feelings representative
Of joys that were forgotten, these same scenes
So beauteous and majestic in themselves,
Though yet the day was distant, did at length
440 Become habitually dear, and all
Their hues and forms were by invisible links
Allied to the affections.
                    I began
My story early, feeling, as I fear,
The weakness of a human love for days
445 Disowned by memory, ere the birth of spring
Planting my snow-drops among winter snows.
Nor will it seem to thee, my Friend,[1] so prompt
In sympathy, that I have lengthened out
With fond and feeble tongue a tedious tale.
450 Meanwhile my hope has been that I might fetch
Reproaches from my former years, whose power
May spur me on, in manhood now mature,
To honourable toil. Yet, should it be
That this is but an impotent desire,
455 That I by such inquiry am not taught
To understand myself, nor thou to know
With better knowledge how the heart was framed
Of him thou lovest, need I dread from thee
Harsh judgements if I am so loath to quit
460 Those recollected hours that have the charm
Of visionary things,[2] and lovely forms
And sweet sensations that throw back our life
And make our infancy a visible scene
On which the sun is shining?

SECOND PART

Thus far my Friend, have we retraced the way
Through which I travelled when I first began
To love the woods and fields: the passion yet

Was in its birth, sustained as might befall
5 By nourishment that came unsought, for still
From week to week, from month to month, we lived
A round of tumult: duly° were our games   *fittingly*
Prolonged in summer till the day-light failed;
No chair remained before the doors, the bench
10 And threshold steps were empty, fast asleep
The labourer and the old man who had sat
A later lingerer, yet the revelry
Continued and the loud uproar: at last
When all the ground was dark, and the huge clouds
15 Were edged with twinkling stars, to bed we went
With weary joints and with a beating mind.
Ah! is there one who ever has been young
And needs a monitory voice to tame
The pride of virtue and of intellect,
20 And is there one, the wisest and the best
Of all mankind, who does not sometimes wish
For things which cannot be, who would not give,
If so he might, to duty and to truth
The eagerness of infantine desire?
25 A tranquillizing spirit presses now
On my corporeal frame, so wide appears
The vacancy between me and those days
Which yet have such self-presence in my heart
That sometimes when I think of them I seem
30 Two consciousnesses, conscious of myself
And of some other being. A grey stone
Of native rock, left midway in the square
Of our small market-village, was the home
And centre of these joys, and when, returned
35 After long absence, thither I repaired,
I found that it was split and gone to build
A smart assembly-room that perked and flared
With wash and rough-cast,[3] elbowing the ground
Which had been ours. But let the fiddle scream
40 And be ye happy! yet I know, my Friends,
That more than one of you will think with me
Of those soft starry nights and that old dame
From whom the stone was named, who there had sat
And watched her table with its huckster's wares,

---

[1] *my Friend* Coleridge.
[2] *visionary things* Things seen in the imagination.
[3] *smart assembly-room* Hawkshead Town Hall, built in 1790; *wash* Whitewash; *rough-cast* Plaster made of lime and gravel.

45 Assiduous, for the length of sixty years.
    —We ran a boisterous race, the year span round
    With giddy motion. But the time approached
    That brought with it a regular desire
    For calmer pleasures, when the beauteous scenes
50 Of nature were collaterally attached
    To every scheme of holiday delight
    And every boyish sport, less grateful° else   *pleasing*
    And languidly pursued.
                          When summer came
    It was the pastime of our afternoons
55 To beat along the plain of Windermere
    With rival oars; and the selected bourn°   *goal*
    Was now an island musical with birds
    That sang for ever, now a sister isle
    Beneath the oak's umbrageous° covert sown   *shady*
60 With lilies of the valley like a field,
    And now a third small island[1] where remained
    An old stone table and one mouldered cave,
    A hermit's history. In such a race,
    So ended, disappointment could be none,
65 Uneasiness, or pain, or jealousy;
    We rested in the shade all pleased alike,
    Conquered and conqueror. Thus our selfishness
    Was mellowed down, and thus the pride of strength
    And the vain-glory of superior skill
70 Were interfused with objects which subdued
    And tempered them, and gradually produced
    A quiet independence of the heart.
    And to my Friend who knows me I may add,
    Unapprehensive of reproof, that hence
75 Ensued a diffidence and modesty,
    And I was taught to feel, perhaps too much,
    The self-sufficing power of solitude.
        No delicate viands sapped our bodily strength;
    More than we wished we knew the blessing then
80 Of vigorous hunger, for our daily meals
    Were frugal, Sabine fare![2] and then exclude

A little weekly stipend, and we lived
Through three divisions of the quartered year
In penniless poverty. But now to school
85 Returned from the half-yearly holidays,
We came with purses more profusely filled,
Allowance which abundantly sufficed
To gratify the palate with repasts
More costly than the Dame of whom I spake,
90 That ancient woman, and her board° supplied,   *table*
Hence inroads into distant vales, and long
Excursions far away among the hills;
Hence rustic dinners on the cool green ground
Or in the woods or by a river-side
95 Or fountain,° festive banquets that provoked   *spring*
The languid action° of a natural scene   *effect*
By pleasure of corporeal appetite.
        Nor is my aim neglected if I tell
How twice in the long length of those half-years
100 We from our funds perhaps with bolder hand
Drew largely, anxious for one day at least
To feel the motion of the galloping steed;
And with the good old Innkeeper in truth
I needs must say that sometimes we have used
105 Sly subterfuge, for the intended bound
Of the day's journey was too distant far
For any cautious man, a Structure famed
Beyond its neighbourhood, the antique walls
Of a large Abbey[3] with its fractured arch,
110 Belfry, and images, and living trees,
A holy scene! Along the smooth green turf
Our horses grazed: in more than inland peace
Left by the winds that overpass the vale
In that sequestered ruin trees and towers
115 Both silent, and both motionless alike,
Hear all day long the murmuring sea that beats
Incessantly upon a craggy shore.
        Our steeds remounted, and the summons given,
With whip and spur we by the Chantry[4] flew

---

[1] *third small island* Island of Lady Holm, where a chapel dedicated
to the Virgin Mary was formerly located.

[2] *Sabine fare* The Sabines were an ancient Italian mountain tribe
known for their austere living habits. "Sabine fare" may also refer to
the sort of rustic food that would have been prepared at the Roman

poet Horace's country estate, often called the "Sabine farm."

[3] *a large Abbey* Furness Abbey, a ruined abbey approximately 25
miles south of Hawkshead.

[4] *Chantry* Altar or chapel which has been endowed for daily masses
to be sung for the donor.

120 In uncouth race, and left the cross-legged Knight
And the stone Abbot, and that single wren
Which one day sang so sweetly in the nave
Of the old church that, though from recent showers
The earth was comfortless, and touched by faint
125 Internal breezes from the roofless walls
The shuddering ivy dripped large drops, yet still
So sweetly 'mid the gloom the invisible bird
Sang to itself that there I could have made
My dwelling-place, and lived for ever there
130 To hear such music. Through the walls we flew
And down the valley, and, a circuit made
In wantonness of heart, through rough and smooth
We scampered homeward. O ye rocks and streams
And that still spirit of the evening air,
135 Even in this joyous time I sometimes felt
Your presence, when with slackened step we breathed[1]
Along the sides of the steep hills, or when,
Lightened by gleams of moonlight from the sea,
We beat with thundering hoofs the level sand.
140   There was a row of ancient trees, since fallen,
That on the margin of a jutting land
Stood near the lake of Coniston and made
With its long boughs above the water stretched
A gloom through which a boat might sail along
145 As in a cloister. An old Hall[2] was near,
Grotesque and beautiful, its gavel° end   *gable*
And huge round chimneys to the top o'ergrown
With fields of ivy. Thither we repaired,
'Twas even a custom with us, to the shore
150 And to that cool piazza. They who dwelt
In the neglected mansion-house supplied
Fresh butter, tea-kettle, and earthen-ware,
And chafing-dish with smoking coals, and so
Beneath the trees we sat in our small boat
155 And in the covert eat° our delicate meal   *ate*
Upon the calm smooth lake. It was a joy
Worthy the heart of one who is full grown
To rest beneath those horizontal boughs
And mark the radiance of the setting sun,

160 Himself unseen, reposing on the top
Of the high eastern hills. And there I said,
That beauteous sight before me, there I said
(Then first beginning in my thoughts to mark
That sense of dim similitude which links
165 Our moral feelings with external forms)
That in whatever region I should close
My mortal life I would remember you,
Fair scenes! that dying I would think on you,
My soul would send a longing look to you:
170 Even as that setting sun while all the vale
Could nowhere catch one faint memorial gleam
Yet with the last remains of his last light
Still lingered, and a farewell lustre threw
On the dear mountain-tops where first he rose.
175   'Twas then my fourteenth summer, and these words
Were uttered in a casual access
Of sentiment, a momentary trance
That far outran the habit of my mind.
         Upon the eastern shore of Windermere,
180 Above the crescent of a pleasant bay,
There was an Inn,[3] no homely-featured shed,
Brother of the surrounding cottages,
But 'twas a splendid place, the door beset
With chaises, grooms, and liveries, and within
185 Decanters, glasses, and the blood-red wine.
In ancient times, or ere the Hall[4] was built
On the large island, had the dwelling been
More worthy of a poet's love, a hut
Proud of its one bright fire and sycamore shade.
190 But though the rhymes were gone which once inscribed
The threshold, and large golden characters
On the blue-frosted sign-board had usurped
The place of the old Lion in contempt
And mockery of the rustic painter's hand,
195 Yet to this hour the spot to me is dear
With all its foolish pomp. The garden lay
Upon a slope surmounted by the plain
Of a small bowling-green; beneath us stood

---

1 *breathed* I.e., let the horses catch their breath.
2 *old Hall* Coniston Hall, built in 1580.

3 *an Inn* The White Lion Inn, which was located in Bowness Village.
4 *the Hall* Built on Belle Isle in Lake Windermere in the early 1780s.

A grove, with gleams of water through the trees
200 And over the tree-tops; nor did we want
Refreshment, strawberries and mellow cream,
And there through half an afternoon we played
On the smooth platform, and the shouts we sent
Made all the mountains ring. But ere the fall
205 Of night, when in our pinnace we returned
Over the dusky lake, and to the beach
Of some small island steered our course with one,
The minstrel of our troop, and left him there
And rowed off gently while he blew his flute
210 Alone upon the rock—oh then the calm
And dead still water lay upon my mind
Even with a weight of pleasure, and the sky,
Never before so beautiful, sank down
Into my heart and held me like a dream.

215   Thus day by day my sympathies increased
And thus the common range of visible things
Grew dear to me: already I began
To love the sun, a Boy I loved the sun
Not, as I since have loved him, as a pledge
220 And surety of my earthly life, a light
Which while I view I feel I am alive,
But for this cause, that I had seen him lay
His beauty on the morning hills, had seen
The western mountain touch his setting orb
225 In many a thoughtless hour, when from excess
Of happiness my blood appeared to flow
With its own pleasure and I breathed with joy.
And from like feelings, humble though intense,
To patriotic and domestic love
230 Analogous, the moon to me was dear,
For I would dream away my purposes
Standing to look upon her while she hung
Midway between the hills as if she knew
No other region but belonged to thee,
235 Yea, appertained by a peculiar right
To thee and thy grey huts,[1] my native vale.

Those incidental charms which first attached
My heart to rural objects day by day
Grew weaker, and I hasten on to tell

240 How nature, intervenient° till this time   *extraneous*
And secondary, now at length was sought
For her own sake. But who shall parcel out
His intellect by geometric rules,
Split like a province into round and square;
245 Who knows the individual hour in which
His habits were first sown, even as a seed;
Who that shall point as with a wand and say,
This portion of the river of my mind
Came from yon fountain? Thou, my Friend, art one
250 More deeply read in thy own thoughts, no slave
Of that false secondary power by which
In weakness we create distinctions, then
Believe our puny boundaries are things
Which we perceive and not which we have made.
255 To thee, unblinded by these outward shows,
The unity of all has been revealed,
And thou wilt doubt with me, less aptly skilled
Than many are to class the cabinet
Of their sensations and in voluble phrase
260 Run through the history and birth of each
As of a single independent thing.
Hard task to analyse a soul in which
Not only general habits and desires
But each most obvious and particular thought,
265 Not in a mystical and idle sense
But in the words of reason deeply weighed,
Hath no beginning.
                    Bless'd the infant Babe
(For with my best conjectures I would trace
The progress of our being) blest the Babe
270 Nursed in his Mother's arms, the Babe who sleeps
Upon his Mother's breast, who when his soul
Claims manifest kindred with an earthly soul
Doth gather passion from his Mother's eye!
Such feelings pass into his torpid life
275 Like an awakening breeze, and hence his mind
Even in the first trial of its powers
Is prompt and watchful, eager to combine
In one appearance all the elements
And parts of the same object, else detached
280 And loath to coalesce. Thus day by day
Subjected to the discipline of love

---

1 *grey huts* Grey stone cottages.

His organs and recipient faculties
Are quickened, are more vigorous, his mind spreads
Tenacious of the forms which it receives.
285   In one beloved presence, nay, and more,
In that most apprehensive habitude[1]
And those sensations which have been derived
From this beloved presence, there exists
A virtue which irradiates and exalts
290   All objects through all intercourse of sense.
No outcast he, bewildered and depressed:
Along his infant veins are interfused
The gravitation and the filial bond
Of nature that connect him with the world.
295   Emphatically such a being lives
An inmate of this *active* universe;
From nature largely he receives, nor so
Is satisfied but largely gives again,
For feeling has to him imparted strength,
300   And powerful in all sentiments of grief,
Of exultation, fear and joy, his mind,
Even as an agent of the one great mind,
Creates, creator and receiver both,
Working but in alliance with the works
305   Which it beholds. Such verily is the first
Poetic spirit of our human life,
By uniform control of after years
In most abated and suppressed, in some
Through every change of growth or of decay
310   Preeminent till death.
                        From early days,
Beginning not long after that first time
In which, a Babe, by intercourse of touch
I held mute dialogues with my Mother's heart,
I have endeavoured to display the means
315   Whereby this infant sensibility,
Great birth-right of our being, was in me
Augmented and sustained. Yet is a path
More difficult before me, and I fear
That in its broken windings we shall need
320   The Chamois'[2] sinews and the Eagle's wing:

For now a trouble came into my mind
From obscure causes. I was left alone
Seeking this visible world, nor knowing why:
The props of my affections were removed[3]
325   And yet the building stood as if sustained
By its own spirit. All that I beheld
Was dear to me, and from this cause it came
That now to Nature's finer influxes°   *influences*
My mind lay open, to that more exact
330   And intimate communion which our hearts
Maintain with the minuter properties
Of objects which already are beloved,
And of those only. Many are the joys
Of youth, but oh! what happiness to live
335   When every hour brings palpable access
Of knowledge, when all knowledge is delight,
And sorrow is not there. The seasons came
And every season brought a countless store
Of modes and temporary qualities
340   Which but for this most watchful power of love
Had been neglected, left a register
Of permanent relations, else unknown:
Hence life, and change, and beauty, solitude
More active even than "best society,"[4]
345   Society made sweet as solitude
By silent inobtrusive sympathies
And gentle agitations of the mind
From manifold distinctions, difference
Perceived in things where to the common eye
350   No difference is: and hence from the same source
Sublimer joy; for I would walk alone
In storm and tempest or in starlight nights
Beneath the quiet heavens, and at that time
Would feel whate'er there is of power in sound
355   To breathe an elevated mood by form
Or image unprofaned: and I would stand
Beneath some rock listening to sounds that are
The ghostly language of the ancient earth
Or make their dim abode in distant winds.

---

[1]   *apprehensive habitude* Disposition most suited to learning.

[2]   *Chamois* Agile goat-antelope found primarily in the mountains of Europe.

[3]   *The props ... removed* Wordsworth's mother died just before his eighth birthday.

[4]   *best society* See Milton, *Paradise Lost* 9.249: "For solitude sometimes is the best society."

360 Thence did I drink the visionary power.
     I deem not profitless these fleeting moods
     Of shadowy exaltation, not for this,
     That they are kindred to our purer mind
     And intellectual life, but that the soul
365 Remembering how she felt, but what she felt
     Remembering not, retains an obscure sense
     Of possible sublimity to which
     With growing faculties she doth aspire,
     With faculties still growing, feeling still
370 That whatsoever point they gain, they still
     Have something to pursue.
                              And not alone
     In grandeur and in tumult, but no less
     In tranquil scenes, that universal power
     And fitness in the latent qualities
375 And essences of things, by which the mind
     Is moved with feelings of delight, to me
     Came strengthened with a superadded soul,
     A virtue not its own. My morning walks
     Were early; oft before the hours of school
380 I travelled round our little lake, five miles
     Of pleasant wandering, happy time more dear
     For this, that one was by my side, a Friend
     Then passionately loved;[1] with heart how full
     Will he peruse these lines, this page, perhaps
385 A blank to other men, for many years
     Have since flowed in between us, and, our minds
     Both silent to each other, at this time
     We live as if those hours had never been.
     Nor seldom did I lift our cottage latch
390 Far earlier, and before the vernal° thrush   *spring-time*
     Was audible, among the hills I sat
     Alone upon some jutting eminence
     At the first hour of morning when the vale
     Lay quiet in an utter solitude.
395 How shall I trace the history, where seek
     The origin of what I then have felt?
     Oft in those moments such a holy calm
     Did overspread my soul that I forgot
     The agency of sight, and what I saw

400 Appeared like something in myself—a dream,
     A prospect° in my mind. 'Twere long to tell   *view*
     What spring and autumn, what the winter-snows
     And what the summer-shade, what day and night,
     The evening and the morning, what my dreams
405 And what my waking thoughts supplied, to nurse
     That spirit of religious love in which
     I walked with nature. But let this at least
     Be not forgotten, that I still retained
     My first creative sensibility,
410 That by the regular action of the world
     My soul was unsubdued. A plastic° power   *formative*
     Abode with me, a forming hand, at times
     Rebellious, acting in a devious mood,
     A local spirit of its own, at war
415 With general tendency, but for the most
     Subservient strictly to the external things
     With which it communed. An auxiliar light
     Came from my mind which on the setting sun
     Bestowed new splendour, the melodious birds,
420 The gentle breezes, fountains that ran on
     Murmuring so sweetly in themselves, obeyed
     A like dominion, and the midnight storm
     Grew darker in the presence of my eye.
     Hence my obeisance, my devotion hence,
425 And *hence* my transport.°   *exaltation*
                              Nor should this perchance
     Pass unrecorded, that I still° had loved   *always*
     The exercise and produce of a toil
     Than analytic industry to me
     More pleasing, and whose character, I deem,
430 Is more poetic, as resembling more
     Creative agency: I mean to speak
     Of that interminable building reared
     By observation of affinities
     In objects where no brotherhood exists
435 To common minds. My seventeenth year was come,
     And whether from this habit rooted now
     So deeply in my mind, or from excess
     Of the great social principle of life
     Coercing all things into sympathy,
440 To unorganic natures I transferred
     My own enjoyments, or, the power of truth

---

[1] *Friend ... loved* John Fleming, Wordsworth's friend at Hawkshead.

Coming in revelation, I conversed
With things that really are. I at this time
Saw blessings spread around me like a sea.
445 Thus did my days pass on, and now at length
From Nature and her overflowing soul
I had received so much that all my thoughts
Were steeped in feeling; I was only then
Contented when with bliss ineffable
450 I felt the sentiment of being spread
O'er all that moves, and all that seemeth still,
O'er all that, lost beyond the reach of thought
And human knowledge, to the human eye
Invisible, yet liveth to the heart,
455 O'er all that leaps, and runs, and shouts and sings
Or beats the gladsome air, o'er all that glides
Beneath the wave, yea, in the wave itself
And mighty depth of waters: wonder not
If such my transports were, for in all things
460 I saw one life and felt that it was joy.
One song they sang, and it was audible,
Most audible then when the fleshly ear,
O'ercome by grosser prelude of that strain,
Forgot its functions, and slept undisturbed.
465   If this be error, and another faith
Find easier access to the pious mind,
Yet were I grossly destitute of all
Those human sentiments which make this earth
So dear, if I should fail with grateful voice
470 To speak of you, ye mountains! and ye lakes
And sounding cataracts! ye mists and winds
That dwell among the hills where I was born.
If, in my youth, I have been pure in heart,
If, mingling with the world, I am content
475 With my own modest pleasures, and have lived
With God and Nature communing, removed
From little enmities and low desires,
The gift is yours: if in these times[1] of fear,

This melancholy waste° of hopes o'erthrown,   *wasteland*
480 If, 'mid indifference and apathy
And wicked exultation, when good men
On every side fall off we know not how
To selfishness disguised in gentle names
Of peace, and quiet, and domestic love,
485 Yet mingled, not unwillingly, with sneers
On visionary minds, if in this time
Of dereliction and dismay I yet
Despair not of our nature, but retain
A more than Roman confidence, a faith
490 That fails not, in all sorrow my support,
The blessing of my life, the gift is yours,
Ye Mountains! thine, O Nature! thou hast fed
My lofty speculations, and in thee
For this uneasy heart of ours I find
495 A never-failing principle of joy
And purest passion.
          Thou, my Friend, wast reared
In the great city 'mid far other scenes,[2]
But we, by different roads, at length have gained
The self-same bourne. And from this cause to thee
500 I speak unapprehensive of contempt,
The insinuated scoff of coward tongues,
And all that silent language which so oft
In conversation betwixt man and man
Blots from the human countenance all trace
505 Of beauty and of love. For thou hast sought
The truth in solitude, and thou art one,
The most intense of Nature's worshippers,
In many things my brother, chiefly here
In this my deep devotion.
                          Fare thee well!
510 Health and the quiet of a healthful mind
Attend thee! seeking oft the haunts of men
But yet more often living with thyself
And for thyself, so haply shall thy days
Be many and a blessing to mankind.

—1799

1 *in these times* I.e., following the failure of the French Revolution. Many radicals were recanting. In a 1799 letter to Wordsworth, Coleridge asks him to write something about those who "have thrown up all hopes of the amelioration of mankind, and are sinking into an almost epicurean selfishness, disguising the same under the soft titles of domestic attachment and contempt for visionary *philosophes*."

2 *Thou … scenes* See Coleridge's "Frost at Midnight" 50–52, in which the speaker addresses his child: "thou shalt learn far other love, / And in far other scenes! For I was reared / In the great city, pent 'mid cloisters dim."

from *The Fourteen-Book Prelude*

from BOOK FIRST
INTRODUCTION, CHILDHOOD, AND SCHOOL-TIME

O there is blessing in this gentle Breeze,
   A visitant that, while he fans my cheek,
Doth seem half-conscious of the joy he brings
From the green fields, and from yon azure sky.
5 Whate'er his mission, the soft breeze can come
To none more grateful than to me; escaped
From the vast City,[1] where I long have pined
A discontented Sojourner—Now free,
Free as a bird to settle where I will.
10 What dwelling shall receive me? in what vale
Shall be my harbour? underneath what grove
Shall I take up my home? and what clear stream
Shall with its murmur lull me into rest?
The earth is all before me:[2] with a heart
15 Joyous, nor scared at its own liberty,
I look about; and should the chosen guide
Be nothing better than a wandering cloud,
I cannot miss my way. I breathe again;
Trances of thought and mountings of the heart
20 Come fast upon me: it is shaken off,
That burthen of my own unnatural self,
The heavy weight of many a weary day
Not mine, and such as were not made for me.
Long months of peace (if such bold word accord
25 With any promises of human life),
Long months of ease and undisturbed delight
Are mine in prospect; whither shall I turn,
By road or pathway, or through trackless field,
Up hill or down, or shall some floating thing
30 Upon the River point me out my course?
Dear Liberty! Yet what would it avail,
But for a gift that consecrates the joy?
For I, methought, while the sweet breath of heaven
Was blowing on my body, felt, within,

35 A correspondent breeze, that gently moved
With quickening virtue, but is now become
A tempest, a redundant° energy,   *abounding*
Vexing its own creation. Thanks to both,
And their congenial powers that, while they join
40 In breaking up a long continued frost,
Bring with them vernal° promises, the hope   *spring-time*
Of active days urged on by flying hours;
Days of sweet leisure taxed with patient thought
Abstruse, nor wanting punctual service high,
45 Matins and vespers, of harmonious verse!
      Thus far, O Friend! did I, not used to make
A present joy the matter of a Song,
Pour forth, that day, my soul in measured strains,
That would not be forgotten, and are here
50 Recorded: to the open fields I told
A prophecy: poetic numbers° came   *verses*
Spontaneously, to clothe in priestly robe
A renovated Spirit singled out,
Such hope was mine, for holy services:
55 My own voice cheered me, and, far more, the mind's
Internal echo of the imperfect sound;
To both I listened, drawing from them both
A cheerful confidence in things to come.
      Content, and not unwilling now to give
60 A respite to this passion, I paced on
With brisk and eager steps; and came at length
To a green shady place where down I sat
Beneath a tree, slackening my thoughts by choice,
And settling into gentler happiness.
65 'Twas Autumn, and a clear and placid day,
With warmth, as much as needed, from a sun
Two hours declined towards the west, a day
With silver clouds, and sunshine on the grass,
And, in the sheltered and the sheltering grove,
70 A perfect stillness. Many were the thoughts
Encouraged and dismissed, till choice was made
Of a known Vale[3] whither my feet should turn,
Nor rest till they had reached the very door
Of the one Cottage which methought I saw.
75 No picture of mere memory ever looked

---

[1] *the vast City* London.

[2] *The earth … me* See Milton, *Paradise Lost* 12.646. Milton writes that following the expulsion of Adam and Eve from Eden, "The world was all before them."

[3] *a known Vale* Grasmere, where Wordsworth and his sister moved in 1799.

So fair; and while upon the fancied scene
I gazed with growing love, a higher power
Than Fancy gave assurance of some work
Of glory, there forthwith to be begun,
80 Perhaps too there performed.[1] Thus long I mused,
Nor e'er lost sight of what I mused upon,
Save where, amid the stately grove of Oaks,
Now here—now there—an acorn, from its cup
Dislodged, through sere leaves rustled, or at once
85 To the bare earth dropped with a startling sound.
     From that soft couch I rose not, till the sun
Had almost touched the horizon; casting then
A backward glance upon the curling cloud
Of city smoke, by distance ruralized,
90 Keen as a Truant or a Fugitive,
But as a Pilgrim resolute, I took,
Even with the chance equipment of that hour,
The road that pointed tow'rd the chosen Vale.
     It was a splendid evening: and my Soul
95 Once more made trial of her strength, nor lacked
Eolian visitations;[2] but the harp
Was soon defrauded, and the banded host
Of harmony dispersed in straggling sounds;
And lastly utter silence! "Be it so;
100 Why think of any thing but present good?"
So, like a Home-bound Labourer, I pursued
My way, beneath the mellowing sun, that shed
Mild influence;[3] nor left in me one wish
Again to bend the sabbath of that time[4]
105 To a servile yoke. What need of many words?
A pleasant loitering journey, through three days
Continued, brought me to my hermitage.
I spare to tell of what ensued, the life
In common things—the endless store of things
110 Rare, or at least so seeming, every day
Found all about me in one neighbourhood;

The self-congratulation,[5] and from morn
To night unbroken cheerfulness serene.
But speedily an earnest longing rose
115 To brace myself to some determined aim,
Reading or thinking; either to lay up
New stores, or rescue from decay the old
By timely interference: and therewith
Came hopes still higher, that with outward life
120 I might endue some airy fantasies
That had been floating loose about for years;
And to such Beings temperately deal forth
The many feelings that oppressed my heart.
That hope hath been discouraged; welcome light
125 Dawns from the East, but dawns—to disappear
And mock me with a sky that ripens not
Into a steady morning: if my mind,
Remembering the bold promise of the past,
Would gladly grapple with some noble theme,
130 Vain is her wish; where'er she turns, she finds
Impediments from day to day renewed.
     And now it would content me to yield up
Those lofty hopes awhile for present gifts
Of humbler industry. But, O dear Friend!
135 The Poet, gentle Creature as he is,
Hath, like the Lover, his unruly times,
His fits when he is neither sick nor well,
Though no distress be near him but his own
Unmanageable thoughts: his mind, best pleas'd
140 While she, as duteous as the Mother Dove,
Sits brooding,[6] lives not always to that end,
But, like the innocent Bird, hath goadings on
That drive her, as in trouble, through the groves:
With me is now such passion, to be blamed
145 No otherwise than as it lasts too long.
     When, as becomes a Man who would prepare
For such an arduous Work, I through myself
Make rigorous inquisition, the report
Is often cheering; for I neither seem

---

[1] *some work ... performed* Wordsworth's poem *The Recluse*, intended to be his major work but never completed.

[2] *Eolian visitations* Influences that act on his soul as winds act on an Aeolian harp, which makes music when touched by a breeze.

[3] *influence* I.e., astrological influence, exerted by the stars over human life.

[4] *sabbath ... time* Time of rest.

[5] *self-congratulation* Self-rejoicing.

[6] *While she ... brooding* See *Paradise Lost* 1.21–22, in which the narrator invokes the Holy Spirit, who, at the time of Creation, "Dovelike satst brooding on the vast Abyss / And madst it pregnant."

150   To lack that first great gift, the vital Soul,
Nor general Truths, which are themselves a sort
Of Elements and Agents, Under-powers,
Subordinate helpers of the living Mind:
Nor am I naked of external things,
155   Forms, images, nor numerous other aids
Of less regard, though won perhaps with toil,
And needful to build up a Poet's praise.
Time, place, and manners° do I seek, and these   *habits*
Are found in plenteous store, but no where such
160   As may be singled out with steady choice:
No little band of yet remembered names
Whom I in perfect confidence might hope
To summon back from lonesome banishment,
And make them dwellers in the hearts of men
165   Now living, or to live in future years.
Sometimes the ambitious Power of choice, mistaking
Proud spring-tide swellings for a regular sea,
Will settle on some British theme, some old
Romantic Tale by Milton left unsung:[1]
170   More often turning to some gentle place
Within the groves of Chivalry, I pipe
To Shepherd Swains,° or seated, harp in hand,   *lovers*
Amid reposing knights by a River side
Or fountain, listen to the grave reports
175   Of dire enchantments faced, and overcome
By the strong mind, and Tales of warlike feats
Where spear encountered spear, and sword with sword
Fought, as if conscious of the blazonry
That the shield bore, so glorious was the strife;
180   Whence inspiration for a song that winds
Through ever changing scenes of votive quest,[2]
Wrongs to redress, harmonious tribute paid
To patient courage and unblemished truth,
To firm devotion, zeal unquenchable,
185   And Christian meekness hallowing faithful loves.[3]
Sometimes, more sternly moved, I would relate
How vanquished Mithridates northward passed,

And, hidden in the cloud of years, became
Odin, the Father of a Race by whom
190   Perished the Roman Empire;[4] how the friends
And followers of Sertorius,[5] out of Spain
Flying, found shelter in the Fortunate Isles;
And left their usages, their arts, and laws
To disappear by a slow gradual death;
195   To dwindle and to perish, one by one,
Starved in those narrow bounds: but not the soul
Of Liberty, which fifteen hundred years
Survived, and, when the European came
With skill and power that might not be withstood,
200   Did, like a pestilence, maintain its hold,
And wasted down by glorious death that Race
Of natural Heroes; or I would record
How, in tyrannic times, some high-souled Man,
Unnamed among the chronicles of Kings,
205   Suffered in silence for truth's sake: or tell
How that one Frenchman,[6] through continued force
Of meditation on the inhuman deeds
Of those who conquered first the Indian isles,
Went, single in his ministry, across
210   The Ocean—not to comfort the Oppressed,
But, like a thirsty wind, to roam about,
Withering the Oppressor: how Gustavus sought
Help at his need in Dalecarlia's mines:[7]

---

[1]   *some old ... unsung*   In *Paradise Lost* 9.24–41, Milton writes that he chose to compose a Biblical rather than a romantic epic.

[2]   *votive quest*   Quest undertaken as the result of a vow.

[3]   *And Christian ... loves*   Reference to Spenser's *Faerie Queene*, line 9: "Fierce warres and faithful loves shall moralize my song."

[4]   *How vanquished ... Empire*   Mithridates was a king of Pontus who was defeated by the Romans in 66 BCE. In *Decline and Fall of the Roman Empire* (1776–88), Edward Gibbon associates the story of King Mithridates's downfall with the tale of Odin, a Goth chieftain who marched towards Rome and who hoped that his descendants would defeat the conquering Romans.

[5]   *Sertorius*   Roman general and ally of Mithridates who conquered much of Spain but was assassinated in 72 BCE. His followers were said to have emigrated to the Canary Island (the "Fortunate Isles") to escape the Romans, and to have survived there until the fifteenth century, when they were defeated by the invading Spaniards.

[6]   [Wordsworth's note]   Dominique de Gourges, a French gentleman who went in 1569 to Florida to avenge the massacre of the French by the Spaniards there.

[7]   *Gustavus ... mines*   Gustavus Vasa led a successful revolt in Sweden against the ruling Danes after gaining support in the mining town of Dalecarlia.

How Wallace[1] fought for Scotland, left the name
215   Of Wallace to be found, like a wild flower,
All over his dear Country, left the deeds
Of Wallace, like a family of Ghosts,
To people the steep rocks and river banks,
Her natural sanctuaries, with a local soul
220   Of independence and stern liberty.
Sometimes it suits me better to invent
A Tale from my own heart, more near akin
To my own passions, and habitual thoughts,
Some variegated Story, in the main
225   Lofty, but the unsubstantial Structure melts
Before the very sun that brightens it,
Mist into air dissolving! Then, a wish,
My last and favourite aspiration, mounts,
With yearning, tow'rds some philosophic Song
230   Of Truth that cherishes our daily life;
With meditations passionate, from deep
Recesses in man's heart, immortal verse
Thoughtfully fitted to the Orphean lyre;[2]
But from this awful° burthen I full soon   *awe-inspiring*
235   Take refuge, and beguile myself with trust
That mellower years will bring a riper mind
And clearer insight. Thus my days are passed
In contradiction; with no skill to part
Vague longing, haply bred by want of power,
240   From paramount impulse—not to be withstood;
A timorous capacity from prudence;
From circumspection, infinite delay.
Humility and modest awe themselves
Betray me, serving often for a cloak
245   To a more subtle selfishness; that now
Locks every function up in blank° reserve,° *total / inaction*
Now dupes me, trusting to an anxious eye
That with intrusive restlessness beats off
Simplicity, and self-presented truth.
250   Ah! better far than this, to stray about
Voluptuously,° through fields and rural walks,   *luxuriously*

And ask no record of the hours, resigned
To vacant musing, unreproved neglect
Of all things, and deliberate holiday:
255   Far better never to have heard the name
Of zeal and just ambition, than to live
Baffled and plagued by a mind that every hour
Turns recreant to her task, takes heart again,
Then feels immediately some hollow thought
260   Hang like an interdict° upon her hopes.   *prohibition*
This is my lot; for either still I find
Some imperfection in the chosen theme;
Or see of absolute accomplishment
Much wanting, so much wanting, in myself
265   That I recoil and droop, and seek repose
In listlessness from vain perplexity;
Unprofitably travelling toward the grave,
Like a false Steward who hath much received,
And renders nothing back.[3] ...

from Book Fifth
Books

... **H**itherto,
In progress through this Work, my mind hath looked
Upon the speaking face of earth and heaven
As her prime Teacher, intercourse with man
15   Established by the sovereign Intellect
Who through that bodily Image hath diffused,
As might appear to the eye of fleeting Time,
A deathless Spirit. Thou also, Man! hast wrought,
For commerce of thy nature with herself,
20   Things that aspire to unconquerable life:
And yet we feel, we cannot choose but feel
That they must perish. Tremblings of the heart
It gives, to think that our immortal being
No more shall need such garments; and yet Man,
25   As long as he shall be the Child of earth,

---

[1] *Wallace* William Wallace (c. 1270–1305), Scottish hero who fought for the freedom of his country but was executed by Edward I in 1305.

[2] *Orphean lyre* Lyre of Orpheus, the poet of Greek myth who could charm all living things with his music.

[3] *false Steward ... back* Reference to the parable of the false steward in Matthew 25.14–30, who wastes what his lord gives him.

Might almost "weep to have"[1] what he may lose,
Nor be himself extinguished; but survive
Abject, depressed, forlorn, disconsolate.
A thought is with me sometimes, and I say—
30 Should the whole frame of earth by inward throes
Be wrenched, or fire come down from far to scorch
Her pleasant habitations, and dry up
Old Ocean in his bed, left singed and bare,
Yet would the living Presence still subsist
35 Victorious; and composure would ensue,
And kindlings like the morning—presage sure
Of day returning, and of life revived.
But all the meditations of mankind,
Yea, all the adamantine° hold° of   *indestructible / fortresses*
      truth,
40 By reason built, or passion, which itself
Is highest reason in a soul sublime;
The consecrated works of Bard and Sage,
Sensuous or intellectual, wrought by men,
Twin labourers, and heirs of the same hopes;
45 Where would they be? Oh! why hath not the Mind
Some element to stamp her image on
In nature somewhat nearer to her own?
Why, gifted with such powers to send abroad
Her spirit, must it lodge in shrines so frail?
50   One day, when from my lips a like complaint
Had fallen in presence of a studious friend,
He with a smile made answer that in truth
'Twas going far to seek disquietude,
But, on the front of his reproof, confessed
55 That he himself had oftentimes given way
To kindred hauntings. Whereupon I told
That once in the stillness of a summer's noon,
While I was seated in a rocky cave
By the sea-side, perusing, so it chanced,
60 The famous history of the errant Knight
Recorded by Cervantes,[2] these same thoughts
Beset me, and to height unusual rose,

While listlessly I sat, and, having closed
The Book, had turned my eyes tow'rd the wide Sea.
65 On Poetry, and geometric truth,
And their high privilege of lasting life,
From all internal injury exempt,
I mused; upon these chiefly: and, at length,
My senses yielding to the sultry air,
70 Sleep seized me, and I passed into a dream.
I saw before me stretched a boundless plain,
Of sandy wilderness, all blank and void;
And as I looked around, distress and fear
Came creeping over me, when at my side,
75 Close at my side, an uncouth Shape appeared
Upon a Dromedary, mounted high.
He seemed an Arab of the Bedouin Tribes:
A Lance he bore, and underneath one arm
A Stone; and, in the opposite hand, a Shell
80 Of a surpassing brightness. At the sight
Much I rejoiced, not doubting but a Guide
Was present, one who with unerring skill
Would through the desert lead me; and while yet
I looked, and looked, self-questioned what this freight
85 Which the New-comer carried through the Waste
Could mean, the Arab told me that the Stone
(To give it in the language of the Dream)
Was Euclid's Elements;[3] "and this," said he,
"This other," pointing to the Shell, "this book
90 Is something of more worth"; and, at the word,
Stretched forth the Shell, so beautiful in shape,
In colour so resplendent, with command
That I should hold it to my ear. I did so—
And heard, that instant, in an unknown tongue,
95 Which yet I understood, articulate sounds,
A loud prophetic blast of harmony—
An Ode, in passion uttered, which foretold
Destruction to the Children of the Earth,
By Deluge now at hand. No sooner ceased
100 The Song than the Arab with calm look declared
That all would come to pass, of which the voice
Had given forewarning, and that he himself
Was going then to bury those two Books:

---

[1] *weep to have* See Shakespeare's Sonnet 64, lines 13–14: "This thought [of the destruction caused by time] is as a death, which cannot choose / But weep to have that which it fears to lose."

[2] *famous history … Cervantes* Miguel de Cervantes's *Don Quixote* (1605).

[3] *Euclid's Elements* Foundational geometry textbook by third century BCE Greek mathematician Euclid.

The One that held acquaintance with the stars,
105 And wedded Soul to Soul in purest bond
Of Reason, undisturbed by space or time:
Th'other, that was a God, yea many Gods,
Had voices more than all the winds, with power
To exhilarate the Spirit, and to soothe,
110 Through every clime, the heart of human kind.
While this was uttering, strange as it may seem,
I wondered not, although I plainly saw
The One to be a Stone, the Other a Shell,
Nor doubted once but that they both were Books;
115 Having a perfect faith in all that passed.
Far stronger now grew the desire I felt
To cleave unto this Man; but when I prayed
To share his enterprize, he hurried on,
Reckless° of me: I followed, not unseen,   *heedless*
120 For oftentimes he cast a backward look,
Grasping his twofold treasure. Lance in rest,
He rode, I keeping pace with him; and now
He to my fancy had become the Knight
Whose tale Cervantes tells; yet not the Knight,
125 But was an Arab of the desert, too,
Of these was neither, and was both at once.
His countenance, meanwhile, grew more disturbed,
And looking backwards when he looked, mine eyes
Saw, over half the wilderness diffused,
130 A bed of glittering light: I asked the cause.
"It is," said he, "the waters of the Deep
Gathering upon us"; quickening then the pace
Of the unwieldy Creature he bestrode,
He left me; I called after him aloud—
135 He heeded not; but with his twofold charge
Still in his grasp, before me, full in view,
Went hurrying o'er the illimitable Waste
With the fleet waters of a drowning World
In chase of him; whereat I waked in terror;
140 And saw the Sea before me, and the Book,
In which I had been reading, at my side.

     Full often, taking from the world of Sleep
This Arab Phantom, which I thus beheld,
This semi-Quixote, I to him have given
145 A substance, fancied him a living man,
A gentle Dweller in the desert, crazed

By love and feeling, and internal thought
Protracted among endless solitudes;
Have shaped him, in the oppression of his brain,
150 And so equipped, wandering upon this quest!
Nor have I pitied him; but rather felt
Reverence was due to a Being thus employed;
And thought that, in the blind and awful lair
Of such a madness, reason did lie couched.
155 Enow° there are on earth to take in charge   *enough*
Their Wives, their Children, and their virgin Loves,
Or whatsoever else the heart holds dear;
Enow to stir for these—yea, will I say,
Contemplating in soberness the approach
160 Of an event so dire, by signs, in earth
Or heaven, made manifest—that I could share
That maniac's fond anxiety, and go
Upon like errand. Oftentimes, at least,
Me hath such strong entrancement overcome,
165 When I have held a volume in my hand,
Poor earthly casket of immortal Verse,
Shakespeare, or Milton, Labourers divine! …

     Here must we pause; this only let me add,
From heart-experience, and in humblest sense
160 Of modesty, that he, who, in his youth,
A daily Wanderer among woods and fields,
With living Nature hath been intimate,
Not only in that raw unpractised time
Is stirred to ecstasy, as others are,
165 By glittering verse; but, further, doth receive,
In measure only dealt out to himself,
Knowledge and increase of enduring joy
From the great Nature that exists in works
Of mighty Poets. Visionary Power
170 Attends the motions of the viewless° winds   *invisible*
Embodied in the mystery of words:
There darkness makes abode, and all the host
Of shadowy things work endless changes there,
As in a mansion like their proper home.
175 Even forms and substances are circumfused
By that transparent veil with light divine;
And, through the turnings intricate of verse,
Present themselves as objects recognized,
In flashes, and with glory not their own.

180   Thus far a scanty record is deduced
Of what I owed to Books in early life;
Their later influence yet remains untold;
But as this work was taking in my mind
Proportions that seemed larger than had first
185   Been meditated, I was indisposed
To any further progress, at a time
When these acknowledgments were left unpaid.

from BOOK SIXTH
CAMBRIDGE, AND THE ALPS [1]

...   'Tis not my present purpose to retrace
490   That variegated journey step by step;
A march it was of military speed,
And earth did change her images and forms
Before us, fast as clouds are changed in heaven.
Day after day, up early and down late,
495   From hill to vale we dropped—from vale to hill
Mounted—from province on to province swept—
Keen hunters in a chase of fourteen weeks,
Eager as birds of prey, or as a Ship
Upon the stretch when winds are blowing fair.
500   Sweet coverts did we cross of pastoral life,
Enticing Valleys, greeted them and left
Too soon, while yet the very flash and gleam
Of salutation were not passed away.
Oh! sorrow for the Youth who could have seen
505   Unchastened, unsubdued, unawed, unraised
To patriarchal dignity of mind
And pure simplicity of wish and will,
Those sanctified Abodes of peaceful Man;
Pleased (though to hardship born, and compassed round
510   With danger, varying as the seasons change),
Pleased with his daily tasks, or, if not pleased,
Contented, from the moment that the Dawn,
Ah! surely not without attendant gleams
Of soul-illumination, calls him forth
515   To industry, by glistenings flung on rocks

Whose evening shadows lead him to repose.
    Well might a Stranger look with bounding heart
Down on a green Recess, the first I saw
Of those deep haunts, an aboriginal Vale,
520   Quiet, and lorded over, and possessed
By naked huts, wood-built and sown like tents,
Or Indian Cabins over the fresh lawns
And by the river side. That very day,
From a bare ridge we also first beheld
525   Unveiled the summit of Mont Blanc, and grieved
To have a soulless image on the eye
Which had usurped upon a living thought
That never more could be. The wondrous Vale
Of Chamouny [2] stretched far below, and soon
530   With its dumb° cataracts, and streams of ice,   *unheard*
A motionless array of mighty waves,
Five rivers broad and vast, made rich amends,
And reconciled us to realities.
There small birds warble from the leafy trees,
535   The eagle soars high in the element;
There doth the Reaper bind the yellow sheaf,
The Maiden spread the hay-cock [3] in the sun,
While Winter like a well-tamed lion walks,
Descending from the Mountain to make sport
540   Among the Cottages by beds of flowers.
    Whate'er in this wide circuit we beheld,
Or heard, was fitted to our unripe state
Of intellect and heart. With such a book
Before our eyes we could not choose but read
545   Lessons of genuine brotherhood, the plain
And universal reason of mankind,
The truths of Young and Old. Nor, side by side
Pacing, two social Pilgrims, or alone
Each with his humour,° could we fail to abound   *disposition*
550   In dreams and fictions pensively composed,
Dejection taken up for pleasure's sake,
And gilded sympathies; the willow [4] wreath,
And sober posies° of funereal flowers   *bouquets*

---

[1]   *from ... Alps* In this passage Wordsworth describes his journey through the Alps, along the Simplon Pass, with Robert Jones, a fellow Cambridge student.

[2]   *Vale of Chamouny* Valley located at the foot of Mont Blanc. (The modern spelling is Chamonix.)

[3]   *hay-cock* Conical pile of hay.

[4]   *willow* Symbol of sadness.

Gathered, among those solitudes sublime,
555 From formal gardens of the Lady Sorrow,
Did sweeten many a meditative hour.
　　Yet still in me with those soft luxuries
Mixed something of stern mood, an under thirst
Of vigor seldom utterly allayed.
560 And from that source how different a sadness
Would issue, let one incident make known.
When from the Vallais we had turned, and
　　clomb°   *climbed*
Along the Simplon's steep and rugged road,
Following a band of Muleteers, we reached
565 A halting-place where all together took
Their noon-tide meal. Hastily rose our Guide,
Leaving *us* at the Board; awhile we lingered,
Then paced the beaten downward way that led
Right to a rough stream's edge and there broke off.
570 The only track now visible was one
That from the torrent's further brink held forth
Conspicuous invitation to ascend
A loft mountain. After brief delay
Crossing the unbridged stream, that road we took
575 And clomb with eagerness, till anxious fears
Intruded, for we failed to overtake
Our Comrades gone before. By fortunate chance,
While every moment added doubt to doubt,
A Peasant met us, from whose mouth we learned
580 That to the Spot which had perplexed us first
We must descend, and there should find the road,
Which in the stony channel of the Stream
Lay a few steps, and then along its banks;
And that our future course, all plain to sight,
585 Was downwards, with the current of that Stream.
Loth to believe what we so grieved to hear,
For still we had hopes that pointed to the clouds,
We questioned him again, and yet again;
But every word that from the Peasant's lips
590 Came in reply, translated by our feelings,
Ended in this, *that we had crossed the Alps....*

from BOOK THIRTEENTH
SUBJECT CONCLUDED

From Nature doth emotion come, and moods
Of calmness equally are Nature's gift:
This is her glory; these two attributes
Are sister horns[1] that constitute her strength.
5 Hence Genius, born to thrive by interchange
Of peace and excitation,°   *stimulus*
finds in her
His best and purest friend, from her receives
That energy by which he seeks the truth,
From her that happy stillness of the mind
10 Which fits him to receive it, when unsought.
　　Such benefit the humblest intellects
Partake of, each in their degree: 'tis mine
To speak of what myself have known and felt.
Smooth task! for words find easy way, inspired
15 By gratitude and confidence in truth.
Long time in search of knowledge did I range
The field of human life, in heart and mind
Benighted, but the dawn beginning now
To reappear, 'twas proved that not in vain
20 I had been taught to reverence a Power
That is the visible quality and shape
And image of right reason,[2] that matures
Her processes by steadfast laws, gives birth
To no impatient or fallacious hopes,
25 No heat of passion or excessive zeal,
No vain conceits, provokes to no quick turns
Of self-applauding intellect—but trains
To meekness, and exalts by humble faith;
Holds up before the mind, intoxicate
30 With present objects, and the busy dance
Of things that pass away, a temperate show
Of objects that endure; and by this course
Disposes her, when over-fondly set
On throwing off incumbrances, to seek
35 In Man, and in the frame of social life,
Whate'er there is desireable and good
Of kindred permanence, unchanged in form
And function, or through strict vicissitude
Of life and death revolving. Above all

---

[1] *horns*   Symbols of strength in the Old Testament.

[2] *right reason*   Type of reason that is in accordance with natural law.

40   Were re-established now those watchful thoughts
Which (seeing little worthy or sublime
In what the Historian's pen so much delights
To blazon, Power and Energy detached
From moral purpose) early tutored me
45   To look with feelings of fraternal love
Upon the unassuming things that hold
A silent station in this beauteous world.

      Thus moderated, thus composed, I found
Once more in Man an object of delight,
50   Of pure imagination, and of love;
And, as the horizon of my mind enlarged,
Again I took the intellectual eye
For my Instructor, studious more to see
Great Truths, than touch and handle little ones.
55   Knowledge was given accordingly; my trust
Became more firm in feelings that had stood
The test of such a trial; clearer far
My sense of excellence—of right and wrong:
The promise of the present time retired
60   Into its true proportion; sanguine° schemes,   *hopeful*
Ambitious projects, pleased me less; I sought
For present good in life's familiar face,
And built thereon my hopes of good to come.

      With settling judgments now of what would last
65   And what must disappear, prepared to find
Presumption, folly, madness, in the Men
Who thrust themselves upon the passive world
As Rulers of the world, to see in these,
Even when the public welfare is their aim,
70   Plans without thought, or built on theories
Vague and unsound, and having brought the Books
Of modern Statists[1] to their proper test,
Life, human life with all its sacred claims
Of sex and age, and heaven-descended rights
75   Mortal, or those beyond the reach of death;
And having thus discerned how dire a thing
Is worshipped in that Idol proudly named
"The Wealth of Nations,"[2] where alone that wealth

Is lodged, and how encreased; and having gained
80   A more judicious knowledge of the worth
And dignity of individual Man,
No composition of the brain, but Man
Of whom we read, the Man whom we behold
With our own eyes—I could not but enquire,
85   Not with less interest than heretofore,
But greater, though in Spirit more subdued,
Why is this glorious Creature to be found
One only in ten thousand? What one is,
Why may not millions be? What bars are thrown
90   By Nature in the way of such a hope?
Our animal appetites, and daily wants,
Are these obstructions insurmountable?
If not, then others vanish into air.
"Inspect the basis of the social Pile:
95   Enquire," said I, "how much of mental Power
And genuine virtue they possess who live
By bodily toil, labour exceeding far
Their due proportion, under all the weight
Of that injustice which upon ourselves
100 Ourselves entail." Such estimate to frame
I chiefly looked (what need to look beyond?)
Among the natural Abodes of men,
Fields with their rural works, recalled to mind
My earliest notices,° with these compared   *observations*
105 The observations made in later youth,
And to that day continued.—For the time
Had never been when throes of mightiest Nations
And the world's tumult unto me could yield,
How far soe'er transported and possessed,
110 Full measure of content; but still I craved
An intermingling of distinct regards°   *sights*
And truths of individual sympathy
Nearer ourselves. Such often might be gleaned
From the great City, else it must have proved
115 To me a heart-depressing wilderness;
But much was wanting; therefore did I turn
To you, ye pathways, and ye lonely roads;
Sought you enriched with every thing I prized,
With human kindness and simple joys.…

---

[1] *Statists* Political theorists.

[2] *The … Nations* Adam Smith's *Inquiry into the Nature and Cause of the Wealth of Nations* (1776), an economic treatise.

from BOOK FOURTEENTH
CONCLUSION

In one of those Excursions (may they ne'er
Fade from remembrance!), through the Northern
        tracts
Of Cambria ranging with a youthful Friend,[1]
I left Bethgellert's huts at couching-time,
5   And westward took my way, to see the sun
Rise from the top of Snowdon. To the door
Of a rude Cottage at the Mountain's base
We came, and roused the Shepherd who attends
The adventurous Stranger's steps, a trusty Guide;
10 Then, cheered by short refreshment, sallied forth.
—It was a close, warm, breezeless summer night,
Wan, dull, and glaring,° with a dripping fog   rainy
Low-hung and thick, that covered all the sky.
But, undiscouraged, we began to climb
15 The mountain-side. The mist soon girt us round,
And, after ordinary Travellers' talk
With our Conductor, pensively we sank
Each into commerce with his private thoughts:
Thus did we breast the ascent, and by myself
20 Was nothing either seen or heard that checked
Those musings or diverted, save that once
The Shepherd's Lurcher,[2] who, among the crags,
Had to his joy unearthed a Hedgehog, teased
His coiled-up Prey with barkings turbulent.
25 This small adventure, for even such it seemed
In that wild place, and at the dead of night,
Being over and forgotten, on we wound
In silence as before. With forehead bent
Earthward, as if in opposition set
30 Against an enemy, I panted up
With eager pace, and no less eager thoughts.
Thus might we wear a midnight hour away,
Ascending at loose distance each from each,

---

[1] *In one ... Friend* This trip was a walking tour through North
Wales (Cambria) with Robert Jones, the same friend with whom he
crossed the Alps. In this passage, they ascend Mount Snowdon, the
highest peak in Wales, from the village of Bethgellert.

[2] *Lurcher* Rabbit-hunting dog.

And I, as chanced, the foremost of the Band:
35 When at my feet the ground appeared to brighten,
And with a step or two seemed brighter still;
Nor was time given to ask, or learn, the cause;
For instantly a light upon the turf
Fell like a flash; and lo! as I looked up,
40 The Moon hung naked in a firmament
Of azure without cloud, and at my feet
Rested a silent sea of hoary mist.
A hundred hills their dusky backs upheaved
All over this still Ocean; and beyond,
45 Far, far beyond, the solid vapours stretched,
In Headlands, tongues, and promontory shapes,
Into the main Atlantic, that appeared
To dwindle, and give up his majesty,
Usurped upon far as the sight could reach.
50 Not so the ethereal Vault; encroachment none
Was there, nor loss; only the inferior stars
Had disappeared, or shed a fainter light
In the clear presence of the full-orbed Moon;
Who, from her sovereign elevation, gazed
55 Upon the billowy ocean, as it lay
All meek and silent, save that through a rift
Not distant from the shore whereon we stood,
A fixed, abysmal, gloomy breathing-place,
Mounted the roar of waters—torrents—streams
60 Innumerable, roaring with one voice!
Heard over earth and sea, and in that hour,
For so it seemed, felt by the starry heavens.
    When into air had partially dissolved
That Vision, given to Spirits of the night,
65 And three chance human Wanderers, in calm thought
Reflected, it appeared to me the type
Of a majestic Intellect, its acts
And its possessions, what it has and craves,
What in itself it is, and would become.
70 There I beheld the emblem of a Mind
That feeds upon infinity, that broods
Over the dark abyss, intent to hear
Its voices issuing forth to silent light
In one continuous stream; a mind sustained
75 By recognitions of transcendent power

In sense, conducting to ideal form;
In soul, of more than mortal privilege.
One function, above all, of such a mind
Had Nature shadowed there, by putting forth,
80 'Mid circumstances awful and sublime,
That mutual domination which she loves
To exert upon the face of outward things,
So moulded, joined, abstracted; so endowed
With interchangeable supremacy,
85 That Men least sensitive see, hear, perceive,
And cannot choose but feel. The power which all
Acknowledge when thus moved, which Nature thus
To bodily sense exhibits, is the express
Resemblance of that glorious faculty[1]
90 That higher minds bear with them as their own.
This is the very spirit in which they deal
With the whole compass of the universe:
They, from their native selves, can send abroad
Kindred mutations; for themselves create
95 A like existence; and whene'er it dawns
Created for them, catch it—or are caught
By its inevitable mastery,
Like angels stopped upon the wing by sound
Of harmony from heaven's remotest spheres.
100 Them the enduring and the transient both
Serve to exalt; they build up greatest things
From least suggestions; ever on the watch,
Willing to work and to be wrought upon,
They need not extraordinary calls
105 To rouse them, in a world of life they live;
By sensible impressions not enthralled,
But, by their quickening impulse, made more prompt
To hold fit converse with the spiritual world,
And with the generations of mankind
110 Spread over time, past, present, and to come,
Age after age, till Time shall be no more.
Such minds are truly from the Deity,
For they are powers; and hence the highest bliss
That flesh can know is theirs—the consciousness
115 Of whom they are, habitually infused
Through every image, and through every thought,

And all affections by communion raised
From earth to heaven, from human to divine.
Hence endless occupation for the Soul,
120 Whether discursive or intuitive;
Hence cheerfulness for acts of daily life,
Emotions which best foresight need not fear,
Most worthy then of trust when most intense:
Hence, amid ills that vex, and wrongs that crush
125 Our hearts, if here the words of Holy Writ[2]
May with fit reverence be applied, that peace
Which passeth understanding[3]—that repose
In moral judgements which from this pure source
Must come, or will by Man be sought in vain. . . .
430   Oh! yet a few short years of useful life,
And all will be complete, thy race be run,
Thy monument of glory will be raised;
Then, though, too weak to tread the ways of truth,
This Age fall back to old idolatry,
435 Though Men return to servitude as fast
As the tide ebbs, to ignominy and shame
By Nations sink together, we shall still
Find solace—knowing what we have learnt to know,
Rich in true happiness if allowed to be
440 Faithful alike in forwarding a day
Of firmer trust, joint laborers in the Work
(Should Providence such grace to us vouchsafe)
Of their deliverance, surely yet to come.
Prophets of Nature, we to them will speak
445 A lasting inspiration, sanctified
By reason, blest by faith: what we have loved
Others will love, and we will teach them how,
Instruct them how the mind of Man becomes
A thousand times more beautiful than the earth
450 On which he dwells, above this Frame of things
(Which 'mid all revolutions in the hopes
And fears of Men doth still remain unchanged)
In beauty exalted, as it is itself
Of quality and fabric more divine.
—1850

[1] *that glorious faculty* I.e., imagination.

[2] *Holy Writ* Scripture.

[3] *that peace … understanding* See Philippians 4.7: "That peace of
God, which passeth all understanding."

Reading, Writing, Publishing

CONTEXTS

During the Romantic period, questions concerning the definition of literature and the nature of its role in society pervaded print culture. Among the topics debated were definitions of intellectual property, the ways in which dissemination of texts should be encouraged or restrained, and the extent to which literature could effect social or political reform. For many, particularly in light of the French Revolution, literature was felt to hold a radical potential to change the world.

Some questioned whether women or members of the laboring classes should be allowed access to political tracts, and feared that less educated or discerning minds could be easily swayed by the persuasive rhetoric of radicals. Daniel Isaac Eaton was among those whose powers of persuasion they feared; he had been tried nine times for publishing or writing radical texts and on one occasion had been sentenced to 18 months in jail. Here he satirizes the anti-revolutionaries' fear of the power of the press and the government's desire to control the circulation of potentially seditious material through legislation and taxes. Eaton's weekly magazine, *Politics for the People* (1793–95), was an important and popular organ of radical journalism; when he was placed in the pillory in 1812 for printing the third part of *Age of Reason*, he was cheered by a large crowd.

Thomas Spence, whose poem on the theme of repression appears next, was also well acquainted with the accusation of libel. He had been arrested four times and imprisoned twice between 1792 and 1794 alone. In the poem reproduced here, his parenthetical denials cleverly serve to protect him from such charges while simultaneously articulating radical criticism of the monarchy and aristocracy. The poem following Spence's, by an anonymous author, uses the sort of animal analogies that were commonly relied upon in political satire at the time. By exploiting traditional moral fables, writers could create poems that were clearly understood by their readers, yet were ambiguous enough to allow their authors to disavow any subversive intent.

The piece that follows emphasizes the importance of literature to revolutionary efforts. While Eaton had mocked anti-radicals' fear of the press, the anonymous author of "On the Characteristics of Poetry" links the feelings excited by poetry to powerful political action, and even to military victory.

The period was what John Stuart Mill called "a reading age"; there were more readers than ever before, and publishing was becoming a major industry. While many viewed this development as beneficial to society, others feared a proliferation of trivial works that would neither improve the minds of readers nor encourage them to pick up more challenging works. If too many books were produced each year for any one person to read, how could people hope to peruse them all and decide which were most worthy of their attention?

Voicing a common fear, the anonymous correspondent to the *Monthly Magazine* whose letter is excerpted here claims that the proliferation of writers has led to a decline in literary standards and a decreased appreciation for writers of true genius. In the following piece, Samuel Pratt proposes an effective solution to this problem in the form of literary journals, whose writers can together provide readers with a balanced critical appraisal. Hannah More, in *Strictures on the Modern System of Female Education*, examines what she sees as the negative effects of the abundant novels and other "alluring little works" on the morals and intellects of young women. In the final excerpt, John Stuart Mill forecasts the downfall of British literature and culture, predicting that its integrity will soon be undermined by commercial society.

⌘ ⌘ ⌘

from Daniel Isaac Eaton, *The Pernicious Effects of the Art of Printing upon Society, Exposed* (1793)

Before this diabolical art was introduced among men, there was social order. ... In the times we are speaking of (the Golden Age), the feudal system prevailed—a system replete with blessings—by it the different orders of society were kept perfectly distinct and separate—there were kings, barons, priests, yeomanry, villains[1] or slaves; and they were, I believe, with regard to rank and power, in the order in which I have named them. The villains, or lowest class, were what Mr. Burke so elegantly terms the *Swinish Multitude*,[2] but of rights or privileges as men they had not an idea; we may with propriety style them the Jackals of the times: they tilled the earth, and performed all manual labour; but in return, their superiors allowed them sufficient of the produce for subsistence—permitted them to take some rest, in order that they might be strong. To bear hardship and fatigue took from them the trouble of thinking—indeed, from the very prudent manner in which they were brought up, I will not say educated, they were little capable of thought, of course exempt from the mental fatigues of study and reflections. The Scriptures having declared gold to be the root of every evil, they were very humanely prevented from possessing any. As to religion, the clergy taught them as much as they thought necessary, and they were without doubt the best judges, being in general good scholars. ...

Since printing has been employed as the medium of diffusing sentiments, &c. government has become more difficult—the governors are frequently and insolently called upon to give an account of the national treasure, its expenditure, &c.—and if they are in any respect tardy, or should circumstances render evasion necessary, it is astonishing, with what boldness some men will dare to revile and insult them.

The lower orders begin to have ideas of rights, as men—to think that one man is as good as another; that society is at present founded upon false principles; that hereditary honours and distinctions are absurd, unjust, and oppressive; that abilities and morals only should recommend to the first officers in a state; that no regard should be paid to rank and titles; that instruction, sufficient to qualify a man for being a member of society, is a debt due to every individual, and that it is the duty of every state to take care that he receive it; that every man has a right to a share in the government, either in his own person, or that of his representative, and that no portion of his property or labour ought to be taxed without his consent, given either by himself, or representative; that everyone should contribute to the support of the state in proportion to his ability, and that all partial exactions are oppressive; that laws should be the same to all, and that no one, whatever may be his rank or station, should be allowed to offend them with impunity; that freedom of speech is the equal right of all, and that the rich have no right to dictate to the poor what sentiments they shall adopt on any subject, or in any wise[3] prevent investigation and inquiry. This, with a great deal more such stuff, is called the rights of man—blessed fruits of the art of printing—the scum of the earth, the swinish multitude, talking of their rights! and insolently claiming, nay, almost demanding, that political liberty shall be the same to all—to the high and the low, the rich and the poor—what audacity!—what unparalleled effrontery!—it ought to meet correction. With similar mistaken notions of liberty, even many women are infatuated; and the press, that grand prolific

---

[1] *villains* I.e., villeins, serfs, or peasants.

[2] *Mr. Burke ... Multitude* Edmund Burke, probably in reference to a particular faction of extremists (rather than all members of the working classes), said that if learning was removed from the hierarchical social order in which it had originated, it would be "cast into the mire, and trodden down under the hoofs of a swinish multitude." Reformers took this comment as proof of the arrogance and superiority with which conservatives regarded the masses.

[3] *wise* Way.

source of evil, that fruitful mother of mischief, has already favoured the public with several female productions on this very popular subject—one in particular, called *Rights of Women*,[1] and in which, as one of their rights, a share in legislation is claimed and asserted —gracious heaven! to what will this fatal delusion lead, and in what will it terminate! ...

For all these, and numberless other evils, the natural consequence of a diffusion of knowledge and science, some remedy must be found; the present administration have made some trifling feeble attempts to check their progress, such as additional duties upon advertisements and newspapers, which almost preclude cheap publications—of the same nature I suppose the late tax upon paper to be—but these remedies are totally inadequate, at least they will be so exceedingly slow in their operation, that the present race have but little prospect of living to see any of their good effects.

To rid ourselves of such a monster, some strong efficient measure must be had recourse to, something that will strike at the root, and have an almost instantaneous effect—such a one, I think, I can point out.

Let all printing presses be committed to the flames, all letter foundries be destroyed, schools and seminaries of learning abolished, dissenters of every denominations double and treble taxed, all discourse upon government and religion prohibited, political clubs and associations of every kind suppressed—excepting those formed for the express purpose of supporting government—and lastly, issue a proclamation against reading, and burn all private libraries. To carry some part of this plan into execution, it will be necessary to employ spies and informers, which by many (Jacobins and Republicans) are thought to be signs either of a weak or wicked and corrupt government; they say that governors, conscious of acting for the public good, of having it only in view in all their measure, would scorn using such unworthy and dishonourable means. I cannot be of this opinion,

but am confident that if the measures I have proposed be but speedily adopted, and rigorously pursued, the happiest consequences would soon be experienced; all the wild, idle theories with which men are at present disturbed, would soon vanish—the lower orders would mind their work, become tractable and docile, and perhaps in less than half a century that desirable state of ignorance and darkness, which formerly prevailed, might again restore to this Island that happy state of society with which it once was blessed.

Thomas Spence, "Examples of Safe Printing," from *Pig's Meat*,[2] Volume 2 (1794)

To prevent misrepresentation in these prosecuting times, it seems necessary to publish every thing relating to tyranny and oppression, though only among brutes, in the most guarded manner.

The following are meant as specimens:

That tyger, or that other salvage wight°   *savage creature*
Is so exceeding furious and fell,°   *fierce*
  As WRONG,
    [*Not meaning our most gracious sovereign Lord the King, or the Government of this country*]
    when it hath arm'd himself with might;
Not fit 'mong men that do with reason mell,°   *mix*
But 'mong wild beasts and salvage woods to dwell;
  Where still the stronger
    [*Not meaning the great men of this country*]
    doth the weak devour,
And they that most in boldness do excell,
  Are dreaded most, and feared by their power.
        —E. Spencer[3]

[1] *Rights of Women* Mary Wollstonecraft's *A Vindication of the Rights of Woman* (1792).

[2] *Pig's Meat* The title is a reference to Burke's term "swinish multitude," which many radical writers adopted as an ironic definition of the working classes.

[3] *E. Spencer* I.e., Renaissance poet Edmund Spenser (1552?–99), whom the poet imitates in order to create historical distance from the referents of the poem.

Joshua,[1] "Sonnet: The Lion," from *Moral and Political Magazine*, Volume 1 (1796)

Why grace we the stern lion with the name
   That marks the chiefs of Europe? More of use
To man's assistance do the kine° produce;   *cattle*
For bulk, behold the elephant's huge frame!
5 For agile beauty see the stately horse.
   King of the forest HE, and doomed to reign,
   Like earthly monarch, o'er the Lybian plain
For fierce pre-eminence in brutal force:
   Before his tyrant rage the fleet° horse flies,   *swift*
10   The patient sheep avoids him, or he dies.
Stern bloody beast! they named thee well: thy right
   Is to this royal title just and good;
Thou gain'dst it by thy savage joy in fight,
Thy brutal fury, and thy thirst for blood.

from Anonymous, "On the Characteristics of Poetry," No. 2, from the *Monthly Magazine* (1797)

In the course of our last discussion, we seemed to be unanimously of opinion that the grand characteristic, the *sine qua non*[2] of poetry, consists in its capacity of pressing the mind with the most vivid pictures. Indeed, the maxim *ut pictura poesis*[3] is amply illustrated whenever poetry is in any shape the subject of investigation. The terms of the painter's art then insensibly creep into the discourse and model our phraseology.

Pursuing, then, this idea, we may perhaps lay it down as the grand and leading end of poetry to make a strong and lively impression on the feelings. In her operations she hurries us far beyond the reach of the voice of sober judgment, and captivates by exciting the aid of the passions. Here, then, we see the cause of the mighty energy of verse, nor wonder at the efficacious-

ness that has been ascribed to the Muses.[4] For how easily are mankind guided by those that possess the happy art of awakening or allaying their feelings. Though all unconscious of being under the guidance of another, they turn obedient to the rein. They are roused to insurrection, or moderated to peace, by him who can touch, with a skilful hand, the master springs that regulate the motions of their minds. When Brutus[5] ascends the rostrum, the words of truth and soberness are heard, and plain integrity convinces the judgment. But, when Anthony[6] displays the bloody robe, and points to the wounds of Caesar, reminding the people that this was once their darling benefactor, the multitude are melted to sorrow, and at last roused from pity to fury and revenge.

Here, then, this essay might, perhaps, with propriety, have been closed. But I must rely upon your candour for the admission of a few more observations, which may, perhaps, tend to illustrate the point to which this enquiry has led us:

The end of poetry, it is said, is an impression upon the feelings. But as there is an intimate connection between feeling and action, so that where the one appears, the other "follows hard upon," if the foregoing observations be true, we may expect to find that the actions of mankind are, in some measure, influenced by the Muses.

And if we look to the simpler ages of society, when we can best distinguish the grand outlines of the human character, where the springs that actuate the conduct of man are, in a manner, bared for inspection, we shall find this to have been the case. In the infancy of states, poetry is a method equally captivating and efficacious of forming the dispositions of the people, and kindling in their hearts that love of glory which is their country's safeguard and defence. Whether we look to the cold regions of Scandinavia, or the delicious clime of Greece, we find that when society has made a certain progress, mankind are strongly influenced by a love of song, and listen, with raptured

---

[1] *Joshua* Biblical lieutenant of Moses who led the Israelites to victory over the Canaanites (see Joshua 1–12).

[2] *sine qua non* Latin: indispensable attribute.

[3] *ut pictura poesis* Latin: "as is painting, so is poetry" (from Horace, *Ars Poetica*).

[4] *Muses* Nine daughters of Zeus and Mnemosyne, each of whom presided over and provided inspiration for an aspect of the arts and sciences.

[5] *Brutus* One of the men who assassinated Julius Caesar, whom had become dictator of Rome for life.

[6] *Anthony* Marc Antony, consul who, after Caesar's assassination, aroused the mob against the conspirators, causing them to be driven from the city.

attention, to the strains that record the tale of other times, and the deeds of heroes of old. They listen till they imbibe the enthusiasm of warfare, and in the day of battle, the hero's arm has not unfrequently been nerved by the rough energy of the early bard. ...

But, indeed, what occasion have we to search into the dust of antiquity for examples of the influence of verse upon human conduct? The transactions of our own times may teach us that as strong feelings generate poetic language, so poetic language inspires the mind with at least a temporary enthusiasm, and thus impels to action. In this country, the fervour or loyalty has of late been blown into a blaze, and for this event the parties interested are not a little indebted to the assistance of the Muses. And when the Marseillaise Hymn[1] echoed through the ranks of the French army at the field of Jemappe,[2] we need not wonder that "the spear of liberty was wielded with classic grace," and that the energy of heroism was communicated with the sound.

from Anonymous, Letter to the *Monthly Magazine* (24 October 1798)

Sir,

Literature is either less cultivated, or less valued in these days than it was in those of our ancestors, for certainly learning does not *now* receive the honours it *then* did. That it is less cultivated, cannot, I think, with any truth be asserted, because the present is denominated a learned age. It must be the universality then, with which it is diffused throughout society, that renders it less valuable—as articles grow cheap, not in proportion to their insignificancy, but their abundance. Great talents, indeed, in any condition of civilized society must inevitably confer a certain degree of power, inasmuch as they render their possessors either useful or formidable; but scarcely any literary attainments would, I apprehend, raise a writer in these days to the same degree of eminence and request as Petrarch, Erasmus,

and Politiano[3] enjoyed in their respective times. We have now amongst us many scholars of great erudition (Parr, Wakefield, Professors Porson and White,[4] &c. &c.), men of distinguished abilities; yet I much question, as haughty as kings were under the feudal system, if any of the princes in being would contend with the same eagerness for their favour, as we learn the various sovereigns of Europe did for that of Petrarch or Erasmus.

It has been questioned by some whether the number of publications, which are annually poured upon the world, have contributed in any proportionable ratio to the increase of literature? In my opinion, they have *not*. To a liberal and cultivated mind there is certainly no indulgence equal to the luxury of books; but, in works of learning, may not the facilities of information be increased, until the powers of application and retention be diminished? After admitting that the present is a learned age, it may appear singular to doubt whether it affords[5] individuals as profoundly learned (at least, as far as Latin and Greek go), as some who flourished in the fifteenth and sixteenth centuries.

From these remarks, I would not be understood as wishing to make invidious comparisons between the learning of different ages, or to depreciate that of our own. Upon a fair investigation, there can be no doubt, I think, to which side the scale of general literature would incline. My object simply is, to show the different direction which letters take, and the different patronage they obtain, in different periods of society. Indeed, learning may more properly be said to *lead* than to *follow* the course of the world: since, though it may, at first, bend to the spirit of the age, it will in the end assuredly direct and govern it. The general stock of

---

[1] *Marseillaise Hymn*   Composed by Claude Joseph Rouget de Lisle on 24 April 1792, "the Marseillaise" celebrated freedom and human rights and became a rallying cry for the French Revolutionaries. It was declared the French national anthem in 1795.

[2] *field of Jemappe*   Where a Revolutionary victory occurred in 1792.

[3] *Petrarch*   Francesco Petrarch, Italian poet and Humanist of the fourteenth century, famous for his sonnets; *Erasmus*   Desidero Erasmus, Dutch Humanist (1466–1536); *Politiano*   Italian poet Angelo Poliziano (1454–95), who also served as professor of Greek and Latin at the University of Florence.

[4] *Parr*   Samuel Parr (1747–1825), a Latin scholar, schoolmaster, minister, and vocal Whig supporter; *Wakefield*   Gilbert Wakefield (1756–1801), a Biblical scholar and religious and political controversialist who also produced an edition of Virgil's *Georgics* (1788); *Professors Porson and White*   Richard Porson (1759–1808), Greek professor at Cambridge, and Gilbert White (1720–93), noted naturalist.

[5] *affords*   Is capable of producing.

genius is, perhaps, always pretty equal; the opportunities of improving it, and the support it receives, vary with the times. Petrarch and Erasmus were caressed by popes and princes; Butler, Otway, and Chatterton,[1] not much inferior in merit, were absolutely starved; and Johnson,[2] whose moral works were calculated to delight and improve the age, lived long in distress, and at length received a scanty pension. In some ages, and upon some occasions, it must be admitted, a genius darts upon the world with intellectual powers that no industry, in the common course of things, can hope to equal. But this is a *particular* case, and is generally compensated some other way. If former times have enjoyed works of more fancy, and sublimity of imagination, than are given to us, we, in return, possess more useful acquisitions. If they have had their Spenser, Tasso, and Shakespeare, we boast Newton, Locke,[3] and Johnson. Science, taste, and correction are indeed the characteristics of the present day. Everything is refined; everything is grand. We are actually misers in luxury and taste, and have left nothing for posterity. "*Venimus ad summum fortunae*"[4]—We learn our Greek from the Pursuits of Literature,[5] and our morality from Parissot, and I do not see how we are to be outdone either in learning or in dress.

I remain, Sir, &c., &c.

Ausonius[6]

---

[1] *Butler, Otway, and Chatterton* Satirical poet Samuel Butler (1612–80), tragic dramatist Thomas Otway (1652–85), and young poet Thomas Chatterton (1752–70) all lived in dire poverty.

[2] *Johnson* Samuel Johnson (1709–84), lexicographer, poet, and author of the journals *The Rambler* and *The Idler*. He struggled for financial security until 1762, when he was granted a pension for his work on the *Dictionary*.

[3] *Spenser* English poet Edmund Spenser (c. 1552–99), author of *The Faerie Queene*; *Tasso* Italian poet Torquato Tasso (1544–95); *Newton* Mathematician and natural philosopher Sir Isaac Newton (1642–1727); *Locke* Philosopher John Locke (1632–1704).

[4] *Venimus ... fortunae* Latin: "We have come to the height of fortune" (Horace, *Epistles* 2.1).

[5] *Pursuits of Literature* Four-part satirical poem by Thomas James Mathias concerning the nature of literature. Its publication (1794–97) aroused much debate.

[6] *Ausonius* I.e., the author's pseudonym, referring to the Latin poet Dicimius Magmus Ausonius (c. 310–c. 393).

from Samuel Pratt, *Gleanings in England: Descriptive of the Countenance, Mind, and Character of the Country* (1799)

There cannot be a doubt but that while the liberty of the press, as to the freedom of publication, shall be sacred—and on this side of licentiousness, it ought to be uncontrolled—it is equally just that the sense and nonsense which indiscriminately issue from the immense vehicle of communication should be subject to vigilant examination, otherwise the whole world would be over-run with abortions of the mind. We want the assistance of some guides who will take upon themselves the trouble of separating the good from the bad and wade through the troubled deep of literature in order, if we may be permitted a continuation of the figure, to collect the pearls and gems, and to describe the useless weeds, whether swimming on the surface or lying at the muddy bottom. A stupendous labour if we consider the great disproportion betwixt the former and the latter. Applying this to the case in point, and it is by no means inapposite, a reader unused to such arduous undertakings can image to himself no task so overwhelming as that of being left unaided to search for instruction in the mass of productions which are every year piled, mountain high, before him.... For this reason, it would be proper that there should be some professional inspectors to direct our choice, even were literary excellence and defect nearly equal. But when the average is on a ratio of at least ninety in the hundred in the scale of compositions *deadweight*, there is not, perhaps, any office so necessary as his, who, with patient circumspection, will examine the great account betwixt wisdom and folly, and settle the balance.

It is not, therefore, possible to conceive a more useful institution than that of a literary journal, when conducted with various ability and inflexible justice; nor can it be denied that a great variety of articles, in every branch of literature, have been analysed on these principles, and a due proportion of good has thence resulted to the community.

We have to boast, even at this day, of great and noble critics; and from most, indeed, in all of our literary journals, we find substantial evidence of unimpeachable judgement and unwarped integrity. It is not, however, to be expected that any human association composed of many members should be conducted on principles uniformly sagacious and correct. Were they to write apart, and consult together ultimately, there must even then often be a clash of sentiment, a dissonance of opinion.

Yet I am persuaded the critics above-described are the very persons who must reprobate the virulences[1] and regret the errors for which they are made responsible. The literary body cannot be supposed to separate, or seem to move a limb independently—much less to commit themselves, and confederate against each other, by deploring the want of candour in some of their colleagues, and of capacity in others. Thus from their not being associated by congeniality, or chosen by consent—and yet under a kind of compact to hold together, and by the good faith that should be preserved in all treaties, bound to support one another in the way of a common cause—the errors, incongruities, adulations, and virulences, which are observed occasionally to disfigure their journals, attach indiscriminately to all.

from Hannah More, *Strictures on the Modern System of Female Education* (1799)

from CHAPTER 8: ON FEMALE STUDY

Will it not be ascribed to a captious singularity, if I venture to remark that real knowledge and real piety, though they may have gained in many instances, have suffered in others from that profusion of little, amusing, sentimental books with which the youthful library overflows? Abundance has its dangers as well as scarcity. In the first place, may not the multiplicity of these alluring little works increase the natural reluctance to those more dry and uninteresting studies, of which, after all, the rudiments of every part of learning *must* consist? And, secondly, is there not some danger (though there are many honourable exceptions) that some of those engaging narratives may serve to infuse into the youthful heart a sort of spurious goodness, a confidence of virtue, a parade of charity? And that the

benevolent actions with the recital of which they abound, when they are not made to flow from any source but *feeling*, may tend to inspire a self-complacency, a self-gratulation, a "stand by, for I am holier than thou?" May not the success with which the good deeds of the little heroes are uniformly crowned, the invariable reward which is made the instant concomitant of well-doing, furnish the young reader with false views of the condition of life, and the nature of the divine dealings with men? May they not help to suggest a false standard of morals, to infuse a love of popularity and an anxiety for praise, in the place of that simple and unostentatious rule of doing whatever good we do *because it is the will of God*? The universal substitution of this principle would tend to purify the worldly morality of many a popular little story. And there are few dangers which good parents will more carefully guard against than that of giving their children a mere political piety—that sort of religion which just goes to make people more respectable, and to stand well with the world; a religion which is to save appearances without inculcating realities; a religion which affects to "preach peace and good will to men," but which forgets to give "glory to God in the highest."[2]

There is a certain precocity of mind which is much helped on by these superficial modes of instruction; for frivolous reading will produce its correspondent effect in much less time than books of solid instruction; the imagination being liable to be worked upon, and the feelings to be set a going, much faster than the understanding can be opened and the judgment enlightened. A talent for conversation should be the result of instruction, not its precursor: it is a golden fruit when suffered to ripen gradually on the tree of knowledge; but if forced in the hot-bed of a circulating library, it will turn out worthless and vapid in proportion as it was artificial and premature. Girls who have been accustomed to devour a multitude of frivolous books will converse and write with a far greater appearance of skill, as to style and sentiment, at twelve or fourteen years old, than those of a more advanced age who are under the discipline of severer studies; but the former having early attained to that low standard which had been held out to them, become stationary; while the latter, quietly

---

[1] *virulences* Incidences of bitter hostility or antagonism.

[2] *preach peace ... the highest* Quotations from Luke 2.14.

progressive, are passing through just gradations to a higher strain of mind; and those who early begin with talking and writing like women, commonly end with thinking and acting like children.

... Who are those ever-multiplying authors that with unparalleled fecundity are overstocking the world with their quick-succeeding progeny? They are NOVEL-WRITERS, the easiness of whose productions is at once the cause of their own fruitfulness, and of the almost infinitely numerous race of imitators to whom they give birth. Such is the frightful facility of this species of composition, that every raw girl, while she reads, is tempted to fancy that she can also write. And as Alexander, on perusing the *Iliad*, found by congenial sympathy the image of Achilles stamped on his own ardent soul,[1] and felt himself the hero he was studying; and as Correggio,[2] on first beholding a picture which exhibited the perfection of the graphic art, prophetically felt all his own future greatness, and cried out in rapture, "And I, too, am a painter!" so a thorough-paced novel-reading Miss, at the close of every tissue of hackneyed adventures, feels within herself the stirring impulse of corresponding genius, and triumphantly exclaims, "And I, too, am an author!" The glutted imagination soon overflows with the redundance of cheap sentiment and plentiful incident, and by a sort of arithmetical proportion is enabled by the perusal of any three novels to produce a fourth; till every fresh production, like the prolific progeny of Banquo, is followed by "Another, and another, and another!"[3] Is a lady, however destitute of talents, education, or knowledge of the world, whose studies have been completed by a circulating library, in any distress of mind? the writing a novel suggests itself as the best soother of her sorrows! Does she labour under any depression of circumstances? writing a novel occurs as the readiest receipt for mending them! and she solaces her imagination with the conviction that the

subscription which has been extorted by her importunity, or given to her necessities, has been offered as a homage to her genius; and this confidence instantly levies a fresh contribution for a succeeding work. Capacity and cultivation are so little taken into the account, that writing a book seems to be now considered as the only sure resource which the idle and the illiterate have always in their power.

from John Stuart Mill, "The Present State of Literature" (16 November 1827)[4]

It is the demand, in literature as in most other things, which calls forth the supply. ... Assuming, therefore, as an indisputable truth, that the writers of every age are for the most part what the readers make them, it becomes important to the present question to consider who formed the reading public formerly, and who compose it now. The present age is very remarkably distinguished from all other ages by the number of persons who can read, and, what is of more consequence, by the number who do. Our working classes have learned to read, and our idle classes have learned to find pleasure in reading, and to devote a part of that time to it which they formerly spent in amusements of a grosser kind. That human nature will be a gainer, and that in a high degree, by this change, no one can be more firmly convinced than I am—but it will perhaps be found that the benefit lies rather in the ultimate than in the immediate effects. Reading is necessary, but no wise or even sensible man was ever made by reading alone. The proper use of reading is to be subservient to thinking. It is by those who read to think that knowledge is advanced, prejudices dispelled, and the physical and moral condition of mankind is improved. I cannot, however, perceive that the general diffusion (so remarkable in our own day) of the taste for reading has yet been accompanied by any marked increase in taste for the severer exercises of the intellect; that such will one day be its effect, may fairly be presumed, but it has not yet declared itself: and it is to the immense multiplication in

---

[1] *Alexander ... ardent soul* Reference to a famous anecdote recounting Alexander the Great's sympathy with Achilles, the Greek hero of Homer's *Iliad*.

[2] *Correggio* Italian Renaissance painter Antonio Allegri (c. 1494–1534), called Correggio after his birthplace.

[3] *prolific progeny ... another* See *Macbeth* 4.1, in which Macbeth is frustrated by a vision of a nearly endless line of Banquo's royal heirs.

[4] *The Present ... 1827* From a speech delivered to the London Debating Society.

the present day of those who read but do not think, that I should be disposed to ascribe what I view as the degeneracy of our literature.

In former days the literati and the learned formed a class apart, and few concerned themselves with literature and philosophy except those who had leisure and inclination to form their philosophical opinions by study and meditation, and to cultivate their literary taste by the assiduous perusal of the most approved models. Those whose sole occupation was pleasure did not seek it in books, but in the gaieties of a court, or in field sports and debauchery. The public for which authors wrote was a small but, to a very considerable degree, an instructed public; and their suffrages were only to be gained by thinking to a certain extent profoundly and by writing well. The authors who were then in highest reputation are chiefly those to whom we now look back as the ablest thinkers and best writers of their time. No doubt there were many blockheads among the reading public in those days, as well as in our own, and the blockheads often egregiously misplaced their admiration, as blockheads are wont, but the applause of the blockheads was not then the object aimed at even by those who obtained it, and they did not constitute so large and so influential a class of readers as to tempt any writer of talent to lay himself out for their admiration. If an author failed of obtaining the suffrages of men of knowledge and taste, it was for want of powers, not from the misapplication of them. The case is now altered. We live in a refined age, and there is a corresponding refinement in our amusements. It is now the height of *mauvais ton*[1] to be drunk, neither is it any longer considered decorous among gentlemen that the staple of their conversation should consist of bawdy. Reading has become one of the most approved and fashionable methods of killing time, and the number of persons who have skimmed the surface of literature is far greater than at any previous period of our history. Our writers therefore find that the greatest success is now to be obtained by writing for the many, and endeavouring all they can to bring themselves down to the level of the many, both in their matter and in the manner of expressing it.

Copyright and the Growth of "a Reading Age"

Changes in copyright restrictions from 1774 onwards are closely connected to the growth of what John Stuart Mill termed "a reading age" in the late eighteenth and early nineteenth centuries. To understand those changes, it is important to understand something of the background. What has come to be called copyright has its roots in the property right held by the stationers or printers who issued books in the sixteenth century. The practice was codified through the granting of a royal charter in 1557 to the Stationers' Company, a body with which printers (and later, booksellers and publishers who commissioned work from printers) could register their new titles as a means of certifying that they were the owners of the intellectual property each work contained. (Until the eighteenth century, authors would typically sell their work to a printer or publisher for a flat fee.) In English practice, these understandings restricted in perpetuity the reproduction of literary works other than by their "owner." The understandings were matters of common practice and of legal precedent; however, much as common practice created something close to monopoly conditions, no formal copyright protection existed in law in England. (In both Scotland and Ireland, intellectual property was far less restricted than in England.) In the early eighteenth century, publishers began to agitate to have perpetual copyright formalized in law. The British Parliament agreed to consider the matter and eventually agreed (in the Statute of Anne, an act passed in 1709 and enacted in 1710) that

---

[1] *mauvais ton* French: bad form.

copyright should be written into law as a specific form of property protection. But rather than declaring it to be a property right that could be held in perpetuity, Parliament restricted it to 14 years from publication (renewable in certain circumstances for a further 14 years). The Act provided for a transitional period of 21 years but decreed that, as of 1731, all literary work that had been published prior to 1711 would come into the public domain. When this newly-established right to publish rival editions began to be tested, however, the publishers who had held possession refused to cede what appeared to be a plainly established right. Arguing in the courts that the Statute of Anne had improperly authorized the compensation of private property, they persuaded a succession of judges to issue injunctions against the publication of rival editions. In defiance of what had been set forward in the Statute of Anne, they managed to maintain an effective monopoly through most of the eighteenth century.

These were changes that had vast effects not only on publishing practice, but also on habits of reading and on literary culture. William St. Clair (whose 2004 book *The Reading Nation in the Romantic Period* is a landmark in the study of this area of literary history) has argued that the success of publishers in preventing the publication of rival editions created an "age of high monopoly." In this view, the restrictions helped to support high prices and thereby to limit the growth of the reading public. At the same time, they encouraged the production of lengthy and handsomely produced volumes, including many works that could be expected to enjoy only a modest sale, but might continue to sell in modest quantity for many years. Together with the ending in 1695 of official state censorship and the gradual withdrawal in the first half of the eighteenth century of other controls on the content of printed matter, the near-monopoly conditions under which British publishers operated fostered something of a golden era for the spread of Enlightenment culture. But the same conditions that favored the publication of lengthy and expensive works of history and philosophy discouraged the spread of popular literature—and tended as well to perpetuate an established literary canon. When the legal case of Donaldson Beckett brought an end to those monopoly conditions in 1774, books started to become smaller and cheaper—and that in turn led to a surge in reading across all social classes. In 1791, bookseller James Lackington described the degree to which things had changed: "According to the best estimation I have been able to make, I suppose that more than four times the number of books are sold now than were sold twenty years since. ... In short, all ranks and degrees now READ." The process of canon formation began to change as well, and by the early nineteenth century the way had opened up for publishers creating libraries of literary classics to include the leading lights of the Romantic period alongside Shakespeare, Milton, and the rest.

That opening, however, began to close quite quickly. Copyright was extended in 1808 to 28 years. It was extended again in 1814 to the life of the author (if he or she lived for more than 28 years after a work had been published), and by the 1830s a bill to extend copyright to 60 years beyond the author's death had been introduced in Parliament. The matter was decided for the remainder of the nineteenth century in 1842 with an extension to whichever turned out to be longer—42 years from publication, or the life of the author plus 7 years. The tides that had created what St. Clair calls "the reading nation" could not be reversed; the flood of cheap editions of out-of-copyright works continued. But new works, now enjoying so much greater copyright protection, became more highly priced—and the established canon, after having been refreshed by the addition of the Romantic poets, now again became more resistant to change.

from Copyright Act of 1709 (the Statute of Anne)

This act (named for the queen under whose reign it was enacted), which came into force in April, 1710, was the world's first copyright law. Although its intent was frustrated by the courts for the better part of the eighteenth century, its importance is difficult to overestimate.

An act for the encouragement of learning, by vesting the copies[1] of printed books in the authors or purchasers of such copies, during the times therein mentioned.

I.   Whereas printers, booksellers, and other persons have of late frequently taken the liberty of printing, reprinting, and publishing, or causing to be printed, reprinted, and published, books and other writings, without the consent of the authors or proprietors of such books and writings, to their very great detriment, and too often to the ruin of them and their families: for preventing therefore such practices for the future, and for the encouragement of learned men to compose and write useful books; may it please your Majesty, that it may be enacted, and be it enacted by the Queen's most excellent majesty, by and with the advice and consent of the lords spiritual and temporal, and commons, in this present parliament assembled, and by the authority of the same;

That from and after the tenth day of April, one thousand seven hundred and ten, the author of any book or books already printed, who hath not transferred to any other the copy or copies of such book or books, share or shares thereof, or the bookseller or booksellers, printer or printers, or other person or persons, who hath or have purchased or acquired the copy or copies of any book or books, in order to print or reprint the same, shall have the sole right and liberty of printing such book and books for the term of one and twenty years, to commence from the said tenth day of April, and no longer; and

That the author of any book or books already composed, and not printed and published, or that shall hereafter be composed, and his assignee or assigns, shall have the sole liberty of printing and reprinting such book and books for the term of fourteen years, to commence from the day of the first publishing the same, and no longer; ...

V.   Provided always, and it is hereby enacted, That nine copies of each book or books, upon the best paper, that from and after the said tenth day of April, one thousand seven hundred and ten, shall be printed and published, as aforesaid, or reprinted and published with additions, shall, by the printer and printers thereof, be delivered to the warehouse keeper of the said company of stationers for the time being, at the hall of the said company, before such publication made, for the use of the royal library, the libraries of the universities of Oxford and Cambridge, the libraries of the four universities in Scotland, the library of Sion College in London, and the library commonly called the library belonging to the faculty of advocates at Edinburgh respectively; ...

XI.   Provided always, that after the expiration of the said term of fourteen years, the sole right of printing or disposing of copies shall return to the authors thereof, if they are then living, for another term of fourteen years.

from Millar v. Taylor (1769)

Lord Mansfield, one of the leading legal minds of the eighteenth century, set out what he saw to be the connection between copyright and property law, in a legal opinion he gave in this 1769 case.

Opinion of Lord Mansfield: Because it is just, that an author should reap the pecuniary profits of his own ingenuity and labour, it is just, that another should not use his name, without his consent. It is fit that he should judge when to publish, or whether he ever will publish. It is fit he should not only choose the time, but the manner of publication; how many; what volume; what print. It is fit, he should choose to whose care he

---

[1]   *copies* Copyright.

will trust the accuracy and correctness of the impression; in whose honesty he will confide, not to foist in additions: with other reasonings of the same effect.

from Hinton *v.* Donaldson (Scotland, 1773); Donaldson *v.* Beckett (England, 1774)

When copyright finally came again to be tested in a meaningful way, one of the works at issue was James Thomson's *The Seasons* (1730), a work that continued to enjoy extraordinary popularity. The London publishers challenged (in both the Scottish and the English courts) the sale of the Scottish editions of such works by booksellers in England. Unlike the English courts, the Scottish courts had always been reluctant to grant injunctions that went against the spirit of the Statute of Anne, and that pattern held in this instance; by a vote of 11–1, the Scots Court of Session rejected the claims of the English publisher. The opinion of one of the judges, Lord Kames, who spoke against monopoly and against treating the printed word in the way that Lord Mansfield had recommended—as private property—became a frequent point of reference in subsequent discussions of copyright.

The English courts saw the matter differently, but the case was referred to the full House of Lords. The arguments of Lord Camden, who addressed the House of Lords after the judges had done so, were regarded as particularly influential, and the Lords ruled decisively that the short period of copyright protection as provided for in the Statute of Anne should be upheld. Following that ruling, the courts ceased to grant injunctions that went against the spirit of that statute—and a new age had begun for publishers, authors, and readers.

*O*pinion of Lord Kames in the case of Hinton Donaldson: ... What may be the law of England, with respect to the question at present under deliberation, I pretend not to know. Nor is it necessary that I should know; because an alleged trespass committed in Scotland against the pursuer, and prosecuted for damages in the court of Session, must be determined by the law of Scotland. ...

... Taking it in all views, no more can be made of [this claim] than to be a privilege or monopoly, which entitles the claimant to the commerce of a certain book, and excludes all others from making money by it. The important question then is, from what source is this monopoly derived, a monopoly that endures for ever, and is effectual against all the world? The act of Queen Anne[1] bestows this monopoly upon authors for a limited time upon certain conditions. But our legislature, far from acknowledging a perpetual monopoly at common law, declares that it shall last no longer than a limited time.

But to follow out[2] the common law. The composer of a valuable book has great merit with respect to the public: his proper reward is approbation and praise, and he seldom fails of that reward. But what is it that entitles him to a pecuniary reward? If he be entitled, the composer of a picture, of a machine, and the inventor of every useful art, is equally entitled. Such a monopoly, so far from being founded on common law, is contradictory to the first principles of society. Why was man made a social being, but to benefit by society, and to partake of all the improvements of society in its progress toward perfection? At the same time, he was made an imitative being, in order to follow what he sees done by others. But to bestow on inventors the monopoly of their productions, would in effect counteract the designs of Providence, in making man a social and imitative being: it would be a miserable cramp upon improvements, and prevent the general use of them. Consider the plough, the loom, the spinning wheel. Would it not sound oddly, that it would be rank injustice for any man to employ these useful machines, without consent of the original inventors and those deriving right from them? ...

Lastly, I shall consider a perpetual monopoly in a commercial view. The act of Queen Anne is contrived with great judgement, not only for the benefit of authors, but for the benefit of learning in general. It excites men of genius to exert their talents for composition; and it multiplies books both of instruction and amusement. And when, upon expiration of the monop-

---

[1] *act of Queen Anne* The Copyright Act of 1709, also known as the Statute of Anne (see above).

[2] *follow out* I.e., continue discussing.

oly, the commerce of these books is laid open to all, their cheapness, from a concurrence of many editors, is singularly beneficial to the public. Attend, on the other hand, to the consequences of a perpetual monopoly. Like all other monopolies, it will unavoidably raise the price of good books beyond the reach of ordinary readers. They will be sold like so many valuable pictures. The sale will be confined to a few learned men who have money to spare, and to a few rich men who buy out of vanity as they buy a diamond or a fine coat. The commerce of books will be in a worse state than before printing was invented. ...

In a word, I have no difficulty to maintain that a perpetual monopoly of books would prove more destructive to learning, and even to authors, than a second irruption of Goths and Vandals.[1] ...

Our booksellers, it is true, aiming at present profit, may not think themselves much concerned about futurity. But it belongs to judges to look forward; and it deserves to be duly pondered whether the interest of literature in general ought to be sacrificed to the pecuniary interest of a few individuals. The greatest profit to them ought to be rejected, unless the monopoly be founded in common law beyond all objection: the most sanguine partisan of the booksellers will not pretend this to be the case. At the same time, it will be founded upon the strictest examination, that the profit of such a monopoly would not rise much above what is afforded by the statute. There are not many books that have so long a run as fourteen years; and the success of books upon the first publication is so uncertain, that a bookseller will give very little more for a perpetuity, than for the temporary privilege bestowed by the statute. This was foreseen by the legislature; and the privilege was wisely confined to fourteen years; a sufficient encouragement to men of genius without hurting the public interest. The best authors write for fame: the more diffused their works are, the more joy they have. The monopoly then is useful only to those who write for money or for bread, who are not always of the most

dignified sort [and even] such writers will gain very little by the monopoly. ...

Opinion of Lord Camden, in the case of Donaldson Beckett: ... If there be any thing in the world common to all mankind, science and learning are in their nature ..., and they ought to be as free and general as air or water. ... Why did we enter into society at all, but to enlighten one another's minds, and improve our faculties, for the common welfare of the species? Those great men, those favoured mortals, those sublime spirits, who share that ray of divinity which we call genius, are entrusted by Providence with the delegated power of imparting to their fellow-creatures that instruction which heaven meant for universal benefit; they must not be niggards to the world, or hoard up for themselves the common stock. ...

Glory is the reward of science, and those who deserve it, scorn all meaner views: I speak not of scribblers for bread, who tease the press with their wretched productions; fourteen years is too long a privilege for their perishable trash. It was not for gain, that Bacon, Newton, Milton, Locke, instructed and delighted the world; it would be unworthy such men to traffic with a dirty bookseller for so much a sheet of a letter press. When the bookseller offered Milton five pound[s] for his Paradise Lost, he did not reject it, and commit his poem to the flames, nor did he accept the miserable pittance as the reward of his labour; he knew that the real price of his work was immortality, and that posterity would pay it. ... [If copyright is held in perpetuity,] All our learning will be locked up in the hands of [unprincipled printers and booksellers], who will set what price upon it their avarice chooses to demand, till the public become as much their slaves, as their own hackney compilers are. ... [E]very valuable author will be as much monopolized by them as Shakespeare is at present. ...

---

[1] *irruption of Goths and Vandals* Barbarian invasion.

from Catharine Macaulay, *A Modest Plea for the Property of Copyright* (1774)

The historian Catharine Macaulay was among those who vigorously opposed the Lords' ruling in Donaldson *v.* Beckett. Macaulay argued that, unlike inventors of machines, for example, authors—and particularly authors of works that may take an extraordinarily long time to reach a large reading public—deserve to expect in perpetuity unrestricted financial compensation for the ongoing sale of their property. Without the promise of such compensation, she suggested, books would be written only by the very rich, or by those dependent on the very rich for patronage. More persuasively, she argued that limiting the term of copyright protection would tend to lower prices—and, along with them, standards of book production.

To be more serious: with the intention of depriving authors of the honest, the dear-bought reward of their labours, they have been … leveled with the inventors of a very inferior order. [Indeed,] the inventor of inferior order would find himself much better rewarded than the author, for his ingenuity. Every common capacity can find out the use of a machine; but it is a length of time before the value of a literary publication is discovered and acknowledged by the vulgar; and … the malice of party prejudice … may for the long term of years keep back the sale of a book which teaches an offensive doctrine, or tells disagreeable truths to the public.

But to come to the last and most important question agitated in the cause between the appellants Donaldson and the independent booksellers: is the rendering of literary property common, advantageous or disadvantageous to the state of literature in this country? The question, I think, is easily answered, that it will be not only disadvantageous, but ruinous to the state of literature.

[What of] a man whom fortune has declined to favour, yet of merit, or genius, and of virtue, sufficient to instruct and enlighten mankind: if such a man is deprived of the necessary lucrative advantage [stemming from] the right of property in his own writings, is he to starve, or live in penury, whilst he is exerting, perhaps

A

MODEST PLEA

FOR THE

PROPERTY

OF

COPY RIGHT.

I SHALL not enter on the subject of those precedents which a noble Lord, in his arguments on this important cause, so properly dismissed: they were very injudiciously used: therefore, I shall only venture a few remarks on the pleas of equity,—of moral fitness,—and public convenience,—which it seems were urged by the council on the side of the respondent booksellers.   B   SIR

The title page of Catharine Macaulay's 1774 pamphlet *A Modest Plea for the Property of Copyright.*

vain endeavours to serve a people who do not desire his services? … Every independent man, not born to an estate being thus, by a hard conjuncture of circumstances, prevented from exerting his talents for the delight and instruction of mankind, this important task can only be the lot of the opulent …; but, alas! genius and learning are, in our days, too humble and too modest to frequent the palaces of the great; therefore, I am afraid, it is from dependent writers alone that we must expect all our future instruction—but can that instruction be edifying which [is] exerted merely to earn the favour of a patron … and [which sets] forth, in false colours, all the prejudices and corrupt views of the man from whose hard-earned bounty the author expects bread?

… In regard to elegant editions, no proprietor of copyright who hold such property … for a small term of years, will find it worthwhile to give a very good edition of works, lest the public, who are fond of pennyworths in the article of books, withhold their purchase 'till the property become common; and in this case the style, if not the sentiments of the author, will be miserably mangled, and the shops full of those wretched editions of works which would disgrace even an Irish press.... This will be the wretched state of literature, and editions of authors, if literary property continues to stand on the footing which the Lords' decision has put it.

from Robert Southey, "Inquiries Concerning the Proposed Alteration of the Laws of Copyright, as It Affects Authors and the Universities," *Quarterly Review* (January 1819)

> The poet Robert Southey was among those authors in the Romantic era who argued that their interests were unfairly damaged by restricting the term of copyright protection.

The question is simply this: upon what principle, with what justice, or under what pretext of public good, are men of letters deprived of a perpetual property in the produce of their own labours, when all other persons enjoy it as their indefeasible right—a right beyond the power of any earthly authority to take away? Is it because their labour is so light, the endowments which it requires so common, the attainments so cheaply and easily acquired, and the present remuneration so adequate, so ample, and so certain?

from Thomas Babington Macaulay, Speech to House of Commons, 5 February 1841

> Macaulay, the famous politician and historian, made his case in the House of Commons for copyright law as a balancing of interests, arguing that a proposed extension of copyright to 60 years following the death of the author would be far too restrictive.

... We may now ... descend from these high regions, where we are in danger of being lost in the clouds, to firm ground and clear light. Let us look at this question like legislators, and after fairly balancing conveniences and inconveniences, pronounce between the existing law of copyright, and the law now proposed to us. The question of copyright, Sir, like most questions of civil prudence, is neither black nor white, but grey. The system of copyright has great advantages and great disadvantages; and it is our business to ascertain what these are, and then to make an arrangement under which the advantages may be as far as possible secured, and the disadvantages as far as possible excluded. The charge which I bring against my honourable and learned friend's bill is this, that it leaves the advantages nearly what they are at present, and increases the disadvantages at least fourfold.

The advantages arising from a system of copyright are obvious. It is desirable that we should have a supply of good books; we cannot have such a supply unless men of letters are liberally remunerated; and the least objectionable way of remunerating them is by means of copyright. You cannot depend for literary instruction and amusement on the leisure of men occupied in the pursuits of active life. Such men may occasionally produce compositions of great merit. But you must not look to such men for works which require deep meditation and long research. Works of that kind you can expect only from persons who make literature the business of their lives. Of these persons few will be found among the rich and the noble.... It is then on men whose profession is literature, and whose private means are not ample, that you must rely for a supply of valuable books. Such men must be remunerated for their literary labour. And there are only two ways in which they can be remunerated. One of those ways is patronage; the other is copyright....

If, as my honourable and learned friend seems to think, ... the real effect of monopoly is to make articles good and cheap, why ... does he limit the operation of so salutary a principle to sixty years? Why does he consent to anything short of a perpetuity? He told us that in consenting to anything short of a perpetuity he was making a compromise between extreme right and expediency. But if his opinion about monopoly be correct, extreme right and expediency would coincide. Or rather, why should we not restore the monopoly of the East India trade to the East India Company? Why should we not revive all those old monopolies which, in

Elizabeth's reign, galled our fathers so severely that, maddened by intolerable wrong, they opposed to their sovereign a resistance before which her haughty spirit quailed for the first and for the last time? ...

Now, I will not affirm that the existing law is perfect, that it exactly hits the point at which the monopoly ought to cease; but this I confidently say, that the existing law is very much nearer that point than the law proposed by my honourable and learned friend. For consider this; the evil effects of the monopoly are proportioned to the length of its duration.... It is by no means the fact that a posthumous monopoly of sixty years gives to an author thrice as much pleasure and thrice as strong a motive as a posthumous monopoly of twenty years. On the contrary, the difference is so small as to be hardly perceptible. We all know how faintly we are affected by the prospect of very distant advantages, even when they are advantages which we may reasonably hope that we shall ourselves enjoy. An advantage that is to be enjoyed more than half a century after we are dead, by somebody, we know not by whom, perhaps by somebody unborn, by somebody utterly unconnected with us, is really no motive at all to action....

The principle of copyright is this. It is a tax on readers for the purpose of giving a bounty to writers. The tax is an exceedingly bad one; it is a tax on one of the most innocent and most salutary of human pleasures; and never let us forget, that a tax on innocent pleasures is a premium on vicious pleasures. I admit, however, the necessity of giving a bounty to genius and learning. In order to give such a bounty, I willingly submit even to this severe and burdensome tax. Nay, I am ready to increase the tax, if it can be shown that by so doing I should proportionally increase the bounty. My complaint is, that my honourable and learned friend doubles, triples, quadruples, the tax, and makes scarcely any perceptible addition to the bounty. ...

But this is not all. I think it right, Sir, to call the attention of the House to an evil, which is perhaps more to be apprehended when an author's copyright remains in the hands of his family, than when it is transferred to

booksellers. I seriously fear that, if such a measure as this should be adopted, many valuable works will be either totally suppressed or grievously mutilated.... Most of us, I am sure, have known persons who, very erroneously as I think, but from the best motives, would not choose to reprint Fielding's novels, or Gibbon's History of the Decline and Fall of the Roman Empire.[1] Some gentlemen may perhaps be of opinion that it would be as well if Tom Jones and Gibbon's History were never reprinted....

I will give another instance. One of the most instructive, interesting, and delightful books in our language is Boswell's Life of Johnson. Now it is well known that Boswell's eldest son considered this book, considered the whole relation of Boswell to Johnson, as a blot in the escutcheon of the family. He thought, not perhaps altogether without reason, that his father had exhibited himself in a ludicrous and degrading light. And thus he became so sore and irritable that at last he could not bear to hear the Life of Johnson mentioned. Suppose that the law had been what my honourable and learned friend wishes to make it. Suppose that the copyright of Boswell's Life of Johnson had belonged, as it well might, during sixty years, to Boswell's eldest son. What would have been the consequence? ...

These are strong cases. ... But ... the books which I have mentioned are singularly inoffensive books, books not touching on any of those questions which drive even wise men beyond the bounds of wisdom. There are books of a very different kind, books which are the rallying points of great political and religious parties. What is likely to happen if the copyright of one of the these books should by descent or transfer come into the possession of some hostile zealot? ...

---

[1] *Fielding's novels ... Roman Empire* Henry Fielding's *The History of Tom Jones, a Foundling* (1749) was attacked by some for its ribald sexual content; similarly, the first volume of Edward Gibbon's six-volume history was attacked by some on publication in 1776 for the author's "pagan" willingness to challenge the accuracy of orthodox Christian histories on such matters as the history of the early martyrs. (Gibbon had relied not on these secondary works but on primary sources.)

THE NATURAL, THE HUMAN, THE SUPERNATURAL, AND THE SUBLIME

CONTEXTS

In "The Two Guides of Life: The Sublime and the Beautiful" (a poem translated into English by Edward Bulwer Lytton in 1844), the German philosopher Friedrich Schiller identifies "two genii," present from birth till death, "to guide thee." These guides structure our existence; we are, the poem maintains, perpetually under their influence, the sway of the beautiful and the sublime. Schiller's notion of aesthetic experience as profoundly powerful, indeed as the central force of human life, would hardly come as a surprise to the Romantics, who placed the beautiful and the sublime, along with the picturesque, at the forefront of their creative and philosophical vision.

Of course, the impulse to catalogue and categorize encounters with the aesthetic has a long history, originating well before the eighteenth century. The ancient Greeks had a great deal to say about the beautiful, connecting beauty with truth—a correspondence famously celebrated in Keats's "Ode on a Grecian Urn" (1820)—and the Platonic ideal. In *Perì Hýpsos*, a treatise on writing, the first-century rhetorician Longinus, deemed extraordinary works "sublime," identifying great thought, powerful emotion, elevated figure of speech, noble diction, and distinguished word arrangement as the sources of sublimity in writing. The sublime, Longinus noted, is a significant source of pleasure, one that is distinguishable from beauty, for the experience of the sublime involves astonishment, alarm, and even fear.

Longinus's commentary was rediscovered in the late sixteenth century, translated into French (in 1674) and subsequently into English (in 1680), and published as *On the Sublime*. The sustained intense interest in the beautiful and the sublime only became a defining feature of the eighteenth century and the Romantic era, however, when a number of important thinkers turned their attentions to the principles and problems of aesthetics. At the same time, what had been formerly identified mainly as aspects of writing became more profoundly associated with the natural world. This evolution is evident in consulting the definition of "sublime" in the *Oxford English Dictionary*, which notes, circa 1700, the first usage of the term as indicating "things in nature" that affect "the mind with a sense of overwhelming grandeur or irresistible power; calculated to inspire awe, deep reverence, or lofty emotion, by reason of its beauty, vastness, or grandeur." English writers, including Joseph Addison, the founder and editor of the popular *Spectator* magazine, and Anthony Ashley Cooper, the Earl of Shaftesbury, undertook the continental tour deemed necessary for learned young men and wrote powerfully of crossing the Alps, extolling the mountains' greatness, and testifying to their personal transformations through such experiences. They wrote, too, of the beauty of nature, remarking on "the pleasures of the imagination" in nature, as in the title of Addison's *Spectator* essays on the subject.

But it was Edmund Burke who, in *A Philosophical Enquiry into the Origin of Our Ideas of the Sublime and Beautiful* (1757), gave the project of categorizing "objects of experience" its most extensive theoretical treatment, initiating the era's myriad investigations into the underpinnings of the sublime and the beautiful. Burke's undertaking is significant in its insistence on the rigorous separation of the two qualities; they are, he proposed, in their effects, virtual opposites. Other thinkers, most notably the German philosopher Immanuel Kant, who wrote extensively on aesthetics, disputed some of Burke's premises, but Burke's ideas were immensely influential, shaping the representation of and reaction to the sublime and the beautiful in the writing of the Romantics. Particularly noteworthy in this context is Burke's focus on the empirical experience of the beauty and grandeur of nature, an emphasis that plays out in much eighteenth-century British poetry and travel writing.

A third aesthetic category bears mentioning. The "picturesque" became an obsession of sorts, a feature of published travelogues and of great interest to travelers everywhere. Here, in a passage from Jane Austen's *Pride and Prejudice* (1813), the novel's spirited heroine Elizabeth Bennet marvels at the picturesque splendor of an estate in Derbyshire:

> They gradually ascended for half a mile, and then found themselves at the top of a considerable eminence, where the wood ceased, and the eye was instantly caught by Pemberley House, situated on the opposite side of a valley, into which the road with some abruptness wound. It was a large, handsome, stone building, standing well on rising ground, and backed by a ridge of high woody hills;—and in front, a stream of some natural importance was swelled into greater, but without any artificial appearance. Its banks were neither formal, nor falsely adorned. Elizabeth was delighted.

Elizabeth so admires, we are told, "a place … where natural beauty had been so little counteracted by an awkward taste." The scene is one of beauty, but its pleasures come from the seeming absence of human intervention. Here, nature, and nature alone, reigns. This appreciation for or awe of nature structures and informs the Romantic mindset. Nature was not simply a matter of inspiration but the object of aspiration, to be emulated and celebrated in its beauty, its sublimity, and its ability to mediate between the two.

* * *

If ideas as to the nature of nature were changing in the Romantic era, nowhere was this more true than in human ideas about non-human animals; a concluding subsection of these "Contexts" materials underscores this point. Through much of the eighteenth century, philosophers debated the question of how non-human animals should be treated. The philosophical background on one side of the issue had been laid out by René Descartes, who asserted in his *Discourse on Method* (1637) that non-human animals "have no reason at all." Even in cases where they show greater ability or dexterity than humans, "it is nature which acts in them" rather than any mental activity of their own, "just as a clock, which is only composed of wheels and weights is able to tell the hours and measure the time more correctly than we can do with all our wisdom." John Locke argued in the other direction in his *Essay Concerning Human Understanding* (1690), asserting that it was far more difficult than Descartes had suggested to draw a clear line separating human and non-human animals. Locke also argued strongly that it was important to educate young people to treat non-human animals with consideration and kindness, which would become a recurring theme of eighteenth- and nineteenth-century writers. In the eighteenth century, Jean-Jacques Rousseau, while accepting that in some sense beasts could be machine-like, also argued that "every animal has ideas, since it has senses; it even combines those ideas in a certain degree; and it is only in degree that man differs, in this respect, from the brute." He, too, felt it important to inculcate in humans—children especially—feelings of kindness towards our fellow creatures.

As the horrific images in William Hogarth's *The Four Stages of Cruelty* suggest, such sentiments were often ignored in the eighteenth century. Indeed, it would be hard to argue that British society as a whole became less cruel toward animals over the course of the century. Animals such as cart horses and donkeys were routinely worked to death by their owners; poor farmers tied horses to plows by their tails to save the expense of a harness; sheep had their wool pulled off instead of sheared; sports such as bullbaiting and cockfighting flourished.

Yet some signs pointed in a different direction. Through the century, it became more and more common among better-off members of society to keep pets (Samuel Johnson's cat Hodge being perhaps the most famous example). In literature, we find powerful (if sometimes inconsistent) expressions of concern for the welfare of non-human animals from the likes of James Thomson, Alexander Pope, William Cowper, and Sarah Scott. In the Romantic era, such voices became more numerous; Anna Laetitia Barbauld was perhaps the most influential among them. As the language of Barbauld's "The Mouse's Petition" suggests, such views were to some degree connected to the revolutionary ferment of the time. Others—perhaps most notably Percy Shelley—went further and strongly advocated vegetarianism, often out of concern for the well-being of human as well as non-human animals. Quite aside from any issues relating to the treatment of animals, there was also the question of what was natural; in Shelley's mind—and that of many others of his time—humans were not naturally meat eaters. (This is also the view suggested in Mary Shelley's *Frankenstein*; the monster decides to live on nuts and berries, thereby choosing a life that is "peaceful and human.")

Beginning with the introduction of a bill against bullbaiting in 1800, a political movement began to take shape, devoted to place legal limits on human cruelty against non-human animals. The movement attracted well-known supporters (including William Wilberforce and Richard Brinsley Sheridan), but it faced extremely strong opposition; the 1800 bill was defeated, and so were numerous others before the first piece of legislation against animal cruelty—An Act to Prevent the Cruel and Improper Treatment of Cattle—was passed in 1822.

⌘ ⌘ ⌘

from Dionysius Longinus, *On the Sublime*[1] (1st Century CE)

Longinus's *On the Sublime* is one of the most significant classical explorations of aesthetics. The treatise's authorship is unknown—the name "Dionysius Longinus" seems to have been the misreading of a medieval copyist—but its importance to the development of ideas about the sublime and their application to literary criticism is undeniable.

In the passage below, "Longinus" explains how the sublime is achieved in writing and elucidates the sources of the sublime.

SECTION I

... But I request you, my dear friend, to give me your opinion on whatever I advance, with that exactness which is due to truth, and that sincerity, which is

natural to yourself. For well did the sage answer the question, *in what do we most resemble the gods?* when he replied, *in doing good and speaking truth.* But since I write, my dear friend, to you, who are versed in every branch of polite learning, there will be little occasion to use many previous words in proving, that the sublime is a certain eminence or perfection of language, and that the greatest writers, both in verse and prose, have by this alone obtained the prize of glory, and filled all time with their renown. For the sublime not only persuades, but even throws an audience into transport. The marvelous always works with more surprising force, than that which barely persuades or delights. In most cases, it is wholly in our own power, either to resist or yield to persuasion. But the sublime, endued with strength irresistible, strikes home, and triumphs over every hearer. Dexterity of invention, and good order and economy in composition, are not to be discerned from one or two passages, nor scarcely sometimes from the whole texture of a discourse; but the sublime, when

[1] *On the Sublime* The translation here is that of William Smith (1743).

seasonably addressed, with the rapid force of lightning has borne down all before it, and shown at one stroke the compacted might of genius. ...

Section 8

There are, if I may so express it, five very copious sources of the sublime, if we presuppose an ability of speaking well, as a common foundation for these five sorts, and indeed without it, any thing besides will avail but little.

1. The first and most excellent of these is a boldness and grandeur in the thoughts, as I have shown in my essay on Xenophon.[1]

2. The second is called the pathetic, or the power of raising the passions to a violent and even enthusiastic degree; and these two being genuine constituents of the sublime, are the gifts of nature, whereas the other sorts depend in some measure upon art.

3. The third consists in a skilful application of figures, which are two-fold, of sentiment and language.

4. The fourth is a noble and graceful manner of expression, which is not only to choose out significant and elegant words, but also to adorn and embellish the style, by the assistance of tropes.

5. The fifth source of the sublime, which completes all the preceding, is the structure or composition of all the periods, in all possible dignity and grandeur. ...

from Joseph Addison, "The Pleasures of the Imagination," *The Spectator* (1712)

Addison (1662–1719), the influential founder of *The Spectator*, contributed to the development of the eighteenth-century discourse on aesthetics and the imagination in a series of papers written in 1712. The essays departed from Addison's usual emphasis on the social and political and inspired later thinkers and poets, most notably Mark Akenside, who published in 1744 his long poem inspired by Addison's thinking and also entitled *The Pleasures of the Imagination*.

---

[1] *Xenophon* Contemporary and admirer of Socrates, Xenophon (c. 430–354 BCE) recorded many of the sayings of Socrates, documenting in the process the history of ancient Greece.

from *The Spectator*, No. 411 (21 June 1712)

Our sight is the most perfect and most delightful of all our senses. It fills the mind with the largest variety of ideas, converses with its objects at the greatest distance, and continues the longest in action without being tired or satiated with its proper enjoyments. The sense of feeling can indeed give us a notion of extension, shape, and all other ideas that enter at the eye, except colours; but at the same time it is very much straitened and confined in its operations, to the number, bulk, and distance of its particular objects. Our sight seems designed to supply all these defects, and may be considered as a more delicate and diffusive kind of touch, that spreads itself over an infinite multitude of bodies, comprehends the largest figures, and brings into our reach some of the most remote parts of the universe.

It is this sense which furnishes the imagination with its ideas; so that by the pleasures of the imagination, or fancy (which I shall use promiscuously), I here mean such as arise from visible objects, either when we have them actually in our view, or when we call up their ideas into our minds by paintings, statues, descriptions, or any the like occasion. We cannot, indeed, have a single image in the fancy that did not make its first entrance through the sight; but we have the power of retaining, altering, and compounding those images, which we have once received, into all the varieties of picture and vision that are most agreeable to the imagination; for by this faculty a man in a dungeon is capable of entertaining himself with scenes and landscapes more beautiful than any that can be found in the whole compass of nature.

There are few words in the English language which are employed in a more loose and uncircumscribed sense than those of the fancy and the imagination. I therefore thought it necessary to fix and determine the notion of these two words, as I intend to make use of them in the thread of my following speculations, that the reader may conceive rightly what is the subject which I proceed upon. I must therefore desire him to remember, that by the pleasures of the imagination, I mean only such pleasures as arise originally from sight, and that I divide these pleasures into two kinds: my design being first of all to discourse of those primary pleasures of the imagination, which entirely proceed from such objects as are before our eyes; and in the next place to speak of those secondary pleasures of the imagination which flow from the ideas of visible objects, when the objects are not actually before the eye, but are called up into our memories, or formed into agreeable visions of things that are either absent or fictitious.

The pleasures of the imagination, taken in their full extent, are not so gross as those of sense, nor so refined as those of the understanding. The last are, indeed, *more preferable*, because they are founded on some new knowledge or improvement in the mind of man; yet it must be confessed, that those of the imagination are as great and as transporting as the other. A beautiful prospect delights the soul, as much as a demonstration; and a description in Homer has charmed more readers than a chapter in Aristotle. Besides, the pleasures of the imagination have this advantage above those of the understanding, that they are more obvious, and more easy to be acquired. It is but opening the eye, and the scene enters. The colours paint themselves on the fancy, with very little attention of thought or application of mind in the beholder. We are struck, we know not how, with the symmetry of anything we see, and immediately assent to the beauty of an object, without inquiring into the particular causes and occasions of it.

A man of polite imagination is let into a great many pleasures, that the vulgar are not capable of receiving. He can converse with a picture, and find an agreeable companion in a statue. He meets with a secret refreshment in a description, and often feels a greater satisfaction in the prospect of fields and meadows, than another does in the possession. It gives him, indeed, a kind of property in everything he sees, and makes the most rude, uncultivated parts of nature administer to his pleasures: so that he looks upon the world, as it were in another light, and discovers in it a multitude of charms, that conceal themselves from the generality of mankind.

There are, indeed, but very few who know how to be idle and innocent, or have a relish of any pleasures that are not criminal: every diversion they take is at the expense of some one virtue or another, and their very first step out of business is into vice or folly. A man should endeavour, therefore, to make the sphere of his innocent pleasures as wide as possible, that he may retire into them with safety, and find in them such a

satisfaction as a wise man would not blush to take. Of this nature are those of the imagination, which do not require such a bent of thought as is necessary to our more serious employments, nor, at the same time, suffer the mind to sink into that negligence and remissness, which are apt to accompany our more sensual delights, but, like a gentle exercise to the faculties, awaken them from sloth and idleness, without putting them upon any labour or difficulty.

We might here add, that the pleasures of the fancy are more conducive to health, than those of the understanding, which are worked out by dint of thinking, and attended with too violent a labour of the brain. Delightful scenes, whether in nature, painting, or poetry, have a kindly influence on the body, as well as the mind, and not only serve to clear and brighten the imagination, but are able to disperse grief and melancholy, and to set the animal spirits in pleasing and agreeable motions. . . .

from *The Spectator*, No. 412 (23 June 1712)

I shall first consider those pleasures of the imagination which arise from the actual view and survey of outward objects; and these, I think, all proceed from the sight of what is *great*, *uncommon*, or *beautiful*. There may indeed be something so terrible or offensive, that horror or loathsomeness of an object may overbear the pleasure which results from its *greatness*, *novelty*, or *beauty*; but still there will be such a mixture of delight in the very disgust it gives us, as any these three qualifications are most conspicuous and prevailing.

By *greatness*, I do not only mean the bulk of any single object, but the largeness of a whole view, considered as one entire piece. Such are the prospects of an open champaign country, a vast uncultivated desert, of huge heaps of mountains, high rocks and precipices, or a wide expanse of waters, where we are not struck with the novelty or beauty of the sight, but with that rude kind of magnificence which appears in many of these stupendous works of nature. Our imagination loves to be filled with an object, or to grasp at anything that is too big for its capacity. We are flung into a pleasing astonishment at such unbounded views, and feel a delightful stillness and amazement in the soul at the apprehension of them. The mind of man naturally hates everything that looks like a restraint upon it, and is apt to fancy itself under a sort of confinement, when the sight is pent up in a narrow compass, and shortened on every side by the neighbourhood of walls or mountains. On the contrary, a spacious horizon is an image of liberty, where the eye has room to range abroad, to expatiate at large on the immensity of its views, and to lose itself amidst the variety of objects that offer themselves to its observation. Such wide and undetermined prospects are as pleasing to the fancy, as the speculations of eternity or infinitude are to the understanding. But if there be a beauty or uncommonness joined with this grandeur, as in a troubled ocean, a heaven adorned with stars and meteors, or a spacious landscape cut out into rivers, woods, rocks, and meadows, the pleasure still grows upon us, as it arises from more than a single principle.

Every thing that is *new* or *uncommon* raises a pleasure in the imagination, because it fills the soul with an agreeable surprise, gratifies its curiosity, and gives it an idea of which it was not before possessed. We are indeed so often conversant with one set of objects, and tired out with so many repeated shows of the same things, that whatever is *new* or *uncommon* contributes a little to vary human life, and to divert our minds for a while with the strangeness of its appearance: it serves us for a kind of refreshment, and takes off from that satiety we are apt to complain of in our usual and ordinary entertainments. It is this that bestows charms on a monster, and makes even the imperfections of nature please us. It is this that recommends variety, where the mind is every instant called off to something new, and the attention not suffered to dwell too long and waste itself on any particular object. It is this, likewise, that improves what is great or beautiful, and makes it afford the mind a double entertainment. Groves, fields, and meadows are at any season of the year pleasant to look upon, but never so much as in the opening of the spring, when they are all new and fresh, with their first gloss upon them, and not yet too much accustomed and familiar to the eye. For this reason there is nothing that more enlivens a prospect than rivers, jetteaus, or falls of water, where the scene is perpetually shifting and entertaining the sight every moment with something that is new. We are quickly tired with looking upon hills and valleys, where everything continues fixed and settled in the same place and posture, but find our thoughts a little agitated and relieved at the sight of such objects as are ever in motion and sliding away from beneath the eye of the beholder.

But there is nothing that makes its way more directly to the soul than *beauty*, which immediately diffuses a secret satisfaction and complacency through the imagination, and gives a finishing to anything that is great or uncommon. The very first discovery of it strikes the mind with an inward joy, and spreads a cheerfulness and delight through all its faculties. There is not perhaps any real beauty or deformity more in one piece of matter than another, because we might have been so made, that whatsoever now appears loathsome to us, might have shown itself agreeable; but we find by experience, that there are several modifications of matter which the mind, without any previous consideration, pronounces at first sight beautiful or deformed. ...

There is a second kind of *beauty* that we find in the several products of art and nature, which does not work in the imagination with that warmth and violence as the beauty that appears in our proper species, but is apt however to raise in us a secret delight, and kind of fondness for the places or objects in which we discover it. This consists either in the gaiety or variety of colours, in the symmetry and proportion parts, in the arrangement and disposition of bodies or in a just mixture and concurrence of all together. Among these several kinds of beauty the eye takes most delight in colours. We nowhere meet with a more glorious or pleasing show in nature, than what appears in the heavens at the rising and setting of the sun which is wholly made up of those different stains of light that show themselves in clouds of a different situation. For this reason we find the poets, who are always addressing themselves to the imagination borrowing more of their epithets from colours than from any other topic.

As the fancy delights in everything that is great, strange, or beautiful, and is still more pleased the more it finds of these perfections in the same object, so it is capable of receiving a new satisfaction by the assistance of another sense. Thus any continued sound, as the music of birds, or a fall of water, awakens every moment the mind of the beholder, and makes him more attentive to the several beauties of the place that lie before him. Thus if there arises a fragrancy of smells or perfumes, they heighten the pleasures of the imagination, and make even the colours and verdure of the landscape appear more agreeable; for the ideas of both senses recommend each other, and are pleasanter together than when they enter the mind separately: as the different colours of a picture, when they are well disposed, set off one another, and receive an additional beauty from the advantage of their situation.

from *The Spectator*, No. 413 (24 June 1712)

... One of the final causes of our delight in anything that is *great*, may be this. The Supreme Author of our being has so formed the soul of man, that nothing but himself can be its last, adequate, and proper happiness. Because, therefore, a great part of our happiness must arise from the contemplation of his being, that he might give our souls a just relish of such a contemplation, he has made them naturally delight in the apprehension of what is great or unlimited. Our admiration, which is a very pleasing motion of the mind, immediately rises at the consideration of any object that takes up a great deal of room in the fancy, and by consequence will improve into the highest pitch of astonishment and devotion when we contemplate his nature, that is neither circumscribed by time nor place, nor to be comprehended by the largest capacity of a created being.

He has annexed a secret pleasure to the idea of anything that is *new* or *uncommon*, that he might encourage us in the pursuit after knowledge, and engage us to search into the wonders of his creation; for every new idea brings such a pleasure along with it, as rewards any pains we have taken in its acquisition, and consequently serves as a motive to put us upon fresh discoveries.

He has made everything that is *beautiful in our own species* pleasant, that all creatures might be tempted to multiply their kind and fill the world with inhabitants; for 'tis very remarkable that wherever nature is crossed in the production of a monster (the result of any unnatural mixture) the breed is incapable of propagating its likeness and of founding a new order of creatures; so that unless all animals were allured by the beauty of their own species, generation would be at an end, and the earth unpeopled.

In the last place, he has made everything that is beautiful in all other objects pleasant, or rather has made so many objects appear beautiful, that he might render the whole creation more gay and delightful. He has given almost everything about us the power of raising an agreeable idea in the imagination: so that it is impossible for us to behold his works with coldness or indifference, and to survey so many beauties without secret satisfaction and complacency. Things would make but a poor appearance to the eye, if we saw them only in their proper figures and motions: and what reason can we assign for their exciting in us many of those ideas which are different from anything that exists in the objects themselves (for such are light and colours), were not it to add supernumerary ornaments to the universe, and make it more agreeable to the imagination? We are everywhere entertained with pleasing shows and apparitions, we discover imaginary glories in the heavens and in the earth, and see some of this visionary beauty poured out upon the whole creation; but what a rough unsightly sketch of nature should we be entertained with, did all her colouring disappear, and the several distinctions of light and shade vanish? In short, our souls are at present delightfully lost and bewildered in a pleasing delusion and we walk about like the enchanted hero of a romance who sees beautiful castles, woods, and meadows, and at the same time hears the warbling of birds and the purling of streams; but upon the finishing of some secret spell the fantastic scene breaks up, and the disconsolate knight finds himself on a barren heath or in a solitary desert. It is not improbable that some thing like this may be the state of the soul after its first separation, in respect of the images it will receive from matter; though indeed the ideas of colours are so pleasing and beautiful in the imagination, that it is possible the soul will not be deprived of them, but perhaps find them excited by some other occasional cause, as they are at present by the different impressions of the subtle matter on the organ of sight. ...

from Sir Jonathan Richardson, the Elder, *An Essay on the Theory of Painting* (1725)

A notable early eighteenth-century portrait painter, Richardson (1667–1745) was also an important critic and theorist of art. In this excerpt from his *Essay on the Theory of Painting*, Richardson discusses the role of the sublime in the creation of art.

OF THE SUBLIME

... By the sublime in general I mean the most excellent of what is excellent, as the excellent is the best of what is good. The dignity of a man consists chiefly in his capacity of thinking, and of communicating his ideas to another; *the greatest, and most noble thoughts, images, or sentiments, conveyed to us in the best chosen words*, I take therefore to be the perfect sublime in writing; the admirable, the marvellous.

But as there may be degrees even in the sublime, something short of the utmost may be also sublime.

Thought, and language are two distinct excellencies: there are few that are capable of adding dignity to a great subject, or even of doing right to such a one; in some cases none: the bulk of mankind conceive not greatly, nor do they know how to utter the conceptions they have to the best advantage; and those that have higher capacities exert them but rarely, and on few occasions: hence it is that we so justly admire what is so excellent, and so uncommon.

The great manner of thinking (as thought in general) is either pure invention, or what arises upon hints suggested from without. ...

As the thoughts, so the language of the sublime must be the most excellent; what that is is the question: whether it be confined to the florid, to magnificent, and sonorous words, tours, figures, &c. or whether brevity, simplicity, or even common, and low words are the best on some occasions.

Poetry, history, declamation, &c. have their peculiar styles, but the sublime (as our high court of parliament is not under the restrictions which inferior courts are) is not limited to any particular style: the best is the sublime language, and that is best that sets the idea in the strongest light; that is the great end, and use of words; but if those that please the ear do equally serve

that purpose, no doubt they are preferable, but not otherwise. Plain and common words paint a great image sometimes stronger than any other. ...

The only reasons that can be given for a peculiarity of style in the sublime are, that as the thought must be great, the language must be so too as best expressing such thought; and because the music of the words serve to the same purpose, and moreover please. I own all this is generally true: why do we use the term *sublime*, and not *the very best*, both which express the same thing, only that one raises, and the other depresses the idea? But I deny it is always thus; and only contend that when low, common words, and a plain style best serves the main end of language, it is then, and only then the sublime style. And when this happens the pleasure that is wanting in the sound is abundantly recompensed by observing the judgment of him who made so wise a choice. ...

But the sublime, as the crown in the state hides all defects; it fills and satisfies the mind, nothing appears to be wanting; nothing to be amiss, or if it does it is easily forgiven. All faults die, and vanish in presence of the sublime, which when it appears is as *the sun traversing the vast desert of the sky*. ...

from Samuel Johnson, *A Dictionary of the English Language* (1755)

Samuel Johnson's (1709–84) famous dictionary offered not only a sense of the meaning of sublime, as it did for all its entries, but it also documented notable instances of the term's literary usage.

SUBLIME. *adj.* [*sublimis*, Latin.]
1. High in place; exalted aloft.
   They furl'd their pens, and soaring th' air *sublime*
   With clang despis'd the ground.   Milton.
   Sublime on these a tow'r of steel is rear'd,
   And dire Tisiphone there keeps the ward. Dryden.
2. High in excellence; exalted by nature.
   My earthly strained to the height
   In that celestial colloquy *sublime*.   Milton.
   Can it be, that souls *sublime*
   Return to visit our terrestrial clime;

And that the gen'rous mind releas'd by death,
Can cover lazy limbs?   Dryden.
3. High in stile or sentiment; lofty; grand.
   Easy in stile, thy work in sense *sublime*.   Prior.
4. Elevated by joy.
   All yet left of that revolted rout,
   Heav'n-fall'n, in station stood or just array,
   Sublime with expectation.   Milton.
      Their hearts were jocund and *sublime*,
   Drunk with idolatry, drunk with wine.   Milton.
5. Haughty; proud.
   He was *sublime*, and almost tumorous in
            his looks and gestures.   Wotton.
SUBLIME. *n.s.* The grand or lofty stile. *The sublime* is a
   Gallicism, but now naturalized.
      Longinus strengthens all his laws,
   And is himself the great *sublime* he draws.   Pope.
   The *sublime* rises from the nobleness of thoughts,
the magnificence of the words, or the harmonious and
lively turn of the phrase; the perfect *sublime* arises from
all three together.   Addison.
TO SUBLIME. *v.a.* [*sublime*, Fr. from the adjective.]
1. To raise by a chemical fire.
      Study our manuscripts, those myriads
   Of letters, which have past 'twixt thee and me,
   Thence write our annals, and in them lessons be
   To all, whom love's *subliming* fire invades.   Donne.
2. To raise on high.
      Although thy trunk be neither large nor strong,
   Nor can thy head, not helpt, itself *sublime*,
   Yet, like a serpent, a tall tree can climb.   Denham.
3. To exalt; to heighten; to improve.
                    Flow'rs, and the fruit,
   Man's nourishment, by gradual scale *sublim'd*
   To vital spirits aspire.   Milton.
   The fancies of most are moved by the inward springs of
the corporeal machine, which even in the most *sublime*
intellectuals is dangerously influential.   Glanville.
   Art being strengthened by the knowledge of things,
may pass into nature by slow degrees, and so be *sublimed*
into a pure genius which is capable of distinguishing
betwixt the beauties of nature and that which is low in
her.   Dryden's *Dufresnoy*.
      Meanly they seek the blessing to confine,
   And force that sun but on a part to shine;

Which not alone the southern wit *sublimes*,
But ripens spirits in cold northern climes.   Pope.
TO SUBLIME. *v.n.* To rise in the chemical vessel by the
force of fire.
   The particles of sal ammoniack in sublimation carry
up the particles of antimony, which will not *sublime*
alone.   Newton's *Optics*.
   This salt is fixed in a gentle fire, and *sublimes* in a
great one.   Arbuthnot on Aliments.
SUBLIMELY. *adv.* [from *sublime*.] Loftily; grandly.
            This fustian's so *sublimely* bad;
   It is not poetry, but prose run mad.   Pope.
SUBLIMITY. *n.s.* [from *sublime*; sublimité, Fr. *sublimita*,
   Lat.]
1. Height of place; local elevation.
2. Height of nature; excellence.
   As religion looketh upon him who in majesty and
power is infinite, as we ought we account not of it,
unless we esteem it even according to that very height of
excellency which our hearts conceive, when divine
sublimity itself is rightly considered.   Hooker.
   In respect of God's incomprehensible *sublimity* and
purity, this is also true, that God is neither a mind, nor
a spirit like other spirits, nor a light such as can be
discerned.   Raleigh.
3. Loftiness of style or sentiment.
   Milton's distinguishing excellence lies in the
sublimity of his thoughts, in the greatness of which he
triumphs over all the poets, modern and ancient,
Homer only excepted.   Addison.

from Edmund Burke, *A Philosophical Enquiry into the Origin of Our Ideas of the Sublime and Beautiful* (1757)

Burke's systematic investigation of the sublime and
the beautiful marks perhaps the first eighteenth-
century attempt to classify aesthetic feeling and
effects. Like Longinus, Burke (1729–97) is interested in how the two categories are produced in
writing; unlike Longinus, Burke fully separates the
sublime and the beautiful, delineating their
respective qualities.

from PART 2

Of the Passion Caused by the Sublime

The passion caused by the great and sublime in nature, when those causes operate most powerfully, is astonishment; and astonishment is that state of the soul, in which all its motions are suspended, with some degree of horror. In this case the mind is so entirely filled with its object, that it cannot entertain any other, nor by consequence reason on that object which employs it. Hence arises the great power of the sublime, that, far from being produced by them, it anticipates our reasonings, and hurries us on by an irresistible force. Astonishment, as I have said, is the effect of the sublime in its highest degree; the inferior effects are admiration, reverence, and respect.

Terror

No passion so effectually robs the mind of all its powers of acting and reasoning as *fear*. For fear being an apprehension of pain or death, it operates in a manner that resembles actual pain. Whatever therefore is terrible, with regard to sight, is sublime too, whether this cause of terror be endued with greatness of dimensions or not; for it is impossible to look on anything as trifling, or contemptible, that may be dangerous. There are many animals, who though far from being large, are yet capable of raising ideas of the sublime, because they are considered as objects of terror. As serpents and poisonous animals of almost all kinds. And to things of great dimensions, if we annex an adventitious idea of terror, they become without comparison greater. A level plain of a vast extent on land, is certainly no mean idea; the prospect of such a plain may be as extensive as a prospect of the ocean: but can it ever fill the mind with anything so great as the ocean itself? This is owing to several causes; but it is owing to none more than this, that the ocean is an object of no small terror. Indeed, terror is in all cases whatsoever, either more openly or latently, the ruling principle of the sublime. Several languages bear a strong testimony to the affinity of these ideas. They frequently use the same word, to signify indifferently the modes of astonishment or admiration, and those of terror.

θάμβος is in Greek, either fear or wonder; δετυος is terrible or respectable; αἰδέω, to reverence or to fear. *Vereor* in Latin, is what αἰδέω is in Greek. The Romans used the verb *stupeo*, a term which strongly marks the state of an astonished mind, to express the effect of either simple fear, or of astonishment; the word *attonitus* (thunder-struck) is equally expressive of the alliance of these ideas; and do not the French *étonnement*, and the English *astonishment* and *amazement*, point out as clearly the kindred emotions which attend fear and wonder? They who have a more general knowledge of languages, could produce, I make no doubt, many other and equally striking examples.

Vastness

Greatness of dimension is a powerful cause of the sublime. This is too evident, and the observation too common, to need any illustration: it is not so common to consider in what ways greatness of dimension, vastness of extent or quantity, has the most striking effect. For certainly, there are ways and modes, wherein the same quantity of extension shall produce greater effects than it is found to do in others. Extension is either in length, height, or depth. Of these the length strikes least; an hundred yards of even ground will never work such an effect as a tower an hundred yards high, or a rock or mountain of that altitude. I am apt to imagine likewise, that height is less grand than depth; and that we are more struck at looking down from a precipice, than looking up at an object of equal height; but of that I am not very positive. A perpendicular has more force in forming the sublime, than an inclined plane; and the effects of a rugged and broken surface seem stronger than where it is smooth and polished. It would carry us out of our way to enter in this place into the cause of these appearances; but certain it is they afford a large and fruitful field of speculation. However, it may not be amiss to add to these remarks upon magnitude, that, as the great extreme of dimension is sublime, so the last extreme of littleness is in some measure sublime likewise: when we attend to the infinite divisibility of matter, when we pursue animal life into these excessively small, and yet organized beings, that escape the nicest inquisition of the sense; when we push our discoveries yet downward, and consider those creatures so many degrees yet smaller, and the still diminishing scale of existence, in tracing which the imagination is lost as well as the sense; we become amazed and confounded at the wonders of minuteness; nor can we distinguish in its effects this extreme of littleness from the vast itself. For division must be infinite as well as addition; because the idea of a perfect unity can no more be arrived at, than that of a complete whole, to which nothing may be added.

from PART 3

Of Beauty

It is my design to consider beauty as distinguished from the sublime; and, in the course of the inquiry, to examine how far it is consistent with it. But previous to this, we must take a short review of the opinions already entertained of this quality; which I think are hardly to be reduced to any fixed principles; because men are used to talk of beauty in a figurative manner, that is to say, in a manner extremely uncertain, and indeterminate. By beauty I mean that quality or those qualities in bodies, by which they cause love, or some passion similar to it. I confine this definition to the merely sensible qualities of things, for the sake of preserving the utmost simplicity in a subject, which must always distract us whenever we take in those various causes of sympathy which attach us to any persons or things from secondary considerations, and not from the direct force which they have merely on being viewed. I likewise distinguish love (by which I mean that satisfaction which arises to the mind upon contemplating anything beautiful, of whatsoever nature it may be) from desire or lust; which is an energy of the mind, that hurries us on to the possession of certain objects, that do not affect us as they are beautiful, but by means altogether different. We shall have a strong desire for a woman of no remarkable beauty; whilst the greatest beauty in men or in other animals, though it causes love, yet excites nothing at all of desire. Which shows that beauty, and the passion caused by beauty, which I call love, is different from desire, though desire may sometimes operate along with

it; but it is to this latter that we must attribute those violent and tempestuous passions, and the consequent emotions of the body, which attend what is called love in some of its ordinary acceptations, and not to the effects of beauty merely as it is such.

The Real Cause of Beauty

Having endeavoured to show what beauty is not, it remains that we should examine, at least with equal attention, in what it really consists. Beauty is a thing much too affecting not to depend upon some positive qualities. And, since it is no creature of our reason, since it strikes us without any reference to use, and even where no use at all can be discerned, since the order and method of nature is generally very different from our measures and proportions, we must conclude that beauty is, for the greater part, some quality in bodies acting mechanically upon the human mind by the intervention of the senses. We ought therefore to consider attentively in what manner those sensible qualities are disposed, in such things as by experience we find beautiful, or which excite in us the passion of love, or some correspondent affection.

The Sublime and Beautiful Compared

On closing this general view of beauty, it naturally occurs, that we should compare it with the sublime; and in this comparison there appears a remarkable contrast. For sublime objects are vast in their dimensions, beautiful ones comparatively small: beauty should be smooth and polished; the great, rugged and negligent; beauty should shun the right line, yet deviate from it insensibly; the great in many cases loves the right line, and when it deviates it often makes a strong deviation: beauty should not be obscure; the great ought to be dark and gloomy: beauty should be light and delicate; the great ought to be solid, and even massive. They are indeed ideas of a very different nature, one being founded on pain, the other on pleasure; and however they may vary afterwards from the direct nature of their causes, yet these causes keep up an eternal distinction between them, a distinction never to be forgotten by any whose business it is to affect the passions. In the infinite variety of natural combinations, we must expect to find the qualities of things the most remote imaginable from each other united in the same object. We must expect also to find combinations of the same kind in the works of art. But when we consider the power of an object upon our passions, we must know that when anything is intended to affect the mind by the force of some predominant property, the affection produced is like to be the more uniform and perfect, if all the other properties or qualities of the object be of the same nature, and tending to the same design, as the principal.

> If black and white blend, soften, and unite
> A thousand ways, are there no black and white?[1]

If the qualities of the sublime and beautiful are sometimes found united, does this prove that they are the same; does it prove that they are any way allied; does it prove even that they are not opposite and contradictory? Black and white may soften, may blend; but they are not therefore the same. Nor, when they are so softened and blended with each other, or with different colours, is the power of black as black, or of white as white, so strong as when each stands uniform and distinguished.

from PART 5

Of Words

Natural objects affect us, by the laws of that connection which Providence has established between certain motions and configurations of bodies, and certain consequent feelings in our mind. Painting affects us in the same manner, but with the superadded pleasure of imitation. Architecture affects by the laws of nature, and the law of reason: from which latter result the rules of proportion, which make a work to be praised or censured, in the whole or in some part, when the end for which it was designed is or is not properly answered. But as to words; they seem to me to affect us in a manner very different from that in which we are affected by natural objects, or by painting or

architecture; yet words have as considerable a share in exciting ideas of beauty and of the sublime as many of those, and sometimes a much greater than any of them: therefore an inquiry into the manner by which they excite such emotions is far from being unnecessary in a discourse of this kind.

Effect of Words

If words have all their possible extent of power, three effects arise in the mind of the hearer. The first is, the *sound*; the second, the *picture*, or representation of the thing signified by the sound; the third is, the *affection* of the soul produced by one or by both of the foregoing. *Compounded abstract* words, of which we have been speaking, (honour, justice, liberty, and the like,) produce the first and the last of these effects, but not the second. *Simple abstracts* are used to signify some one simple idea, without much adverting to others which may chance to attend it, as blue, green, hot, cold, and the like; these are capable of affecting all three of the purposes of words; as the *aggregate* words, man, castle, horse, &c., are in a yet higher degree. But I am of opinion, that the most general effect, even of these words, does not arise from their forming pictures of the several things they would represent in the imagination; because, on a very diligent examination of my own mind, and getting others to consider theirs, I do not find that once in twenty times any such picture is formed, and when it is, there is most commonly a particular effort of the imagination for that purpose. But the aggregate words operate, as I said of the compound-abstracts, not by presenting any image to the mind, but by having from use the same effect on being mentioned, that their original has when it is seen. Suppose we were to read a passage to this effect: "The river Danube rises in a moist and mountainous soil in the heart of Germany, where winding to and fro, it waters several principalities, until, turning into Austria, and leaving the walls of Vienna, it passes into Hungary; there with a vast flood, augmented by the Saave and the Drave, it quits Christendom, and rolling through the barbarous countries which border on Tartary,[2] it enters by many

---

[1] *If black and ... black and white?* Misquoted slightly from Alexander Pope's *An Essay on Man* (1733–34), 2.213–14.

[2] *Tartary* Vast region of eastern Europe and northern Asia controlled by the Mongols in the thirteenth and fourteenth centuries.

mouths in the Black Sea." In this description many things are mentioned, as mountains, rivers, cities, the sea, &c. But let anybody examine himself, and see whether he has had impressed on his imagination any pictures of a river, mountain, watery soil, Germany, &c. Indeed it is impossible, in the rapidity and quick succession of words in conversation to have ideas both of the sound of the word, and of the thing represented: besides, some words, expressing real essences, are so mixed with others of a general and nominal import, that it is impracticable to jump from sense to thought, from particulars to generals, from things to words, in such a manner as to answer the purposes of life; nor is it necessary that we should.

How Words Influence the Passions

Now, as words affect, not by any original power, but by representation, it might be supposed, that their influence over the passions should be but light; yet it is quite otherwise; for we find by experience, that eloquence and poetry are as capable, nay indeed much more capable, of making deep and lively impressions than any other arts, and even than nature itself in very many cases. And this arises chiefly from these three causes. First, that we take an extraordinary part in the passions of others, and that we are easily affected and brought into sympathy by any tokens which are shown of them; and there are no tokens which can express all the circumstances of most passions so fully as words; so that if a person speaks upon any subject, he can not only convey the subject to you, but likewise the manner in which he is himself affected by it. Certain it is, that the influence of most things on our passions is not so much from the things themselves, as from our opinions concerning them; and these again depend very much on the opinions of other men, conveyable for the most part by words only. Secondly, there are many things of a very affecting nature, which can seldom occur in the reality, but the words that represent them often do; and thus they have an opportunity of making a deep impression and taking root in the mind, whilst the idea of the reality was transient; and to some perhaps never really occurred in any shape, to whom it is notwithstanding very affecting, as war, death, famine, &c. Besides, many

ideas have never been at all presented to the senses of any men but by words, as God, angels, devils, heaven, and hell, all of which have, however, a great influence over the passions. Thirdly, by words we have it in our power to make such *combinations* as we cannot possibly do otherwise. By this power of combining, we are able, by the addition of well-chosen circumstances, to give a new life and force to the simple object. In painting we may represent any fine figure we please; but we never can give it those enlivening touches which it may receive from words. To represent an angel in a picture, you can only draw a beautiful young man winged: but what painting can furnish out anything so grand as the addition of one word, "the angel of the *Lord*"? It is true, I have here no clear idea; but these words affect the mind more than the sensible image did; which is all I contend for. A picture of Priam dragged to the altar's foot, and there murdered, if it were well executed, would undoubtedly be very moving, but there are very aggravating circumstances, which it could never represent:

Sanguine fœdantem *quos ipse saeraverat* ignes.[1]

As a further instance, let us consider those lines of Milton, where he describes the travels of the fallen angels through their dismal habitation:

—O'er many a dark and dreary vale
They passed, and many a region dolorous;
O'er many a frozen, many a fiery Alp;
Rocks, caves, lakes, fens, bogs, dens, and shades of
    death,
A universe of death.—[2]

Here is displayed the force of union in

Rocks, caves, lakes, dens, bogs, fens, and shades;

Which yet would lose the greatest part of their effect, if they were not the

---

[1] *Sanguine ... ignes* Cf. Virgil, *Aeneid*, 2.502. Latin: "Polluting with blood the flames that he [Priam, the king of Troy during the Trojan War] himself had sanctified."

[2] *O'er many ... universe of death* See John Milton, *Paradise Lost*, 2.618–22.

Rocks, caves, lakes, dens, bogs, fens, and shades—
——of *Death*.

This idea or this affection caused by a word, which nothing but a word could annex to the others, raises a very great degree of the sublime; and this sublime is raised yet higher by what follows, a *"universe of Death."* Here are again two ideas not presentable but by language; and an union of them great and amazing beyond conception; if they may properly be called ideas which present no distinct image to the mind:—but still it will be difficult to conceive how words can move the passions which belong to real objects, without representing these objects clearly. This is difficult to us, because we do not sufficiently distinguish, in our observations upon language, between a clear expression and a strong expression. These are frequently confounded with each other, though they are in reality extremely different. The former regards the understanding, the latter belongs to the passions. The one describes a thing as it is; the latter describes it as it is felt. Now, as there is a moving tone of voice, an impassioned countenance, an agitated gesture, which affect independently of the things about which they are exerted, so there are words, and certain dispositions of words, which being peculiarly devoted to passionate subjects; and always used by those who are under the influence of any passion, touch and move us more than those which far more clearly and distinctly express the subject matter. We yield to sympathy what we refuse to description. The truth is, all verbal description, merely as naked description, though never so exact, conveys so poor and insufficient an idea of the thing described, that it could scarcely have the smallest effect, if the speaker did not call in to his aid those modes of speech that mark a strong and lively feeling in himself. Then, by the contagion of our passions, we catch a fire already kindled in another, which probably might never have been struck out by the object described. Words, by strongly conveying the passions, by those means which we have already mentioned, fully compensate for their weakness in other respects. It may be observed, that very polished languages, and such as are praised for their superior clearness and perspicuity, are generally deficient in strength. The French language has that perfection and that defect, whereas the Oriental tongues, and in general the languages of most unpolished people, have a great force and energy of expression; and this is but natural. Uncultivated people are but ordinary observers of things, and not critical in distinguishing them; but, for that reason, they admire more, and are more affected with what they see, and therefore express themselves in a warmer and more passionate manner. If the affection be well conveyed, it will work its effect without any clear idea, often without any idea at all of the thing which has originally given rise to it.

It might be expected from the fertility of the subject, that I should consider poetry, as it regards the sublime and beautiful, more at large; but it must be observed that in this light it has been often and well handled already. It was not my design to enter into the criticism of the sublime and beautiful in any art, but to attempt to lay down such principles as may tend to ascertain, to distinguish, and to form a sort of standard for them; which purposes I thought might be best effected by an inquiry into the properties of such things in nature, as raise love and astonishment in us; and by showing in what manner they operated to produce these passions. Words were only so far to be considered, as to show upon what principle they were capable of being the representatives of these natural things, and by what powers they were able to affect us often as strongly as the things they represent, and sometimes much more strongly.

from Immanuel Kant, *Observations on the Feeling of the Beautiful and Sublime* (1764; first English translation 1799)

German philosopher Immanuel Kant (1724–1804) argues that aesthetic experience and pleasure are always subjective; here he presents his observations on the feelings he associates with the beautiful and the sublime. Along with Edmund Burke, Kant is perhaps the most important eighteenth-century thinker on aesthetics.

from Section 1: Of the Distinct Objects
of the Feeling of the Beautiful and Sublime

The various feelings of enjoyment or of displeasure rest not so much upon the nature of the external things that arouse them as upon each person's own disposition to be moved by these to pleasure or pain. This accounts for the joy of some people over things that cause aversion in others, or the amorous passion so often a puzzle to everybody, or the lively antipathy one person feels toward something that to another is quite indifferent. The field of observation of these peculiarities of human nature extends very wide, and still conceals a rich source for discoveries that are just as pleasurable as they are instructive. For the present I shall cast my gaze upon only a few places that seem particularly exceptional in this area, and even upon these more with the eye of an observer than of a philosopher.

Because a person finds himself happy only so far as he gratifies an inclination, the feeling that makes him capable of enjoying great pleasures, without needing exceptional talents to do so, is certainly no trifle. Stout persons, whose favorite authors are their cooks and whose works of fine taste are in their cellars, will thrive on vulgar obscenities and on a coarse jest with just as lively a delight as that upon which persons of noble sensitivity pride themselves. An indolent man who loves having books read aloud to him because it is so pleasant to fall asleep that way, the merchant to whom all pleasures are trifling except those a clever man enjoys when he calculates his profits, one who loves the opposite sex only so far as he counts it among things to enjoy, the lover of the hunt, whether he hunt flies like Domitian[1] or ferocious beasts like A. ... —all these have a feeling that makes them capable of enjoying pleasures after their own fashion, without presuming to envy others or even being able so much as to conceive of other pleasures. But to that kind of feeling, which can take place without any thought whatever, I shall here pay no attention. There is still another feeling of a more delicate sort, so described either because one can enjoy it longer without satiation and exhaustion; or because it presupposes a sensitivity of the soul, so to speak, which

makes the soul fitted for virtuous impulses; or because it indicates talents and intellectual excellences. It is this feeling of which I wish to consider one aspect. I shall moreover exclude from it that inclination that is fixed upon high intellectual insights, and the thrill that was possible to a Kepler,[2] who, as Bayle[3] reports, would not have sold one of his discoveries for a princedom. The latter sensation is quite too delicate to belong in the present sketch, which will concern only the sensuous feeling of which also more ordinary souls are capable.

Finer feeling, which we now wish to consider, is chiefly of two kinds: the feeling of the *sublime* and that of the *beautiful*. The stirring of each is pleasant, but in different ways. The sight of a mountain whose snow-covered peaks rises above the clouds, the description of a raging storm, or Milton's portrayal of the infernal kingdom, arouse enjoyment but with horror; on the other hand, the sight of flower-strewn meadows, valleys with winding brooks and covered with grazing flocks, the description of Elysium, or Homer's portrayal of the girdle of Venus,[4] also occasion a pleasant sensation but one that is joyous and smiling. In order that the former impression could occur to us in due strength, we must have *a feeling of the sublime*, and, in order to enjoy the latter well, a *feeling of the beautiful*. Tall oaks and lonely shadows in a sacred grove are sublime; flower beds, low hedges and trees trimmed in figures are beautiful. Night is sublime, day is beautiful. Temperaments that possess a feeling for the sublime are drawn gradually, by the quiet stillness of a summer evening as the shimmering light of the stars breaks through the brown shadows of night and the lonely moon rises into view, into high feelings of friendship, of disdain for the world, of eternity. The shining day stimulates busy fervor and a feeling of gaiety. The sublime *moves*, the beautiful *charms*. The mien of a man who is undergoing the full

---

[1] *Domitian* Titus Flavius Domitianus (51–96 CE), 11th emperor of Rome.

[2] *Kepler* Johannes Kepler (1571–1630), German mathematician, astronomer, and astrologer best known for articulating the laws of planetary motion, now named after him.

[3] *Bayle* Pierre Bayle (1647–1706), French philosopher who advocated the separation of faith and reason.

[4] *Elysium ... girdle of Venus* In Greek mythology, Elysium, or the Elysian Fields, was the section of the Underworld reserved for the souls of the heroic and the virtuous. In Homer's *Iliad*, Hera thwarts Zeus's design to aid the Trojans by obtaining the magical girdle and seducing him.

feeling of the sublime is earnest, sometimes rigid and astonished. On the other hand the lively sensation of the beautiful proclaims itself through shining cheerfulness in the eyes, through smiling features, and often through audible mirth. The sublime is in turn of different kinds. Its feeling is sometimes accompanied with a certain dread, or melancholy; in some cases merely with quiet wonder; and in still others with a beauty completely pervading a sublime plan. The first I shall call the *terrifying sublime*, the second the *noble*, and the third the *splendid*. Deep loneliness is sublime, but in a way that stirs terror. Hence great far-reaching solitudes, like the colossal Komul Desert in Tartary,[1] have always given us occasion for peopling them with fearsome spirits, goblins, and ghouls.

The sublime must always be great; the beautiful can also be small. The sublime must be simple; the beautiful can be adorned and ornamented. A great height is just as sublime as a great depth, except that the latter is accompanied with the sensation of shuddering, the former with one of wonder. Hence the latter feeling can be the terrifying sublime, and the former the noble. The sight of an Egyptian pyramid, as Hasselquist[2] reports, moves one far more than one can imagine from all the descriptions; but its design is simple and noble. St. Peter's in Rome is splendid; because on its frame, which is large and simple, beauty is so distributed, for example, gold, mosaic work, and so on, that the feeling of the sublime still strikes through with the greatest effect; hence the object is called splendid. An arsenal must be noble and simple, a residence castle splendid, and a pleasure palace beautiful and ornamented.

A long duration is sublime. If it is of time past, then it is noble. If it is projected into an incalculable future, then it has something of the fearsome in it. A building of the remotest antiquity is venerable. Haller's[3] description of the coming eternity stimulates a mild horror, and of the past, transfixed wonder.

---

[1] *Tartary* Vast region of eastern Europe and northern Asia controlled by the Mongols in the thirteenth and fourteenth centuries.

[2] *Hasselquist* Fredric Hasselquist (1722–52), Swedish traveler and naturalist.

[3] *Haller* Albrecht von Haller (1708–77), Swiss anatomist, physiologist, naturalist, and poet.

from SECTION 4: OF NATIONAL CHARACTERISTICS, SO FAR AS THEY DEPEND UPON THE DISTINCT FEELING OF THE BEAUTIFUL AND SUBLIME

Of the peoples of our part of the world, in my opinion those who distinguish themselves among all others by the feeling for the beautiful are the Italians and the French, but by the feeling for the sublime, the Germans, English, and Spanish. Holland can be considered as that land where the finer taste becomes largely unnoticeable. The beautiful itself is either fascinating and moving, or laughing and delightful. The first has something of the sublime in it, and the mind in this feeling is thoughtful and enraptured, but in the second sort of feeling, smiling and joyful. The first sort of beautiful feeling seems to be excellently suited to the Italians, and the second, to the French. In the national character that bears the expression of the sublime, this is either that of the terrifying sort, which is a little inclined to the adventurous, or it is a feeling for the noble, or for the splendid. I believe I have reason to be able to ascribe the feeling of the first sort to the Spaniard, the second to the Englishman, and the third to the German. The feeling for the splendid is not original by nature, like the remaining kinds of taste; and although a spirit of imitation can be united with every other feeling, it really is more peculiar to the glittering sublime; for this is properly a mixed feeling combining the beautiful and the sublime, in which each taken by itself is colder, so that the mind is free enough by means of their combination to attend to examples, and in fact it stands in need of the impulsion of such examples. Accordingly, the German will have less feeling in respect to the beautiful than the Frenchman, and less of what pertains to the sublime than the Englishman; but instances in which both appear in combination will be more suitable to his feeling, as he will fortunately escape the faults into which an excessive strength of either of these sorts of feeling could fall.

from Helen Maria Williams, *A Tour in Switzerland* (1798)

In the following excerpts, Helen Maria Williams (c. 1761–1827)—a novelist, poet, and political radical who was imprisoned in Paris during the Reign of Terror—describes the landscapes she encounters during her travels. Her record is notable for providing a female perspective, both on aesthetic experience and on the continental tour more readily associated with young educated men. The excerpts also demonstrate the possibility for locating both the sublime and the beautiful within the natural landscape.

Chapter 4

... It was not without the most powerful emotion that, for the first time, I cast my eyes on that solemn, that majestic vision, the Alps! How often had the idea of those stupendous mountains filled my heart with enthusiastic awe! So long, so eagerly, had I desired to contemplate that scene of wonders, that I was unable to trace when first the wish was awakened in my bosom—it seemed from childhood to have made a part of my existence—I longed to bid adieu to the gaily-peopled landscapes of Zurich, and wander amidst those regions of mysterious sublimity, the solitudes of nature, where her eternal laws seem at all seasons to forbid more than the temporary visits of man, and where, sometimes, the dangerous passes to her frozen summits are inflexibly barred against mortal footsteps. The pleasure arising from the varying forms of smiling beauty with which we were surrounded, became a cold sensation, while expectation hung upon those vast gigantic shapes, that half-seen chaos which excited the stronger feelings of wonder, mingled with admiration. But I was obliged, with whatever regret, to relinquish for the present a nearer view of those tremendous objects, since private affairs left me only sufficient leisure to visit the cataract of the Rhine before I returned to Basle; whence, however, I soothed myself with the hope of being soon able to depart in search of the terrific scenes of the Alps, and the rich luxuriant graces of the Italian valleys of Switzerland. In the mean time we passed happily through Zurich, in our way to Schaffhausen, for although I had

been assured that the cataract of the Rhine was "but a fall of water," it had excited so tormenting a curiosity, that I found I should be incapable of seeing any thing else with pleasure or advantage, till I had once gazed upon that object.

When we reached the summit of the hill which leads to the fall of the Rhine, we alighted from the carriage, and walked down the steep bank, whence I saw the river rolling turbulently over its bed of rocks, and heard the noise of the torrent, towards which we were descending, increasing as we drew near. My heart swelled with expectation—our path, as if formed to give the scene its full effect, concealed for some time the river from our view; till we reached a wooden balcony, projecting on the edge of the water, and whence, just sheltered from the torrent, it bursts in all its overwhelming wonders on the astonished sight. That stupendous cataract, rushing with wild impetuosity over those broken, unequal rocks, which, lifting up their sharp points amidst its sea of foam, disturb its headlong course, multiply its falls, and make the afflicted waters roar—that cadence of tumultuous sound, which had never till now struck upon my ear—those long feathery surges, giving the element a new aspect—that spray rising into clouds of vapour, and reflecting the prismatic colours, while it disperses itself over the hills—never, never can I forget the sensations of that moment! When with a sort of annihilation of self, with every part impression erased from my memory, I felt as if my heart were bursting with emotions too strong to be sustained—Oh, majestic torrent! which hast conveyed a new image of nature to my soul, the moments I have passed in contemplating thy sublimity will form an epoch in my short span!—thy course is coeval with time, and thou wilt rush down thy rocky walls when this bosom, which throbs with admiration of thy greatness, shall beat no longer!

What an effort does it require to leave, after a transient glimpse, a scene on which, while we meditate, we can take no account of time! Its narrow limits seem too confined for the expanded spirit; such objects appear to belong to immortality; they call the musing mind from all its little cares and vanities, to higher destinies and regions, more congenial than this world to the feelings they excite. I had been often summoned by my fellow-travelers to depart, had often repeated "but one moment more," and many "moments more" had elapsed, before I could resolve to tear myself from the balcony.

We crossed the river, below the fall, in a boat, and had leisure to observe the surrounding scenery. The cataract, however, had for me a sort of fascinating power, which, if I withdrew my eyes for a moment, again fastened them on its impetuous waters. In the background of the torrent a bare mountain lifts its head encircled with its blue vapours; on the right rises a steep cliff, of an enormous height, covered with wood, and upon its summit stands the Castle of Laussen, with its frowning towers, and encircled with its crannied wall; on the left, human industry has seized upon a slender thread of this mighty torrent in its fall, and made it subservient to the purposes of commerce. Foundries, mills, and wheels, are erected on the edge of the river, and a portion of the vast basin into which the cataract falls is confined by a dyke, which preserves the warehouses and the neighbouring huts from its inundations. Sheltered within this little nook, and accustomed to the neighbourhood of the torrent, the boatman unloads his merchandise, and the artisan pursues his toil, regardless of the falling river, and inattentive to those thundering sounds which seem calculated to suspend all human activity in solemn and awful astonishment; while the imagination of the spectator is struck with the comparative littleness of fleeting man, busy with his trivial occupations, contrasted with the view of nature in all her vast, eternal, uncontrollable grandeur. ...

CHAPTER II

After winding for some time among these awful scenes, of which no painting can give an adequate description, and of which an imagination the most pregnant in sublime horrors could form but a very imperfect idea, we came within the sound of these cataracts of the Reuss[1] which announced our approach towards another operation of Satanic power, called the Devil's Bridge.[2] We were more struck with the august drapery of this supernatural work, than with the work itself. It seemed less marvellous than expectation had pictured it, and we were perhaps the more disappointed, as we remembered that "the wonderous art pontifical," was a part of architecture with which his infernal majesty was perfectly well acquainted; and the rocks of the valley of Schellenen were certainly as solid foundations for bridge building as "the aggregated soil solid, or flimsy," which was collected amidst the waste of chaos, and crowded drove "from each side shoaling towards the mouth of hell."[3]

On this spot we loitered for some time to contemplate the stupendous and terrific scenery. The mountainous rocks lifted their heads abrupt, and appeared to fix the limits of our progress at this point, unless we could climb the mighty torrent which was struggling impetuously for passage under our feet, after precipitating its afflicted waters with tremendous roar in successive cascades over the disjointed rocks, and filling the atmosphere with its foam.

Separating ourselves with reluctance from these objects of overwhelming greatness, we turned an angle of the mountain at the end of the bridge, and proceeded along a way of difficult ascent, which led to a rock that seemed inflexibly to bar our passage. A bridge fastened to this rock by iron work, and suspended over the torrent, was formerly the only means of passing, but numerous accidents led the government to seek another outlet. The rock being too high to climb, and too weighty to remove, the engineer took the middle way, and bored a hole in the solid mass two hundred feet along, and about ten or twelve feet broad and high, through which he carried the road. The entrance into this subterranean passage is almost dark, and the little light that penetrates through a crevice in the rock, serves only to make its obscurity more visible. Filled with powerful images of the terrible and sublime, from the enormous objects which I had been contemplating for some hours past, objects, the forms of which were new to my imagination, it was not without a feeling of reluctance that I plunged into this scene of night, whose thick gloom heightened every sensation of terror.

---

[1] *Reuss* River in Switzerland.

[2] *Devil's Bridge* A number of European bridges were believed to have been constructed with the help of the devil.

[3] *the wonderous art ... mouth of hell* Phrases slightly misquoted from John Milton's *Paradise Lost*, 10.312–22, 293–96, and 288. In this Book, Sin and Death enter the world following man's fall and punishment.

After passing through this cavern, the view which suddenly unfolded itself appeared rather a gay illusion of the fancy than real nature. No magical wand was ever fabled to shift more instantaneously the scene, or call up forms of more striking contrast to those on which we had gazed. On the other side of the cavern we seemed amidst the chaos or the overthrow of nature; on this we beheld her dressed in all the loveliness of infancy or renovation, with every charm of soft and tranquil beauty. The rugged and stony interstices between the mountain and the road were here changed into smooth and verdant paths; the abrupt precipice and shagged rock were metamorphosed into gently sloping declivities; the barren and monotonous desert was transformed into a fertile and smiling plain. The long resounding cataract, struggling through the huge masses of granite, here became a calm and limpid current, gliding over fine beds of sand with gentle murmurs, as if reluctant to leave that enchanting abode. ...

CHAPTER 40

... Whether the French Republic will accede to this invitation, and render the Pays de Vaud independent of Berne, is a secret which the book of destiny will perhaps ere long unfold.

In the mean time, it is natural to conclude, that the principles of that mighty revolution which have already diffused themselves over remote regions of the globe, cannot fail to expand in those countries which are placed immediately within their influence. Since the period of the French Revolution, ages have flitted before our eyes, and we have risen suddenly, like the offspring of Deucalion,[1] from infancy to manhood, not without indications it must be confessed, of the hardened origin whence we sprung. Like the traveller, who from the scorching plains, climbs the rocks that lead him to the regions of eternal snow, and finds that in the space of a few hours he has passed through every successive latitude, from burning heat to the confines of the frozen pole, the

journey of months; so the human mind, placed within the sphere of the French Revolution, has bounded over the ruggedness of slow metaphysical researches, and reached at once, with an incredible effort, the highest probable attainments of political discovery. ...

from Mary Wollstonecraft, *A Vindication of the Rights of Men* (1790)

The primary purpose of this pamphlet by Mary Wollstonecraft (1759–97) was the defense of Richard Price, who Edmund Burke described as a radical in his *Reflections on the Revolution in France* (1790). Price, like Wollstonecraft, advocated republicanism, in opposition to Burke's championing of constitutional monarchy. In this excerpt, Wollstonecraft seeks to redefine, recast, and, perhaps most importantly, re-gender ideas about the sublime and the beautiful as they are laid out in Burke's *Enquiry*.

... Had you been in a philosophising mood, had your heart or your reason been at home, you might have been convinced, by ocular demonstration, that madness is only the absence of reason. The ruling angel leaving its seat, wild anarchy ensues. You would have seen that the uncontrolled imagination often pursues the most regular course in its most daring flight; and that the eccentricities are boldly relieved when judgment no longer officiously arranges the sentiments, by bringing them to the test of principles. You would have seen every thing out of nature in that strange chaos of levity and ferocity, and of all sorts of follies jumbled together. You would have seen in that monstrous tragi-comic scene the most opposite passions necessarily succeed, and sometimes mix with each other in the mind; alternate contempt and indignation; alternate laughter and tears; alternate scorn and horror. This is a true picture of that chaotic state of mind, called madness; when reason gone, we know not where, the wild elements of passion clash, and all is horror and confusion. You might have heard the best turned conceits, flash following flash, and doubted whether the rhapsody was not eloquent, if it had not been delivered in an equivocal language, neither verse nor prose, if the sparkling periods had not stood alone,

---

[1] *Deucalion* In Greek mythology, Deucalion is the son of Prometheus who, like Noah, is warned of a coming flood, builds an ark, and so survives the devastation. He is then instructed to re-people the earth with his wife Pyrrha by throwing stones over their shoulders, with the cast stones forming men and women, respectively, according to the thrower's gender.

wanting force because they wanted concatenation.[1]

It is a proverbial observation, that a very thin partition divides wit and madness. Poetry therefore naturally addresses the fancy, and the language of passion is with great felicity borrowed from the heightened picture which the imagination draws of sensible objects concentrated by impassioned reflection. And, during this "fine frenzy," reason has no right to rein-in the imagination, unless to prevent the introduction of supernumerary images; if the passion is real, the head will not be ransacked for stale tropes and cold rodomontade. I now speak of the genuine enthusiasm of genius, which, perhaps, seldom appears, but in the infancy of civilization; for as this light becomes more luminous reason clips the wing of fancy—the youth becomes the man.

Whether the glory of Europe is set, I shall not now enquire; but probably the spirit of romance and chivalry is in the wane; and reason will gain by its extinction.

From observing several cold romantic characters I have been led to confine the term romantic to one definition—false, or rather artificial, feelings. Works of genius are read with a prepossession in their favour, and sentiments imitated, because they were fashionable and pretty, and not because they were forcibly felt.

In modern poetry the understanding and memory often fabricate the pretended effusions of the heart, and romance destroys all simplicity; which, in works of taste, is but a synonymous word for truth. This romantic spirit has extended to our prose, and scattered artificial flowers over the most barren heath; or a mixture of verse and prose producing the strangest incongruities. The turgid bombast of some of your periods fully proves these assertions; for when the heart speaks we are seldom shocked by hyperbole, or dry raptures. ...

Reading your *Reflections* warily over, it has continually and forcibly struck me, that had you been a Frenchman, you would have been, in spite of your respect for rank and antiquity, a violent revolutionist; and deceived, as you now probably are, by the passions that cloud your reason, have termed your romantic enthusiasm an enlightened love of your country, a benevolent respect for the rights of men. Your imagination would have taken fire, and have found arguments, full as ingenious as those you now offer, to prove that the constitution, of which so few pillars remained, that constitution which time had almost obliterated, was not a model sufficiently noble to deserve close adherence. And, for the English constitution, you might not have had such a profound veneration as you have lately acquired; nay, it is not impossible that you might have entertained the same opinion of the English Parliament, that you professed to have during the American war.[2]

Another observation which, by frequently occurring, has almost grown into a conviction, is simply this, that had the English in general reprobated the French Revolution, you would have stood forth alone, and been the avowed Goliath of liberty. But, not liking to see so many brothers near the throne of fame, you have turned the current of your passions, and consequently of your reasoning, another way. Had Dr. Price's sermon[3] not lighted some sparks very like envy in your bosom, I shrewdly suspect that he would have been treated with more candour; nor is it charitable to suppose that any thing but personal pique and hurt vanity could have dictated such bitter sarcasms and reiterated expressions of contempt as occur in your *Reflections*.

But without fixed principles even goodness of heart is no security from inconsistency, and mild affectionate sensibility only renders a man more ingeniously cruel, when the pangs of hurt vanity are mistaken for virtuous indignation, and the gall of bitterness for the milk of Christian charity.

Where is the dignity, the infallibility of sensibility, in the fair ladies, whom, if the voice of rumour is to be credited, the captive negroes curse in all the agony of bodily pain, for the unheard of tortures they invent? It is probable that some of them, after the sight of a flagellation, compose their ruffled spirits and exercise their tender feelings by the perusal of the last imported novel. How true these tears are to nature, I leave you to determine. But these ladies may have read your *Enquiry concerning the origin of our ideas of the Sublime and*

---

[1] *concatenation* I.e., connection.

[2] *American war* Burke argued for American independence in the 1770s, a position many of his opponents in the 1790s found incongruent with his position on the French Revolution.

[3] *Dr. Price's sermon* The sermon, *A Discourse on the Love of Our Country*, was produced in 1789 and published in 1790; Burke's *Reflections* is a response to this text.

Beautiful, and, convinced by your arguments, may have laboured to be pretty, by counterfeiting weakness.

You may have convinced them that *littleness* and *weakness* are the very essence of beauty; and that the Supreme Being, in giving women beauty in the most supereminent degree, seemed to command them, by the powerful voice of Nature, not to cultivate the moral virtues that might chance to excite respect, and interfere with the pleasing sensations they were created to inspire. Thus confining truth, fortitude, and humanity, within the rigid pale of manly morals, they might justly argue, that to be loved, woman's high end and distinction! they should "learn to lisp, to totter in their walk, and nickname God's creatures."[1] Never, they might repeat after you, was any man, much less a woman, rendered amiable by the force of those exalted qualities, fortitude, justice, wisdom, and truth; and thus forewarned of the sacrifice they must make to those austere, unnatural virtues, they would be authorised to turn all their attention to their persons, systematically neglecting morals to secure beauty. Some rational old woman indeed might chance to stumble at this doctrine, and hint, that in avoiding atheism you had not steered clear of the mussulman's[2] creed; but you could readily exculpate yourself by turning the charge on Nature, who made our idea of beauty independent of reason. Nor would it be necessary for you to recollect, that if virtue has any other foundation than worldly utility, you have clearly proved that one half of the human species, at least, have not souls; and that Nature, by making women *little, smooth, delicate, fair* creatures, never designed that they should exercise their reason to acquire the virtues that produce opposite, if not contradictory, feelings. The affection they excite, to be uniform and perfect, should not be tinctured with the respect which moral virtues inspire, lest pain should be blended with pleasure, and admiration disturb the soft intimacy of love. This laxity of morals in the female world is certainly more captivating to a libertine imagination than the cold arguments of reason, that give no sex to virtue. If beautiful weakness be interwoven in a woman's frame, if the chief business of her life be (as you insinuate) to inspire love, and Nature has made an eternal distinction between the qualities that dignify a rational being and this animal perfection, her duty and happiness in this life must clash with any preparation for a more exalted state. So that Plato and Milton were grossly mistaken in asserting that human love led to heavenly, and was only an exaltation of the same affection; for the love of the Deity, which is mixed with the most profound reverence, must be love of perfection, and not compassion for weakness.

To say the truth, I not only tremble for the souls of women, but for the good natured man, whom every one loves. The *amiable* weakness of his mind is a strong argument against its immateriality, and seems to prove that beauty relaxes the *solids* of the soul as well as the body.

It follows then immediately, from your own reasoning, that respect and love are antagonist principles; and that, if we really wish to render men more virtuous, we must endeavour to banish all enervating modifications of beauty from civil society. We must, to carry your argument a little further, return to the Spartan regulations, and settle the virtues of men on the stern foundation of mortification and self-denial; for any attempt to civilize the heart, to make it humane by implanting reasonable principles, is a mere philosophic dream. If refinement inevitably lessens respect for virtue, by rendering beauty, the grand tempter, more seductive; if these relaxing feelings are incompatible with the nervous exertions of morality, the sun of Europe is not set; it begins to dawn, when cold metaphysicians try to make the head give laws to the heart.

But should experience prove that there is a beauty in virtue, a charm in order, which necessarily implies exertion, a depraved sensual taste may give way to a more manly one—and *melting* feelings to rational satisfactions. Both may be equally natural to man; the test is their moral difference, and that point reason alone can decide.

Such a glorious change can only be produced by liberty. Inequality of rank must ever impede the growth of virtue, by vitiating the mind that submits or domineers; that is ever employed to procure nourishment for the body, or amusement for the mind. And if this grand

---

[1] *learn to ... God's creatures* Loosely quoted from Shakespeare's *Hamlet,* 3.1.144–45.

[2] *mussulman* Muslim.

example be set by an assembly of unlettered clowns, if they can produce a crisis that may involve the fate of Europe, and 'more than Europe,' you must allow us to respect unsophisticated reason, and reverence the active exertions that were not relaxed by a fastidious respect for the beauty of rank, or a dread of the deformity produced by any *void* in the social structure. ...

It may be confidently asserted that no man chooses evil, because it is evil; he only mistakes it for happiness, the good he seeks. And the desire of rectifying these mistakes, is the noble ambition of an enlightened understanding, the impulse of feelings that Philosophy invigorates. To endeavour to make unhappy men resigned to their fate, is the tender endeavour of short-sighted benevolence, of transient yearnings of humanity; but to labour to increase human happiness by extirpating error, is a masculine godlike affection. This remark may be carried still further. Men who possess uncommon sensibility, whose quick emotions show how closely the eye and heart are connected, soon forget the most forcible sensations. Not tarrying long enough in the brain to be subject to reflection, the next sensations, of course, obliterate them. Memory, however, treasures up these proofs of native goodness; and the being who is not spurred on to any virtuous act, still thinks itself of consequence, and boasts of its feelings. Why? Because the sight of distress, or an affecting narrative, made its blood flow with more velocity, and the heart, literally speaking, beat with sympathetic emotion. We ought to beware of confounding mechanical instinctive sensations with emotions that reason deepens, and justly terms the feelings of *humanity*. This word discriminates the active exertions of virtue from the vague declamation of sensibility.

The declaration of the National Assembly, when they recognised the rights of men, was calculated to touch the humane heart—the downfall of the clergy; to agitate the pupil of impulse. On the watch to find fault, faults met your prying eye; a different prepossession might have produced a different conviction.

When we read a book that supports our favourite opinions, how eagerly do we suck in the doctrines, and suffer our minds placidly to reflect the images that illustrate the tenets we have previously embraced. We indolently acquiesce in the conclusion, and our spirit animates and corrects the various subjects. But when, on the contrary, we peruse a skilful writer, with whom we do not coincide in opinion, how attentive is the mind to detect fallacy. And this suspicious coolness often prevents our being carried away by a stream of natural eloquence, which the prejudiced mind terms declamation—a pomp of words! We never allow ourselves to be warmed; and, after contending with the writer, are more confirmed in our opinion; as much, perhaps, from a spirit of contradiction as from reason. A lively imagination is ever in danger of being betrayed into error by favourite opinions, which it almost personifies, the more effectually to intoxicate the understanding. Always tending to extremes, truth is left behind in the heat of the chase, and things are viewed as positively good, or bad, though they wear an equivocal face.

Some celebrated writers have supposed that wit and judgment were incompatible; opposite qualities, that, in a kind of elementary strife, destroyed each other: and many men of wit have endeavoured to prove that they were mistaken. Much may be adduced by wits and metaphysicians on both sides of the question. But, from experience, I am apt to believe that they do weaken each other, and that great quickness of comprehension, and facile association of ideas, naturally preclude profundity of research. Wit is often a lucky hit; the result of a momentary inspiration. We know not whence it comes, and it blows where it lists. The operations of judgment, on the contrary, are cool and circumspect; and coolness and deliberation are great enemies to enthusiasm. If wit is of so fine a spirit, that it almost evaporates when translated into another language, why may not the temperature have an influence over it? This remark may be thought derogatory to the inferior qualities of the mind: but it is not a hasty one; and I mention it as a prelude to a conclusion I have frequently drawn, that the cultivation of reason damps fancy. The blessings of Heaven lie on each side; we must choose, if we wish to attain any degree of superiority, and not lose our lives in laborious idleness. If we mean to build our knowledge or happiness on a rational basis, we must learn to distinguish the *possible*, and not fight against the stream. And if we are careful to guard ourselves from imaginary sorrows and vain fears, we must also resign many enchanting illusions: for shallow must be the discernment which fails to discover that raptures and ecstasies arise from error. Whether it will always be so, is not now to be discussed; suffice it to observe, that Truth is seldom arrayed by the Graces; and if she charms, it is only by inspiring a sober satisfaction, which takes its rise from a calm contemplation of proportion and simplicity. But, though it is allowed that one man has by nature more fancy than another, in each individual there is a springtide when fancy should govern and amalgamate materials for the understanding; and a graver period, when those materials should be employed by the judgment. For example, I am inclined to have a better opinion of the heart of an *old* man, who speaks of Sterne[1] as his favourite author, than of his understanding. There are times and seasons for all things: and moralists appear to me to err, when they would confound the gaiety of youth with the seriousness of age; for the virtues of age look not only more imposing, but more natural, when they appear rather rigid. He who has not exercised his judgment to curb his imagination during the meridian of life, becomes, in its decline, too often the prey of childish feelings. Age demands respect; youth love: if this order is disturbed, the emotions are not pure; and when love for a man in his grand climacteric takes place of respect, it, generally speaking, borders on contempt. Judgment is sublime, wit beautiful; and, according to your own theory, they cannot exist together without impairing each other's power. The predominancy of the latter, in your endless Reflections, should lead hasty readers to suspect that it may, in a great degree, exclude the former.

from William Gilpin, *Three Essays on Picturesque Beauty* (1792)

> William Gilpin (1724–1804) articulated the picturesque as "that kind of beauty which is agreeable in a picture" in his *Essay on Prints* (1768). In *Three Essays on Picturesque Beauty*, he further refined and explored the concept that would become of great importance to Romantic poets and painters.

---

[1] *Sterne* Laurence Sterne (1713–68), Irish-born novelist and Anglican member of clergy.

from ESSAY 1

Disputes about beauty might perhaps be involved in less confusion, if a distinction were established, which certainly exists, between such objects as are *beautiful*, and such as are *picturesque*—between those, which please the eye in their *natural state*; and those, which please from some quality, capable of being *illustrated by painting*.

Ideas of beauty vary with the objects, and with the eye of the spectator. The stonemason sees beauties in a well-jointed wall, which escape the architect, who surveys the building under a different idea. And thus the painter, who compares his object with the rules of his art, sees it in a different light from the man of general taste, who surveys it only as simply beautiful.

As this difference therefore between the *beautiful*, and the *picturesque* appears really to exist, and must depend on some peculiar construction of the object; it may be worthwhile to examine, what that peculiar construction is. We inquire not into the *general sources of beauty*, either in nature, or in representation. This would lead into a nice, and scientific discussion, in which it is not our purpose to engage. The question simply is, *What is that quality in objects, which particularly marks them as picturesque?*

In examining the *real object*, we shall find, one source of beauty arises from that species of elegance, which we call *smoothness*, or *neatness*; for the terms are nearly synonymous. The higher the marble is polished, the brighter the silver is rubbed, and the more the mahogany shines, the more each is considered as an object of beauty: as if the eye delighted in gliding smoothly over a surface.

In the class of larger objects the same idea prevails. In a pile of building we wish to see neatness in every part added to the elegance of the architecture. And if we examine a piece of improved pleasure-ground, every thing rough, and slovenly offends.

Mr. Burke, enumerating the properties of beauty, considers *smoothness* as one of the most essential. "A very considerable part of the effect of beauty, says he, is owing to this quality: indeed the most considerable: for take any beautiful object, and give it a broken, and rugged surface, and however well-formed it may be in other respects, it pleases no longer. Whereas, let it want ever so many of the other constituents, if it want not this, it becomes more pleasing, than almost all the others without it."[1] How far Mr. Burke may be right in making smoothness the most considerable source of beauty, I rather doubt. A considerable one it certainly is. Thus then, we suppose, the matter stands with regard to *beautiful objects in general*. But in *picturesque representation* it seems somewhat odd, yet perhaps we shall find it equally true, that the reverse of this is the case; and that the ideas of *neat* and *smooth*, instead of being picturesque, in reality strip the object, in which they reside, of all pretensions to *picturesque beauty*. Nay, farther, we do not scruple to assert, that roughness forms the most essential point of difference between the *beautiful*, and the *picturesque*; as it seems to be that particular quality, which makes objects chiefly pleasing in painting. I use the general term *roughness*; but properly speaking roughness relates only to the surface of bodies: when we speak of their delineation, we use the word *ruggedness*. Both ideas however equally enter into the picturesque; and both are observable in the smaller, as well as in the larger parts of nature—in the outline, and bark of a tree, as in the rude summit, and craggy sides of a mountain. Let us then examine our theory by an appeal to experience; and try how far these qualities enter into the idea of *picturesque beauty*; and how far they mark that difference among objects, which is the ground of our inquiry.

A piece of Palladian architecture[2] may be elegant in the last degree. The proportion of its parts—the propriety of its ornaments—and the symmetry of the whole may be highly pleasing. But if we introduce it in a picture, it immediately becomes a formal object, and ceases to please. Should we wish to give it picturesque beauty, we must use the mallet, instead of the chisel; we must beat down one half of it, deface the other, and throw the mutilated members around in heaps. In short, from a *smooth* building we must turn it into a *rough* ruin. No painter, who had the choice of the two objects, would hesitate which to choose.

Again, why does an elegant piece of garden-ground make no figure on canvas? The shape is pleasing; the combination of the objects, harmonious; and the widening of the walk in the very line of beauty. All this is true, but the *smoothness* of the whole, though right, and as it should be in nature, offends in picture. Turn the lawn into a piece of broken ground: plant rugged oaks instead of flowing shrubs: break the edges of the walk: give it the rudeness of a road; mark it with wheel-tracks; and scatter around a few stones, and brushwood; in a word, instead of making the whole *smooth*, make it rough; and you make it also *picturesque*. All the other ingredients of beauty it already possessed. ...

Painting the Natural, the Human, the Supernatural, and the Sublime

FRENCH

The work of French artists of the Romantic period often displays a passionate flair for the dramatic, whether the subject be political, historical, or mythological; the sublime in nature is more often a backdrop for human drama than it is a subject in itself.

---

[1] *A very considerable ... without it* From Edmund Burke's *A Philosophical Enquiry into the Origin of Our Ideas of the Sublime and Beautiful* (1757).

[2] *Palladian architecture* European architectural style, derived from the work of Andrea Palladio, a sixteenth-century Venetian architect. Palladio's work was in turn based on the classical temple architecture of ancient Greece and Rome.

Jacques-Louis David, *Napoleon Crossing the Alps* (fifth version, c. 1805). This painting (also known as *Napoleon at the Saint-Bernard Pass* and as *Bonaparte Crossing the Alps*), which became the most widely-reproduced image of Napoleon, exists in five different versions. Napoleon had led his army through the Saint-Bernard Pass in the Alps in 1800 as part of a campaign that concluded with the defeat of the Austrian army in the Battle of Marengo later that year. The French victory in Italy led to improved relations between France and Spain, and various gifts were exchanged between the French and Spanish leaders; the first version of *Napoleon Crossing the Alps* was among those. David, an ardent supporter of Napoleon, was commissioned by the French ambassador to Spain to paint the portrait and completed it in January 1801. Napoleon himself asked David to paint three more versions. David painted a fifth on his own initiative and retained it until his death. (Like the second version, it now belongs to the museum of the Palace of Versailles.)

Jean-Antoine Gros, *Napoleon at the Battle of Eylau* (1808). The Battle of Eylau was fought between the French and Russian armies in 1807; it resulted in the loss of between 25,000 and 50,000 lives, but with no clear victory on either side.

Theodore Géricault, *The Raft of the Medusa* (1819). Perhaps the best known of all French paintings of the Romantic era, this work is a monumental depiction (approximately 16 x 24 feet) of an incident that occurred in 1816. The *Medusa* was a French frigate captained by a political appointee lacking in experience; it ran aground on a sandbank some 60 miles from the African coast. The ship had too few lifeboats and almost 150 men and one woman ended up adrift on a makeshift raft with inadequate supplies. By the time the raft was sighted and the survivors rescued by a passing ship, the *Argus*, only 15 remained alive; the others had starved to death or, in some cases, been killed and eaten (Géricault also completed a much smaller work entitled *Cannibalism on the Raft of the Medusa*).

The painting depicts the survivors' despair as the *Argus* has been sighted but has not seen the raft, and is sailing on. By chance, the *Argus* re-appeared again on the horizon some hours later on another tack, at which point the raft was finally sighted. The incident followed the restoration of the French monarchy after the defeat of Napoleon and was widely taken as a sign of the corruption, incompetence, and heartlessness of the new French regime, which had not bothered to instigate any search for the missing ship.

The painting, which was originally hung in Paris under the title *Scène de Naufrage* ("Scene of a Shipwreck"), was also controversial for its inclusion of a black man at the center of the composition; Géricault was an ardent abolitionist. When the work was exhibited in London for several months in 1820, it was received with tremendous enthusiasm and viewed by more than 40,000 people.

Eugene Delacroix, *Liberty Leading the People* (1830). Delacroix's most famous painting celebrates the overthrow of Charles X in 1830, which led to the establishment of a constitutional monarchy under Louis-Phillippe. The figure of Liberty holds a tattered *tricoleur*—the flag of the French Revolution of 1789. The new government bought the painting in 1831; later, it became the inspiration for France's 1886 gift to the United States of the statue *Liberty Enlightening the World*.

GERMAN

The work of such Romantic-era German artists as Philipp Otto Runge and Caspar David Friedrich is infused with symbolism and spirituality; the supernatural (and often specifically the Christian) is portrayed as a deep presence in nature—in plants, in the hours of the day and the changing seasons, and in human nature as well. The nineteenth-century European tradition of painting in this vein has roots in the Academy at Copenhagen in Denmark (where Runge, Friedrich, and the Norwegian Romantic painter Johann Christian Dahl all studied) and in the work of the Danish artist Jens Juel.

Philipp Otto Runge, *The Child in the Meadow*, from *Morning* (1809). *The Child in the Meadow* was conceived of as one part of a larger picture, *Morning*, that was itself planned as part of a still-larger work, *Times of Day*. *Morning* was not quite complete when Runge died (aged 33); before he died he suggested that the unfinished work be cut up and the parts that had been completed be displayed independently. *The Child in the Meadow* was the title given to this fragment. The grand scheme of the larger work is suggestive both of Christian and of classical mythology. The fragment gives a turn to Christian iconography that is also expressive of two other elements central to Runge's vision: a belief in an overriding connection between humans and nature, and a faith in childhood as the human stage that stands closest to the force of creation.

Caspar David Friedrich, *The Wanderer above the Sea of Fog* (1818). The title of this famous painting is also sometimes translated as *The Walker above the Mists*; in German the title is *Der Wanderer über dem Nebelmeer*; the German "Wanderer" can mean either wanderer or hiker.

Caspar David Friedrich, *Arctic Shipwreck* (also known as *Sea of Ice* or *Polar Sea*) (1824).

BRITISH

From the gentle vision of nature expressed in the late eighteenth-century work of Thomas Gainsborough, British artists moved in several directions. The vast scenes depicted by John Martin are dark and theatrical; the Romantic sublime of Philip James de Loutherbourg is strangely unthreatening, even when terrible subjects are depicted; the fiery realism of Joseph Derby locates sublime terror in the human creations of the Industrial Revolution. The work of the two greatest Romantic-era British artists, J.M.W. Turner and John Constable, evolved markedly over the course of several decades.

Thomas Gainsborough, *Peasants Going to Market, Early Morning* (1770).

Thomas Gainsborough, *Cottage Door with Girl and Pigs* (1786).

J.M.W. Turner, *Linlithgow Palace* (1807). The palace where Mary, Queen of Scots had been born was by 1807 a picturesque ruin. The naked nymphs he added in the foreground are reminiscent of artistic styles of an earlier era, but the whole has an unmistakably Romantic cast.

J.M.W. Turner, *The Fighting Temeraire Tugged to Her Last Berth to Be Broken Up* (1839). The *H.M.S. Temeraire* had played an important role in Nelson's victory over the French at Trafalgar in 1805; in 1838, it was towed to a scrap yard at the docks in east London.

J.M.W. Turner, *The Devil's Bridge* (1841)

John Martin, *The Bard* (1817). The term "bard" refers in the first instance to Celtic poets who sang of their people's history and traditions, often with a special focus on heroes and their deeds of bravery. In the Romantic era the term came increasingly to be conflated with "mystic" or "seer."

John Constable, *Dedham Vale* (1802).

John Constable, *Brighton Beach, with Colliers* (1824).

John Constable, *Old Sarum* (1829). Old Sarum, near the site of present-day Salisbury, is the location of some of the earliest evidence of human settlement in Britain; it is known to have been inhabited over 3,000 years ago. By the early nineteenth century, however, the old hill fort was long-abandoned and Old Sarum was uninhabited.

Philip James de Loutherbourg, *Snowdon*, from *The Romantic and Picturesque Scenery of England and Wales* (1805).

Philip James de Loutherbourg, *Storm off Margate*, from *The Romantic and Picturesque Scenery of England and Wales* (1805).

David Cox, *Crossing Lancaster Sands* (1841). Until 1857, when a railway line was built across the bay, people often made their way to Morecamb Bay at low tide across the Lancaster Sands. There were numerous dangers associated with the crossing (including quicksand as well as unpredictable and dangerous tides). The watercolorist David Cox painted the crossing several times; J.M.W. Turner is among the many others to have depicted the crossing of the Lancaster Sands.

The Place of Humans and Non-Human Animals in Nature

from William Godwin, *Fleetwood: or, the New Man of Feeling* (1805)

> *Fleetwood*, William Godwin's (1756–1836) third novel, assesses Rousseau's ideas about the virtue of the "natural man," finding its hero, raised in the natural world, far from ideal.

I loved the country, without feeling any partiality to what are called the sports of the country. My temper, as I have already said, was somewhat unsocial; and so far as related to the intercourse of my species, except when some strong stimulus of humanity called me into action, unenterprising. I was therefore no hunter. I was inaccessible to the pitiful ambition of showing, before a gang of rural squires, that I had a fine horse, and could manage him gracefully. I had not the motive, which ordinarily influences the inhabitants of the country to the cultivation of these sports—the want of occupation. I was young: the world was new to me: I abounded with occupation. In the scenery of Merionethshire I found a source of inexhaustible amusement. Science, history, poetry engaged me by turns, and into each of them my soul plunged itself with an ardour difficult to describe. In the train of these came my visions, my beloved and variegated inventions, the records, which to me appeared voluminous and momentous, of my past life, the plans of my future, the republics I formed, the seminaries of education for which I constructed laws, the figure I proposed hereafter to exhibit in the eyes of a wondering world. I had a still further and more direct reason for my rejection for the sports of the field. I could not with patience regard torture, anguish, and death, as sources of amusement. My natural temper, or my reflective and undebauched habits as a solitaire, prevented me from overlooking the brutality and cruelty of such pursuits. In very early youth I had been seduced, first by a footman of my father, and afterward by my tutor, who was a great lover of the art, to join in an excursion of angling. But, after a short trial, I abjured the amusement for ever; and it was one among the causes of the small respect I entertained for my tutor, that he was devoted to so idle and unfeeling an avocation.

from John Locke, *Some Thoughts Concerning Education* (1693), Section 116

> Locke (1632–1704) had argued in his *Essay Concerning Human Understanding* (1690) that reason is more important to what is human than is physical shape, and that several common human assumptions over how species and essences should be defined and delineated deserved to be challenged. In his influential *Some Thoughts Concerning Education*, he addressed the issue of cruelty toward animals.

Cruelty. One thing I have frequently observed in children, that when they have got possession of any poor creature, they are apt to use it ill: They often torment, and treat very roughly young birds, butterflies, and such other poor animals, which fall into their hands, and that with a seeming kind of pleasure. This I think should be watched in them, and if they incline to any such cruelty they should be taught the contrary usage. For the custom of tormenting and killing of beasts will, by degrees, harden their minds even towards men; and they who delight in the suffering and destruction of inferior creatures, will not be apt to be very compassionate or benign to those of their own kind. Our practice takes notice of this in the exclusion of *butchers* from juries of life and death. Children should from the beginning be bred up in an abhorrence of *killing*, or tormenting any living creature; and be taught not to *spoil* or destroy any thing, unless it be for the preservation or advantage of some other, that is nobler. ...

from William Hogarth, *The Four Stages of Cruelty* (1751)

> In *The Four Stages of Cruelty*, painter, printmaker, satirist, and social critic William Hogarth (1697–1764) depicts four stages in the life of the fictional Tom Nero. In the first plate, Nero is shown as a

child torturing a dog. Subsequent plates show him torturing a horse (Second Stage of Cruelty); engaging in a life of robbery, seduction, and murder (Cruelty in Perfection); and, finally, being mutilated by surgeons in an anatomical theater after he is executed for his crimes (The Reward of Cruelty). Hogarth's engravings thus suggest that childish cruelty to animals can quickly progress to depraved criminality.

Anna Laetitia Barbauld, "The Mouse's Petition" (1773)

Barbauld (1743–1825) was an important participant in late eighteenth-century debates about animal experimentation. The occasion for "The Mouse's Petition" (one of her most popular poems) was a visit she paid to the house of Joseph Priestley in 1771. At the time, Priestley was engaged in what became a famous series of experiments into the nature of air; these experiments compared how various live animal subjects (usually mice) responded to different gaseous environments. Some reviewers of Barbauld's *Poems* (1773) read the poem as an accusation against Priestley of cruelty to animals. Perhaps anxious not to offend her host, Barbauld inserted a footnote to subsequent editions of the book, suggesting that the mouse would have suffered as much or more had it been the victim of "domestic economy" (i.e., a mousetrap), and asserting that she had intended the poem as a petition "of mercy against justice" rather than of "humanity against cruelty." Be that as it may, many continued to read both this and several others of her poems (notably, "The Caterpillar") as expressing opposition to cruelty toward animals.

Barbauld also addresses some of the parallels between human and non-human animals in her influential *Lessons for Children*; an excerpt appears below.

The Mouse's Petition

Oh! Hear a pensive prisoner's prayer,
 For liberty that sighs;
And never let thine heart be shut
Against the wretch's cries.

5 For here forlorn and sad I sit
Within the wiry grate;
And tremble at th'approaching morn,
Which brings impending fate.

If e'er thy breast with freedom glow'd
10 And spurn'd a tyrant's chain,
Let not thy strong oppressive force
A free-born mouse detain.[1]

Oh! do not stain with guiltless blood
Thy hospitable hearth;
15 Nor triumph that thy wiles betrayed
A prize so little worth.

[1] *If e'er ... detain* Barbauld may well be alluding here to political positions Priestley had taken in support of freedom. In 1769, Priestley (who eventually emigrated to the United States) had taken issue with the British government's "enslaving" of the American colonies, and had argued for "a just idea of natural and civil rights."

The scattered gleanings of a feast
My frugal meals supply;
But if thine unrelenting heart
20   That slender boon deny,

The chearful light, the vital air,
Are blessings widely given;
Let nature's commoners enjoy
The common gifts of heaven,

25   The well-taught philosophic mind
To all compassion gives;
Casts round the world an equal eye,
And feels for all that lives.

If mind, as ancient sages taught,
30   A never dying flame,
Still shifts thro' matter's varying forms,
In every form the same.

Beware, lest in the worm you crush,
A brother's soul you find;
35   And tremble lest thy luckless hand
Dislodge a kindred mind.

Or, if this transient gleam of day
Be *all* of life we share,
Let pity plead within thy breast
40   That little *all* to spare.

So may thy hospitable board
With health and peace be crowned;
And every charm of heartfelt ease
Beneath thy roof be found.

45   So, when destruction lurks unseen,
Which men, like mice, may share,
May some kind angel clear thy path,
And break the hidden snare.

from Anna Laetitia Barbauld, *Lessons for Children* (1778–88)

... What has Billy got? He has got a nest of young birds. He has been climbing a high tree for them. Poor little birds! ... Do not let them die. The little birds' papa and mama will be very sorry if they come to die....

... Hark! Somebody is letting off a gun! They are shooting the poor birds. Here is a bird dropped down just at your feet. It is all bloody. Poor thing! How it flutters. Its wing is broken. It cannot fly any further. It is going to die. What bird is it? It is a partridge. Are you not sorry, Charles? It was alive a little while ago....

There was a little girl who loved very dearly to run through the meadows, and catch butterflies that she saw flying about, or resting on the bright gay flowers in the hedges. But she always found that as soon as she touched them, their wings lost all their pretty colour, and were sometimes even rent and broken if she held them ever so gently. She was, as she ought to be, so vexed at this, that she determined to catch no more butterflies, but to be contended with seeing them skim from one flower to another, and to stand and look at them while they opened and shut their beautiful wings in the sun. But though butterflies' wings could be so soon broken and spoiled, birds' she thought could not, and it would be a great deal better, she said to herself, to have pretty young birds in her hand, that might be touched without harm, and would in time sing to her, than the gayest butterflies that were ever seen. And so she persuaded someone to get her a nest-full of young linnets, out of a thick hedge, which she took and put against her bosom, and then fed them, until she thought they would be much happier with her than they were among boughs and leaves of the tree. But when the old bird flew back, after she had been seeking food for her young, and found her nest gone, she made such a sad twittering that the little girl felt very sorry and began to think that though the young ones might be glad to have such a nice warm bed as she made them in a little cage, their mother must be very grieved to lose them, and so she went to bed not half so glad at having the young birds as she was at first. When she got up in the morning she went to look at them, and carry them some food, and she thought, "perhaps the old bird has forgotten them by this time"; but it was no such thing, for she was flying backwards and forwards before the window where the cage stood, and would have come quite near, had not someone frightened her. When she put her hand into the cage with the crumbs of bread she had brought, she hoped the little linnets would put up their beaks and shake their wings, and take the food. But they neither chirped nor moved, and she was very vexed, and touched them with her hand again and again to make them stir, but they would not, and then she thought she would take them out, and so she did, and they were all dead. When she saw this she cried, and found she had been very cruel, and said she would never take poor little birds again from their mother. But after a few days she was again wishing to have something to play with, and to make fond of; and she was so lucky as to find a number of little kittens which an old cat was bringing up in a corner by the kitchen fire. So she begged her mama to let her have one, which she did, and she ran immediately and took the prettiest she could see, and went away with it. But she had not long had it in her arms when the mother came after her, and mewing and looking up at her seemed to beg that she would set it down, and let it go back into the kitchen. And the good little girl remembered the poor birds, and would not for the world be so cruel again; and she let the kitten go, but was soon after rewarded by finding it grown very strong, and that it was ready of its own accord to leave the old cat; and so she had it again, and a faithful little thing it was all its life.

Samuel Taylor Coleridge, "To a Young Ass, Its Mother Being Tethered Near It" (1794)

While at Jesus College, Coleridge (1772–1834) frequently encountered a donkey grazing on the grass; the animal's mother was tethered to a log nearby, apparently unable to move toward fresh grass. Coleridge's pity for animals is consistent with the sympathies of many Romantic intellectuals, but his attraction to the donkey specifically may stem from its association in fable with spiritual merit, patience, humility, lowliness, and suffering that find favor in heaven.

At this stage of his life, Coleridge was in sympathy with the ideas of Barbauld (with whom he corresponded extensively) and others concerning appropriate human attitudes toward non-human animals. Later in life, as he became more conservative, he derided such views as overly sentimental.

Poor little Foal of an oppressèd Race!
I love the languid Patience of thy face:
And oft with gentle hand I give thee bread,
And clap thy ragged Coat, and pat thy head.
5   But what thy dullèd Spirits hath dismayed,
That never thou dost sport along the glade?
And (most unlike the nature of things young)
That earthward still thy moveless head is hung?
Do thy prophetic fears anticipate,
10   Meek Child of Misery! thy future fate?
The starving meal, and all the thousand aches
"Which patient Merit of the Unworthy takes"?[1]
Or is thy sad heart thrilled with filial pain
To see thy wretched Mother's shortened chain?
15   And truly, very piteous is *her* Lot—
Chained to a Log within a narrow spot,
Where the close-eaten Grass is scarcely seen,
While sweet around her waves the tempting Green!

Poor Ass! thy master should have learnt to show
20   Pity—best taught by fellowship of Woe!
For much I fear me that *He* lives like thee,
Half famished in a land of Luxury!
How *askingly* its footsteps hither bend!
It seems to say, "And have I then *one* friend?"
25   Innocent foal! thou poor despised Forlorn!
I hail thee *Brother*—spite of the fool's scorn!
And fain would take thee with me, in the Dell
Of Peace and mild Equality to dwell,
Where Toil shall call the charmer Health his bride,
30   And Laughter tickle Plenty's ribless side!
How thou wouldst toss thy heels in gamesome play,
And frisk about, as lamb or kitten gay!
Yea! and more musically sweet to me
Thy dissonant harsh bray of joy would be,
35   Than warbled melodies that soothe to rest
The aching of pale Fashion's vacant breast!

---

[1]   *Which patient ... Unworthy takes*   From *Hamlet*, 3.1.74.

Percy Bysshe Shelley, *A Vindication of Natural Diet* (1813)

A strong crusader for justice, particularly for the working classes, Shelley (1792–1822) was also an outspoken advocate of vegetarianism. He wrote a number of essays on the topic, of which *A Vindication of Natural Diet* is perhaps the most famous.

I hold that the depravity of the physical and moral nature of man originated in his unnatural habits of life. The origin of man, like that of the universe of which he is a part, is enveloped in impenetrable mystery. His generations either had a beginning, or they had not. The weight of evidence in favour of each of these suppositions seems tolerably equal; and it is perfectly unimportant to the present argument which is assumed. The language spoken however by the mythology of nearly all religions seems to prove, that at some distant period man forsook the path of nature, and sacrificed the purity and happiness of his being to unnatural appetites. The date of this event seems to have also been that of some great change in the climates of the earth, with which it has an obvious correspondence. The allegory of Adam and Eve eating of the tree of evil, and entailing upon their posterity the wrath of God, and the loss of everlasting life, admits of no other explanation, than the disease and crime that have flowed from unnatural diet. Milton was so well aware of this, that he makes Raphael thus exhibit to Adam the consequence of his disobedience:

> Immediately a place,
> Before his eyes appeared: sad, noisome, dark:
> A lazar-house it seemed; wherein were laid
> Numbers of all diseased: all maladies
> Of ghastly spasm, or racking torture, qualms
> Of heart-sick agony, all feverous kinds,
> Convulsions, epilepsies, fierce catarrhs,
> Intestine stone and ulcer, cholic pangs,
> Dæmoniac frenzy, moping melancholy,
> And moon-struck madness, pining atrophy,
> Marasmus, and wide-wasting pestilence,
> Dropsies, and asthmas, and joint-racking rheums.[1]

And how many thousand more might not be added to this frightful catalogue!

The story of Prometheus is one likewise which, although universally admitted to be allegorical, has never been satisfactorily explained. Prometheus stole fire from heaven, and was chained for this crime to mount Caucasus, where a vulture continually devoured his liver, that grew to meet its hunger. Hesiod says, that before the time of Prometheus, mankind were exempt from suffering; that they enjoyed a vigorous youth, and that death, when at length it came, approached like sleep, and gently closed their eyes. Again, so general was this opinion, that Horace, a poet of the Augustan age, writes:

> Audax omnia perpeti,
> Gens humana ruit per vetitum nefas,
> Audax Iapeti genus
> Ignem fraude mala gentibus intulit,
> Post ignem ætheriâ domo
> Subductum, macies et nova febrium
> Terris incubuit cohors
> Semotique prius tarda necessitas,
> Lethi corripuit gradum.[2]

How plain a language is spoken by all this. Prometheus, (who represents the human race) effected some great change in the condition of his nature, and applied fire to culinary purposes; thus inventing an expedient for screening from his disgust the horrors of the shambles. From this moment his vitals were devoured by the vulture of disease. It consumed his being in every shape of its loathsome and infinite variety, inducing the soul-quelling sinkings of premature and violent death. All vice arose from the ruin of healthful innocence. Tyranny, superstition, commerce, and inequality, were then first known, when reason vainly attempted to guide the wanderings of exacerbated passion. I conclude this part of the subject with an extract from Mr. Newton's

---

[1] *Immediately a place ... joint-racking rheums* From *Paradise Lost*, 10. 477–88.

[2] *Audax omnia perpeti ... corripuit gradum* Latin: "Men, ready for anything, are quick / Forbidden wickedness to find; / Prometheus by a dirty trick / Brought ready fire to humankind. / But after fire was brought down to earth / From its heavenly haven, with it a corps / Of new diseases came, and dearth, / So death, remote and slow before, / Sooner than necessary began" (Horace, *Odes*, 1.3.25–32).

Defence of Vegetable Regimen, from whom I have borrowed this interpretation of the fable of Prometheus.

Making allowance for such transposition of the events of the allegory, as time might produce after the important truths were forgotten, which the portion of the ancient mythology was intended to transmit, the drift of the fable seems to be this: Man at his creation was endowed with the gift of perpetual youth; that is, he was not formed to be a sickly suffering creature as we now see him, but to enjoy health, and to sink by slow degrees into the bosom of his parent earth without disease or pain. Prometheus first taught the use of animal food (*primus bovem occidit Prometheus*) and of fire, with which to render it more digestible and pleasing to the taste. Jupiter, and the rest of the gods, foreseeing the consequences of the inventions, were amused or irritated at the short-sighted devices of the newly-formed creature, and left him to experience the sad effects of them. Thirst, the necessary concomitant of a flesh diet, (perhaps of all diet vitiated by culinary preparation) "ensued; water was resorted to, and man forfeited the inestimable gift of health which he had received from heaven: he became diseased, the partaker of a precarious existence, and no longer descended slowly to his grave."[1]

> But just disease to luxury succeeds,
> And every death its own avenger breeds;
> The fury passions from that blood began,
> And turned on man a fiercer savage—Man.[2]

Man, and the animals whom he has infected with his society, or depraved by his dominion, are alone diseased. The wild hog, the mouflon,[3] the bison, and the wolf, are perfectly exempt from malady, and invariably die either from external violence, or natural old age. But the domestic hog, the sheep, the cow, and the dog, are subject to an incredible variety of distempers; and, like the corrupters of their nature, have physicians who thrive upon their miseries. The supereminence of man is like Satan's, a supereminence of pain; and the majority of his species, doomed to penury, disease, and crime, have reason to curse the untoward event, that by enabling him to communicate his sensations, raised him above the level of his fellow animals. But the steps that have been taken are irrevocable. The whole of human science is comprised in one question: How can the advantages of intellect and civilisation be reconciled with the liberty and pure pleasures of natural life? How can we take the benefits, and reject the evils of the system, which is now interwoven with all the fibres of our being? I believe that abstinence from animal food and spirituous liquors would in a great measure capacitate us for the solution of this important question.

Comparative anatomy teaches us that man resembles frugivorous[4] animals in everything, and carnivorous in nothing; he has neither claws wherewith to seize his prey, nor distinct and pointed teeth to tear the living fibre. A Mandarin of the first class, with nails two inches long, would probably find them alone inefficient to hold even a hare. After every subterfuge of gluttony, the bull must be degraded into the ox, and the ram into the wether,[5] by an unnatural and inhuman operation, that the flaccid fibre may offer a fainter resistance to rebellious nature. It is only by softening and disguising dead flesh by culinary preparation that it is rendered susceptible of mastication or digestion, and that the sight of its bloody juices and raw horror, does not excite intolerable loathing and disgust. Let the advocate of animal food, force himself to a decisive experiment on its fitness, and as Plutarch[6] recommends, tear a living lamb with his teeth, and plunging his head into its vitals, slake his thirst with the steaming blood; when fresh from the deed of horror let him revert to the irresistible instincts of nature that would rise in judgment against it, and say, Nature formed me for such work as this. Then, and

---

[1] *Mr. Newton's ... to his grave* John Frank Newton was the author of *Return to Nature, or Defence of Vegetable Regimen* (1811), the work from which the quoted passage is taken. Shelley met Newton in 1812 through the son of William Godwin. Newton's work included an account of his family's successful experiment with a vegetarian diet.

[2] *But just ... Man* From Alexander Pope, *An Essay on Man*, 165–69.

[3] *mouflon* Subspecies of wild sheep.

[4] *frugivorous* Fruit-eating.

[5] *wether* Castrated male sheep or goat.

[6] *Plutarch* Lucius Mestrius Plutarchus (c. 46–120 CE), Greek biographer, historian, and essayist.

then only, would he be consistent.

Man resembles no carnivorous animal. There is no exception, except man be one, to the rule of herbivorous animals having cellulated colons.

The orang-outang perfectly resembles man both in the order and number of his teeth. The orang-outang is the most anthropomorphous of the ape tribe, all of which are strictly frugivorous. There is no other species of animals in which this analogy exists. In many frugivorous animals, the canine teeth are more pointed and distinct than those of man. The resemblance also of the human stomach to that of the orang-outang, is greater than to that of any other animal.

The intestines are also identical with those of herbivorous animals, which present a larger surface for absorption, and have ample and cellulated colons. The cæcum also, though short, is larger than that of carnivorous animals; and even here the orang-outang retains its accustomed similarity. The structure of the human frame then is that of one fitted to a pure vegetable diet, in every essential particular. It is true, that the reluctance to abstain from animal food, in those who have been long accustomed to its stimulus, is so great in some persons of weak minds, as to be scarcely overcome; but this is far from bringing any argument in its favour. A lamb, which was fed for some time on flesh by a ship's crew, refused its natural diet at the end of the voyage. There are numerous instances of horses, sheep, oxen, and even wood-pigeons, having been taught to live upon flesh, until they have loathed their accustomed aliment. Young children evidently prefer pastry, oranges, apples, and other fruit, to the flesh of animals; until, by the gradual depravation of the digestive organs, the free use of vegetables has for a time produced serious inconveniences; *for a time*, I say, since there never was an instance wherein a change from spirituous liquors and animal food, to vegetables and pure water, has failed ultimately to invigorate the body, by rendering its juices bland and consentaneous, and to restore to the mind that cheerfulness and elasticity, which not one in fifty possess on the present system. A love of strong liquors is also with difficulty taught to infants. Almost everyone remembers the wry faces, which the first glass of port produced. Unsophisticated instinct is invariably unerring; but to decide on the fitness of animal food, from

the perverted appetites which its constrained adoption produces, is to make the criminal a judge in his own cause: it is even worse, it is appealing to the infatuated drunkard in a question of the salubrity[1] of brandy.

What is the cause of morbid action in the animal system? Not the air we breathe, for our fellow denizens of nature, breathe the same uninjured; not the water we drink, if remote from the pollutions of man and his inventions, for the animals drink it too; not the earth we tread upon; not the unobscured sight of glorious nature, in the wood, the field, or the expanse of sky and ocean; nothing that we are or do in common, with the undiseased inhabitants of the forest. Something then wherein we differ from them: our habit of altering our food by fire, so that our appetite is no longer a just criterion for the fitness of its gratification. Except in children there remain no traces of that instinct, which determines in all other animals what aliment is natural or otherwise, and so perfectly obliterated are they in the reasoning adults of our species, that it has become necessary to urge considerations drawn from comparative anatomy to prove that we are naturally frugivorous.

Crime is madness. Madness is disease. Whenever the cause of disease shall be discovered, the root from which all vice and misery have so long overshadowed the globe, will lay bare to the axe. All the exertions of man, from that moment, may be considered as tending to the clear profit of his species. No sane mind in a sane body resolves upon a real crime. It is a man of violent passions, blood-shot eyes, and swollen veins, that alone can grasp the knife of murder. The system of a simple diet promises no Utopian advantages. It is no mere reform of legislation, whilst the furious passions and evil propensities of the human heart, in which it had its origin, are still unassuaged. It strikes at the root of all evil, and is an experiment which may be tried with success, not alone by nations, but by small societies, families, and even individuals. In no cases has a return to vegetable diet produced the slightest injury; in most it has been attended with changes undeniably beneficial. Should ever a physician be born with the genius of Locke,[2] I am

---

[1]   *salubrity*   Conduciveness to health and well-being.

[2]   *Locke*   John Locke (1632–1704), English philosopher, physician, and Enlightenment thinker.

persuaded that he might trace all bodily and mental derangements to our unnatural habits, as clearly as that philosopher has traced all knowledge to sensation. What prolific sources of disease are not those mineral and vegetable poisons that have been introduced for its extirpation! How many thousands have become murderers and robbers, bigots and domestic tyrants, dissolute and abandoned adventurers, from the use of fermented liquors; who, had they slaked their thirst only at the mountain stream, would have lived but to diffuse the happiness of their own unperverted feelings. How many groundless opinions and absurd institutions have not received a general sanction, from the sottishness[1] and intemperance of individuals! Who will assert, that had the populace of Paris drank at the pure source of the Seine, and satisfied their hunger at the ever-furnished table of vegetable nature, that they would have lent their brutal suffrage to the proscription-list of Robespierre?[2] Could a set of men, whose passions were not perverted by unnatural stimuli, look with coolness on an auto da fé?[3] Is it to be believed that a being of gentle feelings, rising from his meal of roots, would take delight in sports of blood? Was Nero a man of temperate life? Could you read calm health in his cheek, flushed with ungovernable propensities of hatred for the human race? Did Muley Ismael's[4] pulse beat evenly, was his skin transparent, did his eyes beam with healthfulness, and its invariable concomitants cheerfulness and benignity? Though history has decided none of these questions, a child could not hesitate to answer in the negative. Surely the bile-suffused cheek of Buonaparte,[5] his wrinkled brow, and yellow eye, the ceaseless inquietude of his nervous system, speak no less plainly the character of his unresting ambition than his murders and his victories.

---

[1] *sottishness* Drunkenness.

[2] *Robespierre* Maximilien François Marie Isidore de Robespierre (1758–94), prominent French revolutionary and architect of the Reign of Terror (1793–99).

[3] *auto da fé* Ritual of public penance for heretics and apostates during the Inquisition; literally, it translates to "act of faith." The most common example of auto da fé was burning at the stake.

[4] *Muley Ismael* Moroccan emperor known for his abstemious, ascetic lifestyle.

[5] *Buonaparte* Napoleon Bonaparte (1769–1821), military and political leader of France from 1799 to 1814.

It is impossible, had Buonaparte descended from a race of vegetable feeders, that he could have had either the inclination or the power to ascend the throne of the Bourbons.[6] The desire of tyranny could scarcely be excited in the individual, the power to tyrannize would certainly not be delegated by a society, neither frenzied by inebriation, nor rendered impotent and irrational by disease. Pregnant indeed with inexhaustible calamity, is the renunciation of instinct, as it concerns our physical nature; arithmetic cannot enumerate, nor reason perhaps suspect, the multitudinous sources of disease in civilized life. Even common water, that apparently innoxious pabulum,[7] when corrupted by the filth of populous cities, is a deadly and insidious destroyer. Who can wonder that all the inducements held out by God himself in the Bible to virtue, should have been vainer than a nurse's tale; and that those dogmas, apparently favourable to the intolerant and angry passions, should have alone been deemed essential; whilst Christians are in the daily practice of all those habits, which have infected with disease and crime, not only the reprobate sons, but these favoured children of the common Father's love. Omnipotence itself could not save them from the consequences of this original and universal sin.

There is no disease, bodily or mental, which adoption of vegetable diet and pure water has not infallibly mitigated, wherever the experiment has been fairly tried. Debility is gradually converted into strength, disease into healthfulness; madness in all its hideous variety, from the ravings of the fettered maniac, to the unaccountable irrationalities of ill temper, that make a hell of domestic life, into a calm and considerate evenness of temper, that alone might offer a certain pledge of the future moral reformation of society. On a natural system of diet, old age would be our last and our only malady; the term of our existence would be protracted; we should enjoy life, and no longer preclude others from the enjoyment of it. All sensational delights would be infinitely more exquisite and perfect. The very sense of being would then be a continued pleasure, such as we now feel it in some few and favoured moments of our

---

[6] *Bourbons* Powerful and influential European royal family.

[7] *pabulum* Food, especially as a solution of nutrients suitable for absorption.

youth. By all that is sacred in our hopes for the human race, I conjure those who love happiness and truth, to give a fair trial to the vegetable system. Reasoning is surely superfluous on a subject, whose merits an experience of six months would set for ever at rest. But it is only among the enlightened and benevolent, that so great a sacrifice of appetite and prejudice can be expected, even though its ultimate excellence should not admit of dispute.

It is found easier, by the short-sighted victims of disease, to palliate their torments by medicine, than to prevent them by regimen. The vulgar of all ranks are invariably sensual and indocile; yet I cannot but feel myself persuaded, that when the benefits of vegetable diet are mathematically proved; when it is as clear, that those who live naturally are exempt from premature death, as that nine is not one, the most sottish of mankind will feel a preference towards a long and tranquil, contrasted with a short and painful life. On the average, out of sixty persons, four die in three years. In April 1814, a statement will be given, that sixty persons, all having lived more than three years on vegetables and pure water, are then *in perfect health*. More than two years have now elapsed; *not one of them has died*; no such example will be found in any sixty persons taken at random. Seventeen persons of all ages (the families of Dr. Lambe[1] and Mr. Newton) have lived for seven years on this diet, without a death and almost without the slightest illness. Surely when we consider that some of these were infants, and one a martyr to asthma now nearly subdued, we may challenge any seventeen persons taken at random in this city to exhibit a parallel case. Those who may have been excited to question the rectitude of established habits of diet, by these loose remarks, should consult Mr. Newton's luminous and eloquent essay. It is from that book, and from the conversation of its excellent and enlightened author, that I have derived the materials which I here present to the public.

When these proofs come fairly before the world, and are clearly seen by all who understand arithmetic, it is scarcely possible that abstinence from aliments demonstrably pernicious should not become universal.

In proportion to the number of proselytes, so will be the weight of evidence, and when a thousand persons can be produced living on vegetables and distilled water, who have to dread no disease but old age, the world will be compelled to regard animal flesh and fermented liquors, as slow, but certain poisons. The change which would be produced by simpler habits on political economy is sufficiently remarkable. The monopolizing eater of animal flesh would no longer destroy his constitution by devouring an acre at a meal, and many loaves of bread would cease to contribute to gout, madness and apoplexy,[2] in the shape of a pint of porter, or a dram of gin, when appeasing the long-protracted famine of the hard-working peasant's hungry babes. The quantity of nutritious vegetable matter, consumed in fattening the carcass of an ox, would afford ten times the sustenance, undepraving indeed, and incapable of generating disease, if gathered immediately from the bosom of the earth.

The most fertile districts of the habitable globe are now actually cultivated by men for animals, at a delay and waste of aliment absolutely incapable of calculation. It is only the wealthy that can, to any great degree, even now, indulge the unnatural craving for dead flesh, and they pay for the greater license of the privilege by subjection to supernumerary diseases. Again, the spirit of the nation that should take lead in this great reform, would insensibly become agricultural; commerce, with all its vice, selfishness, and corruption, would gradually decline; more natural habits would produce gentler manners, and the excessive complication of political relations would be so far simplified, that every individual might feel and understand why he loved his country, and took a personal interest in its welfare. How would England, for example, depend on the caprices of foreign rulers, if she contained within herself all the necessaries, and despised whatever they possessed of the luxuries of life? How could they starve her into compliance with their views? Of what consequence would it be, that they refused to take her woolen manufactures, when large and fertile tracts of the island ceased to be allotted to the

---

[1] *Dr. Lambe* William Lambe (1765–1847), author of *Reports on the Effects of Peculiar Regimen in Scirrhous Tumours and Cancerous Ulcers* (1809) and early advocate of a vegetarian diet.

[2] *apoplexy* Stroke.

waste of pasturage? On a natural system of diet, we should require no spices from India; no wines from Portugal, Spain, France, or Madeira; none of those multitudinous articles of luxury, for which every comer of the globe is rifled, and which are the causes of so much individual rivalship, such calamitous and sanguinary national disputes.

In the history of modern times, the avarice of commercial monopoly, no less than the ambition of weak and wicked chiefs, seems to have fomented the universal discord, to have added stubbornness to the mistakes of cabinets, and indocility to the infatuation of the people. Let it ever be remembered, that it is the direct influence of commerce to make the interval between the richest and the poorest man wider and more unconquerable. Let it be remembered, that it is a foe to every thing of real worth and excellence in the human character. The odious and disgusting aristocracy of wealth, is built upon the ruins of all that is good in chivalry or republicanism; and luxury is the forerunner of a barbarism scarce capable of cure. Is it impossible to realize a state of society, where all the energies of man shall be directed to the production of his solid happiness?

Certainly, if this advantage (the object of all political speculation) be in any degree attainable, it is attainable only by a community, which holds out no factitious incentives to the avarice and ambition of the few, and which is internally organized for the liberty, security and comfort of the many. None must be entrusted with power (and money is the completest species of power) who do not stand pledged to use it exclusively for the general benefit. But the use of animal flesh and fermented liquors, directly militates with this equality of the rights of man. The peasant cannot gratify these fashionable cravings without leaving his family to starve. Without disease and war, those sweeping curtailers of population, pasturage would include a waste too great to be afforded. The labour requisite to support a family is far lighter than is usually supposed. The peasantry work, not only for themselves, but for the aristocracy, the army and the manufacturers.

The advantage of a reform in diet is obviously greater than that of any other. It strikes at the root of the evil. To remedy the abuses of legislation, before we annihilate the propensities by which they are produced,

is to suppose, that by taking away the effect, the cause will cease to operate. But the efficacy of this system depends entirely on the proselytism of individuals, and grounds its merits as a benefit to the community, upon the total change of the dietetic habits in its members. It proceeds securely from a number of particular cases, to one that is universal, and has this advantage over the contrary mode, that one error does not invalidate all that has gone before.

Let not too much, however, be expected from this system. The healthiest among us is not exempt from hereditary disease. The most symmetrical, athletic, and long-lived, is a being inexpressibly inferior to what he would have been, had not the unnatural habits of his ancestors accumulated for him a certain portion of malady and deformity. In the most perfect specimen of civilized man, something is still found wanting, by the physiological critic. Can a return to nature, then, instantaneously eradicate predispositions that have been slowly taking root in the silence of innumerable ages? Indubitably not. All that I contend for is, that from the moment of the relinquishing all unnatural habits, no new disease is generated; and that the predisposition to hereditary maladies, gradually perishes, for want of its accustomed supply. In cases of consumption, cancer, gout, asthma, and scrofula, such is the invariable tendency of a diet of vegetables and pure water.

Those who may be induced by these remarks to give the vegetable system a fair trial, should, in the first place, date the commencement of their practice from the moment of their conviction. All depends upon breaking through a pernicious habit, resolutely and at once. Dr. Trotter[1] asserts that no drunkard was ever reformed by gradually relinquishing his dram. Animal flesh in its effects on the human stomach is analogous to a dram. It is similar in the kind, though differing in the degree, of its operation. The proselyte to a pure diet, must be warned to expect a temporary diminution of muscular strength. The subtraction of a powerful stimulus will suffice to account for this event. But it is only temporary, and is succeeded by an equable capability for exertion, far surpassing his former various and fluctuat-

---

[1] *Dr. Trotter* Thomas Trotter (c. 1760–1832), a specialist in the nervous temperament and addiction, was an associate of William Lambe and a fellow advocate of a vegetarian diet.

ing strength. Above all, he will acquire an easiness of breathing, by which the same exertion is performed, with a remarkable exemption from that painful and difficult panting now felt by almost every one, after hastily climbing an ordinary mountain. He will be equally capable of bodily exertion, or mental application, after as before his simple meal. He will feel none of the narcotic effects of ordinary diet. Irritability, the direct consequence, of exhausting stimuli, would yield to the power of natural and tranquil impulses. He will no longer pine under the lethargy of ennui, that unconquerable weariness of life, more dreaded than death itself. He will escape the epidemic madness, that broods over its own injurious notions of the Deity, and "realizes the hell that priests and beldams feign."[1] Every man forms, as it were, his god from his own character; to the divinity of one of simple habits, no offering would be more acceptable than the happiness of his creatures. He would be incapable of hating or persecuting others for the love of God. He will find, moreover, a system of simple diet to be a system of perfect epicurism.[2] He will no longer be incessantly occupied in blunting and destroying those organs, from which he expects his gratification.

The pleasures of taste to be derived from a dinner of potatoes, beans, peas, turnips, lettuce, with a dessert of apples, gooseberries, strawberries, currants, raspberries, and in winter, oranges, apples and pears, is far greater than is supposed. Those who wait until they can eat this plain fare, with the sauce of appetite, will scarcely join with the hypocritical sensualist at a lord mayor's feast, who declaims against the pleasures of the table. Solomon[3] kept a thousand concubines, and owned in despair that all was vanity. The man whose happiness is constituted by the society of one amiable woman, would find some difficulty in sympathizing with the disappointment of this venerable debauchee.

I address myself not only to the young enthusiast: the ardent devotee of truth and virtue; the pure and passionate moralist, yet unvitiated[4] by the contagion of the world. He will embrace a pure system, from its abstract truth, its beauty, its simplicity, and its promise of wide-extended benefit; unless custom has turned poison into food, he will hate the brutal pleasures of the chase by instinct; it will be a contemplation full of horror and disappointment to his mind, that beings capable of the gentlest and most admirable sympathies, should take delight in the death-pangs and last convulsions of dying animals. The elderly man, whose youth has been poisoned by intemperance, or who has lived with apparent moderation, and is afflicted with a variety of painful maladies, would find his account in a beneficial change produced without the risk of poisonous medicines. The mother, to whom the perpetual restlessness of disease, and unaccountable deaths incident to her children, are the causes of incurable unhappiness, would on this diet experience the satisfaction of beholding their perpetual healths and natural playfulness.

The most valuable lives are daily destroyed by diseases, that it is dangerous to palliate and impossible to cure by medicine. How much longer will man continue to pimp for the gluttony of death, his most insidious, implacable, and eternal foe? The proselyte to a simple and natural diet who desires health, must from the moment of his conversion attend to these rules—

NEVER TAKE ANY SUBSTANCE INTO THE STOMACH THAT ONCE HAD LIFE.
DRINK NO LIQUID BUT WATER RESTORED TO ITS ORIGINAL PURITY BY DISTILLATION.

from "An Act to Prevent the Cruel and Improper Treatment of Cattle" (1822)

This law was the first animal protection law passed by a national legislature. Largely the work of Member of Parliament Richard "Humanity Dick" Martin, the Act was the result of many years of effort on the part of Martin and others. It was significant not least of all for treating the offences it named as being against the animals themselves, not against their owners; the implication of the Act was that non-

---

[1] *realizes the hell ... beldams feign* From Shelley's *Queen Mab* (1813), 2.309, a philosophical poem in nine cantos.

[2] *epicurism* Devotion or adaptation to luxurious tastes, especially in drinking and eating.

[3] *Solomon* In the Bible, a king of Israel and son of David.

[4] *unvitiated* Uncorrupted.

human animals could have legal status other than as property. The bill was followed in 1835 and 1849 by other laws relating to the cruel and improper treatment of animals; provisions of those laws included the extension of legal protection to other animals, including bulls and dogs (though not to wild animals).

Whereas it is expedient to prevent the cruel and improper Treatment of Horses, Mares, Geldings, Mules, Asses, Cows, Heifers, Steers, Oxen, Sheep, and other Cattle: May it therefore please Your Majesty, by and with the Advice and Consent of the Lords Spiritual and Temporal, and Commons, in this present Parliament assembled, and by the Authority of the same, That if any person or persons shall wantonly and cruelly beat, abuse, or ill-treat any Horse, Mare, Gelding, Mule, Ass, Ox, Cow, Heifer, Steer, Sheep, or other Cattle, and Complaint on Oath thereof be made to any Justice of the Peace or other Magistrate within whose Jurisdiction such Offence shall be committed, it shall be lawful for such Justice of the Peace or other Magistrate to issue his Summons or Warrant, at his Discretion, to bring the party or parties so complained of before him, or any other Justice of the Peace or other Magistrate of the County, City, or place within which such Justice of the Peace or other Magistrate has Jurisdiction, who shall examine upon Oath any Witness or Witnesses who shall appear or be produced to give Information touching such Offence, (which Oath the said Justice of the Peace or other Magistrate is hereby authorized and required to administer); and if the party or parties accused shall be convicted of any such Offence, either by his, her, or their own Confession, or upon such Information as aforesaid, he, she, or they so convicted shall forfeit and pay any Sum not exceeding Five Pounds, not less than Ten Shillings, to His Majesty, His Heirs and Successors; and if the person or persons so convicted shall refuse or not be able forthwith to pay the Sum forfeited, every such Offender shall, by Warrant under the Hand and Seal of some Justice or Justices of the Peace or other Magistrate within whose Jurisdiction the person offending shall be Convicted, be committed to the House of Correction or some other Prison within the Jurisdiction within which the Offence shall have been committed, there to be kept without Bail or Mainprise[1] for any Time not exceeding Three Months.

---

[1] *Mainprise* Writ to a legal officer directing that security be held in order to ensure the appearance of a prisoner, who would then be released pending trial. Unlike bail, such securities might be other than monetary.

Samuel Taylor Coleridge
1772 – 1834

Samuel Taylor Coleridge is one of the most important figures of English Romanticism. Over the course of a few years, when in his mid-twenties, he composed poems that continue to be regarded as central to the English canon, among them "The Rime of the Ancient Mariner," "Frost at Midnight," and the fragment "Kubla Khan." He wrote few poems during the last thirty-five years of his life, as he was undermined by procrastination and an addiction to opium. Nonetheless, Coleridge's story is in the end one of success. His poetry has remained fresh and affecting for generations of readers, and his later philosophical writing earned him a place as one of the most profound thinkers of the nineteenth century.

Born in 1772, Coleridge was the youngest son of the vicar of Ottery St. Mary, the Rev. John Coleridge, and his wife, Anna Bowdon. He was a voracious reader with a mind that he described as "habituated to *the Vast.*" When his father died, his mother arranged for nine-year-old Samuel to be sent to Christ's Hospital in London, a school founded to educate the promising sons of the poor. Although he received an excellent education at Christ's, Coleridge remained ambivalent about the school long after he left, continuing to feel injured by the fact that he had been a "charity boy."

In 1791, Coleridge entered Jesus College, Cambridge, where his intellectual abilities and academic success were matched only by his facility in running up debts and his increasing despair at his financial situation. He eventually attempted to escape his financial problems by enlisting (under the name Silas Tomkyn Comberbache), but he was rescued by his brother George from both the army and financial distress. In 1794 he met Robert Southey, then an Oxford undergraduate, and the two recognized a shared interest in poetry and radical political ideas. They hatched a plan to found a communitarian settlement in Pennsylvania to be run under a system they called "Pantisocracy." Both the plan and the friendship, however, foundered over the question of what role women and servants should play (Coleridge insisted on a completely egalitarian community; Southey did not). In his early exuberance for the scheme Coleridge became engaged to Sara Fricker, the sister of Southey's fiancée, and he felt bound to honor the commitment even though his feeling for her quickly waned. They married in 1795 but after a brief period of happiness they became progressively more miserable, finally separating in 1807. The marriage produced four children.

Coleridge began a short-lived liberal periodical in 1796 called *The Watchman*. He also published his first poetic collection, *Poems on Various Subjects*, which contained the poem that would later be titled "The Eolian Harp." Almost destitute, he was saved by a yearly pension granted him by Tom and Josiah Wedgwood, sons of the famous potter. The following year he met William Wordsworth and began a troubled but lifelong friendship, the first fruit of which was the joint volume *Lyrical Ballads*, which opened with Coleridge's "The Rime of the Ancyent Marinere" (revised and retitled in 1816). Shortly afterward he accompanied Wordsworth and his sister Dorothy to Germany, where he immersed himself in German philosophy.

Returning to England in 1799, Coleridge joined Wordsworth in the Lake District. Here he met Sara Hutchinson, Wordsworth's future sister-in-law, and became infatuated with her. The relationship between the two remained platonic, but it magnified Coleridge's estrangement from his wife, and the situation was made worse by his increasing dependence on laudanum, the liquid form of opium. From 1802 onward Coleridge spent only brief periods with his family. In 1804 he set off for Malta, where he took a post in the British government. From this time forth he became progressively more conservative, eventually going so far as to deny entirely his early liberal leanings. After a year and a half he returned to England penniless.

From 1808 to 1818, Coleridge intermittently delivered lectures with topics that ranged from German philosophy to current educational controversies. The highlight was a series he gave on Shakespeare and Milton, which displayed all the brilliance of his critical skills. Although frequently sidetracked onto other topics, he also offered incisive analyses of aspects of Shakespeare's plays, from a consideration of love in *Romeo and Juliet* to an anatomization of Hamlet's paradoxical psychology. He ended the series with a masterful examination of *Paradise Lost*.

Coleridge's great talent as a poet lay in his ability to combine Gothicism with complex psychological presentation and to delineate the mind as it explored itself and its relation to the larger world. His more uncanny poems, such as "The Rime of the Ancient Mariner," are haunting both because they excite tension in the reader and because the psychological complexity of the characters and relationships brings to life what might otherwise be clichéd sensationalism. Poems such as "Frost at Midnight" mingle contemplation and description to produce a richly interrelated whole, a style that influenced not only Wordsworth (specifically in "Tintern Abbey"), but poets to the present day.

From the first Coleridge was interested in newspaper writing, in which he could comment on immediate social and cultural issues. The most important of his journalistic ventures was *The Friend* (1809–10), a weekly newspaper he largely wrote himself. In 1813 his drama, *Remorse*, was staged at the Drury Lane Theatre. Three years later he took up residence in Highgate with the family of the young doctor James Gillman. He asked to stay for a month; he remained for the rest of his life. The situation offered a stable environment, and Coleridge began publishing regularly. His Gothic ballad, "Christabel," long known to other writers through private recitation (and an influence on Walter Scott's "The Lay of the Last Minstrel" and Lord Byron's "The Siege of Corinth"), was published in a collection with "Kubla Khan" and "The Pains of Sleep" in 1816, through Byron's enthusiastic support. Soon afterward Coleridge published *Sybilline Leaves*, a collection of his previous poems (including a newly revised *Ancient Mariner* with a marginal gloss) and the long work *Biographia Literaria*.

Although at times rambling and discursive, *Biographia Literaria* is a major literary and philosophical work. Its first volume is autobiographical, detailing (among other events) Coleridge's education and his first involvement with Wordsworth. The volume also begins to delve into literary analysis as, for example, in the famous passage in Chapter 13, in which Coleridge differentiates between imagination and fancy, defining the qualities of each and declaring imagination superior. The second volume consists almost entirely of literary criticism, both formal and philosophical, much of it focusing on Wordsworth's poetry. In both volumes, Coleridge anatomizes both poetry and poetic production, considering not only formal elements but also the psychology of the creative process.

Coleridge's genius and importance were gradually acknowledged by a considerable number of his contemporaries, and the "Sage of Highgate" began to be viewed as an important thinker. This opinion was cemented by the publication of *Aids to Reflection* (1825), which stressed the role of the personal in Christian faith, and *On the Constitution of Church and State* (1830), which emphasized the importance of national culture and defined the class of intellectuals needed to protect it. This latter book in particular had a profound influence on such authors as Matthew Arnold and Thomas Carlyle.

From 1832 onward Coleridge became increasingly ill, although this did not prevent him from helping to prepare *Poetical Works* (1834), a collection of his poetry—he died shortly after its publication. *Table Talk*, a posthumously published collection of his remarks on miscellaneous topics, appeared the following year.

⌘ ⌘ ⌘

The Eolian Harp[1]
Composed at Clevedon, Somersetshire

My pensive Sara![2] thy soft cheek reclined
Thus on mine arm, most soothing sweet it is
To sit beside our Cot,° our Cot o'ergrown   cottage
With white-flower'd Jasmin, and the broad-leav'd Myrtle,
5 (Meet emblems they of Innocence and Love!)
And watch the clouds, that late were rich with light,
Slow saddening round, and mark the star of eve
Serenely brilliant (such should Wisdom be)
Shine opposite! How exquisite the scents
10 Snatch'd from yon bean-field! and the world *so* hush'd!
The stilly murmur of the distant Sea
Tells us of silence.

　　　　And that simplest Lute,
Placed length-ways in the clasping casement, hark!
How by the desultory breeze caress'd,
15 Like some coy maid half yielding to her lover,
It pours such sweet upbraiding, as must needs
Tempt to repeat the wrong! And now, its strings
Boldlier swept, the long sequacious° notes   unvarying
Over delicious surges sink and rise,
20 Such a soft floating witchery of sound
As twilight Elfins make, when they at eve
Voyage on gentle gales from Fairy-Land,
Where Melodies round honey-dropping flowers,
Footless and wild, like birds of Paradise,[3]

25 Nor pause, nor perch, hovering on untam'd wing!
O! the one Life within us and abroad,
Which meets all motion and becomes its soul,
A light in sound, a sound-like power in light,
Rhythm in all thought, and joyance every where—
30 Methinks, it should have been impossible
Not to love all things in a world so fill'd;
Where the breeze warbles, and the mute still air
Is Music slumbering on her instrument.

　　　　And thus, my Love! as on the midway slope
35 Of yonder hill I stretch my limbs at noon,
Whilst through my half-clos'd eye-lids I behold
The sunbeams dance, like diamonds, on the main,
And tranquil muse upon tranquillity;
Full many a thought uncall'd and undetain'd,
40 And many idle flitting phantasies,
Traverse my indolent and passive brain,
As wild and various, as the random gales
That swell and flutter on this subject Lute!
　　　　And what if all of animated nature
45 Be but organic Harps diversely fram'd,
That tremble into thought, as o'er them sweeps
Plastic and vast, one intellectual breeze,
At once the Soul of each, and God of all?
　　　　But thy more serious eye a mild reproof
50 Darts, O beloved Woman! nor such thoughts
Dim and unhallow'd dost thou not reject,
And biddest me walk humbly with my God.
Meek Daughter in the family of Christ!
Well hast thou said and holily disprais'd
55 These shapings of the unregenerate mind;
Bubbles that glitter as they rise and break

[1] *Eolian Harp* Musical instrument named after Æolus, Greek god of the winds; the music of the harp is created by exposure to the wind passing through it.

[2] *Sara* Sara Fricker, whom Coleridge married in 1795.

[3] *birds of Paradise* New Guinean birds of brilliant plumage, thought by Europeans to have no feet.

On vain Philosophy's aye-babbling spring.
For never guiltless may I speak of Him,
The Incomprehensible! save when with awe
60   I praise Him, and with Faith that inly *feels*;
Who with His saving mercies healed me,
A sinful and most miserable man,
Wilder'd and dark, and gave me to possess
Peace, and this Cot, and thee, heart-honour'd Maid!
—1795

Fears in Solitude

Written in April 1798, During the Alarm
of an Invasion[1]

A green and silent spot, amid the hills,
      A small and silent dell! O'er stiller place
No singing sky-lark ever poised himself.
The hills are heathy, save that swelling slope,
5   Which hath a gay and gorgeous covering on,
All golden with the never-bloomless furze,°   *evergreen shrub*
Which now blooms most profusely: but the dell,
Bathed by the mist, is fresh and delicate
As vernal corn-field, or the unripe flax,
10   When, through its half-transparent stalks, at eve,
The level sunshine glimmers with green light.
O! 'tis a quiet spirit-healing nook!
Which all, methinks, would love; but chiefly he,
The humble man, who, in his youthful years,
15   Knew just so much of folly, as had made
His early manhood more securely wise!
Here he might lie on fern or withered heath,
While from the singing lark (that sings unseen
The minstrelsy that solitude loves best),
20   And from the sun, and from the breezy air,
Sweet influences trembled o'er his frame;
And he, with many feelings, many thoughts,
Made up a meditative joy, and found
Religious meanings in the forms of Nature!

25   And so, his senses gradually wrapt
In a half sleep, he dreams of better worlds,
And dreaming hears thee still, O singing lark,
That singest like an angel in the clouds!

      My God! it is a melancholy thing
30   For such a man, who would full fain preserve
His soul in calmness, yet perforce must feel
For all his human brethren—O my God!
It weighs upon the heart, that he must think
What uproar and what strife may now be stirring
35   This way or that way o'er these silent hills—
Invasion, and the thunder and the shout,
And all the crash of onset; fear and rage,
And undetermined conflict—even now,
Even now, perchance, and in his native isle:
40   Carnage and screams beneath this blessed sun!
We have offended, O! my countrymen!
We have offended very grievously,
And have been tyrannous. From east to west
A groan of accusation pierces Heaven!
45   The wretched plead against us; multitudes
Countless and vehement, the sons of God,
Our brethren! like a cloud that travels on,
Steamed up from Cairo's swamps of pestilence,
Even so, my countrymen! have we gone forth
50   And borne to distant tribes slavery and pangs,
And, deadlier far, our vices, whose deep taint
With slow perdition murders the whole man,
His body and his soul! Meanwhile, at home,
All individual dignity and power
55   Engulfed in Courts, Committees, Institutions,
Associations and Societies,
A vain, speech-mounting, speech-reporting Guild,
One Benefit-Club for mutual flattery,
We have drunk up, demure as at a grace,
60   Pollutions from the brimming cup of wealth;
Contemptuous of all honourable rule,
Yet bartering freedom and the poor man's life
For gold, as at a market! The sweet words

---

[1]   *Invasion*   By the French, who threatened an attack on Wales.

Of Christian promise, words that even yet
65 Might stem destruction, were they wisely preached,
Are muttered o'er by men, whose tones proclaim
How flat and wearisome they feel their trade:
Rank scoffers some, but most too indolent
To deem them falsehoods, or to know their truth.
70 O! blasphemous! the Book of Life is made
A superstitious instrument, on which
We gabble o'er the oaths we mean to break,
For all must swear[1]—all and in every place,
College and wharf, council and justice-court;
75 All, all must swear, the briber and the bribed,
Merchant and lawyer, senator and priest,
The rich, the poor, the old man and the young;
All, all make up one scheme of perjury,
That faith doth reel; the very name of God
80 Sounds like a juggler's charm; and bold with joy,
Forth from his dark and lonely hiding-place,
(Portentous sight!) the owlet Atheism,
Sailing on obscene wings athwart the noon,
Drops his blue-fringéd lids, and holds them close,
85 And hooting at the glorious sun in Heaven,
Cries out, "Where is it?"

                Thankless too for peace,
(Peace long preserved by fleets and perilous seas)
Secure from actual warfare, we have loved
To swell the war-whoop, passionate for war!
90 Alas! for ages ignorant of all
Its ghastlier workings, (famine or blue plague,
Battle, or siege, or flight thro' wintry snows,)
We, this whole people, have been clamorous
For war and bloodshed; animating sports,
95 The which we pay for as a thing to talk of,
Spectators and not combatants! No guess
Anticipative of a wrong unfelt,
No speculation on contingency,
However dim and vague, too vague and dim
100 To yield a justifying cause; and forth,

(Stuffed out with big preamble, holy names,
And adjurations° of the God in Heaven,)   *appeal*
We send our mandates for the certain death
Of thousands and ten thousands! Boys and girls,
105 And women, that would groan to see a child
Pull off an insect's leg, all read of war,
The best amusement for our morning meal!
The poor wretch, who has learnt his only prayers
From curses, who knows scarcely words enough
110 To ask a blessing from his Heavenly Father,
Becomes a fluent phraseman, absolute
And technical in victories and defeats,
And all our dainty terms for fratricide;
Terms which we trundle smoothly o'er our tongues
115 Like mere abstractions, empty sounds to which
We join no feeling and attach no form!
As if the soldier died without a wound;
As if the fibres of this godlike frame
Were gored without a pang; as if the wretch,
120 Who fell in battle, doing bloody deeds,
Passed off to Heaven, translated and not killed;
As though he had no wife to pine for him,
No God to judge him! Therefore, evil days
Are coming on us, O my countrymen!
125 And what if all-avenging Providence,
Strong and retributive, should make us know
The meaning of our words, force us to feel
The desolation and the agony
Of our fierce doings?

                Spare us yet awhile,
130 Father and God! O! spare us yet awhile!
Oh! let not English women drag their flight
Fainting beneath the burthen of their babes,
Of the sweet infants, that but yesterday
Laughed at the breast! Sons, brothers, husbands, all
135 Who ever gazed with fondness on the forms
Which grew up with you round the same fire-side,
And all who ever heard the sabbath-bells
Without the infidel's scorn, make yourselves pure!
Stand forth! be men! repel an impious foe,
140 Impious and false, a light yet cruel race,
Who laugh away all virtue, mingling mirth
With deeds of murder; and still promising
Freedom, themselves too sensual to be free,

---

1 *all must swear* According to the Test and Corporation Acts, all
public officials were required to swear allegiance to the Church of
England. (Thus there would be no Catholics, Nonconformists, or
Jews in office.)

Poison life's amities, and cheat the heart
145 Of faith and quiet hope, and all that soothes,
And all that lifts the spirit! Stand we forth;
Render them back upon the insulted ocean,
And let them toss as idly on its waves
As the vile sea-weed, which some mountain-blast
150 Swept from our shores! And oh! may we return
Not with a drunken triumph, but with fear,
Repenting of the wrongs with which we stung
So fierce a foe to frenzy!

                 I have told,
O Britons! O my brethren! I have told
155 Most bitter truth, but without bitterness.
Nor deem my zeal or factious or mistimed;
For never can true courage dwell with them,
Who, playing tricks with conscience, dare not look
At their own vices. We have been too long
160 Dupes of a deep delusion! Some, belike,
Groaning with restless enmity, expect
All change from change of constituted power;
As if a Government had been a robe,
On which our vice and wretchedness were tagged
165 Like fancy-points and fringes, with the robe
Pulled off at pleasure. Fondly these attach
A radical causation to a few
Poor drudges of chastising Providence,
Who borrow all their hues and qualities
170 From our own folly and rank wickedness,
Which gave them birth and nursed them. Others,
    meanwhile,
Dote with a mad idolatry; and all
Who will not fall before their images,
And yield them worship, they are enemies
175 Even of their country!

            Such have I been deemed.—
But, O dear Britain! O my Mother Isle!
Needs must thou prove a name most dear and holy
To me, a son, a brother, and a friend,
A husband, and a father! who revere
180 All bonds of natural love, and find them all
Within the limits of thy rocky shores.
O native Britain! O my Mother Isle!
How shouldst thou prove aught else but dear and holy

To me, who from thy lakes and mountain-hills,
185 Thy clouds, thy quiet dales, thy rocks and seas,
Have drunk in all my intellectual life,
All sweet sensations, all ennobling thoughts,
All adoration of the God in nature,
All lovely and all honourable things,
190 Whatever makes this mortal spirit feel
The joy and greatness of its future being?
There lives nor form nor feeling in my soul
Unborrowed from my country! O divine
And beauteous island! thou hast been my sole
195 And most magnificent temple, in the which
I walk with awe, and sing my stately songs,
Loving the God that made me!—

                      May my fears,
My filial fears, be vain! and may the vaunts
And menace of the vengeful enemy
200 Pass like the gust, that roared and died away
In the distant tree: which heard, and only heard
In this low dell, bowed not the delicate grass.

    But now the gentle dew-fall sends abroad
The fruit-like perfume of the golden furze:
205 The light has left the summit of the hill,
Though still a sunny gleam lies beautiful,
Aslant the ivied beacon. Now farewell,
Farewell, awhile, O soft and silent spot!
On the green sheep-track, up the heathy hill,
210 Homeward I wind my way; and lo! recalled
From bodings that have well-nigh wearied me,
I find myself upon the brow, and pause
Startled! And after lonely sojourning
In such a quiet and surrounded nook,
215 This burst of prospect, here the shadowy main,
Dim tinted, there the mighty majesty
Of that huge amphitheatre of rich
And elmy fields, seems like society—
Conversing with the mind, and giving it
220 A livelier impulse and a dance of thought!
And now, belovéd Stowey![1] I behold
Thy church-tower, and, methinks, the four huge elms
Clustering, which mark the mansion of my friend;

---

[1] *Stowey* Nether Stowey, a village in Somerset where Coleridge
lived for a few years.

And close behind them, hidden from my view,
225 Is my own lowly cottage, where my babe
And my babe's mother dwell in peace! With light
And quickened footsteps thitherward I tend,
Remembering thee, O green and silent dell!
And grateful, that by nature's quietness
230 And solitary musings, all my heart
Is softened, and made worthy to indulge
Love, and the thoughts that yearn for human kind.
—1798

Frost at Midnight

The Frost performs its secret ministry,
Unhelped by any wind. The owlet's cry
Came loud—and hark, again! loud as before.
The inmates of my cottage, all at rest,
5 Have left me to that solitude, which suits
Abstruser musings: save that at my side
My cradled infant slumbers peacefully.
'Tis calm indeed! so calm, that it disturbs
And vexes meditation with its strange
10 And extreme silentness. Sea, hill, and wood,
This populous village! Sea, and hill, and wood,
With all the numberless goings-on of life,
Inaudible as dreams! the thin blue flame
Lies on my low-burnt fire, and quivers not;
15 Only that film,[1] which fluttered on the grate,
Still flutters there, the sole unquiet thing.
Methinks, its motion in this hush of nature
Gives it dim sympathies with me who live,
Making it a companionable form,
20 Whose puny flaps and freaks the idling Spirit
By its own moods interprets, every where
Echo or mirror seeking of itself,
And makes a toy of Thought.

                           But O! how oft,
How oft, at school, with most believing mind,
25 Presageful, have I gazed upon the bars,
To watch that fluttering *stranger*! and as oft

With unclosed lids, already had I dreamt
Of my sweet birth-place, and the old church-tower,
Whose bells, the poor man's only music, rang
30 From morn to evening, all the hot Fair-day,
So sweetly, that they stirred and haunted me
With a wild pleasure, falling on mine ear
Most like articulate sounds of things to come!
So gazed I, till the soothing things, I dreamt,
35 Lulled me to sleep, and sleep prolonged my dreams!
And so I brooded all the following morn,
Awed by the stern preceptor's° face, mine eye   *teacher's*
Fixed with mock study on my swimming book:
Save if the door half opened, and I snatched
40 A hasty glance, and still my heart leaped up,
For still I hoped to see the *stranger's* face,
Townsman, or aunt, or sister more beloved,
My play-mate when we both were clothed alike!

            Dear Babe, that sleepest cradled by my side,
45 Whose gentle breathings, heard in this deep calm,
Fill up the interspersed vacancies
And momentary pauses of the thought!
My babe so beautiful! it thrills my heart
With tender gladness, thus to look at thee,
50 And think that thou shalt learn far other lore,
And in far other scenes! For I was reared
In the great city, pent 'mid cloisters dim,
And saw nought lovely but the sky and stars.
But *thou*, my babe! shalt wander like a breeze
55 By lakes and sandy shores, beneath the crags
Of ancient mountain, and beneath the clouds,
Which image in their bulk both lakes and shores
And mountain crags: so shalt thou see and hear
The lovely shapes and sounds intelligible
60 Of that eternal language, which thy God
Utters, who from eternity doth teach
Himself in all, and all things in himself.
Great universal Teacher! he shall mould
Thy spirit, and by giving make it ask.

            Therefore all seasons shall be sweet to thee,
65 Whether the summer clothe the general earth
With greenness, or the redbreast sit and sing

---

1 [Coleridge's note] In all parts of the kingdom these films are called *strangers* and supposed to portend the arrival of some absent friend.

Betwixt the tufts of snow on the bare branch
Of mossy apple-tree, while the nigh thatch
70 Smokes in the sun-thaw; whether the eave-drops fall
Heard only in the trances of the blast,
Or if the secret ministry of frost
Shall hang them up in silent icicles,
Quietly shining to the quiet Moon.
—1798

The Rime of the Ancient Mariner
In Seven Parts[1]

*Facile credo, plures esse Naturas invisibiles quam visibiles in rerum
universitate. Sed horum omnium familiam quis nobis enarrabit?
et gradus et cognationes et discrimina et singulorum munera? Quid
agunt? quæ loca habitant? Harum rerum notitiam semper ambivit
ingenium humanum, nunquam attigit. Juvat, interea, non
diffiteor, quandoque in animo, tanquam in Tabulâ, majoris et
melioris mundi imaginem contemplari: ne mens assuefacta
hodiernæ vitæ minutiis se contrahat nimis, & tota subsidat in
pusillas cogitationes. Sed veritati interea invigilandum est,
modusque servandus, ut certa ab incertis, diem a nocte,
distinguamus.—T. Burnet. Archaeol. Phil. p. 68.*[2]

PART I

It is an ancient Mariner,
  And he stoppeth one of three.
"By thy long grey beard and glittering eye,
Now wherefore stopp'st thou me?

*An ancient Mariner
meeteth three
Gallants bidden to a
wedding-feast, and
detaineth one.*

5   The Bridegroom's doors are opened wide,
And I am next of kin;
The guests are met, the feast is set:
May'st hear the merry din."

He holds him with his skinny hand,
10 "There was a ship," quoth he.
"Hold off! unhand me, grey-beard loon!"
Eftsoons[3] his hand dropt he.

He holds him with his glittering eye—
The Wedding-Guest stood still,
15 And listens like a three years' child:
The Mariner hath his will.

*The wedding-guest is
spellbound by the eye
of the old sea-faring
man, and constrained
to hear his tale.*

The Wedding-Guest sat on a stone:
He cannot choose but hear;
And thus spake on that ancient man,
20 The bright-eyed Mariner.

"The ship was cheered, the harbour cleared,
Merrily did we drop
Below the kirk,[4] below the hill,
Below the lighthouse top.

25 The Sun came up upon the left,
Out of the sea came he!
And he shone bright, and on the right
Went down into the sea.

*The Mariner tells how
the ship sailed southward
with a good wind and fair
weather, till it reached
the line.*

Higher and higher every day,
30 Till over the mast at noon—"
The Wedding-Guest here beat his breast,
For he heard the loud bassoon.

The bride hath paced into the hall
Red as a rose is she;
35 Nodding their heads before her goes
The merry minstrelsy.

*The wedding-guest
heareth the bridal
music; but the
mariner continueth
his tale.*

The Wedding-Guest he beat his breast,
Yet he cannot choose but hear;

---

1 *The Rime … Parts* This version of the poem was published in 1817.

2 *Facile … distinguamus* From Thomas Burnet's *Archaeologiae
Philosophicae* (1692), translated by Mead and Foxton (1736): "I can
easily believe, that there are more invisible than visible beings in the
universe. But who will declare to us the family of all these, and
acquaint us with the agreements, differences, and peculiar talents
which are to be found among them? It is true, human wit has always
desired a knowledge of these things, though it has never yet attained
it. I will own that it is very profitable, sometimes to contemplate in
the mind, as in a draught, the image of the greater and better world,
lest the soul being accustomed to the trifles of this present life,
should contract itself too much, and altogether rest in mean
cogitations, but, in the meantime, we must take care to keep to the
truth, and observe moderation, that we may distinguish certain from
uncertain things, and day from night."

3 *Eftsoons* At once.

4 *kirk* Church.

And thus spake on that ancient man,
40 The bright-eyed Mariner.

"And now the STORM-BLAST came, and he
Was tyrannous and strong:
He struck with his o'ertaking wings,
And chased us south along.

The ship drawn by a storm toward the south pole.

45 With sloping masts and dipping prow,
As who pursued with yell and blow
Still treads the shadow of his foe,
And forward bends his head,
The ship drove fast, loud roared the blast,
50 And southward aye we fled.

And now there came both mist and snow,
And it grew wondrous cold:
And ice, mast-high, came floating by,
As green as emerald.

55 And through the drifts the snowy clifts
Did send a dismal sheen:
Nor shapes of men nor beasts we ken[1]—
The ice was all between.

The land of ice, and of fearful sounds, where no living thing was to be seen.

The ice was here, the ice was there,
60 The ice was all around:
It cracked and growled, and roared and howled,
Like noises in a swound![2]

At length did cross an Albatross,
Thorough the fog it came;
65 As if it had been a Christian soul,
We hailed it in God's name.

Till a great sea-bird, called the Albatross, came through the snow-fog, and was received with great joy and hospitality.

It ate the food it ne'er had eat,
And round and round it flew.
The ice did split with a thunder-fit;
70 The helmsman steered us through!

And a good south wind sprung up behind;
The Albatross did follow,

And every day, for food or play,
Came to the Mariner's hollo!

75 In mist or cloud, on mast or shroud,
It perched for vespers nine;[3]
Whiles all the night, through fog-smoke white,
Glimmered the white Moon-shine."

And lo! the Albatross proveth a bird of good omen, and followeth the ship as it returned northward, through fog and floating ice.

"God save thee, ancient Mariner!
80 From the fiends, that plague thee thus!—
Why look'st thou so?"—With my cross-bow
I shot the ALBATROSS.

The ancient Mariner inhospitably killed the pious bird of good omen.

PART 2

The Sun now rose upon the right:
Out of the sea came he,
85 Still hid in mist, and on the left
Went down into the sea.

And the good south wind still blew behind,
But no sweet bird did follow,
Nor any day for food or play
90 Came to the mariners' hollo!

And I had done a hellish thing,
And it would work 'em woe:
For all averred, I had killed the bird
That made the breeze to blow.
95 Ah wretch! said they, the bird to slay,
That made the breeze to blow!

His ship mates cry out against the ancient Mariner, for killing the bird of good luck.

Nor dim nor red, like God's own head,
The glorious Sun uprist:
Then all averred, I had killed the bird
100 That brought the fog and mist.
'Twas right, said they, such birds to slay,
That bring the fog and mist.

But when the fog cleared off, they justify the same—and thus make themselves accomplices in the crime.

The fair breeze blew, the white foam flew,
The furrow followed free;
105 We were the first that ever burst
Into that silent sea.

The fair breeze continues;

---

[1] *ken* Recognize.

[2] *swound* Swoon.

[3] *vespers nine* I.e., nine evenings. Vespers are evening prayers.

Down dropt the breeze, the sails dropt down,
'Twas sad as sad could be;
And we did speak only to break
110   The silence of the sea!

All in a hot and copper sky,
The bloody Sun, at noon,
Right up above the mast did stand,
No bigger than the Moon.

115   Day after day, day after day,
We stuck, nor breath nor motion;
As idle as a painted ship
Upon a painted ocean.

Water, water, every where,
120   And all the boards did shrink;
Water, water, every where,
Nor any drop to drink.

The very deep did rot: O Christ!
That ever this should be!
125   Yea, slimy things did crawl with legs
Upon the slimy sea.

About, about, in reel and rout
The death-fires[1] danced at night;
The water, like a witch's oils,
130   Burnt green, and blue and white.

And some in dreams assuréd were
Of the Spirit that plagued us so;
Nine fathom deep he had followed us
From the land of mist and snow.

135   And every tongue, through utter drought,
Was withered at the root;
We could not speak, no more than if
We had been choked with soot.

Ah! well a-day! what evil looks
140   Had I from old and young!
Instead of the cross, the Albatross
About my neck was hung.

The ship enters the Pacific Ocean and sails northward, even till it reaches the Line.

The ship hath been suddenly becalmed.

And the Albatross begins to be avenged.

A spirit has followed them; one of the invisible inhabitants of this planet, neither departed souls nor angels; concerning whom the learned Jew, Josephus, and the Platonic Constantinopolitan, Michael Psellus, may be consulted, and there is no climate or element without one or more.

The shipmates in their sore distress, would fain throw the whole guilt on the ancient Mariner: in sign whereof they hang the dead sea-bird round his neck.

---

[1]   *death-fires* Possibly luminescent plankton.

PART 3

There passed a weary time. Each throat
Was parched, and glazed each eye.
A weary time! a weary time!
How glazed each weary eye,
When looking westward, I beheld
A something in the sky.

At first it seemed a little speck,
150   And then it seemed a mist;
It moved and moved, and took at last
A certain shape, I wist.

A speck, a mist, a shape, I wist!
And still it neared and neared:
155   And as if it dodged a water-sprite,
It plunged and tacked and veered.

With throat unslacked, with black lips baked,
We could nor laugh nor wail;
Through utter drought all dumb we stood!
160   I bit my arm, I sucked the blood,
And cried, A sail! a sail!

With throat unslacked, with black lips baked,
Agape they heard me call:
Gramercy![2] they for joy did grin,
165   And all at once their breath drew in,
As they were drinking all.

See! see! (I cried) she tacks no more!
Hither to work us weal;[3]
Without a breeze, without a tide,
170   She steadies with upright keel!

The western wave was all a-flame.
The day was well nigh done!
Almost upon the western wave
Rested the broad bright Sun;
175   When that strange shape drove suddenly
Betwixt us and the Sun.

The ancient Mariner beholdeth a sign in the element afar off.

At its nearer approach, it seemeth him to be a ship; and at a dear ransom he freeth his speech from the bonds of thirst.

A flash of joy.

And horror follows. For can it be a ship that comes onward without wind or tide?

---

[2]   *Gramercy* Grant mercy, i.e., may God reward you in His mercy.
[3]   *work us weal* Benefit us.

And straight the Sun was flecked with bars,
(Heaven's Mother send us grace!)
As if through a dungeon-grate he peered
180 With broad and burning face.

It seemeth him but the skeleton of a ship.

Alas! (thought I, and my heart beat loud)
How fast she nears and nears!
Are those *her* sails that glance in the Sun,
Like restless gossameres?

And its ribs are seen as bars on the face of the setting Sun. The spectre-woman and her death-mate, and no other on board the skeleton-ship.

185 Are those *her* ribs through which the Sun
Did peer, as through a grate?
And is that Woman all her crew?
Is that a DEATH? and are there two?
Is DEATH that woman's mate?

Her lips were red, *her* looks were free,
190 Her locks were yellow as gold:
Her skin was as white as leprosy,
The Night-mare LIFE-IN-DEATH was she,
Who thicks man's blood with cold.

Like vessel, like crew! Death and Life-in-Death have diced for the ship's crew, and she (the latter) winneth the ancient Mariner.

195 The naked hulk alongside came,
And the twain were casting dice;
"The game is done! I've won! I've won!"
Quoth she, and whistles thrice.

The Sun's rim dips; the stars rush out:
200 At one stride comes the dark;
With far-heard whisper, o'er the sea,
Off shot the spectre-bark.

No twilight within the courts of the sun.

We listened and looked sideways up!
Fear at my heart, as at a cup,
205 My life-blood seemed to sip!
The stars were dim, and thick the night,
The steersman's face by his lamp gleamed white;
From the sails the dews did drip—
Till clomb above the eastern bar
210 The hornéd Moon, with one bright star
Within the nether tip.

At the rising of the Moon,

One after one, by the star-dogged Moon
Too quick for groan or sigh,
Each turned his face with a ghastly pang,
215 And cursed me with his eye.

One after another,

Four times fifty living men,
(And I heard nor sigh nor groan)
With heavy thump, a lifeless lump,
They dropped down one by one.

His ship-mates drop down dead.

220 The souls did from their bodies fly,—
They fled to bliss or woe!
And every soul, it passed me by,
Like the whiz of my cross-bow!

But Life-in-Death begins her work on the ancient Mariner.

PART 4

"I fear thee, ancient Mariner!
225 I fear thy skinny hand!
And thou art long, and lank, and brown,
As is the ribbed sea-sand.¹

The wedding-guest feareth that a spirit is talking to him;

I fear thee and thy glittering eye,
And thy skinny hand, so brown."—
230 Fear not, fear not, thou Wedding-Guest!
This body dropt not down.

But the ancient Mariner assureth him of his bodily life, and proceedeth to relate his horrible penance.

Alone, alone, all, all alone,
Alone on a wide wide sea!
And never a saint took pity on
235 My soul in agony.

The many men, so beautiful!
And they all dead did lie:
And a thousand thousand slimy things
Lived on; and so did I.

He despiseth the creatures of the calm,

240 I looked upon the rotting sea,
And drew my eyes away;
I looked upon the rotting deck,
And there the dead men lay.

And envieth that they should live, and so many lie dead.

I looked to heaven, and tried to pray;
245 But or ever a prayer had gusht,
A wicked whisper came, and made
My heart as dry as dust.

¹ [Coleridge's note] For the two last lines of this stanza, I am indebted to Mr. WORDSWORTH. It was on a delightful walk from Nether Stowey to Dulverton, with him and his sister, in the Autumn of 1797, that this Poem was planned, and in part composed.

I closed my lids, and kept them close,
And the balls like pulses beat;
250 For the sky and the sea, and the sea and the sky
Lay like a load on my weary eye,
And the dead were at my feet.

The cold sweat melted from their limbs,
Nor rot nor reek did they:
255 The look with which they looked on me
Had never passed away.

*But the curse
liveth for him
in the eye of
the dead men.*

An orphan's curse would drag to hell
A spirit from on high;
But oh! more horrible than that
260 Is the curse in a dead man's eye!
Seven days, seven nights, I saw that curse,
And yet I could not die.

*In his loneliness
and fixedness, he
yearneth towards
the journeying Moon,
and the stars that still
sojourn, yet still move
onwards; and every
where the blue sky
belongs to them, and
is their appointed rest,
and their native country,
and their own natural
homes, which they enter
unannounced, as lords
that are certain ex-
pected, and yet there is
a silent joy at their
arrival.*

The moving Moon went up the sky,
And no where did abide:
265 Softly she was going up,
And a star or two beside—

Her beams bemocked the sultry main,
Like April hoar-frost spread;
But where the ship's huge shadow lay,
270 The charméd water burnt alway
A still and awful red.

Beyond the shadow of the ship,
I watched the water-snakes:
They moved in tracks of shining white,
275 And when they reared, the elfish light
Fell off in hoary flakes.

*By the light of the
Moon he beholdeth
God's creatures of
the great calm.*

Within the shadow of the ship
I watched their rich attire:
Blue, glossy green, and velvet black,
280 They coiled and swam; and every track
Was a flash of golden fire.

O happy living things! no tongue
Their beauty might declare:
A spring of love gushed from my heart,
285 And I blessed them unaware:

*Their beauty and
their happiness.*

*He blesseth them in
his heart.*

Sure my kind saint took pity on me,
And I blessed them unaware.

The selfsame moment I could pray;
And from my neck so free
290 The Albatross fell off, and sank
Like lead into the sea.

*The spell begins
to break.*

PART 5

Oh sleep! it is a gentle thing,
Beloved from pole to pole!
To Mary Queen the praise be given!
295 She sent the gentle sleep from Heaven,
That slid into my soul.

The silly[1] buckets on the deck,
That had so long remained,
I dreamt that they were filled with dew;
300 And when I awoke, it rained.

*By grace of the holy
Mother, the ancient
Mariner is refreshed
with rain.*

My lips were wet, my throat was cold,
My garments all were dank;
Sure I had drunken in my dreams,
And still my body drank.

305 I moved, and could not feel my limbs:
I was so light—almost
I thought that I had died in sleep,
And was a blesséd ghost.

And soon I heard a roaring wind:
310 It did not come anear;
But with its sound it shook the sails,
That were so thin and sere.

*He heareth sounds,
and seeth strange
sights and
commotions in
the sky and the
elements.*

The upper air burst into life!
And a hundred fire-flags sheen,
315 To and fro they were hurried about!
And to and fro, and in and out,
The wan stars danced between.

And the coming wind did roar more loud,
And the sails did sigh like sedge;

_____
[1] *silly*   Simple.

320 And the rain poured down from one black cloud;
The Moon was at its edge.

The thick black cloud was cleft, and still
The Moon was at its side:
Like waters shot from some high crag,
325 The lightning fell with never a jag,
A river steep and wide.

The loud wind never reached the ship,
Yet now the ship moved on!
Beneath the lightning and the Moon
330 The dead men gave a groan.

> The bodies of the ship's crew are inspirited, and the ship moves on;

They groaned, they stirred, they all uprose,
Nor spake, nor moved their eyes;
It had been strange, even in a dream,
To have seen those dead men rise.

335 The helmsman steered, the ship moved on;
Yet never a breeze up-blew;
The mariners all 'gan work the ropes,
Where they were wont to do;
They raised their limbs like lifeless tools—
340 We were a ghastly crew.

The body of my brother's son
Stood by me, knee to knee:
The body and I pulled at one rope,
But he said nought to me.

> But not by the souls of the men, nor by dæmons of earth or middle air, but by a blessed troop of angelic spirits, sent down by the invocation of the guardian saint.

345 "I fear thee, ancient Mariner!"
Be calm, thou Wedding-Guest!
'Twas not those souls that fled in pain,
Which to their corses[1] came again,
But a troop of spirits blest:

350 For when it dawned—they dropped their arms,
And clustered round the mast;
Sweet sounds rose slowly through their mouths,
And from their bodies passed.

Around, around, flew each sweet sound,
355 Then darted to the Sun;

Slowly the sounds came back again,
Now mixed, now one by one.

Sometimes a-dropping from the sky
I heard the sky-lark sing;
360 Sometimes all little birds that are,
How they seemed to fill the sea and air
With their sweet jargoning!

And now 'twas like all instruments,
Now like a lonely flute;
365 And now it is an angel's song,
That makes the heavens be mute.

It ceased; yet still the sails made on
A pleasant noise till noon,
A noise like of a hidden brook
370 In the leafy month of June,
That to the sleeping woods all night
Singeth a quiet tune.

Till noon we quietly sailed on,
Yet never a breeze did breathe:
375 Slowly and smoothly went the ship,
Moved onward from beneath.

Under the keel nine fathom deep,
From the land of mist and snow,
The spirit slid: and it was he
380 That made the ship to go.
The sails at noon left off their tune,
And the ship stood still also.

> The lonesome spirit from the south-pole carries on the ship as far as the line, in obedience to the angelic troop, but still requireth vengeance.

The Sun, right up above the mast,
Had fixed her to the ocean:
385 But in a minute she 'gan stir,
With a short uneasy motion—
Backwards and forwards half her length
With a short uneasy motion.

Then like a pawing horse let go,
390 She made a sudden bound:
It flung the blood into my head,
And I fell down in a swound.

---

[1] *corses* Corpses.

How long in that same fit I lay,
I have not to declare;
395 But ere my living life returned,
I heard and in my soul discerned
Two voices in the air.

"Is it he?" quoth one, "Is this the man?
By Him who died on cross,
400 With his cruel bow he laid full low
The harmless Albatross.

The spirit who bideth by himself
In the land of mist and snow,
He loved the bird that loved the man
405 Who shot him with his bow."

The other was a softer voice,
As soft as honey-dew:
Quoth he, "The man hath penance done,
And penance more will do."

PART 6

FIRST VOICE

410 "But tell me, tell me! speak again,
Thy soft response renewing—
What makes that ship drive on so fast?
What is the ocean doing?"

SECOND VOICE

"Still as a slave before his lord,
415 The ocean hath no blast;
His great bright eye most silently
Up to the Moon is cast—

If he may know which way to go;
For she guides him smooth or grim.
420 See, brother, see! how graciously
She looketh down on him."

FIRST VOICE

"But why drives on that ship so fast,
Without or wave or wind?"

The Polar Spirit's fellow-dæmons, the invisible inhabitants of the element, take part in his wrong; and two of them relate, one to the other, that penance long and heavy for the ancient Mariner hath been accorded to the Polar Spirit, who returned southward.

SECOND VOICE

"The air is cut away before,
425 And closes from behind.

Fly, brother, fly! more high, more high!
Or we shall be belated:
For slow and slow that ship will go,
When the Mariner's trance is abated."

430 I woke, and we were sailing on
As in a gentle weather:
'Twas night, calm night, the Moon was high;
The dead men stood together.

All stood together on the deck,
435 For a charnel-dungeon[1] fitter:
All fixed on me their stony eyes,
That in the Moon did glitter.

The pang, the curse, with which they died,
Had never passed away:
440 I could not draw my eyes from theirs,
Nor turn them up to pray.

And now this spell was snapt: once more
I viewed the ocean green,
And looked far forth, yet little saw
445 Of what had else been seen—

Like one, that on a lonesome road
Doth walk in fear and dread,
And having once turned round, walks on,
And turns no more his head;
450 Because he knows, a frightful fiend
Doth close behind him tread.

But soon there breathed a wind on me,
Nor sound nor motion made:
Its path was not upon the sea,
455 In ripple or in shade.

It raised my hair, it fanned my cheek
Like a meadow-gale of spring—

The Mariner hath been cast into a trance; for the angelic power causeth the vessel to drive northward, faster than human life could endure.

The supernatural motion is retarded; the Mariner awakes, and his penance begins anew.

The curse is finally expiated.

---

[1]   *charnel-dungeon* Mortuary; house of death.

It mingled strangely with my fears,
Yet it felt like a welcoming.

460 Swiftly, swiftly flew the ship,
Yet she sailed softly too:
Sweetly, sweetly blew the breeze—
On me alone it blew.

Oh! dream of joy! is this indeed

And the ancient
Mariner beholdeth
his native country.

465 The light-house top I see?
Is this the hill? is this the kirk?
Is this mine own countree?

We drifted o'er the harbour-bar,
And I with sobs did pray—
470 O let me be awake, my God!
Or let me sleep alway.

The harbour-bay was clear as glass,
So smoothly was it strewn!
And on the bay the moonlight lay,
475 And the shadow of the Moon.

The rock shone bright, the kirk no less,
That stands above the rock:
The moonlight steeped in silentness
The steady weathercock.

480 And the bay was white with silent light,

The angelic spirits
leave the dead
bodies,

Till rising from the same,
Full many shapes, that shadows were,
In crimson colours came.

A little distance from the prow

And appear in their
own forms of light.

485 Those crimson shadows were:
I turned my eyes upon the deck—
Oh, Christ! what saw I there!

Each corse lay flat, lifeless and flat,
And, by the holy rood!
490 A man all light, a seraph-man,[1]
On every corse there stood.

This seraph-band, each waved his hand:
It was a heavenly sight!
They stood as signals to the land,
495 Each one a lovely light;

This seraph-band, each waved his hand,
No voice did they impart—
No voice; but oh! the silence sank
Like music on my heart.

500 But soon I heard the dash of oars,
I heard the Pilot's cheer;
My head was turned perforce away
And I saw a boat appear.

The Pilot and the Pilot's boy,
505 I heard them coming fast:
Dear Lord in Heaven! it was a joy
The dead men could not blast.

I saw a third—I heard his voice:
It is the Hermit good!
510 He singeth loud his godly hymns
That he makes in the wood.
He'll shrieve[2] my soul, he'll wash away
The Albatross's blood.

PART 7

This Hermit good lives in that wood

The Hermit of
the Wood.

515 Which slopes down to the sea.
How loudly his sweet voice he rears!
He loves to talk with marineres
That come from a far countree.

He kneels at morn, and noon, and eve—
520 He hath a cushion plump:
It is the moss that wholly hides
The rotted old oak-stump.

The skiff-boat neared: I heard them talk,
"Why, this is strange, I trow![3]
525 Where are those light so many and fair,
That signal made but now?"

---

[1] *rood* Cross; *seraph-man* Angel.

[2] *shrieve* Give absolution to.

[3] *trow* Believe.

"Strange, by my faith!" the Hermit said—
"And they answered not our cheer!
The planks look warped! and see those sails, Approacheth
the ship with
wonder.
530　How thin they are and sere!
I never saw aught like to them,
Unless perchance it were

Brown skeletons of leaves that lag
My forest-brook along;
535　When the ivy-tod[1] is heavy with snow,
And the owlet whoops to the wolf below,
That eats the she-wolf's young."

"Dear Lord! it hath a fiendish look—"
(The Pilot made reply)
540　"I am a-feared"—"Push on, push on!"
Said the Hermit cheerily.

The boat came closer to the ship,
But I nor spake nor stirred;
The boat came close beneath the ship,
545　And straight a sound was heard.

Under the water it rumbled on, The ship
suddenly
sinketh.
Still louder and more dread:
It reached the ship, it split the bay;
The ship went down like lead.

550　Stunned by that loud and dreadful sound, The ancient
Mariner is
saved in the
Pilot's boat.
Which sky and ocean smote,
Like one that hath been seven days drowned
My body lay afloat;
But swift as dreams, myself I found
555　Within the Pilot's boat.

Upon the whirl, where sank the ship,
The boat spun round and round;
And all was still, save that the hill
Was telling of the sound.

560　I moved my lips—the Pilot shrieked
And fell down in a fit;
The holy Hermit raised his eyes,
And prayed where he did sit.

I took the oars: the Pilot's boy,
565　Who now doth crazy go,
Laughed loud and long, and all the while
His eyes went to and fro.
"Ha! ha!" quoth he, "full plain I see,
The Devil knows how to row."

570　And now, all in my own countree,
I stood on the firm land!
The Hermit stepped forth from the boat,
And scarcely he could stand.

"O shrieve me, shrieve me, holy man!" The ancient
Mariner earnestly
entreateth the
Hermit to shrieve
him; and the
penance of life
falls on him.
575　The Hermit crossed his brow.
"Say quick," quoth he, "I bid thee say—
What manner of man art thou?"

Forthwith this frame of mine was wrenched
With a woful agony,
580　Which forced me to begin my tale;
And then it left me free.

Since then, at an uncertain hour, And ever and
anon throughout
his future life an
agony constraineth
him to travel from
land to land.
That agony returns;
And till my ghastly tale is told,
585　This heart within me burns.

I pass, like night, from land to land;
I have strange power of speech;
That moment that his face I see,
I know the man that must hear me:
590　To him my tale I teach.

What loud uproar bursts from that door!
The wedding-guests are there:
But in the garden-bower the bride
And bride-maids singing are:
595　And hark the little vesper bell,
Which biddeth me to prayer!

O Wedding-Guest! this soul hath been
Alone on a wide wide sea:
So lonely 'twas, that God Himself
600　Scarce seeméd there to be.

---

[1] *ivy-tod* Bush.

O sweeter than the marriage-feast,
'Tis sweeter far to me,
To walk together to the kirk
With a goodly company!—

605 To walk together to the kirk,
And all together pray,
While each to his great Father bends,
Old men, and babes, and loving friends
And youth and maidens gay!

610 Farewell, farewell! but this I tell
To thee, thou Wedding-Guest!
He prayeth well, who loveth well
Both man and bird and beast.

And to teach by
his own example,
love and reverence
to all things that
God made and
loveth.

He prayeth best, who loveth best
615 All things both great and small;
For the dear God who loveth us,
He made and loveth all.

The Mariner, whose eye is bright,
Whose beard with age is hoar,[1]
620 Is gone: and now the Wedding-Guest
Turned from the bridegroom's door.

He went like one that hath been stunned,
And is of sense forlorn:
A sadder and a wiser man,
625 He rose the morrow morn.
—1817 (EARLIER VERSION PUBLISHED 1798)

In Context

The Origin of "The Rime of the Ancient Mariner"

from Samuel Taylor Coleridge, *Biographia Literaria*, Chapter 14 (1817)

Almost twenty years after the first publication of "The Rime of the Ancient Mariner," Coleridge gave the following account of the poem's origin and composition.

During the first year that Mr. Wordsworth and I were neighbours, our conversations turned frequently on the two cardinal points of poetry, the power of exciting the sympathy of the reader by a faithful adherence to the truth of nature, and the power of giving the interest of novelty by the modifying colours of imagination. The sudden charm, which accidents of light and shade, which moonlight or sunset diffused over a known and familiar landscape, appeared to represent the practicability of combining both. These are the poetry of nature. The thought suggested itself (to which of us I do not recollect) that a series of poems might be composed of two sorts. In the one, the incidents and agents were to be, in part at least supernatural; and the excellence aimed at was to consist in the interesting of the affections by the dramatic truth of such emotions, as would naturally accompany such situations, supposing them real. And real in *this* sense they have been to every human being who, from whatever source of delusion, has at any time believed himself under supernatural agency. For the second class, subjects were to be chosen from ordinary life; the characters and incidents were to be such, as will be found in every village and its vicinity where there is a meditative and feeling mind to seek after them, or to notice them, when they present themselves. In this idea originated the plan of the *Lyrical Ballads*; in which it was agreed, that my endeavours should be directed to persons and characters supernatural, or at least romantic; yet so as to transfer from our

---

[1]   *hoar*   White, as with frost (hoarfrost).

inward nature a human interest and a semblance of truth sufficient to procure for these shadows of imagination that willing suspension of disbelief for the moment, which constitutes poetic faith. Mr. Wordsworth, on the other hand, was to propose to himself as his object, to give the charm of novelty to things of every day, and to excite a feeling analogous to the supernatural, by awakening the mind's attention from the lethargy of custom, and directing it to the loveliness and the wonders of the world before us; an inexhaustible treasure, but for which, in consequence of the film of familiarity and selfish solicitude we have eyes, yet see not, and hearts that neither feel or understand. With this view I wrote "The Ancient Mariner," and was preparing among other poems, "The Dark Ladie," and the "Christabel" in which I should have more nearly realized my ideal than I had done in my first attempt.

from A Letter from the Rev. Alexander Dyce to Hartley Coleridge (1852)

In this letter to Samuel Taylor Coleridge's eldest son, Hartley, the Reverend Alexander Dyce quotes Wordsworth as saying the following about the inception of "The Rime of the Ancient Mariner":

"The Ancient Mariner" was founded on a strange dream, which a friend of Coleridge had, who fancied he saw a skeleton ship, with figures in it. We had both determined to write some poetry for a monthly magazine, the profits of which were to defer the expenses of a little excursion we were to make together. "The Ancient Mariner" was intended for this periodical, but was too long. I had very little share in the composition of it, for I soon found the style of Coleridge and myself would not assimilate. Beside the lines (in the fourth part) "And thou art long, and lank, and brown, /As in the ribbed sea-sand—" I wrote the stanza (in the first part) "He holds him with his glittering eye— / The Wedding-Guest stood still, / And listens like a three-years child: / The Mariner hath his will" and four or five lines more in different parts of the poem, which I could not now point out. The idea of shooting an albatross was mine; for I had been reading *Shelvocke's Voyages*, which probably Coleridge never saw. I also suggested the reanimation of the dead bodies, to work the ship.

This Lime-Tree Bower My Prison[1]

Addressed to Charles Lamb,
Of the India House, London

Well, they are gone, and here must I remain,
    This lime-tree bower my prison! I have lost
Beauties and feelings, such as would have been
Most sweet to my remembrance even when age
5 Had dimm'd mine eyes to blindness! They, meanwhile,
Friends, whom I never more may meet again,
On springy heath, along the hill-top edge,

Wander in gladness, and wind down, perchance,
To that still roaring dell, of which I told;
10 The roaring dell, o'erwooded, narrow, deep,
And only speckled by the mid-day sun;
Where its slim trunk the ash from rock to rock
Flings arching like a bridge;—that branchless ash,
Unsunn'd and damp, whose few poor yellow leaves
15 Ne'er tremble in the gale, yet tremble still,
Fann'd by the water-fall! and there my friends
Behold the dark green file of long lank weeds,[2]
That all at once (a most fantastic sight!)
Still nod and drip beneath the dripping edge
20 Of the blue clay-stone.

---

[1] [Coleridge's note] In the June of 1797 some long-expected friends [Charles Lamb and William and Dorothy Wordsworth] paid a visit to the author's cottage; and on the morning of their arrival, he met with an accident, which disabled him from walking during the whole time of their stay. One evening, when they had left him for a few hours, he composed the following lines in the garden-bower.

[2] [Coleridge's note] The *Asplenium Scolopendrium*, called in some countries the Adder's Tongue, in others the Hart's Tongue, but Withering gives the Adder's Tongue as the trivial name of the *Ophioglossum* only.

Now, my friends emerge
Beneath the wide wide Heaven—and view again
The many-steepled tract magnificent
Of hilly fields and meadows, and the sea,
With some fair bark, perhaps, whose sails light up
25 The slip of smooth clear blue betwixt two Isles
Of purple shadow! Yes! they wander on
In gladness all; but thou, methinks, most glad,
My gentle-hearted Charles! for thou hast pined
And hunger'd after Nature, many a year,
30 In the great City pent, winning thy way
With sad yet patient soul, through evil and pain
And strange calamity![1] Ah! slowly sink
Behind the western ridge, thou glorious Sun!
Shine in the slant beams of the sinking orb,
35 Ye purple heath-flowers! richlier burn, ye clouds!
Live in the yellow light, ye distant groves!
And kindle, thou blue Ocean! So my friend
Struck with deep joy may stand, as I have stood,
Silent with swimming sense; yea, gazing round
40 On the wide landscape, gaze till all doth seem
Less gross than bodily; and of such hues
As veil the Almighty Spirit, when yet he makes
Spirits perceive his presence.

A delight
Comes sudden on my heart, and I am glad
45 As I myself were there! Nor in this bower,
This little lime-tree bower, have I not mark'd
Much that has sooth'd me. Pale beneath the blaze
Hung the transparent foliage; and I watch'd
Some broad and sunny leaf, and lov'd to see
50 The shadow of the leaf and stem above
Dappling its sunshine! And that walnut-tree
Was richly ting'd, and a deep radiance lay
Full on the ancient ivy, which usurps
Those fronting elms, and now, with blackest mass
55 Makes their dark branches gleam a lighter hue
Through the late twilight: and though now the bat
Wheels silent by, and not a swallow twitters,
Yet still the solitary humble-bee
Sings in the bean-flower! Henceforth I shall know
60 That Nature ne'er deserts the wise and pure;

No plot so narrow, be but Nature there,
No waste so vacant, but may well employ
Each faculty of sense, and keep the heart
Awake to Love and Beauty! and sometimes
65 'Tis well to be bereft of promis'd good,
That we may lift the soul, and contemplate
With lively joy the joys we cannot share.
My gentle-hearted Charles! when the last rook
Beat its straight path along the dusky air
70 Homewards, I blest it! deeming its black wing
(Now a dim speck, now vanishing in light)
Had cross'd the mighty Orb's dilated glory,
While thou stood'st gazing; or, when all was still,
Flew creeking o'er thy head, and had a charm[2]
75 For thee, my gentle-hearted Charles, to whom
No sound is dissonant which tells of Life.
—1800

Christabel

PREFACE

The first part of the following poem was written in the year 1797, at Stowey, in the county of Somerset. The second part, after my return from Germany, in the year 1800, at Keswick, Cumberland. Since the latter date, my poetic powers have been, till very lately, in a state of suspended animation. But as, in my very first conception of the tale, I had the whole present to my mind, with the wholeness, no less than with the liveliness of a vision; I trust that I shall be able to embody in verse the three parts yet to come, in the course of the present year.

It is probable that if the poem had been finished at either of the former periods, or if even the first and second part had been published in the year 1800, the impression of its originality would have been much greater than I dare at present expect. But for this, I have only my own indolence to blame. The dates are men-

---

[1] *strange calamity* Charles Lamb's sister Mary, who suffered from periods of insanity, had fatally stabbed their mother.

[2] [Coleridge's note] Some months after I had written this line, it gave me pleasure to find that Bartram had observed the same circumstance of the Savanna Crane. "When these Birds move their wings in flight, their strokes are slow, moderate and regular; and even when at a considerable distance or high above us, we plainly hear the quill-feathers: their shafts and webs upon one another creak as the joints or working of a vessel in a tempestuous sea."

tioned for the exclusive purpose of precluding charges of plagiarism or servile imitation from myself. For there is among us a set of critics, who seem to hold, that every possible thought and image is traditional; who have no notion that there are such things as fountains in the world, small as well as great; and who would therefore charitably derive every rill[1] they behold flowing from a perforation made in some other man's tank. I am confident however, that as far as the present poem is concerned, the celebrated poets whose writings I might be suspected of having imitated,[2] either in particular passages, or in the tone and the spirit of the whole, would be among the first to vindicate me from the charge, and who, on any striking coincidence, would permit me to address them in this doggerel version of two monkish Latin hexameters:

> 'Tis mine and it is likewise yours,
> But an if this will not do;
> Let it be mine, good friend! for I
> Am the poorer of the two.

I have only to add, that the metre of the Christabel is not, properly speaking, irregular, though it may seem so from its being founded on a new principle: namely, that of counting in each line the accents, not the syllables. Though the latter may vary from seven to twelve, yet in each line the accents will be found to be only four. Nevertheless this occasional variation in the number of syllables is not introduced wantonly, or for the mere ends of convenience, but in correspondence with some transition in the nature of the imagery or passion.

PART I

'Tis the middle of night by the castle clock,
  And the owls have awakened the crowing cock;
Tu—whit!—Tu—whoo!
And hark, again! the crowing cock,
5 How drowsily it crew.

---

[1] *rill* Brook.

[2] *celebrated poets … imitated* Lord Byron and Sir Walter Scott, both of whom had read "Christabel" in manuscript form and had been influenced by it in their own subsequent writings.

Sir Leoline, the Baron rich,
Hath a toothless mastiff bitch;
From her kennel beneath the rock
She maketh answer to the clock,
10 Four for the quarters, and twelve for the hour;
Ever and aye,° by shine and shower,   *always*
Sixteen short howls, not over loud;
Some say, she sees my lady's shroud.

Is the night chilly and dark?
15 The night is chilly, but not dark.
The thin gray cloud is spread on high,
It covers but not hides the sky.
The moon is behind, and at the full;
And yet she looks both small and dull.
20 The night is chill, the cloud is gray:
'Tis a month before the month of May,
And the Spring comes slowly up this way.

The lovely lady, Christabel,
Whom her father loves so well,
25 What makes her in the wood so late,
A furlong from the castle gate?
She had dreams all yesternight
Of her own betrothéd knight;
And she in the midnight wood will pray
30 For the weal° of her lover that's far away.   *well-being*

She stole along, she nothing spoke,
The sighs she heaved were soft and low,
And naught was green upon the oak
But moss and rarest misletoe:[3]
35 She kneels beneath the huge oak tree,
And in silence prayeth she.

The lady sprang up suddenly,
The lovely lady, Christabel!
It moaned as near, as near can be,
40 But what it is she cannot tell.—
On the other side it seems to be,
Of the huge, broad-breasted, old oak tree.

---

[3] *misletoe* Plant considered sacred in ancient Britain when found growing on oak trees.

The night is chill; the forest bare;
Is it the wind that moaneth bleak?
45 There is not wind enough in the air
To move away the ringlet curl
From the lovely lady's cheek—
There is not wind enough to twirl
The one red leaf, the last of its clan,
50 That dances as often as dance it can,
Hanging so light, and hanging so high,
On the topmost twig that looks up at the sky.

Hush, beating heart of Christabel!
Jesu, Maria, shield her well!
55 She folded her arms beneath her cloak,
And stole to the other side of the oak.
        What sees she there?

There she sees a damsel bright,
Dressed in a silken robe of white,
60 That shadowy in the moonlight shone:
The neck that made that white robe wan,
Her stately neck, and arms were bare;
Her blue-veined feet unsandal'd were,
And wildly glittered here and there
65 The gems entangled in her hair.
I guess, 'twas frightful there to see
A lady so richly clad as she—
Beautiful exceedingly!

Mary mother, save me now!
70 (Said Christabel,) And who art thou?

The lady strange made answer meet,
And her voice was faint and sweet:—
Have pity on my sore distress,
I scarce can speak for weariness:
75 Stretch forth thy hand, and have no fear!
Said Christabel, How camest thou here?
And the lady, whose voice was faint and sweet,
Did thus pursue her answer meet:—

My sire is of a noble line,
80 And my name is Geraldine:

Five warriors seized me yestermorn,
Me, even me, a maid forlorn:
They choked my cries with force and fright,
And tied me on a palfrey° white.   *saddle horse*
85 The palfrey was as fleet as wind,
And they rode furiously behind.

They spurred amain,° their steeds were white: *forcefully*
And once we crossed the shade of night.
As sure as Heaven shall rescue me,
90 I have no thought what men they be;
Nor do I know how long it is
(For I have lain entranced, I wis°)   *know*
Since one, the tallest of the five,
Took me from the palfrey's back,
95 A weary woman, scarce alive.
Some muttered words his comrades spoke:
He placed me underneath this oak;
He swore they would return with haste;
Whither they went I cannot tell—
100 I thought I heard, some minutes past,
Sounds as of a castle bell.
Stretch forth thy hand (thus ended she),
And help a wretched maid to flee.

Then Christabel stretched forth her hand,
105 And comforted fair Geraldine:
O well, bright dame! may you command
The service of Sir Leoline;
And gladly our stout° chivalry   *fierce*
Will he send forth and friends withal
110 To guide and guard you safe and free
Home to your noble father's hall.

She rose: and forth with steps they passed
That strove to be, and were not, fast.
Her gracious stars the lady blest,
115 And thus spake on sweet Christabel:
All our household are at rest,
The hall is silent as the cell;
Sir Leoline is weak in health,
And may not well awakened be,
120 But we will move as if in stealth,

And I beseech your courtesy,
This night, to share your couch with me.

They crossed the moat, and Christabel
Took the key that fitted well;
125   A little door she opened straight,
All in the middle of the gate;
The gate that was ironed within and without,
Where an army in battle array had marched out.
The lady sank, belike through pain,
130   And Christabel with might and main
Lifted her up, a weary weight,
Over the threshold of the gate:
Then the lady rose again,
And moved, as she were not in pain.

135   So free from danger, free from fear,
They crossed the court: right glad they were.
And Christabel devoutly cried
To the Lady by her side,
Praise we the Virgin all divine
140   Who hath rescued thee from thy distress!
Alas, alas! said Geraldine,
I cannot speak for weariness.
So free from danger, free from fear,
They crossed the court: right glad they were.

145   Outside her kennel, the mastiff old
Lay fast asleep, in moonshine cold.
The mastiff old did not awake,
Yet she an angry moan did make!
And what can ail the mastiff bitch?
150   Never till now she uttered yell
Beneath the eye of Christabel.
Perhaps it is the owlet's scritch:
For what can aid the mastiff bitch?

They passed the hall, that echoes still
155   Pass as lightly as you will!
The brands° were flat, the brands were dying,   *burning logs*
Amid their own white ashes lying;
But when the lady passed, there came
A tongue of light, a fit of flame;
160   And Christabel saw the lady's eye,
And nothing else saw she thereby,

Save the boss of the shield of Sir Leoline tall,
Which hung in a murky old niche in the wall.
O softly tread, said Christabel,
165   My father seldom sleepeth well.

Sweet Christabel her feet doth bare,
And jealous of the listening air
They steal their way from stair to stair,
Now in glimmer, and now in gloom,
170   And now they pass the Baron's room,
As still as death, with stifled breath!
And now have reached her chamber door;
And now doth Geraldine press down
The rushes of the chamber floor.

175   The moon shines dim in the open air,
And not a moonbeam enters here.
But they without its light can see
The chamber carved so curiously,
Carved with figures strange and sweet,
180   All made out of the carver's brain,
For a lady's chamber meet:°   *suitable*
The lamp with twofold silver chain
Is fastened to an angel's feet.

The silver lamp burns dead and dim;
185   But Christabel the lamp will trim.
She trimmed the lamp, and made it bright,
And left it swinging to and fro,
While Geraldine, in wretched plight,
Sank down upon the floor below.

190   O weary lady, Geraldine,
I pray you, drink this cordial wine!
It is a wine of virtuous powers;
My mother made it of wild flowers.

And will your mother pity me,
195   Who am a maiden most forlorn?
Christabel answered—Woe is me!
She died the hour that I was born.
I have heard the gray-haired friar tell
How on her death-bed she did say,
200   That she should hear the castle-bell
Strike twelve upon my wedding-day.

O mother dear! that thou wert here!
I would, said Geraldine, she were!

But soon with altered voice, said she—
205 "Off, wandering mother! Peak and pine!
I have power to bid thee flee."
Alas! what ails poor Geraldine?
Why stares she with unsettled eye?
Can she the bodiless dead espy?
210 And why with hollow voice cries she,
"Off, woman, off! this hour is mine—
Though thou her guardian spirit be,
Off, woman, off! 'tis given to me."

Then Christabel knelt by the lady's side,
215 And raised to heaven her eyes so blue—
Alas! said she, this ghastly ride—
Dear lady! it hath wildered you!
The lady wiped her moist cold brow,
And faintly said, "'tis over now!"

220 Again the wild-flower wine she drank:
Her fair large eyes 'gan glitter bright,
And from the floor whereon she sank,
The lofty lady stood upright:
She was most beautiful to see,
225 Like a lady of a far countrée.

And thus the lofty lady spake—
"All they who live in the upper sky,
Do love you, holy Christabel!
And you love them, and for their sake
230 And for the good which me befell,
Even I in my degree will try,
Fair maiden, to requite you well.
But now unrobe yourself; for I
Must pray, ere yet in bed I lie."

235 Quoth Christabel, So let it be!
And as the lady bade, did she.
Her gentle limbs did she undress
And lay down in her loveliness.

But through her brain of weal and woe
240 So many thoughts moved to and fro,
That vain it were her lids to close;
So half-way from the bed she rose,
And on her elbow did recline
To look at the lady Geraldine.

245 Beneath the lamp the lady bowed,
And slowly rolled her eyes around;
Then drawing in her breath aloud,
Like one that shuddered, she unbound
The cincture° from beneath her breast: *girdle*
250 Her silken robe, and inner vest,
Dropt to her feet, and full in view,
Behold! her bosom, and half her side—
A sight to dream of, not to tell!
O shield her! shield sweet Christabel!

255 Yet Geraldine nor speaks nor stirs;
Ah! what a stricken look was hers!
Deep from within she seems half-way
To lift some weight with sick assay,°   *attempt*
And eyes the maid and seeks delay;
260 Then suddenly as one defied
Collects herself in scorn and pride,
And lay down by the Maiden's side!—
And in her arms the maid she took,
            Ah wel-a-day!
265 And with low voice and doleful look
These words did say:
"In the touch of this bosom there worketh a spell,
Which is lord of thy utterance, Christabel!
Thou knowest to-night, and wilt know to-morrow
270 This mark of my shame, this seal of my sorrow;
            But vainly thou warrest,
                For this is alone in
            Thy power to declare,
                That in the dim forest
275 Thou heard'st a low moaning,
And found'st a bright lady, surpassingly fair;
And didst bring her home with thee in love and in
            charity,
To shield her and shelter her from the damp air."

THE CONCLUSION TO PART I

It was a lovely sight to see
280   The lady Christabel, when she
Was praying at the old oak tree.
          Amid the jaggéd shadows
          Of mossy leafless boughs,
          Kneeling in the moonlight,
285   To make her gentle vows;
Her slender palms together prest,
Heaving sometimes on her breast;
Her face resigned to bliss or bale°—   grief
Her face, oh call it fair not pale,
290   And both blue eyes more bright than clear.
Each about to have a tear.

With open eyes (ah, woe is me!)
Asleep, and dreaming fearfully,
Fearfully dreaming, yet, I wis,
295   Dreaming that alone, which is—
O sorrow and shame! Can this be she,
The lady, who knelt at the old oak tree?
And lo! the worker of these harms,
That holds the maiden in her arms,
300   Seems to slumber still and mild,
As a mother with her child.

A star hath set, a star hath risen,
O Geraldine! since arms of thine
Have been the lovely lady's prison.
305   O Geraldine! one hour was thine—
Thou'st had thy will! By tairn° and rill,   mountain pool
The night-birds all that hour were still.
But now they are jubilant anew,
From cliff and tower, tu—whoo! tu—whoo!
310   Tu—whoo! tu—whoo! from wood and fell!°   hill

And see! the lady Christabel
Gathers herself from out her trance;
Her limbs relax, her countenance
Grows sad and soft; the smooth thin lids
315   Close o'er her eyes; and tears she sheds—
Large tears that leave the lashes bright!
And oft the while she seems to smile
As infants at a sudden light!

Yea, she doth smile, and she doth weep,
320   Like a youthful hermitess,
Beauteous in a wilderness,
Who, praying always, prays in sleep.
And, if she move unquietly,
Perchance, 'tis but the blood so free
325   Comes back and tingles in her feet.
No doubt, she hath a vision sweet.
What if her guardian spirit 'twere,
What if she knew her mother near?
But this she knows, in joys and woes,
330   That saints will aid if men will call:
For the blue sky bends over all!

PART 2

Each matin° bell, the Baron saith,   morning
Knells us back to a world of death.
These words Sir Leoline first said,
335   When he rose and found his lady dead:
These words Sir Leoline will say
Many a morn to his dying day!

And hence the custom and law began
That still at dawn the sacristan,°   church sexton
340   Who duly pulls the heavy bell,
Five and forty beads° must tell°   rosary beads / count
Between each stroke—a warning knell,
Which not a soul can choose but hear
From Bratha Head to Wyndermere.[1]

345   Saith Bracy the bard, So let it knell!
And let the drowsy sacristan
Still count as slowly as he can!
There is no lack of such, I ween,°   suppose
As well fill up the space between.
350   In Langdale Pike and Witch's Lair,
And Dungeon-ghyll so foully rent,
With ropes of rock and bells of air
Three sinful sextons' ghosts are pent,
Who all give back, one after t'other,
355   The death-note to their living brother;
And oft too, by the knell offended,

---

[1]   *Bratha Head ... Wyndermere*   In the Lake District.

Just as their one! two! three! is ended,
The devil mocks the doleful tale
With a merry peal from Borodale.

360 The air is still! through mist and cloud
That merry peal comes ringing loud;
And Geraldine shakes off her dread,
And rises lightly from the bed;
Puts on her silken vestments white,
365 And tricks her hair in lovely plight,[1]
And nothing doubting of her spell
Awakens the lady Christabel.
"Sleep you, sweet lady Christabel?
I trust that you have rested well."

370 And Christabel awoke and spied
The same who lay down by her side—
O rather say, the same whom she
Raised up beneath the old oak tree!
Nay, fairer yet! and yet more fair!
375 For she belike hath drunken deep
Of all the blessedness of sleep!
And while she spake, her looks, her air
Such gentle thankfulness declare,
That (so it seemed) her girded vests
380 Grew tight beneath her heaving breasts.
"Sure I have sinn'd!" said Christabel,
"Now heaven be praised if all be well!"
And in low faltering tones, yet sweet,
Did she the lofty lady greet
385 With such perplexity of mind
As dreams too lively leave behind.

So quickly she rose, and quickly arrayed
Her maiden limbs, and having prayed
That He, who on the cross did groan,
390 Might wash away her sins unknown,
She forthwith led fair Geraldine
To meet her sire, Sir Leoline.

The lovely maid and the lady tall
Are pacing both into the hall,
395 And pacing on through page and groom,
Enter the Baron's presence-room.

———
[1] *plight* I.e., plait, or braid.

The Baron rose, and while he prest
His gentle daughter to his breast,
With cheerful wonder in his eyes
400 The lady Geraldine espies,
And gave such welcome to the same,
As might beseem so bright a dame!

But when he heard the lady's tale,
And when she told her father's name,
405 Why waxed Sir Leoline so pale,
Murmuring o'er the name again,
Lord Roland de Vaux of Tryermaine?

Alas! they had been friends in youth;
But whispering tongues can poison truth;
410 And constancy lives in realms above;
And life is thorny; and youth is vain;
And to be wroth with one we love,
Doth work like madness in the brain.
And thus it chanced, as I divine,
415 With Roland and Sir Leoline.
Each spake words of high disdain
And insult to his heart's best brother:
They parted—ne'er to meet again!
But never either found another
420 To free the hollow heart from paining—
They stood aloof, the scars remaining,
Like cliffs which had been rent asunder;
A dreary sea now flows between;—
But neither heat, nor frost, nor thunder,
425 Shall wholly do away, I ween,
The marks of that which once hath been.

Sir Leoline, a moment's space,
Stood gazing on the damsel's face:
And the youthful Lord of Tryermaine
430 Came back upon his heart again.

O then the Baron forgot his age,
His noble heart swelled high with rage;
He swore by the wounds in Jesu's side,
He would proclaim it far and wide
435 With trump and solemn heraldry,
That they, who thus had wronged the dame,
Were base as spotted infamy!

"And if they dare deny the same,
My herald shall appoint a week,
440   And let the recreant traitors seek
My tourney° court—that there and then   *tournament*
I may dislodge their reptile souls
From the bodies and forms of men!"
He spake: his eye in lightning rolls!
445   For the lady was ruthlessly seized; and he kenned° *recognized*
In the beautiful lady the child of his friend!

And now the tears were on his face,
And fondly in his arms he took
Fair Geraldine, who met the embrace,
450   Prolonging it with joyous look.
Which when she viewed, a vision fell
Upon the soul of Christabel,
The vision of fear, the touch and pain!
She shrunk and shuddered, and saw again—
455   (Ah, woe is me! Was it for thee,
Thou gentle maid! such sights to see?)

Again she saw that bosom old,
Again she felt that bosom cold,
And drew in her breath with a hissing sound:
460   Whereat the Knight turned wildly round,
And nothing saw, but his own sweet maid
With eyes upraised, as one that prayed.

The touch, the sight, had passed away,
And in its stead that vision blest,
465   Which comforted her after-rest.
While in the lady's arms she lay,
Had put a rapture in her breast,
And on her lips and o'er her eyes
Spread smiles like light!
                              With new surprise,
470   "What ails then my belovéd child?"
The Baron said—His daughter mild
Made answer, "All will yet be well!"
I ween, she had no power to tell
Aught else: so mighty was the spell.

475   Yet he, who saw this Geraldine,
Had deemed her sure a thing divine:
Such sorrow with such grace she blended,

As if she feared she had offended
Sweet Christabel, that gentle maid!
480   And with such lowly tones she prayed
She might be sent without delay
Home to her father's mansion.
                                          "Nay!
Nay, by my soul!" said Leoline.
"Ho! Bracy the bard, the charge be thine!
485   Go thou, with music sweet and loud,
And take two steeds with trappings proud,
And take the youth whom thou lov'st best
To bear thy harp, and learn thy song,
And clothe you both in solemn vest,
490   And over the mountains haste along,
Lest wandering folk, that are abroad,
Detain you on the valley road.

"And when he has crossed the Irthing flood,
My merry bard! he hastes, he hastes
495   Up Knorren Moor, through Halegarth Wood,
And reaches soon that castle good
Which stands and threatens Scotland's wastes.

"Bard Bracy! bard Bracy! your horses are fleet,
Ye must ride up the hall, your music so sweet,
500   More loud than your horses' echoing feet!
And loud and loud to Lord Roland call,
Thy daughter is safe in Langdale hall!
Thy beautiful daughter is safe and free—
Sir Leoline greets thee thus through me!
505   He bids thee come without delay
With all thy numerous array
And take thy lovely daughter home:
And he will meet thee on the way
With all his numerous array
510   White with their panting palfreys' foam:
And, by mine honour! I will say,
That I repent me of the day
When I spake words of fierce disdain
To Roland de Vaux of Tryermaine!—
515   —For since that evil hour hath flown,
Many a summer's sun hath shone;
Yet ne'er found I a friend again
Like Roland de Vaux of Tryermaine."

The lady fell, and clasped his knees,
520 Her face upraised, her eyes o'erflowing;
And Bracy replied, with faltering voice,
His gracious hail on all bestowing!—
"Thy words, thou sire of Christabel,
Are sweeter than my harp can tell;
525 Yet might I gain a boon° of thee,   *request*
This day my journey should not be,
So strange a dream hath come to me,
That I had vowed with music loud
To clear yon wood from thing unblest,
530 Warned by a vision in my rest!
For in my sleep I saw that dove,
That gentle bird, whom thou dost love,
And call'st by thy own daughter's name—
Sir Leoline! I saw the same
535 Fluttering, and uttering fearful moan,
Among the green herbs in the forest alone.
Which when I saw and when I heard,
I wonder'd what might ail the bird;
For nothing near it could I see,
540 Save the grass and herbs underneath the old tree.

"And in my dream methought I went
To search out what might there be found;
And what the sweet bird's trouble meant,
That thus lay fluttering on the ground.
545 I went and peered, and could descry
No cause for her distressful cry;
But yet for her dear lady's sake
I stooped, methought, the dove to take,
When lo! I saw a bright green snake
550 Coiled around its wings and neck.
Green as the herbs on which it couched,
Close by the dove's its head it crouched;
And with the dove it heaves and stirs,
Swelling its neck as she swelled hers!
555 I woke; it was the midnight hour,
The clock was echoing in the tower;
But though my slumber was gone by,
This dream it would not pass away—
It seems to live upon my eye!
560 And thence I vowed this self-same day,
With music strong and saintly song

To wander through the forest bare,
Lest aught unholy loiter there."

Thus Bracy said: the Baron, the while,
565 Half-listening heard him with a smile;
Then turned to Lady Geraldine,
His eyes made up of wonder and love;
And said in courtly accents fine,
"Sweet maid, Lord Roland's beauteous dove,
570 With arms more strong than harp or song,
Thy sire and I will crush the snake!"
He kissed her forehead as he spake,
And Geraldine in maiden wise,
Casting down her large bright eyes,
575 With blushing cheek and courtesy fine
She turned her from Sir Leoline;
Softly gathering up her train,
That o'er her right arm fell again;
And folded her arms across her chest,
580 And couched her head upon her breast,
And looked askance at Christabel—
Jesu, Maria, shield her well!

A snake's small eye blinks dull and shy;
And the lady's eyes they shrunk in her head,
585 Each shrunk up to a serpent's eye,
And with somewhat of malice, and more of dread,
At Christabel she looked askance!—
One moment—and the sight was fled!
But Christabel in dizzy trance
590 Stumbling on the unsteady ground
Shuddered aloud, with a hissing sound;
And Geraldine again turned round,
And like a thing, that sought relief,
Full of wonder and full of grief,
595 She rolled her large bright eyes divine
Wildly on Sir Leoline.

The maid, alas! her thoughts are gone,
She nothing sees—no sight but one!
The maid, devoid of guile and sin,
600 I know not how, in fearful wise,
So deeply had she drunken in
That look, those shrunken serpent eyes,

That all her features were resigned
To this sole image in her mind:
605 And passively did imitate
That look of dull and treacherous hate!
And thus she stood, in dizzy trance,
Still picturing that look askance
With forced unconscious sympathy
610 Full before her father's view—
As far as such a look could be
In eyes so innocent and blue!

And when the trance was o'er, the maid
Paused awhile, and inly prayed:
615 Then falling at the Baron's feet,
"By my mother's soul do I entreat
That thou this woman send away!"
She said: and more she could not say:
For what she knew she could not tell,
620 O'er-mastered by the mighty spell.

Why is thy cheek so wan and wild,
Sir Leoline? Thy only child
Lies at thy feet, thy joy, thy pride,
So fair, so innocent, so mild;
625 The same, for whom thy lady died!
O by the pangs of her dear mother
Think thou no evil of thy child!
For her, and thee, and for no other,
She prayed the moment ere she died:
630 Prayed that the babe for whom she died,
Might prove her dear lord's joy and pride!
    That prayer her deadly pangs beguiled,
        Sir Leoline!
And wouldst thou wrong thy only child,
635   Her child and thine?

Within the Baron's heart and brain
If thoughts, like these, had any share,
They only swelled his rage and pain,
And did but work confusion there.
640 His heart was cleft with pain and rage,
His cheeks they quivered, his eyes were wild,
Dishonored thus in his old age;

Dishonored by his only child,
And all his hospitality
645 To the wronged daughter of his friend
By more than woman's jealousy
Brought thus to a disgraceful end—
He rolled his eye with stern regard
Upon the gentle minstrel bard,
650 And said in tones abrupt, austere—
"Why, Bracy! dost thou loiter here?
I bade thee hence!" The bard obeyed;
And turning from his own sweet maid,
The agéd knight, Sir Leoline,
655 Led forth the lady Geraldine!

The Conclusion to Part 2

A little child, a limber elf,
Singing, dancing to itself,
A fairy thing with red round cheeks,
That always finds, and never seeks,
660 Makes such a vision to the sight
As fills a father's eyes with light;
And pleasures flow in so thick and fast
Upon his heart, that he at last
Must needs express his love's excess
665 With words of unmeant bitterness.
Perhaps 'tis pretty to force together
Thoughts so all unlike each other;
To mutter and mock a broken charm,
To dally with wrong that does no harm.
670 Perhaps 'tis tender too and pretty
At each wild word to feel within
A sweet recoil of love and pity.
And what, if in a world of sin
(O sorrow and shame should this be true!)
675 Such giddiness of heart and brain
Comes seldom save from rage and pain,
So talks as it's most used to do.
    —1801

Dejection: An Ode[1]

Late, late yestreen I saw the new Moon,
With the old Moon in her arms;
And I fear, I fear, my Master dear!
We shall have a deadly storm.
"Ballad of Sir Patrick Spence"[2]

1

Well! If the Bard was weather-wise, who made
    The grand old ballad of Sir Patrick Spence,
This night, so tranquil now, will not go hence
Unroused by winds, that ply a busier trade
5 Than those which mould yon cloud in lazy flakes,
Or the dull sobbing draft, that moans and rakes
Upon the strings of this Æolian lute,[3]
    Which better far were mute.
    For lo! the New-moon winter-bright!
10   And overspread with phantom light,
    (With swimming phantom light o'erspread
    But rimmed and circled by a silver thread)
I see the old Moon in her lap, foretelling
    The coming-on of rain and squally blast.
15 And oh! that even now the gust were swelling,
    And the slant night-shower driving loud and fast!
Those sounds which oft have raised me, whilst they awed,
    And sent my soul abroad,
Might now perhaps their wonted° impulse give,   *usual*
20 Might startle this dull pain, and make it move and live!

2

A grief without a pang, void, dark, and drear,
    A stifled, drowsy, unimpassioned grief,
    Which finds no natural outlet, no relief,
    In word, or sigh, or tear—
25 O Lady! in this wan and heartless mood,
To other thoughts by yonder throstle° woo'd,   *song-thrush*

All this long eve, so balmy and serene,
Have I been gazing on the western sky,
    And its peculiar tint of yellow green:
30 And still I gaze—and with how blank an eye!
And those thin clouds above, in flakes and bars,
That give away their motion to the stars;
Those stars, that glide behind them or between,
Now sparkling, now bedimmed, but always seen:
35 Yon crescent Moon, as fixed as if it grew
In its own cloudless, starless lake of blue;
I see them all so excellently fair,
I see, not feel, how beautiful they are!

3

    My genial spirits fail;
40   And what can these avail
To lift the smothering weight from off my breast?
    It were a vain endeavour,
    Though I should gaze for ever
On that green light that lingers in the west:
45 I may not hope from outward forms to win
The passion and the life, whose fountains are within.

4

O Lady! we receive but what we give,
And in our life alone does Nature live:
Ours is her wedding-garment, ours her shroud!
50   And would we aught behold, of higher worth,
Than that inanimate cold world allowed
To the poor loveless ever-anxious crowd,
    Ah! from the soul itself must issue forth
A light, a glory, a fair luminous cloud
55   Enveloping the Earth—
And from the soul itself must there be sent
    A sweet and potent voice, of its own birth,
Of all sweet sounds the life and element!

5

O pure of heart! thou need'st not ask of me
60 What this strong music in the soul may be!
What, and wherein it doth exist,
This light, this glory, this fair luminous mist,
This beautiful and beauty-making power.
    Joy, virtuous Lady! Joy that ne'er was given,
65 Save to the pure, and in their purest hour,

---

[1] *Dejection: An Ode* Coleridge originally wrote this poem as a verse letter to Sara Hutchinson (Wordsworth's future sister-in-law), with whom he had fallen in love.

[2] *Ballad of Sir Patrick Spence* Anonymous; published in Thomas Percy's *Reliques of Ancient English Poetry* (1765).

[3] *Æolian lute* Musical instrument named after Æolus, Greek god of the winds; the music of the lute, or, rather, harp, is made by exposure to the wind passing through it.

Life, and Life's effluence, cloud at once and shower,
Joy, Lady! is the spirit and the power,
Which wedding Nature to us gives in dower
    A new Earth and new Heaven,
70 Undreamt of by the sensual and the proud—
Joy is the sweet voice, Joy the luminous cloud—
    We in ourselves rejoice!
And thence flows all that charms or ear or sight,
    All melodies the echoes of that voice,
75 All colours a suffusion from that light.

        6
There was a time when, though my path was rough,
    This joy within me dallied with distress,
And all misfortunes were but as the stuff
    Whence Fancy made me dreams of happiness:
80 For hope grew round me, like the twining vine,
And fruits, and foliage, not my own, seemed mine.
But now afflictions bow me down to earth:
Nor care I that they rob me of my mirth;
    But oh! each visitation
85 Suspends what nature gave me at my birth,
    My shaping spirit of Imagination.
For not to think of what I needs must feel,
    But to be still and patient, all I can;
And haply by abstruse research to steal
90   From my own nature all the natural man—
    This was my sole resource, my only plan:
Till that which suits a part infects the whole,
And now is almost grown the habit of my soul.

        7
Hence, viper thoughts, that coil around my mind,
95   Reality's dark dream!
I turn from you, and listen to the wind,
    Which long has raved unnoticed. What a scream
Of agony by torture lengthened out
That lute sent forth! Thou Wind, that rav'st without,
100   Bare crag, or mountain-tairn,[1] or blasted tree,
Or pine-grove whither woodman never clomb,

Or lonely house, long held the witches' home,
    Methinks were fitter instruments for thee,
Mad Lutanist! who in this month of showers,
105 Of dark-brown gardens, and of peeping flowers,
Mak'st Devils' yule, with worse than wintry song,
The blossoms, buds, and timorous leaves among.
    Thou Actor, perfect in all tragic sounds!
Thou mighty Poet, e'en to frenzy bold!
110   What tell'st thou now about?
    'Tis of the rushing of an host in rout,
    With groans, of trampled men, with smarting
        wounds—
At once they groan with pain, and shudder with the cold!
But hush! there is a pause of deepest silence!
115   And all that noise, as of a rushing crowd,
With groans, and tremulous shudderings—all is over—
    It tells another tale, with sounds less deep and loud!
    A tale of less affright,
    And tempered with delight,
120 As Otway's[2] self had framed the tender lay,—
    'Tis of a little child
    Upon a lonesome wild,
Not far from home, but she hath lost her way:
And now moans low in bitter grief and fear,
125 And now screams loud, and hopes to make her
    mother hear.

        8
'Tis midnight, but small thoughts have I of sleep:
Full seldom may my friend such vigils keep!
Visit her, gentle Sleep! with wings of ing,
    And may this storm be but a mountain-birth,
130 May all the stars hang bright above her dwelling,
    Silent as though they watched the sleeping Earth!
    With light heart may she rise,
    Gay fancy, cheerful eyes,
Joy lift her spirit, joy attune her voice;
135 To her may all things live, from the pole to pole,
Their life the eddying of her living soul!
    O simple spirit, guided from above,
Dear Lady! friend devoutest of my choice,
Thus mayest thou ever, evermore rejoice.
—1802

---

[1] [Coleridge's note] Tairn is a small lake, generally if not always applied to the lakes up in the mountains and which are the feeders of those in the valleys. This address to the Storm-wind will not appear extravagant to those who have heard it at night and in a mountainous country.

[2] *Otway* Thomas Otway (1652–85), English playwright known for his tragedies.

Work without Hope

Lines Composed 21st February 1825

All Nature seems at work. Slugs leave their lair—
The bees are stirring—birds are on the wing—
And Winter slumbering in the open air,
Wears on his smiling face a dream of Spring!
5 And I the while, the sole unbusy thing,
Nor honey make, nor pair, nor build, nor sing.

Yet well I ken° the banks where   *recognize*
    amaranths[1] blow,
Have traced the fount whence streams of nectar flow.
Bloom, O ye amaranths! bloom for whom ye may,
10 For me ye bloom not! Glide, rich streams, away!
With lips unbrightened, wreathless brow, I stroll:
And would you learn the spells that drowse my soul?
Work without hope draws nectar in a sieve,
And Hope without an object cannot live.

—1828

Kubla Khan

Or, A Vision in a Dream. A Fragment[2]

In Xanadu did Kubla Khan
A stately pleasure-dome decree:
Where Alph, the sacred river, ran

---

[1] *amaranths* Imaginary flowers, the blossoms of which never fade.

[2] [Coleridge's note] The following fragment is here published at the request of a poet [Lord Byron] of great and deserved celebrity, and as far as the Author's own opinions are concerned, rather as a psychological curiosity, than on the ground of any supposed poetic merits.

In the summer of the year 1797, the Author, then in ill th, had retired to a lonely farmhouse between Porlock and Linton, on the Exmoor confines of Somerset and Devonshire. In consequence of a slight indisposition [dysentery], an anodyne [opium] had been prescribed, from the effects of which he fell asleep in his chair at the moment that he was reading the following sentence, or words of the same substance, in *Purchas's Pilgrimage* [i.e., *Purchas his Pilgrimage* (1613, 1614, 1617, 1626)]: "Here the Khan Kubla commanded a palace to be built, and a stately garden thereunto. And thus ten miles of fertile ground were inclosed with a wall." The author continued for about three hours in a profound sleep, at least of the external senses, during which time he has the most vivid confidence, that he

---

Through caverns measureless to man
5   Down to a sunless sea.
So twice five miles of fertile ground
With walls and towers were girdled round:
And there were gardens bright with sinuous rills,° *brooks*
Where blossomed many an incense-bearing tree;
10 And here were forests ancient as the hills,
Enfolding sunny spots of greenery.

But oh! that deep romantic chasm which slanted
Down the green hill athwart a cedarn cover!
A savage place! as holy and enchanted
15 As e'er beneath a waning moon was haunted
By woman wailing for her demon-lover!
And from this chasm, with ceaseless turmoil seething,
As if this earth in fast thick pants were breathing,

---

could not have composed less than from two to three hundred lines, if that indeed can be called composition in which all the images rose up before him as things, with a parallel production of the correspondent expressions, without any sensation or consciousness of effort. On awaking he appeared to himself to have a distinct recollection of the whole, and taking his pen, ink, and paper, instantly and eagerly wrote down the lines that are here preserved. At this moment he was unfortunately called out by a person on business from Porlock, and detained by him above an hour, and on his return to his room, found to his no small surprise and mortification, that though he still retained some vague and dim recollection of the general purpose of the vision, yet, with the exception of some eight or ten scattered lines and images, all the rest had passed away like the images on the surface of a stream into which a stone has been cast, but, alas! without the after restoration of the latter!

          Then all the charm
  Is broken—all that phantom-world so fair
Vanishes, and a thousand circlets spread,
And each mis-shape the other. Stay awhile,
Poor youth! who scarcely dar'st lift up thine eyes—
The stream will soon renew its smoothness, soon
The visions will return! And lo, he stays,
And soon the fragments dim of lovely forms
Come trembling back, unite, and now once more
The pool becomes a mirror.
[from Coleridge's "The Picture, or the Lover's Resolution" (1802) 69–78]

Yet from the still surviving recollections in his mind, the Author has frequently purposed to finish for himself what had been originally, as it were, given to him. Σαμερον αδιον ασω [from Theocritus's *Idyll* 1.145]: but the tomorrow is yet to come.

As a contrast to this vision, I have annexed a fragment of a very different character [Coleridge's poem "The Pains of Sleep"], describing with equal fidelity the dream of pain and disease.

A mighty fountain momently was forced:
20   Amid whose swift half-intermitted burst
Huge fragments vaulted like rebounding hail,
Or chaffy grain beneath the thresher's flail:
And 'mid these dancing rocks at once and ever
It flung up momently the sacred river.
25   Five miles meandering with a mazy° motion   *labyrinthine*
Through wood and dale the sacred river ran,
Then reached the caverns measureless to man,
And sank in tumult to a lifeless ocean:
And 'mid this tumult Kubla heard from far
30   Ancestral voices prophesying war!
      The shadow of the dome of pleasure
      Floated midway on the waves;
      Where was heard the mingled measure
      From the fountain and the caves.
35   It was a miracle of rare device,
A sunny pleasure-dome with caves of ice!

      A damsel with a dulcimer
      In a vision once I saw:
      It was an Abyssinian maid,
40   And on her dulcimer she played,
      Singing of Mount Abora.
      Could I revive within me
      Her symphony and song,
      To such a deep delight 'twould win me,
45   That with music loud and long,
I would build that dome in air,
That sunny dome! those caves of ice!
And all who heard should see them there,
And all should cry, Beware! Beware!
50   His flashing eyes, his floating hair!
Weave a circle round him thrice,
And close your eyes with holy dread,
For he on honey-dew hath fed,
And drunk the milk of Paradise.
      —1816 (WRITTEN 1798)

from *Biographia Literaria; or Biographical Sketches of My Literary Life and Opinions*

from CHAPTER 4
Mr. Wordsworth's Earlier Poems

... During the last year of my residence at Cambridge, I became acquainted with Mr. Wordsworth's first publication entitled *Descriptive Sketches*,[1] and seldom, if ever, was the emergence of an original poetic genius above the literary horizon more evidently announced. In the form, style, and manner of the whole poem, and in the structure of the particular lines and periods, there is an harshness and acerbity connected and combined with words and images all aglow, which might recall those products of the vegetable world, where gorgeous blossoms rise out of the hard and thorny rind and shell, within which the rich fruit was elaborating. The language was not only peculiar and strong, but at times knotty and contorted, as by its own impatient strength, while the novelty and struggling crowd of images, acting in conjunction with the difficulties of the style, demanded always a greater closeness of attention than poetry (at all events, than descriptive poetry) has a right to claim. It not seldom therefore justified the complaint of obscurity. In the following extract I have sometimes fancied that I saw an emblem of the poem itself, and of the author's genius as it was then displayed.

'Tis storm; and hid in mist from hour to hour,
All day the floods a deepening murmur pour;
The sky is veiled, and every cheerful sight:
Dark is the region as with coming night;
And yet what frequent bursts of overpowering light!
Triumphant on the bosom of the storm,
Glances the fire-clad eagle's wheeling form;
Eastward, in long perspective glittering, shine
The wood-crowned cliffs that o'er the lake recline;
Wide o'er the Alps a hundred streams unfold,
At once to pillars turned that flame with gold;
Behind his sail the peasant strives to shun

---

[1] *Descriptive Sketches* Published 1793 and again in 1815 in an altered version.

The West, that burns like one dilated sun,
Where in a mighty crucible expire
The mountains, glowing hot, like coals of fire.[1]

The poetic psyche, in its process to full development, undergoes as many changes as its Greek namesake, the butterfly.[2] And it is remarkable how soon genius clears and purifies itself from the faults and errors of its earliest products; faults which, in its earliest compositions, are the more obtrusive and confluent, because as heterogeneous elements, which had only a temporary use, they constitute the very *ferment*, by which themselves are carried off. Or we may compare them to some diseases, which must work on the humours, and be thrown out on the surface, in order to secure the patient from their future recurrence. I was in my twenty-fourth year, when I had the happiness of knowing Mr. Wordsworth personally, and while memory lasts, I shall hardly forget the sudden effect produced on my mind, by his recitation of a manuscript poem, which still remains unpublished,[3] but of which the stanza, and tone of style were the same as those of "The Female Vagrant" as originally printed in the first volume of the *Lyrical Ballads*. There was here, no mark of strained thought, or forced diction, no crowd or turbulence of imagery; and, as the poet hath himself well described in his lines "on revisiting the Wye,"[4] manly reflection, and human associations had given both variety, and an additional interest to natural objects, which in the passion and appetite of the first love they had seemed to him neither to need or permit. The occasional obscurities, which had risen from an imperfect control over the resources of his native language, had almost wholly disappeared, together with that worse defect of arbitrary and illogical phrases, at once hackneyed, and fantastic, which hold so distinguished a place in the *technique* of ordinary poetry, and will, more or less, alloy the earlier poems of the truest genius, unless the attention has been specifically directed to their worthlessness and incongruity.[5] I did not perceive anything particular in the mere style of the poem alluded to during its recitation, except indeed such difference as was not separable from the thought and manner; and the Spenserian stanza, which always, more or less, recalls to the reader's mind Spenser's own style, would doubtless have authorized, in my then opinion, a more frequent descent to the phrases of ordinary life, than could without an ill effect have been hazarded in the heroic couplet. It was not however the freedom from false taste, whether as to common defects, or to those more properly his own, which made so unusual an impression on my feelings immediately, and subsequently on my judgement. It was the union of deep feeling with profound thought; the fine balance of truth in observing, with the imaginative faculty in modifying the objects observed; and above all the original gift of spreading the tone, the *atmosphere*, and with it the depth and height of the ideal world around forms, incidents, and situations, of which, for the

---

1 *'Tis storm … fire* From "Descriptive Sketches Taken During a Pedestrian Tour in the Alps" (1815).

2 [Coleridge's note] The fact that in Greek Psyche is the common name for the soul, and the butterfly is thus alluded to in the following stanzas from an unpublished poem ["The Butterfly" (1817)] of the author:

The butterfly the ancient Grecians made
The soul's fair emblem, and its only name—
But of the soul, escaped the slavish trade
Of mortal life! For in this earthly frame
Our's is the reptile's lot, much toil, much blame,
Manifold motions making little speed,
And to deform and kill the things, whereon we feed.

3 *manuscript … unpublished* "Guilt and Sorrow; or, Incidents Upon Salisbury Plain" (1842; written 1793-94).

4 *"on revisiting the Wye"* From Wordsworth's "Lines Composed a Few Miles Above Tintern Abbey," 77–94.

5 [Coleridge's note] Mr. Wordsworth, even in his two earliest, "An Evening Walk" and the "Descriptive Sketches," is more free from this latter defect than most of the young poets his contemporaries. It may, however, be exemplified, together with the harsh and obscure construction, in which he more often offended, in the following lines:

'Mid stormy vapours ever driving by,
Where ospreys, cormorants, and herons cry;
Where hardly given the hopeless waste to cheer,
Denied the bread of life, the foodful ear,
Dwindles the pear on autumn's latest spray,
And *apple sickens* pale in summer's ray;
*Ev'n here content has fixed her smiling reign
With independence, child of high disdain.*

I hope, I need not say, that I have quoted these lines for no other purpose than to make my meaning fully understood. It is to be regretted that Mr. Wordsworth has not republished these two poems entire.

common view, custom had bedimmed all the lustre, had dried up the sparkle and the dew drops. "To find no contradiction in the union of old and new; to contemplate the Ancient of days and all his works with feelings as fresh, as if all had then sprang forth at the first creative fiat;[1] characterizes the mind that feels the riddle of the world, and may help to unravel it. To carry on the feelings of childhood into the powers of manhood; to combine the child's sense of wonder and novelty with the appearances, which every day for perhaps forty years had rendered familiar;

> With sun and moon and stars throughout the year,
> And man and woman;[2]

this is the character and privilege of genius, and one of the marks which distinguish genius from talents. And therefore is it the prime merit of genius and its most unequivocal mode of manifestation, so to represent familiar objects as to awaken in the minds of others a kindred feeling concerning them and that freshness of sensation which is the constant accompaniment of mental, no less than of bodily, convalescence. Who has not a thousand times seen snow fall on water? Who has not watched it with a new feeling, from the time that he has read Burns' comparison of sensual pleasure

> To snow that falls upon a river
> A moment white—then gone for ever![3]

In poems, equally as in philosophic disquisitions, genius produces the strongest impressions of novelty, while it rescues the most admitted truths from the impotence caused by the very circumstance of their universal admission. Truths of all others the most awful and mysterious, yet being at the same time of universal interest, are too often considered as so true, that they lose all the life and efficiency of truth, and lie bedridden in the dormitory of the soul, side by side with the most

---

[1] *fiat* Command.

[2] *With sun ... woman* Milton's sonnet "To Mr. Cyriack Skinner upon his Blindness" (1655) actually reads: "Of sun or moon or star throughout the year, / Or man or woman."

[3] *To snow ... for ever!* Robert Burns's "Tam o'Shanter" (1791) reads: "Or like the snow falls in the river, / A moment white—then melts for ever."

despised and exploded errors."—The Friend,[4] p. 76, No. 5.

This excellence, which in all Mr. Wordsworth's writings is more or less predominant, and which constitutes the character of his mind, I no sooner felt, than I sought to understand. Repeated meditations led me first to suspect (and a more intimate analysis of the human faculties, their appropriate marks, functions, and effects matured my conjecture into full conviction) that fancy and imagination were two distinct and widely different faculties, instead of being, according to the general belief, either two names with one meaning, or, at furthest, the lower and higher degree of one and the same power. It is not, I own, easy to conceive a more apposite translation of the Greek *Phantasia* than the Latin Imaginatio; but it is equally true that in all societies there exists an instinct of growth, a certain collective, unconscious good sense working progressively to desynonymize[5] those words originally of the same

---

[4] [Coleridge's note] As "The Friend" was printed on stampt sheets, and sent only by the poet to a very limited number of subscribers, the author has felt less objection to quote from it, though a work of his own. To the public at large indeed it is the same as a volume in manuscript.

[5] [Coleridge's note] This is effected either by giving to the one word a general, and to the other an exclusive use; as "to put on the back" and "to indorse"; or by an actual distinction of meanings as "naturalist," and "physician"; or by difference of relation as "I" and "Me"; (each of which the rustics of our different provinces still use in all the cases singular of the first personal pronoun). Even the mere difference, or corruption, in the *pronunciation* of the same word, if it have become general, will produce a new word with a distinct signification; thus "property" and "propriety"; the latter of which, even to the time of Charles II was the *written* word for all the senses of both. Thus too "mister" and "master" both hasty pronunciations of the same word "magister," "mistress," and "miss," "if," and "give," &c. &c. There is a sort of *minim immortal* among the *animalcula infusoria* which has not naturally either birth, or death, absolute beginning, or absolute end: for at a certain period a small point appears on its back, which deepens and lengthens till the creature divides into two, and the same process recommences in each of the halves now become integral. This may be a fanciful, but it is by no means a bad emblem of the formation of words, and may facilitate the conception, how immense a nomenclature may be organized from a few simple sounds by rational beings in a social state. For each new application, or excitement of the same sound, will call forth a different sensation, which cannot but affect the pronunciation. The after recollection of the sound, without the same vivid sensation, will modify it still further; till at length all trace of the original likeness is worn away.

meaning, which the conflux of dialects had supplied to the more homogeneous languages, as the Greek and German: and which the same cause, joined with accidents of translation from original works of different countries, occasion in mixed languages like our own. The first and most important point to be proved is, that two conceptions perfectly distinct are confused under one and the same word, and (this done) to appropriate that word exclusively to one meaning, and the synonym (should there be one) to the other. But if (as will be often the case in the arts and sciences) no synonym exists, we must either invent or borrow a word. In the present instance the appropriation has already begun, and been legitimated in the derivative adjective: Milton had a highly *imaginative*, Cowley a very *fanciful* mind. If therefore I should succeed in establishing the actual existences of two faculties generally different, the nomenclature would be at once determined. To the faculty by which I had characterized Milton, we should confine the term *imagination*; while the other would be contra-distinguished as *fancy*. Now were it once fully ascertained, that this division is no less grounded in nature, than that of delirium from mania, or Otway's

Lutes, lobsters, seas of milk, and ships of amber,[1]

from Shakespeare's

What! have his daughters brought him to this pass?[2]

or from the preceding apostrophe to the elements; the theory of the fine arts, and of poetry in particular, could not, I thought, but derive some additional and important light. It would in its immediate effects furnish a torch of guidance to the philosophical critic; and ultimately to the poet himself. In energetic minds, truth soon changes by domestication into power; and from directing in the discrimination and appraisal of the product, becomes influencive in the production. To admire on principle, is the only way to imitate without loss of originality. ...

[1] *Lutes ... amber* From Thomas Otway's play *Venice Preserved* (1682) 5.2; Otway's version has the word "laurel" replacing "lobster."

[2] *What! ... pass?* From *King Lear* 3.4.65.

from CHAPTER 13
On the Imagination, or Esemplastic[3] Power

The IMAGINATION then I consider either as primary, or secondary. The primary IMAGINATION I hold to be the living Power and prime Agent of all human Perception, and as a repetition in the finite mind of the eternal act of creation in the infinite I AM. The secondary I consider as an echo of the former, co-existing with the conscious will, yet still as identical with the primary in the *kind* of its agency, and differing only in *degree,* and in the *mode* of its operation. It dissolves, diffuses, dissipates, in order to re-create; or where this process is rendered impossible, yet still at all events it struggles to idealize and to unify. It is essentially *vital,* even as all objects (as objects) are essentially fixed and dead.

FANCY, on the contrary, has no other counters to play with, but fixities and definites. The Fancy is indeed no other than a mode of Memory emancipated from the order of time and space; and blended with, and modified by that empirical phenomenon of the will, which we express by the word CHOICE. But equally with the ordinary memory it must receive all its materials ready made from the law of association.

Whatever more than this, I shall think it fit to declare concerning the powers and privileges of the imagination in the present work, will be found in the critical essay on the uses of the Supernatural in poetry and the principles that regulate its introduction, which the reader will find prefixed to the poem of *The Ancient Mariner.*

CHAPTER 14
Occasion of the Lyrical Ballads

During the first year that Mr. Wordsworth and I were neighbours, our conversations turned frequently on the two cardinal points of poetry, the power of exciting the sympathy of the reader by a faithful adherence to the truth of nature, and the power of giving the interest of novelty by the modifying colours of imagination. The sudden charm, which accidents of light and shade, which moonlight or sunset diffused over a known and

[3] *Esemplastic* Word coined by Coleridge to mean "moulded into unity."

familiar landscape, appeared to represent the practicability of combining both. These are the poetry of nature. The thought suggested itself (to which of us I do not recollect) that a series of poems might be composed of two sorts. In the one, the incidents and agents were to be, in part at least, supernatural; and the excellence aimed at was to consist in the interesting of the affections by the dramatic truth of such emotions, as would naturally accompany such situations, supposing them real. And real in *this* sense they have been to every human being who, from whatever source of delusion, has at any time believed himself under supernatural agency. For the second class, subjects were to be chosen from ordinary life; the characters and incidents were to be such, as will be found in every village and its vicinity, where there is a meditative and feeling mind to seek after them, or to notice them, when they present themselves.

In this idea originated the plan of the *Lyrical Ballads*, in which it was agreed, that my endeavours should be directed to persons and characters supernatural, or at least romantic; yet so as to transfer from our inward nature a human interest and a semblance of truth sufficient to procure for these shadows of imagination that willing suspension of disbelief for the moment, which constitutes poetic faith. Mr. Wordsworth, on the other hand, was to propose to himself as his object, to give the charm of novelty to things of every day, and to excite a feeling analogous to the supernatural, by awakening the mind's attention from the lethargy of custom, and directing it to the loveliness and the wonders of the world before us; an inexhaustible treasure, but for which in consequence of the film of familiarity and selfish solicitude we have eyes, yet see not, ears that hear not, and hearts that neither feel nor understand.[1]

With this view I wrote *The Ancient Mariner*, and was preparing among other poems, the "Dark Ladie," and the "Christabel," in which I should have more nearly realized my ideal, than I had done in my first attempt. But Mr. Wordsworth's industry had proved so much more successful, and the number of his poems so much

greater, that my compositions, instead of forming a balance, appeared rather an interpolation of heterogeneous matter. Mr. Wordsworth added two or three poems written in his own character, in the impassioned, lofty, and sustained diction, which is characteristic of his genius. In this form the *Lyrical Ballads* were published; and were presented by him, as an *experiment*, whether subjects, which from their nature rejected the usual ornaments and extra-colloquial style of poems in general, might not be so managed in the language of ordinary life as to produce the pleasurable interest, which it is the peculiar business of poetry to impart. To the second edition he added a preface of considerable length, in which notwithstanding some passages of apparently a contrary import, he was understood to contend for the extension of this style to poetry of all kinds, and to reject as vicious and indefensible all phrases and forms of style that were not included in what he (unfortunately, I think, adopting an equivocal expression) called the language of *real* life. From this preface, prefixed to poems in which it was impossible to deny the presence of original genius, however mistaken its direction might be deemed, arose the whole long continued controversy. For from the conjunction of perceived power with supposed heresy I explain the inveteracy[2] and in some instances, I grieve to say, the acrimonious passions, with which the controversy has been conducted by the assailants.

Had Mr. Wordsworth's poems been the silly, the childish things, which they were for a long time described as being; had they been really distinguished from the compositions of other poets merely by meanness of language and inanity of thought; had they indeed contained nothing more than what is found in the parodies and pretended imitations of them; they must have sunk at once, a dead weight, into the slough of oblivion, and have dragged the preface along with them. But year after year increased the number of Mr. Wordsworth's admirers. They were found too not in the lower classes of the reading public, but chiefly among young men of strong sensibility and meditative minds; and their admiration (inflamed perhaps in some degree by opposition) was distinguished by its intensity, I

---

[1]   *we have eyes ... understand*   Cf. Isaiah 6.9: "Hear ye indeed, but understand not; and see ye indeed, but perceive not." See also Matthew 13.13–14.

[2]   *inveteracy*   Deeply rooted prejudice.

might almost say, by its *religious* fervour. These facts, and the intellectual energy of the author, which was more or less consciously felt, where it was outwardly and even boisterously denied, meeting with sentiments of aversion to his opinions, and of alarm at their consequences, produced an eddy of criticism, which would of itself have borne up the poems by the violence with which it whirled them round and round. With many parts of this preface in the sense attributed to them and which the words undoubtedly seem to authorise, I never concurred; but on the contrary objected to them as erroneous in principle, and as contradictory (in appearance at least) both to other parts of the same preface, and to the author's own practice in the greater number of the poems themselves. Mr. Wordsworth in his recent collection[1] has, I find, degraded this prefatory disquisition to the end of his second volume, to be read or not at the reader's choice. But he has not, as far as I can discover, announced any change in his poetic creed. At all events, considering it as the source of a controversy, in which I have been honoured, more than I deserve, by the frequent conjunction of my name with his, I think it expedient to declare once for all, in what points I coincide with his opinions, and what points I altogether differ. But in order to render myself intelligible I must previously, in as few words as possible, explain my ideas, first, of a POEM; and secondly, of POETRY itself, in *kind*, and in *essence*.

The office of philosophical *disquisition* consists in just *distinction*; while it is the privilege of the philosopher to preserve himself constantly aware, that distinction is not division. In order to obtain adequate notions of any truth, we must intellectually separate its distinguishable parts; and this is the technical *process* of philosophy. But having so done, we must then restore them in our conceptions to the unity, in which they actually co-exist; and this is the *result* of philosophy. A poem contains the same elements as a prose composition; the difference therefore must consist in a different combination of them, in consequence of a different object proposed. According to the difference of the object will be the difference of the combination. It is possible, that the object may be merely to facilitate the

recollection of any given facts or observations by artificial arrangement; and the composition will be a poem, merely because it is distinguished from prose by metre, or by rhyme, or by both conjointly. In this, the lowest sense, a man might attribute the name of a poem to the well known enumeration of the days in the several months;

> Thirty days hath September,
> April, June, and November, &c.

and others of the same class and purpose. And as a particular pleasure is found in anticipating the recurrence of sounds and quantities, all compositions that have this charm superadded, whatever be their contents, *may* be entitled poems.

So much for the superficial *form*. A difference of object and contents supplies an additional ground of distinction. The immediate purpose may be the communication of truths; either of truth absolute and demonstrable, as in works of science; or of facts experienced and recorded, as in history. Pleasure, and that of the highest and most permanent kind, may *result* from the *attainment* of the end; but it is not itself the immediate end. In other works the communication of pleasure may be the immediate purpose; and though truth, either moral or intellectual, ought to be the *ultimate* end, yet this will distinguish the character of the author, not the class to which the work belongs. Blest indeed is that state of society, in which the immediate purpose would be baffled by the perversion of the proper ultimate end; in which no charm of diction or imagery could exempt the Bathyllus even of an Anacreon, or the Alexis of Virgil,[2] from disgust and aversion! But the communication of pleasure may be the immediate object of a work not metrically composed; and that object may have been in a high degree attained, as in novels and romances. Would then the mere superaddition of metre, with or without rhyme, entitle *these* to the name of poems? The answer is, that nothing can permanently please, which does not contain in itself the reason why it is so, and not otherwise. If metre be

---

[1] *recent collection* Two volumes entitled *Poems by William Wordsworth* (1815).

[2] *Bathyllus ... Virgil* Both Virgil and Anacreon wrote homoerotic poems. In this period, homosexuality was viewed unfavorably, in a way that we now consider prejudiced and unfair.

superadded, all other parts must be made consonant with it. They must be such, as to justify the perpetual and distinct attention to each part, which an exact correspondent recurrence of accent and sound are calculated to excite. The final definition then, so deduced, may be thus worded. A poem is that species of composition, which is opposed to works of science, by proposing for its *immediate* object pleasure, not truth; and from all other species (having *this* object in common with it) it is discriminated by proposing to itself such delight from the *whole*, as is compatible with a distinct gratification from each component *part*.

Controversy is not seldom excited in consequence of the disputants attaching each a different meaning to the same word; and in few instances has this been more striking, than in disputes concerning the present subject. If a man chooses to call every composition a poem, which is rhyme, or measure, or both, I must leave his opinion uncontroverted. The distinction is at least competent to characterize the writer's intention. If it were subjoined, that the whole is likewise entertaining or affecting, as a tale, or as a series of interesting reflections, I of course admit this as another fit ingredient of a poem, and an additional merit. But if the definition sought for be that of a *legitimate* poem, I answer, it must be one, the parts of which mutually support and explain each other; all in their proportion harmonizing with, and supporting the purpose and known influences of metrical arrangement. The philosophic critics of all ages coincide with the ultimate judgment of all countries, in equally denying the praises of a just poem, on the one hand, to a series of striking lines or distichs,[1] each of which absorbing the whole attention of the reader to itself disjoins it from its context, and makes it a separate whole, instead of an harmonizing part; and on the other hand, to an unsustained composition, from which the reader collects rapidly the general result unattracted by the component parts. The reader should be carried forward, not merely or chiefly by the mechanical impulse of curiosity, or by a restless desire to arrive at the final solution; but by the pleasurable activity of mind excited by the attractions of the journey itself. Like the motion of a serpent, which

the Egyptians made the emblem of intellectual power; or like the path of sound through the air; at every step he pauses and half recedes, and from the retrogressive movement collects the force which again carries him onward. *Præcipitandus est liber spiritus*,[2] says Petronius Arbiter most happily. The epithet, *liber*,[3] here balances the preceding verb; and it is not easy to conceive more meaning condensed in fewer words.

But if this should be admitted as a satisfactory character of a poem, we have still to seek for a definition of poetry. The writings of Plato, and Bishop Taylor, and the *Theoria Sacra* of Burnet,[4] furnish undeniable proofs that poetry of the highest kind may exist without metre, and even without the contra-distinguishing objects of a poem. The first chapter of Isaiah (indeed a very large proportion of the whole book) is poetry in the most emphatic sense; yet it would be not less irrational than strange to assert, that pleasure, and not truth, was the immediate object of the prophet. In short, whatever *specific* import we attach to the word, poetry, there will be found involved in it, as a necessary consequence, that a poem of any length neither can be, or ought to be, all poetry. Yet if an harmonious whole is to be produced, the remaining parts must be preserved *in keeping* with the poetry; and this can be no otherwise effected than by such a studied selection and artificial arrangement, as will partake of *one*, though not a *peculiar*, property of poetry. And this again can be no other than the property of exciting a more continuous and equal attention, than the language of prose aims at, whether colloquial or written.

My own conclusions on the nature of poetry, in the strictest use of the word, have been in part anticipated in the preceding disquisition on the fancy and imagination. What is poetry? is so nearly the same question with, what is a poet? that the answer to the one is involved in the solution of the other. For it is a distinction resulting from the poetic genius itself, which sustains and modifies the images, thoughts, and

---

[1] *distichs* Poetic couplets.

[2] *Præcipitandus est liber spiritus* Latin: from the *Satyricon*: "The free spirit must be hurried along."

[3] *liber* Free.

[4] *Bishop Taylor* English theologian and author Jeremy Taylor (1613–67); *Burnet* English cleric and author Thomas Burnet (1635–1715), who wrote *Sacred Theory of the Earth*.

emotions of the poet's own mind. The poet, described in *ideal* perfection, brings the whole soul of man into activity, with the subordination of its faculties to each other, according to their relative worth and dignity. He diffuses a tone, and spirit of unity, that blends, and (as it were) *fuses*, each into each, by that synthetic and magical power, to which we have exclusively appropriated the name of imagination. This power, first put in action by the will and understanding, and retained under their irremissive, though gentle and unnoticed, controul (*laxis effertur habenis*)[1] reveals itself in the balance or reconciliation of opposite or discordant qualities: of sameness, with difference; of the general, with the concrete; the idea, with the image; the individual, with the representative; the sense of novelty and freshness, with old and familiar objects; a more than usual state of emotion, with more than usual order; judgement ever awake and steady self-possession, with enthusiasm and feeling profound or vehement; and while it blends and harmonizes the natural and the artificial, still subordinates art to nature; the manner to the matter; and our admiration of the poet to our sympathy with the poetry. "Doubtless," as Sir John Davies observes of the soul (and his words may with slight alteration be applied, and even more appropriately to the poetic IMAGINATION):

Doubtless this could not be, but that she turns
Bodies to spirit by sublimation strange,
As fire converts to fire the things it burns,
As we our food into our nature change.

From their gross matter she abstracts their forms,
And draws a kind of quintessence from things;
Which to her proper nature she transforms
To bear them light, on her celestial wings.

Thus does she, when from individual states
She doth abstract the universal kinds;
Which then re-clothed in divers names and fates
Steal access through our senses to our minds.[2]

Finally, GOOD SENSE is the BODY of poetic genius, FANCY its DRAPERY, MOTION its LIFE, and IMAGINATION the SOUL that is everywhere, and in each; and forms all into one graceful and intelligent whole.

from CHAPTER 17
Examination of the Tenets Peculiar to Mr. Wordsworth

As far then as Mr. Wordsworth in his preface contended, and most ably contended, for a reformation in our poetic diction, as far as he has evinced the truth of passion, and the *dramatic* propriety of those figures and metaphors in the original poets, which stript of their justifying reasons, and converted into mere artifices of connection or ornament, constitute the characteristic falsity in the poetic style of the moderns; and as far as he has, with equal acuteness and clearness, pointed out the process in which this change was effected, and the resemblances between that state into which the reader's mind is thrown by the pleasurable confusion of thought from an unaccustomed bain[3] of words and images; and that state which is induced by the natural language of empassioned feeling; he undertook a useful task, and deserves all praise, both for the attempt and for the execution....

My own differences from certain supposed parts of Mr. Wordsworth's theory ground themselves on the assumption, that his words had been rightly interpreted, as purporting that the proper diction for poetry in general consists altogether in a language taken, with due exceptions, from the mouths of men in real life, a language which actually constitutes the natural conversation of men under the influence of natural feelings. My objection is, first, that in *any* sense this rule is applicable only to *certain* classes of poetry; secondly, that even to these classes it is not applicable, except in such a sense, as hath never by any one (as far as I know or have read) been denied or doubted; and lastly, that as far as, and in that degree in which it is *practicable*, yet as a *rule* it is useless, if not injurious, and therefore either need not, or ought not to be practised. The poet informs his reader, that he had generally chosen *low and*

---

[1] *laxis effertur habenis* Latin: moved forward with loosened rein.

[2] *Doubtless ... minds* Adapted from "Nosce Teipsum: Of Human Knowledge" (1599).

[3] *bain* Vessel for water.

rustic life; but not *as* low and rustic, or in order to repeat that pleasure of doubtful moral effect, which persons of elevated rank and of superior refinement oftentimes derive from a happy *imitation* of the rude unpolished manners and discourse of their inferiors. For the pleasure so derived may be traced to three exciting causes. The first is the naturalness, in *fact*, of the things presented. The second is the apparent naturalness of the *representation*, as raised and qualified by an imperceptible infusion of the author's own knowledge and talent, which infusion does, indeed, constitute it an *imitation* as distinguished from a mere *copy*. The third cause may be found in the reader's conscious feeling of his superiority awakened by the contrast presented to him; even as for the same purpose the kings and great barons of yore retained, sometimes *actual* clowns and fools, but more frequently shrewd and witty fellows in that *character*. These, however, were not Mr. Wordsworth's objects. *He* chose low and rustic life, "because in that condition the essential passions of the heart find a better soil, in which they can attain their maturity, are less under restraint, and speak a plainer and more emphatic language; because in that condition of life our elementary feelings coexist in a state of greater simplicity, and consequently may be more accurately contemplated, and more forcibly communicated; because the manners of rural life germinate from those elementary feelings; and from the necessary character of rural occupations are more easily comprehended, and are more durable; and lastly, because in that condition the passions of men are incorporated with the beautiful and permanent forms of nature."[1]

Now it is clear to me, that in the most interesting of the poems, in which the author is more or less dramatic, as the "Brothers," "Michael," "Ruth," the "Mad Mother," &c. the persons introduced are by no means taken *from low or rustic life* in the common acceptation of those words; and it is not less clear, that the sentiments and language, as far as they can be conceived to have been really transferred from the minds and conversation of such persons, are attributable to causes and circumstances not necessarily connected with "their occupations and abode." The thoughts, feelings, language, and manners of the shepherd-farmers in the vales of Cumberland and Westmoreland, as far as they are actually adopted in those poems, may be accounted for from causes, which will and do produce the same results in *every* state of life, whether in town or country. As the two principal I rank that INDEPENDENCE, which raises a man above servitude, or daily toil for the profit of others, yet not above the necessity of industry and a frugal simplicity of domestic life; and the accompanying unambitious, but solid and religious EDUCATION, which has rendered few books familiar, but the Bible, and the liturgy or hymn book. To this latter cause, indeed, which is so far *accidental*, that it is the blessing of particular countries and a particular age, not the product of particular places or employments, the poet owes the shew of probability, that his personages might really feel, think, and talk with any tolerable resemblance to his representation. It is an excellent remark of Dr. Henry More's (*Enthusiasmus triumphatus*, Sec. xxxv) that "a man of confined education, but of good parts, by constant reading of the Bible will naturally form a more winning and commanding rhetoric than those that are learned; the intermixture of tongues and of artificial phrases debasing *their* style."

It is, moreover, to be considered that to the formation of thy feelings, and a reflecting mind, *negations* involve impediments not less formidable, than sophistication intermixture. I am convinced, that for the human soul to prosper in rustic life, a certain vantage-ground is prerequisite. It is not every man, that is likely to be improved by a country life or by country labours. Education, or original sensibility, or both, must pre-exist, if the changes, forms, and incidents of nature are to prove a sufficient stimulant. And where these are not sufficient, the mind contracts and hardens by want of stimulants; and the man becomes selfish, sensual, gross, hard-hearted. Let the management of the POOR LAWS in Liverpool, Manchester, or Bristol be compared with the ordinary dispensation of the poor rates in agricultural villages, where the *farmers* are the overseers and guardians of the poor. ... [The] result would engender more than skepticism concerning the desirable influences of low and rustic life in and for itself. ...

If then I am compelled to doubt the theory, by which the choice of *characters* was to be directed, not

---

[1] "*because ... nature*" From Wordsworth's "Preface" to *Lyrical Ballads* (1800).

only *a priori*,[1] from grounds of reason, but both from the few instances in which the poet himself *need* be supposed to have been governed by it, and from the comparative inferiority of those instances; still more must I hesitate in my assent to the sentence which immediately follows the former citation; and which can neither admit as particular fact, or a general rule. "The language too of these men is adopted (purified indeed from what appear to be its real defects, from all lasting and rational causes of dislike or disgust) because such men hourly communicate with the best objects from which the best part of language is originally derived; and because, from their rank in society, and the sameness and narrow circle of their intercourse, being less under the action of social vanity, they convey their feelings and notions in simple and unelaborated expressions."[2] To this I reply; that a rustic's language, purified from all provincialism and grossness, and so far reconstructed as to be made consistent with the rules of grammar which are in essence no other than the laws of universal logic, applied to psychological materials will not differ from the language of any other man of commonsense, however learned or refined he may be, except as far as the notions, which the rustic has to convey, are fewer and more indiscriminate. This will become still clearer, if we add the consideration (equally important though less obvious) that the rustic, from the more imperfect development of his faculties, and from the lower state of their cultivation, aims almost solely to convey *insulated facts*, either those of his scanty experience or his traditional belief; while the educated man chiefly seeks to discover and express those *connections* of things, or those relative *hearings* of fact to fact, from which some more or less general law is deducible. For *facts* are valuable to a wise man, chiefly as they lead to the discovery of the indwelling *law*, which is the true *being* of things, the sole solution of their modes of existence, and in the knowledge of which consists our dignity and our power. ...

Here let me be permitted to remind the reader, that the positions, which I controvert, are contained in the sentences —"*a selection of the* REAL *language of men*"— "*the language of these men* (i.e., men in low and rustic life) *I propose to myself to imitate, and as far as possible, to adopt the very language of men.*" "*Between the language of prose and that of metrical composition, there neither is, nor can be any essential difference.*"[3] It is against these exclusively, that my opposition is directed.

I object, in the very first instance, to an equivocation in the use of the word "real." Every man's language varies, according to the extent of his knowledge, the activity of his faculties, and the depth or quickness of his feelings. Every man's language has, first, its *individualities*; secondly, the common properties of the *class* to which he belongs; and thirdly, words and phrases of *universal* use. The language of Hooker,[4] Bacon, Bishop Taylor, and Burke,[5] differ from the common language of the learned class only by the superior number and novelty of the thoughts and relations which they had to convey. The language of Algernon Sidney differs not at all from that, which every well educated gentleman would wish to write, and (with due allowances for the undeliberateness, and less connected train, of thinking natural and proper to conversation) such as he would wish to talk. Neither one or the other differ half as much from the general language of cultivated society, as the language of Mr. Wordsworth's homeliest composition differs from that of a common peasant. For "real" therefore, we must substitute *ordinary*, or *lingua communis*.[6] And this, we have proved, is no more to be found in the phraseology of low and rustic life, than in that of any other class. Omit the peculiarities of each, and the result of course must be common to all. And assuredly the omissions and changes to be made in the language of rustics, before it could be transferred to any species of poem, except the drama or other professed imitation, are at least as numerous and weighty, as would be required in adapting to the same purpose the ordinary language of tradesmen and manufacturers. Not

---

[1] *a priori* Latin: without direct experience.

[2] *"The language ... expressions"* From Wordsworth's "Preface" to *Lyrical Ballads* (1800).

[3] *"a selection ... difference"* From Wordsworth's "Preface" to *Lyrical Ballads* (1800).

[4] *Hooker* English clergyman and theologian Richard Hooker (1554–1600).

[5] *Burke* British statesman and political writer Edmund Burke (1729–97).

[6] *lingua communis* Latin: common language.

to mention, that the language so highly extolled by Mr. Wordsworth varies in every county, nay in every village, according to the accidental character of the clergyman, the existence or non-existence of schools; or even, perhaps, as the exciseman, publican, or barber happen to be, or not to be, zealous politicians, and readers of the weekly newspaper *pro bono publico*.[1] Anterior to cultivation the lingua communis of every country, as Dante has well observed, exists everywhere in parts, and nowhere as a whole.

Neither is the case rendered at all more tenable by the addition of the words, "*in a state of excitement.*" For the nature of a man's words, when he is strongly affected by joy, grief, or anger, must necessarily depend on the number and quality of the general truths, conceptions and images, and of the words expressing them, with which his mind had been previously stored. For the property of passion is not to *create*; but to set in increased activity. At least, whatever new connections of thought or images, or (which is equally, if not more than equally, the appropriate effect of strong excitement) whatever generalizations of truth or experience, the heat of passion may produce; yet the terms of their conveyance must have pre-existed in his former conversations, and are only collected and

crowded together by the unusual stimulation. It is indeed very possible to adopt in a poem the unmeaning repetitions, habitual phrases, and other blank counters, which an unfurnished or confused understanding interposes at short intervals, in order to keep hold of his subject which is still slipping from him, and to give him time for recollection; or in mere aid of vacancy, as in the scanty companies of a country stage the same player pops backwards and forwards, in order to prevent the appearance of empty spaces, in the procession of *Macbeth*, or *Henry VIII*. But what assistance to the poet, or ornament to the poem, these can supply, I am at a loss to conjecture. Nothing assuredly can differ either in origin or in mode more widely from the *apparent* tautologies[2] of intense and turbulent feeling, in which the passion is greater and of longer endurance, than to be exhausted or satisfied by a single representation of the image or incident exciting it. Such repetitions I admit to be a beauty of the highest kind; as illustrated by Mr. Wordsworth himself from the song of Deborah. "*At her feet he bowed, he fell, he lay down; at her feet he bowed, he fell; where he bowed, there he fell down dead.*"[3]

—1817

[1] *pro bono publico* Latin: for the good of the public.

[2] *tautologies* Repetitions.

[3] "*At her feet ... dead*" From Wordsworth's note to "The Thorn" (1798).

JANE AUSTEN
1775 – 1817

Jane Austen is considered to be one of the finest novelists in the English language. Her six major novels, along with her shorter fictional works, juvenilia, and surviving correspondence, share a keenness of wit and irony of observation that have ensured her continued popularity among scholars and general readers alike into the twenty-first century. Her fiction scrutinizes the manners and the behavior of ordinary women of the emergent middle class in Georgian England, who need to negotiate between feeling and duty, personal desire and social expectation. As Sir Walter Scott, the most famous novelist of Austen's time, commented in reviewing her favorably in the influential *Quarterly Review*, her writing bears "that exquisite touch which renders ordinary commonplace things and characters interesting." Her work was not as highly esteemed in the middle decades of the nineteenth century, but her popularity rose in the 1870s, and her life and work have for generations been the subject of what is often called an "industry," both scholarly and popular.

Jane Austen was born at Steventon, Hampshire, the sixth child in a family of seven, and the younger of two daughters. Her father, the Reverend George Austen, was a spirited and cultivated man who allowed his daughters free access to his extensive library. Educated mostly at home, she read broadly, including novels by Frances Burney, Laurence Sterne, Henry Fielding, and Samuel Richardson, whose *Sir Charles Grandison* was a particular favorite. Owing in part to the proximity of the boys' school run by Austen's parents from the Steventon Rectory, the household in which Austen grew up was busy and lively, and its members enjoyed and encouraged each others' literary and theatrical pursuits. The young Jane Austen's imagination was fed by family theatricals directed and performed by her elder siblings and cousins for friends and neighbors. Austen's biographer, Claire Tomalin, speculates that the young Jane may have played a minor role in the family production of Richard Brinsley Sheridan's *The Rivals* before she was ten years old. Most importantly, Austen was encouraged to read aloud from her early writing, and her family delighted in the comic stories and burlesques she produced in her teenage years. Fictions such as *Lesley Castle* and *Love & Freindship* (sic), the latter written when Austen was 14, are filled with impertinent and riotous humor, indecorous behavior on the part of young women, and an already astute sense of generic convention. Her father was particularly supportive of her writing: at the front of a notebook he had given her, in which she had composed her *History of England*, a juvenile parody of popular histories, George Austen inscribed the following appreciation: "Effusions of Fancy by a very Young Lady Consisting of Tales in a Style entirely new."

Austen lived a quiet country life among a wide network of relations, friends, and neighbors, an ideal context in which to hone the skills in social observation that informed her writing. She never married, although she had at least two admirers, and even accepted a proposal of marriage in 1802 (retracting her acceptance the following day). In 1795–96 she wrote an epistolary sketch called "Elinor and Marianne," which went through several rewrites in subsequent years before taking its final form as *Sense and Sensibility*. This became Austen's first published work (1811), selling out by 1813 and receiving positive reviews. Three other novels were published in quick succession: *Pride and Prejudice* in 1813, *Mansfield Park* in 1814, and *Emma* in 1816. *Pride and Prejudice*, whose first title was "First Impressions," had initially been rejected in 1797 by the publisher Thomas Cadell, who did not even read the manuscript before returning it. When it finally did appear, *Pride and Prejudice* was an instant hit, and it has since become one of the most widely read novels in the English language. Much of its success is due to the appeal of its heroine, Elizabeth Bennet, whose intelligence, feeling, and independence of thought Austen conveys through sparkling dialogue and pioneering use of narrative techniques that provide for flexibility of viewpoint.

The composition of Austen's major works can be divided into two distinct periods. By 1800 she had written three full-length novels, none of them published. Then followed a ten-year silence: the Austens' decision to quit the family home at Steventon and move to Bath, taking Jane and her elder sister Cassandra with them, meant a break in Austen's writing routine. The family moved often in the next several years, and with the death of several friends and family members in this period, most importantly her father in 1805, Austen seems to have experienced a depression that prevented her from writing. Tomalin points out how easily Austen's existing manuscripts in this decade could have been lost or destroyed. With her settlement at Chawton Cottage in Hampshire late in 1808 with her mother and sister, Austen again found the time and space to write, and it was here that she revised "Elinor and Marianne" into *Sense and Sensibility,* and wrote *Mansfield Park*, *Emma*, and *Persuasion*.

Two of Austen's six major novels were published posthumously in 1818. *Northanger Abbey* had been written under the title "Susan" in 1798–99 and sold to the publisher Richard Crosby in 1803 for the low sum of ten pounds. Although he placed advertisements for the book, he never printed it, and refused to turn over the manuscript or copyright at her request in 1809. *Persuasion*, written in 1815–16, was Austen's last completed novel. Some readers find in it a tone of melancholy, which might be attributable to the fact that she was suffering from illness when it was completed. It is also unique among her major works as the only novel for which any manuscript material survives. Many of her letters were also destroyed by her elder sister Cassandra Austen after her death. The Austen sisters were extremely close, sparing no confidence in their correspondence with each other. Many of Austen's surviving letters to her sister are characterized by harshly honest observations of others' foibles.

Austen wrote fiction at a moment when women were getting their work into print in ever greater numbers, yet faced relentless pressure to think and behave in ways that militated against their attaining, or expressing, social power and authority. Although by 1816 Austen was a critical and popular success (whose most illustrious fan was the Prince Regent himself), she wore her success lightly, famously referring in a letter of that year to her nephew to the "little bit (two inches wide) of Ivory on which I work with so fine a brush." Perhaps the best known description of Austen's writing, the statement has been read by critics as both a disclaimer and a sly celebration of "women's" writing and the domestic novel. But perhaps not too much should be made of a comment made in a spirit of playful banter with a teenager. By the time she wrote this letter she was already seriously ill. She was working on a new novel around this time—*Sanditon*—but it was never finished. Jane Austen died of an undetermined illness on 18 July 1817, and was buried at Winchester Cathedral.

⌘⌘⌘

from *Pride and Prejudice*

CHAPTER I

It is a truth universally acknowledged, that a single man in possession of a good fortune must be in want of a wife.

However little known the feelings or views of such a man may be on his first entering a neighbourhood, this truth is so well fixed in the minds of the surrounding families that he is considered as the rightful property of some one or other of their daughters.

"My dear Mr. Bennet," said his lady to him one day, "have you heard that Netherfield Park is let at last?"

Mr. Bennet replied that he had not.

"But it is," returned she; "for Mrs. Long has just been here, and she told me all about it."

Mr. Bennet made no answer.

"Do not you want to know who has taken it?" cried his wife impatiently.

"*You* want to tell me, and I have no objection to hearing it."

This was invitation enough.

"Why, my dear, you must know, Mrs. Long says that Netherfield is taken by a young man of large fortune from the north of England; that he came down on Monday in a chaise and four[1] to see the place, and was so much delighted with it that he agreed with Mr. Morris immediately; that he is to take possession before Michaelmas,[2] and some of his servants are to be in the house by the end of next week."

"What is his name?"

"Bingley."

"Is he married or single?"

"Oh! single, my dear, to be sure! A single man of large fortune; four or five thousand a year. What a fine thing for our girls!"

"How so? how can it affect them?"

"My dear Mr. Bennet," replied his wife, "how can you be so tiresome! You must know that I am thinking of his marrying one of them."

"Is that his design in settling here?"

"Design! nonsense, how can you talk so! But it is very likely that he *may* fall in love with one of them, and therefore you must visit him as soon as he comes."

"I see no occasion for that. You and the girls may go, or you may send them by themselves, which perhaps will be still better, for as you are as handsome as any of them, Mr. Bingley might like you the best of the party."

"My dear, you flatter me. I certainly *have* had my share of beauty, but I do not pretend to be anything extraordinary now. When a woman has five grown up daughters, she ought to give over thinking of her own beauty."

"In such cases, a woman has not often much beauty to think of."

"But, my dear, you must indeed go and see Mr. Bingley when he comes into the neighbourhood."

"It is more than I engage for,[3] I assure you."

"But consider your daughters. Only think what an establishment it would be for one of them. Sir William and Lady Lucas are determined to go, merely on that account, for in general you know they visit no newcomers. Indeed you must go, for it will be impossible for *us* to visit him, if you do not."

"You are over scrupulous, surely. I dare say Mr. Bingley will be very glad to see you; and I will send a few lines by you to assure him of my hearty consent to his marrying which ever he chooses of the girls, though I must throw in a good word for my little Lizzy."

"I desire you will do no such thing. Lizzy is not a bit better than the others, and I am sure she is not half so handsome as Jane, nor half so good humoured as Lydia. But you are always giving *her* the preference."

"They have none of them much to recommend them," replied he; "they are all silly and ignorant like other girls, but Lizzy has something more of quickness than her sisters."

"Mr. Bennet, how can you abuse your own children in such a way? You take delight in vexing me. You have no compassion on my poor nerves."

"You mistake me, my dear. I have a high respect for your nerves. They are my old friends. I have heard you mention them with consideration these twenty years at least."

---

1   *chaise and four*   Traveling carriage pulled by four horses.

2   *Michaelmas*   The feast of St. Michael, on 29 September.

3   *engage for*   Promise to perform.

"Ah! you do not know what I suffer."

"But I hope you will get over it, and live to see many young men of four thousand a year come into the neighbourhood."

"It will be no use to us if twenty such should come, since you will not visit them."

"Depend upon it, my dear, that when there are twenty, I will visit them all."

Mr. Bennet was so odd a mixture of quick parts, sarcastic humour, reserve, and caprice, that the experience of three and twenty years had been insufficient to make his wife understand his character. *Her* mind was less difficult to develop. She was a woman of mean[1] understanding, little information, and uncertain temper. When she was discontented she fancied herself nervous. The business of her life was to get her daughters married; its solace was visiting and news.

CHAPTER 2

Mr. Bennet was among the earliest of those who waited on Mr. Bingley. He had always intended to visit him, though to the last always assuring his wife that he should not go; and till the evening after the visit was paid, she had no knowledge of it. It was then disclosed in the following manner. Observing his second daughter employed in trimming a hat, he suddenly addressed her with,

"I hope Mr. Bingley will like it, Lizzy."

"We are not in a way to know *what* Mr. Bingley likes," said her mother resentfully, "since we are not to visit."

"But you forget, mama," said Elizabeth, "that we shall meet him at the assemblies, and that Mrs. Long has promised to introduce him."

"I do not believe Mrs. Long will do any such thing. She has two nieces of her own. She is a selfish, hypocritical woman, and I have no opinion[2] of her."

"No more have I," said Mr. Bennet; "and I am glad to find that you do not depend on her serving you."

Mrs. Bennet deigned not to make any reply; but unable to contain herself, began scolding one of her daughters.

"Don't keep coughing so, Kitty, for heaven's sake! Have a little compassion on my nerves. You tear them to pieces."

"Kitty has no discretion in her coughs," said her father; "she times them ill."

"I do not cough for my own amusement," replied Kitty fretfully.

"When is your next ball to be, Lizzy?"

"Tomorrow fortnight."[3]

"Aye, so it is," cried her mother, "and Mrs. Long does not come back till the day before; so, it will be impossible for her to introduce him, for she will not know him herself."

"Then, my dear, you may have the advantage of your friend, and introduce Mr. Bingley to *her*."

"Impossible, Mr. Bennet, impossible, when I am not acquainted with him myself; how can you be so teazing?"

"I honour your circumspection. A fortnight's acquaintance is certainly very little. One cannot know what a man really is by the end of a fortnight. But if *we* do not venture, somebody else will; and after all, Mrs. Long and her nieces must stand their chance; and therefore, as she will think it an act of kindness, if you decline the office, I will take it on myself."

The girls stared at their father. Mrs. Bennet said only, "Nonsense, nonsense!"

"What can be the meaning of that emphatic exclamation?" cried he. "Do you consider the forms of introduction, and the stress that is laid on them, as nonsense? I cannot quite agree with you *there*. What say you, Mary? for you are a young lady of deep reflection I know, and read great books, and make extracts."

Mary wished to say something very sensible, but knew not how.

"While Mary is adjusting her ideas," he continued, "let us return to Mr. Bingley."

"I am sick of Mr. Bingley," cried his wife.

"I am sorry to hear *that*; but why did not you tell me so before? If I had known as much this morning, I certainly would not have called on him. It is very unlucky, but as I have actually paid the visit, we cannot escape the acquaintance now."

---

[1] *mean* Modest.

[2] *have no opinion of her* I.e., have no great opinion of her; regard her as unworthy.

[3] *Tomorrow fortnight* I.e., a fortnight (two weeks) from tomorrow.

The astonishment of the ladies was just what he wished; that of Mrs. Bennet perhaps surpassing the rest; though when the first tumult of joy was over, she began to declare that it was what she had expected all the while.

"How good it was in you, my dear Mr. Bennet! But I knew I should persuade you at last. I was sure you loved your girls too well to neglect such an acquaintance. Well, how pleased I am! and it is such a good joke, too, that you should have gone this morning, and never said a word about it till now."

"Now, Kitty, you may cough as much as you choose," said Mr. Bennet; and, as he spoke, he left the room, fatigued with the raptures of his wife.

"What an excellent father you have, girls," said she, when the door was shut. "I do not know how you will ever make him amends for his kindness; or me either, for that matter. At our time of life, it is not so pleasant, I can tell you, to be making new acquaintance every day; but for your sakes, we would do anything. Lydia, my love, though you *are* the youngest, I dare say Mr. Bingley will dance with you at the next ball."

"Oh!" said Lydia stoutly, "I am not afraid; for though I *am* the youngest, I'm the tallest."

The rest of the evening was spent in conjecturing how soon he would return Mr. Bennet's visit, and determining when they should ask him to dinner.

CHAPTER 3

Not all that Mrs. Bennet, however, with the assistance of her five daughters, could ask on the subject was sufficient to draw from her husband any satisfactory description of Mr. Bingley. They attacked him in various ways: with barefaced questions, ingenious suppositions, and distant surmises; but he eluded the skill of them all, and they were at last obliged to accept the second-hand intelligence of their neighbour Lady Lucas. Her report was highly favourable. Sir William had been delighted with him. He was quite young, wonderfully handsome, extremely agreeable, and to crown the whole, he meant to be at the next assembly with a large party. Nothing could be more delightful! To be fond of dancing was a certain step towards falling in love; and very lively hopes of Mr. Bingley's heart were entertained.

"If I can but see one of my daughters happily settled at Netherfield," said Mrs. Bennet to her husband, "and all the others equally well married, I shall have nothing to wish for."

In a few days Mr. Bingley returned Mr. Bennet's visit, and sat about ten minutes with him in his library. He had entertained hopes of being admitted to a sight of the young ladies, of whose beauty he had heard much; but he saw only the father. The ladies were somewhat more fortunate, for they had the advantage of ascertaining, from an upper window, that he wore a blue coat and rode a black horse.

An invitation to dinner was soon afterwards dispatched; and already had Mrs. Bennet planned the courses that were to do credit to her housekeeping, when an answer arrived which deferred it all. Mr. Bingley was obliged to be in town the following day, and consequently unable to accept the honour of their invitation, &c. Mrs. Bennet was quite disconcerted. She could not imagine what business he could have in town so soon after his arrival in Hertfordshire, and she began to fear that he might be always flying about from one place to another, and never settled at Netherfield as he ought to be. Lady Lucas quieted her fears a little by starting the idea of his being gone to London only to get a large party for the ball; and a report soon followed that Mr. Bingley was to bring twelve ladies and seven gentlemen with him to the assembly. The girls grieved over such a large number of ladies, but were comforted the day before the ball by hearing that, instead of twelve, he had brought only six with him from London, his five sisters and a cousin. And when the party entered the assembly room, it consisted of only five altogether; Mr. Bingley, his two sisters, the husband of the eldest, and another young man.

Mr. Bingley was good looking and gentlemanlike; he had a pleasant countenance, and easy, unaffected manners. His sisters were fine women, with an air of decided fashion. His brother-in-law, Mr. Hurst, merely looked the gentleman; but his friend Mr. Darcy soon drew the attention of the room by his fine, tall person, handsome features, noble mien,[1] and the report which was in general circulation within five minutes after his

---

[1] *mien* Bearing.

entrance, of his having ten thousand a year. The gentlemen pronounced him to be a fine figure of a man, the ladies declared he was much handsomer than Mr. Bingley, and he was looked at with great admiration for about half the evening, till his manners gave a disgust which turned the tide of his popularity; for he was discovered to be proud, to be above his company, and above being pleased; and not all his large estate in Derbyshire could then save him from having a most forbidding, disagreeable countenance, and being unworthy to be compared with his friend.

Mr. Bingley had soon made himself acquainted with all the principal people in the room; he was lively and unreserved, danced every dance, was angry that the ball closed so early, and talked of giving one himself at Netherfield. Such amiable qualities must speak for themselves. What a contrast between him and his friend! Mr. Darcy danced only once with Mrs. Hurst and once with Miss Bingley, declined being introduced to any other lady, and spent the rest of the evening in walking about the room, speaking occasionally to one of his own party. His character was decided. He was the proudest, most disagreeable man in the world, and everybody hoped that he would never come there again. Amongst the most violent against him was Mrs. Bennet, whose dislike of his general behaviour was sharpened into particular resentment by his having slighted one of her daughters.

Elizabeth Bennet had been obliged, by the scarcity of gentlemen, to sit down for two dances; and during part of that time, Mr. Darcy had been standing near enough for her to overhear a conversation between him and Mr. Bingley, who came from the dance for a few minutes to press his friend to join it.

"Come, Darcy," said he, "I must have you dance. I hate to see you standing about by yourself in this stupid manner. You had much better dance."

"I certainly shall not. You know how I detest it, unless I am particularly acquainted with my partner. At such an assembly as this, it would be insupportable. Your sisters are engaged, and there is not another woman in the room whom it would not be a punishment to me to stand up with."

"I would not be so fastidious as you are," cried Bingley, "for a kingdom! Upon my honour, I never met with so many pleasant girls in my life as I have this

evening; and there are several of them you see uncommonly pretty."

"*You* are dancing with the only handsome girl in the room," said Mr. Darcy, looking at the eldest Miss Bennet.

"Oh! she is the most beautiful creature I ever beheld! But there is one of her sisters sitting down just behind you who is very pretty, and, I dare say, very agreeable. Do let me ask my partner to introduce you."

"Which do you mean?" and turning round, he looked for a moment at Elizabeth, till, catching her eye, he withdrew his own and coldly said, "She is tolerable; but not handsome enough to tempt *me*; and I am in no humour at present to give consequence to young ladies who are slighted by other men. You had better return to your partner and enjoy her smiles, for you are wasting your time with me."   Mr. Bingley followed his advice. Mr. Darcy walked off, and Elizabeth remained with no very cordial feelings towards him. She told the story however with great spirit among her friends; for she had a lively, playful disposition, which delighted in anything ridiculous.

The evening altogether passed off pleasantly to the whole family. Mrs. Bennet had seen her eldest daughter much admired by the Netherfield party. Mr. Bingley had danced with her twice, and she had been distinguished by his sisters. Jane was as much gratified by this as her mother could be, though in a quieter way. Elizabeth felt Jane's pleasure. Mary had heard herself mentioned to Miss Bingley as the most accomplished girl in the neighbourhood; and Catherine and Lydia had been fortunate enough to be never without partners, which was all that they had yet learnt to care for at a ball. They returned therefore in good spirits to Longbourn, the village where they lived, and of which they were the principal inhabitants. They found Mr. Bennet still up. With a book he was regardless of time; and on the present occasion he had a good deal of curiosity as to the event of an evening which had raised such splendid expectations. He had rather hoped that all his wife's views on the stranger would be disappointed; but he soon found that he had a very different story to hear.

"Oh! my dear Mr. Bennet," as she entered the room, "we have had a most delightful evening, a most excellent ball. I wish you had been there. Jane was so admired, nothing could be like it. Everybody said how well she looked; and Mr. Bingley thought her quite beautiful, and danced with her twice. Only think of *that* my dear; he actually danced with her twice, and she was the only creature in the room that he asked a second time. First of all, he asked Miss Lucas. I was so vexed to see him stand up with her; but, however, he did not admire her at all—indeed, nobody can, you know—and he seemed quite struck with Jane as she was going down the dance. So, he enquired who she was, and got introduced, and asked her for the two next. Then, the two third he danced with Miss King, and the two fourth with Maria Lucas, and the two fifth with Jane again, and the two sixth with Lizzy, and the Boulanger."[1]

"If he had had any compassion for *me*," cried her husband impatiently, "he would not have danced half so much! For God's sake, say no more of his partners. Oh! that he had sprained his ankle in the first dance!"

"Oh! my dear," continued Mrs. Bennet, "I am quite delighted with him. He is so excessively handsome! and his sisters are charming women. I never in my life saw anything more elegant than their dresses. I dare say the lace upon Mrs. Hurst's gown—"

Here she was interrupted again. Mr. Bennet protested against any description of finery. She was therefore obliged to seek another branch of the subject, and related, with much bitterness of spirit and some exaggeration, the shocking rudeness of Mr. Darcy.

"But I can assure you," she added, "that Lizzy does not lose much by not suiting *his* fancy; for he is a most disagreeable, horrid man, not at all worth pleasing. So high and so conceited that there was no enduring him! He walked here, and he walked there, fancying himself so very great! Not handsome enough to dance with! I wish you had been there, my dear, to have given him one of your set downs. I quite detest the man."

CHAPTER 4

When Jane and Elizabeth were alone, the former, who had been cautious in her praise of Mr. Bingley before, expressed to her sister how very much she admired him.

"He is just what a young man ought to be," said she, "sensible, good humoured, lively; and I never saw such happy manners!—so much ease, with such perfect good breeding!"

"He is also handsome," replied Elizabeth, "which a young man ought likewise to be, if he possibly can. His character is thereby complete."

"I was very much flattered by his asking me to dance a second time. I did not expect such a compliment."

"Did not you? *I* did for you. But that is one great difference between us. Compliments always take *you* by surprise, and *me* never. What could be more natural than his asking you again? He could not help seeing that you were about five times as pretty as every other women in the room. No thanks to his gallantry for that. Well, he certainly is very agreeable, and I give you leave to like him. You have liked many a stupider person."

"Dear Lizzy!"

"Oh! you are a great deal too apt, you know, to like people in general. You never see a fault in anybody. All the world are good and agreeable in your eyes. I never heard you speak ill of a human being in my life."

"I would wish not to be hasty in censuring anyone; but I always speak what I think."

"I know you do; and it is *that* which makes the wonder. With *your* good sense, to be honestly blind to the follies and nonsense of others! Affectation of candour is common enough; one meets it everywhere. But to be candid without ostentation or design—to take the good of everybody's character and make it still better, and say nothing of the bad—belongs to you alone. And so, you like this man's sisters too, do you? Their manners are not equal to his."

"Certainly not, at first. But they are very pleasing women when you converse with them. Miss Bingley is to live with her brother and keep his house; and I am much mistaken if we shall not find a very charming neighbour in her."

Elizabeth listened in silence, but was not convinced; their behaviour at the assembly had not been calculated to please in general; and with more quickness of observation and less pliancy of temper than her sister, and with a judgment too unassailed by any attention to herself, she was very little disposed to approve them. They were in fact very fine ladies; not deficient in good humour when they were pleased, nor in the power of being agreeable where they chose it; but proud and conceited. They were rather handsome, had been educated in one of the first private seminaries in town, had a fortune of twenty thousand pounds, were in the habit of spending more than they ought, and of associating with people of rank; and were therefore in every respect entitled to think well of themselves, and meanly of others. They were of a respectable family in the north of England, a circumstance more deeply impressed on their memories than that their brother's fortune and their own had been acquired by trade.

Mr. Bingley inherited property to the amount of nearly an hundred thousand pounds from his father, who had intended to purchase an estate, but did not live to do it. Mr. Bingley intended it likewise, and sometimes made choice of his county; but as he was now provided with a good house and the liberty of a manor, it was doubtful to many of those who best knew the easiness of his temper, whether he might not spend the remainder of his days at Netherfield, and leave the next generation to purchase.

His sisters were very anxious for his having an estate of his own; but though he was now established only as a tenant, Miss Bingley was by no means unwilling to preside at his table, nor was Mrs. Hurst, who had married a man of more fashion than fortune, less disposed to consider his house as her home when it suited her. Mr. Bingley had not been of age two years when he was tempted by an accidental recommendation to look at Netherfield House. He did look at it and into it for half an hour, was pleased with the situation and the principal rooms, satisfied with what the owner said in its praise, and took it immediately.

Between him and Darcy there was a very steady friendship, in spite of a great opposition of character. Bingley was endeared to Darcy by the easiness, openness, ductility of his temper—though no disposition could offer a greater contrast to his own, and though with his own he never appeared dissatisfied. On the strength of Darcy's regard Bingley had the firmest reliance, and of his judgment the highest opinion. In understanding, Darcy was the superior. Bingley was by no means deficient, but Darcy was clever. He was at the same time haughty, reserved, and fastidious, and his manners, though well bred, were not inviting. In that respect his friend had greatly the advantage. Bingley was sure of being liked wherever he appeared; Darcy was continually giving offence.

The manner in which they spoke of the Meryton assembly was sufficiently characteristic. Bingley had never met with pleasanter people or prettier girls in his life; everybody had been most kind and attentive to him, there had been no formality, no stiffness, he had soon felt acquainted with all the room; and as to Miss Bennet, he could not conceive an angel more beautiful. Darcy, on the contrary, had seen a collection of people in whom there was little beauty and no fashion, for none of whom he had felt the smallest interest, and from none received either attention or pleasure. Miss Bennet he acknowledged to be pretty, but she smiled too much.

Mrs. Hurst and her sister allowed it to be so—but still they admired her and liked her, and pronounced her to be a sweet girl, and one whom they should not object to know more of. Miss Bennet was therefore established as a sweet girl, and their brother felt authorised by such commendation to think of her as he chose.
—1811 (WRITTEN 1796–97)

MARY PRINCE
1788 – 1833

Author of the earliest extant slave narrative by a woman, Mary Prince was born into bondage in the British colony of Bermuda, where for the first twelve years of her life she was spared the cruelty that dominated her adult years. Both her parents were also slaves, the property of Charles Myners. After Myners died, Mary and her mother were sold to a Captain Williams, whose daughter Betsey treated Mary as "her little nigger," yet with relative compassion. Williams sold Prince to another family to raise money for his marriage, and in 1806 she was sent to work in the salt ponds of Turks Island: "This work was perfectly new to me. I was given a half barrel and shovel, and had to stand up to my knees in the water, from four o'clock in the morning till nine, when we were given some Indian corn boiled in water, which we were obliged to swallow as fast as we could for fear the rain should come on and melt the salt." In addition to these intolerable working conditions, Prince also endured physical and probably sexual abuse from her master.

In 1818, Prince was sold for three hundred dollars to John Wood, a plantation owner in Antigua, who beat, overworked, and otherwise abused her. By this time Prince had developed a serious skin problem, and while working for the Woods she became essentially crippled by severe rheumatism; her mistreatment would also eventually lead to damaged eyesight. Prince began attending meetings held at the Moravian Church, where various women taught her to read: "After we had done spelling, we tried to read in the Bible. After reading was over, the missionary gave out a hymn for us to sing." Prince was married in this church to Daniel Jones, a former slave who had purchased his own freedom. Wood horsewhipped Prince when he discovered the marriage. In 1828 Wood took Prince to London as his servant. Abolitionist sympathizers helped her escape and she found employment as a domestic servant (slavery was illegal in England) of Thomas Pringle, a Methodist and secretary of the Society for the Abolition of Slavery.

Pringle encouraged Prince to tell the story of her life and, in 1831, he arranged for the publication of her book, *The History of Mary Prince, a West-Indian Slave, Related by Herself*. In his "Preface" to the work, Pringle wrote: "The idea of writing Mary Prince's history was first suggested by herself. She wished it to be done, she said, that good people in England might hear from a slave what a slave had felt and suffered." Mary Prince told her story to Susanna Strickland (later Moodie), who recorded it in writing. It seems improbable that Strickland—who would later come to be regarded as one of Canada's most accomplished writers in the nineteenth century—would not at a minimum have edited the dictated narrative for grammar and syntax, and some have suggested that Pringle may have had some hand in shaping the manuscript so as to better serve abolitionist ends. (His insistence that the rhetorical flourish at the end of Prince's first paragraph is "given verbatim as uttered by Mary Prince" has struck more than one reader as rather forced.) But most scholars have stopped short of suggesting that material was fabricated by Pringle and Strickland, or that this is not in essence Prince's own narrative. Strickland herself attested that she had "been writing Mr. Pringle's black Mary's life from her own dictation and for her benefit adhering to her own simple story and language without deviating to the paths of flourish or romance."

The book was a great success, and gave rise to considerable controversy. *Blackwood's Magazine* and *The Glasgow Courier* claimed it was fraudulent and propagandistic. A number of libel suits resulted, with Wood suing Pringle and Pringle counter-suing. Wood claimed that the book had "endeavored to injure the character of my family by the most vile and infamous falsehoods." Wood lost the case and the libel scandal served only to make Prince's work more widely known. It reached a third edition in the same year it was published and it has since that time retained its place as one of the most moving, detailed, and comprehensive narratives of the life of a slave.

Slavery was abolished in all British colonies in 1833. Little is known of Prince's life after the publication of her *History*, and we do not know when, where, or how she died.

⌘⌘⌘

The History of Mary Prince
A West Indian Slave
Related by Herself

PREFACE [BY THOMAS PRINGLE[1]]

The idea of writing Mary Prince's history was first suggested by herself. She wished it to be done, she said, that good people in England might hear from a slave what a slave had felt and suffered; and a letter of her late master's, which will be found in the Supplement, induced me to accede to her wish without farther delay. The more immediate object of the publication will afterwards appear.

The narrative was taken down from Mary's own lips by a lady who happened to be at the time residing in my family as a visitor. It was written out fully, with all the narrator's repetitions and prolixities,[2] and afterwards pruned into its present shape; retaining, as far as was practicable, Mary's exact expressions and peculiar phraseology. No fact of importance has been omitted, and not a single circumstance or sentiment has been added. It is essentially her own, without any material alteration farther than was requisite to exclude redundances and gross grammatical errors, so as to render it clearly intelligible.

After it had been thus written out, I went over the whole, carefully examining her on every fact and circumstance detailed; and in all that relates to her resi-

dence in Antigua I had the advantage of being assisted in this scrutiny by Mr. Joseph Phillips, who was a resident in that colony during the same period, and had known her there.

The names of all the persons mentioned by the narrator have been printed in full, except those of Capt. I— and his wife, and that of Mr. D—, to whom conduct of peculiar atrocity is ascribed. These three individuals are now gone to answer at a far more awful tribunal than that of public opinion, for the deeds of which their former bondwoman accuses them; and to hold them up more openly to human reprobation could no longer affect themselves, while it might deeply lacerate the feelings of their surviving and perhaps innocent relatives, without any commensurate public advantage.

Without detaining the reader with remarks on other points which will be adverted to more conveniently in the Supplement, I shall here merely notice farther, that the Anti-Slavery Society have no concern whatever with this publication, nor are they in any degree responsible for the statements it contains. I have published the tract, not as their Secretary, but in my private capacity; and any profits that may arise from the sale will be exclusively appropriated to the benefit of Mary Prince herself.

THOMAS PRINGLE
7, Solly Terrace, Claremont Square,
January 25, 1831

P.S. Since writing the above, I have been furnished by my friend Mr. George Stephen, with the interesting narrative of Asa-Asa, a captured African, now under his protection; and have printed it as a suitable appendix to this little history.

T.P.

---

[1] *Thomas Pringle* Also known as the "father of South African poetry," Pringle (1789–1834) was born in Scotland and lived in South Africa between 1820 and 1826, where he published a newspaper and a magazine. In 1826 he returned to England, where he devoted himself to the antislavery movement as secretary to the Society for the Abolition of Slavery.

[2] *prolixities* Instances of wordiness.

The History of Mary Prince

I was born at Brackish-Pond, in Bermuda, on a farm belonging to Mr. Charles Myners. My mother was a household slave; and my father, whose name was Prince, was a sawyer[1] belonging to Mr. Trimmingham, a shipbuilder at Crow-Lane. When I was an infant, old Mr. Myners died, and there was a division of the slaves and other property among the family. I was bought along with my mother by old Captain Darrel, and given to his grandchild, little Miss Betsey Williams. Captain Williams, Mr. Darrel's son-in-law, was master of a vessel which traded to several places in America and the West Indies, and he was seldom at home long together.

Mrs. Williams was a kind-hearted good woman, and she treated all her slaves well. She had only one daughter, Miss Betsey, for whom I was purchased, and who was about my own age. I was made quite a pet of by Miss Betsey, and loved her very much. She used to lead me about by the hand, and call me her little nigger. This was the happiest period of my life; for I was too young to understand rightly my condition as a slave, and too thoughtless and full of spirits to look forward to the days of toil and sorrow.

My mother was a household slave in the same family. I was under her own care, and my little brothers and sisters were my play-fellows and companions. My mother had us several fine children after she came to Mrs. Williams, three girls and two boys. The tasks given out to us children were light, and we used to play together with Miss Betsey, with as much freedom almost as if she had been our sister.

My master, however, was a very harsh, selfish man; and we always dreaded his return from sea. His wife was herself much afraid of him; and, during his stay at home, seldom dared to show her usual kindness to the slaves. He often left her, in the most distressed circumstances, to reside in other female society, at some place in the West Indies of which I have forgot the name. My poor mistress bore his ill-treatment with great patience, and all her slaves loved and pitied her. I was truly attached to her, and, next to my own mother, loved her better than any creature in the world. My obedience to

her commands was cheerfully given: it sprung solely from the affection I felt for her, and not from fear of the power which the white people's law had given her over me.

I had scarcely reached my twelfth year when my mistress became too poor to keep so many of us at home; and she hired me out to Mrs. Pruden, a lady who lived about five miles off, in the adjoining parish, in a large house near the sea. I cried bitterly at parting with my dear mistress and Miss Betsey, and when I kissed my mother and brothers and sisters, I thought my young heart would break, it pained me so. But there was no help; I was forced to go. Good Mrs. Williams comforted me by saying that I should still be near the home I was about to quit, and might come over and see her and my kindred whenever I could obtain leave of absence from Mrs. Pruden. A few hours after this I was taken to a strange house, and found myself among strange people. This separation seemed a sore trial to me then; but oh! 'twas light, light to the trials I have since endured!—'twas nothing—nothing to be mentioned with them; but I was a child then, and it was according to my strength.

I knew that Mrs. Williams could no longer maintain me; that she was fain to part with me for my food and clothing; and I tried to submit myself to the change. My new mistress was a passionate woman; but yet she did not treat me very unkindly. I do not remember her striking me but once, and that was for going to see Mrs. Williams when I heard she was sick, and staying longer than she had given me leave to do. All my employment at this time was nursing a sweet baby, little Master Daniel; and I grew so fond of my nursling that it was my greatest delight to walk out with him by the sea-shore, accompanied by his brother and sister, Miss Fanny and Master James.—Dear Miss Fanny! She was a sweet, kind young lady, and so fond of me that she wished me to learn all that she knew herself; and her method of teaching me was as follows:—Directly she had said her lessons to her grandmamma, she used to come running to me, and make me repeat them one by one after her; and in a few months I was able not only to say my letters but to spell many small words. But this happy state was not to last long. Those days were too

---

[1] *sawyer* Worker whose job it is to saw timber.

pleasant to last. My heart always softens when I think of them.

At this time Mrs. Williams died. I was told suddenly of her death, and my grief was so great that, forgetting I had the baby in my arms, I ran away directly to my poor mistress's house; but reached it only in time to see the corpse carried out. Oh, that was a day of sorrow—a heavy day! All the slaves cried. My mother cried and lamented her sore; and I (foolish creature!) vainly entreated them to bring my dear mistress back to life. I knew nothing rightly about death then, and it seemed a hard thing to bear. When I thought about my mistress I felt as if the world was all gone wrong; and for many days and weeks I could think of nothing else. I returned to Mrs. Pruden's; but my sorrow was too great to be comforted, for my own dear mistress was always in my mind. Whether in the house or abroad, my thoughts were always talking to me about her.

I stayed at Mrs. Pruden's about three months after this; I was then sent back to Mr. Williams to be sold. Oh, that was a sad sad time! I recollect the day well. Mrs. Pruden came to me and said, "Mary, you will have to go home directly; your master is going to be married, and he means to sell you and two of your sisters to raise money for the wedding." Hearing this I burst out a crying,—though I was then far from being sensible of the full weight of my misfortune, or of the misery that waited for me. Besides, I did not like to leave Mrs. Pruden, and the dear baby, who had grown very fond of me. For some time I could scarcely believe that Mrs. Pruden was in earnest, till I received orders for my immediate return.—Dear Miss Fanny! how she cried at parting with me, whilst I kissed and hugged the baby, thinking I should never see him again. I left Mrs. Pruden's, and walked home with a heart full of sorrow. The idea of being sold away from my mother and Miss Betsey was so frightful, that I dared not trust myself to think about it. We had been bought of Mrs. Myners, as I have mentioned, by Miss Betsey's grandfather, and given to her, so that we were by right *her* property, and I never thought we should be separated or sold away from her.

When I reached the house, I went in directly to Miss Betsey. I found her in great distress; and she cried out as soon as she saw me, "Oh, Mary! my father is going to sell you all to raise money to marry that wicked woman. You are *my* slaves, and he has no right to sell you; but it is all to please her." She then told me that my mother was living with her father's sister at a house close by, and I went there to see her. It was a sorrowful meeting; and we lamented with a great and sore crying our unfortunate situation. "Here comes one of my poor piccaninnies!"[1] she said, the moment I came in, "one of the poor slave-brood who are to be sold to-morrow."

Oh dear! I cannot bear to think of that day,—it is too much.—It recalls the great grief that filled my heart, and the woeful thoughts that passed to and fro through my mind, whilst listening to the pitiful words of my poor mother, weeping for the loss of her children. I wish I could find words to tell you all I then felt and suffered. The great God above alone knows the thoughts of the poor slave's heart, and the bitter pains which follow such separations as these. All that we love taken away from us—oh, it is sad, sad! and sore to be borne!—I got no sleep that night for thinking of the morrow; and dear Miss Betsey was scarcely less distressed. She could not bear to part with her old playmates and she cried sore and would not be pacified.

The black morning at length came; it came too soon for my poor mother and us. Whilst she was putting on us the new osnaburgs[2] in which we were to be sold, she said, in a sorrowful voice, (I shall never forget it!) "See, I am *shrouding* my poor children; what a task for a mother!"—She then called Miss Betsey to take leave of us. "I am going to carry my little chickens to market," (these were her very words) "take your last look of them; may be you will see them no more." "Oh, my poor slaves! my own slaves!" said dear Miss Betsey, "you belong to me; and it grieves my heart to part with you."—Miss Betsey kissed us all, and, when she left us, my mother called the rest of the slaves to bid us good bye. One of them, a woman named Moll, came with her infant in her arms. "Ay!" said my mother, seeing her turn away and look at her child with the tears in her eyes, "your turn will come next." The slaves could say nothing to comfort us; they could only weep and lament

---

[1]   *piccaninnies* Children, usually applied derogatively to black children.

[2]   *osnaburgs* Type of coarse linen used to make clothing.

with us. When I left my dear little brothers and the house in which I had been brought up, I thought my heart would burst.

Our mother, weeping as she went, called me away with the children Hannah and Dinah, and we took the road that led to Hamble Town, which we reached about four o'clock in the afternoon. We followed my mother to the market-place, where she placed us in a row against a large house, with our backs to the wall and our arms folded across our breasts. I, as the eldest, stood first, Hannah next to me, then Dinah; and our mother stood beside, crying over us. My heart throbbed with grief and terror so violently, that I pressed my hands quite tightly across my breast, but I could not keep it still, and it continued to leap as though it would burst out of my body. But who cared for that? Did one of the many bystanders, who were looking at us so carelessly, think of the pain that wrung the hearts of the negro woman and her young ones? No, no! They were not all bad, I dare say, but slavery hardens white people's hearts towards the blacks; and many of them were not slow to make their remarks upon us aloud, without regard to our grief— though their light words fell like cayenne on the fresh wounds of our hearts. Oh those white people have small hearts who can only feel for themselves.

At length the vendue[1] master, who was to offer us for sale like sheep or cattle, arrived, and asked my mother which was the eldest. She said nothing, but pointed to me. He took me by the hand, and led me out into the middle of the street, and, turning me slowly round, exposed me to the view of those who attended the vendue. I was soon surrounded by strange men, who examined and handled me in the same manner that a butcher would a calf or a lamb he was about to purchase, and who talked about my shape and size in like words—as if I could no more understand their meaning than the dumb beasts. I was then put up for sale. The bidding commenced at a few pounds, and gradually rose to fifty-seven, when I was knocked down to the highest bidder; and the people who stood by said that I had fetched a great sum for so young a slave.

I then saw my sisters led forth, and sold to different owners; so that we had not the sad satisfaction of being

partners in bondage. When the sale was over, my mother hugged and kissed us, and mourned over us, begging of us to keep up a good heart, and do our duty to our new masters. It was a sad parting; one went one way, one another, and our poor mammy went home with nothing.

My new master was a Captain I—, who lived at Spanish Point. After parting with my mother and sisters, I followed him to his store, and he gave me into the charge of his son, a lad about my own age, Master Benjy, who took me to my new home. I did not know where I was going, or what my new master would do with me. My heart was quite broken with grief, and my thoughts went back continually to those from whom I had been so suddenly parted. "Oh, my mother! my mother!" I kept saying to myself, "Oh, my mammy and my sisters and my brothers, shall I never see you again!"

Oh, the trials! the trials! they make the salt water come into my eyes when I think of the days in which I was afflicted—the times that are gone; when I mourned and grieved with a young heart for those whom I loved.—It was night when I reached my new home. The house was large, and built at the bottom of a very high hill; but I could not see much of it that night. I saw too much of it afterwards. The stones and the timber were the best things in it; they were not so hard as the hearts of the owners.

Before I entered the house, two slave women, hired from another owner, who were at work in the yard, spoke to me, and asked who I belonged to? I replied, "I am come to live here." "Poor child, poor child!" they both said; "you must keep a good heart, if you are to live here."—When I went in, I stood up crying in a corner. Mrs. I— came and took off my hat, a little black silk hat Miss Pruden made for me, and said in a rough voice, "You are not come here to stand up in corners and cry, you are come here to work." She then put a child into my arms, and, tired as I was, I was forced instantly to take up my old occupation of a nurse.—I could not bear to look at my mistress, her countenance was so stern. She was a stout tall woman with a very dark complexion, and her brows were always drawn together into a frown. I thought of the words of the two slave women when I saw Mrs. I—, and heard the harsh sound of her voice.

[1] *vendue* Sale.

The person I took the most notice of that night was a French Black called Hetty, whom my master took in privateering from another vessel, and made his slave. She was the most active woman I ever saw, and she was tasked to her utmost. A few minutes after my arrival she came in from milking the cows, and put the sweet-potatoes on for supper. She then fetched home the sheep, and penned them in the fold; drove home the cattle, and staked them about the pond side; fed and rubbed down my master's horse, and gave the hog and the fed cow their suppers; prepared the beds, and undressed the children, and laid them to sleep. I liked to look at her and watch all her doings, for her's was the only friendly face I had as yet seen, and I felt glad that she was there. She gave me my supper of potatoes and milk, and a blanket to sleep upon, which she spread for me in the passage before the door of Mrs. I—'s chamber.

I got a sad fright, that night. I was just going to sleep, when I heard a noise in my mistress's room; and she presently called out to inquire if some work was finished that she had ordered Hetty to do. "No, Ma'am, not yet," was Hetty's answer from below. On hearing this, my master started up from his bed, and just as he was, in his shirt, ran down stairs with a long cow-skin in his hand. I heard immediately after, the cracking of the thong, and the house rang to the shrieks of poor Hetty, who kept crying out, "Oh, Massa! Massa! me dead. Massa! have mercy upon me—don't kill me out-right."—This was a sad beginning for me. I sat up upon my blanket, trembling with terror, like a frightened hound, and thinking that my turn would come next. At length the house became still, and I forgot for a little while all my sorrows by falling fast asleep.

The next morning my mistress set about instructing me in my tasks. She taught me to do all sorts of house-hold work; to wash and bake, pick cotton and wool, and wash floors, and cook. And she taught me (how can I ever forget it!) more things than these; she caused me to know the exact difference between the smart of the rope, the cart-whip, and the cow-skin, when applied to my naked body by her own cruel hand. And there was scarcely any punishment more dreadful than the blows I received on my face and head from her hard heavy fist. She was a fearful woman, and a savage mistress to her slaves.

There were two little slave boys in the house, on whom she vented her bad temper in a special manner. One of these children was a mulatto, called Cyrus, who had been bought while an infant in his mother's arms; the other, Jack, was an African from the coast of Guinea, whom a sailor had given or sold to my master. Seldom a day passed without these boys receiving the most severe treatment, and often for no fault at all. Both my master and mistress seemed to think that they had a right to ill-use them at their pleasure; and very often accompanied their commands with blows, whether the children were behaving well or ill. I have seen their flesh ragged and raw with licks.—Lick—lick—they were never secure one moment from a blow, and their lives were passed in continual fear. My mistress was not contented with using the whip, but often pinched their cheeks and arms in the most cruel manner. My pity for these poor boys was soon transferred to myself; for I was licked, and flogged, and pinched by her pitiless fingers in the neck and arms, exactly as they were. To strip me naked—to hang me up by the wrists and lay my flesh open with the cow-skin, was an ordinary punishment for even a slight offence. My mistress often robbed me too of the hours that belong to sleep. She used to sit up very late, frequently even until morning; and I had then to stand at a bench and wash during the greater part of the night, or pick wool and cotton and often I have dropped down overcome by sleep and fatigue, till roused from a state of stupor by the whip, and forced to start up to my tasks.

Poor Hetty, my fellow slave, was very kind to me, and I used to call her my Aunt; but she led a most miserable life, and her death was hastened (at least the slaves all believed and said so,) by the dreadful chastise-ment she received from my master during her preg-nancy. It happened as follows. One of the cows had dragged the rope away from the stake to which Hetty had fastened it, and got loose. My master flew into a terrible passion, and ordered the poor creature to be stripped quite naked, notwithstanding her pregnancy, and to be tied up to a tree in the yard. He then flogged her as hard as he could lick, both with the whip and cow-skin, till she was all over streaming with blood. He rested, and then beat her again and again. Her shrieks were terrible. The consequence was that poor Hetty was brought to bed before her time, and was delivered after severe labour of a dead child. She appeared to recover after her confinement, so far that she was repeatedly flogged by both master and mistress afterwards; but her former strength never returned to her. Ere long her body and limbs swelled to a great size; and she lay on a mat in the kitchen, till the water burst out of her body and she died. All the slaves said that death was a good thing for poor Hetty; but I cried very much for her death. The manner of it filled me with horror. I could not bear to think about it; yet it was always present to my mind for many a day.

After Hetty died all her labours fell upon me, in addition to my own. I had now to milk eleven cows every morning before sunrise, sitting among the damp weeds; to take care of the cattle as well as the children; and to do the work of the house. There was no end to my toils—no end to my blows. I lay down at night and rose up in the morning in fear and sorrow; and often wished that like poor Hetty I could escape from this cruel bondage and be at rest in the grave. But the hand of that God whom then I knew not, was stretched over me; and I was mercifully preserved for better things. It was then, however, my heavy lot to weep, weep, weep, and that for years; to pass from one misery to another, and from one cruel master to a worse. But I must go on with the thread of my story. One day a heavy squall of wind and rain came on suddenly, and my mistress sent me round the corner of the house to empty a large earthen jar. The jar was already cracked with an old deep crack that divided it in the middle, and in turning it upside down to empty it, it parted in my hand. I could not help the accident, but I was dreadfully frightened, looking forward to a severe punishment. I ran crying to my mistress, "O mistress, the jar has come in two." "You have broken it, have you?" she replied; "come directly here to me." I came trembling: she stripped and flogged me long and severely with the cowskin; as long as she had strength to use the lash, for she did not give over till she was quite tired.—When my master came home at night, she told him of my fault; and oh, frightful! how he fell a swearing. After abusing me with every ill name he could think of, (too, too bad to speak in England,) and giving me several heavy blows

with his hand, he said, "I shall come home to-morrow morning at twelve, on purpose to give you a round hundred." He kept his word—Oh sad for me! I cannot easily forget it. He tied me up upon a ladder, and gave me a hundred lashes with his own hand, and master Benjy stood by to count them for him. When he had licked me for some time he sat down to take breath; then after resting, he beat me again and again, until he was quite wearied, and so hot (for the weather was very sultry), that he sank back in his chair, almost like to faint. While my mistress went to bring him drink, there was a dreadful earthquake. Part of the roof fell down, and every thing in the house went—clatter, clatter, clatter. Oh I thought the end of all things near at hand; and I was so sore with the flogging, that I scarcely cared whether I lived or died. The earth was groaning and shaking; every thing tumbling about; and my mistress and the slaves were shrieking and crying out, "The earthquake! the earthquake!" It was an awful day for us all.

During the confusion I crawled away on my hands and knees, and laid myself down under the steps of the piazza, in front of the house. I was in a dreadful state— my body all blood and bruises, and I could not help moaning piteously. The other slaves, when they saw me, shook their heads and said, "Poor child! poor child"—I lay there till the morning, careless of what might happen, for life was very weak in me, and I wished more than ever to die. But when we are very young, death always seems a great way off, and it would not come that night to me. The next morning I was forced by my master to rise and go about my usual work, though my body and limbs were so stiff and sore, that I could not move without the greatest pain.—Nevertheless, even after all this severe punishment, I never heard the last of that jar; my mistress was always throwing it in my face.

Some little time after this, one of the cows got loose from the stake, and eat one of the sweet-potato slips. I was milking when my master found it out. He came to me, and without any more ado, stooped down, and taking off his heavy boot, he struck me such a severe blow in the small of my back, that I shrieked with agony, and thought I was killed; and I feel a weakness in that part to this day. The cow was frightened by his violence, and kicked down the pail and spilt the milk all about. My master knew that this accident was his own fault, but he was so enraged that he seemed glad of an excuse to go on with his ill usage. I cannot remember how many licks he gave me then, but he beat me till I was unable to stand, and till he himself was weary.

After this I ran away and went to my mother, who was living with Mr. Richard Darrel. My poor mother was both grieved and glad to see me; grieved because I had been so ill used, and glad because she had not seen me for a long, long while. She dared not receive me into the house, but she hid me up in a hole in the rocks near, and brought me food at night, after every body was asleep. My father, who lived at Crow-Lane, over the salt-water channel, at last heard of my being hid up in the cavern, and he came and took me back to my master. Oh I was loath, loath to go back; but as there was no remedy, I was obliged to submit.

When we got home, my poor father said to Capt. I—, "Sir, I am sorry that my child should be forced to run away from her owner; but the treatment she has received is enough to break her heart. The sight of her wounds has nearly broke mine.—I entreat you, for the love of God, to forgive her for running away, and that you will be a kind master to her in future." Capt. I— said I was used as well as I deserved, and that I ought to be punished for running away. I then took courage and said that I could stand the floggings no longer; that I was weary of my life, and therefore I had run away to my mother; but mothers could only weep and mourn over their children, they could not save them from cruel masters—from the whip, the rope, and the cow-skin. He told me to hold my tongue and go about my work, or he would find a way to settle me. He did not, however, flog me that day.

For five years after this I remained in his house, and almost daily received the same harsh treatment. At length he put me on board a sloop,[1] and to my great joy sent me away to Turk's Island.[2] I was not permitted to see my mother or father, or poor sisters and brothers, to say good bye, though going away to a strange land, and

might never see them again. Oh the Buckra[3] people who keep slaves think that black people are like cattle, without natural affection. But my heart tells me it is far otherwise.

We were nearly four weeks on the voyage, which was unusually long. Sometimes we had a light breeze, sometimes a great calm, and the ship made no way; so that our provisions and water ran very low, and we were put upon short allowance. I should almost have been starved had it not been for the kindness of a black man called Anthony, and his wife, who had brought their own victuals, and shared them with me.

When we went ashore at the Grand Quay, the captain sent me to the house of my new master, Mr. D—, to whom Captain I— had sold me. Grand Quay is a small town upon a sandbank; the houses low and built of wood. Such was my new master's. The first person I saw, on my arrival, was Mr. D—, a stout sulky looking man, who carried me through the hall to show me to his wife and children. Next day I was put up by the vendue master to know how much I was worth, and I was valued at one hundred pounds currency.

My new master was one of the owners or holders of the salt ponds, and he received a certain sum for every slave that worked upon his premises, whether they were young or old. This sum was allowed him out of the profits arising from the salt works. I was immediately sent to work in the salt water with the rest of the slaves. This work was perfectly new to me. I was given a half barrel and a shovel, and had to stand up to my knees in the water, from four o'clock in the morning till nine, when we were given some Indian corn boiled in water, which we were obliged to swallow as fast as we could for fear the rain should come on and melt the salt. We were then called again to our tasks, and worked through the heat of the day; the sun flaming upon our heads like fire, and raising salt blisters in those parts which were not completely covered. Our feet and legs, from standing in the salt water for so many hours, soon became full of dreadful boils, which eat down in some cases to the very bone, afflicting the sufferers with great torment. We came home at twelve; ate our corn soup, called *blawly,* as fast as we could, and went back to our em-

[1] *sloop* Small ship.
[2] *Turk's Island* The southernmost and easternmost island of the Bahamas.
[3] *Buckra* White.

ployment till dark at night. We then shovelled up the salt in large heaps, and went down to the sea, where we washed the pickle from our limbs, and cleaned the barrows and shovels from the salt. When we returned to the house, our master gave us each our allowance of raw Indian corn, which we pounded in a mortar and boiled in water for our suppers. We slept in a long shed, divided into narrow slips, like the stalls used for cattle. Boards fixed upon stakes driven into the ground, without mat or covering, were our only beds. On Sundays, after we had washed the salt bags, and done other work required of us, we went into the bush and cut the long soft grass, of which we made trusses for our legs and feet to rest upon, for they were so full of the salt boils that we could get no rest lying upon the bare boards.

Though we worked from morning till night, there was no satisfying Mr. D—. I hoped, when I left Capt. I—, that I should have been better off, but I found it was but going from one butcher to another. There was this difference between them: my former master used to beat me while raging and foaming with passion; Mr. D— was usually quite calm. He would stand by and give orders for a slave to be cruelly whipped, and assist in the punishment, without moving a muscle of his face; walking about and taking snuff with the greatest composure. Nothing could touch his hard heart—neither sighs, nor tears, nor prayers, nor streaming blood; he was deaf to our cries, and careless of our sufferings.—Mr. D— has often stripped me naked, hung me up by the wrists, and beat me with the cow-skin, with his own hand, till my body was raw with gashes. Yet there was nothing very remarkable in this; for it might serve as a sample of the common usage of the slaves on that horrible island.

Owing to the boils in my feet, I was unable to wheel the barrow fast through the sand, which got into the sores, and made me stumble at every step; and my master, having no pity for my sufferings from this cause, rendered them far more intolerable, by chastising me for not being able to move so fast as he wished me. Another of our employments was to row a little way off from the shore in a boat, and dive for large stones to build a wall round our master's house. This was very hard work; and the great waves breaking over us continually, made us often so giddy that we lost our footing, and were in danger of being drowned.

Ah, poor me!—my tasks were never ended. Sick or well, it was work—work—work!—After the diving season was over, we were sent to the South Creek, with large bills, to cut up mangoes to burn lime with. Whilst one party of slaves were thus employed, another were sent to the other side of the island to break up coral out of the sea.

When we were ill, let our complaint be what it might, the only medicine given to us was a great bowl of hot salt water, with salt mixed with it, which made us very sick. If we could not keep up with the rest of the gang of slaves, we were put in the stocks,[1] and severely flogged the next morning. Yet, not the less, our master expected, after we had thus been kept from our rest, and our limbs rendered stiff and sore with ill usage, that we should still go through the ordinary tasks of the day all the same.—Sometimes we had to work all night, measuring salt to load a vessel; or turning a machine to draw water out of the sea for the salt-making. Then we had no sleep—no rest—but were forced to work as fast as we could, and go on again all next day the same as usual. Work—work—work—Oh that Turk's Island was a horrible place! The people in England, I am sure, have never found out what is carried on there. Cruel, horrible place!

Mr. D— had a slave called old Daniel, whom he used to treat in the most cruel manner. Poor Daniel was lame in the hip, and could not keep up with the rest of the slaves; and our master would order him to be stripped and laid down on the ground, and have him beaten with a rod of rough briar till his skin was quite red and raw. He would then call for a bucket of salt, and fling upon the raw flesh till the man writhed on the ground like a worm, and screamed aloud with agony. This poor man's wounds were never ed, and I have often seen them full of maggots, which increased his torments to an intolerable degree. He was an object of pity and terror to the whole gang of slaves, and in his wretched case we saw, each of us, our own lot, if we should live to be as old.

---

[1] *stocks* Device for confining the ankles and sometimes the wrists.

Oh the horrors of slavery!—How the thought of it pains my heart! But the truth ought to be told of it; and what my eyes have seen I think it is my duty to relate; for few people in England know what slavery is. I have been a slave—I have felt what a slave feels, and I know what a slave knows; and I would have all the good people in England to know it too, that they may break our chains, and set us free.

Mr. D— had another slave called Ben. He being very hungry, stole a little rice one night after he came in from work, and cooked it for his supper. But his master soon discovered the theft; locked him up all night; and kept him without food till one o'clock the next day. He then hung Ben up by his hands, and beat him from time to time till the slaves came in at night. We found the poor creature hung up when we came home; with a pool of blood beneath him, and our master still licking him, but this was not the worst. My master's son was in the habit of stealing the rice and rum. Ben had seen him do this, and thought he might do the same, and when master found out that Ben had stolen the rice and swore to punish him, he tried to excuse himself by saying that Master Dickey did the same thing every night. The lad denied it to his father, and was so angry with Ben for informing against him, that out of revenge he ran and got a bayonet, and whilst the poor wretch was suspended by his hands and writhing under his wounds, he run it quite through his foot. I was not by when he did it, but I saw the wound when I came home, and heard Ben tell the manner in which it was done.

I must say something more about this cruel son of a cruel father.—He had no heart—no fear of God; he had been brought up by a bad father in a bad path, and he delighted to follow in the same steps. There was a little old woman among the slaves called Sarah, who was nearly past work; and, Master Dickey being the overseer of the slaves just then, this poor creature, who was subject to several bodily infirmities, and was not quite right in her head, did not wheel the barrow fast enough to please him. He threw her down on the ground, and after beating her severely, he took her up in his arms and flung her among the prickly-pear[1] bushes, which are all covered over with sharp venomous prickles. By this her naked flesh was so grievously wounded, that her body swelled and festered all over, and she died in a few days after. In telling my own sorrows, I cannot pass by those of my fellow-slaves—for when I think of my own griefs, I remember theirs.

I think it was about ten years I had worked in the salt ponds at Turk's Island, when my master left off business, and retired to a house he had in Bermuda, leaving his son to succeed him in the island. He took me with him to wait upon his daughters; and I was joyful, for I was sick, sick of Turk's Island, and my heart yearned to see my native place again, my mother, and my kindred.

I had seen my poor mother during the time I was a slave in Turk's Island. One Sunday morning I was on the beach with some of the slaves, and we saw a sloop come in loaded with slaves to work in the salt water. We got a boat and went aboard. When I came upon the deck I asked the black people, "Is there any one here for me?" "Yes," they said, "your mother." I thought they said this in jest—I could scarcely believe them for joy; but when I saw my poor mammy my joy was turned to sorrow, for she had gone from her senses. "Mammy," I said, "is this you!" She did not know me. "Mammy," I said, "what's the matter?" She began to talk foolishly and said that she had been under the vessel's bottom. They had been overtaken by a violent storm at sea. My poor mother had never been on the sea before, and she was so ill, that she lost her senses, and it was long before she came quite to herself again. She had a sweet child with her—a little sister I had never seen, about four years of age, called Rebecca. I took her on shore with me, for I felt I should love her directly; and I kept her with me a week. Poor little thing! her's has been a sad life, and continues so to this day. My mother worked for some years on the island, but was taken back to Bermuda some time before my master carried me again thither.

After I left Turk's Island, I was told by some negroes that came over from it, that the poor slaves had built up a place with boughs and leaves, where they might meet for prayers, but the white people pulled it down twice, and would not allow them even a shed for prayers. A flood came down soon after and washed away many houses, filled the place with sand, and overflowed the

---

[1] *prickly-pear* Type of cactus.

ponds: and I do think that this was for their wickedness; for the Buckra men there were very wicked. I saw and heard much that was very very bad at that place.

I was several years the slave of Mr. D— after I returned to my native place. Here I worked in the grounds. My work was planting and hoeing sweet-potatoes, Indian corn, plaintains, bananas, cabbages, pumpkins, onions, &c. I did all the household work, and attended upon a horse and cow besides,—going also upon all errands. I had to curry the horse—to clean and feed him—and sometimes to ride him a little. I had more than enough to do—but still it was not so very bad as Turk's Island.

My old master often got drunk, and then he would get in a fury with his daughter, and beat her till she was not fit to be seen. I remember on one occasion, I had gone to fetch water, and when I was coming up the hill I heard a great screaming; I ran as fast as I could to the house, put down the water, and went into the chamber, where I found my master beating Miss D— dreadfully. I strove with all my strength to get her away from him; for she was all black and blue with bruises. He had beat her with his fist, and almost killed her. The people gave me credit for getting her away. He turned round and began to lick me. Then I said, "Sir, this is not Turk's Island." I can't repeat his answer, the words were too wicked—too bad to say. He wanted to treat me the same in Bermuda as he had done in Turk's Island.

He had an ugly fashion of stripping himself quite naked and ordering me then to wash him in a tub of water. This was worse to me than all the licks. Some-times when he called me to wash him I would not come, my eyes were so full of shame. He would then come to beat me. One time I had plates and knives in my hand, and I dropped both plates and knives, and some of the plates were broken. He struck me so severely for this, that at last I defended myself, for I thought it was high time to do so. I then told him I would not live longer with him, for he was a very indecent man—very spite-ful, and too indecent; with no shame for his servants, no shame for his own flesh. So I went away to a neighbour-ing house and sat down and cried till the next morning, when I went home again, not knowing what else to do.

After that I was hired to work at Cedar Hills, and every Saturday night I paid the money to my master. I had plenty of work to do there—plenty of washing; but yet I made myself pretty comfortable. I earned two dollars and a quarter a week, which is twenty pence a day.

During the time I worked there, I heard that Mr. John Wood was going to Antigua. I felt a great wish to go there, and I went to Mr. D—, and asked him to let me go in Mr. Wood's service. Mr. Wood did not then want to purchase me; it was my own fault that I came under him, I was so anxious to go. It was ordained to be, I suppose; God led me there. The truth is, I did not wish to be any longer the slave of my indecent master.

Mr. Wood took me with him to Antigua, to the town of St. John's, where he lived. This was about fifteen years ago. He did not then know whether I was to be sold; but Mrs. Wood found that I could work, and she wanted to buy me. Her husband then wrote to my master to inquire whether I was to be sold? Mr. D— wrote in reply, "that I should not be sold to any one that would treat me ill." It was strange he should say this, when he had treated me so ill himself. So I was pur-chased by Mr. Wood for 300 dollars (or £100 Bermuda currency).

My work there was to attend the chambers and nurse the child, and to go down to the pond and wash clothes. But I soon fell ill of the rheumatism, and grew so very lame that I was forced to walk with a stick. I got the Saint Anthony's fire,[1] also, in my left leg, and became quite a cripple. No one cared much to come near me, and I was ill a long long time; for several months I could not lift the limb. I had to lie in a little old out-house, that was swarming with bugs and other vermin, which tormented me greatly; but I had no other place to lie in. I got the rheumatism by catching cold at the pond side, from washing in the fresh water; in the salt water I never got cold. The person who lived in next yard, (a Mrs. Greene,) could not bear to hear my cries and groans. She was kind, and used to send an old slave woman to help me, who sometimes brought me a little soup. When the doctor found I was so ill, he said I must be put into a bath of hot water. The old slave got the bark of some bush that was good for pains, which she boiled in the hot water, and every night she came and put me into the bath, and did what she could for me; I

---

[1] *Saint Anthony's fire* Erysipelas or ergotism, diseases that cause intense redness, swelling of the skin, and severe pain.

MARY PRINCE

don't know what I should have done, or what would have become of me, had it not been for her.—My mistress, it is true, did send me a little food; but no one from our family came near me but the cook, who used to shove my food in at the door, and say, "Molly, Molly, there's your dinner." My mistress did not care to take any trouble about me; and if the Lord had not put it into the hearts of the neighbours to be kind to me, I must, I really think, have lain and died.

It was a long time before I got well enough to work in the house. Mrs. Wood, in the meanwhile, hired a mulatto woman to nurse the child; but she was such a fine lady she wanted to be mistress over me. I thought it very hard for a coloured woman to have rule over me because I was a slave and she was free. Her name was Martha Wilcox; she was a saucy woman, very saucy; and she went and complained of me, without cause, to my mistress, and made her angry with me. Mrs. Wood told me that if I did not mind what I was about, she would get my master to strip me and give me fifty lashes: "You have been used to the whip," she said, "and you shall have it here." This was the first time she threatened to have me flogged; and she gave me the threatening so strong of what she would have done to me, that I thought I should have fallen down at her feet, I was so vexed and hurt by her words. The mulatto woman was rejoiced to have power to keep me down. She was constantly making mischief; there was no living for the slaves—no peace after she came.

I was also sent by Mrs. Wood to be put in the Cage one night, and was next morning flogged, by the magistrate's order, at her desire; and this all for a quarrel I had about a pig with another slave woman. I was flogged on my naked back on this occasion; although I was in no fault after all; for old Justice Dyett, when we came before him, said that I was in the right, and ordered the pig to be given to me. This was about two or three years after I came to Antigua.

When we moved from the middle of the town to the Point, I used to be in the house and do all the work and mind the children, though still very ill with the rheumatism. Every week I had to wash two large bundles of clothes, as much as a boy could help me to lift; but I could give no satisfaction. My mistress was always abusing and fretting after me. It is not possible to tell all

her ill language.—One day she followed me foot after foot scolding and rating me. I bore in silence a great deal of ill words: at last my heart was quite full, and I told her that she ought not to use me so;—that when I was ill I might have lain and died for what she cared; and no one would then come near me to nurse me, because they were afraid of my mistress. This was a great affront. She called her husband and told him what I had said. He flew into a passion: but did not beat me then; he only abused and swore at me; and then gave me a note and bade me go and look for an owner. Not that he meant to sell me; but he did this to please his wife and to frighten me. I went to Adam White, a cooper,[1] a free black who had money, and asked him to buy me. He went directly to Mr. Wood, but was informed that I was not to be sold. The next day my master whipped me.

Another time (about five years ago) my mistress got vexed with me because I fell sick and I could not keep on with my work. She complained to her husband, and he sent me off again to look for an owner. I went to a Mr. Burchell, showed him the note, and asked him to buy me for my own benefit; for I had saved about 100 dollars, and hoped with a little help, to purchase my freedom. He accordingly went to my master: "Mr. Wood," he said, "Molly has brought me a note that she wants an owner. If you intend to sell her, I may as well buy her as another." My master put him off and said that he did not mean to sell me. I was very sorry at this, for I had no comfort with Mrs. Wood, and I wished greatly to get my freedom.

The way in which I made my money was this.— When my master and mistress went from home, as they sometimes did, and left me to take care of the house and premises, I had a good deal of time to myself and made the most of it. I took in washing, and sold coffee and yams and other provisions to the captains of ships. I did not sit still idling during the absence of my owners; for I wanted, by all honest means, to earn money to buy my freedom. Sometimes I bought a hog cheap on board ship, and sold it for double the money on shore; and I also earned a good deal by selling coffee. By this means I by degrees acquired a little cash. A gentleman also lent me some to help to buy my freedom—but when I could

---

[1] *cooper* Barrel- and tub-maker.

not get free he got it back again. His name was Captain Abbot.

My master and mistress went on one occasion into the country, to Date Hill, for a change of air, and carried me with them to take charge of the children, and to do the work of the house. While I was in the country, I saw how the field negroes are worked in Antigua. They are worked very hard and fed but scantily. They are called out to work before daybreak, and come home after dark; and then each has to heave his bundle of grass for the cattle in the pen. Then, on Sunday morning, each slave has to go out and gather a large bundle of grass; and, when they bring it home, they have all to sit at the manager's door and wait till he comes out: often have they to wait there till past eleven o'clock without any breakfast. After that, those that have yams or potatoes, or fire-wood to sell, hasten to market to buy a dog's worth[1] of salt fish, or pork, which is a great treat for them. Some of them buy a little pickle out of the shad barrels, which they call sauce, to season their yams and Indian corn. It is very wrong, I know, to work on Sunday or go to market; but will not God call the Buckra men to answer for this on the great day of judgment—since they will give the slaves no other day?

While we were at Date Hill Christmas came; and the slave woman who had the care of the place (which then belonged to Mr. Roberts the marshal), asked me to go with her to her husband's house, to a Methodist meeting for prayer, at a plantation called Winthorps. I went; and they were the first prayers I ever understood. One woman prayed; and then they all sung a hymn; then there was another prayer and another hymn; and then they all spoke by turns of their own griefs as sinners. The husband of the woman I went with was a black driver. His name was Henry. He confessed that he had treated the slaves very cruelly; but said that he was compelled to obey the orders of his master. He prayed them all to forgive him, and he prayed that God would forgive him. He said it was a horrid thing for a ranger to have sometimes to beat his own wife or sister; but he must do so if ordered by his master.

I felt sorry for my sins also. I cried the whole night, but I was too much ashamed to speak. I prayed God to

forgive me. This meeting had a great impression on my mind, and led my spirit to the Moravian church; so that when I got back to town, I went and prayed to have my name put down in the Missionaries' book; and I followed the church earnestly every opportunity. I did not then tell my mistress about it; for I knew that she would not give me leave to go. But I felt I *must* go. Whenever I carried the children their lunch at school, I ran round and went to hear the teachers.

The Moravian ladies (Mrs. Richter, Mrs. Olufsen, and Mrs. Sauter) taught me to read in the class; and I got on very fast. In this class there were all sorts of people, old and young, grey headed folks and children; but most of them were free people. After we had done spelling, we tried to read in the Bible. After the reading was over, the missionary gave out a hymn for us to sing. I dearly loved to go to the church, it was so solemn. I never knew rightly that I had much sin till I went there. When I found out that I was a great sinner, I was very sorely grieved, and very much frightened. I used to pray God to pardon my sins for Christ's sake, and forgive me for every thing I had done amiss; and when I went home to my work, I always thought about what I had heard from the missionaries, and wished to be good that I might go to heaven. After a while I was admitted a candidate for the holy Communion.—I had been baptized long before this, in August 1817, by the Rev. Mr. Curtin, of the English Church, after I had been taught to repeat the Creed and the Lord's Prayer. I wished at that time to attend a Sunday School taught by Mr. Curtin, but he would not receive me without a written note from my master, granting his permission. I did not ask my owner's permission, from the belief that it would be refused; so that I got no farther instruction at that time from the English Church.

Some time after I began to attend the Moravian Church, I met with Daniel James, afterwards my dear husband. He was a carpenter and cooper to his trade; an honest, hard-working, decent black man, and a widower. He had purchased his freedom of his mistress, old Mrs. Baker, with money he had earned whilst a slave. When he asked me to marry him, I took time to consider the matter over with myself, and would not say yes till he went to church with me and joined the Moravians. He was very industrious after he bought his

---

[1] *dog's worth* 72nd part of a dollar.

freedom; and he had hired a comfortable house, and had convenient things about him. We were joined in marriage, about Christmas 1826, in the Moravian Chapel at Spring Gardens, by the Rev. Mr. Olufsen. We could not be married in the English Church. English marriage is not allowed to slaves; and no free man can marry a slave woman.

When Mr. Wood heard of my marriage, he flew into a great rage, and sent for Daniel, who was helping to build a house for his old mistress. Mr. Wood asked him who gave him a right to marry a slave of his? My husband said, "Sir, I am a free man, and thought I had a right to choose a wife; but if I had known Molly was not allowed to have a husband, I should not have asked her to marry me." Mrs. Wood was more vexed about my marriage than her husband. She could not forgive me for getting married, but stirred up Mr. Wood to flog me dreadfully with his horsewhip. I thought it very hard to be whipped at my time of life for getting a husband—I told her so. She said that she would not have nigger men about the yards and premises, or allow a nigger man's clothes to be washed in the same tub where hers were washed. She was fearful, I think, that I should lose her time, in order to wash and do things for my husband: but I had then no time to wash for myself; I was obliged to put out my own clothes, though I was always at the wash-tub.

I had not much happiness in my marriage, owing to my being a slave. It made my husband sad to see me so ill-treated. Mrs. Wood was always abusing me about him. She did not lick me herself, but she got her husband to do it for her, whilst she fretted the flesh off my bones. Yet for all this she would not sell me. She sold five slaves whilst I was with her; but though she was always finding fault with me, she would not part with me. However, Mr. Wood afterwards allowed Daniel to have a place to live in our yard, which we were very thankful for.

After this, I fell ill again with the rheumatism, and was sick a long time; but whether sick or well, I had my work to do. About this time I asked my master and mistress to let me buy my own freedom. With the help of Mr. Burchell, I could have found the means to pay Mr. Wood; for it was agreed that I should afterwards serve Mr. Burchell a while, for the cash he was to advance for me. I was earnest in the request to my owners; but their hearts were hard—too hard to consent. Mrs. Wood was very angry—she grew quite outrageous—she called me a black devil, and asked me who had put freedom into my head. "To be free is very sweet," I said: but she took good care to keep me a slave. I saw her change colour, and I left the room.

About this time my master and mistress were going to England to put their son in school, and bring their daughters home; and they took me with them to take care of the child. I was willing to come to England: I thought that by going there I should probably get cured of my rheumatism, and should return with my master and mistress, quite well, to my husband. My husband was willing for me to come away, for he had heard that my master would free me,—and I also hoped this might prove true; but it was all a false report.

The steward of the ship was very kind to me. He and my husband were in the same class in the Moravian Church. I was thankful that he was so friendly, for my mistress was not kind to me on the passage; and she told me, when she was angry, that she did not intend to treat me any better in England than in the West Indies—that I need not expect it. And she was as good as her word.

When we drew near to England, the rheumatism seized all my limbs worse than ever, and my body was dreadfully swelled. When we landed at the Tower, I showed my flesh to my mistress, but she took no great notice of it. We were obliged to stop at the tavern till my master got a house; and a day or two after, my mistress sent me down into the wash-house to learn to wash in the English way. In the West Indies we wash with cold water—in England with hot. I told my mistress I was afraid that putting my hands first into the hot water and then into the cold, would increase the pain in my limbs. The doctor had told my mistress long before I came from the West Indies, that I was a sickly body and the washing did not agree with me. But Mrs. Wood would not release me from the tub, so I was forced to do as I could. I grew worse, and could not stand to wash. I was then forced to sit down with the tub before me, and often through pain and weakness was reduced to kneel or to sit down on the floor, to finish my task. When I complained to my mistress of this, she only got into a passion as usual, and said washing in hot water could not hurt any one;—that I was lazy and insolent, and wanted to be free of my work; but that she would make me do it. I thought her very hard on me, and my heart rose up within me. However I kept still at that time, and went down again to wash the child's things; but the English washerwomen who were at work there, when they saw that I was so ill, had pity upon me and washed them for me.

After that, when we came up to live in Leigh Street, Mrs. Wood sorted out five bags of clothes which we had used at sea, and also such as had been worn since we came on shore, for me and the cook to wash. Elizabeth the cook told her, that she did not think that I was able to stand to the tub, and that she had better hire a woman. I also said myself, that I had come over to nurse the child, and that I was sorry I had come from Antigua, since mistress would work me so hard, without compassion for my rheumatism. Mr. and Mrs. Wood, when they heard this, rose up in a passion against me. They opened the door and bade me get out. But I was a stranger, and did not know one door in the street from another, and was unwilling to go away. They made a dreadful uproar, and from that day they constantly kept cursing and abusing me. I was obliged to wash, though I was very ill. Mrs. Wood, indeed once hired a washerwoman, but she was not well treated, and would come no more.

My master quarrelled with me another time, about one of our great washings, his wife having stirred him up to do so. He said he would compel me to do the whole of the washing given out to me, or if I again refused, he would take a short course with me: he would either send me down to the brig in the river, to carry me back to Antigua, or he would turn me at once out of doors, and let me provide for myself. I said I would willingly go back, if he would let me purchase my own freedom. But this enraged him more than all the rest: he cursed and swore at me dreadfully, and said he would never sell my freedom—if I wished to be free, I was free in England, and I might go and try what freedom would do for me, and be d——d. My heart was very sore with this treatment, but I had to go on. I continued to do my work, and did all I could to give satisfaction, but all would not do.

Shortly after, the cook left them, and then matters went on ten times worse. I always washed the child's clothes without being commanded to do it, and any thing else that was wanted in the family; though still I was very sick—very sick indeed. When the great washing came round, which was every two months, my mistress got together again a great many heavy things, such as bed-ticks, bed-coverlets, &c. for me to wash. I told her I was too ill to wash such heavy things that day. She said, she supposed I thought myself a free woman, but I was not; and if I did not do it directly I should be instantly turned out of doors. I stood a long time before I could answer, for I did not know well what to do. I knew that I was free in England, but I did not know where to go, or how to get my living; and therefore, I did not like to leave the house. But Mr. Wood said he would send for a constable to thrust me out; and at last I took courage and resolved that I would not be longer thus treated, but would go and trust to Providence. This was the fourth time they had threatened to turn me out, and, go where I might, I was determined now to take them at their word; though I thought it very hard, after I had lived with them for thirteen years, and worked for them like a horse, to be driven out in this way, like a beggar. My only fault was being sick, and therefore unable to please my mistress, who thought she never could get work enough out of her slaves; and I told them so: but they only abused me and drove me out. This took place from two to three months, I think, after we came to England.

When I came away, I went to the man (one Mash) who used to black the shoes of the family, and asked his wife to get somebody to go with me to Hatton Garden to the Moravian Missionaries: these were the only persons I knew in England. The woman sent a young girl with me to the mission house, and I saw there a gentleman called Mr. Moore. I told him my whole story, and how my owners had treated me, and asked him to take in my trunk with what few clothes I had. The missionaries were very kind to me—they were sorry for my destitute situation, and gave me leave to bring my things to be placed under their care. They were very good people, and they told me to come to the church.

When I went back to Mr. Wood's to get my trunk, I saw a lady, Mrs. Pell, who was on a visit to my mistress. When Mr. and Mrs. Wood heard me come in, they set this lady to stop me, finding that they had gone too far with me. Mrs. Pell came out to me, and said, "Are you really going to leave, Molly? Don't leave, but come into the country with me." I believe she said this because she thought Mrs. Wood would easily get me back again. I replied to her, "Ma'am, this is the fourth time my master and mistress have driven me out, or threatened to drive me—and I will give them no more occasion to bid me go. I was not willing to leave them, for I am a stranger in this country, but now I must go—I can stay no longer to be used." Mrs. Pell then went up stairs to my mistress, and told that I would go, and that she could not stop me. Mrs. Wood was very much hurt and frightened when she found I was determined to go out that day. She said, "If she goes the people will rob her, and then turn her adrift." She did not say this to me, but she spoke it loud enough for me to hear; that it might induce me not to go, I suppose. Mr. Wood also asked me where I was going to. I told him where I had been, and that I should never have gone away had I not been driven out by my owners. He had given me a written paper some time before, which said that I had come with them to England by my own desire; and that was true. It said also that I left them of my own free will, because I was a free woman in England; and that I was idle and would not do my work—which was not true. I gave this paper afterwards to a gentleman who inquired into my case.

I went into the kitchen and got my clothes out. The nurse and the servant girl were there, and I said to the man who was going to take out my trunk, "Stop, before you take up this trunk, and hear what I have to say before these people. I am going out of this house, as I was ordered; but I have done no wrong at all to my owners, neither here nor in the West Indies. I always worked very hard to please them, both by night and day; but there was no giving satisfaction, for my mistress could never be satisfied with reasonable service. I told my mistress I was sick, and yet she has ordered me out of doors. This is the fourth time; and now I am going out."

And so I came out, and went and carried my trunk to the Moravians. I then returned back to Mash the shoeblack's house, and begged his wife to take me in. I had a little West Indian money in my trunk; and they got it changed for me. This helped to support me for a little while. The man's wife was very kind to me. I was very sick, and she boiled nourishing things up for me. She also sent for a doctor to see me, and sent me medicine, which did me good, though I was ill for a long time with the rheumatic pains. I lived a good many months with these poor people, and they nursed me, and did all that lay in their power to serve me. The man was well acquainted with my situation, as he used to go to and fro to Mr. Wood's house to clean shoes and knives; and he and his wife were sorry for me.

About this time, a woman of the name of Hill told me of the Anti-Slavery Society, and went with me to their office, to inquire if they could do any thing to get me my freedom, and send me back to the West Indies. The gentlemen of the Society took me to a lawyer, who examined very strictly into my case; but told me that the laws of England could do nothing to make me free in Antigua. However they did all they could for me: they gave me a little money from time to time to keep me from want; and some of them went to Mr. Wood to try to persuade him to let me return a free woman to my husband; but though they offered him, as I have heard, a large sum for my freedom, he was sulky and obstinate, and would not consent to let me go free.

This was the first winter I spent in England, and I suffered much from the severe cold, and from the rheumatic pains, which still at times torment me. However, Providence was very good to me, and I got many friends—especially some Quaker ladies, who hearing of my case, came and sought me out, and gave me good warm clothing and money. Thus I had great cause to bless God in my affliction.

When I got better I was anxious to get some work to do, as I was unwilling to eat the bread of idleness. Mrs. Mash, who was a laundress, recommended me to a lady for a charwoman. She paid me very handsomely for what work I did, and I divided the money with Mrs. Mash; for though very poor, they gave me food when my own money was done, and never suffered me to want.

In the spring, I got into service with a lady, who saw me at the house where I sometimes worked as a charwoman. This lady's name was Mrs. Forsyth. She had been in the West Indies, and was accustomed to Blacks, and liked them. I was with her six months, and went with her to Margate. She treated me well, and gave me a good character when she left London.

After Mrs. Forsyth went away, I was again out of place, and went to lodgings, for which I paid two shillings a week, and found coals and candle. After eleven weeks, the money I had saved in service was all gone, and I was forced to go back to the Anti-Slavery office to ask a supply, till I could get another situation. I did not like to go back—I did not like to be idle. I would rather work for my living than get it for nothing. They were very good to give me a supply, but I felt shame at being obliged to apply for relief whilst I had strength to work.

At last I went into the service of Mr. and Mrs. Pringle, where I have been ever since, and am as comfortable as I can be while separated from my dear husband, and away from my own country and all old friends and connections. My dear mistress teaches me daily to read the word of God, and takes great pains to make me understand it. I enjoy the great privilege of being enabled to attend church three times on the Sunday; and I have met with many kind friends since I have been here, both clergymen and others. The Rev. Mr. Young, who lives in the next house, has shown me much kindness, and taken much pains to instruct me, particularly while my master and mistress were absent in Scotland. Nor must I forget, among my friends, the Rev. Mr. Mortimer, the good clergyman of the parish, under whose ministry I have now sat for upwards of twelve months. I trust in God I have profited by what I have heard from him. He never keeps back the truth, and I think he has been the means of opening my eyes and ears much better to understand the word of God. Mr. Mortimer tells me that he cannot open the eyes of my heart, but that I must pray to God to change my heart, and make me to know the truth, and the truth will make me free.

I still live in the hope that God will find a way to give me my liberty, and give me back to my husband. I endeavour to keep down my fretting, and to leave all to Him, for he knows what is good for me better than I know myself. Yet, I must confess, I find it a hard and heavy task to do so.

I am often much vexed, and I feel great sorrow when I hear some people in this country say, that the slaves do not need better usage, and do not want to be free. They believe the foreign people, who deceive them, and say slaves are happy. I say, Not so. How can slaves be happy when they have the halter round their neck and the whip upon their back? and are disgraced and thought no more of than beasts?—and are separated from their mothers, and husbands, and children, and sisters, just as cattle are sold and separated? Is it happiness for a driver in the field to take down his wife or sister or child, and strip them, and whip them in such a disgraceful manner?—women that have had children exposed in the open field to shame! There is no modesty or decency shown by the owner to his slaves; men, women, and children are exposed alike. Since I have been here I have often wondered how English people can go out into the West Indies and act in such a beastly manner. But when they go to the West Indies, they forget God and all feeling of shame, I think, since they can see and do such things. They tie up slaves like hogs—moor them up like cattle, and they lick them, so as hogs, or cattle, or horses never were flogged;—and yet they come home and say, and make some good people believe, that slaves don't want to get out of slavery. But they put a cloak about the truth. It is not so. All slaves want to be free—to be free is very sweet. I will say the truth to English people who may read this history that my good friend, Miss S—, is now writing down for me. I have been a slave myself—I know what slaves feel—I can tell by myself what other slaves feel, and by what they have told me. The man that says slaves be quite happy in slavery—that they don't want to be free—that man is either ignorant or a lying person. I never heard a slave say so. I never heard a Buckra man say so, till I heard tell of it in England. Such people ought to be ashamed of themselves. They can't do without slaves they say. What's the reason they can't do without slaves as well as in England? No slaves here—no whips—no stocks—no punishment, except for wicked people. They hire servants in England; and if they don't like them, they send them away: they can't lick them. Let them work ever so hard in England, they are far better off than slaves. If they get a bad master, they give warning and go hire to another. They have their liberty. That's just what *we* want. We don't mind hard work, if we had proper treatment, and proper wages like English servants, and proper time given in the week to keep us from breaking the Sabbath. But they won't give it; they will have work—work—work, night and day, sick or well, till we are quite done up; and we must not speak up nor look amiss, however much we be abused. And then when we are quite done up, who cares for us, more than for a lame horse? This is slavery. I tell it to let English people know the truth; and I hope they will never leave off to pray God, and call loud to the great King of England, till all the poor blacks be given free, and slavery done up for evermore.

—1831

The Abolition of Slavery

CONTEXTS

In the 1750s it was possible for John Newton, the author of the hymn "Amazing Grace," to write that neither he nor any of his friends had had any notion that "slavery could be considered unlawful and wrong." By 1807 the tide had turned sufficiently that the British Parliament (through the Slave Trade Act) prohibited British vessels from participating in the trading of humans. And in 1833 (through the Slavery Abolition Act) slavery in all British territory was ended.

What brought about such a vast change in such a relatively short time? In part the answer lies in the history of ideas; the Enlightenment gave birth to concepts of freedom and equality—of human rights which, as they were thought through, were widely recognized to apply to all humans, regardless of gender, regardless of race. But the abolition first of the slave trade and then of slavery itself was also the result of concerted political pressure. Some have identified the birth of the modern political movement and modern political lobbying in the campaign to abolish slavery. Certainly the Society for Effecting the Abolition of the Slave Trade, formed in 1787 and led by Thomas Clarkson and Granville Sharp, among others, played a hugely important role in acquiring and disseminating information as to the actual conditions endured by slaves, and in pressuring the government to take action. In Parliament, William Wilberforce became the *de facto* leader of the anti-slavery movement: Wilberforce, the author of *Practical Christianity*, was tireless in his efforts. The Society of Friends (also known as the Quakers) also played a leading role, both within the Society for Effecting the Abolition of the Slave Trade and independently, in shaping public opinion and pressing for change. And a number of authors—including William Wordsworth, Samuel Taylor Coleridge, Helen Maria Williams, Anna Laetitia Barbauld, and Mary Robinson—lent their voices to the cause.

The legal system too played an important role in the process. In a landmark 1772 case the owner of one James Somerset lost his legal suit to regain ownership of Somerset, who had run away from servitude while in England. Lord Mansfield, the Lord Chief Justice ruled that, according to the established principles of English law, everyone in England was free. Proponents of slavery had suggested that villeinage, the state of servitude which had existed under feudalism and which had never been declared illegal, provided sufficient legal precedent. Mansfield decided, however, that no such justification could be deemed to exist under English Common Law. If Parliament wished to legalize slavery in England, that would require specific new legislation. Despite Mansfield's *caveat* against taking his ruling to apply to British possessions overseas, abolitionists had some reason to feel confident from that point on that the law would eventually support their arguments universally and unequivocally, in Britain's colonies as well as within Britain itself.

⌘ ⌘ ⌘

from John Newton, *A Slave Trader's Journal* (1751)

John Newton (1725–1807) first went to sea at the age of ten, sailing with his father, the captain of the vessel. By the age of twenty-eight he had wide experience both of the sea and of the slave trade, and was for the first time commanding a vessel himself. The *Duke of Argyll* left England for Bassa in West Africa (in what is now Guinea Bissau) in 1750, made the "middle passage" from Bassa to Antigua in the West Indies between 22 May and 2 July, and returned to Liverpool with a cargo of sugar, arriving in November. The following excerpts are from Newton's journal of that voyage. In later life, Newton came to regret deeply his life as a slave trader (which he had given up for health reasons in 1754). He became a Christian minister and wrote that he would have left the slave trade sooner "had I considered it as I now do to be unlawful and wrong. But I never had a scruple upon this head at the time; nor was such a thought ever suggested to me by any friend." In 1770 Newton wrote the famous hymn "Amazing Grace." He became a strong advocate for the abolition of the slave trade.

Thursday 16 May

… [A] long boat came on board from Grande Bassa. I sent Billinge [the second mate] chiefly to satisfy myself of the state and price of slaves. He says the glut we heard so much of is entirely over, the Brittannia and Ranger having met very few. About Settra Crue there is still plenty (upon the account of a war very probably begun with that view) but extravagantly dear … He brought me a sample of the prices in a woman slave he bought at Bassa, which upon costing up the goods I find cost 96 bars, and I ordered him to get one upon any terms for that reason. That I might not think he gave more than usual, he brought me a list of goods he saw Saunders pay for a man which amounts to 102 bars, and the farther to leeward the dearer still. I think I have sufficient reason not to go down, for setting aside the cost, the assortments in demand there would ruin me soon.

Tuesday 28 May
Secured the after bulkhead of the men's room, for they

had started almost every stantient. Their plot was exceedingly well laid, and had they been let alone an hour longer, must have occasioned us a good deal of trouble and damage. I have reason to be thankful they did not make attempts upon the coast when we had often 7 or 8 of our best men out of the ship at a time and the rest busy. They still look very gloomy and sullen and have doubtless mischief in their heads if they could find every opportunity to vent it. But I hope (by the Divine Assistance) we are fully able to overawe them now. …

Wednesday 12 June
Got the slaves up this morn. Washed them all with fresh water. They complained so much that was obliged to let them go down again when the rooms were cleaned. Buryed a man slave (No. 84) of a flux, which he has been struggling with near 7 weeks. …

Saturday 22 June
Being pretty warm, got up the men and washed all the slaves with fresh water. I am much afraid of another ravage from the flux, for we have had 8 taken within these few days. Have seen 2 or 3 tropick birds and a few flying fish.

Monday 24 June
Buried a girl slave (No. 92). In the afternoon while we were off the deck, William Cooney seduced a woman slave down into the room and lay with her brutelike in view of the whole quarter deck, for which I put him in irons.[1] I hope this has been the first affair of the kind on board and I am determined to keep them quiet if possible. If anything happens to the woman I shall impute it to him, for she was big with child. Her number is 83. …

Friday 28 June
By the favour of Divine Providence made a timely discovery today that the slaves were forming a plot for an insurrection. Surprised 2 of them attempting to get

---

[1] *for which … irons*   In contrast to Newton, some captains actively encouraged their crew to rape the female slaves, since pregnant slaves could be sold at a higher price; mulatto children were especially highly valued as house servants.

off their irons, and upon farther search in their rooms, upon the information of 3 of the boys, found some knives, stones, shot, etc., and a cold chissel. Upon enquiry there appeared 8 principally concerned to move in projecting the mischief and 4 boys in supplying them with the above instruments. Put the boys in irons and slightly in the thumbscrews to urge them to a full confession. We have already 36 men out of our small number. ...

Friday 5 July

... [I]n the morning Mr. Guichard went off with me to view the slaves. When came on shore again, after comparing orders and intelligence, he judged it best for the concern to sell here, if I approved it, without which, he was pleased to say, he would do nothing, tho my letters from the owners referred me wholly to his direction. It seems by all I can learn that this is likely to prove as good a market as any of the neighbouring islands; and as for Jamaica or America, I should be extremely loth to venture so far, for we have had the men slaves so long on board that their patience is just worn out, and I am certain they would drop fast had we another passage to make. Monday is appointed for the sale.

from Quobna Ottobah Cugoano, *Thoughts and Sentiments on the Evil and Wicked Traffic of the Slavery and Commerce of the Human Species* (1787)

> Cugoano was kidnapped in West Africa in 1770 and sold into slavery in the West Indies. His owner traveled with him to England in 1772, and he declared himself a free man on English soil following the landmark Somerset case. His *Thoughts and Sentiments* is the first substantial anti-slavery work by a black writer.

But why should total abolition, and an universal emancipation of slaves, and the enfranchisement of all the Black People employed in the culture of the Colonies, taking place as it ought to do, and without any hesitation, or delay for a moment, even though it might have some seeming appearance of loss either to government or to individuals, be feared at all? Their labour, as freemen, would be as useful in the sugar colonies as any other class of men that could be found; and should it even take place in such a manner that some individuals, at first, would suffer loss as a just reward for their wickedness in slave-dealing, what is that to the happiness and good of doing justice to others; and, I must say, to the great danger, otherwise, that must eventually hang over the whole community? It is certain, that the produce of the labour of slaves, together with all the advantages of the West-India traffic, bring in an immense revenue to government; but let that amount be what it will, there might be as much or more expected from the labour of an equal increase of free people, and without the implication of any guilt attending it, and which, otherwise, must be a greater burden to bear, and more ruinous consequences to be feared from it, than if the whole national debt was to sink at once, and to rest upon the heads of all that might suffer by it. Whereas, if a generous encouragement were to be given to a free people, peaceable among themselves, intelligent and industrious, who by art and labour would improve the most barren situations, and make the most of that which is fruitful; the free and voluntary labour of many, would soon yield to any government, many greater advantages than any thing that slavery can produce. And this should be expected, wherever a Christian government is extended, and the true religion is embraced, that the blessings of liberty should be extended likewise, and that it should diffuse its influences first to fertilize the mind, and then the effects of its benignity would extend, and arise with exuberant blessings and advantages from all its operations. Was this to be the case, every thing would increase and prosper at home and abroad, and ten thousand times greater and greater advantages would arise to the state, and more permanent and solid benefit to individuals from the service of freemen, than ever they can reap, or in any possible way enjoy, by the labour of slaves. ...

from Alexander Falconbridge, *Account of the Slave Trade on the Coast of Africa* (1788)

> Falconbridge sailed aboard slave trading vessels as a surgeon in the 1780s. The work from which the following excerpts are taken was given wide distribution by the Society for Effecting the Abolition of the Slave Trade. In 1789 Falconbridge also testified as to the horrors of the trade before the Parliamentary Committee investigating the issue.

The men negroes, on being brought aboard the ship, are immediately fastened together, two and two, by hand-cuffs on their wrists, and by irons rivetted on their legs. They are then sent down between the decks, and placed in an apartment partitioned off for that purpose. The women likewise are placed in a separate apartment between decks, but without being ironed. And an adjoining room, on the same deck, is besides appointed for the boys. Thus are they all placed in different apartments.

But at the same time, they are frequently stowed so close, as to admit of no other posture than lying on their sides. Neither will the height between decks, unless directly under the grating, permit them the indulgence of an erect posture; especially where there are platforms, which is generally the case. These platforms are a kind of shelf, about eight or nine feet in breadth, extending from the side of the ship towards the centre. They are placed nearly midway between the decks, at the distance of two or three feet from each deck. Upon these the negroes are stowed in the same manner as they are on the deck underneath.

In each of the apartments are placed three or four large buckets, of a conical form, being near two feet in diameter at the bottom, and only one foot at the top, and in depth about twenty-eight inches; to which, when necessary, the negroes have recourse. It often happens, that those who are placed at a distance from the buckets, in endeavouring to get to them, tumble over their companions, in consequence of their being shackled. These accidents, although unavoidable, are productive of continual quarrels, in which some of them are always bruised. In this distressed situation, unable to proceed, and prevented from getting to the tubs, they desist from the attempt; and, as the necessities of nature are not to be repelled, ease themselves as they lie. This becomes a fresh source of broils and disturbances, and tends to render the condition of the poor captive wretches still more uncomfortable. The nuisance arising from these circumstances, is not unfrequently increased by the tubs being much too small for the purpose intended, and their being usually emptied but once every day. The rule for doing this, however, varies in different ships, according to the attention paid to the health and convenience of the slaves by the captain....

The diet of the negroes, while on board, consists chiefly of horse-beans, boiled to the consistence of a pulp; of boiled yams and rice, and sometimes of a small quantity of beef or pork. The latter are frequently taken from the provisions laid in for the sailors. They sometimes make use of a sauce, composed of palm-oil, mixed with flour, water, and pepper, which the sailors call *slabber-sauce*. Yams are the favourite food of the Eboe, or Bight negroes, and rice or corn, of those from the Gold and Windward Coasts; each preferring the produce of their native soil....

They are commonly fed twice a day, about eight o'clock in the morning and four in the afternoon. In most ships they are only fed with their *own food* once a day. Their food is served up to them in tubs, about the size of a small water bucket. They are placed round these tubs in companies of ten to each tub, out of which they feed themselves with wooden spoons. These they soon lose, and when they are not allowed others, they feed themselves with their hands. In favourable weather they are fed upon deck, but in bad weather their food is given them below. Numberless quarrels take place among them during their meals; more especially when they are put upon short allowance ... Their allowance of water is about half a pint each at every meal. It is handed round in a bucket, and given to each negroe in a pannekin; a small utensil with a strait handle, somewhat similar to a sauce-boat....

Upon the negroes refusing to take sustenance, I have seen coals of fire, glowing hot, put on a shovel, and placed so near their lips, as to scorch and burn them. And this has been accompanied with threats, of forcing them to swallow the coals, if they any longer persisted in refusing to eat. These means have generally had the desired effect. I have also been credibly informed, that a certain captain in the slave trade, poured melted lead on such of the negroes as obstinately refused their food.

Exercise being deemed necessary for the preservation of their health, they are sometimes obliged to dance, when the weather will permit their coming on deck. If they go about it reluctantly, or do not move with agility, they are flogged; a person standing by them all the time with a cat-o'-nine-tails[1] in his hand for that purpose. Their musick, upon these occasions consists of a drum, sometimes with only one head; and when that is worn out, they do not scruple to make use of the bottom of one of the tubs before described. The poor wretches are frequently compelled to sing also; but when they do so, their songs are generally, as may naturally be expected, melancholy lamentations of their exile from their native country. ...

On board some ships, the common sailors are allowed to have intercourse with such of the black women whose consent they can procure. And some of them have been known to take the inconstancy of their paramours so much to heart, as to leap overboard and drown themselves. The officers are permitted to indulge their passions among them at pleasure, and sometimes are guilty of such brutal excesses, as disgrace human nature.

Diagram showing allotment of space for slaves on two decks of a late eighteenth-century sailing ship.

---

[1] *cat-o'-nine-tails* Switch with nine ropes attached, used as a beating implement.

William Cowper, "Sweet Meat Has Sour Sauce, or, The Slave-Trader in the Dumps"[2] (1788)

A trader I am to the African shore,
But since that my trading is like to be o'er,
I'll sing you a song that you ne'er heard before,
 Which nobody can deny, deny,
5 Which nobody can deny.

When I first heard the news it gave me a shock,
Much like what they call an electrical knock,
And now I am going to sell off my stock,
 Which nobody, &c.

10 'Tis a curious assortment of dainty regales,
To tickle the negroes with when the ship sails,
Fine chains for the neck, and a cat with nine tails,
 Which nobody, &c.

Here's supple-jack plenty, and store of rat-tan,[3]
15 That will wind itself round the sides of a man,
As close as a hoop round a bucket or can,
 Which nobody, &c.

Here's padlocks and bolts, and screws for the thumbs,
That squeeze them so lovingly till the blood comes,
20 They sweeten the temper like comfits or plums,[4]
 Which nobody, &c.

When a negro his head from his victuals withdraws,
And clenches his teeth and thrusts out his paws,
Here's a notable engine to open his jaws,
25 Which nobody, &c.

Thus going to market, we kindly prepare
A pretty black cargo of African ware,

---

[2] *Sweet Meat ... Dumps* The poem is one of several anti-slavery poems by Cowper. The Society for Effecting the Abolition of the Slave Trade distributed his ballad "The Negro's Complaint" widely; both that poem and this were set to music and sung as well as read.

[3] *supple-jack* Climbing vine; *rat-tan* Palm stem. Both supple-jack and rattan were used for switches or canes.

[4] *comfits or plums* Sweetmeats; sugarplums: fruits preserved with sugar.

For what they must meet with when they get there,
    Which nobody, &c.

30   'Twould do your heart good to see 'em below
Lie flat on their backs all the way as we go,
Like sprats on a gridiron,[1] scores in a row,
    Which nobody, &c.

But ah! if in vain I have studied an art
35   So gainful to me, all boasting apart,
I think it will break my compassionate heart,
    Which nobody, &c.

For oh! how it enters my soul like an awl![2]
This pity, which some people self-pity call,
40   Is sure the most heart-piercing pity of all,
    Which nobody, &c.

So this is my song, as I told you before;
Come buy off my stock, for I must no more
Carry Caesars and Pompeys[3] to Sugar-cane shore,
45   Which nobody can deny, deny,
    Which nobody can deny.

from William Wilberforce, "Speech to the House of Commons," 13 May 1789

> William Wilberforce began his long struggle to have
> the British Parliament abolish the slave trade with
> the speech excerpted below. In April of 1791, a bill
> put forward by Wilberforce was voted down by 163
> votes to 88; not until 1807 were his efforts on this
> score successful. News of the passage of the Slavery
> Abolition Act reached Wilberforce on his deathbed
> in 1833.

A report has been made by his Majesty's Privy
Council, which, I trust, every Gentleman has read,
and which ascertains the Slave Trade to be just such in
practice as we know, from theory, that it must be. What
should we suppose must naturally be the consequence of
our carrying on a Slave Trade with Africa? With a
country, vast in its extent, not utterly barbarous, but
civilized in a very small degree? Does any one suppose a
Slave Trade would *help* their civilization? That Africa
would *profit* by such an intercourse? Is it not plain, that
she must *suffer* from it? That civilization must be
checked; that her barbarous manners must be made
more barbarous; and that the happiness of her millions
of inhabitants must be prejudiced by her intercourse
with Britain? Does not every one see, that a Slave Trade,
carried on around her coasts, must carry violence and
desolation to her very centre? That, in a Continent, just
emerging from barbarism, if a Trade in Men is established—if her men are all converted into goods, and
become commodities that can be bartered, it follows,
they must be subject to ravage just as goods are; and this
too, at a period of civilization, when there is no protecting Legislature to defend this their only sort of property,
in the same manner as the rights of property are maintained by the legislature of every civilized country.

We see then, in the nature of things, how easily all
the practices of Africa are to be accounted for. Her kings
are never compelled to war, that we can hear of, by
public principles,—by national glory—still less by the
love of their people. In Europe it is the extension of
commerce, the maintenance of national honor, or some
great public object, that is ever the motive to war with
every monarch; but, in Africa, it is the personal *avarice*
and *sensuality* of their kings: these two vices of avarice
and sensuality, (the most powerful and predominant in
natures thus corrupt) we tempt, we stimulate in all these
African Princes, and we depend upon these vices for the
very maintenance of the Slave Trade....

Sir, the nature and all the circumstances of this trade
are now laid open to us; we can no longer plead
ignorance,—we cannot evade it,—it is now an object
placed before us,—we cannot pass it; we may spurn it,
we may kick it out of our way, but we cannot turn aside
so as to avoid seeing it; for it is brought now so directly
before our eyes, that this House must decide, and must
justify to all the world, and to their own consciences, the
rectitude of the grounds and principles of their decision.

A Society [the Society for Effecting the Abolition of
the Slave Trade] has been established for the abolition
of this trade, [in 1787] in which Dissenters, Quakers,

---

[1] *sprats on a gridiron* Small fish on a griddle or broiling-pan.

[2] *awl* Tool for piercing holes in leather.

[3] *Caesars and Pompeys* Names commonly given to African slaves.

Churchmen—in which the most conscientious of all persuasions have all united, and made a common cause in this great question. Let not Parliament be the only body that is insensible to the principles of national justice. Let us make reparation to Africa, so far as we can, by establishing a trade upon true commercial principles, and we shall soon find the rectitude of our conduct rewarded, by the benefits of a regular and a growing commerce.

Proponents of Slavery

It is often (and rightly) pointed out that appeals to Christian virtue were central to the abolitionist cause. As some of the following excerpts illustrate, appeals to Christian principles were also made on the other side of the argument—as were appeals of a variety of other sorts.

from Rev. Robert Boncher Nicholls, *Observations, Occasioned by the Attempts Made in England to Effect the Abolition of the Slave Trade* (1788)

[T]he author] thought it incumbent on him first to search the scriptures, to learn whether slavery was inconsistent with the revealed will of the Deity. The result of his enquiry was perfectly satisfactory to himself, and he thought it but right to point out some few of the many passages, to be found in the sacred volumes, which justify that commerce. Since the following observations went to the press the author has the great satisfaction to find, that he might have pursued his original plan without any injury to the cause he has endeavoured to support, as he has seen a pamphlet by the Rev. Mr. Harris, of Liverpool, who has so clearly proved, from the scriptures, that slavery is neither contrary to the law nor gospel, that it is scarcely possible for the most conscientious believer, who reads that tract, to doubt in future; whether the man servant or the maid servant is not as much a man's property as "*his ox or his ass, or any thing that is his.*" ...

About the time of Lord Mansfield's determination in the case of Mr. Stuart's negro, [those in England who were attended by slaves] ... had every right to suppose they were authorised, by the laws of Great Britain, as well as those of the colonies, to consider those people as their property; and that they had a right to their services in Europe, or to send, or accompany them back to the colonies, as they judged proper: They found themselves mistaken, and that it was permitted to debauch their slaves, to encourage or entice them to run away, with impunity. The ideas of liberty, the charms of novelty, and an ignorance of the country they had got to; where they found themselves upon a perfect equality, at least, with the inferior white people, could not fail of having pernicious effects upon their minds, and great numbers ran away from their masters. They in general plunged into vice and debauchery, and many of them, who were desirous of returning to their masters and mistresses, were refused to be received. The whole of those thus lost to their owners, and as to every useful purpose, to the community, cannot have been less in number than from 15,000 to 20,000.—As most of them were prime, young, seasoned, or Creole slaves, the loss to their owners, the planters, have not been less than from 1,000,000 to 1,200,000 sterling. A large sum to be sacrificed, to the mere names of *liberty and humanity*! What has been the result of thus extending *the blessings of liberty* to so many *wretched slaves*. Let any body shew scarce a single instance of any one of these people being in so happy a situation as they were before. The greater part, it is known, died miserably, in a very short time. No parish was willing to receive them, so that the survivors, after begging about the streets of London, and suffering all those evils, and inconveniencies, consequent on idleness and poverty, famine, disease, and the inclemency of the weather; attracted the attention of the public, and government was prevailed upon to undertake the transportation of them to the country from whence they or their ancestors had been ravished *by the wicked traders* of London, Liverpool, and Bristol.

Equal unhappiness would be the lot of the slaves in the islands, if they were set free; what could they do to obtain a livelihood? To suppose they would hire themselves out to work, can only enter into the imagination of those who do not know the people, or the country: What has so lately passed in England is surely sufficient to shew that there can be no idea, they will, any of them, wish to return to their own country. Thousands of negroes have been made free by their masters in the colonies, and it may, with truth, be asserted, that, notwithstanding many of them were very capable of paying for a passage to any part of Africa they thought proper; scarce a single instance can be produced of any one of them desiring to return to the place of his nativity.

The present attempt to cram liberty down the throats of people who are incapable of digesting it, can with propriety, be resembled to nothing, so well as to the account of poor Gulliver, when he was carried out of his little cabinet to the top of the house, by the Brobdignag Monkey.

from Anonymous, *Thoughts on the Slavery of Negroes, as It Affects the British Colonies in the West Indies: Humbly Submitted to the Consideration of Both Houses of Parliament* (1788)

If I am able to shew that the blacks are really happy; that their condition (if the odious name of slave could be forgotten) is preferable to the lower orders of the people in Great Britain and Ireland; and that they enjoy the necessaries, and often the luxuries of life, I trust every honest man will feel a just indignation at any attempt to mislead his judgment, and to impose upon him an opinion of cruelty, which has no existence in any of the British West India islands. ...

Let us take a view of the situation of the Africans, the nature of their country, their climate and government, and the genius and disposition of its inhabitants. The appearance of the slave-coast of Africa, when it was first visited by the Europeans, strongly marked the barbarous state of the people; a rude, inhospitable country, susceptible indeed of cultivation, but almost every way covered with thick, impenetrable forests. The wild luxuriance of nature was here portrayed in rich attire. The pruning hand of man was hardly seen. The peaceful labours of agriculture were little known.

It has been observed, that those countries most favoured by nature, often make the slowest progress to civilization; and that the people always groan under the weight of a cruel despotism. "This is an effect which springs from a natural cause. Great heat enervates the strength and courage of men, while in cold climates they have a certain vigour of body and mind, which renders them capable of long, painful, great, and intrepid actions. We ought not, then, to be astonished, that the effeminacy of the people in hot climates has almost always rendered them slaves; and that the bravery of those in colder regions has enabled them to maintain their liberties."

In those countries between the tropics, and especially under the equator, "the excess of heat renders men so slothful and dispirited, that nothing but the most pressing necessity can induce them to perform any laborious duty." An unconquerable indolence is universally felt and acknowledged. Sunk into the most deplorable degeneracy, they feel no incitements beyond the present moment. In vain may we represent to them the happiness of others. In vain may we attempt to rouse them to a sense of their own weakness. The soul, unwilling to enlarge itself, becomes the prey of every ignoble passion. Strangers to every virtuous and magnanimous sentiment, they are without fame—they are without glory.

The Africans have been always represented as a cruel and perfidious people, lazy, lascivious, faithless in their engagements, innate thieves, without morals, and without any just notion of any one religious duty. Their laws are founded on such principles as naturally flow from so impure a source. The government of the slave-coast of Africa is despotic. The will of the Prince must be obeyed. There is no appeal upon earth from his awful decree. The lives and fortunes of every one are absolutely at his disposal. These tyrants have thought fit to distinguish a number of crimes, but have taken no care to proportionate their degrees of punishment. Every offence is there punished with loss of life or liberty. Captives in war are deliberately murdered, or sold as slaves, as may most indulge the sanguinary caprice of the conqueror. Those convicted of adultery or theft, lose their liberty. He who is in debt, and unable to pay must either sell himself or his children to satisfy the creditor. It may be said, that the loss of life, or liberty, only commences with the injury done to society. I answer, "that in Africa, the civil liberty is already destroyed by the political slavery." A country like this, doomed to bear the weight of human misery, will always present a history of the most shocking cruelties, and of the severest slavery upon earth.

After viewing this melancholy picture, we ought not to be surprised at the extent of the present intercourse between the Africans and Europeans. For want of proper consideration, and from the influence of certain prejudices, the slave-trade has long been considered the scandal and reproach of every nation who have been anywise engaged in it, but without sufficient reason.

Men who enjoy the benefits of civilization, and who are protected in life, liberty, and property, by the wisdom of humane and equal laws, feel that spirit of liberty, and enthusiastic love of their country, which freedom only can inspire. Talk to them of banishment, and it is more terrible than death. Not so the poor African—he has few motives for wishing any longer to behold the distresses of his country; he is, alas! perhaps, the last witness of the sad misfortunes of his house— Already deprived of family, friends, and every other tender endearment, he has no relief but in banishment or death.

It is pleasant to mark the progress of the barbarian, from the moment he is put on shore in an English colony, to the time he becomes the master of a family, and acquires property of his own. He is first of all clothed (a thing unknown to him in his own country) and then instructed in the necessity of cleanliness. When carried to the plantation, he is shewn how to work in common with others. In a little time he chooses himself a wife, and has a house given to him, much better, allowing for the difference of climate, than what the peasants have in this country. When he is sufficiently instructed in the management of ground, a certain portion is allotted to the exclusive use of himself and family, which, with a moderate share of industry, is not only sufficient to supply every personal want, but leave a considerable part to be sent to market, to be sold, or exchanged for either necessaries or luxuries. The African now, finding himself a family man, and in possession of house and land, he begins to rear hogs, poultry, and other small stock, and either sells them to his master at a fair price, or carries them to market, for which one day in the week is allowed him. ...

The African, no longer remembering a country to which he owes nothing but birth, becomes attached to the soil which is so propitious to his wants, and having few cares, and few desires, that are not completely satisfied, there is nothing so terrible to him as a change of situation. The master is the steward, the faithful guardian of all his wants and necessities. In sickness and in health—in youth and in old age, his assiduities are undiminished. The reader will anticipate the happiness of these people—and happy they must be, while their labours are directed by equity and humanity, and not by avarice.

God forbid that I should be an advocate for slavery, or servitude of any description, that can anywise limit the extent of human happiness: at the same time let me caution my countrymen against the weakness and folly of believing that happiness can only be sought in a constitution as free as their own. The history of all nations shew how extremely improper the laws of one country would be for those of another.

from Gordon Turnbull, *An Apology of Negro Slavery; or, the West India Planters Vindicated from the Charge of Inhumanity* (1786)

As a contrast to the horrid and fictitious picture, which has been drawn of the state of the negroes in the West-Indies, I shall here exhibit a true and more pleasing representation, taken from the life.

To begin then with the period of the Guinea negroe's arrival in one of the islands.—As soon as the ship that brings them is at anchor, the master or surgeon goes on shore to procure fresh provisions, fruit, and vegetables of all kinds, which are immediately sent on board for the slaves. Parties of them are sent on shore at different times, and conducted a little way into the country, where they frequently meet with many natives of their own country, who speak the same language, and sometimes with near and dear relations, who all appear very cheerful and happy. These agreeable and unexpected meetings are truly affecting, and excite the most tender and pleasing sensations in the breasts of the bystanders. It is not uncommon for these newly arrived guests, to mingle in the dance, or to join in the song, with their country people. If any of them appear dull or desponding, the old negroes endeavour to enliven them, by the most soothing and endearing expressions, telling them, in their own tongue, not to be afraid of the white men; that the white men are very good; that they will get plenty of *yam, yam,* (their general name for victuals) and that their work will be of the easiest kind. By these means, they are perfectly reconciled to the white men, and to a change of country, and of situation, which many of them declare, to be far superior to that which they had quitted. When the day of sale arrives, they not only meet the planter's looks, and answer his enquiries, by means of an interpreter, with great firmness, but they try, by offering their stout limbs to his inspection, jumping to shew their activity, and other allurements, to induce those, whose appearance pleases them, to buy them, and to engage, if possible, a preference in their favour....

As soon as the new negroes are brought home to the plantation, if a planter has purchased them they are properly clothed.—A sufficient quantity of wholesome food is prepared, and served to them three times a day. They are comfortably lodged in some room of the manager's own house, or in some other convenient place, where they can be immediately under his eye for a few days. During this time they are not put to any kind of labour whatever, but are regularly conducted to bathe in the river, or in the sea, if it is nigh, twice a day. In the evenings they sing and dance, after the manner of their own nation, together with the old negroes who happen to be from the same country, one or two of whom are commonly instrumental performers, in these very noisy, but very joyous assemblies. In a very short time, they are taken into the houses of the principal and best disposed negroes, who adopt one of two of these new subjects into each family, to assist them in all the little domestic offices of cookery, carrying water, wood, &c. This is almost the only work they are employed in for the first two or three months, at the expiration of which, they are put to the easiest kind of labour for some months more....

from Mary Wollstonecraft, *A Vindication of the Rights of Men* (1790)

Wollstonecraft's more famous work, *A Vindication of the Rights of Woman*, was published two years after her much shorter work on the rights of men, which briefly discusses the issue of slavery.

Is it necessary to repeat, that there are rights which we received, at our birth, as men, when we were raised above the brute creation by the power of improving ourselves—and that we receive these not from our forefathers, but from God?

My father may dissipate his property, yet I have no right to complain;—but if he should attempt to sell me for a slave, or fetter me with laws contrary to reason; nature, in enabling me to discern good from evil, teaches me to break the ignoble chain....

But on what principle Mr. Burke[1] could defend American independence, I cannot conceive; for the whole tenor of his ... arguments settles slavery on an everlasting foundation. Allowing his servile reverence for antiquity, and prudent attention to self-interest, to have the force which he insists on, it ought never to be abolished; and, because our ignorant forefathers, not understanding the native dignity of man, sanctioned a traffic that outrages every suggestion of reason and religion, we are to submit to the inhuman custom, and term an atrocious insult to humanity the love of our country and a proper submission to those laws which secure our property.—Security of property! Behold, in a few words, the definition of English liberty. And to this selfish principle every nobler one is sacrificed....

---

[1] *Mr. Burke* Edmund Burke (1729–97), Anglo-Irish statesman, author, and philosopher. Burke famously supported the right of the colonies to self-rule.

Anna Laetitia Barbauld, "Epistle to William Wilberforce, Esq., on the Rejection of the Bill for Abolish-
ing the Slave Trade"[1] (1791)

Cease, Wilberforce, to urge thy generous aim!
　　Thy country knows the sin, and stands the shame!
The preacher, poet, senator in vain
Has rattled in her sight the Negro's chain;
5　With his deep groans assailed her startled ear,
And rent the veil that hid his constant tear;
Forced her averted eyes his stripes[2] to scan,
Beneath the bloody scourge laid bare the man,
Claimed Pity's tear, urged Conscience's strong control,
10　And flashed conviction on her shrinking soul.
The Muse too, soon awaked, with ready tongue
At Mercy's shrine applausive paeans rung;
And Freedom's eager sons, in vain foretold
A new Astraean[3] reign, an age of gold:
15　She knows and she persists—Still Afric bleeds,
Unchecked, the human traffic still proceeds;
She stamps her infamy to future time,
And on her hardened forehead seals the crime.
　　In vain, to thy white standard[4] gathering round,
20　Wit, Worth, and Parts° and Eloquence   *intelligence*
　　　are found:
In vain, to push to birth thy great design,
Contending chiefs, and hostile virtues join;
All, from conflicting ranks, of power possest
To rouse, to melt, or to inform the breast.
25　Where seasoned tools of Avarice prevail,
A nation's eloquence, combined, must fail:
Each flimsy sophistry by turns they try;
The plausive° argument, the daring lie,   *plausible*
The artful gloss,° that moral sense confounds,   *explanation*
30　Th'acknowledged thirst of gain that honour wounds:
Bane of ingenuous minds, th'unfeeling sneer,
Which, sudden, turns to stone the falling tear:
They search assiduous, with inverted skill,

For forms of wrong, and precedents of ill;
35　With impious mockery wrest the sacred page,
And glean up crimes from each remoter age:
Wrung Nature's tortures, shuddering, while you tell,
From scoffing fiends bursts forth the laugh of hell;
In Britain's senate, Misery's pangs give birth
40　To jests unseemly, and to horrid mirth[5]—
Forbear!—thy virtues but provoke our doom,
And swell th'account of vengeance yet to come;
For, not unmarked in Heaven's impartial plan,
Shall man, proud worm, condemn his fellow man?
45　And injured Afric, by herself redrest,
Darts her own serpents at her tyrant's breast.
Each vice, to minds depraved by bondage known,
With sure contagion fastens on his own;
In sickly languors melts his nerveless frame,
50　And blows to rage impetuous Passion's flame:
Fermenting swift, the fiery venom gains
The milky innocence of infant veins;
There swells the stubborn will, damps learning's fire,
The whirlwind wakes of uncontrolled desire,
55　Sears the young heart to images of woe,
And blasts the buds of Virtue as they blow.
　　Lo! where reclined, pale Beauty courts the breeze,
Diffused on sofas of voluptuous ease;
With anxious awe, her menial train around,
60　Catch her faint whispers of half-uttered sound;
See her, in monstrous fellowship, unite
At once the Scythian, and the Sybarite;[6]
Blending repugnant vices, misallied,
Which frugal nature purposed to divide;
65　See her, with indolence to fierceness joined,
Of body delicate, infirm of mind,
With languid tones imperious mandates urge;
With arm recumbent wield the household scourge;
And with unruffled mien,° and placid sounds,   *appearance*
70　Contriving torture, and inflicting wounds.
Nor, in their palmy walks and spicy groves,
The form benign of rural pleasure roves;

---

[1] *William Wilberforce ... Slave Trade* This poem appeared shortly
after the bill put forward by Wilberforce (and supported both by the
Prime Minister, William Pitt, and the leader of the opposition,
Charles Fox) was defeated by a vote of 163 to 88.

[2] *stripes* Open wounds caused by the lash.

[3] *Astraea* Greek goddess of justice.

[4] *standard* Flag.

[5] *To jests ... mirth* Barbauld refers to some Members of Parliament
who laughed in the House of Commons upon hearing of the
suffering of slaves.

[6] *Scythian* Ancient nomadic Europeans: synonym for ferocity;
Sybarite People from the ancient Greek city of Sybaris: synonym
for pleasure-loving.

No milkmaid's song, or hum of village talk,
Soothes the lone poet in his evening walk:
75 No willing arm the flail unwearied plies,
Where the mixed sounds of cheerful labour rise;
No blooming maids, and frolic swains are seen
To pay gay homage to their harvest queen:
No heart-expanding scenes their eyes must prove
80 Of thriving industry, and faithful love:
But shrieks and yells disturb the balmy air,
Dumb sullen looks of woe announce despair,
And angry eyes through dusky features glare.
Far from the sounding lash the Muses fly,
85 And sensual riot drowns each finer joy.
     Nor less from the gay East,° on   *India*
          essenced wings,
Breathing unnamed perfumes, Contagion springs;
The soft luxurious plague alike pervades
The marble palaces, and rural shades;
90 Hence, thronged Augusta° builds her rosy bowers, *London*
And decks in summer wreaths her smoky towers;
And hence, in summer bow'rs, Art's costly hand
Pours courtly splendours o'er the dazzled land:
The manners melt—One undistinguished blaze
95 O'erwhelms the sober pomp of elder days;
Corruption follows with gigantic stride,
And scarce vouchsafes his shameless front to hide:
The spreading leprosy taints ev'ry part,
Infects each limb, and sickens at the heart.
100 Simplicity! most dear of rural maids,
Weeping resigns her violated shades:
Stern Independence from his glebe° retires,   *field*
And anxious Freedom eyes her drooping fires;
By foreign wealth are British morals changed,
105 And Afric's sons, and India's, smile avenged.
     For you, whose tempered ardour long has borne
Untired the labour, and unmoved the scorn;
In Virtue's fasti° be inscribed your fame,   *calendar*
And uttered yours with Howard's[1] honoured name,
110 Friends of the friendless—Hail, ye generous band!
Whose efforts yet arrest Heav'n's lifted hand,
Around whose steady brows, in union bright,
The civic wreath, and Christian's palm unite:
Your merit stands, no greater and no less,

115 Without, or with the varnish of success;
But seek no more to break a nation's fall,
For ye have saved yourselves—and that is all.
Succeeding times your struggles, and their fate,
With mingled shame and triumph shall relate,
120 While faithful History, in her various page,
Marking the features of this motley age,
To shed a glory, and to fix a stain,
Tells how you strove, and that you strove in vain.

William Blake, Images of Slavery

The engravings reproduced below are among sixteen plates prepared by William Blake in 1792–93 as illustrations for John Stedman's *Narrative of Five Years' Expedition against the Revolted Negroes of Surinam* (1796).

---

[1] *Howard* John Howard (1726–90), prison reformer and philanthropist.

from Samuel Taylor Coleridge, *On the Slave Trade* (1796)

The article from which this excerpt is taken was delivered as a lecture in 1795, and published in Coleridge's magazine *The Watchman* the following year.

I have dwelt anxiously on this subject, with a particular view, to the slave-trade, which, I knew, has insinuated in the minds of many, uneasy doubts respecting the existence of a beneficent Deity. And indeed the evils arising from the formation of *imaginary* wants, have in no instance been so dreadfully exemplified, as in this inhuman traffic. We receive from the West-India Islands sugars, rum, cotton, logwood, cocoa, coffee, pimento, ginger, indigo, mahogany, and conserves. Not one of these articles are necessary; indeed with the exception of cotton and mahogany we cannot truly call them even useful: and not one of them is at present attainable by the poor and labouring part of Society. In return we export vast quantities of necessary tools, raiment, and defensive weapons, with great stores of provision. So that in this trade as in most others the poor are employed with unceasing toil first to raise, and

then to send away the comforts, which they themselves absolutely want, in order to procure idle superfluities for their masters. If this trade had never existed, no one human being would have been less comfortably cloathed, housed, or nourished. Such is its value—they who would estimate the price which we pay for it, may consult the evidence delivered before the House of Commons.

from William Earle, *Obi; or, the History of Three-Fingered Jack* (1800)

Earle's novel is set against the background of a slave rebellion in Jamaica; it is based on the true story of Jack Mansong, an escaped slave who was said to have gained strength to lead the rebellion from the religion of "obeah," or "obi." The epistolary novel is for the most part made up of letters from one George Stanford, "a resident of Jamaica," to Charles, "his friend in England." The excerpt that appears here is from the letter with which the book opens.

Jack is a noble fellow, and in spite of every cruel hard-hearted planter, I shall repeat the same to the last hour of my life. "Jack is a Negro," say they. "Jack is a MAN," say I.

—"He is a slave."

—"MAN cannot be a slave to MAN."

—"He is my property."

—"How did you acquire that property?"

—"By paying for it."

—"Paying! Paying whom?"

—"Him who brought him from Africa."

—"How did he get possession of him?"

—"He caught him there."

—"Caught! what? Like a wild beast?"

—"No, but he contrived means to convey him into his ship."

—"Contrived! Then he brought him without his consent?"

—"Very likely."

—"And what is become of that robber?"

—"Robber! He is a very respectable man, who has

left off trade, has married the daughter of a rich planter, and now lives very comfortably, after the fatigues of an industrious life."

—"What! Do they hang a poor hard-labouring man, who, driven by despair at the sight of his numerous family ready to starve for want of a bit of bread, takes advantage of a dark night, goes on the highway and frightens the traveller out of a few pieces of gold; and shall a daring ruffian, who is openly guilty of a crime more heinous in its nature and baneful in its effects, get respected by every body and pass his days in the peaceable enjoyment of riches acquired by such infamous means?"

—"I don't understand you; I never heard that the traffic was infamous. Is it not authorised by all the nations of Europe, Asia and America? Have not regulations been made concerning it by all governments?"

—"Very true, but that does not make it more honorable."

Anti-slavery woodcut (c. 1790s).

Mary Robinson, Poems on Slavery (1798, 1800)

Robinson, one of the best-known writers of the age, published a substantial number of works devoted in whole or in part to anti-slavery themes, including "Captivity: A Poem" (1777), "The African" (1798), and "The Negro Girl" (1800). "The African" was published initially in the *Morning Post*, 2 August 1798 and later incorporated into the long poem *The Progress of Liberty*. "The Negro Girl" appeared in Robinson's collection of *Lyrical Tales*.

The African (1798)

Shall the poor AFRICAN, the passive Slave,
Born in the bland effulgence of broad day,
Cherish'd by torrid splendours, while around
The plains prolific teem with honey'd stores,
5 Sink prematurely to a grave obscure,
No tear to grace his ashes? Or suspire
To wear Submission's long and goading chain,
To drink the tear that down his swarthy cheek
Flows fast, to moisten his toil-fever'd lip
10 Parch'd by the noon-tide blaze? Shall HE endure
The frequent lash, the agonizing scourge,
The day of labour, and the night of pain;
Expose his naked limbs to burning gales;
Faint in the sun, and wither in the storm;
15 Traverse hot sands, imbibe the morbid breeze,
Wing'd with contagion; while his blister'd feet,
Scorch'd by the vertical and raging beam,
Pour the swift life-stream? Shall his frenzied eyes,
Oh! worst of mortal miseries! behold
20 The darling of his heart, his sable love,
Selected from the trembling timid throng,
By the wan TYRANT, whose licentious touch
Seals the dark fiat of the SLAVE's despair!

OH LIBERTY! From thee the suppliant claims
25 The meed of retribution! Thy pure flame
Would light the sense opaque, and warm the spring
Of boundless ecstasy: while Nature's laws,
So violated, plead immortal tongu'd,
For her dark-fated children! Lead them forth
30 From bondage infamous! Bid Reason own

The dignities of MAN, whate'er his clime,
Estate, or colour. And, O sacred TRUTH!
Tell the proud Lords of traffic, that the breast
Thrice ebon-tinted, owns a crimson tide
35 As pure,—as clear, as Europe's Sons can boast.

The Negro Girl (1800)

1

Dark was the dawn, and o'er the deep
The boist'rous whirlwinds blew;
The Sea-bird wheel'd its circling sweep,
And all was drear to view—
5 When on the beach that binds the western shore
The love-lorn ZELMA stood, list'ning the tempest's roar.

2

Her eager Eyes beheld the main,
While on her DRACO dear
She madly call'd, but call'd in vain,
10 No sound could DRACO hear,
Save the shrill yelling of the fateful blast,
While ev'ry Seaman's heart, quick shudder'd as it past.

3

White were the billows, wide display'd
The clouds were black and low;
15 The Bittern shriek'd, a gliding shade
Seem'd o'er the waves to go!
The livid flash illum'd the clam'rous main,
While ZELMA pour'd, unmark'd, her melancholy strain.

4

"Be still!" she cried, "loud tempest cease!
20 O! spare the gallant souls:
The thunder rolls—the winds increase—
The Sea, like mountains, rolls!
While, from the deck, the storm-worn victims leap,
And o'er their struggling limbs, the furious billows sweep.

5

25 "O! barb'rous Pow'r! relentless Fate!
Does Heav'n's high will decree
That some should sleep on beds of state,—

Some, in the roaring Sea?
Some, nurs'd in splendour, deal Oppression's blow,
30 While worth and DRACO pine—in Slavery and woe!

6

"Yon Vessel oft has plough'd the main
With human traffic fraught;
Its cargo,—our dark Sons of pain—
For worldly treasure bought!
35 What had they done?—O Nature tell me why—
Is taunting scorn the lot, of thy dark progeny?

7

"Thou gav'st, in thy caprice, the Soul
Peculiarly enshrin'd;
Nor from the ebon Casket stole
40 The Jewel of the mind!
Then wherefore let the suff'ring Negro's breast
Bow to his fellow, MAN, in brighter colours drest.

8

"Is it the dim and glossy hue
That marks him for despair?—
45 While men with blood their hands embrue,
And mock the wretch's pray'r?
Shall guiltless Slaves the Scourge of tyrants feel,
And, e'en before their GOD! unheard, unpitied kneel.

9

"Could the proud rulers of the land
50 Our Sable race behold;
Some bow'd by torture's Giant hand
And others, basely sold!
Then would they pity Slaves, and cry, with shame,
Whate'er their TINTS may be, their SOULS are still
the same!

10

55 "Why seek to mock the Ethiop's face?
Why goad our hapless kind?
Can features alienate the race—
Is there no kindred mind?
Does not the cheek which vaunts the roseate hue
60 Oft blush for crimes, that Ethiops never knew?

11

"Behold! the angry waves conspire
      To check the barb'rous toil!
While wounded Nature's vengeful ire—
      Roars, round this trembling Isle!
65 And hark! her voice re-echoes in the wind—
Man was not form'd by Heav'n, to trample on his kind!

12

"Torn from my Mother's aching breast,
      My Tyrant sought my love—
But, in the Grave shall ZELMA rest,
70   E'er she will faithless prove—
No DRACO!—Thy companion I will be
To that celestial realm, where Negroes shall be free!

13

"The Tyrant WHITE MAN taught my mind—
      The letter'd page to trace;
75 He taught me in the Soul to find
      No tint, as in the face:
He bade my Reason, blossom like the tree—
But fond affection gave, the ripen'd fruits to thee.

14

"With jealous rage he mark'd my love;
80   He sent thee far away;—
And prison'd in the plantain grove—
      Poor ZELMA pass'd the day—
But ere the moon rose high above the main,
ZELMA, and Love contriv'd, to break the Tyrant's chain.

15

85 "Swift, o'er the plain of burning Sand
      My course I bent to thee;
And soon I reach'd the billowy strand
      Which bounds the stormy Sea.—
DRACO! my Love! Oh yet, thy ZELMA's soul
90 Springs ardently to thee,—impatient of controul.

16

"Again the lightning flashes white—
      The rattling cords among!
Now, by the transient vivid light,

I mark the frantic throng!
95 Now up the tatter'd shrouds my DRACO flies—
While o'er the plunging prow, the curling billows rise.

17

"The topmast falls—three shackled slaves—
      Cling to the Vessel's side!
Now lost amid the madd'ning waves—
100   Now on the mast they ride—
See! on the forecastle my DRACO stands
And now he waves his chain, now clasps his bleeding hands.

18

"Why, cruel WHITE-MAN! when away
      My sable Love was torn,
105 Why did you let poor ZELMA stay,
      On Afric's sands to mourn?
No! ZELMA is not left, for she will prove
In the deep troubled main, her fond—her faithful LOVE."

19

The lab'ring Ship was now a wreck,
110   The Shrouds were flutt'ring wide!
The rudder gone, the lofty deck
      Was rock'd from side to side—
Poor ZELMA's eyes now dropp'd their last big tear,
While, from her tawny cheek, the blood recoil'd with fear.

20

115 Now frantic, on the sands she roam'd,
      Now shrieking stop'd to view
Where high the liquid mountains foam'd,
      Around the exhausted crew—
'Till, from the deck, her DRACO's well known form
120 Sprung mid the yawning waves, and buffeted the Storm.

21

Long, on the swelling surge sustain'd
      Brave DRACO sought the shore,
Watch'd the dark Maid, but ne'er complain'd,
      Then sunk, to gaze no more!
125 Poor ZELMA saw him buried by the wave—
And, with her heart's true Love, plung'd in a wat'ry grave.

George Gordon, Lord Byron
1788 – 1824

George Gordon, Lord Byron, was one of the most influential literary figures of the nineteenth century. His works—the long poems *Childe Harold's Pilgrimage* and *Don Juan* among them—were tremendous popular successes, and the Byronic Hero has become a cultural icon. Byron himself, handsome and charming, sexually unconventional, politically iconoclastic, has been alternately celebrated and reviled from his own time to the present.

Byron's beginnings were inauspicious. He was born in near-poverty on 22 January 1788, lame in one leg (probably the result of a form of cerebral palsy). His father, Captain John ("Mad Jack") Byron, a notorious spendthrift and rake, had married Byron's mother, the Scottish heiress Catherine Gordon, for her money. This he quickly squandered, afterward fleeing to France. Byron and his mother moved to Aberdeen. Here Byron lived out his first ten years, the object of his mother's capricious mixture of love and sudden overwhelming rages, deeply conscious of his lameness, and steeped in Calvinism. Here, too, at ten years old, he was regularly molested by his nursemaid.

In 1798 Byron's great-uncle, the fifth Lord Byron, died childless, and Byron inherited the title. He and his mother moved to the family's ancestral, debt-encumbered home, Newstead Abbey, in Nottinghamshire. Byron was sent to school, first to an academy in Dulwich, then to Harrow in 1801. Around 1801 he also met for the first time his half-sister Augusta, the product of an earlier marriage of his father's. In 1805 Byron entered Trinity College, Cambridge University, where he made the most lasting friendships of his life. He also contracted huge debts to which he would only add in the future.

Byron took a degree from Cambridge in 1807. In the same year, he published his first poetry collection, *Hours of Idleness*. The book was excoriated in the press as pretentious and derivative; Byron responded in 1809 with the verse satire *English Bards and Scotch Reviewers*, in which he attacked the most notable of his critics and many of the leading poets of the day. In that same year, Byron came of age and took possession of Newstead Abbey, where he held riotous parties; as a result of carousing and redecorating, his mountain of debt grew larger. In March he made his first appearance in the House of Lords, and in July, after having incurred more debt to finance himself, he set off on a trip through Europe and the Near East, areas largely closed to the English as a result of the Napoleonic Wars. This journey began an intense attachment to Greece that would color the rest of Byron's life and writing and allowed him to fulfill the homosexual desires that he had been unable to explore in England (where sodomy was a capital crime). During this time he also began *Childe Harold's Pilgrimage,* the work that would make him a celebrity.

Featuring a journey almost identical to that which Byron himself had just completed, undertaken by a mysteriously gloomy hero, *Childe Harold's Pilgrimage*, Cantos I&II, launched both the figure of the "Byronic Hero" and the association between that figure and Byron that the poet would alternately embrace and seek to evade for the remainder of his life. The poem cunningly managed to weave elements from familiar genres such as travel writing, gothic novels, and sentimental literature with experiments in mood and tone. It enthralled its readers. Byron wrote in Spenserian stanzas, but as the poem progressed he began to bend this stiff form so that it became his own. (Harold's discoveries and the narrator's own growing observational and meditative abilities find their mirror in the rhythms of the verse.) With its panoramic focus, high-flown tone, and alluringly aloof protagonist, *Childe Harold's Pilgrimage* marked an important moment in English and European literature.

Now a celebrity, Byron played that role with gusto. He became a darling of Whig society and indulged in a series of affairs, most scandalously with Lady Caroline Lamb. In addition, some time in 1813 Byron became close with his half-sister Augusta. There is some evidence to suggest that this relationship may have been sexual in nature; in any case, it was one of Byron's deepest and most lasting attachments. He also continued writing, producing a collection of hugely popular works ranging from the short lyrics of *Hebrew Melodies* to the "Eastern Tales" produced in 1813 and 1814. In this series of long narrative poems, set in the Near East, he fleshed out the anti-heroic figure he had sketched in *Childe Harold's Pilgrimage*. The protagonists of the "Tales" stood aloof from those who surround them, tortured by a mysterious but deeply felt guilt. Brave, glamorous, and in each case devoted utterly to one woman (who herself was an idealized romantic heroine), they were nonetheless fated to be outcasts. Described most fully in the first of the "Eastern Tales," "The Giaour," the hero reached his final refinement in the last, "Lara." The public embraced this figure, and a literary type entered into the canon with a vengeance: the writing of the next hundred years would be crowded with Byronic Heroes.

In January of 1815, Byron married Annabella Milbanke, a sheltered heiress. The marriage was based on a short courtship and false hopes, and the two participants were utterly unsuited. Byron was psychologically abusive to his wife, whose piety and conventionality were a constant irritant to him. At the end of 1815, a few weeks after the birth of their daughter, Augusta Ada, Annabella left him. A public scandal followed, aided by the unauthorized publication of Byron's poems. Now a social outcast, Byron departed for Europe, never to return. He continued to communicate with his friends in England through a voluminous and revealingly frank series of letters that detailed his sexual adventures, his political and literary beliefs, and his continued involvement with affairs in England. Even if he had written no poetry, the letters would qualify Byron for a place as one of England's foremost authors: urbane, broad-ranging, dazzling, and hilarious, they make for riveting and delightful reading.

Landing in Belgium in April of 1816, Byron made his way through scenes—including a visit to Waterloo—which he would describe in the final two cantos of *Childe Harold*. At Geneva he met Mary and Percy Shelley. They had traveled to Switzerland accompanied by Mary's stepsister Claire Clairmont, who had had a brief sexual relationship with Byron in England. The two poets formed an intimate and intellectually rich friendship, and the four lived in close proximity during the summer. Byron resumed his involvement with Claire; she bore him a daughter, Allegra, in January of 1817.

When the Shelleys departed for England in August, Byron journeyed to Venice, where he lived for the next three years. Here he flung himself into a period of promiscuity (he estimated that he had sex with over two hundred women during this time), but continued to work as well, producing his verse drama *Manfred*, the fourth canto of *Childe Harold*, and the humorous *Beppo*, written in *ottava rima*. This colloquial Italian form was fiendishly ill-adapted to English, but Byron made it his own, also using it to produce his masterpiece, *Don Juan*, which he began in July of 1818.

Don Juan is the creation of an author who has found his *métier*. It is the longest satirical poem in English, a rollicking tale of a young hero who bears the same name as the seducer but resembles him in no other way. Juan, passive and sweet-natured, is seduced by women ranging from a family friend to Catherine the Great. His adventures take him on a journey from Spain to London by way of Greece and Russia. Byron was thus able to mock not only current social mores but also his own previous poems, Don Juan standing as a kind of anti-Byronic Hero. He took as his model for the poem a slight satire written in 1817 by John Hookham Frere in *ottava rima*, but *Don Juan* is also descended from Swift's *Gulliver's Travels*, and Sterne's *Tristram Shandy*. As with the latter, the focus of Byron's poem is not so much what is narrated as its narrator, a garrulous, easily distracted gentleman who at times bears a remarkable resemblance to the author. Byron's publisher, friends, and the critical establishment condemned *Don Juan* for its immorality, but he himself relished it, asserting that he had written it only "to giggle and make giggle"—a comment typically Byronic in its attempt to deny responsibility by invoking comedy. For all its author's disclaimers, *Don Juan* is no mere comic throwaway. It is a text of great cultural and political scope and a work of questing philosophy, arguably the best of its age.

In April of 1819 Byron met Countess Teresa Guiccioli, a young Italian woman married to a much older man. Almost immediately they began a socially sanctioned affair that would last, with reasonable fidelity, until the end of Byron's life. Through her family, Byron was drawn into nationalist schemes to free Italy from the Austrians. When the family was exiled to Pisa in 1821 as a result of this plotting, Byron followed. The Shelleys were now based in Pisa, and Byron became one of their group. Soon, however, this "Pisan circle" fell apart, first because of Shelley's anger over Byron's callous treatment of Allegra (she had joined him in Venice in 1819, only for him first to neglect her and then send her to be brought up in a convent, where she died, unvisited by him, in 1822), then because of Byron's decision to follow the Countess's family to Genoa, and finally because of Shelley's own death in July 1822.

Despite these upheavals, Byron wrote at a furious pace. Between 1819 and 1823 he produced numerous works, including a series of closet dramas (including *Sardanapalus*, *The Two Foscari*, and *Cain*), and his biting satire of England under George III, *The Vision of Judgment*. He also continued *Don Juan*, finishing sixteen cantos by the end of 1823.

In 1824 Byron organized an expedition to assist the Greeks in their fight for independence from the Turks. Settled in the marsh town of Missolonghi, he financed and trained soldiers. Exhausted and worn down, he contracted a fever and died on 19 April, aged thirty-six, his death hastened by copious bloodletting performed by his incompetent doctors.

⌘ ⌘ ⌘

Sun of the Sleepless

Sun of the sleepless! melancholy star!
Whose tearful beam glows tremulously far,
That show'st the darkness thou canst not dispel,
How like art thou to joy remembered well!
5 So gleams the past, the light of other days,
Which shines, but warms not with its powerless rays;
A night-beam Sorrow watcheth to behold,
Distinct, but distant—clear—but, oh how cold!
—1814

She walks in beauty

1

She walks in beauty, like the night
Of cloudless climes and starry skies;
And all that's best of dark and bright
Meet in her aspect and her eyes:
5 Thus mellow'd to that tender light
Which heaven to gaudy day denies.

2

One shade the more, one ray the less,
Had half impair'd the nameless grace
Which waves in every raven tress,

10   Or softly lightens o'er her face;
       Where thoughts serenely sweet express
           How pure, how dear their dwelling place.

                         3

       And on that cheek, and o'er that brow,
           So soft, so calm, yet eloquent,
15   The smiles that win, the tints that glow,
           But tell of days in goodness spent,
       A mind at peace with all below,
           A heart whose love is innocent!
       —1815 [WRITTEN 1814]

When we two parted [1]

                         1

       When we two parted
           In silence and tears,
       Half broken-hearted
           To sever for years,
5   Pale grew thy cheek and cold,
           Colder thy kiss;
       Truly that hour foretold
           Sorrow to this.

                         2

       The dew of the morning
10   Sunk chill on my brow—
       It felt like the warning
           Of what I feel now.
       Thy vows are all broken,
           And light is thy fame;
15   I hear thy name spoken,
           And share in its shame.

                         3

       They name thee before me,
           A knell to mine ear;
       A shudder comes o'er me—
20   Why wert thou so dear?
       They know not I knew thee,
           Who knew thee too well:—
       Long, long shall I rue thee,
           Too deeply to tell.

                         4

25   In secret we met—
           In silence I grieve,
       That thy heart could forget,
           Thy spirit deceive.
       If I should meet thee
30   After long years,
       How should I greet thee!—
           With silence and tears.
       —1816 [WRITTEN 1815]

Stanzas for Music [2]

                         1

       There's not a joy the world can give like that it
           takes away,
       When the glow of early thought declines in feeling's
           dull decay;
       'Tis not on youth's smooth cheek the blush alone,
           which fades so fast,
       But the tender bloom of heart is gone, ere youth
           itself be past.

                         2

5   Then the few whose spirits float above the wreck
           of happiness,
       Are driven o'er the shoals of guilt or ocean of excess:
       The magnet of their course is gone, or only points
           in vain

---

[1] *When we two parted*   This poem has a complex history, at least partially because Byron deliberately misdated its composition as 1816, in order to hide its true subject. In fact, the lines were written in 1815, and their subject is Lady Frances Wedderburn Webster, the wife of a friend of Byron's; Byron had heard gossip about her affair with the Duke of Wellington. Byron himself had had a brief "platonic" affair with Lady Webster in 1813: a heated and exciting chase, kept secret from her husband and ending without consummation.

[2] *Stanzas for Music*   Byron wrote this poem in 1815 to commemorate the death of one of the friends of his youth, the Duke of Dorset. He referred to it in an 1816 letter as "the truest, though the most melancholy, I ever wrote."

The shore to which their shiver'd sail shall never
    stretch again.

3

Then the mortal coldness of the soul like death
    itself comes down;
10 It cannot feel for others' woes, it dare not dream
    its own;
That heavy chill has frozen o'er the fountain of
    our tears,
And tho' the eye may sparkle still, 'tis where the
    ice appears.

4

Tho' wit may flash from fluent lips, and mirth
    distract the breast,
Through midnight hours that yield no more their
    former hope of rest;
15 'Tis but as ivy-leaves around the ruin'd turret wreath,
All green and wildly fresh without but worn and
    grey beneath.

5

Oh could I feel as I have felt,—or be what I have been,
Or weep as I could once have wept, o'er many a
    vanished scene:
As springs in deserts found seem sweet, all
    brackish though they be,
20 So midst the wither'd waste of life, those tears
    would flow to me.
   —1816

Darkness[1]

I had a dream, which was not all a dream.
   The bright sun was extinguish'd, and the stars
Did wander darkling in the eternal space,
Rayless, and pathless, and the icy earth
5 Swung blind and blackening in the moonless air;[2]
Morn came, and went—and came, and brought no day,
And men forgot their passions in the dread
Of this their desolation; and all hearts
Were chill'd into a selfish prayer for light:
10 And they did live by watchfires—and the thrones,
The palaces of crowned kings—the huts,
The habitations of all things which dwell,
Were burnt for beacons; cities were consumed,
And men were gathered round their blazing homes
15 To look once more into each other's face;
Happy were those who dwelt within the eye
Of the volcanos, and their mountain-torch:
A fearful hope was all the world contain'd;
Forests were set on fire—but hour by hour
20 They fell and faded—and the crackling trunks
Extinguish'd with a crash—and all was black.
The brows of men by the despairing light
Wore an unearthly aspect, as by fits
The flashes fell upon them; some lay down
25 And hid their eyes and wept; and some did rest
Their chins upon their clenched hands, and smiled;
And others hurried to and fro, and fed
Their funeral piles with fuel, and looked up
With mad disquietude on the dull sky,
30 The pall of a past world; and then again
With curses cast them down upon the dust,

---

[1] *Darkness* The dust thrown into the atmosphere in 1815 by Mount Tamboro, an Indonesian volcano, made the summer of 1816 the coldest and wettest on record. Influenced by the weather, and perhaps by recent warnings by an Italian astronomer that sunspots might lead to the extinction of the sun, Byron produced this prescient poem, which he labeled "a Fragment." The "last man" theme was a source of fascination for the Romantics, but Byron's poem is distinctive for its absence of a last man, its unrelentingly bleak vision, and its representation of a typically Byronic faithful dog.

[2] *icy earth … moonless air* Cf. Ezekiel 32.7–8; Joel 2.31; Revelation 6.12.

And gnash'd their teeth and howl'd: the wild
   birds shriek'd,
And, terrified, did flutter on the ground,
And flap their useless wings; the wildest brutes
35   Came tame and tremulous; and vipers crawl'd
And twined themselves among the multitude,
Hissing, but stingless—they were slain for food:
And War, which for a moment was no more,
Did glut himself again;—a meal was bought
40   With blood, and each sate sullenly apart
Gorging himself in gloom: no love was left;
All earth was but one thought—and that was death,
Immediate and inglorious; and the pang
Of famine fed upon all entrails—men
45   Died, and their bones were tombless as their flesh;
The meagre by the meagre were devoured,
Even dogs assail'd their masters, all save one,
And he was faithful to a corse,[1] and kept
The birds and beasts and famish'd men at bay,
50   Till hunger clung them, or the dropping dead
Lured their lank jaws; himself sought out no food,
But with a piteous and perpetual moan
And a quick desolate cry, licking the hand
Which answered not with a caress—he died.
55   The crowd was famish'd by degrees; but two
Of an enormous city did survive,
And they were enemies; they met beside
The dying embers of an altar-place
Where had been heap'd a mass of holy things
60   For an unholy usage; they raked up,
And shivering scraped with their cold skeleton hands
The feeble ashes, and their feeble breath
Blew for a little life, and made a flame
Which was a mockery; then they lifted up
65   Their eyes as it grew lighter, and beheld
Each other's aspects—saw, and shriek'd, and died—
Even of their mutual hideousness they died,
Unknowing who he was upon whose brow
Famine had written Fiend. The world was void,
70   The populous and the powerful was a lump,
Seasonless, herbless, treeless, manless, lifeless—
A lump of death—a chaos of hard clay.
The rivers, lakes, and ocean all stood still,
And nothing stirred within their silent depths;

75   Ships sailorless lay rotting on the sea,
And their masts fell down piecemeal; as they dropp'd
They slept on the abyss without a surge—
The waves were dead; the tides were in their grave,
The moon their mistress had expired before;
80   The winds were withered in the stagnant air,
And the clouds perish'd; Darkness had no need
Of aid from them—She was the universe.
   —1816

Prometheus [2]

1

Titan! to whose immortal eyes
   The sufferings of mortality,
     Seen in their sad reality,
Were not as things that gods despise;
5   What was thy pity's recompense?
A silent suffering, and intense;
The rock, the vulture, and the chain,
All that the proud can feel of pain,
The agony they do not show,
10   The suffocating sense of woe,
     Which speaks but in its loneliness,
And then is jealous lest the sky
Should have a listener, nor will sigh
     Until its voice is echoless.

2

15   Titan! to thee the strife was given
     Between the suffering and the will,
     Which torture where they cannot kill;
And the inexorable Heaven,
And the deaf tyranny of Fate,
20   The ruling principle of Hate,
Which for its pleasure doth create
The things it may annihilate,
Refused thee even the boon to die:
The wretched gift eternity
25   Was thine—and thou hast borne it well.

---

1 *corse* Corpse.

2 *Prometheus* The Titan Prometheus stole fire from heaven and gave it to humanity. To punish him, Jupiter, King of the gods, had him chained to a rock in the Caucasus, where a vulture (in some versions, an eagle) tore at his liver. Each night Prometheus's liver grew afresh, to be torn out the next day.

All that the Thunderer[1] wrung from thee
Was but the menace which flung back
On him the torments of thy rack;
The fate thou didst so well foresee
30 But would not to appease him tell;
And in thy Silence was his Sentence,
And in his Soul a vain repentance,
And evil dread so ill dissembled
That in his hand the lightnings trembled.

3

35 Thy Godlike crime was to be kind,
 To render with thy precepts less
 The sum of human wretchedness,
And strengthen Man with his own mind;
But baffled as thou wert from high,
40 Still in thy patient energy,
In the endurance, and repulse
 Of thine impenetrable Spirit,
Which Earth and Heaven could not convulse,
 A mighty lesson we inherit:
45 Thou art a symbol and a sign
 To Mortals of their fate and force;
Like thee, Man is in part divine,
 A troubled stream from a pure source;
And Man in portions can foresee
50 His own funereal destiny;
His wretchedness, and his resistance,
And his sad unallied existence:
To which his Spirit may oppose
Itself—an equal to all woes,
55 And a firm will, and a deep sense,
Which even in torture can descry
 Its own concentered recompense,
Triumphant where it dares defy,
And making Death a Victory.
 —1816

So, we'll go no more a roving[2]

1

So, we'll go no more a roving
 So late into the night,
Though the heart be still as loving,
 And the moon be still as bright.

2

5 For the sword outwears its sheath,
 And the soul wears out the breast,
And the heart must pause to breathe,
 And love itself have rest.

3

Though the night was made for loving,
10 And the day returns too soon,
Yet we'll go no more a roving
 By the light of the moon.
—1817

When a man hath no freedom to fight for at home[3]

When a man hath no freedom to fight for at home,
 Let him combat for that of his neighbors;
Let him think of the glories of Greece and of Rome,
 And get knock'd on the head for his labours.

5 To do good to mankind is the chivalrous plan,
 And is always as nobly requited;
Then battle for freedom wherever you can,
 And, if not shot or hang'd, you'll get knighted.
—1820

[2] *So, we'll … roving* Originally written as part of a letter from Byron to his friend Thomas Moore, 28 February 1817. Just before these lines Byron writes, "The Carnival … knocked me up a little. But it is over—and it is now Lent, with all its abstinence and sacred music. The mumming closed with a masked ball … and, though I did not dissipate much upon the whole, yet I find 'the sword wearing out the scabbard', though I have but just turned the corner of twenty-nine."

[3] *When a man … home* Byron first sent these lines in a letter to his friend Thomas Moore on 5 November 1820. They are based on Byron's activities with the Italian freedom-fighters, the Carbonari, and their abortive attempt to stage an uprising.

[1] *Thunderer* Jupiter.

January 22nd 1842.
Missolonghi
On this day I complete my thirty sixth year [1]

1

'Tis time this heart should be unmoved
　　Since others it hath ceased to move,
Yet though I cannot be beloved
　　　　Still let me love.

2

5　My days are in the yellow leaf [2]
　　The flowers and fruits of love are gone—
The worm—the canker, and the grief
　　　　Are mine alone.

3

The fire that on my bosom preys
10　　Is lone as some Volcanic Isle,
No torch is kindled at its blaze
　　　　A funeral pile!

4

The hope, the fear, the jealous care
　　The exalted portion of the pain
15　And power of Love I cannot share
　　　　But wear the chain.

5

But 'tis not *thus*—and 'tis not *here*
　　Such thoughts should shake my soul, nor *now*

Where Glory decks the hero's bier
20　　　　Or binds his brow.

6

The Sword—the Banner—and the Field
　　Glory and Greece around us see!
The Spartan borne upon his shield [3]
　　　　Was not more free!

7

25　Awake! (not Greece—She *is* awake!)
　　Awake my spirit—think through *whom*
Thy life-blood tracks its parent lake
　　　　And then strike home!

8

Tread those reviving passions down
30　　Unworthy Manhood;—unto thee
Indifferent should the smile or frown
　　　　Of Beauty be.

9

If thou regret'st thy youth, why *live?*
　　The land of honourable Death
35　Is here—up to the Field! and give
　　　　Away thy Breath.

10

Seek out—less often sought than found,
　　A Soldier's Grave—for thee the best,
Then look around and choose thy ground
40　　　　And take thy Rest.

　　—1824

Epistle to Augusta [4]

1

My Sister—my sweet Sister—if a name
　　Dearer and purer were—it should be thine.
Mountains and seas divide us—but I claim

---

[1] *On this ... year* This poem was until recently most commonly
known by its subtitle, but the date and place are the correct title.
Byron wrote it on his 36th birthday, in Greece. A companion who
was with him at the time says, "January 22.—Lord Byron came from
his bedroom into the apartment ... where some friends were
assembled, and said, with a smile, 'You were complaining, the other
day, that I never write any poetry now:—this is my birthday, and I
have just finished something which, I think, is better than what I
usually write.'" The poem is informed by Byron's relationship with
two people, his young Greek companion of the time, Loukas
Chalandritsanos, and a Turkish girl, Hataje, whom he had taken
into his care. Byron's feelings for Chalandritsanos are commonly
understood to be the stronger influence of the two.

[2] *My days ... leaf* See *Macbeth* 5.3.21–22.

[3] [Byron's note] The slain were borne on their shields—witness
the Spartan mother's speech to her son, delivered with his
buckler—"Either *with* this or *on* this."

[4] *Augusta* Byron's half-sister, Augusta Leigh (1783–1857).

No tears, but tenderness to answer mine:
5   Go where I will, to me thou art the same—
        A loved regret which I would not resign—
There yet are two things in my destiny
A world to roam through—and a home with thee.

2

The first were nothing—had I still the last
10   It were the haven of my happiness—
But other claims and other ties thou hast—
        And mine is not the wish to make them less.
A strange doom is thy father's son's and past
        Recalling—as it lies beyond redress—
15   Reversed for him our grandsire's fate of yore
He had no rest at sea—nor I on shore.[1]

3

If my inheritance of storms hath been
        In other elements—and on the rocks
Of perils overlooked or unforeseen
20   I have sustained my share of worldly shocks
The fault was mine—nor do I seek to screen
        My errors with defensive paradox—
I have been cunning in mine overthrow
The careful pilot of my proper woe.

4

25   Mine were my faults—and mine be their reward—
        My whole life was a contest—since the day
That gave me being gave me that which marred
        The gift—a fate, or will that walked astray—
And I at times have found the struggle hard
30   And thought of shaking off my bonds of clay—
But now I fain would for a time survive
If but to see what next can well arrive.

5

Kingdoms and empires in my little day
        I have outlived, and yet I am not old—
35   And when I look on this, the petty spray
        Of my own years of trouble, which have rolled
Like a wild bay of breakers, melts away:—

Something—I know not what—does still uphold
A spirit of slight patience;—not in vain,
40   Even for its own sake—do we purchase pain.

6

Perhaps—the workings of defiance stir
        Within me, or perhaps a cold despair—
Brought on when ills habitually recur,—
        Perhaps a kinder clime—or purer air—
45   For even to this may change of soul refer—
        And with light armour we may learn to bear—
Have taught me a strange quiet which was not
The chief companion of a calmer lot.

7

I feel almost at times as I have felt
50   In happy childhood—trees, and flowers, and brooks
Which do remember me of where I dwelt
        Ere my young mind was sacrificed to books—
Come as of yore upon me—and can melt
        My heart with recognition of their looks—
55   And even at moments I could think I see
Some living thing to love—but none like thee.

8

Here are the Alpine landscapes—which create
        A fund for contemplation;—to admire
Is a brief feeling of a trivial date—
60   But something worthier do such scenes inspire:
Here to be lonely is not desolate—
        For much I view which I could most desire—
And, above all a Lake I can behold—
Lovelier—not dearer than our own of old.

9

65   Oh that thou wert but with me!—but I grow
        The fool of my own wishes—and forget
The solitude which I have vaunted so
        Has lost its praise in this but one regret—
There may be others which I less may show—
70   I am not of the plaintive mood—and yet
I feel an ebb in my philosophy
And the tide rising in my altered eye.

---

[1] *He had no ... on shore* Byron and Augusta's grandfather, Admiral
John Byron, was renowned for never making a sea voyage without
encountering a storm. He was known as "Foulweather Jack."

10

I did remind thee of our own dear lake
　　By the old Hall which may be mine no more—
75 Leman's is fair—but think not I forsake
　　The sweet remembrance of a dearer shore—
Sad havoc Time must with my memory make
　　Ere that or thou can fade these eyes before—
Though like all things which I have loved—they are
80 Resigned for ever—or divided far.

11

The world is all before me—I but ask
　　Of Nature that with which she will comply—
It is but in her Summer's sun to bask—
　　To mingle with the quiet of her sky—
85 To see her gentle face without a mask
　　And never gaze on it with apathy—
She was my early friend—and now shall be
My Sister—till I look again on thee.

12

I can reduce all feelings but this one,
90 　　And that I would not—for at length I see
Such scenes as those wherein my life begun
　　The earliest—were the only paths for me.
Had I but sooner learnt the crowd to shun
　　I had been better than I now can be
95 The passions which have torn me would have slept—
　　I had not suffered—and thou hadst not wept.

13

With false Ambition what had I to do?
　　Little with love, and least of all with fame!
And yet they came unsought and with me grew,
100 　　And made me all which they can make—a Name.
Yet this was not the end I did pursue—

Surely I once beheld a nobler aim.
But all is over—I am one the more
To baffled millions which have gone before.

14

105 And for the future—this world's future may
　　From me demand but little from my care;
I have outlived myself by many a day,
　　Having survived so many things that were—
My years have been no slumber—but the prey
110 　　Of ceaseless vigils;—for I had the share
Of life which might have filled a century
Before its fourth in time had passed me by.

15

And for the remnants which may be to come
　　I am content—and for the past I feel
115 Not thankless—for within the crowded sum
　　Of struggles—happiness at times would steal
And for the present—I would not benumb
　　My feelings farther—nor shall I conceal
That with all this I still can look around
120 And worship Nature with a thought profound.

16

For thee—my own sweet Sister—in thy heart
　　I know myself secure—as thou in mine
We were and are—I am—even as thou art—
　　Beings who ne'er each other can resign
125 It is the same together or apart
　　From Life's commencement to its slow decline—
We are entwined—let death come slow or fast
The tie which bound the first endures the last.
　　—1830

IN CONTEXT

The Byronic Hero

Byron is the only English author to give his name to a specific literary type, one that has been associated with him since he created it. The character now known as the Byronic Hero, although based on attributes present in previous literary characters, was so distilled and reformed by Byron that it became uniquely his own creation. One can see the gradual refinement of the Byronic Hero most clearly in the "Eastern Tales," a term most commonly used to identify the long series of narrative poems Byron wrote between 1813 and 1814. These verse tales, which were extremely popular when they were first published, feature a series of proud, gloomy heroes, each mysteriously tortured and each having as his only redeeming characteristic an enduring love for a single female figure. The extracts below are descriptions of this hero, giving the flavor of his personality and showing the ways in which Byron fine-tuned it as the poems progressed.

from *The Giaour: A Fragment of a Turkish Tale*[1] (1813)

"The Giaour" (the word means "infidel" and is pronounced "Jowr") was the first of Byron's "Eastern Tales." It is written in fragment form, the fragments unconnected to each other and divided between a number of speakers. It tells the story of the young Giaour's love for Leila, a concubine of the sultan Hassan. Leila escapes from the harem: Hassan re-captures her and kills her by sewing her up in a sack and drowning her (at the time, it was believed that Byron had rescued a young woman from just such a fate during his time in the East). The Giaour responds by killing Hassan as he journeys to find a new bride. Years later, the Giaour has taken refuge in a monastery, and the poem ends with his long confession of guilt, anguish, and enduring love for Leila.

180 ...[1] Who thundering comes on blackest steed?
With slacken'd bit and hoof of speed,
Beneath the clattering iron's sound
The cavern'd echoes wake around
In lash for lash, and bound for bound;
185 The foam that streaks the courser's side,
Seems gather'd from the ocean-tide:
Though weary waves are sunk to rest,
There's none within his rider's breast,
And though tomorrow's tempest lower,
190 'Tis calmer than thy heart, young Giaour!
I know thee not, I loathe thy race,
But in thy lineaments I trace
What time shall strengthen, not efface;

---

[1] ... Byron added to this poem in each new edition: the first edition of 1813 was less than 700 lines in length; the seventh, from which these extracts are taken, is almost twice as long.

Though young and pale, that sallow front
195   Is scath'd by fiery passion's brunt,
Though bent on earth thine evil eye
As meteor-like thou glidest by,
Right well I view, and deem thee one
Whom Othman's sons[1] should slay or shun....

Tonight—set Rhamazani's[2] sun
Tonight—the Bairam feast's begun
230   Tonight—but who and what art thou
Of foreign garb and fearful brow?
And what are these to thine or thee,
That thou should'st either pause or flee?
        He stood—some dread was on his face,
235   Soon Hatred settled in its place—
It rose not with the reddening flush
Of transient Anger's hasty blush,
But pale as marble o'er the tomb,
Whose ghastly whiteness aids its gloom.
240   His brow was bent—his eye was glazed—
He raised his arm, and fiercely raised;
And sternly shook his hand on high,
As doubting to return or fly;—
Impatient of his flight delayed
245   Here loud his raven charger neighed—
Down glanced that hand, and grasped his blade—
That sound had burst his waking dream,
As Slumber starts at owlet's scream.—
The spur hath lanced his courser's sides—
250   Away—away—for life he rides—
Swift as the hurled on high jerreed,[3]
Springs to the touch his startled steed,
The rock is doubled—and the shore
Shakes with the clattering tramp no more—
255   The crag is won—no more is seen
His Christian crest and haughty mien.[4]—
'Twas but an instant—he restrained
That fiery barb so sternly reined—
'Twas but a moment that he stood,

---

[1]   *Othman's sons*   Othman I (1258–1324) was the founder of the Turkish Ottoman empire. "Othman's sons" thus means Turks, and by extension, Muslims.

[2]   *Rhamazani*   Ramadhan.

[3]   [Byron's note]   Jeered, or Djerrid, a blunted Turkish Javelin, which darted from horseback with great force and precision. It is a favourite exercise of the Mussulmans [Muslims]; but I know not if it can be called a *manly* one, since the most expert in the art are the Black Eunuchs of Constantinople. I think, next to these, a Mamlouk at Smyrna was the most skilful that came within my observation. [Mamlouks were slave-soldiers, originally from Circassia.]

[4]   *mien*   Appearance.

260   Then sped as if by death pursued;
     But in that instant, o'er his soul
     Winters of Memory seemed to roll,
     And gather in that drop of time
     A life of pain, an age of crime.
265   O'er him who loves, or hates, or fears,
     Such moment pours the grief of years—
     What felt *he* then—at once opprest
     By all that most distracts the breast?
     That pause—which pondered o'er his fate,
270   Oh, who its dreary length shall date!
     Though in Time's record nearly nought,
     It was Eternity to Thought!
     For infinite as boundless space
     The thought that Conscience must embrace,
275   Which in itself can comprehend
     Woe without name—or hope—or end.[1]— …

     Dark and unearthly is the scowl
     That glares beneath his dusky cowl—
     The flash of that dilating eye
835   Reveals too much of times gone by—
     Though varying—indistinct its hue,
     Oft will his glance the gazer rue—
     For in it lurks that nameless spell
     Which speaks—itself unspeakable—
840   A spirit yet unquell'd and high
     That claims and keeps ascendancy,
     And like the bird whose pinions quake,
     But cannot fly the gazing snake,
     Will others quail beneath his look,
845   Nor 'scape the glance they scarce can brook.
     From him the half-affrighted Friar
     When met alone would fain retire—
     As if that eye and bitter smile
     Transferred to others fear and guile—
850   Not oft to smile descendeth he,
     And when he doth 'tis sad to see
     That he but mocks at Misery.
     How that pale lip will curl and quiver!
     Then fix once more as if for ever—
855   As if his sorrow or disdain
     Forbade him e'er to smile again.—
     Well were it so—such ghastly mirth
     From joyaunce ne'er derived its birth.—
     But sadder still it were to trace

---

[1] *Who thundering … or end* The speaker of lines 180–276 is a Turkish fisher.

860　What once were feelings in that face—
　　　Time hath not yet the features fixed,
　　　But brighter traits with evil mixed—
　　　And there are hues not always faded,
　　　Which speak a mind not all degraded
865　Even by the crimes through which it waded—
　　　The common crowd but see the gloom
　　　Of wayward deeds—and fitting doom—
　　　The close observer can espy
　　　A noble soul, and lineage high.—
870　Alas! though both bestowed in vain,
　　　Which Grief could change—and Guilt could stain—
　　　It was no vulgar tenement
　　　To which such lofty gifts were lent,
　　　And still with little less than dread
875　On such the sight is riveted.—
　　　The roofless cot decayed and rent,
　　　　　Will scarce delay the passer by—
　　　The tower by war or tempest bent,
　　　While yet may frown one battlement,
880　　　Demands and daunts the stranger's eye—
　　　Each ivied arch—and pillar lone,
　　　Pleads haughtily for glories gone!
　　　"His floating robe around him folding,
　　　　　Slow sweeps he through the column aisle—
885　With dread beheld—with gloom beholding
　　　　　The rites that sanctify the pile.
　　　But when the anthem shakes the choir,
　　　And kneel the monks—his steps retire—
　　　By yonder lone and wavering torch
890　His aspect glares within the porch;
　　　There will he pause till all is done—
　　　And hear the prayer—but utter none.
　　　See—by the half-illumined wall
　　　His hood fly back—his dark hair fall—
895　That pale brow wildly wreathing round,
　　　As if the Gorgon[1] there had bound
　　　The sablest of the serpent-braid
　　　That o'er her fearful forehead strayed.
　　　For he declines the convent oath,
900　And leaves those locks' unhallowed growth—
　　　But wears our garb in all beside;
　　　And—not from piety but pride
　　　Gives wealth to walls that never heard
　　　Of his one holy vow nor word.—
905　Lo!—mark ye—as the harmony

---

[1] *Gorgon* Medusa, one of the Gorgons, who was once a beautiful maiden whose hair was her chief beauty. Athena turned her hair into a nest of serpents.

Peals louder praises to the sky—
That livid cheek—that stoney air
Of mixed defiance and despair!
Saint Francis! keep him from the shrine!
910   Else may we dread the wrath divine
Made manifest by awful sign.—
If ever evil angel bore
The form of mortal, such he wore—
By all my hope of sins forgiven
915   Such looks are not of earth nor heaven!"[1] ...

"My days, though few, have passed below
In much of joy, but more of woe;
Yet still in hours of love or strife,
985   I've 'scap'd the weariness of life;
Now leagu'd with friends, now girt by foes,
I loath'd the languor of repose;
Now nothing left to love or hate,
No more with hope or pride elate;
990   I'd rather be the thing that crawls
Most noxious o'er a dungeon's walls,[2]
Than pass my dull, unvarying days,
Condemned to meditate and gaze—
Yet, lurks a wish within my breast
995   For rest—but not to feel 'tis rest.
Soon shall my fate that wish fulfil;
        And I shall sleep without the dream
Of what I was, and would be still;
        Dark as to thee my deeds may seem—
1000   My memory now is but the tomb
Of joys long dead—my hope—their doom—
Though better to have died with those
Than bear a life of lingering woes—
My spirit shrunk not to sustain
1005   The searching throes of ceaseless pain;
Nor sought the self-accorded grave
Of ancient fool, and modern knave:
Yet death I have not fear'd to meet,
And in the field it had been sweet
1010   Had danger wooed me on to move
The slave of glory, not of love.
I've brav'd it—not for honour's boast;
I smile at laurels won or lost.—
To such let others carve their way,

---

[1] *"Dark and unearthly ... heaven!"* These lines (832–913) are spoken near the poem's end by a monk of the abbey where the Giaour lives.

[2] *I'd rather ... walls* Cf. Shakespeare, *Othello* 3.3.27–71.

1015   For high renown, or hireling pay;
        But place again before my eyes
        Aught that I deem a worthy prize;—
        The maid I love—the man I hate—
        And I will hunt the steps of fate,
1020   (To save or slay, as these require)
        Through rending steel, and rolling fire;
        Nor need'st thou doubt this speech from one
        Who would but do—what he *hath* done.
        Death is but what the haughty brave—
1025   The weak must bear—the wretch must crave—
        Then let Life go to him who gave:
        I have not quailed to danger's brow—
        When high and happy—need I *now*?"[1] ...

        He pass'd—nor of his name and race
1330   Hath left a token or a trace,
        Save what the father must not say
        Who shrived[2] him on his dying day;
        This broken tale was all we knew
        Of her he lov'd, or him he slew.

from *The Corsair: A Tale* (1814)

The third of the "Eastern Tales," "The Corsair" was also the best-selling—it is said to have
sold 10,000 on its day of publication. It tells the story of the pirate chief Conrad, whose only
virtue is his deep love for the beautiful Medora. During a raid on the court of the Pasha Seyd,
Conrad is captured and condemned to death. Saved by Seyd's concubine Gulnare, who has
fallen in love with Conrad and murders Seyd to rescue him, Conrad returns home
(accompanied by Gulnare), where he finds Medora dead. Destroyed by grief, Conrad
vanishes, never to be seen again.

CANTO I.9

195   Unlike the heroes of each ancient race,
        Demons in act, but Gods at least in face,
        In Conrad's form seems little to admire,
        Though his dark eyebrow shades a glance of fire:
        Robust but not Herculean—to the sight
200   No giant frame sets forth his common height;
        Yet, in the whole, who paused to look again,
        Saw more than marks the crowd of vulgar men;
        They gaze and marvel how—and still confess

---

[1]   *My days ... now*   These lines are part of the Giaour's confession.

[2]   *shrived*   Absolved from sin through the Roman Catholic Sacrament of Extreme Unction, or the Last Rites, which
includes confession.

That thus it is, but why they cannot guess.
205   Sun-burnt his cheek, his forehead high and pale
The sable[1] curls in wild profusion veil;
And oft perforce his rising lip reveals
The haughtier thought it curbs, but scarce conceals.
Though smooth his voice, and calm his general mien,
210   Still seems there something he would not have seen:
His features' deepening lines and varying hue
At times attracted, yet perplexed the view,
As if within that murkiness of mind
Worked feelings fearful, and yet undefined;
215   Such might it be—that none could truly tell—
Too close enquiry his stern glance would quell.
There breathe but few whose aspect might defy
The full encounter of his searching eye;
He had the skill, when Cunning's gaze would seek
220   To probe his heart and watch his changing cheek,
At once the observer's purpose to espy,
And on himself roll back his scrutiny,
Lest he to Conrad rather should betray
Some secret thought, than drag that chief's to day.
225   There was a laughing Devil in his sneer,
That raised emotions both of rage and fear;
And where his frown of hatred darkly fell,
        Hope withering fled—and Mercy sighed farewell!

Canto 1.10

Slight are the outward signs of evil thought,
230   Within—within—'twas there the spirit wrought!
Love shows all changes—Hate, Ambition, Guile,
Betray no further than the bitter smile;
The lip's least curl, the lightest paleness thrown
Along the governed aspect, speak alone
235   Of deeper passions; and to judge their mien,
He, who would see, must be himself unseen.
Then—with the hurried tread, the upward eye,
The clenched hand, the pause of agony,
That listens, starting, lest the step too near
240   Approach intrusive on that mood of fear:
Then—with each feature working from the heart,
With feelings, loosed to strengthen—not depart;
That rise—convulse—contend—that freeze, or glow,
Flush in the cheek, or damp upon the brow;
245   Then—Stranger! if thou canst, and tremblest not,
Behold his soul—the rest that soothes his lot!

---

[1]   *sable*   Black.

Mark—how that lone and blighted bosom sears
The scathing thought of execrated years!
Behold—but who hath seen, or e'er shall see,
250 Man as himself—the secret spirit free?

Canto I.11

Yet was not Conrad thus by Nature sent
To lead the guilty—guilt's worse instrument—
His soul was changed, before his deeds had driven
Him forth to war with man and forfeit heaven.
255 Warped by the world in Disappointment's school,
In words too wise, in conduct *there* a fool;
Too firm to yield, and far too proud to stoop,
Doomed by his very virtues for a dupe,
He cursed those virtues as the cause of ill,
260 And not the traitors who betrayed him still;
Nor deemed that gifts bestowed on better men
Had left him joy, and means to give again.
Feared—shunned—belied—ere youth had lost her force,
He hated man too much to feel remorse,
265 And thought the voice of wrath a sacred call,
To pay the injuries of some on all.
He knew himself a villain—but he deemed
The rest no better than the thing he seemed;
And scorned the best as hypocrites who hid
270 Those deeds the bolder spirit plainly did.
He knew himself detested, but he knew
The hearts that loathed him, crouched and dreaded too.
Lone, wild, and strange, he stood alike exempt
From all affection and from all contempt:
275 His name could sadden, and his acts surprise;
But they that feared him dared not to despise:
Man spurns the worm, but pauses ere he wake
The slumbering venom of the folded snake:
The first may turn—but not avenge the blow;
280 The last expires—but leaves no living foe;
Fast to the doomed offender's form it clings,
And he may crush—not conquer—still it stings!

Canto I.12

None are all evil—quickening round his heart,
One softer feeling would not yet depart;
285 Oft could he sneer at others as beguiled
By passions worthy of a fool or child;
Yet 'gainst that passion vainly still he strove,
And even in him it asks the name of Love!

Yes, it was love—unchangeable—unchanged,
290   Felt but for one from whom he never ranged;
Though fairest captives daily met his eye,
He shunned, nor sought,[1] but coldly passed them by;
Though many a beauty drooped in prisoned bower,
None ever soothed his most unguarded hour.
295   Yes—it was Love—if thoughts of tenderness,
Tried in temptation, strengthened by distress,
Unmoved by absence, firm in every clime,
And yet—oh more than all!—untired by time;
Which nor defeated hope, nor baffled wile,
300   Could render sullen were she[2] ne'er to smile,
Nor rage could fire, nor sickness fret to vent
On her one murmur of his discontent;
Which still would meet with joy, with calmness part,
Lest that his look of grief should reach her heart;
305   Which nought removed, nor menaced to remove—
If there be love in mortals—this was love!
He was a villain—ay—reproaches shower
On him—but not the passion, nor its power,
Which only proved, all other virtues gone,
310   Not guilt itself could quench this loveliest one!

from CANTO 3.24

1855   … And Conrad comes not—came not since that day:
Nor trace, nor tidings of his doom declare
Where lives his grief, or perished his despair!
Long mourned his band whom none could mourn beside;
And fair the monument they gave his bride:
1860   For him they raise not the recording stone—
His death yet dubious, deeds too widely known;
He left a Corsair's name to other times,
Linked with one virtue, and a thousand crimes.

from *Lara: A Tale* (1819)

> *Lara* (the title refers to the hero's last name) was the last of the Eastern Tales. Its hero has
> returned to his homeland after a long, unexplained absence. Haunted by never-revealed events
> in his past, he remains aloof, attended only by his page Kaled. One night at a feast Lara is
> recognized by a fellow guest, who promises to reveal Lara's past the next day. In the morning,
> the guest does not appear, and Lara instead fights a duel with his host. The personal feud
> turns to political rebellion as Lara becomes leader of a serfs' uprising. Wounded in a raid, Lara
> dies in the arms of Kaled, who is then revealed to be a young woman.

---

[1]   *shunned, nor sought*   "Neither" is understood before "shunned."

[2]   *she* I.e., Conrad's beloved.

from Canto 1.5

Whate'er he be, 'twas not what he had been;
 That brow in furrow'd lines had fix'd at last,
And spake of passions, but of passions past;
The pride, but not the fire, of early days,
70 Coldness of mien, and carelessness of praise;
A high demeanour, and glance that took
Their thoughts from others by a single look;
And that sarcastic levity of tongue,
The stinging of a heart the world hath stung,
75 That darts in seeming playfulness around,
And makes those feel who will not own the wound;
All these seem'd his, and something more beneath
Than glance could well reveal, or accent breathe.
Ambition, glory, love, the common aim
80 That some can conquer, and that all would claim,
Within his breast appear'd no more to strive,
Yet seem'd as lately they had been alive;
And some deep feeling it were vain to trace
At moments lighten'd o'er his livid face.

from Canto 1.17

In him inexplicably mix'd appeared
290 Much to be loved and hated, sought and feared;
Opinion varying o'er his hidden lot,
In praise or railing[1] ne'er his name forgot;
His silence formed a theme for others' prate[2]—
They guessed—they gazed—they fain would[3] know his fate.
295 What had he been? what was he, thus unknown,
Who walked their world, his lineage only known?
A hater of his kind? yet some would say,
With them he could seem gay amidst the gay;
But owned that smile if oft observed and near,
300 Waned in its mirth and withered to a sneer;
That smile might reach his lip, but passed not by,
None e'er could trace its laughter to his eye;
Yet there was softness too in his regard,
At times, a heart as not by nature hard,
305 But once perceiv'd, his spirit seemed to chide
Such weakness, as unworthy of its pride,
And steel'd itself, as scorning to redeem

---

[1] *railing* Mockery or abuse.

[2] *prate* Chatter.

[3] *fain would* Longed to.

One doubt from others' half withheld esteem;
In self-inflicted penance of a breast
310   Which tenderness might once have wrung from rest;
In vigilance of grief that would compel
The soul to hate for having lov'd too well.

from CANTO 1.18

There was in him a vital scorn of all:
As if the worst had fall'n which could befall
315   He stood a stranger in this breathing world,
An erring spirit from another hurled;
A thing of dark imaginings, that shaped
By choice the perils he by chance escaped;[1]
But 'scaped in vain, for in their memory yet
320   His mind would half exult and half regret:
With more capacity for love than earth
Bestows on most of mortal mould and birth,
His early dreams of good outstripp'd the truth,
And troubled manhood followed baffled youth;
325   With thought of years in phantom chace misspent,
And wasted powers for better purpose lent;
And fiery passions that had poured their wrath
In hurried desolation o'er his path,
And left the better feelings all at strife
330   In wild reflection o'er his stormy life;
But haughty still, and loth himself to blame,
He called on Nature's self to share the shame,
And charged all faults upon the fleshly form
She gave to clog the soul, and feast the worm;
335   'Till he at last confounded good and ill,
And half mistook for fate the acts of will:[2]
Too high for common selfishness, he could
At times resign his own for others' good,
But not in pity, not because he ought,
340   But in some strange perversity of thought,
That swayed him onward with a secret pride
To do what few or none would do beside;
And this same impulse would in tempting time
Mislead his spirit equally in crime;

---

[1] *A thing of dark ... chance escaped*   Lara imagines that his lucky escapes are the result of choices he made, and thus imagines a control over his fate that he does not really possess.

[2] *But haughty ... acts of will*   These lines may be paraphrased as follows: "unwilling to admit that he has wasted his better self and is responsible for his turn to evil, Lara blames his faults on the fact his (essentially good) soul is trapped in his (earthly and therefore essentially bad) body. By doing this, he confuses the very notions of good and bad, and assumes that his bad acts are the result of fate, rather than choice." Byron here draws on traditional Christian notions of the soul as an immortal and purely good entity, trapped in a body that perverts it through fleshly longings.

345   So much he soared beyond, or sunk beneath
       The men with whom he felt condemned to breathe,
       And longed by good or ill to separate
       Himself from all who shared his mortal state;
       His mind abhorring this had fixed her throne
350   Far from the world, in regions of her own;
       Thus coldly passing all that passed below,
       His blood in temperate seeming now would flow:
       Ah! happier if it ne'er with guilt had glowed,
       But ever in that icy smoothness flowed!
355   'Tis true, with other men their path he walked,
       And like the rest in seeming did and talked,
       Nor outraged Reason's rules by flaw nor start,
       His madness was not of the head, but heart;
       And rarely wandered in his speech, or drew
360   His thoughts so forth as to offend the view.

                     from CANTO 1.19

       With all that chilling mystery of mien,[1]
       And seeming gladness to remain unseen,
       He had (if 'twere not nature's boon) an art
       Of fixing memory on another's heart:
365   It was not love perchance—nor hate—nor aught
       That words can image to express the thought;
       But they who saw him did not see in vain,
       And once beheld, would ask of him again;
       And those to whom he spake remembered well,
370   And on the words, however light, would dwell:
       None knew, nor how, nor why, but he entwined
       Himself perforce around the hearer's mind;
       There he was stamp'd, in liking, or in hate,
       If greeted once; however brief the date
375   That friendship, pity, or aversion knew,
       Still there within the inmost thought he grew.
       You could not penetrate his soul, but found,
       Despite your wonder, to your own he wound;
       His presence haunted still; and from the breast
       He forced an all unwilling interest:
       Vain was the struggle in that mental net,
       His spirit seemed to dare you to forget!

---

[1] *mien* Attitude, appearance.

PERCY BYSSHE SHELLEY
1792 – 1822

Percy Bysshe Shelley's progressive social and political ideas have been an inspiration to many readers, from nineteenth-century socialists such as Marx and Engels to radical thinkers of the 1960s. Although he was born into wealth and privilege, Shelley opposed the powerful, from those who teased and harassed him in school at Eton to the Tory government and press whom he believed were responsible for the oppression of the working classes. He collaborated on *The Necessity of Atheism* (1811), a pamphlet destined to alienate not only his father, but also the bishops and authorities at Oxford, to whom Shelley sent the piece. Antagonistic to kings, priests, judges, the conservative press, and aristocracy, he was called "Mad Shelley" at Oxford. He earned this sobriquet not only for his radicalism but also for his intense interest in science. These intellectual passions underwrite a body of remarkable visionary poetry characterized by an elegance and complexity that is at once very wonderful and very difficult.

Shelley was born in 1792 at Field Place in Sussex, the first of the six children of Elizabeth and Timothy Shelley, a Member of Parliament who became a baronet on the death of his father, Sir Bysshe Shelley. Percy grew up in the affluence befitting his role as heir to the estate and title of his father and grandfather. He spent his early years running free on the estate and entertaining his siblings, so he was unprepared for the rules of the boys' academy he attended, or the bullying he would suffer there. Shelley later attended Eton College, and there the teasing continued, further developing his allegiance to outcasts and the disenfranchised, and nurturing his rebellious spirit. He was still a student at Eton when he published *Zastrozzi* (1810), a Gothic romance novel. He continued to publish during his short stint at Oxford University, from which he and Thomas Jefferson Hogg, his friend and the co-author of *The Necessity of Atheism*, were expelled for writing the pamphlet.

In 1813 Shelley published his first important work: *Queen Mab*, a poetic dream-vision that vilified conventional morality and institutional religion in a utopian picture of humanity returned to a condition of innocence. Shelley's greatest utopian fantasy, *Prometheus Unbound* (1820), would essentially reprise the same picture, imagining a world grown young again as human beings learn to undo the curse of their acquired historical fears and hatreds and replace it with a program based on love, which he called "the great secret" of all morality.

Shelley's personal involvements with love, fueled by his ideals, were also fraught with that inherited curse. In 1811 Shelley married Harriet Westbrook, and the couple had a daughter born to them in 1813. But before long he would fall in love with another young woman, Mary Godwin, the daughter of the radical thinkers William Godwin and Mary Wollstonecraft.

In 1814 Shelley left Harriet and traveled to the continent with Mary and her half sister Claire Clairmont for a six-week tour. When they returned to England Shelley proposed that Harriet should live with Mary and himself as free lovers. When Harriet refused, Shelley, Mary, and Claire again traveled to Europe, where the three met Lord Byron in Switzerland in June. In the meantime, Harriet gave birth to Shelley's second child, a son, in late 1814, and at the end of 1816 she committed suicide. Mary and Percy were then married.

The summer of 1816 is one of the most famous in the history of English letters. Out of it came a series of stunning literary works: Mary's great novel *Frankenstein*; Byron's third canto of *Childe Harold* as well as various apocalyptic works, especially *Manfred*; and a series of key lyric poems by Shelley including "Mont Blanc" and the "Hymn to Intellectual Beauty." Later (1818) Shelley would write "Julian and Maddalo: A Conversation," a brilliant verse dialogue representing the conversations that he and Byron had been having since they met in 1816.

Upon his return to England from Switzerland, his life bristling with personal and political scandals, Shelley was denied custody of his two children from his first marriage. In 1818 the Shelleys moved to the Continent with their baby girl Clara in the hope of joining Byron in Italy and avoiding the judgment of English society. Unfortunately, Clara died in September, and William, born in 1816, died the following year. The only child to survive would be Percy Florence, born in 1819.

Shelley wrote his lyric masterpiece *Prometheus Unbound* that same year, to show how social life might and ought to be, and he wrote the political tragedy *The Cenci* (1819), to show the way it actually was. The distance between the two works is dialectical, as Shelley later attempted to explain in his important prose work, *A Defence of Poetry* (1821). During this prolific period Shelley also responded to the Peterloo Massacre—in which at least eleven people were killed at what was meant to be a peaceful rally in Manchester—by writing "The Mask of Anarchy," "Song: To the Men of England," "A Philosophical View of Reform," and "Ode to the West Wind," a revolutionary lyric that recapitulates, in miniature, the argument and structure of *Prometheus Unbound*. Shelley hoped his verse would undermine the retrograde political institutions of his time and seed the future with a promise of rejuvenation. Enjoying scant fame or immediate influence, he nevertheless concluded his *Defence of Poetry* with the now-famous pronouncement that poets are "the unacknowledged legislators of the world."

In 1822 Shelley—who could not swim—went sailing on the Bay of Spezia in Italy with his friend Edward Williams. They were caught in a sudden squall and drowned. When Shelley's body washed up on the beach a few days later, a copy of Keats's poems was found in his pocket. A funeral pyre was hastily built and his corpse cremated—except for his heart, which was snatched from the pyre by his friend Edward Trelawney.

In a letter to some of his conservative English friends Byron famously declared: "You are all brutally mistaken about Shelley who was without exception—the *best* and least selfish man I ever knew." His ashes were placed near the recently buried Keats in the Protestant Cemetery in Rome. His inconsumable heart remained in Mary Shelley's possession, wrapped in the pages of *Adonais*, Shelley's elegy for Keats, until her death. It is buried with her in her tomb at St. Peter's Churchyard in Bournemouth.

⌘ ⌘ ⌘

To Wordsworth[1]

Poet of Nature, thou hast wept to know
That things depart which never may return:
Childhood and youth, friendship and love's first glow,
Have fled like sweet dreams, leaving thee to mourn.
5   These common woes I feel. One loss is mine
Which thou too feel'st, yet I alone deplore.
Thou wert as a lone star, whose light did shine
On some frail bark in winter's midnight roar:
Thou hast like to a rock-built refuge stood
10 Above the blind and battling multitude:
In honoured poverty thy voice did weave
Songs consecrate to truth and liberty—
Deserting these, thou leavest me to grieve,
Thus having been, that thou shouldst cease to be.
—1816

Alastor; or, The Spirit of Solitude

PREFACE

The poem entitled "Alastor" may be considered as allegorical of one of the most interesting situations of the human mind. It represents a youth of uncorrupted feelings and adventurous genius[2] led forth by an imagination inflamed and purified through familiarity with all that is excellent and majestic, to the contemplation of the universe. He drinks deep of the fountains of knowledge, and is still insatiate. The magnificence and beauty of the external world sinks profoundly into the frame of his conceptions, and affords to their modifications a variety not to be exhausted. So long as it is possible for his desires to point towards objects thus infinite and unmeasured, he is joyous, and tranquil, and self-possessed. But the period arrives when these objects cease to

suffice. His mind is at length suddenly awakened and thirsts for intercourse with an intelligence similar to itself. He images to himself the Being whom he loves. Conversant with speculations of the sublimest and most perfect natures, the vision in which he embodies his own imaginations unites all of wonderful, or wise, or beautiful, which the poet, the philosopher, or the lover could depicture. The intellectual faculties, the imagination, the functions of sense, have their respective requisitions[3] on the sympathy of corresponding powers in other human beings. The Poet is represented as uniting these requisitions, and attaching them to a single image. He seeks in vain for a prototype of his conception. Blasted by his disappointment, he descends to an untimely grave.

The picture is not barren of instruction to actual men. The Poet's self-centred seclusion was avenged by the furies of an irresistible passion pursuing him to speedy ruin. But that Power which strikes the luminaries of the world with sudden darkness and extinction, by awakening them to too exquisite a perception of its influences, dooms to a slow and poisonous decay those meaner spirits that dare to abjure its dominion. Their destiny is more abject and inglorious as their delinquency is more contemptible and pernicious. They who, deluded by no generous error, instigated by no sacred thirst of doubtful knowledge, duped by no illustrious superstition, loving nothing on this earth, and cherishing no hopes beyond, yet keep aloof from sympathies with their kind, rejoicing neither in human joy nor mourning with human grief; these, and such as they, have their apportioned curse. They languish, because none feel with them their common nature. They are morally dead. They are neither friends, nor lovers, nor fathers, nor citizens of the world, nor benefactors of their country. Among those who attempt to exist without human sympathy, the pure and tender-hearted perish through the intensity and passion of their search after its communities, when the vacancy of their spirit suddenly makes itself felt. All else, selfish, blind, and torpid, are those unforeseeing multitudes who constitute, together with their own, the lasting misery and loneliness of the world. Those who love not their fellow-beings live unfruitful lives, and prepare for their old age a miserable grave.

"The good die first,
And those whose hearts are dry as summer dust,
Burn to the socket!"[4]

December 14, 1815

---

[1] *To Wordsworth* As a young man, Wordsworth identified himself as a political radical, but as his career progressed he gradually became more conservative. His 1814 poem *The Excursion* showed a marked change in his political and religious thinking, and was received with disappointment by many of his early admirers, such as Shelley.

[2] *youth of ... genius* This protagonist is unnamed, although because of the poem's title he is often (incorrectly) assumed to be called Alastor. In his *Memoirs of Shelley*, Shelley's friend Thomas Love Peacock explains that Shelley was "at a loss for a title, and I proposed that which he adopted: Alastor, or the Spirit of Solitude. The Greek word *Alastor* is an evil genius."

[3] *requisitions* Claims.

[4] *The ... socket* From Wordsworth's *Excursion*, 1.500–02.

Alastor; or, The Spirit of Solitude

Nondum amabam, et amare amabam, quaerebam quid amarem, amans amare.
—*Confess. St. August.*[1]

Earth, ocean, air, belovèd brotherhood!
If our great Mother[2] has imbued my soul
With aught of natural piety[3] to feel
Your love, and recompense the boon with mine;
5   If dewy morn, and odorous noon, and even,
With sunset and its gorgeous ministers,
And solemn midnight's tingling silentness;
If autumn's hollow sighs in the sere wood,
And winter robing with pure snow and crowns
10 Of starry ice the grey grass and bare boughs;
If spring's voluptuous pantings when she breathes
Her first sweet kisses, have been dear to me;
If no bright bird, insect, or gentle beast
I consciously have injured, but still loved
15 And cherished these my kindred; then forgive
This boast, belovèd brethren, and withdraw
No portion of your wonted favour now!

Mother of this unfathomable world!
Favour my solemn song, for I have loved
20 Thee ever, and thee only; I have watched
Thy shadow, and the darkness of thy steps,
And my heart ever gazes on the depth
Of thy deep mysteries. I have made my bed
In charnels[4] and on coffins, where black death
25 Keeps record of the trophies won from thee,
Hoping to still these obstinate questionings[5]
Of thee and thine, by forcing some lone ghost,

Thy messenger, to render up the tale
Of what we are. In lone and silent hours,
30 When night makes a weird sound of its own stillness,
Like an inspired and desperate alchemist
Staking his very life on some dark hope,
Have I mixed awful talk and asking looks
With my most innocent love, until strange tears
35 Uniting with those breathless kisses, made
Such magic as compels the charmèd night
To render up thy charge: ... and, though ne'er yet
Thou hast unveiled thy inmost sanctuary,
Enough from incommunicable dream,
40 And twilight phantasms, and deep noon-day thought,
Has shone within me, that serenely now
And moveless, as a long-forgotten lyre
Suspended in the solitary dome
Of some mysterious and deserted fane,°   temple
45 I wait thy breath, Great Parent, that my strain
May modulate with murmurs of the air,
And motions of the forests and the sea,
And voice of living beings, and woven hymns
Of night and day, and the deep heart of man.

50   There was a Poet whose untimely tomb
No human hands with pious reverence reared,
But the charmed eddies of autumnal winds
Built o'er his mouldering bones a pyramid
Of mouldering leaves in the waste wilderness:
55 A lovely youth—no mourning maiden decked
With weeping flowers, or votive cypress wreath,[6]
The lone couch of his everlasting sleep:
Gentle, and brave, and generous—no lorn° bard   forlorn
Breathed o'er his dark fate one melodious sigh:
60 He lived, he died, he sung, in solitude.
Strangers have wept to hear his passionate notes,
And virgins, as unknown he passed, have pined
And wasted for fond love of his wild eyes.
The fire of those soft orbs has ceased to burn,
65 And Silence, too enamoured of that voice,
Locks its mute music in her rugged cell.

---

[1] *Nondum ... August* Latin: "I was not yet in love, and I loved to love, I sought what I might love, loving to love." From St. Augustine's *Confessions* 3.1, in which he describes his youthful desire for sexual love, rather than the spiritual love of God that he later found.

[2] *our great Mother* Cybele, goddess of the powers of nature and fertility.

[3] *natural piety* From Wordsworth's "My Heart Leaps Up," line 9.

[4] *charnels* Houses of death, mortuaries.

[5] *obstinate questionings* From Wordsworth's "Ode: Intimations of Immortality," lines 144–45: "Those obstinate questionings / Of sense and outward things."

[6] *cypress wreath* Worn to represent mourning.

By solemn vision, and bright silver dream,
His infancy was nurtured. Every sight
And sound from the vast earth and ambient air,
70 Sent to his heart its choicest impulses.
The fountains of divine philosophy
Fled not his thirsting lips, and all of great,
Or good, or lovely, which the sacred past
In truth or fable consecrates, he felt
75 And knew. When early youth had passed, he left
His cold fireside and alienated home
To seek strange truths in undiscovered lands.
Many a wide waste and tangled wilderness
Has lured his fearless steps; and he has bought
80 With his sweet voice and eyes, from savage men,
His rest and food. Nature's most secret steps
He like her shadow has pursued, where'er
The red volcano overcanopies
Its fields of snow and pinnacles of ice
85 With burning smoke, or where bitumen° lakes   pitch
On black bare pointed islets ever beat
With sluggish surge, or where the secret caves
Rugged and dark, winding among the springs
Of fire and poison, inaccessible
90 To avarice or pride, their starry domes
Of diamond and of gold expand above
Numberless and immeasurable halls,
Frequent with crystal column, and clear shrines
Of pearl, and thrones radiant with chrysolite.[1]
95 Nor had that scene of ampler majesty
Than gems or gold, the varying roof of heaven
And the green earth lost in his heart its claims
To love and wonder; he would linger long
In lonesome vales, making the wild his home,
100 Until the doves and squirrels would partake
From his innocuous hand his bloodless food,
Lured by the gentle meaning of his looks,
And the wild antelope, that starts whene'er
The dry leaf rustles in the brake,° suspend   thicket
105 Her timid steps to gaze upon a form
More graceful than her own.
                    His wandering step
Obedient to high thoughts, has visited
The awful ruins of the days of old:

Athens, and Tyre, and Balbec,[2] and the waste
110 Where stood Jerusalem,[3] the fallen towers
Of Babylon, the eternal pyramids,
Memphis and Thebes,[4] and whatsoe'er of strange
Sculptured on alabaster obelisk,
Or jasper tomb, or mutilated sphynx,
115 Dark Æthiopia in her desert hills
Conceals. Among the ruined temples there,
Stupendous columns, and wild images
Of more than man, where marble daemons[5] watch
The Zodiac's brazen mystery,[6] and dead men
120 Hang their mute thoughts on the mute walls around,
He lingered, poring on memorials
Of the world's youth, through the long burning day
Gazed on those speechless shapes, nor, when the moon
Filled the mysterious halls with floating shades
125 Suspended he that task, but ever gazed
And gazed, till meaning on his vacant mind
Flashed like strong inspiration, and he saw
The thrilling secrets of the birth of time.

Meanwhile an Arab maiden brought his food,
130 Her daily portion, from her father's tent,
And spread her matting for his couch, and stole
From duties and repose to tend his steps—
Enamoured, yet not daring for deep awe
To speak her love—and watched his nightly sleep,
135 Sleepless herself, to gaze upon his lips
Parted in slumber, whence the regular breath
Of innocent dreams arose: then, when red morn
Made paler the pale moon, to her cold home
Wildered,° and wan, and panting, she returned.   bewildered

---

1 *chrysolite* Green gemstone.

2 *Tyre* Ancient capital of Phoenicia, located in present-day Lebanon, that was destroyed by Muslims in 1291; *Balbec* Ancient Phoenician city in eastern Lebanon that is known for its Roman ruins.

3 *Jerusalem* Destroyed by Emperor Titus in 70 CE.

4 *Memphis and Thebes* Ancient cities of lower and upper Egypt, respectively.

5 *daemons* Supernatural beings, or minor deities, of Greek mythology.

6 *Zodiac's brazen mystery* Representations of the Zodiac decorate the ceiling of the temple of Isis (goddess of fertility) at Denderah, in Egypt.

140   The Poet wandering on, through Arabie
And Persia, and the wild Carmanian waste,[1]
And o'er the aërial mountains which pour down
Indus and Oxus[2] from their icy caves,
In joy and exultation held his way;
145 Till in the vale of Cashmire, far within
Its loneliest dell, where odorous plants entwine
Beneath the hollow rocks a natural bower,
Beside a sparkling rivulet he stretched
His languid limbs. A vision on his sleep
150 There came, a dream of hopes that never yet
Had flushed his cheek. He dreamed a veilèd maid
Sate near him, talking in low solemn tones.
Her voice was like the voice of his own soul
Heard in the calm of thought; its music long,
155 Like woven sounds of streams and breezes, held
His inmost sense suspended in its web
Of many-coloured woof[3] and shifting hues.
Knowledge and truth and virtue were her theme,
And lofty hopes of divine liberty,
160 Thoughts the most dear to him, and poesy,
Herself a poet. Soon the solemn mood
Of her pure mind kindled through all her frame
A permeating fire: wild numbers[4] then
She raised, with voice stifled in tremulous sobs
165 Subdued by its own pathos: her fair hands
Were bare alone, sweeping from some strange harp
Strange symphony, and in their branching veins
The eloquent blood told an ineffable tale.
The beating of her heart was heard to fill
170 The pauses of her music, and her breath
Tumultuously accorded with those fits
Of intermitted song. Sudden she rose,
As if her heart impatiently endured
Its bursting burthen: at the sound he turned,
175 And saw by the warm light of their own life
Her glowing limbs beneath the sinuous veil
Of woven wind, her outspread arms now bare,
Her dark locks floating in the breath of night,
Her beamy bending eyes, her parted lips

180 Outstretched, and pale, and quivering eagerly.
His strong heart sunk and sickened with excess
Of love. He reared his shuddering limbs and quelled
His gasping breath, and spread his arms to meet
Her panting bosom … she drew back a while,
185 Then, yielding to the irresistible joy,
With frantic gesture and short breathless cry
Folded his frame in her dissolving arms.
Now blackness veiled his dizzy eyes, and night
Involved and swallowed up the vision; sleep,
190 Like a dark flood suspended in its course,
Rolled back its impulse on his vacant brain.

      Roused by the shock he started from his trance—
The cold white light of morning, the blue moon
Low in the west, the clear and garish hills,
195 The distinct valley and the vacant woods,
Spread round him where he stood. Whither have fled
The hues of heaven that canopied his bower
Of yesternight? The sounds that soothed his sleep,
The mystery and the majesty of Earth,
200 The joy, the exultation? His wan eyes
Gaze on the empty scene as vacantly
As ocean's moon looks on the moon in heaven.
The spirit of sweet human love has sent
A vision to the sleep of him who spurned
205 Her choicest gifts. He eagerly pursues
Beyond the realms of dream that fleeting shade;
He overleaps the bounds. Alas! Alas!
Were limbs, and breath, and being intertwined
Thus treacherously? Lost, lost, for ever lost,
210 In the wide pathless desert of dim sleep,
That beautiful shape! Does the dark gate of death
Conduct to thy mysterious paradise,
O Sleep? Does the bright arch of rainbow clouds,
And pendent mountains seen in the calm lake,
215 Lead only to a black and watery depth,
While death's blue vault, with loathliest vapours hung,
Where every shade which the foul grave exhales
Hides its dead eye from the detested day,
Conducts, O Sleep, to thy delightful realms?
220 This doubt with sudden tide flowed on his heart,
The insatiate hope which it awakened, stung
His brain even like despair.

                  While daylight held

---

[1] *Carmanian waste* Kerman Desert, in present-day Iran.

[2] *Indus and Oxus* Rivers which flow from opposite sides of the Hindu Kush mountains in Asia.

[3] *woof* Thread that crosses from side to side in a web of weaving.

[4] *numbers* Verses, of song or poetry.

The sky, the Poet kept mute conference
With his still soul. At night the passion came,
225 Like the fierce fiend of a distempered dream,
And shook him from his rest, and led him forth
Into the darkness. As an eagle, grasped
In folds of the green serpent, feels her breast
Burn with the poison, and precipitates
230 Through night and day, tempest, and calm, and cloud,
Frantic with dizzying anguish, her blind flight
O'er the wide aëry° wilderness: thus driven   *lofty*
By the bright shadow of that lovely dream,
Beneath the cold glare of the desolate night,
235 Through tangled swamps and deep precipitous dells,
Startling with careless step the moonlight snake,
He fled. Red morning dawned upon his flight,
Shedding the mockery of its vital hues
Upon his cheek of death. He wandered on
240 Till vast Aornos seen from Petra's steep[1]
Hung o'er the low horizon like a cloud;
Through Balk,[2] and where the desolated tombs
Of Parthian kings[3] scatter to every wind
Their wasting dust, wildly he wandered on,
245 Day after day a weary waste of hours,
Bearing within his life the brooding care
That ever fed on its decaying flame.
And now his limbs were lean; his scattered hair
Sered° by the autumn of strange suffering   *made dry*
250 Sung dirges in the wind; his listless hand
Hung like dead bone within its withered skin;
Life, and the lustre that consumed it, shone
As in a furnace burning secretly
From his dark eyes alone. The cottagers,
255 Who ministered with human charity
His human wants, beheld with wondering awe
Their fleeting visitant. The mountaineer,
Encountering on some dizzy precipice
That spectral form, deemed that the Spirit of wind
260 With lightning eyes, and eager breath, and feet
Disturbing not the drifted snow, had paused
In its career: the infant would conceal
His troubled visage in his mother's robe

In terror at the glare of those wild eyes,
265 To remember their strange light in many a dream
Of after-times; but youthful maidens, taught
By nature, would interpret half the woe
That wasted him, would call him with false names
Brother, and friend, would press his pallid hand
270 At parting, and watch, dim through tears, the path
Of his departure from their father's door.

At length upon the lone Chorasmian shore[4]
He paused, a wide and melancholy waste
Of putrid marshes. A strong impulse urged
275 His steps to the sea-shore. A swan was there,
Beside a sluggish stream among the reeds.
It rose as he approached, and with strong wings
Scaling the upward sky, bent its bright course
High over the immeasurable main.
280 His eyes pursued its flight—"Thou hast a home,
Beautiful bird; thou voyagest to thine home,
Where thy sweet mate will twine her downy neck
With thine, and welcome thy return with eyes
Bright in the lustre of their own fond joy.
285 And what am I that I should linger here,
With voice far sweeter than thy dying notes,
Spirit more vast than thine, frame more attuned
To beauty, wasting these surpassing powers
In the deaf air, to the blind earth, and heaven
290 That echoes not my thoughts?" A gloomy smile
Of desperate hope wrinkled his quivering lips.
For sleep, he knew, kept most relentlessly
Its precious charge, and silent death exposed,
Faithless perhaps as sleep, a shadowy lure,
295 With doubtful smile mocking its own strange charms.

Startled by his own thoughts he looked around.
There was no fair fiend near him, not a sight
Or sound of awe but in his own deep mind.
A little shallop[5] floating near the shore
300 Caught the impatient wandering of his gaze.
It had been long abandoned, for its sides
Gaped wide with many a rift, and its frail joints
Swayed with the undulations of the tide.
A restless impulse urged him to embark

---

[1] *Aornos* Mountain on the Indus; *Petra's steep* Probably the Rock of Soghdiana in Uzbekistan. ("Petra" is Latin for "rock.")

[2] *Balk* Balkh, in present-day Afghanistan.

[3] *Parthian kings* Rulers of northern Persia.

[4] *Chorasmian shore* Shore of the Caspian sea.

[5] *shallop* Small open boat or dinghy.

305 And meet lone Death on the drear ocean's waste;
For well he knew that mighty Shadow loves
The slimy caverns of the populous deep.

The day was fair and sunny, sea and sky
Drank its inspiring radiance, and the wind
310 Swept strongly from the shore, blackening the waves.
Following his eager soul, the wanderer
Leaped in the boat, he spread his cloak aloft
On the bare mast, and took his lonely seat,
And felt the boat speed o'er the tranquil sea
315 Like a torn cloud before the hurricane.

As one that in a silver vision floats
Obedient to the sweep of odorous winds
Upon resplendent clouds, so rapidly
Along the dark and ruffled waters fled
320 The straining boat. A whirlwind swept it on,
With fierce gusts and precipitating force,
Through the white ridges of the chafèd sea.
The waves arose. Higher and higher still
Their fierce necks writhed beneath the tempest's scourge
325 Like serpents struggling in a vulture's grasp.
Calm and rejoicing in the fearful war
Of wave ruining on wave, and blast on blast
Descending, and black flood on whirlpool driven
With dark obliterating course, he sate:
330 As if their genii were the ministers
Appointed to conduct him to the light
Of those belovèd eyes, the Poet sate
Holding the steady helm. Evening came on,
The beams of sunset hung their rainbow hues
335 High 'mid the shifting domes of sheeted spray
That canopied his path o'er the waste deep;
Twilight, ascending slowly from the east,
Entwined in duskier wreaths her braided locks
O'er the fair front and radiant eyes of day;
340 Night followed, clad with stars. On every side
More horribly the multitudinous streams
Of ocean's mountainous waste to mutual war
Rushed in dark tumult thundering, as to mock
The calm and spangled sky. The little boat
345 Still fled before the storm; still fled, like foam
Down the steep cataract of a wintry river;
Now pausing on the edge of the riven wave;

Now leaving far behind the bursting mass
That fell, convulsing ocean: safely fled—
350 As if that frail and wasted human form
Had been an elemental god.

At midnight
The moon arose: and lo! the ethereal cliffs
Of Caucasus,[1] whose icy summits shone
Among the stars like sunlight, and around
355 Whose caverned base the whirlpools and the waves
Bursting and eddying irresistibly
Rage and resound for ever. Who shall save?
The boat fled on—the boiling torrent drove—
The crags closed round with black and jaggèd arms,
360 The shattered mountain overhung the sea,
And faster still, beyond all human speed,
Suspended on the sweep of the smooth wave,
The little boat was driven. A cavern there
Yawned, and amid its slant and winding depths
365 Ingulfed the rushing sea. The boat fled on
With unrelaxing speed. "Vision and Love!"
The Poet cried aloud, "I have beheld
The path of thy departure. Sleep and death
Shall not divide us long!"

The boat pursued
370 The windings of the cavern. Daylight shone
At length upon that gloomy river's flow;
Now, where the fiercest war among the waves
Is calm, on the unfathomable stream
The boat moved slowly. Where the mountain, riven,
375 Exposed those black depths to the azure sky,
Ere yet the flood's enormous volume fell
Even to the base of Caucasus, with sound
That shook the everlasting rocks, the mass
Filled with one whirlpool all that ample chasm;
380 Stair above stair the eddying waters rose,
Circling immeasurably fast, and laved°   bathed
With alternating dash the gnarlèd roots
Of mighty trees, that stretched their giant arms
In darkness over it. I' the midst was left,
385 Reflecting, yet distorting every cloud,
A pool of treacherous and tremendous calm.
Seized by the sway of the ascending stream,

---

[1]   *ethereal* Belonging to the upper air; *Caucasus* On the western shore of the Caspian sea, in present-day Georgia.

With dizzy swiftness, round, and round, and round,
Ridge after ridge the straining boat arose,
390   Till on the verge of the extremest curve,
Where, through an opening of the rocky bank,
The waters overflow, and a smooth spot
Of glassy quiet mid those battling tides
Is left, the boat paused shuddering. Shall it sink
395   Down the abyss? Shall the reverting stress
Of that resistless gulf embosom it?
Now shall it fall? A wandering stream of wind,
Breathed from the west, has caught the expanded sail,
And, lo! with gentle motion, between banks
400   Of mossy slope, and on a placid stream,
Beneath a woven grove it sails, and, hark!
The ghastly torrent mingles its far roar
With the breeze murmuring in the musical woods.
Where the embowering trees recede, and leave
405   A little space of green expanse, the cove
Is closed by meeting banks, whose yellow flowers[1]
For ever gaze on their own drooping eyes,
Reflected in the crystal calm. The wave
Of the boat's motion marred their pensive task,
410   Which nought but vagrant bird, or wanton wind,
Or falling spear-grass, or their own decay
Had e'er disturbed before. The Poet longed
To deck with their bright hues his withered hair,
But on his heart its solitude returned,
415   And he forbore. Not the strong impulse hid
In those flushed cheeks, bent eyes, and shadowy frame
Had yet performed its ministry: it hung
Upon his life, as lightning in a cloud
Gleams, hovering ere it vanish, ere the floods
420   Of night close over it.
                The noonday sun
Now shone upon the forest, one vast mass
Of mingling shade, whose brown° magnificence   *dark*
A narrow vale embosoms. There, huge caves,
Scooped in the dark base of their aëry rocks
425   Mocking its moans, respond and roar for ever.
The meeting boughs and implicated° leaves   *entwined*
Wove twilight o'er the Poet's path, as led
By love, or dream, or god, or mightier Death,

He sought in Nature's dearest haunt, some bank,
430   Her cradle, and his sepulchre. More dark
And dark the shades accumulate. The oak,
Expanding its immense and knotty arms,
Embraces the light beech. The pyramids
Of the tall cedar overarching, frame
435   Most solemn domes within, and far below,
Like clouds suspended in an emerald sky,
The ash and the acacia floating hang
Tremulous and pale. Like restless serpents, clothed
In rainbow and in fire, the parasites,
440   Starred with ten thousand blossoms, flow around
The grey trunks, and, as gamesome° infants' eyes,   *playful*
With gentle meanings, and most innocent wiles,
Fold their beams round the hearts of those that love,
These twine their tendrils with the wedded boughs
445   Uniting their close union; the woven leaves
Make net-work of the dark blue light of day,
And the night's noontide clearness, mutable
As shapes in the weird clouds. Soft mossy lawns
Beneath these canopies extend their swells,
450   Fragrant with perfumed herbs, and eyed with blooms
Minute yet beautiful. One darkest glen
Sends from its woods of musk-rose, twined with jasmine,
A soul-dissolving odour, to invite
To some more lovely mystery. Through the dell,
455   Silence and Twilight here, twin-sisters, keep
Their noonday watch, and sail among the shades,
Like vaporous shapes half seen; beyond, a well,
Dark, gleaming, and of most translucent wave,
Images[2] all the woven boughs above,
460   And each depending leaf, and every speck
Of azure sky, darting between their chasms;
Nor aught else in the liquid mirror laves
Its portraiture, but some inconstant star
Between one foliaged lattice twinkling fair,
465   Or, painted bird, sleeping beneath the moon,
Or gorgeous insect floating motionless,
Unconscious of the day, ere yet his wings
Have spread their glories to the gaze of noon.

        Hither the Poet came. His eyes beheld
470   Their own wan light through the reflected lines
Of his thin hair, distinct in the dark depth

---

[1] *yellow flowers* Narcissus flowers. According to Greek mythology, the handsome youth Narcissus fell in love with his own reflection in a pool of water and wasted away pining after his own image.

[2] *Images* Reflects; forms an image of.

Of that still fountain; as the human heart,
Gazing in dreams over the gloomy grave,
Sees its own treacherous likeness there. He heard
475 The motion of the leaves, the grass that sprung
Startled and glanced and trembled even to feel
An unaccustomed presence, and the sound
Of the sweet brook that from the secret springs
Of that dark fountain rose. A Spirit seemed
480 To stand beside him—clothed in no bright robes
Of shadowy silver or enshrining light.
Borrowed from aught the visible world affords
Of grace, or majesty, or mystery—
But, undulating woods, and silent well,
485 And leaping rivulet, and evening gloom
Now deepening the dark shades, for speech assuming,
Held commune with him, as if he and it
Were all that was,—only … when his regard
Was raised by intense pensiveness, … two eyes,
490 Two starry eyes, hung in the gloom of thought,
And seemed with their serene and azure smiles
To beckon him.

        Obedient to the light
That shone within his soul, he went, pursuing
The windings of the dell. The rivulet
495 Wanton and wild through many a green ravine
Beneath the forest flowed. Sometimes it fell
Among the moss with hollow harmony
Dark and profound. Now on the polished stones
It danced; like childhood laughing as it went:
500 Then, through the plain in tranquil wanderings crept,
Reflecting every herb and drooping bud
That overhung its quietness. "O stream!
Whose source is inaccessibly profound,
Whither do thy mysterious waters tend?
505 Thou imagest my life. Thy darksome stillness,
Thy dazzling waves, thy loud and hollow gulfs,
Thy searchless° fountain,° and   *undiscoverable / source*
    invisible course
Have each their type in me: and the wide sky,
And measureless ocean may declare as soon
510 What oozy cavern or what wandering cloud
Contains thy waters, as the universe
Tell where these living thoughts reside, when stretched

Upon thy flowers my bloodless limbs shall waste
I' the passing wind!"

                 Beside the grassy shore
515 Of the small stream he went; he did impress
On the green moss his tremulous step, that caught
Strong shuddering from his burning limbs. As one
Roused by some joyous madness from the couch
Of fever, he did move; yet, not like him,
520 Forgetful of the grave, where, when the flame
Of his frail exultation shall be spent,
He must descend. With rapid steps he went
Beneath the shade of trees, beside the flow
Of the wild babbling rivulet; and now
525 The forest's solemn canopies were changed
For the uniform and lightsome° evening sky.   *luminous*
Grey rocks did peep from the spare moss, and stemmed
The struggling brook: tall spires of windlestrae[1]
Threw their thin shadows down the rugged slope,
530 And nought but gnarled roots[2] of ancient pines,
Branchless and blasted, clenched with grasping roots
The unwilling soil. A gradual change was here,
Yet ghastly. For, as fast years flow away,
The smooth brow gathers, and the hair grows thin
535 And white, and where irradiate° dewy eyes   *illumined*
Had shone, gleam stony orbs: so from his steps
Bright flowers departed, and the beautiful shade
Of the green groves, with all their odorous winds
And musical motions. Calm, he still pursued
540 The stream, that with a larger volume now
Rolled through the labyrinthine dell; and there
Fretted a path through its descending curves
With its wintry speed. On every side now rose
Rocks, which, in unimaginable forms,
545 Lifted their black and barren pinnacles
In the light of evening, and, its precipice
Obscuring the ravine, disclosed above,
Mid toppling stones, black gulfs and yawning caves,
Whose windings gave ten thousand various tongues
550 To the loud stream. Lo! where the pass expands
Its stony jaws, the abrupt mountain breaks,
And seems, with its accumulated crags,
To overhang the world: for wide expand

---

[1] *windlestrae* Windlestraw; withered grass stalks.

[2] *roots* Believed to be a misprint for "trunks" or "knots."

Beneath the wan stars and descending moon
555 Islanded seas, blue mountains, mighty streams,
Dim tracts and vast, robed in the lustrous gloom
Of leaden-coloured even,° and fiery hills   *evening*
Mingling their flames with twilight, on the verge
Of the remote horizon. The near scene,
560 In naked and severe simplicity,
Made contrast with the universe. A pine,
Rock-rooted, stretched athwart the vacancy
Its swinging boughs, to each inconstant blast
Yielding one only response, at each pause
565 In most familiar cadence, with the howl
The thunder and the hiss of homeless streams
Mingling its solemn song, whilst the broad river,
Foaming and hurrying o'er its rugged path,
Fell into that immeasurable void
570 Scattering its waters to the passing winds.

Yet the grey precipice and solemn pine
And torrent, were not all—one silent nook
Was there. Even on the edge of that vast mountain,
Upheld by knotty roots and fallen rocks,
575 It overlooked in its serenity
The dark earth, and the bending vault of stars.
It was a tranquil spot, that seemed to smile
Even in the lap of horror. Ivy clasped
The fissured stones with its entwining arms,
580 And did embower with leaves for ever green,
And berries dark, the smooth and even space
Of its inviolated floor, and here
The children of the autumnal whirlwind bore,
In wanton sport, those bright leaves, whose decay,
585 Red, yellow, or ethereally pale,
Rivals the pride of summer. 'Tis the haunt
Of every gentle wind, whose breath can teach
The wilds to love tranquillity. One step,
One human step alone, has ever broken
590 The stillness of its solitude; one voice
Alone inspired its echoes—even that voice
Which hither came, floating among the winds,
And led the loveliest among human forms
To make their wild haunts the depository
595 Of all the grace and beauty that endued[1]
Its motions, render up its majesty,

Scatter its music on the unfeeling storm,
And to the damp leaves and blue cavern mould,
Nurses of rainbow flowers and branching moss,
600 Commit the colours of that varying cheek,
That snowy breast, those dark and drooping eyes.

The dim and hornèd moon hung low, and poured
A sea of lustre on the horizon's verge
That overflowed its mountains. Yellow mist
605 Filled the unbounded atmosphere, and drank
Wan moonlight even to fulness: not a star
Shone, not a sound was heard; the very winds,
Danger's grim playmates, on that precipice
Slept, clasped in his embrace—O, storm of death!
610 Whose sightless speed divides this sullen night:
And thou, colossal Skeleton, that, still
Guiding its irresistible career
In thy devastating omnipotence,
Art king of this frail world, from the red field
615 Of slaughter, from the reeking hospital,
The patriot's sacred couch, the snowy bed
Of innocence, the scaffold and the throne,
A mighty voice invokes thee. Ruin calls
His brother Death. A rare and regal prey
620 He hath prepared, prowling around the world;
Glutted with which thou mayst repose, and men
Go to their graves like flowers or creeping worms,
Nor ever more offer at thy dark shrine
The unheeded tribute of a broken heart.

625 When on the threshold of the green recess
The wanderer's footsteps fell, he knew that death
Was on him. Yet a little, ere it fled,
Did he resign his high and holy soul
To images of the majestic past,
630 That paused within his passive being now,
Like winds that bear sweet music, when they breathe
Through some dim latticed chamber. He did place
His pale lean hand upon the rugged trunk
Of the old pine. Upon an ivied stone
635 Reclined his languid head, his limbs did rest,
Diffused and motionless, on the smooth brink
Of that obscurest chasm—and thus he lay,
Surrendering to their final impulses
The hovering powers of life. Hope and despair,

---

[1] *endued* Were inherent in.

640 The torturers, slept; no mortal pain or fear
Marred his repose, the influxes of sense,
And his own being unalloyed by pain,
Yet feebler and more feeble, calmly fed
The stream of thought, till he lay breathing there
645 At peace, and faintly smiling—his last sight
Was the great moon, which o'er the western line
Of the wide world her mighty horn suspended,
With whose dun° beams inwoven darkness   *dusky*
    seemed
To mingle. Now upon the jaggèd hills
650 It rests, and still as the divided frame
Of the vast meteor¹ sunk, the Poet's blood,
That ever beat in mystic sympathy
With nature's ebb and flow, grew feebler still:
And when two lessening points² of light alone
655 Gleamed through the darkness, the alternate gasp
Of his faint respiration scarce did stir
The stagnate° night—till the minutest ray   *stagnant*
Was quenched, the pulse yet lingered in his heart.
It paused—it fluttered. But when heaven remained
660 Utterly black, the murky shades involved
An image, silent, cold, and motionless,
As their own voiceless earth and vacant air.
Even as a vapour° fed with golden beams   *cloud*
That ministered on sunlight, ere the west
665 Eclipses it, was now that wondrous frame—
No sense, no motion, no divinity—
A fragile lute, on whose harmonious strings
The breath of heaven did wander—a bright stream
Once fed with many-voicèd waves—a dream
670 Of youth, which night and time have quenched for ever,
Still, dark, and dry, and unremembered now.

    O, for Medea's wondrous alchemy,³
Which wheresoe'er it fell made the earth gleam
With bright flowers, and the wintry boughs exhale

675 From vernal blooms fresh fragrance! O, that God,
Profuse of poisons, would concede the chalice
Which but one living man has drained, who now,
Vessel of deathless wrath, a slave that feels
No proud exemption in the blighting curse
680 He bears, over the world wanders for ever,
Lone as incarnate death!⁴ O, that the dream
Of dark magician in his visioned⁵ cave,
Raking the cinders of a crucible
For life and power, even when his feeble hand
685 Shakes in its last decay, were the true law
Of this so lovely world! But thou art fled
Like some frail exhalation; which the dawn
Robes in its golden beams—ah! thou hast fled!
The brave, the gentle, and the beautiful,
690 The child of grace and genius. Heartless things
Are done and said i'the world, and many worms
And beasts and men live on, and mighty Earth
From sea and mountain, city and wilderness,
In vesper⁶ low or joyous orison,°   *prayer*
695 Lifts still its solemn voice—but thou art fled—
Thou canst no longer know or love the shapes
Of this phantasmal scene, who have to thee
Been purest ministers, who are, alas!
Now thou art not. Upon those pallid lips
700 So sweet even in their silence, on those eyes
That image sleep in death, upon that form
Yet safe from the worm's outrage, let no tear
Be shed—not even in thought. Nor, when those hues
Are gone, and those divinest lineaments,
705 Worn by the senseless° wind, shall live alone   *unfeeling*
In the frail pauses of this simple strain,
Let not high verse, mourning the memory
Of that which is no more, or painting's woe
Or sculpture, speak in feeble imagery
710 Their own cold powers. Art and eloquence,
And all the shows o'the world are frail and vain
To weep a loss that turns their lights to shade.

---

¹ *meteor* Formerly used to refer to any atmospheric phenomenon; here, the moon.

² *two lessening points* The horns, or curved points, of the crescent moon.

³ *Medea's wondrous alchemy* According to Greek myth, the sorceress Medea brewed a magic potion to restore youth to the dying Aeson. In Ovid's version of the tale (*Metamorphoses* 7.275ff), some of the potion spills on the ground and has the effect described in the following lines.

⁴ *one living … death* Reference to the legend of Ahasuerus, the Wandering Jew, who taunted Christ on the way to His crucifixion and as punishment was condemned to wander the earth until Christ's second coming.

⁵ *visioned* I.e., in which he has visions.

⁶ *vesper* Evening prayer.

It is a woe too "deep for tears,"[1] when all
Is reft at once, when some surpassing Spirit,
715 Whose light adorned the world around it, leaves
Those who remain behind, not sobs or groans,
The passionate tumult of a clinging hope;
But pale despair and cold tranquillity,
Nature's vast frame, the web of human things,
720 Birth and the grave, that are not as they were.
    —1816

Mutability

We are as clouds that veil the midnight moon;
    How restlessly they speed, and gleam, and
        quiver,
Streaking the darkness radiantly! Yet soon
Night closes round, and they are lost for ever:

5   Or like forgotten lyres,[2] whose dissonant strings
Give various response to each varying blast,
To whose frail frame no second motion brings
One mood or modulation like the last.

We rest—A dream has power to poison sleep;
10 We rise—One wandering thought pollutes the day;
We feel, conceive or reason, laugh or weep;
Embrace fond woe, or cast our cares away:

It is the same! For, be it joy or sorrow,
The path of its departure still is free:
15 Man's yesterday may ne'er be like his morrow;
Nought may endure but Mutability.
    —1816

Mont Blanc
Lines Written in the Vale of Chamouni [3]

1

The everlasting universe of things
    Flows through the mind, and rolls its rapid waves,
Now dark—now glittering—now reflecting gloom—
Now lending splendour, where from secret springs
5   The source of human thought its tribute brings
Of waters—with a sound but half its own,
Such as a feeble brook will oft assume
In the wild woods, among the mountains lone,
Where waterfalls around it leap for ever,
10 Where woods and winds contend, and a vast river
Over its rocks ceaselessly bursts and raves.

2

Thus thou, Ravine of Arve—dark, deep Ravine—
Thou many-coloured, many-voicèd vale,
Over whose pines, and crags, and caverns sail
15 Fast cloud shadows and sunbeams: awful°   *awe-inspiring*
    scene,
Where Power in likeness of the Arve comes down
From the ice gulfs that gird his secret throne,
Bursting through these dark mountains like the flame
Of lightning through the tempest—thou dost lie,
20 Thy giant brood of pines around thee clinging,
Children of elder time, in whose devotion
The chainless winds still come and ever came
To drink their odours, and their mighty swinging
To hear—an old and solemn harmony;
25 Thine earthly rainbows stretched across the sweep
Of the etherial waterfall, whose veil
Robes some unsculptured[4] image; the strange sleep
Which when the voices of the desert fail

---

[1] *deep for tears* From the last line of Wordsworth's "Ode: Intimations of Immortality": "Thoughts that do often lie too deep for tears."

[2] *lyres* Aeolian harps, stringed instruments that produce music when exposed to wind.

[3] *Mont Blanc … Chamouni* Mont Blanc, located near France's border with Italy, is the highest peak in the Alps. Shelley conceived the idea for the poem when standing on a bridge over the Arve River in the Valley of Chamonix in southeastern France. Of the poem, Shelley wrote, "It was composed under the immediate impression of the deep and powerful feelings excited by the objects which it attempts to describe; and, as an indisciplined overflowing of the soul, rests its claim to approbation on an attempt to imitate the untameable wildness and inaccessible solemnity from which those feelings sprang."

[4] *unsculptured* I.e., not shaped by humans.

Wraps all in its own deep eternity—
30   Thy caverns echoing to the Arve's commotion,
A loud, lone sound no other sound can tame;
Thou art pervaded with that ceaseless motion,
Thou art the path of that unresting sound—
Dizzy Ravine! and when I gaze on thee
35   I seem as in a trance sublime and strange
To muse on my own separate fantasy,
My own, my human mind, which passively
Now renders and receives fast influencings,
Holding an unremitting interchange
40   With the clear universe of things around;
One legion of wild thoughts, whose wandering wings
Now float above thy darkness, and now rest
Where that or thou art no unbidden guest,
In the still cave of the witch Poesy,
45   Seeking among the shadows that pass by,
Ghosts of all things that are, some shade of thee,
Some phantom, some faint image; till the breast
From which they fled recalls them, thou art there!

3

Some say that gleams of a remoter world
50   Visit the soul in sleep—that death is slumber,
And that its shapes the busy thoughts outnumber
Of those who wake and live. I look on high;
Has some unknown omnipotence unfurled
The veil of life and death? or do I lie
55   In dream, and does the mightier world of sleep
Spread far around and inaccessibly
Its circles? For the very spirit fails,
Driven like a homeless cloud from steep to steep
That vanishes among the viewless° gales!   *invisible*
60   Far, far above, piercing the infinite sky,
Mont Blanc appears—still, snowy, and serene—
Its subject mountains their unearthly forms
Pile around it, ice and rock; broad vales between
Of frozen floods, unfathomable deeps,
65   Blue as the overhanging heaven, that spread
And wind among the accumulated steeps;
A desert peopled by the storms alone,
Save when the eagle brings some hunter's bone,
And the wolf tracks her there—how hideously
70   Its shapes are heaped around: rude, bare, and high,
Ghastly, and scarred, and riven. Is this the scene

Where the old Earthquake-daemon[1] taught her young
Ruin? Were these their toys? or did a sea
Of fire envelop once this silent snow?
75   None can reply—all seems eternal now.
The wilderness has a mysterious tongue
Which teaches awful doubt, or faith so mild,
So solemn, so serene, that man may be
But for such faith with nature reconciled;
80   Thou hast a voice, great Mountain, to repeal
Large codes of fraud and woe; not understood
By all, but which the wise, and great, and good
Interpret, or make felt, or deeply feel.

4

The fields, the lakes, the forests, and the streams,
85   Ocean, and all the living things that dwell
Within the daedal[2] earth; lightning, and rain,
Earthquake, and fiery flood, and hurricane,
The torpor of the year when feeble dreams
Visit the hidden buds, or dreamless sleep
90   Holds every future leaf and flower; the bound
With which from that detested trance they leap;
The works and ways of man, their death and birth,
And that of him and all that his may be;
All things that move and breathe with toil and sound
95   Are born and die; revolve, subside and swell.
Power dwells apart in its tranquillity
Remote, serene, and inaccessible:
And *this*, the naked countenance of earth,
On which I gaze, even these primeval mountains
100   Teach the adverting mind. The glaciers creep
Like snakes that watch their prey, from their far
     fountains,
Slow rolling on; there, many a precipice,
Frost and the Sun in scorn of mortal power
Have piled: dome, pyramid, and pinnacle,
105   A city of death, distinct with many a tower
And wall impregnable of beaming ice.
Yet not a city, but a flood of ruin
Is there, that from the boundaries of the sky
Rolls its perpetual stream; vast pines are strewing

---

[1]   *Earthquake-daemon*   In Greek mythology, supernatural being or
minor deity that controls some natural force.

[2]   *daedal*   Skillfully or intricately wrought. (From Daedalus of
classical myth, who built the famous labyrinth in Crete.)

110 Its destined path, or in the mangled soil
    Branchless and shattered stand; the rocks, drawn down
    From yon remotest waste, have overthrown
    The limits of the dead and living world,
    Never to be reclaimed. The dwelling-place
115 Of insects, beasts, and birds, becomes its spoil;
    Their food and their retreat for ever gone,
    So much of life and joy is lost. The race
    Of man flies far in dread; his work and dwelling
    Vanish, like smoke before the tempest's stream,
120 And their place is not known. Below, vast caves
    Shine in the rushing torrent's restless gleam,
    Which from those secret chasms in tumult welling[1]
    Meet in the vale, and one majestic River,
    The breath and blood of distant lands, for ever
125 Rolls its loud waters to the ocean waves,
    Breathes its swift vapours to the circling air.

                          5
    Mont Blanc yet gleams on high—the power is there,
    The still and solemn power of many sights
    And many sounds, and much of life and death.
130 In the calm darkness of the moonless nights,
    In the lone glare of day, the snows descend
    Upon that Mountain; none beholds them there,
    Nor when the flakes burn in the sinking sun,
    Or the star-beams dart through them. Winds contend
135 Silently there, and heap the snow with breath
    Rapid and strong, but silently! Its home
    The voiceless lightning in these solitudes
    Keeps innocently, and like vapour broods
    Over the snow. The secret strength of things
140 Which governs thought, and to the infinite dome
    Of heaven is as a law, inhabits thee!
    And what were thou, and earth, and stars, and sea,
    If to the human mind's imaginings
    Silence and solitude were vacancy?
    —1817

Hymn to Intellectual Beauty[2]

                          1
The awful shadow of some unseen Power
    Floats though unseen amongst us, visiting
        This various world with as inconstant wing
As summer winds that creep from flower to flower.
5 Like moonbeams that behind some piny mountain
        shower,
        It visits with inconstant glance
        Each human heart and countenance;
Like hues and harmonies of evening,
        Like clouds in starlight widely spread,
10   Like memory of music fled,
        Like aught that for its grace may be
Dear, and yet dearer for its mystery.

                          2
Spirit of BEAUTY, that doth consecrate
    With thine own hues all thou dost shine upon
15   Of human thought or form—where art thou gone?
Why dost thou pass away and leave our state,
This dim vast vale of tears, vacant and desolate?
        Ask why the sunlight not forever
        Weaves rainbows o'er yon mountain river,
20 Why aught should fail and fade that once is shown,
        Why fear and dream and death and birth
        Cast on the daylight of this earth
        Such gloom—why man has such a scope
For love and hate, despondency and hope?

                          3
25 No voice from some sublimer world hath ever
        To sage or poet these responses given—
        Therefore the name of God, and ghosts, and Heaven,
Remain the records of their vain endeavour,
Frail spells—whose uttered charm might not avail to
        sever,
30   From all we hear and all we see,
        Doubt, chance, and mutability.

---

[1] *Which from ... welling* Cf. Coleridge's *Kubla Khan*, lines 12–24.

[2] *Hymn ... Beauty* Composed during the summer of 1816, the same summer in which Shelley wrote "Mont Blanc." The concept of "intellectual beauty" is Platonic in origin and was a popular one in contemporary writing. It denotes a beauty of the soul, or the mind and its inventions, that cannot be perceived by the senses and therefore must be grasped intuitively.

Thy light alone—like mist o'er mountains driven,
   Or music by the night wind sent
   Through strings of some still instrument,
35   Or moonlight on a midnight stream,
Gives grace and truth to life's unquiet dream.

4

Love, Hope, and Self-esteem, like clouds depart
   And come, for some uncertain moments lent.
   Man were° immortal, and omnipotent,   *would be*
40 Didst thou,[1] unknown and awful as thou art,
Keep with thy glorious train firm state within his heart.
   Thou messenger of sympathies
   That wax and wane in lovers' eyes—
Thou—that to human thought art nourishment,
45   Like darkness to a dying flame!
   Depart not as thy shadow came,
   Depart not—lest the grave should be,
Like life and fear, a dark reality.

5

While yet a boy I sought for ghosts, and sped
50   Through many a listening chamber, cave and ruin,
   And starlight wood, with fearful steps pursuing
Hopes of high talk with the departed dead.
I called on poisonous names with which our youth is fed,
   I was not heard—I saw them not—
55   When musing deeply on the lot
Of life, at that sweet time when winds are wooing
   All vital things that wake to bring
   News of buds and blossoming—
   Sudden, thy shadow fell on me;
60 I shrieked, and clasped my hands in ecstasy!

6

I vowed that I would dedicate my powers
   To thee and thine—have I not kept the vow?
   With beating heart and streaming eyes, even now
I call the phantoms of a thousand hours
65 Each from his voiceless grave: they have in visioned
    bowers
   Of studious zeal or love's delight
   Outwatched with me the envious night—
They know that never joy illumed my brow

[1] *Didst thou* I.e., "if thou didst."

Unlinked with hope that thou wouldst free
70 This world from its dark slavery,
   That thou—O awful LOVELINESS,
Wouldst give whate'er these words cannot express.

7

The day becomes more solemn and serene
   When noon is past—there is a harmony
75   In autumn, and a lustre in its sky,
Which through the summer is not heard or seen,
As if it could not be, as if it had not been!
   Thus let thy power, which like the truth
   Of nature on my passive youth
80 Descended, to my onward life supply
   Its calm—to one who worships thee,
   And every form containing thee,
   Whom, SPIRIT fair, thy spells did bind
To fear° himself, and love all human kind.   *revere*
—1817

Ozymandias[2]

I met a traveller from an antique land
Who said: Two vast and trunkless legs of stone
Stand in the desert … Near them, on the sand,
Half sunk, a shattered visage lies, whose frown,
5 And wrinkled lip, and sneer of cold command,
Tell that its sculptor well those passions read
Which yet survive, stamped on these lifeless things,
The hand that mocked them, and the heart that fed:
And on the pedestal these words appear:
10 "My name is Ozymandias, king of kings:
Look on my works, ye Mighty, and despair!"
Nothing beside remains. Round the decay
Of that colossal wreck, boundless and bare
The lone and level sands stretch far away.
—1818

[2] *Ozymandias* Greek name for King Ramses II of Egypt (1304–1237 BCE). First century BCE Greek historian Diodorus Siculus records the story of this monument (Ozymandias's tomb was in the shape of a male sphinx) and its inscription, which Diodorus says reads: "King of Kings am I, Ozymandias. If anyone would know how great I am and where I lie, let him surpass one of my exploits."

Ode to the West Wind[1]

I

O Wild West Wind, thou breath[2] of Autumn's
      being,
Thou, from whose unseen presence the leaves dead
Are driven, like ghosts from an enchanter fleeing,

Yellow, and black, and pale, and hectic° red,   *feverish*
5 Pestilence-stricken multitudes: O thou,
Who chariotest to their dark wintry bed

The winged seeds, where they lie cold and low,
Each like a corpse within its grave, until
Thine azure sister of the Spring shall blow

10 Her clarion[3] o'er the dreaming earth, and fill
(Driving sweet buds like flocks to feed in air)
With living hues and odours plain and hill:

Wild Spirit, which art moving everywhere;
Destroyer and Preserver; hear, oh, hear!

2

15 Thou on whose stream, 'mid the steep sky's commotion,
Loose clouds like earth's decaying leaves are shed,
Shook from the tangled boughs of Heaven and Ocean,

Angels° of rain and lightning: there are spread   *harbingers*
On the blue surface of thine aëry surge,
20 Like the bright hair uplifted from the head

Of some fierce Mænad,[4] even from the dim verge
Of the horizon to the zenith's height,
The locks of the approaching storm. Thou dirge

Of the dying year, to which this closing night
25 Will be the dome of a vast sepulchre,
Vaulted with all thy congregated might

Of vapours,° from whose solid atmosphere   *clouds*
Black rain, and fire, and hail will burst: oh, hear!

3

Thou who didst waken from his summer dreams
30 The blue Mediterranean, where he lay,
Lulled by the coil of his chrystàlline streams,[5]

Beside a pumice isle in Baiae's bay,[6]
And saw in sleep old palaces and towers
Quivering within the wave's intenser day,

35 All overgrown with azure moss and flowers
So sweet, the sense faints picturing them! Thou
For whose path the Atlantic's level powers

Cleave themselves into chasms, while far below
The sea-blooms and the oozy woods which wear
40 The sapless foliage of the ocean, know

Thy voice, and suddenly grow gray with fear,
And tremble and despoil themselves:[7] oh, hear!

---

1 [Shelley's note] This poem was conceived and chiefly written in a wood that skirts the Arno, near Florence, and on a day when that tempestuous wind, whose temperature is at once mild and animating, was collecting the vapours which pour down the autumnal rains. They began, as I foresaw, at sunset with a violent tempest of hail and rain, attended by that magnificent thunder and lightning peculiar to the Cispaline regions.

2 *breath* The Latin word for wind, *spiritus*, also means "breath" and "soul," and is the root of the word "inspiration."

3 *clarion* High-pitched trumpet.

4 *Mænad* Female attendant of Bacchus, the Greek god of wine.

5 *coil... streams* Currents of the Mediterranean, the color of which are often different from the surrounding water.

6 *pumice* Porous stone made from cooled lava; *Baiae's bay* Bay west of Naples that contains the ruins of several imperial villas.

7 [Shelley's note] The phenomenon alluded to at the conclusion of the third stanza is well known to naturalists. The vegetation at the bottom of the sea, of rivers, and of lakes, sympathizes with that of the land in the change of seasons, and is consequently influenced by the winds which announce it.

4

If I were a dead leaf thou mightest bear;
If I were a swift cloud to fly with thee;
45   A wave to pant beneath thy power, and share

The impulse of thy strength, only less free
Than thou, O uncontrollable! If even
I were as in my boyhood, and could be

The comrade of thy wanderings over Heaven,
50   As then, when to outstrip thy skiey speed
Scarce seemed a vision; I would ne'er have striven

As thus with thee in prayer in my sore need.
Oh! lift me as a wave, a leaf, a cloud!
I fall upon the thorns of life! I bleed!

55   A heavy weight of hours has chained and bowed
One too like thee: tameless, and swift, and proud.

5

Make me thy lyre,[1] even as the forest is:
What if my leaves are falling like its own!
The tumult of thy mighty harmonies

60   Will take from both a deep, autumnal tone,
Sweet though in sadness. Be thou, Spirit fierce,
My spirit! Be thou me, impetuous one!

Drive my dead thoughts over the universe
Like withered leaves to quicken a new birth!
65   And, by the incantation of this verse,

Scatter, as from an unextinguished hearth
Ashes and sparks, my words among mankind!
Be through my lips to unawakened Earth

The trumpet of a prophecy! O, Wind,
70   If Winter comes, can Spring be far behind?
—1820

The Cloud

I bring fresh showers for the thirsting flowers,
   From the seas and the streams;
I bear light shade for the leaves when laid
   In their noonday dreams.
5   From my wings are shaken the dews that waken
   The sweet buds every one,
When rocked to rest on their mother's breast,
   As she dances about the sun.
I wield the flail of the lashing hail,
10   And whiten the green plains under,
And then again I dissolve it in rain,
   And laugh as I pass in thunder.

I sift the snow on the mountains below,
   And their great pines groan aghast;
15   And all the night 'tis my pillow white,
   While I sleep in the arms of the blast,
Sublime on the towers of my skiey bowers,
   Lightning my pilot sits;
In a cavern under is fettered the thunder,
20   It struggles and howls at fits;[2]
Over earth and ocean, with gentle motion,
   This pilot is guiding me,
Lured by the love of the genii that move
   In the depths of the purple sea;
25   Over the rills, and the crags, and the hills,
   Over the lakes and the plains,
Wherever he dream, under mountain or stream,
   The Spirit he loves remains;
And I all the while bask in Heaven's blue smile,
30   Whilst he is dissolving in rains.

The sanguine Sunrise, with his meteor eyes,
   And his burning plumes outspread,
Leaps on the back of my sailing rack,[3]
   When the morning star shines dead;
35   As on the jag of a mountain crag,
   Which an earthquake rocks and swings,
An eagle alit one moment may sit
   In the light of its golden wings.

---

1 *lyre* Here, Aeolian harp, a stringed instrument that produces music when exposed to wind.

2 *at fits* Fitfully.

3 *rack* Mass of clouds in the upper air.

And when Sunset may breathe, from the lit sea beneath,
40   Its ardours of rest and love,
And the crimson pall[1] of eve may fall
        From the depth of Heaven above,
With wings folded I rest, on mine aëry nest,
        As still as a brooding dove.

45 That orbèd maiden with white fire laden,
        Whom mortals call the Moon,
Glides glimmering o'er my fleece-like floor,
        By the midnight breezes strewn;
And wherever the beat of her unseen feet,
50   Which only the angels hear,
May have broken the woof° of my tent's   weave
        thin roof,
        The stars peep behind her and peer;
And I laugh to see them whirl and flee,
        Like a swarm of golden bees,
55 When I widen the rent in my wind-built tent,
        Till the calm rivers, lakes, and seas,
Like strips of the sky fallen through me on high,
        Are each paved with the moon and these.

I bind the Sun's throne with a burning zone,°   belt
60   And the Moon's with a girdle of pearl;
The volcanoes are dim, and the stars reel and swim,
        When the whirlwinds my banner unfurl.
From cape to cape, with a bridge-like shape,
        Over a torrent sea,
65 Sunbeam-proof, I hand like a roof—
        The mountains its columns be.
The triumphal arch through which I march
        With hurricane, fire, and snow,
When the Powers of the air are chained to my chair,
70   Is the million-coloured bow;
The sphere-fire[2] above its soft colours wove,
        While the moist Earth was laughing below.

I am the daughter of Earth and Water,
        And the nursing of the Sky;
75 I pass through the pores of the ocean and shores;
        I change, but I cannot die.
For after the rain, when with never a stain

The pavilion of Heaven is bare,
And the winds and sunbeams with their convex gleams
80   Build up the blue dome of air,
I silently laugh at my own cenotaph,[3]
        And out of the caverns of rain,
Like a child from the womb, like a ghost from the tomb,
        I arise and unbuild it again.
—1820

To a Skylark[4]

Hail to thee, blithe Spirit!
    Bird thou never wert,
That from Heaven, or near it,
    Pourest thy full heart
5 In profuse strains of unpremeditated art.

Higher still and higher
    From the earth thou springest
Like a cloud of fire;
    The blue deep thou wingest,
10 And singing still dost soar, and soaring ever singest.

In the golden lightning
    Of the sunken sun,
O'er which clouds are bright'ning,
    Thou dost float and run;
15 Like an unbodied joy whose race is just begun.

The pale purple even
    Melts around thy flight;
Like a star of Heaven,
    In the broad daylight
20 Thou art unseen, but yet I hear thy shrill delight,

Keen as are the arrows
    Of that silver sphere,[5]
Whose intense lamp narrows

---

[1] *pall* Rich cloth or canopy.

[2] *sphere-fire* I.e., sunlight.

[3] *cenotaph* Empty sepulcher; monument honoring a dead person
whose body lies elsewhere.

[4] *Skylark* Small bird that sings only when in flight, and often flies
so high that it cannot be easily seen.

[5] *silver sphere* I.e., the morning star.

In the white dawn clear
25   Until we hardly see—we feel that it is there.

All the earth and air
    With thy voice is loud,
As, when night is bare,
    From one lonely cloud
30   The moon rains out her beams, and Heaven is
        overflowed.

What thou art we know not;
    What is most like thee?
From rainbow clouds there flow not
    Drops so bright to see
35   As from thy presence showers a rain of melody.

Like a Poet hidden
    In the light of thought,
Singing hymns unbidden,
    Till the world is wrought
40   To sympathy with hopes and fears it heeded not:

Like a high-born maiden
    In a palace-tower,
Soothing her love-laden
    Soul in secret hour
45   With music sweet as love, which overflows her bower:

Like a glow-worm golden
    In a dell of dew,
Scattering unbeholden
    Its aëreal hue
50   Among the flowers and grass, which screen it from the
        view:

Like a rose embowered
    In its own green leaves,
By warm winds deflowered,
    Till the scent it gives
55   Makes faint with too much sweet these heavy-wingèd
        thieves:

Sound of vernal° showers   *springtime*
    On the twinkling grass,
Rain-awakened flowers,

All that ever was
60   Joyous, and clear, and fresh, thy music doth surpass:

Teach us, Sprite° or Bird,   *fairy*
    What sweet thoughts are thine:
I have never heard
    Praise of love or wine
65   That panted forth a flood of rapture so divine.

Chorus Hymeneal,[1]
    Or triumphal chaunt,°   *chant*
Matched with thine would be all
    But an empty vaunt,
70   A thing wherein we feel there is some hidden want.

What objects are the fountains
    Of thy happy strain?
What fields, or waves, or mountains?
    What shapes of sky or plain?
75   What love of thine own kind? what ignorance of pain?

With thy clear keen joyance
    Languor cannot be:
Shadow of annoyance
    Never came near thee:
80   Thou lovest—but ne'er knew love's sad satiety.

Waking or asleep,
    Thou of death must deem
Things more true and deep
    Than we mortals dream,
85   Or how could thy notes flow in such a crystal stream?

We look before and after,
    And pine for what is not:
Our sincerest laughter
    With some pain is fraught;
90   Our sweetest songs are those that tell of saddest thought.

Yet if we could scorn
    Hate, and pride, and fear;
If we were things born
    Not to shed a tear,
95   I know not how thy joy we ever should come near.

---

[1] *Hymeneal*   Marital (Hymen is the Greek god of marriage).

Better than all measures
    Of delightful sound,
Better than all treasures
    That in books are found,
100 Thy skill to poet were, thou scorner of the ground!

Teach me half the gladness
    That thy brain must know,
Such harmonious madness
    From my lips would flow
105 The world should listen then—as I am listening now.
—1820

Adonais

In this pastoral elegy for fellow poet John Keats, Shelley calls the young poet Adonais after Adonis, the beautiful youth of classical myth who was loved by Venus and killed by a wild boar. In some versions of the story Venus asks Persephone, Queen of the underworld, to allow Adonis to return above ground for four months of every year, while in others she transforms his blood into the bright red anemone, enabling him to live on in this ever-blooming flower.

    Shelley had known Keats only casually, through their mutual acquaintance Leigh Hunt, the editor of the radical *Examiner*, but he admired his poetry and agreed with many of his political views. Hearing of Keats's serious illness in 1820, Shelley had invited Keats to spend the winter with him in Pisa. Keats did journey to Italy, but died in Rome in February of 1821, before he could reach Pisa.

    The beast whom Shelley blames for Keats's death is the anonymous critic who ridiculed Keats's *Endymion* in *The Quarterly Review* (April 1818); Shelley thus gave force to a sentimental myth that Keats's illness and death were brought on by demoralizing reviews, both in *The Quarterly Review* and *Blackwoods Magazine*. For many years after his death, it was commonly maintained that, as Byron said, Keats was "snuffed out by an article." Until the late 1840s, Keats was better known by *Adonais* and the legend of his death than by his own poetry.

Adonais
An Elegy on the Death of John Keats

Αστήρ πρὶν μὲν ἐλαμπες ενι ζωοισιν εωος.
    Νυν δε θανὼν, λαμπεις ἔοπερος εν φθίμενοις.
               PLATO[1]

1

I weep for Adonais—he is dead!
  O, weep for Adonais! though our tears
Thaw not the frost which binds so dear a head!
And thou, sad Hour, selected from all years
5 To mourn our loss, rouse thy obscure compeers,
And teach them thine own sorrow, say: with me
Died Adonais; till the Future dares
Forget the Past, his fate and fame shall be
An echo and a light unto eternity!

2

10 Where wert thou mighty Mother, when he lay,
When thy Son lay, pierced by the shaft which flies
In darkness? Where was lorn° Urania[2]   *forlorn*
When Adonais died? With veiled eyes,
'Mid listening Echoes, in her Paradise
15 She sate, while one, with soft enamoured breath,
Rekindled all the fading melodies,
With which, like flowers that mock the corse°   *body*
    beneath,
He had adorned and hid the coming bulk of death.

3

O, weep for Adonais—he is dead!
20 Wake, melancholy Mother, wake and weep!
Yet wherefore? Quench within their burning bed
Thy fiery tears, and let thy loud heart keep
Like his, a mute and uncomplaining sleep;
For he is gone, where all things wise and fair

---

[1] Αστήρ … *PLATO* [Shelley's translation] Thou wert the morning star among the living, / Ere thy fair light had fled— / Now, having died, thou art as Hesperus, giving / New splendour to the dead. [Translation from the Greek of Plato's *Epigram on Aster*. The planet Venus appears in the sky as both the morning star, Phosphorus, and the evening star, Vesper.]

[2] *Urania* Muse who is invoked near the beginning of Milton's *Paradise Lost*. Urania is also an epithet for the goddess Venus, who loved Adonis.

25 Descend—oh, dream not that the amorous Deep°   abyss
   Will yet restore him to the vital air;
   Death feeds on his mute voice, and laughs at our
       despair.

                          4

   Most musical of mourners, weep again!
   Lament anew, Urania! He[1] died,
30 Who was the Sire of an immortal strain,
   Blind, old, and lonely, when his country's pride,
   The priest, the slave, and the liberticide,
   Trampled and mocked with many a loathed rite
   Of lust and blood; he went, unterrified,
35 Into the gulf of death; but his clear Sprite°   spirit
   Yet reigns o'er earth; the third among the sons of light.

                          5

   Most musical of mourners, weep anew!
   Not all to that bright station dared to climb;
   And happier they their happiness who knew,
40 Whose tapers yet burn through that night of time
   In which suns perished; others more sublime,
   Struck by the envious wrath of man or God,
   Have sunk, extinct in their refulgent° prime;   gleaming
   And some yet live, treading the thorny road,
45 Which leads, through toil and hate, to Fame's serene
       abode.

                          6

   But now, thy youngest, dearest one, has perished,
   The nursling of thy widowhood, who grew,
   Like a pale flower by some sad maiden cherished,
   And fed with true love tears, instead of dew;
50 Most musical of mourners, weep anew!
   Thy extreme hope, the loveliest and the last,
   The bloom, whose petals nipt before they blew,°   bloomed
   Died on the promise of the fruit, is waste;
   The broken lily lies—the storm is overpast.

                          7

55 To that high Capital,[2] where kingly Death
   Keeps his pale court in beauty and decay,
   He came; and bought, with price of purest breath,
   A grave among the eternal. Come away!
   Haste, while the vault of blue Italian day
60 Is yet his fitting charnel°-roof! while still   mortuary
   He lies, as if in dewy sleep he lay;
   Awake him not! surely he takes his fill
   Of deep and liquid rest, forgetful of all ill.

                          8

   He will awake no more, oh, never more!
65 Within the twilight chamber spreads apace,
   The shadow of white Death, and at the door
   Invisible Corruption waits to trace
   His extreme way to her dim dwelling-place;
   The eternal Hunger sits, but pity and awe
70 Soothe her pale rage, nor dares she to deface
   So fair a prey, till darkness, and the law
   Of mortal change, shall fill the grave which is her
       maw.°   stomach

                          9

   O, weep for Adonais! The quick° Dreams,   living
   The passion-winged Ministers of thought,
75 Who were his flocks, whom near the living streams
   Of his young spirit he fed, and whom he taught
   The love which was its music, wander not—
   Wander no more, from kindling brain to brain,
   But droop there, whence they sprung; and mourn their
       lot
80 Round the cold heart, where, after their sweet pain,
   They ne'er will gather strength, or find a home again.

                          10

   And one with trembling hands clasps his cold head,
   And fans him with her moonlight wings, and cries,
   "Our love, our hope, our sorrow, is not dead;
85 See, on the silken fringe of his faint eyes,
   Like dew upon a sleeping flower, there lies
   A tear some Dream has loosened from his brain."
   Lost Angel of a ruined Paradise!

---

[1] *He* Poet John Milton (1608–74), who served in Cromwell's Parliamentary government and, as a result, was imprisoned when the monarchy was restored, although he was released quickly. At the end of this stanza, Shelley places Milton in a triumvirate with the earlier epic poets Homer and Dante ("the third among the sons of light").

---

[2] *high Capital* Rome, where Keats died.

She knew not 'twas her own; as with no stain
90 She faded, like a cloud which had outwept its rain.

11

One from a lucid° urn of starry dew   *resplendent*
Washed his light limbs as if embalming them;
Another clipt her profuse locks, and threw
The wreath upon him, like an anadem,°   *garland*
95 Which frozen tears instead of pearls begem;
Another in her wilful grief would break
Her bow and winged reeds,° as if to stem   *arrows*
A greater loss with one which was more weak;
And dull the barbed fire against his frozen cheek.

12

100 Another Splendour on his mouth alit,
That mouth, whence it was wont to draw the breath
Which gave it strength to pierce the guarded wit,
And pass into the panting heart beneath
With lightning and with music: the damp death
105 Quenched its caress upon his icy lips;
And, as a dying meteor stains a wreath
Of moonlight vapour, which the cold night clips,°   *clasps*
It flushed through his pale limbs, and passed to its
      eclipse.

13

And others came … Desires and Adorations,
110 Winged Persuasions and veiled Destinies,
Splendours, and Glooms, and glimmering Incarnations
Of hopes and fears, and twilight Phantasies;
And Sorrow, with her family of Sighs,
And Pleasure, blind with tears, led by the gleam
115 Of her own dying smile instead of eyes,
Came in slow pomp—the moving pomp might seem
Like pageantry of mist on an autumnal stream.

14

All he had loved, and moulded into thought,
From shape, and hue, and odour, and sweet sound,
120 Lamented Adonais. Morning sought
Her eastern watchtower, and her hair unbound,
Wet with the tears which should adorn the ground,
Dimmed the aerial eyes that kindle day;
Afar the melancholy thunder moaned,

125 Pale Ocean in unquiet slumber lay,
And the wild winds flew round, sobbing in their dismay.

15

Lost Echo sits amid the voiceless mountains,
And feeds her grief with his remembered lay,°   *song*
And will no more reply to winds or fountains,
130 Or amorous birds perched on the young green spray,
Or herdsman's horn, or bell° at closing day;   *church-bell*
Since she can mimic not his lips, more dear
Than those for whose disdain she pined away
Into a shadow of all sounds[1]—a drear
135 Murmur, between their songs, is all the woodmen hear.

16

Grief made the young Spring wild, and she threw down
Her kindling buds, as if she Autumn were,
Or they dead leaves; since her delight is flown
For whom should she have waked the sullen year?
140 To Phoebus was not Hyacinth so dear[2]
Nor to himself Narcissus, as to both
Thou Adonais: wan they stand and sere°   *withered*
Amid the drooping comrades of their youth,
With dew all turned to tears; odour, to sighing ruth.° *pity*

17

145 Thy spirit's sister, the lorn nightingale
Mourns not her mate with such melodious pain;
Not so the eagle, who like thee could scale
Heaven, and could nourish in the sun's domain
Her mighty youth with morning,[3] doth complain,
150 Soaring and screaming round her empty nest,

---

[1] *those for … sounds* Narcissus, whom the nymph Echo loved. Echo had been robbed of her voice by the goddess Hera, and could only repeat what others said. After falling in love with Narcissus, who rejected her in favor of his own reflection, she pined away until only her echoing voice remained.

[2] *To Phoebus … dear* Phoebus Apollo, god of poetry and the sun, loved the beautiful youth Hyacinthus. When Hyacinthus was accidentally slain by a discus the god had thrown, Apollo caused the hyacinth flower to spring up from his spilt blood. It was said that Zephyrus (the west wind), a rejected suitor of Hyacinthus, blew the discus off course so that it would strike the youth. "Zephyr" was also the pen name of the reviewer of *Endymion*.

[3] *nourish … morning* According to legend, the eagle could renew her youth by flying toward the sun until its heat burnt off her old plumage and cleared the film from her eyes.

As Albion[1] wails for thee: the curse of Cain[2]
Light on his head who pierced thy innocent breast,
And scared the angel soul that was its earthly guest!

18

Ah woe is me! Winter is come and gone,
155   But grief returns with the revolving year;
The airs and streams renew their joyous tone;
The ants, the bees, the swallows reappear;
Fresh leaves and flowers deck the dead Seasons' bier;
The amorous birds now pair in every brake,°   *thicket*
160   And build their mossy homes in field and brere;°   *briar*
And the green lizard, and the golden snake,
Like unimprisoned flames, out of their trance awake.

19

Through wood and stream and field and hill and Ocean
A quickening life from the Earth's heart has burst
165   As it has ever done, with change and motion,
From the great morning of the world when first
God dawned on Chaos; in its steam immersed
The lamps of Heaven flash with a softer light;
All baser things pant with life's sacred thirst;
170   Diffuse themselves; and spend in love's delight,
The beauty and the joy of their renewed might.

20

The leprous corpse touched by this spirit tender
Exhales itself in flowers of gentle breath;
Like incarnations of the stars, when splendour
175   Is changed to fragrance, they illumine death
And mock the merry worm that wakes beneath;
Nought we know, dies. Shall that alone which knows[3]
Be as a sword consumed before the sheath
By sightless[4] lightning?—th'intense atom glows
180   A moment, then is quenched in a most cold repose.

21

Alas! that all we loved of him should be,

---

[1] *Albion* England.

[2] *curse of Cain* For murdering his brother Abel, Cain was forced to
wander the earth as a vagabond, unable to farm because no land
would yield crops for him. See Genesis 4.

[3] *that alone which knows* I.e., the mind.

[4] *sightless* Invisible; blind.

But for our grief, as if it had not been,
And grief itself be mortal! Woe is me!
Whence are we, and why are we? of what scene
185   The actors or spectators? Great and mean
Meet massed in death, who lends what life must borrow.
As long as skies are blue, and fields are green,
Evening must usher night, night urge the morrow,
Month follow month with woe, and year wake year to
sorrow.

22

190   *He* will awake no more, oh, never more!
"Wake thou," cried Misery, "childless Mother, rise
Out of thy sleep, and slake,° in thy heart's core,   *ease*
A wound more fierce than his with tears and sighs."
And all the Dreams that watched Urania's eyes,
195   And all the Echoes whom their sister's song
Had held in holy silence, cried: "Arise!"
Swift as a Thought by the snake Memory stung,
From her ambrosial rest the fading Splendour[5] sprung.

23

She rose like an autumnal Night, that springs
200   Out of the East, and follows wild and drear
The golden Day, which, on eternal wings,
Even as a ghost abandoning a bier,
Had left the Earth a corpse. Sorrow and fear
So struck, so roused, so rapt Urania;
205   So saddened round her like an atmosphere
Of stormy mist; so swept her on her way
Even to the mournful place where Adonais lay.

24

Out of her secret Paradise she sped,
Through camps and cities rough with stone, and steel,
210   And human hearts, which to her aery tread
Yielding not, wounded the invisible
Palms of her tender feet where'er they fell:
And barbed tongues, and thoughts more sharp than they
Rent the soft Form they never could repel,
215   Whose sacred blood, like the young tears of May,
Paved with eternal flowers that undeserving way.

---

[5] *ambrosial* Divine (ambrosia is the food of the gods); *the fading
Splendour* Urania.

25

In the death chamber for a moment Death,
Shamed by the presence of that living Might,
Blushed to annihilation, and the breath
220 Revisited those lips, and life's pale light
Flashed through those limbs, so late her dear delight.
"Leave me not wild and drear and comfortless,
As silent lightning leaves the starless night!
Leave me not!" cried Urania: her distress
225 Roused Death: Death rose and smiled, and met her
    vain caress.

26

"Stay yet awhile! speak to me once again;
Kiss me, so long but as a kiss may live;
And in my heartless breast and burning brain
That word, that kiss shall all thoughts else survive,
230 With food of saddest memory kept alive,
Now thou art dead, as if it were a part
Of thee, my Adonais! I would give
All that I am to be as thou now art!
But I am chained to Time, and cannot thence depart!

27

235 "Oh gentle child, beautiful as thou wert,
Why didst thou leave the trodden paths of men
Too soon, and with weak hands though mighty heart
Dare° the unpastured dragon in his den?   *challenge*
Defenceless as thou wert, oh where was then
240 Wisdom the mirrored shield,[1] or scorn the spear?
Or hadst thou waited the full cycle, when
Thy spirit should have filled its crescent sphere,
The monsters of life's waste had fled from thee like deer.

28

"The herded wolves, bold only to pursue;
245 The obscene ravens, clamorous o'er the dead;
The vultures to the conqueror's banner true
Who feed where Desolation first has fed,
And whose wings rain contagion—how they fled,
When like Apollo, from his golden bow,

250 The Pythian of the age[2] one arrow sped
And smiled! The spoilers tempt no second blow,
They fawn on the proud feet that spurn them as they
    go.

29

"The sun comes forth, and many reptiles spawn;
He sets, and each ephemeral insect then
255 Is gathered into death without a dawn,
And the immortal stars awake again;
So is it in the world of living men:
A godlike mind soars forth, in its delight
Making earth bare and veiling heaven, and when
260 It sinks, the swarms that dimmed or shared its light
Leave to its kindred lamps the spirit's awful°   *awe-inspiring*
    night."

30

Thus ceased she: and the mountain shepherds came,
Their garlands sere, their magic mantles rent;
The Pilgrim of Eternity,[3] whose fame
265 Over his living head like Heaven is bent,
An early but enduring monument,
Came, veiling all the lightnings of his song
In sorrow; from her wilds Ierne° sent   *Ireland*
The sweetest lyrist of her saddest wrong,
270 And love taught grief to fall like music from his
    tongue.[4]

31

Midst others of less note, came one frail Form,[5]
A phantom among men; companionless
As the last cloud of an expiring storm
Whose thunder is its knell;° he, as I guess,   *funeral-bell*
275 Had gazed on Nature's naked loveliness,

---

1 *mirrored shield* Because the stare of the Gorgon Medusa would turn men into stone, Perseus fought and defeated her by viewing her reflection in his shield.

2 *Pythian of the age* Byron, who attacked the unfavorable reviewers of his *Hours of Idleness* in his satire *English Bards and Scotch Reviewers* (1809). The epithet "Pythian" was given to the god Apollo when he slew the dragon Python.

3 *Pilgrim of Eternity* Byron.

4 *The sweetest … tongue* Poet Thomas Moore (1779–1852), whose *Irish Melodies* deals with the oppression of his native Ireland by England.

5 *one frail Form* Shelley.

Actæon-like,[1] and now he fled astray
With feeble steps o'er the world's wilderness,
And his own thoughts, along that rugged way,
Pursued, like raging hounds, their father and their prey.

32

280 A pardlike° Spirit beautiful and swift— *leopard-like*
A Love in desolation masked—a Power
Girt round with weakness; it can scarce uplift
The weight of the superincumbent hour;
It is a dying lamp, a falling shower,
285 A breaking billow—even whilst we speak
Is it not broken? On the withering flower
The killing sun smiles brightly: on a cheek
The life can burn in blood, even while the heart may
　　break.

33

His head was bound with pansies overblown,
290 And faded violets, white, and pied, and blue;
And a light spear topped with a cypress cone,
Round whose rude shaft dark ivy tresses grew[2]
Yet dripping with the forest's noonday dew,
Vibrated, as the ever-beating heart
295 Shook the weak hand that grasped it; of that crew
He came the last, neglected and apart;
A herd-abandoned deer struck by the hunter's dart.

34

All stood aloof, and at his partial° moan *sympathetic*
Smiled through their tears; well knew that gentle band
300 Who in another's fate now wept his own;
As in the accents of an unknown land,
He sung new sorrow; sad Urania scanned
The Stranger's mien, and murmured: "who art thou?"
He answered not, but with a sudden hand
305 Made bare his branded and ensanguined° brow, *bloody*
Which was like Cain's or Christ's—Oh! that it should
　　be so!

35

What softer voice is hushed over the dead?
Athwart what brow is that dark mantle thrown?
What form leans sadly o'er the white death-bed,
310 In mockery of monumental stone,
The heavy heart heaving without a moan?
If it be He, who, gentlest of the wise,
Taught, soothed, loved, honoured the departed one;[3]
Let me not vex, with inharmonious sighs
315 The silence of that heart's accepted sacrifice.

36

Our Adonais has drunk poison—oh!
What deaf and viperous murderer could crown
Life's early cup with such a draught of woe?
The nameless worm would now itself disown:
320 It felt, yet could escape the magic tone
Whose prelude held all envy, hate, and wrong,
But what was howling in one breast alone,
Silent with expectation of the song,
Whose master's hand is cold, whose silver lyre unstrung.[4]

37

325 Live thou, whose infamy is not thy fame!
Live! fear no heavier chastisement from me,
Thou noteless blot on a remembered name!
But be thyself, and know thyself to be!
And ever at thy season be thou free
330 To spill the venom when thy fangs o'er flow:
Remorse and Self-contempt shall cling to thee;
Hot Shame shall burn upon thy secret brow,
And like a beaten hound tremble thou shalt—as now.

38

Nor let us weep that our delight is fled
335 Far from these carrion kites[5] that scream below;
He wakes or sleeps with the enduring dead;
Thou canst not soar where he is sitting now.

---

[1] *Actæon-like* Actaeon was a hunter who accidentally came upon Diana, goddess of chastity, bathing naked. Angered, she turned him into a stag, and his own hounds chased him down and tore him apart.

[2] *pansies overblown* Pansies (a symbol of sorrow) past their bloom; *violets* Representing death; *light spear ... tresses grew* Thyrsus, staff borne by Dionysus, the god of fertility, and his followers.

[3] *He, who ... one* Radical journalist Leigh Hunt, to whom Keats dedicated his first volume.

[4] *silver lyre unstrung* On Keats's tomb is engraved the image of a Greek lyre with half its strings broken. According to his friend Joseph Severn, this symbolizes "his classical genius cut off by death before its maturity."

[5] *kites* Falcon-like birds of prey.

Dust to the dust! but the pure spirit shall flow
Back to the burning fountain whence it came,
340 A portion of the Eternal, which must glow
Through time and change, unquenchably the same,
Whilst thy cold embers choke the sordid hearth of
    shame.

39

Peace, peace! he is not dead, he doth not sleep—
He hath awakened from the dream of life—
345 'Tis we who lost in stormy visions keep
With phantoms an unprofitable strife,
And in mad trance, strike with our spirit's knife
Invulnerable nothings. *We* decay
Like corpses in a charnel; fear and grief
350 Convulse us and consume us day by day,
And cold hopes swarm like worms within our living
    clay.

40

He has outsoared the shadow of our night;
Envy and calumny° and hate and pain,   *slander*
And that unrest which men miscall delight,
355 Can touch him not and torture not again;
From the contagion of the world's slow stain
He is secure, and now can never mourn
A heart grown cold, a head grown grey in vain;
Nor, when the spirit's self has ceased to burn,
360 With sparkless ashes load an unlamented urn.

41

He lives, he wakes—'tis Death is dead, not he;
Mourn not for Adonais. Thou young Dawn
Turn all thy dew to splendour, for from thee
The spirit thou lamentest is not gone;
365 Ye caverns and ye forests, cease to moan!
Cease ye faint flowers and fountains, and thou Air
Which like a mourning veil thy scarf hadst thrown
O'er the abandoned Earth, now leave it bare
Even to the joyous stars which smile on its despair!

42

370 He is made one with Nature: there is heard
His voice in all her music, from the moan

Of thunder, to the song of night's sweet bird;[1]
He is a presence to be felt and known
In darkness and in light, from herb and stone,
375 Spreading itself where'er that Power may move
Which has withdrawn his being to its own;
Which wields the world with never wearied love,
Sustains it from beneath, and kindles it above.

43

He is a portion of the loveliness
380 Which once he made more lovely: he doth bear
His part, while the one Spirit's plastic° stress   *formative*
Sweeps through the dull dense world, compelling there,
All new successions to the forms they wear;
Torturing th'unwilling dross° that checks   *impure matter*
    its flight
385 To its own likeness, as each mass may bear;
And bursting in its beauty and its might
From trees and beasts and men into the Heaven's light.

44

The splendours of the firmament of time
May be eclipsed, but are extinguished not;
390 Like stars to their appointed height they climb
And death is a low mist which cannot blot
The brightness it may veil. When lofty thought
Lifts a young heart above its mortal lair,
And love and life contend in it, for what
395 Shall be its earthly doom,° the dead live there   *fate*
And move like winds of light on dark and stormy air.

45

The inheritors of unfulfilled renown
Rose from their thrones, built beyond mortal thought,
Far in the Unapparent. Chatterton[2]
400 Rose pale, his solemn agony had not
Yet faded from him; Sidney,[3] as he fought
And as he fell and as he lived and loved
Sublimely mild, a Spirit without spot,

---

1 *night's sweet bird* I.e., the nightingale, in reference to Keats's "Ode to a Nightingale."

2 *Chatterton* Poet Thomas Chatterton, who committed suicide in 1770 at the age of 17.

3 *Sidney* Sir Philip Sidney (1554–86), who was killed in battle when he was 32.

Arose; and Lucan,[1] by his death approved:
405   Oblivion as they rose shrank like a thing reproved.

46

And many more, whose names on Earth are dark
But whose transmitted effluence cannot die
So long as fire outlives the parent spark,
Rose, robed in dazzling immortality.
410   "Thou art become as one of us," they cry,
"It was for thee yon kingless sphere has long
Swung blind in unascended majesty,
Silent alone amid an Heaven of song.
Assume thy winged throne, thou Vesper[2] of our
            throng!"

47

415   Who mourns for Adonais? Oh come forth
Fond° wretch! and know thyself and him aright.   *foolish*
Clasp with thy panting soul the pendulous Earth;
As from a centre, dart thy spirit's light
Beyond all worlds, until its spacious might
420   Satiate the void circumference: then shrink
Even to a point within our day and night;
And keep thy heart light lest it make thee sink
When hope has kindled hope, and lured thee to the
            brink.

48

Or go to Rome, which is the sepulchre
425   O, not of him, but of our joy: 'tis nought
That ages, empires, and religions there
Lie buried in the ravage they have wrought;
For such as he can lend°—they borrow not   *bestow*
Glory from those who made the world their prey;
430   And he is gathered to the kings of thought
Who waged contention with their time's decay,
And of the past are all that cannot pass away.

49

Go thou to Rome—at once the Paradise,
The grave, the city, and the wilderness;

And where its wrecks like shattered mountains rise,
435   And flowering weeds, and fragrant copses° dress   *thickets*
The bones of Desolation's nakedness
Pass, till the Spirit of the spot shall lead
Thy footsteps to a slope of green access[3]
440   Where, like an infant's smile, over the dead,
A light of laughing flowers along the grass is spread.

50

And gray walls moulder round,[4] on which dull Time
Feeds, like slow fire upon a hoary° brand;[5]   *white*
And one keen pyramid with wedge sublime,
445   Pavilioning the dust of him who planned
This refuge for his memory, doth stand
Like flame transformed to marble; and beneath,
A field is spread, on which a newer band
Have pitched in Heaven's smile their camp of death
450   Welcoming him we lose with scarce extinguished
            breath.

51

Here pause: these graves are all too young as yet
To have outgrown the sorrow which consigned
Its charge to each; and if the seal is set,
Here, on one fountain of a mourning mind,
455   Break it not thou! too surely shalt thou find
Thine own well full, if thou returnest home,
Of tears and gall. From the world's bitter wind
Seek shelter in the shadow of the tomb.
What Adonais is, why fear we to become?

52

460   The One remains, the many change and pass;
Heaven's light forever shines, Earth's shadows fly;
Life, like a dome of many-coloured glass,
Stains the white radiance of Eternity,
Until Death tramples it to fragments. Die,
465   If thou wouldst be with that which thou dost seek!

---

[3] *slope of green access* The Protestant Cemetery in Rome, where Keats is buried. Shelley's son William, who died at age three, is also buried there.

[4] *gray ... round* One of the boundaries of the cemetery incorporates the wall of ancient Rome, while another is formed by the pyramid-tomb of Roman tribune Caius Cestius.

[5] *brand* Burning log.

---

[1] *Lucan* First-century CE Roman poet Marcus Annaeus Lucan, who at the age of twenty-six killed himself to avoid being executed for conspiring against the tyrannical emperor Nero.

[2] *Vesper* The evening star.

Follow where all is fled! Rome's azure sky,
Flowers, ruins, statues, music, words, are weak
The glory they transfuse with fitting truth to speak.

53

Why linger, why turn back, why shrink, my Heart?
470 Thy hopes are gone before: from all things here
They have departed; thou shouldst now depart!
A light is past from the revolving year,
And man, and woman; and what still is dear
Attracts to crush, repels to make thee wither.
475 The soft sky smiles—the low wind whispers near:
'Tis Adonais calls! Oh, hasten thither,
No more let Life divide what Death can join together.

54

That Light whose smile kindles the Universe,
That Beauty in which all things work and move,
480 That Benediction which the eclipsing Curse
Of birth can quench not, that sustaining Love
Which through the web of being blindly wove
By man and beast and earth and air and sea,
Burns bright or dim, as[1] each are mirrors of
485 The fire for which all thirst; now beams on me,
Consuming the last clouds of cold mortality.

55

The breath whose might I have invoked in song
Descends on me; my spirit's bark is driven,
Far from the shore, far from the trembling throng
490 Whose sails were never to the tempest given;
The massy earth and sphered skies are riven!
I am borne darkly, fearfully, afar;
Whilst burning through the inmost veil of Heaven,
The soul of Adonais, like a star,
495 Beacons from the abode where the Eternal are.
—1821

Mutability

1

The flower that smiles to-day
    To-morrow dies;
All that we wish to stay
    Tempts and then flies.
5 What is this world's delight?
Lightning that mocks the night,
    Brief even as bright.

2

Virtue, how frail it is!
    Friendship how rare!
10 Love, how it sells poor bliss
    For proud despair!
But we, though soon they fall,
Survive their joy, and all
    Which ours we call.

3

15 Whilst skies are blue and bright,
    Whilst flowers are gay,
Whilst eyes that change ere night
    Make glad the day;
Whilst yet the calm hours creep,
20 Dream thou—and from thy sleep
    Then wake to weep.
—1824

Stanzas
Written in Dejection – December 1818,
near Naples

1

The sun is warm, the sky is clear,
    The waves are dancing fast and bright,
Blue isles and snowy mountains wear
    The purple noon's transparent might,
5   The breath of the moist earth is light,
Around its unexpanded buds;

---

[1] *as* I.e., to the extent that.

Like many a voice of one delight,
The winds, the birds, the ocean floods,
The City's voice itself, is soft like Solitude's.

2

10 I see the Deep's untrampled floor
With green and purple seaweeds strown;
I see the waves upon the shore,
Like light dissolved in star-showers,[1] thrown:
I sit upon the sands alone—
15 The lightning of the noontide ocean
Is flashing round me, and a tone
Arises from its measured motion,
How sweet! did any heart now share in my emotion.

3

Alas! I have nor hope nor health,
20 Nor peace within nor calm around,
Nor that content surpassing wealth
The sage in meditation found,
And walked with inward glory crowned—
Nor fame, nor power, nor love, nor leisure.
25 Others I see whom these surround—
Smiling they live, and call life pleasure;—
To me that cup has been dealt in another measure.

4

Yet now despair itself is mild,
Even as the winds and waters are;
30 I could lie down like a tired child,
And weep away the life of care
Which I have borne and yet must bear,
Till death like sleep might steal on me,
And I might feel in the warm air
35 My cheek grow cold, and hear the sea
Breathe o'er my dying brain its last monotony.

5

Some might lament that I were cold.
As I, when this sweet day is gone,
Which my lost heart, too soon grown old,
40 Insults with this untimely moan;
They might lament—for I am one
Whom men love not—and yet regret,

Unlike this day, which, when the sun
Shall on its stainless glory set,
45 Will linger, though enjoyed, like joy in memory yet.
—1824

Song to the Men of England[2]

1

Men of England, wherefore plough
For the lords who lay ye low?
Wherefore weave with toil and care
The rich robes your tyrants wear?

2

5 Wherefore feed, and clothe, and save,
From the cradle to the grave,
Those ungrateful drones who would
Drain your sweat—nay, drink your blood?

3

Wherefore, Bees of England, forge
10 Many a weapon, chain, and scourge,
That these stingless drones may spoil
The forced produce of your toil?

4

Have ye leisure, comfort, calm,
Shelter, food, love's gentle balm?
15 Or what is it ye buy so dear
With your pain and with your fear?

5

The seed ye sow, another reaps;
The wealth ye find, another keeps;
The robes ye weave, another wears;
20 The arms ye forge, another bears.

---

[1] *star-showers* Meteor showers.

[2] *Song … England* Composed in 1819, during a time of economic depression and social turmoil following the end of the Napoleonic Wars. In this song, which became a hymn for the British labor movement, Shelley urges the proletariat to force change in the social and economic order.

6

Sow seed—but let no tyrant reap;
Find wealth—let no impostor heap;
Weave robes—let not the idle wear;
Forge arms—in your defence to bear.

7

25 Shrink to your cellars, holes, and cells;
In halls ye deck another dwells.
Why shake the chains ye wrought? Ye see
The steel ye tempered glance on[1] ye.

8

With plough and spade, and hoe and loom,
30 Trace your grave, and build your tomb,
And weave your winding-sheet, till fair
England be your sepulchre.
—1839 (1819)

England in 1819

An old, mad, blind, despised, and dying king,[2]
   Princes, the dregs of their dull race, who flow
Through public scorn—mud from a muddy spring—
Rulers who neither see, nor feel, nor know,
5 But leech-like to their fainting country cling,
Till they drop, blind in blood, without a blow—
A people starved and stabbed in the untilled field[3]—
An army, which liberticide and prey
Makes as a two-edged sword to all who wield—
10 Golden and sanguine laws[4] which tempt and slay;
Religion Christless, Godless—a book sealed;

---

[1] glance on Strike obliquely.

[2] old, mad ... king George III, who was declared insane in 1811. His sons were known for their corruption and their licentious behavior.

[3] A people ... field Reference to the massacre at St. Peter's Field on 16 August 1819 (the Peterloo Massacre), when the militia used undue force to disperse a crowd of men, women, and children who were peacefully demonstrating for political reform. Several people were killed and hundreds more injured (see "The Mask of Anarchy").

[4] Golden ... laws I.e., laws, bought with gold, that lead to bloodshed.

A Senate, Time's worst statute, unrepealed,[5]
Are graves, from which a glorious Phantom[6] may
Burst, to illumine our tempestuous day.
—1839

A Defence of Poetry

This essay, begun in 1822 and never completed, was written in response to an 1820 essay by Shelley's friend Thomas Love Peacock called "The Four Ages of Poetry." In this partially ironic essay, Peacock describes four cycles through which poetry passes: the first is an iron age of crude folk ballads, medieval romances, etc; the second, the gold age, contains the great epics of Homer, Dante, and Milton; the silver age contains the "derivative" poetry of the Augustan poets (who included John Dryden and Alexander Pope); and the fourth stage, the age of brass, is that of Peacock's contemporaries, whom he claimed were markedly inferior. Criticizing Romantic poets such as Byron, Coleridge, and Wordsworth, Peacock urged the men of his generation to apply themselves to new sciences, such as astronomy, economics, politics, mathematics, or chemistry, instead of poetry. Though Shelley recognized Peacock's satirical humor, he also acknowledged that Peacock had put his finger on a common bias of the time—both in the theories of Utilitarian philosophers and in general public opinion—in favor of economic growth and scientific progress over creativity and humanitarian concerns. It was this bias that he attempted to correct in his Defence.

from A Defence of Poetry,
or Remarks Suggested by an Essay Entitled "The Four Ages of Poetry"

According to one mode of regarding those two classes of mental action which are called reason and imagination, the former may be considered as mind contemplating the relations borne by one thought to another, however produced; and the latter, as mind acting upon

---

[5] Time's ... unrepealed Laws against Catholics and Dissenters.

[6] a glorious Phantom I.e., revolution.

those thoughts so as to colour them with its own light, and composing from them, as from elements, other thoughts, each containing within itself the principle of its own integrity. The one is the τὸ ποιειν,[1] or the principle of synthesis, and has for its objects those forms which are common to universal nature and existence itself; the other is the τὸ λογιζειν[2] or principle of analysis, and its action regards the relations of things, simply as relations; considering thoughts, not in their integral unity, but as the algebraical representations which conduct to certain general results. Reason is the enumeration of quantities already known; imagination is the perception of the value of those quantities, both separately and as a whole. Reason respects the differences, and imagination the similitudes of things. Reason is to Imagination as the instrument to the agent, as the body to the spirit, as the shadow to the substance.

Poetry, in a general sense, may be defined to be "the expression of the Imagination": and poetry is connate with the origin of man. Man is an instrument over which a series of external and internal impressions are driven, like the alternations of an ever-changing wind over an Æolian lyre,[3] which move it by their motion to ever-changing melody. But there is a principle within the human being, and perhaps within all sentient beings, which acts otherwise than in the lyre, and produces not melody alone, but harmony, by an internal adjustment of the sounds or motions thus excited to the impressions which excite them. It is as if the lyre could accommodate its chords to the motions of that which strikes them, in a determined proportion of sound; even as the musician can accommodate his voice to the sound of the lyre. A child at play by itself will express its delight by its voice and motions; and every inflexion of tone and every gesture will bear exact relation to a corresponding antitype in the pleasurable impressions which awakened it; it will be the reflected image of that impression; and as the lyre trembles and sounds after the wind has died away, so the child seeks, by prolonging in its voice and motions the duration of the effect, to prolong also a consciousness of the cause. In relation to the objects which delight a child, these expressions are what poetry is to higher objects. The savage (for the savage is to ages what the child is to years) expresses the emotions produced in him by surrounding objects in a similar manner; and language and gesture, together with plastic[4] or pictorial imitation, become the image of the combined effect of those objects, and of his apprehension of them. Man in society, with all his passions and his pleasures, next becomes the object of the passions and pleasures of man; an additional class of emotions produces an augmented treasure of expressions; and language, gesture, and the imitative arts become at once the representation and the medium, the pencil and the picture, the chisel and the statue, the chord and the harmony. The social sympathies, or those laws from which as from its elements society results, begin to develop themselves from the moment that two human beings coexist; the future is contained within the present as the plant within the seed; and equality, diversity, unity, contrast, mutual dependence, become the principles alone capable of affording the motives according to which the will of a social being is determined to action, inasmuch as he is social; and constitute pleasure in sensation, virtue in sentiment, beauty in art, truth in reasoning, and love in the intercourse of kind. Hence men, even in the infancy of society, observe a certain order in their words and actions, distinct from that of the objects and the impressions represented by them, all expression being subject to the laws of that from which it proceeds. But let us dismiss those more general considerations which might involve an enquiry into the principles of society itself, and restrict our view to the manner in which the imagination is expressed upon its forms.

In the youth of the world, men dance and sing and imitate natural objects, observing[5] in these actions, as in all others, a certain rhythm or order. And, although all men observe a similar, they observe not the same order, in the motions of the dance, in the melody of the song, in the combinations of language, in the series of their imitations of natural objects. For there is a certain order or rhythm belonging to each of these classes of mimetic representation, from which the hearer and the spectator

---

[1] τὸ ποιειν   Greek: making.

[2] τὸ λογιζειν   Greek: reasoning.

[3] *Æolian lyre* Stringed instrument that produces music when exposed to wind.

[4] *plastic* Formative.

[5] *observing* Following.

receive an intenser and purer pleasure than from any other: the sense of an approximation to this order has been called taste, by modern writers. Every man in the infancy of art observes an order which approximates more or less closely to that from which this highest delight results: but the diversity is not sufficiently marked, as that its gradations should be sensible, except in those instances where the predominance of this faculty of approximation to the beautiful (for so we may be permitted to name the relation between this highest pleasure and its cause) is very great. Those in whom it exists in excess are poets, in the most universal sense of the word; and the pleasure resulting from the manner in which they express the influence of society or nature upon their own minds, communicates itself to others, and gathers a sort of reduplication from that community. Their language is vitally metaphorical; that is, it marks the before unapprehended relations of things, and perpetuates their apprehension, until the words which represent them, become through time signs for portions or classes of thoughts instead of pictures of integral thoughts; and then if no new poets should arise to create afresh the associations which have been thus disorganized, language will be dead to all the nobler purposes of human intercourse. These similitudes or relations are finely said by Lord Bacon to be "the same footsteps of nature impressed upon the various subjects of the world"[1]—and he considers the faculty which perceives them as the storehouse of axioms common to all knowledge. In the infancy of society every author is necessarily a poet, because language itself is poetry; and to be a poet is to apprehend the true and the beautiful, in a word the good which exists in the relation, subsisting, first between existence and perception, and secondly between perception and expression. Every original language near to its source is in itself the chaos of a cyclic poem:[2] the copiousness of lexicography and the distinctions of grammar are the works of a later age, and are merely the catalogue and the form of the creations of Poetry.

But Poets, or those who imagine and express this indestructible order, are not only the authors of language and of music, of the dance and architecture and statuary and painting: they are the institutors of laws, and the founders of civil society and the inventors of the arts of life and the teachers, who draw into a certain propinquity with the beautiful and the true that partial apprehension of the agencies of the invisible world which is called religion. Hence all original religions are allegorical, or susceptible of allegory, and like Janus have a double face of false and true.[3] Poets, according to the circumstances of the age and nation in which they appeared, were called in the earlier epochs of the world legislators or prophets:[4] a poet essentially comprises and unites both these characters. For he not only beholds intensely the present as it is, and discovers those laws according to which present things ought to be ordered, but he beholds the future in the present, and his thoughts are the germs of the flower and the fruit of latest time. Not that I assert poets to be prophets in the gross sense of the word, or that they can foretell the form as surely as they foreknow the spirit of events: such is the pretence of superstition which would make poetry an attribute of prophecy, rather than prophecy an attribute of poetry. A Poet participates in the eternal, the infinite, and the one; as far as relates to his conceptions, time and place and number are not. The grammatical forms which express the moods of time, and the difference of persons and the distinction of place, are convertible with respect to the highest poetry without injuring it as poetry, and the choruses of Æschylus, and the book of Job, and Dante's Paradise[5] would afford, more than any other writings, examples of this fact, if the limits of this essay did not forbid citation. The

[1] the same ... world   From Francis Bacon's Of the Advancement of Learning (1605) 3.1.

[2] cyclic poem   Set of poems dealing with the same subject (though not always by the same author). The "Arthurian Cycle," a series of poems about the court of King Arthur, is one example of the genre.

[3] like Janus ... true   Janus, the Roman god of war, of doorways, and of beginnings and endings (after whom the month of January is named) is generally depicted with two faces, one looking forward and one back.

[4] were called ... prophets   Cf. Sir Philip Sidney's Defence of Poesy (1595), in which he points out that vates, the Latin word for poet, also means diviner or prophet.

[5] Æschylus   Greek tragic dramatist (c. 525–456 BCE); Dante's Paradise   Reference to Italian poet Dante Alighieri's fourteenth-century work, The Divine Comedy, which describes a journey from Hell, through Purgatory, to Paradise.

creations of sculpture, painting, and music are illustrations still more decisive.

Language, colour, form, and religious and civil habits of action are all the instruments and materials of poetry; they may be called poetry by that figure of speech which considers the effect as a synonym of the cause. But poetry in a more restricted sense expresses those arrangements of language, and especially metrical language, which are created by that imperial faculty whose throne is curtained within the invisible nature of man. And this springs from the nature itself of language, which is a more direct representation of the actions and passions of our internal being, and is susceptible of more various and delicate combinations, than colour, form, or motion, and is more plastic and obedient to the control of that faculty of which it is the creation. For language is arbitrarily produced by the Imagination and has relation to thoughts alone; but all other materials, instruments and conditions of art, have relations among each other, which limit and interpose between conception and expression. The former is as a mirror which reflects, the latter as a cloud which enfeebles, the light of which both are mediums of communication. Hence the fame of sculptors, painters and musicians, although the intrinsic powers of the great masters of these arts, may yield in no degree to that of those who have employed language as the hieroglyphic of their thoughts, has never equalled that of poets in the restricted sense of the term; as two performers of equal skill will produce unequal effects from a guitar and a harp. The fame of legislators and founders of religions, so long as their institutions last, alone seems to exceed that of poets in the restricted sense; but it can scarcely be a question whether, if we deduct the celebrity which their flattery of the gross opinions of the vulgar usually conciliates, together with that which belonged to them in their higher character of poets, any excess will remain.

We have thus circumscribed the meaning of the word Poetry within the limits of that art which is the most familiar and the most perfect expression of the faculty itself. It is necessary however to make the circle still narrower, and to determine the distinction between measured and unmeasured language; for the popular division into prose and verse is inadmissible in accurate philosophy. Sounds as well as thoughts have relation both between each other and towards that which they represent, and a perception of the order of those relations has always been found connected with a perception of the order of the relations of thoughts. Hence the language of poets has ever affected a certain uniform and harmonious recurrence of sound, without which it were not poetry, and which is scarcely less indispensable to the communication of its influence, than the words themselves, without reference to that peculiar order. ...

A poem is the very image of life expressed in its eternal truth. There is this difference between a story and a poem, that a story is a catalogue of detached facts, which have no other bond of connection than time, place, circumstance, cause and effect; the other is the creation of actions according to the unchangeable forms of human nature, as existing in the mind of the creator, which is itself the image of all other minds. The one is partial, and applies only to a definite period of time, and a certain combination of events which can never again recur; the other is universal, and contains within itself the germ of a relation to whatever motives or actions have place in the possible varieties of human nature. ...

Poetry is ever accompanied with pleasure: all spirits on which it falls open themselves to receive the wisdom which is mingled with its delight. In the infancy of the world, neither poets themselves nor their auditors are fully aware of the excellence of poetry: for it acts in a divine and unapprehended manner, beyond and above consciousness; and it is reserved for future generations to contemplate and measure the mighty cause and effect in all the strength and splendour of their union. Even in modern times, no living poet ever arrived at the fulness of his fame; the jury which sits in judgement upon a poet, belonging as he does to all time, must be composed of his peers: it must be impanelled by Time from the selectest of the wise of many generations. A Poet is a nightingale, who sits in darkness and sings to cheer its own solitude with sweet sounds; his auditors are as men entranced by the melody of an unseen musician, who feel that they are moved and softened, yet know not whence or why. The poems of Homer and his contemporaries were the delight of infant Greece; they were the elements of that social system which is the column upon which all succeeding civilization has reposed. Homer embodied the ideal perfection of his age in human character; nor can we doubt that those who read his verses were awakened to an ambition of becoming like to Achilles, Hector and Ulysses:[1] the truth and beauty of friendship, patriotism, and persevering devotion to an object were unveiled to the depths in these immortal creations: the sentiments of the auditors must have been refined and enlarged by a sympathy with such great and lovely impersonations, until from admiring they imitated, and from imitation they identified themselves with the objects of their admiration. ...

The whole objection, however, of the immorality of poetry[2] rests upon a misconception of the manner in which poetry acts to produce the moral improvement of man. Ethical science[3] arranges the elements which poetry has created, and propounds schemes and proposes examples of civil and domestic life: nor is it for want of admirable doctrines that men hate, and despise, and censure, and deceive, and subjugate one another. But Poetry acts in another and diviner manner. It awakens and enlarges the mind itself by rendering it the receptacle of a thousand unapprehended combinations of thought. Poetry lifts the veil from the hidden beauty of the world, and makes familiar objects be as if they were not familiar; it reproduces[4] all that it represents, and the impersonations clothed in its Elysian[5] light stand thenceforward in the minds of those who have once contemplated them, as memorials of that gentle and exalted content which extends itself over all thoughts and actions with which it coexists. The great secret of morals is Love; or a going out of our own nature, and an identification of ourselves with the beautiful which exists in thought, action, or person not our own. A man, to be greatly good, must imagine intensely and comprehensively; he must put himself in the place of another and of many others; the pains and pleasures of his species must become his own. The great instrument of moral good is the imagination; and poetry administers to the effect by acting upon the cause. Poetry enlarges the circumference of the imagination by replenishing it with thoughts of ever new delight, which have the power of attracting and assimilating to their own nature all other thoughts, and which form new intervals and interstices whose void for ever craves fresh food. Poetry strengthens that faculty which is the organ of the moral nature of man, in the same manner as exercise strengthens a limb. A Poet therefore would do ill to embody his own conceptions of right and wrong, which are usually those of his place and time, in his poetical creations, which participate in neither. By this assumption of the inferior office of interpreting the effect, in which perhaps after all he might acquit himself but imperfectly, he would resign the glory in a participation in the cause. There was little danger that Homer, or any of the eternal poets, should have so far misunderstood themselves as to have abdicated this throne of their widest dominion. Those in whom the poetical faculty, though great, is less intense, as Euripides, Lucan, Tasso, Spenser,[6] have frequently affected a moral aim, and the effect of their poetry is diminished in exact proportion to the degree in which they compel us to advert to this purpose. ...

The drama at Athens, or wheresoever else it may have approached to its perfection, coexisted with the moral and intellectual greatness of the age. The tragedies of the Athenian poets are as mirrors in which the spectator beholds himself, under a thin disguise of circumstance, stript of all but that ideal perfection and energy which every one feels to be the internal type of all that he loves, admires, and would become. The imagination is enlarged by a sympathy with pains and passions so mighty that they distend in their conception the capacity of that by which they are conceived; the good affections are strengthened by pity, indignation, terror and sorrow; and an exalted calm is prolonged from the satiety of this high exercise of them into the tumult of familiar life; even crime is disarmed of half its

---

[1] *Achilles, Hector and Ulysses* Trojan and Greek heroes in Homer's *Iliad* and *Odyssey.*

[2] *immorality of poetry* An objection voiced by Plato in his *Republic,* in which he says that poetry often depicts characters who are morally imperfect and whose actions do not provide suitable examples for readers.

[3] *Ethical science* Moral philosophy.

[4] *reproduces* I.e., produces or creates anew.

[5] *Elysian* I.e., paradisical. From Elysium, the paradise where the blessed reside after death, according to Greek myth.

[6] *Euripides* Greek tragedian of the fifth century BCE; *Lucan* Roman poet of the first century CE; *Tasso* Torquato Tasso, Italian epic poet of the sixteenth century; *Spenser* Edmund Spenser, sixteenth-century epic poet, author of *The Faerie Queene.*

horror and all its contagion by being represented as the fatal consequence of the unfathomable agencies of nature; error is thus divested of its wilfulness; men can no longer cherish it as the creation of their choice. In a drama of the highest order there is little food for censure or hatred; it teaches rather self-knowledge and self-respect. Neither the eye nor the mind can see itself, unless reflected upon that which it resembles. The drama, so long as it continues to express poetry, is as a prismatic and many-sided mirror, which collects the brightest rays of human nature and divides and reproduces them from the simplicity of these elementary forms, and touches them with majesty and beauty, and multiplies all that it reflects, and endows it with the power of propagating its like wherever it may fall.

But in periods of the decay of social life, the drama sympathizes with that decay. Tragedy becomes a cold imitation of the form of the great masterpieces of antiquity, divested of all harmonious accompaniment of the kindred arts; and often the very form misunderstood: or a weak attempt to teach certain doctrines, which the writer considers as moral truths; and which are usually no more than specious flatteries of some gross vice or weakness with which the author in common with his auditors are infected. ...

The drama being that form under which a greater number of modes of expression of poetry are susceptible of being combined than any other, the connection of poetry and social good is more observable in the drama than in whatever other form: and it is indisputable that the highest perfection of human society has ever corresponded with the highest dramatic excellence; and that the corruption or the extinction of the drama in a nation where it has once flourished, is a mark of a corruption of manners, and an extinction of the energies which sustain the soul of social life. But, as Machiavelli[1] says of political institutions, that life may be preserved and renewed, if men should arise capable of bringing back the drama to its principles. And this is true with respect to poetry in its most extended sense: all language, institution and form, require not only to be produced but to be sustained: the office and character of

a poet participates in the divine nature as regards providence, no less than as regards creation.

... It is admitted that the exercise of the imagination is most delightful, but it is alleged that that of reason is more useful. Let us examine as the grounds of this distinction, what is here meant by Utility. Pleasure or good, in a general sense, is that which the consciousness of a sensitive and intelligent being seeks, and in which when found it acquiesces. There are two kinds of pleasure, one durable, universal, and permanent; the other transitory and particular. Utility may either express the means of producing the former or the latter. In the former sense, whatever strengthens and purifies the affections, enlarges the imagination, and adds spirit to sense, is useful. But the meaning in which the Author of the Four Ages of Poetry seems to have employed the word utility is the narrower one of banishing the importunity of the wants of our animal nature, the surrounding men with security of life, the dispersing the grosser delusions of superstition, and the conciliating such a degree of mutual forbearance among men as may consist with the motives of personal advantage.

Undoubtedly the promoters of utility in this limited sense have their appointed office in society. They follow the footsteps of poets, and copy the sketches of their creations into the book of common life. They make space, and give time. Their exertions are of the highest value so long as they confine their administration of the concerns of the inferior powers of our nature within the limits due to the superior ones. But whilst the sceptic destroys gross superstitions, let him spare to deface, as some of the French writers have defaced, the eternal truths charactered upon the imaginations of men. Whilst the mechanist abridges, and the political economist combines, labour, let them beware that their speculations, for want of correspondence with those first principles which belong to the imagination, do not tend, as they have in modern England, to exasperate at once the extremes of luxury and want. They have exemplified the saying, "To him that hath, more shall be given; and from him that hath not, the little that he hath shall be taken away."[2] The rich have become richer,

[1] *Machiavelli* Niccolò Machiavelli (1469–1527), author of the political treatise *The Prince*.

[2] *To him ... away* Repeatedly said by Jesus (Matthew 25.29, Mark 4.25, Luke 8.18 and 19.26).

and the poor have become poorer; and the vessel of the state is driven between the Scylla and Charybdis[1] of anarchy and despotism. Such are the effects which must ever flow from an unmitigated exercise of the calculating faculty.

It is difficult to define pleasure in its highest sense; the definition involving a number of apparent paradoxes. For, from an inexplicable defect of harmony in the constitution of human nature, the pain of the inferior is frequently connected with the pleasures of the superior portions of our being. Sorrow, terror, anguish, despair itself are often the chosen expressions of an approximation to the highest good. Our sympathy in tragic fiction depends on this principle; tragedy delights by affording a shadow of the pleasure which exists in pain. This is the source also of the melancholy which is inseparable from the sweetest melody. The pleasure that is in sorrow is sweeter than the pleasure of pleasure itself. And hence the saying, "It is better to go to the house of mourning, than to the house of mirth."[2] Not that this highest species of pleasure is necessarily linked with pain. The delight of love and friendship, the ecstasy of the admiration of nature, the joy of the perception and still more of the creation of poetry is often wholly unalloyed.

The production and assurance of pleasure in this highest sense is true utility. Those who produce and preserve this pleasure are Poets or poetical philosophers.

The exertions of Locke, Hume, Gibbon, Voltaire, Rousseau,[3] and their disciples, in favour of oppressed and deluded humanity, are entitled to the gratitude of mankind. Yet it is easy to calculate the degree of moral and intellectual improvement which the world would have exhibited, had they never lived. A little more nonsense would have been talked for a century or two; and perhaps a few more men, women, and children, burnt as heretics. We might not at this moment have been congratulating each other on the abolition of the Inquisition in Spain.[4] But it exceeds all imagination to conceive what would have been the moral condition of the world if neither Dante, Petrarch, Boccaccio, Chaucer, Shakespeare, Calderon,[5] Lord Bacon, nor Milton, had ever existed; if Raphael and Michael Angelo[6] had never been born; if the Hebrew poetry had never been translated; if a revival of the study of Greek literature had never taken place; if no monuments of ancient sculpture had been handed down to us; and if the poetry of the religion of the ancient world had been extinguished together with its belief. The human mind could never, except by the intervention of these excitements, have been awakened to the invention of the grosser sciences, and that application of analytical reasoning to the aberrations of society, which it is now attempted to exalt over the direct expression of the inventive and creative faculty itself.

… The cultivation of those sciences which have enlarged the limits of the empire of man over the external world, has, for want of the poetical faculty, proportionally circumscribed those of the internal world; and man, having enslaved the elements, remains himself a slave. To what but a cultivation of the mechanical arts in a degree disproportioned to the presence of the creative faculty, which is the basis of all knowledge, is to be attributed the abuse of all invention for abridging and combining labour, to the exasperation of the inequality of mankind? From what other cause has it arisen that the discoveries which should have lightened, have added a weight to the curse imposed on Adam? Poetry, and the principle of Self, of which money is the visible incarnation, are the God and the Mammon of the world.[7]

The functions of the poetical faculty are two-fold; by one it creates new materials of knowledge, and power

---

[1] *Scylla and Charybdis*   A group of rocks and a whirlpool located at the Strait of Messina (between Sicily and mainland Italy).

[2] *It is … mirth*   From Ecclesiastes 7.2.

[3] *Locke … Rousseau*   John Locke, David Hume, Edward Gibbon, François-Marie Arouet Voltaire, and Jean-Jacques Rousseau, noted philosophers of the seventeenth and eighteenth centuries.

[4] *We might … Spain*   The Inquisition was suspended in 1820 (the year before Shelley wrote this essay) and abolished permanently in 1834.

[5] *Petrarch*   Fourteenth-century Italian poet, famous for his love lyrics; *Boccaccio*   Italian poet, author of the *Decameron* (1351–53); *Calderon*   Seventeenth-century Spanish poet and dramatist.

[6] *Raphael and Michael Angelo*   Italian Renaissance painters.

[7] *God and … world*   Cf. Matthew 6.24: "No man can serve two masters: for either he will hate the one, and love the other; or else he will hold to the one, and despise the other. Ye cannot serve God and Mammon," Mammon being the false idol of worldly possessions.

and pleasure; by the other it engenders in the mind a desire to reproduce and arrange them according to a certain rhythm and order which may be called the beautiful and the good. The cultivation of poetry is never more to be desired than at periods when, from an excess of the selfish and calculating principle, the accumulation of the materials of external life exceed the quantity of the power of assimilating them to the internal laws of human nature. The body has then become too unwieldy for that which animates it.

Poetry is indeed something divine. It is at once the centre and circumference of knowledge; it is that which comprehends all science, and that to which all science must be referred. It is at the same time the root and blossom of all other systems of thought: it is that from which all spring, and that which adorns all; and that which, if blighted, denies the fruit and the seed, and withholds from the barren world the nourishment and the succession of the scions[1] of the tree of life. It is the perfect and consummate surface and bloom of things; it is as the odour and the colour of the rose to the texture of the elements which compose it, as the form and the splendour of unfaded beauty to the secrets of anatomy and corruption. What were Virtue, Love, Patriotism, Friendship &c.—what were the scenery of this beautiful Universe which we inhabit—what were our consolations on this side of the grave—and what were our aspirations beyond it—if Poetry did not ascend to bring light and fire from those eternal regions where the owl-winged faculty of calculation dare not ever soar? Poetry is not like reasoning, a power to be exerted according to the determination of the will. A man cannot say, "I will compose poetry." The greatest poet even cannot say it: for the mind in creation is as a fading coal which some invisible influence, like an inconstant wind, awakens to transitory brightness: this power arises from within, like the colour of a flower which fades and changes as it is developed, and the conscious portions of our natures are unprophetic either of its approach or its departure. ...

Poetry is the record of the best and happiest moments of the happiest and best minds. We are aware of evanescent visitations of thought and feeling sometimes associated with place or person, sometimes regarding our own mind alone, and always arising unforeseen and departing unbidden, but elevating and delightful beyond all expression: so that even in the desire and the regret they leave, there cannot but be pleasure, participating as it does in the nature of its object. It is as it were the interpenetration of a diviner nature through our own; but its footsteps are like those of a wind over a sea, which the coming calm erases, and whose traces remain only as on the wrinkled sand which paves it. These and corresponding conditions of being are experienced principally by those of the most delicate sensibility and the most enlarged imagination; and the state of mind produced by them is at war with every base desire. The enthusiasm of virtue, love, patriotism, and friendship is essentially linked with these emotions; and whilst they last, self appears as what it is, an atom to a Universe. Poets are not only subject to these experiences as spirits of the most refined organization, but they can colour all that they combine with the evanescent hues of this ethereal world; a word, a trait in the representation of a scene or a passion, will touch the enchanted chord, and reanimate, in those who have ever experienced these emotions, the sleeping, the cold, the buried image of the past. Poetry thus makes immortal all that is best and most beautiful in the world; it arrests the vanishing apparitions which haunt the interlunations[2] of life, and veiling them or in language or in form sends them forth among mankind, bearing sweet news of kindred joy to those with whom their sisters abide—abide, because there is no portal of expression from the caverns of the spirit which they inhabit into the universe of things. Poetry redeems from decay the visitations of the divinity in man.

Poetry turns all things to loveliness; it exalts the beauty of that which is most beautiful, and it adds beauty to that which is most deformed: it marries exultation and horror, grief and pleasure, eternity and change; it subdues to union under its light yoke all irreconcilable things. It transmutes all that it touches, and every form moving within the radiance of its presence is changed by wondrous sympathy to an incarnation of the spirit which it breathes; its secret

---

[1] *scions* Shoots.

[2] *interlunations* Period between an old and a new moon; period of darkness.

alchemy turns to potable[1] gold the poisonous waters which flow from death through life; it strips the veil of familiarity from the world, and lays bare the naked and sleeping beauty which is the spirit of its forms.

All things exist as they are perceived: at least in relation to the percipient. "The mind is its own place, and of itself can make a heaven of hell, a hell of heaven."[2] But poetry defeats the curse which binds us to be subjected to the accident of surrounding impressions. And whether it spreads its own figured curtain or withdraws life's dark veil from before the scene of things, it equally creates for us a being within our being. It makes us the inhabitants of a world to which the familiar world is a chaos. It reproduces the common universe of which we are portions and percipients, and it purges from our inward sight the film of familiarity which obscures from us the wonder of our being. It compels us to feel that which we perceive, and to imagine that which we know. It creates anew the universe after it has been annihilated in our minds by the recurrence of impressions blunted by reiteration....

The first part of these remarks has related to Poetry in its elements and principles; and it has been shown, as well as the narrow limits assigned them would permit, that what is called poetry, in a restricted sense, has a common source with all other forms of order and of beauty according to which the materials of human life are susceptible of being arranged, and which is poetry in an universal sense.

The second part[3] will have for its object an application of these principles to the present state of the cultivation of Poetry, and a defence of the attempt to idealize the modern forms of manners and opinion, and compel them into a subordination to the imaginative and creative faculty. For the literature of England, an energetic development of which has ever preceded or accompanied a great and free development of the national will, has arisen as it were from a new birth. In spite of the low-thoughted envy which would undervalue contemporary merit, our own will be a memorable age in intellectual achievements, and we live among such philosophers and poets as surpass beyond comparison any who have appeared since the last national struggle for civil and religious liberty.[4] The most unfailing herald, companion, and follower of the awakening of a great people to work a beneficial change in opinion or institution, is Poetry. At such periods there is an accumulation of the power of communicating and receiving intense and impassioned conceptions respecting man and nature. The persons in whom this power resides, may often, as far as regards many portions of their nature, have little apparent correspondence with that spirit of good of which they are the ministers. But even whilst they deny and abjure, they are yet compelled to serve the Power which is seated upon the throne of their own soul. It is impossible to read the compositions of the most celebrated writers of the present day without being startled with the electric life which burns within their words. They measure the circumference and sound the depths of human nature with a comprehensive and all-penetrating spirit, and they are themselves perhaps the most sincerely astonished at its manifestations, for it is less their spirit than the spirit of the age. Poets are the hierophants[5] of an unapprehended inspiration, the mirrors of the gigantic shadows which futurity casts upon the present, the words which express what they understand not; the trumpets which sing to battle, and feel not what they inspire: the influence which is moved not, but moves.[6] Poets are the unacknowledged legislators of the World.

—1820

---

[1] *potable*   Drinkable. Alchemists sought a liquid form of gold that, when consumed, would be the elixir of life.

[2] *The mind ... heaven*   From Satan's speech in Milton's *Paradise Lost* 1.254–55.

[3] *The second part*   Shelley did not complete a second part.

[4] *the last ... liberty*   I.e., the English Civil War of the 1640s.

[5] *hierophants*   Interpreters of sacred mysteries.

[6] *is moved ... moves*   Reference to Greek philosopher Aristotle's description of God as the "Unmoved Mover" of the universe.

FELICIA HEMANS
1793 – 1835

Felicia Hemans was one of the first English poets to earn a living by writing. Her poetry was in many ways representative of the late Romantic and early Victorian eras, with an emphasis on religious, martial, and domestic themes, but several of her poems—perhaps most notably "Casabianca" and "The Homes of England"—remained enormously popular well into the twentieth century. Writing was in Hemans's day still widely considered incompatible with women's domestic bliss; some have argued that Hemans's own marriage failed because of her literary pursuits. It was certainly the case that, while her

work was widely read and widely praised, it was also occasionally mocked, and that gender was at the root of much of the ridicule. (Byron, for example, parodied her as "Mrs. Hewoman.")

Hemans was born Felicia Browne, the fifth of seven children of a Liverpool wine merchant and his wife, the daughter of a foreign diplomat. The failure of her father's business in 1799 caused the family to move to Wales; Felicia adored the country-side and it became the inspiration for much of her poetry. She learned several languages and a great deal about music from her mother, and benefited from a well-stocked family library. She loved Shakespeare as a child and was said to have had an excellent memory for reciting verse. Her own first published volume appeared in 1808, when she was only 14. Although *Poems* received some negative reviews, it sold 1,000 copies and she was encouraged to continue writing. Two of her brothers were then engaged in the British war against Spain and many of the poems are patriotic depictions of Britain in battle. Her brothers passed the volume on to one of their colleagues, Captain Alfred Hemans; he later became her husband. Percy Bysshe Shelley also received her first volume and began a correspondence with the young poet.

Felicia Browne married in 1812, shortly after the publication of her third volume of poetry, *The Domestic Affections and Other Poems*. She and her husband initially lived in her mother's house in Wales, a situation that would eventually prove uncomfortable for Captain Hemans. While Hemans continued to publish and become more popular, Captain Hemans became disillusioned with Wales and moved to Italy in 1818 on grounds of "ill health," never to see his wife again. From this point onwards she supported herself solely by her writing.

Hemans was one of very few British poets to have been in the prime of their writing careers in the 1810s and 1820s. She occupies something of an uneasy position between the Romantics and the Victorians. That she lived into Victoria's era and that her poetry retained a high degree of popularity through the Victorian period may have encouraged modern critics to see Hemans in the light of the standards of a later period; in the past critics perceived her poetry as characterized by powerful rhythms and powerful passions (even by emotional "gush"). And certainly the strength of form and of feeling in poems of patriotic fervor such as "The Homes of England" and "Casabianca" (both of which were learnt by heart by English schoolchildren into the twentieth century) is unquestionable. Yet in her own day, seen against the backdrop of the extravagant passions of Byron and other poets associated with the Romantic Movement, her poetry was praised for its formal and emotional restraint.

Though Hemans's most famous poems are short, she was also successful with longer works, notably the dramatic poem *The Siege of Valencia* (1823), which recounts the epic story of Elmira after her two sons are captured by a Moorish army. And she wrote innovative linked poems, such as those in *Records of Woman* (1828). Though she is often thought of as an important poet of domesticity, Hemans focused at least as much on women acting out their lives on a larger stage.

In 1821 Hemans was awarded the Royal Society of Literature's annual prize of £52.50 (a substantial amount at the time). She was then publishing regularly in British literary magazines, and from 1823, she was earning roughly £200 per year, enough to support herself and her five sons in some comfort. Her work was never out of print, and she was widely read in Britain and in America. The death of her mother in 1827 had a devastating effect on her, however, and from that point onwards she was plagued by poor health.

In her latter years, she rivaled Byron in popularity, and was highly sought after by budding poets and autograph-seekers. She found herself caught, however, between the success she needed to support herself and the masculine characteristics attributed to it, a theme she explores in "Women and Fame." In 1831 Hemans moved to Dublin to live with one of her brothers. She died there in 1835, of a weak heart and the effects of rheumatic fever.

⌘ ⌘ ⌘

The Homes of England

Where's the coward that would not dare
To fight for such a land?
　　　　　　　—MARMION[1]

The stately Homes of England,
　　How beautiful they stand!
Amidst their tall ancestral trees,
　　O'er all the pleasant land.
5　The deer across their greensward° bound　　　　*turf*
　　Thro' shade and sunny gleam,
And the swan glides past them with the sound
　　Of some rejoicing stream.

10　The merry Homes of England!
　　Around their hearths by night,
What gladsome looks of household love
　　Meet, in the ruddy° light!　　　　*red-hued*
There woman's voice flows forth in song,
　　Or childhood's tale is told,
15　Or lips move tunefully along
　　Some glorious page of old.

The blessed Homes of England!
　　How softly on their bowers°　　　　*arbors*
Is laid the holy quietness
20　　That breathes from Sabbath-hours!
Solemn, yet sweet, the church-bell's chime
　　Floats thro' their woods at morn;
All other sounds, in that still time,
　　Of breeze and leaf are born.

25　The Cottage Homes of England!
　　By thousands on her plains,
They are smiling o'er the silvery brooks,
　　And round the hamlet-fanes.[2]
Thro' glowing orchards forth they peep,
30　　Each from its nook of leaves,

---

[1] MARMION Walter Scott's *Marmion: A Tale of Flodden Field* (1808), 4.30. When first published in *Blackwood's Magazine*, the poem had instead the following epigraph from Joanna Baillie, *Ethwald: A Tragedy* (1802) 2.1.2.76–82:

　　A land of peace,
　　Where yellow fields unspoil'd, and pastures green,
　　Mottled with herds and flocks, who crop secure
　　Their native herbage, nor have ever known
　　A stranger's stall, smile gladly.
　　See through its tufted alleys to Heaven's roof
　　The curling smoke of quiet dwellings rise.

[2] *hamlet-fanes* Weather vanes of the village.

And fearless there the lowly sleep,
 As the bird beneath their eaves.

The free, fair Homes of England!
 Long, long, in hut and hall,
35 May hearts of native proof be rear'd
 To guard each hallow'd wall!
And green for ever be the groves,
 And bright the flowery sod,
Where first the child's glad spirit loves
40 Its country and its God!¹
 —1812

The Land of Dreams

 And dreams, in their development, have breath,
 And tears and tortures, and the touch of joy;
 They leave a weight upon our waking thoughts,
 They make us what we were not—what they will,
 And shake us with the vision that's gone by.
     —BYRON.²

Oh spirit land, thou land of dreams!
 A world thou art of mysterious gleams,
Of startling voices, and sounds at strife—
A world of the dead in the hues of life.

5 Like a wizard's magic-glass° thou art   *mirror*
When the wavy shadows float by, and part—
Visions of aspects, now loved, now strange,
Glimmering and mingling in ceaseless change.

Thou art like a city of the past
10 With its gorgeous halls into fragments cast,
Amidst whose ruins there glide and play
Familiar forms of the world's today.

Thou art like the depths where the seas have birth,
Rich with the wealth that is lost from earth—
15 All the sere° flowers of our days gone by,   *dry*
And the buried gems in thy bosom lie.

Yes, thou art like those dim sea-caves,
A realm of treasures, a realm of graves!
And the shapes through thy mysteries that come and go,
20 Are of beauty and terror, of power and woe.

But for me, oh thou picture-land of sleep,
Thou art all one world of affections deep—
And wrung from my heart is each flushing dye
That sweeps o'er thy chambers of imagery.

25 And thy bowers° are fair—even as Eden fair; *arbors*
All the beloved of my soul are there!
The forms my spirit most pines to see,
The eyes whose love hath been life to me:

They are there, and each blessed voice I hear,
30 Kindly, and joyous, and silvery clear;
But undertones are in each, that say,
"It is but a dream; it will melt away!"

I walk with sweet friends in the sunset's glow;
I listen to music of long ago;
35 But one thought, like an omen, breathes faint through
  the lay³—
"It is but a dream; it will melt away!"

I sit by the hearth of my early days;
All the home-faces are met by the blaze,
And the eyes of the mother shine soft, yet say,
40 "It is but a dream; it will melt away!"

And away, like a flower's passing breath, 'tis gone,
And I wake more sadly, more deeply lone—
Oh, a haunted heart is a weight to bear!
Bright faces, kind voices, where are ye, where?

45 Shadow not forth, oh thou land of dreams,
The past, as it fled by my own blue streams!
Make not my spirit within me burn
For the scenes and the hours that may ne'er return!

Call out from the future thy visions bright,
50 From the world o'er the grave, take thy solemn light,
And oh! with the loved, whom no more I see,
Show me my home as it yet may be!

---

¹ [Hemans's note]   Originally published in *Blackwood's Magazine*.
[1828.]

² *And dreams … BYRON* From "The Dream," by George Gordon,
Lord Byron (1788–1824).

³ *lay* Medieval narrative song or poem.

As it yet may be in some purer sphere,
No cloud, no parting, no sleepless fear;
55 So my soul may bear on through the long, long day,
Till I go where the beautiful melts not away!
—1821

Evening Prayer at a Girls' School

Now in thy youth, beseech of Him,
    Who giveth, upbraiding° not,   *sharply scolding*
That his light in thy heart become not dim,
    And his love be unforgot;
And thy God, in the darkest of days, will be
Greenness, and beauty, and strength to thee.[1]
                                    BERNARD BARTON.

Hush! 'tis a holy hour—the quiet room
    Seems like a temple, while yon soft lamp sheds
A faint and starry radiance, through the gloom
    And the sweet stillness, down on bright young heads,
5 With all their clust'ring locks, untouch'd by care,
And bow'd, as flowers are bow'd with night—in prayer.

Gaze on,—'tis lovely!—childhood's lip and cheek,
    Mantling[2] beneath its earnest brow of thought—
Gaze—yet what seest thou in those fair, and meek,
10   And fragile things, as but for sunshine wrought?
—Thou seest what grief must nurture for the sky,
What death must fashion for eternity!

Oh! joyous creatures, that will sink to rest,
    Lightly, when those pure orisons° are done,   *prayers*
15 As birds with slumber's honey-dew oppress'd,
    'Midst the dim folded leaves, at set of sun—
Lift up your hearts!—though yet no sorrow lies
Dark in the summer-heaven of those clear eyes;

Though fresh within your breasts th'untroubled springs
20   Of hope make melody where'er ye tread;
And o'er your sleep bright shadows, from the wings
    Of spirits visiting but youth, be spread;

Yet in those flute-like voices, mingling low,
Is woman's tenderness—how soon her woe!°   *sorrow*

25 Her lot° is on you—silent tears to weep,   *fate*
    And patient smiles to wear through suffering's hour,
And sumless riches, from Affection's deep,
    To pour on broken reeds—a wasted shower!
And to make idols, and to find them clay,[3]
30 And to bewail that worship—therefore pray!

Her lot is on you—to be found untir'd,
    Watching the stars out by the bed of pain,
With a pale cheek, and yet a brow inspir'd,
    And a true heart of hope, though hope be vain.
35 Meekly to bear with wrong, to cheer decay,
And oh! to love through all things—therefore pray!

And take the thought of this calm vesper°   *evening prayer*
    time,
    With its low murmuring sounds and silvery light,
Or through the dark days fading from their prime,
40   As a sweet dew to keep your souls from blight.
Earth will forsake—oh! happy to have given
Th'unbroken heart's first fragrance unto Heaven!
—1825

Casabianca [4]

The boy stood on the burning deck,
    Whence all but him had fled;
The flame that lit the battle's wreck,
    Shone round him o'er the dead.

---

[1] *Now in ... strength to thee* "The Ivy, Addressed to a Young Friend" (1825), 43–48, by Bernard Barton (1784–1849).

[2] *Mantling* Blushing, coloring from emotion.

[3] *And to ... clay* See Daniel 2.31–45.

[4] [Hemans's note] Young Casabianca, a boy about thirteen years old, son to the admiral of the Orient, remained at his post (in the battle of the Nile), after the ship had taken fire, and all the guns had been abandoned; and perished in the explosion of the vessel, when the flames had reached the powder. [The British fleet, commanded by Horatio Nelson, defeated Napoleon's fleet, commanded by Louis de Casabianca, at the battle of the Nile on 1 August 1798. Among those killed when the French flagship, *L'Orient*, exploded were the Admiral and his son, Giacomo Jocante Casabianca (who in fact was only ten). Hemans's source is probably Southey, *Life of Horatio, Lord Nelson* (1813). The poem was first published in the *Monthly Magazine*.]

5   Yet beautiful and bright he stood,
        As born to rule the storm;
    A creature of heroic blood,
        A proud, though child-like form.

    The flames roll'd on—he would not go,
10   Without his father's word;
    That father, faint in death below,
        His voice no longer heard.

    He call'd aloud—"Say, father, say
        If yet my task is done?"
15 He knew not that the chieftain lay
        Unconscious of his son.

    "Speak, Father!" once again he cried,
        "If I may yet be gone!"
    —And but the booming shots replied,
20   And fast the flames roll'd on.

    Upon his brow he felt their breath,
        And in his waving hair;
    And look'd from that lone post of death,
        In still, yet brave despair.

25 And shouted but once more aloud,
        "My father! must I stay?"
    While o'er him fast, through sail and shroud,
        The wreathing fires made way.

    They wrapt the ship in splendor wild,
30   They caught the flag on high,
    And stream'd above the gallant child,
        Like banners in the sky.

    There came a burst of thunder sound—
        The boy—oh! where was he?
35 —Ask of the winds that far around
        With fragments strew'd the sea!

    With mast, and helm, and pennon[1] fair,
        That well had borne their part—
    But the noblest thing that perish'd there,
40   Was that young faithful heart.
    —1826

---

[1]   *pennon* Banner or flag.

Corinne at the Capitol[2]

Les femmes doivent penser qu'il est dans cette carrière
bien peu de sort qui puissent valoir la plus obscure vie
d'une femme aimée et d'une mère heureuse.[3]
                                    —MADAME DE STAËL.

Daughter of th'Italian heaven!
    Thou, to whom its fires are given,
Joyously thy car° hath roll'd   *chariot*
Where the conqueror's pass'd of old;
5   And the festal° sun that shone,   *festive*
O'er three hundred triumphs gone,[4]
Makes thy day of glory bright,
With a shower of golden light.

Now thou tread'st th'ascending road,
10 Freedom's foot so proudly trode;[5]
While, from tombs of heroes borne,
From the dust of empire shorn,
Flowers upon thy graceful head,
Chaplets[6] of all hues, are shed,
15 In a soft and rosy rain,
Touch'd with many a gemlike stain.

Thou hast gain'd the summit now!
Music hails thee from below;
Music, whose rich notes might stir
20 Ashes of the sepulchre;°   *tomb*
Shaking with victorious notes
All the bright air as it floats.

---

[2]   *Corinne at the Capitol* Based on the novel *Corinne, ou l'Italie* (1807), by Germaine de Staël (1766–1817). Corinne is an Italian improvisatrice—a poet who improvises verses in public. The English Lord Nelvil first sees her when she is being honored at the Capitol, in Rome. They fall in love and he offers to marry her, but she declines, preferring her independence. When he marries her half-sister instead, she dies of a broken heart. The poem was first published in *The Literary Souvenir* for 1827 (1826) 189–91.

[3]   *Les femmes … heureuse* French: "Women must reflect that there are in this career [of glory] very few destinies that can equal in worth the most obscure life of a beloved wife and happy mother." See de Staël, *De l'Influence des passions sur le bonheur des individus et des nations* (1796) ch. 3.

[4]   [Hemans's note] The trebly hundred triumphs.—Byron. [See "Childe Harold's Pilgrimage" 4.82 (1818)]; *triumph* Ancient Roman celebration of a military victory; there were a total of 320.

[5]   *trode* Archaic past tense of "tread."

[6]   *Chaplets* Garlands of flowers worn on the head.

Well may woman's heart beat high
  Unto that proud harmony!

25 Now afar it rolls—it dies—
And thy voice is heard to rise
With a low and lovely tone
In its thrilling power alone;
And thy lyre's deep silvery string,
30 Touch'd as by a breeze's wing,
Murmurs tremblingly at first,
Ere° the tide of rapture burst.   *before*

All the spirit of thy sky
Now hath lit thy large dark eye,
35 And thy cheek a flush hath caught
From the joy of kindled thought;
And the burning words of song
From thy lip flow fast and strong,
With a rushing stream's delight
40 In the freedom of its might.

Radiant daughter of the sun!
Now thy living wreath is won.
Crown'd of Rome!—Oh! art thou not
Happy in that glorious lot?°—   *fate*
45 Happier, happier far than thou,
With the laurel on thy brow,[1]
She that makes the humblest hearth
Lovely but to one on earth!
   —1826

The Effigies[2]

Der rasche Kampf verewigt einen Mann:
Er falle gleich, so preiset ihn das Lied.
Allein die Thränen, die unendlichen
Der überbliebnen, der verlass'nen Frau,
Zählt keine Nachwelt.[3]
     —GOETHE

[1] *laurel on ... brow* Poets were traditionally honored with crowns of laurel, which was sacred to Apollo.

[2] *Effigies* Sculptural representations of people, often upon their tombs.

[3] *Der rasche ... Nachwelt* German: "Rash combat oft immortalizes man. / If he should fall, he is renowned in song; / But after ages reckon not the tears / Which ceaseless the forsaken woman sheds." (Goethe, *Iphigenie* 5.6. English translation by Anna Swanwick [1909–14].)

Warrior! whose image on thy tomb,
  With shield and crested head,
Sleeps proudly in the purple gloom
  By the stain'd window shed;
5 The records of thy name and race
  Have faded from the stone,
Yet, through a cloud of years, I trace
  What thou hast been and done.

A banner, from its flashing spear,
10   Flung out o'er many a fight;
A war-cry ringing far and clear,
  And strong to turn the flight;
An arm that bravely bore the lance
  On for the holy shrine;
15 A haughty heart and a kingly glance—
  Chief! were not these things thine?

A lofty place where leaders sate°   *sat*
  Around the council-board;°   *table*
In festive halls a chair of state
20   When the blood-red wine was pour'd;
A name that drew a prouder tone
  From herald, harp, and bard;°   *court poet*
Surely these things were all thine own,—
  So hadst thou thy reward.

25 Woman! whose sculptur'd form at rest
  By the armed knight is laid,
With meek hands folded o'er a breast
  In matron robes array'd;
What was thy tale?—Oh! gentle mate
30   Of him, the bold and free,
Bound unto his victorious fate,
  What bard hath sung of *thee*?

He woo'd a bright and burning star—
  Thine was the void, the gloom,
35 The straining eye that follow'd far
  His fast-receding plume;
The heart-sick listening while his steed
  Sent echoes on the breeze;
The pang—but when did *Fame* take heed
40   Of griefs obscure as these?

Thy silent and secluded hours
    Thro' many a lonely day,
While bending o'er thy broider'd° flowers,   *embroidered*
    With spirit far away;
45 Thy weeping midnight prayers for him
    Who fought on Syrian plains,
Thy watchings till the torch grew dim—
    These fill no minstrel strains.

A still, sad life was thine!—long years
50   With tasks unguerdon'd° fraught,   *unrewarded*
Deep, quiet love, submissive tears,
    Vigils of anxious thought;
Prayer at the cross in fervour pour'd,
    Alms[1] to the pilgrim given—
55 Oh! happy, happier than thy lord,
    In that lone path to heaven!
        —1826

The Image in Lava[2]

Thou thing of years departed!
    What ages have gone by,
Since here the mournful seal was set
    By love and agony!

5   Temple and tower have moulder'd,
    Empires from earth have pass'd,—
And woman's heart hath left a trace
    Those glories to outlast!

And childhood's fragile image
10   Thus fearfully enshrin'd,
Survives the proud memorials rear'd
    By conquerors of mankind.

Babe! wert thou brightly slumbering
    Upon thy mother's breast,
15 When suddenly the fiery tomb
    Shut round each gentle guest?

A strange, dark fate o'ertook you,
    Fair babe and loving heart!
One moment of a thousand pangs—
20   Yet better than to part!

Haply° of that fond bosom,   *by chance*
    On ashes here impress'd,
Thou wert the only treasure, child!
    Whereon a hope might rest.

25 Perchance all vainly lavish'd,
    Its other love had been,
And where it trusted, nought remain'd
    But thorns on which to lean.

Far better then to perish,
30   Thy form within its clasp,
Than live and lose thee, precious one!
    From that impassion'd grasp.

Oh! I could pass all relics
    Left by the pomps of old,
35 To gaze on this rude° monument,   *primitive*
    Cast in affection's mould.

Love, human love! what art thou?
    Thy print upon the dust
Outlives the cities of renown
40   Wherein the mighty trust!

Immortal, oh! immortal
    Thou art, whose earthly glow
Hath given these ashes holiness—
    It must, it must be so!
        —1827

---

1   *Alms* Money given in charity to the poor.

2   [Hemans's note] The impression of a woman's form, with an infant clasped to the bosom, found at the uncovering of Herculaneum. [Herculaneum and Pompeii were destroyed by the eruption of Vesuvius in 79 CE. The image is one of the casts made during the excavations (1763–1820) by pouring plaster into the holes left in the lava by the victims' bodies. The poem was first published in the *New Monthly Magazine* in 1827.]

Properzia Rossi

(Properzia Rossi,[1] a celebrated female sculptor of Bologna, possessed also of talents for poetry and music, died in consequence of an unrequited attachment.—A painting, by Ducis,[2] represents her showing her last work, a basso-relievo of Ariadne,[3] to a Roman knight, the object of her affection, who regards it with indifference.)

> —Tell me no more, no more
> Of my soul's lofty gifts! Are they not vain
> To quench its haunting thirst for happiness?
> Have I not lov'd, and striven, and fail'd to bind
> One true heart unto me, whereon my own
> Might find a resting-place, a home for all
> Its burden of affections? I depart,
> Unknown, tho' Fame goes with me; I must leave
> The earth unknown. Yet it may be that death
> Shall give my name a power to win such tears
> As would have made life precious.[4]

1

O ne dream of passion and of beauty more!
And in its bright fulfilment let me pour
My soul away! Let earth retain a trace
Of that which lit my being, tho' its race
5   Might have been loftier far.—Yet one more dream!
From my deep spirit one victorious gleam
Ere I depart! For thee alone, for thee!
May this last work, this farewell triumph be,
Thou, loved so vainly! I would leave enshrined
10   Something immortal of my heart and mind,
That yet may speak to thee when I am gone,
Shaking thine inmost bosom with a tone
Of lost affection;—something that may prove
What she hath been, whose melancholy love
15   On thee was lavish'd; silent pang and tear,

And fervent song, that gush'd when none were near,
And dream by night, and weary thought by day,
Stealing the brightness from her life away,—
While thou—Awake! not yet within me die,
20   Under the burden and the agony
Of this vain tenderness,—my spirit, wake!
Ev'n for thy sorrowful affection's sake,
Live! in thy work breathe out!—that he may yet,
Feeling sad mastery there, perchance regret
25   Thine unrequited gift.

2

It comes,—the power
Within me born, flows back; my fruitless dower°   *dowry*
That could not win me love. Yet once again
I greet it proudly, with its rushing train
Of glorious images:—they throng—they press—
30   A sudden joy lights up my loneliness,—
I shall not perish all![5]
The bright work grows
Beneath my hand, unfolding, as a rose,
Leaf after leaf, to beauty; line by line,
I fix my thought, heart, soul, to burn, to shine,
35   Thro' the pale marble's veins. It grows—and now
I give my own life's history to thy brow,
Forsaken Ariadne! thou shalt wear
My form, my lineaments;[6] but oh! more fair,
Touch'd into lovelier being by the glow
40   Which in me dwells, as by the summer-light
All things are glorified. From thee my woe
Shall yet look beautiful to meet his sight,
When I am pass'd away. Thou art the mould
Wherein I pour the fervent thoughts, th'untold,
45   The self-consuming! Speak to him of me,
Thou, the deserted by the lonely sea,
With the soft sadness of thine earnest eye,
Speak to him, lorn° one! deeply, mournfully,   *forlorn*
Of all my love and grief! Oh! could I throw
50   Into thy frame a voice, a sweet, and low,
And thrilling voice of song! when he came nigh,
To send the passion of its melody
Thro' his pierced bosom—on its tones to bear
My life's deep feeling, as the southern air

---

[1]   *Properzia Rossi*   Properzia de'Rossi (c.1491–1530), Bolognese sculptor, painter, and poet.

[2]   *Ducis*   Louis Ducis (1775–1847), *Properzia de'Rossi and her Last Bas-relief.*

[3]   *basso-relievo*   Relief sculpture; *Ariadne* Cretan princess who helped Theseus find his way through the labyrinth and kill the Minotaur. They eloped, but he abandoned her on the island of Naxos. See Ovid (43 BCE–17 CE), *Heroides* 10.

[4]   *Tell me ... precious*   The epigraph is by Hemans herself.

[5]   *I shall ... all*   Cf. Horace, *Odes* 3.30.6.

[6]   *lineaments*   Distinctive shapes.

55 Wafts the faint myrtle's[1] breath,—to rise, to swell,
To sink away in accents of farewell,
Winning but one, one gush of tears, whose flow
Surely my parted spirit yet might know,
If love be strong as death!

                    3
                Now fair thou art,
60 Thou form, whose life is of my burning heart!
Yet all the vision that within me wrought,
    I cannot make thee! Oh! I might have given
Birth to creations of far nobler thought,
    I might have kindled, with the fire of heaven,
65 Things not of such as die! But I have been
Too much alone;[2] a heart whereon to lean,
With all these deep affections, that o'erflow
My aching soul, and find no shore below;
An eye to be my star, a voice to bring
70 Hope o'er my path, like sounds that breathe of spring,
These are denied me—dreamt of still in vain,—
Therefore my brief aspirings from the chain,
Are ever but as some wild fitful° song,   *irregular*
Rising triumphantly, to die ere° long   *before*
75 In dirge-like[3] echoes.

                    4
                Yet the world will see
Little of this, my parting work, in thee,
    Thou shalt have fame! Oh, mockery! give the reed
From storms a shelter,—give the drooping vine
Something round, which its tendrils may entwine,—
80   Give the parch'd flower a rain-drop, and the
            meed°   *reward*
Of love's kind words to woman! Worthless fame!
That in *his* bosom wins not for my name
Th'abiding place it ask'd! Yet how my heart,
In its own fairy world of song and art,
85 Once beat for praise!—Are those high longings o'er?
That which I have been can I be no more?—
Never, oh! never more; tho' still thy sky
Be blue as then, my glorious Italy!

And tho' the music, whose rich breathings fill
90 Thine air with soul, be wandering past me still,
And tho' the mantle° of thy sunlight streams,   *cloak*
Unchang'd on forms, instinct with poet-dreams;
Never, oh! never more! Where'er I move,
The shadow of this broken-hearted love
95 Is on me and around! Too well *they* know,
    Whose life is all within, too soon and well,
When there the blight hath settled;—but I go
    Under the silent wings of peace to dwell;
From the slow wasting, from the lonely pain,
100 The inward burning of those words—"*in vain*,"
    Sear'd on the heart—I go. 'Twill soon be past.
Sunshine, and song, and bright Italian heaven,
    And thou, oh! thou, on whom my spirit cast
Unvalued wealth,—who know'st not what was given
105 In that devotedness,—the sad, and deep,
And unrepaid—farewell! If I could weep
Once, only once, belov'd one! on thy breast,
Pouring my heart forth ere I sink to rest!
But that were happiness, and unto me
110 Earth's gift is *fame*. Yet I was form'd to be
So richly blest! With thee to watch the sky,
Speaking not, feeling but that thou wert nigh;
With thee to listen, while the tones of song
Swept ev'n as part of our sweet air along,
115 To listen silently;—with thee to gaze
On forms, the deified of olden days,
This had been joy enough;—and hour by hour,
From its glad well-springs drinking life and power,
How had my spirit soar'd, and made its fame
120   A glory for thy brow!—Dreams, dreams!—the fire
Burns faint within me. Yet I leave my name—
    As a deep thrill may linger on the lyre[4]
When its full chords are hush'd—awhile to live,
And one day haply in thy heart revive
125 Sad thoughts of me:—I leave it, with a sound,
A spell o'er memory, mournfully profound,
I leave it, on my country's air to dwell,—
Say proudly yet—"'Twas hers who lov'd me well!"
    —1828

---

[1] *myrtle's* Belonging to the myrtle, a Mediterranean evergreen
shrub bearing pink flowers and black berries.

[2] *Too … alone* Cf. Byron, *Mazeppa* (1819), 839.

[3] *dirge-like* Like a funeral hymn, solemn and mournful.

---

[4] *lyre* Stringed instrument.

Woman and Fame

Happy—happier far than thou,
With the laurel on thy brow;[1]
She that makes the humblest hearth,
Lovely but to one on earth.[2]

Thou hast a charmed cup, O Fame!
    A draught that mantles[3] high,
And seems to lift this earthly frame
    Above mortality.
5 Away! to me—a woman—bring
Sweet waters from affection's spring.

Thou hast green laurel leaves, that twine
    Into so proud a wreath;
For that resplendent gift of thine,
10   Heroes have smiled in death:
Give *me* from some kind hand a flower,
The record of one happy hour!

15 Thou hast a voice, whose thrilling tone
    Can bid each life-pulse beat
As when a trumpet's note hath blown,
    Calling the brave to meet:
But mine, let mine—a woman's breast,
By words of home-born love be bless'd.

A hollow sound is in thy song,
20 A mockery in thine eye,
To the sick heart that doth but long
    For aid, for sympathy—
For kindly looks to cheer it on,
For tender accents that are gone.

25 Fame, Fame! thou canst not be the stay°   prop
    Unto the drooping reed,
The cool fresh fountain in the day
    Of the soul's feverish need:
Where must the lone one turn or flee?—
30 Not unto thee—oh! not to thee!
                            —1829

---

[1] *laurel on ... brow* Poets were traditionally honored with crowns
of laurel, which was sacred to Apollo.

[2] *Happy—happier ... earth* Paraphrased from Hemans's own
"Corinne at the Capitol" (ll. 45–8).

[3] *mantles* Here, foams.

JOHN KEATS
1795 – 1821

John Keats has come to epitomize the popular conception of the Romantic poet as a passionate dreamer whose intense, sensuous poetry celebrates the world of the imagination over that of everyday life. Keats published only 54 poems in his short lifetime, but his work ranges across a number of poetic genres, including sonnets, odes, romances, and epics. In each of these genres his poetry seeks beauty and truth that will transcend the world of suffering, always questioning its own process of interpretation.

The eldest of four children, John Keats was born in London on 31 October 1795. He lost both his parents by the time he was fourteen—his father in a riding accident and his mother of tuberculosis (then commonly known as consumption). After his mother's death, Keats came under the care of two guardians. He continued to attend Enfield School, a liberal institution where he first became acquainted with Leigh Hunt's radical paper the *Examiner*, and where his interest in poetry grew, particularly after reading the poetry of Edmund Spenser. Keats's friend Charles Brown said it was *The Faerie Queene* that awakened Keats's talent for expressing the "acute sense of beauty" he possessed.

After a promising but incomplete schooling, Keats apprenticed himself in 1815 to a surgeon at Guy's Hospital in London. (He remained licensed as an apothecary until 1817.) Having befriended some of the most prolific artists and critics of his day, among them radical publisher Leigh Hunt, essayist Charles Lamb, painter Benjamin Haydon, and poets John Hamilton Reynolds and Percy Shelley (later to eulogize Keats in *Adonais*), Keats was spurred to further develop his own creative abilities. In 1816, after spending a night reading a translation of Homer with his school friend Cowden Clarke, Keats wrote "On First Looking into Chapman's Homer" (1816), a sonnet that presents a poet reflecting on poetic tradition and discovering his talent, as an explorer surveys "with a wild surmise" another ocean of possibility.

Shortly thereafter, Keats composed "Sleep and Poetry" (1817), a poetic manifesto of sorts in which he proclaims his devotion to a new type of poetry, one in the style of Wordsworth, devoted to nature and the human heart. By aligning himself with Wordsworth's naturalism, Keats ensured the condemnation of critics; nevertheless, that same year he chose to give up surgery and devote himself entirely to poetry. This decision was most likely sealed by Leigh Hunt's first "Young Poets" article (*Examiner*, December 1816), in which he identified Keats, Shelley, and Reynolds as the leaders of a new generation of poets.

Keats's first volume, *Poems* (1817), received little critical attention. The following year he published the long and ambitious romance *Endymion* (1818), about a shepherd-prince who pursues his elusive feminine ideal. The book was sharply criticized in a famous review published in the *Quarterly Review*, where Keats and his friend Hunt were ridiculed as representing "the Cockney school of poetry." Keats endured further criticism when he read "Hymn to Pan" from *Endymion* to the contemporary poet he most admired, Wordsworth; the elder poet ungenerously dismissed it as "a very pretty piece of paganism."

His hopes undimmed, Keats continued to pursue his poetic ideals. In a series of now-famous letters to Benjamin Bailey, he explored his aesthetic ideas and sought to define the purpose of literature for modern life. Keats's letters to his friends and family are justly acclaimed for their intuitions about life, suffering, and poetry. To Keats we owe the concepts of "negative capability," the "chameleon poet," and "the vale of Soul-making." He particularly admired what he saw as Shakespeare's chameleon-like ability to escape from his personality and enter fully into the being of his characters.

During this time, Keats fell in love with the lively and flirtatious Fanny Brawne, who became a kind of muse. Though they became engaged, Keats wanted to gain financial security before marrying. He had begun as well to be haunted by fears of his own early death. (Throat ulcers that had appeared during a walking tour in poor weather the previous summer had become chronic.) It was in this set of tumultuous emotional circumstances that Keats began one of the most extraordinary periods of creativity in the history of English literature. Between January and September of 1819 he composed all of his "great Odes"—"Ode to Psyche," "Ode to a Nightingale," "Ode on a Grecian Urn," "Ode on Indolence," "Ode on Melancholy," and "To Autumn"—as well as "The Eve of St. Agnes," "La Belle Dame sans Merci," "Lamia," and a number of sonnets. "The Eve of St. Agnes" remains Keats's best-known narrative poem. Suffused with amorous feeling and lush imagery, "The Eve of St. Agnes" recounts a romantic story with affinities to the story of Romeo and Juliet. Generations of readers have been seduced by the sensuous immediacy of this poetry.

Keats's largest poetic project was *Hyperion*, a blank-verse epic on Jupiter's dethroning of Saturn and Apollo's overthrow of Hyperion. An intense study of cultural loss, the poem is a self-consciously Miltonic exercise that Keats kept returning to but never completed. He began the poem in the autumn of 1818, but put the manuscript aside in April of the following year. (This first fragmentary version of the poem was published as "Hyperion: A Fragment" in the 1820 volume of his verse.)

In the summer he resumed work on the project, this time casting the story within the frame of a poet's dream vision, but he stopped for a second time in September. (This second version, also fragmentary, was finally published in 1856 as "The Fall of Hyperion.")

When Keats's extraordinary poetic outpouring of 1819 was coming to a close, he began to suspect himself inadequate to the task of undertaking a Miltonic epic. As he wrote to his friend John Reynolds on 21 September 1819:

I have given up Hyperion ... Miltonic verse cannot be written but in an artful or rather artist's humour. I wish to give myself up to other sensations. English ought to be kept up.

Keats wrote little after September of 1819, but he published his third volume of poetry, *Lamia, Isabella, The Eve of St. Agnes, and Other Poems*, in 1820—defiantly advertising himself on the cover as "the author of *Endymion*." Critics were gradually acquiring a taste for Keats's work, but by this time Keats was very ill, having contracted tuberculosis. His lungs weakened and his throat still ulcerating, in August of 1820 Keats declined an invitation to join Shelley and his circle in Pisa, and instead went to Rome, where he died in the house at the base of the Spanish Steps that is now the Keats-Shelley Memorial House. Keats was buried in the Protestant Cemetery in Rome.

In the generations since his death many have wondered what Keats would have accomplished had he lived. Such thoughts, however, focus on the tragedy of the poet's death, rather than on the sustained richness of his achievement. Before his death, Keats asked that his epitaph be "Here lies one whose name was writ in water." (Though his friends complied, they added above, "This Grave contains all that was Mortal of a YOUNG ENGLISH POET, Who on his Death Bed in the Bitterness of his Heart at the Malicious Power of his Enemies, Desired these Words to be incised on his Tomb Stone.") On visiting his gravesite in 1877, Oscar Wilde supplied another epitaph: "A Priest of Beauty slain before his time." But the last sentences of Keats's last letter to Charles Brown are perhaps more evocative: "I can scarcely bid you good bye even in a letter. I always made an awkward bow."

⌘ ⌘ ⌘

On First Looking into Chapman's Homer[1]

Much have I travell'd in the realms of gold,
    And many goodly states and kingdoms seen;
    Round many western islands have I been
Which bards in fealty to Apollo[2] hold.
Oft of one wide expanse had I been told   5
    That deep-brow'd Homer ruled as his demesne;
    Yet never did I breathe its pure serene,
Till I heard Chapman speak out loud and bold:
Then felt I like some watcher of the skies
    When a new planet swims into his ken;[3]   10
Or like stout Cortez[4] when with eagle eyes
    He star'd at the Pacific—and all his men
Look'd at each other with a wild surmise—
    Silent, upon a peak in Darien.
                                    —1816

On the Grasshopper and Cricket

The poetry of earth is never dead:
    When all the birds are faint with the hot sun,
    And hide in cooling trees, a voice will run
From hedge to hedge about the new-mown mead;
That is the Grasshopper's—he takes the lead   5
    In summer luxury—he has never done
    With his delights; for when tired out with fun

He rests at ease beneath some pleasant weed.
The poetry of earth is ceasing never:
    On a lone winter evening, when the frost   10
    Has wrought a silence, from the stove there shrills
The Cricket's song, in warmth increasing ever,
    And seems to one in drowsiness half lost,
    The Grasshopper's among some grassy hills.
                                    —1817

Sleep and Poetry

As I lay in my bed slepe full unmete°   *unallotted*
Was unto me, but why that I ne might
Rest I ne wist,° for there n'as° erthly   *knew / was no*
    wight°   *creature*
[As I suppose] had more of hertis ese°   *heart's ease*
Than I, for I n'ad° sicknesse nor disese.[5]   *had not*
                                            CHAUCER

What is more gentle than a wind in summer?
    What is more soothing than the pretty hummer
That stays one moment in an open flower,
And buzzes cheerily from bower to bower?
What is more tranquil than a musk-rose   5
    blowing°   *blossoming*
In a green island, far from all men's knowing?
More healthful than the leafiness of dales?
More secret than a nest of nightingales?
More serene than Cordelia's[6] countenance?
More full of visions than a high romance?   10
What, but thee Sleep? Soft closer of our eyes!
Low murmurer of tender lullabies!
Light hoverer around our happy pillows!
Wreather of poppy buds, and weeping willows!

---

[1] *On ... Homer* Written in October 1816, on the morning after Keats and his friend and mentor Charles Cowden Clarke had stayed up all night reading the 1614 translation of Homer by George Chapman (1559–1634).

[2] *Apollo* Greek god of poetry.

[3] *a new ... ken* William Herschel had discovered Uranus in 1781.

[4] *Cortez* The first European to see the Pacific (from the Isthmus of Darien in Panama) was not actually Hernán Cortez (1485–1547), the conqueror of Mexico, but Vasco Nuñez de Balboa in 1513 (1475–1519).

[5] *As ... disese* From *The Floure and the Leafe* 17–21, which was then thought to have been written by Chaucer.

[6] *Cordelia* Daughter of King Lear in Shakespeare's *King Lear*.

15 Silent entangler of a beauty's tresses!
Most happy listener! when the morning blesses
Thee for enlivening all the cheerful eyes
That glance so brightly at the new sun-rise.

But what is higher beyond thought than thee?
20 Fresher than berries of a mountain tree?
More strange, more beautiful, more smooth, more
     regal,
Than wings of swans, than doves, than dim-seen eagle?
What is it? And to what shall I compare it?
It has a glory, and naught else can share it:
25 The thought thereof is awful, sweet, and holy,
Chasing away all worldliness and folly;
Coming sometimes like fearful claps of thunder,
Or the low rumblings earth's regions under;
And sometimes like a gentle whispering
30 Of all the secrets of some wond'rous thing
That breathes about us in the vacant air;
So that we look around with prying stare,
Perhaps to see shapes of light, aërial limning,[1]
And catch soft floatings from a faint-heard hymning;
35 To see the laurel wreath,[2] on high suspended,
That is to crown our name when life is ended.
Sometimes it gives a glory to the voice,
And from the heart up-springs, "Rejoice! rejoice!"
Sounds which will reach the Framer of all things,
40 And die away in ardent mutterings.

No one who once the glorious sun has seen,
And all the clouds, and felt his bosom clean
For his great Maker's presence, but must know
What 'tis I mean, and feel his being glow:
45 Therefore no insult will I give his spirit,
By telling what he sees from native merit.

O Poesy! For thee I hold my pen
That am not yet a glorious denizen
Of thy wide heaven—Should I rather kneel
50 Upon some mountain-top until I feel

A glowing splendour round about me hung,
And echo back the voice of thine own tongue?
O Poesy! For thee I grasp my pen
That am not yet a glorious denizen
55 Of thy wide heaven; yet, to my ardent prayer,
Yield from thy sanctuary some clear air,
Smoothed for intoxication by the breath
Of flowering bays, that I may die a death
Of luxury, and my young spirit follow
60 The morning sun-beams to the great Apollo[3]
Like a fresh sacrifice; or, if I can bear
The o'erwhelming sweets, 'twill bring to me the fair
Visions of all places: a bowery nook
Will be elysium[4]—an eternal book
65 Whence I may copy many a lovely saying
About the leaves, and flowers—about the playing
Of nymphs in woods, and fountains; and the shade
Keeping a silence round a sleeping maid;
And many a verse from so strange influence
70 That we must ever wonder how, and whence
It came. Also imaginings will hover
Round my fire-side, and haply there discover
Vistas of solemn beauty, where I'd wander
In happy silence, like the clear Meander[5]
75 Through its lone vales; and where I found a spot
Of awfuller shade, or an enchanted grot,°   grotto
Or a green hill o'erspread with chequered dress
Of flowers, and fearful from its loveliness,
Write on my tablets all that was permitted,
80 All that was for our human senses fitted.
Then the events of this wide world I'd seize
Like a strong giant, and my spirit tease
Till at its shoulders it should proudly see
Wings to find out an immortality.

85 Stop and consider! Life is but a day;
A fragile dew-drop on its perilous way
From a tree's summit; a poor Indian's sleep
While his boat hastens to the monstrous steep

---

[1] *limning* Painting.

[2] *laurel wreath* Wreaths made of leaves of the bay laurel were traditionally bestowed upon those who distinguished themselves in poetry.

[3] *Apollo* Greek god of poetry.

[4] *elysium* State of perfect happiness. From the Elysium of Greek mythology, the place where the blessed reside after death.

[5] *Meander* Winding river in Asia Minor.

Of Montmorenci.[1] Why so sad a moan?
90 Life is the rose's hope while yet unblown;
The reading of an ever-changing tale;
The light uplifting of a maiden's veil;
A pigeon tumbling in clear summer air;
A laughing school-boy, without grief or care,
95 Riding the springy branches of an elm.

O for ten years, that I may overwhelm
Myself in poesy; so I may do the deed
That my own soul has to itself decreed.
Then will I pass the countries that I see
100 In long perspective, and continually
Taste their pure fountains. First the realm I'll pass
Of Flora, and old Pan:[2] sleep in the grass,
Feed upon apples red, and strawberries,
And choose each pleasure that my fancy sees;
105 Catch the white-handed nymphs in shady places,
To woo sweet kisses from averted faces,
Play with their fingers, touch their shoulders white
Into a pretty shrinking with a bite
As hard as lips can make it: till agreed,
110 A lovely tale of human life we'll read
And one will teach a tame dove how it best
May fan the cool air gently o'er my rest;
Another, bending o'er her nimble tread,
Will set a green robe floating round her head,
115 And still will dance with ever varied ease,
Smiling upon the flowers and the trees:
Another will entice me on, and on
Through almond blossoms and rich cinnamon;
Till in the bosom of a leafy world
120 We rest in silence, like two gems upcurl'd
In the recesses of a pearly shell.

And can I ever bid these joys farewell?
Yes, I must pass them for a nobler life,
Where I may find the agonies, the strife
125 Of human hearts: for lo! I see afar,

---

[1] *Montmorenci* Montmorency Falls near Québec City, Canada.

[2] *Flora ... Pan* In Greek mythology, the goddess of flowers and the shepherd god of nature, respectively. The realm of Flora and Pan is that of pastoral poesy, which, according to Virgil, should be the genre with which the aspiring poet begins, eventually working his way up to the epic.

O'er sailing the blue cragginess, a car°   *chariot*
And steeds with streamy manes—the charioteer
Looks out upon the winds with glorious fear:
And now the numerous tramplings quiver lightly
130 Along a huge cloud's ridge; and now with sprightly
Wheel downward come they into fresher skies,
Tipt round with silver from the sun's bright eyes.
Still downward with capacious whirl they glide,
And now I see them on the green-hill's side
135 In breezy rest among the nodding stalks.
The charioteer with wond'rous gesture talks
To the trees and mountains; and there soon appear
Shapes of delight, of mystery, and fear,
Passing along before a dusky space
140 Made by some mighty oaks: as they would chase
Some ever-fleeting music on they sweep.
Lo! how they murmur, laugh, and smile, and weep:
Some with upholden hand and mouth severe;
Some with their faces muffled to the ear
145 Between their arms; some, clear in youthful bloom,
Go glad and smilingly athwart the gloom;
Some looking back, and some with upward gaze;
Yes, thousands in a thousand different ways
Flit onward—now a lovely wreath of girls
150 Dancing their sleek hair into tangled curls;
And now broad wings. Most awfully intent
The driver of those steeds is forward bent,
And seems to listen: O that I might know
All that he writes with such a hurrying glow.

155 The visions all are fled—the car is fled
Into the light of heaven, and in their stead
A sense of real things comes doubly strong,
And, like a muddy stream, would bear along
My soul to nothingness: but I will strive
160 Against all doubtings, and will keep alive
The thought of that same chariot, and the strange
Journey it went.

                    Is there so small a range
In the present strength of manhood, that the high
Imagination cannot freely fly
165 As she was wont of old? prepare her steeds,
Paw up against the light, and do strange deeds
Upon the clouds? Has she not shown us all?

From the clear space of ether, to the small
Breath of new buds unfolding? From the meaning
170 Of Jove's[1] large eyebrow, to the tender greening
Of April meadows? Here her altar shone,
E'en in this isle; and who could paragon
The fervid choir that lifted up a noise
Of harmony, to where it aye will poise
175 Its mighty self of convoluting sound,
Huge as a planet, and like that roll round,
Eternally around a dizzy void?
Ay, in those days the Muses[2] were nigh cloy'd
With honours; nor had any other care
180 Than to sing out and sooth their wavy hair.

Could all this be forgotten? Yes, a schism
Nurtured by foppery and barbarism,
Made great Apollo blush for this his land.
Men were thought wise who could not understand
185 His glories: with a puling infant's force
They sway'd about upon a rocking horse,
And thought it Pegasus.[3] Ah dismal soul'd!
The winds of heaven blew, the ocean roll'd
Its gathering waves—ye felt it not. The blue
190 Bared its eternal bosom, and the dew
Of summer nights collected still to make
The morning precious: beauty was awake!
Why were ye not awake? But ye were dead
To things ye knew not of—were closely wed
195 To musty laws lined out with wretched rule
And compass vile: so that ye taught a school
Of dolts to smooth, inlay, and clip, and fit,
Till, like the certain wands of Jacob's wit,[4]
Their verses tallied. Easy was the task:
200 A thousand handicraftsmen wore the mask
Of Poesy. Ill-fated, impious race!

That blasphemed the bright Lyrist[5] to his face,
And did not know it—no, they went about,
Holding a poor, decrepit standard out
205 Mark'd with most flimsy mottos, and in large
The name of one Boileau![6]

                    O ye whose charge
It is to hover round our pleasant hills!
Whose congregated majesty so fills
My boundly[7] reverence, that I cannot trace
210 Your hallowed names, in this unholy place,
So near those common folk; did not their shames
Affright you? Did our old lamenting Thames°   river
Delight you? Did ye never cluster round
Delicious Avon,° with a mournful sound,   river
215 And weep? Or did ye wholly bid adieu
To regions where no more the laurel grew?
Or did ye stay to give a welcoming
To some lone spirits[8] who could proudly sing
Their youth away, and die? 'Twas even so:
220 But let me think away those times of woe:
Now 'tis a fairer season; ye have breathed
Rich benedictions o'er us; ye have wreathed
Fresh garlands: for sweet music has been heard
In many places—some has been upstirr'd
225 From out its crystal dwelling in a lake,
By a swan's ebon bill;[9] from a thick brake,°   thicket
Nested and quiet in a valley mild,
Bubbles a pipe;[10] fine sounds are floating wild
About the earth: happy are ye and glad.

---

[1] *Jove* Roman king of the gods.

[2] *Muses* In Greek mythology, nine daughters of Zeus and Mnemosyne, each of whom presided over and provided inspiration for an aspect of learning or the arts.

[3] *Pegasus* Great winged horse of Greek mythology. This line is a reference to William Hazlitt's essay "On Milton's Versification" (1815), in which he says, on the use of the heroic couplet by eighteenth-century poets, "Dr. Johnson and Pope would have turned [Milton's] vaulting Pegasus into a rocking-horse."

[4] *Jacob's wit* See Genesis 30.27–43, in which Jacob increases his wealth at the expense of Laban.

[5] *the bright Lyrist* I.e., Apollo.

[6] *Boileau* French literary critic Nicolas Boileau-Despréaux (1636–1711), whose *L'Art Poétique* (1674), a verse treatise on literary aesthetics, was extremely influential among English poets.

[7] *boundly* Term coined by Keats, meaning either "boundless" or "bounden."

[8] *some lone spirits* Reference to poets Thomas Chatterton (1752–70), Henry White (1785–1806), and others, who died young, without receiving the critical attention their work deserved.

[9] *swan's ebon bill* Reference to William Wordsworth (1770–1850), who, along with Coleridge and Southey, was known as a "Lake Poet."

[10] *from a ... pipe* Reference to poet Leigh Hunt (1784–1859).

230 These things are doubtless: yet in truth we've had
    Strange thunders from the potency of song;
    Mingled indeed with what is sweet and strong,
    From majesty: but in clear truth the themes
    Are ugly clubs, the poets Polyphemes[1]
235 Disturbing the grand sea. A drainless shower
    Of light is poesy; 'tis the supreme of power;
    'Tis might half slumb'ring on its own right arm.
    The very archings of her eye-lids charm
    A thousand willing agents to obey,
240 And still she governs with the mildest sway:
    But strength alone though of the Muses born
    Is like a fallen angel: trees uptorn,
    Darkness, and worms, and shrouds, and sepulchres
    Delight it; for it feeds upon the burrs,
245 And thorns of life; forgetting the great end
    Of poesy, that it should be a friend
    To sooth the cares, and lift the thoughts of man.

        Yet I rejoice: a myrtle fairer than
    E'er grew in Paphos,[2] from the bitter weeds
250 Lifts its sweet head into the air, and feeds
    A silent space with ever sprouting green.
    All tenderest birds there find a pleasant screen,
    Creep through the shade with jaunty fluttering,
    Nibble the little cupped flowers and sing.
255 Then let us clear away the choking thorns
    From round its gentle stem; let the young fawns,
    Yeaned° in after times, when we are flown,   *brought forth*
    Find a fresh sward° beneath it, overgrown   *turf*
    With simple flowers: let there nothing be
260 More boisterous than a lover's bended knee;
    Nought more ungentle than the placid look
    Of one who leans upon a closed book;
    Nought more untranquil than the grassy slopes
    Between two hills. All hail delightful hopes!
265 As she was wont, th'imagination
    Into most lovely labyrinths will be gone,
    And they shall be accounted poet kings
    Who simply tell the most heart-easing things.
    O may these joys be ripe before I die.

270 Will not some say that I presumptuously
    Have spoken? that from hastening disgrace
    'Twere better far to hide my foolish face?
    That whining boyhood should with reverence bow
    Ere the dread thunderbolt could reach? How!
275 If I do hide myself, it sure shall be
    In the very fane, the light of Poesy:
    If I do fall, at least I will be laid
    Beneath the silence of a poplar shade;
    And over me the grass shall be smooth shaven;
280 And there shall be a kind memorial graven.
    But off Despondence! miserable bane!
    They should not know thee, who athirst to gain
    A noble end, are thirsty every hour.
    What though I am not wealthy in the dower
285 Of spanning wisdom; though I do not know
    The shiftings of the mighty winds that blow
    Hither and thither all the changing thoughts
    Of man: though no great minist'ring reason sorts
    Out the dark mysteries of human souls
290 To clear conceiving: yet there ever rolls
    A vast idea before me, and I glean
    Therefrom my liberty; thence too I've seen
    The end and aim of Poesy. 'Tis clear
    As any thing most true; as that the year
295 Is made of the four seasons—manifest
    As a large cross, some old cathedral's crest,
    Lifted to the white clouds. Therefore should I
    Be but the essence of deformity,
    A coward, did my very eyelids wink
300 At speaking out what I have dared to think.
    Ah! rather let me like a madman run
    Over some precipice; let the hot sun
    Melt my Dedalian wings,[3] and drive me down
    Convuls'd and headlong! Stay! an inward frown
305 Of conscience bids me be more calm awhile.
    An ocean dim, sprinkled with many an isle,
    Spreads awfully before me. How much toil!
    How many days! what desperate turmoil!
    Ere I can have explored its widenesses.

---

[1] *Polyphemes* One-eyed, club-wielding giant in Homer's *Odyssey*.

[2] *Paphos* City in Cyprus that is the site of a famous temple to Venus, goddess of love and beauty. Myrtle (line 250) is also associated with Venus.

[3] *Dedalian wings* According to Greek mythology, the sculptor Daedalus built wings of wax and feathers so that he and his son Icarus could escape from the island of Crete, where they were imprisoned. Icarus flew too close to the sun, and his wings melted, causing him to fall into the sea.

310 Ah, what a task! upon my bended knees,
I could unsay those—no, impossible!
Impossible!

       For sweet relief I'll dwell
On humbler thoughts, and let this strange assay
Begun in gentleness die so away.
315 E'en now all tumult from my bosom fades:
I turn full hearted to the friendly aids
That smooth the path of honour; brotherhood,
And friendliness the nurse of mutual good.
The hearty grasp that sends a pleasant sonnet
320 Into the brain ere one can think upon it;
The silence when some rhymes are coming out;
And when they're come, the very pleasant rout:
The message certain to be done to-morrow.
'Tis perhaps as well that it should be to borrow
325 Some precious book from out its snug retreat,
To cluster round it when we next shall meet.
Scarce can I scribble on; for lovely airs
Are fluttering round the room like doves in pairs;
Many delights of that glad day recalling,
330 When first my senses caught their tender falling.
And with these airs come forms of elegance
Stooping their shoulders o'er a horse's prance,
Careless, and grand—fingers soft and round
Parting luxuriant curls—and the swift bound
335 Of Bacchus from his chariot, when his eye
Made Ariadne's cheek look blushingly.[1]
Thus I remember all the pleasant flow
Of words at opening a portfolio.

Things such as these are ever harbingers
340 To trains of peaceful images: the stirs
Of a swan's neck unseen among the rushes:
A linnet starting all about the bushes:
A butterfly, with golden wings broad parted,
Nestling a rose, convuls'd as though it smarted
345 With over pleasure—many, many more,
Might I indulge at large in all my store

Of luxuries: yet I must not forget
Sleep, quiet with his poppy coronet:[2]
For what there may be worthy in these rhymes
350 I partly owe to him: and thus, the chimes
Of friendly voices had just given place
To as sweet a silence, when I 'gan retrace
The pleasant day, upon a couch at ease.
It was a poet's house who keeps the keys
355 Of pleasure's temple.[3] Round about were hung
The glorious features of the bards who sung
In other ages—cold and sacred busts
Smiled at each other. Happy he who trusts
To clear Futurity his darling fame!
360 Then there were fauns and satyrs taking aim
At swelling apples with a frisky leap
And reaching fingers, 'mid a luscious heap
Of vine leaves. Then there rose to view a fane°   *temple*
Of liny° marble, and thereto a train   *veined*
365 Of nymphs approaching fairly o'er the sward:
One, loveliest, holding her white hand toward
The dazzling sun-rise: two sisters sweet
Bending their graceful figures till they meet
Over the trippings of a little child:
370 And some are hearing, eagerly, the wild
Thrilling liquidity of dewy piping.
See, in another picture, nymphs are wiping
Cherishingly Diana's[4] timorous limbs;
A fold of lawny mantle dabbling swims
375 At the bath's edge, and keeps a gentle motion
With the subsiding crystal: as when ocean
Heaves calmly its broad swelling smoothness o'er
Its rocky marge, and balances once more
The patient weeds; that now unshent°   *unharmed*
   by foam
380 Feel all about their undulating home.

Sappho's[5] meek head was there half smiling down
At nothing; just as though the earnest frown

---

[1] *Of Bacchus ... blushingly* Ariadne, daughter of King Minos of Crete, was abandoned by her lover, Theseus, on the island of Naxos. Bacchus, god of wine, found her there, consoled her, and married her (Ovid, *Metamorphoses* 8.172–82). Keats would also have been familiar with the painting *Bacchus and Ariadne* (1523) by Venetian painter Titian (1490–1576).

[2] *poppy coronet* The seed capsules of some species of poppy contain opium, and therefore were associated with sleep.

[3] *It was ... temple* Poet Leigh Hunt kept a bed for Keats in his study. Hunt's cottage was filled with busts and pictures, on which the following descriptions are probably based.

[4] *Diana* Roman goddess of chastity, childbirth, and the hunt.

[5] *Sappho* Greek lyric poet of the sixth century BCE.

Of over thinking had that moment gone
From off her brow, and left her all alone.

385   Great Alfred's[1] too, with anxious, pitying eyes,
As if he always listened to the sighs
Of the goaded world; and Kosciusko's[2] worn
By horrid suffrance—mightily forlorn.

Petrarch, outstepping from the shady green,
390   Starts at the sight of Laura;[3] nor can wean
His eyes from her sweet face. Most happy they!
For over them was seen a free display
Of out-spread wings, and from between them shone
The face of Poesy: from off her throne
395   She overlook'd things that I scarce could tell.
The very sense of where I was might well
Keep Sleep aloof: but more than that there came
Thought after thought to nourish up the flame
Within my breast; so that the morning light
400   Surprised me even from a sleepless night;
And up I rose refresh'd, and glad, and gay,
Resolving to begin that very day
These lines; and howsoever they be done,
I leave them as a father does his son.
—1817

On Seeing the Elgin Marbles[4]

My spirit is too weak; mortality
Weighs heavily on me like unwilling sleep,
And each imagined pinnacle and steep
Of godlike hardship, tells me I must die
5   Like a sick Eagle looking at the sky.

Yet 'tis a gentle luxury to weep,
That I have not the cloudy winds to keep
Fresh for the opening of the morning's eye.
Such dim-conceived glories of the brain
10   Bring round the heart an indescribable feud;
So do these wonders a most dizzy pain,
That mingles Grecian grandeur with the rude
Wasting of old Time—with a billowy main,°   sea
A sun, a shadow of a magnitude.
—1817

On Sitting Down to Read
King Lear Once Again

O golden tongued Romance, with serene lute!
Fair plumed Syren![5] Queen of far-away!
Leave melodizing on this wintry day,
Shut up thine olden pages, and be mute:
5   Adieu! for once again the fierce dispute
Betwixt damnation and impassion'd clay
Must I burn through; once more humbly assay
The bitter-sweet of this Shakespearian fruit.
Chief Poet! and ye clouds of Albion,[6]
10   Begetters of our deep eternal theme,
When through the old oak forest I am gone,
Let me not wander in a barren dream,
But when I am consumed in the fire,
Give me new Phœnix[7] wings to fly at my desire.
—1838

When I Have Fears that I May Cease to Be

When I have fears that I may cease to be
Before my pen has glean'd my teeming brain,
Before high piled books, in charact'ry,[8]
Hold like rich garners the full-ripen'd grain;

---

[1] *Great Alfred* Alfred the Great, King of Wessex from 871 to 899.

[2] *Kosciusko* Polish patriot Tadeusz Kosciusko (1746–1817), who led his countrymen in an uprising against Russia, and also fought for the United States Army in the American struggle for independence.

[3] *Petrarch ... Laura* Italian poet Petrarch (1304–74) wrote odes and sonnets in celebration of his beloved, Laura.

[4] *Elgin Marbles* In 1806 Lord Elgin brought friezes and other sculptures that had decorated the exterior of the Parthenon, in Athens, to England. In 1816 the government purchased them for display in the British Museum, where they remain today. See the "In Context" section on this topic available on the companion website.

[5] *Syren* Monster of classical mythology who is half woman, half serpent, and whose enchanted singing lures sailors to their deaths.

[6] *Albion* England.

[7] *Phoenix* Mythical Egyptian bird that is consumed by fire, and then reborn, once every 500 years.

[8] *charact'ry* Symbols or characters.

When I behold, upon the night's starr'd face,
   Huge cloudy symbols of a high romance,
And think that I may never live to trace
   Their shadows, with the magic hand of chance;
And when I feel, fair creature of an hour!
   That I shall never look upon thee more,
Never have relish in the fairy power
   Of unreflecting love—then on the shore
Of the wide world I stand alone, and think
Till love and fame to nothingness do sink.
—1848 (WRITTEN 1818)

Epistle to John Hamilton Reynolds[1]

Dear Reynolds! as last night I lay in bed,
   There came before my eyes that wonted thread
Of shapes, and shadows, and remembrances,
That every other minute vex and please:
Things all disjointed come from north and south—
Two witch's eyes above a cherub's mouth,
Voltaire with casque and shield and habergeon, [2]
And Alexander[3] with his night-cap on;
Old Socrates[4] a-tying his cravat,
And Hazlitt playing with Miss Edgeworth's[5] cat;
And Junius Brutus, pretty well so so,[6]
Making the best of's way towards Soho.[7]

   Few are there who escape these visitings—
Perhaps one or two whose lives have patent wings,
And through whose curtains peeps no hellish nose,
No wild-boar tushes,° and no mermaid's toes;   *tusks*

But flowers bursting out with lusty pride,
And young Æolian harps[8] personified;
Some, Titian[9] colours touch'd into real life—
The sacrifice goes on; the pontiff knife
Gleams in the sun, the milk-white heifer lows,
The pipes go shrilly, the libation flows:
A white sail shows above the green-head cliff,
Moves round the point, and throws her anchor stiff;
The mariners join hymn with those on land.

   You know the Enchanted Castle[10]—it doth stand
Upon a rock, on the border of a lake,
Nested in trees, which all do seem to shake
From some old magic like Urganda's sword.[11]
O Phoebus![12] that I had thy sacred word
To show this Castle, in fair dreaming wise,
Unto my friend, while sick and ill he lies!

   You know it well enough, where it doth seem
A mossy place, a Merlin's Hall,[13] a dream;
You know the clear lake, and the little isles,
The mountains blue, and cold near neighbour rills,
All which elsewhere are but half animate;
There do they look alive to love and hate,
To smiles and frowns; they seem a lifted mound
Above some giant, pulsing underground.

   Part of the building was a chosen see,°   *dwelling-place*
Built by a banish'd Santon° of Chaldee;   *holy man*
The other part, two thousand years from him,
Was built by Cuthbert de Saint Aldebrim;[14]
Then there's a little wing, far from the sun,

---

[1] *John Hamilton Reynolds* Poet and lawyer (1794–1852) who was a close friend of Keats. Reynolds was ill at the time, and Keats sent him this verse letter to cheer him.

[2] *Voltaire* French philosopher François-Marie Arouet de Voltaire (1694–1778); *casque* Helmet; *habergeon* Sleeveless jacket of chain mail.

[3] *Alexander* Poet Alexander Pope (1688–1744).

[4] *Socrates* Greek philosopher of the fifth century BCE.

[5] *Hazlitt* Painter and writer William Hazlitt (1778–1830); *Miss Edgeworth* Novelist Maria Edgeworth (1767–1849).

[6] *Junius Brutus* Actor Junius Brutus Booth (1796–1852); *so so* Tipsy.

[7] *Soho* Area in London, then rather disreputable.

[8] *Æolian harps* Harps that produce sound when exposed to the wind or open air. From Æolus, the Greek god of the winds.

[9] *Titian* I.e, rich; in the style of Titian, a Venetian Renaissance painter whose work was characterized by bold colors. The following lines most likely describe *Sacrifice to Apollo*, by French painter Claude Lorraine (1600–82).

[10] *the Enchanted Castle* Painting by Claude Lorraine.

[11] *Urganda's sword* Enchantress figure in *Amadis of Gaul*, a fifteenth-century romance.

[12] *Phoebus* Apollo, Greek god of poetry and of the sun.

[13] *Merlin's Hall* I.e., a hall built by magicians such as the sorcerer Merlin, from Arthurian legend.

[14] *Cuthbert ... Aldebrim* Character invented by Keats.

Built by a Lapland witch[1] turn'd maudlin nun;
And many other juts of aged stone
Founded with many a mason-devil's groan.

The doors all look as if they oped themselves,
50 The windows as if latched by fays° and elves,   *fairies*
And from them comes a silver flash of light,
As from the westward of a summer's night;
Or like a beauteous woman's large blue eyes
Gone mad through olden songs and poesies.

55 See! what is coming from the distance dim!
A golden galley all in silken trim!
Three rows of oars are lightening, moment whiles,
Into the verd'rous bosoms of those isles;
Towards the shade, under the Castle wall,
60 It comes in silence—now 'tis hidden all.
The clarion sounds, and from a postern-gate
An echo of sweet music doth create
A fear in the poor herdsman, who doth bring
His beasts to trouble the enchanted spring—
65 He tells of the sweet music, and the spot,
To all his friends, and they believe him not.

O that our dreamings all, of sleep or wake,
Would all their colours from the sunset take:
From something of material sublime,
70 Rather than shadow our own soul's daytime
In the dark void of night. For in the world
We jostle—but my flag is not unfurl'd
On the admiral-staff—and to philosophise
I dare not yet! Oh, never will the prize,
75 High reason, and the lore of good and ill,
Be my award! Things cannot to the will
Be settled, but they tease us out of thought;
Or is it that imagination brought
Beyond its proper bound, yet still confin'd,
80 Lost in a sort of Purgatory blind,
Cannot refer to any standard law
Of either earth or heaven? It is a flaw
In happiness, to see beyond our bourn—
It forces us in summer skies to mourn,
85 It spoils the singing of the nightingale.

Dear Reynolds! I have a mysterious tale,
And cannot speak it: the first page I read
Upon a lampit° rock of green sea-weed   *limpet*
Among the breakers; 'twas a quiet eve,
90 The rocks were silent, the wide sea did weave
An untumultuous fringe of silver foam
Along the flat brown sand; I was at home
And should have been most happy—but I saw
Too far into the sea, where every maw°   *throat, gullet*
95 The greater on the less feeds evermore.
But I saw too distinct into the core
Of an eternal fierce destruction,
And so from happiness I far was gone.
Still am I sick of it, and tho', to-day,
100 I've gather'd young spring-leaves, and flowers gay
Of periwinkle and wild strawberry,
Still do I that most fierce destruction see—
The shark at savage prey, the hawk at pounce,
The gentle robin, like a pard° or ounce,°   *leopard / lynx*
105 Ravening a worm—Away, ye horrid moods!
Moods of one's mind! You know I hate them well.
You know I'd sooner be a clapping bell
To some Kamschatkan[2] missionary church,
Than with these horrid moods be left i'the lurch.
110 Do you get health—and Tom the same—I'll dance,
And from detested moods in new romance[3]
Take refuge—Of bad lines a centaine[4] dose
Is sure enough—and so "here follows prose."[5]
—1848

To Homer[6]

Standing aloof in giant ignorance,
Of thee I hear and of the Cyclades,[7]
As one who sits ashore and longs perchance

[1]   *Lapland witch*   Lapland was supposed to be the dwelling-place of witches.

[2]   *Kamschatkan*   From the Kamchatka Peninsula in Siberia.

[3]   *new romance*   Probably Keats's *Isabella* (1820), a romance based on a tale from Italian poet Giovanni Boccaccio's *Decameron* (written 1348–53).

[4]   *centaine*   Company of one hundred.

[5]   *here follows prose*   See Shakespeare's *Twelfth Night* 2.5.154.

[6]   *Homer*   Early Greek poet, believed to be the author of *The Iliad* and *Odyssey*.

[7]   *Cyclades*   Group of islands in the Aegean Sea, off the southeast coast of Greece.

To visit dolphin-coral in deep seas.
5 So thou wast blind!¹—but then the veil was rent;
For Jove² uncurtain'd Heaven to let thee live,
And Neptune³ made for thee a spumy⁴ tent,
And Pan⁵ made sing for thee his forest-hive;
Aye, on the shores of darkness there is light,
10 And precipices show untrodden green;
There is a budding morrow in midnight;
There is a triple sight in blindness keen;
Such seeing hast thou, as it once befell
To Dian, Queen of Earth, and Heaven, and Hell.⁶
—1848 (WRITTEN C. 1818)

The Eve of St. Agnes⁷

1

St. Agnes' Eve—Ah, bitter chill it was!
The owl, for all his feathers, was a-cold;
The hare limp'd trembling through the frozen grass,
And silent was the flock in woolly fold:
5 Numb were the Beadsman's⁸ fingers, while he told
His rosary, and while his frosted breath,
Like pious incense from a censer⁹ old,
Seem'd taking flight for heaven, without a death,

---

¹ thou wast blind Homer was said to have been blind.

² Jove Roman King of the gods.

³ Neptune Roman god of the sea.

⁴ spumy Covered in sea foam.

⁵ Pan Greek shepherd god of nature who was half goat and half man. After the nymph Syrinx turned herself into a bed of reeds in order to escape him, Pan created an instrument (the panpipe) out of the reeds.

⁶ To Dian ... Hell Diana was sometimes envisioned as a multi-figured goddess, presiding over the moon, childbirth, the hunt, and hell.

⁷ St. Agnes Fourth-century Christian martyr, executed at the age of thirteen, who is the patron saint of virgins. It was tradition that young women could obtain a vision of their future husbands if they performed the proper rituals on 20 January, the night before St. Agnes's Feast Day.

⁸ Beadsman Pensioner paid to say prayers for the souls of his benefactors. He "tells," or counts, the beads of his rosary, saying a prayer at each bead.

⁹ censer Incense burner.

Past the sweet Virgin's¹⁰ picture, while his prayer he
saith.

2

10 His prayer he saith, this patient, holy man;
Then takes his lamp, and riseth from his knees,
And back returneth, meagre, barefoot, wan,
Along the chapel aisle by slow degrees:
The sculptur'd dead, on each side, seem to freeze,
15 Emprison'd in black, purgatorial rails:
Knights, ladies, praying in dumb orat'ries,°   chapels
He passeth by; and his weak spirit fails
To think how they may ache in icy hoods and mails.

3

Northward he turneth through a little door,
20 And scarce three steps, ere Music's golden tongue
Flatter'd to tears this aged man and poor;
But no—already had his deathbell rung:
The joys of all his life were said and sung:
His was harsh penance on St. Agnes' Eve:
25 Another way he went, and soon among
Rough ashes sat he for his soul's reprieve,
And all night kept awake, for sinners' sake to grieve.

4

That ancient Beadsman heard the prelude soft;
And so it chanc'd, for many a door was wide,
30 From hurry to and fro. Soon, up aloft,
The silver, snarling trumpets 'gan to chide:
The level chambers, ready with their pride,
Were glowing to receive a thousand guests:
The carved angels, ever eager-eyed,
35 Star'd, where upon their heads the cornice rests,
With hair blown back, and wings put cross-wise on
their breasts.

5

At length burst in the argent¹¹ revelry,
With plume, tiara, and all rich array,
Numerous as shadows haunting fairily
40 The brain, new stuff'd, in youth, with triumphs gay
Of old romance. These let us wish away,

---

¹⁰ Virgin I.e., Mary, virgin mother of Christ.

¹¹ argent Adorned with silver.

And turn, sole-thoughted, to one Lady there,
Whose heart had brooded, all that wintry day,
On love, and wing'd St. Agnes' saintly care,
45 As she had heard old dames full many times declare.

6

They told her how, upon St. Agnes' Eve,
Young virgins might have visions of delight,
And soft adorings from their loves receive
Upon the honey'd middle of the night,
50 If ceremonies due they did aright;°   *arranged properly*
As, supperless to bed they must retire,
And couch supine their beauties, lily white;
Nor look behind, nor sideways, but require
Of Heaven with upward eyes for all that they desire.

7

55 Full of this whim was thoughtful Madeline:
The music, yearning like a God in pain,
She scarcely heard: her maiden eyes divine,
Fix'd on the floor, saw many a sweeping train
Pass by—she heeded not at all: in vain
60 Came many a tiptoe, amorous cavalier,
And back retir'd; not cool'd by high disdain,
But she saw not: her heart was otherwhere:
She sigh'd for Agnes' dreams, the sweetest of the year.

8

She danc'd along with vague, regardless eyes,
65 Anxious her lips, her breathing quick and short:
The hallow'd hour was near at hand: she sighs
Amid the timbrels,° and the throng'd resort   *tambourines*
Of whisperers in anger, or in sport;
'Mid looks of love, defiance, hate, and scorn,
70 Hoodwink'd° with faery fancy; all   *blindfolded*
    amort,°   *dead*
Save to St. Agnes and her lambs unshorn,[1]
And all the bliss to be before to-morrow morn.

9

So, purposing each moment to retire,
She linger'd still. Meantime, across the moors,
75 Had come young Porphyro, with heart on fire

For Madeline. Beside the portal doors,
Buttress'd from moonlight, stands he, and implores
All saints to give him sight of Madeline,
But for one moment in the tedious hours,
80 That he might gaze and worship all unseen;
Perchance speak, kneel, touch, kiss—in sooth such
    things have been.

10

He ventures in: let no buzz'd whisper tell:
All eyes be muffled, or a hundred swords
Will storm his heart, Love's fev'rous citadel:
85 For him, those chambers held barbarian hordes,
Hyena foemen, and hot-blooded lords,
Whose very dogs would execrations howl
Against his lineage: not one breast affords
Him any mercy, in that mansion foul,
90 Save one old beldame,[2] weak in body and in soul.

11

Ah, happy chance! the aged creature came,
Shuffling along with ivory-headed wand,°   *staff*
To where he stood, hid from the torch's flame,
Behind a broad hall-pillar, far beyond
95 The sound of merriment and chorus bland:°   *soft*
He startled her; but soon she knew his face,
And grasp'd his fingers in her palsied hand,
Saying, "Mercy, Porphyro! hie thee from this place;
They are all here to-night, the whole blood-thirsty race!"

12

100 "Get hence! get hence! there's dwarfish Hildebrand;
He had a fever late, and in the fit
He cursed thee and thine, both house and land:
Then there's that old Lord Maurice, not a whit
More tame for his gray hairs—Alas me! flit!
105 Flit like a ghost away."—"Ah, Gossip[3] dear,
We're safe enough; here in this arm-chair sit,
And tell me how"—"Good Saints! not here, not here;
Follow me, child, or else these stones will be thy bier."

13

He follow'd through a lowly arched way,
110 Brushing the cobwebs with his lofty plume,

---

[1] *St. Agnes ... unshorn* The Latin for lamb is *agnus*; thus the traditional association of St. Agnes with lambs, which also carry connotations of whiteness and purity.

[2] *beldame* Grandmother, old woman, or elderly nurse.

[3] *Gossip* Good friend; godmother.

And as she mutter'd "Well-a—well-a-day!"
He found him in a little moonlight room,
Pale, lattic'd, chill, and silent as a tomb.
"Now tell me where is Madeline," said he,
115 "O tell me, Angela, by the holy loom
Which none but secret sisterhood may see,
When they St. Agnes' wool are weaving piously."

14

"St. Agnes! Ah! it is St. Agnes' Eve—
Yet men will murder upon holy days:
120 Thou must hold water in a witch's sieve,
And be liege-lord of all the Elves and Fays,°   *fairies*
To venture so: it fills me with amaze
To see thee, Porphyro!—St. Agnes' Eve!
God's help! my lady fair the conjuror plays
125 This very night: good angels her deceive!
But let me laugh awhile, I've mickle° time to grieve." *much*

15

Feebly she laugheth in the languid moon,
While Porphyro upon her face doth look,
Like puzzled urchin on an aged crone
130 Who keepeth clos'd a wond'rous riddle-book,
As spectacled she sits in chimney nook.
But soon his eyes grew brilliant, when she told
His lady's purpose; and he scarce could brook° *prevent*
Tears, at the thought of those enchantments cold
135 And Madeline asleep in lap of legends old.

16

Sudden a thought came like a full-blown rose,
Flushing his brow, and in his pained heart
Made purple riot: then doth he propose
A stratagem, that makes the beldame start:
140 "A cruel man and impious thou art:
Sweet lady, let her pray, and sleep, and dream
Alone with her good angels, far apart
From wicked men like thee. Go, go!—I deem
Thou canst not surely be the same that thou didst seem."

17

145 "I will not harm her, by all saints I swear,"
Quoth Porphyro: "O may I ne'er find grace
When my weak voice shall whisper its last prayer,
If one of her soft ringlets I displace,

Or look with ruffian passion in her face:
150 Good Angela, believe me by these tears;
Or I will, even in a moment's space,
Awake, with horrid shout, my foemen's ears,
And beard° them, though they be more   *oppose*
    fang'd than wolves and bears."

18

"Ah! why wilt thou affright a feeble soul?
155 A poor, weak, palsy-stricken, churchyard thing,
Whose passing-bell may ere the midnight toll;
Whose prayers for thee, each morn and evening,
Were never miss'd."—Thus plaining,°   *complaining*
    doth she bring
A gentler speech from burning Porphyro;
160 So woeful, and of such deep sorrowing,
That Angela gives promise she will do
Whatever he shall wish, betide her weal or woe.

19

Which was, to lead him, in close secrecy,
Even to Madeline's chamber, and there hide
165 Him in a closet, of such privacy
That he might see her beauty unespied,
And win perhaps that night a peerless bride,
While legion'd fairies pac'd the coverlet,
And pale enchantment held her sleepy-eyed.
170 Never on such a night have lovers met,
Since Merlin paid his Demon all the monstrous debt.[1]

20

"It shall be as thou wishest," said the Dame:
"All cates° and dainties shall be stored there   *delicacies*
Quickly on this feast-night: by the tambour frame[2]
175 Her own lute thou wilt see: no time to spare,
For I am slow and feeble, and scarce dare
On such a catering trust my dizzy head.
Wait here, my child, with patience; kneel in prayer
The while: Ah! thou must needs the lady wed,
180 Or may I never leave my grave among the dead."

---

[1] *Since ... debt* Probably a reference to the episode in Arthurian legend in which the enchanter Merlin falls in love with the enchantress Vivien, or Nimue, who turns one of his spells against him and imprisons him in a cave.

[2] *tambour frame* Circular frame for embroidery.

21

So saying, she hobbled off with busy fear.
The lover's endless minutes slowly pass'd:
The dame return'd, and whisper'd in his ear
To follow her; with aged eyes aghast
185 From fright of dim espial. Safe at last,
Through many a dusky gallery, they gain
The maiden's chamber, silken, hush'd, and chaste;
Where Porphyro took covert, pleas'd amain.°   *completely*
His poor guide hurried back with agues°   *fever*
    in her brain.

22

190 Her falt'ring hand upon the balustrade,
Old Angela was feeling for the stair,
When Madeline, St. Agnes' charmed maid,
Rose, like a mission'd spirit, unaware:
With silver taper's light, and pious care,
195 She turn'd, and down the aged gossip led
To a safe level matting. Now prepare,
Young Porphyro, for gazing on that bed;
She comes, she comes again, like ring-dove
    fray'd° and fled.   *frightened*

23

Out went the taper° as she hurried in;   *candle*
200 Its little smoke, in pallid moonshine, died:
She clos'd the door, she panted, all akin
To spirits of the air, and visions wide:
No uttered syllable, or, woe betide!
But to her heart, her heart was voluble,
205 Paining with eloquence her balmy side;
As though a tongueless nightingale should swell
Her throat in vain, and die, heart-stifled, in her dell.

24

A casement high and triple-arch'd there was,
All garlanded with carven imag'ries
210 Of fruits, and flowers, and bunches of knot-grass,
And diamonded with panes of quaint device,
Innumerable of stains and splendid dyes,
As are the tiger-moth's deep-damask'd wings;
And in the midst, 'mong thousand heraldries,[1]
215 And twilight saints, and dim emblazonings,

A shielded scutcheon blush'd with blood of queens
    and kings.[2]

25

Full on this casement shone the wintry moon,
And threw warm gules[3] on Madeline's fair breast,
As down she knelt for heaven's grace and boon;°   *blessing*
220 Rose-bloom fell on her hands, together prest,
And on her silver cross soft amethyst,
And on her hair a glory, like a saint:
She seem'd a splendid angel, newly drest,
Save wings, for heaven—Porphyro grew faint:
225 She knelt, so pure a thing, so free from mortal taint.

26

Anon his heart revives: her vespers° done,   *evening prayers*
Of all its wreathed pearls her hair she frees;
Unclasps her warmed jewels one by one;
Loosens her fragrant boddice; by degrees
230 Her rich attire creeps rustling to her knees:
Half-hidden, like a mermaid in sea-weed,
Pensive awhile she dreams awake, and sees,
In fancy, fair St. Agnes in her bed,
But dares not look behind, or all the charm is fled.

27

235 Soon, trembling in her soft and chilly nest,
In sort of wakeful swoon, perplex'd[4] she lay,
Until the poppied° warmth of sleep oppress'd   *narcotic*
Her soothed limbs, and soul fatigued away;
Flown, like a thought, until the morrow-day;
240 Blissfully haven'd both from joy and pain;
Clasp'd like a missal[5] where swart Paynims[6] pray;
Blinded alike from sunshine and from rain,
As though a rose should shut, and be a bud again.

28

Stol'n to this paradise, and so entranced,
245 Porphyro gazed upon her empty dress,
And listen'd to her breathing, if it chanced

---

1   *heraldries*   Emblems of rank and genealogy.

2   *scutcheon*   I.e., escutcheon: shield; *blush'd ... kings*   I.e., indicates she is of royal blood.

3   *gules*   Red bars (a heraldic device).

4   *perplex'd*   I.e., between sleep and waking.

5   *missal*   Christian mass- or prayer-book.

6   *swart Paynims*   Dark-skinned pagans.

To wake into a slumberous tenderness;
Which when he heard, that minute did he bless,
And breath'd himself: then from the closet crept,
250 Noiseless as fear in a wide wilderness,
And over the hush'd carpet, silent, stept,
And 'tween the curtains peep'd, where, lo!—how fast
      she slept.

29

Then by the bed-side, where the faded moon
Made a dim, silver twilight, soft he set
255 A table, and, half anguish'd, threw thereon
A cloth of woven crimson, gold, and jet—
O for some drowsy Morphean amulet![1]
The boisterous, midnight, festive clarion,°   *trumpet*
The kettle-drum, and far-heard clarinet,
260 Affray his ears, though but in dying tone—
The hall door shuts again, and all the noise is gone.

30

And still she slept an azure-lidded sleep,
In blanched linen, smooth, and lavender'd,
While he from forth the closet brought a heap
265 Of candied apple, quince, and plum, and gourd;°   *melon*
With jellies soother[2] than the creamy curd,
And lucent° syrops, tinct° with cinnamon;   *clear / imbued*
Manna[3] and dates, in argosy[4] transferr'd
From Fez;[5] and spiced dainties, every one,
270 From silken Samarkand[6] to cedar'd Lebanon.

31

These delicates he heap'd with glowing hand
On golden dishes and in baskets bright
Of wreathed silver: sumptuous they stand
In the retired quiet of the night,
275 Filling the chilly room with perfume light.
"And now, my love, my seraph° fair, awake!   *angel*

---

[1] *Morphean amulet* Sleep-inducing medicine or charm. (Morpheus is the god of dreams.)

[2] *soother* A word of Keats's own invention, meaning more soothing, softer.

[3] *Manna* Dried, sweet gum taken from various plants.

[4] *argosy* Merchant vessels.

[5] *Fez* City in Morocco.

[6] *Samarkand* City in Uzbekistan.

Thou art my heaven, and I thine eremite:°   *hermit*
Open thine eyes, for meek St. Agnes' sake,
Or I shall drowse beside thee, so my soul doth ache."

32

280 Thus whispering, his warm, unnerved arm
Sank in her pillow. Shaded was her dream
By the dusk curtains—'twas a midnight charm
Impossible to melt as iced stream:
The lustrous salvers° in the moonlight gleam;   *trays*
285 Broad golden fringe upon the carpet lies:
It seem'd he never, never could redeem
From such a stedfast spell his lady's eyes;
So mus'd awhile, entoil'd in woofed° phantasies.   *woven*

33

Awakening up, he took her hollow lute—
290 Tumultuous—and, in chords that tenderest be,
He play'd an ancient ditty, long since mute,
In Provence call'd, "La belle dame sans mercy":[7]
Close to her ear touching the melody—
Wherewith disturb'd, she utter'd a soft moan:
295 He ceased—she panted quick—and suddenly
Her blue affrayed eyes wide open shone:
Upon his knees he sank, pale as smooth-sculptured
      stone.

34

Her eyes were open, but she still beheld,
Now wide awake, the vision of her sleep:
300 There was a painful change, that nigh expell'd
The blisses of her dream so pure and deep,
At which fair Madeline began to weep,
And moan forth witless words with many a sigh;
While still her gaze on Porphyro would keep;
305 Who knelt, with joined hands and piteous eye,
Fearing to move or speak, she look'd so dreamingly.

35

"Ah, Porphyro!" said she, "but even now
Thy voice was at sweet tremble in mine ear,
Made tuneable with every sweetest vow;
310 And those sad eyes were spiritual and clear:

---

[7] *La belle ... mercy* French: "The beautiful woman without pity." Title of a long poem by medieval poet Alain Chartier (c. 1385–1433); Keats had not yet written his own poem with this title.

How chang'd thou art! how pallid, chill, and drear!
Give me that voice again, my Porphyro,
Those looks immortal, those complainings° *lamentings*
  dear!
Oh leave me not in this eternal woe,
315 For if thou diest, my Love, I know not where to go."

36

Beyond a mortal man impassion'd far
At these voluptuous accents, he arose,
Ethereal, flush'd, and like a throbbing star
Seen mid the sapphire heaven's deep repose;
320 Into her dream he melted, as the rose
Blendeth its odour with the violet—
Solution sweet: meantime the frost-wind blows
Like Love's alarum° pattering the sharp sleet *warning bell*
Against the window-panes; St. Agnes' moon hath set.

37

325 'Tis dark: quick pattereth the flaw-blown° *gust-driven*
  sleet:
"This is no dream, my bride, my Madeline!"
'Tis dark: the iced gusts still rave and beat:
"No dream, alas! alas! and woe is mine!
Porphyro will leave me here to fade and pine.
330 Cruel! what traitor could thee hither bring?
I curse not, for my heart is lost in thine,
Though thou forsakest a deceived thing—
A dove forlorn and lost with sick unpruned wing."

38

"My Madeline! sweet dreamer! lovely bride!
335 Say, may I be for aye° thy vassal blest? *ever*
Thy beauty's shield, heart-shap'd and
  vermeil° dyed? *vermilion (red)*
Ah, silver shrine, here will I take my rest
After so many hours of toil and quest,
A famish'd pilgrim, saved by miracle.
340 Though I have found, I will not rob thy nest
Saving of thy sweet self; if thou think'st well
To trust, fair Madeline, to no rude infidel.

39

"Hark! 'tis an elfin-storm from faery land,
Of haggard° seeming, but a boon indeed: *wild*
345 Arise—arise! the morning is at hand;
The bloated wassaillers° will never heed— *drinkers*

Let us away, my love, with happy speed;
There are no ears to hear, or eyes to see—
Drown'd all in Rhenish and the sleepy mead:[1]
350 Awake! arise! my love, and fearless be,
For o'er the southern moors I have a home for thee."

40

She hurried at his words, beset with fears,
For there were sleeping dragons all around,
At glaring watch, perhaps, with ready spears—
355 Down the wide stairs a darkling[2] way they found.
In all the house was heard no human sound.
A chain-droop'd lamp was flickering by each door;
The arras,° rich with horseman, hawk, and *tapestries*
  hound,
Flutter'd in the besieging wind's uproar;
360 And the long carpets rose along the gusty floor.

41

They glide, like phantoms, into the wide hall;
Like phantoms, to the iron porch, they glide;
Where lay the Porter, in uneasy sprawl,
With a huge empty flaggon by his side:
365 The wakeful bloodhound rose, and shook his hide,
But his sagacious eye an inmate owns:
By one, and one, the bolts full easy slide—
The chains lie silent on the footworn stones—
The key turns, and the door upon its hinges groans.

42

370 And they are gone: ay, ages long ago
These lovers fled away into the storm.
That night the Baron dreamt of many a woe,
And all his warrior-guests, with shade and form
Of witch, and demon, and large coffin-worm,
375 Were long be-nightmar'd. Angela the old
Died palsy-twitch'd, with meagre face deform;
The Beadsman, after thousand aves[3] told,
For aye unsought for slept among his ashes cold.
—1820

---

[1] *Rhenish* Wine from the Rhine region; *mead* Alcoholic beverage made from fermented honey and water.

[2] *darkling* Obscure, gloomy.

[3] *aves* Latin: abbreviation for *Ave Marias*, or Hail Marys, prayers to the Virgin Mary.

Bright Star

Bright star, would I were steadfast as thou art—
Not in lone splendour hung aloft the night
And watching, with eternal lids apart,
    Like nature's patient, sleepless Eremite,°   *hermit*
5 The moving waters at their priestlike task
    Of pure ablution[1] round earth's human shores,
Or gazing on the new soft fallen mask
    Of snow upon the mountains and the moors—
No—yet still steadfast, still unchangeable,
10   Pillow'd upon my fair love's ripening breast,
To feel for ever its soft fall and swell,
    Awake for ever in a sweet unrest,
Still, still to hear her tender-taken breath,
And so live ever—or else swoon to death.
    —1838 (WRITTEN 1819)

La Belle Dame sans Merci[2]

O what can ail thee, knight-at-arms,
    Alone and palely loitering?
The sedge[3] has wither'd from the lake,
    And no birds sing.

5 O what can ail thee, knight-at-arms,
    So haggard, and so woe-begone?
The squirrel's granary is full,
    And the harvest's done.

I see a lily[4] on thy brow,
10   With anguish moist and fever dew
And on thy cheeks a fading rose
    Fast withereth too.

I met a lady in the meads,°   *meadows*
    Full beautiful—a faery's child,

15 Her hair was long, her foot was light,
    And her eyes were wild.

I made a garland for her head,
    And bracelets too, and fragrant zone;°   *belt*
She look'd at me as she did love,
20   And made sweet moan.

I set her on my pacing steed,
    And nothing else saw all day long,
For sidelong would she bend and sing
    A faery's song.

25 She found me roots of relish sweet,
    And honey wild, and manna dew,[5]
And sure in language strange she said
    "I love thee true."

She took me to her elfin grot,°   *grotto*
30   And there she wept and sigh'd full sore,
And there I shut her wild wild eyes
    With kisses four.

And there she lulled me asleep,
    And there I dream'd—Ah! woe betide!
35 The latest° dream I ever dream'd   *last*
    On the cold hill side.

I saw pale kings and princes too,
    Pale warriors, death-pale were they all;
They cried, "La belle dame sans merci
40   Hath thee in thrall!"°   *captivity*

I saw their starved lips in the gloam,°   *twilight*
    With horrid warning gaped wide,
And I awoke, and found me here,
    On the cold hill's side.

45 And this is why I sojourn here,
    Alone and palely loitering,
Though the sedge is wither'd from the lake,
    And no birds sing.
    —1848 (WRITTEN 1819)

---

[1] *ablution* Religious ritual washing of the body.

[2] *La Belle Dame sans Merci* French: The beautiful lady without pity. This original version of the poem, found in a journal letter to George and Georgiana Keats, was first published in 1848. Keats's revised version was published in 1820.

[3] *sedge* Rush-like grass.

[4] *lily* Flower traditionally symbolic of death.

[5] *manna dew* See Exodus 16, in which God provides the Israelites with a food that falls from heaven, called manna.

La Belle Dame sans Mercy[1]

Ah, what can ail thee, wretched wight,°   *being*
   Alone and palely loitering;
The sedge[2] is wither'd from the lake,
   And no birds sing.

5 Ah, what can ail thee, wretched wight,
   So haggard and so woe-begone?
The squirrel's granary is full,
   And the harvest's done.

I see a lily[3] on thy brow,
10   With anguish moist and fever dew;
And on thy cheek a fading rose
   Fast withereth too.

I met a lady in the meads°   *meadows*
   Full beautiful, a fairy's child;
15 Her hair was long, her foot was light,
   And her eyes were wild.

I set her on my pacing steed,
   And nothing else saw all day long;
For sideways would she lean, and sing
20   A fairy's song.

I made a garland for her head,
   And bracelets too, and fragrant zone:°   *belt*
She look'd at me as she did love,
   And made sweet moan.

25 She found me roots of relish sweet,
   And honey wild, and manna[4] dew;
And sure in language strange she said,
   "I love thee true."

She took me to her elfin grot,°   *grotto*
30   And there she gaz'd and sighed deep.

And there I shut her wild sad eyes—
   So kiss'd to sleep.

And there we slumber'd on the moss,
   And there I dream'd, ah woe betide,
35 The latest dream I ever dream'd
   On the cold hill side.

I saw pale kings, and princes too,
   Pale warriors, death-pale were they all;
Who cry'd—"La belle dame sans mercy
40   Hath thee in thrall!"°   *captivity*

I saw their starv'd lips in the gloom
   With horrid warning gaped wide,
And I awoke, and found me here
   On the cold hill side.

45 And this is why I sojourn here
   Alone and palely loitering,
Though the sedge is wither'd from the lake,
   And no birds sing.
   —1820 (WRITTEN 1819)

Incipit altera Sonneta[5]

I have been endeavouring to discover a better sonnet stanza than we have. The legitimate[6] does not suit the language over-well from the pouncing rhymes—the other kind appears too elegaiac—and the couplet at the end of it has seldom a pleasing effect—I do not pretend to have succeeded—it will explain itself—

If by dull rhymes our English must be chain'd
  And, like Andromeda,[7] the Sonnet sweet
Fetter'd in spite of pained loveliness;
Let us find out, if we must be constrain'd
5 Sandals more interwoven & complete

---

[1] *La Belle … Mercy* French: The beautiful lady without pity. This version of the poem, a revision of "La Belle Dame sans Merci," was published in 1820.

[2] *sedge* Rush-like grass.

[3] *lily* Flower traditionally symbolic of death.

[4] *manna* See Exodus 16, in which God provides the Israelites with a food that falls from heaven, called manna.

[5] *Incipit altera Sonneta* Latin: Another Sonnet Begins.

[6] *The legitimate* I.e., the Petrarchan sonnet. The "other kind" to which Keats refers is the Shakespearean sonnet.

[7] *Andromeda* In Greek myth, Andromeda is tied to a rock to be devoured by a sea serpent after her mother boasts that she is more beautiful than the sea nymphs. Perseus, on his winged horse Pegasus (a symbol of poetic inspiration), rescues her.

To fit the naked foot of Poesy;
Let us inspect the Lyre,[1] & weigh the stress
Of every chord & see what may be gain'd
By ear industrious & attention meet;°   *fitting*
10   Misers of sound & syllable, no less
Than Midas of his coinage,[2] let us be
Jealous of dead leaves in the bay wreath Crown;[3]
So if we may not let the Muse[4] be free,
She will be bound with Garlands of her own.
—1836 (WRITTEN 1819)

Ode to Psyche[5]

O Goddess! hear these tuneless numbers, wrung
   By sweet enforcement and remembrance dear,
And pardon that thy secrets should be sung
   Even into thine own soft-conched[6] ear:
5   Surely I dreamt to-day, or did I see
     The winged Psyche with awaken'd eyes?
I wander'd in a forest thoughtlessly,
     And, on the sudden, fainting with surprise,
Saw two fair creatures, couched side by side
10   In deepest grass, beneath the whisp'ring roof
     Of leaves and trembled blossoms, where there ran
       A brooklet, scarce espied:

'Mid hush'd, cool-rooted flowers, fragrant-eyed,
   Blue, silver-white, and budded Tyrian,[7]

15   They lay calm-breathing on the bedded grass;
     Their arms embraced, and their pinions° too;   *wings*
   Their lips touch'd not, but had not bade adieu,
As if disjoined by soft-handed slumber,
And ready still past kisses to outnumber
20   At tender eye-dawn of aurorean[8] love:
       The winged boy° I knew;   *cupid*
   But who wast thou, O happy, happy dove?
       His Psyche true!

O latest born and liveliest vision far
25   Of all Olympus'[9] faded hierarchy!
Fairer than Phœbe's[10] sapphire-region'd star,
   Or Vesper,[11] amorous glow-worm of the sky;
Fairer than these, though temple thou hast none,
     Nor altar heap'd with flowers;
30   Nor virgin-choir to make delicious moan
     Upon the midnight hours;
No voice, no lute, no pipe, no incense sweet
   From chain-swung censer° teeming;   *incense burner*
No shrine, no grove, no oracle, no heat
35   Of pale-mouth'd prophet dreaming.

O brightest! Though too late for antique vows,
   Too, too late for the fond believing
     lyre,°   *stringed instrument*
When holy were the haunted forest boughs,
   Holy the air, the water, and the fire;
40   Yet even in these days so far retir'd
   From happy pieties, thy lucent fans,°   *wings*
     Fluttering among the faint Olympians,
I see, and sing, by my own eyes inspired.
So let me be thy choir, and make a moan
45   Upon the midnight hours;
Thy voice, thy lute, thy pipe, thy incense sweet
   From swinged censer teeming;
Thy shrine, thy grove, thy oracle, thy heat
   Of pale-mouth'd prophet dreaming.

50   Yes, I will be thy priest, and build a fane°   *temple*
   In some untrodden region of my mind,

---

[1] *Lyre* Stringed instrument.

[2] *Midas ... coinage* In Ovid's *Metamorphoses*, King Midas of Phrygia gets his wish that everything he touches will turn to gold.

[3] *bay wreath Crown* Wreaths made of leaves of the bay laurel were traditionally bestowed upon those who distinguished themselves in poetry.

[4] *Muse* One of nine daughters of Zeus and Mnemosyne, each of whom presided over and provided inspiration for an aspect of learning or the arts.

[5] *Psyche* In classical mythology, a young woman who was beloved by Cupid, winged god of love and son of Venus. After winning over Venus, who was jealous of Psyche's beauty, Psyche was granted immortality by Jupiter. In Greek myth she is often a personification of the soul: her name in Greek means soul or mind as well as butterfly.

[6] *soft-conched* Shaped like a conch shell, but soft.

[7] *Tyrian* Purple. From the Phoenician city of Tyre, where purple or crimson dyes were made in ancient times.

[8] *aurorean* I.e., dawning. Aurora was the goddess of the dawn.

[9] *Olympus* Mount Olympus, home of the gods.

[10] *Phœbe* Diana, goddess of the moon.

[11] *Vesper* Venus, the evening star.

Where branched thoughts, new grown with pleasant
    pain,
    Instead of pines shall murmur in the wind:
Far, far around shall those dark-cluster'd trees
55   Fledge the wild-ridged mountains steep by steep;
And there by zephyrs,° streams, and birds,   *breezes*
    and bees,
    The moss-lain Dryads° shall be lull'd   *wood nymphs*
    to sleep;
    And in the midst of quietness
    A rosy sanctuary will I dress
60 With the wreath'd trellis of a working brain,
    With buds, and bells, and stars without a name,
With all the gardener Fancy e'er could feign,
    Who breeding flowers, will never breed the same:
And there shall be for thee all soft delight
65   That shadowy thought can win,
A bright torch, and a casement ope°   *window opened*
    at night,
To let the warm Love in!
—1820

Ode to a Nightingale [1]

1

My heart aches, and a drowsy numbness pains
    My sense, as though of hemlock° I had   *poison*
    drunk,
Or emptied some dull opiate to the drains
    One minute past, and Lethe-wards[2] had sunk:
5 'Tis not through envy of thy happy lot,
    But being too happy in thine happiness—

That thou, light-winged Dryad°   *wood-nymph*
    of the trees,
    In some melodious plot
Of beechen green, and shadows numberless,
10   Singest of summer in full-throated ease.

2

O, for a draught of vintage! that hath been
    Cool'd a long age in the deep-delved earth,
Tasting of Flora[3] and the country green,
    Dance, and Provençal song,[4] and sunburnt mirth!
15 O for a beaker full of the warm South,
    Full of the true, the blushful Hippocrene,[5]
    With beaded bubbles winking at the brim,
    And purple-stained mouth;
    That I might drink, and leave the world unseen,
20   And with thee fade away into the forest dim:

3

Fade far away, dissolve, and quite forget
    What thou among the leaves hast never known,
The weariness, the fever, and the fret
    Here, where men sit and hear each other groan;
25 Where palsy shakes a few, sad, last gray hairs,
    Where youth grows pale, and spectre-thin, and dies;
    Where but to think is to be full of sorrow
    And leaden-eyed despairs,
    Where Beauty cannot keep her lustrous eyes,
    Or new Love pine at them beyond to-morrow.

4

Away! away! for I will fly to thee,
    Not charioted by Bacchus and his pards,[6]
But on the viewless wings of Poesy,
    Though the dull brain perplexes and retards:
35 Already with thee! tender is the night,
    And haply° the Queen-Moon is on her throne,   *maybe*
    Cluster'd around by all her starry Fays;°   *fairies*

---

[1] *Ode to a Nightingale* Written about 1 May 1819. Twenty years later, Keats's friend and housemate Charles Armitage Brown remembered the composition of the poem: "In the spring of 1819 a nightingale had built her nest near my house. Keats felt a tranquil and continual joy in her song; and one morning he took his chair from the breakfast-table to the grass-plot under a plum-tree, where he sat for two or three hours. When he came into the house, I perceived he had some scraps of paper in his hand, and these he was quietly thrusting behind the books. On enquiry, I found those scraps, four or five in number, contained his poetic feeling on the song of our nightingale."

[2] *Lethe-wards* Towards Lethe, the river of forgetfulness which, in classical mythology, the dead must cross to reach Hades, the underworld.

[3] *Flora* Roman goddess of flowers.

[4] *Provençal song* The region of Provençe, in southern France, was known in the Middle Ages for its poet-singers, or troubadours.

[5] *Hippocrene* Fountain of the Muses (nine sister goddesses who presided over aspects of learning and the arts) located on the sacred Mount Helicon. Its waters were said to provide poetic inspiration.

[6] *Bacchus ... pards* Bacchus, the god of wine, rides a chariot drawn by pards, or leopards.

But here there is no light,
  Save what from heaven is with the breezes blown
40   Through verdurous glooms and winding mossy ways.

5

I cannot see what flowers are at my feet,
  Nor what soft incense hangs upon the boughs,
But, in embalmed° darkness, guess each sweet   *fragrant*
  Wherewith the seasonable month endows
45 The grass, the thicket, and the fruit-tree wild;
  White hawthorn, and the pastoral eglantine;
    Fast fading violets cover'd up in leaves;
      And mid-May's eldest child,
The coming musk-rose, full of dewy wine,
50   The murmurous haunt of flies on summer eves.

6

Darkling[1] I listen; and, for many a time
  I have been half in love with easeful Death,
Call'd him soft names in many a mused rhyme,
  To take into the air my quiet breath;
55 Now more than ever seems it rich to die,
  To cease upon the midnight with no pain,
    While thou art pouring forth thy soul abroad
      In such an ecstasy!
Still wouldst thou sing, and I have ears in vain—
60   To thy high requiem[2] become a sod.

7

Thou wast not born for death, immortal Bird!
  No hungry generations tread thee down;
The voice I hear this passing night was heard
  In ancient days by emperor and clown:°   *rustic*
65 Perhaps the self-same song that found a path
  Through the sad heart of Ruth, when, sick for home,
    She stood in tears amid the alien corn;[3]
      The same that oft-times hath
Charm'd magic casements, opening on the foam
70   Of perilous seas, in faery lands forlorn.

8

Forlorn! the very word is like a bell
  To toll me back from thee to my sole self!
Adieu! the fancy cannot cheat so well
  As she is fam'd to do, deceiving elf.
75 Adieu! adieu! thy plaintive anthem fades
  Past the near meadows, over the still stream,
    Up the hill-side; and now 'tis buried deep
      In the next valley-glades:
Was it a vision, or a waking dream?
80   Fled is that music—Do I wake or sleep?
—1819

Ode on a Grecian Urn

1

Thou still unravish'd bride of quietness,
  Thou foster-child of silence and slow time,
Sylvan° historian, who canst thus express   *woodland*
  A flowery tale more sweetly than our rhyme:
5 What leaf-fring'd legend haunts about thy shape
  Of deities or mortals, or of both,
    In Tempe or the dales of Arcady?[4]
What men or gods are these? What maidens loth?
  What mad pursuit? What struggle to escape?
10   What pipes and timbrels?° What   *tambourines*
    wild ecstasy?

2

Heard melodies are sweet, but those unheard
  Are sweeter; therefore, ye soft pipes, play on;
Not to the sensual° ear, but, more endear'd,   *physical*
  Pipe to the spirit ditties of no tone:
15 Fair youth, beneath the trees, thou canst not leave
  Thy song, nor ever can those trees be bare;
    Bold Lover, never, never canst thou kiss,
Though winning near the goal—yet, do not grieve;
  She cannot fade, though thou hast not thy bliss,
20   For ever wilt thou love, and she be fair!

[1] *Darkling* In the dark.
[2] *requiem* Mass sung for the dead.
[3] *Ruth ... corn* Widow in the Book of Ruth (1-4) who leaves Moab for Judah with her mother-in-law Naomi because of famine.

[4] *Tempe* Valley in ancient Greece renowned for its beauty; *Arcady* Ideal region of rural life, named for a mountainous district in Greece.

3

Ah, happy, happy boughs! that cannot shed
    Your leaves, nor ever bid the Spring adieu;
And, happy melodist, unwearied,
    For ever piping songs for ever new;
25 More happy love! more happy, happy love!
    For ever warm and still to be enjoy'd,
        For ever panting, and for ever young;
All breathing human passion far above,
    That leaves a heart high-sorrowful and cloy'd,
30   A burning forehead, and a parching tongue.

4

Who are these coming to the sacrifice?
    To what green altar, O mysterious priest,
Lead'st thou that heifer lowing at the skies,
    And all her silken flanks with garlands drest?
35 What little town by river or sea shore,
    Or mountain-built with peaceful citadel,
        Is emptied of this folk, this pious morn?
And, little town, thy streets for evermore
    Will silent be; and not a soul to tell
40   Why thou art desolate, can e'er return.

5

O Attic[1] shape! Fair attitude! with brede°   *interwoven design*
    Of marble men and maidens overwrought,°   *overlaid*
With forest branches and the trodden weed;
    Thou, silent form, dost tease us out of thought
45 As doth eternity: Cold Pastoral!
    When old age shall this generation waste,
        Thou shalt remain, in midst of other woe
Than ours, a friend to man, to whom thou say'st,
    "Beauty is truth, truth beauty,"—that is all
50   Ye know on earth, and all ye need to know.[2]
    —1820

---

[1] *Attic*   I.e., Greek. Attica was an ancient region of Greece that had Athens as its capital.

[2] *Beauty is ... know*   The quotation marks in line 49 are present in Keats's 1820 volume of poems, but are absent in transcripts of the poem made by Keats's friends and in the version of the poem published in *Annals of the Fine Arts* in 1820. As a result, their presence has engendered much critical debate. It is unclear whether Keats meant the last line and a half to be spoken by the poet, or whether the entire final two lines are the imagined declaration of the urn.

Ode on Melancholy[3]

I

No, No, go not to Lethe,[4] neither twist
Wolf's-bane,[5] tight-rooted, for its poisonous
    wine;
Nor suffer thy pale forehead to be kiss'd
    By nightshade, ruby grape of Proserpine;[6]
5 Make not your rosary of yew-berries,[7]
    Nor let the beetle, nor the death-moth[8] be
        Your mournful Psyche,[9] nor the downy owl
A partner in your sorrow's mysteries;[10]

---

[3] *Ode on Melancholy*   In the original manuscript version, the poem opened with the following stanza:
Though you should build a bark of dead men's bones,
    And rear a phantom gibbet for a mast,
Stitch creeds together for a sail, with groans
    To fill it out, bloodstained and aghast;
Although your rudder be a Dragon's tail,
    Long sever'd, yet still hard with agony,
Your cordage large uprootings from the skull
Of bald Medusa; certes you would fail
    To find Melancholy, whether she
        Dreameth in any isle of Lethe dull.
(Medusa was one of the Gorgons, three monstrous, winged sisters who had snakes for hair.)

[4] *Lethe*   River in Hades, the classical underworld, whose waters produce forgetfulness.

[5] *Wolf's-bane*   Poisonous plant native to Europe.

[6] *nightshade*   Plants with poisonous berries; *Proserpine* Daughter of Demeter who was abducted by Pluto, god of the underworld, and made queen of Hades. Her mother, goddess of the harvest, mourned for her daughter and so caused an eternal winter until Pluto was prevailed upon to allow Proserpine to return to her mother six months of every year.

[7] *yew-berries*   Poisonous berries of the yew tree, which is commonly planted in graveyards and is therefore often regarded as symbolic of death or sadness.

[8] *beetle*   The scarab, a large black beetle that Egyptians placed in their tombs as a symbol of resurrection; *death-moth* Death's-head moth, whose wings carry a mark resembling a human skull.

[9] *Psyche*   In classical mythology, a young woman who was beloved by Cupid, winged god of love and son of Venus. After winning over Venus, who was jealous of Psyche's beauty, Psyche was granted immortality by Jupiter. In Greek myth she is often a personification of the soul. Her name in Greek means butterfly as well as soul. Psyche was often represented as a butterfly flying out of a dying person's mouth.

[10] *mysteries*   I.e., secret rites or ceremonies.

For shade to shade will come too drowsily,
10   And drown the wakeful anguish of the soul.

2

But when the melancholy fit shall fall
    Sudden from heaven like a weeping cloud,
That fosters the droop-headed flowers all,
    And hides the green hill in an April shroud;
15 Then glut thy sorrow on a morning rose,
    Or on the rainbow of the salt sand-wave,
        Or on the wealth of globed peonies;
Or if thy mistress some rich anger shows,
    Emprison her soft hand, and let her rave,
20   And feed deep, deep upon her peerless eyes.

3

She dwells with Beauty—Beauty that must die;
    And Joy, whose hand is ever at his lips
Bidding adieu; and aching Pleasure nigh,
    Turning to poison while the bee-mouth sips:
25 Ay, in the very temple of Delight
    Veil'd Melancholy has her sovran° shrine,   *sovereign*
        Though seen of none save him whose
            strenuous tongue
Can burst Joy's grape against his palate fine;°   *refined*
    His soul shall taste the sadness of her might,
30   And be among her cloudy trophies hung.
—1820

Ode on Indolence[1]

"They toil not, neither do they spin."[2]

1

One morn before me were three figures seen,
    With bowed necks, and joined hands, side-faced;
And one behind the other stepp'd serene,
    In placid sandals, and in white robes graced;
5 They pass'd, like figures on a marble urn,

When shifted round to see the other side;
    They came again; as when the urn once more
Is shifted round, the first seen shades return;
    And they were strange to me, as may betide
10   With vases, to one deep in Phidian lore.[3]

2

How is it, shadows, that I knew ye not?
    How came ye muffled in so hush a masque?°   *play*
Was it a silent deep-disguised plot
    To steal away, and leave without a task
15 My idle days? Ripe was the drowsy hour;
    The blissful cloud of summer-indolence
        Benumb'd my eyes; my pulse grew less and less;
Pain had no sting, and pleasure's wreath no flower:
    O, why did ye not melt, and leave my sense
20   Unhaunted quite of all but—nothingness?

3

A third time pass'd they by, and, passing, turn'd
    Each one the face a moment whiles to me;
Then faded, and to follow them I burn'd
    And ached for wings because I knew the three;
25 The first was a fair Maid, and Love her name;
    The second was Ambition, pale of cheek,
        And ever watchful with fatigued eye;
The last, whom I love more, the more of blame
    Is heap'd upon her, maiden most unmeek,
30   I knew to be my demon Poesy.

4

They faded, and, forsooth! I wanted wings:
    O folly! What is Love! and where is it?
And for that poor Ambition! It springs
    From a man's little heart's short fever-fit;
35 For Poesy! No—she has not a joy—
    At least for me—so sweet as drowsy noons,
        And evenings steep'd in honeyed indolence;
O, for an age so shelter'd from annoy,°   *harm*
    That I may never know how change the moons,
40   Or hear the voice of busy common sense!

[1] *Ode on Indolence* See the 1819 letter to George and Georgiana Keats, reprinted below, in which Keats describes the bout of indolence that is thought to have inspired this poem.

[2] *They toil ... spin* From Matthew 6.28–89: "Consider the lilies of the field, how they grow; they toil not, neither do they spin: And yet I say unto you, That even Solomon in all his glory was not arrayed like one of these."

[3] *Phidian lore* Lore concerning Phidias, the fifth-century Athenian sculptor of what were later named the Elgin Marbles, the marble sculptures that decorated the outside of the Parthenon and were brought to England by Lord Elgin.

5

A third time came they by—alas! wherefore?
    My sleep had been embroider'd with dim dreams;
My soul had been a lawn besprinkled o'er
    With flowers, and stirring shades, and baffled beams:
45 The morn was clouded, but no shower fell,
    Tho' in her lids hung the sweet tears of May;
        The open casement press'd a new-leav'd vine,
    Let in the budding warmth and
        throstle's° lay;°   *thrush's / song*
        O shadows! 'twas a time to bid farewell!
50   Upon your skirts had fallen no tears of mine.

6

So, ye three ghosts, adieu! Ye cannot raise
    My head cool-bedded in the flowery grass;
For I would not be dieted with praise,
    A pet-lamb in a sentimental farce!
55 Fade softly from my eyes, and be once more
    In masque-like figures on the dreamy urn;
        Farewell! I yet have visions for the night,
    And for the day faint visions there is store;
        Vanish, ye phantoms! from my idle spright,°   *spirit*
60   Into the clouds, and never more return!
—1848 (WRITTEN 1819)

To Autumn

1

Season of mists and mellow fruitfulness,
    Close bosom-friend of the maturing sun;
Conspiring with him how to load and bless
    With fruit the vines that round the thatch-eves run;
5 To bend with apples the moss'd cottage-trees,
    And fill all fruit with ripeness to the core;
        To swell the gourd, and plump the hazel shells
    With a sweet kernel; to set budding more,
        And still more, later flowers for the bees,
10   Until they think warm days will never cease,
        For Summer has o'er-brimm'd their clammy cells.

2

Who hath not seen thee oft amid thy store?
    Sometimes whoever seeks abroad may find
Thee sitting careless on a granary floor,
    Thy hair soft-lifted by the winnowing wind;
15 Or on a half-reap'd furrow sound asleep,
    Drows'd with the fume of poppies, while thy hook[1]
        Spares the next swath and all its twined flowers:
    And sometimes like a gleaner[2] thou dost keep
20   Steady thy laden head across a brook;
        Or by a cider-press, with patient look,
        Thou watchest the last oozings hours by hours.

3

Where are the songs of Spring? Ay, where are they?
    Think not of them, thou hast thy music too—
25 While barred clouds bloom the soft-dying day,
    And touch the stubble-plains with rosy hue;
Then in a wailful choir the small gnats mourn
    Among the river sallows,° borne aloft   *willows*
        Or sinking as the light wind lives or dies;
30 And full-grown lambs loud bleat from hilly bourn;°   *realm*
    Hedge-crickets sing; and now with treble soft
    The red-breast whistles from a
        garden-croft;°   *enclosed garden*
    And gathering swallows twitter in the skies.
—1820

This Living Hand[3]

This living hand, now warm and capable
    Of earnest grasping, would, if it were cold
And in the icy silence of the tomb,
So haunt thy days and chill thy dreaming nights
5 That thou would wish thine own heart dry of blood
So in my veins red life might stream again,
and thou be conscience-calme'd—see here it is—
I hold it towards you—
—1898 (WRITTEN C. 1819)

---

1 *hook* I.e., a reaping-hook or scythe.
2 *gleaner* One who gathers the grain left by the reaper.
3 *This Living Hand* A fragment whose context is unknown.

Selected Letters

To Benjamin Bailey[1]
22 November 1817

My Dear Bailey,

... O I wish I was as certain of the end of all your troubles as that of your momentary start about the authenticity of the Imagination. I am certain of nothing but of the holiness of the Heart's affections and the truth of imagination—What the imagination seizes as Beauty must be truth—whether it existed before or not—for I have the same Idea of all our Passions as of Love they are all in their sublime, creative of essential Beauty—In a Word, you may know my favourite Speculation by my first Book and the little song I sent in my last[2]—which is a representation from the fancy of the probable mode of operating in these Matters—The Imagination may be compared to Adam's dream[3]—he awoke and found it truth. I am the more zealous in this affair, because I have never yet been able to perceive how any thing can be known for truth by consequitive[4] reasoning—and yet it must be—Can it be that even the greatest Philosopher ever arrived at his goal without putting aside numerous objections—However it may be, O for a Life of Sensations rather than of Thoughts! It is "a Vision in the form of Youth" a Shadow of reality to come—and this consideration has further convinced me for it has come as auxiliary to another favourite Speculation of mine, that we shall enjoy ourselves here after by having what we called happiness on Earth repeated in a finer tone and so repeated—And yet such a fate can only befall those who delight in sensation rather than hunger as you do after Truth—Adam's dream will do here and seems to be a conviction that Imagination and its empyreal[5] reflection is the same as human Life and its spiritual repetition. But as I was saying—the simple imaginative Mind may have its rewards in the repetition of its own silent Working coming continually on the spirit with a fine suddenness—to compare great things with small—have you never by being surprised with an old Melody—in a delicious place—by a delicious voice, felt over again your very speculations and surmises at the time it first operated on your soul—do you not remember forming to yourself the singer's face more beautiful [than] it was possible and yet with the elevation of the Moment you did not think so—even then you were mounted on the Wings of Imagination so high—that the Prototype must be here after—that delicious face you will see—What a time! I am continually running away from the subject—sure this cannot be exactly the case with a complex Mind—one that is imaginative and at the same time careful of its fruits—who would exist partly on sensation partly on thought—to whom it is necessary that years should bring the philosophic Mind[6]—such an one I consider yours and therefore it is necessary to your eternal Happiness that you not only have drink this old Wine of Heaven which I shall call the redigestion of our most ethereal Musings on Earth; but also increase in knowledge and know all things. I am glad to hear you are in a fair Way for Easter—you will soon get through your unpleasant reading and then!—but the world is full of troubles and I have not much reason to think myself pestered with many—I think Jane or Marianne has a better opinion of me than I deserve—for really and truly I do not think my Brother's illness connected with mine[7]—you know more of the real Cause than they do—nor have I any chance of being rack'd as you have been[8]—you perhaps at one time thought there was such a thing as Worldly Happiness to be arrived at, at certain periods of time marked out—you have of necessity from your disposition been thus led away—I scarcely remember counting upon any Happiness—I look not for it if it be not in the present hour—nothing startles me

[1] BENJAMIN BAILEY Undergraduate student in Divinity at Oxford University. Keats had stayed with him in September while he was working on Endymion.

[2] my first book I.e., the first book of Endymion; little song ... last The first five stanzas of "Ode to Sorrow," from Book 4 of Endymion, which Keats had enclosed with his previous letter.

[3] Adam's dream See Milton, Paradise Lost 8.460–90, in which Adam dreams about Eve and wakes to find she has been created.

[4] consequitive Consecutive and consequent: a word of Keats's invention.

[5] empyreal Celestial; pertaining to the highest heavens.

[6] philosophic Mind Cf. Wordsworth, Ode: Intimations of Immortality, line 186.

[7] Jane or ... mine Jane and Marianne Reynolds, two friends of Keats, were afraid that his illness was a sign of tuberculosis, from which Keats's youngest brother, Tom, was suffering.

[8] rack'd ... been Bailey was upset over a love affair that had recently ended.

beyond the Moment. The setting sun will always set me to rights—or if a Sparrow come before my Window I take part in its existence and pick about the Gravel. The first thing that strikes me on hearing a Misfortune having befallen another is this. Well it cannot be helped.—he will have the pleasure of trying the resources of his spirit, and I beg now my dear Bailey that hereafter should you observe any thing cold in me not to [put] it to the account of heartlessness but abstraction—for I assure you I sometimes feel not the influence of a Passion or Affection during a whole week—and so long this sometimes continues I begin to suspect myself and the genuineness of my feelings at other times—thinking them a few barren Tragedy-tears—My Brother Tom is much improved—he is going to Devonshire—whither I shall follow him—at present I am just arrived at Dorking to change the Scene—change the Air and give me a spur to wind up my Poem, of which there are wanting 500 Lines. [...]

> Your affectionate friend
> John Keats—

I want to say much more to you—a few hints will set me going
Direct Burford Bridge near dorking

To George and Thomas Keats

21, 27 (?) December 1817
Hampstead Sunday

My Dear Brothers,

... I spent Friday evening with Wells[1] & went the next morning to see *Death on the Pale horse*. It is a wonderful picture, when West's[2] age is considered; But there is nothing to be intense upon; no women one feels mad to kiss; no face swelling into reality. the excellence of every Art is its intensity, capable of making all disagreeables evaporate, from their being in close relationship with Beauty & Truth—Examine *King Lear*[3] & you will find

---

[1] *Wells* Charles Wells, a school friend of Tom Keats.

[2] *West* American painter Benjamin West (1738–1820), who moved to England and became President of the Royal Academy. The painting *Christ Rejected*, mentioned later in this letter, is West's.

[3] *King Lear* Painting by West that depicts the storm scene in Shakespeare's play.

this exemplified throughout; but in this picture we have unpleasantness without any momentous depth of speculation excited, in which to bury its repulsiveness—The picture is larger than *Christ rejected*—I dined with Haydon[4] the sunday after you left, & had a very pleasant day, I dined too (for I have been out too much lately) with Horace Smith[5] & met his two Brothers with Hill & Kingston & one Du Bois, they only served to convince me, how superior humour is to wit in respect to enjoyment—These men say things which make one start, without making one feel, they are all alike; their manners are alike; they all know fashionables; they have a mannerism in their very eating & drinking, in their mere handling a Decanter—They talked of Kean[6] & his low company—Would I were with that company instead of yours said I to myself! I know such like acquaintance will never do for me & yet I am going to Reynolds,[7] on Wednesday—Brown & Dilke[8] walked with me & back from the Christmas pantomime. I had not a dispute but a disquisition[9] with Dilke, on various subjects; several things dovetailed in my mind, & at once it struck me, what quality went to form a Man of Achievement especially in Literature & which Shakespeare possessed so enormously—I mean *Negative Capability*, that is when man is capable of being in uncertainties, Mysteries, doubts, without any irritable reaching after fact & reason—Coleridge, for instance, would let go by a fine isolated verisimilitude caught from the Penetralium[10] of mystery, from being incapable of remaining content with half knowledge. This pursued through Volumes would perhaps take us no further than

---

[4] *Haydon* Painter Benjamin Haydon (1786–1846).

[5] *Horace Smith* Famous literary wit (1779–1849). The other men mentioned are all minor writers or literary critics.

[6] *Kean* Shakespearean actor Edmund Kean (1787–1833).

[7] *Reynolds* Lawyer and poet John Hamilton Reynolds (1796–1852).

[8] *Brown and Dilke* Writers Charles Wentworth Dilke (1789–1864) and Charles Armitage Brown (1786–1842), a close friend and housemate of Keats's who cared for him after he first became ill and who later wrote his biography.

[9] *disquisition* Systematic investigation.

[10] *Penetralium* I.e., the innermost part. From the Latin *penetralia*, the innermost parts of a temple.

Benjamin West, *King Lear* (1788).

this, that with a great poet the sense of Beauty over-comes every other consideration, or rather obliterates all consideration.

Shelley's poem[1] is out, & there are words about its being objected too, as much as Queen Mab was. Poor Shelley I think he has his Quota of good qualities, in sooth la!![2] Write soon to your most sincere friend & affectionate Brother.

John

To John Hamilton Reynolds
3 February 1818
Hampstead

My Dear Reynolds,

I thank you for your dish of Filberts[3]—Would I could get a basket of them by way of dessert every day for the sum of two pence—Would we were a sort of ethe-real Pigs, & turn'd loose to feed upon spiritual Mast[4] & Acorns—which would be merely being a squirrel & feeding upon filberts. For what is a squirrel but an airy pig, or a filbert but a sort of archangelical acorn. About the nuts being worth cracking, all I can say is that where there are a throng of delightful Images ready drawn simplicity is the only thing. The first is the best on

---

[1] *Shelley's poem* Shelley's *Laon and Cythna* (*The Revolt of Islam*), which he was forced to withdraw because readers objected to the poem's description of incestuous love between its hero and heroine.

[2] *in sooth la* In truth.

[3] *Filberts* Hazelnuts.

[4] *Mast* Fruit of certain woodland trees, such as beech, oak, and chestnut.

account of the first line, and the "arrow—foil'd of its antler'd food"[1]—and moreover (and this is the only word or two I find fault with, the more because I have had so much reason to shun it as a quicksand) the last has "tender and true"—We must cut this, and not be rattle-snaked into any more of the like—It may be said that we ought to read our Contemporaries, that Wordsworth &c should have their due from us. But for the sake of a few fine imaginative or domestic passages, are we to be bullied into a certain Philosophy engendered in the whims of an Egotist—Every man has his speculations, but every man does not brood and peacock over them till he makes a false coinage and deceives himself—Many a man can travel to the very bourne[2] of Heaven, and yet want confidence to put down his halfseeing. Sancho[3] will invent a Journey heavenward as well as any body. We hate poetry that has a palpable design upon us—and if we do not agree, seems to put its hand in its breeches pocket.[4] Poetry should be great & unobtrusive, a thing which enters into one's soul, and does not startle it or amaze it with itself but with its subject.—How beautiful are the retired flowers! how would they lose their beauty were they to throng into the highway crying out, "admire me I am a violet! dote upon me I am a primrose!" Modern poets differ from the Elizabethans in this. Each of the moderns like an Elector of Hanover governs his petty state, & knows how many straws are swept daily from the Causeways in all his dominions & has a continual itching that all the Housewives should have their coppers well scoured: the antients were Emperors of vast Provinces, they had only heard of the remote ones and scarcely cared to visit them.—I will cut all this—I will have no more of Wordsworth or Hunt in particular—Why should we be of the tribe of Manasseh, when we can wander with Esau?[5] why should we kick against the Pricks, when we can walk on Roses? Why should we be owls, when we can be Eagles? Why be teased with "nice Eyed wagtails," when we have in sight "the Cherub Contemplation"?[6]—Why with Wordsworths "Matthew with a bough of wilding in his hand" when we can have Jacques "under an oak &c"?[7]—The secret of the Bough of Wilding will run through your head faster than I can write it —Old Matthew spoke to him some years ago on some nothing, & because he happens in an Evening Walk to imagine the figure of the old man—he must stamp it down in black & white, and it is henceforth sacred—I don't mean to deny Wordsworth's grandeur & Hunt's merit, but I mean to say we need not be teazed with grandeur & merit—when we can have them uncontaminated & unobtrusive. Let us have the old Poets, & robin Hood Your letter and its sonnets gave me more pleasure than will the 4th Book of Childe Harold[8] & the whole of any body's life & opinions. In return for your dish of filberts, I have gathered a few Catkins, I hope they'll look pretty.[9]

Yr sincere friend and Coscribbler
John Keats

To JOHN TAYLOR[10]
27 February 1818
Hampstead

My Dear Taylor,

Your alteration strikes me as being a great improvement—the page looks much better. And now I will attend to the Punctuations you speak of—the comma should be at *soberly*, and in the other passage the comma should follow *quiet*.[11] I am extremely indebted to you for this attention and also for your after admoni-

---

[1] *arrow ... food* Keats is commenting on Reynolds's "Sonnet on Robin Hood 1," which Reynolds had sent to Keats.

[2] *bourne* Realm.

[3] *Sancho* Sancho Panza, squire of the naive and idealistic Don Quixote in Miguel de Cervantes's *Don Quixote*.

[4] *put its ... pocket* I.e., refuse to fight (by putting one's fists away).

[5] *Why should ... Esau* In the Old Testament, the tribe of Manasseh lived according to the old way of life, while in Genesis 25 Esau sold his birthright and became an outlaw.

[6] *nice Eyed wagtails* From Leigh Hunt's *The Nymphs* 2.170; *the Cherub Contemplation* From Milton's *Il Penseroso* 54.

[7] *Matthew ... hand* From Wordsworth's *The Two April Mornings* 57–60; *under ... &c* From Shakespeare's *As You Like It* 2.1.31.

[8] *4th ... Harold* Canto 4 of Byron's *Childe Harold's Pilgrimage*, whose publication was eagerly anticipated at the time.

[9] *In return ... pretty* In return for the sonnets on Robin Hood that Reynolds had sent, Keats enclosed two poems of his own, *Robin Hood* and *Lines on the Mermaid Tavern*.

[10] *John Taylor* Partner in the publishing firm of Taylor and Hessey, who were publishing Keats's poem *Endymion* at this time.

[11] *soberly ... quiet* References to *Endymion* 1.149 and 1.247.

tions—It is a sorry thing for me that any one should have to overcome Prejudices in reading my Verses—that affects me more than any hyper-criticism on any particular Passage. In *Endymion* I have most likely but moved into the Go-cart from the leading strings. In Poetry I have a few Axioms, and you will see how far I am from their Centre. 1st I think Poetry should surprise by a fine excess and not by Singularity—it should strike the Reader as a wording of his own highest thoughts, and appear almost a Remembrance—2nd Its touches of Beauty should never be half way thereby making the reader breathless instead of content: the rise, the progress, the setting of imagery should like the Sun come natural to him—shine over him and set soberly although in magnificence leaving him in the Luxury of twilight—but it is easier to think what Poetry should be than to write it—and this leads me on to another axiom. That if Poetry comes not as naturally as the Leaves to a tree it had better not come at all. However it may be with me I cannot help looking into new countries with "O for a Muse of fire to ascend!"[1]— If *Endymion* serves me as a Pioneer perhaps I ought to be content. I have great reason to be content, for thank God I can read and perhaps understand Shakespeare to his depths, and I have I am sure many friends, who, if I fail, will attribute any change in my Life and Temper to Humbleness rather than to Pride—to a cowering under the Wings of great Poets rather than to a Bitterness that I am not appreciated. I am anxious to get *Endymion* printed that I may forget it and proceed. I have copied the 3rd Book and have begun the 4th. On running my Eye over the Proofs—I saw one Mistake I will notice it presently and also any others if there be any—There should be no comma in "the raft branch down sweeping from a tall Ash top"[2]—I have besides made one or two alterations and also altered the 13 Line Page 32 to make sense of it as you will see. I will take care the Printer shall not trip up my Heels—There should be no dash after Dryope in this Line "Dryope's lone lulling of her Child."[3] Remember me to Percy Street.

Your sincere and obligd friend
John Keats—

P.S. You shall have a short *Preface* in good time—

To Benjamin Bailey

13 March 1818
Teignmouth

My dear Bailey,

... I have never had your Sermon[4] from Wordsworth but Mrs. Dilke lent it me—You know my ideas about Religion—I do not think myself more in the right than other people and that nothing in this world is proveable. I wish I could enter into all your feelings on the subject merely for one short 10 Minutes and give you a Page or two to your liking. I am sometimes so very sceptical as to think Poetry itself a mere Jack a lantern to amuse whoever may chance to be struck with its brilliance—As Tradesmen say every thing is worth what it will fetch, so probably every mental pursuit takes its reality and worth from the ardour of the pursuer—being in itself a nothing —Ethereal things may at least be thus real, divided under three heads—Things real—things semireal—and no things—Things real—such as existences of Sun Moon & Stars and passages of Shakespeare—Things semireal such as Love, the Clouds &c which require a greeting of the Spirit to make them wholly exist—and Nothings which are made Great and dignified by an ardent pursuit— Which by the by stamps the burgundy mark on the bottles of our Minds, insomuch as they are able to "*consecrate whate'er they look upon*"[5] I have written a Sonnet here of a somewhat collateral nature—so don't imagine it an a propos des bottes.[6]

[*The Human Seasons* is included here.]

Aye this may be carried—but what am I talking of—it is an old maxim of mine and of course must be well known that every point of thought is the centre of an

---

1 *O for ... ascend* Cf. Shakespeare, *Henry V* Prologue 1: "O for a Muse of fire, that would ascend / The brightest heaven of invention."

2 *the raft ... top* From *Endymion* 1.334–35.

3 *Dryope's ... Child* From *Endymion* 1.495.

4 *your Sermon* Bailey, like many clergymen at the time, had written a memorial sermon for Princess Charlotte, who died in childbirth in 1817.

5 *consecrate ... upon* From Percy Shelley's *Hymn to Intellectual Beauty* 13–14.

6 *a propos des bottes* French: on the subject of boots.

intellectual world—the two uppermost thoughts in a Man's mind are the two poles of his World he revolves on them and every thing is southward or northward to him through their means—We take but three steps from feathers to iron. Now my dear fellow I must once for all tell you I have not one Idea of the truth of any of my speculations—I shall never be a Reasoner because I care not to be in the right, when retired from bickering and in a proper philosophical temper ... My Brother Tom desires to be remember'd to you—he has just this moment had a spitting of blood poor fellow— Remember me to [Gleig] and Whitehead—

Your affectionate friend
John Keats—

TO BENJAMIN BAILEY

18 July 1818

My dear Bailey,

... I am certain I have not a right feeling towards Women—at this moment I am striving to be just to them but I cannot—Is it because they fall so far beneath my Boyish imagination? When I was a Schoolboy I thought a fair Woman a pure Goddess, my mind was a soft nest in which some one of them slept though she knew it not—I have no right to expect more than their reality. I thought them ethereal above Men—I find them perhaps equal.... I do not like to think insults in a Lady's Company—I commit a Crime with her which absence would have not known—is it not extraordinary? When among Men I have no evil thoughts, no malice, no spleen[1]—I feel free to speak or to be silent—I can listen and from every one I can learn—my hands are in my pockets I am free from all suspicion and comfortable. When I am among Women I have evil thoughts, malice spleen—I cannot speak or be silent—I am full of Suspicions and therefore listen to no thing—I am in a hurry to be gone—You must be charitable and put all this perversity to my being disappointed since Boyhood—Yet with such feelings I am happier alone among Crowds of men, by myself or with a friend or two— With all this trust me Bailey I have not the least idea that Men of different feelings and inclinations are more short sighted than myself—I never rejoiced more than

at my Brother's Marriage[2] and shall do so at that of any of my friends—. I must absolutely get over this—but how? The only way is to find the root of evil, and so cure it "with backward mutters of dissevering Power."[3] That is a difficult thing; for an obstinate Prejudice can seldom be produced but from a gordian complication[4] of feelings, which must take time to unravell and care to keep unravelled—I could say a good deal about this but I will leave it in hopes of better and more worthy dispositions—and also content that I am wronging no one, for after all I do think better of Womankind than to suppose they care whether Mister John Keats five feet high likes them or not....

Your affectionate friend
John Keats—

TO RICHARD WOODHOUSE[5]

27 October 1818

My Dear Woodhouse,
Your Letter gave me a great satisfaction; more on account of its friendliness, than any relish of that matter in it which is accounted so acceptable in the "genus irritabile."[6] The best answer I can give you is in a clerklike manner to make some observations on two principle points, which seem to point like indices[7] into the midst of the whole pro and con, about genius, and views and achievements and ambition and coetera.[8] 1st As to the poetical Character itself, (I mean that sort of which, if I am any thing, I am a Member; that sort distinguished from the wordsworthian or egotistical

---

[1] spleen Irritability; ill-humor; melancholy.

[2] my Brother's Marriage Keats's brother George had recently married, as had Bailey.

[3] with ... Power From Milton's Comus 816–17, in which the author describes the spells that will release a lady from the enchantment of Comus.

[4] gordian complication I.e., as difficult to undo as the intricate knot tied by King Gordias.

[5] Richard Woodhouse Young lawyer who worked with Keats's publishers. Woodhouse was struck by Keats's talent and preserved manuscript copies of many of his poems and letters.

[6] genus irritabile Latin: irritable tribe. The complete phrase, from Horace, Epistles 2.2.102, is "irritable race of poets."

[7] indices Pointers.

[8] coetera Latin: the following; the next.

sublime; which is a thing per se and stands alone) it is not itself—it has no self—it is every thing and nothing—It has no character—it enjoys light and shade; it lives in gusto, be it foul or fair, high or low, rich or poor, mean or elevated—It has as much delight in conceiving an Iago as an Imogen.[1] What shocks the virtuous philosopher delights the chameleon Poet. It does no harm from its relish of the dark side of things any more than from its taste for the bright one; because they both end in speculation. A Poet is the most unpoetical of any thing in existence; because he has no Identity—he is continually in for—and filling some other Body—The Sun, the Moon, the Sea and Men and Women who are creatures of impulse are poetical and have about them an unchangeable attribute—the poet has none; no identity—he is certainly the most unpoetical of all God's Creatures. If then he has no self, and if I am a Poet, where is the Wonder that I should say I would write no more? Might I not at that very instant [have] been cogitating on the Characters of Saturn and Ops?[2] It is a wretched thing to confess; but is a very fact that not one word I ever utter can be taken for granted as an opinion growing out of my identical nature—how can it, when I have no nature? When I am in a room with People if I ever am free from speculating on creations of my own brain, then not myself goes home to myself: but the identity of every one in the room begins [so] to press upon me that, I am in a very little time annihilated—not only among Men; it would be the same in a Nursery of children: I know not whether I make myself wholly understood: I hope enough so to let you see that no dependence is to be placed on what I said that day.[3]

In the second place I will speak of my views, and of the life I purpose to myself—I am ambitious of doing the world some good: if I should be spared that may be the work of maturer years—in the interval I will assay to reach to as high a summit in Poetry as the nerve bestowed upon me will suffer. The faint conceptions I have of Poems to come brings the blood frequently into my forehead—All I hope is that I may not lose all interest in human affairs—that the solitary indifference I feel for applause even from the finest Spirits, will not blunt any acuteness of vision I may have. I do not think it will—I feel assured I should write from the mere yearning and fondness I have for the Beautiful even if my night's labours should be burnt every morning and no eye ever shine upon them. But even now I am perhaps not speaking from myself; but from some character in whose soul I now live. I am sure however that this next sentence is from myself. I feel your anxiety, good opinion and friendliness in the highest degree, and am

Yours most sincerely
John Keats

To George and Georgiana Keats[4]
14 February–3 May 1819

My dear Brother & Sister—

... [19 March] Yesterday I got a black eye—the first time I took a Cricket bat—Brown who is always one's friend in a disaster applied a leech to the eyelid, and there is no inflammation this morning though the ball hit me directly on the sight—'t was a white ball—I am glad it was not a clout—This is the second black eye I have had since leaving school—during all my school days I never had one at all—we must eat a peck before we die[5]—This morning I am in a sort of temper indolent and supremely careless: I long after a stanza or two of Thomson's *Castle of indolence*[6]—My passions are all asleep from my having slumbered till nearly eleven and weakened the animal fibre all over me to a delightful sensation about three degrees on this side of faintness—if I had teeth of pearl and the breath of lilies I

---

[1] *gusto* Term used by William Hazlitt to describe expressive vitality in visual arts as well as in poetry. See Hazlitt's essay "On Gusto" (1816); *Iago* Villain of Shakespeare's *Othello*; *Imogen* Heroine of Shakespeare's *Cymbeline*.

[2] *Saturn and Ops* King and queen of the Titans in Keats's *Hyperion* (1820).

[3] *what I ... day* Keats had told Woodhouse that he felt preempted by great poets of the past.

[4] *George and Georgiana Keats* Keats's brother and sister-in-law, who had emigrated to America. Keats would compose long letters to them, each of which spanned several months, and in which he would include transcriptions of his poems.

[5] *eat a peck ... die* Proverbial: everyone must eat a peck of dirt before he or she dies.

[6] *Thomson ... indolence* James Thomson's *The Castle of Indolence*, in which a wizard named Indolence puts a spell of indolence on tired travelers who are lured into his castle.

should call it langour—but as I am[1] I must call it Laziness—In this state of effeminacy the fibres of the brain are relaxed in common with the rest of the body, and to such a happy degree that pleasure has no show of enticement and pain no unbearable frown. Neither Poetry, nor Ambition, nor Love have any alertness of countenance as they pass by me: they seem rather like three figures on a greek vase—a Man and two women—whom no one but myself could distinguish in their disguisement. This is the only happiness; and is a rare instance of advantage in the body overpowering the Mind. I have this moment received a note from Haslam[2] in which he expects the death of his Father who has been for some time in a state of insensibility—his mother bears up he says very well—I shall go to [town] tomorrow to see him. This is the world—thus we cannot expect to give way many hours to pleasure—Circumstances are like Clouds continually gathering and bursting—While we are laughing the seed of some trouble is put into the wide arable land of events—while we are laughing it sprouts [it] grows and suddenly bears a poison fruit which we must pluck—Even so we have leisure to reason on the misfortunes of our friends; our own touch us too nearly for words. Very few men have ever arrived at a complete disinterestedness[3] of Mind: very few have been influenced by a pure desire of the benefit of others—in the greater part of the Benefactors of & to Humanity some meretricious motive has sullied their greatness—some melodramatic scenery has fascinated them—From the manner in which I feel Haslam's misfortune I perceive how far I am from any humble standard of disinterestedness—Yet this feeling ought to be carried to its highest pitch, as there is no fear of its ever injuring society—which it would do I fear pushed to an extremity—For in wild nature the Hawk would loose his Breakfast of Robins and the Robin his of Worms The Lion must starve as well as the swallow—The greater part of Men make their way with the same instinctiveness, the same unwandering eye from their purposes, the same animal eagerness as the Hawk—The Hawk wants a Mate, so does the Man—look at them both they set about it and procure one in the same manner—They want both a

nest and they both set about one in the same manner—they get their food in the same manner—The noble animal Man for his amusement smokes his pipe—the Hawk balances about the Clouds—that is the only difference of their leisures. This it is that makes the Amusement of Life—to a speculative Mind. I go among the Fields and catch a glimpse of a stoat[4] or a fieldmouse peeping out of the withered grass—the creature hath a purpose and its eyes are bright with it—I go amongst the buildings of a city and I see a Man hurrying along—to what? The Creature has a purpose and his eyes are bright with it. But then as Wordsworth says, "we have all one human heart"[5]— there is an electric fire in human nature tending to purify—so that among these human creatures there is continually some birth of new heroism—The pity is that we must wonder at it: as we should at finding a pearl in rubbish—I have no doubt that thousands of people never heard of have had hearts completely disinterested: I can remember but two—Socrates and Jesus—their Histories evince it—What I heard a little time ago, Taylor observe with respect to Socrates, may be said of Jesus—That he was so great a man that though he transmitted no writing of his own to posterity, we have his Mind and his sayings and his greatness handed to us by others. It is to be lamented that the history of the latter was written and revised by Men interested in the pious frauds of Religion. Yet through all this I see his splendour. Even here though I myself am pursuing the same instinctive course as the veriest human animal you can think of—I am however young writing at random—straining at particles of light in the midst of a great darkness—without knowing the bearing of any one assertion of any one opinion. Yet may I not in this be free from sin? May there not be superior beings amused with any graceful, though instinctive attitude my mind may fall into, as I am entertained with the alertness of a Stoat or the anxiety of a Deer? Though a quarrel in the streets is a thing to be hated, the energies displayed in it are fine; the commonest Man shows a grace in his quarrel—By a superior being our reasoning may take the same tone—though erroneous they may be fine—This is the very thing in which consists poetry; and if so it is not so fine a thing as philosophy—For the same reason that an

---

[1]   [Keats's note]   Especially as I have a black eye.

[2]   *Haslam*   Keats's friend William Haslam, a businessman.

[3]   *disinterestedness*   State unmotivated by self-interest.

[4]   *stoat*   Weasel-like animal.

[5]   *we have ... heart*   From *The Old Cumberland Beggar* 152–53.

eagle is not so fine a thing as a truth—Give me this credit—Do you not think I strive—to know myself? Give me this credit— and you will not think that on my own account I repeat Milton's lines

How charming is divine Philosophy
Not harsh and crabbed as dull fools suppose
But musical as is Apollo's lute[1]—

No—no for myself—feeling grateful as I do to have got into a state of mind to relish them properly—Nothing ever becomes real till it is experienced—Even a Proverb is no proverb to you till your Life has illustrated it— ...

[21 April] I have been reading lately two very different books Robertson's *America* and Voltaire's *Siecle De Louis xiv* It is like walking arm and arm between Pizzarro and the great-little Monarch.[2] In How lamentable a case do we see the great body of the people in both instances: in the first, where Men might seem to inherit quiet of Mind from unsophisticated sense; from uncontamination of civilisation; and especially from their being as it were estranged from the mutual helps of Society and its mutual injuries—and thereby more immediately under the Protection of Providence—even there they had mortal pains to bear as bad; or even worse than Baliffs, Debts and Poverties of civilised Life—The whole appears to resolve into this—that Man is originally "a poor forked creature"[3] subject to the same mischances as the beasts of the forest, destined to hardships and disquietude of some kind or other. If he improves by degrees his bodily accommodations and comforts—at each stage, at each accent there are waiting for him a fresh set of annoyances—he is mortal and there is still a heaven with its Stars above his head. The most interesting question that can come before us is, How far by the persevering endeavours of a seldom appearing Socrates Mankind may be made happy—I can imagine such

happiness carried to an extreme—but what must it end in?—Death—and who could in such a case bear with death—the whole troubles of life which are now frittered away in a series of years, would then be accumulated for the last days of a being who instead of hailing its approach, would leave this world as Eve left Paradise—But in truth I do not at all believe in this sort of perfectibility—the nature of the world will not admit of it—the inhabitants of the world will correspond to itself—Let the fish philosophise the ice away from the Rivers in winter time and they shall be at continual play in the tepid delight of summer. Look at the Poles and at the sands of Africa, Whirlpools and volcanoes—Let men exterminate them and I will say that they may arrive at earthly Happiness—The point at which Man may arrive is as far as the parallel state in inanimate nature and no further—For instance suppose a rose to have sensation, it blooms on a beautiful morning it enjoys itself—but there comes a cold wind, a hot sun—it can not escape it, it cannot destroy its annoyances—they are as native to the world as itself: no more can man be happy in spite, the worldly elements will prey upon his nature—The common cognomen of this world among the misguided and superstitious is "a vale of tears" from which we are to be redeemed by a certain arbitrary interposition of God and taken to Heaven—What a little circumscribed straightened notion! Call the world if you Please "The vale of Soul-making" Then you will find out the use of the world (I am speaking now in the highest terms for human nature admitting it to be immortal which I will here take for granted for the purpose of showing a thought which has struck me concerning it) I say "*Soul making*" Soul as distinguished from an Intelligence—There may be intelligences or sparks of the divinity in millions—but they are not Souls till they acquire identities, till each one is personally itself. Intelligences are atoms of perception—they know and they see and they are pure, in short they are God—how then are Souls to be made? How then are these sparks which are God to have identity given them—so as ever to possess a bliss peculiar to each ones individual existence? How, but by the medium of a world like this? This point I sincerely wish to consider because I think it a grander system of salvation than the christian religion—or rather it is a system of Spirit-creation—This is effected by three grand materials acting the

---

[1] *How charming ... lute* Milton's *Comus* 475–77.

[2] *Robertson's ... Monarch* William Robertson's *History of the Discovery and Settlement of America* (1777) describes the Spanish conquistadors, including Francisco Pizarro, who conquered the Incas in the sixteenth century. French philosopher Voltaire's *Le Siècle de Louis XIV* (1751) describes the rule of Louis XIV, who was often called "The Great Monarch."

[3] *a poor forked creature* From *King Lear* 3.4.112–13, in which Lear looks at "Poor Tom" and says "Unaccommodated man is no more but such a poor, bare, forked animal as thou art."

one upon the other for a series of years—These three Materials are the *Intelligence*—the *human heart* (as distinguished from intelligence or Mind) and the *World* or *Elemental space* suited for the proper action of *Mind and Heart* on each other for the purpose of forming the *Soul or Intelligence destined to possess the sense of Identity*. I can scarcely express what I but dimly perceive—and yet I think I perceive it—that you may judge the more clearly I will put it in the most homely form possible—I will call the world a School instituted for the purpose of teaching little children to read—I will call the *human heart* the *horn Book*[1] used in that School—and I will call the *Child able to read, the Soul* made from that *school* and its *hornbook*. Do you not see how necessary a World of Pains and troubles is to school an Intelligence and make it a soul? A Place where the heart must feel and suffer in a thousand diverse ways! Not merely is the Heart a Hornbook, It is the Minds Bible, it is the Minds experience, it is the teat from which the Mind or intelligence sucks its identity—As various as the Lives of Men are—so various become their souls, and thus does God make individual beings, Souls, Identical Souls of the sparks of his own essence—This appears to me a faint sketch of a system of Salvation which does not affront our reason and humanity—I am convinced that many difficulties which christians labour under would vanish before it—there is one which even now Strikes me—the Salvation of Children—In them the Spark or intelligence returns to God without any identity—it having had no time to learn of, and be altered by, the heart—or seat of the human Passions—It is pretty generally suspected that the christian scheme has been copied from the ancient persian and greek Philosophers. Why may they not have made this simple thing even more simple for common apprehension by introducing Mediators and Personages in the same manner as in the heathen mythology abstractions are personified— Seriously I think it probable that this System of Soul-making—may have been the Parent of all the more palpable and personal Schemes of Redemption, among the Zoroastrians the Christians and the Hindus. For as one part of the human species must have their carved Jupiter; so another part must have the palpable and named Mediatior and saviour, their Christ their Oro-

manes and their Vishnu[2]—If what I have said should not be plain enough, as I fear it may not be, I will but [put] you in the place where I began in this series of thoughts—I mean, I began by seeing how man was formed by circumstances—and what are circumstances?—but touchstones of his heart?—and what are touchstones?—but provings of his heart? and what are provings of his heart but fortifiers or alterers of his nature? and what is his altered nature but his soul?—and what was his soul before it came into the world and had These provings and alterations and perfectionings?—An intelligence—without Identity—and how is this Identity to be made? Through the medium of the Heart? And how is the heart to become this Medium but in a world of Circumstances?—There now I think what with Poetry and Theology you may thank your Stars that my pen is not very long winded— …

… this is the 3[d] of May & every thing is in delightful forwardness; the violets are not withered, before the peeping of the first rose; You must let me know every thing, how parcels go &. come, what papers you have, &. what Newspapers you want, & other things—God bless you my dear Brother & Sister

Your ever Affectionate Brother
John Keats—

TO FANNY BRAWNE[3]

25 July 1819
Sunday Night
Isle of Wight

My Sweet Girl,

I hope you did not blame me much for not obeying your request of a Letter on Saturday: we have had four in our small room playing at cards night and morning leaving me no undisturb'd opportunity to write. Now Rice and Martin are gone I am at liberty.

---

[1] *horn Book* Child's primer, originally made of a sheet of paper mounted on wood and protected by a thin sheet of transparent horn.

[2] *Oromanes* Ahriman, the chief evil spirit in Zoroastrianism, who is locked in perpetual struggle with Ahura Mazda; *Vishnu* Hindu deity who protects and preserves the world.

[3] *Fanny Brawne* Young woman whom Keats met in the summer of 1818, and to whom he was engaged by the end of the year (though the couple was waiting to marry until Keats felt he was financially secure). From October to May 1819 Keats stayed in his friend Charles Brown's apartment in Hampstead, which was next door to the Brawnes, who took care of him throughout the summer.

Brown to my sorrow confirms the account you give of your ill health. You cannot conceive how I ache to be with you: how I would die for one hour—for what is in the world? I say you cannot conceive; it is impossible you should look with such eyes upon me as I have upon you: it cannot be. Forgive me if I wander a little this evening, for I have been all day employ'd in a very abstract Poem[1] and I am in deep love with you—two things which must excuse me. I have, believe me, not been an age in letting you take possession of me; the very first week I knew you I wrote myself your vassal; but burnt the Letter as the very next time I saw you I thought you manifested some dislike to me. If you should ever feel for Man at the first sight what I did for you, I am lost. Yet I should not quarrel with you, but hate myself if such a thing were to happen—only I should burst if the thing were not as fine as a Man as you are as a Woman. Perhaps I am too vehement, then fancy me on my knees, especially when I mention a part of your Letter which hurt me; you say speaking of Mr. Severn[2] "but you must be satisfied in knowing that I admired you much more than your friend." My dear love, I cannot believe there ever was or ever could be any thing to admire in me especially as far as sight goes—I cannot be admired, I am not a thing to be admired. You are, I love you; all I can bring you is a swooning admiration of your Beauty. I hold that place among Men which snubnos'd brunettes with meeting eyebrows do among women—they are trash to me—unless I should find one among them with a fire in her heart like the one that burns in mine. You absorb me in spite of myself—you alone: for I look not forward with any pleasure to what is call'd being settled in the world; I tremble at domestic cares—yet for you I would meet them, though if it would leave you the happier I would rather die than do so. I have two luxuries to brood over in my walks, your Loveliness and the hour of my death. O that I could have possession of them both in the same minute. I hate the world: it batters too much the wings of my self-will, and would I could take a sweet poison from your lips to send me out of it. From no others would I take it. I am indeed astonish'd to find myself so careless of all charms but yours—remembering as I do the time when even a bit of ribband was a matter of interest with me. What softer words can I find for you after this—what it is I will not read. Nor will I say more here, but in a Postscript answer any thing else you may have mentioned in your Letter in so many words—for I am distracted with a thousand thoughts. I will imagine you Venus tonight and pray, pray, pray to your star like a Heathen.

Yours ever, fair Star,
John Keats

To Percy Bysshe Shelley[3]

16 August 1820
Hampstead

My Dear Shelley,

I am very much gratified that you, in a foreign country, and with a mind almost over occupied, should write to me in the strain of the Letter beside me. If I do not take advantage of your invitation it will be prevented by a circumstance I have very much at heart to prophesy—There is no doubt that an english winter would put an end to me, and do so in a lingering hateful manner, therefore I must either voyage or journey to Italy as a soldier marches up to a battery. My nerves at present are the worst part of me, yet they feel soothed when I think that come what extreme may, I shall not be destined to remain in one spot long enough to take a hatred of any four particular bedposts. I am glad you take any pleasure in my poor Poem;[4]—which I would willingly take the trouble to unwrite, if possible, did I care so much as I have done about Reputation. I received a copy of the Cenci,[5] as from yourself from Hunt. There is only one part of it I am judge of; the Poetry, and dramatic effect, which by many spirits now a days is considered the mammon.[6] A modern work it is said must have a purpose, which may be the God—*an artist*

---

[1] *very abstract Poem* Most likely *The Fall of Hyperion*.

[2] *Mr. Severn* Joseph Severn, an artist and a friend of Keats. He cared for Keats during his final illness in Rome and was present when he died.

[3] *To … Shelley* This letter is written in response to one from Shelley, in which he, having learned of Keats's serious illness, invites Keats to stay with him in Pisa for the winter.

[4] *my poor Poem* Keats's *Endymion*, which had received several negative reviews but which Shelley had praised in his letter.

[5] *Cenci* Shelley's blank-verse tragedy (1820).

[6] *mammon* Wealth and profit, regarded as a false god. Cf. Matthew 6.24, in which Jesus says, "Ye cannot serve God and Mammon."

must serve Mammon—he must have "self concentration" selfishness perhaps. You I am sure will forgive me for sincerely remarking that you might curb your magnanimity and be more of an artist, and "load every rift" of your subject with ore.[1] The thought of such discipline must fall like cold chains upon you, who perhaps never sat with your wings furl'd for six Months together. And is not this extraordinary talk for the writer of *Endymion*? whose mind was like a pack of scattered cards—I am pick'd up and sorted to a pip.[2] My Imagination is a Monastry and I am its Monk—you must explain my [metaphysics] to yourself. I am in expectation of *Prometheus*[3] every day. Could I have my own wish for its interest effected you would have it still in manuscript—or be but now putting an end to the second act. I remember you advising me not to publish my first-blights, on Hampstead heath—I am returning advice upon your hands. Most of the Poems in the volume I send you[4] have been written above two years, and would never have been publish'd but from a hope of gain; so you see I am inclined enough to take your advice now. I must express once more my deep sense of your kindness, adding my sincere thanks and respects for Mrs. Shelley. In the hope of soon seeing you I remain

most sincerely yours,
John Keats—

To CHARLES BROWN

30 November 1820
Rome

My Dear Brown,

'Tis the most difficult thing in the world to me to write a letter. My stomach continues so bad, that I feel it worse on opening any book,—yet I am much better than I was in Quarantine.[5] Then I am afraid to encounter the proing and conning of any thing interesting to me in England. I have an habitual feeling of my real life having past, and that I am leading a posthumous existence. God knows how it would have been—but it appears to me—however, I will not speak of that subject. I must have been at Bedhampton nearly at the time you were writing to me from Chichester—how unfortunate—and to pass on the river too! There was my star predominant! I cannot answer any thing in your letter, which followed me from Naples to Rome, because I am afraid to look it over again. I am so weak (in mind) that I cannot bear the sight of any hand writing of a friend I love so much as I do you. Yet I ride the little horse,[6]—and, at my worst, even in Quarantine, summoned up more puns, in a sort of desperation, in one week than in any year of my life. There is one thought enough to kill me—I have been well, healthy, alert &c, walking with her[7]and now—the knowledge of contrast, feeling for light and shade, all that information (primitive sense) necessary for a poem are great enemies to the recovery of the stomach. There, you rogue, I put you to the torture,—but you must bring your philosophy to bear—as I do mine, really—or how should I be able to live? D[r] Clarke is very attentive to me; he says, there is very little the matter with my lungs, but my stomach, he says, is very bad. I am well disappointed in hearing good news from George,—for it runs in my head we shall all die young. I have not written to * * * *[8] yet, which he must think very neglectful; being anxious to send him a good account of my health, I have delayed it from week to week. If I recover, I will do all in my power to correct the mistakes made during sickness; and if I should not, all my faults will be forgiven. I shall write to * * * * tomorrow, or next day. I will write to * * * * in the middle of next week. Severn is very well, though he leads so dull a life with me. Remember me to all friends, and tell * * * * I should not have left London without taking leave of

---

[1] *load ... ore*   Reference to Spenser's *Faerie Queene* 2.7.28, in which he describes the Palace of Mammon: "Embost with massy gold of glorious gift, / And with rich metal loaded every rift."

[2] *sorted to a pip*   Put in order. Pips are the markings on playing cards.

[3] *Prometheus*   Shelley's *Prometheus Unbound* (1820), a copy of which he had promised to send to Keats.

[4] *the volume ... you*   Keats's 1820 volume, which Shelley had in his pocket when he drowned.

[5] *in Quarantine*   Keats's ship was quarantined for ten days outside Naples, in extremely hot weather. Keats was writing this letter from Rome, where he was being cared for by Joseph Severn.

[6] *Yet ... horse*   Recommended by Keats's doctor for exercise.

[7] *her*   Fanny Brawne.

[8] * * * *   Brown, whose transcription of this letter is the only surviving copy, deleted the names of Keats's friends in order to conceal their identities.

him, but from being so low in body and mind. Write to George as soon as you receive this, and tell him how I am, as far as you can guess; and also a note to my sister—who walks about my imagination like a ghost— she is so like Tom.[1] I can scarcely bid you good bye even in a letter. I always made an awkward bow.

God bless you!

John Keats.

IN CONTEXT

Politics, Poetry, and the "Cockney School Debate"

As literary journals and magazines of the time demonstrate, in the nineteenth century politics and literary theory were often inextricably intertwined. At the time, only a small minority of adult males had been granted the vote, and the political system was widely perceived to be corrupt. Leigh Hunt, John Keats, William Hazlitt, and Percy Bysshe Shelley were among those who pressed strongly for political reform. Leigh Hunt, with his brothers John and Robert, edited the *Examiner*, a liberal weekly journal that frequently riled the government. After offending the Prince of Wales, Leigh and John spent two years in prison (1813–15) for libel.

In August 1817 the *Edinburgh Review* began to refer to Wordsworth, Coleridge, and Robert Southey as "The Lake School"—all three had lived in and been inspired by England's Lake District. Those poets and some others—Lord Byron in particular—had been identified the previous year by Leigh Hunt as representative of a school of poets "who go directly to Nature for inspiration." Hunt had written his article "Young Poets" to bring to the attention of the public "three young writers [Shelley, Keats, and John Hamilton Reynolds] who appear to us to promise a considerable addition of strength to the new school." Hunt had not named himself as a member of this new group, but it was on him that John Gibson Lockhart focused in launching an attack on the group that was as much political as literary. Lockhart's series of articles on "The Cockney School of Poetry" appeared in *Blackwood's Edinburgh Magazine*, a conservative journal founded in response to the *Edinburgh Review*.

from Leigh Hunt, "Young Poets," *Examiner* (1 December 1816)

In sitting down to this subject, we happen to be restricted by time to a much shorter notice than we could wish: but we mean to take it up again shortly. Many of our readers however have perhaps observed for themselves, that there has been a new school of poetry rising of late, which promises to extinguish the French one that has prevailed among us since the time of Charles the 2d. It began with something excessive, like most revolutions, but this gradually wore away; and an evident aspiration after real nature and original fancy remained, which called to mind the finer times of the English Muse. In fact it is wrong to call it a new school, and still more so to represent it as one of innovation, its only object being to restore the same love of Nature, and of *thinking* instead of mere *talking*, which formerly rendered us real poets, and not merely versifying wits, and bead-rollers of couplets.

We were delighted to see the departure of the old school acknowledged in the number of the *Edinburgh Review* just published—a candour the more generous and spirited, inasmuch as that work has hitherto been the greatest surviving ornament of the same school in prose and criticism, as it is now destined, we trust, to be still the leader in the new.

[1] *my sister ... Tom* Keats's sister Fanny closely resembled his youngest brother Tom, who had died of tuberculosis in December 1818.

We also felt the same delight at the third canto of Lord Byron's *Childe Harold*, in which, to our conceptions at least, he has fairly renounced a certain leaven of the French style, and taken his place where we always said he would be found—among the poets who have a real feeling for numbers,[1] and who go directly to Nature for inspiration. But more of this poem in our next.

The object of the present article is merely to notice three young writers, who appear to us to promise a considerable addition of strength to the new school. Of the first who came before us, we have, it is true, yet seen only one or two specimens, and these were no sooner sent us than we unfortunately mislaid them; but we shall procure what he has published, and if the rest answer to what we have seen, we shall have no hesitation in announcing him for a very striking and original thinker. His name is Percy Bysshe Shelley, and he is the author of a poetical work entitled *Alastor, or the Spirit of Solitude*.

The next with whose name we became acquainted was John Henry Reynolds, author of a tale called *Safie*, written, we believe, in imitation of Lord Byron, and more lately of a small set of poems published by Taylor and Hessey, the principal of which is called the *Naiad*. It opens thus:

> The gold sun went into the west,
> And soft airs sang him to his rest;
> And yellow leaves all loose and dry,
> Play'd on the branches listlessly:
> The sky wax'd palely blue, and high
> A cloud seem'd touch'd upon the sky—
> A spot of cloud—blue, thin, and still,
> And silence bask'd on vale and hill. ...

We shall give another extract or two in a future number. The author's style is too artificial, though he is evidently an admirer of Mr. Wordsworth. Like all young poets too, properly so called, his love of detail is too overwrought and indiscriminate; but still he is a young poet, and only wants a still closer attention to things as opposed to the seduction of words, to realize all that he promises. His nature seems very true and amiable.

The last of these young aspirants who we have met with, and who promise to help the new school to revive Nature and

> "To put a spirit of youth in every thing,"

is, we believe, the youngest of them all, and just of age. His name is John Keats. He has not yet published anything except in a newspaper; but a set of his manuscripts was handed us the other day, and fairly surprised us with the truth of their ambition, and ardent grappling with Nature. In the following sonnet there is one incorrect rhyme, which might be easily altered, but which shall serve in the mean time as a peace-offering to the rhyming critics. The rest of the composition, with the exception of a little vagueness in calling the regions of poetry "the realms of gold," we do not hesitate to pronounce excellent, especially the last six lines. The word *swims* is complete; and the whole conclusion is equally powerful and quiet

[Quotes "On First Looking into Chapman's Homer"]

We have spoken with the less scruple of these poetical promises, because we really are not in the habit of lavishing praises and announcements, and because we have no fear of any pettier vanity on the part of young men who promise to understand human nature so well.

---

[1]   *numbers* I.e., metrical harmony, rhythm.

JOHN KEATS IN CONTEXT 471

from John Lockhart ("Z."),"On the Cockney School of Poetry, No. 1," *Blackwood's Edinburgh Magazine* (October 1817)

> Our talk shall be (a theme we never tire on)
> Of Chaucer, Spenser, Shakespeare, Milton, Byron,
> (Our England's Dante)—Wordsworth—Hunt, and Keats,
> The Muses' son of promise; and of what feats
> He yet may do.
> —CORNELIUS WEBB

While the whole critical world is occupied with balancing the merits, whether in theory or in execution, of what is commonly called The Lake School, it is strange that no one seems to think it at all necessary to say a single word about another new school of poetry which has of late sprung up amongst us. This school has not, I believe, as yet received any name; but if I may be permitted to have the honour of christening it, it may henceforth be referred to by the designation of The Cockney School. Its chief Doctor and Professor is Mr. Leigh Hunt, a man certainly of some talents, of extravagant pretensions both in wit, poetry, and politics, and withal of exquisitely bad taste, and extremely vulgar modes of thinking and manners in all respects. He is a man of little education. He knows absolutely nothing of Greek, almost nothing of Latin, and his knowledge of Italian literature is confined to a few of the most popular of Petrarch's sonnets, and an imperfect acquaintance with Ariosto, through the medium of Mr. Hoole. As to the French poets, he dismisses them in the mass as a set of prim, precise, unnatural pretenders. The truth is, he is in a state of happy ignorance about them and all that they have done. ...

With this stock of knowledge, Mr. Hunt presumes to become the founder of a new school of poetry, and throws away entirely the chance he might have had of gaining some true poetic fame, had he been less lofty in his pretensions. ...

All the great poets of our country have been men of some rank in society, and there is no vulgarity in any of their writings; but Mr. Hunt cannot utter a dedication, or even a note, without betraying the *Shibboleth*[1] of low birth and low habits. He is the ideal of a Cockney Poet. He raves perpetually about "green fields," "jaunty streams," and "o'er-arching leafiness," exactly as a Cheapside shop-keeper does about the beauties of his box[2] on the Camberwell road. Mr. Hunt is altogether unacquainted with the face of nature in her magnificent scenes; he has never seen any mountain higher than Highgate-hill,[3] nor reclined by any stream more pastoral than the Serpentine River.[4] But he is determined to be a poet eminently rural, and he rings the changes—till one is sick of him, on the beauties of the different "high views" which he has taken of God and nature, in the course of some Sunday dinner parties, at which he has assisted in the neighbourhood of London. His books are indeed not known in the country; his fame as a poet (and I might almost say, as a politician too) is entirely confined to the young attorneys and embryo-barristers about town. In the opinion of these competent judges, London is the world—and Hunt is a Homer.

Mr. Hunt is not disqualified by his ignorance and vulgarity alone, for being the founder of a respectable sect in poetry. He labours under the burden of a sin more deadly than either of these. The two great elements of all dignified poetry, religious feeling and patriotic feeling, have no place in his

---

[1] *Shibboleth* Word distinguishing a certain class or party.

[2] *box* Boxwood.

[3] *Highgate-hill* Hill (and district) in the north of London.

[4] *Serpentine River* Lake in Hyde Park, in the center of London.

writings. His religion is a poor tame dilution of the blasphemies of the *Encyclopaedie*[1]—his patriotism a crude, vague, ineffectual, and sour Jacobinism.[2] His works exhibit no reverence either for God or man; neither altar nor throne have any dignity in his eyes. He speaks well of nobody but two or three great dead poets, and in so speaking of them he does well; but alas! Mr. Hunt is no conjurer τεχνη ὅ λανθανει.[3] He pretends, indeed, to be an admirer of Spenser and Chaucer, but what he praises in them is never what is most deserving of praise—it is only that which he humbly conceives bears some resemblance to the more perfect productions of Mr. Leigh Hunt; and we can always discover in the midst of his most violent ravings about the Court of Elizabeth, and the days of Sir Philip Sidney, and the Fairy Queen, that the real objects of his admiration are the Coterie of Hampstead and the Editor of the Examiner. When he talks about chivalry and King Arthur, he is always thinking of himself, and "*a small party of friends, who meet once a week at a Round Table, to discuss the merits of a leg of mutton, and of the subjects upon which we are to write.*"[4]—Mr. Leigh Hunt's ideas concerning the sublime, and concerning his own powers, bear a considerable resemblance to those of his friend Bottom, the weaver, on the same subjects; "I will roar, that it shall do any man's heart good to hear me."—"I will roar you an 'twere any nightingale."[5]

The poetry of Mr. Hunt is such as might be expected from the personal character and habits of its author. As a vulgar man is perpetually labouring to be genteel—in like manner, the poetry of this man is always on the stretch to be grand. He has been allowed to look for a moment from the antechamber into the salon, and mistaken the waving of feathers and the painted floor for the *sine qua non*'s[6] of elegant society. He would fain be always tripping and waltzing, and is sorry that he cannot be allowed to walk about in the morning with yellow breeches and flesh-coloured silk-stockings. He sticks an artificial rosebud into his button hole in the midst of winter. ...

How such an indelicate writer as Mr. Hunt can pretend to be an admirer of Mr. Wordsworth, is to us a thing altogether inexplicable. One great charm of Wordsworth's noble compositions consists in the dignified purity of thought, and the patriarchal simplicity of feeling, with which they are throughout penetrated and imbued. We can conceive a vicious[7] man admiring with distant awe the spectacle of virtue and purity; but if he does so sincerely, he must also do so with the profoundest feeling of the error of his own ways, and the resolution to amend them. His admiration must be humble and silent, not pert and loquacious. Mr. Hunt praises the purity of Wordsworth as if he himself were pure, his dignity as if he also were dignified. ...

The founder of the Cockney School would fain claim poetical kindred with Lord Byron and Thomas Moore.[8] Such a connection would be as unsuitable for them as for William Wordsworth. The days of Mr. Moore's follies are long since over; and, as he is a thorough gentleman, he must necessarily entertain the greatest contempt for such an under-bred person as Mr. Leigh Hunt. But Lord Byron! ... We dare say Mr. Hunt has some fine dreams about the true nobility being the nobility of talent, and flatters himself, that with those who acknowledge only that sort of rank, he

---

[1] *Encylopaedie* Great manifesto of the French *philosophes*, prepared by Denis Diderot and Jean le Rond d'Alembert (1751).

[2] *Jacobinism* Extreme democratic principles; belief in complete equality (after the practice of the French political sect the Jacobins).

[3] τεχνη ὅ λανθανει Greek: his technique does not escape notice.

[4] *a small ... write* From a feature in the *Examiner*, initiated by Leigh Hunt, called "The Round Table."

[5] *I will ... nightingale* From Shakespeare's *A Midsummer Night's Dream* 1.2, in which Bottom the weaver (who is later transformed into an ass) desires to play the lion's part in a play.

[6] *sine qua non* Latin: without which, not.

[7] *vicious* Immoral.

[8] *Thomas Moore* Irish poet (1779–1852).

himself passes for being the *peer* of Byron. He is sadly mistaken. He is as completely a Plebeian[1] in his mind as he is in his rank and station in society. To that highest and unalienable nobility which the great Roman satirist styles "*sola atque unica*,"[2] we fear his pretensions would be equally unavailing.

The shallow and impotent pretensions, tenets, and attempts of this man—and the success with which his influence seems to be extending itself among a pretty numerous, though certainly a very paltry and pitiful, set of readers—have for the last two or three years been considered by us with the most sickening aversion. The very culpable manner in which his chief poem was reviewed in the *Edinburgh Review* (we believe it is no secret, at his own impatient and feverish request, by his partner in the Round Table[3]), was matter of concern to more readers than ourselves. The masterly pen which inflicted such signal chastisement on the early licentiousness of Moore, should not have been idle on that occasion. Mr. Jeffrey[4] does ill, when he delegates his important functions into such hands as those of Mr. Hazlitt. It was chiefly in consequence of that gentleman's allowing Leigh Hunt to pass unpunished through the scene of slaughter, which his execution might so highly have graced, that we came to the resolution of laying before our readers a series of essays on *the Cockney School*—of which here terminates the first.

from John Lockhart ("Z."), "On the Cockney School of Poetry, No. 4," *Blackwood's Edinburgh Magazine* (August 1818)

> Of Keats,
> The Muses' son of promise, and what feats
> He yet may do, &c.
> —CORNELIUS WEBB

Of all the manias of this mad age, the most incurable, as well as the most common, seems to be no other than the *Metromanie*.[5] The just celebrity of Robert Burns and Miss Baillie[6] has had the melancholy effect of turning the heads of we know not how many farm-servants and unmarried ladies; our very footmen compose tragedies, and there is scarcely a superannuated governess in the island that does not leave a roll of lyrics behind her in her band-box. To witness the disease of any human understanding, however feeble, is distressing; but the spectacle of an able mind reduced to a state of insanity is of course ten times more afflicting. It is with such sorrow as this that we have contemplated the case of Mr. John Keats. This young man appears to have received from nature talents of an excellent, perhaps even of a superior order—talents which, devoted to the purpose of any useful profession, must have rendered him a respectable, if not an eminent citizen. His friends, we understand, destined him to the career of medicine, and he was bound apprentice some years ago to a worthy apothecary in town. But all has been undone by a sudden attack of the malady to which we have alluded. Whether Mr. John had been sent home with a diuretic or composing draught to some patient far gone in the poetical mania, we have not heard. This much is certain, that he has caught the infection, and that thoroughly. For some time we were in hopes that he might get off with a

---

[1]   *Plebian*   In ancient Rome, a commoner, a person of low birth or rank.

[2]   *sola atque unica*   Latin: alone and only. See Juvenal's *Satire* 8: "Virtue alone is the only true nobility."

[3]   *partner ... Table*   William Hazlitt, who contributed to both the *Examiner* and the *Edinburgh Review*. Hazlitt frequently wrote for the *Examiner* feature "The Round Table," and his first book-length collection of essays appeared in 1817 under that title.

[4]   *Mr. Jeffrey*   Francis Jeffrey (1773–1850), founder and editor of the *Edinburgh Review*.

[5]   *Metromanie*   Mania for writing poetry.

[6]   *Miss Baillie*   Scottish poet and playwright Joanna Baillie (1762–1851).

violent fit or two; but of late the symptoms are terrible. The frenzy of the "Poems"[1] was bad enough in its way; but it did not alarm us half so seriously as the calm, settled, imperturbable drivelling idiocy of "Endymion." We hope, however, that in so young a person, and with a constitution originally so good, even now the disease is not utterly incurable. Time, firm treatment, and rational restraint, do much for many apparently hopeless invalids; and if Mr. Keats should happen, at some interval of reason, to cast his eye upon our pages, he may perhaps be convinced of the existence of his malady, which in such cases is often all that is necessary to put the patient in a fair way of being cured. ...

[Keats's] Endymion is not a Greek shepherd, loved by a Grecian goddess;[2] he is merely a young Cockney rhymester, dreaming a fantastic dream at the full of the moon. Costume, were it worth while to notice such a trifle, is violated in every page of this goodly octavo. From his prototype Hunt, Keats has acquired a sort of vague idea that the Greeks were a most tasteful people, and that no mythology can be so finely adapted for the purposes of poetry as theirs. It is amusing to see what a hand the two Cockneys make of this mythology; the one confesses that he never read the Greek Tragedians, and the other knows Homer only from Chapman;[3] and both of them write about Apollo, Pan, Nymphs, Muses, and Mysteries, as might be expected from persons of their education. We shall not, however, enlarge at present upon this subject, as we mean to dedicate an entire paper to the classical attainments and attempts of the Cockney poets. As for Mr. Keats' "Endymion," it has just as much to do with Greece as it has with "old Tartary the fierce;" no man whose mind has ever been imbued with the smallest knowledge or feeling of classical poetry or classical history could have stooped to profane and vulgarise every association in the manner which has been adopted by this "son of promise." Before giving any extracts, we must inform our readers that this romance is meant to be written in English heroic rhyme. To those who have read any of Hunt's poems, this hint might indeed be needless. Mr. Keats has adopted the loose, nerveless versification and Cockney rhymes of the poet of *Rimini*;[4] but, in fairness to that gentleman, we must add that the defects of the system are tenfold more conspicuous in his disciple's work than in his own. Mr. Hunt is a small poet, but he is a clever man. Mr. Keats is a still smaller poet, and he is only a boy of pretty abilities, which he has done every thing in his power to spoil.

---

[1] *Poems* Keats's first volume of poetry, which was published in March 1817.

[2] *Endymion ... goddess* "Endymion" retells the story of the goddess of the moon falling in love with a shepherd, as told by the Roman poet Ovid.

[3] *Homer ... Chapman* Keats knew very little Greek, and read it only in translation. George Chapman's edition of Homer's *Iliad* appeared in 1612, and his edition of the *Odyssey* in 1616.

[4] *Rimini* Hunt's long poem *The Story of Rimini* (1816).

MARY SHELLEY
1797 – 1851

As Mary Wollstonecraft Shelley wrote in her introduction to the second edition of *Frankenstein*, readers constantly asked her "How I, then a young girl, came to think of, and to dilate upon, so hideous an idea." At the age of nineteen, Shelley created one of the most extraordinary and powerful horror stories in Western literature, one that continues to pervade our popular culture.

Frankenstein continues to overshadow all her other work, but Shelley has also come to be recognized as having produced a large body of fiction of vivid imaginative power that grapples in penetrating fashion with the political and social concerns of her day.

If Shelley's writing is extraordinary, nor is there anything of the ordinary in her famous parentage or her tumultuous life. She was born Mary Wollstonecraft Godwin in August of 1797. The only child of radical feminist Mary Wollstonecraft and the philosopher, author, and political journalist William Godwin, Shelley felt the weight of her parents' controversial reputations throughout her life. Her mother died just after giving birth, and Shelley came to know her only through her works—in particular the *Vindication of the Rights of Woman* (1792). Godwin, for whom Shelley later said she bore an "excess of attachment," raised Mary and her half-sister Fanny, educating them with the help of several friends and regular visitors—a group of supremely qualified teachers that included poet Samuel Taylor Coleridge, painter Thomas Lawrence, novelist Maria Edgeworth, and scientist Humphrey Davy.

After Godwin married Mary Jane Clairmont in 1801, Mary, who did not get along with her stepmother, spent extended periods of time with family friends in Scotland. On a visit home in 1814, she became acquainted with Percy Bysshe Shelley, a radical poet and admirer of Godwin's principles, who had become a regular visitor to the Godwin home. Although Percy was married at the time, within months the two declared their love for each other and eloped to France, taking Mary's stepsister Claire Clairmont with them. Godwin disowned his daughter upon her elopement and was only slightly mollified when the two married in 1816, following the suicide of Percy's first wife, Harriet.

The couple toured France, Switzerland, and Germany (a trip described in Shelley's first publication, *History of a Six Weeks' Tour*) before eventually settling in Italy near Lord Byron, with whom Claire was having an affair. The subsequent years in Italy were turbulent ones. Two of Shelley's children died in infancy, her three-year-old son William died in 1819, and Claire's daughter by Byron died in a convent in 1822. A life-threatening miscarriage that same year plunged Shelley into severe depression, and she and her husband became increasingly distant. When Percy drowned with his friend Edward Williams in July of 1822, her sorrow at his death was further augmented by her guilt at their estrangement.

Although she wrote some poetry and verse dramas, Shelley's only publication during these years was *Frankenstein, or The Modern Prometheus*, first published in 1818 and revised for a new edition in 1831. This novel about a motherless creature rejected by its father, cast out by society, and parented largely by books has clear points of connection with Shelley's own unusual upbringing and her anxiety concerning familial relationships, origins, and parental responsibility. But the enduring appeal of the novel lies in its narrative power and its ability to stimulate ideas in rich profusion. With its themes of repression and doubling it can be read as a psychodrama, and its unspoken preoccupation with incest allies it with other Gothic thrillers. As a reworking of both Milton's story of the fall of man in *Paradise Lost* and the Greek myth of Prometheus (who stole fire from the gods and gave it to humans, saving them from servility), Shelley's novel shows the consequences of using one's power over others without acknowledging the attendant responsibilities. *Frankenstein* can also be read as a moral tale, advising us to treat others in the way we would like to be treated; if we assume those who are unfamiliar or different are evil, we may ourselves create evil where none existed before. The novel also calls into question the Enlightenment celebration of scientific advancement and articulates a deep-seated fear of the consequences of interfering with the natural order.

As a result of the scandalous events in her past, the radicalism of her parents, and the unsavory reputation of her husband, Shelley felt exiled from society. After the death of Byron in 1824 she found herself without friendship or support. She had a small allowance from her father-in-law, Sir Timothy Shelley, but it was hardly enough to support her, and had been given on the stipulation that she not bring her husband's name before the public. Consequently, although Shelley was eager to see her husband's talent appreciated, his *Posthumous Poems* (1824) had to be withdrawn from circulation only a few months after its release.

Shelley had always felt that "as the daughter of two persons of distinguished literary celebrity" she should be a writer, so she turned to writing for income. She returned to London and began producing book reviews, essays, and short biographies while continuing to write novels. *The Last Man* (1826) presents a view of humanity in which a plague destroys the earth, leaving only one man, Lionel Verney. Shelley's novels *Valperga* (1823) and *The Fortunes of Perkin Warbeck: A Romance* (1830) experiment with the genre of historical fiction—a mode that had recently been made popular by Walter Scott—combining romance and fiction with historical and political analysis. In these novels, as well as in *The Last Man*, critics found evidence of the "unsavory politics" they expected from one of the Godwin circle. Critics and readers alike preferred Shelley's more traditional domestic fictions, such as *Lodore* (1835) and *Falkner* (1837).

In 1844 the concerns that had plagued Shelley since the death of her husband were relieved by the death of his father. Her son, Percy Florence, inherited Sir Thomas's title and estate, and Shelley was free to produce biographical work on her husband. In his final years Sir Thomas had allowed her to publish editions of Percy Shelley's work, and in 1839 she had released his four-volume *Poetical Works*, as well as his *Essays and Letters from Abroad, Translations and Fragments*. In writing about her husband, Shelley endeavored to rationalize his radical attitudes and behavior—particularly his atheism and sedition—in order to mediate his poetry for his audience and redeem his public image. Although she has been accused of altering his manuscripts and misrepresenting his politics, she succeeded in her goal of bringing his work to public notice.

Shelley spent her final years traveling with her son and helping him manage his estate. In 1848 he married Jane St. John, a widow and friend of Shelley. Jane nursed Shelley in the months before her death of a brain tumor in 1851.

⌘ ⌘ ⌘

The Last Man

Other than *Frankenstein*, Mary Shelley's 1824 novel *The Last Man* is the work that has excited the greatest critical interest and enjoyed the most attention from her readership over the past generation. In part this may relate to increased interest in apocalyptic visions around the turn of the millennium; it may also speak to humanity's perpetual fascination with the idea of its own extinction. Additional interest may stem from the parallels between the lives of Shelley and her companions and those of the characters in the novel—the circumstances of Percy Shelley's death are strikingly similar to those surrounding the drowning of Lionel Verney's companions. While Shelley's novel can be seen as a depiction of her own grief on a universal scale, her wistful look back at an idealized, but ultimately untenable, past may also be read as a political critique, and a disillusioned examination of Romanticism.

Shelley's protagonist, Lionel Verney, is the last man in the world, looking back on human history from 2100. During the final years of the twenty-first century the world has been devastated by plague. In its wake, humans have descended into brutality: American survivors have attacked Ireland; the Irish have invaded England; and, finally, small bands of English survivors have been wandering the now-ruined continent of Europe. Lionel Verney and his party suspect themselves to be the last of these groups of survivors. As the final two chapters open, Verney has two remaining companions, Adrian and Clara, the latter distraught after the death of her child. The party has been staying in an abandoned villa at Lake Como in the Alps.

---

from *The Last Man*

CHAPTER 29

Now—soft awhile—have I arrived so near the end? Yes! it is all over now—a step or two over those new-made graves, and the wearisome way is done. Can I accomplish my task? Can I streak my paper with words capacious of the grand conclusion? Arise, black Melancholy! quit thy Cimmerian solitude![1] Bring with thee murky fogs from hell, which may drink up the day; bring blight and pestiferous exhalations, which, entering the hollow caverns and breathing places of earth, may fill her stony veins with corruption, so that not only herbage may no longer flourish, the trees may rot, and the rivers run with gall—but the everlasting mountains be decomposed, and the mighty deep putrify, and the genial atmosphere which clips the globe, lose all powers of generation and sustenance. Do this, sad visaged

power, while I write, while eyes read these pages.

And who will read them? Beware, tender offspring of the re-born world—beware, fair being, with human heart, yet untamed by care, and human brow, yet unploughed by time—beware, lest the cheerful current of thy blood be checked, thy golden locks turn grey, thy sweet dimpling smiles be changed to fixed, harsh wrinkles! Let not day look on these lines, lest garish day waste, turn pale, and die. Seek a cypress grove, whose moaning boughs will be harmony befitting; seek some cave, deep embowered in earth's dark entrails, where no light will penetrate, save that which struggles, red and flickering, through a single fissure, staining thy page with grimmest livery of death.

There is a painful confusion in my brain, which refuses to delineate distinctly succeeding events. Sometimes the irradiation of my friend's gentle smile comes before me; and methinks its light spans and fills eternity—then, again, I feel the gasping throes—

We quitted Como, and in compliance with Adrian's earnest desire, we took Venice in our way to Rome. There was something to the English peculiarly attractive in the idea of this wave-encircled, island-enthroned city.

---

[1] *Cimmerian solitude* Referring to the Cimmerians, mythical people of Homer's *Odyssey* who inhabit the dark, misty fringes of the world.

Adrian had never seen it. We went down the Po and the Brenta[1] in a boat; and, the days proving intolerably hot, we rested in the bordering palaces during the day, travelling through the night, when darkness made the bordering banks indistinct, and our solitude less remarkable; when the wandering moon lit the waves that divided before our prow, and the night-wind filled our sails, and the murmuring stream, waving trees, and swelling canvass, accorded in harmonious strain. Clara, long overcome by excessive grief, had to a great degree cast aside her timid, cold reserve, and received our attentions with grateful tenderness. While Adrian with poetic fervour discoursed of the glorious nations of the dead, of the beauteous earth and the fate of man, she crept near him, drinking in his speech with silent pleasure. We banished from our talk, and as much as possible from our thoughts, the knowledge of our desolation. And it would be incredible to an inhabitant of cities, to one among a busy throng to what extent we succeeded. It was as a man confined in a dungeon, whose small and grated rift at first renders the doubtful light more sensibly obscure, till, the visual orb having drunk in the beam, and adapted itself to its scantiness, he finds that clear noon inhabits his cell. So we, a simple triad on empty earth, were multiplied to each other, till we became all in all. We stood like trees, whose roots are loosened by the wind, which support one another, leaning and clinging with increased fervour while the wintry storms howl.

Thus we floated down the widening stream of the Po, sleeping when the cicale[2] sang, awake with the stars. We entered the narrower banks of the Brenta, and arrived at the shore of the Laguna[3] at sunrise on the sixth of September. The bright orb slowly rose from behind its cupolas and towers, and shed its penetrating light upon the glassy waters. Wrecks of gondolas, and some few uninjured ones, were strewed on the beach at Fusina.[4] We embarked in one of these for the widowed

daughter of ocean,[5] who, abandoned and fallen, sat forlorn on her propping isles, looking towards the far mountains of Greece. We rowed lightly over the Laguna, and entered Canale Grande.[6] The tide ebbed sullenly from out the broken portals and violated halls of Venice: sea weed and sea monsters were left on the blackened marble, while the salt ooze defaced the matchless works of art that adorned their walls, and the sea gull flew out from the shattered window. In the midst of this appalling ruin of the monuments of man's power, nature asserted her ascendancy, and shone more beauteous from the contrast. The radiant waters hardly trembled, while the rippling waves made many sided mirrors to the sun; the blue immensity, seen beyond Lido,[7] stretched far, unspecked by boat, so tranquil, so lovely, that it seemed to invite us to quit the land strewn with ruins, and to seek refuge from sorrow and fear on its placid extent.

We saw the ruins of this hapless city from the height of the tower of San Marco, immediately under us, and turned with sickening hearts to the sea, which, though it be a grave, rears no monument, discloses no ruin. Evening had come apace. The sun set in calm majesty behind the misty summits of the Apennines, and its golden and roseate hues painted the mountains of the opposite shore. "That land," said Adrian, "tinged with the last glories of the day, is Greece." Greece! The sound had a responsive chord in the bosom of Clara. She vehemently reminded us that we had promised to take her once again to Greece, to the tomb of her parents. Why go to Rome? what should we do at Rome? We might take one of the many vessels to be found here, embark in it, and steer right for Albania.

I objected the dangers of ocean, and the distance of the mountains we saw, from Athens; a distance which, from the savage uncultivation of the country, was almost impassable. Adrian, who was delighted with Clara's proposal, obviated these objections. The season was favourable; the north-west that blew would take us transversely across the gulph; and then we might find, in

---

[1] *the Po and the Brenta*   Both rivers flow from the Alps down into the Venetian plain.

[2] *cicale*   Cicada.

[3] *the Laguna*   The Laguna Veneta, which surrounds Venice.

[4] *Fusina*   Located on the coast of the mainland, south of Venice.

[5] *widowed daughter of ocean*   I.e., Venice. In an ancient ceremony, the ruler of Venice threw a ring into the sea each Ascension Day to symbolize the marriage of Venice and the ocean.

[6] *Canale Grande*   Canal that runs through Venice.

[7] *Lido*   Island that forms a breakwater between the sea and the Laguna Veneta.

some abandoned port, a light Greek caique,[1] adapted for such navigation, and run down the coast of the Morea, and, passing over the Isthmus of Corinth, without much land-travelling or fatigue, find ourselves at Athens. This appeared to me wild talk; but the sea, glowing with a thousand purple hues, looked so brilliant and safe; my beloved companions were so earnest, so determined, that, when Adrian said, "Well, though it is not exactly what you wish, yet consent, to please me"—I could no longer refuse. That evening we selected a vessel, whose size just seemed fitted for our enterprize; we bent the sails and put the rigging in order, and, reposing that night in one of the city's thousand palaces, agreed to embark at sunrise the following morning.

When winds that move not its calm surface, sweep
The azure sea, I love the land no more;
The smiles of the serene and tranquil deep
Tempt my unquiet mind—

Thus said Adrian, quoting a translation of Moschus's poem, as, in the clear morning light, we rowed over the Laguna, past Lido, into the open sea—I would have added in continuation,

But, when the roar
Of ocean's gray abyss resounds, and foam
Gathers upon the sea, and vast waves burst[2]—

But my friends declared that such verses were evil augury; so in cheerful mood we left the shallow waters, and, when out at sea, unfurled our sails to catch the favourable breeze. The laughing morning air filled them while sun-light bathed earth, sky and ocean—the placid waves divided to receive our keel, and playfully kissed the dark sides of our little skiff, murmuring a welcome; as land receded, still the blue expanse, most waveless, twin sister to the azure empyrean, afforded smooth conduct to our bark.[3] As the air and waters were tranquil and balmy, so were our minds steeped in quiet. In comparison with the unstained deep, funereal earth appeared a grave, its high rocks and stately mountains

were but monuments, its trees the plumes of a hearse, the brooks and rivers brackish with tears for departed man. Farewell to desolate towns—to fields with their savage intermixture of corn and weeds—to ever multiplying relics of our lost species. Ocean, we commit ourselves to thee—even as the patriarch of old[4] floated above the drowned world, let us be saved, as thus we betake ourselves to thy perennial flood.

Adrian sat at the helm; I attended to the rigging, the breeze right aft filled our swelling canvas, and we ran before it over the untroubled deep. The wind died away at noon; its idle breath just permitted us to hold our course. As lazy, fair-weather sailors, careless of the coming hour, we talked gaily of our coasting voyage, of our arrival at Athens. We would make our home of one of the Cyclades,[5] and there in myrtle-groves, amidst perpetual spring, fanned by the wholesome sea-breezes —we would live long years in beatific union—Was there such a thing as death in the world?—

The sun passed its zenith and lingered down the stainless floor of heaven. Lying in the boat, my face turned up to the sky, I thought I saw on its blue white, marbled streaks, so slight, so immaterial, that now I said—"They are there"—and now, "It is a mere imagination." A sudden fear stung me while I gazed; and, starting up, and running to the prow—as I stood, my hair was gently lifted on my brow—a dark line of ripples appeared to the east, gaining rapidly on us—my breathless remark to Adrian was followed by the flapping of the canvas, as the adverse wind struck it, and our boat lurched—swift as speech, the web of the storm thickened overhead, the sun went down red, the dark sea was strewed with foam, and our skiff rose and fell in its increasing furrows.

Behold us now in our frail tenement, hemmed in by hungry, roaring waves, buffeted by winds. In the inky east two vast clouds, sailing contrary ways, met; the lightning leapt forth, and the hoarse thunder muttered. Again in the south, the clouds replied, and the forked stream of fire, running along the black sky, showed us the appalling piles of clouds, now met and obliterated by the heaving waves. Great God! And we alone—we three—alone—alone—sole dwellers on the sea and on the earth, we three must perish! The vast universe, its

---

[1] *caique* Small row-boat or sail-boat.

[2] *When winds ... burst* From Percy Shelley's sonnet "Translated from the Greek of Moschus" (1816), 2.1–6.

[3] *bark* Boat.

[4] *the patriarch of old* I.e., Noah.

[5] *Cyclades* Group of islands in the Aegean Sea.

myriad worlds, and the plains of boundless earth which we had left—the extent of shoreless sea around—contracted to my view—they and all that they contained, shrunk up to one point, even to our tossing bark, freighted with glorious humanity.

A convulsion of despair crossed the love-beaming face of Adrian, while with set teeth he murmured, "Yet they shall be saved!" Clara, visited by a human pang, pale and trembling, crept near him—he looked on her with an encouraging smile—"Do you fear, sweet girl? O, do not fear, we shall soon be on shore!"

The darkness prevented me from seeing the changes of her countenance; but her voice was clear and sweet, as she replied, "Why should I fear? Neither sea nor storm can harm us, if mighty destiny or the ruler of destiny does not permit. And then the stinging fear of surviving either of you is not here—one death will clasp us undivided."

Meanwhile we took in all our sails, save a jib;[1] and, as soon as we might without danger, changed our course, running with the wind for the Italian shore. Dark night mixed everything; we hardly discerned the white crests of the murderous surges, except when lightning made brief noon, and drank the darkness, showing us our danger, and restoring us to double night. We were all silent, except when Adrian, as steersman, made an encouraging observation. Our little shell obeyed the rudder miraculously well, and ran along on the top of the waves as if she had been an offspring of the sea, and the angry mother sheltered her endangered child.

I sat at the prow, watching our course; when suddenly I heard the waters break with redoubled fury. We were certainly near the shore—at the same time I cried, "About there!" and a broad lightning, filling the concave, showed us for one moment the level beach ahead, disclosing even the sands, and stunted, ooze-sprinkled beds of reeds, that grew at high water mark. Again it was dark, and we drew in our breath with such content as one may, who, while fragments of volcano-hurled rock darken the air, sees a vast mass plowing the ground immediately at his feet. What to do we knew not—the breakers here, there, everywhere, encompassed us—they roared, and dashed, and flung their hated spray in our faces. With considerable difficulty and danger we succeeded at length in altering our course, and stretched out from shore. I urged my companions to prepare for the wreck of our little skiff, and to bind themselves to some oar or spar which might suffice to float them. I was myself an excellent swimmer—the very sight of the sea was wont to raise in me such sensations as a huntsman experiences when he hears a pack of hounds in full cry; I loved to feel the waves wrap me and strive to overpower me; while I, lord of myself, moved this way or that, in spite of their angry bufferings. Adrian also could swim—but the weakness of his frame prevented him from feeling pleasure in the exercise, or acquiring any great expertness.

But what power could the strongest swimmer oppose to the overpowering violence of ocean in its fury? My efforts to prepare my companions were rendered nearly futile—for the roaring breakers prevented our hearing one another speak, and the waves that broke continually over our boat obliged me to exert all my strength in lading the water out, as fast as it came in. The while darkness, palpable and rayless, hemmed us round, dissipated only by the lightning; sometimes we beheld thunderbolts, fiery red, fall into the sea, and at intervals vast spouts stooped from the clouds, churning the wild ocean, which rose to meet them; while the fierce gale bore the rack[2] onwards, and they were lost in the chaotic mingling of sky and sea. Our gunwales had been torn away, our single sail had been rent to ribbands[3] and borne down the stream of the wind. We had cut away our mast, and lightened the boat of all she contained—Clara attempted to assist me in heaving the water from the hold, and, as she turned her eyes to look on the lightning, I could discern by that momentary gleam that resignation had conquered every fear. We have a power given us in any worst extremity, which props the else feeble mind of man, and enables us to endure the most savage tortures with a stillness of soul which in hours of happiness we could not have imagined. A calm, more dreadful in truth than the tempest, allayed the wild beatings of my heart—a calm like that of the gamester, the suicide, and the murderer, when the last die is on the point of being cast—while the poisoned cup is at the lips, as the death-blow is about to be given.

[1] *jib* Triangular sail to the fore of a ship.

[2] *rack* Mass of clouds.

[3] *ribbands* I.e., ribbons.

Hours passed thus—hours which might write old age on the face of beardless youth, and grizzle the silky hair of infancy—hours, while the chaotic uproar continued, while each dread gust transcended in fury the one before, and our skiff hung on the breaking wave, and then rushed into the valley below, and trembled and spun between the watery precipices that seemed most to meet above her. For a moment the gale paused, and ocean sank to comparative silence—it was a breathless interval; the wind which, as a practised leaper, had gathered itself up before it sprung, now with terrific roar rushed over the sea, and the waves struck our stern. Adrian exclaimed that the rudder was gone—"We are lost," cried Clara, "Save yourselves—O save yourselves!" The lightning showed me the poor girl half buried in the water at the bottom of the boat; as she was sinking in it Adrian caught her up, and sustained her in his arms. We were without a rudder—we rushed prow foremost into the vast billows piled up ahead—they broke over and filled the tiny skiff; one scream I heard—one cry that we were gone, I uttered; I found myself in the waters; darkness was around. When the light of the tempest flashed, I saw the keel of our upset boat close to me—I clung to this, grasping it with clenched hand and nails, while I endeavoured during each flash to discover any appearance of my companions. I thought I saw Adrian at no great distance from me, clinging to an oar; I sprung from my hold, and with energy beyond my human strength, I dashed aside the waters as I strove to lay hold of him. As that hope failed, instinctive love of life animated me, and feelings of contention, as if a hostile will combated with mine. I breasted the surges, and flung them from me as I would the opposing front and sharpened claws of a lion about to enfang my bosom. When I had been beaten down by one wave, I rose on another, while I felt bitter pride curl my lip.

Ever since the storm had carried us near the shore, we had never attained any great distance from it. With every flash I saw the bordering coast; yet the progress I made was small, while each wave, as it receded, carried me back into ocean's far abysses. At one moment I felt my foot touch the sand, and then again I was in deep water; my arms began to lose their power of motion; my breath failed me under the influence of the strangling waters—a thousand wild and delirious thoughts crossed

me: as well as I can now recall them, my chief feeling was, how sweet it would be to lay my head on the quiet earth, where the surges would no longer strike my weakened frame, nor the sound of waters ring in my ears—to attain this repose, not to save my life, I made a last effort—the shelving shore suddenly presented a footing for me. I rose, and was again thrown down by the breakers—a point of rock, to which I was enabled to cling, gave me a moment's respite; and then, taking advantage of the ebbing of the waves, I ran forwards—gained the dry sands, and fell senseless on the oozy reeds that sprinkled them.

I must have lain long deprived of life; for when first, with a sickening feeling, I unclosed my eyes, the light of morning met them. Great change had taken place meanwhile: grey dawn dappled the flying clouds, which sped onwards, leaving visible at intervals vast lakes of pure ether. A fountain of light arose in an increasing stream from the east, behind the waves of the Adriatic, changing the grey to a roseate hue, and then flooding sky and sea with aerial gold.

A kind of stupor followed my fainting; my senses were alive, but memory was extinct. The blessed respite was short—a snake lurked near me to sting me into life. On the first retrospective emotion I would have started up, but my limbs refused to obey me; my knees trembled, the muscles had lost all power. I still believed that I might find one of my beloved companions cast like me, half alive, on the beach; and I strove in every way to restore my frame to the use of its animal functions. I wrung the brine from my hair; and the rays of the risen sun soon visited me with genial warmth. With the restoration of my bodily powers, my mind became in some degree aware of the universe of misery, henceforth to be its dwelling. I ran to the water's edge, calling on the beloved names. Ocean drank in and absorbed my feeble voice, replying with pitiless roar. I climbed a near tree: the level sands bounded by a pine forest, and the sea clipped round by the horizon, was all that I could discern. In vain I extended my researches along the beach; the mast we had thrown overboard, with tangled cordage, and remnants of a sail, was the sole relic land received of our wreck. Sometimes I stood still, and wrung my hands. I accused earth and sky—the universal machine and the Almighty power that misdirected it. Again I threw myself on the sands, and then the sighing wind, mimicking a human cry, roused me to bitter, fallacious hope. Assuredly if any little bark or smallest canoe had been near, I should have sought the savage plains of ocean, found the dear remains of my lost ones, and, clinging round them, have shared their grave.

The day passed thus; each moment contained eternity; although when hour after hour had gone by, I wondered at the quick flight of time. Yet even now I had not drunk the bitter potion to the dregs; I was not yet persuaded of my loss; I did not yet feel in every pulsation, in every nerve, in every thought, that I remained alone of my race—that I was the LAST MAN.

The day had clouded over, and a drizzling rain set in at sunset. Even the eternal skies weep, I thought; is there any shame then, that mortal man should spend himself in tears? I remembered the ancient fables, in which human beings are described as dissolving away through weeping into ever-gushing fountains. Ah! that so it were; and then my destiny would be in some sort akin to the watery death of Adrian and Clara. Oh! grief is fantastic; it weaves a web on which to trace the history of its woe from every form and change around; it incorporates itself with all living nature; it finds sustenance in every object; as light, it fills all things, and, like light, it gives its own colours to all.

I had wandered in my search to some distance from the spot on which I had been cast, and came to one of those watch-towers, which at stated distances line the Italian shore. I was glad of shelter, glad to find a work of human hands, after I had gazed so long on nature's drear barrenness; so I entered, and ascended the rough winding staircase into the guard-room. So far was fate kind, that no harrowing vestige remained of its former inhabitants; a few planks laid across two iron tressels, and strewed with the dried leaves of Indian corn, was the bed presented to me; and an open chest, containing some half mouldered biscuit, awakened an appetite, which perhaps existed before, but of which, until now, I was not aware. Thirst also, violent and parching, the result of the sea-water I had drank, and of the exhaustion of my frame, tormented me. Kind nature had gifted the supply of these wants with pleasurable sensations, so that I—even I!—was refreshed and calmed as I ate of this sorry fare, and drank a little of the sour wine which half filled a flask left in this abandoned dwelling. Then I stretched myself on the bed, not to be disdained by the

victim of shipwreck. The earthy smell of the dried leaves was balm to my sense after the hateful odour of seaweed. I forgot my state of loneliness. I neither looked backward nor forward; my senses were hushed to repose; I fell asleep and dreamed of all dear inland scenes, of hay-makers, of the shepherd's whistle to his dog when he demanded his help to drive the flock to fold; of sights and sounds peculiar to my boyhood's mountain life, which I had long forgotten.

I awoke in a painful agony—for I fancied that ocean, breaking its bounds, carried away the fixed continent and deep rooted mountains, together with the streams I loved, the woods, and the flocks—it raged around, with that continued and dreadful roar which had accompanied the last wreck of surviving humanity. As my waking sense returned, the bare walls of the guard room closed round me, and the rain pattered against the single window. How dreadful it is to emerge from the oblivion of slumber and to receive as a good morrow the mute wailing of one's own hapless heart—to return from the land of deceptive dreams to the heavy knowledge of unchanged disaster!—Thus was it with me, now, and for ever! The sting of other griefs might be blunted by time; and even mine yielded sometimes during the day, to the pleasure inspired by the imagination or the senses; but I never look first upon the morning-light but with my fingers pressed tight on my bursting heart, and my soul deluged with the interminable flood of hopeless misery. Now I awoke for the first time in the dead world—I awoke alone—and the dull dirge of the sea, heard even amidst the rain, recalled me to the reflection of the wretch I had become. The sound came like a reproach, a scoff—like the sting of remorse in the soul—I gasped—the veins and muscles of my throat swelled, suffocating me. I put my fingers to my ears, I buried my head in the leaves of my couch, I would have dived to the centre to lose hearing of that hideous moan.

But another task must be mine—again I visited the detested beach, again I vainly looked far and wide, again I raised my unanswered cry, lifting up the only voice that could ever again force the mute air to syllable the human thought.

What a pitiable, forlorn, disconsolate being I was! My very aspect and garb told the tale of my despair. My hair was matted and wild, my limbs soiled with salt ooze; while at sea, I had thrown off those of my garments that encumbered me, and the rain drenched the thin summer-clothing I had retained—my feet were bare, and the stunted reeds and broken shells made them bleed—the while, I hurried to and fro, now looking earnestly on some distant rock which, islanded in the sands, bore for a moment a deceptive appearance—now with flashing eyes reproaching the murderous ocean for its unutterable cruelty.

For a moment I compared myself to that monarch of the waste—Robinson Crusoe.[1] We had been both thrown companionless—he on the shore of a desolate island: I on that of a desolate world. I was rich in the so-called goods of life. If I turned my steps from the near barren scene, and entered any of the earth's million cities, I should find their wealth stored up for my accommodation—clothes, food, books, and a choice of dwelling beyond the command of the princes of former times. Every climate was subject to my selection, while he was obliged to toil in the acquirement of every necessary, and was the inhabitant of a tropical island, against whose heats and storms he could obtain small shelter. Viewing the question thus, who would not have preferred the Sybarite[2] enjoyments I could command, the philosophic leisure, and ample intellectual resources, to his life of labour and peril? Yet he was far happier than I: for he could hope, nor hope in vain—the destined vessel at last arrived to bear him to countrymen and kindred, where the events of his solitude became a fire-side tale. To none could I ever relate the story of my adversity; no hope had I. He knew that, beyond the ocean which begirt his lonely island, thousands lived whom the sun enlightened when it shone also on him: beneath the meridian sun and visiting moon, I alone bore human features; I alone could give articulation to thought; and, when I slept, both day and night were unbeheld of any. He had fled from his fellows, and was transported with terror at the print of a human foot. I would have knelt down and worshipped the same. The wild and cruel Caribbee, the merciless Cannibal[3]—or

worse than these, the uncouth, brute, and remorseless veteran in the vices of civilization, would have been to me a beloved companion, a treasure dearly prized. His nature would be kin to mine; his form cast in the same mould; human blood would flow in his veins; a human sympathy must link us for ever. It cannot be that I shall never behold a fellow being more!—never!—never!—not in the course of years!—Shall I wake, and speak to none, pass the interminable hours, my soul, islanded in the world, a solitary point, surrounded by vacuum? Will day follow day endlessly thus? No! no! a God rules the world—providence has not exchanged its golden sceptre for an aspic's[4] sting. Away! let me fly from the ocean-grave, let me depart from this barren nook, paled in,[5] as it is, from access by its own desolateness; let me tread once again the paved towns; step over the threshold of man's dwellings, and most certainly I shall find this thought a horrible vision—a maddening, but evanescent, dream.

I entered Ravenna[6] (the town nearest to the spot whereon I had been cast) before the second sun had set on the empty world; I saw many living creatures: oxen, and horses, and dogs, but there was no man among them. I entered a cottage, it was vacant; I ascended the marble stairs of a palace, the bats and the owls were nestled in the tapestry; I stepped softly, not to awaken the sleeping town. I rebuked a dog, that by yelping disturbed the sacred stillness; I would not believe that all was as it seemed—The world was not dead, but I was mad; I was deprived of sight, hearing, and sense of touch; I was labouring under the force of a spell, which permitted me to behold all sights of earth, except its human inhabitants; they were pursuing their ordinary labours. Every house had its inmate; but I could not perceive them. If I could have deluded myself into a belief of this kind, I should have been far more satisfied. But my brain, tenacious of its reason, refused to lend itself to such imaginations—and though I endeavoured to play the antic to myself, I knew that I, the offspring of man, during long years one among many—now remained sole survivor of my species.

---

[1] *Robinson Crusoe* Shipwrecked protagonist of Daniel Defoe's *The Life and Adventures of Robinson Crusoe* (1719).

[2] *Sybarite* Luxurious; from the Greek city of Sybaris, noted for its luxury.

[3] *Caribbee* Caribs, inhabitants of the southern West Indies; *Cannibal* Originally also a form of the word "Carib." The fierce inhabitants of this region were rumored to eat human flesh; thus the

evolution of the word "cannibal" to its present meaning.

[4] *aspic* Asp, a poisonous snake.

[5] *paled in* Fenced in.

[6] *Ravenna* Town on the Adriatic Sea, approximately 80 miles south of Venice.

The sun sank behind the western hills; I had fasted since the preceding evening, but, though faint and weary, I loathed food, nor ceased, while yet a ray of light remained, to pace the lonely streets. Night came on, and sent every living creature but me to the bosom of its mate. It was my solace to blunt my mental agony by personal hardship—of the thousand beds around, I would not seek the luxury of one; I lay down on the pavement—a cold marble step served me for a pillow—midnight came; and then, though not before, did my wearied lids shut out the sight of the twinkling stars, and their reflex on the pavement near. Thus I passed the second night of my desolation.

CHAPTER 30

I awoke in the morning, just as the higher windows of the lofty houses received the first beams of the rising sun. The birds were chirping, perched on the window sills and deserted thresholds of the doors. I awoke, and my first thought was, Adrian and Clara are dead. I no longer shall be hailed by their good-morrow, or pass the long day in their society. I shall never see them more. The ocean has robbed me of them—stolen their hearts of love from their breasts, and given over to corruption what was dearer to me than light, or life, or hope.

I was an untaught shepherd-boy when Adrian deigned to confer on me his friendship. The best years of my life had been passed with him. All I had possessed of this world's goods, of happiness, knowledge, or virtue, I owed to him. He had, in his person, his intellect, and rare qualities, given a glory to my life, which without him it had never known. Beyond all other beings he had taught me that goodness, pure and single, can be an attribute of man. It was a sight for angels to congregate to behold, to view him lead, govern, and solace the last days of the human race.

My lovely Clara also was lost to me—she who, last of the daughters of man, exhibited all those feminine and maiden virtues which poets, painters, and sculptors have in their various languages strove to express. Yet, as far as she was concerned, could I lament that she was removed in early youth from the certain advent of misery? Pure she was of soul, and all her intents were holy. But her heart was the throne of love, and the sensibility her lovely countenance expressed was the prophet of many woes, not the less deep and drear because she would have for ever concealed them.

These two wondrously endowed beings had been spared from the universal wreck to be my companions during the last year of solitude. I had felt, while they were with me, all their worth. I was conscious that every other sentiment, regret, or passion had by degrees merged into a yearning, clinging affection for them. I had not forgotten the sweet partner of my youth, mother of my children, my adored Idris; but I saw at least a part of her spirit alive again in her brother;[1] and after, that by Evelyn's[2] death I had lost what most dearly recalled her to me; I enshrined her memory in Adrian's form, and endeavoured to confound the two dear ideas. I sound the depths of my heart, and try in vain to draw thence the expressions that can typify my love for these remnants of my race. If regret and sorrow came athwart me, as well it might in our solitary and uncertain state, the clear tones of Adrian's voice, and his fervent look, dissipated the gloom; or I was cheered unaware by the mild content and sweet resignation Clara's cloudless brow and deep blue eyes expressed. They were all to me—the suns of my benighted soul, repose in my weariness, slumber in my sleepless woe. Ill, most ill, with disjointed words, bare and weak, have I expressed the feeling with which I clung to them. I would have wound myself like ivy inextricably round them, so that the same blow might destroy us. I would have entered and been a part of them—so that

If the dull substance of my flesh were thought,[3]

even now I had accompanied them to their new and incommunicable abode.

Never shall I see them more. I am bereft of their dear converse—bereft of sight of them. I am a tree rent by lightning; never will the bark close over the bared fibres—never will their quivering life, torn by the winds, receive the opiate of a moment's balm. I am alone in the world—but that expression as yet was less pregnant with misery than that Adrian and Clara are dead.

The tide of thought and feeling rolls on for ever the same, though the banks and shapes around, which

---

[1] *her brother* I.e., Adrian.

[2] *Evelyn* Lionel and Idris's youngest son.

[3] *If … thought* From Shakespeare's Sonnet 44, line 1.

govern its course, and the reflection in the wave, vary. Thus the sentiment of immediate loss in some sort decayed, while that of utter, irremediable loneliness grew on me with time. Three days I wandered through Ravenna—now thinking only of the beloved beings who slept in the oozy caves of ocean, now looking forward on the dread blank before me; shuddering to make an onward step, writhing at each change that marked the progress of the hours.

For three days I wandered to and fro in this melancholy town. I passed whole hours in going from house to house, listening whether I could detect some lurking sign of human existence. Sometimes I rang at a bell; it tinkled through the vaulted rooms, and silence succeeded to the sound. I called myself hopeless, yet still I hoped; and still disappointment ushered in the hours, intruding the cold, sharp steel, which first pierced me, into the aching festering wound. I fed like a wild beast, which seizes its food only when stung by intolerable hunger. I did not change my garb, or seek the shelter of a roof, during all those days. Burning heats, nervous irritation, a ceaseless but confused flow of thought, sleepless nights, and days instinct with a frenzy of agitation, possessed me during that time.

As the fever of my blood increased, a desire of wandering came upon me. I remember that the sun had set on the fifth day after my wreck when, without purpose or aim, I quitted the town of Ravenna. I must have been very ill. Had I been possessed by more or less of delirium, that night had surely been my last; for, as I continued to walk on the banks of the Mantone,[1] whose upward course I followed, I looked wistfully on the stream, acknowledging to myself that its pellucid waves could medicine my woes for ever, and was unable to account to myself for my tardiness in seeking their shelter from the poisoned arrows of thought that were piercing me through and through. I walked a considerable part of the night, and excessive weariness at length conquered my repugnance to the availing myself of the deserted habitations of my species. The waning moon, which had just risen, showed me a cottage, whose neat entrance and trim garden reminded me of my own England. I lifted up the latch of the door and entered. A kitchen first presented itself, where, guided by the moon beams, I found materials for striking a light.

Within this was a bed room; the couch was furnished with sheets of snowy whiteness; the wood piled on the hearth, and an array as for a meal might almost have deceived me into the dear belief that I had here found what I had so long sought—one survivor, a companion for my loneliness, a solace to my despair. I steeled myself against the delusion; the room itself was vacant: it was only prudent, I repeated to myself, to examine the rest of the house. I fancied that I was proof against the expectation; yet my heart beat audibly as I laid my hand on the lock of each door, and it sunk again, when I perceived in each the same vacancy. Dark and silent they were as vaults; so I returned to the first chamber, wondering what sightless host had spread the materials for my repast, and my repose. I drew a chair to the table and examined what the viands were of which I was to partake. In truth it was a death feast! The bread was blue and mouldy; the cheese lay a heap of dust. I did not dare examine the other dishes; a troop of ants passed in a double line across the table cloth; every utensil was covered with dust, with cobwebs, and myriads of dead flies. These were object each and all betokening the fallaciousness of my expectations. Tears rushed into my eyes; surely this was a wanton display of the power of the destroyer. What had I done, that each sensitive nerve was thus to be anatomized? Yet why complain more now than ever? This vacant cottage revealed no new sorrow—the world was empty; mankind was dead—I knew it well—why quarrel therefore with an acknowledged and stale truth? Yet, as I said, I had hoped in the very heart of despair, so that every new impression of the hard-cut reality on my soul brought with it a fresh pang, telling me the yet unstudied lesson, that neither change of place nor time could bring alleviation to my misery, but that, as I now was, I must continue, day after day, month after month, year after year, while I lived. I hardly dared conjecture what space of time that expression implied. It is true, I was no longer in the first blush of manhood; neither had I declined far in the vale of years—men have accounted mine the prime of life: I had just entered my thirty-seventh year; every limb was as well knit, every articulation as true, as when I had acted the shepherd on the hills of Cumberland; and with these advantages I was to commence the train of solitary life. Such were the reflections that ushered in my slumber on that night.

---

[1] *Mantone*   River that flows through Ravenna and into the Adriatic.

The shelter, however, and less disturbed repose which I enjoyed, restored me the following morning to a greater portion of health and strength than I had experienced since my fatal shipwreck. Among the stores I had discovered on searching the cottage the preceding night, was a quantity of dried grapes; these refreshed me in the morning as I left my lodging and proceeded towards a town which I discerned at no great distance. As far as I could divine, it must have been Forli. I entered with pleasure its wide and grassy streets. All, it is true, pictured the excess of desolation; yet I loved to find myself in those spots which had been the abode of my fellow creatures. I delighted to traverse street after street, to look up at the tall houses, and repeat to myself, once they contained beings similar to myself—I was not always the wretch I am now. The wide square of Forli, the arcade around it, its light and pleasant aspect, cheered me. I was pleased with the idea, that, if the earth should be again peopled, we, the lost race, would, in the relics left behind, present no contemptible exhibition of our powers to the newcomers.

I entered one of the palaces and opened the door of a magnificent saloon. I started—I looked again with renewed wonder. What wild-looking, unkempt, half-naked savage was that before me? The surprise was momentary.

I perceived that it was I myself whom I beheld in a large mirror at the end of the hall. No wonder that the lover of the princely Idris should fail to recognize himself in the miserable object there portrayed. My tattered dress was that in which I had crawled half alive from the tempestuous sea. My long and tangled hair hung in elf locks on my brow; my dark eyes, now hollow and wild, gleamed from under them; my cheeks were discoloured by the jaundice, which (the effect of misery and neglect) suffused my skin, and were half hid by a beard of many days' growth.

Yet why should I not remain thus, I thought; the world is dead, and this squalid attire is a fitter mourning garb than the foppery of a black suit. And thus, me-thinks, I should have remained, had not hope, without which I do not believe man could exist, whispered to me that in such a plight I should be an object of fear and aversion to the being, preserved I knew not where, but, I fondly trusted, at length to be found by me. Will my readers scorn the vanity that made me attire myself with some care, for the sake of this visionary being? Or will they forgive the freaks of a half crazed imagination? I can easily forgive myself—for hope, however vague, was so dear to me, and a sentiment of pleasure of so rare occurrence, that I yielded readily to any idea that cherished the one, or promised any recurrence of the former to my sorrowing heart.

After such occupation, I visited every street, alley, and nook of Forli. These Italian towns presented an appearance of still greater desolation than those of England or France. Plague had appeared here earlier—it had finished its course and achieved its work much sooner than with us. Probably the last summer had found no human being alive in all the track included between the shores of Calabria and the northern Alps. My search was utterly vain, yet I did not despond. Reason methought was on my side; and the chances were by no means contemptible that there should exist in some part of Italy a survivor like myself—of a wasted, depopulate land. As therefore I rambled through the empty town, I formed my plan for future operations. I would continue to journey on towards Rome. After I should have satisfied myself, by a narrow search, that I left behind no human being in the towns through which I passed, I would write up in a conspicuous part of each, with white paint, in three languages, that "Verney, the last of the race of Englishmen, had taken up his abode in Rome."

In pursuance of this scheme, I entered a painter's shop and procured myself the paint. It is strange that so trivial an occupation should have consoled and even enlivened me. But grief renders one childish, despair fantastic. To this simple inscription, I merely added the adjuration, "Friend, come! I wait for thee!—*Deh, vieni! ti aspetto!*"

On the following morning, with something like hope for my companion, I quitted Forli on my way to Rome. Until now, agonizing retrospect and dreary prospects for the future had stung me when awake, and cradled me to my repose. Many times I had delivered myself up to the tyranny of anguish—many times I resolved a speedy end to my woes; and death by my own hands was a remedy whose practicability was even cheering to me. What could I fear in the other world? If there were a hell, and I were doomed to it, I should come an adept to the sufferance of its tortures—the act were easy, the speedy and certain end of my deplorable tragedy. But now these thoughts faded before the new-born expectation. I went on my way, not as before, feeling each hour, each minute, to be an age instinct with incalculable pain.

As I wandered along the plain, at the foot of the Appennines—through their valleys, and over their bleak summits—my path led me through a country which had been trodden by heroes, visited and admired by thousands. They had, as a tide, receded, leaving me blank and bare in the midst. But why complain? Did I not hope?—so I schooled myself, even after the enliven-ing spirit had really deserted me, and thus I was obliged to call up all the fortitude I could command, and that was not much, to prevent a recurrence of that chaotic and intolerable despair that had succeeded to the miserable shipwreck, that had consummated every fear, and dashed to annihilation every joy.

I rose each day with the morning sun, and left my desolate inn. As my feet strayed through the unpeopled country, my thoughts rambled through the universe, and I was least miserable when I could, absorbed in reverie, forget the passage of the hours. Each evening, in spite of weariness, I detested to enter any dwelling, there to take up my nightly abode—I have sat, hour after hour, at the door of the cottage I had selected, unable to lift the latch and meet face to face blank desertion within. Many nights, though autumnal mists were spread around, I passed under an ilex[1]—many times I have supped on arbutus berries and chestnuts, making a fire, gypsy-like, on the ground—because wild natural scenery reminded me less acutely of my hopeless state of loneliness. I counted the days, and bore with me a peeled willow-wand, on which, as well as I could remember, I had notched the days that had elapsed since my wreck, and each night I added another unit to the melancholy sum.

I had toiled up a hill which led to Spoleto. Around was spread a plain, encircled by the chestnut-covered Apennines. A dark ravine was on one side, spanned by an aqueduct, whose tall arches were rooted in the dell below and attested that man had once deigned to bestow labour and thought here, to adorn and civilize nature. Savage, ungrateful nature, which in wild sport defaced his remains, protruding her easily renewed and fragile growth of wild flowers and parasite plants around his eternal edifices. I sat on a fragment of rock and looked round. The sun had bathed in gold the western atmosphere, and in the east the clouds caught the radiance, and budded into transient loveliness. It set on a world that contained me alone for its inhabitant. I took out my wand—I counted the marks. Twenty-five were already traced—twenty-five days had already elapsed since human voice had gladdened my ears or human countenance met my gaze. Twenty-five long, weary days, succeeded by dark and lonesome nights, had mingled with foregone years and had become a part of the past—the never to be recalled—a real, undeniable portion of my life—twenty-five long, long days.

Why this was not a month!—Why talk of days—or weeks—or months—I must grasp years in my imagina-tion, if I would truly picture the future to my-self—three, five, ten, twenty, fifty anniversaries of that fatal epoch might elapse—every year containing twelve months, each of more numerous calculation in a diary, than the twenty-five days gone by—Can it be? Will it be?—We had been used to look forward to death tremulously—wherefore, but because its place was obscure? But more terrible, and far more obscure, was the unveiled course of my lone futurity. I broke my wand; I threw it from me. I needed no recorder of the inch and barley-corn growth of my life, while my unquiet thoughts created other divisions than those ruled over by the planets—and, in looking back on the age that had elapsed since I had been alone, I disdained to give the name of days and hours to the throes of agony which had in truth portioned it out.

I hid my face in my hands. The twitter of the young birds going to rest, and their rustling among the trees, disturbed the still evening-air—the crickets chirped, the aziolo cooed at intervals. My thoughts had been of death—these sounds spoke to me of life. I lifted up my eyes—a bat wheeled round—the sun had sunk behind the jagged line of mountains, and the paly[2] crescent moon was visible, silver white amidst the orange sunset, and accompanied by one bright star, prolonged thus the twilight. A herd of cattle passed along in the dell below, untended, towards their watering place—the grass was rustled by a gentle breeze, and the olive-woods, mel-lowed into soft masses by the moonlight, contrasted

---

1 *ilex* Evergreen oak.

2 *paly* Pale.

their sea-green with the dark chestnut foliage. Yes, this is the earth; there is no change, no ruin, no rent made in her verdurous expanse; she continues to wheel round and round, with alternate night and day, through the sky, though man is not her adorner or inhabitant. Why could I not forget myself like one of those animals, and no longer suffer the wild tumult of misery that I endure? Yet, ah! what a deadly breach yawns between their state and mine! Have not they companions? Have not they each their mate—their cherished young, their home, which, though unexpressed to us, is, I doubt not, endeared and enriched, even in their eyes, by the society which kind nature has created for them? It is I only that am alone—I, on this little hilltop, gazing on plain and mountain recess; on sky, and its starry population, listening to every sound of earth, and air, and murmuring wave—I only cannot express to any companion my many thoughts, nor lay my throbbing head on any loved bosom, nor drink from meeting eyes an intoxicating dew that transcends the fabulous nectar of the gods. Shall I not then complain? Shall I not curse the murderous engine which has mowed down the children of men, my brethren? Shall I not bestow a malediction on every other of nature's offspring, which dares live and enjoy, while I live and suffer?

Ah, no! I will discipline my sorrowing heart to sympathy in your joys; I will be happy, because ye are so. Live on, ye innocents, nature's selected darlings; I am not much unlike to you. Nerves, pulse, brain, joint, and flesh, of such am I composed, and ye are organized by the same laws. I have something beyond this, but I will call it a defect, not an endowment, if it leads me to misery, while ye are happy. Just then, there emerged from a near copse two goats and a little kid, by the mother's side; they began to browze[1] the herbage of the hill. I approached near to them without their perceiving me; I gathered a handful of fresh grass and held it out; the little one nestled close to its mother, while she timidly withdrew. The male stepped forward, fixing his eyes on me: I drew near, still holding out my lure, while he, depressing his head, rushed at me with his horns. I was a very fool; I knew it, yet I yielded to my rage. I snatched up a huge fragment of rock; it would have crushed my rash foe. I poised it—aimed it—then my heart failed me. I hurled it wide of the mark; it rolled clattering among the bushes into dell. My little visitants, all aghast, galloped back into the covert of the wood; while I, my very heart bleeding and torn, rushed down the hill, and by the violence of bodily exertion sought to escape from my miserable self.

No, no, I will not live among the wild scenes of nature, the enemy of all that lives. I will seek the towns—Rome, the capital of the world, the crown of man's achievements. Among its storied streets, hallowed ruins, and stupendous remains of human exertion, I shall not, as here, find every thing forgetful of man; trampling on his memory, defacing his works, proclaiming from hill to hill, and vale to vale—by the torrents freed from the boundaries which he imposed, by the vegetation liberated from the laws which he enforced, by his habitation abandoned to mildew and weeds—that his power is lost, his race annihilated for ever.

I hailed the Tiber, for that was, as it were, an unalienable possession of humanity. I hailed the wild Campagna,[2] for every rood[3] had been trod by man; and its savage uncultivation, of no recent date, only proclaimed more distinctly his power, since he had given an honourable name and sacred title to what else would have been a worthless, barren track. I entered Eternal Rome by the Porta del Popolo,[4] and saluted with awe its time-honoured space. The wide square, the churches near, the long extent of the Corso, the near eminence of Trinita de' Monti[5] appeared like fairy work, they were so silent, so peaceful, and so very fair. It was evening, and the population of animals which still existed in this mighty city had gone to rest; there was no sound, save the murmur of its many fountains, whose soft monotony was harmony to my soul. The knowledge that I was in Rome soothed me; that wondrous city, hardly more illustrious for its heroes and sages than for the power it exercised over the imaginations of men. I went to rest that night; the eternal burning of my heart quenched, my senses tranquil.

---

1 *browze* Feed on.

2 *Campagna* Plain to the north of Rome through which the Tiber River flows before entering the city.

3 *rood* Measure of land, varying from six to eight yards.

4 *Porta del Popolo* Italian: "Gate of the People."

5 *Corso* Via del Corso, main street of central Rome; a fashionable promenade in Shelley's time; *Trinita de' Monti* Church located at the top of the Spanish Steps.

The next morning I eagerly began my rambles in search of oblivion. I ascended the many terraces of the garden of the Colonna Palace,[1] under whose roof I had been sleeping; and, passing out from it at its summit, I found myself on Monte Cavallo. The fountain sparkled in the sun; the obelisk above pierced the clear dark-blue air. The statues on each side, the works, as they are inscribed, of Phidias and Praxiteles, stood in undiminished grandeur, representing Castor and Pollux,[2] who with majestic power tamed the rearing animal at their side. If those illustrious artists had in truth chiselled these forms, how many passing generations had their giant proportions outlived! and now they were viewed by the last of the species they were sculptured to represent and deify. I had shrunk into insignificance in my own eyes, as I considered the multitudinous beings these stone demigods had outlived, but this after-thought restored me to dignity in my own conception. The sight of the poetry eternized in these statues, took the sting from the thought, arraying it only in poetic ideality.

I repeated to myself—I am in Rome! I behold, and, as it were, familiarly converse with the wonder of the world, sovereign mistress of the imagination, majestic and eternal survivor of millions of generations of extinct men. I endeavoured to quiet the sorrows of my aching heart by even now taking an interest in what in my youth I had ardently longed to see. Every part of Rome is replete with relics of ancient times. The meanest streets are strewed with truncated columns, broken capitals—Corinthian and Ionic—and sparkling fragments of granite or porphyry. The walls of the most penurious dwellings enclose a fluted pillar or ponderous stone, which once made part of the palace of the Caesars; and the voice of dead time, in still vibrations, is breathed from these dumb things, animated and glorified as they were by man.

I embraced the vast columns of the temple of Jupiter Stator,[3] which survives in the open space that was the Forum, and leaning my burning cheek against its cold durability, I tried to lose the sense of present misery and present desertion by recalling to the haunted cell of my brain vivid memories of times gone by. I rejoiced at my success, as I figured Camillus, the Gracchi, Cato, and last the heroes of Tacitus,[4] which shine meteors of surpassing brightness during the murky night of the empire; as the verses of Horace and Virgil, or the glowing periods of Cicero,[5] thronged into the opened gates of my mind, I felt myself exalted by long forgotten enthusiasm. I was delighted to know that I beheld the scene which they beheld—the scene which their wives and mothers, and crowds of the unnamed, witnessed, while at the same time they honoured applauded, or wept for these matchless specimens of humanity. At length, then, I had found a consolation. I had not vainly sought the storied precincts of Rome—I had discovered a medicine for my many and vital wounds.

I sat at the foot of these vast columns. The Coliseum,[6] whose naked ruin is robed by nature in a verdurous and glowing veil, lay in the sunlight on my right. Not far off, to the left, was the Tower of the Capitol.[7] Triumphal arches, the falling walls of many temples, strewed the ground at my feet. I strove, I resolved, to force myself to see the Plebeian multitude and lofty

[1] *Colonna Palace* Located on Monte Cavallo (also called Quirinal Hill), it contains an art gallery of sixteenth- and seventeeth-century paintings.

[2] *The statues ... Pollux* The statues of Castor and Pollux, the twin sons of Zeus and Leda, were then commonly (but incorrectly) ascribed to the fifth- and sixth-century BCE Greek sculptors Phidias and Praxiteles.

[3] *Jupiter Stator* Three large Corinthian columns remain of this temple, which is now thought to belong to Castor, rather than to Jupiter Stator (Jupiter the Stayer, or the Steadfast). The Forum, in which these columns stand, was the location of the marketplace and the center for political, economic, and religious activities.

[4] *Camillus* Roman statesman and general of the fourth century BCE; *the Gracci* Brothers Tiberius and Caius Gracchus, second-century BCE supporters of the plebian cause; *Cato* Either Cato the Elder (234–149 BCE), a famous politician and orator, or Cato the Younger (95–46 BCE), a Roman statesman who committed suicide rather than submit to the tyranny of Julius Caesar; *Tacitus* Roman historian (c. 55–115 CE) whose heroes include Alexander, Julius Caesar, Mithridates, and Seneca.

[5] *Horace ... Cicero* Horace and Virgil were two famous Roman poets of the first century BCE, famous for, respectively, *Odes* and *The Aeneid*. Cicero was a great orator, statesman, and prose writer who was assassinated in 43 BCE.

[6] *Coliseum* Great amphitheater completed in 80 CE and used for gladiatorial combat.

[7] *Tower of the Capitol* Citadel located on Mons Capitolinus, one of the seven hills of Rome.

Patrician forms congregated around; and, as the diorama of ages passed across my subdued fancy, they were replaced by the modern Roman: the Pope, in his white stole, distributing benedictions to the kneeling worshippers; the friar in his cowl; the dark-eyed girl, veiled by her mezzera;[1] the noisy, sun-burnt rustic, leading his herd of buffaloes and oxen to the Campo Vaccino.[2] The romance with which, dipping our pencils in the rainbow hues of sky and transcendent nature, we to a degree gratuitously endow the Italians, replaced the solemn grandeur of antiquity. I remembered the dark monk, and floating figures of "The Italian," and how my boyish blood had thrilled at the description.[3] I called to mind Corinna ascending the Capitol to be crowned,[4] and, passing from the heroine to the author, reflected how the Enchantress Spirit of Rome held sovereign sway over the minds of the imaginative, until it rested on me—sole remaining spectator of its wonders.

I was long wrapt by such ideas; but the soul wearies of a pauseless flight; and, stooping from its wheeling circuits round and round this spot, suddenly it fell ten thousand fathom deep, into the abyss of the present—into self-knowledge—into tenfold sadness. I roused myself—I cast off my waking dreams; and I, who just now could almost hear the shouts of the Roman throng, and was hustled by countless multitudes, now beheld the desert ruins of Rome sleeping under its own blue sky. The shadows lay tranquilly on the ground; sheep were grazing untended on the Palatine, and a buffalo stalked down the Sacred Way[5] that led to the Capitol. I was alone in the Forum; alone in Rome; alone in the world. Would not one living man—one companion in my weary solitude, be worth all the glory and remembered power of this time-honoured city? Double sorrow—sadness, bred in Cimmerian caves, robed my

soul in a mourning garb. The generations I had conjured up to my fancy contrasted more strongly with the end of all—the single point in which, as a pyramid, the mighty fabric of society had ended, while I, on the giddy height, saw vacant space around me.

From such vague laments I turned to the contemplation of the minutiae of my situation. So far, I had not succeeded in the sole object of my desires, the finding a companion for my desolation. Yet I did not despair. It is true that my inscriptions were set up, for the most part, in insignificant towns and villages; yet, even without these memorials, it was possible that the person who, like me, should find himself alone in a depopulate land, should, like me, come to Rome. The more slender my expectation was, the more I chose to build on it, and to accommodate my actions to this vague possibility.

It became necessary, therefore, that for a time I should domesticate myself at Rome. It became necessary that I should look my disaster in the face—not playing the school-boy's part of obedience without submission; enduring life, and yet rebelling against the laws by which I lived.

Yet how could I resign myself? Without love, without sympathy, without communion with any, how could I meet the morning sun, and with it trace its oft repeated journey to the evening shades? Why did I continue to live—why not throw off the weary weight of time, and with my own hand let out the fluttering prisoner from my agonized breast? It was not cowardice that withheld me; for the true fortitude was to endure, and death had a soothing sound accompanying it that would easily entice me to enter its demesne. But this I would not do. I had, from the moment I had reasoned on the subject, instituted myself the subject to fate, and the servant of necessity, the visible laws of the invisible God—I believed that my obedience was the result of sound reasoning, pure feeling, and an exalted sense of the true excellence and nobility of my nature. Could I have seen in this empty earth, in the seasons and their change, the hand of a blind power only, most willingly would I have placed my head on the sod and closed my eyes on its loveliness for ever. But fate had administered life to me when the plague had already seized on its prey—she had dragged me by the hair from out the strangling waves. By such miracles she had bought me for her own; I admitted her authority, and bowed to her

---

[1]   *mezzera*   Mesèro (Italian), a shawl worn by women over the head and shoulders.

[2]   *Campo Vaccino*   Italian: "Cattle Pasture," the original function of the Roman Forum.

[3]   *I remembered ... description*   References to the novel *The Italian* (1797), by Ann Radcliffe.

[4]   *Corinna ... crowned*   Reference to the heroine of Anne-Louise-Germaine de Staël's novel *Corinne, ou l'Italie* (1807).

[5]   *Palatine*   Most important of the seven hills of Rome, it was the location of the earliest Roman settlement; *Sacred Way*   Sacra Via (Latin), the oldest street in Rome.

decrees. If, after mature consideration, such was my resolve, it was doubly necessary that I should not lose the end of life, the improvement of my faculties, and poison its flow by repinings without end. Yet how cease to repine, since there was no hand near to extract the barbed spear that had entered my heart of hearts? I stretched out my hand, and it touched none whose sensations were responsive to mine. I was girded, walled in, vaulted over, by seven-fold barriers of loneliness. Occupation alone, if I could deliver myself up to it, would be capable of affording an opiate to my sleepless sense of woe. Having determined to make Rome my abode, at least for some months, I made arrangements for my accommodation—I selected my home. The Colonna Palace was well adapted for my purpose. Its grandeur—its treasure of paintings, its magnificent halls were objects soothing and even exhilarating.

I found the granaries of Rome well stored with grain, and particularly with Indian corn; this product, requiring less art in its preparation for food, I selected as my principal support. I now found the hardships and lawlessness of my youth turn to account. A man cannot throw off the habits of sixteen years. Since that age, it is true, I had lived luxuriously, or at least surrounded by all the conveniences civilization afforded. But before that time, I had been "as uncouth a savage as the wolf-bred founder of old Rome"[1]—and now, in Rome itself, robber and shepherd propensities, similar to those of its founder, were of advantage to its sole inhabitant. I spent the morning riding and shooting in the Campagna; I passed long hours in the various galleries; I gazed at each statue, and lost myself in a reverie before many a fair Madonna or beauteous nymph. I haunted the Vatican, and stood surrounded by marble forms of divine beauty. Each stone deity was possessed by sacred gladness and the eternal fruition of love. They looked on me with unsympathizing complacency, and often in wild accents I reproached them for their supreme indifference—for they were human shapes, the human form divine was manifest in each fairest limb and lineament. The perfect moulding brought with it the idea of colour and motion; often, half in bitter mockery, half in self-delusion, I clasped their icy proportions, and, coming between

Cupid and his Psyche's lips,[2] pressed the unconceiving marble.

I endeavoured to read. I visited the libraries of Rome. I selected a volume, and, choosing some sequestered, shady nook on the banks of the Tiber, or opposite the fair temple in the Borghese Gardens, or under the old pyramid of Cestius,[3] I endeavoured to conceal me from myself, and immerse myself in the subject traced on the pages before me. As if in the same soil you plant nightshade and a myrtle tree, they will each appropriate the mould, moisture, and air administered, for the fostering their several properties—so did my grief find sustenance, and power of existence, and growth, in what else had been divine manna, to feed radiant meditation. Ah! while I streak this paper with the tale of what my so-named occupations were—while I shape the skeleton of my days—my hand trembles, my heart pants, and my brain refuses to lend expression, or phrase, or idea, by which to image forth the veil of unutterable woe that clothed these bare realities. O worn and beating heart, may I dissect thy fibres, and tell how in each unmitigable misery, sadness dire, repinings, and despair, existed? May I record my many ravings—the wild curses I hurled at torturing nature, and how I have passed days shut out from light and food, from all except the burning hell alive in my own bosom?

I was presented, meantime, with one other occupation, the one best fitted to discipline my melancholy thoughts, which strayed backwards, over many a ruin, and through many a flowery glade, even to the mountain recess from which in early youth I had first emerged.

During one of my rambles through the habitations of Rome, I found writing materials on a table in an author's study. Parts of a manuscript lay scattered about. It contained a learned disquisition on the Italian language; one page an unfinished dedication to posterity, for whose profit the writer had sifted and selected the niceties of this harmonious language—to whose everlasting benefit he bequeathed his labours.

I also will write a book, I cried—for whom to read?—to whom dedicated? And then with silly flourish (what so capricious and childish as despair?) I wrote,

---

[1] *as ... Rome* Romulus, the founder of Rome, and his brother Remus were said to have been reared by a she-wolf. Lionel quotes a statement made earlier by himself, in Chapter 1.

[2] *Cupid ... lips* Cupid, god of love, and his mortal lover, Psyche.

[3] *old ... Cestius* Tomb of Praetor Gaius Cestius Epulo (d. 12 BCE), next to which is the Protestant cemetery in which Percy Shelley was buried.

DEDICATION
TO THE ILLUSTRIOUS DEAD.
SHADOWS, ARISE, AND READ YOUR FALL!
BEHOLD THE HISTORY OF THE
LAST MAN.

Yet, will not this world be re-peopled, and the children of a saved pair of lovers, in some to me unknown and unattainable seclusion, wandering to these prodigious relics of the ante-pestilential race, seek to learn how beings so wondrous in their achievements, with imaginations infinite, and powers godlike, had departed from their home to an unknown country?

I will write and leave in this most ancient city, this "world's sole monument,"[1] a record of these things. I will leave a monument of the existence of Verney, the Last Man. At first I thought only to speak of plague, of death, and last, of desertion; but I lingered fondly on my early years, and recorded with sacred zeal the virtues of my companions. They have been with me during the fulfilment of my task. I have brought it to an end—I lift my eyes from my paper—again they are lost to me. Again I feel that I am alone.

A year has passed since I have been thus occupied. The seasons have made their wonted round, and decked this eternal city in a changeful robe of surpassing beauty. A year has passed; and I no longer *guess* at my state or my prospects—loneliness is my familiar, sorrow my inseparable companion. I have endeavoured to brave the storm—I have endeavoured to school myself to fortitude—I have sought to imbue myself with the lessons of wisdom. It will not do. My hair has become nearly grey—my voice, unused now to utter sound, comes strangely on my ears. My person, with its human powers and features, seem to me a monstrous excrescence of nature. How express in human language a woe human being until this hour never knew! How give intelligible expression to a pang none but I could ever understand!—No one has entered Rome. None will ever come. I smile bitterly at the delusion I have so long nourished, and still more when I reflect that I have exchanged it for another as delusive, as false, but to which I now cling with the same fond trust.

Winter has come again; and the gardens of Rome have lost their leaves—the sharp air comes over the Campagna, and has driven its brute inhabitants to take up their abode in the many dwellings of the deserted city. Frost has suspended the gushing fountains, and Trevi[2] has stilled her eternal music. I had made a rough calculation, aided by the stars, by which I endeavoured to ascertain the first day of the new year. In the old outworn age, the Sovereign Pontiff[3] was used to go in solemn pomp, and mark the renewal of the year by driving a nail in the gate of the temple of Janus.[4] On that day I ascended St. Peter's, and carved on its topmost stone the aera 2100, last year of the world!

My only companion was a dog, a shaggy fellow, half water- and half shepherd's-dog, whom I found tending sheep in the Campagna. His master was dead, but nevertheless he continued fulfilling his duties in expectation of his return. If a sheep strayed from the rest, he forced it to return to the flock, and sedulously kept off every intruder. Riding in the Campagna I had come upon his sheep-walk, and for some time observed his repetition of lessons learned from man, now useless, though unforgotten. His delight was excessive when he saw me. He sprung up to my knees; he capered round and round, wagging his tail, with the short, quick bark of pleasure: he left his fold to follow me, and from that day has never neglected to watch by and attend on me, showing boisterous gratitude whenever I caressed or talked to him. His pattering steps and mine alone were heard when we entered the magnificent extent of nave and aisle of St. Peter's.[5] We ascended the myriad steps together when on the summit I achieved my design, and in rough figures noted the date of the last year. I then turned to gaze on the country, and to take leave of Rome. I had long determined to quit it, and I now formed the plan I would adopt for my future career, after I had left this magnificent abode.

A solitary being is by instinct a wanderer, and that I would become. A hope of amelioration always attends on change of place, which would even lighten the

---

[1] *world's sole monument* From Edmund Spenser's *Ruins of Rome* (1591): "Rome living, was the world's sole ornament, / And dead, is now the world's sole monument" (lines 405–06).

[2] *Trevi* Fountain on the Quirinal Hill, built in 1762 by Nicola Salvi.

[3] *Sovereign Pontiff* I.e., the Pontifex Maximus, the Roman High Priest, a title later given to the pope.

[4] *Janus* Roman god of gates, of doorways, and of the new year.

[5] *nave* Main body of a church; *St Peter's* Basilica of the Vatican.

burden of my life. I had been a fool to remain in Rome all this time: Rome noted for malaria, the famous caterer for death. But it was still possible, that, could I visit the whole extent of earth, I should find in some part of the wide extent a survivor. Methought the sea-side was the most probable retreat to be chosen by such a one. If left alone in an inland district, still they could not continue in the spot where their last hopes had been extinguished; they would journey on, like me, in search of a partner for their solitude, till the watery barrier stopped their further progress.

To that water—cause of my woes—perhaps now to be their cure I would betake myself. Farewell, Italy!—farewell, thou ornament of the world, matchless Rome, the retreat of the solitary one during long months!—to civilized life—to the settled home and succession of monotonous days, farewell! Peril will now be mine; and I hail her as a friend—death will perpetually cross my path, and I will meet him as a benefactor; hardship, inclement weather, and dangerous tempests will be my sworn mates. Ye spirits of storm, receive me! ye powers of destruction, open wide your arms, and clasp me for ever! if a kinder power have not decreed another end, so that after long endurance I may reap my reward, and again feel my heart beat near the heart of another like to me.

Tiber, the road which is spread by nature's own hand, threading her continent, was at my feet, and many a boat was tethered to the banks. I would with a few books, provisions, and my dog, embark in one of these and float down the current of the stream into the sea; and then, keeping near land, I would coast the beauteous shores and sunny promontories of the blue Mediterranean, pass Naples, along Calabria,[1] and would dare the twin perils of Scylla and Charybdis;[2] then with fearless aim, (for what had I to lose?) skim ocean's surface towards Malta and the further Cyclades. I would avoid Constantinople, the sight of whose well-known towers and inlets belonged to another state of existence from my present one; I would coast Asia Minor, and Syria, and, passing the seven-mouthed Nile, steer northward again, till, losing sight of forgotten Carthage and deserted Lybia, I should reach the pillars of Hercules.[3] And then, no matter where—the oozy caves and soundless depths of ocean may be my dwelling before I accomplish this long-drawn voyage, or the arrow of disease find my heart as I float singly on the weltering Mediterranean; or, in some place I touch at, I may find what I seek—a companion; or, if this may not be, to endless time, decrepit and grey headed—youth already in the grave with those I love—the lone wanderer will still unfurl his sail, and clasp the tiller, and, still obeying the breezes of heaven, for ever round another and another promontory, anchoring in another and another bay, still ploughing seedless ocean, leaving behind the verdant land of native Europe, adown the tawny shore of Africa, having weathered the fierce seas of the Cape,[4] I may moor my worn skiff in a creek, shaded by spicy groves of the odorous islands of the far Indian ocean.

These are wild dreams. Yet since, now a week ago, they came on me, as I stood on the height of St. Peter's, they have ruled my imagination. I have chosen my boat, and laid in my scant stores. I have selected a few books; the principal are Homer and Shakespeare—but the libraries of the world are thrown open to me, and in any port I can renew my stock. I form no expectation of alteration for the better; but the monotonous present is intolerable to me. Neither hope nor joy are my pilots—restless despair and fierce desire of change lead me on. I long to grapple with danger, to be excited by fear, to have some task, however slight or voluntary, for each day's fulfilment. I shall witness all the variety of appearance that the elements can assume—I shall read fair augury in the rainbow, menace in the cloud, some lesson or record dear to my heart in everything. Thus around the shores of deserted earth, while the sun is high, and the moon waxes or wanes, angels, the spirits of the dead, and the ever-open eye of the Supreme, will behold the tiny bark, freighted with Verney—the LAST MAN.

THE END

—1826

---

1   *Calabria*   Region of southern Italy.

2   *Scylla and Charybdis*   From Greek mythology, a sea monster, later turned into rock cliffs, and a whirlpool, located in the Straits of Messina.

3   *the pillars of Hercules*   The Rock of Gibraltar and the Hill of Ceuta, two promontories flanking the eastern end to the Strait of Gibraltar, which were considered in ancient times to mark the ends of the earth.

4   *Cape*   Cape of Good Hope.

IN CONTEXT

The "Last Man" Theme in the Nineteenth Century

The theme of "the last man" was one that captured a great many imaginations in the 1820s and 1830s. Shelley's 1826 novel followed on the heels of Thomas Campbell's 1823 poem of the same name (to which, according to Campbell, Byron's poem "Darkness" owes its inspiration). Also in 1826 a number of magazine pieces were published on the same theme, including "The Last Man" (*Blackwoods*) and "The Death of the World" (*European Magazine*). That same year the painter John Martin, whose work often focused on apocalyptic visions, painted an initial study (now lost) of "The Last Man," a watercolor of which he completed in 1832, and an oil painting in 1849. The Campbell poem and the Martin painting are reproduced below; both envisage the end of the world occurring as a result of the sun's light being extinguished, rather than as a result of plague or other natural disaster.

Thomas Campbell, "The Last Man," *New Monthly Magazine 8 (1823)*

All worldly shapes shall melt in gloom,
    The Sun himself must die,
Before this mortal shall assume
      Its Immortality!
5   I saw a vision in my sleep,
That gave my spirit strength to sweep
    Adown the gulf of Time!
I saw the last of human mould,
That shall Creation's death behold,
10   As Adam saw her prime!

The Sun's eye had a sickly glare,
    The Earth with age was wan,
The skeletons of nations were
    Around that lonely man!
15 Some had expir'd in fight—the brands
    Still rusted in their bony hands;
      In plague and famine some!
Earth's cities had no sound nor tread;
And ships were drifting with the dead
20   To shores where all was dumb!

Yet, prophet like, that lone one stood,
   With dauntless words and high,
That shook the sere° leaves from the wood   *withered*
   As if a storm pass'd by,
25 Saying, we are twins in death, proud Sun,
Thy face is cold, thy race is run,
   'Tis Mercy bids thee go.
For thou ten thousand thousand years
Hast seen the tide of human tears,
30   That shall no longer flow.

What though beneath thee man put forth
   His pomp, his pride, his skill;
And arts that made fire, flood, and earth,
   The vassals of his will—
35 Yet mourn I not thy parted sway,
Thou dim discrownèd king of day:
   For all those trophied arts
And triumphs that beneath thee sprang,
Heal'd not a passion or a pang
40   Entail'd on human hearts.

Go, let oblivion's curtain fall
   Upon the stage of men,
Nor with thy rising beams recall
   Life's tragedy again.
45 Its piteous pageants bring not back,
Nor waken flesh, upon the rack
   Of pain anew to writhe;
Stretch'd in disease's shapes abhorr'd,
Or mown in battle by the sword,
50   Like grass beneath the scythe.

Ev'n I am weary in yon skies
   To watch thy fading fire;
Test of all sumless agonies,
   Behold not me expire.
55 My lips that speak thy dirge of death—
Their rounded gasp and gurgling breath
   To see thou shalt not boast.
The eclipse of Nature spreads my pall—
The majesty of Darkness shall
60   Receive my parting ghost!

This spirit shall return to Him
    That gave its heavenly spark;
Yet think not, Sun, it shall be dim
    When thou thyself art dark!
65   No! it shall live again, and shine
In bliss unknown to beams of thine,
    By Him recall'd to breath,
Who captive led captivity,
Who robb'd the grave of Victory—
70   And took the sting from Death!

Go, Sun, while Mercy holds me up
    On Nature's awful waste
To drink this last and bitter cup
    Of grief that man shall taste—
75   Go, tell the night that hides thy face,
Thou saw'st the last of Adam's race,
    On Earth's sepulchral clod,
The dark'ning universe defy
To quench his Immortality,
80   Or shake his trust in God!

John Martin, *The Last Man* (1849).

from Thomas Campbell's letter to the editor of *The Edinburgh Review*, 28 February 1825

... You say that my poem, "The Last Man," seems to have been suggested by Lord Byron's poem "Darkness." Now the truth is, that fifteen, or it may be more, years ago, I called on Lord Byron, who at that time had lodgings near St. James's Street; and we had a long, and to me a very memorable, conversation, from which I have not a doubt that his Lordship imbibed those few ideas in the poem "Darkness" which have any resemblance to mine in "The Last Man." I remember my saying to him that I thought the idea of a being witnessing the extinction of his species and of the Creation, and of his looking, under the fading eye of nature, at desolate cities, ships floating at sea with the dead, would make a striking subject for a poem. I met those very ideas, many years afterwards, when I read Lord Byron's poem "Darkness."

THE VICTORIAN ERA

The word "Victorian" conjures up a series of images that both accurately describe and misrepresent the literature and culture of the last two thirds of the nineteenth century in Britain. Stiff collars and stiff upper lips, draped table legs, exceedingly long novels, and gritty urban squalor have become the iconic images of Victorian Britain. But these images reveal only one dimension of what is a much more complex picture. While it is certainly the case that Victorians tended to place a high value on such qualities as honor, duty, moral seriousness, and sexual propriety—at least officially—it is a mistake to assume that most were humorless or repressed. And while many of the best-known Victorian novels run to many hundreds of pages, we need to remember that Victorian audiences tended to read these in weekly or monthly installments, or in shorter volumes. Although brutal factory conditions, pitiful wages, and crowded cities impoverished many millions of people, the Victorian period also saw the passage of progressive labor laws, unprecedented wealth creation for some, and the first public sewage systems in Britain. And though "Victorian" still suggests "repressed" to many readers, historians and literary scholars alike have increasingly shown that discourses about

Photographer unknown, *Her Majesty the Queen*, 21 June 1887.

sexuality developed and proliferated throughout the period, not least in its literary output.

In fact, it may be fair to say that there was never a single "Victorian mindset" or "Victorian value system" but rather a range of them, and that these shifted throughout the century. Indeed, there is no real consensus about when the Victorian era began and ended. Some point to the passage of the Reform Bill of 1832 as the dawn of a new era, others to the abolition of slavery in the British Empire in 1833. Still others argue for the unity of a longer period,[1] beginning perhaps with the end of the Napoleonic Wars in 1815 and ending

Franz Xavier Winterhalter, *Queen Victoria*, 1842.

---

[1] Some historians have suggested that the period's beginning should perhaps be dated even earlier, with the seeds of "Victorianism" being planted as early as the late eighteenth century, with the reemergence of Evangelicalism and the Methodist revival. The religious movement countered the ideals of the Enlightenment and may thus be said to mark the conclusion of the primary movement of the eighteenth century.

with the outbreak of World War I in 1914. Perhaps the obvious choice is to date the period as starting with Victoria's ascension to the throne in 1837 and concluding with her death in 1901, but the identification of the period so entirely with her reign is ultimately arbitrary and tells us little about the Victorian era.

Photographer unknown, *Queen Victoria*, c. 1897. A picture of Albert is in the background.

Although a great deal of overlap can be found between the Romantic and Victorian periods, most scholars agree that the 1830s was a pivotal decade, marked by the transition of the monarchy from William IV to Victoria and by the spread of a spirit of political and social reform that would characterize the next several decades. During the 1850s and 1860s, Britain emerged from a depressed economy and experienced a level of political and social stability that made these decades the most prosperous of the century. The mid-Victorian period is now often regarded as a kind of high-water mark for Victorian culture, particularly because the 1870s and 1880s saw some decline in the strength of the economy and in Britain's imperial dominance abroad, despite its continued acquisition of colonial possessions. These decades were also marked by the glimmerings of social change, a wave that culminated in the fin-de-siècle spirit of the 1890s, which saw many challenges to the values and conventions of the preceding decades in literature, politics, and everyday life.

A GROWING POWER

During Victoria's reign, Britain was the richest nation and the most powerful empire on the globe, with unchallenged military supremacy until the latter decades of the century and an imperial reach that covered one-quarter of the earth's surface by 1897.[1] As the world's first industrialized country, Britain experienced both the benefits and the horrors of enormous growth throughout the nineteenth century. The census of 1801 put the population of the country at 11 million people; at century's end that number had increased by almost 300 per cent to 37 million. Just as striking was the

Fleet Street, London, c. 1890.

---

[1] The scope of England's imperial holdings was memorably expressed in a popular saying of the period: "The sun never sets on the British empire." (A popular rejoinder to the sentiment was the saying that God did not trust the English in the dark.)

Construction of the sewer beneath Fleet Street, London, early 1860s. By 1858 the stench of sewage from the Thames had become so overwhelming that the Houses of Parliament at Westminster found it impossible to meet; construction of a city-wide underground system of sewers, under the direction of Joseph Bazalgette, began the following year.

Building the Holborn Viaduct across the Fleet valley (*Illustrated Times*, 18 September 1869). The viaduct, carrying both road and rail traffic, was a vast project carried out by the Corporation of the City of London between 1863 and 1869.

movement of this population, from 75 per cent rural distribution in the early decades to nearly the same percentage residing in urban districts by the end of the century. Northern industrial cities grew particularly fast: Manchester, a town of no more than 15,000 people in 1750, had grown to 75,000 by 1800, and to 125,000 by 1820; by 1850 its population was over 300,000. Between 1815 and 1914, more than 20 million people emigrated from Britain to other parts of the world, over half of them to the United States, but millions, too, to Australia and to Canada.

The shift from an agrarian to an industrial wage economy meant an increase in income for many people, creating a sector of the population that was neither rich nor poor and was increasingly termed "middle class." A spirit of entrepreneurship and market thinking—dominated by upwardly mobile males—gradually replaced what had once seemed an entrenched, unchangeable system of aristocratic patronage and paternalism in the world of business and trade. The Reform Bill of 1832 granted political representation in Parliament to certain sectors of the middle-class male population for the first time, although even with its passage, only one in six adult males could vote, and the suffrage was still linked to property ownership. Rail travel, the advent of the telegraph, daily newspapers, and the manufacture and import of goods via steamship from all over the globe collapsed time and space, and flooded the homes of the affluent with new luxuries and conveniences. The Great Exhibition of 1851, the first World's Fair, showcased Britain's industrial dominance with exhibits of new consumer goods and remarkable technologies; the event symbolized Britain's reputation as the "workshop of the world." Thus, for many the overall mood was positive, and Thomas Macaulay's confident assertions of the nation's progress in his bestselling *History of England* rang true for much of his audience.

Alfred Morgan, *An Omnibus Ride to Piccadilly Circus—Mr. Gladstone Travelling with Ordinary Passengers*, 1885. The previous year Prime Minister William Gladstone's government had extended the franchise to working class males, through the Reform Bill of 1884.

GRINDING MILLS, GRINDING POVERTY

The paradox of the economic life of the time was summed up by Thomas Carlyle in 1843: "England is full of wealth," he wrote, "of multifarious produce, supply for human want in every kind; yet England is dying of inanition." For millions of people, low wages, unemployment, and fluctuations in trade created widespread misery in crowded industrial cities such as Manchester and Birmingham. According to one estimate, 70 per cent of the population at mid-century was considered poor. The New Poor Law,[1] passed in 1834, divided and categorized the poor as either "deserving" (the elderly and the physically infirm) or "undeserving" (the able-bodied but unemployed). The poor were now eligible to receive public assistance only in the notorious workhouses, also known as the "Poor Law Bastilles,"[2] which often served to punish and stigmatize rather than relieve. In addition, inadequate housing and slum conditions led to frequent outbreaks of illness and disease. Between 1831 and 1866, four cholera epidemics killed more than 140,000 people, inaugurating Britain's first wide-scale public health movement. Scores of "Blue Books"—statistical investigations, surveys, and government reports on the condition of inner-city neighborhoods—culminated in the Public Health Acts of 1848 and the 1870s. Similarly, between 1802 and 1847, factories and mines producing iron, cotton, and coal, which had been unregulated, employing men, women, and children in conditions that were often dirty and dangerous, were made subject to a series of Factory Acts, designed to force employers to limit work hours—working 14 hours a day had been not uncommon—and prohibit the employment of children under the age of nine in certain industries.

In her poem, "The Cry of the Children" (1843), Elizabeth Barrett Browning drew attention to the problem of child labor, helping to create humanitarian awareness on the part of middle-class readers by asking "How long, O cruel nation, / Will you stand to move

[1] The "Old Poor Law" was passed during the reign of Queen Elizabeth I.
[2] The Paris fortress-prison named the Bastille was stormed on 14 July 1789, initiating the French Revolution.

the world, on a child's heart?"[1] Thomas Hood's "The Song of the Shirt" (1843) focused on the plight of the genteel but impoverished female needle-worker who toils alone in grim conditions for meager wages. Cast in the elevated and stylized "voices" of their victimized speakers, such poems were both wildly popular and highly sentimental, qualities that have until recently served to exclude them from serious study by scholars of English literature. Yet these poems did as much or more than government reports and statistical surveys to shed light on major social issues. So too did Carlyle's *Past and Present* (1843), which called England to responsibility for the many starving workers in the land of "plenty":

> We have more riches than any Nation ever had before: we have less good of them than any Nation had before…. We have forgotten everywhere that *Cash-payment* is not the sole relation of human beings; we think, nothing doubting, that it absolves and liquidates all other engagements.

Even as such voices spoke up in support of the destitute and the working classes, over the course of the century, the voices of working-class people themselves were also increasingly heard. The 1828 publication of Robert Blincoe's *Memoir* of his appalling early life in the mills had a lasting impact; in addition to a direct effect on its readers, Blincoe's memoir provided much of the raw material for Frances Trollope's novel *Michael Armstrong: Factory Boy* (1840), and may also have inspired Charles Dickens's *Oliver Twist* (1838). Blincoe's memoir was followed by a number of other autobiographical narratives of working-class hardship; a particularly notable example of the genre was *A Narrative of the Experience and Sufferings of William Dodd* (1841). Ellen Johnson published a more wide-ranging memoir, *Autobiography of a Factory Girl* (1867), together with her poems and songs. Another prominent working-class poetic voice was that of Ebenezer Elliott, the "Corn-Law Rhymer" from Yorkshire who became an active force first in the Chartist movement and then

in the struggle to repeal the Corn Laws (both of which will be discussed in more detail below). In his *Corn-Law Rhymes* (1831) and in subsequent work Elliott attacked

> The deadly will that takes
> What labour ought to keep;
> It is the deadly power that makes
> Bread dear and labour cheap.

How to best respond to the force of this "deadly power" remained a matter of debate and speculation. If some emphasized the need to continually press for political reform, others appealed emotionally for hearts to change; still others formulated new philosophical approaches to the underlying moral and socio-economic questions. Perhaps the most important of these approaches was Utilitarianism, a broad-reaching philosophy that had first been developed in the late eighteenth century, primarily by Jeremy Bentham, and that was expounded in a more careful, subtle, and thoroughgoing fashion by John Stuart Mill in the nineteenth.[2] Utilitarian thought began to shape governmental policy, including the New Poor Law, in the middle decades of the nineteenth century—and continues to be a shaping force in the social policy of most developed nations today. In its crude form, Utilitarianism holds—in the words of Bentham's 1776 "A Fragment on Government"—that "it is the greatest happiness of the greatest number that is the measure of right and wrong." In other words, the central guiding principle of social morality should be the pursuit of that which is good for all members of society, with no one person or group's interests given special weight. But how does one calculate "the greatest happiness of the greatest number"? Can social, legal, economic, and political problems be resolved by a "moral arithmetic" that evaluates human pain and pleasure according to entirely rationalist principles? According to some crude versions of utilitarian philosophy—though certainly not that of Mill—the answer is yes; imagination, feeling, and individual desire are obsolete impediments to the operation of the "laws" of social improvement, which

---

[1] Many of the poem's details were drawn from the 1842–43 Parliamentary commission report investigating the conditions of child employment in mines and factories. The report's author, R.H. Horne, was a close friend of the poet.

[2] Mill first published *Utilitarianism*, his defense of the utilitarian philosophy in 1861, as a series of three articles in *Fraser's Magazine*. The essays appeared as a one-volume work in 1863.

Thomas Iron Works, London, 1867.

Hatting mill, Manchester, 1890s.

may be derived from empirical observation and calculation.

Writers such as Elizabeth Barrett Browning, Dickens, Carlyle, and John Ruskin were intensely critical of Utilitarianism, taking its crudest forms as representative and regarding it as a morally and spiritually bankrupt response to the human condition. Dickens, in particular, caricatured utilitarian thinking with telling directness in his portrayal of Thomas Gradgrind in *Hard Times* (1854), his tenth novel, aimed at exposing the working conditions in English factories

and initiating reform.[1] However, it may be fitting to understand the intensity of these writers' opposition to Utilitarianism in a larger context: for Mill, "the greatest number" included not only the poor white people of England but also brown and black people in poverty the world over; on the other hand, Dickens, Carlyle, and Ruskin, for all their sympathy for the British poor, looked at those of other races, at best, with condescension and, at worst, with outright loathing. In any case, as the works of writers such as Dickens, Barrett Browning, and Elizabeth Gaskell amply demonstrated, opposition to the cruelties of poverty could be expressed—as plausibly and as powerfully—by means of

---

[1] In a letter to his friend Charles Knight, Dickens accused the utilitarians of seeing "figures and averages, and nothing else."

emotional and aesthetic appeals through literature as it could by means of the philosophical arguments of the Utilitarians.[1]

CORN LAWS, POTATO FAMINE

As the powerful and privileged attempted to confront the range of social crises facing a newly industrialized nation, economic depression, unemployment, political instability in Europe, and a series of crop failures in the 1840s—a decade often dubbed the "Hungry Forties"—caused a disproportionate level of suffering for the poor. Artificial shortages of grain in the country inflated the price of bread beyond the reach of the working class, causing periodic bread riots and a discontented work force. These shortages were in part the result of the Corn Laws, which imposed heavy tariffs on imports of grain, and were intended to protect British agricultural interests and limit dependence on foreign supplies of cereal grains. The Corn Laws were repealed in 1846 under pressure from the Anti-Corn-Law League, an alliance of free-trade advocates and liberal, laissez-faire[2] trade reformers.

In the wake of the repeal of the Corn Laws, three successive crop failures in Ireland led to one of the worst humanitarian disasters of the century, the Irish potato famine of 1845–47. Prime Minister Robert Peel's government attempted to alleviate the situation by importing emergency shipments of grain from the United States in 1845, but when Peel's government was replaced by Lord John Russell's Whig administration in 1846, Russell in effect put a stop to emergency aid; the laissez-faire interests of Russell and his supporters led to the transfer of responsibility for famine relief to the inadequate jurisdiction of the Irish Poor Law. By 1847, between 850,000 and 1,500,000 Irish—from 10 to over 15 per cent of the population, depending on the estimate—had died of starvation; the English government policy toward Ireland, its nearest colonial possession, was in this instance one of such neglect that it may be said to have amounted to extraordinary cruelty.

Inevitably, hostility toward the English, and with it Irish nationalist sentiment, was greatly intensified by the potato famine. The seeds of the Irish independence movement had been effectively sown—and sown not only in Ireland but also in the United States, where hundreds of thousands of Irish emigrated during this period. As these immigrants prospered in America, they provided more and more support for the Fenian movement—which sprang up in the 1850s in support of Irish independence and launched attacks in the 1860s and 1870s, not only in England but also against British possessions in New Brunswick, Upper Canada, and Manitoba—and for subsequent political groups with similar aims. But the road to Irish independence was an extraordinarily rocky one: the Irish won the right to be represented in the British House of Commons, but their greatest Parliamentary spokesman, Charles Parnell,[3] after surviving dozens of scurrilous attempts to discredit him, was finally brought down when his affair with a divorced woman became a public scandal; British Prime Minister William Gladstone became a convert to the cause of Home Rule for the Irish and passed a bill authorizing it through the House of Commons in 1886, only to have the measure killed in the House of Lords; a similar bill in 1893 suffered the same fate; another bill to enact Home Rule was put aside with the outbreak of World War I in 1914. In the end, independence was only achieved after the violent struggles of the 1916 Easter Uprising and the War of Independence of 1919–22. Even then, the British retained possession of a substantial area in Northern Ireland.

---

[1] Although the "social novel" had its origins in the eighteenth century, it was developed and popularized as a genre during the Victorian period.

[2] From the French for "let do," the phrase "laissez-faire" came to be used in the late eighteenth century as a shorthand for the belief that government should intervene as little as possible in the workings of the economy. The term first appeared in English usage in George Whatley's *Principles of Trade* (1774), but it did not become popularized until James Mill's reference in an 1824 entry in *The Encyclopedia Britannica*.

[3] Charles Stewart Parnell (1846–91) was the Irish Protestant founder and leader of the Irish Parliamentary Party and the leading champion of the Irish Home Rule Movement. The movement suffered a serious setback with the revelation of Parnell's affair with Katherine "Kitty" O'Shea, the wife of William O'Shea, another MP. The scandal caused many of Parnell's supporters to turn against him, and he died of a heart attack shortly after marrying Katherine in 1891.

NOTICE
TO
THE EARL OF CHARLEMONT'S TENANTRY.

IN consideration of the extensive failure in the POTATO CROP this Season, willing to bear his share in the general calamity, and anxious to relieve, as far as in him lies, his Poorer Tenants from an undue share of suffering under the Divine Will, LORD CHARLEMONT has directed that the following Scale of Reduction, in Payment of Rent, shall be adopted for this Year, upon his Estates in the COUNTIES of ARMAGH and TYRONE, viz. :—

25 per Cent. on Rents under £5.	10 per Cent. on Rents under £20.
20 per Cent. on Rents under £10	5 per Cent. on Rents under £30.
15 per Cent. on Rents under £15	No Discount on Rents exceeding £30.

Notice of a rent abatement by an Irish landlord, 1846.

Evicted family, Glenbeigh, Ireland, 1888. In the 1880s an economic depression coincided with the election of a substantial number of Irish Home Rule Members of Parliament (under Charles Parnell's leadership), and with a campaign by the Land League to resist the practice of evicting impoverished tenant farmers unable to pay their rent.

"THE TWO NATIONS"

In the 1830s and 1840s, the human costs of the Industrial Revolution—what became known as the "Condition of England" question—were scrutinized by legislators, workers, and writers. Carlyle, Dickens, Gaskell, Harriet Martineau, Benjamin Disraeli, and Henry Mayhew documented the daily existence of poor and working people, and criticized the laws that were intended to address their suffering. The "social problem novel" or "industrial novel," an important subgenre of Victorian fiction, drew attention to class conflict and the social ramifications of laissez-faire economic policies. Prominent examples include Charles Kingsley's *Alton Locke* (1850), Charles Dickens's *Hard Times*, and Elizabeth Gaskell's *Mary Barton* (1848) and *North and South* (1854–55).

In his 1845 novel *Sybil*, future Prime Minister Benjamin Disraeli coined the phrase "the Two Nations" to describe the disparity in Britain between rich and poor. Novelists felt that their work could provoke social reform by exposing their middle-class audiences to the plight of the working classes, who were often portrayed as either vulnerable and victimized by forces beyond their control, or as a violent, angry "mass"; intervention by those of goodwill from other social classes is often implicitly recommended in such fiction as a way of ameliorating the situation and bridging "the Two Nations." The middle-class narrator of Gaskell's novel *Mary Barton*, for example, adopts the role of mediator between Manchester's workers and their industrial "masters" in an attempt to foster understanding and prevent political insurrection.

Non-fiction writing may have been as important as that of any novelist in nurturing the seeds of social change. Henry Mayhew's interviews with working people and street folk for the *Morning Chronicle* newspaper opened a window for its readers onto the daily existence of an often voiceless underclass. It must be said, however, that Mayhew's reports contained no overt political commentary or reform agenda. Friedrich Engels, by contrast, in his chronicle of urban squalor *The Condition of the Working Class in England in 1844*, not only described the extraordinary scale of the human suffering he witnessed but also placed the blame squarely on the shoulders of a class system created by industrial capitalism: "Power lies in the hands of those who own, directly or indirectly, foodstuffs and the

Jabez Hughes, *Benjamin Disraeli*, c. 1877. Disraeli, who led the Conservative Party from 1868 to 1880 (serving as Prime Minister briefly in 1868 and then again from 1874 to 1880), was seen as something of an exotic within the English establishment. His parents were Jewish, but he was baptized as an infant and remained a practicing Anglican throughout his life. Disraeli's prolific literary career, which began with the publication of his first novel, *Vivian Grey*, in 1826, made him a well-known man of letters. A fashionable figure, Disraeli was derided by his strait-laced rival, Liberal leader William Gladstone, as "Asiatic"—a word often used in Victorian times as a synonym for "indulgent and irresponsible." But Disraeli remained a popular figure with much of the general population as well as with much of the establishment—and with the Queen.

means of production. The poor, having no capital, inevitably bear the consequences of defeat in the struggle."[1]

It was not only middle-class writers and observers who were bringing attention to the great divide between Britain's rich and poor. Chartism, a movement that initiated a series of political campaigns in the 1830s and 1840s, was a concrete expression of the desire of working-class people to resist economic and social disparity and press for political reform. The People's Charter of 1838, from which the movement took its name, petitioned the government to adopt a range of key reforms, including annual elections, universal male suffrage, and the abolition of property qualifications for Members of Parliament and of the secret ballot. The mouthpiece of the Chartist movement was the *Northern Star* newspaper, one of many working-class periodicals that flourished in the early decades of the nineteenth century. The Chartist petitions were signed by up to five million people and presented to Parliament by a coalition of workers in 1839, 1842, and 1848, but were rejected each time. A number of middle-class writers sympathetic to the claims of the working classes were nevertheless suspicious of the Chartist movement, particularly in light of the political revolutions taking place in continental Europe in the late 1840s. In his longing for the imagined social order of a feudal past, Carlyle denounced the "mad Chartisms" of the "anarchic multitude," comparing them to the events of the French Revolution and the Reign of Terror. With the defeat of the third petition, Chartism collapsed, but it had helped instigate a new level of class consciousness among ordinary people, and is now considered to be the first independent working-class movement in Britain.

In the 1880s and 1890s various socialist movements emerged, partly on the strength of Karl Marx's theories of capital, which he formulated under the dome of the British Library after moving to London in 1849. The Fabian Society was one of the most influential socialist organizations. Its membership was mainly drawn from the middle class and included such notables as George Bernard Shaw, Sidney Webb and Beatrice Potter Webb, Edith Nesbit, and Annie Besant. The Fabians' tactics

---

[1] Engels's treatise, first published in Germany in 1845, was not translated into English until 1892.

were reformist rather than revolutionary; they advocated public ownership of utilities, affordable housing, improved wages, and greater access to higher education for all.

The Six Points
OF THE
PEOPLE'S
CHARTER.

1. A VOTE for every man twenty-one years of age, of sound mind, and not undergoing punishment for crime.

2. THE BALLOT.—To protect the elector in the exercise of his vote.

3. NO PROPERTY QUALIFICATION for Members of Parliament —thus enabling the constituencies to return the man of their choice, be he rich or poor.

4. PAYMENT OF MEMBERS, thus enabling an honest trades-man, working man, or other person, to serve a constituency, when taken from his business to attend to the interests of the country.

5. EQUAL CONSTITUENCIES, securing the same amount of representation for the same number of electors, instead of allowing small constituencies to swamp the votes of large ones.

6. ANNUAL PARLIAMENTS, thus presenting the most effectual check to bribery and intimidation, since though a constituency might be bought once in seven years (even with the ballot), no purse could buy a constituency (under a system of universal suffrage) in each ensuing twelvemonth; and since members, when elected for a year only, would not be able to defy and betray their constituents as now.

Chartist poster, 1838.

Trade unions and labor movements also grew gradually in scope and strength throughout the century, with the Trade Union Act of 1871 granting legal status to unions for the first time. Newly mobilized workers in the 1880s organized to mount a series of strikes with varying degrees of success. Two of the most highly publicized of these were the match-girls' strike in 1888 and the London dock workers' strike of 1889. Union membership doubled in these years, partly because of the success of these labor actions.

The match-girls' strike began after the dismissal of one of the workers at the Bryant and May Factory in Bow, London, in early July 1888, but its real causes lay in the terrible working conditions at the factory,

The Matchgirl Strike Committee, 1888. A threatened strike by Bryant and May Match Company employees —most of them girls of no more than 15, earning starvation wages and exposed to hazardous phosphorous fumes—became a *cause célèbre* in 1888, and forced the company to change its practices. The action was led by Annie Besant (who had initially become famous during her 1877 trial for obscenity—the charge being based on the distribution of her pamphlet offering practical advice on contraception).

including 14-hour workdays, poor pay and excessive fines, and severe health complications resulting from working with dangerous materials. The strike attracted significant publicity, and factory owners were forced to concede to the strikers' demands for a better working-environment.

The London Dock Strike began on August 14, 1889. At a Parliamentary hearing on the issue, the general manager at the Millwall Docks testified about the physical conditions of the workers, which led to the strike:

The poor fellows are miserably clad, scarcely with a boot on their foot, in a most miserable state ...

These are men who come to work in our docks who come on without having a bit of food in their stomachs, perhaps since the previous day; they have worked for an hour and have earned 5d.; their hunger will not allow them to continue: they take the 5d. in order that they may get food, perhaps the first food they have had for twenty-four hours.

The strike, which had succeeded in garnering strong middle-class support, ended in victory for the workers, whose principal demand had been for increased pay, and the establishment of unions for dock workers.

THE POLITICS OF GENDER

Gender consciousness was central to Victorian England's political scene in a number of significant ways. At the beginning of the Victorian period, middle-class women were shut out of most remunerative employments and institutions of higher education, could not vote, and had few legal rights. By the end of the century, the situation did not, on the surface, look radically different—universal female suffrage, for example, was not achieved in Britain until 1928—but several key developments heralded the changes to come in the twentieth century.

The first major challenges by Victorian "strong-minded women" to patriarchal control were in the area of marriage law. The common-law doctrine of coverture ensured that a woman's legal identity was subsumed in that of her husband's upon marriage. In effect, the law of coverture regarded the husband and wife as "one person": the husband. This meant that upon marriage a husband had full control of his wife's personal property and any earnings she acquired during the marriage; he had absolute authority over their home and children; and he could legally use physical force to discipline the members of his family. If he deserted his wife, she could not sue for divorce and had no custody rights to their children. No viable legal mechanism was available to an average woman to contest her husband's decisions, since husband and wife were "one body"

under the law.[1] The essayist Frances Power Cobbe was among the most effective in pointing out the illogic of such arrangements, as well as the terrible toll they exacted. In contemplating, for example, the situation of "the poor woman whose husband has robbed her earnings, who leaves her and her children to starve, and then goes unpunished because the law can only recognize the relation of husband and wife as ... one before the law," Cobbe observed in her provocative 1868 essay "Criminals, Idiots, Women, and Minors" that

It is one of the numerous anomalies connected with women's affairs, that when they are under debate the same argument which would be held to determine other questions in one way is felt to settle theirs in another. If for instance it be proved of any other class of the community, that it is particularly liable to be injured, imposed upon, and tyrannized over (e.g., the children who work in factories), it is considered to follow as a matter of course that the law must step in for its protection. But it is the alleged *helplessness* of married women which, it is said, makes it indispensable to give all the support of the law, *not* to them, but to the stronger persons with whom they are unequally yoked.

Under pressure from organized networks of reformers, several major pieces of legislation, altering the status and position of married women, were enacted during the period. Perhaps the most economically significant of these was the Married Women's Property Act of 1870,[2]

[1] The tremendous pressures placed on women as a result of coverture are significant to the plot of a number of prominent Victorian novels, perhaps most notably Emily Brontë's *Wuthering Heights* (1847). In the novel, Heathcliff exploits marital coverture to usurp property as part of his plan for vengeance, repeatedly resorting to abuse and exploitation of the authority he is granted as husband.

[2] The Act's full title was "An Act to amend the law relating to the property of married women." Although the Act effectively overturned coverture by allowing women to legally claim their own earnings and property, serious loopholes made it possible to easily evade the law, particularly in regard to inheritance. An additional problem was posed by the fact that the Act was not retroactive, thereby limiting its usefulness for many women. The Act also made it a woman's legal duty to financially maintain her children from profits earned. That is, the Act effectively established both parents as responsible for the financial support of their children.

Cartoon from *Votes for Women III* (7 January 1910).

The movement to win the vote for women began in the 1850s, and articles and petitions on the issue appeared with increasing frequency thereafter. Many of the early arguments drew parallels with other efforts to extend the franchise; as Mary Margaret Dilke observed in an 1889 article, "it is really an interesting study to notice how every argument used to delay the enfranchisement of working men and farm labourers reappears to do duty against women. How often has the question been asked, 'What does Hodge know about finance and foreign policy, colonial affairs and commercial interests?'"

As the suffrage movement grew, differences of opinion developed over the appropriate level of militancy to adopt and over whether the movement should press for universal suffrage or only for certain categories of women to be allowed to vote. The granting of the vote eventually came in two stages, with certain classes of propertied women granted the right to vote in 1918 (the same year the vote was granted to all men of 21 years or more), and all women over the age of 21 finally being granted the franchise in 1928.

which finally allowed married women to legally own the money they earned and the property they inherited. In addition, the Matrimonial Causes Act of 1878 accorded some legal protection to female victims of domestic violence, and the Infant Custody Acts of 1839 and 1886 granted a woman custodial rights to her children.

Although full equality within marriage was not realized in law until the twentieth century, the passage of the aforementioned legislation began to chip away at male patriarchal privilege and challenged the legal and religious "justifications" for women's oppression within the family.

In her 1851 essay "The Enfranchisement of Women" Harriet Taylor Mill addresses those "justifications" one by one, then proceeds to the heart of the matter: "The real question is, whether it is right and expedient that one half of the human race should pass through life in a state of forced subordination to the other half." *The Subjection of Women* (1869),[1] John Stuart Mill's famous extended essay on the topic, grew out of Taylor Mill's essay—the two worked largely collaboratively. "The Enfranchisement of Women" had set out with utmost clarity the ideal that is still being striven for today: "the principle which regulates the existing social relations between the two sexes—the legal subordination of one sex to the other—is wrong in itself and now one of the chief hindrances to human improvement … it ought to be replaced by a principle of perfect equality, admitting no power or privilege on the one side, nor disability on the other."

The principles advocated by Cobbe, Taylor Mill, and Mill were, of course, not only matters of law and politics; they pervaded every aspect of British life, from employment, to educational access, to a variety of cultural matters. The principle of "perfect equality" was far from being realized in any of these areas even at century's end. But, by 1900, some at least were beginning to feel that the slow movement toward acceptance of the principles of gender equality had become inexorable.

EMPIRE

Victorian Britain's internal politics, enormous wealth, and its sense of national and global identity cannot be adequately understood in isolation from its imperial rule abroad. In an address at Oxford in 1870, the highly influential critic and social thinker John Ruskin urged

England to "found colonies as fast and as far as she is able, … seizing every piece of fruitful waste ground she can set her foot on, and there teaching these her colonists that their first aim is to be to advance the power of England by land and sea." And under Victoria's reign such power did indeed grow steadily, with 18 major territories added to the British Empire, which already included India, Canada, Australia, New Zealand, and much of southern Africa and the Caribbean.

Edward Bulwer-Lytton, Viceroy of India, Calcutta, 1877.

If the Empire arose largely from the desire to increase trade and maximize commercial interests, it also increasingly took hold of the political and cultural imagination. The often brutal effects of colonial domination were rationalized by a pseudo-science purporting to demonstrate the inferiority of dark-skinned peoples and by a keenly felt, much-encouraged sense of racial and cultural superiority over other peoples. A paternalistic sense of responsibility for the peoples of the "inferior races" became known as the "white man's burden" in Rudyard Kipling's famous phrasing. Or, as evolutionary theorist Alfred Russel

[1] The essay was completed in 1861, but Mill waited to publish the work until he felt it would be more influential.

Wallace put it, "the relation of a civilized to an uncivilized race, over which it rules, is exactly that of parent to child, or generally adults to infants." In missionary work, travel and exploration, scientific writing, advertising, visual art, and literature, the culture and logic of imperial rule were formulated as part of the everyday "common sense" of the age.

Not everyone was in complete agreement about Britain's imperial policies and practices. Impassioned public debates about the moral and economic injustice of slavery had culminated in the abolition of the slave trade in 1807 and of slavery in all British possessions in 1833. Britain continued to rely on cheap imports of raw materials from its Caribbean colonies, however, and conditions for free workers were sometimes little better than they had been for slaves. Attention to British rule in the West Indies was renewed in 1865 during the controversy that attended Governor Edward Eyre's actions, when black Jamaicans attempted to liberate a black prisoner from a courthouse. Violent clashes between the rebels and white authorities resulted in martial law and the execution of 600 black Jamaicans. The opinions of two of the century's most respected public intellectuals—Thomas Carlyle and John Stuart Mill—represented the opposing poles of the public's response, with Carlyle supporting Eyre's imposition of a harsh law to restore order, and Mill calling for Eyre to be tried for murder.

The "Indian Mutiny" of 1857–58 presented a major challenge to British rule in India, which until that point was still largely under the control of the East India Company. Sepoys—Indian men employed as soldiers by the British—staged a rebellion at Meerut in early 1857, killing British officers. The violence spread throughout northern territories and to Delhi, with massacres of British men, women, and children taking place at Cawnpore and Lucknow. British reprisals were swift and bloody, leading to summary executions, looting, and massacres of Indian civilians. The Indian resistance was motivated by religious, cultural, and political opposition to British policies, and had a lasting impact on British rule in India. One especially significant change was the transfer of colonial governance from the East India Company to the Crown in 1858. In the meantime, the English press was filled with lurid reports of the

Famine Victims, Madras, c. 1877. Famine was a recurrent reality in India throughout the nineteenth century, but the famine of the 1870s was particularly harsh. It gave rise to considerable controversy in Britain, with some (such as Florence Nightingale) pressing for investment in health, sanitation, and irrigation as well as short-term relief measures; others (in sympathy with the harsh approach taken by the Viceroy, Edward Bulwer-Lytton) saw such measures as too expensive or too "lenient."

violence, resulting in greater public fascination with India than ever before. Countless eyewitness accounts, sermons, plays, novels, and poems—some still being written 60 years after the events—expressed moral outrage about the insurgency. There were also those, including the soon-to-be Prime Minister Benjamin Disraeli, who tried to contextualize the violence by criticizing Britain's exploitative attitudes and practices in India, but such dissenting voices remained very much a minority.

Britain participated in few major wars during Victoria's reign; when it did, the results were often less than heroic. In the Crimean War of 1854–56, Britain joined Turkey and France in fighting Russian encroachment into the Middle East, but the war did

Florence Nightingale in the Crimea, c. 1856.

Queen Victoria and her servant, Abdul Karim, 1893.

little to change the balance of power in Europe; it nonetheless resulted in the deaths of 21,000 British troops, 16,000 of whom died of disease.[1] In the Anglo-Zulu War of 1878–79, the Zulus of southern Africa enjoyed considerable initial success against British forces before being subdued, and in the Anglo-Afghan War of 1878–80, the British suffered various reversals before achieving a tenuous hold over Afghanistan. The Boer War of 1899–1902, in South Africa, was fought between the British and the Boers[2] over gold and diamond fields. For the Boers, the war was part of a larger struggle to prevent the influence of foreign powers on agricultural lands they had claimed. A guerilla war ensued, and Britain's image as the greatest military power in the world suffered when the army was unable to defeat the vastly outnumbered Boers.

In England, popular support for the Empire reached its zenith in the 1880s and 1890s as Britain accelerated the pace of its drive to increase its imperial acquisitions to compete with other European powers and with the United States. Queen Victoria's Golden and Diamond Jubilees, during which she celebrated the fiftieth and sixtieth anniversaries of her sovereignty, provided grand occasions for the expression of national pride. As *The Times* crowed, Britain was "the mightiest and most beneficial Empire ever known in the annals of mankind." Much popular reading in these decades was devoted to a celebration of Empire, though warnings of its imminent demise were also increasingly sounded. Boys' adventure stories in such publications as *The Boy's Own Annual* featured tales of manly prowess in the service of Empire and promoted the values of honor, courage, and duty to Queen and country. Travel and exploration narratives were popular, too—particularly those that recounted the heroic journeys of such larger-than-life figures as Richard Burton and David Livingstone. Richard Francis Burton (1821–90) was renowned for his travels throughout Asia and Africa and much celebrated for his mastery of foreign languages, of which he knew 29, by some counts. Perhaps his most famous exploit was traveling to Mecca in disguise, but he was also recognized for translating the complete *One Thousand and One Nights* from Arabic and for bringing

---

[1] When the deplorable conditions of the military's hospitals became public knowledge through reports in *The Times*, Florence Nightingale was dispatched to the Crimea to superintend Britain's female nurses.

[2] White settlers of Dutch descent, also known as Afrikaaners.

the *Kama Sutra* to publication in English. Although he served as a symbol of the Empire's might, Burton was a prominent critic of colonial policies. David Livingstone (1813–73) named Victoria Falls—perhaps the world's most impressive—in honor of the Queen. He was a national hero of sorts during the Victorian era, famed as a missionary, a scientist and explorer, an imperial reformer, who fought against slavery and advocated commercial empire. Speaking to students at Cambridge University in 1857, Livingstone declared,

People talk of the sacrifice I have made in spending so much of my life in Africa. Can that be called a sacrifice which is simply paid back as a small part of a great debt owing to our God, which we can never repay? Is that a sacrifice which brings its own blest reward in healthful activity, the consciousness of doing good, peace of mind, and a bright hope of a glorious destiny hereafter? Away with the word in such a view and with such a thought! It is emphatically no sacrifice. Say rather it is a privilege.

Engraving by G. Durand, after a sketch by H.M. Stanley, "The Meeting of Livingstone and Stanley in Central Africa" (from *The Graphic*, 3 August 1872). By 1869, it had been three years since the renowned missionary and explorer David Livingstone had embarked on an expedition in search of the source of the Nile River. American journalist Henry Morgan Stanley was commissioned in that year by a New York newspaper to find Livingstone; the story of the two finally meeting on the shores of Lake Tanganyika in 1871 became legendary. As Stanley described it, "I ... would have embraced him, only, he being an Englishman, I did not know how he would receive me; so I did what cowardice and false pride suggested was the best thing—walked deliberately to him, took off my hat, and said, 'Dr. Livingstone, I presume?'

"'Yes,' said he, with a kind smile, lifting his cap slightly."

Almost as popular as the narratives of Burton and Livingstone were travel journals by intrepid "lady explorers" such as Mary Kingsley and Isabella Bird, who unsettled conventional notions of Victorian femininity even as they satisfied the public taste for true stories with fictionalized elements. Kingsley (1862–1900) first traveled to Africa in order to complete research for a book left unfinished by her father at the time of his death. She lived with local tribes in Angola. Upon her return to England, she toured the country, giving lectures in which she criticized missionaries for their attempts to change the local people—earning her much censure from the Church of England. She also defended African customs, including polygamy. Her books about her experiences—*Travels in Africa* (1897) and *West African Studies* (1899)—were best-sellers. Bird (1831–1904) traveled extensively, visiting Australia, Hawaii, and Colorado—then the most recent state to join the United States—where she covered more than 800 miles in the Rocky Mountains. The letters she wrote to her sister during this time were published as the immensely popular *A Lady's Life in the Rocky Mountains* (1879).

The imperial romances of some authors were a symptom of the anxieties surrounding Britain's increasingly tenuous grip on its empire. Whereas early and mid-century Victorian fiction tended to imagine the Empire as a fairly static, unknown space to which characters can be exiled in the interests of narrative closure, late-century fiction often represented the Empire in darker, Gothic terms. Incorporating supernatural and psychological elements in their work, writers such as H. Rider Haggard, Arthur Conan Doyle, Rudyard Kipling, and Robert Louis Stevenson used colonial settings to explore themes of racial degeneration and human "savagery." In his 1899 novella, *Heart of Darkness*, Joseph Conrad, a Polish émigré to England, drew on his experience as a member of the merchant marine in his portrayal of imperial greed, exploitation, and corruption among ivory traders in the Congo. Even Kipling, called the "Laureate of Empire" for his energetic—and often jingoistic—portrayals of the glories of British imperialism, was not always unequivocal in his attitudes toward the Empire: in his 1897 poem "Recessional," he sounded a famous warning against imperial hubris: "Far-called, our navies melt

away; / On dune and headland sinks the fire: / Lo, all our pomp of yesterday / Is one with Nineveh and Tyre!"[1]

FAITH AND DOUBT

One of the most unsettling developments for average citizens during the Victorian period was the growing opposition to the authority of Christian faith and the established church. A rapidly changing social order, combined with the growing predominance of scientific rationalism and empiricist method, destabilized Christian certainty, creating a rising tide of secularism and religious skepticism. As critic J.A. Froude put it in 1841, "the very truths which have come forth have produced doubts ... this dazzle has too often ended in darkness."

The poet Arthur Hugh Clough was a central figure in the expression of the religious doubt of the age; in "Easter Day: Naples, 1849"—a poem whose title deliberately invokes the most sacred of days for Christians only to subvert the day's holiness—his verse conveys a strong sense of the passion that could accompany such feelings:

> My heart was hot within me; till at last
> My brain was lightened when my tongue had said—
> Christ is not risen!
> Christ is not risen, no—
> He lies and moulders low.

Biblical scholars in England and Europe in the early decades of the century had begun to question the Scriptures as a source of literal truth and to present the figure of Jesus Christ as a mortal rather than a divine being. The German "higher critics" of the Bible—especially D.F. Strauss in his *Das Leben Jesu* (translated by George Eliot, 1844–46)[2]—were influen-

---

[1] Nineveh, called an "exceeding great city" in the Book of Jonah, was the center of worship of the goddess Ishtar in Assyria; it was captured and razed in 612 BCE, signaling the end of the Assyrian Empire. Tyre—the largest and most important Phoenician city—was sacked by Alexander the Great during his campaign against Persia in 332 BCE.

[2] David Friedrich Strauss (1808–74) shocked and outraged Christian Europe with his depiction of the "historical Jesus." *Das Leben Jesu*, or *The Life of Jesus, Critically Examined*, caused a scandal

tial in this "scientific" discussion of biblical texts. Leading Victorian thinkers such as Carlyle, Eliot, and Martineau wrote of personal religious crises, and wrestled publicly with doubts about the value and meaning of Christian belief. As Matthew Arnold wrote in 1880, "There is not a creed which is not shaken, nor an accredited dogma which is not shown to be questionable, not a received tradition which does not threaten to dissolve." In the climate of uncertainty as to whether the divine could be knowable, Carlyle's arrival, in *Sartor Resartus* (1833–34), at an affirmation of "natural supernaturalism" offers a telling statement of the almost desperate determination to find the divine in both nature and other human beings.

Traditional religious belief received its greatest challenge in the Victorian period from the evidence of the fossil record and Darwinian explanations of the origins of the universe and human beings' place within it. Charles Darwin's theories of evolution and natural selection in *On the Origin of Species* (1859) and *The Descent of Man* (1871) rejected the Christian idea that human beings had been created in God's image and were thus of a different order than the rest of the natural world. In *Descent*, Darwin provoked and challenged his audience by declaring, "He who is not content to look, like a savage, at the phenomena of nature as disconnected, cannot any longer believe that man is the work of a separate act of creation."[1]

And religious controversy and doubt extended further still. Not only were the divinity of Christ, the literal truth of the Bible, and the processes of creation at

issue, so too was the very existence of a creator or divine being. One of Darwin's strongest supporters, the scientist Thomas Henry Huxley, coined the term "agnostic" in 1869 at a party held in connection with the forming of the Metaphysical Society, a learned society that met regularly for over a decade to discuss theological issues, and whose members also included Tennyson, Ruskin, and Gladstone. The term agnostic named a person of a sort unimaginable in most earlier ages—one who neither believes nor disbelieves in the existence of God, holding instead that it is simply impossible for humans to possess knowledge of such matters.[2] It is to such beliefs—or the lack thereof—that Matthew Arnold refers when he writes in "Dover Beach" (1867) of the ebbing tide of the "Sea of Faith." Whereas in the twentieth century that ebbing tide was sometimes welcomed as representing a freeing of human potential, Victorians tended to hear it in the way that Arnold heard it, inextricably associated with an "eternal note of sadness."

The established church of England and Scotland—the Anglican denomination—remained a powerful entity throughout the Victorian era—with the reigning monarch heading the Church as the "Defender of the Faith," as had been the case since Henry VIII's break with Rome in the 1530s—but by century's end its power was more social than political. Though only Anglicans could be admitted to Parliament until the late 1820s, and non-Anglicans were barred from taking degrees at Oxford and Cambridge until 1871, the changes in both policies demonstrated that allegiance to Anglicanism was no longer a necessary criterion for admission to the bastions of power.

The Church was also profoundly influenced by the gradual severance of church-state relations, as well as the increasing popularity of Evangelicalism, a broad-based movement comprising numerous Protestant denominations including Methodism and Presbyterianism. These "Dissenting" or "nonconformist" faiths transformed religious practice in Britain, stressing the importance of an individual's personal relationship with God, of prudence and temperance, of conversion, of missionary work, and of humanitarian activism. In

---

with its insistence on the need to understand the miraculous events depicted in the Gospels as "mythical" in character. Eventually, Strauss's views came to dominate the new epoch of scriptural study, focused on textual interpretation.

[1] Much recent debate has focused on the question of Darwin's own Christian faith. His *Autobiography* (completed in 1876, but first published in 1887, five years after his death) and letters suggest Darwin's growing agnosticism. In the *Autobiography*, Darwin recalls "In my Journal I wrote that whilst standing in the midst of the grandeur of a Brazilian forest, 'it is not possible to give an adequate idea of the higher feelings of wonder, admiration, and devotion, which fill and elevate the mind.' I well remember my conviction that there is more in man than the mere breath of his body." But, toward the end of his life, he wrote to a correspondent, "I am sorry to have to inform you that I do not believe in the Bible as a divine revelation, & therefore not in Jesus Christ as the Son of God."

[2] Among Victorian authors George Eliot is perhaps the most prominent to have described herself as an agnostic.

1878, the Methodist minister William Booth founded the Salvation Army, which ministered to the poor in London's East End and became the center of social purity campaigns stressing chastity and public decency for both sexes. In general, Evangelical congregations were less hierarchical in organization than the traditional Anglican Church, were anti-Catholic in orientation, and attracted both middle- and working-class believers who felt that Anglicanism had lost its spiritual power and become a mere appendage of the state.

Henry Taunt, "Bible Stall at the St. Giles Fair, Oxford," 1880.

Evangelicalism—and the resistance to it—within the Church of England resulted in a split between Anglican Evangelicals (commonly referred to as Low Church), progressives (Broad Church, sometimes called Latitudi-anarians), and Anglo-Catholics (High Church). An important High Church reaction to Evangelicalism took place in the 1830s and 1840s through the Oxford Movement, also called Tractarianism, led by Oxford theologians and intellectuals John Henry Newman, John Keble, and Edward Pusey. Celebrating the mystical and aesthetic elements of worship, they advocated an increased emphasis on religious ritual and a strict

observance of clerical hierarchy within the Anglican communion. Newman's conversion to Roman Catholicism in 1845 spelled the end of the Oxford Movement, heralding a significant Catholic revival that saw many intellectuals rejecting Protestantism to embrace the Catholic faith and tradition. This was a significant religious as well as political development, since Catholics in England and especially in Ireland had for centuries been the objects of persecution. The Catholic Emancipation movement of the 1820s presaged the loosening of political and legal restrictions against members of the Catholic church, the majority of whom were barred from voting, holding office, running for Parliament, or attending the universities.

English Jews were also denied full rights of citizenship until a series of measures granted them access to Parliament, the military, the legal establishment, and institutions of higher learning. Anti-Semitic stereotypes were legion in Victorian novels such as *Oliver Twist*. In at least a few cases the writings of non-Jewish novelists challenged the stereotypes—sometimes tentatively—in ways that to some extent still participated in the culture of prejudice (as in Anthony Trollope's wide-ranging novel of capitalism, marriage, and religion, *The Way We Live Now* [1875]), sometimes more clearly and unequivocally (as in George Eliot's *Daniel Deronda* [1876][1]). And a significant body of Anglo-Jewish literature by writers such as Israel Zangwill and Amy Levy expressed a range of Jewish responses to social prejudice on the part of England's Christian majority.

Though the religious establishment suffered many challenges to its power, it would be a mistake to assume that secularism, Utilitarianism, and Darwinian theory stamped out religious faith or traditional religious

[1] Eliot's novel has been cited by a number of early Zionist leaders—including Emma Lazarus—as highly influential in their decision to embrace Zionism. The narrative's treatment of Jews—contrasting their spirituality and connection to their community to the materialism and corruption of English society—was met with some hostility, and many reviewers remarked that the parts of *Daniel Deronda* focusing on Jewish characters were its weakest.

The critic Edward Said has suggested, in "Zionism from the Standpoint of Its Victims" (1979), that the novel was a propaganda tool, used to encourage patriation of British-controlled Palestine by Jews.

Illustrations by George Cruikshank to Charles Dickens's *Oliver Twist* (1838). The captions identify the figures in the above illustrations as "Fagin and the boys" and as "Monks [another character in the novel] and the Jew." As presented by Dickens and Cruikshank, the character of Fagin is a caricature of evil—and of Jewishness. In passages such as the following, Dickens's descriptions of Fagin give expression to some of the most extreme anti-Semitic stereotypes: "It seemed just the night when it befitted such a being as the Jew to be abroad. As he glided stealthily along, creeping beneath the shelter of the walls and doorways, the hideous old man seemed like some loathsome reptile, engendered in the slime and darkness through which he moved: crawling forth by night, in search of some rich offal for a meal." By repeatedly naming him as "the Jew" Dickens crudely implied that the characteristics of Fagin were also those of Jews in general. Dickens received complaints from readers on this score, and over time he altered his views. Beginning with the edition of 1867 he made revisions to *Oliver Twist*, changing to "Fagin" the previous references to "the Jew." The last novel Dickens completed, *Our Mutual Friend* (1864–65), is notable not least of all for the inclusion of a Jewish character (Riah) who is portrayed by Dickens in a distinctly positive light.

practice: far from it. The Victorian period can be fairly characterized as an age of religious doubt that was also marked by intense religious feeling. As novels such as Anthony Trollope's *Barsetshire Chronicles*—a series of six novels published from 1855 to 1867—vividly convey,

religious affiliation (irrespective of the strength of one's actual faith) shaped most people's sense of personal identity. And the quest for spiritual meaning was itself the driving force behind some of the most moving literary works of the age. One such work, Tennyson's *In*

Memoriam (1849), an elegy for his friend Arthur Henry Hallam, chronicles the spiritual crisis of one man in the aftermath of his friend's death. By the end of the poem, the speaker has reconciled his religious doubts and scientific skepticism to re-embrace a Christian vision of the afterlife. In the closing lines of the poem the speaker exalts "That God, which ever lives and loves, / One God, one law, one element, / And one far-off divine event, / To which the whole creation moves."[1]

Victorian Domesticity: Life and Death

The center of British religious, cultural, and emotional life in the nineteenth century was the family. As industrialization transformed the household from a workspace into its "opposite," the home came to be regarded as an almost sacred space, to be shielded from the aggressive competitiveness of the public world of work. The family, especially among the rising middle class, was increasingly nuclear in structure; the extended networks of friends and relations that had formed strong household connections in pre-industrial society became more and more tenuous. Increasingly, the social arrangement perceived as ideal among the better-off social classes consisted of a male breadwinner, employed outside the home, and his female helpmeet, who nurtured the children, managed the servants, and served as a paragon of domestic virtue. One of the key signs of a man's professional success was his wife's "idleness" within the home. The separation of work and family life was reflected in city planning with the construction of the first modern suburbs, supported by public transportation systems. Middle-class domestic architecture encouraged the display of wealth and the division of sexual labor amongst family members by dividing houses into "public" and "private" spaces. The middle-class family model became the ideal for the working class as well, although economic necessity continued to force many working-class wives and children to contribute to house-hold earnings through paid labor, both inside and outside the home.

Illustration, *Wonders of a Toy-Shop*, c. 1852. Though it is sometimes claimed that children were treated as "little adults" in the nineteenth century, that was far less frequently the case than it had been a century or two earlier. In many respects, indeed, the nineteenth century marks the coming into prominence of "childhood" as a cultural entity. The changing attitudes towards children working in factories was one manifestation of change. Another was the evolution of "toy"—a word used before the nineteenth century to refer to a wide variety of trifles, but increasingly in the nineteenth century applied to playthings for children; toyshops specializing in such items became more and more widespread over the course of the Victorian period.

The domestic ideal and the emphasis on the family circle was shaped and promoted within the most privileged sphere of society. Throughout her reign, Queen Victoria was a paragon of good manners, restraint, and moral uprightness. In this she stood in contrast both to the escapades and excess that had surrounded the monarchies of her predecessors, George IV and William IV, and to the moral hypocrisy that characterized the reign of her son, Edward VII. In 1840, three years after her coronation, she married her first cousin, Prince Albert of Saxe-Coburg-Gotha. Together, they had nine children, and Victoria became the nation's most revered icon of domestic femininity and

---

[1] The importance of Tennyson's poem during the period is well illustrated by Queen Victoria's comment after the death of her husband Prince Albert in 1861 that "Next to the Bible, *In Memoriam* is my comfort."

maternal fecundity. She was a firm believer in separate spheres of influence and authority for men and women, voicing a then-conventional feminine distaste for power: "I am every day more convinced," she at one point declared, "that we women, if we are to be good women, feminine and amiable and domestic, are not fitted to reign." The royal family exemplified an ideal of Victorian domesticity, with Albert exercising much influence over his wife's decisions, and Victoria displaying unwavering devotion to the practical, manly Albert. Yet for all her outwardly conventional feminine attitudes, Victoria privately expressed ambivalence toward childbirth and marriage; she once complained in a letter to her daughter that giving birth made her feel like "a dog or a cow." In 1853, she agreed to undergo anesthesia during the birth of her son Leopold. This was a controversial new medical procedure, not least of all because it challenged the curse laid upon Eve (and therefore all women) in Genesis 1: "In sorrow shalt thou bring forth children."

When Albert died of typhoid in 1861, the entire nation went into a state of mourning. Victoria was overwhelmed with grief, and for 15 years after his death she was rarely seen in public, except at the unveiling of the many public monuments she arranged to have erected to his memory. Eventually many began to regard her seclusion as self-indulgent and excessive, and her popularity among her subjects suffered for several years. Yet Victoria's long widowhood was in many ways a sign of the times; it both reflected and influenced the Victorian vogue for elaborate mourning rituals and conventions governing the public observance of death.

Life expectancy during the Victorian period was almost certainly higher than it was in the late eighteenth century, and it did improve over the period, but for most of the century it was nevertheless extraordinarily low by the standards of the developed world today— probably no higher than 40 years in many areas of the country. The death of relatively young people was far more common than it is today—not only deaths of children but also of young adults—of diseases such as "consumption" (tuberculosis), for example, and of cholera, and very commonly, mothers dying in childbirth.

Romeo gazes at the dead Juliet: photograph of an 1895 production of Shakespeare's *Romeo and Juliet*, with Mrs. Patrick Campbell as Juliet.

It is no exaggeration to say that death became a commercial industry in the nineteenth century; funerals provided a public occasion to mourn the passing of a loved one as much as they offered an opportunity for rich and middle-income people to display wealth. Strict observance of funerary rituals in details of dress and deportment became a social necessity, and commemorative memorabilia, such as tea sets, photographs, and mourning jewelry—often made from the hair of the deceased—could be found in most homes. Many families were prepared to spend the bulk of their savings on the funerals of loved ones. For the poor, the story was of course much different. The indigent were buried with little or no ceremony in unmarked paupers' graves. Many working-class families contributed to burial clubs, an early form of insurance that guaranteed that at least a modest amount of money would be set aside for a respectable funeral for family members.

The obsession with death in the Victorian period is reflected in much of the literature of the period; in Gaskell's novel *Mary Barton*, no fewer than 13 deaths either take place or are recounted within the first ten chapters. Tennyson's famed elegy *In Memoriam* is as much a meditation on death as it is a lament for the loss of a loved one. Countless Victorian novels feature prolonged death scenes, with grieving or greedy family members keeping vigil by the bedside of the dying. One of Dickens's most beloved characters, Little Nell in *The Old Curiosity Shop* (1840–41), was modeled on his sister-in-law, Mary Hogarth, whose death had affected him deeply. Little Nell's death prompted an outpouring of grief from readers, many of whom wrote letters to Dickens in between installments of the novel imploring him to spare her.[1] The beautiful, often eroticized corpse was a favorite image in both visual art and poetry. In Christina Rossetti's "After Death" (1862), a female speaker observes her lover's attitude toward her corpse, and realizes, "He did not love me living; but once dead / He pitied me; and very sweet it is / To know he still is warm tho' I am cold."

Though mortality rates, especially among infants, remained high throughout the century, there were significant medical advances in disease control and sanitation. Prominent among these was the verification of the bacterial theory of disease. Until late in the century, most medical practitioners and lay people believed that disease was spread through miasma, or the spread of harmful odors through the atmosphere. Susceptibility was routinely blamed on moral and social factors such as poverty, overcrowding, and sexual behaviors. During the cholera epidemics of the 1840s, researchers began to make links between incidents of the disease and water sources. Joseph Lister's work in the 1850s and 1860s confirmed the existence of microorganisms, yet the miasma theory of disease was so entrenched that it was not until late in the century that the bacterial theory was fully accepted. By 1890, the pathogens for several diseases, including tuberculosis, cholera, typhoid, rabies, and diphtheria, had been

Advertisement from *The Lady*, 4 October 1900.

identified. Surgical practice was also transformed by Lister's work on antiseptic treatments and the adoption of anesthetics, particularly ether and chloroform.

CULTURAL TRENDS

When the Duke of Wellington died in 1852, a million and a half people lined the streets of London to pay their last respects to the military hero who had defeated Napoleon at Waterloo. The deaths of the eminent were marked by elaborate, theatrical state funerals that fed an increasing appetite for public spectacles, epitomized by the Great Exhibition of 1851. The culture of Victorian Britain was very much a visual one, with public amusements, popular shows, traveling exhibitions,

---

[1] Not all were so moved. Of the death of Dickens's beloved character, Oscar Wilde famously opined, "One would have to have a heart of stone to read the death of little Nell without dissolving into tears … of laughter."

"View of the Grand Entrance to the Great Exhibition, 1851." The idea for what became the Great Exhibition grew out of a proliferation of smaller exhibitions of the products of craft and industry in the 1840s, and out of an awareness that Paris was contemplating its own large-scale international exhibition. Organized largely by Henry Cole, with the strong support of Prince Albert, the "Great Exhibition of the Works of Industry of All Nations" was held in Hyde Park in 1851. The Crystal Palace, centerpiece of the Exhibition, was later dismantled and re-assembled at Sydenham in south London as a home for permanent exhibitions, where it stood until it was destroyed by fire in 1936. (See Contexts: Britain, Empire, and a Wider World.)

circuses, sporting events, holiday resorts, and public gardens to cater to every stratum of a society that had a growing amount of both disposable income and leisure time. London's theaters drew thousands of spectators every night to witness ingenious visual effects created by London's theater impresarios; live animals, underwater sequences, mob scenes, flying machines, sumptuous interiors, and innovations in lighting stoked the public mania for stage realism.[1] Music halls aimed at lower middle- and working-class audiences featured a miscellany of comic songs, dance numbers, and magic shows by popular performers. Many public museums and galleries—which today draw thousands of visitors annually—were established in the Victorian period following the Great Exhibition, including the Victoria and Albert Museum, the National Portrait Gallery, and the Tate Gallery (founded by sugar magnate Henry Tate). Madame Tussaud's Wax Museum found a permanent home in London in 1835. From the 1870s and 1880s onwards, fashionable new shopping arcades and department stores filled with enticing consumer goods made shopping a respectable pastime for middle-class women.

Mass visual culture was inaugurated in the nineteenth century with the advent of a range of technologies, including the kaleidoscope, the daguerreotype, the photograph, and the cinema. As on the stage, visual technologies exploited light and movement in an

---

[1]   Perhaps not coincidentally, this era of special-effects theatricality is now generally said to have marked a nadir in the history of English drama as a literary genre.

William Powell Frith, *The Railway Station* (detail), 1862. The painting depicts a scene at Paddington Station in London.

effort to create the illusion of reality and transport viewers across time and space. Panoramas and dioramas[1] featured foreign cities, battlefields, landscapes, and natural disasters, and anticipated the "moving pictures" of the cinema. Innovations in print technology and the explosion of illustrated print material from the 1830s onwards signaled the public's increasing demand for the pictorial representation of daily events. The popular *Illustrated London News*, established in 1842, was the world's first illustrated weekly paper to hit newsstands; it used increasingly sophisticated technologies—from woodcuts to steel engravings to photographs—in its pictorial coverage of events at home and abroad. Serial novels published in periodicals were accompanied by wood-engraved illustrations intended to heighten the reader's appreciation of the narrative; popular engraver-illustrators such as George Cruikshank and Hablot K. Browne ("Phiz"), both of whom illustrated for Dickens, were initially as celebrated as the author himself.

Victorian painters benefitted both from the emergence of a wealthy middle class able to purchase art for their homes and from the public's fascination with visual representation of contemporary life and historical drama. Scenes of everyday life with a narrative dimension and a moral message were especially popular with the viewing public. Like Victorian novelists and poets, many Victorian visual artists came to document the hardships of an industrial culture and landscape, depicting agricultural laborers, factory workers, and the unemployed in a highly realistic, yet often sentimental mode that has come to be known as social realism. Childhood innocence and scenes of domestic harmony were also common themes for many Victorian artists; new and inexpensive methods of art reproduction meant that such pictures could be sold cheaply to a wide audience that was interested in seeing the values of home and family reflected on its walls. Panoramic views of Victorian life in all its colorful variety were also popular: William Powell Frith's *Derby Day* (1858) and

Railway Station (1862) portrayed scenes of ordinary Victorians in such realistic detail that they caused a great sensation when they were first exhibited at the Royal Academy. Founded in the eighteenth century under George III, the Royal Academy of Arts was institutionalized as the most important mediator of public taste in art in the Victorian period. It offered a free training school to many of the century's most significant artists, and its annual exhibitions of what it deemed the best works of the year drew thousands of spectators and buyers—as well as accusations of bias and preferential treatment on the part of those whose work had been excluded from the exhibitions or poorly hung.

The most influential movement in Victorian painting was the Pre-Raphaelite Brotherhood, composed of the artists John Everett Millais, William Holman Hunt, Thomas Woolner, James Collinson, Frederick George Stephens, and the brothers of Christina Rossetti, artist and poet Dante Gabriel Rossetti, and critic William Michael Rossetti. At mid-century these artists began producing works that challenged the dominant taste for neoclassical style and subject matter by painting in the manner of medieval, pre-Renaissance artists. Close attention to natural detail, flattened perspective, vivid colors, an interest in literary subject matter, and erotically charged images of spiritual and religious devotion were some of the hallmarks of the group. Their paintings of female figures as either ravishing "femmes fatales" or dreamy heroines in historical dress are today instantly recognizable (and are much reproduced). These paintings conveyed both women's power and vulnerability in nineteenth-century culture, and were sometimes twinned, in D.G. Rossetti's work especially, with a companion poem or with a quotation from a literary work. ("The Blessed Damozel" [1846] is one such example, in which the separation of two lovers by death in the poem is conveyed with two separate panels in the painting.) "Pre-Raphaelite," indeed, denotes a style of poetry as well as of painting; sensuous detail and a tendency to link earthly beauty to the divine are as characteristic of the poetry of Rossetti as they are of his paintings.

---

[1] In a diorama, spectators view a partially translucent painting in a specially designed building, with variations of light cast upon the image to simulate the movement of light in a daytime scene. The diorama was first exhibited in London in 1823.

Arthur Hughes, *The Long Engagement* (detail). Hughes (1832–1915) was one of the most prominent of the second wave of Pre-Raphaelite painters.

The Pre-Raphaelites should in part be considered alongside the Gothic Revival, a wave of interest in a medieval and Gothic aesthetic that had begun in the Romantic period and influenced Victorian painting, architecture, design, literature, and religious practice.

The idealization of the Middle Ages is exemplified in the writing of Thomas Carlyle, John Ruskin, William Morris, and Alfred Tennyson. Ruskin, an art critic who championed the work of the Pre-Raphaelites, argued in *The Stones of Venice* (1851–53) for the moral superiority of the Gothic style, in part because it was the product of artisan-workers who were free to use their creativity in their work, and so express their individual and spiritual nature. Ruskin urged his readers to re-examine the "ugly goblins" and "stern statues" of Gothic cathedrals, for "they are the signs of the life and liberty of every workman who struck the stone; a freedom of thought, and rank in scale of being, such as no laws, no charters, no charities can secure."

The Arts and Crafts movement of the last few decades of the century, led by William Morris and influenced by Ruskin's ideas, was dedicated to the production of hand-crafted furniture, glassware, books, and art objects. Design firms such as Morris and Co. and the Century Guild revived the medieval guild system of production, rejecting the mass-produced manufactures of the assembly line in favor of the freedom and spontaneity of craft and its makers. In their critique of the ravages of industrial technology and the drudgery of mechanized labor, the practitioners of Gothic Revival imagined, and to some extent invented, the idea of the medieval past as a time of moral and religious stability, devotion to craft, and harmony with the rhythms of the natural world.

TECHNOLOGY

The technological invention that perhaps best exemplified the industrial age was the steam engine, a source and symbol of power both on land and at sea. Although the steam engine had been in use since the early eighteenth century, it was not until the nineteenth that steam technology helped transform an entire economy and a way of life. Steam engines were adapted for use in the production of coal, textiles, heavy metals, and printing presses, thus becoming indispensable to Britain's industrial growth. Steamships powered the

The Palace of Westminster, home to both Houses of Parliament, was redesigned and rebuilt following the fire of 1834, in a vast project not completed until 1860. It is one of the most striking examples of the Gothic style applied to a secular construction.

British Empire, with several major shipping lines established in the 1840s to serve routes to India, Africa, East Asia, and Australia. Railway steam locomotives epitomized the coming of the Victorian era, with the first local lines built in 1837 and 1838 as Victoria assumed the throne. In the "railway mania" of the 1840s, over 8,000 miles of new track were approved, and, by 1900, over nine hundred million passengers were using Britain's rail system annually. London's underground rail system opened its first line in 1863, though horse-drawn transportation continued to dominate the streetscape until the end of the century.

The convenience and speed of rail travel caught on quickly with everyone from the Queen to the ordinary worker. Rail companies established excursions to special events, such as horse races or the seaside, inaugurating local and national tourism on a mass scale. So important was the advent of railway travel to the development of English daily life, railway stations even became essential to the book trade and the spread of leisure reading; from the 1850s onward, book stalls catering to thousands of daily commuters began to stock their shelves with newspapers, magazines, and cheap, popular fiction, which became known as "railway literature."

Robert Howlett, "Isambard Kingdom Brunel and the Launching Chains of the *Great Eastern*," 1857. The ship (designed largely by Brunel) remained the largest in the world throughout its 31 years on the seas. Brunel, the leading engineer of the age, also played an important role in designing such Victorian landmarks as the Crystal Palace, the new Houses of Parliament, Paddington Station, and the Clifton Suspension Bridge at Bristol.

CULTURAL IDENTITIES

The adoption of new technologies, the reorganization of employment, and the shift in power from the monarchy to the institutions of the modern liberal state revolutionized people's experience of work, family life, civic duty, and leisure time in the Victorian era. Such developments are almost always accompanied by shifts in the way people understand themselves as individuals in relation to their society. In the nineteenth century, the conditions and practices of one's class, gender, race, and sexuality began to acquire new meanings, to take on new importance, and to attract a new kind of attention. Changes in living conditions developed in connection with prescribed gender roles, which began to seem

"natural" and "innate," because they supported the logic of industrial capital and bourgeois family life. Though this process did not begin in the Victorian period, it was majorly extended and thoroughly revised during the time. Victorians tended to think about identity in terms of oppositions: male and female, rich and poor, black and white, and, later in the century, homosexual and heterosexual. Such oppositions had the effect of establishing seemingly stable types and suggesting that the differences were natural and unchangeable. For example, the ideology of separate spheres for men and women proposed that gender and sexual identity were fixed categories and that "true womanhood" was the inherent opposite of normative manliness. Still, in the literary works of the period, the line between "opposites" was constantly crossed and revealed as problematic and variable.

The "Angel in the House"[1] became a common label for the Victorian ideal of respectable middle-class femininity. Quiet beauty, purity, devotion and selflessness were some of the essential features of the domestic wife and mother, who was described and exalted in advice literature and popular domestic novels aimed at female readers. "She must be enduringly, incorruptibly good," advised John Ruskin, "instinctively, infallibly wise—wise, not for self-development, but for self-renunciation; wise, not that she may set herself above her husband, but that she may never fall from his side." The absolute other to this paragon of virtue was the "fallen woman," a label that encompassed any form of female sexual experience deemed improper or immoral. Prostitutes, rape victims, unmarried mothers, adulteresses, homeless women, the insane, and any woman who displayed rebellious passions could be labeled "fallen." Yet the boundary between the domestic

---

1 The phrase originated in the title of Coventry Patmore's long narrative poem. Patmore's "The Angel in the House"—first published in 1854, but revised several times for subsequent publication—was written about the author's wife, Emily, who Patmore exalted as the perfect model of Victorian femininity and domesticity. The poem's opening lines—"Man must be pleased; but him to please / Is woman's pleasure"—rather neatly encapsulate the meaning and the message of the work. In "Professions for Women," a 1942 address given to the Women's Service League, Virginia Woolf argued that "part of the occupation ... of a woman writer" was to kill the "Angel in the House."

angel and the fallen woman was extraordinarily narrow; one false step and innocence became wickedness, followed by ostracism from society, poverty, and almost certain death for the transgressor, at least according to dominant narratives of fallenness.[1] On the other hand, some fallen women were portrayed as penitent victims who embodied the feminine ideal even more fully than their uncorrupted female counterparts. Writers such as Elizabeth Gaskell, Christina Rossetti, George Eliot, Mary Elizabeth Braddon, Augusta Webster, and Thomas Hardy explored the tropes of purity and fallenness, bringing "pure" and "impure" women into each other's (and the reader's) proximity in order to probe the limits of the feminine ideal.

The male counterpart to the domestic angel was the Victorian gentleman, an heir of the chivalric ideal updated for the industrial age. In *The Idea of a University* (a series of lectures published as one volume in 1873), John Henry Newman characterized the gentleman as tender, merciful, prudent, patient, forbearing, resigned, and disciplined. Yet despite Newman's apparent confidence in this description, gentlemanliness was difficult to define: was it based on a man's mode of income or on his behavior? Was it a hereditary, professional, or moral category, or some combination? While eminent men were celebrated with great gusto in biography and prose works such as Carlyle's *On Heroes and Hero Worship* (1841), men were also often regarded as morally inferior to women because of their greater contact with the competition and corruption of the public world. (On the other hand, women could just as easily be pressed into the role of evil temptress in accounting for a man's fall from grace.) Tennyson's dramatic monologue "Ulysses" (1842) wrestles with two competing versions of masculinity: the thwarted Romantic hero, who longs for adventure and freedom from domestic encumbrance, and the reliable, managerial male who faithfully adheres to professional duty.

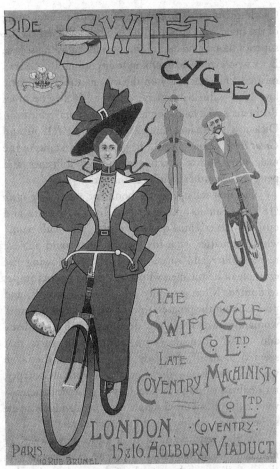

Advertisement for Swift Cycles, c. 1895.

The concepts of the Victorian lady and gentleman were also class categories, serving to both reinforce and blur distinctions between various socio-economic groups. The boarding schools for the sons and daughters of the elite and the middle classes promulgated notions of proper female and male conduct in their curricula; increasingly, it was understood that one was not simply born a lady or a gentleman, but must learn to become one through rigorous training and constant self-scrutiny. As the terms "lady" and "gentleman" gradually lost their association with rank, socio-economic boundaries became increasingly difficult to distinguish, and novelists began to focus on the gendered and class behaviors of individuals for their narrative content. In

---

[1] In a famous moment in Dickens's *David Copperfield*, the narrator's recollection of a dangerous moment in the fallen Emily's early life leads him to wonder if it might not have been far better for her to have died rather to have survived only to later "fall."

Charlotte Brontë's *Jane Eyre* (1847), the moral awakening of the male hero, Edward Rochester, is achieved via the superior moral guidance of the "servant" governess, Jane Eyre, who avoids succumbing to becoming Rochester's mistress, thus teaching him the true nature of domestic love and Christian sacrifice; Jane finally becomes Rochester's wife following his spiritual, moral rebirth. In Dickens's novels, including *David Copperfield* (1850) and *Great Expectations* (1860), the gentlemanly status of the male protagonists is achieved through diligence and perseverance rather than by birthright.

The best-selling advice book for men, *Self Help* (1859) by Samuel Smiles, stressed thrift, hard work, and optimism as essential qualities of the "self-made man," who, no matter what his social status, could achieve respectability and success, in part by following the example of heroic men whose accomplishments Smiles recounted. More generally, advice books, novels, and poems about the progress toward, or the fall from, "true" womanhood or manliness demonstrate that gendered and classed identities were cultural constructs that seemed "natural." The lady, the gentleman, the fallen woman, the hero—these gendered and class types, rationalized through the ideology of separate spheres— were cultural myths through which individuals made sense of their relationship to the social order.

As the century drew to a close, new styles of masculinity and femininity emerged to compete with the prevailing gender models of the previous decades. One of these emergent types was the "New Woman," a term that described a figure of greater sexual, economic, and social independence than the "Angel in the House." Although the term denoted a lifestyle and a literary category more than a political perspective, the figure of the New Woman was in part a product of the gains feminists had made by the 1880s and 1890s in the areas of higher education, employment, political and legal rights, and civic visibility. The New Woman quickly became a flashpoint for opinion makers on either side of the "Woman Question."[1] Smoking, swearing, riding a bicycle, debating in public, wearing men's clothes, and

refusing marriage were some of the trademarks of the New Woman, who figured in novels, short stories, and popular journalism as someone either to emulate or to condemn. A number of male novelists, including George Gissing, George Moore, and Thomas Hardy, created memorable New Woman characters who grapple with the competing demands of personal autonomy and social expectation, while the works of female writers, such as Sarah Grand's *The Heavenly Twins* (1893) and the semi-autobiographical *The Beth Book* (1897), presented New Woman characters who triumph over social convention and the sexual double standard.

For Grand and other feminist writers, such as Mona Caird and Olive Schreiner, the portrayal of the New Woman hinged on a critique of the male sexual privilege that had already come under fire in the 1870s and 1880s during the social purity campaigns and the resistance to the Contagious Diseases Acts. This legislation, enacted in the 1860s, allowed for the forcible confinement and internal examination of prostitutes by doctors in order to prevent the spread of venereal disease, first among the military, and then within civilian communities. Under-writing these Acts was the assumption that because male sexual urges were "uncontrollable," prostitution was a necessary evil that should be regulated because it could not be eradicated. The Act of 1864 decreed that infected women could be held in locked hospitals for three months; the Act of 1869 extended the period of confinement to a year. In 1867, there were proposals to extend the Acts to the north of England and the civilian population. Though the laws were intended to combat the spread of disease by prostitutes, in practice, they essentially meant that any woman passing through a poor neighborhood was subject to compulsory medical examination and arrest. The campaign against the Acts, led by the charismatic Josephine Butler, condemned the sexual double standard and the humiliation of poor and vulnerable women by police and doctors, with Butler comparing the compulsory medical examinations to "instrumental rape." The Acts were struck down in 1886 after much public controversy; the movement to repeal them, led mostly by middle-class women, marked the first instance in which women publicly debated the subject of sex on a broad scale. It was also one of the most visible of the many social purity campaigns of the

[1] The question was largely one of the nature—and consequently, the proper role—of women. The "Woman Question" came to encompass the debates about the rights and responsibilities, as well as the place, of women in Victorian society.

1870s, 1880s, and 1890s, in which moral reformers engaged in the rescue and "reformation" of prostitutes and other "fallen women" and urged men to take a vow of chastity. The mandate of the National Vigilance Association, for example, was to "create a universal ethic of chastity, for all men and women alike." In calling for a single standard of behavior, many of the social purity groups espoused moral coerciveness and interventionist policies, which often ended up stigmatizing and further repressing the women and girls they were attempting to help.

The preoccupations of the purity campaigners were part of a renewed cultural and scientific interest in human sexuality among Victorians, dating from at least the early 1870s and the publication of Darwin's *The Descent of Man*. In that book, Darwin applied the theories from his *On the Origin of Species* to human evolution and behavior, positing that sexual selection among men and women accounted for their mental and physical differences. These "natural differences" were drawn straight from the catalogue of Victorian gender stereotypes, which held that men were inherently courageous, virile, and combative, and women intuitive, passive, and altruistic. The "complementarity" of these traits ensured the survival of the human "race," which evolutionists, anthropologists, and psychologists understood as a hierarchy: white European males at the top, followed by women, children, and the "primitive races." But, scientists wondered, how to explain the fact that some white men—seemingly nature's most civilized specimen—occasionally exhibited traits that resembled those of the women, children, primitives, and even the animals who were understood as biologically and mentally inferior? Such questions were compounded by fears that Britain's empire was crumbling because the purity of the "white race" was being diluted through crossbreeding and racial mingling among English imperialists and the "savages" they ruled in the benighted labyrinths of the Empire. Closer to home, the poverty, crime, and vice of England's urban districts was often racialized: "As there is a darkest Africa is there not also a darkest England?" asked William Booth, founder of the Salvation Army. "Civilisation, which can breed its own barbarians, does it not also breed its own pygmies? May we not find a parallel at our own doors, and

discover within a stone's throw of our cathedrals and palaces similar horrors to those which Stanley[1] has found existing in the great Equatorial forest?"

Social Darwinist theories of atavism (the reappearance of "primitive" characteristics in "advanced" populations) and degeneration (retrograde evolution) were formulated in the second half of the century to account for the "tendencies" of criminals, alcoholics, the poor, the mentally and physically disabled, and homosexuals. It was not until the 1880s that the term "homosexual" entered the English language; before that time homosexual acts among men were illegal (sodomy was punishable by death until 1861), but there was no concept of "the homosexual"—either male or female—as a distinct identity or way of being. With the emergence of a gay male subculture in London in the 1870s and 1880s, homosexuals—also called "sexual inverts"—became subject to increased scientific and legal scrutiny. Although "the lesbian" also emerged as a distinct identity in the 1890s, women were not subject to the same kinds of persecution as gay men, in part because of the belief that women were unmotivated by sexual desire, and that their passionate female "friendships" were therefore innocent, merely temporary diversions from their true calling as wives and mothers.

The Criminal Law Amendment Act of 1885, which raised the age of sexual consent from 13 to 16 under pressure from the social purity campaigners, contained a clause—known as the Labouchère Amendment, after Member of Parliament Henry Labouchère, who had introduced it—that mandated imprisonment for any man found guilty of "gross indecency"—effectively, any sexual act—with another man, even if the "indecency" was conducted entirely in private.[2] The Labouchère Amendment served to demonize gay men as "degenerates" whose "unnatural" desires threatened the stability of marriage, the future of the race, and the strength of the Empire. Feminized male types—the dandy, the aesthete, the fop—surfaced in visual art and

---

[1] Henry Morton Stanley (1841–1904) was a renowned journalist and explorer, best known for his travels in Africa and his successful search for David Livingstone (see above, p. 512).

[2] Many sexual acts were already illegal; in particular, "buggery"—a British term for anal sex—whether between two men or between a man and a woman, had been illegal since the Buggery Act of 1553.

literature alongside the masculinized New Woman figure to characterize a climate of sexual and gender experimentation at the fin-de-siècle that was celebrated by a few and denounced by many. As the popular satirical magazine *Punch* joked, "A new fear my bosom vexes; / Tomorrow there may be no sexes!"

"Two Seated Sicilian Youths," photograph from c. 1893 (Victoria and Albert Museum).

In 1895, celebrity playwright Oscar Wilde[1] was brought to trial under the terms of the Labouchère

Amendment and sentenced to two years in prison for "gross indecency." The highly publicized Wilde trials brought the moral panic of the preceding two decades to a crisis point. Yet Wilde's trial testimony, his writing, and that of his contemporaries such as John Addington Symonds, Algernon Charles Swinburne, "Michael Field," Sarah Grand, Mona Caird, Vernon Lee, and Edward Carpenter signaled a new level of consciousness about sexual and gender identity. With remarkable candor the sexologist Havelock Ellis wrote that while "we may not know exactly what sex is ... we do know that it is mutable, with the possibility of one sex being changed into the other sex, that its frontiers are often mutable, and that there are many stages between a complete male and a complete female." Ellis broke new ground with his multi-volume *The Psychology of Sex* (1897–1910), an early volume of which, *Sexual Inversion* (1897), was particularly noteworthy for treating homosexuality in a purely descriptive fashion, rather than as a pathology. (In other volumes Ellis took a similar approach to many other topics, including "autoerotism," or masturbation, and sado-masochism.) Sexuality and sexual practice had become topics of public conversation in a way that belies twentieth-century stereotypes of Victorian culture as sexually conservative or naïve. The apparent "repression" of sexual behaviors deemed improper or immoral only seemed to prohibit what was in fact an intense interest in the passions, proclivities, and practices of the "other" Victorians.[2]

REALISM

"Art is the nearest thing to life," wrote George Eliot in "The Natural History of German Life" (1856). "It is a mode of amplifying experience and extending our contact with our fellow-men beyond the bounds of our personal lot. All the more sacred is the task of the artist when he undertakes to paint the life of the People." Eliot's essay anticipated the masterpieces of realist

---

[1] Wilde was a married father of two young children, but rumors about his dalliances with men—many of working-class backgrounds, known as "rent-boys"—had abounded as his popularity increased. It was Wilde's involvement with Lord Alfred "Bosie" Douglas, the son of the 9th Marquess of Queensberry, that resulted in the rumors becoming a legal matter. The eccentric Queensberry, who believed his son had been corrupted by the older Wilde, left a note for Wilde at his club, accusing the playwright of "posing as a somdomite [*sic*]." Encouraged by Bosie, who hated his father, Wilde sued for libel; the resulting trial revealed a number of graphic details about Wilde's sexual predilections, and he was subsequently himself tried for acts of gross indecency.

[2] Steven Marcus's seminal exploration of Victorian expressions and repressions of sexuality, *The Other Victorians: A Study of Sexuality and Pornography in Mid-Nineteenth Century England* (1966) helped complicate the sometimes overly simplified early and mid-twentieth-century view of the Victorians as simply repressed and "asexual."

fiction she would begin writing in just a few years—
Adam Bede (1859), *The Mill on the Floss* (1860), and
Middlemarch (1874) among them. For Eliot, as for
many of her contemporaries, the true, even "sacred,"
purpose of art was to present an objective representation
of real life that reflected the habits, desires, and
aspirations of readers. For many novelists, realism
seemed to be the form best suited to this purpose.

Victorian poetry too, especially at mid-century, was
influenced by the predominance of realist fiction; long
narrative poems, such as Tennyson's *Idylls of the King*
(1856–85) and Robert Browning's *The Ring and the
Book* (1868–69), appropriated novelistic forms of storytelling, combining trenchant social critique with formal
experimentation. In Elizabeth Barrett Browning's "verse
novel" and female *Bildungsroman*,[1] *Aurora Leigh*
(1856), the speaker, Aurora Leigh herself, defines and
defends her poetic practice of social engagement with
the contemporary world, sounding very much like Eliot:

> Nay, if there's room for poets in this world
> A little overgrown (I think there is),
> Their sole work is to represent the age,
> Their age, not Charlemagne's …
> …
> … this is living art,
> Which thus presents and thus records true life.

Much realist fiction of the Victorian period tended
to center on the everyday experiences, moral progress,
and inner struggles of an ordinary individual, while
giving a sense of the connections between that
individual and his or her broader social networks. Many
realist novels, including those by Anthony Trollope,
William Thackeray, Dickens, and Eliot contained multiple plot lines and a range of characters across socio-
economic strata, representing both the cohesiveness and
the disintegration of various social communities in an
industrialized, commercializing society. Detailed descriptions of landscapes, city streets, and domestic
interiors and close attention to the emotionally complex
motivations of characters—these too are characteristic of
the realism of the Victorian novel. However, such broad
vision is typically viewed from a single narrative

perspective, whether that of the novel's protagonist or of
an omniscient narrator.

Why did realism hold such appeal for Victorian
novelists and their audiences? One explanation is that
the revolutions of the nineteenth century created a
climate in which people longed for a sense of
verisimilitude in their literature in order to guide them
through the changes and upheavals, both private and
public, which they themselves faced. Many Victorian
readers sought moral and ethical guidance from their
authors, who assumed—or were thrust into—the role of
"secular clerics" with varying degrees of confidence and
authority. Realist fiction, along with other forms of
writing such as biography, criticism, poetry, and history,
was accepted as having a pedagogical function; such
texts not only taught readers how to navigate the
changes they were experiencing, but also how to
imagine sympathetically the authenticity of others'
experience. "We want to be taught to feel," wrote Eliot,
"not for the heroic artisan or the sentimental peasant,
but for the peasant in all his coarse apathy, and the
artisan in all his suspicious selfishness."

In rejecting the heroic and the sentimental, Eliot
positioned the realist novel in opposition to the
heightened, "falsifying" sensibilities of the romantic
mode, as did many others. In 1785, distinguishing
between the romance and the newly emergent genre of
the novel, Clara Reeve had observed that "the Novel is
a picture of real life and manners, and of the times in
which it was written. The Romance in lofty and elevated
language, describes what never happened nor is likely to
happen"; Reeve's description of the novel could be
applied to most Victorian fiction. Nonetheless, many of
the best-known Victorian novels contain elements of the
fantastic, the supernatural, or the mysterious: while
Dickens's *Oliver Twist*—as is true, indeed, of most of
his novels—sets out to realistically document the ravages
of industrial poverty, but the novel's plot depends on
outrageous coincidence, its story peopled with broadly
drawn character types befitting the romantic mode.[2]
The novels of Charlotte and Emily Brontë memorably

---

[1] "Novel of Education" (German).

[2] Oliver Twist is one of many orphans in Dickens's novels. Dickens's orphans inevitably confront the urban nightmares of Victorian
life with well-nigh angelic purity—and, in Oliver's case, perfectly
grammatical English.

Page of advertisements from the eighth number of the 1846 serial publication in ten numbers of Dickens's *Oliver Twist*. (Pages of advertisements appeared at the front and back of each number.)

combine psychological realism with Gothic elements such as female imprisonment and suggestions of ghostly presences. The persistence of romantic elements in Victorian realist novels not only unsettles the confidence of our formal definitions, but also prompts us to consider just whose versions of "the real" were recognized as the most truthful.

Inevitably, realism's dominance in literature and in visual art came under attack. As early as the 1850s, but more widely in the 1880s and 1890s, visual artists, writers, and critics began to question the moral imperatives of realist art in a series of movements that have come to be referred to under the umbrella term "Aestheticism." In poetry, drama, criticism, and fiction, Aestheticism stressed experimentation in form and composition, independence of imagination and expression, and freedom of content, however perverse, morbid, or tawdry. In rebelling against the harsh brutalities of British industrial culture, the Aesthetes sought a "pure" art and formal beauty dissociated from the concerns and surroundings of the everyday. The Aesthetes were not interested in instructing or edifying a mass readership; rather, they advocated aesthetic withdrawal in order to pursue the essential forms of art. "Art for art's sake,"[1] translated from the French by art critic Walter Pater, became the rallying cry of the Aesthetes. "Art never expresses anything but itself," declares one of Oscar Wilde's speakers. "It has an independent life, just as Thought has, and develops purely on its own lines. It is not necessarily realistic in an age of realism, nor spiritual in an age of faith. So far from being a creation of its own time, it is usually in direct opposition to it." Similarly, Wilde concludes his preface to *The Picture of Dorian Gray* (1891) with the assertion that "All art is quite useless," having earlier stated that "There is no such thing as a moral or an immoral book."

By the 1890s, the aesthetic movement had been charged with elitism, hedonism, self-absorption, and homosexuality.[2] Aestheticism by that time had shifted into Decadence, a term of either censure or praise, depending on who wielded it. The Decadents extended the precepts of Aestheticism in their affirmation of the perversity, artificiality, and overindulgence of a culture and a century that was nearing its end, and their works were often taken as evidence of social degeneration; in *Degeneration* (1892), the German critic Max Nordau attacked degenerate, Decadent artists—including Wilde—and argued that social decay is both reflected in and driven by art.

THE VICTORIAN NOVEL

The dominant Victorian literary form was the novel. Although the genre of the novel emerged well in advance of the Victorian period, the literary legitimacy and cultural authority the novel wields today were solidified in the nineteenth century. The novel was a dynamic form, shifting according to popular taste and critical assessments of its potential value to readers, who were offered an ever-expanding list of authors and subgenres from which to choose. The early and mid-Victorian novels of Dickens, Thackeray, and Trollope were wildly successful, both with the critical establishment and the reading public. Female novelists, including the Brontës, Eliot, Braddon, Gaskell, Charlotte Yonge, and Ellen Price Wood were some of the most respected and prolific of the century, and paved the way for legions of other women to enter the field of fiction writing. Although the profession of "novelist" achieved new respectability in the period for both men and women alike, the novel continued in some circles to be maligned as lightweight and "pernicious," associated with frivolous lady scribblers and their female readers. As George Henry Lewes, George Eliot's partner, observed in "The Lady Novelists" (1852), "Of all departments of literature, Fiction is the one to which, by

---

[1] The French writer Théophile Gautier (1811–72) is generally credited with coining the phrase "l'art pour l'art" in the preface to his novel, *Mademoiselle de Maupin* (1836). A number of critics have contended that the idea—if not the precise phrase—dates back to ancient Rome.

[2] Wilde's *The Picture of Dorian Gray*, which first appeared in *Lippincott's Monthly Magazine* in 1890, was immediately accused of having homoerotic overtones and deemed "unclean," "effeminate," and "contaminating." Wilde made a number of changes to the novel before its publication as one volume in 1891, but these were not enough to keep the book from counting against him during Wilde's trial for acts of "gross indecency."

nature and by circumstance, women are best adapted.…
The very nature of fiction calls for that predominance of
Sentiment which we have already attributed to the
feminine mind."

The taste for particular subjects and approaches
shifted regularly: the "silver fork" novels of the 1820s
and 1830s centered on the extravagances and corruptions of the rich and fashionable, while the "social
problem" novels of the 1840s depicted the minute
details of life at the very opposite end of the social scale.
Domestic novels by both the famous and the obscure
focused on the quotidian; George Eliot's *Middlemarch*,
rich in psychological complexity and moral analysis, is
one of the most outstanding examples of domestic
fiction of the Victorian period. A heightened form of
this domestic-centered fiction was the "sensation" novel,
which flourished in the 1860s and 1870s. Strong on
dramatic incident and scandalous subject matter, such
as bigamy, murder, madness, and crime, sensation
novels exposed the hidden corruptions and dirty secrets
of the outwardly respectable middle class; Wilkie
Collins, Braddon, and Wood were some of the leading
practitioners of this wildly popular and much maligned
sub-genre. The immense popular appeal of sensation
novels helped inaugurate the concept of a "mass
readership," much to the chagrin of the critical elite,
who bemoaned the "degradation" of literature as the
century drew to a close. In the latter decades of the
century, mystery novels, detective fiction, horror, and
adventure stories soared in popularity, partly on the
strength of an expanding audience of lower-income
readers, rising literacy rates, and cheaper methods of
book production. The counterpart to these often lurid
and shocking tales were the naturalistic novels of
Thomas Hardy, George Gissing, and George Moore,
whose late-century fiction offers bleak, social Darwinist
portraits of urban class struggle, slum life, rural poverty,
and sexual frustration.

If the vogue for particular kinds of subject matter in
novels shifted regularly, so too did their modes of
publication, distribution, and consumption. One significant mode of publication was the three-volume
edition, known as the "triple-decker." Readers who
could not afford to buy the volumes themselves
borrowed one volume at a time from lending libraries

Cover, *Famous Crimes*, Police Budget Edition, c. 1890.
Sensationalized stories of crime and horror, priced at one
penny each and known as "penny dreadfuls," became
hugely popular in the late nineteenth century.

for a fee, generating huge profits for the most successful
of these, Mudie's Select Library and W.H. Smith and
Son. The triple-decker format was eventually supplanted
by cheap single-volume editions that were sold in
national book chains and at rail stations. Another mode
of publication, one that made the novel a household
word, was the monthly or weekly serial. Monthly
installments of a few chapters, often accompanied by
illustrations and advertisements, were initially published
and purchased in separate parts with paper wrappers,
generally appearing over a period of 19 months. By the
1860s, these serializations were more often appearing in

monthly or weekly literary magazines. Dickens's enormously successful *Pickwick Papers* appeared in installments in 1836–37, launching the serial format as the most important publishing medium for Victorian fiction.[1] Serialization allowed readers with modest incomes to purchase new works when bound volumes were beyond their financial reach, and the regular continuation of a novel over a period of months or years meant that novels and novel reading became woven into the fabric of daily life, mingling with news, opinion, and readers' personal experience. The serialized format also had an influence on the novelistic genre, establishing a particular pace and necessitating "cliff-hangers," ensuring the return of the audience week after week.

POETRY

The novel's predominance and popularity have often meant that the significance of Victorian poetry is overlooked. Victorian poets throughout the century were greatly influenced by poets of the Romantic period, but key departures in form, content, and purpose set the Victorians apart from their predecessors. One of the most important of Victorian innovations was the development of the dramatic monologue, a lyric poem in the voice of a speaker who is not the poet and who occasionally addresses a silent auditor. Although the Victorians did not invent the dramatic monologue, Robert Browning and Alfred Tennyson are typically credited with developing it into a form expressive of psychological complexity. Victorian psychologists were interested in exploring the boundary between sanity and madness, and the possibility of a lucid yet mentally unbalanced narrating persona appealed to Browning and Tennyson, who used the dramatic monologue to expose not only the unstable character of their speakers' passions, but also the social and cultural contexts that either produced or reflected their instability. Browning, in particular, chose a range of unstable, deluded, or even mentally deranged speakers whose self-perception is ironically distanced from the reader's, thus participating

in pre-Freudian ideas about the divided self; perhaps the most famous of these is "My Last Duchess" (1842), which slowly reveals the fate of the speaker's wife. The dramatic monologue was also notably employed by Elizabeth Barrett Browning, D.G. Rossetti, Augusta Webster, Thomas Hardy, Rudyard Kipling, and by many twentieth-century poets.

Many other poetic forms also flourished in the period. Perhaps surprisingly in an "age of realism," epic poems were a feature of the Victorian literary landscape, from Tennyson's *Idylls of the King* to George Eliot's *The Spanish Gypsy* (1868) and William Morris's *The Earthly Paradise* (1868–70). Sonnet sequences too were a popular form, particularly among female poets; notable examples include George Eliot's *Brother and Sister Sonnets* (1869), Christina Rossetti's *Monna Innominata* (1881), Augusta Webster's *Mother and Daughter Sonnets* (1895), and—most popular of all—Elizabeth Barrett Browning's *Sonnets from the Portuguese* (1850), a collection of 44 sonnets chronicling Barrett Browning's courtship with Robert Browning. Through the work of these writers and a host of others—from Felicia Hemans and Letitia Landon at the beginning of the period to Charlotte Mew and Mathilde Blind at its end—the "poetess" became an accepted part of the literary landscape.

The lyric introspection and self-exploration that is the hallmark of much Romantic verse was augmented in both form and content by a Victorian poetry of social engagement that strove to contextualize a speaker's moral and spiritual questions within the vicissitudes of contemporary life. In Tennyson's monologue *Maud* (1855), the tormented speaker's mental deterioration and reawakening are represented as continuous with the effects of industrialization and England's entry into the Crimean War. In Augusta Webster's dramatic monologue *A Castaway* (1870), a high-class prostitute's self-scrutiny illustrates the relationship between political economy and the commodification of female identity, with "coin" as a central metaphor for the connection between the two.

Not all poets accepted the view that poetry should speak to the issues and concerns of the present. In 1853, Matthew Arnold wrote that poets should respond to their world by mining "those elementary feelings which

[1] Long poems and works of non-fiction prose were also sometimes published serially; important examples include Robert Browning's *The Ring and the Book* and Matthew Arnold's *Culture and Anarchy* (serialized in *Cornhill Magazine* in 1867–68).

subsist permanently in the race, and are independent of time." In some of his later poetry, Arnold turned to classical rather than contemporary subjects as a way of rejecting what he saw as the crass materialism and spiritual futility of modern life. Yet for all his melancholia, Arnold did not advocate artistic isolation; whereas many poets of the second half of the century called for the independence of art from the imperative to offer moral instruction, Arnold continued to insist that the aesthetic endeavor necessarily involved ethical responsibility.

In contrast, Swinburne's poetry of sensual experience, his carnal subject matter and verbal pyrotechnics revel in the corporeality of poetry, so much so that he was accused in one famous review of "fleshliness" to the exclusion of "meditation" and "thought."[1] Swinburne's verse was important to the development of Aestheticism, influencing later poets such as Wilde and Symonds, whose poetry tended to emphasize formal beauty, sonic effects, and the momentary over the timeless. Like the Spasmodic poets of the 1840s and 1850s, like Arthur Hugh Clough in the late 1850s and early 1860s, and, at the century's end, like Gerard Manley Hopkins, Swinburne also engaged in many challenging experiments with poetic form and meter, thereby anticipating some of the innovations and deliberate difficulties of modernist writing.

DRAMA

The Victorian period is not remembered for great stage dramas or for penetrating comedies, at least until the last decades of the century. Although Victorian audiences were avid theatergoers, they tended to prefer light-hearted entertainment to more serious fare. Comedies, pantomimes, farces, and musicals attracted audiences from across the social spectrum, but it was melodrama

[1] The charge was made in Robert Buchanan's "The Fleshly School of Poetry," a review essay that first appeared in Volume 18 of *The Contemporary Review* in 1871. The review focused on D.G. Rossetti's *Poems*, citing Swinburne and Morris as other key figures in what Buchanan derisively termed "the Fleshly School," a mode he took to task for its "morbid deviation from the healthy forms of life."

that became the most popular dramatic genre. For most literary critics, melodrama has little or no literary value and is thus easy to dismiss as an aesthetically vacant genre. Yet popular texts can reveal much about a culture because they are so intimately connected with everyday assumptions and values. The melodrama of the Victorian period opens a window onto the nature of power relations within modern market culture and the patriarchal family; sometimes it seems to support, and at other times to contest, these relations. With its sensational plots, stock characters, unadorned language, and a moral economy that unambiguously separates good from evil, melodrama exploited an audience's emotions, and invariably ended on a happy note. (We need look no further than the mass appeal of Hollywood films to begin to understand why stage melodrama was so popular.) Early in the century, melodramas often featured Gothic plots, settings, and characters, but the vogue for such subject matter gave way in the Victorian period to storylines centered on workaday conflicts in familiar settings, such as factories, cottages, and manor houses.

The most prolific and successful writer and adapter of melodramas was Dion Boucicault; his 1852 play *The Corsican Brothers* was such a hit with Queen Victoria that she saw it five times. Tom Taylor's popular *The Ticket-of-Leave Man* (1863) was set in recognizable London locations and featured a sleuth named Jack Hawksure who became a prototype for later stage detectives. Many popular novels, including works by Dickens, Collins, and Braddon, were adapted or pirated for the stage soon after they had been published. Ellen Price Wood's *East Lynne* (1861), a novel with a fallen woman theme, was adapted into several stage versions on the basis of its enormous success as one of the earliest sensation novels.

In 1881, theater impresario Richard D'Oyly Carte opened the Savoy Theatre in London for the express purpose of staging the comic operettas of W.S. Gilbert and Arthur Sullivan, whose collaboration had begun in 1875. Their most popular plays, such as *H.M.S. Pinafore* (1878), *The Mikado* (1885), and *Patience* (1881), are still regularly staged today. Gilbert's storylines and lyrics combined frivolous romance with witty and genial mockery of certain contemporary values,[1] as well as of the formulaic nature of most London stage fare; Sullivan's alternately lilting and bouncy melodies proved irresistible, and "Gilbert and Sullivan" rapidly became a popular phenomenon. The Savoy Operas, as they came to be known, anticipated the new directions in British theater of the 1890s, epitomized in the comic plays of Oscar Wilde and the "problem plays" of George Bernard Shaw; both Wilde and Shaw offered serious critiques of their society while dazzling their audiences with their audacious wit, brilliant dialogue, and shocking candor.

Prose Non-Fiction and Print Culture

Victorian writers of essays, criticism, history, and biography fully embraced the role of the public intellectual, whose particular mission was to instruct and edify readers about the day's key issues. Virtually no subject remained untouched: writers of non-fiction prose, also known as "sages," probed everything, from the latest scientific developments to religious controversies, from political and economic questions to gender issues, from aesthetic developments to social values and mores. In an age of growing religious skepticism, readers looked to their "sages" as latter-day prophets and interpreters who were uniquely qualified to offer an almost divinely inspired wisdom. This role of the secular cleric emerged along with the rise of the professional writer, or "man of letters," who could earn a comfortable living by the pen and maintain a level of gentlemanly respectability. Carlyle, Arnold, Ruskin, Mill, Newman, Pater, and Wilde produced some of the most influential cultural criticism of the age, using a variety of rhetorical techniques, verbal styles, and literary forms.

For female writers, the decision to offer social and cultural critique often came at a price, since women were discouraged from involvement in—and even knowledge

"A Gaiety Girl," Music Hall poster, 1893.

of—political issues. Writers such as Frances Power Cobbe, Florence Nightingale, Harriet Martineau, Caroline Norton, George Eliot, and Harriet Taylor Mill exploited a variety of "voices"—some gendered "male"—in their critiques of the role of women in Victorian society, as well as in their writing on a variety of other topics, from political commentary to literary criticism.

---

[1] *Patience*, for example, satirized Aestheticism, prominently featuring a character known as Bunthorne, an aesthete poet. Though some critics have identified Oscar Wilde as the model for Bunthorne, Wilde's relative obscurity at the time of the operetta's composition suggests that the character is more likely a representation of then-better-known poets such as Swinburne and D.G. Rossetti.

What united most of these writers, male and female, was their simultaneous position as societal outsiders and insiders: in a range of rhetorical styles, from prophetic to disinterested, prose writers typically argued from a marginal position under the assumption that their particular viewpoint had been abandoned or would be resisted by their readers. Yet it was precisely this outsider perspective that guaranteed the sage's unique authority within a society hungry for moral guidance by a voice from "beyond."

The opening of the Manchester Free Library, 1852. In 1845, local governments were given the authority to raise tax revenues to support the establishment of public libraries and museums. Free public libraries were distinguished from fee-charging circulating libraries such as Mudie's and W.H. Smith's.

For every writer or sage celebrated by his or her reading public as a visionary, there were countless, often nameless "hack" writers who also contributed non-fiction prose, or, more properly, journalism, to newspapers and periodicals. Indeed, the periodical and newspaper press afforded both the sages and the hacks, novelists, and poets a space to disseminate their work and reach ever-expanding audiences. In Wilkie Collins's

words, it was "the age of periodicals." Early in the century, prominent literary journals such as the *Edinburgh Review*, *Blackwood's Magazine*, the *Quarterly Review*, *Fraser's Magazine*, and the *Athenaeum* attracted the most eminent writers. In the early Victorian era, writers in these journals generally published anonymously or under a pseudonym, no matter how distinguished they might be; not until the latter half of the century did signatures gradually begin to replace anonymity in many of the periodicals. Throughout the period, the number of periodicals steadily increased, until there was a magazine for every taste, every income level, every hobby group, every political and religious organization. Domestic magazines aimed at female readers, children's magazines, satirical or humor magazines, and monthly and quarterly miscellanies publishing fiction, poetry, criticism, and news all competed with each other for readers' interest, loyalty, and purchasing power in an increasingly diverse literary marketplace. Nearly all of the best-known literary writers across the genres saw their work published in magazines and newspapers: Barrett Browning's "The Cry of the Children" (1843) in *Blackwood's*, Dickens's *Oliver Twist* in *Bentley's Miscellany*, Arnold's *Culture and Anarchy* in the *Cornhill Magazine*, Yonge's *The Clever Woman of the Family* (1865) in the *Churchman's Family Magazine*.

The periodical press was also instrumental in the development of modern literary criticism. Book reviews in influential periodicals, such as the *Athenaeum*, could make or break a writer's reputation; prominent literary reviewers—some of whom, such as Henry James, were also celebrated authors in their own right—both forged a professional identity for themselves as literary critics and formulated principles of literary analysis that are today's tools of the trade.

Victorians were, in general, fascinated with characterizing their "age": Carlyle's "Signs of the Times," Mill's "Spirit of the Age," and Eliza Lynn Linton's "Girl of the Period" became popular catchphrases that signaled a self-conscious awareness of a society in transition. It was the "age of steam," the "age of doubt," and, perhaps most notably for students of literature, the "age of reading." Reading, like many other social institutions and cultural practices, gradually became democratized during Victoria's reign. The 1870 Education Act instituted compulsory elementary education in England and Wales for the first time; adult literacy was nearly universal by century's end. Readers were everywhere: in pubs, on trains, around the family hearth, at gentlemen's clubs, and in reading rooms.[1] The single reader—particularly the female reader—was a common subject for Victorian painters. Reading aloud was also a popular pastime; it was common for middle-class fathers to gather together their dependents, including the servants, at the end of the day or week to read edifying family literature, such as sermons, tracts, and didactic fiction. Drawing on his background in the London theater, Dickens delivered public readings of his novels that attracted huge crowds and increased sales of his books. His performance of Little Nell's death scene famously left audiences weeping.

The explosion of reading and reading cultures in Victorian England went hand in hand with new print technologies, the removal of prohibitive taxes on reading material, the ease of distribution made possible through the rail system, the rise of cheap, mass-produced print, and political, economic, and social reforms that affected people at all levels of their existence. At the beginning of the century, mass literacy was regarded as a recipe for political revolution. From at least the middle of the century onwards, some worried that reading was becoming too popular, that it was a kind of "mania" or "disease" that "consumed" people. Critics such as Matthew Arnold argued that the newly literate but untutored masses lacked the necessary skills to distinguish between the timeless and the trashy, signaling the demise of English culture. Yet there were also those who argued that literacy was a human right, and it was ultimately this viewpoint that prevailed. In 1840, Carlyle wrote, "Books are written by martyr-men, not for rich men alone but for all men. If we consider it, every human being has, by the nature of the case, a *right* to hear what other wise human beings have spoken to him. It is one of the Rights of Men; a very cruel injustice if you deny it to a man." The history of reading—the history of what and how different people read, the expectations that existed about what women and men should read, both in their leisure time and professionally—is ultimately inseparable from the history of the Victorian period.

THE ENGLISH LANGUAGE IN THE VICTORIAN ERA

The English vocabulary continued to expand throughout the period. New words entered the language to name aspects of the changing world of work (*trade-union* is recorded as first having entered the language in 1831, for example; *margin*, used with reference to profit to mean "amount of money available once certain costs are covered," in the 1850s). New words were also needed to name aspects of human nature that were being seen in new ways or acknowledged for the first time (*personality*, used in the modern sense of "distinctive personal identity," in 1835; *sadism* in 1888; *homosexual* in 1892). New words were coined to name new religious movements (such as *evangelicanism*, *disestablishmentarianism*, and its famously long opposite *antidisestablishmentarianism*) and to name new developments in the culture of sports (*caddie* is first recorded in 1857). Less innocuously, new ways kept springing up to express old prejudices; *jew* is first recorded as being used derogatively as a transitive verb in 1845.

The coining of new words from Latin and Greek roots—especially new scientific terms—continued at a quickened pace, from *lithograph* and *locomotive*, to *photograph* and *phonograph*, to *telegraph*, *telephone*, and *dictaphone*. Far fewer new words were entering English from French, however; the flow of new words from French into English,[2] which had continued in the second half of the eighteenth century and the early years of the nineteenth at about the same pace as it had been a century earlier, slowed to a trickle in the Victorian era; it was far more characteristic of the eighteenth-century English to turn to the French for *etiquette* (1750) than it was for Victorians to turn to the French for *élan* (1880).

---

[1]   Private libraries where readers could pay an annual fee for access to current newspapers and the latest books and periodicals.

[2]   The importation of French words into English, often thought of as beginning with the Norman conquest in 1066, in fact did not occur with any great frequency until roughly a century later; the flow reached its peak in the late fourteenth century.

The Western Electric multiple telephone switchboard, the Royal Exchange, Manchester, 1888. The spread of English as the leading language of communication world-wide was aided by the invention of the telegraph in 1837, and of the telephone later in the century.

The expansion of English in the nineteenth century was not restricted to new noun coinages. A lively feature of the growth of the language during this period was an expansion in the use of verb-adverb combinations (e.g., *bring up, hold up, let up, pass up, shut up*—to name only a few of those involving *up*). With the spread of such coinages (as well as of an ever-growing number of slang expressions) into the written language came a gradual reduction in the level of formality of standard English.

A reduction in dialect differences and in range of variation in English pronunciation had begun centuries earlier, with the imposition of English authority over Wales, Scotland, and Ireland; no doubt it was influenced, too, by the inherently stabilizing effects of print culture following the introduction of the printing press to England in the late fifteenth century. This trend toward greater standardization of vocabulary and of pronunciation continued through the nineteenth century. The spread of standardized pronunciation in particular was assisted by the growing influence of the elite boarding schools (known as "public schools") as the preferred sites of education for the privileged classes and for those who aspired to join them. Increasingly, in the late-Victorian period, girls as well as boys were sent to such schools; boarding schools such as St. Andrews (1877) and Roedean (1885) were the first institutions

for girls that paralleled centuries' old boys' schools such as Eton, Harrow, and Rugby.

Perhaps the greatest development relating to the history of the English language in the Victorian period was the initiation of a dictionary "on historical principles"—one that would record not only the various different meanings of words, but also how they had changed over time, and precisely when each meaning was first recorded in surviving written English. *The Oxford English Dictionary*, which was to be among the most ambitious of projects in an age of famously ambitious projects, had its origins in the work of the Philological Society, founded in 1842. In 1858, following the lead of a similar project initiated in Germany[1] and following years of discussion, the society issued a formal "Proposal for the Publication of a New Dictionary by the Philological Society." The society would invite volunteers to assist in sending in records they found of early or significant uses of words; eventually some six million slips with quotations written on them were submitted. By 1879, the Philological Society concluded that the project was so vast that it would not be able to complete it on its own, entering into an agreement with the Oxford University Press. Even with this assistance, it was not until 1884 that it proved possible to publish a volume covering one part of the letter *A*. By 1900, only four and one-half volumes had been published, and it was not until 1928 that a complete version of the full dictionary was available. (By then, of course, much of the early work was outdated; a second edition was published in 1989, and the *OED* is now continually being updated online.)

A less successful Victorian initiative was a multi-faceted campaign to rationalize spelling—a campaign that extended in one form or another through almost the entire period; the prevalence of spellings that bear no relation to phonetic principles increasingly came to be criticized as antiquated and illogical.[2] In the early

[1] The *Deutsches Wörterbuch* was begun by the classicist Franz Passow and the philologists (and compilers of fairy tales) Jacob and Wilhelm Grimm.

[2] As a late-Victorian spelling reformer pointed out, the ways in which English words are spelled often bear so little connection to pronunciation that it would be possible to spell *fish* as *ghoti*, with the *gh* pronounced as we do the *gh* in *cough*; the *o* pronounced as we do the *o* in *women*; and the *ti* pronounced as we do the *ti* in *nation*. This

John Everett Millais, *Ophelia*, 1851–52. The drowning of Ophelia (from Shakespeare's *Hamlet*) was a frequent subject in nineteenth-century painting; the best known representation is that of Millais. As the scene is described in Act 4, Scene 7 of the play, the mentally ill Ophelia comes to a stream "with fantastic garlands" of flowers. Distracted, she falls into the "weeping brook." For a while before she drowns, "her clothes spread wide" and hold her up.

Henry Wallis, *Chatterton*, 1856. The suicide of Thomas Chatterton (1752–70), who died of arsenic poisoning after years of living close to starvation as a struggling poet, captured the imaginations of both Romantics and Victorians. Wallis's painting was widely praised when exhibited in 1856 at the Royal Academy; John Ruskin described it in his notes on the exhibit as "faultless and wonderful."

Thomas Jones Barker, *The Secret of England's Greatness* (detail), c. 1863. Barker's painting depicts the Queen presenting a Bible. The recipient and the specific occasion remain unidentified; in the background are Elizabeth, Duchess of Wellington (who served as Mistress of the Robes to the Queen); Prince Albert; Lord Palmerston (then serving as Prime Minister); and Lord John Russell (then serving as Foreign Secretary). An engraving of the painting was published under the fuller title, *The Bible: The Secret of England's Greatness*.

Franz Xavier Winterhalter, *The Royal Family in 1846* (detail), 1846.

Ford Madox Brown, *Work*, c. 1852–c. 1865. This famous painting (above), which took over twelve years to complete, brings together Victorians from an extraordinary range of backgrounds. The central group of excavators was the painting's starting point—the inspiration coming from the artist observing work on the construction of the London sewers. Less well-off members of society include the flower seller to the left and the motherless children in the foreground, cared for by an older sibling. To the right are two "brain-workers" admired by the artist, Rev. F.D. Maurice (founder of the Working Man's College, where Brown was an art instructor) and Thomas Carlyle. In the background, members of the gentry on horseback observe the scene.

George Clausen,
The Stone Pickers, 1887.

William Holman Hunt, *The Awakening Conscience*, 1853–54. This canvas presents an elaborately coded story. In a letter to *The Times* of London, John Ruskin (signing himself as "The Author of Modern Painters") described the reaction of viewers—and elucidated the painting's intended significance: "… assuredly it is not understood. People gaze at it in a blank wonder, and leave it hopelessly; so that, although it is almost an insult to the painter to explain his thoughts in this instance, I cannot persuade myself to leave it thus misunderstood. The poor girl has been singing with her seducer; some chance words of the song "Oft in the stilly night" have struck upon the numbed places of her heart; she has started up in agony; he, not seeing her face, goes on singing, striking the keys carelessly with his gloved hand." As Ruskin discerned, the woman is evidently the mistress rather than the wife of the man; she wears a ring on every finger of her left hand except the fourth. The piece that has been played, "Oft in the stilly night," is a song in which a woman looks back to the innocence of her childhood. The doubling of the female figure through the use of the mirror suggests the possibility of a brighter future if she follows her awakened conscience and gives up the life of a "kept woman."

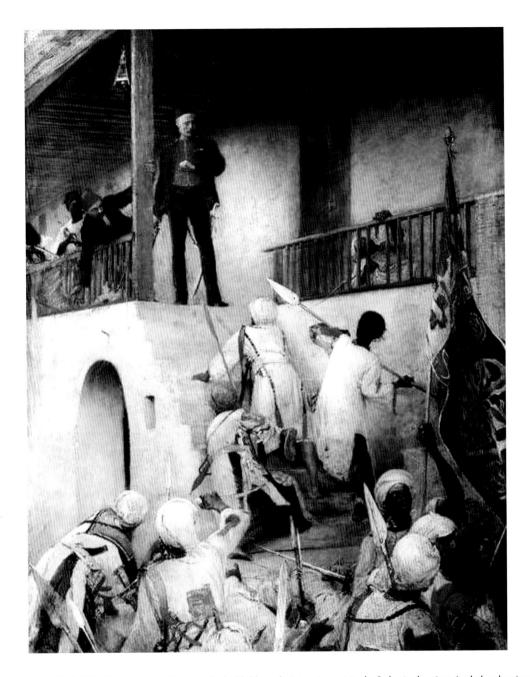

G.W. Joy, *General Gordon's Last Stand*, c. 1893. Gordon, who had held an administrative post in the Sudan in the 1870s (and played an important role during that period in ending the slave trade in the area), was sent again to the Sudan in 1884 on a mission to rescue garrisons of British troops that had been cut off after a rebellion by Mohammed Ahmad (known to the British as "the Mahdi"). Gordon's forces were besieged in Khartoum for ten months and finally overwhelmed, and he was killed during the battle (though almost certainly in the streets of the city, not as he is shown in Joy's iconic painting of the imagined scene). The incident became a *cause célèbre* in Britain, and there were many calls to avenge Gordon's death, but it was not until fourteen years later that the British under General Kitchener re-established British control of the Sudan.

Trade Emblem, Amalgamated Society of Engineers, Machinists, Millwrights, Smiths, and Pattern Makers, c. 1860.

Alfred Concanen, *Modern Advertising: A Railway Station in 1874*, 1874. This colored lithograph appeared as a fold-out frontispiece in the book *A History of Advertising from the Earliest Times*.

John O'Connor, *From Pentonville Road Looking West*, 1884. In the background is St. Pancras, one of the greatest of Victorian railway stations.

Advertisement, 1890s, "Cook's Tours in Scotland." Featured at lower left is the Firth of Forth Bridge (also known as the Forth Rail Bridge). The bridge, built in the wake of the collapse of the Firth of Tay Bridge, in which 75 lives had been lost, pioneered new techniques of cantilever construction; on its completion in 1890 it was by far the longest bridge in the world.

Benjamin Duterrau, *The Conciliation*, 1840. The painting shows a Methodist lay preacher instructing native Tasmanians.

THE OLD FLAG.
THE OLD POLICY.
THE OLD LEADER.

Canadian election poster, 1891. The "Old Leader" was Sir John A. Macdonald, Canadian Prime Minister from 1867 to 1873 and again from 1878 to 1891. "The Old Policy" was Macdonald's National Policy, under the terms of which industries in the Dominion would be protected by a tariff on imports from the United States, but "imperial preference" exempted goods from Britain and her possessions from any tariff.

Emma Brownlow, *The Foundling Restored to Its Mother—An Incident in the Foundling Hospital*, 1858. Foundlings—deserted or abandoned children—were a frequent subject, both in Victorian literature and in the visual arts. The young girl portrayed here was indeed reclaimed soon after Brownlow had painted the picture. Most Victorian-era foundlings (like most orphans) were not so fortunate; they usually ended up not in the Foundling Hospital but in one of the workhouses established under the provisions of the 1834 Poor Law Amendment Act. Brownlow was herself raised in the Foundling Hospital—though not as a foundling; her father held a live-in position as administrator of the Thomas Coram Foundling Hospital.

(above) James Tissot, *Too Early*, 1873. The French painter Jacques-Joseph Tissot moved from Paris to London after being active in the 1871 Paris Commune; he took the Anglicized first name of James, and became both a popular and a highly regarded artist in his adopted home. Over the eleven years until his return to Paris in 1882 he painted many portraits, as well as many canvases depicting social interactions—often suggestive of a narrative. His narrative paintings include scenes of city streets, of harbor life, of garden parties, and of fashionable young women in a variety of sometimes surprising settings. Often dismissed in the twentieth century as a sentimentalist, Tissot is increasingly becoming recognized as an artist who provides a unique window into English social life in the 1870s and early 1880s.

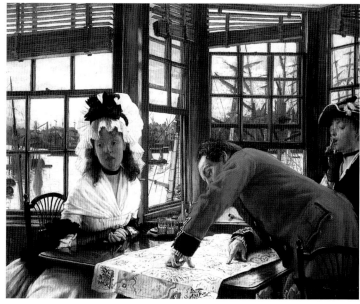

(below) James Tissot, *An Interesting Story*, c. 1872. Of note: Tissot painted a very similar scene from a different angle, and gave it the title *A Tedious History*.

Joseph Nash, *The Great Industrial Exhibition of 1851: The Transept*, 1851. Nash's lithograph, from "his drawing in the possession of Her Majesty," was one of a series. The view was described as follows in the official catalogue: "the whole extent of the transept, interrupted only by the magnificent glass fountain of Messrs. Osler, and the groups of sculpture and tropical plants and trees, ... flashes on the eye more like the fabled palace of Vathek than a structure reared in a few months by mortal hands." (For more on the Crystal Palace see the Contexts section on "Britain, Empire, and a Wider World.")

Franz Xaver Winterhalter, *The First of May, 1851*, 1851. The first of May, 1851 was the opening day of the Great Exhibition at the Crystal Palace; it was also the first birthday of the Queen's third son, Prince Arthur, and the eighty-second birthday of the Duke of Wellington; the "Iron Duke" is here shown presenting a gold casket decorated with jewels to mother and child (who is holding a sprig of lily of the valley). The scene in numerous respects follows traditional Christian iconography; Prince Albert stands behind the Queen, in the position occupied by Joseph in many depictions of Mary and her newborn son.

(For more on the Great Exhibition see the introduction to this volume and the Contexts section, "Britain, Empire, and a Wider World.")

years of the Victorian era, interest in such matters was spurred by the introduction of Isaac Pitman's system of shorthand, with Pitman himself acting as a leading advocate for reform. By the 1850s, the Bible and a number of works were available in phonetic spelling versions, and by the end of the following decade, the Philological Society was taking an active role in airing all sides of the debate. Its American counterpart adopted a less impartial stance, calling in particular for the adoption of simplified phonetic spellings of words such as *tho*, *altho*, and *thruout*. Of their list only two—*program* and *catalog*—became generally adopted in the United States. In Britain resistance to such Americanisms carried the day—and in both countries, the campaign to rationalize spelling faltered by century's end in the face of a growing recognition of the degree to which English had become a written as well as a spoken language, with words comprehended very largely through the appearance on paper of the entire written word.

Resistance to Americanisms generally was felt not only in Britain herself, but also—indeed, perhaps even more strongly—in English Canada, in its unique position as staunchly British by history and by disposition but unavoidably "American" in the geographical sense. Complaints, such as those of a contributor to the *Canadian Journal* in 1857 against words and expressions "imported by travellers, daily circulated by American newspapers, and eagerly incorporated into the language of our Provincial press," were far from uncommon. Words such as *travellers* (in its British spelling; *travelers* according to common practice in the United States) themselves became points of contention. As the American spellings of such words—introduced by Noah Webster in his dictionary in 1825—became entrenched in the United States, Canadians began to develop a hybrid somewhere in between British and American spellings.

Conventions for marking direct speech and quoted material finally stabilized in the Victorian period in something close to their current form, though with what are now established differences between American and British conventions of punctuation still unsettled. Quotation marks themselves are a relatively recent invention; they became widely used only in the eighteenth century. Even in the late eighteenth century a number of different indicators for quoted material were still being used, the most common of which was to include quotation marks not only at the beginning of the quoted passage, but also at the beginning of each subsequent line for as long as the quotation extended. In the early Victorian period, it had become conventional to mark quotations with only an open quotation mark at the beginning of a passage and a closed quotation mark at the end—though it remained acceptable to use either single or double quotation marks.

The period also saw significant changes in the evolution of the paragraph as a primary means of signaling the shape of ideas in prose. The paragraph was originally simply a short horizontal marker added beneath a line in which a break in meaning occurred; in the sixteenth century, it became conventional to mark such shifts by setting off blocks of text through indentation at the beginning of each block. Until the late eighteenth century, however, paragraphs of English prose were often extremely long by modern standards, and one paragraph of expository or argumentative prose might hold a large number of only loosely related ideas. Even in the Romantic era, a paragraph might often run to a page or more. Through the nineteenth century, however, paragraphs gradually but steadily became shorter, and the principle of restricting each paragraph to a set of closely related ideas became much more widely followed.

---

now-famous example is thought to have been first given common currency by Bernard Shaw (who later became a crusader for spelling reform).

HISTORY OF THE LANGUAGE AND OF PRINT CULTURE

In an effort to provide for readers a direct sense of the development of the language and of print culture, examples of texts in their original form (and of illustrations) have been provided in each volume. A list of these within the present volume appears below, arranged in chronological order. Overviews of "prose non-fiction and print culture" and of developments in the history of language during this period appear on pages 539–41.

Gerard Manley Hopkins and Robert Bridges, manuscript versions of "The Windhover," pp. 907–07.

Sidney Paget, illustrations to Sir Arthur Conan Doyle, "The Adventure of the Speckled Band," *The Strand* magazine, pp. 970 ff.

THOMAS CARLYLE
1795 – 1881

Reviewing a book of selections from Thomas Carlyle's writings in 1855, George Eliot evaluated Carlyle's influence on his contemporaries: "There is hardly a superior or active mind of this generation that has not been modified by Carlyle's writings; there has hardly been an English book written for the last ten or twelve years that would not have been different if Carlyle had not lived. The character of his influence is best seen in the fact that many of the men who have the least agreement with his opinions are those to whom the reading of *Sartor Resartus* was an epoch in the history of their minds."

This evaluation stands as essentially correct. Whether it was Charles Dickens or John Ruskin, Robert Browning or William Morris, Matthew Arnold or George Eliot herself, Carlyle's thought and work affected the thinking and perspectives of those around him as few other writers did. This Victorian "sage" who was to become fluent in seven languages and count Johann Wolfgang von Goethe, J.S. Mill, Ralph Waldo Emerson, Alfred Lord Tennyson, Dickens, and Browning among his friends, had very humble beginnings in the village of Ecclefechan, Scotland. Born in 1795, the eldest child of a poor, strict, Calvinist stonemason and a working class, uneducated mother, the young Carlyle showed early promise, and his parents were determined to give their son an education befitting his bright mind. At the age of 14, having attended local schools since he was five, Carlyle walked the nearly 100 miles from his home to enroll in a program at the University of Edinburgh, where he studied mathematics and prepared to enter the ministry. During his years at the University, however, his faith in God was challenged by his studies of skeptics such as David Hume, François-Marie Arouet de Voltaire, and Edward Gibbon. He left Edinburgh at age 19 without attaining a degree, and for some years he taught mathematics at Annan Academy.

He also continued what he began at Edinburgh, his life-long reading and study of German writers, whose work he was to introduce to English readers. In 1823 Carlyle completed a biography of the German poet Schiller, which was published serially in *The London Magazine*; his second publication was a translation of Goethe's *Wilhelm Meister* (1824). In 1827 he published an essay on Jean Paul Richter in the influential *Edinburgh Review*. This sign of recognition was repeated in 1829, when he published his "Signs of the Times" in the *Review*, the first of his essays that focused on the social problems of nineteenth-century England and its "Age of Machinery." With "Signs" and "Characteristics" (1831), the voice of the great social prophet of England emerged. Carlyle's importance increased with the publication of the semiautobiographical *Sartor Resartus* (1833–34), an unconventional and widely influential work.

It is in this period, as well, that Carlyle met and married Jane Baillie Welsh, the brilliant, articulate, talented daughter of a prosperous surgeon. She was well-placed to select from amongst many suitors; why she chose a coarse man from a working-class background was a mystery to her friends and a source of sorrow for her mother. Although their arguments were legendary, their union in 1826 was a true meeting of minds, Carlyle's creative genius and ambition matching Welsh's intellect and drive. In 1834, they moved to London, to a home in Cheyne Row in Chelsea, where

Carlyle began the long career of writing that was to make him the voice of his contemporaries, and where Jane Carlyle continued writing the letters that are amongst the most brilliant of all portraits of nineteenth-century London life.

Carlyle's work shows clearly and urgently the writer's confrontation with the age's dual heritage of religion and Romanticism, of tradition and the "march of mind." Born in a Scottish-Calvinist home in the same year as Keats, Carlyle discovered early in his reading of Gibbon and the Germans that the "old theorem" by which his own father had lived had "passed away," its "immaterialism, mysterious, divine though invisible character" banished by Locke and the mechanical world of the eighteenth century. For Carlyle, claiming that the Bible was factual truth "flatly contradicted all human science and experience." Yet he also believed that the Romantics' response to the passing of the "old beliefs"—the effort he saw in the early Goethe to form "his world out of himself"—led to despair and solipsism. Carlyle's celebration of Goethe's spiritual progress from narcissistic self-focus to a capacious view of man's role in a larger world became one of the main themes of his early work. This estimation was to become one of Carlyle's signature lines: "Close thy Byron, Open thy Goethe," commands Diogenes Teufelsdröckh, the questing protagonist of *Sartor Resartus*.

Carlyle began to achieve great fame with the publication of *The French Revolution* in 1836. His style resembled that of no other historian: highly metaphoric language, sentences that seemed "barbarous" because of their German-inflected structures and jarring syntax, the use of the present tense, representations of men and women so vivid that they seemed like characters from a novel. Carlyle used this style to articulate a sweeping view of history as a continual mingling of past and present and as the unfolding of a divine will.

In *The French Revolution*, Carlyle sees Revolutionary France as a warning to England in the 1830s. He structures the drama of France's Revolution as he had the drama of Teufelsdröckh's life, around the questions forced upon individuals or nations when they lose sight of moral and social accountability. Carlyle sees in France's materialism and its leaders' sense of the life as a "Thespian stage" an emptying of meaning out of all symbols; in this world, proclaiming ideas of Brotherhood—of liberty, equality, fraternity—"will the sooner and the more surely lead to Cannibalism" and a "Brotherhood of Cain."

This exploration of the "Brotherhood of Cain" and how it comes to be the belief of a nation governs Carlyle's greatest social writing, *Past and Present*. By juxtaposing the medieval past of England, with its monks and serfs living in an organic community focused around a monastery, and the industrialism and *laissez-faire* economics of England's present that had produced poverty and starvation, Carlyle created a remarkable picture of the desperate social crises of the hungry forties. The book begins in prison and ends with a vision of a "green flowery world." The landscape between these points is equally polarized: the "formed" world of Abbot Samson and the "enchanted," demonic, "inorganic" world of the industrial present where no one will be his brother's keeper—or his brother's brother—because all have become Cains. This latter-day England is populated by a group of vividly realized demons escaped out of Bunyan and the daily newspapers: Pandarus Dogdraught, Bobus of Houndsditch, Plugson of Undershot (a captain of industry), Sir Jabesh Windbag, the amphibious Pope, and the Dead Sea Apes (who believe that soul and stomach are synonymous). Carlyle does not idealize the medieval world of Abbot Samson; he exonerates his hero from what he sees as the "spiritual rubbish" that characterizes religious exercises then and in Carlyle's own time. In Samson's work, Carlyle finds genuine redemption: "*Laborare est Orare* ... true Work is Worship ... a making of Madness Sane." *Past and Present* constitutes one of the century's great denunciations of the "Gospel of Enlightened Selfishness" that Carlyle and others saw as reducing the connections between human beings to those of a "cash nexus."

In 1840 Carlyle gave, and then published, a series of lectures, *On Heroes and Hero-Worship*. Here again he sets out his religious ideas, finding value in the Norse god Odin and in Mohammad because they understood the divine will at work in the universe (as did Martin Luther, Robert Burns, Samuel Johnson, Oliver Cromwell, and Napoleon). Each man in this unlikely collection of heroes apprehends the workings of the divine and can lead humankind out of darkness—if human beings will listen.

For many readers, Carlyle's exaltation of authority has represented a danger. Certainly this strong-man theme became predominant in his later work, in which he turned towards conservativism and authoritarianism. *The Letters and Speeches of Oliver Cromwell* (1845) and *The History of Friedrich II of Prussia, Called Frederick the Great*, published between 1858 and 1865, furthered Carlyle's doctrine of hero-worship and his principles of order. He strongly opposed the enfranchisement of women and just as vehemently supported the enslavement of black people in the West Indies. (Carlyle's 1849 essay on this topic ended his friendship with Mill, who wrote a spirited reply.) His 1850 publication of *Latter-Day Pamphlet*s, with its corrosively satirical attacks on democracy and its representatives, is an extraordinarily splenetic outburst from a voice that had once challenged England to discover the godlike connections amongst all human beings.

Carlyle remained influential; Charles Dickens, John Ruskin, and Robert Browning all dedicated books to him. In 1874 he turned down a baronetcy offered by British Prime Minister Disraeli; he did, however, accept the Prussian Order of Merit in the same year. After his wife's death in 1866, he wrote little, though he did edit his wife's remarkable letters, *The Letters and Memorials of Jane Welsh Carlyle*, which were published after his death. Carlyle had earlier stated his aversion to the idea of being buried in Westminster Abbey; he was buried in 1881 beside his parents in Ecclefechan, Scotland. George Eliot's estimation of Carlyle is an apt epitaph: "When he is saying the opposite of what we think, he says it so finely, with so hearty conviction—he makes the object about which we differ stand out in such grand relief under the clear light of his strong and honest intellect—he appeals so constantly to our sense of the manly and the truthful—that we are obliged to say 'Hear! Hear!' to the writer before we can give the decorous 'Oh! Oh!' to his opinions."

⌘ ⌘ ⌘

from *Past and Present*[1]

from BOOK 1
CHAPTER 1—MIDAS[2]

[1] *Past and Present*　Carlyle wrote this treatise in seven weeks, in response to the lack of order and leadership that he felt was contributing to the widespread social and economic difficulties England was experiencing at that time. Carlyle blamed both the complacent aristocracy, which sought to maintain the status quo, and the spread of democracy, which he felt did little to provide heroic leaders. In 1837, industry in England entered into a depression that lasted several years. Many factories closed and others were forced to cut wages, which led to rioting in the manufacturing districts. By 1845, approximately one-twelfth of the population was unemployed, and many people ended up in overcrowded poorhouses. When the Chartists organized peaceful protests for social and economic reform, many British citizens began to fear a full-scale revolution.

[2] *MIDAS*　Fabled king of Phrygia who, in one myth, was granted his wish that everything he touched would turn to gold. As a result, he was unable to eat. In another myth, he judges the music of the woodland god Pan to be superior to that of Apollo, god of music.

The condition of England, on which many pamphlets are now in the course of publication, and many thoughts unpublished are going on in every reflective head, is justly regarded as one of the most ominous, and withal one of the strangest, ever seen in this world. England is full of wealth, of multifarious produce, supply for human want in every kind; yet England is dying of inanition. With unabated bounty the land of England blooms and grows; waving with yellow harvests; thick-studded with workshops, industrial implements, with fifteen millions of workers, understood to be the strongest, the cunningest and the willingest our Earth ever had; these men are here; the work they have done, the fruit they have realised is here, abundant, exuberant on every hand of us: and behold, some baleful fiat as of Enchantment has gone forth, saying, "Touch it not, ye workers, ye master-workers, ye master-idlers; none of you can touch it, no man of you

Apollo, offended, changes Midas's ears to those of a donkey.

shall be the better for it; this is enchanted fruit!" On the poor workers such fiat[1] falls first, in its rudest shape; but on the rich master-workers too it falls; neither can the rich master-idlers, nor any richest or highest man escape, but all are like to be brought low with it, and made "poor" enough, in the money sense or a far fataler one.

Of these successful skilful workers some two millions, it is now counted, sit in Workhouses, Poor-law Prisons; or have "out-door relief"[2] flung over the wall to them—the workhouse Bastille[3] being filled to bursting, and the strong Poor-law broken asunder by a stronger. They sit there, these many months now; their hope of deliverance as yet small. In workhouses, pleasantly so-named, because work cannot be done in them. Twelve-hundred-thousand workers in England alone; their cunning right-hand lamed, lying idle in their sorrowful bosom; their hopes, outlooks, share of this fair world, shut-in by narrow walls. They sit there, pent up, as in a kind of horrid enchantment; glad to be imprisoned and enchanted, that they may not perish starved. The picturesque Tourist, in a sunny autumn day, through this bounteous realm of England, descries the Union Workhouse on his path. "Passing by the Workhouse of St. Ives in Huntingdonshire, on a bright day last autumn," says the picturesque Tourist, "I saw sitting on wooden benches, in front of their Bastille and within their ring-wall and its railings, some half-hundred or more of these men. Tall robust figures, young mostly or of middle age; of honest countenance, many of them thoughtful and even intelligent-looking men. They sat there, near by one another; but in a kind of torpor, especially in a silence, which was very striking. In silence: for, alas, what word was to be said? An Earth all lying round, crying, Come and till me, come and reap

me—yet we here sit enchanted! In the eyes and brows of these men hung the gloomiest expression, not of anger, but of grief and shame and manifold inarticulate distress and weariness; they returned my glance with a glance that seemed to say, 'Do not look at us. We sit enchanted here, we know not why. The Sun shines and the Earth calls; and, by the governing Powers and Impotences of this England, we are forbidden to obey. It is impossible, they tell us!' There was something that reminded me of Dante's Hell[4] in the look of all this; and I rode swiftly away."

So many hundred thousands sit in workhouses, and other hundred thousands have not yet got even workhouses; and in thrifty Scotland itself, in Glasgow or Edinburgh City, in their dark lanes, hidden from all but the eye of God, and of rare Benevolence, the minister of God, there are scenes of woe and destitution and desolation, such, as, one may hope, the Sun never saw before in the most barbarous regions where men dwelt. Competent witnesses, the brave and humane Dr. Alison,[5] who speaks what he knows, whose noble Healing Art in his charitable hands becomes once more a truly sacred one, report these things for us. These things are not of this year, or of last year, have no reference to our present state of commercial stagnation, but only to the common state. Not in sharp fever-fits, but in chronic gangrene of this kind is Scotland suffering. A Poor-law, any and every Poor-law, it may be observed, is but a temporary measure; an anodyne, not a remedy. Rich and Poor, when once the naked facts of their condition have come into collision, cannot long subsist together on a mere Poor-law. True enough—and yet, human beings cannot be left to die! Scotland too, till something better come, must have a Poor-law, if Scotland is not to be a byword among the nations. O what a waste is there; of noble and thrice-noble national virtues; peasant Stoicisms, Heroisms; valiant manful habits, soul of a Nation's worth, which all the metal of Potosi[6] cannot purchase back; to which the metal of Potosi, and all you can buy with *it*, is dross and dust!

---

[1] *fiat* Order.

[2] *Workhouses* Established under the Poor Law Amendment Act of 1834 for the relief of the poor. They were designed to be as unpleasant as possible, in order to discourage people from entering them. Living conditions were poor, the work provided was equivalent to prison labor, and families were separated upon entering, with men and women lodged separately; *out-door relief* System, in place prior to the Poor Law Amendment Act, under which each parish would provide its poor with minimum allowances.

[3] *Bastille* Prison. (In reference to the Parisian prison of that name, the destruction of which by the mob in 1789 is commonly held to mark the beginning of the French Revolution.)

[4] *Dante's Hell* Reference to *The Divine Comedy* by thirteenth-century Italian poet Dante Alighieri.

[5] *Dr. Alison* Scottish physician and social reformer who wrote *Observations on the Management of the Poor in Scotland* (1840).

[6] *Potosi* Bolivian city fabled for its riches.

Why dwell on this aspect of the matter? It is too indisputable, not doubtful now to anyone. Descend where you will into the lower class, in Town or Country, by what avenue you will, by Factory Inquiries, Agricultural Inquiries, by Revenue Returns, by Mining-Labourer Committees, by opening your own eyes and looking, the same sorrowful result discloses itself: you have to admit that the working body of this rich English Nation has sunk or is fast sinking into a state, to which, all sides of it considered, there was literally never any parallel. At Stockport Assizes[1]—and this too has no reference to the present state of trade, being of date prior to that—a Mother and a Father are arraigned and found guilty of poisoning three of their children, to defraud a burial-society of some 3l.8s.[2] due on the death of each child. They are arraigned, found guilty; and the official authorities, it is whispered, hint that perhaps the case is not solitary, that perhaps you had better not probe farther into that department of things. This is in the autumn of 1841; the crime itself is of the previous year or season. "Brutal savages, degraded Irish,"[3] mutters the idle reader of Newspapers, hardly lingering on this incident. Yet it is an incident worth lingering on; the depravity, savagery, and degraded Irishism being never so well admitted. In the British land, a human Mother and Father, of white skin and professing the Christian religion, had done this thing; they, with their Irishism and necessity and savagery, had been driven to do it. Such instances are like the highest mountain apex emerged into view, under which lies a whole mountain region and land, not yet emerged. A human Mother and Father had said to themselves, What shall we do to escape starvation? We are deep sunk here, in our dark cellar; and help is far. Yes, in the Ugolino Hunger-tower[4] stern things happen; best-loved little Gaddo fallen dead on his Father's knees! The Stockport Mother and Father think and hint: our poor little starveling Tom, who cries all day for victuals, who will see only evil and not good in this world; if he were out of misery at once; he well dead, and the rest of us perhaps kept alive? It is thought, and hinted; at last it is done. And now Tom being killed, and all spent and eaten, Is it poor little starveling Jack that must go, or poor little starveling Will? What a committee of ways and means!

In starved sieged cities, in the uttermost doomed ruin of old Jerusalem fallen under the wrath of God, it was prophesied and said, "The hands of the pitiful women have sodden their own children."[5] The stern Hebrew imagination could conceive no blacker gulf of wretchedness; that was the ultimatum of degraded god-punished man. And we here, in modern England, exuberant with supply of all kinds, besieged by nothing if it be not by invisible Enchantments, are we reaching that? How come these things? Wherefore are they, wherefore should they be?

Nor are they of the St. Ives workhouses, of the Glasgow lanes, and Stockport cellars, the only unblessed among us. This successful industry of England, with its plethoric wealth, has as yet made nobody rich; it is an enchanted wealth, and belongs yet to nobody. We might ask, Which of us has it enriched? We can spend thousands where we once spent hundreds, but can purchase nothing good with them. In Poor and Rich, instead of noble thrift and plenty, there is idle luxury alternating with mean scarcity and inability. We have sumptuous garnitures for our Life, but have forgotten to *live* in the middle of them. It is an enchanted wealth; no man of us can yet touch it. The class of men who feel that they are truly better off by means of it, let them give us their name!

Many men eat finer cookery, drink dearer liquors—with what advantage they can report, and their Doctors can; but in the heart of them, if we go out of the dyspeptic stomach, what increase of blessedness is there? Are they better, beautifuller, stronger, braver? Are they even what they call "happier"? Do they look with satisfaction on more things and human faces in this God's-Earth; do more things and human faces look with

[1] *Assizes* Court sessions held periodically in the various counties in England.

[2] *3l.8s.* Three pounds, eight shillings.

[3] *"Brutal ... Irish"* This passage reflects the prejudice of many Englishmen and women against the native people of Ireland.

[4] *Ugolino Hunger-tower* In the thirteenth century, Count Ugolino of Pisa and his children and nephews were imprisoned and starved to death when Ugolino betrayed his political allies. According to Dante's *Inferno*, Ugolino ate his children's bodies after they died, in order to stave off starvation. The tower in Pisa's central piazza in which Ugolino was imprisoned has since been called the Tower of Hunger.

[5] *The hands ... children* From Lamentations 4.10; *sodden* Boiled.

satisfaction on them? Not so. Human faces gloom discordantly, disloyally on one another. Things, if it be not mere cotton and iron things, are growing disobedient to man. The Master Worker is enchanted, for the present, like his Workhouse Workman; clamours, in vain hitherto, for a very simple sort of "Liberty"—the liberty "to buy where he finds it cheapest, to sell where he finds it dearest." With guineas jingling in every pocket, he was no whit richer; but now, the very guineas threatening to vanish, he feels that he is poor indeed. Poor Master Worker! And the Master Unworker,[1] is not he in a still fataler situation? Pausing amid his game-preserves, with awful eye—as he well may! Coercing fifty-pound tenants;[2] coercing, bribing, cajoling; "doing what he likes with his own." His mouth full of loud futilities, and arguments to prove the excellence of his Corn-law;[3] and in his heart the blackest misgiving, a desperate half-consciousness that his excellent Corn-law is *in*defensible, that his loud arguments for it are of a kind to strike men too literally *dumb*.

To whom, then, is this wealth of England wealth? Who is it that it blesses, makes happier, wiser, beautifuler, in any way better? Who has got hold of it, to make it fetch and carry for him, like a true servant, not like a false mock-servant, to do him any real service whatsoever? As yet no one. We have more riches than any Nation ever had before; we have less good of them than any Nation ever had before. Our successful industry is hitherto unsuccessful; a strange success, if we stop here! In the midst of plethoric plenty, the people perish; with gold walls, and full barns, no man feels himself safe or satisfied. Workers, Master Workers, Unworkers, all men, come to a pause; stand fixed, and cannot farther. Fatal paralysis spreading inwards, from the extremities, in St. Ives workhouses, in Stockport cellars, through all limbs, as if towards the heart itself. Have we actually got enchanted, then, accursed by some god?

Midas longed for gold, and insulted the Olympians. He got gold, so that whatsoever he touched became gold—and he, with his long ears, was little the better for it. Midas had misjudged the celestial music-tones; Midas had insulted Apollo and the gods. The gods gave him his wish, and a pair of long ears, which also were a good appendage to it. What a truth in these old Fables! ...

CHAPTER 6—HERO-WORSHIP

To the present Editor, not less than to Bobus,[4] a Government of the Wisest, what Bobus calls an Aristocracy of Talent, seems the one healing remedy; but he is not so sanguine as Bobus with respect to the means of realising it. He thinks that we have at once missed realising it, and come to need it so pressingly, by departing far from the inner eternal Laws, and taking-up with the temporary outer semblances of Laws. He thinks that "enlightened Egoism,"[5] never so luminous, is not the rule by which man's life can be led. That "Laissez-faire," "Supply-and-demand," "Cash-payment for the sole nexus,"[6] and so forth, were not, are not and will never be, a practicable Law of Union for a Society of Men. The Poor and Rich, that Governed and Governing, cannot long live together on any such Law of Union. Alas, he thinks that man has a soul in him, *different* from the stomach in any sense of this word; that if said soul be asphyxied, and lie quietly forgotten, the man and his affairs are in a bad way. He thinks that said soul will have to be resuscitated from its asphyxia; that if it prove irresuscitable, the man is not long for this world. In brief, that Midas-eared Mammonism, double-barrelled Dilettantism,[7] and their thousand adjuncts and corollaries, are *not* the Law by which God Almighty has appointed this his Universe to go; that, once for all, these are not the Law; and then, further, that we shall have to return to what *is* the Law—not by smooth flowery paths, it is like, and with "tremendous cheers" in our throat, but over steep untrodden places, through stormclad chasms, waste oceans, and the bosom of tornadoes; thank Heaven, if not through very Chaos and the Abyss! The resuscitating of a soul that has gone to asphyxia is no momentary or pleasant process, but a long and terrible one.

To the present Editor, Hero-worship, as he has else-where named it, means much more than an elected Parliament or stated Aristocracy of the Wisest; for in his dialect it is the summary, ultimate essence, and supreme practical perfection of all manner of worship, and true worthships and noblenesses whatsoever. Such blessed Parliament and, were it once in perfection, blessed Aristocracy of the Wisest, god-honoured and man-honoured, he does look for, more and more per-fected—as the topmost blessed practical apex of a whole world reformed from sham-worship, informed anew with worship, with truth and blessedness! He thinks that Hero-worship, done differently in every different epoch of the world, is the soul of all social business among men; that the doing of it well, or the doing of it ill, measures accurately what degree of well-being or of ill-being there is in the world's affairs. He thinks that we, on the whole, do our Hero-worship worse than any Nation in this world ever did it before; that the Burns an Exciseman, the Byron a Literary Lion,[1] are intrinsi-cally, all things considered, a baser and falser phenome-non than the Odin[2] a God, the Mahomet a Prophet of God. It is this Editor's clear opinion, accordingly, that we must learn to do our Hero-worship better; that to do it better and better means the awakening of the Nation's soul from its asphyxia, and the return of blessed life to

us—Heaven's blessed life, not Mammon's galvanic[3] accursed one. To resuscitate the Asphyxied, apparently now moribund and in the last agony if not resuscitated, such and no other seems the consummation.

"Hero-worship," if you will—yes, friends; but, first of all, by being ourselves of heroic mind. A whole world of Heroes; a world not of Flunkies, where no Hero-King *can* reign: that is what we aim at! We, for our share, will put away all Flunkyism, Baseness, Unveracity from us; we shall then hope to have Noblenesses and Veracities set over us; never till then. Let Bobus and Company sneer, "That is your Reform!" Yes, Bobus, that is our Reform; and except in that, and what will follow out of that, we have no hope at all. Reform, like Charity, O Bobus, must begin at home. Once well at home, how will it radiate outwards, irrepressible, into all that we touch and handle, speak and work; kindling ever new light, by incalculable contagion, spreading in geometric ratio, far and wide—doing good only, wheresoever it spreads, and not evil.

By Reform Bills, Anti-Corn-Law Bills, and thousand other bills and methods, we will demand of our Gover-nors, with emphasis, and for the first time not without effect, that they cease to be quacks, or else depart; that they set no quackeries and block-headisms anywhere to rule over us, that they utter or act no cant to us—it will be better if they do not. For we shall now know quacks when we see them; cant, when we hear it, shall be horrible to us! We will say, with the poor Frenchman at the Bar of the Convention, though in wiser style than he, and "for the space" not "of an hour" but of a life-time: "*Je demands l'arrestation des coquins et des laches.*" "Arrestment of the knaves and dastards." Ah, we know what a work that is; how long it will be before *they* are all or mostly got "arrested"—but here is one; arrest him, in God's name; it is one fewer! We will, in all practicable ways, by word and silence, by act and refusal to act, energetically demand that arrestment—"*je demande cette arrestation-la!*"—and by degrees infallibly attain it. Infallibly, for light spreads; all human souls, never so bedarkened, love light; light once kindled spreads, till all is luminous, till the cry, "*Arrest* your knaves and das-tards" rises imperative from millions of hearts, and rings

---

as an idle pastime, without any serious interest or goal.

[1] *Literary Lion* Poet Robert Burns (1759–96), who worked as an excise officer. Burns came to be regarded as Scotland's national poet; *Byron* Romantic poet George Gordon, Lord Byron (1788–1824).

[2] *Odin* Norse god of war, art, and culture.

---

[3] *galvanic* Applying electricity; having the effect of an electric shock.

and reigns from sea to sea. Nay, how many of them may we not "arrest" with our own hands, even now, we! Do not countenance them, thou there: turn away from their lacquered sumptuosities, their belauded sophistries, their serpent graciosities, their spoken and acted cant, with a sacred horror, with an *Apage Satanas*.[1] Bobus and Company, and all men, will gradually join us. We demand arrestment of the knaves and dastards, and begin by arresting our own poor selves out of that fraternity. There is no other reform conceivable. Thou and I, my friend, can, in the most flunky world, make, each of us, *one* non-flunky, one hero, if we like. That will be two heroes to begin with—Courage! even that is a whole world of heroes to end with, or what we poor Two can do in furtherance thereof!

Yes, friends: Hero-kings, and a whole world not unheroic—there lies the port and happy haven, towards which, through all these stormtost seas, French Revolutions, Chartisms, Manchester Insurrections,[2] that make the heart sick in these bad days, the Supreme Powers are driving us. On the whole, blessed be the Supreme Powers, stern as they are! Towards that haven will we, O friends; let all true men, with what of faculty is in them, bend valiantly, incessantly, with thousandfold endeavour, thither, thither! There, or else in the Ocean-abysses, it is very clear to me, we shall arrive.

Well, here truly is no answer to the Sphinx-question[3]—not the answer a disconsolate public, inquiring at the College of Health, was in hopes of! A total change of regimen, change of constitution and existence from the very centre of it; a new body to be got, with resuscitated soul—not without convulsive travail-throes, as all birth and new-birth presupposes travail! This is sad news to a disconsolate discerning Public, hoping to have got off by some Morrison's Pill,[4] some Saint-John's corrosive mixture and perhaps a little blistery friction on the back! We were prepared to part with our Corn-Law, with various Laws and Unlaws, but this, what is this?

Nor has the Editor forgotten how it fares with your ill-boding Cassandras in Sieges of Troy.[5] Imminent perdition is not usually driven away by words of warning. Didactic Destiny has other methods in store, or these would fail always. Such words should, nevertheless, be uttered, when they dwell truly in the soul of any man. Words are hard, are importunate; but how much harder the importunate events they foreshadow! Here and there a human soul may listen to the words—who knows how many human souls?—whereby the importunate events, if not diverted and prevented, will be rendered *less* hard. The present Editor's purpose is to himself full of hope.

For though fierce travails, though wide seas and roaring gulfs lie before us, is it not something if a Loadstar, in the eternal sky, do once more disclose itself; an everlasting light, shining through all cloud-tempests and roaring billows, ever as we emerge from the trough of the sea; the blessed beacon, far off on the edge of far horizons, towards which we are to steer incessantly for life? Is it not something, O Heavens, is it not all? There lies the Heroic Promised Land; under that Heaven's-light, my brethren, bloom the Happy Isles—there, O there! Thither will we;

"There dwells the great Achilles whom we knew."[6]

---

[1] *Apage Satanas* Latin: Begone, Satan.

[2] *Chartisms* Movements by the Chartists, peaceful democratic reformers whose principles were set out in the "People's Charter," published in 1838; *Manchester Insurrections* Rioting in Manchester in 1842 resulted from the reduction of wages in both the coal mines and the factories. Manchester was also the site of the famous 1819 Peterloo Massacre, at which cavalry charged on an outdoor political meeting, killing at least eleven people and wounding several others.

[3] *Sphinx-question* Riddle, like those posed by the mythological sphinx, a winged half-woman, half-lion who would not allow travelers to pass unless they could correctly answer her riddle. If they answered incorrectly, they would be killed.

[4] *Morrison's Pill* I.e., a cure-all.

[5] *Cassandras … Troy* Cassandra, daughter of the King of Troy, was given the gift of prophecy, but cursed so that nobody would believe her.

[6] *There dwells … knew* Cf. lines 63–64 of Alfred Lord Tennyson's poem "Ulysses": "It may be we shall touch the Happy Isles, / And see the great Achilles, whom we knew." The Happy Isles were the Isles of the Blessed, supposedly (according to Greek myth) located in the Atlantic Ocean.

There dwell all Heroes, and will dwell: thither, all ye heroic-minded! The Heaven's Loadstar once clearly in our eye, how will each true man stand truly to *his* work in the ship; how, with undying hope, will all things be fronted, all be conquered. Nay, with the ship's prow once turned in that direction, is not all, as it were, already well? Sick wasting misery has become noble manful effort with a goal in our eye. The choking Nightmare chokes us no longer, for we *stir* under it; the Nightmare has already fled.

Certainly, could the present Editor instruct men how to know Wisdom, Heroism, when they see it, that they might do reverence to *it* only, and loyally make it ruler over them, yes, he were the living epitome of all Editors, Teachers, Prophets, that now teach and prophesy; he were an *Apollo*-Morrison, a Trismegistus[1] and *effective* Cassandra! Let no Able Editor hope such things. It is to be expected the present laws of copyright, rate of reward per sheet, and other considerations will save him from that peril. Let no Editor hope such things; no—and yet let all Editors aim towards such things, and even towards such alone! One knows not what the meaning of editing and writing is, if even this be not it.

Enough, to the present Editor it has seemed possible some glimmering of light, for here and there a human soul might lie in these confused Paper-Masses now entrusted to him; wherefore he determines to edit the same. Out of old Books, new Writings, and much Meditation not of yesterday, he will endeavour to select a thing or two; and from the Past, in a circuitous way, illustrate the Present and the Future. The Past is a dim indubitable fact: the Future too is one, only dimmer; nay properly it is the *same* fact in new dress and development. For the Present holds it in both the whole Past and the whole Future—as the life-tree Igdrasil,[2] wide-waving, many-toned, has its roots down deep in the Death-kingdoms, among the oldest dead dust of men, and with its boughs reaches always beyond the stars, and in all times and places is one and the same Life-tree! ...

from BOOK 3
CHAPTER 1—PHENOMENA

But, it is said, our religion is gone: we no longer believe in St. Edmund,[3] no longer see the figure of him on the rim of the sky, minatory or confirmatory! God's absolute Laws, sanctioned by an eternal Heaven and an eternal Hell, have become Moral Philosophies, sanctioned by able computations of Profit and Loss, by weak considerations of Pleasures of Virtue and the Moral Sublime.

It is even so. To speak in the ancient dialect, we "have forgotten God"—in the most modern dialect and very truth of the matter, we have taken up the Fact of this Universe as it *is not*. We have quietly closed our eyes to the eternal Substance of things, and opened them only to the Shows and Shams of things. We quietly believe this Universe to be intrinsically a great unintelligible PERHAPS; extrinsically, clear enough, it is a great, most extensive Cattlefold and Workhouse, with most extensive Kitchen-ranges, Dining-tables—whereat he is wise who can find a place! All the Truth of this Universe is uncertain; only the profit and loss of it, the pudding and praise of it, are and remain very visible to the practical man.

There is no longer any God for us! God's Laws are become a Greatest-Happiness Principle, a Parliamentary Expediency. The Heavens overarch us only as an Astronomical Time-keeper, a butt for Herschel-telescopes[4] to shoot science at, to shoot sentimentalities at—in our and old Jonson's[5] dialect, man has lost the *soul* out of him, and now, after the due period, begins to find the want of it! This is verily the plague-spot, centre of the universal Social Gangrene, threatening all modern things with frightful death. To him that will consider it, here is the stem, with its roots and taproot, with its

---

[1] *Apollo* Classical god of poetry, music, and prophecy; *Trismegistus* Greek: thrice great. This is an epithet of the classical god Hermes, the messenger and herald for the other gods.

[2] *Igdrasil* Great tree of Scandinavian mythology, the roots and branches of which stretched through the universe.

[3] *St. Edmund* King of East Anglia (c. 840–70), famous for the miracles attributed to him after his martyrdom.

[4] *Herschel-telescopes* Large telescopes of the sort designed by William Herschel (1738–1822), astronomer who studied the planets and stars with a telescope that had a 40-foot focal length and 48-inch mirror.

[5] *Jonson* Poet and dramatist Ben Jonson (1572–1637).

world-wide upas-boughs[1] and accursed poison-exudations, under which the world lies writhing in atrophy and agony. You touch the focal-centre of all our disease, of our frightful nosology[2] of diseases, when you lay your hand on this. There is no religion; there is no God; man has lost his soul, and vainly seeks antiseptic salt. Vainly: in killing Kings, in passing Reform Bills, in French Revolutions, Manchester Insurrections, is found no remedy. The foul elephantine leprosy, alleviated for an hour, reappears in new force and desperateness next hour.

For actually this is *not* the real fact of the world; the world is not made so, but otherwise! Truly, any Society setting out from this No-God hypothesis will arrive at a result or two. The *Un*veracities, escorted, each Unveracity of them by its corresponding Misery and Penalty; the Phantasms, and Fatuities, and ten-years Corn-Law Debatings, that shall walk the Earth at noonday, must needs be numerous! The Universe *being* intrinsically a Perhaps, being too probably an "infinite Humbug," why should any minor Humbug astonish us? It is all according to the order of Nature, and Phantasms riding with huge clatter along the streets, from end to end of our existence, astonish nobody. Enchanted St. Ives Workhouses and Joe-Manton[3] Aristocracies; giant Working Mammonism near strangled in the partridge-nets of giant-looking Idle Dilettantism—this, in all its branches, in its thousand-thousand modes and figures, is a sight familiar to us.

The Popish Religion,[4] we are told, flourishes extremely in these years; and is the most vivacious-looking religion to be met with at present. "*Elle a trois cents ans dans le ventre*," counts Mr. Jouffroy; "*c'est pourquoi je la respecte!*"[5] The old Pope of Rome, finding it laborious to

kneel so long while they cart him through the streets to bless the people on *Corpus Christi* Day,[6] complains of rheumatism; whereupon his Cardinals consult, construct him, after some study, a stuffed cloaked figure, of iron and wood, with wool or baked hair, and place it in a kneeling posture. Stuffed figure, or rump of a figure; to this stuffed rump he, sitting at his ease on a lower level, joins, by the aid of cloaks and drapery, his living head and outspread hands: the rump with its cloaks kneels, the Pope looks, and holds his hands spread; and so the two in concert bless the Roman population on *Corpus Christi* Day, as well as they can.

I have considered this amphibious Pope, with the wool-and-iron back, with the flesh head and hands, and endeavoured to calculate his horoscope. I reckon him the remarkablest Pontiff that has darkened God's daylight, or painted himself in the human retina, for these several thousand years. Nay, since Chaos first shivered, and "sneezed," as the Arabs say, with the first shaft of sunlight shot through it, "what stranger product was there of Nature and Art working together? Here is a Supreme Priest who believes God to be—What, in the name of God, *does* he believe God to be?—and discerns that all worship of God is a scenic phantasmagory of wax-candles, organ-blasts, Gregorian chants, mass-brayings, purple monsignori,[7] wool-and-iron rumps, artistically spread out—to save the ignorant from worse.

O reader, I say not who are Belial's[8] elect. This poor amphibious Pope too gives loaves to the Poor, has in him more good latent than he is himself aware of. His poor Jesuits, in the late Italian Cholera, were, with a few German Doctors, the only creatures whom dastard terror had not driven mad: they descended fearless into all gulfs and bedlams; watched over the pillow of the dying, with help, with counsel and hope; shone as luminous fixed stars, when all else had gone out in chaotic night: honour to them! This poor Pope—who knows what good is in him? In a Time otherwise too prone to forget, he keeps up the mournfulest ghastly memorial of the Highest, Blessedest, which once was;

---

[1] *upas-boughs* Boughs of the upas tree, a fabled tree of Java said to be so poisonous that it destroyed all life within a fifteen-mile radius.

[2] *nosology* Catalogue.

[3] *Joe-Manton* Prestigious maker of high quality, expensive firearms (1766–1835).

[4] *The Popish Religion* Roman Catholicism.

[5] *Elle a … respecte* French: She [i.e., the Roman Catholic religion] has three hundred years in her stomach, that is why I respect her. Théodore Simon Jouffroy (1796–1842) was a French philosopher and translator.

[6] *Corpus Christi Day* Occasion of the Feast of the Blessed Sacrament, which occurs on the Thursday after Trinity Sunday.

[7] *monsignori* Roman Catholics of ecclesiastical rank. Bishops and lower monsignors wear robes of various shades of purple.

[8] *Belial's* Name for the devil, or for evil personified.

which, in new fit forms, will again partly have to be. Is he not as a perpetual death's-head and cross-bones, with their *Resurgam*,[1] on the grave of a Universal Heroism, grave of a Christianity? Such Noblenesses, purchased by the world's best heart's-blood, must not be lost; we cannot afford to lose them, in what confusions soever. To all of us the day will come, to a few of us it has already come, when no mortal, with his heart yearning for a "Divine Humility," or other "Highest form of Valour," will need to look for it in death's-heads, but will see it round him in here and there a beautiful living head.

Besides, there is in this poor Pope, and his practice of the Scenic Theory of Worship, a frankness which I rather honour. Not half and half, but with undivided heart does *he* set about worshipping by stage-machinery; as if there were now, and could again be, in Nature no other. He will ask you, What other? Under this my Gregorian Chant, and beautiful waxlight Phantasmagory, kindly hidden from you is an Abyss of Black Doubt, Scepticism, nay Sansculottic[2] Jacobinism; an Orcus[3] that has no bottom. Think of that. "Groby Pool *is* thatched with pancakes," as Jeannie Deans's Innkeeper defied it to be![4] The Bottomless of Scepticism, Atheism, Jacobinism, behold, it is thatched over, hidden from your despair, by stage-properties judiciously arranged. This stuffed rump of mine saves not me only from rheumatism but you also from what other *isms*! In this your Life-pilgrimage Nowhither, a fine Squallacci marching-music, and Gregorian Chant, accompanies you, and the hollow Night of Orcus is well hid!

Yes truly, few men that worship by the rotatory Calabash of the Calmucks[5] do it in half so great, frank or effectual a way. Drury Lane,[6] it is said, and that is saying much, might learn from him in the dressing of parts, in the arrangement of lights and shadows. He is the greatest Play-actor that at present draws salary in this world. Poor Pope; and I am told he is fast growing bankrupt too, and will, in a measurable term of years (a great way *within* the "three hundred"), not have a penny to make his pot boil! His old rheumatic back will then get to rest, and himself and his stage-properties sleep well in Chaos forevermore.

Or, alas, why go to Rome for Phantasms walking the streets? Phantasms, ghosts, in this midnight hour, hold jubilee, and screech and jabber; and the question rather were, What high Reality anywhere is yet awake? Aristocracy has become Phantasm-Aristocracy, no longer able to *do* its work, not in the least conscious that it has any work longer to do. Unable, totally careless to *do* its work; careful only to clamour for the *wages* of doing its work—nay for higher, and *palpably* undue wages, and Corn Laws and *increase* of rents, the old rate of wages not being adequate now! In hydra[7]-wrestle, giant "*Millocracy*"[8] so-called, a real giant, though as yet a blind one and but half-awake, wrestles and wrings in choking nightmare, "like to be strangled in the partridge-nets of Phantasm-Aristocracy," as we said, which fancies itself still to be a giant. Wrestles, as under nightmare, till it do awaken, and gasps and struggles thousandfold, we may say, in a truly painful manner, through all fibres of our English Existence, in these hours and years! Is our poor English Existence wholly becoming a Nightmare, full of mere Phantasms?

The Champion of England, cased in iron or tin, rides into Westminster Hall, "being lifted into his saddle with little assistance," and there asks, If in the four quarters of the world, under the cope[9] of Heaven, is any man or demon that dare question the right of this King? Under the cope of Heaven no man makes intelligible answer—as several men ought already to have done. Does not this Champion too know the world; that it is

---

[1] *Resurgam* Latin: I will rise again.

[2] *Sansculottic* Revolutionary. "Sans-culottes" were radical members of the Republican party who refused to wear the short pants ("culottes") and stockings characteristic of the aristocracy, and instead donned the loose pants worn by the working classes.

[3] *Orcus* Underworld.

[4] *Groby Pool ... be* Reference to Sir Walter Scott's *The Heart of Midlothian* (1818), in which the heroine, Jeannie Deans, asks an innkeeper whether there is any bad company on the road. He replies, "Why, when it's clean without them I'll thatch Groby pool wi' pancakes."

[5] *Calabash* Vessel; *Calmucks* Kalmucks, Mongolian people who inhabit the northwest shores of the Caspian Sea.

[6] *Drury Lane* Location of London's Theatre Royal.

[7] *hydra* Many-headed snake of Greek mythology.

[8] *Millocracy* I.e., rule of mill owners.

[9] *cope* Canopy.

a huge Imposture, and bottomless Inanity, thatched over with bright cloth and other ingenious tissues? Him let us leave there, questioning all men and demons.

Him we have left to his destiny; but whom else have we found? From this the highest apex of things, downwards through all strata and breadths, how many fully awakened Realities have we fallen in with—alas, on the contrary, what troops and populations of Phantasms, not God-Veracities but Devil-Falsities, down to the very lowest stratum, which now, by such superincumbent weight of Unveracities, lies enchanted in St. Ives' Workhouses, broad enough, helpless enough! You will walk in no public thoroughfare or remotest byway of English Existence but you will meet a man, an interest of men, that has given up hope in the Everlasting, True, and placed its hope in the Temporary, half or wholly False. The Honourable Member complains unmusically that there is "devil's-dust" in Yorkshire cloth.[1] Yorkshire cloth—why, the very Paper I now write on is made, it seems, partly of plaster-lime well smoothed, and obstructs my writing! You are lucky if you can find now any good Paper, any work really *done*; search where you will, from highest Phantasm apex to lowest Enchanted basis.

Consider, for example, that great Hat seven-feet high, which now perambulates London Streets; which my Friend Sauerteig[2] regarded justly as one of our English notabilities. "The topmost point as yet," said he, "would it were your culminating and returning point, to which English Puffery has been observed to reach!" The Hatter in the Strand of London, instead of making better felt-hats than another, mounts a huge lath-and-plaster Hat, seven-feet high, upon wheels; sends a man to drive it through the streets, hoping to be saved *thereby*. He has not attempted to *make* better hats, as he was appointed by the Universe to do, and as with this ingenuity of his he could very probably have done; but his whole industry is turned to *persuade* us that he has made such! He too knows that the Quack has become God. Laugh not at him, O reader; or do not laugh only. He has ceased to be comic; he is fast becoming tragic. To me this all-deafening blast of Puffery, of poor

Falsehood grown necessitous, of poor Heart-Atheism fallen now into Enchanted Workhouses, sounds too surely like a Doom's-blast! I have to say to myself in old dialect, "God's blessing is not written on all this; His curse is written on all this!" Unless perhaps the Universe *be* a chimera—some old totally deranged eightday clock, dead as brass, which the Maker, if there ever was any Maker, has long ceased to meddle with? To my Friend Sauerteig this poor seven-feet Hat-manufacturer, as the topstone of English Puffery, was very notable.

Alas, that we natives note him little, that we view him as a tiling of course, is the very burden of the misery. We take it for granted, the most rigorous of us, that all men who have made anything are expected and entitled to make the loudest possible proclamation of it, and call on a discerning public to reward them for it. Every man his own trumpeter—that is, to a really alarming extent, the accepted rule. Make loudest possible proclamation of your Hat: true proclamation if that will do; if that will not do, then false proclamation—to such extent of falsity as will serve your purpose, as will not seem too false to be credible! I answer, once for all, that the fact is not so. Nature requires no man to make proclamation of his doings and hat-makings; Nature forbids all men to make such. There is not a man or hat-maker born into the world but feels, or has felt, that he is degrading himself if he speak of his excellencies and prowesses, and supremacy in his craft. His inmost heart says to him, "Leave thy friends to speak of these; if possible, thy enemies to speak of these; but at all events, thy friends!" He feels that he is already a poor braggart, fast hastening to be a falsity and speaker of the Untruth.

Nature's Laws, I must repeat, are eternal: her small still voice, speaking from the inmost heart of us, shall not, under terrible penalties, be disregarded. No one man can depart from the truth without damage to himself—no one million of men, no Twenty-seven Millions of men. Show me a Nation fallen everywhere into this course, so that each expects it, permits it to others and himself, I will show you a Nation travelling with one assent on the broad way. The broad way, however many Banks of England, Cotton Mills, and

---

[1] *Yorkshire cloth* Thick, coarse cloth manufactured in Yorkshire.

[2] *Sauerteig* Gottfried Sauerteig, the fictitious "Picturesque Tourist" who visits the St. Ives workhouse in Book 1, Chapter 1.

Duke's Palaces it may have. Not at happy Elysian fields,[1] and everlasting crowns of victory, earned by silent Valour, will this Nation arrive; but at precipices, devouring gulfs, if it pause not. Nature has appointed happy fields, victorious laurel-crowns,[2] but only to the brave and true. *Un*nature, what we call Chaos, holds nothing in it but vacuities, devouring gulfs. What are Twenty-seven Millions, and their unanimity? Believe them not: the Worlds and the Ages, God and Nature and All Men say otherwise.

"Rhetoric all this?" No, my brother, very singular to say, it is Fact all this. Cocker's Arithmetic[3] is not truer. Forgotten in these days, it is old as the foundations of the Universe, and will endure till the Universe cease. It is forgotten now, and the first mention of it puckers thy sweet countenance into a sneer, but it will be brought to mind again—unless indeed the Law of Gravitation chance to cease, and men find that they *can* walk on vacancy. Unanimity of the Twenty-seven Millions will do nothing; walk not thou with them; fly from them as for thy life. Twenty-seven Millions travelling on such courses, with gold jingling in every pocket, with vivats[4] heaven-high, are incessantly advancing, let me again remind thee, towards the *firm-land's end*—towards the end and extinction of what Faithfulness, Veracity, real Worth, was in their way of life. Their noble ancestors have fashioned for them a "life-road"—in how many thousand senses, this! There is not an old wise Proverb on their tongue, an honest Principle articulated in their hearts into utterance, a wise true method of doing and dispatching any work or commerce of men, but helps yet to carry them forward. Life is still possible to them, because all is not yet Puffery, Falsity, Mammon-worship and Unnature; because somewhat is yet Faithfulness, Veracity, and Valour. With a certain very considerable finite quantity of Unveracity and Phantasm, social life is still possible; not with an infinite quantity! Exceed

your certain quantity, the seven-feet Hat, and all things upwards to the very Champion cased in tin begin to reel and flounder—in Manchester Insurrections, Chartisms, Sliding-scales, the Law of Gravitation not forgetting to act. You advance incessantly towards the land's end; you are, literally enough, "consuming the way." Step after step, Twenty-seven Million unconscious men, till you are *at* the land's end, till there is not Faithfulness enough among you anymore, and the next step now is lifted *not* over land, but into air, over ocean-deeps and roaring abysses—unless perhaps the Law of Gravitation have forgotten to act?

Oh, it is frightful when a whole Nation, as our Fathers used to say, has "forgotten God," has remembered only Mammon, and what Mammon leads to! When your self-trumpeting Hatmaker is the emblem of almost all makers, and workers, and men, that make anything—from soul-overseerships, body-overseerships, epic poems, Acts of Parliament, to hats and shoe-blacking! Not one false man but does uncountable mischief: how much, in a generation or two, will Twenty-seven Millions, mostly false, manage to accumulate? The sum of it, visible in every street, market-place, senate-house, circulating-library, cathedral, cotton-mill, and union-workhouse, fills one *not* with a comic feeling!

CHAPTER 2—GOSPEL OF MAMMONISM

Reader, even Christian Reader as thy title goes, hast thou any notion of Heaven and Hell? I rather apprehend, not. Often as the words are on our tongue, they have got a fabulous or semi-fabulous character for most of us, and pass on like a kind of transient similitude, like a sound signifying little.

Yet it is well worth while for us to know, once and always, that they are not a similitude, nor a fable nor semi-fable; that they are an everlasting highest fact! "No Lake of Sicilian or other sulphur[5] burns now anywhere in these ages," sayest thou? Well, and if there did not! Believe that there does not; believe it if thou wilt; nay, hold by it as a real increase, a rise to higher stages, to

---

[1] *Elysian fields* In Greek mythology, where the blessed reside after death.

[2] *laurel-crowns* Marks of honor conferred upon heroes, poets, and victorious athletes in ancient Greece and Rome.

[3] *Cocker's Arithmetic* Textbook by Edward Cocker (1631–75) that was so widely read and admired it gave rise to the phrase "according to Cocker," meaning "perfectly correct."

[4] *vivats* Expressions of acclamation or approval.

---

[5] *Lake … sulphur* Sulphur, often found near volcanic rocks, was formerly known as "brimstone" (i.e., "burning stone") and was thought to feed the fires of hell. At this time, Sicily was the world's primary source of sulphur.

wider horizons and empires. All this has vanished, or has not vanished; believe as thou wilt as to all this. But that an Infinite of Practical Importance, speaking with strict arithmetical exactness, an *Infinite*, has vanished or can vanish from the Life of any Man, this thou shalt not believe! O brother, the Infinite of Terror, of Hope, of Pity, did it not at any moment disclose itself to thee, indubitable, unnameable? Came it never, like the gleam of eternal Oceans, like the voice of old Eternities, far-sounding through thy heart of hearts? Never? Alas, it was not thy Liberalism, then; it was thy Animalism! The Infinite is more sure than any other fact. But only men can discern it; mere building beavers, spinning arachnes, much more the predatory vulturous and vulpine species, do not discern it well!

"The word Hell," says Sauerteig, "is still frequently in use among the English people, but I could not without difficulty ascertain what they meant by it. Hell generally signifies the Infinite Terror, the thing a man *is* infinitely afraid of, and shudders and shrinks from, struggling with his whole soul to escape from it. There is a Hell, therefore, if you will consider, which accompanies man in all stages of his history and religious or other development. But the Hells of men and Peoples differ notably. With Christians it is the infinite terror of being found guilty before the Just Judge. With old Romans, I conjecture, it was the terror not of Pluto,[1] for whom probably they cared little, but of doing unworthily, doing unvirtuously, which was their word for un*man*fully.[2] And now what is it, if you pierce through his Cants, his oft-repeated Hearsays, what he calls his Worships and so forth, what is it that the modern English soul does, in very truth, dread infinitely, and contemplate with entire despair? What *is* his Hell, after all these reputable, oft-repeated Hearsays, what is it? With hesitation, with astonishment, I pronounce it to be the terror of 'Not succeeding'; of not making money, fame, or some other figure in the world—chiefly of not making money! Is not that a somewhat singular Hell?"

Yes, O Sauerteig, it is very singular. If we do not "succeed," where is the use of us? We had better never have been born. "Tremble intensely," as our friend the Emperor of China says: *there* is the black Bottomless of

Terror, what Sauerteig calls the "Hell of the English!" But indeed this Hell belongs naturally to the Gospel of Mammonism, which also has its corresponding Heaven. For there *is* one Reality among so many Phantasms; about one thing we are entirely in earnest: the making of money. Working Mammonism does divide the world with idle game-preserving Dilettantism—thank Heaven that there is even a Mammonism, *anything* we are in earnest about! Idleness is worst, Idleness alone is without hope: work earnestly at anything, you will by degrees learn to work at almost all things. There is endless hope in work, were it even work at making money.

True, it must be owned, we for the present, with our Mammon-Gospel, have come to strange conclusions. We call it a Society; and go about professing openly the totalest separation, isolation. Our life is not a mutual helpfulness; but rather, cloaked under due laws-of-war, named "fair competition" and so forth, it is a mutual hostility. We have profoundly forgotten everywhere that *Cash payment* is not the sole relation of human beings; we think, nothing doubting, that *it* absolves and liquidates all engagements of man. "My starving workers?" answers the rich mill-owner: "Did not I hire them fairly in the market? Did I not pay them, to the last sixpence, the sum covenanted for? What have I to do with them more?" Verily Mammon-worship is a melancholy creed. When Cain, for his own behoof, had killed Abel, and was questioned, "Where is thy brother?" he too made answer, "Am I my brother's keeper?" Did I not pay my brother *his* wages, the thing he had merited from me?[3]

O sumptuous Merchant Prince, illustrious game-preserving Duke, is there no way of "killing" thy brother but Cain's rude way! "A good man by the very look of him, by his very presence with us as a fellow wayfarer in this Life-pilgrimage, *promises* so much." Woe to him if he forget all such promises, if he never know that they were given! To a deadened soul, seared with the brute Idolatry of Sense, to whom going to Hell is equivalent to not making money, all "promises" and moral duties, that cannot be pleaded for in Courts of Requests,[4] address themselves in vain. Money he can be ordered to pay, but nothing more. I have not heard in all Past History, and expect not to hear in all Future

---

[1] *Pluto* Roman god of the underworld.

[2] *which was ... unmanfully* The Latin word for man is *vir*.

[3] *When Cain ... me* See Genesis 4.9.

[4] *Courts of Requests* Court that examined the petitions of the poor.

History, of any Society anywhere under God's Heaven, supporting itself on such Philosophy. The Universe is not made so; it is made otherwise than so. The man or nation of men that thinks it is made so, marches forward nothing doubting, step after step, but marches—whither we know! In these last two centuries of Atheistic Government (near two centuries now, since the blessed restoration of his Sacred Majesty, and Defender of the Faith, Charles Second), I reckon that we have pretty well exhausted what of "firm earth" there was for us to march on—and are now, very ominously, shuddering, reeling, and let us hope trying to recoil, on the cliff's edge!

For out of this that we call Atheism come so many other *isms* and falsities, each falsity with its misery at its heels! A SOUL is not like wind (*spiritus*, or breath) contained within a capsule; the ALMIGHTY MAKER is not like a Clockmaker that once, in old immemorial ages, having *made* his Horologe of a Universe, sits ever since and sees it go! Not at all. Hence comes Atheism; come, as we say, many other *isms*, and, as the sum of all, comes Valetism,[1] the *reverse* of Heroism—sad root of all woes whatsoever. For indeed, as no man ever saw the above-said wind-element enclosed within its capsule, and finds it at bottom more deniable than conceivable; so too he finds, in spite of Bridgwater Bequests, your Clockmaker Almighty an entirely questionable affair, a deniable affair—and accordingly denies it, and along with it so much else. Alas, one knows not what and how much else! For the faith in an Invisible, Unnameable, Godlike, present everywhere in all that we see and work and suffer, is the essence of all faith whatsoever; and that once denied, or still worse, asserted with lips only, and out of bound prayerbooks only, what other thing remains believable? That Cant well-ordered is marketable Cant; that Heroism means gas-lighted Histrionism;[2] that seen with "clear eyes" (as they call Valet-eyes) no man is a Hero, or ever was a Hero, but all men are Valets and Varlets. The accursed practical quintessence of all sorts of Unbelief! For if there be now no Hero, and the Histrio himself begin to be seen into, what hope is there for the seed of Adam here below? We

are the doomed everlasting prey of the Quack; who, now in this guise, now in that, is to filch us, to pluck and eat us, by such modes as are convenient for him. For the modes and guises I care little. The Quack once inevitable, let him come swiftly, let him pluck and eat me—swiftly, that I may at least have done with him, for in his Quack-world I can have no wish to linger. Though he slay me, yet will I *not* trust in him. Though he conquer nations, and have all the Flunkies of the Universe shouting at his heels, yet will I know well that *he* is an Inanity; that for him and his there is no continuance appointed, save only in Gehenna and the Pool.[3] Alas, the Atheist world, from its utmost summits of Heaven and Westminster Hall,[4] downwards through poor seven-feet Hats and "Unveracities fallen hungry," down to the lowest cellars and neglected hunger-dens of it, is very wretched.

One of Dr. Alison's Scotch facts struck us much. A poor Irish Widow, her husband having died in one of the Lanes of Edinburgh, went forth with her three children, bare of all resource, to solicit help from the Charitable Establishments of that City. At this Charitable Establishment and then at that she was refused, referred from one to the other, helped by none, till she had exhausted them all, till her strength and heart failed her. She sank down in typhus-fever, died, and infected her Lane with fever, so that "seventeen other persons" died of fever there in consequence. The humane Physician asks thereupon, as with a heart too full for speaking, Would it not have been *economy* to help this poor Widow? She took typhus-fever, and killed seventeen of you! Very curious. The forlorn Irish Widow applies to her fellow-creatures, as if saying, "Behold I am sinking, bare of help. Ye must help me! I am your sister, bone of your bone; one God made us. Ye must help me!" They answer, "No, impossible; thou art no sister of ours." But she proves her sisterhood; her typhus-fever kills *them*. They actually were her brothers, though denying it! Had human creature ever to go lower for a proof?

For, as indeed was very natural in such case, all government of the Poor by the Rich has long ago been given over to Supply-and-demand, Laissez-faire and suchlike, and universally declared to be "impossible."

---

[1] *Valetism* I.e., the character of a valet. Carlyle defines valetism in Book 2 as "cloth-worship and quack-worship."

[2] *Histrionism* Acting.

[3] *Gehenna and the Pool* I.e., Hell.

[4] *Westminster Hall* Location of the British Houses of Parliament.

"You are no sister of ours; what shadow of proof is there? Here are our parchments, our padlocks, proving indisputably our money-safes to be *ours*, and you to have no business with them. Depart! It is impossible!" Nay, what wouldst thou thyself have us do? cry indignant readers. Nothing, my friends—till you have got a soul for yourselves again. Till then all things are "impossible." Till then I cannot even bid you buy, as the old Spartans would have done, two-pence worth of powder and lead, and compendiously shoot to death this poor Irish Widow. Even that is "impossible" for you. Nothing is left but that she prove her sisterhood by dying, and infecting you with typhus. Seventeen of you lying dead will not deny such proof that she *was* flesh of your flesh; and perhaps some of the living may lay it to heart.

"Impossible": of a certain two-legged animal with feathers it is said, if you draw a distinct chalk-circle round him, he sits imprisoned, as if girt with the iron ring of Fate, and will die there, though within sight of victuals, or sit in sick misery there, and be fatted to death. The name of this poor two-legged animal is—Goose; and they make of him, when well fattened, *Pâté de foie gras,* much prized by some! …

CHAPTER 13—DEMOCRACY

If the Serene Highnesses and Majesties do not take note of that,[1] then, as I perceive, *that* will take note of itself! The time for levity, insincerity, and idle babble and play-acting, in all kinds, is gone by; it is a serious, grave time. Old long-vexed questions, not yet solved in logical words or parliamentary laws, are fast solving themselves in facts, somewhat unblessed to behold! This largest of questions, this question of Work and Wages, which ought, had we heeded Heaven's voice, to have begun two generations ago or more, cannot be delayed longer without hearing Earth's voice. "Labour" will verily need to be somewhat "organised," as they say—God knows with what difficulty. Man will actually need to have his

debts and earnings a little better paid by man; which, let Parliaments speak of them or be silent of them, are eternally his due from man, and cannot, without penalty and at length not without death penalty,[2] be withheld. How much ought to cease among us straightway, how much ought to begin straightway, while the hours yet are!

Truly they are strange results to which this of leaving all to "Cash," of quietly shutting-up the God's Temple, and gradually opening wide-open the Mammon's Temple, with "Lassez-faire, and Every man for himself," have led us in these days! We have Upper, speaking Classes, who indeed do "speak" as never man spake before; the withered flimsiness, the godless baseness and barrenness of whose Speech might of itself indicate what kind of Doing and practical Governing went on under it! For Speech is the gaseous element out of which most kinds of Practice and Performance, especially all kinds of moral Performance, condense themselves, and take shape; as the one is, so will the other be. Descending, accordingly, into the Dumb Class in its Stockport Cellars and Poor-Law Bastilles, have we not to announce that they also are hitherto unexampled in the History of Adam's Posterity?

Life was never a May-game[3] for men. In all times the lot of the dumb millions born to toil was defaced with manifold sufferings, injustices, heavy burdens, avoidable and unavoidable—not play at all, but hard work that made the sinews sore and the heart sore. As bond-slaves, *villani, bordarii, sochemanni,*[4] nay indeed as dukes, earls, and kings, men were oftentimes made weary of their life, and had to say, in the sweat of their brow and of their soul, Behold, it is not sport, it is grim earnest, and our back can bear no more! Who knows not what massacrings and harryings there have been—grinding, long-continuing, unbearable injustices—till the heart had to rise in madness, and some *"Eu Sachsen, nimith euer sachses,* You Saxons, out with your gully-knives,[5]

---

[1] *that* At the end of the previous chapter, Carlyle urged that "the proper epic of this world" should be "Tools and the Man," rather than "Arms and the Man," a reference to the opening line of Virgil's *Aeneid:* "Arma virumque cano" (Latin: "Of arms and the man I sing").

[2] *death penalty* Reference to the deaths caused by violent revolutions, such as the French Revolution.

[3] *May-game* Entertainment or performance (such as those traditionally making up part of the celebration on the first day of May).

[4] *villani … sochemanni* Classes of peasants in the feudal system.

[5] *gully-knives* Large household knives.

then!" You Saxons, some "arrestment," partial "arrestment of the Knaves and Dastards" has become indispensable! The page of Dryasdust[1] is heavy with such details.

And yet I will venture to believe that in no time, since the beginnings of Society, was the lot of those same dumb millions of toilers so entirely unbearable as it is even in the days now passing over us. It is not to die, or even to die of hunger, that makes a man wretched; many men have died; all men must die—the last exit of us all is in a Fire-Chariot of Pain.[2] But it is to live miserable we know not why; to work sore and yet gain nothing; to be heart-worn, weary, yet isolated, unrelated, girt-in with a cold universal Laissez-faire: it is to die slowly all our life long, imprisoned in a deaf, dead, Infinite Injustice, as in the accursed iron belly of a Phalaris' Bull![3] This is and remains forever intolerable to all men whom God has made. Do we wonder at French Revolutions, Chartisms, Revolts of Three Days? The times, if we will consider them, are really unexampled.

Never before did I hear of an Irish Widow reduced to "prove" her sisterhood by dying of typhus-fever and infecting seventeen "persons," saying in such undeniable way, "You *see* I was your sister!" Sisterhood, brotherhood, was often forgotten; but not till the rise of these ultimate Mammon and Shotbelt Gospels[4] did I ever see it so expressly denied. If no pious Lord or *Law-ward* would remember it, always some pious Lady ("*Hlaf-dig*,"[5] Benefactress, "*Loaf-giveress*," they say she is— blessings on her beautiful heart!) was there, with mild mother-voice and hand, to remember it; some pious thoughtful *Elder*, what we now call "Prester," *Presbyter* or "Priest," was there to put all men in mind of it, in the name of the God who had made all.

Not even in Black Dahomey[6] was it ever, I think, forgotten to the typhus-fever length. Mungo Park,[7] resourceless, had sunk down to die under the Negro Village-Tree, a horrible White object in the eyes of all. But in the poor Black Woman, and her daughter who stood aghast at him, whose earthly wealth and funded capital consisted of one small calabash of rice, there lived a heart richer than *Laissez-faire*: they, with a royal munificence, boiled their rice for him; they sang all night to him, spinning assiduous on their cotton distaffs, as he lay to sleep: "Let us pity the poor white man; no mother has he to fetch him milk, no sister to grind him corn!" Thou poor black Noble One, thou *Lady* too. Did not a God make thee too; was there not in thee too something of a God!

Gurth,[8] born thrall of Cedric the Saxon, has been greatly pitied by Dryasdust and others. Gurth, with the brass collar round his neck, tending Cedric's pigs in the glades of the wood, is not what I call an exemplar of human felicity. But Gurth, with the sky above him, with the free air and tinted boscage and umbrage[9] round him, and in him at least the certainty of supper and social lodging when he came home, Gurth to me seems happy, in comparison with many a Lancashire and Buckinghamshire man of these days, not born thrall of anybody! Gurth's brass collar did not gall him; Cedric *deserved* to be his master. The pigs were Cedric's, but Gurth too would get his parings of them. Gurth had the inexpressible satisfaction of feeling himself related indissolubly, though in a rude brass-collar way, to his fellow-mortals in this Earth. He had superiors, inferiors, equals. Gurth is now "emancipated" long since, has what we call "Liberty." Liberty, I am told, is a divine thing. Liberty when it becomes the "Liberty to die by starvation" is not so divine!

---

[1]　*Dryasdust*　Name given to a dull, pedantic historian, after the fictional antiquarian Dr. Jonas Dryasdust, to whom Walter Scott facetiously dedicated some of his novels.

[2]　*last exit … Pain*　See 2 Kings 2.11–12.

[3]　*Phalaris' Bull*　Phalaris, an ancient Sicilian tyrant, murdered wrong doers by placing them in a brass bull that sat over a fire.

[4]　*Shotbelt Gospels*　I.e., principles of the landed aristocracy who sought to maintain their exclusive right to shoot game.

[5]　*Hlaf-dig*　I.e., loaf-giver.

[6]　*Black Dahomey*　Area of West Africa, formerly belonging to the French, in which human sacrifice and cannibalism were rumored to take place.

[7]　*Mungo Park*　Scottish explorer and author of *Travels in the Interior of Africa* (1799), who was killed by Africans in Bussa in 1806.

[8]　*Gurth*　In Walter Scott's *Ivanhoe* (1819), Gurth is a serf (thrall) of the wealthy farmer Cedric.

[9]　*boscage and umbrage*　Grove and shade.

Liberty? The true liberty of a man, you would say, consisted in his finding out, or being forced to find out, the right path, and to walk thereon. To learn, or to be taught, what work he actually was able for, and then by permission, persuasion, and even compulsion, to set about doing of the same! That is his true blessedness, honour, "liberty," and maximum of wellbeing: if liberty be not that, I for one have small care about liberty. You do not allow a palpable madman to leap over precipices; you violate his liberty, you that are wise, and keep him, were it in strait-waistcoats, away from the precipices! Every stupid, every cowardly and foolish man is but a less palpable madman: his true liberty were that a wiser man, that any and every wiser man, could, by brass collars, or in whatever milder or sharper way, lay hold of him when he was going wrong, and order and compel him to go a little righter. O, if thou really art my *Senior*, Seigneur, my *Elder*, Presbyter or Priest—if thou art in very deed my *Wiser*, may a beneficent instinct lead and impel thee to "conquer" me, to command me! If thou do know better than I what is good and right, I conjure thee in the name of God, force me to do it; were it by never such brass collars, whips and handcuffs, leave me not to walk over precipices! That I have been called, by all the Newspapers, a "free man" will avail me little, if my pilgrimage have ended in death and wreck. O that the Newspapers had called me slave, coward, fool, or what it pleased their *sweet* voices to name me, and I had attained not death, but life! Liberty requires new definitions.

A conscious abhorrence and intolerance of Folly, of Baseness, Stupidity, Poltroonery[1] and all that brood of things, dwells deep in some men; still deeper in others an *unconscious* abhorrence and intolerance, clotted moreover by the beneficent Supreme Powers in what stout appetites, energies, egoisms so-called, are suitable to it. These latter are your Conquerors, Romans, Normans, Russians, Indo-English; Founders of what we call Aristocracies. Which indeed have they not the most "divine right" to found—being themselves very truly Αριστοι[2] BRAVEST, BEST, and conquering generally a confused rabble of WORST, or at lowest, clearly enough, of WORSE? I think their divine right, tried, with affirma-

tory verdict, in the greatest Law-Court known to me, was good! A class of men who are dreadfully exclaimed against by Dryasdust, of whom nevertheless beneficent Nature has oftentimes had need, and may, alas, again have need.

When, across the hundredfold poor scepticisms, trivialisms and constitutional cobwebberies of Dryasdust, you catch any glimpse of a William the Conqueror, a Tancred of Hauteville[3] or suchlike, do you not discern veritably some rude outline of a true God-made King, whom not the Champion of England cased in tin, but all Nature and the Universe were calling to the throne? It is absolutely necessary that he get thither. Nature does not mean her poor Saxon children to perish of obesity, stupor, or other malady, as yet. A stern Ruler and Line of Rulers therefore is called in—a stern but most beneficent *perpetual House-Surgeon* is by Nature herself called in, and even the appropriate *fees* are provided for him! Dryasdust talks lamentably about Hereward and the Fen Counties,[4] fate of Earl Waltheof,[5] Yorkshire and the North reduced to ashes—all which is undoubtedly lamentable. But even Dryasdust apprises me of one fact: "A child, in this William's reign, might have carried a purse of gold from end to end of England." My erudite friend, it is a fact which outweighs a thousand! Sweep away thy constitutional, sentimental, and other cobwebberies; look eye to eye, if thou still have any eye, in the face of this big burly William Bastard.[6] Thou wilt see a fellow of most flashing discernment, of most strong lion-heart, in whom, as it were, within a frame of oak and iron, the gods have planted the soul of "a man of genius"! Dost thou call that nothing? I call it an immense thing! Rage

[1] *Poltroonery* Cowardliness; mean-spiritedness.

[2] Αριστοι Greek: aristocrats.

[3] *William the Conqueror* King William I of England (who ruled from 1066 to 1087) was named "the Conqueror" after he won the throne from King Harold at the Battle of Hastings in 1066; *Tancred of Hauteville* Norman Crusader (1076–1112).

[4] *Hereward … Counties* Anglo-Saxon who rebelled against William I and organized uprisings in Lincolnshire and its surrounding counties (known collectively as the "Fen Counties" because of their marshland).

[5] *Earl Waltheof* Anglo-Saxon who was executed for treason by William I, but was later believed innocent and regarded as a martyr.

[6] *William Bastard* William I was an illegitimate son of Robert I, Duke of Normandy.

enough was in this Willelmus Conquaestor,[1] rage enough for his occasions—and yet the essential element of him, as of all such men, is not scorching *fire*, but shining illuminative *light*. Fire and light are strangely interchangeable; nay, at bottom, I have found them different forms of the same most godlike "elementary substance" in our world—a thing worth stating in these days. The essential element of this Conquaestor is, first of all, the most sun-eyed perception of what *is* really what on this God's-Earth—which, thou wilt find, does mean at bottom "Justice," and "Virtues" not a few—*Conformity* to what the Maker has seen good to make; that, I suppose, will mean Justice and a Virtue or two?

Dost thou think Willelmus Conquaestor would have tolerated ten years' jargon, one hour's jargon, on the propriety of killing Cotton manufactures by partridge[2] Corn Laws? I fancy, this was not the man to knock out of his night's-rest with nothing but a noisy bedlamism[3] in your mouth! "Assist us still better to bush the partridges; strangle Plugson[4] who spins the shirts?"—"*Par la Splendeur de Dieu!*"[5]—Dost thou think Willelmus Conquaestor, in this new time, with Steamengine Captains of Industry on one hand of him, and Joe-Manton Captains of Idleness on the other, would have doubted which *was* really the BEST; which did deserve strangling, and which not?

I have a certain indestructible regard for Willelmus Conquaestor. A resident House-Surgeon, provided by Nature for her beloved English People, and even furnished with the requisite fees, as I said; for he by no means felt himself doing Nature's work, this Willelmus, but his own work exclusively! And his own work withal it was, informed "*par la Splendeur de Dieu!*" I say, it is necessary to get the work out of such a man, however harsh that be! When a world, not yet doomed for death,

is rushing down to ever-deeper Baseness and Confusion, it is a dire necessity of Nature's to bring in her ARISTOCRACIES, her BEST, even by forcible methods. When their descendants or representatives cease entirely to *be* the Best, Nature's poor world will very soon rush down again to Baseness; and it becomes a dire necessity of Nature's to cast them out. Hence French Revolutions, Five-point Charters,[6] Democracies, and a mournful list of *Etceteras*, in these our afflicted times.

To what extent Democracy has now reached, how it advances irresistible with ominous, ever-increasing speed, he that will open his eyes on any province of human affairs may discern. Democracy is everywhere the inexorable demand of these ages, swiftly fulfilling itself. From the thunder of Napoleon battles, to the jabbering of Open-vestry in St. Mary Axe,[7] all things announce Democracy. A distinguished man, whom some of my readers will hear again with pleasure, thus writes to me what in these days he notes from the Wahngasse of Weissnichtwo,[8] where our London fashions seem to be in full vogue. Let us hear the Herr Teufelsdröckh[9] again, were it but the smallest word!

Democracy, which means despair of finding any Heroes to govern you, and contented putting-up with the want of them, alas, thou too, *mein Lieber*,[10] seest well how close it is of kin to *Atheism*, and other sad *Isms*: he who discovers no God whatever, how shall he discover Heroes, the visible Temples of God? Strange enough meanwhile it is to observe with what thoughtlessness, here in our rigidly Conservative Country, men rush into Democracy with full cry. Beyond doubt, his Excellenz the Titular Herr Ritter Kauderwalsch von

---

[1] *Willelmus Conquaestor*   Latin: William the Conqueror.

[2] *partridge*   Reference to the aristocracy's attachment to hunting game.

[3] *bedlamism*   Something characteristic of madness—specifically, of the Hospital of St. Mary of Bethlehem (referred to as "Bedlam"), an overcrowded and frenetic London asylum.

[4] *Plugson*   Fictional industrial firm to which Carlyle refers several times throughout *Past and Present*.

[5] *Par la ... Dieu*   French: By the splendor of God.

[6] *Five-point Charters*   The "People's Charter" (on which the Chartist movement was based) actually had six points, all concerning suffrage.

[7] *jabbering ... Axe*   I.e., the bickering of the rate-paying parishioners, who were generally allowed to express their opinions on temporal affairs of the Church.

[8] *Wahngasse of Weissnichtwo*   German: Delusion alley of I-know-not-where.

[9] *Herr Teufelsdröckh*   Carlyle writes about this fictional German philosopher, Diogenes Teufelsdröckh, in *Sartor Resartus*. He is said to be the author of *Clothes: Their Origin and Influence*, and his name, in German, literally means "God-born devil's dung."

[10] *mein Lieber*   German: my Dear.

Pferdefuss-Quacksalber,[1] he our distinguished Conservative Premier himself, and all but the thicker-headed of his Party discern Democracy to be inevitable as death, and are even desperate of delaying it much!

"You cannot walk the streets without beholding Democracy announce itself. The very Tailor has become, if not properly Sansculottic, which to him would be ruinous, yet a Tailor unconsciously symbolising, and prophesying with his scissors, the reign of Equality. What now is our fashionable coat? A thing of superfinest texture, of deeply meditated cut, with Malines-lace[2] cuffs, quilted with gold; so that a man can carry, without difficulty, an estate of land on his back? *Keineswegs*, By no manner of means! The Sumptuary Laws[3] have fallen into such a state of desuetude[4] as was never before seen. Our fashionable coat is an amphibium between barn-sack and drayman's doublet. The cloth of it is studiously coarse; the colour, a speckled soot-black or rust-brown gray, the nearest approach to a Peasant's. And for shape—thou shouldst see it! The last consummation of the year now passing over us is definable as Three Bags: a big bag for the body, two small bags for the arms, and by way of collar a hem! The first Antique Cheruscan[5] who, of felt-cloth or bear's-hide, with bone or metal needle, set about making himself a coat, before Tailors had yet awakened out of Nothing, did not he make it even so? A loose wide poke for body, with two holes to let out the arms, this was his original coat—to which holes it was soon visible that two small loose pokes, or sleeves, easily appended, would be an improvement.

"Thus has the Tailor-art, so to speak, overset itself, like most other things, changed its centre-of-gravity, whirled suddenly over from zenith to nadir. Your Stulz,[6] with huge somerset,[7] vaults from his high shopboard down to the depths of primal savagery, carrying much

along with him! For I will invite thee to reflect that the Tailor, as topmost ultimate froth of Human Society, is indeed swift-passing, evanescent, slippery to decipher, yet significant of much, nay of all. Topmost evanescent froth, he is churned-up from the very lees, and from all intermediate regions of the liquor. The general outcome he, visible to the eye, of what men aimed to do, and were obliged and enabled to do, in this one public department of symbolising themselves to each other by covering of their skins. A smack of all Human Life lies in the Tailor: its wild struggles towards beauty, dignity, freedom, victory; and how, hemmed-in by Sedan and Huddersfield,[8] by Nescience,[9] Dullness, Prurience,[10] and other sad necessities and laws of Nature, it has attained just to this: Gray savagery of Three Sacks with a hem!

"When the very Tailor verges towards Sansculottism, is it not ominous? The last Divinity of poor mankind dethroning himself, sinking *his* taper too, flame downmost, like the Genius of Sleep or of Death, admonitory that Tailor time shall be no more! For, little as one could advise Sumptuary Laws at the present epoch, yet nothing is clearer than that where ranks do actually exist, strict division of costumes will also be enforced; that if we ever have a new Hierarchy and Aristocracy, acknowledged veritably as such, for which I daily pray Heaven, the Tailor will reawaken, and be, by volunteering and appointment, consciously and unconsciously, a safeguard of that same." Certain farther observations, from the same invaluable pen, on our never-ending changes of mode, our perpetual nomadic and even apelike appetite for change and mere change in all the equipments of our existence, and the "fatal revolutionary character" thereby manifested, we suppress for the present. It may be admitted that Democracy, in all meanings of the word, is in full career; irresistible by any Ritter Kauderwalsch or other Son of Adam, as times go. "Liberty" is a thing men are determined to have.

But truly, as I had to remark in the meanwhile, "the liberty of not being oppressed by your fellow man" is an indispensable, yet one of the most insignificant frac-

---

[1] *Excellenz ... Pferdefuss-Quacksalber* German: Mr. Knight Gibberish Horsefoot-Mountebank. A reference to Sir Robert Peel, the Conservative Prime Minister.

[2] *Malines-lace* Lace made in Malines, a town in Belgium.

[3] *Sumptuary Laws* Laws regulating expenditure on food, dress, etc.

[4] *desuetude* Disuse.

[5] *Cheruscan* Member of an ancient German tribe.

[6] *Stulz* I.e., name of a high-class tailor.

[7] *somerset* Somersault.

[8] *Sedan and Huddersfield* Towns (the first French, the second English) where wool was woven.

[9] *Nescience* Ignorance.

[10] *Prurience* Tendency towards impure or lewd ideas.

tional, parts of Human Liberty. No man oppresses thee, can bid thee fetch or carry, come or go, without reason shown. True, from all men thou art emancipated; but from Thyself and from the Devil—? No man, wiser, unwiser, can make thee come or go; but thy own futilities, bewilderments, thy false appetites for Money, Windsor Georges[1] and suchlike? No man oppresses thee, O free and independent Franchiser; but does not this stupid Porter-pot[2] oppress thee? No Son of Adam can bid thee come or go; but this absurd Pot of Heavy-wet,[3] this can and does! Thou art the thrall not of Cedric the Saxon, but of thy own brutal appetites and this scoured dish of liquor. And thou pratest of thy "liberty"? Thou entire blockhead!

Heavy-wet and gin; alas, these are not the only kinds of thraldom. Thou who walkest in a vain show, looking out with ornamental dilettante sniff and serene suprem-acy at all Life and all Death; and amblest jauntily, perking up thy poor talk into crotchets,[4] thy poor conduct into fatuous somnambulisms; and *art* as an "enchanted Ape" under God's sky, where thou mightest have been a man, had proper Schoolmasters and Con-querors, and Constables with cat-o'-nine tails,[5] been vouchsafed thee—dost thou call that "liberty"? Or your unreposing Mammon-worshipper again, driven, as if by Galvanisms,[6] by Devils and Fixed Ideas, who rises early and sits late, chasing the impossible, straining every faculty to "fill himself with the east wind"[7]—how merciful were it, could you, by mild persuasion, or by the severest tyranny so-called, check him in his mad path, and turn him into a wiser one! All painful tyranny, in that case again, were but mild "surgery," the pain of it cheap, as health and life, instead of galvanism and fixed-idea, are cheap at any price.

Sure enough, of all paths a man could strike into,

there *is*, at any given moment, a *best path* for every man; a thing which, here and now, it were of all things *wisest* for him to do—which, could he be but led or driven to do, he were then doing "like a man," as we phrase it, all men and gods agreeing with him, the whole Universe virtually exclaiming Well-done to him! His success, in such case, were complete; his felicity a maximum. This path, to find this path and walk in it, is the one thing needful for him. Whatsoever forwards him in that, let it come to him even in the shape of blows and spurnings, is liberty; whatsoever hinders him, were it wardmotes,[8] open-vestries, pollbooths, tremendous cheers, rivers of heavy-wet, is slavery.

The notion that a man's liberty consists in giving his vote at election-hustings,[9] and saying, "Behold, now I too have my twenty-thousandth part of a Talker in our National Palaver;[10] will not all the gods be good to me?" is one of the pleasantest! Nature nevertheless is kind at present, and puts it into the heads of many, almost of all. The liberty especially which has to purchase itself by social isolation, and each man standing separate from the other, having no business with him but a cash-account, this is such a liberty as the Earth seldom saw—as the Earth will not long put up with, recom-mend it how you may. This liberty turns out, before it have long continued in action, with all men flinging up their caps round it, to be, for the Working Millions, a liberty to die by want of food; for the Idle Thousands and Units, alas, a still more fatal liberty to live in want of work, to have no earnest duty to do in this God's-World anymore. What becomes of a man in such predicament? Earth's Laws are silent, and Heaven's speak in a voice which is not heard. No work, and the ineradicable need of work, give rise to new very won-drous life-philosophies, new very wondrous life-prac-tices! Dilettantism, Pococurantism, Beau-Brummel-ism,[11] with perhaps an occasional, half-mad, protesting

---

[1] *Windsor Georges*   I.e., the pomp of royalty.

[2] *Porter-pot*   Vessel of porter, a dark beer.

[3] *Heavy-wet*   Malt liquor.

[4] *crotchets*   Odd notions; perverse conceits.

[5] *cat-o'-nine tails*   Whip with nine lashes.

[6] *Galvanisms*   Applications of electricity.

[7] *east wind*   The east wind was proverbially harmful to one's health. In the Bible it is seen as destructive; the wind blowing from the east onto Palestine brings dry, hot air from the desert, and is harmful to crops.

[8] *wardmotes*   Meetings of the citizens of a ward, or area of the city.

[9] *election-hustings*   I.e., election proceedings. The husting was a temporary platform on which candidates for Parliament stood to address electors.

[10] *Palaver*   Rigamarole, prolonged and tedious discussion.

[11] *Pococurantism*   Attitude of indifference or unconcern, from an Italian expression describing an indifferent person; *Beau-Brummel-ism*   Obsession with fashion. George Bryan Brummel (known as

burst of Byronism, establish themselves; at the end of a certain period, if you go back to "the Dead Sea," there is, say our Moslem friends, a very strange "Sabbath day" transacting itself there![1] Brethren, we know but imperfectly yet, after ages of Constitutional Government, what Liberty and Slavery are.

Democracy, the chase of Liberty in that direction shall go its full course, unrestrainable by him of Pferdefuss-Quacksalber, or any of *his* household. The Toiling Millions of Mankind, in most vital need and passionate instinctive desire of Guidance, shall cast away False-Guidance and hope, for an hour, that No-Guidance will suffice them; but it can be for an hour only. The smallest item of human Slavery is the oppression of man by his Mock Superiors; the palpablest, but I say at bottom the smallest. Let him shake off such oppression, trample it indignantly under his feet; I blame him not, I pity and commend him. But oppression by your Mock Superiors well shaken off, the grand problem yet remains to solve: that of finding government by your Real Superiors! Alas, how shall we ever learn the solution of that, benighted, bewildered, sniffing, sneering, god-forgetting unfortunates we are? It is a work for centuries, to be taught us by tribulations, confusions, insurrections, obstructions; who knows if not by conflagration and despair! It is a lesson inclusive of all other lessons; the hardest of all lessons to learn.

One thing I do know: those Apes, chattering on the branches by the Dead Sea, never got it learned, but chatter there to this day. To them no Moses need come a second time; a thousand Moseses would be but so many painted Phantasms, interesting Fellow-Apes of new strange aspect, whom they would "invite to dinner," be glad to meet with in lion-soirées. To them the voice of Prophecy, of heavenly monition, is quite ended. They chatter here, all Heaven shut to them, to the end of the world. The unfortunates! Oh, what is dying of hunger, with honest tools in your hand, with a manful purpose in your heart, and much real labour lying round you done, in comparison? You honestly quit your tools, quit a most muddy confused coil of sore work, short

rations, of sorrow, dispiritments, and contradictions, having now honestly done with it all, and await, not entirely in a distracted manner, what the Supreme Powers, and the Silences and the Eternities may have to say to you.

A second thing I know: this lesson will have to be learned—under penalties! England will either learn it, or England also will cease to exist among Nations. England will either learn to reverence its Heroes, and discriminate them from its Sham-Heroes and Valets and gaslighted Histrios, and to prize them as the audible God's-voice, amid all inane jargons and temporary market-cries, and say to them with heart-loyalty, "Be ye King and Priest, and Gospel and Guidance for us," or else England will continue to worship new and ever-new forms of Quackhood—and so, with what resiliences and reboundings matters little, go down to the Father of Quacks! Can I dread such things of England? Wretched, thickeyed, gross-hearted mortals, why will ye worship lies, and "Stuffed Clothes-suits created by the ninth-parts of men"![2] It is not your purses that suffer, your farm-rents, your commerces, your mill-revenues, loud as ye lament over these; no, it is not these alone, but a far deeper than these: it is your souls that lie dead, crushed down under despicable Nightmares, Atheisms, Brain-fumes, and are not souls at all, but mere succedanea[3] for *salt* to keep your bodies and their appetites from putrefying! Your cotton-spinning and thrice-miraculous mechanism, what is this too, by itself, but a larger kind of Animalism? Spiders can spin, Beavers can build and show contrivance, the Ant lays-up accumulation of capital, and has, for aught I know, a Bank of Antland. If there is no soul in man higher than all that, did it reach to sailing on the cloud-rack and spinning sea-sand, then I say, man is but an animal, a more cunning kind of brute; he has no soul, but only a succedaneum for salt. Whereupon, seeing himself to be truly of the beasts that perish, he ought to admit it, I think—and also straightway universally to kill himself, and so, in a manlike manner at least *end*, and wave these brute-worlds *his* dignified farewell! ...

"Beau Brummel") was a leader of fashion in Regency England.

[1] *there is ... there* According to an Islamic myth, a tribe living on the banks of the Dead Sea were turned into apes after refusing to acknowledge Moses' prophecies.

[2] *the ninth-parts of men* I.e., worthless men.

[3] *succedanea* Substitutes.

from BOOK 4

CHAPTER 4—CAPTAINS OF INDUSTRY

If I believed that Mammonism with its adjuncts was to continue henceforth the one serious principle of our existence, I should reckon it idle to solicit remedial measures from any Government, the disease being insusceptible of remedy. Government can do much, but it can in no wise[1] do all. Government, as the most conspicuous object in Society, is called upon to give signal of what shall be done; and, in many ways, to preside over, further, and command the doing of it. But the Government cannot do, by all its signaling and commanding, what the Society is radically indisposed to do. In the long-run every Government is the exact symbol of its People, with their wisdom and unwisdom; we have to say, Like People like Government. The main substance of this immense Problem of Organising Labour, and first of all of Managing the Working Classes, will, it is very clear, have to be solved by those who stand practically in the middle of it, by those who themselves work and preside over work. Of all that can be enacted by any Parliament in regard to it, the germs must already lie potentially extant in those two Classes, who are to obey such enactment. A Human Chaos *in* which there is no light, you vainly attempt to irradiate by light shed *on* it; order never can arise there.

But it is my firm conviction that the "Hell of England" will *cease* to be that of "not making money," that we shall get a nobler Hell and a nobler Heaven! I anticipate light *in* the Human Chaos, glimmering, shining more and more, under manifold true signals from without That light shall shine. Our deity no longer being Mammon, O Heavens, each man will then say to himself, "Why such deadly haste to make money? I shall not go to Hell, even if I do not make money! There is another Hell, I am told!" Competition, at railway-speed, in all branches of commerce and work will then abate; good felt-hats for the head, in every sense, instead of seven-feet lath-and-plaster hats on wheels, will then be discoverable! Bubble-periods,[2] with their panics and commercial crises, will again become infrequent; steady modest industry will take the place of gambling specula-

tion. To be a noble Master, among noble Workers, will again be the first ambition with some few; to be a rich Master only the second. How the Inventive Genius of England, with the whirr of its bobbins and billy-rollers[3] shoved somewhat into the backgrounds of the brain, will contrive and devise, not cheaper produce exclusively, but fairer distribution of the produce at its present cheapness! By degrees, we shall again have a Society with something of Heroism in it, something of Heaven's Blessing on it; we shall again have, as my German friend asserts, "instead of Mammon-Feudalism with unsold cotton-shirts and Preservation of the Game, noble just Industrialism and Government by the Wisest!"

It is with the hope of awakening here and there a British man to know himself for a man and divine soul, that a few words of parting admonition, to all persons to whom the Heavenly Powers have lent power of any kind in this land, may now be addressed. And first to those same Master-Workers, Leaders of Industry, who stand nearest and in fact powerfulest, though not most prominent, being as yet in too many senses a Virtuality rather than an Actuality.

The Leaders of Industry, if Industry is ever to be led, are virtually the Captains of the World; if there be no nobleness in them, there will never be an Aristocracy more. But let the Captains of Industry consider: once again, are they born of other clay than the old Captains of Slaughter, doomed forever to be no Chivalry, but a mere gold-plated *Doggery*—what the French well name *Canaille,* "Doggery" with more or less gold carrion at its disposal? Captains of Industry are the true Fighters, henceforth recognisable as the only true ones—Fighters against Chaos, Necessity, and the Devils and Jötuns[4]— and lead on Mankind in that great, and alone true and universal warfare; the stars in their courses fighting for them, and all Heaven and all Earth saying audibly, Well done! Let the Captains of Industry retire into their own hearts, and ask solemnly, If there is nothing but vulturous hunger for fine wines, valet reputation, and gilt

---

[1] *wise* Way.

[2] *Bubble-periods* Violent fluctuations in the stock market.

[3] *bobbins* Wooden spools or cylinders on which cotton or thread is wound; *billy-rollers* Machines for preparing cotton or wool for spinning.

[4] *Jötuns* Members of a mythological Norse race of giants.

carriages discoverable there? Of hearts made by the Almighty God I will not believe such a thing. Deep-hidden under wretchedest god-forgetting Cants, Epicurisms,[1] Dead-Sea Apisms, forgotten as under foulest fat Lethe[2] mud and weeds, there is yet, in all hearts born into this God's-World, a spark of the Godlike slumbering. Awake, O nightmare sleepers; awake, arise, or be forever fallen! This is not playhouse poetry, it is sober fact. Our England, our world, cannot live as it is. It will connect itself with a God again, or go down with nameless throes and fire-consummation to the Devils. Thou who feelest aught[3] of such a Godlike stirring in thee, any faintest intimation of it as through heavy-laden dreams, follow *it*, I conjure thee. Arise, save thyself, be one of those that save thy country.

Buccaneers, Chactaw Indians,[4] whose supreme aim in fighting is that they may get the scalps, the money, that they may amass scalps and money—out of such came no Chivalry, and never will! Out of such came only gore and wreck, infernal rage and misery; desperation quenched in annihilation. Behold it, I bid thee; behold there, and consider! What is it that thou have a hundred thousand-pound bills laid-up in thy strong-room, a hundred scalps hung-up in thy wigwam? I value not them or thee. Thy scalps and thy thousand-pound bills are as yet nothing, if no nobleness from within irradiate them; if no Chivalry, in action, or in embryo ever struggling towards birth and action, be there.

Love of men cannot be bought by cash-payment, and without love men cannot endure to be together. You cannot lead a Fighting World without having it regimented, chivalried; the thing, in a day, becomes impossible. All men in it, the highest at first, the very lowest at last, discern consciously, or by a noble instinct,

this necessity. And can you any more continue to lead a Working World unregimented, anarchic? I answer, and the Heavens and Earth are now answering, No! The thing becomes not "in a day" impossible; but in some two generations it does. Yes, when fathers and mothers, in Stockport hunger-cellars, begin to eat their children; and Irish widows have to prove their relationship by dying of typhus-fever; and amid Governing "Corporations of the Best and Bravest," busy to preserve their game by "bushing," dark millions of God's human creatures start up in mad Chartisms, impracticable Sacred-Months, and Manchester Insurrections; and there is a virtual Industrial Aristocracy as yet only half-alive, spell-bound amid money-bags and ledgers; and an actual Idle Aristocracy seemingly near dead in somnolent delusions, in trespasses[5] and double-barrels, "sliding," as on inclined planes, which every new year they *soap* with new Hansard's-jargon[6] under God's sky, and so are "sliding," ever faster, towards a "scale" and balance-scale whereon is written *Thou art found Wanting*—in such days, after a generation or two, I say, it does become, even to the low and simple, very palpably impossible! No Working World, any more than a Fighting World, can be led on without a noble Chivalry of Work, and laws and fixed rules which follow out of that, far nobler than any Chivalry of Fighting was. As an anarchic multitude on mere Supply-and-demand, it is becoming inevitable that we dwindle in horrid suicidal convulsion and self-abrasion, frightful to the imagination, into *Chactaw* Workers. With wigwams and scalps, with palaces and thousand-pound bills, with savagery, depopulation, chaotic desolation! Good Heavens, will not one French Revolution and Reign of Terror suffice us, but must there be two? There will be two if needed; there will be twenty if needed; there will be precisely as many as are needed. The Laws of Nature will have themselves fulfilled. That is a thing certain to me.

Your gallant battle-hosts and work-hosts, as the others did, will need to be made loyally yours; they must and will be regulated, methodically secured in their just

---

[1] *Epicurisms* Pursuits of sensual pleasures, luxury, and ease, so named after the philosophical system of third-century BCE Greek thinker Epicurus.

[2] *Lethe* River of forgetfulness in Hades, the classical underworld.

[3] *aught* Anything.

[4] *Chactaw Indians* The Choctaw, who formerly inhabited central and southern Mississippi and southwest Alabama, and who were known to take as trophies the scalps of enemies killed in battle. The tribe had a friendly relationship with the American settlers; secessions of their eastern land to the settlers allowed Mississippi to become a state. In exchange, they were granted land in present-day Oklahoma, to which they were removed between 1831 and 1903.

[5] *trespasses* I.e., fear of trespassers encroaching on their game preserves.

[6] *Hansard's-jargon* Parliamentary debate (the official report of which is known as "Hansard," after the printer Luke Hansard, who compiled it for many years).

share of conquest under you—joined with you in veritable brotherhood, sonhood, by quite other and deeper ties than those of temporary day's wages! How would mere red-coated regiments, to say nothing of chivalries, fight for you, if you could discharge them on the evening of the battle, on payment of the stipulated shillings—and they discharge you on the morning of it! Chelsea Hospitals,[1] pensions, promotions, rigorous lasting covenant on the one side and on the other, are indispensable even for a hired fighter. The Feudal Baron, much more—how could he subsist with mere temporary mercenaries round him at sixpence a day, ready to go over to the other side, if sevenpence were offered? He could not have subsisted, and his noble instinct saved him from the necessity of even trying! The Feudal Baron had a Man's Soul in him, to which anarchy, mutiny, and the other fruits of temporary mercenaries were intolerable; he had never been a Baron otherwise, but had continued a Chactaw and Buccaneer. He felt it precious, and at last it became habitual, and his fruitful enlarged existence included it as a necessity, to have men round him who in heart loved him; whose life he watched over with rigour yet with love; who were prepared to give their life for him, if need came. It was beautiful; it was human! Man lives not otherwise, nor can live contented, anywhere or anywhen. Isolation is the sum-total of wretchedness to man. To be cut off, to be left solitary; to have a world alien, not your world, all a hostile camp for you, not a home at all, of hearts and faces who are yours, whose you are! It is the frightfulest enchantment, too truly a work of the Evil One. To have neither superior, nor inferior, nor equal, united manlike to you. Without father, without child, without brother. Man knows no sadder destiny. "How is each of us," exclaims Jean Paul,[2] "so lonely in the wide bosom of the All!" Encased each as in his transparent "ice-palace," our brother visible in his, making signals and gesticulations to us—visible, but forever unattainable; on his bosom we shall never rest, nor he on ours. It was not a God that did this; no!

Awake, ye noble Workers, warriors in the one true war; all this must be remedied. It is you who are already half-alive, whom I will welcome into life, whom I will conjure, in God's name, to shake off your enchanted sleep, and live wholly! Cease to count scalps, gold-purses; not in these lies your or our salvation. Even these, if you count only these, will not long be left. Let buccaneering be put far from you; alter, speedily abrogate all laws of the buccaneers, if you would gain any victory that shall endure. Let God's justice, let pity, nobleness and manly valour, with more gold-purses or with fewer, testify themselves in this your brief Life-transit to all the Eternities, the Gods and Silences. It is to you I call; for ye are not dead, ye are already half-alive; there is in you a sleepless dauntless energy, the prime-matter of all nobleness in man. Honour to you in your kind. It is to you I call; ye know at least this, That the mandate of God to His creature man is Work! The future Epic of the World rests not with those that are near dead, but with those that are alive, and those that are coming into life.

Look around you. Your world-hosts are all in mutiny, in confusion, destitution; on the eve of fiery wreck and madness! They will not march farther for you, on the sixpence a day and supply-and-demand principle; they will not, nor ought they, nor can they. Ye shall reduce them to order, begin reducing them. To order, to just subordination; noble loyalty in return for noble guidance. Their souls are driven nigh mad; let yours be sane and ever saner. Not as a bewildered bewildering mob, but as a firm regimented mass, with real captains over them, will these men march any more. All human interests, combined human endeavours, and social growths in this world, have, at a certain stage of their development, required organising; and Work, the grandest of human interests, does now require it.

God knows, the task will be hard; but no noble task was ever easy. This task will wear away your lives, and the lives of your sons and grandsons; but for what purpose, if not for tasks like this, were lives given to men? Ye shall cease to count your thousand-pound scalps; the noble of you shall cease! Nay, the very scalps, as I say, will not long be left if you count only these. Ye shall cease wholly to be barbarous vulturous Chactaws, and become noble European Nineteenth-Century Men. Ye shall know that Mammon, in never such gigs[3] and

---

[1] *Chelsea Hospitals*   Homes such as the Chelsea Royal Hospital, for elderly or disabled veterans.
[2] *Jean Paul*   German writer Jean Paul Richter (1763–1825).
[3] *gigs*   Two-wheeled carriages.

flunky "respectabilities," is not the alone God, that of himself he is but a Devil, and even a Brute-god.

Difficult? Yes, it will be difficult. The short-fibre cotton, that too was difficult. The waste cotton-shrub, long useless, disobedient, as the thistle by the wayside—have ye not conquered it, made it into beautiful bandana webs, white woven shirts for men, bright-tinted air-garments wherein flit goddesses? Ye have shivered mountains asunder, made the hard iron pliant to you as soft putty; the Forest-giants, Marsh-jötuns bear sheaves of golden-grain; Aegir[1] the Sea-demon himself stretches his back for a sleek highway to you, and on Firehorses and Windhorses ye career. Ye are most strong. Thor[2] red-bearded, with his blue sun-eyes, with his cheery heart and strong thunder-hammer, he and you have prevailed. Ye are most strong, ye Sons of the icy North, of the far East—far marching from your rugged Eastern Wildernesses, hitherward from the gray Dawn of Time! Ye are Sons of the *Jötun-land*, the land of Difficulties Conquered. Difficult? You must try this thing. Once try it with the understanding that it will and shall have to be done. Try it as ye try the paltrier thing, making of money! I will bet on you once more, against all Jötuns, Tailor-gods, Double-barrelled Law-wards, and Denizens of Chaos whatsoever!

—1843

---

[1] *Aegir* Norse god of the sea.

[2] *Thor* Norse god of thunder and rain.

WORK AND POVERTY

CONTEXTS

The Industrial Revolution brought rapid, pervasive, and frequently disorienting change to Britain. Manufacturing changed the face of the nation, from its physical appearance to the structure of family life. The Industrial Revolution had begun in the eighteenth century with the invention of new technology for spinning and weaving, and with the invention of the steam engine to power these machines, manufacturers established factories (originally called "mills") for centralized production. Mill towns, such as Manchester boomed as workers crowded into cities seeking employment. There they lived in crowded, unsanitary conditions that bred disease—resulting in frequent epidemics of cholera or typhoid. The second wave of the Industrial Revolution came with the spread of the railway in the 1840s, which allowed the iron and coal industries to flourish. Before legislation began to be passed in the 1840s, workers, including small children, worked long hours in dangerous, unhealthy conditions, without job security, insurance, or benefits. When occasional economic depressions caused factories and mines to close or cut down hours of operation, these workers often starved.

When workers moved from the countryside to the growing cities, they adapted many of their rural traditions to their new surroundings, including those of the bawdy ballad, which laborers often sang while they worked. "The Steam Loom Weaver" is an example from the 1830s. The daily reality for most mill workers, however, was far from amusing, despite the contrary implications of this light-hearted ballad. The next selection is from the testimony of Elizabeth Bentley, one of the few women to speak before the 1832 Sadler Committee on the Labour of Children in Factories. Social reformer Michael Sadler had argued in Parliament for the passing of a Ten Hours Bill (limiting factory work to ten hours a day) and had detailed the suffering of child laborers in order to move his fellow members of Parliament to action. When the government asked for a committee of enquiry into the conditions of child laborers, Sadler chaired it, and the resulting testimony was published in Samuel Kydd's 1857 *History of the Factory Movement*. Bentley was one of thirty-eight workers (only three of whom were female) to be interviewed.

Andrew Ure's *The Philosophy of Manufacturers* was one of the best-known works arguing in favor of the factory system. Ure viewed the factory system as a self-regulating organism that should be beyond government regulation, and into which workers should be introduced at a very young age, when they could be easily disciplined. While Ure speaks of the national wealth and prosperity that the factory system created, William Dodd, a child laborer, gives evidence in the excerpt following of the human costs of such "prosperity." Dodd's narrative of his life, which he published to expose the falsities of "eye-witness" accounts such as Ure's, details the lifetime of suffering and physical deformity that resulted from his early introduction to factory life.

Around the 1840s, Victorians began to take a greater interest in issues of public health, particularly the living conditions of the poor. The very worst of these conditions were being documented in newspapers, books, magazines, and journals by those who sought to arouse public concern and effect change. For many modern readers, it is strange to see the correspondent in Joseph Adshead's *Distress in Manchester* (excerpted here) insisting that the conditions of the poor did not result from any moral failings of their own. At the time, however, such ideas were not readily accepted. Poverty and disease in slums was often assumed to result from moral failings among the poor, and it was somewhat radical to suggest that change could best be effected if reformers focused on improving the environmental, rather than the moral, conditions of the slums. Adshead's text, which combines personal testimony given by those working for the relief of the poor with economic facts about the status of the poor—their numbers, earnings, expenditures, living conditions, etc.—showed that most poor people were not poor out of any fault of their own, but were hapless victims of the Industrial Revolution. The reality for many working-class people was that they would work until they could work no more, at which point they would likely perish—a fate the woman in Thomas Hood's poem "Song of the Shirt" (reprinted below) seems to anticipate eagerly—or live the remainder of their days in a workhouse.

Friedrich Engels, author of *The Condition of the Working Class in England*, excerpted below, sought to expose not only the degrading conditions of the poor, but also the deliberate ways in which the middle classes shielded themselves from the realities of working-class people's suffering. Having come from Germany to study the cotton trade, Engels was struck by the conditions in England's urban centers. In this excerpt, he examines the living conditions of the working-class areas of Manchester (he also examines those of England's other "Great Towns," such as London) and the ways in which these areas are systematically hidden from the view of wealthier citizens. Engels went on to collaborate with Karl Marx on *The Communist Manifesto* (1848), and together the two men laid the foundation of modern Communism.

While laborers in urban centers suffered deplorable living and working conditions, rural laborers also suffered from exploitative wages, long work hours, and poor housing. The philanthropist Reverend Lord Sidney Godolphin Osborne championed various humanitarian causes in a series of letters (1844–84) published in *The Times*; in the letter reproduced below, he draws public attention to the injustices and hardships faced by agricultural workers. Osborne focuses on workers in the farming county of Dorset, in southwest England, where wages for farm labor were among the lowest in the nation. On the whole, rural families made do with dwellings, food, and clothing that were even worse than what their urban counterparts had—but poor people in the countryside nonetheless lived longer than those in the unsanitary, polluted cities and factory towns.

The excerpt following, from Elizabeth Gaskell's novel *Mary Barton: A Tale of Manchester Life*, shows the opposing effects of industrialism on the rich and the poor, and the ways in which the factory system resulted in further alienation between classes. Gaskell contrasts the home lives of the rich and poor and details the private suffering of the latter during the economic depression known as the "hungry forties." *Mary Barton* was part of a developing genre known as the "social problem novel," which focused on the rampant poverty, unemployment, and disease that pervaded the Industrial Revolution. In his slightly later novel *Hard Times*, Charles Dickens details the dehumanizing effects of the factory system and factory managers' lack of recognition of the shared humanity of their employees. The fictional "Coketown" (so called because of the soot that blackens the city), in which his novel is set, is based on Dickens's observations of northern industrial towns such as Manchester and Preston.

Hard Times was first published serially in Dickens's magazine *Household Words*, which often included non-fiction material on social issues. One such article, "Ground in the Mill" by journalist and academic Henry Morley, was part of a series about factory owners' disregard for their employees' lives. A key reference point in Morley's article is the Factories Act of 1844, an important piece of legislation to improve conditions for women, youth, and child workers in cotton mills—but a piece of legislation that did not go far enough, and that was neither thoroughly nor uniformly enforced.

One of the era's most influential depictions of working class and poor people was author and social reformer Henry Mayhew's *London Labour and the London Poor*, excerpted below. Asked by *The Morning Chronicle* to document, as metropolitan correspondent, the lives of the urban poor, Mayhew produced eighty-two articles that he later expanded into a four-volume collection of testimony of the lives of the lower class. He painted the underworld of Victorian society in unprecedented detail, shedding light on the specificities of economic exchange and the economic order that governed the poor. Perhaps more importantly, his work provided Victorians with a personal glimpse into the lives of the poor that helped to shape Victorian social theories. The serial newspaper publications were so popular that they resulted in the establishment of a fund to assist "Labour and the Poor." Mayhew had an ear for individual dialects, slang, and other oddities of speech, and composed each subject's narrative in language that, as closely as possible, imitated the speaker's own words. His characters were so compelling that Mayhew's narratives influenced the depiction of such characters in fiction, and writers such as Charles Dickens drew upon his representations of the poor to bring life to their own characters.

⌘ ⌘ ⌘

Anonymous, "The Steam Loom Weaver" (c. 1830)

O ne morning in summer I did ramble,
   In the pleasant month of June,
The birds did sing the lambkins play,
Two lovers walking in their bloom,
5   The lassie was a steam loom weaver,
The lad an engine driver keen,
All their discourse was about weaving.
And the getting up of steam.

She said my loom is out of fettle,[1]
10   Can you right it yes or no,
You say you are an engine driver,
Which makes the steam so rapid flow;
My lambs and jacks[2] are out of order,
My laith[3] in motion has not been,
15   So work away without delay,
And quickly muster up the steam.

I said fair maid you seem determined,
No longer for to idle be,
Your healds[4] and laith I'll put in motion,
20   Then work you can without delay,
She said young man a pair of pickers,[5]

A shuttle too I want you ween,[6]
Without these three I cannot weave,
So useless would be the steam.

25   Dear lass these things I will provide,
But when to labour will you begin
As soon my lad as things are ready
My loom shop you can enter in.
A shuttle true and pickers too,
30   This young man did provide amain.[7]
And soon her loom was put in tune
So well it was supplied with steam.

Her loom worked well the shuttle flew,
His nickers[8] played the tune nick-nack,
35   Her laith did move with rapid motion,
Her temples, healds, long-lambs and jacks,
Her cloth beam rolled the cloth up tight,
The yarn beam emptied soon its seam,
The young man cried your loom works, light
40   And quickly then off shot the steam.

She said young man another web,
Upon the beam let's get don't strike,
But work away while yet it's day,
This steam loom weaving well I like,
45   He said good lass I cannot stay,
But if a fresh warp you will beam
If ready when I come this way,
I'd strive for to get up the steam.

---

[1] *out of fettle* Out of order.

[2] *lambs and jacks* Lambs are foot pedals that operate the jacks, the oscillating levers that throw the yarn into two alternate sets.

[3] *laith* Loom; or (literally) the supporting stand of the loom.

[4] *healds* Small wires through which the warp passes.

[5] *pickers* Small instrument that moves back and forth in the shuttle-box, driving the shuttle through the warp (the threads that extend lengthwise in the loom).

[6] *ween* Consider; expect.

[7] *amain* At once.

[8] *nickers* Part of a center bit, which nicks a hole to be cut by a tool.

from Elizabeth Bentley, *Testimony before the 1832 Committee on the Labour of Children in Factories* (1857)

"I am twenty-three years of age, and live at Leeds. I began to work at Mr. Busk's flax mill when I was six years old. I was then a little 'doffer.'[1] In that mill we worked from five in the morning till nine at night, when they were 'throng';[2] when they were not so 'throng,' the usual hours of labour were from six in the morning till seven at night. The time allowed for our meals was forty minutes at noon; not any time was allowed for breakfast or 'drinking': these we got as we could. When our work was bad, we had hardly any time to eat them at all: we were obliged to leave them or take them home. When we did not take our uneaten food home, the overlooker took it and gave it to his pigs. I consider 'doffing' to be a laborious employment. When the frames are full, the 'doffers' have to stop them, and take the 'flyers'[3] off, and take the full bobbins off, and carry them to the roller, and then put empty ones on, and set the frame going again. I was kept constantly on my feet; there were so many frames, and they run so quick, the labour was excessive, there was not time for anything. When the 'doffers' flagged[4] a little, or were too late, they were strapped. Those who were last in 'doffing' were constantly strapped—girls as well as boys. I have been strapped severely, and have been hurt by the strap excessively. The overlooker I was under was a very severe man. When I and others have been fatigued and worn out, and had not baskets enough to put the bobbins in, we used to put them in the window bottoms, and that broke the panes sometimes; and I broke one one time, and the overlooker strapped me on the arm, and it rose a blister, and I ran home to my mother. I worked at Mr. Busk's factory three or four years.

"When I left Mr. Busk's, I then went to Benyon's factory; I was about ten years of age, and was employed as a weigher in the card-room.[5] At Benyon's factory we worked from half-past five till eight at night; when they were 'throng,' until nine. The spinners at that mill were allowed forty minutes at noon for meals; no more time throughout the day was allowed. Those employed in the card-rooms had, in addition to the forty minutes at noon, a quarter of an hour allowed for their breakfast, and a quarter of an hour for their 'drinking.' The carding-room is more oppressive than the spinning department: those at work cannot see each other for dust. The 'cards' get so soon filled up with waste and dirt, they must be stopped or they would take fire: the stoppages are as much for the benefit of the employer as for the working people. The children at Benyon's factory were beat up to their labour with a strap.... The girls have many times had black marks upon their skins. Had the parents complained of this excessive ill-usage, the probable consequence would have been the loss of the employment of the child. Of this result the parents were afraid.

"I worked in the card-room; it was so dusty that the dust got upon my lungs, and the work was so hard. I was middling strong when I went there, but the work was so bad; I got so bad in health, that when I pulled the baskets down, I pulled my bones out of their places. The basket I pulled was a very large one; that was full of weights, upheaped, and pulling the basket, pulled my shoulder out of its place, and my ribs have grown over it. That hard work is generally done by women: it is not fit for children. There was no spinning for me, and I therefore did that work....

"I am considerably deformed in person in consequence of this labour. I was about thirteen years old when my deformity began to come on, and it has got worse since. It is five years since my mother died, and she was never able to get me a pair of good stays[6] to hold me up; and when my mother died I had to do for myself, and got me a pair. Before I worked at a mill I was as straight a little girl as ever went up and down town. I was straight until I was thirteen. I have been attended by a medical

---

[1] *doffer* Worker who assists the spinner by removing the full spindles, or bobbins, from the carding machine (which combs the cotton or wool) and replacing them with empty ones.

[2] *throng* Busy.

[3] *flyers* Part of the spinning machine that twists the thread and winds it upon the bobbin.

[4] *flagged* Slowed down.

[5] *card-room* Room that held the carding machines, which combed and cleaned the wool or cotton in preparation for spinning.

[6] *stays* Bodice stiffened with strips of whale-bone that gives support and shape to the figure; a corset.

gentleman, Mr. Hare. He said it was owing to hard labour, and working in the factories. ...

"I have had the misfortune, from being a straight and healthful girl, to become very much otherwise in person. I do not know of any other girls that have become weak and deformed in like manner. I have known others who have been similarly injured in health. I am deformed in the shoulders; it is very common indeed to have weak ankles and crooked knees, that is brought on by stopping the spindle.

"I have had experience in wet spinning—it is very uncomfortable. I have stood before the frames till I have been wet through to my skin; and in winter-time, when myself and others have gone home, our clothes have been frozen, and we have nearly caught our death from cold. We have stopped at home one or two days, just as we were situated in our health; had we stopped away any length of time we should have found it difficult to keep our situation.

"I am now in the poor-house at Hunslet. Not any of my former employers come to see me. When I was at home, Mr. Walker made me a present of 1s. or 2s.,[1] but since I left my work and have gone to the poor-house, no one has come nigh me. I was very willing to have worked as long as I was able, and to have supported my widowed mother. I am utterly incapable now of any exertion of that sort, and am supported by the parish."[2]

from Andrew Ure, *The Philosophy of Manufactures* (1835)

In its precise acceptation, the factory system is of recent origin, and may claim England for its birthplace. The mills for throwing silk, or making organzine,[3] which were mounted centuries ago in several of the Italian states, and furtively transferred to this country by Sir Thomas Lombe in 1718, contained indeed certain elements of a factory, and probably suggested some hints of those grander and more complex combinations of self-acting machines, which were first embodied half a century later in our cotton manufacture by Richard Arkwright, assisted by gentlemen of Derby, well acquainted with its celebrated silk establishment. ...

When the first water-frames for spinning cotton were erected at Cromford, in the romantic valley of the Derwent, about sixty years ago, mankind were little aware of the mighty revolution which the new system of labour was destined by Providence to achieve, not only in the structure of British society, but in the fortunes of the world at large. Arkwright alone had the sagacity to discern, and the boldness to predict in glowing language, how vastly productive human industry would become, when no longer proportioned in its results to muscular effort, which is by its nature fitful and capricious, but when made to consist in the task of guiding the work of mechanical fingers and arms, regularly impelled with great velocity by some indefatigable physical power. What his judgment so clearly led him to perceive, his energy of will enabled him to realize with such rapidity and success, as would have done honour to the most influential individuals, but were truly wonderful in that obscure and indigent artisan. The main difficulty did not, to my apprehension, lie so much in the invention of a proper self-acting mechanism for drawing out and twisting cotton into a continuous thread, as in the distribution of the different members of the apparatus into one cooperative body, in impelling each organ with its appropriate delicacy and speed, and, above all, in training human beings to renounce their desultory[4] habits of work, and to identify themselves with the unvarying regularity of the complex automaton. To devise and administer a successful code of factory discipline, suited to the necessities of factory diligence, was the Herculean enterprise, the noble achievement of Arkwright. Even at the present day, when the system is perfectly organized, and its labour lightened to the utmost, it is found nearly impossible to convert persons past the age of puberty, whether drawn from rural or from handicraft occupations, into useful factory hands. After struggling for a while to conquer their listless or restive habits, they either renounce the employment spontaneously, or are dismissed by the overlookers on account of inattention. ...

---

[1] *s.* Shilling.

[2] *supported by the parish* I.e., with public funds.

[3] *organzine* Silk yarn.

[4] *desultory* Half-hearted, lacking enthusiasm.

It required, in fact, a man of a Napoleon nerve and ambition to subdue the refractory tempers of work-people accustomed to irregular paroxysms of diligence, and to urge on his multifarious and intricate constructions in the face of prejudice, passion, and envy. Such was Arkwright, who, suffering nothing to stay or turn aside his progress, arrived gloriously at the goal, and has for ever affixed his name to a great era in the annals of mankind, an era which has laid open unbounded prospects of wealth and comfort to the industrious, however much they may have been occasionally clouded by ignorance and folly.

... In my recent tour, continued during several months, through the manufacturing districts, I have seen tens of thousands of old, young, and middle-aged of both sexes, many of them too feeble to get their daily bread by any of the former modes of industry, earning abundant food, raiment, and domestic accommodation, without perspiring at a single pore, screened meanwhile from the summer's sun and the winter's frost, in apartments more airy and salubrious[1] than those of the metropolis, in which our legislative and fashionable aristocracies assemble. In those spacious halls the benignant power of steam summons around him his myriads of willing menials, and assigns to each the regulated task, substituting for painful muscular effort on their part, the energies of his own gigantic arm, and demanding in return only attention and dexterity to correct such little aberrations as casually occur in his workmanship. The gentle docility of this moving force qualifies it for impelling the tiny bobbins of the lace-machine with a precision and speed inimitable by the most dexterous hands, directed by the sharpest eyes. Hence, under its auspices, and in obedience to Ark-wright's polity,[2] magnificent edifices, surpassing far in number, value, usefulness, and ingenuity of construction, the boasted monuments of Asiatic, Egyptian, and Roman despotism, have, within the short period of fifty years, risen up in this kingdom, to show to what extent capital, industry, and science may augment the resources of a state, while they meliorate the condition of its citizens. Such is the factory system, replete with prodigies in mechanics and political economy, which promises, in its

future growth, to become the great minister of civilization to the terraqueous[3] globe, enabling this country, as its heart, to diffuse along with its commerce the life-blood of science and religion to myriads of people still lying "in the region and shadow of death."[4] ...

No master would wish to have any wayward children to work within the walls of his factory who do not mind their business without beating, and he therefore usually fines or turns away any spinners who are known to maltreat their assistants. Hence, ill-usage of any kind is a very rare occurrence. I have visited many factories, both in Manchester and in the surrounding districts, during a period of several months, entering the spinning rooms, unexpectedly, and often alone, at different times of the day, and I never saw a single instance of corporal chastisement inflicted on a child, nor indeed did I ever see children in ill-humour. They seemed to be always cheerful and alert, taking pleasure in the light play of their muscles—enjoying the mobility natural to their age. The scene of industry, so far from exciting sad emotions in my mind, was always exhilarating. It was delightful to observe the nimbleness with which they pieced the broken ends, as the mule-carriage[5] began to recede from the fixed roller beam, and to see them at leisure, after a few seconds' exercise of their tiny fingers, to amuse themselves in any attitude they chose, till the stretch and winding-on were once more completed. The work of these lively elves seemed to resemble a sport, in which habit gave them a pleasing dexterity. Conscious of their skill, they were delighted to show it off to any stranger. As to exhaustion by the day's work, they evinced no trace of it on emerging from the mill in the evening; for they immediately began to skip about any neighbouring playground, and to commence their little amusements with the same alacrity as boys issuing from a school. It is moreover my firm conviction that if children are not ill-used by bad parents or guardians, but receive in food and raiment the full benefit of what

___

[1] *salubrious* Favorable to health.

[2] *polity* Mode of administration.

[3] *terraqueous* Consisting of land and water.

[4] *in the ... death* From Matthew 4.16.

[5] *broken ends* I.e., of thread. This was the job of the "piecer," who ensured that the process of spinning could continue uninterrupted; *mule-carriage* The movable part of the mule, a kind of spinning machine, invented in 1779, that could spin yarn of varying thicknesses.

they earn, they would thrive better when employed in our modern factories than if left at home in apartments too often ill-aired, damp, and cold.

from William Dodd, *A Narrative of the Experience and Sufferings of William Dodd, a Factory Cripple, Written by Himself* (1841)

Dear Reader,—I wish it to be distinctly and clearly understood, that, in laying before you the following sheets, I am not actuated by any motive of ill-feeling to any party with whom I have formerly been connected; on the contrary, I have a personal respect for some of my former masters, and am convinced that, had they been in any other line of life, they would have shone forth as ornaments to the age in which they lived; but having witnessed the efforts of some writers (who can know nothing of the factories by experience) to mislead the minds of the public upon a subject of so much importance, I feel it to be my duty to give to the world a fair and impartial account of the working of the factory system, as I have found it in twenty-five years' experience.

… Of four children in our family, I was the only boy; and we were all, at different periods, as we could meet with employers, sent to work in the factories. My eldest sister was ten years of age before she went; consequently, she was, in a manner, out of harm's way, her bones having become firmer and stronger than ours, and capable of withstanding the hardships to which she was exposed much better than we could.… I was born on the 18th of June, 1804; and in the latter part of 1809, being then turned of five years of age, I was put to work at card-making,[1] and about a year after I was sent, with my sisters, to the factories. I was then a fine, strong, healthy, hardy boy, straight in every limb, and remarkably stout and active.…

From six to fourteen years of age, I went through a series of uninterrupted, unmitigated suffering, such as

very rarely falls to the lot of mortals so early in life, except to those situated as I was, and such as I could not have withstood, had I not been strong, and of a good constitution.

My first place in the factories was that of piecer, or the lowest situation: but as the term conveys only a vague idea of the duties to be performed, it will be necessary here to give such explanation as may enable those unacquainted with the business to form a just conception of what those duties are, and to judge of the inadequacy of the remuneration or reward for their performance, and the cruelty of the punishments inflicted for the neglect of those duties.…

The position in which the piecer stands to his work is with his right foot forward, and his right side facing the frame: the motion he makes in going along in front of the frame, for the purpose of piecing, is neither forwards nor backwards, but in a sidling direction, constantly keeping his right side towards the frame. In this position he continues during the day, with his hands, feet, and eyes constantly in motion. It will be easily seen, that the chief weight of his body rests upon his right knee, which is almost always the first joint to give way. The number of cripples with the right knee in, greatly exceed those with the left knee in; a great many have both knees in such as my own from this cause.

Another evil resulting from the position in which the piecer stands, is what is termed "splay-foot," which may be explained thus: in a well-formed foot, there is a finely formed arch of bones immediately under the instep and ankle joint. The continual pressure of the body on this arch, before it is sufficiently strong to bear such pressure (as in the case of boys and girls in the factories) causes it to give way: the bones fall gradually down, the foot then becomes broad and flat, and the owner drags it after him with the broad side first. A great many factory cripples are in this state; this is very often attended with weak ankle and knee joints. I have a brother-in-law exactly thus, who has tried everything likely to do him good, but without success.

---

[1] *card-making* Cards combed and cleansed fibers in preparation for spinning.

A

NARRATIVE

OF THE

EXPERIENCE AND SUFFERINGS

OF

WILLIAM DODD,

A FACTORY CRIPPLE.

WRITTEN BY HIMSELF.

GIVING AN ACCOUNT OF THE HARDSHIPS AND SUFFERINGS
HE ENDURED IN EARLY LIFE, UNDER WHAT DIFFICULTIES HE
ACQUIRED HIS EDUCATION, THE EFFECTS OF FACTORY LABOUR
ON HIS MIND AND PERSON, THE UNSUCCESSFUL EFFORTS MADE
BY HIM TO OBTAIN A LIVELIHOOD IN SOME OTHER LINE OF
LIFE, THE COMPARISON HE DRAWS BETWEEN AGRICULTURAL
AND MANUFACTURING LABOURERS, AND OTHER MATTERS
RELATING TO THE WORKING CLASSES.

SECOND EDITION.

LONDON:
PUBLISHED BY L. & G. SEELEY, 169, FLEET STREET,
AND HATCHARD & SON, 187, PICCADILLY.
1841.

PRICE ONE SHILLING.

Title page from William Dodd, *A Narrative of the Experience and Sufferings of William Dodd, a Factory Cripple, Written by Himself* (1841).

The spinner and the piecer are intimately connected together:[1] the spinner works by the piece, being paid by the stone[2] for the yarn spun; the piecer is hired by the week, and paid according to his abilities. The piecers are the servants of the spinners, and both are under an overlooker; and liable to be dismissed at a week's notice. Being thus circumstanced, it is clearly the advantage of the spinner to have good able piecers, who ought, in return, to be well paid....

In order to induce the piecer to do his work quick and well, the spinner has recourse to many expedients, such as offering rewards of a penny or two-pence for a good week's work inducing them to sing, which, like the music in the army, has a very powerful effect, and keeps them awake and active longer than any other thing; and, as a last resource, when nothing else will do, he takes the strap, or the billy-roller,[3] which are laid on most unmercifully, accompanied by a round volley of oaths; and I pity the poor wretch who has to submit to the infliction of either.

On one occasion, I remember being thrashed with the billy-roller till my back, arms, and legs were covered with ridges as thick as my finger. This was more than I could bear, and, seeing a favourable opportunity, I slipped out and stole off home along some by-ways, so as not to be seen. Mother stripped me, and was shocked at my appearance. The spinner, not meeting with any other to suit him, had the assurance to come and beg that mother would let me go again, and promised not to strike me with the billy-roller any more. He kept his promise, but instead of using the roller, he used his fist.

… A piecer, it will be seen, is an important person in the factories, inasmuch as it is impossible to do without them. Formerly, boys and girls were sent to work in the factories as piecers at the early age of five or six years—as in my own case—but now, owing to the introduction of some wise laws for the regulation of factories,[4] they cannot employ any as piecers before they have attained the age of 9 years; at which age their bones are comparatively strong, generally speaking, and more able to endure the hardships to which they will be exposed.

They now enjoy many privileges that we had not, such as attending schools, limited hours of labour, &c.; but still it is far from being a desirable place for a child. Formerly, it was nothing but work till we could work no longer. I have frequently worked at the frame till I could scarcely get home, and in this state have been stopped by people in the streets who noticed me shuffling along,

---

[1] *The spinner … together* The spinner, who ran the "billy" (or "slubbing," the machine that spins yarn) was dependent on the piecer for the preparation of the wool.

[2] *stone* Unit of measurement equal to 14 pounds.

[3] *billy-roller* Uppermost of a series of wooden rollers through which the wool is moved to the spindles. It was very long and easily removed from the billy; as a result, it was a notorious instrument of punishment to factory children.

[4] *some wise … factories* The 1833 Factory Act, which prevented children under nine from working in any factories except silk mills. It also decreed that children under 11 (and, eventually, under 13) could not work more than 9 hours a day or 48 hours a week, and that all working children had to be provided with education at the expense of the factory owners.

A wood engraving of a child mine-worker included in the *Report of the Commission of the Employment of Children and Young Persons in the Mines* (1842).

and advised me to work no more in the factories: but I was not my own master. Thus year after year passed away, my afflictions and deformities increasing. I could not associate with anybody; on the contrary, I sought every opportunity to rest myself, and to shrink into any corner to screen myself from the prying eye of the curious and scornful! During the day, I frequently counted the clock, and calculated how many hours I had still to remain at work; my evenings were spent in preparing for the following day—in rubbing my knees, ankles, elbows, and wrists with oil, &c., and wrapping them in warm flannel! (for everything was tried to benefit me, except the right one—that of taking me from the work) after which, with a look at, rather than eating my supper (the bad smells of the factory having generally taken my appetite away) I went to bed, to cry myself to sleep, and pray that the Lord would take me to Himself before morning.

... A great many are made cripples by over-exertion. Among those who have been brought up from infancy with me in the factories, and whom death has spared, few have escaped without some injury. My brother-in-law and myself have been crippled by this cause, but in different ways; my sister partly by over-exertion and partly by machinery. On going home to breakfast one

morning, I was much surprised at seeing several of the neighbours and two doctors in our house. On inquiring the cause, I found that my second sister had nearly lost her hand in the machinery. She had been working all night, and, fatigued and sleepy, had not been so watchful as she otherwise would have been; and consequently, her right hand became entangled in the machine which she was attending. Four iron teeth of a wheel, three-quarters of an inch broad, and one-quarter of an inch thick, had been forced through her hand, from the back part, among the leaders, &c.; and the fifth iron tooth fell upon the thumb, and crushed it to atoms. It was thought, for some time, that she would lose her hand. But it was saved; and, as you may be sure, it is stiff and contracted, and is but a very feeble apology for a hand. This accident might have been prevented, if the wheels above referred to had been boxed off,[1] which they might have been for a couple of shillings; and the very next week after this accident, a man had two fingers taken off

---

[1] *the wheels ... boxed off* The Factory Act of 1844 decreed that fly-wheels connected to mechanical parts, such as shafts, had to be boxed off or fenced. However, such a project would cost a few shillings per wheel, which would add up to a considerable expense, and would make it difficult for workers to clean the machinery. As a result, many factory owners ignored the law when it came into effect.

his hand, by the very same wheels—and still they are not boxed off!

Thomas Annan, *Close No. 193, High Street, Glasgow* (1868). Thomas Annan was hired by the Glasgow City Improvement Trust to photograph the city's slums before they were demolished. Many of his pictures show the open sewers and narrow passageways that were features of slum life. (See also Annan's photographs in the Contexts section on photography.)

from Joseph Adshead, *Distress in Manchester. Evidence (Tabular and Otherwise) of the State of the Labouring Classes in 1840–42* (1842)

Chapter 3: Narratives of Suffering

The following painfully interesting report is furnished by a gentleman whose attention was directed to the social and moral condition of the labouring classes, with a view to its improvement. The inquiry was made in January last, and it will be seen that its details are, if possible, more harrowing than any yet given:

January, 1842.

Dear Sir,—An engagement I had made to oblige a friend rendered it necessary that I should visit the inhabitants of several streets in Ancoats and in the neighbourhood of Oldham Road. As this district is not selected as the most destitute, I believe a few cases I shall state will give a very faithful illustration of the condition of tens of thousands of the manufacturing poor.

Upon the first day of our visitation I called at a house occupied by a poor man, a widower with one child, a boy between seven and eight; they were in a state of extreme poverty; the man is about thirty-five years of age, and professed himself able and most anxious to work, but had not been able to obtain any employment for many months; both were living upon what the child could obtain by begging. Upon quitting this house the man called our attention to an adjoining cellar, occupied by a woman who had been deserted by her husband. This cellar was both very dark and very damp, the roof not more than seven feet high, and the area of the floor not more than twelve square yards; its occupants were this woman and her child, a boy six years old, a widow, a lodger with three children, and a second widow with two children, sister of the woman who tenanted the cellar; these nine individuals are all crowded in a place so dark and contracted as to be unfit for the residence of any human being. It was in this abode of wretchedness that we witnessed a remarkable illustration of the sympathy and compassion of the poor for those who are still less favourably circumstanced. On the day previous to our visit, one of these poor women had observed a poor houseless wanderer with two children, ready to sink with hunger and fatigue; this poor creature's husband had left her three months before to seek employment, which she was sure he had not been able to procure, or, as she said, he would soon have found her and let her know. Her poor hostess had no better accommodation to offer than a dark unpaved closet adjoining their cellar, and here, without bed or bedding beyond a handful of dirty shavings which she used as a pillow, the mother and her famishing children were thankful to take shelter: during the night the younger of the children, an infant eleven months old, died, doubtless from long exposure to cold and the want of that support which the breast of the poor, starved, and perishing mother had failed to supply. When we entered the cellar we saw this victim of want laid out upon a board suspended from the roof, and the other children (some of whom were so poorly provided with clothing as to be unfit to quit the cellar without indecent exposure) standing around; the poor mother had left her remaining child and gone out to beg assistance to inter her infant.

In the next house we entered we found two men, one twenty-seven, the other twenty-five, both weavers, and out of work; they both appeared in delicate health, one, however, much worse than the other; neither of them had been able to earn a shilling for several weeks. To our inquiry how they lived, they replied, "We do indeed *exist*, we cannot say we live." One of them produced a dish with potato peelings, which one of their wives had been successful in begging; this they assured us was the only food they had or expected to taste that day. These men were members of a temperance society, were both remarkably intelligent, and we inferred from the kind and patient manner in which they spoke of their poverty and its causes, which they appear perfectly to comprehend, that their minds were considerably under the influence of moral and religious principles. These men were not victims of intemperance, nor improvidence, nor idleness, nor disease, nor anything else which they could have foreseen or provided against; but, reduced and broken-hearted by the impossibility of obtaining work, they and their families are sinking in the midst of misery which they can neither remove nor flee from.

This is a spectacle more calculated than almost any other we can conceive to distress a rightly constituted mind. Men, with physical strength, mental cultivation, and moral principle in active exercise, after having spent their time, and strength, and money, it may be, in learning a trade, starving in the largest manufacturing town in the world for the want of employment! And why? Let the supporters of corn laws[1] answer. ...

Many were the families we visited who assured us they had not tasted food that day. Misery and want,

hunger and nakedness, are not confined to particular localities: they are widely spread, and are spreading more widely. The number of the destitute is daily increasing. The universal testimony is, that there never was any distress equal to that which exists at present—that all other seasons of distress were trifling in comparison. The intemperate and the improvident, indeed, are the first to suffer in all seasons of distress; but it is long since distress has reached the sober, the industrious, the provident, and the respected among the labouring class.

Thomas Hood, "Song of the Shirt" (1843)

With fingers weary and worn,
  With eyelids heavy and red,
A woman sat, in unwomanly rags,
  Plying her needle and thread—
Stitch—stitch—stitch!
  In poverty, hunger, and dirt,
And still with a voice of dolorous pitch
  She sang the "Song of the Shirt."

"Work—work—work
  Till the brain begins to swim;
Work—work—work
  Till the eyes are heavy and dim!
Seam, and gusset,[2] and band,
  Band, and gusset, and seam;
Till over the buttons I fall asleep,
  And sew them on in a dream!

"O! men, with sisters dear!
  O! men, with mothers and wives!
It is not linen you're wearing out,
  But human creatures' lives!
Stitch—stitch—stitch,
  In poverty, hunger, and dirt,
Sewing at once, with a double thread,
  A shroud[3] as well as a shirt.

[1] *corn laws* Laws that kept the prices of grain artificially high to prevent an agricultural depression after the Napoleonic Wars (1803–15). Sir Robert Peel, the Prime Minister, repealed the laws in 1846.

[2] *gusset* Triangular piece of material inserted into a piece of clothing to strengthen or enlarge some part.

[3] *shroud* Sheet in which a corpse is wrapped for burial.

25 "But why do I talk of Death?
    That phantom of grisly bone;
    I hardly fear his terrible shape,
    It seems so like my own—
    It seems so like my own,
30 Because of the fasts I keep:
    Oh! God! that bread should be so dear,
    And flesh and blood so cheap!

    "Work—work—work!
    My labour never flags;
35 And what are its wages? A bed of straw,
    A crust of bread and rags,
    That shatter'd roof, and this naked floor
    A table—a broken chair—
40 A wall so blank, my shadow I thank
    For sometimes falling there!

    "Work—work—work!
    From weary chime to chime,
    Work—work—work
45 As prisoners work for crime!
    Band, and gusset, and seam,
    Seam, and gusset, and band,
    Till the heart is sick, and the brain benumb'd,
    As well as the weary hand.

50 "Work—work—work,
    In the dull December light,
    And work—work—work,
    When the weather is warm and bright—
    While underneath the eaves
55 The brooding swallows cling,
    As if to show me their sunny backs
    And twit me with the spring.

    "Oh! but to breathe the breath
    Of the cowslip and primrose[1] sweet—
60 With the sky above my head,
    And the grass beneath my feet,
    For only one short hour
    To feel as I used to feel,

___
[1] *cowslip ... primrose* Wildflowers.

John Thomson's photograph of "The crawler" (1877). This photograph is taken from Thomson's famous project, *Street Life in London* (1877–78), one of the era's most influential pieces of social documentary. Thomson collaborated with Adolph Smith to create text to accompany the photographs. This picture, one of the best known, shows a destitute woman who told Thomson that she spent her nights on the steps of a workhouse and her days looking after a friend's baby, in exchange for a cup of tea and some bread.

    Before I knew the woes of want
65 And the walk that costs a meal:

    "Oh, but for one short hour!
    A respite, however brief!
    No blessed leisure for Love or Hope,
    But only time for grief!
70 A little weeping would ease my heart,
    But in their briny head

My tears must stop, for every drop
Hinders needle and thread!"

With fingers weary and worn,
75 With eyelids heavy and red,
A woman sat, in unwomanly rags,
Plying her needle and thread—
Stitch—stitch—stitch!
In poverty, hunger, and dirt,
80 And still with a voice of dolorous pitch,
Would that its tone could reach the rich!
She sang this "Song of the Shirt!"

from Friedrich Engels, *The Condition of the Working Class in England in 1844* (1845; trans. Florence Wischnewetzky, 1887)

CHAPTER 3: THE GREAT TOWNS

Manchester lies at the foot of the southern slope of a range of hills, which stretch hither from Oldham, their last peak, Kersallmoor, being at once the racecourse and the Mons Sacer[1] of Manchester. Manchester proper lies on the left bank of the Irwell, between that stream and the two smaller ones, the Irk and the Medlock, which here empty into the Irwell. On the right bank of the Irwell, bounded by a sharp curve of the river, lies Salford, and farther westward Pendleton; northward from the Irwell lie Upper and Lower Broughton; northward of the Irk, Cheetham Hill; south of the Medlock lies Hulme; farther east Chorlton on Medlock; still farther, pretty well to the east of Manchester, Ardwick. The whole assemblage of buildings is commonly called Manchester, and contains about four hundred thousand inhabitants, rather more than less. The town itself is peculiarly built, so that a person may live in it for years, and go in and out daily without coming into contact with a working people's quarter or even with workers, that is, so long as he confines himself to his business or to pleasure walks. This arises chiefly from the fact that by unconscious tacit agreement, as well as with outspoken conscious determination, the working people's quarters are sharply separated from the sections of the city reserved for the middle class; or, if this does not succeed, they are concealed with the cloak of charity. Manchester contains, at its heart, a rather extended commercial district, perhaps half a mile long and about as broad, and consisting almost wholly of offices and warehouses. Nearly the whole district is abandoned by dwellers, and is lonely and deserted at night; only watchmen and policemen traverse its narrow lanes with their dark lanterns. This district is cut through by certain main thoroughfares upon which the vast traffic concentrates, and in which the ground level is lined with brilliant shops. In these streets the upper floors are occupied, here and there, and there is a good deal of life upon them until late at night. With the exception of this commercial district, all Manchester proper, all Salford and Hulme, a great part of Pendleton and Chorlton, two-thirds of Ardwick, and single stretches of Cheetham Hill and Broughton are all unmixed working people's quarters, stretching like a girdle, averaging a mile and a half in breadth, around the commercial district. Outside, beyond this girdle, lives the upper and middle bourgeoisie, the middle bourgeoisie in regularly laid out streets in the vicinity of the working quarters, especially in Chorlton and the lower lying portions of Cheetham Hill; the upper bourgeoisie in remoter villas with gardens in Chorlton and Ardwick, or on the breezy heights of Cheetham Hill, Broughton, and Pendleton, in free, wholesome country air, in fine, comfortable homes, passed once every half or quarter hour by omnibuses going into the city. And the finest part of the arrangements is this, that the members of this money aristocracy can take the shortest road through the middle of all the labouring districts to their places of business, without ever seeing that they are in the midst of the grimy misery that lurks to the right and the left. For the thoroughfares leading from the Exchange in all directions out of the city are lined, on both sides, with an almost unbroken series of shops, and are so kept in the hands of the middle and lower bourgeoisie, which, out of self-interest, cares for a decent and cleanly external appearance and can *care* for it. True, these shops bear some relation to the districts which lie behind them, and are more elegant in the commercial and residential quarters than when they hide grimy working men's dwellings; but they suffice to conceal from the

---

[1] *Mons Sacer* Latin: Sacred Mountain.

eyes of the wealthy men and women of strong stomachs and weak nerves the misery and grime which form the complement to their wealth. So, for instance, Deansgate, which leads from the Old Church directly southward, is lined first with mills and warehouses, then with second-rate shops and alehouses; farther south, when it leaves the commercial district, with less inviting shops, which grow dirtier and more interrupted by beer houses and gin palaces the farther one goes, until at the southern end the appearance of the shops leaves no doubt that workers and workers only are their customers. So Market Street running south-east from the Exchange; at first brilliant shops of the best sort, with counting-houses or warehouses above; in the continuation, Piccadilly, immense hotels and warehouses; in the farther continuation, London Road, in the neighbourhood of the Medlock, factories, beerhouses, shops for the humbler bourgeoisie and the working population; and from this point onward, large gardens and villas of the wealthier merchants and manufacturers. In this way anyone who knows Manchester can infer the adjoining districts, from the appearance of the thoroughfare, but one is seldom in a position to catch from the street a glimpse of the real labouring districts. I know very well that this hypocritical plan is more or less common to all great cities; I know, too, that the retail dealers are forced by the nature of their business to take possession of the great highways; I know that there are more good buildings than bad ones upon such streets everywhere, and that the value of land is greater near them than in remoter districts; but at the same time I have never seen so systematic a shutting out of the working class from the thoroughfares, so tender a concealment of everything which might affront the eye and the nerves of the bourgeoisie, as in Manchester. And yet, in other respects, Manchester is less built according to a plan, after official regulations, is more an outgrowth of accident, than any other city; and when I consider in this connection the eager assurances of the middle class that the working class is doing famously, I cannot help feeling that the liberal manufacturers, the "Big Wigs" of Manchester, are not so innocent after all, in the matter of this sensitive method of construction.

I may mention just here that the mills almost all adjoin the rivers or the different canals that ramify throughout the city, before I proceed at once to describe the labouring quarters. First of all, there is the Old Town of Manchester, which lies between the northern boundary of the commercial district and the Irk. Here the streets, even the better ones, are narrow and winding, like Todd Street, Long Millgate, Withy Grove, and Shude Hill, the houses dirty, old, and tumble-down, and the construction of the side streets utterly horrible. Going from the Old Church to Long Millgate, the stroller has at once a row of old-fashioned houses on the right, of which not one has kept its original level; these are remnants of the old pre-manufacturing Manchester, whose former inhabitants have removed with their descendants into better-built districts, and have left the houses, which were not good enough for them, to a working-class population strongly mixed with Irish blood. Here one is in an almost undisguised working men's quarter, for even the shops and beerhouses hardly take the trouble to exhibit a trifing degree of cleanliness. But all this is nothing in comparison with the courts and lanes which lie behind, to which access can be gained only through covered passages, in which no two human beings can pass at the same time. Of the irregular cramming together of dwellings in ways which defy all rational plan, of the tangle in which they are crowded literally one upon the other, it is impossible to convey an idea. And it is not the buildings surviving from the old times of Manchester which are to blame for this; the confusion has only recently reached its height when every scrap of space left by the old way of building has been filled up and patched over until not a foot of land is left to be further occupied....

The south bank of the Irk is here very steep and between fifteen and thirty feet high. On this abrupt slope there are planted three rows of houses, of which the lowest rise directly out of the river, while the front walls of the highest stand on the crest of the rise in Long Millgate. Among them are mills on the river; in short, the method of construction is as crowded and disorderly here as in the lower part of Long Millgate. Right and left a multitude of covered passages lead from the main street into numerous courts, and he who turns in thither gets into filth and disgusting grime, the equal of which is not to be found—especially in the courts which lead down to the Irk, and which contain unqualifiedly the most horrible dwellings which I have yet beheld. In one of these courts there stands directly at the entrance, at the end of the covered passage, a privy without a door, so dirty that the inhabitants can pass into and out of the court only by passing through foul pools of stagnant urine and excrement. This is the first court on the Irk above Ducie Bridge—in case anyone should care to look into it. Below it on the river there are several tanneries which fill the whole neighbourhood with the stench of animal putrefaction. Below Ducie Bridge the only entrance to most of the houses is by means of narrow, dirty stairs and over heaps of refuse and filth. The first court below Ducie Bridge, known as Allen's Court, was in such a state at the time of the cholera[1] that the sanitary police ordered it evacuated, swept, and disinfected with chloride of lime.... Since then, it seems to have been partially torn down and rebuilt; at least, looking down from Ducie Bridge, the passer-by sees several ruined walls and heaps of debris with some newer houses. The view from this bridge, mercifully concealed from mortals of small stature by a parapet as high as a man, is characteristic for the whole district. At the bottom flows, or rather stagnates, the Irk, a narrow, coal-black, foul-smelling stream, full of debris and refuse, which it deposits on the lower right bank. In dry weather, a lone string of the most disgusting blackish-green slime pools are left standing on this bank, from the depths of which bubbles of miasmatic[2] gas constantly arise and give forth a stench unendurable even on the bridge forty or fifty feet above the surface of the stream. But besides this, the stream itself is checked every few paces by high weirs, behind which slime and refuse accumulate and rot in thick masses. Above the bridge are tanneries, bone mills, and gasworks, from which all drains and refuse find their way into the Irk, which receives further the contents of all the neighbouring sewers and privies. It may be easily imagined, therefore, what sort of residue the stream deposits. Below the bridge you look upon the piles of debris, the refuse, filth, and offal from the courts on the steep left bank; here each house is packed close behind its neighbour and a bit of each is visible, all black, smoky, crumbling, ancient, with broken panes and window-

frames. The background is furnished by old barrack-like factory buildings. On the lower right bank stands a long row of houses and mills, the second row being a ruin without a roof, piled with debris; the third stands so low that the lowest floor is uninhabitable, and therefore without windows or doors. Here the background embraces the pauper burial-ground, the station of the Liverpool and Leeds railway, and, in the rear of this, the workhouse, the "Poor-Law Bastille"[3] of Manchester, which, like a citadel, looks threateningly down from behind its high walls and parapets on the hilltop, upon the working people's quarter below....

Such is the Old Town of Manchester, and, on re-reading my description, I am forced to admit that instead of being exaggerated, it is far from black enough to convey a true impression of the filth, ruin, and uninhabitableness, the defiance of all considerations of cleanliness, ventilation, and health which characterize the construction of this single district, containing at least twenty to thirty thousand inhabitants. And such a district exists in the heart of the second city of England, the first manufacturing city of the world. If anyone wishes to see in how little space a human being can move, how little air—and *such* air—he can breathe, how little of civilization he may share and yet live, it is only necessary to travel hither. True, this is the *Old* Town, and the people of Manchester emphasize the fact whenever anyone mentions to them the frightful condition of this Hell upon Earth; but what does that prove? Everything which here arouses horror and indignation is of recent origin, belongs to the *industrial epoch*. The couple of hundred houses which belong to Old Manchester have been long since abandoned by their original inhabitants; the industrial epoch alone has crammed into them the swarms of workers whom they now shelter; the industrial epoch alone has built up every spot between these old houses to make a covering for the masses whom it has conjured hither from the agricultural districts and from Ireland; the industrial epoch alone enables the owners of these cattle sheds to

---

[1] *the time of the cholera* I.e., 1832.

[2] *miasmatic* Consisting of noxious vapor.

[3] *Poor-Law Bastille* Because of the terrible conditions in the workhouses (established by the Poor Laws in the 1830s), including poor food, monotonous make-work, and the separation of families, workhouses were often compared to prisons such as the famous Bastille in Paris.

A cross-section of working-class low-lodgings. The crowded rooms and open sewer running beneath the building provide examples of the sort of deplorable living conditions described by Engels in his examination of Manchester.

rent them for high prices to human beings, to plunder the poverty of the workers, to undermine the health of thousands, in order that they only, the owners, may grow rich. In the industrial epoch alone has it become possible that the worker scarcely freed from feudal servitude can be used as mere material, a mere chattel; that he must let himself be crowded into a dwelling too bad for every other, which he for his hard-earned wages buys the right to let go utterly to ruin. This is what manufacture has achieved, and, without these workers and their poverty, this slavery would have been impossi-

ble. True, the original construction of this quarter was bad, little good could have been made out of it; but, have the land-owners, has the municipality done anything to improve it when rebuilding? On the contrary, wherever a nook or corner was free, a house has been run up; where a superfluous passage remained, it has been built on; the value of land rose with the blossoming out of manufacture, and the more it rose, the more madly was the work of building carried on, without reference to the health or comfort of the inhabitants, with sole reference to the highest possible profit, on the principle that *no hole is so bad but that some poor creature must take it who can pay for nothing better.* However, it is the Old Town, and with this reflection the bourgeoisie is comforted.

from Reverend Sidney Godolphin Osborne, *Letters of S.G.O.* (1844–84)

24 AUGUST 1846

In London, I believe, there are persons appointed to inspect the markets, and see that unwholesome food is not offered for sale. Newgate has one or more officials whose duty it is to take care that the meat of diseased or improperly killed animals is not sold as food for anything above the grade of a dog or pig. There is a clerk of the fish market, whose nose is supposed to be ever ready and keen to hunt out fish unfit for human food. It may then be fairly assumed that our laws contemplate the protection of the people's health, so far at least as they establish the principle that the sale of unwholesome food is illegal.

The Act of Parliament known as the "Vagrant Act" makes the lodging in the open air, without "visible means of subsistence," penal; here I think we may assume that the law considers every subject of the realm to have shelter and subsistence honestly within reach. There are certain laws in existence directed against the practice of master manufacturers being retailers of goods to their workmen; the evident aim of the law being to secure to the workman liberty of choice in the market at which he purchases the necessaries of life, to protect him from anything like a compulsion to buy where he would be afraid to question the quality or price of the things he needs. Surely, Sir, if it is illegal to offer for sale unwholesome meat in London, to act the truckmaster[1] in Lancashire, although there may be no express enactments to that effect, it is no unfair presumption to say that the *animus*[2] of the law is against such practices wherever practiced.

I am this day returned from a visit to a neighbourhood, in which I found meat which would be condemned in Newgate Market, sold to the labouring poor—in which whole families are living in unroofed houses, without any but invisible means of subsistence, the wages of at least nine out of ten of the labourers in husbandry[3] being paid to them in the shape of goods sold to them by their masters, including meat of the above character.

The parish of Ryme is situated in Dorsetshire, but only divided from Somerset by a brook, it belongs almost entirely to the Duchy of Cornwall;[4] its population is about 200, according to the poor-rate[5] of 1840, its acreage was 978, rented at the sum of 1,108*l*,[6] about rather more than a third of the parish is arable. Two or three years ago a report was made to the union board of the wretched state of the cottages in this parish; a friend favoured me with a copy of it, and means were found to bring it before the council of the Duchy. To their credit be it said, steps have been taken to in some measure mitigate the disgraceful state of the dwellings on their property; six or eight new cottages are either built or are in progress, and some of the old hovels have been destroyed. Though I cannot say much for the substantial nature of the new buildings, they are worthy of all praise, as planned to favour the observation of the common customs of decent life; they have good garden grounds, and are let at a moderate rent. I cannot but hope that in a few years' time the few shameful specimens of dwellings that still exist may also be destroyed, and new ones, fit for human beings, erected in their stead. It is painful, Sir, to see, that where the proprietary[7] of an estate do thus, however late, endeavour to do their duty to those who till the ground on it, their tenantry should be allowed to go on in a course of

---

[1] *truckmaster* I.e., the employer in a truck system, in which workers are paid in goods rather than money.

[2] *animus* Spirit.

[3] *husbandry* Farming.

[4] *Duchy of Cornwall* Large estate, the profits from which belong to the Prince of Wales, the heir apparent to the British throne.

[5] *poor-rate* Assessment for the support of the poor.

[6] *l* Abbreviation for pounds. The abbreviations *s* and *d*, found below, indicate shillings and pence, respectively. There were 12 pence in a shilling and 20 shillings in a pound. See "British Money" on the anthology's website for a discussion of comparative values today.

[7] *proprietary* Owner.

treatment of the labourer which I can only characterise as most wicked and unjust. I was not content to inquire of the labourers themselves as to their condition, but I took no common pains to trace out the truth of their assertions, by obtaining the statements of educated persons in the higher grades of life, who, living on the spot, were, by their professions or business, brought into a thorough acquaintance with the system to which I would now draw attention.

In the parish of Ryme, with one or two exceptions, the wages of able-bodied married men are 7s a week; those of single men and lads, from sixteen to twenty-five or more years of age, are from 2s 6d to 6s. The mowing and harvest afford about two months of task work, at which about 10s a week is earned, besides the allowance of a gallon of cider a day, but the hours then worked are from five in the morning to seven in the evening. The pay for mowing barley is 1s 6d an acre; for reaping and binding wheat 6s an acre, the men finding their own tools. When doing day work the men get about two pints of cider a day, but this is stuff of an inferior quality; it is made on the farms, and costs the farmer but little. At day work they are expected to be on the farm, if the light will permit, at least twelve hours a day. There are no privileges of any kind whatever, that I could discover, afforded by the masters to the men. Thus far, Sir, I have only told of men working for the tenantry of the Prince of Wales for ten months of the year at 7s a week, having to pay 1s out of it for the rent of a cottage, and therefore, as it would appear, having only 6s to bring home to buy food and clothing, for the cider drunk in the field may spur them on to work harder, but it is of no use to their families at home. But now comes the worst part of my story; they are paid almost entirely on the truck system; for a bushel of best wheat they pay 7s the bushel, which is 56s the quarter; for first tailings[1] they pay 6s the bushel, 2c[2] 48s the quarter; for second tailings 5s the bushel, 2c 40s the quarter. If wished for, I shall be happy to supply a sample of this grist,[3] *when any judge will at once say it is charged at least*

1s a bushel too much. Now, Sir, I would have you bear in mind, that, having to pay 1s rent, the labourer needing a bushel of grist a week, and having to pay 6s for it, his wages being only 7s, he is left wholly without money to buy anything else. In justice to the farmer, I will put the 1s overcharge for the grist against the cider he gives in the field. But the farmer makes butter and cheese, there are of these articles inferior qualities, for which there would be no market did not the labourer prove a customer. These, then, are taken by such men as may have children or wives at work on the farm, in lieu of their wages. The cheese is made of skim-milk, is of the colour and hardness of chalk, smells perfectly sour, but is charged for at 3½d a pound. The butter is charged at 10d a pound, is on the average good, but it does again and again occur, that firkins[4] returned by the salesmen as unfit for the market are sold to the men at a price above the market price of good butter. In the neighbouring parish of Yetminster, a tradesman informed me of one farmer who sold his labourers soap and candles, and here let me say I am speaking of large and apparently well-to-do farmers, renting, some of them, 400l a year.

We have found, Sir, that there is a "tailing" as it were of cheese and butter, but what will the public think of a tailing of meat? Three days before I was at Ryme a sheep with the staggers[5] was killed, "just afore he died," and sold to the labourers of one of the principal farmers at 4d the pound. When ewes die in lambing, or as the men express it "are killed afore they are cold dead," the men are sold the meat at 2½d. One woman, who had some of a giddy sheep[6] at 4d the pound, a few days ago, said she would have no more of this "bleeding ewe mutton," for it made her husband ill. It will happen on a dairy farm that a cow will die diseased. There is a complaint called the "quarter evil,"[7] which seems to me the only purveyor of beef to the poor in these parts. When an animal has time, in dying of this disease, to

---

[1] *tailings* Products of inferior quality left over after superior products are made (here, after the high-grade flour is sifted out).

[2] *c* Crown, worth five shillings.

[3] *grist* Batch of grain—here the batch of ground wheat being discussed.

[4] *firkins* Small casks (of butter, in this case).

[5] *with the staggers* Affected with one of many diseases that cause loss of balance in farm animals.

[6] *giddy sheep* Sheep that is ill and staggering or turning around aimlessly.

[7] *"quarter evil"* Bacterial infection affecting livestock; it causes muscular swelling and is often fatal.

have its throat cut, it is retailed at 2½*d* the pound to the labourers. In one instance we had the positive evidence of the man who found it dead, that a sheep's throat was then cut, it was not quite cold, and the meat sold as above. It may be said, are the men compelled to take these things? They answer this question in various ways, but one, I think, will give the sense of all the rest. "They just tell us they can't afford the money to pay us, and therefore axes of us to take the gristing and the cheese of them, many of us must soon get in debt to them, and then you see, Sir, we must go on. As to the dead animals, they just says, 'We can't be expected to take the whole loss,' and they then tells us as we should take some of it off their hands. There may be from twelve to a score of such sheep in the year on my master's farm. 'Tis the only meat we ever sees." Knowing that there was a most respectable and humane man farming largely a few miles off, and that he is rather a fancy sheep breeder, I asked of a man what Mr. P. did with his animals that were so diseased? The answer was, "They be given to the dogs and pigs." As to wages paid in money, I think you would be puzzled to find any one man who had drawn 2*l* in any one year; by the help of clothing clubs, and an occasional job at draining out of the parish, they are alone enabled to get clothes. As a specimen of what life still is in some instances, and was generally for many years, I went into the cottage of a man who it was found had stolen some of his master's wheat. I found the woman, with two of the children, eating a few unwholesome potatoes and some bread; a child, of nine years of age, dead, in a coffin close to them, the only ascent to the bedroom by a broken ladder, the roof so dilapidated that it rains down on the bed. They had five children, all young, she was close to her confinement;[1] the husband earning 7*s*, paying 6*s* for a grist of tailings, of which I procured a sample, and defy anyone to say it is worth 5*s*, the whole building unfit for any human being to live in. Who can wonder that they steal their master's corn? As to drunkenness, the whole system of payment in cider encourages it.

On one side of Ryme is Yetminster, on the other side is Closworth, in Somersetshire, in the former the cottages belong, for the most part, to the parish or to small proprietors. In the latter they are, with the whole parish, the property of a nobleman of known large landed possessions. Your Commissioner made a faint attempt to describe one place in Yetminster in which sixty souls dwell. I went all over it. It is in all truth the very cesspool of everything in which anything human can be recognised—whole families wallowing together at night on filthy rags, in rooms in which they are so packed, and yet so little sheltered, that one's wonder is that the physical existence can survive, as it does, the necessary speedy destruction of all existing moral principle. What matters it that they are the refuse of the parish? It is a refuse pregnant with an eternal life, that requires a care and a preparation for its future birth, which the circumstances of such a place utterly forbid. In a Christian land, divided by law into districts and parishes, professedly each charged with the expense of a moral apparatus, calculated to protect the bodies of the people from the assaults of hunger or violence, their souls from ignorance and heathenism, a vast—almost roofless—manufactory of misery and nursery for vice is allowed to rear its smoke-blackened walls in the very midst of a landscape in which the eye may trace the existence of the mansions and parks of the wealthy, charged to see justice done the body; churches, telling of the existence of an order of men whose duty it is to preach the plain truth boldly, that God will not have the poor oppressed in body or in soul.

If Closworth, the other parish of which I have spoken, is, as I am informed, no worse than two-thirds of the Somerset villages, I can only say that Dorset, bad as it is, I am convinced can show few such specimens of miserable existence. It is no argument to say that most of these wretched, damp, decaying, confined, glassless hovels are the property of little lifeholders.[2] I admit it to be a very general case, though not true in this instance. No one can travel through these districts and not see how every atom of waste ground is seized on for the erection of these dens; but you may go for miles, you may make what inquiry you will, and you will find that those who draw incomes from the soil not only will not, and have not, until lately in a few instances, built any cottages, but they have perseveringly pursued the system of cottage destruction. Hence it is, the dwellings of the peasantry must be thus planted by themselves on the

---

[1]   *confinement*   Delivery date; time of childbirth.

[2]   *lifeholders*   People who hold a tenancy for life.

wastes, or they must become the prey of those who, having little lifeholds, built cabins on them to let at exorbitant rents.

The potato crop is a failure throughout the whole district, I do not believe a third will be fit for food. This is of no small importance, for the only money the poor man can draw to purchase clothing is from the potatoes, either by their sale, or by their consumption enabling him to make shift[1] with a grist once in two instead of every week.

I am well aware, Sir, that the assertions I have made above, of the treatment of the labourers on the Prince of Wales's property, will, as usual, be treated by the parties accused as gross exaggerations. I am, Sir, prepared, at any convenient notice, to meet the agent of the Duchy on the spot, and from my notes, and in the presence of the same witnesses, prove their truth. From what I have learned of the council of the Duchy's proceedings, I believe them to be disposed to act most humanely and to set a most excellent example to their neighbours. I think a very little inquiry, and a very little effort on their part, may put a stop to a state of things disgraceful to so important a proprietary, though common in the case of individual proprietors. For my own part, I can only say that I will shrink from no inquiry into facts I assert in your columns, only claiming, in my own defence, an opportunity to investigate the truth of what my accusers may state. I expect no length of years, I care little how much of them I expend in this cause.

from Elizabeth Gaskell, *Mary Barton* (1848)

CHAPTER 6

John Barton was not far wrong in his idea that the Messrs. Carson would not be over-much grieved for the consequences of the fire in their mill. They were well insured; the machinery lacked the improvements of late years, and worked but poorly in comparison with that which might now be procured. Above all, trade was very slack; cottons could find no market, and goods lay packed and piled in many a warehouse. The mills were merely worked to keep the machinery, human and metal, in some kind of order and readiness for better times. So this was an excellent opportunity, Messrs. Carson thought, for refitting their factory with first-rate improvements, for which the insurance-money would amply pay. They were in no hurry about the business, however. The weekly drain of wages given for labour, useless in the present state of the market, was stopped. The partners had more leisure than they had known for years, and promised wives and daughters all manner of pleasant excursions, as soon as the weather should become more genial. It was a pleasant thing to be able to lounge over breakfast with a review or newspaper in hand; to have time for becoming acquainted with agreeable and accomplished daughters, on whose education no money had been spared, but whose fathers, shut up during a long day with calicoes[2] and accounts, had so seldom had leisure to enjoy their daughters' talents. There were happy family evenings, now that the men of business had time for domestic enjoyments. There is another side to the picture. There were homes over which Carsons' fire threw a deep, terrible gloom; the homes of those who would fain work, and no man gave unto them—the homes of those to whom leisure was a curse. There, the family music was angry wails, when week after week passed by, and there was no work to be had, and consequently no wages to pay for the bread the children cried aloud for in their young impatience of suffering. There was no breakfast to lounge over; their lounge was taken in bed, to try and keep warmth in them that bitter March weather, and, by being quiet, to deaden the gnawing wolf within. Many a penny that would have gone little way enough in oatmeal or potatoes bought opium to still the hungry little ones,[3] and make them forget their uneasiness in heavy troubled sleep. It was mother's mercy. The evil and the good of our nature came out strongly then. There were desperate fathers; there were bitter-tongued mothers (Oh God! what wonder!); there were reckless children; the very closest bonds of nature were snapped in that time of

---

[1] *make shift* Manage.

[2] *calicoes* Cotton cloths.

[3] *opium ... hungry little ones* The apparently common practice among working-class families of giving sick or hungry infants opium or laudanum to help them sleep was frequently discussed at the time.

trial and distress. There was Faith such as the rich can never imagine on earth; there was "Love strong as death"; and, self-denial, among rude, coarse men, akin to that of Sir Philip Sidney's most glorious deed.[1] The vices of the poor sometimes astound us *here*; but when the secrets of all hearts shall be made known, their virtues will astound us in far greater degree. Of this I am certain.

As the cold, bleak spring came on (spring, in name alone), and consequently as trade continued dead, other mills shortened hours, turned off hands,[2] and finally stopped work altogether.

Barton worked short hours; Wilson, of course, being a hand in Carsons' factory, had no work at all. But his son, working at an engineer's, and a steady man, obtained wages enough to maintain all the family in a careful way. Still it preyed on Wilson's mind to be so long indebted to his son. He was out of spirits and depressed. Barton was morose, and soured towards mankind as a body, and the rich in particular. One evening, when the clear light at six o'clock contrasted strangely with the Christmas cold, and when the bitter wind piped down every entry, and through every cranny, Barton sat brooding over his stinted fire, and listening for Mary's step, in unacknowledged trust that her presence would cheer him. The door was opened, and Wilson came breathless in.

"You've not got a bit o' money by you, Barton?" asked he.

"Not I; who has now, I'd like to know. Whatten you want it for?"

"I donnot want it for mysel', tho' we've none to spare. But don[3] you know Ben Davenport as worked at Carsons'? He's down wi' the fever, and ne'er a stick o' fire nor a cowd[4] potato in the house."

"I han got no money, I tell ye," said Barton. Wilson looked disappointed. Barton tried not to be interested,

---

[1] *Sir Philip ... deed* Poet and courtier Sir Philip Sidney (1554–86), who served in many diplomatic missions on the Continent, is said to have refused a glass of water offered to him when he lay dying on the battlefield at Zutphen, in the Netherlands. He instead gave the glass to a less seriously wounded soldier, saying "Thy necessity is greater than mine."

[2] *turned off hands* I.e., laid off workers.

[3] *don* Do.

[4] *cowd* I.e., cold.

but he could not help it in spite of his gruffness. He rose, and went to the cupboard (his wife's pride long ago). There lay the remains of his dinner, hastily put by ready for supper. Bread, and a slice of cold fat boiled bacon. He wrapped them in his handkerchief, put them in the crown of his hat and said—"Come, let's be going."

from Charles Dickens, *Hard Times* (1854)

CHAPTER 5: THE KEY-NOTE

Coketown, to which Messrs. Bounderby and Gradgrind now walked, was a triumph of fact; it had no greater taint of fancy in it than Mrs. Gradgrind herself. Let us strike the key-note, Coketown, before pursuing our tune.

It was a town of red brick, or of brick that would have been red if the smoke and ashes had allowed it; but as matters stood it was a town of unnatural red and black like the painted face of a savage. It was a town of machinery and tall chimneys, out of which interminable serpents of smoke trailed themselves forever and ever, and never got uncoiled. It had a black canal in it, and a river that ran purple with ill-smelling dye, and vast piles of building full of windows where there was a rattling and trembling all day long, and where the piston of the steam-engine worked monotonously up and down, like the head of an elephant in a state of melancholy madness. It contained several large streets all very like one another, and many small streets still more like one another, inhabited by people equally like one another, who all went in and out at the same hours, with the same sound upon the same pavements, to do the same work, and to whom every day was the same as yesterday and tomorrow, and every year the counterpart of the last and the next.

These attributes of Coketown were in the main inseparable from the work by which it was sustained; against them were to be set off, comforts of life which found their way all over the world, and elegancies of life which made, we will not ask how much of the fine lady, who could scarcely bear to hear the place mentioned. The rest of its features were voluntary, and they were these.

You saw nothing in Coketown but what was severely workful. If the members of a religious persuasion built a chapel there—as the members of eighteen religious persuasions had done—they made it a pious warehouse of red brick, with sometimes (but this is only in highly ornamental examples) a bell in a birdcage on the top of it. The solitary exception was the New Church; a stuccoed edifice with a square steeple over the door, terminating in four short pinnacles like florid wooden legs. All the public inscriptions in the town were painted alike, in severe characteristics of black and white. The jail might have been the infirmary, the infirmary might have been the jail, the town hall might have been either, or both, or anything else, for anything that appeared to the contrary in the graces of their construction. Fact, fact, fact, everywhere in the immaterial. The M'Choakumchild school was all fact, and the school of design was all fact, and the relations between master and man were all fact, and everything was fact between the lying-in hospital and the cemetery, and what you couldn't state in figures, or show to be purchaseable in the cheapest market and saleable in the dearest, was not, and never should be, world without end, Amen.[1]

A town so sacred to fact, and so triumphant in its assertion, of course got on well? Why no, not quite well. No? Dear me!

No. Coketown did not come out of its own furnaces, in all respects like gold that had stood the fire. First, the perplexing mystery of the place was, Who belonged to the eighteen denominations? Because, whoever did, the labouring people did not. It was very strange to walk through the streets on a Sunday morning, and note how few of *them* the barbarous jangling of bells that was driving the sick and nervous mad, called away from their own quarter, from their own close rooms, from the corners of their own streets, where they lounged listlessly, gazing at all the church and chapel going, as at a thing with which they had no manner of concern. Nor was it merely the stranger who noticed this, because there was a native organization in Coketown itself, whose members were to be heard of in the House of Commons every session, indignantly petitioning for Acts of Parliament that should make these

people religious by main force.[2] Then came the Teetotal Society, who complained that these same people *would* get drunk, and showed their tabular statements that they did get drunk, and proved at tea parties that no inducement, human or divine (except a medal), would induce them to forego their custom of getting drunk. Then came the chemist and druggist, with other tabular statements, showing that when they didn't get drunk, they took opium. Then came the experienced chaplain of the jail, with more tabular statements, outdoing all the previous tabular statements, and showing that the same people *would* resort to low haunts, hidden from the public eye, where they heard low singing and saw low dancing, and mayhap joined in it; and where A. B., aged twenty-four next birthday, and committed for eighteen months' solitary, had himself said (not that he had ever shown himself particularly worthy of belief) his ruin began, as he was perfectly sure and confident that otherwise he would have been a tip-top moral specimen. Then came Mr. Gradgrind and Mr. Bounderby, the two gentlemen at this present moment walking through Coketown, and both eminently practical, who could, on occasion, furnish more tabular statements derived from their own personal experience, and illustrated by cases they had known and seen, from which it clearly appeared—in short, it was the only clear thing in the case—that these same people were a bad lot altogether, gentlemen; that do what you would for them they were never thankful for it, gentlemen; that they were restless, gentlemen; that they never knew what they wanted; that they lived upon the best, and bought fresh butter; and insisted on Mocha coffee, and rejected all but prime parts of meat, and yet were eternally dissatisfied and unmanageable. In short, it was the moral of the old nursery fable:

There was an old woman, and what do you think
She lived upon nothing but victuals and drink;
Victuals and drink were the whole of her diet,
And yet this old woman would NEVER be quiet.

[1] *never should be ... Amen* From the Anglican Book of Common Prayer: "Glory be to the Father, and to the Son, and to the Holy Ghost; as it was in the beginning, is now, and ever shall be, world without end. Amen."

[2] *members ... main force* See Dickens's pamphlet *Sunday Under Three Heads* (written under the pseudonym "Timothy Sparks"), in which he vehemently opposes the "Sunday Observance Bill." Sir Andrew Agnew and his Evangelical group recommended to Parliament a series of moral reforms focusing on curtailing activities on Sunday, which Dickens contended would severely restrict the ability of the poor to enjoy their one day in the week that was free of labor.

London Nomads by John Thomson, from *Street Life in London* (1877).

from Henry Morley, "Ground in the Mill," *Household Words* No. 213 (22 April 1854)

"It is good when it happens," say the children, "that we die before our time."[1] Poetry may be right or wrong in making little operatives who are ignorant of cowslips[2] say anything like that. We mean here to speak prose. There are many ways of dying. Perhaps it is not good when a factory girl, who has not the whole spirit of play spun out of her for want of meadows, gambols[3] upon bags of wool, a little too near the exposed machinery that is to work it up, and is immediately seized, and punished by the merciless machine that digs its shaft into her pinafore and hoists her up, tears out her left arm at the shoulder joint, breaks her right arm, and beats her on the head. No, that is not good; but it is not a case in point, the girl lives and may be one of those who think that it would have been good for her if she had died before her time.

She had her chance of dying, and she lost it. Possibly it was better for the boy whom his stern master, the machine, caught as he stood on a stool wickedly looking out of window at the sunlight and the flying clouds. These were no business of his, and he was fully punished when the machine he served caught him by one arm and whirled him round and round till he was thrown down dead. There is no lack of such warnings to idle boys and girls. What right has a gamesome[4] youth to display levity before the supreme engine. "Watch me do a trick!" cried such a youth to his fellow, and put his arm familiarly within the arm of the great iron-hearted chief. "I'll show you a trick," gnashed the pitiless monster. A coil of strap fastened his arm to the shaft, and round he went. His leg was cut off, and fell into the room, his arm was broken in three or four places, his ankle was broken, his head was battered; he was not released alive.

Why do we talk about such horrible things? Because they exist, and their existence should be clearly known. Because there have occurred during the last three years more than a hundred such deaths, and more than ten thousand (indeed, nearly twelve thousand) such accidents in our factories, and they are all, or nearly all, preventable.

These few thousands of catastrophes are the results of the administrative kindness so abundant in this country. They are all the fruits of mercy. A man was lime-washing the ceiling of an engine-room: he was seized by a horizontal shaft and killed immediately. A boy was brushing the dust from such a ceiling, before whitewashing: he had a cloth over his head to keep the dirt from falling on him; by that cloth the engine seized and held him to administer a chastisement with rods of iron. A youth while talking thoughtlessly took hold of a strop[5] that hung over the shaft: his hand was wrenched off at the wrist. A man climbed to the top of his machine to put the strap on the drum: he wore a smock which the shaft caught; both of his arms were then torn

---

[1] *It is ... our time*   From Elizabeth Barrett Browning's poem "The Cry of the Children" (1844), included elsewhere in this anthology.

[2] *cowslips*   Wildflowers common in the English countryside; in "The Cry of the Children," working children ask, "Are your cowslips of the meadows / Like our weeds anear the mine?"

[3] *gambols*   Leaps playfully.

[4] *gamesome*   Playful.

[5] *strop*   Band.

out of the shoulder joints, both legs were broken, and his head was severely bruised: in the end, of course, he died. What he suffered was all suffered in mercy. He was rent asunder, not perhaps for his own good, but as a sacrifice to the commercial prosperity of Great Britain. There are few amongst us even among the masters who share most largely in that prosperity—who are willing, we will hope and believe, to pay such a price as all this blood for any good or any gain that can accrue to them. These accidents have arisen in the manner following. By the Factory Act, passed in the seventh year of Her Majesty's reign,[1] it was enacted, among other things, that all parts of the mill-gearing in a factory should be securely fenced. There were no buts and ifs in the Act itself; these were allowed to step in and limit its powers of preventing accidents out of a merciful respect, not for the blood of the operatives, but for the gold of the mill-owners. It was strongly represented that to fence those parts of machinery that were higher than the heads of workmen—more than seven feet above the ground—would be to incur an expense wholly unnecessary. Kind-hearted interpreters of the law, therefore, agreed with mill-owners that seven feet of fencing should be held sufficient. The result of this accommodation—taking only the accounts of the last three years—has been to credit mercy with some pounds and shillings in the books of English manufacturers; we cannot say how many, but we hope they are enough to balance the account against mercy made out on behalf of the English factory workers thus: Mercy debtor to justice, of poor men, women, and children, one hundred and six lives, one hundred and forty-two hands or arms, one thousand two hundred and eighty-seven (or, in bulk, how many bushels of) fingers, for the breaking of one thousand three hundred and forty bones, for five hundred and fifty-nine damaged heads, and for eight thousand two hundred and eighty-two miscellaneous injuries. It remains to be settled how much cash saved to the purses of the manufacturers is a satisfactory and proper off-set to this expenditure of life and limb and this crushing of bone in the persons of their work-people....

We have not spoken too strongly on this subject. We are indignant against no class, but discuss only one section of a topic that concerns, in some form, almost every division of society. Since, however, we now find ourselves speaking about factories, and turning over leaves of the reports of Factory Inspectors, we may as well have our grumble out, or, at any rate, so far prolong it as to make room for one more subject of dissatisfaction. It is important that factory management should be watched by the public; in a friendly spirit indeed—for it is no small part of our whole English mind and body—but with the strictness which every man who means well should exercise in judgment on himself, in scrutiny of his own actions. We are told that in one inspector's district—only in one district—mills and engines have so multiplied during the last three years, in number and in power, that additional work has, in that period, been created for the employment of another forty thousand hands. Every reporter has the same kind of tale to tell. During the last year, in our manufacturing districts, additions to the steam power found employment for an additional army of operatives, nearly thirty thousand strong. The factory system, therefore, is developing itself most rapidly. It grows too fast, perhaps; at present the mills are, for a short time, in excess of the work required, and in many cases lie idle for two days in the week, or for one or two hours in the day. The succession of strikes, too, in Preston, Wigan, Hindley, Burnley, Padiham, and Bacup[2] and the other places, have left a large number of men out of employ, and caused, for a long time, a total sacrifice of wages, to the extent of some twenty thousand pounds a week. These, however, are all temporary difficulties: the great extension of the factory system is a permanent fact, and it must be made to bring good with it, not evil.

The law wisely requires that mill-owners who employ children shall also teach them, and a minimum, as to time, of schooling is assigned. Before this regulation was compulsory, there were some good schools kept as show-places by certain persons; but, when the maintenance of them became a necessity, and schools were no longer exceptional curiosities, these show-places often fell into complete neglect; they were no longer goods that would attract the public. In

---

[1] *seventh year ... reign* I.e., 1844.

[2] *succession of ... and Bacup* During a period of wage-related strikes and lockouts (1853–54), many cotton mills in the industrial towns of northwestern England were closed.

Scotland this part of the Factory Law seems to be well worked; and, for its own sake, as a beneficial requirement. That does not seem, however, to be the case in England. All the inspectors tell us of the lamentable state of the factory schools in this country; allowance being, of course, made for a few worthy exceptions. It is doubtful whether much good will come out of them, unless they be themselves organised by men determined that they shall fulfill their purpose. English factory children have yet to be really taught.

> Let them prove their inward souls against the notion
> — That they live in you, or under you, O wheels!
> Still, all day, the iron wheels go onward,
> Grinding life down from its mark;
> And the children's souls, which God is calling sunward,
> Spin on blindly in the dark.[1]

Here they are left spinning in the dark. Let Mr. Redgrave's account of a factory school visited by him, near Leeds, suffice to show:

> It was held in a large room, and the inspector, visiting it at twenty minutes before twelve, found the children at play in the yard, and the master at work in the school-room, sawing up the black board to make fittings of a house to which he proposed transferring his business. The children being summoned, came in carelessly, their disorderly habits evidently not repressed by their master, but checked slightly by the appearance of a strange gentleman. Two girls lolling in the porch were summoned in, and the teacher then triumphantly drew out of his pocket a whistle, whereupon to blow the order for attention. It was the only whole thing that he had to teach with. There were the twenty children ranged along the wall of a room able to contain seven times the number; there were the bits of black board, the master's arms, with a hand-saw, and a hammer for apparatus, and there were the books, namely, six dilapidated Bibles, some copy books, one slate, and half-a-dozen ragged and odd leaves of a "Reading made Easy." To such a school factory children were being sent to get the hours of education which the law makes necessary.

Doubtless, that sample is a very bad one, but too many resemble it.

"They know the grief of man but not the wisdom,"[2] these poor childish hearts. They are now rescued from day-long ache and toil; we have given them some leisure for learning, though, as yet but little more than the old lesson to learn.

from Henry Mayhew, *London Labour and the London Poor*, "Boy Crossing-Sweepers and Tumblers" (1851)

A remarkably intelligent lad, who, on being spoken to, at once consented to give all the information in his power, told me the following story of his life.

It will be seen from this boy's account, and the one or two following, that a kind of partnership exists among some of these young sweepers. They have associated themselves together, appropriated several crossings to their use, and appointed a captain over them. They have their forms of trial, and "jury-house" for the settlement of disputes; laws have been framed, which govern their commercial proceedings, and a kind of language adopted by the society for its better protection from the arch-enemy, the policeman.

I found the lad who first gave me an insight into the proceedings of the associated crossing-sweepers crouched on the stone steps of a door in Adelaide Street, Strand; and when I spoke to him he was preparing to settle down in a corner and go to sleep—his legs and body being curled round almost as closely as those of a cat on a hearth. The moment he heard my voice he was upon his feet, asking me to "give a halfpenny to poor little Jack."

He was a good-looking lad, with a pair of large mild eyes, which he took good care to turn up with an expression of supplication as he moaned for a halfpenny.

A cap, or more properly a stuff bag, covered a crop of hair which had matted itself into the form of so many paint-brushes, while his face, from its roundness of feature and the complexion of dirt, had an almost Indian look about it; the colour of his hands, too, was

---

[1] *Let them ... the dark* From "The Cry of the Children."

[2] *They know ... the wisdom* From "The Cry of the Children."

such that you could imagine he had been shelling walnuts.

The Boy Crossing Sweepers, from Henry Mayhew's *London Labour and the London Poor* (1861).

He ran before me, treading cautiously with his naked feet, until I reached a convenient spot to take down his statement, which was as follows:

"I've got no mother or father; mother has been dead for two years, and father's been gone for more than that—more nigh five years—he died at Ipswich, in Suffolk. He was a perfumer by trade, and used to make hair-dye, and scent, and pomatum,[1] and all kinds of scents. He didn't keep a shop himself, but he used to serve them as did; he didn't hawk his goods about, neether, but had regular customers, what used to send him a letter, and then he'd take them what they wanted. Yes, he used to serve some good shops: there was H—'s, of London Bridge, what's a large chemist's. He used to make a good deal of money, but he lost it betting; and so his brother, my uncle, did all his. . . .

"After mother died, sister still kept on making nets,[2] and I lived with her for some time. But she was keeping company with a young man, and one day they went out, and came back and said they'd been and got married. It was him as got rid of me.

"He was kind to me for the first two or three months, while he was keeping her company; but before he was married he got a little cross, and after he was married he begun to get more cross, and used to send me to play in the streets, and tell me not to come home again till night. One day he hit me, and I said I wouldn't be hit about by him, and then at tea that night sister gave me three shillings, and told me I must go and get my own living. So I bought a box and brushes (they cost me just the money) and went cleaning boots, and I done pretty well with them, till my box was stole from me by a boy where I was lodging. He's in prison now—got six calendar[3] for picking pockets. . . .

"I was fifteen the 24th of last May, sir, and I've been sweeping crossings now near upon two years. There's a party of six of us, and we have the crossings from St. Martin's Church as far as Pall Mall. I always go along with them as lodges in the same place as I do. In the daytime, if it's dry, we do anythink what we can—open cabs, or anythink; but if it's wet, we separate, and I an' another gets a crossing—those who gets on it first, keeps it—and we stand on each side and take our chance.

"We do it this way: if I was to see two gentlemen coming, I should cry out, 'Two toffs!' and then they are mine; and whether they give me anythink or not they are mine, and my mate is bound not to follow them; for if he did he would get a hiding from the whole lot of us. If we both cry out together, then we share. If it's a lady and a gentleman, then we cries, 'A toff and a doll!' Sometimes we are caught out in this way. Perhaps it is a lady and gentleman and a child; and if I was to see them, and only say, 'A toff and a doll,' and leave out the child, then my mate can add the child; and as he is right and I wrong, then it's his party.

"If there's a policeman coming we musn't ask for money; but we are always on the look-out for policemen, and if we see one, then we calls out 'Phillup!' for that's our signal. One of the policemen at St. Martin's Church—Bandy, we calls him—knows what Phillup means, for he's up to us; so we had to change the word. (At the request of the young crossing-sweeper the present signal is omitted.) . . .

"When we see the rain we say together, 'Oh! there's a jolly good rain! we'll have a good day tomorrow.' If a shower comes on, and we are at our room, which we general are about three o'clock, to get somethink to eat—besides, we general go there to see how much each

---

[1] *pomatum* Scented ointment for the hair.

[2] *nets* Meshwork or network, used for various purposes.

[3] *six calendar* I.e., six months.

other's taken in the day—why, out we run with our brooms.

"At night-time we tumbles[1]—that is, if the policeman ain't nigh. We goes general to Waterloo Place when the opera's on. We sends on one of us ahead, as a looker-out, to look for the policeman, and then we follows. It's no good tumbling to gentlemen *going* to the opera; it's when they're coming back they gives us money. When they've got a young lady on their arm they laugh at us tumbling; some will give us a penny, others threepence, sometimes a sixpence or a shilling, and sometimes a halfpenny. We either do the cat'un wheel, or else we keep before the gentleman and lady, turning head-over-heels, putting our broom on the ground and then turning over it....

"When we are talking together we always talk in a kind of slang. Each policeman we gives a regular name— there's 'Bull's Head,' 'Bandy Shanks,' and 'Old Cherry Legs,' and 'Dot-and-carry-one'; they all knows their names as well as us. We never talks of crossings, but 'fakes.' We don't make no slang of our own, but uses the regular one."

A group of homeless boys just after being admitted to a shelter. (Photograph by John Thomson, c. 1880.)

---

[1]   *tumbles* Perform leaps, somersaults, etc., like acrobats.

JOHN STUART MILL
1806 – 1873

Philosopher, social reformer, economist, and politician, John Stuart Mill was one of the most influential of Victorian thinkers. His breadth of knowledge and interests was staggering, as was his ability to apply his intellect to a wide range of subjects, including women's rights, civil liberties, economic theories, logic, and poetics. Mill's *Utilitarianism* and *On Liberty* are both still regarded as central works in the fields of moral and social philosophy and political science.

Mill seemed destined from an early age to become a polymath—his childhood was practically a monument to over-achievement. He was born in London in 1806, the first child of Harriet Burrow and James Mill, a distinguished psychologist, philosopher, and historian. James was a disciple of Jeremy Bentham, who had founded the philosophical school of utilitarianism, an ethical doctrine whose main premise is that an action ought to be taken only if it produces happiness for all involved (later refined by J.S. Mill into the "greatest happiness principle," which suggests that people ought to act in ways that produce the greatest happiness for all involved). Participating in an experiment devised in part by Bentham, James decided that his eldest son would be a guinea pig for his educational theories, and at a very young age John began a rigorous education aimed at preparing him to become a future leader of the Benthamites.

In his autobiography, Mill described his formal instruction as beginning with Greek at age three; by the age of eight he could translate the works of Socrates and Plato. He then learned Latin well enough to translate such masters as Horace and Ovid, and also studied mathematics, the sciences, and English literature. Not being content to allow his son to learn simply by rote, James heavily emphasized rhetoric and debate, insisting that John make moral decisions about the principles he was learning. By the time he was 14, his father considered him to be ready for university study but felt that an institution would hold him back, and thus Mill began his career a full "quarter of a century before his contemporaries," as he would say in his autobiography.

James's experiment succeeded—John was a brilliant and erudite child, able to converse and debate with adults and to tutor all of his siblings from an early age. The daily ten-hour study regime, however, took a toll on him, and in his early twenties Mill experienced a period of deep depression that was relieved only when he discovered the poetry of William Wordsworth. During this time he pondered the virtues of Bentham's utilitarianism, which seemed to favor the good of the majority at the expense of the individual, who, Mill felt, is the best judge of his or her own happiness. Although he himself was an empiricist, he felt that Bentham's philosophy promoted the "science" of ethics at the expense of real life. Mill said of Bentham's utilitarianism: "It is wholly empirical and the empiricism of one who has had little experience." After reading the Romantic poets—Wordsworth in particular—Mill began to appreciate the therapeutic effects of poetry and the arts and the importance of an emotional life. The essay "What Is Poetry?" (1833) speaks to his concerns about the necessity of individual pleasure.

After studying law for two years, Mill worked for decades in the East India Office, first as a clerk and then as head of his department, but he continued to be an outspoken advocate for individual rights and freedoms (he had been arrested as a teenager for disseminating literature in support of birth control). He published a modification of Bentham's philosophy, later reworked as *Utilitarianism* (1863); his most ambitious early work was *System of Logic*, published in 1843 and still highly regarded in philosophical circles today. The book that followed, *Principles of Political Economy* (1848), commands a similar level of respect in the field of economics. In 1859 Mill wrote another key work: *On Liberty*, a treatise that continued his theme of support for individual rights, deriding democratic majorities that conform to tradition and smother individuality.

In the planning and to some extent the writing of both these and subsequent works, Mill was assisted by Harriet Taylor, an aspiring author whom Mill had first met in 1831 and with whom he began to work closely. (The precise extent of Taylor's involvement remains the subject of debate among scholars.)

After serving as Member of Parliament from 1865 to 1868, Mill published *The Subjection of Women* (1869). He had worked on this book for years, and it had become a passionate subject for both Mill and Taylor. (The two were married in 1851 after her husband's death. Mill and Taylor never moved freely in society together, however; many of his friends, Carlyle and Tennyson included, viewed their relationship as inappropriate.) *The Subjection of Women* spoke to the rights of women, both legally and practically, arguing for government reforms of property and divorce laws, women's enfranchisement, and advocating the end of "slavery" in the home. Mill even argued in Parliament—well ahead of his time—for non-sexist language and the rewording of parliamentary bills to remove gender-specific terms.

Mill died in 1873 in Avignon, France, and was buried beside his wife, who had died prematurely in 1858. In his eloquent and insightful *Autobiography*, published shortly after his death, Mill wrote candidly about his childhood experiences with a demanding father and a thoroughly rational education; about his mental breakdown and his discovery of the value of works of the imagination; about his relationship with Harriet Taylor; and about his writing. The *Autobiography* is one of the great autobiographies in the English language.

⌘⌘⌘

from *The Subjection of Women*

CHAPTER I

If people are mostly so little aware how completely, during the greater part of the duration of our species, the law of force was the avowed rule of general conduct, any other being only a special and exceptional consequence of peculiar ties—and from how very recent a date it is that the affairs of society in general have been even pretended to be regulated according to any moral law; as little do people remember or consider, how institutions and customs which never had any ground but the law of force, last on into ages and states of general opinion which never would have permitted their first establishment. Less than forty years ago, Englishmen might still by law hold human beings in bondage as saleable property: within the present century they might kidnap them and carry them off, and work them literally to death. This absolutely extreme case of the law of force, condemned by those who can tolerate almost every other form of arbitrary power, and which, of all others, presents features the most revolting to the feelings of all who look at it from an impartial position, was the law of civilized and Christian England within the memory of persons now living: and in one half of Anglo-Saxon America three or four years ago, not only did slavery exist, but the slave trade, and the breeding of slaves expressly for it, was a general practice between slave states. Yet not only was there a greater strength of sentiment against it, but, in England at least, a less amount either of feeling or of interest in favour of it, than of any other of the customary abuses of force: for its motive was the love of gain, unmixed and undisguised; and those who profited by it were a very small numerical fraction of the country, while the natural feeling of all who were not personally interested in it, was unmitigated abhorrence. So extreme an instance makes it almost superfluous to refer to any other: but consider the long duration of absolute monarchy. In England at present it is the almost universal conviction that military despotism is a case of the law of force, having no other origin or justification. Yet in all the great nations of Europe except England it either still exists, or has only just ceased to exist, and has even now a strong party favourable to it in all ranks of the people, especially among persons of station and consequence. Such is the power of an established system, even when far from universal; when not only in almost every period of history there have been great and well-known examples of the contrary system, but these have almost invariably been afforded by the most illustrious and most prosperous communities. In this case, too, the possessor of the undue power, the person directly interested in it, is only one person, while those who are subject to it and suffer from it are literally all the rest. The yoke is naturally and necessarily humiliating to all persons, except the one who is on the throne, together with, at most, the one who expects to succeed to it. How different are these cases from that of the power of men over women! I am not now prejudging the question of its justifiableness. I am showing how vastly more permanent it could not but be, even if not justifiable, than these other dominations which have nevertheless lasted down to our own time. Whatever gratification of pride there is in the possession of power, and whatever personal interest in its exercise, is in this case not confined to a limited class, but common to the whole male sex. Instead of being, to most of its supporters, a thing desirable chiefly in the abstract, or, like the political ends usually contended for by factions, of little private importance to any but the leaders; it comes home to the person and hearth of every male head of a family, and of everyone who looks forward to being so. The clodhopper exercises, or is to exercise, his share of

the power equally with the highest nobleman. And the case is that in which the desire of power is the strongest: for everyone who desires power, desires it most over those who are nearest to him, with whom his life is passed, with whom he has most concerns in common, and in whom any independence of his authority is oftenest likely to interfere with his individual preferences. If, in the other cases specified, powers manifestly grounded only on force, and having so much less to support them, are so slowly and with so much difficulty got rid of, much more must it be so with this, even if it rests on no better foundation than those. We must consider, too, that the possessors of the power have facilities in this case, greater than in any other, to prevent any uprising against it. Every one of the subjects lives under the very eye, and almost, it may be said, in the hands, of one of the masters—in closer intimacy with him than with any of her fellow-subjects; with no means of combining against him, no power of even locally overmastering him, and, on the other hand, with the strongest motives for seeking his favour and avoiding to give him offence. In struggles for political emancipation, everybody knows how often its champions are bought off by bribes, or daunted by terrors. In the case of women, each individual of the subject-class is in a chronic state of bribery and intimidation combined. In setting up the standard of resistance, a large number of the leaders, and still more of the followers, must make an almost complete sacrifice of the pleasures or the alleviations of their own individual lot. If ever any system of privilege and enforced subjection had its yoke tightly riveted on the necks of those who are kept down by it, this has. I have not yet shown that it is a wrong system: but everyone who is capable of thinking on the subject must see that even if it is, it was certain to outlast all other forms of unjust authority. And when some of the grossest of the other forms still exist in many civilized countries, and have only recently been got rid of in others, it would be strange if that which is so much the deepest rooted had yet been perceptibly shaken anywhere. There is more reason to wonder that the protests and testimonies against it should have been so numerous and so weighty as they are.

Some will object, that a comparison cannot fairly be made between the government of the male sex and the forms of unjust power which I have adduced in illustration of it, since these are arbitrary, and the effect of mere usurpation, while it on the contrary is natural. But was there ever any domination which did not appear natural to those who possessed it? There was a time when the division of mankind into two classes, a small one of masters and a numerous one of slaves, appeared, even to the most cultivated minds, to be a natural, and the only natural, condition of the human race. No less an intellect, and one which contributed no less to the progress of human thought, than Aristotle,[1] held this opinion without doubt or misgiving; and rested it on the same premises on which the same assertion in regard to the dominion of men over women is usually based, namely that there are different natures among mankind, free natures, and slave natures; that the Greeks were of a free nature, the barbarian races of Thracians[2] and Asiatics of a slave nature. But why need I go back to Aristotle? Did not the slaveowners of the Southern United States maintain the same doctrine, with all the fanaticism with which men cling to the theories that justify their passions and legitimate their personal interests? Did they not call heaven and earth to witness that the dominion of the white man over the black is natural, that the black race is by nature incapable of freedom, and marked out for slavery? some even going so far as to say that the freedom of manual labourers is an unnatural order of things anywhere. Again, the theorists of absolute monarchy have always affirmed it to be the only natural form of government; issuing from the patriarchal, which was the primitive and spontaneous form of society, framed on the model of the paternal, which is anterior to society itself, and, as they contend, the most natural authority of all. Nay, for that matter, the law of force itself, to those who could not plead any other, has always seemed the most natural of all grounds for the exercise of authority. Conquering races hold it to be Nature's own dictate that the conquered should obey the conquerors, or, as they euphoniously paraphrase it, that the feebler and more unwarlike races should submit to the braver and manlier. The smallest acquaintance with human life in the middle ages, shows how supremely natural the

dominion of the feudal nobility over men of low condition appeared to the nobility themselves, and how unnatural the conception seemed, of a person of the inferior class claiming equality with them, or exercising authority over them. It hardly seemed less so to the class held in subjection. The emancipated serfs and burgesses, even in their most vigorous struggles, never made any pretension to a share of authority; they only demanded more or less of limitation to the power of tyrannizing over them. So true is it that unnatural generally means only uncustomary, and that everything which is usual appears natural. The subjection of women to men being a universal custom, any departure from it quite naturally appears unnatural. But how entirely, even in this case, the feeling is dependent on custom, appears by ample experience. Nothing so much astonishes the people of distant parts of the world, when they first learn anything about England, as to be told that it is under a queen: the thing seems to them so unnatural as to be almost incredible. To Englishmen this does not seem in the least degree unnatural, because they are used to it; but they do feel it unnatural that women should be soldiers or members of parliament. In the feudal ages, on the contrary, war and politics were not thought unnatural to women, because not unusual; it seemed natural that women of the privileged classes should be of manly character, inferior in nothing but bodily strength to their husbands and fathers. The independence of women seemed rather less unnatural to the Greeks than to other ancients, on account of the fabulous Amazons[3] (whom they believed to be historical), and the partial example afforded by the Spartan women; who, though no less subordinate by law than in other Greek states, were more free in fact, and being trained to bodily exercises in the same manner with men, gave ample proof that they were not naturally disqualified for them. There can be little doubt that Spartan experience suggested to Plato,[4] among many other of his doctrines, that of the social and political equality of the two sexes.

But, it will be said, the rule of men over women differs from all these others in not being a rule of force: it is accepted voluntarily; women make no complaint, and are consenting parties to it. In the first place, a great

[1]   *Aristotle*   See Aristotle's *Politics*.

[2]   *Thracians*   A warring group of tribes, the Thracians occupied the area north of Greece from 700 BCE to 4 CE.

[3]   *Amazons*   A race of women warriors.

[4]   *Plato*   See Plato's *The Republic*, 5.

number of women do not accept it. Ever since there have been women able to make their sentiments known by their writings (the only mode of publicity which society permits to them), an increasing number of them have recorded protests against their present social condition: and recently many thousands of them, headed by the most eminent women known to the public, have petitioned parliament for their admission to the Parliamentary Suffrage.[1] The claim of women to be educated as solidly, and in the same branches of knowledge, as men, is urged with growing intensity, and with a great prospect of success; while the demand for their admission into professions and occupations hitherto closed against them, becomes every year more urgent. Though there are not in this country, as there are in the United States, periodical Conventions and an organized party to agitate for the Rights of Women, there is a numerous and active Society organized and managed by women, for the more limited object of obtaining the political franchise. Nor is it only in our own country and in America that women are beginning to protest, more or less collectively, against the disabilities under which they labour. France, and Italy, and Switzerland, and Russia now afford examples of the same thing. How many more women there are who silently cherish similar aspirations, no one can possibly know; but there are abundant tokens how many *would* cherish them, were they not so strenuously taught to repress them as contrary to the proprieties of their sex. It must be remembered, also, that no enslaved class ever asked for complete liberty at once. When Simon de Montfort[2] called the deputies of the commons to sit for the first time in parliament, did any of them dream of demanding that an assembly, elected by their constituents, should make and destroy ministries, and dictate to the king in affairs of state? No such thought entered into the imagination of the most ambitious of them. The nobility had already these pretensions; the commons pretended to nothing but to be exempt from arbitrary taxation, and from the gross individual oppres-

sion of the king's officers. It is a political law of nature that those who are under any power of ancient origin, never begin by complaining of the power itself, but only of its oppressive exercise. There is never any want of women who complain of ill usage by their husbands. There would be infinitely more, if complaint were not the greatest of all provocatives to a repetition and increase of the ill usage. It is this which frustrates all attempts to maintain the power but protect the woman against its abuses. In no other case (except that of a child) is the person who has been proved judicially to have suffered an injury, replaced under the physical power of the culprit who inflicted it. Accordingly wives, even in the most extreme and protracted cases of bodily ill usage, hardly ever dare avail themselves of the laws made for their protection: and if, in a moment of irrepressible indignation, or by the interference of neighbours, they are induced to do so, their whole effort afterwards is to disclose as little as they can, and to beg off their tyrant from his merited chastisement.

All causes, social and natural, combine to make it unlikely that women should be collectively rebellious to the power of men. They are so far in a position different from all other subject classes, that their masters require something more from them than actual service. Men do not want solely the obedience of women, they want their sentiments. All men, except the most brutish, desire to have, in the woman most nearly connected with them, not a forced slave but a willing one, not a slave merely, but a favourite. They have therefore put everything in practice to enslave their minds. The masters of all other slaves rely, for maintaining obedience, on fear; either fear of themselves, or religious fears. The masters of women wanted more than simple obedience, and they turned the whole force of education to effect their purpose. All women are brought up from the very earliest years in the belief that their ideal of character is the very opposite to that of men; not self-will, and government by self-control, but submission, and yielding to the control of others. All the moralities tell them that it is the duty of women, and all the current sentimentalities that it is their nature, to live for others; to make complete abnegation of themselves, and to have no life but in their affections. And by their affections are meant the only ones they are allowed to

---

[1] *petitioned ... Parliamentary Suffrage* Mill himself also introduced such a petition to the House of Commons in 1866.

[2] *Simon de Montfort* The Earl of Leicester (c. 1208–65) led a baronial revolt against Henry III and subsequently established a newly representative Parliament.

have—those to the men with whom they are connected, or to the children who constitute an additional and indefeasible tie between them and a man. When we put together three things—first, the natural attraction between opposite sexes; secondly, the wife's entire dependence on the husband, every privilege or pleasure she has being either his gift, or depending entirely on his will; and lastly, that the principal object of human pursuit, consideration, and all objects of social ambition, can in general be sought or obtained by her only through him, it would be a miracle if the object of being attractive to men had not become the polar star of feminine education and formation of character. And, this great means of influence over the minds of women having been acquired, an instinct of selfishness made men avail themselves of it to the utmost as a means of holding women in subjection, by representing to them meekness, submissiveness, and resignation of all individual will into the hands of a man, as an essential part of sexual attractiveness. Can it be doubted that any of the other yokes which mankind have succeeded in breaking, would have subsisted till now if the same means had existed, and had been so sedulously used, to bow down their minds to it? If it had been made the object of the life of every young plebeian to find personal favour in the eyes of some patrician, of every young serf with some seigneur;[1] if domestication with him, and a share of his personal affections, had been held out as the prize which they all should look out for, the most gifted and aspiring being able to reckon on the most desirable prizes; and if, when this prize had been obtained, they had been shut out by a wall of brass from all interests not centering in him, all feelings and desires but those which he shared or inculcated; would not serfs and seigneurs, plebeians and patricians, have been as broadly distinguished at this day as men and women are? and would not all but a thinker here and there, have believed the distinction to be a fundamental and unalterable fact in human nature?

The preceding considerations are amply sufficient to show that custom, however universal it may be, affords in this case no presumption, and ought not to create any prejudice, in favour of the arrangements which place women in social and political subjection to men. But I may go farther, and maintain that the course of history, and the tendencies of progressive human society, afford not only no presumption in favour of this system of inequality of rights, but a strong one against it; and that, so far as the whole course of human improvement up to this time, the whole stream of modern tendencies, warrants any inference on the subject, it is, that this relic of the past is discordant with the future, and must necessarily disappear.

For, what is the peculiar character of the modern world—the difference which chiefly distinguishes modern institutions, modern social ideas, modern life itself, from those of times long past? It is, that human beings are no longer born to their place in life, and chained down by an inexorable bond to the place they are born to, but are free to employ their faculties, and such favourable chances as offer, to achieve the lot which may appear to them most desirable. Human society of old was constituted on a very different principle. All were born to a fixed social position, and were mostly kept in it by law, or interdicted from any means by which they could emerge from it. As some men are born white and others black, so some were born slaves and others freemen and citizens; some were born patricians, others plebeians; some were born feudal nobles, others commoners and *roturiers*.[2] A slave or serf could never make himself free, nor, except by the will of his master, become so. In most European countries it was not till towards the close of the middle ages, and as a consequence of the growth of regal power, that commoners could be ennobled. Even among nobles, the eldest son was born the exclusive heir to the paternal possessions, and a long time elapsed before it was fully established that the father could disinherit him. Among the industrious classes, only those who were born members of a guild, or were admitted into it by its members, could lawfully practise their calling within its local limits; and nobody could practise any calling deemed important, in any but the legal manner—by processes authoritatively prescribed. Manufacturers have stood in the pillory[3] for presuming to carry on their

---

[1] *plebeian* Commoner; *patrician* Aristocrat; *serf* Laborer in a condition of servitude; *seigneur* Feudal lord.

[2] *roturiers* Commoners who owned land in feudal times.

[3] *pillory* Wooden framework in which wrongdoers were locked and exposed to public derision.

business by new and improved methods. In modern Europe, and most in those parts of it which have participated most largely in all other modern improvements, diametrically opposite doctrines now prevail. Law and government do not undertake to prescribe by whom any social or industrial operation shall or shall not be conducted, or what modes of conducting them shall be lawful. These things are left to the unfettered choice of individuals. Even the laws which required that workmen should serve an apprenticeship, have in this country been repealed: there being ample assurance that in all cases in which an apprenticeship is necessary, its necessity will suffice to enforce it. The old theory was, that the least possible should be left to the choice of the individual agent; that all he had to do should, as far as practicable, be laid down for him by superior wisdom. Left to himself he was sure to go wrong. The modern conviction, the fruit of a thousand years of experience, is, that things in which the individual is the person directly interested, never go right but as they are left to his own discretion; and that any regulation of them by authority, except to protect the rights of others, is sure to be mischievous. This conclusion, slowly arrived at, and not adopted until almost every possible application of the contrary theory had been made with disastrous result, now (in the industrial department) prevails universally in the most advanced countries, almost universally in all that have pretensions to any sort of advancement. It is not that all processes are supposed to be equally good, or all persons to be equally qualified for everything; but that freedom of individual choice is now known to be the only thing which procures the adoption of the best processes, and throws each operation into the hands of those who are best qualified for it. Nobody thinks it necessary to make a law that only a strong-armed man shall be a blacksmith. Freedom and competition suffice to make blacksmiths strong-armed men, because the weak-armed can earn more by engaging in occupations for which they are more fit. In consonance with this doctrine, it is felt to be an overstepping of the proper bounds of authority to fix beforehand, on some general presumption, that certain persons are not fit to do certain things. It is now thoroughly known and admitted that if some such presumptions exist, no such presumption is infallible. Even if it

be well grounded in a majority of cases, which it is very likely not to be, there will be a minority of exceptional cases in which it does not hold: and in those it is both an injustice to the individuals, and a detriment to society, to place barriers in the way of their using their faculties for their own benefit and for that of others. In the cases, on the other hand, in which the unfitness is real, the ordinary motives of human conduct will on the whole suffice to prevent the incompetent person from making, or from persisting in, the attempt.

If this general principle of social and economical science is not true; if individuals, with such help as they can derive from the opinion of those who know them, are not better judges than the law and the government, of their own capacities and vocation; the world cannot too soon abandon this principle, and return to the old system of regulations and disabilities. But if the principle is true, we ought to act as if we believed it, and not to ordain that to be born a girl instead of a boy, any more than to be born black instead of white, or a commoner instead of a nobleman, shall decide the person's position through all life—shall interdict people from all the more elevated social positions, and from all, except a few, respectable occupations. Even were we to admit the utmost that is ever pretended as to the superior fitness of men for all the functions now reserved to them, the same argument applies which forbids a legal qualification for members of parliament. If only once in a dozen years the conditions of eligibility exclude a fit person, there is a real loss, while the exclusion of thousands of unfit persons is no gain; for if the constitution of the electoral body disposes them to choose unfit persons, there are always plenty of such persons to choose from. In all things of any difficulty and importance, those who can do them well are fewer than the need, even with the most unrestricted latitude of choice: and any limitation of the field of selection deprives society of some chances of being served by the competent, without ever saving it from the incompetent.

At present, in the more improved countries, the disabilities of women are the only case, save one, in which laws and institutions take persons at their birth, and ordain that they shall never in all their lives be allowed to compete for certain things. The one exception is that of royalty. Persons still are born to the throne; no one, not of the reigning family, can ever occupy it, and no one even of that family can, by any means but the course of hereditary succession, attain it. All other dignities and social advantages are open to the whole male sex: many indeed are only attainable by wealth, but wealth may be striven for by anyone, and is actually obtained by many men of the very humblest origin. The difficulties, to the majority, are indeed insuperable without the aid of fortunate accidents; but no male human being is under any legal ban: neither law nor opinion superadd artificial obstacles to the natural ones. Royalty, as I have said, is excepted: but in this case everyone feels it to be an exception—an anomaly in the modern world, in marked opposition to its customs and principles, and to be justified only by extraordinary special expediencies, which, though individuals and nations differ in estimating their weight, unquestionably do in fact exist. But in this exceptional case, in which a high social function is, for important reasons, bestowed on birth instead of being put up to competition, all free nations contrive to adhere in substance to the principle from which they nominally derogate; for they circumscribe this high function by conditions avowedly intended to prevent the person to whom it ostensibly belongs from really performing it; while the person by whom it is performed, the responsible minister, does obtain the post by a competition from which no full-grown citizen of the male sex is legally excluded. The disabilities, therefore, to which women are subject from the mere fact of their birth, are the solitary examples of the kind in modern legislation. In no instance except this, which comprehends half the human race, are the higher social functions closed against anyone by a fatality of birth which no exertions, and no change of circumstances, can overcome; for even religious disabilities (besides that in England and in Europe they have practically almost ceased to exist) do not close any career to the disqualified person in case of conversion.

The social subordination of women thus stands out an isolated fact in modern social institutions; a solitary breach of what has become their fundamental law; a single relic of an old world of thought and practice exploded in everything else, but retained in the one

thing of most universal interest; as if a gigantic dolmen,[1] or a vast temple of Jupiter Olympius, occupied the site of St. Paul's and received daily worship, while the surrounding Christian churches were only resorted to on fasts and festivals. This entire discrepancy between one social fact and all those which accompany it, and the radical opposition between its nature and the progressive movement which is the boast of the modern world, and which has successively swept away everything else of an analogous character, surely affords, to a conscientious observer of human tendencies, serious matter for reflection. It raises a *prima facie*[2] presumption on the unfavourable side, far outweighing any which custom and usage could in such circumstances create on the favourable; and should at least suffice to make this, like the choice between republicanism and royalty, a balanced question.

The least that can be demanded is, that the question should not be considered as prejudged by existing fact and existing opinion, but open to discussion on its merits, as a question of justice and expediency: the decision on this, as on any of the other social arrangements of mankind, depending on what an enlightened estimate of tendencies and consequences may show to be most advantageous to humanity in general, without distinction of sex. And the discussion must be a real discussion, descending to foundations, and not resting satisfied with vague and general assertions. It will not do, for instance, to assert in general terms, that the experience of mankind has pronounced in favour of the existing system. Experience cannot possibly have decided between two courses, so long as there has only been experience of one. If it be said that the doctrine of the equality of the sexes rests only on theory, it must be remembered that the contrary doctrine also has only theory to rest upon. All that is proved in its favour by direct experience, is that mankind have been able to exist under it, and to attain the degree of improvement and prosperity which we now see; but whether that prosperity has been attained sooner, or is now greater, than it would have been under the other system, experience does not say. On the other hand, experience does say, that every step in improvement has been so invari-

---

[1]   *dolmen*   Celtic monument associated with pagan rituals.

[2]   *prima facie*   Latin: arising at first sight.

ably accompanied by a step made in raising the social position of women, that historians and philosophers have been led to adopt their elevation or debasement as on the whole the surest test and most correct measure of the civilization of a people or an age. Through all the progressive period of human history, the condition of women has been approaching nearer to equality with men. This does not of itself prove that the assimilation must go on to complete equality; but it assuredly affords some presumption that such is the case.

Neither does it avail anything to say that the *nature* of the two sexes adapts them to their present functions and position, and renders these appropriate to them. Standing on the ground of common sense and the constitution of the human mind, I deny that anyone knows, or can know, the nature of the two sexes, as long as they have only been seen in their present relation to one another. If men had ever been found in society without women, or women without men, or if there had been a society of men and women in which the women were not under the control of the men, something might have been positively known about the mental and moral differences which may be inherent in the nature of each. What is now called the nature of women is an eminently artificial thing—the result of forced repression in some directions, unnatural stimulation in others. It may be asserted without scruple, that no other class of dependents have had their character so entirely distorted from its natural proportions by their relation with their masters; for, if conquered and slave races have been, in some respects, more forcibly repressed, whatever in them has not been crushed down by an iron heel has generally been let alone, and if left with any liberty of development, it has developed itself according to its own laws; but in the case of women, a hot-house and stove cultivation has always been carried on of some of the capabilities of their nature, for the benefit and pleasure of their masters. Then, because certain products of the general vital force sprout luxuriantly and reach a great development in this heated atmosphere and under this active nurture and watering, while other shoots from the same root, which are left outside in the wintry air, with ice purposely heaped all round them, have a stunted growth, and some are burnt off with fire and disappear; men, with that inability to recognise their own work which distinguishes the unanalytic mind, indolently believe that the tree grows of itself in the way they have made it grow, and that it would die if one half of it were not kept in a vapour bath and the other half in the snow.

Of all difficulties which impede the progress of thought, and the formation of well-grounded opinions on life and social arrangements, the greatest is now the unspeakable ignorance and inattention of mankind in respect to the influences which form human character. Whatever any portion of the human species now are, or seem to be, such, it is supposed, they have a natural tendency to be: even when the most elementary knowledge of the circumstances in which they have been placed, clearly points out the causes that made them what they are. Because a cottier[1] deeply in arrears to his landlord is not industrious, there are people who think that the Irish are naturally idle. Because constitutions can be overthrown when the authorities appointed to execute them turn their arms against them, there are people who think the French incapable of free government. Because the Greeks cheated the Turks, and the Turks only plundered the Greeks, there are persons who think that the Turks are naturally more sincere: and because women, as is often said, care nothing about politics except their personalities, it is supposed that the general good is naturally less interesting to women than to men. History, which is now so much better understood than formerly, teaches another lesson: if only by showing the extraordinary susceptibility of human nature to external influences, and the extreme variableness of those of its manifestations which are supposed to be most universal and uniform. But in history, as in travelling, men usually see only what they already had in their own minds; and few learn much from history, who do not bring much with them to its study.

Hence, in regard to that most difficult question, what are the natural differences between the two sexes—a subject on which it is impossible in the present state of society to obtain complete and correct knowledge—while almost everybody dogmatizes upon it, almost all neglect and make light of the only means by which any partial insight can be obtained into it. This is, an analytic study of the most important department of

---

[1] *cottier* Tenant who rents a cottage and often works for a landlord in return.

psychology, the laws of the influence of circumstances on character. For, however great and apparently ineradicable the moral and intellectual differences between men and women might be, the evidence of there being natural differences could only be negative. Those only could be inferred to be natural which could not possibly be artificial—the residuum, after deducting every characteristic of either sex which can admit of being explained from education or external circumstances. The profoundest knowledge of the laws of the formation of character is indispensable to entitle anyone to affirm even that there is any difference, much more what the difference is, between the two sexes considered as moral and rational beings; and since no one, as yet, has that knowledge (for there is hardly any subject which, in proportion to its importance, has been so little studied), no one is thus far entitled to any positive opinion on the subject. Conjectures are all that can at present be made; conjectures more or less probable, according as more or less authorized by such knowledge as we yet have of the laws of psychology, as applied to the formation of character.

Even the preliminary knowledge, what the differences between the sexes now are, apart from all question as to how they are made what they are, is still in the crudest and most incomplete state. Medical practitioners and physiologists have ascertained, to some extent, the differences in bodily constitution; and this is an important element to the psychologist: but hardly any medical practitioner is a psychologist. Respecting the mental characteristics of women; their observations are of no more worth than those of common men. It is a subject on which nothing final can be known, so long as those who alone can really know it, women themselves, have given but little testimony, and that little, mostly suborned. It is easy to know stupid women. Stupidity is much the same all the world over. A stupid person's notions and feelings may confidently be inferred from those which prevail in the circle by which the person is surrounded. Not so with those whose opinions and feelings are an emanation from their own nature and faculties. It is only a man here and there who has any tolerable knowledge of the character even of the women of his own family. I do not mean, of their capabilities; these nobody knows, not even themselves, because most

of them have never been called out. I mean their actually existing thoughts and feelings. Many a man thinks he perfectly understands women, because he has had amatory relations with several, perhaps with many of them. If he is a good observer, and his experience extends to quality as well as quantity, he may have learnt something of one narrow department of their nature—an important department, no doubt. But of all the rest of it, few persons are generally more ignorant, because there are few from whom it is so carefully hidden. The most favourable case which a man can generally have for studying the character of a woman, is that of his own wife: for the opportunities are greater, and the cases of complete sympathy not so unspeakably rare. And in fact, this is the source from which any knowledge worth having on the subject has, I believe, generally come. But most men have not had the opportunity of studying in this way more than a single case: accordingly one can, to an almost laughable degree, infer what a man's wife is like, from his opinions about women in general. To make even this one case yield any result, the woman must be worth knowing, and the man not only a competent judge, but of a character so sympathetic in itself, and so well adapted to hers, that he can either read her mind by sympathetic intuition, or has nothing in himself which makes her shy of disclosing it. Hardly anything, I believe, can be more rare than this conjunction. It often happens that there is the most complete unity of feeling and community of interests as to all external things, yet the one has as little admission into the internal life of the other as if they were common acquaintance. Even with true affection, authority on the one side and subordination on the other prevent perfect confidence. Though nothing may be intentionally withheld, much is not shown. In the analogous relation of parent and child, the corresponding phenomenon must have been in the observation of everyone. As between father and son, how many are the cases in which the father, in spite of real affection on both sides, obviously to all the world does not know, nor suspect, parts of the son's character familiar to his companions and equals. The truth is, that the position of looking up to another is extremely unpropitious to complete sincerity and openness with him. The fear of losing ground in his opinion or in his feelings is so strong, that even in an upright character, there is an unconscious tendency to show only the best side, or the side which, though not the best, is that which he most likes to see: and it may be confidently said that thorough knowledge of one another hardly ever exists, but between persons who, besides being intimates, are equals. How much more true, then, must all this be, when the one is not only under the authority of the other, but has it inculcated on her as a duty to reckon everything else subordinate to his comfort and pleasure, and to let him neither see nor feel anything coming from her, except what is agreeable to him. All these difficulties stand in the way of a man's obtaining any thorough knowledge even of the one woman whom alone, in general, he has sufficient opportunity of studying. When we further consider that to understand one woman is not necessarily to understand any other woman; that even if he could study many women of one rank, or of one country, he would not thereby understand women of other ranks or countries; and even if he did, they are still only the women of a single period of history; we may safely assert that the knowledge which men can acquire of women, even as they have been and are, without reference to what they might be, is wretchedly imperfect and superficial, and always will be so, until women themselves have told all that they have to tell.

And this time has not come; nor will it come otherwise than gradually. It is but of yesterday that women have either been qualified by literary accomplishments or permitted by society, to tell anything to the general public. As yet very few of them dare tell anything, which men, on whom their literary success depends, are unwilling to hear. Let us remember in what manner, up to a very recent time, the expression, even by a male author, of uncustomary opinions, or what are deemed eccentric feelings, usually was, and in some degree still is, received; and we may form some faint conception under what impediments a woman, who is brought up to think custom and opinion her sovereign rule, attempts to express in books anything drawn from the depths of her own nature. The greatest woman who has left writings behind her sufficient to give her an eminent rank in the literature of her country, thought it necessary to prefix as a motto to her boldest work, "Un homme peut braver l'opinion; une femme doit s'y

soumettre."[1] The greater part of what women write about women is mere sycophancy to men. In the case of unmarried women, much of it seems only intended to increase their chance of a husband. Many, both married and unmarried, overstep the mark, and inculcate a servility beyond what is desired or relished by any man, except the very vulgarest. But this is not so often the case as, even at a quite late period, it still was. Literary women are becoming more freespoken, and more willing to express their real sentiments. Unfortunately, in this country especially, they are themselves such artificial products, that their sentiments are compounded of a small element of individual observation and consciousness, and a very large one of acquired associations. This will be less and less the case, but it will remain true to a great extent, as long as social institutions do not admit the same free development of originality in women which is possible to men. When that time comes, and not before, we shall see, and not merely hear, as much as it is necessary to know of the nature of women, and the adaptation of other things to it.

I have dwelt so much on the difficulties which at present obstruct any real knowledge by men of the true nature of women, because in this as in so many other things "opinio copiæ inter maximas causas inopiæ est;"[2] and there is little chance of reasonable thinking on the matter, while people flatter themselves that they perfectly understand a subject of which most men know absolutely nothing, and of which it is at present impossible that any man, or all men taken together, should have knowledge which can qualify them to lay down the law to women as to what is, or is not, their vocation. Happily, no such knowledge is necessary for any practical purpose connected with the position of women in relation to society and life. For, according to all the principles involved in modern society, the question rests with women themselves—to be decided by their own experience, and by the use of their own faculties. There are no means of finding what either one person or many

---

[1] [Mill's note] Title-page of Mme. de Staël's *Delphine*. [The French novelist's (1766–1817) words translate as: "A man can brave (public) opinion; a woman must submit to it."]

[2] *"opinio copiæ ... inopiæ est"* Latin: "the belief in sufficiency is one of the greatest causes of insufficiency."

can do, but by trying—and no means by which anyone else can discover for them what it is for their happiness to do or leave undone.

One thing we may be certain of—that what is contrary to women's nature to do, they never will be made to do by simply giving their nature free play. The anxiety of mankind to interfere in behalf of nature, for fear lest nature should not succeed in effecting its purpose, is an altogether unnecessary solicitude. What women by nature cannot do, it is quite superfluous to forbid them from doing. What they can do, but not so well as the men who are their competitors, competition suffices to exclude them from; since nobody asks for protective duties and bounties in favour of women; it is only asked that the present bounties and protective duties in favour of men should be recalled. If women have a greater natural inclination for some things than for others, there is no need of laws or social inculcation to make the majority of them do the former in preference to the latter. Whatever women's services are most wanted for, the free play of competition will hold out the strongest inducements to them to undertake. And, as the words imply, they are most wanted for the things for which they are most fit; by the apportionment of which to them, the collective faculties of the two sexes can be applied on the whole with the greatest sum of valuable result.

The general opinion of men is supposed to be, that the natural vocation of a woman is that of a wife and mother. I say, is supposed to be, because, judging from acts—from the whole of the present constitution of society—one might infer that their opinion was the direct contrary. They might be supposed to think that the alleged natural vocation of women was of all things the most repugnant to their nature; insomuch that if they are free to do anything else—if any other means of living, or occupation of their time and faculties, is open, which has any chance of appearing desirable to them—there will not be enough of them who will be willing to accept the condition said to be natural to them. If this is the real opinion of men in general, it would be well that it should be spoken out. I should like to hear somebody openly enunciating the doctrine (it is already implied in much that is written on the subject)—"It is necessary to society that women should marry and produce children. They will not do so unless they are compelled. Therefore it is necessary to compel them." The merits of the case would then be clearly defined. It would be exactly that of the slaveholders of South Carolina and Louisiana. "It is necessary that cotton and sugar should be grown. White men cannot produce them. Negroes will not, for any wages which we choose to give. *Ergo* they must be compelled." An illustration still closer to the point is that of impressment.[1] Sailors must absolutely be had to defend the country. It often happens that they will not voluntarily enlist. Therefore there must be the power of forcing them. How often has this logic been used! and, but for one flaw in it, without doubt it would have been successful up to this day. But it is open to the retort—First pay the sailors the honest value of their labour. When you have made it as well worth their while to serve you, as to work for other employers, you will have no more difficulty than others have in obtaining their services. To this there is no logical answer except "I will not:" and as people are now not only ashamed, but are not desirous, to rob the labourer of his hire, impressment is no longer advocated. Those who attempt to force women into marriage by closing all other doors against them, lay themselves open to a similar retort. If they mean what they say, their opinion must evidently be, that men do not render the married condition so desirable to women, as to induce them to accept it for its own recommendations. It is not a sign of one's thinking the boon one offers very attractive, when one allows only Hobson's choice,[2] "that or none." And here, I believe, is the clue to the feelings of those men, who have a real antipathy to the equal freedom of women. I believe they are afraid, not lest women should be unwilling to marry, for I do not think that anyone in reality has that apprehension; but lest they should insist that marriage should be on equal conditions; lest all women of spirit and capacity should prefer doing almost anything else, not in their own eyes degrading, rather than marry, when marrying is giving themselves a master, and a master too of all their earthly

---

[1] *impressment* Policy that pressed men into public service, even against their will; this practice was discontinued after 1835.

[2] *Hobson's choice* Expression originating from a Cambridge-London carrier, Thomas Hobson (1544–1630), who refused, when hiring out his horses, to allow any to leave the stable out of turn.

possessions. And truly, if this consequence were necessarily incident to marriage, I think that the apprehension would be very well founded. I agree in thinking it probable that few women, capable of anything else, would, unless under an irresistible *entrainement*,[1] rendering them for the time insensible to anything but itself, choose such a lot, when any other means were open to them of filling a conventionally honourable place in life: and if men are determined that the law of marriage shall be a law of despotism, they are quite right, in point of mere policy, in leaving to women only

Hobson's choice. But, in that case, all that has been done in the modern world to relax the chain on the minds of women, has been a mistake. They never should have been allowed to receive a literary education. Women who read, much more women who write, are, in the existing constitution of things, a contradiction and a disturbing element: and it was wrong to bring women up with any acquirements but those of an odalisque,[2] or of a domestic servant.

—1869

---

[1] *entrainement* Enchantment or charm.

[2] *odalisque* Concubine.

THE PLACE OF WOMEN IN SOCIETY
CONTEXTS

There was much debate concerning the proper place of women and the ideal characteristics of femininity throughout the nineteenth century. In a nation ruled by a female queen who supported education for women but not female suffrage, the lines between traditional masculine and feminine realms were often blurred. The traditional roles of wives, mothers, and daughters; the structure of the family; the nature of marriage; and how society ought to treat those unwilling or unable to conform to its standards of womanhood—all these subjects were open for examination by both men and women, and many writers and thinkers voiced opinions on them.

Sarah Stickney Ellis, the author of *The Women of England*, ran a school for girls but did not support intellectual advancement for women. Instead, she educated her pupils to become capable managers of their homes, from which they could best facilitate the advancement of their husbands and sons. Her numerous guides to female conduct, including *The Daughters of England* (1842), *The Wives of England* (1843), and *The Mothers of England* (1845), were extremely popular.

As the selection from *Fraser's Magazine* shows, the role of the governess in Victorian society posed issues of both gender and class. The growing prosperity of the middle classes enabled more and more families to afford governesses—and the increased emphasis on education (for females as well as for males) led to a widespread acknowledgment of the importance of the role governesses played as educators. In Victorian social hierarchy, the governess was a "lady"; this was *socially* a desirable occupation for many women, especially those daughters of tradespeople who sought to "better themselves." But as a paid employee (albeit often a poorly paid one) the governess was part of the work force—a status that would normally disqualify a woman from being considered a "lady." Consequently, the situation of the governess was rife with tensions, and the daily reality of her life was often very difficult; Charlotte Brontë complained of the "wretched bondage" of being a governess.

The women's suffrage campaign, which began in the 1850s, heightened the debate over women's proper role in society. Suffragists' frustration over the lack of female vote was exacerbated by a series of Reform Acts, which extended the vote to a much greater proportion of men than had previously been entitled, but explicitly excluded all women. There were a variety of arguments used in the effort to justify the political subordination of women to men; these included the scientific argument, which presented evidence for women's supposed intellectual and physical inferiority, and the "divine will" argument, which portrayed female inferiority as part of the natural order established by God in Genesis. In her argument for female suffrage in *The Enfranchisement of Women*, Harriet Taylor presents—and attacks—some additional arguments used to protest women's entrance into politics.

Coventry Patmore's long poem *The Angel in the House*, which became extraordinarily popular in both Britain and the United States, is a sentimental depiction of the ideal female as conceived by many Victorian men of the upper and middle classes. The poem, which celebrated Patmore's first wife (he remarried twice after her death) details their courtship and marriage and epitomizes the view of women held by many men at the time. In the twentieth century the poem became the object of attacks by many feminist critics, notably Virginia Woolf, and the phrase "angel in the house" was commonly used as a sort of shorthand to refer to an oppressive Victorian attitude towards gender roles.

During this era when the "angel in the house" was seen by many as the ideal to which every woman should aspire, growing numbers of women were actually unmarried—an uncomfortable fact that had long been true but began to generate considerable commentary in the latter half of the century. It was generally believed that the "problem" was demographic: there were too many women relative to men, and so some women—commonly referred to as "odd" or "redundant" women—were left without a partner. While emigration and military service occupied many men who might otherwise have started families, the low marriage rate was also a result of individual choice; initially, it was a choice made by men who did not want or could not afford to marry, leaving an abundance of single women (especially those of the middle class) competing for the narrow range of jobs that were considered appropriate for them. But as many in the first generation of "odd women" found single life a viable option, more and more women began to feel free either to postpone marriage or to reject it altogether. To conventional writers such as William Rathbone Greg, who tackles the question in his essay "Why Are Women Redundant?", the "odd women" were to be pitied for their inability—or derided for their refusal—to fulfill their natural destinies as wives and mothers. For feminists such as Frances Power Cobbe, as she argues in a response to Greg's article, the "odd women" were a clear illustration of the problems with a societal model that forced women to choose between marriage and financial desperation. The debate surrounding the "odd women" thus became part of a larger debate raging in the late nineteenth century: the argument over "the woman question."

Conversation about "the woman question" was heated, and the proponents of women's rights were often viciously attacked in print. As the satirical cartoon reproduced below demonstrates, female suffragettes were often viewed as the antithesis of the ideal woman, epitomizing instead traditionally "masculine" characteristics. In the excerpt following, Eliza Lynn Linton, perhaps the most vocal anti-feminist of the period, criticizes what she sees as the unnatural, masculine boldness of the "modern girl," whose unwillingness to serve and support her husband and nurture her children, Linton argues, makes her not only unsuitable for marriage, but a disgrace to England's national character.

The idea that a woman ought to be subordinate to her husband was not only a matter of social expectation; it was also incorporated into English law. For much of the nineteenth century, in most respects the law treated a husband and wife as a single person, with many of the wife's rights—including her right to the possession of her own property—subsumed by her husband's. In her article "Criminals, Idiots, Women, and Minors," Frances Power Cobbe describes and criticizes the common arguments used to justify depriving married women of the legal rights that even convicted felons were afforded. Women began campaigning against these laws in the 1850s, and the Married Women's Property Acts were passed in 1870 and 1884, allowing married women the same property rights as unmarried women.

Within Victorian society's complex network of gender and class distinctions, many citizens relied upon printed material for guidance in matters of conduct and etiquette, as well as for practical advice on household management and professional opportunities. *The Girl's Own Paper*, a weekly paper founded in 1880 as a companion to the very successful *Boy's Own Paper*, provided such information to many female readers. According to its editor, the paper, which was published by the Religious Tract Society, aimed to instruct its readers "in the moral and domestic virtues, preparing them for the responsibility of womanhood and for a heavenly home."

Many women began to reject this traditional paradigm of wifehood and motherhood when "the marriage question" came to occupy a central position in debates concerning women's political rights, their education, and their need for economic independence. Among those who vehemently opposed the change in values was Grant Allen; in some respects a radical thinker, he believed that the institution of marriage required extensive revision, but in his "Plain Words on the Woman Question" he nonetheless attacks the abandonment of traditional gender roles as unnatural and harmful to society. Despite such hostile responses, the new outlook persisted; in her article "The New Aspect of the Woman Question," Sarah Grand coined the phrase "the new woman" to name those of her generation who had embraced the goals of political, educational, and economic equality with men. The importance of these values is defended in Mona Caird's somewhat humorous response to the *Daily Telegraph*'s question "Does Marriage Hinder a Woman's Self-Development?" Her hypothetical reversal of men's and women's roles brings to light how arbitrary—and confining—definitions of "masculine" and "feminine" characteristics could be.

⌘ ⌘ ⌘

from Sarah Stickney Ellis, *The Daughters of England: Their Position in Society, Character and Responsibilities* (1842)

... The sphere upon which a young woman enters on first leaving school, or, to use a popular phrase, on "completing her education," is so entirely new to her, her mind is so often the subject of new impressions, and her attention so frequently absorbed by new motives for exertion, that, if at all accustomed to reflect, we cannot doubt but she will make these, or similar questions, the subject of serious inquiry—"What is my position in society? What do I aim at? And what means do I intend to employ for the accomplishment of my purpose?" ...

As women, then, the first thing of importance is to be content to be inferior to men—inferior in mental power, in the same proportion that you are inferior in bodily strength. Facility of movement, aptitude, and grace, the bodily frame of woman may possess in a higher degree than that of man; just as in the softer touches of mental and spiritual beauty her character may present a lovelier page than his. Yet, as the great attribute of power must still be wanting there, it becomes more immediately her business to inquire how this want may be supplied.

An able and eloquent writer on "Woman's Mission"[1] has justly observed that woman's strength is in her influence. And, in order to render this influence more complete, you will find on examination that you are by nature endowed with peculiar faculties—with a quickness of perception, facility of adaptation, and acuteness

of feeling, which fit you especially for the part you have to act in life; and which, at the same time, render you, in a higher degree than men, susceptible both of pain and pleasure. ...

*   *   *

I have already stated that women, in their position in life, must be content to be inferior to men; but as their inferiority consists chiefly in their want of power, this deficiency is abundantly made up to them by their capability of exercising influence; it is made up to them also in other ways, incalculable in their number and extent; but in none so effectually as by that order of Divine Providence which places them, in a moral and religious point of view, on the same level with man; nor can it be a subject of regret to any right-minded woman that they are not only exempt from the most laborious occupations both of mind and body, but also from the necessity of engaging in those eager pecuniary speculations, and in that fierce conflict of worldly interests by which men are so deeply occupied as to be in a manner compelled to stifle their best feelings, until they become in reality the characters they at first only assumed. Can it be a subject of regret to any kind and feeling woman that her sphere of action is one adapted to the exercise of the affections, where she may love, and trust, and hope, and serve, to the utmost of her wishes? Can it be a subject of regret that she is not called upon, so much as man, to calculate, to compete, to struggle, but rather to occupy a sphere in which the elements of discord cannot with propriety be admitted—in which beauty and order are expected to denote her presence, and where the exercise of benevolence is the duty she is most frequently called upon to perform.

---

[1] *An able ... Mission* Sarah Lewis, whose *Woman's Mission*, a popular book on female conduct, was published in 1839.

Women almost universally consider themselves, and wish to be considered by others, as extremely affectionate; scarcely can a more severe libel be pronounced upon a woman than to say that she is not so. Now the whole law of woman's life is a law of love. I propose, therefore, to treat the subject in this light—to try whether the neglect of their peculiar duties does not imply an absence of love, and whether the principle of love, thoroughly carried out, would not so influence their conduct and feelings as to render them all which their best friends could desire.

Let us, however, clearly understand each other at the outset. To love, is a very different thing from a desire to be beloved. To love, is woman's nature—to be beloved is the consequence of her having properly exercised and controlled that nature. To love, is a woman's duty—to be beloved, is her reward.

* * *

... There is yet another flight of female ambition, another course which the love of distinction is apt to make, more product of folly, and of disappointment, perhaps, than all the rest. It is the ambition of the female author who writes for fame. Could those young aspirants know how little real dignity there is connected with the *trade* of authorship, their harps would be exchanged for distaffs,[1] their rose-tinted paper would be converted into ashes, and their Parnassus[2] would dwindle to a molehill.... The same want of sympathy which so often inspires the first effort of female authorship, might often find a sweet and abundant interchange of kindness in many a faithful heart beside the homely hearth. And after all, there is more true poetry in the fire-side affections of early life than in all those sympathetic associations with unknown and untried developments of mind which ever have existed either amongst the sons or the daughters of men.

Taking a more sober view of the case, there are, unquestionably, subjects of deep interest with which women have opportunities peculiar to themselves of becoming acquainted, and thus of benefiting their fellow creatures through the medium of their writings. But, after all, literature is not the natural channel for a woman's feelings; and pity, not envy, ought to be the meed[3] of her who writes for the public. How much of what with other women is reserved for the select and chosen intercourse of affection, with her must be laid bare to the coarse cavillings,[4] and coarser commendations, of amateur or professional critics. How much of what no woman loves to say, except to the listening ear of domestic affection, by her must be told—nay, blazoned—to the world. And then, in her season of depression, or of wounded feeling, when her spirit yearns to sit in solitude, or even in darkness, so that it may be still; to know and feel that the very essence of that spirit, now embodied in a palpable form, has become an article of sale and bargain, tossed over from the hands of one workman to another, free alike to the touch of the prince and the peasant, and no longer to be reclaimed at will by the original possessor, let the world receive it as it may.

Is such, I ask, an enviable distinction?

from Anonymous, "Hints on the Modern Governess System," *Fraser's Magazine,* November 1844

... To trace the growth of woman's desire after knowledge would be the task of a philosopher; for us, it suffices to see that it is, that is has been from all ages. The barter of Paradise for the means of knowledge is the first recorded act of woman's life; she tempted man to forego all tried blessings, for the untried boon of "knowing good and evil." Thenceforth, man wreaked his vengeance upon woman, for the loss of ease and plenty, by keeping her ignorant, and, consequently, helpless. But since the day that Christianity dawned on the world, an emancipation of the weak out of the power of the strong has been silently progressing. The faint cry, uplifted at intervals, swelled into a chorus; there was a sudden rush; all the world clamoured for a better education for women; no wonder, in such a struggle, that the greater number

---

[1] *distaff* Staff on which wool or flax was wound when spinning.

[2] *Parnassus* Mountain in Greece sacred to the Muses, the nine daughters of Zeus and Mnemosyne, each of whom presided over, and provided inspiration for, a different aspect of the arts and sciences.

[3] *meed* Recompense; reward.

[4] *cavillings* Unfair or petty fault-finding.

mistook chaff and husks[1] for bread. The movement was all too sudden. Education, in as far as it implies intellectual and moral growth, is the work of life; its operations are as secret and as self-derived as the gradual shooting of the green blade into the wheat-ear.

Now, when that cry of women after knowledge pierced the air, a thousand sprang up, mushroomwise, in a night, to answer it. Mothers who had only read their Bibles and receipt-books[2] found themselves unprepared for the emergency—we have so little patience, so little foresight. Then, teaching, that holy vocation of a woman, became a trade. An universal demand creates its own supply. Here was a tempting opening to all aspiring women, who were free to try a new field; the unmarried daughters of the gentry left with scanty portions had, till now, been content to eke out their small incomes in trade; many were the gentlewomen, in our great-grandmothers' days, who lived in honoured independence, though they kept small shops, to which their old friends resorted. They did not lose caste[3] because they sat for part of the day behind the counter. However, this refuge grew insecure from the outward pressure of public opinion in favour of refinement.... Many left their quiet homes for the schoolrooms of halls and castles. As they mounted the stair, others came from a lower rank, and filled the vacant steps. The restless rage to push on had stirred all classes. Those who, disappointed in their new stand, looked wistfully back to the old, found that when they would return they could not. There was no place left for them but that which they had chosen. Like much else, it looked best from a distance. Here, then, was a whole class of women driven into a new line, for which they had received no fitting preparation.... The new generation, thirsting to be taught, found teachers at their mercy, hanging between two ranks. Do the weak desire to learn what they may expect from the strong? Let

them ponder deeply the governess system of the present day. This was the watch-word, "Teach us on our own terms, or work, and cease to be gentlewomen." To the newly risen race of governesses, even such equivocal gentility was preferable to a second change, though it was to be gained at the price of isolation....

The policy of the world is to take advantage of want. It became apparent that a whole family of daughters might be taught by one of these single women, struggling for bread, for less than it formerly cost to send one girl to school. Where competition was so great, there was no difficulty in driving a bargain. The means of instruction might be had so cheaply that the grocer's daughters could be taught to read *Paul and Virginia* in the original tongue, and to strum *The Fall of Paris*.[4] In process of time, therefore, a governess became a necessary appanage[5] in every family.

Whether it be right or wrong, as a general rule, for mothers to delegate their most sacred trust to hired strangers, we are not here to discuss. The fact exists. Is the system carried out fairly for all parties? Is there any question astir as to its abuse? Philanthropic eyes are scanning many social evils. Is it yet considered how far a whole race of women are dragging out weary lives under a mass of trials, the detail of which would fill a "blue book"[6] by themselves? True, if the case were known, "a thousand voices" would be "uplifted."[7] The miseries of the governess may even swell that sickening clamour about the "rights of women," which would never have been raised had women been true to themselves. But that trite saying in this case has its point. The modern governess system is a case between woman and woman. Before one sex demands its due from the other, let it be just to itself.

---

[1] *chaff and husks* Material separated out from grains when threshing cereal crops.

[2] *receipt-books* I.e., recipe books.

[3] *lose caste* I.e., lose their position in society.

[4] *Paul and Virginia* The sentimental French novel *Paul et Virginie* (1787), by Jacques-Henri Bernadin de St. Pierre; *strum* Play poorly on the piano; *The Fall of Paris* Popular song of the period.

[5] *appanage* Possession, perquisite.

[6] *blue book* Parliamentary report.

[7] *a thousand ... uplifted* A reference to the epigraph of this article, from French novelist George Sand's collection of fictional letters, *Lettres à Marcie* (1837): "Society is full of abuses. Women complain of being brutally enslaved, badly brought up, badly educated, badly treated, and badly defended. All this is, unfortunately, true. These complaints are just, and do not doubt but that before long a thousand voices will be uplifted to remedy the evil."

Punch has ably pleaded in the cause of salaries and qualifications.[1] The statistics touching lunatic asylums give a frightful proportion of governesses in the list of the insane.[2] But has the whole life in home schoolrooms ever been investigated? We ask this with a real wish to be informed, with a hope of directing eyes to this unknown page of human life. Have kind, ladylike, cultivated women ever reflected on the relation which subsists between themselves and others of like minds, and, perhaps, formerly in similar circumstances? Have they ever tried to put themselves in the position of the young women devoting themselves to the education of their children, who yet live as strangers in the midst of their homes? ...

... When the lesson-books are closed, and the little ones have capered out of the school-room, what becomes of the teacher, who has not exchanged a thought or a word with any one of congenial mind all day? Hour after hour she has *bent down* her mind, and *raised* the children's to given points, which, however interesting, are exhausting. A young thing, perhaps, still herself, ready to spring up again at one kindly touch. Do not even fond mothers, who teach their own children, feel that after the labours of the day they need some interchange of *mind*? They have often felt refreshed when husband or friend has given them a new thought, or understood an articulated feeling, after the repression of the day, necessary in fulfilling the duty of teaching. Who is there that has not known the dryness of spending time with people of more limited capacities and interests than one's own? ... Let mothers ask if they would not expect their own daughters to languish in spirits and energy, if they had no intercourse with older companions. Whilst the children are with their parents and their guests, the governess, quite as often as not, is expected to remain in the school-room, unless specially invited to join the circle. This is peculiarly the case in large establishments, where the school-room arrangements are distinct from the rest of the family. We believe that most young women of delicate perceptions would prefer their desolate apartment to feeling themselves clogs[3] upon the family party. But do people know what they are about when they leave young creatures alone, long evening after evening, following days of seclusion and exhaustion? Factory-girls, shop-women, teachers of accomplishments, return to their homes at night. The servants gather round the work-table or the hall-fire. Prisoners in gaol[4] may collect together in knots in their yards, look in each other's faces, hear the sound of human voices, tell their troubles and joys, and listen to their neighbours. Solitary confinement, even for felons, is reserved to punish some special offence. It is only the governess, and a certain class of private tutors, who must hear the echoes from the drawing-room and the offices, feeling that, in a house full of people, they dwell alone. Nervous irritability, dejection, loss of energy, are the inevitable results which follow a too solitary life in youth. Yet, without elasticity in her own frame, how can the governess be a fitting companion and teacher of such gay, volatile creatures as children—so easily cowed and spirit-broken by harshness or settled sadness in those who live with them? Would not querulous temper of depression of spirits in the governess be complained of by the parents? Do they consider, when they expect cheerfulness and an even composure of spirits from one fretted with children's restless waywardness, and chilled by the frosty indifference and neglect of the grown-up members of the family, that they ask an impossible thing?

from Harriet Taylor, *The Enfranchisement of Women* (1851)

When a prejudice, which has any hold on the feeling, finds itself reduced to the unpleasant necessity of assigning reasons, it thinks it has done enough when it has re-asserted the very point in the

---

[1] *Punch has ... qualifications* The satirical weekly magazine *Punch* had recently printed numerous articles advocating the improvement of conditions for governesses.

[2] *The statistics ... insane* During the early and mid nineteenth century it was a commonplace that governesses tended toward mental instability as a result of the stressful nature of their employment. While some statistics did show that there was a high percentage of governesses in asylums, this may have been due in part to the fact that private asylums sometimes provided the cheapest respectable accommodation for women without family or employment.

[3] *clogs* Encumbrances. Literally, blocks of wood attached to the leg or neck of a person or animal to prevent escape.

[4] *gaol* I.e., jail.

dispute, in phrases which appeal to the pre-existing feelings. Thus, many persons think they have sufficiently justified the restrictions on women's field of action when they have said that the pursuits from which women are excluded are *unfeminine*, and that the *proper sphere* of women is not politics or publicity, but private and domestic life.

We deny the right of any portion of the species to decide for another portion, or any individual for another individual, what is and what is not their "proper sphere." The proper sphere for all human beings is the largest and highest which they are able to attain to....

We shall follow the very proper convention, in not entering into the question of the alleged differences in physical or mental qualities between the sexes; not because we have nothing to say, but because we have too much.... But if those who assert that the "proper sphere" for women is the domestic, mean by this that they have not shown themselves qualified for any other, the assertion evinces great ignorance of life and of history. Women have shown fitness for the highest social functions, exactly in proportion as they have been admitted to them. By a curious anomaly, though ineligible to even the lowest offices of state, they are in some countries admitted to the highest of all, the regal; and if there is any one function for which they have shown a decided vocation, it is that of reigning....

Concerning the fitness, then, of women for politics, there can be no question: but the dispute is more likely to turn upon the fitness of politics for women. When the reasons alleged for excluding women from active life in all its higher departments are stripped of their garb of declamatory phrases, and reduced to the simple expression of a meaning, they seem to be mainly three: the incompatibility of active life with maternity and with the cares of a household; secondly, its alleged hardening effect on the character; and thirdly, the inexpediency of making an addition to the already excessive pressure of competition in every kind of professional or lucrative employment.

The first, the maternity argument, is usually laid most stress upon: although (it needs hardly be said) this reason, if it be one, can apply only to mothers. It is neither necessary nor just to make imperative on women that they shall be either mothers or nothing; or that if they have been mothers once, they shall be nothing else during the whole remainder of their lives. Neither women nor men need any law to exclude them from an occupation if they have undertaken another which is incompatible with it. No one proposes to exclude the male sex from Parliament because a man may be a soldier or sailor in active service, or a merchant whose business requires all his time and energies. Nine-tenths of the occupations of men exclude them *de facto*[1] from public life, as effectually as if they were excluded by law; but that is no reason for making laws to exclude even the nine-tenths, much less the remaining tenth. The reason of the case is the same for women as for men. There is no need to make provision by law that a woman shall not carry on the active details of a household, or of the education of children, and at the same time practise a profession or be elected to Parliament. Where incompatibility is real, it will take care of itself: but there is gross injustice in making the incompatibility a pretence for the exclusion of those in whose case it does not exist. And these, if they were free to choose, would be a very large proportion. The maternity argument deserts its supporters in the case of single women, a large and increasing class of the population; a fact which, it is not irrelevant to remark, by tending to diminish the excessive competition of numbers, is calculated to assist greatly the prosperity of all. There is no inherent reason or necessity that all women should voluntarily choose to devote their lives to one animal function and its consequences. Numbers of women are wives and mothers only because there is no other career open to them, no other occupation for their feelings or their activities. Every improvement in their education, and enlargement of their faculties—everything which renders them more qualified for any other mode of life, increases the number of those to whom it is an injury and an oppression to be denied the choice. To say that women must be excluded from active life because maternity disqualifies them for it, is in fact to say that every other career should be forbidden them in order that maternity may be their only resource.

But secondly, it is urged that to give the same freedom of occupation to women as to men would be an injurious addition to the crowd of competitors, by

---

[1] *de facto* Latin: in reality; as a matter of fact.

whom the avenues to almost all kinds of employment are choked up, and its remuneration depressed. This argument, it is to be observed, does not reach the political question. It gives no excuse for withholding from women the rights of citizenship. The suffrage, the jury-box, admission to the legislature and to office, it does not touch. It bears only on the industrial branch of the subject. Allowing it, then, in an economical point of view, its full force; assuming that to lay open to women the employments now monopolized by men, would tend, like the breaking down of other monopolies, to lower the rate of remuneration in those employments; let us consider what is the amount of this evil consequence, and what the compensation for it. The worst ever asserted, much worse than is at all likely to be realized, is that if women competed with men, a man and a woman could not together earn more than is now earned by the man alone. Let us make this supposition, the most favourable supposition possible: the joint income of the two would be the same as before, while the woman would be raised from the position of a servant to that of a partner. Even if every woman, as matters now stand, had a claim on some man for support, how infinitely preferable is it that part of the income should be of the woman's earning, even if the aggregate sum were but little increased by it, rather than that she should be compelled to stand aside in order that men may be the sole earners, and the sole dispensers of what is earned. Even under the present laws respecting the property of women, a woman who contributes materially to the support of the family cannot be treated in the same contemptuously tyrannical manner as one who, however she may toil as a domestic drudge, is a dependent on the man for subsistence. As for the depression of wages by increase of competition, remedies will be found for it in time. Palliatives might be applied immediately; for instance, a more rigid exclusion of children from industrial employment, during the years in which they ought to be working only to strengthen their bodies and minds for after life. Children are necessarily dependent, and under the power of others; and their labour, being not for themselves but for the gain of their parents, is a proper subject for legislative regulation. With respect to the future, we neither believe that improvident multiplication, and the

consequent excessive difficulty of gaining a subsistence, will always continue, nor that the division of mankind into capitalists and hired labourers, and the regulation of the reward of labourers mainly by demand and supply, will be for ever, or even much longer, the rule of the world. But so long as competition is the general law of human life, it is tyranny to shut out one half of the competitors. All who have attained the age of self-government have an equal claim to be permitted to sell whatever kind of useful labour they are capable of, for the price which it will bring.

The third objection to the admission of women to political or professional life, its alleged hardening tendency, belongs to an age now past, and is scarcely to be comprehended by people of the present time. There are still, however, persons who say that the world and its avocations render men selfish and unfeeling; that the struggles, rivalries, and collisions of business and of politics make them harsh and unamiable; that if half the species must unavoidably be given up to these things, it is the more necessary that the other half should be kept free from them; that to preserve women from the bad influences of the world is the only chance of preventing men from being wholly given up to them.

There would have been plausibility in this argument when the world was still in the age of violence; when life was full of physical conflict, and every man had to redress his injuries or those of others, by the sword or by the strength of his arm. Women, like priests, by being exempted from such responsibilities, and from some part of the accompanying dangers, may have been enabled to exercise a beneficial influence. But in the present condition of human life, we do not know where those hardening influences are to be found, to which men are subject and from which women are at present exempt. Individuals now-a-days are seldom called upon to fight hand to hand, even with peaceful weapons; personal enmities and rivalries count for little in worldly transactions; the general pressure of circumstances, not the adverse will of individuals, is the obstacle men now have to make head against. That pressure, when excessive, breaks the spirit, and cramps and sours the feelings, but not less of women than of men, since they suffer certainly not less from its evils. There are still quarrels and dislikes, but the sources of them are changed. The feudal chief once found his bitterest enemy in his powerful neighbour, the minister or courtier in his rival for place: but opposition of interest in active life, as a cause of personal animosity, is out of date; the enmities of the present day arise not from great things but small, from what people say of one another, more than from what they do; and if there are hatred, malice, and all uncharitableness, they are to be found among women fully as much as among men. In the present state of civilization, the notion of guarding women from the hardening influences of the world could only be realized by secluding them from society altogether. The common duties of common life, as at present constituted, are incompatible with any other softness in women than weakness. Surely weak minds in weak bodies must ere long cease to be even supposed to be either attractive or amiable.

But, in truth, none of these arguments and considerations touch the foundations of the subject. The real question is, whether it is right and expedient that one half of the human race should pass through life in a state of forced subordination to the other half. If the best state of human society is that of being divided into two parts, one consisting of persons with a will and a substantive existence, the other of humble companions to these persons, attached, each of them to one, for the purpose of bringing up *his* children, and making *his* home pleasant to him; if this is the place assigned to women, it is but kindness to educate them for this; to make them believe that the greatest good fortune which can befall them is to be chosen by some man for this purpose; and that every other career which the world deems happy or honourable is closed to them by the law, not of social institutions, but of nature and destiny.

When, however, we ask why the existence of one-half the species should be merely ancillary to that of the other—why each woman should be a mere appendage to a man, allowed to have no interests of her own, that there may be nothing to compete in her mind with his interests and his pleasure; the only reason which can be given is, that men like it. It is agreeable to them that men should live for their own sake, women for the sake of men: and the qualities and conduct in subjects which are agreeable to rulers, they succeed for a long time in making the subjects themselves consider as their appropriate virtues.

from Coventry Patmore, *The Angel in the House* (1854–56)

THE WIFE'S TRAGEDY

Man must be pleased; but him to please
    Is woman's pleasure; down the gulf
Of his condoled necessities
    She casts her best, she flings herself.
5 How often flings for nought! and yokes
    Her heart to an icicle or whim,
Whose each impatient word provokes
    Another, not from her, but him;
While she, too gentle even to force
10   His penitence by kind replies,
Waits by, expecting his remorse,
    With pardon in her pitying eyes;
And if he once, by shame oppressed,
    A comfortable word confers,
15 She leans and weeps against his breast,
    And seems to think the sin was hers;
And whilst his love has any life,
    Or any eye to see her charms,
At any time, she's still his wife,
20   Dearly devoted to his arms;
She loves with love that cannot tire;
    And when, ah woe, she loves alone,
Through passionate duty love flames higher,
    As grass grows taller round a stone....

THE FOREIGN LAND

A woman is a foreign land,
    Of which, though there he settle young
A man will ne'er quite understand
    The customs, politics, and tongue.
5 The foolish hie° them post-haste through,   *hasten*
    See fashions odd, and prospects fair,
Learn of the language, "How-d'ye do,"
    And go and brag that they've been there.
The most for leave to trade apply,
10   For once, at Empire's seat her heart,
Then get what knowledge ear and eye
    Glean chancewise in the life-long mart.°   *market*

And certain others few and fit,
   Attach them to the Court, and see
15 The country's best, its accent hit,
   And partly sound its polity.

from William Rathbone Greg, "Why Are Women Redundant?" (1862)

... [T]here is an enormous and increasing number of single women in the nation, a number quite disproportionate and quite abnormal; a number which, positively and relatively, is indicative of an unwholesome social state, and is both productive and prognostic of much wretchedness and wrong. There are hundreds of thousands of women—not to speak more largely still—scattered through all ranks, but proportionally most numerous in the middle and upper classes—who have to earn their own living instead of spending and husbanding the earnings of men; who, not having the natural duties and labours of wives and mothers, have to carve out artificial and painfully-sought occupations for themselves; who, in place of completing, sweetening, and embellishing the existence of others, are compelled to lead an independent and incomplete existence of their own. In the manufacturing districts thousands of girls are working in mills and earning ample wages, instead of performing, or preparing and learning to perform, the functions and labours of domestic life. In great cities, thousands, again, are toiling in the ill-paid *métier*[1] of seamstresses and needlewomen, wasting life and soul, gathering the scantiest subsistence, and surrounded by the most overpowering and insidious temptations. As we go a few steps higher in the social scale, we find two classes of similar abnormal existences; women, more or less well educated, spending youth and middle life as governesses, living laboriously, yet perhaps not uncomfortably, but laying by nothing, and retiring to a lonely and destitute old age: and old maids, with just enough income to live upon, but wretched and deteriorating, their minds narrowing, and their hearts withering, because they have nothing to do, and none to love, cherish, and obey. A little further upwards, how many do we daily see, how many have we all known,

who are raised by fortune above the necessity of caring for their own subsistence, but to whom employment is a necessity as imperious as to the milliner or the husbandman,[2] because only employment can fill the dreary void of an unshared existence—beautiful lay nuns, involuntary takers of the veil, who pine for work, who beg for occupation, who pant for interest in life, as the hart panteth after the water-brooks, and dig for it more earnestly than for hid treasures.[3] With most women, probably, this phase comes at some epoch in their course; with numbers, alas, it never passes into any other. Some rush to charity, and do partial good or much mischief; some find solace in literary interests and work, and these, though the fewest, are perhaps the most fortunate of all; some seek in the excessive development of the religious affections a pale ideal substitute for the denied human ones—a substitute of which God forbid that we should speak slightingly, but which is seldom wholly satisfactory or wholly safe. Lastly, as we ascend into the highest ranks of all, we come upon crowds of the same unfulfilled destinies—the same *existences manquées*[4]—women who have gay society,[5] but no sacred or suffering home, whose dreary round of pleasure is yet sadder, less remunerative, and less satisfying, than the dreary round of toil trodden by their humble sisters. The very being of all these various classes is a standing proof of, and protest against, that "something wrong," on which we have a few words to say—that besetting problem which, like the sphinx's,[6] society must solve or die....

... Therefore it is that all those efforts, on which chivalric or compassionate benevolence is now so intent, to render single life as easy, as attractive, and as lucrative to women, as unhappily other influences to which we have alluded have already made it to men, *are efforts in a wrong direction*—spontaneous and natural, no doubt,

---

[1] *métier* French: employment.

[2] *husbandman* Farmer.

[3] *as the hart ... water-brooks* Expression of longing for God in Psalm 42.1; *dig for ... hid treasures* Description of longing for death in Job 3.21.

[4] *existences manquées* French: lost lives.

[5] *gay society* Pleasant, carefree social circle.

[6] *sphinx* Mythical creature said to guard the entrance to the Greek city of Thebes. She posed a riddle to all travelers attempting to enter the city and killed those unable to solve it.

to the tender heart of humanity, which always seeks first to relieve suffering, and only at a later date begins to think of curing disorder—but not to be smiled upon or aided by wise prescribers for the maladies of states. ... To endeavour to make women independent of men; to multiply and facilitate their employments; to enable them to earn a separate and ample subsistence by competing with the hardier sex in those careers and occupations hitherto set apart for that sex alone; to induct them generally into avocations, not only as interesting and beneficent, and therefore *appropriate*, but specially and definitely as *lucrative*; to surround single life for them with so smooth an entrance, and such a pleasant, ornamented, comfortable path, that marriage shall almost come to be regarded, not as their most honourable function and especial calling, but merely as one of many ways open to them, competing on equal terms with other ways for their cold and philosophic choice: this would appear to be the aim and theory of many female reformers. ...

from Frances Power Cobbe, "What Shall We Do with Our Old Maids?" (1862)

... It appears that there is a natural excess of four or five per cent of females over the males in our population. This, then, might be assumed to be the limits within which female celibacy was normal and inevitable.

There is, however, an actual ratio of thirty per cent of women now in England who never marry, leaving one-fourth of both sexes in a state of celibacy. This proportion further appears to be constantly on the increase. It is obvious enough that these facts call for a revision of many of our social arrangements. The old assumption that marriage was the sole destiny of woman, and that it was the business of her husband to afford her support, is brought up short by the statement that one woman in four is certain not to marry, and that three millions of women earn their own living at this moment in England. We may view the case two ways: either—

1st, We must frankly accept this new state of things, and educate women and modify trade in accordance therewith, so as to make the condition of celibacy as little injurious as possible; or—

2nd, We must set ourselves vigorously to stop the current which is leading men and women away from the natural order of Providence. We must do nothing whatever to render celibacy easy or attractive; and we must make the utmost efforts to promote marriage by emigration of women to the colonies,[1] and all other means in our power.

The second of these views we shall in the first place consider. It may be found to colour the ideas of a vast number of writers, and to influence essentially the decisions made on many points—as the admission of women to university degrees, to the medical profession, and generally to free competition in employment. Lately it has met a powerful and not unkindly exposition in an article in a contemporary quarterly, entitled, "Why Are Women Redundant?" Therein it is plainly set forth that all efforts to make celibacy easy for women are labours in a wrong direction, and are to be likened to the noxious exertions of quacks to mitigate the symptoms of disease, and allow the patient to persist in his evil courses. ...

A little deeper reflection, however, discloses a very important point which has been dropped out of the argument. Marriage is, indeed, the happiest and best condition for mankind. But does anyone think that all marriages are so? When we make the assertion that marriage is good and virtuous, do we mean a marriage of interest,[2] a marriage for wealth, for position, for rank, for support? Surely nothing of the kind. Such marriages as these are the sources of misery and sin, not of happiness and virtue, nay, their moral character, to be fitly designated, would require stronger words than we care to use. There is only one kind of marriage which makes good the assertion that it is the right and happy condition for mankind, and that is a marriage founded on free choice, esteem, and affection—in one word, on love. If, then, we seek to promote the happiness and virtue of the community, our efforts must be directed to encouraging *only* marriages which are of the sort to produce them—namely, marriages founded on love. All mar-

---

[1] *emigration of ... the colonies* One course of action recommended in "Why Are Women Redundant?" by William Rathbone Greg, the article to which Cobbe is responding. A selection from Greg's article is reproduced above.

[2] *interest* I.e., self-interest.

riages founded on interest, on the desire for position, support, or the like, we must discourage to the utmost of our power, as the sources of nothing but wretchedness. Where, now, have we reached? Is it not to the conclusion that to make it a woman's *interest* to marry, to force her, by barring out every means of self-support and all fairly remunerative labour, to look to marriage as her sole chance of competency, is precisely to drive her into one of those sinful and unhappy marriages? It is quite clear we can never drive her into *love*. That is a sentiment which poverty, friendlessness, and helplessness can by no means call out. Nor, on the contrary, can competence and freedom in any way check it. It will arise under its natural conditions, if we will but leave the matter alone. A loving marriage can never become a matter of "cold philosophic choice."[1] And if *not* a loving one, then, for Heaven's sake, let us give no motive for choice at all.

Let the employments of women be raised and multiplied as much as possible, let their labour be as fairly remunerated, let their education be pushed as high, let their whole position be made as healthy and happy as possible, and there will come out once more, here as in every other department of life, the triumph of the Divine laws of our nature. Loving marriages are (we cannot doubt) what God has designed, not marriages of interest. When we have made it *less* women's interest to marry, we shall indeed have less and fewer interested marriages, with all their train of miseries and evils. But we shall also have more *loving* ones, more marriages founded on free choice and free affection. Thus we arrive at the conclusion that for the very end of promoting marriage—that is, such marriage as it is alone desirable to promote—we should pursue a precisely opposite course to that suggested by the Reviewer or his party. Instead of leaving single women as helpless as possible, and their labour as ill-rewarded—instead of dinning into their ears from childhood that marriage is their one vocation and concern in life, and securing afterwards if they miss it that they shall find no other vocation or concern—instead of all this, we shall act exactly on the reverse principle. We shall make single life so free and happy that they shall have not one temptation to change it save the only temptation which *ought* to determine them—namely, love. Instead of making marriage a case of "Hobson's choice"[2] for a woman, we shall endeavour to give her such independence of all interested considerations that she may make it a choice, not indeed "cold and philosophic," but warm from the heart, and guided by heart and conscience only.

from Eliza Lynn Linton, "The Girl of the Period," *Saturday Review*, March 1868

Time was when the stereotyped phrase "a fair young English girl" meant the ideal of womanhood, to us, at least, of home birth and breeding. It meant a creature generous, capable, and modest; something franker than a Frenchwoman, more to be trusted than an Italian, as brave as an American but more refined, as domestic as a German and more graceful. It meant a girl who could be trusted alone if need be, because of the innate purity and dignity of her nature, but who was neither bold in bearing nor masculine in mind; a girl who, when she married, would be her husband's friend and companion, but never his rival; one who would consider their interests identical, and not hold him as just so much fair game for spoil; who would make his house his true home and place of rest, not a mere passage-place for vanity and ostentation to go through; a tender mother, an industrious housekeeper, a judicious mistress. We prided ourselves as a nation on our women. We thought we had the pick of creation in this fair young English girl of ours, and envied no other men their own.... This was in the old time, and when English girls were content to be what God and nature had made them. Of late years we have changed the pattern, and have given to the world a race of women as utterly unlike the old insular ideal as if we had created another nation altogether. The girl of the period and the fair young English girl of the past have nothing in common save ancestry and their mother-tongue; and even of this last the modern version makes almost a new language, through the copious additions it has received from the current slang of the day.

---

[1] *cold philosophic choice* Phrase used by Greg in "Why Are Women Redundant?"

[2] *Hobson's choice* Choice in which only one thing is offered, and one must accept it or make do with nothing.

"THE ANGEL IN 'THE HOUSE;'" OR, THE RESULT OF FEMALE SUFFRAGE.

(A Troubled Dream of the Future.)

This cartoon appeared in the 14 June 1884 edition of *Punch*. A satirical representation of the female suffragist, here having gained the vote and a position of political power, speaking in the House of Commons. She is knitting a "blue stocking," an allusion to the term "bluestocking," a derogatory term that began to be applied to free-thinking women in the eighteenth century.

The girl of the period is a creature who dyes her hair and paints her face, as the first articles of her personal religion; whose sole idea of life is plenty of fun and luxury; and whose dress is the object of such thought and intellect as she possesses. Her main endeavour in this is to outvie her neighbours in the extravagance of fashion. No matter whether, as in the time of crinolines, she sacrificed decency, or, as now, in the time of trains, she sacrifices cleanliness; no matter either, whether she makes herself a nuisance and an inconvenience to every one she meets. The girl of the period has done away with such moral muffishness[1] as consideration for others, or regard for counsel and rebuke. It was all very well in old-fashioned times, when fathers and mothers had some authority and were treated with respect, to be tutored and made to obey, but she is far too fast and flourishing to be stopped in mid-career by these slow old morals; and as she dresses to please herself, she does not care if she displeases everyone else. Nothing is too extraordinary and nothing too exaggerated for her

---

[1] *muffishness* Foolishness, often describing someone or something seen as old-fashioned.

vitiated[1] taste; and things which in themselves would be useful reforms if let alone become monstrosities worse than those which they have displaced so soon as she begins to manipulate and improve. If a sensible fashion lifts the gown out of the mud, she raises hers midway to her knee. If the absurd structure of wire and buckram, once called a bonnet, is modified to something that shall protect the wearer's face without putting out the eyes of her companion, she cuts hers down to four straws and a rosebud, or a tag of lace and a bunch of glass beads!… She has blunted the fine edges of feeling so much that she cannot understand why she should be condemned for an imitation of form which does not include imitation of fact; she cannot be made to see that modesty of appearance and virtue ought to be inseparable, and that no good girl can afford to appear bad, under penalty of receiving the contempt awarded to the bad.

This imitation of the *demi-monde*[2] in dress leads to something in manner and feeling, not quite so pronounced perhaps, but far too like to be honourable to herself or satisfactory to her friends. It leads to slang, bold talk, and fastness; to the love of pleasure and indifference to duty; to the desire of money before either love or happiness; to uselessness at home, dissatisfaction with the monotony of ordinary life, and horror of all useful work; in a word, to the worst forms of luxury and selfishness, to the most fatal effects arising from want of high principle and absence of tender feeling…. No one can say of the modern English girl that she is tender, loving, retiring, or domestic. The old fault so often found by keen-sighted Frenchwomen, that she was so fatally *romanesque*,[3] so prone to sacrifice appearances and social advantages for love, will never be set down to the girl of the period. Love indeed is the last thing she thinks of, and the least of the dangers besetting her. Love in a cottage, that seductive dream which used to vex the heart and disturb the calculations of prudent mothers, is now a myth of past ages. The legal barter of herself for so much money, representing so much dash, so much luxury and pleasure—that is her

idea of marriage; the only idea worth entertaining. For all seriousness of thought respecting the duties or the consequences of marriage, she has not a trace. If children come, they find but a stepmother's cold welcome from her; and if her husband thinks that he has married anything that is to belong to him—a *tacens et placens uxor*[4] pledged to make him happy—the sooner he wakes from his hallucination and understands that he has simply married someone who will condescend to spend his money on herself, and who will shelter her indiscretions behind the shield of his name, the less severe will be his disappointment. She has married his house, his carriage, his balance at the bankers, his title; and he himself is just the inevitable condition clogging the wheel of her fortune; at best an adjunct, to be tolerated with more or less patience as may chance. For it is only the old-fashioned sort, not girls of the period *pur sang*,[5] that marry for love, or put the husband before the banker. But she does not marry easily. Men are afraid of her; and with reason. They may amuse themselves with her of an evening, but they do not take her readily for life….

The marvel, in the present fashion of life among women, is how it holds its ground in spite of the disapprobation of men. It used to be an old-time notion that the sexes were made for each other, and that it was only natural for them to please each other, and to set themselves out for that end. But the girl of the period does not please men. She pleases them as little as she elevates them; and how little she does that, the class of women she has taken as her models of itself testifies. All men whose opinion is worth having prefer the simple and genuine girl of the past, with her tender little ways and pretty bashful modesties, to this loud and rampant modernization, with her false red hair and painted skin, talking slang as glibly as a man, and by preference leading the conversation to doubtful subjects. She thinks she is *piquante*[6] and exciting when she thus makes herself the bad copy of a worse original; and she will not see that though men laugh with her they do not respect her, though they flirt with her they do not marry her; she will not believe that she is not the kind of thing they

---

[1] *vitiated* Corrupted.

[2] *demi-monde* French: literally, "half world"; figuratively, the world existing below the level of respectable society. The term was often used to denote the world of the courtesan.

[3] *romanesque* French: romantic.

[4] *tacens … uxor* Latin: silent and pleasing wife.

[5] *pur sang* French: pure-blooded.

[6] *piquante* Stimulating.

want, and that she is acting against nature and her own interests when she disregards their advice and offends their taste. We do not see how she makes out her account, viewing her life from any side; but all we can do is to wait patiently until the national madness has passed, and our women have come back again to the old English ideal, once the most beautiful, the most modest, the most essentially womanly in the world.

from Frances Power Cobbe, "Criminals, Idiots, Women, and Minors," *Fraser's Magazine*, December 1868

There was an allegory rather popular about thirty years ago, whose manifest purpose was to impress on the juvenile mind that tendency which Mr. Matthew Arnold has ingeniously designated "Hebraism."[1] The hero of the tale descends upon earth from some distant planet, and is conducted by a mundane cicerone[2] through one of our great cities, where he beholds the docks and arsenals, the streets and marts, the galleries of art, and the palaces of royalty. The visitor admires everything till he happens to pass a graveyard. "What is that gloomy spot?" he asks of his companion. "It is a cemetery," replies the guide.

"A—what did you say? " inquires the son of the star.

"A graveyard; a place of public interment; where we bury our dead," reiterates the cicerone.

The visitor, pale with awe and terror, learns at last that there is in this world such a thing as *Death*, and (as he is forbidden to return to his own planet) he resolves to dedicate every moment left to him to prepare himself for that fearful event and all that may follow it.

Had that visitor heard for the first time upon his arrival on earth of another incident of human existence—namely, *Marriage*, it may be surmised that his astonishment and awe would also have been considerable. To his eager inquiry whether men and women

earnestly strove to prepare themselves for so momentous an occurrence, he would have received the puzzling reply that women frequently devoted themselves with perfectly Hebraistic singleness of aim to that special purpose; but that men, on the contrary, very rarely included any preparation for the married state among the items of their widest Hellenistic culture. But this anomaly would be trifling compared to others which would be revealed to him. "Ah," we can hear him say to his guide as they pass into a village church. "What a pretty sight is this! What is happening to that sweet young woman in white who is giving her hand to the good-looking fellow beside her, all the company decked in holiday attire, and the joy-bells shaking the old tower overhead? She is receiving some great honour, is she not? The Prize of Virtue, perhaps?"

"Oh, yes," would reply the friend; "an honour certainly. She is being Married." After a little further explanation the visitor would pursue his inquiry:

"Of course, having entered this honourable state of matrimony, she has some privilege above the women who are not chosen by anybody? I notice her husband has just said, 'With all my worldly goods I thee endow.' Does that mean that she will henceforth have the control of his money altogether, or only that he takes her into partnership?"

"*Pas précisément*,[3] my dear sir. By our law it is *her* goods and earnings, present and future, which belong to him from this moment."

"You don't say so? But then, of course, his goods are hers also?"

"Oh dear, no! not at all. He is only bound to find her food; and truth to tell, not very strictly or efficaciously bound to do that."

"How! do I understand you? Is it possible that here in the most solemn religious act, which I perceive your prayer book calls 'The Solemnisation of Holy Matrimony,' every husband makes a generous promise, which promise is not only a mockery, but the actual reverse and parody of the real state of the case: the man who promises giving nothing, and the woman who is silent giving all?"

"Well, yes; I suppose that is something like it, as to the letter of the law. But then, of course, practically—"

---

[1] *Hebraism*   Originally denoting an attribute of the Hebrew people, the term was used by Arnold to describe a moral (rather than intellectual) theory of life. Arnold used the term "Hellenistic," in contrast, to denote the intellectual culture or way of life typified by the ancient Greeks.

[2] *cicerone*   Guide.

[3] *Pas précisément*   French: Not exactly.

"Practically, I suppose few men can really be so unmanly and selfish as the law warrants them in being. Yet some, I fear, may avail themselves of such authority. May I ask another question? As you subject women who enter the marriage state to such very severe penalties as this, what worse have you in store for women who lead a dissolute life, to the moral injury of the community?"

"Oh, the law takes nothing from them. Whatever they earn or inherit is their own. They are able, also, to sue the fathers of their children for their maintenance, which a wife, of course, is not allowed to do on behalf of *her* little ones, because she and her husband are one in the eye of the law."

"One question still further—your criminals? Do they always forfeit their entire property on conviction?"

"Only for the most heinous crimes; felony and murder, for example."

"Pardon me; I must seem to you so stupid! Why is the property of the woman who commits Murder, and the property of the woman who commits Matrimony, dealt with alike by your law?"

Leaving our little allegory and in sober seriousness, we must all admit that the just and expedient treatment of women by men is one of the most obscure problems, alike of equity and of policy. Nor of women only, but of all classes and races of human beings whose condition is temporarily or permanently one of comparative weakness and dependence....

By the common law of England a married woman has no legal existence, so far as property is concerned, independently of her husband. The husband and wife are assumed to be one person, and that person is the husband. The wife can make no contract, and can neither sue nor be sued. Whatever she possess of personal property at the time of her marriage, or whatever she may afterwards earn or inherit, belongs to her husband, without control on her part.... If she possess real estate, so long as her husband lives he receives and spends the income derived from it, being only forbidden to sell it without her consent. From none of her property is he bound to reserve anything, or make any provision for her maintenance or that of her children. This is the law for all, but practically it affects only two

classes of women, *viz.*[1] those who marry hurriedly or without proper advisers, and those whose property at the time of marriage is too small to permit of the expense of a settlement; in other words, the whole middle and lower ranks of women, and a certain portion of the upper ranks. Women of the richer class, with proper advisers, never come under the provisions of the Common Law, being carefully protected therefrom by an intricate system elaborated for the purpose by the courts of Equity, to which the victims of the Common Law have for years applied for redress. That system always involves considerable legal expenses, and an arrangement with trustees which is often extremely inconvenient and injurious to the interests of the married couple; nevertheless it is understood to be so great a boon that none who can afford to avail themselves of it fail to do so.

What then is the principle on which the Common Law mulcts[2] the poorer class of women of their property and earnings, and entails on the rich, if they wish to evade it, the costs and embarrassment of a marriage settlement? There is, of course, a principle in it, and one capable of clear statement. There are grounds for the law; first of Justice, then of Expediency, lastly (and as we believe) most influential of all, of Sentiment.

First, the grounds of Justice.

Man is the natural bread-winner. Woman lives by the bread which man has earned. Ergo, it is fit and right that the man who wins should have absolute disposal, not only of his winnings, but of every other small morsel or fraction of earning or property she may possess. It is a fair return to him for his labour in the joint interests of both.... The woman's case is that of a pauper who enters a workhouse. The ratepayers are bound to support him; but if he have any savings they must be given up to the board. HE cannot claim support and keep independent property.

Then for Expediency. "How can two walk together except they be agreed?" says the Bible. "How can they walk together except one of them have it all his own way?" says the voice of rough and ready practicality. Somebody must rule in a household, or everything will go to rack and ruin; and disputes will be endless. If

---

[1]   *viz.*   Latin: namely; that is to say (an abbreviation of *videlicet*).

[2]   *mulcts*   Swindles.

somebody is to rule it can only be the husband, who is wiser, stronger, knows more of the world, and in any case has not the slightest intention of yielding his predominance. But to give a man such rule he must be allowed to keep the purse. Nothing but the power of the purse—in default of the stick—can permanently and thoroughly secure authority....

Lastly, for the sentimental view. How painful is the notion of a wife holding back her money from him who is every day toiling for her support! How fair is the ideal picture of absolute concession on her part of all she possesses of this world's dross to the man to whom she gives her heart and life!... The young man and maiden, after years of affection, and carefully laying by of provision for the event, take each other at last, to be henceforth no more twain, but one flesh. Both have saved a little money, but it now belongs to the husband alone. He lays it out in the purchase of a cottage where they are henceforth to dwell. Day by day he goes forth to his labour, and weekly he brings home his earnings and places them in his wife's lap, bidding her spend them as she knows best for the supply of their homely board, their clothing which her deft fingers will make and many a time repair, and last for their common treasures, the little children who gather around them. Thus they grow old in unbroken peace and love, the man's will having never once been disputed, the wide yielding alike from choice and from necessity to his superior sense and his legal authority.

Surely this idea of life, for which the Common Law of England has done its utmost to provide, is well worth the pondering before we attempt to meddle with any of its safeguards? Who will suggest anything better in its room?

Alas, there are other scenes besides idylls of domestic peace and obedience promoted by the laws we are considering....

The existing Common Law is not *Just*, because it neither can secure nor actually even attempts to secure for the woman the equivalent support for whose sake she is forced to relinquish her property.

It is not *Expedient*, because while in happy marriages it is superfluous and useless, in unhappy ones it becomes highly injurious; often causing the final ruin of a family which the mother (if upheld by law) might have sup-

ported single-handed. It is also shown not to be considered expedient by the conduct of the entire upper class of the country, and even of the legislature itself in the system of the Court of Chancery. Where no one who can afford to evade the law fails to evade it, the pretence that it is believed to be generally expedient is absurd. Further, the classes which actually evade it, and the countries where it is non-existing, show in no degree less connubial harmony than those wherein it is enforced.

Lastly, it does not tend to fulfil, but to counteract, the *Sentiment* regarding the marriage union, to which it aims to add the pressure of force. Real unanimity is not produced between two parties by forbidding one of them to have any voice at all. The hard mechanical contrivance of the law for making husband and wife of one heart and mind is calculated to produce a precisely opposite result.

from "Between School and Marriage," *The Girl's Own Paper*, Vol. 7 (4 September 1886)

This time in a girl's life corresponds to that in a man's which is passed in a university, or in learning the work of his profession. Too many girls look on it as a *mauvais quart d'heure*,[1] which may be dawdled through in an irresponsible way until they have a house of their own. Marriage represents a home, a position; sometimes even less than that—a trousseau,[2] or a wedding tour. So they hasten through the years of adolescence as well as may be in order to reach the end of a wearisome task.

And yet if the girl is mother to the woman—that is to say, if the woman will be what the girl now is, this time, which is essentially one for settling habits, cannot be anything less than the most important in life. If the girl spend it in thoughtless idleness and discontented trifling, the result will be seen in the character of the woman. It is well for any of us when our work is cut out for us, so to speak, and we have not to look about for a profitable way of passing the time; but this last is the

[1] *mauvais quart d'heure* French: an unpleasant time (literally, an unpleasant quarter of an hour), from the French expression "*passer un mauvais quart d'heure*," meaning "to have a bad time of it."

[2] *trousseau* A bride's collection of clothing and linens.

The Girl's Own Paper, sold weekly for a penny, was mainly marketed to working- and middle-class women, but it was read by women from all classes and age groups and soon after its founding reached a circulation of over 250,000.

miserable condition of many girls belonging to daughter-full houses in easy circumstances. What can they do between school and marriage?

When the financial resources of her father are slender, a girl is quite right to seek for some employment by which she may earn her own living, and perhaps help her brothers and sisters; but when this is not the case, let no feeling of quixotic restlessness induce her to rashly leave home. It may be her plain duty to remain at home, and she may be independent and pay her way quite as much as one who earns and pays current coin. She can pay her way by filling in the little spaces in home life as only a dear daughter can, by lifting the weight of care from her mother, and by slipping in a soft word or a smile where it is like oil on the troubled waters of a father's spirit. What better remuneration can a father have for his expenditure upon his daughters than their laughter, good humour, and sympathy?…

from Emma Brewer, "Our Friends the Servants," *The Girl's Own Paper*, Vol. 14 (25 March 1893)

Among mistresses who earnestly desire the welfare of their servants there is no question which causes more trouble and anxiety than that of allowing visitors in the kitchen, men visitors especially. It is indeed a difficult question, and cannot be solved for every one alike.

I know several ladies who have thought it right that such of their maids as were engaged should be permitted to receive their sweethearts from time to time in the kitchen; but in every case where this has been granted that has come under my notice, the results have been so disastrous as to necessitate the withdrawal of the privilege. It was found utterly destructive of harmony in the kitchen, and gave no real pleasure to anyone. In some cases the fickle men forsook their old love in favour of some younger and more attractive of the fellow-servants, and it is not difficult to imagine the bitterness, anger, and sharp words which became the fashion after such faithlessness.

In others the sweethearts borrowed money of all the foolish girls in order to lay it upon horses in which they were interested; in others, where more stimulant had been taken than was good for them, they have boasted among other men of the beautiful silver, etc., in the houses where their young women lived, with what results may be guessed.

In simple fairness the privilege cannot be granted to one without extending it to all; this, in many houses, would fill the kitchens of an evening; for no maid would acknowledge that she had no young man, and would get one on the spot without considering his character, and such a one would scarcely add to the safety or morality of the kitchen....

There are a few things in the relationship between mistress and maid which distress me greatly, because I know they are utterly destructive of home-peace and comfort; one is a mistress reproving her servant in public, another is a maid answering her mistress rudely, and a third is a mistress finding fault with servants out of the room to one who is waiting in the room.

No good servant would endure the first nor be guilty of the second, but one and all are evil in their result, and it is easy to see that, let the fault be what it may, it cannot be remedied in this fashion.

Servants have feelings to be wounded and rights to be respected, and when these are ignored they feel that their occupation is compromising to their respectability and freedom.

We lose many good servants in this way, and get in their place large importations of very inferior ones from the Continent. It gives one a feeling of sadness that while the mother country stands in increased need of good and trustworthy servants, she cannot retain them or make friends of them, but has to look on while her colonies attract those she herself would so gladly keep.

I do not know if all are aware that every month ships leave England with a number of servants on board; indeed, as many as fourteen vessels go over to Queensland alone, carrying, on an average, two hundred servants on each ship. Any young woman with good health and good character can get a free passage to Queensland if she is under thirty-five years of age. This colony, even above others, values highly our friends the servants, whose success is undoubted. They try to live up to the high opinion formed of them, but it is grievous to see them leaving the old country which wants them even more than the colonies.

from Grant Allen, "Plain Words on the Woman Question," *Fortnightly Review* 46 (October 1889)

... Almost every woman must bear four or five children.[1] In doing so she must on the average use up the ten or twelve best years of her life: the ten or twelve years that immediately succeed her attainment of complete womanhood.... Again, during these ten or twelve years of child-bearing at the very least, the women can't conveniently earn their own livelihood; they must be provided for by the labour of the men.... It is true that in the very lowest state of savagery special provision is seldom made by the men for the women even during the periods of pregnancy, childbirth, and infancy of the offspring. The women must live (as among the Hottentots[2]) over the worst of these periods on their own stored-up stock of fat, like hibernating bears or desert camels. It is true also that among savage races generally the women have to work as hard as the men, though the men bear in most cases the larger share in providing actual food for the entire family. But in civilised communities—and the more so in proportion to their degree of civilisation—the men do most of the hardest work, and in particular take upon themselves the duty of providing for the wives and children. The higher the type, the longer are the wives and children provided for. Analogy would lead one to suppose (with Comte[3]) that in the highest communities the men would do all the work, and the women would be left entirely free to undertake the management and education of the children....

Seeing, then, that these necessities are laid by the very nature of our organization upon women, it would appear as though two duties were clearly imposed upon the women themselves, and upon all those men who sympathize in their welfare: First, to see that their training and education should fit them above everything

[1] *Almost every ... five children* Earlier in the essay, Allen presents statistics to support his argument that women must maintain this average in order for the population to remain stable.

[2] *Hottentots* European term (now recognized as offensive) for the Khoikhoi people of southwestern Africa.

[3] *Comte* French philosopher Auguste Comte (1798–1857) wrote that in an ideal society women would be wholly isolated from political and material concerns in order to serve as parents and moral guardians.

else for this their main function in life; and, second, that in consideration of the special burden they have to bear in connection with reproduction, all the rest of life should be made as light and easy and free for them as possible. We ought frankly to recognise that most women must be wives and mothers: that most women should therefore be trained, physically, morally, socially, and mentally, in the way best fitting them to be wives and mothers; and that all such women have a right to the fullest and most generous support in carrying out their functions as wives and mothers.

And here it is that we seem to come in conflict for a moment with most of the modern Woman-Question agitators. ...

For what is the ideal that most of these modern woman agitators set before them? Is it not clearly the ideal of an unsexed woman? Are they not always talking to us as though it were not the fact that most women must be wives and mothers?... A woman ought to be ashamed to say she has no desire to become a wife and mother. Many such women there are no doubt—it is to be feared, with our existing training, far too many: but instead of boasting of their sexlessness as a matter of pride, they ought to keep it dark, and to be ashamed of it—as ashamed as a man in a like predicament would be of his impotence. They ought to feel they have fallen short of the healthy instincts of their kind, instead of posing as in some sense the cream of the universe, on the strength of what is really a functional aberration.

Unfortunately, however, just at the present moment, a considerable number of the ablest women have been misled into taking this unfeminine side, and becoming real "traitors to their sex" in so far as they endeavour to assimilate women to men in everything, and to put upon their shoulders, as a glory and privilege, the burden of their own support. ...

from Sarah Grand, "The New Aspect of the Woman Question," *North American Review* 158 (March 1894)

... W hat [the new woman] perceived at the outset was the sudden and violent upheaval of the suffering sex in all parts of the world. Women were awakening from their long apathy, and, as they woke, like healthy hungry children unable to articulate, they began to whimper for they knew not what. They might have been easily satisfied at that time had not society, like an ill-conditioned and ignorant nurse, instead of finding out what they lacked, shaken them and beaten them and stormed at them until what was once a little wail became convulsive shrieks and roused up the whole human household. Then man, disturbed by the uproar, came upstairs all anger and irritation, and, without waiting to learn what was the matter, added his own old theories to the din, but, finding they did not act rapidly, formed new ones, and made an intolerable nuisance of himself with his opinions and advice. He was in the state of one who cannot comprehend because he has no faculty to perceive the thing in question, and that is why he was so positive. The dimmest perception that you may be mistaken will save you from making an ass of yourself.

We must look upon man's mistakes, however, with some leniency, because we are not blameless in the matter ourselves. We have allowed him to arrange the whole social system and manage or mismanage it all these ages without ever seriously examining his work with a view to considering whether his abilities or motives were sufficiently good to qualify him for the task. We have listened without a smile to his preachments, about our place in life and all we are good for, on the text that "there is no understanding a woman." We have endured most poignant misery for his sins, and screened him when we should have exposed him and had him punished. We have allowed him to exact all things of us, and have been content to accept the little he grudgingly gave us in return. We have meekly bowed our heads when he called us bad names instead of demanding proofs of the superiority which alone would give him a right to do so. We have listened much edified to man's sermons on the subject of virtue, and have acquiesced uncomplainingly in the convenient arrangement by which this quality has come to be altogether practised for him by us vicariously. We have seen him set up Christ as an example for all men to follow, which argues his belief in the possibility of doing so, and have not only allowed his weakness and hypocrisy in the matter to pass without comment, but, until lately, have not even seen the humor of his pretensions when contrasted with his practices, nor held him up to that wholesome ridicule which is a stimulating corrective. Man deprived us of all proper education, and then jeered at us because we had no knowledge. He narrowed our outlook on life so that our view of it should be all distorted, and then declared that our mistaken impression of it proved us to be senseless creatures. He cramped our minds so that there was no room for reason in them, and then made merry at our want of logic. Our divine intuition was not to be controlled by him, but he did his best to damage it by sneering at it as an inferior feminine method of arriving at conclusions; and finally, after having had his own way until he lost his head completely, he set himself up as a sort of god and required us to worship him, and to our eternal shame be it said, we did so. The truth has all along been in us, but we have cared more for man than for truth, and so the whole human race has suffered. We have failed of our effect by neglecting our duty here, and have deserved much of the obloquy that was cast upon us. All that is over now, however, and while on the one hand man has shrunk to his true proportions in our estimation, we, on the other, have been expanding to our own; and now we come confidently forward to maintain, not that this or that was "intended," but that there are in ourselves, in both sexes, possibilities hitherto suppressed or abused, which, when properly developed, will supply to either what is lacking in the other.

The man of the future will be better, while the woman will be stronger and wiser. To bring this about is the whole aim and object of the present struggle, and with the discovery of the means lies the solution of the Woman Question. Man, having no conception of himself as imperfect from the woman's point of view, will find this difficult to understand, but we know his weakness, and will be patient with him, and help him with his lesson. It is the woman's place and pride and pleasure to teach the child, and man morally is in his infancy. There have been times when there was a doubt as to whether he was to be raised or woman was to be lowered, but we have turned that corner at last; and now woman holds out a strong hand to the child-man, and insists, but with infinite tenderness and pity, upon helping him up....

from Mona Caird, "Does Marriage Hinder a Woman's Self-Development?" *Lady's Realm* (March 1899)

Perhaps it might throw some light on the question whether marriage interferes with a woman's self-development and career, if we were to ask ourselves honestly how a man would fare in the position, say, of his own wife.

We will take a mild case, so as to avoid all risk of exaggeration.

Our hero's wife is very kind to him. Many of his friends have far sadder tales to tell. Mrs. Brown is fond of her home and family. She pats the children on the head when they come down to dessert, and plies them with chocolate creams, much to the detriment of their health; but it amuses Mrs. Brown. Mr. Brown superintends the bilous[1] attacks, which the lady attributes to other causes. As she never finds fault with the children, and generally remonstrates with their father, in a good-natured way, when *he* does so, they are devoted to the indulgent parent, and are inclined to regard the other as second-rate....

John's faded cheeks, the hollow lines under the eyes, and hair out of curl, speak of the struggle for existence as it penetrates to the fireside. If Sophia but knew what it meant to keep going the multitudinous details and departments of a household!...

If incessant vigilance, tact, firmness, foresight, initiative, courage and judgment—in short, all the qualities required for governing a kingdom, and more—have made things go smoothly, the wife takes it as a matter of course; if they go wrong, she naturally lays the blame on the husband. In the same way, if the children are a credit to their parents, that is only as it should be. But if they are naughty, and fretful, and stupid, and untidy, is it not clear that there must be some serious flaw in the system which could produce such results in the offspring of Mrs. Brown? What word in the English language is too severe to describe the man who neglects to watch with sufficient vigilance over his children's health and moral training, who fails to see that his little boys' sailor-suits and knickerbockers are in good repair, that their bootlace ends do not fly out from

[1] *bilous* Angry, peevish.

their ankles at every step, that their hair is not like a hearth-brush, that they do not come down to dinner every day with dirty hands?

To every true man, the cares of fatherhood and home are sacred and all-sufficing. He realizes, as he looks around at his little ones, that they are his crown and recompense.

John often finds that *his* crown-and-recompense gives him a racking headache by war-whoops and stampedes of infinite variety, and there are moments when he wonders in dismay if he is really a true man! He has had the privilege of rearing and training five small crowns and recompenses, and he feels that he could face the future if further privilege, of this sort, were denied him. Not but that he is devoted to his family. Nobody who understands the sacrifices he has made for them could doubt that. Only, he feels that those parts of his nature which are said to distinguish the human from the animal kingdom are getting rather effaced.

He remembers the days before his marriage, when he was so bold, in his ignorant youth, as to cherish a passion for scientific research. He even went so far as to make a chemical laboratory of the family box-room, till attention was drawn to the circumstance by a series of terrific explosions, which shaved off his eyebrows, blackened his scientific countenance, and caused him to be turned out, neck and crop, with his crucibles, and a sermon on the duty that lay nearest him.... His own bent, however, has always been so painfully strong that he even yet tries to snatch spare moments for his researches; but the strain in so many directions has broken down his health. People always told him that a man's constitution was not fitted for severe brain-work. He supposes it is true....

John still hoped, after twenty years of experience, that presently, by some different arrangement, some better management on his part, he would achieve leisure and mental repose to do the work that his heart was in; but that time never came.

No doubt John was not infallible, and made mistakes in dealing with his various problems: do the best of us achieve consummate wisdom? No doubt, if he had followed the advice that we could all have supplied him with, in such large quantities, he might have done rather more than he did. But the question is: Did his marriage interfere with his self-development and career, and would many other Johns, in his circumstances, have succeeded much better?

ELIZABETH BARRETT BROWNING
1806 – 1861

Once considered for the position of poet laureate of England, Elizabeth Barrett Browning was a highly renowned poet in her day, admired by contemporaries such as Wordsworth and Dickinson, critics, and the general public alike. Her poetry fell out of fashion in the first half of the twentieth century, but Barrett Browning began to be lauded once again in the past generation, particularly for her long narrative poem *Aurora Leigh*. Best known among the general public for the romantic vision of her *Sonnets from the Portuguese* ("How do I love thee? Let me count the ways" from "Sonnet XLIII" is one of the most famous lines in English literature), Barrett Browning also addressed significant moral and political issues in her work.

Elizabeth Barrett was the eldest of twelve children born to a wealthy plantation-owning family in Durham, England. Just prior to her birth her parents, Edward Barrett Moulton-Barrett and Mary Graham Clarke Moulton-Barrett, moved from their slave plantation in Jamaica to raise a family in England. The young Barrett grew up in the sheltered environment of a country manor called Hope End, learning languages and studying the classics, at a time when a young woman's education was typically restricted to the domestic sphere. An exceptional and intellectually voracious student, Barrett learned Latin, Greek, and French from her brothers' tutors and studied philosophical, historical, and religious works on her own. She had read Milton's *Paradise Lost* by the time she was 10 years old and, encouraged by her parents, anonymously published her first poem, an epic entitled *The Battle of Marathon*, a few years later. In 1826, she published *An Essay on Mind and Other Poems*. In 1833 she published her translation from the Greek of Aeschylus' *Prometheus Unbound*; she also included some of her own poems in the volume.

Due to the abolition of slavery, the Barretts' fortune began to wane, and in 1832 they were required to sell Hope End, eventually moving to Wimpole Street in London. Her father was overly protective of his children, however, and Barrett fell into semi-seclusion within the family home; her seclusion was compounded by illnesses that had begun to plague her when she was about 12 years old. Critics speculate as to the name of those illnesses, but there is evidence to suggest that Barrett may have suffered from tuberculosis and possibly from a spinal injury. Her maladies were no doubt exacerbated by the opiates prescribed by doctors and the depression that followed the accidental death of her beloved brother Edward, who had accompanied her while she recuperated in the south of England. This tragedy, and Barrett's subsequent feelings of anguish and guilt, inspired some of her best-known poems, including the elegiac sonnet "Grief."

Much has been written about Barrett's middle years, but the image of the bed-ridden recluse remains somewhat at odds with the prolific reader and writer who wrote poetry, essays, reviews, and criticism for magazines and journals and published *The Seraphim and Other Poems* in 1838. The two-volume collection of her *Poems* published in 1844 contains some of her most politically charged poetry, including "The Cry of the Children," which condemned the employment of children in factories. During these years, Barrett kept up an active correspondence with many writers, critics, and artists and accepted occasional visitors in the confines of her family home. It was in this way that she met Robert Browning, who called upon her after the 1844 collection appeared. He visited her after first writing to express his admiration for work that had already made Barrett famous in England and was rapidly gaining recognition in the United States.

The subsequent exchange of 574 letters between Barrett and Browning, six years her junior, and their eventual elopement have received much attention, with some suggesting that Barrett Browning's best work was inspired by this passionate relationship. It is worth noting here that she had already begun to write love poetry, having translated Petrarch's sonnets and written her own before she met Browning. There is no doubt, however, that the force of their relationship inspired some of her most enduring work, notably her famous *Sonnets from the Portuguese*, written during her courtship with Browning and published in 1850. "My little Portuguese," an allusion to her dark skin, was Browning's pet name for his wife.

Her 1846 marriage to Browning and their ensuing life together in Italy were a boon to Barrett Browning's health and her work. Her beloved father, however, who had forbidden his children to marry, refused to speak to or see his daughter again, going so far as to return her letters unopened. In 1849 the Brownings' only child, Robert Wiedemann Barrett Browning (nicknamed "Pen"), was born in Casa Guidi, just outside Florence.

Not long after the publication of *Sonnets*, Barrett Browning published *Casa Guidi Windows*, which promoted the cause of *Risorgimento*, the Italian struggle for unification and independence from foreign domination (the subject also of many of the later *Poems before Congress*). In 1850, she published the abolition poem "The Runaway Slave at Pilgrim's Point," one of the great dramatic monologues and political-protest poems written in English in the nineteenth century. Barrett Browning's comment on Harriet Beecher Stowe's *Uncle Tom's Cabin* summarizes her consistent response to critics who questioned her choice of subjects: "… is it possible you think a woman has no business with questions like the question of slavery? Then she had better use a pen no more. She had better subside into slavery and concubinage herself, I think, as in the times of old, shut herself up with the Penelopes in the 'women's apartment,' and take no rank among thinkers and speakers." The 1856 work *Aurora Leigh* further cemented Barrett Browning's immense popularity, even though its subject matter was deemed scandalous by many at the time. Coventry Patmore, Victorian author of *The Angel in the House*, a book of poems lauding feminine domestic virtues, was among those who attacked Barrett Browning's candor and audacity in *Aurora Leigh*. An ambitious "novel in verse" (as Barrett Browning styled it), *Aurora Leigh* is narrated in nine books of blank verse and is the zenith of Barrett Browning's life work, encompassing her convictions on desire, power, art, love, romance, race, class structures, and the subjugation of women. The independent and progressive heroine of the books is named in part after Barrett Browning's idol, French writer George Sand (née Aurore Dupin), known for her liberal, feminist views and her penchant for wearing men's clothing. Like Sand, and also like Barrett Browning herself, Aurora Leigh is a writer, one who questions her identity as both artist and woman and struggles to achieve independence from subjugation by staid societal mores and manners and yet still preserve the ability to attain love and companionship.

Elizabeth Barrett Browning predeceased her husband by 28 years when she passed away in his arms in 1861; she is buried in the Protestant cemetery in Florence.

⌘ ⌘ ⌘

The Cry of the Children[1]

"Φεῦ, φεῦ, τί προσδέρκεσθέ μ' ὄμμασιν, τέκνα;"[2] —Medea.

1

Do ye hear the children weeping, O my brothers,
    Ere the sorrow comes with years?
They are leaning their young heads against their mothers,
    And *that* cannot stop their tears.
5 The young lambs are bleating in the meadows,
    The young birds are chirping in the nest,
The young fawns are playing with the shadows,
    The young flowers are blowing toward the west—
But the young, young children, O my brothers,
10   They are weeping bitterly!
They are weeping in the playtime of the others,
    In the country of the free.

2

Do you question the young children in the sorrow
    Why their tears are falling so?
15 The old man may weep for his tomorrow
    Which is lost in Long Ago;
The old tree is leafless in the forest,
    The old year is ending in the frost,
The old wound, if stricken, is the sorest,
20   The old hope is hardest to be lost.
But the young, young children, O my brothers,
    Do you ask them why they stand
Weeping sore before the bosoms of their mothers,
    In our happy Fatherland?

3

25 They look up with their pale and sunken faces,
    And their looks are sad to see,
For the man's hoary anguish draws and presses
    Down the cheeks of infancy.

"Your old earth," they say, "is very dreary;
30   Our young feet," they say, "are very weak!
Few paces have we taken, yet are weary—
    Our grave rest is very far to seek.
Ask the aged why they weep, and not the children;
    For the outside earth is cold;
35 And we young ones stand without, in our
        bewildering,
    And the graves are for the old."

4

"True," say the children, "it may happen
    That we die before our time;
Little Alice died last year—her grave is shapen
40   Like a snowball, in the rime.
We looked into the pit prepared to take her:
    Was no room for any work in the close clay!
From the sleep wherein she lieth none will wake her,
    Crying, 'Get up, little Alice! it is day.'
45 If you listen by that grave, in sun and shower,
    With your ear down, little Alice never cries;
Could we see her face, be sure we should not know her,
    For the smile has time for growing in her eyes:
And merry go her moments, lulled and stilled in
50   The shroud by the kirk° chime.   *church*
It is good when it happens," say the children,
    "That we die before our time."

5

Alas, alas, the children! they are seeking
    Death in life, as best to have;
55 They are binding up their hearts away from breaking,
    With a cerement° from the grave.   *shroud*
Go out, children, from the mine and from the city,
    Sing out, children, as the little thrushes do;
Pluck you handfuls of the meadow cowslips pretty,
60   Laugh aloud, to feel your fingers let them through!
But they answer, "Are your cowslips of the meadows
    Like our weeds anear the mine?
Leave us quiet in the dark of the coal shadows,
    From your pleasures fair and fine!

6

65 "For oh," say the children, "we are weary,
    And we cannot run or leap;

---

1 *The Cry of the Children* This poem was written in response to Richard Henry Horne's 1843 "Report of the Children's Employment Commission" regarding child labor in the mining and manufacturing industries (see "In Context: Children in the Mines," on the companion website). Horne was the author of the epic poem *Orion* and the play *Cosmo de' Medici*, as well as *A New Spirit of the Age*, cowritten with Elizabeth Barrett.

2 **Φεῦ ... τέκνα** From Euripides's *Medea* (431 BCE) 1.1040, in which Medea says, upon killing her children: "Alas, why do you gaze at me thus, my children?"

If we cared for any meadows, it were merely
    To drop down in them and sleep.
Our knees tremble sorely in the stooping,
70   We fall upon our faces, trying to go;
And, underneath our heavy eyelids drooping,
    The reddest flower would look as pale as snow;
For, all day, we drag our burden tiring
    Through the coal dark, underground;
75 Or, all day, we drive the wheels of iron
    In the factories, round and round.

7

"For all day, the wheels are droning, turning,
    Their wind comes in our faces,
Till our hearts turn, our heads with pulses burning,
80   And the walls turn in their places:
Turns the sky in the high window blank and reeling,
    Turns the long light that drops adown the wall,
Turn the black flies that crawl along the ceiling,
    All are turning, all the day, and we with all.
85 And all day, the iron wheels are droning,
    And sometimes we could pray,
'O ye wheels,' (breaking out in a mad moaning)
    'Stop! be silent for today!'"

8

Aye, be silent! Let them hear each other breathing
90   For a moment, mouth to mouth!
Let them touch each other's hands, in a fresh wreathing
    Of their tender human youth!
Let them feel that this cold metallic motion
    Is not all the life God fashions or reveals:
95 Let them prove their living souls against the notion
    That they live in you, or under you, O wheels!
Still, all day, the iron wheels go onward,
    Grinding life down from its mark;
And the children's souls, which God is calling sunward,
100   Spin on blindly in the dark.

9

Now tell the poor young children, O my brothers,
    To look up to Him and pray;
So the blessed One who blesseth all the others,
    Will bless them another day.
105 They answer, "Who is God that He should hear us,

While the rushing of the iron wheels is stirred?
When we sob aloud, the human creatures near us
    Pass by, hearing not, or answer not a word.
And *we* hear not (for the wheels in their resounding)
110   Strangers speaking at the door:
Is it likely God, with angels singing round him,
    Hears our weeping any more?

10

"Two words, indeed, of praying we remember,
    And at midnight's hour of harm,
115 'Our Father,' looking upward in the chamber,
    We say softly for a charm.[1]
We know no other words except 'Our Father,'
    And we think that, in some pause of angels' song,
God may pluck them with the silence sweet to gather,
120   And hold both within His right hand which is strong.
'Our Father!' If He heard us, He would surely
    (For they call Him good and mild)
Answer, smiling down the steep world very purely,
    'Come and rest with me, my child.'"

11

125 "But no!" say the children, weeping faster,
    "He is speechless as a stone:
And they tell us, of His image is the master
    Who commands us to work on.
Go to!" say the children,—"up in heaven,
130   Dark, wheel-like, turning clouds are all we find.
Do not mock us; grief has made us unbelieving:
    We look up for God, but tears have made us blind."
Do you hear the children weeping and disproving,
    O my brothers, what ye preach?
135 For God's possible is taught by His world's loving,
    And the children doubt of each.

12

And well may the children weep before you!
    They are weary ere they run;
They have never seen the sunshine, nor the glory

---

1 [Barrett Browning's note] A fact rendered pathetically historical by Mr. Horne's report of his commission. The name of the poet of *Orion* and *Cosmo de' Medici* has, however, a change of associations, and comes in time to remind me that we have some noble poetic heat of literature still, however open to the reproach of being somewhat gelid in our humanity. [*gelid* Cold.]

140   Which is brighter than the sun.
        They know the grief of man, without its wisdom;
            They sink in man's despair, without its calm;
        Are slaves, without the liberty in Christdom,
            Are martyrs, by the pang without the palm;
145   Are worn as if with age, yet unretrievingly
            The harvest of its memories cannot reap,—
        Are orphans of the earthly love and heavenly.
            Let them weep! let them weep!

13

        They look up with their pale and sunken faces,
150   And their look is dread to see,
        For they mind you of their angels in high places,
            With eyes turned on Deity!
        "How long," they say, "how long, O cruel nation,
            Will you stand, to move the world, on a child's
                heart,—
155   Stifle down with a mailed° heel its palpitation,   armored
            And tread onward to your throne amid the mart?
        Our blood splashes upward, O gold-heaper,
            And your purple shows your path!
        But the child's sob in the silence curses deeper
160   Than the strong man in his wrath."
        —1844

To George Sand [1]
A Desire

Thou large-brained woman and large-hearted man,
    Self-called George Sand! whose soul, amid the lions
Of thy tumultuous senses, moans defiance
And answers roar for roar, as spirits can:
5   I would some mild miraculous thunder ran
Above the applauded circus, in appliance
Of thine own nobler nature's strength and science,
Drawing two pinions,° white as wings of swan,   wings
From thy strong shoulders, to amaze the place
10 With holier light! that thou to woman's claim

---

[1] *George Sand* Pseudonym of French author Amandine Aurore
Lucie Dupin (1804–76), who was often condemned for her free-
spirited ways, which included wearing men's clothing. For images of
Sand see "In Context" available on the companion website.

And man's, mightst join beside the angel's grace
Of a pure genius sanctified from blame,
Till child and maiden pressed to thine embrace
To kiss upon thy lips a stainless fame.
—1844

To George Sand
A Recognition

True genius, but true woman! dost deny
    The woman's nature with a manly scorn,
And break away the gauds° and armlets worn   ornaments
By weaker women in captivity?
5   Ah, vain denial! that revolted cry
Is sobbed in by a woman's voice forlorn,—
Thy woman's hair, my sister, all unshorn
Floats back dishevelled strength in agony,
Disproving thy man's name: and while before
10 The world thou burnest in a poet fire,
We see thy woman heart beat evermore
Through the large flame. Beat purer, heart, and higher,
Till God unsex thee on the heavenly shore
Where unincarnate spirits purely aspire!
—1844

A Year's Spinning

1

He listened at the porch that day,
    To hear the wheel go on, and on;
And then it stopped, ran back away,
    While through the door he brought the sun:
    But now my spinning is all done.

2

He sat beside me, with an oath
    That love ne'er ended, once begun;
I smiled—believing for us both,
    What was the truth for only one:
10   And now my spinning is all done.

3

My mother cursed me that I heard
   A young man's wooing as I spun:
Thanks, cruel mother, for that word—
   For I have, since, a harder known!
15   And now my spinning is all done.

4

I thought—O God!—my firstborn's cry
   Both voices to mine ear would drown:
I listened in mine agony—
   It was the *silence* made me groan!
20   And now my spinning is all done.

5

Bury me 'twixt my mother's grave,
   (Who cursed me on her deathbed lone)
And my dead baby's (God it save!)
   Who, not to bless me, would not moan.
25   And now my spinning is all done.

6

A stone upon my heart and head,
   But no name written on the stone!
Sweet neighbours, whisper low instead,
   "This sinner was a loving one—
30   And now her spinning is all done."

7

And let the door ajar remain,
   In case he should pass by anon;
And leave the wheel out very plain,—
   That HE, when passing in the sun,
35   May see the spinning is all done.
     —1850

The Runaway Slave at Pilgrim's Point

1

I stand on the mark beside the shore
   Of the first white pilgrim's bended knee,
Where exile turned to ancestor,
   And God was thanked for liberty.
5   I have run through the night, my skin is as dark,

I bend my knee down on this mark:
   I look on the sky and the sea.

2

O pilgrim-souls, I speak to you!
   I see you come proud and slow
10 From the land of the spirits pale as dew
   And round me and round me ye go.
O pilgrims, I have gasped and run
All night long from the whips of one
   Who in your names works sin and woe!

3

15 And thus I thought that I would come
   And kneel here where you knelt before,
And feel your souls around me hum
   In undertone to the ocean's roar;
And lift my black face, my black hand,
20 Here, in your names, to curse this land
   Ye blessed in freedom's, evermore.

4

I am black, I am black,
   And yet God made me, they say:
But if He did so, smiling back
25   He must have cast His work away
Under the feet of His white creatures,
With a look of scorn, that the dusky features
   Might be trodden again to clay.

5

And yet He has made dark things
30   To be glad and merry as light:
There's a little dark bird sits and sings,
   There's a dark stream ripples out of sight,
And the dark frogs chant in the safe morass,
And the sweetest stars are made to pass
35   O'er the face of the darkest night.

6

But *we* who are dark, we are dark!
   Ah God, we have no stars!
About our souls in care and cark°   *troubles*
   Our blackness shuts like prison bars:
40 The poor souls crouch so far behind

That never a comfort can they find
    By reaching through the prison bars.

7

Indeed we live beneath the sky,
    That great smooth Hand of God stretched out
45 On all his children fatherly,
    To save them from the dread and doubt
Which would be if, from this low place,
All opened straight up to His face
    Into the grand eternity.

8

50 And still God's sunshine and His frost,
    They make us hot, they make us cold,
As if we were not black and lost;
    And the beasts and birds, in wood and fold,
Do fear and take us for very men:
55 Could the whippoorwill or the cat of the glen
    Look into my eyes and be bold?

9

I am black, I am black!
    But, once, I laughed in girlish glee,
For one of my colour stood in the track
60   Where the drivers drove, and looked at me,
And tender and full was the look he gave—
Could a slave look *so* at another slave?—
    I look at the sky and sea.

10

And from that hour our spirits grew
65   As free as if unsold, unbought:
Oh, strong enough, since we were two,
    To conquer the world, we thought.
The drivers drove us day by day;
We did not mind, we went one way,
70   And no better a freedom sought.

11

In the sunny ground between the canes,
    He said "I love you" as he passed;
When the shingle roof rang sharp with the rains,
    I heard how he vowed it fast:
75 While others shook he smiled in the hut,

As he carved me a bowl of the coconut
    Through the roar of the hurricanes.

12

I sang his name instead of a song,
    Over and over I sang his name,
80 Upward and downward I drew it along
    My various notes,—the same, the same!
I sang it low, that the slave girls near
Might never guess, from aught they could hear,
    It was only a name—a name.

13

85 I look on the sky and the sea.
    We were two to love, and two to pray:
Yes, two, O God, who cried to Thee,
    Though nothing didst Thou say!
Coldly Thou sat'st behind the sun:
90 And now I cry who am but one,
    Thou wilt not speak today.

14

We were black, we were black,
    We had no claim to love and bliss,
What marvel if each went to wrack?
95   They wrung my cold hands out of his
They dragged him—where? I crawled to touch
His blood's mark in the dust … not much,
    Ye pilgrim-souls, though plain as this!

15

Wrong, followed by a deeper wrong!
100   Mere grief's too good for such as I:
So the white men brought the shame ere long
    To strangle the sob of my agony.
They would not leave me for my dull
Wet eyes!—it was too merciful
105   To let me weep pure tears and die.

16

I am black, I am black!
    I wore a child upon my breast,
An amulet that hung too slack,
    And, in my unrest, could not rest:
110 Thus we went moaning, child and mother,

One to another, one to another,
    Until all ended for the best.

17

For hark! I will tell you low, low,
    I am black, you see,—
115 And the babe who lay on my bosom so,
    Was far too white, too white for me;
As white as the ladies who scorned to pray
Beside me at church but yesterday,
    Though my tears had washed a place for my knee.

18

120 My own, own child! I could not bear
    To look in his face, it was so white;
I covered him up with a kerchief there,
    I covered his face in close and tight:
And he moaned and struggled, as well might be,
125 For the white child wanted his liberty—
    Ha, ha! he wanted the master right.

19

He moaned and beat with his head and feet,
    His little feet that never grew;
He struck them out, as it was meet,
130   Against my heart to break it through;
I might have sung and made him mild,
But I dared not sing to the white-faced child
    The only song I knew.

20

I pulled the kerchief very close:
135   He could not see the sun, I swear,
More, then, alive, than now he does
    From between the roots of the mango ... where?
I know where. Close! A child and mother
Do wrong to look at one another
140   When one is black and one is fair.

21

Why, in that single glance I had
    Of my child's face, ... I tell you all,
I saw a look that made me mad!
    The master's look, that used to fall
145 On my soul like his lash ... or worse!
And so, to save it from my curse,
    I twisted it round in my shawl.

22

And he moaned and trembled from foot to head,
    He shivered from head to foot;
150 Till after a time, he lay instead
    Too suddenly still and mute.
I felt, beside, a stiffening cold:
I dared to lift up just a fold,
    As in lifting a leaf of the mango fruit.

23

155 But *my* fruit ... ha, ha!—there, had been
    (I laugh to think on't at this hour!)
Your fine white angels (who have seen
    Nearest the secret of God's power)
And plucked my fruit to make them wine,
160 And sucked the soul of that child of mine
    As the hummingbird sucks the soul of the flower.

24

Ha, ha, the trick of the angels white!
    They freed the white child's spirit so.
I said not a word, but day and night
165   I carried the body to and fro,
And it lay on my heart like a stone, as chill.
—The sun may shine out as much as he will:
    I am cold, though it happened a month ago.

25

From the white man's house, and the black man's hut,
170   I carried the little body on;
The forest's arms did round us shut,
    And silence through the trees did run:
They asked no question as I went,
They stood too high for astonishment,
175   They could see God sit on His throne.

26

My little body, kerchiefed fast,
    I bore it on through the forest, on;
And when I felt it was tired at last,
    I scooped a hole beneath the moon:
180 Through the forest tops the angels far,
With a white sharp finger from every star,
    Did point and mock at what was done.

27

Yet when it was all done aright,—
    Earth, 'twixt me and my baby, strewed,—
185 All, changed to black earth,—nothing white,—
    A dark child in the dark!—ensued
Some comfort, and my heart grew young;
I sat down smiling there and sung
    The song I learnt in my maidenhood.

28

190 And thus we two were reconciled,
    The white child and black mother, thus;
For as I sang it soft and wild,
    The same song, more melodious,
Rose from the grave whereon I sat:
195 It was the dead child singing that,
    To join the souls of both of us.

29

I look on the sea and the sky.
    Where the pilgrims' ships first anchored lay
The free sun rideth gloriously,
200   But the pilgrim-ghosts have slid away
Through the earliest streaks of the morn:
My face is black, but it glares with a scorn
    Which they dare not meet by day.

30

Ha!—in their stead, their hunter sons!
205   Ha, ha! they are on me—they hunt in a ring!
Keep off! I brave you all at once,
    I throw off your eyes like snakes that sting!
You have killed the black eagle at nest, I think:
Did you ever stand still in your triumph, and shrink
210   From the stroke of her wounded wing?

31

(Man, drop that stone you dared to lift!—)
    I wish you who stand there five abreast,
Each, for his own wife's joy and gift,
    A little corpse as safely at rest
215 As mine in the mangoes! Yes, but she
May keep live babies on her knee,
    And sing the song she likes the best.

32

I am not mad: I am black.
    I see you staring in my face—
220 I know you staring, shrinking back,
    Ye are born of the Washington race,
And this land is the free America,
And this mark on my wrist—(I prove what I say)
    Ropes tied me up here to the flogging place.

33

225 You think I shrieked then? Not a sound!
    I hung, as a gourd hangs in the sun;
I only cursed them all around
    As softly as I might have done
My very own child: from these sands
230 Up to the mountains, lift your hands,
    O slaves, and end what I begun!

34

Whips, curses; these must answer those!
    For in this UNION you have set
Two kinds of men in adverse rows,
235   Each loathing each; and all forget
The seven wounds in Christ's body fair,
While HE sees gaping everywhere
    Our countless wounds that pay no debt.

35

Our wounds are different. Your white men
240   Are, after all, not gods indeed,
Nor able to make Christs again
    Do good with bleeding. We who bleed
(Stand off!) we help not in our loss!
We are too heavy for our cross,
245   And fall and crush you and your seed.

36

I fall, I swoon! I look at the sky.
    The clouds are breaking on my brain;
I am floated along, as if I should die
    Of liberty's exquisite pain.
250 In the name of the white child waiting for me
In the death dark where we may kiss and agree,
White men, I leave you all curse-free
    In my broken heart's disdain!
              —1850

from *Sonnets from the Portuguese*

1

I thought once how Theocritus[1] had sung
Of the sweet years, the dear and wished-for years,
Who each one in a gracious hand appears
To bear a gift for mortals, old or young:
5 And, as I mused it in his antique tongue,[2]
I saw, in gradual vision through my tears,
The sweet, sad years, the melancholy years,
Those of my own life, who by turns had flung
A shadow across me. Straightway I was 'ware,
10 So weeping, how a mystic Shape did move
Behind me, and drew me backward by the hair;
And a voice said in mastery, while I strove—
"Guess now who holds thee?"—"Death," I said. But, there,
The silver answer rang—"Not Death, but Love."

7

The face of all the world is changed, I think,
Since first I heard the footsteps of thy soul
Move still, oh, still, beside me, as they stole
Betwixt me and the dreadful outer brink
5 Of obvious death, where I, who thought to sink,
Was caught up into love, and taught the whole
Of life in a new rhythm. The cup of dole
God gave for baptism, I am fain to drink,
And praise its sweetness, Sweet, with thee anear.
10 The names of country, heaven, are changed away
For where thou art or shalt be, there or here;
And this … this lute and song … loved yesterday,
(The singing angels know) are only dear
Because thy name moves right in what they say.

13

And wilt thou have me fasten into speech
The love I bear thee, finding words enough,
And hold the torch out, while the winds are rough,
Between our faces, to cast light on each?—
5 I drop it at thy feet. I cannot teach

My hand to hold my spirit so far off
From myself—me—that I should bring thee proof
In words, of love hid in me out of reach.
Nay, let the silence of my womanhood
10 Commend my woman-love to thy belief—
Seeing that I stand unwon, however wooed,
And rend the garment of my life, in brief,
By a most dauntless, voiceless fortitude,
Lest one touch of this heart convey its grief.

21

Say over again, and yet once over again,
That thou dost love me. Though the word repeated
Should seem "a cuckoo-song," as thou dost treat it,
Remember, never to the hill or plain,
5 Valley and wood, without her cuckoo-strain
Comes the fresh Spring in all her green completed.
Belovèd, I, amid the darkness greeted
By a doubtful spirit-voice, in that doubt's pain
Cry, "Speak once more—thou lovest!" Who can fear
10 Too many stars, though each in heaven shall roll,
Too many flowers, though each shall crown the year?
Say thou dost love me, love me, love me—toll
The silver iterance![3]—only minding, Dear,
To love me also in silence with thy soul.

22

When our two souls stand up erect and strong,
Face to face, silent, drawing nigh and nigher,
Until the lengthening wings break into fire
At either curvèd point—what bitter wrong
5 Can the earth do to us, that we should not long
Be here contented? Think. In mounting higher,
The angels would press on us and aspire
To drop some golden orb of perfect song
Into our deep, dear silence. Let us stay
10 Rather on earth, Belovèd—where the unfit
Contrarious moods of men recoil away
And isolate pure spirits, and permit
A place to stand and love in for a day,
With darkness and the death hour rounding it.

---

[1] *Theocritus* Greek poet of the third century BCE who created the genre of the pastoral (characterized by idyllic country life and love between shepherds and shepherdesses).

[2] *antique tongue* Greek language.

[3] *iterance* Repetition.

24

Let the world's sharpness, like a clasping knife,
    Shut in upon itself and do no harm
In this close hand of Love, now soft and warm,
And let us hear no sound of human strife
5 After the click of the shutting. Life to life—
I lean upon thee, Dear, without alarm,
And feel as safe as guarded by a charm
Against the stab of worldlings, who if rife
Are weak to injure. Very whitely still
10 The lilies of our lives may reassure
Their blossoms from their roots, accessible
Alone to heavenly dews that drop not fewer,
Growing straight, out of man's reach, on the hill.
God only, who made us rich, can make us poor.

26

I lived with visions for my company
    Instead of men and women, years ago,
And found them gentle mates, nor thought to know
A sweeter music than they played to me.
5 But soon their trailing purple was not free
Of this world's dust, their lutes did silent grow,
And I myself grew faint and blind below
Their vanishing eyes. Then *thou* didst come—to be,
Belovèd, what they seemed. Their shining fronts,
10 Their songs, their splendours (better, yet the same,
As river water hallowed into fonts),
Met in thee, and from out thee overcame
My soul with satisfaction of all wants:
Because God's gifts put man's best dreams to shame.

28

My letters! all dead paper, mute and white!
    And yet they seem alive and quivering
Against my tremulous hands which loose the string
And let them drop down on my knee tonight.
5 This said—he wished to have me in his sight
Once, as a friend: this fixed a day in spring
To come and touch my hand … a simple thing,
Yet I wept for it!—this, … the paper's light …
Said, *Dear, I love thee;* and I sank and quailed
10 As if God's future thundered on my past.
This said, *I am thine*—and so its ink has paled
With lying at my heart that beat too fast.
And this … O Love, thy words have ill availed
If, what this said, I dared repeat at last!

43

How do I love thee? Let me count the ways.
    I love thee to the depth and breadth and height
My soul can reach, when feeling out of sight
For the ends of Being and ideal Grace.
5 I love thee to the level of every day's
Most quiet need, by sun and candle-light.
I love thee freely, as men strive for Right;
I love thee purely, as they turn from Praise.
I love thee with the passion put to use
10 In my old griefs, and with my childhood's faith.
I love thee with a love I seemed to lose
With my lost saints—I love thee with the breath,
Smiles, tears, of all my life!—and, if God choose,
I shall but love thee better after death.

—1845–47

ALFRED, LORD TENNYSON
1809 – 1892

In 1850, the novelist and critic Charles Kingsley praised Tennyson's dramatic monologue, "Locksley Hall," as the poem that "has had most influence on the minds of the young men of our day." Throughout his long career, Tennyson's poems continued to resonate with Victorian audiences. The self-reflective grief of *In Memoriam* (1850) touched a chord of genuine sympathy in nineteenth-century readers, including Queen Victoria herself, much as Tennyson's re-telling of Arthurian legend in *Idylls of the King* (1859–85) echoed—while also questioning—the nationalistic zeal of the later Victorian period. Britain's poet laureate from 1850 to his death in 1892, Tennyson was the quintessential poet of his age.

He was born in 1809 in Somersby, Lincolnshire, to a privileged family, and his poetic gifts became apparent early on. At age eight, Tennyson was composing pages of blank verse in the style of James Thomson; by ten or eleven he had graduated to studying the work of Alexander pope, imitating hundreds of lines of pope's translation of Homer's *Iliad*. At twelve, Tennyson set to work on his first epic, a six-thousand-line experiment that mimicked Walter Scott's octo-syllabic extravaganzas of war and romance. "I wrote as much as seventy lines at one time," he later recalled, "and used to go shouting them about the fields in the dark." By age fourteen, with an Elizabethan-style drama entitled *The Devil and the Lady*, Tennyson's work was approaching the sonorous agility and understated pathos for which it would be known. His first publication, *Poems by Two Brothers* (1827), a collaborative effort by Tennyson and his two older brothers, Frederick and Charles, was completed just prior to Tennyson's entrance to Trinity College, Cambridge.

Tennyson distinguished himself at Cambridge, establishing his reputation as both a deep thinker and a poet. In June of 1829, he won the chancellor's Gold Medal with a blank-verse poem, *Timbuctoo*. Some time in that year, Tennyson met Arthur Henry Hallam, who was to become the poet's closest friend and companion. It was also in 1829 that Tennyson joined the Cambridge Apostles, an undergraduate debating society of which Hallam and many of Tennyson's other Cambridge friends were a part. The year 1830 saw the publication of Tennyson's first important volume, *Poems, Chiefly Lyrical*, which Hallam reviewed for the *Englishman's Magazine* in an essay entitled "On Some of the characteristics of Modern poetry and on the lyrical poems of Alfred Tennyson." Hallam describes Tennyson as a poet of "sensation," one of a school of poets, including Shelley and Keats, whose "fine organs tremble into emotion at colors, and sounds, and movements" and who translate this physiological sensitivity into their verses. It was precisely such sensitivity that Christopher North (the pseudonym of John Wilson) later attacked in his 1832 *Blackwood's* review of the volume. Subsequently many critics have charted Tennyson's gradual movement away from a poetics of sensation and toward a more restrained poetic style.

The early 1830s were a difficult time for the young poet. Following the death of his father in 1831, Tennyson left Cambridge without taking his degree. Soon afterward, his brother Edward lost his sanity, succumbing to what was known as the "black blood" of the Tennyson family. Finally, and perhaps most devastatingly, Arthur Hallam died suddenly in 1833, apparently of a stroke or a brain hemorrhage. Having published one volume, *Poems*, in 1832, Tennyson would remain silent as a poet for the next ten years, refusing to publish his many works in progress until the *Poems* of 1842, the work that brought him his reputation as both a remarkable poet and a great voice of his age. During the "ten years' silence," however, Tennyson composed much of what many consider his masterwork, *In Memoriam* (1850), in addition to the innovative dramatic monologues of the 1842 *Poems*, including "Ulysses," "Locksley Hall," and "St Simeon Stylites."

In 1847, Tennyson published *The Princess*, a poetic medley that explored, through a wildly improbable narrative, the relations between the sexes and the viability of education for women. Interspersed throughout the work are many of Tennyson's best-known lyrics: "Sweet and low," "The Splendour Falls," and "Tears, Idle Tears," among others. In 1850, Tennyson ascended to the laureateship and married Emily Sellwood, to whom he had been engaged for thirteen years. That same year, Tennyson also published *In Memoriam*, the elegy on which he had been at work since Arthur Hallam's death. The first of many of Tennyson's books to sell in large numbers, *In Memoriam* went into three editions in its first year alone. Amid a rising swell of scientific discovery and industrial transformation, the poem captured the mood of the era, alternating between faith in science and faith in religion, and reflecting the hopes, doubts, and beliefs of the Victorians.

Tennyson's life changed notably as a result of both his marriage and his suddenly public role as poet laureate. The Tennysons had two sons within the next four years, the elder of whom was named Hallam after Tennyson's deceased friend. (After his father's death, Hallam Tennyson wrote a biography entitled *Alfred Lord Tennyson: A Memoir*, and he penned a second volume in 1911, *Tennyson and His Friends*. Alfred Tennyson's grandson Charles also wrote a biography in 1949.)

Many critics have argued that Tennyson's style changed after his appointment as Poet Laureate. Certainly it is true that he assumed a different voice in the occasional poems composed in his role as poet laureate, most notably the "Ode on the death of the duke of Wellington" (1852); likewise "The charge of the light Brigade" (1854) projects an explicit political stance largely absent in his earlier works. But Tennyson continued to evolve as a poet, publishing an experimental "monodrama," *Maud*, in 1855 and the first four segments of his epic, *Idylls of the King*, in 1859. *Maud* was in many ways Tennyson's most controversial publication. critics complained of the poem's irregular rhythms and of the "screed of bombast" that seemed to some like "the rasping of a blacksmith's file." *Idylls of the King*, on the other hand, was largely—though not universally—hailed as a *magnum opus*. Tennyson had contemplated writing an epic from his childhood; the finished *Idylls* reflects the poet's mature thoughts about Victorian life, politics, and culture through the world of Camelot and King Arthur.

Tennyson's later publications include the plays *Queen Mary* (1875), *The Falcon* (1879), and *The Promise of May* (1882), all of which were produced on the Victorian stage, and numerous volumes of poetry, including *Enoch Arden* (1864), *Tiresias, and Other Poems* (1885), *Locksley Hall Sixty Years After* (1886), and *Demeter and Other Poems* (1889). In 1883, Tennyson accepted a barony from the Queen and took a seat in the House of Lords. He died in 1892 at his second home, Aldworth, and is buried beside Robert Browning in the Poets' Corner of Westminster Abbey.

⌘⌘⌘

Julia Margaret Cameron, *Mariana*, 1875.

Mariana

Mariana in the moated grange
(Measure for Measure)[1]

With blackest moss the flower-plots
    Were thickly crusted, one and all:
The rusted nails fell from the knots
    That held the pear to the gable-wall.[2]
5 The broken sheds looked sad and strange:
    Unlifted was the clinking latch;
    Weeded and worn the ancient thatch
Upon the lonely moated grange.
    She only said, "My life is dreary,

10   He cometh not," she said;
    She said, "I am aweary, aweary,
       I would that I were dead!"

Her tears fell with the dews at even;°   *evening*
    Her tears fell ere° the dews were dried;   *before*
15 She could not look on the sweet heaven,
    Either at morn or eventide.
After the flitting of the bats,
    When thickest dark did trance° the sky,   *entrance*
    She drew her casement-curtain by,
20 And glanced athwart the glooming flats.[3]
       She only said, "The night is dreary,
          He cometh not," she said;
       She said, "I am aweary, aweary,
          I would that I were dead!"

25 Upon the middle of the night,
    Waking she heard the night-fowl crow:
The cock sung out an hour ere light:
    From the dark fen° the oxen's low   *lowlands*
Came to her: without hope of change,
30   In sleep she seemed to walk forlorn,
    Till cold winds woke the gray-eyed morn
About the lonely moated grange.
       She only said, "The day is dreary,
          He cometh not," she said;
35   She said, "I am aweary, aweary,
          I would that I were dead!"

About a stone-cast from the wall
    A sluice with blackened waters slept,
And o'er it many, round and small,
40   The clustered marish-mosses[4] crept.
Hard by a poplar shook alway,
    All silver-green with gnarlèd bark:
    For leagues no other tree did mark
The level waste, the rounding gray.
45   She only said, "My life is dreary,
          He cometh not," she said;
       She said, "I am aweary, aweary,
          I would that I were dead!"

---

1 *Mariana ... Measure* Tennyson's epigraph is adapted from the words of the Duke in Shakespeare's *Measure for Measure*, 3.1.277: "There, at the moated grange, lies this dejected Mariana." Earlier in the scene, the Duke has recounted how Mariana, having lost her dowry (and her brother) in a shipwreck, has been deserted by her betrothed; *moated grange* Cottage or small farmhouse surrounded by a moat, or water-filled ditch.

2 *The rusted ... gable-wall* The pear has been espaliered, or trained to grow against a wall on a lattice or framework of stakes.

3 *flats* Flatlands or lowlands.

4 [Tennyson's note] *Marish-mosses*, the little marsh-moss lumps that float on the surface of the water.

And ever when the moon was low,
    50   And the shrill winds were up and away,
In the white curtain, to and fro,
        She saw the gusty shadow sway.
But when the moon was very low,
        And wild winds bound within their cell,[1]
    55   The shadow of the poplar fell
Upon her bed, across her brow.
        She only said, "The night is dreary,
          He cometh not," she said;
        She said, "I am aweary, aweary,
    60   I would that I were dead!"

All day within the dreamy house,
        The doors upon their hinges creaked;
The blue fly sung in the pane; the mouse
        Behind the mouldering wainscot° shrieked,   *paneling*
    65   Or from the crevice peered about.
        Old faces glimmered through the doors,
        Old footsteps trod the upper floors,
Old voices called her from without.
        She only said, "My life is dreary,
    70   He cometh not," she said;
        She said, "I am aweary, aweary,
          I would that I were dead!"

The sparrow's chirrup on the roof,
        The slow clock ticking, and the sound
    75   Which to the wooing wind aloof
        The poplar made, did all confound
Her sense; but most she loathed the hour
        When the thick-moted[2] sunbeam lay
        Athwart the chambers, and the day
    80   Was sloping toward his western bower.
        Then, said she, "I am very dreary,
          He will not come," she said;
        She wept, "I am aweary, aweary,
          Oh God, that I were dead!"

—1830

---

[1] *wild winds ... their cell* Reference to Virgil's *Aeneid*, 1.52, in which Aeolus, god of winds, keeps the winds imprisoned in a cavern.

[2] *thick-moted* I.e., thick with motes of dust.

The Palace of Art

I built my soul a lordly pleasure-house,
    Wherein at ease for aye° to dwell.   *ever*
I said, "O Soul, make merry and carouse,
        Dear soul, for all is well."

    5 A huge crag-platform, smooth as burnished brass
        I chose. The rangèd ramparts bright
From level meadow-bases of deep grass
        Suddenly scaled the light.

Thereon I built it firm. Of ledge or shelf
    10   The rock rose clear, or winding stair.
My soul would live alone unto herself
        In her high palace there.

And "while the world runs round and round," I said,
        "Reign thou apart, a quiet king,
    15 Still as, while Saturn whirls, his steadfast shade
        Sleeps on his luminous ring."

To which my soul made answer readily:
        "Trust me, in bliss I shall abide
In this great mansion, that is built for me,
    20   So royal-rich and wide."

                *

Four courts I made, East, West and South and North,
        In each a squared lawn, wherefrom
The golden gorge of dragons spouted forth
        A flood of fountain-foam.

    25 And round the cool green courts there ran a row
        Of cloisters, branched like mighty woods,
Echoing all night to that sonorous flow
        Of spouted fountain-floods.

And round the roofs a gilded gallery
    30   That lent broad verge° to distant lands,   *view*
Far as the wild swan wings, to where the sky
        Dipped down to sea and sands.

From those four jets four currents in one swell
        Across the mountain streamed below

35   In misty folds, that floating as they fell
       Lit up a torrent-bow.[1]

And high on every peak a statue seemed
       To hang on tiptoe, tossing up
A cloud of incense of all odour steamed
40   From out a golden cup.

So that she thought, "And who shall gaze upon
       My palace with unblinded eyes,
While this great bow will waver in the sun,
       And that sweet incense rise?"

45   For that sweet incense rose and never failed,
       And, while day sank or mounted higher,
The light aerial gallery, golden-railed,
       Burnt like a fringe of fire.

Likewise the deep-set windows, stained and traced,
50   Would seem slow-flaming crimson fires
From shadowed grots° of arches interlaced,   *grottoes*
       And tipped with frost-like spires.

         *

Full of long-sounding corridors it was,
       That over-vaulted grateful° gloom,   *pleasing*
55   Through which the livelong day my soul did pass,
       Well-pleased, from room to room.

Full of great rooms and small the palace stood,
       All various, each a perfect whole
From living Nature, fit for every mood
60   And change of my still soul.

For some were hung with arras° green and blue,   *tapestries*
       Showing a gaudy summer-morn,
Where with puffed cheek the belted hunter blew
       His wreathèd bugle-horn.

65   One seemed all dark and red—a tract of sand,
       And someone pacing there alone,
Who paced forever in a glimmering land,
       Lit with a low large moon.

One showed an iron coast and angry waves.
70   You seemed to hear them climb and fall
And roar rock-thwarted under bellowing caves,
       Beneath the windy wall.

And one, a full-fed river winding slow
       By herds upon an endless plain,
75   The ragged rims of thunder brooding low,
       With shadow-streaks of rain.

And one, the reapers at their sultry toil.
       In front they bound the sheaves. Behind
Were realms of upland, prodigal in oil,
80   And hoary to the wind.[2]

And one a foreground black with stones and slags,
       Beyond, a line of heights, and higher
All barred with long white cloud the scornful crags,
       And highest, snow and fire.

85   And one, an English home—gray twilight poured
       On dewy pastures, dewy trees,
Softer than sleep—all things in order stored,
       A haunt of ancient Peace.

Nor these alone, but every landscape fair,
90   As fit for every mood of mind,
Or gay, or grave, or sweet, or stern, was there
       Not less than truth designed.

         *

Or the maid-mother by a crucifix,
       In tracts of pasture sunny-warm,
95   Beneath branch-work of costly sardonyx[3]
       Sat smiling, babe in arm.

Or in a clear-walled city on the sea,
       Near gilded organ-pipes, her hair
Wound with white roses, slept St. Cecily;[4]
100   An angel looked at her.

---

2 *hoary to the wind* White underside of the olive leaves are exposed by the wind.

3 *sardonyx* Onyx striped with sard, a yellow or orange quartz.

4 *St. Cecily* St. Cecilia, patron saint of music.

---

1 *torrent-bow* Rainbow formed in the spray of a torrent.

Or thronging all one porch of Paradise
  A group of Houris[1] bowed to see
The dying Islamite, with hands and eyes
  That said, We wait for thee.

105 Or mythic Uther's deeply-wounded son[2]
  In some fair space of sloping greens
Lay, dozing in the vale of Avalon,
  And watched by weeping queens.

Or hollowing one hand against his ear,
110 To list° a foot-fall, ere he saw   *hear*
The wood-nymph, stayed the Ausonian king[3] to hear
  Of wisdom and of law.

Or over hills with peaky tops engrailed,° *serrated*
  And many a tract of palm and rice.
115 The throne of Indian Cama[4] slowly sailed
  A summer fanned with spice.

Or sweet Europa's[5] mantle blew unclasped,
  From off her shoulder backward borne:
From one hand drooped a crocus: one hand grasped
120 The mild bull's golden horn.

Or else flushed Ganymede,[6] his rosy thigh
  Half-buried in the Eagle's down,
Sole as a flying star shot through the sky
  Above the pillared town.

125 Nor these alone: but every legend fair
  Which the supreme Caucasian mind

Carved out of Nature for itself, was there,
  Not less than life, designed.

      *

Then in the towers I placed great bells that swung,
130 Moved of themselves, with silver sound;
And with choice paintings of wise men I hung
  The royal dais round.

For there was Milton like a seraph° strong, *angel*
  Beside him Shakespeare bland° and mild; *gentle*
135 And there the world-worn Dante grasped his song,
  And somewhat grimly smiled.

And there the Ionian father[7] of the rest;
  A million wrinkles carved his skin;
A hundred winters snowed upon his breast,
140 From cheek and throat and chin.

Above, the fair hall-ceiling stately-set
  Many an arch high up did lift,
And angels rising and descending met
  With interchange of gift.

145 Below was all mosaic choicely planned
  With cycles of the human tale
Of this wide world, the times of every land
  So wrought, they will not fail.

The people here, a beast of burden slow,
150 Toiled onward, pricked with goads and stings;
Here played, a tiger, rolling to and fro
  The heads and crowns of kings;

Here rose, an athlete, strong to break or bind
  All force in bonds that might endure,
155 And here once more like some sick man declined,
  And trusted any cure.

But over these she trod: and those great bells
  Began to chime. She took her throne:
She sat betwixt the shining Oriels,° *windows*
160 To sing her songs alone.

And through the topmost Oriels' coloured flame
  Two godlike faces gazed below;

---

[1] *Houris* Nymphs of Muslim paradise.

[2] *Uther's deeply-wounded son* King Arthur, son of Uther Pendragon, badly wounded in his last battle and carried to the mystic island of Avalon to heal.

[3] *Ausonian king* Numa, the legendary second king of Rome, who was said to have received the laws of the kingdom from the nymph Egeria; *Ausonia* was an ancient name for Italy often used by poets.

[4] [Tennyson's note] The Hindu God of young love, son of Brahma.

[5] *Europa* In Greek legend, the beautiful daughter of the king of Phoenicia. Zeus fell in love with her and assumed the shape of a bull in order to carry her off.

[6] *Ganymede* In Greek legend, a beautiful youth who was carried up to heaven at the command of Zeus, who made him cupbearer to the gods.

[7] *Ionian father* Homer.

Plato the wise, and large-browed Verulam,[1]
    The first of those who know.

165 And all those names, that in their motion were
    Full-welling fountainheads of change,
Betwixt the slender shafts were blazoned fair
    In diverse raiment° strange: *clothing*

Through which the lights, rose, amber, emerald, blue,
170   Flushed in her temples and her eyes,
And from her lips, as morn from Memnon, drew
    Rivers of melodies.[2]

No nightingale delighteth to prolong
    Her low preamble all alone,
175 More than my soul to hear her echoed song
    Throb through the ribbèd stone;

Singing and murmuring in her feastful mirth,
    Joying to feel herself alive,
Lord over Nature, Lord of the visible earth,
180   Lord of the senses five;

Communing with herself: "All these are mine,
    And let the world have peace or wars,
'Tis one to me." She—when young night divine
    Crowned dying day with stars,

185 Making sweet close of his delicious toils—
    Lit light in wreaths and anadems,°   *garlands*
And pure quintessences of precious oils
    In hollowed moons of gems,

To mimic heaven; and clapped her hands and cried,
190   "I marvel if my still° delight   *constant*
In this great house so royal-rich, and wide,
    Be flattered to the height.

"O all things fair to sate my various eyes!
    O shapes and hues that please me well!
195 O silent faces of the Great and Wise,
    My Gods, with whom I dwell!

"O God-like isolation which art mine,
    I can but count thee perfect gain,
What time I watch the darkening droves of swine
200   That range on yonder plain.

"In filthy sloughs they roll a prurient° skin,   *itching*
    They graze and wallow, breed and sleep;
And oft some brainless devil enters in,
    And drives them to the deep."[3]

205 Then of the moral instinct would she prate
    And of the rising from the dead,
As hers by right of full-accomplished Fate;
    And at the last she said:

"I take possession of man's mind and deed.
210   I care not what the sects may brawl.
I sit as God holding no form of creed,
    But contemplating all."

        *

Full oft the riddle of the painful earth
    Flashed through her as she sat alone,
215 Yet not the less held she her solemn mirth,
    And intellectual throne.

And so she throve and prospered: so three years
    She prospered: on the fourth she fell,
Like Herod, when the shout was in his ears,
220   Struck through with pangs of hell.[4]

Lest she should fail and perish utterly,
    God, before whom ever lie bare
The abysmal deeps of Personality,
    Plagued her with sore despair.

225 When she would think, where'er she turned her sight
    The airy hand confusion wrought,

---

[1] *Oriels' coloured ... Verulam* Recessed stained-glass windows with images of Plato and Francis Bacon, one of whose titles was Baron Verulam.

[2] *morn from ... melodies* The statue of the legendary Ethiopian king Memnon at Thebes was said by the ancient Greeks to produce beautiful music when touched by the rays of the dawning sun.

[3] *oft some ... the deep* See Matthew 8.28–32, in which Jesus casts devils out of two men and into a herd of swine, whereupon the herd stampedes off a cliff into the sea.

[4] *Herod, when ... of hell* See Acts 12.21–23, where King Herod is struck dead as a crowd of his subjects shout that he is a god and not a man.

Wrote, "Mene, mene,"[1] and divided quite
    The kingdom of her thought.

Deep dread and loathing of her solitude
230   Fell on her, from which mood was born
Scorn of herself; again, from out that mood
    Laughter at her self-scorn.

"What! is not this my place of strength," she said,
    "My spacious mansion built for me,
235 Whereof the strong foundation-stones were laid
    Since my first memory?"

But in dark corners of her palace stood
    Uncertain shapes; and unawares
On white-eyed phantasms weeping tears of blood,
240   And horrible nightmares,

And hollow shades enclosing hearts of flame,
    And, with dim fretted foreheads all,
On corpses three-months-old at noon she came,
    That stood against the wall.

245 A spot of dull stagnation, without light
    Or power of movement, seemed my soul,
'Mid onward-sloping motions infinite
    Making for one sure goal.

A still salt pool, locked in with bars of sand,
250   Left on the shore; that hears all night
The plunging seas draw backward from the land
    Their moon-led waters white.

A star that with the choral starry dance
    Joined not, but stood, and standing saw
255 The hollow orb of moving Circumstance
    Rolled round by one fixed law.

Back on herself her serpent pride had curled.
    "No voice," she shrieked in that lone hall,
"No voice breaks through the stillness of this world:
260   One deep, deep silence all!"

She, mouldering with the dull earth's mouldering sod,
    Inwrapt tenfold in slothful shame,
Lay there exilèd from eternal God,
    Lost to her place and name;

265 And death and life she hated equally,
    And nothing saw, for her despair,
But dreadful time, dreadful eternity,
    No comfort anywhere;

Remaining utterly confused with fears,
270   And ever worse with growing time,
And ever unrelieved by dismal tears,
    And all alone in crime:

Shut up as in a crumbling tomb, girt round
    With blackness as a solid wall,
275 Far off she seemed to hear the dully° sound   *faint*
    Of human footsteps fall.

As in strange lands a traveller walking slow,
    In doubt and great perplexity,
A little before moon-rise hears the low
280   Moan of an unknown sea;

And knows not if it be thunder, or a sound
    Of rocks thrown down, or one deep cry
Of great wild beasts; then thinketh, "I have found
    A new land, but I die."

285 She howled aloud, "I am on fire within.
    There comes no murmur of reply.
What is it that will take away my sin,
    And save me lest I die?"

So when four years were wholly finished,
290   She threw her royal robes away.
"Make me a cottage in the vale," she said,
    "Where I may mourn and pray.

"Yet pull not down my palace towers, that are
    So lightly, beautifully built:
295 Perchance I may return with others there
    When I have purged my guilt."
—1832 (REVISED 1842)

---

[1] *"Mene, mene"* The first of the words, seen by the Babylonian king Belshazzar, that are mysteriously written on the wall by a disembodied hand in Daniel 5.25–26. Daniel's interpretation of the words for the frightened king concludes with the phrase "Thy kingdom is divided."

The Lady of Shalott [1]

PART 1

On either side the river lie
Long fields of barley and of rye,
That clothe the wold° and meet the sky;   plain
And through the field the road runs by
5   To many-towered Camelot;
And up and down the people go,
Gazing where the lilies blow
Round an island there below,
        The island of Shalott.

10   Willows whiten,[2] aspens quiver,
Little breezes dusk° and shiver   darken
Through the wave that runs for ever
By the island in the river
        Flowing down to Camelot.
15   Four gray walls, and four gray towers,
Overlook a space of flowers,
And the silent isle imbowers°   encloses
        The Lady of Shalott.

By the margin, willow-veiled,
20   Slide the heavy barges trailed
By slow horses; and unhailed
The shallop[3] flitteth silken-sailed
        Skimming down to Camelot:
But who hath seen her wave her hand?
25   Or at the casement seen her stand?
Or is she known in all the land,
        The Lady of Shalott?

Only reapers, reaping early
In among the bearded barley,
30   Hear a song that echoes cheerly
From the river winding clearly,

Down to towered Camelot:
And by the moon the reaper weary,
Piling sheaves in uplands airy,
35   Listening, whispers "'Tis the fairy
        Lady of Shalott."

PART 2

There she weaves by night and day
A magic web with colours gay.
She has heard a whisper say,
40   A curse is on her if she stay
        To look down to Camelot.
She knows not what the curse may be,
And so she weaveth steadily,
And little other care hath she,
45   The Lady of Shalott.

And moving through a mirror clear
That hangs before her all the year,
Shadows of the world appear.
There she sees the highway near
50   Winding down to Camelot:
There the river eddy whirls,
And there the surly village-churls,
And the red cloaks of market girls,
        Pass onward from Shalott.

55   Sometimes a troop of damsels glad,
An abbot on an ambling pad,°   horse
Sometimes a curly shepherd-lad,
Or long-haired page in crimson clad,
        Goes by to towered Camelot;
60   And sometimes through the mirror blue
The knights come riding two and two:
She hath no loyal knight and true,
        The Lady of Shalott.

But in her web she still delights
65   To weave the mirror's magic sights,
For often through the silent nights
A funeral, with plumes and lights
        And music, went to Camelot:
Or when the moon was overhead,
70   Came two young lovers lately wed;
"I am half sick of shadows," said
        The Lady of Shalott.

---

[1]   *The Lady of Shalott*   The title character is based on the figure of
Elaine in the Arthurian romances, who dies of love for Lancelot; she
is called "the lily maid of Astolat" in Malory's *Morte d'Arthur*.
Tennyson first encountered the story, however, in a medieval Italian
romance called "La Donna di Scalotta" and changed the name to
Shalott for a softer sound.

[2]   *Willows whiten*   I.e., the wind exposes the white undersides of the
leaves.

[3]   *shallop*   Light open boat for use in shallow water.

PART 3

A bow-shot from her bower-eaves,
He rode between the barley-sheaves,
75 The sun came dazzling through the leaves,
And flamed upon the brazen greaves[1]
    Of bold Sir Lancelot.
A red-cross knight for ever kneeled
To a lady in his shield,
80 That sparkled on the yellow field,
    Beside remote Shalott.

The gemmy° bridle glittered free,   *brilliant*
Like to some branch of stars we see
Hung in the golden Galaxy.
85 The bridle bells rang merrily
    As he rode down to Camelot:
And from his blazoned baldric° slung   *shoulder-strap*
A mighty silver bugle hung,
And as he rode his armour rung,
90   Beside remote Shalott.

All in the blue unclouded weather
Thick-jewelled shone the saddle-leather,
The helmet and the helmet-feather
Burned like one burning flame together,
95   As he rode down to Camelot.
As often through the purple night,
Below the starry clusters bright,
Some bearded meteor, trailing light,
    Moves over still Shalott.

100 His broad clear brow in sunlight glowed;
On burnished hooves his war-horse trode;
From underneath his helmet flowed
His coal-black curls as on he rode,
    As he rode down to Camelot.
105 From the bank and from the river
He flashed into the crystal mirror,
"Tirra lirra," by the river
    Sang Sir Lancelot.

She left the web, she left the loom,
110 She made three paces through the room,
She saw the water-lily bloom,
She saw the helmet and the plume,

---

[1] *greaves* Armor worn below the knee.

She looked down to Camelot.
Out flew the web and floated wide;
115 The mirror cracked from side to side;
"The curse is come upon me," cried
    The Lady of Shalott.

PART 4

In the stormy east-wind straining,
The pale yellow woods were waning,
120 The broad stream in his banks complaining,
Heavily the low sky raining
    Over towered Camelot;
Down she came and found a boat
Beneath a willow left afloat,
125 And round about the prow she wrote
    The Lady of Shalott.

And down the river's dim expanse
Like some bold seer in a trance,
Seeing all his own mischance—
130 With a glassy countenance
    Did she look to Camelot.
And at the closing of the day
She loosed the chain, and down she lay;
The broad stream bore her far away,
135   The Lady of Shalott.

Lying, robed in snowy white
That loosely flew to left and right—
The leaves upon her falling light—
Through the noises of the night
140   She floated down to Camelot:
And as the boat-head wound along
The willowy hills and fields among,
They heard her singing her last song,
    The Lady of Shalott.

145 Heard a carol, mournful, holy,
Chanted loudly, chanted lowly,
Till her blood was frozen slowly,
And her eyes were darkened wholly,
    Turned to towered Camelot.
150 For ere she reached upon the tide
The first house by the water-side,
Singing in her song she died,
    The Lady of Shalott.

Under tower and balcony,
155 By garden-wall and gallery,
A gleaming shape she floated by,
Dead-pale between the houses high,
    Silent into Camelot.
Out upon the wharfs they came,
160 Knight and burgher, lord and dame,
And round the prow they read her name,
    The Lady of Shalott.

Who is this? and what is here?
And in the lighted palace near
165 Died the sound of royal cheer;
And they crossed themselves for fear,
    All the knights at Camelot:
But Lancelot mused a little space;
He said, "She has a lovely face;
170 God in his mercy lend her grace,
    The Lady of Shalott."
—1832 (REVISED 1842)

The Lotos-Eaters[1]

"Courage!" he said, and pointed toward the land,
    "This mounting wave will roll us shoreward
        soon."
In the afternoon they came unto a land
In which it seemed always afternoon.
5 All round the coast the languid air did swoon,
Breathing like one that hath a weary dream.
Full-faced above the valley stood the moon;
And like a downward smoke, the slender stream
Along the cliff to fall and pause and fall did seem.

10 A land of streams! some, like a downward smoke,
Slow-dropping veils of thinnest lawn,[2] did go;
And some through wavering lights and shadows broke,
Rolling a slumbrous sheet of foam below.

They saw the gleaming river seaward flow
15 From the inner land: far off, three mountain-tops,
Three silent pinnacles of agèd snow,
Stood sunset-flushed: and, dewed with showery drops,
Up-clomb the shadowy pine above the woven
    copse.°   *thicket*

The charmèd sunset lingered low adown
20 In the red West: through mountain clefts the dale
Was seen far inland, and the yellow down
Bordered with palm, and many a winding vale
And meadow, set with slender galingale;[3]
A land where all things always seemed the same!
25 And round about the keel with faces pale,
Dark faces pale against that rosy flame,
The mild-eyed melancholy Lotos-eaters came.

Branches they bore of that enchanted stem,
Laden with flower and fruit, whereof they gave
30 To each, but whoso did receive of them,
And taste, to him the gushing of the wave
Far far away did seem to mourn and rave
On alien shores; and if his fellow spake,
His voice was thin, as voices from the grave;
35 And deep-asleep he seemed, yet all awake,
And music in his ears his beating heart did make.

They sat them down upon the yellow sand,
Between the sun and moon upon the shore;
And sweet it was to dream of Fatherland,
40 Of child, and wife, and slave; but evermore
Most weary seemed the sea, weary the oar,
Weary the wandering fields of barren foam.
Then some one said, "We will return no more";
And all at once they sang, "Our island home
45 Is far beyond the wave; we will no longer roam."

CHORIC SONG[4]

I

There is sweet music here that softer falls
Than petals from blown roses on the grass,
Or night-dews on still waters between walls
Of shadowy granite, in a gleaming pass;

---

[1] *Lotos-Eaters* In Homer's *Odyssey* (9.82–104), the Lotus Eaters were a race of people who inhabited a remote island; they existed in peaceful apathy because of the narcotic effects of the lotus plants they ate. When Odysseus landed on the island, some of his men ate the lotus plants and wanted to stay on the island, rather than return home to their families. The speaker in line 1 is Odysseus; his men sing the "Choric Song" beginning at line 46.

[2] *lawn* Fine fabric.

[3] *galingale* Species of sedge.

[4] *Choric Song* A song sung in unison (like that performed by the Chorus in an ancient Greek play).

50 Music that gentlier on the spirit lies,
   Than tired eyelids upon tired eyes;
   Music that brings sweet sleep down from the blissful
       skies.
   Here are cool mosses deep,
   And through the moss the ivies creep,
55 And in the stream the long-leaved flowers weep,
   And from the craggy ledge the poppy hangs in sleep.

2

   Why are we weighed upon with heaviness,
   And utterly consumed with sharp distress,
   While all things else have rest from weariness?
60 All things have rest: why should we toil alone,
   We only toil, who are the first of things,
   And make perpetual moan,
   Still from one sorrow to another thrown:
   Nor ever fold our wings,
65 And cease from wanderings,
   Nor steep our brows in slumber's holy balm;
   Nor harken what the inner spirit sings,
   "There is no joy but calm!"
   Why should we only toil, the roof and crown of things?

3

70 Lo! in the middle of the wood,
   The folded leaf is wooed from out the bud
   With winds upon the branch, and there
   Grows green and broad, and takes no care,
   Sun-steeped at noon, and in the moon
75 Nightly dew-fed; and turning yellow
   Falls, and floats adown the air.
   Lo! sweetened with the summer light,
   The full-juiced apple, waxing over-mellow,
   Drops in a silent autumn night.
80 All its allotted length of days,
   The flower ripens in its place,
   Ripens and fades, and falls, and hath no toil,
   Fast-rooted in the fruitful soil.

4

   Hateful is the dark-blue sky,
85 Vaulted o'er the dark-blue sea.
   Death is the end of life; ah, why
   Should life all labour be?
   Let us alone. Time driveth onward fast,
   And in a little while our lips are dumb.

90 Let us alone. What is it that will last?
   All things are taken from us, and become
   Portions and parcels of the dreadful Past.
   Let us alone. What pleasure can we have
   To war with evil? Is there any peace
95 In ever climbing up the climbing wave?
   All things have rest, and ripen toward the grave
   In silence; ripen, fall and cease:
   Give us long rest or death, dark death, or dreamful ease.

5

   How sweet it were, hearing the downward stream,
100 With half-shut eyes ever to seem
   Falling asleep in a half-dream!
   To dream and dream, like yonder amber light,
   Which will not leave the myrrh-bush on the height;
   To hear each other's whispered speech;
105 Eating the Lotos day by day,
   To watch the crisping ripples on the beach,
   And tender curving lines of creamy spray;
   To lend our hearts and spirits wholly
   To the influence of mild-minded melancholy;
110 To muse and brood and live again in memory,
   With those old faces of our infancy
   Heaped over with a mound of grass,
   Two handfuls of white dust,[1] shut in an urn of brass!

6

   Dear is the memory of our wedded lives,
115 And dear the last embraces of our wives
   And their warm tears: but all hath suffered change:
   For surely now our household hearths are cold:
   Our sons inherit us: our looks are strange:
   And we should come like ghosts to trouble joy.
120 Or else the island princes over-bold
   Have eat our substance,[2] and the minstrel sings
   Before them of the ten years' war in Troy,
   And our great deeds, as half-forgotten things.
   Is there confusion in the little isle?
125 Let what is broken so remain.
   The Gods are hard to reconcile:

---

[1] *white dust* I.e., cremated remains.

[2] *Have eat our substance* I.e., have consumed our goods and property.
As the sailors rightly surmise, in the years that they have been away
from their home island of Ithaca (the "little isle" of line 124) following
Odysseus to fight the Trojan War, the other princes of Ithaca and the
neighboring islands have encroached upon their homes.

'Tis hard to settle order once again.
There *is* confusion worse than death,
Trouble on trouble, pain on pain,
130 Long labour unto agèd breath,
Sore task to hearts worn out by many wars
And eyes grown dim with gazing on the pilot-stars.

7

But, propped on beds of amaranth[1] and moly,[2]
How sweet (while warm airs lull us, blowing lowly)
135 With half-dropped eyelid still,
Beneath a heaven dark and holy,
To watch the long bright river drawing slowly
His waters from the purple hill—
To hear the dewy echoes calling
140 From cave to cave through the thick-twinèd vine—
To watch the emerald-coloured water falling
Through many a woven acanthus[3]-wreath divine!
Only to hear and see the far-off sparkling brine,
Only to hear were sweet, stretched out beneath the pine.

8

145 The Lotos blooms below the barren peak:
The Lotos blows by every winding creek:
All day the wind breathes low with mellower tone:
Through every hollow cave and alley lone
Round and round the spicy downs the yellow
Lotos-dust is blown.
150 We have had enough of action, and of motion we,
Rolled to starboard, rolled to larboard,° when   *port*
the surge was seething free,
Where the wallowing monster spouted his foam-
fountains in the sea.
Let us swear an oath, and keep it with an equal mind,
In the hollow Lotos-land to live and lie reclined
155 On the hills like Gods together, careless of mankind.
For they lie beside their nectar, and the bolts are hurled
Far below them in the valleys, and the clouds are
lightly curled
Round their golden houses, girdled with the gleaming
world:
Where they smile in secret, looking over wasted lands,

160 Blight and famine, plague and earthquake, roaring
deeps and fiery sands,
Clanging fights, and flaming towns, and sinking
ships, and praying hands.
But they smile, they find a music centred in a doleful
song
Steaming up, a lamentation and an ancient tale of
wrong,
Like a tale of little meaning though the words are strong;
165 Chanted from an ill-used race of men that cleave the
soil,
Sow the seed, and reap the harvest with enduring toil,
Storing yearly little dues of wheat, and wine and oil;
Till they perish and they suffer—some, 'tis whispered
—down in hell
Suffer endless anguish, others in Elysian[4] valleys dwell,
170 Resting weary limbs at last on beds of asphodel.[5]
Surely, surely, slumber is more sweet than toil, the shore
Than labour in the deep mid-ocean, wind and wave
and oar;
Oh rest ye, brother mariners, we will not wander more.
—1832 (REVISED 1842)

Ulysses[6]

It little profits that an idle king,
By this still hearth, among these barren crags,
Matched with an agèd wife, I mete and dole
Unequal laws unto a savage race,
5 That hoard, and sleep, and feed, and know not me.

I cannot rest from travel: I will drink
Life to the lees:° all times I have enjoyed   *dregs*
Greatly, have suffered greatly, both with those
That loved me, and alone; on shore, and when

---

[1] *amaranth* Mythical flower that never wilted.

[2] *moly* Herb with magical protective powers.

[3] *acanthus* Plant native to Mediterranean shores. The Greeks and
Romans esteemed the plant for the elegance of its leaves.

[4] *Elysian* Heavenly. According to the ancient Greeks, Elysium was
the dwelling place of the blessed after death.

[5] *asphodel* Plant said to cover the Elysian fields.

[6] *Ulysses* Latin name for Odysseus the hero of Homer's *Odyssey*,
which culminates in his reunion (after nearly twenty years) with his
wife Penelope and his only son Telemachus (see line 33) and his
regaining the throne of Ithaca. Here, some time after the adventures
recounted by Homer, the aged yet restless Ulysses prepares to
embark on one last voyage of discovery. Tennyson was inspired by
a passage in Dante's *Inferno* (Canto 26), in which the shade of
Ulysses recounts the story of that final voyage.

10 Thro' scudding drifts the rainy Hyades[1]
Vexed the dim sea: I am become a name;
For always roaming with a hungry heart
Much have I seen and known; cities of men
And manners, climates, councils, governments,
15 Myself not least, but honoured of them all;
And drunk delight of battle with my peers,
Far on the ringing plains of windy Troy.
I am a part of all that I have met;
Yet all experience is an arch wherethrough
20 Gleams that untravelled world, whose margin°   *horizon*
    fades
For ever and for ever when I move.
How dull it is to pause, to make an end,
To rust unburnished, not to shine in use!
As though to breathe were life. Life piled on life
25 Were all too little, and of one to me
Little remains: but every hour is saved
From that eternal silence, something more,
A bringer of new things; and vile it were
For some three suns to store and hoard myself,
30 And this gray spirit yearning in desire
To follow knowledge like a sinking star,
Beyond the utmost bound of human thought.

    This is my son, mine own Telemachus,
To whom I leave the sceptre and the isle—
35 Well-loved of me, discerning to fulfil
This labour, by slow prudence to make mild
A rugged people, and through soft degrees
Subdue them to the useful and the good.
Most blameless is he, centred in the sphere
40 Of common duties, decent not to fail
In offices of tenderness, and pay
Meet adoration to my household gods,
When I am gone. He works his work, I mine.

    There lies the port; the vessel puffs her sail:
45 There gloom the dark broad seas. My mariners,
Souls that have toiled, and wrought, and thought
    with me—
That ever with a frolic welcome took
The thunder and the sunshine, and opposed
Free hearts, free foreheads—you and I are old;

50 Old age hath yet his honour and his toil;
Death closes all: but something ere the end,
Some work of noble note, may yet be done,
Not unbecoming men that strove with Gods.

The lights begin to twinkle from the rocks:
55 The long day wanes: the slow moon climbs: the deep
Moans round with many voices. Come, my friends,
'Tis not too late to seek a newer world.
Push off, and sitting well in order smite
The sounding furrows; for my purpose holds
60 To sail beyond the sunset, and the baths
Of all the western stars, until I die.
It may be that the gulfs will wash us down:
It may be we shall touch the Happy Isles,[2]
And see the great Achilles,[3] whom we knew.
65 Though much is taken, much abides; and though
We are not now that strength which in old days
Moved earth and heaven; that which we are, we are;
One equal temper of heroic hearts,
Made weak by time and fate, but strong in will
70 To strive, to seek, to find, and not to yield.
    —1842 (WRITTEN 1833)

The Epic[4]

At Francis Allen's on the Christmas-eve,—
    The game of forfeits done—the girls all kissed
Beneath the sacred bush[5] and past away—
The parson Holmes, the poet Everard Hall,
5 The host, and I sat round the wassail-bowl,[6]
Then half-way ebbed: and there we held a talk,
How all the old honour had from Christmas gone,
Or gone, or dwindled down to some odd games
In some odd nooks like this; till I, tired out

[1] *Hyades* Group of stars near the constellation Taurus and associated with rainstorms.

[2] *Happy Isles* Elysium, or Isles of the Blessed, where heroes enjoyed the afterlife.

[3] *Achilles* Greek hero of the Trojan War, the central character of Homer's *Iliad*.

[4] *The Epic* Tennyson wrote this poem as a poetic "frame" for the *Morte d'Arthur*, which follows; together the two poems make up a single work. "The Epic" itself consists of the fifty-one lines that precede the "Morte d'Arthur," plus the thirty-one lines that follow.

[5] *sacred bush* Mistletoe.

[6] *wassail-bowl* Punch bowl containing spiced ale.

10 With cutting eights[1] that day upon the pond,
    Where, three times slipping from the outer edge,
    I bumped the ice into three several stars,
    Fell in a doze; and half-awake I heard
    The parson taking wide and wider sweeps,
15 Now harping on the church-commissioners,
    Now hawking at Geology and schism;[2]
    Until I woke, and found him settled down
    Upon the general decay of faith
    Right through the world, "at home was little left,
20 And none abroad: there was no anchor, none,
    To hold by." Francis, laughing, clapped his hand
    On Everard's shoulder, with "I hold by him."
    "And I," quoth Everard, "by the wassail-bowl."
    "Why yes," I said, "we knew your gift that way
25 At college: but another which you had,
    I mean of verse (for so we held it then),
    What came of that?" "You know," said Frank, "he burnt
    His epic, his King Arthur, some twelve books"—
    And then to me demanding why? "Oh, sir,
30 He thought that nothing new was said, or else
    Something so said 'twas nothing—that a truth
    Looks freshest in the fashion of the day:
    God knows: he has a mint of reasons: ask.
    It pleased *me* well enough." "Nay, nay," said Hall,
35 "Why take the style of those heroic times?
    For nature brings not back the Mastodon,[3]
    Nor we those times; and why should any man
    Remodel models? these twelve books of mine
    Were faint Homeric echoes, nothing-worth,
40 Mere chaff and draff,[4] much better burnt." "But I,"
    Said Francis, "picked the eleventh from this hearth
    And have it: keep a thing, its use will come.
    I hoard it as a sugar-plum for Holmes."
    He laughed, and I, though sleepy, like a horse
45 That hears the corn-bin open, pricked my ears;
    For I remembered Everard's college fame
    When we were freshmen: then at my request
    He brought it; and the poet little urged,

But with some prelude of disparagement,
50 Read, mouthing out his hollow oes and aes,
    Deep-chested music, and to this result.
    —1842

Morte d'Arthur[5]

So all day long the noise of battle rolled
    Among the mountains by the winter sea;
Until King Arthur's table, man by man,
Had fallen in Lyonnesse[6] about their Lord,
5 King Arthur: then, because his wound was deep,
The bold Sir Bedivere uplifted him,
Sir Bedivere, the last of all his knights,
And bore him to a chapel nigh the field,
A broken chancel[7] with a broken cross,
10 That stood on a dark strait of barren land.
On one side lay the ocean, and on one
Lay a great water, and the moon was full.

    Then spake King Arthur to Sir Bedivere:
"The sequel of today unsolders all
15 The goodliest fellowship of famous knights
Whereof this world holds record. Such a sleep
They sleep—the men I loved. I think that we
Shall never more, at any future time,
Delight our souls with talk of knightly deeds,
20 Walking about the gardens and the halls
Of Camelot, as in the days that were.
I perish by this people which I made,—
Though Merlin sware° that I should come again   *promised*
To rule once more—but let what will be, be,
25 I am so deeply smitten through the helm
That without help I cannot last till morn.
Thou therefore take my brand° Excalibur,   *sword*
Which was my pride: for thou rememberest how

---

1 *cutting eights* Skating figure-eights.

2 *church-commissioners … Geology … schism* References to contemporary religious and scientific controversies.

3 *Mastadon* An extinct elephant-like mammal; evidence of its existence was first discovered in the eighteenth century, and the name first applied in the early nineteenth.

4 *chaff and draff* Here, refuse, material of little worth.

5 *Morte d'Arthur* French: The Death of [King] Arthur. This poem was later incorporated nearly word for word into the final book of Tennyson's epic *Idylls of the King*. As his kingdom and the knightly Order of the Round Table fall into disorder, Arthur faces a rebellion led by his nephew Modred; in one final battle Arthur defeats Modred, but his knights are almost all killed and Arthur himself gravely wounded by a blow to the head.

6 [Tennyson's note] The country of legend that lay between Cornwall and the Scilly Islands.

7 *chancel* Area around the altar.

In those old days, one summer noon, an arm
30   Rose up from out the bosom of the lake,
Clothed in white samite,° mystic, wonderful,   *silk*
Holding the sword—and how I rowed across
And took it, and have worn it, like a king:
And, wheresoever I am sung or told
35   In aftertime, this also shall be known:
But now delay not: take Excalibur,
And fling him far into the middle mere:[1]
Watch what thou seest, and lightly bring me word."

To him replied the bold Sir Bedivere:
40   "It is not meet,° Sir King, to leave thee thus,   *appropriate*
Aidless, alone, and smitten through the helm.
A little thing may harm a wounded man.
Yet I thy hest° will all perform at full,   *command*
Watch what I see, and lightly bring thee word."

45   So saying, from the ruined shrine he stepped
And in the moon athwart the place of tombs,
Where lay the mighty bones of ancient men,
Old knights, and over them the sea-wind sang
Shrill, chill, with flakes of foam. He, stepping down
50   By zig-zag paths, and juts of pointed rock,
Came on the shining levels of the lake.

There drew he forth the brand Excalibur,
And o'er him, drawing it, the winter moon,
Brightening the skirts of a long cloud, ran forth
55   And sparkled keen with frost against the hilt:
For all the haft° twinkled with diamond sparks,   *handle*
Myriads of topaz-lights, and jacinth[2]-work
Of subtlest jewellery. He gazed so long
That both his eyes were dazzled, as he stood,
60   This way and that dividing the swift mind,
In act to throw: but at the last it seemed
Better to leave Excalibur concealed
There in the many-knotted waterflags,°   *reeds*
That whistled stiff and dry about the marge.°   *shore*
65   So strode he back slow to the wounded King.

Then spake King Arthur to Sir Bedivere:
"Hast thou performed my mission which I gave?
What is it thou hast seen? or what hast heard?"

And answer made the bold Sir Bedivere:
70   "I heard the ripple washing in the reeds,
And the wild water lapping on the crag."

To whom replied King Arthur, faint and pale:
"Thou hast betrayed thy nature and thy name,
Not rendering true answer, as beseemed
75   Thy fealty,° nor like a noble knight: *sworn allegiance*
For surer sign had followed, either hand,
Or voice, or else a motion of the mere.
This is a shameful thing for men to lie.
Yet now, I charge thee, quickly go again
80   As thou art lief° and dear, and do the thing   *beloved*
I bad[3] thee, watch, and lightly bring me word."

Then went Sir Bedivere the second time
Across the ridge, and paced beside the mere,
Counting the dewy pebbles, fix'd in thought;
85   But when he saw the wonder of the hilt,
How curiously and strangely chased,° he smote   *engraved*
His palms together, and he cried aloud,

"And if indeed I cast the brand away,
Surely a precious thing, one worthy note,
90   Should thus be lost for ever from the earth,
Which might have pleased the eyes of many men.
What good should follow this, if this were done?
What harm, undone? deep harm to disobey,
Seeing obedience is the bond of rule.
95   Were it well to obey then, if a king demand
An act unprofitable, against himself?
The King is sick, and knows not what he does.
What record, or what relic of my lord
Should be to aftertime, but empty breath
100   And rumours of a doubt? but were this kept,
Stored in some treasure-house of mighty kings,
Some one might show it at a joust of arms,
Saying, 'King Arthur's sword, Excalibur,
Wrought by the lonely maiden of the Lake.
105   Nine years she wrought it, sitting in the deeps
Upon the hidden bases of the hills.'
So might some old man speak in the aftertime
To all the people, winning reverence.
But now much honour and much fame were lost."

---

1   *middle mere* Middle of the lake.

2   *jacinth* Reddish-orange gem.

3   *bad* I.e., bade, commanded.

110 So spake he, clouded with his own conceit,
And hid Excalibur the second time,
And so strode back slow to the wounded King.

Then spoke King Arthur, breathing heavily:
"What is it thou hast seen? or what hast heard?"
115 And answer made the bold Sir Bedivere:
"I heard the water lapping on the crag,
And the long ripple washing in the reeds."

To whom replied King Arthur, much in wrath:
"Ah, miserable and unkind, untrue,
120 Unknightly, traitor-hearted! Woe is me!
Authority forgets a dying king,
Laid widowed of the power in his eye
That bowed the will. I see thee what thou art,
For thou, the latest-left of all my knights,
125 In whom should meet the offices of all,
Thou wouldst betray me for the precious hilt;
Either from lust of gold, or like a girl
Valuing the giddy pleasure of the eyes.
Yet, for a man may fail in duty twice,
130 And the third time may prosper, get thee hence:
But, if thou spare to fling Excalibur,
I will arise and slay thee with my hands."

Then quickly rose Sir Bedivere, and ran,
And, leaping down the ridges lightly, plunged
135 Among the bulrush-beds, and clutched the sword,
And strongly wheeled and threw it. The great brand
Made lightnings in the splendour of the moon,
And flashing round and round, and whirled in an arch,
Shot like a streamer of the northern morn,[1]
140 Seen where the moving isles of winter[2] shock
By night, with noises of the northern sea.
So flashed and fell the brand Excalibur:
But ere he dipped the surface, rose an arm
Clothed in white samite, mystic, wonderful,
145 And caught him by the hilt, and brandished him
Three times, and drew him under in the mere.
And lightly went the other to the King.

Then spoke King Arthur, drawing thicker breath:
"Now see I by thine eyes that this is done.
150 Speak out: what is it thou hast heard, or seen?"

_____
[1] *northern morn* The aurora borealis.

[2] *isles of winter* Icebergs.

And answer made the bold Sir Bedivere:
"Sir King, I closed mine eyelids, lest the gems
Should blind my purpose, for I never saw,
Nor shall see, here or elsewhere, till I die,
155 Not though I live three lives of mortal men,
So great a miracle as yonder hilt.
Then with both hands I flung him, wheeling him;
But when I looked again, behold an arm,
Clothed in white samite, mystic, wonderful,
160 That caught him by the hilt, and brandished him
Three times, and drew him under in the mere."

And answer made King Arthur, breathing hard:
"My end draws nigh; 'tis time that I were gone.
Make broad thy shoulders to receive my weight,
165 And bear me to the margin; yet I fear
My wound hath taken cold, and I shall die."

So saying, from the pavement he half rose,
Slowly, with pain, reclining on his arm,
And looking wistfully with wide blue eyes
170 As in a picture. Him Sir Bedivere
Remorsefully regarded through his tears,
And would have spoken, but he found not words,
Then took with care, and kneeling on one knee,
O'er both his shoulders drew the languid hands,
175 And rising bore him through the place of tombs.

But, as he walked, King Arthur panted hard,
Like one that feels a nightmare on his bed
When all the house is mute. So sighed the King,
Muttering and murmuring at his ear, "Quick, quick!
180 I fear it is too late, and I shall die."
But the other swiftly strode from ridge to ridge,
Clothed with his breath, and looking, as he walked,
Larger than human on the frozen hills.
He heard the deep behind him, and a cry
185 Before. His own thought drove him, like a goad.
Dry clashed his harness in the icy caves
And barren chasms, and all to left and right
The bare black cliff clanged round him, as he based
His feet on juts of slippery crag that rang
190 Sharp-smitten with the dint of armèd heels—
And on a sudden, lo! the level lake,
And the long glories of the winter moon.
Then saw they how there hove° a dusky barge, *floated*
Dark as a funeral scarf from stem to stern,

195　Beneath them; and descending they were ware°   *aware*
　　　That all the decks were dense with stately forms
　　　Black-stoled,[1] black-hooded, like a dream—by these
　　　Three Queens with crowns of gold—and from them rose
　　　A cry that shivered to the tingling stars,
200　And, as it were one voice, an agony
　　　Of lamentation, like a wind, that shrills
　　　All night in a waste land, where no one comes,
　　　Or hath come, since the making of the world.

　　　　　Then murmured Arthur, "Place me in the barge,"
205　And to the barge they came. There those three Queens
　　　Put forth their hands, and took the King, and wept.
　　　But she, that rose the tallest of them all
　　　And fairest, laid his head upon her lap,
　　　And loosed the shattered casque,° and chafed   *helmet*
　　　　his hands,
210　And called him by his name, complaining loud,
　　　And dropping bitter tears against his brow
　　　Striped with dark blood: for all his face was white
　　　And colourless, and like the withered moon
　　　Smote by the fresh beam of the springing east;
215　And all his greaves and cuisses[2] dashed with drops
　　　Of onset;[3] and the light and lustrous curls—
　　　That made his forehead like a rising sun
　　　High from the dais-throne—were parched with dust;
　　　Or, clotted into points and hanging loose,
220　Mix'd with the knightly growth that fringed his lips.
　　　So like a shattered column lay the King;
　　　Not like that Arthur who, with lance in rest,
　　　From spur to plume a star of tournament,
　　　Shot through the lists[4] at Camelot, and charged
225　Before the eyes of ladies and of kings.

　　　　　Then loudly cried the bold Sir Bedivere,
　　　"Ah! my Lord Arthur, whither shall I go?
　　　Where shall I hide my forehead and my eyes?
　　　For now I see the true old times are dead,
230　When every morning brought a noble chance,
　　　And every chance brought out a noble knight.
　　　Such times have been not since the light that led

The holy Elders[5] with the gift of myrrh.
　　　But now the whole Round Table is dissolved
235　Which was an image of the mighty world;
　　　And I, the last, go forth companionless,
　　　And the days darken round me, and the years,
　　　Among new men, strange faces, other minds."

　　　　　And slowly answered Arthur from the barge:
240　"The old order changeth, yielding place to new,
　　　And God fulfils Himself in many ways,
　　　Lest one good custom should corrupt the world.
　　　Comfort thyself: what comfort is in me?
　　　I have lived my life, and that which I have done
245　May He within Himself make pure! but thou,
　　　If thou shouldst never see my face again,
　　　Pray for my soul. More things are wrought by prayer
　　　Than this world dreams of. Wherefore, let thy voice
　　　Rise like a fountain for me night and day.
250　For what are men better than sheep or goats
　　　That nourish a blind life within the brain,
　　　If, knowing God, they lift not hands of prayer
　　　Both for themselves and those who call them friend?
　　　For so the whole round earth is every way
255　Bound by gold chains about the feet of God.
　　　But now farewell. I am going a long way
　　　With these thou seest—if indeed I go—
　　　(For all my mind is clouded with a doubt)
　　　To the island-valley of Avilion;°   *i.e., Avalon*
260　Where falls not hail, or rain, or any snow,
　　　Nor ever wind blows loudly; but it lies
　　　Deep-meadowed, happy, fair with orchard-lawns
　　　And bowery hollows crown'd with summer sea,
　　　Where I will heal me of my grievous wound."

265　　　So said he, and the barge with oar and sail
　　　Moved from the brink, like some full-breasted swan
　　　That, fluting a wild carol ere her death,[6]
　　　Ruffles her pure cold plume, and takes the flood
　　　With swarthy webs.[7] Long stood Sir Bedivere
270　Revolving many memories, till the hull
　　　Looked one black dot against the verge of dawn,
　　　And on the mere the wailing died away.

---

[1]　*black-stoled*　Wearing black cloaks.

[2]　*greaves and cuisses*　Armor for shins and thighs.

[3]　*onset*　The rush of battle (which has splattered his armor).

[4]　*lists*　Arenas in which jousting and tilting tournaments were held.

[5]　*holy Elders*　The three kings who brought gifts, including myrrh, at the birth of Jesus (Matthew 2.11).

[6]　*swan ... death*　Swans were said to sing only once, at their deaths.

[7]　*webs*　I.e., webbed feet.

Here ended Hall,[1] and our last light, that long
Had winked and threatened darkness, flared and fell:
At which the Parson, sent to sleep with sound,
And waked with silence, grunted "Good!" but we
Sat rapt: it was the tone with which he read—
Perhaps some modern touches here and there
Redeemed it from the charge of nothingness—
Or else we loved the man, and prized his work;
I know not: but we sitting, as I said,
The cock crew loud; as at that time of year
The lusty bird takes every hour for dawn:[2]
Then Francis, muttering, like a man ill-used,
"There now—that's nothing!" drew a little back,
And drove his heel into the smouldered log,
That sent a blast of sparkles up the flue:
And so to bed; where yet in sleep I seemed
To sail with Arthur under looming shores,
Point after point; till on to dawn, when dreams
Begin to feel the truth and stir of day,
To me, methought, who waited with a crowd,
There came a bark° that, blowing forward, bore   *ship*
King Arthur, like a modern gentleman
Of stateliest port;° and all the people cried,   *bearing*
"Arthur is come again: he cannot die."
Then those that stood upon the hills behind
Repeated—"Come again, and thrice as fair;"
And, further inland, voices echoed—"Come
With all good things, and war shall be no more."
At this a hundred bells began to peal,
That with the sound I woke, and heard indeed
The clear church-bells ring in the Christmas-morn.
—1842 (BEGUN 1833)

[*Break, break, break*][3]

Break, break, break,
  On thy cold gray stones, O Sea!
And I would that my tongue could utter
  The thoughts that arise in me.

5 O well for the fisherman's boy,
    That he shouts with his sister at play!
  O well for the sailor lad,
    That he sings in his boat on the bay!

  And the stately ships go on
10   To their haven under the hill;
  But O for the touch of a vanished hand,
    And the sound of a voice that is still![4]

  Break, break, break,
    At the foot of thy crags, O Sea!
15 But the tender grace of a day that is dead
    Will never come back to me.
  —1842 (WRITTEN 1834?)

Locksley Hall

Comrades, leave me here a little, while as yet 'tis
  early morn:
Leave me here, and when you want me, sound upon
  the bugle-horn.

'Tis the place, and all around it, as of old, the curlews[5]
  call,
Dreary gleams about the moorland flying over
  Locksley Hall;

5 Locksley Hall, that in the distance overlooks the
    sandy tracts,
And the hollow ocean-ridges roaring into cataracts.

Many a night from yonder ivied casement, ere I went
  to rest,
Did I look on great Orion[6] sloping slowly to the West.

Many a night I saw the Pleiads,[7] rising through the
  mellow shade,
10 Glitter like a swarm of fire-flies tangled in a silver braid.

---

1 *Here ended Hall* "The Epic" here resumes, as Everard Hall has finished reading out his poem.

2 *The cock … for dawn* For the belief that the rooster crows all night long on Christmas Eve, see Shakespeare, *Hamlet*, I.I.158–60.

3 *Break, break, break* This poem was written not long after the death of Tennyson's closest friend, Arthur Hallam, in 1833.

4 *But … voice that is still* This poem was written not long after the death of Tennyson's closest friend, Arthur Hallam, in 1833.

5 *curlews* Species of shore-dwelling birds.

6 *Orion* The constellation named after the hunter of Greek legend. It sets in November and so was associated with rains and storms.

7 *Pleiads* The constellation commonly known as the Pleiades (named after the seven daughters of Atlas), which rises in May and sets in November.

Here about the beach I wandered, nourishing a
    youth sublime
With the fairy tales of science, and the long result of
    Time;

When the centuries behind me like a fruitful land
    reposed;
When I clung to all the present for the promise that it
    closed:

15 When I dipped into the future far as human eye
    could see;
Saw the Vision of the world, and all the wonder that
    would be.—

In the Spring a fuller crimson comes upon the robin's
    breast;
In the Spring the wanton lapwing gets himself
    another crest;

In the Spring a livelier iris changes on the burnished
    dove;
20 In the Spring a young man's fancy lightly turns to
    thoughts of love.

Then her cheek was pale and thinner than should be
    for one so young,
And her eyes on all my motions with a mute
    observance hung.

And I said, "My cousin Amy, speak, and speak the
    truth to me,
Trust me, cousin, all the current of my being sets to
    thee."

25 On her pallid cheek and forehead came a colour and a
    light,
As I have seen the rosy red flushing in the northern
    night.

And she turned—her bosom shaken with a sudden
    storm of sighs—
All the spirit deeply dawning in the dark of hazel eyes—

Saying, "I have hid my feelings, fearing they should
    do me wrong;"

30 Saying, "Dost thou love me, cousin?" weeping, "I
    have loved thee long."

Love took up the glass of Time,[1] and turned it in
    his glowing hands;
Every moment, lightly shaken, ran itself in golden
    sands.

Love took up the harp of Life, and smote on all the
    chords with might;
Smote the chord of Self, that, trembling, passed in
    music out of sight.

35 Many a morning on the moorland did we hear the
    copses ring,
And her whisper thronged my pulses with the fullness
    of the Spring.

Many an evening by the waters did we watch the
    stately ships,
And our spirits rushed together at the touching of
    the lips.

O my cousin, shallow-hearted! O my Amy, mine no
    more!
40 O the dreary, dreary moorland! O the barren, barren
    shore!

Falser than all fancy fathoms,° false than all   *apprehends*
    songs have sung,
Puppet to a father's threat, and servile to a shrewish
    tongue!

Is it well to wish thee happy?—having known me—to
    decline
On a range of lower feelings and a narrower heart
    than mine!

45 Yet it shall be: thou shalt lower to his level day by day,
What is fine within thee growing coarse to sympathise
    with clay.

As the husband is, the wife is: thou art mated with a
    clown,[2]

---

1 *glass of Time* Hourglass.

2 *clown* Rustic, boorish fellow.

And the grossness of his nature will have weight to
   drag thee down.

He will hold thee, when his passion shall have spent
   its novel force,
50 Something better than his dog, a little dearer than his
   horse.

What is this? his eyes are heavy: think not they are
   glazed with wine.
Go to him: it is thy duty: kiss him: take his hand in
   thine.

It may be my lord is weary, that his brain is
   overwrought:
Soothe him with thy finer fancies, touch him with
   thy lighter thought.

55 He will answer to the purpose, easy things to
   understand—
Better thou wert dead before me, though I slew thee
   with my hand!

Better thou and I were lying, hidden from the heart's
   disgrace,
Rolled in one another's arms, and silent in a last embrace.

Cursèd be the social wants that sin against the
   strength of youth!
60 Cursèd be the social lies that warp us from the
   living truth!

Cursèd be the sickly forms that err from honest
   Nature's rule!
Cursèd be the gold that gilds the straitened forehead
   of the fool![1]

Well—'tis well that I should bluster!—Hadst thou
   less unworthy proved—
Would to God—for I had loved thee more than ever
   wife was loved.

65 Am I mad, that I should cherish that which bears but
   bitter fruit?

I will pluck it from my bosom, though my heart be at
   the root.

Never, though my mortal summers to such length
   of years should come
As the many-wintered crow that leads the clanging
   rookery home.

Where is comfort? in division of the records of the
   mind?
70 Can I part her from herself, and love her, as I knew
   her, kind?

I remember one that perished: sweetly did she speak
   and move:
Such a one do I remember, whom to look at was to love.

Can I think of her as dead, and love her for the love
   she bore?
No—she never loved me truly: love is love for evermore.

75 Comfort? comfort scorned of devils! this is truth the
   poet sings,
That a sorrow's crown of sorrow is remembering
   happier things.[2]

Drug thy memories, lest thou learn it, lest thy heart be
   put to proof,
In the dead unhappy night, and when the rain is on
   the roof.

Like a dog, he hunts in dreams, and thou art staring at
   the wall,
80 Where the dying night-lamp flickers, and the
   shadows rise and fall.

Then a hand shall pass before thee, pointing to his
   drunken sleep,
To thy widowed[3] marriage-pillows, to the tears that
   thou wilt weep.

Thou shalt hear the "Never, never," whispered by the
   phantom years,

---

1 *straitened … fool* Narrow or low foreheads were thought to indicate stupidity.

2 *this is truth … happier things* Cf. Dante, *Inferno* v. 121–23: "No greater grief than to remember joy, when misery is at hand."

3 *widowed* In that she and her husband are emotionally estranged.

And a song from out the distance in the ringing of
thine ears;

85 And an eye shall vex thee, looking ancient kindness on
thy pain.
Turn thee, turn thee on thy pillow: get thee to thy
rest again.

Nay, but Nature brings thee solace; for a tender
voice will cry.
'Tis a purer life than thine; a lip to drain thy trouble dry.

Baby lips will laugh me down: my latest rival brings
thee rest.
90 Baby fingers, waxen touches, press me from the
mother's breast.

O, the child too clothes the father with a dearness not
his due.
Half is thine and half is his: it will be worthy of the two.

O, I see thee old and formal, fitted to thy petty part,
With a little hoard of maxims preaching down a
daughter's heart.

95 "They were dangerous guides the feelings—she[1]
herself was not exempt—
Truly, she herself had suffered"—Perish in thy self-
contempt!

Overlive it—lower yet—be happy! wherefore should I care?
I myself must mix with action, lest I wither by despair.

What is that which I should turn to, lighting upon
days like these?
100 Every door is barred with gold, and opens but to
golden keys.

Every gate is thronged with suitors, all the markets
overflow.
I have but an angry fancy: what is that which I should do?

I had been content to perish, falling on the foeman's
ground,

When the ranks are rolled in vapour, and the winds
are laid with sound.

105 But the jingling of the guinea° helps the hurt   *coin*
that Honour feels,
And the nations do but murmur, snarling at each
other's heels.

Can I but relive in sadness? I will turn that earlier page.
Hide me from my deep emotion, O thou wondrous
Mother-Age!

Make me feel the wild pulsation that I felt before the
strife,
110 When I heard my days before me, and the tumult of
my life;

Yearning for the large excitement that the coming
years would yield,
Eager-hearted as a boy when first he leaves his father's
field,

And at night along the dusky highway near and
nearer drawn,
Sees in heaven the light of London flaring like a
dreary dawn;

115 And his spirit leaps within him to be gone before him
then,
Underneath the light he looks at, in among the
throngs of men:

Men, my brothers, men the workers, ever reaping
something new:
That which they have done but earnest of the things
that they shall do:

For I dipped into the future, far as human eye could see,
120 Saw the Vision of the world, and all the wonder that
would be;

Saw the heavens fill with commerce, argosies[2] of
magic sails,

---

[1] *she* The woman, Amy, is pictured in the future, speaking of
herself in the third person to her daughter.

[2] *argosies* Fleets of merchant ships. In this couplet and the next
the speaker predicts that commerce and warfare will someday be
carried out by aircraft.

Pilots of the purple twilight, dropping down with
   costly bales;

Heard the heavens fill with shouting, and there rained
   a ghastly dew
From the nations' airy navies grappling in the central
   blue;

125 Far along the world-wide whisper of the south-wind
   rushing warm,
With the standards of the peoples plunging through
   the thunder-storm;

Till the war-drum throbbed no longer, and the
   battle-flags were furled
In the Parliament of man, the Federation of the world.

There the common sense of most shall hold a fretful
   realm in awe,
130 And the kindly earth shall slumber, lapped in
   universal law.

So I triumphed ere my passion sweeping through me
   left me dry,
Left me with the palsied heart, and left me with the
   jaundiced eye;

Eye, to which all order festers, all things here are out
   of joint:
Science moves, but slowly slowly, creeping on from
   point to point:

135 Slowly comes a hungry people, as a lion creeping nigher,
Glares at one that nods and winks behind a slowly-
   dying fire.

Yet I doubt not through the ages one increasing
   purpose runs,
And the thoughts of men are widened with the
   process of the suns.

What is that to him that reaps not harvest of his
   youthful joys,
140 Though the deep heart of existence beat forever like a
   boy's?

Knowledge comes, but wisdom lingers, and I linger
   on the shore,
And the individual withers, and the world is more
   and more.

Knowledge comes, but wisdom lingers, and he bears a
   laden breast,
Full of sad experience, moving toward the stillness of
   his rest.

145 Hark, my merry comrades call me, sounding on the
   bugle-horn,
They to whom my foolish passion were a target for
   their scorn:

Shall it not be scorn to me to harp on such a
   mouldered string?
I am shamed through all my nature to have loved so
   slight a thing.

Weakness to be wroth° with weakness!   *angry*
   woman's pleasure, woman's pain—
150 Nature made them blinder motions bounded in a
   shallower brain:

Woman is the lesser man, and all thy passions,
   matched with mine,
Are as moonlight unto sunlight, and as water untwine—

Here at least, where nature sickens, nothing. Ah, for
   some retreat
Deep in yonder shining Orient, where my life began
   to beat;

155 Where in wild Mahratta-battle[1] fell my father evil-
   starred;[2]—
I was left a trampled orphan, and a selfish uncle's ward.

Or to burst all links of habit—there to wander far away,
On from island unto island at the gateways of the day.

Larger constellations burning, mellow moons and
   happy skies,

---

[1] *Mahratta-battle* Conflict between the British and the Mahratta
soldiers from Bombay in 1818.

[2] *evil-starred* Cursed with bad luck.

160   Breadths of tropic shade and palms in cluster, knots of
        Paradise.

Never comes the trader, never floats an European flag,
Slides the bird o'er lustrous woodland, swings the
    trailer[1] from the crag;

Droops the heavy-blossomed bower, hangs the heavy-
    fruited tree—
Summer isles of Eden lying in dark-purple spheres
    of sea.

165   There methinks would be enjoyment more than in
        this march of mind,
In the steamship, in the railway, in the thoughts
    that shake mankind.

There the passions cramped no longer shall have
    scope and breathing space;
I will take some savage woman, she shall rear my
    dusky race.

Iron jointed, supple-sinewed, they shall dive, and they
    shall run,
170   Catch the wild goat by the hair, and hurl their lances
        in the sun;

Whistle back the parrot's call, and leap the rainbows
    of the brooks,
Not with blinded eyesight poring over miserable
    books—

Fool, again the dream, the fancy! but I *know* my
    words are wild,
But I count the gray barbarian lower than the
    Christian child.

175   I, to herd with narrow foreheads, vacant of our
        glorious gains,
Like a beast with lower pleasures, like a beast with
    lower pains!

Mated with a squalid savage—what to me were sun or
    clime?

I the heir of all the ages, in the foremost files[2] of
    time—

I that rather held it better men should perish one
    by one,
180   Than that earth should stand at gaze like Joshua's
        moon in Ajalon![3]

Not in vain the distance beacons. Forward,
    forward let us range,
Let the great world spin forever down the ringing
    grooves of change.

Through the shadow of the globe we sweep into
    the younger day:
Better fifty years of Europe than a cycle of
    Cathay.°   *China*

185   Mother-Age (for mine I knew not) help me as
        when life begun:
Rift° the hills, and roll the waters, flash the   *split open*
    lightnings, weigh the Sun.

O, I see the crescent promise of my spirit hath not set.
Ancient founts of inspiration well through all my
    fancy yet.

Howsoever these things be, a long farewell to Locksley
    Hall!
190   Now for me the woods may wither, now for me the
        roof-tree fall.

Comes a vapour from the margin, blackening over
    heath and holt,°   *wood*
Cramming all the blast before it, in its breast a
    thunderbolt.

Let it fall on Locksley Hall, with rain or hail, or fire or
    snow;
For the mighty wind arises, roaring seaward, and I go.
    —1842

---

1 *trailer*   Vine or hanging branch.

2 *files*   The ages of time pictured as men marching in file.

3 *Joshua's moon in Ajalon*   In Joshua 10.12–13, Joshua makes the
moon and sun stand still during a battle in the valley of Ajalon.

from *The Princess*

[*Sweet and Low*]

Sweet and low, sweet and low,
  Wind of the western sea,
Low, low, breathe and blow,
  Wind of the western sea!
5 Over the rolling waters go,
Come from the dying moon, and blow,
  Blow him again to me;
While my little one, while my pretty one, sleeps.

Sleep and rest, sleep and rest,
10 Father will come to thee soon;
Rest, rest, on mother's breast,
  Father will come to thee soon;
Father will come to his babe in the nest,
Silver sails all out of the west
15 Under the silver moon:
Sleep, my little one, sleep, my pretty one, sleep.

[*The Splendour Falls*]

The splendour falls on castle walls
  And snowy summits old in story:
The long light shakes across the lakes,
  And the wild cataract° leaps in glory.   *waterfall*
5 Blow, bugle, blow, set the wild echoes flying,
Blow, bugle; answer, echoes, dying, dying, dying.

O hark, O hear! how thin and clear,
  And thinner, clearer, farther going!
O sweet and far from cliff and scar[1]
10 The horns of Elfland faintly blowing!
Blow, let us hear the purple glens replying:
Blow, bugle; answer, echoes, dying, dying, dying.

O love, they die in yon rich sky,
  They faint on hill or field or river:
15 Our echoes roll from soul to soul,
  And grow for ever and for ever.
Blow, bugle, blow, set the wild echoes flying,
And answer, echoes, answer, dying, dying, dying.

[1]   *scar* Steep, craggy portion of mountainside.

[*Tears, Idle Tears*]

Tears, idle tears, I know not what they mean,
  Tears from the depth of some divine despair
Rise in the heart, and gather to the eyes,
In looking on the happy Autumn-fields,
5 And thinking of the days that are no more.

Fresh as the first beam glittering on a sail,
That brings our friends up from the underworld,
Sad as the last which reddens over one
That sinks with all we love below the verge;°   *horizon*
10 So sad, so fresh, the days that are no more.

Ah, sad and strange as in dark summer dawns
The earliest pipe of half-awakened birds
To dying ears, when unto dying eyes
The casement° slowly grows a glimmering   *window*
  square;
15 So sad, so strange, the days that are no more.

Dear as remembered kisses after death,
And sweet as those by hopeless fancy feigned
On lips that are for others; deep as love,
Deep as first love, and wild with all regret;
20 O Death in Life, the days that are no more.

[*Now Sleeps the Crimson Petal*]

Now sleeps the crimson petal, now the white;
  Nor waves the cypress in the palace walk;
Nor winks the gold fin in the porphyry[2] font:
The fire-fly wakens: waken thou with me.

5 Now droops the milkwhite peacock like a ghost,
And like a ghost she glimmers on to me.

Now lies the Earth all Danaë[3] to the stars,
And all thy heart lies open unto me.

Now slides the silent meteor on, and leaves
10 A shining furrow, as thy thoughts in me.

[2]   *porphyry* Beautiful, polished purple stone.

[3]   *Danaë* In Greek mythology, a princess visited by Zeus in the form of a shower of gold.

Now folds the lily all her sweetness up,
And slips into the bosom of the lake:
So fold thyself, my dearest, thou, and slip
Into my bosom and be lost in me.

[Come Down, O Maid]

Come down, O maid, from yonder
    mountain height:
What pleasure lives in height (the shepherd sang)
In height and cold, the splendour of the hills?
But cease to move so near the Heavens, and cease
5   To glide a sunbeam by the blasted Pine,
To sit a star upon the sparkling spire;
And come, for Love is of the valley, come,
For Love is of the valley, come thou down
And find him; by the happy threshold, he,
10 Or hand in hand with Plenty in the maize,
Or red with spurted purple of the vats,
Or foxlike in the vine;¹ nor cares to walk
With Death and Morning on the silver horns,
Nor wilt thou snare him in the white ravine,
15 Nor find him dropped upon the firths° of ice,   *juttings*
That huddling slant in furrow-cloven falls
To roll the torrent out of dusky doors:
But follow; let the torrent dance thee down
To find him in the valley; let the wild
20 Lean-headed Eagles yelp alone, and leave
The monstrous ledges there to slope, and spill
Their thousand wreaths of dangling water-smoke,
That like a broken purpose waste in air:
So waste not thou; but come; for all the vales
25 Await thee; azure pillars of the hearth²
Arise to thee; the children call, and I
Thy shepherd pipe, and sweet is every sound,
Sweeter thy voice, but every sound is sweet;
Myriads of rivulets hurrying through the lawn,
30 The moan of doves in immemorial elms,
And murmuring of innumerable bees.

[The Woman's Cause Is Man's³]

"Blame not thyself too much," I said, "nor
    blame
Too much the sons of men and barbarous laws;
These were the rough ways of the world till now.
Henceforth thou hast a helper, me, that know
5   The woman's cause is man's: they rise or sink
Together, dwarfed or godlike, bond or free:
For she that out of Lethe⁴ scales with man
The shining steps of Nature, shares with man
His nights, his days, moves with him to one goal,
10 Stays° all the fair young planet in her hands—   *sustains*
If she be small, slight-natured, miserable,
How shall men grow? but work no more alone!
Our place is much: as far as in us lies
We two will serve them both in aiding her—
15 Will clear away the parasitic forms
That seem to keep her up but drag her down—
Will leave her space to burgeon out of all
Within her—let her make herself her own
To give or keep, to live and learn and be
20 All that not harms distinctive womanhood.
For woman is not undeveloped man,
But diverse:° could we make her as the man,   *different*
Sweet Love were slain: his dearest bond is this,
Not like to like, but like in difference.
25 Yet in the long years liker must they grow;
The man be more of woman, she of man;
He gain in sweetness and in moral height,
Nor lose the wrestling thews° that throw   *muscles*
    the world;
She mental breadth, nor fail in childward care,
30 Nor lose the childlike in the larger mind;
Till at the last she set herself to man,
Like perfect music unto noble words;
And so these twain, upon the skirts° of Time,   *borders*
Sit side by side, full-summed in all their powers,
35 Dispensing harvest, sowing the To-be,
Self-reverent each and reverencing each,

---

¹ *foxlike in the vine*   See Song of Solomon 2.15: "Take us the foxes, the little foxes, that spoil the vines...."

² *azure pillars of the hearth*   Columns of bluish smoke rising from household fires.

---

³ *The Woman's Cause is Man's*   This passage from late in *The Princess* (7.239–291) shows the reconciliation between the princess, a feminist who hoped to live in an environment from which all men were excluded, and the narrator, a prince who wishes to marry her.

⁴ *Lethe*   In Greek myth, one of the rivers of Hades. Drinking its waters caused the souls of the dead to forget their past lives.

Distinct in individualities,
But like each other even as those who love.
Then comes the statelier Eden back to men:
40 Then reign the world's great bridals, chaste and calm:
Then springs the crowning race of humankind.
May these things be!"
                Sighing she spoke "I fear
They will not."
           "Dear, but let us type[1] them now
In our own lives, and this proud watchword rest
45 Of equal; seeing either sex alone
Is half itself, and in true marriage lies
Nor equal, nor unequal: each fulfils
Defect in each, and always thought in thought,
Purpose in purpose, will in will, they grow,
50 The single pure and perfect animal,
The two-celled heart beating, with one full stroke,
Life."
    And again sighing she spoke: "A dream
That once was mine! what woman taught you this ?"
—1847 (REVISED AND SUPPLEMENTED 1850)

The Eagle
[Fragment]

He clasps the crag with crooked hands;
Close to the sun in lonely lands,
Ringed with the azure world, he stands.

The wrinkled sea beneath him crawls;
5 He watches from his mountain walls,
And like a thunderbolt he falls.
—1851 (WRITTEN 1833?)

The Charge of the Light Brigade[2]

1

Half a league,[3] half a league,
Half a league onward,

All in the valley of Death
    Rode the six hundred.[4]
5 "Forward, the Light Brigade!
Charge for the guns!" he said:
Into the valley of Death
    Rode the six hundred.

2

"Forward, the Light Brigade!"
10 Was there a man dismayed?
Not though the soldier knew
    Some one had blundered:
Theirs not to make reply,
Theirs not to reason why,
15 Theirs but to do and die:
Into the valley of Death
    Rode the six hundred.

3

Cannon to right of them,
Cannon to left of them,
20 Cannon in front of them
    Volleyed and thundered;
Stormed at with shot and shell,
Boldly they rode and well,
Into the jaws of Death,
25 Into the mouth of Hell
    Rode the six hundred.

4

Flashed all their sabres bare,
Flashed as they turned in air
Sabring the gunners there,
30 Charging an army, while
    All the world wondered:
Plunged in the battery-smoke
Right through the line they broke;
Cossack and Russian
35 Reeled from the sabre-stroke
    Shattered and sundered.
Then they rode back, but not
    Not the six hundred.

---

[1] *type* Serve as a model for.

[2] *The Charge of the Light Brigade* Written some weeks after a disastrous engagement during the Crimean War. At the Battle of Balaclava on 25 October 1854, the 700 cavalry soldiers of the Light Brigade, acting on a misinterpreted order, directly charged the Russian artillery; a large number were gunned down.

[3] *league* About three miles.

[4] *six hundred* The initial newspaper account read by Tennyson mentioned "607 sabres," and he retained the number even when the correct number was discovered to be considerably higher because "six is much better than seven hundred … metrically" (*Letters* ii.101).

5

Cannon to right of them,
40 Cannon to left of them,
Cannon behind them
      Volleyed and thundered;
Stormed at with shot and shell,
While horse and hero fell,
45 They that had fought so well
Came through the jaws of Death,
Back from the mouth of Hell,
All that was left of them,[1]
      Left of six hundred.

6

50 When can their glory fade?
O the wild charge they made!
      All the world wondered.
Honour the charge they made!
Honour the Light Brigade,
55   Noble six hundred!
                        —1854

[Flower in the Crannied Wall]

Flower in the crannied wall,
I pluck you out of the crannies,
I hold you here, root and all, in my hand,
Little flower—but *if* I could understand
5 What you are, root and all, and all in all,
I should know what God and man is.
                        —1869

Vastness

1

Many a hearth upon our dark globe sighs after many
      a vanished face,
Many a planet by many a sun may roll with the dust
      of a vanished race.

2

Raving politics, never at rest—as this poor earth's
      pale history runs,—

What is it all but a trouble° of ants in the gleam   *agitation*
      of a million million of suns?

3

5 Lies upon this side, lies upon that side, truthless violence
      mourned by the Wise,
Thousands of voices drowning his own in a popular
      torrent of lies upon lies;

4

Stately purposes, valour in battle, glorious annals of army
      and fleet,
Death for the right cause, death for the wrong cause,
      trumpets of victory, groans of defeat;

5

Innocence seethed° in her mother's milk,[2] and   *boiled*
      Charity setting the martyr aflame;
10 Thraldom° who walks with the banner of   *bondage*
      Freedom, and recks not[3] to ruin a realm in her name.

6

Faith at her zenith, or all but lost in the gloom of doubts
      that darken the schools;
Craft with a bunch of all-heal[4] in her hand,
      followed up by her vassal° legion of fools;   *servile*

7

Trade flying over a thousand seas with her spice
      and her vintage, her silk and her corn;
Desolate offing,[5] sailorless harbours, famishing
      populace, wharves forlorn;

8

15 Star of the morning, Hope in the sunrise;
      gloom of the evening, Life at a close;
Pleasure who flaunts on her wide down-way
      with her flying robe and her poisoned rose;

[1] *All ... them* Hundreds of men died or were taken prisoner.

[2] *Innocence ... milk* See Exodus 34.26: "Thou shalt not seethe a
kid in his mother's milk."

[3] *recks not* Is not reluctant.

[4] *all-heal* Name given to various plants believed to have healing
properties.

[5] *offing* Most distant part of the sea visible from shore.

9

Pain, that has crawled from the corpse of Pleasure,
   a worm which writhes all day, and at night
Stirs up again in the heart of the sleeper, and stings
   him back to the curse of the light;

10

Wealth with his wines and his wedded harlots;
   honest Poverty, bare to the bone;
20 Opulent Avarice, lean as Poverty; Flattery gilding
   the rift in a throne;

11

Fame blowing out from her golden trumpet
   a jubilant challenge to Time and to Fate;
Slander, her shadow, sowing the nettle on all the
   laurelled graves of the Great;

12

Love for the maiden, crowned with marriage,
   no regrets for aught that has been,
Household happiness, gracious children,
   debtless competence,° golden mean;   *sufficiency*

13

25 National hatreds of whole generations, and
   pigmy° spites of the village spire;   *trivial*
Vows that will last to the last death-ruckle,°   *death-rattle*
   and vows that are snapped in a moment of fire;

14

He that has lived for the lust of the minute,
   and died in the doing it, flesh without mind;
He that has nailed all flesh to the Cross,
   till Self died out in the love of his kind;

15

Spring and Summer and Autumn and Winter,
   and all these old revolutions of earth;
30 All new-old revolutions of Empire—change of the
   tide—what is all of it worth?

16

What the philosophies, all the sciences, poesy,
   varying voices of prayer?

All that is noblest, all that is basest, all that is filthy
   with all that is fair?

17

What is it all, if we all of us end but in being our own
   corpse-coffins at last,
Swallowed in Vastness, lost in Silence, drowned
   in the deeps of a meaningless Past?

18

35 What but a murmur of gnats in the gloom,
   or a moment's anger of bees in their hive?—

*   *   *

Peace, let it be! for I loved him, and love him for ever:
   the dead are not dead but alive.
—1885; 1889

Crossing the Bar[1]

Sunset and evening star,
   And one clear call for me!
And may there be no moaning of the bar,
   When I put out to sea,

5 But such a tide as moving seems asleep,
   Too full for sound and foam,
When that which drew from out the boundless deep
   Turns again home.

Twilight and evening bell,
10   And after that the dark!
And may there be no sadness of farewell,
   When I embark;

For though from out our bourne° of Time and   *limit*
   Place
   The flood may bear me far,
15 I hope to see my Pilot face to face
   When I have crossed the bar.
—1889

---

[1] *Bar* Sandbank across the mouth of a harbor or estuary.

IN CONTEXT

Images of Tennyson

Particularly in his later years, Tennyson became an iconic figure in Victorian Britain. The best known photographic images of him are those taken by Julia Margaret Cameron, one of which is reproduced, below. (Another appears in the introduction to Tennyson, above.) Tennyson as a younger man is described below by Thomas Carlyle.

Julia Margaret Cameron, *Alfred Tennyson*, 1865. Tennyson nicknamed this photograph "the dirty monk" and claimed that it was his favorite photograph of himself.

from Evert A. Duyckinck, *Portrait Gallery of Eminent Men and Women in Europe and America*, 1873. This portrait appears to be from the 1850s.

from Thomas Carlyle, Letter to Ralph Waldo Emerson, 5 August 1844

Alfred is one of the few British or Foreign Figures (a not increasing number I think!) who are and remain beautiful to me;—a true human soul, or some authentic approximation thereto, to whom your own soul can say, Brother!—However, I doubt[1] he will not come; he often skips me, in these brief visits to Town; skips everybody indeed; being a man solitary and sad, as certain men are, dwelling in an element of gloom,—carrying a bit of Chaos about him, in short, which he is manufacturing into Cosmos!

Alfred is the son of a Lincolnshire Gentleman Farmer, I think; indeed, you see in his verses that he is a native of "moated granges,"[2] and green, fat pastures, not of mountains and their torrents and

---

[1]   *doubt*   Suspect.

[2]   *"moated granges"*   See Tennyson's poem, "Mariana" (above).

storms. He had his breeding at Cambridge, as if for the Law or Church; being master of a small annuity on his Father's decease, he preferred clubbing with his Mother and some Sisters, to live unpromoted and write Poems. In this way he lives still, now here, now there; the family always within reach of London, never in it; he himself making rare and brief visits, lodging in some old comrade's rooms. I think he must be under forty, not much under it.[1] One of the finest-looking men in the world. A great shock of rough dusty-dark hair; bright-laughing hazel eyes; massive aquiline face, most massive yet most delicate; of sallow-brown complexion, almost Indian-looking; clothes cynically loose, free-and-easy;—smokes infinite tobacco. His voice is musical metallic,—fit for loud laughter and piercing wail, and all that may lie between; speech and speculation free and plenteous: I do not meet, in these late decades, such company over a pipe!—We shall see what he will grow to. He is often unwell; very chaotic,—his way is through Chaos and the Bottomless and Pathless; not handy for making out many miles upon.

In Context

Victorian Images of Arthurian Legend

Arthurian romance was a frequent subject of Victorian painting and photography as well as Victorian literature; a sampling is reproduced below.

Julia Margaret Cameron, *The Parting of Lancelot and Guinevere*, 1874.

Julia Margaret Cameron, *Vivien and Merlin*, 1874.

---

[1] *not much under it*   In fact, Tennyson was just about to turn thirty-five when this was written.

John William Waterhouse, *The Lady of Shalott*, 1888.

William Holman Hunt, *The Lady of Shalott*, 1857.

IN CONTEXT

Crimea and the Camera

The Crimean War was the first to be photographed extensively—most notably by Roger Fenton, who spent three months in Crimea in 1855. Both the technology of the time and the demands of Victorian taste militated against shooting scenes of battle directly; unlike Matthew Brady and other photographers of the American Civil War a few years later, Fenton took no pictures of bloody and mangled corpses.

Fenton's most famous photograph of the war, *Valley of the Shadow of Death*, came to be closely associated with Tennyson's famous 1854 poem, "The Charge of the Light Brigade." The connection is not entirely a direct one, however. It was not the valley where the charge occurred that Fenton photographed but another valley in the vicinity—one that had begun to be referred to by soldiers as "the valley of the shadow of death" (in an echo both of Tennyson's poem and of the Bible) because of the frequency with which the Russians shelled it.

Roger Fenton, *General Bosquet Giving Orders to His Staff*, 1855.

Roger Fenton, *Captain Dames*, 1855.

Roger Fenton, *Group of Croat Chiefs*, 1855.

Roger Fenton, *Cookhouse of the 8th Hussars*, 1855.

Roger Fenton, *Valley of the Shadow of Death*, 1855.

CHARLES DARWIN
1809 – 1882

The name Charles Darwin has become synonymous in many minds with the theory of evolution, but theories of evolution did not begin with Darwin. Long before the Victorian era the ancient Greek thinkers Anaximander (611–547 BCE), Empedocles (492–432 BCE), and Aristotle (384–322 BCE) all speculated that life as we know it evolved from sea creatures. In the year Darwin was born, the French biologist Lamarck suggested that species respond and adapt to their environments and then transmit these adaptive traits to their offspring. And in 1850, drawing on the theories of Charles Lyell and Robert Chambers, Tennyson speculated on the idea of evolution in his poetic elegy *In Memoriam*. But when the unassuming British naturalist Charles Darwin articulated his acceptance of the concept of evolution and published his theory of natural selection in 1859 in *On the Origin of Species*, his views provoked comment and controversy internationally. He had offered a detailed, cogent, and plausible theory that many appeared to call into question the idea of divine creation, as well as assumptions about human beings' innate superiority to, and difference from, other creatures.

Charles Robert Darwin was born in 1809 in Shrewsbury, England, to Robert Waring Darwin, a successful doctor (and son of the famous physician, botanist, philosopher, and poet Erasmus Darwin), and Susannah Wedgwood Darwin, daughter of the pottery manufacturer Josiah Wedgwood. Charles distinguished himself neither at school nor at the University of Edinburgh, where his father sent him to study medicine. He often complained throughout his school years of being bored, although he always showed an active interest in and enthusiasm for the natural sciences and for specimen collection. When he left medical school without taking his degree, his father pushed him into a second career track; ironically, the man who would be reviled by religious fundamentalists next studied theology at Cambridge with a view to joining the clergy. Darwin again became bored with his studies, preferring to spend his time collecting and studying beetles. He did make an important friend at Cambridge; his botany professor, John Henslow, recognized Darwin's potential as a natural scientist and recommended him for a position on the H.M.S. Beagle, the ship that would take him around the world to collect biological specimens and data. On this pivotal five-year voyage, Darwin compiled meticulous records of his findings along with an engaging account of his travels and the cultures he encountered, which he subsequently published as *The Voyage of the Beagle* in 1839.

Influenced by James Hutton's geological theories and Charles Lyell's *Principles of Geology*, Darwin also collected fossils and noted the relationship between creatures and their environments, particularly among the unique fauna of the Galapagos Islands. These isolated islands contained species of birds completely unlike those on the mainland, as well as others that closely resembled species of South America. After completing the voyage, Darwin devoted the rest of his career to researching and attempting to explain the differences between such species and their ancestors. After reading Thomas Malthus's *An Essay on the Principle of Population*, he came up with his answer: individuals that are strong enough to survive environmental pressures pass their favorable traits on to successive generations, and thus species adapt and gradually form new species, a process Darwin called "natural selection." Moreover, according to Darwinian theory this process has persisted for millions of years, with all species having evolved from a single life form.

Although he wrote essays on his evolutionary ideas, Darwin did not publish his findings for 20 years, until another naturalist, Alfred Russel Wallace, sent him a paper that included similar conclusions about natural selection. The two agreed to present a joint paper in 1858 to the Linnaean Society in London, and the next year Darwin published *On the Origin of Species. Origin* sold out its entire print run amidst a storm of protest and indignation. In the decade following its publication, responses to the book abounded in the literary world, with authors such as Charles Kingsley and Samuel Butler opposing Darwin, while George Eliot, Thomas Hardy, and Joseph Conrad drew on his theories and modes of explanation.

For the rest of his life, Darwin lived in his country house with his wife, his cousin Emma Wedgwood, whom he had married in 1839, and his many children, studying flora and fauna and publishing his findings. Although the world around him struggled to absorb the impact of his evolutionary theory, Darwin refused to engage in debates about the questions that haunted so many: are humans really evolved from lower life forms, and where does this theory leave the Bible's teachings? In *The Descent of Man, and Selection in Relation to Sex* (1871) Darwin explicitly extended his evolutionary theory to human beings and put forward the notion of sexual selection.

In 1882, after suffering from ill health for many years, quite possibly from a disease acquired during his voyage on the H.M.S. Beagle, Darwin died. He was buried next to Sir Isaac Newton in Westminster Abbey.

⌘ ⌘ ⌘

from *The Voyage of the Beagle*

from CHAPTER 10: TIERRA DEL FUEGO

December 17th, 1832.—Having now finished with Patagonia[1] and the Falkland Islands, I will describe our first arrival in Tierra del Fuego.[2] A little after noon we doubled Cape St. Diego, and entered the famous strait of Le Maire. We kept close to the Fuegian shore, but the outline of the rugged, inhospitable Staten-land was visible amidst the clouds. In the afternoon we anchored in the Bay of Good Success. While entering we were saluted in a manner becoming the inhabitants of this savage land. A group of Fuegians partly concealed by the entangled forest, were perched on a wild point overhanging the sea; and as we passed by, they sprang up and waving their tattered cloaks sent forth a loud and sonorous shout. The savages followed the ship, and just before dark we saw their fire, and again heard their wild cry. The harbour consists of a fine piece of water half surrounded by low rounded mountains of clay-slate, which are covered to the water's edge by one dense gloomy forest. A single glance at the landscape was sufficient to show me how widely different it was from any thing I had ever beheld. At night it blew a gale of wind, and heavy squalls from the mountains swept past us. It would have been a bad time out at sea, and we, as well as others, may call this Good Success Bay.

In the morning the Captain sent a party to communicate with the Fuegians. When we came within hail, one of the four natives who were present advanced to receive us, and began to shout most vehemently, wishing to direct us where to land. When we were on shore the party looked rather alarmed, but continued talking and making gestures with great rapidity. It was without exception the most curious and interesting spectacle I ever beheld. I could not have believed how wide was the difference between savage and civilized man: it is greater than between a wild and domesticated animal, inasmuch as in man there is a greater power of improvement. The chief spokesman was old, and appeared to be the head of the family; the three others were powerful young men, about six feet high. The women and children had been

---

[1]   *Patagonia*   Southern portion of South America.

[2]   *Tierra del Fuego*   Southernmost tip of South America.

sent away. These Fuegians are a very different race from the stunted, miserable wretches farther westward; and they seem closely allied to the famous Patagonians of the Strait of Magellan. Their only garment consists of a mantle made of guanaco[1] skin, with the wool outside; this they wear just thrown over their shoulders, leaving their persons as often exposed as covered. Their skin is of a dirty coppery red colour.

The old man had a fillet of white feathers tied round his head, which partly confined his black, coarse, and entangled hair. His face was crossed by two broad transverse bars; one, painted bright red, reached from ear to ear and included the upper lip; the other, white like chalk, extended above and parallel to the first, so that even his eyelids were thus coloured. The other two men were ornamented by streaks of black powder, made of charcoal. The party altogether closely resembled the devils which come on the stage in plays like Der Freischutz.[2]

Their very attitudes were abject, and the expression of their countenances distrustful, surprised, and startled. After we had presented them with some scarlet cloth, which they immediately tied round their necks, they became good friends. This was shown by the old man patting our breasts, and making a chuckling kind of noise, as people do when feeding chickens. I walked with the old man, and this demonstration of friendship was repeated several times; it was concluded by three hard slaps, which were given me on the breast and back at the same time. He then bared his bosom for me to return the compliment, which being done, he seemed highly pleased. The language of these people, according to our notions, scarcely deserves to be called articulate. Captain Cook[3] has compared it to a man clearing his throat, but certainly no European ever cleared his throat with so many hoarse, guttural, and clicking sounds.

They are excellent mimics: as often as we coughed or yawned, or made any odd motion, they immediately imitated us. Some of our party began to squint and look awry; but one of the young Fuegians (whose whole face was painted black, excepting a white band across his eyes) succeeded in making far more hideous grimaces. They could repeat with perfect correctness each word in any sentence we addressed them, and they remembered such words for some time. Yet we Europeans all know how difficult it is to distinguish apart the sounds in a foreign language. Which of us, for instance, could follow an American Indian through a sentence of more than three words? All savages appear to possess, to an uncommon degree, this power of mimicry. I was told, almost in the same words, of the same ludicrous habit among the Caffres:[4] the Australians, likewise, have long been notorious for being able to imitate and describe the gait of any man, so that he may be recognized. How can this faculty be explained? Is it a consequence of the more practised habits of perception and keener senses, common to all men in a savage state, as compared with those long civilized?

When a song was struck up by our party, I thought the Fuegians would have fallen down with astonishment. With equal surprise they viewed our dancing; but one of the young men, when asked, had no objection to a little waltzing. Little accustomed to Europeans as they appeared to be, yet they knew and dreaded our firearms; nothing would tempt them to take a gun in their hands. They begged for knives, calling them by the Spanish word "cuchilla." They explained also what they wanted, by acting as if they had a piece of blubber in their mouth, and then pretending to cut instead of tear it.

I have not as yet noticed the Fuegians whom we had on board. During the former voyage of the Adventure and Beagle in 1826 to 1830, Captain Fitz Roy[5] seized on a party of natives, as hostages for the loss of a boat, which had been stolen, to the great jeopardy of a party employed on the survey; and some of these natives, as well as a child whom he bought for a pearl-button, he took with him to England, determining to educate them and instruct them in religion at his own expense. To settle these natives in their own country, was one chief inducement to Captain Fitz Roy to undertake our present voyage; and before the Admiralty had resolved to send out this expedition, Captain Fitz Roy had generously chartered a vessel, and would himself have taken them back. The natives were accompanied by a missionary, R. Matthews; of whom and of the natives,

[1] guanaco Wild llama, the coat of which is a red-brown wool.

[2] Der Freischutz 1820 opera by Carl Maria von Weber.

[3] Captain Cook James Cook (1728–79), English explorer.

[4] Caffres Kaffirs, a common term for native Africans (now considered to be derogatory).

[5] Captain Fitz Roy Robert Fitz Roy (1805–65).

Captain Fitz Roy has published a full and excellent account. Two men, one of whom died in England of the smallpox, a boy and a little girl, were originally taken; and we had now on board, York Minster, Jemmy Button (whose name expresses his purchase-money), and Fuegia Basket. York Minster was a full-grown, short, thick, powerful man: his disposition was reserved, taciturn, morose, and when excited violently passionate; his affections were very strong towards a few friends on board; his intellect good. Jemmy Button was a universal favourite, but likewise passionate; the expression of his face at once showed his nice disposition. He was merry and often laughed, and was remarkably sympathetic with any one in pain: when the water was rough, I was often a little seasick, and he used to come to me and say in a plaintive voice, "Poor, poor fellow!" but the notion, after his aquatic life, of a man being sea-sick, was too ludicrous, and he was generally obliged to turn on one side to hide a smile or laugh, and then he would repeat his "Poor, poor fellow!" He was of a patriotic disposition; and he liked to praise his own tribe and country, in which he truly said there were "plenty of trees," and he abused all the other tribes: he stoutly declared that there was no Devil in his land. Jemmy was short, thick, and fat, but vain of his personal appearance; he used to wear gloves, his hair was neatly cut, and he was distressed if his well-polished shoes were dirtied. He was fond of admiring himself in a looking-glass; and a merry-faced little Indian boy from the Rio Negro, whom we had for some months on board, soon perceived this, and used to mock him: Jemmy, who was always rather jealous of the attention paid to this little boy, did not at all like this, and used to say, with rather a contemptuous twist of his head, "Too much skylark." It seems yet wonderful to me, when I think over all his many good qualities, that he should have been of the same race, and doubtless partaken of the same character, with the miserable, degraded savages whom we first met here. Lastly, Fuegia Basket was a nice, modest, reserved young girl, with a rather pleasing but sometimes sullen expression, and very quick in learning anything, especially languages. This she showed in picking up some Portuguese and Spanish, when left on shore for only a short time at Rio de Janeiro and Monte Video, and in her knowledge of English. York Minster was very jealous of any attention paid to her; for it was clear he determined to marry her

as soon as they were settled on shore.

Although all three could both speak and understand a good deal of English, it was singularly difficult to obtain much information from them, concerning the habits of their countrymen: this was partly owing to their apparent difficulty in understanding the simplest alternative. Every one accustomed to very young children, knows how seldom one can get an answer even to so simple a question as whether a thing is black *or* white; the idea of black or white seems alternately to fill their minds. So it was with these Fuegians, and hence it was generally impossible to find out, by cross-questioning, whether one had rightly understood anything which they had asserted. Their sight was remarkably acute: it is well known that sailors, from long practice, can make out a distant object much better than a landsman; but both York and Jemmy were much superior to any sailor on board: several times they have declared what some distant object has been, and though doubted by every one, they have proved right, when it has been examined through a telescope. They were quite conscious of this power; and Jemmy, when he had any little quarrel with the officer on watch, would say, "Me see ship, me no tell."

It was interesting to watch the conduct of the savages, when we landed, towards Jemmy Button: they immediately perceived the difference between him and ourselves, and held much conversation one with another on the subject. The old man addressed a long harangue to Jemmy, which it seems was to invite him to stay with them. But Jemmy understood very little of their language, and was, moreover, thoroughly ashamed of his countrymen. When York Minster afterwards came on shore, they noticed him in the same way, and told him he ought to shave; yet he had not twenty dwarf hairs on his face, whilst we all wore our untrimmed beards. They examined the colour of his skin, and compared it with ours. One of our arms being bared, they expressed the liveliest surprise and admiration at its whiteness, just in the same way in which I have seen the ourang-outang do at the Zoological Gardens. We thought that they mistook two or three of the officers, who were rather shorter and fairer, though adorned with large beards, for the ladies of our party. The tallest among the Fuegians was evidently much pleased at his height being noticed. When placed back to back with the tallest of the boat's crew, he tried his best to edge on higher ground, and to stand on tiptoe. He opened his mouth to show his teeth, and turned his face for a side view; and all this was done with such alacrity, that I dare say he thought himself the handsomest man in Tierra del Fuego. After our first feeling of grave astonishment was over, nothing could be more ludicrous than the odd mixture of surprise and imitation which these savages every moment exhibited. ...

December 25th.—Close by the cove, a pointed hill, called Rater's Peak, rises to the height of 1700 feet. The surrounding islands all consist of conical masses of greenstone, associated sometimes with less regular hills of baked and altered clay-slate. This part of Tierra del Fuego may be considered as the extremity of the submerged chain of mountains already alluded to. The cove takes its name of "Wigwam" from some of the Fuegian habitations; but every bay in the neighbourhood might be so called with equal propriety. The inhabitants, living chiefly upon shell-fish, are obliged constantly to change their place of residence; but they return at intervals to the same spots, as is evident from the piles of old shells, which must often amount to many tons in weight. These heaps can be distinguished at a long distance by the bright green colour of certain plants, which invariably grow on them. Among these may be enumerated the wild celery and scurvy grass, two very serviceable plants, the use of which has not been discovered by the natives.

The Fuegian wigwam resembles, in size and dimensions, a haycock.[1] It merely consists of a few broken branches stuck in the ground, and very imperfectly thatched on one side with a few tufts of grass and rushes. The whole cannot be the work of an hour, and it is only used for a few days. At Goeree Roads I saw a place where one of these naked men had slept, which absolutely offered no more cover than the form of a hare. The man was evidently living by himself, and York Minster said he was "very bad man," and that probably he had stolen something. On the west coast, however, the wigwams are rather better, for they are covered with seal-skins. We were detained here several days by the bad weather. The climate is certainly wretched: the summer solstice was now passed, yet every day snow fell on the hills, and in the valleys there was rain, accompanied by sleet. The thermometer generally stood about 45°, but in the night fell to 38° or 40°. From the damp

and boisterous state of the atmosphere, not cheered by a gleam of sunshine, one fancied the climate even worse than it really was.

While going one day on shore near Wollaston Island, we pulled alongside a canoe with six Fuegians. These were the most abject and miserable creatures I anywhere beheld. On the east coast the natives, as we have seen, have guanaco cloaks, and on the west, they possess seal-skins. Amongst these central tribes the men generally have an otter-skin, or some small scrap about as large as a pocket-handkerchief, which is barely sufficient to cover their backs as low down as their loins. It is laced across the breast by strings, and according as the wind blows, it is shifted from side to side. But these Fuegians in the canoe were quite naked, and even one full-grown woman was absolutely so. It was raining heavily, and the fresh water, together with the spray, trickled down her body. In another harbour not far distant, a woman, who was suckling a recently-born child, came one day alongside the vessel, and remained there out of mere curiosity, whilst the sleet fell and thawed on her naked bosom, and on the skin of her naked baby! These poor wretches were stunted in their growth, their hideous faces bedaubed with white paint, their skins filthy and greasy, their hair entangled, their voices discordant, and their gestures violent. Viewing such men, one can hardly make oneself believe that they are fellow-creatures, and inhabitants of the same world. It is a common subject of conjecture what pleasure in life some of the lower animals can enjoy: how much more reasonably the same question may be asked with respect to these barbarians! At night, five or six human beings, naked and scarcely protected from the wind and rain of this tempestuous climate, sleep on the wet ground coiled up like animals. Whenever it is low water, winter or summer, night or day, they must rise to pick shellfish from the rocks; and the women either dive to collect sea-eggs, or sit patiently in their canoes, and with a baited hairline without any hook, jerk out little fish. If a seal is killed, or the floating carcass of a putrid whale discovered, it is a feast; and such miserable food is assisted by a few tasteless berries and fungi.

They often suffer from famine: I heard Mr. Low, a sealingmaster intimately acquainted with the natives of this country, give a curious account of the state of a party of one hundred and fifty natives on the west coast,

---

[1] *haycock* Haystack.

who were very thin and in great distress. A succession of gales prevented the women from getting shell-fish on the rocks, and they could not go out in their canoes to catch seal. A small party of these men one morning set out, and the other Indians explained to him, that they were going a four days' journey for food: on their return, Low went to meet them, and he found them excessively tired, each man carrying a great square piece of putrid whales-blubber with a hole in the middle, through which they put their heads, like the Gauchos[1] do through their ponchos or cloaks. As soon as the blubber was brought into a wigwam, an old man cut off thin slices, and muttering over them, broiled them for a minute, and distributed them to the famished party, who during this time preserved a profound silence. Mr. Low believes that whenever a whale is cast on shore, the natives bury large pieces of it in the sand, as a resource in time of famine; and a native boy, whom he had on board, once found a stock thus buried. . . .

The different tribes have no government or chief; yet each is surrounded by other hostile tribes, speaking different dialects, and separated from each other only by a deserted border or neutral territory: the cause of their warfare appears to be the means of subsistence. Their country is a broken mass of wild rocks, lofty hills, and useless forests: and these are viewed through mists and endless storms. The habitable land is reduced to the stones on the beach; in search of food they are compelled unceasingly to wander from spot to spot, and so steep is the coast, that they can only move about in their wretched canoes. They cannot know the feeling of having a home, and still less that of domestic affection; for the husband is to the wife as a brutal master to a laborious slave. Was a more horrid deed ever perpetrated, than that witnessed on the west coast by Byron,[2] who saw a wretched mother pick up her bleeding dying infant-boy, whom her husband had mercilessly dashed on the stones for dropping a basket of sea-eggs! How little can the higher powers of the mind be brought into play: what is there for imagination to picture, for reason to compare, for judgment to decide upon? To knock a

limpet from the rock does not require even cunning, that lowest power of the mind. Their skill in some respects may be compared to the instinct of animals; for it is not improved by experience: the canoe, their most ingenious work, poor as it is, has remained the same, as we know from Drake,[3] for the last two hundred and fifty years. Whilst beholding these savages, one asks, whence have they come? What could have tempted, or what change compelled a tribe of men, to leave the fine regions of the north, to travel down the Cordillera or backbone of America, to invent and build canoes, which are not used by the tribes of Chile, Peru, and Brazil, and then to enter on one of the most inhospitable countries within the limits of the globe? Although such reflections must at first seize on the mind, yet we may feel sure that they are partly erroneous. There is no reason to believe that the Fuegians decrease in number; therefore we must suppose that they enjoy a sufficient share of happiness, of whatever kind it may be, to render life worth having. Nature by making habit omnipotent, and its effects hereditary, has fitted the Fuegian to the climate and the productions of his miserable country. . . .

January 19th, 1833—Three whale-boats and the yawl,[4] with a party of twenty-eight, started under the command of Captain Fitz Roy. In the afternoon we entered the eastern mouth of the channel, and shortly afterwards found a snug little cove concealed by some surrounding islets. Here we pitched our tents and lighted our fires. Nothing could look more comfortable than this scene. The glassy water of the little harbour, with the branches of the trees hanging over the rocky beach, the boats at anchor, the tents supported by the crossed oars, and the smoke curling up the wooded valley, formed a picture of quiet retirement. The next day (20th) we smoothly glided onwards in our little fleet, and came to a more inhabited district. Few if any of these natives could ever have seen a white man; certainly nothing could exceed their astonishment at the apparition of the four boats. Fires were lighted on every point (hence the name of Tierra del Fuego, or the land of fire), both to attract our attention and to spread far and wide the news. Some of the men ran for miles along the shore. I shall never forget how wild and savage one

---

[1] *Gauchos* South American horsemen of mixed Native American and European descent.

[2] *Byron* John Byron (1723–86), British vice-admiral and explorer, and grandfather of the poet George Gordon, Lord Byron. See his *Narrative of Great Distresses on the Shores of Patagonia* (1768).

[3] *Drake* Sir Francis Drake (c. 1540–96), English explorer. In 1577 his travels took him past Tierra del Fuego.

[4] *yawl* Small boat.

group appeared: suddenly four or five men came to the edge of an overhanging cliff; they were absolutely naked, and their long hair streamed about their faces; they held rugged staffs in their hands, and, springing from the ground, they waved their arms round their heads, and sent forth the most hideous yells.

At dinner-time we landed among a party of Fuegians. At first they were not inclined to be friendly; for until the Captain pulled in ahead of the other boats, they kept their slings in their hands. We soon, however, delighted them by trifling presents, such as tying red tape round their heads. They liked our biscuit: but one of the savages touched with his finger some of the meat preserved in tin cases which I was eating, and feeling it soft and cold, showed as much disgust at it, as I should have done at putrid blubber. ...

On the last day of February in the succeeding year (1834), the *Beagle* anchored in a beautiful little cove at the eastern entrance of the Beagle Channel. Captain Fitz Roy determined on the bold, and as it proved successful, attempt to beat against the westerly winds by the same route, which we had followed in the boats to the settlement at Woollya. We did not see many natives until we were near Ponsonby Sound, where we were followed by ten or twelve canoes. The natives did not at all understand the reason of our tacking, and, instead of meeting us at each tack, vainly strove to follow us in our zig-zag course. I was amused at finding what a difference the circumstance of being quite superior in force made, in the interest of beholding these savages. While in the boats I got to hate the very sound of their voices, so much trouble did they give us. The first and last word was "yammerschooner." When, entering some quiet little cove, we have looked round and thought to pass a quiet night, the odious word "yammerschooner" has shrilly sounded from some gloomy nook, and then the little signal-smoke has curled up to spread the news far and wide. On leaving some place we have said to each other, "Thank Heaven, we have at last fairly left these wretches!" when one more faint halloo from an all-powerful voice, heard at a prodigious distance, would reach our ears, and clearly could we distinguish— "yammerschooner." But now, the more Fuegians the merrier; and very merry work it was. Both parties laughing, wondering, gaping at each other; we pitying them, for giving us good fish and crabs for rags, *et cetera*;

they grasping at the chance of finding people so foolish as to exchange such splendid ornaments for a good supper. It was most amusing to see the undisguised smile of satisfaction with which one young woman with her face painted black, tied several bits of scarlet cloth round her head with rushes. Her husband, who enjoyed the very universal privilege in this country of possessing two wives, evidently became jealous of all the attention paid to his young wife; and, after a consultation with his naked beauties, was paddled away by them.

Some of the Fuegians plainly showed that they had a fair notion of barter. I gave one man a large nail (a most valuable present) without making any signs for a return; but he immediately picked out two fish, and handed them up on the point of his spear. If any present was designed for one canoe, and it fell near another, it was invariably given to the right owner. The Fuegian boy, whom Mr. Low had on board, showed, by going into the most violent passion, that he quite understood the reproach of being called a liar, which in truth he was. We were this time, as on all former occasions, much surprised at the little notice, or rather none whatever, which was taken of many things, the use of which must have been evident to the natives. Simple circumstances—such as the beauty of scarlet cloth or blue beads, the absence of women, our care in washing ourselves—excited their admiration far more than any grand or complicated object, such as our ship. Bougainville[1] has well remarked concerning these people, that they treat the "chefs d'oeuvres de l'industrie humaine, comme ils traitent les loix de la nature et ses phenomenes."[2]

On the 5th of March, we anchored in the cove at Woollya, but we saw not a soul there. We were alarmed at this, for the natives in Ponsonby Sound showed by gestures, that there had been fighting; and we afterwards heard that the dreaded Oens men had made a descent. Soon a canoe, with a little flag flying, was seen approaching, with one of the men in it washing the paint off his face. This man was poor Jemmy—now a thin haggard savage, with long disordered hair, and naked, except a bit of a blanket round his waist. We did not recognize him till he was close to us; for he was ashamed

---

[1] *Bougainville* Louis de Bougainville (1729–1811), French navigator.

[2] *chefs d'oeuvres ... phenomenes* French: masterworks of human industry as they treat the laws of nature and its phenomena.

684   CHARLES DARWIN

of himself, and turned his back to the ship. We had left him plump, fat, clean, and well dressed—I never saw so complete and grievous a change. As soon however as he was clothed, and the first flurry was over, things wore a good appearance. He dined with Captain Fitz Roy, and ate his dinner as tidily as formerly. He told us he had "too much" (meaning enough) to eat, that he was not cold, that his relations were very good people, and that he did not wish to go back to England: in the evening we found out the cause of this great change in Jemmy's feelings, in the arrival of his young and nice-looking wife. With his usual good feeling, he brought two beautiful otter-skins for two of his best friends, and some spear-heads and arrows made with his own hands for the Captain. He said he had built a canoe for himself, and he boasted that he could talk a little of his own language! But it is a most singular fact, that he appears to have taught all his tribe some English: an old man spontaneously announced "Jemmy Button's wife." Jemmy had lost all his property. He told us that York Minster had built a large canoe, and with his wife Fuegia, had several months since gone to his own country, and had taken farewell by an act of consummate villainy; he persuaded Jemmy and his mother to come with him, and then on the way deserted them by night, stealing every article of their property.

Jemmy went to sleep on shore, and in the morning returned, and remained on board till the ship got under weigh, which frightened his wife, who continued crying violently till he got into his canoe. He returned loaded with valuable property. Every soul on board was heartily sorry to shake hands with him for the last time. I do not now doubt that he will be as happy as, perhaps happier than, if he had never left his own country. Every one must sincerely hope that Captain Fitz Roy's noble hope may be fulfilled, of being rewarded for the many generous sacrifices which he made for these Fuegians, by some shipwrecked sailor being protected by the descendants of Jemmy Button and his tribe! When Jemmy reached the shore, he lighted a signal fire, and the smoke curled up, bidding us a last and long farewell, as the ship stood on her course into the open sea.

The perfect equality among the individuals composing the Fuegian tribes, must for a long time retard their civilization. As we see those animals, whose instinct compels them to live in society and obey a chief, are most capable of improvement, so is it with the races of mankind. Whether we look at it as a cause or a consequence, the more civilized always have the most artificial governments. For instance, the inhabitants of Otaheite,[1] who, when first discovered, were governed by hereditary kings, had arrived at a far higher grade than another branch of the same people, the New Zealanders—who, although benefited by being compelled to turn their attention to agriculture, were republicans in the most absolute sense. In Tierra del Fuego, until some chief shall arise with power sufficient to secure any acquired advantage, such as the domesticated animals, it seems scarcely possible that the political state of the country can be improved. At present, even a piece of cloth given to one is torn into shreds and distributed; and no one individual becomes richer than another. On the other hand, it is difficult to understand how a chief can arise till there is property of some sort by which he might manifest his superiority and increase his power.

I believe, in this extreme part of South America, man exists in a lower state of improvement than in any other part of the world. The South Sea islanders of the two races inhabiting the Pacific, are comparatively civilized. The Esquimaux,[2] in his subterranean hut, enjoys some of the comforts of life, and in his canoe, when fully equipped, manifests much skill. Some of the tribes of southern Africa, prowling about in search of roots, and living concealed on the wild and arid plains, are sufficiently wretched. The Australian, in the simplicity of the arts of life, comes nearest the Fuegian: he can, however, boast of his boomerang, his spear and throwing-stick, his method of climbing trees, of tracking animals, and of hunting. Although the Australian may be superior in acquirements, it by no means follows that he is likewise superior in mental capacity: indeed, from what I saw of the Fuegians when on board, and from what I have read of the Australians, I should think the case was exactly the reverse.

---

[1] *Otaheite* Tahiti.

[2] *Esquimaux* Inuk, or Inuit person.

from CHAPTER 17: GALAPAGOS ARCHIPELAGO[1]

… The natural history of these islands is eminently curious, and well deserves attention. Most of the organic productions are aboriginal creations, found nowhere else; there is even a difference between the inhabitants of the different islands; yet all show a marked relationship with those of America, though separated from that continent by an open space of ocean, between 500 and 600 miles in width. The archipelago is a little world within itself, or rather a satellite attached to America, whence it has derived a few stray colonists, and has received the general character of its indigenous productions. Considering the small size of these islands, we feel the more astonished at the number of their aboriginal beings, and at their confined range. Seeing every height crowned with its crater, and the boundaries of most of the lava-streams still distinct, we are led to believe that within a period, geologically recent, the unbroken ocean was here spread out. Hence, both in space and time, we seem to be brought somewhat near to that great fact—that mystery of mysteries—the first appearance of new beings on this earth. …

The tortoises, when purposely moving towards any point, travel by night and day, and arrive at their journey's end much sooner than would be expected. The inhabitants, from observing marked individuals, consider that they travel a distance of about eight miles in two or three days. One large tortoise, which I watched, walked at the rate of sixty yards in ten minutes, that is 360 yards in the hour, or four miles a day—allowing a little time for it to eat on the road. During the breeding season, when the male and female are together, the male utters a hoarse roar or bellowing, which, it is said, can be heard at the distance of more than a hundred yards. The female never uses her voice, and the male only at these times; so that when the people hear this noise, they know that the two are together. They were at this time (October) laying their eggs. The female, where the soil is sandy, deposits them together, and covers them up with sand; but where the ground is rocky she drops them indiscriminately in any hole: Mr. Bynoe found seven placed in a fissure. The egg is white and spherical; one which I measured was seven inches and three-eighths in circumference, and therefore larger than a hen's egg. The young tortoises, as soon as they are hatched, fall a prey in great numbers to the carrion-feeding buzzard. The old ones seem generally to die from accidents, as from falling down precipices: at least, several of the inhabitants told me, that they had never found one dead without some evident cause. The inhabitants believe that these animals are absolutely deaf; certainly they do not overhear a person walking close behind them. I was always amused when overtaking one of these great monsters, as it was quietly pacing along, to see how suddenly, the instant I passed, it would draw in its head and legs, and uttering a deep hiss fall to the ground with a heavy sound, as if struck dead. I frequently got on their backs, and then giving a few raps on the hinder part of their shells, they would rise up and walk away—but I found it very difficult to keep my balance. The flesh of this animal is largely employed, both fresh and salted; and a beautifully clear oil is prepared from the fat. When a tortoise is caught, the man makes a slit in the skin near its tail, so as to see inside its body, whether the fat under the dorsal plate is thick. If it is not, the animal is liberated; and it is said to recover soon from this strange operation. In order to secure the tortoises, it is not sufficient to turn them like turtle, for they are often able to get on their legs again.

There can be little doubt that this tortoise is an aboriginal inhabitant of the Galapagos; for it is found on all, or nearly all, the islands, even on some of the smaller ones where there is no water; had it been an imported species, this would hardly have been the case in a group which has been so little frequented. …

… [T]his archipelago, though standing in the Pacific Ocean, is zoologically part of America.

If this character were owing merely to immigrants from America, there would be little remarkable in it; but we see that a vast majority of all the land animals, and that more than half of the flowering plants, are aboriginal productions. It was most striking to be surrounded by new birds, new reptiles, new shells, new insects, new plants, and yet by innumerable trifling details of structure, and even by the tones of voice and plumage of the birds, to have the temperate plains of Patagonia, or the hot dry deserts of northern Chile, vividly brought before my eyes. Why, on these small points of land, which

---

[1] *Galapagos Archipelago*   Series of islands off the coast of Ecuador, named after the Spanish word for tortoise.

within a late geological period must have been covered by the ocean, which are formed of basaltic lava, and therefore differ in geological character from the American continent, and which are placed under a peculiar climate—why were their aboriginal inhabitants, associated, I may add, in different proportions both in kind and number from those on the continent, and therefore acting on each other in a different manner—why were they created on American types of organization? It is probable that the islands of the Cape de Verd[1] group resemble, in all their physical conditions, far more closely the Galapagos Islands than these latter physically resemble the coast of America; yet the aboriginal inhabitants of the two groups are totally unlike; those of the Cape de Verd Islands bearing the impress of Africa, as the inhabitants of the Galapagos Archipelago are stamped with that of America.

I have not as yet noticed by far the most remarkable feature in the natural history of this archipelago; it is, that the different islands to a considerable extent are inhabited by a different set of beings. My attention was first called to this fact by the Vice-Governor, Mr. Lawson, declaring that the tortoises differed from the different islands, and that he could with certainty tell from which island any one was brought. I did not for some time pay sufficient attention to this statement, and I had already partially mingled together the collections from two of the islands. I never dreamed that islands, about fifty or sixty miles apart, and most of them in sight of each other, formed of precisely the same rocks, placed under a quite similar climate, rising to a nearly equal height, would have been differently tenanted; but we shall soon see that this is the case. It is the fate of most voyagers, no sooner to discover what is most interesting in any locality, than they are hurried from it; but I ought, perhaps, to be thankful that I obtained sufficient material to establish this most remarkable fact in the distribution of organic beings.

The inhabitants, as I have said, state that they can distinguish the tortoises from the different islands; and that they differ not only in size, but in other characters. Captain Porter[2] has described those from Charles and from the nearest island to it, namely, Hood Island, as having their shells in front thick and turned up like a Spanish saddle, whilst the tortoises from James Island are rounder, blacker, and have a better taste when cooked. M. Bibron,[3] moreover, informs me that he has seen what he considers two distinct species of tortoise from the Galapagos, but he does not know from which islands. The specimens that I brought from three islands were young ones; and probably owing to this cause, neither Mr. Gray[4] nor myself could find in them any specific differences. I have remarked that the marine Amblyrhynchus[5] was larger at Albemarle Island than elsewhere; and M. Bibron informs me that he has seen two distinct aquatic species of this genus; so that the different islands probably have their representative species or races of the Amblyrhynchus, as well as of the tortoise.

—1839

---

[1] *Cape de Verd* Cape Verde, a group of islands off the northwest coast of Africa, due west of Senegal.

[2] *Captain Porter* David Porter (1780–1843), captain of the *Essex*, who recorded his travels in *Journal of a Cruise* (1812).

[3] *M. Bibron* (Monsieur) Gabriel Bibron (1806–48), French zoologist.

[4] *Mr. Gray* Asa Gray (1810–88), a Harvard botanist and one of Darwin's strongest supporters.

[5] *marine Amblyrhynchus* Galapagos marine iguana (*Amblyrhynchus cristatus*).

IN CONTEXT

Images from *The Beagle*

There are extensive visual records of Darwin's voyages—perhaps most notably, the watercolor drawings of Conrad Martens, who was for nine months official artist on the *Beagle*. Several of these drawings were widely circulated in Victorian times in the form of engravings by Thomas Landseer that were based on original sketches by Martens and others sailing with Darwin.

Charles Darwin, 1840 (sketch by George Richmond).

Crossing the Line, 1832 (engraving by T. Landseer after a sketch by A. Earle).
It was a sailors' tradition to celebrate upon crossing the equator with mummery,
roughhousing, and practical jokes.

Fuegian of the Yapoo Tekeenica Tribe,
1832 (watercolor by Conrad Martens).

Fuegians at the Entrance to the Beagle Channel, 1832 (watercolor by Conrad Martens).

The Beagle in Murray Narrow, Tierra del Fuego, 1833 (watercolor by Conrad Martens).

Charles Island, Galapagos, 1835 (watercolor by Conrad Martens).

from *On the Origin of Species*

INTRODUCTION

When on board H.M.S. "Beagle," as naturalist,[1] I was much struck with certain facts in the distribution of the inhabitants of South America, and in the geological relations of the present to the past inhabitants of that continent. These facts seemed to me to throw some light on the origin of species—that mystery of mysteries, as it has been called by one of our greatest philosophers. On my return home, it occurred to me, in 1837, that something might perhaps be made out on this question by patiently accumulating and reflecting on all sorts of facts which could possibly have any bearing on it. After five years' work I allowed myself to speculate on the subject, and drew up some short notes; these I enlarged in 1844 into a sketch of the conclusions, which then seemed to me probable: from that period to the present day I have steadily pursued the same object. I hope that I may be excused for entering on these personal details, as I give them to show that I

have not been hasty in coming to a decision.

My work is now nearly finished; but as it will take me two or three more years to complete it, and as my health is far from strong, I have been urged to publish this abstract. I have more especially been induced to do this, as Mr. Wallace,[2] who is now studying the natural history of the Malay archipelago, has arrived at almost exactly the same general conclusions that I have on the origin of species. Last year he sent to me a memoir on this subject, with a request that I would forward it to Sir Charles Lyell,[3] who sent it to the Linnean Society,[4] and it is published in the third volume of the Journal of that Society. Sir C. Lyell and Dr. Hooker,[5] who both knew of my work—the latter having read my sketch of 1844—honoured me by thinking it advisable to publish, with Mr. Wallace's excellent memoir, some brief extracts from my manuscripts.

---

[1]   *When on board ... naturalist* Darwin traveled on the *Beagle* between 1831 and 1836.

[2]   *Mr. Wallace* Alfred Russel Wallace (1823–1913), English naturalist and social critic.

[3]   *Sir Charles Lyell* British geologist (1797–1875).

[4]   *Linnean Society* Prominent London scientific society.

[5]   *Dr. Hooker* Joseph Dalton Hooker (1817–1911), botanist and friend of Darwin.

This abstract, which I now publish, must necessarily be imperfect. I cannot here give references and authorities for my several statements; and I must trust to the reader reposing some confidence in my accuracy. No doubt errors will have crept in, though I hope I have always been cautious in trusting to good authorities alone. I can here give only the general conclusions at which I have arrived, with a few facts in illustration, but which, I hope, in most cases will suffice. No one can feel more sensible than I do of the necessity of hereafter publishing in detail all the facts, with references, on which my conclusions have been grounded; and I hope in a future work to do this. For I am well aware that scarcely a single point is discussed in this volume on which facts cannot be adduced,[1] often apparently leading to conclusions directly opposite to those at which I have arrived. A fair result can be obtained only by fully stating and balancing the facts and arguments on both sides of each question; and this cannot possibly be here done.

I much regret that want of space prevents my having the satisfaction of acknowledging the generous assistance which I have received from very many naturalists, some of them personally unknown to me. I cannot, however, let this opportunity pass without expressing my deep obligations to Dr. Hooker, who for the last fifteen years has aided me in every possible way by his large stores of knowledge and his excellent judgment.

In considering the origin of species, it is quite conceivable that a naturalist, reflecting on the mutual affinities of organic beings, on their embryological relations, their geographical distribution, geological succession, and other such facts, might come to the conclusion that each species had not been independently created, but had descended, like varieties, from other species. Nevertheless, such a conclusion, even if well founded, would be unsatisfactory, until it could be shown how the innumerable species inhabiting this world have been modified, so as to acquire that perfection of structure and coadaptation which most justly excites our admiration. Naturalists continually refer to external conditions, such as climate, food, *et cetera*, as the only possible cause of variation. In one very limited sense, as we shall hereafter see, this may be true; but it is preposterous to attribute to mere external conditions,

the structure, for instance, of the woodpecker, with its feet, tail, beak, and tongue, so admirably adapted to catch insects under the bark of trees. In the case of the mistletoe, which draws its nourishment from certain trees, which has seeds that must be transported by certain birds, and which has flowers with separate sexes absolutely requiring the agency of certain insects to bring pollen from one flower to the other, it is equally preposterous to account for the structure of this parasite, with its relations to several distinct organic beings, by the effects of external conditions, or of habit, or of the volition of the plant itself.

The author of the "Vestiges of Creation"[2] would, I presume, say that, after a certain unknown number of generations, some bird had given birth to a woodpecker, and some plant to the mistletoe, and that these had been produced perfect as we now see them; but this assumption seems to me to be no explanation, for it leaves the case of the coadaptations of organic beings to each other and to their physical conditions of life, untouched and unexplained.

It is, therefore, of the highest importance to gain a clear insight into the means of modification and coadaptation. At the commencement of my observations it seemed to me probable that a careful study of domesticated animals and of cultivated plants would offer the best chance of making out this obscure problem. Nor have I been disappointed; in this and in all other perplexing cases I have invariably found that our knowledge, imperfect though it be, of variation under domestication, afforded the best and safest clue. I may venture to express my conviction of the high value of such studies, although they have been very commonly neglected by naturalists.

From these considerations, I shall devote the first chapter of this abstract to variation under domestication. We shall thus see that a large amount of hereditary modification is at least possible, and, what is equally or more important, we shall see how great is the power of man in accumulating by his selection successive slight variations. I will then pass on to the variability of species in a state of nature; but I shall, unfortunately, be compelled to treat this subject far too briefly, as it can be

---

[1] *adduced* Brought forth.

[2] *"Vestiges of Creation"* 1844 book, published anonymously but written by Robert Chambers, which suggests that progressive evolution is God's act of creation through geological time.

treated properly only by giving long catalogues of facts. We shall, however, be enabled to discuss what circumstances are most favourable to variation. In the next chapter the struggle for existence amongst all organic beings throughout the world, which inevitably follows from their high geometrical ratio of increase, will be treated of. This is the doctrine of Malthus,[1] applied to the whole animal and vegetable kingdoms. As many more individuals of each species are born than can possibly survive; and as, consequently, there is a frequently recurring struggle for existence, it follows that any being, if it vary however slightly in any manner profitable to itself, under the complex and sometimes varying conditions of life, will have a better chance of surviving, and thus be *naturally selected*. From the strong principle of inheritance, any selected variety will tend to propagate its new and modified form.

This fundamental subject of natural selection will be treated at some length in the fourth chapter; and we shall then see how natural selection almost inevitably causes much extinction of the less improved forms of life and induces what I have called divergence of character. In the next chapter I shall discuss the complex and little known laws of variation and of correlation of growth. In the four succeeding chapters, the most apparent and gravest difficulties on the theory will be given: namely, first, the difficulties of transitions, or in understanding how a simple being or a simple organ can be changed and perfected into a highly developed being or elaborately constructed organ; secondly the subject of instinct, or the mental powers of animals, thirdly, hybridism, or the infertility of species and the fertility of varieties when intercrossed; and fourthly, the imperfection of the geological record. In the next chapter I shall consider the geological succession of organic beings throughout time; in the eleventh and twelfth, their geographical distribution throughout space; in the thirteenth, their classification or mutual affinities, both when mature and in an embryonic condition. In the last chapter I shall give a brief recapitulation of the whole work, and a few concluding remarks.

No one ought to feel surprise at much remaining as yet unexplained in regard to the origin of species and varieties, if he makes due allowance for our profound ignorance in regard to the mutual relations of all the beings which live around us. Who can explain why one species ranges widely and is very numerous, and why another allied species has a narrow range and is rare? Yet these relations are of the highest importance, for they determine the present welfare, and, as I believe, the future success and modification of every inhabitant of this world. Still less do we know of the mutual relations of the innumerable inhabitants of the world during the many past geological epochs in its history. Although much remains obscure, and will long remain obscure, I can entertain no doubt, after the most deliberate study and dispassionate judgment of which I am capable, that the view which most naturalists entertain, and which I formerly entertained—namely, that each species has been independently created—is erroneous. I am fully convinced that species are not immutable; but that those belonging to what are called the same genera[2] are lineal descendants of some other and generally extinct species, in the same manner as the acknowledged varieties of any one species are the descendants of that species. Furthermore, I am convinced that natural selection has been the main but not exclusive means of modification.

from CHAPTER 3: STRUGGLE FOR EXISTENCE

Before entering on the subject of this chapter, I must make a few preliminary remarks, to show how the struggle for existence bears on natural selection. It has been seen in the last chapter that amongst organic beings in a state of nature there is some individual variability; indeed I am not aware that this has ever been disputed. It is immaterial for us whether a multitude of doubtful forms be called species or sub-species or varieties; what rank, for instance, the two or three hundred doubtful forms of British plants are entitled to hold, if the existence of any well-marked varieties be admitted. But the mere existence of individual variability and of some few well-marked varieties, though necessary as the foundation for the work, helps us but little in understanding how species arise in nature. How have all those exquisite adaptations of one part of the organisation to another part, and to the conditions of

---

[1] *Malthus* Thomas Robert Malthus (1766–1834), who theorized in his 1798 work *An Essay on the Principle of Population* that the human population would eventually outstrip its food resources.

[2] *genera* Latin: groupings of species. Plural of "genus."

life, and of one distinct organic being to another being, been perfected? We see these beautiful co-adaptations most plainly in the woodpecker and mistletoe; and only a little less plainly in the humblest parasite which clings to the hairs of a quadruped or feathers of a bird; in the structure of the beetle which dives through the water; in the plumed seed which is wafted by the gentlest breeze; in short, we see beautiful adaptations everywhere and in every part of the organic world.

Again, it may be asked, how is it that varieties, which I have called incipient species, become ultimately converted into good and distinct species, which in most cases obviously differ from each other far more than do the varieties of the same species? How do those groups of species, which constitute what are called distinct genera, and which differ from each other more than do the species of the same genus, arise? All these results, as we shall more fully see in the next chapter, follow inevitably from the struggle for life. Owing to this struggle for life, any variation, however slight and from whatever cause proceeding, if it be in any degree profitable to an individual of any species, in its infinitely complex relations to other organic beings and to external nature, will tend to the preservation of that individual, and will generally be inherited by its offspring. The offspring, also, will thus have a better chance of surviving, for, of the many individuals of any species which are periodically born, but a small number can survive. I have called this principle, by which each slight variation, if useful, is preserved, by the term of natural selection, in order to mark its relation to man's power of selection. We have seen that man by selection can certainly produce great results, and can adapt organic beings to his own uses, through the accumulation of slight but useful variations, given to him by the hand of nature. But natural selection, as we shall hereafter see, is a power incessantly ready for action, and is as immeasurably superior to man's feeble efforts, as the works of nature are to those of art.

We will now discuss in a little more detail the struggle for existence. In my future work this subject shall be treated, as it well deserves, at much greater length. The elder De Candolle[1] and Lyell have largely and philosophically shown that all organic beings are exposed to severe competition. In regard to plants, no one has treated this subject with more spirit and ability than W. Herbert,[2] Dean of Manchester, evidently the result of his great horticultural knowledge. Nothing is easier than to admit in words the truth of the universal struggle for life, or more difficult—at least I have found it so—than constantly to bear this conclusion in mind. Yet unless it be thoroughly engrained in the mind, I am convinced that the whole economy of nature, with every fact on distribution, rarity, abundance, extinction, and variation, will be dimly seen or quite misunderstood. We behold the face of nature bright with gladness, we often see superabundance of food; we do not see, or we forget, that the birds which are idly singing round us mostly live on insects or seeds, and are thus constantly destroying life; or we forget how largely these songsters, or their eggs, or their nestlings, are destroyed by birds and beasts of prey; we do not always bear in mind, that though food may be now superabundant, it is not so at all seasons of each recurring year.

I should premise that I use the term struggle for existence in a large and metaphorical sense, including dependence of one being on another, and including (which is more important) not only the life of the individual, but success in leaving progeny. Two canine animals in a time of dearth, may be truly said to struggle with each other which shall get food and live. But a plant on the edge of a desert is said to struggle for life against the drought, though more properly it should be said to be dependent on the moisture. A plant which annually produces a thousand seeds, of which on an average only one comes to maturity, may be more truly said to struggle with the plants of the same and other kinds which already clothe the ground. The mistletoe is dependent on the apple and a few other trees, but can only in a far-fetched sense be said to struggle with these trees, for if too many of these parasites grow on the same tree, it will languish and die. But several seedling mistletoes, growing close together on the same branch, may more truly be said to struggle with each other. As the mistletoe is disseminated by birds, its existence depends on birds; and it may metaphorically be said to struggle with other fruit-bearing plants, in order to tempt birds to devour and thus disseminate its seeds rather than those of other plants. In these several senses,

---

[1] *The elder De Candolle* Augustin-Pyramus de Candolle (1778–1841), Swiss botanist.

[2] *W. Herbert* William Herbert (1778–1847).

which pass into each other, I use for convenience' sake the general term of struggle for existence.

A struggle for existence inevitably follows from the high rate at which all organic beings tend to increase. Every being, which during its natural lifetime produces several eggs or seeds, must suffer destruction during some period of its life, and during some season or occasional year, otherwise, on the principle of geometrical increase, its numbers would quickly become so inordinately great that no country could support the product. Hence, as more individuals are produced than can possibly survive, there must in every case be a struggle for existence, either one individual with another of the same species, or with the individuals of distinct species, or with the physical conditions of life. It is the doctrine of Malthus applied with manifold force to the whole animal and vegetable kingdoms; for in this case there can be no artificial increase of food, and no prudential restraint from marriage. Although some species may be now increasing, more or less rapidly, in numbers, all cannot do so, for the world would not hold them.

There is no exception to the rule that every organic being naturally increases at so high a rate, that if not destroyed, the earth would soon be covered by the progeny of a single pair. Even slow-breeding man has doubled in twenty-five years, and at this rate, in a few thousand years, there would literally not be standing room for his progeny. Linnaeus[1] has calculated that if an annual plant produced only two seeds—and there is no plant so unproductive as this—and their seedlings next year produced two, and so on, then in twenty years there would be a million plants. The elephant is reckoned to be the slowest breeder of all known animals, and I have taken some pains to estimate its probable minimum rate of natural increase: it will be under the mark to assume that it breeds when thirty years old, and goes on breeding till ninety years old, bringing forth three pair of young in this interval; if this be so, at the end of the fifth century there would be alive fifteen million elephants, descended from the first pair.

But we have better evidence on this subject than mere theoretical calculations, namely, the numerous recorded cases of the astonishingly rapid increase of various animals in a state of nature, when circumstances have been favourable to them during two or three following seasons. Still more striking is the evidence from our domestic animals of many kinds which have run wild in several parts of the world: if the statements of the rate of increase of slow-breeding cattle and horses in South America, and latterly in Australia, had not been well authenticated, they would have been quite incredible. So it is with plants: cases could be given of introduced plants which have become common throughout whole islands in a period of less than ten years. Several of the plants now most numerous over the wide plains of La Plata,[2] clothing square leagues of surface almost to the exclusion of all other plants, have been introduced from Europe; and there are plants which now range in India, as I hear from Dr. Falconer,[3] from Cape Comorin[4] to the Himalaya, which have been imported from America since its discovery. In such cases, and endless instances could be given, no one supposes that the fertility of these animals or plants has been suddenly and temporarily increased in any sensible degree. The obvious explanation is that the conditions of life have been very favourable, and that there has consequently been less destruction of the old and young, and that nearly all the young have been enabled to breed. In such cases the geometrical ratio of increase, the result of which never fails to be surprising, simply explains the extraordinarily rapid increase and wide diffusion of naturalised productions in their new homes.

Many cases are on record showing how complex and unexpected are the checks and relations between organic beings, which have to struggle together in the same country. I will give only a single instance, which, though a simple one, has interested me. In Staffordshire, on the estate of a relation where I had ample means of investigation, there was a large and extremely barren heath, which had never been touched by the hand of man; but several hundred acres of exactly the same nature had been enclosed twenty-five years previously and planted with Scotch fir. The change in the native vegetation of the planted part of the heath was most remarkable, more

[1] *Linnaeus* Carolus Linnaeus (1707–78), Swedish scientist who laid the foundations of modern taxonomy.

[2] *La Plata* Region of Argentina.

[3] *Dr. Falconer* Hugh Falconer (1808–65), one of the pre-eminent British palaeontologists of the time.

[4] *Cape Comorin* Southernmost point of the Indian subcontinent.

than is generally seen in passing from one quite different soil to another: not only the proportional numbers of the heath-plants were wholly changed, but twelve species of plants (not counting grasses and carices[1]) flourished in the plantations, which could not be found on the heath. The effect on the insects must have been still greater, for six insectivorous birds were very common in the plantations, which were not to be seen on the heath; and the heath was frequented by two or three distinct insectivorous birds. Here we see how potent has been the effect of the introduction of a single tree, nothing whatever else having been done, with the exception that the land had been enclosed, so that cattle could not enter. But how important an element enclosure is, I plainly saw near Farnham, in Surrey. Here there are extensive heaths, with a few clumps of old Scotch firs on the distant hill-tops: within the last ten years large spaces have been enclosed, and self-sown firs are now springing up in multitudes, so close together that all cannot live. When I ascertained that these young trees had not been sown or planted, I was so much surprised at their numbers that I went to several points of view, whence I could examine hundreds of acres of the unenclosed heath, and literally I could not see a single Scotch fir, except the old planted clumps. But on looking closely between the stems of the heath, I found a multitude of seedlings and little trees, which had been perpetually browsed down by the cattle. In one square yard, at a point some hundreds yards distant from one of the old clumps, I counted thirty-two little trees; and one of them, judging from the rings of growth, had during twenty-six years tried to raise its head above the stems of the heath, and had failed. No wonder that, as soon as the land was enclosed, it became thickly clothed with vigorously growing young firs. Yet the heath was so extremely barren and so extensive that no one would ever have imagined that cattle would have so closely and effectually searched it for food.

Here we see that cattle absolutely determine the existence of the Scotch fir; but in several parts of the world insects determine the existence of cattle. Perhaps Paraguay offers the most curious instance of this; for here neither cattle nor horses nor dogs have ever run wild, though they swarm southward and northward in a feral state; and Azara and Rengger[2] have shown that this is caused by the greater number in Paraguay of a certain fly, which lays its eggs in the navels of these animals when first born. The increase of these flies, numerous as they are, must be habitually checked by some means, probably by birds. Hence, if certain insectivorous birds (whose numbers are probably regulated by hawks or beasts of prey) were to increase in Paraguay, the flies would decrease—then cattle and horses would become feral, and this would certainly greatly alter (as indeed I have observed in parts of South America) the vegetation: this again would largely affect the insects; and this, as we just have seen in Staffordshire, the insectivorous birds, and so onwards in ever-increasing circles of complexity. We began this series by insectivorous birds, and we have ended with them. Not that in nature the relations can ever be as simple as this. Battle within battle must ever be recurring with varying success; and yet in the long-run the forces are so nicely balanced, that the face of nature remains uniform for long periods of time, though assuredly the merest trifle would often give the victory to one organic being over another. Nevertheless so profound is our ignorance, and so high our presumption, that we marvel when we hear of the extinction of an organic being; and as we do not see the cause, we invoke cataclysms to desolate the world, or invent laws on the duration of the forms of life!

I am tempted to give one more instance showing how plants and animals, most remote in the scale of nature, are bound together by a web of complex relations. I shall hereafter have occasion to show that the exotic *Lobelia fulgens*,[3] in this part of England, is never visited by insects, and consequently, from its peculiar structure, never can set a seed. Many of our orchidaceous plants absolutely require the visits of moths to remove their pollen-masses and thus to fertilise them. I have, also, reason to believe that humble-bees are indispensable to the fertilisation of the heartsease (*Viola tricolor*), for other bees do not visit this flower. From experiments which I have tried, I have found that the

---

[1] *carices* Sedges.

[2] *Azara and Rengger* Félix de Azara (1746–1821), Spanish explorer and naturalist, and Johann Rudolph Rengger (1795–1832), German naturalist. In the early part of the nineteenth century, both published influential studies on Paraguayan fauna.

[3] *Lobelia fulgens* Queen Victoria Cardinal flower.

visits of bees, if not indispensable, are at least highly beneficial to the fertilisation of our clovers; but humble-bees alone visit the common red clover (*Trifolium pratense*), as other bees cannot reach the nectar. Hence I have very little doubt, that if the whole genus of humble-bees became extinct or very rare in England, the heartsease and red clover would become very rare, or wholly disappear. The number of humble-bees in any district depends in a great degree on the number of field-mice, which destroy their combs and nests; and Mr. H. Newman,[1] who has long attended to the habits of humble-bees, believes that "more than two thirds of them are thus destroyed all over England." Now the number of mice is largely dependent, as every one knows, on the number of cats; and Mr. Newman says, "Near villages and small towns I have found the nests of humble-bees more numerous than elsewhere, which I attribute to the number of cats that destroy the mice." Hence it is quite credible that the presence of a feline animal in large numbers in a district might determine, through the intervention first of mice and then of bees, the frequency of certain flowers in that district!

from CHAPTER 14: RECAPITULATION AND CONCLUSION

… I have now recapitulated the chief facts and considerations which have thoroughly convinced me that species have changed, and are still slowly changing by the preservation and accumulation of successive slight favourable variations. Why, it may be asked, have all the most eminent living naturalists and geologists rejected this view of the mutability of species? It cannot be asserted that organic beings in a state of nature are subject to no variation; it cannot be proved that the amount of variation in the course of long ages is a limited quantity; no clear distinction has been, or can be, drawn between species and well-marked varieties. It cannot be maintained that species when intercrossed are invariably sterile, and varieties invariably fertile; or that sterility is a special endowment and sign of creation. The belief that species were immutable productions was almost unavoidable as long as the history of the world was thought to be of short duration; and now that we have acquired some idea of the lapse of time, we are too

apt to assume, without proof, that the geological record is so perfect that it would have afforded us plain evidence of the mutation of species, if they had undergone mutation.

But the chief cause of our natural unwillingness to admit that one species has given birth to other and distinct species, is that we are always slow in admitting any great change of which we do not see the intermediate steps. The difficulty is the same as that felt by so many geologists, when Lyell first insisted that long lines of inland cliffs had been formed, and great valleys excavated, by the slow action of the coast-waves. The mind cannot possibly grasp the full meaning of the term of a hundred million years; it cannot add up and perceive the full effects of many slight variations, accumulated during an almost infinite number of generations.

Although I am fully convinced of the truth of the views given in this volume under the form of an abstract, I by no means expect to convince experienced naturalists whose minds are stocked with a multitude of facts all viewed, during a long course of years, from a point of view directly opposite to mine. It is so easy to hide our ignorance under such expressions as the "plan of creation," "unity of design," *et cetera*, and to think that we give an explanation when we only restate a fact. Any one whose disposition leads him to attach more weight to unexplained difficulties than to the explanation of a certain number of facts will certainly reject my theory. A few naturalists, endowed with much flexibility of mind, and who have already begun to doubt on the immutability of species, may be influenced by this volume; but I look with confidence to the future, to young and rising naturalists, who will be able to view both sides of the question with impartiality. Whoever is led to believe that species are mutable will do good service by conscientiously expressing his conviction; for only thus can the load of prejudice by which this subject is overwhelmed be removed. …

When the views entertained in this volume on the origin of species, or when analogous views are generally admitted, we can dimly foresee that there will be a considerable revolution in natural history. Systematists will be able to pursue their labours as at present; but they will not be incessantly haunted by the shadowy doubt whether this or that form be in essence a species. This I feel sure, and I speak after experience, will be no

---

[1] *Mr. H. Newman* Unidentified.

slight relief. The endless disputes whether or not some fifty species of British brambles are true species will cease. Systematists will have only to decide (not that this will be easy) whether any form be sufficiently constant and distinct from other forms, to be capable of definition; and if definable, whether the differences be sufficiently important to deserve a specific name. This latter point will become a far more essential consideration than it is at present; for differences, however slight, between any two forms, if not blended by intermediate gradations, are looked at by most naturalists as sufficient to raise both forms to the rank of species. Hereafter we shall be compelled to acknowledge that the only distinction between species and well-marked varieties is, that the latter are known, or believed, to be connected at the present day by intermediate gradations, whereas species were formerly thus connected. Hence, without quite rejecting the consideration of the present existence of intermediate gradations between any two forms, we shall be led to weigh more carefully and to value higher the actual amount of difference between them. It is quite possible that forms now generally acknowledged to be merely varieties may hereafter be thought worthy of specific names, as with the primrose and cowslip; and in this case scientific and common language will come into accordance. In short, we shall have to treat species in the same manner as those naturalists treat genera, who admit that genera are merely artificial combinations made for convenience. This may not be a cheering prospect; but we shall at least be freed from the vain search for the undiscovered and undiscoverable essence of the term species.

The other and more general departments of natural history will rise greatly in interest. The terms used by naturalists of affinity, relationship, community of type, paternity, morphology, adaptive characters, rudimentary and aborted organs, et cetera, will cease to be metaphorical, and will have a plain signification. When we no longer look at an organic being as a savage looks at a ship, as at something wholly beyond his comprehension; when we regard every production of nature as one which has had a history; when we contemplate every complex structure and instinct as the summing up of many contrivances, each useful to the possessor, nearly in the same way as when we look at any great mechanical invention as the summing up of the labour, the experience, the reason, and even the blunders of numerous workmen; when we thus view each organic being, how far more interesting, I speak from experience, will the study of natural history become!

A grand and almost untrodden field of inquiry will be opened, on the causes and laws of variation, on correlation of growth, on the effects of use and disuse, on the direct action of external conditions, and so forth. The study of domestic productions will rise immensely in value. A new variety raised by man will be a far more important and interesting subject for study than one more species added to the infinitude of already recorded species. Our classifications will come to be, as far as they can be so made, genealogies; and will then truly give what may be called the plan of creation. The rules for classifying will no doubt become simpler when we have a definite object in view. We possess no pedigrees or armorial bearings; and we have to discover and trace the many diverging lines of descent in our natural genealogies, by characters of any kind which have long been inherited. Rudimentary organs will speak infallibly with respect to the nature of long-lost structures. Species and groups of species, which are called aberrant, and which may fancifully be called living fossils, will aid us in forming a picture of the ancient forms of life. Embryology will reveal to us the structure, in some degree obscured, of the prototypes of each great class.

When we can feel assured that all the individuals of the same species, and all the closely allied species of most genera, have within a not very remote period descended from one parent, and have migrated from some one birthplace; and when we better know the many means of migration, then, by the light which geology now throws, and will continue to throw, on former changes of climate and of the level of the land, we shall surely be enabled to trace in an admirable manner the former migrations of the inhabitants of the whole world. Even at present, by comparing the differences of the inhabitants of the sea on the opposite sides of a continent, and the nature of the various inhabitants of that continent in relation to their apparent means of immigration, some light can be thrown on ancient geography.

The noble science of geology loses glory from the extreme imperfection of the record. The crust of the earth with its embedded remains must not be looked at as a well-filled museum, but as a poor collection made at hazard and at rare intervals. The accumulation of each great fossiliferous formation will be recognised as having depended on an unusual concurrence of circumstances, and the blank intervals between the successive stages as having been of vast duration. But we shall be able to gauge with some security the duration of these intervals by a comparison of the preceding and succeeding organic forms. We must be cautious in attempting to correlate as strictly contemporaneous two formations, which include few identical species, by the general succession of their forms of life. As species are produced and exterminated by slowly acting and still existing causes, and not by miraculous acts of creation and by catastrophes; and as the most important of all causes of organic change is one which is almost independent of altered and perhaps suddenly altered physical conditions, namely, the mutual relation of organism to organism—the improvement of one being entailing the improvement or the extermination of others; it follows, that the amount of organic change in the fossils of consecutive formations probably serves as a fair measure of the lapse of actual time. A number of species, however, keeping in a body might remain for a long period unchanged, whilst within this same period, several of these species, by migrating into new countries and coming into competition with foreign associates, might become modified; so that we must not overrate the accuracy of organic change as a measure of time. During early periods of the earth's history, when the forms of life were probably fewer and simpler, the rate of change was probably slower; and at the first dawn of life, when very few forms of the simplest structure existed, the rate of change may have been slow in an extreme degree. The whole history of the world, as at present known, although of a length quite incomprehensible by us, will hereafter be recognised as a mere fragment of time, compared with the ages which have elapsed since the first creature, the progenitor of innumerable extinct and living descendants, was created.

In the distant future I see open fields for far more important researches. Psychology will be based on a new foundation, that of the necessary acquirement of each mental power and capacity by gradation. Light will be thrown on the origin of man and his history.

Authors of the highest eminence seem to be fully satisfied with the view that each species has been inde-

pendently created. To my mind it accords better with what we know of the laws impressed on matter by the Creator, that the production and extinction of the past and present inhabitants of the world should have been due to secondary causes, like those determining the birth and death of the individual. When I view all beings not as special creations, but as the lineal descendants of some few beings which lived long before the first bed of the Silurian[1] system was deposited, they seem to me to become ennobled. Judging from the past, we may safely infer that not one living species will transmit its unaltered likeness to a distant futurity. And of the species now living very few will transmit progeny of any kind to a far distant futurity; for the manner in which all organic beings are grouped, shows that the greater number of species of each genus, and all the species of many genera, have left no descendants, but have become utterly extinct. We can so far take a prophetic glance into futurity as to foretell that it will be the common and widely-spread species, belonging to the larger and dominant groups, which will ultimately prevail and procreate new and dominant species. As all the living forms of life are the lineal descendants of those which lived long before the Silurian epoch, we may feel certain that the ordinary succession by generation has never once been broken, and that no cataclysm has desolated the whole world. Hence we may look with some confidence to a secure future of equally inappreciable length. And as natural selection works solely by and for the good of each being, all corporeal and mental endowments will tend to progress towards perfection.

It is interesting to contemplate an entangled bank, clothed with many plants of many kinds, with birds singing on the bushes, with various insects flitting about, and with worms crawling through the damp earth, and to reflect that these elaborately constructed forms, so different from each other, and dependent on each other in so complex a manner, have all been produced by laws acting around us. These laws, taken in the largest sense, being growth with reproduction; inheritance which is almost implied by reproduction; variability from the indirect and direct action of the external conditions of life, and from use and disuse; a ratio of increase so high as to lead to a struggle for life, and as a consequence to natural selection,

[1] *Silurian* Geological time period approximately 440 million to 410 million years ago.

entailing divergence of character and the extinction of less-improved forms. Thus, from the war of nature, from famine and death, the most exalted object which we are capable of conceiving, namely, the production of the higher animals, directly follows. There is grandeur in this view of life, with its several powers, having been originally breathed into a few forms or into one; and that, whilst this planet has gone cycling on according to the fixed law of gravity, from so simple a beginning endless forms most beautiful and most wonderful have been, and are being, evolved.

—1859

from *The Descent of Man*

from CHAPTER 19
SECONDARY SEXUAL CHARACTERS OF MAN

With mankind the differences between the sexes are greater than in most species of Quadrumana, but not so great as in some, for instance, the mandrill.[1] Man on an average is considerably taller, heavier, and stronger than woman, with squarer shoulders and more plainly-pronounced muscles. Owing to the relation which exists between muscular development and the projection of the brows, the superciliary ridge[2] is generally more strongly marked in man than in woman. His body, and especially his face, is more hairy, and his voice has a different and more powerful tone. In certain tribes the women are said, whether truly I know not, to differ slightly in tint from the men; and with Europeans, the women are perhaps the more brightly coloured of the two, as may be seen when both sexes have been equally exposed to the weather.

Man is more courageous, pugnacious and energetic than woman, and has a more inventive genius. His brain is absolutely larger, but whether relatively to the larger size of his body, in comparison with woman, has not, I believe, been fully ascertained. In woman the face is rounder; the jaws and the base of the skull smaller; the outlines of the body rounder, in parts more prominent; and her pelvis is broader than in man; but this latter character may perhaps be considered rather as a primary than a secondary sexual character. She comes to maturity at an earlier age than man.

As with animals of all classes, so with man, the distinctive characters of the male sex are not fully developed until he is nearly mature; and if emasculated they never appear. The beard, for instance, is a secondary sexual character, and male children are beardless, though at an early age they have abundant hair on the head. It is probably due to the rather late appearance in life of the successive variations, by which man acquired his masculine characters, that they are transmitted to the male sex alone. Male and female children resemble each other closely, like the young of so many other animals in which the adult sexes differ; they likewise resemble the mature female much more closely than the mature male. The female, however, ultimately assumes certain distinctive characters, and in the formation of her skull is said to be intermediate between the child and the man....

The half-human progenitors of man, and men in a savage state, have struggled together during many generations for the possession of the females. But mere bodily strength and size would do little for victory, unless associated with courage, perseverance, and determined energy. With social animals, the young males have to pass through many a contest before they win a female, and the older males have to retain their females by renewed battles. They have, also, in the case of mankind, to defend their females, as well as their young, from enemies of all kinds, and to hunt for their joint subsistence. But to avoid enemies or to attack them with success, to capture wild animals, and to invent and fashion weapons, requires the aid of the higher mental faculties, namely, observation, reason, invention, or imagination. These various faculties will thus have been continually put to the test and selected during manhood; they will, moreover, have been strengthened by use during this same period of life. Consequently, in accordance with the principle often alluded to,[3] we

---

[1] *Quadrumana* Primates with, literally, "four hands," in that both the hind and forefeet have opposable thumbs. This category, now obsolete, included all primates other than human beings; *mandrill* Earlier, Darwin describes the adult male mandrill (close relative of the baboon) as possessing "extraordinary" bright coloration and facial protuberances that are "scarcely perceptible" in the female.

[2] *superciliary ridge* Ridge of bone above the eye sockets.

[3] *the principle often alluded to* I.e., the principle that characteristics appearing in one sex after maturity will more likely be transmitted to that sex alone.

might expect that they would at least tend to be transmitted chiefly to the male offspring at the corresponding period of manhood.

Now, when two men are put into competition, or a man with a woman, who possess every mental quality with the same perfection, with the exception that the one has the higher energy, perseverance, and courage, this one will generally become more eminent, whatever the object may be, and will gain victory. He may be said to possess genius—for genius has been declared by a great authority to be patience; and patience, in this sense, mean unflinching, undaunted perseverance. But this view of genius is perhaps deficient; for without the higher powers of the imagination and reason, no eminent success in many subjects can be gained. But these latter as well as the former faculties will have developed in man, partly through sexual selection—that is, through the contest of rival males, and partly through natural selection—that is, from success in the general struggle for life; and as in both cases the struggle will have been during maturity, the characters thus gained will have been transmitted more fully to the male than to the female offspring. Thus man has ultimately become superior to woman. It is, indeed, fortunate that the law of the equal transmission of characters to both sexes has commonly prevailed throughout the whole class of mammals; otherwise, it is probable that man would have become as superior in mental endowment to woman, as the peacock is in ornamental plumage to the peahen....

from CHAPTER 21
GENERAL SUMMARY AND CONCLUSION

A brief summary will be sufficient to recall to the reader's mind the more salient points in this work. Many of the views which have been advanced are highly speculative, and some no doubt will prove erroneous; but I have in every case given the reasons which have led me to one view rather than to another. It seemed worthwhile to try how far the principle of evolution would throw light on some or the more complex problems in the natural history of man. False facts are highly injurious to the progress of science, for they often endure long; but false views, if supported by some evidence, do little harm, for every one takes a salutary

pleasure in proving their falseness: and when this is done, one path towards error is closed and the road to truth is often at the same time opened.

The main conclusion here arrived at, and now held by many naturalists who are well competent to form a sound judgment is that man is descended from some less highly organised form. The grounds upon which this conclusion rests will never be shaken, for the close similarity between man and the lower animals in embryonic development, as well as in innumerable points of structure and constitution both of high and of the most trifling importance—the rudiments which he retains, and the abnormal reversions to which he is occasionally liable—are facts which cannot be disputed. They have long been known, but until recently they told us nothing with respect to the origin of man. Now when viewed by the light of our knowledge of the whole organic world, their meaning is unmistakable. The great principle of evolution stands up clear and firm, when these groups or facts are considered in connection with others, such as the mutual affinities of the members of the same group, their geographical distribution in past and present times, and their geological succession. It is incredible that all these facts should speak falsely. He who is not content to look, like a savage, at the phenomena of nature as disconnected, cannot any longer believe that man is the work of a separate act of creation. He will be forced to admit that the close resemblance of the embryo of man to that, for instance, of a dog—the construction of his skull, limbs and whole frame on the same plan with that of other mammals, independently of the uses to which the parts may be put—the occasional re-appearance of various structures, for instance of several muscles, which man does not normally possess, but which are common to the Quadrumana—and a crowd of analogous facts—all point in the plainest manner to the conclusion that man is the co-descendant with other mammals of a common progenitor.

We have seen that man incessantly presents individual differences in all parts of his body and in his mental faculties. These differences or variations seem to be induced by the same general causes, and to obey the same laws as with the lower animals. In both cases similar laws of inheritance prevail. Man tends to increase at a greater rate than his means of subsistence; consequently he is occasionally subjected to a severe struggle for existence, and natural selection will have effected whatever lies within its scope. A succession of strongly-marked variations of a similar nature is by no means requisite; slight fluctuating differences in the individual suffice for the work of natural selection; not that we have any reason to suppose that in the same species, all parts of the organization tend to vary to the same degree. We may feel assured that the inherited effects of the long-continued use or disuse of parts will have done much in the same direction with natural selection. Modifications formerly of importance, though no longer of any special use, are long-inherited. When one part is modified, other parts change through the principle of correlation, of which we have instances in many curious cases of correlated monstrosities. Something may be attributed to the direct and definite action of the surrounding conditions of life, such as abundant food, heat or moisture; and lastly, many characters of slight physiological importance, some indeed of considerable importance, have been gained through sexual selection.

No doubt man, as well as every other animal, presents structures, which seem to our limited knowledge, not to be now of any service to him, nor to have been so formerly, either for the general conditions of life, or in the relations of one sex to the other. Such structures cannot be accounted for by any form of selection, or by the inherited effects of the use and disuse of parts. We know, however, that many strange and strongly-marked peculiarities of structure occasionally appear in our domesticated productions, and if their unknown causes were to act more uniformly, they would probably become common to all the individuals of the species. We may hope hereafter to understand something about the causes of such occasional modifications, especially through the study of monstrosities: hence the labours of experimentalists such as those of M. Camille Dareste,[1] are full of promise for the future. In general we can only say that the cause of each slight variation and of each monstrosity lies much more in the constitution of the organism, than in the nature of the surrounding conditions; though new and changed conditions certainly play an important part in exciting organic changes of many kinds. Through the means just

specified, aided perhaps by others as yet undiscovered, man has been raised to his present state. But since he attained to the rank of manhood, he has diverged into distinct races, or as they may be more fitly called sub-species. Some of these, such as the Negro and European, are so distinct that, if specimens had been brought to a naturalist without any further information, they would undoubtedly have been considered by him as good and true species. Nevertheless all the races agree in so many unimportant details of structure and in so many mental peculiarities that these can be accounted for only by inheritance from a common progenitor; and a progenitor thus characterised would probably deserve to rank as man.

It must not be supposed that the divergence of each race from the other races, and of all from a common stock, can be traced back to any one pair of progenitors. On the contrary, at every stage in the process of modification, all the individuals which were in any way better fitted for their conditions of life, though in different degrees, would have survived in greater numbers than the less well-fitted. The process would have been like that followed by man, when he does not intentionally select particular individuals, but breeds from all the superior individuals, and neglects the inferior. He thus slowly but surely modifies his stock, and unconsciously forms a new strain. So with respect to modifications acquired independently of selection, and due to variations arising from the nature of the organism and the action of the surrounding conditions, or from changed habits of life, no single pair will have been modified much more than the other pairs inhabiting the same country, for all will have been continually blended through free intercrossing.

By considering the embryological structure of man—the homologies[2] which he presents with the lower animals—the rudiments which he retains—and the reversions to which he is liable, we can partly recall in imagination the former condition of our early progenitors; and can approximately place them in their proper place in the zoological series. We thus learn that man is descended from a hairy, tailed quadruped, probably arboreal in its habits, and an inhabitant of the Old World. This creature, if its whole structure had been examined by a naturalist, would have been classed

---

[1] *M. Camille Dareste* (Monsieur) Camille Dareste, French zoologist (1822–99), founder of experimental teratology, the study of abnormalities in plants and animals.

[2] *homologies* Similarities of structure due to common descent.

amongst the Quadrumana, as surely as the still more ancient progenitor of the Old and New World monkeys. The Quadrumana and all the higher mammals are probably derived from an ancient marsupial animal, and this through a long series of diversified forms, from some amphibian-like creature, and this again from some fish-like animal. In the dim obscurity of the past we can see that the early progenitor of all the Vertebrata must have been an aquatic animal provided with branchiae,[1] with the two sexes united in the same individual, and with the most important organs of the body (such as the brain and heart) imperfectly or not at all developed. This animal seems to have been more like the larvae of the existing marine Ascidians[2] than any other known form. ...

The belief in God has often been advanced as not only the greatest, but the most complete of all the distinctions between man and the lower animals. It is however impossible, as we have seen, to maintain that this belief is innate or instinctive in man. On the other hand a belief in all-pervading spiritual agencies seems to be universal; and apparently follows from a considerable advance in man's reason, and from a still greater advance in his faculties of imagination, curiosity and wonder. I am aware that the assumed instinctive belief in God has been used by many persons as an argument for His existence. But this is a rash argument, as we should thus be compelled to believe in the existence of many cruel and malignant spirits, only a little more powerful than man; for the belief in them is far more general than in a beneficent Deity. The idea of a universal and beneficent Creator does not seem to arise in the mind of man, until he has been elevated by long-continued culture.

He who believes in the advancement of man from some low organised form, will naturally ask how does this bear on the belief in the immortality of the soul. The barbarous races of man, as Sir J. Lubbock[3] has shown, possess no clear belief of this kind; but arguments derived from the primeval beliefs of savages are, as we have just seen, of little or no avail. Few persons feel any anxiety from the impossibility of determining at what precise period in the development of the individual, from the first trace of a minute germinal vesicle,[4] man becomes an immortal being; and there is no greater cause for anxiety because the period cannot possibly be determined in the gradually ascending organic scale.

I am aware that the conclusions arrived at in this work will be denounced by some as highly irreligious; but he who denounces them is bound to show why it is more irreligious to explain the origin of man as a distinct species by descent from some lower form, through the laws of variation and natural selection, than to explain the birth of the individual through the laws of ordinary reproduction. The birth both of the species and of the individual are equally parts of that grand sequence of events, which our minds refuse to accept as the result of blind chance. The understanding revolts at such a conclusion, whether or not we are able to believe that every slight variation of structure—the union of each pair in marriage—the dissemination of each seed—and other such events, have all been ordained for some special purpose.

Sexual selection has been treated at great length in this work; for, as I have attempted to show, it has played an important part in the history of the organic world. I am aware that much remains doubtful, but I have endeavoured to give a fair view of the whole case. In the lower divisions of the animal kingdom, sexual selection seems to have done nothing: such animals are often affixed for life to the same spot, or have the sexes combined in the same individual, or what is still more important, their perceptive and intellectual faculties are not sufficiently advanced to allow of the feelings of love and jealousy, or of the exertion of choice. When, however, we come to the Arthropoda[5] and Vertebrata, even to the lowest classes in these two great sub-kingdoms, sexual selection has effected much.

In the several great classes of the animal kingdom—in mammals, birds, reptiles, fishes, insects, and even crustaceans—the differences between the sexes follow nearly the same rules. The males are almost always the wooers; and they alone are armed with special weapons for fighting with their rivals. They are generally stronger and larger than the females, and are endowed with the requisite qualities of courage and pugnacity.

---

[1] *branchiae* Breathing apparatus, gills.

[2] *Ascidians* Molluscs.

[3] *Sir J. Lubbock* John Lubbock, Lord Avebury (1834–1913), in his book *Prehistoric Times* (1865).

[4] *germinal vesicle* Nucleus of animals' permanent ovum.

[5] *Arthropoda* Sub-kingdom which includes insects, spiders, crustaceans, etc.

They are provided, either exclusively or in a much higher degree than the females, with organs for vocal or instrumental music, and with odoriferous glands. They are ornamental with infinitely diversified appendages, and with the most brilliant or conspicuous colours, often arranged in elegant patterns, whilst the females are unadorned. When the sexes differ in more important structures, it is the male which is provided with special sense-organs for discovering the female, with locomotive organs for reaching her, and often with prehensile organs for holding her. These various structures for charming or securing the female are often developed in the male during only part of the year, namely the breeding-season. They have in many cases been more or less transferred to the females; and in the latter case they often appear in her as mere rudiments. They are lost or never gained by the males after emasculation. Generally they are not developed in the male during early youth, but appear a short time before the age for reproduction. Hence in most cases the young of both sexes resemble each other; and the female somewhat resembles her young offspring throughout life. In almost every great class a few anomalous cases occur, where there has been an almost complete transposition of the characters proper to the two sexes; the females assuming characters which properly belong to the males. This surprising uniformity in the laws regulating the differences between the sexes in so many and such widely separated classes, is intelligible if we admit the action of one common cause, namely sexual selection.

Sexual selection depends on the success of certain individuals over others of the same sex, in relation to the propagation of the species; whilst natural selection depends on the success of both sexes, at all ages, in relation to the general conditions of life. The sexual struggle is of two kinds; in the one it is between individuals of the same sex, generally the males, in order to drive away or kill their rivals, the females remaining passive; whilst in the other, the struggle is likewise between the individuals of the same sex, in order to excite or charm those of the opposite sex, generally the females, which no longer remain passive, but select the more agreeable partners. This latter kind of selection is closely analogous to that which man unintentionally, yet effectually, brings to bear on his domesticated productions, when he preserves during a long period the most pleasing or useful individuals, without any wish to modify the breed.

The laws of inheritance determine whether characters gained through sexual selection by either sex shall be transmitted to the same sex, or to both; as well as the age at which they shall be developed. It appears that variations arising late in life are commonly transmitted to one and the same sex. Variability is the necessary basis for the action of selection, and is wholly independent of it. It follows from this, that variations of the same general nature have often been taken advantage of and accumulated through sexual selection in relation to the propagation of the species, as well as through natural selection in relation to the general purposes of life. Hence secondary sexual characters, when equally transmitted to both sexes can be distinguished from ordinary specific characters only by the light of analogy. The modifications acquired through sexual selection are often so strongly pronounced that the two sexes have frequently been ranked as distinct species, or even as distinct genera.[1] Such strongly-marked differences must be in some manner highly important; and we know that they have been acquired in some instances at the cost not only of inconvenience, but of exposure to actual danger.

The belief in the power of sexual selection rests chiefly on the following considerations. Certain characters are confined to one sex; and this alone renders it probable that in most cases they are connected with the act of reproduction. In innumerable instances these characters are fully developed only at maturity, and often during only a part of the year, which is always the breeding-season. The males (passing over a few exceptional cases) are the more active in courtship; they are the better armed, and are rendered the more attractive in various ways. It is to be especially observed that the males display their attractions with elaborate care in the presence of the females; and that they rarely or never display them excepting during the season of love. It is incredible that all this should be purposeless. Lastly we have distinct evidence with some quadrupeds and birds, that the individuals of one sex are capable of feeling a strong antipathy or preference for certain individuals of the other sex.

---

[1] *genera* Latin: groups of species. Plural of "genus."

Bearing in mind these facts, and the marked results of man's unconscious selection, when applied to domesticated animals and cultivated plants, it seems to me almost certain that if the individuals of one sex were during a long series of generations to prefer pairing with certain individuals of the other sex, characterised in some peculiar manner, the offspring would slowly but surely become modified in this same manner. I have not attempted to conceal that, excepting when the males are more numerous than the females, or when polygamy prevails, it is doubtful how the more attractive males succeed in leaving a large number of offspring to inherit their superiority in ornaments or other charms than the less attractive males; but I have shown that this would probably follow from the females—especially the more vigorous ones, which would be the first to breed—preferring not only the more attractive but at the same time the more vigorous and victorious males.

Although we have some positive evidence that birds appreciate bright and beautiful objects, as with the bower-birds of Australia, and although they certainly appreciate the power of song, yet I fully admit that it is astonishing that the females of many birds and some mammals should be endowed with sufficient taste to appreciate ornaments, which we have reason to attribute to sexual selection; and this is even more astonishing in the case of reptiles, fish, and insects. But we really know little about the minds of the lower animals. It cannot be supposed, for instance, that male birds of paradise or peacocks should take such pains in erecting, spreading, and vibrating their beautiful plumes before the females for no purpose. We should remember the fact given on excellent authority in a former chapter, that several peahens, when debarred from an admired male, remained widows during a whole season rather than pair with another bird.

Nevertheless I know of no fact in natural history more wonderful than that of the female Argus pheasant should appreciate the exquisite shading of the ball-and-socket ornaments and the elegant patterns on the wing-feathers of the male. He who thinks that the male was created as he now exists must admit that the great plumes, which prevent the wings from being used for flight, and which are displayed during courtship and at no other time in a manner quite peculiar to this one species, were given to him as an ornament. If so, he must likewise admit that the female was created and endowed with the capacity of appreciating such ornaments. I differ only in the conviction that the male Argus pheasant acquired his beauty gradually, through the preference of the females during many generations for the more highly ornamented males; the aesthetic capacity of the females having been advanced through exercise or habit, just as our own taste is gradually improved. In the male through the fortunate chance of a few feathers, being left, unchanged, we can distinctly trace how simple spots with a little fulvous shading on one side may have been developed by small steps into the wonderful ball-and-socket ornaments; and it is probable that they were actually thus developed.

Everyone who admits the principle of evolution, and yet feels great difficulty in admitting that female mammals, birds, reptiles, and fish, could have acquired the high taste implied by the beauty of the males, and which generally coincides with our own standard, should reflect that the nerve-cells of the brain in the highest as well as in the lowest members of the Vertebrate series, are derived from those of the common progenitor of this great kingdom. For we can thus see how it has come to pass that certain mental faculties, in various and widely distinct groups of animals, have been developed in nearly the same manner and to nearly the same degree.

The reader who has taken the trouble to go through the several chapters devoted to sexual selection, will be able to judge how far the conclusions at which I have arrived are supported by sufficient evidence. If he accepts these conclusions he may, I think, safely extend them to mankind; but it would be superfluous here to repeat what I have so lately said on the manner in which sexual selection apparently has acted on man, both on the male and female side, causing the two sexes to differ in body and mind, and the several races to differ from each other in various characters, as well as from their ancient and lowly-organised progenitors. He who admits the principle of sexual selection will be led to the remarkable conclusion that the nervous system not only regulates most of the existing functions of the body, but has indirectly influenced the progressive development of various bodily structures and of certain mental qualities. Courage, pugnacity, perseverance, strength and size of body, weapons of all kinds, musical organs, both vocal and instrumental, bright colours and ornamental appendages, have all been indirectly gained by the one sex or the other, through the exertion of choice, the influence of love and jealousy, and the appreciation of the beautiful in sound, colour or form; and these powers of the mind manifestly depend on the development of the brain.

Man scans with scrupulous care the character and pedigree of his horses, cattle, and dogs before he matches them; but when he comes to his own marriage he rarely, or never, takes any such care. He is impelled by nearly the same motives as the lower animals, when they are left to their own free choice, though he is in so far superior to them that he highly values mental charms and virtues. On the other hand he is strongly attracted by mere wealth or rank. Yet he might by selection do something not only for the bodily constitution and frame of his offspring, but for their intellectual and moral qualities. Both sexes ought to refrain from marriage if they are in any marked degree inferior in body or mind; but such hopes are Utopian and will never be even partially realised until the laws of inheritance are thoroughly known. Everyone does good service who aids towards this end. When the principles of breeding and inheritance are better understood, we shall not hear ignorant members of our legislature rejecting with scorn a plan for ascertaining whether or not consanguineous marriages[1] are injurious to man.

The advancement of the welfare of mankind is a most intricate problem: all ought to refrain from marriage who cannot avoid abject poverty for their children; for poverty is not only a great evil, but tends to its own increase by leading to recklessness in marriage. On the other hand as Mr. Galton[2] has remarked, if the prudent avoid marriage, whilst the reckless marry, the inferior members tend to supplant the better members of society. Man, like every other animal, has no doubt advanced to his present high condition through a struggle for existence consequent on his rapid multiplication; and if he is to advance still higher, it is to be feared that he must remain subject to a severe struggle. Otherwise he would sink into indolence, and the more gifted men would not be more successful in the battle of life than the less gifted. Hence our natural rate of increase, though leading to many and obvious evils, must not be greatly diminished by any means. There should be open competition for all men; and the most able should not be prevented by laws or customs from succeeding best and rearing the largest number of offspring. Important as the struggle for existence has been and even still is, yet as far as the highest part of man's nature is concerned there are other agencies more important. For the moral qualities are advanced, either directly or indirectly, much more through the effects of habit, the reasoning powers, instruction, religion, *et cetera*, than through natural selection; though to this latter agency may be safely attributed the social instincts, which afforded the basis for the development of the moral sense.

The main conclusion arrived at in this work, namely, that man is descended from some lowly organised form, will, I regret to think, be highly distasteful to many. But there can hardly be a doubt that we are descended from barbarians. The astonishment which I felt on first seeing a party of Fuegians on a wild and broken shore will never be forgotten by me, for the reflection at once rushed into my mind—such were our ancestors. These men were absolutely naked and bedaubed with paint, their long hair was tangled, their mouths frothed with excitement, and their expression was wild, startled, and distrustful. They possessed hardly any arts, and like wild animals lived on what they could catch; they had no government, and were merciless to every one not of their own small tribe. He who has seen a savage in his native land will not feel much shame, if forced to acknowledge that the blood of some more humble creature flows in his veins. For my own part I would as soon be descended from that heroic little monkey, who braved his dreaded enemy in order to save the life of his keeper, or from that old baboon, who descending from the mountains, carried away in triumph his young comrade from a crowd of astonished dogs—as from a savage who delights to torture his enemies, offers up bloody sacrifices, practises infanticide without remorse, treats his wives like slaves, knows no decency, and is haunted by the grossest superstitions.

Man may be excused for feeling some pride at having risen, though not through his own exertions, to the very summit of the organic scale; and the fact of his

---

[1] *consanguineous marriages* Marriages between blood relatives.

[2] *Mr. Galton* Sir Francis Galton (1822–94), Darwin's half cousin, one of the founders of eugenics, the "science" that aimed to improve the human species through selective breeding.

having thus risen, instead of having been aboriginally placed there, may give him hope for a still higher destiny in the distant future. But we are not here concerned with hopes or fears, only with the truth as far as our reason permits us to discover it; and I have given the evidence to the best of my ability. We must, however, acknowledge, as it seems to me, that man with all his noble qualities, with sympathy which feels for the most debased, with benevolence which extends not only to other men but to the humblest living creature, with his god-like intellect which has penetrated into the movements and constitution of the solar system—with all these exalted powers—Man still bears in his bodily frame the indelible stamp of his lowly origin.

—1871

In Context

Defending and Attacking Darwin

One of Darwin's most important defenders was Thomas Henry Huxley (1825–95), a naturalist and essayist who in the 1870s developed the concept of agnosticism. In 1860 he became known as "Darwin's Bulldog" for his aggressive and persuasive efforts to popularize the theory of natural selection—and counter the backlash against it. He continued to write about evolutionary theory throughout the rest of his life.

from Thomas Huxley, "Criticisms on *The Origin of Species*" (1864)

It is singular how differently one and the same book will impress different minds. That which struck the present writer most forcibly on his first perusal of the "Origin of Species" was the conviction that teleology,[1] as commonly understood, had received its deathblow at Mr. Darwin's hands. For the teleological argument runs thus: an organ or organism (A) is precisely fitted to perform a function or purpose (B); therefore it was specially constructed to perform that function. In Paley's[2] famous illustration, the adaptation of all the parts of the watch to the function, or purpose, of showing the time, is held to be evidence that the watch was specially contrived to that end; on the ground, that the only cause we know of, competent to produce such an effect as a watch which shall keep time, is a contriving intelligence adapting the means directly to that end.

Suppose, however, that any one had been able to show that the watch had not been made directly by any person, but that it was the result of the modification of another watch which kept time but poorly; and that this again had proceeded from a structure which could hardly be called a watch at all—seeing that it had no figures on the dial and the hands were rudimentary; and that going back and back in time we came at last to a revolving barrel as the earliest traceable rudiment of the whole fabric. And imagine that it had been possible to show that all these changes had resulted, first, from a tendency of the structure to vary indefinitely; and secondly, from something in the surrounding world which helped all variations in the direction of an accurate time-keeper, and checked all those in other directions; then it is obvious that the force of Paley's argument would be gone. For it would be demonstrated that an apparatus thoroughly well adapted to a particular purpose might be the result of a method of trial and error worked by unintelligent agents, as well as of the direct application of the means appropriate to that end, by an intelligent agent.

[1] *teleology* Study of intelligent design or purpose in nature.

[2] *Paley* William Paley (1743–1805), English philosopher. Huxley refers to Paley's 1802 book, *Natural Theology, or Evidences of the Existence and Attributes of the Deity Collected from the Appearances of Nature.*

Now it appears to us that what we have here, for illustration's sake, supposed to be done with the watch, is exactly what the establishment of Darwin's theory will do for the organic world. For the notion that every organism has been created as it is and launched straight at a purpose, Mr. Darwin substitutes the conception of something which may fairly be termed a method of trial and error. Organisms vary incessantly; of these variations the few meet with surrounding conditions which suit them and thrive; the many are unsuited and become extinguished.

from Thomas Huxley, "Mr. Darwin's Critics" (1871)

The gradual lapse of time has now separated us by more than a decade from the date of the publication of the "Origin of Species"—and whatever may be thought or said about Mr. Darwin's doctrines, or the manner in which he has propounded them, this much is certain, that, in a dozen years, the "Origin of Species" has worked as complete a revolution in biological science as the "Principia"[1] did in astronomy—and it has done so, because, in the words of Helmholtz,[2] it contains "an essentially new creative thought."

And as time has slipped by, a happy change has come over Mr. Darwin's critics. The mixture of ignorance and insolence which, at first, characterised a large proportion of the attacks with which he was assailed, is no longer the sad distinction of anti-Darwinian criticism. Instead of abusive nonsense, which merely discredited its writers, we read essays, which are, at worst, more or less intelligent and appreciative; while, sometimes, like that which appeared in the "North British Review" for 1867, they have a real and permanent value.

The several publications of Mr. Wallace and Mr. Mivart[3] contain discussions of some of Mr. Darwin's views, which are worthy of particular attention, not only on account of the acknowledged scientific competence of these writers, but because they exhibit an attention to those philosophical questions which underlie all physical science, which is as rare as it is needful.

---

[1] *Principia*   Sir Isaac Newton's *Philosophiae Naturalis Principia Mathematica* (1687).

[2] *Helmholtz*   Hermann Ludwig Ferdinand von Helmholtz (1821–94), German professor of physiology and physics.

[3] *Mr. Wallace*   Alfred Russel Wallace (1823–1913), English naturalist and social critic; *Mr. Mivart*   St. George Jackson Mivart (1827–1900), British biologist. His *Genesis of Species* (1871) established him as a leading opponent of Darwin's theory.

from *Punch*

The humor magazine *Punch* continued to lampoon Darwin's theories in its cartoons even after they had become widely accepted in the community at large. The first of the cartoons below (depicting a gorilla as a social "lion"), was published in 1861, the second (a response to Darwin's 1881 *The Formation of Vegetable Mould Through the Action of Worms*) in 1882.

THE LION OF THE SEASON.

MAN·IS·BVT·A·WORM.

IN CONTEXT

Darwin and Human Societies

The term "Social Darwinism" is used to refer to ideas that attempt to apply certain evolutionary notions to social issues. Chief among the Victorian "Social Darwinists" was Herbert Spencer, a wide-ranging thinker who coined the term "survival of the fittest" in an 1852 essay, "A Theory of Population." Like that work, his 1851 book *Social Statics* (from which excerpts are reprinted below) pre-dates Darwin's *On the Origin of Species* by several years. In fact the tenets of Social Darwinism were quite independent of Darwin's biological theories, and were in no way necessarily embraced by the same people. Thomas Henry Huxley, one of Darwin's most dedicated defenders, opposed Spencer's ideas in his 1893 lecture "Evolution and Ethics" (the 1894 revision of which is excerpted below), arguing that the principles of ethics cannot and should not be derived from the principles of evolution.

If Social Darwinists saw in evolution a guide for ethical relations between human beings, some other Victorians were interested in the ethical implications of evolution for relations between human and non-human animals. By the time *On the Origin of Species* was published, a movement opposing the cruel treatment of non-human animals was already underway in Britain, but Darwin's work—with its suggestions of a close biological relationship between humans and other animals—was seen by some to bolster this movement. The poet and novelist Thomas Hardy draws a connection between evolution and animal welfare in a letter (reprinted below) that was originally addressed to the Humanitarian League, a late nineteenth- and early twentieth-century organization dedicated to the prevention of "unnecessary suffering" in "any sentient being."

from Herbert Spencer, *Social Statics: or, the Conditions Essential to Human Happiness Specified, and the First of Them Developed* (1851)

Pervading all nature we may see at work a stern discipline, which is a little cruel that it may be very kind. That state of universal warfare maintained throughout the lower creation, to the great perplexity of many worthy people, is at bottom the most merciful provision which the circumstances admit of. It is much better that the ruminant animal, when deprived by age of the vigour which made its existence a pleasure, should be killed by some beast of prey, than that it should linger out a life made painful by infirmities, and eventually die of starvation. By the destruction of all such, not only is existence ended before it becomes burdensome, but room is made for a younger generation capable of the fullest enjoyment; and, moreover, out of the very act of substitution happiness is derived for a tribe of predatory creatures. Note further, that their carnivorous enemies not only remove from herbivorous herds individuals past their prime, but also weed out the sickly, the malformed, and the least fleet or powerful. By the aid of which purifying process, as well as by the fighting, so universal in the pairing season, all vitiation[1] of the race through the multiplication of its inferior samples is prevented; and the maintenance of a constitution completely adapted to surrounding conditions, and therefore most productive of happiness, is ensured.

---

[1] *vitiation* Impairment.

The development of the higher creation is a progress towards a form of being capable of a happiness undiminished by these drawbacks. It is in the human race that the consummation is to be accomplished. Civilization is the last stage of its accomplishment. And the ideal man is the man in whom all the conditions of that accomplishment are fulfilled. Meanwhile the well-being of existing humanity, and the unfolding of it into this ultimate perfection, are both secured by that same beneficent, though severe discipline, to which the animate creation at large is subject: a discipline which is pitiless in the working out of good: a felicity-pursuing law which never swerves for the avoidance of partial and temporary suffering. The poverty of the incapable, the distresses that come upon the imprudent, the starvation of the idle, and those shoulderings aside of the weak by the strong, which leave so many "in shallows and in miseries,"[1] are the decrees of a large, far-seeing benevolence. It seems hard that an unskilfulness which with all his efforts he cannot overcome, should entail hunger upon the artisan. It seems hard that a labourer incapacitated by sickness from competing with his stronger fellows, should have to bear the resulting privations. It seems hard that widows and orphans should be left to struggle for life or death. Nevertheless, when regarded not separately, but in connection with the interests of universal humanity, these harsh fatalities are seen to be full of the highest beneficence—the same beneficence which brings to early graves the children of diseased parents, and singles out the low-spirited,[2] the intemperate,[3] and the debilitated as the victims of an epidemic.

There are many very amiable people—people over whom in so far as their feelings are concerned we may fitly rejoice—who have not the nerve to look this matter fairly in the face. Disabled as they are by their sympathies with present suffering, from duly regarding ultimate consequences, they pursue a course which is very injudicious, and in the end even cruel. We do not consider it true kindness in a mother to gratify her child with sweetmeats that are certain to make it ill. We should think it a very foolish sort of benevolence which led a surgeon to let his patient's disease progress to a fatal issue, rather than inflict pain by an operation. Similarly, we must call those spurious philanthropists, who, to prevent present misery, would entail greater misery upon future generations. All defenders of a poor-law[4] must, however, be classed amongst such. That rigorous necessity which, when allowed to act on them, becomes so sharp a spur to the lazy, and so strong a bridle to the random, these paupers' friends would repeal, because of the wailings it here and there produces. Blind to the fact, that under the natural order of things society is constantly excreting its unhealthy, imbecile, slow, vacillating, faithless members, these unthinking, though well-meaning, men advocate an interference which not only stops the purifying process, but even increases the vitiation—absolutely encourages the multiplication of the reckless and incompetent by offering them an unfailing provision, and discourages the multiplication of the competent and provident by heightening the prospective difficulty of maintaining a family. And thus, in their eagerness to prevent the really salutary sufferings that surround us, these sigh-wise and groan-foolish people bequeath to posterity a continually increasing curse.

At first sight these considerations seem conclusive against *all* relief to the poor—voluntary as well as compulsory; and it is no doubt true that they imply a condemnation of whatever private charity enables the recipients to elude the necessities of our social existence. With this condemnation, however, no rational man will quarrel. That careless squandering of pence which has fostered into perfection a system of organized begging—which has made skilful mendicancy more profitable than ordinary manual labour—which induces the simulation of palsy, epilepsy, cholera, and no end of

---

[1] *in … miseries*   From Shakespeare's *Julius Caesar* 4.2.70–73: "There is a tide in the affairs of men, / Which taken at the flood leads on to fortune; / Omitted, all the voyage of that life / Is bound in shallows and in miseries."

[2] *low-spirited*   Depressed.

[3] *intemperate*   Heavy drinkers.

[4] *poor-law*   Law providing for the support of the poor at public expense.

diseases and deformities—which has called into existence warehouses for the sale and hire of impostor's dresses—which has given to pity-inspiring babes a market value of *9d.* per day—the unthinking benevolence which has generated all this, cannot but be disapproved by every one. Now it is only against this injudicious charity that the foregoing argument tells. To that charity which may be described as helping men to help themselves, it makes no objection—countenances[1] it rather. And in helping men to help themselves, there remains abundant scope for the exercise of a people's sympathies. Accidents will still supply victims on whom generosity may be legitimately expended. Men thrown upon their backs by unforeseen events, men who have failed for want of knowledge inaccessible to them, men ruined by the dishonesty of others, and men in whom hope long delayed has made the heart sick, may, with advantage to all parties, be assisted. Even the prodigal, after severe hardship has branded his memory with the unbending conditions of social life to which he must submit, may properly have another trial afforded him. And, although by these ameliorations the process of adaptation must be remotely interfered with, yet in the majority of cases, it will not be so much retarded in one direction as it will be advanced in another. ...

Progress ... is not accident, but a necessity. Instead of civilisation being artificial, it is part of nature; all of a piece with the development of the embryo or the unfolding of a flower. The modifications mankind have undergone, and are still undergoing, result from a law underlying the whole organic creation; and provided the human race continues, and the constitution of things remains the same, those modifications must end in completeness. As surely as the trees become bulky when it stands alone, and slender if one of a group ... so surely must things be called evil and immoral disappear; so surely must man become perfect.

from Thomas Huxley, "Evolution and Ethics" (1894)

... **M**an, the animal, ... has worked his way to the headship of the sentient world, and has become the superb animal which he is, in virtue of his success in the struggle for existence. The conditions having been of a certain order, man's organization has adjusted itself to them better than that of his competitors in the cosmic strife. In the case of mankind, the self-assertion, the unscrupulous seizing upon all that can be grasped, the tenacious holding of all that can be kept, which constitute the essence of the struggle for existence, have answered. For his successful progress, throughout the savage state, man has been largely indebted to those qualities which he shares with the ape and the tiger; his exceptional physical organization; his cunning, his sociability, his curiosity, and his imitativeness; his ruthless and ferocious destructiveness when his anger is roused by opposition.

But, in proportion as men have passed from anarchy to social organization, and in proportion as civilization has grown in worth, these deeply ingrained serviceable qualities have become defects. After the manner of successful persons, civilized man would gladly kick down the ladder by which he has climbed. He would be only too pleased to see "the ape and tiger die." But they decline to suit his convenience; and the unwelcome intrusion of these boon companions of his hot youth into the ranged existence of civil life adds pains and griefs, innumerable and immeasurably great, to those which the cosmic process necessarily brings on the mere animal. In fact, civilized man brands all these ape and tiger promptings with the name of sins; he punishes many of the acts which flow from them as crimes; and, in extreme cases, he does his best to put an end to the survival of the fittest of former days by axe and rope.

[1] *countenances* Approves.

I have said that civilized man has reached this point; the assertion is perhaps too broad and general; I had better put it that ethical man has attained thereto. The science of ethics professes to furnish us with a reasoned rule of life; to tell us what is right action and why it is so. Whatever differences of opinion may exist among experts there is a general consensus that the ape and tiger methods of the struggle for existence are not reconcilable with sound ethical principles. ...

The propounders of what are called the "ethics of evolution," when the "evolution of ethics" would usually better express the object of their speculations, adduce a number of more or less interesting facts and more or less sound arguments in favour of the origin of the moral sentiments, in the same way as other natural phenomena, by a process of evolution. I have little doubt, for my own part, that they are on the right track; but as the immoral sentiments have no less been evolved, there is, so far, as much natural sanction for the one as the other. The thief and the murderer follow nature just as much as the philanthropist. Cosmic evolution may teach us how the good and the evil tendencies of man may have come about; but, in itself, it is incompetent to furnish any better reason why what we call good is preferable to what we call evil than we had before. ...

There is another fallacy which appears to me to pervade the so-called "ethics of evolution." It is the notion that because, on the whole, animals and plants have advanced in perfection of organization by means of the struggle for existence and the consequent "survival of the fittest"; therefore men in society, men as ethical beings, must look to the same process to help them towards perfection. I suspect that this fallacy has arisen out of the unfortunate ambiguity of the phrase "survival of the fittest." "Fittest" has a connotation of "best"; and about "best" there hangs a moral flavour. In cosmic nature, however, what is "fittest" depends upon the conditions. Long since,[1] I ventured to point out that if our hemisphere were to cool again, the survival of the fittest might bring about, in the vegetable kingdom, a population of more and more stunted and humbler and humbler organisms, until the "fittest" that survived might be nothing but lichens, diatoms, and such microscopic organisms as those which give red snow its colour; while, if it became hotter, the pleasant valleys of the Thames and Isis might be uninhabitable by any animated beings save those that flourish in a tropical jungle. They, as the fittest, the best adapted to the changed conditions, would survive.

Men in society are undoubtedly subject to the cosmic process. As among other animals, multiplication goes on without cessation, and involves severe competition for the means of support. The struggle for existence tends to eliminate those less fitted to adapt themselves to the circumstances of their existence. The strongest, the most self-assertive, tend to tread down the weaker. But the influence of the cosmic process on the evolution of society is the greater the more rudimentary its civilization. Social progress means a checking of the cosmic process at every step and the substitution for it of another, which may be called the ethical process; the end of which is not the survival of those who may happen to be the fittest, in respect of the whole of the conditions which obtain, but of those who are ethically the best.[2]

---

[1] [Huxley's note]   "Criticisms on the Origin of Species," 1864. *Collected Essays*, vol. ii. p. 91.

[2] [Huxley's note]   Of course, strictly speaking, social life, and the ethical process in virtue of which it advances towards perfection, are part and parcel of the general process of evolution, just as the gregarious habit of innumerable plants and animals, which has been of immense advantage to them, is so. A hive of bees is an organic polity, a society in which the part played by each member is determined by organic necessities. Queens, workers, and drones are, so to speak, castes, divided from one another by marked physical barriers. Among birds and mammals, societies are formed, of which the bond in many cases seems to be purely psychological; that is to say, it appears to depend upon the liking of the individuals for one another's company. The tendency of individuals to over self-assertion is kept down by fighting. Even in these rudimentary forms of society, love and fear come into play, and enforce a greater or less renunciation of self-will. To this extent the general cosmic process begins to be checked by a rudimentary ethical process, which is, strictly speaking, part of the former, just as the "governor" in a steam-engine is part of the mechanism of the engine. [A governor limits an engine's speed.]

As I have already urged, the practice of that which is ethically best—what we call goodness or virtue—involves a course of conduct which, in all respects, is opposed to that which leads to success in the cosmic struggle for existence. In place of ruthless self-assertion it demands self-restraint; in place of thrusting aside, or treading down, all competitors, it requires that the individual shall not merely respect, but shall help his fellows; its influence is directed, not so much to the survival of the fittest, as to the fitting of as many as possible to survive. It repudiates the gladiatorial theory of existence. It demands that each man who enters into the enjoyment of the advantages of a polity shall be mindful of his debt to those who have laboriously constructed it; and shall take heed that no act of his weakens the fabric in which he has been permitted to live. Laws and moral precepts are directed to the end of curbing the cosmic process and reminding the individual of his duty to the community, to the protection and influence of which he owes, if not existence itself, at least the life of something better than a brutal savage.

It is from neglect of these plain considerations that the fanatical individualism[1] of our time attempts to apply the analogy of cosmic nature to society. Once more we have a misapplication of the stoical injunction to follow nature; the duties of the individual to the state are forgotten, and his tendencies to self-assertion are dignified by the name of rights. It is seriously debated whether the members of a community are justified in using their combined strength to constrain one of their number to contribute his share to the maintenance of it; or even to prevent him from doing his best to destroy it. The struggle for existence which has done such admirable work in cosmic nature, must, it appears, be equally beneficent in the ethical sphere. Yet if that which I have insisted upon is true; if the cosmic process has no sort of relation to moral ends; if the imitation of it by man is inconsistent with the first principles of ethics; what becomes of this surprising theory?

Let us understand, once for all, that the ethical progress of society depends, not on imitating the cosmic process, still less in running away from it, but in combating it. It may seem an audacious proposal thus to pit the microcosm against the macrocosm and to set man to subdue nature to his higher ends; but I venture to think that the great intellectual difference between the ancient times ... and our day, lies in the solid foundation we have acquired for the hope that such an enterprise may meet with a certain measure of success.

The history of civilization details the steps by which men have succeeded in building up an artificial world within the cosmos. ...

---

[1] [Huxley's note]   See "Government: Anarchy or Regimentation" [1890], *Collected Essays*, vol. i. pp. 413–418. It is this form of political philosophy to which I conceive the epithet of "reasoned savagery" to be strictly applicable.

Thomas Hardy, "Thomas Hardy on Animals' Rights," *The Times* (3 May 1910)

The Athenæum, Pall Mall, S.W., April 10, 1910.
Sir,

I am glad to think that the Humanitarian League has attained the handsome age of twenty years—the Animals' Defence Department particularly.

Few people seem to perceive fully as yet that the most far-reaching consequence of the establishment of the common origin of all species is ethical; that it logically involved a readjustment of altruistic morals, by enlarging, as a necessity of rightness, the application of what has been called "The Golden Rule" from the area of mere mankind to that of the whole animal kingdom. Possibly Darwin himself did not quite perceive it.

While man was deemed to be a creation apart from all other creations, a secondary or tertiary morality was considered good enough to practise towards the "inferior" races; but no person who reasons nowadays can escape the trying conclusion that this is not maintainable. And though we may not at present see how the principle of equal justice all round is to be carried out in its entirety, I recognize that the League is grappling with the question.

Your obedient servant,
THOMAS HARDY.

Elizabeth Gaskell
1810 – 1865

Mrs. Gaskell, as she was known to nineteenth-century readers, became famous both for her gentle portrayals in fiction of genteel village life and as one of the first authors of the Victorian era to write "social protest" novels dealing with contemporary issues of poverty, industrialization, and social life in both rural and urban England. Gaskell presents brutally honest portrayals of very different sorts of Victorian reality—conditions of poor factory workers in *Mary Barton* and *North and South*, for example, and of the plight of an unwed mother in *Ruth*.

Elizabeth Cleghorn Stevenson was born in 1810 near London to William Stevenson, a Unitarian preacher and civil servant, and Elizabeth Holland, who died soon after childbirth. From the age of one, Elizabeth was raised by a beloved aunt in the village of Knutsford (the model for Gaskell's novel *Cranford*), near Manchester in northern England. She received a liberal, modern education at a boarding school in Warwick, in central England, and when she came of age went to visit a distant relative in Manchester, where she met her future husband, William Gaskell, a Unitarian minister.

According to Unitarian practices, the two lived a fulfilling life together as equals, with Gaskell free to pursue her own interests. For the first twelve years of their marriage, however, she devoted herself to the upbringing and education of her five children and performed many of the duties of her role as a minister's wife, which entailed teaching at a charity school and visiting poor parishioners. By listening to these people's tales of hardship and observing the conditions in factories and homes, Gaskell acquired much of the inspiration for her books. She wrote a small number of short stories and co-authored a poem with her husband while raising her children, but it was not until her infant son died of scarlet fever in 1845 that she began to write novels and stories in earnest, an activity her husband recommended as a partial remedy for the depression brought on by her loss.

Mary Barton, Gaskell's first novel, was published in 1848. In it, she exposed the desperation and hopelessness of poverty-stricken millworkers who toiled in miserable, unhealthy conditions in the industrial city of Manchester. Although the book was originally published under the pseudonym "Cotton Mather Mills, Esq.," it was not long before the public's and critics' curiosity unmasked Gaskell. Even though many society people found her portrayal of factory owners to be harsh and unfair, she became an esteemed guest at literary gatherings and social events. Charles Dickens was so impressed with her writing that he asked her to contribute "a short tale or any number of tales" to his magazine, *Household Words*. Gaskell agreed and contributed numerous stories over the next several years; "Our Society at Cranford" appeared in the 13 December 1851 issue. Eight other humorous tales followed, all concerning the same group of upper and middle-class women and their milieu in a peaceful country village. The tales were extremely well received, and were soon published together as the novel *Cranford* (1853).

Gaskell's next novel was not received as enthusiastically as *Cranford* had been. *Ruth*, also published in 1853, tells the story of a woman who has a child out of wedlock. The subject would have been criticized in any event, but Gaskell's sympathetic portrayal of the woman and her exposure of the hypocrisy of Victorian society deeply angered many people. The book was so controversial that some parishioners burned their copies, and it was banned in many homes, including, ironically, Gaskell's own—even she felt that the subject matter was unsuitable for children. On the other hand, Victorian women writers Elizabeth Barrett Browning, George Eliot, and Charlotte Brontë spoke out in praise of the book. In her next novel, *North and South* (1855), also published in *Household Words* (1854–55), Gaskell returned to issues of factory workers, comparing life in both the rural and urban south with the harsh lives of the working poor in the north. Like *Mary Barton*, *North and South* addressed the need for factory owners to reform workplace conditions and for workers to fight for their rights.

After Charlotte Brontë's death in 1855, Gaskell wrote her biography at the behest of Charlotte's father, Patrick Brontë. Influenced by her close friendship with Charlotte, Gaskell created a very sympathetic portrait of the Brontës, echoing what they had written about various friends and acquaintances. Unfortunately, Gaskell's loyalty to her subject landed her in trouble when one of those maligned by the Brontës threatened legal action. Under pressure from her publisher, Gaskell was forced to apologize publicly, and the questionable material was removed from the book's subsequent editions. *The Life of Charlotte Brontë* (1857) remains, however, a highly readable biography and a masterpiece of characterization.

Gaskell had almost completed her final novel, *Wives and Daughters*, when she collapsed and died suddenly in 1865. Often compared with the novels of Jane Austen and George Eliot, *Wives and Daughters* exposes the social workings of various classes in a small country town, expressing social critique with delicate wit and sly humor for which the author was known. Gaskell was buried beside the Unitarian chapel in Knutsford, the town of her childhood that she had so loved and had immortalized in her stories.

⌘ ⌘ ⌘

Our Society at Cranford [1]

In the first place, Cranford is in possession of the Amazons;[2] all the holders of houses, above a certain rent, are women. If a married couple come to settle in the town, somehow the gentleman disappears; he is either fairly frightened to death by being the only man in the Cranford evening parties, or he is accounted for by being with his regiment, his ship, or closely engaged in business all the week in the great neighbouring commercial town of Drumble, distant only twenty miles on a railroad.[3] In short, whatever does become of the gentlemen, they are not at Cranford. What could they do if they were there? The surgeon has his round of thirty miles, and sleeps at Cranford; but every man cannot be a surgeon. For keeping the trim gardens full of choice flowers without a weed to speck them; for frightening away little boys who look wistfully at the said flowers through the railings; for rushing out at the geese that occasionally venture into the gardens if the gates are left open; for deciding all ques-

---

[1] *Our Society at Cranford*   Published in *Household Words*, a weekly magazine edited by Charles Dickens. Starting in March 1850, *Household Words* was published every Wednesday for nine years. The magazine combined fiction—often serialized novels—and nonfiction; most of the writing was concerned with prominent social issues of the mid-Victorian period. "Our Society at Cranford" was first published in *Household Words* as a stand-alone piece; at Dickens's urging, Gaskell wrote eight more parts, with the concluding section appearing in 1853. The same year, the episodes were collected into the novel *Cranford* and published as a complete volume. Gaskell was apparently working on her novel *Ruth* (1853) concurrently with the publication of *Cranford* in *Household Words*.

[2] *Amazons*   In classical Greek mythology, a legendary tribe of self-sufficient female warriors, often at war with the Greeks. The name has since come to signify "woman warriors" more generally.

[3] *the great neighbouring commercial town … a railroad*   Gaskell's Cranford is modeled on Knutsford, a town in Cheshire that is approximately 20 miles southwest of the city of Manchester.

tions of literature and politics without troubling themselves with unnecessary reasons or arguments; for obtaining clear and correct knowledge of everybody's affairs in the parish; for keeping their neat maid-servants in admirable order; for kindness (somewhat dictatorial) to the poor, and real tender good offices to each other whenever any are in distress, the ladies of Cranford are quite sufficient. "A man," as one of them observed to me once, "is *so* in the way in the house!" Although the ladies of Cranford know all each other's proceedings, they are exceedingly indifferent to each other's opinions. Indeed as each has her own individuality, not to say eccentricity, pretty strongly developed, nothing is so easy as verbal retaliation; but somehow good-will reigns among them to a considerable degree.

The Cranford ladies have only an occasional little quarrel, spirited out in a few peppery words and angry jerks of the head; just enough to prevent the even tenor of their lives from becoming too flat. Their dress is very independent of fashion; as they observe, "What does it signify how we dress here at Cranford, where everybody knows us?" And if they go from home, their reason is equally cogent: "What does it signify how we dress here, where nobody know us?" The materials of their clothes are, in general, good and plain, and most of them are nearly as scrupulous as Miss Tyler, of cleanly[1] memory; but I will answer for it, the last gigot,[2] the last tight and scanty petticoat in war in England, was seen in Cranford—and seen without a smile.

I can testify to a magnificent family red silk umbrella, under which a gentle little spinster, left alone of many brothers and sisters, used to patter to church on rainy days. Have you any red silk umbrellas in London? We had a tradition of the first that had ever been seen in Cranford; and the little boys mobbed it, and called it "a stick in petticoats." It might have been the very red silk one I have described, held by a strong father over a troop of little ones; the poor little lady—the survivor of all—could scarcely carry it.

Then there were rules and regulations for visiting and calls; and they were announced to any young people, who might be staying in the town, with all the solemnity with which the old Manx laws were read once a year on the Tyne-wold.[3]

"Our friends have sent to inquire how you are after your journey tonight, my dear" (fifteen miles, in a gentleman's carriage); "they will give you some rest tomorrow, but the next day, I have no doubt, they will call; so be at liberty after twelve—from twelve to three are our calling-hours."

Then, after they had called, "It is the third day; I dare say your Mamma has told you, my dear, never to let more than three days elapse between receiving a call and returning it; and also, that you are never to stay longer than a quarter of an hour."

"But am I to look at my watch? How am I to find out when a quarter of an hour has passed?"

"You must keep thinking about the time, my dear, and not allow yourself to forget it in conversation."

As everybody had this rule in their minds, whether they received or paid a call, of course no absorbing subject was ever spoken about. We kept ourselves to short sentences of small talk, and were punctual to our time.

I imagine that a few of the gentlefolks of Cranford were poor, and had some difficulty in making both ends meet; but they were like Spartans,[4] and concealed their smart under a smiling face. We none of us spoke of money, because that subject savoured of commerce and trade, and though some might be poor, we were all aristocratic. The Cranfordians had that kindly *esprit de corps*[5] which made them overlook all deficiencies in success when some among them tried to conceal their poverty. When Mrs. Forrester gave a party in her babyhouse of a dwelling, and the little maiden disturbed the ladies on the sofa by a request that she might get the tea-tray out from underneath, every one took this novel proceeding as the most natural thing in the world; and talked on about household forms and ceremonies, as if we all believed that our hostess had a regular servants' hall, second table, with housekeeper and steward;

---

[1] *cleanly* Pure or innocent.

[2] *gigot* Style of sleeve that is very puffy at the shoulder and narrow at the wrist. It was out of fashion by the end of the 1830s, but became popular again towards the end of the century.

[3] *Manx laws* Common law system on the Isle of Man; *Tyne-wold* Tynwald is the name of the Isle of Man parliament.

[4] *Spartans* The ancient inhabitants of Sparta were known for their stoical spirit (as well as for their plainness, scrupulousness, fortitude, and prowess in battle).

[5] *esprit de corps* French: group spirit, comradeship.

instead of the one little charity-school maiden, whose short ruddy arms could never have been strong enough to carry the tray upstairs, if she had not been assisted in private by her mistress, who now sat in state, pretending not to know what cakes were sent up; though she knew, and we knew, and she knew that we knew, and we knew that she knew, she had been busy all the morning making tea-bread and sponge-cakes.

There were one or two consequences arising from this general but unacknowledged poverty, and this very much acknowledged gentility, which were not amiss, and which might be introduced into many circles of society to their great improvement. For instance, the inhabitants of Cranford kept early hours, and clattered home in their pattens,[1] under the guidance of a lantern-bearer, about nine o'clock at night; and the whole town was abed and asleep by half-past ten. Moreover, it was considered "vulgar" (a tremendous word in Cranford) to give anything expensive, in the way of eatable or drinkable, at the evening entertainments. Wafer bread-and-butter and sponge-biscuits were all that the Honourable Mrs. Jamieson gave; and she was sister-in-law to the late Earl of Cranford, although she did practise such "elegant economy."

"Elegant economy!" How naturally one falls back into the phraseology of Cranford! There, economy was always "elegant," and money-spending always "vulgar and ostentatious"; a sort of sour-grapeism, which made us very peaceful and satisfied. I never shall forget the dismay felt when a certain Captain Brown came to live at Cranford, and openly spoke about his being poor. Not in a whisper to an intimate friend, the doors, and windows being previously closed; but, in the public street! in a loud military voice! alleging his poverty as a reason for not taking a particular house. The ladies of Cranford were already rather moaning over the invasion of their territories by a man and a gentleman. He was a half-pay Captain,[2] and had obtained some situation on

a neighbouring railroad, which had been vehemently petitioned against by the little town; and if, in addition to his masculine gender, and his connexion with the obnoxious railroad, he was so brazen as to talk of being poor—why! then, indeed, he must be sent to Coventry.[3] Death was as true and as common as poverty; yet people never spoke about that, loud out in the streets. It was a word not to be mentioned to ears polite. We had tacitly agreed to ignore that any with whom we associated on terms of visiting equality could ever be prevented by poverty from doing anything that they wished. If we walked home to or from a party, it was because the night was *so* fine, or the air *so* refreshing; not because sedan-chairs[4] were expensive. If we wore prints, instead of summer silks, it was because we preferred a washing material; and so on, till we blinded ourselves to the vulgar fact that we were, all of us, people of very moderate means. Of course, then, we did not know what to make of a man who could not speak of poverty as if it was not a disgrace. Yet, somehow Captain Brown made himself respected in Cranford, and was called upon, in spite of all resolutions to the contrary. I was surprised to hear his opinions quoted as authority, at a visit which I paid to Cranford about a year after he had settled in the town. My own friends had been among the bitterest opponents of any proposal to visit Captain Brown and his daughters only twelve months before; and now he was even admitted in the tabooed hours before twelve. True, it was to discover the cause of a smoking chimney, before the fire was lighted; but still Captain Brown walked upstairs, nothing daunted, spoke in a voice too large for the room, and joked quite in the way of a tame man, about the house. He had been blind to all the small slights and omissions of trivial ceremonies with which he had been received. He had been friendly, though the Cranford ladies had been cool: he had answered small sarcastic compliments in good faith; and, with his manly frankness, had overpowered all the shrinking which met him as a man who was not ashamed to be poor. And, at last, his excellent masculine

---

[1] *pattens* Thick-soled shoes, or overshoes, meant to be worn on wet or muddy ground.

[2] *half-pay Captain* Retired officers, as well as those waiting for a new assignment, were given "half-pay." (The term is misleading, as the officers received a great deal more than half of the pay for working officers, whose pay levels were lower on the grounds that they also received room and board; in many cases, the "half-pay" of retired officers was higher than the salary paid those currently in service.)

[3] *sent to Coventry* The expression suggests the refusal to interact with an undesirable member of a group, or the desire to exclude someone from society.

[4] *sedan-chairs* Fashionable vehicles, seating one passenger, carried by two bearers holding on to two poles.

common sense and his facility in devising expedients to overcome domestic dilemmas, had gained him an extraordinary place as authority among the Cranford ladies. He, himself, went on in his course, as unaware of his popularity as he had been of the reverse; and I am sure he was startled one day, when he found his advice so highly esteemed as to make some counsel which he had given in jest, be taken in sober, serious earnest.

It was on this subject—an old lady had an Alderney cow,[1] which she looked upon as a daughter. You could not pay the short quarter-of-an-hour call without being told of the wonderful milk or wonderful intelligence of this animal. The whole town knew and kindly regarded Miss Betsy Barker's Alderney; therefore great was the sympathy and regret when, in an unguarded moment, the poor cow tumbled into a lime-pit.[2] She moaned so loudly that she was soon heard, and rescued; but meanwhile the poor beast had lost most of her hair, and came out looking naked, cold, and miserable, in a bare skin. Everybody pitied the animal, though a few could not restrain their smiles at her droll appearance. Miss Betsy Barker absolutely cried with sorrow and dismay; and it was said she thought of trying a bath of oil. This remedy, perhaps, was recommended by some one of the number whose advice she asked; but the proposal, if ever it was made, was knocked on the head by Captain Brown's decided, "Get her a flannel waistcoat and flannel drawers, Ma'am, if you wish to keep her alive. But my advice is, kill the poor creature at once."

Miss Betsy Barker dried her eyes, and thanked the Captain heartily; she set to work, and by-and-by all the town turned out to see the Alderney meekly going to her pasture, clad in dark grey flannel. I have watched her myself many a time. Do you ever see cows dressed in grey flannel in London?

Captain Brown had taken a small house on the outskirts of the town, where he lived with his two daughters. He must have been upwards of sixty at the time of the first visit I paid to Cranford, after I had left it as a residence. But he had a wiry, well-trained, elastic figure; a stiff military throw-back of his head, and a springing step, which made him appear much younger than he was. His eldest daughter looked almost as old as himself, and betrayed the fact that his real was more than his apparent age. Miss Brown must have been forty; she had a sickly, pained, careworn expression on her face, and looked as if the gaiety of youth had long faded out of sight. Even when young she must have been plain and hard-featured. Miss Jessie Brown was ten years younger than her sister, and twenty shades prettier. Her face was round and dimpled. Miss Jenkyns once said, in a passion against Captain Brown (the cause of which I will tell you presently), "that she thought it was time for Miss Jessie to leave off her dimples, and not always be trying to look like a child." It was true there was something child-like in her face; and there will be, I think, till she dies, though she should live to a hundred. Her eyes were large blue wandering eyes, looking straight at you; her nose was unformed and snub, and her lips were red and dewy; she wore her hair, too, in little rows of curls, which heightened this appearance. I do not know if she was pretty or not; but I liked her face, and so did everybody, and I do not think she could help her dimples. She had something of her father's jauntiness of gait and manner; and any female observer might detect a slight difference in the attire of the two sisters—that of Miss Jessie being about two pounds per annum more expensive than Miss Brown's. Two pounds was a large sum in Captain Brown's annual disbursements.[3]

Such was the impression made upon me by the Brown family, when I first saw them altogether in Cranford church. The Captain I had met before—on the occasion of the smoky chimney, which he had cured by some simple alteration in the flue. In church, he held his double eye-glass to his eyes during the morning hymn, and then lifted up his head erect, and sang out loud joyfully. He made the responses louder than the clerk—an old man with a piping feeble voice, who, I think, felt aggrieved at the Captain's sonorous bass, and quavered higher and higher in consequence.

On coming out of church, the brisk Captain paid the most gallant attention to his two daughters. He nodded and smiled to his acquaintances; but he shook hands with none until he had helped Miss Brown to unfurl her umbrella, had relieved her of her prayer-book, and had waited patiently till she, with trembling nervous hands, had taken up her gown to walk through

---

[1] *Alderney cow* Cow bred in Alderney, one of the Channel Islands.

[2] *lime-pit* Pit used to remove hair from animal hides.

[3] *disbursements* Spending.

the wet roads.

I wondered what the Cranford ladies did with Captain Brown at their parties. We had often rejoiced, in former days, that there was no gentleman to be attended to, and to find conversation for, at the card-parties. We had congratulated ourselves upon the snugness of the evenings; and, in our love for gentility and distaste of mankind, we had almost persuaded ourselves that to be a man was to be "vulgar"; so that when I found my friend and hostess, Miss Jenkyns, was going to have a party in my honour, and that Captain and the Miss Browns were invited, I wondered much what would be the course of the evening. Card-tables, with green baize[1] tops, were set out by daylight, just as usual; it was the third week in November, so the evenings closed in about four. Candles, and clean packs of cards, were arranged on each table. The fire was made up, the neat maid-servant had received her last directions; and, there we stood dressed in our best, each with a candle-lighter in our hands, ready to dart at the candles as soon as the first knock came. Parties in Cranford were solemn festivities, making the ladies feel gravely elated, as they sat together in their best dresses. As soon as three had arrived, we sat down to "Preference,"[2] I being the unlucky fourth. The next four comers were put down immediately to another table; and, presently, the tea-trays, which I had seen set out in the store-room as I passed in the morning, were placed each on the middle of a card-table. The china was delicate egg-shell; the old-fashioned silver glittered with polishing; but the eatables were of the slightest description. While the trays were yet on the tables, Captain and the Miss Browns came in; and I could see, that somehow or other, the Captain was a favourite with all the ladies present. Ruffled brows were smoothed, sharp voices lowered at his approach. Miss Brown looked ill, and depressed almost to gloom. Miss Jessie smiled as usual, and seemed nearly as popular as her father. He immediately and quietly assumed the man's place in the room; attended to every one's wants, lessened the pretty

maid-servant's labour by waiting on empty cups, and bread-and-butterless ladies; and yet did it all in so easy and dignified a manner, and so much as if it were a matter of course for the strong to attend to the weak, that he was a true man throughout. He played for three-penny points with as grave an interest as if they had been pounds; and yet, in all his attention to strangers, he had an eye on his suffering daughter; for suffering I was sure she was, though to many eyes she might only appear to be irritable. Miss Jessie could not play cards; but she talked to the sitters-out, who, before her coming, had been rather inclined to be cross. She sang, too, to an old cracked piano, which I think had been a spinnet[3] in its youth. Miss Jessie sang "Jock of Hazeldean"[4] a little out of tune; but we were none of us musical, though Miss Jenkyns beat time, out of time, by way of appearing to be so.

It was very good of Miss Jenkyns to do this; for I had seen that, a little while before, she had been a good deal annoyed by Miss Jessie Brown's unguarded admission (à-propos of Shetland wool) that she had an uncle, her mother's brother, who was a shopkeeper in Edinburgh. Miss Jenkyns tried to drown this confession by a terrible cough—for the Honourable Mrs. Jamieson was sitting at the card-table nearest Miss Jessie, and what would she say or think if she found out she was in the same room with a shopkeeper's niece! But Miss Jessie Brown (who had no tact, as we all agreed, the next morning) *would* repeat the information, and assure Miss Pole she could easily get her the identical Shetland wool required, "through my uncle, who has the best assortment of Shetland goods of any one in Edinbro'." It was to take the taste of this out of our mouths, and the sound of this out of our ears, that Miss Jenkyns proposed music; so I say again, it was very good of her to beat time to the song.

When the trays reappeared with biscuits and wine, punctually at a quarter to nine, there was conversation; comparing of cards, and talking over tricks; but, by-and-by, Captain Brown sported a bit of literature.

---

[1] *baize* Coarse woolen material, typically used for coverings or linings.

[2] *Preference* Card game, typically involving three players using a thirty-two card deck, in which the trump card is established through bidding.

[3] *spinnet* Musical instrument, resembling a small harpsichord, with each of its strings designed for a single note.

[4] *Jock of Hazeldean* Scottish ballad, with words by Sir Walter Scott.

"Have you seen any numbers of 'Hood's Own?'"[1] said he. (It was then publishing in parts.) "Capital thing!"

Now, Miss Jenkyns was daughter of a deceased rector of Cranford; and, on the strength of a number of manuscript sermons, and a pretty good library of divinity, considered herself literary, and looked upon any conversation about books as a challenge to her. So she answered and said, "Yes, she had seen it; indeed, she might say she had read it."

"And what do you think of it?" exclaimed Captain Brown. "Isn't it famously good?" So urged, Miss Jenkyns could not but speak.

"I must say I don't think it is by any means equal to Dr. Johnson.[2] Still, perhaps, the author is young. Let him persevere, and who knows what he may become if he will take the great Doctor for his model." This was evidently too much for Captain Brown to take placidly; and I saw the words on the tip of his tongue before Miss Jenkyns had finished her sentence.

"It is quite a different sort of thing, my dear madam," he began.

"I am quite aware of that," returned she. "And I make allowances, Captain Brown."

"Just allow me to read you a scene out of this month's number," pleaded he. "I had it only this morning, and I don't think the company can have read it yet."

"As you please," said she, settling herself with an air of resignation. He read the account of the gentleman who was terrified out of his wits by political events, who

"could no more collect himself than the Irish tithes."[3] Some of us laughed heartily. *I* did not dare, because I was staying in the house. Miss Jenkyns sat in patient gravity. When it was ended, she turned to me, and said with mild dignity, "Fetch me 'Rasselas,'[4] my dear, out of the book-room."

When I brought it to her, she turned to Captain Brown: "Now allow *me* to read you a scene, and then the present company can judge between your favourite, Mr. Hood, or Dr. Johnson."

She read one of the conversations between Rasselas and Imlac,[5] in a high-pitched majestic voice; and when she had ended, she said, "I imagine I am now justified in my preference of Dr. Johnson, as a writer of fiction." The Captain screwed his lips up, and drummed on the table, but he did not speak. She thought she would give a finishing blow or two.

"I consider it vulgar, and below the dignity of literature, to publish in numbers."[6]

"How was the 'Rambler'[7] published, Ma'am?" asked Captain Brown, in a low voice; which I think Miss Jenkyns could not have heard.

"Dr. Johnson's style is a model for young beginners. My father recommended it to me when I began to write

[1] *Hood's Own* Thomas Hood (1799–1845), a poet and humorist and publisher of *Comic Annual*, was the author of political satires and caricatures, as well as comic sketches, that appeared monthly and were eventually collected as *Hood's Own, or, Laughter from Year to Year* (1838–39). This reference is one of the alterations made by Charles Dickens; Gaskell's original wording (reinstated in *Cranford*) was "'…any numbers of The Pickwick Papers,' said he"—a reference to Dickens's early work of fiction (published in parts from April 1836 to November 1837). See "In Context" below for further information.

[2] *Dr. Johnson* Samuel Johnson (1709–84), influential poet, essayist, lexicographer (he was responsible for the *Dictionary of the English Language*, published in 1755), and critic. He was frequently held up as a model man of letters during the Victorian period.

[3] *the account… Irish tithes* The Tithe War (1830–36) was a largely nonviolent reaction to the enforcement of a tithe, or tax-like payment, on Irish farmers by the Church of Ireland. The already financially pressed farmers increasingly began resisting making the payments. Although the farmers typically employed civil disobedience, the conflict produced casualties, most notably in 1835, when seventeen people were killed and thirty wounded as part of an enforcement attempt.

This reference was one of the alterations made by Charles Dickens. In Gaskell's original (and in *Cranford*), the text reads as follows: "… the account of the 'swarry' which Sam Weller gave at Bath,"—a reference to Chapter 37 of Dickens's *The Pickwick Papers*.

[4] *Rasselas* Samuel Johnson's *The History of Rasselas, Prince of Abissinia* (1759), an allegorical work on the subject of happiness.

[5] *Rasselas and Imlac* Rasselas is the titular Abissinian prince, confined to a beautiful valley as he awaits ascension to the throne. Eventually, Rasselas flees, accompanied by his faithful friend, the poet Imlac (as well as his sister and her attendant).

[6] *publish in numbers* Publish in parts; serialize.

[7] *Rambler* Samuel Johnson published *The Rambler*, a series of short papers on various topics, every Tuesday and Saturday from 1750 to 1752. Altogether, Johnson produced over two hundred articles, written in an elevated style, on subjects ranging from literature to politics.

letters. I have formed my own style upon it; I recommend it to your favourite."

"I should be very sorry for him to exchange his style
for any such pompous writing," said Captain Brown.

Miss Jenkyns felt this as a personal affront, in a way
of which the Captain had not dreamed. Epistolary
writing, she and her friends considered her *forte*. Many
a copy of many a letter have I seen written and corrected
on the slate, before she "seized the half-hour just previous to post-time to assure" her friends of this or of that;
and Dr. Johnson was, as she said, her model in these
compositions. She drew herself up with dignity, and
only replied to Captain Brown's last remark by saying,
with marked emphasis on every syllable, "I prefer Dr.
Johnson to Mr. Hood."

It is said—I won't vouch for the fact—that Captain
Brown was heard to say, *sotto voce*,[1] "D——n Dr. Johnson!" If he did, he was penitent afterwards, as he showed
by going to stand near Miss Jenkyns's armchair, and
endeavouring to beguile her into conversation on some
more pleasing subject. But she was inexorable. The next
day, she made the remark I have mentioned, about Miss
Jessie's dimples.

It was impossible to live a month at Cranford and
not know the daily habits of each resident; and long
before my visit was ended, I knew much concerning the
whole Brown trio. There was nothing new to be discovered respecting their poverty; for they had spoken
simply and openly about that from the very first. They
made no mystery of the necessity for their being economical. All that remained to be discovered was the
Captain's infinite kindness of heart, and the various
modes in which, unconsciously to himself, he manifested it. Some little anecdotes were talked about for
some time after they occurred. As we did not read
much, and as all the ladies were pretty well suited with
servants, there was a dearth of subjects for conversation.
We, therefore, discussed the circumstance of the Captain taking a poor old woman's dinner out of her hands,
one very slippery Sunday. He had met her returning
from the bakehouse[2] as he came from church, and

noticed her precarious footing; and with the grave
dignity with which he did everything, he relieved her of
her burden, and steered along the street by her side,
carrying her baked mutton and potatoes safely home.
This was thought very eccentric; and it was rather
expected that he would pay a round of calls, on the
Monday morning, to explain and apologise to the
Cranford sense of propriety: but he did no such thing;
and then it was decided that he was ashamed, and was
keeping out of sight. In a kindly pity for him, we began
to say—"After all, the Sunday morning's occurrence
showed great goodness of heart"; and it was resolved
that he should be comforted on his next appearance
amongst us; but, lo! he came down upon us, untouched
by any sense of shame, speaking loud and bass as ever,
his head thrown back, his wig as jaunty and well-curled
as usual, and we were obliged to conclude he had
forgotten all about Sunday.

Miss Pole and Miss Jessie Brown had set up a kind
of intimacy, on the strength of the Shetland wool and
the new knitting stitches; so it happened that when I
went to visit Miss Pole, I saw more of the Browns than
I had done while staying with Miss Jenkyns; who had
never got over what she called Captain Brown's disparaging remarks upon Dr. Johnson, as a writer of light and
agreeable fiction. I found that Miss Brown was seriously
ill of some lingering, incurable complaint, the pain
occasioned by which gave the uneasy expression to her
face that I had taken for unmitigated crossness. Cross,
too, she was at times, when the nervous irritability
occasioned by her disease became past endurance. Miss
Jessie bore with her at these times even more patiently
than she did with the bitter self-upbraidings by which
they were invariably succeeded. Miss Brown used to
accuse herself, not merely of hasty and irritable temper;
but also of being the cause why her father and sister
were obliged to pinch, in order to allow her the small
luxuries which were necessaries in her condition. She
would so fain have made sacrifices for them and have
lightened their cares, that the original generosity of her
disposition added acerbity to her tempter. All this was
borne by Miss Jessie and her father with more than
placidity—with absolute tenderness. I forgave Miss
Jessie her singing out of time, and her juvenility of dress,
when I saw her at home. I came to perceive that Captain

---

[1] *sotto voce* Italian: in a soft voice; under his breath.

[2] *bakehouse* House where bread is baked. The poor could in many
cases take their meals to be heated at the local bakehouse (which
would charge a modest fee for the service).

Brown's dark Brutus wig[1] and padded coat (alas! too often threadbare) were remnants of the military smartness of his youth, which he now wore unconsciously. He was a man of infinite resources, gained in his barrack experience. As he confessed, no one could black his boots to please him except himself; but, indeed, he was not above saving the little maid-servant's labours in every way, feeling probably that his daughter's illness made the place a hard one.

He endeavoured to make peace with Miss Jenkyns soon after the memorable dispute I have named, by a present of a wooden fire-shovel (his own making), having heard her say how much the grating of an iron one annoyed her. She received the present with cool gratitude, and thanked him formally. When he was gone, she bade me put it away in the lumber-room; feeling, probably, that no present from a man who preferred Mr. Hood to Dr. Johnson could be less jarring than an iron fire-shovel.

Such was the state of things when I left Cranford and went to Drumble. I had, however, several correspondents who kept me *au fait*[2] to the proceedings of the dear little town. There was Miss Pole, who was becoming as much absorbed in crochet as she had been once in knitting; and the burden of whose letter was something like, "But don't you forget the white worsted at Flint's," of the old song;[3] for, at the end of every sentence of news came a fresh direction as to some crochet commission which I was to execute for her. Miss Matilda Jenkyns (who did not mind being called Miss Matey, when Miss Jenkyns was not by); wrote nice, kind, rambling letters; now and then venturing into an opinion of her own; but suddenly pulling herself up, and either begging me not to name what she had said, as Deborah thought differently, and *she* knew; or else, putting in a postscript to the effect that, since writing the above, she had been talking over the subject with Deborah, and was quite convinced that, &c.—(here, probably, followed a recantation of every opinion she

had given in the letter). Then came Miss Jenkyns— Deborah, as she liked Miss Matey to call her; her father having once said that the Hebrew name ought to be so pronounced. I secretly think she took the Hebrew prophetess[4] for a model in character; and, indeed, she was not unlike the stern prophetess in some ways; making allowance, of course, for modern customs and difference in dress. Miss Jenkyns wore a cravat, and a little bonnet like a jockey-cap, and altogether had the appearance of a strong-minded woman; therefore, she would have despised the modern idea of women being equal to men. Equal, indeed! She knew they were superior.—But to return to her letters. Everything in them was stately and grand, like herself. I have been looking them over (dear Miss Jenkyns, how I loved her!) and I will give an extract, more especially because it relates to our friend Captain Brown:

"The Honourable Mrs. Jamieson has only just quitted me; and, in the course of conversation she communicated to me the intelligence, that she had yesterday received a call from her revered husband's quondam[5] friend, Lord Mauleverer. You will not easily conjecture what brought his lordship within the precincts of our little town. It was to see Captain Brown, with whom, it appears, his lordship was acquainted in the 'plumed wars,'[6] and who had the privilege of averting destruction from his lordship's head, when some great peril was impending over it, off the misnomered Cape of Good Hope.[7] You know our friend the Honourable Mrs. Jamieson's deficiency in the spirit of innocent curiosity; and you will, therefore, not be so much surprised when I tell you she was quite unable to disclose to me the exact nature of the peril in question. I was anxious, I confess, to ascertain in what manner

[1] *Brutus wig* Wig styled in an uneven crop and named after Lucius Junius Brutus, the Roman Republic's founder.

[2] *au fait* French: up-to-date; fully informed.

[3] *But don't ... old song* The "old song" in question is "Country Commissions," which takes the form of a letter, each verse ending with a reminder to procure a "skein of white worsted at Flint's."

[4] *Deborah ... Hebrew prophetess* Prophet and Judge, or legal and military leader, of the ancient Israelites, Deborah successfully mounted a counterattack against the king of Canaan, a military triumph recounted in the biblical Book of Judges.

[5] *quondam* Latin: former; retired.

[6] *plumed wars* Napoleonic Wars, fought between England and France (1803–15), so-called because of the plumed helmets worn by the soldiers.

[7] *Cape of Good Hope* Part of the Atlantic coast on the Cape Peninsula of South Africa; the rocky terrain was first dubbed "Cape of Tempests" by the Portuguese explorer Bartolomeu Dias, who first rounded it in 1488.

Captain Brown, with his limited establishment, could receive so distinguished a guest; and I discovered that his lordship retired to rest; and, let us hope to refreshing slumbers, at the Angel Hotel; but shared the Brunonian[1] meals during the two days that he honoured Cranford with this august presence. Mrs. Johnson, our civil butcher's wife, informs me that Miss Jessie purchased a leg of lamb; but, besides this, I can hear of no preparation whatever to give a suitable reception to so distinguished a visitor. Perhaps they entertained him with 'the feast of reason and the flow of soul';[2] and to us, who are acquainted with Captain Brown's sad want of relish, for 'the pure wells of English undefiled,'[3] it may be matter for congratulation, that he has had the opportunity of improving his taste by holding converse with an elegant and refined member of the British aristocracy. But from some mundane feelings who is free?"

Miss Pole and Miss Matey wrote to me by the same post. Such a piece of news as Lord Mauleverer's visit was not to be lost on the Cranford letter-writers: they made the most of it. Miss Matey humbly apologised for writing at the same time as her sister, who was so much more capable than she to describe the honour done to Cranford; but, in spite of a little bad spelling, Miss Matey's account gave me the best idea of the commotion occasioned by his lordship's visit, after it had occurred; for, except the people at the Angel, the Browns, Mrs. Jamieson, and a little lad his lordship had sworn at for driving a dirty hoop against the aristocratic legs, I could not hear of any one with whom his lordship had held conversation.

My next visit to Cranford was in the summer. There had been neither births, deaths, nor marriages since I was there last. Everybody lived in the same house, and wore pretty nearly the same well-preserved, old-fashioned clothes. The greatest event was that Miss Jenkyns had purchased a new carpet for the drawing-room. O, the busy work Miss Matey and I had in chasing the sunbeams, as they fell in an afternoon right down on this carpet through the blindless window! We spread newspapers over the places, and sat down to our book or work; and, lo! in a quarter of an hour the sun had moved, and was blazing away on a fresh spot; and down again we went on our knees to alter the position of the newspapers. We were very busy, too, one whole morning before Miss Jenkyns gave her party, in following her directions, and in cutting out and stitching together pieces of newspaper, so as to form little paths to every chair, set for the expected visitors, lest their shoes might dirty or defile the purity of the carpet. Do you make paper paths for every guest to walk upon in London?

Captain Brown and Miss Jenkyns were not very cordial to each other. The literary dispute, of which I had seen the beginning, was a "raw," the slightest touch on which made them wince. It was the only difference of opinion they had ever had; but that difference was enough. Miss Jenkyns could not refrain from talking *at* Captain Brown; and though he did not reply, he drummed with his fingers; which action she felt and resented as very disparaging to Dr. Johnson. He was rather ostentatious in his preference of the writings of Mr. Hood; would walk through the street so absorbed in them, that he all but ran against Miss Jenkyns; and though his apologies were earnest and sincere, and though he did not, in fact, do more than startle her and himself, she owned to me she had rather he had knocked her down, if he had only been reading a higher style of literature. The poor, brave Captain! he looked older, and more worn, and his clothes were very threadbare. But he seemed as bright and cheerful as ever, unless he was asked about his daughter's health.

"She suffers a great deal, and she must suffer more; we do what we can to alleviate her pain—God's will be done!" He took off his hat at these last words. I found, from Miss Pole, that everything had been done, in fact. A medical man, of high repute in that country neighbourhood, had been sent for, and every injunction he had given was attended to, regardless of expense. Miss Pole was sure they denied themselves many things in order to make the invalid comfortable; but they never spoke about it; and as for Miss Jessie! "I really think she's an angel," said poor Miss Pole, quite overcome. "To see her way of bearing with Miss Brown's crossness, and the bright face she puts on after she's been sitting

---

[1] *Brunonian*   Related to Brown.

[2] *the feast ... soul*   Cf. Alexander Pope, *Imitations of Horace,* "The First Satire of the Second Book of Horace, Imitated," 130.

[3] *the pure wells ... undefiled*   The poet Edmund Spenser (c. 1552–99) deemed the works of Geoffrey Chaucer (c. 1343–1400) a "well of English pure and undefiled."

up a whole night and scolded above half of it, is quite beautiful. Yet she looks as neat and as ready to welcome the Captain at breakfast-time, as if she had been asleep in the Queen's bed all night. My dear! you could never laugh at her prim little curls or her pink bows again, if you saw her as I have done." I could only feel very penitent, and greet Miss Jessie with double respect when I met her next. She looked faded and pinched; and her lips began to quiver, as if she was very weak, when she spoke of her sister. But she brightened, and sent back the tears that were glittering in her pretty eyes, as she said:

"But, to be sure, what a town Cranford is for kindness! I don't suppose any one has a better dinner than usual cooked, but the best part of all comes in a little covered basin for my sister. The poor people will leave their earliest vegetables at our door for her. They speak short and gruff, as if they were ashamed of it; but I am sure it often goes to my heart to see their thoughtfulness." The tears now came back and overflowed; but after a minute or two, she began to scold herself, and ended by going away, the same cheerful Miss Jessie as ever.

"But why does not this Lord Mauleverer do something for the man who saved his life?" said I.

"Why, you see, unless Captain Brown has some reason for it, he never speaks about being poor; and he walked along by his lordship, looking as happy and cheerful as a prince; and as they never call attention to their dinner by apologies, and as Miss Brown was better that day, and all seemed bright, I dare say his lordship never knew how much care there was in the background. He did send game in the winter pretty often, but now he is gone abroad."

I had often occasion to notice the use that was made of fragments and small opportunities in Cranford; the rose-leaves that were gathered ere they fell, to make into a potpourri for some one who had no garden; the little bundles of lavender-flowers sent to strew the drawers of some town-dweller, or to burn in the chamber of some invalid. Things that many would despise, and actions which it seemed scarcely worthwhile to perform, were all attended to in Cranford. Miss Jenkyns stuck an apple full of cloves to be heated and smell pleasantly in Miss Brown's room; and as she put in each clove, she uttered

a Johnsonian sentence. Indeed, she never could think of the Browns without talking Johnson; and, as they were seldom absent from her thoughts just then, I heard many a rolling three-piled[1] sentence.

Captain Brown called one day to thank Miss Jenkyns for many little kindnesses, which I did not know until then that she had rendered. He had suddenly become like an old man; his deep bass voice had a quavering in it; his eyes looked dim, and the lines on his face were deep. He did not—could not—speak cheerfully of his daughter's state, but he talked with manly pious resignation, and not much. Twice over he said, "What Jessie has been to us, God only knows!" and after the second time, he got up hastily, shook hands all round without speaking, and left the room.

That afternoon we perceived little groups in the street, all listening with faces aghast to some tale or other. Miss Jenkyns wondered what could be the matter for some time before she took the undignified step of sending Jenny out to inquire.

Jenny came back with a white face of terror. "Oh, Ma'am! oh, Miss Jenkyns, Ma'am! Captain Brown is killed by them nasty cruel railroads!" and she burst into tears. She, along with many others, had experienced the poor Captain's kindness.

"How?—where—where? Good God! Jenny, don't waste time in crying, but tell us something." Miss Matey rushed out into the street at once, and collared the man who was telling the tale.

"Come in—come to my sister at once,—Miss Jenkyns, the rector's daughter. Oh, man, man! say it is not true,"—she cried, as she brought the affrighted carter,[2] sleeking down his hair, into the drawing-room, where he stood with his wet boots on the new carpet, and no one regarded it.

"Please, mum, it is true. I seed it myself," and he shuddered at the recollection. "The Captain was a-reading some new book as he was deep in, a-waiting for the down train;[3] and there was a little lass as wanted to come to its mammy, and gave its sister the slip, and

---

[1] *three-piled* Sophisticated, polished, elegant.

[2] *carter* Cart driver.

[3] *down train* Train headed away from a main terminus (such as London or Manchester); the train headed in the opposite direction may similarly be referred to as the up train.

came toddling across the line. And he looked up sudden at the sound of the train coming, and seed the child, and he darted on the line and cotched it up, and his foot slipped, and the train came over him in no time. Oh Lord, Lord! Mum, it's quite true—and they've come over to tell his daughters. The child's safe, though, with only a bang on its shoulder, as he threw it to its mammy. Poor Captain would be glad of that, mum, would not he, God bless him!" The great rough carter puckered up his manly face, and turned away to hide his tears. I turned to Miss Jenkyns. She looked very ill, as if she were going to faint, and signed to me to open the window.

"Matilda, bring me my bonnet. I must go to those girls. God pardon me if ever I have spoken contemptuously to the Captain!"

Miss Jenkyns arrayed herself to go out, telling Miss Matilda to give the man a glass of wine. While she was away, Miss Matey and I huddled over the fire, talking in a low and awestruck voice. I know we cried quietly all the time.

Miss Jenkyns came home in a silent mood, and we durst not ask her many questions. She told us that Miss Jessie had fainted, and that she and Miss Pole had had some difficulty to bring her round; but that, as soon as she recovered, she begged one of them to go and sit with her sister.

"Dr. Colburn says she cannot live many days, and she shall be spared this shock," said Miss Jessie, shivering with feelings to which she dared not give way.

"But how can you manage, my dear?" asked Miss Jenkyns; "you cannot bear up—she must see your tears."

"God will help me—I will not give way—she was asleep when the news came; she may be asleep yet. She would be so utterly miserable, not merely at my father's death, but to think of what would become of me; she is so good to me." She looked up earnestly in their faces with her soft true eyes, and Miss Pole told Miss Jenkyns afterwards she could hardly bear it, knowing, as she did, how Miss Brown treated her sister.

However, it was settled according to Miss Jessie's wish. Miss Brown was to be told her father had been summoned to take a short journey on railway business. They had managed it in some way—Miss Jenkyns could not exactly say how. Miss Pole was to stop with Miss

Jessie. Mrs. Jamieson had sent to inquire: And this was all we heard that night; and a sorrowful night it was. The next day a full account of the fatal accident was in the country paper, which Miss Jenkyns took in. Her eyes were very weak, she said, and she asked me to read it. When I came to "the gallant gentleman was deeply engaged in the perusal of Hood's Poems,[1] which he had just received," Miss Jenkyns shook her head long and solemnly, and then sighed out, "Poor, dear, infatuated man!"

The corpse was to be taken from the station to the parish church, there to be interred. Miss Jessie had set her heart on following it to the grave; and no dissuasives could alter her resolve. Her restraint upon herself made her almost obstinate; she resisted all Miss Pole's entreaties, and Miss Jenkyns's advice. At last Miss Jenkyns gave up the point; and after a silence, which I feared portended some deep displeasure against Miss Jessie, Miss Jenkyns said she should accompany the latter to the funeral.

"It is not fit for you to go alone. It would be against both propriety and humanity were I to allow it."

Miss Jessie seemed as if she did not half like this arrangement; but her obstinacy, if she had any, had been exhausted in her determination to go to the interment. She longed, poor thing! I have no doubt, to cry alone over the grave of the dear father, to whom she had been all in all; and to give way, for one little half-hour, uninterrupted by sympathy, and unobserved by friendship. But it was not to be. That afternoon Miss Jenkyns sent out for a yard of black crape, and employed herself busily in trimming the little black silk bonnet I have spoken about. When it was finished she put it on, and looked at us for approbation—admiration she despised. I was full of sorrow, but, by one of those whimsical thoughts which come unbidden into our heads, in times of deepest grief, I no sooner saw the bonnet than I was reminded of a helmet; and in that hybrid bonnet, half-helmet, half-jockey cap, did Miss Jenkyns attend Captain Brown's funeral; and I believe supported Miss Jessie with a tender indulgent firmness which was invaluable, allowing her to weep her passionate fill before they left.

[1] *Hood's Poems* One of Dickens's alterations; Gaskell's original reads "a number of Pickwick."

Miss Pole, Miss Matey, and I, meanwhile, attended to Miss Brown: and hard work we found it to relieve her querulous and never-ending complaints. But if we were so weary and dispirited, what must Miss Jessie have been! Yet she came back almost calm, as if she had gained a new strength. She put off her mourning dress, and came in, looking pale and gentle; thanking us each with a soft long pressure of the hand. She could even smile—a faint, sweet, wintry smile, as if to reassure us of her power to endure; but her look made our eyes fill suddenly with tears, more than if she had cried outright.

It was settled that Miss Pole was to remain with her all the watching live-long night; and that Miss Matey and I were to return in the morning to relieve them, and give Miss Jessie the opportunity for a few hours of sleep. But when the morning came, Miss Jenkyns appeared at the breakfast table, equipped in her helmet bonnet, and ordered Miss Matey to stay at home, as she meant to go and help to nurse. She was evidently in state of great friendly excitement, which she showed by eating her breakfast standing, and scolding the household all round.

No nursing—no energetic strong-minded woman could help Miss Brown now. There was that in the room as we entered, which was stronger than us all, and made us shrink into solemn awestruck helplessness. Miss Brown was dying. We hardly knew her voice, it was so devoid of the complaining tone we had always associated with it. Miss Jessie told me afterwards that it, and her face too, were just what they had been formerly, when her mother's death left her the young anxious head of the family, of whom only Miss Jessie survived.

She was conscious of her sister's presence, though not, I think, of ours. We stood a little behind the curtain; Miss Jessie knelt with her face near her sister's, in order to catch the last soft awful whispers.

"Oh, Jessie! Jessie! How selfish I have been! God forgive me for letting you sacrifice yourself for me as you did. I have so loved you—and yet I have thought only of myself. God forgive me!"

"Hush, love! hush!" said Miss Jessie, sobbing.

"And my father! my dear, dear father! I will not complain now, if God will give me strength to be patient. But, oh, Jessie! tell my father how I longed and yearned to see him at last, and to ask his forgiveness. He can never know now how I loved him—oh! if I might but tell him, before I die, what a life of sorrow his has been, and I have done so little to cheer him!"

A light came into Miss Jessie's face. "Would it comfort you, dearest, to think that he does know—would it comfort you, love, to know that his cares, his sorrows—" Her voice quivered, but she steadied it into calmness,—"Mary! he has gone before you to the place where the weary are at rest. He knows now how you loved him."

A strange look, which was not distress, came over Miss Brown's face. She did not speak for some time, but then we saw her lips form the words, rather than heard the sound—"Father, mother, Harry, Archy!"—then, as if it was a new idea throwing a filmy shadow over her darkening mind—"But you will be alone—Jessie!"

Miss Jessie had been feeling this all during the silence, I think; for the tears rolled down her cheeks like rain at these words; and she could not answer at first. Then she put her hands together tight, and lifted them up, and said—but not to us—

"Though He slay me, yet will I trust in Him."[1]

In a few moments more, Miss Brown lay calm and still; never to sorrow or murmur more.

After this second funeral, Miss Jenkyns insisted that Miss Jessie should come to stay with her, rather than go back to the desolate house; which, in fact, we learned from Miss Jessie, must now be given up, as she had not wherewithal to maintain it. She had something about twenty pounds per annum, besides the interest of the money for which the furniture would sell; but she could not live upon that; and so we talked over her qualifications for earning money.

"I can sew neatly," said she, "and I like nursing. I think, too, I could manage a house, if anyone would try me as housekeeper; or I would go into a shop, as saleswoman, if they would have patience with me at first."

Miss Jenkyns declared, in an angry voice, that she should do no such thing; and talked to herself about "some people having no idea of their rank as a Captain's daughter," nearly an hour afterwards, when she brought Miss Jessie up a basin of delicately-made arrow-root, and

---

[1] *Though He ... trust in Him* Cf. Job 13.15.

stood over her like a dragoon[1] until the last spoonful was finished: then she disappeared. Miss Jessie began to tell me some more of the plans which had suggested themselves to her, and insensibly fell into talking of the days that were past and gone, and interested me so much, I neither knew nor heeded how time passed. We were both startled when Miss Jenkyns reappeared, and caught us crying. I was afraid lest she would be displeased, as she often said that crying hindered digestion, and I knew she wanted Miss Jessie to get strong; but, instead, she looked queer and excited, and fidgeted round us without saying anything. At last she spoke. "I have been so much startled—no, I've not been at all startled—don't mind me, my dear Miss Jessie—I've been very much surprised—in fact, I've had a caller, whom you knew once, my dear Miss Jessie—"

Miss Jessie went very white, then flushed scarlet, and looked eagerly at Miss Jenkyns—

"A gentleman, my dear, who wants to know if you would see him."

"Is it?—it is not—" stammered out Miss Jessie—and got no farther.

"This is his card," said Miss Jenkyns, giving it to Miss Jessie; and while her head was bent over it, Miss Jenkyns went through a series of winks and odd faces to me, and formed her lips into a long sentence, of which, of course, I could not understand a word.

"May he come up?" asked Miss Jenkyns, at last.

"Oh, yes! certainly!" said Miss Jessie, as much as to say, this is your house, you may show any visitor where you like. She took up some knitting of Miss Matey's, and began to be very busy, though I could see how she trembled all over.

Miss Jenkyns rang the bell, and told the servant who answered it to show Major Campbell upstairs; and, presently, in walked a tall, fine, frank-looking man of forty, or upwards. He shook hands with Miss Jessie; but he could not see her eyes, she kept them so fixed on the ground. Miss Jenkyns asked me if I would come and help her to tie up the preserves in the store-room; and, though Miss Jessie plucked at my gown and even looked

up at me with begging eye, I durst not refuse to go where Miss Jenkyns asked. Instead of tying up preserves in the store-room, however, we went to talk in the dinning-room; and there Miss Jenkyns told me what Major Campbell had told her—how he had served in the same regiment with Captain Brown, and had become acquainted with Miss Jessie, then a sweet-looking, blooming girl of eighteen; how the acquaintance had grown into love, on his part, though it had been some years before he had spoken; how, on becoming possessed, through the will of an uncle, of a good estate in Scotland, he had offered, and been refused, though with so much agitation, and evident distress, that he was sure she was not indifferent to him; and how he had discovered that the obstacle was the fell disease which was, even then, too surely threatening her sister. She had mentioned that the surgeons foretold intense suffering; and there was no one but herself to nurse her poor Mary, or cheer and comfort her father during the time of illness. They had had long discussions; and, on her refusal to pledge herself to him as his wife, when all should be over, he had grown angry, and broken off entirely, and gone abroad, believing that she was a cold-hearted person, whom he would do well to forget. He had been travelling in the East, and was on his return home when, at Rome, he saw the account of Captain Brown's death in "Galignani."[2]

Just then Miss Matey, who had been out all the morning, and had only lately returned to the house, burst in with a face of dismay and outraged propriety—

"Oh, goodness me!" she said. "Caroline, there's a gentleman sitting in the drawing-room, with his arm round Miss Jessie's waist!" Miss Matey's eyes looked large with terror.

Miss Jenkyns snubbed her down in an instant:

"The most proper place in the world for his arm to be in. Go away, Matilda, and mind your own business." This from her sister, who had hitherto been a model of feminine decorum, was a blow for poor Miss Matey, and with a double shock she left the room.

The last time I ever saw poor Miss Jenkyns was many years after this. Mrs. Campbell had kept up a

---

[1] *arrow-root* Food prepared from the starchy tuberous plant *Maranta*, indigenous to the West Indies; *dragoon* Cavalry soldier, particularly one armed with a musket (which, because it "breathes fire," is sometimes called a "dragoon").

[2] *Galignani* *Galignani's Messenger* was a daily English-language newspaper published in Paris by Giovanni Antonio Galignani (1757–1821), an Italian-born newspaper publisher.

warm and affectionate intercourse with all at Cranford. Miss Jenkyns, Miss Matey, and Miss Pole had all been to visit her, and returned with wonderful accounts of her house, her husband, her dress, and her looks. For, with happiness, something of her early bloom returned; she had been a year or two younger than we had taken her for. Her eyes were always lovely and, as Mrs. Campbell, her dimples were not out of place. At the time to which I have referred, when I last saw Miss Jenkyns, that lady was old and feeble, and had lost something of her strong mind. Little Flora Campbell was staying with the Misses Jenkyns, and when I came in she was reading aloud to Miss Jenkyns, who lay feeble and changed on the sofa. Flora put down the Rambler when I came in. "Ah!" said Miss Jenkyns, "you find me changed, my dear. I can't see as I used to do. If Flora were not here to read to me, I hardly know how I should get through the day. Did you ever read the Rambler? It's a wonderful book—wonderful! and the most improving reading for Flora"—(which I dare say it would have been if she could have read half the words without spelling, and could have understood the meaning of a third)—"better than that strange old book, with the queer name, poor Captain Brown was killed for reading—that book by Mr. Hood, you know—Hood—Admiral Hood; when I was a girl; but that's a long time ago—I wore a cloak with a red Hood"—she babbled on long enough for Flora to get a good long spell at "Miss Kilmansegg and her Golden Leg,"[1] which Miss Matey had left on the table.

Poor, dear Miss Jenkyns! Cranford is Man-less now.[2]
—1851

IN CONTEXT

Charles Dickens and the Publication History of "Our Society at Cranford"

Dickens's editorial interventions in the publication of Gaskell's "Our Society at Cranford" were the subject of some dispute between the two. Dickens evidently felt uncomfortable at the reference to his own works *The Pickwick Papers* and *A Christmas Carol* in the text of Gaskell's story; without consulting her, he edited the piece so as to remove the references. Precisely what other changes may have been in dispute is not clear—Gaskell's letters to Dickens concerning the matter have not survived—but the *Household Words* story includes a final sentence that Gaskell did not include in *Cranford*, in which the second chapter concludes as follows:

> "Ah!" said Miss Jenkyns, "you find me changed, my dear. I can't see as I used to do. If Flora were not here to read to me, I hardly know how I should get through the day. Did you ever read the Rambler? It's a wonderful book—wonderful! and the most improving reading for Flora" (which I daresay it would have been, if she could have read half the words without spelling, and could have understood the meaning of a third), "better than that strange old book, with the queer name, poor Captain Brown was killed for reading—that book by Mr Boz, you know—'Old Poz'; when I was a girl—but that's a long time

---

[1] *Miss Kilmansegg and her Golden Leg* Poem by the popular eighteenth-century writer Thomas Hood. The decision to include this reference was made by Charles Dickens in his capacity as the editor of *Household Words*; Gaskell's original had Flora turn her attention to Dickens's own *Christmas Carol* (1843). (See the "In Context" material below.)

[2] *Poor, dear ... Man-less now* This sentence does not appear in *Cranford*. (See the "In Context" materials below.)

ago—I acted Lucy in Old Poz.'" She babbled on long enough for Flora to get a good long
spell at the Christmas Carol, which Miss Matty had left on the table.

In Gaskell's text Miss Jenkyns confusedly runs together the name under which much of
Dickens's early work appeared—"Boz"—with the name of Maria Edgeworth's 1795
children's play "Old Poz," in which one of the characters is named Lucy. Dickens made a
stab at conveying the same sort of confusion as that which Miss Jenkyns makes between a
work written for adults and one written for children with his reference to a poem by Thomas
Hood and to Little Red Riding Hood, but—not surprisingly—Gaskell was displeased at such
changes having been made without her consent. Though Dickens did manage to placate her
(and to persuade her to publish in *Household Words* the subsequent pieces that together
became *Cranford*), their relationship thereafter was far from entirely smooth.

Included below is Dickens's January 1850 letter inviting Gaskell to contribute to the
magazine, together with two letters to her from December 1851.

LETTER FROM CHARLES DICKENS TO ELIZABETH GASKELL

31 January 1850
Devonshire Terrace

My Dear Mrs. Gaskell,

You may perhaps have seen an announcement in the papers of my intention to start a new cheap
weekly journal of general literature.
I do not know what your literary vows of temperance or abstinence may be, but as I do honestly know
that there is no living English writer whose aid I would desire to enlist in preference to the authoress
of "Mary Barton" (a book that most profoundly affected and impressed me), I venture to ask you
whether you can give me any hope that you will write a short tale, or any number of tales, for the
projected pages.

No writer's name will be used, neither my own nor any other; every paper will be published
without any signature, and all will seem to express the general mind and purpose of the journal, which
is the raising up of those that are down, and the general improvement of our social condition. I should
set a value on your help which your modesty can hardly imagine; and I am perfectly sure that the least
result of your reflection or observation in respect of the life around you, would attract attention and
do good.

Of course I regard your time as valuable, and consider it so when I ask you if you could devote
any of it to this purpose.

If you could and would prefer to speak to me on the subject, I should be very glad indeed to come
to Manchester for a few hours and explain anything you might wish to know. My unaffected and
great admiration of your book makes me very earnest in all relating to you. Forgive my troubling you
for this reason, and believe me ever,
    Faithfully yours.

P.S.—Mrs. Dickens and her sister send their love.

LETTER FROM CHARLES DICKENS TO ELIZABETH GASKELL

Thursday Afternoon, 5 December 1851
Tavistock House

My Dear Mrs. Gaskell,

I write in great haste to tell you that Mr. Wills, in the utmost consternation, has brought me your letter, just received (four o'clock), and that it is <u>too late</u> to recall your tale. I was so delighted with it that I put it first in the number (not hearing of any objection to my proposed alteration by return of post), and the number is now made up and in the printer's hands. I cannot possibly take the tale out—it has departed from me.

I am truly concerned for this, but I hope you will not blame me for what I have done in perfect good faith. Any recollection of me from your pen cannot (as I think you know) be otherwise than truly gratifying to me; but with my name on every page of "Household Words," there would be—or at least I should feel—an impropriety in so mentioning myself. I was particular, in changing the author, to make it "Hood's Poems" in the most important place—I mean where the captain is killed—and I hope and trust that the substitution will not be any serious drawback to the paper in any eyes but yours. I would do anything rather than cause you a minute's vexation arising out of what has given me so much pleasure, and I sincerely beseech you to think better of it, and not to fancy that any shade has been thrown on your charming writing, by

The unfortunate but innocent.

P.S.—I write at a gallop, not to lose another post.

LETTER FROM CHARLES DICKENS TO ELIZABETH GASKELL

Sunday, 21 December 1851
Tavistock House

My Dear Mrs. Gaskell,

If you were not the most suspicious of women, always looking for soft sawder[1] in the purest metal of praise, I should call your paper delightful, and touched in the tenderest and most delicate manner. Being what you are, I confine myself to the observation that I have called it "A Love Affair at Cranford,"[2] and sent it off to the printer.

Faithfully yours ever.

---

[1] *soft sawder* Flattery, insincere or disingenuous praise.

[2] *A Love Affair at Cranford* Title given to the second installment in the series of stories that eventually grew into the novel *Cranford*.

ROBERT BROWNING
1812 – 1889

"The spirit of passionate and imaginative poetry is not dead among us," wrote an exultant R.H. Horne in 1844, while reviewing the poems of the young Robert Browning. But Browning, for all his passion and imagination, was not a popular poet for much of his lifetime. Indeed, until the 1860s, Browning was better known as the husband of Elizabeth Barrett. His own poetry, in the eyes of many of his contemporaries, was far too obscure, littered as it was with recondite historical and literary references and with dubious subject matter—husbands murdering their wives, artists frolicking with prostitutes. Fame did come, however, and scholars now credit Browning for having realized new possibilities in the dramatic monologue, a form of poetry that, like a monologue in a dramatic production, showcases the speech of a character to an implied or imaginary audience. The poems are, in Browning's own words, "so many utterances of so many imaginary persons, not mine." As Browning's dramatic monologues unfold, their speakers reveal levels of psychological complexity that have inspired generations of poets, from the Pre-Raphaelites who were coming of age in the 1840s to Modernists such as Ezra Pound and T.S. Eliot.

Browning was the eldest of two children born in an upper middle-class suburb of London to a scholarly father and a devout, Protestant mother, Sarah Anna Wiedemann. An opponent of slavery, Robert Browning, Sr. rejected employment on his family's plantation in St. Kitts in favor of less lucrative but more morally acceptable work as a clerk for the Bank of England. Both parents helped to shape Browning's religious, social, and intellectual tastes and values, with Browning, Sr. in particular feeding his son's voracious appetite for knowledge. The young Browning composed his first poem at the age of six. He attended Peckham School between the ages of ten and twelve and later some classes at University College in London. But the great majority of his schooling took place at home with tutors, and he spent many hours studying the books in his family's voluminous library. Despite his relative lack of formal schooling, then, Browning had an exceptionally bookish education—which may help to explain the intellectual cast of Browning's poetic vision.

Browning first arrived on the literary scene with the publication in 1833 of *Pauline: A Fragment of a Confession*, a long poem in the style of Shelley's *Alastor* (1816), which John Stuart Mill credited with "considerable poetic powers" that yet revealed "a more intense and morbid self-consciousness than I ever knew in any sane human being." The volume, published with family funds, apparently sold not even a single copy. It was followed in 1835 by *Paracelsus*, which, though similarly obscure, at least made Browning known to a few important critics and ultimately brought him into contact with Carlyle, Dickens, and Wordsworth, among others. With *Sordello* (1840), Browning secured his reputation for writing poetry of bewildering difficulty. Browning claimed that his "stress [in *Sordello*] lay on the incidents in the development of a soul: little else is worth study," and yet few could make sense of such incidents as Browning had chosen to portray them.

In 1842 Browning published a volume of shorter poems, *Dramatic Lyrics*, which marked an important break from his earlier productions. Included were many of the poems on which his reputation came to be based: "My Last Duchess," "Soliloquy of the Spanish Cloister," "Johannes Agricola in Meditation," and "Porphyria's Lover," the last two of which had been published in the

Monthly Repository of 1836 under the heading "Madhouse Cells." With *Dramatic Romances and Lyrics* (1845) and *Men and Women* (1855), Browning confirmed his literary reputation as the foremost innovator of the dramatic monologue; he remained, however, little known among contemporary Victorians. *Men and Women* contained now-canonical poems such as "Fra Lippo Lippi" and "Andrea del Sarto." "Here," wrote George Eliot in the *Westminster Review*, the reader will find "no conventionality, no melodious commonplace, but freshness, originality, sometimes eccentricity of expression; no didactic laying-out of a subject, but dramatic indication, which requires the reader to trace by his own mental activity the underground stream of thought that jets out in elliptical and pithy verse." Eliot's commentary draws attention not only to Browning's unconventional subject matter and dramatic presentation, but also to the range of his accomplishment in poetic form, his lack of "melodious commonplace." Victorian critics noted with varying degrees of wonder and consternation the degree to which Browning experimented with rhythm and meter, an experimentation that in the early twentieth century earned him the nickname "Old Hippety-Hop o' the accents" from Ezra Pound.

In January of 1845 Browning began what became a celebrated correspondence with the already-famous poet Elizabeth Barrett. Even before meeting her personally (an event that took place after four months of writing), Browning praised Barrett's 1844 volume *Poems* with the words, "I do, as I say, love these books with all my heart—and I love you too." Barrett fell in love with Browning after meeting him, and in 1846, despite her semi-invalid state and her father's command never to marry, the two eloped in London and moved to Italy, where they remained for the rest of her life. Their only child, Robert Wiedemann Barrett Browning (nicknamed "Pen"), was born in 1849 in their Florence home, Casa Guidi.

Browning returned to London and society life after his wife's death in 1861. 1864 brought the publication of *Dramatis Personae*, the first of his volumes to be popular among British readers. This was followed in 1868–69 by his twelve-part epic "murder-poem" (as Browning called it), *The Ring and the Book*. Browning conceived the idea of writing this epic in 1860, when in a Florence market he chanced upon a book of documents concerning a 1698 murder trial. He organized the story so that each book in the epic gives voice to a different participant in the event: the murderer, various onlookers, the victim, and even the Pope. In juxtaposing these varying testimonies, Browning suggests the impossibility of ever finding a coherent or truthful narrative and the importance of recognizing the relativity of points of view—something enacted in his dramatic monologues. These "filthy rags of speech," says the Pope, are "tatters all too contaminate for use."

The 1879–80 volumes of *Dramatic Idyls* brought the poet even greater fame, both in England and internationally; the public in the United States flocked to buy his books, and wearing brown articles of clothing in his honor became fashionable. In 1889, on the day his final volume of poems, *Asolando*, was published, Robert Browning died at his son's home in Venice. He is buried next to Alfred, Lord Tennyson, in the Poets' Corner of Westminster Abbey.

⌘ ⌘ ⌘

Porphyria's Lover

The rain set early in tonight,
    The sullen wind was soon awake,
It tore the elm tops down for spite,
    And did its worst to vex the lake:

5   I listened with heart fit to break.
When glided in Porphyria; straight
    She shut the cold out and the storm,
And kneeled and made the cheerless grate
    Blaze up, and all the cottage warm;
10   Which done, she rose, and from her form

Withdrew the dripping cloak and shawl,
    And laid her soiled gloves by, untied
Her hat and let the damp hair fall,
    And, last, she sat down by my side
15   And called me. When no voice replied,
She put my arm about her waist,
    And made her smooth white shoulder bare,
And all her yellow hair displaced,
    And, stooping, made my cheek lie there,
20   And spread, o'er all, her yellow hair,
Murmuring how she loved me—she
    Too weak, for all her heart's endeavour,
To set its struggling passion free
    From pride, and vainer ties dissever,
25   And give herself to me forever.
But passion sometimes would prevail,
    Nor could tonight's gay feast restrain
A sudden thought of one so pale
    For love of her, and all in vain:
30   So, she was come through wind and rain.
Be sure I looked up at her eyes
    Happy and proud; at last I knew
Porphyria worshipped me; surprise
    Made my heart swell, and still it grew
35   While I debated what to do.
That moment she was mine, mine, fair,
    Perfectly pure and good: I found
A thing to do, and all her hair
    In one long yellow string I wound
40   Three times her little throat around,
And strangled her. No pain felt she;
    I am quite sure she felt no pain.
As a shut bud that holds a bee,
    I warily oped her lids: again
45   Laughed the blue eyes without a stain.
And I untightened next the tress
    About her neck; her cheek once more
Blushed bright beneath my burning kiss:
    I propped her head up as before,
50   Only, this time my shoulder bore
Her head, which droops upon it still:
    The smiling rosy little head,
So glad it has its utmost will,
    That all it scorned at once is fled,
55   And I, its love, am gained instead!

Porphyria's love: she guessed not how
    Her darling one wish would be heard.
And thus we sit together now,
    And all night long we have not stirred,
60   And yet God has not said a word!
—1836

Soliloquy of the Spanish Cloister

1

Gr-r-r—there go, my heart's abhorrence!
    Water your damned flowerpots, do!
If hate killed men, Brother Lawrence,
    God's blood, would not mine kill you!
5   What? your myrtle bush wants trimming?
    Oh, that rose has prior claims—
Needs its leaden vase filled brimming?
    Hell dry you up with its flames!

2

At the meal we sit together:
10   *Salve tibi!*[1] I must hear
Wise talk of the kind of weather,
    Sort of season, time of year:
Not a plenteous cork crop: scarcely
    Dare we hope oak galls,[2] I doubt:
15   *What's the Latin name for "parsley"?*
    What's the Greek name for Swine's Snout?[3]

3

Whew! We'll have our platter burnished,
    Laid with care on our own shelf!
With a fire-new spoon we're furnished,
20   And a goblet for ourself,
Rinsed like something sacrificial
    Ere 'tis fit to touch our chaps°—   *jaws*
Marked with L. for our initial!
    (He-he! There his lily snaps!)

---

[1] *Salve tibi*   Hail to thee.

[2] *oak galls*   Growths on oak trees that are used to produce certain inks and tannins.

[3] *Swine's Snout*   Dandelion.

4

25 *Saint*, forsooth! While brown Dolores
        Squats outside the Convent bank
    With Sanchicha, telling stories,
        Steeping tresses in the tank,
    Blue-black, lustrous, thick like horsehairs,
30   —Can't I see his dead eye glow,
    Bright as 'twere a Barbary corsair's?[1]
        (That is, if he'd let it show!)

5

    When he finishes refection,°   *a meal*
        Knife and fork he never lays
35 Crosswise, to my recollection,
        As do I, in Jesu's praise.
    I the Trinity illustrate,
        Drinking watered orange pulp—
    In three sips the Arian[2] frustrate;
40   While he drains his at one gulp.

6

    Oh, those melons? If he's able
        We're to have a feast! so nice!
    One goes to the Abbot's table,
        All of us get each a slice.
45 How go on your flowers? None double?
        Not one fruit-sort can you spy?
    Strange!—And I, too, at such trouble,
        Keep them close-nipped on the sly!

7

    There's a great text in Galatians,
50   Once you trip on it, entails
    Twenty-nine distinct damnations,[3]
        One sure, if another fails:
    If I trip him just a-dying,
        Sure of heaven as sure can be,

55 Spin him round and send him flying
        Off to hell, a Manichee?[4]

8

    Or, my scrofulous° French novel   *morally corrupt*
        On grey paper with blunt type!
    Simply glance at it, you grovel
60   Hand and foot in Belial's° gripe: *the devil's*
    If I double down its pages
        At the woeful sixteenth print,
    When he gathers his greengages,°   *plums*
        Ope a sieve and slip it in't?

9

65 Or, there's Satan!—one might venture
        Pledge one's soul to him, yet leave
    Such a flaw in the indenture
        As he'd miss till, past retrieve,
    Blasted lay that rose acacia
70   We're so proud of! *Hy, Zy, Hine* ...
    'St, there's Vespers![5] *Plena gratiâ
    Ave, Virgo!*[6] Gr-r-r—you swine!
                                                            —1842

My Last Duchess[7]

Ferrara

That's my last Duchess painted on the wall,
    Looking as if she were alive. I call
That piece a wonder, now: Frà° Pandolf's hands   *Brother*

---

[1] *Barbary corsair* Pirate of the Barbary Coast (former name of the Mediterranean coastal region of North Africa).

[2] *Arian* Follower of Arius (256–336), considered a heretic in his day for his disavowal of the notion (inherent in the concept of the Trinity) that Jesus Christ was of the same essence or substance as God.

[3] *Galatians ... damnations* See Galatians 5.19–21 for a list of 17, not 29, sins.

[4] *Manichee* Heretic; follower of the Persian theologian Mani's third-century beliefs in dualism.

[5] *Hy, Zy, Hine ... Vespers* Sound of the bell that rings for Vespers, or evening prayers.

[6] *Plena ... Virgo* Version of the Latin prayer "Ave Maria": "Full of grace / Hail, Virgin."

[7] *My Last Duchess* According to Louis S. Friedland, Browning likely modeled the speaker of this poem on Alfonso II (1533–98), Duke of Ferrara. His first wife, a member of the wealthy Medici family, was only fourteen years old when they married. Only three days after the wedding, Alfonso left his wife for two years, and she died of suspicious causes a year after he returned. Four years later the duke negotiated with a servant to marry the daughter of the Count of Tyrol.

Worked busily a day, and there she stands.
5   Will't please you sit and look at her? I said
"Frà Pandolf" by design, for never read
Strangers like you that pictured countenance,
The depth and passion of its earnest glance,
But to myself they turned (since none puts by
10 The curtain I have drawn for you, but I)
And seemed as they would ask me, if they durst,
How such a glance came there; so, not the first
Are you to turn and ask thus. Sir, 'twas not
Her husband's presence only, called that spot
15 Of joy into the Duchess' cheek: perhaps
Frà Pandolf chanced to say "Her mantle laps
Over my lady's wrist too much," or "Paint
Must never hope to reproduce the faint
Half-flush that dies along her throat": such stuff
20 Was courtesy, she thought, and cause enough
For calling up that spot of joy. She had
A heart—how shall I say?—too soon made glad,
Too easily impressed; she liked whate'er
She looked on, and her looks went everywhere.
25 Sir, 'twas all one! My favour° at her breast,   *gift*
The dropping of the daylight in the West,
The bough of cherries some officious fool
Broke in the orchard for her, the white mule
She rode with round the terrace—all and each
30 Would draw from her alike the approving speech,
Or blush, at least. She thanked men—good! but
     thanked
Somehow—I know not how—as if she ranked
My gift of a nine-hundred-years-old name
With anybody's gift. Who'd stoop to blame
35 This sort of trifling? Even had you skill
In speech—(which I have not)—to make your will
Quite clear to such an one, and say, "Just this
Or that in you disgusts me; here you miss,
Or there exceed the mark"—and if she let
40 Herself be lessoned so, nor plainly set
Her wits to yours, forsooth, and made excuse,
—E'en then would be some stooping; and I choose
Never to stoop. Oh sir, she smiled, no doubt,
Whene'er I passed her; but who passed without

45 Much the same smile? This grew; I gave commands;
Then all smiles stopped together. There she stands
As if alive. Will't please you rise? We'll meet
The company below, then. I repeat,
The Count your master's known munificence
50 Is ample warrant that no just pretence
Of mine for dowry will be disallowed;
Though his fair daughter's self, as I avowed
At starting, is my object. Nay, we'll go
Together down, sir. Notice Neptune,[1] though,
55 Taming a seahorse, thought a rarity,
Which Claus of Innsbruck cast in bronze for me!
—1842

Home-Thoughts, from Abroad

1

Oh, to be in England
Now that April's there,
And whoever wakes in England
Sees, some morning, unaware,
5   That the lowest boughs and the brushwood sheaf
Round the elm-tree bole° are in tiny leaf,   *trunk*
While the chaffinch sings on the orchard bough
In England—now!

2

And after April, when May follows,
10 And the whitethroat builds, and all the swallows!
Hark, where my blossomed pear tree in the hedge
Leans to the field and scatters on the clover
Blossoms and dewdrops—at the bent spray's edge—
That's the wise thrush; he sings each song twice over,
15 Lest you should think he never could recapture
The first fine careless rapture!
And though the fields look rough with hoary dew
All will be gay when noontide wakes anew
The buttercups, the little children's dower—
20 Far brighter than this gaudy melon flower!
—1845

---

[1] *Neptune* Roman god of the sea, who rides in a chariot pulled by seahorses.

The Bishop Orders His Tomb at Saint Praxed's Church

Rome, 15—

Vanity, saith the preacher, vanity![1]
Draw round my bed: is Anselm keeping back?
Nephews—sons mine … ah God, I know not! Well—
She, men would have to be your mother once,
5   Old Gandolf envied me, so fair she was!
What's done is done, and she is dead beside,
Dead long ago, and I am Bishop since,
And as she died so must we die ourselves,
And thence ye may perceive the world's a dream.
10   Life, how and what is it? As here I lie
In this state-chamber, dying by degrees,
Hours and long hours in the dead night, I ask
"Do I live, am I dead?" Peace, peace seems all.
Saint Praxed's ever was the church for peace;
15   And so, about this tomb of mine. I fought
With tooth and nail to save my niche, ye know:
—Old Gandolf cozened me,° despite my care;   *cheated*
Shrewd was that snatch from out the corner south
He graced his carrion with, God curse the same!
20   Yet still my niche is not so cramped but thence
One sees the pulpit o' the epistle side,[2]
And somewhat of the choir, those silent seats,
And up into the aery dome where live
The angels, and a sunbeam's sure to lurk:
25   And I shall fill my slab of basalt there,
And 'neath my tabernacle take my rest,
With those nine columns round me, two and two,
The odd one at my feet where Anselm stands:
Peach-blossom marble all, the rare, the ripe
30   As fresh-poured red wine of a mighty pulse.
—Old Gandolf with his paltry onion-stone,[3]
Put me where I may look at him! True peach,
Rosy and flawless: how I earned the prize!
Draw close: that conflagration of my church

35   —What then? So much was saved if aught were
        missed!
My sons, ye would not be my death? Go dig
The white-grape vineyard where the oil-press stood,
Drop water gently till the surface sink,
And if ye find … Ah God, I know not, I! …
40   Bedded in store of rotten fig leaves soft,
And corded up in a tight olive-frail,°   *basket*
Some lump, ah God, of *lapis lazuli*,[4]
Big as a Jew's head cut off at the nape,
Blue as a vein o'er the Madonna's breast …
45   Sons, all have I bequeathed you, villas, all,
That brave Frascati[5] villa with its bath,
So, let the blue lump poise between my knees,
Like God the Father's globe on both his hands
Ye worship in the Jesu Church[6] so gay,
50   For Gandolf shall not choose but see and burst!
Swift as a weaver's shuttle fleet our years:[7]
Man goeth to the grave, and where is he?[8]
Did I say basalt for my slab, sons? Black—
'Twas ever antique-black° I meant! How else   *black marble*
55   Shall ye contrast my frieze[9] to come beneath?
The bas-relief in bronze ye promised me,
Those Pans and Nymphs[10] ye wot of, and perchance
Some tripod, thyrsus,[11] with a vase or so,
The Saviour at his sermon on the mount,

---

[1] *Vanity, saith the preacher, vanity* From Ecclesiastes 1.2: "Vanity of vanities, saith the Preacher, vanity of vanities; all is vanity."

[2] *epistle side* Right-hand side, where the pulpit is and from which the epistles are read.

[3] *onion-stone* Variety of less expensive marble that is named for its tendency to peel into layers.

[4] *lapis lazuli* Semi-precious blue stone; the altar-tomb of St. Ignatius at Il Gesù (Church of the Holy Name of Jesus) in Rome is decorated with huge columns made from lapis lazuli.

[5] *Frascati* Summer resort near Rome.

[6] *Jesu Church* Il Gesù.

[7] *Swift … years* From Job 7.6: "My days are swifter than a weaver's shuttle, and are spent without hope."

[8] *Man goeth … where is he?* From Job 7.9: "As the cloud is consumed and vanisheth away: so he that goeth down to the grave shall come up no more."

[9] *frieze* Painted or sculpted band on a wall or column.

[10] *bas-relief… Pans and Nymphs* Shallow carvings that depict Greek mythological figures alongside Biblical figures.

[11] *tripod* Vessel on which sat the Oracle at Delphi, where she delivered her prophecies; *thyrsus* Staff adorned with a pine cone and ivy, carried by Dionysus, the Greek god of wine, and his followers.

60 Saint Praxed[1] in a glory,° and one Pan[2]   *halo, lightbeam*
Ready to twitch the Nymph's last garment off,
And Moses with the tables°… but I know   *Ten Commandments*
Ye mark me not! What do they whisper thee,
Child of my bowels, Anselm? Ah, ye hope
65 To revel down my villas while I gasp
Bricked o'er with beggar's mouldy travertine°   *limestone*
Which Gandolf from his tomb top chuckles at!
Nay, boys, ye love me—all of jasper,° then!   *precious stone*
'Tis jasper ye stand pledged to, lest I grieve
70 My bath must needs be left behind, alas!
One block, pure green as a pistachio nut,
There's plenty jasper somewhere in the world—
And have I not Saint Praxed's ear to pray
Horses for ye, and brown Greek manuscripts,
75 And mistresses with great smooth marbly limbs?
—That's if ye carve my epitaph aright,
Choice Latin, picked phrase, Tully's[3] every word,
No gaudy ware like Gandolf's second line—
Tully, my masters? Ulpian[4] serves his need!
80 And then how I shall lie through centuries,
And hear the blessed mutter of the mass,
And see God made and eaten all day long,
And feel the steady candle flame, and taste
Good strong thick stupefying incense smoke!
85 For as I lie here, hours of the dead night,
Dying in state and by such slow degrees,
I fold my arms as if they clasped a crook,°   *bishop's staff*
And stretch my feet forth straight as stone can point,
And let the bedclothes, for a mortcloth,[5] drop
90 Into great laps and folds of sculptor's work:
And as yon tapers dwindle, and strange thoughts
Grow, with a certain humming in my ears,
About the life before I lived this life,
And this life too, popes, cardinals and priests,
95 Saint Praxed at his sermon on the mount,

Your tall pale mother with her talking eyes,
And newfound agate urns as fresh as day,
And marble's language, Latin pure, discreet,
—Aha, *ELUCESCEBAT*[6] quoth our friend?
100 No Tully, said I, Ulpian at the best!
Evil and brief hath been my pilgrimage.[7]
All *lapis*, all, sons! Else I give the Pope
My villas! Will ye ever eat my heart?
Ever your eyes were as a lizard's quick,
105 They glitter like your mother's for my soul,
Or ye would heighten my impoverished frieze,
Piece out its starved design, and fill my vase
With grapes, and add a vizor and a Term,[8]
And to the tripod ye would tie a lynx
110 That in his struggle throws the thyrsus down,
To comfort me on my entablature°   *column*
Whereon I am to lie till I must ask
"Do I live, am I dead?" There, leave me, there!
For ye have stabbed me with ingratitude
115 To death—ye wish it—God, ye wish it! Stone—
Gritstone, a-crumble! Clammy squares which sweat
As if the corpse they keep were oozing through—
And no more lapis to delight the world!
Well go! I bless ye. Fewer tapers° there,   *candles*
120 But in a row: and, going, turn your backs
—Ay, like departing altar ministrants,
And leave me in my church, the church for peace,
That I may watch at leisure if he leers—
Old Gandolf, at me, from his onion-stone,
125 As still he envied me, so fair she was!
—1845

---

[1] *Saint Praxed* Roman virgin of the second century who gave away all of her wealth to the poor.

[2] *Pan* Greek shepherd god of nature, who chased the nymph Syrinx until she turned herself into a bed of reeds.

[3] *Tully* Commonly known as Cicero, Roman orator, philosopher, and statesman of the first century BCE.

[4] *Ulpian* Roman jurist (?–228 CE), whose writings were acknowledged to be of a lower standard than Cicero's.

[5] *mortcloth* Funeral cloth draped over the dead.

[6] *ELUCESCEBAT* Latin: "He was illustrious." *Elucescebat* is a later Latin verb form; Cicero would have written *elucebat*.

[7] *Evil … pilgrimage* Cf. Genesis 47.9: "Jacob said unto Pharaoh … few and evil have the days of the years of my life been, and have not attained unto the days of the years of the life of my fathers in the days of their pilgrimage."

[8] *vizor* Helmet piece represented in Roman sculpture; *Term* Statue of Terminus, Roman god of boundaries.

Fra Lippo Lippi[1]

I am poor brother Lippo, by your leave!
  You need not clap your torches to my face.
Zooks,[2] what's to blame? you think you see a monk!
What, 'tis past midnight, and you go the rounds,
5 And here you catch me at an alley's end
Where sportive ladies leave their doors ajar?
The Carmine's[3] my cloister: hunt it up,
Do—harry out, if you must show your zeal,
Whatever rat, there, haps on his wrong hole,
10 And nip each softling of a wee white mouse,
Weke, weke, that's crept to keep him company!
Aha, you know your betters! Then, you'll take
Your hand away that's fiddling on my throat,
And please to know me likewise. Who am I?
15 Why, one, sir, who is lodging with a friend
Three streets off—he's a certain ... how d'ye call?
Master—a ... Cosimo of the Medici,[4]
I' the house that caps the corner. Boh! you were best!
Remember and tell me, the day you're hanged,
20 How you affected such a gullet's-gripe!°   *stranglehold*
But you, sir, it concerns you that your knaves
Pick up a manner nor discredit you:
Zooks, are we pilchards,[5] that they sweep the streets
And count fair prize what comes into their net?
25 He's Judas to a tittle,[6] that man is!
Just such a face! Why, sir, you make amends.
Lord, I'm not angry! Bid your hangdogs go
Drink out this quarter-florin[7] to the health
Of the munificent House that harbours me

30 (And many more beside, lads! more beside!)
And all's come square again. I'd like his face—
His, elbowing on his comrade in the door
With the pike and lantern—for the slave that holds
John Baptist's head a-dangle by the hair
35 With one hand ("Look you, now," as who should say)
And his weapon in the other, yet unwiped!
It's not your chance to have a bit of chalk,
A wood-coal or the like? or you should see!
Yes, I'm the painter, since you style me so.
40 What, brother Lippo's doings, up and down,
You know them and they take you? like enough!
I saw the proper twinkle in your eye—
'Tell you, I liked your looks at very first.
Let's sit and set things straight now, hip to haunch.
45 Here's spring come, and the nights one makes up bands
To roam the town and sing out carnival,[8]
And I've been three weeks shut within my
    mew,°   *confined space*
A-painting for the great man, saints and saints
And saints again. I could not paint all night—
50 Ouf! I leaned out of window for fresh air.
There came a hurry of feet and little feet,
A sweep of lute strings, laughs, and whifts of song—
Flower o' the broom,
Take away love, and our earth is a tomb![9]
55 *Flower o' the quince,*
I let Lisa go, and what good in life since?
Flower o' the thyme—and so on. Round they went.
Scarce had they turned the corner when a titter
Like the skipping of rabbits by moonlight—three slim
    shapes,
60 And a face that looked up ... zooks, sir, flesh and blood,
That's all I'm made of! Into shreds it went,
Curtain and counterpane and coverlet,
All the bed furniture—a dozen knots,
There was a ladder! Down I let myself,
65 Hands and feet, scrambling somehow, and so dropped,
And after them. I came up with the fun
Hard by Saint Laurence,[10] hail fellow, well met—
Flower o' the rose,

---

1 *Fra Lippo Lippi* Browning extracted details of the life of Florentine painter and Carmelite monk Fra (Brother) Filippo Lippi (1406–69) from Giorgio Vasari's *The Lives of the Painters* (1550); the art theory Lippi propounds, however, is envisioned by Browning.

2 *Zooks* Exclamation of surprise.

3 *Carmine* Lippi was raised an orphan and eventually took his vows in Santa Maria del Carmine, a Carmelite monastery.

4 *Cosimo of the Medici* The wealthy Medici family, headed up by Lippi's patron, Cosimo dé Medici (1389–1464), ruled Florence for many years.

5 *pilchards* Herring-like fish.

6 *to a tittle* Exactly (a "tittle" is a letter stroke or punctuation mark).

7 *florin* Florentine currency.

8 *carnival* Celebrations before Lent.

9 *Flower ... tomb* This song takes the form of a *stornelli*, a three-line Italian folk song about a flower.

10 *Saint Laurence* Church of San Lorenzo in Florence.

If I've been merry, what matter who knows?
70 And so as I was stealing back again
To get to bed and have a bit of sleep
Ere I rise up tomorrow and go work
On Jerome[1] knocking at his poor old breast
With his great round stone to subdue the flesh,
75 You snap me of the sudden. Ah, I see!
Though your eye twinkles still, you shake your head—
Mine's shaved—a monk, you say—the sting's in that!
If Master Cosimo announced himself,
Mum's the word naturally; but a monk!
80 Come, what am I a beast for? tell us, now!
I was a baby when my mother died
And father died and left me in the street.
I starved there, God knows how, a year or two
On fig skins, melon parings, rinds and shucks,
85 Refuse and rubbish. One fine frosty day,
My stomach being empty as your hat,
The wind doubled me up and down I went.
Old Aunt Lapaccia trussed me with one hand,
(Its fellow was a stinger as I knew)
90 And so along the wall, over the bridge,
By the straight cut to the convent. Six words there,
While I stood munching my first bread that month:
"So, boy, you're minded," quoth the good fat father
Wiping his own mouth, 'twas refection°-time—,   *meal*
95 "To quit this very miserable world?
Will you renounce"… "the mouthful of bread?"
    thought I;
By no means! Brief, they made a monk of me;
I did renounce the world, its pride and greed,
Palace, farm, villa, shop and banking-house,
100 Trash, such as these poor devils of Medici
Have given their hearts to—all at eight years old.
Well, sir, I found in time, you may be sure,
'Twas not for nothing—the good bellyful,
The warm serge and the rope that goes all round,[2]
105 And day-long blessed idleness beside!
"Let's see what the urchin's fit for"—that came next.
Not overmuch their way, I must confess.
Such a to-do! They tried me with their books:
Lord, they'd have taught me Latin in pure waste!

110 *Flower o' the clove,*
All the Latin I construe is, "amo," I love!
But, mind you, when a boy starves in the streets
Eight years together, as my fortune was,
Watching folk's faces to know who will fling
115 The bit of half-stripped grape bunch he desires,
And who will curse or kick him for his pains—
Which gentleman processional and fine,
Holding a candle to the Sacrament,
Will wink and let him lift a plate and catch
120 The droppings of the wax to sell again,
Or holla for the Eight[3] and have him whipped—
How say I?—nay, which dog bites, which lets drop
His bone from the heap of offal in the street—
Why, soul and sense of him grow sharp alike,
125 He learns the look of things, and none the less
For admonition from the hunger pinch.
I had a store of such remarks, be sure,
Which, after I found leisure, turned to use.
I drew men's faces on my copy books,
130 Scrawled them within the antiphonary's marge,[4]
Joined legs and arms to the long music notes,
Found eyes and nose and chin for A's and B's,
And made a string of pictures of the world
Betwixt the ins and outs of verb and noun,
135 On the wall, the bench, the door. The monks looked
    black.
"Nay," quoth the Prior, "turn him out, d'ye say?
In no wise. Lose a crow and catch a lark.
What if at last we get our man of parts,[5]
We Carmelites, like those Camaldolese
140 And Preaching Friars,[6] to do our church up fine
And put the front on it that ought to be!"
And hereupon he bade me daub away.
Thank you! my head being crammed, the walls a blank,
Never was such prompt disemburdening.
145 First, every sort of monk, the black and white,
I drew them, fat and lean: then, folk at church,
From good old gossips waiting to confess
Their cribs° of barrel droppings, candle ends—   *pilferings*

1   *Jerome*   The ascetic St. Jerome, who lived many years as a hermit in the Syrian desert.

2   *rope … round*   I.e., rope belt.

3   *Eight*   The eight magistrates who governed Florence.

4   *antiphonary's marge*   Margin of a book of choral—or antiphonal—music, normally sung in harmony by two choirs.

5   *man of parts*   Man of intellect, ability.

6   *Preaching Friars*   Dominican monks.

To the breathless fellow at the altar foot,
150 Fresh from his murder, safe[1] and sitting there
With the little children round him in a row
Of admiration, half for his beard and half
For that white anger of his victim's son
Shaking a fist at him with one fierce arm,
155 Signing himself[2] with the other because of Christ
(Whose sad face on the cross sees only this
After the passion of a thousand years)
Till some poor girl, her apron o'er her head,
(Which the intense eyes looked through) came at eve
160 On tiptoe, said a word, dropped in a loaf,
Her pair of earrings and a bunch of flowers
(The brute took growling), prayed, and so was gone.
I painted all, then cried "'Tis ask and have;
Choose, for more's ready!"—laid the ladder flat,
165 And showed my covered bit of cloister wall.
The monks closed in a circle and praised loud
Till checked, taught what to see and not to see,
Being simple bodies—"That's the very man!
Look at the boy who stoops to pat the dog!
170 That woman's like the Prior's niece who comes
To care about his asthma: it's the life!"
But there my triumph's straw-fire flared and
        funked;°   *smoked*
Their betters took their turn to see and say:
The Prior and the learned pulled a face
175 And stopped all that in no time. "How? what's here?
Quite from the mark of painting, bless us all!
Faces, arms, legs and bodies like the true
As much as pea and pea! it's devil's game!
Your business is not to catch men with show,
180 With homage to the perishable clay,
But lift them over it, ignore it all,
Make them forget there's such a thing as flesh.
Your business is to paint the souls of men—
Man's soul, and it's a fire, smoke ... no, it's not ...
185 It's vapour done up like a newborn babe—
(In that shape when you die it leaves your mouth)
It's ... well, what matters talking, it's the soul!
Give us no more of body than shows soul!

Here's Giotto,[3] with his Saint a-praising God,
190 That sets us praising—why not stop with him?
Why put all thoughts of praise out of our head
With wonder at lines, colours, and what not?
Paint the soul, never mind the legs and arms!
Rub all out, try at it a second time.
195 Oh, that white smallish female with the breasts,
She's just my niece ... Herodias, I would say—
Who went and danced and got men's heads cut off![4]
Have it all out!" Now, is this sense, I ask?
A fine way to paint soul, by painting body
200 So ill, the eye can't stop there, must go further
And can't fare worse! Thus, yellow does for white
When what you put for yellow's simply black,
And any sort of meaning looks intense
When all beside itself means and looks nought.
205 Why can't a painter lift each foot in turn,
Left foot and right foot, go a double step,
Make his flesh liker and his soul more like,
Both in their order? Take the prettiest face,
The Prior's niece ... patron saint—is it so pretty
210 You can't discover if it means hope, fear,
Sorrow or joy? won't beauty go with these?
Suppose I've made her eyes all right and blue,
Can't I take breath and try to add life's flash,
And then add soul and heighten them threefold?
215 Or say there's beauty with no soul at all—
(I never saw it—put the case the same—)
If you get simple beauty and nought else,
You get about the best thing God invents:
That's somewhat: and you'll find the soul you have
        missed,
220 Within yourself, when you return him thanks.
"Rub all out!" Well, well, there's my life, in short,
And so the thing has gone on ever since.
I'm grown a man no doubt, I've broken bounds:
You should not take a fellow eight years old
225 And make him swear to never kiss the girls.
I'm my own master, paint now as I please—

---

[1] *fellow ... safe* Safe from prosecution within the church.

[2] *Signing himself* Making the sign of the cross.

[3] *Giotto* Renowned Florentine artist (1267–1337), whose works
consist mainly of religious paintings and frescoes.

[4] *Herodias ... heads cut off* According to Matthew 14.6–10, King
Herod's niece Salomé (the daughter of his sister Herodias) danced
for the king and then requested that he bring her the head of John
the Baptist, now the patron saint of Florence.

Having a friend, you see, in the Corner-house!
Lord, it's fast holding by the rings in front—
Those great rings serve more purposes than just
230   To plant a flag in, or tie up a horse!
And yet the old schooling sticks, the old grave eyes
Are peeping o'er my shoulder as I work,
The heads shake still—"It's art's decline, my son!
You're not of the true painters, great and old;
235   Brother Angelico's the man, you'll find;
Brother Lorenzo[1] stands his single peer:
Fag on at flesh, you'll never make the third!"
Flower o' the pine,
You keep your mistr ... manners, and I'll stick to mine!
240   I'm not the third, then: bless us, they must know!
Don't you think they're the likeliest to know,
They with their Latin? So, I swallow my rage,
Clench my teeth, suck my lips in tight, and paint
To please them—sometimes do and sometimes don't;
245   For, doing most, there's pretty sure to come
A turn, some warm eve finds me at my saints—
A laugh, a cry, the business of the world—
(*Flower o' the peach,*
Death for us all, and his own life for each!)
250   And my whole soul revolves, the cup runs over,
The world and life's too big to pass for a dream,
And I do these wild things in sheer despite,
And play the fooleries you catch me at,
In pure rage! The old mill-horse, out at grass
255   After hard years, throws up his stiff heels so,
Although the miller does not preach to him
The only good of grass is to make chaff.
What would men have? Do they like grass or no—
May they or mayn't they? all I want's the thing
260   Settled forever one way. As it is,
You tell too many lies and hurt yourself:
You don't like what you only like too much,
You do like what, if given you at your word,
You find abundantly detestable.
265   For me, I think I speak as I was taught;
I always see the garden and God there
A-making man's wife: and, my lesson learned,

The value and significance of flesh,
I can't unlearn ten minutes afterwards.

270   You understand me: I'm a beast, I know.
But see, now—why, I see as certainly
As that the morning star's about to shine,
What will hap some day. We've a youngster here
Comes to our convent, studies what I do,
275   Slouches and stares and lets no atom drop:
His name is Guidi[2]—he'll not mind the monks—
They call him Hulking Tom, he lets them talk—
He picks my practice up—he'll paint apace,
I hope so—though I never live so long,
280   I know what's sure to follow. You be judge!
You speak no Latin more than I, belike;
However, you're my man, you've seen the world
—The beauty and the wonder and the power,
The shapes of things, their colours, lights and shades,
285   Changes, surprises—and God made it all!
—For what? Do you feel thankful, ay or no,
For this fair town's face, yonder river's line,
The mountain round it and the sky above,
Much more the figures of man, woman, child,
290   These are the frame to? What's it all about?
To be passed over, despised? or dwelt upon,
Wondered at? oh, this last of course!—you say.
But why not do as well as say—paint these
Just as they are, careless what comes of it?
295   God's works—paint anyone, and count it crime
To let a truth slip. Don't object, "His works
Are here already; nature is complete:
Suppose you reproduce her—(which you can't)
There's no advantage! you must beat her, then."
300   For, don't you mark? we're made so that we love
First when we see them painted, things we have passed
Perhaps a hundred times nor cared to see;
And so they are better, painted—better to us,
Which is the same thing. Art was given for that;
305   God uses us to help each other so,
Lending our minds out. Have you noticed, now,
Your cullion's° hanging face? A bit of chalk,   *scoundrel's*

---

[1] *Brother Angelico ... Brother Lorenzo* Italian Renaissance artists who painted in the early 1400s in the conventional style, as opposed to Lippi's naturalist style.

[2] *Guidi* Tommaso Guidi (1401–28), who became known as Masaccio, was highly skilled at creating naturalistic portrayals of human figures; he was likely Lippi's teacher, not his student.

And trust me but you should, though! How much
    more,
If I drew higher things with the same truth!
310 That were to take the Prior's pulpit place,
Interpret God to all of you! Oh, oh,
It makes me mad to see what men shall do
And we in our graves! This world's no blot for us,
Nor blank; it means intensely, and means good:
315 To find its meaning is my meat and drink.
"Ay, but you don't so instigate to prayer!"
Strikes in the Prior: "when your meaning's plain
It does not say to folk—remember matins,[1]
Or, mind you fast next Friday!" Why, for this
320 What need of art at all? A skull and bones,
Two bits of stick nailed crosswise, or, what's best,
A bell to chime the hour with, does as well.
I painted a Saint Laurence[2] six months since
At Prato,[3] splashed the fresco in fine style:
325 "How looks my painting, now the scaffold's down?"
I ask a brother: "Hugely," he returns—
"Already not one phiz° of your three slaves   *face*
Who turn the Deacon off his toasted side,
But's scratched and prodded to our heart's content,
330 The pious people have so eased their own
With coming to say prayers there in a rage:
We get on fast to see the bricks beneath.
Expect another job this time next year,
For pity and religion grow i' the crowd—
335 Your painting serves its purpose!" Hang the fools!

—That is—you'll not mistake an idle word
Spoke in a huff by a poor monk, God wot,
Tasting the air this spicy night which turns
The unaccustomed head like Chianti wine!
340 Oh, the church knows! don't misreport me, now!
It's natural a poor monk out of bounds
Should have his apt word to excuse himself:
And hearken how I plot to make amends.
I have bethought me: I shall paint a piece
345 … There's for you! Give me six months, then go, see

Something in Sant'Ambrogio's![4] Bless the nuns!
They want a cast o' my office. I shall paint
God in the midst, Madonna and her babe,
Ringed by a bowery flowery angel brood,
350 Lilies and vestments and white faces, sweet
As puff on puff of grated orris-root[5]
When ladies crowd to Church at midsummer.
And then i' the front, of course a saint or two—
Saint John, because he saves the Florentines,
355 Saint Ambrose, who puts down in black and white
The convent's friends and gives them a long day,
And Job, I must have him there past mistake,
The man of Uz[6] (and Us without the z,
Painters who need his patience). Well, all these
360 Secured at their devotion, up shall come
Out of a corner when you least expect,
As one by a dark stair into a great light,
Music and talking, who but Lippo! I!—
Mazed, motionless and moonstruck—I'm the man!
365 Back I shrink—what is this I see and hear?
I, caught up with my monk's things by mistake,
My old serge gown and rope that goes all round,
I, in this presence, this pure company!
Where's a hole, where's a corner for escape?
370 Then steps a sweet angelic slip of a thing
Forward, puts out a soft palm—"Not so fast!"
—Addresses the celestial presence, "nay—
He made you and devised you, after all,
Though he's none of you! Could Saint John there draw—
375 His camel hair[7] make up a painting brush?
We come to brother Lippo for all that,
Iste perfecit opus!"[8] So, all smile—
I shuffle sideways with my blushing face
Under the cover of a hundred wings

---

[1] *matins* Morning prayer services.

[2] *Saint Laurence* Roman deacon (?–258 CE) who was martyred by being burnt on a gridiron, an instrument of torture.

[3] *Prato* Town west of Florence.

[4] *Sant' Ambrogio's* Lippi painted *Coronation of the Virgin* for the main altar of Florence's Sant' Ambrogio convent.

[5] *orris-root* Roots of the iris flower, used as a fragrant cosmetic powder.

[6] *man of Uz* See Job 1.1: Job was a righteous man who lost everything when God allowed Satan to challenge his faith.

[7] *Saint John … camel hair* St. John the Baptist "was clothed in camel hair," according to Mark 1.6.

[8] *Iste perfecit opus* Latin: He caused the work to be created; inscription on the *Coronation*, placed beside a portrait that Browning (following Vasari) mistakenly took to be Lippi's.

380 Thrown like a spread of kirtles° when you're gay   *skirts*
And play hot cockles,[1] all the doors being shut,
Till, wholly unexpected, in there pops
The hothead husband! Thus I scuttle off
To some safe bench behind, not letting go
385 The palm of her, the little lily thing
That spoke the good word for me in the nick,
Like the Prior's niece … Saint Lucy,[2] I would say.
And so all's saved for me, and for the church
A pretty picture gained. Go, six months hence!
390 Your hand, sir, and goodbye: no lights, no lights!
The street's hushed, and I know my own way back,
Don't fear me! There's the grey beginning. Zooks!
—1855

The Last Ride Together

1

I said—Then, dearest, since 'tis so,
Since now at length my fate I know,
Since nothing all my love avails,
Since all, my life seemed meant for, fails,
5   Since this was written and needs must be—
My whole heart rises up to bless
Your name in pride and thankfulness!
Take back the hope you gave—I claim
Only a memory of the same,
10 —And this beside, if you will not blame,
Your leave for one more last ride with me.

2

My mistress bent that brow of hers;
Those deep dark eyes where pride demurs
When pity would be softening through,
15 Fixed me a breathing-while or two
    With life or death in the balance: right!
The blood replenished me again;
My last thought was at least not vain:
I and my mistress, side by side
20 Shall be together, breathe and ride,

---

[1] *hot cockles* Christmas game played blindfolded.
[2] *Saint Lucy* Virgin martyr of Sicily (? –304? CE).

So, one day more am I deified.
    Who knows but the world may end tonight?

3

Hush! if you saw some western cloud
All billowy-bosomed, over-bowed
25 By many benedictions—sun's
And moon's and evening-star's at once—
    And so, you, looking and loving best,
Conscious grew, your passion drew
Cloud, sunset, moonrise, star-shine too,
30 Down on you, near and yet more near,
Till flesh must fade for heaven was here!—
Thus leant she and lingered—joy and fear!
    Thus lay she a moment on my breast.

4

Then we began to ride. My soul
35 Smoothed itself out, a long-cramped scroll
Freshening and fluttering in the wind.
Past hopes already lay behind.
    What need to strive with a life awry?
Had I said that, had I done this,
40 So might I gain, so might I miss.
Might she have loved me? just as well
She might have hated, who can tell!
Where had I been now if the worst befell?
    And here we are riding, she and I.

5

45 Fail I alone, in words and deeds?
Why, all men strive and who succeeds?
We rode; it seemed my spirit flew,
Saw other regions, cities new,
    As the world rushed by on either side.
50 I thought—All labour, yet no less
Bear up beneath their unsuccess.
Look at the end of work, contrast
The petty done, the undone vast,
This present of theirs with the hopeful past!
55   I hoped she would love me; here we ride.

6

What hand and brain went ever paired?
What heart alike conceived and dared?
What act proved all its thought had been?

What will but felt the fleshly screen?
60   We ride and I see her bosom heave.
There's many a crown for who can reach.
Ten lines, a statesman's life in each!
The flag stuck on a heap of bones,
A soldier's doing! what atones?
65 They scratch his name on the Abbey[1] stones.
        My riding is better, by their leave.

7

What does it all mean, poet? Well,
Your brains beat into rhythm, you tell
What we felt only; you expressed
70 You hold things beautiful the best,
        And pace them in rhyme so, side by side.
'Tis something, nay 'tis much: but then,
Have you yourself what's best for men?
Are you—poor, sick, old ere your time—
75 Nearer one whit your own sublime
Than we who never have turned a rhyme?
        Sing, riding's a joy! For me, I ride.

8

And you, great sculptor—so, you gave
A score of years to Art, her slave,
80 And that's your Venus,[2] whence we turn
To yonder girl that fords the burn!°   *stream*
        You acquiesce, and shall I repine?°   *complain*
What, man of music, you grown grey
With notes and nothing else to say,
85 Is this your sole praise from a friend,
"Greatly his opera's strains intend,
But in music we know how fashions end!"
        I gave my youth; but we ride, *in fine*.[3]

9

Who knows what's fit for us? Had fate
90 Proposed bliss here should sublimate
My being—had I signed the bond—
Still one must lead some life beyond,
        Have a bliss to die with, dim-descried.
This foot once planted on the goal,

95 This glory-garland round my soul,
Could I descry such? Try and test!
I sink back shuddering from the quest.
Earth being so good, would heaven seem best?
        Now, heaven and she are beyond this ride.

10

100 And yet—she has not spoke so long!
What if heaven be that, fair and strong
At life's best, with our eyes upturned
Whither life's flower is first discerned,
        We, fixed so, ever should so abide?
105 What if we still ride on, we two
With life forever old yet new,
Changed not in kind but in degree,
The instant made eternity—
And heaven just prove that I and she
110   Ride, ride together, forever ride?
—1855

Andrea del Sarto[4]
(*Called "The Faultless Painter"*)

But do not let us quarrel any more,
No, my Lucrezia;[5] bear with me for once:
Sit down and all shall happen as you wish.
You turn your face, but does it bring your heart?
5 I'll work then for your friend's friend, never fear,
Treat his own subject after his own way,
Fix his own time, accept too his own price,
And shut the money into this small hand
When next it takes mine. Will it? tenderly?
10 Oh, I'll content him—but tomorrow, Love!
I often am much wearier than you think,
This evening more than usual, and it seems
As if—forgive now—should you let me sit
Here by the window with your hand in mine

---

[1] *Abbey* Westminster Abbey.

[2] *Venus* Roman goddess of love.

[3] *in fine* In the end.

[4] *Andrea del Sarto* Browning's poem explores the life of the painter Andrea del Sarto (1486–1531), as narrated by Giorgio Vasari (once del Sarto's pupil) in *The Lives of the Painters*. In this biography, Vasari speculates as to why del Sarto (translated, this name means "son of a tailor") failed to fulfill the promise of his early paintings.

[5] *Lucrezia* Lucrezia del Fede, del Sarto's wife and model.

15 And look a half-hour forth on Fiesole,[1]
Both of one mind, as married people use,
Quietly, quietly the evening through,
I might get up tomorrow to my work
Cheerful and fresh as ever. Let us try.
20 Tomorrow, how you shall be glad for this!
Your soft hand is a woman of itself,
And mine the man's bared breast she curls inside.
Don't count the time lost, neither; you must serve
For each of the five pictures we require:
25 It saves a model. So! keep looking so—
My serpentining beauty, rounds on rounds!
—How could you ever prick those perfect ears,
Even to put the pearl there! oh, so sweet—
My face, my moon, my everybody's moon,
30 Which everybody looks on and calls his,
And, I suppose, is looked on by in turn,
While she looks—no one's: very dear, no less.
You smile? why, there's my picture ready made,
There's what we painters call our harmony!
35 A common greyness silvers everything—
All in a twilight, you and I alike
—You, at the point of your first pride in me
(That's gone you know)—but I, at every point;
My youth, my hope, my art, being all toned down
40 To yonder sober pleasant Fiesole.
There's the bell clinking from the chapel top;
That length of convent wall across the way
Holds the trees safer, huddled more inside;
The last monk leaves the garden; days decrease,
45 And autumn grows, autumn in everything.
Eh? the whole seems to fall into a shape
As if I saw alike my work and self
And all that I was born to be and do,
A twilight piece. Love, we are in God's hand.
50 How strange now, looks the life he makes us lead;
So free we seem, so fettered° fast we are!   shackled
I feel he laid the fetter: let it lie!
This chamber for example—turn your head—
All that's behind us! You don't understand
55 Nor care to understand about my art,
But you can hear at least when people speak:
And that cartoon,° the second from the door   sketch
—It is the thing, Love! so such things should be—

Behold Madonna!—I am bold to say.
60 I can do with my pencil what I know,
What I see, what at bottom of my heart
I wish for, if I ever wish so deep—
Do easily, too—when I say, perfectly,
I do not boast, perhaps: yourself are judge,
65 Who listened to the Legate's[2] talk last week,
And just as much they used to say in France.
At any rate 'tis easy, all of it!
No sketches first, no studies, that's long past:
I do what many dream of, all their lives,
70 —Dream? strive to do, and agonize to do,
And fail in doing. I could count twenty such
On twice your fingers, and not leave this town,
Who strive—you don't know how the others strive
To paint a little thing like that you smeared
75 Carelessly passing with your robes afloat—
Yet do much less, so much less, Someone says,
(I know his name, no matter)—so much less!
Well, less is more, Lucrezia: I am judged.
There burns a truer light of God in them,
80 In their vexed beating stuffed and stopped-up brain,
Heart, or whate'er else, than goes on to prompt
This low-pulsed forthright craftsman's hand of mine.
Their works drop groundward, but themselves, I know,
Reach many a time a heaven that's shut to me,
85 Enter and take their place there sure enough,
Though they come back and cannot tell the world.
My works are nearer heaven, but I sit here.
The sudden blood of these men! at a word—
Praise them, it boils, or blame them, it boils too.
90 I, painting from myself and to myself,
Know what I do, am unmoved by men's blame
Or their praise either. Somebody remarks
Morello's[3] outline there is wrongly traced,
His hue mistaken; what of that? or else,
95 Rightly traced and well ordered; what of that?
Speak as they please, what does the mountain care?
Ah, but a man's reach should exceed his grasp,
Or what's a heaven for? All is silver-grey
Placid and perfect with my art: the worse!
100 I know both what I want and what might gain,
And yet how profitless to know, to sigh

[1] *Fiesole* Hill town near Florence.
[2] *Legate* Representative of the Pope.
[3] *Morello* Monte Morello, a mountain near Florence.

"Had I been two, another and myself,
Our head would have o'erlooked the world!" No doubt.
Yonder's a work now, of that famous youth
105 The Urbinate[1] who died five years ago.
('Tis copied, George Vasari sent it me.)
Well, I can fancy how he did it all,
Pouring his soul, with kings and popes to see,
Reaching, that heaven might so replenish him,
110 Above and through his art—for it gives way;
That arm is wrongly put—and there again—
A fault to pardon in the drawing's lines,
Its body, so to speak: its soul is right,
He means right—that, a child may understand.
115 Still, what an arm! and I could alter it:
But all the play, the insight and the stretch—
Out of me, out of me! And wherefore out?
Had you enjoined them on me, given me soul,
We might have risen to Rafael, I and you!
120 Nay, Love, you did give all I asked, I think—
More than I merit, yes, by many times.
But had you—oh, with the same perfect brow,
And perfect eyes, and more than perfect mouth,
And the low voice my soul hears, as a bird
125 The fowler's pipe,[2] and follows to the snare—
Had you, with these the same, but brought a mind!
Some women do so. Had the mouth there urged
"God and the glory! never care for gain.
The present by the future, what is that?
130 Live for fame, side by side with Agnolo![3]
Rafael is waiting: up to God, all three!"
I might have done it for you. So it seems:
Perhaps not. All is as God over-rules.
Beside, incentives come from the soul's self;
135 The rest avail not. Why do I need you?
What wife had Rafael, or has Agnolo?
In this world, who can do a thing, will not;
And who would do it, cannot, I perceive:
Yet the will's somewhat—somewhat, too, the power—
140 And thus we half-men struggle. At the end,
God, I conclude, compensates, punishes.

'Tis safer for me, if the award be strict,
That I am something underrated here,
Poor this long while, despised, to speak the truth.
145 I dared not, do you know, leave home all day,
For fear of chancing on the Paris lords.[4]
The best is when they pass and look aside;
But they speak sometimes; I must bear it all.
Well may they speak! That Francis, that first time,
150 And that long festal year at Fontainebleau!
I surely then could sometimes leave the ground,
Put on the glory, Rafael's daily wear,
In that humane great monarch's golden look—
One finger in his beard or twisted curl
155 Over his mouth's good mark that made the smile,
One arm about my shoulder, round my neck,
The jingle of his gold chain in my ear,
I painting proudly with his breath on me,
All his court round him, seeing with his eyes,
160 Such frank French eyes, and such a fire of souls
Profuse, my hand kept plying by those hearts—
And, best of all, this, this, this face beyond,
This in the background, waiting on my work,
To crown the issue with a last reward!
165 A good time, was it not, my kingly days?
And had you not grown restless ... but I know—
'Tis done and past; 'twas right, my instinct said;
Too live the life grew, golden and not grey,
And I'm the weak-eyed bat no sun should tempt
170 Out of the grange whose four walls make his world.
How could it end in any other way?
You called me, and I came home to your heart.
The triumph was—to reach and stay there; since
I reached it ere the triumph, what is lost?
175 Let my hands frame your face in your hair's gold,
You beautiful Lucrezia that are mine!
"Rafael did this, Andrea painted that;
The Roman's is the better when you pray,
But still the other's Virgin was his wife—"
180 Men will excuse me. I am glad to judge
Both pictures in your presence; clearer grows
My better fortune, I resolve to think.
For, do you know, Lucrezia, as God lives,

---

[1] *Urbinate* The painter Raphael (1483–1520), who was born in Urbino.

[2] *fowler's pipe* Call used by hunters to lure fowl.

[3] *Agnolo* I.e., Michelangelo Buonarroti (1475–1564), sculptor and painter.

[4] *For fear ... lords* According to Vasari, del Sarto absconded with funds given to him at Fontainebleau by his patron, King Francis I of France.

Said one day Agnolo, his very self,
185   To Rafael … I have known it all these years …
(When the young man was flaming out his thoughts
Upon a palace wall for Rome to see,
Too lifted up in heart because of it)
"Friend, there's a certain sorry little scrub
190   Goes up and down our Florence, none cares how,
Who, were he set to plan and execute
As you are, pricked on by your popes and kings,
Would bring the sweat into that brow of yours!"
To Rafael's!—And indeed the arm is wrong.
195   I hardly dare … yet, only you to see,
Give the chalk here—quick, thus the line should go!
Ay, but the soul! he's Rafael! rub it out!
Still, all I care for, if he spoke the truth,
(What he? why, who but Michel Agnolo?
200   Do you forget already words like those?)
If really there was such a chance, so lost—
Is, whether you're—not grateful—but more pleased.
Well, let me think so. And you smile indeed!
This hour has been an hour! Another smile?
205   If you would sit thus by me every night
I should work better, do you comprehend?
I mean that I should earn more, give you more.
See, it is settled dusk now; there's a star;
Morello's gone, the watch-lights show the wall,
210   The cue-owls[1] speak the name we call them by.
Come from the window, love—come in, at last,
Inside the melancholy little house
We built to be so gay with. God is just.
King Francis may forgive me: oft at nights
215   When I look up from painting, eyes tired out,
The walls become illumined, brick from brick
Distinct, instead of mortar, fierce bright gold,
That gold of his I did cement them with!
Let us but love each other. Must you go?
220   That cousin here again? he waits outside?
Must see you—you, and not with me? Those loans?
More gaming debts to pay? you smiled for that?
Well, let smiles buy me! have you more to spend?
While hand and eye and something of a heart
225   Are left me, work's my ware, and what's it worth?
I'll pay my fancy. Only let me sit

The grey remainder of the evening out,
Idle, you call it, and muse perfectly
How I could paint, were I but back in France,
230   One picture, just one more—the Virgin's face,
Not yours this time! I want you at my side
To hear them—that is, Michel Agnolo—
Judge all I do and tell you of its worth.
Will you? Tomorrow, satisfy your friend.
235   I take the subjects for his corridor,
Finish the portrait out of hand—there, there,
And throw him in another thing or two
If he demurs; the whole should prove enough
To pay for this same cousin's freak. Beside,
240   What's better and what's all I care about,
Get you the thirteen scudi° for the ruff!   _Italian currency_
Love, does that please you? Ah, but what does he,
The cousin! what does he to please you more?

I am grown peaceful as old age tonight.
245   I regret little, I would change still less.
Since there my past life lies, why alter it?
The very wrong to Francis!—it is true
I took his coin, was tempted and complied,
And built this house and sinned, and all is said.
250   My father and my mother died of want.
Well, had I riches of my own? you see
How one gets rich! Let each one bear his lot.
They were born poor, lived poor, and poor they died:
And I have laboured somewhat in my time
255   And not been paid profusely. Some good son
Paint my two hundred pictures—let him try!
No doubt, there's something strikes a balance. Yes,
You loved me quite enough, it seems tonight.
This must suffice me here. What would one have?
260   In heaven, perhaps, new chances, one more chance—
Four great walls in the New Jerusalem,[2]
Meted on each side by the angel's reed,
For Leonard,[3] Rafael, Agnolo and me
To cover—the three first without a wife,
265   While I have mine! So—still they overcome
Because there's still Lucrezia—as I choose.

Again the cousin's whistle! Go, my Love.
—1855

---

1   *cue-owls* Also known as scops-owls, whose cry sounds like "cue."

2   *Four … Jerusalem* See Revelations 21.10.

3   *Leonard* Artist Leonardo da Vinci (1452–1519).

CHARLES DICKENS
1812 – 1870

Few English novelists have attracted the huge audiences and lasting fame of Charles Dickens. People the world over are familiar with the moral transformation of *A Christmas Carol*'s Ebenezer Scrooge and the life of the orphan Oliver Twist, immortalized in his piteous request for a second bowl of watery gruel: "Please, sir, I want some more." From Pickwick and Sam Weller in *The Pickwick Papers* to Mr. Micawber in *David Copperfield* to Pip in *Great Expectations*, from Mr. Guppy and Mrs. Jellyby in *Bleak House* to Mr. Gradgrind in *Hard Times* and Flora Finching in *Little Dorrit*, Dickens created a panoply of memorable characters. Combining comic genius with astute criticisms of the laws, institutions, and the social order of Victorian society, he created novels that continue to command the attention of critics and the general public alike. His novels still stand as a testament to his stature both as a popular writer and as a social critic.

Dickens's early childhood was signally important as source material for the concerns and themes of his novels. His father worked as a naval office clerk in Portsmouth when Charles was born in 1812, the second of 10 children (two died in infancy). John and Elizabeth Dickens aspired to a middle-class life, but had unending difficulties controlling their spending and were always on the brink of penury. At one time, they served a four-month stint in the Marshalsea debtors' prison. Charles was able to attend school in Chatham, near London, after the family was transferred to the dockyards there, but in 1823 his education was halted, and he joined his parents in Camden Town, London. The young Dickens worked at odd jobs for his parents and was eventually sent off to work at Warren's Boot Blacking Factory at the age of 12. The psychological impact of this environment on Dickens was permanent; he never forgot the humiliation he had suffered or the dismay he had felt at the relatively harsh working conditions under which he and other children were forced to toil.

After the family came into a modest inheritance, Dickens returned to school, but in 1827, at just 15 years of age, he left school again because his father was unable to pay the fees. Working as a clerk in a law firm, he studied shorthand in his spare time, eventually becoming a parliamentary reporter. In 1833, *Monthly Magazine* published Dickens's first story, "A Dinner at Poplar Walk." While working as a newspaper reporter the next year, he launched a highly popular series of articles that were eventually collected and published as *Sketches by Boz* (his journalistic pseudonym) in 1836. The success of this book allowed Dickens to marry Catherine Hogarth and to begin another series that cemented his fame and secured his financial stability. A monthly illustrated serial about the Pickwick Club was commissioned by publishers Chapman and Hall, and the absurd characters of Mr. Pickwick, Mr. Winkle, Mr. Tupman, Mr. Snodgrass, and Sam Weller soon had people all over England clamoring for the latest installment of *The Pickwick Papers*. Dickens consolidated this success by beginning *Oliver Twist* (1837–38) in *Bentley's Miscellany*, which he had begun editing, and then launching *Nicholas Nickleby* (1838–39) as a monthly serial.

In 1837, Dickens and his wife began to raise a family (they eventually had 10 children). In this same year, he lost his beloved sister-in-law, Mary Hogarth, who would become the inspiration for Little Nell in *The Old Curiosity Shop* (1840–41) and for many of the childlike women that constitute the "good angels" of his novels. By the time this book was published, Dickens's fame had spread throughout North America; eager fans would line the piers in New York waiting for the latest installment of a Dickens story to arrive from England.

In 1842, Dickens journeyed to the United States to take advantage of his fame, but the trip turned out to be a disappointment. The hordes that crowded around him relentlessly, trying to speak to, touch, or even just glimpse the famous author were only part of the problem. He scorned, publicly and at any opportunity, the lack of international copyright laws, which meant that Americans could pirate editions of his books without any of the proceeds going to him. Dickens set out his disdain for American habits (such as chewing and spitting tobacco) and for American institutions, such as slavery, and what he thought was a ruthless prison system in a book about his travels, *American Notes* (1842), and made Americans the object of derision in his novel *Martin Chuzzlewit* (1843–44). Americans were incensed and reacted with an outpouring of vindictive editorials in the press. As it happened, *Martin Chuzzlewit* did not sell well on either side of the Atlantic. Americans began to forgive Dickens after the appearance of the overwhelmingly successful *A Christmas Carol* (1843), the first in his Christmas book series and a novel that is all about forgiveness and redemption.

Dickens was an astonishingly energetic and prolific writer, becoming the editor of *Household Words* in 1850, while writing and acting in theatrical works, traveling widely, and working in various social causes. Throughout the 1840s and 1850s, he published at an unprecedented rate: *Dombey and Son* (1846–48), *David Copperfield* (his most autobiographical work, 1849–50), *Bleak House* (1852–53), *Hard Times* (1854), *Little Dorrit* (1855–57), and *A Tale of Two Cities* (1859). Dickens published all of his novels in serial form. The episodic structure of his novels prompted Dickens to develop methods of characterizations that allowed immediate identification of characters by readers waiting for weekly or monthly installments. The Dickens "character" is often recognizable as a type that speaks in a marvelously individualized dialect and may sometimes more closely resemble a caricature from the popular press than a fully rounded character. (George Eliot complained that Dickens's characters had little psychology.) He also wove numerous peripheral stories and characters into the main plotlines, and used coincidence—in which, for example, characters discover long-lost parents and siblings by accident—with Victorian abandon. Yet for Dickens and his readers, coincidence did not undermine reality so much as suggest that divinity shapes our ends.

Dickens not only edited *Household Words*; he also wrote many of the pieces himself. Had he never written a line of fiction, he would still be remembered for the extraordinary body of non-fiction he produced. His essays for the magazine deal with a wide variety of topics, but again and again he returns in one way or another to the condition of the poor—the great issue of his time. The condition of poor children was a particular concern for Dickens—as his 1850 essay "A Walk in the Workhouse" suggests. But, as the 1854 essay "The Quiet Poor" demonstrates, his sympathetic understanding for poor people both *en masse* and as individuals could operate just as keenly for those "who are never to be seen in workhouses and prisons." That essay also illustrates Dickens's abiding interest in public policy; he believed in the power of the human heart to bring change (and he strove in his writing to tug at the heartstrings of his readers), but he was also an advocate for changes to social and economic legislation.

In 1858 Dickens separated from Catherine, an event complicated by his relationship with the actress Ellen Ternan and by the degree of publicity that (partly at Dickens's instigation) attended his change in marital status. In that same year, Dickens began an extensive tour of public readings, a most lucrative but exhausting enterprise that severely compromised his health. He continued touring throughout the 1860s while editing his new journal, *All the Year Round* (begun in 1859), in which he serialized both *A Tale of Two Cities* (1859) and *Great Expectations* (1860–61). During this decade Dickens completed only one other novel, *Our Mutual Friend* (1864–65). He was at work on *The Mystery of Edwin Drood* when he died in 1870 during a grueling schedule of readings. In his will Dickens requested an "unostentatious, and strictly private" burial attended only by a few close friends and family, but throngs gathered later around his grave in Westminster Abbey to mourn his death.

⌘ ⌘ ⌘

A Walk in the Workhouse

On a certain Sunday I formed one of the congrega-tion assembled in the chapel of a large metropoli-tan Workhouse. With the exception of the clergyman and clerk, and a very few officials, there were none but paupers present. The children sat in the galleries; the women in the body of the chapel, and in one of the side aisles; the men in the remaining aisle. The service was decorously performed, though the sermon might have been much better adapted to the comprehension and to the circumstances of the hearers. The usual supplica-tions were offered, with more than the usual significan-cy in such a place, for the fatherless children and wid-ows, for all sick persons and young children, for all that were desolate and oppressed, for the comforting and helping of the weak-hearted, for the raising up of them that had fallen; for all that were in danger, necessity, and tribulation. The prayers of the congregation were desired "for several persons in the various wards danger-ously ill"; and others who were recovering returned their thanks to Heaven.

Among this congregation were some evil-looking young women, and beetle-browed young men; but not many—perhaps that kind of characters kept away. Generally, the faces (those of the children excepted) were depressed and subdued, and wanted colour. Aged people were there in every variety. Mumbling, blear-eyed, spectacled, stupid, deaf, lame; vacantly winking in the gleams of sun that now and then crept in through the open doors, from the paved yard; shading their listening ears, or blinking eyes, with their withered hands; poring over their books, leering at nothing, going to sleep, crouching and drooping in corners. There were weird old women, all skeleton within, all bonnet and cloak without, continually wiping their eyes with dirty dusters of pocket handkerchiefs; and there were ugly old crones, both male and female, with a ghastly kind of contentment upon them which was not at all comfort-ing to see. Upon the whole, it was the dragon, Pauper-ism, in a very weak and impotent condition: toothless, fangless, drawing his breath heavily enough, and hardly worth chaining up.

When the service was over, I walked with the humane and conscientious gentleman whose duty it was to take that walk, that Sunday morning, through the little world of poverty enclosed within the workhouse walls. It was inhabited by a population of some fifteen hundred or two thousand paupers, ranging from the infant newly born or not yet come into the pauper world, to the old man dying on his bed.

In a room opening from a squalid yard, where a number of listless women were lounging to and fro, trying to get warm in the ineffectual sunshine of the tardy May morning—in the "Itch Ward," not to com-promise the truth—a woman such as HOGARTH[1] has often drawn, was hurriedly getting on her gown before a dusty fire. She was the nurse, or wardswoman, of that insalubrious department—herself a pauper—flabby, raw-boned, untidy—unpromising and coarse of aspect as need be. But, on being spoken to about the patients whom she had in charge, she turned round, with her shabby gown half on, half off, and fell a crying with all her might. Not for show, not querulously, not in any mawkish sentiment, but in the deep grief and affliction of her heart; turning away her dishevelled head: sobbing most bitterly, wringing her hands, and letting fall abundance of great tears, that choked her utterance. What was the matter with the nurse of the itch ward? Oh, "the dropped child" was dead! Oh, the child that was found in the street, and she had brought up ever since, had died an hour ago, and see where the little creature lay, beneath this cloth! The dear, the pretty dear!

The dropped child seemed too small and poor a thing for Death to be in earnest with, but Death had taken it; and already its diminutive form was neatly washed, composed, and stretched as if in sleep upon a box. I thought I heard a voice from Heaven saying, It shall be well for thee, O nurse of the itch ward, when some less gentle pauper does those offices to thy cold

---

[1] *HOGARTH* Artist and printmaker William Hogarth (1687–1764) was greatly admired by Dickens for his satirical paintings and prints of eighteenth-century London life.

form, that such as the dropped child are the angels who behold my Father's face!

In another room were several ugly old women crouching, witch-like, round a hearth, and chattering and nodding, after the manner of the monkeys. "All well here? And enough to eat?" A general chattering and chuckling; at last an answer from a volunteer. "Oh yes, gentleman! Bless you, gentleman! Lord bless the Parish of St. So-and-So! It feed the hungry, sir, and give drink to the thusty, and it warm them which is cold, so it do, and good luck to the parish of St. So-and-So, and thankee, gentleman!" Elsewhere, a party of pauper nurses were at dinner. "How do YOU get on?" "Oh pretty well, sir! We works hard, and we lives hard—like the sodgers!"[1]

In another room, a kind of purgatory or place of transition, six or eight noisy madwomen were gathered together, under the superintendence of one sane attendant. Among them was a girl of two or three and twenty, very prettily dressed, of most respectable appearance and good manners, who had been brought in from the house where she had lived as domestic servant (having, I suppose, no friends), on account of being subject to epileptic fits, and requiring to be removed under the influence of a very bad one. She was by no means of the same stuff, or the same breeding, or the same experience, or in the same state of mind, as those by whom she was surrounded; and she pathetically complained that the daily association and the nightly noise made her worse, and was driving her mad—which was perfectly evident. The case was noted for inquiry and redress, but she said she had already been there for some weeks.

If this girl had stolen her mistress's watch, I do not hesitate to say she would have been infinitely better off. We have come to this absurd, this dangerous, this monstrous pass, that the dishonest felon is, in respect of cleanliness, order, diet, and accommodation, better provided for, and taken care of, than the honest pauper.

And this conveys no special imputation on the workhouse of the parish of St. So-and-So, where, on the contrary, I saw many things to commend. It was very agreeable, recollecting that most infamous and atrocious enormity committed at Tooting[2]—an enormity which, a hundred years hence, will still be vividly remembered in the byways of English life, and which has done more to engender a gloomy discontent and suspicion among many thousands of the people than all the Chartist leaders[3] could have done in all their lives—to find the pauper children in this workhouse looking robust and well, and apparently the objects of very great care. In the Infant School—a large, light, airy room at the top of the building—the little creatures, being at dinner, and eating their potatoes heartily, were not cowed by the presence of strange visitors, but stretched out their small hands to be shaken, with a very pleasant confidence. And it was comfortable to see two mangy pauper rocking-horses rampant in a corner. In the girls' school, where the dinner was also in progress, everything bore a cheerful and healthy aspect. The meal was over in the boys' school by the time of our arrival there, and the room was not yet quite rearranged; but the boys were roaming unrestrained about a large and airy yard, as any other schoolboys might have done. Some of them had been drawing large ships upon the schoolroom wall; and if they had a mast with shrouds and stays set up for practice (as they have in the Middlesex House of Correction), it would be so much the better. At present, if a boy should feel a strong impulse upon him to learn the art of going aloft, he could only gratify it, I presume, as the men and women paupers gratify their aspirations after better board and lodging, by smashing as many workhouse windows as possible, and being promoted to prison.

In one place, the Newgate[4] of the workhouse, a company of boys and youths were locked up in a yard alone; their dayroom being a kind of kennel where the casual poor used formerly to be littered down at night. Diverse of them had been there some long time. "Are they never going away?" was the natural inquiry. "Most of them are crippled, in some form or other," said the wardsman, "and not fit for anything." They slunk

---

[1] *sodgers* I.e., soldiers.

[2] *Tooting* In 1849, after four half-starved children had died of cholera in a Tooting workhouse, the proprietor was found guilty of manslaughter.

[3] *Chartist leaders* The Chartist movement pressed for political (and by implication, social and economic) reform from 1836 onwards.

[4] *Newgate* Newgate was London's main prison.

about, like dispirited wolves or hyenas; and made a pounce at their food when it was served out, much as those animals do. The big-headed idiot shuffling his feet along the pavement, in the sunlight outside, was a more agreeable object everyway.

Groves of babies in arms; groves of mothers and other sick women in bed; groves of lunatics; jungles of men in stone-paved downstairs dayrooms, waiting for their dinners; longer and longer groves of old people, in upstairs infirmary wards, wearing out life, God knows how—this was the scenery through which the walk lay, for two hours. In some of these latter chambers, there were pictures stuck against the wall, and a neat display of crockery and pewter on a kind of sideboard; now and then it was a treat to see a plant or two; in almost every ward there was a cat.

In all of these long walks of aged and infirm, some old people were bedridden, and had been for a long time; some were sitting on their beds half naked; some dying in their beds; some out of bed, and sitting at a table near the fire. A sullen or lethargic indifference to what was asked, a blunted sensibility to everything but warmth and food, a moody absence of complaint as being of no use, a dogged silence and resentful desire to be left alone again, I thought were generally apparent. On our walking into the midst of one of these dreary perspectives of old men, nearly the following little dialogue took place, the nurse not being immediately at hand:

"All well here?"

No answer. An old man in a Scotch cap[1] sitting among others on a form at the table, eating out of a tin porringer,[2] pushes back his cap a little to look at us, claps it down on his forehead again with the palm of his hand, and goes on eating.

"All well here?" (repeated).

No answer. Another old man sitting on his bed, paralytically peeling a boiled potato, lifts his head and stares.

"Enough to eat?"

No answer. Another old man, in bed, turns himself and coughs.

"How are YOU today?" To the last old man.

That old man says nothing; but another old man, a tall old man of very good address, speaking with perfect correctness, comes forward from somewhere, and volunteers an answer. The reply almost always proceeds from a volunteer, and not from the person looked at or spoken to.

"We are very old, sir," in a mild, distinct voice. "We can't expect to be well, most of us."

"Are you comfortable?"

"I have no complaint to make, sir." With a half shake of his head, a half shrug of his shoulders, and a kind of apologetic smile.

"Enough to eat?"

"Why, sir, I have but a poor appetite," with the same air as before; "and yet I get through my allowance very easily."

"But," showing a porringer with a Sunday dinner in it; "here is a portion of mutton, and three potatoes. You can't starve on that?"

"Oh dear no, sir," with the same apologetic air. "Not starve."

"What do you want?"

"We have very little bread, sir. It's an exceedingly small quantity of bread."

The nurse, who is now rubbing her hands at the questioner's elbow, interferes with, "It ain't much raly, sir. You see they've only six ounces a day, and when they've took their breakfast, there CAN only be a little left for night, sir." Another old man, hitherto invisible, rises out of his bedclothes, as out of a grave, and looks on.

"You have tea at night?" The questioner is still addressing the well-spoken old man.

"Yes, sir, we have tea at night."

"And you save what bread you can from the morning, to eat with it?"

"Yes, sir—if we can save any."

"And you want more to eat with it?"

"Yes, sir." With a very anxious face.

The questioner, in the kindness of his heart, appears a little discomposed, and changes the subject.

"What has become of the old man who used to lie in that bed in the corner?"

The nurse don't remember what old man is referred to. There has been such a many old men. The well-

---

[1] *Scotch cap* Woolen hat worn in the Highlands.

[2] *porringer* Bowl for porridge, soups, and other runny foods.

spoken old man is doubtful. The spectral old man who has come to life in bed says "Billy Stevens." Another old man who has previously had his head in the fireplace, pipes out, "Charley Walters."

Something like a feeble interest is awakened. I suppose Charley Walters had conversation in him.

"He's dead," says the piping old man.

Another old man, with one eye screwed up, hastily displaces the piping old man, and says.

"Yes! Charley Walters died in that bed, and—and—"

"Billy Stevens," persists the spectral old man.

"No, no! and Johnny Rogers died in that bed, and—and—they're both on 'em dead—and Sam'l Bowyer"; this seems very extraordinary to him; "he went out!"

With this he subsides, and all the old men (having had quite enough of it) subside, and the spectral old man goes into his grave again, and takes the shade of Billy Stevens with him.

As we turn to go out at the door, another previously invisible old man, a hoarse old man in a flannel gown, is standing there, as if he had just come up through the floor.

"I beg your pardon, sir, could I take the liberty of saying a word?"

"Yes, what is it?"

"I am greatly better in my health, sir; but what I want, to get me quite round," with his hand on his throat, "is a little fresh air, sir. It has always done my complaint so much good, sir. The regular leave for going out, comes round so seldom, that if the gentlemen, next Friday, would give me leave to go out walking, now and then—for only an hour or so, sir!—"

Who could wonder, looking through those weary vistas of bed and infirmity, that it should do him good to meet with some other scenes, and assure himself that there was something else on earth? Who could help wondering why the old men lived on as they did; what grasp they had on life; what crumbs of interest or occupation they could pick up from its bare board; whether Charley Walters had ever described to them the days when he kept company with some old pauper woman in the bud, or Billy Stevens ever told them of the time when he was a dweller in the far off foreign land called Home!

The morsel of burnt child, lying in another room, so patiently, in bed, wrapped in lint, and looking steadfastly at us with his bright quiet eyes when we spoke to him kindly, looked as if the knowledge of these things, and of all the tender things there are to think about, might have been in his mind as if he thought, with us, that there was a fellow-feeling in the pauper nurses which appeared to make them more kind to their charges than the race of common nurses in the hospitals—as if he mused upon the future of some older children lying around him in the same place, and thought it best, perhaps, all things considered, that he should die—as if he knew, without fear, of those many coffins, made and unmade, piled up in the store below—and of his unknown friend, "the dropped child," calm upon the box lid covered with a cloth. But there was something wistful and appealing, too, in his tiny face, as if, in the midst of all the hard necessities and incongruities he pondered on, he pleaded, in behalf of the helpless and the aged poor, for a little more liberty—and a little more bread.

—1850

The Quiet Poor

I do not mean the workhouse poor—I have seen plenty of workhouses and tasted many gruels.[1] I do not mean the criminal poor, nor the poor who beg in the streets, but the Quiet Poor: the people who work in their own homes, and are never to be seen in workhouses and prisons,[2] who keep their sorrows, if they have any, quite sacred from the world, and do not exhibit them for pence.[3] Though, to be sure, their shades may "glance and pass before us night and day," to such sorrows, if there be any, "we are blind as they are dumb." I thought, therefore, that I should like to know

---

[1] *workhouse* Establishment for the lodging of the impoverished, who were, if possible, put to work; *gruel* Dish made of oatmeal or fine flour, typical in the diet of invalids and the poor.

[2] *prisons* Persons unable to repay debt were confined in debtors' prisons well into the nineteenth century. (The Debtors' Act of 1869 officially eliminated imprisonment as penalty for unpaid debts.)

[3] *pence* Pennies.

something about them. The last winter has been commonly said to be a very hard one, and I have heard many an old lady cry over the price of bread, "God help the poor!" What does a mere penny a loaf matter? I have thought. A slice of bread less in the day, perhaps; a little hunger, and a little falling-in of cheek. Things not entirely unendurable.

Resolved to see about this for myself, and to find out perhaps what war prices[1] will signify to loyal Britons, I obtained leave to visit the inhabitants of a parochial district in Bethnal Green,[2] remarkable for its poverty, for the struggles made by its inhabitants to keep out of the workhouse, and for the small number of the offences brought home to their doors.

The little district of which I speak, small as it is, contains the population of a country town. To judge by the eye I should imagine that it covers ground about a quarter of a mile wide, and a quarter of a mile long. It is composed wholly of narrow courts and lanes, with a central High Street or Church Street of shops—itself a miserable lane. Although the houses are for the most part but cottages, with two doors and a cellar, there are crammed together in them fourteen thousand people. In the whole quarter there is not one resident whom the world would call respectable; there are not more than about half-a-dozen families able to keep a servant;[3] and there is not one man I believe able to tenant[4] a whole house. The shopkeepers who make a little outside show, fare indoors little better than their neighbours. As a general rule, each room in each house is occupied by a distinct family; they are comparatively wealthy who afford to rent two rooms; but, generally, as the families enlarge, the more they require space, the less they can afford that costly luxury. The natives of this parish chiefly subsist upon potatoes and cheap fish, buying sprats[5] when they are to be had, and, in default of them,

sitting down to dine on potatoes and a herring. They earn money as they can, and all are glad to work hard when there is work for them to do. The majority of the men are either weavers, or they are costermongers and hawkers.[6] These two classes occupy, speaking generally, different portions of the neighbourhood; the weavers earn a trifle more, and hold their heads up better than their neighbours: they are the west end[7] people of the district. The whole place is completely destitute of sewerage; one sewer has been made in a street which forms part of its boundary; it has its share in that, but nothing more. The houses all stand over cesspools; and, before the windows, filth, dead cats, and putrid matter of all sorts run down or stagnate in the open gutters. How do people, who are quiet people, live in such a place?

From a wretched lane, an Egypt watered by a muddy Nile, I turned into a dark house like a catacomb, and after some hazardous climbing reached a chamber in which there were more people than things. Two women sat at work with painful earnestness before the latticed window, three children shivered round an empty grate. Except the broken chairs on which the women sat, there was no seat in the room but an old stool. There was no table, no bed. The larder was the windowsill, its store[8] a couple of potatoes. In one corner was a confused heap of many-coloured rags, in another corner, were a few battered and broken jugs, and pans; there was a little earthen teapot on the cold bars of the grate, and in the middle of the room there was a handsome toy. I saw a household and its home. The father had been some months dead, the mother expected in two or three days to receive from God another child. She had four, and "Have you lost any?" I asked, looking down into the Egypt out of doors. "I have lost nine!"

This woman and her sister were at work together on cloth-tops for boots; each woman could make one in about four hours, and would receive for it threepence, out of which sum she would have expended three farthings[9] on trimming or binding, and a fraction of a

---

[1] *war prices* Great Britain was involved in the Crimean War (popularly known as the "Russian War") against Russia as part of an alliance with France and the Ottoman Empire from 1854 to 1856.

[2] *Bethnal Green* District in London's East End that was considered one of the city's poorest slums.

[3] *families ... a servant* The ability to employ at least one servant was a marker of middle-class identification.

[4] *tenant* Occupy.

[5] *sprats* Small, very oily fish.

[6] *costermongers* Fruit sellers; *hawkers* Itinerant salesmen who carry their goods in a horse cart and loudly advertise their wares.

[7] *west end* Fancy or wealthy part of a town or city.

[8] *store* Food.

[9] *farthing* Quarter-penny coin.

farthing upon thread. She had parted with her furniture piece by piece during the last illness of her husband. I talked to the children, and began to pull the great toy by the string: a monkey riding on a cock. As the wheels rolled, it made music, and up scrambled the fourth child, a great baby boy. "His grandmother gave him that," the mother said. They had sold their bed, their clothes, but they had kept the plaything!

We traced the current of another Nile into another Egypt. These Niles have their inundations, but to their unhappy Egypts such floods only add another plague.[1] In summer time the courts and lanes are rich with exhalation, and in autumn their atmosphere is deadly. When May comes round the poor creatures of this district, pent up as they are, feel the spring blood leaping faintly within them, and are not to be restrained from pressing out in crowds towards the green fields and the hawthorn[2] blossoms. They may be found dancing in the tea-gardens of suburban public-houses,[3] rambling together in suburban meadows, or crawling out to the Essex marshes. That is the stir made by the first warm sunshine of the year, and after that the work goes on; the warm weather is the harvest time of the hawkers and costermongers, who at the best suffer severely during winter.

The summer heat lifts out of the filthy courts a heavy vapour of death, the over-crowded rooms are scarcely tenantable, and the inhabitants, as much as time and weather will permit, turn out into the road before their doors. The air everywhere indeed is stifling, but within doors many of the cottages must be intolerable. I went into one containing four rooms and a cellar, and asked, "How many people live here?" They were counted up for me, and the number came to six and twenty! The present clergyman of this district—whose toil is unremitting in the midst of the vast mass of sorrow to which he is called to minister—dwells upon wholesome ground outside the district. Within it, there is not a parsonage or any house that could be used as one, and

if there were—what man would carry wife or children to a home in which they would drink poison daily? The pastor is very faithful in the performance of his duty; liberal of mind, unsparing of toil; and, although the reward of his office is as little as its toil is great, and he is forced to take new duties on himself to earn a living, yet I know that he pours out his energies, his health, and all the money he can earn beyond what suffices for a frugal maintenance, upon his miserable people. We have need to be thankful that the Church has such sons. The Reverend Theophilus Fitzmumble may be a canon here, a master there, a rector elsewhere, and a vicar of Little Pogis, with a thousand a year for the care of a few hundred farmers and farm labourers, who rarely see his face. Fitzmumble may be a drone, the thousand a year paid for his ministration at Little Pogis might be better paid to a man who has daily to battle with, and to help such misery as that of which I speak in Bethnal Green. But let us, I repeat, be thankful that Fitzmumble is not the whole Church. It has sons content to labour as poor men among the poor, whose hearts ache daily at the sight of wretchedness they cannot help; whose wives fall sick of fevers caught at the sick beds of their unhappy sisters. Of such ministers the tables are luxurious, for they who sit at meat know that their fare is less by the portion that has been sent out to the hungry; such men go richly clad, in threadbare cloth, of which the nap[4] is perhaps represented by small shoes upon the feet of little children who trot to and fro in them to school.

But, though the incumbent[5] of this parochial district about which I speak is truly a Christian gentleman, he has his body to maintain alive, and dares not remain too long in the poison bath of his unsewered district during the hot summer days. He visits then only the dying, and they are not few. "I have seen," he said, "a dead child in a cellar, and its father dying by its side, a living daughter covered with a sack to hide her nakedness when I went in, the rest all hungry and wretched, furniture gone, and an open sewer streaming down into a pool upon the floor." Again he said, "I have seen in the sickly autumn months a ruined household opposite the back premises of a tripe[6] and leather factory, which is a dreadful

---

[1] *another plague* As chronicled in Exodus, Egypt was visited by ten plagues, intended to force the Pharaoh to release the ancient Israelites from their captivity and slavery.

[2] *hawthorn* Small thorny tree, typically bearing white, red, or pink blossoms and small dark red berries.

[3] *public-house* Pub; an inn licensed to sell alcohol.

[4] *nap* Woolly material sheared from the surface of cloth.

[5] *incumbent* Office-holder, especially within the church.

[6] *tripe* Stomach of a cow or other ruminant.

nuisance to its neighbours; it emits a frightful stench, and lays men, women, and children down upon sick beds right and left. In this room opposite the place, I have seen the father of the family and three children hopelessly ill with typhus fever,[1] and the eldest daughter with malignant small pox, while the mother, the one person able to stir about, sat on a chair in the midst of them all deadened with misery. The place by which this household was being murdered has been several times indicted and fined as a nuisance. Every time this has occurred, the proprietors have paid the fine and gone on as before; they regard such fine-paying as only a small item in their trade expenses."

The people in this black spot of London all strive to the last to keep out of the workhouse. The union workhouse planted in a region that is crammed with poor, must be managed strictly, or there will be fearful outcry about keeping down the rates. Are the poor people in the wrong for keeping their arms wound about each other? There is not a house, a room—of all I visited the other day, I did not see one room—in which there was not sickness. Talk of the workhouse, and the mother says, in effect, "who would nurse Johnny like me? Oh, I could not bear to think that he might die, and strangers cover up his face!" Johnny again cries for his mother, or if he be a man, he says that he would die naked and in the streets, rather than not give his last words to his wife.

But, somebody may say, "This is sentimentality. The poor have not such fine feelings. They get to be brutalised." Often it is so; but, quite as often certainly, they are refined by suffering, and have depths of feeling stirred up within them which the more fortunate are only now and then made conscious of in themselves. I went into one room in this unhappy place—this core of all the misery in Bethnal Green—and saw a woman in bed with a three weeks infant on her arm. She was still too weak to rise, and her husband had died when the baby was three days old. She had four other children, and she panted to get up and earn. It eased her heart to tell of her lost love, and the portion of her story that I here repeat was told by her, in the close narrow room, with a more touching emphasis than I can give it here;

with tremblings of the voice and quiverings of the lip that went warm to the hearts of all who listened:—

"The morning before my husband died," she said, "he said to me, 'O Mary, I have had such a beautiful dream!'—'Have you, dear?' says I; 'do you think you feel strong enough to tell it me?'—'Yes,' says he, 'I dreamt that I was in a large place where there was a microscopic clock' (he meant a microscope), 'and I looked through it and saw the seven heavens all full of light and happiness, and straight before me, Mary, I saw a face that was like a face I knew.' 'And whose face was it, love?' says I.—'I do not know,' says he; 'but it was more beautiful than anything I ever saw, and bright and glorious, and I said to it, Shall I be glorified with the same glory that you are glorified with? And the head bowed towards me. And I said, Am I to die soon? And the head bowed towards me. And I said, Shall I die tomorrow? And the face fixed its eyes on me and went away. And now what do you think that means?'—'I do not know,' says I, 'but I think it must mean that God is going to call you away from this world where you have had so much trouble, and your suffering is going to be at an end, but you must wait His time, and that is why the head went away when you said, shall I die tomorrow?'—'I suppose you are right,' says he, 'and I don't mind dying, but O Mary, it goes to my heart to leave you and the young ones' (here the tears spread over the poor woman's eyes, and her voice began to tremble). 'I am afraid to part with you, I am afraid for you after I am gone.'—'You must not think of that,' says I, 'you've been a good husband, and it's God's will you should go.'—'I won't go, Mary, without saying good bye to you,' says he. 'If I can't speak, I'll wave my hand to you,' says he, 'and you'll know when I'm going.' And so it was, for his last hours he could not speak a word, and he went off so gently that I never should have known in what minute he died if I had not seen his hands moving and waving to me Good-bye before he went."

Such dreams and thoughts belong to quiet poverty. I have told this incident just as I heard it; and if I were a daily visitant in Bethnal Green, I should have many tales of the same kind to tell.

The people of this district are not criminal. A lady might walk unharmed at midnight through their

---

[1] *typhus fever* Acute fever, brought on by an infection most commonly associated with crowded, unhealthy living conditions.

wretched lanes. Crime demands a certain degree of energy; but if there were ever any harm in these well-disposed people, that has been tamed out of them by sheer want. They have been sinking for years. Ten years ago, or less, the men were politicians;[1] now, they have sunk below that stage of discontent. They are generally very still and hopeless; cherishing each other; tender not only towards their own kin, but towards their neighbours; and they are subdued by sorrow to a manner strangely resembling the quiet and refined tone of the most polished circles.

By very different roads, Bethnal Green and St. James's[2] have arrived at this result. But there are other elements than poverty that have in some degree assisted to produce it. Many of the weavers have French names, and are descended from French emigrants, who settled hereabouts, as many of their countrymen settled in other places up and down the world after the Revocation of the Edict of Nantes;[3] and at that time there were fields and market gardens near the green[4] of Bethnal. There are here some runlets[5] of the best French blood, and great names may be sometimes met with. The parish clerk, who seemed to have in him a touch of Spanish courtesy, claims to be a descendant from Cervantes.[6] The literary spirit still works in him; for I found his table covered with papers and tickets relating to a penny lecture—twopence to the front seats—that he had been delivering on Nineveh, Palmyra, Babylon,[7]

and other ancient cities, illustrated with little panorama that he had. His lecture had drawn crowds, seventy had been turned from the doors, and he was preparing to repeat it. Then there is a poor fellow in the parish named Racine, who declares that he can prove his descent from Racine the dramatist.[8] There is a Lesage[9] too, to be met with, and many other men whose names are connected with ideas of noble race or noble intellect. The daughters of these handloom weavers dress their hair with care, and will not let themselves be seen in rags. The mothers of the last generation were often to be seen in the old French costumes, and to this day hundreds work in such glazed attics as were used by their forefathers across the sea. Little as they earn, the weaver-households struggle to preserve a decent poverty and hide their cares. They must have some pleasures too. In two or three parts of the parish, there are penny balls; there is a room also for penny concerts, and there is a penny circus, "with a complete change of riders." These places are all quietly and well conducted; but are chiefly supported by the surrounding localities.

The fathers of these families lived when their parents could afford to them the benefit of dame schools.[10] How courteously and sensibly they often talk, and with what well chosen words, I was amazed to hear. A doll-maker, dying of consumption, who certainly believed in long words too devoutly, but who never misapplied them, talked in periods well weighed and rounded, that were in admirable contrast to the slip-slop[11] gossip of my dear friend Sir John Proaser. "One of the weavers," said the clergyman of the district (the Reverend Mr. Trivett), "asked me to lend him *Calvin's Institutes*, and when I told him that mine was a black letter[12] copy, he said that

[1] *politicians* Shrewd, selfish schemers, derogatorily compared to professional politicians.

[2] *St. James* Neighborhood in central London known for its wealthy and aristocratic residents.

[3] *Revocation of the Edict of Nantes* The Edict of Nantes (1598) had granted French Protestants, known as the Huguenots, the right to practice their religion. In 1685, Louis XIV formally cancelled the Edict of Nantes in the Edict of Fontainebleau, which closed all Protestant schools and ordered the destruction of Huguenot churches. Many Huguenots sought asylum abroad, including in England.

[4] *green* Public, grassy piece of land.

[5] *runlets* Small streams.

[6] *Cervantes* Miguel de Cervantes (1547–1616), a Spanish writer and the author of *Don Quixote*.

[7] *Nineveh* Ancient Assyrian city (in present-day Iraq); *Palmyra* Ancient city in present-day Syria, important for its location on the road to Damascus; *Babylon* Ancient Mesopotamian city-state (in present-day Iraq).

[8] *Racine the dramatist* Jean Racine (1639–99) was one of the most renowned French dramatists of the seventeenth century. He is primarily known for his tragedies.

[9] *Lesage* Alain-René Lesage (1668–1747) was a French writer of comedies and satirical adventures.

[10] *dame school* School for young children, maintained by a woman.

[11] *consumption* Tuberculosis; *period* Well-balanced sentence, especially one expressing a complete thought; *slip-slop* Characterized by improper word-usage; conveying weak or careless thinking.

[12] *Calvin's Institutes* The Institutes of the Christian Religion, by John Calvin (1509–64), an introduction to Protestant theology; *black letter* Old-fashioned, heavy, and ornate type associated with early seventeenth-century printing practices—in contrast to the lighter,

he should not mind that in the least. Another asked once for the *Colloquies of Erasmus*, and one who was unmarried and working with his brother, so that he had some shillings to spare, wanted to know what it would cost to get a copy of Smith's *Wealth of Nations*."[1]

I mentioned just now a doll-maker—him I found roasting himself by a large fire—a man wasted and powerless—discussing on what day he should go into Guy's Hospital.[2] There was a heap of bran[3] in a corner, used for doll-stuffing and for a children's bed also, no doubt. Here, as elsewhere, however large the family collected in one room, I never saw more than a single bed. Sleeping places were made usually on the floor. One woman, rich in half-a-dozen chairs, showed me with triumph how she made a first-rate bedstead[4] by putting them artfully together. Before the doll-maker's bran sat a boy at a stool, with a pile of broken tobacco-pipe at his side, and some paste and strips of paper. Each bit of paper as he pasted it he screwed round a fragment of tobacco-pipe. These were, perhaps, to be doll's bones, the basis of their arms and legs. At a deal table[5] near the window a mother, who tottered with ill-health, and a daughter about seventeen years old, were measuring some lengths of calico.[6] The calico was to be cut up for doll's bodies, or skins. The cutting out of bodies requires art and skill. The girl many days before had pricked her thumb, the result was that it had gathered, and was in a poultice.[7] "She is the only one of us, except me, able to make the bodies," said the poor

more modern Roman type.

[1] *Colloquies of Erasmus* The Christian humanist thinker Desiderius Erasmus (1466–1536) published a collection of dialogues examining various contemporary issues in 1518; *shilling* The monetary equivalent of one-twentieth of a pound (£); *Smith's Wealth of Nations* Adam Smith's (1723–90) *Inquiry into the Nature and Causes of the Wealth of Nations* (1766), an examination and endorsement of the free-market economy.

[2] *Guy's Hospital* South-east London hospital, founded in 1721 by Bible publisher Thomas Guy (1645?–1724), that was intended to treat those considered incurable.

[3] *bran* Husk removed from ground grain.

[4] *bedstead* Bed frame.

[5] *deal table* Table made of a plank of pine or fir.

[6] *calico* Cotton cloth, typically imported from the East, but, by the nineteenth century, increasingly manufactured in Europe.

[7] *gathered* Swelled; festered; *poultice* Paste used to treat wounds, sometimes heated and typically applied to the skin using a bandage.

father, "and you see—" He pointed to the crippled thumb, and the mother looked down at it in a maze of sorrow. They looked to its recovery for bread.

In another house I saw a room swept of all furniture, through the distress that such a pricked thumb had occasioned, and two other homes I saw made wretched by the accidental wounding of the husband's hand.

In one of them, an empty room rented at half-a-crown[8] a week, there stood a woman all by herself. She stood because she did not possess a chair, and told us that they—she and her husband—had that morning got some work. They had been living on their furniture for twelve weeks, because her husband, who was a carpenter, had hurt his hand. She had failed to get work until the day before, when she obtained a pair of stays[9] to make, a chance job, for which she would receive fourpence. She was a young woman who would have been pretty if she had been better fed. Alas, for the two young hearts failing there together, for the kisses of the thin and wasted lips that should be full with youth and pleasure! "You earn so little here, and could have a beautiful cottage in the country for the price of this room in Bethnal Green—you scarcely could be worse off if you went into the country." They had done that, but the law of settlement[10] had forced them back again on Bethnal Green.

Why should I make the readers' hearts as heavy as my own was made by the accumulation of these evidences of woe heaped up over woe? I saw families in cellars with walls absolutely wet; in dismantled rooms covered with dust and cobwebs, and containing nothing but a loom almost in ruins; or striving to be clean. One I found papering and whitewashing his home, having obtained means to do so from his landlord after seven years of neglect. In another house a neighbour had dropped in to

[8] *crown* Five-shilling coin; a sum of money worth five shillings.

[9] *pair of stays* Corset or corset-like undergarment, worn by women (and, occasionally, men) for shaping and support.

[10] *law of settlement* Centuries-old legislation in Britain had tied the right to social assistance for those in poverty to "settlement"—the fact of being established in a community. As a result of the complex provisions of the law of settlement as it had evolved by the early 1850s, landholders were discouraged from building and maintaining housing for tenant workers, many rural laborers and their families were effectively forced to live many miles from where they were employed—and many potential rural laborers were forced into the city without employment.

tea in a company dress of old black satin with plenty of cherry-coloured ribbons. The daughter of that house made elaborate and very pretty fringe-tassels at fourteen pence for a hundred and forty-four of them. The father of that house had been two weeks dead. Everywhere I found present sickness, and in many places recent death. Only in one place I found sullen despair, and there the room was full of people—there was no fire in the hearth, and there was no furniture, except a bed from which a woman was roused who spoke hoarsely and looked stupidly wild with ragged dress and hair disordered. She may have been drunk, but she could have sat as she was to Lebrun[1] for a picture of despair. "Why," she was asked, "do none of your children come to school?"—"No money."—"But you need pay nothing—only wash and send them."—"I can't wash them—no fire."

We went into a cellar shared by two families:—the rent of a room or cellar in this district is commonly two shillings a week. One half of this room was occupied by a woman and four children, who had also a husband somewhere working for her; her division contained many bits of furniture and quite a fairy-land of ornaments upon the mantelpiece. The other woman was a widow with a son nineteen years old. They had nothing but a little deal table and two broken chairs; but there were hung up against the wall two coloured pictures in gilt frames, which her son, she said, had lately given her. Perhaps they were a birthday gift; certainly, cheap as they may have been, they were the fruit of a long course of saving; for the poor woman, trembling with ill-health, and supporting her body with both hands upon the little table, said, that her son was then out hawking, and that she expected him in every minute in hope that he might bring home three-halfpence to get their tea.

Account was made of the earnings of a whole lane, and they were found to average threepence farthing a day for the maintenance of each inhabitant, both great and small. There was, I think, one in about six positively disabled by sickness. The dearness[2] of everything during the last winter had been preventing hawkers and others from making their small purchases and sales; the

consequence was to be seen too plainly in many a dismantled room. The spring and summer are for all the harvest time, but some were already beginning to suspect that "the spring must have gone by," for their better times used to begin early in March, and there is still no sign of them. All were, however, trusting more or less that, in the summer, they would be able to recover some of the ground lost during a winter more severe than usual. None seemed to have a suspicion of the fate in store, of the war-prices and causes of privation that probably will make for them this whole year one long winter of distress. It is not only in the dead upon the battle-field, or among the widows and orphans of the fallen, that you may see the miseries of war. Let any one go, five months hence, among these poor people of St. Philip's, Shoreditch (that is the right name of this region of Bethnal Green), when they find that they have lost not their spring only, but their summer—let them be seen fasting under an autumn sun in their close courts and empty rooms, starved by hundreds out of life as well as hope, and he will understand, with a new force, what is the meaning of a war to the poor man.

Something I have neglected to say concerning the dismantled rooms. The absent furniture and clothing has not been pawned, it has gone to a receiving-house.[3] The district is full of miserable people preying upon misery who lend money on goods under the guise of taking care of them, and give no ticket or other surety.[4] It is all made a matter of faith, and an enormous interest is charged for such accommodation in defiance of the law.

And another miserable truth has to be told. The one vice with which misery is too familiar is well-known also here; for on the orders of this wretched land, which they must give up hope who enter,[5] there is a palace hung round outside with eight or ten huge gaslights—inside brilliantly illuminated. That is the house of the dragon at the gate—here lives the gin devil.

What is to be done? Private charity must look on hopelessly when set before an evil so gigantic. Here is

---

1. *Lebrun* Charles Le Brun (1619–90), a French painter and theorist of art.

2. *dearness* High price.

3. *receiving-house* Warehouse.

4. *surety* Assurance on a contract.

5. *this wretched … who enter* Cf. Dante's *Inferno*: Dante, led to the gates of Hell by his guide Virgil, notes the inscription "Abandon all hope, ye who enter here" (III.9).

but a little bit of London, scarcely a quarter of a mile square, we look at it aghast, but there is other misery around it and beyond it. What is to be done? So much drainage and sewerage is to be done, is very certain. All that can be done is to be done to change the character of a Bethnal-Green home. The Society for Improving the Dwellings of the Poor[1] makes nearly five per cent on its rooms for families, though it fails commercially when taking thought for single men. The Society professes pure benevolence, and no care about dividends. Let it abandon that profession, abide by it certainly as a guiding idea, but let it take purely commercial ground before the public, and let its arm be strengthened. They who are now paying from five to seven pounds a year for a filthy room or cellar will be eager enough to pay the same price for a clean and healthy lodging. Let model lodging-houses for such families be multiplied, let them return a percentage to their shareholders; and since the society is properly protected by a charter, let all who would invest a little money wisely look into its plans. I see the need of this so strongly that I shall begin to inquire now very seriously into its affairs, and I exhort others to do the same, with a view to taking shares, if they be found a safe and fit investment.

Private and direct charity may relieve individuals, and console many a private sorrow in this part of London, but it cannot touch—such charity to the extent of thousands of pounds cannot remove—the public evil. Associations for providing any measure of relief are checked by the necessity for charters to protect themselves against the present unjust laws of partnership.

And, after all, the truth remains, that the people are crowded together in a stagnant corner of the world. They are all poor together; no tradesman or employer living among them finds them occupation; they ramble about and toil their lives away painfully to earn threepence farthing a day; while the same people shifted to other quarters in the country, would find men contending for the possession of their labour, glad to give two or three shillings daily for a pair of hands. The

people of the parish hang together like a congealed lump in a solution that needs to be broken up and stirred in with the rest.

Half the men here would be hailed with chants of joy by the manufacturers were they to turn their back upon their handlooms and march to the aid of steam in Preston.[2] I do not say, "Send them to Preston," for in that town one misery can only be relieved because another has been made, but there are very many parts of England in which labour is wanted sorely, and would earn fair pay. Employers in those parts of England should be made fully aware of the existence of such parishes as this, in which hardworking, earnest, quiet people struggle in the dark. Such parishes are banks on which cheques may be drawn to any amount for the capital that can be made of honest labour.

There is room for many of these people in large provincial towns, and in small towns and rural districts. The abolition of the Law of Settlement—a horrible evil and an absolutely frightful cruelty, fully discussed last year in this journal[3]—will remove the chief obstacle to such an attempt to break up little lumps of social misery. The abolition of that law is promised to the country, and whoever strives to make the promise null or to postpone its fulfilment, strives practically—whatever his intent may be—to perpetuate or to prolong some of the worst pains that vex both flesh and spirit of our labourers. When the migrations of the poor cease to be watched with narrow jealousy, as will be the case when this bad law is dead, no corner of our social life in London, or in England, need stagnate or putrefy. There need be no longer six-and-twenty people in a cottage, upon ground that does not find fit work for six. Change will be then possible for Bethnal Green. It may remain the home of poverty and toil, but it may cease to be the home of want.
—15 APRIL 1854[4]

---

[2] *Preston* Parish in Lancashire that saw significant industrialization during the nineteenth century.

[3] *a horrible ... this journal* "How to Kill Labourers," a discussion of the Law of Settlement, appeared in the 2 April 1853 edition of *Household Words*.

[4] *1854* Dickens serialized *Hard Times*, his fictionalized examination of the various social ills of industrialized England, in 1854; an instalment of the novel appeared in the same issue as "The Quiet Poor."

[1] *The Society ... the Poor* Part of Model Dwelling Companies, a group established to provide improved living conditions for the working classes. The companies built new housing with the expectation of a good return on their investment. The combination of social good and private profit became known as "five per cent philanthropy."

THE NEW ART OF PHOTOGRAPHY
CONTEXTS

If the Victorian era was in many ways an "age of realism" in literature, it was also an age in which the "real" was given new definition through the medium of photography. Photography was developed virtually simultaneously by Louis Daguerre and Henry Fox Talbot, with the Frenchman and the Englishman making announcements of their discoveries within three weeks of each other in 1839. As Charles Dickens describes in his essay on "Photography" (excerpted in this section), the technologies developed by the two were quite distinct; the "daguerreotype" resulted in a single image, while the calotype technology developed by Talbot involved paper negatives from which multiple images could be created. Later in the century a variety of other techniques were developed, including glass plate technology, which provided levels of photographic detail that remain virtually unrivaled, even in the twenty-first century. By the 1890s, the advent of the portable "Kodak" camera had put photography into the reach of the middle classes. Not only was it possible for one to obtain a few images of one's loved ones from a professional; one could also take up the activity of photography as an amateur. But even in the 1840s, the new science and art of photography was helping to transform a number of aspects of Victorian culture.

One aspect of culture on which photography had a particularly strong impact was print culture. Engraving had for centuries made possible the reproduction of illustrations, and wood engraving, one of the first methods used to produce illustrations in books, enjoyed a renaissance in the period, as did all things medieval. Metal engravings, a slightly later invention, enjoyed a short revival in popularity during the nineteenth century—particularly steel engravings, which could be used to produce a large number of proofs. This practice was soon superceded, however, by photo-engraving, a photomechanical process by which a photographic image was recorded on a sensitized metal plate, which was then etched in an acid bath and used to reproduce the photograph. The widespread reproduction of actual photographs in newspapers and magazines did not come until the early twentieth century, but these engraving techniques, pioneered in such publications as the satirical magazine *Punch* (founded in 1841), and, especially, in *The Illustrated London News* (founded 14 May 1842), allowed engravings based on photographic images to be reproduced—and to give readers a sense of the world being shown to them as it really was.

The connections between photography and print were not restricted to newspapers and magazines, of course; new technologies such as the engraving machine (created in the 1830s) enabled an unprecedented expansion of book illustration in the Victorian period. And sometimes the connections between literature and photography were entirely direct; Tennyson, for example, commissioned the photographer Julia Margaret Cameron to illustrate his *Idylls of the King*.

Photography interacted just as powerfully with other arts. The connection between photography and painting was an obvious one, and certainly many artists began to use photographs in their work, sometimes merely as an *aide memoire*, sometimes as a "copy text," sometimes as something in-between. For his famous panorama of *Derby Day* (1856–58), for example, the painter William Powell Frith commissioned the photographer Robert Howlett to take photographs not of the entire scene in which Frith was interested (for which Frith relied on his own sketches from life) but of a range of different individuals within it, so that he could fill in human details with greater accuracy and completeness.

Some expressed an outright preference for the newer art over the arts of painting and drawing. In an essay that appeared in the 21 January 1857 issue of the *Journal of the Photographic Society*, for example, "Theta" argued that "what in painting is a tiresome pedantry of observation, becomes in photography an inexhaustible delight, a study, and a piece of instruction. What we cared not for in nature, becomes a joy and wonder in the photographic picture." But when practitioners of the new art began to stake claims for an artistic status that went beyond fidelity to nature and aspired to the condition of "High Art," they met with considerable resistance. A landmark was the exhibition in 1857 at the Art Treasures Exhibition in Manchester (the first major exhibition to showcase photography alongside painting and other traditional visual arts). The most controversial work exhibited was Oscar Rejlander's vast photographic tableau, *The Two Ways of Life*, in which a montage of photographic images of allegorical figures are brought together against an artificial backdrop. To many, the artistic presumption of the work crossed a line; reviewing the exhibition in *The Art-Journal*, Robert Hunt allowed that "the pose of each figure is good and the grouping of the whole as nearly perfect as possible," but nevertheless concluded that "we do not … desire to see many advances in this direction. Works of High Art are not to be executed by a mechanical contrivance. The hand of man, guided by the heaven-born mind, can alone achieve greatness in this direction."

Rejlander was not alone in his desire to create photographs that would be recognized as "High Art," that is, in the same sorts of ways as oil paintings were received. Henry Peach Robinson argued unabashedly in "Pictorial Effect in Photography" (1867) for the use of the photographer's artifice to contrive a pleasing result: "any dodge, trick, and conjuration of any kind is open to the photographer's use. His imperative duty is to avoid the mean, the base, and the ugly, and to aim to elevate his subject, … to correct the unpicturesque. … A great deal can be done and very beautiful pictures made, by a mixture of the real and the artificial in a picture." Robinson's most controversial work of precisely this sort was *Fading Away* (1858), a composition combining images from five negatives, with the full image depicting a girl dying of consumption. Some saw the result of Robinson's artistry as a tasteless exploitation of grief, but the image was extremely popular (Prince Albert was prompted by his admiration of *Fading Away* to place a standing order for a copy of any composite photograph Robinson produced).

A very different approach to the art of photography was taken by Henry Emerson, who strongly criticized the approaches of photographers such as Rejlander, Robinson, and Julia Margaret Cameron. "Photograph people as they really are," he advised in *Naturalistic Photography* (1886). "Do not dress them up. … The photographic technique is perfect." Emerson's recommended photographic techniques, however, were themselves highly original—and in their own way as consciously artistic as those of Robinson or Cameron. In Emerson's view, one should emulate the natural, and "nothing in nature has a hard outline, but everything is seen against something else, and its outlines fade gently into something else, often so subtly that you cannot distinguish clearly where one ends and the other begins." To represent nature as the eye perceives it, then, Emerson recommended shooting photographs slightly out of focus. Emerson's impressionistic approach was popular for a time (and continued to influence some important photographers well into the twentieth century), but by the 1890s it was in painting rather than in photography that impressionism was putting down deep roots. Emerson himself came to recant his earlier views; in "The Death of Naturalistic Photography" (1890), he wrote that he had given up hope of photography being able to compete with painting; and regretting that he had compared "photographs to great works of art, and photographers to great artists … I throw in my lot with those who say Photography is a very limited Art."

But "limited" was by then precisely what photography had proven it was *not*. Within Britain and its colonies alone, the medium had produced the war photographs, nature photographs, and still-lifes of Roger Fenton; the social realism of John Thomson and Thomas Annan; the memorably idealized expressions of female beauty of Julia Margaret Cameron and Lady Clementina Hawarden; suggestive representations of the exotic by Fenton, Thomson, Cameron, Francis Frith, and others; powerful representations by Howlett and others of the vitality of industrial Britain, and Annan's and Thomson's equally powerful images of its brutality; Frank Sutcliffe's and Henry Taunt's evocative images of village and rural life; and the compelling portraiture of Cameron, Lewis Carroll, William Notman, and many others.

The practice of photography was diverse, too. Early on it had become established as a professional pursuit—in the 1851 census there were already 51 British citizens who listed "photographer" as their occupation. But aristocratic amateurs such as Cameron, Hawarden, and Talbot continued to make their marks. With the notable exception of Lady Elizabeth Butler, women remained excluded from the ranks of accepted artists in the medium of painting; in photography, however, Cameron, Hawarden—and, later in the century, Anna Atkins and others—were leading figures.

More generally, it was also true that the sorts of individuals who were attracted to photography formed a diverse group. The barriers that today divide photography as an artistic pursuit from its commercial and scientific applications had for the most part not yet been erected in the Victorian era. Even those who saw photography as an art simultaneously appreciated it as science; Roger Fenton, for example, in his 1852 "Proposal for the Formation of a Royal Photographic Society" (reprinted in this section), refers to photography both as an art and as a "branch of natural science," and proposes to open the society to opticians and chemists as well as artists and "practical photographers, both professional and amateur."

Such breadth was to a large extent characteristic of the age—and should seem less surprising to us in this instance if we remember not only the degree to which photography represented a new technology, but also the degree to which it was initially a severely limited one. No means existed, for example, to enlarge photographic images, and the very long exposure times required in photography's early years meant that it remained impossible for a photograph to "capture a moment"; figures passing quickly in front of the camera would remain entirely unrecorded. (That Fenton's most famous photograph of the Crimean War showed cannon balls in an empty valley was a reflection of Victorian sensibilities, but also a reflection of the limits of technology: he could have depicted dead bodies, but to photograph the action of battle was still impossible.) The diversity and the depth of the achievement of practitioners of the photographic arts in the Victorian era is all the more impressive for the technical obstacles that they faced.

⌘ ⌘ ⌘

Roger Fenton, "Proposal for the Formation of a Photographic Society" (1852)

Roger Fenton, a 32-year-old painter and sometime law student, was among the many in whom the displays at the Great Exhibition of 1851 sparked an interest in the new art of photography. Much of the finest work displayed at the Exhibition was by French photographers (prominent among them Hippolyte Bayard and Gustave Le Gray), and in October of 1851, Fenton traveled to Paris to meet members of the Societé Héliographique, the world's first photographic society. By the summer of 1852, Fenton was becoming prominent in English photographic circles, and later that year he put forward the proposal reprinted here, for the formation of a new society. The Photographic Society came into existence in 1853, with the Queen and Prince Albert as patrons; in 1894 the name was changed to The Royal Photographic Society.

The science of Photography gradually progressing for several years, seems to have advanced at a more rapid pace during and since the Exhibition of 1851. Its lovers and students in all parts of Europe were brought into more immediate and frequent communication.

Ideas of theory and methods of practice were interchanged, the pleasure and the instruction were mutual. In order that this temporary may become the normal condition of the art and of its professors, it is proposed to unite in a common society, with a fixed place of meeting, and a regular official organization, all those gentlemen whose tastes have led them to the cultivation of this branch of natural science.

As the object proposed is not only to form a pleasant and convenient Photographic Club, but a society that shall be as advantageous for the art as is the Geographic Society to the advancement of knowledge in its department, it follows necessarily that it shall include among its members men of all ranks of life; that while men of eminence, from their fortune, social position, or scientific reputation, are welcomed, no photographer of respectability in his particular sphere of life be rejected.

The society then will consist of those eminent in the study of natural philosophy, of opticians, chemists, artists, and practical photographers, professional and amateur. It will admit both town and country members. It is proposed:—

That, after the society has been once organized, persons who may in future wish to become members will have to be proposed and seconded, a majority of votes deciding their election.

That the entrance fee and subscription shall be as small as possible, in order that none may be excluded by the narrowness of their means.

That there shall be an entrance fee of £2.2s.—a subscription of £1.1s.

That the society should have appropriate premises fitted up with laboratory, glass operating room, and salon, in which to hold its meetings.

That such meetings should be periodically held, for the purpose of hearing and discussing written or verbal communications on the subject of Photography, receiving and verifying claims as to priority of invention, exhibiting and comparing pictures produced by different applications of photographic principles; making known improvements in construction of cameras and lenses; and, in fine, promoting by emulation and comparison the progress of the art.

That the proceedings of the society shall be published regularly in some acknowledged organ, which shall be sent to all subscribing members.

That a library of works bearing upon the history or tending to the elucidation of the principles of the science be formed upon the premises, and at the expense of the society, to be used by the members, subject to such rules as may hereafter be agreed upon.

That the society should publish an annual album, of which each member should receive a copy, who had contributed a good negative photograph to its formation, other members having to pay (and the public being charged at the rate of   )?[1]

The heaviest expense attendant upon this plan would be leasing or construction of convenient premises, and this expense might be lessened by the letting off the lower part as a shop for the sale of photographic chemicals, and the upper part to some person who would form a commercial establishment for the printing of positives.

Before any progress can be made in the organization of such a society as the foregoing, it is necessary first to ascertain the amount of support which it would be likely to obtain. If those gentlemen, therefore, who feel inclined to become members of such a society will send in their names and addresses to R. FENTON, Esq., 2, Albert Terrace, and 50, King William Street, City,[2] together with any suggestion which may occur to them individually on the perusal of this outline of a plan, arrangements will be made as soon as a sufficient number of persons have sent in their names, to hold a meeting in some central situation, to which they will be invited to discuss the matter and to elect a committee for the organization of a society.

from Charles Dickens, "Photography," *Household Words*, Volume 7 (1853)

Among Dickens's many contributions to *Household Words* (a widely-circulated miscellany of articles and literary pieces) were installments of his fiction, essays on political issues, and articles on various cultural topics—such as the selection excerpted below.

... Light from the sky is, in fact, the chief part of the stock-in-trade of a photographer. Other light than the sun's can be employed; but, while the sun continues to

---

[1] *rate of   )?* The space left here, together with the question mark, suggest that the specific amount was an issue left for later discussion.

[2] *City* I.e., the City of London.

pour down to us a daily flow of light of the best quality, as cheap as health (we will not say as cheap as dirt, for dirt is a dear article), sunlight will be consumed by the photographers in preference to any other. A diffused, mellow light from the sky, which moderates the darkness of all shadows, is much better suited to the purpose of photography than a direct sunbeam; which creates hard contrasts of light and shade. For in the picture formed by light, whether on metal, glass, or paper, such hard contrasts will be made still harder. Lumpy shadows haunt the chambers of all bad photographers.

He who would not be vexed by them and would produce a portrait in which the features shall be represented with the necessary softness, finds it generally advantageous not only to let the shades be cast upon the face in a room full of diffused rays—that is to say, under a skylight—but also by the waving of large black velvet screens over the head to moderate and stint the quantity of light that falls on features not thrown into shadow. For this reason few very good photographic pictures can be taken from objects illuminated only by a side light, as in a room with ordinary windows. The diffused light of cloudy weather, if the air be free from fog, hinders the process of photography only by lengthening the time occupied in taking impressions. Light, when it is jaundiced by a fog, is quite as liable as jaundiced men to give erroneous views of mankind.

Photography, out of England, has made its most rapid advances, and produced its best results in the United States and in France; but, although both the French and the Americans have the advantage of a much purer and more certain supply of sunlight, it is satisfactory to know that the English photographers have thrown as much light of their own on the new science as any of their neighbours. ...

The den of the photographer, in which he goes through those mysterious operations which are not submitted to the observation of the sitter, is a small room lighted by a window, and communicating into a dark closet, veiled with heavy curtains. Our sense of the supernatural, always associated with dark closets, was excited strongly in this chamber, by the sound of a loud rumbling in the bowels of the house, and the visible departure of a portion of the wall to lower regions. "We thought instinctively of bandits who wind victims up

and down in moveable rooms or turn them up in treacherous screw bedsteads. But, of course, there was no danger to be apprehended. What we saw was, of course, only a contrivance to save labour in conveying pictures up or down for colouring or framing. Our consciences having been satisfied on this point, the expert magician took a plate of the prescribed size, made ready to his hand. Such plates consist of a thin layer of silver fixed upon copper, and are provided to the artist highly polished; but a final and superlative polish is given to each plate, with a "buff" or pad like a double handled razor strop, tinged with a fine mineral powder. Simple as it appears, the final polishing of the plate is an operation that can only succeed well under a practised pair of hands, that regulate their pressure by a refined sense of touch. The plate thus polished was brushed over finally and very lightly, as with the touch of a cat's paw, with a warm pad of black velvet freshly taken from an oven.

To witness the next process we went into the dark closet itself, the very head quarters of spectredom. There, having carefully excluded daylight, the operator lifted up the lid of a small bin, rapidly fixed the plate, silver side downwards, in a place made underneath for its reception, shut down the lid, and began to measure seconds by counting, talking between whiles, thus:—"One—that box—two contains—three—chloride of iodine—four—strewn—five—six—at the bottom. Now!" (Presto, out came the plate in a twinkling, and was held against a sheet of white paper, upon which it reflected a ghastly straw colour by the light of a small jet of gas.) "Ah, tint not deep enough!" The plate was popped into its vapour bath again with magic quickness. "Seven—the action of the iodine" (continued the operator, counting seconds, and teaching us our lesson in the same breath) "rising in vapour upon the surface—eleven—of the plate—twelve—causes it to take in succession—thirteen—fourteen—fifteen—all the colours of the spectrum—sixteen—seventeen; and deposits upon it a film." As he went on solemnly counting, we asked how long he exposed the plate to the visitation of that potent vapour. "A very short time," he replied; "but it varies—thirty—thirty-one—according to the light in the next room—thirty-five—thirty-six—thirty-seven. Adjusting the plate to the weather, thirty-eight—is the result of an acquired instinct—thirty-nine—forty. Now it is ready." The plate was out, and its change to a deeper straw colour was shown. The lid of an adjoining bin was lifted, and the iodized plate was hung in the same way over another vapour; that of the chloride of bromine, that the wraiths of the two vapours might mingle, mingle, mingle as black spirits with white, blue spirits with gray. In this position it remained but a very short time, while we stood watching by in the dark cupboard. The plate having had its temper worked upon by these mysterious agencies was rendered so extremely sensitive, that it was requisite to confine it at once, in a dark hole or solitary cell, made ready for it in a wooden frame; a wooden slide was let down over it, and it was ready to be carried to the camera.

Before quitting this part of the subject, we must add to the preceding description two or three external facts. We have been discussing hitherto the kernel without touching the nutshell in which these, like all other reasonable matters in this country, may be (and usually are) said to lie. The nutshell is in fact as important to a discussion in this country as the small end of the wedge or the British Lion:—In the action of light upon surfaces prepared in a certain manner lies the whole idea of photography. The camera-obscura is an old friend; how to fix chemically the illuminated images formed in the camera by light, was a problem at which Sir Humphrey Davy,[1] half a century ago, was one of the first men who worked. Sir Humphrey succeeded no farther than in the imprinting of a faint image, but as he could not discover how to fix it, the whole subject was laid aside. Between the years 1814 and 1828, two Frenchmen, M. Daguerre and M. Nièpce,[2] were at work upon the problem. In 1827 M. Nièpce produced before the Royal Society what he then called heliographs, sun-pictures, formed and fixed upon glass, copper plated with silver, and well-polished tin. But, as he kept the secret of his processes, no scientific use was made of his discovery. M. Daguerre, working at the same problem,

succeeded about the same time in fixing sun-pictures on paper impregnated with nitrate of silver. M. Daguerre and M. Nièpce having combined their knowledge to increase the value of their art, the French government—in the year 1839—acting nobly, as it has often acted in the interests of science, bought for the free use of the world the details of the new discovery. For the full disclosure of their secrets there was granted to M. Daguerre a life pension of two hundred and forty pounds (he died not many months ago), and a pension of one hundred and sixty pounds to the son of M. Nièpce, with the reversion of one half to their widows.

Six months before the disclosure of the processes in France, Mr. Fox Talbot[3] in England had discovered a process leading to a like result—the fixing of sun-pictures upon paper. As the English parliament buys little for science, nothing unfortunately hindered the patenting of Mr. Talbot's method. That patent in certain respects very much obstructed the advance of photography in this country, and great credit is due to Mr. Talbot for having recently and voluntarily abandoned his exclusive rights, and given his process to the public for all purposes and uses, except that of the portrait-taker. By so doing he acted in the spirit of a liberal art born in our own days, and peculiarly marked with the character of our own time. It does one good to think how photographers, even while exercising the new art for money, have pursued it with a generous ardour for its own sake, and emulate each other in the magnanimity with which they throw their own discoveries into the common heap, and scorn to check the progress of their art for any selfish motive. After the completion of the French discovery two daguerreotype establishments were formed in London armed with patent rights, and their proprietors, Messrs. Claudet and Beard, do in fact still hold those rights, of which they have long cheerfully permitted the infringement. Mr. Beard tried to enforce them only once, we believe; and M. Claudet, with distinguished liberality, never. ...

And we may observe here that another illustration of our vanities was furnished to us on a different occasion. Daguerreotype plates commonly present faces as they would be seen in a looking-glass, that is to say, reversed:

[1] *Sir Humphrey Davy* English scientist. The discoverer of several chemical elements, Davy (1778–1829) also invented a safety lamp for use in mines.

[2] *two Frenchman ... Nièpce* Louis-Jacques-Mandé Daguerre (1787–1851), now more commonly referred to as "Louis Daguerre," inventor of the daguerreotype process of photography, and Nicéphore Nièpce, said by many to have produced the world's first photograph.

[3] *Mr. Fox Talbot* Henry Fox Talbot (1800–77), English scientist and mathematician, inventor of the calotype photographic process.

the left side of the face, in nature, appearing upon the right side of the miniature. That is the ordinary aspect in which every one sees his own face, for it is only possible for him to behold it reflected in a mirror. This reversing, of course, alters in the slightest degree the similitude ... and it is a curious fact that few of us are content to have even our faces shown to us as others see them. The non-inverted daguerreotypes differ too much from the dear images of self that we are used to learn by heart out of our looking-glasses. They invariably please the friend to whom they are to be given, but they frequently displease the sitter.... A daguerreotype, formed in the usual way and inverted, if held before a looking-glass, becomes again inverted, and shows therefore a non-inverted picture of the person whom it represents.

... There are many processes by which photographic impressions may be taken upon paper and glass; a book full of them lies at this moment before us: we have ourselves seen two, and shall confine ourselves to the telling of a part of our experience. We rang the artist's bell of Mr. Henneman in Regent-street, who takes very good portraits upon paper by a process cousin to the Talbotype. By that gentleman we were introduced into a neat little chamber lighted by gas, with a few pans and chemicals upon a counter. His process was excessively simple: he would show it to us. He took a square of glass, cleaned it very perfectly, then holding it up by one corner with the left hand, he poured over the centre of the glass some collodion, which is, as most people know, gun-cotton dissolved in ether. By a few movements of the left hand, which appear easy, but are acquired with trouble, the collodion was caused to flow into an even coat over the surface of the glass, and the excess was poured off at another corner. To do this by a few left-handed movements without causing any ripple upon the collodion adhering to the glass is really very difficult. This done, the plate was left till the ether had almost evaporated, and deposited a film of gun-cotton—which is in fact a delicate paper—spread evenly over the surface of the glass. The glass covered with this delicate paper, before it was yet quite dry, was plunged carefully

into a pan or bath, containing a solution of nitrate of silver, about eight grains of it to every hundred of distilled water. In about two minutes it was taken out, and ready for the camera. It was a sheet of glass covered with a fine film of cotton-paper impregnated with nitrate of silver, a colourless salt blackened by light.

It was removed in a dark frame to the camera. Then an assistant, opening a book, assumed an attitude and sat for his picture. In a few seconds it was taken in the usual way, and the glass carried again into the operator's room. There it was dipped into another bath—a bath of pyrogallic acid—and the impression soon became apparent. To bring it out with greater force it was then dipped into a second and much weaker bath of nitrate of silver. The image was then made perfect; but, as the light parts were all depicted by the blackest shades, and the black parts were left white, the courteous assistant was there represented as a negro.

That negro stage was not of course the finished portrait, it was "the negative"—or stereotype plate, as it were—from which, after it had been fixed with a solution of the sulphate of the peroxyde of iron, any number of impressions could be taken. For it is obvious that if a plate like this be placed on sensitive paper, and exposed to daylight, the whole process will be reversed. The black face will obstruct the passage of the light and leave a white face underneath, the white hair will allow the light to pass, making black hair below, and so on. Impressions thus taken on paper, and afterwards fixed, may either serve for portraits, as they are, or, like the silver plates, they may be coloured.

... Photography already has been found available by the astronomer; the moon has sat for a full-face picture,[1] and there is hope that in a short time photographic paper will become a common auxiliary to the telescope. History will be indebted to photography for facsimiles of documents and volumes that have perished; travellers may bring home incontestible transcripts of inscriptions upon monuments, or foreign scenery. The artist will no longer be delayed in travelling to execute his sketches on

---

[1] *moon has sat for a full-face picture* Amateur photographer John Dillwyn Llewelyn (1810–82) and his daughter Thereza Llewelyn were pioneers in astronomical photography, taking pictures of the moon through the telescope Llewelyn had constructed in 1851 at his estate in Wales.

the spot. He can now wander at his ease, and bring home photographic views, from which to work, as sculptors from the model. Photography is a young art, but from its present aspect we can judge what power it will have in its maturity. The mind may readily become bewildered among expectations, but one thing will suggest many. We understand that a catalogue of the national library of Paris has been commenced, in which each work is designated by a photographic miniature of its title-page.

Photography and Immortality

The following brief extracts are from a letter of poet Elizabeth Barrett (later Elizabeth Barrett Browning) to a friend, and from a speech by one of the first presidents of the photographic society. Pollock's belief was that photography was first and foremost "a *practical science*," but his enthusiasm for it was no less than that of those who valued it more as an art.

from Elizabeth Barrett, Letter to Mary Russell Mitford (1843)

Do you know anything about that wonderful invention of the day, called the Daguerrotype? Think of a man sitting down in the sun and leaving his facsimile in all its full completion of outline and shadow, steadfast on a plate, at the end of a minute and a half! The Mesmeric[1] disembodiment of spirits strikes one as a degree less marvelous. ... It is not merely the likeness which is precious in such cases—but the association and the sense of nearness involved in the thing ... the fact of the very shadow of the person lying there fixed for ever! It is the very sanctification of portraits.

from Sir Frederick Pollock, "Presidential Address," Photographic Society (1855)

The varied objects to which Photography can address itself, its power of rendering permanent that which appears to be as fleeting as the shadows that go across the dial, the power that it possesses of giving fixedness to instantaneous objects, are for the purposes of history ... a matter of the greatest importance. It is not too much to say that no individual—not merely individual man, but no individual substance, no individual matter, nothing that is extraordinary in art, that is celebrated in architecture, that is calculated to excite the imagination of those who behold it, need now perish; but may be rendered immortal by the assistance of Photography.

---

[1] *Mesmeric* Franz Mesmer (1734–1835) claimed to have discovered a mysterious force he termed "animal magnetism"; it was termed *mermerism* by others.

Henry Fox Talbot, *Nelson's Column in Trafalgar Square*, 1843.

Roger Fenton, *The British Museum*, 1857.

Roger Fenton, *Fruit and Flowers*, 1860.

Roger Fenton, *The Long Walk*, 1860.

Oscar Gustav Rejlander, *The Two Ways of Life* (detail), 1857.

Robert Howlett, *The Great Eastern: Isambard Kingdom Brunel Inspecting Construction Work* (detail), 1857.

Oscar Gustav Rejlander, *Homeless*, c. 1860. (This well-known and widely-praised photograph was also sometimes referred to as *A Night in Town* or *Poor Joe*.)

Henry Peach Robinson, *Fading Away*, 1858.

Henry Peach Robinson, *She Never Told Her Love*, 1858.

Francis Frith, *The Pyramids of Dahshoor, From the East*, c. 1858.

Francis Frith, *Crocodile on a Bank of the Nile* (detail), 1857.

Lady Clementina Hawarden, *The Toilette*, c. 1864.

Lady Clementina Hawarden, *Lady Isabella Grace and Clementina Maude, 5 Princes Gardens*, c. 1862–63.

Lewis Carroll, *Ellen Watts* (Ellen Terry), 1865.

Lewis Carroll, *Tuning*, 1876.

Lewis Carroll, *John Everett Millais, His wife, and Two of Their Daughters*, 1865

Francis Bedford, *A Peaceful Village*, 1859.

Julia Margaret Cameron, *Annie—My First Success*, 1864. Cameron maintained that this image was her first successful photograph.

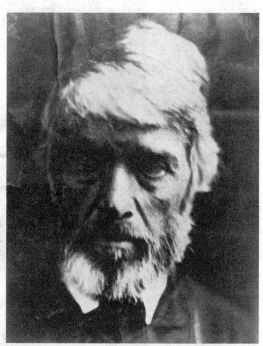

Julia Margaret Cameron, *Thomas Carlyle*, 1867. Carlyle wrote of the photo, "it is as if it suddenly began to speak, terrifically ugly and woebegone!"

Julia Margaret Cameron, *Ophelia*, 1867.

Julia Margaret Cameron, *The Angel at the Sepulchre*, 1869.

Julia Margaret Cameron, *Cingalese Girl*, 1875.

Julia Margaret Cameron, *The Passing of Arthur*, 1875.

Samuel Bourne, *The Rajah of Drangadra*, c. 1868.

Thomas Annan, *Close No. 46, Saltmarket, Glasgow*, 1868.

John Thomson, *Physic Street, Canton*, c. 1869.

William Notman, *Blackfoot Brave, near Calgary, Alberta*, 1889.

William Notman, *Miss Thomas*, 1876.

Peter Henry Emerson, *Gathering Water-lilies*, 1886.

Frederick Evans, *A Sea of Steps*, 1898.   Frederick Evans, *Lincoln Cathedral from the Castle*, 1898.

Frederick Evans, *Portrait of Aubrey Beardsley*, 1893.

John Ruskin
1819 – 1900

John Ruskin was a painter and a poet, author of dozens of books on the arts and sciences, and a dedicated believer in fundamental links between all disciplines. Famous as an art, cultural, and social critic, Ruskin synthesized subjects in fluid and poetic ways, and he exerted an enormous

influence on the aesthetic, philosophical, and political sensibilities of his day. This influence bore heavily on the work of the Pre-Raphaelite painters, notably Dante Gabriel Rossetti, John Everett Millais, and William Holman Hunt. In addition, Ruskin's opposition to industrialization and his ideas about the sacredness of human work inspired William Morris and the Arts and Crafts Movement. Mahatma Gandhi, who translated Ruskin's *Unto the Last* into Gujarati, said about the work's effect on him: "I believe that I discovered some of my deepest convictions reflecting on this great book of Ruskin's, [… which] captured me and made me transform my life."

Ruskin was born in London in 1819 to Margaret Cox and John James Ruskin, a successful wine merchant. Possibly because the couple bore John in midlife and had no other children, the Evangelical Ruskins raised their child in an overprotective and cloistered manner, allowing him neither friends nor toys. The young John's schooling, administered by his mother, was strict and included hours of Bible study every day (the two would read the entire Bible and then resume from the beginning), while his father, also a stern Evangelical, procured tutors for the arts and languages. When Ruskin came of age, he attended Oxford (where he won the Newdigate Prize for poetry), but even then his mother accompanied him, living in rooms nearby, and his father joined the two every weekend.

Even though he had a talent for both poetry and painting, Ruskin realized after graduation that he did not wish to pursue either as a career. His admiration for the British painter J.M.W. Turner, however, led to his first work of art criticism, which evolved into the five-volume *Modern Painters*, published over a period of more than a decade. The first volume of *Modern Painters* was a defense of Turner's "fidelity" to his landscapes and his ability to see and express "truth" in nature. It was not only Ruskin's aesthetic analyses that attracted attention, however, but also his elegant and engaging prose style.

In 1848, Ruskin entered into a disastrous marriage with Euphemia ("Effie") Chalmers, which ended six years later in an annulment on the grounds that the marriage had never been consummated. The following year Effie married the painter John Everett Millais. Throughout his life, Ruskin's relationships with women were fraught, most notably his relationship with Rose La Touche, whom he met (and with whom he apparently fell in love) in 1858 when she was only nine years old. Ruskin proposed marriage to Rose in 1866, but because he had lost his religious faith (he said he had been "unconverted" while attending church in Turin) and she was a strict Evangelical, she ultimately rejected his offer. Not long after her death in 1875, Ruskin suffered an attack of madness, the first of many such episodes he experienced throughout his life.

Although there were times when Ruskin could not function due to mental illness, he was astonishingly prolific: his *Collected Works* fill thirty-nine volumes, and he wrote thousands of letters. His books on architecture, *The Seven Lamps of Architecture* (1849) and the three-volume *Stones of Venice* (1851–53), were so influential that they provoked a revival of Gothic architecture that in some ways ran counter to his philosophies. Ruskin felt that the hand of God was present in those who labored on the stone buildings of the Middle Ages, and that the magnificent Gothic architecture of Venice was a manifestation of a virtuous and honorable people. His writing inspired many to support the preservation and restoration of architectural treasures. Ruskin himself, however, promoted a social, rather than simply an architectural, restoration.

Ruskin's attacks on society became increasingly focused on the effects of modern production, and he became an outspoken challenger of the Industrial Age. His views on economic and social reform, radical at the time, have affected social thinking to this day. Ruskin was strongly opposed to *laissez faire* economics and advocated the organization of labor (the founders of the Labour Party in Britain attributed their ideas to Ruskin), cooperative business ventures, an old-age pension, a minimum wage, public libraries and art galleries, a national health service, equal education opportunities, and pollution control, among many other initiatives. In 1878, Ruskin founded the Guild of St. George, an organization that still exists today, in order to educate the public and to preserve and support small businesses and the production of local crafts.

After writing and lecturing throughout the 1860s, Ruskin was offered the first Slade Professorship of Fine Arts at Oxford, where he delivered (and subsequently published) many famous lectures and speeches to awestruck students, including the young Oscar Wilde. During this decade he also began a series of letters addressed to English laborers, published as *Fors Clavigera*. Ruskin was forced to resign his position at Oxford in 1880 due to mental illness, and although he resumed his professorship for a brief period and published two final books of lectures, *The Pleasures of England* and *The Art of England*, these years were not good to him. He managed to write many installments of his brilliant autobiography, *Praeterita*, but it remained unfinished. After a long illness he died in 1900. Although Westminster Abbey offered a resting place, Ruskin's last wishes were honored, and he was buried near his home in the Coniston graveyard. For the great Russian writer Leo Tolstoy, and for many others, Ruskin's legacy remained alive: "Ruskin was one of the most remarkable of men, not only of England and our time but of all countries and all times. He was one of those rare men who think with their hearts, and so he thought and said not only what he himself had seen and felt, but what everyone will think and say in the future."

⌘ ⌘ ⌘

from *Modern Painters*

A DEFINITION OF GREATNESS IN ART

Painting, or art generally, as such, with all its technicalities, difficulties, and particular ends, is nothing but a noble and expressive language, invaluable as the vehicle of thought, but by itself nothing. He who has learned what is commonly considered the whole art of painting, that is, the art of representing any natural object faithfully, has as yet only learned the language by which his thoughts are to be expressed. He has done just as much towards being that which we ought to respect as a great painter, as a man who has learned how to express himself grammatically and melodiously has towards being a great poet. The language is, indeed, more difficult of acquirement in the one case than in the other, and possesses more power of delighting the sense, while it speaks to the intellect; but it is, nevertheless, nothing more than language, and all those excellences which are peculiar to the painter as such, are merely what rhythm, melody, precision, and force are in the words of the orator and the poet, necessary to their greatness, but not the tests of their greatness. It is not by the mode of representing and saying, but by what is represented and said, that the respective greatness either of the painter or the writer is to be finally determined. ...

So that, if I say that the greatest picture is that which conveys to the mind of the spectator the greatest number of the greatest ideas, I have a definition which will include as subjects of comparison every pleasure which art is capable of conveying. If I were to say, on the contrary, that the best picture was that which most closely imitated nature, I should assume that art could only please by imitating nature; and I should cast out of the pale of criticism those parts of works of art which are not imitative, that is to say, intrinsic beauties of colour and form, and those works of art wholly, which, like the Arabesques of Raffaelle[1] in the Loggias,[2] are not imitative at all. Now, I want a definition of art wide enough to include all its varieties of aim. I do not say, therefore, that the art is greatest which gives most pleasure, because perhaps there is some art whose end is to teach, and not to please. I do not say that the art is greatest which teaches us most, because perhaps there is some art whose end is to please, and not to teach. I do not say that the art is greatest which imitates best, because perhaps there is some art whose end is to create and not to imitate. But I say that the art is greatest which conveys to the mind of the spectator, by any means whatsoever, the greatest number of the greatest ideas; and I call an idea great in proportion as it is received by a higher faculty of the mind, and as it more fully occupies, and in occupying, exercises and exalts, the faculty by which it is received.

If this, then, be the definition of great art, that of a great artist naturally follows. He is the greatest artist who has embodied, in the sum of his works, the greatest number of the greatest ideas. ...

---

[1] *Raffaelle* I.e., Raphael (1483–1520), Italian Renaissance painter.

[2] *Loggias* Open-air galleries.

OF TRUTH OF WATER

I believe it is a result of the experience of all artists, that it is the easiest thing in the world to give a certain degree of depth and transparency to water; but that it is next to impossible, to give a full impression of surface. If no reflection be given, a ripple being supposed, the water looks like lead: if reflection be given, it, in nine cases out of ten, looks *morbidly* clear and deep, so that we always go down *into* it, even when the artist most wishes us to glide *over* it. Now, this difficulty arises from the very same circumstance which occasions the frequent failure in effect of the best-drawn foregrounds ... the change, namely, of focus necessary in the eye in order to receive rays of light coming from different distances. Go to the edge of a pond in a perfectly calm day, at some place where there is duckweed floating on the surface, not thick, but a leaf here and there. Now, you may either see in the water the reflection of the sky, or you may see the duckweed; but you cannot, by any effort, see both together. If you look for the reflection, you will be sensible of a sudden change or effort in the eye, by which it adapts itself to the reception of the rays which have come all the way from the clouds, have struck on the water, and so been sent up again to the eye. The focus you adopt is one fit for great distance; and, accordingly, you will feel that you are looking down a great way under the water, while the leaves of the duckweed, though they lie upon the water at the very spot on which you are gazing so intently, are felt only as a vague uncertain interruption, causing a little confusion in the image below, but entirely undistinguishable as leaves, and even their colour unknown and unperceived. Unless you think of them, you will not even feel that anything interrupts your sight, so excessively slight is their effect. If, on the other hand, you make up your mind to look for the leaves of the duckweed, you will perceive an instantaneous change in the effort of the eye, by which it becomes adapted to receive near rays, those which have only come from the surface of the pond. You will then see the delicate leaves of the duckweed with perfect clearness, and in vivid green; but, while you do so, you will be able to perceive nothing of the reflections in the very water on which they float, nothing but a vague flashing and melting of light and dark hues, without form or meaning, which to investigate, or find out what they mean or are, you must quit your hold of the duckweed, and plunge down.

Hence it appears, that whenever we see plain reflections of comparatively distant objects, in near water, we cannot possibly see the surface, and *vice versa;* so that when in a painting we give the reflections with the same clearness with which they are visible in nature, we presuppose the effort of the eye to look under the surface, and, of course, destroy the surface, and induce an effect of clearness which, perhaps, the artist has not particularly wished to attain, but which he has found himself forced into, by his reflections, in spite of himself. And the reason of this effect of clearness appearing preternatural is, that people are not in the habit of looking at water with the distant focus adapted to the reflections, unless by particular effort. We invariably, under ordinary circumstances, use the surface focus; and, in consequence, receive nothing more than a vague and confused impression of the reflected colours and lines, however clearly, calmly, and vigorously all may be defined underneath, if we choose to look for them. We do not look for them, but glide along over the surface, catching only playing light and capricious colour for evidence of reflection, except where we come to images of objects close to the surface, which the surface focus is of course adapted to receive; and these we see clearly, as of the weeds on the shore, or of sticks rising out of the water, etc. Hence, the ordinary effect of water is only to be rendered by giving the reflections of the *margin* clear and distinct (so clear they usually are in nature, that it is impossible to tell where the water begins); but the moment we touch the reflection of distant objects, as of high trees or clouds, that instant we must become vague and uncertain in drawing, and, though vivid in colour and light as the object itself, quite indistinct in form and feature. If we take such a piece of water as that in the foreground of Turner's[1] Château of Prince Albert, the first impression from it is, "What a wide *surface!*" We glide over it a quarter of a mile into the picture before we know where we are, and yet the water is as calm and crystalline as a mirror; but we are not allowed to tumble into it, and gasp for breath as we go down, we are kept upon the surface, though

that surface is flashing and radiant with every hue of cloud, and sun, and sky, and foliage. But the secret is in the drawing of these reflections. We cannot tell, when we look *at* them and *for* them, what they mean. They have all character, and are evidently reflections of something definite and determined; but yet they are all uncertain and inexplicable; playing colour and palpitating shade, which, though we recognize them in an instant for images of something, and feel that the water is bright, and lovely, and calm, we cannot penetrate nor interpret; we are not allowed to go down to them, and we repose, as we should in nature, upon the lustre of the level surface. It is in this power of saying everything, and yet saying nothing too plainly, that the perfection of art here, as in all other cases, consists.

—1843

from *The Stones of Venice*

THE NATURE OF GOTHIC

. . . In the definition proposed, I shall only endeavour to analyze the idea which I suppose already to exist in the reader's mind. We all have some notion, most of us a very determined one, of the meaning of the term Gothic, but I know that many persons have this idea in their minds without being able to define it: that is to say, understanding generally that Westminster Abbey is Gothic, and St. Paul's is not, that Strasburg Cathedral is Gothic, and St. Peter's is not, they have, nevertheless, no clear notion of what it is that they recognize in the one or miss in the other, such as would enable them to say how far the work at Westminster or Strasburg is good and pure of its kind; still less to say of any nondescript building, like St. James's Palace or Windsor Castle, how much right Gothic element there is in it, and how much wanting. And I believe this inquiry to be a pleasant and profitable one; and that there will be found something more than usually interesting in tracing out this grey, shadowy, many-pinnacled image of the Gothic spirit within us; and discerning what fellowship there is between it and our Northern hearts. And if, at any point of the inquiry, I should interfere with any of the reader's

---

[1] *Turner* J.M.W. Turner (1775–1851), English landscape artist.

previously formed conceptions, and use the term Gothic in any sense which he would not willingly attach to it, I do not ask him to accept, but only to examine and understand, my interpretation, as necessary to the intelligibility of what follows in the rest of the work. ...

I believe, then, that the characteristic or moral elements of Gothic are the following, placed in the order of their importance:

1. Savageness.
2. Changefulness.
3. Naturalism.
4. Grotesqueness.
5. Rigidity.
6. Redundance.

These characters are here expressed as belonging to the building; as belonging to the builder, they would be expressed thus: —1. Savageness or Rudeness. 2. Love of Change. 3. Love of Nature. 4. Disturbed Imagination. 5. Obstinacy. 6. Generosity. And I repeat, that the withdrawal of any one, or any two, will not at once destroy the Gothic character of a building, but the removal of a majority of them will. I shall proceed to examine them in their order.

(1.) Savageness. I am not sure when the word "Gothic" was first generically applied to the architecture of the North; but I presume that, whatever the date of its original usage, it was intended to imply reproach, and express the barbaric character of the nations among whom that architecture arose. It never implied that they were literally of Gothic lineage, far less that their architecture had been originally invented by the Goths themselves; but it did imply that they and their buildings together exhibited a degree of sternness and rudeness, which, in contradistinction to the character of Southern and Eastern nations, appeared like a perpetual reflection of the contrast between the Goth and the Roman in their first encounter. And when that fallen Roman, in the utmost impotence of his luxury, and insolence of his guilt, became the model for the imitation of civilized Europe, at the close of the so-called Dark ages, the word Gothic became a term of unmitigated contempt, not unmixed with aversion. From that contempt, by the exertion of the antiquaries

and architects of this century, Gothic architecture has been sufficiently vindicated; and perhaps some among us, in our admiration of the magnificent science of its structure, and sacredness of its expression, might desire that the term of ancient reproach should be withdrawn, and some other, of more apparent honourableness, adopted in its place. There is no chance, as there is no need, of such a substitution. As far as the epithet was used scornfully, it was used falsely; but there is no reproach in the word, rightly understood; on the contrary, there is a profound truth, which the instinct of mankind almost unconsciously recognizes. It is true, greatly and deeply true, that the architecture of the North is rude and wild; but it is not true, that, for this reason, we are to condemn it, or despise. Far otherwise: I believe it is in this very character that it deserves our profoundest reverence.

The charts of the world which have been drawn up by modern science have thrown into a narrow space the expression of a vast amount of knowledge, but I have never yet seen any one pictorial enough to enable the spectator to imagine the kind of contrast in physical character which exists between Northern and Southern countries. We know the differences in detail, but we have not that broad glance and grasp which would enable us to feel them in their fulness. We know that gentians[1] grow on the Alps, and olives on the Apennines; but we do not enough conceive for ourselves that variegated mosaic of the world's surface which a bird sees in its migration, that difference between the district of the gentian and of the olive which the stork and the swallow see far off, as they lean upon the sirocco wind.[2] Let us, for a moment, try to raise ourselves even above the level of their flight, and imagine the Mediterranean lying beneath us like an irregular lake, and all its ancient promontories sleeping in the sun: here and there an angry spot of thunder, a grey stain of storm, moving upon the burning field; and here and there a fixed wreath of white volcano smoke, surrounded by its circle of ashes; but for the most part a great peacefulness of light, Syria and Greece, Italy and Spain, laid like pieces of a golden pavement into the sea-blue, chased, as we stoop nearer to them, with bossy beaten work of

---

[1] *gentians* Flowers.

[2] *sirocco wind* Hot, moist wind from North Africa.

mountain chains, and glowing softly with terraced gardens, and flowers heavy with frankincense, mixed among masses of laurel, and orange, and plumy palm, that abate with their grey-green shadows the burning of the marble rocks, and of the ledges of porphyry[1] sloping under lucent sand. Then let us pass farther towards the north, until we see the orient colours change gradually into a vast belt of rainy green, where the pastures of Switzerland, and poplar valleys of France, and dark forests of the Danube and Carpathians stretch from the mouths of the Loire to those of the Volga, seen through clefts in grey swirls of rain-cloud and flaky veils of the mist of the brooks, spreading low along the pasture lands: and then, farther north still, to see the earth heave into mighty masses of leaden rock and heathy moor, bordering with a broad waste of gloomy purple that belt of field and wood, and splintering into irregular and grisly islands amidst the northern seas, beaten by storm, and chilled by ice-drift, and tormented by furious pulses of contending tide, until the roots of the last forests fail from among the hill ravines, and the hunger of the north wind bites their peaks into barrenness; and, at last, the wall of ice, durable like iron, sets, deathlike, its white teeth against us out of the polar twilight. And, having once traversed in thought this gradation of the zoned iris of the earth in all its material vastness, let us go down nearer to it, and watch the parallel change in the belt of animal life; the multitudes of swift and brilliant creatures that glance in the air and sea, or tread the sands of the southern zone; striped zebras and spotted leopards, glistening serpents, and birds arrayed in purple and scarlet. Let us contrast their delicacy and brilliancy of colour, and swiftness of motion, with the frost-cramped strength, and shaggy covering, and dusky plumage of the northern tribes; contrast the Arabian horse with the Shetland, the tiger and leopard with the wolf and bear, the antelope with the elk, the bird of paradise with the osprey; and then, submissively acknowledging the great laws by which the earth and all that it bears are ruled throughout their being, let us not condemn, but rejoice in the expression by man of his own rest in the statutes of the lands that gave him birth. Let us watch him with reverence as he sets side by side the burning gems, and smoothes with soft sculpture the

jasper pillars, that are to reflect a ceaseless sunshine, and rise into a cloudless sky: but not with less reverence let us stand by him, when, with rough strength and hurried stroke, he smites an uncouth animation out of the rocks which he has torn from among the moss of the moorland, and heaves into the darkened air the pile of iron buttress and rugged wall, instinct with work of an imagination as wild and wayward as the northern sea; creatures of ungainly shape and rigid limb, but full of wolfish life; fierce as the winds that beat, and changeful as the clouds that shade them. ...

In ... the first volume of this work, it was noticed that the systems of architectural ornament, properly so called, might be divided into three:—1. Servile ornament, in which the execution or power of the inferior workman is entirely subjected to the intellect of the higher;—2. Constitutional ornament, in which the executive inferior power is, to a certain point, emancipated and independent, having a will of its own, yet confessing its inferiority and rendering obedience to higher powers;—and 3. Revolutionary ornament, in which no executive inferiority is admitted at all. I must here explain the nature of these divisions at somewhat greater length.

Of Servile ornament, the principal schools are the Greek, Ninevite, and Egyptian; but their servility is of different kinds. The Greek master-workman was far advanced in knowledge and power above the Assyrian or Egyptian. Neither he nor those for whom he worked could endure the appearance of imperfection in anything; and, therefore, what ornament he appointed to be done by those beneath him was composed of mere geometrical forms—balls, ridges, and perfectly symmetrical foliage—which could be executed with absolute precision by line and rule, and were as perfect in their way, when completed, as his own figure sculpture. The Assyrian and Egyptian, on the contrary, less cognizant of accurate form in anything, were content to allow their figure sculpture to be executed by inferior workmen, but lowered the method of its treatment to a standard which every workman could reach, and then trained him by discipline so rigid, that there was no chance of his falling beneath the standard appointed. The Greek gave to the lower workman no subject which he could not perfectly execute. The

---

[1] *porphyry* Red crystalline rock.

Assyrian gave him subjects which he could only execute imperfectly, but fixed a legal standard for his imperfection. The workman was, in both systems, a slave.

But in the mediaeval, or especially Christian, system of ornament, this slavery is done away with altogether; Christianity having recognized, in small things as well as great, the individual value of every soul. But it not only recognizes its value; it confesses its imperfection, in only bestowing dignity upon the acknowledgment of unworthiness. That admission of lost power and fallen nature, which the Greek or Ninevite felt to be intensely painful, and, as far as might be, altogether refused, the Christian makes daily and hourly, contemplating the fact of it without fear, as tending, in the end, to God's greater glory. Therefore, to every spirit which Christianity summons to her service, her exhortation is: Do what you can, and confess frankly what you are unable to do; neither let your effort be shortened for fear of failure, nor your confession silenced for fear of shame. And it is, perhaps, the principal admirableness of the Gothic schools of architecture, that they thus receive the results of the labour of inferior minds; and out of fragments full of imperfection, and betraying that imperfection in every touch, indulgently raise up a stately and unaccusable whole. ...

And now, reader, look round this English room of yours, about which you have been proud so often, because the work of it was so good and strong, and the ornaments of it so finished. Examine again all those accurate mouldings, and perfect polishings, and unerring adjustments of the seasoned wood and tempered steel. Many a time you have exulted over them, and thought how great England was, because her slightest work was done so thoroughly. Alas! if read rightly, these perfectnesses are signs of a slavery in our England a thousand times more bitter and more degrading than that of the scourged African, or helot[1] Greek. Men may be beaten, chained, tormented, yoked like cattle, slaughtered like summer flies, and yet remain in one sense, and the best sense, free. But to smother their souls with them, to blight and hew into rotting pollards[2] the

suckling branches of their human intelligence, to make the flesh and skin which, after the worm's work on it, is to see God, into leathern thongs to yoke machinery with—this is to be slave-masters indeed; and there might be more freedom in England, though her feudal lords' lightest words were worth men's lives, and though the blood of the vexed husbandman dropped in the furrows of her fields, than there is while the animation of her multitudes is sent like fuel to feed the factory smoke, and the strength of them is given daily to be wasted into the fineness of a web, or racked into the exactness of a line.

And, on the other hand, go forth again to gaze upon the old cathedral front, where you have smiled so often at the fantastic ignorance of the old sculptors: examine once more those ugly goblins, and formless monsters, and stern statues, anatomiless and rigid; but do not mock at them, for they are signs of the life and liberty of every workman who struck the stone; a freedom of thought, and rank in scale of being, such as no laws, no charters, no charities can secure; but which it must be the first aim of all Europe at this day to regain for her children. ...

We have much studied and much perfected, of late, the great civilized invention of the division of labour; only we give it a false name. It is not, truly speaking, the labour that is divided; but the men: divided into mere segments of men—broken into small fragments and crumbs of life; so that all the little piece of intelligence that is left in a man is not enough to make a pin, or a nail, but exhausts itself in making the point of a pin or the head of a nail. Now it is a good and desirable thing, truly, to make many pins in a day; but if we could only see with what crystal sand their points were polished—sand of human soul, much to be magnified before it can be discerned for what it is—we should think there might be some loss in it also. And the great cry that rises from all our manufacturing cities, louder than their furnace blast, is all in very deed for this—that we manufacture everything there except men; we blanch cotton, and strengthen steel, and refine sugar, and shape pottery; but to brighten, to strengthen, to refine, or to form a single living spirit, never enters into our estimate of advantages. And all the evil to which that cry is urging our myriads can be met only in one way: not by

---

[1] *helot* Of a class of serfs, falling between slave and citizen in the Spartan social hierarchy.

[2] *pollards* Trees whose branches have been lopped off to shape them.

teaching nor preaching, for to teach them is but to show them their misery, and to preach to them, if we do nothing more than preach, is to mock at it. It can be met only by a right understanding, on the part of all classes, of what kinds of labour are good for men, raising them, and making them happy; by a determined sacrifice of such convenience, or beauty, or cheapness as is to be got only by the degradation of the workman; and by equally determined demand for the products and results of healthy and ennobling labour.

And how, it will be asked, are these products to be recognized, and this demand to be regulated? Easily: by the observance of three broad and simple rules:

1. Never encourage the manufacture of any article not absolutely necessary, in the production of which *Invention* has no share.

2. Never demand an exact finish for its own sake, but only for some practical or noble end.

3. Never encourage imitation or copying of any kind, except for the sake of preserving records of great works.

The second of these principles is the only one which directly rises out of the consideration of our immediate subject; but I shall briefly explain the meaning and extent of the first also, reserving the enforcement of the third for another place.

1. Never encourage the manufacture of anything not necessary, in the production of which invention has no share.

For instance. Glass beads are utterly unnecessary, and there is no design or thought employed in their manufacture. They are formed by first drawing out the glass into rods; these rods are chopped up into fragments of the size of beads by the human hand, and the fragments are then rounded in the furnace. The men who chop up the rods sit at their work all day, their hands vibrating with a perpetual and exquisitely timed palsy, and the beads dropping beneath their vibration like hail. Neither they, nor the men who draw out the rods or fuse the fragments, have the smallest occasion for the use of any single human faculty; and every young lady, therefore, who buys glass beads is engaged in the slave-trade, and in a much more cruel one than that which we have so long been endeavouring to put down. ...

[One example to] show the reader what I mean [comes] from the manufacture already alluded to, that

of glass. Our modern glass is exquisitely clear in its substance, true in its form, accurate in its cutting. We are proud of this. We ought to be ashamed of it. The old Venice glass was muddy, inaccurate in all its forms, and clumsily cut, if at all. And the old Venetian was justly proud of it. For there is this difference between the English and Venetian workman, that the former thinks only of accurately matching his patterns, and getting his curves perfectly true and his edges perfectly sharp, and becomes a mere machine for rounding curves and sharpening edges; while the old Venetian cared not a whit whether his edges were sharp or not, but he invented a new design for every glass that he made, and never moulded a handle or a lip without a new fancy in it. And therefore, though some Venetian glass is ugly and clumsy enough when made by clumsy and uninventive workmen, other Venetian glass is so lovely in its forms that no price is too great for it; and we never see the same form in it twice. Now you cannot have the finish and the varied form too. If the workman is thinking about his edges, he cannot be thinking of his design; if of his design, he cannot think of his edges. Choose whether you will pay for the lovely form or the perfect finish, and choose at the same moment whether you will make the worker a man or a grindstone.

Nay, but the reader interrupts me—"If the workman can design beautifully, I would not have him kept at the furnace. Let him be taken away and made a gentleman, and have a studio, and design his glass there, and I will have it blown and cut for him by common workmen, and so I will have my design and my finish too."

All ideas of this kind are founded upon two mistaken suppositions: the first, that one man's thoughts can be, or ought to be, executed by another man's hands; the second, that manual labour is a degradation, when it is governed by intellect.

On a large scale, and in work determinable by line and rule, it is indeed both possible and necessary that the thoughts of one man should be carried out by the labour of others; in this sense I have already defined the best architecture to be the expression of the mind of manhood by the hands of childhood. But on a smaller scale, and in a design which cannot be mathematically defined, one man's thoughts can never be expressed by another: and the difference between the spirit of touch of the man who is inventing, and of the man who is obeying directions, is often all the difference between a great and a common work of art. How wide the separation is between original and second-hand execution, I shall endeavour to show elsewhere; it is not so much to our purpose here as to mark the other and more fatal error of despising manual labour when governed by intellect; for it is no less fatal an error to despise it when thus regulated by intellect, than to value it for its own sake. We are always in these days endeavouring to separate the two; we want one man to be always thinking, and another to be always working, and we call one a gentleman, and the other an operative; whereas the workman ought often to be thinking, and the thinker often to be working, and both should be gentlemen, in the best sense. As it is, we make both ungentle, the one envying, the other despising, his brother; and the mass of society is made up of morbid thinkers, and miserable workers. Now it is only by labour that thought can be made healthy, and only by thought that labour can be made happy, and the two cannot be separated with impunity. It would be well if all of us were good handicraftsmen in some kind, and the dishonour of manual labour done away with altogether; so that though there should still be a trenchant distinction of race between nobles and commoners, there should not, among the latter, be a trenchant distinction of employment, as between idle and working men, or between men of liberal and illiberal professions. All professions should be liberal, and there should be less pride felt in peculiarity of employment, and more in excellence of achievement. And yet more, in each several profession, no master should be too proud to do its hardest work. The painter should grind his own colours; the architect work in the mason's yard with his men. ... Hitherto I have used the words imperfect and perfect merely to distinguish between work grossly unskilful, and work executed with average precision and science; and I have been pleading that any degree of unskilfulness should be admitted, so only that the labourer's mind had room for expression. But, accurately speaking, no good work whatever can be perfect, and *the demand for perfection is always a sign of a misunderstanding of the ends of art.*

This for two reasons, both based on everlasting laws.

The first, that no great man ever stops working till he has reached his point of failure: that is to say, his mind is always far in advance of his powers of execution, and the latter will now and then give way in trying to follow it; ... And therefore, if we are to have great men working at all, or less men doing their best, the work will be imperfect, however beautiful. Of human work none but what is bad can be perfect, in its own bad way.

The second reason is, that imperfection is in some sort essential to all that we know of life. It is the sign of life in a mortal body, that is to say, of a state of progress and change. Nothing that lives is, or can be, rigidly perfect; part of it is decaying, part nascent. The foxglove blossom—a third part bud, a third part past, a third part in full bloom—is a type of the life of this world. And in all things that live there are certain irregularities and deficiencies which are not only signs of life, but sources of beauty. No human face is exactly the same in its lines on each side, no leaf perfect in its lobes, no branch in its symmetry. All admit irregularity as they imply change; and to banish imperfection is to destroy expression, to check exertion, to paralyze vitality. All things are literally better, lovelier, and more beloved for the imperfections which have been divinely appointed, that the law of human life may be Effort, and the law of human judgment, Mercy.

Accept this then for a universal law, that neither architecture nor any other noble work of man can be good unless it be imperfect; and let us be prepared for the otherwise strange fact, which we shall discern clearly as we approach the period of the Renaissance, that the first cause of the fall of the arts of Europe was a relentless requirement of perfection, incapable alike either of being silenced by veneration for greatness, or softened into forgiveness of simplicity.

Thus far then of the Rudeness or Savageness, which is the first mental element of Gothic architecture. It is an element in many other healthy architectures also, as the Byzantine and Romanesque; but true Gothic cannot exist without it.

The second mental element above named was Changefulness, or Variety.

I have already enforced the allowing independent operation to the inferior workman, simply as a duty *to him,* and as ennobling the architecture by rendering it more Christian. We have now to consider what reward we obtain for the performance of this duty, namely, the perpetual variety of every feature of the building.

Wherever the workman is utterly enslaved, the parts of the building must of course be absolutely like each other; for the perfection of his execution can only be reached by exercising him in doing one thing, and giving him nothing else to do. The degree in which the workman is degraded may be thus known at a glance, by observing whether the several parts of the building are similar or not; and if, as in Greek work, all the capitals are alike, and all the mouldings unvaried, then the degradation is complete; if, as in Egyptian or Ninevite work, though the manner of executing certain figures is always the same, the order of design is perpetually varied, the degradation is less total; if, as in Gothic work, there is perpetual change both in design and execution, the workman must have been altogether set free.

How much the beholder gains from the liberty of the labourer may perhaps be questioned in England, where one of the strongest instincts in nearly every mind is that love of order which makes us desire that our house windows should pair like our carriage horses, and allows us to yield our faith unhesitatingly to architectural theories which fix a form for everything, and forbid variation from it. I would not impeach love of order: it is one of the most useful elements of the English mind; it helps us in our commerce and in all purely practical matters; and it is in many cases one of the foundation stones of morality. Only do not let us suppose that love of order is love of art. It is true that order, in its highest sense, is one of the necessities of art, just as time is a necessity of music; but love of order has no more to do with our right enjoyment of architecture or painting, than love of punctuality with the appreciation of an opera. ...

From these general uses of variety in the economy of the world, we may at once understand its use and abuse in architecture. The variety of the Gothic schools is the more healthy and beautiful, because in many cases it is entirely unstudied, and results, not from mere love of change, but from practical necessities. For in one point of view Gothic is not only the best, but the *only rational* architecture, as being that which can fit itself most easily

to all services, vulgar or noble. Undefined in its slope of roof, height of shaft, breadth of arch, or disposition of ground plan, it can shrink into a turret, expand into a hall, coil into a staircase, or spring into a spire, with undegraded grace and unexhausted energy; and whenever it finds occasion for change in its form or purpose, it submits to it without the slightest sense of loss either to its unity or majesty,—subtle and flexible like a fiery serpent, but ever attentive to the voice of the charmer. And it is one of the chief virtues of the Gothic builders, that they never suffered ideas of outside symmetries and consistencies to interfere with the real use and value of what they did. If they wanted a window, they opened one; a room, they added one; a buttress, they built one; utterly regardless of any established conventionalities of external appearance, knowing (as indeed it always happened) that such daring interruptions of the formal plan would rather give additional interest to its symmetry than injure it. ....

The third constituent element of the Gothic mind was stated to be Naturalism; that is to say, the love of natural objects for their own sake, and the effort to represent them frankly, unconstrained by artistical laws.

This characteristic of the style partly follows in necessary connection with those named above. For, so soon as the workman is left free to represent what subjects he chooses, he must look to the nature that is round him for material, and will endeavour to represent it as he sees it, with more or less accuracy according to the skill he possesses, and with much play of fancy, but with small respect for law. There is, however, a marked distinction between the imaginations of the Western and Eastern races, even when both are left free; the Western, or Gothic, delighting most in the representation of facts, and the Eastern (Arabian, Persian, and Chinese) in the harmony of colours and forms. ...

Now the noblest art is an exact unison of the abstract value, with the imitative power, of forms and colours. It is the noblest composition, used to express the noblest facts. But the human mind cannot in general unite the two perfections: it either pursues the fact to the neglect of the composition, or pursues the composition to the neglect of the fact.

And it is intended by the Deity that it *should* do this: the best art is not always wanted. Facts are often wanted without art, as in a geological diagram; and art often without facts, as in a Turkey carpet. And most men have been made capable of giving either one or the other, but not both; only one or two, the very highest, can give both....

We have now, I believe, obtained a sufficiently accurate knowledge both of the spirit and form of Gothic architecture; but it may, perhaps, be useful to the general reader, if, in conclusion, I set down a few plain and practical rules for determining, in every instance, whether a given building be good Gothic or not, and, if not Gothic, whether its architecture is of a kind which will probably reward the pains of careful examination.

First, look if the roof rises in a steep gable, high above the walls. If it does not do this, there is something wrong: the building is not quite pure Gothic, or has been altered.

Secondly, look if the principal windows and doors have pointed arches with gables over them. If not pointed arches, the building is not Gothic; if they have not any gables over them, it is either not pure, or not first-rate.

If, however, it has the steep roof, the pointed arch, and gable all united, it is nearly certain to be a Gothic building of a very fine time....

... See if it looks as if it had been built by strong men; if it has the sort of roughness, and largeness, and nonchalance, mixed in places with the exquisite tenderness which seems always to be the sign-manual of the broad vision, and massy[1] power of men, who can see *past* the work they are doing, and betray here and there something like disdain for it....

The Ducal Palace—Bird's Eye View.

Secondly, observe if it be irregular, its different parts fitting themselves to different purposes, no one caring what becomes of them, so that they do their work. If one part always answers accurately to another part, it is sure to be a bad building; and the greater and more conspicuous the irregularities, the greater the chances are that it is a good one. For instance, in the Ducal Palace,[2] of which a rough woodcut [appears here], the general idea is sternly symmetrical; but two windows are lower than the rest of the six; and if the reader will count the arches of the small arcade as far as to the great balcony, he will find it is not in the centre, but set to the right-hand side by the whole width of one of those arches. We may be pretty sure that the building is a good one; none but a master of his craft would have ventured to do this.

—1853

---

[1] *massy* Heavy.

[2] *Ducal Palace* Gothic palace in Venice.

MATTHEW ARNOLD
1822 – 1888

Nicknamed "the Emperor" by his friends and family, Matthew Arnold was an ardent and, in the view of some Victorians, arrogant critic of modernity. Arnold embodied both the idealist expectations and the apocalyptic anxieties of the approaching *fin-de-siécle* in his poetry and prose. In the face of an increasingly materialistic mass culture, dominated by the vacuity of what he called "the average man" or "Philistine" of the democratized middle classes, Arnold sought to revive culture in the image of liberal humanism. Only an education in the ostensibly timeless and universal works of masters like Marcus Aurelius, Tolstoy, Homer, and Wordsworth, Arnold believed, could cure the *malaise* of modern life.

"For the creation of a masterwork of literature, two powers must concur," Arnold wrote in 1865, "The power of the man and the power of the moment, and the man is not enough without the moment." Arnold believed that modern industrial life and the materialism it had made possible were radically indisposed towards artistic genius and indeed had created a climate of psychological and moral enervation that poetry was powerless to heal. The *Zeitgeist* (one of his terms for the powerful work of modern popular culture) was profoundly "unpoetical," and was best anatomized through prose. His own career shows symptoms of the fragmentation he analyzed. Arnold incisively broke with the often melancholic poetry of his early years in order to pursue prose criticism, for him the best possible literary work, he believed, in an era that he saw as spiritually bankrupt. Modern society was in no condition to produce great poets; the best that modern life could muster, according to Arnold, were powerful critics—*if* they stayed away from the politics of the passing moment.

The River Thames ran past the village of Laleham where Matthew Arnold was born in 1822. Arnold was the eldest son of Mary Penrose Arnold and Dr. Thomas Arnold. His father, a clergyman and headmaster of Rugby School, was celebrated for reforming the school's curriculum to foreground Christian values, classical languages, and competitive games. Ironically, Arnold, who in later life would come to resemble his father by valuing above all else great humanist texts and a classical education, was lazy, laconic, and flippant as a student. Upon meeting the young dilettante, Charlotte Brontë wrote that "his manner displeases, from its seeming foppery." Yet, in spite of a flamboyant indifference to academia and a studied attempt to dissociate himself from all that his father represented, he amazed family and friends by winning a scholarship to Oxford's Balliol College in 1840, the prodigious Newdigate Prize for poetry in 1843, and a Fellowship at Oriel College in 1845.

Wordsworth, a friend of the family, was one of the most tangible influences on Arnold's poetry. When Wordsworth died, Arnold wondered sadly, "Who will teach us how to feel?" He frequently fled from classes to wander the countryside around the Lake District or to hike in the Alps, landscapes memorialized by Wordsworth and Coleridge. Many critics claim that Arnold was most accomplished as a poet of nature. The "simple joy the country yields," rendered in poems like "Thyrsis," reveals a surprising affinity with the quiet style of Thomas Gray; his "Resignation" speaks to Wordsworth's "Tintern Abbey." Arnold's personal manner, reminiscent of his idols Lord Byron and Goethe, did not cancel out a heartfelt relation to nature, whose unadorned expression modeled the "high seriousness" he admired in Sophocles and Aeschylus.

In 1847, Arnold obtained employment in London as a private secretary to the liberal politician Lord Lansdowne, a period during which he produced most of his poetry. In 1849 the publication of *The Strayed Reveller, and Other Poems*, by "A," was followed by *Empedocles on Etna, and Other Poems* (1852). The controversial preface to *Poems* (1853) provoked heated debate. Here Arnold focused on the ponderous force of the "unpoetical" nineteenth century writ large over his earlier work and damned the "dialogue of the mind with itself" that his *Empedocles on Etna* exhibited. Great poetry, Arnold claimed, must be distinguished from verse produced by a restless intellect fragmented by attempts to address the problems of contemporary life. Poetry should create works of beauty and unity that rise above the historical moment to "inspirit and rejoice" readers.

Letters to his best friend and fellow poet Arthur Hugh Clough, who did address the intellectual issues of the current moment, provide valuable insight into the demanding standards Arnold set for poetry. "I am glad you like the *Gypsy Scholar*," he wrote, "—but what does it *do* for you? Homer *animates*—Shakespeare *animates*—in its poor way I think *Sohrab and Rustum animates*—the *Gypsy Scholar* at best awakens a pleasing melancholy." Considered an often biting critic of the work of his contemporaries, including Clough, Arnold's harshest criticisms were first addressed to his own work. His poem "Dover Beach," probably written in 1851, but published in 1867, is one of English literature's profound expressions of modernity's disaffection with itself. Yet perceiving that his own poetry seemed passively ensnared in the "continual state of mental distress" that he took to task in the preface to *Poems*, he largely ceased writing poetry from the mid-1850s onward. After *New Poems* (1867), Arnold would refashion himself as a prose writer. According to Lionel Trilling, Arnold "perceived in himself the poetic power, but knew that his genius was not of the greatest, that the poetic force was not irresistible in him," not enough, at any rate, to act as a transformative agent in an age of disillusionment.

In 1851, Arnold married Frances Lucy Wightman and to support his family accepted a position as a public school inspector. Initially thinking the job would suffice "for the next three or four years," Arnold continued to be employed in the public service for thirty-five years. In contrast to writers like Tennyson or Carlyle, Arnold had to work for a living, writing only in his spare time. He believed that his inspections of schools in Britain and across Europe gave him first-hand experience to support his conviction that educating the public in a classical humanist tradition was key to "civilizing the next generation of the lower classes."

Arnold was elected Professor of Poetry at Oxford University in 1857, where he delivered public lectures for the following ten years. Though a proponent of an exacting standard of classical scholarship, Arnold was the first to lecture in English rather than Latin, altering an elitist institutional practice that acted as a barrier to the kind of education that the nineteenth century urgently needed, in his opinion. Arnold turned many of his lectures into essays and books, including *On Translating Homer* (1861) and *Friendship's Garland* (1871).

Though by his own standards of greatness Arnold could not *transform* society as a poet, as a critic he was determined to *reform* it. In his famous essay "The Function of Criticism at the Present Time," published in *Essays in Criticism* (1865), Arnold helped raise the value of criticism from its status as a "baneful and injurious employment" to a creative activity in its own right. Deftly juxtaposing snatches from tabloids alongside texts of high culture, Arnold's critical methodology foreshadowed the kind of work pursued in cultural studies today. While few have unanimously agreed with Arnold's pronouncements on literature and society, he has influenced almost every significant English-speaking critic since his time, including T.S. Eliot, F.R. Leavis, Lionel Trilling, and Raymond Williams.

In *Culture and Anarchy* (1869), arguably his most important work of social criticism, Arnold proposed that antagonistic factions of British society could learn to overcome their differences through an education in "disinterested" and universal human values. The differences allowed expression in democratic societies would disintegrate into anarchic disorder, thought Arnold, unless tethered to the "higher" ideals of the humanist tradition. His witty veneer and Apollonian appeal to transcendent virtues of "sweetness and light" sometimes enamored, and sometimes exasperated, a public whose prominent figures he often singled out by name for critical interrogation. Leslie Stephen, Virginia Woolf's father, remarked drily: "I often wished ... that I too had a little sweetness and light that I might be able to say such nasty things of my enemies."

During the 1870s, Arnold published a series of attacks on orthodox religion: *St. Paul and Protestantism* (1870), *Literature and Dogma* (1873), and *God and the Bible* (1875). Even in a period that witnessed the challenges to traditional religious belief posed by Darwin's theories, the work of geologists, and the "higher criticism" of the Bible that came from Germany and elsewhere, Arnold's religious critiques scandalized many Victorians. He recommended that Victorians exchange their faith in a religion founded on the assumption of the truth of the Bible for faith in a transcendent, secular humanism. When he returned to literary criticism in "The Study of Poetry" (1880), he claimed, as Thomas Carlyle had before him in the 1830s, that "most of what now passes for religion and philosophy will be replaced by poetry."

Like Dickens and Thackeray before him, Arnold embarked on a lecture tour of the United States, in 1883. Tired and burdened by debts, Arnold saw the trip as a money-making venture that would also allow him to visit a daughter who had married an American. He was loved in Washington but received with mixed success in other cities. He compiled his lectures in *Discourses in America* (1885), which contains his discussion of Emerson as well as the essay "Literature and Science." Here Arnold responds to Thomas Huxley's claim in "Science and Culture" (1881) that "for the purpose of attaining real culture, an exclusively scientific education is at least as effectual as an exclusively literary education." Especially in America, Arnold argued, where the democratic impulse to glorify "the average man" was particularly enthusiastic, education must safeguard the guiding ideals of the Western tradition, "the best that is known and thought."

Arnold died suddenly of a heart attack in 1888, leaving behind him a remarkable body of cultural criticism and a few poems familiar to all readers of English poetry. His statement about Oxford and modernity in *Culture and Anarchy* may well be taken as fitting epitaph: "We in Oxford ... have not failed to seize one truth,—the truth that beauty and sweetness are essential characters of a complete human perfection. ... We have not won our political battles, we have not carried our main points, we have not stopped our adversaries' advance, we have not marched victoriously with the modern world; but we have told silently upon the mind of the century, we have prepared currents of feeling which sap our adversaries' position when it seems gained, we have kept up our communications with the future."

⌘⌘⌘

The Buried Life

Light flows our war of mocking words, and yet,
  Behold, with tears mine eyes are wet!
I feel a nameless sadness o'er me roll.
Yes, yes, we know that we can jest,
5 We know, we know that we can smile!
But there's a something in this breast,
To which thy light words bring no rest,

And thy gay smiles no anodyne.°   *remedy*
Give me thy hand, and hush awhile,
10 And turn those limpid eyes on mine,
And let me read there, love! thy inmost soul.

Alas! is even love too weak
To unlock the heart, and let it speak?
Are even lovers powerless to reveal
15 To one another what indeed they feel?

I knew the mass of men concealed
Their thoughts, for fear that if revealed
They would by other men be met
With blank indifference, or with blame reproved;
20 I knew they lived and moved
Tricked in disguises, alien to the rest
Of men, and alien to themselves—and yet
The same heart beats in every human breast!

But we, my love!—doth a like spell benumb
25 Our hearts, our voices?—must we too be dumb?

Ah! well for us, if even we,
Even for a moment, can get free
Our heart, and have our lips unchained;
For that which seals them hath been deep-ordained!
30 Fate, which foresaw
How frivolous a baby man would be—
By what distractions he would be possessed,
How he would pour himself in every strife,
And well-nigh change his own identity—
35 That it might keep from his capricious play
His genuine self, and force him to obey
Even in his own despite his being's law,
Bade through the deep recesses of our breast
The unregarded river of our life
40 Pursue with indiscernible flow its way;
And that we should not see
The buried stream, and seem to be
Eddying at large in blind uncertainty,
Though driving on with it eternally.

45 But often, in the world's most crowded streets,
But often, in the din of strife,
There rises an unspeakable desire
After the knowledge of our buried life;
A thirst to spend our fire and restless force
50 In tracking out our true, original course;
A longing to inquire
Into the mystery of this heart which beats
So wild, so deep in us—to know
Whence our lives come and where they go.
55 And many a man in his own breast then delves,
But deep enough, alas! none ever mines.
And we have been on many thousand lines,

And we have shown, on each, spirit and power;
But hardly have we, for one little hour,
60 Been on our own line, have we been ourselves—
Hardly had skill to utter one of all
The nameless feelings that course through our breast,
But they course on for ever unexpressed.
And long we try in vain to speak and act
65 Our hidden self, and what we say and do
Is eloquent, is well—but 'tis not true!
And then we will no more be racked
With inward striving, and demand
Of all the thousand nothings of the hour
70 Their stupefying power;
Ah yes, and they benumb us at our call!
Yet still, from time to time, vague and forlorn,
From the soul's subterranean depth upborne
As from an infinitely distant land,
75 Come airs, and floating echoes, and convey
A melancholy into all our day.

Only—but this is rare—
When a beloved hand is laid in ours,
When, jaded with the rush and glare
80 Of the interminable hours,
Our eyes can in another's eyes read clear,
When our world-deafened ear
Is by the tones of a loved voice caressed—
A bolt is shot back somewhere in our breast,
85 And a lost pulse of feeling stirs again.
The eye sinks inward, and the heart lies plain,
And what we mean, we say, and what we would, we
    know.
A man becomes aware of his life's flow,
And hears its winding murmur; and he sees
90 The meadows where it glides, the sun, the breeze.

And there arrives a lull in the hot race
Wherein he doth for ever chase
That flying and elusive shadow, rest.
An air of coolness plays upon his face,
95 And an unwonted calm pervades his breast.
And then he thinks he knows
The hills where his life rose,
And the sea where it goes.
—1852

The Scholar-Gipsy[1]

Go, for they call you, shepherd, from the hill;
  Go, shepherd, and untie the wattled cotes![2]
    No longer leave thy wistful flock unfed,
    Nor let thy bawling fellows rack their throats,
5   Nor the cropped herbage shoot another head.
      But when the fields are still,
    And the tired men and dogs all gone to rest,
     And only the white sheep are sometimes seen
     Cross and recross the strips of moon-blanched green,
10   Come, shepherd, and again begin the quest!

Here, where the reaper was at work of late—
  In this high field's dark corner, where he leaves
    His coat, his basket, and his earthen cruse,°   *jug*
    And in the sun all morning binds the sheaves,
15   Then here, at noon, comes back his stores to use—
      Here will I sit and wait,
    While to my ear from uplands far away
     The bleating of the folded° flocks is borne,   *enclosed*
     With distant cries of reapers in the corn—
20   All the live murmur of a summer's day.

Screened is this nook o'er the high, half-reaped field,
  And here till sun-down, shepherd! will I be.
    Through the thick corn the scarlet poppies peep,
    And round green roots and yellowing stalks I see
25   Pale pink convolvulus[3] in tendrils creep;
      And air-swept lindens yield
    Their scent, and rustle down their perfumed showers
     Of bloom on the bent grass where I am laid,
     And bower me from the August sun with shade;
30   And the eye travels down to Oxford's towers.

And near me on the grass lies Glanvil's book—
  Come, let me read the oft-read tale again!
    The story of the Oxford scholar poor,
    Of pregnant[4] parts and quick inventive brain,
35   Who, tired of knocking at preferment's door,
      One summer-morn forsook
    His friends, and went to learn the gipsy-lore,
     And roamed the world with that wild brotherhood,
     And came, as most men deemed, to little good,
40   But came to Oxford and his friends no more.

But once, years after, in the country-lanes,
  Two scholars, whom at college erst he knew,
    Met him, and of his way of life enquired;
    Whereat he answered, that the gipsy-crew,
45   His mates, had arts to rule as they desired
      The workings of men's brains,
    And they can bind them to what thoughts they will.
     "And I," he said, "the secret of their art,
     When fully learned, will to the world impart;
50   But it needs heaven-sent moments for this skill."

This said, he left them, and returned no more.
  But rumours hung about the country-side,
    That the lost Scholar long was seen to stray,
    Seen by rare glimpses, pensive and tongue-tied,
55   In hat of antique shape, and cloak of grey,
      The same the gypsies wore.

---

[1] *The Scholar-Gipsy* Arnold said this poem was inspired by the following passage in Joseph Glanville's *Vanity of Dogmatizing* (1661): "There was very lately a lad in the University of Oxford, who was by his poverty forced to leave his studies there; and at last to join himself to a company of vagabond gypsies. Among these extravagant people, by the insinuating subtilty of his carriage, he quickly got so much of their love and esteem as that they discovered to him their mystery. After he had been a pretty while exercised in the trade, there chanced to ride by a couple of scholars, who had formerly been of his acquaintance. They quickly spied out their old friend among the gypsies; and he gave them an account of the necessity which drove him to that kind of life, and told them that the people he went with were not such imposters as they were taken for, but that they had a traditional kind of learning among them, and could do wonders by the power of imagination, their fancy binding that of others; that he himself had learned much of their art, and when he had compassed the whole secret, he intended, he said, to leave their company, and give the world an account of what he had learned." Arnold imagines this student still roaming the area surrounding Oxford, where Arnold spent "the freest and most delightful part, perhaps, of my life."

[2] *wattled cotes* Sheepfolds made of woven sticks.

[3] *convolvulus* Morning-glory.

[4] *pregnant* Full of ideas.

Shepherds had met him on the Hurst[1] in spring;
   At some lone alehouse in the Berkshire moors,
      On the warm ingle-bench,[2] the smock-frocked
         boors°   *rustics*
60   Had found him seated at their entering,

But, 'mid their drink and clatter, he would fly.
   And I myself seem half to know thy looks,
      And put the shepherds, wanderer! on thy trace;
      And boys who in lone wheatfields scare the rooks
65   I ask if thou hast passed their quiet place;
         Or in my boat I lie
   Moored to the cool bank in the summer-heats,
      'Mid wide grass meadows which the sunshine
         fills,
      And watch the warm, green-muffled Cumner
         hills,
70   And wonder if thou haunt'st their shy retreats.

For most, I know, thou lov'st retired ground!
   Thee at the ferry Oxford riders blithe,
      Returning home on summer-nights, have met
   Crossing the stripling Thames at Bab-lock-hithe,
75   Trailing in the cool stream thy fingers wet,
        As the punt's[3] rope chops round;
   And leaning backward in a pensive dream,
      And fostering in thy lap a heap of flowers
      Plucked in shy fields and distant Wychwood
         bowers,
80   And thine eyes resting on the moonlit stream.

And then they land, and thou art seen no more!
   Maidens, who from the distant hamlets come
      To dance around the Fyfield elm in May,
   Oft through the darkening fields have seen thee
        roam,
85   Or cross a stile into the public way.
       Oft thou hast given them store
   Of flowers—the frail-leafed, white anemone,
      Dark bluebells drenched with dews of summer
         eves,

And purple orchises with spotted leaves—
90   But none hath words she can report of thee.

And, above Godstow Bridge, when hay-time's here
   In June, and many a scythe in sunshine flames,
      Men who through those wide fields of breezy
         grass
   Where black-winged swallows haunt the glittering
         Thames,
95   To bathe in the abandoned lasher pass,[4]
       Have often passed thee near
   Sitting upon the river bank o'ergrown;
      Marked thine outlandish garb, thy figure
         spare,
      Thy dark vague eyes, and soft abstracted air—
100   But, when they came from bathing, thou wast gone!

At some lone homestead in the Cumner hills,
   Where at her open door the housewife darns,
      Thou hast been seen, or hanging on a gate
   To watch the threshers in the mossy barns.
105   Children, who early range these slopes and late
       For cresses from the rills,
   Have known thee eyeing, all an April-day,
      The springing pastures and the feeding kine;° *cows*
      And marked thee, when the stars come out
         and shine,
110   Through the long dewy grass move slow away.

In autumn, on the skirts of Bagley Wood—
   Where most the gypsies by the turf-edged way
      Pitch their smoked tents, and every bush you
         see
   With scarlet patches tagged and shreds of grey,[5]
115   Above the forest-ground called Thessaly—
       The blackbird, picking food,
   Sees thee, nor stops his meal, nor fears at all;
      So often has he known thee past him stray,
      Rapt, twirling in thy hand a withered spray,
120   And waiting for the spark from heaven to fall.

---

[1] *the Hurst* Hill outside Oxford. All the places mentioned in the stanzas following are located in the area surrounding Oxford.

[2] *ingle-bench* Fireside bench.

[3] *punt* Small, shallow boat propelled with a long pole pushed against the river bottom.

[4] *lasher pass* Place where water collects after spilling over a dam.

[5] *With scarlet ... grey* Reference to the clothes of the gypsies, which they hang on the bushes to dry.

And once, in winter, on the causeway chill
  Where home through flooded fields foot-travellers
      go,
    Have I not passed thee on the wooden bridge,
  Wrapt in thy cloak and battling with the snow,
125   Thy face toward Hinksey and its wintry ridge?
      And thou hast climbed the hill,
  And gained the white brow of the Cumner range;
    Turned once to watch, while thick the
      snowflakes fall,
    The line of festal light in Christ-Church hall[1]—
130 Then sought thy straw in some sequestered grange.

But what—I dream! Two hundred years are flown
  Since first thy story ran through Oxford halls,
    And the grave Glanvil did the tale inscribe
  That thou wert wandered from the studious walls
135   To learn strange arts, and join a gipsy-tribe;
      And thou from earth art gone
  Long since, and in some quiet churchyard laid—
    Some country-nook, where o'er thy unknown
      grave
    Tall grasses and white flowering nettles wave,
140 Under a dark, red-fruited yew-tree's shade.

—No, no, thou hast not felt the lapse of hours!
  For what wears out the life of mortal men?
    'Tis that from change to change their being
      rolls;
  'Tis that repeated shocks, again, again,
145   Exhaust the energy of strongest souls
      And numb the elastic powers.
  Till having used our nerves with bliss and
    teen,°   *vexation*
    And tired upon a thousand schemes our wit,
    To the just-pausing Genius[2] we remit
150 Our worn-out life, and are—what we have been.

Thou hast not lived, why should'st thou perish, so?
  Thou hadst *one* aim, *one* business, *one* desire;

Else wert thou long since numbered with the
    dead!
Else hadst thou spent, like other men, thy fire!
155   The generations of thy peers are fled,
      And we ourselves shall go;
  But thou possessest an immortal lot,
    And we imagine thee exempt from age
    And living as thou liv'st on Glanvil's page,
160 Because thou hadst—what we, alas! have not.

For early didst thou leave the world, with powers
  Fresh, undiverted to the world without,
    Firm to their mark, not spent on other things;
  Free from the sick fatigue, the languid doubt,
165   Which much to have tried, in much been
      baffled, brings.
      O life unlike to ours!
  Who fluctuate idly without term or scope,
    Of whom each strives, nor knows for what he
      strives,
    And each half lives a hundred different lives;
170 Who wait like thee, but not, like thee, in hope.

Thou waitest for the spark from heaven! and we,
  Light half-believers of our casual creeds,
    Who never deeply felt, nor clearly willed,
  Whose insight never has borne fruit in deeds,
175   Whose vague resolves never have been fulfilled;
      For whom each year we see
  Breeds new beginnings, disappointments new;
    Who hesitate and falter life away,
    And lose tomorrow the ground won today—
180 Ah! do not we, wanderer! await it too?

Yes, we await it!—but it still delays,
  And then we suffer! and amongst us one,
    Who most has suffered,[3] takes dejectedly
  His seat upon the intellectual throne;
185   And all his store of sad experience he
      Lays bare of wretched days;
  Tells us his misery's birth and growth and signs,

---

[1] *Christ-Church hall* Dining hall of Christ Church, an Oxford College.

[2] *Genius* Attendant spirit that accompanies a soul from birth to death and shapes his or her character.

[3] *one ... suffered* Reference probably either to Tennyson—whose *In Memoriam* appeared in 1850, the year he succeeded Wordsworth as Poet Laureate—or to German philosopher Johann Wolfgang von Goethe (1749–1832).

And how the dying spark of hope was fed,
And how the breast was soothed, and how the
head,
190   And all his hourly varied anodynes.

This for our wisest! and we others pine,
And wish the long unhappy dream would end,
And waive all claim to bliss, and try to bear;
With close-lipped patience for our only friend,
195   Sad patience, too near neighbour to despair—
But none has hope like thine!
Thou through the fields and through the woods
dost stray,
Roaming the country-side, a truant boy,
Nursing thy project in unclouded joy,
200   And every doubt long blown by time away.

O born in days when wits were fresh and clear,
And life ran gaily as the sparkling Thames;
Before this strange disease of modern life,
With its sick hurry, its divided aims,
205   Its heads o'ertaxed, its palsied hearts, was rife—
Fly hence, our contact fear!
Still fly, plunge deeper in the bowering wood!
Averse, as Dido did with gesture stern
From her false friend's approach in Hades turn,[1]
210   Wave us away, and keep thy solitude!

Still nursing the unconquerable hope,
Still clutching the inviolable shade,
With a free, onward impulse brushing through,
By night, the silvered branches of the glade—
215   Far on the forest-skirts, where none pursue.
On some mild pastoral slope
Emerge, and resting on the moonlit pales
Freshen thy flowers as in former years
With dew, or listen with enchanted ears,
220   From the dark dingles,[2] to the nightingales!

But fly our paths, our feverish contact fly!
For strong the infection of our mental strife,
Which, though it gives no bliss, yet spoils for rest;
And we should win thee from thy own fair life,
225   Like us distracted, and like us unblest.
Soon, soon thy cheer would die,
Thy hopes grow timorous, and unfixed thy powers,
And thy clear aims be cross and shifting made;
And then thy glad perennial youth would fade,
230   Fade, and grow old at last, and die like ours.

Then fly our greetings, fly our speech and smiles!
—As some grave Tyrian[3] trader, from the sea,
Descried at sunrise an emerging prow
Lifting the cool-haired creepers stealthily,
235   The fringes of a southward-facing brow
Among the Aegean isles;
And saw the merry Grecian coaster come,
Freighted with amber grapes, and Chian wine,
Green, bursting figs, and tunnies°   tuna fish
steeped in brine—
240   And knew the intruders on his ancient home,

The young light-hearted masters of the waves—
And snatched his rudder, and shook out more sail;
And day and night held on indignantly
O'er the blue Midland waters with the gale,
245   Betwixt the Syrtes[4] and soft Sicily,
To where the Atlantic raves
Outside the western straits; and unbent sails
There, where down cloudy cliffs, through
sheets of foam,
Shy traffickers, the dark Iberians[5] come;
250   And on the beach undid his corded bales.
—1853

---

[3]   *Tyrian*   From Tyre, ancient capital of Phoenicia.

[4]   *Syrtes*   Two treacherous gulfs off the coast of northern Africa.

[5]   *dark Iberians*   Inhabitants of Spain or Portugal. The story of these "shy traffickers" comes from fifth-century BCE Greek historian Herodotus's *History*, in which he explains that the Carthaginians would sail through the Strait of Gibraltar to trade with the West Africans. In a unique trading process, these Carthaginians would leave their goods on the beach, withdrawing to their ships. The Africans would come out of their hiding places and leave gold beside the goods they wished to purchase. After they had retreated, the Carthaginians would return and decide if this was adequate payment. The process would be repeated until the two sides reached an agreement.

---

[1]   *as Dido … turn*   In Virgil's *Aeneid*, Dido, Queen of Carthage, commits suicide when her lover, Aeneas, deserts her. When he encounters her in Hades, she turns away from him.

[2]   *dingles*   Wooded dales.

Stanzas from The Grande Chartreuse[1]

Through Alpine meadows soft-suffused
    With rain, where thick the crocus blows,
Past the dark forges long disused,
    The mule-track from Saint Laurent goes.
5   The bridge is crossed, and slow we ride,
    Through forest, up the mountain-side.

The autumnal evening darkens round,
    The wind is up, and drives the rain;
While, hark! far down, with strangled sound
10   Doth the Dead Guier's[2] stream complain,
    Where that wet smoke, among the woods,
    Over his boiling cauldron broods.

Swift rush the spectral vapours white
    Past limestone scars with ragged pines,
15   Showing—then blotting from our sight!—
    Halt—through the cloud-drift something shines!
    High in the valley, wet and drear,
    The huts of Courrerie appear.

Strike leftward! cries our guide; and higher
20   Mounts up the stony forest-way.
At last the encircling trees retire;
    Look! through the showery twilight grey
    What pointed roofs are these advance?
    A palace of the Kings of France?

25   Approach, for what we seek is here!
    Alight, and sparely sup, and wait
For rest in this outbuilding near;
    Then cross the sward[3] and reach that gate.
    Knock; pass the wicket! Thou art come
30   To the Carthusians' world-famed home.

The silent courts, where night and day
    Into their stone-carved basins cold
The splashing icy fountains play—
    The humid corridors behold!
35   Where, ghostlike in the deepening night,
    Cowled forms brush by in gleaming white.

The chapel, where no organ's peal
    Invests the stern and naked prayer—
With penitential cries they kneel
40   And wrestle; rising then, with bare
    And white uplifted faces stand,
    Passing the Host from hand to hand;

Each takes, and then his visage wan
    Is buried in his cowl once more.
45   The cells!—the suffering Son of Man
    Upon the wall—the knee-worn floor—
    And where they sleep, that wooden bed,
    Which shall their coffin be, when dead![4]

The library, where tract and tome
50   Not to feed priestly pride are there,
To hymn the conquering march of Rome,
    Nor yet to amuse, as ours are!
    They paint of souls the inner strife,
    Their drops of blood, their death in life.

55   The garden, overgrown—yet mild,
    See, fragrant herbs[5] are flowering there!
Strong children of the Alpine wild
    Whose culture is the brethren's care;
    Of human tasks their only one,
60   And cheerful works beneath the sun.

Those halls, too, destined to contain
    Each its own pilgrim-host of old,
    From England, Germany, or Spain—

---

[1] *Grande Chartreuse* Carthusian monastery in a nearly inaccessible valley in the French Alps, established by Saint Bruno in 1804. Arnold visited the monastery on his honeymoon in 1851. The Carthusians are known for their austerity, and devote their time to fasting, solitary contemplation, and prayer.

[2] *Dead Guier* Guiers Mort, a river that flows down past the monastery and into the Guiers Vif (French: "Living Guiers").

[3] *sward* Stretch of grass.

[4] *that wooden ... dead* Carthusians are buried on wooden planks. They are sometimes (incorrectly) thought to sleep in their coffins.

[5] *fragrant herbs* From which the Carthusians make the liqueur Chartreuse, the sales of which provide their primary source of income.

All are before me! I behold
65 The House, the Brotherhood austere!
—And what am I, that I am here?

For rigorous teachers seized my youth,
And purged its faith, and trimmed its fire,
Showed me the high, white star of Truth,
70 There bade me gaze, and there aspire.
Even now their whispers pierce the gloom:
What dost thou in this living tomb?

Forgive me, masters of the mind!
At whose behest I long ago
75 So much unlearnt, so much resigned—
I come not here to be your foe!
I seek these anchorites, not in ruth,°   remorse
To curse and to deny your truth;

Not as their friend, or child, I speak!
80 But as, on some far northern strand,
Thinking of his own Gods, a Greek
In pity and mournful awe might stand
Before some fallen Runic[1] stone—
For both were faiths, and both are gone.

85 Wandering between two worlds, one dead,
The other powerless to be born,
With nowhere yet to rest my head,
Like these, on earth I wait forlorn.
Their faith, my tears, the world deride—
90 I come to shed them at their side.

Oh, hide me in your gloom profound,
Ye solemn seats of holy pain!
Take me, cowled forms, and fence me round,
Till I possess my soul again;
95 Till free my thoughts before me roll,
Not chafed by hourly false control!

For the world cries your faith is now
But a dead time's exploded dream;
My melancholy, sciolists[2] say,
100 Is a passed mode, an outworn theme—

As if the world had ever had
A faith, or sciolists been sad!

Ah, if it *be* passed, take away,
At least, the restlessness, the pain;
105 Be man henceforth no more a prey
To these out-dated stings again!
The nobleness of grief is gone—
Ah, leave us not the fret alone!

But—if you cannot give us ease—
110 Last of the race of them who grieve
Here leave us to die out with these
Last of the people who believe!
Silent, while years engrave the brow;
Silent—the best are silent now.

115 Achilles[3] ponders in his tent,
The kings of modern thought are dumb;
Silent they are, though not content,
And wait to see the future come.
They have the grief men had of yore,
120 But they contend and cry no more.

Our fathers[4] watered with their tears
This sea of time whereon we sail,
Their voices were in all men's ears
Who passed within their puissant° hail.   powerful
125 Still the same ocean round us raves,
But we stand mute, and watch the waves.

For what availed it, all the noise
And outcry of the former men?
Say, have their sons achieved more joys,
130 Say, is life lighter now than then?
The sufferers died, they left their pain—
The pangs which tortured them remain.

What helps it now, that Byron bore,
With haughty scorn which mocked the smart,

---

[1]   *Runic*   Carved with runes (early Norse letters).

[2]   *sciolists*   Pretenders to knowledge.

[3]   *Achilles*   Greek warrior who, during the Trojan War, stayed in his tent, refusing to participate, until the death of his best friend, Patroclus, in battle, moved him to action.

[4]   *Our fathers*   I.e., the previous generation of writers.

135 Through Europe to the Aetolian shore[1]
The pageant of his bleeding heart?
That thousands counted every groan,
And Europe made his woe her own?

What boots it, Shelley! that the breeze
140 Carried thy lovely wail away,
Musical through Italian trees
Which fringe thy soft blue Spezzian bay?[2]
Inheritors of thy distress
Have restless hearts one throb the less?

145 Or are we easier, to have read,
O Obermann![3] the sad, stern page,
Which tells us how thou hidd'st thy head
From the fierce tempest of thine age
In the lone brakes of Fontainebleau,
150 Or chalets near the Alpine snow?

Ye slumber in your silent grave!
The world, which for an idle day
Grace to your mood of sadness gave,
Long since hath flung her weeds[4] away.
155 The eternal trifler breaks your spell;
But we—we learnt your lore too well!

Years hence, perhaps, may dawn an age,
More fortunate, alas! than we,
Which without hardness will be sage,
160 And gay without frivolity.
Sons of the world, oh, speed those years;
But, while we wait, allow our tears!

Allow them! We admire with awe
The exulting thunder of your race;
165 You give the universe your law,
You triumph over time and space!

Your pride of life, your tireless powers,
We laud them, but they are not ours.

We are like children reared in shade
170 Beneath some old-world abbey wall,
Forgotten in a forest-glade,
And secret from the eyes of all.
Deep, deep the greenwood round them waves,
Their abbey, and its close° of graves!   enclosure

175 But, where the road runs near the stream,
Oft through the trees they catch a glance
Of passing troops in the sun's beam—
Pennon,[5] and plume, and flashing lance!
Forth to the world those soldiers fare,
180 To life, to cities, and to war!

And through the wood, another way,
Faint bugle-notes from far are borne,
Where hunters gather, staghounds bay,
Round some fair forest-lodge at morn.
185 Gay dames are there, in sylvan green;
Laughter and cries—those notes between!

The banners flashing through the trees
Make their blood dance and chain their eyes;
That bugle-music on the breeze
190 Arrests them with a charmed surprise.
Banner by turns and bugle woo:
Ye shy recluses, follow too!

O children, what do ye reply?
"Action and pleasure, will ye roam
195 Through these secluded dells to cry
And call us?—but too late ye come!
Too late for us your call ye blow,
Whose bent was taken long ago.

"Long since we pace this shadowed nave;
200 We watch those yellow tapers shine,
Emblems of hope over the grave,
In the high altar's depth divine;

---

[1] *Aetolian shore* In Greece, where the English poet George Gordon, Lord Byron, died.

[2] *Spezzian bay* Where English poet Percy Bysshe Shelley drowned, in Italy.

[3] *Obermann* Protagonist of the 1804 novel of that name by Étienne Pivert de Senancour (1770–1846).

[4] *weeds* Mourning garments.

---

[5] *Pennon* Narrow triangular flag, usually borne on the head of a lance.

The organ carries to our ear
Its accents of another sphere.

205 "Fenced early in this cloistral round
Of reverie, of shade, of prayer,
How should we grow in other ground?
How should we flower in foreign air?
—Pass, banners, pass, and bugles, cease;
210 And leave our desert to its peace!"
—1855

Dover Beach

The sea is calm tonight.
    The tide is full, the moon lies fair
Upon the straits—on the French coast the light
Gleams and is gone; the cliffs of England stand,
5 Glimmering and vast, out in the tranquil bay.
Come to the window, sweet is the night-air!
Only, from the long line of spray
Where the sea meets the moon-blanched land,
Listen! you hear the grating roar
10 Of pebbles which the waves draw back, and fling,
At their return, up the high strand,°   shore
Begin, and cease, and then again begin,
With tremulous cadence slow, and bring
The eternal note of sadness in.

15 Sophocles long ago
Heard it on the Aegean, and it brought
Into his mind the turbid ebb and flow
Of human misery;[1] we
Find also in the sound a thought,
20 Hearing it by this distant northern sea.

The Sea of Faith
Was once, too, at the full, and round earth's shore

Lay like the folds of a bright girdle furled.
But now I only hear
25 Its melancholy, long, withdrawing roar.
Retreating, to the breath
Of the night-wind, down the vast edges drear
And naked shingles[2] of the world.

Ah, love, let us be true
30 To one another! for the world, which seems
To lie before us like a land of dreams,
So various, so beautiful, so new,
Hath really neither joy, nor love, nor light,
Nor certitude, nor peace, nor help for pain;
35 And we are here as on a darkling plain
Swept with confused alarms of struggle and flight,
Where ignorant armies clash by night.[3]
—1867

East London[4]

'Twas August, and the fierce sun overhead
    Smote on the squalid streets of Bethnal Green,
And the pale weaver, through his windows seen
In Spitalfields, looked thrice dispirited.

5 I met a preacher there I knew, and said:
"Ill and o'erworked, how fare you in this scene?"
"Bravely!" said he; "for I of late have been
Much cheered with thoughts of Christ, *the living bread.*"

O human soul! as long as thou canst so
10 Set up a mark of everlasting light,
Above the howling senses' ebb and flow,

To cheer thee, and to right thee if thou roam—
Not with lost toil thou labourest through the night!

---

[1] *Sophocles ... misery* Cf. Sophocles's *Antigone* 583–91: "Blest are those whose days have not tasted of evil. For when a house has once been shaken by the gods, no form of ruin is lacking, but it spreads over the bulk of the race, just as, when the surge is driven over the darkness of the deep by the fierce breath of Thracian sea-winds, it rolls up the black sand from the depths, and the wind-beaten headlands that front the blows of the storm give out a mournful roar."

[2] *shingles* Water-worn pebbles.

[3] *as on ... night* Reference to Thucydides's *History of the Peloponnesian War*, in which the invading Athenians became confused as night fell on the battle at Epipolae. Combatants could not tell friend from foe in the moonlight.

[4] *East London* Working-class area of the city. Bethnal Green and Spitalfields are districts in East London.

Thou mak'st the heaven thou hop'st indeed thy
    home.
—1867

West London[1]

Crouched on the pavement, close by Belgrave
    Square,
A tramp I saw, ill, moody, and tongue-tied.
A babe was in her arms, and at her side
A girl; their clothes were rags, their feet were bare.

5 Some labouring men, whose work lay somewhere
        there,
    Passed opposite; she touched her girl, who hied°   hastened
    Across, and begged, and came back satisfied.
    The rich she had let pass with frozen stare.

    Thought I: "Above her state this spirit towers;
10 She will not ask of aliens, but of friends,
    Of sharers in a common human fate.

    "She turns from that cold succour, which attends
    The unknown little from the unknowing great,
    And points us to a better time than ours."
    —1867

from *The Function of Criticism at the Present Time*

Many objections have been made to a proposition
which, in some remarks of mine on translating
Homer,[2] I ventured to put forth; a proposition about
criticism, and its importance at the present day. I said:
"Of the literature of France and Germany, as of the
intellect of Europe in general, the main effort, for now
many years, has been a critical effort; the endeavour, in
all branches of knowledge, theology, philosophy,
history, art, science, to see the object as in itself it really
is." I added, that owing to the operation in English

literature of certain causes, "almost the last thing for
which one would come to English literature is just that
very thing which now Europe most desires—criticism";
and that the power and value of English literature was
thereby impaired. More than one rejoinder declared that
the importance I here assigned to criticism was excessive,
and asserted the inherent superiority of the creative
effort of the human spirit over its critical effort. And the
other day, having been led by a Mr. Shairp's excellent
notice of Wordsworth[3] to turn again to his biography,
I found, in the words of this great man, whom I, for
one, must always listen to with the profoundest respect,
a sentence passed on the critic's business, which seems
to justify every possible disparagement of it. Wordsworth says in one of his letters:

> The writers in these publications [the reviews], while
> they prosecute their inglorious employment, can not
> be supposed to be in a state of mind very favourable
> for being affected by the finer influences of a thing
> so pure as genuine poetry.

And a trustworthy reporter of his conversation
quotes a more elaborate judgement to the same effect:

> Wordsworth holds the critical power very low,
> infinitely lower than the inventive; and he said today
> that if the quantity of time consumed in writing
> critiques on the works of others were given to
> original composition, of whatever kind it might be,
> it would be much better employed; it would make a
> man find out sooner his own level, and it would do
> infinitely less mischief. A false or malicious criticism
> may do much injury to the minds of others, a stupid
> invention, either in prose or verse, is quite harmless.

---

[1] *West London* Wealthy end of the city. Belgrave Square was (and
is) a particularly affluent district.

[2] *in some ... Homer* In Arnold's *On Translating Homer* (1861).

[3] [Arnold's note] I cannot help thinking that a practice, common
in England during the last century, and still followed in France, of
printing a notice of this kind—a notice by competent critics—to
serve as an introduction to an eminent author's works, might be
revived among us with advantage. To introduce all succeeding
editions of Wordsworth, Mr. Shairp's notice might, it seems it me,
excellently serve; it is written from the point of view of an admirer,
nay, or a disciple, and that is right; but then the disciple must also
be, as in this case he is, a critic, a man of letters, not, as too often
happens, some relation or friend with no qualification for his task
except affection for his author. [Arnold refers to J.C. Shairp's essay
Wordsworth: The Man and the Poet (1864).]

It is almost too much to expect of poor human nature, that a man capable of producing some effect in one line of literature, should, for the greater good of society, voluntarily doom himself to impotence and obscurity in another. Still less is this to be expected from men addicted to the composition of the "false or malicious criticism" of which Wordsworth speaks. However, everybody would admit that a false or malicious criticism had better never been written. Everybody, too, would be willing to admit, as a general proposition, that the critical faculty is lower than the inventive. But is it true that criticism is really, in itself, a baneful and injurious employment; is it true that all time given to writing critiques on the works of others would be much better employed if it were given to original composition of whatever kind this may be? Is it true Johnson had better have gone on producing more *Irenes* instead of writing his *Lives of the Poets*;[1] nay, is it certain that Wordsworth himself was better employed in making his Ecclesiastical Sonnets than when he made his celebrated Preface,[2] so full of criticism, and criticism of the works of others? Wordsworth was himself a great critic, and it is to be sincerely regretted that he has not left us more criticism; Goethe[3] was one of the greatest of critics, and we may sincerely congratulate ourselves that he has left us so much criticism. Without wasting time over the exaggeration which Wordsworth's judgement on criticism clearly contains, or over an attempt to trace the causes—not difficult, I think, to be traced—which may have led Wordsworth to this exaggeration, a critic may with advantage seize an occasion for trying his own conscience, and for asking himself of what real service at any given moment the practice of criticism either is or may be made to his own mind and spirit, and to the minds and spirits of others.

The critical power is of lower rank than the creative. True; but in assenting to this proposition, one or two things are to be kept in mind. It is undeniable that the exercise of a creative power, that a free creative activity, is the highest function of man; it is proved to be so by man's finding in it his true happiness. But it is undeniable, also, that men may have the sense of exercising this free creative activity in other ways than in producing great words of literature or art; if it were not so, all but a very few men would be shut out from the true happiness of all men. They may have it in well-doing, they may have it in learning, they may have it even in criticising. This is one thing to be kept in mind. Another is, that the exercise of the creative power in the production of great works of literature or art, however high this exercise of it may rank, is not at all epochs and under all conditions possible; and that therefore labour may be vainly spent in attempting it, which might with more fruit be used in preparing for it, in rendering it possible. This creative power works with elements, with materials; what if it has not those materials, those elements, ready for its use? In that case it must surely wait till they are ready. Now in literature—I will limit myself to literature, for it is about literature that the question arises—the elements with which the creative power works are ideas; the best ideas, on every matter which literature touches, current at the time. At any rate we may lay it down as certain that in modern literature no manifestation of the creative power not working with these can be very important or fruitful. And I say current at the time, not merely accessible at the time; for creative literary genius does not principally show itself in discovering new ideas; that is rather the business of the philosopher. The grand work of literary genius is a work of synthesis and exposition, not of analysis and discovery; its gift lies in the faculty of being happily inspired by a certain intellectual and spiritual atmosphere, by a certain order of ideas, when it finds itself in them; of dealing divinely with these ideas, presenting them in the most effective and attractive combinations—making beautiful works with them, in short. But it must have the atmosphere, it must find itself amidst the order of ideas, in order to work freely; and these it is not so easy to command. This is why great creative epochs in literature are so rare, this is why there is so much that is unsatisfactory in the productions of many men of real genius; because, for the creation of

---

[1] *Johnson ... Poets* In the nineteenth century Samuel Johnson was perhaps most celebrated for his biographical and critical work *Lives of the English Poets* (1779–81), while his play *Irene* (1736) has never been highly regarded.

[2] *Preface* To Wordsworth and Coleridge's *Lyrical Ballads* (1800). His *Ecclesiastical Sonnets* is not his best-known work.

[3] *Goethe* German poet and dramatist Johann Wolfgang von Goethe (1749–1832).

a masterwork of literature two powers must concur, the power of the man and the power of the moment, and the man is not enough without the moment; the creative power has, for its happy exercise, appointed elements, and those elements are not in its own control.

Nay, they are more within the control of the critical power. It is the business of the critical power, as I said in the words already quoted, "in all branches of knowledge, theology, philosophy, history, art, science, to see the object as in itself it really is." Thus it tends, at last, to make an intellectual situation of which the creative power can profitably avail itself. It tends to establish an order of ideas, if not absolutely true, yet true by comparison with that which it displaces; to make the best ideas prevail. Presently these new ideas reach society, the touch of truth is the touch of life, and there is a stir and growth everywhere; out of this stir and growth come the creative epochs of literature.

Or, to narrow our range, and quit these considerations of the general march of genius and of society—considerations which are apt to become too abstract and impalpable—every one can see that a poet, for instance, ought to know life and the world before dealing with them in poetry; and life and the world being in modern times very complex things, the creation of a modern poet, to be worth much, implies a great critical effort behind it; else it must be a comparatively poor, barren, and short-lived affair. This is why Byron's poetry had so little endurance in it, and Goethe's so much; both Byron and Goethe had a great productive power, but Goethe's was nourished by a great critical effort providing the true materials for it, and Byron's was not; Goethe knew life and the world, the poet's necessary subjects, much more comprehensively and thoroughly than Byron. He knew a great deal more of them, and he knew them much more as they really are.

It has long seemed to me that the burst of creative activity in our literature, through the first quarter of this century, had about it in fact something premature; and that from this cause its productions are doomed, most of them, in spite of the sanguine hopes which accompanied and do still accompany them, to prove hardly more lasting than the productions of far less splendid epochs. And this prematureness comes from its having proceeded without having its proper data, without sufficient materials to work with. In other words, the English poetry of the first quarter of this century, with plenty of energy, plenty of creative force, did not know enough. This makes Byron so empty of matter, Shelley so incoherent, Wordsworth even, profound as he is, yet so wanting in completeness and variety. Wordsworth cared little for books, and disparaged Goethe. I admire Wordsworth, as he is, so much that I cannot wish him different; and it is vain, no doubt, to imagine such a man different from what he is, to suppose that he could have been different. But surely the one thing wanting to make Wordsworth an even greater poet than he is—his thought richer, and his influence of wider application—was that he should have read more books, among them, no doubt, those of that Goethe whom he disparaged without reading him.

But to speak of books and reading may easily lead to a misunderstanding here. It was not really books and reading that lacked to our poetry at this epoch; Shelley had plenty of reading, Coleridge had immense reading. Pindar[1] and Sophocles—as we all say so glibly, and often with so little discernment of the real import of what we are saying—had not many books; Shakespeare was no deep reader. True; but in the Greece of Pindar and Sophocles, in the England of Shakespeare, the poet lived in a current of ideas in the highest degree animating and nourishing to the creative power; society was, in the fullest measure, permeated by fresh thought, intelligent and alive. And this state of things is the true basis for the creative power's exercise, in this it finds its data, its materials, truly ready for its hand; all the books and reading in the world are only valuable as they are helps to this. Even when this does not actually exist, books and reading may enable a man to construct a kind of semblance of it in his own mind, a world of knowledge and intelligence in which he may live and work. This is by no means an equivalent to the artist for the nationally diffused life and thought of the epochs of Sophocles or Shakespeare; but, besides that it may be a means of preparation for such epochs, it does really constitute, if many share in it, a quickening and sustaining atmosphere of great value. Such an atmosphere the many-sided learning and the long and widely combined critical effort of Germany formed for Goethe, when he

---

[1] *Pindar*   Greek lyric poet of the fifth century BCE.

lived and worked. There was no national glow of life and thought there, as in the Athens of Pericles[1] or the England of Elizabeth. That was the poet's weakness. But there was a sort of equivalent for it in the complete culture and unfettered thinking of a large body of Germans. That was his strength. In the England of the first quarter of this century there was neither a national glow of life and thought, such as we had in the age of Elizabeth, nor yet a culture and a force of learning and criticism such as were to be found in Germany. Therefore the creative power of poetry wanted, for success in the highest sense, materials and a basis; a thorough interpretation of the world was necessarily denied to it.

... The Englishman has been called a political animal, and he values what is political and practical so much that ideas easily become objects of dislike in his eyes, and thinkers "miscreants," because ideas and thinkers have rashly meddled with politics and practice. This would be all very well if the dislike and neglect confined themselves to ideas transported out of their own sphere, and meddling rashly with practice; but they are inevitably extended to ideas as such, and to the whole life of intelligence; practice is everything, a free play of the mind is nothing. The notion of the free play of the mind upon all subjects being a pleasure in itself, being an object of desire, being an essential provider of elements without which a nation's spirit, whatever compensations it may have for them, must, in the long run, die of inanition, hardly enters into an Englishman's thoughts. It is noticeable that the word *curiosity*, which in other languages is used in a good sense, to mean, as a high and fine quality of man's nature, just this disinterested love of a free play of the mind on all subjects, for its own sake—it is noticeable, I say, that this word has in our language no sense of the kind, no sense but a rather bad and disparaging one. But criticism, real criticism, is essentially the exercise of this very quality; it obeys an instinct prompting it to try to know the best that is known and thought in the world, irrespectively of practice, politics, and everything of the kind; and to value knowledge and thought as they approach this best, without the intrusion of any other considerations whatever. This is an instinct for which there is, I think, little original sympathy in the practical English nature, and what there was of it has undergone a long benumbing period of blight and suppression in the epoch of concentration which followed the French Revolution.

But epochs of concentration cannot well endure for ever; epochs of expansion, in the due course of things, follow them. Such an epoch of expansion seems to be opening in this country. In the first place all danger of a hostile forcible pressure of foreign ideas upon our practice has long disappeared; like the traveller in the fable, therefore, we begin to wear our cloak a little more loosely.[2] Then, with a long peace, the ideas of Europe steal gradually and amicably in, and mingle, though in infinitesimally small quantities at a time, with our own notions. Then, too, in spite of all that is said about the absorbing and brutalising influence of our passionate material progress, it seems to me indisputable that this progress is likely, though not certain, to lead in the end to an apparition of intellectual life; and that man, after he has made himself perfectly comfortable and has now to determine what to do with himself next, may begin to remember that he has a mind, and that the mind may be made the source of great pleasure. I grant it is mainly the privilege of faith, at present, to discern this end to our railways, our business, and our fortune-making; but we shall see if, here as elsewhere, faith is not in the end the true prophet. Our ease, our travelling, and our unbounded liberty to hold just as hard and securely as we please to the practice to which our notions have given birth, all tend to beget an inclination to deal a little more freely with these notions themselves, to canvass them a little, to penetrate a little into their real nature. Flutterings of curiosity, in the foreign sense of the word, appear amongst us, and it is in these that criticism must look to find its account. Criticism first; a time of true creative activity, perhaps—which, as I

---

[1]   *Athens of Pericles* Pericles was a leading Athenian statesman of the early fifth century BCE and was responsible for the construction of the Parthenon.

[2]   *like the ... loosely* In one of Aesop's fables, the wind and the sun compete to see who is more powerful, betting on which of them can cause a traveler to take his cloak off first. The wind attempts to use force, but the fierce gusts only cause the traveler to clutch his cloak more tightly. When the sun shines on him, however, the traveler is persuaded to take off his cloak.

have said, must inevitably be preceded amongst us by a time of criticism—hereafter, when criticism has done its work.

It is of the last importance that English criticism should clearly discern what rule for its course, in order to avail itself of the field now opening to it, and to produce fruit for the future, it ought to take. The rule may be summed up in one word—*disinterestedness*.[1] And how is criticism to show disinterestedness? By keeping aloof from what is called "the practical view of things"; by resolutely following the law of its own nature, which is to be a free play of the mind on all subjects which it touches. By steadily refusing to lend itself to any of those ulterior, political, practical considerations about ideas, which plenty of people will be sure to attach to them, which perhaps ought often to be attached to them, which in this country at any rate are certain to be attached to them quite sufficiently, but which criticism has really nothing to do with. Its business is, as I have said, simply to know the best that is known and thought in the world, and by in its turn making this known, to create a current of true and fresh ideas. Its business is to do this with inflexible honesty, with due ability; but its business is to do no more, and to leave alone all questions of practical consequences and applications, questions which will never fail to have due prominence given to them. Else criticism, besides being really false to its own nature, merely continues in the old rut which it has hitherto followed in this country, and will certainly miss the chance now given to it. For what is at present the bane of criticism in this country? It is that practical considerations cling to it and stifle it. It subserves interests not its own. Our organs of criticism are organs of men and parties having practical ends to serve, and with them those practical ends are the first thing and the play of the mind the second; so much play of mind as is compatible with the prosecution of those practical ends is all that is wanted. An organ like the *Revue des Deux Mondes*,[2] having for its main function to understand and utter the best that is known and thought in the world, existing, it may be said, as just an organ for a free play of the mind, we have not. But we have the *Edinburgh Review*, existing as an organ of the old Whigs, and for as much play of the mind as may suit its being that; we have the *Quarterly Review*, existing as an organ of the Tories, and for as much play of mind as may suit its being that; we have the *British Quarterly Review*, existing as an organ of the political Dissenters, and for as much play of mind as may suit its being that; we have *The Times*, existing as an organ of the common, satisfied, well-to-do Englishman, and for as much play of mind as may suit its being that. And so on through all the various fractions, political and religious, of our society; every fraction has, as such, its organ of criticism, but the notion of combining all fractions in the common pleasure of a free disinterested play of mind meets with no favour. Directly this play of mind wants to have more scope, and to forget the pressure of practical considerations a little, it is checked, it is made to feel the chain. We saw this the other day in the extinction, so much to be regretted, of the *Home and Foreign Review*.[3] Perhaps in no organ of criticism in this country was there so much knowledge, so much play of mind; but these could not save it. The *Dublin Review* subordinates play of mind to the practical business of English and Irish Catholicism, and lives. It must needs be that men should act in sects and parties, that each of these sects and parties should have its organ, and should make this organ subserve the interests of its action; but it would be well, too, that there should be a criticism, not the minister of these interests, not their enemy, but absolutely and entirely independent of them. No other criticism will ever attain any real authority or make any real way towards its end—the creating a current of true and fresh ideas.

It is because criticism has so little kept in the pure intellectual sphere, has so little detached itself from practice, has been so directly polemical and controversial, that it has so ill accomplished, in this country, its best spiritual work; which is to keep man from a self-satisfaction which is retarding and vulgarizing, to lead him towards perfection, by making his mind dwell upon what is excellent in itself, and the absolute beauty and fitness of things. A polemical practical criticism makes men blind even to the ideal

---

[1] *disinterestedness* I.e., objectivity.

[2] *Revue ... Mondes* International magazine founded in Paris in 1829.

[3] *Home ... Review* Liberal, predominantly Catholic periodical (1862–64).

imperfection of their practice, makes them willingly assert its ideal perfection, in order the better to secure it against attack; and clearly this is narrowing and baneful for them. If they were reassured on the practical side, speculative considerations of ideal perfection they might be brought to entertain, and their spiritual horizon would thus gradually widen. Sir Charles Adderley[1] says to the Warwickshire farmers—

> Talk of the improvement of breed! Why, the race we ourselves represent, the men and women, the old Anglo-Saxon race, are the best breed in the whole world…The absence of a too enervating climate, too unclouded skies, and a too luxurious nature, has produced so vigorous a race of people, and has rendered us so superior to all the world.

Mr. Roebuck says to the Sheffield cutlers—

> I look around me and ask what is the state of England? Is not property safe? Is not every man able to say what he likes? Can you not walk from one end of England to the other in perfect security? I ask you whether, the world over or in past history, there is anything like it? Nothing. I pray that our unrivaled happiness may last.

Now obviously there is a peril for poor human nature in words and thoughts of such exuberant self-satisfaction, until we find ourselves safe in the streets of the Celestial City.

> *Das wenige verschwindet leicht dem Blicke*
> *Der vorwärts sieht, wie viel noch übrig bleibt*[2]—

says Goethe; "the little that is done seems nothing when we look forward and see how much we have yet to do." Clearly this is a better line of reflection for weak humanity, so long as it remains on this earthly field of labour and trial.

But neither Sir Charles Adderley nor Mr. Roebuck is by nature inaccessible to considerations of this sort. They only lose sight of them owing to the controversial

life we all lead, and the practical from which all speculation takes with us. They have in view opponents whose aim is not ideal, but practical; and in their zeal to uphold their own practice against these innovators, they go so far as even to attribute to this practice an ideal perfection. Somebody has been wanting to introduce a six-pound franchise, or to abolish church-rates,[3] or to collect agricultural statistics by force, or to diminish local self-government. How natural, in reply to such proposals, very likely improper or ill-timed, to go a little beyond the mark and to say stoutly, "such a race of people as we stand, so superior to all the world! The Old Anglo-Saxon race, the best breed in the whole world! I pray that our unrivaled happiness may last! I ask you whether, the world over or in past history, there is anything like it?" And so long as criticism answers this dithyramb by insisting that the old Anglo-Saxon race would be still more superior to all others if it had no church-rates, or that our unrivalled happiness would last yet longer with a six-pound franchise, so long will the strain, "The best breed in the whole world!" swell louder and louder, everything ideal and refining will be lost out of sight, and both the assailed and their critics will remain in a sphere, to say the truth, perfectly unvital, a sphere in which spiritual progression is impossible. But let criticism leave church-rates and the franchise alone, and in the most candid spirit, without a single lurking thought of practical innovation, confront with our dithyramb this paragraph on which I stumbled in a newspaper immediately after reading Mr. Roebuck:

> A shocking child murder has just been committed at Nottingham. A girl named Wragg left the workhouse there on Saturday morning with her young illegitimate child. The child was soon afterwards found dead on Mapperly Hills, having been strangled. Wragg is in custody.

Nothing but that; but, in juxtaposition with the absolute eulogies of Sir Charles Adderley and Mr. Roebuck, how eloquent, how suggestive are those few lines! "Our old Anglo-Saxon breed, the best in the

---

[1]   *Sir Charles Adderley*   Conservative member of Parliament and landowner (1814–1905).

[2]   *Das wenige … bleibt*   Goethe's *Iphigenie auf Tauris* 1.291–92.

[3]   *six-pound franchise*   Proposal to extend voting rights to anyone whose property was worth six pounds or more annual rent—a radical idea at the time; *church-rates*   Taxes paid to support the Church of England.

whole world!"—how much that is harsh and ill-favoured there is in this best! *Wragg*! If we are to talk of ideal perfection of "the best in the whole world," has any one reflected what a touch of grossness in our race, what an original shortcoming in the more delicate spiritual perceptions, is shown by the natural growth amongst us of such hideous names—Higginbottom, Stiggins, Bugg! In Ionia and Attica they were luckier in this respect than "the best race in the world"; by the Ilissus[1] there was no Wragg, poor thing! And "our unrivaled happiness"—what an element of grimness, bareness, and hideousness mixes with it and blurs it; the workhouse, the dismal Mapperly Hills[2]—how dismal those who have seen them will remember—the gloom, the smoke, the cold, the strangled illegitimate child! "I ask you whether, the world over or in past history, there is anything like it?" Perhaps not, one is inclined to answer; but at any rate, in that case, the world is very much to be pitied. And the final touch—short, bleak, and inhuman: *Wragg is in custody*. The sex lost in the confusion of our unrivalled happiness; or (shall I say?) the superfluous Christian name lopped off by the straightforward vigour of our old Anglo-Saxon breed! There is profit for the spirit in such contrasts as this; criticism serves the cause of perfection by establishing them. By eluding sterile conflict, by refusing to remain in the sphere where alone narrow and relative conceptions have any worth and validity, criticism may diminish its momentary importance, but only in this way has it a chance of gaining admittance for those wider and more perfect conceptions to which all its duty is really owed. Mr. Roebuck will have a poor opinion of an adversary who replies to his defiant songs of triumph only by murmuring under his breath, *Wragg is in custody*; but in no other way will these songs of triumph be induced gradually to moderate themselves, to get rid of what in them is excessive and offensive, and to fall into a softer and truer key.

It will be said that it is a very subtle and indirect action which I am thus prescribing for criticism, and that, by embracing in this manner the Indian virtue of detachment and abandoning the sphere of practical life,

it condemns itself to a slow and obscure work. Slow and obscure it may be, but it is the only proper work of criticism. The mass of mankind will never have any ardent zeal for seeing things as they are; very inadequate ideas will always satisfy them. On these inadequate ideas reposes, and must repose, the general practice of the world. That is as much as saying that whoever sets himself to see things as they are will find himself one of a very small circle; but it is only by this small circle resolutely doing its own work that adequate ideas will ever get current at all. The rush and roar of practical life will always have a dizzying and attracting effect upon the most collected spectator, and tend to draw him into its vortex; most of all will this be the case where that life is so powerful as it is in England. But it is only by remaining collected, and refusing to lend himself to the point of view of the practical man, that the critic can do the practical man any service; and it is only by the greatest sincerity in pursuing his own course, and by at last convincing even the practical man of his sincerity, that he can escape misunderstandings which perpetually threaten him.

For the practical man is not apt for fine distinctions, and yet in these distinctions truth and the highest culture greatly find their account. But it is not easy to lead a practical man—unless you reassure him as to your practical intentions, you have no chance of leading him—to see a thing which he has always been used to look at from one side only, which he greatly values, and which, looked at from that side, quite deserves, perhaps, all the prizing and admiring which he bestows upon it—that this thing, looked at from another side, may appear much less beneficent and beautiful, and yet retain all its claims to our practical allegiance. Where shall we find language innocent enough, how shall we make the spotless purity of our intentions evident enough, to enable us to say to the political Englishman that the British Constitution itself, which, seen from the practical side, looks such a magnificent organ of progress and virtue, seen from the speculative side—with its compromises, its love of facts, its horror of theory, its studied avoidance of clear thoughts—that, seen from this side, our august Constitution sometimes looks—

---

[1] *Ilissus* River in Attica.

[2] *Mapperly Hills* Located near the coal-mining, industrial area of Nottingham.

forgive me, shade of Lord Somers![1]—a colossal machine for the manufacture of Philistines?[2] How is Cobbett[3] to say this and not be misunderstood, blackened as he is with the smoke of a lifelong conflict in the field of political practice? How is Mr. Carlyle to say it and not be misunderstood, after his furious raid into this field with his Latter-day Pamphlets?[4] How is Mr. Ruskin, after his pugnacious political economy?[5] I say, the critic must keep out of the region of immediate practice in the political, social, humanitarian sphere, if he wants to make a beginning for that more free speculative treatment of things, which may perhaps one day make its benefits felt even in this sphere, but in a natural and thence irresistible manner. ...

If I have insisted so much on the course which criticism must take where politics and religion are concerned, it is because, where these burning matters are in question, it is most likely to go astray. I have wished, above all, to insist on the attitude which criticism should adopt towards things in general; on its right tone and temper of mind. But then comes another question as to the subject-matter which literary criticism should most seek. Here, in general, its course is determined for it by the idea which is the law of its being; the idea of a disinterested endeavour to learn and propagate the best that is known and thought in the world, and thus to establish a current of fresh and true ideas. By the very nature of things, as England is not all the world, much of the best that is known and thought in the world cannot be of English growth, must be foreign; by the nature of things, again, it is just this that we are least likely to know, while English thought is streaming in upon us from all sides, and takes excellent care that we

shall not be ignorant of its existence. The English critic of literature, therefore, must dwell much on foreign thought, and with particular heed on any part of it, which, while significant and fruitful in itself, is for any reason specially likely to escape him. Again, judging is often spoken of as the critic's one business, and so in some sense it is; but the judgement which almost insensibly forms itself in a fair and clear mind, along with fresh knowledge, is the valuable one; and thus knowledge, and ever fresh knowledge, must be the critic's great concern for himself. And it is by communicating fresh knowledge, and letting his own judgement pass along with it—but insensibly, and in the second place, not the first, as a sort of companion and clue, not as an abstract lawgiver—that the critic will generally do most good to his readers. Sometimes, no doubt, for the sake of establishing an author's place in literature, and his relation to a central standard (and if this is not done, how are we to get at our best in the world?) criticism may have to deal with a subject-matter so familiar that fresh knowledge is out of the question, and then it must be all judgement; an enunciation and detailed application of principles. Here the great safeguard is never to let oneself become abstract, always to retain an intimate and lively consciousness of the truth of what one is saying, and, the moment this fails us, to be sure that something is wrong. Still, under all circumstances, this mere judgement and application of principles is, in itself, not the most satisfactory work to the critic; like mathematics, it is tautological, and cannot well give us, like fresh learning, the sense of creative activity.

But stop, someone will say; all this talk is of no practical use to us whatever; this criticism of yours is not what we have in our minds when we speak of criticism; when we speak of critics and criticism, we mean critics and criticism of the current English literature of the day; when you offer to tell criticism of its function, it is to this criticism that we expect you to address yourself. I am sorry for it, for I am afraid I must disappoint these expectations. I am bound by my own definition of criticism: a disinterested endeavour to learn and propagate the best that is known and thought in the world. How much of current English literature comes into this "best that is known and thought in the world"? Not very much, I fear; certainly less, at this moment,

---

[1] *Lord Somers* Statesman who presided over the creation of the Declaration of Rights (1689).

[2] *Philistines* Members of the Biblical tribe that fought against the Israelites. Here Arnold uses the term humorously to denote the unenlightened middle classes; "the enemy."

[3] *Cobbett* William Cobbett (1762–1835), farmer and radical political writer.

[4] *Latter-day Pamphlets* Satirical pamphlets, published in 1850, in which Thomas Carlyle expressed vehement anti-democratic views.

[5] *Mr. Ruskin ... economy* In his *Unto the Last* (1862), John Ruskin moved away from art criticism and attacked laissez-faire economics.

than of the current literature of France or Germany. Well, then, am I to alter my definition of criticism, in order to meet the requirements of a number of practising English critics, who, after all, are free in their choice of a business? That would be making criticism lend itself just to one of those alien practical considerations, which, I have said, are so fatal to it. One may say, indeed, to those who have to deal with the mass—so much better disregarded—of current English literature, that they may at all events endeavour, in dealing with this, to try it, so far as they can, by the standard of the best that is known and thought in the world; one may say, that to get anywhere near this standard, every critic should try and possess one great literature, at least, besides his own; and the more unlike his own, the better. But, after all, the criticism I am really concerned with—the criticism which alone can much help us for the future, the criticism which, throughout Europe, is at the present day meant, when so much stress is laid on the importance of criticism and the critical spirit—is a criticism which regards Europe as being, for intellectual and spiritual purposes, one great confederation, bound to a joint action and working to a common result; and whose members have, for their proper outfit, a knowledge of Greek, Roman, and Eastern antiquity, and of one another. Special, local, and temporary advantages being put out of account, that modern nation will in the intellectual and spiritual sphere make most progress, which most thoroughly carries out this programme. And what is that but saying that we too, all of us, as individuals, the more thoroughly we carry it out, shall make the more progress?

There is so much inviting us!—what are we to take? what will nourish us in growth towards perfection? That is the question which, with the immense field of life and of literature lying before him, the critic has to answer; for himself first, and afterwards for others. In this idea of the critic's business the essays brought together in the following pages have had their origin; in this idea, widely different as are their subjects, they have, perhaps, their unity.

I conclude with what I said at the beginning: to have the sense of creative activity is the great happiness and the great proof of being alive, and it is not denied to criticism to have it; but then criticism must be sincere,

simple, flexible, ardent, ever widening its knowledge. Then it may have, in no contemptible measure, a joyful sense of creative activity; a sense which a man of insight and conscience will prefer to what he might derive from a poor, starved, fragmentary, inadequate creation. And at some epochs no other creation is possible.

Still, in full measure, the sense of creative activity belongs only to genuine creation; in literature we must never forget that. But what true man of letters ever can forget it? It is no such common matter for a gifted nature to come into possession of a current of true and living ideas, and to produce amidst the inspiration of them, that we are likely to underrate it. The epochs of Aeschylus and Shakespeare make us feel their pre-eminence. In an epoch like those is, no doubt, the true life of literature; there is the promised land, towards which criticism can only beckon. That promised land it will not be ours to enter, and we shall die in the wilderness: but to have desired to enter it, to have saluted it from afar, is already, perhaps, the best distinction among contemporaries; it will certainly be the best title to esteem with posterity.
—1864

from *Culture and Anarchy*[1]

from CHAPTER I: SWEETNESS AND LIGHT

The disparagers of culture make its motive curiosity; sometimes, indeed, they make its motive mere exclusiveness and vanity. The culture which is supposed to plume itself on a smattering of Greek and Latin is a culture which is begotten by nothing so intellectual as

[1] *Culture and Anarchy* This work grew out of Arnold's last Oxford lecture, in 1869, and responds to the political climate surrounding the passage of the Second Reform Bill in 1867. Arnold feared that the individualism, or self-serving attitude, that seemed to fuel much of laissez-faire capitalism would lead to a state of anarchy—a state in which no culture could flourish. "Sweetness and light" is taken from a fable in Jonathan Swift's *The Battle of the Books* (1704). In this fable, the bee (who represents ancient culture) travels far to fill its hive with honey and wax (which is used to make candles). The bee thus provides "the two noblest things, which are sweetness and light," while the spider (representing modern culture) stays at home and forms its own web, producing "nothing at all but flybane and cobweb."

curiosity; it is valued either out of sheer vanity and ignorance or else as an engine of social and class distinction, separating its holder, like a badge or title, from other people who have not got it. No serious man would call this *culture*, or attach any value to it, as culture, at all. To find the real ground for the very different estimate which serious people will set upon culture, we must find some motive for culture in the terms of which may lie a real ambiguity; and such a motive the word *curiosity* gives us.

I have before now pointed out that we English do not, like the foreigners, use this word in a good sense as well as in a bad sense. With us the word is always used in a somewhat disapproving sense. A liberal and intelligent eagerness about the things of the mind may be meant by a foreigner when he speaks of curiosity, but with us the word always conveys a certain notion of frivolous and unedifying activity. In the *Quarterly Review*, some little time ago, was an estimate of the celebrated French critic, M. Sainte-Beuve,[1] and a very inadequate estimate it in my judgement was. And its inadequacy consisted chiefly in this: that in our English way it left out of sight the double sense really involved in the word *curiosity*, thinking enough was said to stamp M. Sainte-Beuve with blame if it was said that he was impelled in his operations as a critic by curiosity, and omitting either to perceive that M. Sainte-Beuve himself, and many other people with him, would consider that this was praiseworthy and not blameworthy, or to point out why it ought really to be accounted worthy of blame and not of praise. For as there is a curiosity about intellectual matters which is futile, and merely a disease, so there is certainly a curiosity—a desire after the things of the mind simply for their own sakes and for the pleasure of seeing them as they are— which is, in an intelligent being, natural and laudable. Nay, and the very desire to see things as they are implies a balance and regulation of mind which is not often attained without fruitful effort, and which is the very opposite of the blind and diseased impulse of mind which is what we mean to blame when we blame curiosity. Montesquieu[2] says: "The first motive which ought to impel us to study is the desire to augment the excellence of our nature, and to render an intelligent being yet more intelligent." This is the true ground to assign for the genuine scientific passion, however manifested, and for culture, viewed simply as a fruit of this passion; and it is a worthy ground, even though we let the term *curiosity* stand to describe it.

But there is of culture another view, in which not solely the scientific passion, the sheer desire to see things as they are, natural and proper in an intelligent being, appears as the ground of it. There is a view in which all the love of our neighbour, the impulses towards action, help, and beneficence, the desire for removing human error, clearing human confusion, and diminishing human misery, the noble aspiration to leave the world better and happier than we found it—motives eminently such as are called social—come in as part of the grounds of culture, and the main and pre-eminent part. Culture is then properly described not as having its origin in curiosity, but as having its origin in the love of perfection; it is *a study of perfection*. It moves by the force, not merely or primarily of the scientific passion for pure knowledge, but also of the moral and social passion for doing good. As, in the first view of it, we took for its worthy motto Montesquieu's words: "To render an intelligent being yet more intelligent!" so, in the second view of it, there is no better motto which it can have than these words of Bishop Wilson:[3] "To make reason and the will of God prevail!"...

Nothing is more common than for people to confound the inward peace and satisfaction which follows the subduing of the obvious faults of our animality with what I may call absolute inward peace and satisfaction—the peace and satisfaction which are reached as we draw near to complete spiritual perfection, and not merely to moral perfection, or rather to relative moral perfection. No people in the world have done more and struggled more to attain this relative moral perfection than our English race has. For no people in the world has the command to *resist the devil, to overcome the wicked one*, in the nearest and most obvious sense of those words, had such a pressing force and reality. And we have had our reward, not only in the great worldly prosperity which our obedience to this

---

[1]   *M. Sainte-Beuve* French critic Augustine Saint-Beuve (1804–69).

[2]   *Montesquieu* French political philosopher (1689–1755).

[3]   *Bishop Wilson* Church of England clergyman (1601–53) whose *Maxims* Arnold admired.

command has brought us, but also, and far more, in great inward peace and satisfaction. But to me few things are more pathetic than to see people, on the strength of the inward peace and satisfaction which their rudimentary efforts towards perfection have brought them, employ, concerning their incomplete perfection and the religious organisations within which they have found it, language which properly applies only to complete perfection, and is a far-off echo of the human soul's prophecy of it. Religion itself, I need hardly say, supplies them in abundance with this grand language. And very freely do they use it; yet it is really the severest possible criticism of such an incomplete perfection as alone we have yet reached through our religious organisations.

The impulse of the English race towards moral development and self-conquest has nowhere so powerfully manifested itself as in Puritanism. Nowhere has Puritanism found so adequate an expression as in the religious organisation of the Independents.[1] The modern Independents have a newspaper, the *Nonconformist*, written with great sincerity and ability. The motto, the standard, the profession of faith which this organ of theirs carries aloft, is: "The Dissidence of Dissent and the Protestantism of the Protestant religion." There is sweetness and light, and an ideal of complete harmonious human perfection! One need not go to culture and poetry to find language to judge it. Religion, with its instinct for perfection, supplies language to judge it, language, too, which is in our mouths every day. "Finally, be of one mind, united in feeling," says St. Peter.[2] There is an ideal which judges the Puritan ideal: "The Dissidence of Dissent and the Protestantism of the Protestant religion!" And religious organisations like this are what people believe in, rest in, would give their lives for! Such, I say, is the wonderful virtue of even the beginnings of perfection, of having conquered even the plain faults of our animality, that the religious organisation which has helped us to do it can seem to us something precious, salutary, and to be propagated, even when it wears such a brand of imperfection on its forehead as this. And men have got such a habit of giving to the language of religion a

special application, of making it a mere jargon, that for the condemnation which religion itself passes on the shortcomings of their religious organisations they have no ear; they are sure to cheat themselves and to explain this condemnation away. They can only be reached by the criticism which culture, like poetry, speaking a language not to be sophisticated, and resolutely testing these organisations by the ideal of a human perfection complete on all sides, applies to them.

But men of culture and poetry, it will be said, are again and again failing, and failing conspicuously, in the necessary first stage to a harmonious perfection, in the subduing of the great obvious faults of our animality, which it is the glory of these religious organisations to have helped us to subdue. True, they do often so fail. They have often been without the virtues as well as the faults of the Puritan; it has been one of their dangers that they so felt the Puritan's faults that they too much neglected the practice of his virtues. I will not, however, exculpate them at the Puritan's expense. They have often failed in morality, and morality is indispensable. And they have been punished for their failure, as the Puritan has been rewarded for his performance. They have been punished wherein they erred; but their ideal of beauty, of sweetness and light, and a human nature complete on all its sides, remains the true ideal of perfection still; just as the Puritan's ideal of perfection remains narrow and inadequate, although for what he did well he has been richly rewarded. Notwithstanding the mighty results of the Pilgrim Fathers' voyage, they and their standard of perfection are rightly judged when we figure to ourselves Shakespeare or Virgil—souls in whom sweetness and light, and all that in human nature is most humane, were eminent—accompanying them on their voyage, and think what intolerable company Shakespeare and Virgil would have found them! In the same way let us judge the religious organisations which we see all around us. Do not let us deny the good and the happiness which they have accomplished; but do not let us fail to see clearly that their idea of human perfection is narrow and inadequate, and that the Dissidence of Dissent and the Protestantism of the

---

[1] *Independents* Members of a seventeenth-century Puritan sect.

[2] *Finally ... Peter* From 1 Peter 3.8.

Protestant religion will never bring humanity to its true goal. As I said with regard to wealth: Let us look at the life of those who live in and for it—so I say with regard to the religious organisations. Look at the life imaged in such a newspaper as the *Nonconformist*—a life of jealousy of the Establishment,[1] disputes, tea-meetings, openings of chapels, sermons; and then think of it as an ideal of a human life completing itself on all sides, and aspiring with all its organs after sweetness, light, and perfection!

Another newspaper, representing, like the *Nonconformist*, one of the religious organisations of this country, was a short time ago giving an account of the crowd at Epsom on the Derby day,[2] and of all the vice and hideousness which was to be seen in that crowd; and then the writer turned suddenly round upon Professor Huxley,[3] and asked him how he proposed to cure all this vice and hideousness without religion. I confess I felt disposed to ask the asker this question: and how do you propose to cure it with such a religion as yours? How is the ideal of a life so unlovely, so unattractive, so incomplete, so narrow, so far removed from a true and satisfying ideal of human perfection, as is the life of your religious organisation as you yourself reflect it, to conquer and transform all this vice and hideousness? Indeed, the strongest plea for the study of perfection as pursued by culture, the clearest proof of the actual inadequacy of the idea of perfection held by the religious organisations—expressing, as I have said, the most widespread effort which the human race has yet made after perfection—is to be found in the state of our life and society with these in possession of it, and having been in possession of it I know not how many hundred years. We are all of us included in some religious organisation or other; we all call ourselves, in the sublime and aspiring language of religion which I have before noticed, children of God. Children of God—it is an immense pretension!—and how are we to

justify it? By the works which we do, and the words which we speak. And the work which we collective children of God do, our grand centre of life, our city which we have builded for us to dwell in, is London! London, with its unutterable external hideousness, and with its internal canker of *publice egestas, privatim opulentia*—to use the words which Sallust puts into Cato's[4] mouth about Rome—unequalled in the world! The word, again, which we children of God speak, the voice which most hits our collective thought, the newspaper with the largest circulation in England, nay, with the largest circulation in the whole world, is the *Daily Telegraph*! I say that when our religious organisations—which I admit to express the most considerable effort after perfection that our race has yet made—land us in no better result than this, it is high time to examine carefully their idea of perfection, to see whether it does not leave out of account sides and forces of human nature which we might turn to great use; whether it would not be more operative if it were more complete. And I say that English reliance on our religious organisations and on their ideas of human perfection just as they stand, is like our reliance on freedom, on muscular Christianity, on population, on coal, on wealth—mere belief in machinery, and unfruitful; and that it is wholesomely counteracted by culture, bent on seeing things as they are, and on drawing the human race onwards to a more complete, a harmonious perfection.

Culture, however, shows its single-minded love of perfection, its desire simply to make reason and the will of God prevail, its freedom from fanaticism, by its attitude towards all this machinery, even while it insists that it is machinery. Fanatics, seeing the mischief men do themselves by their blind belief in some machinery or other—whether it is wealth and industrialism, or whether it is the cultivation of bodily strength and activity, or

---

[1] *Establishment* I.e., the established Church, the Church of England.

[2] *Epsom ... day* The Derby Stakes, a thoroughbred horse race, is held every June in Epsom, Surrey.

[3] *Professor Huxley* Thomas Huxley (1825–95), biologist, educator, and vocal supporter of the theory of evolution.

[4] *publice ... opulentia* Latin: public poverty; private opulence; *Sallust* First-century BCE Roman historian; *Cato* Roman statesman Cato the Younger (95–46 BCE).

whether it is a political organisation—or whether it is a religious organisation—oppose with might and main the tendency to this or that political and religious organisation, or to games and athletic exercises, or to wealth and industrialism, and try violently to stop it. But the flexibility which sweetness and light give, and which is one of the rewards of culture pursued in good faith, enables a man to see that a tendency may be necessary, and even, as a preparation for something in the future, salutary, and yet that the generations or individuals who obey this tendency are sacrificed to it, that they fall short of the hope of perfection by following it; and that its mischiefs are to be criticised, lest it should take too firm a hold and last after it has served its purpose....

—1868

DANTE GABRIEL ROSSETTI
1828 – 1882

"Youth and Death, Destiny and Fortune, Fame, Poetic Fame, Memory, Oblivion"—these, according to Walter Pater, are among the "mysterious powers" at the center of Dante Gabriel Rossetti's work. But "enthroned" among these, Pater wrote, is "the ideal intensity of love." The ethereal yet sensuous aesthetic Rossetti developed to evoke these mysteries in painting as well as poetry exerted a strong influence on poets and artists of the late nineteenth and early twentieth centuries.

Stylized and radiant scenes of knights, maidens, and lovers—soon synonymous with Rossetti's name—found their original inspiration in works of early Italian, Christian, and medieval iconography. The subject of "The Blessed Damozel," one of Rossetti's finest poems, glows with the spiritually luminous effects associated with the religious poetry of Dante (Rossetti's namesake). Yet Rossetti also endowed his damsel with an earthly voluptuousness. Borrowing from Dantesque and Arthurian mythology, Rossetti created fantasies whose "stained glass" quality reflects both the literary outlines of religious allegory and the sensual strokes of an artist enraptured by the female figure. It was an artistic approach that ran the risk of causing offense at a time when soul and body, love and sex, were separate compartments of Victorian life, and Rossetti's work was frequently attacked in the later half of his career for trying to solder spiritual to "fleshly" desires.

Born in 1828 into an erudite family, Rossetti was the third of four children. He was a competitive yet fiercely fond older brother to his sister, the future poet Christina. His mother, Frances Polidori Rossetti, was Anglo-Italian; his father, Gabriele Rossetti, an exiled Italian patriot, was a Professor at King's College, London. The Rossetti's childhood home, with its assortment of orthodox and unorthodox books, was a meeting place where politicized ex-patriots spent many an evening debating the past and future of Italy. From the stream of sketches and literary compositions issuing from the temperamental imaginations of Dante Gabriel and Christina, it was apparent early on that the two youngest Rossettis were extraordinarily gifted. Their parents held high hopes that Dante Gabriel would become a great painter, even though his schooling in painting and his knowledge of European painting were not extensive.

Rossetti was a moody student at the Royal Academy of Arts in 1848 when he co-founded the Pre-Raphaelite Brotherhood with fellow painters William Holman Hunt, John Everett Millais, James Collinson, Frederic George Stephens, Thomas Woolner, and Dante Gabriel's brother, critic William Michael Rossetti. In a letter to his sister Christina, Rossetti spoke of the group as a "Round Table" whose knights shared a mutual love of Keats. They also adored Malory's *Morte Darthur*, the novels of Walter Scott, and the work of Blake, Dante, Tennyson, and Browning. By referencing early Florentine and Sienese schools (dubbed "the Italian Primitives" because they predated the High Renaissance), the Pre-Raphaelites sought to reform what they saw as the florid emptiness of Victorian art and its lack of truth to nature. "Sincerity" as a quality of near-devotional feeling communicated through purity of line and color was more important to the Pre-Raphaelites than mere technical virtuosity. As one critic put it, the Pre-Raphaelites favored "primitive but vital imperfection, as opposed to lifeless perfection." A movement in both literature and painting, Pre-Raphaelitism was identified with a vivid palette, formal patterning, and symbolic details woven into exotic scenes of religious or romantic love whose settings evoked a sumptuous "elsewhere." In Pre-Raphaelite poetry and painting, there was always a "definiteness of sensible imagery," as Pater said of "The Blessed Damozel."

When sixteen-year old Christina published *Verses* in 1847, Rossetti was compelled to try with meter what he was doing with color. "Colour and metre," Rossetti claimed, "are the true parents of nobility in painting and poetry." In 1850, the Pre-Raphaelite Brotherhood published a journal of poems and illustrations entitled *The Germ*, in which Rossetti's "The Blessed Damozel" first appeared. The publication gained Rossetti a small group of admirers that would steadily increase. Ruskin, who helped turn the tide in his favor by praising the art of the Pre-Raphaelites in *The Times* in 1851, became one of Rossetti's prominent patrons and closest friends. Rossetti cherished intellectual friendships with Robert Browning and William Morris, and socialized with the flamboyant Algernon Swinburne. He obtained stable employment teaching art at the Working Men's College. Stumbling across a book of William Blake's poems and paintings, Rossetti discovered another kindred spirit, albeit one who had died a year before he was born. Having secured his own reputation, Rossetti was able to rescue Blake from near oblivion, rediscovering him for a Victorian audience. In 1861, he also published *The Early Italian Poets*, which introduced, through his translations of the *Vita Nuova* and other poems by Dante and his predecessors and contemporaries, many poets whose work had been unknown in England.

Rossetti was also prone to what one biographer calls "rescue missions" of unknown beauties. Elizabeth Gaskell wrote that Rossetti was "hair-mad," with a penchant for the wavy tresses of women he and his friends called "stunners." On the one hand, Rossetti supported the equality and independence of working-class women like Elizabeth Siddal, whom he eventually married. On the other hand, his rescue of beautiful women from their class obscurity dramatized a sexual imbalance of power that was titillating; like many Victorian men, Rossetti enjoyed the license to "fall in love" with working-class women without seriously compromising his reputation, a license prohibited to women under the double standards of Victorian society.

Siddal, a model for the Pre-Raphaelites and an artist and poet in her own right, committed suicide in 1862, two years after her marriage to Rossetti. Invoking Dante's dead beloved, Beatrice, Rossetti memorialized Siddal in a painting entitled *Beata Beatrix* (c.1863). Seized with remorse at her funeral, he tucked a manuscript of poems into her coffin. He had them exhumed years later in order to publish his first collection of verse, *Poems* (1870). Though Rossetti afterwards lived with Fanny Cornforth, he fell in love with Jane Burden, the wife of William Morris. Both Fanny and "Janey" came from working-class backgrounds and modeled for Rossetti, becoming sensuously stylized objects of desire in paintings such as *Proserpine* (1874).

Soon after the appearance of Rossetti's *The House of Life*, a sequence of sonnets that appeared in his first volume of poetry, the poet Robert Buchanan denounced its "animalism" in a scalding critique entitled *The Fleshly School of Poetry* (1871). According to Buchanan, Rossetti's "house of life" was suggestive of a brothel and his sonnets bore the stamp of "the same sense of weary, wasting, yet exquisite sensuality." Rossetti counterattacked with *The Stealthy School of Criticism* (1872), but many readers since have felt that there was a germ of truth in Buchanan's criticisms: the spiritual impulse that strove to unite love and sexuality in Rossetti's art seems at times overshadowed by a carnal undergrowth verging upon the fetishistic.

Rossetti had always been temperamental, and Buchanan's attack temporarily deranged him. Though Yeats's youthful claim that he was "in all things Pre-Raphaelite" was proof of Rossetti's influence on the next generation of poets, Rossetti himself never fully recovered from being "stigmatized as a sensualist," in the words of one critic. He continued to paint and write, however, publishing *Ballads and Sonnets* in 1881. Bouts of nervous depression, made worse by the consumption of whiskey and narcotics, led to a decline in Rossetti's health; he died in 1882.

⌘ ⌘ ⌘

The Blessed Damozel [1]

The blessed damozel leaned out
    From the gold bar of Heaven;
Her eyes were deeper than the depth
    Of waters stilled at even;
5   She had three lilies in her hand,
    And the stars in her hair were seven.

Her robe, ungirt from clasp to hem,
    No wrought flowers did adorn,
But a white rose of Mary's gift,
10   For service meetly worn;
Her hair that lay along her back
    Was yellow like ripe corn.

Herseemed she scarce had been a day
    One of God's choristers;
15   The wonder was not yet quite gone
    From that still look of hers;
Albeit, to them she left, her day
    Had counted as ten years.

(To one, it is ten years of years.
20   ... Yet now, and in this place,
Surely she leaned o'er me—her hair
    Fell all about my face....
Nothing: the autumn-fall of leaves.
    The whole year sets apace.)

25   It was the rampart of God's house
    That she was standing on;
By God built over the sheer depth
    The which is Space begun;
So high, that looking downward thence
30   She scarce could see the sun.

It lies in Heaven, across the flood
    Of ether, as a bridge.

Beneath, the tides of day and night
    With flame and darkness ridge
35   The void, as low as where this earth
    Spins like a fretful midge.[2]

Around her, lovers, newly met
    'Mid deathless love's acclaims,
Spoke evermore among themselves
40   Their heart-remembered names;
And the souls mounting up to God
    Went by her like thin flames.

And still she bowed herself and stooped
    Out of the circling charm;
45   Until her bosom must have made
    The bar she leaned on warm,
And the lilies lay as if asleep
    Along her bended arm.

From the fixed place of Heaven she saw
50   Time like a pulse shake fierce
Through all the worlds. Her gaze still strove
    Within the gulf to pierce
Its path; and now she spoke as when
    The stars sang in their spheres.[3]

55   The sun was gone now; the curled moon
    Was like a little feather
Fluttering far down the gulf; and now
    She spoke through the still weather.
Her voice was like the voice the stars
60   Had when they sang together.

(Ah sweet! Even now, in that bird's song,
    Strove not her accents there,
Fain to be hearkened? When those bells
    Possessed the mid-day air,
65   Strove not her steps to reach my side
    Down all the echoing stair?)

---

[1] *The Blessed Damozel*   After the poem's publication, Rossetti told novelist Hall Caine that he had written it as something of a sequel to Edgar Allen Poe's poem "The Raven" (1845): "I saw that Poe had done the utmost it was possible to do with the grief of the lover on earth, and so determined to reverse the conditions, and give utterance to the yearning of the loved one in heaven." A "damozel" is a damsel, a young, unmarried woman.

---

[2] *midge*   Small fly.

[3] *as when ... spheres*   See Job 38.7, in which the morning stars sing on creation day. Rossetti probably also refers to the Pythagorean concept of the music of the spheres, inaudible to those on earth.

Dante Gabriel Rossetti, *The Blessed Damozel* (1875–78).

"We two will stand beside that shrine,
80   Occult,° withheld, untrod,   *secret*
Whose lamps are stirred continually
     With prayer sent up to God;
And see our old prayers, granted, melt
     Each like a little cloud.

85   "We two will lie i'the shadow of
     That living mystic tree[1]
Within whose secret growth the Dove[2]
     Is sometimes felt to be,
While every leaf that His plumes touch
90   Saith His Name audibly.

"And I myself will teach to him,
     I myself, lying so,
The songs I sing here; which his voice
     Shall pause in, hushed and slow,
95 And find some knowledge at each pause,
     Or some new thing to know."

(Alas! We two, we two, thou say'st!
     Yea, one wast thou with me
That once of old. But shall God lift
100   To endless unity
The soul whose likeness with thy soul
     Was but its love for thee?)

"We two," she said, "will seek the groves
     Where the lady Mary is,
105 With her five handmaidens, whose names
     Are five sweet symphonies,
Cecily, Gertrude, Magdalen,
     Margaret and Rosalys.

"Circlewise sit they, with bound locks
110   And foreheads garlanded;
Into the fine cloth white like flame
     Weaving the golden thread,
To fashion the birth-robes for them
     Who are just born, being dead.

"I wish that he were come to me,
     For he will come," she said.
"Have I not prayed in Heaven?—on earth,
70   Lord, Lord, has he not prayed?
Are not two prayers a perfect strength?
     And shall I feel afraid?

"When round his head the aureole° clings,   *halo*
     And he is clothed in white,
75 I'll take his hand and go with him
     To the deep wells of light;
As unto a stream we will step down,
     And bathe there in God's sight.

---

1 *living mystic tree* Tree of life (See Revelation 22.2).

2 *Dove* Holy Spirit.

"He shall fear, haply,° and be dumb: *perchance*
    Then will I lay my cheek
To his, and tell about our love,
    Not once abashed or weak:
And the dear Mother will approve
    My pride, and let me speak.

"Herself shall bring us, hand in hand,
    To him round whom all souls
Kneel, the clear-ranged unnumbered heads
    Bowed with their aureoles:
And angels meeting us shall sing
    To their citherns and citoles.[1]

"There will I ask of Christ the Lord
    Thus much for him and me:
Only to live as once on earth
    With Love—only to be,
As then awhile, for ever now
    Together, I and he."

She gazed and listened and then said,
    Less sad of speech than mild—
"All this is when he comes." She ceased.
    The light thrilled towards her, filled
With angels in strong level flight.
    Her eyes prayed, and she smiled.

(I saw her smile.) But soon their path
    Was vague in distant spheres:
And then she cast her arms along
    The golden barriers,
And laid her face between her hands,
    And wept. (I heard her tears.)
—1850

(line numbers: 115, 120, 125, 130, 135, 140)

The Woodspurge [2]

The wind flapped loose, the wind was still,
    Shaken out dead from tree and hill:
I had walked on at the wind's will—
I sat now, for the wind was still.

Between my knees my forehead was—
My lips, drawn in, said not Alas!
My hair was over in the grass,
My naked ears heard the day pass.

My eyes, wide open, had the run
Of some ten weeds to fix upon;
Among those few, out of the sun,
The woodspurge flowered, three cups in one.

From perfect grief there need not be
Wisdom or even memory:
One thing then learnt remains to me—
The woodspurge has a cup of three.
—1870

(line numbers: 5, 10, 15)

Jenny

"Vengeance of Jenny's case! Fie on her!
Never name her, child"

               (Mrs. Quickly.)[3]

Lazy laughing languid Jenny,
    Fond of a kiss and fond of a guinea,[4]
Whose head upon my knee to-night
Rests for a while, as if grown light
With all our dances and the sound
To which the wild tunes spun you round:
Fair Jenny mine, the thoughtless queen
Of kisses which the blush between
Could hardly make much daintier;

(line number: 5)

---

1   *citherns* Guitar-like instruments strung with wire and played with a quill, popular in the sixteenth and seventeenth centuries; *citoles* Stringed instruments common in the thirteenth to fifteenth centuries.

2   *Woodspurge* Wildflower with cup-like, yellowish-green flowers that excrete a milky juice.

3   *Vengeance ... Quickly* From Shakespeare's *The Merry Wives of Windsor* 1.1. The rest of Mistress Quickly's speech reads, "if she be a whore."

4   *guinea* English gold coin.

10 Whose eyes are as blue skies, whose hair
Is countless gold incomparable;
Fresh flower, scarce touched with signs that tell
Of Love's exuberant hotbed—Nay,
Poor flower left torn since yesterday
15 Until to-morrow leave you bare;
Poor handful of bright spring-water
Flung in the whirlpool's shrieking face;
Poor shameful Jenny, full of grace
Thus with your head upon my knee—
20 Whose person or whose purse may be
The lodestar[1] of your reverie?

This room of yours, my Jenny, looks
A change from mine so full of books,
Whose serried[2] ranks hold fast, forsooth,
25 So many captive hours of youth—
The hours they thieve from day and night
To make one's cherished work come right,
And leave it wrong for all their theft,
Even as to-night my work was left:
30 Until I vowed that since my brain
And eyes of dancing seemed so fain,
My feet should have some dancing too—
And thus it was I met with you.
Well, I suppose 'twas hard to part,
35 For here I am. And now, sweetheart,
You seem too tired to get to bed.

It was a careless life I led
When rooms like this were scarce so strange
Not long ago. What breeds the change—
40 The many aims or the few years?
Because to-night it all appears
Something I do not know again.

The cloud's not danced out of my brain—
The cloud that made it turn and swim
45 While hour by hour the books grew dim.
Why, Jenny, as I watch you there,
For all your wealth of loosened hair,
Your silk ungirdled and unlaced
And warm sweets open to the waist,

50 All golden in the lamplight's gleam,
You know not what a book you seem,
Half-read by lightning in a dream!
How should you know, my Jenny? Nay,
And I should be ashamed to say—
55 Poor beauty, so well worth a kiss!
But while my thought runs on like this
With wasteful whims more than enough,
I wonder what you're thinking of.

If of myself you think at all,
60 What is the thought?—conjectural
On sorry matters best unsolved?—
Or inly° is each grace revolved   *inwardly*
To fit me with a lure?—or (sad
To think!) perhaps you're merely glad
65 That I'm not drunk or ruffianly
And let you rest upon my knee.

For sometimes, were the truth confessed,
You're thankful for a little rest—
Glad from the crush to rest within,
70 From the heart-sickness and the din
Where envy's voice at virtue's pitch
Mocks you because your gown is rich;
And from the pale girl's dumb rebuke,
Whose ill-clad grace and toil-worn look
75 Proclaim the strength that keeps her weak
And other nights than yours bespeak;
And from the wise unchildish elf,
To schoolmate lesser than himself
Pointing you out, what thing you are—
80 Yes, from the daily jeer and jar,
From shame and shame's outbraving too,
Is rest not sometimes sweet to you?
But most from the hatefulness of man
Who spares not to end what he began,
85 Whose acts are ill and his speech ill,
Who, having used you at his will,
Thrusts you aside, as when I dine
I serve the dishes and the wine.

Well, handsome Jenny mine, sit up,
90 I've filled our glasses, let us sup,
And do not let me think of you,

---

1   *lodestar*   Pole star; i.e., guiding star.

2   *serried*   Pressed close together.

Lest shame of yours suffice for two.
What, still so tired? Well, well then, keep
Your head there, so you do not sleep;
95 But that the weariness may pass
And leave you merry, take this glass.
Ah! lazy lily hand, more blessed
If ne'er in rings it had been dressed
Nor ever by a glove concealed!

100   Behold the lilies of the field,
They toil not neither do they spin;[1]
(So doth the ancient text begin—
Not of such rest as one of these
Can share.) Another rest and ease
105 Along each summer-sated path
From its new lord the garden hath,
Than that whose spring in blessings ran
Which praised the bounteous husbandman,
Ere yet, in days of hankering breath,
110 The lilies sickened unto death.

     What, Jenny, are your lilies dead?
Aye, and the snow-white leaves are spread
Like winter on the garden-bed.
But you had roses left in May—
115 They were not gone too. Jenny, nay,
But must your roses die, and those
Their purfled[2] buds that should unclose?
Even so; the leaves are curled apart,
Still red as from the broken heart,
120 And here's the naked stem of thorns.

     Nay, nay, mere words. Here nothing warns
As yet of winter. Sickness here
Or want alone could waken fear—
Nothing but passion wrings a tear.
125 Except when there may rise unsought
Haply° at times a passing thought   *perchance*
Of the old days which seem to be
Much older than any history
That is written in any book;

When she would lie in fields and look
130 Along the ground through the blown grass,
And wonder where the city was,
Far out of sight, whose broil° and bale°   *tumult / woe*
They told her then for a child's tale.

135   Jenny, you know the city now.
A child can tell the tale there, how
Some things which are not yet enrolled
In market-lists are bought and sold
Even till the early Sunday light,
140 When Saturday night is market-night
Everywhere, be it dry or wet,
And market-night in the Haymarket.
Our learned London children know,
Poor Jenny, all your pride and woe;
145 Have seen your lifted silken skirt
Advertise dainties through the dirt;
Have seen your coach-wheels splash rebuke
On virtue; and have learned your look
When, wealth and health slipped past, you stare
150 Along the streets alone, and there,
Round the long park, across the bridge,
The cold lamps at the pavement's edge
Wind on together and apart,
A fiery serpent for your heart.

155   Let the thoughts pass, an empty cloud!
Suppose I were to think aloud—
What if to her all this were said?
Why, as a volume seldom read
Being opened halfway shuts again,
160 So might the pages of her brain
Be parted at such words, and thence
Close back upon the dusty sense.
For is there hue or shape defined
In Jenny's desecrated mind,
165 Where all contagious currents meet,
A Lethe[3] of the middle street?
Nay, it reflects not any face,
Nor sound is in its sluggish pace,
But as they coil those eddies clot,
170 And night and day remember not.

---

[1] *Behold ... spin* Reference to Matthew 6.28: "And why take ye thought for raiment? Consider the lilies of the field, how they grow; they toil not, neither do they spin."

[2] *purfled* Edged with another color.

[3] *Lethe* River in Hades (the underworld of classical mythology) whose waters bring forgetfulness to those who drink from them.

Why, Jenny, you're asleep at last!
Asleep, poor Jenny, hard and fast—
So young and soft and tired; so fair,
With chin thus nestled in your hair,
175   Mouth quiet, eyelids almost blue
As if some sky of dreams shone through!

Just as another woman sleeps!
Enough to throw one's thoughts in heaps
Of doubt and horror—what to say
180   Or think—this awful secret sway,
The potter's power over the clay!
Of the same lump (it has been said)
For honour and dishonour made,
Two sister vessels.[1] Here is one.

185   My cousin Nell is fond of fun,
And fond of dress, and change, and praise,
So mere a woman in her ways:
And if her sweet eyes rich in youth
Are like her lips that tell the truth,
190   My cousin Nell is fond of love.
And she's the girl I'm proudest of.
Who does not prize her, guard her well?
The love of change, in cousin Nell,
Shall find the best and hold it dear:
195   The unconquered mirth turn quieter
Not through her own, through others' woe:
The conscious pride of beauty glow
Beside another's pride in her,
One little part of all they share.
200   For Love himself shall ripen these
In a kind soil to just increase
Through years of fertilizing peace.

Of the same lump (as it is said)
For honour and dishonour made,
205   Two sister vessels. Here is one.

It makes a goblin of the sun.

So pure—so fallen! How dare to think
Of the first common kindred link?
Yet, Jenny, till the world shall burn
210   It seems that all things take their turn;
And who shall say but this fair tree
May need, in changes that may be,
Your children's children's charity?
Scorned then, no doubt, as you are scorned!
215   Shall no man hold his pride forewarned
Till in the end, the Day of Days,
At Judgment, one of his own race,
As frail and lost as you, shall rise—
His daughter, with his mother's eyes?

220   How Jenny's clock ticks on the shelf!
Might not the dial scorn itself
That has such hours to register?
Yet as to me, even so to her
Are golden sun and silver moon,
225   In daily largesse of earth's boon,
Counted for life-coins to one tune.
And if, as blindfold fates are tossed,
Through some one man this life be lost,
Shall soul not somehow pay for soul?

230   Fair shines the gilded aureole°   halo
In which our highest painters place
Some living woman's simple face.
And the stilled features thus descried
As Jenny's long throat droops aside—
235   The shadows where the cheeks are thin,
And pure wide curve from ear to chin—
With Raffael's, Leonardo's[2] hand
To show them to men's souls, might stand,
Whole ages long, the whole world through,
240   For preachings of what God can do.
What has man done here? How atone,
Great God, for this which man has done?
And for the body and soul which by
Man's pitiless doom must now comply
245   With lifelong hell, what lullaby
Of sweet forgetful second birth
Remains? All dark. No sign on earth

---

[1] *The potter's ... vessels* Reference to Romans 9.21: "Hath not the potter power over the clay, of the same lump to make one vessel unto honor, and another unto dishonor?"

[2] *Raffael's, Leonardo's* I.e., Italian painters Raphael (1483–1520) and Leonardo da Vinci (1452–1519).

What measure of God's rest endows
The many mansions of his house.

250   If but a woman's heart might see
Such erring heart unerringly
For once! But that can never be.

Like a rose shut in a book
In which pure women may not look,
255   For its base pages claim control
To crush the flower within the soul;
Where through each dead rose-leaf that clings,
Pale as transparent psyche-wings,
To the vile text, are traced such things
260   As might make lady's cheek indeed
More than a living rose to read;
So nought save foolish foulness may
Watch with hard eyes the sure decay;
And so the life-blood of this rose,
265   Puddled with shameful knowledge, flows
Through leaves no chaste hand may unclose:
Yet still it keeps such faded show
Of when 'twas gathered long ago,
That the crushed petals' lovely grain,
270   The sweetness of the sanguine stain,
Seen of a woman's eyes, must make
Her pitiful heart, so prone to ache,
Love roses better for its sake—
Only that this can never be:
275   Even so unto her sex is she.

Yet, Jenny, looking long at you,
The woman almost fades from view.
A cipher of man's changeless sum
Of lust, past, present, and to come,
280   Is left. A riddle that one shrinks
To challenge from the scornful sphinx.[1]

Like a toad within a stone
Seated while Time crumbles on;[2]

Which sits there since the earth was cursed
285   For Man's transgression at the first;
Which, living through all centuries,
Not once has seen the sun arise;
Whose life, to its cold circle charmed,
The earth's whole summers have not warmed;
290   Which always—whitherso the stone
Be flung—sits there, deaf, blind, alone;
Aye, and shall not be driven out
Till that which shuts him round about
Break at the very Master's stroke,
295   And the dust thereof vanish as smoke,
And the seed of Man vanish as dust—
Even so within this world is Lust.

Come, come, what use in thoughts like this?
Poor little Jenny, good to kiss—
300   You'd not believe by what strange roads
Thought travels, when your beauty goads
A man to-night to think of toads!
Jenny, wake up ... Why, there's the dawn!

And there's an early wagon drawn
305   To market, and some sheep that jog
Bleating before a barking dog;
And the old streets come peering through
Another night that London knew;
And all as ghostlike as the lamps.

310   So on the wings of day decamps
My last night's frolic. Glooms begin
To shiver off as lights creep in
Past the gauze curtains half drawn-to,
And the lamp's doubled shade grows blue—
315   Your lamp, my Jenny, kept alight,
Like a wise virgin's, all one night!
And in the alcove coolly spread
Glimmers with dawn your empty bed;

---

[1]   *sphinx* Winged creature of Greek mythology who killed those who could not answer its riddles.

[2]   *Like a ... on* Phenomenon of living toads, frogs, or other creatures trapped in stone or wood is one that has been occasionally reported. One such instance occurred in 1865, when workers excavating in Hartlepool, England, split open a magnesium lime-stone rock found 25 feet underground to discover a living toad. The *Hartlepool Free Press* reported, "The cavity was no larger than its body, and presented the appearance of being cast for it." There was no evidence as to how the toad could have gotten into the stone or survived in it for any length of time. But, from its appearance and the age of the rock in which it was found, the toad was estimated to be over 6000 years old.

And yonder your fair face I see
320 Reflected lying on my knee,
Where teems with first foreshadowings
Your pier-glass[1] scrawled with diamond rings:
And on your bosom all night worn
Yesterday's rose now droops forlorn
325 But dies not yet this summer morn.

And now without, as if some word
Had called upon them that they heard,
The London sparrows far and nigh
Clamour together suddenly;
330 And Jenny's cage-bird grown awake
Here in their song his part must take,
Because here too the day doth break.

And somehow in myself the dawn
Among stirred clouds and veils withdrawn
335 Strikes greyly on her. Let her sleep.
But will it wake her if I heap
These cushions thus beneath her head
Where my knee was? No—there's your bed,
My Jenny, while you dream. And there
340 I lay among your golden hair
Perhaps the subject of your dreams,
These golden coins.

For still one deems
That Jenny's flattering sleep confers
345 New magic on the magic purse—
Grim web, how clogged with shrivelled flies!
Between the threads fine fumes arise
And shape their pictures in the brain.
There roll no streets in glare and rain,
350 Nor flagrant man-swine whets his tusk;
But delicately sighs in musk
The homage of the dim boudoir;
Or like a palpitating star
Thrilled into song, the opera-night
355 Breathes faint in the quick pulse of light;
Or at the carriage-window shine
Rich wares for choice; or, free to dine,
Whirls through its hour of health (divine

For her) the concourse of the Park.
360 And though in the discounted dark
Her functions there and here are one,
Beneath the lamps and in the sun
There reigns at least the acknowledged belle
Apparelled beyond parallel.
365 Ah Jenny, yes, we know your dreams.

For even the Paphian Venus[2] seems
A goddess o'er the realms of love,
When silver-shrined in shadowy grove:
Aye, or let offerings nicely placed
370 But hide Priapus[3] to the waist,
And whoso looks on him shall see
An eligible deity.

Why, Jenny, waking here alone
May help you to remember one,
375 Though all the memory's long outworn
Of many a double-pillowed morn.
I think I see you when you wake,
And rub your eyes for me, and shake
My gold, in rising, from your hair,
380 A Danaë[4] for a moment there.

Jenny, my love rang true! for still
Love at first sight is vague, until
That tinkling makes him audible.

And must I mock you to the last,
385 Ashamed of my own shame—aghast
Because some thoughts not born amiss
Rose at a poor fair face like this?
Well, of such thoughts so much I know:
In my life, as in hers, they show,

---

[1] *pier-glass* Large, tall mirror.

[2] *Paphian Venus* Venus, goddess of love, was said to have been born of sea-form, but emerged on the island of Paphos, Cyprus.

[3] *Priapus* God of procreation, and a personification of an erect phallus.

[4] *Danaë* According to Greek mythology, Acrisius imprisoned his daughter Danaë in a room of bronze to ensure she would never conceive a son. Zeus, however, fell in love with Danaë and came to her through the ceiling as a shower of gold that fell in her lap.

390 By a far gleam which I may near,
A dark path I can strive to clear.

Only one kiss. Goodbye, my dear.
—1848

My Sister's Sleep

She fell asleep on Christmas Eve:
At length the long-ungranted shade
Of weary eyelids overweighed
The pain nought else might yet relieve.

5 Our mother, who had leaned all day
Over the bed from chime to chime,
Then raised herself for the first time,
And as she sat her down, did pray.

Her little work-table was spread
10 With work to finish. For the glare
Made by her candle, she had care
To work some distance from the bed.

Without, there was a cold moon up,
Of winter radiance sheer and thin;
15 The hollow halo it was in
Was like an icy crystal cup.

Through the small room, with subtle sound
Of flame, by vents the fireshine drove
And reddened. In its dim alcove
20 The mirror shed a clearness round.

I had been sitting up some nights,
And my tired mind felt weak and blank;
Like a sharp strengthening wine it drank
The stillness and the broken lights.

25 Twelve struck. That sound, by dwindling years
Heard in each hour, crept off; and then
The ruffled silence spread again,
Like water that a pebble stirs.

Our mother rose from where she sat:
30 Her needles, as she laid them down,
Met lightly, and her silken gown
Settled: no other noise than that.

"Glory unto the Newly Born!"
So, as said angels, she did say;
35 Because we were in Christmas Day,
Though it would still be long till morn.

Just then in the room over us
There was a pushing back of chairs,
As some who had sat unawares
40 So late, now heard the hour, and rose.

With anxious softly-stepping haste
Our mother went where Margaret lay,
Fearing the sounds o'erhead—should they
Have broken her long watched-for rest!

45 She stopped an instant, calm, and turned;
But suddenly turned back again;
And all her features seemed in pain
With woe, and her eyes gazed and yearned.

For my part, I but hid my face,
50 And held my breath, and spoke no word:
There was none spoken; but I heard
The silence for a little space.

Our mother bowed herself and wept:
And both my arms fell, and I said,
55 "God knows I knew that she was dead."
And there, all white, my sister slept.

Then kneeling, upon Christmas morn
A little after twelve o'clock
We said, ere the first quarter struck,
60 "Christ's blessing on the newly born!"
—1850

Sibylla Palmifera[1]

Under the arch of Life, where love and death,
  Terror and mystery, guard her shrine, I saw
  Beauty enthroned; and though her gaze struck awe,
I drew it in as simply as my breath.
Hers are the eyes which, over and beneath,
  The sky and sea bend on thee—which can draw,
  By sea or sky or woman, to one law,
The allotted bondman of her palm and wreath.

This is that Lady Beauty, in whose praise
  Thy voice and hand shake still—long known to thee
  By flying hair and fluttering hem—the beat
  Following her daily of thy heart and feet,
How passionately and irretrievably,
In what fond flight, how many ways and days!
—1868

Dante Gabriel Rossetti, *Sybilla Palmifera* (1868).

[1] *Sibylla Palmifera* This sonnet was composed to accompany the painting of the same title, included above; the poem later appeared under the title "Soul's Beauty" in the 1881 version of Rossetti's sonnet sequence *The House of Life*. The Sibyl (prophet) of Cumae wrote her prophesies on palm leaves.

Lady Lilith[1]

Of Adam's first wife, Lilith, it is told
      (The witch he loved before the gift of Eve)
      That, ere the snake's, her sweet tongue could deceive,
And her enchanted hair was the first gold.
5   And still she sits, young while the earth is old,
      And, subtly of herself contemplative,
      Draws men to watch the bright web she can weave,
Till heart and body and life are in its hold.

Rose, foxglove, poppy are her flowers: for where
10   Is he not found, O Lilith, whom shed scent
And soft-shed fingers and soft sleep shall snare?
      Lo! as that youth's eyes burned at thine, so went
      Thy spell through him, and left his straight neck
            bent
And round his heart one strangling golden hair.
—1868

Mary Magdalene at the Door of Simon the Pharisee [2]

(For a Drawing)[3]

"Why wilt thou cast the roses from thine hair?
      Nay, be thou all a rose—wreath, lips, and
            cheek.

Dante Gabriel Rossetti, *Mary Magdalene at the Door of Simon the Pharisee* (1858).

Nay, not this house—that banquet-house we seek;
See how they kiss and enter; come thou there.
5   This delicate day of love we two will share
      Till at our ear love's whispering night shall speak.
      What, sweet one—hold'st thou still the foolish
            freak?°   whim
Nay, when I kiss thy feet they'll leave the stair."

"Oh loose me! See'st thou not my Bridegroom's face
10   That draws me to Him? For His feet my kiss,
            My hair, my tears He craves to-day—and oh!
What words can tell what other day and place
      Shall see me clasp those blood-stained feet of His?
            He needs me, calls me, loves me: let me go!"
—1870

1   *Lady Lilith*   Like "Sibylla Palmifera," this sonnet was composed to accompany a painting (*Lady Lilith*). In the extended version of Rossetti's sonnet sequence *The House of Life* (1881), the two poems appeared together with the titles "Soul's Beauty" and "Body's Beauty." Lilith was the first wife of Adam; according to Talmudic legend, she rejected Adam when she refused to accept a subservient position in sexual intercourse. She left the Garden of Eden and mated with various demons.

2   *Mary … Pharisee*   See Luke 7.36–50, which tells how an anonymous penitent, often assumed to be Mary Magdalene, burst into the house of Simon, a Pharisee, where Jesus was dining. She prostrated herself at his feet, which she then washed with her tears and dried with her hair.

3   [Rossetti's note]   In the drawing Mary has left a procession of revellers, and is ascending by a sudden impulse the steps of the house where she sees Christ. Her lover has followed her and is trying to turn her back.

from *The House of Life*
The Sonnet

A Sonnet is a moment's monument—
    Memorial from the Soul's eternity
  To one dead deathless hour. Look that it be,
Whether for lustral° rite or dire portent,   *purification*
5   Of its own arduous fulness reverent:
      Carve it in ivory or in ebony,
      As Day or Night may rule; and let Time see
  Its flowering crest impearled and orient.

  A Sonnet is a coin: its face reveals
10   The soul—its converse, to what Power 'tis due—
  Whether for tribute to the august appeals
      Of Life, or dower in Love's high retinue,
  It serve; or, 'mid the dark wharf's cavernous breath,
  In Charon's[1] palm it pay the toll to Death.
—1881

6a. Nuptial Sleep[2]

At length their long kiss severed, with sweet smart:
    And as the last slow sudden drops are shed
  From sparkling eaves when all the storm has fled,
So singly flagged the pulses of each heart.
5   Their bosoms sundered, with the opening start
      Of married flowers to either side outspread
      From the knit stem; yet still their mouths, burnt red,
  Fawned on each other where they lay apart.

  Sleep sank them lower than the tide of dreams,
10   And their dreams watched them sink, and slid away.
  Slowly their souls swam up again, through gleams
      Of watered light and dull drowned waifs of day;
  Till from some wonder of new woods and streams
      He woke, and wondered more: for there she lay.
—1870

10. The Portrait

O Lord of all compassionate control,
    O Love! let this my lady's picture glow
  Under my hand to praise her name, and show
Even of her inner self the perfect whole:
5   That he who seeks her beauty's furthest goal,
      Beyond the light that the sweet glances throw
      And refluent wave of the sweet smile, may know
The very sky and sea-line of her soul.

  Lo! it is done. Above the enthroning throat
10   The mouth's mould testifies of voice and kiss,
      The shadowed eyes remember and foresee.
  Her face is made her shrine. Let all men note
      That in all years (O Love, thy gift is this!)
      They that would look on her must come to me.
—1870

97. A Superscription

Look in my face; my name is Might-have-been;
    I am also called No-more, Too-late, Farewell;
    Unto thine ear I hold the dead-sea shell
Cast up thy Life's foam-fretted feet between;
5   Unto thine eyes the glass where that is seen
      Which had Life's form and Love's, but by my spell
      Is now a shaken shadow intolerable,
  Of ultimate things unuttered the frail screen.

  Mark me, how still I am! But should there dart
10   One moment through thy soul the soft surprise
      Of that winged Peace which lulls the breath of
        sighs—
  Then shalt thou see me smile, and turn apart
  Thy visage to mine ambush at thy heart
      Sleepless with cold commemorative eyes.
—1870

---

1   *Charon* In Greek mythology, ferryman of the river Styx who, for
a fee, transports dead souls into Hades.

2   *Nuptial Sleep* This sonnet was published in Rossetti's 1870
volume, *Poems*, but was omitted from the 1881 edition of *The House
of Life* after Robert Buchanan, in his review *The Fleshly School of
Poetry* (1871), attacked its depiction of "shameless nakedness."

101. The One Hope

When vain desire at last and vain regret
  Go hand in hand to death, and all is vain,
  What shall assuage the unforgotten pain
And teach the unforgetful to forget?
5 Shall Peace be still a sunk stream long unmet—
  Or may the soul at once in a green plain
  Stoop through the spray of some sweet life-fountain
And cull the dew-drenched flowering amulet?[1]

Ah! when the wan soul in that golden air
10 Between the scriptured petals softly blown
  Peers breathless for the gift of grace unknown—
Ah! let none other alien spell soe'er
But only the one Hope's one name be there—
  Not less nor more, but even that word alone.
—1870

---

[1] *amulet* Charm against evil, sickness, harm, etc.

CHRISTINA ROSSETTI
1830 – 1894

To the late-Victorian critic Edmund Gosse, Christina Rossetti was "one of the most perfect poets of the age." Of her works, Rossetti's fellow-poet Algernon Charles Swinburne claimed that "nothing more glorious in poetry has ever been written." Although Rossetti may have been less popular than contemporaries such as Alfred Tennyson and Elizabeth Barrett Browning, her melding

of sensuous imagery and stringent form earned her the admiration and devotion of many nineteenth-century readers. Her lyricism elicited praise for being, as one critic wrote in 1862, "remarkably fresh and free," as well as "true and most genuine." The ease of Rossetti's lyric voice remains apparent in works as diverse as the sensual *Goblin Market* and the subtle religious hymns she penned throughout her career.

She was born in London in 1830, the youngest of four children. Her father, Gabriel Rossetti, was a scholar and an Italian exile, and her mother, Frances Polidori, was the English-Italian daughter of another Italian exile. Italian revolutionaries-in-exile frequented the Rossetti home, creating a provocative and unconventional environment for the Rossetti children. Other influences included their mother's devotion to Christianity and visits to their maternal grandfather's rural home. "If any one thing schooled me in the direction of poetry," Rossetti was later to write, "it was perhaps the delightful idle liberty to prowl all alone about my grandfather's cottage-grounds some thirty miles from London."

Rossetti's grandfather Polidori printed her first volume of poems, *Verses: Dedicated to Her Mother*, in 1847. Though immature in light of the works that would follow, the poems of the sixteen-year-old Rossetti already exhibited many of the qualities for which her work would later be known: directness of expression and simplicity of narrative colored with vivid and often sensuous detail. In 1850 several of her poems were published in *The Germ*, the journal of the Pre-Raphaelite Brotherhood founded in part by her two brothers, Dante Gabriel and William Michael. Although she was not formally a member of the Brotherhood, Rossetti's aesthetic sense—and especially her attention to color and detail—link her to the movement. Other Pre-Raphaelite values were also central to Rossetti's poetic vision, including a devotion to the faithful representation of nature and, at the same time, a penchant for symbolic representation.

The 1850s were a difficult time for Rossetti. Early in the decade she rejected, most likely on religious grounds, a suitor to whom she had been engaged for two years, the Pre-Raphaelite painter James Collinson. Collinson had converted to Anglicanism to please Rossetti, but he ultimately returned to his original faith, Catholicism. (In 1866 Rossetti appears to have rejected a second suitor, Charles Bagot Cayley, perhaps because he was an agnostic.) In 1854 Rossetti volunteered to join Florence Nightingale's nursing efforts in the Crimean War, but she was rejected for being too young. She volunteered instead at the Highgate Penitentiary for "fallen women." Throughout this period, she lived with her mother, sister, and brother William in the family home.

Rossetti first gained attention in the literary world with her 1862 publication of *Goblin Market and Other Poems*. Before publication of the volume, the eminent critic John Ruskin had declared the poems irregular in both their rhyme schemes and meters. Ruskin advised Rossetti to "exercise herself in the severest commonplace of metre until she [could] write as the public like." Rossetti nevertheless went ahead with publication, and the vast majority of her Victorian critics praised the volume for what one reviewer called its "very decided character and originality, both in theme and treatment." "Here," notes the *Eclectic Review*, "is a volume of really true poetry." "Goblin Market" remains among her most discussed works. Few readers have believed William Michael Rossetti's insistence that his sister "did not mean anything profound" by "Goblin Market," but many have found the precise nature of its deep suggestiveness elusive.

More volumes followed, among the most important of which were *The Prince's Progress and Other Poems* (1866), *Sing-Song* (1872), *A Pageant and Other Poems* (1881), and *Verses* (1893). In *Sing-Song* Rossetti proved herself a talented writer of children's verses. With "Monna Innominata," the "sonnet of sonnets" published in *A Pageant and Other Poems*, Rossetti offered her own bold contribution to the sonnet-sequence tradition. In the prose preface to "Monna Innominata," Rossetti notes that women such as Dante's Beatrice and Petrarch's Laura were denied the opportunity to speak for themselves. If either had spoken in her own voice, Rossetti writes, "the portrait left us might have appeared more tender, if less dignified, than any drawn even by a devoted friend." According to Rossetti, even the *Sonnets from the Portuguese* of the "Great Poetess" Elizabeth Barrett Browning do not offer us a voice "drawn from feeling": her circumstances, that is, her happy love-story, precluded her from giving her speaker such a voice. Rossetti's sonnets, in contrast, speak of unfulfilled yearning and painful loss, bringing to the sonnet form the voice of a woman's suffering such as Rossetti believed had never before been written. Critics have often read the poem in biographical terms, following from William Michael Rossetti's suggestion that the "introductory prose-note … is a blind … interposed to draw off attention from the writer in her proper person." But such readings, however tempting, limit interpretation of the poems and fail to account for the deep complexities of Rossetti's work.

In 1871, Rossetti was stricken with exophthalmic bronchocele, or Graves's disease, a disease causing protrusion of the eyeballs, which led her to retreat even further into an already quiet life. Rossetti continued to live with and care for her mother and two aunts. She lived to see editions of her collected poems published in 1875 and then again in 1890, and in 1892 she was among those mentioned as a possible successor to Tennyson as England's Poet Laureate. She died in 1894 from cancer, having undergone surgery for breast cancer in 1892.

⌘⌘⌘

Goblin Market

Morning and evening
Maids heard the goblins cry:
"Come buy our orchard fruits,
Come buy, come buy:
5   Apples and quinces,
Lemons and oranges,
Plump unpecked cherries,
Melons and raspberries,
Bloom-down-cheeked peaches,
10   Swart°-headed mulberries,   *dark*
Wild free-born cranberries,
Crabapples, dewberries,
Pine-apples, blackberries,
Apricots, strawberries;—
15   All ripe together
In summer weather,—
Morns that pass by,
Fair eves that fly;
Come buy, come buy:
20   Our grapes fresh from the vine,
Pomegranates full and fine,
Dates and sharp bullaces,
Rare pears and greengages,

Damsons[1] and bilberries
25 Taste them and try:
Currants and gooseberries,
Bright-fire-like barberries,
Figs to fill your mouth,
Citrons from the South,
30 Sweet to tongue and sound to eye;
Come buy, come buy."

Evening by evening
Among the brookside rushes,
Laura bowed her head to hear,
35 Lizzie veiled her blushes:
Crouching close together
In the cooling weather,
With clasping arms and cautioning lips,
With tingling cheeks and finger tips.
40 "Lie close," Laura said,
Pricking up her golden head:
"We must not look at goblin men,
We must not buy their fruits:
Who knows upon what soil they fed
45 Their hungry thirsty roots?"
"Come buy," call the goblins
Hobbling down the glen.
"Oh," cried Lizzie, "Laura, Laura,
You should not peep at goblin men."
50 Lizzie covered up her eyes,
Covered close lest they should look;
Laura reared her glossy head,
And whispered like the restless brook:
"Look, Lizzie, look, Lizzie,
55 Down the glen tramp little men.
One hauls a basket,
One bears a plate,
One lugs a golden dish
Of many pounds weight.
60 How fair the vine must grow
Whose grapes are so luscious;
How warm the wind must blow
Through those fruit bushes."
"No," said Lizzie: "No, no, no;
65 Their offers should not charm us,

Their evil gifts would harm us."
She thrust a dimpled finger
In each ear, shut eyes and ran:
Curious Laura chose to linger
70 Wondering at each merchant man.
One had a cat's face,
One whisked a tail,
One tramped at a rat's pace,
One crawled like a snail,
75 One like a wombat prowled obtuse and furry,
One like a ratel° tumbled hurry skurry.   *badger*
She heard a voice like voice of doves
Cooing all together:
They sounded kind and full of loves
80 In the pleasant weather.

Laura stretched her gleaming neck
Like a rush-imbedded swan,
Like a lily from the beck,°   *stream*
Like a moonlit poplar branch,
85 Like a vessel at the launch
When its last restraint is gone.

Backwards up the mossy glen
Turned and trooped the goblin men,
With their shrill repeated cry,
90 "Come buy, come buy."
When they reached where Laura was
They stood stock still upon the moss,
Leering at each other,
Brother with queer brother;
95 Signalling each other,
Brother with sly brother.
One set his basket down,
One reared his plate;
One began to weave a crown
100 Of tendrils, leaves, and rough nuts brown
(Men sell not such in any town);
One heaved the golden weight
Of dish and fruit to offer her:
"Come buy, come buy," was still their cry.
105 Laura stared but did not stir,
Longed but had no money:
The whisk-tailed merchant bade her taste
In tones as smooth as honey,

---

[1] *bullaces ... Damsons* Bullaces, greengages, and damsons are all
varieties of plums.

The cat-faced purr'd,
110 The rat-paced spoke a word
Of welcome, and the snail-paced even was heard;
One parrot-voiced and jolly
Cried "Pretty Goblin" still for "Pretty Polly";—
One whistled like a bird.

115 But sweet-tooth Laura spoke in haste:
"Good Folk, I have no coin;
To take were to purloin:
I have no copper in my purse,
I have no silver either,
120 And all my gold is on the furze°   *evergreen shrub*
That shakes in windy weather
Above the rusty heather."
"You have much gold upon your head,"
They answered all together:
125 "Buy from us with a golden curl."
She clipped a precious golden lock,
She dropped a tear more rare than pearl,
Then sucked their fruit globes fair or red.
Sweeter than honey from the rock,[1]
130 Stronger than man-rejoicing wine,
Clearer than water flowed that juice;
She never tasted such before,
How should it cloy with length of use?
She sucked and sucked and sucked the more
135 Fruits which that unknown orchard bore;
She sucked until her lips were sore;
Then flung the emptied rinds away
But gathered up one kernel-stone,
And knew not was it night or day
140 As she turned home alone.

Lizzie met her at the gate
Full of wise upbraidings:
"Dear, you should not stay so late,
Twilight is not good for maidens;
145 Should not loiter in the glen
In the haunts of goblin men.
Do you not remember Jeanie,
How she met them in the moonlight,
Took their gifts both choice and many,
150 Ate their fruits and wore their flowers

Plucked from bowers
Where summer ripens at all hours?
But ever in the noonlight
She pined and pined away;
155 Sought them by night and day,
Found them no more but dwindled and grew grey;
Then fell with the first snow,
While to this day no grass will grow
Where she lies low:
160 I planted daisies there a year ago
That never blow.
You should not loiter so."
"Nay, hush," said Laura:
"Nay, hush, my sister:
165 I ate and ate my fill,
Yet my mouth waters still;
Tomorrow night I will
Buy more": and kissed her:
"Have done with sorrow;
170 I'll bring you plums tomorrow
Fresh on their mother twigs,
Cherries worth getting;
You cannot think what figs
My teeth have met in,
175 What melons icy cold
Piled on a dish of gold
Too huge for me to hold,
What peaches with a velvet nap,
Pellucid° grapes without one seed: *translucent*
180 Odorous indeed must be the mead
Whereon they grow, and pure the wave they drink
With lilies at the brink,
And sugar-sweet their sap."

Golden head by golden head,
185 Like two pigeons in one nest
Folded in each other's wings,
They lay down in their curtained bed:
Like two blossoms on one stem,
Like two flakes of new-fall'n snow,
190 Like two wands of ivory
Tipped with gold for awful° kings.   *awe-inspiring*
Moon and stars gazed in at them,
Wind sang to them lullaby,

---

[1] *honey from the rock* See Deuteronomy 32.13.

Lumbering owls forbore to fly,
195　Not a bat flapped to and fro
Round their rest:
Cheek to cheek and breast to breast
Locked together in one nest.

Early in the morning
200　When the first cock crowed his warning,
Neat like bees, as sweet and busy,
Laura rose with Lizzie:
Fetched in honey, milked the cows,
Aired and set to rights the house,
205　Kneaded cakes of whitest wheat,
Cakes for dainty mouths to eat,
Next churned butter, whipped up cream,
Fed their poultry, sat and sewed;
Talked as modest maidens should:
210　Lizzie with an open heart,
Laura in an absent dream,
One content, one sick in part;
One warbling for the mere bright day's delight,
One longing for the night.

215　At length slow evening came:
They went with pitchers to the reedy brooks;
Lizzie most placid in her look,
Laura most like a leaping flame.
They drew the gurgling water from its deep.
220　Lizzie plucked purple and rich golden flags,
Then turning homeward said: "The sunset flushes
Those furthest loftiest crags;
Come Laura, not another maiden lags.
No wilful squirrel wags,
225　The beasts and birds are fast asleep."
But Laura loitered still among the rushes,
And said the bank was steep.

And said the hour was early still,
The dew not fall'n, the wind not chill;
230　Listening ever, but not catching
The customary cry,
"Come buy, come buy,"
With its iterated jingle
Of sugar-baited words:
235　Not for all her watching

Once discerning even one goblin
Racing, whisking, tumbling, hobbling—
Let alone the herds
That used to tramp along the glen,
240　In groups or single,
Of brisk fruit-merchant men.
Till Lizzie urged, "O Laura, come;
I hear the fruit-call, but I dare not look:
You should not loiter longer at this brook:
245　Come with me home.
The stars rise, the moon bends her arc,
Each glowworm winks her spark,
Let us get home before the night grows dark:
For clouds may gather
250　Though this is summer weather,
Put out the lights and drench us thro';
Then if we lost our way what should we do?"

Laura turned cold as stone
To find her sister heard that cry alone,
255　That goblin cry,
"Come buy our fruits, come buy."
Must she then buy no more such dainty fruit?
Must she no more such succous° pasture find,   *juicy*
Gone deaf and blind?
260　Her tree of life drooped from the root:
She said not one word in her heart's sore ache;
But peering through the dimness, nought discerning,
Trudged home, her pitcher dripping all the way;
So crept to bed, and lay
265　Silent till Lizzie slept;
Then sat up in a passionate yearning,
And gnashed her teeth for baulked desire, and wept
As if her heart would break.

Day after day, night after night,
270　Laura kept watch in vain
In sullen silence of exceeding pain.
She never caught again the goblin cry,
"Come buy, come buy"—
She never spied the goblin men
275　Hawking their fruits along the glen:
But when the noon waxed bright
Her hair grew thin and grey;
She dwindled, as the fair full moon doth turn

To swift decay and burn
280 Her fire away.

One day remembering her kernel-stone
She set it by a wall that faced the south;
Dewed it with tears, hoped for a root,
Watched for a waxing shoot,
285 But there came none.
It never saw the sun,
It never felt the trickling moisture run:
While with sunk eyes and faded mouth
She dreamed of melons, as a traveller sees
290 False waves in desert drouth
With shade of leaf-crowned trees,
And burns the thirstier in the sandful breeze.

She no more swept the house,
Tended the fowl or cows,
295 Fetched honey, kneaded cakes of wheat,
Brought water from the brook:
But sat down listless in the chimney-nook
And would not eat.

Tender Lizzie could not bear
300 To watch her sister's cankerous care,
Yet not to share.
She night and morning
Caught the goblins' cry:
"Come buy our orchard fruits,
305 Come buy, come buy:"—
Beside the brook, along the glen,
She heard the tramp of goblin men,
The voice and stir
Poor Laura could not hear;
310 Longed to buy fruit to comfort her,
But feared to pay too dear.
She thought of Jeanie in her grave,
Who should have been a bride;
But who for joys brides hope to have
315 Fell sick and died
In her gay prime,
In earliest winter time,
With the first glazing rime,
With the first snow-fall of crisp Winter time.

320 Till Laura dwindling
Seemed knocking at Death's door.
Then Lizzie weighed no more
Better and worse;
But put a silver penny in her purse,
325 Kissed Laura, crossed the heath with clumps of furze
At twilight, halted by the brook:
And for the first time in her life
Began to listen and look.

Laughed every goblin
330 When they spied her peeping:
Came towards her hobbling,
Flying, running, leaping,
Puffing and blowing,
Chuckling, clapping, crowing.
335 Clucking and gobbling,
Mopping and mowing,
Full of airs and graces,
Pulling wry faces,
Demure grimaces,
340 Cat-like and rat-like,
Ratel- and wombat-like,
Snail-paced in a hurry,
Parrot-voiced and whistler,
Helter skelter, hurry skurry,
345 Chattering like magpies,
Fluttering like pigeons,
Gliding like fishes,—
Hugged her and kissed her:
Squeezed and caressed her:
350 Stretched up their dishes,
Panniers, and plates:
"Look at our apples
Russet and dun,
Bob at our cherries,
355 Bite at our peaches,
Citrons and dates,
Grapes for the asking,
Pears red with basking
Out in the sun,
360 Plums on their twigs;
Pluck them and suck them,—
Pomegranates, figs."

"Good folk," said Lizzie,
Mindful of Jeanie:
365 "Give me much and many"—
Held out her apron,
Tossed them her penny.
"Nay, take a seat with us,
Honour and eat with us,"
370 They answered grinning:
"Our feast is but beginning.
Night yet is early,
Warm and dew-pearly,
Wakeful and starry:
375 Such fruits as these
No man can carry;
Half their bloom would fly,
Half their dew would dry,
Half their flavour would pass by.
380 Sit down and feast with us,
Be welcome guest with us,
Cheer you and rest with us."—
"Thank you," said Lizzie: "But one waits
At home alone for me:
385 So without further parleying,°   discussion
If you will not sell me any
Of your fruits though much and many,
Give me back my silver penny
I tossed you for a fee."—
390 They began to scratch their pates,°   heads
No longer wagging, purring,
But visibly demurring,
Grunting and snarling.
One called her proud,
395 Cross-grained, uncivil;
Their tones waxed loud,
Their looks were evil.
Lashing their tails
They trod and hustled her,
400 Elbowed and jostled her,
Clawed with their nails,
Barking, mewing, hissing, mocking,
Tore her gown and soiled her stocking,
Twitched her hair out by the roots,
405 Stamped upon her tender feet,
Held her hands and squeezed their fruits
Against her mouth to make her eat.

White and golden Lizzie stood,
Like a lily in a flood,—
410 Like a rock of blue-veined stone
Lashed by tides obstreperously,—
Like a beacon left alone
In a hoary roaring sea,
Sending up a golden fire,—
415 Like a fruit-crowned orange tree
White with blossoms honey-sweet
Sore beset by wasp and bee,—
Like a royal virgin town
Topped with gilded dome and spire
420 Close beleaguered by a fleet
Mad to tug her standard down.

One may lead a horse to water,
Twenty cannot make him drink.
Though the goblins cuffed and caught her,
425 Coaxed and fought her,
Bullied and besought her,
Scratched her, pinched her black as ink,
Kicked and knocked her,
Mauled and mocked her,
430 Lizzie uttered not a word;
Would not open lip from lip
Lest they should cram a mouthful in:
But laughed in heart to feel the drip
Of juice that syruped all her face,
435 And lodged in dimples of her chin,
And streaked her neck which quaked like curd.
At last the evil people,
Worn out by her resistance,
Flung back her penny, kicked their fruit
440 Along whichever road they took,
Not leaving root or stone or shoot;
Some writhed into the ground,
Some dived into the brook
With ring and ripple,
445 Some scudded on the gale without a sound,
Some vanished in the distance.

In a smart, ache, tingle,
Lizzie went her way;
Knew not was it night or day;
450 Sprang up the bank, tore through the furze,

Threaded copse and dingle,°   *dell*
And heard her penny jingle
Bouncing in her purse,—
Its bounce was music to her ear.
455 She ran and ran
As if she feared some goblin man
Dogged her with gibe or curse
Or something worse:
But not one goblin skurried after,
460 Nor was she pricked by fear;
The kind heart made her windy-paced
That urged her home quite out of breath with haste
And inward laughter.

She cried, "Laura," up the garden,
465 "Did you miss me?
Come and kiss me.
Never mind my bruises,
Hug me, kiss me, suck my juices
Squeezed from goblin fruits for you,
470 Goblin pulp and goblin dew.
Eat me, drink me, love me;
Laura, make much of me;
For your sake I have braved the glen
And had to do with goblin merchant men."
475 Laura started from her chair,
Flung her arms up in the air,
Clutched her hair:
"Lizzie, Lizzie, have you tasted
For my sake the fruit forbidden?
480 Must your light like mine be hidden,
Your young life like mine be wasted,
Undone in mine undoing,
And ruined in my ruin,
Thirsty, cankered, goblin-ridden?"—
485 She clung about her sister,
Kissed and kissed and kissed her:
Tears once again
Refreshed her shrunken eyes,
Dropping like rain
490 After long sultry drouth;
Shaking with aguish[1] fear, and pain,
She kissed and kissed her with a hungry mouth.

Her lips began to scorch,
That juice was wormwood to her tongue,
495 She loathed the feast:
Writhing as one possessed she leaped and sung,
Rent all her robe, and wrung
Her hands in lamentable haste,
And beat her breast.
500 Her locks streamed like the torch
Borne by a racer at full speed,
Or like the mane of horses in their flight,
Or like an eagle when she stems the light
Straight toward the sun,
505 Or like a caged thing freed,
Or like a flying flag when armies run.

Swift fire spread through her veins, knocked at her
    heart,
Met the fire smouldering there
And overbore its lesser flame;
510 She gorged on bitterness without a name:
Ah! fool, to choose such part
Of soul-consuming care!
Sense failed in the mortal strife:
Like the watchtower of a town
515 Which an earthquake shatters down,
Like a lightning-stricken mast,
Like a wind-uprooted tree
Spun about,
Like a foam-topped waterspout
520 Cast down headlong in the sea,
She fell at last;
Pleasure past and anguish past,
Is it death or is it life?

Life out of death.
525 That night long Lizzie watched by her,
Counted her pulse's flagging stir,
Felt for her breath,
Held water to her lips, and cooled her face
With tears and fanning leaves.
530 But when the first birds chirped about their eaves,
And early reapers plodded to the place
Of golden sheaves,
And dew-wet grass
Bowed in the morning winds so brisk to pass,

---

[1] *aguish* Feverish.

535 And new buds with new day
Opened of cup-like lilies on the stream,
Laura awoke as from a dream,
Laughed in the innocent old way,
Hugged Lizzie but not twice or thrice;
540 Her gleaming locks showed not one thread of grey,
Her breath was sweet as May,
And light danced in her eyes.

Days, weeks, months, years
Afterwards, when both were wives
545 With children of their own;
Their mother-hearts beset with fears,
Their lives bound up in tender lives;
Laura would call the little ones
And tell them of her early prime,
550 Those pleasant days long gone
Of not-returning time:

Would talk about the haunted glen,
The wicked quaint fruit-merchant men,
Their fruits like honey to the throat
555 But poison in the blood;
(Men sell not such in any town):
Would tell them how her sister stood
In deadly peril to do her good,
And win the fiery antidote:
560 Then joining hands to little hands
Would bid them cling together,—
"For there is no friend like a sister
In calm or stormy weather;
To cheer one on the tedious way,
565 To fetch one if one goes astray,
To lift one if one totters down,
To strengthen whilst one stands."
—1862

In Context

Illustrating *Goblin Market*

The first edition of *Goblin Market* appeared in 1862 with a frontispiece by the author's brother, the Pre-Raphaelite painter and poet Dante Gabriel Rossetti. The round inset above the drawing of sisters Laura and Lizzie depicts the goblins carrying their fruits to market. Another notable edition was that of 1893, with art nouveau illustrations by artist and writer Laurence Housman (brother of poet A.E. Housman).

1862 Macmillan edition—illustration by D.G. Rossetti.

Illustration by Laurence Housman from the 1893
Macmillan edition.

A Triad

Three sang of love together: one with lips
    Crimson, with cheeks and bosom in a glow,
Flushed to the yellow hair and finger tips;
    And one there sang who soft and smooth as snow
5   Bloomed like a tinted hyacinth at a show;

And one was blue with famine after love,
    Who like a harpstring snapped rang harsh and low
The burden of what those were singing of.
One shamed herself in love; one temperately
10   Grew gross in soulless love, a sluggish wife;
One famished died for love. Thus two of three
    Took death for love and won him after strife;
One droned in sweetness like a fattened bee:
    All on the threshold, yet all short of life.
—1862

Remember

Remember me when I am gone away,
    Gone far away into the silent land;
    When you can no more hold me by the hand,
Nor I half turn to go yet turning stay.
5   Remember me when no more day by day
    You tell me of our future that you planned:
    Only remember me; you understand
It will be late then to counsel or to pray.
Yet if you should forget me for a while
10   And afterwards remember, do not grieve:
    For if the darkness and corruption leave
    A vestige of the thoughts that once I had,
Better by far you should forget and smile
    Than that you should remember and be sad.
—1862

A Birthday

My heart is like a singing bird
    Whose nest is in a watered shoot;
My heart is like an apple tree
    Whose boughs are bent with thickset fruit;
5   My heart is like a rainbow shell
    That paddles in a halcyon° sea;   calm
My heart is gladder than all these
    Because my love is come to me.

Raise me a dais of silk and down;
10   Hang it with vair° and purple dyes;   squirrel fur
Carve it in doves and pomegranates,

And peacocks with a hundred eyes;
Work it in gold and silver grapes,
    In leaves, and silver fleurs-de-lys;
15 Because the birthday of my life
    Is come, my love is come to me.
—1861

After Death

The curtains were half drawn, the floor was swept
    And strewn with rushes, rosemary and may
Lay thick upon the bed on which I lay,
Where thro' the lattice ivy-shadows crept.
5 He leaned above me, thinking that I slept
    And could not hear him; but I heard him say:
    "Poor child, poor child": and as he turned away
Came a deep silence, and I knew he wept.
He did not touch the shroud, or raise the fold
10   That hid my face, or take my hand in his,
    Or ruffle the smooth pillows for my head:
    He did not love me living; but once dead
He pitied me; and very sweet it is
To know he still is warm tho' I am cold.
—1862

An Apple-Gathering

I plucked pink blossoms from mine apple tree
    And wore them all that evening in my hair:
Then in due season when I went to see
    I found no apples there.

5 With dangling basket all along the grass
    As I had come I went the selfsame track:
My neighbours mocked me while they saw me pass
    So empty-handed back.

Lilian and Lilias smiled in trudging by,
10   Their heaped-up basket teazed me like a jeer;
Sweet-voiced they sang beneath the sunset sky,
    Their mother's home was near.

Plump Gertrude passed me with her basket full,
    A stronger hand than hers helped it along;
15 A voice talked with her thro' the shadows cool
    More sweet to me than song.

Ah Willie, Willie, was my love less worth
    Than apples with their green leaves piled above?
I counted rosiest apples on the earth
20   Of far less worth than love.

So once it was with me you stooped to talk
    Laughing and listening in this very lane;
To think that by this way we used to walk
    We shall not walk again!

25 I let my neighbours pass me, ones and twos
    And groups; the latest said the night grew chill,
And hastened: but I loitered, while the dews
    Fell fast I loitered still.
—1862

Echo

Come to me in the silence of the night;
    Come in the speaking silence of a dream;
Come with soft rounded cheeks and eyes as bright
    As sunlight on a stream;
        Come back in tears,
5 O memory, hope, love of finished years.

O dream how sweet, too sweet, too bitter sweet,
    Whose wakening should have been in Paradise,
Where souls brimfull of love abide and meet;
    Where thirsting longing eyes
10   Watch the slow door
That opening, letting in, lets out no more.

Yet come to me in dreams, that I may live
    My very life again tho' cold in death:
Come back to me in dreams, that I may give
15   Pulse for pulse, breath for breath:
        Speak low, lean low,
As long ago, my love, how long ago.
—1862

Winter: My Secret

I tell my secret? No indeed, not I:
  Perhaps some day, who knows?
But not today; it froze, and blows, and snows,
And you're too curious: fie!
5   You want to hear it? well:
  Only, my secret's mine, and I won't tell.

Or, after all, perhaps there's none:
Suppose there is no secret after all,
  But only just my fun.
10 Today's a nipping day, a biting day;
  In which one wants a shawl,
A veil, a cloak, and other wraps:
I cannot ope to every one who taps,
And let the draughts come whistling thro' my hall;
15 Come bounding and surrounding me,
Come buffeting, astounding me,
Nipping and clipping thro' my wraps and all.
I wear my mask for warmth: who ever shows
  His nose to Russian snows
20 To be pecked at by every wind that blows?
You would not peck? I thank you for good will,
Believe, but leave that truth untested still.

Spring's an expansive time: yet I don't trust
  March with its peck of dust,
25 Nor April with its rainbow-crowned brief showers,
  Nor even May, whose flowers
One frost may wither thro' the sunless hours.

Perhaps some languid summer day,
  When drowsy birds sing less and less,
30 And golden fruit is ripening to excess,
If there's not too much sun nor too much cloud,
And the warm wind is neither still nor loud,
  Perhaps my secret I may say,
    Or you may guess.
  —1862

"No, Thank You, John"

I never said I loved you, John:
  Why will you teaze me day by day,
And wax a weariness to think upon
  With always "do" and "pray"?

5   You know I never loved you, John;
  No fault of mine made me your toast:[1]
Why will you haunt me with a face as wan
  As shows an hour-old ghost?

I dare say Meg or Moll would take
10   Pity upon you, if you'd ask:
And pray don't remain single for my sake
  Who can't perform that task.

I have no heart?—Perhaps I have not;
  But then you're mad to take offence
15 That I don't give you what I have not got:
  Use your own common sense.

Let bygones be bygones:
  Don't call me false, who owed not to be true:
I'd rather answer "No" to fifty Johns
20   Than answer "Yes" to you.

Let's mar our pleasant days no more,
  Songbirds of passage, days of youth:
Catch at today, forget the days before:
  I'll wink at your untruth.

25 Let us strike hands as hearty friends;
  No more, no less; and friendship's good:
Only don't keep in view ulterior ends,
  And points not understood

In open treaty. Rise above
30   Quibbles and shuffling off and on:
Here's friendship for you if you like; but love,—
  No, thank you, John.
  —1862

---

[1] *your toast* I.e., the woman to whom John would raise a glass when toasting his lady.

A Pause of Thought

I looked for that which is not, nor can be,
    And hope deferred made my heart sick in truth:
But years must pass before a hope of youth
    Is resigned utterly.

5 I watched and waited with a steadfast will:
    And though the object seemed to flee away
That I so longed for, ever day by day
    I watched and waited still.

Sometimes I said, "This thing shall be no more;
10   My expectation wearies and shall cease;
I will resign it now and be at peace:"
    Yet never gave it o'er.

Sometimes I said, "It is an empty name
    I long for; to a name why should I give
15 The peace of all the days I have to live?"—
    Yet gave it all the same.

Alas, thou foolish one! alike unfit
    For healthy joy and salutary pain:
Thou knowest the chase useless, and again
20   Turnest to follow it.
    —1848

Song

She sat and sang alway
    By the green margin of a stream,
Watching the fishes leap and play
    Beneath the glad sunbeam.

5 I sat and wept alway
    Beneath the moon's most shadowy beam,
Watching the blossoms of the May
    Weep leaves into the stream.

I wept for memory;
10   She sang for hope that is so fair:
My tears were swallowed by the sea;
    Her songs died on the air.
    —1862

Song

When I am dead, my dearest,
    Sing no sad songs for me;
Plant thou no roses at my head,
    Nor shady cypress tree.
5 Be the green grass above me
    With showers and dewdrops wet;
And if thou wilt, remember,
    And if thou wilt, forget.

I shall not see the shadows,
10   I shall not feel the rain;
I shall not hear the nightingale
    Sing on as if in pain.
And dreaming through the twilight
    That doth not rise nor set,
15 Haply° I may remember,   *by chance*
    And haply may forget.
    —1862

Dead before Death

Ah! changed and cold, how changed and very cold!
    With stiffened smiling lips and cold calm eyes:
    Changed, yet the same; much knowing, little wise;
This was the promise of the days of old!
5 Grown hard and stubborn in the ancient mould,
    Grown rigid in the sham of lifelong lies:
    We hoped for better things as years would rise,
But it is over as a tale once told.
All fallen the blossom that no fruitage bore,
10   All lost the present and the future time,
All lost, all lost, the lapse that went before:
So lost till death shut-to the opened door,
    So lost from chime to everlasting chime,
So cold and lost for ever evermore.
    —1862

Monna Innominata [1]
A Sonnet of Sonnets

Beatrice, immortalized by "*altissimo poeta ... cotanto amante*";[2] Laura, celebrated by a great though an inferior bard[3]—have alike paid the exceptional penalty of exceptional honour, and have come down to us resplendent with charms, but (at least, to my apprehension) scant of attractiveness.

These heroines of worldwide fame were preceded by a bevy of unnamed ladies "*donne innominate*" sung by a school of less conspicuous poets; and in that land and that period which gave simultaneous birth to Catholics, to Albigenses, and to Troubadours,[4] one can imagine many a lady as sharing her lover's poetic aptitude, while the barrier between them might be one held sacred by both, yet not such as to render mutual love incompatible with mutual honour.

Had such a lady spoken for herself, the portrait left us might have appeared more tender, if less dignified, than any drawn even by a devoted friend. Or had the Great Poetess[5] of our own day and nation only been unhappy instead of happy, her circumstances would have invited her to bequeath to us, in lieu of the "Portuguese Sonnets," an inimitable "*donna innominata*" drawn not from fancy but from feeling, and worthy to occupy a niche beside Beatrice and Laura.

1

"Lo dì che han detto a' dolci amici addio."—DANTE
"Amor, con quanto sforzo oggi mi vinci!"—PETRARCA [6]

Come back to me, who wait and watch for you:—
    Or come not yet, for it is over then,
        And long it is before you come again,
So far between my pleasures are and few.

---

[1] *Monna Innominata*   Italian: Unnamed Lady.

[2] *altissimo poeta ... cotanto amante*   Italian: loftiest poet ... equally great lover (Italian). Rossetti refers to Italian poet Dante Alighieri (1265–1321), whose muse was Beatrice.

[3] *great ... bard*   Italian poet Francesco Petrarca (1304–74) wrote many love songs to Laura.

[4] *Albigenses*   Albigensians were members of a religious sect of the twelfth and thirteenth centuries; *Troubadours* Wandering lyric poets of the eleventh to thirteenth centuries.

[5] *Great Poetess*   Elizabeth Barrett Browning.

[6] *DANTE*   From *Purgatorio* 8.3: "Who in the morn have bid sweet friends farewell"; *PETRARCA* From *Canzone* 85.12: "Love, with what forces you conquer me now!"

5 While, when you come not, what I do I do
        Thinking "Now when he comes," my sweetest "when":
        For one man is my world of all the men
This wide world holds; O love, my world is you.
    Howbeit, to meet you grows almost a pang
10   Because the pang of parting comes so soon;
        My hope hangs waning, waxing, like a moon
            Between the heavenly days on which we meet:
    Ah me, but where are now the songs I sang
    When life was sweet because you called them sweet?

2

"Era già l'ora che volge il desio."—DANTE
"Ricorro al tempo ch' io vi vidi prima."—PETRARCA [7]

I wish I could remember that first day,
    First hour, first moment of your meeting me,
    If bright or dim the season, it might be
Summer or winter for aught I can say;
5 So unrecorded did it slip away,
        So blind was I to see and to foresee,
        So dull to mark the budding of my tree
That would not blossom yet for many a May.
    If only I could recollect it, such
10   A day of days! I let it come and go
        As traceless as a thaw of bygone snow;
    It seemed to mean so little, meant so much;
    If only now I could recall that touch,
        First touch of hand in hand—Did one but know!

3

"O ombre vane, fuor che ne l'aspetto!"—DANTE
"Immaginata guida la conduce."—PETRARCA [8]

I dream of you to wake: would that I might
    Dream of you and not wake but slumber on;
        Nor find with dreams the dear companion gone,
As summer ended summer birds take flight.
5 In happy dreams I hold you full in sight,
        I blush again who waking look so wan;

---

[7] *DANTE*   From *Purgatorio* 8.1: "Now was the hour that wakens fond desire"; *PETRARCA* From Sonnet 20.3: "I remember when I saw you for the first time."

[8] *DANTE*   From *Purgatorio* 2.79: "Oh vain shadows, except in outward aspect"; *PETRARCA* From *Canzone* 277.9: "An imagined guide leads her."

Brighter than sunniest day that ever shone,
In happy dreams your smile makes day of night.
Thus only in a dream we are at one,
    Thus only in a dream we give and take
        The faith that maketh rich who take or give;
    If thus to sleep is sweeter than to wake,
        To die were surely sweeter than to live,
Tho' there be nothing new beneath the sun.

10

4

"Poca favilla gran fiamma seconda."—DANTE
"Ogni altra cosa, ogni pensier va fore,
    E sol ivi con voi rimansi amore."—PETRARCA[1]

I loved you first: but afterwards your love,
    Outsoaring mine, sang such a loftier song
As drowned the friendly cooings of my dove.
    Which owes the other most? My love was long,
        And yours one moment seemed to wax more strong;
    I loved and guessed at you, you construed me
And loved me for what might or might not be—
    Nay, weights and measures do us both a wrong.
For verily love knows not "mine" or "thine";
    With separate "I" and "thou" free love has done,
        For one is both and both are one in love:
Rich love knows nought of "thine that is not mine";
    Both have the strength and both the length
        thereof,
    Both of us, of the love which makes us one.

5

10

5

"Amor che a nullo amato amar perdona."—DANTE
"Amor m'addusse in sì gioiosa spene."—PETRARCA[2]

O my heart's heart, and you who are to me
    More than myself myself, God be with you,
    Keep you in strong obedience leal° and true   loyal
To Him whose noble service setteth free;
    Give you all good we see or can foresee,
        Make your joys many and your sorrows few,

5

Bless you in what you bear and what you do,
Yea, perfect you as He would have you be.
So much for you; but what for me, dear friend?
    To love you without stint and all I can
Today, tomorrow, world without an end;
        To love you much and yet to love you more,
    As Jordan at his flood sweeps either shore;
Since woman is the helpmeet made for man.

10

6

"Or puoi la quantitate
Comprender de l'amor che a te mi scalda."—DANTE
"Non vo' che da tal nodo amor mi sciolglia."—PETRARCA[3]

Trust me, I have not earned your dear rebuke,
    I love, as you would have me, God the most;
        Would lose not Him, but you, must one be lost,
Nor with Lot's wife cast back a faithless look,[4]
Unready to forego what I forsook;
    This say I, having counted up the cost,
        This, tho' I be the feeblest of God's host,
The sorriest sheep Christ shepherds with His crook.
Yet while I love my God the most, I deem
    That I can never love you overmuch;
        I love Him more, so let me love you too;
    Yea, as I apprehend it, love is such
I cannot love you if I love not Him,
    I cannot love Him if I love not you.

5

10

7

"Qui primavera sempre ed ogni frutto."—DANTE
"Ragionando con meco ed io con lui."—PETRARCA[5]

"Love me, for I love you"—and answer me,
    "Love me, for I love you": so shall we stand
    As happy equals in the flowering land
Of love, that knows not a dividing sea.
Love builds the house on rock and not on sand,
    Love laughs what while the winds rave desperately;

5

---

[1] *DANTE* From *Paradiso* 1.34: "From a small spark a great flame rises"; *PETRARCA* From *Canzone* 72.44–45: "All other hopes, all other thoughts are gone, and love with you remains there alone."

[2] *DANTE* From *Inferno* 5.103: "Love, that denial takes from none beloved"; *PETRARCA* From Sonnet 56.11: "Love urged me in this gladness to believe."

[3] *DANTE* From *Purgatorio* 21.133–34: "Now has thou proved the force and ardor of the love I bear thee"; *PETRARCA* From *Canzone* 59.17: "I do not wish love to release me from this knot."

[4] *Lot's wife … look* See Genesis 19.26: "[Lot's] wife looked back from behind him, and she became a pillar of salt."

[5] *DANTE* From *Purgatorio* 28.143: "Perpetual spring and every fruit"; *PETRARCA* From *Canzone* 35.14: "Speaking with me and I with him."

And who hath found love's citadel unmanned?
　　And who hath held in bonds love's liberty?—
My heart's a coward tho' my words are brave—
10　　We meet so seldom, yet we surely part
　　So often; there's a problem for your art!
Still I find comfort in his Book, who saith,
Tho' jealousy be cruel as the grave,
And death be strong, yet love is strong as death.[1]

8

"Come dicesse a Dio, D'altro non calme."—DANTE
"Spero trovar pietà non che perdono."—PETRARCA[2]

"I, if I perish, perish"—Esther spake:[3]
　　And bride of life or death she made her fair
　　In all the lustre of her perfumed hair
And smiles that kindle longing but to slake.
5　She put on pomp of loveliness, to take
　　Her husband through his eyes at unaware;
　　She spread abroad her beauty for a snare,
Harmless as doves and subtle as a snake.
She trapped him with one mesh of silken hair,
10　　She vanquished him by wisdom of her wit,
　　　　And built her people's house that it should
　　　　　　stand:—
　　　　If I might take my life so in my hand,
And for my love to Love put up my prayer,
And for love's sake by Love be granted it!

9

"O dignitosa coscienza e netta!"—DANTE
"Spirto più acceso di virtuti ardenti."—PETRARCA[4]

Thinking of you, and all that was, and all
　　That might have been and now can never be,
　　I feel your honoured excellence, and see
Myself unworthy of the happier call:
5　For woe is me who walk so apt to fall,
　　So apt to shrink afraid, so apt to flee,
　　Apt to lie down and die (ah woe is me!)
Faithless and hopeless turning to the wall.
And yet not hopeless quite nor faithless quite,
10　Because not loveless; love may toil all night,
　　But take at morning; wrestle till the break
　　　　Of day, but then wield power with God and
　　　　　　man:—
　　　　So take I heart of grace as best I can,
Ready to spend and be spent for your sake.

10

"Con miglior corso e con migliore stella."—DANTE
"La vita fugge e non s'arresta un' ora."—PETRARCA[5]

Time flies, hope flags, life plies a wearied wing;
　　Death following hard on life gains ground apace;
　　Faith runs with each and rears an eager face,
Outruns the rest, makes light of everything,
5　Spurns earth, and still finds breath to pray and sing;
　　While love ahead of all uplifts his praise,
　　Still asks for grace and still gives thanks for grace,
Content with all day brings and night will bring.
Life wanes; and when love folds his wings above
10　　Tired hope, and less we feel his conscious pulse,
　　　　Let us go fall asleep, dear friend, in peace:
　　　　A little while, and age and sorrow cease;
　　A little while, and life reborn annuls
Loss and decay and death, and all is love.

---

[1] *his Book ... death* See The Song of Solomon 6: "Set me as a seal upon your heart, as a seal upon your arm; for love is strong as death, passion fierce as the grave."

[2] *DANTE* From *Purgatorio* 8.12: "As if telling God, 'I care for nothing else'"; *PETRARCA* From *Canzone* 1.8: "I hope to find pity, not just forgiveness."

[3] *I ... spake* From Esther 4.16, in which Queen Esther says to Mordecai, before donning beautiful robes and appealing to her husband to cease his mission to kill her people, the Jews: "Go, gather together all the Jews ... and neither eat nor drink three days, night or day: I also and my maidens will fast likewise; and so will I go in unto the king, which is not according to the law: and if I perish, I perish."

[4] *DANTE* From *Purgatorio* 3.8: "Oh conscience clear and upright!"; *PETRARCA* From *Canzone* 283.3: "Spirit dazzling with blazing virtues."

[5] *DANTE* From *Paradiso* 1.40: "In best course and in happiest constellation"; *PETRARCA* From *Canzone* 272.1: "Life flies and doesn't stay for an hour."

11

"Vien dietro a me e lascia dir le genti."—DANTE
"Contando i casi della vita nostra."—PETRARCA[1]

Many in aftertimes will say of you
    "He loved her"—while of me what will they say?
    Not that I loved you more than just in play,
For fashion's sake as idle women do.
5   Even let them prate; who know not what we knew
    Of love and parting in exceeding pain,
    Of parting hopeless here to meet again,
Hopeless on earth, and heaven is out of view.
But by my heart of love laid bare to you,
10   My love that you can make not void nor vain,
Love that foregoes you but to claim anew
        Beyond this passage of the gate of death,
    I charge you at the Judgment make it plain
        My love of you was life and not a breath.

12

"Amor, che ne la mente mi ragiona."—DANTE
"Amor vien nel bel viso di costei."—PETRARCA[2]

If there be any one can take my place
    And make you happy whom I grieve to grieve,
    Think not that I can grudge it, but believe
I do commend you to that nobler grace,
5   That readier wit than mine, that sweeter face;
    Yea, since your riches make me rich, conceive
    I too am crowned, while bridal crowns I weave,
And thread the bridal dance with jocund° pace.   merry
For if I did not love you, it might be
10   That I should grudge you some one dear delight;
        But since the heart is yours that was mine own,
    Your pleasure is my pleasure, right my right,
    Your honourable freedom makes me free,
        And you companioned I am not alone.

13

"E drizzeremo glí occhi al Primo Amore."—DANTE
"Ma trovo peso non de le mie braccia."—PETRARCA[3]

If I could trust mine own self with your fate,
    Shall I not rather trust it in God's hand?
    Without Whose Will one lily doth not stand,
Nor sparrow fall at His appointed date;
5   Who numbereth the innumerable sand,
Who weighs the wind and water with a weight,
To Whom the world is neither small nor great,
    Whose knowledge foreknew every plan we planned.
Searching my heart for all that touches you,
10   I find there only love and love's goodwill
Helpless to help and impotent to do,
        Of understanding dull, of sight most dim;
        And therefore I commend you back to Him
    Whose love your love's capacity can fill.

14

"E la Sua Volontade è nostra pace."—DANTE
"Sol con questi pensier, con altre chiome."—PETRARCA[4]

Youth gone, and beauty gone if ever there
    Dwelt beauty in so poor a face as this;
    Youth gone and beauty, what remains of bliss?
I will not bind fresh roses in my hair,
5   To shame a cheek at best but little fair,—
    Leave youth his roses, who can bear a thorn,—
I will not seek for blossoms anywhere,
    Except such common flowers as blow with corn.[5]
Youth gone and beauty gone, what doth remain?
10   The longing of a heart pent up forlorn,
        A silent heart whose silence loves and longs;
        The silence of a heart which sang its songs
    While youth and beauty made a summer morn,
Silence of love that cannot sing again.
—1881

---

[1]   *DANTE*   From *Purgatorio* 5.13: "Come after me, and leave behind the people's babblings"; *PETRARCA* From *Canzone* 285.12: "Telling of the changes in our lives."

[2]   *DANTE*   From *Purgatorio* 2.112: "Love that discourses in my thoughts"; *PETRARCA* From *Canzone* 13.2: "Love appears in the beautiful face of this lady."

[3]   *DANTE*   From *Paradiso* 32.142: "And our eyes will turn unto the first Love"; *PETRARCA* From Sonnet 20.5: "The burden I find too great a weight for my arms."

[4]   *DANTE*   From *Paradiso* 3.85: "And in his will is our tranquility"; *PETRARCA* From *Canzone* 30.32: "Alone with these thoughts, with time-altered locks of hair."

[5]   *corn*   Grain.

Cobwebs

It is a land with neither night nor day,
Nor heat nor cold, nor any wind, nor rain,
   Nor hills nor valleys; but one even plain
Stretches thro' long unbroken miles away:
5 While thro' the sluggish air a twilight grey
   Broodeth; no moons or seasons wax and wane,
   No ebb and flow are there along the main,
No bud-time no leaf-falling there for aye,°   *any*
No ripple on the sea, no shifting sand,
10   No beat of wings to stir the stagnant space,
No pulse of life thro' all the loveless land:
And loveless sea; no trace of days before,
   No guarded home, no toil-won resting place
No future hope no fear for evermore.
        —1896 (WRITTEN 1855)

In an Artist's Studio

One face[1] looks out from all his canvasses,
  One selfsame figure sits or walks or leans:
   We found her hidden just behind those screens,
That mirror gave back all her loveliness.
5 A queen in opal or in ruby dress,
   A nameless girl in freshest summer-greens,
   A saint, an angel;—every canvass means
The same one meaning, neither more nor less.
He feeds upon her face by day and night,
10   And she with true kind eyes looks back on him,
Fair as the moon and joyful as the light:
   Not wan with waiting, nor with sorrow dim;
Not as she is, but was when hope shone bright;
   Not as she is, but as she fills his dream.
        —1896

Dante Gabriel Rossetti's *Beata Beatrix* (1864–70).

Promises like Pie-Crust [2]

Promise me no promises,
  So will I not promise you;
Keep we both our liberties,
  Never false and never true:
5 Let us hold the die uncast,
   Free to come as free to go;
For I cannot know your past,
  And of mine what can you know?

---

[1] *One face*   I.e., Elizabeth (Lizzie) Siddal's. Siddal (1829–62) was
D.G. Rossetti's model for *Beata Beatrix* and many other paintings;
the two eventually married. She was a poet and artist in her own
right.

[2] *Promises like Pie-Crust*   See Jonathan Swift's comment: "Promises
and pie-crust are made to be broken."

You, so warm, may once have been
10   Warmer towards another one;
I, so cold, may once have seen
    Sunlight, once have felt the sun:
Who shall show us if it was
    Thus indeed in time of old?
15 Fades the image from the glass
    And the fortune is not told.

If you promised, you might grieve
    For lost liberty again;
If I promised, I believe
20   I should fret to break the chain:
Let us be the friends we were,
    Nothing more but nothing less;
Many thrive on frugal fare
    Who would perish of excess.
—1896 (WRITTEN 1861)

In Progress

Ten years ago it seemed impossible
    That she should ever grow so calm as this,
    With self-remembrance in her warmest kiss
And dim dried eyes like an exhausted well.
5 Slow-speaking when she has some fact to tell,
    Silent with long-unbroken silences,
    Centred in self yet not unpleased to please,

Gravely monotonous like a passing bell.
Mindful of drudging daily common things,
10   Patient at pastime, patient at her work,
Wearied perhaps but strenuous certainly.
Sometimes I fancy we may one day see
    Her head shoot forth seven stars from where they
        lurk
And her eyes lightnings and her shoulders wings.
—1896

Sleeping at Last

Sleeping at last, the trouble & tumult over,
  Sleeping at last, the struggle & horror past,
Cold & white out of sight of friend & of lover
Sleeping at last.

5 No more a tired heart downcast or overcast,
No more pangs that wring or shifting fears that hover,
Sleeping at last in a dreamless sleep locked fast.

Fast asleep. Singing birds in their leafy cover
Cannot wake her, nor shake her gusty blast.
10 Under the purple thyme & the purple clover
Sleeping at last.
—1896

LEWIS CARROLL
1832 – 1898

Lewis Carroll (the pseudonym of Charles Dodgson) created some of the most beloved and enduring literature for children ever written in English. *Alice's Adventures in Wonderland* and *Through the Looking-Glass* have remained perennially popular since their first publication. His famously frustrated protagonist, who engages in bewildering exchanges with such memorable characters as the Mad Hatter, the Cheshire Cat, the March Hare, and the Mock Turtle, is as familiar a figure as any character in nineteenth-century fiction.

Charles Lutwidge Dodgson was the third of eleven children born to Frances Jane Lutwidge and the Reverend Charles Dodgson, who was a mathematician and later a curate in Daresbury, Cheshire. Because they lived in a remote village, the Dodgson children were largely schooled at home and relied on one another for amusement; Charles contributed many stories and drawings to their various family magazines. He became a fine student when he later entered boarding school, winning many awards and scholarships.

Dodgson continued to excel at Oxford University, where he followed in his father's footsteps and took first place honors in mathematics. He thereafter spent almost his entire life as a lecturer in mathematics at Oxford, where he was given a lifetime fellowship, with the stipulation that he enter the ministry and refrain from marrying. During his early years there, he took up the then-new art of photography as a hobby and devoted himself to taking exquisite photographs—primarily of children, although he later also became known for his portraits of famous literary figures, Alfred, Lord Tennyson and Dante Gabriel Rossetti among them.

Dodgson eventually became acquainted with the family of Henry Liddell, who was then Dean of Christ Church College. As he had done with many other children, Dodgson endeared himself to the three Liddell daughters by weaving elaborate tales for their amusement. On one occasion, Dodgson and a friend took advantage of a beautiful summer's day to go boating down the Thames with the Liddell girls. During the outing Dodgson began making up the story of Alice's adventures underground, wherein Alice goes down a rabbit hole and meets various characters that both fascinate and confound her. He later often looked back upon this day wistfully, as when he wrote of the "birth" of the Alice of his tales: "I can call it up almost as clearly as if it were yesterday—the cloudless blue above, the watery mirror below, the boat drifting idly on its way, the tinkle of the drops that fell from the oars … the three eager faces, hungry for news of fairy-land, and who would not be said 'nay' to: from whose lips 'Tell us a story, please,' had all the stern immutability of Fate!" The poet W.H. Auden later called July 4, the day of this 1862 outing, "as memorable a day in the history of literature as it is in American history."

After Dodgson had complied with Alice Liddell's request to write up the story for her, Henry Kingsley (brother of novelist Charles Kingsley) saw the manuscript and persuaded him to publish it. Having already published several books on mathematics under his own name, he took the name Lewis, which he anglicized from "Ludovicus," the Latin word for "Lutwidge," and Carroll from "Carolus," Latin for "Charles." *Alice's Adventures in Wonderland* appeared in 1865 with illustrations by *Punch* cartoonist John Tenniel. From that point on, Lewis Carroll's fame far surpassed that of

Charles Dodgson. In 1872 he published the sequel *Through the Looking-Glass and What Alice Found There*, which continued the tale of Alice as she passes through a mirror and finds herself engaged as a pawn in a topsy-turvy game of chess. (By this time, sadly, he was entirely estranged from the Liddells.)

Carroll later wrote three books of nonsense poems including *The Hunting of the Snark* (1876). He also published *Sylvie and Bruno* and *Sylvie and Bruno Concluded* (1889 and 1893), but the novel and its sequel never achieved the fame of the Alice series. The author died of bronchitis in 1898; he is buried in a cemetery near the home he bought for his family in Surrey.

⌘ ⌘ ⌘

Verses Recited by Humpty Dumpty[1]

In winter when the fields are white,
I sing this song for your delight.

In spring, when woods are getting green,
I'll try and tell you what I mean.

5   In summer, when the days are long,
Perhaps you'll understand the song.

In autumn, when the leaves are brown,
Take pen and ink and write it down.

I sent a message to the fish:
10   I told them "This is what I wish."

The little fishes of the sea,
They sent an answer back to me.

The little fishes' answer was
"We cannot do it, sir, because."

15   I sent to them again to say
"It will be better to obey."

The fishes answered with a grin,
"Why, what a temper you are in!"

I told them once, I told them twice;
20   They would not listen to advice.

I took a kettle large and new,
Fit for the deed I had to do.

My heart went hop, my heart went thump;
I filled the kettle at the pump.

25   Then someone came to me and said,
"The little fishes are in bed."

I said to him, I said it plain,
"Then you must wake them up again."

I said it very loud and clear;
30   I went and shouted in his ear.

But he was very stiff and proud;
He said, "You needn't shout so loud!"

And he was very proud and stiff;
He said, "I'd go and wake them, if ——"

35   I took a corkscrew from the shelf;
I went to wake them up myself.

And when I found the door was locked,
I pulled and pushed and kicked and knocked.

And when I found the door was shut,
40   I tried to turn the handle, but ——
("That's all," said Humpty Dumpty.)
      —1872

---

[1] *Verses ... Dumpty* From *Through the Looking-Glass and What Alice Found There*, Ch. 6: "Humpty Dumpty."

Jabberwocky[1]

'Twas brillig and the slithy toves
    Did gyre and gimble in the wabe;
All mimsy were the borogroves,
    And the mome raths outgrabe.

5 "Beware the Jabberwock, my son!
    The jaws that bite, the claws that catch!
Beware the Jubjub bird, and shun
    The frumious Bandersnatch!"

He took his vorpal sword in hand:
10   Long time the manxome foe he sought—
So rested he by the Tumtum tree.
    And stood awhile in thought.

And as in uffish thought he stood,
    The Jabberwock, with eyes of flame,

15 Came whiffling through the tulgey wood,
    And burbled as it came!

One, two! One, two! And through and through
    The vorpal blade went snicker-snack!
He left it dead, and with its head
20   He went galumphing back.

"And hast thou slain the Jabberwock?
    Come to my arms, my beamish boy!
O frabjous day! Callooh! Callay!"
    He chortled in his joy.

25 'Twas brillig and the slithy toves
    Did gyre and gimble in the wabe;
All mimsy were the borogroves,
    And the mome raths outgrabe.
                                    —1872

_____

IN CONTEXT

"Jabberwocky"

The poem "Jabberwocky" appears in the first chapter of *Through the Looking-Glass and What Alice Found There*. The first of the following excerpts provides the surrounding context in that chapter; the second is an excerpt from later in the book, when the poem is again discussed.

from Lewis Carroll, *Through the Looking-Glass and What Alice Found There* (1872)

from CHAPTER 1: LOOKING-GLASS HOUSE

There was a book lying near Alice on the table, and while she sat watching the White King (for she was still a little anxious about him, and had the ink all ready to throw over him, in case he fainted again), she turned over the leaves, to find some part that she could read, "—for it's all in some language I don't know," she said to herself.

It was like this.

        YKCOWREBBAJ

    sevot yhtils eht dna ,gillirb sawT'
    ebaw eht ni elbmig dna eryg diD
    ,sevorgorob eht erew ysmim llA
    .ebargtuo shtar emom eht dnA

_____

[1] *Jabberwocky* From *Through the Looking-Glass and What Alice Found There*, Ch. 1: "Looking-Glass House."

She puzzled over this for some time, but at last a bright thought struck her. "Why, it's a looking-glass book, of course! And if I hold it up to a glass, the words will all go the right way again."

This was the poem that Alice read.

[Here the poem appears.]

"It seems very pretty," she said when she had finished it, "but it's rather hard to understand." (You see she didn't like to confess, even to herself, that she couldn't make it out at all.) "Somehow it seems to fill my head with ideas—only I don't exactly know what they are! However, somebody killed something: that's clear, at any rate—."

from CHAPTER 6: HUMPTY DUMPTY

"You seem very clever at explaining words, sir," said Alice. "Would you kindly tell me the meaning of the poem called 'Jabberwocky'?"

"Let's hear it," said Humpty Dumpty. "I can explain all the poems that ever were invented—and a good many that haven't been invented just yet."

This sounded very hopeful, so Alice repeated the first verse:

"'Twas brillig, and the slithy toves
    Did gyre and gimble in the wabe;
All mimsy were the borogroves,
    And the mome raths outgrabe."

"That's enough to begin with," Humpty Dumpty interrupted: "there are plenty of hard words there. '*Brillig*' means four o'clock in the afternoon—the time when you begin *broiling* things for dinner."

"That'll do very well," said Alice: "and '*slithy*'?"

"Well, '*slithy*' means 'lithe and slimy.' 'Lithe' is the same as 'active.' You see it's like a portmanteau[1]—there are two meanings packed up into one word."

"I see it now," Alice remarked thoughtfully: "and what about '*toves*'?"

"Well, '*toves*' are something like badgers—they're something like lizards—and they're something like corkscrews."

"They must be very curious-looking creatures."

"They are that," said Humpty Dumpty: "also they made their nests under sundials—also they live on cheese."

"And what's to '*gyre*' and to '*gimble*'?"

"To '*gyre*' is to go round and round like a gyroscope. To '*gimble*' is to make holes like a gimlet."[2]

"And 'the *wabe*' is the grass plot round a sundial, I suppose?" said Alice, surprised at her own ingenuity.

"Of course it is. It's called '*wabe*,' you know, because it goes a long way before it, and a long way behind it——"

"And a long way beyond it on each side," Alice added.

"Exactly so. Well, then, '*mimsy*' is 'flimsy and miserable' (there's another portmanteau for you). And a '*borogrove*' is a thin, shabby-looking bird with its feathers sticking out all round—something like a live mop."

"And then '*mome raths*'?" said Alice. "If I'm not giving you too much trouble."

---

[1] *portmanteau* Leather carrying case; "portmanteau" has since entered the English language in the sense to which Humpty Dumpty refers, i.e., a blended word.

[2] *gimlet* Small tool used for boring holes.

"Well, a '*rath*' is a sort of green pig; but '*mome*' I'm not certain about. I think it's short for '*from home*'—meaning that they'd lost their way, you know."

"And what does '*outgrabe*' mean?"

"Well, '*outgribing*' is something between bellowing and whistling, with a kind of sneeze in the middle: however, you'll hear it done, maybe—down in the wood yonder—and when you've once heard it you'll be *quite* content. Who's been repeating all that hard stuff to you?"

"I read it in a book," said Alice.

IN CONTEXT

The Photographs of Lewis Carroll

Though as a photographer Carroll is best known for his images of children—and of Alice Liddell in particular—he was among the most accomplished of Victorian portrait photographers. Like many photographers of the time, he often portrayed his subjects in dramatic roles.

Alice, Lorina, Harry, and Edith Liddell, 1860.

Alice Liddell as "The Beggar Maid," 1858.

Alexander Munro, the sculptor, with
his wife, Mary, 1863.

George Macdonald and his daughter
Lily, 1863.

Ella Chlora Monier-William, 1866.   "Andromeda," 1865.   "Captive Princess," 1875.

AUGUSTA WEBSTER
1837 – 1894

Augusta Webster is best known for bold poetic portraits that give dramatic voice to social issues in Victorian culture. Despite the considerable reputation she enjoyed when alive, for nearly a hundred years after her death she went missing from the English canon; the unstinting support of Victorian literary critic Theodore Watts-Gunn, who declared it "a monstrous thing that such a poet as Augusta Webster should be unknown," was not enough to prevent the politics of twentieth-century canon-formation from ignoring Webster. She lacked any powerful connections to secure her reputation, and the genres she favored—longer dramatic monologues and verse poems—do not lend themselves to anthologization. It was not until the 1980s and '90s that feminist scholarship rediscovered Webster.

Born in 1837 to Julia Hume Davies and Vice-Admiral George Davies of the British Navy in Poole, Dorset, Julia Augusta Davies spent her earliest years on board her father's ship, the *Griper*. It is said that Webster learned Greek at a young age to help her brother with his lessons; her mastery of a classical language traditionally reserved for male education may also have been motivated by literary ambitions, anticipating a career which included two translations of Greek plays. Webster attended the Cambridge School of Art and was admitted to the South Kensington Art School where, according to Ray Strachey, she "nearly dashed the prospects of women art students for ever by being expelled for whistling." In 1863 she married Thomas Webster, a fellow and law lecturer at Trinity College in Cambridge. Their only child, Margaret, is memorialized in one of Webster's finest works, the posthumously published sonnet sequence *Mother and Daughter*. While no personal documents exist to shed light on the Websters' marriage, the couple's decision to move to London suggests that it was not conventionally patriarchal; giving up a prestigious position in Cambridge, Webster's husband supported a move which would enable his wife to develop professionally in proximity to some of her literary models.

In London, Webster was poetry reviewer for the *Athenaeum* for a decade, and wrote regular columns for the *Examiner*. At a time when the dominant ideology of the British Medical Association warned against education for women on the grounds that it would sap the vital energy needed for reproduction, Webster campaigned on behalf of women's suffrage and education, becoming one of the first women to be elected to the London School Board.

Webster's writing is rich with social commentary. Her poem "A Castaway," praised by Robert Browning and called "her masterpiece" by Watts-Dunn, presents through the persona of a prostitute a powerful critique of the Victorian "economy of love" (to borrow the phrase of Webster scholar Christine Sutphin). "A Castaway," like "The Happiest Girl in the World" and "Jeanne D'Arc," is written in the poetic genre in which Webster excelled, the dramatic monologue. Two collections of monologues, *Dramatic Studies* (1866) and *Portraits* (1870), mark Webster's most lasting contribution to English poetry. In contrast to the psychological interiors dramatized by Robert Browning in monologues such as "Fra Lippo Lippi," Webster skillfully crafted the monologue to speak to external social circumstances. Webster was able to give voice to a sensual and political potency prohibited Victorian women by speaking through mythological surrogates in "Medea in Athens" and "Circe." While the implied, silent listener addressed within conventional dramatic monologues is often absent from Webster's treatments (leading the *London Review* to describe *Dramatic Studies* as "a set of soliloquies"), her monologues stage a voice whose message is a moving social performance.

The essays on love and marriage that Webster regularly contributed to the *Examiner* were, like most submissions to Victorian periodicals, anonymous. The editor of the *Examiner* held Webster's essay "A Translation and a Transcription" in high esteem, ranking it "the best article which ever appeared in its pages." Webster's first two books, *Blanche Lisle and Other Poems* (1860) and a narrative poem in blank verse entitled *Lilian Gray* (1864), were published under the pseudonym Cecil Home. All subsequent work, ranging from lyrics to verse dramas, appeared under Webster's own name. She even daringly attached her own name to her translations of *The Medea of Euripides* and *The Prometheus Bound of Aeschylus* at a time when scholarship in classical languages was considered to be strictly the province of "gentlemen."

Webster brought something of the unconventional to whatever genre she attempted. Whereas sonnet sequences had traditionally been vehicles for the expression of romantic love, her sonnet sequence *Mother and Daughter* (1894) took the love between a mother and a daughter as its subject.

When she died in 1894 Webster left behind no diaries or family letters, and only scanty evidence of correspondence with Christina Rossetti, Oliver Wendell Holmes, and a few other prominent writers of the day. Her poetic legacy, however, is increasingly regarded as being of very considerable substance.

⌘ ⌘ ⌘

A Castaway

Poor little diary, with its simple thoughts,
Its good resolves, its "Studied French an hour,"
"Read Modern History," "Trimmed up my grey hat,"
"Darned stockings," "Tatted,"[1] "Practiced my new song,"
5 "Went to the daily service," "Took Bess soup,"
"Went out to tea." Poor simple diary!
And did *I* write it? Was I this good girl,
This budding colourless young rose of home?
Did I so live content in such a life,
10 Seeing no larger scope, nor asking it,
Than this small constant round—old clothes to mend,
New clothes to make, then go and say my prayers,
Or carry soup, or take a little walk
And pick the ragged-robins[2] in the hedge?
15 Then, for ambition, (was there ever life
That could forego that?) to improve my mind

And know French better and sing harder songs;
For gaiety, to go, in my best white
Well washed and starched and freshened with new bows,
20 And take tea out to meet the clergyman.
No wishes and no cares, almost no hopes,
Only the young girl's hazed and golden dreams
That veil the future from her.

                              So long since:
And now it seems a jest to talk of me
25 As if I could be one with her, of me
Who am ... me.

                    And what is that? My looking-glass
Answers it passably; a woman sure,
No fiend, no slimy thing out of the pools,
A woman with a ripe and smiling lip
30 That has no venom in its touch I think,
With a white brow on which there is no brand;
A woman none dare call not beautiful,
Not womanly in every woman's grace.

---

[1] *Tatted* Made lace.

[2] *ragged-robin* Common English flower.

Aye, let me feed upon my beauty thus,
35 Be glad in it like painters when they see
At last the face they dreamed but could not find
Look from their canvas on them, triumph in it,
The dearest thing I have. Why, 'tis my all,
Let me make much of it: is it not this,
40 This beauty, my own curse at once and tool
To snare men's souls (I know what the good say
Of beauty in such creatures), is it not this
That makes me feel myself a woman still,
With still some little pride, some little—

Stop!
45 "Some little pride, some little"—Here's a jest!
What word will fit the sense but modesty?
A wanton I, but modest!

Modest, true;
I'm not drunk in the streets, ply not for hire
At infamous corners with my likenesses
50 Of the humbler kind; yes, modesty's my word—
'Twould shape my mouth well too, I think I'll try:
"Sir, Mr. What-you-will, Lord Who-knows-what,
My present lover or my next to come,
Value me at my worth, fill your purse full,
55 For I am modest; yes, and honour me
As though your schoolgirl sister or your wife
Could let her skirts brush mine or talk of me;
For I am modest."

Well, I flout myself:
But yet, but yet—

Fie, poor fantastic fool,
60 Why do I play the hypocrite alone,
Who am no hypocrite with others by?
Where should be my "But yet"? I am that thing
Called half a dozen dainty names, and none
Dainty enough to serve the turn and hide
65 The one coarse English worst that lurks beneath:
Just that, no worse, no better.

And, for me,
I say let no one be above her trade;

I own my kindredship with any drab[1]
Who sells herself as I, although she crouch
70 In fetid garrets and I have a home
All velvet and marqueterie and pastilles,[2]
Although she hide her skeleton in rags
And I set fashions and wear cobweb lace:
The difference lies but in my choicer ware,
75 That I sell beauty and she ugliness;
Our traffic's one—I'm no sweet slaver-tongue
To gloze[3] upon it and explain myself
A sort of fractious angel misconceived—
Our traffic's one: I own it. And what then?
80 I know of worse that are called honourable.
Our lawyers, who with noble eloquence
And virtuous outbursts lie to hang a man,
Or lie to save him, which way goes the fee:
Our preachers, gloating on your future hell
85 For not believing what they doubt themselves:
Our doctors, who sort poisons out by chance
And wonder how they'll answer, and grow rich:
Our journalists, whose business is to fib
And juggle truths and falsehoods to and fro:
90 Our tradesmen, who must keep unspotted names
And cheat the least like stealing that they can:
Our —— all of them, the virtuous worthy men
Who feed on the world's follies, vices, wants,
And do their businesses of lies and shams
95 Honestly, reputably, while the world
Claps hands and cries "good luck," which of their
        trades,
Their honourable trades, barefaced like mine,
All secrets brazened out, would show more white?

And whom do I hurt more than they? as much?
100 The wives? Poor fools, what do I take from them
Worth crying for or keeping? If they knew
What their fine husbands look like seen by eyes
That may perceive there are more men than one!
But, if they can, let them just take the pains
105 To keep them: 'tis not such a mighty task
To pin an idiot to your apron-string;

---

[1] *drab*   Common prostitute.

[2] *marqueterie*   Inlaid mosaic work decorating furniture; *pastilles*
Aromatic pastes burnt as perfumes.

[3] *gloze*   Interpret deceitfully or flatteringly.

And wives have an advantage over us,
(The good and blind ones have) the smile or pout
Leaves them no secret nausea at odd times.
110 Oh, they could keep their husbands if they cared,
But 'tis an easier life to let them go,
And whimper at it for morality.

      Oh! those shrill carping virtues, safely housed
From reach of even a smile that should put red
115 On a decorous cheek, who rail at us
With such a spiteful scorn and rancorousness,
(Which maybe is half envy at the heart)
And boast themselves so measurelessly good
And us so measurelessly unlike them,
120 What is their wondrous merit that they stay
In comfortable homes whence not a soul
Has ever thought of tempting them, and wear
No kisses but a husband's upon lips
There is no other man desires to kiss—
125 Refrain in fact from sin impossible?
How dare they hate us so? what have they done,
What borne, to prove them other than we are?
What right have they to scorn us—glass-case saints,
Dianas[1] under lock and key—what right
130 More than the well-fed helpless barn-door fowl
To scorn the larcenous wild-birds?

          Pshaw, let be!
Scorn or no scorn, what matter for their scorn?
I have outfaced my own—that's harder work.
Aye, let their virtuous malice dribble on—
135 Mock snowstorms on the stage—I'm proof long since:
I have looked coolly on my what and why,
And I accept myself.

          Oh I'll endorse
The shamefullest revilings mouthed at me,
Cry "True! Oh perfect picture! Yes, that's I!"
140 And add a telling blackness here and there,
And then dare swear you, every nine of ten,
My judges and accusers, I'd not change
My conscience against yours, you who tread out
Your devil's pilgrimage along the roads

145 That take in church and chapel, and arrange
A roundabout and decent way to hell.

      Well, mine's a short way and a merry one:
So says my pious hash of ohs and ahs,
Choice texts and choicer threats, appropriate names,
150 (Rahabs and Jezebels[2]) some fierce Tartuffe[3]
Hurled at me through the post. We had rare fun
Over that tract[4] digested with champagne.
Where is it? where's my rich repertory
Of insults Biblical?[5] "I prey on souls"—
155 Only my men have oftenest none I think:
"I snare the simple ones"—but in these days
There seem to be none simple and none snared
And most men have their favourite sinnings planned
To do them civilly and sensibly:
160 "I braid my hair"—but braids are out of date:
"I paint my cheeks"—I always wear them pale:
"I—"

      Pshaw! the trash is savourless today:
One cannot laugh alone. There, let it burn.
What, does the windy dullard think one needs
165 His wisdom dove-tailed on to Solomon's,[6]
His threats out-threatening God's, to teach the news
That those who need not sin have safer souls?
We know it, but we've bodies to save too;
And so we earn our living.

<hr>

[1] *Diana* Roman goddess of virginity.

[2] *Rahabs and Jezebels* I.e., harlots. Rahab was a Biblical harlot whose family was saved from the destruction of Jericho because she hid messengers that had been sent by Joshua to spy on the city. (See Joshua 6.17–25.) Jezebel was a Phoenician princess who married Ahab, King of Israel. She refused to worship Yahweh, continuing to practice her country's traditional worship instead, and murdered Yahweh's prophets. Her name is often used to denote a cruel, sexually predatory woman. (See 1 Judges 16 and 18.)

[3] *Tartuffe* Hypocritical character who feigned virtue in Molière's 1664 play of that name.

[4] *tract* Religious pamphlet.

[5] *insults Biblical* See Ecclesiastes 7.26: "And I find more bitter than death the woman, whose heart is snares and nets, and her hands as bands: whoso pleaseth God shall escape from her; but the sinner shall be taken by her," and 1 Timothy 2.9–10, which advises women to "adorn themselves in modest apparel, with shamefacedness and sobriety; not with braided hair, or gold, or pearls, or costly array; / But (which becometh women professing godliness) with good works."

[6] *Solomon* Biblical king of Israel who was known for his wisdom.

Well lit, tract!
170 At least you've made me a good leaping blaze.
Up, up, how the flame shoots! and now 'tis dead.
Oh proper finish, preaching to the last—
No such bad omen either; sudden end,
And no sad withering horrible old age.
175 How one would clutch at youth to hold it tight!
And then to know it gone, to see it gone,
Be taught its absence by harsh careless looks,
To live forgotten, solitary, old—
The cruellest word that ever woman learns.
180 Old—that's to be nothing, or to be at best
A blurred memorial that in better days
There was a woman once with such a name.
No, no, I could not bear it: death itself
Shows kinder promise ... even death itself,
185 Since it must come one day—

Oh this grey gloom!
This rain, rain, rain, what wretched thoughts it brings!
Death: I'll not think of it.

Will no one come?
'Tis dreary work alone.

Why did I read
That silly diary? Now, sing-song, ding-dong,
190 Come the old vexing echoes back again,
Church bells and nursery good-books, back again
Upon my shrinking ears that had forgotten—
I hate the useless memories: 'tis fools' work
Singing the hackneyed° dirge of "better days":   *stale*
195 Best take Now kindly, give the past good-bye,
Whether it were a better or a worse.

Yes, yes, I listened to the echoes once,
The echoes and the thoughts from the old days.
The worse for me: I lost my richest friend,
200 And that was all the difference. For the world,
I would not have that flight known. How they'd roar:
"What! Eulalie, when she refused us all,
'Ill' and 'away,' was doing Magdalene,[1]

Tears, ashes, and her Bible, and then off
205 To hide her in a Refuge[2] ... for a week!"

A wild whim that, to fancy I could change
My new self for my old because I wished!
Since then, when in my languid days there comes
That craving, like homesickness, to go back
210 To the good days, the dear old stupid days,
To the quiet and the innocence, I know
'Tis a sick fancy and try palliatives.

What is it? You go back to the old home,
And 'tis not *your* home, has no place for you,
215 And, if it had, you could not fit you in it.
And could I fit me to my former self?
If I had had the wit, like some of us,
To sow my wild-oats into three per cents,[3]
Could I not find me shelter in the peace
220 Of some far nook where none of them would come,
Nor whisper travel from this scurrilous world
(That gloats, and moralizes through its leers)
To blast me with my fashionable shame?
There I might—oh my castle in the clouds!
225 And where's its rent?—but there, were there a there,
I might again live the grave blameless life
Among such simple pleasures, simple cares:
But could they be my pleasures, be my cares?
The blameless life, but never the content—
230 Never. How could I henceforth be content
With any life but one that sets the brain
In a hot merry fever with its stir?
What would there be in quiet rustic days,
Each like the other, full of time to think,
235 To keep one bold enough to live at all?
Quiet is hell, I say—as if a woman
Could bear to sit alone, quiet all day,
And loathe herself and sicken on her thoughts.

They tried it at the Refuge, and I failed:
240 I could not bear it. Dreary hideous room,
Coarse pittance, prison rules, one might bear these

---

1   *doing Magdalene* Becoming a reformed prostitute, so called after Mary Magdalene of the New Testament, one of Jesus' disciples. The houses in Victorian England to which prostitutes could come to reform were known as "Magdalene houses."

2   *Refuge* Shelter.

3   *three per cents* British government stocks, which returned three per cent interest annually.

And keep one's purpose; but so much alone,
And then made faint and weak and fanciful
By change from pampering to half-famishing—
245 Good God, what thoughts come! Only one week more
And 'twould have ended: but in one day more
I must have killed myself. And I loathe death,
The dreadful foul corruption with who knows
What future after it.

　　　　　　　　Well, I came back,
250 Back to my slough.[1] Who says I had my choice?
Could I stay there to die of some mad death?
And if I rambled out into the world
Sinless but penniless, what else were that
But slower death, slow pining shivering death
255 By misery and hunger? Choice! what choice
Of living well or ill? could I have that?
And who would give it me? I think indeed
If some kind hand, a woman's—I hate men—
Had stretched itself to help me to firm ground,
260 Taken a chance and risked my falling back,
I could have gone my way not falling back:
But, let her be all brave, all charitable,
How could she do it? Such a trifling boon—
A little work to live by, 'tis not much—
265 And I might have found will enough to last:
But where's the work? More seamstresses than shirts;
And defter hands at white work[2] than are mine
Drop starved at last: dressmakers, milliners,
Too many too they say; and then their trades
270 Need skill, apprenticeship. And who so bold
As hire me for their humblest drudgery?
Not even for scullery[3] slut; not even, I think,
For governess although they'd get me cheap.
And after all it would be something hard,
275 With the marts for decent women overfull,
If I could elbow in and snatch a chance
And oust some good girl so, who then perforce
Must come and snatch her chance among our crowd.

　　　　Why, if the worthy men who think all's done
280 If we'll but come where we can hear them preach,

Could bring us all, or any half of us,
Into their fold, teach all us wandering sheep,
Or only half of us, to stand in rows
And baa them hymns and moral songs, good lack,[4]
285 What would they do with us? what could they do?
Just think! with were't but half of us on hand
To find work for … or husbands. Would they try
To ship us to the colonies for wives?[5]

　　　Well, well, I know the wise ones talk and talk:
290 "Here's cause, here's cure": "No, here it is, and here":
And find society to blame, or law,
The Church, the men, the women, too few schools,
Too many schools, too much, too little taught:
Somewhere or somehow someone is to blame:
295 But I say all the fault's with God Himself
Who puts too many women in the world.
We ought to die off reasonably and leave
As many as the men want, none to waste.
Here's cause; the woman's superfluity:
300 And for the cure, why, if it were the law,
Say, every year, in due percentages,
Balancing them with males as the times need,
To kill off female infants, 'twould make room;
And some of us would not have lost too much,
305 Losing life ere we know what it *can* mean.

　　　The other day I saw a woman weep
Beside her dead child's bed: the little thing
Lay smiling, and the mother wailed half mad,
Shrieking to God to give it back again.
310 I could have laughed aloud: the little girl
Living had but her mother's life to live;
There she lay smiling, and her mother wept
To know her gone!

　　　　　　　　My mother would have wept.

　　　Oh, mother, mother, did you ever dream,
315 You good grave simple mother, you pure soul

---

[1] *slough*   State of moral degradation.

[2] *white work*   White-thread embroidery on white cloth.

[3] *scullery*   Room, adjoining the kitchen, in which dishes were washed.

[4] *good lack*   A polite exclamation.

[5] *ship … wives*   Reference to Sir Sidney Herbert's proposal to send half a million "surplus" women, such as those driven to prostitution by a lack of employment, to the colonies, where there was a shortage of women from whom to choose for settlers who wished to marry.

No evil could come nigh, did you once dream
In all your dying cares for your lone girl
Left to fight out her fortune helplessly
That there would be *this* danger?—for *your* girl,
320 Taught by you, lapped in a sweet ignorance,
Scarcely more wise of what things sin could be
Than some young child a summer six months old,
Where in the north the summer makes a day,
Of what is darkness ... darkness that will come
325 Tomorrow suddenly. Thank God at least
For this much of my life, that when you died,
That when you kissed me dying, not a thought
Of this made sorrow for you, that I too
Was pure of even fear.

                              Oh yes, I thought,
330 Still new in my insipid treadmill life,
(My father so late dead), and hopeful still,
There might be something pleasant somewhere in it,
Some sudden fairy come, no doubt, to turn
My pumpkin to a chariot, I thought then
335 That I might plod and plod and drum the sounds
Of useless facts into unwilling ears,
Tease children with dull questions half the day
Then con dull answers in my room at night
Ready for next day's questions, mend quill pens
340 And cut my fingers, add up sums done wrong
And never get them right; teach, teach, and teach—
What I half knew, or not at all—teach, teach
For years, a lifetime—*I*!

                              And yet, who knows?
It might have been, for I was patient once,
345 And willing, and meant well; it might have been
Had I but still clung on in my first place—
A safe dull place, where mostly there were smiles
But never merry-makings; where all days
Jogged on sedately busy, with no haste;
350 Where all seemed measured out, but margins broad:
A dull home but a peaceful, where I felt
My pupils would be dear young sisters soon,
And felt their mother take me to her heart,
Motherly to all lonely harmless things.
355 But I must have a conscience, must blurt out
My great discovery of my ignorance!

And who required it of me? And who gained?
What did it matter for a more or less
The girls learnt in their schoolbooks, to forget
360 In their first season?[1] We did well together:
They loved me and I them: but I went off
To housemaid's pay, six crossgrained[2] brats to teach,
Wrangles and jangles, doubts, disgrace ... then this;
And they had a perfection found for them,
Who has all ladies' learning in her head
Abridged and scheduled, speaks five languages,
385 Knows botany and conchology[3] and globes,
Draws, paints, plays, sings, embroiders, teaches all
On a patent method never known to fail:
And now they're finished and, I hear, poor things,
Are the worst dancers and worst dressers out.[4]
390 And where's their profit of those prison years
All gone to make them wise in lesson-books?
Who wants his wife to know weeds' Latin names?
Who ever chose a girl for saying dates?
Or asked if she had learned to trace a map?

395   Well, well, the silly rules this silly world
Makes about women! This is one of them.
Why must there be pretence of teaching them
What no one ever cares that they should know,
What, grown out of the schoolroom, they cast off
400 Like the schoolroom pinafore,[5] no better fit
For any use of real grown-up life,
For any use to her who seeks or waits
The husband and the home, for any use,
For any shallowest pretence of use,
405 To her who has them? Do I not know this,
I, like my betters, that a woman's life,
Her natural life, her good life, her one life,
Is in her husband, God on earth to her,
And what she knows and what she can and is
410 Is only good as it brings good to him?

---

[1] *first season* The London social season, when Parliament is in session and everyone of social importance is in the city.

[2] *crossgrained* Difficult to manage.

[3] *conchology* The study of sea-shells.

[4] *out* I.e., appearing in society. Young girls did not attend public social functions, so it was said that they "came out" when they became old enough to do so.

[5] *pinafore* Garment worn by little girls.

Oh God, do I not know it? I the thing
Of shame and rottenness, the animal
That feeds men's lusts and preys on them, I, I,
Who should not dare to take the name of wife
415   On my polluted lips, who in the word
Hear but my own reviling, I know that.
I could have lived by that rule, how content:
My pleasure to make him some pleasure, pride
To be as he would have me, duty, care,
420   To fit all to his taste, rule my small sphere
To his intention; then to lean on him,
Be guided, tutored, loved—no not that word,
That *loved* which between men and women means
All selfishness, all cloying talk, all lust,
425   All vanity, all idiocy—not loved,
But cared for. I've been loved myself, I think,
Some once or twice since my poor mother died,
But *cared for*, never—that's a word for homes,
Kind homes, good homes, where simple children come
430   And ask their mother is this right or wrong,
Because they know she's perfect, cannot err;
Their father told them so, and he knows all,
Being so wise and good and wonderful,
Even enough to scold even her at times
435   And tell her everything she does not know.
Ah the sweet nursery logic!

               Fool! thrice fool!
Do I hanker after that too? Fancy me
Infallible nursery saint, live code of law!
Me preaching! teaching innocence to be good!
440   A mother!

            Yet the baby thing that woke
And wailed an hour or two, and then was dead,
Was mine, and had he lived ... why then my name
Would have been mother. But 'twas well he died:
I could have been no mother, I, lost then
445   Beyond his saving. Had he come before
And lived, come to me in the doubtful days
When shame and boldness had not grown one sense,
For his sake, with the courage come of him,
I might have struggled back.

                  But how? But how?

450   His father would not then have let me go:
His time had not yet come to make an end
Of my "forever" with a hireling's fee
And civil light dismissal. None but him
To claim a bit of bread of if I went,
455   Child or no child: would he have given it me?
He! no; he had not done with me. No help,
No help, no help. Some ways can be trodden back,
But never our way, we who one wild day
Have given goodbye to what in our deep hearts
460   The lowest woman still holds best in life,
Good name—good name though given by the world
That mouths and garbles with its decent prate,
And wraps it in respectable grave shams,
And patches conscience partly by the rule
465   Of what one's neighbour thinks, but something more
By what his eyes are sharp enough to see.
How I could scorn it with its Pharisees,[1]
If it could not scorn me: but yet, but yet—
Oh God, if I could look it in the face!

470   Oh I am wild, am ill, I think, tonight:
Will no one come and laugh with me? No feast,
No merriment tonight. So long alone!
Will no one come?

             At least there's a new dress
To try, and grumble at—they never fit
475   To one's ideal. Yes, a new rich dress,
With lace like this too, that's a soothing balm
For any fretting woman, cannot fail;
I've heard men say it ... and they know so well
What's in all women's hearts, especially
480   Women like me.

           No help! no help! no help!
How could it be? It was too late long since—
Even at the first too late. Whose blame is that?
There are some kindly people in the world,
But what can *they* do? If one hurls oneself
485   Into a quicksand, what can be the end,
But that one sinks and sinks? Cry out for help?
Ah yes, and, if it came, who is so strong
To strain from the firm ground and lift one out?

---

[1] *Pharisees* I.e., hypocrites.

And how, so firmly clutching the stretched hand
490 As death's pursuing terror bids, even so,
How can one reach firm land, having to foot
The treacherous crumbling soil that slides and gives
And sucks one in again? Impossible path!
No, why waste struggles, I or anyone?
495 What is must be. What then? I where I am,
Sinking and sinking; let the wise pass by
And keep their wisdom for an apter use,
Let me sink merrily as I best may.

  Only, I think my brother—I forgot;
500 He stopped his brotherhood some years ago—
But if he had been just so much less good
As to remember mercy. Did he think
How once I was his sister, prizing him
As sisters do, content to learn for him
505 The lesson girls with brothers all must learn,
To do without?

        I have heard girls lament
That doing so without all things one would,
But I saw never aught to murmur at,
For men must be made ready for their work
510 And women all have more or less their chance
Of husbands to work for them, keep them safe
Like summer roses in soft greenhouse air
That never guess 'tis winter out of doors:
No, I saw never aught to murmur at,
515 Content with stinted fare and shabby clothes
And cloistered silent life to save expense,
Teaching myself out of my borrowed books,
While he for some one pastime (needful, true,
To keep him of his rank; 'twas not his fault)
520 Spent in a month what could have given me
My teachers for a year.

        'Twas no one's fault:
For could he be launched forth on the rude sea
Of this contentious world and left to find
Oars and the boatman's skill by some good chance?
525 'Twas no one's fault: yet still he might have thought
Of our so different youths and owned at least
'Tis pitiful when a mere nerveless girl
Untutored must put forth upon that sea,

Not in the woman's true place, the wife's place,
530 To trust a husband and be borne along,
But impotent blind pilot to herself.

  Merciless, merciless—like the prudent world
That will not have the flawed soul prank[1] itself
With a hoped second virtue, will not have
535 The woman fallen once lift up herself ...
Lest she should fall again. Oh how his taunts,
His loathing fierce reproaches, scarred and seared
Like branding iron hissing in a wound!
And it was true—*that* killed me: and I felt
540 A hideous hopeless shame burn out my heart,
And knew myself forever that he said,
That which I was—Oh it was true, true, true.

  No, not true then. I was not all that then.
Oh, I have drifted on before mad winds
545 And made ignoble shipwreck; not today
Could any breeze of heaven prosper me
Into the track again, nor any hand
Snatch me out of the whirlpool I have reached;
But then?

        Nay, he judged very well: he knew
550 Repentance was too dear a luxury
For a beggar's buying, knew it earns no bread—
And knew me a too base and nerveless thing
To bear my first fault's sequel and just die.
And how could he have helped me? Held my hand,
555 Owned me for his, fronted the angry world
Clothed with my ignominy? Or maybe
Taken me to his home to damn him worse?
What did I look for? for what less would serve
That he could do, a man without a purse?
560 He meant me well, he sent me that five pounds,
Much to him then; and, if he bade me work
And never vex him more with news of me,
We both knew him too poor for pensioners.
I see he did his best; I could wish now
565 Sending it back I had professed some thanks.

  But there! I was too wretched to be meek:
It seemed to me as if he, everyone,

---

[1] *prank* Dress up, adorn.

The whole great world, were guilty of my guilt,
Abettors and avengers: in my heart
570   I gibed them back their gibings; I was wild.

I see clear now and know one has one's life
In hand at first to spend or spare or give
Like any other coin; spend it, or give,
Or drop it in the mire, can the world see
575   You get your value for it, or bar off
The hurrying of its marts to grope it up
And give it back to you for better use?
And if you spend or give, that is your choice;
And if you let it slip, that's your choice too,
580   You should have held it firmer. Yours the blame,
And not another's, not the indifferent world's
Which goes on steadily, statistically,
And count by censuses not separate souls—
And if it somehow needs to its worst use
585   So many lives of women, useless else,
It buys us of ourselves; we could hold back,
Free all of us to starve, and some of us,
(Those who have done no ill, and are in luck)
To slave their lives out and have food and clothes
590   Until they grow unserviceably old.

Oh, I blame no one—scarcely even myself.
It was to be: the very good in me
Has always turned to hurt; all I thought right
At the hot moment, judged of afterwards,
595   Shows reckless.

Why, look at it, had I taken
The pay my dead child's father offered me
For having been its mother, I could then
Have kept life in me—many have to do it,
That swarm in the back alleys, on no more,
600   Cold sometimes, mostly hungry, but they live—
I could have gained a respite trying it,
And maybe found at last some humble work
To eke the pittance out. Not I, forsooth,
I must have spirit, must have womanly pride,
605   Must dash back his contemptuous wages, I
Who had not scorned to earn them, dash them back
The fiercer that he dared to count our boy
In my appraising: and yet now I think

I might have taken it for my dead boy's sake;
610   It would have been *his* gift.

But I went forth
With my fine scorn, and whither did it lead?
Money's the root of evil do they say?
Money is virtue, strength: money to me
Would then have been repentance: could I live
615   Upon my idiot's pride?

Well, it fell soon.
I had prayed Clement might believe me dead,
And yet I begged of him—That's like me too,
Beg of him and then send him back his alms!
What if he gave as to a whining wretch
620   That holds her hand and lies? I am less to him
Than such a one; her rags do him no wrong,
But I, I wrong him merely that I live,
Being his sister. Could I not at least
Have still let him forget me? But 'tis past:
625   And naturally he may hope I am long dead.

Good God! to think that we were what we were
One to the other … and now!

He has done well;
Married a sort of heiress, I have heard,
A dapper little madam dimple cheeked
630   And dimple brained, who makes him a good wife—
No doubt she'd never own but just to him,
And in a whisper, she can even suspect
That we exist, we other women things:
What would she say if she could learn one day
635   She has a sister-in-law? So he and I
Must stand apart till doomsday.

But the jest,
To think how she would look! Her fright, poor thing!
The notion! I could laugh outright … or else,
For I feel near it, roll on the ground and sob.

640   Well, after all, there's not much difference
Between the two sometimes.

Was that the bell?

Someone at last, thank goodness. There's a voice,
And that's a pleasure. Whose though? Ah, I know.
Why did she come alone, the cackling goose?
645   Why not have brought her sister? She tells more
And titters less. No matter; half a loaf

Is better than no bread.

                              Oh, is it you?
Most welcome, dear: one gets so moped alone.
—1870, 1893

ALGERNON CHARLES SWINBURNE
1837 – 1909

Victorian poet and critic Algernon Swinburne was physically slight, but he had a powerful personality, and he left behind a vast literary output. Much of his writing, however, on topics such as incest, cannibalism, sadomasochism, and necrophilia, was too outrageous for "respectable" Victorian tastes. Although he was born into a distinguished family of British aristocracy, Swinburne's opinions on politics, religion, and sexuality were offensive enough to have earned him the nickname "Swineborn" in *Punch* magazine. Swinburne's poetry, however, was also metrically innovative, musical, and often erudite. Oscar Wilde claimed him as his literary master but said of Swinburne's writing, "Words seem to dominate him. Alliteration tyrannizes over him. Mere sound often becomes his lord. He is so eloquent that whatever he touches becomes unreal." This "diffuseness" was, according to T.S. Eliot, one of his "glories." Although few have disputed the musicality of Swinburne's poetry, some critics have accused him of being vague and soporific.

Algernon Swinburne was born in 1837 into a highly respectable aristocratic family. His father, Admiral Charles Henry Swinburne, was the son of a baronet, and his mother, Lady Jane, was the daughter of an earl. Raised a devout Anglo-Catholic, Swinburne read profusely and acquired an intimate knowledge of the Bible, as well as a proficiency in French and Italian. His early years at Eton, however, were troubled ones; as a result of disciplinary problems, he was removed from the school before he graduated. After private tutoring, he entered Balliol College at Oxford in 1856. During his first two years there, Swinburne excelled in the Classics and won a scholarship for French and Italian; his unruliness got the better of him again, and he was forced to leave Balliol without a degree. He nevertheless made many important friends at Oxford, including Benjamin Jowett (then master of Balliol) and the Pre-Raphaelites Edward Burne-Jones, William Morris, and Dante Gabriel Rossetti (with whom he lived in London after Rossetti's wife, Elizabeth Siddal, died).

London saw the best and the worst of Swinburne. During the 1860s, he gained notoriety for his wild, drunken revelries and experiments with flagellation, as much as for the publication of two important works, *Atalanta in Calydon* (1865) and *Poems and Ballads* (1866). The classical Greek tragic form of the verse-play *Atalanta* and its concentration on fate and divine intervention belied the long poem's modern revolt against religious institutions and its sympathy, instead, with the "holy spirit of man." While Victorians might have been expected to rail against Swinburne's chastisement of religious orthodoxy, the lyrical and mellifluous tragedy held many in its sway, and won accolades from reviewers. John Ruskin said that it was the "grandest thing ever done by a youth—though he is a Demoniac youth," and Tennyson wrote to Swinburne praising the metrical creativity of *Atalanta*.

Poems and Ballads, on the other hand, had the public (Ruskin included) up in arms. In such poems as "The Triumph of Time," "Dolores," "The Leper," "Hymn to Prosperine," and "Laus Veneris," Swinburne explored themes of sexual perversion, paganism, and moral and spiritual decay. One reviewer said the author was an "unclean, fiery imp from the pit," while another, referring to Swinburne's association with the Aesthetes, called him the "libidinous laureate of a pack of satyrs." Amid this outcry, the publishing house withdrew the book from publication, angering Swinburne and prompting his eloquent riposte in *Notes on Poems and Reviews*. *Poems and Ballads* was re-released shortly afterward by another publisher.

Swinburne's notoriety continued into the late 1860s and 1870s, as he cultivated his image as a "scandalous poet," to use his own words. He wrote at a feverish rate—even though his alcoholism was by then prompting seizures and blackouts—and produced such works as *A Song of Italy* (1867), a defense of Italian liberation; *Ave Atque Vale* (1868), an elegy to Baudelaire; the brilliant essay *William Blake* (1868); and *Songs Before Sunrise* (1871), which continued the theme of spiritual and political revolution. By the end of the 1870s, however, Swinburne was near death, his nerves destroyed by alcohol, and his body depleted from overwork. Luckily, in 1879, his friend Theodore Watts-Dunton took him to his house in Putney and helped nurse him back to health. There Swinburne lived in quiet solitude for the remaining 30 years of his life, writing and publishing prolifically, and finally succumbing to pneumonia in 1909.

In those final decades, Swinburne won the respect of many Victorians. Although the *Guardian* noted upon his death that his verse could be "careless, trivial, or inharmonious," the newspaper also acknowledged that "the greatest poet lately living is dead … and we cannot doubt that much of his poetry will live by virtue of its exquisite music."

⌘ ⌘ ⌘

Hymn to Proserpine[1]
(*After the Proclamation in Rome of the Christian Faith*[2])

Vicisti, Galilæe[3]

I have lived long enough, having seen one thing, that
    love hath an end;
Goddess and maiden and queen, be near me now and
    befriend.
Thou art more than the day or the morrow, the
    seasons that laugh or that weep;
For these give joy and sorrow; but thou, Proserpina,
    sleep.

5   Sweet is the treading of wine, and sweet the feet of the
    dove;
But a goodlier gift is thine than foam of the grapes or
    love.
Yea, is not even Apollo,[4] with hair and harpstring of
    gold,
A bitter God to follow, a beautiful God to behold?
I am sick of singing: the bays burn deep and chafe: I
    am fain
10   To rest a little from praise and grievous pleasure and
    pain.
For the Gods we know not of, who give us our daily
    breath,
We know they are cruel as love or life, and lovely as
    death.
O Gods dethroned and deceased, cast forth, wiped
    out in a day!
From your wrath is the world released, redeemed from
    your chains, men say.
15   New Gods are crowned in the city; their flowers have
    broken your rods;
They are merciful, clothed with pity, the young
    compassionate Gods.
But for me their new device is barren, the days are bare;

---

[1]   *Proserpine*   In Roman mythology, daughter of Jupiter and Ceres and wife of Pluto, King of the underworld, who stole her from her mother.

[2]   *Proclamation … Faith*   Roman Emperor Constantine the Great legalized the Christian faith when he proclaimed the Edict of Milan in 313 CE.

[3]   *Vicisti, Galilæe*   Latin: "Thou hast conquered, Galilee," said to be the dying words in 363 of Julian the Apostate, half-brother of Constantine the Great. Julian eventually became emperor after the deaths of Constantine I and II; he was a pagan who opposed instituting Christianity as the state religion (as it was eventually proclaimed by Emperor Theodosius in 380).

[4]   *Apollo*   Greek sun god; also god of the arts.

Things long past over suffice, and men forgotten that
    were.
Time and the Gods are at strife; ye dwell in the midst
    thereof,
20 Draining a little life from the barren breasts of love.
I say to you, cease, take rest; yea, I say to you all, be at
    peace,
Till the bitter milk of her breast and the barren bosom
    shall cease.
Wilt thou yet take all, Galilean? but these thou shalt
    not take,
The laurel, the palms and the pæan,[1] the breast of the
    nymphs in the brake;[2]
25 Breasts more soft than a dove's that tremble with
    tenderer breath;
And all the wings of the Loves,[3] and all the joy before
    death;
All the feet of the hours that sound as a single lyre,
Dropped and deep in the flowers, with strings that
    flicker like fire.
More than these wilt thou give, things fairer than all
    these things?
30 Nay, for a little we live, and life hath mutable wings.
A little while and we die; shall life not thrive as it may?
For no man under the sky lives twice, outliving his day.
And grief is a grievous thing, and a man hath enough
    of his tears:
Why should he labour, and bring fresh grief to
    blacken his years?
35 Thou hast conquered, O pale Galilean; the world has
    grown grey from thy breath;
We have drunken of things Lethean,[4] and fed on the
    fullness of death.
Laurel is green for a season, and love is sweet for a day;
But love grows bitter with treason, and laurel outlives
    not May.
Sleep, shall we sleep after all? for the world is not
    sweet in the end;

---

[1] *pæan* Hymn of praise.

[2] *brake* Ferns.

[3] *Loves* Cupids or other gods representing sexual love.

[4] *Lethean* Of the Greek mythological river Lethe in Hades (the
underworld), the waters of which cause the dead to forget the past;
also called the "River of Oblivion."

40 For the old faiths loosen and fall, the new years ruin
    and rend.
Fate is a sea without shore, and the soul is a rock that
    abides;
But her ears are vexed with the roar and her face with
    the foam of the tides.
O lips that the live blood faints in, the leavings of
    racks and rods!
O ghastly glories of saints, dead limbs of gibbeted
    Gods!
45 Though all men abase them before you in spirit, and
    all knees bend,
I kneel not neither adore you, but standing, look to
    the end.
All delicate days and pleasant, all spirits and sorrows
    are cast
Far out with the foam of the present that sweeps to
    the surf of the past:
Where beyond the extreme sea-wall, and between the
    remote sea-gates,
50 Waste water washes, and tall ships founder, and deep
    death waits:
Where, mighty with deepening sides, clad about with
    the seas as with wings,
And impelled of invisible tides, and fulfilled of
    unspeakable things,
White-eyed and poisonous-finned, shark-toothed and
    serpentine-curled,
Rolls, under the whitening wind of the future, the
    wave of the world.
55 The depths stand naked in sunder behind it, the
    storms flee away;
In the hollow before it the thunder is taken and
    snared as a prey;
In its sides is the north-wind bound; and its salt is of
    all men's tears;
With light of ruin, and sound of changes, and pulse of
    years:
With travail of day after day, and with trouble of hour
    upon hour;
60 And bitter as blood is the spray; and the crests are as
    fangs that devour:
And its vapour and storm of its steam as the sighing of
    spirits to be;

And its noise as the noise in a dream; and its depth as
the roots of the sea:
And the height of its heads as the height of the utmost
stars of the air:
And the ends of the earth at the might thereof
tremble, and time is made bare.
65 Will ye bridle the deep sea with reins, will ye chasten
the high sea with rods?
Will ye take her to chain her with chains, who is older
than all ye Gods?
All ye as a wind shall go by, as a fire shall ye pass and
be past;
Ye are Gods, and behold, ye shall die, and the waves
be upon you at last.
In the darkness of time, in the deeps of the years, in
the changes of things,
70 Ye shall sleep as a slain man sleeps, and the world shall
forget you for kings.
Though the feet of thine high priests tread where thy
lords and our forefathers trod,
Though these that were Gods are dead, and thou
being dead art a God,
Though before thee the throned Cytherean[1] be fallen,
and hidden her head,
Yet thy kingdom shall pass, Galilean, thy dead shall go
down to thee dead.
75 Of the maiden thy mother men sing as a goddess with
grace clad around;
Thou art throned where another was king; where
another was queen she is crowned.
Yea, once we had sight of another: but now she is
queen, say these.
Not as thine, not as thine was our mother, a blossom
of flowering seas,
Clothed round with the world's desire as with
raiment, and fair as the foam,
80 And fleeter than kindled fire, and a goddess, and
mother of Rome.
For thine came pale and a maiden, and sister to
sorrow; but ours,

Her deep hair heavily laden with odour and colour of
flowers,
White rose of the rose-white water, a silver splendour,
a flame,
Bent down unto us that besought her, and earth grew
sweet with her name.
85 For thine came weeping, a slave among slaves, and
rejected; but she
Came flushed from the full-flushed wave, and
imperial, her foot on the sea.
And the wonderful waters knew her, the winds and
the viewless ways,
And the roses grew rosier, and bluer the sea-blue
stream of the bays.
Ye are fallen, our lords, by what token? we wist[2] that
ye should not fall.
90 Ye were all so fair that are broken; and one more fair
than ye all.
But I turn to her still, having seen she shall surely
abide in the end;
Goddess and maiden and queen, be near me now and
befriend.
O daughter of earth, of my mother, her crown and
blossom of birth,
I am also, I also, thy brother; I go as I came unto earth.
95 In the night where thine eyes are as moons are in
heaven, the night where thou art,
Where the silence is more than all tunes, where sleep
overflows from the heart,
Where the poppies[3] are sweet as the rose in our world,
and the red rose is white,
And the wind falls faint as it blows with the fume of
the flowers of the night.
And the murmur of spirits that sleep in the shadow of
Gods from afar
100 Grows dim in thine ears and deep as the deep dim
soul of a star,
In the sweet low light of thy face, under heavens
untrod by the sun,
Let my soul with their souls find place, and forget
what is done and undone.
Thou art more than the Gods who number the days
of our temporal breath;

[1] *throned Cytherean* Venus, Roman goddess of love and beauty (Aphrodite in Greek mythology), who was born of the foam of the sea and, according to some accounts, came ashore on the Greek island of Cythera.

[2] *wist* Know.

[3] *poppies* Flowers representing sleep, sacred to Proserpine.

For these give labour and slumber; but thou,
    Proserpina, death.
105 Therefore now at thy feet I abide for a season in
    silence. I know
I shall die as my fathers died, and sleep as they sleep;
    even so.
For the glass of the years is brittle wherein we gaze for
    a span;
A little soul for a little bears up this corpse which is
    man.[1]
So long I endure, no longer; and laugh not again,
    neither weep.
110 For there is no God found stronger than death; and
    death is a sleep.
—1866

A Forsaken Garden

In a coign° of the cliff between lowland and   *wedge*
    highland,
  At the sea-down's edge between windward and lee,
Walled round with rocks as an inland island,
  The ghost of a garden fronts the sea.
5 A girdle of brushwood and thorn encloses
    The steep square slope of the blossomless bed
Where the weeds that grew green from the graves of
    its roses
    Now lie dead.

The fields fall southward, abrupt and broken,
10   To the low last edge of the long lone land.
If a step should sound or a word be spoken,
    Would a ghost not rise at the strange guest's hand?
So long have the grey bare walks lain guestless,
    Through branches and briars if a man make way,
15 He shall find no life but the sea-wind's, restless
    Night and day.

The dense hard passage is blind and stifled
    That crawls by a track none turn to climb
To the strait° waste place that the years have   *narrow*
    rifled

20 Of all but the thorns that are touched not of time.
The thorns he spares when the rose is taken;
    The rocks are left when he wastes the plain.
The wind that wanders, the weeds wind-shaken,
    These remain.

25 Not a flower to be pressed of the foot that falls not;
    As the heart of a dead man the seed-lots are dry;
From the thicket of thorns whence the nightingale
    calls not,
    Could she call, there were never a rose to reply.
Over the meadows that blossom and wither
    Rings but the note of a sea-bird's song;
30 Only the sun and the rain come hither
    All year long.

The sun burns sere and the rain dishevels
    One gaunt bleak blossom of scentless breath.
35 Only the wind here hovers and revels
    In a round where life seems barren as death.
Here there was laughing of old, there was weeping,
    Haply, of lovers none ever will know,
Whose eyes went seaward a hundred sleeping
40   Years ago.

Heart handfast in heart as they stood, "Look thither,"
    Did he whisper? "look forth from the flowers to
    the sea;
For the foam-flowers endure when the rose-blossoms
    wither,
    And men that love lightly may die—but we?"
45 And the same wind sang and the same waves
    whitened,
    And or ever the garden's last petals were shed,
In the lips that had whispered, the eyes that had
    lightened,
    Love was dead.

Or they loved their life through, and then went whither?
50   And were one to the end—but what end who knows?
Love deep as the sea as a rose must wither,
    As the rose-red seaweed that mocks the rose.
Shall the dead take thought for the dead to love them?
    What love was ever as deep as a grave?

---

[1] [Swinburne's note] ψυχάριον εἶ βαστάζον νεκρόν.—Epictetus
[Greek: "You are a little soul, carrying around a corpse."]

55 They are loveless now as the grass above them
        Or the wave.

    All are at one now, roses and lovers,
        Not known of the cliffs and the fields and the sea.
    Not a breath of the time that has been hovers
60   In the air now soft with a summer to be.
    Not a breath shall there sweeten the seasons hereafter
        Of the flowers or the lovers that laugh now or weep,
    When as they that are free now of weeping and
            laughter
        We shall sleep.

65 Here death may deal not again forever;
        Here change may come not till all change end.
    From the graves they have made they shall rise up
            never,

    Who have left nought living to ravage and rend.
    Earth, stones, and thorns of the wild ground growing,
70   While the sun and the rain live, these shall be;
    Till a last wind's breath upon all these blowing
        Roll the sea.

    Till the slow sea rise and the sheer cliff crumble,
        Till terrace and meadow the deep gulfs drink,
75 Till the strength of the waves of the high tides humble
        The fields that lessen, the rocks that shrink,
    Here now in his triumph where all things falter,
        Stretched out on the spoils that his own hand
            spread,
    As a god self-slain on his own strange altar,
80   Death lies dead.
    —1876

THOMAS HARDY
1840 – 1928

The work of Thomas Hardy—highly original and yet intimately connected with centuries-old traditions—is as important to the history of English poetry as it is to that of the novel in English, and as central to twentieth-century literature as it is to that of the Victorian era. Hardy was born in 1840 in Dorset, where much of his fiction was later set. A frail child, he did not attend the local school until the age of eight. However, his ill health fostered his love of reading. In his walks in the area, Hardy also came into contact with the local farmers and laborers, whose hardship and poverty deeply touched him. At the age of 15, he was apprenticed to a local architect, a career that would sustain him until he became established as a writer.

In 1862 Hardy moved to London to work with another architect. Always driven, he would rise at five in the morning to complete three or four hours of reading—in Homer, the Greek Testament, the Renaissance poets—before going to the office. On his return from work, he would often stay up reading and writing until midnight. It was during this time that he began writing poetry and short stories. Although he submitted many pieces to various magazines and the editors often wrote that he showed promise, his work was consistently rejected. The hectic schedule that Hardy was following caused his health to deteriorate, and he was forced to return to the countryside in 1867 to recuperate. In Dorchester, he worked as an architect during the day and wrote in his spare time. It was in the course of his employment that he met his first wife, Emma Gifford. He had been sent to St. Juliot to draw plans for a church restoration, and Emma was the sister-in-law of the rector. The two struck up a close friendship and Emma was very supportive of his writing. With Emma's encouragement, Hardy published his first novel, *Desperate Remedies* (1871). The novel, which has much in common with sensation fiction, a popular sub-genre of the 1860s, met with mixed reviews, but he continued to write. *Under the Greenwood Tree*, published in 1872, brought him popular acclaim.

In his early novels, Hardy began to include real places from the Dorset area, renamed Wessex— and to be praised for his portrayal of the countryside and the people of the region. *A Pair of Blue Eyes* appeared in 1873, and mirrored his own courtship with Emma. The two were married in 1874. That year also saw the publication of *Far from the Madding Crowd*, the first of what are now regarded as his classic novels. It depicts the life and loves of Bathsheba Everdene, and provides a convincing portrait of rural life. The novel also includes one of Hardy's "fallen women"; the case of Fanny Robin, who is seduced and eventually dies in a workhouse, shocked many readers. Despite this, the novel was very popular, and allowed him to give up his architectural work and concentrate solely on writing.

The Return of the Native, published in 1878, was also very successful. All of Hardy's novels were by now appearing in serialized form in monthly family magazines—a development which affected both the way that he wrote and the content of his fiction. Like most serialized writers, Hardy incorporated a steady flow of incidents in his novels; he was catering to an audience that needed to be encouraged to keep reading and buy the next issue. The "family" nature of the magazines often led his editors (one of whom was Leslie Stephen, the father of Virginia Woolf) to caution him to tone down the racier scenes and rewrite large sections. Because of the strict morality that dominated editorial policy, for example, Hardy could not state explicitly that some of his characters might have been involved in extra-marital activities.

Censure of Hardy's depiction of "immoral" subject matter reached its peak with the publication of his next two major novels, *Tess of the d'Urbervilles* (1891) and *Jude the Obscure* (1895). In the first of these, the aristocratic Alec d'Urberville forces himself upon Tess, who then bears his illegitimate child. Both the "seduction" itself and Tess's attempt to have the illegitimate child baptized shocked readers. Hardy rewrote many of the novel's explicit or controversial sections for serialization in *Longman's Magazine*, but when the novel was published as a complete volume, the controversial sections were restored.

Jude the Obscure depicts the thwarted life of Jude Fawley, a village mason who dreams of attending university but whose hopes are derailed by romantic entanglements—first with Arabella Dunn and later with Sue Bridehead—and by the deadening exclusions of class-conscious English society of the later nineteenth century. Hardy's marriage was on shaky ground at the time, and his wife Emma attempted to halt the publication of the novel. Publication went forward, but criticism of the book was swift and cruel. The Bishop of Wakefield, for one, said he had "bought one of Mr. Hardy's novels, but was so disgusted with its insolence and indecency" that he "threw it into the fire." Unfavorable and uncomprehending responses to *Jude* encouraged Hardy to give up fiction; this was the last novel he wrote.

Hardy's stories—of which he considered "The Son's Veto" to be his best—are, like his novels, frequently rooted in the details of traditional rural and small town life, although they often touch on highly contemporary issues. Also like his novels, they often take in the broad sweep of his characters' lives, which are typically subject to remorseless twists of fate; the gods may haunt his texts, but no God is there. Ongoing tensions between the city and the countryside, the educated and the uneducated, and the rich and the poor frequently contribute to the tragedy that lies at the heart of the life of a typical Hardy character, although these material factors frequently combine with a more philosophically grounded pessimism.

From the mid 1890s, Hardy concentrated on composing poetry, continuing in a different genre the portrayal of the Wessex region he had made famous in the novels. *Wessex Poems* appeared in 1898, *Satires of Circumstance* in 1914, and *Moments of Vision* in 1917. Hardy's poems form a body of work strongly rooted in the physical details of place—but even more than that, one strongly rooted in the past. Hardy often borrows from traditional poetic forms (such as the ballad), and he often employs archaic diction. In subject matter, too, the poems tend to be strongly rooted in the past—more often than not a very personal past, with love and the loss of love being recalled by the speaker; in very many of Hardy's poems an elegiac tone is pervasive.

Hardy's poetry is sometimes discussed as constituting a reaction to modernism; perhaps it would be more accurate to think of it standing as a strong counterweight to modernism. Certainly the simplicity and emotional resonance of his poetry have exerted a strong influence on the works of many subsequent poets (Philip Larkin perhaps most prominent among them). So too has Hardy's formal approach. His rhythms, his rhymes, and the way in which he varies quantity are all tightly controlled and finely modulated; the extraordinary degree of technical accomplishment in much of Hardy's poetry does not call attention to itself, and is perhaps all the more impressive for so often being unobtrusive.

Hardy's reputation continues to rest on his lyrics and ballads—most of them tightly compact works. His most ambitious poetic work is much longer; *The Dynasts* is an extraordinary epic poem set in the Napoleonic Wars. It was published in three parts between 1903 and 1908.

The death of Emma in 1912, and Hardy's subsequent remorse for what had become of their relationship, resulted in some of his finest poetry and love poems, which appeared in *Satires of*

Circumstance (1914). Hardy remarried in 1914; his second wife, Florence, is listed as the author of a two-volume biography that appeared in 1928 and 1930, but it has since been established that Hardy wrote the work himself. Hardy was awarded the Order of Merit in 1910 and the Gold Medal of the Royal Society of Literature in 1912. When he died in 1928, his ashes were interred in Poets' Corner at Westminster Abbey, but his heart was buried with Emma in Stinsford, in southern England.

⌘ ⌘ ⌘

The Son's Veto

I

To the eyes of a man viewing it from behind, the nut-brown hair was a wonder and a mystery. Under the black beaver hat, surmounted by its tuft of black feathers, the long locks, braided and twisted and coiled like the rushes of a basket, composed a rare, if somewhat barbaric, example of ingenious art. One could understand such weavings and coiling being wrought to last intact for a year, or even a calendar month; but that they should be all demolished regularly at bedtime, after a single day of permanence, seemed a reckless waste of successful fabrication.

And she had done it all herself, poor thing. She had no maid, and it was almost the only accomplishment she could boast of. Hence the unstinted pains.

She was a young invalid lady—not so very much of an invalid—sitting in a wheeled chair, which had been pulled up in the front part of a green enclosure, close to a band-stand, where a concert was going on, during a warm June afternoon. It had place in one of the minor parks or private gardens that are to be found in the suburbs of London, and was the effort of a local association to raise money for some charity. There were worlds within worlds in the great city, and though nobody outside the immediate district had ever heard of the charity, or the band, or the garden, the enclosure was filled with an interested audience sufficiently informed of all these.

As the trains proceeded many of the listeners observed the chaired lady, whose back hair, by reason of her prominent position, so challenged inspection. Her face was not easily discernible, but the aforesaid cunning tress-weavings, the white ear and poll,[1] and the curve of a cheek which was neither flaccid nor sallow, were signals that led to the expectation of good beauty in front. Such expectations are not infrequently disappointed as soon as the disclosure comes; and in the present case, when the lady, by a turn of the head, at length revealed herself, she was not so handsome as the people behind her had supposed, and even hoped—they did not know why.

For one thing (alas! the commonness of this complaint), she was less young than they had fancied her to be. Yet attractive her face unquestionably was, and not at all sickly. The revelation of its details came each time she turned to talk to a boy of twelve or thirteen who stood beside her, and the shape of whose hat and jacket implied that he belonged to a well-known public school.[2] The immediate by-standers could hear that he called her "Mother."

When the end of the programme was reached, and the audience withdrew, many chose to find their way out by passing at her elbow. Almost all turned their heads to take a full and near look at the interesting woman, who remained stationary in the chair till the way should be clear enough for her to be wheeled out without obstruction. As if she expected their glances, and did not mind gratifying their curiosity, she met the eyes of several of her observers by lifting her own, showing these to be soft, brown, and affectionate orbs, a little plaintive in their regard.

She was conducted out of the garden, and passed along the pavement till she disappeared from view, the school-boy walking beside her. To inquiries made by some persons who watched her away, the answer came that she was the second wife of the incumbent of a neighbouring parish, and that she was lame. She was generally believed to be a woman with a story—an

---

[1] *poll* Nape of the neck.

[2] *public school* In England, private school.

innocent one, but a story of some sort or other.

In conversing with her on their way home the boy who walked at her elbow said that he hoped his father had not missed them.

"He have been so comfortable these last few hours that I am sure he cannot have missed us," she replied.

"*Has,* dear mother—not *have*!" exclaimed the public-school boy, with an impatient fastidiousness that was almost harsh. "Surely you know that by this time!"

His mother hastily adopted the correction, and did not resent his making it, or retaliate, as she might well have done, by bidding him to wipe that crumby mouth of his, whose condition had been caused by surreptitious attempts to eat a piece of cake without taking it out of the pocket wherein it lay concealed. After this the pretty woman and the boy went onward in silence.

That question of grammar bore upon her history, and she fell into reverie, of a somewhat sad kind to all appearance. It might have been assumed that she was wondering if she had done wisely in shaping her life as she had shaped it, to bring out such a result as this.

In a remote nook in North Wessex, forty miles from London, near the thriving county-town of Aldbrickham, there stood a pretty village with its church and parsonage, which she knew well enough, but her son had never seen. It was her native village, Gaymead, and the first event bearing upon her present situation had occurred at that place when she was only a girl of nineteen.

How well she remembered it, that first act in her little tragi-comedy, the death of her reverend husband's first wife. It happened on a spring evening, and she who now and for many years had filled that first wife's place was then parlor-maid in the parson's house.

When everything had been done that could be done, and the death was announced, she had gone out in the dusk to visit her parents, who were living in the same village, to tell them the sad news. As she opened the white swing-gate and looked towards the trees which rose westward, shutting out the pale light of the evening sky, she discerned, without much surprise, the figure of a man standing in the hedge, though she roguishly exclaimed, as a matter of form, "Oh Sam, how you frightened me!"

He was a young gardener of her acquaintance. She told him the particulars of the late event, and they stood

silent, these two young people, in that elevated, calmly philosophic mind which is engendered when a tragedy has happened close at hand, and has not happened to the philosophers themselves. But it had its bearings upon their relations.

"And will you stay on now at the Vicarage, just the same?" asked he.

She had hardly thought of that. "Oh yes—I suppose," she said. "Everything will be just as usual, I imagine."

He walked beside her towards her mother's. Presently his arm stole round her waist. She gently removed it; but he placed it there again, and she yielded the point. "You see, dear Sophy, you don't know that you'll stay on; you may want a home; and I shall be ready to offer one some day, though I may not be ready just yet."

"Why, Sam, how can you be so fast? I've never even said I liked 'ee; and it is all your own doing, coming after me."

"Still, it is nonsense to say I am not to have a try at you, like the rest." He stooped to kiss her a farewell, for they had reached her mother's door.

"No, Sam; you sha'nt!" she cried, putting her hand over his mouth. "You ought to be more serious on such a night as this." And she bade him adieu without allowing him to kiss her or to come indoors.

The vicar just left a widower was at this time a man about forty years of age, of good family, and childless. He had led a secluded existence in this college living, partly because there were no resident landowners; and his loss now intensified his habit of withdrawal from outward observation. He was still less seen than heretofore, kept himself still less in time with the rhythm and racket of the movements called progress in the world without. For many months after his wife's decease the economy of his household remained as before; the cook, the house-maid, the parlor-maid, and the man out-of-doors performed their duties or left them undone, just as nature prompted them—the vicar knew not which. It was then represented to him that his servants seemed to have nothing to do in his small family of one. He was struck with the truth of this representation, and decided to cut down his establishment. But he was forestalled by Sophy, the parlor-maid, who said one evening that she wished to leave him.

"And why?" said the parson.

"Sam Hobson has asked me to marry him, sir."

"Well—do you want to marry?"

"Not much. But it would be a home for me. And we have heard that one of us will have to leave."

A day or two after she said: "I don't want to leave just yet, sir, if you don't wish it. Sam and I have quarreled."

He looked at her. He had hardly ever observed her before, though he had been frequently conscious of her soft presence in the room. What a kitten-like, flexuous, tender creature she was! She was the only one of the servants with whom he came into immediate and continuous relation. What should he do if Sophy were gone?

Sophy did not go, but one of the others did, and things proceeded quietly again.

When Mr. Twycott, the vicar, was ill, Sophy brought up his meals to him, and she had no sooner left the room one day than he heard a noise on the stairs. She had slipped down with the tray, and so twisted her foot that she could not stand. The village surgeon was called in; the vicar got better, but Sophy was incapacitated for a long time; and she was informed that she must never again walk much or engage in any occupation which required her to stand long on her feet. As soon as she was comparatively well she spoke to him alone. Since she was forbidden to walk and bustle about, and, indeed could not do so, it became her duty to leave. She could very well work at something sitting down, and she had an aunt, a seamstress.

The parson had been very greatly moved by what she had suffered on his account, and he exclaimed, "No, Sophy; lame or not lame, I cannot let you go. You must never leave me again."

He came close to her, and, though she could never exactly tell how it happened, she became conscious of his lips upon her cheek. He then asked her to marry him. Sophy did not exactly love him, but she had a respect for him which almost amounted to veneration. Even if she had wished to get away from him she hardly dared refuse a personage so reverend and august in her eyes, and she assented forthwith to be his wife.

Thus it happened that one fine morning, when the doors of the church were naturally open for ventilation, and the singing birds fluttered in and alighted on the tie-beams of the rood, there was a marriage-service at the communion rails which hardly a soul knew of. The parson and a neighbouring curate had entered at one door, and Sophy at another, followed by two necessary persons, whereupon in a short time there emerged a newly-made husband and wife.

Mr. Twycott knew perfectly well that he had committed social suicide by this step, despite Sophy's spotless character, and he had taken his measures accordingly. An exchange of livings had been arranged with an acquaintance who was incumbent of a church in the south of London, and as soon as possible the couple removed thither, abandoning their pretty country home with trees and shrubs and glebe[1] for a narrow, dusty house in a long, straight street, and their fine peal of bells for the wretchedest one-tongue clangor that ever tortured mortal ears. It was all on her account. They were, however, away from every one who had known her former position, and also under less observation from without than they would have had to put up with in any country parish.

Sophy the woman was as charming a partner as a man could possess, though Sophy the lady had her deficiencies. She showed a natural aptitude for little domestic refinements, so far as related to things and manners; but in what is called culture she was less intuitive. She had now been married more than fourteen years, and her husband had taken much trouble with her education; but she still held confused ideas on the use of "was" and "were", which did not beget a respect for her among the few acquaintances she made. Her great grief in this relation was that her only child, on whose education no expense had been or would be spared, was now old enough to perceive these deficiencies in his mother, and not only to see them but to feel irritated at their existence.

Thus she lived on in the city, and wasted hours in braiding her beautiful hair, till her once apple cheeks waned to pink of the very faintest. Her foot had never regained its natural strength after the accident, and she was mostly obliged to avoid walking altogether. Her husband had grown to like London for its freedom and its domestic privacy; but he was twenty years his Sophy's senior, and had latterly been seized with a serious illness. On this day, however, he had seemed to be well enough to justify her accompanying her son Randolph to the concert.

---

[1] *glebe* Land granted to clergyman.

2

The next time we get a glimpse of her is when she appears in the mournful attire of a widow.

Mr. Twycott had never rallied, and now lay in a well-packed cemetery to the south of the great city, where, if all the dead it contained had stood erect and alive, not one would have known him or recognized his name. The boy had dutifully followed him to the grave, and was now again at school.

Throughout these changes Sophy had been treated like the child she was in nature though not in years. She was left with no control over anything that had been her husband's beyond her modest personal income. In his anxiety lest her inexperience should be overreached he had safeguarded with trustees all he possibly could. The completion of the boy's course at the public school, to be followed in due time by Oxford and ordination, had been all provisioned and arranged, and she really had nothing to occupy her in the world but to eat and drink, and make a business of indolence, and go on weaving and coiling the nut-brown hair, merely keeping a home open for the son whenever he came to her during vacations.

Foreseeing his probable decease long years before her, her husband in his lifetime had purchased for her use a semi-detached villa in the same long, straight road whereon the church and parsonage faced, which was to be hers as long as she chose to live in it. Here she now resided, looking out upon the fragment of lawn in front, and through the railings at the ever-flowing traffic; or, bending forward over the window-sill on the first floor, stretching her eyes far up and down the vista of sooty trees, hazy air, and drab house façades, along which echoed the noises common to a suburban main thoroughfare.

Somehow, her boy, with his aristocratic school-knowledge, his grammar, and his aversions, was losing those wide infantile sympathies, extending as far as to the sun and moon themselves, with which he, like other children, had been born, and which his mother, a child of nature herself, had loved in him; he was reducing their compass to a population of a few thousand wealthy and titled people, the mere veneer of a thousand million or so of others who did not interest him at all. He drifted further and further away from her. Sophy's *milieu* being a suburb of minor tradesmen and under-clerks, and her almost only companions the two servants

of her own house, it was not surprising that after her husband's death she soon lost the little artificial tastes she had acquired from him, and became—in her son's eyes—a mother whose mistakes and origin it was his painful lot as a gentleman to blush for. As yet he was far from being man enough—if he ever would be—to rate these sins of hers at their true infinitesimal value beside the yearning fondness that welled up and remained penned in her heart till it should be more fully accepted by him, or by some other person or thing. If he had lived at home with her he would have had all of it; but he seemed to require so very little in present circum-stances, and it remained stored.

Her life became insupportably dreary; she could not take walks, and had no interest in going for drives, or, indeed, in traveling anywhere. Nearly two years passed without an event, and still she looked on that suburban road, thinking of the village in which she had been born, and whither she would have gone back—oh, how gladly!—even to work in the fields.

Taking no exercise, she often could not sleep, and would rise in the night or early morning and look out upon the then vacant thoroughfare, where the lamps stood like sentinels waiting for some procession to go by. An approximation to such a procession was indeed made every early morning about one o'clock, when the country vehicles passed up with loads of vegetables for Covent Garden market. She often saw them creeping along at this silent and dusky hour—wagon after wagon, bearing green bastions of cabbages nodding to their fall, yet never falling; walls of baskets enclosing masses of beans and pease; pyramids of snow-white turnips, swaying howdahs[1] of mixed produce—creeping along behind aged night-horses, who seemed ever patiently wondering between their hollow coughs why they had always to work at that still hour when all other sentient creatures were privileged to rest. Wrapped in a cloak, it was soothing to watch and sympathize with them when depression and nervousness hindered sleep, and to see how the fresh green-stuff brightened to life as it came opposite the lamp, and how the sweating animals steamed and shone with their miles of travel.

They had an interest, almost a charm, for Sophy, these semi-rural people and vehicles moving in an urban

---

[1]   *howdahs*   Seats carried by elephants.

atmosphere, leading a life quite distinct from that of the daytime toilers on the same road. One morning a man who accompanied a wagon-load of potatoes gazed rather hard at the house fronts as he passed, and with a curious emotion she thought his form was familiar to her. She looked out for him again. His being an old-fashioned conveyance with a yellow front, it was easily recognizable, and on the third night after she saw it a second time. The man alongside was, as she had fancied, Sam Hobson, formerly gardener at Gaymead, who would at one time have married her.

She had occasionally thought of him, and wondered if life in a cottage with him would not have been a happier lot than the life she had accepted. She had not thought of him passionately, but her now dismal situation lent an interest to his resurrection—a tender interest which it is impossible to exaggerate. She went back to bed, and began thinking. When did these market-gardeners, who traveled up to town so regularly at one or two in the morning, come back? She dimly recollected seeing their empty wagons, hardly noticeable among the ordinary day-traffic, passing down at some hour before noon.

It was only April, but that morning, after breakfast, she had the window opened, and sat looking out, the feeble sun shining full upon her. She affected to sew, but her eyes never left the street. Between ten and eleven the desired wagon, now unladen, reappeared on its return journey. But Sam was not looking round him then, and drove on in a reverie.

"Sam!" cried she.

Turning with a start, his face lighted up. He called to him a little boy to hold the horse, alighted, and came and stood under her window.

"I can't come down easily, Sam, or I would!" she said. "Did you know I lived here?"

"Well, Mrs. Twycott, I knew you lived along here somewhere. I have often looked out for 'ee."

He briefly explained his own presence on the scene. He had long since given up his gardening in the village near Aldbrickham, and was now manager at a market-gardener's on the south side of London, it being part of his duty to go up to Covent Garden with wagon-loads of produce two or three times a week. In answer to her curious inquiry, he admitted that he had come to this particular district because he had seen in the Aldbrickham paper a year or two before the announcement of the death in South London of the aforetime vicar of Gaymead, which had revived an interest in her dwelling-place that he could not extinguish, leading him to hover about the locality till his present post had been secured.

Hobson came and stood under her window.[1]

They spoke of their native village in dear old North Wessex, the spots in which they had played together as children. She tried to feel that she was a dignified personage now, that she must not be too confidential with Sam. But she could not keep it up, and the tears hanging in her eyes were indicated in her voice.

"You are not happy, Mrs. Twycott, I'm afraid," he said.

---

[1] The illustrations that appear here and on page 890 accompanied "The Son's Veto" when it was first published in the *Illustrated London News,* 1 December 1891.

"Oh, of course not! I lost my husband only the year before last."

"Ah! I meant in another way. You'd like to be home again!"

"This is my home—for life. The house belongs to me. But I understand"—She let it out then.

"Yes, Sam. I long for home—*our* home! I *should* like to be there, and never leave it, and die there." But she remembered herself. "That's only a momentary feeling. I have a son, you know, a dear boy. He's at school now."

"Somewhere handy, I suppose? I see there's lots of 'em along this road."

"Oh no! Not in one of these wretched holes! At a public school—one of the most distinguished in England."

"Chok' it all! of course! I forgot, ma'am, that you've been a lady for so many years."

"No, I am not a lady," she said, sadly. "I never shall be. But he's a gentleman, and that—makes it—oh, how difficult for me!"

3

The acquaintance thus oddly reopened proceeded apace. She often looked out to get a few words with him by night or by day. Her sorrow was that she could not accompany her one old friend on foot a little way, and talk more freely than she could do while he paused before the house. One night, at the beginning of June, when she was again on the watch after an absence of some days from the window, he entered the gate and said, softly, "Now, wouldn't some air do you good? I've only half a load this morning. Why not ride up to Covent Garden with me? There's a nice seat on the cabbages, where I've spread a sack. You can be home again in a cab before anybody is up."

She refused at first, and then, trembling with excitement, hastily finished her dressing, and wrapped herself up in cloak and veil, afterwards sidling downstairs by the aid of the handrail, in a way she could adopt on an emergency. When she had opened the door she found Sam on the step, and he lifted her bodily on his strong arm across the little forecourt into his vehicle. Not a soul was visible or audible in the infinite length of the straight, flat highway, with its ever-waiting lamps converging to points in each direction. The air was fresh as country air at this hour, and the stars shone, except to the north-eastward, where there was a whitish light—the dawn. Sam carefully placed her in the seat and drove on.

They talked as they had talked in old days, Sam pulling himself up now and then, when he thought himself too familiar. More than once she said with misgiving that she wondered if she ought to have indulged in the freak. "But I am so lonely in my house," she added, "and this makes me so happy!"

"You must come again, dear Mrs. Twycott. There is no time o' day for taking the air like this."

It grew lighter and lighter. The sparrows became busy in the streets, and the city waxed denser around them. When they approached the river it was day, and on the bridge they beheld the full blaze of morning sunlight in the direction of St. Paul's, the river glistening towards it, and not a craft stirring.

Near Covent Garden he put her into a cab, and they parted, looking into each other's faces like the very old friends they were. She reached home without adventure, limped to the door, and let herself in with her latch-key unseen.

The air and Sam's presence had revived her; her cheeks were quite pink—almost beautiful. She had something to live for in addition to her son. A woman of pure instincts, she knew there had been nothing really wrong in the journey, but supposed it conventionally to be very wrong indeed.

Soon, however, she gave way to the temptation of going with him again, and on this occasion their conversation was distinctly tender, and Sam said he never should forget her, notwithstanding that she had served him rather badly at one time. After much hesitation he told her of a plan it was in his power to carry out, and one he should like to take in hand, since he did not care for London work; it was to set up as a master gardener down at Aldbrickham, the county-town of their native place. He knew of an opening—a shop kept by aged people who wished to retire.

"And why don't you do it, then, Sam?" she asked, with a slight heart-sinking.

"Because I'm not sure if—you'd join me. I know you wouldn't—couldn't! Such a lady as ye've been so long, you couldn't be a wife to a man like me."

"I hardly suppose I could!" she assented, also frightened at the idea.

"If you could," he said, eagerly, "you'd on'y have to sit in the back parlor and look through the glass partition when I was away sometimes—just to keep an eye on things. The lameness wouldn't hinder that. I'd keep you as genteel as ever I could, dear Sophy—if I might think of it," he pleaded.

"Sam, I'll be frank," she said, putting her hand on his. "If it were only myself I would do it, and gladly, though everything I possess would be lost to me by marrying again."

"I don't mind that. It's more independent."

"That's good of you, dear, dear Sam. But there's something else. I have a son. I almost fancy when I am miserable sometimes that he is not really mine, but one I hold in trust for my late husband. He seems to belong so little to me personally, so entirely to his dead father. He is so much educated and I so little that I do not feel dignified enough to be his mother. Well, he would have to be told."

"Yes. Unquestionably." Sam saw her thought and her fear. "Still, you can do as you like, Sophy—Mrs. Twycott," he added. "It is not you who are the child, but he."

"Ah, you don't know! Sam, if I could, I would marry you, some day. But you must wait awhile, and let me think."

It was enough for him, and he was blithe at their parting. Not so she. To tell Randolph seemed impossible. She could wait till he had gone up to Oxford, when what she did would affect his life but little. But would he ever tolerate the idea? And if not, could she defy him?

She had not told him a word when the yearly cricket-match came on at Lord's[1] between the public schools, though Sam had already gone back to Aldbrickham. Mrs. Twycott felt stronger than usual. She went to the match with Randolph, and was able to leave her chair and walk about occasionally. The bright idea occurred to her that she could casually broach the subject while moving round among the spectators, when the boy's spirits were high with interest in the game, and

he would weigh domestic matters as feathers in the scale beside the day's victory. They promenaded under the lurid July sun, this pair, so wide apart, yet so near, and Sophy saw the large proportion of boys like her own, in their broad white collars and dwarf hats, and all around the rows of great coaches under which was jumbled the débris of luxurious luncheons—bones, pie-crusts, champagne-bottles, glasses, plates, napkins, and the family silver; while on the coaches sat the proud fathers and mothers; but never a poor mother like her. If Randolph had not appertained to these, had not centred all his interests in them, had not cared exclusively for the class they belonged to, how happy would things have been! A great huzza at some small performance with the bat burst from the multitude of relatives, and Randolph jumped wildly into the air to see what had happened. Sophy fetched up the sentence that had been already shaped; but she could not get it out. The occasion was, perhaps, an inopportune one. The contrast between her story and the display of fashion to which Randolph had grown to regard himself as akin would be fatal. She awaited a better time.

It was on an evening when they were alone in their plain suburban residence, where life was not blue but brown, that she ultimately broke silence, qualifying her announcement of a probable second marriage by assuring him that it would not take place for a long time to come, when he would be living quite independently of her.

The boy thought the idea a very reasonable one, and asked if she had chosen anybody. She hesitated; and he seemed to have a misgiving. He hoped his step-father would be a gentleman, he said.

"Not what you call a gentleman," she answered, timidly. "He'll be much as I was before I knew your father;" and by degrees she acquainted him with the whole. The youth's face remained fixed for a moment; then he flushed, leaned on the table, and burst into passionate tears.

His mother went up to him, kissed all of his face that she could get at, and patted his back as if he were still the baby he once had been, crying herself the while. When he had somewhat recovered from his paroxysm he went hastily to his own room and fastened the door.

Parleyings were attempted through the key-hole, outside which she waited and listened. It was long

[1] *yearly cricket-match … Lord's* Lord's cricket ground in London has been the site of an annual cricket match between two of the most prestigious public schools in England, Eton and Harrow, since 1805.

before he would reply, and when he did it was to say sternly at her from within: "I am ashamed of you! It will ruin me! A miserable boor! a churl! a clown! It will degrade me in the eyes of all the gentlemen of England!"

"Say no more—perhaps I am wrong! I will struggle against it!" she cried, miserably.

Before Randolph left her that summer a letter arrived from Sam to inform her that he had been unexpectedly fortunate in obtaining the shop. He was in possession; it was the largest in the town, combining fruit with vegetables, and he thought it would form a home worthy even of her some day. Might he not run up to town to see her?

She met him by stealth, and said he must still wait for her final answer. The autumn dragged on, and when Randolph was home at Christmas for the holidays she broached the matter again. But the young gentleman was inexorable.

It was dropped for months; renewed again; abandoned under his repugnance; again attempted, and thus the gentle creature reasoned and pleaded till four or five long years had passed. Then the faithful Sam revived his suit with some peremptoriness. Sophy's son, now an undergraduate, was down from Oxford one Easter, when she again opened the subject. As soon as he was ordained, she argued, he would have a home of his own, wherein she, with her bad grammar and her ignorance, would be an encumbrance to him. Better obliterate her as much as possible.

He showed a more manly anger now, but would not agree. She on her side was more persistent, and he had doubts whether she could be trusted in his absence. But by indignation and contempt for her taste he completely maintained his ascendancy; and finally taking her before a little cross and shrine that he had erected in his bedroom for his private devotions, there bade her kneel, and swear that she would not wed Samuel Hobson without his consent. "I owe this to my father!" he said.

The poor woman swore, thinking he would soften as soon as he was ordained and in full swing of clerical work. But he did not. His education had by this time sufficiently ousted his humanity to keep him quite firm; though his mother might have led an idyllic life with her faithful fruiterer and green-grocer, and nobody have been anything the worse in the world.

He made her swear before a little cross and shrine in his bed-room that she would not wed Samuel Hobson without his consent.

Her lameness became more confirmed as time went on, and she seldom or never left the house in the long southern thoroughfare, where she seemed to be pining her heart away. "Why mayn't I say to Sam that I'll marry him? Why mayn't I?" she would murmur plaintively to herself when nobody was near.

Some four years after this date a middle-aged man was standing at the door of the largest fruiterer's shop in Aldbrickham. He was the proprietor, but to-day, instead of his usual business attire, he wore a neat suit of black; and his window was partly shuttered. From the railway station a funeral procession was seen approaching; it passed his door and went out of the town towards the village of Gaymead. The man, whose eyes were wet, held his hat in his hand as the vehicles moved by; while from the mourning coach a young smooth-shaven priest in a high waistcoat looked black as a cloud at the shopkeeper standing there.

—DECEMBER 1891

IN CONTEXT

Hardy's Notebooks and Memoranda

Hardy's notebooks and memoranda for the years during which "The Son's Veto" and other short stories were written contain an interesting mixture of observations on daily life, reflections on broader issues, and thoughts regarding the writing of fiction. The following entries, for example, give a vivid sense of aspects of Hardy's life in the autumn of 1892:

"*End of September*. In London. This is the time to realize London as an old city, all the pulsing excitements of May being absent."

"Drove home from dining with McIlvaine at the Café Royal, behind a horse who had no interest in me, was going a way he had no interest in going, and was whipped on by a man who had no interest in me, or the horse, or the way. Amid this string of compulsions reached home."

"*October*. At Great Fawley, Berks. Entered a ploughed vale which might be called the Valley of Brown Melancholy. The silence is remarkable .... Though I am alive with the living I can only see the dead here, and am scarcely conscious of the happy children at play."

"*October 7*. Tennyson died yesterday morning."

"*October 12*. Tennyson's funeral in Westminster Abbey. The music was sweet impressive, but as a funeral the scene was less penetrating than a plain country interment would have been."

Hardy's notations regarding specific stories are generally unrevealing (e.g., "January 13th. *The Fiddler of the Reels* posted to Messrs Scribner, New York," "December [no date]. Found and touched up a short story called 'An Imaginative Woman'.") They do include, however, several interesting comments about writing in general. On 24 October 1892, for example, Hardy reflected that "the best tragedy—highest tragedy in short—is that of the *worthy* encompassed by the *inevitable*. The tragedies of immoral and worthless people are not of the best." Four months later he made a note that is of particular relevance to his own fiction writing:

"*February 23*. A story must be exceptional enough to justify its telling. We tale-tellers are all Ancient Mariners, and none of us is warranted in stopping Wedding Guests (in other words, the hurrying public) unless he has something more unusual to relate than the ordinary experience of every average man and woman.

"The whole secret of fiction and the drama—in the constructional part—lies in the adjustment of things unusual to things eternal and universal. The writer who knows exactly how exceptional, and how non-exceptional, his events should be made, possesses the key to the art."

(The quotations from Hardy's notebooks and memoranda are as reproduced in Florence Hardy, *The Life of Thomas Hardy, Volume 2: The Later Years of Thomas Hardy, 1892–1928* [London: Macmillan, 1930] 13, 15, 26, 15–16.)

Hap°   *chance*

If but some vengeful god would call to me
From up the sky, and laugh: "Thou suffering thing,
Know that thy sorrow is my ecstasy,
That thy love's loss is my hate's profiting!"

5 Then would I bear it, clench myself, and die,
Steeled by the sense of ire unmerited;
Half-eased in that a Powerfuller than I
Had willed and meted° me the tears I shed.   *allotted*

But not so. How arrives it joy lies slain,
10 And why unblooms the best hope ever sown?
—Crass Casualty obstructs the sun and rain,
And dicing Time for gladness casts a moan....
These purblind Doomsters[1] had as readily strown
Blisses about my pilgrimage as pain.
—1898 (WRITTEN 1866)

Neutral Tones

We stood by a pond that winter day,
And the sun was white, as though chidden of God,
And a few leaves lay on the starving sod;
—They had fallen from an ash, and were gray.

5 Your eyes on me were as eyes that rove
Over tedious riddles of years ago;
And some words played between us to and fro
On which lost the more by our love.

The smile on your mouth was the deadest thing
10 Alive enough to have strength to die;
And a grin of bitterness swept thereby
Like an ominous bird a-wing ...

Since then, keen° lessons that love deceives,   *sharp*
And wrings with wrong, have shaped to me
15 Your face, and the God-curst sun, and a tree,
And a pond edged with grayish leaves.
—1898 (WRITTEN 1867)

---

[1] *purblind Doomsters* Half-blind judges.

The Darkling° Thrush   *in the dark*

I leant upon a coppice gate[2]
When Frost was spectre-grey,
And Winter's dregs made desolate
The weakening eye of day.
5 The tangled bine[3]-stems scored the sky
Like strings of broken lyres,
And all mankind that haunted nigh
Had sought their household fires.

The land's sharp features seemed to be
10 The Century's corpse outleant,[4]
His crypt the cloudy canopy,
The wind his death-lament.
The ancient pulse of germ and birth
Was shrunken hard and dry,
15 And every spirit upon earth
Seemed fervorless as I.

At once a voice arose among
The bleak twigs overhead
In a full-hearted evensong
20 Of joy illimited;
An aged thrush, frail, gaunt, and small,
In blast-beruffled plume,[5]
Had chosen thus to fling his soul
Upon the growing gloom.

25 So little cause for carolings
Of such ecstatic sound
Was written on terrestrial things
Afar or nigh around,
That I could think there trembled through
30 His happy good-night air
Some blessed Hope, whereof he knew
And I was unaware.
—1901 (WRITTEN 31 DECEMBER 1900)

---

[2] *coppice gate* Gate leading to a thicket or small forest.

[3] *bine* Hop, a climbing plant.

[4] *The Century's corpse outleant* I.e., as if the century were leaning out of its coffin.

[5] *plume* I.e., feathers.

The Ruined Maid

"O'Melia, my dear, this does everything crown!¹
   Who could have supposed I should meet you
      in Town?
And whence such fair garments, such prosperi-ty?"—
"O didn't you know I'd been ruined?" said she.

5   —"You left us in tatters, without shoes or socks,
Tired of digging potatoes, and spudding up docks;²
And now you've gay bracelets and bright feathers three!"—
"Yes: that's how we dress when we're ruined," said she.

   —"At home in the barton° you said 'thee' and 'thou,'   *barnyard*
10 And 'thik oon,' and 'theäs oon,' and 't'other'; but now
Your talking quite fits 'ee for high compa-ny!"—
"Some polish is gained with one's ruin," said she.

   —"Your hands were like paws then, your face blue
      and bleak
But now I'm bewitched by your delicate cheek,
15 And your little gloves fit as on any la-dy!"—
"We never do work when we're ruined," said she.

   —"You used to call home-life a hag-ridden dream,
And you'd sigh, and you'd sock;³ but at present you seem
To know not of megrims° or melancho-ly!"—   *depression*
20 "True. One's pretty lively when ruined," said she.

   —"I wish I had feathers, a fine sweeping gown,
And a delicate face, and could strut about Town!"—
"My dear—a raw country girl, such as you be,
Cannot quite expect that. You ain't ruined," said she.
—1901 (WRITTEN 1866)

A Broken Appointment

You did not come.
And marching Time drew on, and wore me numb.—
Yet less for loss of your dear presence there
Than that I thus found lacking in your make

5   That high compassion which can overbear
Reluctance for pure lovingkindness' sake
Grieved I, when, as the hope-hour stroked its sum,
      You did not come.

      You love not me,
10 And love alone can lend you loyalty;
—I know and knew it. But, unto the store
Of human deeds divine in all but name,
Was it not worth a little hour or more
To add yet this: Once you, a woman, came
15 To soothe a time-torn man; even though it be
      You love not me?

—1902

Shut Out That Moon

Close up the casement, draw the blind,
   Shut out that stealing moon,
She wears too much the guise she wore
      Before our lutes were strewn
5 With years-deep dust, and names we read
      On a white stone were hewn.

Step not out on the dew-dashed lawn
      To view the Lady's Chair,
Immense Orion's glittering form,
10   The Less and Greater Bear:⁴
Stay in; to such sights we were drawn
      When faded ones were fair.

Brush not the bough for midnight scents
      That come forth lingeringly,
15 And wake the same sweet sentiments
      They breathed to you and me
When living seemed a laugh, and love
      All it was said to be.

Within the common lamp-lit room
20   Prison my eyes and thought;
Let dingy details crudely loom,
      Mechanic° speech be wrought: *low, vulgar*

---

¹ *this does everything crown* This surpasses everything.

² *spudding up docks* Uprooting weeds.

³ *sock* Mouth your displeasure.

⁴ *Lady's Chair ... Greater Bear* Constellations.

Too fragrant was Life's early bloom,
  Too tart the fruit it brought!
—1909

The Convergence of the Twain

(Lines on the Loss of the "Titanic"[1])

1

In a solitude of the sea
  Deep from human vanity,
And the Pride of Life that planned her, stilly couches she.

2

Steel chambers, late the pyres
5   Of her salamandrine fires,[2]
Cold currents thrid,[3] and turn to rhythmic tidal lyres.

3

Over the mirrors meant
  To glass the opulent
The sea-worm crawls—grotesque, slimed, dumb,
    indifferent.

4

10   Jewels in joy designed
  To ravish the sensuous mind
Lie lightless, all their sparkles bleared and black and blind.

5

Dim moon-eyed fishes near
  Gaze at the gilded gear
15 And query: "What does this vaingloriousness down
    here?" ...

6

Well: while was fashioning
  This creature of cleaving wing,
The Immanent Will[4] that stirs and urges everything

7

Prepared a sinister mate
20   For her—so gaily great—
A Shape of Ice, for the time far and dissociate.

8

And as the smart ship grew
  In stature, grace, and hue,
In shadowy silent distance grew the Iceberg too.

9

25   Alien they seemed to be:
  No mortal eye could see
The intimate welding of their later history,

10

Or sign that they were bent
  By paths coincident
30 On being anon twin halves of one august event,

11

Till the Spinner of the Years
  Said "Now!" And each one hears,
And consummation comes, and jars two hemispheres.
—1914

Channel Firing[5]

That night your great guns, unawares,
  Shook all our coffins as we lay,
And broke the chancel[6] window-squares,
We thought it was the Judgment-day

---

[1] *the "Titanic"* At the time the largest ship ever built, the ocean liner *Titanic* had been described as unsinkable, but on its maiden voyage in 1912 it collided with an iceberg; over 1,400 people drowned when it sank.

[2] *salamandrine fires* According to mythology, salamanders are able to survive any heat.

[3] *thrid* Thread.

[4] *The Immanent Will* The force that pervades and determines human existence.

[5] *Channel Firing* In the months leading up to the First World War both the British and the German navies practiced firing in the English Channel. (This poem was written in April 1914; the First World War began in August of the same year.)

[6] *chancel* Eastern part of a church, used by those who officiate at services.

5   And sat upright. While drearisome
    Arose the howl of wakened hounds:
    The mouse let fall the altar-crumb,
    The worms drew back into the mounds,

    The glebe¹ cow drooled. Till God called, "No;
10 It's gunnery practice out at sea
    Just as before you went below;
    The world is as it used to be:

    "All nations striving strong to make
    Red war yet redder. Mad as hatters²
15 They do no more for Christès° sake   Christ's
    Than you who are helpless in such matters.

    "That this is not the judgment-hour
    For some of them's a blessed thing,
    For if it were they'd have to scour
20 Hell's floor for so much threatening. . . .

    "Ha, ha. It will be warmer when
    I blow the trumpet (if indeed
    I ever do; for you are men,
    And rest eternal sorely need)."

25 So down we lay again. "I wonder,
    Will the world ever saner be,"
    Said one, "than when He sent us under
    In our indifferent century!"

    And many a skeleton shook his head.
30 "Instead of preaching forty year,"
    My neighbour Parson Thirdly said,
    "I wish I had stuck to pipes and beer."

    Again the guns disturbed the hour,
    Roaring their readiness to avenge,

35 As far inland as Stourton Tower,
    And Camelot, and starlit Stonehenge.³
    —1914

The Voice

Woman much missed, how you call to me, call to me,
    Saying that now you are not as you were
When you had changed from the one who was all to me,
    But as at first, when our day was fair.

5   Can it be you that I hear? Let me view you, then,
    Standing as when I drew near to the town
Where you would wait for me: yes, as I knew you then,
    Even to the original air-blue gown!

Or is it only the breeze, in its listlessness
10 Travelling across the wet mead° to me here,   meadow
You being ever dissolved to wan wistlessness,
    Heard no more again far or near?

        Thus I; faltering forward,
        Leaves around me falling,
15 Wind oozing thin through the thorn from norward,
        And the woman calling.
    —1914 (WRITTEN DECEMBER 1912)

Transformations

Portion of this yew⁴
    Is a man my grandsire knew,
Bosomed here at its foot:
This branch may be his wife,
5   A ruddy human life
Now turned to a green shoot.

These grasses must be made
Of her who often prayed,

---

¹ *glebe* Field, especially a field belonging to a church.

² *Mad as hatters* Makers of felt hats in the late eighteenth and early nineteenth century frequently went insane as a result of breathing in mercury compounds used in the manufacture of the hats.

³ *Stourton Tower … Stonehenge* Stourton Tower was built to commemorate the victory of King Alfred over the Danes; Camelot was the site of King Arthur's court; Stonehenge is the famous prehistoric stone monument near Salisbury.

⁴ *yew* Traditionally, yew trees have been planted beside churches and near graveyards.

Last century, for repose;
10 And the fair girl long ago
Whom I vainly tried to know
May be entering this rose.

So, they are not underground,
But as nerves and veins abound
15 In the growths of upper air,
And they feel the sun and rain,
And the energy again
That made them what they were!
—1915

In Time of "The Breaking of Nations"[1]

1

Only a man harrowing clods
    In a slow silent walk
With an old horse that stumbles and nods
    Half asleep as they stalk.

2

5 Only thin smoke without flame
    From the heaps of couch-grass;
Yet this will go onward the same
    Though Dynasties pass.

3

Yonder a maid and her wight[2]
10   Come whispering by:
War's annals will fade into night
    Ere their story die.
—1916

The Photograph

The flame crept up the portrait line by line
    As it lay on the coals in the silence of night's profound,
    And over the arm's incline,

And along the marge of the silkwork superfine,
5 And gnawed at the delicate bosom's defenceless round.

Then I vented a cry of hurt, and averted my eyes;
The spectacle was one that I could not bear,
        To my deep and sad surprise;
But, compelled to heed, I again looked furtivewise
10 Till the flame had eaten her breasts, and mouth, and hair.

"Thank God, she is out of it now!" I said at last,
In a great relief of heart when the thing was done
        That had set my soul aghast,
And nothing was left of the picture unsheathed from
        the past
15 But the ashen ghost of the card it had figured on.

She was a woman long hid amid packs of years,
She might have been living or dead; she was lost to
        my sight,
        And the deed that had nigh drawn tears
Was done in a casual clearance of life's arrears;
20 But I felt as if I had put her to death that night! …

—Well; she knew nothing thereof did she survive,
And suffered nothing if numbered among the dead;
        Yet—yet—if on earth alive
Did she feel a smart, and with vague strange anguish
        strive?
25 If in heaven, did she smile at me sadly and shake her
        head?
—1917

During Wind and Rain

They sing their dearest songs—
    He, she, all of them—yea,
Treble and tenor and bass,
    And one to play;
5 With the candles mooning each face....
    Ah, no; the years O!
How the sick leaves reel down in throngs!

They clear the creeping moss—
    Elders and juniors—aye,

---

[1] *In Time of "The Breaking of Nations"* See Jeremiah 51.20: "Thou art my battleaxe and weapons of war: for with thee will I break in pieces the nations. ..."

[2] *wight* I.e., man.

10 Making the pathways neat
    And the garden gay;
And they build a shady seat. . . .
    Ah, no; the years, the years;
See, the white storm-birds wing across.

15 They are blithely breakfasting all—
Men and maidens—yea,
Under the summer tree,
    With a glimpse of the bay,
While pet fowl come to the knee. . . .
20   Ah, no; the years O!
And the rotten rose is ript from the wall.

They change to a high new house,
He, she, all of them—aye,
Clocks and carpets and chairs
25   On the lawn all day,
And brightest things that are theirs. . . .
    Ah, no; the years, the years;
Down their carved names the rain-drop ploughs.
—1917

The Oxen

Christmas Eve, and twelve of the clock.
  "Now they are all on their knees,"[1]
An elder said as we sat in a flock
    By the embers in hearthside ease.

5 We pictured the meek mild creatures where
    They dwelt in their strawy pen,
Nor did it occur to one of us there
    To doubt they were kneeling then.

So fair a fancy few would weave
10   In these years! Yet, I feel,
If someone said on Christmas Eve,
    "Come; see the oxen kneel,

In the lonely barton° by yonder coomb°   *barnyard / valley*
    Our childhood used to know,"
15 I should go with him in the gloom,
    Hoping it might be so.
—1917

Going and Staying

1

The moving sun-shapes on the spray,
  The sparkles where the brook was flowing,
Pink faces, plightings, moonlit May—
These were the things we wished would stay;
5   But they were going.

2

Seasons of blankness as of snow,
The silent bleed of a world decaying,
The moan of multitudes in woe—
These were the things we wished would go;
10   But they were staying.

3

Then we looked closelier at Time,
And saw his ghostly arms revolving
To sweep off woeful things with prime,
Things sinister with things sublime
15   Alike dissolving.
—1920

---

[1] *Now they are all on their knees* It was once widely believed that oxen would kneel at the appointed time on Christmas every year in imitation of the ox in the manger kneeling when Christ was born.

In Context

Hardy's Reflections on the Writing of Poetry

The Life of Thomas Hardy, published under the name of his second wife, Florence Hardy, was later discovered to have been written by Hardy himself. When this third-person autobiography discusses Hardy's poetic career in relation to his fiction writing, the author reveals his sensitivity to suggestions that he had taken up poetry only as a result of the reaction against his later novels:

> In the early weeks of this year [1899] the poems were reviewed in the customary periodicals— mostly in a friendly tone, even in a tone of respect, and with praise for many pieces in the volume; though by some critics not without umbrage at Hardy's having taken the liberty to adopt another vehicle of expression than prose fiction without consulting them....
>
> Almost all the fault-finding was, in fact, based on the one great antecedent conclusion that an author who has published prose first, and that largely, must necessarily express himself badly in verse, no reservation being added to except cases in which he may have published prose for temporary or compulsory reasons, or prose of a poetical kind, or have written verse first of all, or for a long time intermediately.... In the present case, although it was shown that many of the verses had been written before their author dreamt of novels, the critics' view was very little affected that he had "at the eleventh hour," as they untruly put it, taken up a hitherto uncared-for art.

A few pages on, the account is again at pains to emphasize the purity of Hardy's motives in abandoning prose fiction and devoting himself to poetry:

> When one considers how he might have made himself a man of affluence by taking the current of popularity as it served, writing "best sellers," and ringing changes upon the novels he had already written, his bias towards poetry must have been instinctive and disinterested.

Hardy includes few reflections on the nature of his own poetry, but he does take issue with Wordsworth's famous strictures against poetic diction, asserting that Wordsworth "should have put the matter somewhat like this: in works of *passion and sentiment* (not 'imagination and sentiment') the language of verse is the language of prose. In works of *fancy* (or *imagination*), 'poetic diction' (of the real kind) is proper, and even necessary." Here and there Hardy also makes interesting comments on the origin of particular poems. Here, for example, are his remarks concerning "In Time of 'The Breaking of Nations'":

> I believe it would be said by people who knew me well that I have a faculty (perhaps not uncommon) for burying an emotion in my heart or brain for forty years, and exhuming it at the end of that time as fresh as when interred. For instance, the poem entitled "The Breaking of Nations" contains a feeling that moved me in 1870, during the Franco-Prussian war, when I chanced to be looking at such an agricultural incident in Cornwall. But I did not write the verses till during the war with Germany of 1914, and onwards.

GERARD MANLEY HOPKINS
1844 – 1889

The Victorian priest and poet Gerard Manley Hopkins lived only 45 years, but his work spans three eras of literary history. A Romantic in his notions of the beauty and power of the natural world and of the importance of the imagination and the individual's connection with nature, Hopkins shared some affinities with Keats and other poets of the Romantic period. He also shared affinities with the Victorian Pre-Raphaelites, and like them was very influenced by the writings of John Ruskin. But because his poems and letters, in which he outlined his innovative poetic theories, were not published until 1918, some 30 years after his death, he is sometimes grouped with such Modernists as T.S. Eliot and Ezra Pound. Indeed these poets were influenced by Hopkins's experimental verse, with its unconventional syntax, dense alliteration, and "sprung rhythm" (the term Hopkins coined to describe his unique metric style).

Hopkins was born in Essex of affluent parents and showed promise as a scholar from an early age, but he was clearly also talented in music and the visual arts. His early schooling was at Highgate, where he studied under, and formed a lifelong friendship with, the Pre-Raphaelite poet R.W. Dixon. Hopkins went on to study classics at Oxford, where he became known as the "Star of Balliol [College]" and was educated by such luminaries as Benjamin Jowett and Walter Pater. While Pater's aestheticism was indeed an influence on Hopkins's artistic philosophies, no one at Oxford had a greater impact on him than did John Henry Newman. A convert to Roman Catholicism who later became a Cardinal, Newman was one of the leaders of the "Oxford Movement" of the 1830s and early 1840s, a Tractarian movement (because of the "Tracts for the Times" that Newman and others wrote) that called for the Church of England to recognize points of communion with the Roman Catholic Church.

Hopkins's conversion to Roman Catholicism in 1866 estranged him from his devout Anglican parents, who wrote "terrible" letters to try to dissuade him from his decision to become a Jesuit priest. He replied to his father's concerns by saying: "I am surprised you shd. say fancy and aesthetic tastes have led me to my present state of mind: these wd. be better satisfied in the Church of England, for bad taste is always meeting one in the accessories of Catholicism." Hopkins served the Catholic Church for the rest of his life, and for many of those years he renounced his own poetry, burning much of it in the belief that, with the exception of sermons, authorship was not becoming for a priest. It was obvious, however, that he did not cease thinking about the techniques of writing, as his journals and letters, many written to his Oxford friend and poet (later Poet Laureate) Robert Bridges, attest.

After a famous shipwreck in 1875, Hopkins's superiors encouraged him to write of the fate of five Franciscan nuns, exiled from Germany by the Falk Laws, who had drowned in the disaster. In the long ode *The Wreck of the Deutschland* he began experimenting with the rhythms he had been thinking about for so long. According to Hopkins, every object in the natural world has a unique and fluid identity, or "inscape," an essence that comprises its form and its meaning. Hopkins also coined the term "instress" to describe the way in which objects or people perceive "inscape." Instress is a powerful burst of energy that allows an observer to penetrate and experience the object's essence. Poetry, for Hopkins, is instress, and that which it seeks to penetrate is the divine.

In creating a poetic sound that would present the inscape of objects and of speech itself, Hopkins was inspired by the rhythms of Welsh nursery rhymes and Old English poetry. "Sprung rhythm" was the result, a syntactically disjunctive, highly alliterative, and densely rhyming style that reconfigured the nature of stresses and line length. The poems in this style that followed *Deutschland*—among them the famous "God's Grandeur"—often aimed to celebrate the spiritual and the divine. Notably, Hopkins added the dedication "*To Christ our Lord*" to "The Windhover."

Hopkins continued to write poetry, but his duties as a priest took priority. He served from 1877 to 1879 in various parishes in Sheffield, Oxford, and London, and then went on to fulfill demanding duties in the dreary slums of Manchester, Liverpool, and Glasgow. In 1881 he began teaching at Stonyhurst College in Lancashire, and in 1884 was appointed Professor of Greek and Latin at University College in Dublin. Hopkins disliked both his duties at this university and the city itself, which was still recovering from the Great Famine. Years of illness and depression followed, combined with doubts about his ability to give himself completely to God. During these years of angst, Hopkins composed what are now called his "terrible sonnets," among them "Carrion Comfort" and "No Worst, There is None," named for their themes of anguish and desolation.

Hopkins was not to live long in Ireland; he contracted typhoid fever and died in 1889 at the age of 45. Robert Bridges edited a volume of his poetry, *The Poems of Gerard Manley Hopkins*, and released it to the public thirty years after Hopkins's death, presumably waiting until the world was ready to hear the sound of the poet who acknowledged his "oddness" by saying: "The effect of studying masterpieces is to make me admire and do otherwise." Although his output was relatively small, the poet who "did otherwise" made an enormous impact on the literary world, and has influenced several generations of poets.

⌘ ⌘ ⌘

God's Grandeur

The world is charged with the grándeur of God.
　　It will flame out, like shining from shook foil;[1]
It gathers to a greatness, like the ooze of oil
Crushed.[2] Why do men then now not reck°　　　　*regard*
　　his rod?
5　Génerátions have trod, have trod, have trod;
　　And all is seared with trade; bleared, smeared, with
　　　　toil;
　　And wears man's smudge and shares man's smell:
　　　　the soil
Is bare now, nor can foot feel, being shod.

Ánd, for° all this, náture is never spent;　　　　*despite*
10　There lives the dearest freshness deep down things;
And though the last lights off the black West went
　　Oh, morning, at the brown brink eastward,
　　　　springs—
Because the Holy Ghost óver the bent
　　World broods with warm breast and with ah!
　　　　bright wings.
　　　　　　—1918 (WRITTEN 1877)

The Windhover[3]
To Christ Our Lord

I caught this morning morning's minion, king-
　　dom of daylight's dauphin,[4] dapple-dáwn-drawn
　　　　Falcon, in his riding
Of the rólling level úndernéath him steady air, and
　　　　striding
High there, how he rung upon the rein of a
　　wimpling° wing　　　　　　　　　　　　*rippling*
5　In his écstasy! then off, off forth on swing,

As a skate's heel sweeps smooth on a bow-bend:
　　the hurl and gliding
Rebuffed the bíg wind. My heart in hiding
Stírred for a bird,—the achieve of, the mástery of the
　　thing!

Brute beauty and valour and act, oh, air, pride, plŭme,
　　here
10　Buckle! AND the fire that breaks from thee then, a
　　billion
Tímes told lovelier, more dangerous, O my
　　chevalier!°　　　　　　　　　　　　　*horseman*

No wŏnder of it: shéer plód makes plóugh down
　　síllion°　　　　　　　　　　　　　　*furrows*
Shíne, and blue-bleak embers, ah my dear,
　　Fall, gáll themsélves, and gásh gŏld-vermílion.
　　　　—1918 (WRITTEN 1877)

Pied[5] Beauty

Glóry be to God for dappled things—
　　For skies of couple-colour as a brinded° cow;　*spotted*
　　　　For rose-moles all in stipple upon trout that
　　　　　　swim;
Fresh-firecoal chestnut-fálls;[6] fínches' wings;
5　Lándscape plotted and pieced—fold,°　　　　*pasture*
　　　　fallow, and plough;
　　　　And áll trádes, their gear and tackle and
　　　　　　trim.°　　　　　　　　　　　*equipment*

Áll things counter,° original, spáre,° stránge;　*contrary / rare*
　　Whatever is fickle, frecklèd (who knows how?)
　　　　With swíft, slów; sweet, soŭr; adázzle, dím;
10　He fathers-forth whose beauty is pást chánge:
　　　　　　　　　　Práise hím.
　　　　—1918 (WRITTEN 1877)

1　[Hopkins's note] I mean foil in its sense of leaf or tinsel. … Shaken
goldfoil gives off broad glares like sheet lightning and also, and this
is true of nothing else, owing to its zigzag dints and creasings and
network of small many cornered facets, a sort of fork lightning too.

2　*oil / Crushed*　I.e., as olive oil.

3　*Windhover*　Another name for a kestrel, a small falcon that
appears to hover in the wind.

4　*dauphin*　Title of the eldest son of the King of France—the heir.

5　*Pied*　Multicolored.

6　*Fresh … fálls*　Freshly fallen, brightly colored chestnuts.

Felix Randal

Félix Rándal the fárrier,[1] O is he déad then? my
  dúty all énded,
Who have watched his mould of man, big-bóned and
  hardy-handsome
Pining, píning, till time when reason rámbled in it
  and some
Fatal four disorders, fléshed there, all contended?

5 Síckness bróke him. Impatient, he cursed at first, but
  mended
Being anointed[2] and all; though a heavenlier heart
  began some
Mónths éarlier, since I had our swéet repríeve and
  ránsom[3]
Téndered to him. Áh well, God rést him áll road
  éver[4] he offénded!

This séeing the síck endéars them tó us, us tóo it
  endéars.
10 My tongue had taught thee comfort, touch had
  quenchèd thy tears,
Thy tears that touched my heart, child, Félix, poor
  Felix Randal;

How far from then forethought of, all thy more
  boisterous years,
When thou at the random[5] grim fórge, pówerful
  amídst péers,
Didst fettle° for the great grey drayhorse[6]   *prepare*
his bright and battering sandal!
    —1918 (WRITTEN 1880)

Spring and Fall: To a Young Child

Márgarét, áre you gríeving
  Over Goldengrove unleaving?
Leáves, like the thíngs of mán, you
With your fresh thoughts care for, can you?
5 Ah! ás the héart grows ólder
It will come to such sights colder
By and by, nor spare a sigh
Though worlds of wanwood leafmeal[7] lie;
And yet you *will* weep and know why.
10 Now no matter, child, the name:
Sórrow's spríngs áre the sáme.
Nor mouth had, no nor mind, expressed
What héart héard of, ghóst° guéssed: *spirit*
It ís the blíght mán was bórn for,
15 It is Margaret you mourn for.
    —1918 (WRITTEN 1880)

[As kingfishers catch fire]

As kingfishers catch fire, dragonflies draw flame;
  As tumbled over rim in roundy wells
    Stones ring; like each tucked° string   *plucked*
    tells, each hung bell's
Bow swung finds tongue to fling out broad its name;
5 Each mortal thing does one thing and the same:
    Deals out that being indoors each one dwells;
    Selves—goes its self; *myself* it speaks and spells,
Crying *What I do is me: for that I came.*

I say more: the just man justices;
10   Keeps grace: that keeps all his goings graces;
Ácts in God's eye what in God's eye he is—

    Chríst. For Christ plays in ten thousand places,
Lovely in limbs, and lovely in eyes not his
    To the Father through the features of men's faces.
    —1918 (WRITTEN 1879–82)

---

[1] *fárrier* One who shoes horses.

[2] *anointed* As in the sacrament of Extreme Unction, performed for the dying.

[3] *had our swéet repríeve and ránsom* I.e., had received Holy Communion.

[4] *áll road éver* However.

[5] *random* Roughly built.

[6] *drayhorse* Powerful horse used for drawing a sled.

[7] *wanwood leafmeal* Decaying wood and leaves.

[*No worst, there is none*]

No worst, there is none. Pitched past pitch of grief,
   More pangs will, schooled at forepangs, wilder wring.
Comforter, where, where is your comforting?
Mary, mother of us, where is your relief?
5 My cries heave, herds-long; huddle in a main, a chief—
Woe, world-sorrow; on an áge-old ánvil wínce and
      síng—
Then lull, then leave off. Fury had shrieked "No ling-
Ering! Let me be fell:° force[1] I must be brief."   *fierce*
O the mind, mind has mountains; cliffs of fall
10 Frightful, sheer, no-man-fathomed. Hold them cheap
May who ne'er hung there. Nor does long our small
Durance deal with that steep or deep. Here! creep,
Wretch, under a comfort serves in a whirlwind: all
Life death does end and each day dies with sleep.
—1918 (WRITTEN 1884–85)

[*I wake and feel the fell[2] of dark, not day*]

I wake and feel the fell of dark, not day
   What hours, O what black hours we have spent
This night! what sights you, heart, saw, ways you went!
And more must, in yet longer light's delay.

5 With witness I speak this. But where I say
Hours I mean years, mean life. And my lament
Is cries countless, cries like dead letters sent
To dearest him that lives alas! away.

I am gall, I am heartburn. God's most deep decree
10 Bitter would have me taste: my taste was me;
Bones built in me, flesh filled, blood brimmed the curse.

Selfyeast of spirit a dull dough sours. I see
The lost are like this, and their scourge to be
As I am mine, their sweating selves; but worse.
—1918

[*Not, I'll not, carrion[3] comfort*]

Not, I'll not, carrion comfort, Despair, not feast on
   thee;
Not untwist—slack they may be—these last strands of
   man
In me ór, most weary, cry *I can no more*. I can;
Can something, hope, wish day come, not choose not
   to be.

5 But ah, but O thou terrible, why wouldst thou rude
   on me[4]
Thy wring-world right foot rock? lay a lionlimb
   against me? scan
With darksome devouring eyes my bruisèd bones? and
   fan,
O in turns of tempest, me heaped there; me frantic to
   avoïd thee and flee?

Why? That my chaff might fly; my grain lie, sheer and
   clear.
10 Nay in all that toil, that coil,° since (seems)   *tumult*
   I kissed the rod,
Hand rather, my heart lo! lapped strength, stole joy,
   would laugh, cheer.
Cheer whóm though? The hero whose héaven-
   handling flúng me, fóot tród
Me? or mé that fóught him? O which one? is it éach
   one? That níght, that yéar
Of now done darkness I wretch lay wrestling with (my
   God!) my God.
—1918

---

[1] *force* Perforce, or out of necessity.

[2] *fell* Bitterness; also an animal hide, used as a covering.

[3] *carrion* Dead flesh.

[4] *rude on me* Roughly against me.

That Nature Is a Heraclitean Fire[1] *and of the Comfort of the Resurrection*

Cloud-puffball, torn tufts, tossed pillows | flaunt
    forth, then chevy° on an air—   *race*
Built thoroughfare: heaven-roysterers,[2] in gay-gangs |
    they throng; they glitter in marches.
Down roughcast,[3] down dazzling whitewash, |
    wherever an elm arches,
Shivelights[4] and shadowtackle[5] in long | lashes lace,
    lance, and pair.
5   Delightfully the bright wind boisterous | ropes,
    wrestles, beats earth bare
Of yestertempest's creases; in pool and rut peel
    parches
Squandering ooze to squeezed | dough, crúst, dust;
    stánches,° stárches   *reinforces*
Squadroned masks and manmarks | treadmire toil
    there
Fóotfretted in it. Million-fuelèd, | nature's bonfire
    burns on.
10   But quench her bonniest, dearest | to her, her
    clearest-selvèd spark
Mán, how fást his fíredint, | his mark on mind, is
    gone!
Bóth are in an ŭnfáthomable, áll is in an enórmous
    dárk
Drowned. O pity and indig | nation! Manshape, that
    shone
Sheer off, disseveral,° a star, death blots
    black out; nor mark   *separate*
15   Is any of him at all so stark
But vastness blurs and time | beats level. Enough! the
    Resurrection,
A héart's-clarion! Awáy grief's gásping, | joyless days,
    dejection.
          Across my foundering deck shone

A beacon, an eternal beam. | Flesh fade, and mortal
    trash
20   Fáll to the residuary worm; | world's wildfire, leave
    but ash:
          In a flash, at a trumpet crash,
I am all at once what Christ is, | since he was what I
    am, and
This Jack,° jóke, poor pótsherd,[6] | patch,[7]   *fellow*
    matchwood,° immortal diamond,   *kindling*
          Is immortal diamond.
—1918 (WRITTEN 1888)

[*Thou art indeed just, Lord*]

Justus quidem tu es, Domine, si disputem tecum:
verumtamen justa loquar ad te: Quare via impiorum
prosperatur?[8] *etc.*

Thou art indeed just, Lord, if I contend
    With thee; but, sir, so what I plead is just.
   Whý do sínners' ways prosper? and why must
Dísappóintment all I endeavour end?
5   Wert thou my enemy, O thou my friend,
How wouldst thou worse, I wonder, than thou dost
Defeat, thwart me? Oh, the sots° and thralls   *drunkards*
   of lust
Do in spare hours more thrive than I that spend,
Sir, life upon thy cause. See, banks and brakes°   *thickets*
10 Now, leavèd how thick! lacèd they are again
With fretty chervil,[9] look, and fresh wind shakes
Them; birds build—but not I build; no, but strain,
Time's eunuch, and not breed one work that wakes.
Mine, O thou lord of life, send my roots rain.
—1918 (WRITTEN 1889)

---

[1] *Heraclitean Fire* Heraclitus (c. 535–475 BCE), a Greek philosopher, taught that everything is derived from fire, and therefore in a
constant state of change.

[2] *roysterers* Noisy party-goers.

[3] *roughcast* Wall plastering made of lime and gravel.

[4] *Shivelights* Strips of light.

[5] *shadowtackle* Shadows which resemble a ship's rigging.

[6] *pótsherd* Piece of broken pottery.

[7] *patch* Simpleton.

[8] *Justus ... prosperatur* Latin: You are always righteous, O Lord,
when I bring a case before you. Yet I would speak with you about
your justice: why does the way of the wicked prosper? (Jeremiah
12.1).

[9] *fretty chervil* Interlaced leaves and stems of a garden herb.

IN CONTEXT

The Growth of "The Windhover"

Manuscript copies of Hopkins's poems open a remarkable window on his unique approach to poetic rhythm—and to poetic composition; "The Windhover" is a particularly interesting example.

The first page reproduced here (headed "Another version") is entirely in Hopkins's hand, and probably dates from 1877. The second dates from 1883; it is from an album of "fair copy" transcriptions of Hopkins's (often not very legible) manuscripts that was prepared by his friend and mentor, the poet Robert Bridges, and then corrected by Hopkins in 1884. According to Hopkins scholar Norman H. Mackenzie, the corrections and revisions here in Hopkins's handwriting include the addition of ": to Christ our Lord" to the title; the alteration of "o air" to "oh, air"; the replacement of the ampersand with the word "AND" in line 10; the addition of stress marks in lines two, 3, 12, and 14; the addition of a "slur" between "the" and "hurl" in line 6, and the addition of seven "outrides" (as Hopkins termed the curved marks below the line).

Adding marks to indicate particularly strong stresses and adding "slurs" and "outrides" were among the many ways Hopkins endeavored to direct the reading of his poems according to the principles of what he termed "sprung rhythm" (see the Glossary at the back of this volume for a definition). The meaning of the "slur" mark is fairly straightforward; it indicates where two syllables should be compressed together so as to be pronounced as one—much as in this case an apostrophe might be used to do (*th'hurl*). The "outride" denotes a much less familiar concept, and it may be best to quote Hopkins directly here. At one point he writes that "the outride under one or more syllables makes them extrametrical: a slight pause follows as if the voice were silently making its way back to the highroad of the verse." Elsewhere he describes syllables so marked as "hangers or outriders," meaning "one, two or three slack syllables added to a foot and not counted in the nominal scanning. They are so called because they seem to hang below the line or ride forward or backward from it in another dimension than the line itself, according to a principle needless to explain here."

When entering corrections and revisions in 1884 Hopkins also added at lower right the date and place of the poem's original composition. The marginal notes, however, were evidently added by Bridges when he transcribed them; "= A", for example, indicates that the hyphen Bridges has added to line 6 is taken from an early manuscript of the poem (referred to as manuscript A).

The windhover (Another version) : to Christ our Lord.

I caught this morning morning's minion, king-   96
    Of daylight's dauphin, dapple-dawn-drawn Fal-
        con, in his riding   [and striding
    Of the rolling level underneath him steady air,
O how he rung upon the rein of a wimpling wing
In his ecstacy! then off, ; forth on swing,
    As a skate's heel sweeps smooth on a bow-bend:
        the hurl and gliding
    Rebuffed the big : wind . my heart in hiding
Stirred for a bird — for the mastery of the thing !

Brute beauty and valour and act, ; air, pride, plume,
                here   [then, a billion
    Buckle ! And the fire that breaks from thee
: times told lovelier , more dangerous, , O my
        chevalier !

    no wonder f it : sheer ; plod makes plough down
            sillion
Shine, and blue-bleak embers, ah my dear,
    Fall, gall themselves, and gash : gold-vermilion.

(8)

The Windhover : to Christ our Lord

I caught this morning morning's minion, king-
dom of daylight's dauphin, dapple-dawn-drawn Falcon, in his riding
Of the rolling, level underneath him steady air, & striding
High there, how he rung upon the rein of a wimpling wing
In his ecstasy! then off, off forth on swing
As a skate's heel sweeps smooth on a bow-bend: the hurl & gliding   = A
Rebuffed the big wind. My heart in hiding
Stirred for a bird, — the achieve of, the mastery of the thing!   , A, A.

Brute beauty & valour & act, oh, air, pride, plume, here
Buckle! AND the fire that breaks from thee then, a billion
Times told lovelier, more dangerous, o my chevalier!
No wonder of it: sheer plód makes plough down sillion
Shine, & blue-bleak embers, ah my dear,
Fall, gall themselves, & gash gold-vermilion.

St. Beuno's. May 30 1877

from *Journal* 1870–74

[*"Inscape" and "Instress"*]

[April 15] The white violets are broader and smell; the blue, scentless and finer made, have sharper whelking[1] and a more winged recoil in the leaves.

Take a *few* primroses in a glass and the instress[2] of—brilliancy, sort of starriness: I have not the right word—so simple a flower gives is remarkable. It is, I think, due to the strong swell given by the deeper yellow middle.

"The young lambs bound As to the tabour's sound."[3]

They toss and toss: it is as if it were the earth that flung them, not themselves. It is the pitch of graceful agility when we think that.

April 16—Sometimes they rest a little space on the hind legs and the fore-feet drop curling in on the breast, not so liquidly as we see it in the limbs of foals though.

Bright afternoon; clear distances; Pendle[4] dappled with tufted shadow; west wind; interesting clouding, flat and lying in the warp of the heaved but the pieces with rounded outline and dolphin-backs showing in places and all was at odds and at Z's, one piece with another. Later beautifully delicate crisping. Later rippling....

April 21—We have had other such afternoons, one today—the sky a beautiful grained blue, silky lingering clouds in flat-bottomed loaves, others a little browner in ropes or in burly-shouldered ridges swany and lustrous, more in the Zenith[5] stray packs of a sort of violet paleness. White-rose cloud formed fast, not in the same density—some caked and swimming in a wan whiteness, the rest soaked with the blue and like the leaf of a flower held against the light and diapered out by the worm or veining of deeper blue between rosette and rosette. Later / moulding, which brought rain: in perspective it was vaulted in very regular ribs with fretting between: but these are not ribs; they are a "wracking" install made of these two realities—the frets, which are scarves of rotten cloud bellying upwards and drooping at their ends and shaded darkest at the brow or tropic where they double to the eye, and the whiter field of sky showing between: the illusion looking down the "wagon" is complete. These swaths of fretted cloud move in rank, not in file.

April 22—But such a lovely damasking in the sky as today I never felt before. The blue was charged with simple instress, the higher, zenith sky earnest and frowning, lower more light and sweet. High up again, breathing through woolly coats of cloud or on the quains[6] and branches of the flying pieces it was the true exchange of crimson, nearer the earth / against the sun / it was turquoise, and in the opposite south-western bay below the sun it was like clear oil but just as full of colour, shaken over with slanted flashing "travellers," all in flight, stepping one behind the other, their edges tossed with bright ravelling,[7] as if white napkins were thrown up in the sun but not quite at the same moment so that they were all in a scale down the air falling one after the other to the ground....

[May 9] This day and May 11 the bluebells in the little wood between the College[8] and the highroad and in one of the Hurst Green[9] cloughs.[10] In the little wood / opposite the light / they stood in blackish spreads or sheddings like the spots on a snake. The heads are then like thongs and solemn in grain and grape-colour. But in the clough / through the light / they came in falls of sky-colour washing the brows and slacks of the ground

---

[1] *whelking* Ridges.

[2] *instress* Hopkins's own term, meaning the force or energy which sustains an inscape, which is the individual or essential quality of a thing.

[3] *"The ... sound."* From William Wordsworth's *Ode: Intimations of Immortality*, line 20–21; *tabour's* Drum's.

[4] *Pendle* Pendle Hill in Lancashire, England.

[5] *Zenith* Point in the sky directly overhead.

[6] *quains* Angles (Hopkins's own term).

[7] *ravelling* Frayed edges.

[8] *College* Stonyhurst College, the seminary where Hopkins studied, in Lancashire, England.

[9] *Hurst Green* Village in Blackburn, Lancashire, England.

[10] *cloughs* Ravines.

with vein-blue, thickening at the double, vertical themselves and the young grass and brake fern combed vertical, but the brake struck the upright of all this with light winged transomes.[1] It was a lovely sight.—The bluebells in your hand baffle you with their inscape, made to every sense: if you draw your fingers through them they are lodged and struggle / with a shock of wet heads; the long stalks rub and click and flatten to a fan on one another like your fingers themselves would when you passed the palms hard across one another, making a brittle rub and jostle like the noise of a hurdle strained by leaning against; then there is the faint honey smell and in the mouth the sweet gum when you bite them. But this is easy, it is the eye they baffle. They give one a fancy of panpipes and of some wind instrument with stops—a trombone perhaps. The overhung necks—for growing they are little more than a staff with a simple crook but in water, where they stiffen, they take stronger turns, in the head like sheephooks[2] or, when more waved throughout, like the waves riding through a whip that is being smacked—what with these overhung necks and what with the crisped ruffled bells dropping mostly on one side and the gloss these have at their footstalks they have an air of the knights at chess. Then the knot or "knoop" of buds some shut, some just gaping, which makes the pencil of the whole spike, should be noticed: the inscape of the flower most finely carried out in the siding of the axes, each striking a greater and greater slant, is finished in these clustered buds, which for the most part are not straightened but rise to the end like a tongue and this and their tapering and a little flattening they have made them look like the heads of snakes.

[July 19, 1872] Stepped into a barn of ours, a great shadowy barn, where the hay had been stacked on either side, and looking at the great rudely arched timber-frames—principals(?) and tie-beams, which make them look like bold big *As* with the cross-bar high up—I thought how sadly beauty of inscape was unknown and buried away from simple people and yet how near at hand it was if they had eyes to see it and it could be called out everywhere again....

After the examinations we went for our holiday out to Douglas in the Isle of Man. Aug. 3—At this time I had first begun to get hold of the copy of Scotus[3] on the Sentences in the Baddely library and was flush with a new stroke of enthusiasm. It may come to nothing or it may be a mercy from God. But just then when I took in any inscape of the sky or sea I thought of Scotus. ...

Aug. 10—I was looking at high waves. The breakers always are parallel to the coast and shape themselves to it except where the curve is sharp however the wind blows. They are rolled out by the shallowing shore just as a piece of putty between the palms whatever its shape runs into a long roll. The slant ruck[4] or crease one sees in them shows the way of the wind. The regularity of the barrels surprised and charmed the eye; the edge behind the comb or crest was as smooth and bright as glass. It may be noticed to be green behind and silver white in front: the silver marks where the air begins, the pure white is foam, the green / solid water. Then looked at to the right or left they are scrolled over like mould-boards[5] or feathers or jibsails seen by the edge. It is pretty to see the hollow of the barrel disappearing as the white combs on each side run along the wave gaining ground till the two meet at a pitch and crush and over-lap each other.

About all the turns of the scaping[6] from the break and flooding of wave to its run out again I have not yet satisfied myself. The shores are swimming and the eyes have before them a region of milky surf but it is hard for them to unpack the huddling and gnarls of the water and law out the shapes and the sequence of the running: I catch however the looped or forked wisp made by every big pebble the backwater runs over—if it were clear and smooth there would be a network from their overlapping, such as can in fact be seen on smooth sand after the tide is out; then I saw it run browner, the foam dwindling and twitched into long chains of suds, while

---

[1] *transomes* Crossbeams.

[2] *sheephooks* Shepherds' crooks.

[3] *Scotus* Duns Scotus (c. 1266–1308), Scottish-born theologian and philosopher. In his *Lectura*, he analyzes Thomas Lombard's *Sentences*.

[4] *ruck* Ridge.

[5] *mouldboards* Boards attached to plows, used to form furrows.

[6] *scaping* Hopkins's term for a reflection or impression of the individual quality of a thing or action.

the strength of the backdraught shrugged the stones together and clocked them one against another. ...

April 8 [1873]—The ashtree growing in the corner of the garden was felled. It was lopped first: I heard the sound and looking out and seeing it maimed there came at that moment a great pang and I wished to die and not to see the inscapes of the world destroyed any more. ...

July 23—To Beaumont: it was the rector's day. It was a lovely day: shires-long of pearled cloud under cloud, with a grey stroke underneath marking each row; beautiful blushing yellow in the straw of the uncut rye fields, the wheat looking white and all the ears making a delicate and very true crisping along the top and with just enough air stirring for them to come and go gently; then there were fields reaping. All this I would have looked at again in returning but during dinner I talked too freely and unkindly and had to do penance going home. One field I saw from the balcony of the house behind an elmtree, which it threw up, like a square of pale goldleaf, as it might be, catching the light. (WRITTEN 1871–73)

from *Letter to Robert Bridges*

St. Giles's, Oxford.
25 February 1879

... No doubt my poetry errs on the side of oddness. I hope in time to have a more balanced and Miltonic[1] style. But as air, melody, is what strikes me most of all in music and design in painting, so design, pattern or what I am in the habit of calling "inscape" is what I above all aim at in poetry. Now it is the virtue of design, pattern, or inscape to be distinctive and it is the virtue of distinctiveness to become queer. This vice I cannot have escaped. ...
(WRITTEN 1879)

---

[1] *Miltonic* In the manner of John Milton (1608–74), English poet.

Author's Preface[2]

The poems in this book are written some in Running Rhythm, the common rhythm in English use, some in Sprung Rhythm, and some in a mixture of the two. And those in the common rhythm are some counter-pointed,[3] some not.

Common English rhythm, called Running Rhythm above, is measured by feet[4] of either two or three syllables and (putting aside the imperfect feet at the beginning and end of lines and also some unusual measures in which feet seem to be paired together and double or composite feet to arise) never more or less.

Every foot has one principal stress or accent, and this or the syllable it falls on may be called the Stress of the foot and the other part, the one or two unaccented syllables, the Slack. Feet (and the rhythms made out of them) in which the stress comes first are called Falling Feet and Falling Rhythms, feet and rhythm in which the slack comes first are called Rising Feet and Rhythms, and if the stress is between two slacks there will be Rocking Feet and Rhythms. These distinctions are real and true to nature; but for purposes of scanning it is a great convenience to follow the example of music and take the stress always first, as the accent or the chief accent always comes first in a musical bar. If this is done there will be in common English verse only two possible feet—the so-called accentual Trochee[5] and Dactyl,[6] and correspondingly only two possible uniform rhythms, the so-called Trochaic and Dactylic. But they may be mixed and then what the Greeks called a Logaoedic Rhythm[7] arises. These are the facts and according to these the scanning of ordinary regularly-written English verse is very simple indeed and to bring in other principles is here unnecessary.

---

[2] *Author's Preface* Prefatory to accompany Hopkins's manuscript poems.

[3] *counterpointed* Containing two types of rhythm in a line of verse.

[4] *feet* Metrical units.

[5] *Trochee* Metrical foot consisting of an accented syllable followed by an unaccented syllable.

[6] *Dactyl* Metrical foot consisting of an accented syllable followed by two unaccented syllables.

[7] *Logaoedic Rhythm* Rhythm in which dactyls are combined with trochees.

But because verse written strictly in these feet and by these principles will become same and tame the poets have brought in licences and departures from rule to give variety, and especially when the natural rhythm is rising, as in the common ten-syllable or five-foot verse, rhymed or blank. These irregularities are chiefly Reversed Feet and Reversed or Counterpoint Rhythm, which two things are two steps or degrees of licence in the same kind. By a reversed foot I mean the putting the stress where, to judge by the rest of the measure, the slack should be and the slack where the stress, and this is done freely at the beginning of a line and, in the course of a line, after a pause; only scarcely ever in the second foot or place and never in the last, unless when the poet designs some extraordinary effect; for these places are characteristic and sensitive and cannot well be touched. But the reversal of the first foot and of some middle foot after a strong pause is a thing so natural that our poets have generally done it, from Chaucer down, without remark and it commonly passes unnoticed and cannot be said to amount to a formal change of rhythm, but rather is that irregularity which all natural growth and motion shows. If however the reversal is repeated in two feet running, especially so as to include the sensitive second foot, it must be due either to great want of ear or else is a calculated effect, the super-inducing or *mounting* of a new rhythm upon the old; and since the new or mounted rhythm is actually heard and at the same time the mind naturally supplies the natural or standard foregoing rhythm, for we do not forget what the rhythm is that by rights we should be hearing, two rhythms are in some manner running at once and we have something answerable to counterpoint in music, which is two or more strains of tune going on together, and this is Counterpoint Rhythm. Of this kind of verse Milton is the great master and the choruses of *Samson Agonistes*[1] are written throughout in it—but with the disadvantage that he does not let the reader clearly know what the ground-rhythm is meant to be and so they have struck most readers as merely irregular. And in fact if you counterpoint throughout, since only one of the counter rhythms is actually heard, the other is really destroyed or cannot come to exist, and what is written

is one rhythm only and probably Sprung Rhythm, of which I now speak.

Sprung Rhythm, as used in this book, is measured by feet of from one to four syllables, regularly, and for particular effects any number of weak or slack syllables may be used. It has one stress, which falls on the only syllable, if there is only one, or, if there are more, then scanning as above, on the first, and so gives rise to four sorts of feet, a monosyllable and the so-called accentual Trochee, Dactyl, and the First Paeon.[2] And there will be four corresponding natural rhythms; but nominally the feet are mixed and any one may follow any other. And hence Sprung Rhythm differs from Running Rhythm in having or being only one nominal rhythm, a mixed or "logaoedic" one, instead of three, but on the other hand in having twice the flexibility of foot, so that any two stresses may either follow one another running or be divided by one, two, or three slack syllables. But strict Sprung Rhythm cannot be counterpointed. In Sprung Rhythm, as in logaoedic rhythm generally, the feet are assumed to be equally long or strong and their seeming inequality is made up by pause or stressing.

Remark also that it is natural in Sprung Rhythm for the lines to be *rove over*, that is for the scanning of each line immediately to take up that of the one before, so that if the first has one or more syllables at its end the other must have so many the less at its beginning; and in fact the scanning runs on without break from the beginning, say, of a stanza to the end and all the stanza is one long strain, though written in lines asunder.

Two licences are natural to Sprung Rhythm. The one is rests, as in music; but of this an example is scarcely to be found in this book, unless in the *Echos*, second line. The other is *hangers* or *outrides*, that is one, two, or three slack syllables added to a foot and not counting in the nominal scanning. They are so called because they seem to hang below the line or ride forward or backward from it in another dimension than the line itself, according to a principle needless to explain here. These outriding half feet or hangers are marked by a loop underneath them, and plenty of them will be found.

---

[1] *Samson Agonistes*   Dramatic poem published by Milton in 1671.

[2] *Paeon*   Metrical foot consisting of one stressed and three un-stressed syllables.

The other marks are easily understood, namely accents, where the reader might be in doubt which syllable should have the stress; slurs, that is loops *over* syllables, to tie them together into the time of one; little loops at the end of a line to show that the rhyme goes on to the first letter of the next line; what in music are called pauses ⌒, to show that the syllable should be dwelt on; and twirls ~, to mark reversed or counter-pointed rhythm.

Note on the nature and history of Sprung Rhythm —Sprung Rhythm is the most natural of things. For (1) it is the rhythm of common speech and of written prose, when rhythm is perceived in them. (2) It is the rhythm of all but the most monotonously regular music, so that in the words of choruses and refrains and in songs written closely to music it arises. (3) It is found in nursery rhymes, weather saws, and so on; because, however these may have been once made in running rhythm, the terminations having dropped off by the change of language, the stresses come together and so

the rhythm is sprung. (4) It arises in common verse when reversed or counterpointed, for the same reason.

But nevertheless in spite of all this and though Greek and Latin lyric verse, which is well known, and the old English verse seen in "Pierce Ploughman"[1] are in sprung rhythm, it has in fact ceased to be used since the Elizabethan age, Greene[2] being the last writer who can be said to have recognized it. For perhaps there was not, down to our days, a single, even short, poem in English in which sprung rhythm is employed—not for single effects or in fixed places—but as the governing principle of the scansion. I say this because the contrary has been asserted: if it is otherwise the poem should be cited. . . . —1883

---

[1] *Pierce Ploughman* I.e., *Piers Plowman*, by William Langland (written c. 1360–99).

[2] *Greene* Robert Greene (1558–92).

"MICHAEL FIELD"
KATHARINE BRADLEY AND EDITH COOPER
1846 – 1914   1862 – 1913

In May 1884, a volume of two plays by an unknown author, Michael Field, was published to critical acclaim. One reviewer wrote in *The Spectator*: "We know nothing of the author, but we have found a wealth of surprises in the strength, the simplicity, and the terseness of the imaginative feeling.... [The work] has the true poetic voice of fire in it. If this is the work of a young author, it is the work of the highest possible promise." The two authors who had taken the pen name "Michael Field," Katharine Bradley (her first name is spelled various ways, but she signed her name "Katharine") and Edith Cooper had wished to receive the serious criticism accorded to male authors and also to conceal their relationship as lovers. The authors' identities did become widely known during their lifetimes, but "Michael" (Bradley) and "Field" (Cooper), as they called themselves, continued to collaborate on many books of plays and poetry, sometimes as "Michael Field," sometimes under other pseudonyms.

Bradley's father, a tobacco manufacturer, died in 1848, when she was two. Her mother educated her at home, and she later attended Newnham College, the new women's college at Cambridge. When her older sister, Emma, married James Cooper, the family stayed together with the married couple in Kenilworth, near Birmingham in central England. Bradley's mother died when she was twenty-two, and not long afterward Emma also passed away. Bradley stayed on to help raise her sister's children, Amy and Edith; Edith was then six years old. Katharine and her niece Edith shared a love of literature and writing, evident from the time Edith was young, and the two later attended Bristol University together.

Bradley wrote one volume of poetry on her own in 1875 (*The New Minnesinger*, published under the pseudonym Arran Leigh), but thereafter published only in collaboration with Cooper. A stanza from their poem "It Was Deep April" describes their moment of decision: "The world was on us, pressing sore; / My love and I took hands and swore, / Against the world, to be / Poets and lovers evermore." The two eventually wrote some 30 plays and 11 volumes of poetry together in such a close collaboration that they later claimed in their journals that when they reviewed their work they could not distinguish who had written what. When their first collaborative work was published, the plays *Callirrhoë* and *Fair Rosamund*, they sent a copy to Robert Browning and revealed their true identities. Browning loved their work and became a close friend, but unfortunately he let slip to the public the authorship of the plays, a move that Bradley wrote back to tell him would "dwarf and enfeeble our work.... We cannot be stifled in drawing room conventionalities."

But even after their identities were exposed, Bradley and Cooper did not allow themselves to be stifled. They lived and traveled together and wrote poems about love between women; their first joint volume of poetry was inspired by Henry Wharton's translation of the ancient Greek Sappho's fragments of poetry, in which her love object was a woman. Their 1889 volume *Long Ago* was called by the journal *The Academy* "one of the most exquisite lyrical productions of the latter half of the nineteenth century."

Bradley and Cooper kept a journal that they called *Works and Days*, in which they described their daily lives and their abiding love for each other: "closer married" than the Brownings, they said, because they also shared an artistic partnership. The younger, Cooper, was the first to die, of cancer, in 1913; eight months later Bradley died of the same disease.

⌘ ⌘ ⌘

The Magdalen

Timoteo Viti[1]

This tender sylph[2] of a maid
Is the Magdalen—this figure lone:
Her attitude is swayed
By the very breath she breathes,
5   The prayer of her being that takes no voice.
Boulders, the grass enwreathes,
Arch over her as a cave
That of old an earthquake clave
And filled with stagnant gloom:
10   Yet a woman has strength to choose it for her room.

Her long, fair hair is allowed
To wander in its thick simpleness;
The graceful tresses crowd
Unequal, yet close enough
15   To have woven about her neck and breast
A wimple of golden stuff.
Though the rock behind is rude,
The sweetness of solitude
Is on her face, the soft
20   Withdrawal that in wildflowers we have loved so oft.

Her mantle is scarlet red
In folds of severe resplendency;
Her hair beneath is spread
Full length; from its lower flakes
25   Her feet come forth in their naked charm:
A wind discreetly shakes
The scarlet raiment,° the hair.   *dress*
Her small hands, a tranquil pair,

Are laid together; her book
30   And cup of ointment furnish scantily her nook.

She is happy the livelong day,
Yet her thoughts are often with the past;
Her sins are done away,
They can give her no annoy.
35   She is white—oh! infinitely clean
And her heart throbs with joy;

[1] *The Magdalen Timoteo Viti* Painting of the Biblical Mary Magdalene by Renaissance painter Timoteo Viti (reproduced here as an illustration).

[2] *sylph* Slight, graceful woman.

Besides, there is joy in heaven
That her sins are thus forgiven;
And she thinks till even-fall°   *dusk*
40 Of the grace, the strangeness, the wonder of it all.

She is shut from fellowship;
How she loved to mingle with her friends!
To give them eyes and lip;
She lived for their sake alone;
45 Not a braid of her hair, not a rose
Of her cheek was her own:
And she loved to minister
To any in want of her,
All service was so sweet:
50 Now she must stand all day on lithe, unsummoned feet.

Among the untrodden weeds
And moss she is glad to be remote;
She knows that when God needs
From the sinning world relief,
55 He will find her thus with the wild bees,
The doves and the plantain leaf,
Waiting in a perfect peace
For His kingdom's sure increase,
Waiting with a deeper glow
60 Of patience every day, because He tarrieth so.

By her side the box of nard[1]
Unbroken … God is a great way off;
She loves Him: it is hard
That she may not now even spread
65 The burial spice, who would gladly keep
The tomb where He lay dead,
As it were her rocky cave;
And fold the linen and lave°   *wash*
The napkin that once bound
70 His head; no place for her pure arts is longer found.

And these are the things that hurt;
For the rest she gives herself no pain:
She wears no camel shirt,

She uses nor scourge, nor rod;
75 But bathes her fair body in the well
And keeps it pure for God:
The beauty, that He hath made
So bright, she guards in the shade,
For, as an angel's dress,
80 Spotless she must preserve her newborn loveliness.

Day by day and week by week,
She lives and muses and makes no sound;
She has no words to speak
The joy that her desert brings:
85 In her heart there is a song
And yet no song she sings.
Since the word *Rabboni*[2] came
Straightway at the call of her name
And the Master reproved,
90 It seems she has no choice—her lips have never moved.

She stole away when the pale
Light was trembling on the garden ground
And others told the tale,
Christ was risen; she roamed the wide,
95 Fearful countries of the wilderness
And many a riverside,
Till she found her destined grot,°   *grotto*
South, in France, a woody spot,
Where she is often glad,
100 Musing on those great days when she at first grew sad.
—1892

La Gioconda[3]

Leonardo Da Vinci

Historic, sidelong, implicating eyes;
A smile of velvet's lustre on the cheek;
Calm lips the smile leads upward; hand that lies
Glowing and soft, the patience in its rest
5 Of cruelty that waits and doth not seek

---

[1] *nard* Ointment made from the aromatic plant of the same name.

[2] *Rabboni* Hebrew: master, teacher.
[3] *La Gioconda* Da Vinci's painting, the *Mona Lisa*.

For prey; a dusky forehead and a breast
Where twilight touches ripeness amorously:
Behind her, crystal rocks, a sea and skies
Of evanescent blue on cloud and creek;
10   Landscape that shines suppressive of its zest
For those vicissitudes by which men die.
—1892

A girl

A girl,
Her soul a deep-wave pearl
Dim, lucent of all lovely mysteries;
    A face flowered for heart's ease,
    A brow's grace soft as seas
5   Seen through faint forest trees:
    A mouth, the lips apart,
Like aspen leaflets trembling in the breeze
From her tempestuous heart.
10   Such: and our souls so knit,
I leave a page half-writ—
    The work begun
Will be to heaven's conception done,
    If she come to it.
—1893

It was deep April, and the morn

It was deep April, and the morn
    Shakespeare was born;[1]
The world was on us, pressing sore;
My Love and I took hands and swore,
5   Against the world, to be
Poets and lovers evermore,
To laugh and dream on Lethe's[2] shore
To sing to Charon[3] in his boat,
Heartening the timid souls afloat;
10   Of judgment never to take heed,
But to those fast-locked souls to speed,
Who never from Apollo fled,
Who spent no hour among the dead;
        Continually
15   With them to dwell,
Indifferent to heaven and hell.
—1893

---

[1] *morn ... was born* It is traditional to celebrate Shakespeare's birthday on 23 April, St. George's Day.

[2] *Lethe* In Greek mythology, a river in Hades (the underworld), the waters of which cause the dead to forget the past.

[3] *Charon* Greek mythological ferryman of the underworld who transports the souls of the dead across the River Styx.

To Christina Rossetti

Lady, we would behold thee moving bright
  As Beatrice or Matilda[1] mid the trees,
Alas! thy moan was as a moan for ease
And passage through cool shadows to the night:
Fleeing from love, hadst thou not poet's right   5
To slip into the universe? The seas
Are fathomless to rivers drowned in these,
And sorrow is secure in leafy light.
Ah, had this secret touched thee, in a tomb   10
Thou hadst not buried thy enchanting self,
As happy Syrinx[2] murmuring with the wind,
Or Daphne,[3] thrilled through all her mystic bloom,
From safe recess as genius or as elf,
Thou hadst breathed joy in earth and in thy kind.
—1896

---

[1] *Beatrice* From Dante's *Divine Comedy*, Book 3, *Paradise*: a woman who personifies love and acts as Dante's guide through Paradise; *Matilda* From Book 2, *Purgatory*: a beautiful virgin who meets Dante in the Garden of Eden and leads him to the river Lethe to wash away his sins.

[2] *Syrinx* In Greek mythology, the nymph Syrinx turned herself into a bed of reeds in order to escape Pan's advances.

[3] *Daphne* In Greek mythology, the nymph Daphne fled from the god Apollo's advances and was transformed into a laurel tree in her escape.

OSCAR WILDE
1854 – 1900

For his epigrammatic genius, his challenges to bourgeois sensibilities, and his dazzling essays, dramas, and other writings, Oscar Wilde has been both reverenced and reviled for more than a century. Notorious for his flamboyance and wit before he had ever published a word, Wilde established himself in the literary world with his sole novel, *The Picture of Dorian Gray*, and even more with such sparkling social comedies as *An Ideal Husband* and *The Importance of Being Earnest*. He was a vocal advocate of aestheticism; Wilde saw in art the possibility for a life beyond the day-to-day monotony of ordinary existence. The "aesthetic movement," he writes, "produced certain colours, subtle in their loveliness and fascinating in their almost mystical tone. They were, and are, our reaction against the crude primaries of a doubtless more respectable but certainly less cultivated age."

Wilde began his life as Oscar Fingal O'Flahertie Wills Wilde. His parents, themselves no strangers to controversy, were Lady Jane Francesca Elgee and Dr. (later Sir) William Wilde. Both were accomplished writers. William, an ear and eye surgeon, wrote a book on medical and literary institutions in Austria and another about his voyage to North Africa and the Middle East. He achieved fame for his work on the Irish Census, for which he conducted a groundbreaking demographic study of the Great Famine, earning a knighthood in 1864. His reputation was somewhat tainted, however, by his womanizing; he fathered three children out of wedlock. Lady Wilde was also a prominent figure. Born Jane Frances Agnes Elgee, she adopted the more Italian-sounding "Francesca" to reinforce the family's claim that they were descended from Dante Alighieri (truth never stood in the way of a good Wilde family story). Lady Wilde took yet another name, "Speranza," when she published poems in *The Nation*, a weekly Dublin newspaper published by an anti-British revolutionary group called the Young Irelanders.

Wilde grew up in the colorful environment of his mother's famous salon, where she hosted leading Dublin artists and writers. Once when Wilde returned from college, he invited a friend to Lady Wilde's weekly "conversazione," saying: "I want to introduce you to my mother. We have founded a society for the suppression of virtue." Wilde was a brilliant student at Trinity College, graduating in 1874 with the Berkeley Gold Medal for Classics and receiving a scholarship to study at Oxford. Before long, he was celebrated at Oxford's Magdalen College for his wit, decadence, and ostentatious appearance. He was most influenced in his academic years by two rivals at Oxford, John Ruskin and Walter Pater. From Ruskin, perhaps the most influential art critic of the century, Wilde took counsel on what the older scholar believed to be the spiritual, ethical, and moral nature of art. From Pater, who was already infamous following the publication of his *Studies in the History of the Renaissance* (1873), Wilde picked up elements of aestheticism he would eventually transform into his own theories of art. Wilde would later describe Pater's *Renaissance* as "the holy writ of beauty."

After winning the Newdigate prize for poetry and graduating with first class honors, Wilde moved to London and began his career as a divisive public figure. He was known, for example, for a formal jacket, called his "cello coat," that he wore to the opening of the Grosvenor Gallery in 1877, and for being more generally a poster-boy of the emerging aesthetic movement. By the time he published a book of poems in 1881, he had already become the butt of many caricatures in *Punch* magazine; he had taken to modeling his look on the character of Bunthorne in Gilbert and Sullivan's satirical comic opera *Patience*. For the next few years Wilde delivered lectures in the United States and Great Britain about the aesthetic movement, for which he had ambitious plans: "I want to make this artistic movement the basis for a new civilization." In Boston he voiced some of the ideas about art and life for which he would best be known: "The supreme object of life is to live. Few people live. It is true life only to realize one's own perfection, to make one's every dream a reality. Even this is possible."

In 1884 Wilde married Constance Lloyd, with whom he would have two sons, Cyril and Vyvyan. From 1887 to 1889 he edited *Woman's World*, a popular magazine. Through the late 1880s, Wilde wrote reviews of many of his most famous contemporaries, including the painter James Whistler and the poets D.G. Rossetti, William Morris, Algernon Swinburne. He was also at work on the volume that would ultimately constitute the most thorough account of his aesthetic philosophy, *Intentions* (1891), which included the essays "The Decay of Lying" and "The Critic as Artist." The essays argue for the paramount importance of art in human life: "[Arts] are ... the great archetypes of which things that have existence are but unfinished copies." Rather than artists copying from the world about them, writes Wilde, we as individuals interpret the world *through art*, through the "archetypes" presented to us by works of art. Hence "[T]here may have been fogs for centuries in London," but "no one saw them .... till Art had invented them." The early 1890s also saw the publication of Wilde's novel, *The Picture of Dorian Gray*, which both puts forward Wilde's aesthetic beliefs and suggests some of the dangers of a life given over to aesthetic consumption.

Wilde was clearly at his very best in the early 1890s. In addition to *Intentions*, *Dorian Gray*, and poems such as "Helas," Wilde penned a string of brilliant social comedies, including *Lady Windermere's Fan* (1892), *A Woman of No Importance* (1893), and *An Ideal Husband* (1895). His final comedy was his masterpiece of farce, *The Importance of Being Earnest*; it first played in 1895 to wildly enthusiastic crowds at the St. James Theatre in London. Success came to an end only through Wilde's ill-fated affair with a young aristocrat, Lord Alfred Douglas ("Bosie"). Douglas's father, the mentally unstable Marquis of Queensbury, was infuriated by the relationship, and in 1895 he publicly accused Wilde of sodomy. Convinced he had to defend his own and Douglas's honor, Wilde sued the Marquis for libel. After Wilde failed in his suit against Queensbury, the government used evidence from the trial to launch a criminal investigation against Wilde because homosexuality was a criminal offense. Wilde was found guilty of "gross indecency" and sentenced to two years of imprisonment with hard labor.

Prison left Wilde financially and emotionally broken. The horrid conditions of late-Victorian prison life—including a poor diet, enforced silence, and physically taxing labor—were especially difficult to handle. From prison Wilde wrote a moving autobiographical letter to Bosie, later entitled *De Profundis*, that accuses the younger man of heartless and selfish behavior. (Bosie had treated Wilde poorly all along, and he abandoned Wilde during his imprisonment.) Even from his cell, however, Wilde wrote of seeing "new developments in Art and Life." Upon his release he composed "The Ballad of Reading Gaol" (1898), a heartfelt indictment of the prison system and capital punishment, as well as a meditation on the universal characteristics of human nature.

Wilde's last years were spent in Italy and France. He seems never to have recovered fully from his prison experience, and by late in 1900 he was quite ill. He died and was buried in Paris before the year ended; the immediate cause of his death has never been conclusively established. In 1995 a window in the Poets' Corner of Westminster Abbey was dedicated in his honor.

⌘ ⌘ ⌘

Impression du Matin[1]

The Thames nocturne of blue and gold[2]
Changed to a harmony in gray:
    A barge with ochre-coloured hay
Dropped from the wharf: and chill and cold

5 The yellow fog came creeping down
    The bridges, till the houses' walls
    Seemed changed to shadows and St. Paul's
Loomed like a bubble o'er the town.

Then suddenly arose the clang
10   Of waking life; the streets were stirred
    With country wagons: and a bird
Flew to the glistening roofs and sang.

But one pale woman all alone,
    The daylight kissing her wan hair,
15   Loitered beneath gas lamps' flare,
With lips of flame and heart of stone.
    —1881

---

[1] *Impression du Matin*   French: Impression of the Morning.

[2] *gold* Cf. James McNeill Whistler's series of paintings, the "Nocturnes." Two of the most famous of these are "Nocturne in Blue and Gold: Old Battersea Bridge" and "Nocturne in Black and Gold: The Falling Rocket," both of which were painted in the 1870s. These and other similar paintings were important precursors of the movement that came to be known as Impressionism; painters such as Claude Monet and Edgar Degas, like Whistler, strove to capture the transitory effects of light both on the landscape and on human figures. Much as Wilde was moved to write his own "impressions" in verse (this is one of several Wilde poems that include the word "impression" in their title), he did not respond positively to Whistler's radical experiments with impressions on canvas. His response to "Nocturne in Black and Gold: The Falling Rocket" on seeing it exhibited at the Grosvenor Gallery in 1877 was to call it "worth looking at for about as long as one looks at a real rocket, that is, for something less than a quarter of a minute." This judgment concurred with that of the famous art critic John Ruskin (who had been a teacher of Wilde's at Oxford). Ruskin criticized Whistler for "flinging a pot of paint in the public's face" with works such as "Nocturne in Black and Gold: The Falling Rocket"—an insult for which Whistler sued him in a famous trial. (Whistler won the case, but was awarded only one farthing in damages and had to pay the costs of the trial, which contributed to his eventual bankruptcy.)

E Tenebris[3]

Come down, O Christ, and help me! Reach thy hand,
    For I am drowning in a stormier sea
    Than Simon on thy lake of Galilee:[4]
The wine of life is spilt upon the sand,
5 My heart is as some famine-murdered land
    Whence all good things have perished utterly,
    And well I know my soul in Hell must lie
If I this night before God's throne should stand.
"He sleeps perchance, or rideth to the chase,
10   Like Baal, when his prophets howled that name
    From morn to noon on Carmel's smitten height."[5]
Nay, peace, I shall behold, before the night,
    The feet of brass,[6] the robe more white than flame,
The wounded hands, the weary human face.
    —1881

To Milton

Milton! I think thy spirit hath passed away
    From these white cliffs and high-embattled
        towers;
This gorgeous fiery-coloured world of ours
Seems fallen into ashes dull and grey,
5 And the age changed unto a mimic play
Wherein we waste our else too-crowded hours:
For all our pomp and pageantry and powers
We are but fit to delve the common clay,
Seeing this little isle on which we stand,
10 This England, this sea-lion of the sea,
By ignorant demagogues is held in fee,

---

[3] *E Tenebris*   Latin: Out of the darkness.

[4] *Simon ... Galilee* In Matthew 14.24–31, Simon Peter, one of the twelve apostles, nearly drowns in a storm at sea when Christ bids him to walk across the water to him. Christ reaches out his hand and saves him, saying "O thou of little faith, wherefore didst thou doubt?"

[5] *"He sleeps ... height"* In 1 Kings 18.19–40, Elijah mocks the priests of Baal (who had called upon their God all day in vain) by saying, "either he is talking, or he is pursuing, or he is in a journey, or peradventure he sleepeth, and must be awaked." Here the speaker imagines a similar voice taunting him.

[6] *feet of brass* Revelation 1.13–16 describes a vision of the Son of man in which his feet are "like unto fine brass."

Who love her not: Dear God! is this the land
Which bare a triple empire in her hand
When Cromwell spake the word "Democracy!"
—1881

from "The Critic as Artist" [1]

ERNEST.   ... [S]urely, the higher you place the creative artist, the lower must the critic rank.

GILBERT.   Why so?

ERNEST.   Because the best that he can give us will be but an echo of rich music, a dim shadow of clear-outlined form. It may, indeed, be that life is chaos, as you tell me that it is; that its martyrdoms are mean and its heroisms ignoble; and that it is the function of Literature to create, from the rough material of actual existence, a new world that will be more marvellous, more enduring, and more true than the world that common eyes look upon, and through which common natures seek to realize their perfection. But surely, if this new world has been made by the spirit and touch of a great artist, it will be a thing so complete and perfect that there will be nothing left for the critic to do. I quite understand now, and indeed admit most readily, that it is far more difficult to talk about a thing than to do it. But it seems to me that this sound and sensible maxim, which is really extremely soothing to one's feelings, and should be adopted as its motto by every Academy of Literature all over the world, applies only to the relations that exist between Art and Life, and not to any relations that there may be between Art and Criticism.

GILBERT.   But, surely, Criticism is itself an art. And just as artistic creation implies the working of the critical faculty, and, indeed, without it cannot be said to exist at all, so Criticism is really creative in the highest sense of the word. Criticism is, in fact, both creative and independent.

ERNEST.   Independent?

GILBERT.   Yes; independent. Criticism is no more to be judged by any low standard of imitation or resemblance than is the work of poet or sculptor. The critic occupies the same relation to the work of art that he criticizes as the artist does to the visible world of form and colour, or the unseen world of passion and of thought. He does not even require for the perfection of his art the finest materials. Anything will serve his purpose. And just as out of the sordid and sentimental amours of the silly wife of a small country doctor in the squalid village of Yonville-l'Abbaye, near Rouen, Gustave Flaubert was able to create a classic and make a masterpiece of style,[2] so, from subjects of little or no importance, such as the pictures in this year's Royal Academy, or in any year's Royal Academy for that matter, Mr. Lewis Morris's poems, M. Ohnet's novels, or the plays of Mr. Henry Arthur Jones,[3] the true critic can, if it be his pleasure so to direct or waste his faculty of contemplation, produce work that will be flawless in beauty and instinct with intellectual subtlety. Why not? Dullness is always an irresistible temptation for brilliancy, and stupidity is the permanent *Bestia Trionfans*[4] that calls wisdom from its cave. To an artist so creative as the critic, what does subject matter signify? No more and no less than it does to the novelist and the painter. Like them, he can find his motives everywhere. Treatment is the test. There is nothing that has not in it suggestion or challenge.

ERNEST.   But is Criticism really a creative art?

GILBERT.   Why should it not be? It works with materials, and puts them into a form that is at once new and delightful. What more can one say of poetry? Indeed, I would call criticism a creation within a creation. For just as the great artists, from Homer and Aeschylus down to Shakespeare and Keats,[5] did not go directly to life for

---

[1]   *The Critic as Artist*   In this dialogue, the two men debate the merits of art criticism. Earlier, Ernest had questioned the usefulness of criticism, asking, "Why should the artist be troubled by the shrill clamour of criticism? Why should those who cannot create take it upon themselves to estimate the value of creative work?" In response, Gilbert argued that criticism is itself an art, that "there is no fine art without self-consciousness, and self-consciousness and the critical spirit are one," and, furthermore, that it is "very much more difficult to talk about a thing than to do it."

[2]   *masterpiece of style*   I.e., Flaubert's *Madame Bovary*.

[3]   *Mr. Lewis Morris*   Popular Anglo-Welsh poet; *M. Ohnet* Georges Ohnet, nineteenth-century French novelist, many of whose works were successfully dramatized; *Mr. Henry Arthur Jones* Innovative playwright of the late nineteenth century.

[4]   *Bestia Trionfans*   Latin: Triumphant Beast. From the title of sixteenth-century philosopher Giordano Bruno's allegory *Spacio della Bestia Trionfante* (*Expulsion of the Triumphant Beast*).

[5]   *Homer*   Greek poet to whom the authorship of *The Iliad* and *The Odyssey* is attributed (?850 BCE); *Shakespeare* William Shakespeare, English poet and playwright (1564–1616); *Keats* John Keats,

their subject-matter, but sought for it in myth, and legend, and ancient tale, so the critic deals with materials that others have, as it were, purified for him, and to which imaginative form and colour have been already added. Nay, more, I would say that the highest Criticism, being the purest form of personal impression, is in its way more creative than creation, as it has least reference to any standard external to itself, and is, in fact, its own reason for existing, and, as the Greeks would put it, in itself, and to itself, an end. Certainly, it is never trammelled by any shackles of verisimilitude. No ignoble considerations of probability, that cowardly concession to the tedious repetitions of domestic or public life, affect it ever. One may appeal from fiction unto fact. But from the soul there is no appeal.

ERNEST.   From the soul?

GILBERT.   Yes, from the soul. That is what the highest criticism really is, the record of one's own soul. It is more fascinating than history, as it is concerned simply with oneself. It is more delightful than philosophy, as its subject is concrete and not abstract, real and not vague. It is the only civilized form of autobiography, as it deals not with the events, but with the thoughts of one's life; not with life's physical accidents of deed or circumstance, but with the spiritual moods and imaginative passions of the mind. I am always amused by the silly vanity of those writers and artists of our day who seem to imagine that the primary function of the critic is to chatter about their second-rate work. The best that one can say of most modern creative art is that it is just a little less vulgar than reality, and so the critic, with his fine sense of distinction and sure instinct of delicate refinement, will prefer to look into the silver mirror or through the woven veil, and will turn his eyes away from the chaos and clamour of actual existence, though the mirror be tarnished and the veil be torn. His sole aim is to chronicle his own impressions. It is for him that pictures are painted, books written, and marble hewn into form.

ERNEST.   I seem to have heard another theory of Criticism.

GILBERT.   Yes: it has been said by one whose gracious memory we all revere, and the music of whose pipe once lured Proserpina from her Sicilian fields, and made those white feet stir, and not in vain, the Cumnor cowslips, that the proper aim of Criticism is to see the object as in itself it really is.[1] But this is a very serious error, and takes no cognizance of Criticism's most perfect form, which is in its essence purely subjective, and seeks to reveal its own secret and not the secret of another. For the highest Criticism deals with art not as expressive but as impressive purely.

ERNEST.   But is that really so?

GILBERT.   Of course it is. Who cares whether Mr. Ruskin's views on Turner[2] are sound or not? What does it matter? That mighty and majestic prose of his, so fervid and so fiery-coloured in its noble eloquence, so rich in its elaborate symphonic music, so sure and certain, at its best, in subtle choice of word and epithet, is at least as great a work of art as any of those wonderful sunsets that bleach or rot on their corrupted canvases in England's Gallery;[3] greater indeed, one is apt to think at times, not merely because its equal beauty is more enduring, but on account of the fuller variety of its appeal, soul speaking to soul in those long-cadenced lines, not through form and colour alone, though through these, indeed, completely and without loss, but with intellectual and emotional utterance, with lofty passion and with loftier thought, with imaginative insight, and with poetic aim; greater, I always think, even as Literature is the greater art.

—1890

English poet (1795–1821).

---

[1] *it has … really is*   Matthew Arnold, whose poem *Thyrsis* attempts to summon the goddess Proserpine from the pastoral landscape of Sicily to the Cumnor hills of England. Arnold discusses the aim of criticism in his essay *The Function of Criticism at the Present Time.*

[2] *Turner*   English landscape painter Joseph Mallord William Turner. Cf. John Ruskin's *Modern Painters.*

[3] *England's Gallery*   The Tate Gallery in London, upon which a major bequest of Turner's paintings was bestowed in 1856.

from "The Decay of Lying[1]"

CYRIL. ... [I]n order to avoid making any error I want you to tell me briefly the doctrines of the new aesthetics.

VIVIAN. Briefly, then, they are these. Art never expresses anything but itself. It has an independent life, just as Thought has, and develops purely on its own lines. It is not necessarily realistic in an age of realism, nor spiritual in an age of faith. So far from being the creation of its time, it is usually in direct opposition to it, and the only history that it preserves for us is the history of its own progress. Sometimes it returns upon its footsteps, and revives some antique form, as happened in the archaistic movement of late Greek Art, and in the Pre-Raphaelite movement of our own day. At other times it entirely anticipates its age, and produces in one century work that it takes another century to understand, to appreciate, and to enjoy. In no case does it reproduce its age. To pass from the art of a time to the time itself is the great mistake that all historians commit.

The second doctrine is this. All bad art comes from returning to Life and Nature and elevating them into ideals. Life and Nature may sometimes be used as part of Art's rough material, but before they are of any real service to art they must be translated into artistic conventions. The moment Art surrenders its imaginative medium it surrenders everything. As a method Realism is a complete failure, and the two things that every artist should avoid are modernity of form and modernity of subject matter. To us, who live in the nineteenth century, any century is a suitable subject for art except our own. The only beautiful things are the things that do not concern us. It is, to have the pleasure of quoting myself, exactly because Hecuba is nothing to us that her sorrows are so suitable a motive for a tragedy.[2] Besides, it is only the modern that ever becomes old-fashioned. M. Zola[3] sits down to give us a picture of the Second Empire. Who cares for the Second Empire now? It is out of date. Life goes faster than Realism, but Romanticism is always in front of Life.

The third doctrine is that Life imitates Art far more than Art imitates Life. This results not merely from Life's imitative instinct, but from the fact that the self-conscious aim of Life is to find expression, and that Art offers it certain beautiful forms through which it may realize that energy. It is a theory that has never been put forward before, but it is extremely fruitful, and throws an entirely new light upon the history of Art.

It follows, as a corollary from this, that external Nature also imitates Art. The only effects that she can show us are effects that we have already seen through poetry, or in paintings. This is the secret of Nature's charm, as well as the explanation of Nature's weakness.

The final revelation is that Lying, the telling of beautiful untrue things, is the proper aim of Art. But of this I think I have spoken at sufficient length. And now let us go out on the terrace, where "droops the milk-white peacock like a ghost,"[4] while the evening star "washes the dusk with silver."[5] At twilight nature becomes a wonderfully suggestive effect, and is not without loveliness, though perhaps its chief use is to illustrate quotations from the poets. Come! We have talked long enough.

—1889

[1] *The Decay of Lying* In this Platonic dialogue, Wilde sets out a new theory of aesthetics through the conversation of two characters, Vivian and Cyril (named after Wilde's two sons). Vivian, prompted by Cyril's questioning, has been reading from his essay in progress, called "The Decay of Lying," which explores and confirms Plato's claim in *The Republic* that art is falsehood, yet challenges his assertion that art is a mere imitation of life, and that the lies of art are morally repugnant. On the contrary, Vivian celebrates the lies of art, declaring, "if something cannot be done to check, or at least modify, our monstrous worship of facts, Art will become sterile and Beauty will pass from the land." At the heart of this work is a challenge to the Victorian adherence to realism and advocacy of faithful imitation of nature.

[2] *Hecuba ... tragedy* Hecuba, Queen of Troy when that city was conquered by the Greeks, saw her husband and her sons murdered. In Shakespeare's *Hamlet*, one of the players performing for Hamlet recites an emotional monologue on the terrible fate of Hecuba, prompting Hamlet to wonder, "What's Hecuba to him, or he to Hecuba, / That he should weep for her?" (2.2.).

[3] *M. Zola* (Monsieur) Émile Zola, French novelist (1840–1902).

[4] *"droops ... ghost"* From "The Princess" by Alfred, Lord Tennyson.

[5] *"washes ... silver"* From "To the Evening Star" by William Blake.

Preface[1] to *The Picture of Dorian Gray*

The artist is the creator of beautiful things.

To reveal art and conceal the artist is art's aim.

The critic is he who can translate into another medium or a new material his impression of beautiful things.

The highest as the lowest form of criticism is a mode of autobiography.

Those who find ugly meanings in beautiful things are corrupt without being charming. This is a fault.

Those who find beautiful meanings in beautiful things are cultivated. For these there is hope.

They are the elect to whom beautiful things mean only beauty.

There is no such thing as a moral or an immoral book. Books are well written, or badly written. That is all.

The nineteenth century dislike of Realism is the rage of Caliban[2] seeing his own face in a glass.

The nineteenth century dislike of Romanticism is the rage of Caliban not seeing his own face in a glass.

The moral life of man forms part of the subject matter of the artist, but the morality of art consists in the perfect use of an imperfect medium.

No artist desires to prove anything. Even things that are true can be proved.

No artist has ethical sympathies. An ethical sympathy in an artist is an unpardonable mannerism of style.

No artist is ever morbid. The artist can express everything.

Thought and language are to the artist instruments of an art.

Vice and virtue are to the artist materials for an art.

From the point of view of form, the type of all the arts is the art of the musician.

From the point of view of feeling, the actor's craft is the type.

All art is at once surface and symbol.

Those who go beneath the surface do so at their peril.

Those who read the symbol do so at their peril.

It is the spectator, and not life, that art really mirrors.

Diversity of opinion about a work of art shows that the work is new, complex, and vital.

When critics disagree the artist is in accord with himself.

We can forgive a man for making a useful thing as long as he does not admire it. The only excuse for making a useless thing is that one admires it intensely.

All art is quite useless.

—1891

The Importance of Being Earnest
A Trivial Comedy for Serious People

THE PERSONS IN THE PLAY

John Worthing, J.P.[3]
Algernon Moncrieff
Rev. Canon Chasuble, D.D.[4]
Merriman, *Butler*
Lane, *Manservant*
Lady Bracknell
Hon.[5] Gwendolen Fairfax
Cecily Cardew
Miss Prism, *Governess*

THE SCENES IN THE PLAY

ACT 1. Algernon Moncrieff's Flat in Half-Moon Street,[6] W.
ACT 2. The Garden at the Manor House, Woolton.[7]
ACT 3. Drawing-Room at the Manor House, Woolton.

TIME: The Present.

1 *Preface* Published in 1891, the year after the novel's first appearance, this preface was a response to the charges of immorality leveled at the novel by numerous critics.

2 *Caliban* The "monster" of Shakespeare's *The Tempest*, Caliban is a native of the island and has been enslaved by Prospero.

3 *J.P.* Justice of the Peace.

4 *D.D.* Doctor of Divinity.

5 *Hon.* I.e., The Honorable. The honorific in this case designates the daughter of a peer below the rank of Earl.

6 *Half-Moon Street* Street located in a fashionable area of London.

7 *Woolton* A fictional location.

ACT 1

SCENE

(*Morning-room in Algernon's flat in Half-Moon Street. The room is luxuriously and artistically furnished. The sound of a piano is heard in the adjoining room.*)

(*Lane is arranging afternoon tea on the table, and after the music has ceased, Algernon enters.*)

ALGERNON.   Did you hear what I was playing, Lane?

LANE.   I didn't think it polite to listen, sir.

ALGERNON.   I'm sorry for that, for your sake. I don't play accurately—any one can play accurately—but I
5 play with wonderful expression. As far as the piano is concerned, sentiment is my forte. I keep science for Life.

LANE.   Yes, sir.

ALGERNON.   And, speaking of the science of Life, have you got the cucumber sandwiches[1] cut for Lady
10 Bracknell?

LANE.   Yes, sir. (*Hands them on a salver.*[2])

ALGERNON.   (*Inspects them, takes two, and sits down on the sofa.*) Oh! … by the way, Lane, I see from your book that on Thursday night, when Lord Shoreman and Mr.
15 Worthing were dining with me, eight bottles of champagne are entered as having been consumed.

LANE.   Yes, sir; eight bottles and a pint.

ALGERNON.   Why is it that at a bachelor's establishment the servants invariably drink the champagne? I ask
20 merely for information.

LANE.   I attribute it to the superior quality of the wine, sir. I have often observed that in married households the champagne is rarely of a first-rate brand.

ALGERNON.   Good heavens! Is marriage so demoralising
25 as that?

LANE.   I believe it is a very pleasant state, sir. I have had very little experience of it myself up to the present. I have only been married once. That was in consequence of a misunderstanding between myself and a young
30 person.

ALGERNON.   (*Languidly.*) I don't know that I am much interested in your family life, Lane.

LANE.   No, sir; it is not a very interesting subject. I never think of it myself.

35 ALGERNON. Very natural, I am sure. That will do, Lane, thank you.

LANE.   Thank you, sir. (*Lane goes out.*)

ALGERNON.   Lane's views on marriage seem somewhat lax. Really, if the lower orders don't set us a good
40 example, what on earth is the use of them? They seem, as a class, to have absolutely no sense of moral responsibility.

(*Enter Lane.*)

LANE.   Mr. Ernest Worthing.

(*Enter Jack. Lane goes out.*)

ALGERNON. How are you, my dear Ernest? What brings
45 you up to town?

JACK.   Oh, pleasure, pleasure! What else should bring one anywhere? Eating as usual, I see, Algy!

ALGERNON.   (*Stiffly.*) I believe it is customary in good society to take some slight refreshment at five o'clock.
50 Where have you been since last Thursday?

JACK.   (*Sitting down on the sofa.*) In the country.

ALGERNON.   What on earth do you do there?

JACK.   (*Pulling off his gloves.*) When one is in town[3] one amuses oneself. When one is in the country one amuses
55 other people. It is excessively boring.

ALGERNON.   And who are the people you amuse?

JACK.   (*Airily.*) Oh, neighbours, neighbours.

ALGERNON.   Got nice neighbours in your part of Shropshire?

60 JACK.   Perfectly horrid! Never speak to one of them.

ALGERNON.   How immensely you must amuse them! (*Goes over and takes sandwich.*) By the way, Shropshire is your county, is it not?

JACK.   Eh? Shropshire? Yes, of course. Hallo! Why all
65 these cups? Why cucumber sandwiches? Why such reckless extravagance in one so young? Who is coming to tea?

---

1 *cucumber sandwiches* Small sandwiches of cucumber on thinly-sliced bread, a staple of afternoon tea in polite English society.

2 *salver* Serving tray, typically silver.

3 *in town* In London.

ALGERNON. Oh! merely Aunt Augusta and Gwendolen.

JACK. How perfectly delightful!

70 ALGERNON. Yes, that is all very well; but I am afraid Aunt Augusta won't quite approve of your being here.

JACK. May I ask why?

ALGERNON. My dear fellow, the way you flirt with Gwendolen is perfectly disgraceful. It is almost as bad as

75 the way Gwendolen flirts with you.

JACK. I am in love with Gwendolen. I have come up to town expressly to propose to her.

ALGERNON. I thought you had come up for pleasure? … I call that business.

80 JACK. How utterly unromantic you are!

ALGERNON. I really don't see anything romantic in proposing. It is very romantic to be in love. But there is nothing romantic about a definite proposal. Why, one may be accepted. One usually is, I believe. Then the

85 excitement is all over. The very essence of romance is uncertainty. If ever I get married, I'll certainly try to forget the fact.

JACK. I have no doubt about that, dear Algy. The Divorce Court was specially invented for people whose

90 memories are so curiously constituted.

ALGERNON. Oh! there is no use speculating on that subject. Divorces are made in Heaven—(*Jack puts out his hand to take a sandwich. Algernon at once interferes.*) Please don't touch the cucumber sandwiches. They are

95 ordered specially for Aunt Augusta. (*Takes one and eats it.*)

JACK. Well, you have been eating them all the time.

ALGERNON. That is quite a different matter. She is my aunt. (*Takes plate from below.*) Have some bread and

100 butter. The bread and butter is for Gwendolen. Gwendolen is devoted to bread and butter.

JACK. (*Advancing to table and helping himself.*) And very good bread and butter it is too.

ALGERNON. Well, my dear fellow, you need not eat as if

105 you were going to eat it all. You behave as if you were married to her already. You are not married to her already, and I don't think you ever will be.

JACK. Why on earth do you say that?

ALGERNON. Well, in the first place girls never marry the

110 men they flirt with. Girls don't think it right.

JACK. Oh, that is nonsense!

ALGERNON. It isn't. It is a great truth. It accounts for the extraordinary number of bachelors that one sees all over the place. In the second place, I don't give my consent.

115 JACK. Your consent!

ALGERNON. My dear fellow, Gwendolen is my first cousin. And before I allow you to marry her, you will have to clear up the whole question of Cecily. (*Rings bell.*)

120 JACK. Cecily! What on earth do you mean? What do you mean, Algy, by Cecily! I don't know any one of the name of Cecily.

(*Enter Lane.*)

ALGERNON. Bring me that cigarette case Mr. Worthing left in the smoking-room the last time he dined here.

125 LANE. Yes, sir.

(*Lane goes out.*)

JACK. Do you mean to say you have had my cigarette case all this time? I wish to goodness you had let me know. I have been writing frantic letters to Scotland Yard about it. I was very nearly offering a large reward.

130 ALGERNON. Well, I wish you would offer one. I happen to be more than usually hard up.

JACK. There is no good offering a large reward now that the thing is found.

(*Enter Lane with the cigarette case on a salver. Algernon takes it at once. Lane goes out.*)

ALGERNON. I think that is rather mean of you, Ernest,

135 I must say. (*Opens case and examines it.*) However, it makes no matter, for, now that I look at the inscription inside, I find that the thing isn't yours after all.

JACK. Of course it's mine. (*Moving to him.*) You have seen me with it a hundred times, and you have no right

140 whatsoever to read what is written inside. It is a very ungentlemanly thing to read a private cigarette case.

ALGERNON. Oh! it is absurd to have a hard and fast rule about what one should read and what one shouldn't. More than half of modern culture depends on what one

145 shouldn't read.

JACK. I am quite aware of the fact, and I don't propose to discuss modern culture. It isn't the sort of thing one should talk of in private. I simply want my cigarette case back.

150 ALGERNON. Yes; but this isn't your cigarette case. This cigarette case is a present from some one of the name of Cecily, and you said you didn't know any one of that name.

JACK. Well, if you want to know, Cecily happens to be
155   my aunt.

ALGERNON. Your aunt!

JACK. Yes. Charming old lady she is, too. Lives at Tunbridge Wells. Just give it back to me, Algy.

ALGERNON. (*Retreating to back of sofa.*) But why does
160   she call herself little Cecily if she is your aunt and lives at Tunbridge Wells? (*Reading.*) "From little Cecily with her fondest love."

JACK. (*Moving to sofa and kneeling upon it.*) My dear fellow, what on earth is there in that? Some aunts are
165   tall, some aunts are not tall. That is a matter that surely an aunt may be allowed to decide for herself. You seem to think that every aunt should be exactly like your aunt! That is absurd! For Heaven's sake give me back my cigarette case. (*Follows Algernon round the room.*)

170 ALGERNON. Yes. But why does your aunt call you her uncle? "From little Cecily, with her fondest love to her dear Uncle Jack." There is no objection, I admit, to an aunt being a small aunt, but why an aunt, no matter what her size may be, should call her own nephew her
175   uncle, I can't quite make out. Besides, your name isn't Jack at all; it is Ernest.

JACK. It isn't Ernest; it's Jack.

ALGERNON. You have always told me it was Ernest. I have introduced you to every one as Ernest. You answer
180   to the name of Ernest. You look as if your name was Ernest. You are the most earnest-looking person I ever saw in my life. It is perfectly absurd your saying that your name isn't Ernest. It's on your cards. Here is one of them. (*Taking it from case.*) "Mr. Ernest Worthing, B.
185   4, The Albany." I'll keep this as a proof that your name is Ernest if ever you attempt to deny it to me, or to Gwendolen, or to any one else. (*Puts the card in his pocket.*)

JACK. Well, my name is Ernest in town and Jack in the
190   country, and the cigarette case was given to me in the country.

ALGERNON. Yes, but that does not account for the fact that your small Aunt Cecily, who lives at Tunbridge Wells, calls you her dear uncle. Come, old boy, you had
195   much better have the thing out at once.

JACK. My dear Algy, you talk exactly as if you were a dentist. It is very vulgar to talk like a dentist when one isn't a dentist. It produces a false impression.

ALGERNON. Well, that is exactly what dentists always
200   do. Now, go on! Tell me the whole thing. I may mention that I have always suspected you of being a confirmed and secret Bunburyist; and I am quite sure of it now.

JACK. Bunburyist? What on earth do you mean by a
205   Bunburyist?

ALGERNON. I'll reveal to you the meaning of that incomparable expression as soon as you are kind enough to inform me why you are Ernest in town and Jack in the country.

210 JACK. Well, produce my cigarette case first.

ALGERNON. Here it is. (*Hands cigarette case.*) Now produce your explanation, and pray make it improbable. (*Sits on sofa.*)

JACK. My dear fellow, there is nothing improbable about
215   my explanation at all. In fact it's perfectly ordinary. Old Mr. Thomas Cardew, who adopted me when I was a little boy, made me in his will guardian to his grand-daughter, Miss Cecily Cardew. Cecily, who addresses me as her uncle from motives of respect that you could
220   not possibly appreciate, lives at my place in the country under the charge of her admirable governess, Miss Prism.

ALGERNON. Where in that place in the country, by the way?

225 JACK. That is nothing to you, dear boy. You are not going to be invited ... I may tell you candidly that the place is not in Shropshire.

ALGERNON. I suspected that, my dear fellow! I have Bunburyed all over Shropshire on two separate
230   occasions. Now, go on. Why are you Ernest in town and Jack in the country?

JACK. My dear Algy, I don't know whether you will be able to understand my real motives. You are hardly serious enough. When one is placed in the position of guardian, one has to adopt a very high moral tone on all subjects. It's one's duty to do so. And as a high moral tone can hardly be said to conduce very much to either one's health or one's happiness, in order to get up to town I have always pretended to have a younger brother of the name of Ernest, who lives in the Albany, and gets into the most dreadful scrapes. That, my dear Algy, is the whole truth pure and simple.

ALGERNON. The truth is rarely pure and never simple. Modern life would be very tedious if it were either, and modern literature a complete impossibility!

JACK. That wouldn't be at all a bad thing.

ALGERNON. Literary criticism is not your forte, my dear fellow. Don't try it. You should leave that to people who haven't been at a University. They do it so well in the daily papers. What you really are is a Bunburyist. I was quite right in saying you were a Bunburyist. You are one of the most advanced Bunburyists I know.

JACK. What on earth do you mean?

ALGERNON. You have invented a very useful younger brother called Ernest, in order that you may be able to come up to town as often as you like. I have invented an invaluable permanent invalid called Bunbury, in order that I may be able to go down into the country whenever I choose. Bunbury is perfectly invaluable. If it wasn't for Bunbury's extraordinary bad health, for instance, I wouldn't be able to dine with you at Willis's to-night, for I have been really engaged to Aunt Augusta for more than a week.

JACK. I haven't asked you to dine with me anywhere to-night.

ALGERNON. I know. You are absurdly careless about sending out invitations. It is very foolish of you. Nothing annoys people so much as not receiving invitations.

JACK. You had much better dine with your Aunt Augusta.

ALGERNON. I haven't the smallest intention of doing anything of the kind. To begin with, I dined there on Monday, and once a week is quite enough to dine with one's own relations. In the second place, whenever I do dine there I am always treated as a member of the family, and sent down[1] with either no woman at all, or two. In the third place, I know perfectly well whom she will place me next to, to-night. She will place me next Mary Farquhar, who always flirts with her own husband across the dinner-table. That is not very pleasant. Indeed, it is not even decent … and that sort of thing is enormously on the increase. The amount of women in London who flirt with their own husbands is perfectly scandalous. It looks so bad. It is simply washing one's clean linen in public. Besides, now that I know you to be a confirmed Bunburyist I naturally want to talk to you about Bunburying. I want to tell you the rules.

JACK. I'm not a Bunburyist at all. If Gwendolen accepts me, I am going to kill my brother, indeed I think I'll kill him in any case. Cecily is a little too much interested in him. It is rather a bore. So I am going to get rid of Ernest. And I strongly advise you to do the same with Mr. … with your invalid friend who has the absurd name.

ALGERNON. Nothing will induce me to part with Bunbury, and if you ever get married, which seems to me extremely problematic, you will be very glad to know Bunbury. A man who marries without knowing Bunbury has a very tedious time of it.

JACK. That is nonsense. If I marry a charming girl like Gwendolen, and she is the only girl I ever saw in my life that I would marry, I certainly won't want to know Bunbury.

ALGERNON. Then your wife will. You don't seem to realise, that in married life three is company and two is none.

JACK. (*Sententiously.*) That, my dear young friend, is the theory that the corrupt French Drama has been propounding for the last fifty years.

ALGERNON. Yes; and that the happy English home has proved in half the time.

JACK. For heaven's sake, don't try to be cynical. It's perfectly easy to be cynical.

ALGERNON. My dear fellow, it isn't easy to be anything nowadays. There's such a lot of beastly competition about. (*The sound of an electric bell is heard.*) Ah! that must be Aunt Augusta. Only relatives, or creditors, ever ring in that Wagnerian[2] manner. Now, if I get her out

---

[1] *sent down* I.e., sent from the drawing-room (typically upstairs) down to the dining-room (typically on a lower floor).

[2] *Wagnerian* Suggesting the music of German composer Richard Wagner (1813–83), known for dramatic, stirring compositions such as *Tannhäuser, Lohengrin,* and *Der Ring des Nibelungen.*

of the way for ten minutes, so that you can have an
opportunity for proposing to Gwendolen, may I dine
with you to-night at Willis's?

JACK. I suppose so, if you want to.

ALGERNON. Yes, but you must be serious about it. I hate
people who are not serious about meals. It is so shallow
of them.

(*Enter Lane.*)

Lady Bracknell and Miss Fairfax.

(*Algernon goes forward to meet them. Enter Lady Bracknell
and Gwendolen.*)

LADY BRACKNELL. Good afternoon, dear Algernon, I
hope you are behaving very well.

ALGERNON. I'm feeling very well, Aunt Augusta.

LADY BRACKNELL. That's not quite the same thing. In
fact the two things rarely go together. (*Sees Jack and
bows to him with icy coldness.*)

ALGERNON. (*To Gwendolen.*) Dear me, you are smart!

GWENDOLEN. I am always smart! Am I not, Mr. Worthing?

JACK. You're quite perfect, Miss Fairfax.

GWENDOLEN. Oh! I hope I am not that. It would leave
no room for developments, and I intend to develop in
many directions.

(*Gwendolen and Jack sit down together in the corner.*)

LADY BRACKNELL. I'm sorry if we are a little late,
Algernon, but I was obliged to call on dear Lady Harbury. I hadn't been there since her poor husband's
death. I never saw a woman so altered; she looks quite
twenty years younger. And now I'll have a cup of tea,
and one of those nice cucumber sandwiches you
promised me.

ALGERNON. Certainly, Aunt Augusta. (*Goes over to tea-
table.*)

LADY BRACKNELL. Won't you come and sit here,
Gwendolen?

GWENDOLEN. Thanks, mamma, I'm quite comfortable
where I am.

ALGERNON. (*Picking up empty plate in horror.*) Good
heavens! Lane! Why are there no cucumber sandwiches?
I ordered them specially.

LANE. (*Gravely.*) There were no cucumbers in the
market this morning, sir. I went down twice.

ALGERNON. No cucumbers!

LANE. No, sir. Not even for ready money.

ALGERNON. That will do, Lane, thank you.

LANE. Thank you, sir. (*Goes out.*)

ALGERNON. I am greatly distressed, Aunt Augusta,
about there being no cucumbers, not even for ready
money.

LADY BRACKNELL. It really makes no matter, Algernon.
I had some crumpets with Lady Harbury, who seems to
me to be living entirely for pleasure now.

ALGERNON. I hear her hair has turned quite gold from
grief.

LADY BRACKNELL. It certainly has changed its colour.
From what cause I, of course, cannot say. (*Algernon
crosses and hands tea.*) Thank you. I've quite a treat for
you to-night, Algernon. I am going to send you down
with Mary Farquhar. She is such a nice woman, and so
attentive to her husband. It's delightful to watch them.

ALGERNON. I am afraid, Aunt Augusta, I shall have to
give up the pleasure of dining with you to-night after
all.

LADY BRACKNELL. (*Frowning.*) I hope not, Algernon. It
would put my table completely out. Your uncle would
have to dine upstairs. Fortunately he is accustomed to
that.

ALGERNON. It is a great bore, and, I need hardly say, a
terrible disappointment to me, but the fact is I have just
had a telegram to say that my poor friend Bunbury is
very ill again. (*Exchanges glances with Jack.*) They seem
to think I should be with him.

LADY BRACKNELL. It is very strange. This Mr. Bunbury
seems to suffer from curiously bad health.

ALGERNON. Yes; poor Bunbury is a dreadful invalid.

LADY BRACKNELL. Well, I must say, Algernon, that I
think it is high time that Mr. Bunbury made up his
mind whether he was going to live or to die. This shilly-
shallying with the question is absurd. Nor do I in any
way approve of the modern sympathy with invalids. I
consider it morbid. Illness of any kind is hardly a thing
to be encouraged in others. Health is the primary duty
of life. I am always telling that to your poor uncle, but

he never seems to take much notice … as far as any
improvement in his ailment goes. I should be much
obliged if you would ask Mr. Bunbury, from me, to be
kind enough not to have a relapse on Saturday, for I rely
on you to arrange my music for me. It is my last
reception, and one wants something that will encourage
conversation, particularly at the end of the season when
every one has practically said whatever they had to say,
which, in most cases, was probably not much.

ALGERNON. I'll speak to Bunbury, Aunt Augusta, if he
is still conscious, and I think I can promise you he'll be
all right by Saturday. Of course the music is a great
difficulty. You see, if one plays good music, people don't
listen, and if one plays bad music people don't talk. But
I'll run over the programme I've drawn out, if you will
kindly come into the next room for a moment.

LADY BRACKNELL. Thank you, Algernon. It is very
thoughtful of you. (*Rising, and following Algernon.*) I'm
sure the programme will be delightful, after a few
expurgations. French songs I cannot possibly allow.
People always seem to think that they are improper, and
either look shocked, which is vulgar, or laugh, which is
worse. But German sounds a thoroughly respectable
language, and indeed, I believe is so. Gwendolen, you
will accompany me.

GWENDOLEN. Certainly, mamma.

(*Lady Bracknell and Algernon go into the music-room,
Gwendolen remains behind.*)

JACK. Charming day it has been, Miss Fairfax.

GWENDOLEN. Pray don't talk to me about the weather,
Mr. Worthing. Whenever people talk to me about the
weather, I always feel quite certain that they mean
something else. And that makes me so nervous.

JACK. I do mean something else.

GWENDOLEN. I thought so. In fact, I am never wrong.

JACK. And I would like to be allowed to take advantage
of Lady Bracknell's temporary absence …

GWENDOLEN. I would certainly advise you to do so.
Mamma has a way of coming back suddenly into a
room that I have often had to speak to her about.

JACK. (*Nervously.*) Miss Fairfax, ever since I met you I
have admired you more than any girl … I have ever met
since … I met you.

GWENDOLEN. Yes, I am quite well aware of the fact.
And I often wish that in public, at any rate, you had
been more demonstrative. For me you have always had
an irresistible fascination. Even before I met you I was
far from indifferent to you. (*Jack looks at her in
amazement.*) We live, as I hope you know, Mr.
Worthing, in an age of ideals. The fact is constantly
mentioned in the more expensive monthly magazines,
and has reached the provincial[1] pulpits, I am told; and
my ideal has always been to love some one of the name
of Ernest. There is something in that name that inspires
absolute confidence. The moment Algernon first
mentioned to me that he had a friend called Ernest, I
knew I was destined to love you.

JACK. You really love me, Gwendolen?

GWENDOLEN. Passionately!

JACK. Darling! You don't know how happy you've made
me.

GWENDOLEN. My own Ernest!

JACK. But you don't really mean to say that you couldn't
love me if my name wasn't Ernest?

GWENDOLEN. But your name is Ernest.

JACK. Yes, I know it is. But supposing it was something
else? Do you mean to say you couldn't love me then?

GWENDOLEN. (*Glibly.*) Ah! that is clearly a metaphysical
speculation, and like most metaphysical speculations has
very little reference at all to the actual facts of real life, as
we know them.

JACK. Personally, darling, to speak quite candidly, I
don't much care about the name of Ernest … I don't
think the name suits me at all.

GWENDOLEN. It suits you perfectly. It is a divine name.
It has a music of its own. It produces vibrations.

JACK. Well, really, Gwendolen, I must say that I think
there are lots of other much nicer names. I think Jack,
for instance, a charming name.

GWENDOLEN. Jack? … No, there is very little music in
the name Jack, if any at all, indeed. It does not thrill. It
produces absolutely no vibrations … I have known
several Jacks, and they all, without exception, were more
than usually plain. Besides, Jack is a notorious
domesticity for John! And I pity any woman who is

[1] *provincial* "Province" does not indicate a formal British jurisdiction; "the provinces" is a colloquial term for all areas of the country that are some distance from London.

married to a man called John. She would probably never be allowed to know the entrancing pleasure of a single moment's solitude. The only really safe name is Ernest.

485 JACK. Gwendolen, I must get christened at once—I mean we must get married at once. There is no time to be lost.

GWENDOLEN. Married, Mr. Worthing?

JACK. (Astounded.) Well … surely. You know that I love
490 you, and you led me to believe, Miss Fairfax, that you were not absolutely indifferent to me.

GWENDOLEN. I adore you. But you haven't proposed to me yet. Nothing has been said at all about marriage. The subject has not even been touched on.

495 JACK. Well … may I propose to you now?

GWENDOLEN. I think it would be an admirable opportunity. And to spare you any possible disappointment, Mr. Worthing, I think it only fair to tell you quite frankly before-hand that I am fully
500 determined to accept you.

JACK. Gwendolen!

GWENDOLEN. Yes, Mr. Worthing, what have you got to say to me?

JACK. You know what I have got to say to you.

505 GWENDOLEN. Yes, but you don't say it.

JACK. Gwendolen, will you marry me? (Goes on his knees.)

GWENDOLEN. Of course I will, darling. How long you have been about it! I am afraid you have had very little
510 experience in how to propose.

JACK. My own one, I have never loved any one in the world but you.

GWENDOLEN. Yes, but men often propose for practice. I know my brother Gerald does. All my girl-friends tell
515 me so. What wonderfully blue eyes you have, Ernest! They are quite, quite, blue. I hope you will always look at me just like that, especially when there are other people present. (Enter Lady Bracknell.)

LADY BRACKNELL. Mr. Worthing! Rise, sir, from this
520 semi-recumbent posture. It is most indecorous.

GWENDOLEN. Mamma! (He tries to rise; she restrains him.) I must beg you to retire. This is no place for you. Besides, Mr. Worthing has not quite finished yet.

LADY BRACKNELL. Finished what, may I ask?

525 GWENDOLEN. I am engaged to Mr. Worthing, mamma.

(They rise together.)

LADY BRACKNELL. Pardon me, you are not engaged to any one. When you do become engaged to some one, I, or your father, should his health permit him, will inform you of the fact. An engagement should come on a young
530 girl as a surprise, pleasant or unpleasant, as the case may be. It is hardly a matter that she could be allowed to arrange for herself … And now I have a few questions to put to you, Mr. Worthing. While I am making these inquiries, you, Gwendolen, will wait for me below in
535 the carriage.

GWENDOLEN. (Reproachfully.) Mamma!

LADY BRACKNELL. In the carriage, Gwendolen!

(Gwendolen goes to the door. She and Jack blow kisses to each other behind Lady Bracknell's back. Lady Bracknell looks vaguely about as if she could not understand what the noise was. Finally turns round.)

Gwendolen, the carriage!

GWENDOLEN. Yes, mamma. (Goes out, looking back at
540 Jack.)

LADY BRACKNELL. (Sitting down.) You can take a seat, Mr. Worthing. (Looks in her pocket for note-book and pencil.)

JACK. Thank you, Lady Bracknell, I prefer standing.

545 LADY BRACKNELL. (Pencil and note-book in hand.) I feel bound to tell you that you are not down on my list of eligible young men, although I have the same list as the dear Duchess of Bolton has. We work together, in fact. However, I am quite ready to enter your name, should
550 your answers be what a really affectionate mother requires. Do you smoke?

JACK. Well, yes, I must admit I smoke.

LADY BRACKNELL. I am glad to hear it. A man should always have an occupation of some kind. There are far
555 too many idle men in London as it is. How old are you?

JACK. Twenty-nine.

LADY BRACKNELL. A very good age to be married at. I have always been of opinion that a man who desires to get married should know either everything or nothing.
560 Which do you know?

JACK. (After some hesitation.) I know nothing, Lady Bracknell.

LADY BRACKNELL. I am pleased to hear it. I do not approve of anything that tampers with natural ignorance. Ignorance is like a delicate exotic fruit; touch it and the bloom is gone. The whole theory of modern education is radically unsound. Fortunately in England, at any rate, education produces no effect whatsoever. If it did, it would prove a serious danger to the upper classes, and probably lead to acts of violence in Grosvenor Square.[1] What is your income?

JACK. Between seven and eight thousand a year.

LADY BRACKNELL. (*Makes a note in her book.*) In land, or in investments?

JACK. In investments, chiefly.

LADY BRACKNELL. That is satisfactory. What between the duties[2] expected of one during one's lifetime, and the duties exacted from one after one's death, land has ceased to be either a profit or a pleasure. It gives one position, and prevents one from keeping it up. That's all that can be said about land.

JACK. I have a country house with some land, of course, attached to it, about fifteen hundred acres, I believe; but I don't depend on that for my real income. In fact, as far as I can make out, the poachers are the only people who make anything out of it.

LADY BRACKNELL. A country house! How many bedrooms? Well, that point can be cleared up afterwards. You have a town house, I hope? A girl with a simple, unspoiled nature, like Gwendolen, could hardly be expected to reside in the country.

JACK. Well, I own a house in Belgrave Square, but it is let by the year to Lady Bloxham. Of course, I can get it back whenever I like, at six months' notice.

LADY BRACKNELL. Lady Bloxham? I don't know her.

JACK. Oh, she goes about very little. She is a lady considerably advanced in years.

LADY BRACKNELL. Ah, nowadays that is no guarantee of respectability of character. What number in Belgrave Square?

JACK. 149.

LADY BRACKNELL. (*Shaking her head.*) The unfashionable side. I thought there was something. However, that could easily be altered.

JACK. Do you mean the fashion, or the side?

LADY BRACKNELL. (*Sternly.*) Both, if necessary, I presume. What are your politics?

JACK. Well, I am afraid I really have none. I am a Liberal Unionist.[3]

LADY BRACKNELL. Oh, they count as Tories. They dine with us. Or come in the evening, at any rate. Now to minor matters. Are your parents living?

JACK. I have lost both my parents.

LADY BRACKNELL. To lose one parent, Mr. Worthing, may be regarded as a misfortune; to lose both looks like carelessness. Who was your father? He was evidently a man of some wealth. Was he born in what the Radical papers call the purple of commerce,[4] or did he rise from the ranks of the aristocracy?

JACK. I am afraid I really don't know. The fact is, Lady Bracknell, I said I had lost my parents. It would be nearer the truth to say that my parents seem to have lost me … I don't actually know who I am by birth. I was … well, I was found.

LADY BRACKNELL. Found!

JACK. The late Mr. Thomas Cardew, an old gentleman of a very charitable and kindly disposition, found me, and gave me the name of Worthing, because he happened to have a first-class ticket for Worthing in his pocket at the time. Worthing is a place in Sussex. It is a seaside resort.

LADY BRACKNELL. Where did the charitable gentleman who had a first-class ticket for this seaside resort find you?

JACK. (*Gravely.*) In a hand-bag.

LADY BRACKNELL. A hand-bag?

JACK. (*Very seriously.*) Yes, Lady Bracknell. I was in a hand-bag—a somewhat large, black leather hand-bag, with handles to it—an ordinary hand-bag in fact.

LADY BRACKNELL. In what locality did this Mr. James, or Thomas, Cardew come across this ordinary hand-bag?

JACK. In the cloak-room at Victoria Station. It was given

---

[1] *Grosvenor Square* Located in a fashionable part of central London.

[2] *duties* Taxes.

[3] *Liberal Unionist* The Liberal Unionists, who in 1886 had broken away from the Liberal party in reaction to Prime Minister William Gladstone's support for Irish Home Rule, occupied the political center between the two large parties, the Liberals and the Conservatives.

[4] *Was he born … the purple of commerce* I.e., was he born into a wealthy merchant or trading family. (The color purple is traditionally associated with royalty.)

to him in mistake for his own.

LADY BRACKNELL.   The cloak-room at Victoria Station?

645 JACK.   Yes. The Brighton line.

LADY BRACKNELL.   The line is immaterial. Mr. Worth-ing, I confess I feel somewhat bewildered by what you have just told me. To be born, or at any rate bred, in a hand-bag, whether it had handles or not, seems to me to
650 display a contempt for the ordinary decencies of family life that reminds one of the worst excesses of the French Revolution. And I presume you know what that unfortunate movement led to? As for the particular locality in which the hand-bag was found, a cloak-room
655 at a railway station might serve to conceal a social indiscretion—has probably, indeed, been used for that purpose before now—but it could hardly be regarded as an assured basis for a recognised position in good society.

660 JACK.   May I ask you then what you would advise me to do? I need hardly say I would do anything in the world to ensure Gwendolen's happiness.

LADY BRACKNELL.   I would strongly advise you, Mr. Worthing, to try and acquire some relations as soon as
665 possible, and to make a definite effort to produce at any rate one parent, of either sex, before the season[1] is quite over.

JACK.   Well, I don't see how I could possibly manage to do that. I can produce the hand-bag at any moment. It
670 is in my dressing-room at home. I really think that should satisfy you, Lady Bracknell.

LADY BRACKNELL.   Me, sir! What has it to do with me? You can hardly imagine that I and Lord Bracknell would dream of allowing our only daughter—a girl
675 brought up with the utmost care—to marry into a cloak-room, and form an alliance with a parcel? Good morning, Mr. Worthing!

(*Lady Bracknell sweeps out in majestic indignation.*)

JACK.   Good morning! (*Algernon, from the other room, strikes up the Wedding March. Jack looks perfectly furious,*
680 *and goes to the door.*) For goodness' sake don't play that ghastly tune, Algy. How idiotic you are!

---

1   *the season*   The London social season, which ran while Parliament was sitting. Many wealthy families spent the rest of the year at their country homes.

(*The music stops and Algernon enters cheerily.*)

ALGERNON.   Didn't it go off all right, old boy? You don't mean to say Gwendolen refused you? I know it is a way she has. She is always refusing people. I think it is
685 most ill-natured of her.

JACK.   Oh, Gwendolen is as right as a trivet.[2] As far as she is concerned, we are engaged. Her mother is perfectly unbearable. Never met such a Gorgon[3] ... I don't really know what a Gorgon is like, but I am quite sure that
690 Lady Bracknell is one. In any case, she is a monster, without being a myth, which is rather unfair ... I beg your pardon, Algy, I suppose I shouldn't talk about your own aunt in that way before you.

ALGERNON.   My dear boy, I love hearing my relations
695 abused. It is the only thing that makes me put up with them at all. Relations are simply a tedious pack of people, who haven't got the remotest knowledge of how to live, nor the smallest instinct about when to die.

JACK.   Oh, that is nonsense!

700 ALGERNON.   It isn't!

JACK.   Well, I won't argue about the matter. You always want to argue about things.

ALGERNON.   That is exactly what things were originally made for.

705 JACK.   Upon my word, if I thought that, I'd shoot myself ... (*A pause.*) You don't think there is any chance of Gwendolen becoming like her mother in about a hundred and fifty years, do you, Algy?

ALGERNON.   All women become like their mothers. That
710 is their tragedy. No man does. That's his.

JACK.   Is that clever?

ALGERNON.   It is perfectly phrased! and quite as true as any observation in civilized life should be.

JACK.   I am sick to death of cleverness. Everybody is
715 clever nowadays. You can't go anywhere without meeting clever people. The thing has become an absolute public nuisance. I wish to goodness we had a few fools left.

ALGERNON.   We have.

---

2   *as right as a trivet*   Proverbial expression indicating stability (a trivet is a three-footed stand or support).

3   *Gorgon*   In Greek mythology the three Gorgons are sisters who have repulsive features (including snakes growing out of their heads instead of hair); anyone who looks at them turns into stone.

720 JACK. I should extremely like to meet them. What do they talk about?

ALGERNON. The fools? Oh! about the clever people, of course.

JACK. What fools!

725 ALGERNON. By the way, did you tell Gwendolen the truth about your being Ernest in town, and Jack in the country?

JACK. (*In a very patronising manner.*) My dear fellow, the truth isn't quite the sort of thing one tells to a nice, sweet, refined girl. What extraordinary ideas you have about the way to behave to a woman!

730

ALGERNON. The only way to behave to a woman is to make love to her, if she is pretty, and to some one else, if she is plain.

735 JACK. Oh, that is nonsense.

ALGERNON. What about your brother? What about the profligate Ernest?

JACK. Oh, before the end of the week I shall have got rid of him. I'll say he died in Paris of apoplexy.[1] Lots of people die of apoplexy, quite suddenly, don't they?

740

ALGERNON. Yes, but it's hereditary, my dear fellow. It's a sort of thing that runs in families. You had much better say a severe chill.

JACK. You are sure a severe chill isn't hereditary, or anything of that kind?

745

ALGERNON. Of course it isn't!

JACK. Very well, then. My poor brother Ernest is carried off suddenly, in Paris, by a severe chill. That gets rid of him.

750 ALGERNON. But I thought you said that … Miss Cardew was a little too much interested in your poor brother Ernest? Won't she feel his loss a good deal?

JACK. Oh, that is all right. Cecily is not a silly romantic girl, I am glad to say. She has got a capital appetite, goes on long walks, and pays no attention at all to her lessons.

755

ALGERNON. I would rather like to see Cecily.

JACK. I will take very good care you never do. She is excessively pretty, and she is only just eighteen.

ALGERNON. Have you told Gwendolen yet that you have an excessively pretty ward who is only just eighteen?

760

JACK. Oh! one doesn't blurt these things out to people. Cecily and Gwendolen are perfectly certain to be extremely great friends. I'll bet you anything you like that half an hour after they have met, they will be calling each other sister.

765

ALGERNON. Women only do that when they have called each other a lot of other things first. Now, my dear boy, if we want to get a good table at Willis's, we really must go and dress. Do you know it is nearly seven?

770

JACK. (*Irritably.*) Oh! It always is nearly seven.

ALGERNON. Well, I'm hungry.

JACK. I never knew you when you weren't …

ALGERNON. What shall we do after dinner? Go to a theatre?

775

JACK. Oh no! I loathe listening.

ALGERNON. Well, let us go to the Club?

JACK. Oh, no! I hate talking.

ALGERNON. Well, we might trot round to the Empire[2] at ten?

780

JACK. Oh, no! I can't bear looking at things. It is so silly.

ALGERNON. Well, what shall we do?

JACK. Nothing!

ALGERNON. It is awfully hard work doing nothing. However, I don't mind hard work where there is no definite object of any kind.

785

(*Enter Lane.*)

LANE. Miss Fairfax.

(*Enter Gwendolen. Lane goes out.*)

ALGERNON. Gwendolen, upon my word!

GWENDOLEN. Algy, kindly turn your back. I have something very particular to say to Mr. Worthing.

790

ALGERNON. Really, Gwendolen, I don't think I can allow this at all.

GWENDOLEN. Algy, you always adopt a strictly immoral attitude towards life. You are not quite old enough to do that. (*Algernon retires to the fireplace.*)

795

JACK. My own darling!

GWENDOLEN. Ernest, we may never be married. From the expression on mamma's face I fear we never shall. Few parents nowadays pay any regard to what their children say to them. The old-fashioned respect for the young is fast dying out. Whatever influence I ever had

800

---

[1] *apoplexy* Stroke.

[2] *the Empire* Theater that often featured risqué variety shows.

over mamma, I lost at the age of three. But although she may prevent us from becoming man and wife, and I may marry some one else, and marry often, nothing that
805 she can possibly do can alter my eternal devotion to you.

JACK.   Dear Gwendolen!

GWENDOLEN.   The story of your romantic origin, as related to me by mamma, with unpleasing comments, has naturally stirred the deeper fibres of my nature. Your
810 Christian name has an irresistible fascination. The simplicity of your character makes you exquisitely incomprehensible to me. Your town address at the Albany[1] I have. What is your address in the country?

JACK.   The Manor House, Woolton, Hertfordshire.

(*Algernon, who has been carefully listening, smiles to himself, and writes the address on his shirt-cuff. Then picks up the Railway Guide.*)

815 GWENDOLEN.   There is a good postal service, I suppose? It may be necessary to do something desperate. That of course will require serious consideration. I will communicate with you daily.

JACK.   My own one!

820 GWENDOLEN.   How long do you remain in town?

JACK.   Till Monday.

GWENDOLEN.   Good! Algy, you may turn round now.

ALGERNON.   Thanks, I've turned round already.

GWENDOLEN.   You may also ring the bell.

825 JACK.   You will let me see you to your carriage, my own darling?

GWENDOLEN.   Certainly.

JACK.   (*To Lane, who now enters.*) I will see Miss Fairfax out.

830 LANE.   Yes, sir. (*Jack and Gwendolen go off.*)

(*Lane presents several letters on a salver to Algernon. It is to be surmised that they are bills, as Algernon, after looking at the envelopes, tears them up.*)

ALGERNON.   A glass of sherry, Lane.

LANE.   Yes, sir.

ALGERNON.   To-morrow, Lane, I'm going Bunburying.

LANE.   Yes, sir.

835 ALGERNON.   I shall probably not be back till Monday.

You can put up my dress clothes, my smoking jacket, and all the Bunbury suits …

LANE.   Yes, sir. (*Handing sherry.*)

ALGERNON.   I hope to-morrow will be a fine day, Lane.

840 LANE.   It never is, sir.

ALGERNON.   Lane, you're a perfect pessimist.

LANE.   I do my best to give satisfaction, sir.

(*Enter Jack. Lane goes off.*)

JACK.   There's a sensible, intellectual girl! the only girl I ever cared for in my life. (*Algernon is laughing
845 immoderately.*) What on earth are you so amused at?

ALGERNON.   Oh, I'm a little anxious about poor Bunbury, that is all.

JACK.   If you don't take care, your friend Bunbury will get you into a serious scrape some day.

850 ALGERNON.   I love scrapes. They are the only things that are never serious.

JACK.   Oh, that's nonsense, Algy. You never talk anything but nonsense.

ALGERNON.   Nobody ever does.

(*Jack looks indignantly at him, and leaves the room. Algernon lights a cigarette, reads his shirt-cuff, and smiles.*)

ACT DROP

ACT 2

SCENE

(*Garden at the Manor House. A flight of grey stone steps leads up to the house. The garden, an old-fashioned one, full of roses. Time of year, July. Basket chairs, and a table covered with books, are set under a large yew-tree. Miss Prism discovered seated at the table. Cecily is at the back watering flowers.*)

MISS PRISM.   (*Calling.*) Cecily, Cecily! Surely such a utilitarian occupation as the watering of flowers is rather Moulton's duty than yours? Especially at a moment when intellectual pleasures await you. Your German
5 grammar is on the table. Pray open it at page fifteen. We will repeat yesterday's lesson.

---

[1]   *the Albany*   Fashionable men's club in London.

CECILY. (*Coming over very slowly.*) But I don't like German. It isn't at all a becoming language. I know perfectly well that I look quite plain after my German
10 lesson.

MISS PRISM. Child, you know how anxious your guardian is that you should improve yourself in every way. He laid particular stress on your German, as he was leaving for town yesterday. Indeed, he always lays stress
15 on your German when he is leaving for town.

CECILY. Dear Uncle Jack is so very serious! Sometimes he is so serious that I think he cannot be quite well.

MISS PRISM. (*Drawing herself up.*) Your guardian enjoys the best of health, and his gravity of demeanour is
20 especially to be commended in one so comparatively young as he is. I know no one who has a higher sense of duty and responsibility.

CECILY. I suppose that is why he often looks a little bored when we three are together.

25 MISS PRISM. Cecily! I am surprised at you. Mr. Worthing has many troubles in his life. Idle merriment and triviality would be out of place in his conversation. You must remember his constant anxiety about that unfortunate young man his brother.

30 CECILY. I wish Uncle Jack would allow that unfortunate young man, his brother, to come down here sometimes. We might have a good influence over him, Miss Prism. I am sure you certainly would. You know German, and geology, and things of that kind influence a man very
35 much. (*Cecily begins to write in her diary.*)

MISS PRISM. (*Shaking her head.*) I do not think that even I could produce any effect on a character that according to his own brother's admission is irretrievably weak and vacillating. Indeed I am not sure that I would desire to
40 reclaim him. I am not in favour of this modern mania for turning bad people into good people at a moment's notice. As a man sows so let him reap.[1] You must put away your diary, Cecily. I really don't see why you should keep a diary at all.

45 CECILY. I keep a diary in order to enter the wonderful secrets of my life. If I didn't write them down, I should probably forget all about them.

MISS PRISM. Memory, my dear Cecily, is the diary that we all carry about with us.

50 CECILY. Yes, but it usually chronicles the things that have never happened, and couldn't possibly have happened. I believe that Memory is responsible for nearly all the three-volume novels that Mudie sends us.[2]

MISS PRISM. Do not speak slightingly of the three-
55 volume novel, Cecily. I wrote one myself in earlier days.

CECILY. Did you really, Miss Prism? How wonderfully clever you are! I hope it did not end happily? I don't like novels that end happily. They depress me so much.

MISS PRISM. The good ended happily, and the bad
60 unhappily. That is what Fiction means.

CECILY. I suppose so. But it seems very unfair. And was your novel ever published?

MISS PRISM. Alas! no. The manuscript unfortunately was abandoned. (*Cecily starts.*) I use the word in the
65 sense of lost or mislaid. To your work, child, these speculations are profitless.

CECILY. (*Smiling.*) But I see dear Dr. Chasuble coming up through the garden.

MISS PRISM. (*Rising and advancing.*) Dr. Chasuble! This
70 is indeed a pleasure.

(*Enter Canon Chasuble.*)

CHASUBLE. And how are we this morning? Miss Prism, you are, I trust, well?

CECILY. Miss Prism has just been complaining of a slight headache. I think it would do her so much good to have
75 a short stroll with you in the Park, Dr. Chasuble.

MISS PRISM. Cecily, I have not mentioned anything about a headache.

CECILY. No, dear Miss Prism, I know that, but I felt instinctively that you had a headache. Indeed I was
80 thinking about that, and not about my German lesson, when the Rector came in.

CHASUBLE. I hope, Cecily, you are not inattentive.

CECILY. Oh, I am afraid I am.

CHASUBLE. That is strange. Were I fortunate enough to
85 be Miss Prism's pupil, I would hang upon her lips. (*Miss Prism glares.*) I spoke metaphorically.—My metaphor was drawn from bees. Ahem! Mr. Worthing, I suppose, has not returned from town yet?

---

[1] *As a man sows so let him reap* Galatians 6.7: "whatsoever a man soweth, that shall he also reap."

[2] *nearly all … Mudie sends us* Commercial lending libraries of the time, such as Mudie's, specialized in lending novels that were published in three volumes.

MISS PRISM. We do not expect him till Monday
afternoon.

CHASUBLE. Ah yes, he usually likes to spend his Sunday in London. He is not one of those whose sole aim is enjoyment, as, by all accounts, that unfortunate young man his brother seems to be. But I must not disturb Egeria and her pupil any longer.

MISS PRISM. Egeria? My name is Lætitia, Doctor.

CHASUBLE. (*Bowing.*) A classical allusion merely, drawn from the Pagan authors.[1] I shall see you both no doubt at Evensong?[2]

MISS PRISM. I think, dear Doctor, I will have a stroll with you. I find I have a headache after all, and a walk might do it good.

CHASUBLE. With pleasure, Miss Prism, with pleasure. We might go as far as the schools and back.

MISS PRISM. That would be delightful. Cecily, you will read your Political Economy in my absence. The chapter on the Fall of the Rupee you may omit. It is somewhat too sensational. Even these metallic problems have their melodramatic side.[3]

(*Goes down the garden with Dr. Chasuble.*)

CECILY. (*Picks up books and throws them back on table.*) Horrid Political Economy! Horrid Geography! Horrid, horrid German!

(*Enter Merriman with a card on a salver.*)

MERRIMAN. Mr. Ernest Worthing has just driven over from the station. He has brought his luggage with him.

CECILY. (*Takes the card and reads it.*) "Mr. Ernest Worthing, B. 4, The Albany, W." Uncle Jack's brother! Did you tell him Mr. Worthing was in town?

MERRIMAN. Yes, Miss. He seemed very much disappointed. I mentioned that you and Miss Prism were in the garden. He said he was anxious to speak to you privately for a moment.

CECILY. Ask Mr. Ernest Worthing to come here. I suppose you had better talk to the housekeeper about a room for him.

MERRIMAN. Yes, Miss.

(*Merriman goes off.*)

CECILY. I have never met any really wicked person before. I feel rather frightened. I am so afraid he will look just like every one else. (*Enter Algernon, very gay and debonair.*) He does!

ALGERNON. (*Raising his hat.*) You are my little cousin Cecily, I'm sure.

CECILY. You are under some strange mistake. I am not little. In fact, I believe I am more than usually tall for my age. (*Algernon is rather taken aback.*) But I am your cousin Cecily. You, I see from your card, are Uncle Jack's brother, my cousin Ernest, my wicked cousin Ernest.

ALGERNON. Oh! I am not really wicked at all, cousin Cecily. You mustn't think that I am wicked.

CECILY. If you are not, then you have certainly been deceiving us all in a very inexcusable manner. I hope you have not been leading a double life, pretending to be wicked and being really good all the time. That would be hypocrisy.

ALGERNON. (*Looks at her in amazement.*) Oh! Of course I have been rather reckless.

CECILY. I am glad to hear it.

ALGERNON. In fact, now you mention the subject, I have been very bad in my own small way.

CECILY. I don't think you should be so proud of that, though I am sure it must have been very pleasant.

ALGERNON. It is much pleasanter being here with you.

CECILY. I can't understand how you are here at all. Uncle Jack won't be back till Monday afternoon.

ALGERNON. That is a great disappointment. I am obliged to go up by the first train on Monday morning. I have a business appointment that I am anxious ... to miss!

CECILY. Couldn't you miss it anywhere but in London?

ALGERNON. No: the appointment is in London.

---

[1] *A classical allusion ... Pagan authors* In Roman mythology, the nymph Egeria taught Numa, the second King of Rome, the lessons of wisdom and law which he then used to found the institutions of Rome.

[2] *Evensong* The evening service in the Anglican church (and various other Christian denominations).

[3] *The chapter ... melodramatic side* The rupee (India's currency) declined dramatically in the early 1890s as a result of a variety of disasters, including an outbreak of plague.

CECILY. Well, I know, of course, how important it is not to keep a business engagement, if one wants to retain any sense of the beauty of life, but still I think you had better wait till Uncle Jack arrives. I know he wants to
165 speak to you about your emigrating.

ALGERNON. About my what?

CECILY. Your emigrating. He has gone up to buy your outfit.

ALGERNON. I certainly wouldn't let Jack buy my outfit.
170 He has no taste in neckties at all.

CECILY. I don't think you will require neckties. Uncle Jack is sending you to Australia.[1]

ALGERNON. Australia! I'd sooner die.

CECILY. Well, he said at dinner on Wednesday night,
175 that you would have to choose between this world, the next world, and Australia.

ALGERNON. Oh, well! The accounts I have received of Australia and the next world are not particularly encouraging. This world is good enough for me, cousin Cecily.

180 CECILY. Yes, but are you good enough for it?

ALGERNON. I'm afraid I'm not that. That is why I want you to reform me. You might make that your mission, if you don't mind, cousin Cecily.

CECILY. I'm afraid I've no time, this afternoon.

185 ALGERNON. Well, would you mind my reforming myself this afternoon?

CECILY. It is rather Quixotic of you. But I think you should try.

ALGERNON. I will. I feel better already.

190 CECILY. You are looking a little worse.

ALGERNON. That is because I am hungry.

CECILY. How thoughtless of me. I should have remembered that when one is going to lead an entirely new life, one requires regular and wholesome meals. Won't you
195 come in?

ALGERNON. Thank you. Might I have a buttonhole[2] first? I never have any appetite unless I have a buttonhole first.

CECILY. A Maréchal Niel?[3] (Picks up scissors.)

200 ALGERNON. No, I'd sooner have a pink rose.

CECILY. Why? (Cuts a flower.)

ALGERNON. Because you are like a pink rose, Cousin Cecily.

CECILY. I don't think it can be right for you to talk to
205 me like that. Miss Prism never says such things to me.

ALGERNON. Then Miss Prism is a short-sighted old lady. (Cecily puts the rose in his buttonhole.) You are the prettiest girl I ever saw.

CECILY. Miss Prism says that all good looks are a snare.

210 ALGERNON. They are a snare that every sensible man would like to be caught in.

CECILY. Oh, I don't think I would care to catch a sensible man. I shouldn't know what to talk to him about.

(They pass into the house. Miss Prism and Dr. Chasuble return.)

215 MISS PRISM. You are too much alone, dear Dr. Chasuble. You should get married. A misanthrope I can understand—a womanthrope,[4] never!

CHASUBLE. (With a scholar's shudder.) Believe me, I do not deserve so neologistic a phrase. The precept as well
220 as the practice of the Primitive Church[5] was distinctly against matrimony.

MISS PRISM. (Sententiously.) That is obviously the reason why the Primitive Church has not lasted up to the present day. And you do not seem to realize, dear
225 Doctor, that by persistently remaining single, a man converts himself into a permanent public temptation. Men should be more careful; this very celibacy leads weaker vessels astray.

CHASUBLE. But is a man not equally attractive when
230 married?

MISS PRISM. No married man is ever attractive except to his wife.

CHASUBLE. And often, I've been told, not even to her.

MISS PRISM. That depends on the intellectual sympa-
235 thies of the woman. Maturity can always be depended on. Ripeness can be trusted. Young women are green. (Dr. Chasuble starts.) I spoke horticulturally. My metaphor was drawn from fruits. But where is Cecily?

---

[1] *Australia* A former penal colony, at the time still considered to be largely composed of wilderness.

[2] *buttonhole* Boutonniere, flower for one's lapel.

[3] *Maréchal Niel* Variety of yellow rose.

[4] *misanthrope ... womanthrope* The correct word for someone who hates women is a "misogynist"; a "misanthrope" is someone who hates all humanity.

[5] *Primitive Church* Early Christian church.

CHASUBLE. Perhaps she followed us to the schools.

(*Enter Jack slowly from the back of the garden. He is dressed in the deepest mourning, with crepe hatband and black gloves.*)

240 MISS PRISM. Mr. Worthing!

CHASUBLE. Mr. Worthing?

MISS PRISM. This is indeed a surprise. We did not look for you till Monday afternoon.

JACK. (*Shakes Miss Prism's hand in a tragic manner.*) I
245 have returned sooner than I expected. Dr. Chasuble, I hope you are well?

CHASUBLE. Dear Mr. Worthing, I trust this garb of woe does not betoken some terrible calamity?

JACK. My brother.

250 MISS PRISM. More shameful debts and extravagance?

CHASUBLE. Still leading his life of pleasure?

JACK. (*Shaking his head.*) Dead!

CHASUBLE. Your brother Ernest dead?

JACK. Quite dead.

255 MISS PRISM. What a lesson for him! I trust he will profit by it.

CHASUBLE. Mr. Worthing, I offer you my sincere condolence. You have at least the consolation of knowing that you were always the most generous and forgiv-
260 ing of brothers.

JACK. Poor Ernest! He had many faults, but it is a sad, sad blow.

CHASUBLE. Very sad indeed. Were you with him at the end?

265 JACK. No. He died abroad; in Paris, in fact. I had a telegram last night from the manager of the Grand Hotel.

CHASUBLE. Was the cause of death mentioned?

JACK. A severe chill, it seems.

270 MISS PRISM. As a man sows, so shall he reap.

CHASUBLE. (*Raising his hand.*) Charity, dear Miss Prism, charity! None of us are perfect. I myself am peculiarly susceptible to draughts. Will the interment take place here?

275 JACK. No. He seems to have expressed a desire to be buried in Paris.

CHASUBLE. In Paris! (*Shakes his head.*) I fear that hardly points to any very serious state of mind at the last. You

would no doubt wish me to make some slight allusion
280 to this tragic domestic affliction next Sunday. (*Jack presses his hand convulsively.*) My sermon on the meaning of the manna in the wilderness[1] can be adapted to almost any occasion, joyful, or, as in the present case, distressing. (*All sigh.*) I have preached it at harvest
285 celebrations, christenings, confirmations,[2] on days of humiliation and festal days. The last time I delivered it was in the Cathedral, as a charity sermon on behalf of the Society for the Prevention of Discontent among the Upper Orders. The Bishop, who was present, was much
290 struck by some of the analogies I drew.

JACK. Ah! that reminds me, you mentioned christenings I think, Dr. Chasuble? I suppose you know how to christen all right? (*Dr. Chasuble looks astounded.*) I mean, of course, you are continually christening, aren't you?

295 MISS PRISM. It is, I regret to say, one of the Rector's most constant duties in this parish. I have often spoken to the poorer classes on the subject. But they don't seem to know what thrift is.

CHASUBLE. But is there any particular infant in whom
300 you are interested, Mr. Worthing? Your brother was, I believe, unmarried, was he not?

JACK. Oh yes.

MISS PRISM. (*Bitterly.*) People who live entirely for pleasure usually are.

305 JACK. But it is not for any child, dear Doctor. I am very fond of children. No! the fact is, I would like to be christened myself, this afternoon, if you have nothing better to do.

CHASUBLE. But surely, Mr. Worthing, you have been
310 christened already?

JACK. I don't remember anything about it.

CHASUBLE. But have you any grave doubts on the subject?

JACK. I certainly intend to have. Of course I don't know
315 if the thing would bother you in any way, or if you think I am a little too old now.

CHASUBLE. Not at all. The sprinkling, and, indeed, the

---

1 *manna in the wilderness* See Exodus 16.

2 *christenings, confirmations* Whereas a christening formally admits a person to the Christian church through baptism (usually as an infant), in many Christian denominations a person's standing as a full member of the church must be confirmed at a later ceremony (typically as a young adult).

immersion of adults is a perfectly canonical practice.

JACK. Immersion!

320 CHASUBLE. You need have no apprehensions. Sprinkling is all that is necessary, or indeed I think advisable. Our weather is so changeable. At what hour would you wish the ceremony performed?

JACK. Oh, I might trot round about five if that would

325 suit you.

CHASUBLE. Perfectly, perfectly! In fact I have two similar ceremonies to perform at that time. A case of twins that occurred recently in one of the outlying cottages on your own estate. Poor Jenkins the carter,[1] a

330 most hard-working man.

JACK. Oh! I don't see much fun in being christened along with other babies. It would be childish. Would half-past five do?

CHASUBLE. Admirably! Admirably! (*Takes out watch.*)

335 And now, dear Mr. Worthing, I will not intrude any longer into a house of sorrow. I would merely beg you not to be too much bowed down by grief. What seem to us bitter trials are often blessings in disguise.

MISS PRISM. This seems to me a blessing of an extremely

340 obvious kind.

(*Enter Cecily from the house.*)

CECILY. Uncle Jack! Oh, I am pleased to see you back. But what horrid clothes you have got on! Do go and change them.

MISS PRISM. Cecily!

345 CHASUBLE. My child! my child!

(*Cecily goes towards Jack; he kisses her brow in a melancholy manner.*)

CECILY. What is the matter, Uncle Jack? Do look happy! You look as if you had toothache, and I have got such a surprise for you. Who do you think is in the dining-room? Your brother!

350 JACK. Who?

CECILY. Your brother Ernest. He arrived about half an hour ago.

JACK. What nonsense! I haven't got a brother.

CECILY. Oh, don't say that. However badly he may have

355 behaved to you in the past he is still your brother. You couldn't be so heartless as to disown him. I'll tell him to come out. And you will shake hands with him, won't you, Uncle Jack? (*Runs back into the house.*)

CHASUBLE. These are very joyful tidings.

360 MISS PRISM. After we had all been resigned to his loss, his sudden return seems to me peculiarly distressing.

JACK. My brother is in the dining-room? I don't know what it all means. I think it is perfectly absurd.

(*Enter Algernon and Cecily hand in hand. They come slowly up to Jack.*)

JACK. Good heavens! (*Motions Algernon away.*)

365 ALGERNON. Brother John, I have come down from town to tell you that I am very sorry for all the trouble I have given you, and that I intend to lead a better life in the future. (*Jack glares at him and does not take his hand.*)

370 CECILY. Uncle Jack, you are not going to refuse your own brother's hand?

JACK. Nothing will induce me to take his hand. I think his coming down here disgraceful. He knows perfectly well why.

375 CECILY. Uncle Jack, do be nice. There is some good in every one. Ernest has just been telling me about his poor invalid friend Mr. Bunbury whom he goes to visit so often. And surely there must be much good in one who is kind to an invalid, and leaves the pleasures of London

380 to sit by a bed of pain.

JACK. Oh! he has been talking about Bunbury, has he?

CECILY. Yes, he has told me all about poor Mr. Bunbury, and his terrible state of health.

JACK. Bunbury! Well, I won't have him talk to you

385 about Bunbury or about anything else. It is enough to drive one perfectly frantic.

ALGERNON. Of course I admit that the faults were all on my side. But I must say that I think that Brother John's coldness to me is peculiarly painful. I expected a more

390 enthusiastic welcome, especially considering it is the first time I have come here.

CECILY. Uncle Jack, if you don't shake hands with Ernest I will never forgive you.

JACK. Never forgive me?

395 CECILY. Never, never, never!

---

[1] *carter* Cart driver.

JACK.   Well, this is the last time I shall ever do it. (*Shakes hands with Algernon and glares.*)

CHASUBLE.   It's pleasant, is it not, to see so perfect a reconciliation? I think we might leave the two brothers
400 together.

MISS PRISM.   Cecily, you will come with us.

CECILY.   Certainly, Miss Prism. My little task of reconciliation is over.

CHASUBLE.   You have done a beautiful action to-day,
405 dear child.

MISS PRISM.   We must not be premature in our judgments.

CECILY.   I feel very happy.

(*They all go off except Jack and Algernon.*)

JACK.   You young scoundrel, Algy, you must get out of
410 this place as soon as possible. I don't allow any Bunburying here.

(*Enter Merriman.*)

MERRIMAN.   I have put Mr. Ernest's things in the room next to yours, sir. I suppose that is all right?

JACK.   What?

415 MERRIMAN.   Mr. Ernest's luggage, sir. I have unpacked it and put it in the room next to your own.

JACK.   His luggage?

MERRIMAN.   Yes, sir. Three portmanteaus, a dressing-case, two hat-boxes, and a large luncheon-basket.

420 ALGERNON.   I am afraid I can't stay more than a week this time.

JACK.   Merriman, order the dog-cart[1] at once. Mr. Ernest has been suddenly called back to town.

MERRIMAN.   Yes, sir. (*Goes back into the house.*)

425 ALGERNON.   What a fearful liar you are, Jack. I have not been called back to town at all.

JACK.   Yes, you have.

ALGERNON.   I haven't heard any one call me.

JACK.   Your duty as a gentleman calls you back.

430 ALGERNON.   My duty as a gentleman has never interfered with my pleasures in the smallest degree.

---

1 *dog-cart* Small horse-drawn carriage in which the occupants would sit back-to-back; a box for conveying hunting dogs was also typically part of the contraption.

JACK.   I can quite understand that.

ALGERNON.   Well, Cecily is a darling.

JACK.   You are not to talk of Miss Cardew like that. I
435 don't like it.

ALGERNON.   Well, I don't like your clothes. You look perfectly ridiculous in them. Why on earth don't you go up and change? It is perfectly childish to be in deep mourning for a man who is actually staying for a whole
440 week with you in your house as a guest. I call it grotesque.

JACK.   You are certainly not staying with me for a whole week as a guest or anything else. You have got to leave ... by the four-five train.

445 ALGERNON.   I certainly won't leave you so long as you are in mourning. It would be most unfriendly. If I were in mourning you would stay with me, I suppose. I should think it very unkind if you didn't.

JACK.   Well, will you go if I change my clothes?

450 ALGERNON.   Yes, if you are not too long. I never saw anybody take so long to dress, and with such little result.

JACK.   Well, at any rate, that is better than being always over-dressed as you are.

ALGERNON.   If I am occasionally a little over-dressed, I
455 make up for it by being always immensely over-educated.

JACK.   Your vanity is ridiculous, your conduct an outrage, and your presence in my garden utterly absurd. However, you have got to catch the four-five, and I
460 hope you will have a pleasant journey back to town. This Bunburying, as you call it, has not been a great success for you. (*Goes into the house.*)

ALGERNON.   I think it has been a great success. I'm in love with Cecily, and that is everything.

(*Enter Cecily at the back of the garden. She picks up the can and begins to water the flowers.*)

465 But I must see her before I go, and make arrangements for another Bunbury. Ah, there she is.

CECILY.   Oh, I merely came back to water the roses. I thought you were with Uncle Jack.

ALGERNON.   He's gone to order the dog-cart for me.

470 CECILY.   Oh, is he going to take you for a nice drive?

ALGERNON.   He's going to send me away.

CECILY.   Then have we got to part?

ALGERNON. I am afraid so. It's a very painful parting.

CECILY. It is always painful to part from people whom
475 one has known for a very brief space of time. The
absence of old friends one can endure with equanimity.
But even a momentary separation from anyone to
whom one has just been introduced is almost unbearable.

480 ALGERNON. Thank you.

(*Enter Merriman.*)

MERRIMAN. The dog-cart is at the door, sir.

(*Algernon looks appealingly at Cecily.*)

CECILY. It can wait, Merriman for … five minutes.

MERRIMAN. Yes, Miss.

(*Exit Merriman.*)

ALGERNON. I hope, Cecily, I shall not offend you if I
485 state quite frankly and openly that you seem to me to be
in every way the visible personification of absolute
perfection.

CECILY. I think your frankness does you great credit,
Ernest. If you will allow me, I will copy your remarks
490 into my diary. (*Goes over to table and begins writing in
diary.*)

ALGERNON. Do you really keep a diary? I'd give anything to look at it. May I?

CECILY. Oh no. (*Puts her hand over it.*) You see, it is
495 simply a very young girl's record of her own thoughts
and impressions, and consequently meant for publication. When it appears in volume form I hope you will
order a copy. But pray, Ernest, don't stop. I delight in
taking down from dictation. I have reached "absolute
500 perfection." You can go on. I am quite ready for more.

ALGERNON. (*Somewhat taken aback.*) Ahem! Ahem!

CECILY. Oh, don't cough, Ernest. When one is dictating
one should speak fluently and not cough. Besides, I
don't know how to spell a cough. (*Writes as Algernon
505 speaks.*)

ALGERNON. (*Speaking very rapidly.*) Cecily, ever since I
first looked upon your wonderful and incomparable
beauty, I have dared to love you wildly, passionately,
devotedly, hopelessly.

510 CECILY. I don't think that you should tell me that you
love me wildly, passionately, devotedly, hopelessly.
Hopelessly doesn't seem to make much sense, does it?

ALGERNON. Cecily!

(*Enter Merriman.*)

MERRIMAN. The dog-cart is waiting, sir.

515 ALGERNON. Tell it to come round next week, at the
same hour.

MERRIMAN. (*Looks at Cecily, who makes no sign.*) Yes, sir.

(*Merriman retires.*)

CECILY. Uncle Jack would be very much annoyed if he
knew you were staying on till next week, at the same
520 hour.

ALGERNON. Oh, I don't care about Jack. I don't care for
anybody in the whole world but you. I love you, Cecily.
You will marry me, won't you?

CECILY. You silly boy! Of course. Why, we have been
525 engaged for the last three months.

ALGERNON. For the last three months?

CECILY. Yes, it will be exactly three months on Thursday.

ALGERNON. But how did we become engaged?

530 CECILY. Well, ever since dear Uncle Jack first confessed
to us that he had a younger brother who was very
wicked and bad, you of course have formed the chief
topic of conversation between myself and Miss Prism.
And of course a man who is much talked about is always
535 very attractive. One feels there must be something in
him, after all. I daresay it was foolish of me, but I fell in
love with you, Ernest.

ALGERNON. Darling! And when was the engagement
actually settled?

540 CECILY. On the 14th of February last. Worn out by
your entire ignorance of my existence, I determined to
end the matter one way or the other, and after a long
struggle with myself I accepted you under this dear old
tree here. The next day I bought this little ring in your
545 name, and this is the little bangle with the true lover's
knot I promised you always to wear.

ALGERNON. Did I give you this? It's very pretty, isn't it?

CECILY. Yes, you've wonderfully good taste, Ernest. It's the excuse I've always given for your leading such a bad life. And this is the box in which I keep all your dear letters. (*Kneels at table, opens box, and produces letters tied up with blue ribbon.*)

ALGERNON. My letters! But, my own sweet Cecily, I have never written you any letters.

CECILY. You need hardly remind me of that, Ernest. I remember only too well that I was forced to write your letters for you. I wrote always three times a week, and sometimes oftener.

ALGERNON. Oh, do let me read them, Cecily?

CECILY. Oh, I couldn't possibly. They would make you far too conceited. (*Replaces box.*) The three you wrote me after I had broken off the engagement are so beautiful, and so badly spelled, that even now I can hardly read them without crying a little.

ALGERNON. But was our engagement ever broken off?

CECILY. Of course it was. On the 22nd of last March. You can see the entry if you like. (*Shows diary.*) "To-day I broke off my engagement with Ernest. I feel it is better to do so. The weather still continues charming."

ALGERNON. But why on earth did you break it off? What had I done? I had done nothing at all. Cecily, I am very much hurt indeed to hear you broke it off. Particularly when the weather was so charming.

CECILY. It would hardly have been a really serious engagement if it hadn't been broken off at least once. But I forgave you before the week was out.

ALGERNON. (*Crossing to her, and kneeling.*) What a perfect angel you are, Cecily.

CECILY. You dear romantic boy. (*He kisses her, she puts her fingers through his hair.*) I hope your hair curls naturally, does it?

ALGERNON. Yes, darling, with a little help from others.

CECILY. I am so glad.

ALGERNON. You'll never break off our engagement again, Cecily?

CECILY. I don't think I could break it off now that I have actually met you. Besides, of course, there is the question of your name.

ALGERNON. Yes, of course. (*Nervously.*)

CECILY. You must not laugh at me, darling, but it had always been a girlish dream of mine to love some one whose name was Ernest. (*Algernon rises, Cecily also.*) There is something in that name that seems to inspire absolute confidence. I pity any poor married woman whose husband is not called Ernest.

ALGERNON. But, my dear child, do you mean to say you could not love me if I had some other name?

CECILY. But what name?

ALGERNON. Oh, any name you like—Algernon—for instance …

CECILY. But I don't like the name of Algernon.

ALGERNON. Well, my own dear, sweet, loving little darling, I really can't see why you should object to the name of Algernon. It is not at all a bad name. In fact, it is rather an aristocratic name. Half of the chaps who get into the Bankruptcy Court are called Algernon. But seriously, Cecily … (*Moving to her*) … if my name was Algy, couldn't you love me?

CECILY. (*Rising.*) I might respect you, Ernest, I might admire your character, but I fear that I should not be able to give you my undivided attention.

ALGERNON. Ahem! Cecily! (*Picking up hat.*) Your Rector here is, I suppose, thoroughly experienced in the practice of all the rites and ceremonials of the Church?

CECILY. Oh, yes. Dr. Chasuble is a most learned man. He has never written a single book, so you can imagine how much he knows.

ALGERNON. I must see him at once on a most important christening—I mean on most important business.

CECILY. Oh!

ALGERNON. I shan't be away more than half an hour.

CECILY. Considering that we have been engaged since February the 14th, and that I only met you to-day for the first time, I think it is rather hard that you should leave me for so long a period as half an hour. Couldn't you make it twenty minutes?

ALGERNON. I'll be back in no time.

(*Kisses her and rushes down the garden.*)

CECILY. What an impetuous boy he is! I like his hair so much. I must enter his proposal in my diary.

(*Enter Merriman.*)

MERRIMAN. A Miss Fairfax has just called to see Mr. Worthing. On very important business, Miss Fairfax states.

CECILY. Isn't Mr. Worthing in his library?

MERRIMAN. Mr. Worthing went over in the direction of
635 the Rectory some time ago.

CECILY. Pray ask the lady to come out here; Mr. Worthing is sure to be back soon. And you can bring tea.

MERRIMAN. Yes, Miss. (*Goes out.*)

CECILY. Miss Fairfax! I suppose one of the many good
640 elderly women who are associated with Uncle Jack in
some of his philanthropic work in London. I don't quite
like women who are interested in philanthropic work. I
think it is so forward of them.

(*Enter Merriman.*)

MERRIMAN. Miss Fairfax.

(*Enter Gwendolen. Exit Merriman.*)

645 CECILY. (*Advancing to meet her.*) Pray let me introduce
myself to you. My name is Cecily Cardew.

GWENDOLEN. Cecily Cardew? (*Moving to her and
shaking hands.*) What a very sweet name! Something tells
me that we are going to be great friends. I like you
650 already more than I can say. My first impressions of
people are never wrong.

CECILY. How nice of you to like me so much after we
have known each other such a comparatively short time.
Pray sit down.

655 GWENDOLEN. (*Still standing up.*) I may call you Cecily,
may I not?

CECILY. With pleasure!

GWENDOLEN. And you will always call me Gwendolen,
won't you?

660 CECILY. If you wish.

GWENDOLEN. Then that is all quite settled, is it not?

CECILY. I hope so. (*A pause. They both sit down together.*)

GWENDOLEN. Perhaps this might be a favourable
opportunity for my mentioning who I am. My father is
665 Lord Bracknell. You have never heard of Papa, I suppose?

CECILY. I don't think so.

GWENDOLEN. Outside the family circle, Papa, I am glad
to say, is entirely unknown. I think that is quite as it
670 should be. The home seems to me to be the proper

sphere for the man. And certainly once a man begins to
neglect his domestic duties he becomes painfully effeminate, does he not? And I don't like that. It makes men
so very attractive. Cecily, Mamma, whose views on
675 education are remarkably strict, has brought me up to be
extremely short-sighted; it is part of her system; so do
you mind my looking at you through my glasses?

CECILY. Oh! not at all, Gwendolen. I am very fond of
being looked at.

680 GWENDOLEN. (*After examining Cecily carefully through
a lorgnette.*) You are here on a short visit, I suppose.

CECILY. Oh no! I live here.

GWENDOLEN. (*Severely.*) Really? Your mother, no
doubt, or some female relative of advanced years, resides
685 here also?

CECILY. Oh no! I have no mother, nor, in fact, any
relations.

GWENDOLEN. Indeed?

CECILY. My dear guardian, with the assistance of Miss
690 Prism, has the arduous task of looking after me.

GWENDOLEN. Your guardian?

CECILY. Yes, I am Mr. Worthing's ward.

GWENDOLEN. Oh! It is strange he never mentioned to
me that he had a ward. How secretive of him! He grows
695 more interesting hourly. I am not sure, however, that
the news inspires me with feelings of unmixed delight.
(*Rising and going to her.*) I am very fond of you, Cecily;
I have liked you ever since I met you! But I am bound
to state that now that I know that you are Mr. Worth-
700 ing's ward, I cannot help expressing a wish you were—
well, just a little older than you seem to be—and not
quite so very alluring in appearance. In fact, if I may
speak candidly—

CECILY. Pray do! I think that whenever one has anything
705 unpleasant to say, one should always be quite candid.

GWENDOLEN. Well, to speak with perfect candour,
Cecily, I wish that you were fully forty-two, and more
than usually plain for your age. Ernest has a strong
upright nature. He is the very soul of truth and honour.
710 Disloyalty would be as impossible to him as deception.
But even men of the noblest possible moral character are
extremely susceptible to the influence of the physical
charms of others. Modern, no less than Ancient History,
supplies us with many most painful examples of what I
715 refer to. If it were not so, indeed, History would be

quite unreadable.

CECILY. I beg your pardon, Gwendolen, did you say Ernest?

GWENDOLEN. Yes.

720 CECILY. Oh, but it is not Mr. Ernest Worthing who is my guardian. It is his brother—his elder brother.

GWENDOLEN. (*Sitting down again.*) Ernest never mentioned to me that he had a brother.

CECILY. I am sorry to say they have not been on good
725 terms for a long time.

GWENDOLEN. Ah! that accounts for it. And now that I think of it I have never heard any man mention his brother. The subject seems distasteful to most men. Cecily, you have lifted a load from my mind. I was
730 growing almost anxious. It would have been terrible if any cloud had come across a friendship like ours, would it not? Of course you are quite, quite sure that it is not Mr. Ernest Worthing who is your guardian?

CECILY. Quite sure. (*A pause.*) In fact, I am going to be
735 his.

GWENDOLEN. (*Inquiringly.*) I beg your pardon?

CECILY. (*Rather shy and confidingly.*) Dearest Gwendolen, there is no reason why I should make a secret of it to you. Our little county newspaper is sure to chronicle
740 the fact next week. Mr. Ernest Worthing and I are engaged to be married.

GWENDOLEN. (*Quite politely, rising.*) My darling Cecily, I think there must be some slight error. Mr. Ernest Worthing is engaged to me. The announcement will
745 appear in the *Morning Post* on Saturday at the latest.

CECILY. (*Very politely, rising.*) I am afraid you must be under some misconception. Ernest proposed to me exactly ten minutes ago. (*Shows diary.*)

GWENDOLEN. (*Examines diary through her lorgnette
750 carefully.*) It is certainly very curious, for he asked me to be his wife yesterday afternoon at 5:30. If you would care to verify the incident, pray do so. (*Produces diary of her own.*) I never travel without my diary. One should always have something sensational to read in the train.
755 I am so sorry, dear Cecily, if it is any disappointment to you, but I am afraid I have the prior claim.

CECILY. It would distress me more than I can tell you, dear Gwendolen, if it caused you any mental or physical anguish, but I feel bound to point out that since Ernest
760 proposed to you he clearly has changed his mind.

GWENDOLEN. (*Meditatively.*) If the poor fellow has been entrapped into any foolish promise I shall consider it my duty to rescue him at once, and with a firm hand.

CECILY. (*Thoughtfully and sadly.*) Whatever unfortunate
765 entanglement my dear boy may have got into, I will never reproach him with it after we are married.

GWENDOLEN. Do you allude to me, Miss Cardew, as an entanglement? You are presumptuous. On an occasion of this kind it becomes more than a moral duty to speak
770 one's mind. It becomes a pleasure.

CECILY. Do you suggest, Miss Fairfax, that I entrapped Ernest into an engagement? How dare you? This is no time for wearing the shallow mask of manners. When I see a spade I call it a spade.

775 GWENDOLEN. (*Satirically.*) I am glad to say that I have never seen a spade. It is obvious that our social spheres have been widely different.

(*Enter Merriman, followed by the footman. He carries a salver, table cloth, and plate stand. Cecily is about to retort. The presence of the servants exercises a restraining influence, under which both girls chafe.*)

MERRIMAN. Shall I lay tea here as usual, Miss?

CECILY. (*Sternly, in a calm voice.*) Yes, as usual.

(*Merriman begins to clear table and lay cloth. A long pause. Cecily and Gwendolen glare at each other.*)

780 GWENDOLEN. Are there many interesting walks in the vicinity, Miss Cardew?

CECILY. Oh! yes! a great many. From the top of one of the hills quite close one can see five counties.

GWENDOLEN. Five counties! I don't think I should like
785 that; I hate crowds.

CECILY. (*Sweetly.*) I suppose that is why you live in town?

(*Gwendolen bites her lip, and beats her foot nervously with her parasol.*)

GWENDOLEN. (*Looking round.*) Quite a well-kept garden this is, Miss Cardew.

790 CECILY. So glad you like it, Miss Fairfax.

GWENDOLEN. I had no idea there were any flowers in

the country.

CECILY. Oh, flowers are as common here, Miss Fairfax, as people are in London.

795 GWENDOLEN. Personally I cannot understand how anybody manages to exist in the country, if anybody who is anybody does. The country always bores me to death.

CECILY. Ah! This is what the newspapers call agricultural

800 depression,[1] is it not? I believe the aristocracy are suffering very much from it just at present. It is almost an epidemic amongst them, I have been told. May I offer you some tea, Miss Fairfax?

GWENDOLEN. (*With elaborate politeness.*) Thank you.

805 (*Aside.*) Detestable girl! But I require tea!

CECILY. (*Sweetly.*) Sugar?

GWENDOLEN. (*Superciliously.*) No, thank you. Sugar is not fashionable any more. (*Cecily looks angrily at her, takes up the tongs and puts four lumps of sugar into the*

810 *cup.*)

CECILY. (*Severely.*) Cake or bread and butter?

GWENDOLEN. (*In a bored manner.*) Bread and butter, please. Cake is rarely seen at the best houses nowadays.

CECILY. (*Cuts a very large slice of cake, and puts it on the*

815 *tray.*) Hand that to Miss Fairfax.

(*Merriman does so, and goes out with footman. Gwendolen drinks the tea and makes a grimace. Puts down cup at once, reaches out her hand to the bread and butter, looks at it, and finds it is cake. Rises in indignation.*)

GWENDOLEN. You have filled my tea with lumps of sugar, and though I asked most distinctly for bread and butter, you have given me cake. I am known for the gentleness of my disposition, and the extraordinary

820 sweetness of my nature, but I warn you, Miss Cardew, you may go too far.

CECILY. (*Rising.*) To save my poor, innocent, trusting boy from the machinations of any other girl there are no lengths to which I would not go.

825 GWENDOLEN. From the moment I saw you I distrusted you. I felt that you were false and deceitful. I am never deceived in such matters. My first impressions of people are invariably right.

---

[1] *agricultural depression* The British economy in general was in depression from 1873 until the mid-1890s; the agricultural sector was depressed from 1875 until the mid-1890s.

CECILY. It seems to me, Miss Fairfax, that I am trespass-

830 ing on your valuable time. No doubt you have many other calls of a similar character to make in the neighbourhood.

(*Enter Jack.*)

GWENDOLEN. (*Catching sight of him.*) Ernest! My own Ernest!

835 JACK. Gwendolen! Darling! (*Offers to kiss her.*)

GWENDOLEN. (*Draws back.*) A moment! May I ask if you are engaged to be married to this young lady? (*Points to Cecily.*)

JACK. (*Laughing.*) To dear little Cecily! Of course not!

840 What could have put such an idea into your pretty little head?

GWENDOLEN. Thank you. You may! (*Offers her cheek.*)

CECILY. (*Very sweetly.*) I knew there must be some misunderstanding, Miss Fairfax. The gentleman whose

845 arm is at present round your waist is my guardian, Mr. John Worthing.

GWENDOLEN. I beg your pardon?

CECILY. This is Uncle Jack.

GWENDOLEN. (*Receding.*) Jack! Oh!

(*Enter Algernon.*)

850 CECILY. Here is Ernest.

ALGERNON. (*Goes straight over to Cecily without noticing any one else.*) My own love! (*Offers to kiss her.*)

CECILY. (*Drawing back.*) A moment, Ernest! May I ask you—are you engaged to be married to this young lady?

855 ALGERNON. (*Looking round.*) To what young lady? Good heavens! Gwendolen!

CECILY. Yes! to good heavens, Gwendolen, I mean to Gwendolen.

ALGERNON. (*Laughing.*) Of course not! What could

860 have put such an idea into your pretty little head?

CECILY. Thank you. (*Presenting her cheek to be kissed.*) You may.

(*Algernon kisses her.*)

GWENDOLEN. I felt there was some slight error, Miss Cardew. The gentleman who is now embracing you is

865 my cousin, Mr. Algernon Moncrieff.

CECILY. (*Breaking away from Algernon.*) Algernon Moncrieff! Oh!

(*The two girls move towards each other and put their arms round each other's waists as if for protection.*)

CECILY. Are you called Algernon?

ALGERNON. I cannot deny it.

870 CECILY. Oh!

GWENDOLEN. Is your name really John?

JACK. (*Standing rather proudly.*) I could deny it if I liked. I could deny anything if I liked. But my name certainly is John. It has been John for years.

875 CECILY. (*To Gwendolen.*) A gross deception has been practised on both of us.

GWENDOLEN. My poor wounded Cecily!

CECILY. My sweet wronged Gwendolen!

GWENDOLEN. (*Slowly and seriously.*) You will call me
880 sister, will you not? (*They embrace. Jack and Algernon groan and walk up and down.*)

CECILY. (*Rather brightly.*) There is just one question I would like to be allowed to ask my guardian.

GWENDOLEN. An admirable idea! Mr. Worthing, there
885 is just one question I would like to be permitted to put to you. Where is your brother Ernest? We are both engaged to be married to your brother Ernest, so it is a matter of some importance to us to know where your brother Ernest is at present.

890 JACK. (*Slowly and hesitatingly.*) Gwendolen—Cecily—it is very painful for me to be forced to speak the truth. It is the first time in my life that I have ever been reduced to such a painful position, and I am really quite inexperienced in doing anything of the kind. However, I will
895 tell you quite frankly that I have no brother Ernest. I have no brother at all. I never had a brother in my life, and I certainly have not the smallest intention of ever having one in the future.

CECILY. (*Surprised.*) No brother at all?

900 JACK. (*Cheerily.*) None!

GWENDOLEN. (*Severely.*) Had you never a brother of any kind?

JACK. (*Pleasantly.*) Never. Not even of any kind.

GWENDOLEN. I am afraid it is quite clear, Cecily, that
905 neither of us is engaged to be married to any one.

CECILY. It is not a very pleasant position for a young girl suddenly to find herself in. Is it?

GWENDOLEN. Let us go into the house. They will hardly venture to come after us there.

910 CECILY. No, men are so cowardly, aren't they?

(*They retire into the house with scornful looks.*)

JACK. This ghastly state of things is what you call Bunburying, I suppose?

ALGERNON. Yes, and a perfectly wonderful Bunbury it is. The most wonderful Bunbury I have ever had in my
915 life.

JACK. Well, you've no right whatsoever to Bunbury here.

ALGERNON. That is absurd. One has a right to Bunbury anywhere one chooses. Every serious Bunburyist knows that.

920 JACK. Serious Bunburyist! Good heavens!

ALGERNON. Well, one must be serious about something, if one wants to have any amusement in life. I happen to be serious about Bunburying. What on earth you are serious about I haven't got the remotest idea. About
925 everything, I should fancy. You have such an absolutely trivial nature.

JACK. Well, the only small satisfaction I have in the whole of this wretched business is that your friend Bunbury is quite exploded. You won't be able to run
930 down to the country quite so often as you used to do, dear Algy. And a very good thing too.

ALGERNON. Your brother is a little off colour, isn't he, dear Jack? You won't be able to disappear to London quite so frequently as your wicked custom was. And not
935 a bad thing either.

JACK. As for your conduct towards Miss Cardew, I must say that your taking in a sweet, simple, innocent girl like that is quite inexcusable. To say nothing of the fact that she is my ward.

940 ALGERNON. I can see no possible defence at all for your deceiving a brilliant, clever, thoroughly experienced young lady like Miss Fairfax. To say nothing of the fact that she is my cousin.

JACK. I wanted to be engaged to Gwendolen, that is all.
945 I love her.

ALGERNON. Well, I simply wanted to be engaged to Cecily. I adore her.

JACK. There is certainly no chance of your marrying Miss Cardew.

950 ALGERNON. I don't think there is much likelihood, Jack, of you and Miss Fairfax being united.

JACK. Well, that is no business of yours.

ALGERNON. If it was my business, I wouldn't talk about it. (*Begins to eat muffins.*) It is very vulgar to talk about 955 one's business. Only people like stock-brokers do that, and then merely at dinner parties.

JACK. How can you sit there, calmly eating muffins when we are in this horrible trouble, I can't make out. You seem to me to be perfectly heartless.

960 ALGERNON. Well, I can't eat muffins in an agitated manner. The butter would probably get on my cuffs. One should always eat muffins quite calmly. It is the only way to eat them.

JACK. I say it's perfectly heartless your eating muffins at 965 all, under the circumstances.

ALGERNON. When I am in trouble, eating is the only thing that consoles me. Indeed, when I am in really great trouble, as any one who knows me intimately will tell you, I refuse everything except food and drink. At 970 the present moment I am eating muffins because I am unhappy. Besides, I am particularly fond of muffins. (*Rising.*)

JACK. (*Rising.*) Well, that is no reason why you should eat them all in that greedy way. (*Takes muffins from* 975 *Algernon.*)

ALGERNON. (*Offering tea-cake.*) I wish you would have tea-cake instead. I don't like tea-cake.

JACK. Good heavens! I suppose a man may eat his own muffins in his own garden.

980 ALGERNON. But you have just said it was perfectly heartless to eat muffins.

JACK. I said it was perfectly heartless of you, under the circumstances. That is a very different thing.

ALGERNON. That may be. But the muffins are the same.

(*He seizes the muffin-dish from Jack.*)

985 JACK. Algy, I wish to goodness you would go.

ALGERNON. You can't possibly ask me to go without having some dinner. It's absurd. I never go without my dinner. No one ever does, except vegetarians and people like that. Besides I have just made arrangements with 990 Dr. Chasuble to be christened at a quarter to six under the name of Ernest.

JACK. My dear fellow, the sooner you give up that nonsense the better. I made arrangements this morning with Dr. Chasuble to be christened myself at 5:30, 995 and I naturally will take the name of Ernest. Gwendolen would wish it. We can't both be christened Ernest. It's absurd. Besides, I have a perfect right to be christened if I like. There is no evidence at all that I have ever been christened by anybody. I should think it 1000 extremely probable I never was, and so does Dr. Chasuble. It is entirely different in your case. You have been christened already.

ALGERNON. Yes, but I have not been christened for years.

1005 JACK. Yes, but you have been christened. That is the important thing.

ALGERNON. Quite so. So I know my constitution can stand it. If you are not quite sure about your ever having been christened, I must say I think it rather 1010 dangerous your venturing on it now. It might make you very unwell. You can hardly have forgotten that some one very closely connected with you was very nearly carried off this week in Paris by a severe chill.

JACK. Yes, but you said yourself that a severe chill was 1015 not hereditary.

ALGERNON. It usen't to be, I know—but I daresay it is now. Science is always making wonderful improvements in things.

JACK. (*Picking up the muffin-dish.*) Oh, that is non-1020 sense; you are always talking nonsense.

ALGERNON. Jack, you are at the muffins again! I wish you wouldn't. There are only two left. (*Takes them.*) I told you I was particularly fond of muffins.

JACK. But I hate tea-cake.

1025 ALGERNON. Why on earth then do you allow tea-cake to be served up for your guests? What ideas you have of hospitality!

JACK. Algernon! I have already told you to go. I don't want you here. Why don't you go!

1030 ALGERNON. I haven't quite finished my tea yet! and there is still one muffin left. (*Jack groans, and sinks into a chair. Algernon still continues eating.*)

ACT DROP

ACT 3

SCENE

(Morning-room at the Manor House. Gwendolen and Cecily are at the window, looking out into the garden.)

GWENDOLEN.   The fact that they did not follow us at once into the house, as any one else would have done, seems to me to show that they have some sense of shame left.

5   CECILY.   They have been eating muffins. That looks like repentance.

GWENDOLEN.   *(After a pause.)* They don't seem to notice us at all. Couldn't you cough?

CECILY.   But I haven't got a cough.

10   GWENDOLEN.   They're looking at us. What effrontery!

CECILY.   They're approaching. That's very forward of them.

GWENDOLEN.   Let us preserve a dignified silence.

CECILY.   Certainly. It's the only thing to do now.

(Enter Jack followed by Algernon. They whistle some dreadful popular air from a British Opera.)

15   GWENDOLEN.   This dignified silence seems to produce an unpleasant effect.

CECILY.   A most distasteful one.

GWENDOLEN.   But we will not be the first to speak.

CECILY.   Certainly not.

20   GWENDOLEN.   Mr. Worthing, I have something very particular to ask you. Much depends on your reply.

CECILY.   Gwendolen, your common sense is invaluable. Mr. Moncrieff, kindly answer me the following question. Why did you pretend to be my guardian's brother?

25   ALGERNON.   In order that I might have an opportunity of meeting you.

CECILY.   *(To Gwendolen.)* That certainly seems a satisfactory explanation, does it not?

GWENDOLEN.   Yes, dear, if you can believe him.

30   CECILY.   I don't. But that does not affect the wonderful beauty of his answer.

GWENDOLEN.   True. In matters of grave importance, style, not sincerity is the vital thing. Mr. Worthing, what explanation can you offer to me for pretending to have a brother? Was it in order that you might have an

35   opportunity of coming up to town to see me as often as possible?

JACK.   Can you doubt it, Miss Fairfax?

GWENDOLEN.   I have the gravest doubts upon the

40   subject. But I intend to crush them. This is not the moment for German scepticism.[1] *(Moving to Cecily.)* Their explanations appear to be quite satisfactory, especially Mr. Worthing's. That seems to me to have the stamp of truth upon it.

45   CECILY.   I am more than content with what Mr. Moncrieff said. His voice alone inspires one with absolute credulity.

GWENDOLEN.   Then you think we should forgive them?

CECILY.   Yes. I mean no.

50   GWENDOLEN.   True! I had forgotten. There are principles at stake that one cannot surrender. Which of us should tell them? The task is not a pleasant one.

CECILY.   Could we not both speak at the same time?

GWENDOLEN.   An excellent idea! I nearly always speak at

55   the same time as other people. Will you take the time from me?

CECILY.   Certainly.

(Gwendolen beats time with uplifted finger.)

GWENDOLEN and CECILY.   *(Speaking together.)* Your Christian names are still an insuperable barrier. That is

60   all!

JACK and ALGERNON.   *(Speaking together.)* Our Christian names! Is that all? But we are going to be christened this afternoon.

GWENDOLEN.   *(To Jack.)* For my sake you are prepared

65   to do this terrible thing?

JACK.   I am.

CECILY.   *(To Algernon.)* To please me you are ready to face this fearful ordeal?

ALGERNON.   I am!

70   GWENDOLEN.   How absurd to talk of the equality of the sexes! Where questions of self-sacrifice are concerned, men are infinitely beyond us.

JACK.   We are. *(Clasps hands with Algernon.)*

CECILY.   They have moments of physical courage of

75   which we women know absolutely nothing.

---

[1]   *German scepticism* According to the school of philosophy deriving from Immanuel Kant, we do not always perceive the true state of things-in-themselves.

GWENDOLEN. (*To Jack.*) Darling!
ALGERNON. (*To Cecily.*) Darling! (*They fall into each other's arms.*)

(*Enter Merriman. When he enters he coughs loudly, seeing the situation.*)

MERRIMAN. Ahem! Ahem! Lady Bracknell!
80 JACK. Good heavens!

(*Enter Lady Bracknell. The couples separate in alarm. Exit Merriman.*)

LADY BRACKNELL. Gwendolen! What does this mean?
GWENDOLEN. Merely that I am engaged to be married to Mr. Worthing, Mamma.
LADY BRACKNELL. Come here. Sit down. Sit down
85 immediately. Hesitation of any kind is a sign of mental decay in the young, of physical weakness in the old. (*Turns to Jack.*) Apprised, sir, of my daughter's sudden flight by her trusty maid, whose confidence I purchased by means of a small coin, I followed her at once by a
90 luggage train. Her unhappy father is, I am glad to say, under the impression that she is attending a more than usually lengthy lecture by the University Extension Scheme on the Influence of a permanent income on Thought. I do not propose to undeceive him. Indeed I
95 have never undeceived him on any question. I would consider it wrong. But of course, you will clearly understand that all communication between yourself and my daughter must cease immediately from this moment. On this point, as indeed on all points, I am firm.
100 JACK. I am engaged to be married to Gwendolen, Lady Bracknell!
LADY BRACKNELL. You are nothing of the kind, sir. And now, as regards Algernon!… Algernon!
ALGERNON. Yes, Aunt Augusta.
105 LADY BRACKNELL. May I ask if it is in this house that your invalid friend Mr. Bunbury resides?
ALGERNON. (*Stammering.*) Oh! No! Bunbury doesn't live here. Bunbury is somewhere else at present. In fact, Bunbury is dead.
110 LADY BRACKNELL. Dead! When did Mr. Bunbury die? His death must have been extremely sudden.
ALGERNON. (*Airily.*) Oh! I killed Bunbury this after-

noon. I mean poor Bunbury died this afternoon.
LADY BRACKNELL. What did he die of?
115 ALGERNON. Bunbury? Oh, he was quite exploded.
LADY BRACKNELL. Exploded! Was he the victim of a revolutionary outrage? I was not aware that Mr. Bunbury was interested in social legislation. If so, he is well punished for his morbidity.
120 ALGERNON. My dear Aunt Augusta, I mean he was found out! The doctors found out that Bunbury could not live, that is what I mean—so Bunbury died.
LADY BRACKNELL. He seems to have had great confidence in the opinion of his physicians. I am glad,
125 however, that he made up his mind at the last to some definite course of action, and acted under proper medical advice. And now that we have finally got rid of this Mr. Bunbury, may I ask, Mr. Worthing, who is that young person whose hand my nephew Algernon is now
130 holding in what seems to me a peculiarly unnecessary manner?
JACK. That lady is Miss Cecily Cardew, my ward.

(*Lady Bracknell bows coldly to Cecily.*)

ALGERNON. I am engaged to be married to Cecily, Aunt Augusta.
135 LADY BRACKNELL. I beg your pardon?
CECILY. Mr. Moncrieff and I are engaged to be married, Lady Bracknell.
LADY BRACKNELL. (*With a shiver, crossing to the sofa and sitting down.*) I do not know whether there is anything
140 peculiarly exciting in the air of this particular part of Hertfordshire, but the number of engagements that go on seems to me considerably above the proper average that statistics have laid down for our guidance. I think some preliminary inquiry on my part would not be out
145 of place. Mr. Worthing, is Miss Cardew at all connected with any of the larger railway stations in London? I merely desire information. Until yesterday I had no idea that there were any families or persons whose origin was a Terminus.

(*Jack looks perfectly furious, but restrains himself.*)

150 JACK. (*In a clear, cold voice.*) Miss Cardew is the granddaughter of the late Mr. Thomas Cardew of 149 Bel-

grave Square, S.W.; Gervase Park, Dorking, Surrey; and the Sporran, Fifeshire, N.B.

LADY BRACKNELL. That sounds not unsatisfactory. Three addresses always inspire confidence, even in tradesmen. But what proof have I of their authenticity?

JACK. I have carefully preserved the Court Guides[1] of the period. They are open to your inspection, Lady Bracknell.

LADY BRACKNELL. (*Grimly.*) I have known strange errors in that publication.

JACK. Miss Cardew's family solicitors are Messrs. Markby, Markby, and Markby.

LADY BRACKNELL. Markby, Markby, and Markby? A firm of the very highest position in their profession. Indeed I am told that one of the Mr. Markbys is occasionally to be seen at dinner parties. So far I am satisfied.

JACK. (*Very irritably.*) How extremely kind of you, Lady Bracknell! I have also in my possession, you will be pleased to hear, certificates of Miss Cardew's birth, baptism, whooping cough, registration, vaccination, confirmation, and the measles; both the German and the English variety.

LADY BRACKNELL. Ah! A life crowded with incident, I see; though perhaps somewhat too exciting for a young girl. I am not myself in favour of premature experiences. (*Rises, looks at her watch.*) Gwendolen! the time approaches for our departure. We have not a moment to lose. As a matter of form, Mr. Worthing, I had better ask you if Miss Cardew has any little fortune?

JACK. Oh! about a hundred and thirty thousand pounds in the Funds. That is all. Goodbye, Lady Bracknell. So pleased to have seen you.

LADY BRACKNELL. (*Sitting down again.*) A moment, Mr. Worthing. A hundred and thirty thousand pounds! And in the Funds! Miss Cardew seems to me a most attractive young lady, now that I look at her. Few girls of the present day have any really solid qualities, any of the qualities that last, and improve with time. We live, I regret to say, in an age of surfaces. (*To Cecily.*) Come over here, dear. (*Cecily goes across.*) Pretty child! your dress is sadly simple, and your hair seems almost as Nature might have left it. But we can soon alter all that.

A thoroughly experienced French maid produces a really marvellous result in a very brief space of time. I remember recommending one to young Lady Lancing, and after three months her own husband did not know her.

JACK. And after six months nobody knew her.

LADY BRACKNELL. (*Glares at Jack for a few moments. Then bends, with a practised smile, to Cecily.*) Kindly turn round, sweet child. (*Cecily turns completely round.*) No, the side view is what I want. (*Cecily presents her profile.*) Yes, quite as I expected. There are distinct social possibilities in your profile. The two weak points in our age are its want of principle and its want of profile. The chin a little higher, dear. Style largely depends on the way the chin is worn. They are worn very high, just at present. Algernon!

ALGERNON. Yes, Aunt Augusta!

LADY BRACKNELL. There are distinct social possibilities in Miss Cardew's profile.

ALGERNON. Cecily is the sweetest, dearest, prettiest girl in the whole world. And I don't care twopence about social possibilities.

LADY BRACKNELL. Never speak disrespectfully of Society, Algernon. Only people who can't get into it do that. (*To Cecily.*) Dear child, of course you know that Algernon has nothing but his debts to depend upon. But I do not approve of mercenary marriages. When I married Lord Bracknell I had no fortune of any kind. But I never dreamed for a moment of allowing that to stand in my way. Well, I suppose I must give my consent.

ALGERNON. Thank you, Aunt Augusta.

LADY BRACKNELL. Cecily, you may kiss me!

CECILY. (*Kisses her.*) Thank you, Lady Bracknell.

LADY BRACKNELL. You may also address me as Aunt Augusta for the future.

CECILY. Thank you, Aunt Augusta.

LADY BRACKNELL. The marriage, I think, had better take place quite soon.

ALGERNON. Thank you, Aunt Augusta.

CECILY. Thank you, Aunt Augusta.

LADY BRACKNELL. To speak frankly, I am not in favour of long engagements. They give people the opportunity of finding out each other's character before marriage, which I think is never advisable.

JACK. I beg your pardon for interrupting you, Lady

---

[1] *Court Guides* Directory of names and addresses of those members of the nobility, gentry, and society who have been presented at court.

Bracknell, but this engagement is quite out of the
question. I am Miss Cardew's guardian, and she cannot
marry without my consent until she comes of age. That
consent I absolutely decline to give.

LADY BRACKNELL.　Upon what grounds may I ask?
Algernon is an extremely, I may almost say an ostentatiously, eligible young man. He has nothing, but he
looks everything. What more can one desire?

JACK.　It pains me very much to have to speak frankly to
you, Lady Bracknell, about your nephew, but the fact is
that I do not approve at all of his moral character. I
suspect him of being untruthful.

(*Algernon and Cecily look at him in indignant amazement.*)

LADY BRACKNELL.　Untruthful! My nephew Algernon?
Impossible! He is an Oxonian.[1]

JACK.　I fear there can be no possible doubt about the
matter. This afternoon during my temporary absence in
London on an important question of romance, he
obtained admission to my house by means of the false
pretence of being my brother. Under an assumed name
he drank, I've just been informed by my butler, an
entire pint bottle of my Perrier-Jouet, Brut, '89; wine I
was specially reserving for myself. Continuing his
disgraceful deception, he succeeded in the course of the
afternoon in alienating the affections of my only ward.
He subsequently stayed to tea, and devoured every
single muffin. And what makes his conduct all the more
heartless is, that he was perfectly well aware from the
first that I have no brother, that I never had a brother,
and that I don't intend to have a brother, not even of
any kind. I distinctly told him so myself yesterday
afternoon.

LADY BRACKNELL.　Ahem! Mr. Worthing, after careful
consideration I have decided entirely to overlook my
nephew's conduct to you.

JACK.　That is very generous of you, Lady Bracknell. My
own decision, however, is unalterable. I decline to give
my consent.

LADY BRACKNELL.　(*To Cecily.*) Come here, sweet child.
(*Cecily goes over.*) How old are you, dear?

CECILY.　Well, I am really only eighteen, but I always

admit to twenty when I go to evening parties.

LADY BRACKNELL.　You are perfectly right in making
some slight alteration. Indeed, no woman should ever be
quite accurate about her age. It looks so calculating …
(*In a meditative manner.*) Eighteen, but admitting to
twenty at evening parties. Well, it will not be very long
before you are of age and free from the restraints of
tutelage. So I don't think your guardian's consent is,
after all, a matter of any importance.

JACK.　Pray excuse me, Lady Bracknell, for interrupting
you again, but it is only fair to tell you that according to
the terms of her grandfather's will Miss Cardew does not
come legally of age till she is thirty-five.

LADY BRACKNELL.　That does not seem to me to be a
grave objection. Thirty-five is a very attractive age.
London society is full of women of the very highest
birth who have, of their own free choice, remained
thirty-five for years. Lady Dumbleton is an instance in
point. To my own knowledge she has been thirty-five
ever since she arrived at the age of forty, which was
many years ago now. I see no reason why our dear
Cecily should not be even still more attractive at the age
you mention than she is at present. There will be a large
accumulation of property.

CECILY.　Algy, could you wait for me till I was thirty-
five?

ALGERNON.　Of course I could, Cecily. You know I
could.

CECILY.　Yes, I felt it instinctively, but I couldn't wait all
that time. I hate waiting even five minutes for anybody.
It always makes me rather cross. I am not punctual
myself, I know, but I do like punctuality in others, and
waiting, even to be married, is quite out of the question.

ALGERNON.　Then what is to be done, Cecily?

CECILY.　I don't know, Mr. Moncrieff.

LADY BRACKNELL.　My dear Mr. Worthing, as Miss
Cardew states positively that she cannot wait till she is
thirty-five—a remark which I am bound to say seems to
me to show a somewhat impatient nature—I would beg
of you to reconsider your decision.

JACK.　But my dear Lady Bracknell, the matter is entirely
in your own hands. The moment you consent to my
marriage with Gwendolen, I will most gladly allow your
nephew to form an alliance with my ward.

LADY BRACKNELL.　(*Rising and drawing herself up.*) You

---

[1] *Oxonian*　One who has attended Oxford University.

must be quite aware that what you propose is out of the
question.
JACK.   Then a passionate celibacy is all that any of us can
look forward to.
LADY BRACKNELL.   That is not the destiny I propose for
Gwendolen. Algernon, of course, can choose for himself. (*Pulls out her watch.*) Come, dear, (*Gwendolen rises*)
we have already missed five, if not six, trains. To miss
any more might expose us to comment on the platform.

(*Enter Dr. Chasuble.*)

CHASUBLE.   Everything is quite ready for the christenings.
LADY BRACKNELL.   The christenings, sir! Is not that
somewhat premature?
CHASUBLE.   (*Looking rather puzzled, and pointing to Jack
and Algernon.*) Both these gentlemen have expressed a
desire for immediate baptism.
LADY BRACKNELL.   At their age? The idea is grotesque
and irreligious! Algernon, I forbid you to be baptized. I
will not hear of such excesses. Lord Bracknell would be
highly displeased if he learned that that was the way in
which you wasted your time and money.
CHASUBLE.   Am I to understand then that there are to be
no christenings at all this afternoon?
JACK.   I don't think that, as things are now, it would be
of much practical value to either of us, Dr. Chasuble.
CHASUBLE.   I am grieved to hear such sentiments from
you, Mr. Worthing. They savour of the heretical views
of the Anabaptists,[1] views that I have completely
refuted in four of my unpublished sermons. However,
as your present mood seems to be one peculiarly
secular, I will return to the church at once. Indeed, I
have just been informed by the pew-opener[2] that for
the last hour and a half, Miss Prism has been waiting
for me in the vestry.
LADY BRACKNELL.   (*Starting.*) Miss Prism! Did I hear

you mention a Miss Prism?
CHASUBLE.   Yes, Lady Bracknell. I am on my way to join
her.
LADY BRACKNELL.   Pray allow me to detain you for a
moment. This matter may prove to be one of vital
importance to Lord Bracknell and myself. Is this Miss
Prism a female of repellent aspect, remotely connected
with education?
CHASUBLE.   (*Somewhat indignantly.*) She is the most
cultivated of ladies, and the very picture of respectabil-
ity.
LADY BRACKNELL.   It is obviously the same person. May
I ask what position she holds in your household?
CHASUBLE.   (*Severely.*) I am a celibate, madam.
JACK.   (*Interposing.*) Miss Prism, Lady Bracknell, has
been for the last three years Miss Cardew's esteemed
governess and valued companion.
LADY BRACKNELL.   In spite of what I hear of her, I must
see her at once. Let her be sent for.
CHASUBLE.   (*Looking off.*) She approaches; she is nigh.

(*Enter Miss Prism hurriedly.*)

MISS PRISM.   I was told you expected me in the vestry,
dear Canon. I have been waiting for you there for an
hour and three-quarters.

(*Catches sight of Lady Bracknell, who has fixed her with a
stony glare. Miss Prism grows pale and quails. She looks
anxiously round as if desirous to escape.*)

LADY BRACKNELL.   (*In a severe, judicial voice.*) Prism!
(*Miss Prism bows her head in shame.*) Come here, Prism!
(*Miss Prism approaches in a humble manner.*) Prism!
Where is that baby? (*General consternation. The Canon
starts back in horror. Algernon and Jack pretend to be
anxious to shield Cecily and Gwendolen from hearing the
details of a terrible public scandal.*) Twenty-eight years
ago, Prism, you left Lord Bracknell's house, Number
104, Upper Grosvenor Street, in charge of a perambulator that contained a baby of the male sex. You never
returned. A few weeks later, through the elaborate
investigations of the Metropolitan police, the perambulator was discovered at midnight, standing by itself in a
remote corner of Bayswater. It contained the manuscript

---

[1]   *heretical views … Anabaptists* Although Anabaptists, members of
a Protestant sect that rejects Anglican doctrine, believe in baptism,
they reject the Anglican custom of baptizing infants. Dr. Chasuble
is suggesting that Jack is heretical in denying the value of baptism in
the Anglican church.

[2]   *pew-opener* One assigned to open the doors of pews for privileged
churchgoers.

of a three-volume novel of more than usually revolting sentimentality. (*Miss Prism starts in involuntary indignation.*) But the baby was not there! (*Every one looks at Miss Prism.*) Prism! Where is that baby? (*A pause.*)

400 MISS PRISM.   Lady Bracknell, I admit with shame that I do not know. I only wish I did. The plain facts of the case are these. On the morning of the day you mention, a day that is for ever branded on my memory, I prepared as usual to take the baby out in its perambulator. I had

405 also with me a somewhat old, but capacious hand-bag in which I had intended to place the manuscript of a work of fiction that I had written during my few unoccupied hours. In a moment of mental abstraction, for which I never can forgive myself, I deposited the manuscript in

410 the bassinette, and placed the baby in the hand-bag.

JACK.   (*Who has been listening attentively.*) But where did you deposit the hand-bag?

MISS PRISM.   Do not ask me, Mr. Worthing.

JACK.   Miss Prism, this is a matter of no small impor-

415 tance to me. I insist on knowing where you deposited the hand-bag that contained that infant.

MISS PRISM.   I left it in the cloak-room of one of the larger railway stations in London.

JACK.   What railway station?

420 MISS PRISM.   (*Quite crushed.*) Victoria. The Brighton line. (*Sinks into a chair.*)

JACK.   I must retire to my room for a moment. Gwendolen, wait here for me.

GWENDOLEN.   If you are not too long, I will wait here

425 for you all my life.

(*Exit Jack in great excitement.*)

CHASUBLE.   What do you think this means, Lady Bracknell?

LADY BRACKNELL.   I dare not even suspect, Dr. Chasuble. I need hardly tell you that in families of high

430 position strange coincidences are not supposed to occur. They are hardly considered the thing.

(*Noises heard overhead as if some one was throwing trunks about. Every one looks up.*)

CECILY.   Uncle Jack seems strangely agitated.

CHASUBLE.   Your guardian has a very emotional nature.

LADY BRACKNELL.   This noise is extremely unpleasant.

435 It sounds as if he was having an argument. I dislike arguments of any kind. They are always vulgar, and often convincing.

CHASUBLE.   (*Looking up.*) It has stopped now. (*The noise is redoubled.*)

440 LADY BRACKNELL.   I wish he would arrive at some conclusion.

GWENDOLEN.   This suspense is terrible. I hope it will last.

(*Enter Jack with a hand-bag of black leather in his hand.*)

JACK.   (*Rushing over to Miss Prism.*) Is this the handbag,

445 Miss Prism? Examine it carefully before you speak. The happiness of more than one life depends on your answer.

MISS PRISM.   (*Calmly.*) It seems to be mine. Yes, here is the injury it received through the upsetting of a Gower

450 Street omnibus[1] in younger and happier days. Here is the stain on the lining caused by the explosion of a temperance beverage,[2] an incident that occurred at Leamington. And here, on the lock, are my initials. I had forgotten that in an extravagant mood I had had

455 them placed there. The bag is undoubtedly mine. I am delighted to have it so unexpectedly restored to me. It has been a great inconvenience being without it all these years.

JACK.   (*In a pathetic voice.*) Miss Prism, more is restored

460 to you than this hand-bag. I was the baby you placed in it.

MISS PRISM.   (*Amazed.*) You?

JACK.   (*Embracing her.*) Yes ... mother!

MISS PRISM.   (*Recoiling in indignant astonishment.*) Mr.

465 Worthing! I am unmarried!

JACK.   Unmarried! I do not deny that is a serious blow. But after all, who has the right to cast a stone against one who has suffered? Cannot repentance wipe out an act of folly? Why should there be one law for men, and

470 another for women? Mother, I forgive you. (*Tries to embrace her again.*)

---

[1] *Gower Street omnibus* Public horse-drawn bus on a route in central London.

[2] *temperance beverage* Non-alcoholic drink. (The temperance movement aimed to prohibit all alcoholic beverages.)

MISS PRISM. (*Still more indignant.*) Mr. Worthing, there is some error. (*Pointing to Lady Bracknell.*) There is the lady who can tell you who you really are.

475 JACK. (*After a pause.*) Lady Bracknell, I hate to seem inquisitive, but would you kindly inform me who I am?

LADY BRACKNELL. I am afraid that the news I have to give you will not altogether please you. You are the son of my poor sister, Mrs. Moncrieff, and consequently

480 Algernon's elder brother.

JACK. Algy's elder brother! Then I have a brother after all. I knew I had a brother! I always said I had a brother! Cecily,—how could you have ever doubted that I had a brother? (*Seizes hold of Algernon.*) Dr. Chasuble, my

485 unfortunate brother. Miss Prism, my unfortunate brother. Gwendolen, my unfortunate brother. Algy, you young scoundrel, you will have to treat me with more respect in the future. You have never behaved to me like a brother in all your life.

490 ALGERNON. Well, not till to-day, old boy, I admit. I did my best, however, though I was out of practice. (*Shakes hands.*)

GWENDOLEN. (*To Jack.*) My own! But what own are you? What is your Christian name, now that you have

495 become some one else?

JACK. Good heavens! ... I had quite forgotten that point. Your decision on the subject of my name is irrevocable, I suppose?

GWENDOLEN. I never change, except in my affections.

500 CECILY. What a noble nature you have, Gwendolen!

JACK. Then the question had better be cleared up at once. Aunt Augusta, a moment. At the time when Miss Prism left me in the hand-bag, had I been christened already?

505 LADY BRACKNELL. Every luxury that money could buy, including christening, had been lavished on you by your fond and doting parents.

JACK. Then I was christened! That is settled. Now, what name was I given? Let me know the worst.

510 LADY BRACKNELL. Being the eldest son you were naturally christened after your father.

JACK. (*Irritably.*) Yes, but what was my father's Christian name?

LADY BRACKNELL. (*Meditatively.*) I cannot at the present

515 moment recall what the General's Christian name was. But I have no doubt he had one. He was eccentric, I admit. But only in later years. And that was the result of the Indian climate, and marriage, and indigestion, and other things of that kind.

520 JACK. Algy! Can't you recollect what our father's Christian name was?

ALGERNON. My dear boy, we were never even on speaking terms. He died before I was a year old.

JACK. His name would appear in the Army Lists[1] of the

525 period, I suppose, Aunt Augusta?

LADY BRACKNELL. The General was essentially a man of peace, except in his domestic life. But I have no doubt his name would appear in any military directory.

JACK. The Army Lists of the last forty years are here.

530 These delightful records should have been my constant study. (*Rushes to bookcase and tears the books out.*) M. Generals ... Mallam, Maxbohm, Magley, what ghastly names they have—Markby, Migsby, Mobbs, Moncrieff! Lieutenant 1840, Captain, Lieutenant-Colonel, Colo-

535 nel, General 1869, Christian names, Ernest John. (*Puts book very quietly down and speaks quite calmly.*) I always told you, Gwendolen, my name was Ernest, didn't I? Well, it is Ernest after all. I mean it naturally is Ernest.

LADY BRACKNELL. Yes, I remember now that the

540 General was called Ernest, I knew I had some particular reason for disliking the name.

GWENDOLEN. Ernest! My own Ernest! I felt from the first that you could have no other name!

JACK. Gwendolen, it is a terrible thing for a man to find

545 out suddenly that all his life he has been speaking nothing but the truth. Can you forgive me?

GWENDOLEN. I can. For I feel that you are sure to change.

JACK. My own one!

550 CHASUBLE. (*To Miss Prism.*) Laetitia! (*Embraces her.*)

MISS PRISM. (*Enthusiastically.*) Frederick! At last!

ALGERNON. Cecily! (*Embraces her.*) At last!

JACK. Gwendolen! (*Embraces her.*) At last!

LADY BRACKNELL. My nephew, you seem to be display-

555 ing signs of triviality.

JACK. On the contrary, Aunt Augusta, I've now realized for the first time in my life the vital Importance of Being Earnest.

TABLEAU

—1895

---

[1] *Army Lists* Directories of officers.

IN CONTEXT

Wilde and "The Public"

Interview with Oscar Wilde, *St. James Gazette*, January 1895

I found Mr. Oscar Wilde (writes a Representative) making ready to depart on a short visit to Algiers, and reading—of course, nothing so obvious as a time-table, but a French newspaper which contained an account of the first night of *The Ideal Husband*[1] and its author's appearance after the play.

"How well the French appreciate these brilliant willful moments in an artist's life," remarked Mr. Wilde, handing me the article as if he considered the interview already at an end.

"Does it give you any pleasure," I inquired, "to appear before the curtain after the production of your plays?"

"None whatsoever. No artist finds any interest in seeing the public. The public is very much interested in seeing an artist. Personally, I prefer the French custom, according to which the name of the dramatist is announced to the public by the oldest actor in the piece."

"Would you advocate," I asked, "this custom in England?"

"Certainly. The more the public is interested in artists, the less it is interested in art. The personality of the artist is not a thing the public should know anything about. It is too accidental." Then, after a pause—

"It might be more interesting if the name of the author were announced by the *youngest* actor present."

"It is only in deference, then, to the imperious mandate of the public that you have appeared before the curtain?"

"Yes; I have always been very good-natured about that. The public has always been so appreciative of my work I felt it would be a pity to spoil its evening."

"I notice some people have found fault with the character of your speeches."

"Yes, the old-fashioned idea was that the dramatist should appear and merely thank his kind friends for their patronage and presence. I am glad to say I have altered all that. The artist cannot be degraded into the servant of the public. While I have always recognized the cultured appreciation that actors and audience have shown for my work, I have equally recognized that humility is for the hypocrite, modesty for the incompetent. Assertion is at once the duty and privilege of the artist."

"To what do you attribute, Mr. Wilde, the fact that so few men of letters besides yourself have written plays for public presentation?"

"Primarily the existence of an irresponsible censorship. The fact that my *Salomé* cannot be performed is sufficient to show the folly of such an institution. If painters were obliged to show their pictures to clerks at Somerset House, those who think in form and colour would adopt some other mode of expression. If every novel had to be submitted to a police magistrate, those whose passion is fiction would seek some new mode of realization. No art ever survived censorship; no art ever will."

"And secondly?"

"Secondly to the rumour persistently spread abroad by journalists for the last thirty years, that the duty of the dramatist was to please the public. The aim of art is no more to give pleasure than to give

---

[1]   *The Ideal Husband*   I.e., Wilde's play *An Ideal Husband*. The play, which had opened on 3 January 1895, was currently enjoying a very successful run at the Haymarket Theatre.

pain. The aim of art is to be art. As I said once before, the work of art is to dominate the spectator—the spectator is not to dominate art."

"You admit no exceptions?"

"Yes. Circuses where it seems the wishes of the public might be reasonably carried out."

"Do you think," I inquired, "that French dramatic criticism is superior to our own?"

"It would be unfair to confuse French dramatic criticism with English theatrical criticism. The French dramatic critic is always a man of culture and generally a man of letters. In France poets like Gautier[1] have been dramatic critics. In England they are drawn from a less distinguished class. They have neither the same capacities nor the same opportunities. They have all the moral qualities, but none of the artistic qualifications. For the criticism of such a complex mode of art as the drama the highest culture is necessary. No one can criticize drama who is not capable of receiving impressions from the other arts also."

"You admit they are sincere?"

"Yes; but their sincerity is little more than stereotyped stupidity. The critic of the drama should be versatile as the actor. He should be able to change his mood at will and should catch the colour of the moment."

"At least they are honest?"

"Absolutely. I don't believe there is a single dramatic critic in London who would deliberately set himself to misrepresent the work of any dramatist—unless, of course, he personally disliked the dramatist, or had some play of his own he wished to produce at the same theatre, or had an old friend among the actors, or some natural reasons of that kind. I am speaking, however, of London dramatic critics. In the provinces both audience and critics are cultured. In London it is only the audience who are cultured."

"I fear you do not rate our dramatic critics very highly, Mr. Wilde; but, at all events, they are incorruptible?"

"In a market where there are no bidders."

"Still their memories stand them in good stead," I pleaded.

"The old talk of having seen Macready[;][2] that must be a very painful memory. The middle-aged boast that they can recall Diplomacy;[3] hardly a pleasant reminiscence."

"You deny them, then, even a creditable past?"

"They have no past and no future, and are incapable of realizing the colour of the moment that finds them at the play."

"What do you propose should be done?"

"They should be pensioned off, and only allowed to write on politics or theology or bimetallism, or some subject easier than art."

"In fact," I said, carried away by Mr. Wilde's aphorisms, "they should be seen and not heard."

"The old should neither be seen nor heard," said Mr. Wilde with some emphasis.

"You said the other day there were only two dramatic critics in London. May I ask—"

"They must have been greatly gratified by such an admission from me; but I am bound to say that since last week I have struck one of them from the list."

"Whom have you left in?"

"I think I had better not mention his name. It might make him too conceited. Conceit is the privilege of the creative."

"How would you define ideal dramatic criticism?"

[1] *Gautier* Théophile Gautier (1811–72), French poet, novelist, and dramatist.

[2] *Macready* William Charles Macready (1793–1873), English actor and theater manager.

[3] *Diplomacy* An English adaptation of the French play *Dora* (1878), by Victorien Sardou (1831–1908).

"As far as my work is concerned[,] unqualified appreciation."

"And whom have you omitted?"

"Mr. William Archer, of the *World*."[1]

"What do you chiefly object to in his article?"

"I object to nothing in the article, but I grieve at everything in it. It is bad taste in him to write of me by my Christian name, and he need not have stolen his vulgarisms from the *National Observer* in its most impudent and impotent days."

"Mr. Archer asked whether[,] if it was agreeable to you to be hailed by your Christian name when the enthusiastic spectators called you before the curtain."

"To be so addressed by enthusiastic spectators is as great a compliment as to be written of by one's Christian name is, in a journalist, bad manners. Bad manners make a journalist."

"Do you think French actors, like French criticism, superior to our own?"

"The English actors act quite as well; but they act best between the lines. They lack the superb elocution of the French—so clear, so cadenced, and so musical. A long sustained speech seems to exhaust them. At the Théâtre Français we go to listen, to an English theatre we go to look. There are, of course, exceptions. Mr. George Alexander, Mr. Lewis Waller, Mr. Forbes Robertson, and others I might mention, have superb voices and know how to use them. I wish I could say the same of the critics; but in the case of the literary drama in England there is too much of what is technically known as 'business.' Yet there is more than one of our English actors who is capable of producing a wonderful dramatic effect by aid of a monosyllable and two cigarettes."

For a moment Mr. Wilde was silent, and then added, "Perhaps, after all, that is acting."

"But are you satisfied with the interpreters of *The Ideal Husband*?"

"I am charmed with all of them. Perhaps they are a little too fascinating. The stage is the refuge of the too fascinating."

"Have you heard it said that all the characters in your play talk as you do?"

"Rumours of that kind have reached me from time to time," said Mr. Wilde, lighting a cigarette, "and I should fancy that some such criticism has been made. The fact is that it is only in the last few years that the dramatic critic has had the opportunity of seeing plays written by anyone who has a mastery of style. In the case of a dramatist, also an artist, it is impossible not to feel that the work of art, to be a work of art, must be dominated by the artist. Every play of Shakespeare is dominated by Shakespeare. Ibsen and Dumas[2] dominate their works. My works are dominated by myself."

"Have you ever been influenced by any of your predecessors?"

"It is enough for me to state definitely, and I hope once for all, that not a single dramatist in this century has ever in the smallest degree influenced me. Only two have interested me."

"And they are?"

"Victor Hugo and Maeterlinck."[3]

"Other writers surely have influenced your other works?"

"Setting aside the prose and poetry of Greek and Latin authors, the only writers who have influenced me are Keats, Flaubert, and Walter Pater;[4] and before I came across them I had already

[1] *Mr. William ... World* For Archer's criticism of Wilde, see "*An Ideal Husband*," *The World*, 9 January 1895, 26–27.

[2] *Ibsen* Norwegian playwright Henrik Ibsen (1828–1906); *Dumas* French author and playwright Alexandre Dumas, *fils* (1824–95).

[3] *Maeterlinck* Maurice Maeterlinck (1862–1949), Belgian poet and playwright who was awarded the Nobel Prize for Literature in 1911.

[4] *Keats* John Keats, English poet (1795–1821); *Flaubert* French novelist Gustave Flaubert (1821–80), celebrated author of *Madame Bovary* (1867); *Walter Pater* English critic and scholar; he had reviewed some of Wilde's works.

gone more than halfway to meet them. Style must be in one's soul before one can recognize it in others."

"And do you consider *The Ideal Husband* the best of your plays?"

A charming smile crossed Mr. Wilde's face.

"Have you forgotten my classical expression—that only mediocrities improve? My three plays are to each other, as a wonderful young poet has beautifully said,

> as one white rose
> On one green stalk to another one.

They form a perfect cycle, and in their delicate sphere complete both life and art."

"Do you think that the critics will understand your new play,[1] which Mr. George Alexander has secured?"

"I hope not."

"I dare not ask, I suppose, if it will please the public?"

"When a play that is a work of art is produced on the stage, what is being tested is not the play, but the stage; when a play that is *not* a work of art is produced on the stage, what is being tested is not the play, but the public."

"What sort of play are we to expect?"

"It is exquisitely trivial, a delicate bubble of fancy, and it has its philosophy."

"Its philosophy!"

"That we should treat all the trivial things of life very seriously, and all the serious things of life with sincere and studied triviality."[2]

"You have no leanings towards realism?"

"None whatever. Realism is only a background; it cannot form an artistic motive for a play that is to be a work of art."

"Still I have heard you congratulated on your pictures of London society."

"If Robert Chiltern, the Ideal Husband, were a common clerk, the humanity of his tragedy would be none the less poignant. I have placed him in the higher ranks of life merely because that is the side of social life with which I am best acquainted. In a play dealing with actualities to write with ease one must write with knowledge."

"Then you see nothing suggestive of treatment in the tragedies of everyday existence?"

"If a journalist is run over by a four-wheeler in the Strand, an incident I regret to say I have never witnessed, it suggests nothing to me from a dramatic point of view. Perhaps I am wrong; but the artist must have his limitations."

"Well," I said, rising to go, "I have enjoyed myself immensely."

"I was sure you would," said Mr. Wilde. "But tell me how you manage your interviews."

"Oh, Pitman," I said carelessly.

"Is that your name? It's not a very *nice* name."

Then I left.

---

[1] *new play*   *The Importance of Being Earnest*, which opened on 14 February 1895.

[2] *It is … triviality*   The full title of the play is *The Importance of Being Earnest: A Trivial Comedy for Serious People*.

IN CONTEXT

The First Wilde Trial (1895)

The following is an excerpt from the transcripts of the cross examination of Wilde by Edward Carson, the attorney defending the Marquess of Queensberry in the libel action[1] Wilde had brought against him.

from *The Transcripts of the Trial*

Portrait of Oscar Wilde at the time of his trial, by Henri de Toulouse-Lautrec.

CARSON.   You stated that your age was thirty-nine. I think you are over forty. You were born on 16th October 1854?

WILDE.   I have no wish to pose as being young. I am thirty-nine or forty. You have my certificate and that settles the matter.

CARSON.   But being born in 1854 makes you more than forty?

WILDE.   Ah! Very well.

CARSON.   What age is Lord Alfred Douglas?

WILDE.   Lord Alfred Douglas is about twenty-four, and was between twenty and twenty-one years

---

[1]   *Marquess ... libel action*   The Marquess of Queensberry, offended at the close friendship Wilde had formed with his son, Lord Alfred Douglas, had left a card at Wilde's club addressed to "Oscar Wilde posing as a sodomnite [sic]." Wilde felt that he had little choice but to prosecute, or to become publicly known as a man who was unable to deny such a charge. It was this prosecution which eventually led to his imprisonment and the exile of Lord Alfred Douglas.

of age when I first knew him. Down to the time of the interview in Tite Street, Lord Queensberry was friendly. I did not receive a letter on 3rd April in which Lord Queensberry desired that my acquaintance with his son should cease. After the interview I had no doubt that such was Lord Queensberry's desire. Notwithstanding Lord Queensberry's protest, my intimacy with Lord Alfred Douglas has continued down to the present moment.

CARSON.   You have stayed with him at many places?

WILDE.   Yes.

CARSON.   At Oxford? Brighton on several occasions? Worthing?

WILDE.   Yes.

CARSON.   You never took rooms for him?

WILDE.   No.

CARSON.   Were you at other places with him?

WILDE.   Yes; at Cromer and at Torquay.

CARSON.   And in various hotels in London?

WILDE.   Yes; at one in Albemarle Street, and in Dover Street, and at the Savoy.

CARSON.   Did you ever take rooms yourself in addition to your house in Tite Street?

WILDE.   Yes; at 10 and 11 St. James's Place. I kept the rooms from the month of October 1893 to the end of March 1894. Lord Alfred Douglas has stayed in those chambers, which are not far from Piccadilly. I have been abroad with him several times and even lately to Monte Carlo. With reference to the writings which have been mentioned, it was not at Brighton, in 20 King's Road, that I wrote my article for *The Chameleon*.[1] I observed that there were also contributions from Lord Alfred Douglas, but these were not written at Brighton. I have seen them. I thought them exceedingly beautiful poems. One was "In Praise of Shame" and the other "Two Loves."

CARSON.   These loves. They were two boys?

WILDE.   Yes.

CARSON.   One boy calls his love "true love," and the other boy calls his love "shame"?

WILDE.   Yes.

CARSON.   Did you think that made any improper suggestion?

WILDE.   No, none whatever.

CARSON.   You read "The Priest and the Acolyte"?

WILDE.   Yes.

CARSON.   You have no doubt whatever that that was an improper story?

WILDE.   From the literary point of view it was highly improper. It is impossible for a man of literature to judge it otherwise; by literature, meaning treatment, selection of subject, and the like. I thought the treatment rotten and the subject rotten.

CARSON.   You are of opinion, I believe, that there is no such thing as an immoral book?

WILDE.   Yes.

CARSON.   May I take it that you think "The Priest and the Acolyte" was not immoral?

WILDE.   It was worse; it was badly written.

CARSON.   Was not the story that of a priest who fell in love with a boy who served him at the altar, and was discovered by the rector in the priest's room, and a scandal arose?

WILDE.   I have read it only once, in last November, and nothing will induce me to read it again. I don't care for it. It doesn't interest me.

---

[1] *The Chameleon* Oxford undergraduate magazine, of which there was only one issue, that of December 1894 to which Wilde refers. In this issue Wilde's "Phrases and Philosophies for the Use of the Young" appeared, as well as an anonymous story about male homosexuality (actually written not by Wilde but by the editor), called "The Priest and the Acolyte." Though Wilde was not the author, the mere fact that a piece signed by him appeared juxtaposed to this story proved damaging to his reputation.

CARSON.   Do you think the story blasphemous?

WILDE.   I think it violated every artistic canon of beauty.

CARSON.   That is not an answer?

WILDE.   It is the only one I can give.

CARSON.   I want to see the position you pose in?

WILDE.   I do not think you should say that.

CARSON.   I have said nothing out of the way. I wish to know whether you thought the story blasphemous?

WILDE.   The story filled me with disgust. The end was wrong.

CARSON.   Answer the question, sir. Did you or did you not consider the story blasphemous?

WILDE.   I thought it disgusting.

CARSON.   I am satisfied with that. You know that when the priest in the story administers poison to the boy, he uses the words of the sacrament of the Church of England?

WILDE.   That I entirely forgot.

CARSON.   Do you consider that blasphemous?

WILDE.   I think it is horrible. "Blasphemous" is not a word of mine.

[*Carson then read the following passage from "The Priest and the Acolyte."*]:

> Just before the consecration the priest took a tiny phial from the pocket of his cassock, blessed it, and poured the contents into the chalice.
>
> When the time came for him to receive from the chalice, he raised it to his lips, but did not taste of it.
>
> He administered the sacred wafer to the child, and then he took his hand; he turned towards him; but when he saw the light in the beautiful face he turned again to the crucifix with a low moan. For one instant his courage failed him; then he turned to the little fellow again, and held the chalice to his lips:
>
> "The Blood of our Lord Jesus Christ, which was shed for thee, preserve thy body and soul unto everlasting life."

CARSON.   Do you approve of those words?

WILDE.   I think them disgusting, perfect twaddle.

CARSON.   I think you will admit that anyone who would approve of such an article would pose as guilty of improper practices?

WILDE.   I do not think so in the person of another contributor to the magazine. It would show very bad literary taste. I strongly objected to the whole story. I took no steps to express disapproval of *The Chameleon* because I think it would have been beneath my dignity as a man of letters to associate myself with an Oxford undergraduate's productions. I am aware that the magazine may have been circulated among the undergraduates of Oxford. I do not believe that any book or work of art ever had any effect whatever on morality.

CARSON.   Am I right in saying that you do not consider the effect in creating morality or immorality?

WILDE.   Certainly, I do not.

CARSON.   So far as your works are concerned, you pose as not being concerned about morality or immorality?

WILDE.   I do not know whether you use the word "pose" in any particular sense.

CARSON.   It is a favorite word of your own?

WILDE.   Is it? I have no pose in this matter. In writing a play or a book, I am concerned entirely with literature—that is, with art. I aim not at doing good or evil, but in trying to make a thing that will have some quality of beauty.

CARSON.   Listen, sir. Here is one of the "Phrases and Philosophies for the Use of the Young" which you contributed: "Wickedness is a myth invented by good people to account for the curious attractiveness of others." You think that true?

WILDE.   I rarely think that anything I write is true.

CARSON.   Did you say "rarely"?

WILDE.   I said "rarely." I might have said "never"—not true in the actual sense of the word.

CARSON.   "Religions die when they are proved to be true." Is that true?

WILDE.   Yes; I hold that. It is a suggestion towards a philosophy of the absorption of religions by science, but it is too big a question to go into now.

CARSON.   Do you think that was a safe axiom to put forward for the philosophy of the young?

WILDE.   Most stimulating.

CARSON.   "If one tells the truth, one is sure, sooner or later, to be found out"?

WILDE.   That is a pleasing paradox, but I do not set very high store on it as an axiom.

CARSON.   Is it good for the young?

WILDE.   Anything is good that stimulates thought in whatever age.

CARSON.   Whether moral or immoral?

WILDE.   There is no such thing as morality or immorality in thought. There is immoral emotion.

CARSON.   "Pleasure is the only thing one should live for"?

WILDE.   I think that the realization of oneself is the prime aim of life, and to realize oneself through pleasure is finer than to do so through pain. I am, on that point, entirely on the side of the ancients—the Greeks. It is a pagan idea.

CARSON.   "A truth ceases to be true when more than one person believes in it"?

WILDE.   Perfectly. That would be my metaphysical definition of truth; something so personal that the same truth could never be appreciated by two minds.

CARSON.   "The condition of perfection is idleness: the aim of perfection is youth"?

WILDE.   Oh, yes; I think so. Half of it is true. The life of contemplation is the highest life, and so recognized by the philosopher.

CARSON.   "There is something tragic about the enormous number of young men there are in England at the present moment who start life with perfect profiles, and end by adopting some useful profession"?

WILDE.   I should think that the young have enough sense of humour.

CARSON.   You think that is humourous?

WILDE.   I think it is an amusing paradox, an amusing play on words.

CARSON.   What would anyone say would be the effect of "Phrases and Philosophies" taken in connection with such an article as "The Priest and the Acolyte"?

WILDE.   Undoubtedly it was the idea that might be formed that made me object so strongly to the story. I saw at once that maxims that were perfectly nonsensical, paradoxical, or anything you like, might be read in conjunction with it.

CARSON.   After the criticisms that were passed on *Dorian Gray*, was it modified a good deal?

WILDE.   No. Additions were made. In one case it was pointed out to me—not in a newspaper or anything of that sort, but by the only critic of the century whose opinion I set high, Mr. Walter Pater—that a certain passage was liable to misconstruction, and I made an addition.

CARSON.   This is in your introduction to *Dorian Gray*: "There is no such thing as a moral or an immoral book. Books are well written, or badly written." That expresses your view?

WILDE.   My view on art, yes.

CARSON.   Then I take it that no matter how immoral a book may be, if it is well written, it is, in your opinion, a good book?

WILDE.   Yes, if it were well written so as to produce a sense of beauty, which is the highest sense of which a human being can be capable. If it were badly written, it would produce a sense of disgust.
CARSON.   Then a well-written book putting forward perverted moral views may be a good book?
WILDE.   No work of art ever puts forward views. Views belong to people who are not artists.
CARSON.   A perverted novel might be a good book?
WILDE.   I don't know what you mean by a "perverted" novel.
CARSON.   Then I will suggest *Dorian Gray* as open to the interpretation of being such a novel?
WILDE.   That could only be to brutes and illiterates. The views of Philistines on art are incalculably stupid.
CARSON.   An illiterate person reading *Dorian Gray* might consider it such a novel?
WILDE.   The views of illiterates on art are unaccountable. I am concerned only with my view of art. I don't care twopence what other people think of it.
CARSON.   The majority of persons would come under your definition of Philistines and illiterates?
WILDE.   I have found wonderful exceptions.
CARSON.   Do you think that the majority of people live up to the position you are giving us?
WILDE.   I am afraid they are not cultivated enough.
CARSON.   Not cultivated enough to draw the distinction between a good book and a bad book?
WILDE.   Certainly not.
CARSON.   The affection and love of the artist of *Dorian Gray* might lead an ordinary individual to believe that it might have a certain tendency?
WILDE.   I have no knowledge of the views of ordinary individuals.
CARSON.   You did not prevent the ordinary individual from buying your book?
WILDE.   I have never discouraged him.

[*Carson then read a long passage from Chapter 1 of* The Picture of Dorian Gray *(from "The story is simply this …" to "I must see Dorian Gray").*]

CARSON.   Now I ask you, Mr. Wilde, do you consider that that description of the feeling of one man towards a youth just grown up was a proper or an improper feeling?
WILDE.   I think it is the most perfect description of what an artist would feel on meeting a beautiful personality that was in some way necessary to his art and life.
CARSON.   You think that is a feeling a young man should have towards another?
WILDE.   Yes, as an artist.

[*Carson then read a long passage from Chapter 9 of* The Picture of Dorian Gray *(from "Let us sit down, Dorian" to "You are made to be worshipped").*]

CARSON.   Do you mean to say that that passage describes the natural feeling of one man towards another?
WILDE.   It would be the influence produced by a beautiful personality.
CARSON.   A beautiful person?
WILDE.   I said a "beautiful personality." You can describe it as you like. Dorian Gray's was a most remarkable personality.
CARSON.   May I take it that you, as an artist, have never known the feeling described here?
WILDE.   I have never allowed any personality to dominate my art.
CARSON.   Then you have never known the feeling you described?
WILDE.   No. It is a work of fiction.
CARSON.   So far as you are concerned you have no experience as to its being a natural feeling?

WILDE.   I think it is perfectly natural for any artist to admire intensely and love a young man. It is an incident in the life of almost every artist.

CARSON.   But let us go over it phrase by phrase. "I quite admit that I adored you madly." What do you say to that? Have you ever adored a young man madly?

WILDE.   No, not madly; I prefer love—that is a higher form.

CARSON.   Never mind about that. Let us keep down to the level we are at now?

WILDE.   I have never given adoration to anybody except myself. (*Loud laughter.*)

CARSON.   I suppose you think that a very smart thing?

WILDE.   Not at all.

CARSON.   Then you have never had that feeling?

WILDE.   No. The whole idea was borrowed from Shakespeare, I regret to say—yes, from Shakespeare's sonnets.

CARSON.   I believe you have written an article to show that Shakespeare's sonnets were suggestive of unnatural vice?

WILDE.   On the contrary I have written an article to show that they are not.[1] I objected to such a perversion being put upon Shakespeare.

CARSON.   "I have adored you extravagantly"?

WILDE.   Do you mean financially?

CARSON.   Oh, yes, financially! Do you think we are talking about finance?

WILDE.   I don't know what you are talking about.

CARSON.   Don't you? Well, I hope I shall make myself very plain before I have done. "I was jealous of everyone to whom you spoke." Have you ever been jealous of a young man?

WILDE.   Never in my life.

CARSON.   "I wanted to have you all to myself." Did you ever have that feeling?

WILDE.   No; I should consider it an intense nuisance, an intense bore.

CARSON.   "I grew afraid that the world would know of my idolatry." Why should he grow afraid that the world should know of it?

WILDE.   Because there are people in the world who cannot understand the intense devotion, affection, and admiration that an artist can feel for a wonderful and beautiful personality. These are the conditions under which we live. I regret them.

CARSON.   These unfortunate people, that have not the high understanding that you have, might put it down to something wrong?

WILDE.   Undoubtedly; to any point they chose. I am not concerned with the ignorance of others.

CARSON.   In another passage Dorian Gray receives a book. Was the book to which you refer a moral book?

WILDE.   Not well written, but it gave me an idea.

CARSON.   Was not the book you have in mind of a certain tendency?

WILDE.   I decline to be cross-examined upon the work of another artist. It is an impertinence and a vulgarity.

[*Wilde then stated the book Carson referred to was* A Rebours, *by J.K. Huysmans; and, following an appeal by Sir Edward Clarke, Wilde's attorney, the judge ruled against further reference to it. Carson then read a long passage from Chapter 12 of* The Picture of Dorian Gray *(from "… I think it right that you should know the most dreadful things are being said about you in London" to "Dorian, your reputation is infamous … ").*]

---

[1] *an article … not*   Cf. "The Portrait of Mr. W.H." first published in *Blackwood's Edinburgh Magazine*, 146.885 (July 1889), and then again in a limited edition in 1921.

CARSON.   Does not this passage suggest a charge of unnatural vice?

WILDE.   It describes Dorian Gray as a man of very corrupt influence, though there is no statement as to the nature of the influence. But as a matter of fact I do not think that one person influences another, nor do I think there is any bad influence in the world.

CARSON.   A man never corrupts a youth?

WILDE.   I think not.

CARSON.   Nothing could corrupt him?

WILDE.   If you are talking of separate ages.

CARSON.   No, sir, I am talking common sense.

WILDE.   I do not think one person influences another.

CARSON.   You don't think that flattering a young man, making love[1] to him, in fact, would be likely to corrupt him?

WILDE.   No.

CARSON.   Where was Lord Alfred Douglas staying when you wrote that letter to him?

WILDE.   At the Savoy; and I was at Babbacombe, near Torquay.

CARSON.   It was a letter in answer to something he had sent you?

WILDE.   Yes, a poem.

CARSON.   Why should a man of your age address a boy nearly twenty years younger as "My own boy"?

WILDE.   I was fond of him. I have always been fond of him.

CARSON.   Do you adore him?

WILDE.   No, but I have always liked him. I think it is a beautiful letter. It is a poem. I was not writing an ordinary letter. You might as well cross-examine me as to whether *King Lear* or a sonnet of Shakespeare was proper.

CARSON.   Apart from art, Mr. Wilde?

WILDE.   I cannot answer apart from art.

CARSON.   Suppose a man who was not an artist had written this letter, would you say it was a proper letter?

WILDE.   A man who was not an artist could not have written that letter.

CARSON.   Why?

WILDE.   Because nobody but an artist could write it. He certainly could not write the language unless he were a man of letters.

CARSON.   I can suggest, for the sake of your reputation, that there is nothing very wonderful in this "red rose-leaf lips of yours"?

WILDE.   A great deal depends on the way it is read.

CARSON.   "Your slim gilt soul walks between passion and poetry." Is that a beautiful phrase?

WILDE.   Not as you read it, Mr. Carson. You read it very badly.

CARSON.   I do not profess to be an artist; and when I hear you give evidence, I am glad I am not—

SIR EDWARD CLARKE.   I don't think my friend should talk like that. (*To witness*) Pray, do not criticize my friend's reading again.

CARSON.   Is that not an exceptional letter?

WILDE.   It is unique, I should say.

CARSON.   Was that the ordinary way in which you carried on your correspondence?

WILDE.   No; but I have often written to Lord Alfred Douglas, though I never wrote to another young man in the same way.

CARSON.   Have you often written letters in the same style as this?

---

[1]   *making love* Until the 1960s this expression was generally used to refer to the process of wooing or courtship, not to any physical act of lovemaking.

WILDE.   I don't repeat myself in style.

CARSON.   Here is another letter which I believe you also wrote to Lord Alfred Douglas. Will you read it?

WILDE.   No; I decline. I don't see why I should.

CARSON.   Then I will.

> Savoy Hotel,
> Victoria Embankment, London.
> Dearest of all Boys,
> Your letter was delightful, red and yellow wine to me; but I am sad and out of sorts. Bosie,[1] you must not make scenes with me. They kill me, they wreck the loveliness of life. I cannot see you, so Greek and gracious, distorted with passion. I cannot listen to your curved lips saying hideous things to me. I would sooner——than have you bitter, unjust, hating.... I must see you soon. You are the divine thing I want, the thing of grace and beauty; but I don't know how to do it. Shall I come to Salisbury? My bill here is £49 for a week. I have also got a new sitting-room.... Why are you not here, my dear, my wonderful boy? I fear I must leave—no money, no credit, and a heart of lead.
> Your own Oscar. ...

Is that an ordinary letter?

WILDE.   Everything I write is extraordinary. I do not pose as being ordinary, great heavens! Ask me any question you like about it.

CARSON.   Is it the kind of letter a man writes to another?

WILDE.   It was a tender expression of my great admiration for Lord Alfred Douglas. It was not, like the other, a prose poem.

---

[1]   *Bosie* Lord Alfred Douglas's nickname.

Sir Arthur Conan Doyle
1859 – 1930

British Detective Sherlock Holmes is so renowned that his fame outstrips that of his creator, Sir Arthur Conan Doyle. Conan Doyle wrote many other sorts of fiction, as well as books on history, war, and supernatural subjects, and although some were very successful, they never roused the interest generated by the man with the deerstalker cap, calabash pipe, and magnifying glass, who solved crimes using "elementary" deductions, abetted by the faithful Dr. Watson. When Conan Doyle grew bored with his creation and tried to kill off Holmes and his evil nemesis Professor Moriarty, his reading public wore arm bands to display their mourning, and publishers offered such enormous sums to have Holmes revived that Conan Doyle eventually succumbed to pressure and brought his character back to life.

For Conan Doyle, life began in Edinburgh, Scotland, in 1859. His father, Charles Altamont Doyle, was a civil servant with artistic aspirations, but alcoholism and epilepsy eventually caused him to be institutionalized. Conan Doyle's mother, Mary Foley Doyle, encouraged her son's voluminous appetite for books and his literary aspirations, even though unrelieved poverty made educating her ten children a financial struggle. When Conan Doyle came of age, he studied medicine at Edinburgh University—where he met Dr. Joseph Bell, the man who became the model for Sherlock Holmes—and earned his medical degree in 1881. During a subsequent medical stint in Southsea near Portsmouth, where his practice was undemanding and left him ample spare time, he began writing; he devoted himself to it full-time beginning in 1891.

Conan Doyle's first Sherlock Holmes adventure, *A Study in Scarlet*, was written in Southsea and published in the 1887 *Beeton Christmas Annual*. After he had published his second Holmes story, *The Sign of the Four*, in *Lippincott's Magazine* in 1890, *The Strand Magazine* began featuring "The Adventures of Sherlock Holmes." (The illustrations by Sidney Paget that accompany "The Adventure of the Speckled Band," below, are from its original publication in *The Strand* in 1892.) In an age of great scientific discovery, the public became captivated by Holmes's cool, rational, almost superhuman reasoning skills, but readers also responded to his all-too-human problems, such as his fear of emotional ties and his cocaine habit. Conan Doyle created other memorable characters in such books as *Micah Clarke* (1889) and *The Lost World* (1912), but none attained Holmes's cachet, much to Conan Doyle's chagrin. In 1891 he complained that the Sherlock Holmes adventures held back his writing career: "I'm thinking of slaying Holmes," he said in a letter to his mother, "He takes my mind from better things."

Whether or not these other "things" were better, Conan Doyle penned much fine work alongside his Sherlock Holmes adventures, including the historical novel *The White Company* (1891) and the science-fiction novella *The Poison Belt* (1913). He also adapted some of his Holmes stories, such as "The Adventure of the Speckled Band," for the stage. After serving in the Boer War in South Africa, he was knighted in recognition of two treatises he had written in support of the war. In the final decades of his life, most notably after the death of his son in World War I, Conan Doyle became immersed in spiritualism and the occult, writing and lecturing extensively on the subject.

After returning from an exhaustive lecture tour in 1929, Conan Doyle suffered a heart attack. He never regained his health and he died in 1930. He is buried in the rose garden at Windlesham, his home in Sussex, where he had lived with his second wife (his first wife had died in 1906) and children.

⌘ ⌘ ⌘

The Adventure of the Speckled Band

In glancing over my notes of the seventy odd cases in which I have during the last eight years studied the methods of my friend Sherlock Holmes, I find many tragic, some comic, a large number merely strange, but none commonplace; for, working as he did rather for the love of his art than for the acquirement of wealth, he refused to associate himself with any investigation which did not tend towards the unusual, and even the fantastic. Of all these varied cases, however, I cannot recall any which presented more singular features than that which was associated with the well-known Surrey family of the Roylotts of Stoke Moran. The events in question occurred in the early days of my association with Holmes, when we were sharing rooms as bachelors, in Baker Street. It is possible that I might have placed them upon record before, but a promise of secrecy was made at the time, from which I have only been freed during the last month by the untimely death of the lady to whom the pledge was given. It is perhaps as well that the facts should now come to light, for I have reasons to know there are widespread rumours as to the death of Dr. Grimesby Roylott which tend to make the matter even more terrible than the truth.

It was early in April, the year '83, that I woke one morning to find Sherlock Holmes standing, fully dressed, by the side of my bed. He was a late riser as a rule, and, as the clock on the mantelpiece showed me that it was only a quarter past seven, I blinked up at him in some surprise, and perhaps just a little resentment, for I was myself regular in my habits.

"Very sorry to knock you up,[1] Watson," said he, "but it's the common lot this morning. Mrs. Hudson has

been knocked up, she retorted upon me, and I on you."

"What is it, then? A fire?"

"No, a client. It seems that a young lady has arrived in a considerable state of excitement, who insists upon seeing me. She is waiting now in the sitting room. Now, when young ladies wander about the metropolis at this hour of the morning, and knock sleepy people up out of their beds, I presume that it is something very pressing which they have to communicate. Should it prove to be an interesting case, you would, I am sure, wish to follow it from the outset. I thought at any rate that I should call you, and give you the chance."

"My dear fellow, I would not miss it for anything."

I had no keener pleasure than in following Holmes in his professional investigations, and in admiring the rapid deductions, as swift as intuitions, and yet always founded on a logical basis, with which he unravelled the problems which were submitted to him. I rapidly threw on my clothes, and was ready in a few minutes to accompany my friend down to the sitting room. A lady dressed in black and heavily veiled, who had been sitting in the window, rose as we entered.

"Good morning, madam," said Holmes cheerily. "My name is Sherlock Holmes. This is my intimate friend and associate, Dr. Watson, before whom you can speak as freely as before myself. Ha, I am glad to see that Mrs. Hudson has had the good sense to light the fire. Pray draw up to it, and I shall order you a cup of hot coffee, for I observe that you are shivering."

"It is not cold which makes me shiver," said the woman in a low voice, changing her seat as requested.

"What then?"

"It is fear, Mr. Holmes. It is terror." She raised her veil as she spoke, and we could see that she was indeed in a pitiable state of agitation, her face all drawn and grey, with restless, frightened eyes, like those of some

[1] *knock you up* I.e., "wake you up with a knock at the door." (This usage remains current in some parts of Britain.)

hunted animal. Her features and figure were those of a woman of thirty, but her hair was shot with premature grey, and her expression was weary and haggard. Sherlock Holmes ran her over with one of his quick, all-comprehensive glances.[1]

"She raised her veil."

"You must not fear," said he soothingly, bending forward and patting her forearm. "We shall soon set matters right, I have no doubt. You have come in by train this morning, I see."

"You know me, then?"

"No, but I observe the second half of a return ticket in the palm of your left glove. You must have started early, and yet you had a good drive in a dog-cart, along heavy roads, before you reached the station."

The lady gave a violent start, and stared in bewilderment at my companion.

"There is no mystery, my dear madam," said he, smiling. "The left arm of your jacket is spattered with mud in no less than seven places. The marks are perfectly fresh. There is no vehicle save a dog-cart which throws up mud in that way, and then only when you sit on the left-hand side of the driver."

"Whatever your reasons may be, you are perfectly correct," said she. "I started from home before six, reached Leatherhead at twenty past, and came in by the first train to Waterloo. Sir, I can stand this strain no

longer, I shall go mad if it continues. I have no one to turn to—none, save only one, who cares for me, and he, poor fellow, can be of little aid. I have heard of you, Mr. Holmes; I have heard of you from Mrs. Farintosh, whom you helped in the hour of her sore need. It was from her that I had your address. Oh, sir, do you not think you could help me too, and at least throw a little light through the dense darkness which surrounds me? At present it is out of my power to reward you for your services, but in a month or two I shall be married, with the control of my own income, and then at least you shall not find me ungrateful."

Holmes turned to his desk, and unlocking it, drew out a small casebook which he consulted.

"Farintosh," said he. "Ah, yes, I recall the case; it was concerned with an opal tiara. I think it was before your time, Watson. I can only say, madam, that I shall be happy to devote the same care to your case as I did to that of your friend. As to reward, my profession is its reward; but you are at liberty to defray whatever expenses I may be put to, at the time which suits you best. And now I beg that you will lay before us everything that may help us in forming an opinion upon the matter."

"Alas!" replied our visitor. "The very horror of my situation lies in the fact that my fears are so vague, and my suspicions depend so entirely upon small points, which might seem trivial to another, that even he to whom of all others I have a right to look for help and advice looks upon all that I tell him about it as the fancies of a nervous woman. He does not say so, but I can read it from his soothing answers and averted eyes. But I have heard, Mr. Holmes, that you can see deeply into the manifold wickedness of the human heart. You may advise me how to walk amid the dangers which encompass me."

"I am all attention, madam."

"My name is Helen Stoner, and I am living with my stepfather, who is the last survivor of one of the oldest Saxon families in England, the Roylotts of Stoke Moran, on the western border of Surrey."

Holmes nodded his head. "The name is familiar to me," said he.

"The family was at one time among the richest in England, and the estate extended over the borders into Berkshire in the north, and Hampshire in the west. In

[1] *She raised her veil ... glances* The illustration of this scene is by Sidney Paget; it accompanied the story's original publication in *The Strand Magazine* in 1892. Paget's eight other original illustrations are also included in these pages.

the last century, however, four successive heirs were of a dissolute and wasteful disposition, and the family ruin was eventually completed by a gambler, in the days of the Regency.[1] Nothing was left save a few acres of ground and the two-hundred-year-old house, which is itself crushed under a heavy mortgage. The last squire dragged out his existence there, living the horrible life of an aristocratic pauper; but his only son, my stepfather, seeing that he must adapt himself to the new conditions, obtained an advance from a relative, which enabled him to take a medical degree, and went out to Calcutta, where, by his professional skill and his force of character, he established a large practice. In a fit of anger, however, caused by some robberies which had been perpetrated in the house, he beat his native butler to death, and narrowly escaped a capital sentence. As it was, he suffered a long term of imprisonment, and afterwards returned to England a morose and disappointed man.

"When Dr. Roylott was in India he married my mother, Mrs. Stoner, the young widow of Major-General Stoner, of the Bengal Artillery. My sister Julia and I were twins, and we were only two years old at the time of my mother's re-marriage. She had a considerable sum of money, not less than a thousand a year, and this she bequeathed to Dr. Roylott entirely whilst we resided with him, with a provision that a certain annual sum should be allowed to each of us in the event of our marriage. Shortly after our return to England my mother died—she was killed eight years ago in a railway accident near Crewe. Dr. Roylott then abandoned his attempts to establish himself in practice in London, and took us to live with him in the ancestral house at Stoke Moran. The money which my mother had left was enough for all our wants, and there seemed no obstacle to our happiness.

"But a terrible change came over our stepfather about this time. Instead of making friends and exchanging visits with our neighbours, who had at first been overjoyed to see a Roylott of Stoke Moran back in the old family seat, he shut himself up in his house, and seldom came out save to indulge in ferocious quarrels with whoever might cross his path. Violence of temper approaching to mania has been hereditary in the men of the family, and in my stepfather's case it had, I believe, been intensified by his long residence in the tropics. A series of disgraceful brawls took place, two of which ended in the police-court, until at last he became the terror of the village, and the folks would fly at his approach, for he is a man of immense strength, and absolutely uncontrollable in his anger.

"He hurled the blacksmith over a parapet."

"Last week he hurled the local blacksmith over a parapet[2] into a stream and it was only by paying over all the money that I could gather together that I was able to avert another public exposure. He had no friends at all save the wandering gypsies, and he would give these vagabonds leave to encamp upon the few acres of bramble-covered land which represent the family estate, and would accept in return the hospitality of their tents, wandering away with them sometimes for weeks on end. He has a passion also for Indian animals, which are sent over to him by a correspondent, and he has at this moment a cheetah and a baboon, which wander freely over his grounds, and are feared by the villagers almost as much as their master.

---

[1] *the Regency* I.e., 1810–20, the period in which George, Prince of Wales, acted as regent for his father, George III, who was incapacitated by mental illness.

[2] *parapet* Stone embankment.

"You can imagine from what I say that my poor sister Julia and I had no great pleasure in our lives. No servant would stay with us, and for a long time we did all the work of the house. She was but thirty at the time of her death, and yet her hair had already begun to whiten, even as mine has."

"Your sister is dead, then?"

"She died just two years ago, and it is of her death that I wish to speak to you. You can understand that, living the life which I have described, we were little likely to see anyone of our own age and position. We had, however, an aunt, my mother's maiden sister, Miss Honoria Westphail, who lives near Harrow, and we were occasionally allowed to pay short visits at this lady's house. Julia went there at Christmas two years ago, and met there a half-pay Major[1] of Marines, to whom she became engaged. My stepfather learned of the engagement when my sister returned, and offered no objection to the marriage; but within a fortnight of the day which had been fixed for the wedding, the terrible event occurred which has deprived me of my only companion."

Sherlock Holmes had been leaning back in his chair with his eyes closed, and his head sunk in a cushion, but he half opened his lids now, and glanced across at his visitor.

"Pray be precise as to details," said he.

"It is easy for me to be so, for every event of that dreadful time is seared into my memory. The manor house is, as I have already said, very old, and only one wing is now inhabited. The bedrooms in this wing are on the ground floor, the sitting rooms being in the central block of the buildings. Of these bedrooms, the first is Dr. Roylott's, the second my sister's, and the third my own. There is no communication between them, but they all open out into the same corridor. Do I make myself plain?"

"Perfectly so."

"The windows of the three rooms open out upon the lawn. That fatal night Dr. Roylott had gone to his room early, though we knew that he had not retired to rest, for my sister was troubled by the smell of the strong Indian cigars which it was his custom to smoke. She left her room, therefore, and came into mine, where she sat for some time, chatting about her approaching wedding.

---

[1] *half-pay Major*   When retired or not in service, officers were paid half their wages.

At eleven o'clock she rose to leave me, but she paused at the door and looked back. 'Tell me, Helen,' said she, 'have you ever heard anyone whistle in the dead of the night?'

"'Never,' said I.

"'I suppose that you could not possibly whistle yourself in your sleep?'

"'Certainly not. But why?'

"'Because during the last few nights I have always, about three in the morning, heard a low clear whistle. I am a light sleeper, and it has awakened me. I cannot tell where it came from—perhaps from the next room, perhaps from the lawn. I thought that I would just ask you whether you had heard it.'

"'No, I have not. It must be those wretched gypsies in the plantation.'

"'Very likely. And yet if it were on the lawn I wonder that you did not hear it also.'

"'Ah, but I sleep more heavily than you.'

"'Well, it is of no great consequence, at any rate,' she smiled back at me, closed my door, and a few moments later I heard her key turn in the lock."

"Indeed," said Holmes. "Was it your custom always to lock yourselves in at night?"

"Always."

"And why?"

"I think that I mentioned to you that the doctor kept a cheetah and a baboon. We had no feeling of security unless our doors were locked."

"Quite so. Pray proceed with your statement."

"I could not sleep that night. A vague feeling of impending misfortune impressed me. My sister and I, you will recollect, were twins, and you know how subtle are the links which bind two souls which are so closely allied. It was a wild night. The wind was howling outside, and the rain was beating and splashing against the windows. Suddenly, amidst all the hubbub of the gale, there burst forth the wild scream of a terrified woman. I knew that it was my sister's voice. I sprang from my bed, wrapped a shawl round me, and rushed into the corridor. As I opened my door I seemed to hear a low whistle, such as my sister described, and a few moments later a clanging sound, as if a mass of metal had fallen. As I ran down the passage my sister's door was unlocked, and revolved slowly upon its hinges. I stared at it horror-stricken, not knowing what was about

"Her face blanched with terror."

to issue from it. By the light of the corridor lamp I saw my sister appear at the opening, her face blanched with terror, her hands groping for help, her whole figure swaying to and fro like that of a drunkard. I ran to her and threw my arms round her, but at that moment her knees seemed to give way and she fell to the ground. She writhed as one who is in terrible pain, and her limbs were dreadfully convulsed. At first I thought that she had not recognized me, but as I bent over her she suddenly shrieked out in a voice which I shall never forget, 'O, my God! Helen! It was the band! The speckled band!' There was something else which she would fain have said, and she stabbed with her finger into the air in the direction of the doctor's room, but a fresh convulsion seized her and choked her words. I rushed out, calling loudly for my stepfather, and I met him hastening from his room in his dressing gown. When he reached my sister's side she was unconscious, and though he poured brandy down her throat, and sent for medical aid from the village, all efforts were in vain, for she slowly sank and died without having recovered her consciousness. Such was the dreadful end of my beloved sister."

"One moment," said Holmes; "are you sure about this whistle and metallic sound? Could you swear to it?"

"That was what the county coroner asked me at the inquiry. It was my strong impression that I heard it, and yet among the crash of the gale, and the creaking of an old house, I may possibly have been deceived."

"Was your sister dressed?"

"No, she was in her nightdress. In her right hand was found the charred stump of a match, and in her left a matchbox."

"Showing that she had struck a light and looked about her when the alarm took place. That is important. And what conclusions did the coroner come to?"

"He investigated the case with great care, for Dr. Roylott's conduct had long been notorious in the county, but he was unable to find any satisfactory cause of death. My evidence showed that the door had been fastened upon the inner side, and the windows were blocked by old-fashioned shutters with broad iron bars, which were secured every night. The walls were carefully sounded, and were shown to be quite solid all round, and the flooring was also thoroughly examined, with the same result. The chimney is wide, but is barred up by four large staples. It is certain, therefore, that my sister was quite alone when she met her end. Besides, there were no marks of any violence upon her."

"How about poison?"

"The doctors examined her for it, but without success."

"What do you think that this unfortunate lady died of, then?"

"It is my belief that she died of pure fear and nervous shock, though what it was which frightened her I cannot imagine."

"Were there gypsies in the plantation at the time?"

"Yes, there are nearly always some there."

"Ah, and what did you gather from this allusion to a band—a speckled band?"

"Sometimes I have thought that it was merely the wild talk of delirium, sometimes that it may have referred to some band of people, perhaps to these very gypsies in the plantation. I do not know whether the spotted handkerchiefs which so many of them wear over their heads might have suggested the strange adjective which she used."

Holmes shook his head like a man who is far from being satisfied.

"These are very deep waters," said he; "pray go on with your narrative."

"Two years have passed since then, and my life has been until lately lonelier than ever. A month ago, however, a dear friend, whom I have known for many years, has done me the honour to ask my hand in marriage. His name is Armitage—Percy Armitage—the second son of Mr. Armitage, of Crane Water, near Reading. My stepfather has offered no opposition to the match, and we are to be married in the course of the spring. Two days ago some repairs were started in the west wing of the building, and my bedroom wall has been pierced, so that I have had to move into the chamber in which my sister died, and to sleep in the very bed in which she slept. Imagine, then, my thrill of terror when last night, as I lay awake, thinking over her terrible fate, I suddenly heard in the silence of the night the low whistle which had been the herald of her own death. I sprang up and lit the lamp, but nothing was to be seen in the room. I was too shaken to go to bed again, however, so I dressed, and as soon as it was daylight I slipped down, got a dog-cart at the Crown Inn, which is opposite, and drove to Leatherhead, from whence I have come on this morning, with the one object of seeing you and asking your advice."

"You have done wisely," said my friend. "But have you told me all?"

"Yes, all."

"Miss Stoner, you have not. You are screening your stepfather."

"Why, what do you mean?"

For answer Holmes pushed back the frill of black lace which fringed the hand that lay upon our visitor's knee. Five little livid spots, the marks of four fingers and a thumb, were printed upon the white wrist.

"You have been cruelly used," said Holmes.

The lady coloured deeply, and covered over her injured wrist. "He is a hard man," she said, "and perhaps he hardly knows his own strength."

There was a long silence, during which Holmes leaned his chin upon his hands and stared into the crackling fire.

"This is very deep business," he said at last. "There are a thousand details which I should desire to know before I decide upon our course of action. Yet we have not a moment to lose. If we were to come to Stoke Moran today, would it be possible for us to see over these rooms without the knowledge of your stepfather?"

"As it happens, he spoke of coming into town today upon some most important business. It is probable that he will be away all day, and that there would be nothing to disturb you. We have a housekeeper now, but she is old and foolish, and I could easily get her out of the way."

"Excellent. You are not averse to this trip, Watson?"

"By no means."

"Then we shall both come. What are you going to do yourself?"

"I have one or two things which I would wish to do now that I am in town. But I shall return by the twelve o'clock train, so as to be there in time for your coming."

"And you may expect us early in the afternoon. I have myself some small business matters to attend to. Will you not wait and breakfast?"

"No, I must go. My heart is lightened already since I have confided my trouble to you. I shall look forward to seeing you again this afternoon." She dropped her thick black veil over her face, and glided from the room.

"And what do you think of it all, Watson?" asked Sherlock Holmes, leaning back in his chair.

"It seems to me to be a most dark and sinister business."

"Dark enough and sinister enough."

"Yet if the lady is correct in saying that the flooring and walls are sound, and that the door, window, and chimney are impassable, then her sister must have been undoubtedly alone when she met her mysterious end."

"What becomes, then, of these nocturnal whistles, and what of the very peculiar words of the dying woman?"

"I cannot think."

"When you combine the ideas of whistles at night, the presence of a band of gypsies who are on intimate terms with this old doctor, the fact that we have every reason to believe that the doctor has an interest in preventing his stepdaughter's marriage, the dying allusion to a band, and finally, the fact that Miss Helen Stoner heard a metallic clang, which might have been caused by one of those metal bars which secured the shutters falling back into their place, I think there is good ground to think that the mystery may be cleared along these lines."

"But what, then, did the gypsies do?"

"I cannot imagine."

"I see many objections to any such a theory."

"And so do I. It is precisely for that reason that we are going to Stoke Moran this day. I want to see whether the objections are fatal, or if they may be explained away. But what, in the name of the devil!"

The ejaculation had been drawn from my companion by the fact that our door had been suddenly dashed open, and that a huge man framed himself in the aperture. His costume was a peculiar mixture of the professional and of the agricultural, having a black top hat, a long frock-coat, and a pair of high gaiters,[1] with a hunting-crop swinging in his hand. So tall was he that his hat actually brushed the crossbar of the doorway, and his breadth seemed to span it across from side to side. A large face, seared with a thousand wrinkles, burned yellow with the sun, and marked with every evil passion, was turned from one to the other of us, while his deep-set, bile-shot eyes, and the high thin fleshless nose, gave him somewhat the resemblance to a fierce old bird of prey.

"Which of you is Holmes?"

"Which of you is Holmes?" asked this apparition.

"My name, sir, but you have the advantage of me," said my companion quietly.

"I am Dr. Grimesby Roylott, of Stoke Moran."

"Indeed, Doctor," said Holmes blandly. "Pray take a seat."

"I will do nothing of the kind. My stepdaughter has been here. I have traced her. What has she been saying to you?"

"It is a little cold for the time of the year," said Holmes.

"What has she been saying to you?" screamed the old man furiously.

"But I have heard that the crocuses promise well," continued my companion imperturbably.

"Ha! You put me off, do you?" said our new visitor, taking a step forward, and shaking his hunting crop. "I know you, you scoundrel! I have heard of you before. You are Holmes the meddler."

My friend smiled.

"Holmes the busybody!"

His smile broadened.

"Holmes the Scotland Yard jack-in-office."[2]

Holmes chuckled heartily. "Your conversation is most entertaining," said he. "When you go out close the door, for there is a decided draught."

"I will go when I have had my say. Don't you dare to meddle with my affairs. I know that Miss Stoner has been here—I traced her! I am a dangerous man to fall foul of! See here." He stepped swiftly forward, seized the poker, and bent it into a curve with his huge brown hands.

"See that you keep yourself out of my grip," he snarled, and hurling the twisted poker into the fireplace, he strode out of the room.

"He seems a very amiable person," said Holmes, laughing. "I am not quite so bulky, but if he had remained I might have shown him that my grip was not much more feeble than his own." As he spoke he picked up the steel poker, and with a sudden effort straightened it out again.

"Fancy his having the insolence to confound me with the official detective force! This incident gives zest to our investigation, however, and I only trust that our little friend will not suffer from her imprudence in allowing this brute to trace her. And now, Watson, we shall order breakfast, and afterwards I shall walk down

---

[1] *gaiters* Coverings of cloth or leather for the lower legs.

[2] *jack-in-office* Insolent minor official.

to Doctors' Commons,[1] where I hope to get some data which may help us in this matter."

It was nearly one o'clock when Sherlock Holmes returned from his excursion. He held in his hand a sheet of blue paper, scrawled over with notes and figures.

"I have seen the will of the deceased wife," said he. "To determine its exact meaning I have been obliged to work out the present prices of the investments with which it is concerned. The total income, which at the time of the wife's death was little short of £1,100, is now through the fall in agricultural prices not more than £750. Each daughter can claim an income of £250, in case of marriage. It is evident, therefore, that if both girls had married this beauty would have had a mere pittance, while even one of them would cripple him to a serious extent. My morning's work has not been wasted, since it has proved that he has the very strongest motives for standing in the way of anything of the sort. And now, Watson, this is too serious for dawdling, especially as the old man is aware that we are interesting ourselves in his affairs, so if you are ready we shall call a cab and drive to Waterloo. I should be very much obliged if you would slip your revolver into your pocket. An Eley's No. 2[2] is an excellent argument with gentlemen who can twist steel pokers into knots. That and a toothbrush are, I think, all that we need."

At Waterloo we were fortunate in catching a train for Leatherhead, where we hired a trap[3] at the station inn, and drove for four or five miles through the lovely Surrey lanes. It was a perfect day, with a bright sun and a few fleecy clouds in the heavens. The trees and wayside hedges were just throwing out their first green shoots, and the air was full of the pleasant smell of the moist earth. To me at least was a strange contrast between the sweet promise of the spring and this sinister quest upon which we were engaged. My companion sat in front of the trap, his arms folded, his hat pulled down over his eyes, and his chin sunk upon his breast, buried in the deepest thought.

Suddenly, however, he started, tapped me on the shoulder, and pointed over the meadows.

"Look there!" said he.

A heavily timbered park stretched up in a gentle slope, thickening into a grove at the highest point. From amidst the branches there jutted out the grey gables and high roof-tree[4] of a very old mansion.

"Stoke Moran?" said he.

"Yes, sir, that be the house of Dr. Grimesby Roylott," remarked the driver.

"There is some building going on there," said Holmes; "that is where we are going."

"There's the village," said the driver, pointing to a cluster of roofs some distance to the left; "but if you want to get to the house, you'll find it shorter to go over this stile,[5] and so by the footpath over the fields. There it is, where the lady is walking."

"And the lady, I fancy, is Miss Stoner," observed Holmes, shading his eyes. "Yes, I think we had better do as you suggest."

We got off, paid our fare, and the trap rattled back on its way to Leatherhead.

"We got off, paid our fare."

"I thought it as well," said Holmes, as we climbed the stile, "that this fellow should think we had come here as architects, or on some definite business. It may stop his gossip. Good afternoon, Miss Stoner. You see that we have been as good as our word."

---

1 *Doctors' Commons* Buildings that housed the association of Doctors of Civil Law in London.

2 *Eley's No. 2* Conan Doyle is likely referring to a small but powerful pistol called a "Webley No. 2," which could be loaded with cartridges made by the ammunition manufacturer Eley.

3 *trap* Small, two-wheeled carriage.

4 *roof-tree* Ridge pole.

5 *stile* Set of steps passing over a fence.

Our client of the morning had hurried forward to meet us with a face which spoke her joy. "I have been waiting so eagerly for you," she cried, shaking hands with us warmly. "All has turned out splendidly. Dr. Roylott has gone to town, and it is unlikely that he will be back before evening."

"We have had the pleasure of making the doctor's acquaintance," said Holmes, and in a few words he sketched out what had occurred. Miss Stoner turned white to the lips as she listened.

"Good heavens!" she cried, "he has followed me, then."

"So it appears."

"He is so cunning that I never know when I am safe from him. What will he say when he returns?"

"He must guard himself, for he may find that there is someone more cunning than himself upon his track. You must lock yourself from him tonight. If he is violent, we shall take you away to your aunt's at Harrow. Now, we must make the best use of our time, so kindly take us at once to the rooms which we are to examine."

The building was of grey, lichen-blotched stone, with a high central portion, and two curving wings, like the claws of a crab, thrown out on each side. In one of these wings the windows were broken and blocked with wooden boards, while the roof was partly caved in, a picture of ruin. The central portion was in little better repair, but the right-hand block was comparatively modern, and the blinds in the windows, with the blue smoke curling up from the chimneys, showed that this was where the family resided. Some scaffolding had been erected against the end wall, and the stonework had been broken into, but there were no signs of any workmen at the moment of our visit. Holmes walked slowly up and down the ill-trimmed lawn, and examined with deep attention the outsides of the windows.

"This, I take it, belongs to the room in which you used to sleep, the centre one to your sister's, and the one next to the main building to Dr. Roylott's chamber?"

"Exactly so. But I am now sleeping in the middle one."

"Pending the alterations, as I understand. By the way, there does not seem to be any very pressing need for repairs at that end wall."

"There were none. I believe that it was an excuse to move me from my room."

"Ah! that is suggestive. Now, on the other side of this narrow wing runs the corridor from which these three rooms open. There are windows in it, of course?"

"Yes, but very small ones. Too narrow for anyone to pass through."

"As you both locked your doors at night, your rooms were unapproachable from that side. Now, would you have the kindness to go into your room, and to bar your shutters."

Miss Stoner did so, and Holmes, after a careful examination through the open window, endeavoured in every way to force the shutter open, but without success. There was no slit through which a knife could be passed to raise the bar. Then with his lens[1] he tested the hinges, but they were of solid iron, built firmly into the massive masonry. "Hum!" said he, scratching his chin in some perplexity, "my theory certainly presents some difficulties. No one could pass these shutters if they were bolted. Well, we shall see if the inside throws any light upon the matter."

A small side door led into the white-washed corridor from which the three bedrooms opened. Holmes refused to examine the third chamber, so we passed at once to the second, that in which Miss Stoner was now sleeping, and in which her sister had met her fate. It was a homely[2] little room, with a low ceiling and a gaping fireplace, after the fashion of old country houses. A brown chest of drawers stood in one corner, a narrow white-counterpaned bed in another, and a dressing-table on the left-hand side of the window. These articles, with two small wicker-work chairs, made up all the furniture in the room, save for a square of Wilton carpet[3] in the centre. The boards round and the panelling of the walls were brown, worm-eaten oak, so old and discoloured that it may have dated from the original building of the house. Holmes drew one of the chairs into a corner and

---

[1] *lens* Magnifying glass.

[2] *homely* Simple, unsophisticated.

[3] *Wilton carpet* Brand of carpet made in Wilton, England.

sat silent, while his eyes travelled round and round and up and down, taking in every detail of the apartment.

"Where does that bell communicate with?" he asked at last, pointing to a thick bell-rope which hung down beside the bed, the tassel actually lying upon the pillow.

"It goes to the housekeeper's room."

"It looks newer than the other things?"

"Yes, it was only put there a couple of years ago."

"Your sister asked for it, I suppose?"

"No, I never heard of her using it. We used always to get what we wanted for ourselves."

"Indeed, it seemed unnecessary to put so nice a bell-pull there. You will excuse me for a few minutes while I satisfy myself as to this floor." He threw himself down upon his face with his lens in his hand, and crawled swiftly backwards and forwards, examining minutely the cracks between the boards. Then he did the same with the woodwork with which the chamber was panelled. Finally he walked over to the bed and spent some time in staring at it, and in running his eye up and down the wall. Finally he took the bell-rope in his hand and gave it a brisk tug.

"Why, it's a dummy," said he.

"Won't it ring?"

"No, it is not even attached to a wire. This is very interesting. You can see now that it is fastened to a hook just above where the little opening of the ventilator is."

"How very absurd! I never noticed that before."

"Very strange!" muttered Holmes, pulling at the rope. "There are one or two very singular points about this room. For example, what a fool a builder must be to open a ventilator in another room, when, with the same trouble, he might have communicated with the outside air!"

"That is also quite modern," said the lady.

"Done about the same time as the bell-rope," remarked Holmes.

"Yes, there were several little changes carried out about that time."

"They seem to have been of a most interesting character—dummy bell-ropes, and ventilators which do not ventilate. With your permission, Miss Stoner, we shall now carry our researches into the inner apartment."

Dr. Grimesby Roylott's chamber was larger than that of his stepdaughter, but was as plainly furnished. A camp bed, a small wooden shelf full of books, mostly of a technical character, an armchair beside the bed, a plain wooden chair against the wall, a round table, and a large iron safe were the principal things which met the eye. Holmes walked slowly round and examined each and all of them with the keenest interest.

"What's in here?" he asked, tapping the safe.

"My stepfather's business papers."

"Oh! you have seen inside, then?"

"Only once, some years ago. I remember that it was full of papers."

"There isn't a cat in it, for example?"

"No. What a strange idea!"

"Well, look at this!" He took up a small saucer of milk which stood on the top of it.

"Well, look at this."

"No; we don't keep a cat. But there is a cheetah and a baboon."

"Ah, yes, of course! Well, a cheetah is just a big cat, and yet a saucer of milk does not go very far in satisfying its wants, I daresay. There is one point which I should wish to determine." He squatted down in front of the wooden chair, and examined the seat of it with the greatest attention.

"Thank you. That is quite settled," said he, rising and putting his lens in his pocket. "Hullo! Here is something interesting!"

The object which had caught his eye was a small dog lash hung on one corner of the bed. The lash, however, was curled upon itself, and tied so as to make a loop of whipcord.

"What do you make of that, Watson?"

"It's a common enough lash. But I don't know why it should be tied."

"That is not quite so common, is it? Ah, me! It's a wicked world, and when a clever man turns his brain to crime it is the worst of all. I think that I have seen enough now, Miss Stoner, and, with your permission, we shall walk out upon the lawn."

I had never seen my friend's face so grim, or his brow so dark, as it was when we turned from the scene of this investigation. We had walked several times up and down the lawn, neither Miss Stoner nor myself liking to break in upon his thoughts before he roused himself from his reverie. "It is very essential, Miss Stoner," said he, "that you should absolutely follow my advice in every respect."

"I shall most certainly do so."

"The matter is too serious for any hesitation. Your life may depend upon your compliance."

"I assure you that I am in your hands."

"In the first place, both my friend and I must spend the night in your room."

Both Miss Stoner and I gazed at him in astonishment.

"Yes, it must be so. Let me explain. I believe that that is the village inn over there?"

"Yes, that is the Crown."

"Very good. Your windows would be visible from there?"

"Certainly."

"You must confine yourself to your room, on pretence of a headache, when your stepfather comes back. Then when you hear him retire for the night, you must open the shutters of your window, undo the hasp, put your lamp there as a signal to us, and then withdraw with everything which you are likely to want into the room which you used to occupy. I have no doubt that, in spite of the repairs, you could manage there for one night."

"Oh, yes, easily."

"The rest you will leave in our hands."

"But what will you do?"

"We shall spend the night in your room, and we shall investigate the cause of this noise which has disturbed you."

"I believe, Mr. Holmes, that you have already made up your mind," said Miss Stoner, laying her hand upon my companion's sleeve.

"Perhaps I have."

"Then for pity's sake tell me what was the cause of my sister's death."

"I should prefer to have clearer proofs before I speak."

"You can at least tell me whether my own thought is correct, and if she died from some sudden fright."

"Good-bye, and be brave."

"No, I do not think so. I think that there was probably some more tangible cause. And now, Miss Stoner, we must leave you, for if Dr. Roylott returned and saw us, our journey would be in vain. Goodbye, and be brave, for if you will do what I have told you, you may rest assured that we shall soon drive away the dangers that threaten you."

Sherlock Holmes and I had no difficulty in engaging a bedroom and sitting room at the Crown Inn. They were on the upper floor, and from our window we could command a view of the avenue gate, and of the inhabited wing of Stoke Moran Manor House. At dusk we saw Dr. Grimesby Roylott drive past, his huge form looming up beside the little figure of the lad who drove him. The boy had some slight difficulty in undoing the heavy iron gates, and we heard the hoarse roar of the doctor's voice, and saw the fury with which he shook his clenched fists at him. The trap drove on, and a few minutes later we saw a sudden light spring up among the trees as the lamp was lit in one of the sitting rooms.

"Do you know, Watson," said Holmes, as we sat together in the gathering darkness, "I have really some scruples as to taking you tonight. There is a distinct element of danger."

"Can I be of assistance?"

"Your presence might be invaluable."

"Then I shall certainly come."

"It is very kind of you."

"You speak of danger. You have evidently seen more in these rooms than was visible to me."

"No, but I fancy that I may have deduced a little more. I imagine that you saw all that I did."

"I saw nothing remarkable save the bell-rope, and what purpose that could answer I confess is more than I can imagine."

"You saw the ventilator, too?"

"Yes, but I do not think that it is such a very unusual thing to have a small opening between two rooms. It was so small that a rat could hardly pass through."

"I knew that we should find a ventilator before ever we came to Stoke Moran."

"My dear Holmes!"

"Oh, yes, I did. You remember in her statement she said that her sister could smell Dr. Roylott's cigar. Now, of course that suggests at once that there must be a communication between the two rooms. It could only be a small one, or it would have been remarked upon at the coroner's inquiry. I deduced a ventilator."

"But what harm can there be in that?"

"Well, there is at least a curious coincidence of dates. A ventilator is made, a cord is hung, and a lady who sleeps in the bed dies. Does not that strike you?"

"I cannot as yet see any connection."

"Did you observe anything very peculiar about that bed?"

"No."

"It was clamped to the floor. Did you ever see a bed fastened like that before?"

"I cannot say that I have."

"The lady could not move her bed. It must always be in the same relative position to the ventilator and to the rope—for so we may call it, since it was clearly never meant for a bell-pull."

"Holmes," I cried, "I seem to see dimly what you are hitting at. We are only just in time to prevent some subtle and horrible crime."

"Subtle enough and horrible enough. When a doctor does go wrong he is the first of criminals. He has nerve and he has knowledge. Palmer and Pritchard[1] were among the heads of their profession. This man strikes even deeper, but I think, Watson, that we shall be able to strike deeper still. But we shall have horrors enough before the night is over; for goodness' sake let us have a quiet pipe, and turn our minds for a few hours to something more cheerful."

About nine o'clock the light among the trees was extinguished, and all was dark in the direction of the Manor House. Two hours passed slowly away, and then, suddenly, just at the stroke of eleven, a single bright light shone out right in front of us.

"That is our signal," said Holmes, springing to his feet; "it comes from the middle window."

As we passed out he exchanged a few words with the landlord, explaining that we were going on a late visit to an acquaintance, and that it was possible that we might spend the night there. A moment later we were out on

---

[1]   *Palmer and Pritchard*   Both men were doctors who, in unrelated cases, were executed in the mid-1800s for murdering people using poison.

the dark road, a chill wind blowing in our faces, and one yellow light twinkling in front of us through the gloom to guide us on our sombre errand. There was little difficulty in entering the grounds, for unrepaired breaches gaped in the old park wall. Making our way among the trees, we reached the lawn, crossed it, and were about to enter through the window, when out from a clump of laurel bushes there darted what seemed to be a hideous and distorted child, who threw itself on the grass with writhing limbs, and then ran swiftly across the lawn into the darkness.

"My God!" I whispered, "did you see it?"

Holmes was for the moment as startled as I. His hand closed like a vice upon my wrist in his agitation. Then he broke into a low laugh, and put his lips to my ear.

"It is a nice household," he murmured, "that is the baboon."

I had forgotten the strange pets which the doctor affected. There was a cheetah, too; perhaps we might find it upon our shoulders at any moment. I confess that I felt easier in my mind when, after following Holmes's example and slipping off my shoes, I found myself inside the bedroom. My companion noiselessly closed the shutters, moved the lamp on to the table, and cast his eyes round the room. All was as we had seen it in the daytime. Then creeping up to me and making a trumpet of his hand, he whispered into my ear again so gently that it was all that I could do to distinguish the words:

"The least sound would be fatal to our plans."

I nodded to show that I had heard.

"We must sit without a light. He would see it through the ventilator."

I nodded again.

"Do not go to sleep; your very life may depend upon it. Have your pistol ready in case we should need it. I will sit on the side of the bed, and you in that chair."

I took out my revolver and laid it on the corner of the table. Holmes had brought up a long thin cane, and this he placed upon the bed beside him. By it he laid the box of matches and the stump of a candle. Then he turned down the lamp and we were left in darkness.

How shall I ever forget that dreadful vigil? I could not hear a sound, not even the drawing of a breath, and yet I knew that my companion sat open-eyed, within a few feet of me, in the same state of nervous tension in which I was myself. The shutters cut off the least ray of light, and we waited in absolute darkness. From outside came the occasional cry of a night bird, and once at our very window a long drawn, cat-like whine, which told us that the cheetah was indeed at liberty. Far away we could hear the deep tones of the parish clock, which boomed out every quarter of an hour. How long they seemed, those quarters! Twelve o'clock, and one, and two, and three, and still we sat waiting silently for whatever might befall.

Suddenly there was the momentary gleam of a light up in the direction of the ventilator, which vanished immediately, but was succeeded by a strong smell of burning oil and heated metal. Someone in the next room had lit a dark lantern.[1] I heard a gentle sound of movement, and then all was silent once more, though the smell grew stronger. For half an hour I sat with straining ears. Then suddenly another sound became audible—a very gentle, soothing sound, like that of a small jet of steam escaping continually from a kettle. The instant that we heard it, Holmes sprang from the bed, struck a match, and lashed furiously with his cane at the bell-pull.

"Holmes lashed furiously."

"You see it, Watson?" he yelled. "You see it?"

But I saw nothing. At the moment when Holmes struck the light I heard a low, clear whistle, but the

---

[1] *dark lantern* Lantern with a slide so that its light can be hidden.

sudden glare flashing into my weary eyes made it impossible for me to tell what it was at which my friend lashed so savagely. I could, however, see that his face was deadly pale, and filled with horror and loathing.

He had ceased to strike, and was gazing up at the ventilator, when suddenly there broke from the silence of the night the most horrible cry to which I have ever listened. It swelled up louder and louder, a hoarse yell of pain and fear and anger all mingled in the one dreadful shriek. They say that away down in the village, and even in the distant parsonage, that cry raised the sleepers from their beds. It struck cold to our hearts, and I stood gazing at Holmes, and he at me, until the last echoes of it had died away into the silence from which it rose.

"What can it mean?" I gasped.

"It means that it is all over," Holmes answered. "And perhaps, after all, it is for the best. Take your pistol, and we shall enter Dr. Roylott's room."

With a grave face he lit the lamp, and led the way down the corridor. Twice he struck at the chamber door without any reply from within. Then he turned the handle and entered, I at his heels, with the cocked pistol in my hand.

"He made neither sound nor motion."

It was a singular sight which met our eyes. On the table stood a dark lantern with the shutter half open, throwing a brilliant beam of light upon the iron safe, the door of which was ajar. Beside this table, on the wooden chair, sat Dr. Grimesby Roylott, clad in a long grey dressing gown, his bare ankles protruding beneath, and his feet thrust into red heelless Turkish slippers. Across

his lap lay the short stock with the long lash which we had noticed during the day. His chin was cocked upwards, and his eyes were fixed in a dreadful rigid stare at the corner of the ceiling. Round his brow he had a peculiar yellow band, with brownish speckles, which seemed to be bound tightly round his head. As we entered he made neither sound nor motion.

"The band! The speckled band!" whispered Holmes.

I took a step forward. In an instant his strange headgear began to move, and there reared itself from among his hair the squat diamond-shaped head and puffed neck of a loathsome serpent.

"It is a swamp adder!" cried Holmes—"the deadliest snake in India. He has died within ten seconds of being bitten. Violence does, in truth, recoil upon the violent, and the schemer falls into the pit which he digs for another. Let us thrust this creature back into its den, and we can then remove Miss Stoner to some place of shelter, and let the county police know what has happened."

As he spoke he drew the dog whip swiftly from the dead man's lap, and throwing the noose round the reptile's neck, he drew it from its horrid perch, and, carrying it at arm's length, threw it into the iron safe, which he closed upon it.

Such are the true facts of the death of Dr. Grimesby Roylott, of Stoke Moran. It is not necessary that I should prolong a narrative which has already run to too great a length, by telling how we broke the sad news to the terrified girl, how we conveyed her by the morning train to the care of her good aunt at Harrow, of how the slow process of official inquiry came to the conclusion that the doctor met his fate while indiscreetly playing with a dangerous pet. The little which I had yet to learn of the case was told me by Sherlock Holmes as we travelled back next day.

"I had," said he, "come to an entirely erroneous conclusion, which shows, my dear Watson, how dangerous it always is to reason from insufficient data. The presence of the gypsies, and the use of the word 'band,' which was used by the poor girl, no doubt, to explain the appearance which she had caught a horrid glimpse of by the light of her match, were sufficient to put me upon an entirely wrong scent. I can only claim the merit that I instantly reconsidered my position when, however, it became clear to me that whatever danger threatened an occupant of the room could not come either from the window or the door. My attention was speedily drawn, as I have already remarked to you, to this ventilator, and to the bell-rope which hung down to the bed. The discovery that this was a dummy, and that the bed was clamped to the floor, instantly gave rise to the suspicion that the rope was there as a bridge for something passing through the hole, and coming to the bed. The idea of a snake instantly occurred to me, and when I coupled it with my knowledge that the doctor was furnished with a supply of creatures from India, I felt that I was probably on the right track. The idea of using a form of poison which could not possibly be discovered by any chemical test was just such a one as would occur to a clever and ruthless man who had had an Eastern training. The rapidity with which such a poison would take effect would also, from his point of view, be an advantage. It would be a sharp-eyed coroner indeed who could distinguish the two little dark punctures which would show where the poison fangs had done their work. Then I thought of the whistle. Of course, he must recall the snake before the morning light revealed it to the victim. He had trained it, probably by the use of the milk which we saw, to return to him when summoned. He would put it through the ventilator at the hour that he thought best, with the certainty that it would crawl down the rope, and land on the bed. It might or might not bite the occupant, perhaps she might escape every night for a week, but sooner or later she must fall a victim.

"I had come to these conclusions before ever I had entered his room. An inspection of his chair showed me that he had been in the habit of standing on it, which, of course, would be necessary in order that he should reach the ventilator. The sight of the safe, the saucer of milk, and the loop of whipcord were enough to finally dispel any doubts which may have remained. The metallic clang heard by Miss Stoner was obviously caused by her father hastily closing the door of his safe upon its terrible occupant. Having once made up my mind, you know the steps which I took in order to put the matter to the proof. I heard the creature hiss, as I have no doubt that you did also, and I instantly lit the light and attacked it."

"With the result of driving it through the ventilator."

"And also with the result of causing it to turn upon its master at the other side. Some of the blows of my cane came home, and roused its snakish temper, so that it flew upon the first person it saw. In this way I am no doubt indirectly responsible for Dr. Grimesby Roylott's death, and I cannot say that it is likely to weigh very heavily upon my conscience."

—1892

RUDYARD KIPLING
1865 – 1936

The name "Rudyard Kipling" evokes images of the Raj in India, a time when Britannia ruled the waves and the sun never set on the British Empire. Indeed his life spanned most of the duration of British Colonial Office rule in India (1858–1947). Kipling, for many years considered England's unofficial poet laureate, was a strong proponent of imperialism; he believed it was Britain's duty to govern and civilize colonized lands. Though he was also capable of offering serious critiques of empire—and though he acknowledged that colonized people were "captives"—Kipling gave frequent voice to his belief that the British were in India to serve the native people. His famous 1899 poem, "The White Man's Burden," published in *McClure's Magazine*, aroused a storm of controversy, coming out at a time when many people were beginning to question the right of imperialist powers to subjugate foreigners. Yet, for more than a half century Kipling's poems, short stories, and novels were wildly popular in India, Great Britain, and the United States, and in 1907 the Nobel Foundation honored him "in consideration of the power of observation, originality of imagination, virility of ideas and remarkable talent for narration which characterize the creations of this world-famous author." Thus Kipling became the first British writer to be awarded the Nobel Prize for Literature.

Kipling was named after Rudyard Lake in England, but he was born in Bombay (now Mumbai), India. Both his father, John Lockwood Kipling, professor of architectural sculpture at the University of Bombay, and his mother, Alice Macdonald, were children of Methodist ministers. Macdonald and her sisters were all associated with distinguished people—one sister married the neoclassical painter Sir Edward Poynter; another was the mother of Stanley Baldwin, who became Prime Minister of England in 1923; and another was the wife of the Pre-Raphaelite painter Sir Edward Burne-Jones. Kipling spent his first six years with his parents, learning the languages of his Indian friends and imbibing the cultural wealth of India. Of his school years, however, Kipling would say in his autobiography that his only happy moments were spent at the Burne-Jones home. Like many children of expatriates, he and his sister were sent to England for their education, where they spent five miserable years with severe, Calvinist foster parents in a home that Kipling would later call the House of Desolation. In 1878 he transferred to a boarding school in Devon (depicted in *Stalky and Co.*), which was also brutal at times, but where he acquired his schoolboy ethos (the sense of loyalty to and camaraderie with his peers so evident in his work) and began to write in earnest.

Upon graduation, Kipling moved back to India, working first as a newspaper journalist for the *Civil and Military Gazette* in Lahore (now part of Pakistan) and then as an editor of *Pioneer* in Allahabad. Many of the poems and stories he wrote during that time were collected in *Departmental Ditties* (1886) and *Plain Tales from the Hills* (1888), in which Kipling wrote about the moral and psychological difficulties of integrating Indian and British cultures. The Indian Railway Library also published collections of Kipling's stories, notably *The Phantom Rickshaw and other Eerie Tales* and *Wee Willie Winkie and Other Child Stories* (1888). The first of these collections included "The Man Who Would Be King," which has remained one of Kipling's most popular stories. By the time he returned to England in 1889, Kipling was a well-established author in India and had become very popular in Britain as well. The public loved his "tales of the exotic," which took them to worlds they could scarcely imagine and introduced them to cultures they would likely never experience first-hand.

Kipling published several collections of short stories and poems in the early 1890s; the volume *Barrack-Room Ballads and Other Verses* (1892), which included such well-known poems as "Mandalay" and "Gunga Din," went into more than 50 editions in the 30 years following. Two early novels, *The Light that Failed* (1891) and *The Naulahka* (1892), did not fare as well. Nevertheless, in this period Kipling acquired a reputation as a spokesman for the people. With lyrics often inspired by street ballads and music hall ditties, he wrote using everyday language and expressed the thoughts of soldiers and other working people.

In 1892 Kipling married an American, Caroline Balestier, and the couple settled in Vermont. Although Kipling was unhappy in the United States, he wrote some of his most esteemed works during his five-year stay there, including *The Jungle Book* (1894), *The Second Jungle Book* (1895), and *Captains Courageous* (1897).

The family eventually settled in Sussex, England, but Kipling continued to travel the world as a newspaper correspondent. He covered the Boer War in South Africa in 1899 and returned to the region annually thereafter, staying in a house given to him by Cecil Rhodes, the famous British imperialist and business magnate. Kipling's own imperialist political sentiments were disseminated widely at the turn of the century, most notably in the London *Times*, which published "Recessional," composed in honor of Queen Victoria's Diamond Jubilee, and "The White Man's Burden." The latter poem was soon afterward countered in the London magazine *Truth* with a poem by Henry Labouchère, which changed Kipling's opening refrain from "Take up the white man's burden," to "Pile on the brown man's burden." Amid the controversy that ensued, a letter to the editor was published that read: "There is something almost sickening in this 'imperial' talk of assuming and bearing burdens for the good of others. They are never assumed or held where they are not found to be of material advantage or ministering to honor or glory." Kipling himself suggested that his poem offered neither a noble call to arms nor a justification for colonization, but rather a warning of the costs involved on both sides of imperialist missions abroad.

Kipling's least controversial and best-loved novel appeared in 1901. *Kim* is a picaresque adventure tale of a British beggar boy, the orphaned son of an Irish soldier. Raised in Lahore by an opium-addicted, half-caste woman, Kim O'Hare comes to believe he is destined for greatness and eventually travels through India with a holy man in search of his glorious future. In 1907, the Nobel committee said that in *Kim* "there is an elevated diction as well as a tenderness and charm.... In sketching a personality he makes clear, almost in his first words, the peculiar traits of that person's character and temper.... [Kipling is] capable of reproducing with astounding accuracy the minutest detail from real life."

In the decades following his Nobel Prize, Kipling's literary output dwindled somewhat amid controversy over his politics and grief over the loss of two of his three children. Even former admirers, such as W.B. Yeats and T.S. Eliot, began to be critical of Kipling's unwavering allegiance to British imperialism. Nevertheless, the last half century has seen a resurgence of interest in his work.

Sir Ian Hamilton said that Kipling's death in January 1936 (two days before the death of Kipling's friend, King George V) placed "a full stop to the period when war was a romance and the expansion of our Empire a duty." When his ashes were interred in Poets' Corner of Westminster Abbey, Kipling's pallbearers included the then-prime minister of England, a field marshal, and the admiral of the fleet; the poem "Recessional" was sung as a hymn. Kipling's unfinished autobiography, *Something of Myself*, was published a year after his death.

⌘ ⌘ ⌘

Gunga Din

You may talk o' gin and beer
When you're quartered safe out 'ere,
An' you're sent to penny-fights° an' Aldershot[1] it;   *skirmishes*
But when it comes to slaughter
5   You will do your work on water,
An' you'll lick the bloomin' boots of 'im that's got it.
Now in Injia's sunny clime,
Where I used to spend my time
A-servin' of 'Er Majesty the Queen,
10   Of all them blackfaced crew
The finest man I knew
Was our regimental bhisti,° Gunga Din.   *water carrier*
            He was "Din! Din! Din!
        You limpin' lump o' brick-dust, Gunga Din!
15   Hi! Slippy *hitherao*![2]
            Water, get it! *Panee lao*,[3]
        You squidgy-nosed old idol, Gunga Din."

The uniform 'e wore
Was nothin' much before,
20   An' rather less than 'arf o' that be'ind,
For a piece o' twisty rag
An' a goatskin water bag
Was all the field equipment 'e could find.
When the sweatin' troop train lay
25   In a sidin' through the day,
Where the 'eat would make your bloomin' eyebrows crawl,
We shouted "Harry By!"[4]
Till our throats were bricky-dry,
Then we wopped 'im 'cause 'e couldn't serve us all.
30   It was "Din! Din! Din!
        You 'eathen, where the mischief 'ave you been?
            You put some *juldee*[5] in it
            Or I'll *marrow*[6] you this minute
        If you don't fill up my helmet, Gunga Din!"

35   'E would dot an' carry one[7]
Till the longest day was done;
An' 'e didn't seem to know the use o' fear.
If we charged or broke or cut,
You could bet your bloomin' nut,
40   'E'd be waitin' fifty paces right flank rear.
With 'is mussick° on 'is back,   *waterbag*
'E would skip with our attack,
An' watch us till the bugles made "Retire,"
An' for all 'is dirty 'ide
45   'E was white, clear white, inside
When 'e went to tend the wounded under fire!
            It was "Din! Din! Din!"
        With the bullets kickin' dust spots on the green.
            When the cartridges ran out,
50   You could hear the front ranks shout,
        "Hi! ammunition mules an' Gunga Din!"

I shan't forgit the night
When I dropped be'ind the fight
With a bullet where my belt plate should 'a' been.
55   I was chokin' mad with thirst,
An' the man that spied me first
Was our good old grinnin,' gruntin' Gunga Din.
'E lifted up my 'ead,
An' he plugged me where I bled,
60   An' 'e guv me 'arf-a-pint o' water green.
It was crawlin' and it stunk,
But of all the drinks I've drunk,
I'm gratefullest to one from Gunga Din.
            It was "Din! Din! Din!
65   'Ere's a beggar with a bullet through 'is spleen;
            'E's chawin' up the ground,
            An' 'e's kickin' all around:
        For Gawd's sake git the water, Gunga Din!"

'E carried me away
70   To where a dooli° lay,   *stretcher*
An' a bullet come an' drilled the beggar clean.
'E put me safe inside,
An' just before 'e died,
"I 'ope you liked your drink," sez Gunga Din.
75   So I'll meet 'im later on
At the place where 'e is gone—

---

[1] *Aldershot* Town southwest of London, site of a military training center.

[2] *Slippy hitherao* I.e., *idhar ao.* Urdu: Come here!

[3] *Panee lao* Urdu: Bring water.

[4] *Harry By* I.e., *arré bhai!* Urdu: in this context, Hey, you!

[5] *juldee* I.e., *juldee karo.* Urdu: hurry!

[6] *marrow* I.e., *maro.* Urdu: hit.

[7] *dot an' carry one* From mathematics: calculate.

Where it's always double drill and no canteen.
'E'll be squattin' on the coals
Givin' drink to poor damned souls,
80   An' I'll get a swig in hell from Gunga Din!
        Yes, Din! Din! Din!
    You Lazarushian[1]-leather Gunga Din!
        Though I've belted you and flayed you,
        By the livin' Gawd that made you,
85   You're a better man than I am, Gunga Din!
—1890

The Widow at Windsor [2]

'Ave you 'eard o' the Widow at Windsor
    With a hairy gold crown on 'er 'ead?
She 'as ships on the foam—she 'as millions at 'ome,
    An' she pays us poor beggars in red.[3]
5   (Ow, poor beggars in red!)
There's 'er nick[4] on the cavalry 'orses,
    There's 'er mark[5] on the medical stores—
An' 'er troopers° you'll find with a fair wind be'ind   *troop-ships*
    That takes us to various wars.
10   (Poor beggars!—barbarious wars!)
        Then 'ere's to the Widow at Windsor,
            An 'ere's to the stores an' the guns,
        The men an' the 'orses what makes up the
                forces
            O' Missis Victorier's sons.
15   (Poor beggars! Victorier's sons!)

Walk wide o' the Widow at Windsor,
    For 'alf o' Creation she owns:
We 'ave bought 'er the same with the sword an' the flame,
    An' we've salted it down with our bones.
20   (Poor beggars!—it's blue with our bones!)
Hands off o' the sons o' the Widow,

Hands off o' the goods in 'er shop,
For the kings must come down an' the emperors frown
    When the Widow at Windsor says "Stop!"
25   (Poor beggars!—we're sent to say "Stop!")
        Then 'ere's to the lodge o' the Widow,
            From the pole to the tropics it runs—
        To the lodge that we tile with the rank an' the file,
            An' open in form with the guns.
30   (Poor beggars!—it's always they guns!)

We 'ave 'eard o' the Widow at Windsor,
    It's safest to leave 'er alone:
For 'er sentries we stand by the sea an' the land
    Wherever the bugles are blown.
35   (Poor beggars!—an' don't we get blown!)
Take 'old o' the Wings o' the Mornin',[6]
    An' flop round the earth till you're dead;
But you won't get away from the tune that they play
    To the bloomin' old rag over'ead.
40   (Poor beggars!—it's 'ot over'ead!)
        Then 'ere's to the sons o' the Widow,
            Wherever, 'owever they roam.
        'Ere's all they desire, an' if they require
            A speedy return to their 'ome.
45   (Poor beggars! they'll never see 'ome!)
—1890

Recessional [7]

God of our fathers, known of old,
    Lord of our far-flung battle-line,
Beneath whose awful Hand we hold
    Dominion over palm and pine—
5   Lord God of Hosts, be with us yet,
Lest we forget[8]—lest we forget!

---

[1] *Lazarushian* Cf. Luke 16; the good Lazarus was a leper/beggar.

[2] *The Widow at Windsor* Queen Victoria, who, upon losing her husband in 1861, went into permanent mourning. (See the "In Context" section below for more information.)

[3] *red* Red coats of British soldiers.

[4] *'er nick* Mark distinguishing animals as belonging to the queen.

[5] *'er mark* "V.R.I.," the Queen's identification mark.

[6] *Wings o' the Mornin'* From Psalm 139.9–10: "If I take the wings of the morning, and dwell in the uttermost parts of the sea; / Even there shall thy hand lead me, and thy right hand shall hold me."

[7] *Recessional* Hymn written for Queen Victoria's sixtieth anniversary Jubilee.

[8] *Lest we forget* Cf. Deuteronomy 4.9: "[T]ake heed to thyself, and keep thy soul diligently, lest thou forget the things which thine eyes have seen, and lest they depart from thy heart all the days of thy life: but teach them thy sons, and thy sons' sons."

The tumult and the shouting dies;
    The captains and the kings depart:
Still stands Thine ancient sacrifice,
10   An humble and a contrite heart.[1]
Lord God of Hosts, be with us yet,
Lest we forget—lest we forget!

Far-called, our navies melt away;
    On dune and headland sinks the fire:
15 Lo, all our pomp of yesterday
    Is one with Nineveh and Tyre![2]
Judge of the nations, spare us yet,
Lest we forget—lest we forget!

If, drunk with sight of power, we loose
20   Wild tongues that have not Thee in awe,
Such boastings as the Gentiles use,
    Or lesser breeds without the law[3]—
Lord God of Hosts, be with us yet,
Lest we forget—lest we forget!

25 For heathen heart that puts her trust
    In reeking tube and iron shard,
All valiant dust that builds on dust,
    And guarding, calls not Thee to guard,
For frantic boast and foolish word—
30 Thy mercy on Thy people, Lord!
    —1897

The White Man's Burden

THE UNITED STATES AND THE PHILIPPINE ISLANDS[4]

Take up the White Man's burden—
    Send forth the best ye breed—
Go bind your sons to exile
    To serve your captives' need;
5 To wait in heavy harness
    On fluttered folk and wild—
Your new-caught, sullen peoples,
    Half devil and half child.

Take up the White Man's burden—
10   In patience to abide,
To veil the threat of terror
    And check the show of pride;
By open speech and simple,
    An hundred times made plain.
15 To seek another's profit,
    And work another's gain.

Take up the White Man's burden—
    The savage wars of peace—
Fill full the mouth of Famine
20   And bid the sickness cease;
And when your goal is nearest
    The end for others sought,
Watch Sloth and heathen Folly
    Bring all your hope to nought.

25 Take up the White Man's burden—
    No tawdry rule of kings,
But toil of serf and sweeper—
    The tale of common things.
The ports ye shall not enter,
30   The roads ye shall not tread,
Go make them with your living,
    And mark them with your dead!

---

[1] *contrite heart* Cf. Psalms 51.17: "The sacrifices of God are a broken spirit: a broken and a contrite heart."

[2] *Nineveh and Tyre* Ruined cities that were once capitals of empires.

[3] *Gentiles ... law* Cf. Romans 2.14: "For when the Gentiles, which have not the law, do by nature the things contained in the law, these, having not the law, are a law unto themselves."

[4] *UNITED STATES AND THE PHILIPPINE ISLANDS* Response to the American takeover of the Philippines after the Spanish American War of 1898. (See the "In Context" section below for more information.)

Take up the White Man's burden—
    And reap his old reward:
35 The blame of those ye better,
    The hate of those ye guard—
The cry of hosts ye humour
    (Ah, slowly!) toward the light:—
"Why brought ye us from bondage,
40   Our loved Egyptian night?"

Take up the White Man's burden—
    Ye dare not stoop to less—
Nor call too loud on Freedom
    To cloak your weariness;
45 By all ye cry or whisper,
    By all ye leave or do,
The silent, sullen peoples
    Shall weigh your gods and you.

Take up the White Man's burden—
50   Have done with childish days—
The lightly proffered laurel,[1]
    The easy, ungrudged praise.
Comes now, to search your manhood
    Through all the thankless years,
55 Cold-edged with dear-bought wisdom,
    The judgment of your peers!
—1899

If[2]—

If you can keep your head when all about you
    Are losing theirs and blaming it on you,
If you can trust yourself when all men doubt you,
    But make allowance for their doubting too;
5 If you can wait and not be tired by waiting,
    Or being lied about, don't deal in lies,
Or being hated, don't give way to hating,
    And yet don't look too good, nor talk too wise:

If you can dream—and not make dreams your master;
10   If you can think—and not make thoughts your aim;
If you can meet with Triumph and Disaster
    And treat those two impostors just the same;
If you can bear to hear the truth you've spoken
    Twisted by knaves to make a trap for fools,
15 Or watch the things you gave your life to, broken,
    And stoop and build 'em up with worn out tools:

If you can make one heap of all your winnings
    And risk it on one turn of pitch-and-toss,[3]
And lose, and start again at your beginnings
20   And never breathe a word about your loss;
If you can force your heart and nerve and sinew
    To serve your turn long after they are gone,
And so hold on when there is nothing in you
    Except the Will which says to them: "Hold on!"

25 If you can talk with crowds and keep your virtue,
    Or walk with kings—nor lose the common touch,
If neither foes nor loving friends can hurt you,
    If all men count with you, but none too much;
If you can fill the unforgiving minute
30   With sixty seconds' worth of distance run,
Yours is the earth and everything that's in it,
    And—which is more—you'll be a man, my son!
—1910

---

[2] *If* It has been suggested that this poem may have been written in celebration of Dr. Leander Starr Jameson. Jameson launched the failed Jameson Raid of British troops against the Boers in South Africa in 1895, which ultimately led to the Boer War (1899–1902). Jameson went on to serve as Premier of the Cape Colony from 1904 to 1908.

[3] *pitch-and-toss* Coin tossing game.

---

[1] *laurel* Leaves of the bay laurel tree are a symbol of victory.

IN CONTEXT

Victoria and Albert

Queen Victoria was widowed when Prince Albert died on 14 December 1861. His partnership with the Queen had been an extraordinarily successful one—as a professional partnership as well as in family life. For many years after his death the Queen was a recluse, so much so that the public began to lose patience with and sympathy for Victoria in her mourning. It was not until the early 1870s that the Queen began to re-emerge. As she did so she gradually regained public favor, and by the time Kipling's "The Widow at Windsor" was published in 1890 she was widely revered. Her 60th Anniversary Jubilee in 1897—for which Kipling composed "Recessional"—was a massive national celebration.

Frederick Shuckard's painting of an idealized 18-year-old Princess Victoria receiving news of her accession to the throne in 1837.

Queen Victoria and Prince Albert in the early 1850s.
(Photograph by Roger Fenton.)

Queen Victoria in mourning, 1867.

Queen Victoria with John Brown, a servant who had been personal ghillie (the term applied to the attendant to a Highland Chief) to Prince Albert and who later served Queen Victoria; Brown is credited with helping to bring the Queen out from seclusion. (Photo by W & D Downy.)

The Queen with Princess Beatrice, Princess Victoria, and great-grand daughter Alice, 1867. (Photographer unknown.)

Queen Victoria in the Gold Jubilee procession, 1897.

Victoria holding the future Edward VIII on the occasion of his baptism; her son Edward (later Edward VII) and grandson George (later George V) are in the background.

IN CONTEXT

The "White Man's Burden" in the Philippines

The Philippine Islands had long been a Spanish colony, but Spain's defeat in 1898 at the hands of American Admiral George Dewey during the Spanish-American War was followed by an agreement ceding the islands to the United States for $20 million. Local forces (under Emilio Agninaldo) had been rebelling against the Spanish, and, expecting the American victory to lead to liberation, declared a republic. The Americans, however, deciding that the natives were not ready for independence, ruthlessly suppressed the insurrection of Agninaldo's forces (which continued until 1905). Not until 1946 was the Republic of the Philippines granted full independence. The American annexation of the islands in 1899 was widely popular in the United States, but a significant minority loudly protested the expression of American imperialism that was the occasion for Kipling's famous poem. Following are excerpts from the platform adopted by one American organization at their founding meeting in Chicago, 17 October 1899.

Platform of the American Anti-Imperialist League

We hold that the policy known as imperialism is hostile to liberty and tends toward militarism, an evil from which it has been our glory to be free. We regret that it has become necessary in the land of Washington and Lincoln to reaffirm that all men, of whatever race or color, are entitled to life, liberty, and the pursuit of happiness. We maintain that governments derive their just powers from the consent of the governed. We insist that the subjugation of any people is "criminal aggression" and open disloyalty to the distinctive principles of our government.

We earnestly condemn the policy of the present national administration in the Philippines. It seeks to extinguish the spirit of 1776 in those islands. We deplore the sacrifice of our soldiers and sailors, whose bravery deserves admiration even in an unjust war. We denounce the slaughter of the Filipinos as a needless horror. We protest against the extension of American sovereignty by Spanish methods.

We demand the immediate cessation of the war against liberty, begun by Spain and continued by us. We urge that Congress be promptly convened to announce to the Filipinos our purpose to concede to them the independence for which they have so long fought and which of right is theirs.

The United States have always protested against the doctrine of international law which permits the subjugation of the weak by the strong. A self-governing state cannot accept sovereignty over an unwilling people. The United States cannot act upon the ancient heresy that might makes right.

Imperialists assume that with the destruction of self-government in the Philippines by American hands, all opposition here will cease. This is a grievous error. Much as we abhor the war of "criminal aggression" in the Philippines, greatly as we regret that the blood of the Filipinos is on American hands, we more deeply resent the betrayal of American institutions at home. The real firing line is not in the suburbs of Manila. The foe is of our own household. The attempt of 1861 was to divide the country. That of 1899 is to destroy its fundamental principles and noblest ideals.

Whether the ruthless slaughter of the Filipinos shall end next month or next year is but an incident in a contest that must go on until the Declaration of Independence and the Constitution of the United States are rescued from the hands of their betrayers. Those who dispute about standards of value while the Republic is undermined will be listened to as little as those who would wrangle about the small economies of the household while the house is on fire. The training of a great people for a century, the aspiration for liberty of a vast immigration are forces that will hurl aside those who in the delirium of conquest seek to destroy the character of our institutions.

We deny that the obligation of all citizens to support their Government in times of grave national peril applies to the present situation. If an administration may with impunity ignore the issues upon which it was chosen, deliberately create a condition of war anywhere on the face of the globe, debauch the civil service for spoils to promote the adventure, organize a truth suppressing censorship and demand of all citizens a suspension of judgement and their unanimous support while it chooses to continue the fighting, representative government itself is imperiled.

We propose to contribute to the defeat of any person or party that stands for the forcible subjugation of any people. We shall oppose for reelection all who in the White House or in Congress betray American liberty in pursuit of un-American gains. We still hope that both of our great political parties will support and defend the Declaration of Independence in the closing campaign of the century.

We hold, with Abraham Lincoln, that "no man is good enough to govern another man without that other's consent. When the white man governs himself, that is self-government, but when he governs himself and also governs another man, that is more than self-government—that is despotism." "Our reliance is in the love of liberty which God has planted in us. Our defense is in the spirit which prizes liberty as the heritage of all men in all lands. Those who deny freedom to others deserve it not for themselves, and under a just God cannot long retain it."

We cordially invite the co-operation of all men and women who remain loyal to the Declaration of Independence and the Constitution of the United States.

BRITAIN, EMPIRE, AND A WIDER WORLD
CONTEXTS

In the Victorian era colonies in the British Empire were divided into two broad categories. In one category were crown colonies ruled by governments with no direct responsibility to the people they ruled, but only to the Foreign Office and the home country as a whole. The vast majority of the populace in such colonies did not share in the history, religion, or traditions of England or other European cultures, and were brown or black in color; in this category were the bulk of British possessions in Africa, Asia, and the Caribbean. In areas of the Empire where emigration from Britain and other European nations had created a majority or a substantial minority of a population sharing the cultural and racial makeup of "the old country," on the other hand, responsible government became the norm. Under the terms of Imperial arrangements in the latter category, administration was still overseen by British authority, but governments with a substantial degree of real power were elected by and responsible to the local populace, and were composed of local leaders rather than temporary appointees from abroad. Canada, the Australian colonies, and New Zealand were prominent in this second category.

India was in many ways a special case, with local hereditary rulers in some cases maintaining considerable authority under an umbrella of British rule over the subcontinent, and with Imperial rule complicated both by the existence of the India Office as a separate government department in Britain, and by the authority wielded (until 1858) by the East India Company. The latter was the last such entity to hold substantial power in a British colony. In the seventeenth century, the East India Company, the Hudson's Bay Company, and the Royal Africa Company were among the commercial entities given royal charters, empowering them not only to trade commercially in particular parts of the globe but also to exercise political authority over the local people. Beginning in the eighteenth century, such authority began to be transferred to government of a more conventional sort.

Throughout the history of the British Empire various notions of "Empire" competed with one another. Perhaps the least complicated was the notion that Empire should be based purely on the commercial interests of the Imperial power. It was this notion that was foremost in the minds of many commercial adventurers staking out an Imperial claim—but also in the minds of many "little Englanders" in the nineteenth century who did not necessarily have any desire to abandon the Empire as a whole, but felt it would be expedient and appropriate to "cut loose" colonies that were perceived to represent a net drain on Britain's resources, financial and otherwise. For others, though, the Empire was a vital symbol of the nation's importance in the world—and of its "greatness" (a word in which power and morality came to be inextricably entangled). Finally, there were those whose notions of Empire were shaped by a hope and a confidence that Britain would improve the lot of her subject peoples—improve their economic conditions, certainly, but also bring to them literacy and an appropriate level of education, what were perceived to be the benefits of Christianity, and a broader set of cultural benefits, as well. It is easy to be cynical about this last set of ideas, and there was surely much in these "enlightened" notions of Empire that was hypocritical, patronizing, and racist. That there was also frequently some kernel of altruism in the "enlightened imperialism" of the likes of William Gladstone or David Livingstone, however, is difficult to doubt, even as it must now be plain to all how horrifically misguided such impulses often were.

There was no pretense made that the greatest of horrors endured by subject peoples under British imperialism was a civilizing mission. After a long struggle, outright slavery had been abolished in all British possessions in 1833, but in certain British colonies in the Caribbean, practices tantamount to slavery continued for decades thereafter—prompting incidents such as the uprising against British Governor Edward Eyre in Jamaica in 1865. Nor was there anything civilizing in the unspeakable atrocities meted out during the suppression of the Indian rebellion in 1857–58, or the brutal treatment accorded the aboriginal peoples of Australia, New Zealand, and (to a somewhat lesser extent) Canada; all these represented Imperialism stripped of any veneer of civilization.

The feelings of cultural and racial superiority on which rationalizations of the subjugation of other peoples were founded took a variety of forms. The sort of anthropological theorizing that Adam Smith and other eighteenth-century thinkers had engaged in was comparatively benign, and remained popular throughout the nineteenth century. According to this way of thinking, other peoples were not inherently inferior; they were simply at a less fully advanced stage of social and economic organization than were European peoples. An anthropological "stages of development" approach often led to an assumption by the British and other Europeans of a "childish" mentality among peoples elsewhere in the globe, but it also left room for the moral anthropology of Rousseau and others that ascribed to the "noble savage" the attribute of an innocence largely lost to "higher" stages of civilization. (It is this view with which Charles Dickens takes vehement issue in the essay from *Household Words* excerpted in this section.)

Although this approach was widely held throughout the Victorian era, pseudo-scientific claims of a biological sort were increasingly made. According to many making such claims, other peoples were not at a lower stage of development (from which they could, with assistance, be raised over the course of time to the level of Europeans); rather they were inherently, biologically inferior, and it would thus always be appropriate to treat them as creatures of a lower order.

Through most of the twentieth century little direct attention was paid to the attitudes of leading Victorian literary figures towards these issues, and it came to be widely assumed that writers who had deplored, for example, the brutality of conditions for workers in industry in England would also have deplored oppression and brutality overseas. As Edward Said and others were instrumental in demonstrating, in the late twentieth century, however, this was simply not the case. While John Stuart Mill and some others did indeed hold what we now acknowledge to be relatively enlightened views on the subject of race and culture, the list of those espousing views which today can only be described as racist (tellingly, neither the word "racialist" or the word "racist" is recorded as having been used before the twentieth century) is a long one, and includes such major figures as Thomas Carlyle, William Thackeray, John Ruskin, and Walter Bagehot. It is difficult to read the pronouncements of many of these figures on such matters without feeling a sense of revulsion. Again, though, we should be wary of presuming ourselves to be at a moral pinnacle; it may well be that in another 150 years we will look back on the views that predominate in our own time—our willingness to ignore genocide so long as it is happening in faraway lands, for example—with as much revulsion as we feel toward the racism of many of the most renowned Victorians.

⌘ ⌘ ⌘

Thomas Pringle, "Afar in the Desert" (1824)

Born and raised in Scotland, Thomas Pringle spent six years in South Africa; much of his work, including the poem below, is inspired by his experiences there. "Afar in the Desert" was first published in Pringle's own literary journal in South Africa, but it was very well received abroad—Samuel Taylor Coleridge counted it "among the two or three most perfect lyric poems in our language." Pringle witnessed slavery in South Africa and became deeply opposed to the practice; after his return to the British Isles he devoted much of his time to campaigning for abolition as secretary to the Anti-Slavery Society.

Afar in the desert I love to ride,
　With the silent Bush-boy[1] alone by my side:
When the sorrows of life the soul o'ercast,
And, sick of the Present, I cling to the Past;
5　When the eye is suffused with regretful tears,
From the fond recollections of former years;
And shadows of things that have long since fled
Flit over the brain, like the ghosts of the dead:
Bright visions of glory—that vanished too soon;
10　Day-dreams—that departed ere manhood's noon;
Attachments—by fate or by falsehood reft;°　　*taken away*
Companions of early days—lost or left;
And my Native Land—whose magical name
Thrills to the heart like electric flame;
15　The home of my childhood; the haunts of my prime;
All the passions and scenes of that rapturous time
When the feelings were young and the world was new,
Like the fresh bowers of Eden unfolding to view;
All—all now forsaken—forgotten—foregone!
20　And I—a lone exile remembered of none—
My high aims abandoned, my good acts undone,
Aweary of all that is under the sun,
With that sadness of heart which no stranger may scan,
I fly to the Desert afar from man!

25　　Afar in the Desert I love to ride,
With the silent Bush-boy alone by my side:
When the wild turmoil of this wearisome life,

With its scenes of oppression, corruption, and strife—
The proud man's frown, and the base man's fear,
30　The scorner's laugh, and the sufferer's tear—
And malice, and meanness, and falsehood, and folly,
Dispose me to musing and dark melancholy;
When my bosom is full, and my thoughts are high,
And my soul is sick with the bondman's° sigh—　　*slave's*
35　Oh! then there is freedom, and joy, and pride,
Afar in the Desert alone to ride!
There is rapture to vault on the champing steed,
And to bound away with the eagle's speed,
With the death-fraught firelock° in my hand—　　*musket*
40　The only law of the Desert Land!

　　Afar in the Desert I love to ride,
With the silent Bush-boy alone by my side:
Away—away from the dwellings of men,
By the wild deer's haunt, by the buffalo's glen;
45　By valleys remote where the oribi[2] plays,
Where the gnu,° the gazelle, and the　　*wildebeest*
　　hartèbeest[3] graze,
And the kùdù and eland[4] unhunted recline
By the skirts of grey forests o'erhung with wild-vine;
Where the elephant browses at peace in his wood,
50　And the river-horse° gambols[5] unscared　　*hippopotamus*
　　in the flood,
And the mighty rhinoceros wallows at will
In the fen where the wild-ass is drinking his fill.

　　Afar in the Desert I love to ride,
With the silent Bush-boy alone by my side:
55　O'er the brown Karroo,[6] where the bleating cry
Of the springbok's[7] fawn sounds plaintively;
And the timorous quagga's[8] shrill whistling neigh
Is heard by the fountain at twilight grey;

1　*Bush-boy*　Term for a native person living in the wilderness.

2　*oribi*　Type of small brown antelope.

3　*hartèbeest*　Another type of antelope, common to South Africa.

4　*kùdù and eland*　Two other types of African antelope.

5　*gambols*　Bounds playfully.

6　*Karroo*　Semi-desert area in central South Africa.

7　*springbok*　Type of antelope known for springing straight upward when startled.

8　*quagga*　Type of zebra that was native to southern Africa; it is now extinct.

Where the zebra wantonly tosses his mane,
60 With wild hoof scouring the desolate plain;
And the fleet-footed ostrich over the waste
Speeds like a horseman who travels in haste,
Hying° away to the home of her rest,   hastening
Where she and her mate have scooped their nest,
65 Far hid from the pitiless plunderer's view
In the pathless depths of the parched Karroo.

　　Afar in the Desert I love to ride,
With the silent Bush-boy alone by my side:
Away—away—in the Wilderness vast,
70 Where the White Man's foot hath never passed,
And the quivered Coránna or Bechuán[1]
Hath rarely crossed with his roving clan:
A region of emptiness, howling and drear,
Which Man hath abandoned from famine and fear;
75 Which the snake and the lizard inhabit alone,
With the twilight bat from the yawning stone;
Where grass, nor herb, nor shrub takes root,
Save poisonous thorns that pierce the foot;
And the bitter-melon, for food and drink,
80 Is the pilgrim's fare by the salt lake's brink:
A region of drought, where no river glides,
Nor rippling brook with osiered[2] sides;
Where sedgy[3] pool, nor bubbling fount,
Nor tree, nor cloud, nor misty mount,
85 Appears, to refresh the aching eye:
But the barren earth, and the burning sky,
And the black horizon, round and round,
Spread—void of living sight or sound.

　　And here, while the night-winds round me sigh,
90 And the stars burn bright in the midnight sky,
As I sit apart by the desert stone,
Like Elijah at Horeb's cave alone,[4]
"A still small voice" comes through the wild
(Like a Father consoling his fretful Child),

---

[1] *Coránna or Bechuán* Two native tribes.

[2] *osiered* Covered in osiers, or willow trees.

[3] *sedgy* Filled with sedge—coarse grass or rushes.

[4] *Like Elijah … cave alone* Reference to 1 Kings 19, which tells the story of Elijah, who journeyed for 40 days and nights to Horeb, the mount of God. After a great wind, an earthquake, and a fire, the Lord spoke to Elijah in "a still, small voice."

95 Which banishes bitterness, wrath, and fear,
Saying—MAN IS DISTANT, BUT GOD IS NEAR!

from Frances Trollope, *Domestic Manners of the Americans* (1832)

The novelist Frances Trollope's account of her visit to the United States features a number of reflections on the direction taken by the American character in the decades since America became independent from Britain.

from CHAPTER 1: ENTRANCE OF THE MISSISSIPPI

On the 4th of November, 1827, I sailed from London, accompanied by my son and two daughters; and after a favourable, though somewhat tedious voyage, arrived on Christmas-day at the mouth of the Mississippi.

The first indication of our approach to land was the appearance of this mighty river pouring forth its muddy mass of waters, and mingling with the deep blue of the Mexican Gulf. The shores of this river are so utterly flat, that no object upon them is perceptible at sea, and we gazed with pleasure on the muddy ocean that met us, for it told us we were arrived, and seven weeks of sailing had wearied us; yet it was not without a feeling like regret that we passed from the bright blue waves, whose varying aspect had so long furnished our chief amusement, into the murky stream which now received us.

Large flights of pelicans were seen standing upon the long masses of mud which rose above the surface of the waters, and a pilot came to guide us over the bar, long before any other indication of land was visible.

I never beheld a scene so utterly desolate as this entrance of the Mississippi. Had Dante seen it, he might have drawn images of another Bolgia[5] from its horrors. One only object rears itself above the eddying waters; this is the mast of a vessel long since wrecked in attempting to cross the bar, and it still stands, a dismal

---

[5] *Dante* Italian poet Dante Alighieri (1265–1321), author of the epic poem *The Divine Comedy*, composed of three sections describing Heaven (*Paradiso*), Purgatory (*Purgatorio*), and Hell (*Inferno*); *Bolgia* Level of Hell in Dante's *Inferno*.

witness of the destruction that has been, and a boding prophet of that which is to come. …

By degrees bulrushes of enormous growth become visible, and a few more miles of mud brought us within sight of a cluster of huts called the Balize, by far the most miserable station that I ever saw made the dwelling of man, but I was told that many families of pilots and fishermen lived there.

For several miles above its mouth, the Mississippi presents no objects more interesting than mud banks, monstrous bulrushes, and now and then a huge crocodile luxuriating in the slime. Another circumstance that gives to this dreary scene an aspect of desolation, is the incessant appearance of vast quantities of drift wood, which is ever finding its way to the different mouths of the Mississippi. Trees of enormous length, sometimes still bearing their branches, and still oftener their uptorn roots entire, the victims of the frequent hurricane, come floating down the stream. Sometimes several of these, entangled together, collect among their boughs a quantity of floating rubbish, that gives the mass the appearance of a moving island, bearing a forest, with its roots mocking the heavens; while the dishonoured branches lash the tide in idle vengeance: this, as it approaches the vessel, and glides swiftly past, looks like the fragment of a world in ruins. …

from CHAPTER 3: COMPANY ON BOARD THE STEAM BOAT

The weather was warm and bright, and we found the guard of the boat, as they call the gallery that runs round the cabins, a very agreeable station; here we all sat as long as light lasted, and sometimes wrapped in our shawls, we enjoyed the clear bright beauty of American moonlight long after every passenger but ourselves had retired. We had a full complement of passengers on board. The deck, as is usual, was occupied by the Kentucky flat-boat men, returning from New Orleans, after having disposed of the boat and cargo which they had conveyed thither, with no other labour than that of steering her, the current bringing her down at the rate of four miles an hour. We had about two hundred of these men on board, but the part of the vessel occupied by them is so distinct from the cabins, that we never saw them, except when we stopped to take in wood; and

then they ran, or rather sprung and vaulted over each other's heads to the shore, whence they all assisted in carrying wood to supply the steam engine; the performance of this duty being a stipulated part of the payment of their passage.

From the account given by a man servant we had on board, who shared their quarters, they are a most disorderly set of persons, constantly gambling and wrangling, very seldom sober, and never suffering a night to pass without giving practical proof of the respect in which they hold the doctrines of equality, and community of property. The clerk of the vessel was kind enough to take our man under his protection, and assigned him a berth in his own little nook; but as this was not inaccessible, he told him by no means to detach his watch or money from his person during the night. Whatever their moral characteristics may be, these Kentuckians are a very noble-looking race of men; their average height considerably exceeds that of Europeans, and their countenances, excepting when disfigured by red hair, which is not unfrequent, extremely handsome.

The gentlemen in the cabin (we had no ladies) would certainly neither, from their language, manners, nor appearance, have received that designation in Europe; but we soon found their claim to it rested on more substantial ground, for we heard them nearly all addressed by the titles of general, colonel, and major. On mentioning these military dignities to an English friend some time afterwards, he told me that he too had made the voyage with the same description of company, but remarking that there was not a single captain among them; he made the observation to a fellow-passenger, and asked how he accounted for it. "Oh, sir, the captains are all on deck," was the reply.

… I know it is equally easy and invidious[1] to ridicule the peculiarities of appearance and manner in people of a different nation from ourselves; we may, too, at the same moment, be undergoing the same ordeal in their estimation; and, moreover, I am by no means disposed to consider whatever is new to me as therefore objectionable; but, nevertheless, it was impossible not to feel repugnance to many of the novelties that now surrounded me.

---

[1] *invidious* Tending to incite ill-feeling or unpopularity against others.

The total want of all the usual courtesies of the table, the voracious rapidity with which the viands[1] were seized and devoured, the strange uncouth phrases and pronunciation; the loathsome spitting, from the contamination of which it was absolutely impossible to protect our dresses; the frightful manner of feeding with their knives, till the whole blade seemed to enter into the mouth; and the still more frightful manner of cleaning the teeth afterwards with a pocket knife, soon forced us to feel that we were not surrounded by the generals, colonels, and majors of the old world; and that the dinner hour was to be any thing rather than an hour of enjoyment.

The little conversation that went forward while we remained in the room, was entirely political, and the respective claims of Adams and Jackson[2] to the presidency were argued with more oaths and more vehemence than it had ever been my lot to hear. Once a colonel appeared on the verge of assaulting a major, when a huge seven-foot Kentuckian gentleman horse-dealer, asked of the heavens to confound them both, and bade them sit still and be d———d. We too thought we should share this sentence; at least sitting still in the cabin seemed very nearly to include the rest of it, and we never tarried[3] there a moment longer than was absolutely necessary to eat.

from CHAPTER 34: RETURN TO NEW YORK—CONCLUSION

… Nothing could be more beautiful than our passage down the Hudson on the following day, as I thought of some of my friends in England, dear lovers of the picturesque; … not even a moving panoramic view, gliding before their eyes for an hour together, in all the scenic splendour of Drury Lane, or Covent Garden,[4] could give them an idea of it. They could only see one side at a time. The change, the contrast, the ceaseless variety of beauty, as you skim from side to side, the liquid smoothness of the broad mirror that reflects the scene, and most of all, the clear bright air through which you look at it; all this can only be seen and believed by crossing the Atlantic.

As we approached New York the burning heat of the day relaxed, and the long shadows of evening fell coolly on the beautiful villas we passed. I really can conceive nothing more exquisitely lovely than this approach to the city. The magnificent boldness of the Jersey shore on the one side, and the luxurious softness of the shady lawns on the other, with the vast silvery stream that flows between them, altogether form a picture which may well excuse a traveller for saying, once and again, that the Hudson River can be surpassed in beauty by none on the outside of Paradise.

It was nearly dark when we reached the city, and it was with great satisfaction that we found our comfortable apartments in Hudson Street unoccupied; and our pretty, kind (Irish) hostess willing to receive us again. We passed another fortnight there; and again we enjoyed the elegant hospitality of New York, though now it was offered from beneath the shade of their beautiful villas. In truth, were all America like this fair city, and all, no, only a small proportion of its population like the friends we left there, I should say, that the land was the fairest in the world.

It is a matter of historical notoriety that the original stock of the white population now inhabiting the United States, were persons who had banished themselves, or were banished from the mother country. The land they found was favourable to their increase and prosperity; the colony grew and flourished. Years rolled on, and the children, the grand-children, and the great grand-children of the first settlers, replenished the land, and found it flowing with milk and honey. That they should wish to keep this milk and honey to themselves, is not very surprising. What did the mother country do for them? She sent them out gay and gallant officers to guard their frontier; the which they thought they could guard as well themselves; and then she taxed their tea. Now, this was disagreeable; and to atone for it, the distant colony had no great share in her mother's grace and glory. It was not from among them that her high

---

[1] *viands* Food.

[2] *Adams* John Quincy Adams (1767–1848) won a controversial majority in the American election of 1824 by joining forces with third candidate Henry Clay, whom he later named Secretary of State; *Jackson* Andrew Jackson (1767–1845) contested Adams's government and went on to win the 1829 election.

[3] *tarried* Delayed.

[4] *Drury Lane* Street in London, England, location of the famous theater of that name; *Covent Garden* Theater and entertainment district in central London, England.

and mighty were chosen; the rays which emanated from that bright sun of honour, the British throne, reached them but feebly. They knew not, they cared not, for her kings nor her heroes; their thriftiest trader was their noblest man; the holy seats of learning were but the cradles of superstition; the splendour of the aristocracy, but a leech that drew their "golden blood." The wealth, the learning, the glory of Britain, was to them nothing; the having their own way every thing. Can any blame their wish to obtain it? Can any lament that they succeeded?…

As long as their governments are at peace with each other, the individuals of every nation in Europe make it a matter of pride, as well as of pleasure, to meet each other frequently, to discuss, compare, and reason upon their national varieties, and to vote it a mark of fashion and good taste to imitate each other in all the external embellishments of life.

The consequence of this is most pleasantly perceptible at the present time, in every capital of Europe. The long peace has given time for each to catch from each what was best in customs and manners, and the rapid advance of refinement and general information has been the result.

To those who have been accustomed to this state of things, the contrast upon crossing to the new world is inconceivably annoying; and it cannot be doubted that this is one great cause of the general feeling of irksomeness, and fatigue of spirits, which hangs upon the memory while recalling the hours passed in American society.

A single word indicative of doubt, that any thing, or every thing, in that country is not the very best in the world, produces an effect which must be seen and felt to be understood. If the citizens of the United States were indeed the devoted patriots they call themselves, they would surely not thus encrust themselves in the hard, dry, stubborn persuasion, that they are the first and best of the human race, that nothing is to be learnt, but what they are able to teach, and that nothing is worth having, which they do not possess.

The art of man could hardly discover a more effectual antidote to improvement, than this persuasion; and yet I never listened to any public oration, or read any work, professedly addressed to the country, in which

they did not labour to impress it on the minds of the people.

from Thomas Babington Macaulay, "Minute on Indian Education" (1835)

In this 1835 speech, Macaulay, then a member of the Council of India, argued that the sum set aside by the British Parliament for the education of Indian citizens should be used to teach the English language and the scientific and cultural advancements of Britain, rather than to promote the study of India's native cultures and languages. In the paragraphs immediately preceding this excerpt, Macaulay put forward the claim that the people of India should not be taught in any of their native languages, as the various dialects are "poor and rude," and "contain neither literary nor scientific information." In addition, he asserted, the historical, philosophical, and literary achievements of works written in European languages far surpassed their Sanskrit and Arabic equivalents.

from "Minute on Indian Education"

…

How, then, stands the case? We have to educate a people who cannot at present be educated by means of their mother-tongue. We must teach them some foreign language. The claims of our own language it is hardly necessary to recapitulate. It stands pre-eminent even among the languages of the west. It abounds with works of imagination not inferior to the noblest which Greece has bequeathed to us; with models of every species of eloquence; with historical compositions, which, considered merely as narratives, have seldom been surpassed, and which, considered as vehicles of ethical and political instruction, have never been equalled; with just and lively representations of human life and human nature; with the most profound speculations on metaphysics, morals, government, jurisprudence,[1] and trade; with full and correct information respecting every experimental science which tends to preserve the health, to increase the comfort, or to

---

[1] *jurisprudence* Law.

expand the intellect of man. Whoever knows that language has ready access to all the vast intellectual wealth which all the wisest nations of the earth have created and hoarded in the course of ninety generations. It may safely be said that the literature now extant in that language is of far greater value than all the literature which three hundred years ago was extant in all the languages of the world together. Nor is this all. In India, English is the language spoken by the ruling class. It is spoken by the higher class of natives at the seats of government. It is likely to become the language of commerce throughout the seas of the East. It is the language of two great European communities which are rising, the one in the south of Africa, the other in Australasia; communities which are every year becoming more important, and more closely connected with our Indian Empire. Whether we look at the intrinsic value of our literature, or at the particular situation of this country, we shall see the strongest reason to think that, of all foreign tongues, the English tongue is that which would be the most useful to our native subjects.

The question now before us is simply whether, when it is in our power to teach this language, we shall teach languages in which, by universal confession, there are no books on any subject which deserve to be compared to our own; whether, when we can teach European science, we shall teach systems which, by universal confession, whenever they differ from those of Europe, differ for the worse; and whether, when we can patronize sound philosophy and true history, we shall countenance, at the public expense, medical doctrines which would disgrace an English farrier,[1] astronomy which would move laughter in girls at an English boarding-school, history abounding with kings thirty feet high, and reigns thirty thousand years long, and geography made up of seas of treacle and seas of butter.

We are not without experience to guide us. History furnishes several analogous cases, and they all teach the same lesson. There are in modern times, to go no further, two memorable instances of a great impulse given to the mind of a whole society—of prejudices overthrown, of knowledge diffused, of taste purified, of arts and sciences planted in countries which had recently been ignorant and barbarous.

The first instance to which I refer is the great revival of letters among the western nations at the close of the fifteenth, and the beginning of the sixteenth, century. At that time almost everything that was worth reading was contained in the writings of the ancient Greeks and Romans. Had our ancestors acted as the Committee of Public Instruction has hitherto acted;[2] had they neglected the language of Cicero and Tacitus;[3] had they confined their attention to the old dialects of our own island; had they printed nothing, and taught nothing at the universities, but chronicles in Anglo-Saxon, and romances in Norman-French, would England have been what she now is? What the Greek and Latin were to the contemporaries of More and Ascham,[4] our tongue is to the people of India. The literature of England is now more valuable than that of classical antiquity. I doubt whether the Sanskrit literature be as valuable as that of our Saxon and Norman progenitors. In some departments—in history, for example—I am certain that it is much less so.

Another instance may be said to be still before our eyes. Within the last hundred and twenty years, a nation which had previously been in a state as barbarous as that in which our ancestors were before the crusades, has gradually emerged from the ignorance in which it was sunk, and has taken its place among civilized communities—I speak of Russia. There is now in that country a large educated class, abounding with persons fit to serve the state in the highest functions, and in no wise inferior to the most accomplished men who adorn the best circles of Paris and London. There is reason to hope that this vast empire, which in the time of our grandfathers was probably behind the Punjab, may, in the time of our grandchildren, be pressing close on France and Britain in the career of improvement. And how was this

---

[1] *farrier* One who shoes or cares for horses.

[2] *Committee ... acted* The Committee of Public Instruction had hitherto used the allocated funds solely for promoting the study of Arabic and Sanskrit literature and for encouraging those "learned natives" who studied the science, religions, and histories of their native cultures.

[3] *Cicero* Roman orator of the first century BCE; *Tacitus* First-century CE author of two works of Roman history, *Histories* and *Annals*.

[4] *More* Sir Thomas More (1478–1535), English statesman and humanist scholar, author of *Utopia*; *Ascham* Roger Ascham (1515–68), Latin Secretary to Edward VI, Mary I, and Elizabeth I.

change effected? Not by flattering national prejudices; not by feeding the mind of the young Muscovite[1] with old women's stories which his rude fathers had believed; not by filling his head with lying legends about St. Nicholas;[2] not by encouraging him to study the great question, whether the world was or was not created on the 13th of September; not by calling him "a learned native," when he has mastered all these points of knowledge: but by teaching him those foreign languages in which the greatest mass of information had been laid up, and thus putting all that information within his reach. The languages of Western Europe civilized Russia. I cannot doubt that they will do for the Hindu what they have done for the Tartar.[3] ...

It is impossible for us, with our limited means, to attempt to educate the body of the people. We must at present do our best to form a class who may be interpreters between us and the millions whom we govern; a class of persons, Indian in blood and colour, but English in taste, in opinions, in morals, and in intellect. To that class we may leave it to refine the vernacular dialects of the country, to enrich those dialects with terms of science borrowed from the Western nomenclature, and to render them by degrees fit vehicles for conveying knowledge to the great mass of the population.

from Report of a Speech by William Charles Wentworth, Australian Legislative Council (1844)

In 1844 the aboriginal populace in Australia probably still outnumbered that of the whites. Official policy called for "amity and kindness" and forbade "any unnecessary interruption" of aboriginal existence, but, as the excerpt below suggests, attitudes towards native peoples that prevailed were often brutally harsh.

He could not see if the whites in this colony were to go out into the land and possess it, that the Government had much to do with them. No doubt there

would be battles between the settlers and the border tribes; but they might be settled without the aid of the Government. The civilized people had come in and the savage must go back. They must go on progressing until their dominancy was established, and therefore he could think that no measure was wise or merciful to the blacks which clothed them with a degree of seeming protection, which their position would not allow them to maintain.... It was not the policy of a wise Government to attempt the perpetuation of the aboriginal race of New South Wales.... They must give way before the arms, aye! even the diseases of civilized nations—they must give way before they attain the power of those nations.

from William H. Smith, *Smith's Canadian Gazetteer* (1846)

Smith states in his preface that he was "induced to undertake the task" of writing his gazetteer by the "great ignorance" which he found to exist respecting the province of Canada West (now Ontario), "not only amongst persons in Great Britain, or newly arrived emigrants, but even amongst many of those who had been for years resident in the country." The *Gazetteer* included information on all towns and geographical areas in the province. The following excerpts are taken from the section of general reflections with which the work concludes.

It is most extraordinary, so long as Canada has been settled, that its great natural advantages should still be so little known; that so many persons who are either compelled by necessity to emigrate, or who do so from choice, should continue to pass it by and go on to the west of the United States, or otherwise emigrate to the more distant colonies of the Cape, New South Wales, or New Zealand and yet such is the case....

In what respects will the advocates of emigration to the United States pretend to say that any portion of that country is superior to Canada. Is it in the climate? A tree may be judged of by its fruits, and very many of the native Canadians, in point of robust appearance and complexion, might be taken for English emigrants. Will any one venture to make the same assertion respecting a native of Ohio, Indiana, Illinois, or Missouri? And of

[1] *Muscovite* Resident of Moscow.

[2] *St. Nicholas* Patron saint of sailors, revered in Christian Orthodox tradition.

[3] *Tartar* Here, Russian.

what avail is it that the climate will grow cotton and tobacco, if the settler neither has the strength to cultivate them, nor a market in which to dispose of them, when grown? In the winter and spring of 1841–2, pork (a staple article of the State) was selling in Illinois, at from a dollar to a dollar and a half per 100 lbs.; and at that price it was almost impossible to obtain cash for it; wheat at a quarter dollar, and Indian corn from five to ten cents per bushel; butter, fifteen and sixteen pounds for a dollar; fowls, half a dollar per dozen; and other farming produce in proportion. At such prices farming could not be very profitable. A man certainly might live cheaply, and cram himself with bacon and corn bread till he brought on bilious fever;[1] but he could *make nothing* of what he raised. And a farmer having a fat ox, has even been known after killing it, to take from it the hide and tallow, and drag the carcass into the woods to be devoured by the wolves; finding from the small price the beef would fetch, that it was more profitable to do so than to sell the whole animal!

Is it from the nature of the government, that the States are so much more desirable as a place of residence—where the only law is mob law, and the bowie knife is the constant companion of the citizens, and is used even in the halls of legislature themselves? Or is New Zealand much to be preferred, where the settler in taking his morning ramble, to acquire an appetite for his breakfast, frequently receives a "settler" himself, and instead of returning to his morning's meal, is roasted for the breakfast of some native chief, and his interesting family. Canada, on the contrary, suffers under none of these disadvantages and annoyances. The government and constitution of the country are English; the laws English; the climate is fine and healthy; the Indians are tolerably civilized, none of them at any rate are cannibals, and few of them are even thieves; and bowie knives are not "the fashion." The settler, unless he has been guilty of the folly of planting himself down beyond the bounds of civilization and of roads, may always command a fair price and cash for whatever he can raise—he need never be beyond the reach of medical attendance, churches, and schools—he can obtain as much land as he need wish to purchase, at a fair and moderate

rate—he knows that whatever property he acquires is as secure as if he had it in England—his landed property, if he possesses any, is gradually increasing in value—and if he is only moderately careful and industrious, he need have no anxiety for the future—his sons, growing up in and with the country, and as they grow, acquiring a knowledge of the country and its customs, and the various modes of doing business in it, if steady, will have no difficulty in succeeding in any business they may select, or may be qualified for.

Much has been written on the subject of emigration, and many speculations entered into as to *who* are the proper persons to emigrate? The only answer that can be given to this question is—*those who are obliged to do so.* Let no person who is doing *well* at home, no matter what may be his profession or occupation, emigrate with the expectation of doing *better,*—let him not leave his home and travel over the world, in search of advantages which he may not find elsewhere. But those who are *not* doing well, who find it difficult to struggle against increasing competition, who fear the loss in business of what little property they possess, or who find it difficult with an increasing family to keep up appearances as they have been accustomed to do, and find it necessary to make a change—all these may safely emigrate, with a fair prospect of improving their condition. Persons of small, independent incomes may live cheaply in Canada, particularly in the country, and enjoy many comforts, and even luxuries, that were not within their reach at home. Retired military men do not generally make good settlers. They usually, when they leave the army, sell out, instead of retiring on half pay; and when they emigrate they are apt to squander their property in purchasing land and in building, till at length they come to a stand for want of the means to proceed, frequently with their buildings half-finished, from being planned on too large a scale; although, if they had been asked in the commencement how they intended to *live* when the ready money was expended, they would have been unable to give an intelligible answer. If they succeed in getting some government office, the emoluments[2] of which are sufficient for their support, they will manage to get along very well; otherwise they will sink gradually

---

[1] *bilious fever* Over-secretion of bile, causing indigestion.

[2] *emoluments* Salary, remuneration.

lower and lower, and their children are apt to get into idle and dissipated habits. The idle and inactive life to which they have been accustomed while in the army, particularly during these "piping times of peace,"[1] totally incapacitates them for making good settlers in the backwoods. *A lounger, unless independent, has no business in Canada.* Naval officers, on the contrary, make settlers of a very different character. They have been accustomed, when on service, to a life of activity; and if they have been long on service, they have generally seen a great deal of the world—they have their half-pay to fall back on, which fortunately for them they cannot sell—and they generally make very excellent settlers. Lawyers are not wanted: Canada swarms with them; and they multiply in the province so fast, that the demand is not by any means equal to the supply. Medical men may find many openings in the country, where they will have no difficulty in making a tolerable living; but they will have to work hard for it, having frequently to ride fifteen, twenty-five, or even thirty miles to see a patient! And in the towns, the competition is as great as in England....

Carlyle, Mill, and "The Negro Question"

In the wake of the abolition of slavery in all British possessions in 1837, and of the ending of the preferential tariff on sugar in 1846, plantation owners in the British West Indies complained vociferously about their situation, arguing that they were placed in the unfair position of having to compete against sugar produced in countries such as Brazil where slavery was still permitted. Amongst the many in Britain who supported their arguments was Thomas Carlyle, who sets out his position in the essay excerpted below. Shortly thereafter, John Stuart Mill delivered a stinging reply, also excerpted below. Carlyle reprinted a revised version of the essay in 1853 under the more incendiary title "Occasional Discourse on the Nigger Question."[2] In the 1860s the two also disagreed

publicly over the Eyre rebellion (an uprising in Jamaica against the oppressive conditions under which black Jamaicans were forced to work, which became a *cause célèbre* in England when the rebellion was suppressed, with extraordinary brutality, by Governor Edward John Eyre).

from Thomas Carlyle, "Occasional Discourse on the Negro Question," *Fraser's Magazine* (1849)

West Indian affairs, as we all know, and some of us know to our cost, are in a rather troublous condition this good while. In regard to West Indian affairs, however, Lord John Russell[3] is able to comfort us with one fact, indisputable where so many are dubious, that the negroes are all very happy and doing well. A fact very comfortable indeed. West Indian whites, it is admitted, are far enough from happy; West Indian colonies not unlike sinking wholly into ruin; at home, too, the British whites are rather badly off—several millions of them hanging on the verge of continual famine—and, in single towns, many thousands of them very sore put to it, at this time ... to live at all—these, again, are uncomfortable facts; and they are extremely extensive and important ones. But ... how pleasant to have always this fact to fall back upon; our beautiful black darlings are at last happy; with little labor except to the teeth, *which*, surely, in those excellent horse-jaws of theirs, will not fail!

Exeter Hall,[4] my philanthropic friends, has had its way in this matter. The twenty millions, a mere trifle, despatched with a single dash of the pen, are paid; and, far over the sea, we have a few black persons rendered extremely "free" indeed. Sitting yonder, with their beautiful muzzles up to the ears in pumpkins, imbibing

---

[1] *piping ... peace* See William Shakespeare's *Richard III* 1.1.24: "Why, I, in this weak piping time of peace, / Have no delight to pass away the time."

[2] *more incendiary ... Nigger Question* From the late sixteenth century into the eighteenth, the term "nigger" was generally used in a more or less neutral fashion, and rarely in a way that directly

expressed hostility towards blacks. In the late eighteenth and early nineteenth centuries the word began to be used more and more frequently to express contempt. An example from the same period at which Carlyle was writing is Hartley Coleridge's 1849 complaint against turning Othello "into a rank wooly-pated, thick-lipped nigger."

[3] *Lord John Russell* Russell (1792–1878) was British Prime Minister from 1846 to 1852 and from 1865 to 1866.

[4] *Exeter Hall* Exeter Hall, on the Strand, in London, was built in 1830 to serve as a meeting place for a variety of religious groups, benevolent associations, and other charitable institutions.

sweet pulps and juices; the grinder and incisor teeth ready for every new work, and the pumpkins cheap as grass in those rich climates; while the sugar crops rot round them, uncut, because labor cannot be hired. ... A state of matters lovely to contemplate, in these emancipated epochs of the human mind, which has earned us, not only the praises of Exeter Hall, and loud, long-eared hallelujahs of laudatory psalmody[1] from the friends of freedom everywhere, but lasting favor (it is hoped) from the heavenly powers themselves; which may, at least, justly appeal to the heavenly powers, and ask them, if ever, in terrestrial procedure, they saw the match of it! Certainly, in the past history of the human species, it has no parallel; nor, one hopes, will it have in the future. ...

Truly, my philanthropic friends, Exeter Hall philanthropy is wonderful; and the social science ... which finds the secret of this universe in "supply and demand," and reduces the duty of human governors to that of letting men alone, is also wonderful. A dreary, desolate and, indeed, quite abject and distressing one; what we might call, by way of eminence, the *dismal science.*[2] These two, Exeter Hall philanthropy and the Dismal Science, led by any sacred cause of black emancipation, or the like, to fall in love and make a wedding of it—will give birth to progenies and prodigies: dark extensive moon-calves, unnameable abortions, wide-coiled monstrosities, such as the world has not seen hitherto!...

My philanthropic friends, can you discern no fixed headlands in this wide-weltering[3] deluge of benevolent twaddle and revolutionary grapeshot that has burst forth on us—no sure bearings at all? Fact and nature, it seems to me, say a few words to us, if, happily, we have still an ear for fact and nature. Let us listen a little, and try. And first, with regard to the West Indies, it may be laid down as a principle, which no eloquence in Exeter Hall, or Westminster Hall,[4] or elsewhere, can invalidate or hide, except for a short time only, that no black man,

who will not work according to what ability the gods have given him for working, has the smallest right to eat pumpkin, or to any fraction of land that will grow pumpkin, however plentiful such land may be, but has an indisputable and perpetual *right* to be compelled, by the real proprietors of said land, to do competent work for his living. This is the everlasting duty of all men, black or white, who are born into this world. To do competent work, to labor honestly according to the ability given them; for that, and for no other purpose, was each one of us sent into this world; and woe is to every man who by friend or by foe, is prevented from fulfilling this, the end of his being....

The idle black man in the West Indies had, not long since, the right, and will again, under better form, if it please Heaven, have the right (actually the first "right of man" for an indolent person) to be *compelled* to work as he was fit, and to *do* the Maker's will, who had constructed him with such and such prefigurements of capability....

And now observe, my friends, it was not Black Quashee,[5] or those he represents, that made those West India islands what they are, or can, by any hypothesis, be considered to have the right of growing pumpkins there. For countless ages, since they first mounted oozy on the back of earthquakes, from their dark bed in the ocean deeps, and reeking, saluted the tropical sun, and ever onward, till the European white man first saw them, some three short centuries ago, those islands had produced mere jungle, savagery, poison reptiles and swamp malaria till the white European first saw them, they were, as if not yet created; their noble elements of cinnamon—sugar, coffee, pepper, black and gray, lying all asleep, waiting the white Enchanter, who should say to them, awake! Till the end of human history, and the sounding of the trump of doom, they might have lain so, had Quashee, and the like of him, been the only artists in the game. Swamps, fever-jungles, man-eating caribs, rattle-snakes, and reeking waste and putrefaction: this had been the produce of them under the incompetent caribal[6] (what we call cannibal) possessors till that

---

[1] *psalmody* Singing of psalms.

[2] *dismal science* This famous phrase describing the science now known as economics has often been cited as first used by Carlyle in his "Latter Day Pamphlet" (1850), rather than in the present essay.

[3] *wide-weltering* State of turmoil, often used to describe the sea.

[4] *Westminster Hall* Location of British Parliament.

[5] *Quashee* African first name, used by some eighteenth- and nineteenth-century writers to stand for all black people.

[6] *caribal* Insulting combination of "Carib," indigenous person of the West Indies, and "cannibal."

time; and Quashee knows, himself, whether ever he could have introduced an improvement. Him, had he, by a miraculous chance, been wafted thither, the caribals would have eaten, rolling him as a fat morsel under their tongue—for him, till the sounding of the trump of doom, the rattlesnakes and savageries would have held on their way. It was not he, then—it was another than he! ... Quashee, if he will not help in bringing out the spices, will get himself made a slave again (which state will be a little less ugly than his present one), and with beneficent whip, since other methods avail not, will be compelled to work. ... The gods are long-suffering; but the law, from the beginning, was, He that will not work shall perish from the earth—and the patience of the gods has limits!

Before the West Indies could grow a pumpkin for any negro, how much European heroism had to spend itself in obscure battle; to sink, in mortal agony, before the jungles, the putrescences and waste savageries could become arable, and the devils be, in some measure, chained there! The West Indies grow pineapples, and sweet fruits, and spices; we hope they will, one day, grow beautiful, heroic human lives too, which is surely the ultimate object they were made for; beautiful souls and brave; sages, poets, what not—making the earth nobler round them, as their kindred from of old have been doing; ... heroic white men, worthy to be called old Saxons, browned with a mahogany tint in those new climates and conditions. But under the soil of Jamaica, before it could even produce spices, or any pumpkin, the bones of many thousand British men had to be laid. ...

Already one hears of black *Adscripti glebae*;[1] which seems a promising arrangement, one of the first to suggest itself in such a complicacy. It appears the Dutch blacks, in Java, are already a kind of *Adscripts*, after the manner of the old European serfs; bound by royal authority, to give so many days of work a year. Is not this something like a real approximation; the first step toward all manner of such? Wherever, in British territory, there exists a black man, and needful work to the just extent is not to be got out of him, such a law, in defect of better, should be brought to bear upon said black man! ...

from John Stuart Mill, "The Negro Question," *Fraser's Magazine* (1850)

TO THE EDITOR OF *Fraser's Magazine*

Sir:

Your last month's number contains a speech against the "rights of Negroes," the doctrines and spirit of which ought not to pass without remonstrance. The author issues his opinions, or rather ordinances, under imposing auspices no less than those of the "immortal gods." "The Powers," "the Destinies," announce, through him, not only what *will* be, but what *shall* be done; what they "have decided upon, passed their eternal act of Parliament for." This is speaking "as one having authority"; but authority from whom? If by the quality of the message we may judge of those who sent it, not from any powers to whom just or good men acknowledge allegiance. This so-called "eternal act of Parliament" is no new law, but the old law of the strongest—a law against which the great teachers of mankind have in all ages protested—it is the law of force and cunning; the law that whoever is more powerful than an other, is "born lord" of that other, the other being born his "servant," who must be "compelled to work" for him by "beneficent whip," if "other methods avail not." I see nothing divine in this injunction. If "the gods" will this, it is the first duty of human beings to resist such gods. Omnipotent these "gods" are *not*, for powers which demand *human* tyranny and injustice cannot accomplish their purpose unless human beings cooperate. The history of human improvement is the record of a struggle by which inch after inch of ground has been wrung from these maleficent[2] powers, and more and more of human life rescued from the iniquitous[3] dominion of the law of might. Much, very much of this work still remains to do; but the progress made in it is the best and greatest achievement yet performed by mankind, and it was hardly to be expected at this period of the world that we should be enjoined, by way of a great reform in human affair, to begin *un*doing it.

... I must first set my anti-philanthropic opponent right on a matter of fact. He entirely misunderstands the

---

1 *Adscripti glebae* Latin: Permanently tied to the land; serf.

2 *maleficent* Harmful, evil.

3 *iniquitous* Unjust, unrighteous.

great national revolt of the conscience of this country against slavery and the slave-trade if he supposes it to have been an affair of sentiment. It depended no more on humane feelings than any cause which so irresistibly appealed to them must necessarily do: Its first victories were gained while the lash yet ruled uncontested in the barrack-yard, and the rod in schools, and while men were still hanged by dozens for stealing to the value of forty shillings. It triumphed because it was the cause of justice; and, in the estimation of the great majority of its supporters, of religion. Its originators and leaders were persons of a stern sense of moral obligation, who, in the spirit of the religion of their time, seldom spoke much of benevolence and philanthropy, but often of duty, crime, and sin. For nearly two centuries had negroes, many thousands annually, been seized by force or treachery and carried off to the West Indies to be worked to death, literally to death; for it was the received maxim, the acknowledged dictate of good economy, to wear them out quickly and import more. In this fact every other possible cruelty, tyranny, and wanton oppression was by implication included. And the motive on the part of the slave-owners was the love of gold; or, to speak more truly, of vulgar and puerile ostentation. I have yet to learn that anything more detestable than this has been done by human beings towards human beings in any part of the earth....

After fifty years of toil and sacrifice, the object was accomplished, and the negroes, freed from the despotism of their fellow-beings, were left to themselves, and to the chances which the arrangements of existing society provide for these who have no resource but their labour. These chances proved favorable to them, and, for the last ten years, they afford the unusual spectacle of a labouring class whose labour bears so high a price that they can exist in comfort on the wages of a comparatively small quantity of work. This, to the ex-slave-owners, is an inconvenience; but I have not yet heard that any of them has been reduced to beg his bread, or even to dig for it, as the negro, however scandalously he enjoys himself, still must.... If the [plantation owners] cannot continue to realize their large incomes without more labourers, let them find them, and bring them from where they can best be procured, only not by force. Not so, thinks your anti-philanthropic contribu-

tor. That negroes should exist, and enjoy existence, on so little work, is a scandal, in his eyes, worse than their former slavery. It must be put a stop to at any price. He does not "wish to see" them slaves again "if it can be avoided"; but "decidedly" they "will have to be servants," "servants to the whites," "compelled to labour," and "not to go idle another minute." "Black Quashee," "up to the ears in pumpkins," and "working about half an hour a day," is to him the abomination of abominations.

... To give it a rational meaning, it must first be known what he means by work. Does work mean everything which people *do*? No; or he would not reproach people with doing no work. Does it mean laborious exertion? No; for many a day spent in killing game, includes more muscular fatigue than a day's ploughing. Does it mean *useful* exertion? But your contributor always scoffs at the idea of utility. Does he mean that all persons ought to earn their living? But some earn their living by doing nothing, and some by doing mischief; and the negroes, whom he despises, still do earn by labour the "pumpkins" they consume and the finery they wear.

Work, I imagine, is not a good in itself. There is nothing laudable in work for work's sake. To work voluntarily for a worthy object is laudable; but what constitutes a worthy object? On this matter, the oracle of which your contributor is the prophet[1] has never yet been prevailed on to declare itself. He revolves in an eternal circle round the idea of work, as if turning up the earth, or driving a shuttle or a quill, were ends in themselves, and the ends of human existence. Yet, even in the case of the most sublime service to humanity, it is not because it is work that it is worthy; the worth lies in the service itself, and in the will to render it—the noble feelings of which it is the fruit; and if the nobleness of will is proved by other evidence than work, as for instance by danger or sacrifice, there is the same worthiness. While we talk only of work, and not of its object, we are far from the root of the matter; or, if it may be called the root, it is a root without flower or fruit.

---

[1] *prophet* With the publication of *Past and Present* in 1843, Carlyle began to be considered a visionary, even a prophetic voice, of social and cultural commentary in England.

In the present case, it seems, a noble object means "spices."——"The gods wish, besides pumpkins, that spices and valuable products be grown in their West Indies"——the "noble elements of cinnamon, sugar, coffee, pepper black and gray," "things far nobler than pumpkins." Why so? Is what supports life inferior in dignity to what merely gratifies the sense of taste? Is it the verdict of the "immortal gods" that pepper is noble, freedom (even freedom from the lash) contemptible? But spices lead "towards commerces, arts, polities, and social developments." Perhaps so; but of what sort? When they must be produced by slaves, the "polities and social developments" they lead to are such as the world, I hope, will not choose to be cursed with much longer.

The worth of work does not surely consist in its leading to other work, and so on to work upon work without end. On the contrary, the multiplication of work, for purposes not worth caring about, is one of the evils of our present condition. When justice and reason shall be the rule of human affairs, one of the first things to which we may expect them to be applied is the question. How many of the so-called luxuries, conveniences, refinements, and ornaments of life, are *worth* the labour which must be undergone as the condition of producing them? The beautifying of existence is as worthy and useful an object as the sustaining of it; but only a vitiated[1] taste can see any such result in those fopperies[2] of so-called civilization, which myriads of hands are now occupied and lives wasted in providing. In opposition to the "gospel of work," I would assert the gospel of leisure, and maintain that human beings *cannot* rise to the finer attributes of their nature compatibly with a life filled with labour. I do not include under the name labour such work, if work it be called, as is done by writers and afforders of "guidance," an occupation which, let alone the vanity of the thing, cannot be called by the same name with the real labour, the exhausting, stiffening, stupefying toil of many kinds of agricultural and manufacturing labourers. To reduce very greatly the quantity of work required to carry on existence is as needful as to distribute it more equally; and the progress of science, and the increasing ascendency of justice and good sense, tend to this result.

There is a portion of work rendered necessary by the fact of each person's existence: no one could exist unless work, to a certain amount, were done either by or for him. Of this each person is bound, in justice, to perform his share; and society has an incontestable right to declare to every one, that if he work not, at this work of necessity, neither shall he eat. Society has not enforced this right, having in so far postponed the rule of justice to other considerations. But there is an ever-growing demand that it be enforced, so soon as any endurable plan can be devised for the purpose. If this experiment is to be tried in the West Indies, let it be tried impartially; and let the whole produce belong to those who do the work which produces it. We would not have black labourers compelled to grow spices which they do not want, and white proprietors who do not work at all exchanging the spices for houses in Belgrave Square.[3] We would not withhold from the whites, any more than from the blacks, the "divine right" of being compelled to labour. Let them have exactly the same share in the produce that they have in the work. If they do not like this, let them remain as they are, so long as they are permitted, and make the best of supply and demand.

Your contributor's notions of justice and proprietary right are of another kind than these. According to him, the whole West Indies belong to the whites: the negroes have no claim there, to either land or food, but by their sufferance. "It was not Black Quashee, or those he represents, that made those West India islands what they are." I submit, that those who furnished the thews[4] and sinews really had something to do with the matter.

But the great ethical doctrine of the discourse, ... than which a doctrine more damnable, I should think, never was propounded by a professed moral reformer, is, that one kind of human beings are born servants to another kind. "You will have to be servants," he tells the negroes, "to those that are born wiser than you, that are born lords of you—servants to the whites, if they are (as what mortal can doubt that they are?) born wiser than you." I do not hold him to the absurd letter of his dictum; it belongs to the mannerism in which he is enthralled like a child in swaddling clothes. By "born wiser," I will suppose him to mean, born more capable

[1] *vitiated* Corrupted.

[2] *fopperies* Here, useless consumer goods.

[3] *Belgrave Square* Fashionable area of London.

[4] *thews* Muscles.

of wisdom: a proposition which, he says, no mortal can doubt, but which, I will make bold to say, that a full moiety[1] of all thinking persons, who have attended to the subject, either doubt or positively deny.

Among the things for which your contributor professes entire disrespect, is the analytical examination of human nature. It is by analytical examination that we have learned whatever we know of the laws of external nature; and if he had not disdained to apply the same mode of investigation to the laws of the formation of character, he would have escaped the vulgar error of imputing every difference which he finds among human beings to an original difference of nature. As well might it be said, that of two trees, sprung from the same stock one cannot be taller than another but from greater vigor in the original seedling. Is nothing to be attributed to soil, nothing to climate, nothing to difference of exposure—has no storm swept over the one and not the other, no lightning scathed it, no beast browsed on it, no insects preyed on it, no passing stranger stripped off its leaves or its bark? If the trees grew near together, may not the one which, by whatever accident, grew up first, have retarded the other's development by its shade? Human beings are subject to an infinitely greater variety of accidents and external influences than trees, and have infinitely more operation in impairing the growth of one another; since those who begin by being strongest, have almost always hitherto used their strength to keep the others weak. What the original differences are among human beings, I know no more than your contributor, and no less; it is one of the questions not yet satisfactorily answered in the natural history of the species. This, however, is well known—that spontaneous improvement, beyond a very low grade—improvement by internal development, without aid from other individuals or peoples—is one of the rarest phenomena in history; and whenever known to have occurred, was the result of an extraordinary combination of advantages; in addition doubtless to many accidents of which all trace is now lost. No argument against the capacity of negroes for improvement, could be drawn from their not being one of these rare exceptions. It is curious, withal, that the earliest known civilization was, we have the strongest reason to believe, a negro civilization. The original Egyptians are inferred, from the evidence of their sculptures, to have been a negro race: it was from negroes, therefore, that the Greeks learnt their first lessons in civilization; … but I again renounce all advantage from facts: [even if it *were* true that] whites [were] born ever so superior in intelligence to the blacks, and competent by nature to instruct and advise them, it would not be the less monstrous to assert that they had therefore a right either to subdue them by force, or circumvent them by superior skill; to throw upon them the toils and hardships of life, reserving for themselves, under the misapplied name of work, its agreeable excitements. …

Though we cannot extirpate[2] all pain, we can, if we are sufficiently determined upon it, abolish all tyranny; one of the greatest victories yet gained over that enemy is slave-emancipation and all Europe is struggling, with various success, towards further conquests over it. If, in the pursuit of this, we lose sight of any object equally important; if we forget that freedom is not the only thing necessary for human beings, let us be thankful to any one who points out what is wanting; but let us not consent to turn back. That this country should turn back, in the matter of negro slavery, I have not the smallest apprehension.

There is, however, another place where that tyranny still flourishes, but now for the first time finds itself seriously in danger. At this crisis of American slavery, when the decisive conflict between right and iniquity seems about to commence, your contributor steps in, and flings this missile, loaded with the weight of his reputation, into the abolitionist camp. The words of English writers of celebrity are words of power on the other side of the ocean; and the owners of human flesh, who probably thought they had not an honest man on their side between the Atlantic and the Vistula,[3] will welcome such an auxiliary. Circulated as his dissertation will probably be, by those whose interests profit by it, from one end of the American Union to the other, I hardly know of an act by which one person could have done so much mischief as this may possibly do; and I

---

1   *moiety*   Half.

2   *extirpate*   To remove, literally pull out roots.

3   *between the Atlantic and the Vistula*   I.e., in Britain or in Continental Europe. (The Vistula is a river in Poland.)

hold that by thus acting, he has made himself an instrument of what an able writer in the *Inquirer* justly calls "a true work of the devil."[1]

The Great Exhibition of 1851

No single event is more expressive of the place Britain saw itself and its Empire occupying in the world than the Great Exhibition of the Industry of all Nations of 1851. It was intended as a celebration of the achievements of the entire world, but also of the special place that Britain saw itself occupying in the world—economic engine, most powerful nation, moral leader. The brainchild very largely of the Prince Consort, the event attracted exhibitors from throughout the Empire and from many other nations; more than 6,200,000 people visited what came to be regarded as the first world's fair. The exhibition hall—popularly known as the Crystal Palace—occupied over twenty-one acres in Hyde Park in central London over a six month period (after which it was disassembled and rebuilt in a suburban location). The Exhibition was a success in every respect, not least of all financially; revenues helped to fund the construction of both the Albert Hall and the Victoria and Albert Museum.

Prince Albert, Speech Delivered at the Lord Mayor's Banquet, London, 1849 (as reprinted in *The Illustrated London News*, 11 October 1849)

I conceive it to be the duty of every educated person closely to study and watch the time in which he lives; and as far as in him lies, to add his might of individual exertion to further the accomplishment of what he believes Providence to have ordained. Nobody, however, who has paid any attention to the features of our present era, will doubt for a moment that we are living at a period of most wonderful transition which tends rapidly to the accomplishment of that great end to which indeed, all history points—the realization of the unity of mankind. Not a unity which breaks down the limits and levels the peculiar characteristics of the different nations of the earth, but rather a unity, the result and product of those very national varieties and antagonistic qualities. The distances which separated the different nations and parts of the globe are gradually vanishing before the achievements of modern invention, and we can traverse them with incredible ease; the languages of all nations are known and their acquirements placed within the reach of everybody; thought is communicated with the rapidity and even by the power of lightning.

On the other hand, the great principle of the division of labour which may be called the moving power of civilization, is being extended to all branches of science, industry and art. Whilst formerly the greatest mental energies strove at universal knowledge, and that knowledge was confined to a few, now they are directed to specialities, and in these again, even to the minutest points; but the knowledge acquired becomes at once the property of the community at large. Whilst formerly discovery was wrapped in secrecy, the publicity of the present day causes, that no sooner is a discovery or invention made, than it is already improved upon and surpassed by competing efforts: the products of all quarters of the globe are placed at our disposal, and we have only to choose what is the cheapest and best for our purposes, and the powers of production are entrusted to the stimulus of competition and capital.

So man is approaching a more complete fulfillment of that great and sacred mission which he has to perform in this world. His reason being created after the image of God, he has to use it to discover the laws by which the Almighty governs His creation, and, by making these laws his standard of action, to conquer nature to his use—himself a divine instrument. Science discovers these laws of power, motion and transformation; industry applies them to raw matter which the earth yields us in abundance, but which becomes valuable only by knowledge; art teaches us the immutable laws of beauty and symmetry, and gives to our productions forms in accordance with them.

Gentlemen, the Exhibition of 1851 is to give us a true test and a living picture of the point of development at which the whole of mankind has arrived in this

---

[1] *writer ... devil* From an article responding to Carlyle in *London Inquirer*: "It is a true work of the Devil, the fostering of a tyrannical prejudice."

Engraving by H. Bibby of a daguerreotype by John J.E. Mayall, *Great Exhibition, Main Avenue Looking East*, 1851.

great task, and a new starting point from which all nations will be able to direct their further exertions.

Joseph Paxton, first sketch for the Great Exhibition Building, 1850. From this initial sketch, drawn on blotting paper during a railway board meeting, Paxton developed the design of the Crystal Palace.

London Dining Rooms, 1851
Waiter (to Chinaman). "Very nice birds'-nest soup, Sir!—Yes, Sir!—Rat pie, Sir, just up—yes, Sir!—and a nice little dog to foller—yes, Sir!"

Cartoon from *Punch*, 1851. The Great Exhibition brought an unprecedented influx of foreign visitors to London—most from Europe, but some from much farther afield. The satirical magazine *Punch* was far from alone in engaging in casually racist ridicule of the cultural practices of foreigners. The original caption is reproduced above.

from *The Art Journal Illustrated Catalogue of the Great Exhibition of The Industry of All Nations* (1851)

We commence this illustrated catalogue of the principal contents of the Great Exhibition with a brief but succinct History of the Building—and of the Project from its commencement up to the present time.

The experiment of an Exhibition of the Industry of all the civilised Nations of the World has been tried, and has succeeded beyond the most sanguine expectations of its projectors. It is, indeed, scarcely possible to instance any great enterprise of modern date which has so completely satisfied the anticipations which had been formed of its results…. Other nations have devised means for the display and encouragement of their own arts and manufactures; but it has been reserved for England to provide an arena for the exhibition of the industrial triumphs of the whole world. She has offered an hospitable invitation to surrounding nations to bring the choicest products of their industry to her capital, and there to enter into an amicable competition with each other and with herself; and she has endeavoured to secure to them the certainty of an impartial verdict on their efforts. Whatever be the extent of the benefit which this great demonstration may confer upon the Industrial Arts of the world, it cannot fail to soften, if not to eradicate altogether, the prejudices and animosities which have so long retarded the happiness of nations; and to promote those feelings of "peace and good will" which are among the surest antecedents of their prosperity; a peace, which Shakespeare has told us—

Is of the nature of a conquest;
For then both parties nobly are subdued,
And neither party loses.

It forms no part of our present object to enter, with any degree of minuteness, into the history of exhibitions of this class; but a brief glance at the origin and progress of such associations in France and England may not be considered irrelevant….

The great success which attended the French Industrial Exposition of 1844 had caused representations to be made to the English government of the advantages which would accrue to our commerce from a similar exhibition in this country; but the efforts which were made to obtain its cooperation appear to have been wholly unsuccessful. In 1848, a proposal to establish a self-supporting exhibition of the products of British industry, to be directed by a Royal Commission, was submitted by H.R.H. Prince Albert to the government, but with no better success; and it then became apparent that no reliance whatever could be placed upon the active support of Her Majesty's ministers for any such plan. They had, in all probability, no objection to see the experiment tried, but were evidently unwilling to commit themselves to any responsibility in behalf of a scheme which seemed to be beset by so many difficulties. Meanwhile, the popular feeling in favour of such an undertaking was rapidly strengthening, and the success which has attended the experiment may, in a great measure, be referred to the freedom of action which this dissociation from the timid councils of the government secured for its projectors. It may be proper, in this place, to remark that, excepting in facilitating its correspondence with foreign nations; the provision of a site for the building; and the organisation of the police; no assistance has been either sought or obtained from the government for the present Exhibition; whilst, in every case in which it has been attended by expense, the cost has been defrayed out of the funds at the disposal of the Executive Committee....

H.R.H. Prince Albert ... on the termination of the Parliamentary session of 1849, took the subject under his immediate superintendence. But, indeed, for his indefatigable perseverance, his courageous defiance of all risks of failure, his remarkable sagacity in matters of business, and the influence which attached to his support, the whole project, notwithstanding the great exertions which had been made to secure its realisation, must have fallen to the ground. The maturely considered views of his Royal Highness, and the patriotic objects he proposed in making this great peace-offering to mankind, are admirably set forth in the speech delivered by him on the occasion of the banquet given by Mr. Alderman Farncomb, then Lord Mayor of London, to the municipal authorities of the United Kingdom in support of the project. "The Exhibition of 1851 would," he said, "afford

a true test of the point of development at which the whole of mankind has arrived in this great task, and a new starting point from which all nations would be able to direct their further exertions."...

On the 29th of June, 1849, at a meeting, at Buckingham Palace, of several of the gentlemen who afterwards became members of the Royal Commission, and Prince Albert, his Royal Highness communicated his plan for the formation of a great collection of works of Industry and Art in London, in 1851, for the purposes of exhibition, of competition, and of encouragement; when he proposed that these contributions should consist of four great divisions, namely: raw materials; machinery and mechanical inventions; manufactures; and sculpture and plastic art generally....

Impressed with the truth of the proverb, *Ce n'est que le premier pas qui coûte*,[1] the council of the Society of Arts, after much fruitless negotiation with other parties, entered into an engagement with Messrs. Munday, the well-known contractors, by which those gentlemen undertook to deposit a prize fund of 20,000 *l.*; to erect a suitable building; to find offices; to advance the money requisite for all preliminary expenses; and to take the whole risk of loss; on the following conditions: The 20,000 *l.* prize fund, the cost of the building, and five percent on all advances, to be repaid out of the first receipts; the residue to be divided into three equal parts; one part to be paid over at once to the Society of Arts, in aid of future exhibitions; and out of the other two parts all other incidental costs, such as those of general management and preliminary expenses; the residue, if any, to be remuneration of the contractors for their outlay, trouble, and risk....

With a view to give Foreign nations as much time for preparation as possible, the Commissioners resolved, long before they had decided on the size and character of the building, to divide a certain large extent of space among foreign countries, amounting in the whole to 210,000 superficial feet, or rather more than the entire space which France had occupied for its two expositions of 1844 and 1849. Subsequently, the quantities of space allotted to foreign nations was increased; France obtaining 65,000 feet instead of 50,000. A definite amount of

---

[1]   *Ce ... coûte*   French: It is only the first step that costs.

space proportioned to their presumed wants was also allotted to each of the British Colonies....

Every class appears, however, to have been satisfied with the final allocations, which were the best that could have been made under the circumstances.

When the time arrived for making definite arrangements for the erection of the building, the Commissioners had only 35,000 *l*. in hand; and, notwithstanding the guarantee to which they had themselves largely subscribed, they must have felt themselves committed to a very deep responsibility. Nothing daunted, however, an invitation was addressed, through the public prints, to architects of all nations, to furnish designs for an edifice, the roof of which was to cover 700,000 square feet; and the area of which, including the open spaces, was not to exceed 900,000 feet. Other conditions were enumerated which showed that the whole of the details had been carefully and judiciously considered. Although the time allowed for the preparation of the drawings was only a month, there were no fewer than two hundred and thirty-three competitors, many of whom sent in designs of a highly elaborate character. Of these, thirty-eight, or one-sixth of the whole, were from foreigners; 128 from London and its vicinity; and 51 from the provincial towns of England....

Among the contractors who had accepted the invitation of the Building Committee, was the firm of Fox & Henderson, who, availing themselves of the permission to alter and amend the plan of the Committee, contained in the latter part of the report, presented a tender for a building of an entirely different character from that which had been suggested by the Committee. This, we need scarcely add, was the plan which, with certain modifications and additions, was ultimately adopted; and for which, notwithstanding all that has been said to the contrary, the public is wholly indebted to Mr. Paxton....

[A]nd if it be correct, as stated by Mr. Paxton at the dinner given to him at Derby, on the 6th of August, that his original sketch on a sheet of blotting paper indicates the principal features of the building as it now stands as much as the most finished drawings which have been made since, there can be no excuse for attempting to deprive him of any portion of the merit of the invention. But he appears to have done considerably

more than merely furnish the idea. In nine days from that on which he had made the blotting paper sketch, he was in possession of nine plans, all, with a single exception, prepared by his own hand. And although his suggestion to Messrs. Fox & Henderson was offered so late as the 2nd June, 1850, his plan was engraved and published in the Illustrated News of the 6th July....

Tests had, as we have shown, been applied in the course of the work which had satisfied the scientific men who witnessed them that the iron girders would bear a strain upon them four times as great as they could ever be called upon to bear; but it was resolved to subject them to a still severer ordeal.

The first of these more elaborate experiments, which took place in the presence of Her Majesty, Prince Albert, and several scientific persons, was to ascertain the extent of oscillation that would be produced in the galleries by the regular motion of large bodies of persons. Three hundred workmen were accordingly deployed over the platform, and then crowded together as closely as possible. The load borne by the planks laid across the platform represented the degree of pressure that would be occasioned by the crowding of the bays of the galleries. The amount of deflection produced by this experiment was scarcely perceptible. The men next walked regularly and irregularly, and finally ran over the temporary floor, with little more effect. Even when packed in the closest order, and jumping simultaneously for several minutes, the play of the timbers and the wrought-iron work, was admirably developed, and the extreme deflection of any one girder did not exceed a quarter of an inch. As, however, the workmen were unable to keep military time in their step, the whole corps of Sappers and Miners employed on the ground, arranged in close order, marched several times over and around the bays without producing any other effect than is observable in a house in which dancing is going on. The crowning experiment suggested by Messrs. Maudslay & Field, the eminent civil engineers, rendered any further test wholly unnecessary. Seven frames, each capable of holding 36 cannon-balls, of 68 lbs. each, were constructed, and drawn with their contents over the floor. In this way a pressure on the flooring of seven and a half tons was obtained; the probable pressure from a crowd not exceeding 95 lb. The pressure of an ordinary

EXTERIOR OF THE BUILDING FOR THE GREAT EXHIBITION (SOUTH SIDE).

crowd, however, at a public meeting or a theatre does not exceed 60 lbs. to the square foot....

The site of the Great Exhibition is the one originally proposed for it by H.R.H. Prince Albert. It consists of a rectangular piece of ground in Hyde Park, situated between the Queen's Drive and Rotten Row,[1] and contains about 26 acres, being 2300 feet in length by 500 feet in breadth. Its principal frontage extends from east to west. Several lofty trees which stretch across the centre of its length have been allowed to remain, and it is to them we are indebted for the magnificent transept and semicircular roof, suggested after the first plans had received the approval of the Commissioners. The ground, although apparently level, has a fall from 1 to 250 inches from west to east. Among the most striking advantages of the spot were the facilities of access from all parts which it presented, and the ease with which it could be drained and supplied with gas and water; whilst the beauty of the neighbourhood can scarcely be exceeded within the same convenient distance from the metropolis. Indeed, however strong may have been the private objections urged against the adoption of this site, in the first instance, it is now universally admitted that

a more desirable locality for the purpose to which it has been converted could not have been selected....

Two ... groups of trees, whose immolation was also interdicted, have rendered open courts necessary; but they are, nevertheless, included within the building. The entire area enclosed and roofed over comprises no fewer than 772,784 square feet, or about 19 acres; thus presenting an edifice about four times the size of St. Peter's, at Rome, and six times that of St. Paul's.[2] We have already described the principal entrance at the south front. Besides this, there is one at each end, and, at convenient intervals, no fewer than fifteen places of egress....

The first impression conveyed to the mind of a visitor, inexperienced in the science of architecture, on entering the building, is a sense of insecurity, arising from the apparent lightness of its supports as compared with the vastness of its dimensions. But this feeling is soon dissipated when he is informed how severely the strength of every separate part has been tested, and with what extreme care the connexion of all the supports

[1]   *Queen's Drive and Rotten Row* Carriage paths.

[2]   *St. Peter's, at Rome* St. Peter's Basilica, among the world's largest churches; *St. Paul's* St. Paul's Cathedral in London, then the largest church in England.

with each other has been considered, so as to present the greatest possible combination of strength....

Among other striking examples of the ingenuity of the originators and constructors of the Crystal Palace is the ridge-and-furrow roof, by which the rain water is distributed into equal portions, and all ordinary chances of overflow averted; and the peculiar formation of the floor, which is a "trellised wooden pathway," with spaces between each board through which, on sweeping, "the dust at once disappears, and falls into the vacuity below." It may also be thoroughly washed without discomfort, for the water disappears as fast as the dust through the interstices; and the boards become fit for visitors almost immediately afterwards....

Such was the extraordinary eagerness of the public to be present at its inauguration, that upwards of 40,000 *l.* of season tickets were disposed of on the 29th of April; and but for the restriction that the holders of season tickets only should be admitted to this ceremony, the place would doubtless have overflowed with visitors. It is not our intention to enter into minute details of the circumstances which attended its inauguration; they were in every respect worthy of the occasion. It was opened by Her Majesty in person, accompanied by the Royal Family, and attended by the members of her cabinet, and by all the officers and ladies of her court. So soon as the music which hailed her entry had ceased, H.R.H. Prince Albert, as President of the Royal Commissioners, read a report of their proceedings since their appointment. This manifesto mentions that "for the suggestions of the principle of this structure, the Commissioners are indebted to Mr. Joseph Paxton, and expresses a hope that the undertaking, which has for its end the promotion of all branches of human industry, and the strengthening of the bonds of peace and friendship among all nations of the earth, may, under God's blessing, conduce to the welfare of Her Majesty's people, and be long remembered among the brightest incidents of her peaceful and happy reign."

To this address, Her Majesty returned a most gracious answer, and the Archbishop of Canterbury having invoked the blessing of the Almighty on the undertaking, the ceremony terminated with the performance of the Hallelujah chorus by the united choirs of the Chapel Royal, St. Paul's, Westminster Abbey, and St. George's Chapel, Windsor. The procession included all the persons who had been officially engaged in the work; the royal and foreign commissioners, Her Majesty's ministers, the whole of the lords and ladies of the court in waiting, and the foreign ambassadors. The vast but elegant proportions of the building, the richness and tastefulness of the costumes, and the large number (25,000) of well-dressed persons assembled on the occasion, rendered its inauguration one of the most imposing sights that had ever been witnessed in this country. But it is not in her regal capacity alone that Her Majesty has deigned to honour the Great Exhibition with her countenance. Day after day, accompanied by her children, and often at much personal inconvenience, has she flattered the various exhibitors by careful examinations of their productions; until it may fairly be presumed that there is scarcely one of her subjects who has more thoroughly inspected all that is worthy of attention within its walls than she has done. Whatever may have been the weather, or however crowded the interior, Her Majesty has devoted, almost daily, until the close of the session of parliament released her from attendance in London, several hours to visits to the Crystal Palace; inspecting each department in succession, and selecting from many of them such objects as gratified her taste, or were, for other reasons, considered to possess claims upon her attention.

On entering the building, for the first time, the eye is completely dazzled by the rich variety of hues which burst upon it on every side; and it is not until this partial bewilderment has subsided, that we are in a condition to appreciate as it deserves its real magnificence and the harmonious beauty of effect produced by the artistical arrangement of the glowing and varied hues which blaze along its grand and simple lines. After passing through the southern entrance, the whole extent of the transept, interrupted only by the magnificent glass fountain of Messrs. Osler,[1] and the groups of sculpture and tropical plants and trees, that are

---

[1] *Messrs. Osler* Follett and Clarkson Osler, England's leading glass manufacturers.

intermixed throughout, flashes on the eye more like the fabled palace of Vathek,[1] than a structure reared in a few months by mortal hands....

Forming the centre, or nearly so, of the entire building, and dividing alike the transept and the nave, rises the gigantic fountain of Messrs. Osler, the culminating point of view from every quarter of the building; whilst at the northern end the eye is relieved by the verdure of tropical plants and the lofty and overshadowing branches of forest trees.

On the right, looking from Messrs. Osler's glass fountain up the Eastern Division of the Nave, towards the American organ and its enormous eagle, a combination of splendours bursts upon the sight of overpowering magnificence....

The Western Division of the Nave, devoted to the products of England and her Colonies, if less showy, on a superficial view, than its rival, has much of sterling merit to recommend it. Here, too, are interspersed statues, fountains, mirrors, organs, and other large ornamental objects.

Crossing the Transept, and pursuing our course to the left, we enter the western division of the nave. We have here the Indian Court, Africa, Canada, the West Indies, the Cape of Good Hope, the Medieval Court, and the English Sculpture Court.... To these succeed Birmingham, the great British Furniture Court, Sheffield, and its hardware, the woollen and mixed fabrics, shawls, flax, and linens, and printing and dyeing. The long avenue leading from the Medieval Court to the end of the building is devoted to general hardware, brass and iron-work of all kinds, locks, grates, etc.; whilst behind it, and parallel with it, but occupying three times its breadth, is the department for agricultural machines and implements. At the back of this division is the long narrow gallery occupied by the mineral products of England. Passing the small compartment of glass which runs transversely under the great organ gallery, across the nave, we have the cotton fabric and carriage courts, leather, furs, and hair, minerals and mineral manufactures, and machinery; including cotton and woollen

power-looms in motion. The next is the largest compartment in the building, comprising machinery in motion, flax, silk, and lace, rope-making lathes, tools, and mills; minerals and mineral manufactures, furniture, marine engines, ceilings, hydraulic presses, steam hammers, fire engines, etc. Then follow paper and stationery; Jersey, Ceylon, and Malta, with the Fine Arts Court behind them; railway and steam machinery in motion; building contrivances, printing, and French machinery, occupying the whole of the last compartments on both sides of the nave, as well as those which face the transept. Crossing to the left of the Crystal Fountain, we have Persia, Greece, Egypt, and Turkey, Spain, Portugal, Madeira, and Italy, musical instruments, and chemicals; France, its tapestry, machinery, arms and instruments, occupying two large courts;

---

[1] *palace of Vathek* In William Beckford's French novel *Vathek* (1782; first English translation 1786), the title character expands his already magnificent palace to incorporate five new wings, each for the satisfaction of one of the five senses.

Belgium her furniture, carpets, and machinery; Austria, with her gorgeous furniture courts, and machinery furniture; the Zollverein, with its octagon room, the most tastefully-arranged compartment in the building; North of Germany and Hanse Towns; Russia, with its malachite doors, vases, and ornaments; and the United States, with its agricultural implements, raw materials, etc., occupying all that part of the nave which terminates with its organ, if we except a small gallery on the north-east side, devoted to English paper-hangings. From this extremity of the building, and from the organ gallery more especially, the finest *coup d'œil*[1] of the nave and its adjoining galleries may be obtained....

Among the more striking objects in the southeastern gallery, in the British half of the nave, are the silks and shawls, abutting on the transept; lace and embroideries, jewellery, and clocks and watches; and behind them military arms and models, raw produce, substances used as food, and chemicals. Traversing the gallery for naval architecture, by the organ, we have philosophical instruments, civil engineering, architecture and building models, musical instruments, anatomical models, glass chandeliers, decorations, etc.; china and pottery above the left side of the northern part of the transept. On the opposite side, in the north-eastern gallery, are perfumery, toys, fishing materials, miscellaneous articles, wax flowers, stained glass, British, French, Austrian, Belgian, Prussian, Bavarian, and American products.

Clear passages under the galleries, of eight and ten feet broad, run the whole length of the building. Upon the extreme north and south sides, there are also longitudinal passages of similar width; the former interrupted by the offices of the commissioners and the entrances, and the latter by the refreshment rooms. With the exception of the offices, staircases, entrances, refreshment courts, and the various avenues and passages, including the transept, the whole of the ground-floor and galleries are available for exhibitors. As we have already shown, foreign countries, including the United States of America, occupy the east side of the transept above and below; whilst the United Kingdom, the East Indies, and the British Colonies are confined to the west side; with the exception of the United Kingdom, which

extends into parts of the north and south galleries, on the east side of the transept. The productions of England and her Colonies occupy thirty separate sections....

In retiring from the contemplation of this magnificent edifice, the extraordinary expedition with which it was constructed must be regarded as one of the marvels of the age.

---

from Henry Mayhew, *London Labour and the London Poor* (1851)

> Mayhew's work is known primarily for the sympathetic attention it drew to the plight of poor Londoners. When the poor were not of "English stock," however, Mayhew was decidedly less sympathetic—as the following excerpt from his section on "Hindo Beggars" illustrates.

HINDO BEGGARS

[These] are those spare, snake-eyed Asiatics who walk the streets, coolly dressed in Manchester cottons, or chintz of a pattern commonly used for bed-furniture, to which the resemblance is carried out by the dark, polished colour of the thin limbs which it envelopes. They very often affect to be converts to the Christian religion, and give away tracts; with the intention of entrapping the sympathy of elderly ladies. They assert that they have been high-caste Brahmins,[2] but as untruth, even when not acting professionally, is habitual to them, there is not the slightest dependence to be placed on what they say. Sometimes, in the winter, they "do shallow," that is, stand on the kerb-stone of the pavement, in their thin, ragged clothes, and shiver as with cold and hunger, or crouch against a wall and whine like a whipped animal; at others they turn out with a small, barrel-shaped drum, on which they make a monotonous noise with their fingers, to which music they sing and dance. Or they will "stand pad with a fakement," i.e., wear a placard upon their breasts, that describes them as natives of Madagascar, in distress, converts to Christianity, anxious to get to a seaport where they can work their

---

[1]   *coup d'œil*   Here, line of sight.

[2]   *Brahmins*   Members of the highest Hindu class or caste.

passage back. This is a favourite artifice with Lascars[1]— or they will sell lucifers,[2] or sweep a crossing, or do anything where their picturesque appearance, of which they are proud and conscious, can be effectively displayed. They are as cunning as they look, and can detect a sympathetic face among a crowd. They never beg of soldiers, or sailors, to whom they always give a wide berth as they pass them in the streets. . . .

Dickens and Thackeray on the Race Question

Charles Dickens and William Makepeace Thackeray, widely regarded as the two greatest novelists of the age, were also great friends. And, as the excerpts below show, they held similar views on the question of race.

from Charles Dickens, "The Noble Savage," *Household Words* (1853)

To come to the point at once, I beg to say that I have not the least belief in the Noble Savage.[3] I consider him a prodigious nuisance, and an enormous superstition. His calling rum firewater, and me a pale face, wholly fail to reconcile me to him. I don't care what he calls me. I call him a savage, and I call a savage a something highly desirable to be civilised off the face of the earth. I think a mere gent (which I take to be the lowest form of civilisation) better than a howling, whistling, clucking, stamping, jumping, tearing savage. It is all one to me, whether he sticks a fish-bone through his visage, or bits of trees through the lobes of his ears, or bird's feathers in his head; whether he flattens his hair between two boards, or spreads his nose over the breadth of his face, or drags his lower lip down by great weights, or blackens his teeth, or knocks them out, or paints one

cheek red and the other blue, or tattoos himself, or oils himself, or rubs his body with fat, or crimps it with knives. Yielding to whichsoever of these agreeable eccentricities, he is a savage cruel, false, thievish, murderous; addicted more or less to grease, entrails, and beastly customs; a wild animal with the questionable gift of boasting; a conceited, tiresome, bloodthirsty, monotonous humbug.

Yet it is extraordinary to observe how some people will talk about him, as they talk about the good old times; how they will regret his disappearance, in the course of this world's development, from such and such lands where his absence is a blessed relief and an indispensable preparation for the sowing of the very first seeds of any influence that can exalt humanity; how, even with the evidence of himself before them, they will either be determined to believe, or will suffer themselves to be persuaded into believing, that he is something which their five senses tell them he is not.

There was Mr. Catlin,[4] some few years ago, with his Ojibbeway Indians. Mr. Catlin was an energetic, earnest man, who had lived among more tribes of Indians than I need reckon up here, and who had written a picturesque and glowing book about them. With his party of Indians squatting and spitting on the table before him, or dancing their miserable jigs after their own dreary manner, he called, in all good faith, upon his civilised audience to take notice of their symmetry and grace, their perfect limbs, and the exquisite expression of their pantomime; and his civilised audience, in all good faith, complied and admired. Whereas, as mere animals, they were wretched creatures, very low in the scale and very poorly formed; and as men and women possessing any power of truthful dramatic expression by means of action, they were no better than the chorus at an Italian Opera in England—and would have been worse if such a thing were possible.

Mine are no new views of the noble savage. The greatest writers on natural history found him out long ago. Buffon[5] knew what he was, and showed why he is

[1] *Lascars* East Indian sailors.

[2] *lucifers* Cheap matches sold by street peddlers.

[3] *Noble Savage* The notion of the "noble savage" is associated with the ideas of the French philosopher Jean-Jacques Rousseau (1712–78), who held that human beings are naturally innocent and good, but become corrupted by civilized society. According to this way of thinking, indigenous peoples were seen as inherently nobler because they were closer to a "state of nature."

[4] *Mr. Catlin* George Catlin (1796–1872), pioneered the Wild West Show, which brought indigenous peoples and cultures from the American West to the American east coast and to Europe.

[5] *Buffon* George-Louis Leclerc, Comte de Buffon (1707–88), French naturalist and mathematician.

the sulky tyrant that he is to his women, and how it happens (Heaven be praised!) that his race is spare in numbers. For evidence of the quality of his moral nature, pass himself for a moment and refer to his "faithful dog." Has he ever improved a dog, or attached a dog, since his nobility first ran wild in woods, and was brought down (at a very long shot) by Pope?[1] Or does the animal that is the friend of man, always degenerate in his low society?

It is not the miserable nature of the noble savage that is the new thing; it is the whimpering over him with maudlin admiration, and the affecting to regret him, and the drawing of any comparison of advantage between the blemishes of civilisation and the tenor of his swinish life. There may have been a change now and then in those diseased absurdities, but there is none in him.

Think of the Bushmen.[2] Think of the two men and the two women who have been exhibited about England for some years. Are the majority of persons—who remember the horrid little leader of that party in his festering bundle of hides, with his filth and his antipathy to water, and his straddled legs, and his odious eyes shaded by his brutal hand, and his cry of "Qu-u-u-u-aaa!" (Bosjesman[3] for something desperately insulting I have no doubt)—conscious of an affectionate yearning towards that noble savage, or is it idiosyncratic in me to abhor, detest, abominate, and abjure him? I have no reserve on this subject, and will frankly state that, setting aside that stage of the entertainment when he counterfeited the death of some creature he had shot, by laying his head on his hand and shaking his left leg—at which time I think it would have been justifiable homicide to slay him—I have never seen that group sleeping, smoking, and expectorating round their brazier, but I have sincerely desired that something might happen to the charcoal smouldering therein, which would cause the immediate suffocation of the whole of the noble strangers.

There is at present a party of Zulu Kaffirs[4] exhibiting at the St. George's Gallery, Hyde Park Corner, London. These noble savages are represented in a most agreeable manner; they are seen in an elegant theatre, fitted with appropriate scenery of great beauty, and they are described in a very sensible and unpretending lecture, delivered with a modesty which is quite a pattern to all similar exponents. Though extremely ugly, they are much better shaped than such of their predecessors as I have referred to; and they are rather picturesque to the eye, though far from odoriferous to the nose. What a visitor left to his own interpretings and imaginings might suppose these noblemen to be about, when they give vent to that pantomimic expression which is quite settled to be the natural gift of the noble savage, I cannot possibly conceive; for it is so much too luminous for my personal civilisation that it conveys no idea to my mind beyond a general stamping, ramping, and raving, remarkable (as everything in savage life is) for its dire uniformity. But let us—with the interpreter's assistance, of which I for one stand so much in need—see what the noble savage does in Zulu Kaffirland.

The noble savage sets a king to reign over him, to whom he submits his life and limbs without a murmur or question, and whose whole life is passed chin deep in a lake of blood; but who, after killing incessantly, is in his turn killed by his relations and friends, the moment a grey hair appears on his head. All the noble savage's wars with his fellow-savages (and he takes no pleasure in anything else) are wars of extermination—which is the best thing I know of him, and the most comfortable to my mind when I look at him. He has no moral feelings of any kind, sort, or description; and his "mission" may be summed up as simply diabolical.

The ceremonies with which he faintly diversifies his life are, of course, of a kindred nature. If he wants a wife he appears before the kennel of the gentleman whom he has selected for his father-in-law, attended by a party of male friends of a very strong flavour, who screech and whistle and stamp an offer of so many cows for the young lady's hand. The chosen father-in-law—also supported by a high-flavoured party of male friends—screeches, whistles, and yells (being seated on the ground, he can't stamp) that there never was such a daughter in the market as his daughter, and that he must have six more cows. The son-in-law and his select circle of backers screech, whistle, stamp, and yell in reply, that they will give three more cows. The father-in-

[1] *Pope* Alexander Pope (1688–1744), British poet.
[2] *Bushmen* European name for peoples of the Kalahari desert.
[3] *Bosjesman* Language of the "Bushmen."
[4] *Kaffirs* Derogatory term for Africans.

law (an old deluder, overpaid at the beginning) accepts four, and rises to bind the bargain. The whole party, the young lady included, then falling into epileptic convulsions, and screeching, whistling, stamping, and yelling together—and nobody taking any notice of the young lady (whose charms are not to be thought of without a shudder)—the noble savage is considered married, and his friends make demoniacal leaps at him by way of congratulation.

When the noble savage finds himself a little unwell, and mentions the circumstance to his friends, it is immediately perceived that he is under the influence of witchcraft. A learned personage, called an Imyanger or Witch Doctor, is immediately sent for to Nooker the Umtargartie, or smell out the witch. The male inhabitants of the kraal[1] being seated on the ground, the learned doctor, got up like a grizzly bear, appears, and administers a dance of a most terrific nature, during the exhibition of which remedy he incessantly gnashes his teeth, and howls:—"I am the original physician to Nooker the Umtargartie. Yow yow yow! No connexion with any other establishment. Till till till! All other Umtargarties are feigned Umtargarties, Boroo Boroo! but I perceive here a genuine and real Umtargartie, Hoosh Hoosh Hoosh! in whose blood I, the original Imyanger and Nookerer, Blizzerum Boo! will wash these bear's claws of mine. O yow yow yow!" All this time the learned physician is looking out among the attentive faces for some unfortunate man who owes him a cow, or who has given him any small offence, or against whom, without offence, he has conceived a spite. Him he never fails to Nooker as the Umtargartie, and he is instantly killed. In the absence of such an individual, the usual practice is to Nooker the quietest and most gentlemanly person in company. But the nookering is invariably followed on the spot by the butchering.

Some of the noble savages in whom Mr. Catlin was so strongly interested, and the diminution of whose numbers, by rum and smallpox, greatly affected him, had a custom not unlike this, though much more appalling and disgusting in its odious details.

The women being at work in the fields, hoeing the Indian corn, and the noble savage being asleep in the shade, the chief has sometimes the condescension to come forth, and lighten the labour by looking at it. On these occasions, he seats himself in his own savage chair, and is attended by his shield-bearer: who holds over his head a shield of cowhide—in shape like an immense mussel shell fearfully and wonderfully, after the manner of a theatrical supernumerary. But lest the great man should forget his greatness in the contemplation of the humble works of agriculture, there suddenly rushes in a poet, retained for the purpose, called a Praiser. This literary gentleman wears a leopard's head over his own, and a dress of tigers' tails; he has the appearance of having come express on his hind legs from the Zoological Gardens; and he incontinently strikes up the chief's praises, plunging and tearing all the while. There is a frantic wickedness in this brute's manner of worrying the air, and gnashing out, "O what a delightful chief he is! O what a delicious quantity of blood he sheds! O how majestically he laps it up! O how charmingly cruel he is! O how he tears the flesh of his enemies and crunches the bones! O how like the tiger and the leopard and the wolf and the bear he is! O, row row row row, how fond I am of him!" which might tempt the Society of Friends to charge at a hand-gallop into the Swartz-Kop location and exterminate the whole kraal.

When war is afoot among the noble savages—which is always—the chief holds a council to ascertain whether it is the opinion of his brothers and friends in general that the enemy shall be exterminated. On this occasion, after the performance of an Umsebeuza, or war song,—which is exactly like all the other songs, the chief makes a speech to his brothers and friends, arranged in single file. No particular order is observed during the delivery of this address, but every gentleman who finds himself excited by the subject, instead of crying "Hear, hear!" as is the custom with us, darts from the rank and tramples out the life, or crushes the skull, or mashes the face, or scoops out the eyes, or breaks the limbs, or performs a whirlwind of atrocities on the body, of an imaginary enemy. Several gentlemen becoming thus excited at once, and pounding away without the least regard to the orator, that illustrious person is rather in the position of an orator in an Irish House of Commons. But, several of these scenes of savage life bear a strong generic resemblance to an Irish election, and I think would be

---

[1] *kraal* A community of indigenous people in southern or central Africa, typically dwelling in huts surrounded by a stockade.

extremely well received and understood at Cork.[1]

In all these ceremonies the noble savage holds forth to the utmost possible extent about himself; from which (to turn him to some civilised account) we may learn, I think, that as egotism is one of the most offensive and contemptible littlenesses a civilised man can exhibit, so it is really incompatible with the interchange of ideas; inasmuch as if we all talked about ourselves we should soon have no listeners, and must be all yelling and screeching at once on our own separate accounts: making society hideous. It is my opinion that if we retained in us anything of the noble savage, we could not get rid of it too soon. But the fact is clearly otherwise. Upon the wife and dowry question, substituting coin for cows, we have assuredly nothing of the Zulu Kaffir left. The endurance of despotism is one great distinguishing mark of a savage always. The improving world has quite got the better of that too. In like manner, Paris is a civilised city, and the Théâtre Français a highly civilised theatre; and we shall never hear, and never have heard in these later days (of course) of the Praiser THERE. No, no, civilised poets have better work to do. As to Nookering Umtargarties, there are no pretended Umtargarties in Europe, and no European powers to Nooker them; that would be mere spydom, subordination, small malice, superstition, and false pretence. And as to private Umtargarties, are we not in the year eighteen hundred and fifty-three, with spirits rapping at our doors?

To conclude as I began. My position is, that if we have anything to learn from the Noble Savage, it is what to avoid. His virtues are a fable; his happiness is a delusion; his nobility, nonsense.

We have no greater justification for being cruel to the miserable object, than for being cruel to a WILLIAM SHAKESPEARE or an ISAAC NEWTON; but he passes away before an immeasurably better and higher power than ever ran wild in any earthly woods, and the world will be all the better when his place knows him no more.

from William Makepeace Thackeray, Letters to Mrs. Carmichael-Smyth

TO MRS. CARMICHAEL-SMYTH, 26 JANUARY 1853

... I don't believe Blacky *is* my man and my brother, though God forbid I should own him or flog him, or part him from his wife and children. But the question is a much longer [one than] is set forth in Mrs. Stowe's philosophy:[2] and I shan't speak about it, till I know it, or till it's my business, or I think I can do good.

TO MRS. CARMICHAEL-SMYTH, 13 FEBRUARY 1853

... They are not my men and brethren,[3] these strange people with retreating foreheads, with great obtruding lips and jaws: with capacities for thought, pleasure, endurance quite different to mine. They are not suffering as you are impassioning yourself for their wrongs as you read Mrs. Stowe, they are grinning and joking in the sun; roaring with laughter as they stand about the streets in squads; very civil, kind and gentle, even winning in their manner when you accost them at gentlemen's houses, where they do all the service. But they don't seem to me to be the same as white men, any more than asses are the same animals as horses; I don't mean this disrespectfully, but simply that there is such a difference of colour, habits, conformation of brains, that we must acknowledge it, and can't by any rhetorical phrase get it over; Sambo[4] is not my man and my brother; the very aspect of his face is grotesque and inferior. ... As soon as the cheap substitute is found, depend on it the Planter, who stoutly pleads humanity now as the one of the reasons why he can't liberate his people, will get rid of them quickly enough; & the price of the slave-goods will fall so that owners won't care to hold such an unprofitable & costly stock.

[1] *Several gentlemen ... Cork* Dickens is displaying his prejudice against the Irish, who had historically been held, by many in England, to have been "savages."

[2] *Mrs. Stowe's philosophy* Reference to Harriet Beecher Stowe's anti-slavery novel, *Uncle Tom's Cabin* (1852).

[3] *They are ... brethren* Reference to abolitionist materials that featured a slave in chains accompanied by the caption "Am I not a man and your brother?"

[4] *Sambo* Common slave name which became a derogatory term for any black person.

Conservatives, Liberals, and Empire

The following excerpts from speeches by Liberal Prime Minister William Gladstone, Conservative Prime Minister Benjamin Disraeli, and business-person, mining magnate, politician, and colonizer Cecil Rhodes provide three different perspectives on the attitudes taken by Britain's two main political parties towards issues of Empire in the second half of the nineteenth century.

from William Gladstone, "Our Colonies" (1855)

But an idea far more important and effective to a far greater extent has been the idea that the colonies ought to be maintained for the purpose of establishing an exclusive trade, the whole profit of which should be confined to the mother country, and should be enjoyed by the mother country. This was in fact the basis of the modern colonial system of Europe. I do not speak now of the political system, but it was the basis of the commercial laws of the countries which had colonies: that the industry of the colonists, instead of having a fair field and equal favour given to it, was attempted to be made entirely subservient to the interests and the profit of the mother country. It was placed in an unfair position. People were told in fact that they might go to the colonies, but that whatever they produced in the colonies must be sent to the British market—nay, that it must be sent in British vessels to the British market—nay, that whatever was produced must be sent to the British market in British vessels and in the state of raw produce, because if sent in other vessels, although it were sent better and cheaper, it would not be for the interest of the British shipowner, and if sent in a manufactured state it would not be for the interest of the British manufacturer....

Now, as I repudiate any and all of these reasons for desiring the possession of colonies, it is but fair that I should endeavour to state why I think colonies are desirable for a country circumstanced as England is. I have stated, that I do not think them desirable simply to puff up our reputation, apart from the basis and substance on which it rests. It is plain that they are not to be desired for revenue, because they do not yield it. It is

plain that they are not to be desired for trading monopoly, because that we have entirely abandoned. It is plain they are not to be desired for patronage, properly so called, within their limits, because they will not allow us to exercise patronage, and I am bound to say, I do not think the public men of this country have any desire so to exercise it. With respect to territory, it is perfectly plain that mere extension of territory is not a legitimate object of ambition, unless you can show that you are qualified to make use of that territory for the purposes for which God gave the earth to man. Why then are colonies desirable? In my opinion, and I submit it to you with great respect, they are desirable both for the material and for the moral and social results which a wise system of colonisation is calculated to produce. As to the first, the effect of colonisation undoubtedly is to increase the trade and employment of the mother country. Take the case of the emigrant going across the Atlantic. Why does he go across the Atlantic? Because he expects—and in general he is the best judge of his own interests—to get better wages across the Atlantic than he can get at home. If he goes across the Atlantic to get better wages, he leaves in the labour market at home fewer persons than before, and consequently raises the rate of wages at home by carrying himself away from the competition with his fellows. By going to the colony and supplying it with labour he likewise creates a demand for capital there, and by this means he creates a trade between the colony and the mother country. The capital and labour thus employed in the colony raise and export productions, for which commodities are wanted in return....

But I do not concede that the material benefit of colonies is the only consideration which we are able to plead. Their moral and social advantage is a very great one. If we are asked why, on these grounds, it is desirable that colonies should be founded and possessed, I answer by asking another question—Why is it desirable that your population at home should increase? Why is it that you rejoice, always presuming that the increase of population goes hand in hand with equally favourable or more favourable conditions of existence for the mass of the people—why is it that you rejoice in an increase of population at home? Because an increase of population is an increase of power, an increase of strength and stability to the state, and because it multiplies the number of people who, as we hope, are living under good laws, and belong to a country to which it is an honour and an advantage to belong. That is the great moral benefit that attends the foundation of British colonies. We think that our country is a country blessed with laws and a constitution that are eminently beneficial to mankind, and if so, what can be more to be desired than that we should have the means of reproducing in different portions of the globe something as like as may be to that country which we honour and revere? I think it is in a work by Mr. Roebuck that the expression is used, "that the object of colonisation is the creation of so many happy Englands." It is the reproduction of the image and likeness of England—the reproduction of a country in which liberty is reconciled with order, in which ancient institutions stand in harmony with popular freedom, and a full recognition of popular rights, and in which religion and law have found one of their most favoured homes....

from Benjamin Disraeli, "Conservative and Liberal Principles" (1872)

Gentlemen, there is another and second great object of the Tory party. If the first is to maintain the institutions of the country, the second is, in my opinion, to uphold the Empire of England. If you look to the history of this country since the advent of Liberalism—forty years ago—you will find that there has been no effort so continuous, so subtle, supported by so much energy, and carried on with so much ability and acumen, as the attempts of Liberalism to effect the disintegration of the Empire of England.

And, gentlemen, of all its efforts, this is the one which has been the nearest to success. Statesmen of the highest character, writers of the most distinguished ability, the most organised and efficient means, have been employed in this endeavour. It has been proved to all of us that we have lost money by our colonies. It has been shown with precise, with mathematical demonstration, that there never was a jewel in the Crown of England that was so truly costly as the possession of India. How often has it been suggested that we should

at once emancipate ourselves from this incubus.[1] Well, that result was nearly accomplished. When those subtle views were adopted by the country under the plausible plea of granting self-government to the colonies, I confess that I myself thought that the tie was broken. Not that I for one object to self-government. I cannot conceive how our distant colonies can have their affairs administered except by self-government. But self-government, in my opinion, when it was conceded, ought to have been conceded as part of a great policy of Imperial consolidation. It ought to have been accompanied by an Imperial tariff, by securities for the people of England for the enjoyment of the unappropriated lands which belonged to the Sovereign as their trustee, and by a military code which should have precisely defined the means and the responsibilities by which the colonies should be defended, and by which, if necessary, this country should call for aid from the colonies themselves. It ought, further, to have been accompanied by the institution of some representative council in the metropolis, which would have brought the colonies into constant and continuous relations with the Home Government. All this, however, was omitted because those who advised that policy—and I believe their convictions were sincere —looked upon the colonies of England, looked even upon our connection with India, as a burden upon this country, viewing everything in a financial aspect, and totally passing by those moral and political considerations which make nations great, and by the influence of which alone men are distinguished from animals.

Well, what has been the result of this attempt during the reign of Liberalism for the disintegration of the Empire? It has entirely failed. But how has it failed? Through the sympathy of the colonies with the Mother Country. They have decided that the Empire shall not be destroyed, and in my opinion no minister in this country will do his duty who neglects any opportunity of reconstructing as much as possible our Colonial Empire, and of responding to those distant sympathies which may become the source of incalculable strength and happiness to this land....

---

[1] *incubus* Mythical demon said to rape sleeping women, and in so doing to drain their life force to sustain itself. Figuratively, an evil that drains vital energy.

THE RHODES COLOSSUS

STRIDING FROM CAPE TOWN TO CAIRO.

Cecil Rhodes (1858–1902), nowadays best known for having endowed the Rhodes Scholarships for study at Oxford University, was the leading Briton in Southern Africa in the late nineteenth century—and a leading backer of the extension of British commercial and political interests in Africa as a whole. (The statue of the Colossus in the ancient city of Rhodes to which this cartoon alludes is said to have straddled the entrance to the harbor.)

from Cecil Rhodes, Speech Delivered in Cape Town, 18 July 1899

And, sir, my people have changed. I speak of the English people, with their marvellous common sense, coupled with their powers of imagination—all thoughts of a Little England are over. They are tumbling over each other, Liberals and Conservatives, to show which side are the greatest and most enthusiastic Imperialists. The people have changed, and so do all the parties, just like the Punch and Judy show[1] at a country fair. The people have found out that England is small, and her trade is large, and they have also found out that other people are taking their share of the world, and enforcing hostile tariffs. The people of England are finding out that "trade follows the flag,"[2] and they have all become Imperialists. They are not going to part with any territory. And the bygone ideas of nebulous republics are over. The English people intend to retain every inch of land they have got, and perhaps, sir, they intend to secure a few more inches. ...

from David Livingstone, "Cambridge Lecture Number 1" (1858)

The following excerpts are from a speech delivered at Cambridge University by the famous missionary; it was received with extended cheering.

When I went to Africa about seventeen years ago I resolved to acquire an accurate knowledge of the native tongues; and as I continued, while there, to speak generally in the African languages, the result is that I am not now very fluent in my own; but if you will excuse my imperfections under that head, I will endeavour to give you as clear an idea of Africa as I can....

My object in going into the country south of the desert was to instruct the natives in a knowledge of Christianity, but many circumstances prevented my living amongst them more than seven years, amongst

[1] *Punch and Judy show* Puppet show involving Mr. Punch and his wife Judy.

[2] *trade ... flag* Popular dictum of the period, meant to encourage colonization.

which were considerations arising out of the slave system carried on by the Dutch Boers. I resolved to go into the country beyond, and soon found that, for the purposes of commerce, it was necessary to have a path to the sea. I might have gone on instructing the natives in religion, but as civilization and Christianity must go on together, I was obliged to find a path to the sea, in order that I should not sink to the level of the natives. The chief was overjoyed at the suggestion, and furnished me with twenty-seven men, and canoes, and provisions, and presents for the tribes through whose country we had to pass. We might have taken a shorter path to the sea than that to the north, and then to the west, by which we went; but along the country by the shorter route, there is an insect called the tsetse, whose bite is fatal to horses, oxen, and dogs, but not to men or donkeys. You seem to think there is a connexion between the two. The habitat of that insect is along the shorter route to the sea. The bite of it is fatal to domestic animals, not immediately, but certainly in the course of two or three months; the animal grows leaner and leaner, and gradually dies of emaciation: a horse belonging to Gordon Cumming died of a bite five or six months after it was bitten.

On account of this insect, I resolved to go to the north, and then westwards to the Portuguese settlement of Loanda. Along the course of the river which we passed, game was so abundant that there was no difficulty in supplying the wants of my whole party: antelopes were so tame that they might be shot from the canoe. But beyond 14 degrees of south latitude the natives had guns, and had themselves destroyed the game, so that I and my party had to live on charity. The people, however, in that central region were friendly and hospitable: but they had nothing but vegetable productions: the most abundant was the cassava, which, however nice when made into tapioca pudding, resembles in its more primitive condition nothing so much as a mess of laundress's starch. There was a desire in the various villages through which we passed to have intercourse with us, and kindness and hospitality were shown us; but when we got near the Portuguese settlement of Angola the case was changed, and payment was demanded for every thing. But I had nothing to pay with. Now the people had been in the habit of trading

David Livingstone, 1864. Photo by Thomas Annan.

with the slavers, and so they said I might give one of my men in payment for what I wanted. When I shewed them that I could not do this, they looked upon me as an interloper, and I was sometimes in danger of being murdered.

As we neared the coast, the name of England was recognized, and we got on with ease. Upon one occasion, when I was passing through the parts visited by slave-traders, a chief who wished to shew me some kindness offered me a slave-girl: upon explaining that I had a little girl of my own, whom I should not like my own chief to give to a black man, the chief thought I was displeased with the size of the girl, and sent me one a head taller. By this and other means I convinced my men of my opposition to the principle of slavery; and when we arrived at Loanda I took them on board a British vessel, where I took a pride in showing them that those countrymen of mine and those guns were there for the purpose of putting down the slave-trade. They were convinced from what they saw of the honesty of Englishmen's intentions; and the hearty reception they met with from the sailors made them say to me, "We see they are your countrymen, for they have hearts like you." On the journey, the men had always looked forward to reaching the coast: they had seen Manchester prints and other articles imported therefrom, and they could not believe they were made by mortal hands. On reaching the sea, they thought that they had come to the end of the world. They said, "We marched along with our father, thinking the world was a large plain without limit; but all at once the land said 'I am finished, there is no more of me'"; and they called themselves the true old men—the true ancients—having gone to the end of the world. On reaching Loanda, they commenced trading in firewood, and also engaged themselves at sixpence a day in unloading coals, brought by a steamer for the supply of the cruiser lying there to watch the slave-vessels. On their return, they told their people "we worked for a whole moon, carrying away the stones that burn." By the time they were ready to go back to their own country, each had secured a large bundle of goods. On the way back, however, fever detained them, and their goods were all gone, leaving them on their return home, as poor as when they started....

A prospect is now before us of opening Africa for commerce and the Gospel. Providence has been preparing the way, for even before I proceeded to the Central basin it had been conquered and rendered safe by a chief named Sebituane, and the language of the Bechuanas made the fashionable tongue, and that was one of the languages into which Mr. Moffat had translated the Scriptures. Sebituane also discovered Lake Ngami some time previous to my explorations in that part. In going back to that country my object is to open up traffic along the banks of the Zambesi, and also to preach the Gospel. The natives of Central Africa are very desirous of trading, but their only traffic is at present in slaves, of which the poorer people have an unmitigated horror; it is therefore most desirable to encourage the former principle, and thus open a way for the consumption of free productions, and the introduction of Christianity and commerce. By encouraging the native propensity for trade, the advantages that might be derived in a commercial point of view are incalculable; nor should we lose sight of the inestimable blessings it is in our power to bestow upon the unenlightened African, by giving him the light of Christianity. Those two pioneers of civilization—Christianity and commerce—should ever be inseparable; and Englishmen should be warned by the fruits of neglecting that principle as exemplified in the result of the management of Indian affairs. By trading with Africa, also, we should at length be independent of slave labour, and thus discountenance practices so obnoxious to every Englishman.

Though the natives are not absolutely anxious to receive the Gospel, they are open to Christian influences. Among the Bechuanas the Gospel was well received. These people think it a crime to shed a tear, but I have seen some of them weep at the recollection of their sins when God had opened their hearts to Christianity and repentance....

I beg to direct your attention to Africa; I know that in a few years I shall be cut off in that country, which is now open; do not let it be shut again! I go back to Africa to try to make an open path for commerce and Christianity; do you carry out the work which I have begun. I LEAVE IT WITH YOU!

Eliza M., "Account of Cape Town," *King William's Town Gazette* (1863)

The following account (brought to light by M.J. Daymond et al. and the *Women Writing Africa Project*[1]) is one of the most remarkable literary descriptions we have of the world of nineteenth-century British colonialism from the point of view of one of the colonized. King William's Town was a small town some 500 miles east of Cape Town, and Eliza M., as she was identified in the *King William's Town Gazette*, had attended school at St. Matthew's Mission in the area. As Daymond et al. suggest, such a piece as this would in all likelihood have "been written as a school exercise." It would have been published, they speculate, "partly because its naiveté was amusing to the whites, but also because it was proof of the civilizing policies of the missionaries. It was translated from Xhosa into English by an unknown translator." What may have seemed "amusing naiveté" to nineteenth-century settlers is more likely to strike the modern reader as a style of elemental freshness.

We left East London on the Sunday, while it was raining; the sea was fighting very much, and there were soldiers going to England and their wives. On the Tuesday we arrived at Algoa Bay, and boats came to fetch the people who were going there, and other people came in. The ship went off the same day. A great wind blew, and I thought myself that if it had been another ship, it would not have been able to go on, but in its going, it kept twisting about, it did not go straight, but

---

[1] *Women Writing Africa Project*   M.J. Daymond et al., eds., *Women Writing Africa: The Southern Region* (New York: The Feminist Press, 2003), 98–104.

it went well on the day of our arrival, for the wind was good. We arrived on the Friday. While I was in the ship, I forgot I was on the water, it was like a house inside, but outside it was not like a house. There is everything that is kept at home; there were fowls and sheep and pigs, and slaughtering every day. I kept looking at the thing which makes the ship go. There are two horses inside, made of iron, which make it go; and when I looked inside, it was very frightful. There are many bed-rooms inside. The ship we were in is named the *Norman*, it is a steamer. It was unpleasant when nothing appeared, but when we left the Bay, we saw the mountains till we got to the Cape. One mountain is called the Lion's Head, and another is called Green Point, and I myself saw those mountains. That which is called the Lion's Head, is like a lion asleep. And another mountain above the town is that called Table Mountain; nevertheless it is not like a table, still that name is proper for it.

Before I came into the town, my heart said, "this place is not large," but when I entered it, I wondered, and was afraid. Oh, we slept that day. I have forgotten to relate something I saw the day I arrived. I saw black people, and I thought they were our kind, but they are not; they are Slams, called in English, Malays. Also, I was astonished at their large hats, pointed at the top, and large below. I saw some making baskets of reeds, and I wished I knew how to do it. On the Saturday evening, we went to a shop to buy butter and bread. At night lights were hung up throughout the whole town. I had thought we were going to walk in the darkness. I have not yet seen houses built with grass, like those we live in, they are high beautiful houses. The roads where people walk, are very fine. I have not yet seen a dirty, muddy place in the whole town. On the Sunday, bells sounded; there is one big one, and other small ones; we went to service in the great church.

Early on the Monday, wagons came about to sell things. Really people here get these things for nothing from their owners. A person can get men's trousers for three shillings each, yet in other places a person can never get them for that money. You can get three pairs of stockings for a shilling, a child's cap for a penny; you can get a width of a dress for threepence, if it is five widths, it is a shilling and threepence. There are little

wagons, the man who drives the horses sits behind, the proprietor does nothing, he sits so.

Another thing. The shoes of the Malays astonished me. There is a heel, and yonder on before a piece of wood sticks out, and they put it between their toes, and so make a clattering like the Germans. As things are to be got for such little money, how cheap must they be in England!

On Friday I saw a man riding in a wagon, there was a barrel inside and a cross-bar, and the water came out there. I don't know how it came out. It watered the new road, which is being made. And on Tuesday I saw people working at slates, taking off their ends—it was a great heap; the people who were at work were four. On the day of our arrival, a house was burnt, the people escaped, but I don't know whether the goods escaped. There are carts which go every day, carrying earth to throw on the road which is being mended, drawn by one horse.

There is a house where there are all kinds of beasts, and there are figures of black people, as if they were alive; their blackness is very ugly; also the bones of a man when he is dead, and birds and elephants, and lions, and tigers and sea-shells. I was afraid of those people, and the skeleton. There is also an ape holding Indian Corn, and there are monkeys.

In the evening we went out again, we went to the houses of the Malays; we went to see their decorations, for they were rejoicing because their days of fasting were ended. They were very beautiful; they had made flowers of paper, you would never think they were made of paper. We went for the sole purpose of seeing these works. They made a great noise, singing as they walked; you would laugh to see the children dancing outside and clapping their hands.

There are also wagons there for the sale of fish. The proprietors sound a thing like a horn to announce that he who wishes to buy let him buy. There are others for collecting dust-heaps, they ring a bell. There are vehicles to convey two people, he who drives the horses, and he who sits inside. In some there are windows and lights lit at night: those windows are two.

There are not many trees in the town; in some places there are not many at all, but in one place it is like the bush; it is pleasant underneath the trees; there are stools to sit on when a person is tired. That path is very long; I saw two Newfoundland dogs. I did not know that I should ever come to see them when I heard them spoken of. They are dogs with large heads and great long ears; the hair is like sheep's wool, and they have great claws; they are suited to assist people. It seemed as if they could swallow me without chewing; I was very much afraid, but one was not very big, it was about the size of the dogs of black people, when it barks, it says so with a great voice. Also, I saw sheep rather unlike others, in the tail here it was very large, the head was small, and the body was large and fat.

I have forgotten to mention something which I ought to have said before; when I came out of the ship and walked on land the earth seemed to move, and when I entered a house, it seemed to imitate the sailing of a ship, and when I lay down it seemed to move.

I saw an ox-wagon here, but I had not imagined that I should see a wagon.

We go to a very large beautiful Church; I don't forget the people who sing, the English; the prayers are said with thin voices as if it were singing; but the chief thing done is singing frequently, all the while there is continually singing, and then sitting. There is a Kafir school here; I went one day, they were reading; they can read well; there are also carpenters &c.

There is another place besides that which I said is like the bush, and in that place there are trees and flowers, and two fountains; a thing is stuck in, and the water comes out above. I saw the date-tree when it is young; it is one leaf, yet when it is grown, it is a very large tree. In that place there are wild birds, doves are there, and those birds which the English call canaries, and a very beautiful bird, its tail is long, its bill is red.

Yesterday the soldiers had sports, the music-band played, and when they finished playing they fired. They were many, and they fired together. And as we were walking, they fired; I was very much startled and afraid. And to-day they are playing the music. It seems to-day it exceeds in sweetness, I mean its sound.

There came a person here who is a Kafir. I rejoiced very much when I heard that he too was one. He asked me what I had come to do here; I said "I am only travelling." He asked whether I was a prisoner, and I said "No." He said he was very glad, he had thought I was a prisoner. I told him that I was going away again, and he said "May you go in peace, the Lord preserve you well till you arrive whence you came." I never saw a person like him of such kindness; he said he had come here to learn, he came from where I did; but I should not have known him to be a Kafir, and he did not know that I was one.

There are creatures which are eaten; they come from the sea, their name is called crawfish, they are frightful in appearance, yet their flesh is very fine and white.

The person of this house is a dyer of clothes, the white he makes red, and the red green, and the brown he makes black. I saw the wood with which they dye. Soap is cut in pieces, and put in water, and heated and boiled well, and continually stirred. This thing—dyeing clothes, is a great work. Water is even in the house; I don't know where it comes from, a person turns a thing, and fresh water comes out as if it were of a river.

There are also carts for selling meat, and for selling bread. I saw the fire-wagon, I did nothing but wonder. I did not know that it was such a big thing. It is long, with many wheels, they are not so large as those of an ox-wagon; people sit in places inside. The wheels run on metal; I say I could do nothing but wonder very much. I had not thought that it was such a great thing. And when it is about to proceed it says "Sh!" I don't know whether it is the boiling of the water; it hastens exceedingly, a person would be unable to notice it well, yet now some people say that this is a small one which I have seen. If it treads on anything, it must smash it, it is a very great thing. I shall never forget it. Where I saw it, the place was fenced on both sides, and I beheld it from the outside. I entered it another week after I had seen it; we went to Somerset West and slept one night. In the morning we returned by it: when I was inside, the earth seemed to move; it is pleasant to ride inside. I end now although this is not all the news about it. When I was in it, I saw a sugar plant; it is not a large plant, it is short with red flowers. I saw other trees at Somerset West which I had never seen before.

One day I saw people going to a burial, the carriages were black, but that people should wear black clothes is done also among the natives where a person has died; there were stuck up black feathers, and on the graves were placed stones with writing; the name of the person was written, and the years of his age, and the year in which he died.

I have seen to-day another thing which I did not know of, that thing which is said to be always done by white people in this month of May. They make themselves black people, they smear themselves with something black, with red patches on the cheeks; a thing is made with evergreens, and a man is put inside, and two people carry it, and another man carries a pan, and goes begging for money.

Another thing which I saw during the past month, was people going to the Governor's house—little chiefs, and chiefs of the soldiers, some had hats with red and white feathers, and silver coats, and gold swords, and the bishop went too. I heard it said that they were going to hear the things which were about to be spoken by people who had come from Graham's Town, King William's Town, Beaufort, and other places; it was said that these people were going to speak of the state of those towns and the doings of the people who live there. I do not say that those coats were really of gold, I say there was gold on some parts of them, on the arms and the back.

Also I have seen the fruit of the tree which the English call the chestnut; I did not see what the tree is like, the fruit is nice, the outside of it is hard; when you eat it it is sweet and edible like the potato, you can roast it or boil it. There is another fruit called Banana in English, it also is a nice fruit; it is not boiled or roasted, it is eaten like other fruits. There is a great white sweet potato, it is called Sweet Potato; those potatoes are very large, I had never seen them before, they are nearly all long: I do not know whether they are the potatoes named "Medicine" by the Fingoes.

I am puzzled to know how to begin to relate what was done yesterday, but I will try. Yesterday was said to be the wedding-day of the Great Son of Victoria, but it was not really the day of his marriage, for he has been married some time. The thing first done was arranging the children of the schools and I was there too. All walked in threes, going from one street to another. When we left the school-house we took up our station on an open piece of ground, other people climbed on the houses, and others looked on from below. On one house where we were standing there was the figure of a man like a king, a red cloth was put as if it were held by him, it is called in English a flag. Amongst all of us there were flags of different beautiful kinds; we stood there a great while, till we saw a multitude of soldiers and their officers and little chiefs and different sorts of people: one set wore clothes all alike, another had different clothes and ancient hats which were worn by the people of that time. All these now went in front, a very long line, then followed the ranks of another school, and we came after them. When we had finished going through many streets, we went to stand in another open spot of ground. All the time we were walking we were singing the song of Victoria. And there we saw the Governor and his wife; we all saluted. Although it seems that I have written a great deal I have not yet wondered at the things done at night, but let me finish those of the day. We were given food. We saw boats going along with people inside and boys wearing red clothes; there followed one with an old man, his hairs were long and white. There was a woman at his side wearing short clothes. Other boats followed with people in them, all the time they were appearing the drum and trumpets were sounded. I don't know how I shall make myself understood. I never saw such a beautiful thing; some of the men wore short dresses and short coats, and others wore short trousers like those of the French. All these things were red. When we had finished walking we went to stand in an open piece of ground, then we all went home. I do not know if any other things were done.

We went out again in the evening to see the fireworks. First we went into the gardens, where there were what I shall call candles; but nevertheless they are not called so in English. They were lights put inside little red and green glasses—When I was at a distance I thought they were little round things, all these were hung up and fastened in the trees,—there were some large ones and there were others not put in glasses.

We walked and went to a great crowd of people, we could not tell what we should do to see that which we came to see. There we saw a tall man with a high hat, I did not understand how it was made, and another man wearing women's clothes continually playing with that tall man. All these things have their names in English, some were called *Punch & Judy*, *Spectre*, *Father of the Doomed Arm-chair*, or the *Maid, the Murderer and the Midnight Avenger*,[1] and many other plays besides these. We passed on from that woman and man and went to see white people smeared with soot, they went into a house made of a tent where there were stools, and two came out and spoke to the people saying, "Ladies and gentlemen, come in and see what we have got here inside." Some went in and others did not, afterwards they opened that the people might see; there were black people sitting on chairs and singing. So we left; at the entrance of the garden there was written in letters of fire, "GOD bless Albert and Alexandra." In another place there were other things of fire, that place is called in English the Parade, where there was a thing like a light-house, on all sides there were candles. Some people sent up fire from Table Mountain, others from Green Point, others sent up fire in the midst of the town, it went up and came down again.

Besides these things there was another thing done, an ox was baked whole, the legs were not removed, only the inside and the hoofs. Many tables were set underneath the trees; that ox was intended for the poor people.

I am going to end now; I am very glad that I was brought here to see things which I never thought I should see.

There is another thing which has lately taken place, the birthday of Queen Victoria. Two balloons were made, no one went in them, there were only lights. That sort is called fire-balloons. The first was sent up; it rose very high till it was like a star: I did not see it again where it went. The other reappeared, it did not rise high like the first, it burnt, and fire came down like two stars.

I saw where newspapers are printed; four people were at work. I do not know what I shall say to tell about it. There is a thing which folds the papers and another thing which continually receives them. It made us sleepy.

E.M.
Translator unknown

from Agnes Macdonald, "By Car and Cowcatcher," *Murray's Magazine* (1887)

The essay from which the passages below are excerpted describes Macdonald's trip across Canada by train with her husband, Canadian Prime Minister Sir John A. Macdonald.

... The description of a cow-catcher is less easy. To begin with, it is misnamed, for it catches no cows at all. Sometimes, I understand, it throws up on the buffer-beam whatever maimed or mangled animal it has struck, but in most cases it clears the line by shoving forward, or tossing aside, any removable obstruction. It is best described as a sort of barred iron beak, about six feet long, projecting close over the track in a V shape, and attached to the buffer-beam by very strong bolts. It is sometimes sheathed with thin iron plates in winter, and acts then as a small snow-plough.

Behold me now, enthroned on the candle-box, with a soft felt hat well over my eyes, and a linen carriage-cover tucked round me from waist to foot. Mr. E.[2] had seated himself on the other side of the headlight. He had succumbed to the inevitable, ceased further expostulation, disclaimed all responsibility, and, like the jewel of a Superintendent he was, had decided on sharing my peril! I turn to him, peeping round the headlight, with my best smile. "This is *lovely*," I triumphantly announce, seeing that a word of comfort is necessary, "*quite lovely*; I shall travel on this cowcatcher from summit to sea!"

Mr. Superintendent, in his turn, peeps round the headlight and surveys me with solemn and resigned surprise. "I—suppose—you—will," he says slowly, and I see that he is hoping, at any rate, that I shall live to do it!

With a mighty snort, a terribly big throb, and shrieking whistle, No. 374 moves slowly forward. The very small population of Laggan have all come out to see. They stand in the hot sunshine, and shade their eyes as the stately engine moves on. "It is an awful thing to do!" I hear a voice say, as the little group lean forward; and for a moment I feel a thrill that is very like fear; but it is gone at once, and I can think of nothing but the

---

[1] *Spectre ... Avenger* Popular plays of the period.

[2] *Mr. E.* John M. Egan, general superintendent of the western division of the Canadian Pacific Railroad at the time.

novelty, the excitement, and the fun of this mad ride in glorious sunshine and intoxicating air, with magnificent mountains before and around me, their lofty peaks smiling down on us, and never a frown on their grand faces!

The pace quickens gradually, surely, swiftly, and then we are rushing up to the summit. We soon stand on the "Great Divide"—5300 feet above sea-level—between the two great oceans. As we pass, Mr. E. by a gesture, points out a small river (called Bath Creek, I think) which, issuing from a lake on the narrow summit-level, winds near the track. I look, and lo! the water, flowing *eastward* towards the Atlantic side, turns in a moment as the Divide is passed, and pours *westward* down the Pacific slope!

Another moment and a strange silence has fallen round us. With steam shut off and brakes down, the 60-ton engine, by its own weight and impetus alone, glides into the pass of the Kicking Horse River, and begins a descent of 2800 feet in twelve miles. We rush onward through the vast valley stretching before us, bristling with lofty forests, dark and deep, that, clinging to the mountain side, are reared up into the sky. The river, widening, grows white with dashing foam, and rushes downwards with tremendous force. Sunlight flashes on glaciers, into gorges, and athwart[1] huge, towering masses of rock crowned with magnificent tree crests that rise all round us of every size and shape. Breathless—almost awe-stricken—but with a wild triumph in my heart, I look from farthest mountain peak, lifted high before me, to the shining pebbles at my feet! Warm wind rushes past; a thousand sunshine colours dance in the air. With a firm right hand grasping the iron stanchion, and my feet planted on the buffer beam, there was not a yard of that descent in which I faltered for a moment. If I had, then assuredly in the wild valley of the Kicking Horse River, on the western slope of the Rocky Mountains, a life had gone out that day! I did not think of danger, or remember what a giddy post I had. I could only gaze at the glaciers that the mountains held so closely, 5000 feet above us, at the trace of snow avalanches which had left a space a hundred feet wide massed with torn and prostrate trees; on the shadows that played over the distant peaks; and on a hundred rainbows made by the foaming, dashing river, which

swirls with tremendous rapidity down the gorge on its way to the Columbia in the valley below....

Halted at Palliser. The Chief and his friends walked up to the cow-catcher to make a morning call. I felt a little "superior" and was rather condescending. Somewhat flushed with excitement, but still anxious to be polite, I asked "would the Chief step up and take a drive?" To the horror of the bystanders he carelessly consented, and in another moment had taken the place of Mr. E., the latter seating himself at our feet on the buffer-beam. There was a general consternation among our little group of friends and the few inhabitants of Palliser—the Chief rushing through the flats of the Columbia on a cow-catcher! and, worse still, possibly even among the wild Selkirk Mountains—those mountains of which scarcely three years before, in his charming book, "From Old Westminster to New," my friend Mr. Sandford Fleming[2] had said, "no one had been through the western slope of the Selkirks"! Every one is horrified. It is a comfort to the other occupant of the buffer to find some one else wilful, and as we steamed away towards Donald, at the eastern base of the Selkirks, I felt not so bad after all!...

Henry Lawson, "The Drover's[3] Wife" (1892)

> Australian-born poet and prose writer Henry Lawson is best known for short stories like the one below, depicting the harshness of life in the Australian bush.

The two-roomed house is built of round timber, slabs, and stringy bark, and floored with split slabs. A big bark kitchen standing at one end is larger than the house itself, veranda included.

Bush all round—bush with no horizon, for the country is flat. No ranges in the distance. The bush consists of stunted, rotten native apple trees. No undergrowth. Nothing to relieve the eye save the darker green of a few she-oaks which are sighing above the narrow, almost waterless creek. Nineteen miles to the nearest sign of civilization—a shanty on the main road.

---

[1] *athwart* Run across in oblique direction.

[2] *Sandford Fleming* Canadian engineer and inventor (1827–1915).

[3] *Drover* Person who drives livestock to market, often over great distances.

The drover, an ex-squatter,[1] is away with sheep. His wife and children are left here alone.

Four ragged, dried-up-looking children are playing about the house. Suddenly one of them yells: "Snake! Mother, here's a snake!"

The gaunt, sun-browned bushwoman dashes from the kitchen, snatches her baby from the ground, holds it on her left hip, and reaches for a stick.

"Where is it?"

"Here! Gone into the wood-heap!" yells the eldest boy—a sharp-faced urchin of eleven. "Stop there, mother! I'll have him. Stand back! I'll have the beggar!"

"Tommy, come here, or you'll be bit. Come here at once when I tell you, you little wretch!"

The youngster comes reluctantly, carrying a stick bigger than himself. Then he yells, triumphantly:

"There it goes—under the house!" and darts away with club uplifted. At the same time the big, black, yellow-eyed dog-of-all-breeds, who has shown the wildest interest in the proceedings, breaks his chain and rushes after that snake. He is a moment late, however, and his nose reaches the crack in the slabs just as the end of its tail disappears. Almost at the same moment the boy's club comes down and skins the aforesaid nose. Alligator takes small notice of this, and proceeds to undermine the building; but he is subdued after a struggle and chained up. They cannot afford to lose him.

The drover's wife makes the children stand together near the dog-house while she watches for the snake. She gets two small dishes of milk and sets them down near the wall to tempt it to come out; but an hour goes by and it does not show itself.

It is near sunset, and a thunderstorm is coming. The children must be brought inside. She will not take them into the house, for she knows the snake is there, and may at any moment come up through the cracks in the rough slab floor; so she carries several armfuls of firewood into the kitchen, and then takes the children there. The kitchen has no floor—or, rather, an earthen one—called a "ground floor" in this part of the bush. There is a large, roughly made table in the centre of the place. She brings

the children in, and makes them get on this table. They are two boys and two girls—mere babies. She gives them some supper, and then, before it gets dark, she goes into the house, and snatches up some pillows and bed-clothes— expecting to see or lay her hand on the snake any minute. She makes a bed on the kitchen table for the children, and sits down beside it to watch all night.

She has an eye on the corner, and a green sapling club laid in readiness on the dresser by her side, together with her sewing basket and a copy of the *Young Ladies' Journal*. She has brought the dog into the room.

Tommy turns in, under protest, but says he'll lie awake all night and smash that blinded snake.

His mother asks him how many times she has told him not to swear.

He has his club with him under the bedclothes, and Jacky protests:

"Mummy! Tommy's skinnin' me alive wif his club. Make him take it out."

Tommy: "Shet up you little—! D'yer want to be bit with the snake?"

Jacky shuts up.

"If yer bit," says Tommy, after a pause, "you'll swell up, an smell, an' turn red an' green an' blue all over till yer bust. Won't he mother?"

"Now then, don't frighten the child. Go to sleep," she says.

The two younger children go to sleep, and now and then Jacky complains of being "skeezed." More room is made for him. Presently Tommy says: "Mother! Listen to them (adjective) little 'possums. I'd like to screw their blanky necks."

And Jacky protests drowsily:

"But they don't hurt us, the little blanks!"

Mother: "There, I told you you'd teach Jacky to swear." But the remark makes her smile. Jacky goes to sleep.

Presently Tommy asks:

"Mother! Do you think they'll ever extricate the (adjective) kangaroo?"

"Lord! How am I to know, child? Go to sleep."

"Will you wake me if the snake comes out?"

"Yes. Go to sleep."

Near midnight. The children are all asleep and she sits there still, sewing and reading by turns. From time

---

[1] *squatter* Someone who settles with livestock on government land. Initially, squatters struggled to establish themselves, but some eventually became wealthy as owners of large-scale grazing operations.

to time she glances round the floor and wall-plate, and whenever she hears a noise she reaches for the stick. The thunderstorm comes on, and the wind, rushing through the cracks in the slab wall, threatens to blow out her candle. She places it on a sheltered part of the dresser and fixes up a newspaper to protect it. At every flash of lightning, the cracks between the slabs gleam like polished silver. The thunder rolls, and the rain comes down in torrents.

Alligator lies at full length on the floor, with his eyes turned towards the partition. She knows by this that the snake is there. There are large cracks in that wall opening under the floor of the dwelling-house.

She is not a coward, but recent events have shaken her nerves. A little son of her brother-in-law was lately bitten by a snake, and died. Besides, she has not heard from her husband for six months, and is anxious about him.

He was a drover, and started squatting here when they were married. The drought of 18— ruined him. He had to sacrifice the remnant of his flock and go droving again. He intends to move his family into the nearest town when he comes back, and, in the meantime, his brother, who keeps a shanty on the main road, comes over about once a month with provisions. The wife has still a couple of cows, one horse, and a few sheep. The brother-in-law kills one of the sheep occasionally, gives her what she needs of it, and takes the rest in return for other provisions.

She is used to being left alone. She once lived like this for eighteen months. As a girl she built the usual castles in the air; but all her girlish hopes and aspirations have long been dead. She finds all the excitement and recreation she needs in the *Young Ladies' Journal*, and, Heaven help her! takes a pleasure in the fashion plates.

Her husband is an Australian, and so is she. He is careless, but a good enough husband. If he had the means he would take her to the city and keep her there like a princess. They are used to being apart, or at least she is. "No use fretting," she says. He may forget sometimes that he is married; but if he has a good cheque when he comes back he will give most of it to her. When he had money he took her to the city several times—hired a railway sleeping compartment, and put up at the best hotels. He also bought her a buggy, but they had to sacrifice that along with the rest.

The last two children were born in the bush—one while her husband was bringing a drunken doctor, by force, to attend to her. She was alone on this occasion, and very weak. She had been ill with a fever. She prayed to God to send her assistance. God sent Black Mary— the "whitest" gin[1] in all the land. Or, at least, God sent "King Jimmy" first, and he sent Black Mary. He put his black face round the door post, took in the situation at a glance, and said cheerfully: "All right, missus—I bring my old woman, she down alonga creek."

One of her children died while she was here alone. She rode nineteen miles for assistance, carrying the dead child.

It must be near one or two o'clock. The fire is burning low. Alligator lies with his head resting on his paws, and watches the wall. He is not a very beautiful dog to look at, and the light shows numerous old wounds where the hair will not grow. He is afraid of nothing on the face of the earth or under it. He will tackle a bullock[2] as readily as he will tackle a flea. He hates all other dogs— except kangaroo-dogs[3]—and has a marked dislike to friends or relations of the family. They seldom call, however. He sometimes makes friends with strangers. He hates snakes and has killed many, but he will be bitten some day and die; most snake-dogs end that way.

Now and then the bushwoman lays down her work and watches, and listens, and thinks. She thinks of things in her own life, for there is little else to think about.

The rain will make the grass grow, and this reminds her how she fought a bush-fire once while her husband was away. The grass was long, and very dry, and the fire threatened to burn her out. She put on an old pair of her husband's trousers and beat out the flames with a green bough, till great drops of sooty perspiration stood out on her forehead and ran in streaks down her blackened arms. The sight of his mother in trousers greatly amused Tommy, who worked like a little hero by her side, but the terrified baby howled lustily for his "mummy." The fire would have mastered her but for four excited bushmen who arrived in the nick of time.

---

[1] *gin* Derogatory term used by white Australians to refer to an Aboriginal woman.

[2] *bullock* Young or castrated bull.

[3] *kangaroo-dogs* Large dogs used to hunt kangaroo.

It was a mixed-up affair all round; when she went to take up the baby he screamed and struggled convulsively, thinking it was a "blackman"; and Alligator, trusting more to the child's sense than his own instinct, charged furiously, and (being old and slightly deaf) did not in his excitement at first recognize his mistress's voice, but continued to hang on to the moleskins[1] until choked off by Tommy with a saddle-strap. The dog's sorrow for his blunder, and his anxiety to let it be known that it was all a mistake, was as evident as his ragged tail and a twelve-inch grin could make it. It was a glorious time for the boys; a day to look back to, and talk about, and laugh over for many years.

She thinks how she fought a flood during her husband's absence. She stood for hours in the drenching downpour, and dug an overflow gutter to save the dam across the creek. But she could not save it. There are things that a bushwoman cannot do. Next morning the dam was broken, and her heart was nearly broken too, for she thought how her husband would feel when he came home and saw the result of years of labour swept away. She cried then.

She also fought the pleuropneumonia[2]—dosed and bled the few remaining cattle, and wept again when her two best cows died.

Again, she fought a mad bullock that besieged the house for a day. She made bullets and fired at him through cracks in the slabs with an old shotgun. He was dead in the morning. She skinned him and got seventeen-and-six[3] for the hide.

She also fights the crows and eagles that have designs on her chickens. Her plan of campaign is very original. The children cry "Crows, mother!" and she rushes out and aims a broomstick at the birds as though it were a gun, and says, "Bung!" The crows leave in a hurry; they are cunning, but a woman's cunning is greater.

Occasionally a bushman in the horrors,[4] or a villainous-looking sundowner,[5] comes and nearly scares the life out of her. She generally tells the suspicious-looking stranger that her husband and two sons are at work below the dam, or over at the yard, for he always cunningly inquires for the boss.

Only last week a gallows-faced swagman[6]—having satisfied himself that there were no men on the place—threw his swag down on the veranda, and demanded tucker.[7] She gave him something to eat; then he expressed his intention of staying for the night. It was sundown then. She got a batten[8] from the sofa, loosened the dog, and confronted the stranger, holding the batten in one hand and the dog's collar with the other. "Now you go!" she said. He looked at her and at the dog, said "All right, mum," in a cringing tone, and left. She was a determined-looking woman, and Alligator's yellow eyes glared unpleasantly—besides, the dog's chawing-up apparatus greatly resembled that of the reptile he was named after.

She has few pleasures to think of as she sits here alone by the fire, on guard against a snake. All days are much the same to her; but on Sunday afternoon she dresses herself, tidies the children, smartens up baby, and goes for a lonely walk along the bush-track, pushing an old perambulator[9] in front of her. She does this every Sunday. She takes as much care to make herself and the children look smart as she would if she were going to do the block in the city. There is nothing to see, however, and not a soul to meet. You might walk for twenty miles along this track without being able to fix a point in your mind, unless you are a bushman. This is because of the everlasting, maddening sameness of the stunted trees—that monotony which makes a man long to break away and travel as far as trains can go, and sail as far as ships can sail—and further.

But this bushwoman is used to the loneliness of it. As a girl-wife she hated it, but now she would feel strange away from it.

She is glad when her husband returns, but she does not gush or make a fuss about it. She gets him something good to eat, and tidies up the children.

---

[1] *moleskins* Trousers.

[2] *pleuropneumonia* Highly infectious disease afflicting cattle.

[3] *seventeen-and-six* Seventeen shillings and sixpence.

[4] *in the horrors* I.e., extremely drunk.

[5] *sundowner* Vagrant who arrives at sundown to avoid working in exchange for requested shelter.

[6] *swagman* Australian: man who travels the countryside in search of work.

[7] *tucker* Australian: food.

[8] *batten* I.e., board.

[9] *perambulator* Baby carriage.

She seems contented with her lot. She loves her children, but has no time to show it. She seems harsh to them. Her surroundings are not favourable to the development of the "womanly" or sentimental side of nature.

It must be near morning now; but the clock is in the dwelling-house. Her candle is nearly done; she forgot that she was out of candles. Some more wood must be got to keep the fire up, and so she shuts the dog inside and hurries round to the wood-heap. The rain has cleared off. She seizes a stick, pulls it out, and—crash! The whole pile collapses.

Yesterday she bargained with a stray blackfellow[1] to bring her some wood, and while he was at work she went in search of a missing cow. She was absent an hour or so, and the native black made good use of his time. On her return she was so astonished to see a good heap of wood by the chimney, that she gave him an extra fig of tobacco, and praised him for not being lazy. He thanked her, and left with head erect and chest well out. He was the last of his tribe and a King; but he had built that wood-heap hollow.

She is hurt now, and tears spring to her eyes as she sits down again by the table. She takes up a handkerchief to wipe the tears away, but pokes her eyes with her bare fingers instead. The handkerchief is full of holes, and she finds that she has put her thumb through one, and her forefinger through another.

This makes her laugh, to the surprise of the dog. She has a keen, very keen, sense of the ridiculous; and some time or other she will amuse bushmen with the story.

She has been amused before like that. One day she sat down "to have a good cry," as she said—and the old cat rubbed against her dress and "cried too." Then she had to laugh.

It must be near daylight. The room is very close and hot because of the fire. Alligator still watches the wall from time to time. Suddenly he becomes greatly interested; he draws himself a few inches nearer the partition, and a thrill runs though his body. The hair on the back of his neck begins to bristle, and the battle-light is in his yellow eyes. She knows what this means, and lays her hand on the stick. The lower end of one of the partition slabs has a large crack on both sides. An evil pair of small, bright, bead-like eyes glisten at one of these holes. The snake—a black one—comes slowly out, about a foot, and moves its head up and down. The dog lies still, and the woman sits as one fascinated. The snake comes out a foot further. She lifts her stick, and the reptile, as though suddenly aware of danger, sticks his head in through the crack on the other side of the slab, and hurries to get his tail round after him. Alligator springs, and his jaws come together with a snap. He misses, for his nose is large and the snake's body down in the angle formed by the slabs and the floor. He snaps again as the tail comes round. He has the snake now, and tugs it out eighteen inches. Thud, thud comes the woman's club on the ground. Alligator pulls again. Thud, thud. Alligator gives another pull and he has the snake out—a black brute, five feet long. The head rises to dart about, but the dog has the enemy close to the neck. He is a big, heavy dog, but quick as a terrier. He shakes the snake as though he felt the original curse in common with mankind. The eldest boy wakes up, seizes his stick, and tries to get out of bed, but his mother forces him back with a grip of iron. Thud, thud—the snake's back is broken in several places. Thud, thud—its head is crushed, and Alligator's nose skinned again.

She lifts the mangled reptile on the point of her stick, carries it to the fire, and throws it in; then piles on the wood, and watches the snake burn. The boy and dog watch, too. She lays her hand on the dog's head, and all the fierce, angry light dies out of his yellow eyes. The younger children are quieted, and presently go to sleep. The dirty-legged boy stands for a moment in his shirt, watching the fire. Presently he looks up at her, sees the tears in her eyes, and, throwing his arms around her neck, exclaims:

"Mother, I won't never go drovin'; blast me if I do!"

And she hugs him to her worn-out breast and kisses him; and they sit thus together while the sickly daylight breaks over the bush.

---

[1]   *blackfellow*   Offensive Australian term for an Aboriginal man.

THE EARLY TWENTIETH CENTURY: FROM 1900 TO MID-CENTURY

The first half of the twentieth century saw a fracturing of almost every aspect of British life. At the beginning of the century, Queen Victoria, monarch for 63 years, still reigned over a nation that had become the world's greatest economic and political power. Over the course of the nineteenth century, the industrial revolution had transformed the economy and Great Britain had become "factory to the world." Despite a high level of religious anxiety among the educated classes of the late Victorian period, the established church retained its authority over a God-fearing society. The working class was not always contented with its lot—and with reason—but the class hierarchy remained extraordinarily stable. So, too, did gender roles; a small minority of women was pressing to be given the vote, but they were regarded as extremists by the vast majority of the population. Expressions of sexuality were tightly circumscribed, and the possibility of having an orientation other than heterosexual was unmentioned (except for occasional veiled references to difficulties or scandals "of the Oscar Wilde sort"). And the British Empire had reached its zenith. The vast dominions of Canada and Australia had become semi-autonomous (in 1867 and 1901 respectively), but overwhelmingly their people were proud to call themselves British subjects. Despite a lively debate in the latter half of the nineteenth century as to whether Britain's imperial ambitions were truly benefitting either the colonizers or the colonized, the majority of British citizens were not "little Englanders" looking to reduce Britain's overseas commitments; they were pleased that British rule extended over all of India, a very large part of Africa, and a considerable amount of the rest of the world. England was seen by the English, in the words of the popular poet W.E. Henley, as the "Chosen daughter of the Lord." Britain had certainly not been immune to change in the second half the nineteenth century—indeed, many of the lines along which twentieth-century society would fracture were in place in the late Victorian era. Political and ideological strains that would shake class structure were already forming; categories of gender and sexuality were already becoming far less stable than they had been a decade or two earlier; and the "Aesthetes" had begun in the 1890s to break free of characteristically Victorian patterns of anxiety over the religious, the moral, and the aesthetic. But for most British people the world in 1900 seemed recognizably the same world as that of 1850, and Britain held a central place within it.

By 1950 that world had been distinctly altered. The four years of World War I had resulted in the deaths of millions and had had a catastrophic effect on the nation's spirit; the great economic depression of the 1930s had bred poverty and despair; the seven years of World War II had threatened Britain's survival and left the nation exhausted, even in victory; and immediately in its wake, with Britain still physically and emotionally devastated, had begun a new war, a "Cold War" against the Soviet Union. Exhausted by these struggles, Britain in 1950 had lost its place as the world's leading power to the United States. Daily life had been radically altered by the radio, the telephone, and the automobile. Church-going was in decline, and the nation was well on its way to becoming a secular society. Though Britain remained more class-conscious than North America or Australia, the class structure itself had seen great change; only the wealthy had servants, and all social classes partook of the same culture to an unprecedented extent. The Labour Party government of Clement Attlee, elected in 1945 in a clean break from Winston Churchill and the glorious but conservative path that he represented, had for five years been building a welfare state; this was Britain's first avowedly socialist government. "Votes for women"—to most minds a far-fetched notion in 1900—had in 1950 been a reality for over 20 years; women had done "men's work" during two long world wars, and were starting to wonder if winning the vote might represent the beginning rather than the end of the struggle for gender equality. Much

King Edward VII.

The streets of London decorated for the Coronation of Edward VII, 1902.

of Britain was as repressed sexually as it had been in 1900—but more and more people were starting to see the awkwardness that surrounded sexual matters as an obstacle to be overcome rather than as the expression of a necessary and appropriate sense of modesty. And the sun was rapidly setting on the British Empire. The dominions were now fully independent and beginning to drift away from the mother country culturally; India had been partitioned in 1947 into two independent nations; and in Britain's African and Caribbean possessions the stirrings of unrest that would lead to independence had already begun. In literature Britain had in the years between 1900 and 1950 undergone the Modernist revolution.[1] The sometimes fractured, some-

times free-flowing approaches to form that the poetry of T.S. Eliot, the plays of Samuel Beckett, and the prose fiction of James Joyce and Virginia Woolf represented had not been taken up by the majority of writers. Yet many serious writers in 1950 were aware of the expanded possibilities of literary form that modernism had revealed—and many wrote with a sense that the world was not the ordered and coherent whole that it had been widely assumed to be at the dawn of the twentieth century.

THE EDWARDIAN PERIOD

If it is true to say that the first half of the twentieth century may be characterized as a period in which the old Britain and the old world broke apart, it is also true that much of that fracturing did not begin to be readily visible until the years after 1910. 1910 was marked by the death of Edward VII, but more significantly this was the time of the first explosions of Modernism—Cubism in painting, Imagism in poetry, in music such groundbreaking works as Stravinsky's *The Rite of Spring* (1913). With these began the fracturing of form that would become a dominant theme in the cultural history of much of the rest of the century. With 1914 came the

---

[1] "Modernist" and "Modernism" are commonly used as umbrella terms to describe a wide range of inter-connected intellectual and aesthetic developments of the first half of the twentieth century that occurred in France, Italy, the United States and other areas as well as in Britain. A connecting thread is that expressions of Modernism tend to shun the linear, the decorative, and the sentimental. They tend too towards the presentation of reality fractured into its component pieces—and conversely, towards a rejection of aesthetic traditions through which reality is represented through the construction of conventionally unified wholes, through a single point of view, or through a single, unbroken narrative. Modernism is discussed more fully later in this introduction.

outbreak of World War I, and with 1915 and 1916—the years of the gruesomely drawn-out battles of Ypres and of the Somme—came a more visceral sense of fracturing as the full horror of the war's unprecedented carnage began to sink home.

The deaths of Victoria in 1901 and of her son Edward nine years later have often been seen as defining moments in the change from the Victorian to the modern world. Edwardian Britain liked to see itself as highly distinct from its Victorian predecessor. And certainly there were some changes; architectural style became rather less ornate, for example, and social style rather less formal. But at its core the Edwardian era was as much a continuation from the Victorian one as a break with it. Established religion, a hierarchy of social class, a largely inflexible set of attitudes towards gender roles, a complacent confidence in Britain's dominant position in the world—all these remained largely unchanged.

In some respects a "Victorian" sense of Empire carried on into the 1920s and 1930s. Here Queen Mary (wife of George V) is shown visiting the Burma pavilion at the British Empire Exhibition, London, 1924. Though some complained that the Exhibition's strongly patriotic flavor was excessively self-congratulatory, it was highly popular with most Londoners.

A sternwheel steamer and trading canoes at Okopedi on the Eyong River, Nigeria, 1909. Nigeria was among the last British possessions to be governed through a trading company; in 1900, control was transferred from the Royal Niger Company to the government, and the territory became the Protectorate of Southern Nigeria. The Niger Company continued as the leading trading entity in the region.

In the literary world Victorian traditions were being carried forward by novelists such as George Moore and Arnold Bennett, dramatists such as Arthur Wing Pinero, and poets such as Robert Bridges and W.E. Henley, the immensely popular author of "Invictus" and "Pro Rege Nostro" ("England, My England"). And even much of the literature that we now think of as recognizably modern may as readily be seen as connecting with that of the late Victorian era as anticipating the later literature of the century. The prose fiction of Joseph Conrad, for example, with its laying bare of the dark corners of the human soul (and of the dark realities of colonialism), touches the nerves of the reader in ways that we think of as distinctively modern. Indeed, the cry "that was no more than a breath" of the dying ivory agent

Kurtz in Conrad's *Heart of Darkness* (1899, 1902)—"The horror! The horror!"—is often regarded as a defining expression of the anguish that came to be felt as characteristic of the twentieth century. And some of Conrad's narrative techniques break ground that would become heavily tilled in the twentieth century; through layering of viewpoints (stories within stories, multiple narrators) Conrad found ways to create a narrative density that at once intensifies and destabilizes the reader's experience of the events being recounted. But Conrad was an extraordinary innovator, not a revolutionary; however original, the threads of most of his fiction are still woven through a storytelling art that draws on the conventions of fiction writing that held sway through the nineteenth century—conventions of realism through which implausible coincidences or exotic adventures could be made believable to the reader. As a *New York Times* reviewer put it in 1903, "the adventures he describes are little short of miraculous and are laid among scenes wholly alien to commonplace life, [but] they are wrought into a tissue of truth so firm and so tough as to resist the keenest scepticism.... Not even his Kurtz, the man of impenetrable darkness of soul, is either a bloodless or an incredible figure."

The novelist E.M. Forster is recognizably an author of the twentieth century in his treatment not only of the sexual (see below for a discussion of his novel *Maurice*) but also of the spiritual; his approach to the spiritual realities that transcend everyday life connects to the work of later twentieth-century writers such as Elizabeth Bowen, Graham Greene, and Kazuo Ishiguro. And in some stylistic respects (notably, the shifting, ironic narrative voice of *A Passage to India* [1924]), his fiction has affinities with modernism. But the texture of his work—most notably of the novels *A Room With a View* (1908) and *Howard's End* (1910)—is woven of nuances of social interaction and of subtle modulations of feeling, and relates at least as strongly to the conventions of Victorian realism as it does to those of Modernism. Forster is above all a social novelist, whose work recognizably connects with the traditions of his nineteenth-century predecessors.

Much of H.G. Wells's fiction was forward-looking in a more precise sense. Beginning in 1895 with the publication of *The Time Machine*, and continuing with *The Island of Dr. Moreau* (1896), *The Invisible Man* (1897), and *The War of the Worlds* (1898), Wells had founded the genre of science fiction as we still know it today. He continued in this vein in the new century with such works as *The First Men in the Moon* (1901) and *The War in the Air* (1908). But in the style of his fiction Wells, too, was a traditional storyteller. And, though he is remembered today primarily for his science fiction, he wrote in a vein of social comedy with at least as much frequency, and with even greater success in his own lifetime. *Love and Mr. Lewisham* (1900), *Kipps: The Story of a Simple Soul* (1905), and *The History of Mr. Polly* (1910) are comic novels that draw on Wells's own struggles, in painting an entertaining but strongly critical picture of the English social class system.

Like many writers of the time—playwright Bernard Shaw perhaps most prominent among them—Wells became a committed socialist in the early years of the twentieth century. The chief vehicle of socialist response in Britain at the time was the Fabian society, founded in 1884 to promote *evolutionary* socialism (thus disavowing violent class struggle). The Fabian Society, led by Shaw, Sidney Webb, and Beatrice Potter Webb, was instrumental in forming the Labour Representation Committee in 1900; that committee, with substantial input as well from the Trades Union Congress, transformed itself into a political party in 1906, and over the course of the next generation the Labour Party managed to displace the Liberal Party as the main political alternative to Britain's Conservative Party. *Mrs Warren's Profession* is among the earliest of a long series of plays that give dramatic life to Shaw's progressive views; among its most memorable successors are *Major Barbara* (1905) and *Pygmalion* (1913). Shaw continued to write for the stage well into the 1920s (and lived until 1950), but he too expressed a powerful sense of change more in the content of his work than in its form. And other writers of the Edwardian era—including novelists and dramatists of thoroughly modern views such as Sarah Grand, Ella Hepworth Dixon, and Cicely Hamilton (all of whom expressed their strong feminist views through their work), for the most part structured their texts in traditional ways.

Members of a slum-dwelling family in London, c. 1913. Though Britain was the world's wealthiest nation, the poor often lived in appalling conditions of hardship.

David Lloyd George, 1906. Lloyd George was a leading advocate of the interests of the working class in the early years of the century. As Chancellor of the Exchequer, he introduced the "Peoples' Budget" of 1909, calling for new taxes on the better-off to pay for measures to improve the lot of the poor, including an old age pension. The Old Age Pensions Act was resisted so strongly by the House of Lords that the Liberal Government acted to reduce the power of the House; both that Act and the Parliament Act, which established the supremacy of the House of Commons, became law in 1911. Lloyd George was also responsible for the National Insurance Act (1911), which provided some protection for workers who lost earnings through illness or unemployment.

Workers share a paper to read the news during the General Strike of 1926. The condition of the working class had improved somewhat by the 1920s, but in some sectors—notably coal mining—efforts were being made to roll back improvements in wages and working conditions. The 1926 General Strike in support of the coal miners lasted nine days.

The World Wars

As Lord Earl Grey, the British Foreign Secretary, watched the streetlights being lit from his office window one evening just before the outbreak of war in August 1914, he is famously reported to have remarked to a friend, "The lamps are going out all over Europe; we shall not see them lit again in our lifetime." At the time such thinking went against the grain; at the outset of the "Great War," many in England firmly expected their soldiers to be home before Christmas. But over the next thirty years many came to believe that the moment at which the First World War broke out had heralded nothing less than the collapse of civilization as it had long been known. At the outset of the Second World War in 1940, George Orwell adopted this vein of apocalyptic pessimism in his long essay "Inside the Whale":

The war of 1914–1918 was only a heightened moment in an almost continuous crisis. At this date it hardly needs a war to bring home to us the disintegration of our society and the increasing helplessness of all decent people.... While I have been writing this book another European war has broken out. It will either last several years and tear western civilization to pieces, or it will end inconclusively and prepare the way for yet another war that will do the job once and for all.

Western civilization has proved to be rather more resilient than Orwell had feared, but his view of the period beginning in 1914 as "an almost continuous crisis" is now widely shared by historians; increasingly the two world wars of the twentieth century are being seen as part of a continuum. From more than one angle this makes sense. In both wars, Britain and her Empire/Commonwealth allies, joined belatedly by the United States, were fighting against a militaristic and expansionist Germany. In both wars much of the rest of the world was drawn into the conflict, though there was no parallel in World War I to the crucial importance of the Pacific theater and the struggle between the Allies and Japan in World War II.

The two wars are also linked through a chain of causation. Though all authorities agree that both wars had multiple causes, it is also universally agreed that one vitally important cause of the Second World War was the decision by the allies after World War I to demand reparations—a decision that had the effect in the short term of crippling Germany economically—and that had the even more pernicious effect over the longer term of so embittering the German people as to make a majority highly receptive to Hitler's appeals to nationalism, expansionism, anti-Semitism, and hate. The British economist John Maynard Keynes had been among those prescient enough to foresee the problem early on. In his chapter on "Europe After the Treaty" in *The Economic Consequences of the Peace* (1919), he summarized the matter with blunt eloquence:

This chapter must be one of pessimism. The treaty includes no provisions for the economic rehabilitation of Europe—nothing to make the defeated ... into good neighbours, nothing to stabilise the new states of Europe; … Nor does it promote in any way a compact of economic solidarity amongst the Allies themselves … It is an extraordinary fact that the fundamental economic problem of a Europe starving and disintegrating before their eyes, was the one question in which it was impossible to arouse the interest of the Four [powers that imposed the peace treaty].

Hitler's eventual rise to power, then, was partly fueled by the hardships imposed on the Germans by the Allies at the conclusion of World War I.

The Western Front in World War I, 1915.

If there are similarities and connections between the two world wars, there are also important differences. There are differences in the way the wars were fought, to start with—the trench warfare, stagnation, and machine gun carnage of World War I contrasts with the tanks, submarines, airplanes, and bombs of World War II. There is usually also agreed to be a substantial difference in the moral context in which the two wars were fought. Many have suggested that ethically there

Londoners sleeping in the Elephant and Castle underground station during the bombing raids of 1940. These raids, popularly referred to as "the Blitz," were intended by the Nazis to "soften up" the English in preparation for a German invasion. Though much of London (and of other cities) was destroyed, the efforts of the British Air Force against superior numbers in what came to be known as the "Battle of Britain" were highly successful, and Hitler eventually decided against attempting an invasion of the British Isles; only the two Channel Islands fell to the Nazi forces. The Battle of Britain during the Blitz subsequently became a defining event in the British national consciousness.

was little to choose between the two sides in World War I—that the essential nature of the conflict was simply a power struggle between Britain and Germany as co-aggressors. And it has often (and rightly) been suggested that the tangle of old world alliances that existed prior to the First World War did much to facilitate the sort of stumbling into war that occurred in the wake of the assassination of Archduke Franz Ferdinand of Austria on 28 June 1914. In fact there probably was to some degree a legitimate moral case to be made on the side of Britain at the outset of World War I—much as the jingoism of the time on all sides may now strike us as repulsive. There is no question, though, that the moral imperative that lay behind the Allies' decision to go to war with Germany in 1939 was far stronger than it was at any time during World War I. Nazi atrocities against the Jews had in 1939 not yet reached their full extent, but already Hitler had shown that he was a dictator willing to persecute minorities ruthlessly and to invade neighboring countries on the flimsiest of pretexts.

This image of the 1940 Battle of Britain was taken from the cockpit of a German fighter plane. It shows a British Hurricane fighter with its left wing torn off; the wing is visible in the top right of the photo, and the pilot, parachuting to safety, is seen in the top left.

World War II, then, was driven far more persuasively than was the first by a moral imperative, and there was thus much less of a disconnect than there had been in World War I between idealistic calls for sacrifice and the reality as it was sensed by the ordinary soldier; few looked at Nazi Germany in the autumn of 1939 with the detached tone that the poet W.H. Auden famously adopted in "September 1, 1939" in seeking to explain the phenomenon of Hitler, the "psychopathic god": "Those to whom evil is done / Do evil in return." To most it seemed clear that both in the case of Hitler as an individual and in the case of the people of Nazi Germany as a whole, the evil that was being done was far disproportionate to whatever evil had been committed against them. (Even today, many who admire Auden's poem as an affirmation of the humane in the face of the more basely human and in the face of war as a general proposition find the feelings the poem expresses odd or inappropriate in the moral context of World War II.)

A crucial difference between the experience of World War I and II was that in World War II the horrors of war had less shock value. Paul Fussell, whose *The Great War and Modern Memory* is a landmark study of the connections between wartime experience and literature, was a soldier himself in World War II; by the time of World War II, as he put it, "we didn't need to be told by people like Remarqué [author of *All Quiet on the Western Front*] and Siegfried Sassoon how nasty war was. We knew that already, and we just had to pursue it in a sort of controlled despair. It didn't have the ironic shock value of the Great War." It should perhaps not surprise us, then, that the body of serious literature that arose *directly* from the experience of World War II turned out to be slighter than the body of such literature that emerged during and after World War I. Certainly works such as Robert Graves's *Goodbye to All That*, Siegfried Sassoon's *Memoirs of an Infantry Officer*, David Jones's *In Parenthesis*, and the poetry of Wilfred Owen, Isaac Rosenberg, and others all seem to have secured a place in the canon of British literature, whereas few if any works emerging directly out of the combat experience of World War II have staked such a claim. Indeed, Auden's "September 1, 1939" and Virginia Woolf's *Between the Acts* are among the few works still widely read from that time on themes that relate to the experience of the war even tangentially.

Two aspects of the 1939–45 conflict have come to be seen as defining elements of twentieth-century experience. The first of these was the planned extermination of an entire people—the event that resulted in the murder of approximately six million Jews (as well as significant numbers of other groups deemed "undesirables" by the Nazis, notably homosexuals and Roma), and that has come to be known as "The Holocaust." The second is the use of the atomic bomb against Japan by the United States in 1945—and the consequent dawning among the world's population of an awareness that humans now had the capacity to destroy the entire human race. From those most horrific aspects of World War II has emerged a literature that will surely be lasting (including the works of Primo Levi, the diaries of Anne Frank, John Hersey's *Hiroshima*)—but few if any of its most important works are by British writers.

Brighton Rock (1938), Graham Greene's "entertainment" about the lives of young British gangsters, was first issued in a Penguin paperback in 1943. The price of 2 shillings is equivalent to a little under £4 in UK 2013 currency.

THIS IS A WARTIME BOOK

THIS POCKET BOOK INCLUDES EVERY WORD CONTAINED IN THE ORIGINAL, HIGHER-PRICED EDITION. IT IS PRINTED FROM BRAND-NEW PLATES MADE FROM COMPLETELY RESET, LARGE, CLEAR, EASY-TO-READ TYPE, AND IS PRODUCED IN FULL COMPLIANCE WITH THE GOVERNMENT'S REGULATIONS FOR CONSERVING PAPER AND OTHER ESSENTIAL MATERIALS.

F-1

Printed in Canada

Notice from copyright page of a 1945 printing of the paperback edition of Mazo de la Roche's *Jalna*, one volume of the family saga that has remained extraordinarily popular from its publication in 1927.

As in World War I, however, there was a rich body of literary work produced in Britain during World War II that was not directly *about* the war. Works of this sort in the years 1914–18 include T.S. Eliot's *Prufrock and Other Observations* (1917) and James Joyce's *Portrait of the Artist as a Young Man* (1916). In the years 1939–45, the list of such works is both long and remarkably diverse, and includes the exuberant verse of Dylan Thomas's *The Map of Love* (1939); Eliot's *Four Quartets* (which he regarded as his finest work); many of Auden's finest lyrics, including "Lay Your Sleeping Head, My Love," "Musee des Beaux Arts," and "Song (As I Walked Out One Evening)" (all first published in 1940); the bubbling hilarity of Noel Coward's play about the afterlife, *Blithe Spirit* (1942); the memorably self-deprecating and socially observant light comedy of Monica Dickens's memoir *One Pair of Hands* (1939); now-classic memoirs by Vera Brittain (*Testament of Friendship*, 1940) and Flora Thompson (*Lark Rise to Candleford*, 1940); Joyce Cary's novel of the memorable artist and outsider Gulley Jimson, *The Horse's Mouth* (1944); Graham Greene's tragic novel of a disillusioned "whisky priest" in revolutionary Mexico, *The Power and the Glory* (1940); and two very different but equally devastating fictional treatments of the horrors of totalitarian communism, Arthur Koestler's grim novel of the suffering endured by a "deviationist," *Darkness at Noon* (1940), and Orwell's fable of a collectivist society that comes to be based on the principle that "all animals are equal, but some are more equal than others," *Animal Farm* (1945). In writing the following comments in 1940 about the literature of World War I, Orwell clearly also had World War II in mind:

> In 1917 there was nothing a thinking and sensitive person could do, except remain human, if possible. ... By simply staying aloof and keeping in touch with pre-war emotions, Eliot [in publishing *Prufrock* in 1917] was carrying on the human heritage.... So different from bayonet drill! After the bombs and the food queues and the recruiting posters, a human voice! What a relief!

Marx, Einstein, Freud, and Modernism

Several towering figures in the intellectual and cultural life of the twentieth century played a key part in shaping the world view according to which human life was subject to forces over which, individually, humans could have little control, and of which they would often be entirely unaware. The first of these figures—Karl Marx—died 17 years before the end of the nineteenth century. But his vision of economic forces and class struggles saturated with historical inevitability continued to shape political and social attitudes (as well as a good many literary ones) throughout the twentieth century. An intellectual underpinning derived from Marx is, to a large extent, what differentiates the attitudes of social realist writers such as Shaw, Wells, and George Gissing from those of predecessors such as Charles Dickens and Elizabeth Gaskell. Much as Dickens and Gaskell had deplored the conditions of inequality that beset Victorian Britain, they believed that the actions and the goodwill of individual human beings could ameliorate social problems. The approach of 1890s and early

twentieth-century socially progressive writers, in contrast, derived largely from the Marxist view that individuals are typically caught in a web of large social and economic forces over which they have no control; that class oppression is a systemic matter; and that mass struggle and political action (rather than appeals to the higher natures of the ruling classes) are the appropriate means of bringing about a better world. Thus for Shaw, for example, the "fundamental condition of the existence" of prostitution was that "a large class of women are more highly paid and better treated as prostitutes than they would be as respectable women." The activist writer and publisher Nancy Cunard was equally alert to the interactions of class, gender, money—and race. Author of some of a number of important essays on colonialism (and publisher of such key modernist works as Samuel Beckett's *Whoroscope* and Pound's *Cantos*), Cunard spoke of the British Empire in unvarnished terms of class and race as few had before: when writing in *Negro* of the system of British rule in Jamaica, for example, she understood it clearly as having been purposefully structured as "white at the top, mulatto in the centre and back at the bottom of the economic and social scale" so as to rule by dividing "the peoples of African and semi-African descent."[1]

If the socially progressive literature of the early twentieth century had intellectual underpinnings derived largely from Marx, the intellectual underpinnings of twentieth-century modernist literature are intimately connected with the ideas of physicist Albert Einstein, of philosophers of language such as Bertrand Russell, and of the psychoanalyst Sigmund Freud. Einstein's paper, "The Electrodynamics of Moving Bodies" (1905), later to become known as his Special Theory of Relativity, posited that both time and motion are not absolute but rather relative to the observer. In the same year, he completed his thesis on "A New Determination of Molecular Dimension," a major step forward in the development of quantum theory in which he postulated (among other things) that light was

---

[1] *The activist ... descent* Cunard was greatly assisted in these endeavors by George Padmore (1902–59), a Trinidadian-born writer and activist who later lived in the United States and in Britain and who played an important role in various progressive causes in the 1930s. A strong pan-Africanist, Padmore eventually became personal advisor to Kwame Nkrumah, Ghana's first President.

both waves and tiny particles of light quanta, or photons. Much as they may have been imperfectly understood, the broad outlines of Einstein's theories became widely disseminated in subsequent years, and clearly contributed to a growing sense of a world that was being discovered to be in a far less stable form that it had been thought.

New language-based trends in analytic philosophy were also undermining certainties. The ideas developed by Gottlob Frege, Bertrand Russell, and Ludwig Wittgenstein in the late nineteenth and early twentieth century had the effect of destabilizing what had been thought of as largely fixed relationships between words and meanings. The focus of these philosophers was on analyzing the content of what we mean when we make statements, whether they be statements referring to objects in the "real" world or statements involving claims of a more abstract sort. They endeavored to design symbolic systems that could convey meaning more reliably than words, for their work suggested that relationships between a word and a presumed referent were exceedingly complex and inherently unstable; Wittgenstein's work, in particular, suggested that it was in the nature of language for words to float largely free of fixed referents in any world of "objective truth." Indeed, Wittgenstein suggested in his groundbreaking 1921 work *Tractatus Logico-Philosophicus* that "Language disguises thought. So much so, that from the outward form of the clothing it is impossible to infer the form of the thought beneath it, because the outward form of the clothing is not designed to reveal the form of the body, but for entirely different purposes."

The perceived unreliability and instability of language and of meaning affected the realm of ethics as much as it did those of metaphysics and epistemology, and from about 1910 onward, moral relativism was a subject of lively debate. (G.E. Moore's *Ethics*, an influential attempt to hold such relativism at bay, was published in 1912; T.S. Eliot read a paper on "The Relativity of the Moral Judgement" in the Cambridge rooms of his friend Bertrand Russell in 1915.) Russell became famous as a result of his pacifism (for which he was jailed in 1918), his efforts to undermine the authority of Christianity over Western society, and his challenge to societal constrictions on sexual behavior. But

the changes that he helped to bring about to the foundations of analytic philosophy may have been even more revolutionary—and more influential in the literary realm—than his shocking views on social issues.

Just as important as the work of Marx, Einstein, or the philosophers of language to the intellectual shape of the twentieth century was that of several explorers of the human psyche. Of these, pride of place is traditionally accorded to Sigmund Freud, an Austrian psychiatrist who advanced revolutionary notions of the importance and complexity of sexuality in the human psyche, and of the importance of the unconscious in human thought and behavior. Both notions had an enormous effect on twentieth-century intellectual life in general and on imaginative literature in particular, as writers sought ways to represent sexuality as a much more central element of human experience than had been the habit of the Victorians, and sought ways in which to represent the richness of the human unconscious.[1]

Another key pioneer in the study of the human mind was the American William James (brother of novelist Henry James). Among James's most important contributions was his conceptualization of the fluidity of consciousness. James entitled a chapter in his *Principles of Psychology* (1892) "The Stream of Consciousness," beginning by observing that "within each personal consciousness states are always changing" and that "each personal consciousness is sensibly continuous." The connections between the ideas of James and twentieth-century literary developments are not difficult to discern. Most obviously, the "stream of consciousness" technique of prose fiction that features so prominently in core Modernist texts such as Dorothy Richardson's *Pilgrimage* (1915–67), Virginia Woolf's *Mrs. Dalloway* (1925), and James Joyce's *Ulysses* (1922) represents a

---

[1] Though Freud's important work began in the 1890s, he began to become well known in the English-speaking world only after 1910, with the publication of a series of lectures he had given at Clark University in the United States on *The Origin and Development of Psychoanalysis*. Of his most important works, *The Interpretation of Dreams* (1900) was translated in 1913, *The Psychopathology of Everyday Life* (1901) in 1914; soon after, his work came to the attention of the Bloomsbury Group in England, and both Leonard Woolf and Lytton Strachey wrote reviews of or commentaries on Freud's work. (In the 1920s the Woolfs' Hogarth Press became for a time the leading publisher of English translations of Freud's work.)

new form of realism that is psychological rather than social in character. These writers aim at an increased awareness of the ways in which the mind associates freely, in which "irrelevant" thoughts may connect with repressed impulses or emotions that are central to the psyche, and in which unpredictable but meaningful details are constantly jostling together with the quotidian.

A similar apparent disconnectedness is also an obvious feature of Modernist poetry—most obviously in the disjunctions that characterize many of the poems of Ezra Pound and T.S. Eliot. To be sure, many have argued persuasively that a unity both of thought and of feeling emerges from the extended allusive density of poems such as *The Waste Land*. But it is abundantly clear that any such unity is very different in character from the unity that emerges, say, from a defining long poem of the Victorian period such as Tennyson's *In Memoriam*, just as whatever unity emerges from Joyce's *Ulysses* is very different in character from that of the classic realism of Victorian novels such as George Eliot's *Middlemarch* or Anthony Trollope's *The Way We Live Now*.

Less frequently discussed is the modernity of Eliot's later poetry—most notably, *Four Quartets* (1935–43), an extended poetic expression of the search for meaning and truth in a context of instability. Much as the poem is infused with the Anglo-Catholicism to which Eliot had converted in 1927, it is also deeply colored by the sorts of destabilizing awareness that were so central to the habits of thought that came to the fore in the first half of the twentieth century. The poet continually struggles to conceptualize the movements of time, but finds that

> Words strain,
> Crack, and sometimes break, under the burden,
> Under the tension, slip, slide, perish,
> Decay with imprecision, will not stay in place,
> Will not stay still.

Samuel Beckett, one of the first to appreciate that most disconnected of all Joyce's works, *Finnegans Wake* (1939), became the last great figure of Modernist literature. It was Beckett, above all, who pioneered the expression in action of the psychological insights of Modernism and the despair that so often accompanied

them. It is perhaps the case that "action" should here be put in quotation marks, however, for Beckett's plays—perhaps most notably *Waiting for Godot* (1952), *Krapp's Last Tape* (1958), and *Endgame* (1957)—are informed by an unprecedented awareness of the degree to which a *lack* of action may be as expressive as action, just as silences may be as expressive as words. Beckett extended the Modernist project in his prose fiction as well as in his plays—and in French as well as in English through to the 1970s; it is perhaps due more to his influence than that of any of the other great figures of Modernism that ripples from the Modernist tradition have continued to radiate in British literature even into the twenty-first century.

A common tendency is to assume that what is aesthetically revolutionary will substantially overlap with what is politically revolutionary (or at least with what is progressive). In fact there is no necessary connection between the two—and, indeed, a striking feature of twentieth-century Modernism is that many of its key figures were politically conservative or even reactionary.[1] During his lifetime, T.S. Eliot was probably almost as influential for his political, religious, and cultural conservatism as he was for his revolutionary aesthetic. Writer and artist Wyndham Lewis, whose concept of Vorticism was for a time central to the intellectual currents of Modernism, embraced political views that could fairly be characterized as reactionary rather than conservative. Ezra Pound, for his part, who was even more revolutionary than Eliot in his Modernist aesthetic, ended even further to the right politically—notoriously lending his support to the fascist cause, and calling for the extermination of Jews during World War II. Eliot and Pound were also far from progressive in their attitudes on gender and sex; many have suggested that a dark sense of sexuality is a fundamental aspect of Eliot's world view—and almost as many have suggested that a disturbing element of misogyny lurks not far below the surface of much of his writing (his early writing in particular).

---

[1] The roots of this conservatism are in part to be found in various nineteenth-century political and ideological developments—especially a strain of ultra-conservatism in France that developed in the second half of the century and that connects both with Pound and the Symbolists and with twentieth-century fascisms.

Leading modernist women writers, by contrast, more often combined the freedom of modernist forms with progressive, unconventional, or even revolutionary political and social views. The futurist poet Mina Loy, for example, was a strong feminist and decidedly left of center politically; Nancy Cunard was a pioneer of left-of-center class analysis as well as of modernist publishing; and Virginia Woolf, though she rarely shared the unqualified sense of political conviction that came to motivate her husband Leonard (who ran for Parliament as a Labour Party candidate in 1920), was herself not only a powerful voice for feminism but also a Labour Party member and a supporter of a variety of socialist and progressive causes.

It was Woolf who famously assigned a specific point in time to the great change that Modernism represented: "on or about December 1910," she commented in a 1924 essay, "human character changed." She was, of course, exaggerating for effect; few in her era were more acutely aware of how erratically change may occur, and of the ways in which the characteristics of one era may extend into the next. In that connection it is worth reminding ourselves that, much as the Modernism of Eliot, Joyce, and Woolf has come to take on the character of the defining spirit of British literature in the 1910s and 1920s, its centrality was far from obvious at the time. For every admirer of the Cubist paintings of Picasso and Braque, there were many who reacted with contempt or ridicule. For every gallery-goer who was stirred by the modernist sculptures of Jacob Epstein (such as the young colonial P.K. Page, as recounted in her poem "Ecce Homo"), there were many chuckling over the way in which such sculpture was lampooned in the pages of the satirical magazine *Punch*. And for every dedicated reader of *The Waste Land* or *To the Lighthouse* there were dozens of readers of the ballads of Robert Service, and of the traditionally structured novels of Arnold Bennett and John Galsworthy. Not until 1948 and 1969 respectively were T.S. Eliot and Samuel Beckett awarded the Nobel Prize for literature; the only British writers to receive the award before 1940 were Rudyard Kipling (1907), W.B. Yeats (1923), George Bernard Shaw (1925), and Galsworthy (1932).

Illustration by Ernest H. Shepard from the chapter "The Further Adventures of Toad" in Kenneth Grahame's *The Wind in the Willows* (1908). The early decades of the twentieth century are remembered for the dawn of Modernism, but they were also something of a golden age for children's literature; in addition to Grahame's work, Sir J.M. Barrie's *Peter Pan* (1906), Lucy Maud Montgomery's *Anne of Green Gables* (1908), and A.A. Milne's *Winnie the Pooh* (1926) and *The House at Pooh Corner* (1928) all remain popular classics.

THE PLACE OF WOMEN

As well as being a central figure of Modernism in the British literary tradition, Woolf is central to what is arguably the most important historical development of the twentieth century, the attempt to free women from the dense network of social, economic, and legal restrictions that had always ensured male dominance and control. If *To the Lighthouse* (1927) and *Mrs. Dalloway* (1925), with their psychological realism, are key documents of Modernism, *A Room of One's Own* (1929) is a key document of the struggle by women in the twentieth century for full equality. Woolf's call for change, and also her evocation of personal experience in a male-dominated social and literary milieu, continue to resonate with readers in the present century.

Illustration accompanying the article "Presentation Day at London University," by "A Lady Graduate" in *The Girl's Own Paper*, July 1898. The University of London had begun to admit women as full degree students at the undergraduate level in 1878.

As the twentieth century opened, women were still second-class citizens in almost every respect—unable to vote, subject to a variety of employment limitations, restricted for the most part from higher education, and restricted too in myriad intangible ways by social nuance and convention. Oppression in the workplace in the context of the industrial revolution has long been widely acknowledged; at least as pervasive in the late nineteenth and early twentieth centuries was the exploitation of retail workers, as the Report of the Royal Commission on Labour detailed:

The maximum salary in addition to board and lodging ever paid to women in the shop working 70 3/4 hours was stated at 35 to 40 shillings [equivalent to roughly £200 in 2015]; in the other shops 30 shillings was stated as the maximum salary ever given. The girls declared that they had nothing to complain of, except the long hours of work and the short time allowed for meals, which had seriously affected their health. No one closed earlier than 11:00 p.m. on Saturdays, 9:30 on Fridays, and 9:00 on Mondays, Tuesdays, and Wednesdays, beginning in each case at 8:30 a.m.

For decades, those in the suffrage movement and other women's groups struggled to bring change. In 1903, Emmeline Pankhurst, together with others frustrated with the pace of change and with the "lady-like" tone of the protests by other women's groups, formed The Women's Social and Political Union, taking as their motto "Deeds Not Words." As Pankhurst recalled in 1914,

From the very first, in those early London days, when … we were few in numbers and very poor in purse, we made the public aware of the woman suffrage movement as it had never been before. We adopted Salvation Army methods and went out into the highways and byways after converts.

Real change finally began to take effect just before the end of the war in 1918, with the Representation of the People Act granting the vote to all men over the age of 21 and to women over the age of 30 who also met one or more of several restrictive criteria regarding marital status and property.[1] (Not until 1928 were all such restrictions lifted and all women over 21 granted the franchise.) The London *Times* provided a (doubtless oversimplified) summary of the effect of the war on the suffrage movement in an article on the occasion of the 1930 commemoration by Prime Minister Stanley Baldwin of a statue of Pankhurst:

The World War came. In the twinkling of an eye … the militant suffragettes laid aside their banners. They put on their overalls and went into the factory and into the field; they were nursing, they made

---

[1] Two "Contexts" sections ("War and Revolution," elsewhere in the volume, and "Gender and Sexual Orientation," available on the website) document the events of World War I and the ways in which they hastened the move towards equality.

munitions, and they endured sacrifices with the men, and the effective opposition to the movement melted in the furnace of the War.

The success of the suffrage movement and the change in the role women played in the workplace were the most dramatic gender-related changes during this period, but there were many other important developments; the era was also characterized by changing notions regarding gender and education, contraception and reproductive technology, and the nature of masculinity.

The arrest of Emmeline Pankhurst during a suffragette demonstration near Buckingham Palace, 1914.

Sylvia Pankhurst (daughter of suffragette leader Emmeline Pankhurst) painting the slogan "Votes for Women" on the front of the Women's Social Defence League offices in London, 1912.

Women's contingent to the 1930 "Hunger March," a demonstration in London's Hyde Park.

Avant-Garde and Mass Culture

The concept of the avant-garde, of a tiny minority far in advance of the popular taste in culture (or of the majority view politically) came into its own in the twentieth century. No doubt it may have resonated with particular force simply because of the degree to which cultural activity was being extended to "the masses"; with primary education having been made compulsory in Britain through the Education Act of 1870, the twentieth century was the first in which the vast majority of British people were fully literate. The expansion of libraries had helped to spread the habit of reading through the nineteenth century, and with the publishing industry's shift in the 1890s away from "triple deckers" intended for purchase by libraries and toward one-volume novels of modest length aimed at individual buyers, the habit of book-buying began to spread at a comparable rate. In the early years of the century, publishers introduced series of relatively affordable hardcover editions of literary classics, aimed at a broad popular market (chief among them the Everyman's Library series from Dent and the World's Classics series from Oxford University Press).

The British film industry was competitive with that of the United States in the 1920s and early 1930s. In this 1920s photograph a scene from the (now lost) film *The Thrill* is being shot on a beach near Brighton.

THE PUBLISHERS OF *EVERYMAN'S LIBRARY* WILL BE PLEASED TO SEND FREELY TO ALL APPLICANTS A LIST OF THE PUBLISHED AND PROJECTED VOLUMES TO BE COMPRISED UNDER THE FOLLOWING THIRTEEN HEADINGS:

TRAVEL ❧ SCIENCE ❧ FICTION
THEOLOGY & PHILOSOPHY
HISTORY ❧ CLASSICAL
FOR YOUNG PEOPLE
ESSAYS ❧ ORATORY
POETRY & DRAMA
BIOGRAPHY
REFERENCE
ROMANCE

IN FOUR STYLES OF BINDING: CLOTH, FLAT BACK, COLOURED TOP; LEATHER, ROUND CORNERS, GILT TOP; LIBRARY BINDING IN CLOTH, & QUARTER PIGSKIN

LONDON: J. M. DENT & SONS, LTD.
NEW YORK: E. P. DUTTON & CO.

Preliminary advertising page from *Captain Cook's Voyages of Discovery*, one of the Everyman's Library volumes published in 1906, the year the series was founded. Eventually its list grew to include over 1,000 titles.

An even more revolutionary step came in 1936, with the introduction of Penguin Books' series of affordable paperback editions. "The Penguin books are splendid value for sixpence," wrote George Orwell in reviewing Penguin's third batch of ten titles, "so splendid that if the other publishers had any sense they could combine against them and suppress them. [If instead] the other publishers follow suit, the result may be a flood of cheap reprints which will cripple the lending libraries … and check the output of new novels." Within a few years the paperback novel had indeed become ubiquitous in British society, but with none of the disastrous effects Orwell had feared; the size of the market for books had been expanded sufficiently by the arrival of the paperback to more than compensate authors and publishers for the lower revenue per copy sold.

Along with the spread of a mass literary culture—and the spread as well of the cinema and of radio—came huge social and cultural changes. If Modernism was a cultural movement concentrated in a small elite, modernity swept through every corner of society in the 1920s and 1930s. The social and cultural attitudes of the late Victorian age may have persisted through to the end of the Edwardian era, but within 10 years "Victorian" had

World War I and the years that followed brought huge changes in women's fashion, with shorter skirts and dresses and more freedom of movement. This photograph, from the 1920s, shows two London models.

become a synonym for "stuffy and old fashioned." The book that set the tone more than any other was Lytton Strachey's *Eminent Victorians* (1918), a series of biographical essays on four leading members of Victorian society (Henry Edward Cardinal Manning, Florence Nightingale, Matthew Arnold, and General Charles George Gordon). Strachey's work is often characterized as "satirical," but "irreverent" is perhaps a better adjective. He writes in a breezy, brilliant, style, but he is interested in the depths of human emotion as well as the surfaces. He pokes fun at his subjects, to be sure, but he is more interested in exploring the workings of what he sees as pretension, hypocrisy, ambition, and

self-deception than he is in ridiculing them. Here is how Strachey begins his essay on Florence Nightingale:

> Everyone knows the popular conception of Florence Nightingale. The saintly, self-sacrificing woman, the delicate maiden of high degree who threw aside the pleasures of a life of ease to succour the afflicted, the Lady with the Lamp, gliding through the horrors of the hospital at Scutari, and consecrating with the radiance of her goodness the dying soldier's couch—the vision is familiar to all. But the truth was different. The Miss Nightingale of fact was not as facile fancy painted her. She worked in another fashion, and towards another end; she moved under the stress of an impetus which finds no place in the popular imagination. A Demon possessed her. Now demons, whatever else they may be, are full of interest. And so it happens that in the real Miss Nightingale there was more that was interesting than in the legendary one; there was also less that was agreeable.

The deft touch of Strachey's satire became simplified and coarsened in the ridicule popularly directed at Victorian styles—and, in particular, at Victorian attitudes towards sexuality—as an emerging mass society sought to define itself against the backdrop of supposed Victorian narrowness and prudery. The reaction may have been overdone, and certainly the characterization of the Victorians was simplistic, but there could be no doubt that the short skirts, jazz music, and sexual attitudes of the 1920s and 1930s were as far removed from those of only fifteen or twenty years before as those of 1905 or 1910 had been from the attitudes and styles of a full century earlier. Virginia Woolf's recollections of a Bloomsbury scene from the 1920s in which Woolf, her sister Vanessa Bell, and Vanessa's husband Clive Bell are together in the drawing room at 46 Gordon Square give something of the flavor of the time:

> Suddenly the door opened and the long and sinister figure of Mr. Lytton Strachey stood on the threshold. He pointed a finger at a stain on Vanessa's white dress.
> "Semen?" he said.

Can one really say it? I thought, and we burst out laughing. With that one word all barriers of reticence and reserve went down.... So there was now nothing that one could not say, nothing that one could not do, at 46 Gordon Square.

Few places in Britain in the 1920s and 1930s had left Victorian conventions of respectability so firmly behind as had 46 Gordon Square; few others had traveled so far in the same direction, or so fast, as had the "bohemians" of the Bloomsbury Group.

Indeed, the literary portrayal even of heterosexual love (let alone of homosexuality) remained largely off limits through to the 1960s. A litmus test was D.H. Lawrence's *Lady Chatterley's Lover*, which was published in 1928, but with certain passages, which were considered objectionable on account of their sexual content, removed. Not until 1960, after a high profile court case, was the unexpurgated text of the novel (by today's standards still far from explicit in its portrayal of sexuality) finally published. Despite such strictures, however, change was occurring throughout society, and "Victorian" attitudes seemed to many to be part of the distant past.

A commuter chooses *Lady Chatterley's Lover* over *The Times*, London, 1960.

Two women, outside a London bookshop, holding copies of the newly-published paperback edition of *Lady Chatterley's Lover* (1960).

SEXUAL ORIENTATION

The number of leading writers in the first half of the twentieth century who acknowledged a same-sex sexual orientation, at least among their circle of friends, was probably greater than it had been in any previous era of British history—certainly greater than at any time since the early years of the seventeenth century. The list of writers and intellectuals who are now known to have been gay, lesbian, or bisexual includes not only W.H. Auden and Christopher Isherwood, but also A.E. Housman, Nancy Cunard, E.M. Forster, Radclyffe Hall, John Maynard Keynes, Lytton Strachey, Sylvia Townsend-Warner, and a number of others.

It should be emphasized here that sexual identities are far from being stable, trans-historical categories. As a "Contexts" section available in the online portion of this anthology details, notions of and attitudes towards same-sex orientation were in flux throughout the late nineteenth and early twentieth centuries. Until well into the second half of the twentieth century, however (interestingly, at about the time that the word *gay* began to be used to identify those with a same-sex sexual orientation), there was little or no tolerance of same-sex sexuality in most sectors of society. As Auden and his friend and sometime literary collaborator Isherwood tacitly recognized when they moved to the United States, Britain in the 1920s and 1930s was even less ready than was America to openly acknowledge the legitimacy of same-sex relationships. Famously, the novelist and playwright Oscar Wilde had been tried and imprisoned in 1895 for "acts of gross indecency," and homosexuality continued to be widely regarded (in a somewhat contradictory fashion) both as a sin and as a disease throughout the first half of the century. E.M. Forster's novel on the theme of homosexual love, *Maurice*, which was not published until after his death in 1971, but which he had completed in 1914, gives a strong sense of the reality. When Maurice, having realized that "he loved men and had always loved them," confesses to his doctor that he is "an unspeakable of the Oscar Wilde sort," he is met with disgust and denial:

> "Rubbish, rubbish!…Now listen to me, Maurice, never let that evil hallucination, that temptation from the devil, occur to you again."
>
> The voice impressed him; was not science speaking?
>
> "Who put that lie into your head? You whom I see and know to be a decent fellow! We'll never mention it again. No—I'll not discuss. I'll not discuss. The worst thing I could do for you is to discuss it."

Maurice eventually does accept his sexual identity, but not before a further consultation, this one with a Mr. Lasker-Jones, who claims a fifty-per cent rate of "cure" by means of hypnotism for what he terms "congenital homosexuality."

If male homosexuality remained "unspeakable" through much of this period, female homosexuality remained for many unimaginable. In 1921 the British Parliament debated adding "acts of gross indecency between women" to the list of acts prohibited in the criminal statutes, but elected not to do so for fear of advertising homosexuality to "innocent" women. A few years later Hall's novel *The Well of Loneliness* was the occasion for the greatest literary storm of the era, over its alleged "obscenity." The novel recounts the story of a young woman named Stephen (whose parents had hoped for and expected a boy, and gone forward with the planned name regardless when the baby turned out

to be a girl), and the romantic relationships she forms with other women. That the book could have been deemed obscene is astonishing to many readers today. In many ways the book is striking for the sense of normalcy it evokes as to the quotidian aspects of love:

> And now for the first time the old house was home. Mary went quickly from room to room humming a little tune as she did so, feeling that she saw with a new understanding the intimate objects that filled those rooms—were they not Stephen's? Every now and again she must pause to touch them because they were Stephen's.

Even when the novel's prose becomes effusive over the physical and spiritual aspects of the union, the most specific suggestions of the expression of sexual love between two women are passages such as the following: "Stephen bent down and kissed Mary's hands very humbly, for now she could find no words any more … and that night they were not divided."

Radclyffe Hall, c. 1920.

Such effusive attestations of the rapturous purity of unions at once physical and spiritual as one finds in *Maurice* and *The Well of Loneliness* may seem unexceptionable today, and even at the time many people were supportive; *The Well of Loneliness* was published to a generally favorable reception in the press. In the view of *The Sunday Times*, Hall's novel was written "with distinction, with a lively sense of characterization, and with a feeling for the background of her subject which makes her work delightful reading. And, first and last, she has courage and honesty." *The Daily Herald* asserted that there was "nothing pornographic" in the book:

> The evil minded will seek in vain in these pages for any stimulant to sexual excitement. The lustful [figures] of popular fiction may continue their sadistic course unchecked in those pornographic novels which are sold by the million, but Miss Radclyffe Hall has entirely ignored these crude and violent figures of sexual melodrama. She has given to English literature a profound and moving study of a profound and moving problem.

The Daily Express was the lone dissenter; a 19 August 1928 article headed "A Book That Must Be Suppressed" accused the novel of "devastating young souls" with its story of "sexual inversion and perversion." It seems probable that the *Express* represented popular feeling at the time more accurately than did the *Sunday Times* or the *Daily Herald*; soon after the *Express* article appeared, the Home Office advised the publishers to discontinue publication, and the police then charged the publishers under the 1857 Obscene Publications Act. Despite the support of dozens of high-profile authors and intellectuals, the magistrate Sir Charles Biron ruled against *The Well of Loneliness*:

> Unfortunately these women exist, and the book asks that their existence and vices should be recognised and tolerated, and not treated with condemnation, as they are at present by all decent people. This being the tenor of the book I have no hesitation in saying it is an … offence against public decency, and an obscene libel, and I shall order it to be destroyed.

The inevitable focus of history on landmark cases such as those of Oscar Wilde and *The Well of Loneliness* has to a considerable degree sensationalized and darkened our sense of late nineteenth- and early twentieth-century life outside the heterosexual mainstream. That it could be a dark and depressing existence there can be no doubt—the pessimism that Forster expressed even as late as 1960 ("police prosecutions will continue …") is surely understandable. But, as documents such as the letters exchanged between Strachey and Keynes attest, it could also be one of self-assured candor, zestful comedy, and a wholehearted enjoyment of life. "Our time will come," declared Strachey, speaking confidently in an 8 April 1906 letter to Keynes of the situation of homosexuals in Britain, "about a hundred years hence." A hundred years later it is beginning to seem that Strachey's optimism may have been at least as well founded as Forster's more pessimistic view.

IRELAND

If a remarkable amount of memorable literature emerged in Britain from the years of turmoil between the two World Wars in the first half of the twentieth century, the same statement could be made of Ireland, as the Irish endured the state of turmoil that remained a constant throughout the first half of the century. The fiction of James Joyce and the plays of Samuel Beckett have already been mentioned as central to the evolution of Modernist literature. The other important Irish literary work of the period includes J.M. Synge's vivid portrayals of the elemental life of the Aran Islanders on the coast of western Ireland in plays such as *Riders of the Sea* (1904) and *The Playboy of the Western World* (1907); the plays of Lady Augusta Gregory; the sweeping expressiveness of Sean O'Casey's great dramas *Juno and the Paycock* (1924) and *The Plough and the Stars* (1926); and the extraordinary range of the poetry of William Butler Yeats from the 1890s through the 1930s—lyrical, Romantic, Symbolist, mystical, political, Existential, and perhaps above all, passionate.

To this list should be added the plays of Bernard Shaw, who was born in Dublin and lived there for the first twenty years of his life. Shaw has often been called the most important dramatist in English after Shakespeare; he was a socially committed writer who understood, as he puts it in the "Preface" to his 1905 play *Major Barbara*, that "it is difficult to make people realise that an evil is an evil." Shaw *was* able to make people realize such things, not only through effective polemic but also (and more memorably) through the sparkling wit of his plays. Shaw's important work extends from brilliantly biting works of the 1890s and early 1900s such as *Mrs Warren's Profession*, *Arms and the Man*, and *Major Barbara* (on the topics of prostitution, militaristic attitudes, and religion and social reform, respectively); to *Pygmalion* (1912), a satire of attitudes toward social class and its expression through language, on which the 1950s musical *My Fair Lady* was based; to the epic historical drama *Saint Joan* (1923).

Cover, *Major Barbara: A Screen Version*, Penguin, 1945. This early "film tie-in" publication (number 500 in the Penguin series) was still in the standard early Penguin format; not until the 1960s did it become common for book publishers to employ a different cover design in such situations.

If the Irish Shaw is arguably the greatest "British" dramatist of the twentieth century, one of the greatest "British" writers of the 1890s, Oscar Wilde, had also been born and raised in Ireland before moving to London. Indeed, many have judged the literary outpouring from Irish writers during the period 1890–1960 to amount to a more important body of work than the entire literature of Britain over the same period—despite the fact that the combined population of England, Scotland, and Wales, at almost 50 million, was more than ten times that of Ireland.

But how are Britain and Ireland to be defined? Here matters become tangled, for during this period Ireland, for centuries a predominantly Catholic (and mostly unwilling) component of the United Kingdom, finally achieved the status of an independent republic. In the process, however, it became geographically split, with several largely Protestant counties of Northern Ireland remaining a political unit of the United Kingdom.

The Irish had been treated as second-class citizens throughout the centuries of English rule over Ireland. But the hardships they endured in the nineteenth century were particularly severe; the potato famine of 1845–51 alone is estimated to have killed almost a million Irish—almost 10 per cent of the population. By the 1880s and 1890s political pressure in Ireland for radical change had become extremely powerful. And there was pressure for cultural change too; the Celtic Revival (also known as the Irish Literary revival), begun in 1896 by Irishmen and women such as Yeats and Lady Augusta Gregory, was remarkably successful both in increasing appreciation for the traditions of Irish culture and in encouraging the creation of new works in those traditions.

In the late nineteenth century, too, many in England became more sympathetic to Irish aspirations. In an effort to end the long history of oppression and resistance in British-controlled Ireland, Liberal governments twice introduced bills providing for one form or another of "Home Rule" (the term used to refer to limited Irish self-government) in the British House of Commons. The second of these was passed by the House of Commons but defeated in the Conservative-dominated House of Lords. In 1912, another Home Rule Bill was passed, and again the House of Lords rejected it. But now the rules had been changed; as a result of the previous year's Parliament Act, a veto by the House of Lords retained force for only three years. As the date in 1914 approached when the veto was due to expire and Home Rule would thus come into effect, tension rose to such a pitch that many felt civil war to be a real possibility. Substantial areas of the north of Ireland that had been forcibly settled by the English in earlier eras were now staunchly Protestant and vowed resistance to any government order to allow an Ireland dominated by "Papists" to become independent of Britain. And since Protestants from Ulster, in the north of Ireland, were heavily represented in the British army's contingent of troops stationed in Ireland, the military could not be relied on to carry out orders. With the onset of World War I, however, the implementation of the Home Rule Bill was postponed until after the war—and in a fateful move, Prime Minister Herbert Asquith promised that the British government would never force Ulster Protestants to accept Home Rule involuntarily.

Given the long history of vetoes and postponements—and given that the promised self-government in any case was to bring only a limited independence from Britain—it is unsurprising that Irish nationalists were impatient. On Easter Monday, 1916, rebels stormed public buildings in Dublin and proclaimed a republic. In the struggle, as Yeats famously wrote in "Easter, 1916," the Irish were "transformed utterly" and "a terrible beauty" was born. The uprising was brutally suppressed, but the nationalist Sinn Fein continued to wage a guerrilla opposition to British rule. Yet another Home Rule Bill was passed in 1920, providing for six counties of Ulster to be partitioned at independence, and the remainder of the island to remain a part of the British Empire but to be granted Dominion status (parallel to that of Canada, Australia, New Zealand, and South Africa) as the Irish Free State. That limited form of independence came into effect in 1922, but many Irish Republicans refused to accept any form of subservience to the British Crown, and the Irish Republican

Army continued a clandestine struggle. In 1937 a new constitution changed the status of the country to that of a sovereign state within the British Commonwealth—a status sufficiently independent of Britain that Ireland was able to remain neutral in World War II—and in 1949 an Irish Republic was finally proclaimed, with the nation withdrawing from the Commonwealth. But the long struggle was still not fully over; tensions within Northern Ireland would continue to haunt Britain into the twenty-first century.

A young boy sings nationalist songs to a crowd outside Mountjoy Prison, Dublin, where an Irish Republican Army prisoner is about to be executed (1921).

An understanding of the politics and religion of Ireland is essential background for an understanding of Irish history—and Irish literary history—during this period. But it gives little sense of the daily reality of Catholics and Protestants who lived largely in isolation from each other, Catholics overwhelmingly the majority in Ireland, Protestants forming the majority in Northern

Wyndham Lewis, *Workshop*, c. 1915.

The Canadian-born writer and artist Wyndham Lewis (1882–1957) lived largely in England from 1908 onwards. In the period 1912–15 he was a leader among those painters variously described as Futurist, Cubist, and "Vorticist"—the last of these a term that Lewis himself coined. Though his writing—like that of Pound and others in their circle—is tainted by anti-Semitism, misogyny, and, in Lewis's case, venomous portrayals of homosexuals, Lewis is unquestionably a figure central to British Modernism. *Workshop* is one of the works that extend furthest his vision of harsh lines and fragmented shapes conveying a sense of the modern city, and of modernity itself.

World War I recruiting poster used in Ireland, c. 1915.

"Dig for Victory" poster,
distributed in Britain's West African colonies, 1940.

A bombed street in London, 1940. The photographer is unknown.

Sirkka-Liisa Konttinen, *Kendal Street*, 1969. A member of the Amber collective, between 1969 and 1983 Finnish-born Konttinen documented the life and eventual demolition of Byker, a terraced community in Newcastle upon Tyne in northern England. In 2003 she and Amber returned to document the Byker Wall Estate that replaced it.

Bill Brandt, *The Lambeth Walk*, 1936. This photo, originally published in the illustrated weekly magazine *Picture Post*, was taken in the Bethnal Green area of London. The girl performs a dance popular at the time.

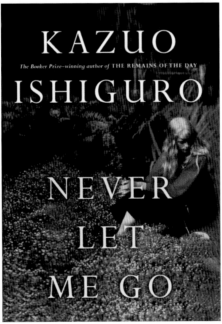

A sampling of book covers: Graham Greene's *Journey Without Maps* (1936; Pan paperback edition, 1948), Roddy Doyle's *The Van* (Secker & Warburgh), and Kazuo Ishiguro's *Never Let Me Go* (2005). The image on the Ishiguro cover is "Christina," from a famous 1912–13 series of photographs by Lieutenant-Colonel Mervyn O'Gorman of his daughters, whom he photographed both in autochrome color and in black and white, sometimes on a beach near their Dorset home, sometimes (as here) in a garden setting.

THE
BEATLES.. LONDON PALLADIUM
.. ROYAL COMMAND PERFORMANCE. 1963

Poster, The Beatles London Palladium Royal Command Performance, 1963. The Royal Variety Performance (also known as the Royal Command Performance) is a gala variety show held every year, the proceeds of which go to charity. When The Beatles performed at the show on 4 November 1963, the audience included the Queen Mother, Princess Margaret, and Lord Snowdon, but not the Queen. As the group was about to play their hit song "Twist and Shout," John Lennon made a request: "Will the people in the cheaper seats clap their hands? And the rest of you, if you'll just rattle your jewelry."

David Hockney, *My Mother, Bolton Abbey, Yorkshire*, 1982. Painter and photographer David Hockney (b. 1937) has long maintained his reputation as one of Britain's leading visual artists. Hockney initially created controversy with his open homosexuality, and in recent years he has incited debate with his views on art history, arguing strenuously that the old Masters employed camera-like techniques in order to achieve realistic effects. A native of Bradford, Hockney has lived largely in California since the 1970s.

Tim Smith, Peel Square, Bradford, c. 1995.
From the 1950s onwards many immigrants
from Asia have settled in Bradford.

Notting Hill Carnival, Notting Hill, London,
1979. The Carnival was started in 1964 to celebrate Caribbean culture within Britain.

Ireland. The novelist Elizabeth Bowen, who was raised mainly in Dublin in an Irish Protestant family (she "was taught to say 'Church of Ireland,' not 'Protestant'") later described her experiences in *Seven Winters: Memories of a Dublin Childhood* (1943):

> It was not until the end of those seven winters that I understood that we Protestants were a minority, and that the unquestioned rules of our being came, in fact, from the closeness of a minority world.... I took the existence of Roman Catholics for granted but met few and was not interested in them. They were, simply, "the others," whose world lay alongside ours but never touched. As to the difference between the two religions, I was too discreet to ask questions—if I wanted to know. This appeared to share a delicate, awkward aura with those two other differences—of sex, of class. So quickly in a child's mind does prudery seed itself and make growth that I remember, even, an almost sexual shyness on the subject of Roman Catholics. I walked with hurried steps and averted cheek past porticos of churches that were "not ours," uncomfortably registering in my nostrils the pungent, unlikely smell [of incense] that came round curtains, through swinging doors.

IDEOLOGY AND ECONOMICS IN THE 1930S AND 1940S

How do ideologies differ from ideas? In part they are simply sets of ideas, but the question goes beyond that: an ideology is a systematic set of beliefs that is shared widely, and that prescribes a program of political action in association with those beliefs. In the twentieth century, such ideologies as communism, socialism, fascism, and liberalism all exerted enormous power. The central concepts of liberal democracy took shape in the nineteenth century, and by the end of the twentieth century had spread to much of the world. But for much of the twentieth century they were powerfully challenged by those of other ideologies: socialism (and its relative, communism) and fascism.

Fascism is identified as an ideology of the far right and it has indeed often co-existed with capitalist eco-

nomic structures. But the strength of its appeal is—like that of communism—collectivist in nature. As the official name of the Nazi party in Germany (the National Socialist Party) suggests, fascism is "socialist" in its appeal to the egalitarian instincts of the populace. But whereas socialism and communism are (in theory at least) internationalist, appealing to the fellow-feeling of humans *as humans*, fascism appeals strongly to nationalist feeling—to the instinct of the population to pull together *as a nation*. More broadly, the egalitarian ideals of fascist societies are never inclusive; the nation defines itself not only against other nations, but typically also against a backdrop of a perceived "other" within its midst. Whether the "other" be immigrants, those of a different skin color, those of a different religion, or a group such as the Jews that is defined by race, culture, and religion, the otherness is typically used as a focal point for defining the nation's identity, and for lending intensity to the ideological allegiance of the fascist core.

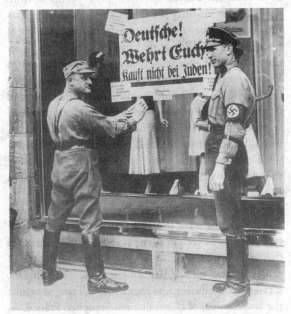

Nazi authorities affix a poster to a shop as part of their campaign of persecution, 1935. The sign reads "Buy nothing from Jews!"

If fascism weirdly approaches socialism from one direction, communism departs from socialist ideals in another. Socialist ideals are above all those of fairness and equality in a society in which government is prepared to intervene consistently on behalf of the greater good—to control capitalism, in socialism's weaker version (social democracy), or to replace it with a system of government ownership of the means of production on behalf of the entire population, in the full-fledged socialist model. Such ideals are built on foundations very similar to those of communist ideology, but the differences turn out in practice to be crucial. Perhaps the most important difference is that communist ideology—especially as it attained full force in the twentieth century—embodied the paradoxical notion that an elite could act as the "vanguard" for the masses, and that a "dictatorship of the proletariat" could reasonably act on behalf of all the people, without the people in practice having a direct say in who was to govern, or how. With the benefit of hindsight, it seems obvious that such an ideology was likely to result in almost as much oppression and cruelty as was the ideology of fascism. But in a Russia that had been laboring under the inequalities of a semi-feudal system, or indeed in Depression-era North America or Great Britain, when the engines of capitalism seemed to be merciless and unrestrained by government, to many communism seemed the only realistic path toward a society that would be both more free and more fair for all citizens.

The greatest ideological struggles of the first half of the century were unquestionably those that unfolded in Russia in 1917 and in Germany and Italy in the 1930s, but an ideologically charged climate was a worldwide reality. In some ways, the twentieth-century ideological tapestry may be seen in sharpest focus in the context of the Spanish Civil War (1936–39). Under the banner of those fighting for the Republican cause were liberals, socialists, communists, and anarchists—all ranged against the fascist forces of Generalissimo Francisco Franco. As George Orwell details in his account of the ideological and physical battles of the war, *Homage to Catalonia* (1938), the Spanish Civil War became a battleground not only between democracy and fascism, but also between the various factions on the Republican side, with idealism all too often being trumped by self-

interest or by the dictates of outside governments lending support. In the end, the Communist government of the Soviet Union was as reluctant as were the capitalist governments of Britain or the United States to stand in the way of the anticipated "stable" government that the fascist General Franco represented.

The Spanish Civil War is often regarded as central to 1930s intellectual currents, and certainly the degree to which intellectuals from Britain (and indeed, from throughout the western world) rallied to the Republican side was remarkable. Sylvia Townsend Warner was among the leading British writers in Spain during the war; as she reported in a 1937 magazine article, the conflict was extraordinary not least of all for the bond that grew up between intellectuals and common citizens: "It is unusual for writers to hear words such as 'Here come the Intellectuals' spoken by working-class people and common soldiers in tones of kindliness and enthusiasm."

Others spoke out not only against fascism but against all forms of militarism—and against war itself. Notably, Virginia Woolf's polemic *Three Guineas* (1938) inquired into the role that women could play in the prevention of war, concluding that war is not merely a public issue—that, rather, "the public and the private worlds are inseparably connected; that the tyrannies and servilities of the one are the tyrannies and servilities of the other."

Even before the Spanish Civil War became a focal point for literature and politics, literature in the 1930s had become more highly political than that of the 1920s. Writers such as Auden (in his early work), Christopher Isherwood, C. Day Lewis, Louis MacNeice, Stephen Spender, and Edward Upward were all, in the view of MacNeice in his *Modern Poetry* (1932), "unlike Yeats and Eliot ... emotionally partisan":

> Yeats [in the 1930s] proposed to turn his back on desire and hatred; Eliot sat back and watched other people's emotions with ennui and ironical self-pity. ... The whole poetry, on the other hand, of Auden, Spender, and Day Lewis implies that they have desires and hatreds of their own and, further, that they think some things *ought* to be desired and others hated.

Many of these writers joined or were sympathetic to the Communist Party through much of the 1930s. In the later twentieth century it would have been unimaginable for most of the important writers of a generation to be sympathetic to "the Party," as it came to be called, but in the early 1930s the brutality of Soviet communism under Stalin was not yet public knowledge—and the mainstream parties in Britain (Labour as well as the Conservatives) were dealing timorously and ineffectively with an economic downturn of unprecedented severity.

A young woman takes aim during target practice, Spain, 1936.

The Great Depression that began late in 1929 and lasted until the outbreak of war ten years later was a worldwide phenomenon—and one exacerbated in Britain (as in North America) by the determination of governments not to go into debt in order to provide support for the unemployed and otherwise impoverished, or to invest in getting the economy moving. Individuals, too, reacted with fear, and strove to increase their savings, thereby contributing to what British economist John Maynard Keynes termed "the paradox of thrift": when people saved rather than spending what little they had, they further reduced the demand for goods, which in turn led to further reductions in production, more unemployment, lower wages for those still working—and so the cycle continued. By the end of 1930, some 20% of the British workforce was unemployed, and by the mid-1930s it was estimated that a quarter of the population had been reduced to a subsistence diet.

Keynes—an important figure in the Bloomsbury Group, and something of a cultural icon as well as one of the most important twentieth-century economists—broke new ground with his arguments for government intervention in the economy—recommending both that governments intervene to control inflation and that they act to "even out" the imbalances of the economic cycle by spending more during downturns. Conservatives argued that such imbalances would right themselves in the long run in any case, and should not be tampered with; Keynes's response was that "the long run is a misleading guide to current affairs. In the long run we are all dead." It was not until after World War II, though, that governments in Britain and elsewhere adopted Keynes's prescriptions for smoothing out the business cycle; although economic conditions improved somewhat in the south of Britain in the late 1930s, it was not until the war that economic growth resumed throughout the country.

A turn toward the political left is to be expected during any severe and prolonged economic downturn; given that the Great Depression was more severe and prolonged a downturn than any in the twentieth century, it is unsurprising that writers and intellectuals moved further to the left politically during the 1930s than at any other time during the century. But why did they embrace, in such large numbers, the relatively rigid doctrines of the Communist Party? As Orwell looked back in 1940, he took the view that the ideological coloring of the intellectual life of the 1930s had been as broadly connected to cultural as it had been to economic trends:

> By 1930 ... the debunking of western civilization had reached its climax.... How many of the values by which our grandfathers lived could now be taken seriously? Patriotism, religion, the Empire, the family, the sanctity of marriage, the Old School Tie, birth, breeding, honour, discipline—anyone of ordinary education could turn the whole lot of them inside out in three minutes. But what do you achieve, after all, by getting rid of such primal things as patriotism and religion? You have not necessarily gotten rid of the need for something to believe in.... It is significant that [those intellectuals who did embrace religion in these years] went almost invariably to the Roman Church.... They went, that is, to the church with a world-wide organization, the

one with a rigid discipline, the one with power and prestige behind it. ... I do not think one need look farther than this for the reason the young writers of the thirties flocked into or towards the Communist Party. It was simply something to believe in. Here was a church, an army, an orthodoxy, a discipline.

With World War II, however, another form of discipline inevitably took hold; even though Britain and the United States became allies, the ties between the British and American intellectual communities and the Soviet Communist Party steadily loosened. With the beginning of the "Cold War" between the West and the USSR immediately following the end of World War II (and a new sense of purpose in the Labour Party under Clement Attlee), the link between British intellectuals and the Communist Party had for the most part come to an end.

THE LITERATURE OF THE 1930S AND 1940S

George Orwell may be seen as one of the writers who most fully expresses the ideological conflicts over socialism, communism, fascism, and liberal democracy that were at the heart of so much of twentieth-century life. His earlier works detail the appalling toll that capitalism was exacting on the working class. In *Down and Out in Paris and London* (1933), he recounts from personal experience the reality of the life of a vagrant, and of the life of the lowest of workers in the Paris hotel and restaurant industry. In *The Road to Wigan Pier* (1937), Orwell details the hardships of miners in the north of England, and of the working-class population throughout the country. Orwell was an avowed socialist; ironically enough, however, the two works for which he remains best known have often been portrayed as attacks on socialism; they are both novels in which he attacks the corruption of socialist ideals under Soviet-style communism. *Animal Farm* is a fable that shows the ways in which power may readily be seized by the most powerful and unprincipled in a "collectivist" system; *1984* is a futurist view of a society in which "Big Brother" controls people's minds as much as their actions.

Like Orwell's *1984*, Aldous Huxley's *Brave New World* (1932) is a dystopia in which the State effectively controls the minds of its citizens, who are convinced that they are expressing human potential to its fullest.

Another writer of central importance to twentieth-century literature who was initially defined against a backdrop of ideology is the poet W.H. Auden. Auden first became famous as a political poet, particularly with his memorable call to arms against fascism in "Spain 1937": "But today the struggle." Auden quickly became disenchanted with political polemic, however, not least of all his own. He became disillusioned with the Republican side in the Spanish Civil War after witnessing the persecution of Catholic priests by members of the Republican army, and after traveling through China in the wake of the 1937–38 Nanking Massacre he became convinced that violence is a disease that lurks within every human heart. "The act of taking sides," he became convinced, "spelled out the death of free culture and the triumph ... of its enemies." Auden's poetic response to the outbreak of World War II, "September 1, 1939," was famously equivocal, the emphasis being placed on the expiration of the 1930s—dubbed by Auden "a low, dishonest decade"—rather than on the imminence of the fascist threat to freedom.

"Spain 1937" and "September 1, 1939" were among those poems that Auden refused to allow to be printed in later volumes of his poetry. Even in the 1930s, his work was extraordinarily diverse, and more and more as the years went by his name became paired with that of T.S. Eliot; after the death of Yeats in 1939, Eliot and Auden were almost universally regarded as the leading poets of the day. But the two may in more than one respect be seen as polar opposites. Whereas Eliot had moved permanently from the United States to England as a young man, Auden moved permanently from Britain to New York to 1939. Eliot's first marriage had failed in the face of the mental illness of his wife, Vivienne; she was eventually confined in a mental institution, and Eliot embraced the stiff collar traditions of the Church and of respectable society with ever-greater conviction. Auden's marriage to novelist Thomas Mann's daughter Erica also ended, but it could hardly have been said to have "failed," since it had been entered into only to protect Erica from persecution at the hands of the Nazis. Auden made no secret of his same-sex sexual orientation (at a time when it took considerable courage to do so), and felt stifled by the society of which Eliot was a pillar; he moved in 1939 to New York, where he soon entered into a lifelong relationship with the poet Chester Kallman, and where his rumpled figure became a quiet fixture on the literary scene. If Eliot was a central figure of Modernism, Auden's connections to the forms of Modernism were more tenuous. His skill with poetic forms was extraordinarily wide ranging, but unlike Eliot he kept returning to accentual-syllabic meters, and to the use of rhyme.

The explosive sexuality of D.H. Lawrence's fiction has been touched on above. If sexual love was one of the great themes of his work, the other was surely the corrosive effect that the British class system exerted on human relationships. In the 1930s that became a theme more and more widely taken up by novelists, in works such as Henry Green's *Living* (1929), Walter Greenwood's *Love on the Dole* (1933), and J.B. Priestley's *Angel Pavement* (1930). With the notable exception of the novels and stories of Edward Upward, however, expressions of outrage against the capitalist order of things tended to be fewer in number and milder in tone in the prose fiction of the time than they were in its poetry.

Somerset Maugham's *The Razor's Edge* (1944), a novel of romance and spirituality, became one of the twentieth century's bestselling novels both in Britain and in North America. It was issued in paperback editions on both sides of the Atlantic in 1946. Pocket Books, which had followed Penguin's lead and introduced mass market paperbacks into the United States in 1941, published the American paperback edition (shown here).

At least as numerous and at least as popular in Britain during this era were fiction writers of a more conservative political stripe, including Somerset Maugham, with his tightly crafted novels and short stories; Evelyn Waugh, with his bitingly satirical novels; and P.G. Wodehouse, with his more light-hearted brand of satirical fiction. Many have seen an inherent conservatism, too, in what was then a new genre of popular fiction, the detective novel. The genre saw few if any worthy successors to Sir Arthur Conan Doyle's nineteenth-century creation, Sherlock Holmes, until Agatha Christie introduced her detective Hercule Poirot and the equally astute Jane Marple to readers in the late 1920s and 1930s. Together with the Father Brown novels of the Catholic conservative G.K. Chesterton,

Christie's works founded an enduring tradition of English mystery novels.

The revolutionary experiments of Modernism that are so central to the literary history of the 1910s and 1920s were for the most part not extended in the following decades. To this generalization, David Jones's *In Parenthesis* (1937) is a notable exception; written partly in prose, partly in free verse, Jones's epic of World War I bears the unmistakable stamp of Modernism. And some other authors continued to experiment with literary form. Henry Green's *Living*, for example, is written with an economy of expression that mirrors the economies of the working-class life it depicts, with articles and nouns frequently omitted from the normal syntactical flow. But most fiction writers of the period adopted a traditional approach to narrative, and even T.S. Eliot seemed to be backing away from Modernism with his ritualized play *Murder in the Cathedral* (1935) —and, following World War II, with a series of drawing room comedies.

From the late 1930s well into the 1970s one of the leading figures of British literature was unquestionably Graham Greene. Greene exploded onto the literary scene in 1938 with the publication of *Brighton Rock*, a tautly written exploration of the seediness and cruelty that lurked not far below the surface of much of British life. In subsequent novels, perhaps most notable among them *The Power and the Glory* (1940) and *The Heart of the Matter* (1948), Greene went on to explore the same qualities in human life generally. The setting of Greene's novels might be colonial Africa, rural Mexico, or war-torn London, but it is always recognizably "Greeneland"; always in the background is a sense of anguished Catholicism tinged with a bleak sense of despair.

LITERATURE AND EMPIRE

No matter how widely Greene's geographical imagination ranged, the human souls he was interested in exploring were mostly those of white males from the Western world. Other British writers of the time, however, were beginning to reach for an understanding of the world that would take fuller account of the lives and the souls of those who lived under British rule in Africa, India, and much of the rest of the world. The essays of Nancy Cunard, along with those of Orwell, expressed a wide-ranging understanding of the mechanisms of Imperial rule, and of the reality of life for many who suffered under it. In fiction, the novelist Joyce Cary broke new ground with his *Mr. Johnson* (1939), a comic novel with a Nigerian clerk as its protagonist. The novel represents the Nigerian in ways that are bound to make today's reader wince. Yet it also gives expression to a specifically Nigerian sense of humor, and conveys a genuinely sympathetic understanding of the situation both of Johnson and of Nigerians generally under British rule. *Mr. Johnson* is a long way from the literature of the last few decades of the twentieth century in its approach to colonial and multicultural realities (let alone the debates of the late twentieth century over "appropriation of voice"). Yet in a very real sense it marks a step forward for British literature in the possibilities it demonstrates for the British imagination of connecting with the rest of the world. In a very direct sense there is also a connection between *Mr. Johnson* and the explosion of African literature later in the century (in the first half of the century exceedingly few African writers were published). As Chinua Achebe later recalled, reading the Cary novel was one of the things that led him to become a writer; "in spite of [Cary's] ability, in spite of his sympathy and understanding, he could not get under the skin of his African. They just did not communicate. And I felt if a good [English white] writer could make this mess perhaps we ought to try our hand."

The twentieth century had begun for Britain with a war in South Africa that had ended with a Pyrrhic victory. In a struggle against white colonists of Dutch background (Afrikaaners, or "Boers") that came to involve the Zulus and other native populations, the superior firepower of the British prevailed—but not without the adoption of a variety of brutally oppressive measures as the British struggled to control a guerrilla campaign by the Afrikaaners. At the time, the war seemed an extension of the British struggle against the Afrikaaners that had been continuing on and off for more than fifty years—and, as with previous conflicts, this one resulted in an expansion of the size of the British Empire. The war aroused objections to the

Imperial project to an unprecedented degree, however; more than a century later, it is difficult not to see in it a foreshadowing of the loss of Empire. The brutalities in which the British allowed themselves to engage as they struggled to assert control seem a foretaste of the struggles against the Independence Movement in India in the 1930s and 1940s that would end with the independence of India in 1947, and of the struggles in Kenya and elsewhere in Africa in the 1950s that could be resolved only through the independence of those colonies. In one of his most famous speeches during the dark days of the Battle of Britain in 1940, Prime Minister Winston Churchill alluded to the possibility of the British Empire lasting for "a thousand years." Even then its foundations had crumbled, and within another 20 years the edifice of Empire would be almost entirely dismantled.

THE ENGLISH LANGUAGE IN THE EARLY TWENTIETH CENTURY

Many trends in the development of the English language that had begun in the nineteenth century or earlier continued through the first half of the twentieth. Punctuation became simpler: whereas, for example, it remained common in Britain through to the end of the nineteenth century and into the twentieth to precede a dash with a comma, by mid-century the norm was always to use one or the other, never both. Long periodic sentences had been on the decline through most of the nineteenth century, and this trend continued into the twentieth; on both sides of the Atlantic, sentences became shorter. Paragraphs also became shorter. To these generalizations, however, there were significant exceptions. With the growth of universities and the expansion of business, government, and political bureaucracies came an increase in academic, administrative, and political jargon of the sort of which Orwell complained in his famous essay "Politics and the English Language" (1946). While the majority of people (including most writers of fiction) were using shorter sentences, in other quarters writers were, in Orwell's words, "gumming together long strips of words which have already been set in order by someone else, and making the results presentable by sheer humbug."

In the twentieth century spelling was largely stable on both sides of the Atlantic; though shortened forms of some of the more archaic spellings in standard English became common in down-market forms of advertising, particularly in the United States (*thru*, *donut*), even there few of these came close to displacing the longer traditional forms. Conventions for marking direct speech also stabilized on both sides of the Atlantic, with the British using single quotation marks and the Canadians adopting the American convention of using double quotation marks.

Vocabulary, of course, continued to expand, with many new coinages entering the language as the result of new developments in science and technology. Interestingly, Britain and the United States developed largely separate terminologies regarding that most influential of twentieth century developments in technology, the automobile; in Britain cars run on *petrol*, the engine is under the *bonnet*, the luggage goes in the *boot*, and you drive on the *motorway*—without much noise unless there is a hole in your *silencer*. In numerous other areas in which new coinages were necessary, British usage developed as quite distinct from that in the United States—from television *presenters* (hosts); to *breeze block* construction (concrete block), to battery-powered *torches* (flashlights), to *Wellingtons* (rubber boots), to *hire purchase plans* (installment plans), British English remained distinct from American English. (Former British possessions such as Canada and Australia partook of both in forming their own national patterns.)

Perhaps the greatest structural shift in English in the first half of the twentieth century was the simplification or elimination of forms marking the subjunctive mood. In constructions such as "If I were to travel through time I would…," for example, the old subjunctive form came to be largely replaced by the simple past form of the verb ("If I traveled through time I would …").

Throughout the nineteenth century, the spread of literacy and of mass transportation led to a steady decrease in the distinctiveness of the various dialects of English spoken in Britain, and in the distinctiveness of regional accents. That movement toward standardization continued in the twentieth century, with radio and television as its new vehicles. In 1922, the government set up the BBC (at first the initials stood for British

Broadcasting Company, but the name was soon changed to British Broadcasting Corporation), and it remained the dominant force in British radio—and, from the 1950s on, British television—for most of the century. In 1926, John Reith, the BBC's managing director, created an Advisory Committee on Spoken English, chaired by Robert Bridges, then the Poet Laureate, with the task of making recommendations to facilitate a standard of pronunciation over the air. Reith specifically asked that the committee seek a "style or quality of English that would not be laughed at in any part of the country." In practice, the standardized pronunciations recommended by the committee—which remained largely mandatory for announcers until 1989—were broadly similar to the pronunciations taught in the nation's elite "public" schools (see the glossary at the back of this volume for a

discussion of this term) in southern England. Indeed, the three terms "public school pronunciation," "BBC pronunciation," and "Received Standard Pronunciation" (a term introduced by Henry Cecil Wyld in the early twentieth century to denote "the form which ... is heard with practically no variation among speakers of the better class all over the country") are all roughly synonymous. Despite the ongoing trend towards standardization of speech in the twentieth century, however, the varieties of British English remained extraordinarily diverse throughout the century—so much so that someone from London could at century's end still have great difficulty understanding the accent of a Glaswegian or a "Geordie" (a native of the Newcastle area).

HISTORY OF THE LANGUAGE
AND OF PRINT CULTURE

In an effort to provide for readers a direct sense of the development of the language and of print culture, examples of texts in their original form, of illustrations, and of other materials related to book culture have been provided in each volume. A list of these within the present volume, arranged chronologically, appears below. An overview of developments in the history of language during the first half of the century appears on pages 1067 to 1068; material on developments in the history of language since World War II appears on pages 1409, 1416–17, and 1419–21.

Bernard Shaw
1856 – 1950

Considered by many to be the greatest dramatist of his age, George Bernard Shaw was at times revered by, at times alienated from, the London society he criticized through his plays. A committed socialist, Shaw often used his plays to expound his views on the rights of women, on

numerous social injustices, or on the deleterious effects of capitalism. In some cases he treated topics (such as prostitution and religion) in ways that caused his plays to be banned in England for many years, but Shaw himself always remained in the public eye. In the end he wrote more than 50 plays, and was awarded the Nobel Prize for Literature, the prize money for which he directed be used for the translation of Swedish works into English. He is the only Nobel laureate to have won an Academy Award (for his screenplay *Pygmalion*). The adjective "Shavian" was coined to describe his witty dialogue and epigrams.

Shaw was born into somewhat shabby gentility in Dublin in 1856, the son of a failing corn merchant and alcoholic father and a music teacher and singer mother. Shaw spent a great deal of time with the servants, one of whom exposed him to the realities of working-class life in Dublin when she was supposed to be taking him for air. The poverty and hardship he saw, and the ragtag characters with whom he came into contact, stayed with him for life and greatly influenced his later work. He and his two older sisters had a governess for their early education, but neither parent showed a particular interest in their children's formal education. As a result, Shaw flitted from school to school, attending irregularly; he finally gave it all up at age 15 to work as a clerk in a land surveyor's office. One of his duties was to collect rent from poor tenants. Shaw hated his work, but it provided material for his plays, the first of which, *Widowers' Houses* (1892), dealt with slum landlords. It was also during this time that Shaw dropped the "George" from his name, and became known as Bernard Shaw.

In 1876 Shaw moved to London to join his mother, who had moved there in 1873 with her music teacher. For the next nine years, Shaw honed his writing skills, building a successful career as a music and art critic. It was also during this time that he began to develop his creative writing. From 1879 to 1883 Shaw wrote five novels, none of which was published at the time. (Shaw eventually gave up writing novels; he said he had come to dislike the form, and called it clumsy and unreal.) From 1891 onward, Shaw dedicated himself to work as a playwright. His family background—a music-filled home, a mother who had been a performer—had helped foster a love of the stage, and he had become particularly interested in theater while still in Dublin, where he had frequented the Theatre Royal.

From 1891 to 1903 Shaw wrote 12 plays, some of which had very short runs in London, while others premiered in America (e.g., *The Devil's Disciple*) or Germany (*Caesar and Cleopatra*). By 1898 he was earning enough in royalties from his plays to be financially secure; it was also in that year that he married Charlotte Payne Townshend, a marriage that brought still greater financial stability.

Shaw created several categories for his plays: his *Plays Unpleasant* engage with various social issues. In addition to *Widowers' Houses*, these include *The Philanderer* (1905) and *Mrs Warren's Profession* (1902), which explored the topic of prostitution and was banned from public performance in England for 30 years. His next set of plays, *Plays Pleasant*, received better reviews and gave him his first commercial successes. These plays include *Candida*, *Arms and the Man*, *The Man of Destiny*, and *You Never Can Tell*. He termed various of his other plays "Comedies," "Chronicles," and "Political Extravaganzas." During Shaw's lifetime his most highly acclaimed plays included *Man and Superman* (1905), *Major Barbara* (1905), *Pygmalion* (1913), *Heartbreak House* (1920), and *Saint Joan* (1923). Throughout his long career Shaw remained very involved in the production of his plays, often arranging the casting, direction, and staging.

In awarding Shaw the Nobel Prize for 1925, the selection committee commended him for his "work which is marked by both idealism and humanity, its stimulating satire often being infused with a singular poetic beauty." He was offered a knighthood in 1926, but declined it, as he did many other honors. Shaw died in 1950, after falling from a tree he had been pruning. Throughout his life he had remained an eccentric, distinguished not only by his literary reputation but also by his vegetarianism, his discordant political views (he opposed Britain's involvement in World War I), and odd clothing (he wore an unbleached wool suit through much of his life for its perceived health benefits). In almost every way Shaw was an original.

⌘ ⌘ ⌘

Mrs Warren's Profession

A Note on the Text of *Mrs Warren's Profession*

Mrs Warren's Profession was first published in 1898 in volume 1 (*Plays Unpleasant*) of *Plays Pleasant and Unpleasant*, in London by Grant Richards, and in Chicago and New York by Herbert S. Stone. The other plays in *Plays Unpleasant* were *Widowers' Houses* and *The Philanderer*. The first separate edition of *Mrs Warren's Profession* was published in London by Grant Richards in 1902 in an identical text, but with a new preface by Shaw and photographs of the Stage Society production of 5–6 January 1902. Shaw revised *Mrs Warren's Profession* for the *Plays Unpleasant* volume (1930) of *The Works of Bernard Shaw: Collected Edition*, published in London by Constable between 1930 and 1938. This was the text of *Mrs Warren's Profession* used for *Bernard Shaw: Collected Plays with Their Prefaces* published in seven volumes by Max Reinhardt between 1970 and 1974 under the editorial supervision of Dan H. Laurence, and subsequently by Penguin Books, again under the editorial supervision of Dan H. Laurence. The definitive Penguin text is the copytext for the Broadview edition on which the text printed here is based.

Shaw made numerous revisions in the 1898 text for the 1930 edition. Many are relatively minor, but those that suggest significant changes in Shaw's thinking about a character or situation are recorded here in footnotes in this edition.

Shaw had strong opinions on matters of spelling, punctuation, and typography. He retained some archaic spellings (e.g., *shew* for *show*), and dropped the "u" in "our" spellings such as *honor*, *labor*, and *neighbor*. He preferred to reserve the use of italics for stage directions and descriptions of settings and characters (which are detailed and elaborate for the benefit of readers who might never have the opportunity of seeing his plays), electing to indicate emphasis of a word by spacing the letters (e.g., d e a r for *dear*, v e r y for *very*). He had no choice but to use italics for stressing *I*, and he sometimes chose to use small capital letters for stressing some words (e.g., ME for *me*).

Shaw disliked the apostrophe, believing it to be redundant (and ugly) in most instances. He eliminated it whenever he could (e.g., in *Ive, youve, thats, werent, dont, wont*), though it was necessary to retain it where its omission might cause confusion (e.g., *I'll, it's, he'll*).

For some readers Shaw's rationale for these practices is unconvincing, and the idiosyncrasies are irritating. They are, however, Shaw's clear preferences, and serve if nothing else as a frequent reminder of his nonconformity—the essence of the man and his work—and have, therefore, been retained in this anthology.

⌘ ⌘ ⌘

Mrs Warren's Profession [1]

ACT 1

(*Summer afternoon in a cottage garden on the eastern slope of a hill a little south of Haslemere[2] in Surrey. Looking up the hill, the cottage is seen in the left hand corner of the garden, with its thatched roof and porch, and a large lattice[3] window to the left of the porch. A paling[4] completely shuts in the garden, except for a gate on the right. The common rises uphill beyond the paling to the sky line. Some folded canvas garden chairs are leaning against the side bench in the porch. A lady's bicycle is propped against the wall, under the window. A little to the right of the porch a hammock is slung from two posts. A big canvas umbrella, stuck in the ground, keeps the sun off the hammock, in which a young lady lies reading and making notes, her head towards the cottage and her feet towards the gate. In front of the hammock, and within reach of her hand, is a common kitchen chair, with a pile of serious-looking books and a supply of writing paper on it.*

A gentleman walking on the common comes into sight from behind the cottage. He is hardly past middle age, with something of the artist about him, unconventionally but carefully dressed and clean-shaven except for a moustache, with an eager susceptible face and very amiable and considerate manners. He has silky black hair, with waves of grey and white in it. His eyebrows are white, his moustache black. He seems not certain of his way. He looks over the paling; takes stock of the place; and sees the young lady.*)

THE GENTLEMAN. (*Taking off his hat.*) I beg your pardon. Can you direct me to Hindhead View—Mrs Alison's?

THE YOUNG LADY. (*Glancing up from her book.*) This is
5 Mrs Alison's. (*She resumes her work.*)

THE GENTLEMAN.   Indeed! Perhaps—may I ask are you Miss Vivie Warren?

THE YOUNG LADY. (*Sharply, as she turns on her elbow to get a good look at him.*) Yes.

10 THE GENTLEMAN. (*Daunted and conciliatory.*) I'm afraid I appear intrusive. My name is Praed.[5] (*Vivie at once throws her books upon the chair, and gets out of the hammock.*) Oh, pray dont[6] let me disturb you.

VIVIE. (*Striding to the gate and opening it for him.*) Come
15 in, Mr Praed. (*He comes in.*) Glad to see you. (*She proffers her hand and takes his with a resolute and hearty grip. She is an attractive specimen of the sensible, able, highly-educated young middle-class Englishwoman. Age 22. Prompt, strong, confident, self-possessed. Plain business-like
20 dress, but not dowdy. She wears a chatelaine[7] at her belt, with a fountain pen and a paper knife among its pendants.*)

---

1 *Mrs Warren's Profession* Shaw took the name of Mrs Warren from Warren Street, near one of his early London homes in Fitzroy Square, Bloomsbury. Mrs Warren's profession—prostitution—is never explicitly identified in the play.

2 *Haslemere* Market town about 40 miles southwest of London.

3 *lattice* Divided by strips into square or diamond-shaped sections.

4 *paling* Fence.

5 *Praed* Praed's name is perhaps an allusion to Winthrop Mackworth Praed (1802–39), a Cambridge-educated politician and poet. His portrait hung in the National Gallery in London. Praed St. is just north of Hyde Park in west-central London.

6 *dont* Shaw often omits the apostrophe in contractions such as "dont," "Ive," and "doesnt." See above, "A Note on the Text."

7 *chatelaine* Set of short chains attached to a woman's belt used for carrying small items (such as Vivie's fountain pen and paper knife).

PRAED. Very kind of you indeed, Miss Warren. (*She shuts the gate with a vigorous slam. He passes in to the middle of the garden, exercising his fingers, which are slightly numbed by her greeting.*) Has your mother arrived?

VIVIE. (*Quickly, evidently scenting aggression.*) Is she coming?

PRAED. (*Surprised.*) Didnt you expect us?

VIVIE. No.

PRAED. Now, goodness me, I hope Ive not mistaken the day. That would be just like me, you know. Your mother arranged that she was to come down from London and that I was to come over from Horsham[1] to be introduced to you.

VIVIE. (*Not at all pleased.*) Did she? Hm! My mother has rather a trick of taking me by surprise—to see how I behave myself when she's away, I suppose. I fancy I shall take my mother very much by surprise one of these days, if she makes arrangements that concern me without consulting me beforehand. She hasnt come.

PRAED. (*Embarrassed.*) I'm really very sorry.

VIVIE. (*Throwing off her displeasure.*) It's not your fault, Mr Praed, is it? And I'm very glad youve come. You are the only one of my mother's friends I have ever asked her to bring to see me.

PRAED. (*Relieved and delighted.*) Oh, now this is really very good of you, Miss Warren!

VIVIE. Will you come indoors; or would you rather sit out here and talk?

PRAED. It will be nicer out here, dont you think?

VIVIE. Then I'll go and get you a chair. (*She goes to the porch for a garden chair.*)

PRAED. (*Following her.*) Oh, pray, pray! Allow me. (*He lays hands on the chair.*)

VIVIE. (*Letting him take it.*) Take care of your fingers, theyre rather dodgy things, those chairs. (*She goes across to the chair with the books on it; pitches them into the hammock; and brings the chair forward with one swing.*)

PRAED. (*Who has just unfolded his chair.*) Oh, now do let me take that hard chair. I like hard chairs.

VIVIE. So do I. Sit down, Mr Praed. (*This invitation she gives with genial peremptoriness, his anxiety to please her*

clearly striking her as a sign of weakness of character on his part. But he does not immediately obey.*)

PRAED. By the way, though, hadnt we better go to the station to meet your mother?

VIVIE. (*Coolly.*) Why? She knows the way.

PRAED. (*Disconcerted.*) Er—I suppose she does. (*He sits down.*)

VIVIE. Do you know, you are just like what I expected. I hope you are disposed to be friends with me.

PRAED. (*Again beaming.*) Thank you, my d e a r[2] Miss Warren: thank you. Dear me! I'm so glad your mother hasnt spoilt you!

VIVIE. How?

PRAED. Well, in making you too conventional. You know, my dear Miss Warren, I am a born anarchist. I hate authority. It spoils the relations between parent and child: even between mother and daughter. Now I was always afraid that your mother would strain her authority to make you very conventional. It's such a relief to find that she hasnt.

VIVIE. Oh! have I been behaving unconventionally?

PRAED. Oh no: oh dear no. At least not conventionally unconventionally, you understand. (*She nods and sits down. He goes on, with a cordial outburst.*) But it was so charming of you to say that you were disposed to be friends with me! You modern young ladies are splendid: perfectly splendid!

VIVIE. (*Dubiously.*) Eh? (*Watching him with dawning disappointment as to the quality of his brains and character.*)

PRAED. When I was your age, young men and women were afraid of each other: there was no good fellowship. Nothing real. Only gallantry copied out of novels, and as vulgar and affected as it could be. Maidenly reserve! gentlemanly chivalry! always saying no when you meant yes! simple purgatory[3] for shy and sincere souls.

VIVIE. Yes, I imagine there must have been a frightful waste of time. Especially women's time.

PRAED. Oh, waste of life, waste of everything. But things are improving. Do you know, I have been in a positive state of excitement about meeting you ever

---

[1] *Horsham* Market town about 38 miles southwest of London (about 15 miles east of Haslemere).

[2] *d e a r* The spacing between letters is Shaw's way of indicating an emphasis on the word. See above, "A Note on the Text."

[3] *purgatory* In Catholic doctrine, a place for spiritual cleansing of the dead before entry to heaven.

since your magnificent achievements at Cambridge: a thing unheard of in my day. It was perfectly splendid, your tieing with the third wrangler.[1] Just the right place, you know. The first wrangler is always a dreamy, morbid fellow, in whom the thing is pushed to the length of a disease.

VIVIE.   It doesnt pay. I wouldnt do it again for the same money!

PRAED.   (*Aghast*.) The same money!

VIVIE.   I did it for £50.[2]

PRAED.   Fifty pounds!

VIVIE.   Yes. Fifty pounds. Perhaps you dont know how it was. Mrs Latham, my tutor at Newnham,[3] told my mother that I could distinguish myself in the mathematical tripos[4] if I went in for it in earnest. The papers were full just then of Phillipa Summers[5] beating the senior wrangler. You remember about it, of course.

PRAED.   (*Shakes his head energetically*) !!!

VIVIE.   Well anyhow she did: and nothing would please my mother but that I should do the same thing. I said flatly it was not worth my while to face the grind since I was not going in for teaching; but I offered to try for fourth wrangler or thereabouts for £50. She closed with me at that, after a little grumbling; and I was better than my bargain. But I wouldnt do it again for that. £200 would have been better near the mark.

PRAED.   (*Much damped*.) Lord bless me! Thats a very practical way of looking at it.

VIVIE.   Did you expect to find me an unpractical person?

PRAED.   But surely its practical to consider not only the work these honors cost, but also the culture they bring.

VIVIE.   Culture! My dear Mr Praed: do you know what the mathematical tripos means? It means grind, grind, grind for six to eight hours a day at mathematics, and nothing but mathematics. I'm supposed to know something about science; but I know nothing except the mathematics it involves. I can make calculations for engineers, electricians, insurance companies, and so on; but I know next to nothing about engineering or electricity or insurance. I dont even know arithmetic well. Outside mathematics, lawn-tennis, eating, sleeping, cycling, and walking, I'm a more ignorant barbarian than any woman could possibly be who hadnt gone in for the tripos.

PRAED.   (*Revolted*.) What a monstrous, wicked, rascally system! I knew it! I felt at once that it meant destroying all that makes womanhood beautiful.

VIVIE.   I dont object to it on that score in the least. I shall turn it to very good account, I assure you.

PRAED.   Pooh! in what way?

VIVIE.   I shall set up chambers[6] in the City, and work at actuarial calculations and conveyancing.[7] Under cover of that I shall do some law, with one eye on the Stock Exchange all the time. Ive come down here by myself to read law: not for a holiday, as my mother imagines. I hate holidays.

PRAED.   You make my blood run cold. Are you to have no romance, no beauty in your life?

VIVIE.   I dont care for either, I assure you.

PRAED.   You cant mean that.

VIVIE.   Oh yes I do. I like working and getting paid for it. When I'm tired of working, I like a comfortable chair, a cigar, a little whisky, and a novel with a good detective story in it.

PRAED.   (*Rising in a frenzy of repudiation*.) I dont believe it. I am an artist; and I cant believe it: I refuse to believe

---

[1]   *wrangler*   Wranglers were those who achieved a first-class honors degree in mathematics at Cambridge. Vivie had placed equal third among the wranglers in her year. The top student was designated senior wrangler.

[2]   *£50*   It would have taken most working-class women in England at this time two years to earn this amount.

[3]   *Newnham*   Newnham College was founded as a women's college of Cambridge University in 1871. The first Cambridge college for women, Girton, was founded in 1869. All other colleges of the University admitted men only.

[4]   *tripos*   The Tripos was (and is) the honors course at Cambridge, so-called because of the medieval tradition of the candidate sitting on a three-legged stool.

[5]   *Phillipa Summers*   Allusion to Philippa Fawcett, daughter of Henry Fawcett (1833–84), Professor of Political Economy at Cambridge and Liberal Member of Parliament, and Millicent Fawcett (1847–1929), leader of the women's suffrage movement and strong proponent of women's education at Cambridge. Philippa Fawcett gained the highest mark in the mathematical tripos in June 1890 (*The Times*, 9 June 1890), the first woman to do so.

[6]   *chambers*   Law office.

[7]   *conveyancing*   Vivie will specialize as an actuary (compiling and analyzing statistics to calculate insurance risks and premiums) and a conveyancer (transferring ownership of property).

it. It's only that you havnt discovered yet what a wonderful world art can open up to you.

VIVIE.   Yes I have. Last May I spent six weeks in London with Honoria Fraser. Mamma thought we were doing a round of sightseeing together; but I was really at Honoria's chambers in Chancery Lane[1] every day, working away at actuarial calculations for her, and helping her as well as a greenhorn could. In the evenings we smoked and talked, and never dreamt of going out except for exercise. And I never enjoyed myself more in my life. I cleared all my expenses, and got initiated into the business without a fee into the bargain.

PRAED.   But bless my heart and soul, Miss Warren, do you call that discovering art?

VIVIE.   Wait a bit. That wasnt the beginning. I went up to town on an invitation from some artistic people in Fitzjohn's Avenue:[2] one of the girls was a Newnham chum. They took me to the National Gallery[3]—

PRAED.   (*Approving.*) Ah ! ! (*He sits down, much relieved.*)

VIVIE.   (*Continuing.*) —to the Opera—

PRAED.   (*Still more pleased.*) Good!

VIVIE.   —and to a concert where the band played all the evening: Beethoven and Wagner[4] and so on. I wouldnt go through that experience again for anything you could offer me. I held out for civility's sake until the third day; and then I said, plump out, that I couldnt stand anymore of it, and went off to Chancery Lane. Now you know the sort of perfectly splendid modern young lady I am. How do you think I shall get on with my mother?

PRAED.   (*Startled.*) Well, I hope—er—

VIVIE.   It's not so much what you hope as what you believe, that I want to know.

PRAED.   Well, frankly, I am afraid your mother will be a little disappointed. Not from any shortcoming on your part, you know: I dont mean that. But you are so different from her ideal.

VIVIE.   Her what?!

PRAED.   Her ideal.

VIVIE.   Do you mean her ideal of ME?

PRAED.   Yes.

VIVIE.   What on Earth is it like?

PRAED.   Well, you must have observed, Miss Warren, that people who are dissatisfied with their own bringing-up generally think that the world would be all right if everybody were to be brought up quite differently. Now your mother's life has been—er—I suppose you know—

VIVIE.   Dont suppose anything, Mr Praed. I hardly know my mother. Since I was a child I have lived in England, at school or college, or with people paid to take charge of me. I have been boarded out all my life. My mother has lived in Brussels or Vienna and never let me go to her. I only see her when she visits England for a few days. I dont complain: it's been very pleasant; for people have been very good to me; and there has always been plenty of money to make things smooth. But dont imagine I know anything about my mother. I know far less than you do.

PRAED.   (*Very ill at ease.*) In that case—(*He stops, quite at a loss. Then, with a forced attempt at gaiety.*) But what nonsense we are talking! Of course you and your mother will get on capitally. (*He rises, and looks abroad at the view.*) What a charming little place you have here!

VIVIE.   (*Unmoved.*) Rather a violent change of subject, Mr Praed. Why wont my mother's life bear being talked about?

PRAED.   Oh, you really musnt say that. Isnt it natural that I should have a certain delicacy in talking to my old friend's daughter about her behind her back? You and she will have plenty of opportunity of talking about it when she comes.

VIVIE.   No: s h e wont talk about it either. (*Rising.*) However, I daresay you have good reasons for telling me nothing. Only, mind this, Mr Praed. I expect there will be a battle royal when my mother hears of my Chancery Lane project.

PRAED.   (*Ruefully.*) I'm afraid there will.

VIVIE.   Well, I shall win because I want nothing but my fare to London to start there to-morrow earning my

[1] *Chancery Lane*   Street in west-central London, the location of many legal offices and related businesses.

[2] *Fitzjohn's Avenue*   Street in the fashionable district of Hampstead, northwest of central London.

[3] *National Gallery*   Founded in 1824, the National Gallery moved to its current location on the north side of Trafalgar Square in 1838. The Gallery holds one of the world's finest collections of European paintings. Shaw was a frequent visitor.

[4] *Beethoven and Wagner*   German composers Ludwig van Beethoven (1770–1827) and Wilhelm Richard Wagner (1813–83) were Shaw's favorite composers.

own living by devilling[1] for Honoria. Besides, I have no mysteries to keep up; and it seems she has. I shall use that advantage over her if necessary.

PRAED. (*Greatly shocked.*) Oh no! No, pray. Youd not do such a thing.

VIVIE. Then tell me why not.

PRAED. I really cannot. I appeal to your good feeling. (*She smiles at his sentimentality.*) Besides, you may be too bold. Your mother is not to be trifled with when she's angry.

VIVIE. You can't frighten me, Mr Praed. In that month at Chancery Lane I had opportunities of taking the measure of one or two women v e r y like my mother. You may back me to win. But if I hit harder in my ignorance than I need, remember that it is you who refuse to enlighten me. Now, let us drop the subject. (*She takes her chair and replaces it near the hammock with the same vigorous swing as before.*)

PRAED. (*Taking a desperate resolution.*) One word, Miss Warren. I had better tell you. It's very difficult; but –

(*Mrs Warren and Sir George Crofts arrive at the gate. Mrs Warren is between 40 and 50, formerly pretty, showily dressed in a brilliant hat and a gay blouse fitting tightly over her bust and flanked by fashionable sleeves. Rather spoilt and domineering, and decidedly vulgar, but, on the whole, a genial and fairly presentable old blackguard[2] of a woman.*

Crofts is a tall powerfully-built man of about 50, fashionably dressed in the style of a young man. Nasal voice, reedier than might be expected from his strong frame. Clean-shaven bulldog jaws, large flat ears, and thick neck: gentlemanly combination of the most brutal types of city man, sporting man, and man about town.)

VIVIE. Here they are. (*Coming to them as they enter the garden.*) How do, mater?[3] Mr Praed's been here this half hour waiting for you.

MRS WARREN. Well, if youve been waiting, Praddy, it's your own fault: I thought youd have had the gumption[4] to know I was coming by the 3:10 train. Vivie: put your hat on, dear: youll get sunburnt. Oh, I forgot to introduce you. Sir George Crofts: my little Vivie.

(*Crofts advances to Vivie with his most courtly manner. She nods, but makes no motion to shake hands.*)

CROFTS. May I shake hands with a young lady whom I have known by reputation very long as the daughter of one of my oldest friends?

VIVIE. (*Who has been looking him up and down sharply.*) If you like. (*She takes his tenderly proffered hand and gives it a squeeze that makes him open his eyes; then turns away and says to her mother*) Will you come in, or shall I get a couple more chairs? (*She goes into the porch for the chairs.*)

MRS WARREN. Well, George, what do you think of her?

CROFTS. (*Ruefully.*) She has a powerful fist. Did you shake hands with her, Praed?

PRAED. Yes: it will pass off presently.

CROFTS. I hope so. (*Vivie reappears with two more chairs. He hurries to her assistance.*) Allow me.

MRS WARREN. (*Patronizingly.*) Let Sir George help you with the chairs, dear.

VIVIE. (*Pitching them into his arms.*) Here you are. (*She dusts her hands and turns to Mrs Warren.*) Youd like some tea, wouldnt you?

MRS WARREN. (*Sitting in Praed's chair and fanning herself.*) I'm dying for a drop to drink.

VIVIE. I'll see about it. (*She goes into the cottage.*)

(*Sir George has by this time managed to unfold a chair and plant it beside Mrs Warren, on her left. He throws the other on the grass and sits down, looking dejected and rather foolish, with the handle of his stick in his mouth. Praed, still very uneasy, fidgets about the garden on their right.*)

MRS WARREN. (*To Praed, looking at Crofts.*) Just look at him, Praddy: he looks cheerful, dont he? He's been worrying my life out these three years to have that little

[1] *devilling* Serve as a barrister's (i.e., lawyer's) junior assistant.

[2] *blackguard* Person characterized by dishonorable behavior; here used by Shaw more as a term of endearment. In the 1898 text Mrs Warren is still "good-looking" (not just "formerly pretty"), and she is not described as "decidedly vulgar."

[3] *mater* Latin: mother. University slang.

[4] *gumption* Common sense.

305 girl of mine shewn to him; and now that Ive done it, he's quite out of countenance. (*Briskly.*) Come! Sit up, George; and take your stick out of your mouth. (*Crofts sulkily obeys.*)

PRAED. I think, you know—if you dont mind my
310 saying so—that we had better get out of the habit of thinking of her as a little girl. You see she has really distinguished herself; and I'm not sure, from what I have seen of her, that she is not older than any of us.

MRS WARREN. (*Greatly amused.*) Only listen to him,
315 George! Older than any of us! Well, she h a s been stuffing you nicely with her importance.

PRAED. But young people are particularly sensitive about being treated in that way.

MRS WARREN. Yes; and young people have to get all
320 that nonsense taken out of them, and a good deal more besides. Dont you interfere, Praddy: I know how to treat my own child as well as you do. (*Praed, with a grave shake of his head, walks up the garden with his hands behind his back. Mrs Warren pretends to laugh, but looks
325 after him with perceptible concern. Then she whispers to Crofts.*) Whats the matter with him? What does he take it like that for?

CROFTS. (*Morosely.*) Youre afraid of Praed.

MRS WARREN. What! Me! Afraid of dear old Praddy!
330 Why, a fly wouldnt be afraid of him.

CROFTS. Youre afraid of him.

MRS WARREN. (*Angry.*) I'll trouble you to mind your own business, and not try any of your sulks on me. I'm not afraid of y o u, anyhow. If you cant make yourself
335 agreeable, youd better go home. (*She gets up, and, turning her back on him, finds herself face to face with Praed.*) Come, Praddy, I know it was only your tender-heartedness. Youre afraid I'll bully her.

PRAED. My dear Kitty: you think I'm offended. Dont
340 imagine that: pray dont. But you know I often notice things that escape you; and though you never take my advice, you sometimes admit afterwards that you ought to have taken it.

MRS WARREN. Well, what do you notice now?
345 PRAED. Only that Vivie is a grown woman. Pray, Kitty, treat her with every respect.

MRS WARREN. (*With genuine amazement.*) Respect! Treat my own daughter with respect! What next, pray!

VIVIE. (*Appearing at the cottage door and calling to Mrs
350 Warren.*) Mother: will you come to my room before tea?

MRS WARREN. Yes, dearie. (*She laughs indulgently at Praed's gravity, and pats him on the cheek as she passes him on her way to the porch.*) Dont be cross, Praddy. (*She follows Vivie into the cottage.*)

355 CROFTS. (*Furtively.*) I say, Praed.

PRAED. Yes.

CROFTS. I want to ask you a rather particular question.

PRAED. Certainly. (*He takes Mrs Warren's chair and sits close to Crofts.*)

360 CROFTS. Thats right: they might hear us from the window. Look here: did Kitty ever tell you who that girl's father is?

PRAED. Never.

CROFTS. Have you any suspicion of who it might be?

365 PRAED. None.

CROFTS. (*Not believing him.*) I know, of course, that you perhaps might feel bound not to tell if she had said anything to you. But it's very awkward to be uncertain about it now that we shall be meeting the girl every day.
370 We wont exactly know how we ought to feel towards her.

PRAED. What difference can that make? We take her on her own merits. What does it matter who her father was?

375 CROFTS. (*Suspiciously.*) Then you know who he was?

PRAED. (*With a touch of temper.*) I said no just now. Did you not hear me?

CROFTS. Look here, Praed. I ask you as a particular favor. If you d o know (*Movement of protest from
380 Praed.*)—I only say, if you know, you might at least set my mind at rest about her. The fact is, I feel attracted.

PRAED. (*Sternly.*) What do you mean?

CROFTS. Oh, dont be alarmed: it's quite an innocent feeling. Thats what puzzles me about it. Why, for all I
385 know I might be her father.

PRAED. You! Impossible!

CROFTS. (*Catching him up cunningly.*) You know for certain that I'm not?

PRAED. I know nothing about it, I tell you, anymore
390 than you. But really, Crofts—oh no, it's out of the question. Theres not the least resemblance.

CROFTS. As to that, theres no resemblance between her and her mother that I can see. I suppose she's not y o u r daughter, is she?

395 PRAED. (*Rising indignantly.*) Really, Crofts—!

CROFTS. No offence, Praed. Quite allowable as between two men of the world.

PRAED. (*Recovering himself with an effort and speaking gently and gravely.*) Now listen to me, my dear Crofts.

400 (*He sits down again.*) I have nothing to do with that side of Mrs Warren's life, and never had. She has never spoken to me about it; and of course I have never spoken to her about it. Your delicacy will tell you that a handsome woman needs some friends who are

405 not—well, not on that footing with her. The effect of her own beauty would become a torment to her if she could not escape from it occasionally. You are probably on much more confidential terms with Kitty than I am. Surely you can ask her the question yourself.

410 CROFTS. I h a v e asked her, often enough. But she's so determined to keep the child all to herself that she would deny that it ever had a father if she could. (*Rising.*) I'm thoroughly uncomfortable about it, Praed.

PRAED. (*Rising also.*) Well, as you are, at all events, old

415 enough to be her father, I dont mind agreeing that we both regard Miss Vivie in a parental way, as a young girl whom we are bound to protect and help. What do you say?

CROFTS. (*Aggressively.*) I'm no older than you, if you

420 come to that.

PRAED. Yes you are, my dear fellow: you were born old. I was born a boy: Ive never been able to feel the assurance of a grown-up man in my life. (*He folds his chair and carries it to the porch.*)

425 MRS WARREN. (*Calling from within the cottage.*) Prad-dee! George! Tea-ea-ea-ea!

CROFTS. (*Hastily.*) She's calling us. (*He hurries in.*)

(*Praed shakes his head bodingly, and is following Crofts when he is hailed by a young gentleman who has just appeared on the common, and is making for the gate. He is pleasant, pretty, smartly dressed, cleverly good-for-nothing, not long turned 20, with a charming voice and agreeably disrespectful manners. He carries a light sporting magazine rifle.[1]*)

---

[1]   *magazine rifle*   Rifle with attached device holding ammunition.

THE YOUNG GENTLEMAN. Hallo! Praed!

PRAED. Why, Frank Gardner! (*Frank comes in and*

430 *shakes hands cordially.*) What on earth are you doing here?

FRANK. Staying with my father.

PRAED. The Roman father?[2]

FRANK. He's rector here. I'm living with my people this

435 autumn for the sake of economy. Things came to a crisis in July: the Roman father had to pay my debts. He's stony broke in consequence; and so am I. What are you up to in these parts? Do you know the people here?

PRAED. Yes: I'm spending the day with a Miss Warren.

440 FRANK. (*Enthusiastically.*) What! Do you know Vivie? Isnt she a jolly girl? I'm teaching her to shoot with this (*putting down the rifle*). I'm so glad she knows you: youre just the sort of fellow she ought to know. (*He smiles, and raises the charming voice almost to a singing*

445 *tone as he exclaims:*) It's e v e r so jolly to find you here, Praed.

PRAED. I'm an old friend of her mother. Mrs Warren brought me over to make her daughter's acquaintance.

FRANK. The mother! Is s h e here?

450 PRAED. Yes: inside, at tea.

MRS WARREN. (*Calling from within.*) Prad-dee-ee-ee-eee! The tea-cake'll be cold.

PRAED. (*Calling.*) Yes, Mrs Warren. In a moment. Ive just met a friend here.

455 MRS WARREN. A what?

PRAED. (*Louder.*) A friend.

MRS WARREN. Bring him in.

PRAED. (*To Frank.*) Will you accept the invitation?

FRANK. (*Incredulous, but immensely amused.*) Is that

460 Vivie's mother?

PRAED. Yes.

FRANK. By Jove! What a lark! Do you think she'll like me?

PRAED. Ive no doubt youll make yourself popular as

465 usual. Come in and try. (*Moving toward the house.*)

FRANK. Stop a bit. (*Seriously.*) I want to take you into my confidence.

---

[2]   *Roman father*   This might be thought to suggest that Frank's father is a Catholic priest, but he is in fact a clergyman of the Church of England. It is more likely an ironic reference to supposed "Roman" qualities of strictness and integrity.

PRAED. Pray dont. It's only some fresh folly, like the barmaid at Redhill.[1]

470 FRANK.   Its ever so much more serious than that. You say youve only just met Vivie for the first time?

PRAED. Yes.

FRANK. (*Rhapsodically.*) Then you can have no idea what a girl she is. Such character! Such sense! And her cleverness! Oh, my eye, Praed, but I can tell you she is clever! And—need I add?—she loves me.

CROFTS. (*Putting his head out of the window.*) I say, Praed: what are you about? Do come along. (*He disappears.*)

480 FRANK. Hallo! Sort of chap that would take a prize at a dog show, aint he? Who's he?

PRAED. Sir George Crofts, an old friend of Mrs Warren's. I think we had better come in.

(*On their way to the porch they are interrupted by a call from the gate. Turning, they see an elderly clergyman looking over it.*)

THE CLERGYMAN. (*Calling.*) Frank!

485 FRANK. Hallo! (*To Praed.*) The Roman father. (*To The Clergyman.*) Yes, gov'nor: all right: presently. (*To Praed.*) Look here, Praed: youd better go in to tea. I'll join you directly.

PRAED. Very good. (*He goes into the cottage.*)

(*The Clergyman remains outside the gate, with his hands on the top of it. The Rev. Samuel Gardner, a beneficed[2] clergyman of the Established Church,[3] is over 50. Externally he is pretentious, booming, noisy, important. Really he is that obsolescent social phenomenon the fool of the family dumped on the Church by his father the patron, clamorously asserting himself as father and clergyman without being able to command respect in either capacity.*)

490 REV. S. Well, sir. Who are your friends here, if I may ask?

FRANK. Oh, it's all right, gov'nor! Come in.

REV. S. No, sir; not until I know whose garden I am entering.

495 FRANK. It's all right. It's Miss Warren's.

REV. S. I have not seen her at church since she came.

FRANK. Of course not: she's a third wrangler. Ever so intellectual. Took a higher degree than you did; so why should she go to hear you preach?

500 REV. S. Dont be disrespectful, sir.

FRANK. Oh, it dont matter: nobody hears us. Come in. (*He opens the gate, unceremoniously pulling his father with it into the garden.*) I want to introduce you to her. Do you remember the advice you gave me last July, gov'nor?

505 REV. S. (*Severely.*) Yes. I advised you to conquer your idleness and flippancy, and to work your way into an honorable profession and live on it and not upon me.

FRANK. No: thats what you thought of afterwards. What you actually said was that since I had neither brains nor money, I'd better turn my good looks to account by marrying somebody with both. Well, look here, Miss Warren has brains: you cant deny that.

REV. S. Brains are not everything.

FRANK. No, of course not: theres the money—

515 REV. S. (*Interrupting him austerely.*) I was not thinking of money sir. I was speaking of higher things. Social position, for instance.

FRANK. I dont care a rap about that.

REV. S. But I do, sir.

520 FRANK. Well, nobody wants y o u to marry her. Anyhow, she has what amounts to a high Cambridge degree;[4] and she seems to have as much money as she wants.

REV. S. (*Sinking into a feeble vein of humor.*) I greatly doubt whether she has as much money as you will want.

FRANK. Oh, come: I havnt been so very extravagant. I live ever so quietly; I dont drink; I dont bet much; and I never go regularly on the razzle-dazzle as you did when you were my age.

530 REV. S. (*Booming hollowly.*) Silence, sir.

FRANK. Well, you told me yourself, when I was making ever such an ass of myself about the barmaid at Redhill,

---

[1] *Redhill* Small town about 25 miles south of London. Frank's "folly" with the barmaid is not further explained, but it hints at the nature of his pre-Vivie relationships.

[2] *beneficed* Supported by the church (with house and salary).

[3] *Established Church* Church of England.

[4] *Cambridge degree* Vivie has not actually been awarded a degree by Cambridge, only, as Frank says, "what amounts to one." Although women were allowed to attend lectures and sit examinations at Cambridge in the nineteenth century, they were not awarded degrees until 1921.

that you once offered a woman £50 for the letters you wrote to her when—

535 REV. S. (*Terrified.*) Sh-sh-sh, Frank, for Heaven's sake! (*He looks around apprehensively. Seeing no one within earshot he plucks up courage to boom again, but more subduedly.*) You are taking an ungentlemanly advantage of what I confided to you for your own good, to save

540 you from an error you would have repented all your life long. Take warning by your father's follies, sir; and dont make them an excuse for your own.

FRANK. Did you ever hear the story of the Duke of Wellington and his letters?

545 REV. S. No, sir; and I dont want to hear it.

FRANK. The old Iron Duke didnt throw away £50: not he. He just wrote: "Dear Jenny: publish and be damned! Yours affectionately, Wellington." Thats what you should have done.[1]

550 REV. S. (*Piteously.*) Frank, my boy: when I wrote those letters I put myself into that woman's power. When I told you about them I put myself, to some extent, I am sorry to say, in your power. She refused my money with these words, which I shall never forget. "Knowledge is

555 power," she said; "and I never sell power." Thats more than twenty years ago; and she has never made use of her power or caused me a moment's uneasiness. You are behaving worse to me than she did, Frank.

FRANK. Oh yes I dare say! Did you ever preach at her

560 the way you preach at me every day?

REV. S. (*Wounded almost to tears.*) I leave you, sir. You are incorrigible. (*He turns toward the gate.*)

FRANK. (*Utterly unmoved.*) Tell them I shant be home to tea, will you, gov'nor, like a good fellow? (*He moves*

565 *towards the cottage door and is met by Praed and Vivie coming out.*)

VIVIE. (*To Frank.*) Is that your father, Frank? I do so want to meet him.

FRANK. Certainly. (*Calling after his father.*) Gov'nor.

570 Youre wanted. (*The parson turns at the gate, fumbling*

nervously at his hat. *Praed crosses the garden to the opposite side, beaming in anticipation of civilities.*) My father: Miss Warren.

VIVIE. (*Going to The Clergyman. and shaking his hand.*)

575 Very glad to see you here, Mr Gardner. (*Calling to the cottage.*) Mother: come along: youre wanted.

(*Mrs Warren appears on the threshold, and is immediately transfixed recognizing The Clergyman.*)

VIVIE. (*Continuing.*) Let me introduce—

MRS WARREN. (*Swooping on the Reverend Samuel.*) Why, it's Sam Gardner, gone into the church! Well, I

580 never! Dont you know us, Sam? This is George Crofts, as large as life and twice as natural. Dont you remember me?

REV. S. (*Very red.*) I really—er—

MRS WARREN. Of course you do. Why, I have a whole

585 album of your letters still: I came across them only the other day.

REV. S. (*Miserably confused.*) Miss Vavasour,[2] I believe.

MRS WARREN. (*Correcting him quickly in a loud whisper.*) Tch! Nonsense! Mrs Warren: Don't you see

590 my daughter there?

ACT 2

(*Inside the cottage after nightfall. Looking eastward from within instead of westward from without, the latticed window, with its curtains drawn, is now seen in the middle of the front wall of the cottage, with the porch door to the left of it. In the left-hand side wall is the door leading to the kitchen. Farther back against the same wall is a dresser with a candle and matches on it, and Frank's rifle standing beside them, with the barrel resting in the plate-rack. In the centre a table stands with a lighted lamp on it. Vivie's books and writing materials are on a table to the right of the window, against the wall. The fireplace is on the right with a settle:[3] there is no fire. Two of the chairs are set right*

---

[1] *Thats what you should have done* Arthur Wellesley, 1st Duke of Wellington (1769–1852), defeated Napoleon at Waterloo in 1815. He later served as Prime Minister, 1828–30. His comment "Publish and be damned" was in response to a blackmail letter concerning a London courtesan well-known to Wellington. Wellington's iron-fisted discipline in military matters caused him to be known as the Iron Duke.

[2] *Miss Vavasour* Name used by Mrs Warren at the time the Reverend Samuel knew her. A vavasour was a medieval vassal owing allegiance to a great lord.

[3] *settle* A wooden bench with high back and arms, and a box or draw under the seat.

and left of the table.

    The cottage door opens, shewing a fine starlit night without; and Mrs Warren, her shoulders wrapped in a shawl borrowed from Vivie, enters, followed by Frank, who throws his cap on the window seat. She has had enough of walking, and gives a gasp of relief as she unpins her hat; takes it off; sticks the pin through the crown; and puts it on the table.)

MRS WARREN.   O Lord! I dont know which is the worst of the country, the walking or the sitting at home with nothing to do. I could do with a whisky and soda now very well, if only they had such a thing in this place.

5 FRANK.   Perhaps Vivie's got some.

MRS WARREN.   Nonsense! What would a young girl like her be doing with such things! Never mind: it dont matter. I wonder how she passes her time here! I'd a good deal rather be in Vienna.

10 FRANK.   Let me take you there. (*He helps her to take off her shawl, gallantly giving her shoulders a very perceptible squeeze*[1] *as he does so.*)

MRS WARREN.   Ah! would you? I'm beginning to think youre a chip of the old block.[2]

15 FRANK.   Like the gov'nor, eh? (*He hangs the shawl on the nearest chair and sits down.*)

MRS WARREN.   Never you mind. What do you know about such things? Youre only a boy. (*She goes to the hearth, to be farther from temptation.*)

20 FRANK.   Do come to Vienna with me. It'd be ever such larks.

MRS WARREN.   No, thank you. Vienna is no place for you—at least not until youre a little older. (*She nods at him to emphasize this piece of advice. He makes a mock-*
25 *piteous face, belied by his laughing eyes. She looks at him; then comes back to him.*) Now, look here, little boy. (*Taking his face in her hands and turning it up to her.*) I know you through and through by your likeness to your father, better than you know yourself. Dont you go
30 taking any silly ideas into your head about me. Do you hear?

FRANK.   (*Gallantly wooing her with his voice.*) Cant help it, my dear Mrs Warren: it runs in the family.

(*She pretends to box his ears; then looks at the pretty laughing upturned face for a moment, tempted. At last she kisses him, and immediately turns away, out of patience with herself.*)

35 MRS WARREN.   There! I shouldnt have done that. I am wicked. Never mind, my dear: it's only a motherly kiss. Go and make love to Vivie.

FRANK.   So I have.

MRS WARREN.   (*Turning on him with a sharp note of alarm in her voice.*) What!

40 FRANK.   Vivie and I are ever such chums.

MRS WARREN.   What do you mean? Now see here: I wont have any young scamp tampering with my little girl. Do you hear? I wont have it.

FRANK.   (*Quite unabashed.*) My dear Mrs Warren: dont
45 you be alarmed. My intentions are honorable: ever so honorable; and your little girl is jolly well able to take care of herself. She dont need looking after half so much as her mother. She aint so handsome, you know.

MRS WARREN.   (*Taken aback by his assurance.*) Well, you
50 have got a nice healthy two inches thick of cheek all over you. I dont know where you got it. Not from your father, anyhow.

CROFTS.   (*In the garden.*) The gipsies, I suppose?

REV. S.   (*Replying.*) The broomsquires[3] are far worse.

55 MRS WARREN.   (*To Frank.*) Sh-sh! Remember! youve had your warning.

(*Crofts and the Reverend Samuel come in from the garden, The Clergyman continuing his conversation as he enters.*)

REV. S.   The perjury at the Winchester assizes[4] is deplorable.

MRS WARREN.   Well? what became of you two? And
60 wheres Praddy and Vivie?

---

[1] *squeeze*   In the 1898 text Frank's "*very perceptible squeeze*" is "*the most delicate possible little caress.*"

[2] *chip of the old block*   "Chip *off* the old block" is relatively recent usage. "Chip *of* the old block" was standard in Shaw's time.

[3] *broomsquires*   Itinerant makers and vendors of brooms made from a bunch of heather or twigs.

[4] *Winchester assizes*   Courts of law held periodically in Winchester, as in other counties in England, for the administering of civil and criminal justice. Shaw may have had a particular case in mind, but it has not been traced. The line does not appear in the 1898 text.

CROFTS. (*Putting his hat on the settle and his stick in the chimney corner.*) They went up the hill. We went to the village. I wanted a drink. (*He sits down on the settle, putting his legs up along the seat.*)

65 MRS WARREN. Well she oughtnt go off like that without telling me. (*To Frank.*) Get your father a chair, Frank: where are your manners? (*Frank springs up and gracefully offers his father his chair; then takes another from the wall and sits down at the table, in the middle, with his*

70 *father on his right and Mrs Warren on his left.*) George: where are you going to stay tonight? You cant stay here. And whats Praddy going to do?

CROFTS. Gardner'll put me up.

MRS WARREN. Oh, no doubt youve taken care of

75 yourself! But what about Praddy?

CROFTS. Dont know. I suppose he can sleep at the inn.

MRS WARREN. Havnt you room for him, Sam?

REV. S. Well—er—you see, as rector here, I am not free to do as I like. Er—what is Mr Praed's social position?

80 MRS WARREN. Oh, he's all right: he's an architect. What an old stick-in-the-mud you are, Sam!

FRANK. Yes, it's all right, gov'nor. He built that place down in Wales for the Duke. Caernarvon Castle they call it. You must have heard of it. (*He winks with*

85 *lightning smartness at Mrs Warren, and regards his father blandly.*)

REV. S. Oh, in that case, of course we shall only be too happy. I suppose he knows the Duke personally.

FRANK. Oh, ever so intimately! We can stick him in

90 Georgina's old room.

MRS WARREN. Well, thats settled. Now if only those two would only come in and let us have supper. Theyve no right to stay out after dark like this.

CROFTS. (*Aggressively.*) What harm are they doing you?

95 MRS WARREN. Well, harm or not, I dont like it.

FRANK. Better not wait for them, Mrs Warren. Praed will stay out as long as possible. He has never known before what it is to stray over the heath on a summer night with my Vivie.

100 CROFTS. (*Sitting up in some consternation.*) I say, you know! Come!

REV. S. (*Rising, startled out of his professional manner into real force and sincerity.*) Frank, once for all, it's out of the question. Mrs Warren will tell you that it's not to be

105 thought of.

CROFTS. Of course not.

FRANK. (*With enchanting placidity.*) Is that so, Mrs Warren?

MRS WARREN. (*Reflectively.*) Well, Sam, I dont know.

110 If the girl wants to get married, no good can come of keeping her unmarried.

REV. S. (*Astounded.*) But married to h i m!—your daughter to my son! Only think: it's impossible.

CROFTS. Of course it's impossible. Dont be a fool,

115 Kitty.

MRS WARREN. (*Nettled.*) Why not? Isnt my daughter good enough for your son?

REV. S. But surely, my dear Mrs Warren, you know the reasons—

120 MRS WARREN. (*Defiantly.*) I know no reasons. If you know any, you can tell them to the lad, or to the girl, or to your congregation, if you like.

REV. S. (*Collapsing helplessly into his chair.*) You know very well that I couldnt tell anyone the reasons. But my

125 boy will believe me when I tell him there a r e reasons.

FRANK. Quite right, Dad: he will. But has your boy's conduct ever been influenced by your reasons?

CROFTS. You cant marry her; and thats all about it. (*He gets up and stands on the hearth, with his back to the*

130 *fireplace, frowning determinedly.*)

MRS WARREN. (*Turning on him sharply.*) What have you got to do with it, pray?

FRANK. (*With his prettiest lyrical cadence.*) Precisely what I was going to ask myself, in my own graceful fashion.

135 CROFTS. (*To Mrs Warren.*) I suppose you dont want to marry the girl to a man younger than herself and without either a profession or twopence to keep her on. Ask Sam, if you dont believe me. (*To the parson.*) How much more money are you going to give him?

140 REV. S. Not another penny. He has had his patrimony and he spent the last of it in July. (*Mrs Warren's face falls.*)

CROFTS. (*Watching her.*) There! I told you. (*He resumes his place on the settle and puts his legs on the seat again, as*

145 *if the matter were finally disposed of.*)

FRANK. (*Plaintively.*) This is ever so mercenary. Do you suppose Miss Warren's going to marry for money? If we love one another—

MRS WARREN. Thank you. Your love's a pretty cheap

150 commodity, my lad. If you have no means of keeping a

wife, that settles it: you cant have Vivie.

FRANK.   (*Much amused.*) What do y o u say, gov'nor, eh?

REV. S.   I agree with Mrs Warren.

FRANK.   And good old Crofts has already expressed his
155   opinion.

CROFTS.   (*Turning angrily on his elbow.*) Look here: I
want none of y o u r cheek.

FRANK.   (*Pointedly.*) I'm e v e r so sorry to surprise you,
Crofts, but you allowed yourself the liberty of speaking
160   to me like a father a moment ago. One father is enough,
thank you.

CROFTS.   (*Contemptuously.*)   Yah! (*He turns away again.*)

FRANK.   (*Rising.*) Mrs Warren: I cannot give my Vivie
up, even for your sake.

165   MRS WARREN.   (*Muttering.*) Young scamp!

FRANK.   (*Continuing.*) And as you no doubt intend to
hold out other prospects to her, I shall lose no time in
placing my case before her. (*They stare at him, and he
begins to declaim gracefully*)

170   He either fears his fate too much,
            Or his deserts are small,
            That dares not put it to the touch
            To gain or lose it all.[1]

(*The cottage door opens whilst he is reciting; and Vivie and
Praed come in. He breaks off. Praed puts his hat on the
dresser. There is an immediate improvement in the
company's behavior. Crofts takes down his legs from the
settle and pulls himself together as Praed joins him at the
fireplace. Mrs Warren loses her ease of manner and takes
refuge in querulousness.[2]*)

MRS WARREN.   Wherever have you been, Vivie?

175   VIVIE.   (*Taking off her hat and throwing it carelessly on the
table.*) On the hill.

MRS WARREN.   Well, you shouldnt go off like that
without letting me know. How could I tell what had
become of you? And night coming on too!

180   VIVIE.   (*Going to the door of the kitchen and opening it,
ignoring her mother.*) Now, about supper? (*All rise except
Mrs Warren.*) We shall be rather crowded in here, I'm
afraid.

MRS WARREN.   Did you hear what I said, Vivie?

185   VIVIE.   (*Quietly.*) Yes, mother. (*Reverting to the supper
difficulty.*) How many are we? (*Counting.*) One, two,
three, four, five, six. Well, two will have to wait until
the rest are done: Mrs Alison has only plates and knives
for four.

190   PRAED.   Oh, it doesnt matter about me. I—

VIVIE.   You have had a long walk and are hungry, Mr
Praed: you shall have your supper at once. I can wait
myself. I want one person to wait with me. Frank: are
you hungry?

195   FRANK.   Not the least in the world. Completely off my
peck,[3] in fact.

MRS WARREN.   (*To Crofts.*) Neither are you, George.
You can wait.

CROFTS.   Oh, hang it, Ive eaten nothing since tea-time.
200   Cant Sam do it?

FRANK.   Would you starve my poor father?

REV. S.   (*Testily.*) Allow me to speak for myself, sir. I am
perfectly willing to wait.

VIVIE.   (*Decisively.*) Theres no need. Only two are
205   wanted. (*She opens the door of the kitchen.*) Will you take
my mother in, Mr Gardner. (*The parson takes Mrs
Warren; and they pass into the kitchen. Praed and Crofts
follow. All except Praed clearly disapprove of the
arrangement, but do not know how to resist it. Vivie stands
210   at the door looking in at them.*) Can you squeeze past to
that corner, Mr Praed: it's a rather tight fit. Take care of
your coat against the white-wash: thats right. Now, are
you all comfortable?

PRAED.   (*Within.*) Quite, thank you.

215   MRS WARREN.   (*Within.*) Leave the door open, dearie.
(*Vivie frowns; but Frank checks her with a gesture, and
steals to the cottage door, which he softly sets wide open.*)
Oh Lor, what a draught! Youd better shut it, dear.

---

[1]   *He either ... all*   From "My Dear and Only Love," a poem by the
Scottish soldier and writer James Graham, Marquess of Montrose
(1612–50). Frank slightly misquotes. "He either fears his fate too
much, / Or his deserts are small, / That puts it not unto the touch
/ To win or lose it all."

[2]   *querulousness*   Petulance.

[3]   *off my peck*   Not hungry.

(Vivie shuts it with a slam,[1] and then, noting with disgust that her mother's hat and shawl are lying about, takes them tidily to the window seat, whilst Frank noiselessly shuts the cottage door.)

FRANK.   (*Exulting.*) Aha! Got rid of em. Well, Vivvums: what do you think of my governor?

VIVIE.   (*Preoccupied and serious.*) Ive hardly spoken to him. He doesnt strike me as being a particularly able person.

FRANK.   Well, you know, the old man is not altogether such a fool as he looks. You see, he was shoved into the church rather; and in trying to live up to it he makes a much bigger ass of himself than he really is. I dont dislike him as much as you might expect. He means well. How do you think youll get on with him?

VIVIE.   (*Rather grimly.*) I dont think my future life will be much concerned with him, or with any of that old circle of my mother's, except perhaps Praed. (*She sits down on the settle.*) What do you think of my mother?

FRANK.   Really and truly?

VIVIE.   Yes, really and truly.

FRANK.   Well, she's ever so jolly. But she's rather a caution,[2] isnt she? And Crofts! oh, my eye, Crofts! (*He sits beside her.*)

VIVIE.   What a lot, Frank!

FRANK.   What a crew!

VIVIE.   (*With intense contempt for them.*) If I thought that *I* was like that—that I was going to be a waster, shifting along from one meal to another with no purpose, and no character, and no grit in me, I'd open an artery and bleed to death without one moment's hesitation.

FRANK.   Oh no, you wouldnt. Why should they take any grind when they can afford not to? I wish I had their luck. No: what I object to is their form. It isnt the thing: it's slovenly, ever so slovenly.

VIVIE.   Do you think your form will be any better when youre as old as Crofts, if you dont work?

FRANK.   Of course I do. Ever so much better. Vivvums musnt lecture: her little boy is incorrigible. (*He attempts to take her face caressingly in his hands.*)

VIVIE.   (*Striking his hands down sharply.*) Off with you: Vivvums is not in a humor for petting her little boy this evening. (*She rises and comes forward to the other side of the room.*)

FRANK.   (*Following her.*) How unkind!

VIVIE.   (*Stamping at him.*) Be serious. I'm serious.

FRANK.   Good. Let us talk learnedly. Miss Warren: do you know that all the most advanced thinkers are agreed that half the diseases of modern civilization are due to starvation of the affections in the young. Now, I—

VIVIE.   (*Cutting him short.*) You are very tiresome. (*She opens the inner door.*) Have you room for Frank there? He's complaining of starvation.

MRS WARREN.   (*Within.*) Of course there is (*Clatter of knives and glasses as she moves the things on the table.*)

Here! theres room now beside me. Come along, Mr Frank.

FRANK.   Her little boy will be ever so even with his Vivvums for this. (*He passes into the kitchen.*)

MRS WARREN.   (*Within.*) Here, Vivie: come on you too, child. You must be famished. (*She enters, followed by Crofts, who holds the door open for Vivie with marked deference. She goes out without looking at him; and shuts the door after her.*) Why, George, you cant be done: youve eaten nothing. Is there anything wrong with you?

CROFTS.   Oh, all I wanted was a drink. (*He thrusts his hands in his pockets, and begins prowling around the room, restless and sulky.*)

MRS WARREN.   Well, I like enough to eat. But a little of that cold beef and cheese and lettuce goes a long way. (*With a sigh of only half repletion she sits down lazily on the settle.*)

CROFTS.   What do you go encouraging that young pup for?

MRS WARREN.   (*On the alert at once.*) Now see here, George: what are you up to about that girl? Ive been watching your way of looking at her. Remember: I know you and what your looks mean.

CROFTS.   Theres no harm in looking at her, is there?

MRS WARREN.   I'd put you out and pack you back to London pretty soon if I saw any of your nonsense. My girl's little finger is more to me than any of your body and soul. (*Crofts receives this with a sneering grin. Mrs Warren, flushing a little at her failure to impose on him in the character of a theatrically devoted mother, adds in a*

---

[1]   *with a slam*   In the 1898 text Vivie merely shuts the door "promptly."

[2]   *a caution*   Eccentric person; a "bit of a character."

300 lower key.) Make your mind easy: the young pup has no more chance than you have.

CROFTS. Maynt a man take an interest in a girl?

MRS WARREN. Not a man like you.

CROFTS. How old is she?

305 MRS WARREN. Never you mind how old she is.

CROFTS. Why do you make such a secret of it?

MRS WARREN. Because I choose.

CROFTS. Well, I'm not fifty yet; and my property is as good as ever it was—

310 MRS WARREN. (*Interrupting him.*) Yes, because youre as stingy as youre vicious.

CROFTS. (*Continuing.*) And a baronet[1] isnt to be picked up every day. No other man in my position would put up with you for a mother-in-law. Why shouldnt she

315 marry me?

MRS WARREN. You!

CROFTS. We three could live together quite comfortably: I'd die before her and leave her a bouncing widow with plenty of money. Why not? It's been growing in

320 my mind all the time Ive been walking with that fool inside there.

MRS WARREN. (*Revolted.*) Yes: it's the sort of thing that w o u l d grow in your mind.

(*He halts in his prowling; and the two look at one another, she steadfastly, with a sort of awe behind her contemptuous disgust: he stealthily, with a carnal gleam in his eye and a loose grin.*)

325 CROFTS. (*Suddenly becoming anxious and urgent as he sees no sign of sympathy in her.*) Look here, Kitty: youre a sensible woman: you neednt put on any moral airs. I'll ask no more questions; and you need answer none. I'll settle the whole property on her; and if you want a cheque for yourself on the wedding day, you can name

330 any figure you like—in reason.

MRS WARREN. So it's come to that with you, George, like all the other worn-out old creatures!

CROFTS. (*Savagely.*) Damn you!

(*Before she can retort[2] the door of the kitchen is opened; and the voices of the others are heard returning. Crofts, unable to recover his presence of mind, hurries out of the cottage. The Clergyman appears at the kitchen door.*)

REV. S. (*Looking around.*) Where is Sir George?

335 MRS WARREN. Gone out to have a pipe. (*The Clergyman takes his hat from the table, and joins Mrs Warren at the fireside. Meanwhile Vivie comes in, followed by Frank, who collapses into the nearest chair with an air of extreme exhaustion. Mrs Warren looks round at Vivie

340 and says, with her affectation of maternal patronage ever more forced than usual.*) Well, dearie, have you had a good supper?

VIVIE. You know what Mrs Alison's suppers are. (*She turns to Frank and pets him.*) Poor Frank! was all the beef

345 gone? did it get nothing but bread and cheese and ginger beer? (*Seriously, as if she had done quite enough trifling for one evening.*) Her butter is really awful. I must get some down from the stores.

FRANK. Do, in Heaven's name!

(*Vivie goes to the writing-table and makes a memorandum to order the butter. Praed comes in from the kitchen, putting up his handkerchief, which he has been using as a napkin.*)

350 REV. S. Frank, my boy: it is time for us to be thinking of home. Your mother does not know yet that we have visitors.

PRAED. I'm afraid we're giving trouble.

FRANK. (*Rising.*) Not the least in the world: my mother

355 will be delighted to see you. She's a genuinely intellectual artistic woman; and she sees nobody here from one year's end to another except the gov'nor; so you can imagine how jolly dull it pans out for her. (*To his father.*) Y o u r e not intellectual or artistic: are you

360 pater? So take Praed home at once; and I'll stay here and entertain Mrs Warren. Youll pick up Crofts in the garden. He'll be excellent company for the bull-pup.[3]

PRAED. (*Taking his hat from the dresser, and coming close

---

1 *baronet* The lowest of Britain's hereditary titles, established in 1611. It confers a knighthood, however: hence, *Sir* George Crofts. His wife would be titled *Lady* Crofts.

2 *Before she can retort* In the 1898 text Mrs Warren is given more time: "*She rises and turns fiercely on him.*"

3 *bull-pup* Sarcastic reference to Praed. He's not a bull-*dog*.

to Frank.) Come with us, Frank. Mrs Warren has not
seen Miss Vivie for a long time; and we have prevented
them from having a moment together yet.

FRANK. (*Quite softened and looking at Praed with romantic admiration.*) Of course. I forgot. Ever so thanks for reminding me. Perfect gentleman, Praddy. Always were. My ideal through life. (*He rises to go, but pauses a moment between the two older men, and puts his hand on Praed's shoulder.*) Ah, if you had only been my father instead of this unworthy old man! (*He puts his other hand on his father's shoulder.*)

REV. S. (*Blustering.*) Silence, sir, silence: you are profane.

MRS WARREN. (*Laughing heartily.*) You should keep him in better order, Sam. Goodnight. Here: take George his hat and stick with my compliments.

REV. S. (*Taking them.*) Goodnight. (*They shake hands. As he passes Vivie he shakes hands with her also and bids her goodnight. Then, in booming command, to Frank.*) Come along, sir, at once. (*He goes out.*)

MRS WARREN. Byebye, Praddy.

PRAED. Byebye, Kitty.

(*They shake hands affectionately and go out together, she accompanying him to the garden gate.*)

FRANK. (*To Vivie.*) Kissums?

VIVIE. (*Fiercely.*) No. I hate you.[1] (*She takes a couple of books and some paper from the writing-table, and sits down with them at the middle table, at the end next the fireplace.*)

FRANK. (*Grimacing.*) Sorry. (*He goes for his cap and rifle. Mrs Warren returns. He takes her hand.*) Goodnight, d e a r Mrs Warren. (*He kisses her hand.[2] She snatches it away, her lips tightening, and looks more than half disposed to box his ears. He laughs mischievously and runs off, clapping-to[3] the door behind him.*)

MRS WARREN. (*Resigning herself to an evening of boredom now that the men are gone.*) Did you ever in your life hear anyone rattle on so? Isnt he a tease? (*She

sits at the table.*) Now that I think of it, dearie, dont you go encouraging him. I'm sure he's a regular good-for-nothing.

VIVIE. (*Rising to fetch more books.*) I'm afraid so. Poor Frank! I shall have to get rid of him; but I shall feel sorry for him, though he's not worth it. That man Crofts does not seem to me to be good for much either: is he? (*She throws the books on the table rather roughly.*)

MRS WARREN. (*Galled by Vivie's indifference.[4]*) What do you know of men, child, to talk that way about them? Youll have to make up your mind to see a good deal of Sir George Crofts, as he's a friend of mine.

VIVIE. (*Quite unmoved.*) Why? (*She sits down and opens a book.*) Do you expect that we shall be much together? You and I, I mean?

MRS WARREN. (*Staring at her.*) Of course: until youre married. Youre not going back to college again.

VIVIE. Do you think my way of life would suit you? I doubt it.

MRS WARREN. Y o u r way of life! What do you mean?

VIVIE. (*Cutting a page[5] of her book with the paper knife on her chatelaine.*) Has it really never occurred to you, mother, that I have a way of life like other people?

MRS WARREN. What nonsense is this youre trying to talk? Do you want to shew your independence, now that youre a great little person at school? Dont be a fool, child.

VIVIE. (*Indulgently.*) Thats all you have to say on the subject, is it, mother?

MRS WARREN. (*Puzzled, then angry.*) Dont you keep on asking me questions like that. (*Violently.*) Hold your tongue. (*Vivie works on, losing no time, and saying nothing.*) You and your way of life, indeed! What next? (*She looks at Vivie again. No reply.*) Your way of life will be what I please, so it will. (*Another pause.*) Ive been noticing these airs in you ever since you got that tripos or whatever you call it. If you think I'm going to put up with them youre mistaken; and the sooner you find it out, the better. (*Muttering.*) All I have to say on the subject, indeed! (*Again raising her voice angrily.*) Do you know who youre speaking to, Miss?

VIVIE. (*Looking across at her without raising her head

---

[1] *I hate you* In the 1898 text Frank "*silently begs a kiss,*" and receives in return from Vivie "*a stern glance,*" rather than her fierce comment.

[2] *kisses her hand* In the 1898 text Frank "*squeezes*" Mrs Warren's hand.

[3] *clapping-to* Slamming.

[4] *Vivie's indifference* In the 1898 text Mrs Warren is galled by Vivie's "*cool tone,*" rather than her indifference.

[5] *Cutting a page* Books were sold with their pages uncut, that is, as folded by the binder.

440 *from her book*.) No. Who are you? What are you?

MRS WARREN. (*Rising breathless*.) You young imp!

VIVIE. Everybody knows my reputation, my social standing, and the profession I intend to pursue. I know nothing about you. What is that way of life which you

445 invite me to share with you and Sir George Crofts, pray?

MRS WARREN. Take care. I shall do something I'll be sorry for after, and you too.

VIVIE. (*Putting aside her books with cool decision*.) Well, let us drop the subject until you are better able to face it.

450 (*Looking critically at her mother*.) You want some good walks and a little lawn tennis to set you up. You are shockingly out of condition: you were not able to manage twenty yards uphill today without stopping to pant; and your wrists are mere rolls of fat. Look at mine.

455 (*She holds out her wrists*.)

MRS WARREN. (*After looking at her helplessly, begins to whimper*.) Vivie—

VIVIE. (*Springing up sharply*.) Now pray dont begin to cry. Anything but that. I really cannot stand

460 whimpering. I will go out of the room if you do.

MRS WARREN. (*Piteously*.) Oh, my darling, how can you be so hard on me? Have I no rights over you as your mother?

VIVIE. A r e you my mother?

465 MRS WARREN. (*Appalled*.) A m I your mother! Oh, Vivie!

VIVIE. Then where are our relatives? my father? our family friends? You claim the rights of a mother: the right to call me fool and child; to speak to me as no

470 woman in authority over me at college dare speak to me; to dictate my way of life; and to force on me the acquaintance of a brute whom any one can see to be the most vicious sort of London man about town. Before I give myself the trouble to resist such claims, I may as

475 well find out whether they have any real existence.

MRS WARREN. (*Distracted, throwing herself on her knees*.) Oh no, no. Stop, stop. I a m your mother, I swear it. Oh, you cant mean to turn on me—my own child! it's not natural. You believe me, dont you? Say you believe

480 me.

VIVIE. Who was my father?

MRS WARREN. You dont know what youre asking. I cant tell you.

VIVIE. (*Determinedly*.) Oh yes you can, if you like. I

485 have a right to know; and you know very well that I have that right. You can refuse to tell me, if you please; but if you do you will see the last of me tomorrow morning.

MRS WARREN. Oh, it's too horrible to hear you talk like

490 that. You wouldnt—you c o u l d n t leave me.

VIVIE. (*Ruthlessly*.) Yes, without a moment's hesitation, if you trifle with me about this. (*Shivering with disgust*.) How can I feel sure that I may not have the contaminated blood of that brutal waster in my veins?

495 MRS WARREN. No, no. On my oath it's not he, nor any of the rest that you have ever met. I'm certain of that, at least.

(*Vivie's eyes fasten sternly on her mother as the significance of this flashes on her*.)

VIVIE. (*Slowly*.) You are certain of that, at l e a s t. Ah! You mean that that is all you are certain of. (*Thoughtfully*.) I see. (*Mrs Warren buries her face in her*

500 *hands*.) Dont do that, mother: you know you dont feel it a bit. (*Mrs Warren takes down her hands and looks up deplorably at Vivie, who takes out her watch and says*) Well, that is enough for tonight. At what hour would

505 you like breakfast? Is half-past eight too early for you?

MRS WARREN. (*Wildly*.) My God, what sort of woman are you?

VIVIE. (*Coolly*.) The sort the world is mostly made of, I should hope. Otherwise I dont understand how it gets

510 its business done. Come (*taking her mother by the wrist, and pulling her up pretty resolutely*): pull yourself together. Thats right.

MRS WARREN. (*Querulously*.) Youre very rough with me, Vivie.

515 VIVIE. Nonsense. What about bed? It's past ten.

MRS WARREN. (*Passionately*.) Whats the use of my going to bed? Do you think I could sleep?

VIVIE. Why not? I shall.

MRS WARREN. You! youve no heart. (*She suddenly*

520 *breaks out vehemently in her natural tongue—the dialect of a woman of the people—with all her affectations of maternal authority and conventional manners gone, and an overwhelming inspiration of true conviction and scorn in her*.) Oh, I wont bear it: I wont put up with the

525 injustice of it. What right have you to set yourself up

above m e like this? You boast of what you are to me—to me, who gave you the chance of being what you are. What chance had I? Shame on you for a bad daughter and a stuck-up prude!

530 VIVIE. (*Sitting down with a shrug,*[1] *no longer confident; for her replies, which have sounded sensible and strong to her so far, now begin to ring rather woodenly and even priggishly against the new tone of her mother.*) Dont think for a moment I set myself up against you in any way.
535 You attacked me with the conventional authority of a mother: I defended myself with the conventional superiority of a respectable woman. Frankly, I am not going to stand any of your nonsense; and when you drop it I shall not expect you to stand any of mine. I
540 shall always respect your right to your own opinions and your own way of life.

MRS WARREN. My own opinions and my own way of life! Listen to her talking! Do you think I was brought up like you? able to pick and choose my own way of life?
545 Do you think I did what I did because I liked it, or thought it right, or wouldnt rather have gone to college and been a lady if I'd had the chance?

VIVIE. Everybody has some choice, mother. The poorest girl alive may not be able to choose between being
550 Queen of England or Principal of Newnham; but she can choose between ragpicking and flowerselling, according to her taste. People are always blaming their circumstances for what they are. I dont believe in circumstances. The people who get on in this world are
555 the people who get up and look for the circumstances they want, and, if they cant find them, make them.

MRS WARREN. Oh, it's easy to talk, very easy, isnt it? Here! would you like to know what m y circumstances were?

560 VIVIE. Yes: you had better tell me. Wont you sit down?

MRS WARREN. Oh, I'll sit down: dont you be afraid. (*She plants her chair farther forward with brazen energy, and sits down. Vivie is impressed in spite of herself.*) D'you know what your gran'mother was?

565 VIVIE. No.

MRS WARREN. No, you dont. I do. She called herself a widow and had a fried-fish shop down by the Mint,[2] and kept herself and four daughters out of it. Two of us were sisters: that was me and Liz; and we were both
570 good-looking and well made. I suppose our father was a well-fed man: mother pretended he was a gentleman; but I dont know. The other two were only half sisters: undersized, ugly, starved looking, hard working, honest poor creatures: Liz and I would have half-murdered
575 them if mother hadnt half-murdered u s to keep our hands off them. They were the respectable ones. Well, what did they get by their respectability? I'll tell you. One of them worked in a whitelead factory[3] twelve hours a day for nine shillings a week until she died of
580 lead poisoning. She only expected to get her hands a little paralyzed; but she died. The other was always held up to us as a model because she married a Government laborer in the Deptford victualling yard,[4] and kept his room and the three children neat and tidy on eighteen
585 shillings a week—until he took to drink. That was worth being respectable for, wasnt it?

VIVIE. (*Now thoughtfully attentive.*) Did you and your sister think so?

MRS WARREN. Liz didnt, I can tell you: she had more
590 spirit. We both went to a church school—that was part of the ladylike airs we gave ourselves to be superior to the children that knew nothing and went nowhere— and we stayed there until Liz went out one night and never came back. I know the schoolmistress thought I'd
595 soon follow her example; for the clergyman was always warning me that Lizzie'd end by jumping off Waterloo Bridge.[5] Poor fool: that was all he knew about it! But I was more afraid of the whitelead factory than I was of

---

1 *with a shrug* In the 1898 text Vivie is still "*cool and determined*" at this point.

2 *the Mint* The Royal Mint is the official manufacturer of British coinage. In Shaw's time it was located in working-class East End London. It moved in 1968 to its present location in Llantrisant, South Wales.

3 *whitelead factory* Whitelead is a mixture of lead carbonate and hydrated lead oxide used as a white pigment in paint.

4 *Deptford victualling yard* The Royal Victualling Yard—for providing supplies and provisions for the Royal Navy—was established at Deptford (on the River Thames) in 1742.

5 *Waterloo Bridge* Waterloo Bridge connects Victoria Embankment with Waterloo on the south bank of the Thames in London. The original bridge (built in 1817) was demolished in 1936 and replaced with the present structure.

the river; and so would you have been in my place. That clergyman got me a situation as scullery[1] maid in a temperance restaurant[2] where they sent out for anything you liked. Then I was waitress; and then I went to the bar at Waterloo station:[3] fourteen hours a day serving drinks and washing glasses for four shillings a week and my board. That was considered a great promotion for me. Well, one cold, wretched night, when I was so tired I could hardly keep myself awake, who should come up for a half of scotch[4] but Lizzie, in a long fur cloak, elegant and comfortable, with a lot of sovereigns[5] in her purse.

VIVIE. (*Grimly.*) My aunt Lizzie!

MRS WARREN.   Yes; and a very good aunt to have, too. She's living down at Winchester[6] now, close to the cathedral, one of the most respectable ladies there. Chaperones girls at the county ball, if you please. No river for Liz, thank you! You remind me of Liz a little: she was a first-rate business woman—saved money from the beginning—never let herself look too like what she was—never lost her head or threw away a chance. When she saw I'd grown up good-looking she said to me across the bar "What are you doing there, you little fool? wearing out your health and your appearance for other people's profit!" Liz was saving money then to take a house for herself in Brussels; and she thought we two could save faster than one. So she lent me some money and gave me a start; and I saved steadily and first paid her back, and then went into business with her as her partner. Why shouldnt I have done it? The house in Brussels was real high class: a much better place for a woman to be in than the factory where Anne Jane got poisoned. None of our girls were ever treated as I was treated in the scullery of that temperance place, or at the Waterloo bar, or at home. Would you have had me stay in them and become a worn-out old drudge before I was

forty?

VIVIE.   (*Intensely interested by this time.*) No, but why did you choose that business? Saving money and good management will succeed in any business.

MRS WARREN.   Yes, saving money. But where can a woman get the money to save in any other business? Could you save out of four shillings a week and keep yourself dressed as well? Not you. Of course, if youre a plain woman and cant earn anything more; or if you have a turn for music, or the stage, or newspaper-writing: thats different. But neither Liz nor I had any turn for such things: all we had was our appearance and our turn for pleasing men. Do you think we were such fools as to let other people trade in our good looks by employing us as shopgirls, or barmaids, or waitresses, when we could trade in them ourselves and get all the profits instead of starvation wages? Not likely.

VIVIE.   You were certainly quite justified—from the business point of view.

MRS WARREN.   Yes; or any other point of view. What is any respectable girl brought up to do but to catch some rich man's fancy and get the benefit of his money by marrying him?—as if a marriage ceremony could make any difference in the right or wrong of the thing! Oh, the hypocrisy of the world makes me sick! Liz and I had to work and save and calculate just like other people; elseways[7] we should be as poor as any good-for-nothing drunken waster of a woman that thinks her luck will last forever. (*With great energy.*) I despise such people: theyve no character; and if theres a thing I hate in a woman, it's want of character.

VIVIE.   Come now, mother: Frankly! Isn't it part of what you call character in a woman that she should greatly dislike such a way of making money?

MRS WARREN.   Why, of course. Everybody dislikes having to work and make money; but they have to do it all the same. I'm sure Ive often pitied a poor girl, tired out and in low spirits, having to try to please some man that she doesnt care two straws for—some half-drunken fool that thinks he's making himself agreeable when he's teasing and worrying and disgusting a woman so that hardly any money could pay her for putting up with it. But she has to bear with disagreeables and take the

---

[1] *scullery* Small room adjacent to the kitchen used mainly for washing dishes.

[2] *temperance restaurant* Restaurant that does not serve alcohol.

[3] *Waterloo station* Then, and now, one of London's principal railway stations.

[4] *half of scotch* Large glass of Scotch whisky.

[5] *sovereigns* Gold coins worth £1.

[6] *Winchester* City about 65 miles southwest of London.

[7] *elseways* Otherwise.

rough with the smooth, just like a nurse in a hospital or anyone else. It's not work that any woman would do for pleasure, goodness knows; though to hear the pious people talk you would suppose it was a bed of roses.

VIVIE. Still, you consider it worth while. It pays.

MRS WARREN. Of course it's worth while to a poor girl, if she can resist temptation and is good-looking and well conducted and sensible. It's far better than any other employment open to her. I always thought that oughtnt to be. It c a n t be right, Vivie, that there shouldnt be better opportunities for women. I stick to that: it's wrong. But it's so, right or wrong; and a girl must make the best of it. But of course it's not worth while for a lady. If you took to it youd be a fool; but I should have been a fool if I'd taken to anything else.

VIVIE. (More and more deeply moved.) Mother: suppose we were both as poor as you were in those wretched old days, are you quite sure that you wouldnt advise me to try the Waterloo bar, or marry a laborer, or even go into the factory?

MRS WARREN. (Indignantly.) Of course not. What sort of mother do you take me for! How could you keep your self-respect in such starvation and slavery? And whats a woman worth? whats life worth? without self-respect! Why am I independent and able to give my daughter a first-rate education, when other women that had just as good opportunities are in the gutter? Because I always knew how to respect myself and control myself. Why is Liz looked up to in a cathedral town? The same reason. Where would we be now if we'd minded the clergyman's foolishness? Scrubbing floors for one and sixpence a day and nothing to look forward to but the workhouse infirmary.[1] Dont you be led astray by people who dont know the world, my girl. The only way for a woman to provide for herself decently is for her to be good to some man that can afford to be good to her. If she's in his own station of life, let her make him marry her; but if she's far beneath him she cant expect it: why should she? it wouldnt be for her own happiness. Ask

___

[1] *workhouse infirmary* Workhouses, which supported the sick and the indigent, had existed in England since the early seventeenth century. The Poor Law Amendment Act of 1834 limited assistance to the able-bodied poor and made conditions as uncomfortable as possible. Most workhouses had their own infirmaries where rudimentary medical help was provided. Workhouses were phased out in England by about 1930.

any lady in London society that has daughters; and she'll tell you the same, except that I tell you straight and she'll tell you crooked. Thats all the difference.

VIVIE. (Fascinated, gazing at her.) My dear mother: you are a wonderful woman: you are stronger than all England. And are you really and truly not one wee bit doubtful—or—or—ashamed?

MRS WARREN. Well, of course, dearie, it's only good manners to be ashamed of it: it's expected from a woman. Women have to pretend to feel a great deal that they dont feel. Liz used to be angry with me for plumping out the truth about it. She used to say that when every woman could learn enough from what was going on in the world before her eyes, there was no need to talk about it to her. But then Liz was such a perfect lady! She had the true instinct of it; while I was always a bit of a vulgarian. I used to be so pleased when you sent me your photos to see that you were growing up like Liz: youve just her ladylike, determined way. But I cant stand saying one thing when everyone knows I mean another. Whats the use in such hypocrisy? If people arrange the world that way for women, there's no good pretending it's arranged the other way. No: I never was a bit ashamed really. I consider I had a right to be proud of how we managed everything so respectably, and never had a word against us, and how the girls were so well taken care of. Some of them did very well: one of them married an ambassador. But of course now I darent talk about such things: whatever would they think of us! (She yawns.) Oh dear! I do believe I'm getting sleepy after all. (She stretches herself lazily, thoroughly relieved by her explosion, and placidly ready for her night's rest.)

VIVIE. I believe it is I who will not be able to sleep now. (She goes to the dresser and lights the candle. Then she extinguishes the lamp, darkening the room a good deal.) Better let in some fresh air before locking up. (She opens the cottage door, and finds that it is a broad moonlight.) What a beautiful night! Look! (She draws aside the curtains of the window. The landscape is seen bathed in the radiance of the harvest moon rising over Blackdown.[2])

MRS WARREN. (With a perfunctory glance of the scene.) Yes, dear; but take care you dont catch your death of

___

[2] *Blackdown* Prominent hill about three miles south of Haslemere.

760 cold from the night air.

VIVIE. (*Contemptuously.*) Nonsense.

MRS WARREN. (*Querulously.*) Oh yes: everything I say is nonsense, according to you.

VIVIE. (*Turning to her quickly.*) No: really that is not so, 765 mother. You have got completely the better of me tonight, though I intended it to be the other way. Let us be good friends now.

MRS WARREN. (*Shaking her head a little ruefully.*) So it has been the other way. But I suppose I must give in to 770 it. I always got the worst of it from Liz; and now I suppose it'll be the same with you.

VIVIE. Well, never mind. Come: goodnight, dear old mother. (*She takes her mother in her arms.*)

MRS WARREN. (*Fondly.*) I brought you up well, didnt I, 775 dearie?

VIVIE. You did.

MRS WARREN. And youll be good to your poor old mother for it, wont you?

VIVIE. I will, dear. (*Kissing her.*) Goodnight.

780 MRS WARREN. (*With unction.*) Blessings on my own dearie darling! a mother's blessing!

(*She embraces her daughter protectingly, instinctively looking upward for divine sanction.*)

ACT 3

(*In the Rectory garden next morning, with the sun shining from a cloudless sky. The garden wall has a five-barred wooden gate, wide enough to admit a carriage, in the middle. Beside the gate hangs a bell on a coiled spring, communicating with a pull outside. The carriage drive comes down the middle of the garden and then swerves to its left, where it ends in a little gravelled circus[1] opposite the Rectory porch. Beyond the gate is seen the dusty high road, parallel with the wall, bounded on the farther side by a strip of turf and an unfenced pine wood. On the lawn, between the house and the drive, is a clipped yew tree, with a garden bench in its shade. On the opposite side the garden is shut in by a box hedge; and there is a sundial on the turf, with an iron chair near it. A little path leads off through*)

the box hedge, behind the sundial.

Frank, seated on the chair near the sundial, on which he has placed the morning papers, is reading The Standard.[2] His father comes from the house, red-eyed and shivery, and meets Frank's eye with misgiving.)

FRANK. (*Looking at his watch.*) Half-past eleven. Nice hour for a rector to come down to breakfast!

REV. S. Dont mock, Frank: dont mock. I am a little— er—(*Shivering.*)—

5 FRANK. Off color?

REV. S. (*Repudiating the expression.*) No, sir: u n w e l l this morning. Wheres your mother?

FRANK. Dont be alarmed: she's not here. Gone to town by the 11.13 with Bessie. She left several messages for 10 you. Do you feel equal to receiving them now, or shall I wait til you have breakfasted?

REV. S. I h a v e breakfasted, sir. I am surprised at your mother going to town when we have people staying with us. Theyll think it very strange.

15 FRANK. Possibly she has considered that. At all events, if Crofts is going to stay here, and you are going to sit up every night with him until four, recalling the incidents of your fiery youth, it is clearly my mother's duty, as a prudent housekeeper, to go up to the stores 20 and order a barrel of whisky and a few hundred siphons.[3]

REV. S. I did not observe that Sir George drank excessively.

FRANK. You were not in a condition to, gov'nor.

25 REV. S. Do you mean to say that I—?

FRANK. (*Calmly.*) I never saw a beneficed clergyman less sober. The anecdotes you told about your past career were so awful that I really dont think Praed would have passed the night under your roof if it hadnt been for the 30 way my mother and he took to one another.

REV. S. Nonsense, sir. I am Sir George Crofts' host. I must talk to him about something; and he has only one subject. Where is Mr Praed now?

FRANK. He is driving my mother and Bessie to the 35 station.

---

[1] *circus* Circular driveway.

[2] *The Standard* A leading London daily newspaper, first published in 1827.

[3] *siphons* Bottles of soda (to mix with the whisky).

REV. S.   Is Crofts up yet?

FRANK.   Oh, long ago. He hasnt turned a hair: he's in much better practice than you. He has kept it up ever since, probably. He's taken himself off somewhere to smoke.

(*Frank resumes his paper. The parson turns disconsolately towards the gate; then comes back irresolutely.*)

REV. S.   Er—Frank.

FRANK.   Yes.

REV. S.   Do you think the Warrens will expect to be asked here after yesterday afternoon?

FRANK.   Theyve been asked already.

REV. S.   (*Appalled.*) What!!!

FRANK.   Crofts informed us at breakfast that you told him to bring Mrs Warren and Vivie over here today, and to invite them to make this house their home. My mother then found she must go to town by the 11.13 train.

REV. S.   (*With despairing vehemence.*) I never gave any such invitation. I never thought of such a thing.

FRANK.   (*Compassionately.*) How do you know, gov'nor, what you said and thought last night?

PRAED.   (*Coming in through the hedge.*) Good morning.

REV. S.   Good morning. I must apologize for not having met you at breakfast. I have a touch of—of—

FRANK.   Clergyman's sore throat, Praed. Fortunately not chronic.

PRAED.   (*Changing the subject.*) Well, I must say your house is in a charming spot here. Really most charming.

REV. S.   Yes: it is indeed. Frank will take you for a walk, Mr Praed, if you like. I'll ask you to excuse me: I must take the opportunity to write my sermon while Mrs Gardner is away and you are all amusing yourself. You wont mind, will you?

PRAED.   Certainly not. Dont stand on the slightest ceremony with me.

REV. S.   Thank you. I'll—er—er—(*He stammers his way to the porch and vanishes into the house.*)

PRAED.   Curious thing it must be writing a sermon every week.

FRANK.   Ever so curious, if h e did it. He buys em. He's gone for some soda water.

PRAED.   My dear boy: I wish you would be more respectful to your father. You know you can be so nice when you like.

FRANK.   My dear Praddy: you forget that I have to live with the governor. When two people live together—it dont matter whether theyre father and son or husband and wife or brother and sister—they cant keep up the polite humbug thats so easy for ten minutes on an afternoon call. Now the governor, who unites to many admirable domestic qualities the irresoluteness of a sheep and the pompousness and aggressiveness of a jackass—

PRAED.   No, pray, pray, my dear Frank, remember! He is your father.

FRANK.   I give him due credit for that. (*Rising and flinging down his paper.*) But just imagine his telling Crofts to bring the Warrens over here! He must have been ever so drunk. You know, my dear Praddy, my mother wouldnt stand Mrs Warren for a moment. Vivie mustnt come here until she has gone back to town.

PRAED.   But your mother doesnt know anything about Mrs Warren, does she? (*He picks up the paper and sits down to read it.*)

FRANK.   I dont know. Her journey to town looks as if she did. Not that my mother would mind in the ordinary way: she has stuck like a brick to lots of women who had got into trouble. But they were all nice women. Thats what makes the real difference. Mrs Warren, no doubt, has her merits; but she's ever so rowdy; and my mother simply wouldnt put up with her. So—hallo! (*This exclamation is provoked by the reappearance of the clergyman, who comes out of the house in haste and dismay.*)

REV. S.   Frank: Mrs Warren and her daughter are coming across the heath with Crofts: I saw them from the study windows. What a m I to say about your mother?

FRANK.   Stick on your hat and go out and say how delighted you are to see them; and that Frank's in the garden; and that mother and Bessie have been called to the bedside of a sick relative, and were ever so sorry that they couldnt stop; and that you hope Mrs Warren slept well; and—and—say any blessed thing except the truth, and leave the rest to Providence.

REV. S.   But how are we to get rid of them afterwards?

FRANK.   Theres no time to think of that now. Here! (*He

bounds into the house.)

REV. S.   He's so impetuous. I dont know what to do with him, Mr Praed.

125   FRANK.   (*Returning with a clerical felt hat, which he claps on his father's head.*) Now: off with you. (*Rushing him through the gate.*) Praed and I'll wait here, to give the thing an unpremeditated air. (*The clergyman, dazed but obedient, hurries off.*)

130   FRANK.   We must get the old girl back to town somehow, Praed. Come! Honestly, dear Praddy, do you like seeing them together?

PRAED.   Oh, why not?

FRANK.   (*His teeth on edge.*) Dont it make your flesh

135   creep ever so little? that wicked old devil, up to every villainy under the sun, I'll swear, and Vivie—ugh!

PRAED.   Hush, pray. Theyre coming.

(*The clergyman and Crofts are seen coming along the road, followed by Mrs Warren and Vivie walking affectionately together.*)

FRANK.   Look: she actually has her arm round the old woman's waist. It's her right arm: she began it. She's

140   gone sentimental, by God! Ugh! ugh! Now do you feel the creeps? (*The clergyman opens the gate; and Mrs Warren and Vivie pass him and stand in the middle of the garden looking at the house. Frank, in an ecstasy of dissimulation, turns gaily to Mrs Warren, exclaiming*) Ever

145   so delighted to see you, Mrs Warren. This quiet old rectory garden becomes you perfectly.

MRS WARREN.   Well, I never! Did you hear that, George? He says I look well in a quiet old rectory

150   garden.

REV. S.   (*Still holding the gate for Crofts who loafs through it, heavily bored.*) You look well everywhere, Mrs Warren.

FRANK.   Bravo, gov'nor! Now look here: lets have a treat before lunch. First lets see the church. Everyone has to

155   do that. It's a regular old thirteenth century church, you know: the gov'nor's ever so fond of it, because he got up a restoration fund and had it completely rebuilt six years ago. Praed will be able to shew its points.

PRAED.   (*Rising.*) Certainly, if the restoration has left any

160   to shew.

REV. S.   (*Mooning[1] hospitably at them.*) I shall be pleased, I'm sure, if Sir George and Mrs Warren really care about it.

MRS WARREN.   Oh, come along and get it over.

165   CROFTS.   (*Turning back towards the gate.*) Ive no objection.

REV. S.   Not that way. We go through the fields, if you dont mind. Round here. (*He leads the way by the little path through the box hedge.*)

170   CROFTS.   Oh, all right. (*He goes with the parson.*)

(*Praed follows with Mrs Warren. Vivie does not stir: she watches them until they have gone, with all the lines of purpose in her face marking it strongly.*)

FRANK.   Aint you coming?

VIVIE.   No. I want to give you a warning, Frank. You were making fun of my mother just now when you said that about the rectory garden. That is barred in the

175   future. Please treat my mother with as much respect as you treat your own.

FRANK.   My dear Viv: she wouldnt appreciate it: the two cases require different treatment. But what on earth has happened to you? Last night we were perfectly agreed as

180   to your mother and her set. This morning I find you attitudinizing sentimentally with your arm round your parent's waist.

VIVIE.   (*Flushing.*) Attitudinizing!

FRANK.   That was how it struck me. First time I ever saw

185   you do a second-rate thing.

VIVIE.   (*Controlling herself.*) Yes, Frank: there has been a change; but I dont think it a change for the worse. Yesterday I was a little prig.

FRANK.   And today?

190   VIVIE.   (*Wincing; then looking at him steadily.*) Today I know my mother better than you do.

FRANK.   Heaven forbid!

VIVIE.   What do you mean?

FRANK.   Viv: theres a freemasonry among thoroughly

195   immoral people that you know nothing of. Youve too much character. T h a t s the bond between your mother and me: thats why I know her better than youll ever know her.

---

[1]   *Mooning*   Listlessly, without energy (he has a hangover).

VIVIE.   You are wrong: you know nothing about her. If
you knew the circumstances against which my mother
had to struggle—

FRANK.   (*Adroitly finishing the sentence for her.*) I should
know why she is what she is, shouldnt I? What
difference would that make? Circumstances or no
circumstances, Viv, you wont be able to stand your
mother.

VIVIE.   (*Very angrily.*) Why not?

FRANK.   Because she's an old wretch, Viv. If you ever
put your arm round her waist in my presence again, I'll
shoot myself there and then as a protest against an
exhibition which revolts me.

VIVIE.   Must I choose between dropping your acquaintance and dropping my mother's?

FRANK.   (*Gracefully.*) That would put the old lady at ever
such a disadvantage. No, Viv; your infatuated little boy
will have to stick to you in any case. But he's all the
more anxious that you shouldnt make mistakes. It's no
use, Viv: your mother's impossible. She may be a good
sort; but she's a bad lot, a very bad lot.

VIVIE.   (*Hotly.*) Frank—! (*He stands his ground. She turns
away and sits down on the bench under the yew tree,
struggling to recover her self-command. Then she says*) Is
she to be deserted by all the world because she's what
you call a bad lot? Has she no right to live?

FRANK.   No fear of that, Viv: she wont ever be deserted.
(*He sits on the bench beside her.*)

VIVIE.   But I am to desert her, I suppose.

FRANK.   (*Babyishly, lulling her and making love to her
with his voice.*) Musnt go live with her. Little family
group of mother and daughter wouldnt be a success.
Spoil o u r little group.

VIVIE.   (*Falling under the spell.*) What little group?

FRANK.   The babes in the wood: Vivie and little Frank.
(*He nestles against her like a weary child.*) Lets go and get
covered up with leaves.

VIVIE.   (*Rhythmically, rocking him like a nurse.*) Fast
asleep, hand in hand, under the trees.

FRANK.   The wise little girl with her silly little boy.

VIVIE.   The dear little boy with his dowdy little girl.

FRANK.   Ever so peaceful, and relieved from the
imbecility of the little boy's father and the
questionableness of the little girl's—

VIVIE.   (*Smothering the word against her breast.*) Sh-sh-sh-

sh! little girl wants to forget all about her mother. (*They
are silent for some moments, rocking one another. Then
Vivie wakes up with a shock, exclaiming*) What a pair of
fools we are! Come: sit up. Gracious! your hair. (*She
smooths it.*) I wonder do all grown up people play in that
childish way when nobody is looking. I never did it
when I was a child.

FRANK.   Neither did I. You are my first playmate. (*He
catches her hand to kiss it, but checks himself to look round
first. Very unexpectedly, he sees Crofts emerging from the
box hedge.*) Oh damn!

VIVIE.   Why damn, dear?

FRANK.   (*Whispering.*) Sh! Heres this brute Crofts. (*He
sits farther away from her with an unconcerned air.*)[1]

CROFTS.   Could I have a few words with you, Miss
Vivie?

VIVIE.   Certainly.

CROFTS.   (*To Frank.*) Youll excuse me, Gardner. Theyre
waiting for you in the church, if you dont mind.

FRANK.   (*Rising.*) Anything to oblige you, Crofts—
except church. If you should happen to want me,
Vivvums, ring the gate bell. (*He goes into the house with
unruffled suavity.*)

CROFTS.   (*Watching him with a crafty air as he disappears,
and speaking to Vivie with an assumption of being on
privileged terms with her.*) Pleasant young fellow that,
Miss Vivie. Pity he has no money, isnt it?

VIVIE.   Do you think so?

CROFTS.   Well, whats he to do? No profession. No
property. Whats he good for?

VIVIE.   I realize his disadvantages, Sir George.

CROFTS.   (*A little taken aback at being so precisely
interpreted.*) Oh, it's not that. But while we're in this
world, we're in it; and money's money. (*Vivie does not
answer.*) Nice day, isnt it?

VIVIE.   (*With scarcely veiled contempt for this effort at
conversation.*) Very.

CROFTS.   (*With brutal good humor, as if he liked her
pluck.*) Well, thats not what I came to say. (*Sitting down
beside her.*) Now listen, Miss Vivie I'm quite aware that
I'm not a young lady's man.

VIVIE.   Indeed, Sir George?

[1]   At this point in the 1898 text Vivie says: "Dont be rude to him,
Frank. I particularly want to be polite to him. It will please my
mother."

CROFTS. No; and to tell you the honest truth I dont want to be either. But when I say a thing I mean it; when I feel a sentiment I feel it in earnest; and what I value I pay hard money for. Thats the sort of man I am.

290 VIVIE. It does you great credit, I'm sure.

CROFTS. Oh, I dont mean to praise myself. I have my faults, Heaven knows: no man is more sensible of[1] that than I am. I know I'm not perfect; thats one of the advantages of being a middle-aged man; for I'm not a

295 young man, and I know it. But my code is a simple one, and, I think, a good one. Honor between man and man; fidelity between man and woman; and no cant about this religion or that religion, but an honest belief that things are making for good on the whole.

300 VIVIE. (With biting irony.) "A power, not ourselves, that makes for righteousness,"[2] eh?

CROFTS. (Taking her seriously.) Oh certainly. Not ourselves, of course. You understand what I mean. Well, now as to practical matters. You may have an idea that

305 I have flung my money about; but I havnt: I'm richer today than when I first came into the property. Ive used my knowledge of the world to invest my money in ways that other men have overlooked; and whatever else I may be, I'm a safe man from the money point of view.

310 VIVIE. It's very kind of you to tell me all this.

CROFTS. Oh well, come, Miss Vivie: you neednt pretend you dont see what I'm driving at. I want to settle down with a Lady Crofts. I suppose you think me very blunt, eh?

315 VIVIE. Not at all: I am much obliged to you for being so definite and business-like. I quite appreciate the offer: the money, the position, L a d y C r o f t s and so on. But I think I will say no, if you dont mind. I'd rather not. (She rises, and strolls across to the sundial to get out of

320 his immediate neighborhood.)

CROFTS. (Not at all discouraged, and taking advantage of the additional room left him on the seat to spread himself comfortably, as if a few preliminary refusals were part of the inevitable routine of courtship.) I'm in no hurry. It

325 was only just to let you know in case young Gardner should try to trap you. Leave the question open.

---

[1] sensible of Aware of.

[2] A power ... righteousness Matthew Arnold, Literature and Dogma (1873), chapter 8: "The eternal not ourselves that makes for righteousness."

VIVIE. (Sharply.) My no is final. I wont go back from it.

(Crofts is not impressed. He grins; leans forward with his elbows on his knees to prod with his stick at some unfortunate insect in the grass; and looks cunningly at her. She turns away impatiently.)

CROFTS. I'm a good deal older than you. Twenty-five years: quarter of a century. I shant live forever; and I'll

330 take care that you shall be well off when I'm gone.

VIVIE. I am proof against even that inducement, Sir George. Dont you think youd better take your answer? There is not the slightest chance of my altering it.

CROFTS. (Rising, after a final slash at a daisy, and coming

335 nearer to her.) Well, no matter. I could tell you some things that would change your mind fast enough; but I wont, because I'd rather win you by honest affection. I was a good friend to your mother: ask her whether I wasnt. She'd never have made the money that paid for

340 your education if it hadnt been for my advice and help, not to mention the money I advanced her. There are not many men who would have stood by her as I have. I put not less than £40,000 into it, from first to last.

VIVIE. (Staring at him.) Do you mean to say you were

345 my mother's business partner?

CROFTS. Yes. Now just think of all the trouble and the explanations it would save if we were to keep the whole thing in the family, so to speak. Ask your mother whether she'd like to have to explain all her affairs to a

350 perfect stranger.

VIVIE. I see no difficulty, since I understand that the business is wound up, and the money invested.

CROFTS. (Stopping short, amazed.) Wound up! Wind up a business thats paying 35 per cent in the worst years!

355 Not likely. Who told you that?

VIVIE. (Her color quite gone.) Do you mean that it is still—? (She stops abruptly, and puts her hand on the sundial to support herself. Then she gets quickly to the iron chair and sits down.) What business are you talking

360 about?

CROFTS. Well, the fact is it's not what would be considered exactly a high-class business in my set—the country set, you know—o u r set it will be if you think better of my offer. Not that theres any mystery about it:

365 dont think that. Of course you know by your mother's being in it that it's perfectly straight and honest. Ive

known her for many years; and I can say of her that she'd cut off her hands sooner than touch anything that was not what it ought to be. I'll tell you all about it if you like. I dont know whether youve found in travelling how hard it is to find a really comfortable private hotel.

VIVIE. (*Sickened, averting her face.*) Yes: go on.

CROFTS. Well, thats all it is. Your mother has a genius for managing such things. Weve got two in Brussels, one in Ostend, one in Vienna and two in Budapest.[1] Of course there are others besides ourselves in it: but we hold most of the capital; and your mother's indispensable as managing director. Youve noticed, I dare say, that she travels a good deal. But you see you cant mention such things in society. Once let out the word hotel and everybody says you keep a public-house. You wouldnt like people to say that of your mother, would you? Thats why we're so reserved about it. By the way, youll keep it to yourself, wont you? Since its been a secret so long, it had better remain so.

VIVIE. And this is the business you invite me to join you in?

CROFTS. Oh, no. My wife shant be troubled with business. Youll not be in it more than youve always been.

VIVIE. *I* always been! What do you mean?

CROFTS. Only that youve always lived on it. It paid for your education and the dress you have on your back. Dont turn up your nose at business, Miss Vivie; where would your Newnhams and Girtons be without it?

VIVIE. (*Rising, almost beside herself.*) Take care. I know what this business is.

CROFTS. (*Starting, with a suppressed oath.*) Who told you?

VIVIE. Your partner. My mother.

CROFTS. (*Black with rage.*) The old—

VIVIE. Just so.

(*He swallows the epithet and stands for a moment swearing and raging foully to himself. But he knows that his cue is to be sympathetic. He takes refuge in generous indignation.*)

CROFTS. She ought to have had more consideration

for you. *I'd* never have told you.

VIVIE. I think you would probably have told me when we were married: it would have been a convenient weapon to break me in with.

CROFTS. (*Quite sincerely.*) I never intended that. On my word as a gentleman I didnt.

(*Vivie wonders at him. Her sense of the irony of his protest cools and braces her. She replies with contemptuous self-possession.*)

VIVIE. It does not matter. I suppose you understand that when we leave here today our acquaintance ceases.

CROFTS. Why? Is it for helping your mother?

VIVIE. My mother was a very poor woman who had no reasonable choice but to do as she did. You were a rich gentleman; and you did the same for the sake of 35 per cent. You are a pretty common sort of scoundrel, I think. That is my opinion of you.

CROFTS. (*After a stare: not at all displeased, and much more at his ease on these frank terms than on their former ceremonious ones.*) Ha! ha! ha! ha! Go it, little missie, go it; it doesnt hurt me and it amuses you. Why the devil shouldnt I invest my money that way? I take the interest on my capital like other people: I hope you dont think I dirty my own hands with the work. Come! you wouldnt refuse the acquaintance of my mother's cousin the Duke of Belgravia[2] because some of the rents he gets are earned in queer ways. You wouldnt cut the Archbishop of Canterbury,[3] I suppose, because the Ecclesiastical Commissioners[4] have a few publicans and sinners among their tenants. Do you remember your Crofts scholarship at Newnham? Well, that was founded by my brother the M.P. He gets his 22 per cent out of a factory with 600 girls in it, and not one of them

---

[1] *Weve got … Budapest* In the 1898 text the count of brothels is slightly different: two in Brussels, one in Berlin, one in Vienna, and two in Budapest.

[2] *Belgravia* Belgravia was (and is) a fashionable and expensive residential area of London. The title "Duke of Belgravia" is fictitious.

[3] *Archbishop of Canterbury* The Archbishop of Canterbury in office at the time that Shaw was writing *Mrs Warren's Profession* was Edward White Benson (1829–96), Archbishop from 1882 to his death.

[4] *Ecclesiastical Commissioners* A body established in 1836 to buy, sell, and manage land and property and oversee other business operations for the Church of England. It consisted of leading ecclesiastics, politicians, and judges.

getting wages enough to live on. How d'ye suppose they manage when they have no family to fall back on? Ask your mother. And do you expect me to turn my back on 35 per cent when all the rest are pocketing what they can, like sensible men? No such fool! If youre going to pick and choose your acquaintances on moral principles, youd better clear out of this country, unless you want to cut yourself out of all decent society.

VIVIE. (*Conscience stricken.*) You might go on to point out that I myself never asked where the money I spent came from. I believe I am just as bad as you.

CROFTS. (*Greatly reassured.*) Of course you are; and a very good thing too! What harm does it do after all? (*Rallying her jocularly.*) So you dont think me such a scoundrel now you come to think it over. Eh?

VIVIE. I have shared profits with you; and I admitted you just now to the familiarity of knowing what I think of you.

CROFTS. (*With serious friendliness.*) To be sure you did. You wont find me a bad sort: I dont go in for being superfine intellectually: but Ive plenty of honest human feeling; and the old Crofts breed comes out in a sort of instinctive hatred of anything low, in which I'm sure youll sympathize with me. Believe me, Miss Vivie, the world isnt such a bad place as the croakers[1] make out. As long as you dont fly openly in the face of society, society doesnt ask any inconvenient questions; and it makes precious short work of the cads who do. There are no secrets better kept than the secrets everybody guesses. In the class of people I can introduce you to, no lady or gentleman would so far forget themselves as to discuss my business affairs or your mother's. No man can offer you a safer position.

VIVIE. (*Studying him curiously.*) I suppose you really think youre getting on famously with me.

CROFTS. Well, I hope I may flatter myself that you think better of me than you did at first.

VIVIE. (*Quietly.*[2]) I hardly find you worth thinking about at all now. When I think of the society that tolerates you, and the laws that protect you! when I think of how helpless nine out of ten young girls would be in the hands of you and my mother! the unmentionable woman and her capitalist bully—

CROFTS. (*Livid.*) Damn you!

VIVIE. You need not. I feel among the damned already.

(*She raises the latch of the gate to open it and go out. He follows her and puts his hand heavily on the top bar to prevent its opening.*)

CROFTS. (*Panting with fury.*) Do you think I'll put up with this from you, you young devil?

VIVIE. (*Unmoved.*) Be quiet. Some one will answer the bell. (*Without flinching a step she strikes the bell with the back of her hand. It clangs harshly; and he starts back involuntarily. Almost immediately Frank appears at the porch with his rifle.*)

FRANK. (*With cheerful politeness.*) Will you have the rifle, Viv; or shall I operate?

VIVIE. Frank: have you been listening?

FRANK. (*Coming down into the garden.*) Only for the bell, I assure you; so that you shouldnt have to wait. I think I shewed great insight into your character, Crofts.

CROFTS. For two pins I'd take that gun from you and break it across your head.

FRANK. (*Stalking him cautiously.*) Pray dont. I'm ever so careless in handling firearms. Sure to be a fatal accident, with a reprimand from the coroner's jury for my negligence.

VIVIE. Put the rifle away, Frank; it's quite unnecessary.

FRANK. Quite right, Viv. Much more sportsmanlike to catch him in a trap. (*Crofts, understanding the insult, makes a threatening movement.*) Crofts: there are fifteen cartridges in the magazine here; and I am a dead shot at the present distance and at an object of your size.

CROFTS. Oh, you neednt be afraid. I'm not going to touch you.

FRANK. Ever so magnanimous of you under the circumstances! Thank you!

CROFTS. I'll just tell you this before I go. It may interest you, since youre so fond of one another. Allow me, Mr Frank, to introduce you to your half-sister, the eldest daughter of the Reverend Samuel Gardner. Miss Vivie: your half-brother. Good morning. (*He goes out through the gate along the road.*)

FRANK. (*After a pause of stupefaction, raising the rifle.*)

---

[1] *croakers* Those who speak dismally, forebodingly.

[2] *Quietly* The 1898 text specifies that Vivie speaks to Crofts "*almost gently, but with intense conviction.*"

515 Youll testify before the coroner that its an accident, Viv. (*He takes aim at the retreating figure of Crofts. Vivie seizes the muzzle and pulls it round against her breast.*)

VIVIE. Fire now. You may.

FRANK. (*Dropping his end of the rifle hastily.*) Stop! take
520 care. (*She lets it go. It falls on the turf.*) Oh, youve given your little boy such a turn. Suppose it had gone off! ugh! (*He sinks on the garden seat overcome.*)

VIVIE.   Suppose it had: do you think it would not have been a relief to have some sharp physical pain tearing
525 through me?

FRANK. (*Coaxingly.*) Take it ever so easy, dear Viv. Remember: even if the rifle scared that fellow into telling the truth for the first time in his life, that only makes us the babes in the wood in earnest. (*He holds out
530 his arms to her.*) Come and be covered up with leaves again.

VIVIE. (*With a cry of disgust.*) Ah, not that, not that. You make all my flesh creep.

FRANK.   Why, whats the matter?

535 VIVIE. Goodbye. (*She makes for the gate.*)

FRANK. (*Jumping up.*) Hallo! Stop! Viv! Viv! (*She turns in the gateway.*) Where are you going to? Where shall we find you?

VIVIE. At Honoria Fraser's chambers, 67 Chancery
540 Lane, for the rest of my life. (*She goes off quickly in the opposite direction to that taken by Crofts.*)

FRANK.   But I say—wait dash it! (*He runs after her.*)

ACT 4

(*Honoria Fraser's chambers in Chancery Lane. An office at the top of New Stone Buildings, with a plate-glass window, distempered[1] walls, electric light, and a patent stove.[2] Saturday afternoon. The chimneys of Lincoln's Inn[3] and the western sky beyond are seen through the window. There is a double writing table in the middle of the room, with a*

cigar box, ash pans,[4] *and a portable electric reading lamp almost snowed up in heaps of papers and books. This table has knee holes and chairs right and left and is very untidy. The clerk's desk, closed and tidy, with its high stool, is against the wall, near a door communicating with the inner rooms. In the opposite wall is the door leading to the public corridor. Its upper panel is of opaque glass, lettered in black on the outside,* Fraser and Warren. *A baize screen hides the corner between this door and the window.*

Frank, in a fashionable light-colored coaching suit, with his stick, gloves, and white hat in his hands, is pacing up and down the office. Somebody tries the door with a key.)

FRANK. (*Calling.*) Come in. It's not locked.

(*Vivie comes in, in her hat and jacket. She stops and stares at him.*)

VIVIE. (*Sternly.*) What are you doing here?

FRANK.   Waiting to see you. Ive been here for hours. Is this the way you attend to your business? (*He puts his hat
5 and stick on the table, and perches himself with a vault on the clerk's stool looking at her with every appearance of being in a specially restless, teasing, flippant mood.*)

VIVIE.   Ive been away exactly twenty minutes for a cup of tea. (*She takes off her hat and jacket and hangs them up
10 behind the screen.*) How did you get in?

FRANK.   The staff had not left when I arrived. He's gone to play cricket on Primrose Hill.[5] Why dont you employ a woman, and give your sex a chance?

VIVIE.   What have you come for?

15 FRANK. (*Springing off the stool and coming close to her.*) Viv: lets go and enjoy the Saturday half-holiday somewhere, like the staff. What do you say to Richmond,[6] and then a music hall,[7] and a jolly supper?

VIVIE.   Cant afford it. I shall put in another six hours
20 work before I go to bed.

---

[1] *distempered* Painted.

[2] *patent stove* Open stove.

[3] *Lincoln's Inn* One of four (Lincoln's Inn, Gray's Inn, Inner Temple, Middle Temple) institutions, all located in London, that have exercised the exclusive right since the Middle Ages of admitting barristers (lawyers) to the bar (i.e., to practice law). Lincoln's Inn is located just off Chancery Lane, near to Honoria Fraser's chambers.

[4] *ash pans* I.e., ashtrays.

[5] *Primrose Hill* Parkland area northwest of central London, frequently visited by Shaw.

[6] *Richmond* Town on the Thames, a few miles southwest of central London.

[7] *music hall* Music halls were popular places of entertainment in Victorian England, featuring songs, comedy, dances, and novelty acts.

FRANK. Cant afford it, cant we? Aha! Look here. (*He takes out a handful of sovereigns and makes them chink.*) Gold, Viv: gold!

VIVIE. Where did you get it?

FRANK. Gambling, Viv: gambling. Poker.

VIVIE. Pah! It's meaner than stealing it. No: I'm not coming. (*She sits down to work at the table, with her back to the glass door, and begins turning over the papers.*)

FRANK. (*Remonstrating piteously.*) But, my dear Viv, I want to talk to you ever so seriously.

VIVIE. Very well: sit down in Honoria's chair and talk here. I like ten minutes chat after tea. (*He murmurs.*) No use groaning: I'm inexorable. (*He takes the opposite seat disconsolately.*) Pass that cigar box, will you?

FRANK. (*Pushing the cigar box across.*) Nasty womanly habit. Nice men dont do it any longer.

VIVIE. Yes: they object to the smell in the office; and weve had to take to cigarets. See! (*She opens the box and takes out a cigaret, which she lights. She offers him one; but he shakes his head with a wry face. She settles herself comfortably in her chair, smoking.*) Go ahead.

FRANK. Well, I want to know what youve done—what arrangements youve made.

VIVIE. Everything was settled twenty minutes after I arrived here. Honoria has found the business too much for her this year; and she was on the point of sending for me and proposing partnership when I walked in and told her I hadnt a farthing[1] in the world. So I installed myself and packed her off for a fortnight's holiday. What happened at Haslemere when I left?

FRANK. Nothing at all. I said you had gone to town on particular business.

VIVIE. Well?

FRANK. Well, either they were too flabbergasted to say anything, or else Crofts had prepared your mother. Anyhow, she didnt say anything; and Crofts didnt say anything; and Praddy only stared. After tea they got up and went; and Ive not seen them since.

VIVIE. (*Nodding placidly with one eye on a wreath of smoke.*) Thats all right.

FRANK. (*Looking round disparagingly.*) Do you intend to stick in this confounded place?

[1] *farthing* A bronze coin, the smallest denomination of British currency (one quarter of a penny). The farthing was withdrawn from circulation in 1961.

VIVIE. (*Blowing the wreath decisively away, and sitting straight up.*) Yes. These two days have given me back all my strength and self-possession. I will never take a holiday again as long as I live.

FRANK. (*With a very wry face.*) Mps! You look quite happy. And as hard as nails.

VIVIE. (*Grimly.*) Well for me that I am!

FRANK. (*Rising.*) Look here, Viv: we must have an explanation. We parted the other day under a complete misunderstanding. (*He sits on the table, close to her.*)

VIVIE. (*Putting away the cigaret.*) Well: clear it up.

FRANK. You remember what Crofts said?

VIVIE. Yes.

FRANK. That revelation was supposed to bring about a complete change in the nature of our feeling for one another. It placed us on the footing of brother and sister.

VIVIE. Yes.

FRANK. Have you ever had a brother?

VIVIE. No.

FRANK. Then you dont know what being brother and sister feels like? Now I have lots of sisters; and the fraternal feeling is quite familiar to me. I assure you my feeling for you is not the least in the world like it. The girls will go their way; I will go mine; and we shant care if we never see one another again. Thats brother and sister. But as to you, I cant be easy if I have to pass a week without seeing you. Thats not brother and sister. It's exactly what I felt an hour before Crofts made his revelation. In short, dear Viv, it's love's young dream.

VIVIE. (*Bitingly.*) The same feeling, Frank, that brought your father to my mother's feet. Is that it?

FRANK. (*So revolted that he slips off the table for a moment.*) I very strongly object, Viv, to have my feelings compared to any which the Reverend Samuel is capable of harboring; and I object still more to a comparison of you to your mother. (*Resuming his perch.*) Besides, I dont believe the story. I have taxed my father with it, and obtained from him what I consider tantamount to a denial.

VIVIE. What did he say?

FRANK. He said he was sure there must be some mistake.

VIVIE. Do you believe him?

FRANK. I am prepared to take his word as against

Crofts'.

VIVIE.   Does it make any difference? I mean in your imagination or conscience; for of course it makes no real difference.

FRANK.   (*Shaking his head.*) None whatever to m e.

VIVIE.   Nor to me.

FRANK.   (*Staring.*) But this is ever so surprising! (*He goes back to his chair.*) I thought our whole relations were altered in your imagination and conscience, as you put it, the moment those words were out of that brute's muzzle.

VIVIE.   No: it was not that. I didnt believe him. I only wish I could.

FRANK.   Eh?

VIVIE.   I think brother and sister would be a very suitable relation for us.

FRANK.   You really mean that?

VIVIE.   Yes. It's the only relation I care for, even if we could afford any other. I mean that.

FRANK.   (*Raising his eyebrows like one on whom a new light has dawned, and rising with quite an effusion of chivalrous sentiment.*) My dear Viv: why didnt you say so before? I am ever so sorry for persecuting you. I understand, of course.

VIVIE.   (*Puzzled.*) Understand what?

FRANK.   Oh, I'm not a fool in the ordinary sense: only in the Scriptural sense of doing all the things the wise man declared to be folly, after trying them himself on the most extensive scale.[1] I see I am no longer Vivvum's little boy. Dont be alarmed: I shall never call you Vivvums again—at least unless you get tired of your new little boy, whoever he may be.

VIVIE.   My new little boy!

FRANK.   (*With conviction.*) Must be a new little boy. Always happens that way. No other way, in fact.

VIVIE.   None that you know of, fortunately for you.

(*Someone knocks at the door.*)

FRANK.   My curse upon yon caller, whoe'er he be!

VIVIE.   It's Praed. He's going to Italy and wants to say goodbye. I asked him to call this afternoon. Go and let him in.

FRANK.   We can continue our conversation after his departure for Italy. I'll stay him out. (*He goes to the door and opens it.*) How are you, Praddy? Delighted to see you. Come in.

(*Praed, dressed for travelling, comes in, in high spirits.*)

PRAED.   How do you do, Miss Warren? (*She presses his hand cordially, though a certain sentimentality in his high spirits jars on her.*) I start in an hour from the Holborn Viaduct.[2] I wish I could persuade you to try Italy.

VIVIE.   What for?

PRAED.   Why, to saturate yourself with beauty and romance, of course.

(*Vivie, with a shudder, turns her chair to the table, as if the work waiting for her there were a support to her. Praed sits opposite to her. Frank places a chair near Vivie, and drops lazily and carelessly into it, talking at her over his shoulder.*)

FRANK.   No use, Praddy. Viv is a little Philistine.[3] She is indifferent to my romance, and insensible to my beauty.

VIVIE.   Mr Praed: once for all, there is no beauty and no romance in life for me. Life is what it is; and I am prepared to take it as it is.

PRAED.   (*Enthusiastically.*) You will not say that if you come with me to Verona and on to Venice. You will cry with delight at living in such a beautiful world.

FRANK.   This is most eloquent, Praddy. Keep it up.

PRAED.   Oh, I assure you *I* have cried—I shall cry again, I hope—at fifty! At your age, Miss Warren, you would not need to go so far as Verona. Your spirits would absolutely fly up at the mere sight of Ostend. You would be charmed with the gaiety, the vivacity, the happy air of Brussels.

VIVIE.   (*Springing up with an exclamation of loathing.*) Agh!

PRAED.   (*Rising.*) Whats the matter?

---

[1]   *extensive scale*   Perhaps a reference to Solomon's comments on folly throughout the Book of Proverbs.

[2]   *Holborn Viaduct*   The Holborn Viaduct opened in London in 1869 as a route for trains over the valley of the Fleet River (which had been covered over since the middle of the eighteenth century).

[3]   *Philistine*   From the historical Philistines, enemies of the Israelites; the modern sense of the word denotes someone hostile or indifferent to culture and the arts.

FRANK. (*Rising.*) Hallo, Viv!

VIVIE. (*To Praed, with deep reproach.*) Can you find no better example of your beauty and romance than Brussels to talk to me about?

PRAED. (*Puzzled.*) Of course it's very different from Verona. I dont suggest for a moment that—

VIVIE. (*Bitterly.*) Probably the beauty and romance come to much the same in both places.

PRAED. (*Completely sobered and much concerned.*) My dear Miss Warren: I—(*Looking inquiringly at Frank.*) Is anything the matter?

FRANK. She thinks your enthusiasm frivolous, Praddy. She's had ever such a serious call.[1]

VIVIE. (*Sharply.*) Hold your tongue, Frank. Dont be silly.

FRANK. (*Sitting down.*) Do you call this good manners, Praed?

PRAED. (*Anxious and considerate.*) Shall I take him away, Miss Warren? I feel sure we have disturbed you at your work.

VIVIE. Sit down: I'm not ready to go back to work yet. (*Praed sits.*) You both think I have an attack of nerves. Not a bit of it. But there are two subjects I want dropped, if you dont mind. One of them (*To Frank.*) is love's young dream in any shape or form: the other (*To Praed.*) is the romance and beauty of life, especially Ostend and the gaiety of Brussels. You are welcome to any illusions you have left on these subjects: I have none. If we three are to remain friends, I must be treated as a woman of business, permanently single (*To Frank.*) and permanently unromantic (*To Praed.*).

FRANK. I shall also remain permanently single until you change your mind. Praddy: change the subject. Be eloquent about something else.

PRAED. (*Diffidently.*) I'm afraid theres nothing else in the world I c a n talk about. The Gospel of Art is the only one I can preach. I know Miss Warren is a great devotee of the Gospel of Getting On; but we cant discuss that without hurting your feelings, Frank, since you are determined not to get on.

FRANK. Oh, dont mind my feelings. Give me some improving advice by all means: it does me ever so much good. Have another try to make a successful man of me,

Viv. Come: lets have it all: energy, thrift, foresight, self-respect, character. Dont you hate people who have no character, Viv?

VIVIE. (*Wincing.*) Oh, stop, stop: let us have no more of that horrible cant. Mr Praed: if there are really only those two gospels in the world, we had better all kill ourselves; for the same taint is in both, through and through.

FRANK. (*Looking critically at her.*) There is a touch of poetry about you today, Viv, which has hitherto been lacking.

PRAED. (*Remonstrating.*) My dear Frank: arnt you a little unsympathetic?

VIVIE. (*Merciless to herself.*) No: it's good for me. It keeps me from being sentimental.

FRANK. (*Bantering her.*) Checks your strong natural propensity that way, dont it?

VIVIE. (*Almost hysterically.*) Oh yes: go on: dont spare me. I was sentimental for one moment in my life—beautifully sentimental—by moonlight; and now—

FRANK. (*Quickly.*) I say, Viv: take care. Dont give yourself away.

VIVIE. Oh, do you think Mr Praed does not know all about my mother? (*Turning on Praed.*) You had better have told me that morning, Mr Praed. You are very old fashioned in your delicacies, after all.

PRAED. Surely it is you who are a little old fashioned in your prejudices, Miss Warren. I feel bound to tell you, speaking as an artist, and believing that the most intimate human relationships are far beyond and above the scope of the law, that though I know that your mother is an unmarried woman, I do not respect her the less on that account. I respect her more.

FRANK. (*Airily.*) Hear! Hear!

VIVIE. (*Staring at him.*) Is that a l l you know?

PRAED. Certainly that is all.

VIVIE. Then you neither of you know anything. Your guesses are innocence itself compared to the truth.

PRAED. (*Rising, startled and indignant, and preserving his politeness with an effort.*) I hope not. (*More empathetically.*) I hope not, Miss Warren.

FRANK. (*Whistles.*) Whew!

VIVIE. You are not making it easy for me to tell you, Mr Praed.

---

1 *call* I.e., divine prompting to service.

PRAED.   (*His chivalry drooping before their conviction.*) If there i s anything worse—that is, anything else—are you sure you are right to tell us, Miss Warren?

VIVIE.   I am sure that if I had the courage I should spend the rest of my life in telling everybody—stamping and branding it into them until they all felt their part in its abomination as I feel mine. There is nothing I despise more than the wicked convention that protects these things by forbidding a woman to mention them. And yet I cant tell you. The two infamous words[1] that describe what my mother is are ringing in my ears and struggling on my tongue; but I cant utter them: the shame of them is too horrible for me. (*She buries her face in her hands. The two men, astonished, stare at one another and then at her. She raises her head again desperately and snatches a sheet of paper and a pen.*) Here: let me draft you a prospectus.

FRANK.   Oh, she's mad. Do you hear, Viv? mad. Come! pull yourself together.

VIVIE.   You shall see. (*She writes.*) "Paid up capital: not less than £40,000 standing in the name of Sir George Crofts, Baronet, the chief shareholder. Premises at Brussels, Ostend, Vienna and Budapest. Managing director: Mrs Warren"; and now dont let us forget her qualifications: the two words. (*She writes the words and pushes the paper to them.*) There! Oh no: dont read it: dont! (*She snatches it back and tears it to pieces; then seizes her head in her hands and hides her face on the table.*)

(*Frank, who has watched the writing over her shoulder, and opened his eyes very widely at it, takes a card from his pocket; scribbles the two words on it; and silently hands it to Praed, who reads it with amazement, and hides it hastily in his pocket.*)

FRANK.   (*Whispering tenderly.*) Viv, dear: thats all right. I read what you wrote: so did Praddy. We understand. And we remain, as this leaves us at present, yours ever so devotedly.

PRAED.   We do indeed, Miss Warren. I declare you are the most splendidly courageous woman I ever met.

(*This sentimental compliment braces Vivie. She throws it away from her with an impatient shake, and forces herself to stand up, though not without some support from the table.*)

FRANK.   Dont stir, Viv, if you dont want to. Take it easy.

VIVIE.   Thank you. You can always depend on me for two things: not to cry and not to faint. (*She moves a few steps toward the door of the inner room, and stops close to Praed to say*) I shall need much more courage than that when I tell my mother that we have come to the parting of the ways. Now I must go into the next room for a moment to make myself neat again, if you dont mind.

PRAED.   Shall we go away?

VIVIE.   No: I'll be back presently. Only for a moment. (*She goes into the other room, Praed opening the door for her.*)

PRAED.   What an amazing revelation! I'm extremely disappointed in Crofts: I am indeed.

FRANK.   I'm not in the least. I feel he's perfectly accounted for at last. But what a facer[2] for me, Praddy! I cant marry her now.

PRAED.   (*Sternly.*) Frank! (*The two look at one another, Frank unruffled, Praed deeply indignant.*) Let me tell you, Gardner, that if you desert her now you will behave very despicably.

FRANK.   Good old Praddy! Ever chivalrous! But you mistake: it's not the moral aspect of the case: it's the money aspect. I really cant bring myself to touch the old woman's money now.

PRAED.   And was that what you were going to marry on?

FRANK.   What else? *I* havnt any money, nor the smallest turn for making it. If I married Viv now she would have to support me; and I should cost her more than I am worth.

PRAED.   But surely a clever bright fellow like you can make something by your own brains.

FRANK.   Oh yes, a little. (*He takes out his money again.*) I made all that yesterday in an hour and a half. But I made it in a highly speculative business. No, dear Praddy: even if Bessie and Georgina[3] marry millionaires

---

[1] *two infamous words*   Having read the page proofs of *Mrs Warren's Profession* in July 1897, actress Ellen Terry asked Shaw what the "two infamous words" were. Shaw replied, "Prostitute and Procuress."

[2] *facer*   A blow in the face (figuratively); a sudden difficulty.

[3] *Bessie and Georgina*   Frank's sisters. In the 1898 text Bessie is Jessie, and Frank has other (unnamed) sisters.

and the governor dies after cutting them off with a shilling,[1] I shall have only four hundred a year. And he wont die until he's three score and ten.[2] He hasnt originality enough. I shall be on short allowance for the next twenty years. No short allowance for Viv, if I can help it. I withdraw gracefully and leave the field to the guilded youth of England. So thats settled. I shant worry her about it: I'll just send her a little note after we're gone. She'll understand.

PRAED. (*Grasping his hand.*) Good fellow, Frank! I heartily beg your pardon. But must you never see her again?

FRANK.   Never see her again! Hang it all, be reasonable. I shall come along as often as possible, and be her brother. I can n o t understand the absurd consequences you romantic people expect from the most ordinary transactions. (*A knock at the door.*) I wonder who this is. Would you mind opening the door? If it's a client it will look more respectable than if I appeared.

PRAED. Certainly. (*He goes to the door, and opens it. Frank sits down in Vivie's chair to scribble a note.*) My dear Kitty: come in: come in.

(*Mrs Warren comes in, looking apprehensively round for Vivie. She has done her best to make herself matronly and dignified. The brilliant hat is replaced by a sober bonnet, and the gay blouse covered by a costly black silk mantle. She is pitiably anxious and ill at ease: evidently panic-stricken.*)

MRS WARREN. (*To Frank.*) What! Y o u r e here, are you?

FRANK. (*Turning in his chair from his writing, but not rising.*) Here, and charmed to see you. You come like a breath of spring.

MRS WARREN. Oh, get out with your nonsense. (*In a low voice.*) Wheres Vivie?

(*Frank points expressively to the door of the inner room, but says nothing.*)

MRS WARREN. (*Sitting down suddenly and almost beginning to cry.*) Praddy: wont she see me, dont you think?

PRAED. My dear Kitty: dont distress yourself. Why should she not?

MRS WARREN. Oh, you never can see why not: youre too innocent.[3] Mr Frank: did she say anything to you?

FRANK. (*Folding his note.*) She m u s t see you, if (*very expressively*) you wait til she comes in.

MRS WARREN. (*Frightened.*) Why shouldnt I wait?

(*Frank looks quizzically at her; puts his note carefully on the ink bottle, so that Vivie cannot fail to find it when next she dips her pen; then rises and devotes his attention to her.*)

FRANK. My dear Mrs Warren: suppose you were a sparrow—ever so tiny and pretty a sparrow hopping in the roadway—and you saw a steam roller coming in your direction, would you wait for it?

MRS WARREN. Oh, dont bother me with your sparrows. What did she run away from Haslemere like that for?

FRANK. I'm afraid she'll tell you if you rashly await her return.

MRS WARREN. Do you want me to go away?

FRANK. No: I always want you to stay. But I a d v i s e you to go away.

MRS WARREN. What! And never see her again!

FRANK. Precisely.

MRS WARREN. (*Crying again.*) Praddy: dont let him be cruel to me. (*She hastily checks her tears and wipes her eyes.*) She'll be so angry if she sees Ive been crying.

FRANK. (*With a touch of real compassion in his airy tenderness.*) You know that Praddy is the soul of kindness, Mrs Warren. Praddy: what do y o u say? Go or stay?

PRAED. (*To Mrs Warren.*) I really should be very sorry to cause you unnecessary pain; but I think perhaps you had better not wait. The fact is—(*Vivie is heard at the inner door.*)

FRANK. Sh! Too late. She's coming.

MRS WARREN. Dont tell her I was crying. (*Vivie comes in. She stops gravely on seeing Mrs Warren, who greets her with hysterical cheerfulness.*) Well, dearie. So here you are

1   *shilling* A shilling was one-twentieth part of £1 in the British currency system prior to decimilization in 1971.

2   *three score and ten* From Psalms 90.10: "The days of our years are three-score years and ten …" I.e., the number of years traditionally allotted to human beings.

3   *too innocent* In the 1898 text Praed is "too amiable."

VIVIE.   I am glad you have come. I want to speak to you. You said you were going, Frank, I think.

405 FRANK.   Yes. Will you come with me, Mrs Warren? What do you say to a trip to Richmond, and the theatre in the evening? There is safety in Richmond. No steam roller there.

VIVIE.   Nonsense, Frank. My mother will stay here.

410 MRS WARREN.   (*Scared.*) I dont know: perhaps I'd better go. We're disturbing you at your work.

VIVIE.   (*With quiet decision.*) Mr Praed: please take Frank away. Sit down, mother. (*Mrs Warren obeys helplessly.*)

PRAED.   Come, Frank. Goodbye, Miss Vivie.

415 VIVIE.   (*Shaking hands.*) Goodbye. A pleasant trip.

PRAED.   Thank you: thank you. I hope so.

FRANK.   (*To Mrs Warren.*) Goodbye: youd ever so much better have taken my advice. (*He shakes hands with her. Then airily to Vivie.*) Byebye, Viv.

420 VIVIE.   Goodbye. (*He goes out gaily without shaking hands with her.*)

PRAED.   (*Sadly.*) Goodbye, Kitty.

MRS WARREN.   (*Snivelling.*) —oobye!

(*Praed goes. Vivie, composed and extremely grave, sits down in Honoria's chair, and waits for her mother to speak. Mrs Warren, dreading a pause, loses no time in beginning.*)

MRS WARREN.   Well, Vivie, what did you go away like
425 that for without saying a word to me? How could you do such a thing! And what have you done to poor George? I wanted him to come with me; but he shuffled out of it. I could see that he was quite afraid of you. Only fancy: he wanted me not to come. As if (*Trem-*
430 *bling.*) I should be afraid of you, dearie. (*Vivie's gravity deepens.*) But of course I told him it was all settled and comfortable between us, and that we were on the best of terms. (*She breaks down.*) Vivie: whats the meaning of this? (*She produces a commercial envelope, and fumbles at
435 the enclosure with trembling fingers.*) I got it from the bank this morning.

VIVIE.   It is my month's allowance. They sent it to me as usual the other day. I simply sent it back to be placed to your credit, and asked them to send you the lodgment
440 receipt.[1] In future I shall support myself.

MRS WARREN.   (*Not daring to understand.*) Wasnt it enough? Why didnt you tell me? (*With a cunning gleam in her eye.*) I'll double it: I was intending to double it. Only let me know how much you want.

445 VIVIE.   You know very well that that has nothing to do with it. From this time I go my own way in my own business and among my own friends. And you will go yours. (*She rises.*) Goodbye.

MRS WARREN.   (*Rising, appalled.*) Goodbye?

450 VIVIE.   Yes: Goodbye. Come: dont let us make a useless scene: you understand perfectly well. Sir George Crofts has told me the whole business.

MRS WARREN.   (*Angrily.*) Silly old—(*She swallows an epithet, and turns white at the narrowness of her escape
455 from uttering it.*)

VIVIE.   Just so.

MRS WARREN.   He ought to have his tongue cut out. But I thought it was ended: you said you didnt mind.

VIVIE.   (*Steadfastly.*) Excuse me: I d o mind.

460 MRS WARREN. But I explained—

VIVIE.   You explained how it came about. You did not tell me that it is still going on. (*She sits.*)

(*Mrs Warren, silenced for a moment, looks forlornly at Vivie, who waits, secretly hoping that the combat is over. But the cunning expression comes back into Mrs Warren's face; and she bends across the table, sly and urgent, half whispering.*)

MRS WARREN.   Vivie: do you know how rich I am?

VIVIE.   I have no doubt you are very rich.

465 MRS WARREN.   But you dont know all that that means: youre too young. It means a new dress every day; it means theatres and balls every night; it means having the pick of all the gentlemen in Europe at your feet; it means a lovely house and plenty of servants; it means
470 the choicest of eating and drinking; it means everything you like, everything you want, everything you can think of. And what are you here? A mere drudge, toiling and moiling[2] early and late for your bare living and two cheap dresses a year. Think over it. (*Soothingly.*) Youre
475 shocked, I know. I can enter into your feelings; and I think they do you credit; but trust me, nobody will

---

1 *lodgment receipt* Deposit receipt.

2 *toiling and moiling* Working extremely hard.

blame you: you may take my word for that. I know what young girls are; and I know youll think better of it when youve turned it over in your mind.

480 VIVIE. So thats how it's done, is it? You must have said all that to many a woman, mother, to have it so pat.

MRS WARREN. (*Passionately.*) What harm am I asking you to do? (*Vivie turns away contemptuously. Mrs Warren continues desperately.*) Vivie: listen to me: you dont

485 understand: youve been taught wrong on purpose: you dont know what the world is really like.

VIVIE. (*Arrested.*) Taught wrong on purpose! What do you mean?

MRS WARREN. I mean that youre throwing away all

490 your chances for nothing. You think that people are what they pretend to be: that the way you were taught at school and college to think right and proper is the way things really are. But it's not: it's all only a pretence, to keep the cowardly slavish common run of people

495 quiet. Do you want to find that out, like other women, at forty when youve thrown yourself away and lost your chances; or wont you take it in good time now from your own mother, that loves you and swears to you that it's truth: gospel truth? (*Urgently.*) Vivie: the big people,

500 the clever people, the managing people, all know it. They do as I do, and think what I think. I know plenty of them. I know them to speak to, to introduce you to, to make friends of for you. I dont mean anything wrong: thats what you dont understand: your head is

505 full of ignorant ideas about me. What do the people that taught you know about life or about people like me? When did they ever meet me, or speak to me, or let anyone tell them about me? the fools! Would they ever have done anything for you if I hadnt paid them? Havnt

510 I told you that I want you to be respectable? Havnt I brought you up to be respectable? And how can you keep it up without my money and my influence and Lizzie's friends? Cant you see that youre cutting your own throat as well as breaking my heart in turning your

515 back on me?

VIVIE. I recognize the Crofts philosophy of life, mother. I heard it all from him that day at the Gardners'.

MRS WARREN. You think I want to force that played-out old sot on you! I dont, Vivie: on my oath I dont.

520 VIVIE. It would not matter if you did: you would not succeed. (*Mrs Warren winces, deeply hurt by the implied*

indifference towards her affectionate intention. Vivie, neither understanding this nor concerning herself about it, goes on calmly.) Mother: you dont at all know the sort of

525 person I am. I dont object to Crofts more than to any other coarsely built man of his class. To tell you the truth, I rather admire him for being strongminded enough to enjoy himself in his own way and make plenty of money instead of living the usual shooting,

530 hunting, dining-out, tailoring, loafing life of his set merely because all the rest do it. And I'm perfectly aware that if I'd been in the same circumstances as my aunt Liz, I'd have done exactly what she did. I dont think I'm more prejudiced or straightlaced than you: I think I'm

535 less. I'm certain I'm less sentimental. I know very well that fashionable morality is all a pretence, and that if I took your money and devoted the rest of my life to spending it fashionably, I might be as worthless and vicious and the silliest woman could possibly want to be

540 without having a word said to me about it. But I dont want to be worthless. I shouldnt enjoy trotting about the park to advertise my dressmaker and carriage builder, or being bored at the opera to shew off a shopwindowful of diamonds.

545 MRS WARREN. (*Bewildered.*) But—

VIVIE. Wait a moment. Ive not done. Tell me why you continue your business now that you are independent of it. Your sister, you told me, has left all that behind her. Why dont you do the same?

550 MRS WARREN. Oh, it's all very easy for Liz: she likes good society, and has the air of being a lady. Imagine m e in a cathedral town! Why, the very rooks in the trees would find me out even if I could stand the dulness of it. I must have work and excitement, or I

555 should go melancholy mad. And what else is there for me to do? The life suits me: I'm fit for it and not for anything else. If I didnt do it, somebody else would; so I dont do any real harm by it. And then it brings in money; and I like making money. No: it's no use: I cant

560 give it up—not for anybody. But what need you know about it? I'll never mention it. I'll keep Crofts away. I'll not trouble you much: you see I have to be constantly running about from one place to another. Youll be quit of me altogether when I die.

565 VIVIE. No: I am my mother's daughter. I am like you: I must have work, and must make more money than I

spend. But my work is not your work, and my way not your way. We must part. It will not make much difference to us: instead of meeting one another for perhaps a few months in twenty years, we shall never meet: thats all.

MRS WARREN.   (*Her voice stifled in tears.*) Vivie: I meant to have been more with you: I did indeed.

VIVIE.   It's no use, mother: I am not to be changed by a few cheap tears and entreaties any more than you are, I daresay.

MRS WARREN.   (*Wildly.*) Oh, you call a mother's tears cheap.

VIVIE.   They cost you nothing; and you ask me to give you the peace and quietness of my whole life in exchange for them. What use would my company be to you if you could get it? What have we two in common that could make either of us happy together?

MRS WARREN.   (*Lapsing recklessly into her dialect.*) We're mother and daughter. I want my daughter. Ive a right to you. Who is to care for me when I'm old? Plenty of girls have taken to me like daughters and cried at leaving me; but I let them all go because I had you to look forward to. I kept myself lonely for you. Youve no right to turn on me now and refuse to do your duty as daughter.

VIVIE.   (*Jarred and antagonized by the echo of the slums in her mother's voice.*) My duty as a daughter! I thought we should come to that presently. Now once for all, mother, you want a daughter and Frank wants a wife. I dont want a mother; and I dont want a husband. I have spared neither Frank nor myself in sending him about his business. Do you think I will spare y o u?

MRS WARREN.   (*Violently.*) Oh, I know the sort you are: no mercy for yourself or anyone else. *I* know. My experience has done that for me anyhow: I can tell the pious, canting, hard, selfish woman when I meet her. Well, keep yourself to yourself: *I* dont want you. But listen to this. Do you know what I would do with you if you were a baby again? aye, as sure as theres a Heaven above us.

VIVIE.   Strangle me, perhaps.

MRS WARREN.   No: I'd bring you up to be a real daughter to me, and not what you are now, with your pride and your prejudices and the college education you stole from me: yes, stole: deny it if you can: what was it but stealing? I'd bring you up in my own house, I

would.

VIVIE.   (*Quietly.*) In one of your own houses.

MRS WARREN.   (*Screaming.*) Listen to her! listen to how she spits on her mother's grey hairs! Oh, may you live to have your own daughter tear and trample on you as you have trampled on me. And you will: you will. No woman ever had luck with a mother's curse on her.

VIVIE.   I wish you wouldnt rant, mother. It only hardens me. Come: I suppose I am the only young woman you ever had in your power that you did good to. Dont spoil it all now.

MRS WARREN.   Yes, Heaven forgive me, it's true; and you are the only one that ever turned on me. Oh, the injustice of it! the injustice! the injustice! I always wanted to be a good woman. I tried honest work; and I was slave-driven until I cursed the day I ever heard of honest work. I was a good mother; and because I made my daughter a good woman she turns me out as if I was a leper. Oh, if I only had my life to live over again! I'd talk to that lying clergyman in the school. From this time forth, so help me Heaven in my last hour, I'll do wrong and nothing but wrong. And I'll prosper on it.

VIVIE.   Yes: it's better to choose your line and go through with it. If I had been you, mother, I might have done as you did: but I should not have lived one life and believed in another. You are a conventional woman at heart. That is why I am bidding you goodbye now. I am right, am I not?

MRS WARREN.   (*Taken aback.*) Right to throw away all my money?

VIVIE.   No: right to get rid of you! I should be a fool not to. Isnt that so?

MRS WARREN.   (*Sulkily.*) Oh well, yes, if you come to that, I suppose you are. But Lord help the world if everybody took to doing the right thing! And now I'd better go than stay where I'm not wanted. (*She turns to the door.*)

VIVIE.   (*Kindly.*) Wont you shake hands?

MRS WARREN.   (*After looking at her fiercely for a moment with a savage impulse to strike her.*) No, thank you. Goodbye.

VIVIE.   (*Matter-of-factly.*) Goodbye. (*Mrs Warren goes out, slamming the door behind her. The strain on Vivie's face relaxes; her grave expression breaks up into one of joyous content; her breath goes out in a half sob, half laugh* of intense relief. She goes buoyantly to her place at the writing-table; pushes the electric lamp out of the way; pulls over a great sheaf of papers; and is in the act of dipping her pen in the ink when she finds Frank's note. She opens it unconcernedly and reads it quickly, giving a little laugh at some quaint turn of expression in it.) And goodbye, 660

Frank. (She tears the note up and tosses the pieces into the waste paper basket without a second thought. Then she goes at her work with a plunge, and soon becomes absorbed in its figures.) 665

—1898, 1930

JOSEPH CONRAD
1857 – 1924

Joseph Conrad has long been recognized as one of the twentieth century's greatest writers of fiction in English—an extraordinary fact given that English was his third language, and that a significant portion of his early adult life was spent in nautical, rather than literary, pursuits. He did not become a British citizen until he was almost 30 years old, and did not begin his career as an author until he was almost 40. Yet in spite of his status as an outsider to the vibrant literary circles of late nineteenth-century British society, Conrad soon established himself as one of the finest literary craftsmen of his

age. Initially many regarded him as an able seaman who simply turned his colorful experiences into material for his novels; it soon became evident that Joseph Conrad was an exceptional writer whose work demonstrated a careful and deliberate attention to political, psychological, and social nuances.

Joseph Conrad was born Jozef Teodor Konrad Nalecz Korzeniowski on 3 December 1857, in Poland (then under Russian rule). His parents, Apollo and Evalina, were members of the educated, landed gentry who opposed Czarist Russian control in Poland. Apollo was arrested for revolutionary conspiracy, and, in 1862, the family was exiled to Vologda in northern Russia and forced to endure years of hardship and illness; Conrad's mother died in 1865 and his father in 1868.

Following the death of his parents, Conrad came under the guardianship of his maternal uncle in Kraków, Poland; he spent much of the next few years reading translations of Shakespeare, Dickens, and Victor Hugo. Yet Conrad seemed to dislike school life; he was bored and restless. At the age of fifteen, he expressed his desire to go to sea. He spent the next two years pressing his family for permission against strong opposition. His pleas were eventually heard, and in 1874, nearing his seventeenth birthday, Conrad traveled to Marseilles and joined the French merchant navy.

From 1874 to 1877, Conrad made a number of voyages to Martinique and the West Indies aboard French ships, where he quickly acquired great skill as a sailor. During these years he spent time engaged in illicit gunrunning on behalf of the Carlist Royalists in Spain. In 1878, due to huge debts acquired through smuggling and gambling, Conrad shot himself in the chest. He long claimed that this injury was the result of a duel, rather than what seems to have been a suicide attempt. Whatever the case, Conrad recovered from his injury and escaped his creditors by joining the British merchant navy. Knowing just a few words in English, Conrad began to learn the language in voyages between the ports of Lowescroft and Newcastle, aboard a coal schooner.

Over the next sixteen years, Conrad traveled to Australia, South America, India, Borneo, and the South Pacific in the service of the British merchant navy. In 1886, he achieved several important milestones: he received his certificate as a master mariner, became a British citizen, and changed his name to Joseph Conrad. In 1888, Conrad was given his only sea command as captain of the *Otago*; he spent the next 15 months journeying from Bangkok to Singapore, about the Malay Archipelago, and to Australia and Mauritius. Conrad would later use his experiences aboard the *Otago* as inspiration for *The Secret Sharer*. In 1890 he took a steamboat up the Congo River to take command of a

Belgian steamer—a journey that was an unmitigated disaster and yet would form the template for his best known work, *Heart of Darkness*. It was also while in the Congo that Conrad contracted malaria, the effects of which would plague him for years. In ill health and with his interest in writing increasing steadily, Conrad retired from seafaring and settled permanently in England in 1894; his first published novel was *Almayer's Folly* in 1895. He would dedicate the rest of his life to literary pursuits, writing prolifically until his death of a heart attack, near Canterbury, in 1924.

Conrad wrote 13 novels, two volumes of memoirs, and 28 short stories, but suffered from persistent doubts as to the quality of his creative output and from constant financial pressure. His experiences at sea form the background for many of his stories; his major interest is the profound moral and psychological ambiguities of the human experience. In *Lord Jim* (1900) he explores the concept of personal honor by presenting the hero's history as a life spent in atonement for an act of cowardice as a young marine officer. In *The Nigger of the "Narcissus"* (1897), Conrad shows how a single black seaman's plight affects the morale of an entire ship's crew. In *Heart of Darkness* (1902), Conrad revisits his own terrifying journey to the Congo as he explores the extent of human corruptibility.

In his later works, Conrad shifted his attention away from the sea and toward the complexities of politics. With *Nostromo* (1904), he explored the effects of politics and "material interests" on human relationships and the futility of human attempts at change. *The Secret Agent* (1906) concerns an anarchist bomb plot in London, and *Under Western Eyes* (1911) presents a story of betrayal and a search for redemption amidst antigovernment violence in Czarist Russia.

Conrad has long been considered a master of English prose—an extraordinary feat for a man who was twenty-one years of age before he began speaking a word of English. In part, however, his distanced relationship with the language may have helped free him to make English prose do new things. Words are carefully chosen for their evocative and symbolic functions and his often poetic prose style seems to float free of local idiosyncrasies.

Like much of Conrad's work, *The Secret Sharer* (1912) reflects his own personal experience—in this case, his experience as a new captain aboard the *Otago,* when he felt like an interloper aboard his own ship. The story features a *doppelgänger*, in the character of Leggatt; in addition to being a real character and contributor to the events of the story, Leggatt functions as the Captain's second self or alter ego. The work may be best viewed in the context of the late nineteenth- and early twentieth-century preoccupation with the unconscious and "true self." Like much of Conrad's work, it displays a tendency to regard society and the individual in terms of dualisms: good and evil, savagery and civilization, emotion and intellect. But whereas for many others of the time such dualisms fostered simplistic habits of thought, in Conrad's work they give rise to complexity and ambiguity.

In the "Preface" to *The Nigger of the "Narcissus,"* Conrad outlined his aims as an artist. The "Preface" was written a few months after finishing the work itself, and first appeared in the 1898 version of the book, at a time when Conrad had fully dedicated himself to his writing and found himself (in his own words) "done with the sea."

⌘⌘⌘

The Preface to *The Nigger of the "Narcissus"*[1]
[The Task of the Artist]

A work that aspires, however humbly, to the condition of art should carry its justification in every line. And art itself may be defined as a single-minded attempt to render the highest kind of justice to the visible universe, by bringing to light the truth, manifold and one, underlying its every aspect. It is an attempt to find in its forms, in its colours, in its light, in its shadows, in the aspects of matter and in the facts of life, what of each is fundamental, what is enduring and essential—their one illuminating and convincing quality—the very truth of their existence. The artist, then, like the thinker or the scientist, seeks the truth and makes his appeal. Impressed by the aspect of the world the thinker plunges into ideas, the scientist into facts—whence, presently, emerging they make their appeal to those qualities of our being that fit us best for the hazardous enterprise of living. They speak authoritatively to our common-sense, to our intelligence, to our desire of peace or to our desire of unrest; not seldom to our prejudices, sometimes to our fears, often to our egoism—but always to our credulity. And their words are heard with reverence, for their concern is with weighty matters: with the cultivation of our minds and the proper care of our bodies; with the attainment of our ambitions; with the perfection of the means and the glorification of our precious aims.

It is otherwise with the artist.

Confronted by the same enigmatical spectacle the artist descends within himself, and in that lonely region of stress and strife, if he be deserving and fortunate, he finds the terms of his appeal. His appeal is made to our less obvious capacities: to that part of our nature which, because of the warlike conditions of existence, is necessarily kept out of sight within the more resisting and hard qualities—like the vulnerable body within the steel armour. His appeal is less loud, more profound, less distinct, more stirring—and sooner forgotten. Yet its effect endures for ever. The changing wisdom of successive generations discards ideas, questions facts, demolishes theories. But the artist appeals to that part of our being which is not dependent on wisdom: to that in us which is a gift and not an acquisition—and, therefore, more permanently enduring. He speaks to our capacity for delight and wonder, to the sense of mystery surrounding our lives; to our sense of pity, and beauty, and pain; to the latent feeling of fellowship with all creation—and to the subtle but invincible, conviction of solidarity that knits together the loneliness of innumerable hearts: to the solidarity in dreams, in joy, in sorrow, in aspirations, in illusions, in hope, in fear, which binds men to each other, which binds together all humanity—the dead to the living and the living to the unborn.

It is only some such train of thought, or rather of feeling, that can in a measure explain the aim of the attempt, made in the tale which follows, to present an unrestful episode in the obscure lives of a few individuals out of all the disregarded multitude of the bewildered, the simple and the voiceless. For, if there is any part of truth in the belief confessed above, it becomes evident that there is not a place of splendour or a dark corner of the earth that does not deserve, if only a passing glance of wonder and pity. The motive, then, may be held to justify the matter of the work; but this preface, which is simply an avowal of endeavour, cannot end here—for the avowal is not yet complete.

Fiction—if it at all aspires to be art—appeals to temperament. And in truth it must be, like painting, like music, like all art, the appeal of one temperament to all the other innumerable temperaments whose subtle and resistless power endows passing events with their true meaning, and creates the moral, the emotional atmosphere of the place and time. Such an appeal, to be effective, must be an impression conveyed through the senses; and, in fact, it cannot be made in any other way,

---

[1] *Preface … Narcissus* Conrad's novella *The Nigger of the "Narcissus"* was first published in *The New Review* in 1897. Conrad added the preface when it came out in book form in 1898. The novella deals with the death of a black seaman aboard a merchant ship called the *Narcissus*. Conrad had served as first mate on a ship bearing that name in 1883. The pejorative term "nigger" was not used in the American edition, which at the suggestion of the publisher was entitled *Children of the Sea*. The reason given for the change, however, was not that the term was inherently offensive but rather that a book perceived to be about a black man would not interest many readers. Surprisingly, the term "nigger" continued for decades to appear in book titles in Britain; the Agatha Christie mystery novel now known by its original American title, *And Then There Were None*, first appeared in the UK in 1939 as *Ten Little Niggers*.

because temperament, whether individual or collective, is not amenable to persuasion. All art, therefore, appeals primarily to the senses, and the artistic aim when expressing itself in written words must also make its appeal through the senses, if its high desire is to reach the secret spring of responsive emotions. It must strenuously aspire to the plasticity of sculpture, to the colour of painting, and to the magic suggestiveness of music—which is the art of arts. And it is only through complete, unswerving devotion to the perfect blending of form and substance; it is only through an unremitting, never-discouraged care for the shape and ring of sentences that an approach can be made to plasticity, to colour; and the light of magic suggestiveness may be brought to play for an evanescent instant over the commonplace surface of words: of the old, old words, worn thin, defaced by ages of careless usage.

The sincere endeavour to accomplish that creative task, to go as far on that road as his strength will carry him, to go undeterred by faltering, weariness or reproach, is the only valid justification for the worker in prose. And if his conscience is clear, his answer to those who, in the fulness of a wisdom which looks for immediate profit, demand specifically to be edified, consoled, amused; who demand to be promptly improved, or encouraged, or frightened, or shocked, or charmed, must run thus:—My task which I am trying to achieve is, by the power of the written word, to make you hear, to make you feel—it is, before all, to make you *see*. That—and no more, and it is everything. If I succeed, you shall find there according to your deserts: encouragement, consolation, fear, charm—all you demand; and, perhaps, also that glimpse of truth for which you have forgotten to ask.

To snatch in a moment of courage, from the remorseless rush of time, a sapping phase of life is only the beginning of the task. The task approached in tenderness and faith is to hold up unquestioningly, without choice and without fear, the rescued fragment before all eyes and in the light of a sincere mood. It is to show its vibration, its colour, its form; and through its movement, its form, and its colour, reveal the substance of its truth—disclose its inspiring secret: the stress and passion within the core of each convincing moment. In a single-minded attempt of that kind, if one be

deserving and fortunate, one may perchance attain to such clearness of sincerity that at last the presented vision of regret or pity, of terror or mirth, shall awaken in the hearts of the beholders that feeling of unavoidable solidarity; of the solidarity in mysterious origin, in toil, in joy, in hope, in uncertain fate, which binds men to each other and all mankind to the visible world.

It is evident that he who, rightly or wrongly, holds by the convictions expressed above cannot be faithful to any one of the temporary formulas of his craft. The enduring part of them—the truth which each only imperfectly veils—should abide with him as the most precious of his possessions, but they all: Realism, Romanticism, Naturalism, even the unofficial sentimentalism (which, like the poor, is exceedingly difficult to get rid of[1]); all these gods must, after a short period of fellowship, abandon him—even on the very threshold of the temple—to the stammerings of his conscience and to the outspoken consciousness of the difficulties of his work. In that uneasy solitude the supreme cry of Art for Art, even, loses the exciting ring of its apparent immorality. It sounds far off. It has ceased to be a cry, and is heard only as a whisper, often incomprehensible, but at times, and faintly, encouraging.

Sometimes, stretched at ease in the shade of a roadside tree, we watch the motions of a labourer in a distant field, and after a time, begin to wonder languidly as to what the fellow may be at. We watch the movements of his body, the waving of his arms, we see him bend down, stand up, hesitate, begin again. It may add to the charm of an idle hour to be told the purpose of his exertions. If we know he is trying to lift a stone, to dig a ditch, to uproot a stump, we look with a more real interest at his efforts; we are disposed to condone the jar of his agitation upon the restfulness of the landscape; and even, if in a brotherly frame of mind, we may bring ourselves to forgive his failure. We understood his object, and, after all, the fellow has tried, and perhaps he had not the strength, and perhaps he had not the knowledge. We forgive, go on our way—and forget.

---

[1] *like the poor … get rid of* The reference is to John 12.8: "for the poor always you have with you."

And so it is with the workman of art. Art is long and life is short,[1] and success is very far off. And thus, doubtful of strength to travel so far, we talk a little about the aim—the aim of art, which, like life itself, is inspiring, difficult—obscured by mists. It is not in the clear logic of a triumphant conclusion; it is not in the unveiling of one of those heartless secrets which are called the Laws of Nature. It is not less great, but only more difficult.

To arrest, for the space of a breath, the hands busy about the work of the earth, and compel men entranced by the sight of distant goals to glance for a moment at the surrounding vision of form and colour, of sunshine and shadows; to make them pause for a look, for a sigh, for a smile—such is the aim, difficult and evanescent, and reserved only for a very few to achieve. But sometimes, by the deserving and the fortunate, even that task is accomplished. And when it is accomplished—behold!—all the truth of life is there: a moment of vision, a sigh, a smile—and the return to an eternal rest.
—1898

The Secret Sharer

I

On my right hand there were lines of fishing stakes resembling a mysterious system of half-submerged bamboo fences, incomprehensible in its division of the domain of tropical fishes, and crazy of aspect as if abandoned forever by some nomad tribe of fishermen now gone to the other end of the ocean; for there was no sign of human habitation as far as the eye could reach. To the left a group of barren islets, suggesting ruins of stone walls, towers, and blockhouses, had its foundations set in a blue sea that itself looked solid, so still and stable did it lie below my feet; even the track of light from the westering sun shone smoothly, without that animated glitter which tells of an imperceptible ripple. And when I turned my head to take a parting glance at the tug which had just left us anchored outside the bar, I saw the straight line of the flat shore joined to the stable sea, edge to edge, with a perfect and unmarked closeness, in one leveled floor half brown, half blue under the enormous dome of the sky. Corresponding in their insignificance to the islets of the sea, two small clumps of trees, one on each side of the only fault in the impeccable joint, marked the mouth of the river Meinam[2] we had just left on the first preparatory stage of our homeward journey; and, far back on the inland level, a larger and loftier mass, the grove surrounding the great Paknam pagoda,[3] was the only thing on which the eye could rest from the vain task of exploring the monotonous sweep of the horizon. Here and there gleams as of a few scattered pieces of silver marked the windings of the great river; and on the nearest of them, just within the bar, the tug steaming right into the land became lost to my sight, hull and funnel and masts, as though the impassive earth had swallowed her up without an effort, without a tremor. My eye followed the light cloud of her smoke, now here, now there, above the plain, according to the devious curves of the stream, but always fainter and farther away, till I lost it at last behind the miter-shaded hill of the great pagoda. And then I was left alone with my ship, anchored at the head of the Gulf of Siam.[4]

She floated at the starting point of a long journey, very still in an immense stillness, the shadows of her spars[5] flung far to the eastward by the setting sun. At that moment I was alone on her decks. There was not a sound in her—and around us nothing moved, nothing lived, not a canoe on the water, not a bird in the air, not a cloud in the sky. In this breathless pause at the threshold of a long passage we seemed to be measuring our fitness for a long and arduous enterprise, the appointed task of both our existences to be carried out,

---

[1] *Art is long and life is short* The Latin proverb *ars longa, vita brevis* derives from a saying of the Greek physician Hippocrates.

[2] *the river Meinam* Conrad may have been referring to the Chao Phraya river in the city of Samut Prakan, Thailand. Located just south of Bangkok, Samut Prakan is a port city on the Gulf of Thailand.

[3] *Paknam pagoda* Located in Samut Prakan, the Phra Samut Chedi pagoda was originally built in the middle of the river. Today it adjoins the west bank due to silt accumulation.

[4] *Siam* Thailand.

[5] *spars* Mast attachments securing the sail; also called booms or gaffs.

far from all human eyes, with only sky and sea for spectators and for judges.

There must have been some glare in the air to interfere with one's sight, because it was only just before the sun left us that my roaming eyes made out beyond the highest ridges of the principal islet of the group something which did away with the solemnity of perfect solitude. The tide of darkness flowed on swiftly; and with tropical suddenness a swarm of stars came out above the shadowy earth, while I lingered yet, my hand resting lightly on my ship's rail as if on the shoulder of a trusted friend. But, with all that multitude of celestial bodies staring down at one, the comfort of quiet communion with her was gone for good. And there were also disturbing sounds by this time—voices, footsteps forward; the steward flitted along the main-deck, a busily ministering spirit; a hand bell tinkled urgently under the poop deck[1]…

I found my two officers waiting for me near the supper table, in the lighted cuddy.[2] We sat down at once, and as I helped the chief mate, I said:

"Are you aware that there is a ship anchored inside the islands? I saw her mastheads above the ridge as the sun went down."

He raised sharply his simple face, overcharged by a terrible growth of whisker, and emitted his usual ejaculations: "Bless my soul, sir! You don't say so!"

My second mate was a round-cheeked, silent young man, grave beyond his years, I thought; but as our eyes happened to meet I detected a slight quiver on his lips. I looked down at once. It was not my part to encourage sneering on board my ship. It must be said, too, that I knew very little of my officers. In consequence of certain events of no particular significance, except to myself, I had been appointed to the command only a fortnight before. Neither did I know much of the hands forward. All these people had been together for eighteen months or so, and my position was that of the only stranger on board. I mention this because it has some bearing on what is to follow. But what I felt most was my being a stranger to the ship; and if all the truth must be told, I was somewhat of a stranger to myself. The youngest

man on board (barring the second mate), and untried as yet by a position of the fullest responsibility, I was willing to take the adequacy of the others for granted. They had simply to be equal to their tasks; but I wondered how far I should turn out faithful to that ideal conception of one's own personality every man sets up for himself secretly.

Meantime the chief mate, with an almost visible effect of collaboration on the part of his round eyes and frightful whiskers, was trying to evolve a theory of the anchored ship. His dominant trait was to take all things into earnest consideration. He was of a painstaking turn of mind. As he used to say, he "liked to account to himself" for practically everything that came in his way, down to a miserable scorpion he had found in his cabin a week before. The why and the wherefore of that scorpion—how it got on board and came to select his room rather than the pantry (which was a dark place and more what a scorpion would be partial to), and how on earth it managed to drown itself in the inkwell of his writing desk—had exercised him infinitely. The ship within the islands was much more easily accounted for; and just as we were about to rise from table he made his pronouncement. She was, he doubted not, a ship from home lately arrived. Probably she drew too much water to cross the bar except at the top of spring tides. Therefore she went into that natural harbour to wait for a few days in preference to remaining in an open roadstead.

"That's so," confirmed the second mate, suddenly, in his slightly hoarse voice. "She draws over twenty feet. She's the Liverpool ship *Sephora* with a cargo of coal. Hundred and twenty-three days from Cardiff."

We looked at him in surprise.

"The tugboat skipper told me when he came on board for your letters, sir," explained the young man. "He expects to take her up the river the day after tomorrow."

After thus overwhelming us with the extent of his information he slipped out of the cabin. The mate observed regretfully that he "could not account for that young fellow's whims." What prevented him telling us all about it at once, he wanted to know.

---

1 *poop deck* Highest and hindmost deck on a ship.
2 *cuddy* Small ship-board cabin.

I detained him as he was making a move. For the last two days the crew had had plenty of hard work, and the night before they had very little sleep. I felt painfully that I—a stranger—was doing something unusual when I directed him to let all hands turn in without setting an anchor watch. I proposed to keep on deck myself till one o'clock or thereabouts. I would get the second mate to relieve me at that hour.

"He will turn out the cook and the steward at four," I concluded, "and then give you a call. Of course at the slightest sign of any sort of wind we'll have the hands up and make a start at once."

He concealed his astonishment. "Very well, sir." Outside the cuddy he put his head in the second mate's door to inform him of my unheard-of caprice to take a five hours' anchor watch on myself. I heard the other raise his voice incredulously—"What? The Captain himself?" Then a few more murmurs, a door closed, then another. A few moments later I went on deck.

My strangeness, which had made me sleepless, had prompted that unconventional arrangement, as if I had expected in those solitary hours of the night to get on terms with the ship of which I knew nothing, manned by men of whom I knew very little more. Fast alongside a wharf, littered like any ship in port with a tangle of unrelated things, invaded by unrelated shore people, I had hardly seen her yet properly. Now, as she lay cleared for sea, the stretch of her main-deck seemed to me very fine under the stars. Very fine, very roomy for her size, and very inviting. I descended the poop and paced the waist, my mind picturing to myself the coming passage through the Malay Archipelago, down the Indian Ocean, and up the Atlantic. All its phases were familiar enough to me, every characteristic, all the alternatives which were likely to face me on the high seas—everything!... except the novel responsibility of command. But I took heart from the reasonable thought that the ship was like other ships, the men like other men, and that the sea was not likely to keep any special surprises expressly for my discomfiture.

Arrived at that comforting conclusion, I bethought myself of a cigar and went below to get it. All was still down there. Everybody at the after end of the ship was sleeping profoundly. I came out again on the quarter-deck, agreeably at ease in my sleeping suit on that warm breathless night, barefooted, a glowing cigar in my teeth, and, going forward, I was met by the profound silence of the fore end of the ship. Only as I passed the door of the forecastle, I heard a deep, quiet, trustful sigh of some sleeper inside. And suddenly I rejoiced in the great security of the sea as compared with the unrest of the land, in my choice of that untempted life presenting no disquieting problems, invested with an elementary moral beauty by the absolute straightforwardness of its appeal and by the singleness of its purpose.

The riding light in the forerigging burned with a clear, untroubled, as if symbolic, flame, confident and bright in the mysterious shades of the night. Passing on my way aft along the other side of the ship, I observed that the rope side ladder, put over, no doubt, for the master of the tug when he came to fetch away our letters, had not been hauled in as it should have been. I became annoyed at this, for exactitude in some small matters is the very soul of discipline. Then I reflected that I had myself peremptorily dismissed my officers from duty, and by my own act had prevented the anchor watch being formally set and things properly attended to. I asked myself whether it was wise ever to interfere with the established routine of duties even from the kindest of motives. My action might have made me appear eccentric. Goodness only knew how that absurdly whiskered mate would "account" for my conduct, and what the whole ship thought of that informality of their new captain. I was vexed with myself.

Not from compunction certainly, but, as it were mechanically, I proceeded to get the ladder in myself. Now a side ladder of that sort is a light affair and comes in easily, yet my vigorous tug, which should have brought it flying on board, merely recoiled upon my body in a totally unexpected jerk. What the devil!... I was so astounded by the immovableness of that ladder that I remained stockstill, trying to account for it to myself like that imbecile mate of mine. In the end, of course, I put my head over the rail.

The side of the ship made an opaque belt of shadow on the darkling glassy shimmer of the sea. But I saw at once something elongated and pale floating very close to the ladder. Before I could form a guess a faint flash of phosphorescent light, which seemed to issue suddenly from the naked body of a man, flickered in the sleeping water with the elusive, silent play of summer lightning in a night sky. With a gasp I saw revealed to my stare a pair of feet, the long legs, a broad livid back immersed right up to the neck in a greenish cadaverous glow. One hand, awash, clutched the bottom rung of the ladder. He was complete but for the head. A headless corpse! The cigar dropped out of my gaping mouth with a tiny plop and a short hiss quite audible in the absolute stillness of all things under heaven. At that I suppose he raised up his face, a dimly pale oval in the shadow of the ship's side. But even then I could only barely make out down there the shape of his black-haired head. However, it was enough for the horrid, frost-bound sensation which had gripped me about the chest to pass off. The moment of vain exclamations was past, too. I only climbed on the spare spar and leaned over the rail as far as I could, to bring my eyes nearer to that mystery floating alongside.

As he hung by the ladder, like a resting swimmer, the sea lightning played about his limbs at every stir; and he appeared in it ghastly, silvery, fishlike. He remained as mute as a fish, too. He made no motion to get out of the water, either. It was inconceivable that he should not attempt to come on board, and strangely troubling to suspect that perhaps he did not want to. And my first words were prompted by just that troubled incertitude.

"What's the matter?" I asked in my ordinary tone, speaking down to the face upturned exactly under mine.

"Cramp," it answered, no louder. Then slightly anxious, "I say, no need to call anyone."

"I was not going to," I said.

"Are you alone on deck?"

"Yes."

I had somehow the impression that he was on the point of letting go the ladder to swim away beyond my ken—mysterious as he came. But, for the moment, this being appearing as if he had risen from the bottom of the sea (it was certainly the nearest land to the ship) wanted only to know the time. I told him. And he, down there, tentatively:

"I suppose your captain's turned in?"

"I am sure he isn't," I said.

He seemed to struggle with himself, for I heard something like the low, bitter murmur of doubt.

"What's the good?" His next words came out with a hesitating effort.

"Look here, my man. Could you call him out quietly?"

I thought the time had come to declare myself.

"I am the captain."

I heard a "By Jove!" whispered at the level of the water. The phosphorescence flashed in the swirl of the water all about his limbs, his other hand seized the ladder.

"My name's Leggatt."

The voice was calm and resolute. A good voice. The self-possession of that man had somehow induced a corresponding state in myself. It was very quietly that I remarked:

"You must be a good swimmer."

"Yes. I've been in the water practically since nine o'clock. The question for me now is whether I am to let go this ladder and go on swimming till I sink from exhaustion, or—to come on board here."

I felt this was no mere formula of desperate speech, but a real alternative in the view of a strong soul. I should have gathered from this that he was young; indeed, it is only the young who are ever confronted by such clear issues. But at the time it was pure intuition on my part. A mysterious communication was established already between us two—in the face of that silent, darkened tropical sea. I was young, too; young enough to make no comment. The man in the water began suddenly to climb up the ladder, and I hastened away from the rail to fetch some clothes.

Before entering the cabin I stood still, listening in the lobby at the foot of the stairs. A faint snore came through the closed door of the chief mate's room. The second mate's door was on the hook, but the darkness in there was absolutely soundless. He, too, was young and could sleep like a stone. Remained the steward, but he was not likely to wake up before he was called. I got a sleeping suit out of my room and, coming back on deck, saw the naked man from the sea sitting on the main hatch, glimmering white in the darkness, his elbows on his knees and his head in his hands. In a moment he had concealed his damp body in a sleeping suit of the same gray-stripe pattern as the one I was wearing and followed me like my double on the poop. Together we moved right aft, barefooted, silent.

"What is it?" I asked in a deadened voice, taking the lighted lamp out of the binnacle,[1] and raising it to his face.

"An ugly business."

He had rather regular features; a good mouth; light eyes under somewhat heavy, dark eyebrows; a smooth, square forehead; no growth on his cheeks; a small, brown mustache, and a well-shaped, round chin. His expression was concentrated, meditative, under the inspecting light of the lamp I held up to his face; such as a man thinking hard in solitude might wear. My sleeping suit was just right for his size. A well-knit young fellow of twenty-five at most. He caught his lower lip with the edge of white, even teeth.

"Yes," I said, replacing the lamp in the binnacle. The warm, heavy tropical night closed upon his head again.

"There's a ship over there," he murmured.

"Yes, I know. The *Sephora*. Did you know of us?"

"Hadn't the slightest idea. I am the mate of her—" He paused and corrected himself. "I should say I *WAS*."

"Aha! Something wrong?"

"Yes. Very wrong indeed. I've killed a man."

"What do you mean? Just now?"

"No, on the passage. Weeks ago. Thirty-nine south. When I say a man—"

"Fit of temper," I suggested, confidently.

The shadowy, dark head, like mine, seemed to nod imperceptibly above the ghostly gray of my sleeping suit. It was, in the night, as though I had been faced by my own reflection in the depths of a somber and immense mirror.

"A pretty thing to have to own up to for a Conway boy," murmured my double, distinctly.

"You're a Conway boy?"

"I am," he said, as if startled. Then, slowly... "Perhaps you too—"

It was so; but being a couple of years older I had left before he joined. After a quick interchange of dates a silence fell; and I thought suddenly of my absurd mate with his terrific whiskers and the "Bless my soul—you don't say so" type of intellect. My double gave me an inkling of his thoughts by saying: "My father's a parson in Norfolk. Do you see me before a judge and jury on that charge? For myself I can't see the necessity. There are fellows that an angel from heaven—And I am not that. He was one of those creatures that are just simmering all the time with a silly sort of wickedness. Miserable devils that have no business to live at all. He wouldn't do his duty and wouldn't let anybody else do theirs. But what's the good of talking! You know well enough the sort of ill-conditioned snarling cur—"

He appealed to me as if our experiences had been as identical as our clothes. And I knew well enough the pestiferous danger of such a character where there are no means of legal repression. And I knew well enough also that my double there was no homicidal ruffian. I did not think of asking him for details, and he told me the story roughly in brusque, disconnected sentences. I needed no more. I saw it all going on as though I were myself inside that other sleeping suit.

"It happened while we were setting a reefed foresail,[2] at dusk. Reefed foresail! You understand the sort of weather. The only sail we had left to keep the ship running; so you may guess what it had been like for days. Anxious sort of job, that. He gave me some of his cursed insolence at the sheet. I tell you I was overdone with this terrific weather that seemed to have no end to it. Terrific, I tell you—and a deep ship. I believe the fellow himself was half crazed with funk. It was no time for gentlemanly reproof, so I turned round and felled him like an ox. He up and at me. We closed just as an awful sea made for the ship. All hands saw it coming and took to the rigging, but I had him by the throat, and went on shaking him like a rat, the men above us yelling, 'Look out! look out!' Then a crash as if the sky had fallen on my head. They say that for over ten minutes hardly anything was to be seen of the ship— just the three masts and a bit of the forecastle head and of the poop all awash driving along in a smother of foam. It was a miracle that they found us, jammed together behind the forebitts. It's clear that I meant business, because I was holding him by the throat still when they picked us up. He was black in the face. It was too much for them. It seems they rushed us aft together, gripped as we were, screaming 'Murder!' like a lot of

---

1   *binnacle*   Box, or stand, containing a compass and lantern.

2   *reefed foresail*   The sail set furthest forward; also known as the jib. A reefed sail has been tied back to reduce the sail area.

lunatics, and broke into the cuddy. And the ship running for her life, touch and go all the time, any minute her last in a sea fit to turn your hair gray only a-looking at it. I understand that the skipper, too, started raving like the rest of them. The man had been deprived of sleep for more than a week, and to have this sprung on him at the height of a furious gale nearly drove him out of his mind. I wonder they didn't fling me overboard after getting the carcass of their precious shipmate out of my fingers. They had rather a job to separate us, I've been told. A sufficiently fierce story to make an old judge and a respectable jury sit up a bit. The first thing I heard when I came to myself was the maddening howling of that endless gale, and on that the voice of the old man. He was hanging on to my bunk, staring into my face out of his sou'wester.[1]

"'Mr. Leggatt, you have killed a man. You can act no longer as chief mate of this ship.'"

His care to subdue his voice made it sound monotonous. He rested a hand on the end of the skylight to steady himself with, and all that time did not stir a limb, so far as I could see. "Nice little tale for a quiet tea party," he concluded in the same tone.

One of my hands, too, rested on the end of the skylight; neither did I stir a limb, so far as I knew. We stood less than a foot from each other. It occurred to me that if old "Bless my soul—you don't say so" were to put his head up the companion and catch sight of us, he would think he was seeing double, or imagine himself come upon a scene of weird witchcraft; the strange captain having a quiet confabulation by the wheel with his own gray ghost. I became very much concerned to prevent anything of the sort. I heard the other's soothing undertone.

"My father's a parson in Norfolk," it said. Evidently he had forgotten he had told me this important fact before. Truly a nice little tale.

"You had better slip down into my stateroom now," I said, moving off stealthily. My double followed my movements; our bare feet made no sound; I let him in, closed the door with care, and, after giving a call to the second mate, returned on deck for my relief.

"Not much sign of any wind yet," I remarked when he approached.

"No, sir. Not much," he assented, sleepily, in his hoarse voice, with just enough deference, no more, and barely suppressing a yawn.

"Well, that's all you have to look out for. You have got your orders."

"Yes, sir."

I paced a turn or two on the poop and saw him take up his position face forward with his elbow in the ratlines of the mizzen[2] rigging before I went below. The mate's faint snoring was still going on peacefully. The cuddy lamp was burning over the table on which stood a vase with flowers, a polite attention from the ship's provision merchant—the last flowers we should see for the next three months at the very least. Two bunches of bananas hung from the beam symmetrically, one on each side of the rudder casing. Everything was as before in the ship—except that two of her captain's sleeping suits were simultaneously in use, one motionless in the cuddy, the other keeping very still in the captain's stateroom.

It must be explained here that my cabin had the form of the capital letter L, the door being within the angle and opening into the short part of the letter. A couch was to the left, the bed place to the right; my writing desk and the chronometers' table faced the door. But anyone opening it, unless he stepped right inside, had no view of what I call the long (or vertical) part of the letter. It contained some lockers surmounted by a bookcase; and a few clothes, a thick jacket or two, caps, oilskin coat, and such like, hung on hooks. There was at the bottom of that part a door opening into my bathroom, which could be entered also directly from the saloon. But that way was never used.

The mysterious arrival had discovered the advantage of this particular shape. Entering my room, lighted strongly by a big bulkhead lamp swung on gimbals above my writing desk, I did not see him anywhere till he stepped out quietly from behind the coats hung in the recessed part.

"I heard somebody moving about, and went in there at once," he whispered.

---

[1] *sou'wester* Waterproof, often oilskin, hat with a wide slanting brim that is longer in back than in front.

[2] *mizzen* The shorter mast behind the main mast aboard a ketch or yawl.

I, too, spoke under my breath.

"Nobody is likely to come in here without knocking and getting permission."

He nodded. His face was thin and the sunburn faded, as though he had been ill. And no wonder. He had been, I heard presently, kept under arrest in his cabin for nearly seven weeks. But there was nothing sickly in his eyes or in his expression. He was not a bit like me, really; yet, as we stood leaning over my bed place, whispering side by side, with our dark heads together and our backs to the door, anybody bold enough to open it stealthily would have been treated to the uncanny sight of a double captain busy talking in whispers with his other self.

"But all this doesn't tell me how you came to hang on to our side ladder," I inquired, in the hardly audible murmurs we used, after he had told me something more of the proceedings on board the *Sephora* once the bad weather was over.

"When we sighted Java Head I had had time to think all those matters out several times over. I had six weeks of doing nothing else, and with only an hour or so every evening for a tramp on the quarter-deck."

He whispered, his arms folded on the side of my bed place, staring through the open port. And I could imagine perfectly the manner of this thinking out—a stubborn if not a steadfast operation; something of which I should have been perfectly incapable.

"I reckoned it would be dark before we closed with the land," he continued, so low that I had to strain my hearing near as we were to each other, shoulder touching shoulder almost. "So I asked to speak to the old man. He always seemed very sick when he came to see me—as if he could not look me in the face. You know, that foresail saved the ship. She was too deep to have run long under bare poles. And it was I that managed to set it for him. Anyway, he came. When I had him in my cabin—he stood by the door looking at me as if I had the halter round my neck already—I asked him right away to leave my cabin door unlocked at night while the ship was going through Sunda Straits.[1] There would be the Java coast within two or three miles, off Angier Point. I wanted nothing more.

I've had a prize for swimming my second year in the Conway."

"I can believe it," I breathed out.

"God only knows why they locked me in every night. To see some of their faces you'd have thought they were afraid I'd go about at night strangling people. Am I a murdering brute? Do I look it? By Jove! If I had been he wouldn't have trusted himself like that into my room. You'll say I might have chucked him aside and bolted out, there and then—it was dark already. Well, no. And for the same reason I wouldn't think of trying to smash the door. There would have been a rush to stop me at the noise, and I did not mean to get into a confounded scrimmage. Somebody else might have got killed—for I would not have broken out only to get chucked back, and I did not want any more of that work. He refused, looking more sick than ever. He was afraid of the men, and also of that old second mate of his who had been sailing with him for years—a gray-headed old humbug; and his steward, too, had been with him devil knows how long—seventeen years or more—a dogmatic sort of loafer who hated me like poison, just because I was the chief mate. No chief mate ever made more than one voyage in the *Sephora*, you know. Those two old chaps ran the ship. Devil only knows what the skipper wasn't afraid of (all his nerve went to pieces altogether in that hellish spell of bad weather we had)—of what the law would do to him—of his wife, perhaps. Oh, yes! she's on board. Though I don't think she would have meddled. She would have been only too glad to have me out of the ship in any way. The 'brand of Cain' business, don't you see. That's all right. I was ready enough to go off wandering on the face of the earth—and that was price enough to pay for an Abel of that sort. Anyhow, he wouldn't listen to me. 'This thing must take its course. I represent the law here.' He was shaking like a leaf. 'So you won't?' 'No!' 'Then I hope you will be able to sleep on that,' I said, and turned my back on him. 'I wonder that *you* can,' cries he, and locks the door.

"Well after that, I couldn't. Not very well. That was three weeks ago. We have had a slow passage through the Java Sea; drifted about Carimata for ten days. When we anchored here they thought, I suppose, it was all right. The nearest land (and that's five miles) is the

---

[1] *Sunda Straits* Located between the islands of Sumatra and Java in Indonesia.

ship's destination; the consul would soon set about catching me; and there would have been no object in holding to these islets there. I don't suppose there's a drop of water on them. I don't know how it was, but tonight that steward, after bringing me my supper, went out to let me eat it, and left the door unlocked. And I ate it—all there was, too. After I had finished I strolled out on the quarter-deck. I don't know that I meant to do anything. A breath of fresh air was all I wanted, I believe. Then a sudden temptation came over me. I kicked off my slippers and was in the water before I had made up my mind fairly. Somebody heard the splash and they raised an awful hullabaloo. 'He's gone! Lower the boats! He's committed suicide! No, he's swimming.' Certainly I was swimming. It's not so easy for a swimmer like me to commit suicide by drowning. I landed on the nearest islet before the boat left the ship's side. I heard them pulling about in the dark, hailing, and so on, but after a bit they gave up. Everything quieted down and the anchorage became still as death. I sat down on a stone and began to think. I felt certain they would start searching for me at daylight. There was no place to hide on those stony things—and if there had been, what would have been the good? But now I was clear of that ship, I was not going back. So after a while I took off all my clothes, tied them up in a bundle with a stone inside, and dropped them in the deep water on the outer side of that islet. That was suicide enough for me. Let them think what they liked, but I didn't mean to drown myself. I meant to swim till I sank—but that's not the same thing. I struck out for another of these little islands, and it was from that one that I first saw your riding light. Something to swim for. I went on easily, and on the way I came upon a flat rock a foot or two above water. In the daytime, I dare say, you might make it out with a glass from your poop. I scrambled up on it and rested myself for a bit. Then I made another start. That last spell must have been over a mile."

His whisper was getting fainter and fainter, and all the time he stared straight out through the porthole, in which there was not even a star to be seen. I had not interrupted him. There was something that made comment impossible in his narrative, or perhaps in himself; a sort of feeling, a quality, which I can't find a name for. And when he ceased, all I found was a futile

whisper: "So you swam for our light?"

"Yes—straight for it. It was something to swim for. I couldn't see any stars low down because the coast was in the way, and I couldn't see the land, either. The water was like glass. One might have been swimming in a confounded thousand-feet deep cistern with no place for scrambling out anywhere; but what I didn't like was the notion of swimming round and round like a crazed bullock before I gave out; and as I didn't mean to go back … No. Do you see me being hauled back, stark naked, off one of these little islands by the scruff of the neck and fighting like a wild beast? Somebody would have got killed for certain, and I did not want any of that. So I went on. Then your ladder—"

"Why didn't you hail the ship?" I asked, a little louder.

He touched my shoulder lightly. Lazy footsteps came right over our heads and stopped. The second mate had crossed from the other side of the poop and might have been hanging over the rail for all we knew.

"He couldn't hear us talking—could he?" My double breathed into my very ear, anxiously.

His anxiety was in answer, a sufficient answer, to the question I had put to him. An answer containing all the difficulty of that situation. I closed the porthole quietly, to make sure. A louder word might have been overheard.

"Who's that?" he whispered then.

"My second mate. But I don't know much more of the fellow than you do."

And I told him a little about myself. I had been appointed to take charge while I least expected anything of the sort, not quite a fortnight ago. I didn't know either the ship or the people. Hadn't had the time in port to look about me or size anybody up. And as to the crew, all they knew was that I was appointed to take the ship home. For the rest, I was almost as much of a stranger on board as himself, I said. And at the moment I felt it most acutely. I felt that it would take very little to make me a suspect person in the eyes of the ship's company.

He had turned about meantime; and we, the two strangers in the ship, faced each other in identical attitudes.

"Your ladder—" he murmured, after a silence. "Who'd have thought of finding a ladder hanging over at night in a ship anchored out here! I felt just then a very unpleasant faintness. After the life I've been leading for nine weeks, anybody would have got out of condition. I wasn't capable of swimming round as far as your rudder chains. And, lo and behold! there was a ladder to get hold of. After I gripped it I said to myself, 'What's the good?' When I saw a man's head looking over I thought I would swim away presently and leave him shouting—in whatever language it was. I didn't mind being looked at. I—I liked it. And then you speaking to me so quietly—as if you had expected me—made me hold on a little longer. It had been a confounded lonely time—I don't mean while swimming. I was glad to talk a little to somebody that didn't belong to the *Sephora*. As to asking for the captain, that was a mere impulse. It could have been no use, with all the ship knowing about me and the other people pretty certain to be round here in the morning. I don't know—I wanted to be seen, to talk with somebody, before I went on. I don't know what I would have said.... 'Fine night, isn't it?' or something of the sort."

"Do you think they will be round here presently?" I asked with some incredulity.

"Quite likely," he said, faintly.

He looked extremely haggard all of a sudden. His head rolled on his shoulders.

"H'm. We shall see then. Meantime get into that bed," I whispered. "Want help? There."

It was a rather high bed place with a set of drawers underneath. This amazing swimmer really needed the lift I gave him by seizing his leg. He tumbled in, rolled over on his back, and flung one arm across his eyes. And then, with his face nearly hidden, he must have looked exactly as I used to look in that bed. I gazed upon my other self for a while before drawing across carefully the two green serge curtains which ran on a brass rod. I thought for a moment of pinning them together for greater safety, but I sat down on the couch, and once there I felt unwilling to rise and hunt for a pin. I would do it in a moment. I was extremely tired, in a peculiarly intimate way, by the strain of stealthiness, by the effort of whispering and the general secrecy of this excitement.

It was three o'clock by now and I had been on my feet since nine, but I was not sleepy; I could not have gone to sleep. I sat there, fagged out, looking at the curtains, trying to clear my mind of the confused sensation of being in two places at once, and greatly bothered by an exasperating knocking in my head. It was a relief to discover suddenly that it was not in my head at all, but on the outside of the door. Before I could collect myself the words "Come in" were out of my mouth, and the steward entered with a tray, bringing in my morning coffee. I had slept, after all, and I was so frightened that I shouted, "This way! I am here, steward," as though he had been miles away. He put down the tray on the table next the couch and only then said, very quietly, "I can see you are here, sir." I felt him give me a keen look, but I dared not meet his eyes just then. He must have wondered why I had drawn the curtains of my bed before going to sleep on the couch. He went out, hooking the door open as usual.

I heard the crew washing decks above me. I knew I would have been told at once if there had been any wind. Calm, I thought, and I was doubly vexed. Indeed, I felt dual more than ever. The steward reappeared suddenly in the doorway. I jumped up from the couch so quickly that he gave a start.

"What do you want here?"

"Close your port, sir—they are washing decks."

"It is closed," I said, reddening.

"Very well, sir." But he did not move from the doorway and returned my stare in an extraordinary, equivocal manner for a time. Then his eyes wavered, all his expression changed, and in a voice unusually gentle, almost coaxingly:

"May I come in to take the empty cup away, sir?"

"Of course!" I turned my back on him while he popped in and out. Then I unhooked and closed the door and even pushed the bolt. This sort of thing could not go on very long. The cabin was as hot as an oven, too. I took a peep at my double, and discovered that he had not moved, his arm was still over his eyes; but his chest heaved; his hair was wet; his chin glistened with perspiration. I reached over him and opened the port.

"I must show myself on deck," I reflected.

Of course, theoretically, I could do what I liked, with no one to say nay to me within the whole circle of the horizon; but to lock my cabin door and take the key away I did not dare. Directly I put my head out of the companion I saw the group of my two officers, the second mate barefooted, the chief mate in long India-rubber boots, near the break of the poop, and the steward halfway down the poop ladder talking to them eagerly. He happened to catch sight of me and dived, the second ran down on the main-deck shouting some order or other, and the chief mate came to meet me, touching his cap.

There was a sort of curiosity in his eye that I did not like. I don't know whether the steward had told them that I was "queer" only, or downright drunk, but I know the man meant to have a good look at me. I watched him coming with a smile which, as he got into point-blank range, took effect and froze his very whiskers. I did not give him time to open his lips.

"Square the yards by lifts and braces before the hands go to breakfast."

It was the first particular order I had given on board that ship; and I stayed on deck to see it executed, too. I had felt the need of asserting myself without loss of time. That sneering young cub got taken down a peg or two on that occasion, and I also seized the opportunity of having a good look at the face of every foremast man as they filed past me to go to the after braces. At breakfast time, eating nothing myself, I presided with such frigid dignity that the two mates were only too glad to escape from the cabin as soon as decency permitted; and all the time the dual working of my mind distracted me almost to the point of insanity. I was constantly watching myself, my secret self, as dependent on my actions as my own personality, sleeping in that bed, behind that door which faced me as I sat at the head of the table. It was very much like being mad, only it was worse because one was aware of it.

I had to shake him for a solid minute, but when at last he opened his eyes it was in the full possession of his senses, with an inquiring look.

"All's well so far," I whispered. "Now you must vanish into the bathroom."

He did so, as noiseless as a ghost, and then I rang for the steward, and facing him boldly, directed him to tidy up my stateroom while I was having my bath—"and be quick about it." As my tone admitted of no excuses, he

said, "Yes, sir," and ran off to fetch his dustpan and brushes. I took a bath and did most of my dressing, splashing, and whistling softly for the steward's edification, while the secret sharer of my life stood drawn up bolt upright in that little space, his face looking very sunken in daylight, his eyelids lowered under the stern, dark line of his eyebrows drawn together by a slight frown.

When I left him there to go back to my room the steward was finishing dusting. I sent for the mate and engaged him in some insignificant conversation. It was, as it were, trifling with the terrific character of his whiskers; but my object was to give him an opportunity for a good look at my cabin. And then I could at last shut, with a clear conscience, the door of my stateroom and get my double back into the recessed part. There was nothing else for it. He had to sit still on a small folding stool, half smothered by the heavy coats hanging there. We listened to the steward going into the bathroom out of the saloon, filling the water bottles there, scrubbing the bath, setting things to rights, whisk, bang, clatter—out again into the saloon—turn the key—click. Such was my scheme for keeping my second self invisible. Nothing better could be contrived under the circumstances. And there we sat; I at my writing desk ready to appear busy with some papers, he behind me out of sight of the door. It would not have been prudent to talk in daytime; and I could not have stood the excitement of that queer sense of whispering to myself. Now and then, glancing over my shoulder, I saw him far back there, sitting rigidly on the low stool, his bare feet close together, his arms folded, his head hanging on his breast—and perfectly still. Anybody would have taken him for me.

I was fascinated by it myself. Every moment I had to glance over my shoulder. I was looking at him when a voice outside the door said:

"Beg pardon, sir."

"Well!" ... I kept my eyes on him, and so when the voice outside the door announced, "There's a ship's boat coming our way, sir," I saw him give a start—the first movement he had made for hours. But he did not raise his bowed head.

"All right. Get the ladder over."

I hesitated. Should I whisper something to him? But what? His immobility seemed to have been never disturbed. What could I tell him he did not know already?... Finally I went on deck.

2

The skipper of the *Sephora* had a thin red whisker all round his face, and the sort of complexion that goes with hair of that colour; also the particular, rather smeary shade of blue in the eyes. He was not exactly a showy figure; his shoulders were high, his stature but middling—one leg slightly more bandy than the other. He shook hands, looking vaguely around. A spiritless tenacity was his main characteristic, I judged. I behaved with a politeness which seemed to disconcert him. Perhaps he was shy. He mumbled to me as if he were ashamed of what he was saying; gave his name (it was something like Archbold—but at this distance of years I hardly am sure), his ship's name, and a few other particulars of that sort, in the manner of a criminal making a reluctant and doleful confession. He had had terrible weather on the passage out—terrible—terrible—wife aboard, too.

By this time we were seated in the cabin and the steward brought in a tray with a bottle and glasses. "Thanks! No." Never took liquor. Would have some water, though. He drank two tumblerfuls. Terrible thirsty work. Ever since daylight had been exploring the islands round his ship.

"What was that for—fun?" I asked, with an appearance of polite interest.

"No!" He sighed. "Painful duty."

As he persisted in his mumbling and I wanted my double to hear every word, I hit upon the notion of informing him that I regretted to say I was hard of hearing.

"Such a young man, too!" he nodded, keeping his smeary blue, unintelligent eyes fastened upon me. "What was the cause of it—some disease?" he inquired, without the least sympathy and as if he thought that, if so, I'd got no more than I deserved.

"Yes; disease," I admitted in a cheerful tone which seemed to shock him. But my point was gained, because he had to raise his voice to give me his tale. It is not worth while to record his version. It was just over two months since all this had happened, and he had thought so much about it that he seemed completely muddled as

to its bearings, but still immensely impressed.

"What would you think of such a thing happening on board your own ship? I've had the *Sephora* for these fifteen years. I am a well-known shipmaster."

He was densely distressed—and perhaps I should have sympathized with him if I had been able to detach my mental vision from the unsuspected sharer of my cabin as though he were my second self. There he was on the other side of the bulkhead, four or five feet from us, no more, as we sat in the saloon. I looked politely at Captain Archbold (if that was his name), but it was the other I saw, in a gray sleeping suit, seated on a low stool, his bare feet close together, his arms folded, and every word said between us falling into the ears of his dark head bowed on his chest.

"I have been at sea now, man and boy, for seven-and-thirty years, and I've never heard of such a thing happening in an English ship. And that it should be my ship. Wife on board, too."

I was hardly listening to him.

"Don't you think," I said, "that the heavy sea which, you told me, came aboard just then might have killed the man? I have seen the sheer weight of a sea kill a man very neatly, by simply breaking his neck."

"Good God!" he uttered, impressively, fixing his smeary blue eyes on me. "The sea! No man killed by the sea ever looked like that." He seemed positively scandalized at my suggestion. And as I gazed at him certainly not prepared for anything original on his part, he advanced his head close to mine and thrust his tongue out at me so suddenly that I couldn't help starting back.

After scoring over my calmness in this graphic way he nodded wisely. If I had seen the sight, he assured me, I would never forget it as long as I lived. The weather was too bad to give the corpse a proper sea burial. So next day at dawn they took it up on the poop, covering its face with a bit of bunting; he read a short prayer, and then, just as it was, in its oilskins and long boots, they launched it amongst those mountainous seas that seemed ready every moment to swallow up the ship herself and the terrified lives on board of her.

"That reefed foresail saved you," I threw in.

"Under God—it did," he exclaimed fervently. "It was by a special mercy, I firmly believe, that it stood some of those hurricane squalls."

"It was the setting of that sail which—" I began.

"God's own hand in it," he interrupted me. "Nothing less could have done it. I don't mind telling you that I hardly dared give the order. It seemed impossible that we could touch anything without losing it, and then our last hope would have been gone."

The terror of that gale was on him yet. I let him go on for a bit, then said, casually—as if returning to a minor subject:

"You were very anxious to give up your mate to the shore people, I believe?"

He was. To the law. His obscure tenacity on that point had in it something incomprehensible and a little awful; something, as it were, mystical, quite apart from his anxiety that he should not be suspected of "countenancing any doings of that sort." Seven-and-thirty virtuous years at sea, of which over twenty of immaculate command, and the last fifteen in the *Sephora*, seemed to have laid him under some pitiless obligation.

"And you know," he went on, groping shame-facedly amongst his feelings, "I did not engage that young fellow. His people had some interest with my owners. I was in a way forced to take him on. He looked very smart, very gentlemanly, and all that. But do you know—I never liked him, somehow. I am a plain man. You see, he wasn't exactly the sort for the chief mate of a ship like the *Sephora*."

I had become so connected in thoughts and impressions with the secret sharer of my cabin that I felt as if I, personally, were being given to understand that I, too, was not the sort that would have done for the chief mate of a ship like the *Sephora*. I had no doubt of it in my mind.

"Not at all the style of man. You understand," he insisted, superfluously, looking hard at me.

I smiled urbanely. He seemed at a loss for a while.

"I suppose I must report a suicide."

"Beg pardon?"

"Suicide! That's what I'll have to write to my owners directly I get in."

"Unless you manage to recover him before tomorrow," I assented, dispassionately... "I mean, alive."

He mumbled something which I really did not catch, and I turned my ear to him in a puzzled manner. He fairly bawled:

"The land—I say, the mainland is at least seven miles off my anchorage."

"About that."

My lack of excitement, of curiosity, of surprise, of any sort of pronounced interest, began to arouse his distrust. But except for the felicitous pretense of deafness I had not tried to pretend anything. I had felt utterly incapable of playing the part of ignorance properly, and therefore was afraid to try. It is also certain that he had brought some ready-made suspicions with him, and that he viewed my politeness as a strange and unnatural phenomenon. And yet how else could I have received him? Not heartily! That was impossible for psychological reasons, which I need not state here. My only object was to keep off his inquiries. Surlily? Yes, but surliness might have provoked a point-blank question. From its novelty to him and from its nature, punctilious courtesy was the manner best calculated to restrain the man. But there was the danger of his breaking through my defense bluntly. I could not, I think, have met him by a direct lie, also for psychological (not moral) reasons. If he had only known how afraid I was of his putting my feeling of identity with the other to the test! But, strangely enough—(I thought of it only afterwards)—I believe that he was not a little disconcerted by the reverse side of that weird situation, by something in me that reminded him of the man he was seeking—suggested a mysterious similitude to the young fellow he had distrusted and disliked from the first.

However that might have been, the silence was not very prolonged. He took another oblique step.

"I reckon I had no more than a two-mile pull to your ship. Not a bit more."

"And quite enough, too, in this awful heat," I said.

Another pause full of mistrust followed. Necessity, they say, is mother of invention, but fear, too, is not barren of ingenious suggestions. And I was afraid he would ask me point-blank for news of my other self.

"Nice little saloon, isn't it?" I remarked, as if noticing for the first time the way his eyes roamed from one closed door to the other. "And very well fitted out, too. Here, for instance," I continued, reaching over the back of my seat negligently and flinging the door open, "is my bathroom."

He made an eager movement, but hardly gave it a glance. I got up, shut the door of the bathroom, and invited him to have a look round, as if I were very proud of my accommodation. He had to rise and be shown round, but he went through the business without any raptures whatever.

"And now we'll have a look at my stateroom," I declared, in a voice as loud as I dared to make it, crossing the cabin to the starboard side with purposely heavy steps.

He followed me in and gazed around. My intelligent double had vanished. I played my part.

"Very convenient—isn't it?"

"Very nice. Very comf … " He didn't finish and went out brusquely as if to escape from some unrighteous wiles of mine. But it was not to be. I had been too frightened not to feel vengeful; I felt I had him on the run, and I meant to keep him on the run. My polite insistence must have had something menacing in it, because he gave in suddenly. And I did not let him off a single item; mate's room, pantry, storerooms, the very sail locker which was also under the poop—he had to look into them all. When at last I showed him out on the quarter-deck he drew a long, spiritless sigh, and mumbled dismally that he must really be going back to his ship now. I desired my mate, who had joined us, to see to the captain's boat.

The man of whiskers gave a blast on the whistle which he used to wear hanging round his neck, and yelled, "*Sephora's* away!" My double down there in my cabin must have heard, and certainly could not feel more relieved than I. Four fellows came running out from somewhere forward and went over the side, while my own men, appearing on deck too, lined the rail. I escorted my visitor to the gangway ceremoniously, and nearly overdid it. He was a tenacious beast. On the very ladder he lingered, and in that unique, guiltily conscientious manner of sticking to the point:

"I say … you … you don't think that—"

I covered his voice loudly:

"Certainly not … I am delighted. Good-by."

I had an idea of what he meant to say, and just saved

myself by the privilege of defective hearing. He was too shaken generally to insist, but my mate, close witness of that parting, looked mystified and his face took on a thoughtful cast. As I did not want to appear as if I wished to avoid all communication with my officers, he had the opportunity to address me.

"Seems a very nice man. His boat's crew told our chaps a very extraordinary story, if what I am told by the steward is true. I suppose you had it from the captain, sir?"

"Yes. I had a story from the captain."

"A very horrible affair—isn't it, sir?"

"It is."

"Beats all these tales we hear about murders in Yankee ships."

"I don't think it beats them. I don't think it resembles them in the least."

"Bless my soul—you don't say so! But of course I've no acquaintance whatever with American ships, not I so I couldn't go against your knowledge. It's horrible enough for me…. But the queerest part is that those fellows seemed to have some idea the man was hidden aboard here. They had really. Did you ever hear of such a thing?"

"Preposterous—isn't it?"

We were walking to and fro athwart the quarter-deck. No one of the crew forward could be seen (the day was Sunday), and the mate pursued:

"There was some little dispute about it. Our chaps took offense. 'As if we would harbour a thing like that,' they said. 'Wouldn't you like to look for him in our coal-hole?' Quite a tiff. But they made it up in the end. I suppose he did drown himself. Don't you, sir?"

"I don't suppose anything."

"You have no doubt in the matter, sir?"

"None whatever."

I left him suddenly. I felt I was producing a bad impression, but with my double down there it was most trying to be on deck. And it was almost as trying to be below. Altogether a nerve-trying situation. But on the whole I felt less torn in two when I was with him. There was no one in the whole ship whom I dared take into my confidence. Since the hands had got to know his story, it would have been impossible to pass him off for anyone else, and an accidental discovery was to be dreaded now more than ever....

The steward being engaged in laying the table for dinner, we could talk only with our eyes when I first went down. Later in the afternoon we had a cautious try at whispering. The Sunday quietness of the ship was against us; the stillness of air and water around her was against us; the elements, the men were against us—everything was against us in our secret partnership; time itself—for this could not go on forever. The very trust in Providence was, I suppose, denied to his guilt. Shall I confess that this thought cast me down very much? And as to the chapter of accidents which counts for so much in the book of success, I could only hope that it was closed. For what favourable accident could be expected?

"Did you hear everything?" were my first words as soon as we took up our position side by side, leaning over my bed place.

He had. And the proof of it was his earnest whisper, "The man told you he hardly dared to give the order."

I understood the reference to be to that saving foresail.

"Yes. He was afraid of it being lost in the setting."

"I assure you he never gave the order. He may think he did, but he never gave it. He stood there with me on the break of the poop after the main topsail blew away, and whimpered about our last hope—positively whimpered about it and nothing else—and the night coming on! To hear one's skipper go on like that in such weather was enough to drive any fellow out of his mind. It worked me up into a sort of desperation. I just took it into my own hands and went away from him, boiling, and—But what's the use telling you? YOU know!... Do you think that if I had not been pretty fierce with them I should have got the men to do anything? Not it! The bo's'n[1] perhaps? Perhaps! It wasn't a heavy sea—it was a sea gone mad! I suppose the end of the world will be something like that; and a man may have the heart to see it coming once and be done with it—but to have to face it day after day—I don't blame anybody. I was precious little better than the rest. Only—I was an officer of that old coal wagon, anyhow—"

[1] *bo's'n* Boatswain (petty officer in charge of ship's rigging, sails, anchors, and deck crew).

"I quite understand," I conveyed that sincere assurance into his ear. He was out of breath with whispering; I could hear him pant slightly. It was all very simple. The same strung-up force which had given twenty-four men a chance, at least, for their lives, had, in a sort of recoil, crushed an unworthy mutinous existence.

But I had no leisure to weigh the merits of the matter—footsteps in the saloon, a heavy knock. "There's enough wind to get under way with, sir." Here was the call of a new claim upon my thoughts and even upon my feelings.

"Turn the hands up," I cried through the door. "I'll be on deck directly."

I was going out to make the acquaintance of my ship. Before I left the cabin our eyes met—the eyes of the only two strangers on board. I pointed to the recessed part where the little campstool awaited him and laid my finger on my lips. He made a gesture—somewhat vague—a little mysterious, accompanied by a faint smile, as if of regret.

This is not the place to enlarge upon the sensations of a man who feels for the first time a ship move under his feet to his own independent word. In my case they were not unalloyed. I was not wholly alone with my command; for there was that stranger in my cabin. Or rather, I was not completely and wholly with her. Part of me was absent. That mental feeling of being in two places at once affected me physically as if the mood of secrecy had penetrated my very soul. Before an hour had elapsed since the ship had begun to move, having occasion to ask the mate (he stood by my side) to take a compass bearing of the pagoda, I caught myself reaching up to his ear in whispers. I say I caught myself, but enough had escaped to startle the man. I can't describe it otherwise than by saying that he shied. A grave, preoccupied manner, as though he were in possession of some perplexing intelligence, did not leave him henceforth. A little later I moved away from the rail to look at the compass with such a stealthy gait that the helmsman noticed it—and I could not help noticing the unusual roundness of his eyes. These are trifling instances, though it's to no commander's advantage to be suspected of ludicrous eccentricities. But I was also more seriously affected. There are to a seaman certain words, gestures, that should in given conditions come as naturally, as instinctively as the winking of a menaced eye. A certain order should spring on to his lips without thinking; a certain sign should get itself made, so to speak, without reflection. But all unconscious alertness had abandoned me. I had to make an effort of will to recall myself back (from the cabin) to the conditions of the moment. I felt that I was appearing an irresolute commander to those people who were watching me more or less critically.

And, besides, there were the scares. On the second day out, for instance, coming off the deck in the afternoon (I had straw slippers on my bare feet) I stopped at the open pantry door and spoke to the steward. He was doing something there with his back to me. At the sound of my voice he nearly jumped out of his skin, as the saying is, and incidentally broke a cup.

"What on earth's the matter with you?" I asked, astonished.

He was extremely confused. "Beg your pardon, sir. I made sure you were in your cabin."

"You see I wasn't."

"No, sir. I could have sworn I had heard you moving in there not a moment ago. It's most extraordinary … very sorry, sir."

I passed on with an inward shudder. I was so identified with my secret double that I did not even mention the fact in those scanty, fearful whispers we exchanged. I suppose he had made some slight noise of some kind or other. It would have been miraculous if he hadn't at one time or another. And yet, haggard as he appeared, he looked always perfectly self-controlled, more than calm—almost invulnerable. On my suggestion he remained almost entirely in the bathroom, which, upon the whole, was the safest place. There could be really no shadow of an excuse for anyone ever wanting to go in there, once the steward had done with it. It was a very tiny place. Sometimes he reclined on the floor, his legs bent, his head sustained on one elbow. At others I would find him on the campstool, sitting in his gray sleeping suit and with his cropped dark hair like a patient, unmoved convict. At night I would smuggle him into my bed place, and we would whisper together, with the regular footfalls of the officer of the watch passing and repassing over our heads. It was an infinitely

miserable time. It was lucky that some tins of fine preserves were stowed in a locker in my stateroom; hard bread I could always get hold of; and so he lived on stewed chicken, *paté de foie gras*, asparagus, cooked oysters, sardines—on all sorts of abominable sham delicacies out of tins. My early-morning coffee he always drank; and it was all I dared do for him in that respect.

Every day there was the horrible maneuvering to go through so that my room and then the bathroom should be done in the usual way. I came to hate the sight of the steward, to abhor the voice of that harmless man. I felt that it was he who would bring on the disaster of discovery. It hung like a sword over our heads.

The fourth day out, I think (we were then working down the east side of the Gulf of Siam, tack for tack, in light winds and smooth water)—the fourth day, I say, of this miserable juggling with the unavoidable, as we sat at our evening meal, that man, whose slightest movement I dreaded, after putting down the dishes ran up on deck busily. This could not be dangerous. Presently he came down again; and then it appeared that he had remembered a coat of mine which I had thrown over a rail to dry after having been wetted in a shower which had passed over the ship in the afternoon. Sitting stolidly at the head of the table I became terrified at the sight of the garment on his arm. Of course he made for my door. There was no time to lose.

"Steward," I thundered. My nerves were so shaken that I could not govern my voice and conceal my agitation. This was the sort of thing that made my terrifically whiskered mate tap his forehead with his forefinger. I had detected him using that gesture while talking on deck with a confidential air to the carpenter. It was too far to hear a word, but I had no doubt that this pantomime could only refer to the strange new captain.

"Yes, sir," the pale-faced steward turned resignedly to me. It was this maddening course of being shouted at, checked without rhyme or reason, arbitrarily chased out of my cabin, suddenly called into it, sent flying out of his pantry on incomprehensible errands, that accounted for the growing wretchedness of his expression.

"Where are you going with that coat?"

"To your room, sir."

"Is there another shower coming?"

"I'm sure I don't know, sir. Shall I go up again and see, sir?"

"No! never mind."

My object was attained, as of course my other self in there would have heard everything that passed. During this interlude my two officers never raised their eyes off their respective plates; but the lip of that confounded cub, the second mate, quivered visibly.

I expected the steward to hook my coat on and come out at once. He was very slow about it; but I dominated my nervousness sufficiently not to shout after him. Suddenly I became aware (it could be heard plainly enough) that the fellow for some reason or other was opening the door of the bathroom. It was the end. The place was literally not big enough to swing a cat in. My voice died in my throat and I went stony all over. I expected to hear a yell of surprise and terror, and made a movement, but had not the strength to get on my legs. Everything remained still. Had my second self taken the poor wretch by the throat? I don't know what I could have done next moment if I had not seen the steward come out of my room, close the door, and then stand quietly by the sideboard.

"Saved," I thought. "But, no! Lost! Gone! He was gone!"

I laid my knife and fork down and leaned back in my chair. My head swam. After a while, when sufficiently recovered to speak in a steady voice, I instructed my mate to put the ship round at eight o'clock himself.

"I won't come on deck," I went on. "I think I'll turn in, and unless the wind shifts I don't want to be disturbed before midnight. I feel a bit seedy."

"You did look middling bad a little while ago," the chief mate remarked without showing any great concern.

They both went out, and I stared at the steward clearing the table. There was nothing to be read on that wretched man's face. But why did he avoid my eyes, I asked myself. Then I thought I should like to hear the sound of his voice.

"Steward!"

"Sir!" Startled as usual.

"Where did you hang up that coat?"

"In the bathroom, sir." The usual anxious tone. "It's not quite dry yet, sir."

For some time longer I sat in the cuddy. Had my double vanished as he had come? But of his coming there was an explanation, whereas his disappearance would be inexplicable ... I went slowly into my dark room, shut the door, lighted the lamp, and for a time dared not turn round. When at last I did I saw him standing bolt-upright in the narrow recessed part. It would not be true to say I had a shock, but an irresistible doubt of his bodily existence flitted through my mind. Can it be, I asked myself, that he is not visible to other eyes than mine? It was like being haunted. Motionless, with a grave face, he raised his hands slightly at me in a gesture which meant clearly, "Heavens! what a narrow escape!" Narrow indeed. I think I had come creeping quietly as near insanity as any man who has not actually gone over the border. That gesture restrained me, so to speak.

The mate with the terrific whiskers was now putting the ship on the other tack. In the moment of profound silence which follows upon the hands going to their stations I heard on the poop his raised voice: "Hard alee!"[1] and the distant shout of the order repeated on the main-deck. The sails, in that light breeze, made but a faint fluttering noise. It ceased. The ship was coming round slowly: I held my breath in the renewed stillness of expectation; one wouldn't have thought that there was a single living soul on her decks. A sudden brisk shout, "Mainsail haul!" broke the spell, and in the noisy cries and rush overhead of the men running away with the main brace we two, down in my cabin, came together in our usual position by the bed place.

He did not wait for my question. "I heard him fumbling here and just managed to squat myself down in the bath," he whispered to me. "The fellow only opened the door and put his arm in to hang the coat up. All the same—"

"I never thought of that," I whispered back, even more appalled than before at the closeness of the shave, and marveling at that something unyielding in his character which was carrying him through so finely. There was no agitation in his whisper. Whoever was

---

[1] *Hard alee* "Hard a lee" (meaning "hard towards the leeward side") is the command given when a ship comes about.

being driven distracted, it was not he. He was sane. And the proof of his sanity was continued when he took up the whispering again.

"It would never do for me to come to life again."

It was something that a ghost might have said. But what he was alluding to was his old captain's reluctant admission of the theory of suicide. It would obviously serve his turn—if I had understood at all the view which seemed to govern the unalterable purpose of his action.

"You must maroon me as soon as ever you can get amongst these islands off the Cambodge[1] shore," he went on.

"Maroon you! We are not living in a boy's adventure tale," I protested. His scornful whispering took me up.

"We aren't indeed! There's nothing of a boy's tale in this. But there's nothing else for it. I want no more. You don't suppose I am afraid of what can be done to me? Prison or gallows or whatever they may please. But you don't see me coming back to explain such things to an old fellow in a wig and twelve respectable tradesmen, do you? What can they know whether I am guilty or not— or of *what* I am guilty, either? That's my affair. What does the Bible say? 'Driven off the face of the earth.' Very well, I am off the face of the earth now. As I came at night so I shall go."

"Impossible!" I murmured. "You can't."

"Can't? … Not naked like a soul on the Day of Judgment. I shall freeze on to this sleeping suit. The Last Day is not yet—and … you have understood thoroughly. Didn't you?"

I felt suddenly ashamed of myself. I may say truly that I understood—and my hesitation in letting that man swim away from my ship's side had been a mere sham sentiment, a sort of cowardice.

"It can't be done now till next night," I breathed out. "The ship is on the off-shore tack and the wind may fail us."

"As long as I know that you understand," he whispered. "But of course you do. It's a great satisfaction to have got somebody to understand. You seem to have been there on purpose." And in the same whisper, as if we two whenever we talked had to say things to each

other which were not fit for the world to hear, he added, "It's very wonderful."

We remained side by side talking in our secret way—but sometimes silent or just exchanging a whispered word or two at long intervals. And as usual he stared through the port. A breath of wind came now and again into our faces. The ship might have been moored in dock, so gently and on an even keel she slipped through the water, that did not murmur even at our passage, shadowy and silent like a phantom sea.

At midnight I went on deck, and to my mate's great surprise put the ship round on the other tack. His terrible whiskers flitted round me in silent criticism. I certainly should not have done it if it had been only a question of getting out of that sleepy gulf as quickly as possible. I believe he told the second mate, who relieved him, that it was a great want of judgment. The other only yawned. That intolerable cub shuffled about so sleepily and lolled against the rails in such a slack, improper fashion that I came down on him sharply.

"Aren't you properly awake yet?"

"Yes, sir! I am awake."

"Well, then, be good enough to hold yourself as if you were. And keep a lookout. If there's any current we'll be closing with some islands before daylight."

The east side of the gulf is fringed with islands, some solitary, others in groups. On the blue background of the high coast they seem to float on silvery patches of calm water, arid and gray, or dark green and rounded like clumps of evergreen bushes, with the larger ones, a mile or two long, showing the outlines of ridges, ribs of gray rock under the dark mantle of matted leafage. Unknown to trade, to travel, almost to geography, the manner of life they harbour is an unsolved secret. There must be villages—settlements of fishermen at least—on the largest of them, and some communication with the world is probably kept up by native craft. But all that forenoon, as we headed for them, fanned along by the faintest of breezes, I saw no sign of man or canoe in the field of the telescope I kept on pointing at the scattered group.

At noon I gave no orders for a change of course, and the mate's whiskers became much concerned and seemed to be offering themselves unduly to my notice. At last I said:

---

[1] *Cambodge* Cambodia.

"I am going to stand right in. Quite in—as far as I can take her."

The stare of extreme surprise imparted an air of ferocity also to his eyes, and he looked truly terrific for a moment.

"We're not doing well in the middle of the gulf," I continued, casually. "I am going to look for the land breezes tonight."

"Bless my soul! Do you mean, sir, in the dark amongst the lot of all them islands and reefs and shoals?"

"Well—if there are any regular land breezes at all on this coast one must get close inshore to find them, mustn't one?"

"Bless my soul!" he exclaimed again under his breath. All that afternoon he wore a dreamy, contemplative appearance which in him was a mark of perplexity. After dinner I went into my stateroom as if I meant to take some rest. There we two bent our dark heads over a half-unrolled chart lying on my bed.

"There," I said. "It's got to be Koh-ring. I've been looking at it ever since sunrise. It has got two hills and a low point. It must be inhabited. And on the coast opposite there is what looks like the mouth of a biggish river—with some towns, no doubt, not far up. It's the best chance for you that I can see."

"Anything. Koh-ring let it be."

He looked thoughtfully at the chart as if surveying chances and distances from a lofty height—and following with his eyes his own figure wandering on the blank land of Cochin-China, and then passing off that piece of paper clean out of sight into uncharted regions. And it was as if the ship had two captains to plan her course for her. I had been so worried and restless running up and down that I had not had the patience to dress that day. I had remained in my sleeping suit, with straw slippers and a soft floppy hat. The closeness of the heat in the gulf had been most oppressive, and the crew were used to seeing me wandering in that airy attire.

"She will clear the south point as she heads now," I whispered into his ear. "Goodness only knows when, though, but certainly after dark. I'll edge her in to half a mile, as far as I may be able to judge in the dark—"

"Be careful," he murmured, warningly—and I realized suddenly that all my future, the only future for

which I was fit, would perhaps go irretrievably to pieces in any mishap to my first command.

I could not stop a moment longer in the room. I motioned him to get out of sight and made my way on the poop. That unplayful cub had the watch. I walked up and down for a while thinking things out, then beckoned him over.

"Send a couple of hands to open the two quarter-deck ports," I said, mildly.

He actually had the impudence, or else so forgot himself in his wonder at such an incomprehensible order, as to repeat:

"Open the quarter-deck ports! What for, sir?"

"The only reason you need concern yourself about is because I tell you to do so. Have them open wide and fastened properly."

He reddened and went off, but I believe made some jeering remark to the carpenter as to the sensible practice of ventilating a ship's quarter-deck. I know he popped into the mate's cabin to impart the fact to him because the whiskers came on deck, as it were by chance, and stole glances at me from below—for signs of lunacy or drunkenness, I suppose.

A little before supper, feeling more restless than ever, I rejoined, for a moment, my second self. And to find him sitting so quietly was surprising, like something against nature, inhuman.

I developed my plan in a hurried whisper.

"I shall stand in as close as I dare and then put her round. I will presently find means to smuggle you out of here into the sail locker, which communicates with the lobby. But there is an opening, a sort of square for hauling the sails out, which gives straight on the quarter-deck and which is never closed in fine weather, so as to give air to the sails. When the ship's way is deadened in stays and all the hands are aft at the main braces you will have a clear road to slip out and get overboard through the open quarter-deck port. I've had them both fastened up. Use a rope's end to lower yourself into the water so as to avoid a splash—you know. It could be heard and cause some beastly complication."

He kept silent for a while, then whispered, "I understand."

"I won't be there to see you go," I began with an effort. "The rest … I only hope I have understood, too."

"You have. From first to last"—and for the first time there seemed to be a faltering, something strained in his whisper. He caught hold of my arm, but the ringing of the supper bell made me start. He didn't though; he only released his grip.

After supper I didn't come below again till well past eight o'clock. The faint, steady breeze was loaded with dew; and the wet, darkened sails held all there was of propelling power in it. The night, clear and starry, sparkled darkly, and the opaque, lightless patches shifting slowly against the low stars were the drifting islets. On the port bow there was a big one more distant and shadowily imposing by the great space of sky it eclipsed.

On opening the door I had a back view of my very own self looking at a chart. He had come out of the recess and was standing near the table.

"Quite dark enough," I whispered.

He stepped back and leaned against my bed with a level, quiet glance. I sat on the couch. We had nothing to say to each other. Over our heads the officer of the watch moved here and there. Then I heard him move quickly. I knew what that meant. He was making for the companion; and presently his voice was outside my door.

"We are drawing in pretty fast, sir. Land looks rather close."

"Very well," I answered. "I am coming on deck directly."

I waited till he was gone out of the cuddy, then rose. My double moved too. The time had come to exchange our last whispers, for neither of us was ever to hear each other's natural voice.

"Look here!" I opened a drawer and took out three sovereigns. "Take this anyhow. I've got six and I'd give you the lot, only I must keep a little money to buy some fruit and vegetables for the crew from native boats as we go through Sunda Straits."

He shook his head.

"Take it," I urged him, whispering desperately. "No one can tell what—"

He smiled and slapped meaningly the only pocket of the sleeping jacket. It was not safe, certainly. But I produced a large old silk handkerchief of mine, and tying the three pieces of gold in a corner, pressed it on him. He was touched, I supposed, because he took it at

last and tied it quickly round his waist under the jacket, on his bare skin.

Our eyes met; several seconds elapsed, till, our glances still mingled, I extended my hand and turned the lamp out. Then I passed through the cuddy, leaving the door of my room wide open…"Steward!"

He was still lingering in the pantry in the greatness of his zeal, giving a rub-up to a plated cruet stand the last thing before going to bed. Being careful not to wake up the mate, whose room was opposite, I spoke in an undertone.

He looked round anxiously. "Sir!"

"Can you get me a little hot water from the galley?"

"I am afraid, sir, the galley fire's been out for some time now."

"Go and see."

He flew up the stairs.

"Now," I whispered, loudly, into the saloon—too loudly, perhaps, but I was afraid I couldn't make a sound. He was by my side in an instant—the double captain slipped past the stairs—through a tiny dark passage … a sliding door. We were in the sail locker, scrambling on our knees over the sails. A sudden thought struck me. I saw myself wandering barefooted, bareheaded, the sun beating on my dark poll. I snatched off my floppy hat and tried hurriedly in the dark to ram it on my other self. He dodged and fended off silently. I wonder what he thought had come to me before he understood and suddenly desisted. Our hands met gropingly, lingered united in a steady, motionless clasp for a second … No word was breathed by either of us when they separated.

I was standing quietly by the pantry door when the steward returned.

"Sorry, sir. Kettle barely warm. Shall I light the spirit lamp?"

"Never mind."

I came out on deck slowly. It was now a matter of conscience to shave the land as close as possible—for now he must go overboard whenever the ship was put in stays. Must! There could be no going back for him. After a moment I walked over to leeward and my heart flew into my mouth at the nearness of the land on the bow. Under any other circumstances I would not have held on a minute longer. The second mate had followed me anxiously.

I looked on till I felt I could command my voice.

"She will weather," I said then in a quiet tone.

"Are you going to try that, sir?" he stammered out incredulously.

I took no notice of him and raised my tone just enough to be heard by the helmsman.

"Keep her good full."

"Good full, sir."

The wind fanned my cheek, the sails slept, the world was silent. The strain of watching the dark loom of the land grow bigger and denser was too much for me. I had shut my eyes—because the ship must go closer. She must! The stillness was intolerable. Were we standing still?

When I opened my eyes the second view started my heart with a thump. The black southern hill of Koh-ring seemed to hang right over the ship like a towering fragment of everlasting night. On that enormous mass of blackness there was not a gleam to be seen, not a sound to be heard. It was gliding irresistibly towards us and yet seemed already within reach of the hand. I saw the vague figures of the watch grouped in the waist, gazing in awed silence.

"Are you going on, sir?" inquired an unsteady voice at my elbow.

I ignored it. I had to go on.

"Keep her full. Don't check her way. That won't do now," I said warningly.

"I can't see the sails very well," the helmsman answered me, in strange, quavering tones.

Was she close enough? Already she was, I won't say in the shadow of the land, but in the very blackness of it, already swallowed up as it were, gone too close to be recalled, gone from me altogether.

"Give the mate a call," I said to the young man who stood at my elbow as still as death. "And turn all hands up."

My tone had a borrowed loudness reverberated from the height of the land. Several voices cried out together: "We are all on deck, sir."

Then stillness again, with the great shadow gliding closer, towering higher, without a light, without a sound. Such a hush had fallen on the ship that she might have been a bark of the dead floating in slowly

under the very gate of Erebus.[1]

"My God! Where are we?"

It was the mate moaning at my elbow. He was thunderstruck, and as it were deprived of the moral support of his whiskers. He clapped his hands and absolutely cried out, "Lost!"

"Be quiet," I said, sternly.

He lowered his tone, but I saw the shadowy gesture of his despair. "What are we doing here?"

"Looking for the land wind."

He made as if to tear his hair, and addressed me recklessly.

"She will never get out. You have done it, sir. I knew it'd end in something like this. She will never weather, and you are too close now to stay. She'll drift ashore before she's round. O my God!"

I caught his arm as he was raising it to batter his poor devoted head, and shook it violently.

"She's ashore already," he wailed, trying to tear himself away.

"Is she? … Keep good full there!"

"Good full, sir," cried the helmsman in a frightened, thin, childlike voice.

I hadn't let go the mate's arm and went on shaking it. "Ready about, do you hear? You go forward"—shake—"and stop there"—shake—"and hold your noise"—shake—"and see these head-sheets properly overhauled"—shake, shake—shake.

And all the time I dared not look towards the land lest my heart should fail me. I released my grip at last and he ran forward as if fleeing for dear life.

I wondered what my double there in the sail locker thought of this commotion. He was able to hear everything—and perhaps he was able to understand why, on my conscience, it had to be thus close—no less. My first order "Hard alee!" re-echoed ominously under the towering shadow of Koh-ring as if I had shouted in a mountain gorge. And then I watched the land intently. In that smooth water and light wind it was impossible to feel the ship coming-to. No! I could not feel her. And my second self was making now ready to ship out and lower himself overboard. Perhaps he was gone already…?

---

[1] *Erebus* In classical myth, a place of darkness between earth and Hades, the underworld.

The great black mass brooding over our very mastheads began to pivot away from the ship's side silently. And now I forgot the secret stranger ready to depart, and remembered only that I was a total stranger to the ship. I did not know her. Would she do it? How was she to be handled?

I swung the mainyard and waited helplessly. She was perhaps stopped, and her very fate hung in the balance, with the black mass of Koh-ring like the gate of the everlasting night towering over her taffrail.[1] What would she do now? Had she way on her yet? I stepped to the side swiftly, and on the shadowy water I could see nothing except a faint phosphorescent flash revealing the glassy smoothness of the sleeping surface. It was impossible to tell—and I had not learned yet the feel of my ship. Was she moving? What I needed was something easily seen, a piece of paper, which I could throw overboard and watch. I had nothing on me. To run down for it I didn't dare. There was no time. All at once my strained, yearning stare distinguished a white object floating within a yard of the ship's side. White on the black water. A phosphorescent flash passed under it. What was that thing?… I recognized my own floppy hat. It must have fallen off his head … and he didn't bother. Now I had what I wanted—the saving mark for my eyes. But I hardly thought of my other self, now gone from the ship, to be hidden forever from all friendly faces, to be a fugitive and a vagabond on the earth, with no brand of the curse on his sane forehead to stay a slaying hand … too proud to explain.

And I watched the hat—the expression of my sudden pity for his mere flesh. It had been meant to save his homeless head from the dangers of the sun. And now—behold—it was saving the ship, by serving me for a mark to help out the ignorance of my strangeness. Ha! It was drifting forward, warning me just in time that the ship had gathered sternaway.

"Shift the helm," I said in a low voice to the seaman standing still like a statue.

The man's eyes glistened wildly in the binnacle light as he jumped round to the other side and spun round the wheel.

I walked to the break of the poop. On the over-shadowed deck all hands stood by the forebraces waiting for my order. The stars ahead seemed to be gliding from right to left. And all was so still in the world that I heard the quiet remark, "She's round," passed in a tone of intense relief between two seamen.

"Let go and haul."

The foreyards ran round with a great noise, amidst cheery cries. And now the frightful whiskers made themselves heard giving various orders. Already the ship was drawing ahead. And I was alone with her. Nothing! no one in the world should stand now between us, throwing a shadow on the way of silent knowledge and mute affection, the perfect communion of a seaman with his first command.

Walking to the taffrail, I was in time to make out, on the very edge of a darkness thrown by a towering black mass like the very gateway of Erebus—yes, I was in time to catch an evanescent glimpse of my white hat left behind to mark the spot where the secret sharer of my cabin and of my thoughts, as though he were my second self, had lowered himself into the water to take his punishment: a free man, a proud swimmer striking out for a new destiny.

—1912

[1] *taffrail* Stern rail.

A.E. HOUSMAN
1859 – 1936

During his lifetime, A.E. Housman published only two slim volumes of poetry, *A Shropshire Lad* and *Last Poems*. Yet his poems were widely read by both popular and academic audiences, and these two books continue to receive substantial critical attention. In 1996, as part of the festivities commemorating the centenary of the publication of *A Shropshire Lad*, a window in the Poets' Corner of Westminster Abbey was dedicated to Housman. Tom Stoppard's play about Housman, *The Invention of Love*, was produced at the National Theatre, London, in 1997, and debuted in the United States in the winter of 1999–2000.

Although Housman is now known primarily for his poetry, he considered his life's work to be classical scholarship. By the time he was appointed Professor of Latin at Cambridge, Housman had published 99 classical papers, the first volume of his edition of Manilius, an edition of Juvenal, and an edition of Ovid's *Ibis*. In a testimony to Housman's scholarly writings, T.S. Eliot commented in 1933 that Housman "is one of the few living masters of English prose."

The eldest of seven children, Alfred Edward Housman was born on 26 March 1859 to Sarah Jane Williams, a clergyman's daughter, and Edward Housman, a lawyer. As a young child, Housman took great pleasure in words, and was writing verse by the age of eight. He frequently directed the younger children in playacting and wrote out a family magazine that he circulated among friends and relatives. His happy childhood at the family home in Bromsgrove, Worcestershire was dramatically interrupted by the news, in 1869, that his mother had breast cancer. In a sad coincidence, she died on 26 March 1871, on Housman's twelfth birthday. During his wife's illness, Edward Housman began to drink heavily; the family maintained respectable appearances but his drinking worsened, as did their financial situation.

In 1870, a scholarship enabled Housman to enter Bromsgrove School as a day-boy. He was serious and quiet, nicknamed "Mouse" by his classmates, but also a gifted student, winning prizes for English verse, freehand drawing, French, and Latin and Greek verse. These successes resulted in a scholarship to study Classics at St. John's College, Oxford, in 1877 where Housman initially excelled, passing the required second-year examinations with First Class Honours. During this time, his poetry began to be published by *Waifs and Strays*, an Oxford magazine. In 1880, Housman moved out of the college buildings to share a residence with A.W. Pollard and Moses Jackson. Some biographers have argued that Jackson was the love of Housman's life; if so, however, his feelings were apparently never reciprocated. Housman's Oxford career ended in disappointment when, in May 1881, he failed the final set of examinations required of undergraduates. Housman returned to Oxford in 1882 so that he could take another exam and receive the lesser "pass" degree.

With his father's health in decline and the family finances in a shambles, Housman passed the Civil Service exam in June 1882 in order to qualify himself for employment. Shortly after, he accepted a position as clerk in the Patent Office in London, where Moses Jackson also worked. Housman toiled for ten years in the Patent Office, all the while continuing his study of Classics by reading in the evenings at the British Museum. His first scholarly article appeared in 1882 in the *Journal of Philology*; during his time at the Patent Office he would publish 25 essays, although many of his colleagues were unaware of his scholarly pursuits. By 1892, when Housman applied for the position of Professor of Latin at University College, London, he was a well-respected classical scholar with an international reputation.

Housman's first book of poetry, *A Shropshire Lad*, has never been out of print. The manuscript was originally rejected by the Macmillan publishing company, as well as several others, and Housman published it at his own expense with the firm of Kegan Paul in 1896. Housman composed most of the poems in *A Shropshire Lad* in the wake of two deaths—that of his friend Adalbert Jackson in 1892, and that of his father in 1894. Coincidentally, the period of the poems' composition was also the period of Oscar Wilde's trial and conviction under the Labouchere Amendment that outlawed homosexuality in England. Housman carefully guarded his own sexuality in his life and his work, no doubt aware that he would have risked prison and exile if he had chosen to express himself openly. Several modern critics have pointed to the ways in which Housman expresses same-sex love through various poetic codes, and certainly he left ample scope for a broader public to read his poems as expressing a love that was entirely conventional. In form, Housman tends to choose straightforward iambic rhythms and simple rhymes, and in its subject matter his poetry returns again and again to themes of loss, of pastoral beauty, of idealized (and often unrequited) love, and of patriotism. Much as Housman was an intellectual in his approach to classical literature—meticulous in his scholarship, and scathing in his criticism of those less careful or competent—he was fundamentally a Romantic in his own poetry; he argued in his essay *The Name and Nature of Poetry* (1933) that poetry should appeal more to the emotions than to the intellect, and his own work embodies that belief. It was an approach that went against the grain of the intellectual currents of modernism, but that was entirely in line with early twentieth-century popular sentiment.

A Shropshire Lad was followed, in 1922, by the publication of *Last Poems*. As with Housman's first book of poetry, this new collection immediately found a wide audience. In 1911, after nineteen years as Professor of Latin at University College, Housman was appointed Professor of Latin at Trinity College, Cambridge, and for the next 25 years he occupied the Kennedy Chair in Latin. On 24 April 1936, Housman gave his last lecture at Cambridge, and six days later he died. After Housman's death, his brother Laurence produced *More Poems* from the finished poems contained within Housman's notebooks. Many of these pieces, as well as *Additional Poems*, published in Laurence's biography of his brother, contain explicitly homosexual material that Housman dared not publish within his lifetime. (The propriety of publishing poems that Housman had, in his will, instructed his brother to destroy has been extensively debated by biographers and scholars.)

⌘ ⌘ ⌘

Loveliest of Trees

Loveliest of trees, the cherry now
  Is hung with bloom along the bough,
And stands about the woodland ride
  Wearing white for Eastertide.

5 Now, of my threescore years and ten,
  Twenty will not come again,

And take from seventy springs a score,
  It only leaves me fifty more.

And since to look at things in bloom
10 Fifty springs are little room,
About the woodlands I will go
  To see the cherry hung with snow.

—1896

To an Athlete Dying Young

The time you won your town the race
We chaired you through the market-place;
Man and boy stood cheering by,
And home we brought you shoulder-high.

5 Today, the road all runners come,
Shoulder-high we bring you home,
And set you at your threshold down,
Townsman of a stiller town.

Smart lad, to slip betimes away
10 From fields where glory does not stay,
And early though the laurel[1] grows
It withers quicker than the rose.

Eyes the shady night has shut
Cannot see the record cut,°   broken
15 And silence sounds no worse than cheers
After earth has stopped the ears:

Now you will not swell the rout°   group
Of lads that wore their honours out,
Runners whom renown outran
20 And the name died before the man.

So set, before its echoes fade,
The fleet foot on the sill of shade,
And hold to the low lintel[2] up
The still-defended challenge-cup.

25 And round that early laurelled head
Will flock to gaze the strengthless dead
And find unwithered on its curls
The garland briefer than a girl's.
—1896

1 *laurel* Evergreen bush or tree whose branches were used to crown victorious athletes in ancient Greece.

2 *lintel* Horizontal support beam, often running across a doorway or window.

Terence, This Is Stupid Stuff

"Terence,[3] this is stupid stuff:
You eat your victuals fast enough;
There can't be much amiss, 'tis clear,
To see the rate you drink your beer.
5 But oh, good Lord, the verse you make,
It gives a chap the belly-ache.
The cow, the old cow, she is dead;
It sleeps well, the hornèd head:
We poor lads, 'tis our turn now
10 To hear such tunes as killed the cow.
Pretty friendship 'tis to rhyme
Your friends to death before their time
Moping melancholy mad:
Come, pipe a tune to dance to, lad."

15 Why, if 'tis dancing you would be,
There's brisker pipes than poetry.
Say, for what were hop-yards[4] meant,
Or why was Burton built on Trent?[5]
Oh many a peer[6] of England brews
20 Livelier liquor than the Muse,[7]
And malt does more than Milton can
To justify God's ways to man.[8]
Ale, man, ale's the stuff to drink
For fellows whom it hurts to think:
25 Look into the pewter pot°   mug
To see the world as the world's not.
And faith, 'tis pleasant till 'tis past:
The mischief is that twill not last.

3 *Terence* This poem is from Housman's *The Shropshire Lad* (originally titled *The Poems of Terence Hearsay*), a series of poems that tell the story of a central character, Terence Hearsay, who leaves his hometown and moves to London.

4 *hop-yards* Or hop-gardens: areas of land upon which hops are grown.

5 *Burton … Trent* Burton-on-Trent, a town in East Staffordshire, is the historical center of the British brewing industry. Brewing was first begun there by Benedictine monks in the eleventh century.

6 *peer* Member of the British nobility. Brewers were among those raised to the peerage, and were thus referred to as "beer barons."

7 *Muse* One of nine Greek goddesses of arts and learning; here, the source of poetic inspiration.

8 *Milton … man* Cf. John Milton's *Paradise Lost* (1667), Book 1.26.

Oh I have been to Ludlow[1] fair
30   And left my necktie God knows where,
And carried half-way home, or near,
Pints and quarts of Ludlow beer:
Then the world seemed none so bad,
And I myself a sterling lad;
35   And down in lovely muck I've lain,
Happy till I woke again.
Then I saw the morning sky:
Heigho, the tale was all a lie;
The world, it was the old world yet,
40   I was I, my things were wet,
And nothing now remained to do
But begin the game anew.

Therefore, since the world has still
Much good, but much less good than ill,
45   And while the sun and moon endure
Luck's a chance, but trouble's sure,
I'd face it as a wise man would,
And train for ill and not for good.
'Tis true the stuff I bring for sale
50   Is not so brisk a brew as ale:
Out of a stem that scored the hand
I wrung it in a weary land.
But take it: if the smack is sour,
The better for the embittered hour;
55   It should do good to heart and head
When your soul is in my soul's stead;
And I will friend you, if I may,
In the dark and cloudy day.

There was a king reigned in the East:
60   There, when kings will sit to feast,
They get their fill before they think
With poisoned meat and poisoned drink.
He gathered all that springs to birth
From the many-venomed earth;
65   First a little, thence to more,
He sampled all her killing store;
And easy, smiling, seasoned sound,

Sate the king when healths went round.
They put arsenic in his meat
70   And stared aghast to watch him eat;
They poured strychnine in his cup
And shook to see him drink it up:
They shook, they stared as white's their shirt:
Them it was their poison hurt.
75   —I tell the tale that I heard told.
Mithridates, he died old.[2]
—1896

The Chestnut Casts His Flambeaux[3]

The chestnut casts his flambeaux, and the flowers
    Stream from the hawthorn in the wind away,
The doors clap to, the pane is blind with showers.
    Pass me the can,[4] lad; there's an end of May.

5   There's one spoilt spring to scant° our mortal lot,   reduce
    One season ruined of our little store.
May will be fine next year as like as not:
    Oh ay, but then we shall be twenty-four.

We for a certainty are not the first
10   Have sat in taverns while the tempest hurled
Their hopeful plans to emptiness, and cursed
    Whatever brute and blackguard[5] made the world.

It is in truth iniquity on high
    To cheat our sentenced souls of aught they crave,
15   And mar the merriment as you and I
    Fare on our long fool's-errand to the grave.

Iniquity it is; but pass the can.
    My lad, no pair of kings our mothers bore;

[2] *There was ... died old* According to Pliny's *Natural History*, Mithridates, king of Pontus from approximately 114 to 63 BCE, gradually built up a tolerance to all known poisons by ingesting a small amount of each daily, starting in childhood.

[3] *Flambeaux* French: torch or candlestick. The horse chestnut is known for its long, upright clusters (or "candles") of flowers, usually white in color with a reddish tinge.

[4] *can* I.e., of beer; mug or tankard.

[5] *blackguard* Scoundrel.

[1] *Ludlow* Market town in Shropshire.

Our only portion is the estate of man:
20   We want the moon, but we shall get no more.

If here today the cloud of thunder lours[1]
    Tomorrow it will hie° on far behests;°   *hasten / commands*
The flesh will grieve on other bones than ours
    Soon, and the soul will mourn in other breasts.

25 The troubles of our proud and angry dust
    Are from eternity, and shall not fail.
Bear them we can, and if we can we must.
    Shoulder the sky, my lad, and drink your ale.
            —1922

Epitaph on an Army of Mercenaries[2]

These, in the day when heaven was falling,
    The hour when earth's foundations fled,
Followed their mercenary calling
    And took their wages and are dead.

5   Their shoulders held the sky suspended;
    They stood, and earth's foundations stay;
What God abandoned, these defended,
    And saved the sum of things for pay.
            —1922

---

[1] *lours* Looks dark and ominous.

[2] *Epitaph ... Mercenaries* Housman published this poem in *The Times* on 31 October 1917, the third anniversary of the First Battle of Ypres, in order to honor the bravery of the professional soldiers who fought and died in the battle.

SIEGFRIED SASSOON
1886 – 1967

Siegfried Sassoon gained his reputation during and after World War I as a poet who stridently protested the war. Shocked by the realities of the front, he transformed his horror and disgust into accusatory, didactic verse meant to confront those at home with the atrocities of war.

Sassoon was born into a wealthy merchant family, and his privileged upbringing that included horseback riding, fox hunting, a Cambridge education, and London socializing left him little prepared for war. Having decided to become a poet, however, he found that because he was without ambition or direction in life his poetry lacked passion. On the morning that war was declared, he enlisted.

When Sassoon was first commissioned into the Royal Welch Fusiliers, his poetry was neither satirical nor disillusioned; like many young poets of the day, he gave voice to patriotic sentiments. His perception changed dramatically after surviving the Battle of the Somme on 1 July 1916—the day on which 19,000 British men were killed and 38,000 wounded. Sassoon distinguished himself with his fierce courage in this battle—earning himself a Military Cross (which he later threw away) and the nickname "Mad Jack"—but the experience purged him of any romantic notions as to the glory of war.

In a new, starkly realistic voice, Sassoon attacked commanding officers, Church, and State, and all those back home who were ignorant of or indifferent to the conditions of war. His compressed, intense verses use graphic descriptions, colloquial language, and explosive direct speech to convey the brutalities of war. They often also rely on simple oppositions—such as between innocent and guilty, home and front, men and women—to achieve ironic effect.

In April 1917, Sassoon was sent home to recover from a sniper wound. There he drafted his famous public protest, published in *The Times* on 31 July 1917, in which he declared that the war had become a mere matter of "aggression and conquest" and that it was being deliberately prolonged. Sassoon was saved from prison only by the intervention of his friend Robert Graves, a fellow poet and Welch Fusilier, who testified that Sassoon was shell-shocked. Eager to avoid making a martyr of Sassoon, a medical board sent him to Edinburgh's Craiglockhart War Hospital instead.

While at Craiglockhart (where he met Wilfred Owen, another poet), Sassoon began to experiment with longer, dramatic-narrative poems that evoked the physical details of the trench. He was declared fit for active duty in 1918, but was on the front lines only a month before he received a shot in the head that sent him back to England for good. His war poems were published—to little critical acclaim—in *The Old Huntsman* (1917) and *Counter-Attack and Other Poems* (1918). After the war, Sassoon continued to launch vociferous poetic salvos, now directed against the Allies' vindictive treatment of Germany and the British government's neglect of returned soldiers. Gradually, however, anger subsided into disillusionment with and alienation from a world he could not change.

Sassoon retreated into his own memories, beginning a six-volume autobiography that took nearly twenty years to complete. The first three volumes, *Memoirs of a Fox-Hunting Man* (1928), *Memoirs of an Infantry Officer* (1930), and *Sherston's Progress* (1936), revisit the past under the guise of a fictional persona, George Sherston, while the second three, *The Old Century and Seven More Years* (1938), *The Weald of Youth* (1942), and *Siegfried's Journey: 1916–1920* (1945) are autobiography in the conventional sense. In all six of these volumes, however, Sassoon noticeably distanced himself from his most traumatic experiences as he attempted to deal with the war and its after-effects. Sassoon's posthumously published diaries make clear exactly how much he had omitted, including the turbulent events surrounding his marriage in 1933, the birth of his son George in 1936, the dissolution of his marriage in 1941, and a long period of anguish over his homosexuality.

Sassoon continued to write, but he published most of his later poetry collections privately. He felt his work was frequently misunderstood, particularly as his religious faith increased and he became a self-proclaimed "religious poet" in the years preceding his conversion to Roman Catholicism in 1957. After this point Sassoon wrote very little poetry, and he spent the remainder of his life in relative seclusion at his home in Wiltshire, where he died in 1967.

⌘ ⌘ ⌘

They

The Bishop tells us: "When the boys come back
    They will not be the same; for they'll have fought
In a just cause: they lead the last attack
On Anti-Christ; their comrades' blood has bought
5 New right to breed an honourable race,
They have challenged Death and dared him face to face."
"We're none of us the same!" the boys reply.
"For George lost both his legs; and Bill's stone blind;
Poor Jim's shot through the lungs and like to die;
10 And Bert's gone syphilitic: you'll not find
A chap who's served that hasn't found *some* change."
And the Bishop said: "The ways of God are strange!"
    —1917 (WRITTEN 31 OCTOBER 1916)

Glory of Women

You love us when we're heroes, home on leave,
    Or wounded in a mentionable place.
You worship decorations; you believe
That chivalry redeems the war's disgrace.
5 You make us shells. You listen with delight,
By tales of dirt and danger fondly thrilled.
You crown our distant ardours while we fight,

10 And mourn our laurelled memories when we're killed.
You can't believe that British troops "retire"
When hell's last horror breaks them, and they run,
Trampling the terrible corpses—blind with blood.
O German mother dreaming by the fire,
While you are knitting socks to send your son
His face is trodden deeper in the mud.
    —1918 (WRITTEN 1917)

Everyone Sang

Everyone suddenly burst out singing;
    And I was filled with such delight
As prisoned birds must find in freedom,
Winging wildly across the white
5 Orchards and dark-green fields; on—on—and out of
        sight.

Everyone's voice was suddenly lifted;
And beauty came like the setting sun:
My heart was shaken with tears; and horror
Drifted away ... O, but Everyone
10 Was a bird; and the song was wordless; the singing
        will never be done.
    —1919

from *Memoirs of an Infantry Officer*[1]

On July the first, the weather, after an early morning mist, was of the kind commonly called heavenly. Down in our frowsty[2] cellar we breakfasted at six, unwashed and apprehensive. Our table, appropriately enough, was an empty ammunition box. At six-forty-five the final bombardment began, and there was nothing for us to do except sit round our candle until the tornado ended. For more than forty minutes the air vibrated and the earth rocked and shuddered. Through the sustained uproar the tap and rattle of machine-guns could be identified; but except for the whistle of bullets no retaliation came our way until a few 5.9 shells[3] shook the roof of our dugout. Barton and I sat speechless, deafened and stupefied by the seismic state of affairs, and when he lit a cigarette the match flame staggered crazily. Afterwards I asked him what he had been thinking about. His reply was "Carpet slippers and Kettle-holders." My own mind had been working in much the same style, for during that cannonading cataclysm the following refrain was running in my head:

> They come as a boon and a blessing to men,
> The Something, the Owl, and the Waverley Pen.[4]

For the life of me I couldn't remember what the first one was called. Was it the Shakespeare? Was it the Dickens? Anyhow it was an advertisement which I'd often seen in smoky railway stations. Then the bombardment lifted and lessened, our vertigo abated, and we looked at one another in dazed relief. Two brigades of our division were now going over the top on our right. Our brigade was to attack "when the main assault had reached its final objective." In our fortunate role of privileged spectators Barton and I went up the stairs to see what we could from Kingston Road Trench. We left

Jenkins crouching in a corner, where he remained most of the day. His haggard blinking face haunts my memory. He was an example of the paralysing effect which such an experience could produce on a nervous system sensitive to noise, for he was a good officer both before and afterwards. I felt no sympathy for him at the time, but I do now. From the support-trench, which Barton called "our opera box," I observed as much of the battle as the formation of the country allowed, the rising ground on the right making it impossible to see anything of the attack towards Mametz. A small shiny black notebook contains my pencilled particulars, and nothing will be gained by embroidering them with afterthoughts. I cannot turn my field-glasses on to the past....

7.45. The barrage is now working to the right of Fricourt and beyond. I can see the 21st Division advancing about three-quarters of a mile away on the left and a few Germans coming to meet them, apparently surrendering. Our men in small parties (not extended in line) go steadily on to the German front-line. Brilliant sunshine and a haze of smoke drifting along the landscape. Some Yorkshires[5] a little way below on the left, watching the show and cheering as if at a football match. The noise almost as bad as ever.

9.30. Came back to dug-out and had a shave. 21st Division still going across the open, apparently without casualties. The sunlight flashes on bayonets as the tiny figures move quietly forward and disappear beyond mounds of trench debris. A few runners come back and ammunition parties go across. Trench-mortars[6] are knocking hell out of Sunken Road Trench and the ground where the Manchesters will attack soon. Noise not so bad now and very little retaliation.

9.50. Fricourt half-hidden by clouds of drifting smoke, blue, pinkish and grey. Shrapnel bursting in small bluish-white puffs with tiny flashes. The birds seem bewildered; a lark begins to go up and then flies feebly along, thinking better of it. Others flutter above the trench with querulous cries, weak on the wing. I can

---

[1] *from ... Officer* The following excerpt, which describes the beginning of the Battle of the Somme in 1916, is taken from Section 4, Chapter 2, entitled "Battle."

[2] *frowsty* Musty; stale or unpleasant smelling.

[3] *5.9 shells* 5.9-caliber shells.

[4] *They come ... Pen* This then-popular slogan of MacNiven and Cameron, Ltd. (a producer of pen nibs) advertised three types of nibs: the Pickwick (the missing term) the Owl, and the Waverley.

[5] *Yorkshires* I.e., men belonging to one of the battalions of the Yorkshire Regiment that fought at the Battle of the Somme.

[6] *Trench-mortars* Small mortars used to propel bombs into enemy trenches.

see seven of our balloons,[1] on the right. On the left our men still filing across in twenties and thirties. Another huge explosion in Fricourt and a cloud of brown-pink smoke. Some bursts are yellowish.

10.5. I can see the Manchesters down in New Trench, getting ready to go over. Figures filing down the trench. Two of them have gone out to look at our wire gaps![2] Have just eaten my last orange.... I am staring at a sunlit picture of Hell, and still the breeze shakes the yellow weeds, and the poppies glow under Crawley Ridge where some shells fell a few minutes ago. Manchesters are sending forward some scouts. A bayonet glitters. A runner comes back across the open to their Battalion Headquarters, close here on the right. 21st Division still trotting along the sky line toward La Boisselle. Barrage going strong to the right of Contalmaison Ridge. Heavy shelling toward Mametz.

12.15. Quieter the last two hours. Manchesters still waiting. Germans putting over a few shrapnel shells. Silly if I got hit! Weather cloudless and hot. A lark singing confidently overhead.

1.30. Manchesters attack at 2.30. Mametz and Montauban reported taken. Mametz consolidated.

2.30. Manchesters left New Trench and apparently took Sunken Road Trench, bearing rather to the right. Could see about 400. Many walked casually across with sloped arms. There were about forty casualties on the left (from machine-gun in Fricourt). Through my glasses I could see one man moving his left arm up and down as he lay on his side; his face was a crimson patch. Others lay still in the sunlight while the swarm of figures disappeared over the hill. Fricourt was a cloud of pinkish smoke. Lively machine-gun fire on the far side of the hill. At 2.50 no one to be seen in No Man's Land except the casualties (about half-way across). Our dug-out shelled again since 2.30.

5.0. I saw about thirty of our A Company crawl across to Sunken Road from New Trench. Germans put a few big shells on the cemetery and traversed Kingston Road with machine-gun. Manchester wounded still out

there. Remainder of A Company went across—about 100 altogether. Manchesters reported held up in Bois Français Support. Their Colonel went across and was killed.

8.0. Staff Captain of our brigade has been along. Told Barton that Seventh Division has reached its objectives with some difficulty, except on this brigade front. Manchesters are in trouble, and Fricourt attack has failed. Several hundred prisoners brought in on our sector.

9.30. Our A Company holds Rectangle and Sunken Road. Jenkins gone off in charge of a carrying-party.[3] Seemed all right again. C Company now reduced to six runners, two stretcher-bearers, Company-Sergeant-Major, signallers, and Barton's servant. Flook away on carrying-party. Sky cloudy westward. Red sunset. Heavy gunfire on the left.

2.30. (Next afternoon.) Adjutant[4] has just been up here, excited, optimistic, and unshaven. He went across last night to ginger up A Company who did very well, thanks to the bombers. About 40 casualties; only 4 killed. Fricourt and Rose Trench occupied this morning without resistance. I am now lying out in front of our trench in the long grass, basking in sunshine where yesterday there were bullets. Our new front-line on the hill is being shelled. Fricourt is full of troops wandering about in search of souvenirs. The village was a ruin and is now a dust heap. A gunner (Forward Observation Officer) has just been along here with a German helmet in his hand. Said Fricourt is full of dead; he saw one officer lying across a smashed machine-gun with his head bashed in—"a fine looking chap," he said, with some emotion, which rather surprised me.

8.15. Queer feeling, seeing people moving about freely between here and Fricourt. Dumps being made. Shacks and shelters being put up under skeleton trees and all sorts of transport arriving at Cemetery Cross Roads. We stay here till to-morrow morning. Feel a bit of a fraud.

—1930 (WRITTEN 1916)

---

[1] *balloons* As a defense against hostile aircraft, troops set up a series of connected balloons attached to long wire cables.

[2] *wire gaps* Holes made in the protective barbed wire by enemy shells.

[3] *carrying-party* Party sent to deliver supplies.

[4] *Adjutant* Military officer whose role is to communicate the orders of superior officers.

WILFRED OWEN
1893 – 1918

Wilfred Owen's humane responses to World War I, his compassionate depictions of the suffering that war engendered, and his critique of nationalism challenged the imperialist rhetoric of honor, glory, and patriotic duty, prompting Dylan Thomas later to declare him "a poet of all times, all places, and all wars."

Owen was the first-born son and of Thomas Owen and Susan Shaw of Shropshire, and the favorite of his mother, who hoped to see him become a clergyman. When Owen left school in 1911 he took a post as lay assistant to the Vicar of Dunsden, who would help him prepare for his university entrance exam in exchange for parish work. Owen, however, became increasingly critical of the Church's response to the suffering of the poor, and found his passion for poetry eclipsed his religious faith. He left the vicarage and, having failed to win a university scholarship, departed for France to work as a private tutor.

Though Owen had little intention of joining up when war broke out, pressure to do so increased as the fighting continued. In 1915 he returned to England, enlisted in the Artists' Rifles, and was commissioned lieutenant in the Manchester Regiment. Owen crossed the channel in December of 1916 to join his men on the Somme, where he began recording his impressions in letters and poems immediately. His use of a pastoral mode owed much to the influence of Keats, but his powerful descriptions of death, wounded bodies, and the weapons of war, which coupled startling images and shifting angles of vision, subverted the traditional pastoral. Owen also developed his own approach to rhyme, in which half rhymes (pararhymes) and assonance featured prominently. This gave his poetry a discordant, mournful quality that echoed his pessimistic warnings of further suffering to come, and helped create haunting elegies for the generation he shows being slaughtered like cattle in "Anthem for Doomed Youth" (1920).

Owen had been at the front only four months when a shell exploded a few feet from his head, resulting in his nearly being buried alive. A few weeks later he was removed to Craiglockhart War Hospital, outside Edinburgh, and treated for shell shock. There he met Siegfried Sassoon, another war poet whose stridently satirical poetry Owen greatly admired. It was during this time, while recovering from his trauma, that Owen wrote most of his poems. The influence of Sassoon is evident in his more didactic work, such as "Dulce et Decorum Est" (1920), which uses graphic descriptions of the battlefield and powerful direct speech to attack the classic dictum that it is sweet and fitting to die for one's country.

In his expressions of pity for his fellow soldiers, Owen occasionally fell into the trap of romanticizing death and sacrifice for which he criticized both Church and State, at times portraying soldiers as Christ-figures crucified by those in charge. The men of his poems, regardless of nationality, are usually victims passively laying down their lives, never killing. Several of Owen's strongest poems—such as "Strange Meeting" (1920)—attempt to confront and explore these contradictions.

Owen faced a similar incongruity in his own attitude towards war. Though he opposed the fighting in principle, he was glad to be able to return to the front in August 1918 and to resume serving with his men in battle. He was, he said, "a conscientious objector with a very seared conscience." Owen was killed less than three months after returning to his regiment—only a week before the war's end—while leading an offensive on the banks of the Sambre Canal.

⌘ ⌘ ⌘

A Terre

(Being the philosophy of many Soldiers.)

Sit on the bed, I'm blind, and three parts shell,
Be careful; can't shake hands now; never shall.
Both arms have mutinied against me—brutes.
My fingers fidget like ten idle brats.

5 I tried to peg out° soldierly—no use!   *die*
One dies of war like any old disease.
This bandage feels like pennies on my eyes.[1]
I have my medals?—Discs to make eyes close,
My glorious ribbons?—Ripped from my own back
10 In scarlet shreds. (That's for your poetry book.)

A short life and a merry one, my brick!°   *reliable chum*
We used to say we'd hate to live dead old—
Yet now ... I'd willingly be puffy, bald,
And patriotic. Buffers[2] catch from boys
15 At least the jokes hurled at them. I suppose
Little I'd ever teach a son, but hitting,
Shooting, war, hunting, all the arts of hurting.
Well, that's what I learnt—that, and making money.

Your fifty years ahead seem none too many?
20 Tell me how long I've got? God! For one year
To help myself to nothing more than air!
One Spring! Is one too good to spare, too long?
Spring wind would work its own way to my lung,
And grow me legs as quick as lilac-shoots.

25 My servant's lamed, but listen how he shouts!
When I'm lugged out, he'll still be good for that.
Here in this mummy-case, you know, I've thought
How well I might have swept his floors for ever,
I'd ask no night off when the bustle's over,
30 Enjoying so the dirt. Who's prejudiced
Against a grimed hand when his own's quite dust,
Less live than specks that in the sun-shafts turn,
Less warm than dust that mixes with arms' tan?
I'd love to be a sweep,[3] now, black as Town,
35 Yes, or a muckman. Must I be his load?

O Life, Life, let me breathe—a dug-out rat!
Not worse than ours the existences rats lead—
Nosing along at night down some safe vat,
They find a shell-proof home before they rot.
40 Dead men may envy living mites in cheese,
Or good germs even. Microbes have their joys,
And subdivide, and never come to death,
Certainly flowers have the easiest time on earth.
"I shall be one with nature, herb, and stone,"
45 Shelley[4] would tell me. Shelley would be stunned;
The dullest Tommy° hugs that fancy now.   *British soldier*
"Pushing up daisies," is their creed you know.
To grain, then, go my fat, to buds my sap,
For all the usefulness there is in soap.
50 D'you think the Boche° will ever stew man-soup?   *Germans*
Some day, no doubt, if ...
                              Friend, be very sure
I shall be better off with plants that share
More peaceably the meadow and the shower.
Soft rains will touch me—as they could touch once,
55 And nothing but the sun shall make me ware.°   *aware*

---

[1] *pennies on my eyes*   Reference to the ancient practice of placing coins on the eyes of the dead.

[2] *Buffers*   Old men who are out of touch with present times.

[3] *sweep*   Chimney sweep.

[4] *Shelley*   Romantic poet Percy Shelley; the above line is paraphrased from his *Adonais: An Elegy on the Death of John Keats* (1821).

Your guns may crash around me. I'll not hear;
Or, if I wince, I shall not know I wince.
Don't take my soul's poor comfort for your jest.
Soldiers may grow a soul when turned to fronds,
60   But here the thing's best left at home with friends.

My soul's a little grief, grappling your chest,
To climb your throat on sobs; easily chased
On other sighs and wiped by fresher winds.

Carry my crying spirit till it's weaned
65   To do without what blood remained these wounds.
              —1919

The Sentry

We'd found an old Boche° dug-out, and   *German*
      he knew,
And gave us hell, for shell on frantic shell
Hammered on top, but never quite burst through.
Rain, guttering down in waterfalls of slime
5   Kept slush waist high, that rising hour by hour,
Choked up the steps too thick with clay to climb.
What murk of air remained stank old, and sour
With fumes of whizz-bangs,[1] and the smell of men
Who'd lived there years, and left their curse in the den,
10   If not their corpses …
         There we herded from the blast
Of whizz-bangs, but one found our door at last.
Buffeting eyes and breath, snuffing the candles.
And thud! flump! thud! down the steep steps came
         thumping
15   And splashing in the flood, deluging muck—
The sentry's body; then his rifle, handles
Of old Boche bombs, and mud in ruck on ruck.
We dredged him up, for killed, until he whined
"O sir, my eyes—I'm blind—I'm blind, I'm blind!"
20   Coaxing, I held a flame against his lids
And said if he could see the least blurred light
He was not blind; in time he'd get all right.
"I can't," he sobbed. Eyeballs, huge-bulged like squids
Watch my dreams still; but I forgot him there

In posting next for duty, and sending a scout
To beg a stretcher somewhere, and floundering about
To other posts under the shrieking air.
              *   *   *
Those other wretches, how they bled and spewed,
And one who would have drowned himself for good—
30   I try not to remember these things now.
Let dread hark back for one word only: how
Half-listening to that sentry's moans and jumps,
And the wild chattering of his broken teeth,
Renewed most horribly whenever crumps[2]
35   Pummelled the roof and slogged the air beneath—
Through the dense din, I say, we heard him shout
"I see your lights!" But ours had long died out.
              —1919

Disabled

He sat in a wheeled chair, waiting for dark,
      And shivered in his ghastly suit of grey,
Legless, sewn short at elbow. Through the park
Voices of boys rang saddening like a hymn,
5   Voices of play and pleasure after day,
Till gathering sleep had mothered them from him.

About this time Town used to swing so gay
When glow-lamps budded in the light-blue trees
And girls glanced lovelier as the air grew dim,
10   — In the old times, before he threw away his knees.
Now he will never feel again how slim
Girls' waists are, or how warm their subtle hands,
All of them touch him like some queer disease.

There was an artist silly for his face,
15   For it was younger than his youth, last year.
Now he is old; his back will never brace;
He's lost his colour very far from here,
Poured it down shell-holes till the veins ran dry,
And half his life-time lapsed in the hot race,
20   And leap of purple spurted from his thigh.
One time he liked a bloodsmear down his leg,
After the matches carried shoulder-high.

---

1   *whizz-bangs*   Shells fired by small-caliber, high-velocity guns.

2   *crumps*   Sounds of exploding shells.

It was after football, when he'd drunk a peg,[1]
He thought he'd better join. He wonders why.…
25 Someone had said he'd look a god in kilts.[2]

That's why; and maybe, too, to please his Meg,
Aye, that was it, to please the giddy jilts[3]
He asked to join. He didn't have to beg;
Smiling they wrote his lie; aged nineteen years.
30 Germans he scarcely thought of; all their guilt
And Austria's,[4] did not move him. And no fears
Of Fear came yet. He thought of jewelled hilts
For daggers in plaid socks; of smart salutes;
And care of arms; and leave; and pay arrears;
35 *Esprit de corps*,[5] and hints for young recruits.
And soon, he was drafted out with drums and cheers.

Some cheered him home, but not as crowds cheer Goal.
Only a solemn man who brought him fruits
Thanked him; and then enquired about his soul.

40 Now, he will spend a few sick years in institutes,
And do what things the rules consider wise,
And take whatever pity they may dole.
To-night he noticed how the women's eyes
Passed from him to the strong men that were whole.
45 How cold and late it is! Why don't they come
And put him into bed? Why don't they come?
—1919

Strange Meeting

It seemed that out of battle I escaped
Down some profound dull tunnel, long since
   scooped
Through granites which titanic wars had groined.
Yet also there encumbered sleepers groaned,
5 Too fast in thought or death to be bestirred.

Then, as I probed them, one sprang up, and stared
With piteous recognition in fixed eyes,
Lifting distressful hands as if to bless.
And by his smile, I knew that sullen hall,
10 By his dead smile I knew we stood in Hell.
With a thousand pains that vision's face was grained;
Yet no blood reached there from the upper ground,
And no guns thumped, or down the flues made moan.
"Strange friend," I said, "here is no cause to mourn."
15 "None," said the other, "save the undone years,
The hopelessness. Whatever hope is yours,
Was my life also; I went hunting wild
After the wildest beauty in the world,
Which lies not calm in eyes, or braided hair,
20 But mocks the steady running of the hour,
And if it grieves, grieves richlier than here.
For of my glee might many men have laughed,
And of my weeping something had been left,
Which must die now. I mean the truth untold,
25 The pity of war, the pity war distilled.
Now men will go content with what we spoiled.
Or, discontent, boil bloody, and be spilled.
They will be swift with swiftness of the tigress,
None will break ranks, though nations trek from progress.
30 Courage was mine, and I had mystery,
Wisdom was mine, and I had mastery;
To miss the march of this retreating world
Into vain citadels that are not walled.
Then, when much blood had clogged their chariot-
   wheels,
35 I would go up and wash them from sweet wells,
Even with truths that lie too deep for taint.
I would have poured my spirit without stint
But not through wounds; not on the cess° of war.   *bog*
Foreheads of men have bled where no wounds were.
40 I am the enemy you killed, my friend.
I knew you in this dark; for so you frowned
Yesterday through me as you jabbed and killed.
I parried; but my hands were loath and cold.
Let us sleep now.…"
—1920

---

1 *peg* Quantity of alcohol.

2 *kilts* Part of the uniform for Scottish soldiers during World War I.

3 *giddy jilts* Scottish slang: flirtatious young women.

4 *Austria* Ally of Germany during World War I.

5 *Esprit de corps* Fellowship within a group.

Parable of the Old Man and the Young

So Abram rose, and clave the wood, and went,
And took the fire with him, and a knife.[1]
And as they sojourned both of them together,
Isaac the first-born spake and said, My Father,
5 Behold the preparations, fire and iron,
But where the lamb for this burnt-offering?
Then Abram bound the youth with belts and straps,
And builded parapets[2] and trenches there,
And stretchèd forth the knife to slay his son.
10 When lo! an angel called him out of heaven,
Saying, Lay not thy hand upon the lad,
Neither do anything to him. Behold,
A ram caught in a thicket by its horns;
Offer the Ram of Pride instead of him.
15 But the old man would not so, but slew his son,
And half the seed of Europe, one by one.[3]
—1920

Arms and the Boy

Let the boy try along this bayonet-blade
How cold steel is, and keen with hunger of blood;
Blue with all malice, like a madman's flash;
And thinly drawn with famishing for flesh.

5 Lend him to stroke these blind, blunt bullet-heads
Which long to nuzzle in the hearts of lads,
Or give him cartridges of fine zinc teeth,
Sharp with the sharpness of grief and death.

For his teeth seem for laughing round an apple.
10 There lurk no claws behind his fingers supple;

And God will grow no talons at his heels,
Nor antlers through the thickness of his curls.
—1920

Anthem for Doomed Youth

What passing-bells for these who die as cattle?
Only the monstrous anger of the guns.
Only the stuttering rifles' rapid rattle
Can patter out their hasty orisons.°   prayers
5 No mockeries for them from prayers or bells,
Nor any voice of mourning save the choirs,—
The shrill, demented choirs of wailing shells;
And bugles calling for them from sad shires.

What candles may be held to speed them all?
10 Not in the hands of boys, but in their eyes
Shall shine the holy glimmers of good-byes.
The pallor of girls' brows shall be their pall;[4]
Their flowers the tenderness of silent minds,
And each slow dusk a drawing-down of blinds.
—1920

The Send-Off

Down the close, darkening lanes they sang their way
To the siding-shed,
And lined the train with faces grimly gay.

Their breasts were stuck all white with wreath and spray
5 As men's are, dead.

Dull porters watched them, and a casual tramp
Stood staring hard,
Sorry to miss them from the upland camp.

Then, unmoved, signals nodded, and a lamp
10 Winked to the guard.

---

1 *So Abram ... a knife* Cf. Genesis 22. In the biblical story, God instructs Abraham to sacrifice his son Isaac as a burnt offering. Abraham is about to kill his son when the angel of the Lord appears to stop him; Abraham finds a ram and sacrifices it in Isaac's stead.

2 *parapets* Defenses of earth built in front of military trenches.

3 *And half ... by one* This line is absent from some published versions of the poem.

4 *pall* Cloth spread over a coffin, hearse, or tomb.

So secretly, like wrongs hushed-up, they went.
They were not ours:
We never heard to which front these were sent.

Nor there if they yet mock what women meant
15 Who gave them flowers.

Shall they return to beatings of great bells
In wild trainloads?
A few, a few, too few for drums and yells,

May creep back, silent, to still village wells
20 Up half-known roads.
                —1920

Dulce et Decorum Est[1]

Bent double, like old beggars under sacks,
Knock-kneed, coughing like hags, we cursed
            through sludge,
Till on the haunting flares we turned our backs,
And towards our distant rest began to trudge.
5 Men marched asleep. Many had lost their boots,
But limped on, blood-shod. All went lame, all blind;
Drunk with fatigue; deaf even to the hoots
Of gas-shells dropping softly behind.

Gas! GAS! Quick, boys!—An ecstasy of fumbling,
10 Fitting the clumsy helmets just in time,
But someone still was yelling out and stumbling
And flound'ring like a man in fire or lime—
Dim, through the misty panes[2] and thick green light,
As under a green sea, I saw him drowning.

15 In all my dreams before my helpless sight
He plunges at me, guttering, choking, drowning.

If in some smothering dreams, you too could pace
Behind the wagon that we flung him in,
And watch the white eyes writhing in his face,
20 His hanging face, like a devil's sick of sin;
If you could hear, at every jolt, the blood
Come gargling from the froth-corrupted lungs,
Bitter as the cud
Of vile, incurable sores on innocent tongues,—
25 My friend, you would not tell with such high zest
To children ardent for some desperate glory,
The old Lie: Dulce et decorum est
Pro patria mori.
                —1920

Futility

Move him into the sun—
Gently its touch awoke him once,
At home, whispering of fields half-sown.
Always it woke him, even in France,
5 Until this morning and this snow.
If anything might rouse him now
The kind old sun will know.

Think how it wakes the seeds—
Woke once the clays of a cold star.
10 Are limbs, so dear achieved, are sides
Full-nerved, still warm, too hard to stir?
Was it for this the clay grew tall?
—O what made fatuous sunbeams toil
To break earth's sleep at all?
                —1920

---

[1] *Dulce et Decorum Est*   Owen's poem takes its title from a famous
line from the Roman poet Horace's *Odes* (3.2): "Dulce et decorum
est pro patria mori" (Latin: "Sweet and fitting it is to die for one's
country").

[2] *panes*   Visors of the gas masks.

WAR AND REVOLUTION
CONTEXTS

Britain declared war on Germany on 4 August 1914, and nearly every family in England had lost someone before the Armistice on 11 November 1918. Roughly one million British soldiers died (and roughly ten million soldiers overall)—nearly one in every eight who enlisted. Eighteen million more were wounded. While soldiers and civilians alike began the war filled with idealism, there was little room for glory in the trench warfare that became the dominant mode of conflict during the war. The battle line on the Western Front remained virtually unmoved for three years, with both sides making attempted advancements at great loss of life. The German use of poison gas at the second battle of Ypres (1915), the British landing at Gallipoli (1915), and the British introduction of tanks at the Somme (1916) were all launched in the hope they would lead to a victorious break-through—and all ended horrifically. Indeed, the "Great War," as it was called at the time, was characterized from first to last by extreme disillusionment, from the misplaced hope at its outset that the fighting would end by Christmas 1914, to the confidence voiced by Woodrow Wilson (the American President who brought the United States into the war in 1917) that the conflict would lead nations to come together in a new League of Nations that would make this "a war to end all wars." After the war the British people would never again recapture the idealism and firm faith in technology, progress, and traditional values that had been prevalent earlier in the century. In stark contrast to Wilson's optimism, many were persuaded by the war's end that technological progress and failed humanity were driving civilization towards a perpetual state of war. Subsequent years were filled with unrest as the British people struggled to make sense of the sweeping changes war had brought.

The war was certainly unprecedented in its technology—airplanes as well as tanks were used for the first time in warfare, and machine guns facilitated new levels of mass slaughter. And the industrial nature of the war meant that civilians were relied upon nearly as much as soldiers for military success. Morale was thus important almost as much at home as on the front, and artists, photographers, poets, actors, and performers became important participants in the manufacture of patriotism. This section opens with a testament to the importance of patriotic poetry during wartime, and a sampling of popular poems and songs. There was little that was heroic or romantic about the daily life of soldiers in the trenches, but through songs such as "I Learned to Wash in Shell-holes" and "Oh, It's a Lovely War" soldiers might keep up morale by viewing their deplorable living conditions with humor. ("Oh, It's a Lovely War," by J.P. Long and Maurice Scott, became once again widely known after the 1960s stage production *Oh, What a Lovely War!* and the film that took its title from the play's.)

The war was unprecedented too in its geographic scope; the fighting extended into Africa and the Middle East as well as across Europe and into Asia. The British Empire fought as one, with troops from all areas serving under imperial command. Canadian troops were particularly influential at Vimy Ridge, where in April 1917 they forced German troops to retreat from their dominant position on the northern part of the Western front. Soldiers from Australia and New Zealand were vitally important in offensives at the Somme and Gallipoli, where they sustained heavy losses.

War transformed everyday life and affected every aspect of society. Everyone was at risk, and everyone had a part to play in the war effort. While Victorian society had been characterized by rigid boundaries—between public and private space, between masculine and feminine realms and duties, and between classes—the war forced a sudden breakdown of these categories. After the war they were partially restored, but society was forever transformed. In her essay "The Cordite Makers," Rebecca West (the pen name of Cicily Fairfield) highlights the parallels between the daily lives of soldiers on the home front and that of many women working in the arms industry—particularly in terms of the personal sacrifices that they made and the dangers that they faced.

Ivor Gurney's poem "To His Love" and Vince Palmer's "The Farmer Remembers the Somme," both of which appear below, provide a grim sense of how firm a grip the memory of horror and of loss took upon those who had experienced the fighting at first hand. Less focused on the horror of battle is the excerpt below from poet Robert Graves's *Goodbye to All That*. Graves's description of his war years as an officer in the Royal Welch Fusiliers, is among the most vivid and detailed prose accounts of life on the front. The passage excerpted here gives among other things a clear sense of the stark differences between civilians' and soldiers' perceptions of the war.

If the Great War revolutionized the way in which British people saw the world, it also helped to bring full-scale revolution to Britain's largest ally. The Russian Revolution was the product of many causes, but not the least of these was the hardship and desperation brought on by the war itself. Ultimately, the Revolution proved to be one of the central events of the twentieth century; over the course of the next two generations, the ideological models of Marx and Lenin and the institutional models of Lenin and Stalin would spread through much of the world. The excerpt included in these pages highlights the conflict between communist idealism and totalitarian realism that came to a head almost immediately following the Bolshevik "October Revolution" of 1917.

⌘ ⌘ ⌘

from Anonymous, Introduction to *Songs and Sonnets for England in War Time* (1914)

The *Songs and Sonnets for England in War Time* anthology was the first of a genre that became common in World War I, the popular anthology of war poetry. The introduction provides a straightforward statement of the rationale for such volumes.

In the stress of a nation's peril, the poet at last comes into his own again, and with clarion call he rouses the sleeping soul of the Empire. Prophet he is, champion and consoler.

If in these later times the poet has been neglected, now in our infinite need, in our pride and our sorrow, he is here to strengthen, comfort and inspire. The poet is vindicated.

What can so nobly uplift the hearts of a people facing war with its unspeakable agony as music and poetry? The sound of martial music steels men's hearts before battle. The sound of martial words inspires human souls to do and to endure. God, His poetry, and His music are the Holy Trinity of war.

… The greatest songs [have not always been those] that have sent men on to victory. Sometimes it has been a modest verse that has found refuge in the heart of the soldier ready for the ultimate sacrifice, cheered on his way by the lilt of a humble song. Who else, indeed, can take the place of a poet?

Recruitment poster for South Australia, 1914.

Recruitment poster for Canada, 1914.

"In Flanders Fields": The Poem and Some Responses

Canadian physician John McCrae's "In Flanders Fields," scribbled in twenty minutes while he was sitting on the back of an ambulance just north of the field of Ypres, remains the most widely recited poem of the war. McCrae, not satisfied with the poem, would have thrown it away, but a fellow officer sent it to London, where it was published by *Punch* (after being rejected by *The Spectator*). The responses to the poem reproduced below are only three of many—a testimony to the strength of emotion the poem evoked in readers. Elizabeth Daryush's more personal description of loss provides a sharp contrast to the two more patriotic poems by Mitchell and Armstrong.

John McCrae, "In Flanders Fields" (1915)

In Flanders Fields the poppies blow
Between the crosses, row on row,
That mark our place; and in the sky
The larks, still bravely singing, fly
5 Scarce heard amid the guns below.

We are the Dead. Short days ago
We lived, felt dawn, saw sunset glow,
Loved and were loved, and now we lie
In Flanders Fields.

10 Take up our quarrel with the foe:
To you from failing hands we throw
The torch; be yours to hold it high.

In Flanders Fields

—

In Flanders fields the poppies grow
Between the crosses, row on row
That mark our place : and in the sky
The larks still bravely singing, fly
Scarce heard amid the guns below.

We are the Dead . Short days ago
We lived, felt dawn, saw sunset glow,
Loved, and were loved, and now we lie
In Flanders fields.

Take up our quarrel with the foe :
To you from failing hands we throw
The torch : be yours to hold it high !
If ye break faith with us who die
We shall not sleep, though poppies grow
In Flanders fields.

John McCrae

An autograph copy of McCrae's famous poem. Note that in this version he has replaced "blow" with "grow" in the first line.

If ye break faith with us who die
We shall not sleep, though poppies grow
15   In Flanders Fields.

John Mitchell, "Reply to 'In Flanders Fields'" (1916)

Oh! sleep in peace where poppies grow;
The torch your falling hands let go
Was caught by us, again held high,
A beacon light in Flanders sky
5   That dims the stars to those below.
You are our dead, you held the foe,
And ere the poppies cease to blow,
We'll prove our faith in you who lie
In Flanders Fields.

10   Oh! rest in peace, we quickly go
To you who bravely died, and know
In other fields was heard the cry,
For freedom's cause, of you who lie,
So still asleep where poppies grow,
15   In Flanders Fields.

As in rumbling sound, to and fro,
The lightning flashes, sky aglow,
The mighty hosts appear, and high
Above the din of battle cry,
20   Scarce heard amidst the guns below,
Are fearless hearts who fight the foe,
And guard the place where poppies grow.
Oh! sleep in peace, all you who lie
In Flanders Fields.

25   And still the poppies gently blow,
Between the crosses, row on row.
The larks, still bravely soaring high,
Are singing now their lullaby
To you who sleep where poppies grow
30   In Flanders Fields.

German troops in a tench on the Western Front, 1918.

J.A. Armstrong, "Another Reply to 'In Flanders Fields'" (1916)

In Flanders Fields the cannons boom,
And fitful flashes light the gloom;
While up above, like eagles, fly
The fierce destroyers of the sky;
5   With stains the earth wherein you lie
Is redder than the poppy bloom,
In Flanders Fields.
Sleep on, ye brave! The shrieking shell,
The quaking trench, the startling yell,
10   The fury of the battle hell
Shall wake you not, for all is well;
Sleep peacefully, for all is well.
Your flaming torch aloft we bear,
With burning heart and oath we swear
15   To keep the faith, to fight it through,
To crush the foe, or sleep with you,
In Flanders Fields.

Elizabeth Daryush, "Flanders Fields" (1916)

Here the scented daisy glows
Glorious as the carmined° rose;   *reddened*
Here the hill-top's verdure mean
Fair is with unfading green;
Here, where sorrow still must tread,   5
All her graves are garlanded.

And still, O glad passer-by
Of the fields of agony,
Lower laughter's voice, and bare
Thy head in the valley where   10
Poppies bright and rustling wheat
Are a desert to love's feet.

———————————

Anonymous, "I Learned to Wash in Shell-Holes"

I learned to wash in shell-holes and to shave myself in
    tea,
While the fragments of a mirror did a balance on my knee;
I learned to dodge the whizzbangs[1] and the flying lumps
    of lead,
And to keep a foot of earth between the snipers and my
    head.

I learned to keep my haversack[2] well filled with   5
    buckshee[3] food,
To take my army issue and to pinch what else I could;
I learned to cook Maconochie[4] with candle ends and
    string,
With four-by-two[5] and sardine oil and any old darn thing.

I learned to use my bayonet according, as you please,
For a bread-knife or a chopper or a prong for toasting   10
    cheese;
I learned to gather souvenirs that home I hoped to send,

Shells inscribed by soldiers. (Imperial War
Museum, London.)

And hump them round for months and months and
    dump them in the end.

I never used to grumble after breakfast in the line
That the eggs were cooked too lightly or the bacon cut
    too fine;
I never told the sergeant just exactly what I thought;   15
I never did a pack-drill[6] for I never quite got caught.
I never stopped a whizzbang though I've stopped a lot
    of mud,
But the one that Fritz[7] sent over with my name on was
    a dud.

J.P. Long and Maurice Scott, "Oh! It's a Lovely
War" (1917)

Up to your waist in water, up to your eyes in slush,
Using the kind of language that makes the sergeant
    blush,
Who wouldn't join the army? That's what we all
    enquire.
Don't we pity the poor civilians sitting beside the fire.

(*Chorus*)

———————————

[1] *whizzbangs* Shells fired by small-caliber, high-velocity German
guns.

[2] *haversack* Stout canvas bag for carrying daily rations.

[3] *buckshee* Extra, spare.

[4] *Maconochie* Tinned vegetable stew (named after its inventor).

[5] *four-by-two* Rag for cleaning the barrel of a rifle.

[6] *pack-drill* Form of drill used as punishment, in which soldiers
had to march in full uniform while carrying a heavy pack.

[7] *Fritz* Nickname for a German soldier.

5   *Oh, oh, oh it's a lovely war.*
Who wouldn't be a soldier, eh? Oh it's a shame to take the
   pay.
As soon as reveille[1] has gone we feel just as heavy as lead,
But we never get up till the sergeant brings our breakfast up
   to bed.
Oh, oh, oh it's a lovely war.
10   *What do we want with eggs and ham when we've got plum*
   and apple jam?
Form fours. Right turn. How shall we spend the money we
   earn?
Oh, oh, oh it's a lovely war.

When does a soldier grumble? When does he make a
   fuss?
No one is more contented in all the world than us.
15   *Oh it's a cushy life, boys, really we love it so:*
Once a fellow was sent on leave and simply refused to
   go.

Come to the cookhouse door, boys, sniff at the lovely
   stew.
Who is it says the colonel gets better grub than you?
Any complaints this morning? Do we complain? Not
   we.
20   *What's the matter with lumps of onion floating around*
   the tea?

from Rebecca West, "The Cordite Makers" (1916)

The world was polished to brightness by an east wind when I visited the cordite[2] factory, and shone with hard colours like a German toy-landscape. The marshes were very green and the scattered waters very blue, and little white clouds roamed one by one across the sky like grazing sheep on a meadow. On the hills around stood elms, and grey churches and red farms and yellow ricks,[3] painted bright by the sharp sunshine. And very distinct on the marshes there lay the village which is always full of people, and yet is the home of nothing except death.

---

1 *reveille*   Morning drum beat or bugle call to wake the soldiers.

2 *cordite*   Type of smokeless explosive.

3 *ricks*   Haystacks.

A ship full of Australian and New Zealand troops on their way to the Turkish peninsula of Gallipoli in the summer of 1915. The Gallipoli offensive was disastrous. Winston Churchill (then First Lord of the Admiralty) had hoped Gallipoli would provide an alternative to the trench warfare of the sort endured in Flanders, but the offensive was doomed by poor planning, insufficient knowledge of the terrain, and an underestimation of the enemy's strength.

In the glare it showed that like so many institutions of the war it has the disordered and fantastic quality of a dream. It consists of a number of huts, some like the government-built cottages for Irish labourers, and some like the open-air shelters in a sanatorium, scattered over five hundred acres; they are connected by raised wooden gangways and interspersed with green mounds and rush ponds. It is of such vital importance to the State that it is ringed with barbed-wire entanglements and patrolled by sentries, and its products must have sent tens of thousands of our enemies to their death. And it is inhabited chiefly by pretty young girls clad in a Red-Riding-Hood fancy dress of khaki and scarlet.

Every morning at six, when the night mist still hangs over the marshes, 250 of these girls are fetched by a light railway from their barracks on a hill two miles away. When I visited the works they had already been at work for nine hours, and would work for three more. This twelve-hour shift is longer than one would wish, but it is not possible to introduce three shifts, since the girls would find an eight-hour day too light and would complain of being debarred from the opportunity of making more money; and it is not so bad as it sounds, for in these airy and isolated huts there is neither the orchestra of rattling machines nor the sense of a confined area crowded with tired people which make the ordinary factory such a fatiguing place. Indeed, these girls, working in teams of six or seven in those clean and tidy rooms, look as if they were practising a neat domestic craft rather than a deadly domestic process. . . .

But how deceptive this semblance of normal life is; what extraordinary work this is for women and how extraordinarily they are doing it, is made manifest in a certain row of huts where the cordite is being pressed through wire mesh. This, in all the world, must be the place where war and grace are closest linked. Without, a strip of garden runs beside the huts, gay with shrubs and formal with a sundial. Within there is a group of girls that composes into so beautiful a picture that one remembers that the most glorious painting in the world, Velasquez's[1] *The Weavers*, shows women working just like this.

One girl stands high on a platform against the wall, filling the cordite paste into one of the two great iron presses, and when she has finished with that she swings round the other one on a swivel with a fine free gesture. The other girls stand round the table laying out the golden cords in graduated sizes from the thickness of rope to the thinness of macaroni, the clear khaki and scarlet of their dresses shining back from the wet floor in a perpetually changing pattern as they move quickly about their work. They look very young in their pretty, childish dresses, and one thinks them good children for working so diligently. And it occurs to one as something incredible that they are now doing the last three hours of a twelve-hour shift.

If one asks the manager whether this zeal can possibly be normal, whether it is not perhaps the result of his presence, one is confronted by the awful phenomenon, beside which a waterspout or a volcano in eruption would be a little thing, of a manager talking about his employees with reverence. It seems that the girls work all day with a fury which mounts to a climax in the last three hours before the other 250 girls step

into their places for the twelve-hour night shift. In these hours spies are sent out to walk along the verandah to see how the teams in the other huts are getting on, and their reports set the girls on to an orgy of competitive industry. Here again it was said that for attention, enthusiasm and discipline, there could not be better workmen than these girls.

There is matter connected with these huts, too, that showed the khaki and scarlet hoods to be no fancy dress, but a military uniform. They are a sign, for they have been dipped in a solution that makes them fireproof, that the girls are ready to face an emergency, which had arisen in those huts only a few days ago. There had been one of those incalculable happenings of which high explosives are so liable, an inflammatory mixture of air with acetone, and the cordite was ignited. Two huts were instantly gutted, and the girls had to walk out through the flame. In spite of the uniform one girl lost a hand. These, of course, are the everyday dangers of the high-explosives factory. There is very little to be feared by our enemies by land, and it is the sentries' grief and despair that their total bag for the eighteen months of their patrol of the marshes consists of one cow.

Surely, never before in modern history can women have lived a life so completely parallel to that of the regular Army. The girls who take up this work sacrifice almost as much as men who enlist; for although they make on an average 30s[2] a week they are working much harder than most of them, particularly the large number who were formerly domestic servants, would ever have dreamed of working in peacetime. And, although their colony of wooden huts has been well planned by their employers, and is pleasantly administered by the Young Women's Christian Association, it is, so far as severance of home-ties goes, barrack life. For although they are allowed to go home for Sunday, travelling is difficult from this remote village, and the girls are so tired that most of them spend the day in bed.

And there are two things about the cordite village which the State ought never to forget, and which ought to be impressed upon the public mind by the bestowal of military rank upon the girls. First of all there is the cold fact that they face more danger every day than any

---

[1] *Velasquez* Spanish painter Diego Velásquez (1599–1660).

[2] *s* Shillings.

soldier on home defence has seen since the beginning of the war. And secondly, there is the fact—and one wishes it could be expressed in terms of the saving of English and the losing of German life—that it is because of this army of cheerful and disciplined workers that this cordite factory has been able to increase its output since the beginning of the war by something over 1,500 per cent. It was all very well for the Army to demand high explosives, and for Mr. Lloyd George[1] to transmit the demand to industry; in the last resort the matter lay in the hands of the girls in the khaki and scarlet hoods, and the State owes them a very great debt for the way in which they have handled it.

from Francis Marion Beynon, *Aleta Day* (1919)

The following excerpt is from Francis Marion Beynon's autobiographical novel *Aleta Day*, which recounts the heroine's childhood in a small town in Manitoba, Canada, and her subsequent love for a man who enlists when World War I begins. Beynon herself was a journalist known for her feminist views and her pacifism—a stance that lost her her job in 1917. This excerpt, however, expresses the idealism that permeated the nation in the months after the declaration of war, before the realities of trench warfare were realized.

from CHAPTER 24: WAR

Then the war came. It burst like a cloud upon our holidaying world, and set us all a-tremble and a-thrill.

Germany had broken the peace of the world and plunged us into night. Very well, we would collect a few Canadians and send them over and they would settle the matter in a few months and come home, and we would give them a banquet, and allow them to die in the poor-house, as had been done to the heroes of other wars.

What days those were! An extra[2] every half-hour! War maps in every hand! A half mile towards Paris—

Female workers at a Birmingham airplane factory in September 1918.

gloom for two days! A great ship sunk—gloom for a week! Our hearts were sensitive to suffering then and the death of a hundred thousand men meant something to us. The blood reeked in our nostrils.

Yet for all that we [were] women, old men and cripples, how we did shout our patriotism from the housetops, so that nobody should miss our voice in the great songs.

What days those were!

The even tramp of troops along the streets! The morning call of the bugle! The thrill of an hourly excitement! The awful torment of soul as one read of rivers full of dead bodies. Human bodies! It broke our hearts to read of men with their legs and arms blown off; with their faces shattered to pieces; men who would go on living under the most horrible physical limitations. That was early in the war before we had grown callous to the pain of other human beings.

And yet, mixed with our horror, there was a thrill, a feeling that something had really happened in our time.

What days those were!

---

[1] *Mr. Lloyd George* David Lloyd George (1863–1945), British Prime Minister.

[2] *extra* Additional issue of a newspaper.

Ivor Gurney, "To His Love" (1919)

Ivor Gurney (1890–1937) fought on the Western front from May 1916 to October 1917 (when he was poisoned by gas). He published two collections of war poems, as well as other work, but was increasingly affected by severe mental illness, and in 1922 was certified as insane.

He's gone, and all our plans
    Are useless indeed.
We'll walk no more on Cotswold[1]
    Where the sheep feed
5   Quietly and take no heed.

His body that was so quick
    Is not as you
Knew it, on Severn River
    Under the blue
10   Driving our small boat through.

You would not know him now....
    But still he died
Nobly, so cover him over
    With violets of pride
15   Purple from Severn side.

Cover him, cover him soon!
    And with thick-set
Masses of memoried flowers
    Hide that red wet
20   Thing I must somehow forget.

Vance Palmer, "The Farmer Remembers the Somme" (1920)

Both Vance Palmer (1885–1959), who was better known as a writer of fiction than as a poet, and his wife, Nettie Palmer, a leading critic as well as a poet, played central roles in Australian cultural life from the 1920s through to the 1950s. Vance Palmer joined the Australian Army in 1918, but never saw active service.

Will they never fade or pass!
    The mud, and the misty figures endlessly coming
In file through the foul morass,°   *marsh*
And the grey flood-water lipping the reeds and grass,
5 And the steel wings drumming.

The hills are bright in the sun:
There's nothing changed or marred in the well-known
    places;
When work for the day is done
There's talk, and quiet laughter, and gleams of fun
10 On the old folks' faces.

I have returned to these:
The farm, and the kindly Bush, and the young calves
    lowing;
But all that my mind sees
Is a quaking bog in a mist—stark, snapped trees,
15 and the dark Somme flowing.

---

[1] *Cotswold* Range of hills in western England.

11th Month NOVEMBER 1917	1917 NOVEMBER 30 Days
4 Sun—22nd after Trinity	
5 Mon	8 Th
6 Tues—(Last Quarter, 5.4 P.M.	9 Fri
7 Wed	10 Sat—s. R. 7.10, s. s. 4.18

NEWLY-DUG TRENCHES.   Apart from uniforms,
there are times when soldiers have no chance of disguising
their whereabouts from an enemy. A hastily-prepared
trench may indicate your position more clearly than the
brightest accoutrements.
    Suppose, as in the sketch on opposite page, you have only
just had time to throw up an entrenchment, the newly-turned
earth, AA, will stand up in the shape of a very distinct wall
against a green background, and so your enemy will quickly
"spot" you.

A page from the *Soldier's Own Diary*, copies of which were widely distributed to troops during
the war.

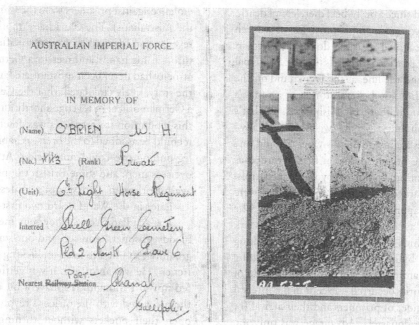

Memorial card for an Australian soldier killed and buried at Gallipoli. After the war, when the process of gathering the remains of soldiers and of constructing cemeteries began, Gallipoli became the final resting place for many New Zealand and Australian soldiers. Because most families could not arrange a visit to their loved one's grave, pictures were supplied to these families upon request.

from Robert Graves, *Good-Bye to All That* (1929, revised 1957)

from CHAPTER 17

We[1] once discussed which were the cleanest troops in trenches, taken by nationalities. We agreed on a descending-order list like this: English and German Protestants; Northern Irish, Welsh and Canadians; Irish and German Catholics; Scots, with certain higher-ranking exceptions; Mohammedan Indians; Algerians; Portuguese; Belgians; French. We put the Belgians and French there for spite; they could not have been dirtier than the Algerians and the Portuguese.

Propaganda reports of atrocities were, it was agreed, ridiculous. We remembered that while the Germans *could* commit atrocities against enemy civilians, Ger-

many itself, except for an early Russian cavalry raid, had never had the enemy on her soil. We no longer believed the highly-coloured accounts of German atrocities in Belgium; knowing the Belgians now at first-hand. By atrocities we meant, specifically, rape, mutilation and torture—not summary shootings of suspected spies, harbourers of spies, *francs-tireurs*,[2] or disobedient local officials. If the atrocity-list had to include the accidental-on-purpose bombing or machine-gunning of civilians from the air, the Allies were now committing as many atrocities as the Germans. French and Belgian civilians had often tried to win our sympathy by exhibiting mutilations of children—stumps of hands and feet, for instance—representing them as deliberate, fiendish atrocities when, as likely as not, they were merely the result of shell-fire. We did not believe rape to be any more common on the German side of the line than on

---

[1] *We* Graves, who was an officer in the Royal Welch Fusiliers, is here recounting his discussions with other British officers.

[2] *francs-tireurs* French: irregular soldiers.

the Allied side. And since a bully-beef diet, fear of death, and absence of wives made ample provision of women necessary in the occupied areas, no doubt the German Army authorities provided brothels in the principal French towns behind the line, as the French did on the Allied side. We did not believe stories of women's forcible enlistment in these establishments. "What's wrong with the voluntary system?" we asked cynically.

As for atrocities against soldiers—where should one draw the line? The British soldier, at first, regarded as atrocious the use of bowie-knives[1] by German patrols. After a time, he learned to use them himself; they were cleaner killing weapons than revolvers or bombs. The Germans regarded as equally atrocious the British Mark VII rifle-bullet, which was more apt to turn on striking than the German bullet. For true atrocities, meaning personal rather than military violations of the code of war, few opportunities occurred—except in the interval between the surrender of prisoners and their arrival (or non-arrival) at Headquarters. Advantage was only too often taken of this opportunity. Nearly every instructor in the Mess could quote specific instances of prisoners having been murdered on the way back. The commonest motives were, it seems, revenge for the death of friends or relatives, jealousy of the prisoner's trip to a comfortable prison camp in England, military enthusiasm, fear of being suddenly overpowered by the prisoners or, more simply, impatience with the escorting job. In any of these cases the conductors would report on arrival at Headquarters that a German shell had killed the prisoners; and no questions would be asked. We had every reason to believe that the same thing happened on the German side, where prisoners, as useless mouths to feed in a country already short of rations, would be even less welcome. None of us had heard of German prisoners being more than threatened at Headquarters to get military information from them. The sort that they could give was not of sufficient importance to make torture worth while; and anyhow, it had been found that, when treated kindly, prisoners were anxious in gratitude to tell as much as they knew. German intelligence officers had probably discovered that too.

The troops with the worst reputation for acts of violence against prisoners were the Canadians (and later the Australians). The Canadians' motive was said to be revenge for a Canadian found crucified with bayonets through his hands and feet in a German trench. This atrocity had never been substantiated; nor did we believe the story, freely circulated, that the Canadians crucified a German officer in revenge shortly afterwards. How far this reputation for atrocities was deserved, and how far it could be ascribed to the overseas habit of bragging and leg-pulling, we could not decide. At all events, most overseas men, and some British troops, made atrocities against prisoners a boast, not a confession.

Later in the War, I heard two first-hand accounts.

A Canadian-Scot: "They sent me back with three bloody prisoners, you see, and one started limping and groaning, so I had to keep on kicking the sod down the trench. He was an officer. It was getting dark and I felt fed up, so I thought: 'I'll have a bit of a game.' I had them covered with the officer's revolver and made 'em open their pockets without turning round. Then I dropped a Mills bomb[2] in each, with the pin out, and ducked behind a traverse. Bang, bang, bang! No more bloody prisoners. No good Fritzes[3] but dead 'uns."

An Australian: "Well, the biggest lark I had was at Morlancourt, when we took it the first time. There were a lot of Jerries[4] in a cellar, and I said to 'em: 'Come out, you Camarades!' So out they came, a dozen of 'em, with their hands up. 'Turn out your pockets,' I told 'em. They turned 'em out. Watches, and gold and stuff, all dinkum.[5] Then I said: 'Now back to your cellar, you sons of bitches!' For I couldn't be bothered with 'em. When they were all safely down I threw half a dozen Mills bombs in after 'em. I'd got the stuff all right, and we weren't taking prisoners that day."

An old woman at Cardonette on the Somme gave me my first-hand account of large-scale atrocities. I was billeted with her in July 1916. Close to her home, a battalion of French Turcos[6] overtook the rear-guard of

---

[1] *bowie-knives* Curved, double-edged knives of about 15 inches in length.

[2] *Mills bomb* Type of hand grenade made to form shrapnel on explosion.

[3] *Fritzes* Nickname for German soldiers.

[4] *Jerries* Nickname for German soldiers.

[5] *dinkum* Australian slang: genuine, authentic.

[6] *French Turcos* Algerians serving in the French infantry.

a German division retreating from the Marne in September 1914. The Turcos surprised the dead-weary Germans while still marching in column. The old woman went, with gestures, through the pantomime of slaughter, and ended: "*Et enfin, ces animaux leur ont arraché les oreilles et les ont mis à la poche!*"[1] …

We discussed the continuity of regimental morale. A captain in a Line battalion of a Surrey regiment said: "Our battalion has never recovered from the first Battle of Ypres. What's wrong is that we have a rotten depot. The drafts are bad, and so we get a constant re-infection." He told me one night in our sleeping hut: "In both the last two shows I had to shoot a man of my company to get the rest out of the trench. It was so bloody awful, I couldn't stand it. That's why I applied to be sent down here." This was the truth, not the usual loose talk that one heard at the base. I felt sorrier for him than for any other man I met in France. He deserved a better regiment.

The boast of every good battalion was that it had never lost a trench; both our Line battalions made it—meaning, that they had never been forced out of a trench without recapturing it before the action ended. Capturing a German trench and being unable to hold it for lack of reinforcements did not count; nor did retirement by order from Headquarters, or when the battalion next door had broken and left a flank in the air. And, towards the end of the War, trenches could be honourably abandoned as being wholly obliterated by bombardment, or because not really trenches at all, but a line of selected shell-craters.

We all agreed on the value of arms-drill as a factor in morale. "Arms-drill as it should be done," someone said, "is beautiful, especially when the company feels itself as a single being, and each movement is not a synchronized movement of every man together, but the single movement of one large creature." I used to get big bunches of Canadians to drill: four or five hundred at a time. Spokesmen stepped forward once and asked what sense there was in sloping and ordering arms, and fixing and unfixing bayonets. They said they had come across to fight, and not to guard Buckingham Palace. I told them that in every division of the four in which I had

served—the First, Second, Seventh and Eighth—there had been three different kinds of troops. Those that had guts but were no good at drill; those that were good at drill but had no guts; and those that had guts and were good at drill. These last, for some reason or other, fought by far the best when it came to a show—I didn't know why, and I didn't care. I told them that when they were better at fighting than the Guards they could perhaps afford to neglect their arms-drill.

We often theorized in the Mess about drill. I held that the best drill never resulted from being bawled at by a sergeant-major: that there must be perfect respect between the man who gives the order and the men who carry it out. The test of drill came, I said, when the officer gave an incorrect word of command. If his company could, without hesitation, carry out the order intended or, if the order happened to be impossible, could stand absolutely still, or continue marching, without confusion in the ranks, that was good drill. Some instructors regarded the corporate spirit that resulted from drilling together as leading to loss of initiative in the men drilled.

Others argued that it acted just the other way round: "Suppose a section of men with rifles get isolated from the rest of the company, without an N.C.O.[2] in charge, and meet a machine-gun. Under the stress of danger this section will have that all-one-body feeling of drill, and obey an imaginary word of command. There may be no communication between its members, but there will be a drill movement, with two men naturally opening fire on the machine-gun while the remainder work round, part on the left flank and part on the right; and the final rush will be simultaneous. Leadership is supposed to be the perfection for which drill has been instituted. That's wrong. Leadership is only the first stage. Perfection of drill is communal action. Though drill may seem to be antiquated parade-ground stuff, it's the foundation of tactics and musketry. Parade-ground musketry won all the battles in our regimental histories; this War, which is unlikely to open out, and must end with the collapse, by 'attrition,' of one side or the other, will be won by parade-ground tactics—by the simple drill tactics of small units fighting in limited spaces, and in noise and

[1] *Et enfin … poche* French: And finally, these animals tore off their ears [i.e., the ears of their prisoners] and put them in their pockets.

[2] *N.C.O.* Non-commissioned officer.

confusion so great that leadership is quite impossible." Despite variance on this point we all agreed that regimental pride remained the strongest moral force that kept a battalion going as an effective fighting unit; contrasting it particularly with patriotism and religion.

Patriotism, in the trenches, was too remote a sentiment, and at once rejected as fit only for civilians, or prisoners. A new arrival who talked patriotism would soon be told to cut it out. As "Blighty,"[1] a geographical concept, Great Britain was a quiet, easy place for getting back to out of the present foreign misery; but as a nation it included not only the trench-soldiers themselves and those who had gone home wounded, but the staff, Army Service Corps, lines-of-communication troops, base units, home-service units, and all civilians down to the detested grades of journalists, profiteers, "starred" men exempted from enlistment, conscientious objectors, and members of the Government. The trench-soldier, with this carefully graded caste-system of honour, never considered that the Germans opposite might have built up exactly the same system themselves. He thought of Germany as a nation in arms, a unified nation inspired with the sort of patriotism that he himself despised. He believed most newspaper reports on conditions and sentiments in Germany, though believing little or nothing of what he read about similar conditions and sentiments in England. Yet he never under-rated the German as a soldier. Newspaper libels on Fritz's courage and efficiency were resented by all trench-soldiers of experience.

Hardly one soldier in a hundred was inspired by religious feeling of even the crudest kind. It would have been difficult to remain religious in the trenches even if one had survived the irreligion of the training battalion at home. A regular sergeant at Montagne, a Second Battalion man, had recently told me that he did not hold with religion in time of war. He said that the "niggers" (meaning the Indians) were right in officially relaxing their religious rules while fighting. "And all this damn nonsense, Sir—excuse me, Sir—that we read in the papers, Sir, about how miraculous it is that the wayside crucifixes are always getting shot at, but the figure of our Lord Jesus somehow don't get hurt, it

fairly makes me sick, Sir." This was his explanation why, when giving practice fire-orders from the hill-top, he had shouted, unaware that I stood behind him: "Seven hundred, half left, bloke on cross, five rounds, concentrate, FIRE!" And why, for "concentrate," he had humorously substituted "consecrate." His platoon, including the two unusual "Bible-wallahs" whose letters home always began in the same formal way: "Dear Sister in Christ," or "Dear Brother in Christ," blazed away.

Women celebrating on Armistice Day, London, 1918.

from May Wedderburn Cannan, *Grey Ghosts and Voices* (1976)

The following is taken from the autobiography of May Wedderburn Cannan, daughter of the head of the Oxford University Press. During the war Cannan worked at the Press and as a volunteer nurse, participating in the mobilization of the Red Cross. She also went to France to volunteer in a soldiers' canteen in Rouen, an experience she describes in the excerpt below. Cannan gives a sense of the change of attitude—from optimism to cynicism—among both poets and the general public as the war progressed when she explains the popular expression at the time, "Went to the war with Rupert Brooke and came home with Siegfried Sassoon." While Brooke was an idealistic poet whose verse celebrated his country and its cause, Sassoon's verse painted in grim detail the horrors of a war the senseless atrocities of which could not be idealized. After years of trench warfare, the poems of Brooke seemed naive and simplistic to many.

---

[1]   *Blighty*   England; home.

I suppose it is difficult for anyone to realise now what "France" meant to us. In the Second War I met a young man of the Left who assured me that Rupert Brooke's[1] verse was of no account, phoney, because it was "impossible that anyone should have thought like that." I turned and rent him, saying that he was entitled to his own opinion of Rupert Brooke's verse, but not entitled to say that no one could have thought like that. How could he know how we had thought?—All our hopes and all our loves, and God knew, all our fears, were in France; to get to France, if only to stand on her soil, was something; to share, in however small a way, in what was done there was Heart's Desire.

I asked my Father could I take all my holidays in one and go for four weeks to France—I did not want holidays, I said, but I did want France. It was dark and we were walking home through the confines of Little Clarendon Street; my voice, I knew, shook; he took his pipe out of his mouth, halted his step for a moment and looked down at me. "Ah! France" he said, "France, yes, I think you should go. We'll manage." I stammered thanks and we walked home in silence, understanding each other.

The Canteen was started at Rouen because Lord Brassey's yacht *The Sunbeam* had made two or three journeys there during the shortage of hospital ships bringing wounded home. Lady Mabelle Egerton, his daughter, looking round the desolate railway yards beyond the quays asked the R.T.O.[2] if there was anything that could be done for the troops; drafts going up the line to Railhead, who had to spend a long day there, and sometimes a long night.

He said that the men brought their rations, including tea, but that there was no means of making hot water. (It was long before the days of another war when motorised infantry "brewed up" with their petrol cans) —Could she find some philanthropic person to take on the job? She could find no one—and decided to do it herself, and so the Canteen, later known affectionately

to thousands of the B.E.F. and the New Armies[3] as "the Coffee Shop," was born....

Along the length of railway line ran a row of sheds with huge sliding doors. In the first, and smaller one, was established a boiler room where enormous vats of hot water forever boiled. Beyond, steps led to a room where we ate our own meals when there was time and kept books for anyone who asked for something to read going up the Line. And across the whole of the great sheds ran heavy tables; ours with shelves under which at night held guttering candles and trays for change. Behind were the steaming cauldrons where we washed, (when a draft had left), the unbelievably pink French bowls in which we served coffee.

Coffee had proved more possible to get than tea and to it was added ham sandwiches. We had hundreds of someone's "Handy Hams" enclosed in a kind of scaly protection. In cold weather when we could not peel them we flung them with violence onto the stone floor to crack them; then endlessly we cut slices of ham.

I remember at the end of a long cutting session my left hand could not close itself; it had held the ham steady against the knife for so long, but we did have two machines for cutting bread. Butter in the cold weather was hard and stiff to spread, and when it was hot it dripped.

We were wanted because there had been an epidemic of measles among the staff; one girl had died of pneumonia, and another was home on sick leave—we were gapfillers only, but we were wanted—they needed us....

When the big trains were due in we opened the sliding doors of the sheds, the train doors banged and banged down the long line of the corridors and some 2,000 men would surge in. Barricaded behind our heavy table, and thankful for it when the pressure was heavy or a draft had somehow got hold of some drink, we handed out bowls of coffee and sandwiches, washed dirty bowls till the water in the tall vats was chocolate brown, and served again.

Someone would play the piano; Annie Laurie; Loch Lomond. Blurred lanterns lit the scene as best they might when it rained and our candles in the tills under

---

[1] *Rupert Brooke* Poet (1887–1915) known for his patriotic, idealistic verse. Brooke died of blood poisoning on the way to Gallipoli in 1915.

[2] *R.T.O.* Railroad Transportation Officer.

[3] *B.E.F.* British Expeditionary Force; *New Armies* Forces assembled from the 1914 volunteer recruitment campaign of the Earl of Kitchener, Secretary of State for War.

the tables guttered in the wind. One was hot or horrid cold, harried, dirty, and one's feet ached with the stone floors. When the smaller drafts came one could distinguish faces, and regimental badges; have a word or two. Two men told me with impressment that they were "the New Army, Kitchener's!" I said yes, and we had been expecting them, and thought of the old Army and the T.A.[1] Worried young officers asked one to change a pound note and frowned over getting "25 shillings" (francs) to the pound. Twice I came on an old friend but there was no time save for a brief greeting and a "good bye and good luck."

When the whistle blew they stood to save the King[2] and the roof came off the sheds. Two thousand men, maybe, singing—it was the most moving thing I knew. Then there'd be the thunder of seats pushed back, the stamp of army boots on the pave, and as the train went out they sang Tipperary[3]—

No one seemed to know how the song, written and first sung at Stalybridge in 1912, had become the song of the B.E.F. My brother-in-law, a Mons man,[4] said they did not sing it till they read in the papers that they were—then they learned it! ...

That spring I collected such verse as I thought "possible," got my Father to "cast an eye over it," and set forth to see Mr. Blackwell.[5] He had a small office up an uncarpeted stair at the back of the famous bookshop in the Broad.[6] At the last moment my Father said he would come with me. I think that he wanted to make sure that I was not published in any series or involved in any clique.

Mr. Blackwell was, I remember, very kind, but as I was practically blind and deaf with nerves I have a blurred recollection of what happened. We walked up the Broad together afterwards, and, suddenly realising that his ridiculous daughter was struggling with tears, he

stopped dead. "Why are you crying?" "I'm not," I said, using the old formula; "It's all right only I did think he might take it." "But he has!" "Has he?" I asked astounded. "Yes, of course" said my Father, and continuing up the street; "The trouble with you and that young man is that you have both got the Oxford manner so badly you can't understand each other." He seemed amused. As I have never been able to discover what the Oxford manner is I have never known what he meant. ...

I was lucky for after the Somme there was a change of heart among poets. Siegfried Sassoon wrote to the Press from France saying that the war was now a war of conquest and without justification,[7] and declared himself to be a conscientious objector. He was rescued from trouble by Robert Graves and his friends who claimed a breakdown. C.E. Montague wrote *Disenchantment* and Wilfred Owen[8] was much influenced by him. A saying went round, "Went to the war with Rupert Brooke and came home with Siegfried Sassoon."

I had much admired some of Sassoon's verse but I was not coming home with him. Someone must go on writing for those who were still convinced of the right of the cause for which they had taken up arms.

The conscription tribunals were often ruthless and sometimes, rather horrible; but by no means always (after all the army did not want unwilling, and therefore bad, soldiers), and, testifying their conscientious objections, persistent defenders of culture and antiwar writers were excused active service and able to do other work. There was a colony of them at Garsington near Oxford where Philip and Lady Ottoline Morrell[9] had their

---

[1] *T.A.*   Territorial Army.

[2] *to save the King*   I.e., they stood to sing the national anthem, "God Save the King."

[3] *Tipperary*   The song "It's a Long Way to Tipperary."

[4] *Mons man*   I.e., a man who had fought at the Battle of Mons, in Belgium, the first battle of World War I (23 August 1914).

[5] *Blackwell*   The publisher Basil Blackwell (1889–1984).

[6] *bookshop in the Broad*   I.e., Blackwell's, Broad Street, Oxford.

[7] *Siegfried Sassoon ... justification*   Sassoon's letter, in which he condemned the war as a mere matter of "aggression and conquest," was published in *The Times* on 31 July 1917. After his friend and fellow poet Robert Graves testified that Sassoon was suffering from shell-shock, a medical board sent Sassoon to Craiglockhart War Hospital, Edinburgh, rather than to prison.

[8] *C.E. Montague*   Journalist and novelist Charles Edward Montague (1867–1928), whose *Disenchantment* comprised a series of articles he had published in the *Manchester Guardian* in 1920 and 1921 on the impact of the war; *Wilfred Owen*   War poet (1893–1918).

[9] *Philip and Lady Ottoline Morrell*   Solicitor and politician Philip Morrell (1870–1943) and his wife Ottoline (1873–1938), a well-known literary hostess. Both were pacifists, and their Oxford home, Garsington Manor, provided a refuge for conscientious objectors during the war.

home and entertained such people as Middleton Murry, Katherine Mansfield, Lawrence, Bertrand Russell,[1] my cousin Gilbert Cannan and others of the intellectual élite who stayed there talking of art and verse and genius and pure intellect....

from "Proceedings" of the All-Russian Central Executive Committee of Soviets of Workers', Soldiers', and Peasants' Deputies[2] (17 November 1917)

In March of 1917 (February according to the old Julian calendar, which the Russians used until 1918, when they adopted the Gregorian calendar), with Russia suffering from extreme poverty and in the midst of the war against Germany, the autocratic regime of Czar Nicholas II crumbled as troops refused orders to suppress workers' risings in Moscow and St. Petersburg. The Czar was replaced by a provisional government led by Alexander Kerensky, a democratic socialist. In November (October, according to the Julian calendar), a second revolution occurred when the more radical Bolsheviks, led by V.I. Lenin, seized power. Between June 1917 and January of the following year, representatives of councils of workers (or "soviets") met in Petrograd (St. Petersburg). The discussions shed interesting light on the connections between the revolution and World War I and touch on vitally important issues such as the degree to which the new government would tolerate free speech and the ways in which it contemplated interacting with the rest of the world. The way in which many of the issues discussed here were handled by the Communist government would shape a great deal of twentieth-century history.

The speakers in the excerpts below are V.A. Avanesov, soon to become Secretary of the Central Executive Committee of the new government; A.L. Kalegayev and V.A. Karelin, leaders of the Socialist-Revolutionary Party; Soviet representative S.M. Zaks; Vladimir Lenin, leader of the Bolshevik Party (forerunner of the Communist Party, which domi-

nated the country from 1917 until the collapse of the USSR in 1989–91); and Leon Trotsky, Lenin's second-in-command. (Trotsky later broke with Communist Party authorities after Joseph Stalin came to power; he was murdered while living in exile in Mexico.)

AVANESOV. The question of press freedom must be seen in the context of the current political situation in the country as a whole. It seems that no one objects to closure of bourgeois newspapers during an insurrection, when fighting is in progress. If this is so, [we must ask ourselves] whether the struggle is indeed over and the moment has come when we can pass on to a normal mode of life. Having silenced the bourgeois press, [the revolutionary authorities] would be very naive if they were to let slip from their hands such a powerful means of influencing the ideals of all workers, soldiers, and peasants. All these measures are designed to facilitate the creation of a new regime, free from capitalist oppression, in which a socialist press will ensure freedom of speech for all citizens and for all tendencies of thought.

We defend freedom of the press [in principle], but this concept must be divorced from old petty-bourgeois or bourgeois notions of liberty. If the new government has had the strength to abolish private landed property, thereby infringing the rights of the landlords, it would be ridiculous for Soviet power to stand up for antiquated notions about liberty of the press. First the newspapers must be freed from capitalist oppression, just as we have freed the land from the landlords, and then we can promulgate new socialist laws and norms enshrining a liberty that will serve the whole toiling people, and not just capital....

KALEGAYEV. ... [T]here is a profound disagreement between our position and that of the Bolsheviks. [The latter argue:] previously we defended all civil liberties, but now we are prepared to muzzle our opponents. However, one cannot emancipate society from the fetters of capitalism by taking repressive measures against newspapers. Nor is it possible to carve up freedom of the press like a loaf of bread, allocating so much freedom to each group according to the influence exerted by its ideas. When the Bolsheviks talk of poisoning the people's consciousness by the printed word, they

[1]   *Middleton Murry* Writer and editor John Middleton Murry (1889–1957), husband of author Katherine Mansfield (1888–1923); *Lawrence* Writer D.H. Lawrence (1885–1930); *Bertrand Russell* Philosopher and journalist (1872–1970).

[2]   *Proceedings ... Deputies* Translated by H.L. Keep.

are adopting the viewpoint of [the editors of] *Zemshchina*.[1]

TROTSKY. One should distinguish between the situation during a civil war and the situation once victory is complete. To demand that all repressive measures should be abandoned during a civil war is equivalent to demanding that the war itself should cease. Such a demand could come only from adversaries of the proletariat. Our opponents are not offering us peace. No one can provide a guarantee against [a victory of] the Kornilovites.[2] During a civil war it is legitimate to suppress newspapers that support the other side. But when we are finally victorious our attitude toward the press will be analogous to that on freedom of trade. Then we shall naturally move on to a [regular] regime in press matters. In our party press we have for a long time been accustomed to take a non-proprietorial view of press freedom. Measures taken against [suspect] individuals should also be taken against press organs. We should confiscate and socialize printing-presses and stocks of newsprint … (*Shouts from the floor:* "And Bolshevik ones too?") Yes, all these stocks should be transferred to public ownership. Any group of [workers,] soldiers, or peasants will be able to submit an application for [access to supplies of] newsprint and to a printing-press. …

KARELIN. It is a Hottentot[3] morality which holds that it's bad if someone steals my wife but good if I steal someone else's. I say this because Trotsky has been critical of our party. It is surprising that we should hear [such arguments] from a party which itself now enjoys freedom of the press. We cannot have double standards of morality.

But I would rather discuss this question in terms of political expediency. Is it expedient to muzzle the expression of any trend of opinion? History teaches that whenever this is done it only makes such opinions more

attractive. Forbidden fruit is sweet. I agree with Trotsky that we have to eliminate capitalist oppression in regard to the press. But the measures [he proposes] are risky. One can attain this objective without muzzling opinion, simply by undertaking a wide range of protective actions in the distribution of material. The [Bolshevik] resolution proposes that parties and groups should have [the right to publish] newspapers in proportion to the number of their supporters, but such calculations will scarcely be practicable. It would be absurd to distribute [opportunities to publish] in proportion to [the strength of various currents of] opinion; this would be like socializing thought itself.

I should make it clear that in advocating freedom of opinion we do not seek to extend it to the weakest sector [in terms of popular support]. Trotsky alleges that we are arguing from the standpoint of capital. I say that whoever puts the question in such terms is arguing from the standpoint of his own ministerial portfolio. Genuine representatives of the people should not be afraid of minority opinions. Such fear betrays an awareness that one's own opinions are weak. "Who wants press freedom?" Trotsky asks. The answer is: everyone who cherishes the [revolutionary] movement of our people. …

ZAKS. [I]f we burn our bridges will we not be entirely isolated? After all, we have won precious little support so far. Western Europe is shamefully silent. One can't build socialism by decree and by relying solely upon a single party.

LENIN. The phrase "the west is shamefully silent" is impermissible from the lips of an internationalist.[4] One would have to be blind not to notice the ferment that has gripped the working classes of Germany and the west [in general]. The leaders of the German proletariat, the socialist intelligentsia, consist in main of defensists, as they do everywhere else, but their proletarian followers are prepared to desert them and to respond to our call. The savage discipline that prevails in the German army and navy has not prevented elements opposed [to the war] from taking action. The revolutionary sailors in the German navy, knowing that their enterprise was

---

[1] *Zemshchina* Russian newspaper whose title translates as "lands of the state," i.e., lands where the workers live (as opposed to the *oprichnina*, which was the personal domain of the Tsar).

[2] *Kornilovites* Supporters of General Kornilov, who attempted to replace Kerensky with a military government.

[3] *Hottentot* I.e., ignorant; inferior. (A derogatory term deriving from the name then given to members of a Southwest African people.)

[4] *internationalist* Socialist who supported an international workers' rebellion, and who thought such a movement should take precedence over the war.

doomed to fail, went to meet their fate heroically, in the hope that their sacrifice would awaken the spirit of insurrection among the people. …

We believe in a revolution in the west. We know that this is inevitable, but of course we can't bring it about to order. Did we know last December what was to happen in February? Did we know for sure in September that next month Russian revolutionary democracy would bring off the greatest overturn in world [history]? We knew that the old government was sitting on a volcano and we could guess from many signs that beneath the surface a great change was occurring in people's ideas. We could feel the electricity in the air, we knew that it would inevitably discharge itself in a purifying storm. But we could not predict the day and hour when the storm would break. It is exactly the same now in the case of Germany. There too the people's sullen discontent is growing and is bound to erupt in the form of a broad mass movement. We cannot decree the revolution, but we can at least help it along. We shall organize fraternization in the trenches and help the western peoples to launch the invincible socialist revolution.

Revolutionary soldiers during the March 1917 uprising in Petrograd.

Vladimir Lenin and Leon Trotsky, c. 1917.

WILLIAM BUTLER YEATS
_1865 – 1939_

In *On Poetry and Poets* (1957), fellow poet and contemporary T.S. Eliot wrote of William Butler Yeats: "Born into a world in which the doctrine of 'Art for Art's Sake' was generally accepted, and living on into one in which art has been asked to be instrumental to social purposes, he held firmly to the right view which is between these, though not in any way a compromise between them, and showed that an artist, by serving his art with entire integrity, is at the same time rendering the greatest service he can to his own nation and to the whole world." In truth, few poets of the twentieth century have contributed as much to the cultural, political, and social framework of their own country, and to English literature in general. An analysis of Yeats's poetry, however, is impossible without understanding the deeply personal and biographical nature of his writing, and Yeats's own endeavor to shape his entire canon of work into a unified body of art.

William Butler Yeats was born in the Dublin suburb of Sandymount on 13 June 1865. His father, John Butler Yeats, had given up law to take up portrait painting, a decision that, though artistically and intellectually stimulating, led to many years of uprooted existence and strained finances for his family. When William was two, the family moved to London, yet much of his childhood was spent moving between schooling in London and retreats to the family home of his mother, Susan Pollexfen, in County Sligo, Ireland. In County Sligo, Yeats would find inspiration in the beauty of the countryside, the local folklore, and Irish tradition. In 1880, the family returned permanently to Ireland and settled in Howth, close to Dublin. In 1883, having completed high school, Yeats decided to become an artist and enrolled in the Metropolitan School of Art, but he soon left to pursue his true passion, poetry. His first published poems appeared in the *Dublin University Review* in 1885; three years later he wrote "The Lake Isle of Innisfree" (first published in 1890), which established his reputation as a poet of powerful emotions deeply rooted in Irish tradition and in the Irish landscape.

Also at an early age, influenced by his father's religious skepticism, Yeats developed a strong interest in occultism, folklore, and theosophism, a system of philosophical thought based on the direct and immediate experience of the divine. In 1885 he joined with friends to form the Dublin Hermetic Society, a group devoted to discussion of occult sciences and pseudo-sciences of the day. This group was predominantly influenced by a more famous mystical society, The Theosophical Society, founded in New York by Madame Helena Blavatsky. In 1887, Yeats met with Madame Blavatsky and later joined the Esoteric section of the London chapter of The Theosophical Society. In 1890, Yeats left the Society to join the Hermetic Order of the Golden Dawn, an occult society that drew upon astrology, tarot, kabbala, and Eastern mysticism for its teachings. Throughout his life and career, Yeats would turn to mythology and the occult as tools for developing his own vision of history and imagination. In much of his poetry, this vision is evident in an elaborate system of images and symbols that Yeats would continually investigate and refine.

In 1889 Yeats's first collection, *The Wanderings of Oisin and Other Poems*, was published. The collection was well received, but the attention of one reader in particular would be responsible for what Yeats would term "the troubling of my life." The beautiful actress and Irish nationalist Maud Gonne was introduced to Yeats by a mutual friend, John O'Leary, shortly after the collection was published. The meeting marked a fateful moment in the life of Yeats, as Gonne would become his obsession for the next quarter-century, and his poetry would resonate with his love and despair for her in poems such as "No Second Troy" (1910) and "A Prayer for My Daughter" (1921). She also helped to inspire him in two new cultural endeavors: the establishment of an Irish national theater and the development of a public voice for the Irish nationalist movement for independence.

Through the 1890s Yeats continued to gain literary prominence with further collections of poetry—among them *The Rose* (1893) and *Poems* (1895)—as well as anthologies, works of prose fiction, and studies of Irish folklore and fairy tales. The vivid lushness that characterizes much of Yeats's early poetry reaches a high point with poems such as "The Secret Rose" in the 1899 collection *The Wind Among the Reeds.*

In 1896 Yeats met Lady Augusta Gregory, a fellow writer and promoter of Irish literature, who invited him to stay in her country house at Coole Park. Through her influence, Yeats became involved in the founding of the Irish National Theatre in 1899. In writing for the theater, Yeats found a new voice for his interest in mythology, mysticism, and Irish nationalism. In 1904, the Irish National Theatre's permanent home, The Abbey Theatre, opened with Yeats's play *On Baile's Strand.* As the Abbey's director and dramatist, Yeats helped develop it into one of the world's leading theaters and, perhaps more importantly to him, into the center of the Irish literary renaissance.

The publication of *The Green Helmet and Other Poems* in 1910 marks Yeats's transition into the second phase of his poetic career. Where his early poems often offered romantic melancholy and idyllic meditations on pagan themes, the poetry of this second phase became more direct in its analysis of the events and attitudes of the period. As Yeats became embittered by the small-minded nationalism of The Abbey's middle-class audiences, and as he watched with horror the growing violence in the struggle for Irish independence, he began to write poems such as "Easter 1916" and "Nineteen Hundred and Nineteen," reflecting his distrust of popular judgment and concern for the future of his country.

At the same time, Yeats continued to develop his complex system of symbolism and esoteric theories regarding the movement of history and human intellect. In 1917, having exhausted his proposals to Maud Gonne and suffered another humiliating refusal by Gonne's daughter Iseult, Yeats married Georgie Hyde-Lees, whom he had met in 1911. On their honeymoon, Hyde-Lees delighted Yeats with her gift for automatic writing (believed by Yeats to be dictated by spirits), and for several years her writings inspired Yeats to refine his symbolic system, as described in his book *A Vision* (1925). Although Yeats's later poetry is by no means unintelligible without an understanding of *A Vision*, many of his poems refer directly to the patterns and imagery examined within its pages. According to Yeats, the progress of art and thought is directly interwoven through the spirals, or gyres, of human history, represented in *A Vision* by two interpenetrating cones that make up antithetical cycles of 2000 years. These ideas became increasingly evident in his poetic works, particularly later poems such as "Byzantium" and "Sailing to Byzantium."

In 1922 Yeats was elected Senator of the Irish Free State; a year later, he was awarded the Nobel Prize for Literature, becoming the first Irish writer to receive the award. Yeats continued to produce major poetry well into his later years. As his health began to decline, his poetry took on a defiant tone, reflecting an awareness of his own mortality. Poems of this period, such as "Lapis Lazuli" and "The Circus Animals' Desertion," rage against old age while reflecting on his life and body of work. Poems published in *The Tower* (1928), *The Winding Stair* (1933), and *Last Poems* (1939) are thought by many critics to be among his finest.

Following a long period of heart trouble, Yeats died on 28 January 1939; he was buried in Roquebrune, France, where he had been spending the winter. In 1948, his remains were reinterred, as he had wished, in Drumcliff, County Sligo. Also according to his wishes, his epitaph is taken from "Under Ben Bulben": "Cast a cold eye / On life, on death. / Horseman, pass by!"

⌘ ⌘ ⌘

The Lake Isle of Innisfree[1]

I will arise and go now, and go to Innisfree,
And a small cabin build there, of clay and wattles[2]
    made;
Nine bean-rows will I have there, a hive for the honey
    bee,
And live alone in the bee-loud glade.

5   And I shall have some peace there, for peace comes
        dropping slow,
Dropping from the veils of the morning to where the
    cricket sings;
There midnight's all a glimmer, and noon a purple glow,
And evening full of the linnet's° wings.   *small songbird's*

I will arise and go now, for always night and day
10 I hear lake water lapping with low sounds by the shore;
While I stand on the roadway, or on the pavements grey,
I hear it in the deep heart's core.
—1890

When You Are Old[3]

When you are old and gray and full of sleep,
And nodding by the fire, take down this book,
And slowly read, and dream of the soft look
Your eyes had once, and of their shadows deep;

5 How many loved your moments of glad grace,
And loved your beauty with love false or true,
But one man loved the pilgrim soul in you,
And loved the sorrows of your changing face;

And bending down beside the glowing bars,
10 Murmur, a little sadly, how Love fled
And paced upon the mountains overhead
And hid his face amid a crowd of stars.
—1892

The Secret Rose[4]

Far-off, most secret, and inviolate Rose,
Enfold me in my hour of hours; where those
Who sought thee in the Holy Sepulchre,[5]
Or in the wine vat, dwell beyond the stir
5 And tumult of defeated dreams; and deep
Among pale eyelids, heavy with the sleep
Men have named beauty. Thy great leaves enfold
The ancient beards, the helms of ruby and gold

---

[1] *Lake Isle of Innisfree*   A small island in Lough Gill, County Sligo; Innisfree (*Inis Fraoigh* in Gaelic) means "Heather Island."

[2] *wattles*   Poles and reeds interwoven to create a thatched wall or roof.

[3] *When You Are Old*   Based on one of Pierre de Ronsard's (1524–85) *Sonnets pour Hélène*, "*Quand vous serez bien vieille, au soir, à la chandelle,*" which translates to: "When you are very old, sitting by the candlelight at night."

[4] *The Secret Rose*   First published under the title "O'Sullivan Rua to the Secret Rose."

[5] *Holy Sepulchre*   Cave in which Jesus Christ's body was placed before his resurrection.

Of the crowned Magi;[1] and the king whose eyes
10 Saw the Pierced Hands and Rood° of elder rise   *cross*
In druid vapour and make the torches dim;
Till vain frenzy awoke and he died;[2] and him
Who met Fand walking among flaming dew
By a grey shore where the wind never blew,
15 And lost the world and Emer for a kiss;[3]
And him who drove the gods out of their liss,[4]
And till a hundred morns had flowered red,
Feasted, and wept the barrows° of his dead;   *grave mounds*
And the proud dreaming king who flung the crown
20 And sorrow away, and calling bard and clown
Dwelt among wine-stained wanderers in deep woods:[5]
And him who sold tillage,° and house,   *farmland*
    and goods,
And sought through lands and islands numberless years,
Until he found with laughter and with tears,
25 A woman, of so shining loveliness
That men threshed corn at midnight by a tress,°   *lock of hair*
A little stolen tress.[6] I, too, await
The hour of thy great wind of love and hate.

---

[1] *Magi* Three wise men who came from the East to bring gifts to the baby Jesus.

[2] *the king ... he died* King Conchobar, who was said to have the same birth date and death date as Jesus Christ. Conchobar had an object embedded in his head, an injury from a past battle; when he was told of Christ's execution, he grew so angry that the object burst out of his skull and he died. Here, Yeats imagines Conchobar witnessing the crucifixion in a vision brought by Druids, priests of Celtic religion. Yeats identifies this and the poem's other references to Irish myth and folktale in an extensive note accompanying some editions of the poem.

[3] *and him ... a kiss* In Irish myth, the great hero Cúchulainn became a lover to the goddess Fand and accompanied her to the otherworld, leaving his wife Emer.

[4] *And him ... their liss* Caoilte, a hero of Irish legend. Seized by rage after almost all of his friends were killed in a battle, he drove the nearby gods out of their home; *liss* Circular fort common in iron-age Ireland.

[5] *And the proud ... deep woods* Legendary Irish king Fergus. According to Yeats, he fell so deeply in love with a woman that he was motivated to give up his throne to her son Conchobar, and he spent the rest of his days feasting and hunting in the forest.

[6] *And him who sold ... stolen tress* Reference to an Irish folktale in which a working man, while traveling on the road in the dark, discovers a box containing a brightly glowing lock of hair. He uses it as a lamp to work at night until the king learns of the hair and sends him to find the woman to whom it belongs.

When shall the stars be blown about the sky,
30 Like the sparks blown out of a smithy,°   *blacksmith's forge*
    and die?
Surely thine hour has come, thy great wind blows,
Far-off, most secret, and inviolate Rose?
—1896

No Second Troy[7]

Why should I blame her[8] that she filled my days
    With misery, or that she would of late[9]
Have taught to ignorant men most violent ways,
Or hurled the little streets upon the great,
5 Had they but courage equal to desire?
What could have made her peaceful with a mind
That nobleness made simple as a fire,
With beauty like a tightened bow, a kind
That is not natural in an age like this,
10 Being high and solitary and most stern?
Why, what could she have done being what she is?
Was there another Troy for her to burn?
—1910

Easter 1916[10]

I have met them at close of day
    Coming with vivid faces
From counter or desk among grey
Eighteenth-century houses.
5 I have passed with a nod of the head
Or polite meaningless words,
Or have lingered awhile and said
Polite meaningless words,

---

[7] *Troy* During the Trojan War, the Greeks besieged and destroyed the city of Troy in an effort to retrieve Helen, who had been abducted by the Trojan, Paris, from her husband, the Greek Menelaus.

[8] *her* Maud Gonne.

[9] *of late* Gonne ceased her political work in 1905.

[10] *Easter 1916* On Easter Monday, 24 April 1916, Irish nationalists instigated an unsuccessful rebellion against the British government (which was then at war with Germany); the Easter rebellion lasted until 29 April. Many of the Irish nationalist leaders were executed that May.

And thought before I had done
10 Of a mocking tale or a gibe
To please a companion
Around the fire at the club,
Being certain that they and I
But lived where motley° is worn: *jester's costume*
15 All changed, changed utterly:
A terrible beauty is born.

That woman's days were spent
In ignorant good-will,
Her nights in argument
20 Until her voice grew shrill.[1]
What voice more sweet than hers
When, young and beautiful,
She rode to harriers?
This man had kept a school
25 And rode our wingèd horse;[2]
This other his helper and friend[3]
Was coming into his force;
He might have won fame in the end,
So sensitive his nature seemed,
30 So daring and sweet his thought.
This other man I had dreamed
A drunken, vainglorious lout.[4]
He had done most bitter wrong
To some who are near my heart,
35 Yet I number him in the song;
He, too, has resigned his part
In the casual comedy;
He, too, has been changed in his turn,

Transformed utterly:
40 A terrible beauty is born.

Hearts with one purpose alone
Through summer and winter seem
Enchanted to a stone
To trouble the living stream.
45 The horse that comes from the road,
The rider, the birds that range
From cloud to tumbling cloud,
Minute by minute they change;
A shadow of cloud on the stream
50 Changes minute by minute;
A horse-hoof slides on the brim,
And a horse plashes within it;
The long-legged moor-hens dive,
And hens to moor-cocks call;
55 Minute by minute they live:
The stone's in the midst of all.

Too long a sacrifice
Can make a stone of the heart.
O when may it suffice?
60 That is Heaven's part, our part
To murmur name upon name,
As a mother names her child
When sleep at last has come
On limbs that had run wild.
65 What is it but nightfall?
No, no, not night but death;
Was it needless death after all?
For England may keep faith
For all that is done and said.[5]
70 We know their dream; enough
To know they dreamed and are dead;
And what if excess of love
Bewildered them till they died?
I write it out in a verse—
75 MacDonagh and MacBride

---

[1] *That woman's ... shrill* Countess Markiewicz, née Constance Gore-Booth (1868–1927), played a central role in the Easter Rebellion; she was arrested and sentenced to death (though the death sentence was later commuted). Yeats later wrote a poem about her and her Irish-nationalist sister, "In Memory of Eva Gore-Booth and Con Markiewicz" (1929).

[2] *This man ... wingèd horse* Pádraic Pearse (1879–1916) founded St. Enda's School near Dublin. He was a leader in the effort to revive the Gaelic language, and wrote both Irish and English poetry; the "wingèd horse" refers to Pegasus, the horse of the Muses.

[3] *This other his helper and friend* Thomas MacDonagh (1878–1916), an Irish poet and playwright who also taught school.

[4] *vainglorious lout* Major John MacBride (1865–1916), estranged husband of Irish nationalist Maud Gonne; their separation just two years after marriage was due in part to his drinking bouts.

[5] *For England ... said* England had originally granted Ireland Home Rule in 1913, but then postponed it due to World War I, promising to institute it after the war.

And Connolly[1] and Pearse[2]
Now and in time to be,
Wherever green is worn,
Are changed, changed utterly:
80 A terrible beauty is born.
—1916

The Wild Swans at Coole[3]

The trees are in their autumn beauty,
   The woodland paths are dry,
Under the October twilight the water
Mirrors a still sky;
5 Upon the brimming water among the stones
Are nine-and-fifty swans.

The nineteenth autumn[4] has come upon me
Since I first made my count;
I saw, before I had well finished,
10 All suddenly mount
And scatter wheeling in great broken rings
Upon their clamorous wings.

I have looked upon those brilliant creatures,
And now my heart is sore.
15 All's changed since I, hearing at twilight,
The first time on this shore,
The bell-beat of their wings above my head,
Trod with a lighter tread.

Unwearied still, lover by lover,
20 They paddle in the cold
Companionable streams or climb the air;
Their hearts have not grown old;
Passion or conquest, wander where they will,
Attend upon them still.

25 But now they drift on the still water,
Mysterious, beautiful;
Among what rushes will they build,
By what lake's edge or pool
Delight men's eyes, when I awake some day
30 To find they have flown away?
—1917

In Memory of Major Robert Gregory[5]

1

Now that we're almost settled in our house[6]
   I'll name the friends that cannot sup with us
Beside a fire of turf[7] in th' ancient tower,
And having talked to some late hour
5 Climb up the narrow winding stair to bed:
Discoverers of forgotten truth
Or mere companions of my youth,
All, all are in my thoughts tonight being dead.

2

Always we'd have the new friend meet the old
10 And we are hurt if either friend seem cold,
And there is salt to lengthen out the smart
In the affections of our heart,
And quarrels are blown up upon that head;
But not a friend that I would bring
15 This night can set us quarrelling,
For all that come into my mind are dead.

3

Lionel Johnson[8] comes the first to mind,
That loved his learning better than mankind,
Though courteous to the worst; much falling he
20 Brooded upon sanctity

---

[1] *Connolly* James Connolly (1868–1916), Irish Socialist.

[2] *MacDonagh ... Pearse* All four men were executed for their involvement in the Easter Uprising of 1916.

[3] *Coole* Coole Park, County Galway estate of Lady Gregory, friend and patron of Yeats.

[4] *nineteenth autumn* Yeats first visited Coole Park in 1897, nineteen years before he wrote this poem.

[5] [Yeats's note] Major Robert Gregory [Lady Gregory's only son (1881–1918)], R.F.C. [Royal Flying Corps], M.C. [Military Cross], Legion of Honour, was killed in action on the Italian Front, January 23, 1918.

[6] *our house* Yeats had bought a section of Lady Gregory's estate at Coole Park; Thoor Ballylee, an ancient Norman tower situated there, became his home.

[7] *turf* Dried peat used for fuel.

[8] *Lionel Johnson* English poet and scholar (1867–1902).

Till all his Greek and Latin learning seemed
A long blast upon the horn that brought
A little nearer to his thought
A measureless consummation that he dreamed.

4

25 And that enquiring man John Synge[1] comes next,
That dying chose the living world for text
And never could have rested in the tomb
But that, for long travelling, he had come
Towards nightfall upon certain set apart
30 In a most desolate stony place,[2]
Towards nightfall upon a race
Passionate and simple like his heart.

5

And then I think of old George Pollexfen,[3]
In muscular youth well known to Mayo[4] men
35 For horsemanship at meets or at racecourses,
That could have shown how pure-bred horses
And solid men, for all their passion, live
But as the outrageous stars incline
By opposition, square and trine;[5]
40 Having grown sluggish and contemplative.

6

They were my close companions many a year,
A portion of my mind and life, as it were,
And now their breathless faces seem to look
Out of some old picture-book;
45 I am accustomed to their lack of breath,
But not that my dear friend's dear son,
Our Sidney[6] and our perfect man,
Could share in that discourtesy of death.

7

For all things the delighted eye now sees
50 Were loved by him; the old storm-broken trees
That cast their shadows upon road and bridge;
The tower set on the stream's edge;
The ford where drinking cattle make a stir
Nightly, and startled by that sound
55 The water-hen must change her ground;
He might have been your heartiest welcomer.

8

When with the Galway foxhounds he would ride
From Castle Taylor to the Roxborough side
Or Esserkelly plain, few kept his pace;
60 At Mooneen[7] he had leaped a place
So perilous that half the astonished meet
Had shut their eyes; and where was it
He rode a race without a bit?
And yet his mind outran the horses' feet.

9

65 We dreamed that a great painter had been born
To cold Clare[8] rock and Galway rock and thorn,
To that stern colour and that delicate line
That are our secret discipline
Wherein the gazing heart doubles her might.
70 Soldier, scholar, horseman, he,
And yet he had the intensity
To have published all to be a world's delight.

10

What other could so well have counselled us
In all lovely intricacies of a house
75 As he that practised or that understood
All work in metal or in wood,
In moulded plaster or in carven stone?
Soldier, scholar, horseman, he,
And all he did done perfectly
80 As though he had but that one trade alone.

---

[1] *John Synge* Irish playwright (1871–1909), co-director, along with Yeats and Lady Gregory, of the Abbey Theatre.

[2] *set apart … place* Synge had set some of his plays in the Aran Islands, off the west coast of Ireland.

[3] *George Pollexfen* Yeats's maternal uncle, an astrologer.

[4] *Mayo* County north of Galway.

[5] *opposition, square and trine* Astrological terms used to describe angles between heavenly bodies.

[6] *Sidney* Elizabethan poet Sir Philip Sidney (1554–86), who, like Gregory, was an artist, scholar, and statesman who died young in battle.

[7] *Castle … Mooneen* Country manors in the County of Galway: Roxborough was Lady Gregory's childhood home; Moneen is beside Esserkelly, which is near Ardrahan in County Galway.

[8] *Clare* County to the south of Galway.

11

Some burn faggots,° others may consume   *bundles of twigs*
The entire combustible world in one small room
As though dried straw, and if we turn about
The bare chimney is gone black out
85 Because the work had finished in that flare.
Soldier, scholar, horseman, he,
As 'twere all life's epitome,
What made us dream that he could comb grey hair?

12

I had thought, seeing how bitter is that wind
90 That shakes the shutter, to have brought to mind
All those that manhood tried, or childhood loved
Or boyish intellect approved,
With some appropriate commentary on each;
Until imagination brought
95 A fitter welcome; but a thought
Of that late death took all my heart for speech.
—1918

Nineteen Hundred and Nineteen[1]

I

Many ingenious lovely things are gone
That seemed sheer miracle to the multitude,
Protected from the circle of the moon
That pitches common things about. There stood
5 Amid the ornamental bronze and stone
An ancient image made of olive wood[2]—
And gone are Phidias' famous ivories[3]
And all the golden grasshoppers and bees.[4]

We too had many pretty toys when young;
10 A law indifferent to blame or praise,
To bribe or threat; habits that made old wrong
Melt down, as it were wax in the sun's rays;
Public opinion ripening for so long
We thought it would outlive all future days.
15 O what fine thought we had because we thought
That the worst rogues and rascals had died out.

All teeth were drawn, all ancient tricks unlearned,
And a great army but a showy thing;
What matter that no cannon had been turned
20 Into a ploughshare?[5] Parliament and king
Thought that unless a little powder burned
The trumpeters might burst with trumpeting
And yet it lack all glory; and perchance
The guardsmen's drowsy chargers would not prance.

25 Now days are dragon-ridden, the nightmare
Rides upon sleep: a drunken soldiery
Can leave the mother, murdered at her door,
To crawl in her own blood, and go scot-free;
The night can sweat with terror as before
30 We pieced our thoughts into philosophy,
And planned to bring the world under a rule,
Who are but weasels fighting in a hole.

He who can read the signs nor sink unmanned
Into the half-deceit of some intoxicant
35 From shallow wits; who knows no work can stand,
Whether health, wealth or peace of mind were spent
On master-work of intellect or hand,
No honour leave its mighty monument,
Has but one comfort left: all triumph would
40 But break upon his ghostly solitude.

But is there any comfort to be found?
Man is in love and loves what vanishes,
What more is there to say? That country round
None dared admit, if such a thought were his,
45 Incendiary or bigot could be found
To burn that stump on the Acropolis,

---

[1] *Nineteen Hundred and Nineteen* 1919 was a year of increasing armed confrontation between the Irish Republican Army and the Irish government, which was controlled by Britain.

[2] *ancient ... wood* Statue of Athena, patron goddess of Athens, was carved out of the wood of the sacred olive tree and stood on the Acropolis; the statue was later destroyed in a fire.

[3] *Phidias' famous ivories* Phidias (sometimes spelled "Pheidias" or "Phideas," c. 500–c. 432 BCE) was a celebrated Greek sculptor who created an ivory- and gold-encrusted statue of Athena (since destroyed) in the Parthenon.

[4] *golden grasshoppers and bees* Offerings to the gods in the form of golden trinkets; Thucydides wrote of the Athenian custom of tying up a lock of hair with a golden grasshopper.

[5] *no cannon ... ploughshare* Cf. Isaiah 2.4: "They shall beat their swords into plowshares ... nation shall not lift up sword against nation, neither shall they learn war anymore."

Or break in bits the famous ivories
Or traffic in the grasshoppers or bees.

2

When Loie Fuller's[1] Chinese dancers enwound
50 A shining web, a floating ribbon of cloth,
It seemed that a dragon of air
Had fallen among dancers, had whirled them round
Or hurried them off on its own furious path;
So the Platonic Year[2]
55 Whirls out new right and wrong,
Whirls in the old instead;
All men are dancers and their tread
Goes to the barbarous clangour of a gong.

3

Some moralist or mythological poet
60 Compares the solitary soul to a swan;
I am satisfied with that,
Satisfied if a troubled mirror show it,
Before that brief gleam of its life be gone,
An image of its state;
65 The wings half spread for flight,
The breast thrust out in pride
Whether to play, or to ride
Those winds that clamour of approaching night.

A man in his own secret meditation
70 Is lost amid the labyrinth that he has made
In art or politics;
Some Platonist affirms that in the station
Where we should cast off body and trade
The ancient habit sticks,
75 And that if our works could
But vanish with our breath
That were a lucky death,
For triumph can but mar our solitude.

The swan has leaped into the desolate heaven:
80 That image can bring wildness, bring a rage
To end all things, to end

---

1 *Loie Fuller* An American dancer and choreographer (1862–1928); her dancers were Japanese, not Chinese.

2 *Platonic Year* Full revolution of the constellations in relation to the equinoxes, approximately 26,000 years.

What my laborious life imagined, even
The half-imagined, the half-written page;
O but we dreamed to mend
85 Whatever mischief seemed
To afflict mankind, but now
That winds of winter blow
Learn that we were crack-pated when we dreamed.

4

We, who seven years ago
90 Talked of honour and of truth,
Shriek with pleasure if we show
The weasel's twist, the weasel's tooth.

5

Come let us mock at the great
That had such burdens on the mind
95 And toiled so hard and late
To leave some monument behind,
Nor thought of the levelling wind.

Come let us mock at the wise;
With all those calendars whereon
100 They fixed old aching eyes,
They never saw how seasons run,
And now but gape at the sun.

Come let us mock at the good
That fancied goodness might be gay,
105 And sick of solitude
Might proclaim a holiday:
Wind shrieked—and where are they?

Mock mockers after that
That would not lift a hand maybe
110 To help good, wise or great
To bar that foul storm out, for we
Traffic in mockery.

6

Violence upon the roads: violence of horses;
Some few have handsome riders, are garlanded
115 On delicate sensitive ear or tossing mane,
But wearied running round and round in their courses
All break and vanish, and evil gathers head:

Herodias' daughters have returned again,[1]
A sudden blast of dusty wind and after
120 Thunder of feet, tumult of images,
Their purpose in the labyrinth of the wind;
And should some crazy hand dare touch a daughter
All turn with amorous cries, or angry cries,
According to the wind, for all are blind.
125 But now wind drops, dust settles; thereupon
There lurches past, his great eyes without thought
Under the shadow of stupid straw-pale locks,
That insolent fiend Robert Artisson[2]
To whom the love-lorn Lady Kyteler brought
130 Bronzed peacock feathers, red combs of her cocks.[3]
—1919

A Prayer for My Daughter [4]

Once more the storm is howling, and half hid
Under this cradle-hood and coverlid
My child sleeps on. There is no obstacle
But Gregory's wood[5] and one bare hill
5 Whereby the haystack- and roof-levelling wind,
Bred on the Atlantic, can be stayed;
And for an hour I have walked and prayed
Because of the great gloom that is in my mind.

I have walked and prayed for this young child an hour
10 And heard the sea-wind scream upon the tower,[6]
And under the arches of the bridge, and scream
In the elms above the flooded stream;

Imagining in excited reverie
That the future years had come,
15 Dancing to a frenzied drum,
Out of the murderous innocence of the sea.

May she be granted beauty and yet not
Beauty to make a stranger's eye distraught,
Or hers before a looking-glass, for such,
20 Being made beautiful overmuch,
Consider beauty a sufficient end,
Lose natural kindness and maybe
The heart-revealing intimacy
That chooses right, and never find a friend.

25 Helen[7] being chosen found life flat and dull
And later had much trouble from a fool,
While that great Queen, that rose out of the spray,[8]
Being fatherless could have her way
Yet chose a bandy-leggèd smith[9] for man.
30 It's certain that fine women eat
A crazy salad with their meat
Whereby the Horn of Plenty is undone.

In courtesy I'd have her chiefly learned;
Hearts are not had as a gift but hearts are earned
35 By those that are not entirely beautiful;
Yet many, that have played the fool
For beauty's very self, has charm made wise,
And many a poor man that has roved,
Loved and thought himself beloved,
40 From a glad kindness cannot take his eyes.

May she become a flourishing hidden tree
That all her thoughts may like the linnet be,
And have no business but dispensing round
Their magnanimities of sound,
45 Nor but in merriment begin a chase,
Nor but in merriment a quarrel.

---

[1] *Herodias' ... again* The reference here is not to the Biblical character (whose daughter was Salomé) but rather to the eponymous witch-goddess of Germanic mythology. Her daughters are associated with violently whirling winds.

[2] [Yeats's note] My last symbol, Robert Artisson, was an evil spirit much run after in Kilkenny at the start of the fourteenth century.

[3] *To whom ... cocks* It was said that Artisson seduced Lady Kyteler, who supposedly sacrificed cocks and peacocks to him and was accused of poisoning her husbands; *combs* Pronounced ridges on cocks' crowns.

[4] *My Daughter* Anne Butler Yeats, born 26 February 1919.

[5] *Gregory's wood* Lady Gregory's wood at Coole Park, her estate in western Ireland.

[6] *tower* Thoor Ballylee, the ancient Norman tower on the land Yeats bought from Lady Gregory in June 1917.

[7] *Helen* Wife of Menelaus. She was abducted by Paris, the son of the king of Troy; the Greeks besieged the city for ten years to save her, finally bringing her back to her husband.

[8] *that great Queen ... spray* Aphrodite, the Greek goddess of love, beauty, and fecundity, rose out of the sea at birth.

[9] *bandy-leggèd smith* Hephaestus, god of fire and husband of Aphrodite, was born lame.

O may she live like some green laurel
Rooted in one dear perpetual place.

My mind, because the minds that I have loved,
50 The sort of beauty that I have approved,
Prosper but little, has dried up of late,
Yet knows that to be choked with hate
May well be of all evil chances chief.
If there's no hatred in a mind
55 Assault and battery of the wind
Can never tear the linnet from the leaf.

An intellectual hatred is the worst,
So let her think opinions are accursed.
Have I not seen the loveliest woman[1] born
60 Out of the mouth of Plenty's horn,
Because of her opinionated mind
Barter that horn and every good
By quiet natures understood
For an old bellows full of angry wind?

65 Considering that, all hatred driven hence,
The soul recovers radical innocence
And learns at last that it is self-delighting,
Self-appeasing, self-affrighting,
And that its own sweet will is Heaven's will;
70 She can, though every face should scowl
And every windy quarter howl
Or every bellows burst, be happy still.

And may her bridegroom bring her to a house
Where all's accustomed, ceremonious;
75 For arrogance and hatred are the wares
Peddled in the thoroughfares.
How but in custom and in ceremony
Are innocence and beauty born?
Ceremony's a name for the rich horn,
80 And custom for the spreading laurel tree.
—1919

An Irish Airman Foresees His Death

I know that I shall meet my fate
Somewhere among the clouds above;
Those that I fight I do not hate
Those that I guard I do not love;
5 My country is Kiltartan Cross,[2]
My countrymen Kiltartan's poor,
No likely end could bring them loss
Or leave them happier than before.
Nor law, nor duty bade me fight,
10 Nor public man, nor cheering crowds,
A lonely impulse of delight
Drove to this tumult in the clouds;
I balanced all, brought all to mind,
The years to come seemed waste of breath,
15 A waste of breath the years behind
In balance with this life, this death.
—1919

The Second Coming[3]

Turning and turning in the widening gyre[4]
The falcon cannot hear the falconer;
Things fall apart; the centre cannot hold;
Mere anarchy is loosed upon the world,
5 The blood-dimmed tide is loosed, and everywhere
The ceremony of innocence is drowned;
The best lack all conviction, while the worst
Are full of passionate intensity.

Surely some revelation is at hand;
10 Surely the Second Coming is at hand.
The Second Coming! Hardly are those words out
When a vast image out of *Spiritus Mundi*[5]

---

[1] *loveliest woman* Maud Gonne, whom Yeats had loved, was an important Irish liberation activist; she married Major John MacBride in 1903.

[2] *Kiltartan Cross* In County Galway, Ireland.

[3] *The Second Coming* The return of Christ, as predicted in the New Testament. See Revelation 1.7: "Behold, he cometh with clouds; and every eye shall see him."

[4] *gyre* Spiral formed from concentric circles.

[5] *Spiritus Mundi* Universal spirit that houses the images of civilization's past memories and provides divine inspiration for the poet; the human race is a connected whole in the *spiritus mundi*.

Troubles my sight: somewhere in sands of the desert
A shape with lion body and the head of a man,[1]
15   A gaze blank and pitiless as the sun,
Is moving its slow thighs, while all about it
Reel shadows of the indignant desert birds.
The darkness drops again; but now I know
That twenty centuries of stony sleep
20   Were vexed to nightmare by a rocking cradle,[2]
And what rough beast, its hour come round at last,
Slouches towards Bethlehem to be born?
—1920

Leda and the Swan[3]

A sudden blow: the great wings beating still
Above the staggering girl, her thighs caressed
By the dark webs, her nape caught in his bill,
He holds her helpless breast upon his breast.

5   How can those terrified vague fingers push
The feathered glory from her loosening thighs?
And how can body, laid in that white rush,
But feel the strange heart beating where it lies?

A shudder in the loins engenders there
10   The broken wall, the burning roof and tower
And Agamemnon dead.[4]
                              Being so caught up,
So mastered by the brute blood of the air,
Did she put on his knowledge with his power
Before the indifferent beak could let her drop?
—1924

Among School Children

1

I walk through the long schoolroom questioning;
A kind old nun in a white hood replies;
The children learn to cipher and to sing,
To study reading-books and history,
5   To cut and sew, be neat in everything
In the best modern way—the children's eyes
In momentary wonder stare upon
A sixty-year-old smiling public man.

2

I dream of a Ledaean[5] body, bent
10   Above a sinking fire, a tale that she
Told of a harsh reproof, or trivial event
That changed some childish day to tragedy—
Told, and it seemed that our two natures blent
Into a sphere from youthful sympathy,
15   Or else, to alter Plato's parable,
Into the yolk and white of the one shell.[6]

3

And thinking of that fit of grief or rage
I look upon one child or t'other there
And wonder if she stood so at that age—
20   For even daughters of the swan[7] can share
Something of every paddler's heritage—
And had that colour upon cheek or hair,
And thereupon my heart is driven wild:
She stands before me as a living child.

4

25   Her present image floats into the mind—
Did Quattrocento finger[8] fashion it
Hollow of cheek as though it drank the wind

---

1   *shape ... man*   The Egyptian Sphinx.

2   *rocking cradle*   Cradle of the Christ Child.

3   *Leda and the Swan*   Zeus came to Leda in the form of a swan and raped her; she then gave birth to Helen of Troy (whose abduction from her husband, King Menelaus, by Paris, initiated the Trojan War) and the twins, Castor and Pollux.

4   *broken wall ... Agamemnon dead*   Events of the Trojan War.

5   *Ledaean*   Like that of Leda (see note on Leda below).

6   *Plato's parable ... shell*   A speaker in Plato's *Symposium* explains that man was originally both male and female in one form, but was then divided into two; love was the reunion of man with his other half.

7   *daughters of the swan*   Leda, raped by Zeus in the form of a swan, gave birth to Helen of Troy.

8   *Quattrocento finger*   Skillful hand of a fifteenth-century Italian artist.

And took a mess of shadows for its meat?
And I though never of Ledaean kind
30   Had pretty plumage once—enough of that,
Better to smile on all that smile, and show
There is a comfortable kind of old scarecrow.

5

What youthful mother, a shape upon her lap
Honey of generation[1] had betrayed,
35   And that must sleep, shriek, struggle to escape
As recollection or the drug decide,
Would think her son, did she but see that shape
With sixty or more winters on its head,
A compensation for the pang of his birth,
40   Or the uncertainty of his setting forth?

6

Plato thought nature but a spume that plays
Upon a ghostly paradigm of things;[2]
Solider Aristotle played the taws
Upon the bottom of a king of kings;[3]
45   World-famous golden-thighed Pythagoras
Fingered upon a fiddle-stick or strings[4]
What a star sang and careless Muses heard:
Old clothes upon old sticks to scare a bird.

7

Both nuns and mothers worship images,

But those the candles light are not as those
50   That animate a mother's reveries,
But keep a marble or a bronze repose.
And yet they too break hearts—O Presences
That passion, piety or affection knows,
55   And that all heavenly glory symbolise—
O self-born mockers of man's enterprise;

8

Labour is blossoming or dancing where
The body is not bruised to pleasure soul,
Nor beauty born out of its own despair,
60   Nor blear-eyed wisdom out of midnight oil.
O chestnut tree, great-rooted blossomer,
Are you the leaf, the blossom, or the bole?°   trunk
O body swayed to music, O brightening glance,
How can we know the dancer from the dance?
—1927

Sailing to Byzantium [5]

1

That is no country for old men. The young
In one another's arms, birds in the trees
—Those dying generations—at their song,
The salmon-falls, the mackerel-crowded seas,
5   Fish, flesh, or fowl, commend all summer long
Whatever is begotten, born, and dies.
Caught in that sensual music all neglect
Monuments of unageing intellect.

2

An aged man is but a paltry thing,
10   A tattered coat upon a stick, unless
Soul clap its hands and sing, and louder sing
For every tatter in its mortal dress,
Nor is there singing school but studying
Monuments of its own magnificence;

---

[1]   [Yeats's note] I have taken the "honey of generation" from Porphyry's essay on "The Cave of the Nymphs," but find no warrant in Porphyry for considering it the "drug" that destroys the "recollection" of prenatal freedom. [The Neoplatonic philosopher Porphyry (233–c. 304) stated that the pleasure of sexual intercourse, like the sweetness of honey, drugs infants, thereby causing them to forget prenatal bliss before being born into this mortal world.]

[2]   Plato ... things   Plato argued that the appearance of nature was merely an imitation of the real world; therefore, nature itself was unreal, but provided a "ghostly" image of the real "paradigm of things."

[3]   Solider ... kings   Unlike Plato, Aristotle believed that reality took form in the image of nature; therefore, nature was reality itself. Aristotle tutored Alexander the Great, the son of King Philip of Macedonia; taws Leather whip.

[4]   golden-thighed ... strings   Pythagoras, a Greek philosopher of the sixth century BCE, developed a theory of the mathematical regularity of the universe and the mathematical origins of musical harmony. He was said to have a golden thigh.

[5]   Byzantium   Ancient city eventually renamed Constantinople (now Istanbul), capital of the Eastern Roman Empire. In A Vision, Yeats envisioned Byzantium as a center for artists: "The painter, the mosaic worker, the worker in gold and silver, the illuminator of sacred books were almost impersonal, almost perhaps without the consciousness of individual design, absorbed in their subject matter and that the vision of a whole people."

15 And therefore I have sailed the seas and come
To the holy city of Byzantium.

3

O sages standing in God's holy fire
As in the gold mosaic of a wall,
Come from the holy fire, perne in a gyre,[1]
20 And be the singing-masters of my soul.
Consume my heart away; sick with desire
And fastened to a dying animal
It knows not what it is; and gather me
Into the artifice of eternity.

4

25 Once out of nature I shall never take
My bodily form from any natural thing,
But such a form as Grecian goldsmiths make
Of hammered gold and gold enamelling
To keep a drowsy Emperor awake;
30 Or set upon a golden bough to sing[2]
To lords and ladies of Byzantium
Of what is past, or passing, or to come.

—1927

Byzantium[3]

The unpurged images of day recede;
The Emperor's drunken soldiery are abed;
Night resonance recedes, night walkers'[4] song
After great cathedral[5] gong;

5 A starlit or a moonlit dome disdains
All that man is,
All mere complexities,
The fury and the mire of human veins.

Before me floats an image, man or shade,
10 Shade more than man, more image than a shade;
For Hades'[6] bobbin° bound in mummy-cloth   spool
May unwind the winding path;
A mouth that has no moisture and no breath
Breathless mouths may summon;
15 I hail the superhuman;
I call it death-in-life and life-in-death.[7]

Miracle, bird or golden handiwork,
More miracle than bird or handiwork,
Planted on the star-lit golden bough,
20 Can like the cocks of Hades crow,[8]
Or, by the moon embittered, scorn aloud
In glory of changeless metal
Common bird or petal
And all complexities of mire or blood.

25 At midnight on the Emperor's pavement flit
Flames that no faggot feeds, nor steel has lit,
Nor storm disturbs, flames begotten of flame,
Where blood-begotten spirits come
And all complexities of fury leave,
30 Dying into a dance,
An agony of trance,
An agony of flame that cannot singe a sleeve.

Astraddle on the dolphin's mire and blood,[9]
Spirit after spirit! The smithies break the flood,
35 The golden smithies of the Emperor!

---

1 *perne in a gyre* Rotate in a spiral; the literal definition of "perne" is bobbin.

2 [Yeats's note] I have read somewhere that in the Emperor's palace at Byzantium was a tree made of gold and silver, and artificial birds that sang.

3 *Byzantium* Constantinople (today, Istanbul); Yeats recorded "the subject for a poem" in his diary of 1930: "Describe Byzantium as it is in the system towards the end of the first Christian millennium… Flames at the street corners where the soul is purified, birds of hammered gold singing in the golden trees, in the harbour [dolphins] offering their backs to the wailing dead that they may carry them to Paradise."

4 *night walkers* Prostitutes.

5 *great cathedral* Church of St. Sophia, built in Byzantium by the emperor Justinian I in 532–37.

6 *Hades* Greek god of the underworld.

7 *death-in-life and life-in-death* Cf. Tennyson's "Tears, Idle Tears," 20: "O Death in Life" and Coleridge's *The Rime of the Ancient Mariner* 3.193: "The Nightmare LIFE-IN-DEATH was she."

8 *the cocks of Hades crow* Because cocks symbolized rebirth and resurrection, they appeared on Roman tombstones as a sign of the continuation of human life.

9 *Astraddle … blood* According to Neoplatonism, dolphins symbolize the soul in transition, as they transport the recently departed to the Islands of the Blest.

Marbles of the dancing floor
Break bitter furies of complexity,
Those images that yet
Fresh images beget,
40   That dolphin-torn, that gong-tormented sea.
　　　　　—1930

Crazy Jane Talks with the Bishop

I met the Bishop on the road
And much said he and I.
"Those breasts are flat and fallen now,
Those veins must soon be dry;
5   Live in a heavenly mansion,
Not in some foul sty."

"Fair and foul are near of kin,
And fair needs foul," I cried.
"My friends are gone, but that's a truth
10   Nor grave nor bed denied,
Learned in bodily lowliness
And in the heart's pride.

"A woman can be proud and stiff
When on love intent;
15   But Love has pitched his mansion in
The place of excrement;
For nothing can be sole or whole
That has not been rent."
　　　　　—1933

Lapis Lazuli [1]
(For Harry Clifton) [2]

I have heard that hysterical women say
They are sick of the palette and fiddle-bow,
Of poets that are always gay,
For everybody knows or else should know
5   That if nothing drastic is done
Aeroplane and Zeppelin [3] will come out,
Pitch like King Billy bomb-balls [4] in
Until the town lie beaten flat.

All perform their tragic play,
10   There struts Hamlet, there is Lear,
That's Ophelia, that Cordelia; [5]
Yet they, should the last scene be there,
The great stage curtain about to drop,
If worthy their prominent part in the play,
15   Do not break up their lines to weep.
They know that Hamlet and Lear are gay;
Gaiety transfiguring all that dread.
All men have aimed at, found and lost;
Black out; Heaven blazing into the head:
20   Tragedy wrought to its uttermost.
Though Hamlet rambles and Lear rages,
And all the drop-scenes drop at once

---

[1] *Lapis Lazuli* Yeats received a carving made of lapis lazuli (semiprecious blue stone) on his birthday, 13 June 1935. Yeats described the stone in a letter to Dorothy Wellesley (English poet and friend): "Ascetic, pupil, hard stone, eternal theme of the sensual east. The heroic cry in the midst of despair. But no, I am wrong, the east has its solutions always and therefore knows nothing of tragedy. It is we, not the east, that must raise the heroic cry."

[2] *Harry Clifton* Yeats's apprentice, who gave the elder poet a gift made of lapis lazuli for his seventieth birthday.

[3] *Zeppelin* German airship used to bomb London during World War I; in 1938 another war with Germany seemed imminent.

[4] *King Billy bomb-balls* King William III (William of Orange) overcame the soldiers of the deposed king James II at the Battle of the Boyne in Ireland, 1690. An anonymous ballad describes the fight: "King William he threw his bomb-balls in, / And set them on fire." Also a nickname for Kaiser Wilhelm II, German emperor and king of Prussia during World War I.

[5] *There struts ... Cordelia* References to tragedies by Shakespeare: *Hamlet* tells the story of the death of Ophelia, beloved of Prince Hamlet, and then of Hamlet himself; *King Lear* tells of the death first of Lear's daughter Cordelia, then of Lear himself.

Upon a hundred thousand stages,
It cannot grow by an inch or an ounce.

25 On their own feet they came, or on shipboard,
Camel-back, horse-back, ass-back, mule-back,
Old civilisations put to the sword.
Then they and their wisdom went to rack:
No handiwork of Callimachus,[1]
30 Who handled marble as if it were bronze,
Made draperies that seemed to rise
When sea-wind swept the corner, stands;
His long lamp-chimney shaped like the stem
Of a slender palm, stood but a day;
35 All things fall and are built again,
And those that build them again are gay.

Two Chinamen, behind them a third,
Are carved in lapis lazuli,
Over them flies a long-legged bird,
40 A symbol of longevity;
The third, doubtless a serving-man,
Carries a musical instrument.

Every discoloration of the stone,
Every accidental crack or dent,
45 Seems a water-course or an avalanche,
Or lofty slope where it still snows
Though doubtless plum or cherry-branch
Sweetens the little half-way house
Those Chinamen climb towards, and I
50 Delight to imagine them seated there;
There, on the mountain and the sky,
On all the tragic scene they stare.
One asks for mournful melodies;
Accomplished fingers begin to play.
55 Their eyes mid many wrinkles, their eyes,
Their ancient, glittering eyes, are gay.
     —1938

The Circus Animals' Desertion

1

I sought a theme and sought for it in vain,
I sought it daily for six weeks or so.
Maybe at last, being but a broken man,
I must be satisfied with my heart, although
5 Winter and summer till old age began
My circus animals were all on show,
Those stilted boys, that burnished chariot,[2]
Lion and woman and the Lord knows what.

2

What can I but enumerate old themes?
10 First that sea-rider Oisín[3] led by the nose
Through three enchanted islands, allegorical dreams,
Vain gaiety, vain battle, vain repose,
Themes of the embittered heart, or so it seems,
That might adorn old songs or courtly shows;
15 But what cared I that set him on to ride,
I, starved for the bosom of his faery bride?

And then a counter-truth filled out its play,
The Countess Cathleen[4] was the name I gave it;
She, pity-crazed, had given her soul away,
20 But masterful Heaven had intervened to save it.
I thought my dear must her own soul destroy,
So did fanaticism and hate enslave it,
And this brought forth a dream and soon enough
This dream itself had all my thought and love.

---

1 *Callimachus* Greek sculptor of the fifth century BCE.

2 *Those stilted ... chariot* Yeats may be alluding to the ancient Irish heroes of his first works; the chariot may refer to the carriage built on the stage of his play, *The Unicorn from the Stars* (1908).

3 *Oisín* Irish warrior of Yeats's *The Wanderings of Oisín* (1889); Oisín is led by the fairy, Niamh, to three islands—called Delight, Many Fears, Forgetfulness—purported to be paradisiacal. When he returns to Ireland 150 years later he finds his friends dead and his country converted to Christianity.

4 *The Countess Cathleen* Play written by Yeats in 1892; an Irish countess, modeled on the Irish activist Maud Gonne, sells her soul to the devil to save the starving peasantry, but in the end is saved by God for her magnanimous motives.

25 And when the Fool and Blind Man stole the bread
Cuchulain fought the ungovernable sea;[1]
Heart-mysteries there, and yet when all is said
It was the dream itself enchanted me:
Character isolated by a deed
30 To engross the present and dominate memory.
Players and painted stage took all my love,
And not those things that they were emblems of.

3

Those masterful images because complete
Grew in pure mind, but out of what began?

35 A mound of refuse or the sweepings of a street,
Old kettles, old bottles, and a broken can,
Old iron, old bones, old rags, that raving slut[2]
Who keeps the till. Now that my ladder's gone,
I must lie down where all the ladders start,
40 In the foul rag-and-bone shop of the heart.
—1939

---

[1] *And when ... sea* In Yeats's play *On Baile's Strand* (1904), Cuchulain goes mad after he discovers that he has killed his own son. He runs out to the sea to fight the waves; meanwhile, the fool and the blind man steal bread from the ovens of the townspeople watching Cuchulain's sea-battle.

[2] *slut* Foul or unkempt woman. (Here the word has no connotation of sexual looseness.)

VIRGINIA WOOLF
1882 – 1941

A towering figure in the history of twentieth-century feminist thought, Virginia Woolf also occupies a central place in the development of the twentieth-century novel. Woolf, along with contemporaries such as James Joyce and Dorothy Richardson, rejected the traditional conventions of fiction, which included narrative coherence, omniscient narration, and emphasis on external settings and events. Instead, she explored the everyday, internal lives of her characters in a style—often called stream-of-consciousness—that mimics the flow of her characters' thoughts. In her fiction and essays alike, she examined the ways in which social roles and values are constructed and the effects these have on the lives and interactions of individuals.

Virginia Woolf was born Adeline Virginia Stephen, the third child of an illustrious, upper-middle-class London family. Her father, Leslie Stephen, a philosopher and literary critic, was primarily known as editor of the *Dictionary of National Biography* and President of the London Library. Her mother, born Julia Jackson, had been married into the Duckworth publishing family, and then married Stephen some time after the death of her first husband. Deeply connected to Victorian literary circles, the Stephen family included among its friends Henry James, Matthew Arnold, and George Eliot. From childhood, Woolf was drawn to a literary career, and her father in particular encouraged her, as she says, "to read what one liked because one liked it, never to pretend to admire what one did not. ... To write in the fewest possible words, as clearly as possible, exactly what one meant."

Surrounded by her father's impressive library, Woolf immersed herself in the study of languages and literary classics. While her brothers Thoby and Adrian went to public schools and eventually to university at Cambridge, Woolf and her sister Vanessa were educated at home by their father and private tutors. The lack of formal education for women would become a pervasive issue in Woolf's novels and later essays such as *A Room of One's Own* (1929) and *Three Guineas* (1938). A frequent exploration into the emotional effects of death in her later writing would also stem from Woolf's youthful experience. In 1895, her mother died of influenza; a few months later, at the age of thirteen, Woolf suffered a mental breakdown, symptoms of which included hearing voices, avoiding food, and experiencing extreme anxiety. Her mother's death was followed by that of her beloved half-sister and maternal substitute, Stella Duckworth, in childbirth, and then by that of her father, from cancer, in 1904. A second breakdown resulted. These breakdowns were harbingers of Woolf's lifelong struggle with manic and depressive episodes, which were generally brought about by stress—such as the emotional and mental anxiety that accompanied the completion of a book.

Despite Woolf's emotional turmoil in the year following her father's death, the event freed her from her family's inhibiting influence and facilitated her emergence amongst London's intelligentsia. With an unsigned review, she received her first publication in *The Guardian*, and against her extended family's attempts to introduce her into polite society, Woolf and several of her siblings moved to the Bloomsbury area of London. There they began associating with her brother Thoby's Cambridge friends, and what began as a social gathering of casual friends for drinks and conversation eventually came to be known as the Bloomsbury Group, a cultural circle bound together by an intense interest in current literary, philosophical, artistic, sexual, and political issues. Its members included novelist E.M. Forster, biographer and essayist Lytton Strachey, painter Duncan Grant, art critics Roger Fry and Clive Bell (the future husband of Woolf's sister Vanessa), economist John Maynard Keynes, and political theorist Leonard Woolf. Although Thoby Stephen died of typhoid in 1906, the group continued to meet throughout Woolf's lifetime. It attracted a certain amount of controversy as a result of the new ideas (particularly concerning sexuality) and frank artistic expression it fostered, and also because of the class snobbery it was perceived to exhibit (to the extent that the word *Bloomsbury* later became widely used to connote an insular and patronizing aestheticism).

In 1912, Virginia Stephen married Leonard Woolf, who throughout her life provided her with the time, encouragement, and emotional support necessary for her to continue writing as she alternated between periods of stability and intense productivity and episodes of immobilizing emotional collapse. In 1915, *The Voyage Out*, Woolf's first major novel, was published, introducing her readers for the first time to the character of Clarissa Dalloway, whom Woolf would make central to her later novel *Mrs. Dalloway* (1925). *The Voyage Out* and its successor, *Night and Day* (1919), are Woolf's most conventional works.

In 1917, Woolf and her husband Leonard bought a hand press and established Hogarth Press at their London home, intending to publish their own works and those of their friends. The Hogarth Press soon became a highly successful enterprise, publishing the early works of authors such as E.M. Forster, Katherine Mansfield, and T.S. Eliot, as well as English translations of the works of Sigmund Freud.

Woolf's 1922 novel *Jacob's Room*, based on the life and death of Woolf's brother Thoby, represented a stylistic breakthrough for her. In this novel, she tried an entirely different approach, ignoring much of the framework of external events and descriptions present in her earlier work. In this novel, she said, there was "no scaffolding; scarcely a brick to be seen; all crepuscular." By 1925, Woolf had completed *Mrs. Dalloway*, the culmination of many years' experimentation with narrative technique. Originally titled *The House*, *Mrs. Dalloway* takes place in a twenty-four hour period in London, and explores the subjectivities of characters who never meet, but whose observations, experiences, and memories reveal a curious kinship between them. Describing her new method of characterization, Woolf said, "I dig out beautiful caves behind my characters.... The idea is that the caves shall connect and each come to daylight at the present moment."

In her next novel, *To the Lighthouse* (1927), Woolf further developed her stream-of-consciousness style, relying heavily on imagery and rich symbolism to convey meaning. Divided into three distinct parts that take place against the backdrop of ordinary domestic events, the novel experiments with the passage of time through the consciousness of its various characters. By alternating between various viewpoints, Woolf demonstrates how rare, tenuous, and fleeting the moments of real connection between people are.

In 1929, Woolf's best-known work of non-fiction was published. Originally constructed as lecture notes for talks to be given at Newnham and Girton Colleges at Cambridge, the work was expanded and published as *A Room of One's Own*. The essay, which has become a foundational text of literary feminism, explores the traditional barriers and prejudices faced by women writers. At the core of Woolf's argument is her conclusion that a woman must have financial independence and privacy (a room of her own) if she is to write fiction successfully. In presenting the concept of the androgynous mind, Woolf also provides insight into her own literary process. As defined by Woolf, the successful author of whatever sex must possess the ability to draw creative forces from all facets of his or her emotional and intellectual being—regardless of whether these facets are traditionally classified as "masculine" or "feminine." To do so, the author must move beyond any awareness of his or her own gender role as dictated by social customs; as Woolf says, "It is fatal for anyone who writes to think of their sex." In her novel of the previous year, *Orlando*, Woolf had celebrated what she saw as the androgynous creative mind of her friend Vita Sackville-West. Subtitled *A Biography*, *Orlando* plays overtly with the form of genre as Woolf follows her main character—who is able to change sex as the times and his or her desires demanded—across several hundred years of British history.

For the next twelve years, Woolf continued to pursue more radical experiments with form while developing her ideas about writing, genre, and gender roles in numerous essays (most of which are collected in two volumes of her *Common Readers*). Woolf's next novel, *The Waves* (1931), is a poem-novel written "to a rhythm and not to a plot" that focuses on the mutability of life. In 1938, Woolf extended the feminist critique of male privilege begun in *A Room of One's Own* with *Three Guineas*, which implicitly links the values of patriarchal society with those of fascism. Less popular at the time than its predecessor, *Three Guineas*, and the pacifism it advocates, have found a more receptive audience in the later twentieth and early twenty-first centuries.

Just as *The Waves* sought to combine poetry and the novel, Woolf described her 1937 work *The Years* as an "essay-novel," and her final novel, *Between the Acts* (1941), is something of a drama-novel, focusing on the audience reception of an amateur pageant that takes place as the threat of war is imminent. Woolf herself, discouraged by the progress of World War II and its implications for herself and her Jewish husband, and dreading the critical reception this work would receive, faced another emotional breakdown. Before she could complete the revisions of *Between the Acts*, she began to feel mental illness engulf her. She composed a note to her husband explaining that she felt that this time she would not recover, filled her pockets with stones, and drowned herself in the River Ouse near her home.

Throughout her lifetime, Woolf was offered numerous honors, all of which she refused because of her avowed contempt for patriarchal society. After declining an honorary degree from Manchester University, she wrote in her diary, "It is an utterly corrupt society ..., and I will take nothing that it can give me." She did not want to be condescended to or used as a "token woman." Nevertheless, the honors continued to be offered, and, after her death, the loss of her unique vision and style were greatly mourned. She has since been hailed as a pioneer of the modernist novel, a central early figure in the development of feminist theory, and a central figure in the twentieth-century world of letters. Her personal diaries and letters, published posthumously in several volumes, provide unique insight into her aims as an artist and her intellectual development in a remarkable literary and artistic milieu.

⌘ ⌘ ⌘

The Mark on the Wall

Perhaps it was the middle of January in the present year that I first looked up and saw the mark on the wall. In order to fix a date it is necessary to remember what one saw. So now I think of the fire; the steady film of yellow light upon the page of my book; the three chrysanthemums in the round glass bowl on the mantel-piece. Yes, it must have been the winter time, and we had just finished our tea, for I remember that I was smoking a cigarette when I looked up and saw the mark on the wall for the first time. I looked up through the smoke of my cigarette and my eye lodged for a moment upon the burning coals, and that old fancy of the crimson flag flapping from the castle tower came into my mind, and I thought of the cavalcade of red knights riding up the side of the black rock. Rather to my relief the sight of the mark interrupted the fancy, for it is an old fancy, an automatic fancy, made as a child perhaps. The mark was a small round mark, black upon the white wall, about six or seven inches above the mantelpiece.

How readily our thoughts swarm upon a new object, lifting it a little way, as ants carry a blade of straw so feverishly, and then leave it.… If that mark was made by a nail, it can't have been for a picture, it must have been for a miniature—the miniature of a lady with white powdered curls, powder-dusted cheeks, and lips like red carnations. A fraud of course, for the people who had this house before us would have chosen pictures in that way—an old picture for an old room. That is the sort of people they were—very interesting people, and I think of them so often, in such queer places, because one will never see them again, never know what happened next. They wanted to leave this house because they wanted to change their style of furniture, so he said, and he was in process of saying that in his opinion art should have ideas behind it when we were torn asunder, as one is torn from the old lady about to pour out tea and the young man about to hit the tennis ball in the back garden of the suburban villa as one rushes past in the train.

But as for that mark, I'm not sure about it; I don't believe it was made by a nail after all; it's too big, too round, for that. I might get up, but if I got up and looked at it, ten to one I shouldn't be able to say for certain; because once a thing's done, no one ever knows how it happened. Oh! dear me, the mystery of life! The inaccuracy of thought! The ignorance of humanity! To show how very little control of our possessions we have—what an accidental affair this living is after all our civilization—let me just count over a few of the things lost in our lifetime, beginning, for that seems always the most mysterious of losses—what cat would gnaw, what rat would nibble—three pale blue canisters of book-binding tools? Then there were the bird cages, the iron hoops, the steel skates, the Queen Anne coal-scuttle, the bagatelle board,[1] the hand organ—all gone, and jewels too. Opals and emeralds, they lie about the roots of turnips. What a scraping paring affair it is to be sure! The wonder is that I've any clothes on my back, that I sit surrounded by solid furniture at this moment. Why, if one wants to compare life to anything, one must liken it to being blown through the Tube[2] at fifty miles an hour—landing at the other end without a single hairpin in one's hair! Shot out at the feet of God entirely naked! Tumbling head over heels in

the asphodel[3] meadows like brown paper parcels pitched down a shoot in the post office! With one's hair flying back like the tail of a racehorse. Yes, that seems to express the rapidity of life, the perpetual waste and repair; all so casual, all so haphazard.…

But after life. The slow pulling down of thick green stalks so that the cup of the flower, as it turns over, deluges one with purple and red light. Why, after all, should one not be born there as one is born here, helpless, speechless, unable to focus one's eyesight, groping at the roots of the grass, at the toes of the Giants? As for saying which are trees, and which are men and women, or whether there are such things, that one won't be in a condition to do for fifty years or so. There will be nothing but spaces of light and dark, intersected by thick stalks, and rather higher up perhaps, rose-shaped blots of an indistinct colour—dim pinks and blues—which will, as time goes on, become more definite, become—I don't know what.…

And yet the mark on the wall is not a hole at all. It may even be caused by some round black substance, such as a small rose leaf, left over from the summer, and I, not being a very vigilant housekeeper—look at the dust on the mantelpiece, for example, the dust which, so they say, buried Troy three times over, only fragments of pots utterly refusing annihilation, as one can believe.

The tree outside the window taps very gently on the pane … I want to think quietly, calmly, spaciously, never to be interrupted, never to have to rise from my chair, to slip easily from one thing to another, without any sense of hostility, or obstacle. I want to sink deeper and deeper, away from the surface, with its hard separate facts. To steady myself, let me catch hold of the first idea that passes … Shakespeare … Well, he will do as well as another. A man who sat himself solidly in an arm-chair, and looked into the fire, so—A shower of ideas fell perpetually from some very high Heaven down through his mind. He leant his forehead on his hand, and people, looking in through the open door—for this scene is supposed to take place on a summer's evening—But how dull this is, this historical fiction! It doesn't interest me at all. I wish I could hit upon a pleasant track of thought, a

---

[1] *bagatelle board*   Playing surface for a game similar to billiards.

[2] *Tube*   Nickname for the London Underground, the system of subway lines that underlies the city of London.

[3] *asphodel*   Genus of liliaceous flowers; said to cover the Elysian fields, the paradise where (according to Greek mythology) the blessed would reside after death.

track indirectly reflecting credit upon myself, for those are the pleasantest thoughts, and very frequent even in the minds of modest mouse-coloured people, who believe genuinely that they dislike to hear their own praises. They are not thoughts directly praising oneself; that is the beauty of them; they are thoughts like this:

"And then I came into the room. They were discussing botany. I said how I'd seen a flower growing on a dust heap on the site of an old house in Kingsway. The seed, I said, must have been sown in the reign of Charles the First. What flowers grew in the reign of Charles the First?" I asked—(but I don't remember the answer). Tall flowers with purple tassels to them perhaps. And so it goes on. All the time I'm dressing up the figure of myself in my own mind, lovingly, stealthily, not openly adoring it, for if I did that, I should catch myself out, and stretch my hand at once for a book in self-protection. Indeed, it is curious how instinctively one protects the image of oneself from idolatry or any other handling that could make it ridiculous, or too unlike the original to be believed in any longer. Or is it not so very curious after all? It is a matter of great importance. Suppose the looking-glass smashes, the image disappears, and the romantic figure with the green of forest depths all about it is there no longer, but only that shell of a person which is seen by other people—what an airless, shallow, bald, prominent world it becomes! A world not to be lived in. As we face each other in omnibuses and underground railways we are looking into the mirror; that accounts for the vagueness, the gleam of glassiness, in our eyes. And the novelists in future will realise more and more the importance of these reflections, for of course there is not one reflection but an almost infinite number; those are the depths they will explore, those the phantoms they will pursue, leaving the description of reality more and more out of their stories, taking a knowledge of it for granted, as the Greeks did and Shakespeare perhaps—but these generalisations are very worthless. The military sound of the word is enough. It recalls leading articles, cabinet ministers—a whole class of things indeed which as a child one thought the thing itself, the standard thing, the real thing, from which one could not depart save at the risk of nameless damnation. Generalisations bring back somehow Sunday in London, Sunday afternoon walks, Sunday luncheons, and also ways of speaking of the dead, clothes, and habits—like the habit of sitting all together in one room until a certain hour, although nobody liked it. There was a rule for everything. The rule for tablecloths at that particular period was that they should be made of tapestry with little yellow compartments marked upon them, such as you may see in photographs of the carpets in the corridors of the royal palaces. Tablecloths of a different kind were not real tablecloths. How shocking, and yet how wonderful it was to discover that these real things, Sunday luncheons, Sunday walks, country houses, and tablecloths were not entirely real, were indeed half phantoms, and the damnation which visited the disbeliever in them was only a sense of illegitimate freedom. What now takes the place of those things I wonder, those real standard things? Men perhaps, should you be a woman; the masculine point of view which governs our lives, which sets the standard, which establishes Whitaker's Table of Precedency,[1] which has become, I suppose, since the war half a phantom to many men and women, which soon, one may hope, will be laughed into the dustbin where the phantoms go, the mahogany sideboards and the Landseer prints,[2] Gods and Devils, Hell and so forth, leaving us all with an intoxicating sense of illegitimate freedom—if freedom exists. . . .

In certain lights that mark on the wall seems actually to project from the wall. Nor is it entirely circular. I cannot be sure, but it seems to cast a perceptible shadow, suggesting that if I ran my finger down that strip of the wall it would, at a certain point, mount and descend a small tumulus, a smooth tumulus like those barrows on the South Downs[3] which are, they say, either tombs or camps. Of the two I should prefer them to be tombs, desiring melancholy like most English people, and finding it natural at the end of a walk to think of the bones stretched beneath the turf . . . There must be some book about it. Some antiquary[4] must have dug up those bones and given them a name . . . What sort of

---

[1] *Table of Precedency* Table in *Whitaker's Almanac* that illustrates the hierarchy of the various ranks of the British social order.

[2] *Landseer prints* Edwin Henry Landseer (1802–73) produced paintings and engravings of animals.

[3] *South Downs* Range of chalk hills in southeastern England; *barrows* Mounds of earth or stone.

[4] *antiquary* Collector of antiquities, usually a non-professional.

a man is an antiquary, I wonder? Retired Colonels for the most part, I daresay, leading parties of aged labourers to the top here, examining clods of earth and stone, and getting into correspondence with the neighbouring clergy, which, being opened at breakfast time, gives them a feeling of importance, and the comparison of arrowheads necessitates cross-country journeys to the country towns, an agreeable necessity both to them and to their elderly wives, who wish to make plum jam or to clean out the study, and have every reason for keeping that great question of the camp or the tomb in perpetual suspension, while the Colonel himself feels agreeably philosophic in accumulating evidence on both sides of the question. It is true that he does finally incline to believe in the camp; and, being opposed, indites a pamphlet which he is about to read at the quarterly meeting of the local society when a stroke lays him low, and his last conscious thoughts are not of wife or child, but of the camp and that arrowhead there, which is now in the case at the local museum, together with the foot of a Chinese murderess, a handful of Elizabethan nails, a great many Tudor clay pipes, a piece of Roman pottery, and the wine-glass that Nelson drank out of—proving I really don't know what.

No, no, nothing is proved, nothing is known. And if I were to get up at this very moment and ascertain that the mark on the wall is really—what shall I say?—the head of a gigantic old nail, driven in two hundred years ago, which has now, owing to the patient attrition of many generations of housemaids, revealed its head above the coat of paint, and is taking its first view of modern life in the sight of a white-walled fire-lit room, what should I gain? Knowledge? Matter for further speculation? I can think sitting still as well as standing up. And what is knowledge? What are our learned men save the descendants of witches and hermits who crouched in caves and in woods brewing herbs, interrogating shrew-mice and writing down the language of the stars? And the less we honour them as our superstitions dwindle and our respect for beauty and health of mind increases ... Yes, one could imagine a very pleasant world. A quiet spacious world, with the flowers so red and blue in the open fields. A world without professors or specialists or house-keepers with the profiles of policemen, a world which one could slice with one's thought as a fish slices the water with his fin, grazing the stems of the water-lilies, hanging suspended over nests of white sea eggs.... How peaceful it is down here, rooted in the centre of the world and gazing up through the grey waters, with their sudden gleams of light, and their reflections—if it were not for Whitaker's Almanack—if it were not for the Table of Precedency!

I must jump up and see for myself what that mark on the wall really is—a nail, a rose-leaf, a crack in the wood?

Here is Nature once more at her old game of self-preservation. This train of thought, she perceives, is threatening mere waste of energy, even some collision with reality, for who will ever be able to lift a finger against Whitaker's Table of Precedency? The Archbishop of Canterbury is followed by the Lord High Chancellor; the Lord High Chancellor is followed by the Archbishop of York. Everybody follows somebody, such is the philosophy of Whitaker; and the great thing is to know who follows whom. Whitaker knows, and let that, so Nature counsels, comfort you, instead of enraging you; and if you can't be comforted, if you must shatter this hour of peace, think of the mark on the wall.

I understand Nature's game—her prompting to take action as a way of ending any thought that threatens to excite or to pain. Hence, I suppose, comes our slight contempt for men of action—men, we assume, who don't think. Still, there's no harm in putting a full stop to one's disagreeable thoughts by looking at a mark on the wall.

Indeed, now that I have fixed my eyes upon it, I feel that I have grasped a plank in the sea; I feel a satisfying sense of reality which at once turns the two Archbishops and the Lord High Chancellor to the shadows of shades. Here is something definite, something real. Thus, waking from a midnight dream of horror, one hastily turns on the light and lies quiescent, worshipping the chest of drawers, worshipping solidity, worshipping reality, worshipping the impersonal world which is proof of some existence other than ours. That is what one wants to be sure of. ... Wood is a pleasant thing to think about. It comes from a tree; and trees grow, and we don't know how they grow. For years and years they grow, without paying any attention to us, in meadows, in forests, and by the side of rivers—all things one likes to think about. The cows swish their tails beneath them on hot afternoons; they paint rivers so green that when a moorhen dives one expects to see its feathers all green when it comes up again. I like to think of the fish balanced against the stream like flags blown out; and of water-beetles slowly raising domes of mud upon the bed of the river. I like to think of the tree itself: first the close dry sensation of being wood; then the grinding of the storm; then the slow, delicious ooze of sap. I like to think of it, too, on winter's nights standing in the empty field with all leaves close-furled, nothing tender exposed to the iron bullets of the moon, a naked mast upon an earth that goes tumbling, tumbling all night long. The song of birds must sound very loud and strange in June; and how cold the feet of insects must feel upon it, as they make laborious progresses up the creases of the bark, or sun themselves upon the thin green awning of the leaves, and look straight in front of them with diamond-cut red eyes.... One by one the fibres snap beneath the immense cold pressure of the earth, then the last storm comes and, falling, the highest branches drive deep into the ground again. Even so, life isn't done with; there are a million patient, watchful lives still for a tree, all over the world, in bedrooms, in ships, on the pavement, lining rooms, where men and women sit after tea, smoking cigarettes. It is full of peaceful thoughts, happy thoughts, this tree. I should like to take each one separately—but something is getting in the way.... Where was I? What has it all been about? A tree? A river? The Downs? Whitaker's Almanack? The fields of asphodel? I can't remember a thing. Everything's moving, falling, slipping, vanishing.... There is a vast upheaval of matter. Someone is standing over me and saying—

"I'm going out to buy a newspaper."

"Yes?"

"Though it's no good buying newspapers.... Nothing ever happens. Curse this war; God damn this war! ... All the same, I don't see why we should have a snail on our wall."

Ah, the mark on the wall! It was a snail.

—1921

Blue & Green

GREEN

The pointed fingers of glass hang downwards. The light slides down the glass, and drops a pool of green. All day long the ten fingers of the lustre drop green upon the marble. The feathers of parakeets—their harsh cries—sharp blades of palm trees—green, too; green needles glittering in the sun. But the hard glass drips on to the marble; the pools hover above the desert sand; the camels lurch through them; the pools settle on the marble; rushes edge them; weeds clog them; here and there a white blossom; the frog flops over; at night the stars are set there unbroken. Evening comes, and the shadow sweeps the green over the mantelpiece; the ruffled surface of ocean. No ships come; the aimless waves sway beneath the empty sky. It's night; the needles drip blots of blue. The green's out.

BLUE

The snub-nosed monster rises to the surface and spouts through his blunt nostrils two columns of water, which, fiery-white in the centre, spray off into a fringe of blue beads. Strokes of blue line the black tarpaulin of his hide. Slushing the water through mouth and nostrils he sinks, heavy with water, and the blue closes over him dowsing the polished pebbles of his eyes. Thrown upon the beach he lies, blunt, obtuse, shedding dry blue scales. Their metallic blue stains the rusty iron on the beach. Blue are the ribs of the wrecked rowing boat. A wave rolls beneath the blue bells. But the cathedral's different, cold, incense laden, faint blue with the veils of madonnas.

—1921

Kew Gardens

From the oval-shaped flower-bed there rose perhaps a hundred stalks spreading into heart-shaped or tongue-shaped leaves half way up and unfurling at the tip red or blue or yellow petals marked with spots of colour raised upon the surface; and from the red, blue or yellow gloom of the throat emerged a straight bar, rough with gold dust and slightly clubbed at the end. The petals were voluminous enough to be stirred by the summer breeze, and when they moved, the red, blue, and yellow lights passed one over the other, staining an inch of the brown earth beneath with a spot of the most intricate colour. The light fell either upon the smooth grey back of a pebble, or the shell of a snail with its brown circular veins, or, falling into a raindrop, it expanded with such intensity of red, blue, and yellow the thin walls of water that one expected them to burst and disappear. Instead, the drop was left in a second silver grey once more, and the light now settled upon the flesh of a leaf, revealing the branching thread of fibre beneath the surface, and again it moved on and spread its illumination in the vast green spaces beneath the dome of the heart-shaped and tongue-shaped leaves. Then the breeze stirred rather more briskly overhead and the colour was flashed into the air above, into the eyes of the men and women who walk in Kew Gardens in July.

The figures of these men and women straggled past the flower-bed with a curiously irregular movement not unlike that of the white and blue butterflies who crossed the turf in zig-zag flights from bed to bed. The man was about six inches in front of the woman, strolling carelessly, while she bore on with greater purpose, only turning her head now and then to see that the children were not too far behind. The man kept this distance in front of the woman purposely, though perhaps unconsciously, for he wanted to go on with his thoughts.

"Fifteen years ago I came here with Lily," he thought. "We sat somewhere over there by a lake, and I begged her to marry me all through the hot afternoon. How the dragon-fly kept circling round us: how clearly I see the dragon-fly and her shoe with the square silver buckle at the toe. All the time I spoke I saw her shoe and when it moved impatiently I knew without looking up what she was going to say: the whole of her seemed to be in her shoe. And my love, my desire, were in the dragon-fly; for some reason I thought that if it settled there, on that leaf, the broad one with the red flower in the middle of it, if the dragonfly settled on the leaf she would say 'Yes' at once. But the dragon-fly went round and round: it never settled anywhere—of course not, happily not, or I shouldn't be walking here with Eleanor and the children—Tell me, Eleanor, d'you ever think of the past?"

"Why do you ask, Simon?"

"Because I've been thinking of the past. I've been thinking of Lily, the woman I might have married … Well, why are you silent? Do you mind my thinking of the past?"

"Why should I mind, Simon? Doesn't one always think of the past, in a garden with men and women lying under the trees? Aren't they one's past, all that remains of it, those men and women, those ghosts lying under the trees … one's happiness, one's reality?"

"For me, a square silver shoe-buckle and a dragon-fly—"

"For me, a kiss. Imagine six little girls sitting before their easels twenty years ago, down by the side of a lake, painting the water-lilies, the first red water-lilies I'd ever seen. And suddenly a kiss, there on the back of my neck. And my hand shook all the afternoon so that I couldn't paint. I took out my watch and marked the hour when I would allow myself to think of the kiss for five minutes only—it was so precious—the kiss of an old grey-haired woman with a wart on her nose, the mother of all my kisses all my life. Come Caroline, come Hubert."

They walked on past the flower-bed, now walking four abreast, and soon diminished in size among the trees and looked half transparent as the sunlight and shade swam over their backs in large trembling irregular patches.

In the oval flower-bed the snail, whose shell had been stained red, blue and yellow for the space of two minutes or so, now appeared to be moving very slightly in its shell, and next began to labour over the crumbs of loose earth which broke away and rolled down as it passed over them. It appeared to have a definite goal in front of it, differing in this respect from the singular high-stepping angular green insect who attempted to cross in front of it, and waited for a second with its antennae trembling as if in deliberation, and then stepped off as rapidly and strangely in the opposite direction. Brown cliffs with deep green lakes in the hollows, flat blade-like trees that waved from root to tip, round boulders of grey stone, vast crumpled surfaces of a thin crackling texture—all these objects lay across the snail's progress between one stalk and another to his goal. Before he had decided whether to circumvent the arched tent of a dead leaf or to breast it there came past the bed the feet of other human beings.

This time they were both men. The younger of the two wore an expression of perhaps unnatural calm; he raised his eyes and fixed them very steadily in front of him while his companion spoke, and directly his companion had done speaking he looked on the ground again and sometimes opened his lips only after a long pause and sometimes did not open them at all. The elder man had a curiously uneven and shaky method of walking, jerking his hand forward and throwing up his head abruptly, rather in the manner of an impatient carriage horse tired of waiting outside a house; but in the man these gestures were irresolute and pointless. He talked almost incessantly; he smiled to himself and again began to talk, as if the smile had been an answer. He was talking about spirits—the spirits of the dead, who, according to him, were even now telling him all sorts of odd things about their experiences in Heaven.

"Heaven was known to the ancients as Thessaly, William, and now, with this war, the spirit matter is rolling between the hills like thunder." He paused, seemed to listen, smiled, jerked his head and continued:—

"You have a small electric battery and a piece of rubber to insulate the wire—isolate?—insulate?—well, we'll skip the details, no good going into details that wouldn't be understood—and in short the little machine stands in any convenient position by the head of the bed, we will say, on a neat mahogany stand. All arrangements being properly fixed by workmen under my direction, the widow applies her ear and summons the spirit by sign as agreed. Women! Widows! Women in black—"

Here he seemed to have caught sight of a woman's dress in the distance, which in the shade looked a purple black. He took off his hat, placed his hand upon his heart, and hurried towards her muttering and gesticulating feverishly. But William caught him by the sleeve and touched a flower with the tip of his walking-stick in order to divert the old man's attention. After looking at it for a moment in some confusion the old man bent his ear to it and seemed to answer a voice speaking from it, for he began talking about the forests of Uruguay which he had visited hundreds of years ago in company with the most beautiful young woman in Europe. He could be heard murmuring about forests of Uruguay blanketed with the wax petals of tropical roses, nightingales, sea beaches, mermaids and women drowned at sea, as he suffered himself to be moved on by William, upon whose face the look of stoical patience grew slowly deeper and deeper.

Following his steps so closely as to be slightly puzzled by his gestures came two elderly women of the lower middle class, one stout and ponderous, the other rosy-cheeked and nimble. Like most people of their station[1] they were frankly fascinated by any signs of eccentricity betokening a disordered brain, especially in the well-to-do; but they were too far off to be certain whether the gestures were merely eccentric or genuinely mad. After they had scrutinised the old man's back in silence for a moment and given each other a queer, sly look, they went on energetically piecing together their very complicated dialogue:

"Nell, Bert, Lot, Cess, Phil, Pa, he says, I says, she says, I says, I says, I says—"

"My Bert, Sis, Bill, Grandad, the old man, sugar,

Sugar, flour, kippers, greens

Sugar, sugar, sugar."

The ponderous woman looked through the pattern of falling words at the flowers standing cool, firm and upright in the earth, with a curious expression. She saw them as a sleeper waking from a heavy sleep sees a brass candlestick reflecting the light in an unfamiliar way, and closes his eyes and opens them, and seeing the brass candlestick again, finally starts broad awake and stares at the candlestick with all his powers. So the heavy woman came to a standstill opposite the oval-shaped flower-bed, and ceased even to pretend to listen to what the other

---

[1] *their station* I.e., their position in English society.

woman was saying. She stood there letting the words fall over her, swaying the top part of her body slowly backwards and forwards, looking at the flowers. Then she suggested that they should find a seat and have their tea.

The snail had now considered every possible method of reaching his goal without going round the dead leaf or climbing over it. Let alone the effort needed for climbing a leaf, he was doubtful whether the thin texture which vibrated with such an alarming crackle when touched even by the tip of his horns would bear his weight; and this determined him finally to creep beneath it, for there was a point where the leaf curved high enough from the ground to admit him. He had just inserted his head in the opening and was taking stock of the high brown roof and was getting used to the cool brown light when two other people came past outside on the turf. This time they were both young, a young man and a young woman. They were both in the prime of youth, or even in that season which precedes the prime of youth, the season before the smooth pink folds of the flower have burst their gummy case, when the wings of the butterfly, though fully grown, are motionless in the sun.

"Lucky it isn't Friday," he observed.

"Why? D'you believe in luck?"

"They make you pay sixpence on Friday."

"What's sixpence anyway? Isn't it worth sixpence?"

"What's 'it'—what do you mean by 'it'?"

"O anything—I mean—you know what I mean."

Long pauses came between each of these remarks: they were uttered in toneless and monotonous voices. The couple stood still on the edge of the flower-bed, and together pressed the end of her parasol deep down into the soft earth. The action and the fact that his hand rested on the top of hers expressed their feelings in a strange way, as these short insignificant words also expressed something, words with short wings for their heavy body of meaning, inadequate to carry them far and thus alighting awkwardly upon the very common objects that surrounded them and were to their inexperienced touch so massive: but who knows (so they thought as they pressed the parasol into the earth) what precipices aren't concealed in them, or what slopes of ice don't shine in the sun on the other side? Who knows?

Who has ever seen this before? Even when she wondered what sort of tea they gave you at Kew, he felt that something loomed up behind her words, and stood vast and solid behind them; and the mist very slowly rose and uncovered—O Heavens,—what were those shapes?—little white tables, and waitresses who looked first at her and then at him; and there was a bill that he would pay with a real two shilling piece, and it was real, all real, he assured himself, fingering the coin in his pocket, real to everyone except to him and to her; even to him it began to seem real; and then—but it was too exciting to stand and think any longer, and he pulled the parasol out of the earth with a jerk and was impatient to find the place where one had tea with other people, like other people.

"Come along, Trissie; it's time we had our tea."

"Wherever does one have one's tea?" she asked with the oddest thrill of excitement in her voice, looking vaguely round and letting herself be drawn on down the grass path, trailing her parasol, turning her head this way and that way, forgetting her tea, wishing to go down there and then down there, remembering orchids and cranes among wild flowers, a Chinese pagoda and a crimson-crested bird; but he bore her on.

Thus one couple after another with much the same irregular and aimless movement passed the flower-bed and were enveloped in layer after layer of green-blue vapour, in which at first their bodies had substance and a dash of colour, but later both substance and colour dissolved in the green-blue atmosphere. How hot it was! So hot that even the thrush chose to hop, like a mechanical bird, in the shadow of the flowers, with long pauses between one movement and the next; instead of rambling vaguely the white butterflies danced one above another, making with their white shifting flakes the outline of a shattered marble column above the tallest flowers; the glass roofs of the palm house shone as if a whole market full of shiny green umbrellas had opened in the sun; and in the drone of the aeroplane the voice of the summer sky murmured its fierce soul. Yellow and black, pink and snow white, shapes of all these colours, men, women, and children, were spotted for a second upon the horizon, and then, seeing the breadth of yellow that lay upon the grass, they wavered and sought shade beneath the trees, dissolving like drops of water in the yellow and green atmosphere, staining it faintly with red and blue. It seemed as if all gross and heavy bodies had sunk down in the heat motionless and lay huddled upon the ground, but their voices went wavering from them as if they were flames lolling from the thick waxen bodies of candles. Voices, yes, voices, wordless voices, breaking the silence suddenly with such depth of contentment, such passion of desire, or, in the voices of children, such freshness of surprise; breaking the silence? But there was no silence; all the time the motor omnibuses were turning their wheels and changing their gear; like a vast nest of Chinese boxes all of wrought steel turning ceaselessly one within another the city murmured; on the top of which the voices cried aloud and the petals of myriads of flowers flashed their colours into the air.

—1921

Mrs. Dalloway in Bond Street

Mrs. Dalloway said she would buy the gloves herself. Big Ben was striking as she stepped out into the street. It was eleven o'clock and the unused hour was fresh as if issued to children on a beach. But there was something solemn in the deliberate swing of the repeated strokes; something stirring in the murmur of wheels and the shuffle of footsteps.

No doubt they were not all bound on errands of happiness. There is much more to be said about us than that we walk the streets of Westminster. Big Ben too is nothing but steel rods consumed by rust were it not for the care of H.M.'s Office of Works. Only for Mrs. Dalloway the moment was complete; for Mrs. Dalloway June was fresh. A happy childhood—and it was not to his daughters only that Justin Parry had seemed a fine fellow (weak of course on the Bench); flowers at evening, smoke rising; the caw of rooks falling from ever so high, down down through the October air—there is nothing to take the place of childhood. A leaf of mint brings it back: or a cup with a blue ring.

Poor little wretches, she sighed, and pressed forward. Oh, right under the horses' noses, you little demon! and there she was left on the kerb stretching her hand out, while Jimmy Dawes grinned on the further side.

A charming woman, poised, eager, strangely white-haired for her pink cheeks, so Scope Purvis, C.B.,[1] saw her as he hurried to his office. She stiffened a little, waiting for Durtnall's van to pass. Big Ben struck the tenth; struck the eleventh stroke. The leaden circles dissolved in the air. Pride held her erect, inheriting, handing on, acquainted with discipline and with suffering. How people suffered, how they suffered, she thought, thinking of Mrs. Foxcroft at the Embassy last night decked with jewels, eating her heart out, because that nice boy was dead, and now the old Manor House (Durtnall's van passed) must go to a cousin.

"Good morning to you!" said Hugh Whitbread raising his hat rather extravagantly by the china shop, for they had known each other as children. "Where are you off to?"

"I love walking in London," said Mrs. Dalloway. "Really it's better than walking in the country!"

"We've just come up," said Hugh Whitbread. "Unfortunately to see doctors."

"Milly?" said Mrs. Dalloway, instantly compassionate.

"Out of sorts," said Hugh Whitbread. "That sort of thing. Dick all right?"

"First rate!" said Clarissa.

Of course, she thought, walking on, Milly is about my age—fifty—fifty-two. So it is probably that, Hugh's manner had said so, said it perfectly—dear old Hugh, thought Mrs. Dalloway, remembering with amusement, with gratitude, with emotion, how shy, like a brother—one would rather die than speak to one's brother—Hugh had always been, when he was at Oxford, and came over, and perhaps one of them (drat the thing!) couldn't ride. How then could women sit in Parliament? How could they do things with men? For there is this extraordinarily deep instinct, something inside one; you can't get over it; it's no use trying; and men like Hugh respect it without our saying it, which is what one loves, thought Clarissa, in dear old Hugh.

She had passed through the Admiralty Arch and saw at the end of the empty road with its thin trees Victo-

1 *C.B.* Companion of the Bath. The Order of the Bath is an order of chivalry conferred by the sovereign of England.

ria's white mound,[1] Victoria's billowing motherliness, amplitude and homeliness, always ridiculous, yet how sublime, thought Mrs. Dalloway, remembering Kensington Gardens and the old lady in horn spectacles and being told by Nanny to stop dead still and bow to the Queen. The flag flew above the Palace. The King and Queen were back then. Dick had met her at lunch the other day—a thoroughly nice woman. It matters so much to the poor, thought Clarissa, and to the soldiers. A man in bronze stood heroically on a pedestal with a gun on her left hand side—the South African war. It matters, thought Mrs. Dalloway walking towards Buckingham Palace. There it stood four-square, in the broad sunshine, uncompromising, plain. But it was character, she thought; something inborn in the race; what Indians respected. The Queen went to hospitals, opened bazaars—the Queen of England, thought Clarissa, looking at the Palace. Already at this hour a motor car passed out at the gates; soldiers saluted; the gates were shut. And Clarissa, crossing the road, entered the Park,[2] holding herself upright.

June had drawn out every leaf on the trees. The mothers of Westminster with mottled breasts gave suck to their young. Quite respectable girls lay stretched on the grass. An elderly man, stooping very stiffly, picked up a crumpled paper, spread it out flat and flung it away. How horrible! Last night at the Embassy Sir Dighton had said, "If I want a fellow to hold my horse, I have only to put up my hand." But the religious question is far more serious than the economic, Sir Dighton had said, which she thought extraordinarily interesting, from a man like Sir Dighton. "Oh, the country will never know what it has lost," he had said, talking of his own accord, about dear Jack Stewart.

She mounted the little hill lightly. The air stirred with energy. Messages were passing from the Fleet to the Admiralty. Piccadilly and Arlington Street and the Mall[3] seemed to chafe the very air in the Park and lift its leaves hotly, brilliantly, upon waves of that divine vitality which Clarissa loved. To ride; to dance; she had

adored all that. Or going long walks in the country, talking, about books, what to do with one's life, for young people were amazingly priggish—oh, the things one had said! But one had conviction. Middle age is the devil. People like Jack'll never know that, she thought; for he never once thought of death, never, they said, knew he was dying. And now can never mourn—how did it go?—a head grown grey ... From the contagion of the world's slow stain[4] ... have drunk their cup a round or two before.[5] ... From the contagion of the world's slow stain! She held herself upright.

But how Jack would have shouted! Quoting Shelley, in Piccadilly! "You want a pin," he would have said. He hated frumps. "My God Clarissa! My God Clarissa!"—she could hear him now at the Devonshire House[6] party, about poor Sylvia Hunt in her amber necklace and that dowdy old silk. Clarissa held herself upright for she had spoken aloud and now she was in Piccadilly, passing the house with the slender green columns, and the balconies; passing club windows full of newspapers; passing old Lady Burdett-Coutts's house where the glazed white parrot used to hang; and Devonshire House, without its gilt leopards; and Claridge's,[7] where she must remember Dick wanted her to leave a card on Mrs. Jepson or she would be gone. Rich Americans can be very charming. There was St. James's Palace; like a child's game with bricks; and now—she had passed Bond Street—she was by Hatchard's book shop. The stream was endless—endless—endless. Lords, Ascot, Hurlingham—what was it? What a duck, she thought, looking at the frontispiece of some book of memoirs spread wide in the bow window, Sir Joshua perhaps or Romney;[8] arch, bright, demure; the sort of girl—like her

---

[1]   *Victoria's white mound*   Monument to Queen Victoria at the entrance to Buckingham Palace.

[2]   *the Park*   St. James's Park, London.

[3]   *the Mall*   Walk bordered by trees in St. James's Park.

[4]   *how did it ... stain*   See Percy Shelley's *Adonais* (1821): "From the contagion of the world's slow stain / He is secure, and now can never mourn. / A heart grown cold, a head grown grey in vain" (lines 356–58).

[5]   *have drunk ... before*   See Edward Fitzgerald's *The Rubáiyát of Omar Khayyám* (1859): "Lo! some we loved, the loveliest and best / That Time and Fate of all their Vintage prest / Have drunk their Cup a Round or two before / And one by one crept silently to Rest."

[6]   *Devonshire House*   London home of the Duke of Devonshire.

[7]   *Claridge's*   Claridge's Hotel.

[8]   *Sir Joshua ... Romney*   Sir Joshua Reynolds (1723–92) and George Romney (1734–1802), English painters.

own Elizabeth—the only real sort of girl. And there was that absurd book, Soapy Sponge,[1] which Jim used to quote by the yard; and Shakespeare's Sonnets. She knew them by heart. Phil and she had argued all day about the Dark Lady, and Dick had said straight out at dinner that night that he had never heard of her. Really, she had married him for that! He had never read Shakespeare! There must be some little cheap book she could buy for Milly—*Cranford*[2] of course! Was there ever anything so enchanting as the cow in petticoats? If only people had that sort of humour, that sort of self-respect now, thought Clarissa, for she remembered the broad pages; the sentences ending; the characters—how one talked about them as if they were real. For all the great things one must go to the past, she thought. From the contagion of the world's slow stain ... Fear no more the heat o' the sun.[3]... And now can never mourn, can never mourn, she repeated, her eyes straying over the window; for it ran in her head; the test of great poetry; the moderns had never written anything one wanted to read about death, she thought; and turned.

Omnibuses joined motor cars; motor cars vans; vans taxicabs, taxicabs motor cars—here was an open motor car with a girl, alone. Up till four, her feet tingling, I know, thought Clarissa, for the girl looked washed out, half asleep, in the corner of the car after the dance. And another car came; and another. No! No! No! Clarissa smiled good-naturedly. The fat lady had taken every sort of trouble, but diamonds! orchids! at this hour of the morning! No! No! No! The excellent policeman would, when the time came, hold up his hand. Another motor car passed. How utterly unattractive! Why should a girl of that age paint black round her eyes? And a young man, with a girl, at this hour, when the country—The admirable policeman raised his hand and Clarissa acknowledging his sway, taking her time, crossed,

walked towards Bond Street; saw the narrow crooked street, the yellow banners; the thick notched telegraph wires stretched across the sky.

A hundred years ago her great-great-grandfather, Seymour Parry, who ran away with Conway's daughter, had walked down Bond Street. Down Bond Street the Parrys had walked for a hundred years, and might have met the Dalloways (Leighs on the mother's side) going up. Her father got his clothes from Hill's. There was a roll of cloth in the window, and here just one jar on a black table, incredibly expensive; like the thick pink salmon on the ice block at the fishmonger's. The jewels were exquisite—pink and orange stars, paste, Spanish, she thought, and chains of old gold; starry buckles, little brooches which had been worn on sea-green satin by ladies with high head-dresses. But no good looking! One must economise. She must go on past the picture dealer's where one of the odd French pictures hung, as if people had thrown confetti—pink and blue—for a joke. If you had lived with pictures (and it's the same with books and music) thought Clarissa, passing the Aeolian Hall, you can't be taken in by a joke.

The river of Bond Street was clogged. There, like a Queen at a tournament, raised, regal, was Lady Bexborough. She sat in her carriage, upright, alone, looking through her glasses. The white glove was loose at her wrist. She was in black, quite shabby, yet, thought Clarissa, how extraordinarily it tells, breeding, self-respect, never saying a word too much or letting people gossip; an astonishing friend; no one can pick a hole in her after all these years, and now, there she is, thought Clarissa, passing the Countess who waited powdered, perfectly still, and Clarissa would have given anything to be like that, the mistress of Clarefield, talking politics, like a man. But she never goes anywhere, thought Clarissa, and it's quite useless to ask her, and the carriage went on and Lady Bexborough was borne past like a Queen at a tournament, though she had nothing to live for and the old man is failing and they say she is sick of it all, thought Clarissa and the tears actually rose to her eyes as she entered the shop.

"Good morning," said Clarissa in her charming voice. "Gloves," she said with her exquisite friendliness and putting her bag on the counter began, very slowly, to undo the buttons. "White gloves," she said. "Above

1 *Soapy Sponge* The nickname of the protagonist of R.S. Surtees's novel *Mr. Sponge's Sporting Tour* (1853).

2 *Cranford* Novel by Elizabeth Gaskell (1853). In the book, Miss Betsy Barker dresses her cow in grey flannel after a fall into a lime pit removes all its hair.

3 *Fear ... sun* From Shakespeare's *Cymbeline*, 4.2: "Fear no more the heat o' the sun / Nor the furious winter's rages / Thou thy worldly task hast done / Home art gone, and ta'en thy wages / Golden lads and girls all must / As chimney-sweepers, come to dust."

the elbow," and she looked straight into the shop-woman's face—but this was not the girl she remembered? She looked quite old. "These really don't fit," said Clarissa. The shop-girl looked at them. "Madame wears bracelets?" Clarissa spread out her fingers. "Perhaps it's my rings." And the girl took the grey gloves with her to the end of the counter.

Yes, thought Clarissa, if it's the girl I remember, she's twenty years older .... There was only one other customer, sitting sideways at the counter, her elbow poised, her bare hand drooping, vacant; like a figure on a Japanese fan, thought Clarissa, too vacant perhaps, yet some men would adore her. The lady shook her head sadly. Again the gloves were too large. She turned round the glass. "Above the wrist," she reproached the grey-headed woman; who looked and agreed.

They waited; a clock ticked; Bond Street hummed, dulled, distant; the woman went away holding gloves. "Above the wrist," said the lady, mournfully, raising her voice. And she would have to order chairs, ices, flowers, and cloak-room tickets, thought Clarissa. The people she didn't want would come; the others wouldn't. She would stand by the door. They sold stockings—silk stockings. A lady is known by her gloves and her shoes, old Uncle William used to say. And through the hanging silk stockings quivering silver she looked at the lady, sloping shouldered, her hand drooping, her bag slipping, her eyes vacantly on the floor. It would be intolerable if dowdy women came to her party! Would one have liked Keats[1] if he had worn red socks? Oh, at last—she drew into the counter and it flashed into her mind:

"Do you remember before the war you had gloves with pearl buttons?"

"French gloves, Madame?"

"Yes, they were French," said Clarissa. The other lady rose very sadly and took her bag, and looked at the gloves on the counter. But they were all too large—always too large at the wrist.

"With pearl buttons," said the shop-girl, who looked ever so much older. She split the lengths of tissue paper apart on the counter. With pearl buttons, thought Clarissa, perfectly simple—how French!

[1] *Keats*   John Keats (1795–1821), English Romantic poet.

"Madame's hands are so slender," said the shop-girl, drawing the glove firmly, smoothly, down over her rings. And Clarissa looked at her arm in the looking-glass. The glove hardly came to the elbow. Were there others half an inch longer? Still it seemed tiresome to bother her—perhaps the one day in the month, thought Clarissa, when it's an agony to stand. "Oh, don't bother," she said. But the gloves were brought.

"Don't you get fearfully tired," she said in her charming voice, "standing? When d'you get your holiday?"

"In September, Madame, when we're not so busy."

When we're in the country thought Clarissa. Or shooting. She has a fortnight at Brighton. In some stuffy lodging. The landlady takes the sugar. Nothing would be easier than to send her to Mrs. Lumley's right in the country (and it was on the tip of her tongue). But then she remembered how on their honeymoon Dick had shown her the folly of giving impulsively. It was much more important, he said, to get trade with China. Of course he was right. And she could feel the girl wouldn't like to be given things. There she was in her place. So was Dick. Selling gloves was her job. She had her own sorrows quite separate, "and now can never mourn, can never mourn," the words ran in her head. "From the contagion of the world's slow stain," thought Clarissa holding her arm stiff, for there are moments when it seems utterly futile (the glove was drawn off leaving her arm flecked with powder)—simply one doesn't believe, thought Clarissa, any more in God.

The traffic suddenly roared; the silk stockings brightened. A customer came in.

"White gloves," she said, with some ring in her voice that Clarissa remembered.

It used, thought Clarissa, to be so simple. Down down through the air came the caw of the rooks. When Sylvia died, hundreds of years ago, the yew hedges looked so lovely with the diamond webs in the mist before early church. But if Dick were to die tomorrow, as for believing in God—no, she would let the children choose, but for herself, like Lady Bexborough, who opened the bazaar, they say, with the telegram in her hand—Roden, her favourite, killed—she would go on. But why, if one doesn't believe? For the sake of others, she thought, taking the glove in her hand. The girl would be much more unhappy if she didn't believe.

"Thirty shillings," said the shop-woman. "No, pardon me Madame, thirty-five. The French gloves are more."

For one doesn't live for oneself, thought Clarissa.

And then the other customer took a glove, tugged it, and it split.

"There!" she exclaimed.

"A fault of the skin," said the grey-headed woman hurriedly. "Sometimes a drop of acid in tanning. Try this pair, Madame."

"But it's an awful swindle to ask two pound ten!"

Clarissa looked at the lady; the lady looked at Clarissa.

"Gloves have never been quite so reliable since the war," said the shop-girl, apologising, to Clarissa.

But where had she seen the other lady?—elderly, with a frill under her chin; wearing a black ribbon for gold eyeglasses; sensual, clever, like a Sargent[1] drawing. How one can tell from a voice when people are in the habit, thought Clarissa, of making other people—"It's a shade too tight," she said—obey. The shop-woman went off again. Clarissa was left waiting. Fear no more she repeated, playing her finger on the counter. Fear no more the heat o' the sun. Fear no more she repeated. There were little brown spots on her arm. And the girl crawled like a snail. Thou thy worldly task hast done. Thousands of young men had died that things might go on. At last! Half an inch above the elbow; pearl buttons; five and a quarter. My dear slow coach, thought Clarissa, do you think I can sit here the whole morning? Now you'll take twenty-five minutes to bring me my change!

There was a violent explosion in the street outside. The shop-women cowered behind the counters. But Clarissa, sitting very upright, smiled at the other lady. "Miss Anstruther!" she exclaimed.

—1923

Modern Fiction

In making any survey, even the freest and loosest, of modern fiction, it is difficult not to take it for granted that the modern practice of the art is somehow an improvement upon the old. With their simple tools and primitive materials, it might be said, Fielding did well and Jane Austen even better,[2] but compare their opportunities with ours! Their masterpieces certainly have a strange air of simplicity. And yet the analogy between literature and the process, to choose an example, of making motor cars scarcely holds good beyond the first glance. It is doubtful whether in the course of the centuries, though we have learnt much about making machines, we have learnt anything about making literature. We do not come to write better; all that we can be said to do is to keep moving, now a little in this direction, now in that, but with a circular tendency should the whole course of the track be viewed from a sufficiently lofty pinnacle. It need scarcely be said that we make no claim to stand, even momentarily, upon that vantage ground. On the flat, in the crowd, half blind with dust, we look back with envy to those happier warriors, whose battle is won and whose achievements wear so serene an air of accomplishment that we can scarcely refrain from whispering that the fight was not so fierce for them as for us. It is for the historian of literature to decide; for him to say if we are now beginning or ending or standing in the middle of a great period of prose fiction, for down in the plain little is visible. We only know that certain gratitudes and hostilities inspire us; that certain paths seem to lead to fertile land, others to the dust and the desert; and of this perhaps it may be worth while to attempt some account.

Our quarrel, then, is not with the classics, and if we speak of quarrelling with Mr. Wells, Mr. Bennett, and Mr. Galsworthy,[3] it is partly that by the mere fact of their existence in the flesh their work has a living, breathing, everyday imperfection which bids us take what liberties with it we choose. But it is also true that, while we thank them for a thousand gifts, we reserve our unconditional gratitude for Mr. Hardy, for Mr. Conrad, and in a much lesser degree for the Mr. Hudson of *The Purple Land, Green Mansions,* and *Far Away and Long*

---

[1] *Sargent* John Singer Sargent (1856–1925), the celebrated American artist, was (and is) known for his portraits of women of fashion.

[2] *Fielding ... better* Henry Fielding (1707–54) and Jane Austen (1775–1817), British novelists.

[3] *Mr. Wells ... Galsworthy* H.G. Wells (1866–1946), Arnold Bennett (1867–1931), and John Galsworthy (1867–1933), three popular novelists at the time.

Ago.[1] Mr. Wells, Mr. Bennett, and Mr. Galsworthy have excited so many hopes and disappointed them so persistently that our gratitude largely takes the form of thanking them for having shown us what they might have done but have not done; what we certainly could not do, but as certainly, perhaps, do not wish to do. No single phrase will sum up the charge or grievance which we have to bring against a mass of work so large in its volume and embodying so many qualities, both admirable and the reverse. If we tried to formulate our meaning in one word we should say that these three writers are materialists. It is because they are concerned not with the spirit but with the body that they have disappointed us, and left us with the feeling that the sooner English fiction turns its back upon them, as politely as may be, and marches, if only into the desert, the better for its soul. Naturally, no single word reaches the centre of three separate targets. In the case of Mr. Wells it falls notably wide of the mark. And yet even with him it indicates to our thinking the fatal alloy in his genius, the great clod of clay that has got itself mixed up with the purity of his inspiration. But Mr. Bennett is perhaps the worst culprit of the three, inasmuch as he is by far the best workman. He can make a book so well constructed and solid in its craftsmanship that it is difficult for the most exacting of critics to see through what chink or crevice decay can creep in. There is not so much as a draught between the frames of the windows, or a crack in the boards. And yet—if life should refuse to live there? That is a risk which the creator of *The Old Wives' Tale*, George Cannon, Edwin Clayhanger,[2] and hosts of other figures, may well claim to have surmounted. His characters live abundantly, even unexpectedly, but it remains to ask how do they live, and what do they live for? More and more they seem to us, deserting even the

well-built villa in the Five Towns,[3] to spend their time in some softly padded first-class railway carriage, pressing bells and buttons innumerable; and the destiny to which they travel so luxuriously becomes more and more unquestionably an eternity of bliss spent in the very best hotel in Brighton. It can scarcely be said of Mr. Wells that he is a materialist in the sense that he takes too much delight in the solidity of his fabric. His mind is too generous in its sympathies to allow him to spend much time in making things shipshape and substantial. He is a materialist from sheer goodness of heart, taking upon his shoulders the work that ought to have been discharged by Government officials, and in the plethora of his ideas and facts scarcely having leisure to realise, or forgetting to think important, the crudity and coarseness of his human beings. Yet what more damaging criticism can there be both of his earth and of his Heaven than that they are to be inhabited here and hereafter by his Joans and his Peters? Does not the inferiority of their natures tarnish whatever institutions and ideals may be provided for them by the generosity of their creator? Nor, profoundly though we respect the integrity and humanity of Mr. Galsworthy, shall we find what we seek in his pages.

If we fasten, then, one label on all these books, on which is one word materialists, we mean by it that they write of unimportant things; that they spend immense skill and immense industry making the trivial and the transitory appear the true and the enduring.

We have to admit that we are exacting, and, further, that we find it difficult to justify our discontent by explaining what it is that we exact. We frame our question differently at different times. But it reappears most persistently as we drop the finished novel on the crest of a sigh—Is it worth while? What is the point of it all? Can it be that, owing to one of those little deviations which the human spirit seems to make from time to time, Mr. Bennett has come down with his magnificent apparatus for catching life just an inch or two on the wrong side? Life escapes; and perhaps without life nothing else is worth while. It is a confession of vagueness to have to make use of such a figure as this, but we

---

[1] *Mr. Hardy ... Ago* Thomas Hardy (1840–1928), author of *Tess of the d'Urbervilles* and *Jude the Obscure*; Joseph Conrad (1857–1924), author of *Heart of Darkness*; William Henry Hudson (1841–1922), Argentinean author and naturalist who lived in London. *The Purple Land* and *Green Mansions* are romances set in Argentina, and *Far Away and Long Ago* is an account of Hudson's early life in Argentina.

[2] *George ... Clayhanger* Characters from Bennett's novels *The Roll-Call* and *Clayhanger*.

[3] *the Five Towns* Five towns in Staffordshire that comprise the center of England's pottery industry and that provide the setting for many of Bennett's novels.

scarcely better the matter by speaking, as critics are prone to do, of reality. Admitting the vagueness which afflicts all criticism of novels, let us hazard the opinion that for us at this moment the form of fiction most in vogue more often misses than secures the thing we seek. Whether we call it life or spirit, truth or reality, this, the essential thing, has moved off, or on, and refuses to be contained any longer in such ill-fitting vestments as we provide. Nevertheless, we go on perseveringly, conscientiously, constructing our two and thirty chapters after a design which more and more ceases to resemble the vision in our minds. So much of the enormous labour of proving the solidity, the likeness to life, of the story is not merely labour thrown away but labour misplaced to the extent of obscuring and blotting out the light of the conception. The writer seems constrained, not by his own free will but by some powerful and unscrupulous tyrant who has him in thrall, to provide a plot, to provide comedy, tragedy, love interest, and an air of probability embalming the whole so impeccable that if all his figures were to come to life they would find themselves dressed down to the last button of their coats in the fashion of the hour. The tyrant is obeyed; the novel is done to a turn. But sometimes, more and more often as time goes by, we suspect a momentary doubt, a spasm of rebellion, as the pages fill themselves in the customary way. Is life like this? Must novels be like this?

Look within and life, it seems, is very far from being "like this." Examine for a moment an ordinary mind on an ordinary day. The mind receives a myriad impressions—trivial, fantastic, evanescent, or engraved with the sharpness of steel. From all sides they come, an incessant shower of innumerable atoms; and as they fall, as they shape themselves into the life of Monday or Tuesday, the accent falls differently from of old; the moment of importance came not here but there; so that, if a writer were a free man and not a slave, if he could write what he chose, not what he must, if he could base his work upon his own feeling and not upon convention, there would be no plot, no comedy, no tragedy, no love interest or catastrophe in the accepted style, and perhaps not a single button sewn on as the Bond Street tailors would have it. Life is not a series of gig lamps symmetrically arranged; life is a luminous halo, a semitransparent envelope surrounding us from the beginning

of consciousness to the end. Is it not the task of the novelist to convey this varying, this unknown and uncircumscribed spirit, whatever aberration or complexity it may display, with as little mixture of the alien and external as possible? We are not pleading merely for courage and sincerity; we are suggesting that the proper stuff of fiction is a little other than custom would have us believe it.

It is, at any rate, in some such fashion as this that we seek to define the quality which distinguishes the work of several young writers, among whom Mr. James Joyce[1] is the most notable, from that of their predecessors. They attempt to come closer to life, and to preserve more sincerely and exactly what interests and moves them, even if to do so they must discard most of the conventions which are commonly observed by the novelist. Let us record the atoms as they fall upon the mind in the order in which they fall, let us trace the pattern, however disconnected and incoherent in appearance, which each sight or incident scores upon the consciousness. Let us not take it for granted that life exists more fully in what is commonly thought big than in what is commonly thought small. Any one who has read *The Portrait of the Artist as a Young Man* or, what promises to be a far more interesting work, *Ulysses*,[2] now appearing in the *Little Review*, will have hazarded some theory of this nature as to Mr. Joyce's intention. On our part, with such a fragment before us, it is hazarded rather than affirmed; but whatever the intention of the whole, there can be no question but that it is of the utmost sincerity and that the result, difficult or unpleasant as we may judge it, is undeniably important. In contrast with those whom we have called materialists, Mr. Joyce is spiritual; he is concerned at all costs to reveal the flickerings of that innermost flame which flashes its messages through the brain, and in order to preserve it he disregards with complete courage whatever seems to him adventitious, whether it be probability, or coherence, or any other of these signposts which for generations have served to support the imagination of a reader when called upon to imagine what he can neither

---

[1]   *Mr. James Joyce*   James Joyce (1882–1941), Irish novelist.

[2]   [Woolf's note]   Written in April, 1919.

touch nor see. The scene in the cemetery,[1] for instance, with its brilliancy, its sordidity, its incoherence, its sudden lightning flashes of significance, does undoubtedly come so close to the quick of the mind that, on a first reading at any rate, it is difficult not to acclaim a masterpiece. If we want life itself, here surely we have it. Indeed, we find ourselves fumbling rather awkwardly if we try to say what else we wish, and for what reason a work of such originality yet fails to compare, for we must take high examples, with *Youth* or *The Mayor of Casterbridge*.[2] It fails because of the comparative poverty of the writer's mind, we might say simply and have done with it. But it is possible to press a little further and wonder whether we may not refer our sense of being in a bright yet narrow room, confined and shut in, rather than enlarged and set free, to some limitation imposed by the method as well as by the mind. Is it the method that inhibits the creative power? Is it due to the method that we feel neither jovial nor magnanimous, but centred in a self which, in spite of its tremor of susceptibility, never embraces or creates what is outside itself and beyond? Does the emphasis laid, perhaps didactically, upon indecency, contribute to the effect of something angular and isolated? Or is it merely that in any effort of such originality it is much easier, for contemporaries especially, to feel what it lacks than to name what it gives? In any case it is a mistake to stand outside examining "methods." Any method is right, every method is right, that expresses what we wish to express, if we are writers; that brings us closer to the novelist's intention if we are readers. This method has the merit of bringing us closer to what we were prepared to call life itself; did not the reading of *Ulysses* suggest how much of life is excluded or ignored, and did it not come with a shock to open *Tristram Shandy* or even *Pendennis*[3] and be by them convinced that there are not only other aspects of life, but more important ones into the bargain.

However this may be, the problem before the novelist at present, as we suppose it to have been in the past, is to contrive means of being free to set down what he chooses. He has to have the courage to say that what interests him is no longer "this" but "that": out of "that" alone must he construct his work. For the moderns "that," the point of interest, lies very likely in the dark places of psychology. At once, therefore, the accent falls a little differently; the emphasis is upon something hitherto ignored; at once a different outline of form becomes necessary, difficult for us to grasp, incomprehensible to our predecessors. No one but a modern, no one perhaps but a Russian, would have felt the interest of the situation which Tchekov[4] has made into the short story which he calls "Gusev."[5] Some Russian soldiers lie ill on board a ship which is taking them back to Russia. We are given a few scraps of their talk and some of their thoughts; then one of them dies and is carried away; the talk goes on among the others for a time, until Gusev himself dies, and looking "like a carrot or a radish" is thrown overboard. The emphasis is laid upon such unexpected places that at first it seems as if there were no emphasis at all; and then, as the eyes accustom themselves to twilight and discern the shapes of things in a room we see how complete the story is, how profound, and how truly in obedience to his vision Tchekov has chosen this, that, and the other, and placed them together to compose something new. But it is impossible to say "this is comic," or "that is tragic," nor are we certain, since short stories, we have been taught, should be brief and conclusive, whether this, which is vague and inconclusive, should be called a short story at all.

The most elementary remarks upon modern English fiction can hardly avoid some mention of the Russian influence, and if the Russians are mentioned one runs the risk of feeling that to write of any fiction save theirs is waste of time. If we want understanding of the soul and heart where else shall we find it of comparable profundity? If we are sick of our own materialism the least considerable of their novelists has by right of birth a natural reverence for the human spirit. "Learn to make yourself akin to people .... But let this sympathy be not with the mind—for it is easy with the mind—but with the heart, with love towards them." In every great

---

[1] *The scene ... cemetery* In the "Hades" section of *Ulysses*.

[2] *Youth ... Casterbridge* By Joseph Conrad and Thomas Hardy, respectively.

[3] *Tristram ... Pendennis* Novels by Laurence Sterne (1713–68) and William Makepeace Thackeray (1811–68), respectively.

[4] *Tchekov* Russian playwright and short story writer Anton Chekhov (1860–1904).

[5] *"Gusev"* Published in 1890.

Russian writer we seem to discern the features of a saint, if sympathy for the sufferings of others, love towards them, endeavour to reach some goal worthy of the most exacting demands of the spirit constitute saintliness. It is the saint in them which confounds us with a feeling of our own irreligious triviality, and turns so many of our famous novels to tinsel and trickery. The conclusions of the Russian mind, thus comprehensive and compassionate, are inevitably, perhaps, of the utmost sadness. More accurately indeed we might speak of the inconclusive-ness of the Russian mind. It is the sense that there is no answer, that if honestly examined life presents question after question which must be left to sound on and on after the story is over in hopeless interrogation that fills us with a deep, and finally it may be with a resentful, despair. They are right perhaps; unquestionably they see further than we do and without our gross impediments of vision. But perhaps we see something that escapes them, or why should this voice of protest mix itself with our gloom? The voice of protest is the voice of another and an ancient civilisation which seems to have bred in us the instinct to enjoy and fight rather than to suffer and understand. English fiction from Sterne to Meredith[1] bears witness to our natural delight in humour and comedy, in the beauty of earth, in the activities of the intellect, and in the splendour of the body. But any deductions that we may draw from the comparison of two fictions so immeasurably far apart are futile save indeed as they flood us with a view of the infinite possibilities of the art and remind us that there is no limit to the horizon, and that nothing—no "method," no experiment, even of the wildest—is forbidden, but only falsity and pretence. "The proper stuff of fiction" does not exist; everything is the proper stuff of fiction, every feeling, every thought; every quality of brain and spirit is drawn upon; no perception comes amiss. And if we can imagine the art of fiction come alive and standing in our midst, she would undoubtedly bid us break her and bully her, as well as honour and love her, for so her youth is renewed and her sovereignty assured.

—1925

---

[1] *Meredith* George Meredith, novelist and poet (1828–1909).

from *A Room of One's Own*[2]

CHAPTER 1

But, you may say, we asked you to speak about women and fiction—what has that got to do with a room of one's own? I will try to explain. When you asked me to speak about women and fiction I sat down on the banks of a river and began to wonder what the words meant. They might mean simply a few remarks about Fanny Burney; a few more about Jane Austen; a tribute to the Brontës and a sketch of Haworth Parsonage under snow; some witticisms if possible about Miss Mitford; a respectful allusion to George Eliot; a reference to Mrs. Gaskell[3] and one would have done. But at second sight the words seemed not so simple. The title women and fiction might mean, and you may have meant it to mean, women and what they are like; or it might mean women and the fiction that they write; or it might mean women and the fiction that is written about them; or it might mean that somehow all three are inextricably mixed together and you want me to consider them in that light. But when I began to consider the subject in this last way, which seemed the most interesting, I soon saw that it had one fatal drawback. I should never be able to come to a conclusion. I should never be able to fulfil what is, I understand, the first duty of a lecturer—to hand you after an hour's discourse a nugget of pure truth to wrap up between the pages of your notebooks and keep on the mantel-piece for ever. All I could do was to offer you an opinion upon one minor point—a woman must have money and a room

---

[2] [Woolf's note] This essay is based upon two papers read to the Arts Society at Newnham and the Odtaa at Girton in October 1928. The papers were too long to be read in full, and have since been altered and expanded. [Newnham and Girton are women's colleges at Cambridge University, and Odtaa (an acronym for "One Damn Thing After Another") was a literary society whose name was taken from John Masefield's 1926 novel of that title.]

[3] *Fanny Burney* (1752–1840) Novelist, diarist, and dramatist; *Haworth Parsonage* The family home of novelists Charlotte (1816–55), Emily (1818–48), and Anne (1820–49) Brontë; *Miss Mitford* Mary Russell Mitford (1787–1855), poet; *George Eliot* Pseudonym of Mary Anne Evans (1819–80), author of many novels, including *The Mill on the Floss* (1860) and *Adam Bede* (1859); *Mrs. Gaskell* Elizabeth Gaskell (1810–65), author of *Cranford* and *Mary Barton*.

of her own if she is to write fiction; and that, as you will see, leaves the great problem of the true nature of woman and the true nature of fiction unsolved. I have shirked the duty of coming to a conclusion upon these two questions—women and fiction remain, so far as I am concerned, unsolved problems. But in order to make some amends I am going to do what I can to show you how I arrived at this opinion about the room and the money. I am going to develop in your presence as fully and freely as I can the train of thought which led me to think this. Perhaps if I lay bare the ideas, the prejudices, that lie behind this statement you will find that they have some bearing upon women and some upon fiction. At any rate, when a subject is highly controversial—and any question about sex is that—one cannot hope to tell the truth. One can only show how one came to hold whatever opinion one does hold. One can only give one's audience the chance of drawing their own conclusions as they observe the limitations, the prejudices, the idiosyncrasies of the speaker. Fiction here is likely to contain more truth than fact. Therefore I propose, making use of all the liberties and licences of a novelist, to tell you the story of the two days that preceded my coming here—how, bowed down by the weight of the subject which you have laid upon my shoulders, I pondered it, and made it work in and out of my daily life. I need not say that what I am about to describe has no existence; Oxbridge is an invention; so is Fernham;[1] "I" is only a convenient term for somebody who has no real being. Lies will flow from my lips, but there may perhaps be some truth mixed up with them; it is for you to seek out this truth and to decide whether any part of it is worth keeping. If not, you will of course throw the whole of it into the wastepaper basket and forget all about it.

Here then was I (call me Mary Beton, Mary Seton, Mary Carmichael[2] or by any name you please—it is not a matter of any importance) sitting on the banks of a river a week or two ago in fine October weather, lost in thought. That collar I have spoken of, women and fiction, the need of coming to some conclusion on a subject that raises all sorts of prejudices and passions, bowed my head to the ground. To the right and left bushes of some sort, golden and crimson, glowed with the colour, even it seemed burnt with the heat, of fire. On the further bank the willows wept in perpetual lamentation, their hair about their shoulders. The river reflected whatever it chose of sky and bridge and burning tree, and when the undergraduate had oared his boat through the reflections they closed again, completely, as if he had never been. There one might have sat the clock round lost in thought. Thought—to call it by a prouder name than it deserved—had let its line down into the stream. It swayed, minute after minute, hither and thither among the reflections and the weeds, letting the water lift it and sink it, until—you know the little tug—the sudden conglomeration of an idea at the end of one's line: and then the cautious hauling of it in, and the careful laying of it out? Alas, laid on the grass how small, how insignificant this thought of mine looked; the sort of fish that a good fisherman puts back into the water so that it may grow fatter and be one day worth cooking and eating. I will not trouble you with that thought now, though if you look carefully you may find it for yourselves in the course of what I am going to say.

But however small it was, it had, nevertheless, the mysterious property of its kind—put back into the mind, it became at once very exciting, and important; and as it darted and sank, and flashed hither and thither, set up such a wash and tumult of ideas that it was impossible to sit still. It was thus that I found myself walking with extreme rapidity across a grass plot. Instantly a man's figure rose to intercept me. Nor did I at first understand that the gesticulations of a curious-looking object, in a cut-away coat and evening shirt, were aimed at me. His face expressed horror and indignation. Instinct rather than reason came to my help; he was a Beadle;[3] I was a woman. This was the turf; there was the path. Only the Fellows and Scholars are allowed here; the gravel is the place for me. Such thoughts were the work of a moment. As I regained the path the arms

---

[1] *Oxbridge* Amalgamation of the names of the Universities of Oxford and Cambridge, a term used to describe the two collectively; *Fernham* Woolf combines characteristics of Newnham and Girton in her description of this fictional college.

[2] *Mary Beton … Carmichael* See the "Ballad of Mary Hamilton," in which the companions of Mary, Queen of Scots were "Mary Beton and Mary Seton, / Mary Carmichael and me."

[3] *Beadle* Minor church or college official.

of the Beadle sank, his face assumed its usual repose, and though turf is better walking than gravel, no very great harm was done. The only charge I could bring against the Fellows and Scholars of whatever the college might happen to be was that in protection of their turf, which has been rolled for 300 years in succession, they had sent my little fish into hiding.

What idea it had been that had sent me so audaciously trespassing I could not now remember. The spirit of peace descended like a cloud from heaven, for if the spirit of peace dwells anywhere, it is in the courts and quadrangles of Oxbridge on a fine October morning. Strolling through those colleges past those ancient halls the roughness of the present seemed smoothed away; the body seemed contained in a miraculous glass cabinet through which no sound could penetrate, and the mind, freed from any contact with facts (unless one trespassed on the turf again), was at liberty to settle down upon whatever meditation was in harmony with the moment. As chance would have it, some stray memory of some old essay about revisiting Oxbridge in the long vacation brought Charles Lamb[1] to mind— Saint Charles, said Thackeray,[2] putting a letter of Lamb's to his forehead. Indeed, among all the dead (I give you my thoughts as they came to me), Lamb is one of the most congenial; one to whom one would have liked to say, Tell me then how you wrote your essays? For his essays are superior even to Max Beerbohm's,[3] I thought, with all their perfection, because of that wild flash of imagination, that lightning crack of genius in the middle of them which leaves them flawed and imperfect, but starred with poetry. Lamb then came to Oxbridge perhaps a hundred years ago. Certainly he wrote an essay—the name escapes me—about the manuscript of one of Milton's poems which he saw here. It was Lycidas perhaps, and Lamb wrote how it shocked him to think it possible that any word in Lycidas could have been different from what it is. To think of Milton changing the words in that poem

seemed to him a sort of sacrilege. This led me to remember what I could of Lycidas and to amuse myself with guessing which word it could have been that Milton had altered, and why. It then occurred to me that the very manuscript itself which Lamb had looked at was only a few hundred yards away, so that one could follow Lamb's footsteps across the quadrangle to that famous library[4] where the treasure is kept. Moreover, I recollected, as I put this plan into execution, it is in this famous library that the manuscript of Thackeray's Esmond is also preserved. The critics often say that Esmond is Thackeray's most perfect novel. But the affectation of the style, with its imitation of the eighteenth century, hampers one, so far as I remember; unless indeed the eighteenth-century style was natural to Thackeray—a fact that one might prove by looking at the manuscript and seeing whether the alterations were for the benefit of the style or of the sense. But then one would have to decide what is style and what is meaning, a question which—but here I was actually at the door which leads into the library itself. I must have opened it, for instantly there issued, like a guardian angel barring the way with a flutter of black gown instead of white wings, a deprecating, silvery, kindly gentleman, who regretted in a low voice as he waved me back that ladies are only admitted to the library if accompanied by a Fellow of the College or furnished with a letter of introduction.

That a famous library has been cursed by a woman is a matter of complete indifference to a famous library. Venerable and calm, with all its treasures safe locked within its breast, it sleeps complacently and will, so far as I am concerned, so sleep for ever. Never will I wake those echoes, never will I ask for that hospitality again, I vowed as I descended the steps in anger. Still an hour remained before luncheon, and what was one to do? Stroll on the meadows? Sit by the river? Certainly it was a lovely autumn morning; the leaves were fluttering red to the ground; there was no great hardship in doing either. But the sound of music reached my ear. Some service or celebration was going forward. The organ complained magnificently as I passed the chapel door. Even the sorrow of Christianity sounded in that serene

[1] *Charles Lamb* English essayist (1775–1834). The essay referred to later in this paragraph is "Oxford in the Vacation" (1820).

[2] *Thackeray* William Makepeace Thackeray, English novelist (1811–63).

[3] *Max Beerbohm* English parodist, essayist, and cartoonist (1872–1956).

[4] *that famous library* The manuscript of Milton's *Lycidas* held by the library of Trinity College, Cambridge.

air more like the recollection of sorrow than sorrow itself; even the groanings of the ancient organ seemed lapped in peace. I had no wish to enter had I the right, and this time the verger[1] might have stopped me, demanding perhaps my baptismal certificate, or a letter of introduction from the Dean. But the outside of these magnificent buildings is often as beautiful as the inside. Moreover, it was amusing enough to watch the congregation assembling, coming in and going out again, busying themselves at the door of the chapel like bees at the mouth of a hive. Many were in cap and gown; some had tufts of fur on their shoulders; others were wheeled in bath-chairs;[2] others, though not past middle age, seemed creased and crushed into shapes so singular that one was reminded of those giant crabs and crayfish who heave with difficulty across the sand of an aquarium. As I leant against the wall the University indeed seemed a sanctuary in which are preserved rare types which would soon be obsolete if left to fight for existence on the pavement of the Strand.[3] Old stories of old deans and old dons came back to mind, but before I had summoned up courage to whistle—it used to be said that at the sound of a whistle old Professor ——— instantly broke into a gallop—the venerable congregation had gone inside. The outside of the chapel remained. As you know, its high domes and pinnacles can be seen, like a sailing-ship always voyaging never arriving, lit up at night and visible for miles, far away across the hills.[4] Once, presumably, this quadrangle with its smooth lawns, its massive buildings, and the chapel itself was marsh too, where the grasses waved and the swine rootled.[5] Teams of horses and oxen, I thought, must have hauled the stone in wagons from far countries, and then with infinite labour the grey blocks in whose shade I was now standing were poised in order one on top of another, and then the painters brought their glass for the windows, and the masons were busy for centuries up

on that roof with putty and cement, spade and trowel. Every Saturday somebody must have poured gold and silver out of a leathern purse into their ancient fists, for they had their beer and skittles[6] presumably of an evening. An unending stream of gold and silver, I thought, must have flowed into this court perpetually to keep the stones coming and the masons working; to level, to ditch, to dig and to drain. But it was then the age of faith, and money was poured liberally to set these stones on a deep foundation, and when the stones were raised, still more money was poured in from the coffers of kings and queens and great nobles to ensure that hymns should be sung here and scholars taught. Lands were granted; tithes were paid. And when the age of faith was over and the age of reason had come, still the same flow of gold and silver went on; fellowships were founded; lectureships endowed; only the gold and silver flowed now, not from the coffers of the king, but from the chests of merchants and manufacturers, from the purses of men who had made, say, a fortune from industry, and returned, in their wills, a bounteous share of it to endow more chairs, more lectureships, more fellowships in the university where they had learnt their craft. Hence the libraries and laboratories; the observatories; the splendid equipment of costly and delicate instruments which now stands on glass shelves, where centuries ago the grasses waved and the swine rootled. Certainly, as I strolled round the court, the foundation of gold and silver seemed deep enough; the pavement laid solidly over the wild grasses. Men with trays on their heads went busily from staircase to staircase. Gaudy blossoms flowered in window-boxes. The strains of the gramophone blared out from the rooms within. It was impossible not to reflect—the reflection whatever it may have been was cut short. The clock struck. It was time to find one's way to luncheon.

It is a curious fact that novelists have a way of making us believe that luncheon parties are invariably memorable for something very witty that was said, or for something very wise that was done. But they seldom spare a word for what was eaten. It is part of the novelist's convention not to mention soup and salmon and ducklings, as if soup and salmon and ducklings were of

---

[1] *verger* Church attendant.

[2] *bath-chairs* Large chairs on wheels for invalids, so named for Bath, an English spa city, and retreat for ill and elderly people.

[3] *the Strand* Busy street in London that runs parallel to the northern bank of the Thames.

[4] *As you … hills* Description of the chapel of King's College, Cambridge, which was built from 1446 to 1547.

[5] *rootled* Rooted about.

[6] *skittles* Game resembling bowling. The expression "all beer and skittles" denotes pure enjoyment.

no importance whatsoever, as if nobody ever smoked a cigar or drank a glass of wine. Here, however, I shall take the liberty to defy that convention and to tell you that the lunch on this occasion began with soles, sunk in a deep dish, over which the college cook had spread a counterpane of the whitest cream, save that it was branded here and there with brown spots like the spots on the flanks of a doe. After that came the partridges, but if this suggests a couple of bald, brown birds on a plate you are mistaken. The partridges, many and various, came with all their retinue of sauces and salads, the sharp and the sweet, each in its order; their potatoes, thin as coins but not so hard; their sprouts, foliated as rosebuds but more succulent. And no sooner had the roast and its retinue been done with than the silent serving-man, the Beadle himself perhaps in a milder manifestation, set before us, wreathed in napkins, a confection which rose all sugar from the waves. To call it pudding and so relate it to rice and tapioca would be an insult. Meanwhile the wineglasses had flushed yellow and flushed crimson; had been emptied; had been filled. And thus by degrees was lit, halfway down the spine, which is the seat of the soul, not that hard little electric light which we call brilliance, as it pops in and out upon our lips, but the more profound, subtle and subterranean glow, which is the rich yellow flame of rational intercourse. No need to hurry. No need to sparkle. No need to be anybody but oneself. We are all going to heaven and Vandyck is of the company[1]—in other words, how good life seemed, how sweet its rewards, how trivial this grudge or that grievance, how admirable friendship and the society of one's kind, as, lighting a good cigarette, one sunk among the cushions in the window-seat.

If by good luck there had been an ashtray handy, if one had not knocked the ash out of the window in default, if things had been a little different from what they were, one would not have seen, presumably, a cat without a tail. The sight of that abrupt and truncated animal padding softly across the quadrangle changed by some fluke of the subconscious intelligence the emo-

tional light for me. It was as if some one had let fall a shade. Perhaps the excellent hock[2] was relinquishing its hold. Certainly, as I watched the Manx cat pause in the middle of the lawn as if it too questioned the universe, something seemed lacking, something seemed different. But what was lacking, what was different, I asked myself, listening to the talk. And to answer that question I had to think myself out of the room, back into the past, before the war indeed, and to set before my eyes the model of another luncheon party held in rooms not very far distant from these; but different. Everything was different. Meanwhile the talk went on among the guests, who were many and young, some of this sex, some of that; it went on swimmingly, it went on agreeably, freely, amusingly. And as it went on I set it against the background of that other talk, and as I matched the two together I had no doubt that one was the descendant, the legitimate heir of the other. Nothing was changed; nothing was different save only—here I listened with all my ears not entirely to what was being said, but to the murmur or current behind it. Yes, that was it—the change was there. Before the war at a luncheon party like this people would have said precisely the same things but they would have sounded different, because in those days they were accompanied by a sort of humming noise, not articulate, but musical, exciting, which changed the value of the words themselves. Could one set that humming noise to words? Perhaps with the help of the poets one could. A book lay beside me and, opening it, I turned casually enough to Tennyson. And here I found Tennyson was singing:

> There has fallen a splendid tear
>   From the passion-flower at the gate.
> She is coming, my dove, my dear;
>   She is coming, my life, my fate;
> The red rose cries, "She is near, she is near;"
>   And the white rose weeps, "She is late;"
> The larkspur listens, "I hear, I hear;"
>   And the lily whispers, "I wait."[3]

Was that what men hummed at luncheon parties before the war? And the women?

[1] *We are all ... company* These were said to be the last words of English portrait and landscape painter Thomas Gainsborough (1727–88); *Vandyck* Sir Anthony Van Dyck (1599–1641), portrait artist.

[2] *hock* I.e., Hochheimer, a German white wine.

[3] *There has ... wait* From Alfred, Lord Tennyson's *Maud* (1855), 1.22.10.

> *My heart is like a singing bird*
> *Whose nest is in a water'd shoot;*
> *My heart is like an apple tree*
> *Whose boughs are bent with thick-set fruit;*
> *My heart is like a rainbow shell*
> *That paddles in a halcyon sea;*
> *My heart is gladder than all these*
> *Because my love is come to me.*[1]

Was that what women hummed at luncheon parties before the war?

There was something so ludicrous in thinking of people humming such things even under their breath at luncheon parties before the war that I burst out laughing, and had to explain my laughter by pointing at the Manx cat, who did look a little absurd, poor beast, without a tail, in the middle of the lawn. Was he really born so, or had he lost his tail in an accident? The tailless cat, though some are said to exist in the Isle of Man, is rarer than one thinks. It is a queer animal, quaint rather than beautiful. It is strange what a difference a tail makes—you know the sort of things one says as a lunch party breaks up and people are finding their coats and hats.

This one, thanks to the hospitality of the host, had lasted far into the afternoon. The beautiful October day was fading and the leaves were falling from the trees in the avenue as I walked through it. Gate after gate seemed to close with gentle finality behind me. Innumerable beadles were fitting innumerable keys into well-oiled locks; the treasure-house was being made secure for another night. After the avenue one comes out upon a road—I forget its name—which leads you, if you take the right turning, along to Fernham. But there was plenty of time. Dinner was not till half-past seven. One could almost do without dinner after such a luncheon. It is strange how a scrap of poetry works in the mind and makes the legs move in time to it along the road. Those words—

> *There has fallen a splendid tear*
> *From the passion-flower at the gate.*
> *She is coming, my dove, my dear—*

sang in my blood as I stepped quickly along towards Headingley. And then, switching off into the other measure, I sang, where the waters are churned up by the weir:

> *My heart is like a singing bird*
> *Whose nest is in a water'd shoot;*
> *My heart is like an apple tree ....*

What poets, I cried aloud, as one does in the dusk, what poets they were!

In a sort of jealousy, I suppose, for our own age, silly and absurd though these comparisons are, I went on to wonder if honestly one could name two living poets now as great as Tennyson and Christina Rossetti were then. Obviously it is impossible, I thought, looking into those foaming waters, to compare them. The very reason why the poetry excites one to such abandonment, such rapture, is that it celebrates some feeling that one used to have (at luncheon parties before the war perhaps), so that one responds easily, familiarly, without troubling to check the feeling, or to compare it with any that one has now. But the living poets express a feeling that is actually being made and torn out of us at the moment. One does not recognize it in the first place; often for some reason one fears it; one watches it with keenness and compares it jealously and suspiciously with the old feeling that one knew. Hence the difficulty of modern poetry; and it is because of this difficulty that one cannot remember more than two consecutive lines of any good modern poet. For this reason—that my memory failed me—the argument flagged for want of material. But why, I continued, moving on towards Headingley, have we stopped humming under our breath at luncheon parties? Why has Alfred ceased to sing

> *She is coming, my dove, my dear?*

Why has Christina ceased to respond

> *My heart is gladder than all these*
> *Because my love is come to me?*

Shall we lay the blame on the war? When the guns fired in August 1914, did the faces of men and women show so plain in each other's eyes that romance was killed?

---

[1] *My heart ... me* The opening stanza of Christina Rossetti's "A Birthday" (1861).

Certainly it was a shock (to women in particular with their illusions about education, and so on) to see the faces of our rulers in the light of the shell-fire. So ugly they looked—German, English, French—so stupid. But lay the blame where one will, on whom one will, the illusion which inspired Tennyson and Christina Rossetti to sing so passionately about the coming of their loves is far rarer now than then. One has only to read, to look, to listen, to remember. But why say "blame"? Why, if it was an illusion, not praise the catastrophe, whatever it was, that destroyed illusion and put truth in its place? For truth … those dots mark the spot where, in search of truth, I missed the turning up to Fernham. Yes indeed, which was truth and which was illusion, I asked myself. What was the truth about these houses, for example, dim and festive now with their red windows in the dusk, but raw and red and squalid, with their sweets and their boot-laces, at nine o'clock in the morning? And the willows and the river and the gardens that run down to the river, vague now with the mist stealing over them, but gold and red in the sunlight—which was the truth, which was the illusion about them? I spare you the twists and turns of my cogitations, for no conclusion was found on the road to Headingley, and I ask you to suppose that I soon found out my mistake about the turning and retraced my steps to Fernham.

As I have said already that it was an October day, I dare not forfeit your respect and imperil the fair name of fiction by changing the season and describing lilacs hanging over garden walls, crocuses, tulips and other flowers of spring. Fiction must stick to facts, and the truer the facts the better the fiction—so we are told. Therefore it was still autumn and the leaves were still yellow and falling, if anything, a little faster than before, because it was now evening (seven twenty-three to be precise) and a breeze (from the southwest to be exact) had risen. But for all that there was something odd at work:

> My heart is like a singing bird
> Whose nest is in a water'd shoot;
> My heart is like an apple tree
> Whose boughs are bent with thick-set fruit—

perhaps the words of Christina Rossetti were partly responsible for the folly of the fancy—it was nothing of course but a fancy—that the lilac was shaking its flowers over the garden walls, and the brimstone butterflies were scudding hither and thither, and the dust of the pollen was in the air. A wind blew, from what quarter I know not, but it lifted the half-grown leaves so that there was a flash of silver grey in the air. It was the time between the lights when colours undergo their intensification and purples and golds burn in window-panes like the beat of an excitable heart; when for some reason the beauty of the world revealed and yet soon to perish (here I pushed into the garden, for, unwisely, the door was left open and no beadles seemed about), the beauty of the world which is so soon to perish, has two edges, one of laughter, one of anguish, cutting the heart asunder. The gardens of Fernham lay before me in the spring twilight, wild and open, and in the long grass, sprinkled and carelessly flung, were daffodils and bluebells, not orderly perhaps at the best of times, and now wind-blown and waving as they tugged at their roots. The windows of the building, curved like ships' windows among generous waves of red brick, changed from lemon to silver under the flight of the quick spring clouds. Somebody was in a hammock, somebody, but in this light they were phantoms only, half guessed, half seen, raced across the grass—would no one stop her?—and then on the terrace, as if popping out to breathe the air, to glance at the garden, came a bent figure, formidable yet humble, with her great forehead and her shabby dress—could it be the famous scholar, could it be J —— H ——[1] herself? All was dim, yet intense too, as if the scarf which the dusk had flung over the garden were torn asunder by star or sword—the flash of some terrible reality leaping, as its way is, out of the heart of the spring. For youth—

Here was my soup. Dinner was being served in the great dining-hall. Far from being spring it was in fact an evening in October. Everybody was assembled in the big dining-room. Dinner was ready. Here was the soup. It was a plain gravy soup. There was nothing to stir the fancy in that. One could have seen through the transparent liquid any pattern that there might have been on the plate itself. But there was no pattern. The plate was plain. Next came beef with its attendant greens and potatoes—a homely trinity, suggesting the rumps of cattle in a muddy market, and sprouts curled and

---

[1] *J —— H ——* Jane Harrison (1850–1928), cultural anthropologist and archaeologist who was a Fellow at Newnham College.

yellowed at the edge, and bargaining and cheapening, and women with string bags on Monday morning. There was no reason to complain of human nature's daily food, seeing that the supply was sufficient and coal-miners doubtless were sitting down to less. Prunes and custard followed. And if any one complains that prunes, even when mitigated by custard, are an unchari-table vegetable (fruit they are not), stringy as a miser's heart and exuding a fluid such as might run in misers' veins who have denied themselves wine and warmth for eighty years and yet not given to the poor, he should reflect that there are people whose charity embraces even the prune. Biscuits and cheese came next, and here the water-jug was liberally passed round, for it is the nature of biscuits to be dry, and these were biscuits to the core. That was all. The meal was over. Everybody scraped their chairs back; the swing-doors swung violently to and fro; soon the hall was emptied of every sign of food and made ready no doubt for breakfast next morning. Down corridors and up staircases the youth of England went banging and singing. And was it for a guest, a stranger (for I had no more right here in Fernham than in Trinity or Somerville or Girton or Newnham or Christchurch[1]), to say, "The dinner was not good," or to say (we were now, Mary Seton and I, in her sitting-room), "Could we not have dined up here alone?" for if I had said anything of the kind I should have been prying and searching into the secret economies of a house which to the stranger wears so fine a front of gaiety and courage. No, one could say nothing of the sort. Indeed, conversation for a moment flagged. The human frame being what it is, heart, body and brain all mixed together, and not contained in separate compart-ments as they will be no doubt in another million years, a good dinner is of great importance to good talk. One cannot think well, love well, sleep well, if one has not dined well. The lamp in the spine does not light on beef and prunes. We are all *probably* going to heaven, and Vandyck is, we *hope*, to meet us round the next corner—that is the dubious and qualifying state of mind that beef and prunes at the end of the day's work breed between them. Happily my friend, who taught science,

had a cupboard where there was a squat bottle and little glasses—(but there should have been sole and partridge to begin with)—so that we were able to draw up to the fire and repair some of the damages of the day's living. In a minute or so we were slipping freely in and out among all those objects of curiosity and interest which form in the mind in the absence of a particular person, and are naturally to be discussed on coming together again—how somebody has married, another has not; one thinks this, another that; one has improved out of all knowledge, the other most amazingly gone to the bad—with all those speculations upon human nature and the character of the amazing world we live in which spring naturally from such beginnings. While these things were being said, however, I became shamefacedly aware of a current setting in of its own accord and carrying everything forward to an end of its own. One might be talking of Spain or Portugal, or book or racehorse, but the real interest of whatever was said was none of those things, but a scene of masons on a high roof some five centuries ago. Kings and nobles brought treasure in huge sacks and poured it under the earth. This scene was for ever coming alive in my mind and placing itself by another of lean cows and a muddy market and withered greens and the stringy hearts of old men—these two pictures, disjointed and disconnected and nonsensical as they were, were for ever coming together and combating each other and had me entirely at their mercy. The best course, unless the whole talk was to be distorted, was to expose what was in my mind to the air, when with good luck it would fade and crumble like the head of the dead king when they opened the coffin at Windsor. Briefly, then, I told Miss Seton about the masons who had been all those years on the roof of the chapel, and about the kings and queens and nobles bearing sacks of gold and silver on their shoulders, which they shovelled into the earth; and then how the great financial magnates of our own time came and laid cheques and bonds, I suppose, where the others had laid ingots and rough lumps of gold. All that lies beneath the colleges down there, I said; but this college, where we are now sitting, what lies beneath its gallant red brick and the wild unkempt grasses of the garden? What force is behind the plain china off which we dined, and (here it popped out of my mouth before I

---

[1] *Trinity... Christchurch* Somerville and Christchurch are colleges at Oxford, while Trinity, Girton, and Newnham are Cambridge colleges.

could stop it) the beef, the custard and the prunes?

Well, said Mary Seton, about the year 1860—Oh, but you know the story, she said, bored, I suppose, by the recital. And she told me—rooms were hired. Committees met. Envelopes were addressed. Circulars were drawn up. Meetings were held; letters were read out; so-and-so has promised so much; on the contrary, Mr. —— won't give a penny. The *Saturday Review* has been very rude. How can we raise a fund to pay for offices? Shall we hold a bazaar? Can't we find a pretty girl to sit in the front row? Let us look up what John Stuart Mill[1] said on the subject. Can any one persuade the editor of the —— to print a letter? Can we get Lady —— to sign it? Lady —— is out of town. That was the way it was done, presumably, sixty years ago, and it was a prodigious effort, and a great deal of time was spent on it. And it was only after a long struggle and with the utmost difficulty that they got thirty thousand pounds together.[2] So obviously we cannot have wine and partridges and servants carrying tin dishes on their heads, she said. We cannot have sofas and separate rooms. "The amenities," she said, quoting from some book or other, "will have to wait."[3]

At the thought of all those women working year after year and finding it hard to get two thousand pounds together, and as much as they could do to get thirty thousand pounds, we burst out in scorn at the reprehensible poverty of our sex. What had our mothers been doing then that they had no wealth to leave us? Powdering their noses? Looking in at shop windows? Flaunting in the sun at Monte Carlo? There were some photographs on the mantel-piece. Mary's mother—if that was her picture—may have been a wastrel[4] in her

spare time (she had thirteen children by a minister of the church), but if so her gay and dissipated life had left too few traces of its pleasures on her face. She was a homely body; an old lady in a plaid shawl which was fastened by a large cameo; and she sat in a basket-chair, encouraging a spaniel to look at the camera, with the amused, yet strained expression of one who is sure that the dog will move directly the bulb is pressed. Now if she had gone into business; had become a manufacturer of artificial silk or a magnate on the Stock Exchange; if she had left two or three hundred thousand pounds to Fernham, we could have been sitting at our ease tonight and the subject of our talk might have been archaeology, botany, anthropology, physics, the nature of the atom, mathematics, astronomy, relativity, geography. If only Mrs. Seton and her mother and her mother before her had learnt the great art of making money and had left their money, like their fathers and their grandfathers before them, to found fellowships and lectureships and prizes and scholarships appropriated to the use of their own sex, we might have dined very tolerably up here alone off a bird and a bottle of wine; we might have looked forward without undue confidence to a pleasant and honourable lifetime spent in the shelter of one of the liberally endowed professions. We might have been exploring or writing; mooning about the venerable places of the earth; sitting contemplative on the steps of the Parthenon, or going at ten to an office and coming home comfortably at half-past four to write a little poetry. Only, if Mrs. Seton and her like had gone into business at the age of fifteen, there would have been— that was the snag in the argument—no Mary. What, I asked, did Mary think of that? There between the curtains was the October night, calm and lovely, with a star or two caught in the yellowing trees. Was she ready to resign her share of it and her memories (for they had been a happy family, though a large one) of games and quarrels up in Scotland, which she is never tired of praising for the fineness of its air and the quality of its cakes, in order that Fernham might have been endowed with fifty thousand pounds or so by a stroke of the pen? For, to endow a college would necessitate the suppression of families altogether. Making a fortune and bearing thirteen children—no human being could stand it. Consider the facts, we said. First there are nine

---

[1] *John Stuart Mill* English philosopher and economist (1806–73) who was interested in the status and treatment of women; author of *The Subjection of Women*.

[2] [Woolf's note] "We are told that we ought to ask for 30,000 at least…. It is not a large sum, considering that there is to be but one college of this sort for Great Britain, Ireland, and the Colonies, and considering how easy it is to raise immense sums for boys' schools. But considering how few people really wish women to be educated, it is a good deal."—Lady Stephen, *Life of Miss Emily Davies*.

[3] [Woolf's note] "Every penny which could be scraped together was set aside for building, and the amenities had to be postponed." —R. Strachey, *The Cause*.

[4] *wastrel* Spendthrift.

months before the baby is born. Then the baby is born. Then there are three or four months spent in feeding the baby. After the baby is fed there are certainly five years spent in playing with the baby. You cannot, it seems, let children run about the streets. People who have seen them running wild in Russia say that the sight is not a pleasant one. People say, too, that human nature takes its shape in the years between one and five. If Mrs. Seton, I said, had been making money, what sort of memories would you have had of games and quarrels? What would you have known of Scotland, and its fine air and cakes and all the rest of it? But it is useless to ask these questions, because you would never have come into existence at all. Moreover, it is equally useless to ask what might have happened if Mrs. Seton and her mother and her mother before her had amassed great wealth and laid it under the foundations of college and library, because, in the first place, to earn money was impossible for them, and in the second, had it been possible, the law denied them the right to possess what money they earned. It is only for the last forty-eight years that Mrs. Seton has had a penny of her own.[1] For all the centuries before that it would have been her husband's property—a thought which, perhaps, may have had its share in keeping Mrs. Seton and her mothers off the Stock Exchange. Every penny I earn, they may have said, will be taken from me and disposed of according to my husband's wisdom—perhaps to found a scholarship or to endow a fellowship in Balliol or Kings,[2] so that to earn money, even if I could earn money, is not a matter that interests me very greatly. I had better leave it to my husband.

At any rate, whether or not the blame rested on the old lady who was looking at the spaniel, there could be no doubt that for some reason or other our mothers had mismanaged their affairs very gravely. Not a penny could be spared for "amenities"; for partridges and wine, beadles and turf, books and cigars, libraries and leisure. To raise bare walls out of the bare earth was the utmost they could do.

So we talked standing at the window and looking, as so many thousands look every night, down on the domes and towers of the famous city beneath us. It was very beautiful, very mysterious in the autumn moonlight. The old stone looked very white and venerable. One thought of all the books that were assembled down there; of the pictures of old prelates and worthies hanging in the panelled rooms; of the painted windows that would be throwing strange globes and crescents on the pavement; of the tablets and memorials and inscriptions; of the fountains and the grass; of the quiet rooms looking across the quiet quadrangles. And (pardon me the thought) I thought, too, of the admirable smoke and drink and the deep armchairs and the pleasant carpets: of the urbanity, the geniality, the dignity which are the offspring of luxury and privacy and space. Certainly our mothers had not provided us with anything comparable to all this—our mothers who found it difficult to scrape together thirty thousand pounds, our mothers who bore thirteen children to ministers of religion at St. Andrews.

So I went back to my inn, and as I walked through the dark streets I pondered this and that, as one does at the end of the day's work. I pondered why it was that Mrs. Seton had no money to leave us; and what effect poverty has on the mind; and what effect wealth has on the mind; and I thought of the queer old gentlemen I had seen that morning with tufts of fur upon their shoulders; and I remembered how if one whistled one of them ran; and I thought of the organ booming in the chapel and of the shut doors of the library; and I thought how unpleasant it is to be locked out; and I thought how it is worse perhaps to be locked in; and, thinking of the safety and prosperity of the one sex and of the poverty and insecurity of the other and of the effect of tradition and of the lack of tradition upon the mind of a writer, I thought at last that it was time to roll up the crumpled skin of the day, with its arguments and its impressions and its anger and its laughter, and cast it into the hedge. A thousand stars were flashing across the blue wastes of the sky. One seemed alone with an inscrutable society. All human beings were laid asleep—prone, horizontal, dumb. Nobody seemed stirring in the streets of Oxbridge. Even the door of the hotel sprang

---

[1] *It is ... own* Reference to the Married Women's Property Acts of 1870 and 1882, which allowed married women the same rights to their property that single women enjoyed.

[2] *Balliol or Kings* Two colleges, the first at Oxford and the second at Cambridge.

open at the touch of an invisible hand—not a boots[1] was sitting up to light me to bed, it was so late.

Chapter 2

The scene, if I may ask you to follow me, was now changed. The leaves were still falling, but in London now, not Oxbridge; and I must ask you to imagine a room, like many thousands, with a window looking across people's hats and vans and motor-cars to other windows, and on the table inside the room a blank sheet of paper on which was written in large letters WOMEN AND FICTION, but no more. The inevitable sequel to lunching and dining at Oxbridge seemed, unfortunately, to be a visit to the British Museum. One must strain off what was personal and accidental in all these impressions and so reach the pure fluid, the essential oil of truth. For that visit to Oxbridge and the luncheon and the dinner had started a swarm of questions. Why did men drink wine and women water? Why was one sex so prosperous and the other so poor? What effect has poverty on fiction? What conditions are necessary for the creation of works of art?—a thousand questions at once suggested themselves. But one needed answers, not questions; and an answer was only to be had by consulting the learned and the unprejudiced, who have removed themselves above the strife of tongue and the confusion of body and issued the result of their reasoning and research in books which are to be found in the British Museum. If truth is not to be found on the shelves of the British Museum, where, I asked myself, picking up a notebook and a pencil, is truth?

Thus provided, thus confident and enquiring, I set out in the pursuit of truth. The day, though not actually wet, was dismal, and the streets in the neighbourhood of the Museum were full of open coal-holes, down which sacks were showering; four-wheeled cabs were drawing up and depositing on the pavement corded boxes containing, presumably, the entire wardrobe of some Swiss or Italian family seeking fortune or refuge or some other desirable commodity which is to be found in the

boarding-houses of Bloomsbury[2] in the winter. The usual hoarse-voiced men paraded the streets with plants on barrows. Some shouted; others sang. London was like a workshop. London was like a machine. We were all being shot backwards and forwards on this plain foundation to make some pattern. The British Museum was another department of the factory. The swing-doors swung open; and there one stood under the vast dome, as if one were a thought in the huge bald forehead which is so splendidly encircled by a band of famous names. One went to the counter; one took a slip of paper; one opened a volume of the catalogue, and ..... the five dots here indicate five separate minutes of stupefaction, wonder, and bewilderment. Have you any notion of how many books are written about women in the course of one year? Have you any notion how many are written by men? Are you aware that you are, perhaps, the most discussed animal in the universe? Here had I come with a notebook and pencil proposing to spend a morning reading, supposing that at the end of the morning I should have transferred the truth to my notebook. But I should need to be a herd of elephants, I thought, and a wilderness of spiders, desperately referring to the animals that are reputed longest lived and most multitudinously eyed, to cope with all this. I should need claws of steel and beak of brass even to penetrate the husk. How shall I ever find the grains of truth embedded in all this mass of paper, I asked myself, and in despair began running my eye up and down the long list of titles. Even the names of the books gave me food for thought. Sex and its nature might well attract doctors and biologists; but what was surprising and difficult of explanation was the fact that sex—woman, that is to say—also attracts agreeable essayists, light-fingered novelists, young men who have taken the M.A. degree; men who have taken no degree; men who have no apparent qualification save that they are not women. Some of these books were, on the face of it, frivolous and facetious; but many, on the other hand, were serious and prophetic, moral and hortatory. Merely to read the titles suggested innumerable schoolmasters, innumerable clergymen mounting their platforms and

---

[1] *boots* I.e., hotel servant, because one of a servant's chores was to clean the guests' boots.

[2] *Bloomsbury* Area of London in which the British Museum is located and in which many of Woolf's circle (known collectively as "The Bloomsbury Group") lived.

pulpits and holding forth with a loquacity which far exceeded the hour usually allotted to such discourse on this one subject. It was a most strange phenomenon; and apparently—here I consulted the letter M—one confined to male sex. Women do not write books about men—a fact that I could not help welcoming with relief, for if I had first to read all that men have written about women, then all that women have written about men, the aloe that flowers once in a hundred years would flower twice before I could set pen to paper. So, making a perfectly arbitrary choice of a dozen volumes or so, I sent my slips of paper to lie in the wire tray, and waited in my stall, among the other seekers for the essential oil of truth.

What could be the reason, then, of this curious disparity, I wondered, drawing cart-wheels on the slips of paper provided by the British taxpayer for other purposes. Why are women, judging from this catalogue, so much more interesting to men than men are to women? A very curious fact it seemed, and my mind wandered to picture the lives of men who spend their time in writing books about women; whether they were old or young, married or unmarried, red-nosed or humpbacked—anyhow, it was flattering, vaguely, to feel oneself the object of such attention, provided that it was not entirely bestowed by the crippled and the in-firm—so I pondered until all such frivolous thoughts were ended by an avalanche of books sliding down on to the desk in front of me. Now the trouble began. The student who has been trained in research at Oxbridge has no doubt some method of shepherding his question past all distractions till it runs into its answer as a sheep runs into its pen. The student by my side, for instance, who was copying assiduously from a scientific manual was, I felt sure, extracting pure nuggets of the essential ore every ten minutes or so. His little grunts of satisfac-tion indicated so much. But if, unfortunately, one has had no training in a university, the question far from being shepherded into its pen flies like a frightened flock hither and thither, helter-skelter, pursued by a whole pack of hounds. Professors, schoolmasters, sociologists, clergymen, novelists, essayists, journalists, men who had no qualification save that they were not women, chased my simple and single question—Why are women poor?—until it became fifty questions; until the fifty

questions leapt frantically into mid-stream and were carried away. Every page in my notebook was scribbled over with notes. To show the state of mind I was in, I will read you a few of them, explaining that the page was headed quite simply, WOMEN AND POVERTY, in block letters; but what followed was something like this:

Condition in Middle Ages of,
Habits in the Fiji Islands of,
Worshipped as goddesses by,
Weaker in moral sense than,
Idealism of,
Greater conscientiousness of,
South Sea Islanders, age of puberty among,
Attractiveness of,
Offered as sacrifice to,
Small size of brain of,
Profounder sub-consciousness of,
Less hair on the body of,
Mental, moral and physical inferiority of,
Love of children of,
Greater length of life of,
Weaker muscles of,
Strength of affections of,
Vanity of,
Higher education of,
Shakespeare's opinion of,
Lord Birkenhead's[1] opinion of,
Dean Inge's[2] opinion of,
La Bruyère's[3] opinion of,
Dr. Johnson's[4] opinion of,
Mr. Oscar Browning's[5] opinion of, …

Here I drew breath and added, indeed, in the margin, Why does Samuel Butler[6] say, "Wise men never say

---

[1] *Lord Birkenhead* Frederick Elwin Smith, Earl of Birkenhead, who was Lord Chancellor from 1919 to 1922 and an opponent of women's suffrage.

[2] *Dean Inge* William Ralph Inge, Dean of St. Paul's Cathedral from 1911 to 1934.

[3] *La Bruyère* Jean de La Bruyère, French essayist and moralist (1645–96).

[4] *Dr. Johnson* Samuel Johnson (1709–84), British lexicographer, critic, poet, and essayist.

[5] *Mr. Oscar Browning* History lecturer at King's College, Cam-bridge (1837–1923).

[6] *Samuel Butler* Nineteenth-century English author (1835–1902).

what they think of women?" Wise men never say anything else apparently. But, I continued, leaning back in my chair and looking at the vast dome in which I was a single but by now somewhat harassed thought, what is so unfortunate is that wise men never think the same thing about women. Here is Pope:

Most women have no character at all.[1]

And here is La Bruyère:

Les femmes sont extrêmes; elles sont meilleures ou pires que les hommes[2]—

a direct contradiction by keen observers who were contemporary. Are they capable of education or incapable? Napoleon thought them incapable. Dr. Johnson thought the opposite.[3] Have they souls or have they not souls? Some savages say they have none. Others, on the contrary, maintain that women are half divine and worship them on that account.[4] Some sages hold that they are shallower in the brain; others that they are deeper in the consciousness. Goethe[5] honoured them; Mussolini[6] despises them. Wherever one looked men thought about women and thought differently. It was impossible to make head or tail of it all, I decided, glancing with envy at the reader next door who was making the neatest abstracts, headed often with an A or a B or a C, while my own notebook rioted with the wildest scribble of contradictory jottings. It was distressing, it was bewildering, it was humiliating. Truth had run through my fingers. Every drop had escaped.

I could not possibly go home, I reflected, and add as a serious contribution to the study of women and fiction that women have less hair on their bodies than men, or that the age of puberty among the South Sea Islanders is nine—or is it ninety?—even the handwriting had become in its distraction indecipherable. It was disgraceful to have nothing more weighty or respectable to show after a whole morning's work. And if I could not grasp the truth about W. (as for brevity's sake I had come to call her) in the past, why bother about W. in the future? It seemed pure waste of time to consult all those gentlemen who specialise in woman and her effect on whatever it may be—politics, children, wages, morality—numerous and learned as they are. One might as well leave their books unopened.

But while I pondered I had unconsciously, in my listlessness, in my desperation, been drawing a picture where I should, like my neighbour, have been writing a conclusion. I had been drawing a face, a figure. It was the face and the figure of Professor von X. engaged in writing his monumental work entitled *The Mental, Moral, and Physical Inferiority of the Female Sex*. He was not in my picture a man attractive to women. He was heavily built; he had a great jowl; to balance that he had very small eyes; he was very red in the face. His expression suggested that he was labouring under some emotion that made him jab his pen on the paper as if he were killing some noxious insect as he wrote, but even when he had killed it that did not satisfy him; he must go on killing it; and even so, some cause for anger and irritation remained. Could it be his wife, I asked, looking at my picture. Was she in love with a cavalry officer? Was the cavalry officer slim and elegant and dressed in astrachan?[7] Had he been laughed at, to adopt the Freudian theory, in his cradle by a pretty girl? For even in his cradle the professor, I thought, could not have been an attractive child. Whatever the reason, the professor was made to look very angry and very ugly in my sketch, as he wrote his great book upon the mental,

---

[1] *Most ... all* From the opening of English poet and satirist Alexander Pope's Epistle 2, "To a Lady" from his *Moral Essays*: "Nothing so true as what you once let fall, / 'Most women have no character at all.'"

[2] *Les ... hommes* "Women are extreme: they are better or worse than men." From La Bruyère's *Les Caractères* (1688).

[3] [Woolf's note] "'Men know that women are an overmatch for them, and therefore they choose the weakest or the most ignorant. If they did not think so, they never would be afraid of women knowing as much as themselves.' ... In justice to the sex, I think it but candid to acknowledge that, in a subsequent conversation, he told me that he was serious in what he said."—Boswell, *The Journal of a Tour to the Hebrides*.

[4] [Woolf's note] "The ancient Germans believed that there was something holy in women, and accordingly consulted them as oracles."—Frazer, *Golden Bough*.

[5] *Goethe* German writer Johann Wolfgang von Goethe (1749–1832).

[6] *Mussolini* Benito Mussolini (1883–1945), Italian Fascist dictator.

[7] *astrachan* I.e., astrakhan, wool of very young lambs.

moral and physical inferiority of women. Drawing pictures was an idle way of finishing an unprofitable morning's work. Yet it is in our idleness, in our dreams, that the submerged truth sometimes comes to the top. A very elementary exercise in psychology, not to be dignified by the name of psycho-analysis, showed me, on looking at my notebook, that the sketch of the angry professor had been made in anger. Anger had snatched my pencil while I dreamt. But what was anger doing there? Interest, confusion, amusement, boredom—all these emotions I could trace and name as they succeeded each other throughout the morning. Had anger, the black snake, been lurking among them? Yes, said the sketch, anger had. It referred me unmistakably to the one book, to the one phrase, which had roused the demon; it was the professor's statement about the mental, moral and physical inferiority of women. My heart had leapt. My cheeks had burnt. I had flushed with anger. There was nothing specially remarkable, however foolish, in that. One does not like to be told that one is naturally the inferior of a little man—I looked at the student next me—who breathes hard, wears a ready-made tie, and has not shaved this fortnight. One has certain foolish vanities. It is only human nature, I reflected, and began drawing cart-wheels and circles over the angry professor's face till he looked like a burning bush or a flaming comet—anyhow, an apparition without human semblance or significance. The professor was nothing now but a faggot[1] burning on the top of Hampstead Heath.[2] Soon my own anger was explained and done with; but curiosity remained. How explain the anger of the professors? Why were they angry? For when it came to analysing the impression left by these books there was always an element of heat. This heat took many forms; it showed itself in satire, in sentiment, in curiosity, in reprobation. But there was another element which was often present and could not immediately be identified. Anger, I called it. But it was anger that had gone underground and mixed itself with all kinds of other emotions. To judge from its odd effects, it was anger disguised and complex, not anger simple and open.

Whatever the reason, all these books, I thought, surveying the pile on the desk, are worthless for my purposes. They were worthless scientifically, that is to say, though humanly they were full of instruction, interest, boredom, and very queer facts about the habits of the Fiji Islanders. They had been written in the red light of emotion and not in the white light of truth. Therefore they must be returned to the central desk and restored each to his own cell in the enormous honeycomb. All that I had retrieved from that morning's work had been the one fact of anger. The professors—I lumped them together thus—were angry. But why, I asked myself, having returned the books, why, I repeated, standing under the colonnade among the pigeons and the prehistoric canoes, why are they angry? And, asking myself this question, I strolled off to find a place for luncheon. What is the real nature of what I call for the moment their anger? I asked. Here was a puzzle that would last all the time that it takes to be served with food in a small restaurant somewhere near the British Museum. Some previous luncher had left the lunch edition of the evening paper on a chair, and, waiting to be served, I began idly reading the headlines. A ribbon of very large letters ran across the page. Somebody had made a big score in South Africa. Lesser ribbons announced that Sir Austen Chamberlain was at Geneva.[3] A meat axe with human hair on it had been found in a cellar. Mr. Justice —— commented in the Divorce Courts upon the Shamelessness of Women. Sprinkled about the paper were other pieces of news. A film actress had been lowered from a peak in California and hung suspended in mid-air. The weather was going to be foggy. The most transient visitor to this planet, I thought, who picked up this paper could not fail to be aware, even from this scattered testimony, that England is under the rule of a patriarchy. Nobody in their senses could fail to detect the dominance of the professor. His was the power and the money and the influence. He was the proprietor of the paper and its editor and sub-editor. He was the Foreign Secretary and the Judge. He was the cricketer; he owned the race-horses and the yachts. He was the director of the company that pays two hundred

---

[1] *faggot* Bundle of sticks for fuel.

[2] *Hampstead Heath* Natural area in north London and the highest point in the city.

[3] *Sir Austin Chamberlain* Statesman, member of the British House of Commons and Secretary of State of Foreign Affairs from 1924 to 1929; *Geneva* Location of the League of Nations headquarters.

per cent to its shareholders. He left millions to charities and colleges that were ruled by himself. He suspended the film actress in mid-air. He will decide if the hair on the meat axe is human; he it is who will acquit or convict the murderer, and hang him, or let him go free. With the exception of the fog he seemed to control everything. Yet he was angry. I knew that he was angry by this token. When I read what he wrote about women I thought, not of what he was saying, but of himself. When an arguer argues dispassionately he thinks only of the argument; and the reader cannot help thinking of the argument too. If he had written dispassionately about women, had used indisputable proofs to establish his argument and had shown no trace of wishing that the result should be one thing rather than another, one would not have been angry either. One would have accepted the fact, as one accepts the fact that a pea is green or a canary yellow. So be it, I should have said. But I had been angry because he was angry. Yet it seemed absurd, I thought, turning over the evening paper, that a man with all this power should be angry. Or is anger, I wondered, somehow, the familiar, the attendant sprite on power? Rich people, for example, are often angry because they suspect that the poor want to seize their wealth. The professors, or patriarchs, as it might be more accurate to call them, might be angry for that reason partly, but partly for one that lies a little less obviously on the surface. Possibly they were not "angry" at all; often, indeed, they were admiring, devoted, exemplary in the relations of private life. Possibly when the professor insisted a little too emphatically upon the inferiority of women, he was concerned not with their inferiority, but with his own superiority. That was what he was protecting rather hot-headedly and with too much emphasis, because it was a jewel to him of the rarest price. Life for both sexes—and I looked at them, shouldering their way along the pavement—is arduous, difficult, a perpetual struggle. It calls for gigantic courage and strength. More than anything, perhaps, creatures of illusion as we are, it calls for confidence in oneself. Without self-confidence we are as babes in the cradle. And how can we generate this imponderable quality, which is yet so invaluable, most quickly? By thinking that other people are inferior to oneself. By feeling that one has some innate superiority—it may be

wealth, or rank, a straight nose, or the portrait of a grandfather by Romney[1]—for there is no end to the pathetic devices of the human imagination—over other people. Hence the enormous importance to a patriarch who has to conquer, who has to rule, of feeling that great numbers of people, half the human race indeed, are by nature inferior to himself. It must indeed be one of the chief sources of his power. But let me turn the light of this observation on to real life, I thought. Does it help to explain some of those psychological puzzles that one notes in the margin of daily life? Does it explain my astonishment the other day when Z, most humane, most modest of men, taking up some book by Rebecca West[2] and reading a passage in it, exclaimed, "The arrant feminist! She says that men are snobs!" The exclamation, to me so surprising—for why was Miss West an arrant feminist for making a possibly true if uncomplimentary statement about the other sex?—was not merely the cry of wounded vanity; it was a protest against some infringement of his power to believe in himself. Women have served all these centuries as looking-glasses possessing the magic and delicious power of reflecting the figure of man at twice its natural size. Without that power probably the earth would still be swamp and jungle. The glories of all our wars would be unknown. We should still be scratching the outlines of deer on the remains of mutton bones and bartering flints for sheepskins or whatever simple ornament took our unsophisticated taste. Supermen and Fingers of Destiny would never have existed. The Czar and the Kaiser would never have worn their crowns or lost them. Whatever may be their use in civilised societies, mirrors are essential to all violent and heroic action. That is why Napoleon and Mussolini both insist so emphatically upon the inferiority of women, for if they were not inferior, they would cease to enlarge. That serves to explain in part the necessity that women so often are to men. And it serves to explain how restless they are under her criticism; how impossible it is for her to say to them this book is bad, this picture is feeble, or whatever it may be, without giving far more pain and rousing far

---

[1] *Romney* George Romney, eighteenth-century British painter and portraitist.

[2] *Rebecca West* Assumed name of Cecily Isabel Andrews (1892–1983), English novelist, critic, and journalist.

more anger than a man would do who gave the same criticism. For if she begins to tell the truth, the figure in the looking-glass shrinks; his fitness for life is diminished. How is he to go on giving judgement, civilising natives, making laws, writing books, dressing up and speechifying at banquets, unless he can see himself at breakfast and at dinner at least twice the size he really is? So I reflected, crumbling my bread and stirring my coffee and now and again looking at the people in the street. The looking-glass vision is of supreme importance because it charges the vitality; it stimulates the nervous system. Take it away and man may die, like the drug fiend deprived of his cocaine. Under the spell of that illusion, I thought, looking out of the window, half the people on the pavement are striding to work. They put on their hats and coats in the morning under its agreeable rays. They start the day confident, braced, believing themselves desired at Miss Smith's tea party; they say to themselves as they go into the room, I am the superior of half the people here, and it is thus that they speak with that self-confidence, that self-assurance, which have had such profound consequences in public life and lead to such curious notes in the margin of the private mind.

But these contributions to the dangerous and fascinating subject of the psychology of the other sex—it is one, I hope, that you will investigate when you have five hundred a year of your own—were interrupted by the necessity of paying the bill. It came to five shillings and ninepence. I gave the waiter a ten-shilling note and he went to bring me change. There was another ten-shilling note in my purse; I noticed it, because it is a fact that still takes my breath away—the power of my purse to breed ten-shilling notes automatically. I open it and there they are. Society gives me chicken and coffee, bed and lodging, in return for a certain number of pieces of paper which were left me by an aunt, for no other reason than that I share her name.

My aunt, Mary Beton, I must tell you, died by a fall from her horse when she was riding out to take the air in Bombay. The news of my legacy reached me one night about the same time that the act was passed that gave votes to women. A solicitor's letter fell into the post-box and when I opened it I found that she had left me five hundred pounds a year for ever. Of the

two—the vote and the money—the money, I own, seemed infinitely the more important. Before that I had made my living by cadging odd jobs from newspapers, by reporting a donkey show here or a wedding there; I had earned a few pounds by addressing envelopes, reading to old ladies, making artificial flowers, teaching the alphabet to small children in a kindergarten. Such were the chief occupations that were open to women before 1918. I need not, I am afraid, describe in any detail the hardness of the work, for you know perhaps women who have done it; nor the difficulty of living on the money when it was earned, for you may have tried. But what still remains with me as a worse infliction than either was the poison of fear and bitterness which those days bred in me. To begin with, always to be doing work that one did not wish to do, and to do it like a slave, flattering and fawning, not always necessarily perhaps, but it seemed necessary and the stakes were too great to run risks; and then the thought of that one gift which it was death to hide—a small one but dear to the possessor—perishing and with it myself, my soul—all this became like a rust eating away the bloom of the spring, destroying the tree at its heart. However, as I say, my aunt died; and whenever I change a ten-shilling note a little of that rust and corrosion is rubbed off; fear and bitterness go. Indeed, I thought, slipping the silver into my purse, it is remarkable, remembering the bitterness of those days, what a change of temper a fixed income will bring about. No force in the world can take from me my five hundred pounds. Food, house, and clothing are mine for ever. Therefore not merely do effort and labour cease, but also hatred and bitterness. I need not hate any man; he cannot hurt me. I need not flatter any man; he has nothing to give me. So imperceptibly I found myself adopting a new attitude towards the other half of the human race. It was absurd to blame any class or any sex, as a whole. Great bodies of people are never responsible for what they do. They are driven by instincts which are not within their control. They too, the patriarchs, the professors, had endless difficulties, terrible drawbacks to contend with. Their education had been in some ways as faulty as my own. It had bred in them defects as great. True, they had money and power, but only at the cost of harbouring in their breasts an eagle, a vulture, for ever tearing the liver out and plucking at the lungs—the instinct for possession, the rage for acquisition which drives them to desire other people's fields and goods perpetually; to make frontiers and flags; battleships and poison gas; to offer up their own lives and their children's lives. Walk through the Admiralty Arch[1] (I had reached that monument), or any other avenue given up to trophies and cannon, and reflect upon the kind of glory celebrated there. Or watch in the spring sunshine the stockbroker and the great barrister going indoors to make money and more money and more money when it is a fact that five hundred pounds a year will keep one alive in the sunshine. These are unpleasant instincts to harbour, I reflected. They are bred of the conditions of life; of the lack of civilisation, I thought, looking at the statue of the Duke of Cambridge, and in particular at the feathers in his cocked hat, with a fixity that they have scarcely ever received before. And, as I realised these drawbacks, by degrees fear and bitterness modified themselves into pity and toleration; and then in a year or two, pity and toleration went, and the greatest release of all came, which is freedom to think of things in themselves. That building, for example, do I like it or not? Is that picture beautiful or not? Is that in my opinion a good book or a bad? Indeed my aunt's legacy unveiled the sky to me, and substituted for the large and imposing figure of a gentleman, which Milton recommended for my perpetual adoration,[2] a view of the open sky.

So thinking, so speculating, I found my way back to my house by the river. Lamps were being lit and an indescribable change had come over London since the morning hour. It was as if the great machine after labouring all day had made with our help a few yards of something very exciting and beautiful—a fiery fabric flashing with red eyes, a tawny monster roaring with hot breath. Even the wind seemed flung like a flag as it lashed the houses and rattled the hoardings.

In my little street, however, domesticity prevailed. The house painter was descending his ladder; the nursemaid was wheeling the perambulator carefully in and out back to nursery tea; the coal-heaver was folding his empty sacks on top of each other; the woman who keeps the green-grocer's shop was adding up the day's takings with her hands in red mittens. But so engrossed was I with the problem you have laid upon my shoulders that I could not see even these usual sights without referring them to one centre. I thought how much harder it is now than it must have been even a century ago to say which of these employments is the higher, the more necessary. Is it better to be a coal-heaver or a nursemaid; is the charwoman[3] who has brought up eight children of less value to the world than the barrister who has made a hundred thousand pounds? It is useless to ask such questions; for nobody can answer them. Not only do the comparative values of charwomen and lawyers rise and fall from decade to decade, but we have no rods with which to measure them even as they are at the moment. I had been foolish to ask my professor to furnish me with "indisputable proofs" of this or that in his argument about women. Even if one could state the value of any one gift at the moment, those values will change; in a century's time very possibly they will have changed completely. Moreover, in a hundred years, I thought, reaching my own doorstep, women will have ceased to be the protected sex. Logically they will take part in all the activities and exertions that were once denied them. The nursemaid will heave coal. The shopwoman will drive an engine. All assumptions founded on the facts observed when women were the protected sex will have disappeared—as, for example (here a squad of soldiers marched down the street), that women and clergymen and gardeners live longer than other people. Remove that protection, expose them to the same exertions and activities, make them soldiers and sailors and engine-drivers and dock labourers, and will not women die off so much younger, so much quicker, than men that one will say, "I saw a woman today," as one used to say, "I saw an aeroplane." Anything may happen when womanhood has ceased to be a protected occupation, I thought, opening the door. But what bearing has all this upon the subject of my paper, Women and Fiction? I asked, going indoors.

---

[1] *Admiralty Arch* Triple arch leading from Trafalgar Square into the Mall in London, forming part of the ceremonial approach to Buckingham Palace.

[2] *gentleman ... adoration* In *Paradise Lost* (1667), Milton suggests that man (Adam) was formed "for God only" and woman (Eve) "for God in him" (4.299).

[3] *charwoman* Cleaning woman.

CHAPTER 3

It was disappointing not to have brought back in the evening some important statement, some authentic fact. Women are poorer than men because—this or that. Perhaps now it would be better to give up seeking for the truth, and receiving on one's head an avalanche of opinion hot as lava, discoloured as dish-water. It would be better to draw the curtains; to shut out distractions; to light the lamp; to narrow the enquiry and to ask the historian, who records not opinions but facts, to describe under what conditions women lived, not throughout the ages, but in England, say in the time of Elizabeth.

For it is a perennial puzzle why no woman wrote a word of that extraordinary literature when every other man, it seemed, was capable of song or sonnet. What were the conditions in which women lived, I asked myself; for fiction, imaginative work that is, is not dropped like a pebble upon the ground, as science may be; fiction is like a spider's web, attached ever so lightly perhaps, but still attached to life at all four corners. Often the attachment is scarcely perceptible; Shakespeare's plays, for instance, seem to hang there complete by themselves. But when the web is pulled askew, hooked up at the edge, torn in the middle, one remembers that these webs are not spun in mid-air by incorporeal creatures, but are the work of suffering human beings, and are attached to grossly material things, like health and money and the houses we live in.

I went, therefore, to the shelf where the histories stand and took down one of the latest, Professor Trevelyan's *History of England*.[1] Once more I looked up Women, found "position of," and turned to the pages indicated. "Wife-beating," I read, "was a recognised right of man, and was practised without shame by high as well as low.... Similarly," the historian goes on, "the daughter who refused to marry the gentleman of her parents' choice was liable to be locked up, beaten and flung about the room, without any shock being inflicted on public opinion. Marriage was not an affair of personal affection, but of family avarice, particularly in the 'chivalrous' upper classes.... Betrothal often took place while one or both of the parties was in the cradle, and

marriage when they were scarcely out of the nurses' charge." That was about 1470, soon after Chaucer's time. The next reference to the position of women is some two hundred years later, in the time of the Stuarts. "It was still the exception for women of the upper and middle class to choose their own husbands, and when the husband had been assigned, he was lord and master, so far at least as law and custom could make him. Yet even so," Professor Trevelyan concludes, "neither Shakespeare's women nor those of authentic seventeenth-century memoirs, like the Verneys and the Hutchinsons,[2] seem wanting in personality and character." Certainly, if we consider it, Cleopatra must have had a way with her; Lady Macbeth, one would suppose, had a will of her own; Rosalind, one might conclude, was an attractive girl.[3] Professor Trevelyan is speaking no more than the truth when he remarks that Shakespeare's women do not seem wanting in personality and character. Not being a historian, one might go even further and say that women have burnt like beacons in all the works of all the poets from the beginning of time—Clytemnestra, Antigone, Cleopatra, Lady Macbeth, Phedre, Cressida, Rosalind, Desdemona, the Duchess of Malfi, among the dramatists;[4] then among the prose writers: Millamant, Clarissa, Becky Sharp, Anna Karenina, Emma Bovary, Madame de Guermantes[5]—the names flock to mind, nor do they recall women "lacking in personality and character." Indeed, if woman had no existence save in the fiction written by

2 *Verneys* The *Memoirs of the Verney Family* (published 1892) is a family history that records, as one of its authors boasted, "an ordinary gentleman's family of the higher class" consisting of "good average specimens of hundreds of men or women of their age"; *Hutchinsons* Lucy Hutchinson's *Memoirs of the Life of Colonel Hutchinson* (published 1806) detailed the life of her husband, John Hutchinson, and his experiences in the civil war.

3 *Cleopatra ... girl* Cleopatra, Lady Macbeth, and Rosalind are the heroines of Shakespeare's *Antony and Cleopatra*, *Macbeth*, and *As You Like It*, respectively.

4 *Clytemnestra ... dramatists* Heroines from Aeschylus's *Agamemnon*; Sophocles's *Antigone*; Shakespeare's *Antony and Cleopatra* and *Macbeth*; Racine's *Phèdre*; Shakespeare's *Troilus and Cressida*, *As You Like It*, and *Othello*; and Webster's *The Duchess of Malfi*.

5 *then ... Guermantes* Characters from, respectively, Congreve's *Way of the World*; Richardson's *Clarissa*; Thackeray's *Vanity Fair*; Tolstoy's *Anna Karenina*; Flaubert's *Madame Bovary*; and Proust's *À la recherche du temps perdu*.

1 *Professor ... England* George Macaulay Trevelyan's *History of England* (1929).

men, one would imagine her a person of the utmost importance; very various; heroic and mean; splendid and sordid; infinitely beautiful and hideous in the extreme; as great as a man, some think even greater.[1] But this is woman in fiction. In fact, as Professor Trevelyan points out, she was locked up, beaten and flung about the room.

A very queer, composite being thus emerges. Imaginatively she is of the highest importance; practically she is completely insignificant. She pervades poetry from cover to cover; she is all but absent from history. She dominates the lives of kings and conquerors in fiction; in fact she was the slave of any boy whose parents forced a ring upon her finger. Some of the most inspired words, some of the most profound thoughts in literature fall from her lips; in real life she could hardly read, could scarcely spell, and was the property of her husband.

It was certainly an odd monster that one made up by reading the historians first and the poets afterwards—a worm winged like an eagle; the spirit of life and beauty in a kitchen chopping up suet. But these monsters, however amusing to the imagination, have no existence in fact. What one must do to bring her to life was to think poetically and prosaically at one and the same moment, thus keeping in touch with fact—that she is Mrs. Martin, aged thirty-six, dressed in blue, wearing a black hat and brown shoes; but not losing sight of fiction either—that she is a vessel in which all sorts of spirits and forces are coursing and flashing perpetually.

The moment, however, that one tries this method with the Elizabethan woman, one branch of illumination fails; one is held up by the scarcity of facts. One knows nothing detailed, nothing perfectly true and substantial about her. History scarcely mentions her. And I turned to Professor Trevelyan again to see what history meant to him. I found by looking at his chapter headings that it meant—"The Manor Court and the Methods of Open-field Agriculture ... The Cistercians and Sheep-farming ... The Crusades ... The University ... The House of Commons ... The Hundred Years' War ... The War of the Roses ... The Renaissance Scholars ... The Dissolution of the Monasteries ... Agrarian and Religious Strife ... The Origin of English Sea-power ... The Armada ... " and so on. Occasionally an individual woman is mentioned, an Elizabeth, or a Mary; a queen or a great lady. But by no possible means could middle-class women with nothing but brains and character at their command have taken part in any one of the great movements which, brought together, constitute the historian's view of the past. Nor shall we find her in any collection of anecdotes. Aubrey[2] hardly mentions her. She never writes her own life and scarcely keeps a diary; there are only a handful of her letters in existence. She left no plays or poems by which we can judge her. What one wants, I thought—and why does not some brilliant student at Newnham or Girton supply it?—is a mass of information; at what age did she marry; how many children had she as a rule; what was her house like; had she a room to herself; did she do the cooking; would she be likely to have a servant? All these facts lie somewhere, presumably, in parish registers and account books; the life of the average Elizabethan woman must be scattered about somewhere, could one collect it and make a book of it. It would be ambitious beyond my daring, I thought, looking about the shelves for books that were not there, to suggest to the students of those famous colleges that they should re-write history, though I own that it often seems a little queer as it is, unreal, lop-sided; but why should they not add a supplement to history? calling it, of course, by some inconspicuous name so that women might figure there without impropriety? For one often catches a glimpse of them in the

1. [Woolf's note] "It remains a strange and almost inexplicable fact that in Athena's city, where women were kept in almost Oriental suppression as odalisques or drudges, the stage should yet have produced figures like Clytemnestra and Cassandra, Atossa and Antigone, Phèdre and Medea, and all the other heroines who dominate play after play of the 'misogynist' Euripides. But the paradox of this world where in real life a respectable woman could hardly show her face alone in the street, and yet on the stage woman equals or surpasses man, has never been satisfactorily explained. In modern tragedy the same predominance exists. At all events, a very cursory survey of Shakespeare's work (similarly with Webster, though not with Marlowe or Jonson) suffices to reveal how this dominance, this initiative of women, persists from Rosalind to Lady Macbeth. So too in Racine; six of his tragedies bear their heroines' names; and what male characters of his shall we set against Hermione and Andromaque, Bérénice and Roxane, Phèdre and Athalie? So again with Ibsen; what men shall we match with Solveig and Nora, Hedda and Hilda Wangel and Rebecca West?"—F.L. Lucas, Tragedy, pp. 114–15.

2. Aubrey John Aubrey (1626–97), writer and antiquary known for his Brief Lives, a collection of short, informal biographies.

lives of the great, whisking away into the background, concealing, I sometimes think, a wink, a laugh, perhaps a tear. And, after all, we have lives enough of Jane Austen; it scarcely seems necessary to consider again the influence of the tragedies of Joanna Baillie[1] upon the poetry of Edgar Allen Poe; as for myself, I should not mind if the homes and haunts of Mary Russell Mitford[2] were closed to the public for a century at least. But what I find deplorable, I continued, looking about the bookshelves again, is that nothing is known about women before the eighteenth century. I have no model in my mind to turn about this way and that. Here I am asking why women did not write poetry in the Elizabethan age, and I am not sure how they were educated; whether they were taught to write; whether they had sitting-rooms to themselves; how many women had children before they were twenty-one; what, in short, they did from eight in the morning till eight at night. They had no money evidently; according to Professor Trevelyan they were married whether they liked it or not before they were out of the nursery, at fifteen or sixteen very likely. It would have been extremely odd, even upon this showing, had one of them suddenly written the plays of Shakespeare, I concluded, and I thought of that old gentleman, who is dead now, but was a bishop, I think, who declared that it was impossible for any woman, past, present, or to come, to have the genius of Shakespeare. He wrote to the papers about it. He also told a lady who applied to him for information that cats do not as a matter of fact go to heaven, though they have, he added, souls of a sort. How much thinking those old gentlemen used to save one! How the borders of ignorance shrank back at their approach! Cats do not go to heaven. Women cannot write the plays of Shakespeare.

Be that as it may, I could not help thinking, as I looked at the works of Shakespeare on the shelf, that the bishop was right at least in this; it would have been impossible, completely and entirely, for any woman to

have written the plays of Shakespeare in the age of Shakespeare. Let me imagine, since facts are so hard to come by, what would have happened had Shakespeare had a wonderfully gifted sister, called Judith, let us say. Shakespeare himself went, very probably—his mother was an heiress—to the grammar school, where he may have learnt Latin—Ovid, Virgil, and Horace—and the elements of grammar and logic. He was, it is well known, a wild boy who poached rabbits, perhaps shot a deer, and had, rather sooner than he should have done, to marry a woman in the neighbourhood, who bore him a child rather quicker than was right. That escapade sent him to seek his fortune in London. He had, it seemed, a taste for the theatre; he began by holding horses at the stage door. Very soon he got work in the theatre, became a successful actor, and lived at the hub of the universe, meeting everybody, knowing everybody, practising his art on the boards, exercising his wits in the streets, and even getting access to the palace of the queen. Meanwhile his extraordinarily gifted sister, let us suppose, remained at home. She was as adventurous, as imaginative, as agog to see the world as he was. But she was not sent to school. She had no chance of learning grammar and logic, let alone of reading Horace and Virgil. She picked up a book now and then, one of her brother's perhaps, and read a few pages. But then her parents came in and told her to mend the stockings or mind the stew and not moon about with books and papers. They would have spoken sharply but kindly, for they were substantial people who knew the conditions of life for a woman and loved their daughter—indeed, more likely than not she was the apple of her father's eye. Perhaps she scribbled some pages up in an apple loft on the sly, but was careful to hide them or set fire to them. Soon, however, before she was out of her teens, she was to be betrothed to the son of a neighbouring wool-stapler.[3] She cried out that marriage was hateful to her, and for that she was severely beaten by her father. Then he ceased to scold her. He begged her instead not to hurt him, not to shame him in this matter of her marriage. He would give her a chain of beads or a fine petticoat, he said; and there were tears in his eyes. How could she disobey him? How could she break his heart?

---

[1] *Joanna Baillie* Romantic Scottish poet and dramatist (1762–1851).

[2] *Mary Russell Mitford* Poet, novelist, and playwright whose correspondence with notable authors, including Elizabeth Barrett Browning, Charles Lamb, and Harriet Martineau, provides insight into the literary world of the early nineteenth century.

[3] *wool-stapler* Dealer in wool.

The force of her own gift alone drove her to it. She made up a small parcel of her belongings, let herself down by a rope one summer's night and took the road to London. She was not seventeen. The birds that sang in the hedge were not more musical than she was. She had the quickest fancy, a gift like her brother's, for the tune of words. Like him, she had a taste for the theatre. She stood at the stage door; she wanted to act, she said. Men laughed in her face. The manager—a fat, loose-lipped man—guffawed. He bellowed something about poodles dancing and women acting[1]—no woman, he said, could possibly be an actress. He hinted—you can imagine what. She could get no training in her craft. Could she even seek her dinner in a tavern or roam the streets at midnight? Yet her genius was for fiction and lusted to feed abundantly upon the lives of men and women and the study of their ways. At last—for she was very young, oddly like Shakespeare the poet in her face, with the same grey eyes and rounded brows—at last Nick Greene the actor-manager took pity on her; she found herself with child by that gentleman and so—who shall measure the heat and violence of the poet's heart when caught and tangled in a woman's body?—killed herself one winter's night and lies buried at some cross-roads where the omnibuses now stop outside the Elephant and Castle.[2]

That, more or less, is how the story would run, I think, if a woman in Shakespeare's day had had Shakespeare's genius. But for my part, I agree with the deceased bishop, if such he was—it is unthinkable that any woman in Shakespeare's day should have had Shakespeare's genius. For genius like Shakespeare's is not born among labouring, uneducated, servile people. It was not born in England among the Saxons and the Britons. It is not born today among the working classes. How, then, could it have been born among women whose work began, according to Professor Trevelyan, almost

before they were out of the nursery, who were forced to it by their parents and held to it by all the power of law and custom? Yet genius of a sort must have existed among women as it must have existed among the working classes. Now and again an Emily Brontë or a Robert Burns blazes out and proves its presence. But certainly it never got itself on to paper. When, however, one reads of a witch being ducked, of a woman possessed by devils, of a wise woman selling herbs, or even of a very remarkable man who had a mother, then I think we are on the track of a lost novelist, a suppressed poet, of some mute and inglorious Jane Austen,[3] some Emily Brontë who dashed her brains out on the moor or mopped and mowed about the highways crazed with the torture that her gift had put her to. Indeed, I would venture to guess that Anon, who wrote so many poems without signing them, was often a woman. It was a woman Edward Fitzgerald,[4] I think, suggested who made the ballads and the folk-songs, crooning them to her children, beguiling her spinning with them, or the length of the winter's night.

This may be true or it may be false—who can say?—but what is true in it, so it seemed to me, reviewing the story of Shakespeare's sister as I had made it, is that any woman born with a great gift in the sixteenth century would certainly have gone crazed, shot herself, or ended her days in some lonely cottage outside the village, half witch, half wizard, feared and mocked at. For it needs little skill in psychology to be sure that a highly gifted girl who had tried to use her gift for poetry would have been so thwarted and hindered by other people, so tortured and pulled asunder by her own contrary instincts, that she must have lost her health and sanity to a certainty. No girl could have walked to London and stood at a stage door and forced her way into the presence of actor-managers without doing herself a violence and suffering an anguish which may have been irrational—for chastity may be a fetish invented by certain societies for unknown reasons—but were none the less inevitable. Chastity had then, it has

1 *He ... acting* Reference to Samuel Johnson's infamous statement, recorded by Boswell, that "a woman's preaching is like a dog's walking on its hinder legs. It is not done well; but you are surprised to find it done at all" (James Boswell, *Life of Samuel Johnson*, 31 July 1763).

2 *lies buried ... Castle* It was common practice to bury victims of suicide at crossroads. The Elephant and Castle was a pub located south of the Thames.

3 *some ... Austen* See Thomas Gray, "Elegy Written in a Country Church-Yard" (1751): "Some mute and inglorious Milton here may rest" (line 59).

4 *Edward Fitzgerald* Author of *The Rubáiyát of Omar Khayyám* (1859).

even now, a religious importance in a woman's life, and has so wrapped itself round with nerves and instincts that to cut it free and bring it to the light of day demands courage of the rarest. To have lived a free life in London in the sixteenth century would have meant for a woman who was poet and playwright a nervous stress and dilemma which might well have killed her. Had she survived, whatever she had written would have been twisted and deformed, issuing from a strained and morbid imagination. And undoubtedly, I thought, looking at the shelf where there are no plays by women, her work would have gone unsigned. That refuge she would have sought certainly. It was the relic of the sense of chastity that dictated anonymity to women even so late as the nineteenth century. Currer Bell, George Eliot, George Sand,[1] all the victims of inner strife as their writings prove, sought ineffectively to veil themselves by using the name of a man. Thus they did homage to the convention, which if not implanted by the other sex was liberally encouraged by them (the chief glory of a woman is not to be talked of, said Pericles,[2] himself a much-talked-of man), that publicity in women is detestable. Anonymity runs in their blood. The desire to be veiled still possesses them. They are not even now as concerned about the health of their fame as men are, and, speaking generally, will pass a tombstone or a signpost without feeling an irresistible desire to cut their names on it, as Alf, Bert, or Chas. must do in obedience to their instinct, which murmurs if it sees a fine woman go by, or even a dog, Ce chien est à moi.[3] And, of course, it may not be a dog, I thought, remembering Parliament Square, the Sièges Allée[4] and other avenues; it may be a piece of land or a man with curly black hair. It is one of the great advantages of being a woman that one can pass even a very fine negress without wishing to make an Englishwoman of her.

That woman, then, who was born with a gift of poetry in the sixteenth century, was an unhappy woman, a woman at strife against herself. All the conditions of her life, all her own instincts, were hostile to the state of mind which is needed to set free whatever is in the brain. But what is the state of mind that is most propitious to the act of creation, I asked. Can one come by any notion of the state that furthers and makes possible that strange activity? Here I opened the volume containing the Tragedies of Shakespeare. What was Shakespeare's state of mind, for instance, when he wrote *Lear* and *Antony and Cleopatra?* It was certainly the state of mind most favourable to poetry that there has ever existed. But Shakespeare himself said nothing about it. We only know casually and by chance that he "never blotted a line."[5] Nothing indeed was ever said by the artist himself about his state of mind until the eighteenth century perhaps. Rousseau[6] perhaps began it. At any rate, by the nineteenth century self-consciousness had developed so far that it was the habit for men of letters to describe their minds in confessions and autobiographies. Their lives also were written, and their letters were printed after their deaths. Thus, though we do not know what Shakespeare went through when he wrote *Lear*, we do know what Carlyle went through when he wrote the *French Revolution*; what Flaubert went through when he wrote *Madame Bovary*; what Keats was going through when he tried to write poetry against the coming of death and the indifference of the world.[7]

And one gathers from this enormous modern literature of confession and self-analysis that to write a work of genius is almost always a feat of prodigious difficulty. Everything is against the likelihood that it will come from the writer's mind whole and entire. Generally material circumstances are against it. Dogs will bark; people will interrupt; money must be made; health will break down. Further, accentuating all these difficulties and making them harder to bear is the world's notorious indifference. It does not ask people to write poems and novels and histories; it does not need them. It does not

---

[1] *Currer ... Sand*   Male pseudonyms under which female authors Charlotte Brontë, Mary Anne Evans, and Amandine Dupin published.

[2] *Pericles*   Athenian statesman (d. 429 BCE).

[3] *Ce ... moi*   French: This dog is mine.

[4] *Sièges Allée*   Victory Avenue, in Berlin.

[5] *never ... line*   Ben Jonson, *Timber:* "I remember, the players have often mentioned it as an honour to Shakespeare that in his writing (whatsoever he penned) he never blotted out a line."

[6] *Rousseau*   French philosopher Jean-Jacques Rousseau (1712–87).

[7] *we do ... world*   Philosopher Thomas Carlyle provided this autobiographical information in his *Reminiscences* (1881), while French novelist Gustave Flaubert and English Romantic poet John Keats wrote extensively about their writing experiences in their letters.

care whether Flaubert finds the right word or whether Carlyle scrupulously verifies this or that fact. Naturally, it will not pay for what it does not want. And so the writer, Keats, Flaubert, Carlyle, suffers, especially in the creative years of youth, every form of distraction and discouragement. A curse, a cry of agony, rises from those books of analysis and confession. "Mighty poets in their misery dead"[1]—that is the burden of their song. If anything comes through in spite of all this, it is a miracle, and probably no book is born entire and uncrippled as it was conceived.

But for women, I thought, looking at the empty shelves, these difficulties were infinitely more formidable. In the first place, to have a room of her own, let alone a quiet room or a sound-proof room, was out of the question, unless her parents were exceptionally rich or very noble, even up to the beginning of the nineteenth century. Since her pin money, which depended on the good will of her father, was only enough to keep her clothed, she was debarred from such alleviations as came even to Keats or Tennyson or Carlyle, all poor men, from a walking tour, a little journey to France, from the separate lodging which, even if it were miserable enough, sheltered them from the claims and tyrannies of their families. Such material difficulties were formidable; but much worse were the immaterial. The indifference of the world which Keats and Flaubert and other men of genius have found so hard to bear was in her case not indifference but hostility. The world did not say to her as it said to them, Write if you choose; it makes no difference to me. The world said with a guffaw, Write? What's the good of your writing? Here the psychologists of Newnham and Girton might come to our help, I thought, looking again at the blank spaces on the shelves. For surely it is time that the effect of discouragement upon the mind of the artist should be measured, as I have seen a dairy company measure the effect of ordinary milk and Grade A milk upon the body of the rat. They set two rats in cages side by side, and of the two one was furtive, timid, and small, and the other was glossy, bold, and big. Now what food do we feed women as artists upon? I asked, remembering, I suppose, that dinner of prunes and custard. To answer that

question I had only to open the evening paper and to read that Lord Birkenhead[2] is of opinion—but really I am not going to trouble to copy out Lord Birkenhead's opinion upon the writing of women. What Dean Inge[3] says I will leave in peace. The Harley Street[4] specialist may be allowed to rouse the echoes of Harley Street with his vociferations without raising a hair on my head. I will quote, however, Mr. Oscar Browning, because Mr. Oscar Browning was a great figure in Cambridge at one time, and used to examine the students at Girton and Newnham. Mr. Oscar Browning was wont to declare "that the impression left on his mind, after looking over any set of examination papers, was that, irrespective of the marks he might give, the best woman was intellectually the inferior of the worst man." After saying that Mr. Browning went back to his rooms—and it is this sequel that endears him and makes him a human figure of some bulk and majesty—he went back to his rooms and found a stable-boy lying on the sofa—"a mere skeleton, his cheeks were cavernous and sallow, his teeth were black, and he did not appear to have the full use of his limbs. ... 'That's Arthur' [said Mr. Browning]. 'He's a dear boy really and most high-minded.'"[5] The two pictures always seem to me to complete each other. And happily in this age of biography the two pictures often do complete each other, so that we are able to interpret the opinions of great men not only by what they say, but by what they do.

But though this is possible now, such opinions coming from the lips of important people must have been formidable enough even fifty years ago. Let us suppose that a father from the highest motives did not wish his daughter to leave home and become writer, painter or scholar. "See what Mr. Oscar Browning says," he would say; and there was not only Mr. Oscar Browning; there was the *Saturday Review*; there was Mr. Greg—the "essentials of a woman's being," said Mr.

---

[1] *Mighty ... dead* William Wordsworth, *Resolution and Independence* (1807).

[2] *Lord Birkenhead* Lord Chancellor from 1919 to 1922.

[3] *Dean Inge* Dean of St. Paul's Cathedral, London.

[4] *Harley Street* Street upon which many of the most highly regarded or fashionable medical practices were located.

[5] *Mr. Oscar Browning ... high-minded* Oscar Browning (1837–1923), history lecturer at King's College, Cambridge.

Greg[1] emphatically, "are that *they are supported by, and they minister to, men*"—there was an enormous body of masculine opinion to the effect that nothing could be expected of women intellectually. Even if her father did not read out loud these opinions, any girl could read them for herself; and the reading, even in the nineteenth century, must have lowered her vitality, and told profoundly upon her work. There would always have been that assertion—you cannot do this, you are incapable of doing that—to protest against, to overcome. Probably for a novelist this germ is no longer of much effect; for there have been women novelists of merit. But for painters it must still have some sting in it; and for musicians, I imagine, is even now active and poisonous in the extreme. The woman composer stands where the actress stood in the time of Shakespeare. Nick Greene, I thought, remembering the story I had made about Shakespeare's sister, said that a woman acting put him in mind of a dog dancing. Johnson repeated the phrase two hundred years later of women preaching. And here, I said, opening a book about music, we have the very words used again in this year of grace, 1928, of women who try to write music. "Of Mlle. Germaine Tailleferre one can only repeat Dr. Johnson's dictum concerning a woman preacher, transposed into terms of music. 'Sir, a woman's composing is like a dog's walking on his hind legs. It is not done well, but you are surprised to find it done at all.'"[2] So accurately does history repeat itself.

Thus, I concluded, shutting Mr. Oscar Browning's life and pushing away the rest, it is fairly evident that even in the nineteenth century a woman was not encouraged to be an artist. On the contrary, she was snubbed, slapped, lectured, and exhorted. Her mind must have been strained and her vitality lowered by the need of opposing this, of disproving that. For here again we come within range of that very interesting and obscure masculine complex which has had so much influence upon the woman's movement; that the deep-seated desire, not so much that *she* shall be inferior as that *he* shall be superior, which plants him wherever one looks, not only in front of the arts, but barring the way to politics too, even when the risk to himself seems infinitesimal and the suppliant humble and devoted. Even Lady Bessborough,[3] I remembered, with all her passion for politics, must humbly bow herself and write to Lord Granville Leveson-Gower: " … notwithstanding all my violence in politics and talking so much on that subject, I perfectly agree with you that no woman has any business to meddle with that or any other serious business, farther than giving her opinion (if she is ask'd)." And so she goes on to spend her enthusiasm where it meets with no obstacle whatsoever upon that immensely important subject, Lord Granville's maiden speech in the House of Commons. The spectacle is certainly a strange one, I thought. The history of men's opposition to women's emancipation is more interesting perhaps than the story of that emancipation itself. An amusing book might be made of it if some young student at Girton or Newnham would collect examples and deduce a theory—but she would need thick gloves on her hands, and bars to protect her of solid gold.

But what is amusing now, I recollected, shutting Lady Bessborough, had to be taken in desperate earnest once. Opinions that one now pastes in a book labelled cock-a-doodle-dum and keeps for reading to select audiences on summer nights once drew tears, I can assure you. Among your grandmothers and great-grandmothers there were many that wept their eyes out. Florence Nightingale shrieked aloud in her agony.[4] Moreover, it is all very well for you, who have got yourselves to college and enjoy sitting-rooms—or is it only bed-sitting-rooms?—of your own to say that genius should disregard such opinions; that genius should be above caring what is said of it. Unfortunately, it is precisely the men or women of genius who mind most what is said of them. Remember Keats. Remember the words he had cut on his tombstone.[5] Think of Tennyson; think—but I need hardly multiply instances of the undeniable, if very unfortunate, fact that it is the nature of the artist to mind excessively what is said about him.

---

1   *Mr. Greg*   Probably W.H. Greg, a well-known journalist of the era.

2   [Woolf's note]   *A Survey of Contemporary Music*, Cecil Gray, p.246.

3   *Lady Bessborough*   Henrietta Elizabeth, daughter of the first Earl Spencer, later Lady Bessborough (1761–1821). Lady Bessborough had an affair with Lord Granville.

4   [Woolf's note]   *See Cassandra*, by Florence Nightingale, printed in *The Cause*, by R. Strachey.

5   *Remember … tombstone*   "Here lies one whose name was writ in water."

Literature is strewn with the wreckage of men who have minded beyond reason the opinions of others.

And this susceptibility of theirs is doubly unfortunate, I thought, returning again to my original enquiry into what state of mind is most propitious for creative work, because the mind of an artist, in order to achieve the prodigious effort of freeing whole and entire the work that is in him, must be incandescent, like Shakespeare's mind, I conjectured, looking at the book which lay open at *Antony and Cleopatra*. There must be no obstacle in it, no foreign matter unconsumed.

For though we say that we know nothing about Shakespeare's state of mind, even as we say that, we are saying something about Shakespeare's state of mind. The reason perhaps why we know so little of Shakespeare—compared with Donne or Ben Jonson or Milton—is that his grudges and spites and antipathies are hidden from us. We are not held up by some "revelation" which reminds us of the writer. All desire to protest, to preach, to proclaim an injury, to pay off a score, to make the world the witness of some hardship or grievance was fired out of him and consumed. Therefore his poetry flows from him free and unimpeded. If ever a human being got his work expressed completely, it was Shakespeare. If ever a mind was incandescent, unimpeded, I thought, turning again to the bookcase, it was Shakespeare's mind.

—1929

from *A Sketch of the Past*[1]

—I begin: the first memory.

This was of red and purple flowers on a black ground—my mother's dress; and she was sitting either in a train or in an omnibus, and I was on her lap. I therefore saw the flowers she was wearing very close; and can still see purple and red and blue, I think, against the black; they must have been anemones, I suppose. Perhaps we were going to St. Ives;[2] more probably, for

from the light it must have been evening, we were coming back to London. But it is more convenient artistically to suppose that we were going to St. Ives, for that will lead to my other memory, which also seems to be my first memory, and in fact it is the most important of all my memories. If life has a base that it stands upon, if it is a bowl that one fills and fills and fills—then my bowl without a doubt stands upon this memory. It is of lying half asleep, half awake, in bed in the nursery at St. Ives. It is of hearing the waves breaking, one, two, one, two, and sending a splash of water over the beach; and then breaking, one, two, one, two, behind a yellow blind. It is of hearing the blind draw its little acorn[3] across the floor as the wind blew the blind out. It is of lying and hearing this splash and seeing this light, and feeling, it is almost impossible that I should be here; of feeling the purest ecstasy I can conceive.

I could spend hours trying to write that as it should be written, in order to give the feeling which is even at this moment very strong in me. But I should fail (unless I had some wonderful luck); I dare say I should only succeed in having the luck if I had begun by describing Virginia herself.

Here I come to one of the memoir writer's difficulties—one of the reasons why, though I read so many, so many are failures. They leave out the person to whom things happened. The reason is that it is so difficult to describe any human being. So they say. "This is what happened"; but they do not say what the person was like to whom it happened. And the events mean very little unless we know first to whom they happened. Who was I then? Adeline Virginia Stephen, the second daughter of Leslie and Julia Prinsep Stephen, born on 25th January 1882, descended from a great many people, some famous, others obscure; born into a large connection, born not of rich parents, but of well-to-do parents, born into a very communicative, literate, letter writing, visiting, articulate, late nineteenth century world; so that I could if I liked to take the trouble, write a great deal here not only about my mother and father but about uncles and aunts, cousins, and friends. But I do not know how much of this, or what part of this, made me feel what I felt in the nursery at St. Ives. I do not know

---

[1] *A Sketch of the Past* An essay that was published as part of *Moments of Being* (1976), a collection of Woolf's autobiographical writings the title of which has its origins in this excerpt.

[2] *St. Ives* Town in Cornwall at which Woolf's family spent holidays. It is the setting of Woolf's novel *To the Lighthouse*.

[3] *acorn* I.e., acorn-shaped bead on the end of a curtain pull.

how far I differ from other people. That is another memoir writer's difficulty. Yet to describe oneself truly one must have some standard of comparison; was I clever, stupid, good looking, ugly, passionate, cold—? Owing partly to the fact that I was never at school, never competed in any way with children of my own age, I have never been able to compare my gifts and defects with other people's. But of course there was one external reason for the intensity of this first impression: the impression of the waves and the acorn on the blind; the feeling, as I describe it sometimes to myself, of lying in a grape and seeing through a film of semi-transparent yellow—it was due partly to the many months we spent in London. The change of nursery was a great change. And there was the long train journey; and the excitement. I remember the dark; the lights; the stir of the going up to bed.

But to fix my mind upon the nursery—it had a balcony; there was a partition, but it joined the balcony of my father's and mother's bedroom. My mother would come out onto her balcony in a white dressing gown. There were passion flowers growing on the wall; they were great starry blossoms, with purple streaks, and large green buds, part empty, part full.

If I were a painter I should paint these first impressions in pale yellow, silver, and green. There was the pale yellow blind; the green sea; and the silver of the passion flowers. I should make a picture that was globular; semi-transparent. I should make a picture of curved petals; of shells; of things that were semi-transparent; I should make curved shapes, showing the light through, but not giving a clear outline. Everything would be large and dim; and what was seen would at the same time be heard; sounds would come through this petal or leaf—sounds indistinguishable from sights. Sound and sight seem to make equal parts of these first impressions. When I think of the early morning in bed I also hear the caw of rooks falling from a great height. The sound seems to fall through an elastic, gummy air; which holds it up; which prevents it from being sharp and distinct.... The rooks cawing is part of the waves breaking—one, two, one, two—and the splash as the wave drew back and then it gathered again, and I lay there half awake, half asleep, drawing in such ecstasy as I cannot describe.

The next memory—all these colour-and-sound memories hang together at St. Ives—was much more robust; it was highly sensual. It was later. It still makes me feel warm; as if everything were ripe; humming; sunny; smelling so many smells at once; and all making a whole that even now makes me stop—as I stopped then going down to the beach; I stopped at the top to look down at the gardens. They were sunk beneath the road. The apples were on a level with one's head. The gardens gave off a murmur of bees; the apples were red and gold; there were also pink flowers; and grey and silver leaves. The buzz, the croon, the smell, all seemed to press voluptuously against some membrane; not to burst it; but to hum round one such a complete rapture of pleasure that I stopped, smelt; looked. But again I cannot describe that rapture. It was rapture rather than ecstasy. ...

But the peculiarity of these two strong memories is that each was very simple. I am hardly aware of myself, but only of the sensation. I am only the container of the feeling of ecstasy, of the feeling of rapture. Perhaps this is characteristic of all childhood memories; perhaps it accounts for their strength. Later we add to feelings much that makes them more complex; and therefore less strong; or if not less strong, less isolated, less complete. But instead of analysing this, here is an instance of what I mean—my feeling about the looking-glass in the hall.

There was a small looking-glass in the hall at Talland House.[1] It had, I remember, a ledge with a brush on it. By standing on tiptoe I could see my face in the glass. When I was six or seven perhaps, I got into the habit of looking at my face in the glass. But I only did this if I was sure that I was alone. I was ashamed of it. A strong feeling of guilt seemed naturally attached to it. But why was this so? One obvious reason occurs to me—Vanessa[2] and I were both what was called tomboys; that is, we played cricket, scrambled over rocks, climbed trees, were said not to care for clothes and so on. Perhaps therefore

---

[1] *Talland House* Name of the Stephens's summer house.

[2] *Vanessa* Woolf's older sister; later Vanessa Bell.

to have been found looking in the glass would have been against our tomboy code. But I think that my feeling of shame went a great deal deeper. I am almost inclined to drag in my grandfather—Sir James, who once smoked a cigar, liked it, and so threw away his cigar and never smoked another. I am almost inclined to think that I inherited a streak of the puritan, of the Clapham Sect.[1] At any rate, the looking-glass shame has lasted all my life, long after the tomboy phase was over. I cannot now powder my nose in public. Everything to do with dress—to be fitted, to come into a room wearing a new dress—still frightens me; at least makes me shy, self-conscious, uncomfortable. "Oh to be able to run, like Julian Morrell, all over the garden in a new dress," I thought not many years ago at Garsington;[2] when Julian undid a parcel and put on a new dress and scampered round and round like a hare. Yet femininity was very strong in our family. We were famous for our beauty—my mother's beauty, Stella's[3] beauty, gave me as early as I can remember, pride and pleasure. What then gave me this feeling of shame, unless it were that I inherited some opposite instinct? My father was spartan, ascetic, puritanical. He had I think no feeling for pictures; no ear for music; no sense of the sound of words. This leads me to think that my—I would say "our" if I knew enough about Vanessa, Thoby and Adrian[4]—but how little we know even about brothers and sisters—this leads me to think that my natural love for beauty was checked by some ancestral dread. Yet this did not prevent me from feeling ecstasies and raptures spontaneously and intensely and without any shame or the least

sense of guilt, so long as they were disconnected with my own body. I thus detect another element in the shame which I had in being caught looking at myself in the glass in the hall. I must have been ashamed or afraid of my own body. Another memory, also of the hall, may help to explain this. There was a slab outside the dining room door for standing dishes upon. Once when I was very small Gerald Duckworth lifted me onto this, and as I sat there he began to explore my body. I can remember the feel of his hand going under my clothes; going firmly and steadily lower and lower. I remember how I hoped that he would stop; how I stiffened and wriggled as his hand approached my private parts. But it did not stop. His hand explored my private parts too. I remember resenting, disliking it—what is the word for so dumb and mixed a feeling? It must have been strong, since I still recall it. This seems to show that a feeling about certain parts of the body; how they must not be touched; how it is wrong to allow them to be touched; must be instinctive. It proves that Virginia Stephen was not born on the 25th January 1882, but was born many thousands of years ago; and had from the very first to encounter instincts already acquired by thousands of ancestresses in the past.

And this throws light not merely on my own case, but upon the problem that I touched on the first page; why it is so difficult to give any account of the person to whom things happen. The person is evidently immensely complicated. Witness the incident of the looking-glass. Though I have done my best to explain why I was ashamed of looking at my own face I have only been able to discover some possible reasons; there may be others; I do not suppose that I have got at the truth; yet this is a simple incident; and it happened to me personally; and I have no motive for lying about it. In spite of all this, people write what they call "lives" of other people; that is, they collect a number of events, and leave the person to whom it happened unknown. Let me add a dream; for it may refer to the incident of the looking-glass. I dreamt that I was looking in a glass when a horrible face—the face of an animal—suddenly showed over my shoulder. I cannot be sure if this was a dream, or if it happened. Was I looking in the glass one day when something in the background moved, and seemed to me alive? I cannot be sure. But I have always

[1] *Clapham Sect* Group of wealthy English social reformers based in the town of Clapham. Its members, mostly evangelical Anglicans, devoted their time and money to worthy Christian causes, primarily the abolition of slavery. Woolf's grandfather, James Stephen, married Jane Catherine Venn, whose father and grandfather, John and Henry Venn, were the rector and curate of Clapham.

[2] *Julian Morrell* The daughter of Philip Morrell, a member of Parliament, and Ottoline Morrell, prominent member of literary society; *Garsington* Morrell family home.

[3] *Stella* Stella Duckworth, Woolf's half-sister. Stella's brother Gerald is mentioned later in this paragraph.

[4] *Thoby and Adrian* Woolf's brothers.

remembered the other face in the glass, whether it was a dream or a fact, and that it frightened me.

These then are some of my first memories. But of course as an account of my life they are misleading, because the things one does not remember are as important; perhaps they are more important. If I could remember one whole day I should be able to describe, superficially at least, what life was like as a child. Unfortunately, one only remembers what is exceptional. And there seems to be no reason why one thing is exceptional and another not. Why have I forgotten so many things that must have been, one would have thought, more memorable than what I do remember? Why remember the hum of bees in the garden going down to the beach, and forget completely being thrown naked by father into the sea? (Mrs. Swanwick says she saw that happen.)[1]

This leads to a digression, which perhaps may explain a little of my own psychology; even of other people's. Often when I have been writing one of my so-called novels I have been baffled by this same problem; that is, how to describe what I call in my private shorthand—"non-being." Every day includes much more non-being than being. Yesterday for example, Tuesday the 18th of April, was it happened a good day; above the average in "being." It was fine; I enjoyed writing these first pages; my head was relieved of the pressure of writing about Roger;[2] I walked over Mount Misery[3] and along the river; and save that the tide was out, the country, which I notice very closely always, was coloured and shaded as I like—there were the willows, I remember, all plumy and soft green and purple against the blue. I also read Chaucer with pleasure; and began a book—the memoirs of Madame de la Fayette—which interested me. These separate moments of being were however embedded in many more moments of non-being. I have already forgotten what Leonard and I

talked about at lunch; and at tea; although it was a good day the goodness was embedded in a kind of nondescript cotton wool. This is always so. A great part of every day is not lived consciously. One walks, eats, sees things, deals with what has to be done; the broken vacuum cleaner; ordering dinner; writing orders to Mabel;[4] washing; cooking dinner; bookbinding. When it is a bad day the proportion of non-being is much larger. I had a slight temperature last week; almost the whole day was non-being. The real novelist can somehow convey both sorts of being. I think Jane Austen can; and Trollope; perhaps Thackeray and Dickens and Tolstoy. I have never been able to do both. I tried—in *Night and Day*; and in *The Years*. But I will leave the literary side alone for the moment.

As a child then, my days, just as they do now, contained a large proportion of this cotton wool, this non-being. Week after week passed at St. Ives and nothing made any dint upon me. Then, for no reason that I know about, there was a sudden violent shock; something happened so violently that I have remembered it all my life. I will give a few instances. The first: I was fighting with Thoby on the lawn. We were pommelling each other with our fists. Just as I raised my fist to hit him, I felt: why hurt another person? I dropped my hand instantly, and stood there, and let him beat me. I remember the feeling. It was a feeling of hopeless sadness. It was as if I became aware of something terrible; and of my own powerlessness. I slunk off alone, feeling horribly depressed. The second instance was also in the garden at St. Ives. I was looking at the flower bed by the front door; "That is the whole," I said. I was looking at a plant with a spread of leaves; and it seemed suddenly plain that the flower itself was a part of the earth; that a ring enclosed what was the flower; and that was the real flower; part earth; part flower. It was a thought I put away as being likely to be very useful to me later. The third case was also at St. Ives. Some people called Valpy had been staying at St. Ives, and had left. We were waiting at dinner one night, when somehow I overheard my father or my mother say that Mr. Valpy had killed himself. The next thing I remember is being in the garden at night and walking on the path by

[1] *Mrs. Swanwick ... happen*   In her autobiography, *I Have Been Young* (1935), Helena Sickert Swanwick, who became acquainted with Leslie Stephen at St. Ives, remembers watching "with delight his naked babies running around the beach or being towed into the sea between his legs."

[2] *Roger*   Woolf was working on *Roger Fry: A Biography*, which was published in 1940.

[3] *Mount Misery*   The nickname given to two cottages located between Piddinghow and Southease in the Ouse River valley.

[4] *Mabel*   The Woolfs's maid.

the apple tree. It seemed to me that the apple tree was connected with the horror of Mr. Valpy's suicide. I could not pass it. I stood there looking at the grey-green creases of the bark—it was a moonlit night—in a trance of horror. I seemed to be dragged down, hopelessly, into some pit of absolute despair from which I could not escape. My body seemed paralysed.

These are three instances of exceptional moments. I often tell them over, or rather they come to the surface unexpectedly. But now that for the first time I have written them down, I realise something that I have never realised before. Two of these moments ended in a state of despair. The other ended, on the contrary, in a state of satisfaction. When I said about the flower "That is the whole," I felt that I had made a discovery. I felt that I had put away in my mind something that I should go back, to turn over and explore. It strikes me now that this was a profound difference. It was the difference in the first place between despair and satisfaction. This difference I think arose from the fact that I was quite unable to deal with the pain of discovering that people hurt each other; that a man I had seen had killed himself. The sense of horror held me powerless. But in the case of the flower I found a reason; and was thus able to deal with the sensation. I was not powerless. I was conscious—if only at a distance—that I should in time explain it. I do not know if I was older when I saw the flower than I was when I had the other two experiences. I only know that many of these exceptional moments brought with them a peculiar horror and a physical collapse; they seemed dominant; myself passive. This suggests that as one gets older one has a greater power through reason to provide an explanation; and that this explanation blunts the sledge-hammer force of the blow. I think this is true, because though I still have the peculiarity that I receive these sudden shocks, they are now always welcome; after the first surprise, I always feel instantly that they are particularly valuable. And so I go on to suppose that the shock-receiving capacity is what makes me a writer. I hazard the explanation that a shock is at once in my case followed by the desire to explain it. I feel that I have had a blow; but it is not, as I thought as a child, simply a blow from an enemy hidden behind the cotton wool of daily life; it is or will become a revelation of some order; it is a token of some real thing behind appearances; and I make it real by putting it into words. It is only by putting it into words that I make it whole; this wholeness means that it has lost its power to hurt me; it gives me, perhaps because by doing so I take away the pain, a great delight to put the severed parts together. Perhaps this is the strongest pleasure known to me. It is the rapture I get when in writing I seem to be discovering what belongs to what; making a scene come right; making a character come together. From this I reach what I might call a philosophy; at any rate it is a constant idea of mine; that behind the cotton wool is hidden a pattern; that we—I mean all human beings—are connected with this; that the whole world is a work of art; that we are parts of the work of art. *Hamlet* or a Beethoven quartet is the truth about this vast mass that we call the world. But there is no Shakespeare, there is no Beethoven; certainly and emphatically there is no God; we are the words; we are the music; we are the thing itself. And I see this when I have a shock.

This intuition of mine—it is so instinctive that it seems given to me, not made by me—has certainly given its scale to my life ever since I saw the flower in the bed by the front door at St. Ives. . . .

—1979 (WRITTEN 1939–40)

IN CONTEXT

Woolf and Bloomsbury[1]

Virginia Woolf was a central figure in a group of talented and influential friends that came to be known as the "Bloomsbury Group" after the part of London in which many of them lived. In addition to Woolf and her husband Leonard, the group included Woolf's sister Vanessa Bell, historian and intellectual Lytton Strachey, economist John Maynard Keynes, artist Duncan Grant, art critic Roger Fry, and novelist E.M. Forster. On the fringes of the group were such other leading figures as T.S. Eliot; since many of the group's central figures were widely connected, the social circle that revolved around Bloomsbury was a large one. As Eliot put it after she died, Woolf "was the center not merely of an esoteric group, but of the literary life of London.…With the death of Virginia Woolf, a whole pattern of culture is broken."[2]

Vanessa Bell, *Virginia Woolf*, 1912.

---

[1] *Woolf and Bloomsbury* Unless otherwise specified, all quotations are from *Recollections of Virginia Woolf*, edited by Joan Russell Noble (1972).

[2] *was the … broken* From T.S. Eliot's obituary of Woolf in *Horizon*, May 1941, 313–16.

The Woolfs were publishers as well as writers; small though it was, Hogarth Press published several of the most important books of the era, including Eliot's *Poems*, Katherine Mansfield's *Prelude*, and the first English edition of several of Sigmund Freud's works, as well as Woolf's own fiction. One of their friends, John Lehman, has given a good sense of the press's physical operations:

> The Hogarth Press was named after Hogarth house in Richmond where [the Woolfs] were living when they began printing and publishing. In 1924 they moved to No. 52 Tavistock Square in Bloomsbury. Leonard and Virginia lived upstairs, and the activities of the Press were concentrated in the basement—a rather ramshackle basement, as was the case with any of the old Bloomsbury houses. The front room, looking on to the square, was the general office, in which there were as a rule not more than two or three girls at work, whose business it was to deal with the order, make out the invoices, pack up the books and handle the general correspondence. Leading out of the basement front room was a longish, dark corridor, piled with binders' packets of recently published books. On one side was the former scullery, in which Leonard had installed the treadle[1] printing press, still used for occasional small and special books.

Of Woolf herself, many have left vivid recollections—many of them touching on the strong sense of *joie de vivre* that she often radiated. In the context of the frequent depression that she experienced this may seem surprising, but the accounts are too numerous to be doubted. For Clive Bell, a sense of fun is the most lasting impression left by Woolf:[2]

> Writing was her passion and her joy and her poison. Yet, I repeat, hers was a happy nature. … My children, from the time they were old enough to enjoy anything beyond their animal satisfactions, enjoyed beyond anything a visit from Virginia: "Virginia's coming, what fun we shall have." That is what they said and felt when they were children and went on saying and feeling to the end. And so said all of us. So said everyone who knew her. … She might be divinely witty or outrageously fanciful; she might retail village gossip or tell stories of her London friends; always she was indescribably entertaining.

Bell also speaks of how Woolf sometimes "grew angry and lashed out" when she suspected she was being condescended to. She often felt resentful of "the way in which men, as she thought, patronized women, especially women who were attempting to create works of art or succeed in what were once considered manly professions. Assuredly Virginia did not wish to be a man, or to be treated as a man: she wished to be treated as an equal—just possibly as a superior."

Others describe a similar mixture in Woolf's personality. According to the novelist Elizabeth Bowen, Woolf could be "awfully naughty," even "fiendish." "She could say things about people, all in a flash, which remained with one. Fleetingly malicious, rather than outright cruel." Bowen also recalled a streak of superciliousness: "I was reminded sometimes of 'The Lord thy God is a jealous God: Thou shalt have no other God but me.' There was a touch of that about her." But, like Bell, Bowen recalls more strongly her exuberant and joyful spirit: "I was aware, one could not but be aware, of an undertow often of sadness, of melancholy, of great fear. But the main impression was of a creature of laughter and movement. … And her laughter was entrancing, it was outrageous laughter, almost like a child's laughter." Bowen has also likened Woolf's inquisitiveness to that of a child:

---

1   *treadle*   Lever worked by the foot.
2   *Clive Bell … Woolf*   All Clive Bell's recollections are from his *Old Friends: Personal Recollections* (1956).

She wanted to know all the details of people's lives.… She would say to anybody, to me, or anyone to whom she was talking, "Now what did you do, *exactly* what did you do? … You say you went to a party, where was it, who was there, what were they wearing?" Or, "You walked down the street, now *why* did you walk down the street? Who were you with? What did you see? Did you see a cat, did you see a dog?" It was that sort of inquisitiveness—almost childish. I never knew her to probe *deeply* into anything, and I don't know whether she really took much interest in people's affairs of the heart or not. … Past a point, her own imagination took over.

Bowen is one of many to have remarked on Woolf's intensity as a writer; another is E.M. Forster. As he put it when comparing her to many of her contemporaries, "she liked writing with an intensity which few writers have attained or desired":

Most of them write with half an eye on their royalties, half an eye on their critics, and a third half eye on improving the world, which leaves them with only half an eye for the task on which she concentrated her entire vision. She would not look elsewhere, and her circumstances combined with her temperament to focus her. Money she had not to consider, because she possessed a private income, and though financial independence is not always a safeguard against commercialism, it was in her case.

Anonymous, *Virginia Woolf and T.S. Eliot*, 1920s.

Even those who were not always sympathetic to Woolf or to Bloomsbury recognized that her approach both to those around her and to the craft of writing was in many respects extraordinary. The poet Stephen Spender was among those who sniped at Bloomsbury, calling it a "clique" rather than a group, and suggesting that Woolf "moved in a very limited social world." Yet even he felt obliged to remark on the "undiluted purity of one of those uncorrupted natures which seem set aside from the world for a special task by a strange conjunction of fortune and misfortune."[1] With Woolf, he ventured, "style, form, and material are indivisible."

---

[1] *undiluted ... misfortune* This and the following quotation are from Stephen Spender's obituary of Woolf in the *Listener*, 10 April 1941, 533.

JAMES JOYCE

1882 – 1941

Irish novelist James Joyce's prose style and subject matter were so innovative and influential that fellow writer T.S. Eliot was prompted to declare that Joyce had helped to make "the modern world possible for art" by discovering "a way of controlling, or ordering, of giving a shape and a significance to the panorama of futility and anarchy which is contemporary history." Joyce's works as a whole redefined realism as they sought to access reality as perceived by the mind—whether awake or dreaming. Although throughout his life Joyce battled publishers, critics, and readers who objected to his frank treatment of the more "vulgar" aspects of his characters' thoughts and actions, Joyce became a literary figure of the first magnitude during his lifetime, and has remained so since.

James Augustus Aloysius Joyce was born in the middle-class Dublin suburb of Rathgar and was the first surviving son in a family of twelve siblings. Through his father's fecklessness, Joyce's family situation would eventually devolve into poverty. John Joyce's increasing dependence on alcohol created strains both on the family's finances and on its morale. On the other hand, Joyce's mother, Mary Jane Joyce, exposed the young Joyce to the arts and to religion, as she was both accomplished in music and devout in her Catholicism. The former he would embrace with as much fervor as he rejected the latter.

At the age of 6, Joyce started his studies under the tutorship of the Jesuits. During the course of his schooling, however, he became increasingly cynical about the Church. His intellectual and spiritual rebelliousness grew so that by the time he entered university he had begun to believe that religion, family, and nation were all traps of conventionality that the true artist must avoid.

While at University College, Joyce attempted to write poetry and enjoyed writing articles parodying various literary styles. A penchant for experimentation with form stayed with him, from the economy of voice exhibited in *Dubliners*, to the variety of narrative expressions created for *A Portrait of the Artist as a Young Man* and *Ulysses*, to the radical linguistic experimentation of *Finnegans Wake*. In political matters, he rejected the single-minded nationalism of his peers and wrote outspoken articles that were published privately after the school advisory board barred publication in the school newspaper. Meanwhile, he was very successful in his chosen field of study—modern languages.

Joyce originally moved to Paris in 1902 to study medicine, but it was not until about 1904 that he took up his artistic mission in earnest and decided to leave Ireland. Apart from some brief periods, Joyce remained an exile from the country about which he would spend his life writing. For Joyce, exile was a prerequisite for artistic objectivity and freedom; he believed that his self-imposed exile allowed him to see the truth of Ireland and Irishness with clarity, precision, and detachment.

In June 1904, Joyce was invited by the paper *The Irish Homestead* to submit a short story. In the end he wrote a series of fifteen stories that were published in 1914 under the title *Dubliners*. Along the way Joyce had a series of arguments with publishers that would also dog and delay the publication of *A Portrait of the Artist as a Young Man*, as editors objected to what they saw as the inappropriate subject matter and language of his work. In 1909, he wrote to London publisher Grant Richards, with whom he was in negotiations for *Dubliners*, "I seriously believe that you will retard the course of civilization in Ireland by preventing the Irish people from having one good look at themselves in my nicely polished looking-glass." Richards, however, was in no financial position to advance the course of Irish civilization, and the book was rejected, not to be published until 1914.

Joyce described *Dubliners* as "a chapter of the moral history of my country." The book is divided—according to a letter Joyce wrote to his publisher—into four sections, representing childhood, adolescence, maturity, and public life. The fifteenth story, "The Dead," was not part of Joyce's original manuscript. This story, the longest in the collection, became the showpiece of the book upon its publication. Thematically, each of the stories in *Dubliners* deals with the lives of ordinary people, many of whom suffer from a sort of emotional paralysis—as a result of internal or external forces or moral decay—that makes them unable to move forward.

Many of these stories have as their focus a moment of self-recognition on the part of a character, a moment Joyce referred to as an "epiphany." The triggers to an epiphany are often accidental, "little errors and gestures—mere straws in the wind," as Joyce described them in a letter to his brother Stanislaus. The sharp focus allowed by a sudden flash of clarity is fleeting but allows characters a moment in which to see above their particular circumstances.

In 1904 Joyce also met the woman who would be his lifelong partner. As legend has it, it was on 16 June, or "Bloomsday" (the day on which the events in *Ulysses* take place), that James Joyce first went out walking with Nora Barnacle, a chambermaid from Galway. Uninterested in literature, but with a fresh charm and wit and, like Joyce, an interest in music, she followed Joyce to the city of Pola, in the Austro-Hungarian Empire, four months after their meeting. They lived there a short time, without the sanction of marriage, and later moved to Trieste, Italy, where Joyce continued to write and eked out a meager living teaching English. The couple produced two children, Lucia and Georgio, and ultimately married, in 1931.

During their time in Trieste, in the fall of 1907, Joyce started editing, cutting, and reshaping the almost 1,000 pages of *Stephen Hero*, a novel he had begun in 1904. The result would be *A Portrait of the Artist as a Young Man*, on which Joyce continued to work intermittently for the next nine years. The novel-in-progress began to be published serially in *The Egoist* in 1914. It was not published as a volume until 1916, by the New York publisher B.W. Huebsch. It had been rejected by every London publisher to whom Joyce had sent it, despite the support of some major literary figures of the day, including W.B. Yeats, H.G. Wells, and Ezra Pound.

The hero of *Portrait*, Stephen Dedalus, bears a striking similarity to Joyce himself. The novel details the artistic growth of a writer, from childhood to the age of twenty, and outlines Joyce's artistic mission in life: to "record ... with extreme care" epiphanic moments of sublime self-awareness; it also extends Joyce's experiments with style. The voice of the implied narrator changes and develops in correspondence with the development of the central character.

Ulysses details a day in Dublin life. Events in the novel follow the comings and goings of Stephen Dedalus, continuing the artistic journey on which Joyce set him in *A Portrait of the Artist as a Young Man*, and Leo Bloom, the Jewish-Irish Everyman who is the hero of the novel. *Ulysses* takes as its model Homer's *Odyssey*; an everyday journey through the neighborhoods of Dublin becomes highly symbolic as Leo Bloom follows a path that parallels that of Homer's hero. Meanwhile, Stephen Dedalus plays the role of Homer's Telemachus; Joyce imagines him an artist and visionary cut off from society. Joyce believed that Odysseus was perhaps the most well-rounded character in Western literature, embodying the best and the worst in human behavior: he was both brave and cowardly, a liar and an intellectual. Joyce's endeavors to portray these traits in his hero make Leo Bloom one of the most warmly compelling characters in all of twentieth-century literature.

In form, each chapter is an ironic rewriting of a chapter from Homer's *Odyssey*, and is written in a broadly different literary style from the one that precedes it. The novel adopts a stream-of-consciousness approach that makes little or no distinction between what is happening externally and what takes place in a character's mind. Perspectives move fluidly from internal to external dialogue, from character to character, and from event to event, with little to indicate the change. The novel's central themes are those that recur in Joyce's work: the inner life of Dublin in all its beauty and hollowness, and the outsider status of Leo Bloom (because of his Jewishness) and Stephen Dedalus (because of his artistic mission). This shared experience of Leo and Stephen, and Stephen's figurative search for an absent father, link the two thematically throughout the story.

Ulysses began to be published serially in the *Little Review* beginning in 1918, but in 1920 publication ceased in the face of obscenity charges. Not until 1922 was *Ulysses* published, and even then it was printed in Paris, not Britain. An American edition was published in 1934, after a landmark court case decided the book was not pornography. The weary judge at the time acquiesced to the view that the book was a work of art, even if many readers would not understand it. A British edition of *Ulysses* finally appeared in 1937.

It was not until about 1920 that the Joyce family began to attain a modest level of financial security, largely the result of the support and patronage of a number of people who had as much faith in Joyce's genius as he himself did. The family moved from Trieste to Zurich in 1914, then to Paris in 1920, then back to Zurich in 1940, where Joyce died of a perforated ulcer, just after seeing the publication of his final—and perhaps least understood—novel, *Finnegans Wake* (1939). In stylistic terms, the novel goes beyond the playful, self-conscious mode of *Ulysses* and enters a far more obscure territory. The title refers to a common folk song in which a laborer, Finnegan, falls and hits his head. His friends assume he is dead and hold a wake for him; he finally awakens after having whiskey spilled on him. *Finnegans Wake* is ostensibly the dream of Finnegan's successor, a Dublin Everyman with the initials H.C.E. (which stand for a variety of names, including Humphrey Chimpden Earwicker and Here Comes Everybody), and also features H.C.E.'s wife, A.L.P. (Anna Livia Plurabelle, Amnis Limina Permanent) and their twin sons, Shem and Shaun. Everything that occurs, and all the characters present, belong at least partially to the realm of dream. The novel's form relies on the cyclical view of history set out by Italian philosopher Giambattista Vico. The narrative is largely composed of multi-leveled puns that are fraught with symbolic meaning. Joyce used elements of English and seven other languages to create the texture of the novel, reinventing not just the form of the novel but the structure of language itself in order to escape the stifling traditions in which he felt conventional language was steeped.

During his lifetime Joyce promised his writing would "keep the professors busy," and in this he has succeeded, and continues to succeed, to an extent that even he might not have expected. For many years scholars were occupied with historical, cultural, and anthropological research into the background of Joyce's Dublin. While this research continues, developments in critical theory (such as postcolonialism) have also opened up many new ways to interpret Joyce's texts. During his lifetime much of his work was, as one of Joyce's friends said, "outside of literature"; "literature" has since shifted to accommodate Joyce.

⌘ ⌘ ⌘

Araby[1]

North Richmond Street, being blind,[2] was a quiet street except at the hour when the Christian Brothers' School set the boys free. An uninhabited house of two storeys stood at the blind end, detached from its neighbours in a square ground. The other houses of the street, conscious of decent lives within them, gazed at one another with brown imperturbable faces.

The former tenant of our house, a priest, had died in the back drawingroom. Air, musty from having been long enclosed, hung in all the rooms and the waste room behind the kitchen was littered with old useless papers. Among these I found a few papercovered books, the pages of which were curled and damp: *The Abbot* by Walter Scott, *The Devout Communicant* and *The Memoirs of Vidocq*.[3] I liked the last best because its leaves were yellow. The wild garden behind the house contained a central apple tree and a few straggling bushes under one of which I found the late tenant's rusty bicycle pump. He had been a very charitable priest; in his will he had left all his money to institutions and the furniture of his house to his sister.

When the short days of winter came dusk fell before we had well eaten our dinners. When we met in the street the houses had grown sombre. The space of sky above us was the colour of everchanging violet and towards it the lamps of the street lifted their feeble lanterns. The cold air stung us and we played till our bodies glowed. Our shouts echoed in the silent street. The career of our play brought us through the dark muddy lanes behind the houses where we ran the gantlet of the rough tribes from the cottages, to the back doors of the dark dripping gardens where odours arose from the ashpits, to the dark odorous stables where a coachman smoothed and combed the horse or shook music from the buckled harness. When we returned to the street light from the kitchen windows had filled the

areas.[4] If my uncle was seen turning the corner we hid in the shadow until we had seen him safely housed. Or if Mangan's sister came out on the doorstep to call her brother in to his tea we watched her from our shadow peer up and down the street. We waited to see whether she would remain or go in and if she remained we left our shadow and walked up to Mangan's steps resignedly. She was waiting for us, her figure defined by the light from the half-opened door. Her brother always teased her before he obeyed and I stood by the railings looking at her. Her dress swung as she moved her body and the soft rope of her hair tossed from side to side.

Every morning I lay on the floor in the front parlour watching her door. The blind was pulled down to within an inch of the sash so that I could not be seen. When she came out on the doorstep my heart leaped. I ran to the hall, seized my books and followed her. I kept her brown figure always in my eye and when we came near the point at which our ways diverged I quickened my pace and passed her. This happened morning after morning. I had never spoken to her except for a few casual words and yet her name was like a summons to all my foolish blood.

Her image accompanied me even in places the most hostile to romance. On Saturday evenings when my aunt went marketing I had to go to carry some of the parcels. We walked through the flaring streets, jostled by drunken men and bargaining women, amid the curses of labourers, the shrill litanies of shop boys who stood on guard by the barrels of pigs' cheeks, the nasal chanting of street singers who sang a *come-all-you* about O'Donovan Rossa[5] or a ballad about the troubles in our native land. These noises converged in a single sensation of life for me: I imagined that I bore my chalice safely through a throng of foes. Her name sprang to my lips at moments in strange prayers and praises which I myself did not understand. My eyes were often full of tears (I could not tell why) and at times a flood from my heart seemed to pour itself out into my bosom. I thought little

---

[1] *Araby* Charity bazaar held in Dublin in 1894.

[2] *blind* A dead end.

[3] *The Devout Communicant* Catholic religious manual published in 1831; *The Memoirs of Vidocq* Written by François-Eugène Vidocq (1775–1857), a career criminal who was appointed chief of a French detective force.

[4] *areas* Spaces between the railings and the fronts of houses, below street level.

[5] *come-all-you* Ballad (so called because many ballads started with this phrase); *O'Donovan Rossa* Jeremiah Donovan, Irish nationalist who was sentenced to a lifetime of penal servitude but was granted amnesty and departed for America.

of the future. I did not know whether I would ever speak to her or not or, if I spoke to her, how I could tell her of my confused adoration. But my body was like a harp and her words and gestures were like fingers running upon the wires.

One evening I went into the back drawingroom in which the priest had died. It was a dark rainy evening and there was no sound in the house. Through one of the broken panes I heard the rain impinge upon the earth, the fine incessant needles of water playing in the sodden beds. Some distant lamp or lighted window gleamed below me. I was thankful that I could see so little. All my senses seemed to desire to veil themselves and, feeling that I was about to slip from them, I pressed the palms of my hands together until they trembled, murmuring: *O love! O love!* many times.

At last she spoke to me. When she addressed the first words to me I was so confused that I did not know what to answer. She asked me was I going to *Araby*. I forget whether I answered yes or no. It would be a splendid bazaar, she said; she would love to go.

—And why can't you? I asked.

While she spoke she turned a silver bracelet round and round her wrist. She could not go, she said, because there would be a retreat that week in her convent.[1] Her brother and two other boys were fighting for their caps and I was alone at the railings. She held one of the spikes, bowing her head towards me. The light from the lamp opposite our door caught the white curve of her neck, lit up the hair that rested there and, falling, lit up the hand upon the railing. It fell over one side of her dress and caught the white border of a petticoat, just visible as she stood at ease.

—It's well for you, she said.

—If I go, I said, I will bring you something.

What innumerable follies laid waste my waking and sleeping thoughts after that evening! I wished to annihilate the tedious intervening days. I chafed against the work of school. At night in my bedroom and by day in the classroom her image came between me and the page I strove to read. The syllables of the word *Araby* were called to me through the silence in which my soul luxuriated and cast an eastern enchantment over me. I

asked for leave to go to the bazaar on Saturday night. My aunt was surprised and hoped it was not some freemason affair.[2] I answered few questions in class. I watched my master's face pass from amiability to sternness; he hoped I was not beginning to idle. I could not call my wandering thoughts together. I had hardly any patience with the serious work of life which, now that it stood between me and my desire, seemed to me child's play, ugly monotonous child's play.

On Saturday morning I reminded my uncle that I wished to go to the bazaar in the evening. He was fussing at the hallstand, looking for the hatbrush, and answered me curtly:

—Yes, boy, I know.

As he was in the hall I could not go into the front parlour and lie at the window. I left the house in bad humour and walked slowly towards the school. The air was pitilessly raw and already my heart misgave me.

When I came home to dinner my uncle had not yet been home. Still it was early. I sat staring at the clock for some time and when its ticking began to irritate me I left the room. I mounted the staircase and gained the upper part of the house. The high cold empty gloomy rooms liberated me and I went from room to room singing. From the front window I saw my companions playing below in the street. Their cries reached me weakened and indistinct and, leaning my forehead against the cool glass, I looked over at the dark house where she lived. I may have stood there for an hour seeing nothing but the brownclad figure cast by my imagination, touched discreetly by the lamplight at the curved neck, at the hand upon the railings and at the border below the dress.

When I came downstairs again I found Mrs. Mercer sitting at the fire. She was an old garrulous woman, a pawnbroker's widow who collected used stamps for some pious purpose. I had to endure the gossip of the teatable. The meal was prolonged beyond an hour and still my uncle did not come. Mrs. Mercer stood up to go: she was sorry she couldn't wait any longer but it was

---

[1]   *convent*   I.e., convent school.

[2]   *freemason affair*   Affiliated with the Freemasons, a secret society originally made up of skilled stone-workers. The society was said to be anti-Catholic, and the Archbishop of Dublin had decreed that any Catholics caught at a freemason bazaar could be excommunicated.

after eight o'clock and she did not like to be out late as the night air was bad for her. When she had gone I began to walk up and down the room, clenching my fists. My aunt said:

—I'm afraid you may put off your bazaar for this night of Our Lord.

At nine o'clock I heard my uncle's latchkey in the halldoor. I heard him talking to himself and heard the hallstand rocking when it had received the weight of his overcoat. I could interpret these signs. When he was midway through his dinner I asked him to give me the money to go to the bazaar. He had forgotten.

—The people are in bed and after their first sleep now, he said.

I did not smile. My aunt said to him energetically:

—Can't you give him the money and let him go? You've kept him late enough as it is.

My uncle said he was very sorry he had forgotten. He said he believed in the old saying: *All work and no play makes Jack a dull boy.* He asked me where I was going and when I had told him a second time he asked me did I know *The Arab's Farewell to his Steed.*[1] When I left the kitchen he was about to recite the opening lines of the piece to my aunt.

I held a florin tightly in my hand as I strode down Buckingham Street towards the station. The sight of the streets thronged with buyers and glaring with gas recalled to me the purpose of my journey. I took my seat in a third class carriage of a deserted train. After an intolerable delay the train moved out of the station slowly. It crept onward among ruinous houses and over the twinkling river. At Westland Row Station a crowd of people pressed at the carriage doors; but the porters moved them back, saying that it was a special train for the bazaar. I remained alone in the bare carriage. In a few minutes the train drew up beside an improvised wooden platform. I passed out on to the road and saw by the lighted dial of a clock that it was ten minutes to ten. In front of me was a large building which displayed the magical name.

I could not find any sixpenny entrance and, fearing that the bazaar would be closed, I passed in quickly through a turnstile, handing a shilling to a wearylooking man. I found myself in a big hall girdled at half its height by a gallery. Nearly all the stalls were closed and the greater part of the hall was in darkness. I recognised a silence like that which pervades a church after a service. I walked into the centre of the bazaar timidly. A few people were gathered about the stalls which were still open. Before a curtain over which the words *Café Chantant*[2] were written in coloured lamps two men were counting money on a salver. I listened to the fall of the coins.

Remembering with difficulty why I had come I went over to one of the stalls and examined porcelain vases and flowered teasets. At the door of the stall a young lady was talking and laughing with two young gentlemen. I remarked their English accents and listened vaguely to their conversation.

—O, I never said such a thing!

—O, but you did!

—O, but I didn't!

—Didn't she say that?

—She did. I heard her.

—O, there's a … fib!

Observing me the young lady came over and asked me did I wish to buy anything. The tone of her voice was not encouraging: she seemed to have spoken to me out of a sense of duty. I looked humbly at the great jars that stood like eastern guards at either side of the dark entrance to her stall and murmured:

—No, thank you.

The young lady changed the position of one of the vases and went back to the two young men. They began to talk of the same subject. Once or twice the young lady glanced at me over her shoulder.

I lingered before her stall, though I knew my stay was useless, to make my interest in her wares seem the more real. Then I turned away slowly and walked down the middle of the bazaar. I allowed the two pennies to fall against the sixpence in my pocket. I heard a voice call from one end of the gallery that the light was out. The upper part of the hall was now completely dark.

Gazing up into the darkness I saw myself as a creature driven and derided by vanity: and my eyes burned with anguish and anger.

—1914

---

[1] *The Arab's … Steed* Popular romantic poem by Caroline Norton (1808–77).

[2] *Café Chantant* Café that provides musical entertainment.

Eveline

She sat at the window watching the evening invade the avenue. Her head was leaned against the window curtains and in her nostrils was the odour of dusty cretonne.[1] She was tired.

Few people passed. The man out of the last house passed on his way home; she heard his footsteps clacking along the concrete pavement and afterwards crunching on the cinder path before the new red houses. One time there used to be a field there in which they used to play every evening with other people's children. Then a man from Belfast bought the field and built houses in it—not like their little brown houses but bright brick houses with shining roofs. The children of the avenue used to play together in that field—the Devines, the Waters, the Dunns, little Keogh the cripple, she and her brothers and sisters. Ernest, however, never played: he was too grown up. Her father used often to hunt them in out of the field with his blackthorn stick but usually little Keogh used to keep nix[2] and call out when he saw her father coming. Still they seemed to have been rather happy then. Her father was not so bad then, and besides her mother was alive. That was a long time ago; she and her brothers and sisters were all grown up; her mother was dead. Tizzie Dunn was dead, too, and the Waters had gone back to England. Everything changes. Now she was going to go away like the others, to leave her home.

Home! She looked round the room reviewing all its familiar objects which she had dusted once a week for so many years, wondering where on earth all the dust came from. Perhaps she would never see again those familiar objects from which she had never dreamed of being divided. And yet during all those years she had never found out the name of the priest whose yellowing photograph hung on the wall above the broken harmonium[3] beside the coloured print of the promises made to Blessed Margaret Mary Alacoque.[4] He had been a school friend of her father's. Whenever he showed the photograph to a visitor her father used to pass it with a casual word:

—He is in Melbourne now.

She had consented to go away, to leave her home. Was that wise? She tried to weigh each side of the question. In her home anyway she had shelter and food; she had those whom she had known all her life about her. Of course she had to work hard both in the house and at business. What would they say of her in the stores when they found out that she had run away with a fellow? Say she was a fool, perhaps; and her place would be filled up by advertisement. Miss Gavan would be glad. She had always had an edge on her, especially whenever there were people listening.

—Miss Hill, don't you see these ladies are waiting?

—Look lively, Miss Hill, please.

She would not cry many tears at leaving the stores.

But in her new home, in a distant unknown country, it would not be like that. Then she would be married—she, Eveline. People would treat her with respect then. She would not be treated as her mother had been. Even now, though she was over nineteen, she sometimes felt herself in danger of her father's violence. She knew it was that that had given her the palpitations. When they were growing up he had never gone for her, like he used to go for Harry and Ernest, because she was a girl; but latterly he had begun to threaten her and say what he would do to her only for her dead mother's sake. And now she had nobody to protect her. Ernest was dead and Harry, who was in the church decorating business, was nearly always down somewhere in the country. Besides, the invariable squabble for money on Saturday nights had begun to weary her unspeakably. She always gave her entire wages—seven shillings—and Harry always sent up what he could but the trouble was to get any money from her father. He said she used to

1 *cretonne* Thick, unglazed, cotton fabric often used for chair covers and curtains.

2 *keep nix* Keep watch.

3 *harmonium* Type of reed organ.

4 *Blessed Margaret Mary Alacoque* Seventeenth-century French nun whose devotion led her to perform extreme acts of penance, such as drinking water in which laundry had been washed and carving the name of Jesus into her chest.

squander the money, that she had no head, that he wasn't going to give her his hard earned money to throw about the streets and much more for he was usually fairly bad of a Saturday night. In the end he would give her the money and ask her had she any intention of buying Sunday's dinner. Then she had to rush out as quickly as she could and do her marketing, holding her black leather purse tightly in her hand as she elbowed her way through the crowds and returning home late under her load of provisions. She had hard work to keep the house together and to see that the two young children who had been left to her charge went to school regularly and got their meals regularly. It was hard work—a hard life—but now that she was about to leave it she did not find it a wholly undesirable life.

She was about to explore another life with Frank. Frank was very kind, manly, openhearted. She was to go away with him by the night boat to be his wife and to live with him in Buenos Ayres where he had a home waiting for her. How well she remembered the first time she had seen him; he was lodging in a house on the main road where she used to visit. It seemed a few weeks ago. He was standing at the gate, his peaked cap pushed back on his head and his hair tumbled forward over a face of bronze. Then they had come to know each other. He used to meet her outside the stores every evening and see her home. He took her to see the *Bohemian Girl*[1] and she felt elated as she sat in an unaccustomed part of the theatre with him. He was awfully fond of music and sang a little. People knew that they were courting and when he sang about the lass that loves a sailor she always felt pleasantly confused. He used to call her Poppens out of fun. First of all it had been an excitement for her to have a fellow and then she had begun to like him. He had tales of distant countries. He had started as a deck boy at a pound a month on a ship of the Allan line[2] going out to Canada. He told her the names of the ships he had been on and the names of the different services. He had sailed through the Straits of

Magellan and he told her stories of the terrible Patagonians.[3] He had fallen on his feet in Buenos Ayres, he said, and had come over to the old country just for a holiday. Of course, her father had found out the affair and had forbidden her to have anything to say to him:

—I know these sailor chaps, he said.

One day he had quarrelled with Frank and after that she had to meet her lover secretly.

The evening deepened in the avenue. The white of two letters in her lap grew indistinct. One was to Harry, the other was to her father. Ernest had been her favourite but she liked Harry too. Her father was becoming old lately, she noticed; he would miss her. Sometimes he could be very nice. Not long before, when she had been laid up for a day, he had read her out a ghost story and made toast for her at the fire. Another day, when their mother was alive, they had all gone for a picnic to the Hill of Howth.[4] She remembered her father putting on her mother's bonnet to make the children laugh.

Her time was running out but she continued to sit by the window, leaning her head against the window curtain, inhaling the odour of dusty cretonne. Down far in the avenue she could hear a street organ playing. She knew the air. Strange that it should come that very night to remind her of the promise to her mother, her promise to keep the home together as long as she could. She remembered the last night of her mother's illness; she was again in the close dark room at the other side of the hall and outside she heard a melancholy air of Italy. The organ player had been ordered to go away and given sixpence. She remembered her father strutting back into the sickroom saying:

—Damned Italians! coming over here!

As she mused the pitiful vision of her mother's life laid its spell on the very quick of her being—that life of commonplace sacrifices closing in final craziness. She trembled as she heard again her mother's voice saying constantly with foolish insistence:

---

[1] *Bohemian Girl* 1843 opera by Dubliner Michael Balfe (1808–70).

[2] *the Allan line* The Allan Steamship Company, founded in 1852 by Sir Hugh Allan, made weekly departures from Liverpool to the Western coast of Canada (with stops along the way, including at Cape Horn and Buenos Aires).

[3] *the terrible Patagonians* Refers either to the strong, unpredictable Patagonian winds in the Strait of Magellan, or to a group of South American natives that early explorers had claimed were giants. By the beginning of the nineteenth century, this rumor was discredited.

[4] *Hill of Howth* Located northeast of Dublin, on the Howth peninsula.

—Derevaun Seraun! Derevaun Seraun![1]

She stood up in a sudden impulse of terror. Escape! She must escape! Frank would save her. He would give her life, perhaps love too. But she wanted to live. Why should she be unhappy? She had a right to happiness. Frank would take her in his arms, fold her in his arms. He would save her.

She stood among the swaying crowd in the station at the North Wall. He held her hand and she knew that he was speaking to her, saying something about the passage over and over again. The station was full of soldiers with brown baggages. Through the wide doors of the sheds she caught a glimpse of the black mass of the boat lying in beside the quay wall, with illumined portholes. She answered nothing. She felt her cheek pale and cold and out of a maze of distress she prayed to God to direct her, to show her what was her duty. The boat blew a long mournful whistle into the mist. If she went, tomorrow she would be on the sea with Frank, steaming towards Buenos Ayres. Their passage had been booked. Could she still draw back after all he had done for her? Her distress awoke a nausea in her body and she kept moving her lips in silent fervent prayer.

A bell clanged upon her heart. She felt him seize her hand:

—Come!

All the seas of the world tumbled about her heart. He was drawing her into them: he would drown her. She gripped with both hands at the iron railing.

—Come!

No! No! No! It was impossible. Her hands clutched the iron in frenzy. Amid the seas she sent a cry of anguish.

—Eveline! Evvy!

He rushed beyond the barrier and called to her to follow. He was shouted at to go on but he still called to her. She set her white face to him, passive, like a helpless animal. Her eyes gave him no sign of love or farewell or recognition.

—1914

---

[1] *Derevaun Seraun* The meaning of this phrase, if there is one, is uncertain. While some scholars believe it to be garbled Irish, others assert it is gibberish.

The Dead

Lily, the caretaker's daughter, was literally run off her feet. Hardly had she brought one gentleman into the little pantry behind the office on the ground floor and helped him off with his overcoat when the wheezy hall-door bell clanged again and she had to scamper along the bare hallway to let in another guest. It was well for her she had not to attend to the ladies also. But Miss Kate and Miss Julia had thought of that and had converted the bathroom upstairs into a ladies' dressing-room. Miss Kate and Miss Julia were there, gossiping and laughing and fussing, walking after each other to the head of the stairs, peering down over the banisters and calling down to Lily to ask her who had come.

It was always a great affair, the Misses Morkan's annual dance. Everybody who knew them came to it, members of the family, old friends of the family, the members of Julia's choir, any of Kate's pupils that were grown up enough and even some of Mary Jane's pupils too. Never once had it fallen flat. For years and years it had gone off in splendid style as long as anyone could remember, ever since Kate and Julia, after the death of their brother Pat, had left the house in Stony Batter and taken Mary Jane, their only niece, to live with them in the dark gaunt house on Usher's Island, the upper part of which they had rented from Mr. Fullam, the corn factor[2] on the ground floor. That was a good thirty years ago if it was a day. Mary Jane, who was then a little girl in short clothes, was now the main prop of the household for she had the organ in Haddington Road. She had been through the academy[3] and gave a pupils' concert every year in the upper room of the Antient Concert Rooms. Many of her pupils belonged to better class families on the Kingstown and Dalkey line. Old as they were, her aunts also did their share. Julia, though she was quite grey, was still the leading soprano in Adam and Eve's[4] and Kate, being too feeble to go about much, gave music lessons to beginners on the old square piano in the back room. Lily, the caretaker's daughter, did housemaid work for them. Though their life was modest

---

[2] *corn factor* Grain merchant.

[3] *the academy* Royal Irish Academy of Music.

[4] *Adam and Eve's* Roman Catholic church in Dublin.

they believed in eating well, the best of everything: diamond bone sirloins, three shilling tea and the best bottled stout. But Lily seldom made a mistake in the orders so that she got on well with her three mistresses. They were fussy, that was all. But the only thing they would not stand was back answers.[1]

Of course they had good reason to be fussy on such a night. And then it was long after ten o'clock and yet there was no sign of Gabriel and his wife. Besides they were dreadfully afraid that Freddy Malins might turn up screwed.[2] They would not wish for worlds that any of Mary Jane's pupils should see him under the influence: and when he was like that it was sometimes very hard to manage him. Freddy Malins always came late but they wondered what could be keeping Gabriel: and that was what brought them every two minutes to the banisters to ask Lily had Gabriel or Freddy come.

—O, Mr. Conroy, said Lily to Gabriel when she opened the door for him, Miss Kate and Miss Julia thought you were never coming. Good night, Mrs. Conroy.

—I'll engage they did, said Gabriel, but they forget that my wife here takes three mortal hours to dress herself.

He stood on the mat, scraping the snow from his goloshes, while Lily led his wife to the foot of the stairs and called out:

—Miss Kate, here's Mrs. Conroy.

Kate and Julia came toddling down the dark stairs at once. Both of them kissed Gabriel's wife, said she must be perished alive and asked was Gabriel with her.

—Here I am as right as the mail, Aunt Kate! Go on up. I'll follow, called out Gabriel from the dark.

He continued scraping his feet vigorously while the three women went upstairs, laughing, to the ladies' dressingroom. A light fringe of snow lay like a cape on the shoulders of his overcoat and like toecaps on the toes of his goloshes; and, as the buttons of his overcoat slipped with a squeaking noise through the snow-stiffened frieze,[3] a cold fragrant air from out of doors escaped from crevices and folds.

—Is it snowing again, Mr. Conroy? asked Lily.

She had preceded him into the pantry to help him off with his overcoat. Gabriel smiled at the three syllables she had given his surname and glanced at her. She was a slim growing girl, pale in complexion and with haycoloured hair. The gas in the pantry made her look still paler. Gabriel had known her when she was a child and used to sit on the lowest step nursing[4] a rag doll.

—Yes, Lily, he answered, and I think we're in for a night of it. He looked up at the pantry ceiling which was shaking with the stamping and shuffling of feet on the floor above, listened for a moment to the piano and then glanced at the girl who was folding his overcoat carefully at the end of a shelf.

—Tell me, Lily, he said in a friendly tone, do you still go to school?

—O no, sir, she answered, I'm done schooling this year and more.

—O then, said Gabriel gaily, I suppose we'll be going to your wedding one of these fine days with your young man—eh?

The girl glanced back at him over her shoulder and said with great bitterness:

—The men that is now is only all palaver[5] and what they can get out of you.

Gabriel coloured as if he felt he had made a mistake and, without looking at her, kicked off his goloshes and flicked actively with his muffler at his patent leather shoes.

He was a stout tallish young man. The high colour of his cheeks pushed upwards even to his forehead where it scattered itself in a few formless patches of pale red; and on his hairless face there scintillated restlessly the polished lenses and bright gilt rims of the glasses which screened his delicate and restless eyes. His glossy black hair was parted in the middle and brushed in a long curve behind his ears where it curled slightly beneath the groove left by his hat.

When he had flicked lustre into his shoes he stood up and pulled his waistcoat down more tightly on his plump body. Then he took a coin rapidly from his pocket.

[1] *back answers* Rudeness; back-talk.

[2] *screwed* Drunk.

[3] *frieze* Coarse woolen cloth.

[4] *nursing* Here, taking care of.

[5] *palaver* Flattering talk.

—O Lily, he said, thrusting it into her hand, it's Christmas time, isn't it? Just ... here's a little ...

He walked rapidly towards the door.

—O no, sir! cried the girl, following him. Really, sir, I wouldn't take it.

—Christmas time! Christmas time! said Gabriel, almost trotting to the stairs and waving his hand to her in deprecation.

The girl, seeing that he had gained the stairs, called out after him:

—Well, thank you, sir.

He waited outside the drawingroom door until the waltz should finish, listening to the skirts that swept against it and to the shuffling of feet. He was still discomposed by the girl's bitter and sudden retort. It had cast a gloom over him which he tried to dispel by arranging his cuffs and the bows of his tie. Then he took from his waistcoat pocket a little paper and glanced at the headings he had made for his speech. He was undecided about the lines from Robert Browning[1] for he feared they would be above the heads of his hearers. Some quotation that they could recognise from Shakespeare or from the Melodies[2] would be better. The indelicate clacking of the men's heels and the shuffling of their soles reminded him that their grade of culture differed from his. He would only make himself ridiculous by quoting poetry to them which they could not understand. They would think that he was airing his superior education. He would fail with them just as he had failed with the girl in the pantry. He had taken up a wrong tone. His whole speech was a mistake from first to last, an utter failure.

Just then his aunts and his wife came out of the ladies' dressingroom. His aunts were two small plainly dressed old women. Aunt Julia was an inch or so the taller. Her hair, drawn low over the tops of her ears, was grey; and grey also, with darker shadows, was her large flaccid face. Though she was stout in build and stood erect her slow eyes and parted lips gave her the appearance of a woman who did not know where she was or where she was going. Aunt Kate was more vivacious. Her face, healthier than her sister's, was all puckers and

creases like a shrivelled red apple and her hair, braided in the same oldfashioned way, had not lost its ripe nut colour.

They both kissed Gabriel frankly. He was their favourite nephew, the son of their dead elder sister Ellen who had married T.J. Conroy of the Port and Docks.[3]

—Gretta tells me you're not going to take a cab back to Monkstown tonight, Gabriel, said Aunt Kate.

—No, said Gabriel, turning to his wife, we had quite enough of that last year, hadn't we? Don't you remember, Aunt Kate, what a cold Gretta got out of it? Cab windows rattling all the way and the east wind blowing in after we passed Merrion. Very jolly it was. Gretta caught a dreadful cold.

Aunt Kate frowned severely and nodded her head at every word.

—Quite right, Gabriel, quite right, she said. You can't be too careful.

—But as for Gretta there, said Gabriel, she'd walk home in the snow if she were let.

Mrs. Conroy laughed.

—Don't mind him, Aunt Kate, she said. He's really an awful bother, what with green shades for Tom's eyes at night and making him do the dumbbells and forcing Lottie to eat the stirabout.[4] The poor child! And she simply hates the sight of it! ... O, but you'll never guess what he makes me wear now!

She broke out into a peal of laughter and glanced at her husband whose admiring and happy eyes had been wandering from her dress to her face and hair. The two aunts laughed heartily too for Gabriel's solicitude was a standing joke with them.

—Goloshes! said Mrs. Conroy. That's the latest. Whenever it's wet underfoot I must put on my goloshes. Tonight even he wanted me to put them on but I wouldn't. The next thing he'll buy me will be a diving suit.

Gabriel laughed nervously and patted his tie reassuringly while Aunt Kate nearly doubled herself so heartily did she enjoy the joke. The smile soon faded from Aunt Julia's face and her mirthless eyes were directed towards her nephew's face. After a pause she asked:

—And what are goloshes, Gabriel?

[1] *Robert Browning* English poet (1812–89).

[2] *Melodies* Thomas Moore's collection of poetry and songs, *Irish Melodies*.

[3] *Port and Docks* Dublin Port and Docks Board, an essential part of Dublin's commercial life.

[4] *stirabout* Porridge.

—Goloshes, Julia! exclaimed her sister. Goodness me, don't you know what goloshes are? You wear them over your ... over your boots, Gretta, isn't it?

—Yes, said Mrs. Conroy. Guttapercha[1] things. We both have a pair now. Gabriel says everyone wears them on the continent.[2]

—O, on the continent, murmured Aunt Julia, nodding her head slowly.

Gabriel knitted his brows and said, as if he were slightly angered:

—It's nothing very wonderful but Gretta thinks it very funny because she says the word reminds her of christy minstrels.[3]

—But tell me, Gabriel, said Aunt Kate with brisk tact. Of course you've seen about the room. Gretta was saying ...

—O, the room is all right, replied Gabriel. I've taken one in the Gresham.[4]

—To be sure, said Aunt Kate, by far the best thing to do. And the children, Gretta, you're not anxious about them?

—O, for one night, said Mrs. Conroy. Besides Bessie will look after them.

—To be sure, said Aunt Kate again. What a comfort it is to have a girl like that, one you can depend on! There's that Lily, I'm sure I don't know what has come over her lately. She's not the girl she was at all.

Gabriel was about to ask his aunt some questions on this point but she broke off suddenly to gaze after her sister who had wandered down the stairs and was craning her neck over the banisters.

—Now, I ask you, she said almost testily, where is Julia going. Julia! Julia! Where are you going?

Julia who had gone half way down one flight came back and announced blandly:

—Here's Freddy!

At the same moment a clapping of hands and a final flourish of the pianist told that the waltz had ended. The drawingroom door was opened from within and

some couples came out. Aunt Kate drew Gabriel aside hurriedly and whispered into his ear:

—Slip down, Gabriel, like a good fellow and see if he's all right and don't let him up if he's screwed. I'm sure he's screwed. I'm sure he is.

Gabriel went to the stairs and listened over the banisters. He could hear two persons talking in the pantry. Then he recognised Freddy Malins' laugh. He went down the stairs noisily.

—It's such a relief, said Aunt Kate to Mrs. Conroy, that Gabriel is here. I always feel easier in my mind when he's here ...

—Julia, there's Miss Daly and Miss Power will take some refreshment. Thanks for your beautiful waltz, Miss Daly. It made lovely time.

A tall wizenfaced man with a stiff grizzled moustache and swarthy skin who was passing out with his partner said:

—And may we have some refreshment too, Miss Morkan?

—Julia, said Aunt Kate summarily, and here's Mr. Browne and Miss Furlong. Take them in, Julia, with Miss Daly and Miss Power.

—I'm the man for the ladies, said Mr. Browne, pursing his lips until his moustache bristled and smiling in all his wrinkles. You know, Miss Morkan, the reason they are so fond of me is ...

He did not finish his sentence but, seeing that Aunt Kate was out of earshot, at once led the three young ladies into the back room. The middle of the room was occupied by two square tables placed end to end and on these Aunt Julia and the caretaker were straightening and smoothing a large cloth. On the sideboard were arrayed dishes and plates and glasses and bundles of knives and forks and spoons. The top of the closed square piano served also as a sideboard for viands and sweets. At a smaller sideboard in one corner two young men were standing, drinking hop bitters.[5]

Mr. Browne led his charges thither and invited them all, in jest, to some ladies' punch, hot, strong and sweet. As they said they never took anything strong he opened three bottles of lemonade for them. Then he asked one of the young men to move aside and, taking hold of the decanter, filled out for himself a goodly measure of

---

[1] *Guttapercha* Substance similar to rubber and used for waterproofing.

[2] *continent* I.e., Europe.

[3] *christy minstrels* Minstrel show. From the nineteenth-century minstrel show founded by George Christy.

[4] *Gresham* One of Dublin's top hotels.

[5] *hop bitters* Unfermented liquor flavored with hops.

whisky. The young men eyed him respectfully while he took a trial sip.

—God help me, he said smiling, it's the doctor's orders.

His wizened face broke into a broader smile and the three young ladies laughed in musical echo to his pleasantry, swaying their bodies to and fro, with nervous jerks of their shoulders. The boldest said:

—O, now, Mr. Browne, I'm sure the doctor never ordered anything of the kind.

Mr. Browne took another sip of his whisky and said, with sidling mimicry:

—Well, you see, I'm like the famous Mrs. Cassidy who is reported to have said: *Now, Mary Grimes, if I don't take it make me take it for I feel I want it.*

His hot face had leaned forward a little too confidentially and he had assumed a very low Dublin accent so that the young ladies, with one instinct, received his speech in silence. Miss Furlong, who was one of Mary Jane's pupils, asked Miss Daly what was the name of the pretty waltz she had played; and Mr. Browne, seeing that he was ignored, turned promptly to the two young men who were more appreciative.

A redfaced young woman, dressed in pansy, came into the room, excitedly clapping her hands and crying:

—Quadrilles![1] Quadrilles!

Close on her heels came Aunt Kate, crying:

—Two gentlemen and three ladies, Mary Jane!

—O, here's Mr. Bergin and Mr. Kerrigan, said Mary Jane. Mr. Kerrigan, will you take Miss Power. Miss Furlong, may I get you a partner, Mr. Bergin. O, that'll just do now.

—Three ladies, Mary Jane, said Aunt Kate.

The two young gentlemen asked the ladies if they might have the pleasure and Mary Jane turned to Miss Daly.

—O, Miss Daly, you're really awfully good after playing for the last two dances but really we're so short of ladies tonight.

—I don't mind in the least, Miss Morkan.

—But I've a nice partner for you, Mr. Bartell D'Arcy, the tenor. I'll get him to sing later on. All Dublin is raving about him.

—Lovely voice, lovely voice! said Aunt Kate.

As the piano had twice begun the prelude to the first figure Mary Jane led her recruits quickly from the room. They had hardly gone when Aunt Julia wandered slowly into the room, looking behind her at something.

—What is the matter, Julia? asked Aunt Kate anxiously. Who is it?

Julia, who was carrying in a column of table-napkins, turned to her sister and said simply, as if the question had surprised her:

—It's only Freddy, Kate, and Gabriel with him.

In fact right behind her Gabriel could be seen piloting Freddy Malins across the landing. The latter, a young man of about forty, was of Gabriel's size and build with very round shoulders. His face was fleshy and pallid, touched with colour only at the thick hanging lobes of his ears and at the wide wings of his nose. He had coarse features, a blunt nose, a convex and receding brow, tumid and protruded lips. His heavylidded eyes and the disorder of his scanty hair made him look sleepy. He was laughing heartily in a high key at a story which he had been telling Gabriel on the stairs and at the same time rubbing the knuckles of his left fist backwards and forwards into his left eye.

—Good evening, Freddy, said Aunt Julia.

Freddy Malins bade the Misses Morkan good evening in what seemed an offhand fashion by reason of the habitual catch in his voice and then, seeing that Mr. Browne was grinning at him from the sideboard, crossed the room on rather shaky legs and began to repeat in an undertone the story he had just told to Gabriel.

—He's not so bad, is he? said Aunt Kate to Gabriel.

Gabriel's brows were dark but he raised them quickly and answered:

—O no, hardly noticeable.

—Now, isn't he a terrible fellow! she said. And his poor mother made him take the pledge[2] on New Year's Eve. But come on, Gabriel, into the drawingroom.

Before leaving the room with Gabriel she signalled to Mr. Browne by frowning and shaking her forefinger in warning to and fro. Mr. Browne nodded in answer and, when she had gone, said to Freddy Malins:

—Now then, Teddy, I'm going to fill you out a good glass of lemonade just to buck you up.

---

[1] *Quadrilles* Type of square dance.

[2] *take the pledge* I.e., pledge to abstain from alcoholic beverages.

Freddy Malins, who was nearing the climax of his story, waved the offer aside impatiently but Mr. Browne, having first called Freddy Malins' attention to a disarray in his dress, filled out and handed him a full glass of lemonade. Freddy Malins' left hand accepted the glass mechanically, his right hand being engaged in the mechanical readjustment of his dress. Mr. Browne, whose face was once more wrinkling with mirth, poured out for himself a glass of whisky while Freddy Malins exploded, before he had well reached the climax of his story, in a kink of highpitched bronchitic laughter and, setting down his untasted and overflowing glass, began to rub the knuckles of his left fist backwards and forwards into his left eye, repeating words of his last phrase as well as his fit of laughter would allow him.

Gabriel could not listen while Mary Jane was playing her academy piece, full of runs and difficult passages, to the hushed drawingroom. He liked music but the piece she was playing had no melody for him and he doubted whether it had any melody for the other listeners though they had begged Mary Jane to play something. Four young men, who had come from the refreshment room to stand in the doorway at the sound of the piano, had gone away quietly in couples after a few minutes. The only persons who seemed to follow the music were Mary Jane herself, her hands racing along the keyboard or lifted from it at the pauses like those of a priestess in momentary imprecation, and Aunt Kate standing at her elbow to turn the page.

Gabriel's eyes, irritated by the floor which glittered with beeswax under the heavy chandelier, wandered to the wall above the piano. A picture of the balcony scene in *Romeo and Juliet* hung there and beside it was a picture of the two murdered princes in the tower[1] which Aunt Julia had worked[2] in red, blue and brown wools when she was a girl. Probably in the school they had gone to as girls that kind of work had been taught, for one year his mother had worked for him as a birthday present a waistcoat of purple tabinet[3] with little foxes'

heads upon it, lined with brown satin and having round mulberry buttons. It was strange that his mother had had no musical talent though Aunt Kate used to call her the brainscarrier of the Morkan family. Both she and Julia had always seemed a little proud of their serious and matronly sister. Her photograph stood before the pierglass.[4] She held an open book on her knees and was pointing out something in it to Constantine who, dressed in a man-o'-war suit,[5] lay at her feet. It was she who had chosen the names for her sons for she was very sensible of the dignity of family life. Thanks to her, Constantine was now senior curate in Balbriggan and, thanks to her, Gabriel himself had taken his degree in the Royal University. A shadow passed over his face as he remembered her sullen opposition to his marriage. Some slighting phrases she had used still rankled in his memory. She had once spoken of Gretta as being country cute and that was not true of Gretta at all. It was Gretta who had nursed her all during her last long illness in their house at Monkstown.

He knew that Mary Jane must be near the end of her piece for she was playing again the opening melody with runs of scales after every bar and while he waited for the end the resentment died down in his heart. The piece ended with a trill of octaves in the treble and a final deep octave in the bass. Great applause greeted Mary Jane as, blushing and rolling up her music nervously, she escaped from the room. The most vigorous clapping came from the four young men in the doorway who had gone away to the refreshment room at the beginning of the piece but had come back when the piano had stopped.

Lancers[6] were arranged. Gabriel found himself partnered with Miss Ivors. She was a frankmannered talkative young lady with a freckled face and prominent brown eyes. She did not wear a lowcut bodice and the large brooch which was fixed in the front of her collar bore on it an Irish device.

When they had taken their places she said abruptly:

—I have a crow to pluck with you.

—With me? said Gabriel.

---

[1] *the two ... tower* Edward IV's two sons were murdered in the Tower of London in about 1483–84, allegedly at the instigation of their uncle, the future Richard III.

[2] *worked* I.e., wrought; made.

[3] *tabinet* Fabric made of silk and wool, similar to poplin.

[4] *pierglass* Tall mirror.

[5] *man-o'-war suit* Sailor suit, frequently worn by children.

[6] *Lancers* Type of quadrille.

She nodded her head gravely.

—What is it? asked Gabriel, smiling at her solemn manner.

—Who is G.C.? answered Miss Ivors turning her eyes upon him.

Gabriel coloured and was about to knit his brows as if he did not understand when she said bluntly:

—O, innocent Amy! I have found out that you write for the *Daily Express*. Now aren't you ashamed of yourself?

—Why should I be ashamed of myself? asked Gabriel blinking his eyes and trying to smile.

—Well, I'm ashamed of you, said Miss Ivors frankly. To say you'd write for a rag like that. I didn't think you were a west Briton.[1]

A look of perplexity appeared on Gabriel's face. It was true that he wrote a literary column every Wednesday in the *Daily Express* for which he was paid fifteen shillings. But that did not make him a west Briton surely. The books he received for review were almost more welcome than the paltry cheque. He loved to feel the covers and turn over the pages of newly printed books. Nearly every day when his teaching in the college was ended he used to wander down the quays to the secondhand booksellers, to Hickey's on Bachelor's Walk, to Webb's or Massey's on Aston's Quay or to Clohissey's in the bystreet. He did not know how to meet her charge. He wanted to say that literature was above politics. But they were friends of many years' standing and their careers had been parallel, first at the university and then as teachers: he could not risk a grandiose phrase with her. He continued blinking his eyes and trying to smile and murmured lamely that he saw nothing political in writing reviews of books.

When their turn to cross had come he was still perplexed and inattentive. Miss Ivors promptly took his hand in a warm grasp and said in a soft friendly tone:

—Of course, I was only joking. Come, we cross now. When they were together again she spoke of the university question[2] and Gabriel felt more at ease. A

friend of hers had shown her his review of Browning's poems. That was how she had found out the secret: but she liked the review immensely. Then she said suddenly:

—O, Mr. Conroy, will you come for an excursion to the Aran Isles[3] this summer? We're going to stay there a whole month. It will be splendid out in the Atlantic. You ought to come. Mr. Clancy is coming and Mr. Kilkelly and Kathleen Kearney. It would be splendid for Gretta too if she'd come. She's from Connacht,[4] isn't she?

—Her people are, said Gabriel shortly.

—But you will come, won't you? said Miss Ivors, laying her warm hand eagerly on his arm.

—The fact is, said Gabriel, I have already arranged to go …

—Go where? asked Miss Ivors.

—Well, you know, every year I go for a cycling tour with some fellows and so …

—But where? asked Miss Ivors.

—Well, we usually go to France or Belgium or perhaps Germany, said Gabriel awkwardly.

—And why do you go to France and Belgium, said Miss Ivors, instead of visiting your own land?

—Well, said Gabriel, it's partly to keep in touch with the languages and partly for a change.

—And haven't you your own language to keep in touch with, Irish? asked Miss Ivors.

—Well, said Gabriel, if it comes to that, you know, Irish is not my language.

Their neighbours had turned to listen to the cross-examination. Gabriel glanced right and left nervously and tried to keep his good humour under the ordeal which was making a blush invade his forehead.

—And haven't you your own land to visit, continued Miss Ivors, that you know nothing of, your own people and your own country?

—O, to tell you the truth, retorted Gabriel suddenly, I'm sick of my own country, sick of it!

—Why? asked Miss Ivors.

Gabriel did not answer for his retort had heated him.

---

1   *west Briton*   Colloquial term for an Irish person who sees Ireland as the western part of Great Britain, rather than as a separate nation.

2   *university question*   Concerning the establishment of an Irish national university, the representation of "Irish" values in universities, and the provision of equal access to education for Catholics

(Trinity College was open only to Protestants).

3   *Aran Isles*   Three islands off the coast of County Galway, on Ireland's west coast.

4   *Connacht*   Connaught, in west Ireland.

—Why? repeated Miss Ivors.

They had to go visiting[1] together and, as he had not answered her, Miss Ivors said warmly:

—Of course, you've no answer.

Gabriel tried to cover his agitation by taking part in the dance with great energy. He avoided her eyes for he had seen a sour expression on her face. But when they met in the long chain he was surprised to feel his hand firmly pressed. She looked at him from under her brows for a moment quizzically until he smiled. Then, just as the chain was about to start again, she stood on tiptoe and whispered into his ear:

—West Briton!

When the lancers were over Gabriel went away to a remote corner of the room where Freddy Malins' mother was sitting. She was a stout feeble old woman with white hair. Her voice had a catch in it like her son's and she stuttered slightly. She had been told that Freddy had come and that he was nearly all right. Gabriel asked her whether she had had a good crossing. She lived with her married daughter in Glasgow and came to Dublin on a visit once a year. She answered placidly that she had had a beautiful crossing and that the captain had been most attentive to her. She spoke also of the beautiful house her daughter kept in Glasgow and of the nice friends they had there. While her tongue rambled on Gabriel tried to banish from his mind all memory of the unpleasant incident with Miss Ivors. Of course the girl or woman or whatever she was was an enthusiast but there was a time for all things. Perhaps he ought not to have answered her like that. But she had no right to call him a west Briton before people, even in joke. She had tried to make him ridiculous before people, heckling him and staring at him with her rabbit's eyes.

He saw his wife making her way towards him through the waltzing couples. When she reached him she said into his ear:

—Gabriel, Aunt Kate wants to know won't you carve the goose as usual. Miss Daly will carve the ham and I'll do the pudding.

—All right, said Gabriel.

—She's sending in the younger ones first as soon as this waltz is over so that we'll have the table to ourselves.

—Were you dancing? asked Gabriel.

—Of course I was. Didn't you see me? What words had you with Molly Ivors?

—No words. Why! Did she say so?

—Something like that. I'm trying to get that Mr. D'Arcy to sing. He's full of conceit, I think.

—There were no words, said Gabriel moodily, only she wanted me to go for a trip to the west of Ireland and I said I wouldn't.

His wife clasped her hands excitedly and gave a little jump.

—O, do go, Gabriel, she cried. I'd love to see Galway again.

—You can go if you like, said Gabriel coldly.

She looked at him for a moment, then turned to Mrs. Malins and said:

—There's a nice husband for you, Mrs. Malins.

While she was threading her way back across the room Mrs. Malins, without adverting to the interruption, went on to tell Gabriel what beautiful places there were in Scotland and beautiful scenery. Her son-in-law brought them every year to the lakes and they used to go fishing. Her son-in-law was a splendid fisher. One day he caught a fish, a beautiful big big fish: and the man in the hotel boiled it for their dinner.

Gabriel hardly heard what she said. Now that supper was coming near he began to think again about his speech and about the quotation. When he saw Freddy Malins coming across the room to visit his mother Gabriel left the chair free for him and retired into the embrasure of the window. The room had already cleared and from the back room came the clatter of plates and knives. Those who still remained in the drawingroom seemed tired of dancing and were conversing quietly in little groups. Gabriel's warm trembling fingers tapped the cold pane of the window. How cool it must be outside! How pleasant it would be to walk out alone, first along by the river and then through the park! The snow would be lying on the branches of the trees and forming a bright cap on the top of the Wellington monument.[2] How much more pleasant it would be there than at the supper table!

He ran over the headings of his speech: Irish hospi-

---

[1] *go visiting* Reference to the part of the dance in which the partners cross the floor together and meet another couple.

[2] *Wellington monument* Monument to the Duke of Wellington, an English military hero born in Ireland.

tality, sad memories, the Three Graces, Paris,[1] the quotation from Browning. He repeated to himself a phrase he had written in his review: *One feels that one is listening to a thought-tormented music.* Miss Ivors had praised the review. Was she sincere? Had she really any life of her own behind all her propagandism? There had never been any ill feeling between them until that night. It unnerved him to think that she would be at the supper table, looking up at him while he spoke with her critical quizzing eyes. Perhaps she would not be sorry to see him fail in his speech. An idea came into his mind and gave him courage. He would say, alluding to Aunt Kate and Aunt Julia: *Ladies and gentlemen, the generation which is now on the wane among us may have had its faults but for my part I think it had certain qualities of hospitality, of humour, of humanity, which the new and very serious and hypereducated generation that is growing up around us seems to me to lack.* Very good: that was one for Miss Ivors. What did he care that his aunts were only two ignorant old women?

A murmur in the room attracted his attention. Mr. Browne was advancing from the door, gallantly escorting Aunt Julia who leaned upon his arm, smiling and hanging her head. An irregular musketry of applause escorted her also as far as the piano and then, as Mary Jane seated herself on the stool and Aunt Julia, no longer smiling, half turned so as to pitch her voice fairly into the room, gradually ceased. Gabriel recognised the prelude. It was that of an old song of Aunt Julia's, *Arrayed for the Bridal.*[2] Her voice strong and clear in tone attacked with great spirit the runs which embellish the air and, though she sang very rapidly, she did not miss even the smallest of the grace notes. To follow the voice, without looking at the singer's face, was to feel and share the excitement of swift and secure flight.

Gabriel applauded loudly with all the others at the close of the song and loud applause was borne in from the invisible supper table. It sounded so genuine that a little colour struggled into Aunt Julia's face as she bent to replace in the music stand the old leatherbound songbook that had her initials on the cover. Freddy Malins, who had listened with his head perched sideways to hear the better, was still applauding when everyone else had ceased and talking animatedly to his mother who nodded her head gravely and slowly in acquiescence. At last, when he could clap no more, he stood up suddenly and hurried across the room to Aunt Julia, whose hand he seized and held in both his hands, shaking it when words failed him or the catch in his voice proved too much for him.

—I was just telling my mother, he said, I never heard you sing so well, never. No, I never heard your voice so good as it is tonight. Now! Would you believe that now? That's the truth. Upon my word and honour that's the truth. I never heard your voice sound so fresh and so ... so clear and fresh, never.

Aunt Julia smiled broadly and murmured something about compliments as she released her hand from his grasp. Mr. Browne extended his open hand towards her and said to those who were near him in the manner of a showman introducing a prodigy to an audience:

—Miss Julia Morkan, my latest discovery!

He was laughing very heartily at this himself when Freddy Malins turned to him and said:

—Well, Browne, if you're serious you might make a worse discovery. All I can say is I never heard her sing half so well as long as I am coming here. And that's the honest truth.

—Neither did I, said Mr. Browne. I think her voice has greatly improved.

Aunt Julia shrugged her shoulders and said with meek pride:

—Thirty years ago I hadn't a bad voice as voices go.

—I often told Julia, said Aunt Kate emphatically, that she was simply thrown away in that choir. But she never would be said by[3] me.

She turned as if to appeal to the good sense of the others against a refractory child while Aunt Julia gazed

---

[1]   *Three Graces* In Greek mythology, the three daughters of Zeus and Eurynome who embodied the qualities of beauty and charm; *Paris* In Greek mythology, Paris was asked by the gods to judge a beauty contest between Hera, Athena, and Aphrodite. All three goddesses offered Paris a bribe. When he chose Aphrodite, she rewarded him by granting him the most beautiful woman in the world, who was Helen of Troy. Paris's abduction of Helen from her husband, Menelaus, is the putative cause of the Trojan War.

[2]   *Arrayed ... Bridal* Popular and challenging song from Bellini's opera *I Puritani* (1835) that begins with the words "Arrayed for the bridal, in beauty behold her."

[3]   *be said by* Be ruled by; submit to.

in front of her, a vague smile of reminiscence playing on her face.

—No, continued Aunt Kate, she wouldn't be said or led by anyone, slaving there in that choir night and day, night and day. Six o'clock on Christmas morning! And all for what?

—Well, isn't it for the honour of God, Aunt Kate? asked Mary Jane twisting round on the piano stool and smiling.

Aunt Kate turned fiercely on her niece and said:

—I know all about the honour of God, Mary Jane, but I think it's not at all honourable for the pope to turn out the women out of the choirs that have slaved there all their lives and put little whippersnappers of boys over their heads. I suppose it is for the good of the church if the pope does it. But it's not just, Mary Jane, and it's not right.[1]

She had worked herself into a passion and would have continued in defence of her sister for it was a sore subject with her but Mary Jane, seeing that all the dancers had come back, intervened pacifically:

—Now, Aunt Kate, you're giving scandal to Mr. Browne who is of the other persuasion.[2]

Aunt Kate turned to Mr. Browne, who was grinning at this allusion to his religion, and said hastily:

—O, I don't question the pope's being right. I'm only a stupid old woman and I wouldn't presume to do such a thing. But there's such a thing as common everyday politeness and gratitude. And if I were in Julia's place I'd tell that Father Healy straight up to his face …

—And besides, Aunt Kate, said Mary Jane, we really are all hungry and when we are hungry we are all very quarrelsome.

—And when we are thirsty we are also quarrelsome, added Mr. Browne.

—So that we had better go to supper, said Mary Jane, and finish the discussion afterwards.

On the landing outside the drawingroom Gabriel found his wife and Mary Jane trying to persuade Miss Ivors to stay for supper. But Miss Ivors, who had put on her hat and was buttoning her cloak, would not stay. She did not feel in the least hungry and she had already overstayed her time.

—But only for ten minutes, Molly, said Mrs. Conroy. That won't delay you.

—To take a pick itself,[3] said Mary Jane, after all your dancing.

—I really couldn't, said Miss Ivors.

—I am afraid you didn't enjoy yourself at all, said Mary Jane hopelessly.

—Ever so much, I assure you, said Miss Ivors, but you really must let me run off now.

—But how can you get home? asked Mrs. Conroy.

—O, it's only two steps up the quay. Gabriel hesitated a moment and said:

—If you will allow me, Miss Ivors, I'll see you home if you really are obliged to go.

But Miss Ivors broke away from them.

—I won't hear of it, she cried. For goodness' sake go in to your suppers and don't mind me. I'm quite well able to take care of myself.

—Well, you're the comical girl, Molly, said Mrs. Conroy frankly.

—*Beannacht libh*,[4] cried Miss Ivors with a laugh as she ran down the staircase.

Mary Jane gazed after her, a moody puzzled expression on her face, while Mrs. Conroy leaned over the banisters to listen for the hall door. Gabriel asked himself was he the cause of her abrupt departure. But she did not seem to be in ill humour: she had gone away laughing. He stared blankly down the staircase.

At that moment Aunt Kate came toddling out of the supper room, almost wringing her hands in despair.

—Where is Gabriel? she cried. Where on earth is Gabriel? There's everyone waiting in there, stage to let, and nobody to carve the goose!

—Here I am, Aunt Kate! cried Gabriel with sudden animation, ready to carve a flock of geese, if necessary.

---

1 *I know … right* On 22 November 1903, Pope Pius X issued a papal bull, in which he announced that the singing of Church music constituted a liturgical function for which women were ineligible and that, henceforth, soprano and alto voices would be produced by young boys.

2 *of the other persuasion* I.e., a Protestant.

3 *a pick itself* I.e., a little bit.

4 *Beannacht libh* An Irish farewell; literally, "my blessings go with you."

A fat brown goose lay at one end of the table and at the other end, on a bed of creased paper strewn with sprigs of parsley, lay a great ham, stripped of its outer skin and peppered over with crust crumbs, a neat paper frill round its shin, and beside this was a round of spiced beef. Between these rival ends ran parallel lines of side dishes: two little minsters of jelly, red and yellow, a shallow dish full of blocks of blancmange[1] and red jam, a large green leafshaped dish with a stalkshaped handle on which lay bunches of purple raisins and peeled almonds, a companion dish on which lay a solid rectangle of Smyrna figs, a dish of custard topped with grated nutmeg, a small bowl full of chocolates and sweets wrapped in gold and silver papers and a glass vase in which stood some tall celery stalks. In the centre of the table there stood, as sentries to a fruit stand which upheld a pyramid of oranges and American apples, two squat oldfashioned decanters of cut glass, one containing port and the other dark sherry. On the closed square piano a pudding in a huge yellow dish lay in waiting and behind it were three squads of bottles of stout and ale and minerals drawn up according to the colours of their uniforms, the first two black with brown and red labels, the third and smallest squad white, with transverse green sashes.

Gabriel took his seat boldly at the head of the table and, having looked to the edge of the carver, plunged his fork firmly into the goose. He felt quite at ease now for he was an expert carver and liked nothing better than to find himself at the head of a well laden table.

—Miss Furlong, what shall I send you? he asked. A wing or a slice of the breast?

—Just a small slice of the breast.

—Miss Higgins, what for you?

—O, anything at all, Mr. Conroy.

While Gabriel and Miss Daly exchanged plates of goose and plates of ham and spiced beef Lily went from guest to guest with a dish of hot floury potatoes wrapped in a white napkin. This was Mary Jane's idea and she had also suggested apple sauce for the goose but Aunt Kate had said that plain roast goose without any apple sauce had always been good enough for her and she hoped she might never eat worse. Mary Jane waited on her pupils and saw that they got the best slices and

Aunt Kate and Aunt Julia opened and carried across from the piano bottles of stout and ale for the gentlemen and bottles of minerals for the ladies. There was a great deal of confusion and laughter and noise, the noise of orders and counterorders, of knives and forks, of corks and glass stoppers. Gabriel began to carve second helpings as soon as he had finished the first round without serving himself. Everyone protested loudly so that he compromised by taking a long draught of stout for he had found the carving hot work. Mary Jane settled down quietly to her supper but Aunt Kate and Aunt Julia were still toddling round the table, walking on each other's heels, getting in each other's way and giving each other unheeded orders. Mr. Browne begged of them to sit down and eat their supper and so did Gabriel but they said there was time enough so that, at last, Freddy Malins stood up and, capturing Aunt Kate, plumped her down on her chair amid general laughter.

When everyone had been well served Gabriel said smiling:

—Now if anyone wants a little more of what vulgar people call stuffing let him or her speak.

A chorus of voices invited him to begin his own supper and Lily came forward with three potatoes which she had reserved for him.

—Very well, said Gabriel amiably as he took another preparatory draught, kindly forget my existence, ladies and gentlemen, for a few minutes.

He set to his supper and took no part in the conversation with which the table covered Lily's removal of the plates. The subject of talk was the opera company which was then at the Theatre Royal. Mr. Bartell D'Arcy, the tenor, a dark-complexioned young man with a smart moustache, praised very highly the leading contralto of the company but Miss Furlong thought she had a rather vulgar style of production. Freddy Malins said there was a negro chieftain singing in the second part of the Gaiety pantomime who had one of the finest tenor voices he had ever heard.

—Have you heard him? he asked Mr. Bartell D'Arcy across the table.

—No, answered Mr. Bartell D'Arcy carelessly.

—Because, Freddy Malins explained, now I'd be curious to hear your opinion of him. I think he has a grand voice.

---

[1] blancmange   Milk jelly.

—It takes Teddy to find out the really good things, said Mr. Browne familiarly to the table.

—And why couldn't he have a voice too? asked Freddy Malins sharply. Is it because he's only a black?

Nobody answered this question and Mary Jane led the table back to the legitimate opera. One of her pupils had given her a pass for *Mignon*.[1] Of course, it was very fine, she said, but it made her think of poor Georgina Burns.[2] Mr. Browne could go back farther still to the old Italian companies that used to come to Dublin, Tietjens, Trebelli, Ilma de Murzka, Campanini, the great Giuglini, Ravelli, Aramburo. Those were the days, he said, when there was something like singing to be heard in Dublin. He told too of how the top gallery of the old Royal used to be packed night after night, of how one night an Italian tenor had sung five encores to *Let Me Like a Soldier Fall*, introducing a high C every time, and of how the gallery boys would sometimes in their enthusiasm unyoke the horses from the carriage of some great *prima donna* and pull her themselves through the streets to her hotel. Why did they never play the grand old operas now, he asked. *Dinorah, Lucrezia Borgia*?[3] Because they could not get the voices to sing them: that was why.

—O, well, said Mr. Bartell D'Arcy, I presume there are as good singers today as there were then.

—Where are they? asked Mr. Browne defiantly.

—In London, Paris, Milan, said Mr. Bartell D'Arcy warmly. I suppose Caruso,[4] for example, is quite as good, if not better than any of the men you have mentioned.

—Maybe so, said Mr. Browne. But I may tell you I doubt it strongly.

—O, I'd give anything to hear Caruso sing, said Mary Jane.

—For me, said Aunt Kate, who had been picking a bone, there was only one tenor. To please me, I mean. But I suppose none of you ever heard of him.

—Who was he, Miss Morkan? asked Mr. Bartell D'Arcy politely.

—His name, said Aunt Kate, was Parkinson. I heard him when he was in his prime and I think he had then the purest tenor voice that was ever put into a man's throat.

—Strange, said Mr. Bartell D'Arcy. I never even heard of him.

—Yes, yes, Miss Morkan is right, said Mr. Browne. I remember hearing of old Parkinson but he's too far back for me.

—A beautiful pure sweet mellow English tenor, said Aunt Kate with enthusiasm.

Gabriel having finished, the huge pudding was transferred to the table. The clatter of forks and spoons began again. Gabriel's wife served out spoonfuls of the pudding and passed the plates down the table. Midway down they were held up by Mary Jane who replenished them with raspberry or orange jelly or with blancmange and jam. The pudding was of Aunt Julia's making and she received praises for it from all quarters. She herself said that it was not quite brown enough.

—Well, I hope, Miss Morkan, said Mr. Browne, that I'm brown enough for you because, you know, I'm all brown.

All the gentlemen, except Gabriel, ate some of the pudding out of compliment to Aunt Julia. As Gabriel never ate sweets the celery had been left for him. Freddy Malins also took a stalk of celery and ate it with his pudding. He had been told that celery was a capital thing for the blood and he was just then under doctor's care. Mrs. Malins, who had been silent all through the supper, said that her son was going down to Mount Melleray[5] in a week or so. The table then spoke of Mount Melleray, how bracing the air was down there, how hospitable the monks were and how they never asked for a penny-piece from their guests.

—And do you mean to say, asked Mr. Browne incredulously, that a chap can go down there and put up there as if it were a hotel and live on the fat of the land and then come away without paying a farthing?

—O, most people give some donation to the monastery when they leave, said Mary Jane.

---

[1] *Mignon* 1866 opera by Ambroise Thomas.

[2] *Georgina Burns* Famous soprano who made her Dublin début in 1878.

[3] *Dinorah* 1859 comic opera by Giacomo Meyerbeer; *Lucrezia Borgia* 1833 opera by Gaetano Donizetti.

[4] *Caruso* Tenor Enrico Caruso (1874–1921).

[5] *Mount Melleray* Site of the Abbey of St. Bernard de Trappe, founded in 1831 by the Cistercian monks.

—I wish we had an institution like that in our church, said Mr. Browne candidly.

He was astonished to hear that the monks never spoke, got up at two in the morning and slept in their coffins.[1] He asked what they did it for.

—That's the rule of the order, said Aunt Kate firmly.

—Yes, but why? asked Mr. Browne.

Aunt Kate repeated that it was the rule, that was all. Mr. Browne still seemed not to understand. Freddy Malins explained to him, as best he could, that the monks were trying to make up for the sins committed by all the sinners in the outside world. The explanation was not very clear for Mr. Browne grinned and said:

—I like that idea very much but wouldn't a comfortable spring bed do them as well as a coffin?

—The coffin, said Mary Jane, is to remind them of their last end.

As the subject had grown lugubrious it was buried in a silence of the table during which Mrs. Malins could be heard saying to her neighbour in an indistinct undertone:

—They are very good men, the monks, very pious men.

The raisins and almonds and figs and apples and oranges and chocolates and sweets were now passed about the table and Aunt Julia invited all the guests to have either port or sherry. At first Mr. Bartell D'Arcy refused to take either but one of his neighbours nudged him and whispered something to him upon which he allowed his glass to be filled. Gradually as the last glasses were being filled the conversation ceased. A pause followed, broken only by the noise of the wine and by unsettlings of chairs. The Misses Morkan, all three, looked down at the tablecloth. Someone coughed once or twice and then a few gentlemen patted the table gently as a signal for silence. The silence came and Gabriel pushed back his chair and stood up.

The patting at once grew louder in encouragement and then ceased altogether. Gabriel leaned his ten trembling fingers on the tablecloth and smiled nervously at the company. Meeting a row of upturned faces he raised his eyes to the chandelier. The piano was playing a waltz tune and he could hear the skirts sweeping against the drawingroom door. People perhaps were standing in the snow on the quay outside, gazing up at the lighted windows and listening to the waltz music. The air was pure there. In the distance lay the park where the trees were weighted with snow. The Wellington monument wore a gleaming cap of snow that flashed westward over the white field of Fifteen Acres.

He began:

—Ladies and gentlemen.

It has fallen to my lot this evening as in years past to perform a very pleasing task, but a task for which I am afraid my poor powers as a speaker are all too inadequate.

—No, no, said Mr. Browne.

—But, however that may be, I can only ask you tonight to take the will for the deed and to lend me your attention for a few moments while I endeavour to express to you in words what my feelings are on this occasion.

—Ladies and gentlemen. It is not the first time that we have gathered together under this hospitable roof, around this hospitable board. It is not the first time that we have been the recipients—or, perhaps I had better say, the victims—of the hospitality of certain good ladies.

He made a circle in the air with his arm and paused. Everyone laughed or smiled at Aunt Kate and Aunt Julia and Mary Jane who all turned crimson with pleasure. Gabriel went on more boldly:

—I feel more strongly with every recurring year that our country has no tradition which does it so much honour and which it should guard so jealously as that of its hospitality. It is a tradition that is unique so far as my experience goes (and I have visited not a few places abroad) among the modern nations. Some would say, perhaps, that with us it is rather a failing than anything to be boasted of. But granted even that, it is, to my mind, a princely failing and one that I trust will long be cultivated among us. Of one thing, at least, I am sure. As long as this one roof shelters the good ladies aforesaid—and I wish from my heart it may do so for many and many a long year to come—the tradition of genuine warmhearted courteous Irish hospitality, which our forefathers have handed down to us and which we in

---

[1] *slept in their coffins* Though commonly believed, this is not a real custom of the Cistercians.

turn must hand down to our descendants, is still alive among us.

A hearty murmur of assent ran round the table. It shot through Gabriel's mind that Miss Ivors was not there and that she had gone away discourteously: and he said with confidence in himself:

—Ladies and gentlemen.

—A new generation is growing up in our midst, a generation actuated by new ideas and new principles. It is serious and enthusiastic for these new ideas and its enthusiasm, even when it is misdirected, is, I believe, in the main sincere. But we are living in a sceptical and, if I may use the phrase, a thought-tormented age: and sometimes I fear that this new generation, educated or hypereducated as it is, will lack those qualities of humanity, of hospitality, of kindly humour which belonged to an older day. Listening tonight to the names of all those great singers of the past it seemed to me, I must confess, that we were living in a less spacious age. Those days might without exaggeration be called spacious days: and if they are gone beyond recall let us hope, at least, that in gatherings such as this we shall still speak of them with pride and affection, still cherish in our hearts the memory of those dead and gone great ones whose fame the world will not willingly let die.

—Hear! hear! said Mr. Browne loudly.

—But yet, continued Gabriel, his voice falling into a softer inflection, there are always in gatherings such as this sadder thoughts that will recur to our minds: thoughts of the past, of youth, of changes, of absent faces that we miss here tonight. Our path through life is strewn with many such sad memories: and were we to brood upon them always we could not find the heart to go on bravely with our work among the living. We have all of us living duties and living affections which claim, and rightly claim, our strenuous endeavours.

—Therefore I will not linger on the past. I will not let any gloomy moralising intrude upon us here tonight. Here we are gathered together for a brief moment from the bustle and rush of our everyday routine. We are met here as friends, in the spirit of good fellowship, as colleagues also, to a certain extent, in the true spirit of camaraderie, and as the guests of—what shall I call them?—the three Graces of the Dublin musical world.

The table burst into applause and laughter at this sally. Aunt Julia vainly asked each of her neighbours in turn to tell her what Gabriel had said.

—He says we are the three Graces, Aunt Julia, said Mary Jane. Aunt Julia did not understand but she looked up, smiling, at Gabriel who continued in the same vein:

—Ladies and gentlemen.

—I will not attempt to play tonight the part that Paris played on another occasion. I will not attempt to choose between them. The task would be an invidious one and one beyond my poor powers. For when I view them in turn, whether it be our chief hostess herself, whose good heart, whose too good heart, has become a byword with all who know her, or her sister, who seems to be gifted with perennial youth and whose singing must have been a surprise and a revelation to us all tonight, or, last but not least, when I consider our youngest hostess, talented, cheerful, hard-working and the best of nieces, I confess, ladies and gentlemen, that I do not know to which of them I should award the prize.

Gabriel glanced down at his aunts and, seeing the large smile on Aunt Julia's face and the tears which had risen to Aunt Kate's eyes, hastened to his close. He raised his glass of port gallantly while every member of the company fingered a glass expectantly and said loudly:

—Let us toast them all three together. Let us drink to their health, wealth, long life, happiness and prosperity and may they long continue to hold the proud and self-won position which they hold in their profession and the position of honour and affection which they hold in our hearts.

All the guests stood up, glass in hand and, turning towards the three seated ladies, sang in unison with Mr. Browne as leader:

—For they are jolly gay fellows,
For they are jolly gay fellows,
For they are jolly gay fellows
Which nobody can deny.

Aunt Kate was making frank use of her handkerchief and even Aunt Julia seemed moved. Freddy Malins beat time with his pudding fork and the singers turned towards one another as if in melodious conference, while they sang with emphasis:

—Unless he tells a lie,
Unless he tells a lie.

Then turning once more towards their hostesses they sang:

—For they are jolly gay fellows,
For they are jolly gay fellows,
For they are jolly gay fellows
Which nobody can deny.

The acclamation which followed was taken up beyond the door of the supper room by many of the other guests and renewed time after time, Freddy Malins acting as officer with his fork on high.

The piercing morning air came into the hall where they were standing so that Aunt Kate said:

—Close the door, somebody. Mrs. Malins will get her death of cold.

—Browne is out there, Aunt Kate, said Mary Jane.

—Browne is everywhere, said Aunt Kate lowering her voice.

Mary Jane laughed at her tone.

—Really, she said archly, he is very attentive.

—He has been laid on here like the gas, said Aunt Kate in the same tone, all during the Christmas.

She laughed herself this time good-humouredly and then added quickly:

—But tell him to come in, Mary Jane, and close the door. I hope to goodness he didn't hear me.

At that moment the hall door was opened and Mr. Browne came in from the doorstep, laughing as if his heart would break. He was dressed in a long green overcoat with mock astrakhan[1] cuffs and collar and wore on his head an oval fur cap. He pointed down the snowcovered quay whence the sound of shrill prolonged whistling was borne in.

—Teddy will have all the cabs in Dublin out, he said. Gabriel advanced from the little pantry behind the office, struggling into his overcoat and, looking round the hall, said:

—Gretta not down yet?

—She's getting on her things, Gabriel, said Aunt Kate.

—Who's playing up there? asked Gabriel.

—Nobody. They're all gone.

—O no, Aunt Kate, said Mary Jane. Bartell D'Arcy and Miss O'Callaghan aren't gone yet.

—Someone is strumming at the piano, anyhow, said Gabriel. Mary Jane glanced at Gabriel and Mr. Browne and said with a shiver:

—It makes me feel cold to look at you two gentlemen muffled up like that. I wouldn't like to face your journey home at this hour.

—I'd like nothing better this minute, said Mr. Browne stoutly, than a rattling fine walk in the country or a fast drive with a good spanking goer between the shafts.

—We used to have a very good horse and trap[2] at home, said Aunt Julia sadly.

—The never-to-be-forgotten Johnny, said Mary Jane laughing. Aunt Kate and Gabriel laughed too.

—Why, what was wonderful about Johnny? asked Mr. Browne.

—The late lamented Patrick Morkan, our grandfather that is, explained Gabriel, commonly known in his later years as the old gentleman, was a glue boiler.

—O now, Gabriel, said aunt Kate laughing, he had a starch mill.

—Well, glue or starch, said Gabriel, the old gentleman had a horse by the name of Johnny. And Johnny used to work in the old gentleman's mill walking round and round in order to drive the mill. That was all very well; but now comes the tragic part about Johnny. One fine day the old gentleman thought he'd like to drive out with the quality to a military review in the park.

—The Lord have mercy on his soul, said Aunt Kate compassionately.

—Amen, said Gabriel. So the old gentleman, as I said, harnessed Johnny and put on his very best tall hat and his very best stock collar and drove out in grand

---

[1]   *astrakhan* Lambskin.

[2]   *trap* Small, two-wheeled carriage on springs.

style from his ancestral mansion somewhere near Back Lane, I think.

Everyone laughed, even Mrs. Malins, at Gabriel's manner and Aunt Kate said:

—O now, Gabriel, he didn't live in Back Lane really. Only the mill was there.

—Out from the mansion of his forefathers, continued Gabriel, he drove with Johnny. And everything went on beautifully until Johnny came in sight of King Billy's[1] statue: and whether he fell in love with the horse King Billy sits on or whether he thought he was back again in the mill, anyhow he began to walk round the statue.

Gabriel paced in a circle round the hall in his goloshes amid the laughter of the others.

—Round and round he went, said Gabriel, and the old gentleman, who was a very pompous old gentleman, was highly indignant. *Go on, sir! What do you mean, sir? Johnny! Johnny! Most extraordinary conduct! Can't understand the horse!*

The peals of laughter which followed Gabriel's imitation of the incident were interrupted by a resounding knock at the hall door. Mary Jane ran to open it and let in Freddy Malins. Freddy Malins, with his hat well back on his head and his shoulders humped with cold, was puffing and steaming after his exertions.

—I could only get one cab, he said.

—O, we'll find another along the quay, said Gabriel.

—Yes, said Aunt Kate. Better not keep Mrs. Malins standing in the draught.

Mrs. Malins was helped down the front steps by her son and Mr. Browne and, after many manoeuvres, hoisted into the cab. Freddy Malins clambered in after her and spent a long time settling her on the seat, Mr. Browne helping him with advice. At last she was settled comfortably and Freddy Malins invited Mr. Browne into the cab. There was a good deal of confused talk, then Mr. Browne got into the cab. The cabman settled his rug over his knees and bent down for the address. The confusion grew greater and the cabman was directed differently by Freddy Malins and Mr. Browne, each of whom had his head out through a window of the cab. The difficulty was to know where to drop Mr.

Browne along the route and Aunt Kate, Aunt Julia and Mary Jane helped the discussion from the doorstep with cross-directions and contradictions and abundance of laughter. As for Freddy Malins he was speechless with laughter. He popped his head in and out of the window every moment, to the great danger of his hat, and told his mother how the discussion was progressing till at last Mr. Browne shouted to the bewildered cabman above the din of everybody's laughter:

—Do you know Trinity College?

—Yes, sir, said the cabman.

—Well, drive bang up against Trinity College gates, said Mr. Browne, and then we'll tell you where to go. You understand now?

—Yes, sir, said the cabman.

—Make like a bird for Trinity College.

—Right, sir, cried the cabman.

The horse was whipped up and the cab rattled off along the quay amid a chorus of laughter and adieus.

Gabriel had not gone to the door with the others. He was in a dark part of the hall gazing up the staircase. A woman was standing near the top of the first flight in the shadow also. He could not see her face but he could see the terracotta and salmonpink panels of her skirt which the shadow made appear black and white. It was his wife. She was leaning on the banisters listening to something. Gabriel was surprised at her stillness and strained his ear to listen also. But he could hear little save the noise of laughter and dispute on the front steps, a few chords struck on the piano and a few notes of a man's voice singing.

He stood still in the gloom of the hall, trying to catch the air that the voice was singing and gazing up at his wife. There was grace and mystery in her attitude as if she were a symbol of something. He asked himself what is a woman standing on the stairs in the shadow, listening to distant music, a symbol of. If he were a painter he would paint her in that attitude. Her blue felt hat would show off the bronze of her hair against the darkness and the dark panels of her skirt would show off the light ones. *Distant Music* he would call the picture if he were a painter.

The hall door was closed and Aunt Kate, Aunt Julia and Mary Jane came down the hall, still laughing.

—Well, isn't Freddy terrible? said Mary Jane. He's

[1] *King Billy* King William III (William of Orange), who took the British throne in the Glorious Revolution of 1688.

really terrible.

Gabriel said nothing but pointed up the stairs towards where his wife was standing. Now that the hall door was closed the voice and the piano could be heard more clearly. Gabriel held up his hand for them to be silent. The song seemed to be in the old Irish tonality and the singer seemed uncertain both of his words and of his voice. The voice made plaintive by the distance and by the singer's hoarseness faintly illuminated the cadence of the air with words expressing grief:

—*O, the rain falls on my heavy locks*
And the dew wets my shin,
My babe lies cold …

—O, exclaimed Mary Jane. It's Bartell D'Arcy singing and he wouldn't sing all the night. O, I'll get him to sing a song before he goes.

—O do, Mary Jane, said Aunt Kate.

Mary Jane brushed past the others and ran to the staircase but before she reached it the singing stopped and the piano was closed abruptly.

—O, what a pity! she cried. Is he coming down, Gretta? Gabriel heard his wife answer yes and saw her come down towards them. A few steps behind her were Mr. Bartell D'Arcy and Miss O'Callaghan.

—O, Mr. D'Arcy, cried Mary Jane, it's downright mean of you to break off like that when we were all in raptures listening to you.

—I have been at him all the evening, said Miss O'Callaghan, and Mrs. Conroy too, and he told us he had a dreadful cold and couldn't sing.

—O, Mr. D'Arcy, said Aunt Kate, now that was a great fib to tell.

—Can't you see that I'm as hoarse as a crow? said Mr. D'Arcy roughly.

He went into the pantry hastily and put on his overcoat. The others, taken aback by his rude speech, could find nothing to say. Aunt Kate wrinkled her brows and made signs to the others to drop the subject. Mr. D'Arcy stood swathing his neck carefully and frowning.

—It's the weather, said Aunt Julia after a pause.

—Yes, everybody has colds, said Aunt Kate readily, everybody.

—They say, said Mary Jane, we haven't had snow like it for thirty years: and I read this morning in the newspaper that the snow is general all over Ireland.

—I love the look of snow, said Aunt Julia sadly.

—So do I, said Miss O'Callaghan. I think Christmas is never really Christmas unless we have the snow on the ground.

—But poor Mr. D'Arcy doesn't like the snow, said Aunt Kate smiling.

Mr. D'Arcy came from the pantry, fully swathed and buttoned, and in a repentant tone told them the history of his cold. Everyone gave him advice and said it was a great pity and urged him to be very careful of his throat in the night air. Gabriel watched his wife who did not join in the conversation. She was standing right under the dusty fanlight and the flame of the gas lit up the rich bronze of her hair which he had seen her drying at the fire a few days before. She was in the same attitude and seemed unaware of the talk about her. At last she turned towards them and Gabriel saw that there was colour on her cheeks and that her eyes were shining. A sudden tide of joy went leaping out of his heart.

—Mr. D'Arcy, she said, what is the name of that song you were singing?

—It's called *The Lass of Aughrim*,[1] said Mr. D'Arcy, but I couldn't remember it properly. Why? Do you know it?

—*The Lass of Aughrim*, she repeated. I couldn't think of the name.

—It's a very nice air, said Mary Jane. I'm sorry you were not in voice tonight.

—Now, Mary Jane, said Aunt Kate, don't annoy Mr. D'Arcy. I won't have him annoyed.

Seeing that all were ready to start she shepherded them to the door where goodnight was said:

—Well, goodnight Aunt Kate, and thanks for the pleasant evening.

—Goodnight, Gabriel. Goodnight, Gretta!

—Goodnight, Aunt Kate, and thanks ever so much. Goodnight, Aunt Julia.

—O, goodnight, Gretta, I didn't see you.

—Goodnight, Mr. D'Arcy. Goodnight, Miss

---

[1] *The Lass of Aughrim* Irish ballad about a peasant girl who commits suicide when her noble seducer refuses to recognize her when she arrives at his door pregnant with his child.

O'Callaghan.

—Goodnight, Miss Morkan.

—Goodnight again.

—Goodnight all. Safe home.

—Goodnight. Goodnight.

The morning was still dark. A dull yellow light brooded over the houses and the river and the sky seemed to be descending. It was slushy underfoot and only streaks and patches of snow lay on the roofs, on the parapets of the quay and on the area railings. The lamps were still burning redly in the murky air and, across the river, the palace of the Four Courts[1] stood out menacingly against the heavy sky.

She was walking on before him with Mr. Bartell D'Arcy, her shoes in a brown parcel tucked under one arm and her hands holding her skirt up from the slush. She had no longer any grace of attitude but Gabriel's eyes were still bright with happiness. The blood went bounding along his veins and the thoughts went rioting through his brain, proud, joyful, tender, valorous.

She was walking on before him so lightly and so erect that he longed to run after her noiselessly, catch her by the shoulders and say something foolish and affectionate into her ear. She seemed to him so frail that he longed to defend her against something and then to be alone with her. Moments of their secret life together burst like stars upon his memory. A heliotrope envelope was lying beside his breakfast cup and he was caressing it with his hand. Birds were twittering in the ivy and the sunny web of the curtain was shimmering along the floor: he could not eat for happiness. They were standing on the crowded platform and he was placing a ticket inside the warm palm of her glove. He was standing with her in the cold, looking in through a grated window at a man making bottles in a roaring furnace. It was very cold. Her face, fragrant in the cold air, was quite close to his and suddenly she called out to the man at the furnace:

—Is the fire hot, sir?

But the man could not hear her with the noise of the furnace. It was just as well. He might have answered rudely.

A wave of yet more tender joy escaped from his heart and went coursing in warm flood along his arteries. Like the tender fire of stars moments of their life together, that no one knew of or would ever know of, broke upon and illumined his memory. He longed to recall to her those moments, to make her forget the years of their dull existence together and remember only their moments of ecstasy. For the years, he felt, had not quenched his soul or hers. Their children, his writing, her household cares had not quenched all their souls' tender fire. In one letter that he had written to her then he had said: *Why is it that words like these seem to me so dull and cold? Is it because there is no word tender enough to be your name?*

Like distant music these words that he had written years before were borne towards him from the past. He longed to be alone with her. When the others had gone away, when he and she were in their room in the hotel, then they would be alone together. He would call her softly:

—Gretta!

Perhaps she would not hear at once: she would be undressing. Then something in his voice would strike her. She would turn and look at him …

At the corner of Winetavern Street they met a cab. He was glad of its rattling noise as it saved him from conversation. She was looking out of the window and seemed tired. The others spoke only a few words, pointing out some building or street. The horse galloped along wearily under the murky morning sky, dragging his old rattling box after his heels, and Gabriel was again in a cab with her, galloping to catch the boat, galloping to their honeymoon.

As the cab drove across O'Connell bridge Miss O'Callaghan said:

—They say you never cross O'Connell bridge without seeing a white horse.

—I see a white man this time, said Gabriel.

—Where? asked Mr. Bartell D'Arcy.

Gabriel pointed to the statue[2] on which lay patches of snow. Then he nodded familiarly to it and waved his hand.

—Goodnight, Dan, he said gaily.

When the cab drew up before the hotel Gabriel

---

[1] *palace … Courts* Judicial building; home of the four traditional divisions of the judicial system in Ireland.

[2] *the statue* The O'Connell Memorial, commemorating Irish nationalist Daniel O'Connell (1775–1847).

jumped out and, in spite of Mr. Bartell D'Arcy's protest, paid the driver. He gave the man a shilling over his fare. The man saluted and said:

—A prosperous new year to you, sir.

—The same to you, said Gabriel cordially.

She leaned for a moment on his arm in getting out of the cab and while standing at the kerbstone bidding the others goodnight. She leaned lightly on his arm, as lightly as when she had danced with him a few hours before. He had felt proud and happy then, happy that she was his, proud of her grace and wifely carriage. But now after the kindling again of so many memories, the first touch of her body, musical and strange and perfumed, sent through him a keen pang of lust. Under cover of her silence he pressed her arm closely to his side: and, as they stood at the hotel door, he felt that they had escaped from their lives and duties, escaped from home and friends and run away together with wild and radiant hearts to a new adventure.

An old man was dozing in a great hooded chair in the hall. He lit a candle in the office and went before them to the stairs. They followed him in silence, their feet falling in soft thuds on the thickly carpeted stairs. She mounted the stairs behind the porter, her head bowed in the ascent, her frail shoulders curved as with a burden, her skirt girt tightly about her. He could have flung his arms about her hips and held her still for his arms were trembling with desire to seize her and only the stress of his nails against the palms of his hands held the wild impulse of his body in check. The porter halted on the stairs to settle his guttering candle. They halted too on the steps below him. In the silence Gabriel could hear the falling of the molten wax into the tray and the thumping of his own heart against his ribs.

The porter led them along a corridor and opened a door. Then he set his unstable candle down on a toilet table and asked at what hour they were to be called in the morning.

—Eight, said Gabriel.

The porter pointed to the tap of the electric light and began a muttered apology but Gabriel cut him short.

—We don't want any light. We have light enough from the street. And, I say, he added pointing to the candle, you might remove that handsome article, like a

good man.

The porter took up his candle again, but slowly, for he was surprised by such a novel idea. Then he mumbled goodnight and went out. Gabriel shot the lock to.

A ghostly light from the street lamp lay in a long shaft from one window to the door. Gabriel threw his overcoat and hat on a couch and crossed the room towards the window. He looked down into the street in order that his emotion might calm a little. Then he turned and leaned against a chest of drawers with his back to the light. She had taken off her hat and cloak and was standing before a large swinging mirror, unhooking her waist. Gabriel paused for a few moments, watching her, and then said:

—Gretta!

She turned away from the mirror slowly and walked along the shaft of light towards him. Her face looked so serious and weary that the words would not pass Gabriel's lips. No, it was not the moment yet.

—You look tired, he said.

—I am a little, she answered.

—You don't feel ill or weak?

—No, tired: that's all.

She went on to the window and stood there, looking out. Gabriel waited again and then, fearing that diffidence was about to conquer him, he said abruptly:

—By the way, Gretta!

—What is it?

—You know that poor fellow Malins? he said quickly.

—Yes, what about him?

—Well, poor fellow, he's a decent sort of chap after all, continued Gabriel in a false voice. He gave me back that sovereign I lent him and I didn't expect it really. It's a pity he wouldn't keep away from that Browne because he's not a bad fellow at heart.

He was trembling now with annoyance. Why did she seem so abstracted? He did not know how he could begin. Was she annoyed too about something? If she would only turn to him or come to him of her own accord! To take her as she was would be brutal. No, he must see some ardour in her eyes first. He longed to be master of her strange mood.

—When did you lend him the pound? she asked after a pause. Gabriel strove to restrain himself from breaking out into brutal language about the sottish Malins and his pound. He longed to cry to her from his soul, to crush her body against his, to overmaster her. But he said:

—O, at Christmas, when he opened that little Christmas card shop in Henry Street.

He was in such a fever of rage and desire that he did not hear her come from the window. She stood before him for an instant looking at him strangely. Then, suddenly raising herself on tiptoe and resting her hands lightly on his shoulders, she kissed him.

—You are a very generous person, Gabriel, she said.

Gabriel, trembling with delight at her sudden kiss and at the quaintness of her phrase, put his hands on her hair and began smoothing it back, scarcely touching it with his fingers. The washing had made it fine and brilliant. His heart was brimming over with happiness. Just when he was wishing for it she had come to him of her own accord. Perhaps her thoughts had been running with his. Perhaps she had felt the impetuous desire that was in him and then the yielding mood had come upon her. Now that she had fallen to him so easily he wondered why he had been so diffident.

He stood, holding her head between his hands. Then, slipping one arm swiftly about her body and drawing her towards him, he said softly:

—Gretta dear, what are you thinking about?

She did not answer nor yield wholly to his arm. He said again softly:

—Tell me what it is, Gretta. I think I know what is the matter. Do I know?

She did not answer at once. Then she said in an outburst of tears:

—O, I am thinking about that song, *The Lass of Aughrim*.

She broke loose from him and ran to the bed and, throwing her arms across the bedrail, hid her face. Gabriel stood stockstill for a moment in astonishment and then followed her. As he passed in the way of the cheval glass he caught sight of himself in full length, his broad, wellfilled shirtfront, the face whose expression always puzzled him when he saw it in a mirror and his glimmering gilt-rimmed eyeglasses. He halted a few paces from her and said:

—What about the song? Why does that make you cry?

She raised her head from her arms and dried her eyes with the back of her hand like a child. A kinder note than he had intended went into his voice.

—Why, Gretta? he asked.

—I am thinking about a person long ago who used to sing that song.

—And who was the person long ago? asked Gabriel smiling.

—It was a person I used to know in Galway when I was living with my grandmother, she said.

The smile passed away from Gabriel's face. A dull anger began to gather again at the back of his mind and the dull fires of his lust began to glow angrily in his veins.

—Someone you were in love with? he asked ironically.

—It was a young boy I used to know, she answered, named Michael Furey. He used to sing that song, *The Lass of Aughrim*. He was very delicate.

Gabriel was silent. He did not wish her to think that he was interested in this delicate boy.

—I can see him so plainly, she said after a moment. Such eyes as he had, big dark eyes! And such an expression in them—an expression! ...

—O, then you were in love with him? said Gabriel.

—I used to go out walking with him, she said, when I was in Galway.

A thought flew across Gabriel's mind.

—Perhaps that was why you wanted to go to Galway with that Ivors girl? he said coldly.

She looked at him and asked in surprise:

—What for?

Her eyes made Gabriel feel awkward. He shrugged his shoulders and said:

—How do I know? To see him, perhaps.

She looked away from him along the shaft of light towards the window in silence.

—He is dead, she said at length. He died when he was only seventeen. Isn't it a terrible thing to die so young as that?

—What was he? asked Gabriel, still ironically.

—He was in the gasworks, she said.

Gabriel felt humiliated by the failure of his irony and by the evocation of this figure from the dead, a boy in the gasworks. The irony of his mood soured into sarcasm. While he had been full of memories of their secret life together, full of tenderness and joy and desire, she had been comparing him in her mind with another. A shameful consciousness of his own person assailed him. He saw himself as a ludicrous figure, acting as a pennyboy for his aunts, a nervous wellmeaning sentimentalist, orating to vulgarians and idealising his own clownish lusts, the pitiable fatuous fellow he had caught a glimpse of in the mirror. Instinctively he turned his back more to the light lest she might see the shame that burned upon his forehead.

He tried to keep up his tone of cold interrogation but his voice when he spoke was humble and indifferent.

—I suppose you were in love with this Michael Furey, Gretta, he said.

—I was great with him at that time, she said.

Her voice was veiled and sad. Gabriel, feeling now how vain it would be to try to lead her whither he had purposed, caressed one of her hands and said also sadly:

—And what did he die of so young, Gretta? Consumption, was it?

—I think he died for me, she answered.

A vague terror seized Gabriel at this answer as if, at that hour when he had hoped to triumph, some impalpable and vindictive being was coming against him, gathering forces against him in its vague world. But he shook himself free of it with an effort of reason and continued to caress her hand. He did not question her again for he felt that she would tell him of herself. Her hand was warm and moist: it did not respond to his touch but he continued to caress it just as he had caressed her first letter to him that spring morning.

—It was in the winter, she said, about the beginning of the winter when I was going to leave my grandmother's and come up here to the convent. And he was ill at the time in his lodgings in Galway and wouldn't be let out and his people in Oughterard were written to. He was in decline, they said, or something like that. I never knew rightly.

She paused for a moment and sighed.

—Poor fellow, she said, he was very fond of me and he was such a gentle boy. We used to go out together walking, you know, Gabriel, like the way they do in the country. He was going to study singing only for his health. He had a very good voice, poor Michael Furey.

—Well, and then? asked Gabriel.

—And then when it came to the time for me to leave Galway and come up to the convent he was much worse and I wouldn't be let see him so I wrote him a letter saying I was going up to Dublin and would be back in the summer and hoping he would be better then.

She paused for a moment to get her voice under control and then went on:

—Then the night before I left I was in my grandmother's house in Nun's Island, packing up, and I heard gravel thrown up against the window. The window was so wet I couldn't see so I ran downstairs as I was and slipped out the back into the garden and there was the poor fellow at the end of the garden shivering.

—And did you not tell him to go back? asked Gabriel.

—I implored of him to go home at once and told him he would get his death in the rain. But he said he did not want to live. I can see his eyes as well as well![1] He was standing at the end of the wall where there was a tree.

—And did he go home? asked Gabriel.

—Yes, he went home. And when I was only a week in the convent he died and he was buried in Oughterard where his people came from. O, the day I heard that, that he was dead! …

She stopped, choking with sobs and, overcome by emotion, flung herself face downward on the bed, sobbing in the quilt. Gabriel held her hand for a moment longer, irresolutely, and then, shy of intruding on her grief, let it fall gently and walked quietly to the window. She was fast asleep.

Gabriel, leaning on his elbow, looked for a few moments unresentfully at her tangled hair and half open mouth, listening to her deep drawn breath. So she had had that romance in her life: a man had died for her sake. It hardly pained him now to think how poor a part he, her husband, had played in her life. He watched her while she slept as though he and she had never lived together as man and wife. His curious eyes rested long

---

[1]   *as well as well* I.e., as well as well can be.

upon her face and on her hair: and as he thought of what she must have been then, in that time of her first girlish beauty, a strange friendly pity for her entered his soul. He did not like to say even to himself that her face was no longer beautiful but he knew that it was no longer the face for which Michael Furey had braved death.

Perhaps she had not told him all the story. His eyes moved to the chair over which she had thrown some of her clothes. A petticoat string dangled to the floor. One boot stood upright, its limp upper fallen down: the fellow of it lay upon its side. He wondered at his riot of emotions of an hour before. From what had it proceeded? From his aunts' supper, from his own foolish speech, from the wine and dancing, the merrymaking when saying goodnight in the hall, the pleasure of the walk along the river in the snow. Poor Aunt Julia! She too would soon be a shade[1] with the shade of Patrick Morkan and his horse. He had caught that haggard look upon her face for a moment when she was singing *Arrayed for the Bridal.* Soon perhaps he would be sitting in that same drawingroom, dressed in black, his silk hat on his knees. The blinds would be drawn down and Aunt Kate would be sitting beside him, crying and blowing her nose and telling him how Julia had died. He would cast about in his mind for some words that might console her and would find only lame and useless ones. Yes, yes: that would happen very soon.

The air of the room chilled his shoulders. He stretched himself cautiously along under the sheets and lay down beside his wife. One by one they were all becoming shades. Better pass boldly into that other world, in the full glory of some passion, than fade and wither dismally with age. He thought of how she who lay beside him had locked in her heart for so many years that image of her lover's eyes when he had told her that he did not wish to live.

Generous tears filled Gabriel's eyes. He had never felt like that himself towards any woman but he knew that such a feeling must be love. The tears gathered more thickly in his eyes and in the partial darkness he imagined he saw the form of a young man standing under a dripping tree. Other forms were near. His soul had approached that region where dwell the vast hosts of the dead. He was conscious of, but could not apprehend, their wayward and flickering existence. His own identity was fading out into a grey impalpable world: the solid world itself which these dead had one time reared and lived in was dissolving and dwindling.

A few light taps upon the pane made him turn to the window. It had begun to snow again. He watched sleepily the flakes, silver and dark, falling obliquely against the lamplight. The time had come for him to set out on his journey westward. Yes, the newspapers were right: snow was general all over Ireland. It was falling on every part of the dark central plain, on the treeless hills, falling softly upon the Bog of Allen and, farther westward, softly falling into the dark mutinous Shannon waves. It was falling, too, upon every part of the lonely churchyard on the hill where Michael Furey lay buried. It lay thickly drifted on the crooked crosses and headstones, on the spears of the little gate, on the barren thorns. His soul swooned slowly as he heard the snow falling faintly through the universe and faintly falling, like the descent of their last end, upon all the living and the dead.

—1914

---

[1] *shade* Ghost.

IN CONTEXT

Joyce's Dublin

The Custom House and the River Liffey, 1885.

Above: View from the O'Connell Bridge along what is now O'Connell Street (then Sackville Street), c. 1905. Daniel O'Connell (1775–1847), known as the Great Liberator, was a nationalist leader to whom Joyce claimed a family connection. The statue of O'Connell referred to in "The Dead" stands in front of Nelson's Pillar (in the background in this photograph).

Right: View of O'Connell Bridge and the Liffey, c. 1895.

D.H. LAWRENCE
1885 – 1930

D.H. Lawrence declared that "one sheds one's sicknesses in books." That claim suggests not only the sufferings of a man whose fierce desire to live was helplessly incarcerated in a body wasting away from tuberculosis, but also the broader afflictions associated with British modernization: the rise of machine culture, the devastating loss of life in World War I, and the outmoded moral values governing relations between the sexes and the classes. A prolific writer, Lawrence "shed" a staggering array of novels, short stories, essays, and poems that relentlessly—and usually scandalously—broke cultural prohibitions to pioneer a new language of sexual and social possibility.

Some critics claim that Lawrence's only lasting allegiance was to his mother, an omnipresent figure who haunted his thoughts long after her death from cancer when he was twenty-five. David Herbert Lawrence, the fourth of five children born in the English mining town of Eastwood, Nottinghamshire, was his mother's favorite. Lawrence's parents were miserably mismatched. Lydia Lawrence felt she had married beneath herself, and struggled to cultivate more than working-class sensibilities in her children. Arthur Lawrence, the miner father, felt belittled by his own family. Marital tensions remembered from childhood percolate through Lawrence's works. If at first he villainized his father in the guise of various literary characters, Lawrence slowly gained sympathy for his father's awkward role in the family and for his earthy vitality. Scenes of an educated woman being sexually liberated through a liaison with a virile working-class man—most controversially explicit in *Lady Chatterley's Lover* (1928)—are seen throughout the works of Lawrence. His early novel *Sons and Lovers* (1913), while often interpreted as an Oedipal tale of mother-love, has also been read as a story of matricide. Feminist critics have noted how his texts encode both adoration and dread of the primal power Lawrence imagined that the female held over the male.

Lawrence worked as a clerk and an elementary-school teacher to pay for his studies at Nottingham University College, and obtained his teacher's certificate in 1908. He secured a good teaching position at the Davidson Road School in Croydon, one of England's spacious new turn-of-the-century state schools. But two severe attacks of pneumonia, at ages sixteen and twenty-six, nearly killed Lawrence and led him to give up his teaching career. His close encounters with death left him, in the words of one critic, "with a heightened awareness of the physical world and a messianic tendency to preach." A suspected if not yet confirmed consumptive, Lawrence broke off an uninspired engagement to Louie Burrows on the grounds that his doctor advised against marriage.

Ford Madox Ford, editor of *The English Review* when the prestigious journal published Lawrence's first poems in 1909, introduced Lawrence to literati who were fascinated by the idea of meeting a young working-class genius in the flesh. A "primitivism" that at the time was prompting writers and artists to seek a remedy for European modernity in non-European cultures also supported fantasies about the curative raw talent of the working class. (Lawrence, romanticized for his class background, would himself exoticize Mexican culture in his 1926 novel, *The Plumed Serpent*.)

Though Lawrence castigated homosexual desire throughout his life (most sharply in his introduction to Maurice Magnus's steamy *Memoirs of the Foreign Legion*, 1924), a homoerotic element in his work makes its appearance in the first of his novels, *The White Peacock* (1910). The figure of "Cyril" in the novel, based upon his childhood friend Alan Chambers, may have represented one of the loves of Lawrence's life. Soon after his second illness, however, Lawrence was to have a fateful encounter with Frieda von Richthofen at the home of Ernest Weekley, one of Lawrence's favorite professors from college. Lawrence was by now rebelling against the universe of Christian guilt and glorifying an animal instinct in its place; he quickly came to worship the sensuality of Weekley's wife, a German baroness (and cousin of the WWI German flying ace Manfred von Richthofen, the "Red Baron"). Though Frieda left her husband and three children to be with Lawrence, she had little intention of re-marrying; it was Lawrence who pressured Frieda into marriage and cut her off from her young children, fearful that he could not compete with the force of maternal love which he himself knew so well.

Before meeting Lawrence, Frieda had been the lover of Otto Gross, a Freudian disciple who believed in sexually revolutionizing society to a degree never endorsed by Freud, and the indomitable Frieda continued to have countless lovers after marrying Lawrence. Lawrence's commitment to monogamy was in conflict with his goal of transcending sexual possessiveness. The Lawrences' many arguments were recorded by many visitors, yet the two remained together until Lawrence's death. To an acquaintance who asked what his ultimate message was, Lawrence wrote, "You shall love your wife completely and implicitly and in entire nakedness of body and spirit." Yet as one biographer dryly noted, "Lawrence's complete love included throttling her and covering her with bruises."

Lawrence's second major work of fiction, *The Rainbow*, was published in 1915, but its descriptions of sex and its coarse language led not only to its suppression, but also to legal difficulties for Lawrence. Persecuted, as well, during the war years, on account of his German wife and his provocative views, Lawrence felt exiled. Embracing a tramp-like lifestyle with Frieda, Lawrence set up house successively in Italy, Australia, the United States, Mexico, and France. World War I bred in Lawrence a fierce desire to form a community of the like-minded in tune with archetypal life forces, and the Lawrences' nomadic lifestyle was largely fueled by his restless utopian desires.

If Lawrence's sexual frankness created controversy, his radical dissolution of conventional narrative voice also disturbed many contemporaries. By the time he published *Women in Love* (1921), a story of two sisters who leave the countryside in pursuit of modern careers and sexual freedom, Lawrence no longer put any stock in individual subjectivity. His fiction strove to capture poetically the impersonal forces of nature that work through individuals but are in themselves vast and impersonal. To many minds, *Women in Love* succeeds magnificently in conveying a sense of individuals caught in the struggle with larger forces.

The publication of *Lady Chatterley's Lover* (1928) further scandalized the British public. The novel graphically depicts the primal sexuality awakened in Constance Chatterley by her working-class lover, Mellors. An anonymous critic who reviewed the novel in *John Bull* famously called it "a cesspool, the most obscene book in the English language." The publication of the book provoked censorship debates in the British Parliament in 1929, and the novel's label of "obscene" was not officially lifted until 1960.

Both Lawrence and his wife refused to admit that he was dying of tuberculosis until the disease was too advanced to deny. He died in 1930 at the age of 45 in the south of France.

⌘⌘⌘

Snake

A Snake came to my water-trough
   On a hot, hot day, and I in pyjamas for the heat,
To drink there.

In the deep, strange-scented shade of the great dark
   carob-tree
5 I came down the steps with my pitcher
And must wait, must stand and wait, for there he was
   at the trough before me.

He reached down from a fissure in the earth-wall in
   the gloom
And trailed his yellow-brown slackness soft-bellied
   down, over the edge of the stone trough
And rested his throat upon the stone bottom,
10 And where the water had dripped from the tap, in a
   small clearness,
He sipped with his straight mouth,
Softly drank through his straight gums, into his slack
   long body,
Silently.

Someone was before me at my water-trough,
15 And I, like a second comer, waiting.

He lifted his head from his drinking, as cattle do,
And looked at me vaguely, as drinking cattle do,
And flickered his two-forked tongue from his lips, and
   mused a moment,
And stooped and drank a little more,
20 Being earth-brown, earth-golden from the burning
   bowels of the earth
On the day of Sicilian July, with Etna[1] smoking.

The voice of my education said to me
He must be killed,
For in Sicily the black, black snakes are innocent, the
   gold are venomous.

25 And voices in me said, If you were a man
You would take a stick and break him now, and finish
   him off.

But must I confess how I liked him,
How glad I was he had come like a guest in quiet, to
   drink at my water-trough
And depart peaceful, pacified, and thankless,
30 Into the burning bowels of this earth?

Was it cowardice, that I dared not kill him?
Was it perversity, that I longed to talk to him?
Was it humility, to feel so honoured?
I felt so honoured.

35 And yet those voices:
If you were not afraid, you would kill him!

And truly I was afraid, I was most afraid,
But even so, honoured still more
That he should seek my hospitality
40 From out the dark door of the secret earth.

He drank enough
And lifted his head, dreamily, as one who has
   drunken,
And flickered his tongue like a forked night on the
   air, so black,
Seeming to lick his lips,
45 And looked around like a god, unseeing, into the air,
And slowly turned his head,
And slowly, very slowly, as if thrice adream,
Proceeded to draw his slow length curving round
And climb again the broken bank of my wall-face.

50 And as he put his head into that dreadful hole,
And as he slowly drew up, snake-easing his shoulders,
   and entered farther,
A sort of horror, a sort of protest against his
   withdrawing into that horrid black hole,

---

[1] *Etna* Volcano in Sicily.

Deliberately going into the blackness, and slowly
    drawing himself after,
Overcame me now his back was turned.

55 I looked round, I put down my pitcher,
I picked up a clumsy log
And threw it at the water-trough with a clatter.

I think it did not hit him,
But suddenly that part of him that was left behind
    convulsed in undignified haste,
60 Writhed like lightning, and was gone
Into the black hole, the earth-lipped fissure in the
    wall-front,
At which, in the intense still noon, I stared with
    fascination.

And immediately I regretted it.
I thought how paltry, how vulgar, what a mean act!
65 I despised myself and the voices of my accursed
    human education.

And I thought of the albatross,[1]
And I wished he would come back, my snake.

For he seemed to me again like a king,
Like a king in exile, uncrowned in the underworld,
70 Now due to be crowned again.

And so, I missed my chance with one of the lords
Of life.
And I have something to expiate;
A pettiness.
    —1923

---

[1] *albatross* Reference to Samuel Taylor Coleridge's *Rime of the Ancient Mariner* (1798), in which a sailor needlessly and thoughtlessly kills an albatross.

Bavarian Gentians

Not every man has gentians[2] in his house
in soft September, at slow, sad Michaelmas.[3]

Bavarian gentians, big and dark, only dark
darkening the day-time, torch-like with the smoking
    blueness of Pluto's[4] gloom,
5 ribbed and torch-like, with their blaze of darkness
    spread blue
down flattening into points, flattened under the sweep
    of white day
torch-flower of the blue-smoking darkness, Pluto's
    dark-blue daze,
black lamps from the halls of Dis, burning dark blue,
giving off darkness, blue darkness, as Demeter's pale
    lamps give off light,
10 lead me then, lead the way.

Reach me a gentian, give me a torch!
let me guide myself with the blue, forked torch of this
    flower
down the darker and darker stairs, where blue is
    darkened on blueness
even where Persephone goes, just now, from the
    frosted September
15 to the sightless realm where darkness is awake upon
    the dark
and Persephone herself is but a voice
or a darkness invisible enfolded in the deeper dark
of the arms Plutonic, and pierced with the passion of
    dense gloom,

---

[2] *gentians* Herb that bears blue flowers.

[3] *Michaelmas* Feast of St. Michael the Archangel, on September 29.

[4] *Pluto* Greek God of the underworld (Roman Dis). He abducted Persephone, daughter of Demeter (the goddess of agriculture), and brought her to Hades to be his queen. Her mother grieved for her loss, putting the earth into an eternal winter. Finally she was allowed to return to earth for half the year (the reason for spring and summer) if she returned to Hades for the other half (the reason for fall and winter).

among the splendour of torches of darkness, shedding darkness on the lost bride and her groom.[1]

—1933

Odour of Chrysanthemums

I

The small locomotive engine, Number 4, came clanking, stumbling down from Selston with seven full wagons. It appeared round the corner with loud threats of speed, but the colt that it startled from among the gorse,[2] which still flickered indistinctly in the raw afternoon, out-distanced it at a canter. A woman, walking up the railway line to Underwood, drew back into the hedge, held her basket aside, and watched the footplate of the engine advancing. The trucks thumped heavily past, one by one, with slow inevitable movement, as she stood insignificantly trapped between the jolting black wagons and the hedge; then they curved away towards the coppice[3] where the withered oak leaves dropped noiselessly, while the birds, pulling at the scarlet hips[4] beside the track, made off into the dusk that had already crept into the spinney.[5] In the open, the smoke from the engine sank and cleaved to the rough grass. The fields were dreary and forsaken, and in the marshy strip that led to the whimsey,[6] a reedy pit-pond, the fowls had already abandoned their run among the alders, to roost in the tarred fowl-house. The pit-bank loomed up beyond the pond, flames like red sores licking its ashy sides, in the afternoon's stagnant light. Just beyond rose the tapering chimneys and the clumsy black headstocks of Brinsley Colliery.[7] The two wheels

were spinning fast up against the sky, and the winding engine rapped out its little spasms. The miners were being turned up.

The engine whistled as it came into the wide bay of railway lines beside the colliery, where rows of trucks stood in harbour.

Miners, single, trailing and in groups, passed like shadows diverging home. At the edge of the ribbed level of sidings squat a low cottage, three steps down from the cinder track. A large bony vine clutched at the house, as if to claw down the tiled roof. Round the bricked yard grew a few wintry primroses. Beyond, the long garden sloped down to a bush-covered brook course. There were some twiggy apple trees, winter-crack trees, and ragged cabbages. Beside the path hung dishevelled pink chrysanthemums, like pink cloths hung on bushes. A woman came stooping out of the felt-covered fowl-house, halfway down the garden. She closed and pad-locked the door, then drew herself erect, having brushed some bits from her white apron.

She was a tall woman of imperious mien,[8] handsome, with definite black eyebrows. Her smooth black hair was parted exactly. For a few moments she stood steadily watching the miners as they passed along the railway: then she turned towards the brook course. Her face was calm and set, her mouth was closed with disillusionment. After a moment she called:

"John!" There was no answer. She waited, and then said distinctly:

"Where are you?"

"Here!" replied a child's sulky voice from among the bushes. The woman looked piercingly through the dusk.

"Are you at that brook?" she asked sternly.

For answer the child showed himself before the raspberry-canes that rose like whips. He was a small, sturdy boy of five. He stood quite still, defiantly.

"Oh!" said the mother, conciliated. "I thought you were down at that wet brook—and you remember what I told you—"

The boy did not move or answer.

"Come, come on in," she said more gently, "it's getting dark. There's your grandfather's engine coming down the line!"

---

[1] *among...groom*   In another, longer version of the poem (thought to be an earlier version), the following three lines follow: "Give me a flower on a tall stem, and three dark flames, / for I will go to the wedding, and be wedding-guest / at the marriage of the living dark."

[2] *gorse*   Prickly shrub.

[3] *coppice*   Thicket of small trees.

[4] *hips*   Fruits (of wild roses).

[5] *spinney*   Small copse.

[6] *whimsey*   Machine used to raise water or ore from a mine.

[7] *headstocks*   Supports of revolving machine parts; *Colliery* Coal mine.

[8] *mien*   Bearing.

The lad advanced slowly, with resentful, taciturn movement. He was dressed in trousers and waistcoat of cloth that was too thick and hard for the size of the garments. They were evidently cut down from a man's clothes.

As they went slowly towards the house he tore at the ragged wisps of chrysanthemums and dropped the petals in handfuls among the path.

"Don't do that—it does look nasty," said his mother. He refrained, and she, suddenly pitiful, broke off a twig with three or four wan flowers and held them against her face. When mother and son reached the yard her hand hesitated, and instead of laying the flower aside, she pushed it in her apron-band. The mother and son stood at the foot of the three steps looking across the bay of lines at the passing home of the miners. The trundle of the small train was imminent. Suddenly the engine loomed past the house and came to a stop opposite the gate.

The engine-driver, a short man with round grey beard, leaned out of the cab high above the woman.

"Have you got a cup of tea?" he said in a cheery, hearty fashion.

It was her father. She went in, saying she would mash.[1] Directly, she returned.

"I didn't come to see you on Sunday," began the little grey-bearded man.

"I didn't expect you," said his daughter.

The engine-driver winced; then, reassuming his cheery, airy manner, he said:

"Oh, have you heard then? Well, and what do you think—?"

"I think it is soon enough," she replied.

At her brief censure the little man made an impatient gesture, and said coaxingly, yet with dangerous coldness:

"Well, what's a man to do? It's no sort of life for a man of my years, to sit at my own hearth like a stranger. And if I'm going to marry again it may as well be soon as late—what does it matter to anybody?"

The woman did not reply, but turned and went into the house. The man in the engine-cab stood assertive, till she returned with a cup of tea and a piece of bread and butter on a plate. She went up the steps and stood near the footplate of the hissing engine.

"You needn't 'a' brought me bread an' butter," said her father. "But a cup of tea"—he sipped appreciatively—"it's very nice." He sipped for a moment or two, then: "I hear as Walter's got another bout[2] on," he said.

"When hasn't he?" said the woman bitterly.

"I heerd tell of him in the 'Lord Nelson'[3] braggin' as he was going to spend that b—— afore he went: half a sovereign[4] that was."

"When?" asked the woman.

"A' Sat'day night—I know that's true."

"Very likely," she laughed bitterly. "He gives me twenty-three shillings."

"Aye, it's a nice thing, when a man can do nothing with his money but make a beast of himself!" said the grey-whiskered man. The woman turned her head away. Her father swallowed the last of his tea and handed her the cup.

"Aye," he sighed, wiping his mouth. "It's a settler,[5] it is—"

He put his hand on the lever. The little engine strained and groaned, and the train rumbled towards the crossing. The woman again looked across the metals. Darkness was settling over the spaces of the railway and trucks: the miners, in grey sombre groups, were still passing home. The winding engine pulsed hurriedly, with brief pauses. Elizabeth Bates looked at the dreary flow of men, then she went indoors. Her husband did not come.

The kitchen was small and full of firelight; red coals piled glowing up the chimney mouth. All the life of the room seemed in the white, warm hearth and the steel fender reflecting the red fire. The cloth was laid for tea; cups glinted in the shadows. At the back, where the lowest stairs protruded into the room, the boy sat struggling with a knife and a piece of white wood. He was almost hidden in the shadow. It was half-past four. They had but to await the father's coming to begin tea. As the mother watched her son's sullen little struggle

---

with the wood, she saw herself in his silence and pertinacity; she saw the father in her child's indifference to all but himself. She seemed to be occupied by her husband. He had probably gone past his home, slunk past his own door, to drink before he came in, while his dinner spoiled and wasted in waiting. She glanced at the clock, then took the potatoes to strain them in the yard. The garden and fields beyond the brook were closed in uncertain darkness. When she rose with the saucepan, leaving the drain steaming into the night behind her, she saw the yellow lamps were lit along the high road that went up the hill away beyond the space of the railway lines and the field.

Then again she watched the men trooping home, fewer now and fewer.

Indoors the fire was sinking and the room was dark red. The woman put her saucepan on the hob, and set a batter-pudding near the mouth of the oven. Then she stood unmoving. Directly, gratefully, came quick young steps to the door. Someone hung on the latch a moment, then a little girl entered and began pulling off her outdoor things, dragging a mass of curls, just ripening from gold to brown, over her eyes with her hat.

Her mother chid her for coming late from school, and said she would have to keep her at home the dark winter days.

"Why, mother, it's hardly a bit dark yet. The lamp's not lighted, and my father's not home."

"No, he isn't. But it's a quarter to five! Did you see anything of him?"

The child became serious. She looked at her mother with large, wistful blue eyes.

"No, mother, I've never seen him. Why? Has he come up an' gone past, to Old Brinsley? He hasn't, mother, 'cos I never saw him."

"He'd watch that," said the mother bitterly, "he'd take care as you didn't see him. But you may depend upon it, he's seated in the 'Prince o' Wales.' He wouldn't be this late."

The girl looked at her mother piteously.

"Let's have our teas, mother, should we?" said she.

The mother called John to table. She opened the door once more and looked out across the darkness of the lines. All was deserted: she could not hear the winding-engines.

"Perhaps," she said to herself, "he's stopped to get some ripping[1] done."

They sat down to tea. John, at the end of the table near the door, was almost lost in the darkness. Their faces were hidden from each other. The girl crouched against the fender slowly moving a thick piece of bread before the fire. The lad, his face a dusky mark on the shadow, sat watching her who was transfigured in the red glow.

"I do think it's beautiful to look in the fire," said the child.

"Do you?" said her mother. "Why?"

"It's so red, and full of little caves—and it feels so nice, and you can fair smell it."

"It'll want mending directly," replied her mother, "and then if your father comes he'll carry on and say there never is a fire when a man comes home sweating from the pit. A public-house is always warm enough."

There was silence till the boy said complainingly: "Make haste, our Annie."

"Well, I am doing! I can't make the fire do it no faster, can I?"

"She keeps wafflin' it about so's to make 'er slow," grumbled the boy.

"Don't have such an evil imagination, child," replied the mother.

Soon the room was busy in the darkness with the crisp sound of crunching. The mother ate very little. She drank her tea determinedly, and sat thinking. When she rose her anger was evident in the stern unbending of her head. She looked at the pudding in the fender, and broke out:

"It is a scandalous thing as a man can't even come home to his dinner! If it's crozzled[2] up to a cinder I don't see why I should care. Past his very door he goes to get to a public-house, and here I sit with his dinner waiting for him—"

She went out. As she dropped piece after piece of coal on the red fire, the shadows fell on the walls, till the room was almost in total darkness.

"I canna see," grumbled the invisible John. In spite of herself, the mother laughed.

---

[1] *ripping* Cutting away coal.

[2] *crozzled* Curled; burnt.

"You know the way to your mouth," she said. She set the dust-pan outside the door. When she came again like a shadow on the hearth, the lad repeated, complaining sulkily:

"I canna see."

"Good gracious!" cried the mother irritably, "you're as bad as your father if it's a bit dusk!"

Nevertheless, she took a paper spill[1] from a sheaf on the mantelpiece and proceeded to light the lamp that hung from the ceiling in the middle of the room. As she reached up, her figure displayed itself just rounding with maternity.

"Oh, mother—!" exclaimed the girl.

"What?" said the woman, suspended in the act of putting the lamp-glass over the flame. The copper reflector shone handsomely on her, as she stood with uplifted arm, turning to face her daughter.

"You've got a flower in your apron!" said the child, in a little rapture at this unusual event.

"Goodness me!" exclaimed the woman, relieved. "One would think the house was afire." She replaced the glass and waited a moment before turning up the wick. A pale shadow was seen floating vaguely on the floor.

"Let me smell!" said the child, still rapturously, coming forward and putting her face to her mother's waist.

"Go along, silly!" said the mother, turning up the lamp. The light revealed their suspense so that the woman felt it almost unbearable. Annie was still bending at her waist. Irritably, the mother took the flowers out from her apron-band.

"Oh, mother—don't take them out!" Annie cried, catching her hand and trying to replace the sprig.

"Such nonsense!" said the mother, turning away. The child put the pale chrysanthemums to her lips, murmuring:

"Don't they smell beautiful!"

Her mother gave a short laugh.

"No," she said, "not to me. It was chrysanthemums when I married him, and chrysanthemums when you were born, and the first time they ever brought him home drunk, he'd got brown chrysanthemums in his button-hole."

She looked at the children. Their eyes and their parted lips were wondering. The mother sat rocking in silence for some time. Then she looked at the clock.

"Twenty minutes to six!" In a tone of fine bitter carelessness she continued: "Eh, he'll not come now till they bring him. There he'll stick! But he needn't come rolling in here in his pit-dirt, for *I* won't wash him. He can lie on the floor—Eh, what a fool I've been, what a fool! And this is what I came here for, to this dirty hole, rats and all, for him to slink past his very door. Twice last week—he's begun now—"

She silenced herself, and rose to clear the table. While for an hour or more the children played, subduedly intent, fertile of imagination, united in fear of the mother's wrath, and in dread of their father's home-coming, Mrs. Bates sat in her rocking-chair making a "singlet"[2] of thick cream-coloured flannel, which gave a dull wounded sound as she tore off the grey edge. She worked at her sewing with energy, listening to the children, and her anger wearied itself, lay down to rest, opening its eyes from time to time and steadily watching, its ears raised to listen. Sometimes even her anger quailed and shrank, and the mother suspended her sewing, tracing the footsteps that thudded along the sleepers outside; she would lift her head sharply to bid the children "hush," but she recovered herself in time, and the footsteps went past the gate, and the children were not flung out of their play-world.

But at last Annie sighed, and gave in. She glanced at her wagon of slippers, and loathed the game. She turned plaintively to her mother.

"Mother!"—but she was inarticulate.

John crept out like a frog from under the sofa. His mother glanced up.

"Yes," she said, "just look at those shirt-sleeves!"

The boy held them out to survey them, saying nothing. Then somebody called in a hoarse voice away down the line, and suspense bristled in the room, till two people had gone by outside, talking.

"It is time for bed," said the mother.

"My father hasn't come," wailed Annie plaintively. But her mother was primed with courage.

---

[1] *paper spill* Folded or twisted paper used for lighting candle, fire, lamp, etc.

[2] *singlet* Undershirt.

"Never mind. They'll bring him when he does come—like a log." She meant there would be no scene. "And he may sleep on the floor till he wakes himself. I know he'll not go to work tomorrow after this!"

The children had their hands and faces wiped with a flannel. They were very quiet. When they had put on their nightdresses, they said their prayers, the boy mumbling. The mother looked down at them, at the brown silken bush of intertwining curls in the nape of the girl's neck, at the little black head of the lad, and her heart burst with anger at their father, who caused all three such distress. The children hid their faces in her skirts for comfort.

When Mrs. Bates came down, the room was strangely empty, with a tension of expectancy. She took up her sewing and stitched for some time without raising her head. Meantime her anger was tinged with fear.

2

The clock struck eight and she rose suddenly, dropping her sewing on her chair. She went to the stair-foot door, opened it, listening. Then she went out, locking the door behind her.

Something scuffled in the yard, and she started, though she knew it was only the rats with which the place was over-run. The night was very dark. In the great bay of railway lines, bulked with trucks, there was no trace of light, only away back she could see a few yellow lamps at the pit-top, and the red smear of the burning pit-bank on the night. She hurried along the edge of the track, then, crossing the converging lines, came to the stile by the white gates, whence she emerged on the road. Then the fear which had led her shrank. People were walking up to New Brinsley; she saw the lights in the houses; twenty yards farther on were the broad windows of the "Prince of Wales," very warm and bright, and the loud voices of men could be heard distinctly. What a fool she had been to imagine that anything had happened to him! He was merely drinking over there at the "Prince of Wales." She faltered. She had never yet been to fetch him, and she never would go. So she continued her walk towards the long straggling line of houses, standing back on the highway. She entered a passage between the dwellings.

"Mr. Rigley?—Yes! Did you want him? No, he's not in at this minute."

The raw-boned woman leaned forward from her dark scullery and peered at the other, upon whom fell a dim light through the blind of the kitchen window.

"Is it Mrs. Bates?" she asked in a tone tinged with respect.

"Yes. I wondered if your Master was at home. Mine hasn't come yet."

"'Asn't 'e! Oh, Jack's been 'ome an' 'ad 'is dinner an' gone out. 'E's just gone for 'alf an hour afore bed-time. Did you call at the 'Prince of Wales'?"

"No—"

"No, you didn't like—! It's not very nice." The other woman was indulgent. There was an awkward pause. "Jack never said nothink about—about your Master," she said.

"No!—I expect he's stuck in there!"

Elizabeth Bates said this bitterly, and with recklessness. She knew that the woman across the yard was standing at her door listening, but she did not care. As she turned:

"Stop a minute! I'll just go an' ask Jack if 'e knows anythink," said Mrs. Rigley.

"Oh no—I wouldn't like to put——!"

"Yes, I will, if you'll just step inside an' see as th' childer doesn't come downstairs and set theirselves afire."

Elizabeth Bates, murmuring a remonstrance, stepped inside. The other woman apologised for the state of the room.

The kitchen needed apology. There were little frocks and trousers and childish undergarments on the squab[1] and on the floor, and a litter of playthings everywhere. On the black American cloth[2] of the table were pieces of bread and cake, crusts, slops, and a teapot with cold tea.

"Eh, ours is just as bad," said Elizabeth Bates, looking at the woman, not at the house. Mrs. Rigley put a shawl over her head and hurried out, saying:

"I shanna be a minute."

The other sat, noting with faint disapproval the general untidiness of the room. Then she fell to count-

[1]   *squab* Sofa.

[2]   *American cloth* Flexible enameled cloth used for covering furniture.

ing the shoes of various sizes scattered over the floor. There were twelve. She sighed and said to herself: "No wonder!"—glancing at the litter. There came the scratching of two pairs of feet on the yard, and the Rigleys entered. Elizabeth Bates rose. Rigley was a big man, with very large bones. His head looked particularly bony. Across his temple was a blue scar, caused by a wound got in the pit, a wound in which the coal-dust remained blue like tattooing.

"'Asna 'e come whoam yit?" asked the man, without any form of greeting, but with deference and sympathy. "I couldna say wheer he is—'e's non ower theer!"—he jerked his head to signify the "Prince of Wales."

"'E's 'appen gone up to th' 'Yew,'" said Mrs. Rigley. There was another pause. Rigley had evidently something to get off his mind:

"Ah left 'im finishin' a stint," he began. "Loose-all[1] 'ad bin gone about ten minutes when we com'n away, an' I shouted: 'Are ter comin', Walt?' an' 'e said: 'Go on, Ah shanna be but a'ef a minnit,' so we com'n ter th' bottom, me an' Bowers, thinkin' as 'e wor just behint, an' 'ud come up i' th' next bantle[2]—"

He stood perplexed, as if answering a charge of deserting his mate. Elizabeth Bates, now again certain of disaster, hastened to reassure him:

"I expect 'e's gone up to th' 'Yew Tree,' as you say. It's not the first time. I've fretted myself into a fever before now. He'll come home when they carry him."

"Ay, isn't it too bad!" deplored the other woman.

"I'll just step up to Dick's an' see if 'e *is* theer," offered the man, afraid of appearing alarmed, afraid of taking liberties.

"Oh, I wouldn't think of bothering you that far," said Elizabeth Bates, with emphasis, but he knew she was glad of his offer.

As they stumbled up the entry, Elizabeth Bates heard Rigley's wife run across the yard and open her neighbour's door. At this, suddenly all the blood in her body seemed to switch away from her heart.

"Mind!" warned Rigley. "Ah've said many a time as Ah'd fill up them ruts in this entry, sumb'dy 'll be breakin' their legs yit."

She recovered herself and walked quickly along with the miner.

"I don't like leaving the children in bed, and nobody in the house," she said.

"No, you dunna!" he replied courteously. They were soon at the gate of the cottage.

"Well, I shanna be many minnits. Dunna you be frettin' now, 'e'll be all right," said the butty.[3]

"Thank you very much, Mr. Rigley," she replied.

"You're welcome!" he stammered, moving away. "I shanna be many minnits."

The house was quiet. Elizabeth Bates took off her hat and shawl, and rolled back the rug. When she had finished, she sat down. It was a few minutes past nine. She was startled by the rapid chuff of the winding-engine at the pit, and the sharp whirr of the brakes on the rope as it descended. Again she felt the painful sweep of her blood, and she put her hand to her side, saying aloud: "Good gracious!—it's only the nine o'clock deputy going down," rebuking herself.

She sat still, listening. Half an hour of this, and she was wearied out.

"What am I working myself up like this for?" she said pitiably to herself, "I s'll only be doing myself some damage."

She took out her sewing again.

At a quarter to ten there were footsteps. One person! She watched for the door to open. It was an elderly woman, in a black bonnet and a black woollen shawl—his mother. She was about sixty years old, pale, with blue eyes, and her face all wrinkled and lamentable. She shut the door and turned to her daughter-in-law peevishly.

"Eh, Lizzie, whatever shall we do, whatever shall we do!" she cried.

Elizabeth drew back a little, sharply.

"What is it, mother?" she said.

The elder woman seated herself on the sofa.

"I don't know, child, I can't tell you!"—she shook her head slowly. Elizabeth sat watching her, anxious and vexed.

"I don't know," replied the grandmother, sighing very deeply. "There's no end to my troubles, there isn't.

[1] *Loose-all* Signal to finish working in the pits.

[2] *bantle* Group.

[3] *butty* Buddy; workmate.

The things I've gone through, I'm sure it's enough—!" She wept without wiping her eyes, the tears running.

"But, mother," interrupted Elizabeth, "what do you mean? What is it?"

The grandmother slowly wiped her eyes. The fountains of her tears were stopped by Elizabeth's directness. She wiped her eyes slowly.

"Poor child! Eh, you poor thing!" she moaned. "I don't know what we're going to do, I don't—and you as you are—it's a thing, it is indeed!"

Elizabeth waited.

"Is he dead?" she asked, and at the words her heart swung violently, though she felt a slight flush of shame at the ultimate extravagance of the question. Her words sufficiently frightened the old lady, almost brought her to herself.

"Don't say so, Elizabeth! We'll hope it's not as bad as that; no, may the Lord spare us that, Elizabeth. Jack Rigley came just as I was sittin' down to a glass afore going to bed, an' 'e said: ''Appen you'll go down th' line, Mrs. Bates. Walt's had an accident. 'Appen you'll go an' sit wi' 'er till we can get him home.' I hadn't time to ask him a word afore he was gone. An' I put my bonnet on an' come straight down, Lizzie. I thought to myself: 'Eh, that poor blessed child, if anybody should come an' tell her of a sudden, there's no knowin' what'll 'appen to 'er.' You mustn't let it upset you, Lizzie—or you know what to expect. How long is it, six months—or is it five, Lizzie? Ay!"—the old woman shook her head—"time slips on, it slips on! Ay!"

Elizabeth's thoughts were busy elsewhere. If he was killed—would she be able to manage on the little pension and what she could earn?—she counted up rapidly. If he was hurt—they wouldn't take him to the hospital—how tiresome he would be to nurse!—but perhaps she'd be able to get him away from the drink and his hateful ways. She would—while he was ill. The tears offered to come to her eyes at the picture. But what sentimental luxury was this she was beginning? She turned to consider the children. At any rate she was absolutely necessary for them. They were her business.

"Ay!" repeated the old woman, "it seems but a week or two since he brought me his first wages. Ay—he was a good lad, Elizabeth, he was, in his way. I don't know why he got to be such a trouble, I don't. He was a happy

lad at home, only full of spirits. But there's no mistake he's been a handful of trouble, he has! I hope the Lord'll spare him to mend his ways. I hope so, I hope so. You've had a sight o' trouble with him, Elizabeth, you have indeed. But he was a jolly enough lad wi' me, he was, I can assure you. I don't know how it is. ..."

The old woman continued to muse aloud, a monotonous irritating sound, while Elizabeth thought concentratedly, startled once, when she heard the winding-engine chuff quickly, and the brakes skirr with a shriek. Then she heard the engine more slowly, and the brakes made no sound. The old woman did not notice. Elizabeth waited in suspense. The mother-in-law talked, with lapses into silence.

"But he wasn't your son, Lizzie, an' it makes a difference. Whatever he was, I remember him when he was little, an' I learned to understand him and to make allowances. You've got to make allowances for them—"

It was half-past ten, and the old woman was saying: "But it's trouble from beginning to end; you're never too old for trouble, never too old for that—" when the gate banged back, and there were heavy feet on the steps.

"I'll go, Lizzie, let me go," cried the old woman, rising. But Elizabeth was at the door. It was a man in pit-clothes.

"They're bringin' 'im, Missis," he said. Elizabeth's heart halted a moment. Then it surged on again, almost suffocating her.

"Is he—is it bad?" she asked.

The man turned away, looking at the darkness:

"The doctor says 'e'd been dead hours. 'E saw 'im i' th' lamp-cabin."

The old woman, who stood just behind Elizabeth, dropped into a chair, and folded her hands, crying: "Oh, my boy, my boy!"

"Hush!" said Elizabeth, with a sharp twitch of a frown. "Be still, mother, don't waken th' children: I wouldn't have them down for anything!"

The old woman moaned softly, rocking herself. The man was drawing away. Elizabeth took a step forward.

"How was it?" she asked.

"Well, I couldn't say for sure," the man replied, very ill at ease. "'E wor finishin' a stint an' th' butties 'ad gone, an' a lot o' stuff come down atop 'n 'im."

"And crushed him?" cried the widow, with a shudder.

"No," said the man, "it fell at th' back of 'im. 'E wor under th' face, an' it niver touched 'im. It shut 'im in. It seems 'e wor smothered."

Elizabeth shrank back. She heard the old woman behind her cry:

"What?—what did 'e say it was?"

The man replied, more loudly: "'E wor smothered!"

Then the old woman wailed aloud, and this relieved Elizabeth.

"Oh, mother," she said, putting her hand on the old woman, "don't waken th' children, don't waken th' children."

She wept a little, unknowing, while the old mother rocked herself and moaned. Elizabeth remembered that they were bringing him home, and she must be ready. "They'll lay him in the parlour," she said to herself, standing a moment pale and perplexed.

Then she lighted a candle and went into the tiny room. The air was cold and damp, but she could not make a fire, there was no fireplace. She set down the candle and looked round. The candlelight glittered on the lustre-glasses, on the two vases that held some of the pink chrysanthemums, and on the dark mahogany. There was a cold, deathly smell of chrysanthemums in the room. Elizabeth stood looking at the flowers. She turned away, and calculated whether there would be room to lay him on the floor, between the couch and the chiffonier. She pushed the chairs aside. There would be room to lay him down and to step round him. Then she fetched the old red tablecloth, and another old cloth, spreading them down to save her bit of carpet. She shivered on leaving the parlour; so, from the dresser drawer she took a clean shirt and put it at the fire to air. All the time her mother-in-law was rocking herself in the chair and moaning.

"You'll have to move from there, mother," said Elizabeth. "They'll be bringing him in. Come in the rocker."

The old mother rose mechanically, and seated herself by the fire, continuing to lament. Elizabeth went into the pantry for another candle, and there, in the little pent-house[1] under the naked tiles, she heard them coming. She stood still in the pantry doorway, listening. She heard them pass the end of the house, and come awkwardly down the three steps, a jumble of shuffling footsteps and muttering voices. The old woman was silent. The men were in the yard.

Then Elizabeth heard Matthews, the manager of the pit, say: "You go in first, Jim. Mind!"

The door came open, and the two women saw a collier[2] backing into the room, holding one end of a stretcher, on which they could see the nailed pit-boots of the dead man. The two carriers halted, the man at the head stooping to the lintel[3] of the door.

"Wheer will you have him?" asked the manager, a short, white-bearded man.

Elizabeth roused herself and came from the pantry carrying the unlighted candle.

"In the parlour," she said.

"In there, Jim!" pointed the manager, and the carriers backed round into the tiny room. The coat with which they had covered the body fell off as they awkwardly turned through the two doorways, and the women saw their man, naked to the waist, lying stripped for work. The old woman began to moan in a low voice of horror.

"Lay th' stretcher at th' side," snapped the manager, "an' put 'im on th' cloths. Mind now, mind! Look you now—!"

One of the men had knocked off a vase of chrysanthemums. He stared awkwardly, then they set down the stretcher. Elizabeth did not look at her husband. As soon as she could get in the room, she went and picked up the broken vase and the flowers.

"Wait a minute!" she said.

The three men waited in silence while she mopped up the water with a duster.

"Eh, what a job, what a job, to be sure!" the manager was saying, rubbing his brow with trouble and perplexity. "Never knew such a thing in my life, never! He'd no business to ha' been left. I never knew such a thing in

[1] *pent-house* Subsidiary structure with a sloping roof, attached to the wall of the main building.

[2] *collier* Coal miner.

[3] *lintel* Horizontal support beam.

my life! Fell over him clean as a whistle, an' shut him in. Not four foot of space, there wasn't—yet it scarce bruised him."

He looked down at the dead man, lying prone, half naked, all grimed with coal-dust.

"'Sphyxiated,' the doctor said. It *is* the most terrible job I've ever known. Seems as if it was done o' purpose. Clean over him, an' shut 'im in, like a mouse-trap"—he made a sharp, descending gesture with his hand.

The colliers standing by jerked aside their heads in hopeless comment.

The horror of the thing bristled upon them all.

Then they heard the girl's voice upstairs calling shrilly:

"Mother, mother—who is it? Mother, who is it?"

Elizabeth hurried to the foot of the stairs and opened the door:

"Go to sleep!" she commanded sharply. "What are you shouting about? Go to sleep at once—there's nothing—"

Then she began to mount the stairs. They could hear her on the boards, and on the plaster floor of the little bedroom. They could hear her distinctly:

"What's the matter now?—what's the matter with you, silly thing?"—her voice was much agitated, with an unreal gentleness.

"I thought it was some men come," said the plaintive voice of the child. "Has he come?"

"Yes, they've brought him. There's nothing to make a fuss about. Go to sleep now, like a good child."

They could hear her voice in the bedroom, they waited whilst she covered the children under the bedclothes.

"Is he drunk?" asked the girl, timidly, faintly.

"No! No—he's not! He—he's asleep."

"Is he asleep downstairs?"

"Yes—and don't make a noise."

There was silence for a moment, then the men heard the frightened child again:

"What's that noise?"

"It's nothing, I tell you, what are you bothering for?"

The noise was the grandmother moaning. She was oblivious of everything, sitting on her chair rocking and moaning. The manager put his hand on her arm and bade her "Sh—sh!!"

The old woman opened her eyes and looked at him. She was shocked by this interruption, and seemed to wonder.

"What time is it?" the plaintive thin voice of the child, sinking back unhappily into sleep, asked this last question.

"Ten o'clock," answered the mother more softly. Then she must have bent down and kissed the children.

Matthews beckoned to the men to come away. They put on their caps and took up the stretcher. Stepping over the body, they tiptoed out of the house. None of them spoke till they were far from the wakeful children.

When Elizabeth came down she found her mother alone on the parlour floor, leaning over the dead man, the tears dropping on him.

"We must lay him out," the wife said. She put on the kettle, then returning knelt at the feet, and began to unfasten the knotted leather laces. The room was clammy and dim with only one candle, so that she had to bend her face almost to the floor. At last she got off the heavy boots and put them away.

"You must help me now," she whispered to the old woman. Together they stripped the man.

When they arose, saw him lying in the naïve dignity of death, the woman stood arrested in fear and respect. For a few moments they remained still, looking down, the old mother whimpering. Elizabeth felt countermanded. She saw him, how utterly inviolable he lay in himself. She had nothing to do with him. She could not accept it. Stooping, she laid her hand on him, in claim. He was still warm, for the mine was hot where he had died. His mother had his face between her hands, and was murmuring incoherently. The old tears fell in succession as drops from wet leaves; the mother was not weeping, merely her tears flowed. Elizabeth embraced the body of her husband, with cheek and lips. She seemed to be listening, inquiring, trying to get some connection. But she could not. She was driven away. He was impregnable.

She rose, went into the kitchen, where she poured warm water into a bowl, brought soap and flannel and a soft towel.

"I must wash him," she said.

Then the old mother rose stiffly, and watched Elizabeth as she carefully washed his face, carefully brushing the big blond moustache from his mouth with the flannel. She was afraid with a bottomless fear, so she ministered to him. The old woman, jealous, said:

"Let me wipe him!"—and she kneeled on the other side drying slowly as Elizabeth washed, her big black bonnet sometimes brushing the dark head of her daughter-in-law. They worked thus in silence for a long time. They never forgot it was death, and the touch of the man's dead body gave them strange emotions, different in each of the women; a great dread possessed them both, the mother felt the lie was given to her womb, she was denied; the wife felt the utter isolation of the human soul, the child within her was a weight apart from her.

At last it was finished. He was a man of handsome body, and his face showed no traces of drink. He was blond, full-fleshed, with fine limbs. But he was dead.

"Bless him," whispered his mother, looking always at his face, and speaking out of sheer terror. "Dear lad—bless him!" She spoke in a faint, sibilant ecstasy of fear and mother love.

Elizabeth sank down again to the floor, and put her face against his neck, and trembled and shuddered. But she had to draw away again. He was dead, and her living flesh had no place against his. A great dread and weariness held her: she was so unavailing. Her life was gone like this.

"White as milk he is, clear as a twelve-month baby, bless him, the darling!" the old mother murmured to herself. "Not a mark on him, clear and clean and white, beautiful as ever a child was made," she murmured with pride. Elizabeth kept her face hidden.

"He went peaceful, Lizzie—peaceful as sleep. Isn't he beautiful, the lamb? Ay—he must ha' made his peace, Lizzie. 'Appen he made it all right, Lizzie, shut in there. He'd have time. He wouldn't look like this if he hadn't made his peace. The lamb, the dear lamb. Eh, but he had a hearty laugh. I loved to hear it. He had the heartiest laugh, Lizzie, as a lad—"

Elizabeth looked up. The man's mouth was fallen back, slightly open under the cover of the moustache.

The eyes, half shut, did not show glazed in the obscurity. Life with its smoky burning gone from him, had left him apart and utterly alien to her. And she knew what a stranger he was to her. In her womb was ice of fear, because of this separate stranger with whom she had been living as one flesh. Was this what it all meant—utter, intact separateness, obscured by heat of living? In dread she turned her face away. The fact was too deadly. There had been nothing between them, and yet they had come together, exchanging their nakedness repeatedly. Each time he had taken her, they had been two isolated beings, far apart as now. He was no more responsible than she. The child was like ice in her womb. For as she looked at the dead man, her mind, cold and detached, said clearly: "Who am I? What have I been doing? I have been fighting a husband who did not exist. *He* existed all the time. What wrong have I done? What was that I have been living with? There lies the reality, this man." And her soul died in her for fear: she knew she had never seen him, he had never seen her, they had met in the dark and had fought in the dark, not knowing whom they met nor whom they fought. And now she saw, and turned silent in seeing. For she had been wrong. She had said he was something he was not; she had felt familiar with him. Whereas he was apart all the while, living as she never lived, feeling as she never felt.

In fear and shame she looked at his naked body, that she had known falsely. And he was the father of her children. Her soul was torn from her body and stood apart. She looked at his naked body and was ashamed, as if she had denied it. After all, it was itself. It seemed awful to her. She looked at his face, and she turned her own face to the wall. For his look was other than hers, his way was not her way. She had denied him what he was—she saw it now. She had refused him as himself. And this had been her life, and his life. She was grateful to death, which restored the truth. And she knew she was not dead.

And all the while her heart was bursting with grief and pity for him. What had he suffered? What stretch of horror for this helpless man! She was rigid with agony. She had not been able to help him. He had been cruelly injured, this naked man, this other being, and she could make no reparation. There were the children—but the children belonged to life. This dead man had nothing to do with them. He and she were only channels through which life had flowed to issue in the children. She was a mother—but how awful she knew it now to have been a wife. And he, dead now, how awful he must have felt it to be a husband. She felt that in the next world he would be a stranger to her. If they met there, in the beyond, they would only be ashamed of what had been before. The children had come, for some mysterious reason, out of both of them. But the children did not unite them. Now he was dead, she knew how eternally he was apart from her, how eternally he had nothing more to do with her. She saw this episode of her life closed. They had denied each other in life. Now he had withdrawn. An anguish came over her. It was finished then: it had become hopeless between them long before he died. Yet he had been her husband. But how little!

"Have you got his shirt, 'Lizabeth?"

Elizabeth turned without answering, though she strove to weep and behave as her mother-in-law expected. But she could not, she was silenced. She went into the kitchen and returned with the garment.

"It is aired," she said, grasping the cotton shirt here and there to try. She was almost ashamed to handle him; what right had she or anyone to lay hands on him; but her touch was humble on his body. It was hard work to clothe him. He was so heavy and inert. A terrible dread gripped her all the while: that he could be so heavy and utterly inert, unresponsive, apart. The horror of the distance between them was almost too much for her—it was so infinite a gap she must look across.

At last it was finished. They covered him with a sheet and left him lying, with his face bound. And she fastened the door of the little parlour, lest the children should see what was lying there. Then, with peace sunk heavy on her heart, she went about making tidy the kitchen. She knew she submitted to life, which was her immediate master. But from death, her ultimate master, she winced with fear and shame.

—1914

WORK AND WORKING-CLASS LIFE

CONTEXTS

D.H. Lawrence presents a bleak picture of life in the mining communities of the English Midlands (in novels such as *Sons and Lovers* as well as stories such as "The Odour of Chrysanthemums") but does not exaggerate the hardships of the working class. The materials in this section—chief among them excerpts from two of the most important non-fictional accounts of working-class life in northern England in the first half of the twentieth century (George Orwell's *The Road to Wigan Pier* and Robert Roberts's *The Classic Slum*)—provide a broader picture of such hardships.

⌘ ⌘ ⌘

Anonymous, "Armoured cars at Hyde Park Corner," 1926. A convoy of armored cars assembles at Hyde Park Corner in London. During the General Strike of 1926, troops were called on to maintain Britain's food supply—and no doubt to intimidate the strikers. The spark that set off the General Strike was the dissatisfaction coal miners' felt about their working conditions. When, following World War I, a reviving coal industry in Germany had caused the price of coal in Britain to tumble, mine owners had responded by reducing the already-low wages of their workers. On May 1, one million coal miners went on strike in protest, and the five-million-strong Trades Union Congress backed them; transport-ation, the steel industry, and many other sectors of the economy were paralyzed. The government, led by Prime Minister Stanley Baldwin and Chan-cellor of the Exchequer Winston Churchill, took

a strong stand against the workers, and within twelve days the General Strike had ended. The miners continued to strike for several more months, but eventually acceded to the demands of the owners that they work longer hours for lower pay.

from George Orwell, *The Road to Wigan Pier* (1937)

George Orwell's *The Road to Wigan Pier* was com-missioned by the Left Book Club as a report on the state of the unemployed in northern England. Characteristically, Orwell did not do exactly as he had been instructed or had expected to do; he wrote extensively about the conditions of workers as well as those of the unemployed, and he wrote frankly and not always flatteringly about the working class (as well as writing scathingly about the privileged classes).

Our civilization, *pace* Chesterton,[1] *is* founded on coal, more completely than one realises until one stops to think about it. The machines that keep us alive, and the machines that make the machines, are all

---

[1] *pace Chesterton* Despite what Chesterton said. See the exchange below involving G.K. Chesterton, George Bernard Shaw, and Hilaire Belloc.

directly or indirectly dependent upon coal. In the metabolism of the Western world the coal-miner is second in importance only to the man who ploughs the soil. He is a sort of grimy caryatid[1] upon whose shoulders nearly everything that is *not* grimy is supported. For this reason the actual process by which coal is extracted is well worth watching, if you get the chance and are willing to take the trouble.

When you go down a coal-mine it is important to try and get to the coal face when the "fillers"[2] are at work.... On a Sunday, for instance, a mine seems almost peaceful. The time to go there is when the machines are roaring and the air is black with coal dust, and when you can actually see what the miners have to do. At those times the place is like hell, or at any rate like my own mental picture of hell. Most of the things one imagines in hell are there—heat, noise, confusion, darkness, foul air, and, above all, unbearably cramped space. Everything except the fire, for there is no fire down there except the feeble beams of Davy lamps[3] and electric torches which scarcely penetrate the clouds of coal dust.

When you have finally got there ... you crawl through the last line of pit props and see opposite you a shiny black wall three or four feet high. This is the coal face. Overhead is the smooth ceiling made by the rock from which the coal has been cut; underneath is the rock again, so that the gallery you are in is only as high as the ledge of coal itself, probably not much more than a yard. The first impression of all, overmastering everything else for a while, is the frightful, deafening din from the conveyor belt which carries the coal away. You cannot see very far, because the fog of coal dust throws back the beam of your lamp, but you can see on either side of you the line of half-naked kneeling men, one to every four or five yards, driving their shovels under the fallen coal and flinging it swiftly over their left shoulders. They are feeding it on to the conveyor belt, a moving rubber belt a couple of feet wide which runs a yard or two behind them. Down this belt a glittering

river of coal races constantly. In a big mine it is carrying away several tons of coal every minute. It bears it off to some place in the main roads where it is shot into tubs holding half a ton, and thence dragged to the cages and hoisted to the outer air.

It is impossible to watch the "fillers" at work without feeling a pang of envy for their toughness. It is a dreadful job that they do, an almost superhuman job by the standards of an ordinary person. For they are not only shifting monstrous quantities of coal, they are also doing it in a position that doubles or trebles the work. They have got to remain kneeling all the while—they could hardly rise from their knees without hitting the ceiling—and you can easily see by trying it what a tremendous effort this means. Shovelling is comparatively easy when you are standing up, because you can use your knee and thigh to drive the shovel along; kneeling down, the whole of the strain is thrown upon your arm and belly muscles. And the other conditions do not exactly make things easier. There is the heat—it varies, but in some mines it is suffocating—and the coal dust that stuffs up your throat and nostrils and collects along your eyelids, and the unending rattle of the conveyor belt, which in that confined space is rather like the rattle of a machine gun. ...

It is not long since conditions in the mines were worse than they are now. There are still living a few very old women who in their youth have worked underground, with a harness round their waists and a chain that passed between their legs, crawling on all fours and dragging tubs of coal. They used to go on doing this even when they were pregnant....

The adjustments a miner's family have to make when he is changed from one shift to another must be tiresome in the extreme. If he is on the night shift he gets home in time for breakfast, on the morning shift he gets home in the middle of the afternoon, and on the afternoon shift he gets home in the middle of the night; and in each case, of course, he wants his principal meal of the day as soon as he returns. I notice that the Rev. W.R. Inge, in his book *England*, accuses the miners of gluttony. From my own observation I should say that they eat astonishingly little. Most of the miners I stayed with ate slightly less than I did. Many of them declare that they cannot do their day's work if they have had a

---

[1] *caryatid* Supporting column carved in the shape of a female.

[2] *fillers* Miners who load coal onto conveyor belts.

[3] *Davy lamps* Glass cylinder-shaped lamps. The flame in the lamps was encased in wire gauze, which allowed air in, but prevented the flame from escaping and igniting flammable gases in the mine.

heavy meal beforehand, and the food they take with them is only a snack, usually bread-and-dripping[1] and cold tea....

Every miner of long standing that I have talked to had either been in a fairly serious accident himself or had seen some of his mates killed, and in every mining family they tell you tales of fathers, brothers or uncles killed at work. ("And he fell seven hundred feet, and they wouldn't never have collected t'pieces only he were wearing a new suit of oilskins," etc., etc., etc.) ...

Anyone who wants to see the effects of the housing shortage at their very worst should visit the dreadful caravan-dwellings that exist in numbers in many of the northern towns. Ever since the war, in the complete impossibility of getting houses, parts of the population have overflowed into supposedly temporary quarters in fixed caravans.... One [caravan] measuring fourteen feet long, had seven people in it—seven people in about 450 cubic feet of space; which is to say that each person had for his entire dwelling a space *a good deal* smaller than one compartment of a public lavatory. The dirt and congestion of these places is such that you cannot well imagine it unless you have tested it with your own eyes and more particularly your nose....

Talking once with a miner I asked him when the housing shortage first became acute in his district; he answered, "When we were told about it," meaning that till recently people's standards were so low that they took almost any degree of overcrowding for granted. He added that when he was a child his family had slept eleven in a room and thought nothing of it, and that later, when he was grown-up, he and his wife had lived in one of the old-style back to back houses[2] in which you not only had to walk a couple of hundred yards to the lavatory but often had to wait in a queue when you got there, the lavatory being shared by thirty-six people....

[But nowadays] the middle classes—yes, even the bridge clubs in the country towns—are beginning to realise that there is such a thing as unemployment. The "My dear, I don't *believe* in all this nonsense about unemployment. Why, only last week we wanted a man to weed the garden, and we simply couldn't get one. They don't *want* to work, that's all it is!" which you heard at every decent tea-table five years ago, is growing perceptibly less frequent. As for the working class themselves, they have gained immensely in economic knowledge. I believe that the *Daily Worker* has accomplished a great deal here: its influence is out of all proportion to its circulation....

[Anywhere in the North] there is immense and systematic thieving of coal by the unemployed. I call it thieving because technically it is that, though it does no harm to anybody. In the "dirt" that is sent up from the pits there is a certain amount of broken coal, and unemployed people spend a lot of time in picking it out of the slag-heaps. All day long over those strange grey mountains you see people wandering to and fro with sacks and baskets among the sulphurous smoke (many slag-heaps are on fire under the surface), prising out the tiny nuggets of coal which are buried here and there. You meet men coming away, wheeling strange and wonderful homemade bicycles—bicycles made of rusty parts picked off refuse-tips, without saddles, without chains and almost always without tyres—across which are slung bags containing perhaps half a hundredweight of coal, fruit of half a day's searching. In times of strikes, when everybody is short of fuel, the miners turn out with pick and shovel and burrow into the slag-heaps, whence the hummocky appearance which most slag-heaps have. During long strikes, in places where there are outcrops of coal, they have sunk surface mines and carried them scores of yards into the earth.

---

[1] *dripping* Fat from cooked meat.

[2] *back to back houses* Terraced houses (with communal lavatories).

Coal Searchers (Illustration to *The Road to Wigan Pier*, 1937).

Caravan Dwellers Near a Durham Quarry (Illustration to *The Road to Wigan Pier*, 1937).

A South Wales Miner Takes His Bath (Illustration to *The Road to Wigan Pier*, 1937).

Stepney, Shadwell District (Illustration to *The Road to Wigan Pier*, 1937).

from "A Debate Between G.B. Shaw and G.K. Chesterton, Chaired by Hilaire Belloc" (1928)

As the following excerpts from this 1928 exchange illustrate, the exploitation of coal miners was sufficiently extreme as to motivate even some conservative thinkers (Chesterton notable among them) to advocate nationalization of the industry. Shaw, a longtime socialist, saw nationalization of the coal industry as a necessary first step towards a much broader program. Belloc, a renowned writer of humorous sketches, attempted to keep the tone light. Coal was one of several major industries nationalized by Clement Atlee's Labour Government when it took power after World War II.

SHAW.   ... You have to begin with the question of the distribution of wealth. The other day a man died and the Government took four and a half million pounds as death duty on his property. That man made all his money by the labour of men who received twenty-six shillings a week after years of qualifying for their work. Was that a reasonable distribution of wealth between them?

... Let us come down to facts. Mr. Chesterton has formed the Distributist League[1] which organized this meeting. What was the very first thing the League said must be done? It said the coal-mines must be nationalized. Instead of saying that the miner's means of production must be made his own property, it was forced to advocate making national property of the coal mines. These coal-mines, when nationalized, will not be managed by the House of Commons: if they were you would very soon have no coal. But neither will they be managed by the miners. If you ask the man working in the mine to manage the mine he will say, "Not me, governor! That is your job." I would like Mr. Chesterton to consider what he understands by the means of production. He has spoken of them in rather a nineteenth-century manner. He has been talking as though the means of production were machines. I submit to you that the real means of production in this country are men and women, and that consequently you always have the maximum control of the individual over the means of production, because it means self-control over his own person. But he must surrender that control to the manager of the mine because he does not know how to manage it himself. Under the present capitalistic system he has to surrender it to the manager appointed by the proprietors of the mine. Under Socialism he would have to surrender it to the manager appointed by the Coalmaster-General. That would not prevent the product of the mine being equally distributed among the people. There is no difficulty here. In a sense Mr. Chesterton really does not disagree with me in this matter, since he does see that in the matter of fuel in this country you have to come to nationalization. Fuel must be controlled equally for the benefit of all the people. Since we agreed upon that, I am not disposed to argue the matter further. Now that Mr. Chesterton agreed that the coal-mines will have to be nationalized he will be led by the same pressure of facts to agree to the nationalization of everything else. I have to allow for the pressure of facts because, as a playwright, I think of all problems in terms of actual men and women. Mr. Chesterton lets himself idealize them sometimes as virtuous peasant proprietors and self-managing petty capitalists. The capitalist and the landlord have their own particular ways of robbing the poor; but their legal rights are quite different. It is a very direct way on the part of the landlord. He may do exactly what he likes with the land he owns. If I own a large part of Scotland I can turn the people off the land practically into the sea, or across the sea. I can take women in child-bearing and throw them into the snow and leave them there. That has been done. I can do it for no better reason than I think it is better to shoot deer on the land than allow people to live on it....

CHESTERTON.   ... We have said again and again that in our human state of society there must be a class of things called exceptions. We admit that upon the whole in the very peculiar case of coal it is desirable and about the best way out of the difficulty that it should be controlled by the officials of the State, just in the same way as postage stamps are controlled. No one says anything else about postage stamps. I cannot imagine that anyone wants to have his own postage stamps, of

---

[1] *Distributist League* Founded in 1926, the Distributist League advocated broad ownership of property and capital within society.

perhaps more picturesque design and varied colours. I can assure you that Distributists are perfectly sensible and sane people, and they have always recognized that there are institutions in the State in which it is very difficult to apply the principle of individual property, and that one of these cases is the discovery under the earth of valuable minerals. Socialists are not alone in believing this. Charles I, who, I suppose, could not be called a Socialist, pointed out that certain kinds of minerals ought to belong to the State, that is, to the Commons. We have said over and over again that we support the nationalization of the coal-mines, not as a general example of Distribution but as a common-sense admission of an exception. The reason why we make it an exception is because it is not very easy to see how the healthy principle of personal ownership can be applied. If it could we should apply it with the greatest pleasure. We consider personal ownership infinitely more healthy. If there were a way in which a miner could mark out one particular piece of coal and say, "This is mine, and I am proud of it," we should have made an enormous improvement upon State management. There are cases in which it is very difficult to apply the principle, and that is one of them. It is the reverse of the truth for Mr. Shaw to say that the logic of that fact will lead me to the application of the same principle to other cases, like the ownership of the land....

Belloc. .... I was told when I accepted this onerous office that I was to sum up. I shall do nothing of the sort. In a very few years from now this debate will be antiquated. I will now recite you a poem: "Our civilization Is built upon coal. Let us chant in rotation Our civilization That lump of damnation Without any soul, Our civilization Is built upon coal. In a very few years, It will float upon oil. Then give three hearty cheers, In a very few years We shall mop up our tears And have done with our toil. In a very few years It will float upon oil." In I do not know how many years—five, ten, twenty—this debate will be as antiquated as crinolines are. I am surprised that neither of the two speakers pointed out that one of three things is going to happen. One of three things: not one of two. It is always one of three things. This industrial civilization which, thank God, oppresses only the small part of the world in which we are most inextricably bound up, will break down and therefore end from its monstrous wickedness, folly, ineptitude, leading to a restoration of sane, ordinary human affairs, complicated but based as a whole upon the freedom of the citizens. Or it will break down and lead to nothing but a desert. Or it will lead the mass of men to become contented slaves, with a few rich men controlling them. Take your choice. You will all be dead before any of the three things comes off. One of the three things is going to happen, or a mixture of two, or possibly a mixture of the three combined.

Construction workers, London, 1920s.

An English bedspring factory, unidentified
location, 1920s.

Cleaning and maintenance for a steam engine,
England, unidentified location, 1920s.

Louis MacNeice, "Birmingham" (1935)

Northern Irish poet Louis MacNeice (1907–63) was
part of a loosely defined cohort of poets that shared
a tendency toward left-wing values during the
1930s. Some members of this group—sometimes
called the "Auden group" for its central figure,
W.H. Auden—belonged to the Communist Party,
but MacNeice did not fully embrace a specific
ideology, writing that he sympathized with the
concerns of the working classes "on paper and in the
soul. But not in my heart or my guts." In poems
such as "Birmingham," MacNeice portrays the
everyday environment of ordinary city-dwellers in
1930s Britain.

Smoke from the train-gulf hid by hoardings
   blunders upward, the brakes of cars
Pipe as the policeman pivoting round raises his flat
      hand, bars
With his figure of a monolith Pharaoh the queue of
      fidgety machines
(Chromium dogs on the bonnet, faces behind the
      triplex[1] screens).
5   Behind him the streets run away between the proud
      glass of shops,
Cubical scent-bottles artificial legs arctic foxes[2] and
      electric mops,
But beyond this centre the slumward vista thins like a
      diagram:
There, unvisited, are Vulcan's[3] forges who doesn't care
      a tinker's damn.

Splayed outwards through the suburbs houses, houses
      for rest
10   Seducingly rigged by the builder, half-timbered
      houses with lips pressed
So tightly and eyes staring at the traffic through bleary
      haws
And only a six-inch grip of the racing earth in their
      concrete claws;

---

[1]   *triplex*   Single building containing three homes.
[2]   *arctic foxes*   I.e., furs.
[3]   *Vulcan*   Roman god of fire, associated with volcanoes and
blacksmiths.

In these houses men as in a dream pursue the Platonic
    Forms[1]
With wireless and cairn terriers and gadgets
    approximating to the fickle norms
15   And endeavour to find God and score one over the
    neighbour
By climbing tentatively upward on jerry-built beauty
    and sweated labour.

The lunch hour: the shops empty, shopgirls' faces
    relax
Diaphanous as green glass, empty as old almanacs
As incoherent with ticketed gewgaws tiered behind
    their heads
20   As the Burne-Jones windows in St. Philip's[2] broken by
    crawling leads;
Insipid colour, patches of emotion, Saturday thrills
(This theatre is sprayed with 'June')—the gutter take
    our old playbills,
Next week-end it is likely in the heart's funfair we
    shall pull
Strong enough on the handle to get back our money;
    or at any rate it is possible.

25   On shining lines the trams like vast sarcophagi move
Into the sky, plum after sunset, merging to duck's egg,
    barred with mauve
Zeppelin clouds, and Pentecost[3]-like the cars'
    headlights bud
Out from sideroads and the traffic signals, crème-de-
    menthe or bull's blood,
Tell one to stop, the engine gently breathing, or to go
    on
30   To where like black pipes of organs in the frayed and
    fading zone

---

[1] *Platonic Forms* In the philosophy of Plato, Forms are abstract,
ideal concepts; a Form exists for every quality and for every type of
object, and things in the material world are imperfect reflections of
their corresponding Forms.

[2] *Burne-Jones … St. Philip's* St Philip's Cathedral in Birmingham
features four stained glass windows (1885–91) by the Birmingham-
born artist Edward Burne-Jones.

[3] *Pentecost* Major Christian feast day commemorating the day on
which the Holy Spirit granted the twelve disciples the gift of
speaking many languages (see Acts 2).

Of the West the factory chimneys on sullen sentry
    will all night wait
To call, in the harsh morning, sleep-stupid faces
    through the daily gate.

from Louis MacNeice, *Autumn Journal* (1939)

Often considered Louis MacNeice's most significant
work, the long poem *Autumn Journal* documents
the poet's thoughts and experiences in the fall of
1938, incorporating personal matters alongside
observations regarding political ideology and the
world events that would lead to the declaration of
World War II the following year.

from 3

… Now the till and the typewriter call the fingers,
    The workman gathers his tools
For the eight-hour day but after that the solace
    Of films or football pools
5   Or of the gossip or cuddle, the moments of self-glory
    Or self-indulgence, blinkers on the eyes of doubt,
The blue smoke rising and the brown lace sinking
    In the empty glass of stout.
Most are accepters, born and bred to harness,
10   And take things as they come,
But some refusing harness and more who are refused it
    Would pray that another and a better Kingdom
    come,[4]
Which now is sketched in the air or travestied in
    slogans
    Written in chalk or tar on stucco or plaster-board
15   But in time may find its body in men's bodies,
    Its law and order in their heart's accord,
Where skill will no longer languish nor energy be
    trammelled
    To competition and graft,[5]
Exploited in subservience but not allegiance
20   To an utterly lost and daft
System that gives a few at fancy prices
    Their fancy lives

---

[4] *Kingdom come* Cf. Matthew 6.10.

[5] *graft* Corruption in politics or business.

While ninety-nine in the hundred who never attend
    the banquet
  Must wash the grease of ages off the knives. ...

from Margaret Powell, *Below Stairs* (1968)

Margaret Powell (1907–84) was compelled by poverty to work in the homes of wealthy English families—first as a kitchen maid, then as a cook—until marriage enabled her to leave domestic service. When she was in her early sixties, she published the autobiography *Below Stairs*, a frank and unromantic depiction of the grueling work life and restricted personal freedom typically experienced by servants in 1920s England. The popular success of *Below Stairs* led Powell to a career as a memoirist, novelist, and television personality.

from CHAPTER 7

... They were tremendous houses in Adelaide Crescent; they started off with a basement and went right up to an attic, there were a hundred and thirty-two stairs in all, and the basements were dark and like dungeons. The front of the basement, with iron bars all down the bay windows, was the servants' hall. When you were sitting in there all you saw going by was people's legs, and when you were on the other side of the basement hall, which was the kitchen, a big conservatory overhung that, so you saw nothing at all. It had one tiny window high up in the wall which you couldn't see through unless you got a ladder. The light had to be on all day long.

The Crescent is one of the most imposing in Hove.[1] The houses were Regency style, and even now, although they are all flats, they haven't altered the façade, and it still looks very much as it did with gardens right down the centre. Of course, at that time only the residents had keys and were allowed to use the gardens, but that certainly didn't apply to the servants, I can assure you.

When my mother and I arrived at this house for the interview we went to the front door. In all the time I worked there, that was the only time I ever went in by the front door. But the front door it was on this particu-

lar day. We were ushered into a hall that I thought was the last word in opulence. There was a lovely carpet on the floor, and tremendously wide stairs carpeted right across, not like the tiny little bit of lino in the middle we had on our stairs. There was a great mahogany table in the hall and a mahogany hallstand, and huge mirrors with gilt frames. The whole thing breathed an aura of wealth to me. I thought they must be millionaires. I'd never seen anything like it.

A butler opened the door to us and my mother said that this was Margaret Langley who had come for the interview as a kitchen maid. A very tiny little butler he was. I'd always thought that butlers were tall, imposing men. In the hall we saw a rather elderly gentleman and the lady who was to interview us. We were shown into what was obviously a nursery—a day nursery.

My mother did all the talking because I was overcome with wonder at this room, for although it was only a nursery, you could have put all the three rooms that we lived in into it. Also I was overcome with shyness; I suffered agonies of self-consciousness in those days. And the lady, Mrs. Clydesdale, looked me up and down as though I was something at one of those markets, you know, one of those slave markets. She seemed to be weighing up all my points.

My mother told her that I had been doing daily jobs.[2] She didn't mention the laundry because she didn't think that was any recommendation. People thought that laundries were hotbeds of vice in those days because of the obscene language of the girls who worked there.

Mrs. Clydesdale decided that because I was strong and healthy I would do. I was to have twenty-four pounds a year, paid monthly. I was to have one afternoon and evening off from four o'clock to ten o'clock, and alternate Sundays off the same hours, and I was never to be in later than ten o'clock under any circumstances. I was to have three print dresses, blue or green; four white aprons with bibs, and four caps; stockings, and black strapped shoes. I was always to say "Sir" and "Madam" if I was spoken to by Mr. and Mrs. Clydesdale, and I was to treat the upper servants with great respect and do everything the cook asked me to do. To all these things my mother said, "Yes, Madam, no, Madam," and all these things she promised on my

---

[1] *Hove* Coastal town in southwest England, adjoining Brighton.

[2] *daily jobs* As opposed to live-in employment.

behalf that I would do. My spirits sank lower and lower. I felt I was in jail at the finish.

When we got outside I told Mum how I felt but she'd decided that the job would do for me. So that was that.

The trouble was the uniform. My mother worked it out that it couldn't be done—all these things that had to be bought for me—under two pounds. I know that it sounds a ridiculously small sum now, but two pounds was untold wealth to us then. We hadn't got two pounds but anyway she managed to borrow it and she fitted me out.

On the day I was due to go there she got her old, battered tin trunk that she'd been all through domestic service with, and I packed the few things that I had in it. Apart from the uniform my own clothes were very few indeed. I was dressed up in a blouse and skirt and a coat that had belonged to my grandmother.

I said to Mum, "How are we going to get the tin trunk down to Adelaide Crescent? Are we going to have a taxi?" She said, "You must be stark, raving mad. Where do you think we are going to get the money from? Dad's going to borrow the barrow." Dad worked for a decorator at that time, so he was going to load the trunk on to the barrow and wheel it down there. We must have looked a peculiar lot—my Dad walking in the road with the tin trunk on the barrow, and Mum and I trailing along on the pavement. When we got there Dad carried the tin trunk down to the basement.

As she said goodbye my Mum put her arms around me, which was very unusual because in our family we didn't indulge in any outward show of affection. I felt as if I could have howled and howled. And yet they weren't going miles away, they lived in the same town, but to me it was a terrible thing to see my mother and father retreating and leaving me in this alien environment. I thought, "Oh, no, I can't stay here," but I wouldn't say so. I knew I'd got to work as my parents couldn't afford to keep me. . . .

from Chapter 9

But to get back to my daily round. I found that what I had thought was work for six was, in fact, work for one, and that one was me from now on.

Up I got at five-thirty, dragged myself downstairs, and presented myself to the kitchen range.[1] I lit it, cleaned it, and lit the fire in the servants' hall.

Then I'd tear upstairs to do the front door, which was all white paint and brass—a thankless task, particularly in the winter, for when I'd got it all bright and shiny the wind from the sea tarnished it again. So by the time Madam saw it, it was something to find fault with.

Then there were fourteen wide stone steps to be scrubbed. Back downstairs again, and there was Mary waiting with all the boots and shoes.

I remember the first morning. She said, "Carrie" (that was the head housemaid) "says she hopes you know how to clean boots and shoes." "Well, of course I do," I said. After all, I'd done them at home. But I didn't know how to do them the way they wanted them done.

The Reverend, he used to wear boots all day; black boots in the week and brown boots on Sundays. In the evenings he changed into black patent shoes. Madam wore black or brown, often both during the course of the day. Then there were the governess's, and Leonora's.[2] These I did and I thought they looked very nice indeed. Well, the toes shone anyway.

When Mary came down for them she said, "Oh, they won't do. They won't do at all." I said, "What's the matter with them? They look all right to me." "All right," she said, "I'll take them up if you like but Carrie will only sling them back at me."

About two minutes afterwards down she came again and said, "It's like I said, they won't do. You haven't done the insteps." "The insteps?" I said. "I never knew you had to clean underneath the shoes." So I did that, gave them another polish, and Mary took them up again.

Seconds later back she came and said, "You haven't done the bootlaces." I said, "Haven't done the bootlaces!" "Don't you know?" she said. "You have to iron all the bootlaces, take them all out and iron them." I thought she was joking. "Iron the bootlaces?" I said. She said, "Yes." You see in those days they weren't the narrow little bootlaces they are now, they were quite half an inch wide. In fact Mrs. Clydesdale's and Leonora's were nearly an inch wide.

---

[1] *range* Stove.

[2] *Leonora* The Clydesdales's young daughter.

So I had to take the laces out of the shoes and iron them. Of course, there were no electric irons, just flat irons. They had to be heated in front of the fire and that took nearly a quarter of an hour. Never in all my life have I seen such a footling procedure.

After that I had to clean the knives because there were no stainless ones in those days. I did this with a large round knife-machine; it had three holes into which I shook the knife-powder, a sort of emery powder. Then I put a knife into each of these holes and turned the handle....

By now it was time to take Mrs. McIlroy[1] a cup of tea. Then I laid up breakfast in the servants' hall, and at eight o'clock the staff had their meal.

After we'd had our breakfast it was time for Mrs. McIlroy and me to cook for upstairs.

Like most of the meals this was very different from what we had. Mrs. Clydesdale thought only about our nourishment, so we used to have things like herrings and cod and stews and milk puddings, but none of these nourishing foods ever found their way upstairs. So I was forced to the conclusion that even their internal organs differed from ours, inasmuch as what nourished us did them no good at all.

There were always economies which had to be made. During my years in domestic service I noticed that all economies began with the servants and always ended with them too.

The breakfasts they had upstairs were always huge, whether they had visitors or whether they didn't; there were bacon and eggs, sausages, kidneys, either finnan haddock or kedgeree[2]—not one or two of these things but every one.

I couldn't help thinking of my poor father and mother at home. All they had was toast. And all this food going up to them, who never worked. I just couldn't help thinking of the unfairness of life.

If I said so to Mrs. McIlroy she couldn't see it, she just accepted her lot. She thought there ought to be the people who had the money and the people who didn't. "Because," she said, "if there weren't the people who had the money, what would there be for people like us

to do?" "But," I said, "couldn't it be equalled out more—more equitably—for them not to have so much, and for us to have a little bit more? Why do you and I have to work in this dungeon with the barest of comforts while they have everything upstairs? After all," I said, "don't forget, Mrs. McIlroy, our board and our lodging is part of our wages. The two pounds a month that I have in money is supposed to be supplemented by the board and lodging. If the lodging is of the kind that Mary and I have in that attic, and the food is meagre, and the outings are so small," I said, "how are we getting an equitable wage?" ...

from CHAPTER 12

In my first months there I made one mistake after another. I particularly remember one day when I was doing the front door—I was a bit late this particular morning—the newsboy came with the papers. As I went to put them on the hall table, Mrs. Clydesdale came down the stairs. I went to hand her the papers. She looked at me as if I were something subhuman. She didn't speak a word, she just stood there looking at me as though she could hardly believe that someone like me could be walking and breathing. I thought, what's the matter? I've got my cap on, I've got my apron on, I've got my black stockings and shoes; I couldn't think what was wrong. Then at last she spoke. She said, "Langley, never, never on any occasion ever hand anything to me in your bare hands, always use a silver salver. Surely you know better than that. Your mother was in service, didn't she teach you anything?" I thought it was terrible. Tears started to trickle down my cheeks; that someone could think that you were so low that you couldn't even hand them anything out of your hands without it first being placed on a silver salver.

I was so miserable about this that I wanted to go home; it seemed the last straw. I thought, I can't stand domestic service. I don't think I ever felt so wretched before or after that. But I knew I couldn't go home, because we had only three rooms—we lived in the bottom half of a house, two rooms on the ground floor and one in the middle—and since I had come into service, my mother's father had died, and my grandmother had to come and live with us. So now there just wasn't room. I didn't even say anything to my mother

---

[1] *Mrs. McIlroy* The cook.

[2] *finnan haddock* Scottish smoked haddock; *kedgeree* Dish made of rice, eggs, and fish, usually finnan haddock.

about it. What was the good of making them unhappy as well? In any case I think she'd just have said, "Take no notice." She'd have been right. That's what you had to do if you wanted to keep any pride at all—just take no notice.

Although we weren't forced to attend church, it was taken for granted that we went at least once on Sunday, preferably in the evening. It interfered less with their comfort if we went in the evening. One day the Reverend asked me if I had been confirmed. I said, "No, I haven't." He wanted to know why; so I said, "Well, my mother didn't bother about it, she never mentioned it to me, and now I'm fifteen I don't think it's worth bothering about." After all I couldn't see what it had to do with being a kitchen maid whether I was confirmed or not, I mean it made no difference to my work; but of course the Reverend was greatly concerned with my religion and with my moral affairs.

In fact, all my life in domestic service I've found that employers were always greatly concerned with your moral welfare. They couldn't have cared less about your physical welfare; so long as you were able to do the work, it didn't matter in the least to them whether you had back-ache, stomach-ache, or what ache, but anything to do with your morals they considered their concern. That way they called it "looking after the servants," taking an interest in those below. They didn't worry about the long hours you put in, the lack of freedom and the poor wages, so long as you worked hard and knew that God was in Heaven and that He'd arranged for it that you lived down below and laboured, and that they lived upstairs in comfort and luxury, that was all right with them. I used to think how incongruous it was when the Reverend used to say morning prayers and just before they were over he'd say, "Now let us all count our blessings." I thought, well, it would take a lot longer to count yours than it would ours. ...

from Chapter 14

Living in such close contact with the other servants, a lot of quarrels went on. You can't coop up a lot of females, perhaps it even applies to men, without words passing, and what words too. But it didn't matter how much we servants quarrelled among ourselves, a united front was always presented to them upstairs.

We always called them "Them." "Them" was the enemy, "Them" overworked us, and "Them" underpaid us, and to "Them" servants were a race apart, a necessary evil.

As such we were their main topic of conversation. The parlourmaids used to come down and tell us. It would go something like this. "You know if I lived in a little country place I wouldn't bother about servants at all, they are only a nuisance to me; they quarrel among themselves, they want more money, and they don't want to work hard, and they don't do the things the way you want them, but there, you see, I have a certain position to keep up and so I must employ them."

Mrs. Cutler[1] certainly looked upon us as necessary evils, so in that house we were always united against "Them" upstairs. In the opinion of "Them," we servants must never get ill, we must never dress too well, and we must never have an opinion that differed from theirs. After all it was perfectly obvious, wasn't it, that if you'd only stayed in school until you were thirteen or fourteen, your knowledge was very small in comparison to what they knew upstairs. So if you had to have opinions why not take them from those upstairs who knew more than you did?

It was the opinion of "Them" upstairs that servants couldn't appreciate good living or comfort, therefore they must have plain fare, they must have dungeons to work in and to eat in, and must retire to cold spartan bedrooms to sleep. After all, what's the point of spending money making life easier and more comfortable for a lot of ungrateful people who couldn't care less what you do for them? They never tried, mind, to find out if we would have cared more by making our conditions good and our bedrooms nice places in which to rest. No, it wasn't worth spending your money because servants never stayed with you, no matter what you did for them. After all was said and done, only "Them" upstairs needed luxury living, only "Them" could grace the dining-room table and make witty conversation. I mean there's got to be a stratum of society in which people can move around graciously and indulge in witty conversation, and no one can do this if they work hard.

1   *Mrs. Cutler*   Powell's employer; after spending a year working for the Clydesdales in Hove, Powell moved to London and worked for the Cutler family.

So make life harder for those who work for you, and the less inclined they'll feel for any kind of conversation.

But if "Them" upstairs could have heard the conversation the parlourmaids carried down from upstairs, they would have realized that our impassive expressions and respectful demeanours hid scorn, and derision.

from Robert Roberts, *The Classic Slum* (1971)

Though it was not published until 1971, *The Classic Slum* is a largely first-hand account of working class life in the early twentieth century; Robert Roberts (1905–74) had grown up in the same area of the northern English city of Salford that Frederic Engels had described in 1844 as "the classic slum."

Every industrial city, of course, folds within itself a clutter of loosely defined overlapping "villages." Those in the Great Britain of seventy years ago were almost self-contained communities. Our own consisted of some thirty streets and alleys locked along the north and south by two railway systems a furlong[1] apart. About twice that distance to the east lay another slum which turned on its farther side into a land of bonded warehouses and the city proper. West of us, well beyond the tramlines, lay the middle classes, bay-windowed and begardened. We knew them not.

In the city as a whole our village rated indubitably low. "The children of this school," wrote one of King Edward VII's inspectors, commenting on our only seat of learning, "are of the poorest class; so, too, is the teaching." With cash, or on tick,[2] our villagers, about three thousand in all, patronized fifteen beer-houses, a hotel and two off-licences,[3] nine grocery and general shops, three greengrocers (forever struggling to survive against the street hawker), two tripe shops, three barbers, three cloggers, two cook shops, one fish and chip shop (*déclassé*), an old clothes store, a couple of pawnbrokers and two loan offices.

Religion was served by two chapels (Primitive Methodist and Congregationalist), one "tin" mission (Church of England) and one sinister character who held spiritualist seances in his parlour and claimed from the window to cure "Female Bad Legs." (Through overwork innumerable women suffered from burst varicose veins.) Culture, pleasure and need found outlet through one theatre (and, later, three cinemas), a dancing room ("low"), two coy brothels, eight bookmakers, and a private moneylender. ... Over one quarter of a mile industry stood represented by a dying brickworks and an iron foundry. Several gasholders on the south side polluted the air, sometimes for days together. Little would grow; even the valiant aspidistra pined. We possessed besides two coal yards, a corn[4] store, a cattle wharf and perhaps as closed an urban society as any in Europe.

In our community, as in every other of its kind, each street had the usual social rating; one side or one end of that street might be classed higher than another. Weekly rents varied from 2s 6d[5] for the back-to-back to 4s 6d for a "two up and two down."[6] End houses often had special status. Every family, too, had a tacit ranking, and even individual members within it; neighbours would consider a daughter in one household as "dead common" while registering her sister as "refined," a word much in vogue. (Young women with incipient consumption were often thought "refined.") Class divisions were of the greatest consequence, though their implications remained unrealized: the many looked upon social and economic inequality as the law of nature. Division in our own society ranged from an elite at the peak, composed of the leading families, through recognized strata to a social base whose members one damned as the "lowest of the low," or simply "no class." Shopkeepers, publicans[7] and skilled tradesmen occupied the premier positions, each family having its own sphere of influence. A few of these aristocrats, while sharing working-class culture, had aspirations. From their ranks the lower middle class, then clearly defined, drew most of its

---

[1] *furlong* Unit of distance. (One furlong equals 660 feet.)

[2] *on tick* On credit.

[3] *off-licences* Originally, permits that allowed the sale of alcoholic beverages; here, a shop at which alcohol is sold by permit.

[4] *corn* I.e., grain.

[5] *2s 6d* Two shillings sixpence.

[6] *two up and two down* House consisting of two rooms downstairs and two upstairs.

[7] *publicans* Owners of pubs.

recruits—clerks and, in particular, schoolteachers (struggling hard at that time for social position). Well before translation those striving to "get on" tried to ape what they believed were "real" middle-class manners and customs. Publicans' and shopkeepers' daughters, for instance, set the fashion in clothes for a district. Some went to private commercial colleges in the city, took music lessons or perhaps studied elocution—that short cut, it was felt, to "culture"—at two shillings an hour, their new "twang" tried out later over the bar and counter, earning them a deal of covert ridicule....

Many women and girls in the district worked in some branch of the textile industry. Of these, we accepted weavers as "top" in their class, followed by winders and drawers-in. Then came spinners. They lacked standing on several counts: first, the trade contained a strong Irish Catholic element, and wages generally were lower than in other sections. Again, because of the heat and slippery floors, women worked barefoot, dressed in little more than calico shifts. These garments, the respectable believed, induced in female spinners a certain moral carelessness. They came home, too, covered in dust and fluff; all things which combined to depress their social prestige. Women employees of dye works, however, filled the lowest bracket: their work was dirty, wet and heavy and they paid due penalty for it. Clogs and shawls were, of course, standard wear for all. The girl who first defied this tradition in one of Lancashire's largest mills remembered the "stares, skits and sneers" of fellow workers sixty years afterwards. Her parents, urgently in need of money, had put her to weaving, where earnings for girls were comparatively good. They lived, however, in one of the newer suburbs with its parloured houses and small back gardens. To be seen in such a district returning from a mill in clogs and shawl would have meant instant social demotion for the whole family. She was sent to the weaving shed wearing coat and shoes and thereby shocked a whole establishment. Here was a "forward little bitch," getting above herself. So clearly, in fact, did headwear denote class that, in Glasgow, separate clubs existed for "hat" girls and "shawl" girls. Nevertheless, before 1914 even, continued good wages in weaving and the consequent urge to bolster status had persuaded not a few to follow the lone teenager's example. By the end of the war, in

the big town cotton mills at least, coats and shoes could be worn without comment....

Position in our Edwardian community was judged not only by what one possessed but also by what one pawned. Through agreement with the local broker the back room of our corner shop served as a depot for those goods pledged by the week which owners had been unable to redeem before nine o'clock on Saturday, when the local pawnshop closed. Our service gave women waiting on drunken or late-working husbands a few hours' grace in which to redeem shoes and clothing before the Sabbath, and so maintain their social stake in the English Sunday. Towards our closing time there was always a great scurrying shopwards to get the "bundle." Housewives after washday on Monday pledged what clean clothes could be spared until weekend and returned with cash to buy food. Often they stood in the shop and thanked God that *they* were not as certain others who, having no clothes but what they stood in, had sunk low enough to pawn ashpans, hearth rugs or even the "pots off the table." Other customers tut-tutted in disgust. News of domestic distress soon got around. Inability to redeem basic goods was a sure sign of a family's approaching destitution, and credit dried up fast in local tick shops. Naturally, the gulf between those households who patronized "Uncle," even if only occasionally, and those who did not gaped wide. Some families would go hungry rather than pledge their belongings.

The interest charged on articles pawned was usually a penny in the shilling per week, one half being paid at pledging time (Monday) and the other on redemption of the goods (Saturday). ...

A working-class woman, if she went even a short distance from her own door, would slip on a shawl. In public without it she was said to be "in her figure," and to be seen that way too often caused comment. With their graceful hair styles, sweeping gowns, narrow waists and curving forms, women seem to have held more feminine allure then than at any time since. But realists among the old working class today remember, and with sadness, not King Edward's "lovely ladies" and tea on the lawn at Hurlingham, but the many women broken and aged with childbearing well before their own youth was done. They remember the spoiled complexions, the mouths full of rotten teeth, the varicose veins, the ignorance of simple hygiene, the intelligence stifled and the endless battle merely to keep clean. Unlike many in the middle and upper classes, fondly looking back, they see no "glory gleaming." They weep no tears for the past. What things the poor did own then, most made gallant use of. The tragedy was that in the most opulent country in the world so many possessed so little....

Whenever status was being assessed in shop or street group, one marked with puzzlement that one or two households were dismissed with ominous brevity, and this not for any obvious reason, social or economic. Only in late teenage did we discover that the closed community, like the family, could hold skeletons in its cupboard. The damned houses were those where, neighbours knew, incestuous relationship had borne a fruit which walked the streets before their very eyes. Here stood a hazard that faced all poor parents of large adolescent families sleeping together, perhaps with older relatives, in two small bedrooms. In their hearts they harboured a dread of what seemed to a respectable household the ultimate disgrace. Such sin, of course, had to be recognized in whispered *tête à tête;* but I don't recall a single prosecution: strict public silence saved miscreants from the rigours of the law.

The matriarchy presided in judgement over the public behaviour of both children and young teenagers. Mothers round washing lines or going to the shop half a dozen times a day would inevitably hear of the peccadilloes of their offspring. Punishment followed, often unjustly, since the word of an adult was accepted almost always against that of a child. With some people a child had no "word"; only too often he was looked upon as an incomplete human being whose opinions and feelings were of little or no account—until he began to earn money! It is true that a much more indulgent attitude towards the young had already developed among the middle classes, but it had not yet spread far down the social scale. In the lower working class "manners" were imposed upon children with the firmest hand: adults recognized that if anything was to be got from "above" one should learn early to ask for it with a proper measure of humble politeness. There was besides, of course, the desire to imitate one's betters....

Among women in shop talk the confinement of daily life was often a subject for bitter complaint. Some did manage an occasional visit to the cemetery, or an hour in a balding park on the edge of the village, but many were denied even this. One, I recall, spoke wearily of never having been more than five minutes' walk from her home in eighteen years of married life. Husbands were luckier: at least once a year a beer-house picnic would take them for a long boozing day in the country. Children too got intense pleasure from the outings that charity or the Sunday school provided. Our top people paid annual visits to Blackpool, New Brighton and Southport and made sure that everybody knew, especially about their first ride in a motor car. At Southport quite early in the century an enterprising young man was doing excellent business with his Daimler open saloon,[1] taking half a dozen passengers a time for five-minute trips round the lake.

In general, slum life was far from being the jolly hive of communal activity that some romantics have claimed. They forget, perhaps, or never knew of the dirt that hung over all, of the rubbish that lay for months in the back alleys, of the "entries" or ginnels[2] with open middens[3] where starving cats and dogs roamed or died and lay for weeks unmoved. They did not know those houses that stank so badly through an open doorway that one stepped off the pavement to pass them by. That people stayed scrupulously clean in such surroundings—and many did—only proves the tenacity of the human spirit.

On the light evenings after a day's work many men, even if they had the desire, possessed no means of occupying body or mind. Ignorance and poverty combined to breed, for the most part, tedium, a dumb accidie[4] of the back streets to which only brawling brought relief. Summer evening leisure for men without the few coppers to go into a tavern meant long, empty hours lounging between kitchen chair and threshold. How familiar one grew in childhood with those silent figures leaning against door jambs, staring into vacancy waiting for bedtime.

---

[1] *saloon* Here, a car with passenger room for four or more.

[2] *ginnels* Narrow passages between homes.

[3] *open middens* Garbage heaps.

[4] *accidie* Sloth.

KATHERINE MANSFIELD
1888 – 1923

In her short life, Katherine Mansfield managed to secure a reputation as one of the world's most gifted writers of short fiction. Her later stories in particular are important for their experimentation with style and atmosphere. Instead of a conventional storyline, these stories present a series of loosely linked moments, portraying the small details of human life as a means of illuminating a specific character at a specific point of crisis or epiphany. Among Mansfield's favorite devices are internal monologues, daydreams, the flexible manipulation of time and tense, and the use of rhythm and sound to convey mood and meaning. Her stories also often feature a variety of viewpoints, with language and syntax specific to each. Mansfield also experimented with the short story cycle, linking character and/or setting and utilizing repeating images and motifs. In "The Garden Party," for instance, the Sheridan family maintains the ongoing family chronicle Mansfield created in her earlier works (using the name "Burnell").

Kathleen Mansfield Beauchamp was born in Wellington, New Zealand, the third of six children of Harold Beauchamp and Annie Burnell Dyer Beauchamp. Her father was of working-class origins, but became a successful industrialist and later chairman of the Bank of New Zealand; his rise in the financial and commercial world was rewarded with a knighthood in the year of Mansfield's death. Dyer Beauchamp was a genteel woman of delicate persuasion, for whom the regimens of household management and child rearing seemed both too taxing and beneath her social ambitions. As a result, Mansfield's memories of her mother were more frequently detached than affectionate.

Mansfield's school years were divided between the country village of Karori and the capital, Wellington, where the family moved to a mansion at Tinakori Road (the setting for "The Garden Party"). In 1903, she and her sisters entered Queen's College in London. She immersed herself in French and German while contemplating a career as a cellist. Mansfield also advanced her literary career as she became a contributor to and editor of the College's magazine. It was at Queen's College that she developed a close relationship with Ida Baker (to whom she referred as Leslie Moore)—a relationship Mansfield would depend upon for the rest of her life. By this time, the young author and musician Kathleen Beauchamp had decided to adopt the professional name of "Katherine Mansfield."

At the conclusion of her studies in London, Mansfield returned unwillingly to Wellington. Having flourished artistically in the cosmopolitan environment of London, she despised the provincial lifestyle of her home, and for nearly two years she exhausted her parents with constant pleas to return to England. In 1908, with the support of Baker, she was given leave to return to London and never saw New Zealand again.

Within weeks of returning, Mansfield fell in love with a fellow musician, Garnett Trowell. When their relationship collapsed within a few months, she impulsively married G.C. Bowden, a singing teacher whose name she bore for the next nine years, despite having left him on their wedding night. She returned to Trowell and traveled with his opera company until she became pregnant and was sent by her mother to an unfashionable Bavarian spa for the duration of her pregnancy, which ended in miscarriage. During her stay in Germany, she wrote a series of satirical sketches of German characters that were published individually in *The New Age*; they were later collected and published as *In a German Pension* (1911). On her return to London Mansfield was diagnosed with rheumatic fever; it was later discovered to be gonorrhea, a condition that contributed to her failing health for the rest of her life.

By late 1911, Mansfield had begun contributing to *Rhythm*, an avant-garde quarterly edited by John Middleton Murry. A year later she became *Rhythm*'s editor and began a lifelong, tumultuous love affair with Murry. The "Two Tigers," as they were known, cultivated several close relationships within literary circles, most notably with D.H. Lawrence (a friendship that would end bitterly in 1920), Virginia Woolf, and Aldous Huxley. In 1913, *Rhythm* became *The Blue Review* after the publisher absconded, leaving Mansfield and Murry with considerable debts. *The Blue Review* folded after only three months, despite an impressive list of contributors including Lawrence, H.G. Wells, Hugh Walpole, and T.S. Eliot.

In 1915, Mansfield's youngest brother Leslie was killed in France. Her profound grief sent her into self-imposed exile in that country, where in an effort to console herself she began writing stories about her childhood in New Zealand; thus began her most productive and successful period as a writer. That same year Mansfield finally divorced G.C. Bowden and married John Murry. Later in the year she was diagnosed with tuberculosis; for the remaining years of her life she traveled between London, Switzerland, and the French Riviera in search of modern treatments and salubrious climates.

In 1919 Mansfield began reviewing novels for the *Athenaeum*, the editor of which was Murry, and a year later she published *Bliss, and Other Stories*. In the next two years she wrote many of her most notable works, several of which are included in *The Garden Party and Other Stories* (1922). In October of that year she entered the Gurdjieff Institute in France for controversial therapy under the guidance of mystic George Ivanovich Gurdjieff. In early 1923, overexcited by a visit from her husband, Mansfield suffered a severe lung hemorrhage upon rapidly climbing the steps to her room; she died later that evening. Although Mansfield had requested in her will that Murry publish as little of her work as possible, two further collections of her stories were published, as well as a collection of poetry and other works.

The relatively small body of work that Mansfield left behind addresses grand themes such as the evolution of the self, the terrors of childhood, the solitude of the outsider, and the reality of death. Malcolm Cowley, a contemporary of Mansfield, wrote that her stories "have a thesis: namely, that life is a very wonderful spectacle, but disagreeable for the actors."

⌘ ⌘ ⌘

The Garden Party

And after all the weather was ideal. They could not have had a more perfect day for a garden party if they had ordered it. Windless, warm, the sky without a cloud. Only the blue was veiled with a haze of light gold, as it is sometimes in early summer. The gardener had been up since dawn, mowing the lawns and sweeping them, until the grass and the dark flat rosettes where the daisy plants had been seemed to shine. As for the roses, you could not help feeling they understood that roses are the only flowers that impress people at garden parties, the only flowers that everybody is certain of knowing. Hundreds, yes, literally hundreds, had come out in a single night; the green bushes bowed down as though they had been visited by archangels.

Breakfast was not yet over before the men came to put up the marquee.

"Where do you want the marquee put, mother?"

"My dear child, it's no use asking me. I'm determined to leave everything to you children this year. Forget I am your mother. Treat me as an honoured guest."

But Meg could not possibly go and supervise the men. She had washed her hair before breakfast, and she sat drinking her coffee in a green turban, with a dark wet curl stamped on each cheek. Jose, the butterfly, always came down in a silk petticoat and a kimono jacket.

"You'll have to go, Laura; you're the artistic one."

Away Laura flew, still holding her piece of bread and butter. It's so delicious to have an excuse for eating out of doors and, besides, she loved having to arrange things; she always felt she could do it so much better than anybody else.

Four men in their shirt sleeves stood grouped together on the garden path. They carried staves[1] covered with rolls of canvas and they had big toolbags slung on their backs. They looked impressive. Laura wished now that she was not holding that piece of bread and butter, but there was nowhere to put it and she couldn't possibly throw it away. She blushed and tried to look severe and even a little bit shortsighted as she came up to them.

"Good morning," she said, copying her mother's voice. But that sounded so fearfully affected that she was ashamed, and stammered like a little girl, "Oh—er—have you come—is it about the marquee?"

"That's right, miss," said the tallest of the men, a lanky, freckled fellow, and he shifted his tool bag, knocked back his straw hat and smiled down at her. "That's about it."

His smile was so easy, so friendly, that Laura recovered. What nice eyes he had, small, but such a dark blue! And now she looked at the others, they were smiling too. "Cheer up, we won't bite," their smile seemed to say. How very nice workmen were! And what a beautiful morning! She mustn't mention the morning; she must be businesslike. The marquee.

"Well, what about the lily lawn? Would that do?"

And she pointed to the lily lawn with the hand that didn't hold the bread and butter. They turned, they stared in the direction. A little fat chap thrust out his underlip and the tall fellow frowned.

"I don't fancy it," said he. "Not conspicuous enough. You see, with a thing like a marquee"—and he turned to Laura in his easy way—"you want to put it somewhere where it'll give you a bang slap in the eye, if you follow me."

Laura's upbringing made her wonder for a moment whether it was quite respectful of a workman to talk to her of bangs slap in the eye. But she did quite follow him.

"A corner of the tennis court," she suggested. "But the band's going to be in one corner."

"H'm, going to have a band, are you?" said another of the workmen. He was pale. He had a haggard look as his dark eyes scanned the tennis court. What was he thinking?

"Only a very small band," said Laura gently. Perhaps he wouldn't mind so much if the band was quite small. But the tall fellow interrupted.

"Look here, miss, that's the place. Against those trees. Over there. That'll do fine."

Against the karakas. Then the karaka trees would be hidden. And they were so lovely, with their broad, gleaming leaves, and their clusters of yellow fruit. They were like trees you imagined growing on a desert island, proud, solitary, lifting their leaves and fruits to the sun in a kind of silent splendour. Must they be hidden by a marquee?

They must. Already the men had shouldered their staves and were making for the place. Only the tall fellow was left. He bent down, pinched a sprig of lavender, put his thumb and forefinger to his nose and snuffed up the smell. When Laura saw that gesture she forgot all about the karakas in her wonder at him caring for things like that—caring for the smell of lavender. How many men that she knew would have done such a thing? Oh, how extraordinarily nice workmen were, she thought. Why couldn't she have workmen for friends rather than the silly boys she danced with and who came to Sunday night supper? She would get on much better with men like these.

It's all the fault, she decided, as the tall fellow drew something on the back of an envelope, something that was to be looped up or left to hang, of these absurd class

---

[1] *staves* Rods.

distinctions. Well, for her part, she didn't feel them. Not a bit, not an atom.... And now there came the chock-chock of wooden hammers. Someone whistled, someone sang out, "Are you right there, matey?" "Matey!" The friendliness of it, the—the— Just to prove how happy she was, just to show the tall fellow how at home she felt, and how she despised stupid conventions, Laura took a big bite of her bread and butter as she stared at the little drawing. She felt just like a work girl.

"Laura, Laura, where are you? Telephone, Laura!" a voice cried from the house.

"Coming!" Away she skimmed, over the lawn, up the path, up the steps, across the veranda and into the porch. In the hall her father and Laurie were brushing their hats ready to go to the office.

"I say, Laura," said Laurie very fast, "you might just give a squiz[1] at my coat before this afternoon. See if it wants pressing."

"I will," said she. Suddenly she couldn't stop herself. She ran at Laurie and gave him a small, quick squeeze. "Oh, I do love parties, don't you?" gasped Laura.

"Ra—ther," said Laurie's warm, boyish voice, and he squeezed his sister too and gave her a gentle push. "Dash off to the telephone, old girl."

The telephone. "Yes, yes; oh yes. Kitty? Good morning, dear. Come to lunch? Do, dear. Delighted, of course. It will only be a very scratch[2] meal—just the sandwich crusts and broken meringue shells and what's left over. Yes, isn't it a perfect morning? Your white? Oh, I certainly should. One moment—hold the line. Mother's calling." And Laura sat back. "What, mother? Can't hear."

Mrs. Sheridan's voice floated down the stairs. "Tell her to wear that sweet hat she had on last Sunday."

"Mother says you're to wear that sweet hat you had on last Sunday. Good. One o'clock. Bye-bye."

Laura put back the receiver, flung her arms over her head, took a deep breath, stretched and let them fall. "Huh," she sighed, and the moment after the sigh she sat up quickly. She was still, listening. All the doors in the house seemed to be open. The house was alive with soft, quick steps and running voices. The green baize door[3] that led to the kitchen regions swung open and shut with a muffled thud. And now there came a long, chuckling absurd sound. It was the heavy piano being moved on its stiff castors. But the air! If you stopped to notice, was the air always like this? Little faint winds were playing chase in at the tops of the windows, out at the doors. And there were two tiny spots of sun, one on the inkpot, one on a silver photograph frame, playing too. Darling little spots. Especially the one on the inkpot lid. It was quite warm. A warm little silver star. She could have kissed it.

The front door bell pealed and there sounded the rustle of Sadie's print skirt on the stairs. A man's voice murmured; Sadie answered, careless, "I'm sure I don't know. Wait. I'll ask Mrs. Sheridan."

"What is it, Sadie?" Laura came into the hall.

"It's the florist, Miss Laura."

It was, indeed. There, just inside the door, stood a wide, shallow tray full of pots of pink lilies. No other kind. Nothing but lilies—canna lilies, big pink flowers, wide open, radiant, almost frighteningly alive on bright crimson stems.

"O–oh, Sadie!" said Laura, and the sound was like a little moan. She crouched down as if to warm herself at that blaze of lilies; she felt they were in her fingers, on her lips, growing in her breast.

"It's some mistake," she said faintly. "Nobody ever ordered so many. Sadie, go and find mother."

But at that moment Mrs. Sheridan joined them.

"It's quite right," she said calmly. "Yes, I ordered them. Aren't they lovely?" She pressed Laura's arm. "I was passing the shop yesterday, and I saw them in the window. And I suddenly thought for once in my life I shall have enough canna lilies. The garden party will be a good excuse."

"But I thought you said you didn't mean to interfere," said Laura. Sadie had gone. The florist's man was still outside at his van. She put her arm round her mother's neck and gently, very gently, she bit her mother's ear.

"My darling child, you wouldn't like a logical mother, would you? Don't do that. Here's the man."

---

[1] *squiz* Glance.

[2] *scratch* Quickly thrown together.

[3] *baize door* Door, covered with a green felt-like material, that separates the kitchen from the rest of the house in large English homes.

He carried more lilies still, another whole tray.

"Bank them up, just inside the door, on both sides of the porch, please," said Mrs. Sheridan. "Don't you agree, Laura?"

"Oh, I *do*, mother."

In the drawing room Meg, Jose and good little Hans had at last succeeded in moving the piano.

"Now, if we put this chesterfield against the wall and move everything out of the room except the chairs, don't you think?"

"Quite."

"Hans, move these tables into the smoking room, and bring a sweeper to take these marks off the carpet and—one moment, Hans—" Jose loved giving orders to the servants and they loved obeying her. She always made them feel they were taking part in some drama. "Tell mother and Miss Laura to come here at once."

"Very good, Miss Jose."

She turned to Meg. "I want to hear what the piano sounds like, just in case I'm asked to sing this afternoon. Let's try over 'This Life is Weary.'"

Pom! Ta-ta-ta *Tee*-ta! The piano burst out so passionately that Jose's face changed. She clasped her hands. She looked mournfully and enigmatically at her mother and Laura as they came in.

This Life is *Wee*-ary,
A Tear—a Sigh.
A Love that *Chan*-ges,
    This Life is *Wee*-ary,
A Tear—a Sigh.
A Love that *Chan*-ges,
And then ... Goodbye!

But at the word "Goodbye," and although the piano sounded more desperate than ever, her face broke into a brilliant, dreadfully unsympathetic smile.

"Aren't I in good voice, mummy?" she beamed.

This Life is *Wee*-ary,
Hope comes to Die.
A Dream—a *Wa*-kening.

But now Sadie interrupted them. "What is it, Sadie?"

"If you please, m'm, cook says have you got the flags for the sandwiches?"

"The flags for the sandwiches, Sadie?" echoed Mrs. Sheridan dreamily. And the children knew by her face that she hadn't got them. "Let me see." And she said to Sadie firmly, "Tell cook I'll let her have them in ten minutes."

Sadie went.

"Now, Laura," said her mother quickly, "come with me into the smoking room. I've got the names somewhere on the back of an envelope. You'll have to write them out for me. Meg, go upstairs this minute and take that wet thing off your head. Jose, run and finish dressing this instant. Do you hear me, children, or shall I have to tell your father when he comes home tonight? And—and, Jose, pacify cook if you do go into the kitchen, will you? I'm terrified of her this morning."

The envelope was found at last behind the dining room clock, though how it had got there Mrs. Sheridan could not imagine.

"One of you children must have stolen it out of my bag, because I remember vividly—cream cheese and lemon curd. Have you done that?"

"Yes."

"Egg and—" Mrs. Sheridan held the envelope away from her. "It looks like mice. It can't be mice, can it?"

"Olive, pet," said Laura, looking over her shoulder.

"Yes, of course, olive. What a horrible combination it sounds. Egg and olive."

They were finished at last, and Laura took them off to the kitchen. She found Jose there pacifying the cook, who did not look at all terrifying.

"I have never seen such exquisite sandwiches," said Jose's rapturous voice. "How many kinds did you say there were, cook? Fifteen?"

"Fifteen, Miss Jose."

"Well, cook, I congratulate you."

Cook swept up crusts with the long sandwich knife, and smiled broadly.

"Godber's has come," announced Sadie, issuing out of the pantry. She had seen the man pass the window.

That meant the cream puffs had come. Godber's were famous for their cream puffs. Nobody ever thought of making them at home.

"Bring them in and put them on the table, my girl," ordered cook.

Sadie brought them in and went back to the door. Of course Laura and Jose were far too grown up to really care about such things. All the same, they couldn't help agreeing that the puffs looked very attractive. Very. Cook began arranging them, shaking off the extra icing sugar.

"Don't they carry one back to all one's parties?" said Laura.

"I suppose they do," said practical Jose, who never liked to be carried back. "They look beautifully light and feathery, I must say."

"Have one each, my dears," said cook in her comfortable voice. "Yer ma won't know."

Oh, impossible. Fancy cream puffs so soon after breakfast. The very idea made one shudder. All the same, two minutes later Jose and Laura were licking their fingers with that absorbed inward look that only comes from whipped cream.

"Let's go into the garden, out by the back way," suggested Laura. "I want to see how the men are getting on with the marquee. They're such awfully nice men."

But the back door was blocked by cook, Sadie, Godber's man and Hans.

Something had happened.

"Tuk-tuk-tuk," clucked cook like an agitated hen. Sadie had her hand clapped to her cheek as though she had toothache. Han's face was screwed up in the effort to understand. Only Godber's man seemed to be enjoying himself; it was his story.

"What's the matter? What's happened?"

"There's been a horrible accident," said cook. "A man killed."

"A man killed! Where? How? When?"

But Godber's man wasn't going to have his story snatched from under his very nose.

"Know those little cottages just below here, miss?" Know them? Of course she knew them. "Well, there's a young chap living there, name of Scott, a carter. His horse shied at a traction engine, corner of Hawke Street this morning, and he was thrown out on the back of his head. Killed."

"Dead!" Laura stared at Godber's man.

"Dead when they picked him up," said Godber's man with relish. "They were taking the body home as I come up here." And he said to the cook, "He's left a wife and five little ones."

"Jose, come here." Laura caught hold of her sister's sleeve and dragged her through the kitchen to the other side of the green baize door. There she paused and leaned against it. "Jose!" she said, horrified, "however are we going to stop everything?"

"Stop everything, Laura!" cried Jose in astonishment. "What do you mean?"

"Stop the garden party, of course." Why did Jose pretend?

But Jose was still more amazed. "Stop the garden party? My dear Laura, don't be so absurd. Of course we can't do anything of the kind. Nobody expects us to. Don't be so extravagant."

"But we can't possibly have a garden party with a man dead just outside the front gate."

That really was extravagant, for the little cottages were in a lane to themselves at the very bottom of a steep rise that led up to the house. A broad road ran between. True, they were far too near. They were the greatest possible eyesore and they had no right to be in that neighbourhood at all. They were little mean dwellings painted a chocolate brown. In the garden patches there was nothing but cabbage stalks, sick hens and tomato cans. The very smoke coming out of their chimneys was poverty stricken. Little rags and shreds of smoke, so unlike the great silvery plumes that uncurled from the Sheridans' chimneys. Washerwomen lived in the lane and sweeps and a cobbler and a man whose house front was studded all over with minute birdcages. Children swarmed. When the Sheridans were little they were forbidden to set foot there because of the revolting language and of what they might catch. But since they were grown up Laura and Laurie on their prowls sometimes walked through. It was disgusting and sordid. They came out with a shudder. But still one must go everywhere; one must see everything. So through they went.

"And just think of what the band would sound like to that poor woman," said Laura.

"Oh, Laura!" Jose began to be seriously annoyed. "If you're going to stop a band playing every time someone has an accident, you'll lead a very strenuous life. I'm every bit as sorry about it as you. I feel just as sympathetic." Her eyes hardened. She looked at her sister just as she used to when they were little and fighting together. "You won't bring a drunken workman back to life by being sentimental," she said softly.

"Drunk! Who said he was drunk?" Laura turned furiously on Jose. She said just as they had used to say on those occasions, "I'm going straight up to tell mother."

"Do, dear," cooed Jose.

"Mother, can I come into your room?" Laura turned the big glass doorknob.

"Of course, child. Why, what's the matter? What's given you such a colour?" And Mrs. Sheridan turned round from her dressing table. She was trying on a new hat.

"Mother, a man's been killed," began Laura.

"*Not* in the garden?" interrupted her mother.

"No, no!"

"Oh, what a fright you gave me!" Mrs. Sheridan sighed with relief and took off the big hat and held it on her knees.

"But listen, mother," said Laura. Breathless, half choking, she told the dreadful story. "Of course, we can't have our party, can we?" she pleaded. "The band and everybody arriving. They'd hear us, mother; they're nearly neighbours!"

To Laura's astonishment her mother behaved just like Jose; it was harder to bear because she seemed amused. She refused to take Laura seriously.

"But, my dear child, use your common sense. It's only by accident we've heard of it. If someone had died there normally—and I can't understand how they keep alive in those poky little holes—we should still be having our party, shouldn't we?"

Laura had to say "yes" to that, but she felt it was all wrong. She sat down on her mother's sofa and pinched the cushion frill.

"Mother, isn't it really terribly heartless of us?" she asked.

"Darling!" Mrs. Sheridan got up and came over to her, carrying the hat. Before Laura could stop her she had popped it on. "My child!" said her mother, "the hat is yours. It's made for you. It's much too young for me. I have never seen you look such a picture. Look at yourself!" And she held up her hand-mirror.

"But, mother," Laura began again. She couldn't look at herself; she turned aside.

This time Mrs. Sheridan lost patience just as Jose had done.

"You are being very absurd, Laura," she said coldly. "People like that don't expect sacrifices from us. And it's not very sympathetic to spoil everybody's enjoyment as you're doing now."

"I don't understand," said Laura, and she walked quickly out of the room into her own bedroom. There, quite by chance, the first thing she saw was this charming girl in the mirror, in her black hat trimmed with gold daisies and a long black velvet ribbon. Never had she imagined she could look like that. Is mother right? she thought. And now she hoped her mother was right. Am I being extravagant? Perhaps it was extravagant. Just for a moment she had another glimpse of that poor woman and those little children and the body being carried into the house. But it all seemed blurred, unreal, like a picture in the newspaper. I'll remember it again after the party's over, she decided. And somehow that seemed quite the best plan. . . .

Lunch was over by half-past one. By half-past two they were all ready for the fray. The green-coated band had arrived and was established in a corner of the tennis court.

"My dear!" trilled Kitty Maitland, "aren't they too like frogs for words? You ought to have arranged them round the pond with the conductor in the middle on a leaf."

Laurie arrived and hailed them on his way to dress. At the sight of him Laura remembered the accident again. She wanted to tell him. If Laurie agreed with the others, then it was bound to be all right. And she followed him into the hall.

"Laurie!"

"Hallo!" He was halfway upstairs, but when he turned round and saw Laura he suddenly puffed out his cheeks and goggled his eyes at her. "My word, Laura! You do look stunning," said Laurie. "What an absolutely topping hat!"

Laura said faintly "Is it?" and smiled up at Laurie and didn't tell him after all.

Soon after that people began coming in streams. The band struck up; the hired waiters ran from the house to the marquee. Wherever you looked there were couples strolling, bending to the flowers, greeting, moving on over the lawn. They were like bright birds that had alighted in the Sheridans' garden for this one afternoon, on their way to—where? Ah, what happiness it is to be with people who all are happy, to press hands, press cheeks, smile into eyes.

"Darling Laura, how well you look!"

"What a becoming hat, child!"

"Laura, you look quite Spanish. I've never seen you look so striking."

And Laura, glowing, answered softly, "Have you had tea? Won't you have an ice? The passion fruit ices really are rather special." She ran to her father and begged him: "Daddy darling, can't the band have something to drink?"

And the perfect afternoon slowly ripened, slowly faded, slowly its petals closed.

"Never a more delightful garden party ..." "The greatest success ..." "Quite the most ..."

Laura helped her mother with the goodbyes. They stood side by side in the porch till it was all over.

"All over, all over, thank heaven," said Mrs. Sheridan. "Round up the others, Laura. Let's go and have some fresh coffee. I'm exhausted. Yes, it's been very successful. But oh, these parties, these parties! Why will you children insist on giving parties!" And they all of them sat down in the deserted marquee.

"Have a sandwich, daddy dear. I wrote the flag."

"Thanks." Mr. Sheridan took a bite and the sandwich was gone. He took another. "I suppose you didn't hear of a beastly accident that happened today?" he said.

"My dear," said Mrs. Sheridan, holding up her hand, "we did. It nearly ruined the party. Laura insisted we should put it off."

"Oh, mother!" Laura didn't want to be teased about it.

"It was a horrible affair all the same," said Mr. Sheridan. "The chap was married too. Lived just below in the lane, and leaves a wife and half a dozen kiddies, so they say."

An awkward little silence fell. Mrs. Sheridan fidgeted with her cup. Really, it was very tactless of father....

Suddenly she looked up. There on the table were all those sandwiches, cakes, puffs, all uneaten, all going to be wasted. She had one of her brilliant ideas.

"I know," she said. "Let's make up a basket. Let's send that poor creature some of this perfectly good food. At any rate, it will be the greatest treat for the children. Don't you agree? And she's sure to have neighbours calling in and so on. What a point to have it all ready prepared. Laura!" She jumped up. "Get me the big basket out of the stairs cupboard."

"But, mother, do you really think it's a good idea?" said Laura.

Again, how curious, she seemed to be different from them all. To take scraps from their party. Would the poor woman really like that?

"Of course! What's the matter with you today? An hour or two ago you were insisting on us being sympathetic."

Oh well! Laura ran for the basket. It was filled, it was now heaped by her mother.

"Take it yourself, darling," said she. "Run down just as you are. No, wait, take the arum lilies too. People of that class are so impressed by arum lilies."

"The stems will ruin her lace frock," said practical Jose.

So they would. Just in time. "Only the basket, then. And, Laura!"—her mother followed her out of the marquee—"don't on any account—"

"What, mother?"

No, better not put such ideas into the child's head! "Nothing! Run along."

It was just growing dusky as Laura shut their garden gates. A big dog ran by like a shadow. The road gleamed white, and down below in the hollow the little cottages were in deep shade. How quiet it seemed after the afternoon. Here she was going down the hill to somewhere where a man lay dead, and she couldn't realise it. Why couldn't she? She stopped a minute. And it seemed to her that kisses, voices, tinkling spoons, laughter, the smell of crushed grass were somehow inside her. She had no room for anything else. How strange! She looked up at the pale sky, and all she thought was, "Yes, it was the most successful party."

Now the broad road was crossed. The lane began, smoky and dark. Women in shawls and men's tweed caps hurried by. Men hung over the palings; the children played in the doorways. A low hum came from the mean little cottages. In some of them there was a flicker of light, and a shadow, crab-like, moved across the window. Laura bent her head and hurried on. She wished now she had put on a coat. How her frock shone! And the big hat with the velvet streamer—if only it was another hat! Were the people looking at her? They must be. It was a mistake to have come; she knew all along it was a mistake. Should she go back even now?

No, too late. This was the house. It must be. A dark knot of people stood outside. Beside the gate an old, old woman with a crutch sat in a chair, watching. She had her feet on a newspaper. The voices stopped as Laura drew near. The group parted. It was as though she was expected, as though they had known she was coming here.

Laura was terribly nervous. Tossing the velvet ribbon over her shoulder, she said to a woman standing by, "Is this Mrs. Scott's house?" and the woman, smiling queerly, said, "It is, my lass."

Oh, to be away from this! She actually said, "Help me, God," as she walked up the tiny path and knocked. To be away from those staring eyes, or to be covered up in anything, one of those women's shawls even. I'll just leave the basket and go, she decided. I shan't even wait for it to be emptied.

Then the door opened. A little woman in black showed in the gloom.

Laura said, "Are you Mrs. Scott?" But to her horror the woman answered, "Walk in, please, miss," and she was shut in the passage.

"No," said Laura, "I don't want to come in. I only want to leave this basket. Mother sent—"

The little woman in the gloomy passage seemed not to have heard her. "Step this way, please, miss," she said in an oily voice, and Laura followed her.

She found herself in a wretched little low kitchen, lighted by a smoky lamp. There was a woman sitting before the fire.

"Em," said the little creature who had let her in. "Em! It's a young lady." She turned to Laura. She said meaningly, "I'm 'er sister, miss. You'll excuse 'er, won't you?"

"Oh, but of course!" said Laura. "Please, please don't disturb her. I—I only want to leave—"

But at that moment the woman at the fire turned round. Her face, puffed up, red, with swollen eyes and swollen lips, looked terrible. She seemed as though she couldn't understand why Laura was there. What did it mean? Why was this stranger standing in the kitchen with a basket? What was it all about? And the poor face puckered up again.

"All right, my dear," said the other. "I'll thenk the young lady."

And again she began, "You'll excuse her, miss, I'm sure," and her face, swollen too, tried an oily smile.

Laura only wanted to get out, to get away. She was back in the passage. The door opened. She walked straight through into the bedroom, where the dead man was lying.

"You'd like a look at 'im, wouldn't you?" said Em's sister, and she brushed past Laura over to the bed. "Don't be afraid, my lass"—and now her voice sounded fond and sly, and fondly she drew down the sheet—"'e looks a picture. There's nothing to show. Come along, my dear."

Laura came.

There lay a young man, fast asleep—sleeping so soundly, so deeply, that he was far, far away from them both. Oh, so remote, so peaceful. He was dreaming. Never wake him up again. His head was sunk in the pillow, his eyes were closed; they were blind under the closed eyelids. He was given up to his dream. What did garden parties and baskets and lace frocks matter to him? He was far from all those things. He was wonderful, beautiful. While they were laughing and while the band was playing, this marvel had come to the lane. Happy … happy…. All is well, said that sleeping face. This is just as it should be. I am content.

But all the same you had to cry, and she couldn't go out of the room without saying something to him. Laura gave a loud childish sob.

"Forgive my hat," she said.

And this time she didn't wait for Em's sister. She found her way out of the door, down the path past all those dark people. At the corner of the lane she met Laurie.

He stepped out of the shadow. "Is that you, Laura?"

"Yes."

"Mother was getting anxious. Was it all right?"

"Yes, quite, Oh, Laurie!" She took his arm, she pressed up against him.

"I say, you're not crying, are you?" asked her brother.

Laura shook her head. She was.

Laurie put his arm round her shoulder. "Don't cry," he said in his warm, loving voice. "Was it awful?"

"No," sobbed Laura. "It was simply marvellous. But, Laurie—" She stopped, she looked at her brother. "Isn't life," she stammered, "isn't life—" But what life was she couldn't explain. No matter. He quite understood.

"*Isn't* it, darling?" said Laurie.

—1922

T.S. ELIOT
1888 – 1965

The poetry and prose of T.S. Eliot probably did more than that of any other writer to transform the face of twentieth-century English writing. His Modernist poems of the 1910s and 1920s (*The Waste Land* chief among them) were revolutionary both in their form and in their content—yet Eliot himself, the most unlikely of revolutionaries, became an icon of the literary establishment. He voiced in unique fashion the bleakness and despair that was characteristically felt by many in the early twentieth century—yet he became a leading voice of traditional Christianity. He embraced difficulty as the literary strategy most consonant with the character of his era—yet he also wrote a succession of highly accessible plays for the popular stage. He strove for Christian virtue, but has been strongly criticized for alleged hostility towards women and towards Jews. In short, he is a central figure of the twentieth century not only because his works are central documents of its literature, but also because they embody many of the paradoxes of the age.

Thomas Stearns Eliot was born in St. Louis, Missouri, in 1888, the youngest son in a distinguished New England family that traced its roots back to the first Puritan settlers of

Massachusetts. Eliot followed his older brother to Harvard in 1906, where he joined the board of Harvard's literary magazine and started a lifelong friendship with Conrad Aiken, a fellow board member. In 1909, the year before he completed his MA, Eliot began drafting the poems that would become "The Love Song of J. Alfred Prufrock," "Preludes," "Portrait of a Lady," and "Rhapsody on a Windy Night." He spent a postgraduate year at the Sorbonne in Paris and then began doctoral studies in philosophy at Harvard. His dissertation was on the ideas of the then-influential French philosopher Henri Bergson, whose emphasis on the intuitive and subjective aspects of reality and on the importance of change may have influenced Eliot's poetic explorations of the human psyche. Certainly a strong awareness of the subjectivity of perception, of the importance of the unconscious, and of alienation and social claustrophobia in an unpredictably changing world are all powerful elements in Eliot's early poetry.

While both Eliot and Aiken were in London in 1914, Aiken showed the manuscript of "Prufrock" to American poet and critic Ezra Pound (then living abroad), who immediately recognized it as extraordinary work. The alliance of Pound and Eliot marked the beginning not only of Eliot's career as a poet (Pound and his wife financed the 1917 publication of *Prufrock and Other Observations*), but of a literary collaboration that profoundly influenced the development of modern literature.

"The Love Song of J. Alfred Prufrock," as critic James F. Knapp said, changed "our conception of what kind of shape a poem might take." With little connecting or transitional material, the poem juxtaposes disparate thoughts and scenes and combines classical literary references with images of urban, industrial twentieth-century life. Eliot was heavily influenced by French Symbolist poets Charles Baudelaire and Jules Laforgue. Their powerful, disconnected imagery, their ironic, detached tones, and their themes of alienation helped Eliot discover his own poetic voice. With strong rhythms that blend formal and informal speech and striking metaphors, Eliot creates an ironic love song in the frustrated inner voice of "Prufrock"'s central figure, who, in the face of his bleak physical and spiritual life, is unable to act on his love.

Inspired by what he referred to as "the mind of Europe," and with some persuasion by Pound, Eliot chose England as his permanent home. His decision was solidified by an impulsive decision in 1915 to marry Vivienne Haigh-Wood, an Englishwoman whom he had met that spring. In England, Eliot balanced writing and editorial work for the avant-garde magazine *The Egoist* with more reliable employment as a schoolteacher and then as a bank clerk at Lloyd's Bank in London.

Eliot's first book of criticism, *The Sacred Wood* (1920), established him as a discerning and erudite literary critic and introduced a new set of critical precepts that would become highly influential. Eliot placed a high value on "impersonality" in poetry, and on the idea of an "objective correlative" as a means of expressing emotion through a set of objects, circumstances, or chain of events. Eliot's introduction of these ideas to the literary world helped pave the way for the critical approach known as "New Criticism." In the writings of I.A. Richards and others of this school, the focus was on the work itself as an artefact independent of authorial intention. Eliot's essays also examined his sense of the necessary difficulty of modern writing, which he believed had the nearly impossible task of synthesizing the seemingly unrelated, chaotic experiences of modern citizens.

By 1921, affected by the strain of overwork and the increasing pressure of his wife's failing physical and mental health, Eliot had a nervous breakdown. During a three-month-long rest cure, he was finally able to complete *The Waste Land*, a project he had begun in 1914. Originally composed as a series of narrative poems, *The Waste Land* was considerably longer in its original version; Pound helped Eliot pare down and fuse the diverse materials into a rhythmically coherent whole. Published in 1922, *The Waste Land* deviated far more decisively than had "Prufrock" from accepted notions of what constituted poetry. Written in fragmented form, this poem of complex imagery, multiple voices, jazz rhythms, and dense literary and mythological allusions jumps between perspectives and scenes without connective or transitional passages. With its radical break from established conventions in structure, theme, and expression, and its blending of western and of non-western ideologies, *The Waste Land* can be disorienting for readers—so much so, in fact, that when the poem first appeared some writers and critics wondered if the poem was a hoax orchestrated by Eliot and his literary friends.

Much as *The Waste Land* was derided in some quarters, in others it established Eliot as a groundbreaking writer. Meanwhile, his critical writing in the international literary journal *The Criterion* (which Eliot founded in 1922) helped to round out his reputation as one of London's leading literary figures. In 1925, Eliot was recruited by the publishing firm Faber and Gwyer (later Faber and Faber) as a literary editor and board member. The position, which he held for many years, further extended Eliot's influence, as he was able to cultivate young writers—such as W.H. Auden—whose work he found promising.

Eliot's next long poem, *The Hollow Men* (1925), in some ways extends *The Waste Land*'s articulation of alienation and despair, but it also deals with more transcendent themes of what Eliot called "the salvation of the soul." Eliot's Christian faith continued to strengthen, and in 1927, the same year he was naturalized as a British citizen, Eliot was baptized into the Church of England. Religion thereafter became central to his life, and in 1933 he moved to Glenville Place presbytery, where he served as a church warden for seven years. He wrote a series of poetic meditations on religious themes and scenarios, including *Journey of the Magi* (1927) and *Marina* (1930). Steeped in Eliot's studies of Shakespeare and Dante, these works meditate on spiritual growth while experimenting with more traditional dramatic forms. The dramatic monologue form in which *Journey of the Magi* is constructed, for example, is reminiscent of Robert Browning's work.

Much of Eliot's later career focused on dramatic writing. For many years he worked on *Sweeney Agonistes*, an unfinished experimental play of modern life, written in rhythmic prose accented by drum beats. He then published two ecclesiastical dramas, one of which was *Murder in the Cathedral* (1935), a ritual drama based on the murder of Thomas à Becket, before turning to clever West End social dramas like *The Cocktail Party* (1950). Though innovative in their attempts to reconcile classical drama with modern themes, these plays have not been successfully revived in recent decades. Ironically, however, a book of playful children's verse that Eliot wrote for his godchildren, *Old Possum's Book of Practical Cats* (1939), has been much more successful on the stage than any of Eliot's plays; it was adapted by British composer Andrew Lloyd Webber into the hit musical *Cats* (1980).

Despite a busy lecturing schedule and a marriage that was increasingly taxing (Vivienne was institutionalized in 1938), Eliot produced four long poems in the late 1930s and early 1940s that together, published as *Four Quartets* (1943), he considered his crowning achievement. Comprising "Burnt Norton," "The Dry Salvages," "East Coker," and "Little Gidding," *Four Quartets* was in part inspired by the later string quartets of Beethoven. With its powerfully suggestive imagery and elaborate patterns of sound, it is among Eliot's most complex and technically masterful works. It also gives voice to Eliot's conviction that, in a world otherwise devoid of meaning, submission to God is essential. *Four Quartets* for a time took pride of place over *The Waste Land* as Eliot's most celebrated work.

The late years of Eliot's life were filled with personal happiness and public recognition of his contribution to modern literature. He was awarded eighteen honorary degrees, and in 1948 he was awarded both a Nobel Prize for Literature and the British Order of Merit. Vivienne having died in 1947, in 1957 Eliot married Valerie Fletcher and enjoyed what he described as the only happy period of his life since childhood. He died in London in 1965 and was buried, according to his wishes, in his ancestors' parish church at East Coker. The plaque on the church wall bears his chosen epitaph, from *Four Quartets*: "In my beginning is my end, in my end is my beginning."

Near the end of his life Eliot commented, with sly irony, that he would "perhaps have a certain historical place in the literary history of our period." And indeed, he was lauded on his death as a unique literary figure; his obituary in *Life* magazine declared that "our age beyond any doubt has been, and will continue to be, the Age of Eliot." In subsequent decades the praise has been less effusive, and in two respects Eliot's work has been sharply criticized: most critics now acknowledge elements of misogyny and of anti-Semitism in his writing. But the impact of his poetic innovation is lasting, and a sense of the centrality of Eliot's work to the literary history of the twentieth century has remained constant. As Northrop Frye observed, "Whether he is liked or disliked is of no importance, but he must be read."

⌘ ⌘ ⌘

The Love Song of J. Alfred Prufrock [1]

S'io credesse che mia risposta fosse
A persona che mai tornasse al mondo,
Questa fiamma staria senza piu scosse.
Ma perciocche giammai di questo fondo
Non torno viva alcun, s'i'odo il vero,
Senza tema d'infamia ti rispondo. [2]

Let us go then, you and I,
When the evening is spread out against the sky
Like a patient etherized upon a table;
Let us go, through certain half-deserted streets,
5 The muttering retreats
Of restless nights in one-night cheap hotels
And sawdust restaurants with oyster-shells:
Streets that follow like a tedious argument
Of insidious intent
10 To lead you to an overwhelming question ...
Oh, do not ask, "What is it?"
Let us go and make our visit.

In the room the women come and go
Talking of Michelangelo.

15 The yellow fog that rubs its back upon the
       window-panes,
The yellow smoke that rubs its muzzle on the
       window-panes
Licked its tongue into the corners of the evening,
Lingered upon the pools that stand in drains,
Let fall upon its back the soot that falls from chimneys,
20 Slipped by the terrace, made a sudden leap,
And seeing that it was a soft October night,
Curled once about the house, and fell asleep.

And indeed there will be time
For the yellow smoke that slides along the street,
25 Rubbing its back upon the window panes;
There will be time, there will be time [3]
To prepare a face to meet the faces that you meet
There will be time to murder and create,
And time for all the works and days [4] of hands
30 That lift and drop a question on your plate;
Time for you and time for me,
And time yet for a hundred indecisions,
And for a hundred visions and revisions,
Before the taking of a toast and tea.

35 In the room the women come and go
Talking of Michelangelo.

And indeed there will be time
To wonder, "Do I dare?" and, "Do I dare?"
Time to turn back and descend the stair,
40 With a bald spot in the middle of my hair—
(They will say: "How his hair is growing thin!")
My morning coat, [5] my collar mounting firmly to the
       chin,
My necktie rich and modest, but asserted by a simple
       pin—
(They will say: "But how his arms and legs are thin!")
45 Do I dare
Disturb the universe?
In a minute there is time
For decisions and revisions which a minute will reverse.

For I have known them all already, known them
       all—
50 Have known the evenings, mornings, afternoons,
I have measured out my life with coffee spoons;
I know the voices dying with a dying fall [6]

---

1 *J. Alfred Prufrock* The name is likely taken from the The
Prufrock-Littau Company, a furniture dealer located in St. Louis,
Eliot's birthplace.

2 *S'io credesse ... ti rispondo* Italian: "If I thought that my reply
were given to anyone who might return to the world, this flame
would stand forever still; but since never from this deep place has
anyone ever returned alive, if what I hear is true, without fear of
infamy I answer thee," Dante's *Inferno* 27.61–66; Guido da Monte-
feltro's speech as he burns in Hell.

3 *there will be time* See Ecclesiastes 3.1–8. "To everything there is
a season, and a time to every purpose under heaven: A time to be
born, and a time to die; a time to plant, and a time to pluck up that
which is planted; a time to kill, and a time to heal ..."

4 *works and days* Title of a poem by eighth-century BCE Greek poet
Hesiod.

5 *morning coat* A formal coat with tails.

6 *with a dying fall* In Shakespeare's *Twelfth Night* 1.1.1–15. Duke
Orsino commands, "That strain again, it had a dying fall."

Beneath the music from a farther room.
    So how should I presume?

55 And I have known the eyes already, known them
    all—
The eyes that fix you in a formulated phrase,
And when I am formulated, sprawling on a pin,
When I am pinned and wriggling on the wall,
Then how should I begin
60 To spit out all the butt-ends of my days and ways?
    And how should I presume?

And I have known the arms already, known them
    all—
Arms that are braceleted and white and bare
(But in the lamplight, downed with light brown hair!)
65 Is it perfume from a dress
That makes me so digress?
Arms that lie along a table, or wrap about a shawl.
    And should I then presume?
    And how should I begin?

      *   *   *

70 Shall I say, I have gone at dusk through narrow streets
And watched the smoke that rises from the pipes
Of lonely men in shirt-sleeves, leaning out of
    windows? ...[1]
    I should have been a pair of ragged claws
Scuttling across the floors of silent seas.[2]

      *   *   *

75 And the afternoon, the evening, sleeps so peacefully!
Smoothed by long fingers,
Asleep ... tired ... or it malingers,
Stretched on the floor, here beside you and me.
Should I, after tea and cakes and ices,
80 Have the strength to force the moment to its crisis?

But though I have wept and fasted, wept and prayed,
Though I have seen my head (grown slightly bald)
    brought in upon a platter,[3]
I am no prophet[4]—and here's no great matter;
I have seen the moment of my greatness flicker,
85 And I have seen the eternal Footman hold my coat,
    and snicker,
And in short, I was afraid.

And would it have been worth it, after all,
After the cups, the marmalade, the tea,
Among the porcelain, among some talk of you and me,
90 Would it have been worth while,
To have bitten off the matter with a smile,
To have squeezed the universe into a ball[5]
To roll it toward some overwhelming question,
To say: "I am Lazarus,[6] come from the dead,
95 Come back to tell you all, I shall tell you all"—
If one, settling a pillow by her head,
    Should say: "That is not what I meant at all;
    That is not it, at all."

And would it have been worth it, after all,
100 Would it have been worth while,
After the sunsets and the dooryards and the sprinkled
    streets,[7]
After the novels, after the teacups, after the skirts that
    trail along the floor—
And this, and so much more?—
It is impossible to say just what I mean!
105 But as if a magic lantern[8] threw the nerves in patterns
    on a screen:

---

1 ... The ellipsis here makes note of a 38 line insertion written by Eliot, entitled *Prufrock's Pervigilium*. The subtitle and 33 of the lines were later removed.

2 *I should ... seas* See Shakespeare's *Hamlet* 2.2, in which Hamlet tells Polonius, "for you yourself, sir, should be old as I am, if like a crab you could go backwards."

3 *brought in upon a platter* Reference to Matthew 14.1–12, in which the prophet John the Baptist is beheaded at the command of Herod, and his head presented to Salomé upon a platter.

4 *I am no prophet* See Amos 7.14. When commanded by King Amiziah not to prophesy, the Judean Amos answered; "I was no prophet, neither was I a prophet's son; but I was a herdsman, and a farmer of sycamore fruit."

5 *squeezed ... ball* See Andrew Marvell's "To His Coy Mistress" 41–42: "Let us roll our strength and all / Our sweetness up into one ball."

6 *Lazarus* Raised from the dead by Jesus in John 11.1–44.

7 *sprinkled streets* Streets sprayed with water to keep dust down.

8 *magic lantern* In Victorian times, a device used to project images painted on glass onto a blank screen or wall.

Would it have been worth while
If one, settling a pillow or throwing off a shawl,
And turning toward the window, should say:
　　"That is not it at all,
110　　That is not what I meant, at all."

　　　　*　　　*　　　*

No! I am not Prince Hamlet, nor was meant to be;
Am an attendant lord, one that will do
To swell a progress,[1] start a scene or two,
Advise the prince; no doubt, an easy tool,
115 Deferential, glad to be of use,
Politic, cautious, and meticulous;
Full of high sentence,[2] but a bit obtuse;
At times, indeed, almost ridiculous—
Almost, at times, the Fool.

120 I grow old … I grow old …
I shall wear the bottoms of my trousers rolled.

Shall I part my hair behind? Do I dare to eat a peach?
I shall wear white flannel trousers, and walk upon the
　　beach.
I have heard the mermaids singing,[3] each to each.

125 I do not think that they will sing to me.

I have seen them riding seaward on the waves
Combing the white hair of the waves blown back
When the wind blows the water white and black.

We have lingered in the chambers of the sea
130 By sea-girls wreathed with seaweed red and brown
Till human voices wake us, and we drown.
　　　—1915, 1917[4]

---

[1] *progress* Journey made by royalty through the country.

[2] *high sentence* Serious, elevated sentiments or opinions.

[3] *I have … singing* See John Donne's "Song": "Teach me to hear
the mermaids singing."

[4] *1915, 1917* The poem was first published in the Chicago
magazine *Poetry* in 1915. Lines 15–34 were added when it appeared
in *Prufrock and Other Observations* in 1917.

Preludes[5]

1

The winter evening settles down
With smell of steaks in passageways.
Six o'clock.
The burnt-out ends of smoky days.
5 And now a gusty shower wraps
The grimy scraps
Of withered leaves about your feet
And newspapers from vacant lots;
The showers beat
10 On broken blinds and chimney-pots,
And at the corner of the street
A lonely cab-horse steams and stamps.
And then the lighting of the lamps.

2

The morning comes to consciousness
15 Of faint stale smells of beer
From the sawdust-trampled[6] street
With all its muddy feet that press
To early coffee-stands.
With the other masquerades
20 That time resumes,
One thinks of all the hands
That are raising dingy shades
In a thousand furnished rooms.

3

You tossed a blanket from the bed,
25 You lay upon your back, and waited;
You dozed, and watched the night revealing
The thousand sordid images
Of which your soul was constituted;
They flickered against the ceiling.
30 And when all the world came back
And the light crept up between the shutters,
And you heard the sparrows in the gutters,
You had such a vision of the street

---

[5] *Preludes* In Parts 3 and 4 of this poem, many of the images and
details of setting are taken from Charles-Louis Philippe's novel
Bubu-de-Montparnasse (1898).

[6] *sawdust-trampled* Sawdust was placed on the floors of bars and
restaurants to absorb dirt.

As the street hardly understands;
35   Sitting along the bed's edge, where
You curled the papers from your hair,[1]
Or clasped the yellow soles of feet
In the palms of both soiled hands.

4

His soul stretched tight across the skies
40   That fade behind a city block,
Or trampled by insistent feet
At four and five and six o'clock;
And short square fingers stuffing pipes,
And evening newspapers, and eyes
45   Assured of certain certainties,
The conscience of a blackened street
Impatient to assume the world.

I am moved by fancies that are curled
Around these images, and cling:
50   The notion of some infinitely gentle
Infinitely suffering thing.

Wipe your hand across your mouth, and laugh;
The worlds revolve like ancient women
Gathering fuel in vacant lots.
    —1915

Burbank with a Baedeker: Bleistein[2] with a Cigar

Tra-la- la- la- la- la-laire—nil nisi divinum stabile est;
caetera fumus[3]*—the gondola stopped, the old palace was*
there, how charming its grey and pink[4]*—goats and monkeys,*

---

[1] *papers ... hair* I.e., "curl papers," used to curl hair.

[2] *Baedeker* Popular line of guide-books; *Bleistein* Jewish-German name literally meaning "Leadstone,"

[3] *nil ... fumus* Latin: nothing but the divine endures; all the rest is smoke.

[4] *the gondola ... pink* From Henry James's *Aspern Papers* (1888), Chapter 1. The passage is narrated by an American woman living in Venice who is giving her visiting friend a tour of the city: "The gondola stopped, the old palace was there. ... 'How charming! It's grey and pink!' my companion exclaimed."

with such hair too![5]*—so the countess passed on until she came*
through the little park, where Niobe presented her with a
cabinet, and so departed.[6]

Burbank crossed a little bridge
Descending at a small hotel;
Princess Volupine arrived,
    They were together, and he fell.[7]

5   Defunctive° music under sea   *dying*
    Passed seaward with the passing bell
Slowly: the God Hercules
    Had left him, that had loved him well.[8]

The horses, under the axletree
10   Beat up the dawn from Istria[9]
With even feet. Her shuttered barge
    Burned on the water all the day.

But this or such was Bleistein's way:
    A saggy bending of the knees
15   And elbows, with the palms turned out,
    Chicago Semite Viennese.

A lustreless protrusive eye
    Stares from the protozoic slime

---

[5] *goats and monkeys* An exclamation made by Othello in Shakespeare's *Othello* 4.1 (set in Venice) when he becomes convinced his wife is having an affair; *with such hair too* From Robert Browning's "A Toccata of Galuppi's," about the eighteenth-century Venetian composer Baldassare Galuppi (1706–85).

[6] *so the ... departed* From the stage directions of *Entertainment of Alice, Dowager Countess of Derby* by John Marston (c.1575–1634); *Niobe* Mother in Greek myth who boasted that she had more children than Zeus.

[7] *They were ... fell* From Alfred Tennyson's "The Sisters" (Eliot has changed the pronoun from "she" to "he").

[8] *Defunctive music ... well* See Shakespeare's *Antony and Cleopatra* 4.3, in which Cleopatra's soldiers hear music just before they are defeated by Caesar's army. "'Tis the god Hercules, whom Antony lov'd, / Now leaves him," one soldier says.

[9] *horses ... dawn* In classical myth, the sun is a chariot pulled across the sky; *Istria* Peninsula that juts into the northeast Adriatic.

At a perspective of Canaletto.[1]
20   The smoky candle end of time

Declines. On the Rialto[2] once.
    The rats are underneath the piles.
The jew is underneath the lot.[3]
    Money in furs.[4] The boatman smiles,

25 Princess Volupine extends
    A meagre, blue-nailed, phthisic° hand   *consumptive*
To climb the waterstair. Lights, lights,
    She entertains Sir Ferdinand

Klein. Who clipped the lion's wings[5]
30   And flea'd his rump and pared his claws?
Thought Burbank, meditating on
    Time's ruins, and the seven laws.[6]
                                    —1919

Gerontion[7]

Thou hast nor youth nor age
But as it were an after dinner sleep
Dreaming of both.[8]

Here I am, an old man in a dry month,
    Being read to by a boy, waiting for rain.[9]
I was neither at the hot gates[10]
Nor fought in the warm rain
5   Nor knee deep in the salt marsh, heaving a cutlass,
Bitten by flies, fought.
My house is a decayed house,
And the jew squats on the window sill, the owner,
Spawned in some estaminet[11] of Antwerp,
10 Blistered in Brussels, patched and peeled in London.[12]
The goat coughs at night in the field overhead;
Rocks, moss, stonecrop,[13] iron, merds.°   *feces*
The woman keeps the kitchen, makes tea,
Sneezes at evening, poking the peevish gutter.[14]
15   I an old man,
A dull head among windy spaces.

    Signs are taken for wonders. "We would see a
        sign!"
The word within a word, unable to speak a word,
Swaddled with darkness.[15] In the juvescence°   *youth*
    of the year
20 Came Christ the tiger

---

[9] *Here I ... rain* These two lines are based on a sentence in A.C. Benson's biography *Edward Fitzgerald* (1905), in which the poet is described as sitting "in a dry month, old and blind, being read to by a country boy, longing for rain."

[10] *hot gates* Literal translation of the Greek *Thermopylae*, a pass between northern and central Greece and the location of several historical battles, including that between the Greeks and the Persians in 480 BCE.

[11] *estaminet* French: café.

[12] *the jew ... London* The association of Jews with images of squalor, decay, and disgusting physicality was one of the many ways in which anti-Semitism was expressed in British literary tradition. For more on the controversy over such elements as they appear in Eliot's verse see the "In Context" section below.

[13] *stonecrop* Herb with yellow flowers that grows on rocks or old walls.

[14] *gutter* Sputtering fire.

[15] *Signs are ... darkness* Reference to two Biblical passages. The first is Matthew 12.39: "An evil and adulterous generation seeketh after a sign; and there shall no sign be given to it, but the sign of the prophet Jonas," and the second is John 1.1: "In the beginning was the Word, and the Word was with God, and the Word was God." Both of these passages were sources for a Christmas sermon given by Anglican preacher Lancelot Andrewes in 1618.

[1] *Canaletto* Italian painter Antonio Canale (1697–1768), famous for his paintings of Venice and London.

[2] *Rialto* Island in Venice, containing the old mercantile quarter of the medieval city.

[3] *The jew ... lot* For a discussion of the controversy over Eliot's attitudes towards Jewish people, see the "In Context" section on "Eliot and Anti-Semitism" later in this volume.

[4] *Money in furs* Venice was a center for fur trade from the Black Sea.

[5] *lion's wings* The winged lion was a symbol of the Venetian Republic.

[6] *seven laws* Either the seven laws of architecture that John Ruskin outlined in his *Seven Lamps of Architecture* (1849), which describes Venice's Gothic style as the ideal, or the Noachian Laws, the Seven Commandments of the Sons of Noah from the Jewish Talmud.

[7] *Gerontion* Greek: little old man. Eliot originally planned to print this poem as a prelude to *The Waste Land*, but when Ezra Pound advised against this he published it separately.

[8] *Thou hast ... both* From Shakespeare's *Measure for Measure* 3.1.32–34.

In depraved May, dogwood and chestnut,
    flowering judas,[1]
To be eaten, to be divided, to be drunk
Among whispers; by Mr. Silvero
With caressing hands, at Limoges[2]
25 Who walked all night in the next room;

     By Hakagawa, bowing among the Titians;[3]
By Madame de Tornquist, in the dark room
Shifting the candles; Fraulein von Kulp
Who turned in the hall, one hand on the door.
30   Vacant shuttles
Weave the wind. I have no ghosts,
An old man in a draughty house
Under a windy knob.[4]

     After such knowledge, what forgiveness? Think now
35 History has many cunning passages, contrived
     corridors
And issues, deceives with whispering ambitions,
Guides us by vanities. Think now
She gives when our attention is distracted
And what she gives, gives with such supple confusions
40 That the giving famishes the craving. Gives too late
What's not believed in, or if still believed,
In memory only, reconsidered passion. Gives too soon
Into weak hands,[5] what's thought can be dispensed with
Till the refusal propagates a fear. Think
45 Neither fear nor courage saves us. Unnatural vices
Are fathered by our heroism. Virtues
Are forced upon us by our impudent crimes.
These tears are shaken from the wrath-bearing tree.

The tiger springs in the new year. Us he devours.
    Think at last
50 We have not reached conclusion, when I
Stiffen in a rented house. Think at last
I have not made this show purposelessly
And it is not by any concitation°   *stirring up*
Of the backward devils.[6]
55 I would meet you upon this honestly.
I that was near your heart was removed therefrom
To lose beauty in terror, terror in inquisition.
I have lost my passion: why should I need to keep it
Since what is kept must be adulterated?
60 I have lost my sight, smell, hearing, taste and touch:
How should I use them for your closer contact?

     These with a thousand small deliberations
Protract the profit of their chilled delirium,
Excite the membrane, when the sense has cooled,
65 With pungent sauces, multiply variety
In a wilderness of mirrors. What will the spider do,
Suspend its operations, will the weevil
Delay? De Bailhache, Fresca, Mrs. Cammel, whirled
Beyond the circuit of the shuddering Bear[7]
70 In fractured atoms. Gull against the wind, in the
     windy straits
Of Belle Isle, or running on the Horn,[8]
White feathers in the snow, the Gulf[9] claims,
And an old man driven by the Trades[10]
To a sleepy corner.

75   Tenants of the house,
Thoughts of a dry brain in a dry season.
    —1920

---

[1] *judas* Purple-flowered tree of southern Europe named after Judas, who was said to have hanged himself from a tree of this type after betraying Jesus.

[2] *Limoges* French town known for its china of the same name.

[3] *Titians* Paintings by Venetian painter Titian (1485–1576).

[4] *Vacant shuttles ... knob* See Job 7.6–7: "My days are swifter than a weaver's shuttle, and are spent without hope. O remember that my life is wind: mine eye shall no more see good"; *knob* Knoll.

[5] *too soon ... hands* See Percy Shelley's *Adonais* (1821), in which he describes Keats's death: "Too soon, and with weak hands."

[6] *backward devils* In Dante's *Inferno*, tellers of the future were punished by being forced to walk backwards.

[7] *Bear* Constellation Ursa Major (the Great Bear).

[8] *Belle Isle* Channel between Labrador and Newfoundland at the entrance to the Gulf of St. Lawrence; *the Horn* Cape Horn, the southernmost tip of South America.

[9] *Gulf* Gulf stream, a warm ocean current in the North Atlantic.

[10] *Trades* Trade winds, which blow, almost constantly, towards the equator.

The Waste Land

The title and plan of Eliot's groundbreaking poem *The Waste Land* were substantially influenced by Jessie Weston's *From Ritual to Romance* (1920), which details the various legends of the Holy Grail and explores the influence of pre-Christian religions on these legends. According to most accounts of the Grail, the sacred vessel lies in the heart of a (formerly fertile) Waste Land that is now stricken with drought and presided over by a Fisher King who is cursed with impotence. The land and its king can be saved only from permanent sterility by a knight who is able to pass several tests and attain the Grail, thus bringing about regeneration. Overlaying this myth with a modern setting and numerous cultural references, Eliot shows that a similar sterility plagues a contemporary society characterized by casual sexuality, blatant materialism, and industrial exploitation of nature.

With its disparate images, ever-shifting narrative events, and seemingly random structure, *The Waste Land* embraces the fragmented present while looking back to a more coherent past. Allusions to seventeenth-century poets, to Chaucer, to Shakespeare, to Dante, to pre-Socratic philosophers, and to works of history and anthropology, such as James Frazer's twelve-volume anthropological study *The Golden Bough* (1890–1915), gesture towards the presence of a recurring order beneath contemporary history and indicate the possibility of regeneration. The poem's disconnected and highly allusive character (which gives it a sense of difficulty more often heightened than alleviated by Eliot's copious notes) provoked charges of intentional obscurity upon the poem's publication, but Eliot maintained that any poetry developed out of such a complex and various society must itself be various and complex.

By its very nature, *The Waste Land* seems to resist order and any cohesive account of meaning; its complexity and ambiguity make possible a variety of interpretations. Even the identity of its narrator is unclear: are all the disparate voices filtered through any single voice? And, if so, is the voice that of the blind prophet Tiresias, or some other nameless narrator, or is the speaker Eliot himself? This very complexity may in large part be responsible for the continued vitality of the poem, however. Eliot's friend Conrad Aiken maintained that the poem was important primarily for its private "emotional value," and that readers should rely as much on their first responses to the diverse elements of the poem as on the copious and ever-expanding body of scholarship surrounding it. As much as *The Waste Land* has taken its place as a central document of the modernist movement, it retains as well the ability to speak directly to readers.

The Waste Land [1]

"Nam Sibyllam quidem Cumis ego ipse oculis meis vidi in ampulla pendere, et cum illi pueri dicerent: Σίβυλλα τί θέλεις; respondebat illa: ἀποθανεῖν θέλω." [2]

For Ezra Pound
il miglior fabbro. [3]

---

[1] [Eliot's note] Not only the title, but the plan and a good deal of the incidental symbolism of the poem were suggested by Miss Jessie L. Weston's book on the Grail legend: *From Ritual to Romance* (Cambridge). Indeed, so deeply am I indebted, Miss Weston's book will elucidate the difficulties of the poem much better than my notes can do; and I recommend it (apart from the great interest of the book itself) to any who think such elucidation of the poem worth the trouble. To another work of anthropology I am indebted in general, one which has influenced our generation profoundly; I mean [Sir James Frazer's 1890 to 1915 twelve-volume] *The Golden Bough*; I have used especially the two volumes *Adonis, Attis, Osiris*. Anyone who is acquainted with these works will immediately recognise in the poem certain references to vegetation ceremonies.

[2] *Nam … θέλω* Latin and Greek: "For once I saw with my own eyes the Sybil at Cumae hanging in a cage, and when the boys asked her, 'Sybil, what do you want?' she responded, 'I want to die.'" From the *Satyricon* of Petronius Arbiter (first-century CE Roman writer). The most famous of the prophetic Sibyls of Greek mythology, the Cumaean Sibyl received immortality from the god Apollo, but neglected to ask him for eternal youth.

[3] *il miglior fabbro* Italian: the better craftsman. This compliment was originally paid by Dante, in his *Purgatorio* (26.117), to the Provençal poet, Arnaut Daniel. Eliot adopts it for his dedication to fellow expatriate and Modernist American poet, Ezra Pound (1885–1972), who played a key editorial role in the poem's production.

1. The Burial of the Dead[1]

April is the cruellest month, breeding
Lilacs out of the dead land, mixing
Memory and desire, stirring
Dull roots with spring rain.
5 Winter kept us warm, covering
Earth in forgetful snow, feeding
A little life with dried tubers.
Summer surprised us, coming over the Starnbergersee[2]
With a shower of rain; we stopped in the colonnade,
10 And went on in sunlight, into the Hofgarten,[3]
And drank coffee, and talked for an hour.
Bin gar keine Russin, stamm' aus Litauen, echt
deutsch.[4]
And when we were children, staying at the archduke's,
My cousin's, he took me out on a sled,
15 And I was frightened. He said, Marie,
Marie, hold on tight. And down we went.
In the mountains, there you feel free.
I read, much of the night, and go south in the winter.

What are the roots that clutch, what branches grow
20 Out of this stony rubbish? Son of man,[5]
You cannot say, or guess, for you know only
A heap of broken images, where the sun beats,
And the dead tree gives no shelter, the cricket no
relief,[6]
And the dry stone no sound of water. Only

25 There is shadow under this red rock,[7]
(Come in under the shadow of this red rock),
And I will show you something different from either
Your shadow at morning striding behind you
Or your shadow at evening rising to meet you;
30 I will show you fear in a handful of dust.
    Frisch weht der Wind
    Der Heimat zu
    Mein Irisch Kind,
    Wo weilest du?[8]
35 "You gave me hyacinths first a year ago;
They called me the hyacinth girl."
—Yet when we came back, late, from the Hyacinth
garden,
Your arms full, and your hair wet, I could not
Speak, and my eyes failed, I was neither
40 Living nor dead, and I knew nothing,
Looking into the heart of light, the silence.
Oed' und leer das Meer.[9]

Madame Sosostris,[10] famous clairvoyante,
Had a bad cold, nevertheless
45 Is known to be the wisest woman in Europe,
With a wicked pack of cards.[11] Here, said she,

---

[1] THE BURIAL OF THE DEAD Reference to the Anglican Order for the Burial of the Dead.

[2] Starnbergersee Lake near Munich, Germany.

[3] Hofgarten Public park in Munich.

[4] Bin ... deutsch German: I'm not Russian at all, I come from Lithuania, a pure German.

[5] Son of man Eliot's note cites Ezekiel 2.1, in which God addresses Ezekiel, whose mission will be to preach the coming of the Messiah to unbelievers, saying, "Son of man, stand upon thy feet, and I will speak unto thee."

[6] cricket no relief Eliot's note cites Ecclesiastes 12.5, in which the preacher speaks of the fearful deprivations of old age: "Also when they shall be afraid of that which is high, and fears shall be in the way, and the almond tree shall flourish, and the grasshopper shall be a burden, and desire shall fail: because man goeth to his long home, and the mourners go about the streets ..."

[7] There is shadow ... rock See Isaiah 32.2, in which the blessings of Christ's kingdom are described: "And a man shall be as an hiding place from the wind, and a covert from the tempest; as rivers of water in a dry place, as the shadow of a great rock in a weary land."

[8] Frisch ... du? German: "Fresh blows the wind to the homeland—my Irish child, where do you tarry?" From Richard Wagner's opera Tristan und Isolde (1865), 1.5–8, this is a sailor's lament for the girl he has left behind in Ireland.

[9] Oed' ... Meer German: "Desolate and empty is the sea." Eliot's note cites Tristan und Isolde 3.24, in which Tristan lies dying, waiting for his beloved, Isolde, to come to him, but there is no sign of her ship on the sea.

[10] Madame Sosostris This name is often thought to have been "unconsciously" borrowed by Eliot from the name of the fortune-teller Madame Sesostris in Aldous Huxley's novel Crome Yellow (1921). It may more plausibly have derived from the Greek word for saviour, soteros.

[11] [Eliot's note] I am not familiar with the exact constitution of the Tarot pack of cards, from which I have obviously departed to suit my own convenience. The Hanged Man, a member of the traditional pack, fits my purpose in two ways: because he is associated in my mind with the Hanged God of Frazer, and because I associate him with the hooded figure in the passage of the disciples to Emmaus in Part V. The Phoenician Sailor and the Merchant appear later; also the "crowds of people," and Death by Water is executed in Part IV.

Is your card, the drowned Phoenician Sailor,
(Those are pearls that were his eyes.[1] Look!)
Here is Belladonna, the Lady of the Rocks,[2]
50 The lady of situations.
Here is the man with three staves, and here the Wheel,[3]
And here is the one-eyed merchant, and this card,
Which is blank, is something he carries on his back,
Which I am forbidden to see. I do not find
55 The Hanged Man.[4] Fear death by water.
I see crowds of people, walking round in a ring.
Thank you. If you see dear Mrs. Equitone,
Tell her I bring the horoscope myself:
One must be so careful these days.

60 Unreal City,[5]
Under the brown fog of a winter dawn,
A crowd flowed over London Bridge, so many,
I had not thought death had undone so many.[6]
Sighs, short and infrequent, were exhaled,
65 And each man fixed his eyes before his feet.

The Man with Three Staves (an authentic member of the Tarot
pack) I associate, quite arbitrarily, with the Fisher King himself.
[The Tarot pack, generally used for fortune-telling, consists of 78
cards in four suits—cups, wands, swords, and pentangles. It
originated in France and Italy in the fourteenth century.]

[1] *Those are … eyes* From Ariel's song in Shakespeare's *The Tempest*
1.2.397–403: "Full fathom five thy father lies: / Of his bones are
coral made; / Those are pearls that were his eyes; / Nothing of him
that doth fade / But doth suffer a sea-change / Into something rich
and strange: / Sea nymphs hourly ring his knell: / *Burden*. Ding-
dong. / Hark! Now I hear them—ding-dong bell."

[2] *Belladonna* Italian: beautiful woman. Also another name for the
poisonous plant deadly nightshade, once used for cosmetic purposes
by Italian women; *Lady of the Rocks* Possible ironic reference to
Leonardo da Vinci's painting *Madonna of the Rocks*.

[3] *Wheel* Wheel of Fortune.

[4] *Hanged Man* This man's self-sacrifice in the role of fertility god
is necessary for the annual rejuvenation of the land.

[5] *Unreal City* Eliot's note cites the following lines from the 1859
poem "Les sept vieillards" by poet Charles Baudelaire: "Fourmillante
cité, cité pleine de rêves, / Où le spectre en plein jour raccroche le
passant!" (French: "Swarming city, city full of dreams, / Where the
daylight specter intercepts the passerby.") "The City" is the name for
London's financial district, located north of London Bridge.

[6] *so many … so many* Eliot's note cites Dante's *Inferno* 3.55–57:
"such a long stream / of people, that I would not have thought / that
death had undone so many." This is spoken by Dante soon after he
has entered the Gates of Hell in the company of Virgil, his guide
through the underworld.

Flowed up the hill and down King William Street,
To where Saint Mary Woolnoth[7] kept the hours
With a dead sound on the final stroke of nine.[8]
There I saw one I knew, and stopped him, crying
"Stetson![9]
70 You who were with me in the ships at Mylae![10]
That corpse you planted last year in your garden,
Has it begun to sprout? Will it bloom this year?
Or has the sudden frost disturbed its bed?
Oh keep the Dog far hence, that's friend to men,
75 Or with his nails he'll dig it up again![11]
You! hypocrite lecteur!—mon semblable,—mon frère!"[12]

2. A GAME OF CHESS[13]

The Chair she sat in, like a burnished throne,[14]
Glowed on the marble, where the glass
Sustained by standards wrought with fruited vines
80 From which a golden Cupidon peeped out
(Another hid his eyes behind his wing)
Doubled the flames of sevenbranched candelabra

[7] *Saint Mary Woolnoth* Church in King William Street. Eliot
joined a campaign to have this church, and others like it that were
slated for demolition, preserved.

[8] [Eliot's note] A phenomenon which I have often noticed.

[9] *Stetson* Eliot, when questioned, maintained this was a reference
to the average City clerk, and not, as some had suggested, to Ezra
Pound, whose nickname was "Buffalo Bill."

[10] *Mylae* The Battle of Mylae (260 BCE) took place in the trade-
based First Punic War between the Romans and the Carthaginians.

[11] *Oh keep … again* Eliot's note cites the dirge in John Webster's
play *The White Devil* (1612) 5.4: "But keep the wolf far thence,
that's foe to men, / For with his nails he'll dig them up again."
Sirius, the Dog Star, heralded the annual flooding of the Nile in
Egyptian mythology.

[12] *hypocrite … mon frère* French: "Hypocrite reader—my double—my brother!" Eliot's note cites the preface of Baudelaire's *Fleurs
du Mal*.

[13] *A GAME OF CHESS* Title of Thomas Middleton's 1624 satirical
political drama. In Middleton's play *Women Beware Women*, a game
of chess distracts a mother-in-law, preventing her from noticing that
her daughter-in-law is being seduced upstairs. Each move in the
chess game mirrors a move in the seduction.

[14] [Eliot's note] Cf. Antony and Cleopatra, 2.2.190. [This is the
beginning of Enorbarbus's description of the first meeting of Antony
and Cleopatra: "The barge she sat in, like a burnished throne, /
Burned on the water."]

Reflecting light upon the table as
The glitter of her jewels rose to meet it,
From satin cases poured in rich profusion;
In vials of ivory and coloured glass
Unstoppered, lurked her strange synthetic perfumes,
Unguent, powdered, or liquid—troubled, confused
And drowned the sense in odours; stirred by the air
That freshened from the window, these ascended
In fattening the prolonged candle-flames,
Flung their smoke into the laquearia,[1]
Stirring the pattern on the coffered ceiling.
Huge sea-wood fed with copper
Burned green and orange, framed by the coloured
    stone,
In which sad light a carved dolphin swam.
Above the antique mantel was displayed
As though a window gave upon the sylvan scene[2]
The change of Philomel, by the barbarous king
So rudely forced;[3] yet there the nightingale
Filled all the desert with inviolable voice
And still she cried, and still the world pursues,
"Jug Jug"[4] to dirty ears.
And other withered stumps of time
Were told upon the walls; staring forms
Leaned out, leaning, hushing the room enclosed.
Footsteps shuffled on the stair.
Under the firelight, under the brush, her hair
Spread out in fiery points
Glowed into words, then would be savagely still.

"My nerves are bad to-night. Yes, bad. Stay with me.
Speak to me. Why do you never speak? Speak.
     What are you thinking of? What thinking? What?
I never know what you are thinking. Think."

I think we are in rats' alley[5]
Where the dead men lost their bones.

  "What is that noise?"
                The wind under the door.[6]
"What is that noise now? What is the wind doing?"
             Nothing again nothing.
                          "Do
You know nothing? Do you see nothing? Do you
    remember
Nothing?"

  I remember
Those are pearls that were his eyes.
"Are you alive, or not? Is there nothing in your head?"
                               But

O O O O that Shakespeherian Rag[7]—
It's so elegant
So intelligent
"What shall I do now? What shall I do?"
I shall rush out as I am, and walk the street
With my hair down, so. What shall we do to-morrow?
What shall we ever do?"
              The hot water at ten.
And if it rains, a closed car at four.
And we shall play a game of chess,
Pressing lidless eyes and waiting for a knock upon the
    door.[8]

When Lil's husband got demobbed,[9] I said—
I didn't mince my words, I said to her myself,
HURRY UP PLEASE ITS TIME[10]
Now Albert's coming back, make yourself a bit smart.

---

[1] *laquearia* Latin: paneled ceiling. Eliot's note cites Virgil's *Aeneid* 1,726, describing a banquet given by Queen Dido of Carthage for her soon-to-be lover, Aeneas: "Burning lamps hang from the gold-paneled ceiling, and torches dispel the night with their flames."

[2] *sylvan scene* Eliot's note cites Milton's *Paradise Lost* 4.140, which describes the Garden of Eden seen through Satan's eyes.

[3] *The change ... forced* Eliot's notes for this passage cite Greek poet Ovid's *Metamorphoses* 6, which tells the Greek myth of Philomela, who was raped by King Tereus of Thrace (her sister's husband) and had her tongue cut out before being changed into a nightingale.

[4] *Jug Jug* In Elizabethan poetry, a conventional representation of a nightingale's song. Also, a crude reference to sexual intercourse.

[5] [Eliot's note] Cf. part 3, line 195 [of *Metamorphoses* 6].

[6] *The wind ... door* Eliot's note cites a line from John Webster's *The Devil's Law Case* (3.2.162). A patient who is believed to have been stabbed to death groans in pain, prompting the surgeon to ask, "Is the wind in that door still?"

[7] *O ... Rag* Reference to a popular American ragtime song performed in Ziegfield's Follies in 1912.

[8] [Eliot's note] Cf. the game of chess in Middleton's *Women Beware Women*.

[9] *demobbed* Demobilized; released from military service.

[10] *HURRY ... TIME* Expression used by bartenders in Britain to announce closing time.

He'll want to know what you done with that money he
    gave you
To get yourself some teeth. He did, I was there.
145 You have them all out, Lil, and get a nice set,
He said, I swear, I can't bear to look at you.
And no more can't I, I said, and think of poor Albert,
He's been in the army four years, he wants a good time,
And if you don't give it him, there's others will, I said.
150 Oh is there, she said. Something o' that, I said.
Then I'll know who to thank, she said, and give me a
    straight look.
HURRY UP PLEASE ITS TIME
If you don't like it you can get on with it, I said.
Others can pick and choose if you can't.
155 But if Albert makes off, it won't be for lack of telling.
You ought to be ashamed, I said, to look so antique.
(And her only thirty-one.)
I can't help it, she said, pulling a long face,
It's them pills I took, to bring it off, she said.
160 (She's had five already, and nearly died of young
    George.)
The chemist° said it would be alright,   *pharmacist*
    but I've never been the same.
You are a proper fool, I said.
Well, if Albert won't leave you alone, there it is, I said,
What you get married for if you don't want children?
165 HURRY UP PLEASE ITS TIME
Well, that Sunday Albert was home, they had a hot
    gammon,°   *smoked ham*
And they asked me in to dinner, to get the beauty of it
    hot—
HURRY UP PLEASE ITS TIME
HURRY UP PLEASE ITS TIME
170 Goonight Bill. Goonight Lou. Goonight May. Goonight.
Ta ta. Goonight. Goonight.
Good night, ladies, good night, sweet ladies, good night,
    good night.[1]

---

1 *Good night ... night* Ophelia's last words in Shakespeare's *Hamlet* (4.5.72–3) before she drowns herself. These words are taken by her father as evidence that she had been driven insane by Hamlet's seeming indifference to her.

3. THE FIRE SERMON [2]

The river's tent is broken: the last fingers of leaf
Clutch and sink into the wet bank. The wind
175 Crosses the brown land, unheard. The nymphs are
    departed.
Sweet Thames, run softly, till I end my song.[3]
The river bears no empty bottles, sandwich papers,
Silk handkerchiefs, cardboard boxes, cigarette ends
Or other testimony of summer nights. The nymphs
    are departed.
180 And their friends, the loitering heirs of city directors;
Departed, have left no addresses.
By the waters of Leman I sat down and wept ...[4]
Sweet Thames, run softly till I end my song,
Sweet Thames, run softly, for I speak not loud or long.
185 But at my back in a cold blast I hear
The rattle of the bones, and chuckle spread from ear
    to ear.[5]

A rat crept softly through the vegetation
Dragging its slimy belly on the bank
While I was fishing in the dull canal
190 On a winter evening round behind the gashouse
Musing upon the king my brother's wreck
And on the king my father's death before him.[6]
White bodies naked on the low damp ground

---

2 *THE FIRE SERMON* Sermon preached by the Buddha against passions (such as lust, anger, and envy) that consume people and prevent their regeneration.

3 *Sweet Thames ... song* Eliot's note cites the refrain of Edmund Spenser's *Prothalamion* (1596), a poem that celebrates the ideals of marriage, written to commemorate the joint marriages of the two daughters of the Earl of Worcester.

4 *By the ... wept* Reference to Psalm 137, in which the Hebrews lament their exile in Babylon and their lost homeland: "By the rivers of Babylon, there sat we down, yea, we wept, when we remembered Zion." For Babylon Eliot substitutes "Leman," the French name for Lake Geneva. "Leman" is also a medieval word meaning sweetheart.

5 *But at ... ear* Eliot's note cites Andrew Marvell's "To His Coy Mistress": "But at my back I always hear / Time's wingèd chariot hurrying near" (lines 21–22).

6 *And on ... him* Eliot's note cites Shakespeare's *The Tempest* 1.2.388–93, in which Ferdinand, shipwrecked on the shore, is prompted by Ariel's music to ponder the supposed drowning of his father, King Alonso: "Sitting on a bank, / Weeping again the king my father's wrack / This music crept by me upon the waters, / Allaying both their fury and my passion / With its sweet air." Eliot also quotes from this passage on line 257.

And bones cast in a little low dry garret,
195   Rattled by the rat's foot only, year to year.
But at my back from time to time I hear
The sound of horns and motors, which shall bring[1]
Sweeney[2] to Mrs. Porter in the spring.
O the moon shone bright on Mrs. Porter
200   And on her daughter
They wash their feet in soda water[3]
Et O ces voix d'enfants, chantant dans la coupole![4]

Twit twit twit
Jug jug jug jug jug jug
205   So rudely forc'd.
Tereu[5]

Unreal City
Under the brown fog of a winter noon
Mr. Eugenides, the Smyrna[6] merchant
210   Unshaven, with a pocket full of currants
C.i.f. London: documents at sight,[7]
Asked me in demotic[8] French

To luncheon at the Cannon Street Hotel[9]
Followed by a weekend at the Metropole.[10]

215   At the violet hour, when the eyes and back
Turn upward from the desk, when the human engine waits
Like a taxi throbbing waiting,
I Tiresias,[11] though blind, throbbing between two lives,
Old man with wrinkled female breasts, can see
220   At the violet hour, the evening hour that strives
Homeward, and brings the sailor home from sea,[12]
The typist home at teatime, clears her breakfast, lights
Her stove, and lays out food in tins.
Out of the window perilously spread
225   Her drying combinations[13] touched by the sun's last rays,

---

[1] [Eliot's note] Cf. [John] Day, *Parliament of Bees*: "When of the sudden, listening, you shall hear, / A noise of horns and hunting, which shall bring / Actaeon to Diana in the spring, / Where all shall see her naked skin … " [According to classical myth, when the hunter Actaeon saw Diana, goddess of chastity and the hunt, bathing naked with her nymphs, she changed him into a stag and set his dogs upon him.]

[2] *Sweeney* Character in two earlier poems by Eliot, "Sweeney Erect" and "Sweeney Among the Nightingales."

[3] [Eliot's note] I do not know the origin of the ballad from which these are taken: it was reported to me from Sydney, Australia. [One version of this ballad, which was sung by Australian soldiers in World War I, is as follows: "O the moon shone bright on Mrs. Porter / And on the daughter / Of Mrs. Porter / They wash their feet in soda water / And so they oughter / To keep them clean."]

[4] *Et O … coupole* French: "And O those children's voices singing under the cupola." Eliot's note indicates that this is the last line of French poet Paul Verlaine's sonnet "Parsifal" (1886). Verlaine refers to the opera *Parsifal* (1882) by Richard Wagner, in which a choir of children sings while the innocent knight Parsifal has his feet washed before entering the Castle of the Grail.

[5] *Tereu* Latin vocative form of Tereus, who raped Philomela.

[6] *Smyrna* Port city in western Turkey.

[7] *C.i.f. … sight* Eliot's note explains that "C.i.f." means that the price includes "cost, insurance, freight to London," and that "documents on sight" indicates that "the Bill of Lading, etc., were to be handed to the buyer upon payment of the sight draft."

[8] *demotic* Popular; vulgar.

[9] *Cannon Street Hotel* Hotel near the Cannon Street train station, a terminus for travelers to and from the continent.

[10] *Metropole* Large hotel on the seashore at Brighton.

[11] [Eliot's note] Tiresias, although a mere spectator and not indeed a "character," is yet the most important personage in the poem, uniting all the rest. Just as the one-eyed merchant, seller of currants, melts into the Phoenician Sailor, and the latter is not wholly distinct from Ferdinand Prince of Naples, so all the women are one woman, and the two sexes meet in Tiresias. What Tiresias sees, in fact, is the substance of the poem. The whole passage from Ovid is of great anthropological interest. [Eliot then quotes in Latin the passage from *Metamorphoses* that describes Tiresias's sex change. Jove, who had drunk a great deal, "jested with Juno. He said, 'Your pleasure in love is really greater than that enjoyed by men.' She denied it; so they decided to seek the opinion of the wise Tiresias, for he knew both aspects of love. For once, with a blow of his staff, he had committed violence on two huge snakes as they copulated in the green forest; and—wonderful to tell—was turned into a woman and thus spent seven years. In the eighth year he saw the same snakes again and said: 'If a blow struck at you is so powerful that it changes the sex of the giver, I will now strike at you again.' With these words she struck the snakes, and again became a man. So he was appointed arbiter in the playful quarrel, and supported Jove's statement. It is said that Saturnia [Juno] was quite disproportionately upset, and condemned the arbiter to perpetual blindness. But the almighty father (for no god may undo what has been done by another god), in return for the sight that was taken away, gave him the power to know the future and so lightened the penalty paid by the honor."]

[12] [Eliot's note] This may not appear as exact as Sappho's lines but I had in mind the "longshore" or "dory" fisherman, who returns at nightfall. [Eliot refers to seventh-century BCE Greek poet Sappho's poem, known as Fragment 149, in which Hesperus, the evening star, brings home "all things the bright dawn disperses," including "the sheep, the goat, the child to its mother."]

[13] *combinations* Undergarments that combined the chemise and panties.

On the divan are piled (at night her bed)
Stockings, slippers, camisoles, and stays.°   *corset*
I Tiresias, old man with wrinkled dugs°   *breasts*
Perceived the scene, and foretold the rest—
230 I too awaited the expected guest.
He, the young man carbuncular,° arrives,   *pimply*
A small house agent's clerk, with one bold stare,
One of the low on whom assurance sits
As a silk hat on a Bradford[1] millionaire.
235 The time is now propitious, as he guesses,
The meal is ended, she is bored and tired,
Endeavours to engage her in caresses
Which still are unreproved, if undesired.
Flushed and decided, he assaults at once;
240 Exploring hands encounter no defence;
His vanity requires no response,
And makes a welcome of indifference.
(And I Tiresias have foresuffered all
Enacted on this same divan or bed;
245 I who have sat by Thebes below the wall
And walked among the lowest of the dead.[2])
Bestows one final patronising kiss,
And gropes his way, finding the stairs unlit …

She turns and looks a moment in the glass,
250 Hardly aware of her departed lover;
Her brain allows one half-formed thought to pass:
"Well now that's done: and I'm glad it's over."
When lovely woman stoops to folly and[3]
Paces about her room again, alone,
255 She smoothes her hair with automatic hand,
And puts a record on the gramophone.

"This music crept by me upon the waters"[4]
And along the Strand, up Queen Victoria Street.
O City city, I can sometimes hear
260 Beside a public bar in Lower Thames Street,
The pleasant whining of a mandoline
And a clatter and a chatter from within
Where fishmen lounge at noon: where the walls
Of Magnus Martyr[5] hold
265 Inexplicable splendour of Ionian white and gold.[6]

The river sweats[7]
Oil and tar
The barges drift
With the turning tide
270 Red sails
Wide
To leeward, swing on the heavy spar.
The barges wash
Drifting logs
275 Down Greenwich reach
Past the Isle of Dogs.[8]
          Weialala leia
          Wallala leialala[9]

Elizabeth and Leicester[10]

---

[1] *Bradford* Textile center in industrial Yorkshire, many of whose residents became extremely wealthy during the textile boom that accompanied World War I.

[2] *I who … dead* In *Oedipus Rex*, by fifth-century BCE Greek dramatist Sophocles, Tiresias perceives that the curse of infertility that plagues the people and land of Thebes has been brought upon them by the unwitting marriage of Oedipus to his mother, Queen Jocasta. In book 9 of Homer's *Odyssey*, Odysseus journeys to the underworld, where he consults Tiresias.

[3] *When … and* Eliot's note cites Oliver Goldsmith's novel *The Vicar of Wakefield* (1762), in which Olivia, returning to the place where she was seduced, sings: "When lovely woman stoops to folly / And finds too late that men betray / What charm can soothe her melancholy, / What art can wash her guilt away? / The only art her guilt to cover, / To hide her shame from every eye, / To give repentance to her lover, / And wring his bosom—is to die."

[4] [Eliot's note] V. [I.e., "see," from the Latin *vide*.] *The Tempest*, as above.

[5] [Eliot's note] The interior of St. Magnus Martyr is to my mind one of the finest among [Sir Christopher] Wren's interiors. See *The Proposed Demolition of Nineteen City Churches* (P.S. King & Son, Ltd.).

[6] *Inexplicable … gold* Reference to the slender Ionic columns inside the church.

[7] [Eliot's note] The Song of the (three) Thames-daughters begins here. From line 292 to 306 inclusive they speak in turn. V. *Gotter-dammerung*, 3.1: the Rhine-daughters. [Eliot refers to Wagner's opera *The Twilight of the Gods*, in which the Rhine maidens lament the theft of the Rhine's gold, which has also robbed the river of its beauty.]

[8] *Isle of Dogs* Peninsula formed by a bend in the river Thames. Opposite this peninsula, on the south side of the Thames, lies the London borough of Greenwich.

[9] *Weialala … leialala* In Wagner's opera, this is the ecstatic cry repeated by the maidens as they guard the lump of gold in the river.

[10] [Eliot's note] V. Froude, *Elizabeth*, Vol. 1, ch. 4, letter of De Quadra to Philip of Spain: "In the afternoon we were in a barge, watching the games on the river. (The queen) was alone with Lord Robert and myself on the poop, when they began to talk nonsense,

280 Beating oars
The stern was formed
A gilded shell
Red and gold
The brisk swell
285 Rippled both shores
Southwest wind
Carried down stream
The peal of bells
White towers
290 Weialala leia
Wallala leialala

"Trams and dusty trees.
Highbury bore me. Richmond and Kew
Undid me. By Richmond I raised my knees
295 Supine on the floor of a narrow canoe."[1]

"My feet are at Moorgate,[2] and my heart
Under my feet. After the event
He wept. He promised 'a new start.'
I made no comment. What should I resent?"

300 "On Margate Sands.[3]
I can connect
Nothing with nothing.
The broken fingernails of dirty hands.
My people humble people who expect
305 Nothing."
         la la

To Carthage then I came[4]

Burning burning burning burning[5]
O Lord Thou pluckest me out[6]
310 O Lord Thou pluckest

burning

4. DEATH BY WATER

Phlebas the Phoenician, a fortnight dead,
Forgot the cry of gulls, and the deep sea swell
And the profit and loss.
315   A current under sea
Picked his bones in whispers. As he rose and fell
He passed the stages of his age and youth
Entering the whirlpool.
             Gentile or Jew
320 O you who turn the wheel and look to windward,
Consider Phlebas, who was once handsome and tall as
     you.

5. WHAT THE THUNDER SAID [7]

After the torchlight red on sweaty faces
After the frosty silence in the gardens
After the agony in stony places

---

and went so far that Lord Robert at last said, as I was on the spot there was no reason why they should not be married if the queen pleased." [Eliot refers to *History of England from the Fall of Wolsey to the Death of Elizabeth* (1856–70), by James Anthony Froude. Froude quotes from a letter by Alvarez de Quadra, Bishop of Aquila and Spanish Ambassador to Queen Elizabeth's court. De Quadra believed the young queen would marry Lord Dudley.]

[1]   *Trams and ... canoe*   Eliot's note cites the lines from Dante's *Purgatorio* (5.130–36) that he parodies: "Remember me, who am La Pia [Piety]; / Sienna made me and the Maremma undid me"; *Highbury* Middle-class suburb in north London; *Richmond and Kew* Areas of London located on the Thames in southwest London. Between them lies Kew Gardens.

[2]   *Moorgate*   Area in the east of the City.

[3]   *Margate Sands*   Primary beach in the Kent seaside resort of Margate.

[4]   *To Carthage ... came*   Eliot's note cites the opening of Book 3 of *The Confessions of Saint Augustine*: "To Carthage then I came, where a cauldron of unholy loves sang all about mine ears."

[5]   [Eliot's note]   The complete text of the Buddha's Fire Sermon (which corresponds in importance to the Sermon on the Mount) from which these words are taken, will be found translated in the late Henry Clarke Warren's *Buddhism in Translation* (Harvard Oriental Series). Mr. Warren was one of the great pioneers of Buddhist studies in the Occident.

[6]   [Eliot's note]   From St. Augustine's *Confessions* again. The collocation of these two representatives of eastern and western asceticism, as the culmination of this part of the poem, is not an accident. [Eliot refers to 10.237–38 of the Confessions: "I entangle my steps with these outward beauties, but thou pluckest me out, O Lord, thou pluckest me out."]

[7]   [Eliot's note]   In the first part of Part 5 three themes are employed: the journey to Emmaus, the approach to the Chapel Perilous (see Miss Weston's book), and the present decay of eastern Europe. [*journey to Emmaus* See Luke 24.13–31, in which Jesus, after being resurrected, joins two of his disciples on the road to Emmaus, but they do not recognize him; *Chapel Perilous* The final stage of the Grail quest.]

325 The shouting and the crying
Prison and palace and reverberation
Of thunder of spring over distant mountains
He who was living is now dead[1]
We who were living are now dying
330 With a little patience

Here is no water but only rock
Rock and no water and the sandy road
The road winding above among the mountains
Which are mountains of rock without water
335 If there were water we should stop and drink
Amongst the rock one cannot stop or think
Sweat is dry and feet are in the sand
If there were only water amongst the rock
Dead mountain mouth of carious[2] teeth that cannot spit
340 Here one can neither stand nor lie nor sit
There is not even silence in the mountains
But dry sterile thunder without rain
There is not even solitude in the mountains
But red sullen faces sneer and snarl
345 From doors of mudcracked houses
                    If there were water

        And no rock
        If there were rock
        And also water
350   And water
        A spring
        A pool among the rock
        If there were the sound of water only
        Not the cicada[3]
355   And dry grass singing
        But sound of water over a rock
        Where the hermit-thrush sings in the pine trees[4]

Drip drop drip drop drop drop drop
But there is no water

360 Who is the third who walks always beside you?[5]
When I count, there are only you and I together
But when I look ahead up the white road
There is always another one walking beside you
Gliding wrapt in a brown mantle, hooded
365 I do not know whether a man or a woman
—But who is that on the other side of you?

What is that sound high in the air
Murmur of maternal lamentation
Who are those hooded hordes swarming
370 Over endless plains, stumbling in cracked earth
Ringed by the flat horizon only
What is the city over the mountains
Cracks and reforms and bursts in the violet air
Falling towers
375 Jerusalem Athens Alexandria
Vienna London
Unreal[6]

A woman drew her long black hair out tight
And fiddled whisper music on those strings
380 And bats with baby faces in the violet light
Whistled, and beat their wings
And crawled head downward down a blackened wall

---

[1] *After the torchlight ... dead* References to the events from the betrayal of Christ to His death.

[2] *carious* Decayed.

[3] *cicada* Grasshopper. See Ecclesiastes 12.4: "Also when they shall be afraid of that which is high, and fears shall be in the way, and the almond tree shall flourish, and the grasshopper shall be a burden, and desire shall fail: because man goeth to his long home, and the mourners go about the streets."

[4] [Eliot's note]   This is *Turdus aonalaschkae pallasii,* the hermit-thrush which I have heard in Quebec Province. Chapman says (*Handbook of Birds of Eastern North America*) "it is most at home in secluded woodland and thickety retreats. ... Its notes are not remarkable for variety or volume, but in purity and sweetness of tone and exquisite modulation they are unequalled." Its "water-dripping song" is justly celebrated.

[5] [Eliot's note]   The following lines were stimulated by the account of one of the Antarctic expeditions (I forget which, but I think one of Shackleton's): it was related that the party of explorers, at the extremity of their strength, had the constant delusion that there was *one more member* than could actually be counted. [Eliot refers to Sir Ernest Shackleton's third journey to the Antarctic (1914–17), during which he and his men attempted to cross the Antarctic ice cap on foot. See *South: The Story of Shackleton's Last Expedition, 1914-1917* (1919).]

[6] *What is that ... Unreal* Eliot's note for these lines quotes in German Herman Hesse, *Blick ins Chaos: Drei Aufsätze* (*A Glimpse into Chaos: Three Essays*). "Already half of Europe, already at least half of Eastern Europe, on the way to chaos, drives drunk in sacred infatuation along the edge of the precipice, singing drunkenly, as though singing hymns, as Dmitri Karamazov sang. The offended bourgeois laughs at the songs; the saint and the seer hear them with tears." Dmitri Karamazov is a character in Fyodor Dostoevsky's *The Brothers Karamazov* (1879–80).

And upside down in air were towers
Tolling reminiscent bells, that kept the hours
385 And voices singing out of empty cisterns and exhausted
    wells.

In this decayed hole among the mountains
In the faint moonlight, the grass is singing
Over the tumbled graves, about the chapel
There is the empty chapel, only the wind's home.[1]
390 It has no windows, and the door swings,
Dry bones can harm no one.
Only a cock stood on the rooftree
Co co rico co co rico[2]
In a flash of lightning. Then a damp gust
395 Bringing rain

Ganga[3] was sunken, and the limp leaves
Waited for rain, while the black clouds
Gathered far distant, over Himavant.[4]
The jungle crouched, humped in silence.
400 Then spoke the thunder
DA[5]
Datta: what have we given?
My friend, blood shaking my heart
The awful daring of a moment's surrender

405 Which an age of prudence can never retract
By this, and this only, we have existed
Which is not to be found in our obituaries
Or in memories draped by the beneficent spider[6]
Or under seals broken by the lean solicitor
410 In our empty rooms
DA
Dayadhvam: I have heard the key[7]
Turn in the door once and turn once only
We think of the key, each in his prison
415 Thinking of the key, each confirms a prison
Only at nightfall, aetherial rumours
Revive for a moment a broken Coriolanus[8]
DA
Damyata: The boat responded
420 Gaily, to the hand expert with sail and oar
The sea was calm, your heart would have responded
Gaily, when invited, beating obedient
To controlling hands

                          I sat upon the shore
425 Fishing, with the arid plain behind me[9]

---

1 *There is ... home* The Chapel Perilous appeared to be surrounded by death and decay; these nightmare visions were meant to induce despair in the questing knight. Once inside the Chapel, the knight's courage would be tested with further horrors.

2 *Only a ... rico* The crowing of the cock signals the coming of the morning and the departure of ghosts and evil spirits, as in *Hamlet* 1.1, when Hamlet's father's ghost disappears with its call. Also, in the Gospels Peter repents his repudiation of Christ after the cock crows.

3 *Ganga* The Ganges, a sacred river in India.

4 *Himavant* Sanskrit: snowy. Adjective used to describe the Himalayas.

5 [Eliot's note] "Datta, dayadhvam, damyata" (Give, sympathise, control). The fable of the meaning of the Thunder is found in the *Brihadaranyaka—Upanishad*, 5, 1. A translation is found in Deussen's *Sechzig Upanishads des Veda*, p. 489. [Eliot refers to the Hindu fable in which gods, men, and demons, each in turn ask the Lord of Creation, Prajapati, "Please instruct us, Sir." To each he utters the syllable "Da," and each group interprets the answer differently: "Damyata," practice self-control; "Datta," give alms; "Dayadhvam," have compassion. According to the fable, "This very thing is repeated even today by the heavenly voice, in the form of thunder, as 'Da,' 'Da,' 'Da,' which means: 'Control yourselves,' 'Give,' and 'Have compassion.'"]

6 [Eliot's note] Cf. [John] Webster, *The White Devil*, 5, 6: "... they'll remarry / Ere the worm pierce your winding-sheet, ere the spider / Make a thin curtain for your epitaphs." [In this excerpt from the play, the villain Flamineo urges men never to trust their wives.]

7 *I have ... key* Eliot's note cites the passage in Dante's *Inferno* 33.46, in which Ugolino della Gherardesca remembers being locked up with his children in the tower, where they all starved to death. Eliot also quotes philosopher Francis Herbert Bradley's *Appearance and Reality: A Metaphysical Essay* (1893), p. 346: "My external sensations are no less private to myself than are my thoughts or my feelings. In either case my experience falls within my own circle, a circle closed on the outside; and, with all its elements alike, every sphere is opaque to the others which surround it.... In brief, regarded as an existence which appears in a soul, the whole world for each is peculiar and private to that soul."

8 *Coriolanus* Roman general of Shakespeare's play of that name. A character who is motivated by pride rather than duty, Coriolanus leads the enemy against Rome, the city from which he has been exiled.

9 *Fishing... me* Eliot's note refers readers to Weston's *From Ritual to Romance*, chapter 9, "The Fisher King." In this chapter, Weston comments upon the Fisher King's intimate relation with his people and his land, "a relation mainly dependent upon the identification of the King with the Divine principle of Life and Fertility." Weston also argues that "the Fish is a Life symbol of immemorial antiquity, and that the title of Fisher has, from the earliest ages, been associated with Deities who were held to be specially connected with the origin and preservation of life."

Shall I at least set my lands in order?[1]
London Bridge is falling down falling down falling
    down
Poi s'ascose nel foco che gli affina[2]
Quando fiam ceu chelidon[3]—O swallow swallow
430 *Le Prince d'Aquitaine à la tour abolie*[4]
These fragments I have shored against my ruins
Why then Ile fit you. Hieronymo's mad againe.[5]
Datta. Dayadhvam. Damyata.
        Shantih shantih shantih[6]

—1922

---

[1] *Shall I … order* See Isaiah 38.1, in which the prophet Isaiah counsels the sickly King Hezekiah, whose kingdom has been destroyed by the conquering Assyrians, "Thus saith the Lord, Set thine house in order: for thou shalt die, and not live."

[2] *Poi … affina* Italian: "Then he vanished into the fire that refines them" (Dante's *Purgatorio* 26.148). Eliot's note quotes, in Italian, the three lines of the *Purgatorio* immediately preceding, in which the poet Arnaut Daniel, who is in Purgatory for lust, says to Dante "Now I pray you, by the goodness that guides you to the top of the staircase [of purgatory], be mindful in time of my suffering."

[3] *Quando … chelidon* Latin: "When shall I be as the swallow?" Eliot's note cites an anonymous Latin poem about Venus and the spring, "The Vigil of Venus," as well as the story of Philomela, whose sister Procne (the wife of Tereus) was turned into a swallow. "The Vigil of Venus" refers to Philomela and Procne in its closing lines.

[4] *Le Prince … abolie* French: "The Prince of Aquitaine in the ruined tower." Eliot's note cites French poet Gerard de Nerval's sonnet "El Desdichado" (1853). One of the Tarot cards shows a tower struck by lightning.

[5] *Why then … againe* Eliot's note cites Thomas Kyd's *The Spanish Tragedy: Hieronymo Is Mad Againe* (1592). In the play, Hieronymo, whose son has been murdered, is asked to write a play for the court. He responds "Why then Ile fit you (i.e., "I'll accommodate you," or "I'll give you your due"). He writes the play and persuades the murderers to act in it. During the course of the play, his son's murder is avenged.

[6] [Eliot's note] Shantih. Repeated as here, a formal ending to an Upanishad. "The Peace which passeth understanding" is our equivalent to this word. [The Upanishads are poetic dialogues that comment on the Vedas, the ancient Hindu scriptures. Eliot's phrasing derives from Paul's letter to the early Christians in Philippians 4.7: "And the peace of God, which passeth all understanding, shall keep your hearts and minds through Jesus Christ."]

Journey of the Magi [7]

"A cold coming we had of it,
    Just the worst time of the year
For a journey, and such a long journey:
The ways deep and the weather sharp,
5 The very dead of winter."[8]
And the camels galled, sore-footed, refractory,
Lying down in the melting snow.
There were times we regretted
The summer palaces on slopes, the terraces,
10 And the silken girls bringing sherbet.
Then the camel men cursing and grumbling
And running away, and wanting their liquor and
    women,
And the night-fires going out, and the lack of shelters,
And the cities hostile and the towns unfriendly
15 And the villages dirty and charging high prices:
A hard time we had of it.
At the end we preferred to travel all night,
Sleeping in snatches,
With the voices singing in our ears, saying
20 That this was all folly.

Then at dawn we came down to a temperate valley,
Wet, below the snow line, smelling of vegetation;
With a running stream and a water-mill beating the
    darkness,
And three trees[9] on the low sky,
25 And an old white horse[10] galloped away in the meadow.
Then we came to a tavern with vine-leaves over the
    lintel,[11]
Six hands at an open door dicing for pieces of silver,[12]
And feet kicking the empty wine-skins.
But there was no information, and so we continued

---

[7] *Magi* Three wise men who journeyed to Bethlehem to honor Jesus at His birth (see Matthew 2.1–12).

[8] *A cold … winter* Adapted from a sermon given by Anglican preacher Lancelot Andrewes on Christmas Day, 1622.

[9] *three trees* Suggests the three crosses on Calvary, on which Christ and two criminals were crucified (see Luke 23.32–43).

[10] *white horse* Ridden by Christ in Revelation 6.2 and 19.11–14.

[11] *lintel* Doorframe.

[12] *dicing … silver* Allusion to Judas' betrayal of Jesus for thirty pieces of silver, and to the soldiers who throw dice for the robes of Christ at His crucifixion (Matthew 26.14 and 27.35).

30   And arrived at evening, not a moment too soon
      Finding the place; it was (you may say) satisfactory.

      All this was a long time ago, I remember,
      And I would do it again, but set down
      This set down
35   This: were we led all that way for
      Birth or Death? There was a Birth, certainly,
      We had evidence and no doubt. I had seen birth and
          death,
      But had thought they were different; this Birth was
      Hard and bitter agony for us, like Death, our death.
40   We returned to our places, these Kingdoms,
      But no longer at ease here, in the old dispensation,
      With an alien people clutching their gods.
      I should be glad of another death.
          —1927

Marina[1]

Quis hic locus, quae regio, quae mundi plaga?[2]

What seas what shores what grey rocks and what
      islands
What water lapping the bow
And scent of pine and the woodthrush singing
      through the fog
What images return
5   O my daughter.

      Those who sharpen the tooth of the dog, meaning
Death
Those who glitter with the glory of the humming-
      bird, meaning

Death
10   Those who sit in the stye of contentment, meaning
Death
Those who suffer the ecstasy of the animals, meaning
Death

      Are become unsubstantial, reduced by a wind,
15   A breath of pine, and the woodsong fog
By this grace dissolved in place

      What is this face, less clear and clearer
The pulse in the arm, less strong and stronger—
Given or lent? more distant than stars and nearer than
      the eye

20   Whispers and small laughter between leaves and
      hurrying feet
Under sleep, where all the waters meet.

      Bowsprit[3] cracked with ice and paint cracked
      with heat.
I made this, I have forgotten
And remember.
25   The rigging weak and the canvas rotten
Between one June and another September.
Made this unknowing, half conscious, unknown, my
      own.
The garboard strake[4] leaks, the seams need caulking.
This form, this face, this life
30   Living to live in a world of time beyond me; let me
Resign my life for this life, my speech for that
      unspoken,
The awakened, lips parted, the hope, the new ships.

      What seas what shores what granite islands
      towards my timbers
And woodthrush calling through the fog
35   My daughter.
      —1930

---

[1] *Marina* In Shakespeare's *Pericles*, the daughter of the title
character. She is born during a storm at sea and her mother dies
giving birth to her. Pericles gives her to the governor of Tarsus and
his wife to raise. Through a series of plot twists, Marina is believed,
by age sixteen, to have died. Pericles, maddened by grief, becomes
a wanderer. During his travels he finds Marina and they are restored
to one another.

[2] *Quis hic … plaga* Latin: "What place is this, what region, what
corner of the world?" Spoken by Hercules in Seneca's *Hercules
Furens (The Mad Hercules)* after he regains his senses following a
period of madness during which he murders his children and wife.

[3] *Bowsprit* Large spar projecting from the front of a boat.

[4] *garboard strake* Thick wooden plank forming a ridge along the
keel of a boat.

Burnt Norton

τοῦ λόλου δ᾽ἐόντος ξυνοῦ ζώουσιν οἱ πολλοί
ὡς ἰδίαν ἔχοντες φρόνησιν.

1. p. 77. Fr. 2

ὁδὸς ἄνω κάτω μία καὶ ὠυτή.

1. p. 89. Fr. 60

Diels: *Die Fragmente der Vorsokratiker (Herakleitos).*[1]

1

Time present and time past
Are both perhaps present in time future,
And time future contained in time past.
If all time is eternally present
5 All time is unredeemable.
What might have been is an abstraction
Remaining a perpetual possibility
Only in a world of speculation.
What might have been and what has been
10 Point to one end, which is always present.
Footfalls echo in the memory
Down the passage which we did not take
Towards the door we never opened
Into the rose-garden. My words echo
15 Thus, in your mind.
    But to what purpose
Disturbing the dust on a bowl of rose-leaves
I do not know.
    Other echoes
20 Inhabit the garden. Shall we follow?
Quick, said the bird, find them, find them,
Round the corner. Through the first gate,
Into our first world, shall we follow

The deception of the thrush? Into our first world.
25 There they were, dignified, invisible,
Moving without pressure, over the dead leaves,
In the autumn heat, through the vibrant air,
And the bird called, in response to
The unheard music hidden in the shrubbery,
30 And the unseen eyebeam crossed, for the roses
Had the look of flowers that are looked at.
There they were as our guests, accepted and accepting.
So we moved, and they, in a formal pattern,
Along the empty alley, into the box circle,
35 To look down into the drained pool.
Dry the pool, dry concrete, brown edged,
And the pool was filled with water out of sunlight,
And the lotos[2] rose, quietly, quietly,
The surface glittered out of heart of light,
40 And they were behind us, reflected in the pool.
Then a cloud passed, and the pool was empty.
Go, said the bird, for the leaves were full of children,
Hidden excitedly, containing laughter.
Go, go, go, said the bird: human kind
45 Cannot bear very much reality.
Time past and time future
What might have been and what has been
Point to one end, which is always present.

2

Garlic and sapphires in the mud
50 Clot the bedded axle-tree.
The trilling wire in the blood
Sings below inveterate scars
And reconciles forgotten wars.
The dance along the artery
55 The circulation of the lymph
Are figured in the drift of stars
Ascend to summer in the tree
We move above the moving tree
In light upon the figured leaf
60 And hear upon the sodden floor
Below, the boarhound and the boar
Pursue their pattern as before
But reconciled among the stars.

---

[1] *Burnt Norton ... (Herakleitos)* Name of a large country house in Gloucestershire, England, that was built on the site of an earlier home that had burned down in the seventeenth century. Eliot visited the home in 1934. This poem was first published in 1935, and then republished in 1943 as one of the *Four Quartets*. Eliot modeled the structure of this long poem on one of Beethoven's final quartets, particularly the A Minor Quartet (Beethoven's last), which Eliot found "quite inexhaustible to study. There is some sort of heavenly or at least more than human gaiety about some of his later things which one imagines must come to oneself as the fruit of reconciliation and relief after immense suffering; I should like to get something of that into verse before I die." The epigraphs are from the writings of sixth-century BCE philosopher Heraclitus: τοῦ ... φρόνησιν Greek: "Although the Word governs all things, most people live as though they had wisdom of their own." ὁδὸς ... ὠυτή Greek: "The way up and the way down are the same."

[2] *lotos* Plant whose flowers, according to Greek myth, produced dreamy forgetfulness in those who ate them.

At the still point of the turning world. Neither
flesh nor fleshless;
65 Neither from nor towards; at the still point, there the
dance is,
But neither arrest nor movement. And do not call it
fixity,
Where past and future are gathered. Neither
movement from nor towards,
Neither ascent nor decline. Except for the point, the
still point,
There would be no dance, and there is only the dance.
70 I can only say, *there* we have been: but I cannot say where.
And I cannot say, how long, for that is to place it in time.

The inner freedom from the practical desire,
The release from action and suffering, release from the
inner
And the outer compulsion, yet surrounded
75 By a grace of sense, a white light still and moving,
Erhebung[1] without motion, concentration
Without elimination, both a new world
And the old made explicit, understood
In the completion of its partial ecstasy,
80 The resolution of its partial horror.
Yet the enchainment of past and future
Woven in the weakness of the changing body,
Protects mankind from heaven and damnation
Which flesh cannot endure.
85   Time past and time future
Allow but a little consciousness.
To be conscious is not to be in time
But only in time can the moment in the rose-garden,
The moment in the arbour where the rain beat,
90 The moment in the draughty church at smokefall
Be remembered; involved with past and future.
Only through time time is conquered.

3

Here is a place of disaffection
Time before and time after
95 In a dim light: neither daylight
Investing form with lucid stillness
Turning shadow into transient beauty

With slow rotation suggesting permanence
Nor darkness to purify the soul
100 Emptying the sensual with deprivation
Cleansing affection from the temporal.
Neither plenitude nor vacancy. Only a flicker
Over the strained time-ridden faces
Distracted from distraction by distraction
105 Filled with fancies and empty of meaning
Tumid apathy with no concentration
Men and bits of paper, whirled by the cold wind
That blows before and after time,
Wind in and out of unwholesome lungs
110 Time before and time after.
Eructation° of unhealthy souls   *belching*
Into the faded air, the torpid
Driven on the wind that sweeps the gloomy hills of
London,
Hampstead and Clerkenwell, Campden and Putney,
115 Highgate, Primrose and Ludgate. Not here
Not here the darkness, in this twittering world.

Descend lower, descend only
Into the world of perpetual solitude,
World not world, but that which is not world,
120 Internal darkness, deprivation
And destitution of all property,
Desiccation of the world of sense,
Evacuation of the world of fancy,
Inoperancy of the world of spirit;
125 This is the one way, and the other
Is the same, not in movement
But abstention from movement; while the world moves
In appetency,[2] on its metalled ways
Of time past and time future.

4

130 Time and the bell have buried the day,
The black cloud carries the sun away.
Will the sunflower turn to us, will the clematis[3]
Stray down, bend to us; tendril and spray
Clutch and cling?
135 Chill
Fingers of yew be curled
Down on us? After the kingfisher's wing

---

[1] *Erhebung* German: Lifting up. Term used by the German philosopher Georg Wilhelm Friedrich Hegel (1770–1831) to denote a new level of understanding.

[2] *appetency* Instinctive inclination.

[3] *clematis* Type of twining shrub.

Has answered light to light, and is silent, the light is still
At the still point of the turning world.

5

140 Words move, music moves
Only in time; but that which is only living
Can only die. Words, after speech, reach
Into the silence. Only by the form, the pattern,
Can words or music reach
145 The stillness, as a Chinese jar still
Moves perpetually in its stillness.
Not the stillness of the violin, while the note lasts,
Not that only, but the co-existence,
Or say that the end precedes the beginning,
150 And the end and the beginning were always there
Before the beginning and after the end.
And all is always now. Words strain,
Crack and sometimes break, under the burden,
Under the tension, slip, slide, perish,
155 Decay with imprecision, will not stay in place,
Will not stay still. Shrieking voices
Scolding, mocking, or merely chattering,
Always assail them. The Word in the desert
Is most attacked by voices of temptation,
160 The crying shadow in the funeral dance,
The loud lament of the disconsolate chimera.[1]

The detail of the pattern is movement,
As in the figure of the ten stairs.[2]
Desire itself is movement
165 Not in itself desirable;
Love is itself unmoving,
Only the cause and end of movement,
Timeless, and undesiring
Except in the aspect of time
170 Caught in the form of limitation
Between un-being and being.
Sudden in a shaft of sunlight
Even while the dust moves
There rises the hidden laughter

175 Of children in the foliage
Quick now, here, now, always—
Ridiculous the waste sad time
Stretching before and after.
—1935, 1943

Tradition and the Individual Talent

I

In English writing we seldom speak of tradition, though we occasionally apply its name in deploring its absence. We cannot refer to "the tradition" or to "a tradition"; at most, we employ the adjective in saying that the poetry of So-and-so is "traditional" or even "too traditional." Seldom, perhaps, does the word appear except in a phrase of censure. If otherwise, it is vaguely approbative, with the implication, as to the work approved, of some pleasing archaeological reconstruction. You can hardly make the word agreeable to English ears without this comfortable reference to the reassuring science of archaeology.

Certainly the word is not likely to appear in our appreciations of living or dead writers. Every nation, every race, has not only its own creative, but its own critical turn of mind; and is even more oblivious of the shortcomings and limitations of its critical habits than of those of its creative genius. We know, or think we know, from the enormous mass of critical writing that has appeared in the French language, the critical method or habit of the French; we only conclude (we are such unconscious people) that the French are "more critical than we," and sometimes even plume ourselves a little with the fact, as if the French were the less spontaneous. Perhaps they are; but we might remind ourselves that criticism is as inevitable as breathing, and that we should be none the worse for articulating what passes in our minds when we read a book and feel an emotion about it, for criticizing our own minds in their work of criticism. One of the facts that might come to light in this process is our tendency to insist, when we praise a poet, upon those aspects of his work in which he least resembles anyone else. In these aspects or parts of his work we pretend to find what is individual, what is the peculiar essence of the man. We dwell with satisfaction upon the poet's difference from his predecessors, especially his

---

[1] *chimera* Fire-breathing monster of Greek mythology that was usually represented as part goat, part lion, and part serpent. Hence, any fantastic monster of disparate parts or fanciful illusion.

[2] *ten stairs* According to Spanish poet and mystic St. John of the Cross (1542–91), there are ten steps on the mystical ladder of divine love.

immediate predecessors; we endeavour to find something that can be isolated in order to be enjoyed. Whereas if we approach a poet without this prejudice we shall often find that not only the best, but the most individual parts of his work may be those in which the dead poets, his ancestors, assert their immortality most vigorously. And I do not mean the impressionable period of adolescence, but the period of full maturity.

Yet if the only form of tradition, of handing down, consisted in following the ways of the immediate generation before us in a blind or timid adherence to its successes, "tradition" should positively be discouraged. We have seen many such simple currents soon lost in the sand; and novelty is better than repetition. Tradition is a matter of much wider significance. It cannot be inherited, and if you want it you must obtain it by great labour. It involves, in the first place, the historical sense, which we may call nearly indispensable to anyone who would continue to be a poet beyond his twenty-fifth year; and the historical sense involves a perception, not only of the pastness of the past, but of its presence; the historical sense compels a man to write not merely with his own generation in his bones, but with a feeling that the whole of the literature of Europe from Homer[1] and within it the whole of the literature of his own country has a simultaneous existence and composes a simultaneous order. This historical sense, which is a sense of the timeless as well as of the temporal and of the timeless and of the temporal together, is what makes a writer traditional. And it is at the same time what makes a writer most acutely conscious of his place in time, of his own contemporaneity.

No poet, no artist of any art, has his complete meaning alone. His significance, his appreciation is the appreciation of his relation to the dead poets and artists. You cannot value him alone; you must set him, for contrast and comparison, among the dead. I mean this as a principle of aesthetic, not merely historical, criticism. The necessity that he shall conform, that he shall cohere, is not one-sided; what happens when a new work of art is created is something that happens simultaneously to all the works of art which preceded it. The existing monuments form an ideal order among themselves, which is modified by the introduction of the new

(the really new) work of art among them. The existing order is complete before the new work arrives; for order to persist after the supervention of novelty, the *whole* existing order must be, if ever so slightly, altered; and so the relations, proportions, values of each work of art toward the whole are readjusted; and this is conformity between the old and the new. Whoever has approved this idea of order, of the form of European, of English literature will not find it preposterous that the past should be altered by the present as much as the present is directed by the past. And the poet who is aware of this will be aware of great difficulties and responsibilities.

In a peculiar sense he will be aware also that he must inevitably be judged by the standards of the past. I say judged, not amputated, by them; not judged to be as good as, or worse or better than, the dead; and certainly not judged by the canons of dead critics. It is a judgement, a comparison, in which two things are measured by each other. To conform merely would be for the new work not really to conform at all; it would not be new, and would therefore not be a work of art. And we do not quite say that the new is more valuable because it fits in; but its fitting in is a test of its value—a test, it is true, which can only be slowly and cautiously applied, for we are none of us infallible judges of conformity. We say: it appears to conform, and is perhaps individual, or it appears individual, and may conform; but we are hardly likely to find that it is one and not the other.

To proceed to a more intelligible exposition of the relation of the poet to the past: he can neither take the past as a lump, an indiscriminate bolus,[2] nor can he form himself wholly on one or two private admirations, nor can he form himself wholly upon one preferred period. The first course is inadmissible, the second is an important experience of youth, and the third is a pleasant and highly desirable supplement. The poet must be very conscious of the main current, which does not at all flow invariably through the most distinguished reputations. He must be quite aware of the obvious fact that art never improves, but that the material of art is never quite the same. He must be aware that the mind of Europe—the mind of his own country—a mind which he learns in time to be much more important than his own private mind—is a mind which changes, and that this change is a development which abandons

[1] *Homer* Greek poet (c. 700 BCE), author of the *Iliad* and the *Odyssey*.

[2] *bolus* Round mass.

nothing *en route*, which does not superannuate either Shakespeare, or Homer, or the rock drawing of the Magdalenian draughtsmen.[1] That this development, refinement perhaps, complication certainly, is not, from the point of view of the artist, any improvement. Perhaps not even an improvement from the point of view of the psychologist or not to the extent which we imagine; perhaps only in the end based upon a complication in economics and machinery. But the difference between the present and the past is that the conscious present is an awareness of the past in a way and to an extent which the past's awareness of itself cannot show. Someone said: "The dead writers are remote from us because we *know* so much more than they did." Precisely, and they are that which we know.

I am alive to a usual objection to what is clearly part of my programme for the *métier* of poetry. The objection is that the doctrine requires a ridiculous amount of erudition (pedantry), a claim which can be rejected by appeal to the lives of poets in any pantheon. It will even be affirmed that much learning deadens or perverts poetic sensibility. While, however, we persist in believing that a poet ought to know as much as will not encroach upon his necessary receptivity and necessary laziness, it is not desirable to confine knowledge to whatever can be put into a useful shape for examinations, drawing rooms, or the still more pretentious modes of publicity. Some can absorb knowledge, the more tardy must sweat for it. Shakespeare acquired more essential history from Plutarch[2] than most men could from the whole British Museum. What is to be insisted upon is that the poet must develop or procure the consciousness of the past and that he should continue to develop this consciousness throughout his career.

What happens is a continual surrender of himself as he is at the moment to something which is more valuable. The progress of an artist is a continual self-sacrifice, a continual extinction of personality.

There remains to define this process of depersonalization and its relation to the sense of tradition. It is in this depersonalization that art may be said to approach the condition of science. I therefore invite you to consider, as a suggestive analogy, the action which takes place when a bit of finely filiated[3] platinum is introduced into a chamber containing oxygen and sulphur dioxide.

2.

Honest criticism and sensitive appreciation is directed not upon the poet but upon the poetry. If we attend to the confused cries of the newspaper critics and the susurrus[4] of popular repetition that follows, we shall hear the names of poets in great numbers; if we seek not Blue-book[5] knowledge but the enjoyment of poetry, and ask for a poem, we shall seldom find it. I have tried to point out the importance of the relation of the poem to other poems by other authors, and suggested the conception of poetry as a living whole of all the poetry that has ever been written. The other aspect of this Impersonal theory of poetry is the relation of the poem to its author. And I hinted, by an analogy, that the mind of the mature poet differs from that of the immature one not precisely in any valuation of "personality," not being necessarily more interesting, or having "more to say," but rather by being a more finely perfected medium in which special, or very varied, feelings are at liberty to enter into new combinations.

The analogy was that of the catalyst. When the two gases previously mentioned are mixed in the presence of a filament of platinum, they form sulphurous acid. This combination takes place only if the platinum is present; nevertheless, the newly formed acid contains no trace of platinum, and the platinum itself is apparently unaffected: has remained inert, neutral, and unchanged. The mind of the poet is the shred of platinum. It may partly or exclusively operate upon the experience of the man himself; but, the more perfect the artist, the more completely separate in him will be the man who suffers and the mind which creates; the more perfectly will the mind digest and transmute the passions which are its material.

The experience, you will notice, the elements which enter the presence of the transforming catalyst, are of

---

[1] *Magdalenian draughtsmen* Magdalenian cave paintings of the Paleolithic period are among the first known works of art.

[2] *Plutarch* Greek biographer of the first century CE who had a strong influence on English literature; Shakespeare drew some of his characters in plays such as *Coriolanus, Antony and Cleopatra*, and *Julius Caesar* from Plutarch's biographies.

[3] *filiated* Made into filament, or fine thread.

[4] *susurrus* Whispering or muttering.

[5] *Blue-book* Official reports of the British Government.

two kinds: emotions and feelings. The effect of a work of art upon the person who enjoys it is an experience different in kind from any experience not of art. It may be formed out of one emotion, or may be a combination of several; and various feelings, inhering for the writer in particular words or phrases or images, may be added to compose the final result. Or great poetry may be made without the direct use of any emotion whatever: composed out of feelings solely. Canto XV of the *Inferno*[1] (Brunetto Latini) is a working up of the emotion evident in the situation; but the effect, though single as that of any work of art, is obtained by considerable complexity of detail. The last quatrain gives an image, a feeling attaching to an image, which "came," which did not develop simply out of what precedes, but which was probably in suspension in the poet's mind until the proper combination arrived for it to add itself to. The poet's mind is in fact a receptacle for seizing and storing up numberless feelings, phrases, images, which remain there until all the particles which can unite to form a new compound are present together.

If you compare several representative passages of the greatest poetry you see how great is the variety of types of combination, and also how completely any semi-ethical criterion of "sublimity" misses the mark. For it is not the "greatness," the intensity, of the emotions, the components, but the intensity of the artistic process, the pressure, so to speak, under which the fusion takes place, that counts. The episode of Paolo and Francesca[2] employs a definite emotion, but the intensity of the poetry is something quite different from whatever intensity in the supposed experience it may give the impression of. It is no more intense, furthermore, than Canto XXVI, the voyage of Ulysses, which has not the direct dependence upon an emotion. Great variety is possible in the process of transmutation of emotion: the

murder of Agamemnon,[3] or the agony of Othello,[4] gives an artistic effect apparently closer to a possible original than the scenes from Dante. In the *Agamemnon,* the artistic emotion approximates to the emotion of an actual spectator; in *Othello* to the emotion of the protagonist himself. But the difference between art and the event is always absolute; the combination which is the murder of Agamemnon is probably as complex as that which is the voyage of Ulysses. In either case there has been a fusion of elements. The ode of Keats contains a number of feelings which have nothing particular to do with the nightingale, but which the nightingale, partly perhaps because of its attractive name, and partly because of its reputation, served to bring together.

The point of view which I am struggling to attack is perhaps related to the metaphysical theory of the substantial unity of the soul: for my meaning is, that the poet has, not a "personality" to express, but a particular medium, which is only a medium and not a personality, in which impressions and experiences combine in peculiar and unexpected ways. Impressions and experiences which are important for the man may take no place in the poetry, and those which become important in the poetry may play quite a negligible part in the man, the personality.

I will quote a passage which is unfamiliar enough to be regarded with fresh attention in the light—or darkness—of these observations:

> *And now methinks I could e'en chide myself*
> *For doting on her beauty, though her death*
> *Shall be revenged after no common action.*
> *Does the silkworm expend her yellow labours*
> *For thee? For thee does she undo herself?*
> *Are lordships sold to maintain ladyships*
> *For the poor benefit of a bewildering minute?*
> *Why does yon fellow falsify highways,*
> *And put his life between the judge's lips,*

---

[1] *Canto XV of the Inferno* In this canto, Dante meets an old acquaintance, Brunetto Latini, who is in Hell for being a Sodomite.

[2] *episode of Paolo and Francesca* Two illicit lovers (Paolo is Francesca's husband's brother).

[3] *murder of Agamemnon* In Aeschylus's play, Clytemnestra kills her husband Agamemnon after he sacrifices their daughter to the god Artemis.

[4] *agony of Othello* In the play by Shakespeare, Othello mistakenly thinks that his wife is unfaithful, kills her, and then, upon learning the truth, commits suicide.

To refine such a thing—keeps horse and men
To beat their valours for her?...[1]

In this passage (as is evident if it is taken in its context) there is a combination of positive and negative emotions: an intensely strong attraction toward beauty and an equally intense fascination by the ugliness which is contrasted with it and which destroys it. This balance of contrasted emotion is in the dramatic situation to which the speech is pertinent, but that situation alone is inadequate to it. This is, so to speak, the structural emotion, provided by the drama. But the whole effect, the dominant tone, is due to the fact that a number of floating feelings, having an affinity to this emotion by no means superficially evident, have combined with it to give us a new art emotion.

It is not in his personal emotions, the emotions provoked by particular events in his life, that the poet is in anyway remarkable or interesting. His particular emotions may be simple, or crude, or flat. The emotion in his poetry will be a very complex thing, but not with the complexity of the emotions of people who have very complex or unusual emotions in life. One error, in fact, of eccentricity in poetry is to seek for new human emotions to express; and in this search for novelty in the wrong place it discovers the perverse. The business of the poet is not to find new emotions, but to use the ordinary ones and, in working them up into poetry, to express feelings which are not in actual emotions at all. And emotions which he has never experienced will serve his turn as well as those familiar to him. Consequently, we must believe that "emotion recollected in tranquillity"[2] is an inexact formula. For it is neither emotion, nor recollection, nor, without distortion of meaning, tranquillity. It is a concentration, and a new thing resulting from the concentration, of a very great number of experiences which to the practical and active person would not seem to be experiences at all; it is a concen-

tration which does not happen consciously or of deliberation. These experiences are not "recollected," and they finally unite in an atmosphere which is "tranquil" only in that it is a passive attending upon the event. Of course this is not quite the whole story. There is a great deal, in the writing of poetry, which must be conscious and deliberate. In fact, the bad poet is usually unconscious where he ought to be conscious, and conscious where he ought to be unconscious. Both errors tend to make him "personal." Poetry is not a turning loose of emotion, but an escape from emotion; it is not the expression of personality, but an escape from personality. But, of course, only those who have personality and emotions know what it means to want to escape from these things.

3

ὁ δὲ νοῦς ἴσως θειότερόν τι καὶ ἀπαθές ἐστιν[3]

This essay proposes to halt at the frontier of metaphysics or mysticism, and confine itself to such practical conclusions as can be applied by the responsible person interested in poetry. To divert interest from the poet to the poetry is a laudable aim: for it would conduce to a juster estimation of actual poetry, good and bad. There are many people who appreciate the expression of sincere emotion in verse, and there is a smaller number of people who can appreciate technical excellence. But very few know when there is an expression of *significant* emotion, emotion which has its life in the poem and not in the history of the poet. The emotion of art is impersonal. And the poet cannot reach this impersonality without surrendering himself wholly to the work to be done. And he is not likely to know what is to be done unless he lives in what is not merely the present, but the present moment of the past, unless he is conscious, not of what is dead, but of what is already living.

—1919

---

[1] *And now ... for her* From *The Revenger's Tragedy* (1607), a play variously ascribed to Cyril Tourneur and to Thomas Middleton.

[2] *"emotion ... tranquillity"* From William Wordsworth's Preface to *Lyrical Ballads* (1800): "Poetry is the spontaneous overflow of powerful feelings: it takes its origin from emotion recollected in tranquillity: the emotion is contemplated till by a species of reaction the tranquillity gradually disappears, and an emotion, kindred to that which was before the subject of contemplation, is gradually produced, and does itself actually exist in the mind."

[3] *ὁ δὲ ... ἐστιν* Greek: "The mind is doubtless something more divine and unaffected." From Aristotle's *De Anima* (Latin: On the Soul) 1.4.

The Metaphysical Poets[1]

By collecting these poems from the work of a generation more often named than read, and more often
read than profitably studied, Professor Grierson has
rendered a service of some importance. Certainly the
reader will meet with many poems already preserved in
other anthologies, at the same time that he discovers
poems such as those of Aurelian Townshend or Lord
Herbert of Cherbury here included. But the function of
such an anthology as this is neither that of Professor
Saintsbury's admirable edition of Caroline poets nor
that of *The Oxford Book of English Verse*. Mr. Grierson's
book is in itself a piece of criticism, and a provocation of
criticism; and we think that he was right in including so
many poems of Donne, elsewhere (though not in many
editions) accessible, as documents in the case of "metaphysical poetry." The phrase has long done duty as a term
of abuse, or as the label of a quaint and pleasant taste. The
question is to what extent the so-called metaphysicals
formed a school (in our own time we should say a
"movement"), and how far this so-called school or
movement is a digression from the main current.

Not only is it extremely difficult to define metaphysical poetry, but difficult to decide what poets practise it
and in which of their verses. The poetry of Donne (to
whom Marvell and Bishop King are sometimes nearer
than any of the other authors) is late Elizabethan, its
feeling often very close to that of Chapman. The
"courtly" poetry is derivative from Jonson, who borrowed liberally from the Latin; it expires in the next
century with the sentiment and witticism of Prior.
There is finally the devotional verse of Herbert,
Vaughan, and Crashaw (echoed long after by Christina
Rossetti and Francis Thompson); Crashaw, sometimes
more profound and less sectarian than the others, has a
quality which returns through the Elizabethan period to
the early Italians. It is difficult to find any precise use of
metaphor, simile, or other conceit, which is common to
all the poets and at the same time important enough as
an element of style to isolate these poets as a group.
Donne, and often Cowley, employ a device which is
sometimes considered characteristically "metaphysical";
the elaboration (contrasted with the condensation) of a
figure of speech to the furthest stage to which ingenuity
can carry it. Thus Cowley develops the commonplace
comparison of the world to a chess-board through long
stanzas ("To Destiny"[2]), and Donne, with more grace,
in "A Valediction,"[3] the comparison of two lovers to a
pair of compasses. But elsewhere we find, instead of the
mere explication of the content of a comparison, a
development by rapid association of thought which
requires considerable agility on the part of the reader.

> *On a round ball*
> *A workeman that hath copies by, can lay*
> *An Europe, Afrique, and an Asia,*
> *And quickly make that, which was nothing, All,*
> *   So doth each teare,*
> *   Which thee doth weare,*
> *A globe, yea world by that impression grow,*
> *Till thy tears mixt with mine doe overflow*
> *This world, by waters sent from thee, my heaven*
> *   dissolved so.*[4]

Here we find at least two connexions which are not
implicit in the first figure, but are forced upon it by the
poet: from the geographer's globe to the tear, and the
tear to the deluge. On the other hand, some of Donne's
most successful and characteristic effects are secured by
brief words and sudden contrasts:

> *A bracelet of bright hair about the bone,*[5]

where the most powerful effect is produced by the
sudden contrast of associations of "bright hair" and of
"bone." This telescoping of images and multiplied
associations is characteristic of the phrase of some of the
dramatists of the period which Donne knew: not to
mention Shakespeare, it is frequent in Middleton,
Webster, and Tourneur, and is one of the sources of the
vitality of their language.

---

[1] *The Metaphysical Poets*   Originally published in the *Times Literary
Supplement* as a review of the Clarendon Press volume *Metaphysical
Lyrics and Poems of the Seventeenth Century: Donne to Butler* (1921),
edited by Herbert J.C. Grierson.

[2] *"To Destiny"* Abraham Cowley's "Destiny" (1656).

[3] *"A Valediction"* Donne's poem "A Valediction: Forbidding
Mourning" (1633).

[4] *On a round ... dissolved so* From Donne's "A Valediction: Of
Weeping," 10–18.

[5] *A bracelet ... bone* From "The Relic" (1633), 6.

Johnson, who employed the term "metaphysical poets," apparently having Donne, Cleveland, and Cowley chiefly in mind, remarks of them that "the most heterogeneous ideas are yoked by violence together."[1] The force of this impeachment lies in the failure of the conjunction, the fact that often the ideas are yoked but not united; and if we are to judge of styles of poetry by their abuse, enough examples may be found in Cleveland to justify Johnson's condemnation. But a degree of heterogeneity of material compelled into unity by the operation of the poet's mind is omnipresent in poetry. We need not select for illustration such a line as

Notre ame est un trois-mats cherchant son Icarie;[2]

we may find it in some of the best lines of Johnson himself (*The Vanity of Human Wishes*):

> *His fate was destined to a barren strand,*
> *A petty fortress, and a dubious hand;*
> *He left a name at which the world grew pale,*
> *To point a moral, or adorn a tale—*

where the effect is due to a contrast of ideas, different in degree but the same in principle, as that which Johnson mildly reprehended. And in one of the finest poems of the age (a poem which could not have been written in any other age), the *Exequy* of Bishop King, the extended comparison is used with perfect success: the idea and the simile become one, in the passage in which the Bishop illustrates his impatience to see his dead wife, under the figure of a journey:

> *Stay for me there; I will not faile*
> *To meet thee in that hollow Vale.*
> *And think not much of my delay;*
> *I am already on the way,*
> *And follow thee with all the speed*
> *Desire can make, or sorrows breed.*
> *Each minute is a short degree,*
> *And ev'ry houre a step towards thee.*
> *At night when I betake to rest,*
> *Next morn I rise nearer my West*
> *Of life, almost by eight houres sail,*

> *Than when sleep breath'd his drowsy gale. . . .*
> *But heark! My Pulse, like a soft Drum*
> *Beats my approach, tells Thee I come;*
> *And slow howere my marches be,*
> *I shall at last sit down by Thee.*

(In the last few lines there is that effect of terror which is several times attained by one of Bishop King's admirers, Edgar Poe.) Again, we may justly take these quatrains from Lord Herbert's "Ode,"[3] stanzas which would, we think, be immediately pronounced to be of the metaphysical school:

> *So when from hence we shall be gone,*
> *And be no more, nor you, nor I,*
> *As one another's mystery,*
> *Each shall be both, yet both but one.*

> *This said, in her up-lifted face,*
> *Her eyes, which did that beauty crown,*
> *Were like two starrs, that having faln down,*
> *Look up again to find their place:*

> *While such a moveless silent peace*
> *Did seize on their becalmed sense,*
> *One would have thought some influence*
> *Their ravished spirits did possess.*

There is nothing in these lines (with the possible exception of the stars, a simile not at once grasped, but lovely and justified) which fits Johnson's general observations on the metaphysical poets in his essay on Cowley. A good deal resides in the richness of association which is at the same time borrowed from and given to the word "becalmed"; but the meaning is clear, the language simple and elegant. It is to be observed that the language of these poets is as a rule simple and pure; in the verse of George Herbert this simplicity is carried as far as it can go—a simplicity emulated without success by numerous modern poets. The *structure* of the sentences, on the other hand, is sometimes far from simple, but this is not a vice; it is a fidelity to thought and feeling. The effect, at its best, is far less artificial than that of an ode by Gray. And as this fidelity induces variety of thought and

---

[1] *"the most ... together"* Samuel Johnson in his "Life of Cowley" (1779).

[2] *Notre ... Icarie* French: "Our soul is a three-masted ship seeking its Icarie." From Charles Baudelaire's *Le Voyage.*

[3] *Lord Herbert's "Ode"* Edward Herbert, Lord Cherbury's "An Ode Upon a Question Moved, Whether Love Should Continue Forever?" (1664).

feeling, so it induces variety of music. We doubt whether, in the eighteenth century, could be found two poems in nominally the same metre, so dissimilar as Marvell's "Coy Mistress" and Crashaw's "Saint Teresa"; the one producing an effect of great speed by the use of short syllables, and the other an ecclesiastical solemnity by the use of long ones:

> Love, thou art absolute sole lord
> Of life and death.

If so shrewd and sensitive (though so limited) a critic as Johnson failed to define metaphysical poetry by its faults, it is worthwhile to inquire whether we may not have more success by adopting the opposite method: by assuming that the poets of the seventeenth century (up to the Revolution[1]) were the direct and normal development of the precedent age; and, without prejudicing their case by the adjective "metaphysical," consider whether their virtue was not something permanently valuable, which subsequently disappeared, but ought not to have disappeared. Johnson has hit, perhaps by accident, on one of their peculiarities, when he observes that "their attempts were always analytic"; he would not agree that, after the dissociation, they put the material together again in a new unity.

It is certain that the dramatic verse of the later Elizabethan and early Jacobean poets expresses a degree of development of sensibility which is not found in any of the prose, good as it often is. If we except Marlowe, a man of prodigious intelligence, these dramatists were directly or indirectly (it is at least a tenable theory) affected by Montaigne. Even if we except also Jonson and Chapman, these two were notably erudite, and were notably men who incorporated their erudition into their sensibility: their mode of feeling was directly and freshly altered by their reading and thought. In Chapman especially there is a direct sensuous apprehension of thought, or a re-creation of thought into feeling, which is exactly what we find in Donne:

> in this one thing, all the discipline
> Of manners and of manhood is contained;
> A man to join himself with th' Universe
> In his main sway, and make in all things fit

> One with that All, and go on, round as it;
> Not plucking from the whole his wretched part,
> And into straits, or into nought revert,
> Wishing the complete Universe might be
> Subject to such a rag of it as he;
> But to consider great Necessity.[2]

We compare this with some modern passage:

> No, when the fight begins within himself,
> A man's worth something. God stoops o'er his head
> Satan looks up between his feet—both tug—
> He's left, himself, i' the middle; the soul wakes
> And grows. Prolong that battle through his life![3]

It is perhaps somewhat less fair, though very tempting (as both poets are concerned with the perpetuation of love by offspring), to compare with the stanzas already quoted from Lord Herbert's "Ode" the following from Tennyson:

> One walked between his wife and child,
> With measured footfall firm and mild,
> And now and then he gravely smiled.
>
> The prudent partner of his blood
> Leaned on him, faithful, gentle,
> Wearing the rose of womanhood.
>
> And in their double love secure,
> The little maiden walked demure,
> Pacing with downward eyelids pure.
>
> These three made unity so sweet,
> My frozen heart began to beat,
> Remembering its ancient beat.[4]

The difference is not a simple difference of degree between poets. It is something which had happened to the mind of England between the time of Donne or Lord Herbert of Cherbury and the time of Tennyson and Browning; it is the difference between the intellec-

---

[1] Revolution I.e., the English Revolution, 1640–60.

[2] in this one ... Necessity From The Revenge of Bussy d'Ambois (1613), 4.1.

[3] No ... life From Robert Browning's "Bishop Blougram's Apology" (1855), 693–97.

[4] One walked ... beat From "The Two Voices" (1833), 412–23.

tual poet and the reflective poet. Tennyson and Browning are poets, and they think; but they do not feel their thought as immediately as the odour of a rose. A thought to Donne was an experience; it modified his sensibility. When a poet's mind is perfectly equipped for its work, it is constantly amalgamating disparate experience; the ordinary man's experience is chaotic, irregular, fragmentary. The latter falls in love, or reads Spinoza, and these two experiences have nothing to do with each other, or with the noise of the typewriter or the smell of cooking; in the mind of the poet these experiences are always forming new wholes.

We may express the difference by the following theory: The poets of the seventeenth century, the successors of the dramatists of the sixteenth, possessed a mechanism of sensibility which could devour any kind of experience. They are simple, artificial, difficult, or fantastic, as their predecessors were; no less nor more than Dante, Guido Cavalcanti, Guinicelli, or Cino. In the seventeenth century a dissociation of sensibility set in, from which we have never recovered; and this dissociation, as is natural, was aggravated by the influence of the two most powerful poets of the century, Milton and Dryden. Each of these men performed certain poetic functions so magnificently well that the magnitude of the effect concealed the absence of others. The language went on and in some respects improved; the best verse of Collins, Gray, Johnson, and even Goldsmith satisfies some of our fastidious demands better than that of Donne or Marvell or King. But while the language became more refined, the feeling became more crude. The feeling, the sensibility, expressed in the "Country Churchyard"[1] (to say nothing of Tennyson and Browning) is cruder than that in the "Coy Mistress."[2]

The second effect of the influence of Milton and Dryden followed from the first, and was therefore slow in manifestation. The sentimental age began early in the eighteenth century, and continued. The poets revolted against the ratiocinative, the descriptive; they thought and felt by fits, unbalanced; they reflected. In one or two passages of Shelley's "Triumph of Life," in the second *Hyperion*,[3] there are traces of a struggle toward unification of sensibility. But Keats and Shelley died, and Tennyson and Browning ruminated.

After this brief exposition of a theory—too brief, perhaps, to carry conviction—we may ask, what would have been the fate of the "metaphysical" had the current of poetry descended in a direct line from them, as it descended in a direct line to them? They would not, certainly, be classified as metaphysical. The possible interests of a poet are unlimited; the more intelligent he is the better; the more intelligent he is the more likely that he will have interests: our only condition is that he turn them into poetry, and not merely meditate on them poetically. A philosophical theory which has entered into poetry is established, for its truth or falsity in one sense ceases to matter, and its truth in another sense is proved. The poets in question have, like other poets, various faults. But they were, at best, engaged in the task of trying to find the verbal equivalent for states of mind and feeling. And this means both that they are more mature, and that they wear better, than later poets of certainly not less literary ability.

It is not a permanent necessity that poets should be interested in philosophy, or in any other subject. We can only say that it appears likely that poets in our civilization, as it exists at present, must be *difficult*. Our civilization comprehends great variety and complexity, and this variety and complexity, playing upon a refined sensibility, must produce various and complex results. The poet must become more and more comprehensive, more allusive, more indirect, in order to force, to dislocate if necessary, language into his meaning. (A brilliant and extreme statement of this view, with which it is not requisite to associate oneself, is that of M. Jean Epstein,[4] *La Poésie d'aujourd'hui*.) Hence we get something which looks very much like the conceit—we get, in fact, a method curiously similar to that of the "metaphysical poets," similar also in its use of obscure words and of simple phrasing.

O géraniums diaphanes, guerroyeurs sortilèges,
Sacrilèges monomanes!
Emballages, dévergondages, douches! O pressoirs

[1] *"Country Churchyard"* "Elegy Written in a Country Churchyard," by Thomas Gray (1716–71).

[2] *"Coy Mistress"* "To His Coy Mistress," by Andrew Marvell (1621–78).

[3] *Hyperion* John Keats began his epic fragment in 1818; in 1819 he revised the poem and wrote *The Fall of Hyperion, A Dream*.

[4] *M. Jean Epstein* French intellectual (1897–1953).

Des vendanges des grands soirs!
Layettes aux abois,
Thyrses au fond des bois!
Transfusions, représailles,
Relevailles, compresses et l'éternel potion,
Angélus! n'en pouvoir plus
De débâcles nuptiales! de débâcles nuptiales![1]

The same poet could write also simply:

Elle est bien loin, elle pleure,
Le grand vent se lamente aussi ...[2]

Jules Laforgue, and Tristan Corbière in many of his poems, are nearer to the "school of Donne" than any modern English poet. But poets more classical than they have the same essential quality of transmuting ideas into sensations, of transforming an observation into a state of mind.

Pour l'enfant, amoureux de cartes et d'estampes,
L'univers est égal à son vaste appétit.
Ah, que le monde est grand à la clarté des lampes!
Aux yeux du souvenir que le monde est petit![3]

In French literature the great master of the seventeenth century—Racine—and the great master of the nineteenth—Baudelaire—are in some ways more like each other than they are like anyone else. The greatest two masters of diction are also the greatest two psychologists, the most curious explorers of the soul. It is interesting to speculate whether it is not a misfortune that two of the greatest masters of diction in our language, Milton and Dryden, triumph with a dazzling disregard of the soul. If we continued to produce Miltons and Drydens it might not so much matter, but as things are it is a pity that English poetry has remained so incomplete. Those who object to the "artificiality" of Milton or Dryden sometimes tell us to "look into our hearts and write." But that is not looking deep enough; Racine or Donne looked into a good deal more than the heart. One must look into the cerebral cortex, the nervous system, and the digestive tracts.

May we not conclude, then, that Donne, Crashaw, Vaughan, Herbert and Lord Herbert, Marvell, King, Cowley at his best, are in the direct current of English poetry, and that their faults should be reprimanded by this standard rather than coddled by antiquarian affection? They have been enough praised in terms which are implicit limitations because they are "metaphysical" or "witty," "quaint" or "obscure," though at their best they have not these attributes more than other serious poets. On the other hand, we must not reject the criticism of Johnson (a dangerous person to disagree with) without having mastered it, without having assimilated the Johnsonian canons of taste. In reading the celebrated passage in his essay on Cowley we must remember that by wit he clearly means something more serious than we usually mean today; in his criticism of their versification we must remember in what a narrow discipline he was trained, but also how well trained; we must remember that Johnson tortures chiefly the chief offenders, Cowley and Cleveland. It would be a fruitful work, and one requiring a substantial book, to break up the classification of Johnson and exhibit these poets in all their difference of kind and of degree, from the massive music of Donne to the faint, pleasing tinkle of Aurelian Townshend.

—1921

---

[1] *O géraniums ... nuptiales* French: "O diaphanous geraniums, warrior magic spells, / Monomaniacal sacrileges! / Packing materials, licentiousness, showers! O presses / Of the great evening grape harvests! / Pressed baby clothes, / Thyrsis deep in the woods! / Transfusions, reprisals, / Reawakenings, compresses, and the eternal potion, / Angélus! No longer able / Marriage debacles! Marriage debacles!" From Jules Laforgue's *Derniers vers* (1890).

[2] *Elle est bien ... aussi* French: "She is far away, she cries, / The high wind also laments." From *Derniers vers.*

[3] *Pour l'enfant ... est petit* French: "For the child, loving maps and stamps, / The universe is his vast appetite. / Ah, how large the world is by the clear light of the lamps! / To eyes remembering that the world is small." From Baudelaire's *Le Voyage.*

IN CONTEXT

T.S. Eliot and Anti-Semitism

Considerable controversy occurred in the latter years of the twentieth century over the issue of T.S. Eliot and anti-Semitism. The issue had been raised here and there during Eliot's lifetime: J.V. Healy raised the matter in correspondence with Eliot in 1940; a letter of George Orwell's in 1948 reveals that some were then suggesting in conversation that Eliot was anti-Semitic, and so on. Orwell no doubt gave voice to a then-common view in dismissing the suggestion:

> It is nonsense what Fyvel said about Eliot being anti-Semitic. Of course you can find what would now be called antisemitic remarks in his early work, but who didn't say such things at that time? (Letter to Julian Symons, 29 October 1948)

That anti-Semitism was widespread in the 1910s and 1920s in both the USA and Britain is certain, and to some extent Eliot's views on the question were no doubt those of the majority at the time. But few published literary works displayed the consistency of association that one finds in Eliot's early poetry between what is Jewish and what is squalid and distasteful. Still, leading critics and scholars did not begin to air the matter publicly until 1971, when the issue of anti-Semitism in Eliot's works was raised by a leading critic, George Steiner, in a letter to *The Listener*:

> The obstinate puzzle is Eliot's uglier touches tend to occur at the heart of very good poetry (which is *not* the case with Pound). One thinks of the notorious "the Jew squats on the window-sill ... Spawned in some estaminet of Antwerp" in "Geron-tion"; of
>
>> The rats are underneath the piles.
>> The Jew is underneath the lot.
>
> In "Burbank with a Baedeker: Bleistein with a Cigar"; of
>
>> Rachel nee Rabinovich
>> tears at the grapes with murderous paws
>
> in "Sweeney among the Nightingales." (*The Listener*, 29 April 1971)

The question Steiner raised as to how the uglier touches in Eliot's work connected with the aesthetic quality of the whole is one that has continued to interest scholars and critics. In an important 1988 book, another leading scholar, Christopher Ricks, put forward an extended analysis of the ways in which various forms of prejudice may have animated both Eliot's work itself and responses to it. Ricks begins his study with a look at prejudice against women; he notes how the critics had picked up on the latent element of misogyny in two famous lines from "The Love Song of J. Alfred Prufrock":

> John Crowe Ransom [puts a] rhetorical question: "How could they ['the women'] have had any inkling of that glory which Michaelangelo had put into his marbles and his paintings?"

Helen Gardner does not as a woman have any different sense of the women: "The absurdity of discussing his giant art, in high-pitched feminine voices, drifting through a drawing room, adds merely extra irony to the underlying sense of the lines."

[T]he critics miss ... one of the things that is salutory in the lines

> In the room the women come and go
> Talking of Michaelangelo.

What none of the critics will own is how much their sense of the lines is incited by prejudice.... Grover Smith [writes that] "the women meanwhile are talking, no doubt tediously and ignorantly, of Michaelangelo." For all we know, as against suspect (perhaps justifiably, but still), the women could be talking as invaluably as [renowned art historian] Kenneth Clark (*T.S. Eliot and Prejudice*, 10–11).

Ricks analyzes at length and with considerable subtlety the "uglier touches" in Eliot's poetry, noting how these are associative rather than unequivocally prejudicial or inciteful. A line such as "The Jew is underneath the lot," he comments, does not "come clean, since the effect of the article 'The Jew' is to disparage all Jews ... while nevertheless leaving open a bolt-hole for the disingenuous reply that a particular Jew only is meant" (35).

As Ricks pointed out, some of Eliot's other writings are at least as disturbing as the published poems. Particularly troubling are an unpublished poem, "Dirge," that was part of an early draft of *The Waste Land*, and a passage from *After Strange Gods*, a series of lectures given by Eliot in Virginia in 1933, and published in book form a year later. (Eliot never allowed the book to be reprinted.) In the passage Eliot is describing what he feels is to be striven for in a society that properly values tradition:

The population should be homogenous.... What is still more important is unity of religious background; and reasons of race and religion combine to make any large number of free-thinking Jews undesirable. There must be a proper balance between urban and rural, industrial and agricultural development. And a spirit of excessive tolerance is to be deprecated (*After Strange Gods*, 20).

If Ricks's focus was primarily a literary one, that of Anthony Julius in his *T.S. Eliot, Anti-Semitism, and Literary Form* (1995) was more broadly social—and more clearly provocative. With his searing indictment both of the anti-Semitism of Eliot's age and its memorable expressions in Eliot's verse, Julius touched a raw nerve. Whereas Ricks's criticisms are often elliptical, and his tone generally reserved, Julius is direct and unrelenting:

"Women," "jews," and "negroes" are not interchangeable "aliens" in Eliot's work. They are, respectively, intimidating, sightless, and transparent; their deaths are respectively longed for, delighted in, and noted without emotion....

... However, this does not amount to an argument for suppression. I censure; I do not wish to censor.... Eliot's anti-Semitic poems are integral to his oeuvre, an oeuvre which is to be valued and preserved.... One can teach anti-Semitism from such texts; one can also teach poetry. One reads them, appalled, and impressed.

Like Steiner a generation earlier, Julius concludes that Eliot is "able to place his anti-Semitism at the service of his art." A storm of controversy followed the publication of Julius's book, with many defending Julius but many others continuing to argue either that Eliot was not anti-Semitic or that anti-Semitism was irrelevant to his work. A further camp held that anti-Semitism was in fact a significant presence, but that the poetry succeeds despite such "uglier touches" rather than in any way because of them. Today there remains no consensus on these issues, but there can be no doubt that the controversy has left a mark; it is unlikely that extended discussion of Eliot's poetry will again be able to take place without any reference to this troubling issue.

JEAN RHYS
1890 – 1979

Jean Rhys, born Ella Gwendolyn Rees Williams, was a West Indies-born writer whose works are strongly marked by her cultural background and by her experience of life as a white Creole woman in the heavily colonized Caribbean and later in metropolitan London. Although she published four novels early in her career, she was not recognized as a major literary figure until the publication of *Wide Sargasso Sea* (1966), which won the prestigious W.H. Smith Literary Award and became one of the most widely read novels of the late twentieth century. The novel is a "prequel" to Charlotte

Brontë's *Jane Eyre* (1847), in which Rhys gives a voice to Rochester's insane and confined wife, Bertha Mason. Rhys made no secret of her motive for writing the book; as she remarked in an interview, "I was convinced Charlotte Brontë must have had something against the West Indies, and I was angry about it." She was thus led to explore the conflict of cultures between colonizer and colonized as she cast in a different light the central motif of *Jane Eyre*—that of a helpless female outsider, powerless and victimized, who relies on older European men for protection. In doing so, Rhys anticipated by a decade or more many of the insights of postcolonialism, the literary movement examining the repercussions of imperialism on subject nations and their citizens that became prevalent in the 1990s. She was one of the first to explicitly connect the marginalization of women with issues of race and class.

Rhys was born in 1890 in Roseau, Dominica, in the West Indies. Her father was a Welsh doctor, and her mother a Dominican Creole of Scottish lineage. She began her education in Roseau, in a convent school. As a white Creole in a predominantly black area, she often felt socially isolated, despite identifying with the black community from an early age. At sixteen she traveled to England, attending the prestigious Perse Prepatory girls' school in Cambridge. While there, Rhys excelled academically, taking first prize in Roman literature in the exams for Cambridge and Oxford. She attended one term at the Royal Academy of Dramatic Art in London in 1909, though she never made it to university; her father died in 1910, leaving Rhys in severely reduced circumstances. Alone and destitute in England, Rhys lived a drifter's life, taking on a variety of jobs: chorus girl (under the stage name Vivian Gray), actress, volunteer cook during World War I, secretary, and ghostwriter of a book about furniture.

In 1919 Rhys married the first of her three husbands. The pair had two children—a son who died as an infant and a daughter—and lived a largely itinerant existence, residing sporadically in Vienna, Budapest, and Paris. During this period she acquainted herself with works of modern art and literature, and began to suffer from the alcoholism that would plague her for the rest of her life. In Paris in 1922, she met Modernist novelist Ford Madox Ford (1873–1939) under whose patronage she began to write. She published her first short story, "Vienne," in Ford's magazine *The Transatlantic Review* in 1924, and followed this with her first collection, *The Left Bank and Other Stories*, in 1927. She continued to publish steadily during the 1930s. Her first novel, *Postures* (1928; *Quartet*, 1929, in the United States), further developed the typical Rhys heroine: sexually alluring, sensitive, and dependent. She followed this with a trio of critically acclaimed semi-autobiographical novels, *After*

Leaving Mr. Mackenzie (1930), *Voyage in the Dark* (1934), and *Good Morning, Midnight* (1939). For some time these publications allowed her to enjoy moderate literary recognition and financial security, but the late 1940s and 50s were marked for Rhys by near-poverty, continuing alcoholism, and trouble with the authorities. Her second husband was jailed in the 1950s for financial misdoing, and she herself spent time in London's Holloway Prison in 1949 after an altercation with neighbors. Rhys brings this period to vivid life in her story of the displaced black drifter, Selina, "Let Them Call It Jazz."

Rhys fell into relative obscurity during the 1940s and 50s, but interest in her work revived with the radio production of *Good Morning, Midnight* in 1958. She followed this with her 1966 masterpiece, *Wide Sargasso Sea*, which she had begun to write over twenty years earlier. The rest of her career was devoted to her memoirs, *Smile Please* (published posthumously in 1979), and her collections *Tigers Are Better-Looking* (1968) and *Sleep It Off, Lady* (1976). Rhys died in Devonshire, England, in 1979, at the age of 88.

⌘ ⌘ ⌘

Let Them Call It Jazz

One bright Sunday morning in July I have trouble with my Notting Hill[1] landlord because he ask for a month's rent in advance. He tell me this after I live there since winter, settling up[2] every week without fail. I have no job at the time, and if I give the money he want there's not much left. So I refuse. The man drunk already at that early hour, and he abuse me—all talk, he can't frighten me. But his wife is a bad one—now she walk in my room and say she must have cash. When I tell her no, she give my suitcase one kick and it burst open. My best dress fall out, then she laugh and give another kick. She say month in advance is usual, and if I can't pay find somewhere else.

Don't talk to me about London. Plenty people there have heart like stone. Any complaint—the answer is "prove it." But if nobody see and bear witness for me, how to prove anything? So I pack up and leave, I think better not have dealings with that woman. She too cunning, and Satan don't lie worse.

I walk about till a place nearby is open where I can have coffee and a sandwich. There I start talking to a man at my table. He talk to me already, I know him, but I don't know his name. After a while he ask, "What's the matter? Anything wrong?" and when I tell

him my trouble he say I can use an empty flat[3] he own till I have time to look around.

This man is not at all like most English people. He see very quick, and he decide very quick. English people take long time to decide—you three-quarter dead before they make up their mind about you. Too besides, he speak very matter of fact, as if it's nothing. He speak as if he realize well what it is to live like I do—that's why I accept and go.

He tell me somebody occupy the flat till last week, so I find everything all right, and he tell me how to get there—three-quarters of an hour from Victoria Station,[4] up a steep hill, turn left, and I can't mistake the house. He give me the keys and an envelope with a telephone number on the back. Underneath is written "After 6 p.m. ask for Mr. Sims."

In the train that evening I think myself lucky, for to walk about London on a Sunday with nowhere to go—that take the heart out of you.

I find the place and the bedroom of the downstairs flat is nicely furnished—two looking glass, wardrobe, chest of drawers, sheets, everything. It smell of jasmine scent, but it smell strong of damp too.

I open the door opposite and there's a table, a couple chairs, a gas stove and a cupboard, but this room so big it look empty. When I pull the blind up I notice the

---

[1] *Notting Hill* At this time, an unfashionable and relatively cheap district in London.

[2] *settling up* Paying.

[3] *flat* Apartment.

[4] *Victoria Station* Major railway station in London.

paper peeling off and mushrooms growing on the walls—you never see such a thing.

The bathroom the same, all the taps rusty. I leave the two other rooms and make up the bed. Then I listen, but I can't hear one sound. Nobody come in, nobody go out of that house. I lie awake for a long time, then I decide not to stay and in the morning I start to get ready quickly before I change my mind. I want to wear my best dress, but it's a funny thing—when I take up that dress and remember how my landlady kick it I cry. I cry and I can't stop. When I stop I feel tired to my bones, tired like old woman. I don't want to move again—I have to force myself. But in the end I get out in the passage and there's a postcard for me. "Stay as long as you like. I'll be seeing you soon—Friday probably. Not to worry." It isn't signed, but I don't feel so sad and I think, "All right, I wait here till he come. Perhaps he know of a job for me."

Nobody else live in the house but a couple on the top floor—quiet people and they don't trouble me. I have no word to say against them.

First time I meet the lady she's opening the front door and she give me a very inquisitive look. But next time she smile a bit and I smile back—once she talk to me. She tell me the house very old, hundred and fifty year old, and she and her husband live there since long time. "Valuable property," she says, "it could have been saved, but nothing done of course." Then she tells me that as to the present owner—if he is the owner—well he have to deal with local authorities and she believe they make difficulties. "These people are determined to pull down all the lovely old houses—it's shameful."

So I agree that many things shameful. But what to do? What to do? I say it have an elegant shape, it make the other houses in the street look cheap trash, and she seem pleased. That's true too. The house sad and out of place, especially at night. But it have style. The second floor shut up, and as for my flat, I go in the two empty rooms once, but never again.

Underneath was the cellar, full of old boards and broken-up furniture—I see a big rat there one day. It was no place to be alone in I tell you, and I get the habit of buying a bottle of wine most evenings, for I don't like whisky and the rum here no good. It don't even *taste* like rum. You wonder what they do to it.

After I drink a glass or two I can sing and when I sing all the misery goes from my heart. Sometimes I make up songs but next morning I forget them, so other times I sing the old ones like *Tantalizin'* or *Don't Trouble Me Now.*

I think I go but I don't go. Instead I wait for the evening and the wine and that's all. Everywhere else I live—well, it doesn't matter to me, but this house is different—empty and no noise and full of shadows, so that sometimes you ask yourself what make all those shadows in an empty room.

I eat in the kitchen, then I clean up everything nice and have a bath for coolness. Afterwards I lean my elbows on the windowsill and look at the garden. Red and blue flowers mix up with the weeds and there are five-six apple trees. But the fruit drop and lie in the grass, so sour nobody want it. At the back, near the wall, is a bigger tree—this garden certainly take up a lot of room, perhaps that's why they want to pull the place down.

Not much rain all the summer, but not much sunshine either. More of a glare. The grass get brown and dry, the weeds grow tall, the leaves on the trees hang down. Only the red flowers—the poppies—stand up to that light, everything else look weary.

I don't trouble about money, but what with wine and shillings for the slot-meters,[1] it go quickly; so I don't waste much on food. In the evening I walk outside—not by the apple trees but near the street—it's not so lonely.

There's no wall here and I can see the woman next door looking at me over the hedge. At first I say good evening, but she turn away her head, so afterwards I don't speak. A man is often with her, he wear a straw hat with a black ribbon and goldrim spectacles. His suit hang on him like it's too big. He's the husband it seems and he stare at me worse than his wife—he stare as if I'm wild animal let loose. Once I laugh in his face because why these people have to be like that? I don't bother them. In the end I get that I don't even give them one single glance. I have plenty other things to worry about.

---

[1] *shillings* Coins used in the United Kingdom prior to 1971, each worth 1/20th of a pound; *slot-meters* Meters, here for hot water, operated by inserting a coin into a slot, often used to provide gas heating.

To show you how I felt. I don't remember exactly. But I believe it's the second Saturday after I come that when I'm at the window just before I go for my wine I feel somebody's hand on my shoulder and it's Mr. Sims. He must walk very quiet because I don't know a thing till he touch me.

He says hullo, then he tells me I've got terrible thin, do I ever eat. I say of course I eat but he goes on that it doesn't suit me at all to be so thin and he'll buy some food in the village. (That's the way he talk. There's no village here. You don't get away from London so quick.)

It don't seem to me he look very well himself, but I just say bring a drink instead, as I am not hungry.

He come back with three bottles—vermouth, gin and red wine. Then he ask if the little devil who was here last smash all the glasses and I tell him she smash some, I find the pieces. But not all. "You fight with her, eh?"

He laugh, and he don't answer. He pour out the drinks then he says, "Now, you eat up those sandwiches."

Some men when they are there you don't worry so much. These sort of men you do all they tell you blindfold because they can take the trouble from your heart and make you think you're safe. It's nothing they say or do. It's a feeling they can give you. So I don't talk with him seriously—I don't want to spoil that evening. But I ask about the house and why it's so empty and he says:

"Has the old trout upstairs been gossiping?"

I tell him, "She suppose they make difficulties for you."

"It was a damn bad buy," he says and talks about selling the lease or something. I don't listen much.

We were standing by the window then and the sun low. No more glare. He puts his hand over my eyes. "Too big—much too big for your face," he says and kisses me like you kiss a baby. When he takes his hand away I see he's looking out at the garden and he says this—"It gets you. My God it does."

I know very well it's not me he means, so I ask him, "Why sell it then? If you like it, keep it."

"Sell what?" he says. "I'm not talking about this damned house."

I ask what he's talking about. "Money," he says. "Money. That's what I'm talking about. Ways of

making it."

"I don't think so much of money. It don't like me and what do I care?" I was joking, but he turns around, his face quite pale and he tells me I'm a fool. He tells me I'll get push around all my life and die like a dog, only worse because they'd finish off a dog, but they'll let me live till I'm a caricature of myself. That's what he say, "Caricature of yourself." He say I'll curse the day I was born and everything and everybody in this bloody world before I'm done.

I tell him, "No I'll never feel like that," and he smiles, if you can call it a smile, and says he's glad I'm content with my lot. "I'm disappointed in you, Selina. I thought you had more spirit."

"If I contented that's all right," I answer him, "I don't see very many looking contented over here." We're standing staring at each other when the door bell rings. "That's a friend of mine," he says. "I'll let him in."

As to the friend, he's all dressed up in stripe pants and a black jacket and he's carrying a brief-case. Very ordinary looking but with a soft kind of voice.

"Maurice, this is Selina Davis," says Mr. Sims, and Maurice smiles very kind but it don't mean much, then he looks at his watch and says they ought to be getting along.

At the door Mr. Sims tells me he'll see me next week and I answer straight out, "I won't be here next week because I want a job and I won't get one in this place."

"Just what I'm going to talk about. Give it a week longer, Selina."

I say, "Perhaps I stay a few more days. Then I go. Perhaps I go before."

"Oh no you won't go," he says.

They walk to the gates quickly and drive off in a yellow car. Then I feel eyes on me and it's the woman and her husband in the next door garden watching. The man make some remark and she look at me so hateful, so hating I shut the front door quick.

I don't want more wine. I want to go to bed early because I must think. I must think about money. It's true I don't care for it. Even when somebody steal my savings—this happen soon after I get to the Notting Hill house—I forget it soon. About thirty pounds they steal. I keep it roll up in a pair of stockings, but I go to the drawer one day, and no money. In the end I have to tell the police. They ask me exact sum and I say I don't count it lately, about thirty pounds. "You don't know how much?" they say. "When did you count it last? Do you remember? Was it before you move or after?"

I get confuse, and I keep saying, "I don't remember," though I remember well I see it two days before. They don't believe me and when a policeman come to the house I hear the landlady tell him, "She certainly had no money when she came here. She wasn't able to pay a month's rent in advance for her room though it's a rule in this house." "These people terrible liars," she say and I think "it's you a terrible liar, because when I come you tell me weekly or monthly as you like." It's from that time she don't speak to me and perhaps it's she take it. All I know is I never see one penny of my savings again, all I know is they pretend I never have any, but as it's gone, no use to cry about it. Then my mind goes to my father, for my father is a white man and I think a lot about him. If I could see him only once, for I too small to remember when he was there. My mother is fair coloured woman, fairer than I am they say, and she don't stay long with me either. She have a chance to go to Venezuela when I three-four year old and she never come back. She send money instead. It's my grandmother take care of me. She's quite dark and what we call "country-cookie" but she's the best I know.

She save up all the money my mother send, she don't keep one penny for herself—that's how I get to England. I was a bit late in going to school regular, getting on for twelve years, but I can sew very beautiful, excellent—so I think I get a good job—in London perhaps.

However here they tell me all this fine handsewing take too long. Waste of time—too slow. They want somebody to work quick and to hell with the small stitches. Altogether it don't look so good for me, I must say, and I wish I could see my father. I have his name—Davis. But my grandmother tell me, "Every word that come out of that man's mouth a damn lie. He is certainly first class liar, though no class otherwise." So perhaps I have not even his real name.

Last thing I see before I put the light out is the postcard on the dressing table. "Not to worry."

Not to worry! Next day is Sunday, and it's on the Monday the people next door complain about me to the police. That evening the woman is by the hedge, and

when I pass her she says in very sweet quiet voice, "*Must* you stay? *Can't* you go?" I don't answer. I walk out in the street to get rid of her. But she run inside her house to the window, she can still see me. Then I start to sing, so she can understand I'm not afraid of her. The husband call out: "If you don't stop that noise I'll send for the police." I answer them quite short. I say, "You go to hell and take your wife with you." And I sing louder.

The police come pretty quick—two of them. Maybe they just round the corner. All I can say about police, and how they behave is I think it all depend who they dealing with. Of my own free will I don't want to mix up with police. No.

One man says, you can't cause this disturbance here. But the other asks a lot of questions. What is my name? Am I tenant of a flat in No. 17? How long have I lived there? Last address and so on. I get vexed the way he speak and I tell him, "I come here because somebody steal my savings. Why you don't look for my money instead of bawling at me? I work hard for my money. All-you don't do one single thing to find it."

"What's she talking about?" the first one says, and the other one tells me, "You can't make that noise here. Get along home. You've been drinking."

I see that woman looking at me and smiling, and other people at their windows, and I'm so angry I bawl at them too. I say, "I have absolute and perfect right to be in the street same as anybody else, and I have absolute and perfect right to ask the police why they don't even look for my money when it disappear. It's because a dam' English thief take it you don't look," I say. The end of all this is that I have to go before a magistrate, and he fine me five pounds for drunk and disorderly, and he give me two weeks to pay.

When I get back from the court I walk up and down the kitchen, up and down, waiting for six o'clock because I have no five pounds left, and I don't know what to do. I telephone at six and a woman answers me very short and sharp, then Mr. Sims comes along and he don't sound too pleased either when I tell him what happen. "Oh Lord!" he says, and I say I'm sorry. "Well don't panic," he says, "I'll pay the fine. But look, I don't think … " Then he breaks off and talk to some other person in the room. He goes on, "Perhaps better not stay at No. 17. I think I can arrange something else. I'll call for you Wednesday—Saturday latest. Now behave till then." And he hang up before I can answer that I don't want to wait till Wednesday, much less Saturday. I want to get out of that house double quick and with no delay. First I think I ring back, then I think better not as he sound so vex.

I get ready, but Wednesday he don't come, and Saturday he don't come. All the week I stay in the flat. Only once I go out and arrange for bread, milk and eggs to be left at the door, and seems to me I meet up with a lot of policemen. They don't look at me, but they see me all right. I don't want to drink—I'm all the time listening, listening and thinking, how can I leave before I know if my fine is paid? I tell myself the police let me know, that's certain. But I don't trust them. What they care? The answer is Nothing. Nobody care. One afternoon I knock at the old lady's flat upstairs, because I get the idea she give me good advice. I can hear her moving about and talking, but she don't answer and I never try again.

Nearly two weeks pass like that, then I telephone. It's the woman speaking and she say, "Mr. Sims is not in London at present." I ask, "When will he be back—it's urgent," and she hang up. I'm not surprised. Not at all. I knew that would happen. All the same I feel heavy like lead. Near the phone box is a chemist's shop, so I ask him for something to make me sleep, the day is bad enough, but to lie awake all night—Ah no! He gives me a little bottle marked *"One or two tablets only"* and I take three when I go to bed because more and more I think that sleeping is better than no matter what else. However, I lie there, eyes wide open as usual, so I take three more. Next thing I know the room is full of sunlight, so it must be late afternoon, but the lamp is still on. My head turn around and I can't think well at all. At first I ask myself how I get to the place. Then it comes to me, but in pictures—like the landlady kicking my dress, and when I take my ticket at Victoria Station, and Mr. Sims telling me to eat the sandwiches, but I can't remember everything clear, and I feel very giddy and sick. I take in the milk and eggs at the door, go in the kitchen, and try to eat but the food hard to swallow.

It's when I'm putting the things away that I see the bottles—pushed back on the lowest shelf in the cupboard.

There's a lot of drink left, and I'm glad I tell you. Because I can't bear the way I feel. Not any more. I mix

a gin and vermouth and I drink it quick, then I mix another and drink it slow by the window. The garden looks different, like I never see it before. I know quite well what I must do, but it's late now—tomorrow. I have one more drink, of wine this time, and then a song come in my head, I sing it and I dance it, and more I sing, more I am sure this is the best tune that has ever come to me in all my life.

The sunset light from the window is gold colour. My shoes sound loud on the boards. So I take them off, my stockings too and go on dancing but the room feel shut in, I can't breathe, and I go outside still singing. Maybe I dance a bit too. I forget all about that woman till I hear her saying, "Henry, look at this." I turn around and I see her at the window. "Oh yes, I wanted to speak with you," I say, "Why bring the police and get me in bad trouble? Tell me that."

"And you tell *me* what you're doing here at all," she says. "This is a respectable neighbourhood."

Then the man come along. "Now young woman, take yourself off. You ought to be ashamed of this behaviour."

"It's disgraceful," he says, talking to his wife, but loud so I can hear, and she speaks loud too—for once. "At least the other tarts[1] that crook installed here were *white* girls," she says.

"You a dam' fouti[2] liar," I say. "Plenty of those girls in your country already. Numberless as the sands on the shore. You don't need me for that."

"You're not a howling success at it certainly." Her voice sweet sugar again. "And you won't be seeing much more of your friend Mr. Sims. He's in trouble too. Try somewhere else. Find somebody else. If you can, of course." When she say that my arm moves of itself. I pick up a stone and bam! through the window. Not the one they are standing at but the next, which is of coloured glass, green and purple and yellow.

I never see a woman look so surprise. Her mouth fall open she so full of surprise. I start to laugh, louder and louder—I laugh like my grandmother, with my hands on my hips and my head back. (When she laugh like that you can hear her to the end of our street.) At last I say, "Well, I'm sorry. An accident. I get it fixed tomorrow early." "That glass is irreplaceable," the man says.

---

[1] *tarts* Women considered sexually promiscuous.

[2] *fouti* Crazy.

"Irreplaceable." "Good thing," I say, "those colours look like they sea-sick to me. I buy you a better window-glass."

He shake his fist at me. "You won't be let off with a fine this time," he says. Then they draw the curtains. I call out at them. "You run away. Always you run away. Ever since I come here you hunt me down because I don't answer back. It's you shameless." I try to sing "Don't trouble me now."

> Don't trouble me now
> You without honour.
> Don't walk in my footstep
> You without shame.

But my voice don't sound right, so I get back indoors and drink one more glass of wine—still wanting to laugh, and still thinking of my grandmother for that is one of her songs.

It's about a man whose doudou[1] give him the go-by when she find somebody rich and he sail away to Panama. Plenty people die there of fever when they make that Panama canal so long ago. But he don't die. He come back with dollars and the girl meet him on the jetty, all dressed up and smiling. Then he sing to her, "You without honour, you without shame." It sound good in Martinique patois[2] too: "Sans honte."

Afterwards I ask myself, "Why I do that? It's not like me. But if they treat you wrong over and over again the hour strike when you burst out that's what."

Too besides, Mr. Sims can't tell me now I have no spirit. I don't care, I sleep quickly and I'm glad I break the woman's ugly window. But as to my own song it go *right* away and it never come back. A pity.

Next morning the doorbell ringing wake me up. The people upstairs don't come down, and the bell keeps on like fury self. So I go to look, and there is a policeman and a policewoman outside. As soon as I open the door the woman put her foot in it. She wear sandals and thick stockings and I never see a foot so big or so bad. It look like it want to mash up the whole world. Then she come in after the foot, and her face not so pretty either. The policeman tell me my fine is not

paid and people make serious complaints about me, so they're taking me back to the magistrate. He show me a paper and I look at it, but I don't read it. The woman push me in the bedroom, and tell me to get dress quickly, but I just stare at her, because I think perhaps I wake up soon. Then I ask her what I must wear. She say she suppose I had some clothes on yesterday. Or not? "What's it matter, wear anything," she says. But I find clean underclothes and stockings and my shoes with high heels and I comb my hair. I start to file my nails, because I think they too long for magistrate's court but she get angry. "Are you coming quietly or aren't you?" she says. So I go with them and we get in a car outside.

I wait for a long time in a room full of policemen. They come in, they go out, they telephone, they talk in low voices. Then it's my turn, and first thing I notice in the court room is a man with frowning black eyebrows. He sit below the magistrate, he dressed in black and he so handsome I can't take my eyes off him. When he see that he frown worse than before.

First comes a policeman to testify I cause disturbance, and then comes the old gentleman from next door. He repeat that bit about nothing but the truth so help me God. Then he says I make dreadful noise at night and use abominable language, and dance in obscene fashion. He says when they try to shut the curtains because his wife so terrify of me, I throw stones and break a valuable stain-glass window. He say his wife get serious injury if she'd been hit, and as it is she in terrible nervous condition and the doctor is with her. I think, "Believe me, if I aim at your wife I hit your wife—that's certain." "There was no provocation," he says. "None at all." Then another lady from across the street says this is true. She heard no provocation whatsoever, and she swear that they shut the curtains but I go on insulting them and using filthy language and she saw all this and heard it.

The magistrate is a little gentleman with a quiet voice, but I'm very suspicious of these quiet voices now. He ask me why I don't pay my fine, and I say because I haven't the money. I get the idea they want to find out all about Mr. Sims—they listen so very attentive. But they'll find out nothing from me. He ask how long I have the flat and I say I don't remember. I know they want to trip me up like they trip me up about my

---

[1]   *doudou*   Sweetheart.

[2]   *Martinique*   West Indian island colonized by the French; *patois* Regional dialect, in this case the Creole dialect of Martinique.

savings so I won't answer. At last he ask if I have any-thing to say as I can't be allowed to go on being a nuisance. I think, "I'm nuisance to you because I have no money that's all." I want to speak up and tell him how they steal all my savings, so when my landlord asks for month's rent I haven't got it to give. I want to tell him the woman next door provoke me since long time and call me bad names but she have a soft sugar voice and nobody hear—that's why I broke her window, but I'm ready to buy another after all. I want to say all I do is sing in that old garden, and I want to say this in decent quiet voice. But I hear myself talking loud and I see my hands wave in the air. Too besides it's no use, they won't believe me, so I don't finish. I stop, and I feel the tears on my face. "Prove it." That's all they will say. They whisper, they whisper. They nod, they nod.

Next thing I'm in a car again with a different policewoman, dressed very smart. Not in uniform. I ask her where she's taking me and she says "Holloway"[1] just that "Holloway."

I catch hold of her hand because I'm afraid. But she takes it away. Cold and smooth her hand slide away and her face is china face—smooth like a doll and I think, "This is the last time I ask anything from anybody. So help me God."

The car come up to a black castle and little mean streets are all round it. A lorry[2] was blocking up the castle gates. When it get by we pass through and I am in jail. First I stand in a line with others who are waiting to give up handbags and all belongings to a woman behind bars like in a post office. The girl in front bring out a nice compact, look like gold to me, lipstick to match and a wallet full of notes. The woman keep the money, but she give back the powder and lipstick and she half-smile. I have two pounds seven shillings and sixpence in pennies. She take my purse, then she throw me my compact (which is cheap) my comb and my handker-chief like everything in my bag is dirty. So I think, "Here too, here too." But I tell myself, "Girl, what you expect, eh? They all like that. All."

Some of what happen afterwards I forget, or perhaps better not remember. Seems to me they start by trying to frighten you. But they don't succeed with me for I don't care for nothing now, it's as if my heart hard like

a rock and I can't feel.

Then I'm standing at the top of a staircase with a lot of women and girls. As we are going down I notice the railing very low on one side, very easy to jump, and a long way below there's the grey stone passage like it's waiting for you.

As I'm thinking this a uniform woman step up alongside quick and grab my arm. She say, "Oh no you don't."

I was just noticing the railing very low that's all—but what's the use of saying so.

Another long line waits for the doctor. It move forward slowly and my legs terrible tired. The girl in front is very young and she cry and cry. "I'm scared," she keeps saying. She's lucky in a way—as for me I never will cry again. It all dry up and hard in me now. That, and a lot besides. In the end I tell her to stop, because she doing just what these people want her to do.

She stop crying and start a long story, but while she is speaking her voice get very far away, and I find I can't see her face clear at all.

Then I'm in a chair, and one of those uniform women is pushing my head down between my knees, but let her push—everything go away from me just the same.

They put me in the hospital because the doctor say I'm sick. I have cell by myself and it's all right except I don't sleep. The things they say you mind I don't mind.

When they clang the door on me I think, "You shut me in, but you shut all those other dam' devils *out*. They can't reach me now."

At first it bothers me when they keep on looking at me all through the night. They open a little window in the doorway to do this. But I get used to it and get used to the night chemise[3] they give me. It very thick, and to my mind it not very clean either—but what's that matter to me? Only the food I can't swallow—especially the porridge. The woman ask me sarcastic, "Hunger striking?" But afterwards I can leave most of it, and she don't say nothing.

One day a nice girl comes around with books and she give me two, but I don't want to read so much. Beside one is about a murder, and the other is about a ghost and I don't think it's at all like those books tell you.

1 *Holloway* Notorious women's prison in London.
2 *lorry* Truck.
3 *night chemise* Nightgown.

There is nothing I want now. It's no use. If they leave me in peace and quiet that's all I ask. The window is barred but not small, so I can see a little thin tree through the bars, and I like watching it.

After a week they tell me I'm better and I can go out with the others for exercise. We walk round and round one of the yards in that castle—it is fine weather and the sky is a kind of pale blue, but the yard is a terrible sad place. The sunlight fall down and die there. I get tired walking in high heels and I'm glad when that's over.

We can talk, and one day an old woman come up and ask me for dog-ends. I don't understand, and she start muttering at me like she very vexed. Another woman tell me she mean cigarette ends, so I say I don't smoke. But the old woman still look angry, and when we're going in she give me one push and I nearly fall down. I'm glad to get away from these people, and hear the door clang and take my shoes off.

Sometimes I think, "I'm here because I wanted to sing" and I have to laugh. But there's a small looking glass in my cell and I see myself and I'm like somebody else. Like some strange new person. Mr. Sims tell me I too thin, but what he say now to this person in the looking glass? So I don't laugh again.

Usually I don't think at all. Everything and everybody seem small and far away, that is the only trouble.

Twice the doctor come to see me. He don't say much and I don't say anything, because a uniform woman is always there. She look like she thinking, "Now the lies start." So I prefer not to speak. Then I'm sure they can't trip me up. Perhaps I there still, or in a worse place. But one day this happen.

We were walking round and round in the yard and I hear a woman singing—the voice come from high up, from one of the small barred windows. At first I don't believe it. Why should anybody sing here? Nobody want to sing in jail, nobody want to do anything. There's no reason, and you have no hope. I think I must be asleep, dreaming, but I'm awake all right and I see all the others are listening too. A nurse is with us that afternoon, not a policewoman. She stop and look up at the window.

It's a smoky kind of voice, and a bit rough sometimes, as if those old dark walls theyselves are complaining, because they see too much misery—too much. But it don't fall down and die in the courtyard; seems to me it could jump the gates of the jail easy and travel far, and

nobody could stop it. I don't hear the words—only the music. She sing one verse and she begin another, then she break off sudden. Everybody starts walking again, and nobody says one word. But as we go in I ask the woman in front who was singing. "That's the Holloway song," she says. "Don't you know it yet? She was singing from the punishment cells, and she tell the girls cheerio and never say die." Then I have to go one way to the hospital block and she goes another so we don't speak again.

When I'm back in my cell I can't just wait for bed. I walk up and down and I think. "One day I hear that song on trumpets and these walls will fall and rest."[1] I want to get out so bad I could hammer on the door, for I know now that anything can happen, and I don't want to stay lock up here and miss it.

Then I'm hungry. I eat everything they bring and in the morning I'm still so hungry I eat the porridge. Next time the doctor come he tells me I seem much better. Then I say a little of what really happen in that house. Not much. Very careful.

He look at me hard and kind of surprised. At the door he shake his finger and says, "Now don't let me see you here again."

That evening the woman tells me I'm going, but she's so upset about it I don't ask questions. Very early, before it's light she bangs the door open and shouts at me to hurry up. As we're going along the passages I see the girl who gave me the books. She's in a row with others doing exercises. Up Down, Up Down, Up. We pass quite close and I notice she's looking very pale and tired. It's crazy, it's all crazy. This up down business and everything else too. When they give me my money I remember I leave my compact in the cell, so I ask if I can go back for it. You should see that policewoman's face as she shoo me on.

There's no car, there's a van and you can't see through the windows. The third time it stop I get out with one other, a young girl, and it's the same magistrates' court as before.

The two of us wait in a small room, nobody else there, and after a while the girl say, "What the hell are they doing? I don't want to spend all day here." She go to the bell and she keep her finger press on it. When I

---

[1] *One day ... rest* Cf. Joshua 6, in which the sound of trumpets brings down the walls of Jericho.

look at her she say, "Well, what are they *for?*" That girl's face is hard like a board—she could change faces with many and you wouldn't know the difference. But she get results certainly. A policeman come in, all smiling, and we go in the court. The same magistrate, the same frowning man sits below, and when I hear my fine is paid I want to ask who paid it, but he yells at me. "Silence."

I think I will never understand the half of what happen, but they tell me I can go, and I understand that. The magistrate ask if I'm leaving the neighbourhood and I say yes, then I'm out in the streets again, and it's the same fine weather, same feeling I'm dreaming.

When I get to the house I see two men talking in the garden. The front door and the door of the flat are both open. I go in, and the bedroom is empty, nothing but the glare streaming inside because they take the Venetian blinds away. As I'm wondering where my suitcase is, and the clothes I leave in the wardrobe, there's a knock and it's the old lady from upstairs carrying my case packed, and my coat is over her arm. She says she sees me come in. "I kept your things for you." I start to thank her but she turn her back and walk away. They like that here, and better not expect too much. Too besides, I bet they tell her I'm terrible person.

I go in the kitchen, but when I see they are cutting down the big tree at the back I don't stay to watch.

At the station I'm waiting for the train and a woman asks if I feel well. "You look so tired," she says. "Have you come a long way?" I want to answer, "I come so far I lose myself on that journey." But I tell her, "Yes, I am quite well. But I can't stand the heat." She says she can't stand it either, and we talk about the weather till the train come in.

I'm not frightened of them any more—after all what else can they do ? I know what to say and everything go like a clock works.

I get a room near Victoria where the landlady accept one pound in advance, and next day I find a job in the kitchen of a private hotel close by. But I don't stay there

long. I hear of another job going in a big store—altering ladies' dresses and I get that. I lie and tell them I work in very expensive New York shop. I speak bold and smooth faced, and they never check up on me. I make a friend there—Clarice—very light coloured, very smart, she have a lot to do with the customers and she laugh at some of them behind their backs. But I say it's not their fault if the dress don't fit. Special dress for one person only—that's very expensive in London. So it's take in, or let out all the time. Clarice have two rooms not far from the store. She furnish them herself gradual and she gives parties sometimes Saturday nights. It's there I start whistling the Holloway Song. A man comes up to me and says, "Let's hear that again." So I whistle it again (I never sing now) and he tells me "Not bad." Clarice have an old piano somebody give her to store and he plays the tune, jazzing it up. I say, "No, not like that," but everybody else say the way he do it is first class. Well I think no more of this till I get a letter from him telling me he has sold the song and as I was quite a help he encloses five pounds with thanks.

I read the letter and I could cry. For after all, that song was all I had. I don't belong nowhere really, and I haven't money to buy my way to belonging. I don't want to either.

But when that girl sing, she sing to me, and she sing for me. I was there because I was *meant* to be there. It was *meant* I should hear it—this I *know.*

Now I've let them play it wrong, and it will go from me like all the other songs—like everything. Nothing left for me at all.

But then I tell myself all this is foolishness. Even if they played it on trumpets, even if they played it just right, like I wanted—no walls would fall so soon. "So let them call it jazz," I think, and let them play it wrong. That won't make no difference to the song I heard.

I buy myself a dusty pink dress with the money.

—1962

SYLVIA TOWNSEND WARNER
1893 – 1978

Sylvia Townsend Warner's career spanned over fifty years and included novels, short stories, poetry, essays, translations, and biography writing. Though she is associated with British Modernism, she has long been overshadowed by her contemporary Virginia Woolf, but her writing has gained greater recognition in recent years. Her work attracted the notice of feminist scholars in the 1970s for its depictions of female autonomy and passionate relationships between women, and in the 1980s and 1990s the publication of diaries and of several biographies captured the interest of a broader public. In 2000, the Sylvia Townsend Warner Society was created in order to support scholarship and further the recognition of Warner's influence and large body of work.

Warner was born in Harrow-on-the-Hill, north London, the only child of Nora and George Townsend Warner. George was a well-liked housemaster at Harrow School; he had a close bond with his daughter, and inspired her to develop an early interest in a variety of intellectual activities. Educated at home, Warner pursued a passion for music, planning to study with Austrian composer and music theorist Arnold Shoenberg—an arrangement prevented by the outbreak of World War I. In 1917, opportunity came closer to home with a position on a committee assembling ten volumes of Tudor Church music for Oxford University Press. It is through this association that Warner became close to Percy Buck, music director at her father's school and married father of five; the two became involved in a secret relationship that lasted until 1929.

In 1922, Warner visited the marshes in Essex and experienced an artistic awakening; she started a novel, began writing poems, and experimented with a play. In Chaldon Herring, Dorset, she visited writer Theodore Powyrs, and there she became a part of an active circle of writers and intellectuals, including Stephen Tomlin and David Garnett. Warner published her first book of verse, *The Espalier*, in 1925; in 1926 she finished *Lolly Willowes*, a novel centered on a protagonist who escapes the rigid society into which she is born for a natural world of freedom and magic. Popular in her own country and across the Atlantic, the book charmed readers with its realistic characters and its elements of fantasy. A chance to be the guest editor of the *New York Herald Tribune* followed in 1929, and at the same time as this professional success, Warner also experienced a personal transformation. While staying in Chaldron Herring, she became acquainted with the poet Valentine Ackland. Ackland, thirteen years younger than Warner, had recently had her marriage annulled and changed her name from Molly to the androgynous Valentine; she and Warner would begin a life-long passionate and often tumultuous relationship. The couple frequently returned to Dorset in between professional opportunities in London and elsewhere, and often worked or shared projects, including the publication of a joint poetry collection, *Whether a Dove or Seagull*, in 1933.

Through her interactions with Ackland, who was an occasional contributor to the *Left Review*, Warner began to define her own evolving political beliefs. The pair joined the Communist party in 1935 and threw their efforts into activism: fundraising, writing, and working for the Republican cause during the Spanish Civil War, first with the Red Cross in Barcelona and later as part of the Second Congress of the International Association of Writers for the Defence of Culture in Madrid and Valencia. Warner's fiction reflected her political concerns; in 1938 she published *After the Death of*

Don Juan, a novel critics considered to be heavily influenced by the Civil War. Though Warner would eventually become disillusioned with the Communist party, she continued to express her concern for the oppressed and the excluded through her writing.

The novels Warner wrote after the 1920s were less commercially popular, but her short stories were consistently well received. Published in the *New Yorker* over a span of almost fifty years, her stories display great diversity both of subject matter and of style. Her fiction is by turns realistic and dreamlike. It can focus as strongly on the supernatural as it often does on human psychology. Warner emphasizes the individuality of her characters but returns repeatedly to certain themes: class, the process of aging, and the sense of isolation that so many long to escape but are unable to. She published seven novels in all, with settings as diverse as Paris during the 1848 revolution (*Summer Will Show,* 1936), a medieval convent (*The Corner that Held Them,* 1948), and a mission in the South Seas (*Mr. Fortune's Maggot,* 1926). She wrote more than 150 short stories, translated two texts from French, and produced a biography of T.H. White (1967).

Working on the story of White's life may have inspired Warner to think about her own personal and literary legacy. Ackland suffered from poor health for many years and as they grew older, Warner began collecting and annotating diaries and compiling the letters exchanged between the two. She released her last collection of stories, *Kingdoms of Elfin,* in 1977. At her death at age eighty-four, Warner's ashes were placed with Ackland's in a church yard in Chaldon. Warner's archive, *I'll Stand by You: The Letters of Sylvia Townsend & Valentine Ackland,* was published in 1998, and Warner's other diaries and archives have since been published, giving contemporary and future readers a view of her unique imagination and perspective.

⌘ ⌘ ⌘

I Saw Spain

It was our first day in Spain. We were at Port-Bou, in Catalonia,[1] the little frontier fishing town. Our passports had been visaed by the Workers' Committee, we had only to wait for the afternoon train to Barcelona.

We sat drinking coffee and staring at the profound Mediterranean blue of the bay, the pale slopes of the Pyrenees,[2] and trying to read the newspaper in Catalan. One of the members of the Committee, a grave grey haired man, speaking a slow, very pure French, came to our table, saying that he had a quarter of an hour to himself, and would have his coffee with us. He helped us with the newspaper, and told us of the situation of the town, its fishers and small holders enrolled in the militia.

He apologised for yawning, saying he had been up all night. There was so much to be done, he said. He looked as though he had been up for many nights. "Do you ever sleep?" I asked him.

"With one eye," he answered.

THE PATROL TUG

Just then we heard the hoot of a siren. The children ran to the water's edge, four or five militiamen with old-fashioned muskets or revolvers joined the children, women came out of the houses and stood shading their eyes, looking towards the sea.

"Something abnormal," said our friend. We too got up and walked down to the water's edge. The siren hooted again, a small tug came round the headland.

"She patrols this coast," he said, "She must have

---

[1] *Catalonia*   Region of northeastern Spain that was a stronghold for the Republican (i.e., anti-fascist) side in the Spanish Civil War (1936–39). The war officially began when a conservative military uprising, led by Francisco Franco, attempted to remove a recently elected leftist government; Franco would eventually win the war with military support from other fascist leaders. Many European and North American volunteers came to Spain to fight against fascism as members of International Brigades.

[2] *Pyrenees*   Mountain range between Spain and France.

something to report, she does not usually come in at this hour."

While we stood watching he pointed to a little hut on the headland. Look-out men were stationed there, day and night. If they saw and enemy ship, or the Italian planes coming from Majorca,[1] they blew a whistle. The alarm would be taken up by other watchers blowing a siren fixed in the church tower, and at that warning the people of Port-Bou would be ready to take shelter.

"We shelter," he said, smiling rather satirically, pointing to the dark hole in the hillside, the railway track leading into it, "we shelter in the International Tunnel."

"Is there any defence for the town?" I asked. He looked at the handful of militiamen, the children, grave and alert, silently watching the tug coming in.

"What you see."

That group of men and children on the shingle,[2] watchful and resolute, that half-dozen of poor arms, the old tug, hooting like a mother bird giving its warning note … this was our first sight of the Workers' Spain against which the weight of Europe is actively or passively engaged. Our friend, bleached with fatigue, haggard with responsibility, nothing bright about him except his clear eyes and the scarlet of the badge in his buttonhole (PSUC, United Socialist Party of Catalonia) was one of those brutal Marxists who endanger, so we are told, the whole régime of civilisation.

RAMONA, A MILITIA GIRL

Bright-eyed Ramona, militia girl, aged twenty-four, her solid thighs and round bosom filling out her brown dungaree uniform, a revolver in her belt, her quartermaster's badge on her breast, was, when we met her, already a veteran. She had taken part in the ill-fated expedition to Majorca[3] when volunteer troops were landed on an island where they expected to confront only Spanish Fascism, and found instead the superior forces of international Fascism. The position taken in the first

rush was held for three weeks, it was hunger at last which forced it to be evacuated. "When we saw a cat …" said Ramona. "But at last there was not another cat to be found."

Above the bright eyes, which had looked death so steadfastly in the face, were a pair of plucked eyebrows. Ramona the veteran, Ramona who could take a machine gun to pieces and reassemble it without a bungle, had not been long enough in the army to grow her natural eyebrows again.

"Before I joined the army I was a shop girl," she said.

"What did you sell?"

"Mothers of God and ice-creams," she replied.

"A religious place," she explained. "A village in the mountains, like a little Lourdes.[4] It belonged, all of it, to a Fascist, he exploited it, it was his property.

"So were we," she continued. "We girls, who sold at his shop and waited at his restaurant. If a girl was young, that was enough for him, he would seduce her. But she must be young. When she had a baby, then his mother would dismiss her. She was religious, that old mother, she loved just three things, the church, and money and her son. All night she would pray and weep because her son was a sinner. Then in the morning she would hire another young girl."

"Were you seduced, Ramona?"

"Not I! I was in my Trade Union, I was a Socialist, I had ideas. And I was old, too—too old for him. They would not have kept me only I was smart and a good saleswoman, and made money for them.

"I used to talk to the other girls, argue with them, you know, but they were too tired to listen to me, or too much afraid of the boss and the old woman. We slept all in one attic, like in a barracks. At five in the morning she would come in, scolding us for lying so long in bed.

"And they got away," she exclaimed, beating her brown fist on the table. "I ran all the way to the Committee in the town, I said to them, 'This man is a Fascist, the woman is religious, all their money will go to buy arms to kill us if we do not get it now.' And they sent men. But it was too late, they were off, both of them, with their money. Nothing was left but the rosaries and the images, and the girls with their unborn babies.

---

[1] *Majorca* Island off the east coast of Spain. During the Spanish Civil War, the fascist military used it as an air force base.

[2] *shingle* Beach.

[3] *ill-fated expedition to Majorca* I.e., the Battle of Majorca (1936), a failed attempt by Republican forces to capture the island from the fascist military. The Republicans had greater numbers but insufficient supplies and inferior airpower.

[4] *Lourdes* Town in southwest France that attracts many Roman Catholic pilgrims.

"All that money," she said furiously. "Shooting us down!" She talked as candidly as a bird sings, there was only one subject from which she would flinch aside, become preoccupied and reserved. It did not do to ask her when the Centuria[1] to which she belonged might go again into the fighting line. For recently the military authorities of loyal Spain had been discountenancing the *milicianas*, no more women were permitted to enlist, those already in the militia were being weeded out. Ramona would need all her prowess and her persuasion, her skill with machine guns, her reputation as a superb quartermaster, if she were to go into the fight again. This unwomaning of the Workers' Militia was given great prominence in the capitalist newspapers of Europe, and attributed by them to one of two causes: that the *milicianas* ran away, or that they spread venereal disease. The actual reason was different, a something unsuspected by the ruling class. It had been found that the sight of a dead or wounded woman tended to set up curious reactions in the men fighting, men, one must remember, untrained in warfare, and for the most part deprived of the rallying effect of being officered by people of the ruling class. These men, seeing their women fellow-soldiers fall dead, or lie writhing, lost their heads. Horror, or furious rage, took possession of them; forgetting caution, forgetting rather that military version of caution which is called discipline, they would rush upon the enemy, calling them Butchers, and Fascists, and get needlessly killed themselves. And since there was no time to train away this working-class chivalry, it was thought best to withdraw the women from the fighting ranks.

So now, though the fascists have still a good chance of killing Ramona, she is likeliest to be shot in a captured town, or killed as a civilian in an air raid. To the fascists this will make little difference, a worker dead is a worker dead to them. But it will make a considerable difference to Ramona, so proud in her uniform, wearing her forage cap so jauntily with the tassel dangling above her bright eyes.

A LONG WALK FROM SWITZERLAND

I met him at the Department of Strangers, the office which deals with the affairs of all extra-nationals in Barcelona. He was a large raw-boned man with small grey eyes, his clothes were shabby, his boots were torn. He was sitting on a small gold chair with a red velvet seat (for the Department of Strangers is housed in what used to be a luxury hotel), grim as a man of stone, and in a furious temper.

As I neared him he said in a rasping voice:

"Do you speak French? Well, listen to this. This place is not businesslike."

"They are very busy," I said appeasingly.

"Bah! I came here yesterday, and told them that I want to enlist myself in the International Legion. They told me to come again this morning, when they would have made my arrangements. I came this morning, half an hour ago, and I am still waiting." Leaning forward, squawking his elegant chair on the parquet, he added, "I find it very irksome."

"Other people are waiting, too," I said. "You must take your turn, even to enlist."

Locking his bony hands, he went on:

"I came here to fight, not to wait. I walk here from Switzerland …"

"From Switzerland?"

The exclamation was startled out of me. I had a ridiculous vision of this angry man stalking out of a chalet, setting out on his walk, saying abruptly over his shoulder, in answer to a question cried from within the chalet, "To Spain."

He strode over my question.

"I was unemployed, I had no money for trains, so I walked. We have Fascists in Switzerland too, I know them. I come here to fight them, and I am kept waiting. Thirty five minutes, now."

My name was called. The man for whom I was translating had been summoned for his interview. As I got up the angry man said, in a tone of even profounder resentment:

"If you get a chance, you might mention in there that I have come here to fight."

When I came out again into the waiting room I looked round for my angry man, to assure him that the word had been spoken, that his affair was already in hand. But he was gone, my angry man. Instead, I saw a beaming stranger, who had borrowed his boots and his travel stained clothes, and who was filling out a form

[1] *Centuria* Military company.

and signing his name in a handwriting full of exultant and stately flourishes.

"It's all right," he said, recognising me vaguely as something recalled from a nightmare. "It's all right. I'm going to the Karl Marx Barracks right away."
—1937

A Love Match

It was Mr. Pilkington who brought the Tizards to Hallowby. He met them, a quiet couple, at Carnac,[1] where he had gone for a schoolmasterly Easter holiday to look at the monoliths. After two or three meetings at a café, they invited him to their rented chalet. It was a cold, wet afternoon and a fire of pine cones crackled on the hearth. "We collect them on our walks," said Miss Tizard. "It's an economy. And it gives us object." The words, and the formal composure of her manner, made her seem like a Frenchwoman. Afterwards, he learned that the Tizards were a Channel Island family and had spent their childhood in Jersey.[2] The ancestry that surfaced in Miss Tizard's brisk gait and erect carriage, brown skin and compact sentences, did not show in her brother. His fair hair, his red face, his indecisive remarks, his diffident movements—as though with the rest of his body he were apologising for his stiff leg—were entirely English. He ought not, thought Mr. Pilkington, to be hanging about in France. He'd done more than enough for France already. For this was in 1923 and Mr. Pilkington, with every intention of preserving a historian's impartiality, was nevertheless infected by the current mood of disliking the French.[3]

The weather continued cold and wet; there was a sameness about the granite avenues. Mr. Pilkington's mind became increasingly engaged with the possibility,

the desirability, the positive duty of saving that nice fellow Tizard from wasting his days in exile. He plied him with hints, with suggestions, with tactful inquiries. Beyond discovering that money was not the obstacle to return, he got no further. Tizard, poor fellow, must be under his sister's thumb. Yet it was from the sister that he got his first plain answer. "Justin would mope if he had nothing to do." Mr. Pilkington stopped himself from commenting on the collection of pine cones as an adequate lifework. As though she had read his thought, she went on, "There is a difference between idling in a foreign country and being an idler in your own." At that moment Tizard limped into the room with crayfish bristling from his shopping basket. "It's begun," he said ruefully. "La Jeune France[4] has arrived. I've just seen two young men in pink trousers with daisy chains round their necks, riding through the town on donkeys." Mr. Pilkington asked if this was a circus. Miss Tizard explained that it was the new generation, and would make Carnac a bedlam[5] till the summer's end. "Of course, there's a certain amount of that sort of thing in England, too," observed Mr. Pilkington. "But only in the South. It doesn't trouble us at Hallowby." As he spoke, he was conscious of playing a good card; then the immensity of the trump he held broke upon him. He was too excited to speak. Inviting them to dine at his hotel on the following night, he went away.

By next evening, more of La Jeune France had arrived, and was mustered outside the hotel extemporising[6] a bullfight ballet in honour of St Cornély, patron saint of cattle and of the parish church. Watching Tizard's look of stoically endured embarrassment Mr. Pilkington announced that he had had a blow; the man who had almost promised to become curator of the Beelby Military Museum had written to say he couldn't take up the post. "He didn't say why. But I know why. Hallowby is too quiet for him."

---

[1] *Carnac* Town in northwestern France known for its large number of prehistoric stone monuments.

[2] *Channel Island family* The Tizards come from the Channel Islands, a group of British islands located in the English Channel; *Jersey* Largest of the Channel Islands.

[3] *current ... French* Relations between England and France, allies during World War I, were strained in the years after the war as both countries tried to recover from economic devastation and often took opposing stances towards international relations, especially regarding Germany.

[4] *La Jeune France* Literally, "Young France"; the term was first applied to young men of nineteenth-century Paris who adopted an unconventional, rebellious style of dress and behavior.

[5] *bedlam* Chaotic scene; the word derives from the common name given to a famously overcrowded asylum for the emotionally disturbed.

[6] *extemporising* Improvising.

"But I thought Hallowby had blast furnaces and strikes[1] and all that sort of thing," said Tizard.

"That is Hallowby juxta Mare,"[2] replied Mr. Pilkington. "We are Old Hallowby. Very quiet; quite old, too. The school was founded in 1623. We shall be having our modest tercentenary[3] this summer. That is why I am so put out by Dalsover's not taking up the curatorship. I hoped to have the museum all in order. It would have been something to visit, if it rains during the Celebrations." He allowed a pause.

Tizard, staring at the toothpicks, inquired, "Is it a wet climate?"

But Mr. Pilkington was the headmaster of a minor public school, a position of command. As if the pause had not taken place, raising his voice above the bullfight he told how fifty years earlier Davenport Beelby, a rich man's sickly son, during a lesson on the Battle of Minden[4] awoke to military glory and began to collect regimental buttons. Buttons, badges, pikes, muskets and bayonets, shakos and helmets, despatches,[5] newspaper cuttings, stones from European battlefields, sand from desert campaigns—his foolish collection grew into the lifework of a devoted eccentric and, as such collections sometimes do, became valuable and authoritative, though never properly catalogued. Two years ago he had died, bequeathing the collection to his old school, with a fund sufficient for upkeep and the salary of a curator.

"I wish you'd consider coming as our curator," said Mr. Pilkington. "I'm sure you would find it congenial. Beelby wanted an Army man. Three mornings a week would be quite enough."

Tizard shifted his gaze from the toothpicks to the mustard jar. "I am not an Army man," he said. "I just fought. Not the same thing, you know."

Miss Tizard exclaimed, "No! Not at all," and changed the subject.

But later that evening she said to her brother, "Once we were there, we shouldn't see much of him. It's a possibility."

"Do you want to go home, Celia?"

"I think it's time we did. We were both of us born for a sober, conventional, taxpaying life, and if—'

"Voici Noël!" sang the passing voices. "Voici Noël! Voici Noël, petits enfants!"[6]

She composed her twitching hands and folded them on her lap. "We were young rowdies once," he said placatingly.

A fortnight[7] later, they were Mr. Pilkington's guests at Hallowby. A list of empty houses had been compiled by Miss Robson, the secretary. All were variously suitable; each in turn was inspected by Miss Tizard and rejected. Mr. Pilkington felt piqued that his offer of a post should dance attendance on the aspect of a larder or the presence of decorative tiles. Miss Tizard was a disappointment to him; he had relied on her support. Now it was the half-hearted Tizard who seemed inclined to root, while she flitted from one eligible residence to another, appearing, as he remarked to the secretary, to expect impossibilities. Yet when she settled as categorically as a queen bee the house she chose had really nothing to be said for it. A square, squat mid-Victorian box, Newton Lodge was one of the ugliest houses in Hallowby; though a high surrounding wall with a green door in it hid the totality of its ugliness from passers-by, its hulking chimneys proclaimed what was below. It was not even well situated. It stood in a deteriorating part of the town, and was at some distance from the school buildings and the former gymnasium—Victorian also—which had been assigned to the Beelby Collection. But the house having been chosen, the curatorship was bestowed and the move made. Justin Tizard, rescued from wasting his days in exile—though too late for the tercentenary celebrations—began his duties as curator by destroying a quantity of cobwebs and sending for a window-cleaner.

[1] blast furnaces Large furnaces used for smelting ores; strikes After World War I, tension between British industrial workers and their employers increased; the conflict culminated in a nine-day general strike in 1926.

[2] juxta Mare Latin: By the sea. Though this town is fictitious, several English towns (e.g., Bradwell Juxta Mare, Weston Super Mare) have names that include similar Latin components.

[3] tercentenary Three hundred year anniversary.

[4] Battle of Minden 1759 British defeat of French forces during the Seven Years' War (1756–63).

[5] bayonets Steel-bladed weapons attached to guns and used to slash an opponent; shakos Tall, cylindrical military hats; despatches Official correspondences.

[6] Voici Noël Song by French composer Jean-Baptiste Weckerlin (1821–1910); Voici Noël, petits enfants! French: It is Christmas, little children!

[7] fortnight Period of two weeks.

All through the summer holidays he worked on, sorting things into heaps, subdividing the heaps into lesser heaps. Beelby's executors must have given carte-blanche to the packers, who had acted on the principle of filling up with anything that came handy, and the unpackers had done little more than tumble things out and scatter them with notices saying "DO NOT DIS-TURB." The largest heap consisted of objects he could not account for, but unaccountably it lessened, till the day came when he could look round on tidiness. Ambition seized him. Tidiness is not enough; no one looks twice at tidiness. There must also be parade and ostentation. He bought stands, display cases, dummies for the best uniforms. Noticing a decayed wooden horse in the saddler's shop, he bought that, too; trapped, with its worser side to the wall and with a cavalry dummy astride, it made a splendid appearance. He combed plumes, shook out bearskins, polished holsters and gunstocks, oiled the demi-culverin,[1] sieved the desert sand. At this stage, his sister came and polished with him, mended, refurbished, sewed on loose buttons. Of the two, she had more feeling for the exhibits them-selves, for the discolouring glory and bloodshed they represented. It was the housewife's side that appealed to him. Sometimes, hearing him break into the whistle of a contented mind, she would look up from her work and stare at him with the unbelief of thankfulness.

Early in the autumn term, Mr. Pilkington made time to visit the museum. He did not expect much and came prepared with speeches of congratulation and encouragement. They died on his lips when he saw the transformation. Instead, he asked how much the display cases had cost, and the dummies, and the horse, and how much of the upkeep fund remained after all this expenditure. He could not find fault; there was no reason to do so. He was pleased to see Tizard so well established as master in his own house. Perhaps he was also pleased that there was no reason to find fault. Though outwardly unchanged, the Tizard of Carnac appeared to have been charged with new contents—with something obstinately reckless beneath the easy-going manner, with watchfulness beneath the diffi-dence. But this, reflected Mr. Pilkington, might well be accounted for by the startling innovations in the mu-seum. He stayed longer than he meant, and only after

leaving remembered that he had omitted to say how glad he was that Tizard had accepted the curatorship. This must be put right; he did not want to discourage the young man who had worked so hard and so effi-ciently, and also he must get into the way of remember-ing that Tizard was in fact a young man—under thirty. Somehow, one did not think of him as a young man.

Justin Tizard, newly a captain in an infantry regiment, came on leave after the battle of the Somme.[2] His sister met the train at Victoria. There were some pigeons strutting on the platform and he was watching them when a strange woman in black came up to him, touched his shoulder, and said, "Justin!" It was as though Celia were claiming a piece of lost luggage, he thought. She had a taxi waiting, and they drove to her flat. She asked about his health, about his journey; then she congratulated him on his captaincy. "Practical reasons," he said. "My habit of not getting killed. They were bound to notice it sooner or later." After this, they fell silent. He looked out of the window at the streets so clean and the people so busy with their own affairs. "That's a new Bovril[3] poster, isn't it?" he inquired. Her answer was so slow in coming that he didn't really take in whether it was yes or no.

Her flat was new, anyway. She had only been in it since their mother's remarriage. It was up a great many flights of stairs, and she spoke of moving to somewhere with a lift, now that Tim's legacy had made a rich woman of her. The room smelled of polish and flowers. There was a light-coloured rug on the floor and above this was the blackness of Celia's skirts. She was wearing black for her fiancé. The news of his death had come to her in this same room, while she was still sorting books and hanging pictures. Looking round the room, still not looking at Celia, he saw Tim's photograph on her desk. She saw his glance, and hers followed it. "Poor Tim!" they said, both speaking at once, the timbre of their voices relating them. "They say he was killed instantaneously," she went on. "I hope it's true—though I suppose they always say that."

---

1   *demi-culverin*   Type of cannon.

2   *battle of the Somme*   July–November 1916 offensive of the Allied forces against the Germans, who were positioned at the Somme River in northern France. With more than a million casualties, it was one of the bloodiest battles of the First World War.

3   *Bovril*   Beef extract product popular in Britain.

"I'm sure it is," he replied. He knew that Tim had been blown to pieces. Compassion made it possible to look at her. Dressed in black, possessing these new surroundings, she seemed mature and dignified beyond her actual three years' seniority. For the first time in his life he saw her not as a sister but as an individual. But he could not see her steadily for long. There was a blur on his sight, a broth of mud and flame and frantic unknown faces and writhing entrails. When she showed him to his bedroom she stepped over mud that heaved with the bodies of men submerged in it. She had drawn the curtains. There was a bed with sheets turned back, and a bedside lamp shed a serene, unblinking light on the pillows. "Bed!" he exclaimed, and heard the spontaneity die in his voice. "Wonderful to see a bed!"

"And this is the bathroom. I've got everything planned. First of all, you must have a bath, lie and soak in it. And then put on these pyjamas and the dressing gown, and we will have supper."

Left to himself, he was violently sick. Shaking with fatigue, he sat in a hot scented bath and cleaned his knees with scrupulous care, like a child. Outside was the noise of London.

The pyjamas were silk, the dressing gown was quilted and wrapped him round like a caress. In the sitting room was Celia, still a stranger, though now a stranger without a hat. There was a table sparkling with silver and crystal, smoked salmon, a bottle of champagne. It was all as she had planned it for Tim—Oh, poor Celia!

They discussed their mother's remarriage. It had been decided on with great suddenness, and appeared inexplicable. Though they refrained from saying much, their comments implied that her only reason for marrying a meat king from the Argentine was to get away from England and the war. "There he was, at eleven in the morning, with a carnation—a foot shorter than she," said Celia, describing the return from the registry office.

"In that case, he must be four foot three."

"He is exactly four foot three. I stole up and measured him."

Spoken in her imperturbable voice, this declaration struck him as immensely funny, as funny as a nursery joke. They laughed hilariously, and after this their evening went almost naturally.

Turning back after his unadorned, brotherly "Good night, Celia," he exclaimed, "But where are you sleeping?"

"In here." Before he could demur[1] she went on, "The sofa fits me. It would be far too short for you."

He told her how balmily[2] he had slept, one night behind the lines, with his head on a bag of nails.

"Exactly! That is why tonight you are going to sleep properly. In a bed."

She heard him get into bed, heard the lamp switched off. Almost immediately she heard his breathing lengthen into slumber. Then, a few minutes later, he began to talk in his sleep.

Perhaps a scruple—the dishonourableness of being an eavesdropper, a Peeping Tom—perhaps mere craven terror, made her try not to listen. She began to read, and when she found that impossible she repeated poems she had learned at school, and when that failed she polished the silver cigarette box. But Justin's voice was raised, and the partition wall was thin, and the ghastly confidences went on and on. She could not escape them. She was dragged, a raw recruit, into battle.

In the morning she thought she would not be able to look him in the face. But he was cheerful, and so was she. She had got off from the canteen, she explained, while he was on leave; they had nothing to do but enjoy themselves. They decided to have some new experiences, so they went up the Monument.[3] If he wants to throw himself off, she thought, I won't stop him. They looked down on London; on the curve of the Thames, the shipping, the busy lighters.[4] They essayed[5] how many City churches they could identify by their spires. They talked about Pepys.[6] She would be surprised, Justin said, how many chaps carried a copy of the Diary, and she asked if bullets also glanced off Pepys carried in a breast

---

[1] *demur* I.e., protest.

[2] *balmily* Relaxedly, refreshingly.

[3] *the Monument* Column commemorating the Great Fire of London and offering tourists a panoramic view of the city.

[4] *lighters* Flat-bottomed barges used to load ships.

[5] *essayed* Tested, tried.

[6] *Pepys* Samuel Pepys (1633–1703), naval official whose *Diary* detailing life in seventeenth-century England became popular reading in the centuries after his death.

pocket.[1] So they made conversation quite successfully. And afterwards, when they had decided to go for a walk down Whitechapel High Street and lunch off winkles[2] at a stall, many people glanced at them with kindness and sentimentality, and an old woman patted Celia's back, saying, "God bless you, dearie! Isn't it lovely to have him home?"

Whitechapel was a good idea. The throng of people carried some of the weight of self-consciousness for them; the wind blowing up-river and the hooting of ships' sirens made them feel they were in some foreign port of call, taking a stroll till it was time to re-embark. He was less aware that she had grown strange to him, and she was momentarily able to forget the appalling stranger who had raved in her bed all night.

They dined at a restaurant, and went on to a music hall.[3] That night he took longer to fall asleep. She had allowed herself a thread of hope, when he began to talk again. Three Justins competed, thrusting each other aside: a cold, attentive observer, a debased child, a devil bragging in hell. At intervals they were banished by a recognisable Justin interminably muttering to himself, "Here's a sword for Toad, here's a sword for Rat, here's a sword for Mole, here's a sword for Badger." The reiteration from that bible of their childhood[4] would stick on the word, "Rat." "Got you!" And he was off again.

The next day they went to the Zoo. The Zoo was not so efficacious as Whitechapel. It was feeling the pinch, the animals looked shabby and dejected, many cages were empty. Two sleepless nights had made Celia's feet swell. It was pain to walk, pain to stand. She wondered how much longer she could keep it up, this

"God bless you, dearie" pretence of a lovely leave. The day accumulated its hours like a windlass.[5] The load grew heavier; the windlass baulked under it, but wound on. He went to bed with the usual "Good night, Celia." As usual, she undressed and put on that derision[6] of a nightdress, and wrapped herself in an eiderdown and lay down to wait under the smiling gaze of Tim's photograph. She felt herself growing icy cold, couldn't remember if she had wound her watch, couldn't remember what diversion she had planned for the morrow, was walking over Richmond Bridge[7] in a snowstorm, when she noticed he had begun again. *She noticed.* It had come to that. Two nights of a vicarious endurance of what was being endured, had been endured, would continue to be endured by a cancelled generation, had so exhausted her that now she felt neither horror nor despair, merely a bitter acquiescence. Justin went on with his Hail Devil Rosary, and in France the guns went on and on,[8] and the mud dried into dust and slumped back into mud again. People went down to Kent to listen to the noise of the guns:[9] the people in Kent said that they had grown used to it, didn't hear it any longer. The icy cold sensation bored into her midriff, nailed her down in sleep.

Some outcry, some exclamation (she could not afterwards remember what it was), woke her. Before she knew what she was doing she was in the next room, trying to waken the man who lay so rigidly in her bed, who, if she could awaken him, would be Justin, her brother Justin. "Oh, poor Justin, my poor Justin!" Throwing herself on the bed, she clasped him in her arms, lifted his head to lie against her breast, kissed his chattering lips. "There, there!" She felt him relax, waken, drag her towards him. They rushed into the

---

[1] *bullets also … breast pocket* Reference to popular stories of soldiers who survived a bullet because its force was slowed by a bible carried in a fortuitous place.

[2] *Whitechapel High Street* Famous street running through London's East End; *winkles* Periwinkles, any of several types of shellfish eaten in Europe.

[3] *music hall* Theater where variety shows were performed.

[4] *bible … childhood* Kenneth Grahame's children's book *The Wind in the Willows* (1908), which depicts the lives of four friends: Toad, Rat, Mole, and Badger. In the climactic episode, the friends take up arms against a horde of weasels and stoats who have invaded Toad Hall; the quotation regarding swords is from the scene in which weapons are distributed. During the battle itself Rat utters gleeful exclamations as he strikes down various stoats and weasels.

[5] *windlass* Horizontal spool with a crank, used to lift large objects by winding a hoisting rope around the spool.

[6] *derision* Object of scorn.

[7] *Richmond Bridge* Bridge crossing the Thames at Richmond, in southwest London.

[8] *Hail Devil Rosary* Play on the Roman Catholic Rosary, a sequence of prayers in which the "Hail Mary" devotion features; *in France … and on* A great deal of fighting during World War I took place on the battlefields of France.

[9] *Kent … guns* As England's south-easternmost county, Kent is the part of England closest to France.

escape of love like winter-starved cattle rushing into a spring pasture.

When light came into the room, they drew a little apart and looked at each other.

"Now we've done it," he said; and hearing the new note in his voice she replied, "A good thing, don't you think?"

Their release left them no option. After a few hours they were not even astonished. They were mated for life, that was all—for a matter of days, so they made the most of it. At the end of his leave they parted in exaltation, he convinced that he was going off to be killed, she that she would bear his child, to which she would devote the remainder of her existence.

A little later she knew she was not pregnant.

Early in the new year Justin, still panoplied[1] in this legendary and by now rather ludicrous charmed life, was made a major. In April, he was wounded in the leg. "Nothing to worry about," he wrote; "just a few splinters. I am in bed, as peaceful as a pincushion." Later, she heard that he had been moved to a hospital on the outskirts of London. One of the splinters had escaped notice, and gas gangrene[2] had developed in the wound.

I shall be a peg leg, he thought. It's not decent for a peg leg to make love; even to his sister. He was ravaged with fret and behaving with perfect decorum when Celia was shown in—dressed all in leaf green, walking like an empress, smelling delicious. For a moment the leaf-green Celia was almost as much of a stranger as the Celia all in black had been. When she kissed him, he discovered that she was shaking from head to foot. "There, there," he said, patting her. Still holding his hand, she addressed herself to charming Nurse Painter. Nurse Painter was in favour of sisters. They weren't so much trouble, didn't upset a patient, as sweethearts or wives did—and you didn't have to be hanging round all the time, ready to shoo them off. When Celia came next day, Nurse Painter congratulated her on having done the Major no end of good. There had been a lot of pus; she liked to see a lot of pus.

They continued to give satisfaction; when Justin left hospital with a knee that would always be stiff and from time to time cause him pain, Nurse Painter's approval went with them. A sister was just what he wanted—there would be no silly excitement; and as Miss Tizard was a trifle older than the Major, there would be a restraining hand if called for. If Nurse Painter had known what lay beneath this satisfactory arrangement, it is probable that her approval would not have been seriously withdrawn. The war looked like going on for ever; the best you could hope for was a stalemate. Potatoes were unobtainable, honesty was no more, it was hate and muddle wherever you looked. If a gentleman and lady could pluck up heart enough to love and be happy—well, good luck to them!

Justin and Celia went to Oxfordshire, where they compared the dragonflies on the Windrush with the dragonflies on the Evenlode.[3] Later, they went to France.

Beauty cannot be suborned.[4] Never again did Justin see Celia quivering with beauty as she had done on the day she came to him in hospital. But he went on thinking she had a charming face and the most entertaining eyebrows in the world. Loving each other criminally and sincerely, they took pains to live together happily and to safeguard their happiness from injuries of their own infliction or from outside. It would have been difficult for them to be anything but inconspicuous, or to be taken for anything but a brother and sister—the kind of brother and sister of whom one says, "It will be rather hard for her when he marries." Their relationship, so conveniently obvious to the public eye, was equally convenient in private life, for it made them unusually intuitive about each other's feelings. Brought up to the same standard of behaviour, using the same vocabulary, they felt no need to impress each other and were not likely to be taken aback by each other's likes and dislikes. Even the fact of remembering the same foxed copy of *The Swiss Family Robinson*[5] with the tear across the picture of the boa constrictor was a reassuring bond. During the first years in France they felt they would like to have a child—or for the sake of the other's happiness ought to have a child—and discussed the possibilities of

1 *panoplied* Adorned in formal or ceremonial dress.

2 *gas gangrene* Progressive wound infection caused by bacteria that produce gases in the affected tissue.

3 *Windrush ... Evenlode* Windrush and Evenlode are tributaries of the Thames.

4 *suborned* Persuaded to bear false witness.

5 *foxed* Stained or aged; *The Swiss Family Robinson* 1812–27 children's adventure novel by Johann Wyss.

a child put out to nurse, learning French as its native speech, and then being adopted as a postwar orphan, since it was now too late for it to be a war orphan. But however the child was dated, it would be almost certain to declare its inheritance of Grandfather Tizard's nose, and as a fruitful incest is thought even worse of than a barren one, they sensibly gave up the idea; though regretting it.

Oddly enough, after settling in Hallowby they regretted it no longer. They had a home in England, a standing[1] and things to do. Justin had the Beelby Museum; Celia had a household. In Hallowby it was not possible to stroll out to a restaurant or to bring home puddings from the pastry cook, fillets of veal netted into bolsters by the butcher. Celia had to cook seriously, and soon found that if she was to cook meals worth eating she must go shopping too. This was just what was needed for their peace and quiet, since to be seen daily shopping saved a great deal of repetitious explanation that she and Justin could not afford to keep a servant in the house but must be content with Mrs. Mugthwaite coming in three afternoons a week, and a jobbing[2] gardener on Fridays. True, it exposed her to a certain amount of condolence and amazement from the school wives, but as they, like Mrs. Mugthwaite, came only in the afternoons, she could bear with it. Soon they came more sparingly; for, as Justin pointed out, poverty is the sturdiest of all shelters, since people feel it to be rather sad and soon don't think about it, whereas her first intention of explaining that ever since her Aunt Dinah had wakened in the middle of the night to see an angered cook standing over her with a meat hatchet she had been nervous of servants sleeping under the same roof would only provoke gossip, surmise and insistent recommendations of cooks without passions. Justin was more long-sighted than Celia. She always knew what to do or say at the moment. He could look ahead, foresee dangers, and take steps to dodge them.

They did not see as much of Mr. Pilkington as they had apprehended, and members of the staff were in no hurry to take up with another of Pilkington's Pets. Celia grew alarmed; if you make no friends, you become odd. She decided that they must occasionally go to church, though not too often or too enthusiastically, as it would

then become odd that they did not take the Sacrament.[3] No doubt a great many vicious church attenders took the Sacrament, and the rubric only forbids it to "open and notorious evil-livers," which they had every intention of not being; but she could see a scruple of honour at work in Justin, so she did not labour this argument. There was a nice, stuffy pitch-pine St. Cuthbert's near by, and at judicious intervals they went there for evensong[4]—thereby renewing another bond of childhood: the pleasure of hurrying home on a cold evening to eat baked potatoes hot from the oven. How old Mr. Gillespie divined from Justin's church demeanour that he was a whist[5] player was a mystery never solved. But he divined it. He had barely saved Celia's umbrella from being blown inside out, remarking, "You're newcomers, aren't you? You don't know the east wind at this corner," before he was saying to Justin, "You don't play whist, by any chance?" But probably he would have asked this of anyone not demonstrably a raving maniac, for since Colin Colbeck's death he, Miss Colbeck and Canon Pendarves were desperate for a fourth player. Canon Pendarves gave dinner parties, with a little music afterwards. Celia, driven into performance and remembering how Becky Sharp had wooed Lady Steyne[6] by singing the religious songs of Mozart, sat down at the piano and played "The Carmen's Whistle,"[7] one of the few things she reliably knew by heart. This audacious antiquarianism delighted the Canon, who kept her at his side for the rest of the evening, relating how he had once tried to get up a performance of Tallis's forty-part motet.[8]

The Tizards were no longer odd. Their new friends were all considerably older than they; the middle-aged had more conscience about the war and were readier to make friends with a disabled major and his devoted

---

[1] *standing* Social position.

[2] *jobbing* Working occasionally rather than as a full-time employee.

[3] *the Sacrament* Christian ritual of the Eucharist, the consuming of consecrated bread and wine in memory of Christ's sacrifice.

[4] *evensong* Evening prayer.

[5] *whist* Card game similar to bridge.

[6] *Becky Sharp ... Lady Steyne* Reference to William Thackeray's novel *Vanity Fair* (1848), which depicts the ruthless social climbing of the calculating Becky Sharp.

[7] *The Carmen's Whistle* Sixteenth-century song by English composer William Byrd.

[8] *Tallis's ... motet* Thomas Tallis's *Spem in alium* (c. 1573), a famous choral composition for forty voices.

maiden sister. In time, members of the staff overlooked their prejudice against Pilkington Pets and found the Tizard couple agreeable, if slightly boring.

Returning from their sober junketings[1] Justin and Celia, safe within their brick wall, cast off their weeds of middle age, laughed, chattered and kissed with an intensified delight in their scandalous immunity from blame. They were a model couple, the most respectable couple in Hallowby, treading hand in hand the thornless path to fogydom. They began to give small dinner parties themselves. They set up a pug and a white cat. During their fifth summer in Hallowby they gave an evening party in the Beelby Museum. This dashing event almost carried them too far. It was such a success that they were begged to make an annual thing of it; and Celia was so gay, and her dress so fashionable, that she was within an inch of being thought a dangerous woman. Another party being expected of them, another had to be given. But this was a very different set-out: a children-and-parents party with a puppet show, held in St. Cuthbert's Church Room, with Canon Pendarves speaking on behalf of the Save the Children Fund[2] and a collection taken at the door. The collection was a master stroke. It put the Tizards back in their place as junior fogies—where Justin, for his part, was thankful to be. He had got there a trifle prematurely, perhaps, being in his mid-thirties, but it was where he intended to end his days.

He was fond of gardening, and had taken to gardening seriously, having an analysis made of the Newton Lodge soil—too acid, as he suspected—buying phosphates and potash and lime and kainite,[3] treating different plots with different mixtures and noting the results in a book. He could not dig, but he limpingly mowed and rolled the lawn, trained climbing roses and staked delphiniums. Within the shelter of the wall, delphiniums did magnificently. Every year he added new varieties and when the original border could be lengthened no further a parallel bed was dug, with a grass walk in between. Every summer evening he walked there, watching the various blues file off, some to darkness, some to pallor, as the growing dusk took

possession of them, while the white cat flitted about his steps like a moth. Because one must not be wholly selfish, from time to time he would invite a pair of chosen children to tea, cut each of them a long delphinium lance (cutting only those which were going over, however) and set them to play jousting matches on the lawn. Most of them did no more than thwack, but the two little Semples, the children of the school chaplain, fought with system, husbanding[4] their strokes and aiming at each other's faces. Even when they had outgrown jousting they still came to Newton Lodge, hunting snails, borrowing books, helping him weigh out basic slag,[5] addressing him as "Justin."

"Mary is just the age our child would have been," remarked Celia after one of these visits. Seeing him start at the words, she went on, "When you went back to be killed, and I was quite sure I would have a baby."

"I wouldn't stand being called Justin—if she were."

"You might have to. They're Bright Young Things[6] from the cradle on, nowadays." By now the vogue for being a Bright Young Thing had reached even to Hallowby, its ankles growing rather muddied and muscular on the way. It was not like Celia to prefer an inferior article, and Justin wondered to see her tolerance of this anglicisation of the *Jeune France* when the original movement had so exasperated her. He hoped she wasn't mellowing; mellowness is not the food of love. A quite contrary process, however, was at work in Celia. At Carnac, even when accepting Pilkington as a way out of it, the exaltation of living in defiance of social prohibitions and the absorbing manoeuvres of seeming to live in compliance with them had been stimulus enough; she had had no mercy for less serious rebels. But during the last few years the sense of sinking month by month into the acquiescence of Hallowby, eating its wholesome lotus[7] like cabbage, conforming with the inattentiveness of habit—and aware that if she overlooked a conformity the omission would be re-

---

[1] *junketings* Appearances at social events.

[2] *Save the Children Fund* Charitable organization founded in 1919 in England to benefit children suffering the after-effects of the war.

[3] *phosphates … kainite* Fertilizers.

[4] *husbanding* Carefully regulating.

[5] *slag* Byproduct of metal-refining processes that is used as a fertilizer.

[6] *Bright Young Things* Social circle of young people in 1920s London who became known for their lifestyles of hedonism and glamor.

[7] *lotus* In mythology, fruit that induces a state of dreamy obliviousness when eaten.

dressed by the general conviction that Justin Tizard, though in no way exciting, was always so nice and had a sister who devoted her life to him, so nice for them both, etc. etc.—had begun to pall, and the sight of any rebellion, however puerile, however clumsy, roused up her partisanship. Since she could not shock Hallowby to its foundations, she liked to see these young creatures trying to, and wished them luck. From time to time she even made approaches to them, solicited their trust, indicated that she was ranged on their side. They accepted, confided, condescended—and dropped her.

When one is thus put back in one's place, one finds one has grown out of it, and is a misfit. Celia became conscious how greatly she disliked Hallowby society. The school people nauseated her with their cautious culture and breezy heartiness. The indigenous inhabitants were more bearable, because they were less pretentious; but they bored her. The Church, from visiting bishops down to Salvation Army cornet[1] players, she loathed for its hypocrisy. Only in Hallowby's shabbiest quarter—in Edna Road, Gladstone Terrace and Gas Lane—could she find anyone to love. Mr. Newby the fishmonger in his malodorous den; old Mrs. Foe among her sallowing cabbages and bruised apples; Mr. Raby, the grocer, who couldn't afford to buy new stock because he hadn't the heart to call in the money his poorer customers owed him, and so had none but the poorest customers—these people were good. Probably it was only by their goodness that they survived and had not cut their throats in despair long ago. Celia began to shop in Gas Lane. It was not a success. Much as she might love Mr. Newby she loved Justin better, and when a dried haddock gave him food poisoning she had to remove her custom—since the cat wouldn't touch Newby's fish anyhow. These disheartening experiences made her dislike respectable Hallowby even more. She wanted to cast it off, as someone tossing in fever wants to cast off a blanket.

The depression[2] began. The increase of Mr. Raby's customers drove him out of business: he went bankrupt and closed the shop. Groups of unemployed men from Hallowby juxta Mare appeared in Gas Lane and Edna Road and sang at street corners—for misfortune always resorts to poor neighbourhoods for succour. People began to worry about their investments and to cut down subscriptions to such examples of conspicuous waste as the Chamber Music Society. Experts on nutrition wrote to the daily papers, pointing out the wastefulness of frying, and explaining how, by buying cheaper cuts of meat and cooking them much longer, the mothers of families on the dole[3] would be able to provide wholesome adequate meals. Celia's uneasy goodwill and smouldering resentment found their outlet. As impetuously as she had flung herself into Justin's bed, she flung herself into relief work at Hallowby juxta Mare. Being totally inexperienced in relief work she exploded there like a nova.[4] Her schemes were so outrageous that people in authority didn't think them worth contesting even; she was left to learn by experience, and made the most of this valuable permission. One of her early outrages was to put on a revue composed and performed by local talent. Local talent ran to the impromptu, and when it became known what scarification[5] of local reputations could be expected, everyone wanted to hear what might be said of everyone else and Celia was able to raise the price of admission, which had been sixpence, to as much as half a guinea for the best seats. Her doings became a joke; you never knew what that woman wouldn't be up to next. Hadn't she persuaded Wilson & Beck to take on men they had turned off, because now, when half the factory stood idle, was the moment to give it a spring cleaning? Celia worked herself to the bone, and probably did a considerable amount of good, but her great service to Hallowby juxta Mare was that she made the unemployed interested in their plight instead of dulled by it, so that helpers came to her from the unemployed themselves. If she was not so deeply impressed by their goodness as she had been by the idealised goodness of Mr. Newby and Mrs. Foe, she was impressed by their arguments; she became political, and

---

[1] *Salvation Army* Evangelical Christian organization with a military structure and a strong commitment to charity. Music plays an important role in Salvation Army worship; *cornet* Valved instrument similar to a trumpet.

[2] *the depression* The Great Depression (1929–39), a period of worldwide economic decline.

[3] *dole* Financial support provided by the government to unemployed individuals.

[4] *nova* Star that abruptly becomes immensely brighter and then fades to its previous brightness within months or years.

[5] *scarification* I.e., painfully scathing criticism.

by 1936 she was marching in Communist demonstrations, singing:

Twenty-five years of hunger and war
And they call it a glorious Jubilee.[1]

Inland Hallowby was also looking forward to the Jubilee. The school was rehearsing a curtailed version of Purcell's *King Arthur*, with Mary Semple, now home from her finishing school, coming on in a chariot to sing "Fairest Isle."[2] There was to be folk dancing by Scouts and Guides, a tea for the old people, a fancy-dress[3] procession; and to mark the occasion Mr. Harvey, J.P.,[4] one of the school governors, had presented the Beelby Museum with a pair of buckskin breeches worn by the Duke of Wellington on the field of Talavera.[5] "I shall be expected to make a speech about them," groaned Justin. "I think I shall hire a deputy and go away for the day."

Celia jumped at this. "We'll both go away. Not just for the day but for a fortnight. We'll go to Jersey, because you must attend the Jubilee celebrations on your native island—a family obligation. Representative of one of the oldest families. And if we find the same sort of fuss going on there, we can nip over to France in the Escudiers' boat and be quit of the whole thing. It's foolproof, it's perfect. The only thing needed to make it perfectly perfect is to make it a month. Justin, it's the answer." She felt indeed that it was the answer. For some time now, Justin had seemed distrait[6] and out of humour. Afraid he was unwell, she told herself he was stale and knew that he had been neglected. An escapade would put all right. Talavera had not been fought in

vain. But she couldn't get him to consent. She was still persuading when the first letter arrived. It was typed and had been posted in Hallowby. It was unsigned, and began, "Hag."

Reading what followed, Celia tried to hold on to her first impression that the writer was some person in Hallowby juxta Mare. "You think you're sitting pretty, don't you? You think no one has found you out." She had made many enemies there; this must come from one of them. Several times she had been accused of misappropriating funds. Yes, that was it: "...and keep such a tight hold on him." But why *him*? It was as though two letters lay on the flimsy page—the letter she was bent on reading and the letter that lay beneath and glared through it. It was a letter about her relations with Justin that she tore into bits and dropped in the waste-paper basket as he came down to breakfast.

She could hardly contain her impatience to get the bits out again, stick them on a backing sheet, make sure. Nothing is ever quite what it first was; the letter was viler, but it was also feebler. It struck her as amateurish.

The letter that came two days later was equally vile but better composed; the writer must be getting his or her hand in. A third was positively elegant. Vexatiously, there was no hint of a demand for hush money. Had there been, Celia could have called in the police, who would have set those ritual springes[7] into which black-mailers—at any rate, blackmailers one reads of in newspapers—walk so artlessly. But the letters did not blackmail, did not even threaten. They stated that what the writer knew was common knowledge. After two letters, one on the heels of the other, which taunted Celia with being ugly, ageing and sexually ridiculous—letters that ripped through her self-control and made her cry with mortification—the writer returned to the theme of common knowledge and concluded with an "It may interest you to hear that the following know all about your loathsome performances" and a list of half a dozen Hallowby names. Further letters laconically listed more names. From the outset, Celia had decided to keep all this to herself, and still held to the decision; but she hoped she wouldn't begin to talk in her sleep. There was less chance of this, as by now she was sleeping scarcely at all.

---

[1] *Jubilee* I.e., the twenty-fifth anniversary of King George V's reign, celebrated throughout England in 1935.

[2] *King Arthur* 1691 semi-opera composed by Henry Purcell, with libretti by John Dryden; *Fairest Isle* Soprano aria that appears in the fifth act of *King Arthur*.

[3] *Scouts and Guides* I.e., members of the Boy Scouts and Girl Guides; *fancy-dress* Masquerade costume.

[4] *J.P.* Justice of the Peace.

[5] *Duke of Wellington* Arthur Wellesley, 1st Duke of Wellington (1769–1852), successful military leader who became Prime Minister of Great Britain; *Talavera* Site of an 1809 battle of the Peninsular War (1808–14), in which the British and Spanish armies joined forces against the French.

[6] *distrait* Preoccupied with distracting anxieties.

[7] *springes* Snares.

It was a Sunday morning and she and Justin were spraying roses for greenfly[1] when Justin said, "Puss, what are you concealing?" She syringed Mme Alfred Carrière[2] so violently that the jet bowed the rose, went beyond it, and deluged a robin. Justin took the syringe out of her hand and repeated the question.

Looking at him, she saw his face was drawn with woe. "No, no, it's nothing like that," she exclaimed. "I'm perfectly well. It's just that some poisen-pen imbecile..."

When he had read through the letters, he said thoughtfully, "I'd like to wring that little bitch's neck."

"Yes, it is some woman or other, isn't it? I felt sure of that."

"Some woman or other? It's Mary Semple."

"That pretty little Mary Semple?"

"That pretty little Mary Semple. Give me the letters. I'll soon settle her." He looked at his watch. "No, I can't settle her yet. She'll still be in church."

"But I don't understand why."

"You do, really."

"Justin! Have you been carrying on with Mary Semple?"

"No, I wouldn't say that. She's got white eyelashes. But ever since she came home Mary Semple has been doing all she could to carry on with me. There I was in the Beelby, you see, like a bull at the stake. No one comes near the place now; I was at her mercy. And in she tripped, and talked about the old days, telling me her little troubles, showing me poems, pitying me for my hard lot. I tried to cool her down, I tried to taper it off. But she was bent on rape, and one morning I lost all patience, told her she bored me and that if she came again I'd empty the fire bucket over her. She wept and wailed, and I paid no attention, and when there was silence I looked cautiously round and she was gone. And a day or so after"—he looked at the mended letter— "yes, a couple of days after, she sat her down to take it out of you."

"But, Justin—how did she know about us?"

"No fire without smoke, I suppose. I dare say she overheard her parents cheering each other along the way with Christian surmises. Anyhow, children nowadays are brought up on that sort of useful knowledge."

"No fire without smoke," she repeated. "And what about those lists?"

"Put in to make your flesh creep, most likely. Even if they do know, they weren't informed at a public meeting. Respectable individuals are too wary about libel and slander to raise their respectable voices individually. It's like that motet Pendarves used to talk about, when he could never manage to get them all there at once. Extraordinary ambitions people have! Fancy wanting to hear forty singers simultaneously yelling different tunes."

"It can be done. There was a performance at Newcastle—he was dead by then. But, Justin—"

"That will do, Celia. I am now going off to settle Mary Semple."

"How will you manage to see her alone?"

"I shall enter her father's dwelling. Mary will manage the rest."

The savagery of these last words frightened her. She had not heard that note in his voice since he cried out in his sleep. She watched him limp from the room as though she were watching an incalculable stranger. A moment later he reappeared, took her hand, and kissed it. "Don't worry, Puss. If need be, we'll fly the country."

Whatever danger might lie ahead, it was the thought of the danger escaped that made her tremble. If she had gone on concealing those letters—and she had considered it her right and duty to do so—a wedge would have been driven between her and Justin, bruising the tissue of their love, invisibly fissuring them, as a wedge of ice does in the living tree. And thus a scandal about their incest would have found them without any spontaneity of reaction and distracted by the discovery of how long she had been arrogating to herself a thing that concerned them both. "Here and now," she exclaimed, "I give up being an elder sister who knows best." Justin, on his way to the Semples', was muttering to himself, "Damn and blast it, why couldn't she have told me sooner? If she had it would all be over by now." It did not occur to him to blame himself for a lack of openness. This did not occur to Celia, either. It was Justin's constancy that mattered, not his fidelity—which was his own business.

When he reappeared, washed and brushed and ready for lunch, and told her there would be no more billets-

---

[1]   *greenfly*   Type of aphid, a garden pest.

[2]   *Mme Alfred Carrière*   Variety of cream or pink-colored rose.

doux[1] from Mary, it was with merely tactical curiosity that she asked, "Did you have to bribe her?" And as he did not answer at once, she went on to ask, "Would you like potted shrimps or mulligatawny?[2] There's both."

They did not have to fly the country. Mary Semple disposed of the rest of her feelings by quarrelling with everyone in the cast of *King Arthur* and singing "Fairest Isle" with such venom that her hearers felt their blood run cold, and afterwards remarked that stage fright had made her sing out of tune. The people listed by Mary as cognisant showed no more interest in the Tizards than before. The tradesmen continued to deliver. Not a cold shoulder was turned. But on that Sunday morning the balance between Justin and Celia had shifted, and never returned to its former adjustment. Both of them were aware of this, so neither of them referred to it, though at first Celia's abdication made her rather insistent that Justin should know best, make decisions, assert his authority. Justin asserted his authority by knowing what decisions could be postponed till the moment when there was no need to make them at all. Though he did not dislike responsibility, he was not going to be a slave to it. Celia's abdication also released elements in her character which till then had been penned back by her habit of common sense and efficiency. She became slightly frivolous, forgetful and timid. She read novels before lunch, abandoned all social conscience about bores, mislaid bills, took second helpings of *risotto*[3] and mashed potatoes and began to put on weight. She lost her aplomb as a driver and had one or two small accidents. She discovered the delights of needing to be taken away for pick-me-up holidays. Mrs. Mugthwaite, observing, all this, knew it was the Change,[4] and felt sorry for poor Mr. Tizard; the Change wasn't a thing that a brother should be expected to deal with. From time to time, Justin and Celia discussed leaving Hallowby and going to live somewhere away from the east-coast climate and the east wind at the corner by St Cuthbert's, but they put off moving, because the two animals had grown old, were set in their ways, and would be happier dying in their own home. The pug died just before the Munich crisis,[5] the cat lived on into the war.[6]

So did Mr. Pilkington, who died from overwork two months before the first air raid on Hallowby juxta Mare justified his insistence on constructing an air-raid shelter under the school playing fields. This first raid was concentrated on the ironworks, and did considerable damage. All next day, inland Hallowby heard the growl of demolition explosives. In the second raid, the defences were better organised. The enemy bombers were driven off their target before they could finish their mission. Two were brought down out to sea. A third, twisting inland, jettisoned its remaining bombs on and around Hallowby. One dropped in Gas Lane, another just across the road from Newton Lodge. The blast brought down the roof and dislodged a chimney stack. The rescue workers, turning the light of their torches here and there, noting the usual disparities between the havocked and the unharmed, the fireplace blown out, the portrait smiling above it, followed the trail of bricks and rubble upstairs and into a bedroom whose door slanted from its hinges. A cold air met them; looking up, they saw the sky. The floor was deep in rubble; bits of broken masonry, clots of brickwork, stood up from it like rocks on a beach. A dark bulk crouched on the hearth, and was part of the chimney stack, and a torrent of slates had fallen on the bed, crushing the two bodies that lay there.

The wavering torchlights wandered over the spectacle. There was a silence. Then young Foe spoke out. "He must have come in to comfort her. That's my opinion." The others concurred. Silently, they disentangled Justin and Celia, and wrapped them in separate tarpaulin sheets. No word of what they had found got out. Foe's hypothesis was accepted by the coroner and became truth.

—1961

---

[1] *billets-doux* Love letters.

[2] *potted shrimps* Shrimp cooked in butter; *mulligatawny* Curried soup.

[3] *risotto* Italian rice dish.

[4] *the Change* Change of life, a colloquial term for menopause.

[5] *Munich Crisis* The Munich Agreement, made in September 1938 between Great Britain, France, Italy, and Germany, was an attempt to prevent another world war by allowing Germany to occupy part of Czechoslovakia, which it had threatened to invade.

[6] *the war* I.e., World War II.

STEVIE SMITH
1902 – 1971

The poetry Stevie Smith produced in the years surrounding World War II has been considered some of the most original of its time. Sharing elements with the work of such diverse poets as William Blake, Robert Browning, Edward Lear, and Ogden Nash, Smith's poetry fits into no established genres and follows no known conventions. So unusual is her work, with its weighty themes explored in deceptively simple tones, that for many years her critical reputation remained ambiguous—she was for the most part not regarded as a "serious" poet. Smith experienced immense popularity during her lifetime, but her writing has only recently received substantial critical attention.

Stevie Smith was born in Hull on 20 September 1902. (Christened Florence Margaret, Smith was many years later nicknamed Stevie—after the then-famous jockey Steve Donaghue—when horseback riding with friends one day.) Shortly after her birth, her father abandoned the family, and her mother took Smith and her sister to live with their unmarried aunt in Palmer's Green, a London suburb. After Smith's mother died in 1919 she was raised by her aunt, whom she affectionately called "The Lion Aunt of Hull." Smith and her aunt lived together in the house in Palmer's Green until the Lion Aunt's death in 1968, after which point Smith remained in the house alone.

After completing school, Smith pursued a secretarial course and acquired a position in 1922 as private secretary to Sir Neville Pearson, Chairman of the leading publishing firm of Pearson, Newness; she retained this position until her retirement in 1953. Smith had begun writing poetry in her twenties and in 1935 she collected several pieces and approached the publisher Chatto and Windus. The firm's editor turned down the poems, advising her to write a novel instead. The result, completed six weeks later, was *Novel on Yellow Paper* (1936), thus named because Smith had typed it while at work, on Pearson's yellow carbon-copy paper.

Novel on Yellow Paper was widely and favorably reviewed. Readers were astonished by the deft insights and frantic pace of its chatty-voiced narrator, who tells her story in a stream-of-consciousness style which many have compared to that of Virginia Woolf. Although Smith wrote two sequels to her first novel, *Over the Frontier* (1938) and *The Holiday* (1949), she preferred writing poetry to the novel. With the commercial success of *Novel on Yellow Paper*, Smith was able to ensure the publication of her first volume of poems, *A Good Time Was Had by All* (1937). This was soon followed by the collections *Tender Only to One* (1938) and *Mother, What Is Man?* (1942).

Readers appreciated the unique sense of humor that characterized Smith's neat, economical poems. The simple language, often-ridiculous rhymes, odd syntax, and repetitive, singsong rhythms conveyed the sense of a child-like sensibility—a sense that was accentuated by the bizarre doodles she published alongside the poems. When she began holding her own poetry readings after the war, Smith emphasized the nursery-rhyme quality of her poems; she would arrive in her customary schoolgirl's frocks and pageboy haircut and proceed to sing her poems in a loud, off-key voice to the tunes of well-known hymns or children's songs.

Underneath the apparent frivolity of Smith's poems, however, lie powerful themes. She frequently rewrote common myths and legends and satirized accepted ideas or conventions. In "The Blue from

Heaven" (1957), for example, she isolates and dissects one image from the myth of King Arthur, while in "The New Age" (1957) she mocks the often-heard lament over the decline of culture and civilization. Though she called herself an agnostic, Smith had a lifelong attachment to the Church of England, and many of her poems deal with Christian themes; she once called the main business of her life "death, loneliness, God, and the devil." Her fascination with death—a subject of many of her poems—has been much commented upon. She claimed to find comfort in the knowledge that death was always an option, and in poems such as "Thoughts About a Person from Porlock" (1962) and "Is It Wise?" (1937) she contemplates the release that death would bring. But Smith's poetry also celebrates life, even at its most bizarre and unpleasant. She possessed a remarkable ability to see the comic in tragic events, as is evident in the black humor of "Not Waving but Drowning"(1957).

By the 1960s Stevie Smith had published numerous collections of poetry and was something of a cult figure, idolized by her younger peers for her indifference to established conventions, her cynicism, and her fierce honesty. When she died in 1971 she was at the height of her popularity, having recently been honored with the Cholmondeley Award for Poetry (1966) and the Queen's Medal for Poetry (1969). Smith herself did not believe that poets should occupy a privileged position in society. On the contrary, she said a poet should "be just made to get on with his writing: put in a room with pencils and pen or a typewriter; and then if his poems are no good, then he must just be thrown out."

⌘⌘⌘

Mother, Among the Dustbins

Mother, among the dustbins and the manure
I feel the measure of my humanity, an allure
As of the presence of God. I am sure

In the dustbins, in the manure, in the cat at play,
5 Is the presence of God, in a sure way
He moves there. Mother, what do you say?

I too have felt the presence of God in the broom
I hold, in the cobwebs in the room,
But most of all in the silence of the tomb.

10 Ah! but that thought that informs the hope of our kind
Is but an empty thing, what lies behind?—
Naught but the vanity of a protesting mind

That would not die. This is the thought that bounces
Within a conceited head and trounces
15 Inquiry. Man is most frivolous when he pronounces.

Well Mother, I shall continue to feel as I do,
And I think you would be wise to do so too,

Can you question the folly of man in the creation of God?
  Who are you?
—1938

The River God

I may be smelly, and I may be old,
  Rough in my pebbles, reedy in my pools,
But where my fish float by I bless their swimming
And I like the people to bathe in me, especially women.
5 But I can drown the fools
Who bathe too close to the weir,[1] contrary to rules.
And they take a long time drowning
As I throw them up now and then in a spirit of clowning.
Hi yih, yippity-yap, merrily I flow,
10 O I may be an old foul river but I have plenty of go.
Once there was a lady who was too bold
She bathed in me by the tall black cliff where the
    water runs cold,
So I brought her down here
To be my beautiful dear.
15 Oh will she stay with me will she stay
This beautiful lady, or will she go away?

1 *weir* Barrier or dam to hold back water.

She lies in my beautiful deep river bed with many a weed
To hold her, and many a waving reed.
Oh who would guess what a beautiful white face lies there
20 Waiting for me to smooth and wash away the fear
She looks at me with. Hi yih, do not let her
Go. There is no one on earth who does not forget her
Now. They say I am a foolish old smelly river
But they do not know of my wide original bed
25 Where the lady waits, with her golden sleepy head.
If she wishes to go I will not forgive her.
—1950

Not Waving but Drowning

Nobody heard him, the dead man,
    But still he lay moaning:
I was much further out than you thought
And not waving but drowning.

5 Poor chap, he always loved larking
And now he's dead
It must have been too cold for him his heart gave way,
They said.

Oh, no no no, it was too cold always
10 (Still the dead one lay moaning)
I was much too far out all my life
And not waving but drowning.
—1957

The New Age

Shall I tell you the signs of a New Age coming?
    It is a sound of drubbing and sobbing
Of people crying, We are old, we are old
And the sun is going down and becoming cold
5 Oh sinful and sad and the last of our kind
If we turn to God now do you think He will mind?
Then they fall on their knees and begin to whine
That the state of Art itself presages decline
As if Art has anything or ever had
10 To do with civilization whether good or bad.

Art is wild as a cat and quite separate from civilization
But that is another matter that is not now under
    consideration.
Oh these people are fools with their sighing and sinning
Why should Man be at an end? he is hardly beginning.
15 This New Age will slip in under cover of their cries
And be upon them before they have opened their eyes.
Well, say geological time is a one-foot rule
Then Man's only been here about half an inch to play
    the fool
Or be wise if he likes, as he often has been
20 Oh heavens how these crying people spoil the
    beautiful geological scene.
—1957

Away, Melancholy

Away, melancholy,
    Away with it, let it go.

Are not the trees green,
The earth as green?
5 Does not the wind blow,
Fire leap and the rivers flow?
Away melancholy.

The ant is busy
He carrieth his meat,
10 All things hurry
To be eaten or eat.
Away, melancholy.

Man, too, hurries,
Eats, couples, buries,
15 He is an animal also
With a hey ho melancholy,
Away with it, let it go.

Man of all creatures
Is superlative
20 (Away melancholy)
He of all creatures alone
Raiseth a stone
(Away melancholy)
Into the stone, the god

25   Pours what he knows of good
     Calling, good, God.
     Away melancholy, let it go.

     Speak not to me of tears,
     Tyranny, pox, wars,
30   Saying, Can God
     Stone of man's thought, be good?

     Say rather it is enough
     That the stuffed
     Stone of man's good, growing,
35   By man's called God.
     Away, melancholy, let it go.

     Man aspires
     To good,
     To love
40   Sighs;

     Beaten, corrupted, dying
     In his own blood lying
     Yet heaves up an eye above
     Cries, Love, love.
45   It is his virtue needs explaining,
     Not his failing.

     Away, melancholy,
     Away with it, let it go.
     —1957

The Blue from Heaven

A legend of King Arthur of Britain.

King Arthur rode in another world
And his twelve knights rode behind him
And Guinevere was there
Crying: Arthur, where are you dear?

5   Why is the King so blue
     Why is he this blue colour?
     It is because the sun is shining
     And he rides under the blue cornflowers.

     High wave the cornflowers
10   That shed the pale blue light
     And under the tall cornflowers
     Rides King Arthur and his twelve knights.

     And Guinevere is there
     Crying: Arthur, where are you dear?

15   First there were twelve knights riding
     And then there was only one
     And King Arthur said to the one knight,
     Be gone.

     All I wish for now, said Arthur,
20   Is the beautiful colour blue
     And to ride in the blue sunshine
     And Guinevere I do not wish for you.

     Oh Lord, said Guinevere
     I do not see the colour blue
25   And I wish to ride where our knights rode,
     After you.

     Go back, go back, Guinevere,
     Go back to the palace, said the King.
     So she went back to the palace
30   And her grief did not seem to her a small thing.

     The Queen has returned to the palace
     Crying: Arthur, where are you dear?
     And every day she speaks of Arthur's grandeur
     To the knights who are there.

35   That Arthur has fallen from the grandeur
     Of his powers all agree
     And the falling off of Arthur
     Becomes their theme presently.

     As if it were only temporarily
40   And it was not for ever
     They speak, but the Queen knows
     He will come back never.

     Yes, Arthur has passed away
     Gladly he has laid down his reigning powers

45   He has gone to ride in the blue light
     Of the peculiar towering cornflowers.
     —1957

Pretty

Why is the word pretty so underrated?
  In November the leaf is pretty when it falls
The stream grows deep in the woods after rain
And in the pretty pool the pike stalks

5   He stalks his prey, and this is pretty too,
    The prey escapes with an underwater flash
    But not for long, the great fish has him now
    The pike is a fish who always has his prey

    And this is pretty. The water rat is pretty
10 His paws are not webbed, he cannot shut his nostrils
    As the otter can and the beaver, he is torn between
    The land and water. Not "torn," he does not mind.

    The owl hunts in the evening and it is pretty
    The lake water below him rustles with ice
15 There is frost coming from the ground, in the air mist
    All this is pretty, it could not be prettier.

     Yes, it could always be prettier, the eye abashes
     It is becoming an eye that cannot see enough,
     Out of the wood the eye climbs. This is prettier
20   A field in the evening, tilting up.

     The field tilts to the sky. Though it is late
     The sky is lighter than the hill field
     All this looks easy but really it is extraordinary
     Well, it is extraordinary to be so pretty.

25   And it is careless, and that is always pretty
     This field, this owl, this pike, this pool are careless,
     As Nature is always careless and indifferent
     Who sees, who steps, means nothing, and this is pretty.

     So a person can come along like a thief—pretty!—
30   Stealing a look, pinching the sound and feel,
     Lick the icicle broken from the bank
     And still say nothing at all, only cry pretty.

     Cry pretty, pretty, pretty and you'll be able
     Very soon not even to cry pretty
35   And so be delivered entirely from humanity
     This is prettiest of all, it is very pretty.
     —1962

GEORGE ORWELL
1903 – 1950

George Orwell struggled throughout his life to live his convictions as well as to write from them. His most famous novels, *Animal Farm* (1945) and *1984* (1949), have been translated into more than sixty languages and have sold over forty million copies. While his writerly craftsmanship and strongly articulated views on the importance of linguistic integrity (most directly expressed in his 1946 essay "Politics and the English Language") are admired and respected, he is recognized even more widely for his moral integrity, independence of mind, and scope of vision.

Born Eric Arthur Blair in Motihari, India on 25 June 1903, Orwell came from a family with strong colonial ties on both sides. His father, Richard Blair, worked as an opium agent for the British Imperial government; his mother, Ida Limouzin, grew up in Burma surrounded by a large staff of native servants, taking work as a governess in India when her father lost his wealth. Although the baby Eric returned to England with his mother and older sister in 1904, his sense of identity was moulded by the colonial experience. He was also strongly marked by his experiences as an economically poor but culturally middle-class student in English boarding schools, first at St. Cyprian's School (an experience later immortalized in his 1953 *Such, Such Were the Joys*) and then as a scholarship student at Eton.

Despite his evident abilities as a scholar, Eric did not apply himself while at Eton and was ultimately discouraged from pursuing university-level studies; in fact, he was himself more interested in returning to his colonial roots and pursuing a more adventurous career. After sitting eight days of qualifying examinations, he was selected to travel to Burma to join the Imperial Police. He served there from 1922 to 1927 in an array of posts around the country before deciding that the work was not suited to his character or his ideals; it had also taken its toll physically. His experiences left him feeling profoundly ambivalent about the colonial presence of the British, and about the nature of imperialist authority in general. He resigned his assignment upon his return to England, filled with a profound sense of guilt.

Although he was at this point determined to become a writer, he had not written much of anything while in Burma, nor published any adult work. Nevertheless, he decided that living in poverty, first in the East End of London, then in Paris, taking various low-paying jobs here and there, would help provide him with suitable material and would also condition his mind for the task of writing. He spent the years 1928–29 in Paris, taking menial jobs in restaurants and hotels and contracting pneumonia in the process, and then returned to England where he spent some time living as a tramp. His first book, *Down and Out in Paris and London*, appeared in 1933 under the pseudonym of George Orwell, chosen to protect his family and to distance himself from them and from his own earlier life.

Orwell spent nine months in 1934 living with his parents while he finished his second book, the novel *A Clergyman's Daughter* (1935). He then moved out, took work in a bookshop, and continued to write; his *Burmese Days*, which drew on his experiences in Burma and expressed his sense of indignation about imperialism, appeared in 1934. *A Clergyman's Daughter* was published the following year; in it Orwell attempted to use his tramping experiences as material for fiction, but was himself dissatisfied with the results. In later years he did his best to keep this and his next autobiographical novel, *Keep the Aspidistra Flying* (1936), out of view, preventing their reissues; the latter did not appear in the United States until 1956.

In 1936, emboldened by an advance for his next, nonfictional project, Orwell married Eileen O'Shaughnessy. Eileen abandoned her graduate studies in Educational Psychology at University College in London to move with Orwell into a tiny, isolated, and primitive cottage in Wallington, Hertfordshire, where they kept a garden, goats, and chickens, and managed a small shop, and where Orwell continued to write. His study of the dismal lives of the poor and unemployed in the industrial towns of the north of England took him tramping once again; *The Road to Wigan Pier* (1937) gave voice to his socialist views and established his reputation as a political writer.

Orwell's political idealism was severely tested when he fought for the Republicans in the Spanish Civil War. He witnessed first-hand the intense in-fighting amongst the various factions of the Left, and he became an intense critic of all political orthodoxies as a result. His next book, *Homage to Catalonia*, combined personal recollection with biting political analysis; it was as critical of the Soviet-influenced Communist faction in Spain as it was of Franco's Fascists. It received a mixed reception when it appeared in 1938. Today, however, it is recognized as an eloquent illustration of Orwell's passionate intellectual and political independence of mind.

World War II broke out three months after the publication of Orwell's next novel, *Coming Up for Air* (1939); unable to join the army due to his poor health, Orwell worked for two years for the BBC's Eastern Service, in addition to writing various essays and reviews. In 1944, Orwell and his wife adopted a son, Richard Horatio Blair, to whom they were both deeply devoted. But in 1945, Orwell's life changed: Eileen died (and her death devastated Orwell), and *Animal Farm* was published and brought overnight literary and financial success. This short novel is a fable that satirizes the corruption of socialist ideals that had by then occurred in the Soviet Union under Joseph Stalin; everyone was supposedly equal but "some animals are more equal than others," in Orwell's famous phrase.

Orwell spent most of the last years of his life in an isolated cottage on the island of Jura, off the coast of Scotland, with Richard, a nanny, and his sister Avril for company. As he gradually succumbed to tuberculosis, he wrote *1984*, widely considered his most ambitious and important work. This dark novel imagines a totalitarian future in which absolute conformity is rigidly enforced; "Big Brother is watching you" is the catchword of a society in which privacy and individual freedom have all but disappeared. In 1949 that book was published, and Orwell entered a sanatorium in England. Three months before his death on 21 January 1950, he married Sonia Brownell.

⌘ ⌘ ⌘

Politics and the English Language

Most people who bother with the matter at all would admit that the English language is in a bad way, but it is generally assumed that we cannot by conscious action do anything about it. Our civilization is decadent and our language—so the argument runs—must inevitably share in the general collapse. It follows that any struggle against the abuse of language is a sentimental archaism, like preferring candles to electric light or hansom cabs to aeroplanes. Underneath this lies the half-conscious belief that language is a natural growth and not an instrument which we shape for our own purposes.

Now, it is clear that the decline of a language must ultimately have political and economic causes: it is not due simply to the bad influence of this or that individual writer. But an effect can become a cause, reinforcing the original cause and producing the same effect in an intensified form, and so on indefinitely. A man may take to drink because he feels himself to be a failure, and then fail all the more completely because he drinks. It is rather the same thing that is happening to the English language. It becomes ugly and inaccurate because our thoughts are foolish, but the slovenliness of our language makes it easier for us to have foolish thoughts. The point is that the process is reversible. Modern English, especially written English, is full of bad habits which spread by imitation and which can be avoided if one is willing to take the necessary trouble. If one gets rid of these habits one can think more clearly, and to think clearly is a necessary first step towards political regeneration: so that the fight against bad English is not frivolous and is not the exclusive concern of professional writers. I will come back to this presently, and I hope that by that time the meaning of what I have said here will have become clearer. Meanwhile, here are five specimens of the English language as it is now habitually written.

These five passages have not been picked out because they are especially bad—I could have quoted far worse if I had chosen—but because they illustrate various of the mental vices from which we now suffer. They are a little below the average, but are fairly representative samples. I number them so that I can refer back to them when necessary:

1. I am not, indeed, sure whether it is not true to say that the Milton who once seemed not unlike a seventeenth-century Shelley had not become, out of an experience ever more bitter in each year, more alien (*sic*) to the founder of that Jesuit sect which nothing could induce him to tolerate.

Professor Harold Laski
(Essay in *Freedom of Expression*).

2. Above all, we cannot play ducks and drakes with a native battery of idioms which prescribes such egregious collocations of vocables as the Basic *put up with* for *tolerate* or *put at a loss* for *bewilder*.

Professor Lancelot Hogben (*Interglossa*).

3. On the one side we have the free personality: by definition it is not neurotic, for it has neither conflict nor dream. Its desires, such as they are, are transparent, for they are just what institutional approval keeps in the forefront of consciousness; another institutional pattern would alter their number and intensity; there is little in them that is natural, irreducible, or culturally dangerous. But *on the other side*, the social bond itself is nothing but the mutual reflection of these self-secure integrities. Recall the definition of love. Is not this the very picture of a small academic? Where is there a place in this hall of mirrors for either personality or fraternity?

Essay on psychology in *Politics* (New York).

4. All the "best people" from the gentlemen's clubs, and all the frantic Fascist captains, united in common hatred of Socialism and bestial horror of the rising tide of the mass revolutionary movement, have turned to acts of provocation, to foul incendiarism, to medieval legends of poisoned wells, to legalise their own destruction to proletarian organisations, and rouse the agitated petty-bourgeoisie to chauvinistic fervour on behalf of the fight against the revolutionary way out of the crisis.

Communist pamphlet.

5. If a new spirit *is* to be infused into this old country, there is one thorny and contentious reform which must be tackled, and that is the humanisation and galvanisation of the BBC.[1] Timidity here will bespeak canker and atrophy of the soul. The heart of Britain may be sound and of strong beat, for instance, but the British lion's roar at present is like that of Bottom in Shakespeare's *Midsummer Night's Dream*—as gentle as any sucking dove. A virile new Britain cannot continue indefinitely to be traduced in the eyes, or rather ears, of the world by the effete languors of Langham Place,[2] brazenly masquerading as "standard English." When the Voice of Britain is heard at nine o'clock, better far and infinitely less ludicrous to hear aitches honestly dropped than the present priggish, inflated, inhibited, school-ma'amish arch braying of blameless bashful mewing maidens!

Letter in *Tribune*.

Each of these passages has faults of its own, but, quite apart from avoidable ugliness, two qualities are common to all of them. The first is staleness of imagery: the other is lack of precision. The writer either has a meaning and cannot express it, or he inadvertently says something else, or he is almost indifferent as to whether

---

[1] *BBC*   British Broadcasting Corporation.

[2] *Langham Place*   Location of the main office of the BBC.

his words mean anything or not. This mixture of vagueness and sheer incompetence is the most marked characteristic of modern English prose, and especially of any kind of political writing. As soon as certain topics are raised, the concrete melts into the abstract and no one seems able to think of turns of speech that are not hackneyed: prose consists less and less of *words* chosen for the sake of their meaning, and more of *phrases* tacked together like the sections of a prefabricated hen-house. I list below, with notes and examples, various of the tricks by means of which the work of prose construction is habitually dodged:

Dying metaphors. A newly invented metaphor assists thought by evoking a visual image, while on the other hand a metaphor which is technically "dead" (e.g., *iron resolution*) has in effect reverted to being an ordinary word and can generally be used without loss of vividness. But in between these two classes there is a huge dump of worn-out metaphors which have lost all evocative power and are merely used because they save people the trouble of inventing phrases for themselves. Examples are: *Ring the changes on, take up the cudgels for, toe the line, ride roughshod over, stand shoulder to shoulder with, play into the hands of, no axe to grind, grist to the mill, fishing in troubled waters, rift within the lute, on the order of the day, Achilles' heel, swan song, hotbed.* Many of these are used without knowledge of their meaning (What is a "rift," for instance?), and incompatible metaphors are frequently mixed, a sure sign that the writer is not interested in what he is saying. Some metaphors now current have been twisted out of their original meaning without those who use them even being aware of the fact. For example, *toe the line* is sometimes written *tow the line.* Another example is *the hammer and the anvil,* now always used with the implication that the anvil gets the worst of it. In real life it is always the anvil that breaks the hammer, never the other way about: a writer who stopped to think what he was saying would be aware of this, and would avoid perverting the original phrase.

Operators, or *verbal false limbs.* These save the trouble of picking out appropriate verbs and nouns, and at the same time pad each sentence with extra syllables which give it an appearance of symmetry. Characteristic phrases are: *render inoperative, militate against, prove unacceptable, make contact with, be subjected to, give rise to, give grounds for, have the effect of, play a leading part (role) in, make itself felt, take effect, exhibit a tendency to, serve the purpose of,* etc., etc. The keynote is the elimination of simple verbs. Instead of being a single word, such as *break, stop, spoil, mend, kill,* a verb becomes a *phrase,* made up of a noun or adjective tacked on to some general-purposes verb such as *prove, serve, form, play, render.* In addition, the passive voice is wherever possible used in preference to the active, and noun constructions are used instead of gerunds (*by examination of* instead of *by examining*). The range of verbs is further cut down by means of the *-ise* and *de-* formations, and banal statements are given an appearance of profundity by means of the *not un-* formation. Simple conjunctions and prepositions are replaced by such phrases as *with respect to, having regard to, the fact that, by dint of, in view of, in the interests of, on the hypothesis that;* and the ends of sentences are saved from anticlimax by such resounding commonplaces as *greatly to be desired, cannot be left out of account, a development to be expected in the near future, deserving of serious consideration, brought to a satisfactory conclusion,* and so on and so forth.

Pretentious diction. Words like *phenomenon, element, individual* (as noun), *objective, categorical, effective, virtual, basic, primary, promote, constitute, exhibit, exploit, utilise, eliminate, liquidate,* are used to dress up simple statements and give an air of scientific impartiality to biassed judgements. Adjectives like *epoch-making, epic, historic, unforgettable, triumphant, age-old, inevitable, inexorable, veritable,* are used to dignify the sordid processes of international politics, while writing that aims at glorifying war usually takes on an archaic colour, its characteristic words being: *realm, throne, chariot, mailed fist, trident, sword, shield, buckler, banner, jackboot, clarion.* Foreign words and expressions such as *cul de sac, ancien régime, deus ex machina, mutatis mutandis, status quo, Gleichschaltung, Weltanschauung,*[1]

---

[1] *ancien ... Weltanschauung* Phrases meaning, respectively, old system of government (French), god from the machine (Latin), the necessary changes being made (Latin), the state of things (Latin), enforced political conformity (German), philosophy of life (German).

are used to give an air of culture and elegance. Except for the useful abbreviation *i.e., e.g.,* and *etc.,* there is no real need for any of the hundreds of foreign phrases now current in English. Bad writers, and especially scientific, political, and sociological writers, are nearly always haunted by the notion that Latin or Greek words are grander than Saxon ones, and unnecessary words like *expedite, ameliorate, predict, extraneous, deracinated, clandestine, sub-aqueous* and hundreds of others constantly gain ground from their Anglo-Saxon opposite numbers.[1] The jargon peculiar to Marxist writing (*hyena, hangman, cannibal, petty bourgeois, these gentry, lacquey, flunkey, mad dog, White Guard,* etc.) consists largely of words and phrases translated from Russian, German, or French; but the normal way of coining a new word is to use a Latin or Greek root with the appropriate affix and, where necessary, the *-ise* formation. It is often easier to make up words of this kind (*deregionalise, impermissible, extramarital, non-fragmentatory* and so forth) than to think up the English words that will cover one's meaning. The result, in general, is an increase in slovenliness and vagueness.

Meaningless words. In certain kinds of writing, particularly in art criticism and literary criticism, it is normal to come across long passages which are almost completely lacking in meaning.[2] Words like *romantic, plastic, values, human, dead, sentimental, natural, vitality,* as used in art criticism, are strictly meaningless, in the sense that they not only do not point to any discoverable object, but are hardly even expected to do so by the reader.

When one critic writes, "The outstanding features of Mr. X's work is its living quality," while another writes,

"The immediately striking thing about Mr. X's work is its peculiar deadness," the reader accepts this as a simple difference of opinion. If words like *black* and *white* were involved, instead of the jargon words *dead* and *living,* he would see at once that language was being used in an improper way. Many political words are similarly abused. The word *Fascism* has now no meaning except in so far as it signifies "something not desirable." The words *democracy, socialism, freedom, patriotic, realistic, justice,* have each of them several different meanings which cannot be reconciled with one another. In the case of a word like *democracy,* not only is there no agreed definition, but the attempt to make one is resisted from all sides. It is almost universally felt that when we call a country democratic we are praising it: consequently the defenders of every kind of regime claim that it is a democracy, and fear that they might have to stop using the word if it were tied down to any one meaning. Words of this kind are often used in a consciously dishonest way. That is, the person who uses them has his own private definition, but allows his hearer to think he means something quite different. Statements like *Marshal Pétain*[3] *was a true patriot, The Soviet press is the freest in the world, The Catholic Church is opposed to persecution,* are almost always made with intent to deceive. Other words used in variable meanings, in most cases more or less dishonestly, are: *class, totalitarian, science, progressive, reactionary, bourgeois, equality.*

Now that I have made this catalogue of swindles and perversions, let me give another example of the kind of writing that they lead to. This time it must of its nature be an imaginary one. I am going to translate a passage of good English into modern English of the worst sort. Here is a well-known verse from *Ecclesiastes*:

I returned and saw under the sun, that the race is not to the swift, nor the battle to the strong, neither yet bread to the wise, nor yet riches to men of understanding, nor yet favour to men of skill; but time and chance happeneth to them all.

Here it is in modern English:

---

[1] [Orwell's note] An interesting illustration of this is the way in which the English flower names which were in use till very recently are being ousted by Greek ones, *snapdragon* becoming *atirrhinum, forget-me-not* becoming *myosotis,* etc. It is hard to see any practical reason for this change in fashion: it is probably due to an instinctive turning-away from the more homely word and a vague feeling that the Greek word is scientific.

[2] [Orwell's note] Example: "Comfort's catholicity of perception and image, strangely Whitmanesque in range, continues to evoke that trembling atmospheric accumulative hinting at a cruel, an inexorably serene timelessness ... Wrey Gardiner scores by aiming at simple bullseyes with precision. Only they are not so simple, and through this contented sadness runs more than the surface bitter-sweet of resignation" (*Poetry Quarterly*).

[3] *Marshal Pétain* French general (1856–1951) who was appointed head of the Vichy government, which ruled Occupied France during World War II in collaboration with the Nazis.

Objective considerations of contemporary phenomena compels the conclusion that success or failure
in competitive activities exhibits no tendency to be
commensurate with innate capacity, but that a
considerable element of the unpredictable must
invariably be taken into account.

This is a parody, but not a very gross one. Exhibit 3,
above, for instance, contains several patches of the same
kind in English. It will be seen that I have not made a
full translation. The beginning and ending of the
sentence follow the original meaning fairly closely, but
in the middle the concrete illustrations—race, battle,
bread—dissolve into the vague phrase "success or failure
in competitive activities." This had to be so, because no
modern writer of the kind I am discussing—no one
capable of using phrases like "objective consideration of
contemporary phenomena"—would ever tabulate his
thoughts in that precise and detailed way. The whole
tendency of modern prose is away from concreteness.
Now analyse these two sentences a little more closely.
The first contains forty-nine words but only sixty
syllables, and all its words are those of everyday life. The
second contains thirty-eight words of ninety syllables:
eighteen of its words are from Latin roots, and one from
Greek. The first sentence contains six vivid images, and
only one phrase ("time and chance") that could be called
vague. The second contains not a single fresh, arresting
phrase, and in spite of its ninety syllables it gives only a
shortened version of the meaning contained in the first.
Yet without a doubt it is the second kind of sentence
that is gaining ground in modern English. I do not want
to exaggerate. This kind of writing is not yet universal,
and outcrops of simplicity will occur here and there in
the worst-written page. Still, if you or I were told to
write a few lines on the uncertainty of human fortunes,
we should probably come much nearer to my imaginary
sentence than to the one from *Ecclesiastes*.

As I have tried to show, modern writing at its worst
does not consist in picking out words for the sake of
their meaning and inventing images in order to make
the meaning clearer. It consists in gumming together
long strips of words which have already been set in order
by someone else, and making the results presentable by
sheer humbug. The attraction of this way of writing is
that it is easy. It is easier—even quicker, once you have
the habit—to say *In my opinion it is a not unjustifiable
assumption that* than to say *I think*. If you use ready-
made phrases, you not only don't have to hunt about for
words; you also don't have to bother with the rhythms
of your sentences, since these phrases are generally so
arranged as to be more or less euphonious. When you
are composing in a hurry—when you are dictating to a
stenographer, for instance, or making a public speech—
it is natural to fall into a pretentious, Latinized style.
Tags like *a consideration which we should do well to bear
in mind* or *a conclusion to which all of us would readily
assent* will save many a sentence from coming down
with a bump. By using stale metaphors, similes, and
idioms, you save much mental effort, at the cost of
leaving your meaning vague, not only for your reader but
for yourself. This is the significance of mixed metaphors.
The sole aim of a metaphor is to call up a visual image.
When these images clash—as in *The Fascist octopus has
sung its swan song, the jackboot is thrown into the melting
pot*—it can be taken as certain that the writer is not seeing
a mental image of the objects he is naming; in other
words he is not really thinking.

Look again at the examples I gave at the beginning
of this essay. Professor Laski (1) uses five negatives in 53
words. One of these is superfluous, making nonsense of
the whole passage, and in addition there is the slip *alien*
for akin, making further nonsense, and several avoidable
pieces of clumsiness which increase the general
vagueness. Professor Hogben (2) plays ducks and drakes
with a battery which is able to write prescriptions, and,
while disapproving of the everyday phrase *put up with*,
is unwilling to look *egregious* up in the dictionary and
see what it means. (3), if one takes an uncharitable
attitude towards it, is simply meaningless: probably one
could work out its intended meaning by reading the
whole of the article in which it occurs. In (4) the writer
knows more or less what he wants to say, but an
accumulation of stale phrases chokes him like tea-leaves
blocking a sink. In (5) words and meaning have almost
parted company. People who write in this manner
usually have a general emotional meaning—they dislike
one thing and want to express solidarity with
another—but they are not interested in the detail of
what they are saying. A scrupulous writer, in every
sentence that he writes, will ask himself at least four
questions, thus: What am I trying to say? What words
will express it? What image or idiom will make it

clearer? Is this image fresh enough to have an effect? And he will probably ask himself two more: Could I put it more shortly? Have I said anything that is avoidably ugly? But you are not obliged to go to all this trouble. You can shirk it by simply throwing your mind open and letting the ready-made phrases come crowding in. They will construct your sentences for you—even think your thoughts for you, to a certain extent—and at need they will perform the important service of partially concealing your meaning even from yourself. It is at this point that the special connection between politics and the debasement of language becomes clear.

In our time it is broadly true that political writing is bad writing. Where it is not true, it will generally be found that the writer is some kind of rebel, expressing his private opinions, and not a "party line." Orthodoxy, of whatever colour, seems to demand a lifeless, imitative style. The political dialects to be found in pamphlets, leading articles, manifestos, White Papers,[1] and the speeches of Under-Secretaries do, of course, vary from party to party, but they are all alike in that one almost never finds in them a fresh, vivid, homemade turn of speech. When one watches some tired hack on the platform mechanically repeating the familiar phrases—*bestial atrocities, iron heel, blood-stained tyranny, free peoples of the world, stand shoulder to shoulder*—one often has a curious feeling that one is not watching a live human being but some kind of dummy: a feeling which suddenly becomes stronger at moments when the light catches the speaker's spectacles and turns them into blank discs which seem to have no eyes behind them. And this is not altogether fanciful. A speaker who uses that kind of phraseology has gone some distance towards turning himself into a machine. The appropriate noises are coming out of his larynx, but his brain is not involved as it would be if he were choosing his words for himself. If the speech he is making is one that he is accustomed to make over and over again, he may be almost unconscious of what he is saying, as one is when one utters the responses in church. And this reduced state of consciousness, if not indispensable, is at any rate favourable to political conformity.

In our time, political speech and writing are largely the defence of the indefensible. Things like the continuance of British rule in India, the Russian purges and deportations, the dropping of the atom bombs on Japan, can indeed be defended, but only by arguments which are too brutal for most people to face, and which do not square with the professed aims of political parties. Thus political language has to consist largely of euphemism, question-begging and sheer cloudy vagueness. Defenceless villages are bombarded from the air, the inhabitants driven out into the countryside, the cattle machine-gunned, the huts set on fire with incendiary bullets: this is called *pacification*. Millions of peasants are robbed of their farms and sent trudging along the roads with no more than they can carry: this is called *transfer of population* or *rectification of frontiers*. People are imprisoned for years without trial, or shot in the back of the neck, or sent to die of scurvy in Arctic lumber camps: this is called *elimination of unreliable elements*. Such phraseology is needed if one wants to name things without calling up mental pictures of them. Consider for instance some comfortable English professor defending Russian totalitarianism. He cannot say outright, "I believe in killing off your opponents when you can get good results by doing so." Probably, therefore, he will say something like this:

> While freely conceding that the Soviet regime exhibits certain features which the humanitarian may be inclined to deplore, we must, I think, agree that a certain curtailment of the right to political opposition is an unavoidable concomitant of transitional periods, and that the rigours which the Russian people have been called upon to undergo have been amply justified in the sphere of concrete achievement.

The inflated style is itself a kind of euphemism. A mass of Latin words falls upon the facts like soft snow, blurring the outlines and covering up all the details. The great enemy of clear language is insincerity. When there is a gap between one's real and one's declared aims, one turns as it were instinctively to long words and exhausted idioms, like a cuttlefish[2] squirting out ink. In our age there is no such thing as "keeping out of politics." All issues are political issues, and politics itself is a mass of lies, evasions, folly, hatred and schizophrenia. When the general atmosphere is bad, language must suffer. I should expect to find—this is a

---

[1] *White Papers* Parliamentary documents.

[2] *cuttlefish* Octopus.

guess which I have not sufficient knowledge to verify—that the German, Russian, and Italian languages have all deteriorated in the last ten or fifteen years, as a result of dictatorship.

But if thought corrupts language, language can also corrupt thought. A bad usage can spread by tradition and imitation, even among people who should and do know better. The debased language that I have been discussing is in some ways very convenient. Phrases like *a not unjustifiable assumption, leaves much to be desired, would serve no good purpose, a consideration which we should do well to bear in mind*, are a continuous temptation, a packet of aspirins always at one's elbow. Look back through this essay, and for certain you will find that I have again and again committed the very faults I am protesting against. By this morning's post I have received a pamphlet dealing with conditions in Germany. The author tells me that he "felt impelled" to write it. I open it at random, and here is almost the first sentence that I see: "(The Allies) have an opportunity not only of achieving a radical transformation of Germany's social and political structure in such a way as to avoid a nationalistic reaction in Germany itself, but at the same time of laying the foundations of a co-operative and unified Europe." You see, he "feels impelled" to write—feels, presumably, that he has something new to say—and yet his words, like cavalry horses answering the bugle, group themselves automatically into the familiar dreary pattern. This invasion of one's mind by ready-made phrases (*lay the foundations, achieve a radical transformation*) can only be prevented if one is constantly on guard against them, and every such phrase anaesthetises a portion of one's brain.

I said earlier that the decadence of our language is probably curable. Those who deny this would argue, if they produced an argument at all, that language merely reflects existing social conditions, and that we cannot influence its development by any direct tinkering with words and constructions. So far as the general tone or spirit of a language goes, this may be true, but it is not true in detail. Silly words and expressions have often disappeared, not through any evolutionary process but owing to the conscious action of a minority. Two recent examples were *explore every avenue* and *leave no stone unturned*, which were killed by the jeers of a few journalists. There is a long list of flyblown metaphors which could similarly be got rid of if enough people would interest themselves in the job; and it should also be possible to laugh the *not un-* formation out of existence,[1] to reduce the amount of Latin and Greek in the average sentence, to drive out foreign phrases and strayed scientific words, and, in general, to make pretentiousness unfashionable. But all these are minor points. The defence of the English language implies more than this, and perhaps it is best to start by saying what it does *not* imply.

To begin with it has nothing to do with archaism, with the salvaging of obsolete words and turns of speech, or with the setting up of a "standard English" which must never be departed from. On the contrary, it is especially concerned with the scrapping of every word or idiom which has outworn its usefulness. It has nothing to do with correct grammar and syntax, which are of no importance so long as one makes one's meaning clear, or with the avoidance of Americanisms, or with having what is called a "good prose style." On the other hand it is not concerned with fake simplicity and the attempt to make written English colloquial. Nor does it even imply in every case preferring the Saxon word to the Latin one, though it does imply using the fewest and shortest words that will cover one's meaning. What is above all needed is to let the meaning choose the word, and not the other way about. In prose, the worst thing one can do with words is to surrender to them. When you think of a concrete object, you think wordlessly, and then, if you want to describe the thing you have been visualizing you probably hunt about till you find the exact words that seem to fit it. When you think of something abstract you are more inclined to use words from the start, and unless you make a conscious effort to prevent it, the existing dialect will come rushing in and do the job for you, at the expense of blurring or even changing your meaning. Probably it is better to put off using words as long as possible and get one's meaning as clear as one can through pictures or sensations. Afterwards one can choose—not simply accept—the phrases that will best cover the meaning, and then switch round and decide what impression

---

[1] [Orwell's note]   One can cure oneself of the *not un-* formation by memorizing this sentence: *A not unblack dog was chasing a not unsmall rabbit across a not ungreen field.*

one's words are likely to make on another person. This last effort of the mind cuts out all stale or mixed images, all prefabricated phrases, needless repetitions, and humbug and vagueness generally. But one can often be in doubt about the effect of a word or a phrase, and one needs rules that one can rely on when instinct fails. I think the following rules will cover most cases:

(i) Never use a metaphor, simile, or other figure of speech which you are used to seeing in print.

(ii) Never use a long word where a short one will do.

(iii) If it is possible to cut a word out, always cut it out.

(iv) Never use the passive where you can use the active.

(v) Never use a foreign phrase, a scientific word, or a jargon word if you can think of an everyday English equivalent.

(vi) Break any of these rules sooner than say anything outright barbarous.

These rules sound elementary, and so they are, but they demand a deep change of attitude in anyone who has grown used to writing in the style now fashionable. One could keep all of them and still write bad English, but one could not write the kind of stuff that I quoted in those five specimens at the beginning of this article.

I have not here been considering the literary use of language, but merely language as an instrument for expressing and not for concealing or preventing thought. Stuart Chase and others have come near to claiming that all abstract words are meaningless, and have used this as a pretext for advocating a kind of political quietism. Since you don't know what Fascism is, how can you struggle against Fascism? One need not swallow such absurdities as this, but one ought to recognise that the present political chaos is connected with the decay of language, and that one can probably bring about some improvement by starting at the verbal end. If you simplify your English, you are freed from the worst follies of orthodoxy. You cannot speak any of the necessary dialects, and when you make a stupid remark its stupidity will be obvious, even to yourself. Political language—and with variations this is true of all political parties, from Conservatives to Anarchists—is designed to make lies sound truthful and murder

respectable, and to give an appearance of solidity to pure wind. One cannot change this all in a moment, but one can at least change one's own habits, and from time to time one can even, if one jeers loudly enough, send some worn-out and useless phrase—some *jackboot, Achilles' heel, hotbed, melting pot, acid test, veritable inferno* or other lump of verbal refuse—into the dustbin where it belongs.

—1946

Shooting an Elephant

In Moulmein, in Lower Burma, I was hated by large numbers of people—the only time in my life that I have been important enough for this to happen to me. I was sub-divisional police officer of the town, and in an aimless, petty kind of way anti-European feeling was very bitter. No one had the guts to raise a riot, but if a European woman went through the bazaars alone somebody would probably spit betel juice over her dress. As a police officer I was an obvious target and was baited whenever it seemed safe to do so. When a nimble Burman tripped me up on the football field and the referee (another Burman) looked the other way, the crowd yelled with hideous laughter. This happened more than once. In the end the sneering yellow faces of young men that met me everywhere, the insults hooted after me when I was at a safe distance, got badly on my nerves. The young Buddhist priests were the worst of all. There were several thousands of them in the town and none of them seemed to have anything to do except stand on street corners and jeer at Europeans.

All this was perplexing and upsetting. For at that time I had already made up my mind that imperialism was an evil thing and the sooner I chucked up my job and got out of it the better. Theoretically—and secretly, of course—I was all for the Burmese and all against their oppressors, the British. As for the job I was doing, I hated it more bitterly than I can perhaps make clear. In a job like that you see the dirty work of Empire at close quarters. The wretched prisoners huddling in the stinking cages of the lock-ups, the grey, cowed faces of the long-term convicts, the scarred buttocks of the men who had been flogged with bamboos—all these oppressed me with an intolerable sense of guilt. But I could get nothing into perspective. I was young and ill-educated and I had had to think out my problems in the utter silence that is imposed on every Englishman in the East. I did not even know that the British Empire is dying, still less did I know that it is a great deal better than the younger empires that are going to supplant it. All I knew was that I was stuck between my hatred of the empire I served and my rage against the evil-spirited little beasts who tried to make my job impossible. With one part of my mind I thought of the British Raj as an unbreakable tyranny, as something clamped down, *in saecula saeculorum*,[1] upon the will of prostrate peoples; with another part I thought that the greatest joy in the world would be to drive a bayonet into a Buddhist priest's guts. Feelings like these are the normal by-products of imperialism; ask any Anglo-Indian official, if you can catch him off duty.

One day something happened which in a roundabout way was enlightening. It was a tiny incident in itself, but it gave me a better glimpse than I had had before of the real nature of imperialism—the real motives for which despotic governments act. Early one morning the sub-inspector at a police station the other end of the town rang me up on the 'phone and said that an elephant was ravaging the bazaar. Would I please come and do something about it? I did not know what I could do, but I wanted to see what was happening and I got on to a pony and started out. I took my rifle, an old .44 Winchester and much too small to kill an elephant, but I thought the noise might be useful *in terrorem*.[2] Various Burmans stopped me on the way and told me about the elephant's doings. It was not, of course, a wild elephant, but a tame one which had gone "must."[3] It had been chained up, as tame elephants always are when their attack of "must" is due, but on the previous night it had broken its chain and escaped. Its mahout,[4] the only person who could manage it when it was in that state, had set out in pursuit, but had taken the wrong direction and was now twelve hours' journey away, and in the morning the elephant had suddenly reappeared in the town. The Burmese population had

no weapons and were quite helpless against it. It had already destroyed somebody's bamboo hut, killed a cow, and raided some fruit-stalls and devoured the stock; also it had met the municipal rubbish van, and, when the driver jumped out and took to his heels, had turned the van over and inflicted violences upon it.

The Burmese sub-inspector and some Indian constables were waiting for me in the quarter where the elephant had been seen. It was a very poor quarter, a labyrinth of squalid bamboo huts, thatched with palm-leaf, winding all over a steep hillside. I remember that it was a cloudy, stuffy morning at the beginning of the rains. We began questioning the people as to where the elephant had gone, and, as usual, failed to get any definite information. That is invariably the case in the East; a story always sounds clear enough at a distance, but the nearer you get to the scene of events the vaguer it becomes. Some of the people said that the elephant had gone in one direction, some said that he had gone in another, some professed not even to have heard of any elephant. I had almost made up my mind that the whole story was a pack of lies, when we heard yells a little distance away. There was a loud, scandalized cry of "Go away, child! Go away this instant!" and an old woman with a switch in her hand came round the corner of a hut, violently shooing away a crowd of naked children. Some more women followed, clicking their tongues and exclaiming; evidently there was something that the children ought not to have seen. I rounded the hut and saw a man's dead body sprawling in the mud. He was an Indian, a black Dravidian coolie, almost naked, and he could not have been dead many minutes. The people said that the elephant had come suddenly upon him round the corner of the hut, caught him with its trunk, put its foot on his back and ground him into the earth. This was the rainy season and the ground was soft, and his face had scored a trench a foot deep and a couple of yards long. He was lying on his belly with arms crucified and head sharply twisted to one side. His face was coated with mud, the eyes wide open, the teeth bared and grinning with an expression of unendurable agony. (Never tell me, by the way, that the dead look peaceful. Most of the corpses I have seen looked devilish.) The friction of the great beast's foot had stripped the skin from his back as neatly as one skins a rabbit. As soon as I saw the dead man I sent an orderly

---

[1] *in saecula saeculorum* Latin: for centuries upon centuries; forever.

[2] *terrorem* Latin: in fright, terror, or alarm.

[3] *"must"* I.e., condition characterized by aggressive behavior brought on by a surge in testosterone.

[4] *mahout* Elephant trainer or keeper.

to a friend's house nearby to borrow an elephant rifle. I had already sent back the pony, not wanting it to go mad with fright and throw me if it smelt the elephant.

The orderly came back in a few minutes with a rifle and five cartridges, and meanwhile some Burmans had arrived and told us that the elephant was in the paddy fields below, only a few hundred yards away. As I started forward practically the whole population of the quarter flocked out of the houses and followed me. They had seen the rifle and were all shouting excitedly that I was going to shoot the elephant. They had not shown much interest in the elephant when he was merely ravaging their homes, but it was different now that he was going to be shot. It was a bit of fun to them, as it would be to an English crowd; besides they wanted the meat. It made me vaguely uneasy. I had no intention of shooting the elephant—I had merely sent for the rifle to defend myself if necessary—and it is always unnerving to have a crowd following you. I marched down the hill, looking and feeling a fool, with the rifle over my shoulder and an ever-growing army of people jostling at my heels. At the bottom, when you got away from the huts, there was a metalled road and beyond that a miry waste of paddy fields a thousand yards across, not yet ploughed but soggy from the first rains and dotted with coarse grass. The elephant was standing eight yards from the road, his left side towards us. He took not the slightest notice of the crowd's approach. He was tearing up bunches of grass, beating them against his knees to clean them and stuffing them into his mouth.

I had halted on the road. As soon as I saw the elephant I knew with perfect certainty that I ought not to shoot him. It is a serious matter to shoot a working elephant—it is comparable to destroying a huge and costly piece of machinery—and obviously one ought not to do it if it can possibly be avoided. And at that distance, peacefully eating, the elephant looked no more dangerous than a cow. I thought then and I think now that his attack of "must" was already passing off; in which case he would merely wander harmlessly about until the mahout came back and caught him. Moreover, I did not in the least want to shoot him. I decided that I would watch him for a little while to make sure that he did not turn savage again, and then go home.

But at that moment I glanced round at the crowd that had followed me. It was an immense crowd, two thousand at the least and growing every minute. It blocked the road for a long distance on either side. I looked at the sea of yellow faces above the garish clothes—faces all happy and excited over this bit of fun, all certain that the elephant was going to be shot. They were watching me as they would watch a conjurer about to perform a trick. They did not like me, but with the magical rifle in my hands I was momentarily worth watching. And suddenly I realized that I should have to shoot the elephant after all. The people expected it of me and I had got to do it; I could feel their two thousand wills pressing me forward, irresistibly. And it was at this moment, as I stood there with the rifle in my hands, that I first grasped the hollowness, the futility of the white man's dominion in the East. Here was I, the white man with his gun, standing in front of the unarmed native crowd—seemingly the leading actor of the piece; but in reality I was only an absurd puppet pushed to and fro by the will of those yellow faces behind. I perceived in this moment that when the white man turns tyrant it is his own freedom that he destroys. He becomes a sort of hollow, posing dummy, the conventionalized figure of a sahib. For it is the condition of his rule that he shall spend his life in trying to impress the "natives," and so in every crisis he has got to do what the "natives" expect of him. He wears a mask, and his face grows to fit it. I had got to shoot the elephant. I had committed myself to doing it when I sent for the rifle. A sahib has got to act like a sahib; he has got to appear resolute, to know his own mind and do definite things. To come all that way, rifle in hand, with two thousand people marching at my heels, and then to trail feebly away, having done nothing—no, that was impossible. The crowd would laugh at me. And my whole life, every white man's life in the East, was one long struggle not to be laughed at.

But I did not want to shoot the elephant. I watched him beating his bunch of grass against his knees, with that preoccupied grandmotherly air that elephants have. It seemed to me that it would be murder to shoot him. At that age I was not squeamish about killing animals, but I had never shot an elephant and never wanted to. (Somehow it always seems worse to kill a *large* animal.) Besides, there was the beast's owner to be considered. Alive, the elephant was worth at least a hundred pounds; dead, he would only be worth the value of his tusks, five pounds, possibly. But I had got to act quickly. I turned to some experienced-looking Burmans who had been there when we arrived, and asked them how the elephant had been behaving. They all said the same thing: he took no notice of you if you left him alone, but he might charge if you went too close to him.

It was perfectly clear to me what I ought to do. I ought to walk up to within, say, twenty-five yards of the elephant and test his behaviour. If he charged I could shoot, if he took no notice of me it would be safe to leave him until the mahout came back. But also I knew that I was going to do no such thing. I was a poor shot with a rifle and the ground was soft mud into which one would sink at every step. If the elephant charged and I missed him, I should have about as much chance as a toad under a steam-roller. But even then I was not thinking particularly of my own skin, only of the watchful yellow faces behind. For at that moment, with the crowd watching me, I was not afraid in the ordinary sense, as I would have been if I had been alone. A white man mustn't be frightened in front of "natives"; and so, in general, he isn't frightened. The sole thought in my mind was that if anything went wrong those two thousand Burmans would see me pursued, caught, trampled on and reduced to a grinning corpse like that Indian up the hill. And if that happened it was quite probable that some of them would laugh. That would never do. There was only one alternative. I shoved the cartridges into the magazine and lay down on the road to get a better aim.

The crowd grew very still, and a deep, low, happy sigh, as of people who see the theatre curtain go up at last, breathed from innumerable throats. They were going to have their bit of fun after all. The rifle was a beautiful German thing with cross-hair sights. I did not then know that in shooting an elephant one would shoot to cut an imaginary bar running from ear-hole to ear-hole. I ought, therefore, as the elephant was sideways on, to have aimed straight at his ear-hole; actually I aimed several inches in front of this, thinking the brain would be further forward.

When I pulled the trigger I did not hear the bang or feel the kick—one never does when a shot goes home —but I heard the devilish roar of glee that went up from the crowd. In that instant, in too short a time, one would have thought, even for the bullet to get there, a mysterious, terrible change had come over the elephant. He neither stirred nor fell, but every line of his body had altered. He looked suddenly stricken, shrunken, immensely old, as though the frightful impact of the bullet had paralysed him without knocking him down. At last, after what seemed a long time—it might have been five seconds, I dare say—he sagged flabbily to his knees. His mouth slobbered. An enormous senility seemed to have settled upon him. One could have imagined him thousands of years old. I fired again into the same spot. At the second shot he did not collapse but climbed with desperate slowness to his feet and stood weakly upright, with legs sagging and head drooping. I fired a third time. That was the shot that did for him. You could see the agony of it jolt his whole body and knock the last remnant of strength from his legs. But in falling he seemed for a moment to rise, for as his hind legs collapsed beneath him he seemed to tower upwards like a huge rock toppling, his trunk reaching skywards like a tree. He trumpeted, for the first and only time. And then down he came, his belly towards me, with a crash that seemed to shake the ground even where I lay.

I got up. The Burmans were already racing past me across the mud. It was obvious that the elephant would never rise again, but he was not dead. He was breathing very rhythmically with long rattling gasps, his great mound of a side painfully rising and falling. His mouth was wide open—I could see far down into caverns of pale pink throat. I waited a long time for him to die, but his breathing did not weaken. Finally I fired my two remaining shots into the spot where I thought his heart must be. The thick blood welled out of him like red velvet, but still he did not die. His body did not even jerk when the shots hit him, the tortured breathing continued without a pause. He was dying, very slowly and in great agony, but in some world remote from me where not even a bullet could damage him further. I felt that I had got to put an end to that dreadful noise. It seemed dreadful to see the great beast lying there, powerless to move and yet powerless to die, and not even to be able to finish him. I sent back for my small rifle and poured shot after shot into his heart and down his throat. They seemed to make no impression. The tortured gasps continued as steadily as the ticking of a clock.

In the end I could not stand it any longer and went

away. I heard later that it took him half an hour to die. Burmans were bringing dahs[1] and baskets even before I left, and I was told they had stripped his body almost to the bones by the afternoon.

Afterwards, of course, there were endless discussions about the shooting of the elephant. The owner was furious, but he was only an Indian and could do nothing. Besides, legally I had done the right thing, for a mad elephant has to be killed, like a mad dog, if its owner fails to control it. Among the Europeans opinion was divided. The older men said I was right, the younger men said it was a damn shame to shoot an elephant for killing a coolie, because an elephant was worth more than any damn Coringhee coolie. And afterwards I was very glad that the coolie had been killed; it put me legally in the right and it gave me a sufficient pretext for shooting the elephant. I often wondered whether any of the others grasped that I had done it solely to avoid looking a fool.

—1950

In Context

Elephants in Asia

There are two types of elephant: the African elephant is by definition a wild animal, but the smaller Asian (or Indian) elephant may be tamed. The latter has long been employed as a beast of burden in many parts of Asia, used for transport, logging, and various other tasks—including hunting, as in the photograph below, of a royal expedition to India in 1912, illustrates.

---

[1] *dahs* Short swords or knives.

SAMUEL BECKETT
1906 – 1989

Though Samuel Beckett was a prolific writer of poetry, prose fiction, and criticism, he remains best known for two of his plays, *Waiting for Godot* and *Endgame*, which are credited with having revolutionized theater, and which continue to be performed worldwide today. Fragmented, filled with absences and silences, and sparing of plot, characterization, and setting, Beckett's work is broadly innovative; it attempts to dispense with elements previously thought to be essential to dramatic productions. By paring down his writing to the bare necessities, Beckett created new possibilities of form and produced works whose brevity and lack of structure leaves them open to a variety of critical interpretations.

Beckett was born on 13 April 1906 in Foxrock, an upper-class, Protestant suburb of Dublin. He attended a boarding school in Northern Ireland and from there continued on (in 1923) to Trinity College, Dublin, where he studied French and Italian. Upon graduation, having excelled academically, Beckett was offered a two-year position as an exchange lecturer in Paris, and it was there that his writing career began. Within months of arriving in Paris he had been introduced to fellow Dublin writer James Joyce, whose writing Beckett greatly admired. Beckett established himself as part of Joyce's circle of literary friends in Paris, and in 1928 was commissioned to write an essay on Joyce's *Finnegans Wake*, which was still a work in progress at the time; that essay and a short story of Beckett's were published simultaneously in the Paris literary magazine *transition*. Shortly thereafter his first poem, *Whoroscope* (1930), was published by Nancy Cunard's Hours Press. Beckett had been encouraged by a friend to submit a poem to Cunard's competition for the best short poem on the subject of time. Using existing notes, he composed the prize-winning poem about French philosopher René Descartes in one night.

After living in Paris for two years, Beckett was loath to return to Ireland. He found the atmosphere and literary community in Paris far more conducive to his writing, but largely as a result of financial pressures, he spent the following seven years (1930–37) in Ireland, moving between his family home in Foxrock and Dublin, where he taught at Trinity College for two years immediately following his departure from Paris. Beckett also spent some time in London undergoing therapy for recurring panic attacks and bouts of depression. During these seven years he worked on several projects, including his first novel, *Dream of Fair to Middling Women*; the series of short stories *More Pricks than Kicks* (1934); the novel *Murphy*; and a small collection of poems. This early work was not well received: his collection of poetry barely sold, *Dream* (1992) was not published during his lifetime, *More Pricks* received mixed reviews, and *Murphy* was rejected dozens of times before finally being accepted in 1938, two years after its completion.

In October 1937 Beckett returned to Paris, intending to settle there permanently and devote himself to his writing. This writer's life, however, was not without incident. Walking home late one night in January 1938, Beckett was stabbed in the chest and spent months recovering in hospital. There he was visited by Suzanne Deschevaux-Dumesnil, the woman who eventually became his wife. (Though the two were living together less than a year later, they did not marry until 1961.) Beckett and Deschevaux-Dumesnil were forced to leave Paris twice during World War II. The first time, in

1940, they escaped the city days before it fell to German forces. Upon returning to Paris a few months later, Beckett began working for the French Resistance (for which service he was decorated by the French government after the war). In 1942 the two had to flee Paris again when Beckett's Resistance cell was betrayed. They escaped their apartment only hours before the Gestapo arrived.

Though Beckett was able to do some writing while in hiding in the south of France, his most prolific period occurred after his return to his Paris flat in 1945. Between 1946 and 1950 he underwent what he referred to as "the siege in the room," composing four novellas, two plays, and four novels. Three of these novels—*Molloy* (1951), *Malone Dies* (*Malone meurt*, 1951), and *The Unnamable* (*L'innommable*, 1953)—comprise a trilogy and are perhaps his most highly regarded prose works. All the prose from this period departs from his earlier work in several ways. First, Beckett had decided to write entirely in French, translating his work back into English once it was completed. This helped him to avoid lyricism and enhanced the distinctive sparseness of his writing style. He also abandoned the omniscient narration of his earlier novels in favor of a first-person point of view. Frequently, as in *Texts for Nothing* (*Textes pour rien*, 1955) these narratives are more like fragmented meditations or monologues than stories. In fact, Beckett's prose, like his plays, tended towards monologue as his writing career progressed, to the point where the distinction between the two sometimes becomes blurred; many of his later works of short prose, such as *Imagination Dead Imagine* (*Imagination morte imaginez*, 1965), have been given stage performances.

To take a break from his trilogy, Beckett began working on *Waiting for Godot* (*En attendant Godot*, 1952), the two-act play in which, as Irish critic Vivian Mercier famously said, "Nothing happens, twice." The lack of progression in this play about two men waiting for someone called Godot (who never arrives) is characteristic of the majority of Beckett's drama. Set on practically bare stages, lacking significant character development, and consisting of plots with neither climax nor resolution, Beckett's plays have been referred to as more "anti-theater" than theater. The spareness of the setting of *Godot* ("A country road. A tree.") is exceeded by that of the setting of *Endgame* (*Fin de partie*, 1957)—a nearly empty room. In *Endgame*, which Beckett called "more inhuman than *Godot*," the characters are also waiting, though for nothing in particular, except the inevitable end. The frequently nonsensical dialogue of this play, like that of Beckett's others, often doubles back on itself and is interrupted by long silences; Beckett believed the role of theater was not to give "meaning" but to provide an "experience" from which audience members could generate their own meaning if they so desired.

Beckett's characters are largely of a piece. They tend to be aging, homeless, in mental and physical pain, and isolated from those around them yet desperately trying to maintain a sense of connection. Their bodies are sources of anguish, and they are constantly plagued by some difficulty or other. Their sense of disconnection from the outside world and from one another is a source of anxiety, as is the seemingly tenuous nature of their sterile existence. They attempt to alleviate this anxiety and give meaning to their existence through action, but to little avail. The dialogue, movements, and choices of these characters are rarely shown to have logic or consequence, and the result is by turns painful and funny to watch. Beckett's plays, like those of Eugène Ionesco and Jean Genet, are central texts to any discussion of absurdist theater—they present the absurdity and futility of the human condition as a given. Though often bleak, absurdist drama can also be highly comic; as Nell says in *Endgame*, "Nothing is funnier than unhappiness."

At no point in his career did Beckett demonstrate any concern for audience expectations, or feel the need to write in any currently popular style. Perhaps as a result, his work pushed the limits of what was thought possible. His willingness to experiment with new ideas, new media, and new technology resulted in a remarkably rich and diverse body of work. In 1958, shortly after reel-to-reel tape recorders were invented, Beckett incorporated one into a ground-breaking short play, *Krapp's Last Tape* (*La dernière bande*, 1958), in which a man conducts a "conversation" with a recording of his own voice from years before. In 1964 Beckett forayed into the world of film, writing a script for a film (titled simply *Film*) and traveling to New York to assist in making it.

As he aged, Beckett increasingly despaired of the ability of language to express anything meaningful about the nature of human existence. His 1969 play *Breath* is the most extreme manifestation of such feelings; it lasts less than one minute and includes sounds but no articulated words.

The extraordinary importance of Beckett's work was acknowledged in 1969 when he was awarded the Nobel Prize for Literature. He continued to direct many of his plays and to assist in their production for television up until only a few years before his death in 1989.

⌘ ⌘ ⌘

Krapp's Last Tape

A late evening in the future.

Krapp's den.

Front centre a small table, the two drawers of which open towards audience.

Sitting at the table, facing front, i.e. across from the drawers, a wearish old man: Krapp.

Rusty black narrow trousers too short for him. Rusty black sleeveless waistcoat, four capacious pockets. Heavy silver watch and chain. Grimy white shirt open at neck, no collar. Surprising pair of dirty white boots, size ten at least, very narrow and pointed.

White face. Purple nose. Disordered grey hair. Unshaven.

Very near-sighted (but unspectacled). Hard of hearing.

Cracked voice. Distinctive intonation.

Laborious walk.

On the table a tape-recorder with microphone and a number of cardboard boxes containing reels of recorded tapes.

Table and immediately adjacent area in strong white light. Rest of stage in darkness.

Krapp remains a moment motionless, heaves a great sigh, looks at his watch, fumbles in his pockets, takes out an envelope, puts it back, fumbles, takes out a small bunch of keys, raises it to his eyes, chooses a key, gets up and moves to front of table. He stoops, unlocks first drawer, peers into it, feels about inside it, takes out a reel of tape, peers at it, puts it back, locks drawer, unlocks second drawer, peers into it, feels about inside it, takes out a large banana, peers at it, locks drawer, puts keys back in his pocket. He turns, advances to edge of stage, halts, strokes banana, peels it, drops skin at his feet, puts end of banana in his mouth and remains motionless, staring vacuously before him. Finally he bites off the end, turns aside and begins pacing to and fro at edge of stage, in the light, i.e. not more than four or five paces either way, meditatively eating banana. He treads on skin, slips, nearly falls, recovers himself, stoops and peers at skin and finally pushes it, still stooping, with his foot over the edge of stage into pit. He resumes his pacing, finishes banana, returns to table, sits down, remains a moment motionless, heaves a great sigh, takes keys from his pockets, raises them to his eyes, chooses key, gets up and moves to front of table, unlocks second drawer, takes out a second large banana, peers at it, locks drawer, puts back keys in his pocket, turns, advances to edge of stage, halts, strokes banana, peels it, tosses skin into pit, puts end of banana in his mouth and remains motionless, staring vacuously before him. Finally he has an idea, puts banana in his waistcoat pocket, the end emerging, and goes with all the speed he can muster backstage into darkness. Ten seconds. Loud pop of cork. Fifteen seconds. He comes back into light carrying an old ledger and sits down at table. He lays ledger on table, wipes his mouth, wipes his hands on the front of his waistcoat, brings them smartly together and rubs them.

KRAPP. (*Briskly.*) Ah! (*He bends over ledger, turns the pages, finds the entry he wants, reads.*) Box … thrree … spool … five. (*He raises his head and stares front. With relish.*) Spool! (*Pause.*) Spoool! (*Happy smile. Pause. He bends over table, starts peering and poking at the boxes.*) Box … thrree … thrree … four … two … (*With surprise.*) nine! good God! … seven … ah! the little rascal! (*He takes up box, peers at it.*) Box thrree. (*He lays it on table, opens it and peers at spools inside.*) Spool … (*He peers at ledger.*) … five … (*He peers at spools.*) … five … five …ah! the little scoundrel! (*He takes out a spool, peers at it.*) Spool five. (*He lays it on table, closes box three, puts it back with the others, takes up the spool.*) Box thrree, spool five. (*He bends over the machine, looks up. With relish.*) Spoool! (*Happy smile. He bends, loads spool on machine, rubs his hands.*) Ah! (*He peers at ledger, reads entry at foot of page.*) Mother at rest at last … Hm … The black ball … (*He raises his head, stares blankly front. Puzzled.*) Black ball? … (*He peers again at ledger, reads.*) The dark nurse … (*He raises his head, broods, peers again at ledger, reads.*) Slight improvement in bowel condition … Hm … Memorable … what? (*He peers closer.*) Equinox, memorable equinox. (*He raises his head, stares blankly front. Puzzled.*) Memorable equinox? … (*Pause. He shrugs his shoulders, peers again at ledger, reads.*) Farewell to—(*He turns the page.*—) love.

(*He raises his head, broods, bends over machine, switches on and assumes listening posture, i.e. leaning forward, elbows on table, hand cupping ear towards machine, face front.*)

TAPE. (*Strong voice, rather pompous, clearly Krapp's at a much earlier time.*) Thirty-nine today, sound as a—(*Settling himself more comfortably he knocks one of the boxes off the table, curses, switches off, sweeps boxes and ledger violently to the ground, winds tape back to beginning, switches on, resumes posture.*) Thirty-nine today, sound as a bell, apart from my old weakness, and intellectually I have now every reason to suspect at the … (*Hesitates.*) … crest of the wave—or thereabouts. Celebrated the awful occasion, as in recent years, quietly at the Winehouse. Not a soul. Sat before the fire with closed eyes, separating the grain from the husks. Jotted down a few notes, on the back of an envelope. Good to be back in my den, in my old rags. Have just eaten I regret to say three bananas and only with difficulty refrained from a fourth. Fatal things for a man with my condition. (*Vehemently.*) Cut 'em out! (*Pause.*) The new light above my table is a great improvement. With all this darkness round me I feel less alone. (*Pause.*) In a way. (*Pause.*) I love to get up and move about in it, then back here to … (*Hesitates.*) … me. (*Pause.*) Krapp.

(*Pause.*)

The grain, now what I wonder do I mean by that, I mean … (*Hesitates.*) … I suppose I mean those things worth having when all the dust has—when all *my* dust has settled. I close my eyes and try and imagine them.

(*Pause. Krapp closes his eyes briefly.*)

Extraordinary silence this evening, I strain my ears and do not hear a sound. Old Miss McGlome always sings at this hour. But not tonight. Songs of her girlhood, she says. Hard to think of her as a girl. Wonderful woman though. Connaught,[1] I fancy. (*Pause.*) Shall I sing when I am her age, if I ever am? No. (*Pause.*) Did I sing as a boy? No. (*Pause.*) Did I ever sing? No.

(*Pause.*)

Just been listening to an old year, passages at random. I did not check in the book, but it must be at least ten or twelve years ago. At that time I think I was still living on and off with Bianca in Kedar Street. Well out of that, Jesus yes! Hopeless business. (*Pause.*) Not much about her, apart from a tribute to her eyes. Very warm. I suddenly saw them again. (*Pause.*) Incomparable! (*Pause.*) Ah well … (*Pause.*) These old P.M.s are gruesome, but I often find them——(*Krapp switches off, broods, switches on.*)—a help before embarking on a new … (*Hesitates.*) … retrospect. Hard to believe I was ever that young whelp. The voice! Jesus! And the aspirations! (*Brief laugh in which Krapp joins.*) And the resolutions! (*Brief laugh in which Krapp joins.*) To drink less, in

---

[1] *Connaught* Western province of Ireland.

particular. (*Brief laugh of Krapp alone.*) Statistics. Seven-teen hundred hours, out of the preceding eight thou-sand odd, consumed on licensed premises alone. More than 20%, say 40% of his waking life. (*Pause.*) Plans for a less … (*Hesitates.*) … engrossing sexual life. Last illness of his father. Flagging pursuit of happiness. Unattain-able laxation.[1] Sneers at what he calls his youth and thanks to God that it's over. (*Pause.*) False ring there. (*Pause.*) Shadows of the opus … magnum. Closing with a—(*Brief laugh.*)—yelp to Providence. (*Prolonged laugh in which Krapp joins.*) What remains of all that misery? A girl in a shabby green coat, on a railway-station platform? No?

(*Pause.*)

When I look—

(*Krapp switches off, broods, looks at his watch, gets up, goes backstage into darkness. Ten seconds. Pop of cork. Ten seconds. Second cork. Ten seconds. Third cork. Ten seconds. Brief burst of quavering song.*)

KRAPP.   (*Sings.*)   Now the day is over,
                 Night is drawing nigh-igh,
                 Shadows—[2]

(*Fit of coughing. He comes back into light, sits down, wipes his mouth, switches on, resumes his listening posture.*)

TAPE.   —back on the year that is gone, with what I hope is perhaps a glint of the old eye to come, there is of course the house on the canal where mother lay a-dying, in the late autumn, after her long viduity (*Krapp gives a start.*), and the—(*Krapp switches off, winds back tape a little, bends his ear closer to machine, switches on.*)—a-dying, after her long viduity, and the—

(*Krapp switches off, raises his head, stares blankly before him. His lips move in the syllables of "viduity." No sound. He gets up, goes backstage into darkness, comes back with an enormous dictionary, lays it on table, sits down and looks up the word.*)

KRAPP.   (*Reading from dictionary.*) State—or condition of being—or remaining—a widow—or widower. (*Looks up. Puzzled.*) Being—or remaining? … (*Pause. He peers again at dictionary. Reading.*) "Deep weeds of viduity" … Also of an animal, especially a bird … the vidua or weaver-bird … Black plumage of male … (*He looks up. With relish.*) The vidua-bird!

(*Pause. He closes dictionary, switches on, resumes listening posture.*)

TAPE.   —bench by the weir from where I could see her window. There I sat, in the biting wind, wishing she were gone. (*Pause.*) Hardly a soul, just a few regulars, nursemaids, infants, old men, dogs. I got to know them quite well—oh by appearance of course I mean! One dark young beauty I recollect particularly, all white and starch, incomparable bosom, with a big black hooded perambulator, most funereal thing. Whenever I looked in her direction she had her eyes on me. And yet when I was bold enough to speak to her—not having been introduced—she threatened to call a policeman. As if I had designs on her virtue! (*Laugh. Pause.*) The face she had! The eyes! Like … (*Hesitates.*) … chrysolite![3] (*Pause.*) Ah well … (*Pause.*) I was there when—(*Krapp switches off, broods, switches on again.*)—the blind went down, one of those dirty brown roller affairs, throwing a ball for a little white dog, as chance would have it. I happened to look up and there it was. All over and done with, at last. I sat on for a few moments with the ball in my hand and the dog yelping and pawing at me. (*Pause.*) Moments. Her moments, my moments. (*Pause.*) The dog's moments. (*Pause.*) In the end I held it out to him and he took it in his mouth, gently, gently. A small, old, black, hard, solid rubber ball. (*Pause.*) I shall feel it, in my hand, until my dying day. (*Pause.*) I might have kept it. (*Pause.*) But I gave it to the dog.

(*Pause.*)

Ah well …

(*Pause.*)

---

[1] *laxation*   Relaxed state.

[2] *Now … Shadows*   From an old hymn, words by Sabine Baring-Gould (1865).

[3] *chrysolite*   Green gem.

Spiritually a year of profound gloom and indigence until that memorable night in March, at the end of the jetty, in the howling wind, never to be forgotten, when suddenly I saw the whole thing. The vision, at last. This I fancy is what I have chiefly to record this evening, against the day when my work will be done and perhaps no place left in my memory, warm or cold, for the miracle that … (*Hesitates.*) … for the fire that set it alight. What I suddenly saw then was this, that the belief I had been going on all my life, namely—(*Krapp switches off impatiently, winds tape forward, switches on again.*)—great granite rocks the foam flying up in the light of the lighthouse and the wind-gauge spinning like a propeller, clear to me at last that the dark I have always struggled to keep under is in reality my most—(*Krapp curses, switches off, winds tape forward, switches on again.*)—unshatterable association until my dissolution of storm and night with the light of the understanding and the fire—(*Krapp curses louder, switches off, winds tape forward, switches on again.*)—my face in her breasts and my hand on her. We lay there without moving. But under us all moved, and moved us, gently, up and down, and from side to side.

(*Pause.*)

Past midnight. Never knew such silence. The earth might be uninhabited.

(*Pause.*)

Here I end—

(*Krapp switches off, winds tape back, switches on again.*)

—upper lake, with the punt,[1] bathed off the bank, then pushed out into the stream and drifted. She lay stretched out on the floorboards with her hands under her head and her eyes closed. Sun blazing down, bit of a breeze, water nice and lively. I noticed a scratch on her thigh and asked her how she came by it. Picking gooseberries, she said. I said again I thought it was hopeless and no good going on, and she agreed, without opening her eyes. (*Pause.*) I asked her to look at me and after a few moments—(*Pause.*)—after a few moments she did,

but the eyes just slits, because of the glare. I bent over her to get them in the shadow and they opened. (*Pause. Low.*) Let me in. (*Pause.*) We drifted in among the flags[2] and stuck. The way they went down, sighing, before the stem! (*Pause.*) I lay down across her with my face in her breasts and my hand on her. We lay there without moving. But under us all moved, and moved us, gently, up and down, and from side to side.

(*Pause.*)

Past midnight. Never knew—

(*Krapp switches off, broods. Finally he fumbles in his pockets, encounters the banana, takes it out, peers at it, puts it back, fumbles, brings out the envelope, fumbles, puts back envelope, looks at his watch, gets up and goes backstage into darkness. Ten seconds. Sound of bottle against glass, then brief siphon. Ten seconds. Bottle against glass alone. Ten seconds. He comes back a little unsteadily into light, goes to front of table, takes out keys, raises them to his eyes, chooses key, unlocks first drawer, peers into it, feels about inside, takes out reel, peers at it, locks drawer, puts keys back in his pocket, goes and sits down, takes reel off machine, lays it on dictionary, loads virgin reel on machine, takes envelope from his pocket, consults back of it, lays it on table, switches on, clears his throat and begins to record.*)

KRAPP. Just been listening to that stupid bastard I took myself for thirty years ago, hard to believe I was ever as bad as that. Thank God that's all done with anyway. (*Pause.*) The eyes she had! (*Broods, realizes he is recording silence, switches off, broods. Finally.*) Everything there, everything, all the—(*Realizes this is not being recorded, switches on.*) Everything there, everything on this old muckball, all the light and dark and famine and feasting of … (*Hesitates.*) … the ages! (*In a shout.*) Yes! (*Pause.*) Let that go! Jesus! Take his mind off his homework! Jesus! (*Pause. Weary.*) Ah well, maybe he was right. (*Pause.*) Maybe he was right. (*Broods. Realizes. Switches off. Consults envelope.*) Pah! (*Crumples it and throws it away. Broods. Switches on.*) Nothing to say, not a squeak. What's a year now? The sour cud and the iron stool. (*Pause.*) Revelled in the word spool. (*With relish.*)

---

[1] punt Shallow, flat-bottomed boat.

[2] flags Irises.

Spooool! Happiest moment of the past half million. (*Pause.*) Seventeen copies sold, of which eleven at trade price to free circulating libraries beyond the seas. Getting known. (*Pause.*) One pound six and something, eight I have little doubt. (*Pause.*) Crawled out once or twice, before the summer was cold. Sat shivering in the park, drowned in dreams and burning to be gone. Not a soul. (*Pause.*) Last fancies. (*Vehemently.*) Keep 'em under! (*Pause.*) Scalded the eyes out of me reading *Effie*[1] again, a page a day, with tears again. Effie … (*Pause.*) Could have been happy with her, up there on the Baltic, and the pines, and the dunes. (*Pause.*) Could I? (*Pause.*) And she? (*Pause.*) Pah! (*Pause.*) Fanny came in a couple of times. Bony old ghost of a whore. Couldn't do much, but I suppose better than a kick in the crutch. The last time wasn't so bad. How do you manage it, she said, at your age? I told her I'd been saving up for her all my life. (*Pause.*) Went to Vespers[2] once, like when I was in short trousers. (*Pause. Sings.*)

> Now the day is over,
> Night is drawing nigh-igh,
> Shadows—(*Coughing, then almost inaudible.*) —of
>   the evening
> Steal across the sky.

(*Gasping.*) Went to sleep and fell off the pew. (*Pause.*) Sometimes wondered in the night if a last effort mightn't—(*Pause.*) Ah finish your booze now and get to your bed. Go on with this drivel in the morning. Or leave it at that. (*Pause.*) Leave it at that. (*Pause.*) Lie propped up in the dark—and wander. Be again in the dingle[3] on a Christmas Eve, gathering holly, the redberried. (*Pause.*) Be again on Croghan[4] on a Sunday morning, in the haze, with the bitch, stop and listen to the bells. (*Pause.*) And so on. (*Pause.*) Be again, be again.

(*Pause.*) All that old misery. (*Pause.*) Once wasn't enough for you. (*Pause.*) Lie down across her.

(*Long pause. He suddenly bends over machine, switches off, wrenches off tape, throws it away, puts on the other, winds it forward to the passage he wants, switches on, listens staring front.*)

TAPE.   —gooseberries, she said. I said again I thought it was hopeless and no good going on, and she agreed, without opening her eyes. (*Pause.*) I asked her to look at me and after a few moments—(*Pause.*)—after a few moments she did, but the eyes just slits, because of the glare. I bent over her to get them in the shadow and they opened. (*Pause. Low.*) Let me in. (*Pause.*) We drifted in among the flags and stuck. The way they went down, sighing, before the stem! (*Pause.*) I lay down across her with my face in her breasts and my hand on her. We lay there without moving. But under us all moved, and moved us, gently, up and down, and from side to side.

(*Pause. Krapp's lips move. No sound.*)

Past midnight. Never knew such silence. The earth might be uninhabited.

(*Pause.*)

Here I end this reel. Box—(*Pause.*)—three, spool—(*Pause.*)—five. (*Pause.*) Perhaps my best years are gone. When there was a chance of happiness. But I wouldn't want them back. Not with the fire in me now. No, I wouldn't want them back.

(*Krapp motionless staring before him. The tape runs on in silence.*)

CURTAIN
—1958

---

[1] *Effie* Effi Briest (1895), a sentimental novel by Theodor Fontane about a failed love affair.

[2] *Vespers* Evening prayer service.

[3] *dingle* Valley.

[4] *Croghan* Croghan Hill in County Wicklow, Ireland.

W.H. Auden

1907 — 1973

W.H. Auden's poetry documents the changing political, social, and psychological landscape of his time, using language firmly rooted in the world around him. In describing the physical and spiritual ills of society and seeking order and clarity in human existence, he developed a poetry that couples contemporary speech with more traditional, structured verse forms. "Auden was an epoch-making poet on public themes," Seamus Heaney said, "the register of a new sensibility."

Born in York, England, in 1907, Wystan Hugh Auden was the youngest of three sons. His chief childhood interests were scientific: he was fascinated by engineering, mineralogy, and geology, and won a scholarship to study natural science at Oxford. A developing passion for poetry, however, led him to transfer to English, although his interest in science—and his experiences growing up in industrial England (he spent his childhood in Birmingham)—remain evident in the themes that permeate his poetry. He became a central member of a group of writers known as the "Oxford Group," which included Cecil Day Lewis, Stephen Spender, and Louis MacNeice. Auden published numerous poems in undergraduate magazines, and when he had assembled a first volume, he sent it to T.S. Eliot at the publishing house of Faber and Gwyer (later Faber and Faber). The volume was rejected, and Auden had it printed privately on Spender's handpress. Eliot had expressed interest in Auden's work, however, and in 1930 he

published Auden's *Poems*. Heavily colored by a sense of political commitment, *Poems* addresses concrete social problems, such as the poverty in depressed areas of industrial England. Many poems are experiments with tone and form—for example, Auden melded Anglo-Saxon sound patterns with modern subject matter.

After graduating from Oxford, Auden spent a year in Germany with a university friend, Christopher Isherwood, and was influenced by German music, literature, and theater—particularly the leftist political theater of Bertolt Brecht and Kurt Weill. When he returned to England, Auden worked variously as a schoolmaster, a university lecturer, a writer of experimental drama, and a verse commentator on documentary films. In this last position he worked with composer Benjamin Britten, who became a close friend and artistic collaborator. Collaborative work appealed to Auden, who went on to co-write three plays with Isherwood: *The Dog Beneath the Skin* (1935), *The Ascent of F6* (1936), and *On the Frontier* (1938). A trip to Iceland with MacNeice, funded by Auden's publishers, resulted in the collaborative travel book *Letters from Iceland* (1937), an unconventional collection of essays, poems, letters, and notes on everything from touring the country to contemporary politics.

Although Auden was openly homosexual, he agreed in 1935 to marry German novelist Thomas Mann's daughter Erika, whose passport was about to be revoked by the Nazis. When the Spanish Civil War began a year later, he volunteered for the Spanish Republic as a medical worker, but the authorities instead gave him work in the censor's office, writing government propaganda. He was disturbed by the extent to which Stalin's government controlled the Republic and also by the fact that the government had forced the churches to close. Although Auden had abandoned his religious beliefs after childhood, the experience caused him to reconsider the importance of spirituality.

Auden later traveled with Isherwood to China and Japan to observe the Sino-Japanese war. There they wrote *Journey to a War* (1939), largely about the complexity of political writing. In his poems of this period Auden developed his characteristically sparse, terse, and often fragmented style, relying on concrete images and colloquial language to create a sense of immediacy and intensity. His explicitly political poems of this period, such as "Spain 1937," had helped to establish his reputation as a poet, but in 1939, the year he moved to New York, he decided he would never again write anything that resembled propaganda, regardless of cause. In fact, in later years he often rewrote and even suppressed his earlier, more left-wing poems.

In New York, where Auden settled for most of his later life, he devoted himself to his poetry with renewed energy. He became involved in a serious relationship with Chester Kallman, a nineteen-year-old student who would become his lifelong companion and an important literary collaborator. The 1940 volume *Another Time* signals his desire to move on to explore new subjects and modes of expression. *Another Time* meticulously measures the social pulse of the thirties—which Auden characterized as "the age of anxiety"—and includes some of his best-known works, including "Musée des Beaux Arts," "September 1, 1939" (his response to the declaration of war), and elegies to poets Matthew Arnold, A.E. Housman, and W.B. Yeats, all of whom had been significant influences on his poetic development.

From then on, Auden's poetry began to take on more intimate and subjective overtones, often with religious themes. In 1941 he began attending the Anglican church regularly and experienced a renewal of religious faith. While his earlier poetry examined concrete social ills, his later poetry developed a more complex worldview, often focusing on spiritual aspects of society and casting social problems in terms of personal responsibility. His next major collection, *For the Time Being* (1944), includes the Christmas Oratorio "For the Time Being" and "The Sea and the Mirror," a poetic commentary on Shakespeare's *The Tempest* that explored Auden's ideas of poetry in the light of Christianity. With *The Collected Poetry* (1945), Auden began revising and retitling his earlier work, a task he would continue, almost compulsively, throughout his life.

In 1948, Auden was awarded the Pulitzer Prize for *The Age of Anxiety* (1947), a verse dialogue between four people in a New York bar. *The Shield of Achilles* (1955), which won the National Book Award, displays the influence of Anglo-Catholic theology and rituals, which Auden increasingly explored in verse. During these years he also wrote a considerable body of criticism and taught at various universities. In 1956 he became a Professor of Poetry at Oxford, where he gave three lectures per year for five years. These lectures, together with numerous reviews and essays, were collected in *The Dyer's Hand* (1962).

In his later years, with volumes such as *About the House* (1965) and *City Without Walls* (1969), Auden cemented his reputation as one of the leading poets of his day. After awarding him the National Medal for Literature in 1967, the National Book Committee declared that Auden's poetry "has illuminated our lives and times with grace, wit, and vitality. His work, branded by the moral and ideological fires of our age, breathes with eloquence, perception, and intellectual power." In 1972, seeking to return to a small community in which he could live peacefully as a writer, Auden accepted an honorary studentship at Christ Church, Oxford, his alma mater. He died there the following year. A final volume of poetry, *Thank You, Fog*, was published posthumously in 1974. Auden's careful attention to poetic form and meter, his sensitivity to language and to the music of words, and his concern with eternal questions of spirituality, love, and humanity's place in the world have all served to secure his current standing as one of the twentieth century's most significant poetic voices.

⌘ ⌘ ⌘

[At last the secret is out]

At last the secret is out, as it always must come in
   the end,
The delicious story is ripe to tell to the intimate friend;
Over the tea-cups and into the square the tongue has
   its desire;
Still waters run deep, my dear, there's never smoke
   without fire.

5   Behind the corpse in the reservoir, behind the ghost
      on the links,[1]
Behind the lady who dances and the man who madly
      drinks,
Under the look of fatigue the attack of migraine and
      the sigh
There is always another story, there is more than
      meets the eye.

For the clear voice suddenly singing, high up in the
      convent wall,
10   The scent of the elder bushes, the sporting prints in
      the hall,
The croquet matches in summer, the handshake, the
      cough, the kiss,
There is always a wicked secret, a private reason for this.
—1936

[Funeral Blues][2]

Stop all the clocks, cut off the telephone,
   Prevent the dog from barking with a juicy bone,
Silence the pianos and with muffled drum
Bring out the coffin, let the mourners come.

5   Let aeroplanes circle moaning overhead
Scribbling on the sky the message He Is Dead,

Put crêpe bows[3] round the white necks of the public
      doves,
Let the traffic policemen wear black cotton gloves.

He was my North, my South, my East and West,
10   My working week and my Sunday rest,
My noon, my midnight, my talk, my song;
I thought that love would last for ever; I was wrong.

The stars are not wanted now: put out every one;
Pack up the moon and dismantle the sun;
15   Pour away the ocean and sweep up the wood;
For nothing now can ever come to any good.
—1936, 1940

Spain 1937[4]

Yesterday all the past. The language of size
   Spreading to China along the trade-routes; the
      diffusion
         Of the counting-frame and the cromlech;[5]
Yesterday the shadow-reckoning in the sunny climates.

---

[3] *crêpe bows*   Black crepe, a woven fabric with a wrinkled surface,
is the traditional fabric of mourning clothes.

[4] *Spain 1937*   In the 1930s, Spain was a nation in which wealthy
landowners and a conservative Roman Catholic Church hierarchy
controlled much of society, and much inequality existed. The
election of a left-of-center government in 1936 signaled a break with
the past; the new government promised to enact a substantial
program of land reform and a variety of other progressive changes.
Almost immediately following the government's election, conservative forces began to plan its overthrow. An attempted coup was
launched by army factions on 18 July 1936, but faced stiff resistance.
This was the beginning of the Spanish Civil War, which ended with
the victory of Francisco Franco's Nationalists—a Fascist party—and
the installation of Franco as commander-in-chief and Head of State.
Progressives, liberal democrats, communists, and anarchists from
around the world were drawn to the Republican cause, and many
came to Spain to fight with the forces loyal to the democratically
elected government. On the other side the fascist dictatorships of
Hitler in Germany, Mussolini in Italy, and Salazar in Portugal all
provided support for Franco's army. Sympathetic to the Republicans, Auden went to Spain in January 1937 with a medical unit. He
wrote this poem in March 1937, after he had returned to Britain,
and had it printed as a separate pamphlet, the proceeds of which
went to aid Spanish medical work.

[5] *cromlech*   Ancient Celtic stone structure.

---

[1] *links*   Undulating, sandy ground near a shore.

[2] *[Funeral Blues]*   This poem first appeared in *The Ascent of F6*, a
play co-written by Auden and Christopher Isherwood. It then
appeared, in a revised version and with this present title, in Auden's
1940 collection *Another Time*.

5   Yesterday the assessment of insurance by cards,
The divination of water; yesterday the invention
        Of cart-wheels and clocks, the taming of
Horses; yesterday the bustling world of the navigators.

Yesterday the abolition of fairies and giants;
10   The fortress like a motionless eagle eyeing the valley,
        The chapel built in the forest;
Yesterday the carving of angels and of frightening
    gargoyles.

The trial of heretics among the columns of stone;
Yesterday the theological feuds in the taverns
15   And the miraculous cure at the fountain;
Yesterday the Sabbath of Witches.[1] But today the
    struggle.

Yesterday the installation of dynamos[2] and turbines;
The construction of railways in the colonial desert;
        Yesterday the classic lecture
20   On the origin of Mankind. But today the struggle.

Yesterday the belief in the absolute value of Greek;
The fall of the curtain upon the death of a hero;
        Yesterday the prayer to the sunset,
And the adoration of madmen. But today the struggle.

25   As the poet whispers, startled among the pines
Or, where the loose waterfall sings, compact, or upright
        On the crag by the leaning tower:
"O my vision. O send me the luck of the sailor."

And the investigator peers through his instruments
30   At the inhuman provinces, the virile bacillus
        Or enormous Jupiter finished:
"But the lives of my friends. I inquire, I inquire."

And the poor in their fireless lodgings dropping the
    sheets

Of the evening paper: "Our day is our loss. O show us
35   History the operator, the
Organiser, Time the refreshing river."

And the nations combine each cry, invoking the life
That shapes the individual belly and orders
        The private nocturnal terror:
40   "Did you not found once the city state of the sponge,

"Raise the vast military empires of the shark
And the tiger, establish the robin's plucky
        canton?°   *territory*
        Intervene. O descend as a dove or
A furious papa or a mild engineer: but descend."

45   And the life, if it answers at all, replies from the heart
And the eyes and the lungs, from the shops and
        squares of the city:
        "O no, I am not the Mover,
Not today, not to you. To you I'm the

"Yes-man, the bar-companion, the easily-duped:
50   I am whatever you do; I am your vow to be
        Good, your humorous story;
I am your business voice; I am your marriage.

"What's your proposal? To build the Just City?[3] I will.
I agree. Or is it the suicide pact, the romantic
55   Death? Very well, I accept, for
I am your choice, your decision: yes, I am Spain."

Many have heard it on remote peninsulas,
On sleepy plains, in the aberrant fishermen's islands,
        In the corrupt heart of the city;
60   Have heard and migrated like gulls or the seeds of a
    flower.

They clung like burrs to the long expresses that lurch
Through the unjust lands, through the night, through
        the alpine tunnel;
        They floated over the oceans;
They walked the passes: they came to present their lives.

---

[1] *Sabbath of Witches* Nocturnal gathering of witches believed by medieval Christians to be a demonic orgy or a heretical parody of the Mass.

[2] *dynamos* Machines that rotate copper wire coils in a magnetic field to convert mechanical into electrical energy.

---

[3] *the Just City* In Plato's *Republic*, Socrates discusses what is required to make a just city, and recommends rule by a "philosopher-king."

65 On that arid square, that fragment nipped off from hot
Africa, soldered so crudely to inventive Europe,
      On that tableland scored by rivers,
Our fever's menacing shapes are precise and alive.

To-morrow, perhaps, the future: the research on fatigue
70 And the movements of packers; the gradual exploring
      of all the
      Octaves of radiation;
To-morrow the enlarging of consciousness by diet and
      breathing.

To-morrow the rediscovery of romantic love;
The photographing of ravens; all the fun under
75   Liberty's masterful shadow;
To-morrow the hour of the pageant-master and the
      musician.

To-morrow, for the young, the poets exploding like
      bombs,
The walks by the lake, the winter of perfect communion;
      To-morrow the bicycle races
80 Through the suburbs on summer evenings: but today
      the struggle.

To-day the inevitable increase in the chances of death;
The conscious acceptance of guilt in the fact of murder;
      To-day the expending of powers
On the flat ephemeral pamphlet and the boring meeting.

85 To-day the makeshift consolations; the shared cigarette;
The cards in the candle-lit barn and the scraping concert,
      The masculine jokes; today the
Fumbled and unsatisfactory embrace before hurting.

The stars are dead; the animals will not look:
90 We are left alone with our day, and the time is short and
      History to the defeated
May say Alas but cannot help or pardon.
      —1937

[Lullaby]

Lay your sleeping head, my love,
      Human on my faithless arm;
Time and fevers burn away
Individual beauty from
5 Thoughtful children, and the grave
Proves the child ephemeral:
But in my arms till break of day
Let the living creature lie,
Mortal, guilty, but to me
10 The entirely beautiful.

Soul and body have no bounds:
To lovers as they lie upon
Her tolerant enchanted slope
In their ordinary swoon,
15 Grave the vision Venus[1] sends
Of supernatural sympathy,
Universal love and hope;
While an abstract insight wakes
Among the glaciers and the rocks
20 The hermit's carnal ecstasy.

Certainty, fidelity
On the stroke of midnight pass
Like vibrations of a bell,
And fashionable madmen raise
25 Their pedantic boring cry:
Every farthing of the cost,
All the dreaded cards foretell,
Shall be paid, but from this night
Not a whisper, not a thought,
30 Not a kiss nor look be lost.

Beauty, midnight, vision dies:
Let the winds of dawn that blow
Softly round your dreaming head
Such a day of sweetness show
35 Eye and knocking heart may bless,
Find the mortal world enough;
Noons of dryness see you fed

---

[1] *Venus* Roman goddess of beauty and love, mother of Cupid.

By the involuntary powers,
    Nights of insult let you pass
40 Watched by every human love.
    —1937

[As I walked out one evening]

As I walked out one evening,
    Walking down Bristol Street,
The crowds upon the pavement
    Were fields of harvest wheat.

5 And down by the brimming river
    I heard a lover sing
Under an arch of the railway:
    "Love has no ending.

"I'll love you, dear, I'll love you
10   Till China and Africa meet,
And the river jumps over the mountain
    And the salmon sing in the street,

"I'll love you till the ocean
    Is folded and hung up to dry
15 And the seven stars[1] go squawking
    Like geese about the sky.

"The years shall run like rabbits,
    For in my arms I hold
The Flower of the Ages,
20   And the first love of the world."

But all the clocks in the city
    Began to whirr and chime:
"O let not Time deceive you,
    You cannot conquer Time.

25 "In the burrows of the Nightmare
    Where Justice naked is,
Time watches from the shadow
    And coughs when you would kiss.

"In headaches and in worry
30   Vaguely life leaks away,
And Time will have his fancy
    To-morrow or to-day.

"Into many a green valley
    Drifts the appalling snow;
35 Time breaks the threaded dances
    And the diver's brilliant bow.

"O plunge your hands in water,
    Plunge them in up to the wrist;
Stare, stare in the basin
40   And wonder what you've missed.

"The glacier knocks in the cupboard,
    The desert sighs in the bed,
And the crack in the tea-cup opens
    A lane to the land of the dead.

45 "Where the beggars raffle the banknotes
    And the Giant is enchanting to Jack,[2]
And the Lily-white Boy is a Roarer,[3]
    And Jill goes down on her back.

"O look, look in the mirror,
50   O look in your distress:
Life remains a blessing
    Although you cannot bless.

"O stand, stand at the window
    As the tears scald and start;
55 You shall love your crooked neighbour
    With your crooked heart."

It was late, late in the evening,
    The lovers they were gone;
The clocks had ceased their chiming,
60   And the deep river ran on.
    —1938

---

[1] *seven stars* Pleiades, seven daughters of Atlas who, according to Greek mythology, were transformed into stars by Zeus.

[2] *Giant ... Jack* Auden alters the story of Jack and the Beanstalk.

[3] *Lily-white ... Roarer* Allusion to the English folk song, "Green Grow the Rushes, O": "Two, two lily-white boys / Clothèd all in green, O." A "roarer" is a riotous or disorderly person.

Musée des Beaux Arts[1]

About suffering they were never wrong,
The Old Masters: how well they understood
Its human position; how it takes place
While someone else is eating or opening a window or
    just walking dully along;
5 How, when the aged are reverently, passionately waiting
For the miraculous birth, there always must be
Children who did not specially want it to happen,
    skating
On a pond at the edge of the wood:
They never forgot
10 That even the dreadful martyrdom must run its course
Anyhow in a corner, some untidy spot
Where the dogs go on with their doggy life and the
    torturer's horse
Scratches its innocent behind on a tree.

In Brueghel's *Icarus*, for instance: how everything
    turns away
15 Quite leisurely from the disaster;[2] the ploughman may
Have heard the splash, the forsaken cry,
But for him it was not an important failure; the sun
    shone
As it had to on the white legs disappearing into the
    green
Water; and the expensive delicate ship that must have
    seen
20 Something amazing, a boy falling out of the sky,
Had somewhere to get to and sailed calmly on.
    —1939, 1940

In Memory of W.B. Yeats[3]
(d. Jan. 1939)

I

He disappeared in the dead of winter:
The brooks were frozen, the airports almost
    deserted,
And snow disfigured the public statues;
The mercury sank in the mouth of the dying day.
5 O all the instruments agree[4]
The day of his death was a dark cold day.

Far from his illness
The wolves ran on through the evergreen forests,
The peasant river was untempted by the fashionable
    quays;
10 By mourning tongues
The death of the poet was kept from his poems.

But for him it was his last afternoon as himself,
An afternoon of nurses and rumours;
The provinces of his body revolted,
15 The squares of his mind were empty,
Silence invaded the suburbs,
The current of his feeling failed: he became his
    admirers.

Now he is scattered among a hundred cities
And wholly given over to unfamiliar affections;
20 To find his happiness in another kind of wood
And be punished under a foreign code of conscience.
The words of a dead man
Are modified in the guts of the living.

But in the importance and noise of to-morrow
25 When the brokers are roaring like beasts on the floor
    of the Bourse,[5]
And the poor have the sufferings to which they are
    fairly accustomed,
And each in the cell of himself is almost convinced of
    his freedom;

---

[1] *Musée des Beaux Arts*   The Royal Museum of Fine Arts in Brussels owns several paintings by Flemish painter Pieter Brueghel (1525–69), including *Landscape with the Fall of Icarus*. According to Greek myth, Icarus and his father, Daedalus, escaped from the island of Crete, where they were imprisoned, by constructing wings with feathers and wax. Icarus flew too close to the sun, however, and the wax of his wings melted, causing him to plummet into the sea.

[2] *how everything ... disaster*   In Brueghel's painting, a shepherd, a farmer, and a fisher carry on with their respective jobs, ignoring Icarus's legs disappearing into the water in the picture's lower right corner.

[3] *W.B. Yeats*   Irish poet William Butler Yeats (1865–1939).

[4] *O all ... agree*   Auden later changed this line to read "What instruments we have agree."

[5] *Bourse*   Paris Stock Exchange.

A few thousand will think of this day
As one thinks of a day when one did something
   slightly unusual.

30   O all the instruments agree
The day of his death was a dark cold day.

2

You were silly like us: your gift survived it all;
The parish of rich women, physical decay,
Yourself. Mad Ireland hurt you into poetry.
35   Now Ireland has her madness and her weather still,
For poetry makes nothing happen: it survives
In the valley of its saying where executives
Would never want to tamper, flows on south
From ranches of isolation and the busy griefs,
40   Raw towns that we believe and die in; it survives,
A way of happening, a mouth.

3

Earth, receive an honoured guest;
William Yeats is laid to rest:
Let the Irish vessel lie
45   Emptied of its poetry.

Time that is intolerant
Of the brave and innocent,
And indifferent in a week
To a beautiful physique,

50   Worships language and forgives
Everyone by whom it lives;
Pardons cowardice, conceit,
Lays its honours at their feet.

Time that with this strange excuse
55   Pardoned Kipling and his views,[1]
And will pardon Paul Claudel,[2]
Pardons him for writing well.

In the nightmare of the dark
All the dogs of Europe bark,

60   And the living nations wait,
Each sequestered in its hate;

Intellectual disgrace
Stares from every human face,
And the seas of pity lie
65   Locked and frozen in each eye.

Follow, poet, follow right
To the bottom of the night,
With your unconstraining voice
Still persuade us to rejoice;

70   With the farming of a verse
Make a vineyard of the curse,
Sing of human unsuccess
In a rapture of distress;

In the deserts of the heart
75   Let the healing fountain start,
In the prison of his days
Teach the free man how to praise.

—1939

September 1, 1939[3]

I sit in one of the dives
  On Fifty-Second Street
Uncertain and afraid
As the clever hopes expire
5   Of a low dishonest decade:
Waves of anger and fear
Circulate over the bright
And darkened lands of the earth,
Obsessing our private lives;
10   The unmentionable odour of death
Offends the September night.

Accurate scholarship can
Unearth the whole offence
From Luther[4] until now

---

[1] *Kipling ... views* Rudyard Kipling (1865–1936) was an Indian-born English writer whose work often celebrated imperialism.

[2] *Paul Claudel* French-Catholic poet, playwright, and diplomat (1868–1955) who was widely criticized for supporting Franco's fascist insurgency in the Spanish Civil War.

[3] *September 1, 1939* Date of Hitler's invasion of Poland; Britain and France declared war on Germany two days later. Auden had moved to New York in January 1939.

[4] *Luther* Martin Luther (1483–1546), German monk whose attempts to reform the Catholic Church were instrumental in bringing about the Protestant Reformation. Luther's writings grew

15 That has driven a culture mad,
  Find what occurred at Linz,[1]
  What huge imago[2] made
  A psychopathic god:
  I and the public know
20 What all schoolchildren learn,
  Those to whom evil is done
  Do evil in return.

  Exiled Thucydides[3] knew
  All that a speech can say
25 About Democracy,
  And what dictators do,
  The elderly rubbish they talk
  To an apathetic grave;
  Analysed all in his book,
30 The enlightenment driven away,
  The habit-forming pain,
  Mismanagement and grief:
  We must suffer them all again.

  Into this neutral air
35 Where blind skyscrapers use
  Their full height to proclaim
  The strength of Collective Man,
  Each language pours its vain
  Competitive excuse:
40 But who can live for long
  In an euphoric dream;
  Out of the mirror they stare,
  Imperialism's face
  And the international wrong.

45 Faces along the bar
  Cling to their average day:
  The lights must never go out,
  The music must always play,
  All the conventions conspire
50 To make this fort assume
  The furniture of home;
  Lest we should see where we are,
  Lost in a haunted wood,
  Children afraid of the night
55 Who have never been happy or good.

  The windiest militant trash
  Important Persons shout
  Is not so crude as our wish:
  What mad Nijinsky wrote
60 About Diaghilev[4]
  Is true of the normal heart;
  For the error bred in the bone
  Of each woman and each man
  Craves what it cannot have,
65 Not universal love
  But to be loved alone.

  From the conservative dark
  Into the ethical life
  The dense commuters come,
70 Repeating their morning vow,
  "I *will* be true to the wife,
  I'll concentrate more on my work,"
  And helpless governors wake
  To resume their compulsory game:
75 Who can release them now,
  Who can reach the deaf,
  Who can speak for the dumb?

  All I have is a voice
  To undo the folded lie,
  The romantic lie in the brain
80 Of the sensual man-in-the-street

markedly more anti-Semitic as he aged; in *Mein Kampf*, Hitler ranks Martin Luther as one of three great German cultural heroes, along with Frederick the Great and Richard Wagner.

[1] *Linz* Town in Austria in which Hitler grew up; he returned in 1938 to announce Germany's annexation of Austria.

[2] *imago* According to psychiatrist and founder of analytical psychology C.G. Jung (1875–1961), an idealized image of a person formed in childhood.

[3] *Thucydides* Greek historian and general (c. 460–c. 400 BCE) and author of *The History of the Peloponnesian War* who was exiled at the war's end for failing to prevent the surrender of Amphipolis to the Spartans. One of the speeches in Thucydides's *History*, Pericles's funeral oration for the dead Athenian soldiers, outlines the dangers and benefits of democracy. Elected 16 times to the position of general, Pericles instituted many democratic reforms while retaining a significant degree of personal power.

[4] *Nijinsky ... Diaghilev* Vaslav Nijinsky (1890–1950), Russian ballet dancer and choreographer who was diagnosed with schizophrenia in 1919. In 1936, Nijinsky's wife published a heavily edited version of her husband's 1919 diary, in which he said of his former lover, founder of the Ballets Russes Sergei Pavlovich Diaghilev, "Some politicians are hypocrites like Diaghilev, who does not want universal love, but to be loved alone."

And the lie of Authority
Whose buildings grope the sky:
There is no such thing as the State
85 And no one exists alone;
Hunger allows no choice
To the citizen of the police;
We must love one another or die.[1]

Defenceless under the night
90 Our world in stupor lies;
Yet, dotted everywhere,
Ironic points of light
Flash out wherever the Just
Exchange their messages:
95 May I, composed like them
Of Eros[2] and of dust,
Beleaguered by the same
Negation and despair,
Show an affirming flame.
—1939

from *The Sea and the Mirror*

[Song of the Master and Boatswain][3]

At Dirty Dick's and Sloppy Joe's
    We drank our liquor straight,
Some went upstairs with Margery,
    And some, alas, with Kate;
5 And two by two like cat and mouse
The homeless played at keeping house.

There Wealthy Meg, the Sailor's Friend,
    And Marion, cow-eyed,
Opened their arms to me but I
10   Refused to step inside;
I was not looking for a cage
In which to mope in my old age.

The nightingales[4] are sobbing in
    The orchards of our mothers,
15 And hearts that we broke long ago
    Have long been breaking others;
Tears are round, the sea is deep:
Roll them overboard and sleep.
—1944

[3] *Song ... Boatswain* Auden's *The Sea and the Mirror* is a poetic response to Shakespeare's *The Tempest*. "The Master and Boatswain" refers to the prostitutes mentioned by a drunken Stephano in 2.2.46–54:
    The master, the swabber, the boatswain, and I,
    The gunner and his mate,
    Loved Mall, Meg, and Marian, and Margery,
    But none of us cared for Kate;
    For she had a tongue with a tang,
    Would cry to a sailor, "Go hang!"
    She loved not the savour of tar nor of pitch,
    Yet a tailor might scratch her where e'er she did itch.
    Then to sea, boys, and let her go hang!

[4] *nightingales* In Greek myth, Philomela, the daughter of the king of Athens, was transformed into a nightingale after being raped by her brother-in-law, Tereus, King of Thrace, who had cut out her tongue to prevent her from talking. A "nightingale" is also a slang term for a prostitute.

[1] *All I have ... die* In a revised edition of this poem, printed in *The Collected Poetry of W.H. Auden* (1945), this stanza is removed.

[2] *Eros* In contrast to The New Testament *agape*, or Christian love, *eros* represents earthly, or sexual love. In Greek myth, the winged Eros, son of Aphrodite, is the god of love.

The Late Twentieth Century and Beyond: From 1945 to the Twenty-First Century

The End of the War and the Coming of the Welfare State

Winston Churchill had inspired the nation—many said saved the nation—in the dark days of 1940, and remained over the following five years, by all accounts, one of the greatest war leaders in British history. Yet in 1945, the electorate unceremoniously dumped him and the Conservative Party from office, and installed the Labour Party under Clement Attlee in its place. Much as people were grateful to Churchill for his leadership in the war effort, he was seen very much as a war leader and a figure of the past at a time when people felt strongly that they had fought not so much to preserve the world of the past as for their right to make a better world.[1] All too clearly, voters had seen that Churchill's fondest wish at the end of the war was to return to the peacetime Britain of earlier days—a Britain with a vast Empire abroad and a rigid class system at home. Unlike the Prime Minister, at war's end the British people were increasingly seeing Imperial possessions as a drain on the nation's scarce resources, and the class system as an impediment to prosperity and an affront to notions of equality. With remarkably little fanfare, the old British world of masters and servants had already largely disappeared, but its husk still gave shape to many social attitudes; it remained almost impossibly difficult to "get ahead" if one came from a working-class background and had the "wrong accent," one could never be fully accepted in many social milieus if one's background was "in trade," and so on.

Quite aside from the issue of increasingly anachronistic social attitudes, the working class and the lower middle class continued to face great obstacles simply in their daily physical existence. For many, conditions at the end of World War II were little better than they had been at the end of World War I; with its calls to redistribute wealth and to engage the forces of government throughout the economy on behalf of general good, Labour represented a real change. And unquestionably, the various measures enacted by the Attlee government (many of them following on the recommendations of the 1942 and 1944 Reports to Parliament of William Beveridge) made Britain a much fairer society than it had been at any time previously in its history. The new initiatives included the establishment of the National Health Service and the National Insurance Act, which provided a measure of protection against poverty resulting from unemployment—or indeed from any other source.

If British life became more egalitarian during the Attlee years, however, much of what was being shared was still hardship. In a fifty-years-on retrospective, Doug Saunders memorably summarized the situation in postwar Britain:

> Food rationing during the war was bad. After the war it was terrible. Posters were put up reading "Eat Less Bread: Eat Potatoes Instead." Then, in the spring of 1946, those posters went down: there was no bread at all. ... Coal supplies were cut back to almost nil, so that in the winter of 1947, the coldest in British history, people were ordered not to heat their homes. ... If the economies and buildings and cities were fractured, even worse damage was done to families. About four million children had been shipped away from their parents to unknown locations and with almost no contact, for years. Children and parents alike returned from the war to find things utterly different. ... Susan Goodman, who was ten years old at the end of the war, had lived in

---

[1] Churchill might still have been elected had it not been for his veer to the extreme ideological right during the course of the campaign. Apparently strongly influenced by having read F.A. Hayek's polemic against socialism, in his speech on 4 June 1945 Churchill likened Britain's Labour Party to Hitler's secret police, suggesting that no Labour government "could afford to allow free expression of public discontent.... They would have to fall back on some sort of Gestapo."

the countryside, with her mother in London and her father in the armed forces. She recalls the moment when "this man got off the train—he was very tall and very yellow. He came up and said, 'Hello Sue, I'm Daddy,' and I put out my hand and said 'How do you do.' It was not auspicious."

Even into the 1950s, food and fuel shortages persisted—and as the hardships continued, people grew as tired of Attlee and Labour as they had been of Churchill and the Conservatives in 1945. With the 1950 election Churchill was returned to office, and he presided over a period of relative calm from 1950 to 1955. In terms of the ideological direction of the nation, however, it was the election of 1945 that had represented the great turning point. From the late 1940s through to the late 1970s, periods of Labour rule (first under Attlee, later under Prime Ministers Harold Wilson and James Callaghan) alternated with periods of Conservative rule (first under Churchill again, later under Prime Ministers Harold Macmillan and Edward Heath). Under Labour, the growth of what came to be known as the "welfare state" was fostered, while under the Conservatives, the social activism of Labour was eschewed—but even while the Conservatives were in power, little attempt was made to dismantle the structures through which Labour was attempting to reshape British society; for thirty years the domestic agenda for Britain remained one of building a more egalitarian society.

If the political shape of the 1950s, 1960s, and 1970s in Britain has something of a unity to it, the same cannot be said for the shape of its economic and cultural life over that period. Britain recovered far more slowly economically after World War II than did North America and many other parts of the world. The 1950s in North America are thought of as years of contentment in the midst of robust economic growth. Not so in Britain; for many, through much of that decade British life remained dreary and unsatisfying. The major literary movement of the era—the writings of the so-called "angry young men"—represented a reaction against the dreariness and lack of opportunity that characterized so much of British life. John Osborne's play *Look Back in Anger* (1956), which depicted the struggles of the rebellious Jimmy Porter, became the touchstone in discussions of the movement, but works of prose fiction such as John Braine's *Room at the Top* (1957) and Alan

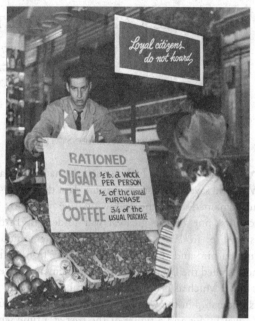

Wartime rationing in Montreal, 1942. Unlike in Britain, hardships on the home front ended soon after the war in countries such as Canada and Australia.

The "London fog" for which the city became famous in the nineteenth and twentieth centuries was primarily created by air pollution. From December 1953 to March 1954, conditions became worse than ever, and there were more than 12,000 smog-related deaths. Since the 1950s air (and water) quality in London has improved dramatically as a result of anti-pollution measures.

Sillitoe's *Saturday Night and Sunday Morning* (1958) and *The Loneliness of the Long Distance Runner* (1959), which also dealt with the conflicts and resentments of young working-class or lower middle-class males struggling to get on in society, had almost as great an impact.

Two other writers—Kingsley Amis and Philip Larkin—were initially often mentioned in the same breath as Osborne and Sillitoe, but even in the 1950s these two were on quite different literary paths, and, in the 1960s and 1970s, their work diverged even further both from that of angry young men and from each other's (though the two remained lifelong friends). With *Lucky Jim* (1954), a social satire about class distinctions, romantic bungling, and university life, Amis achieved literary celebrity at an early age. His subsequent novels written in a similar vein—social satire bordering on farce—but as the years went on, the humor was tinged more with bitterness than with insight, and was discolored by misogyny. Larkin, too, tried his hand early on in his career with social satire— *A Girl in Winter* (1947) being the more notable of his two novels—but with Larkin, the satire was more gentle, and did not sit entirely at ease with his evident aim of achieving a high degree of psychological realism. It was as a poet that Larkin made a lasting mark; poetry turned out to be the perfect medium for his unique variety of psychological understanding, his sometimes wry biting wit, and his bleak honesty about old age and death. Like Amis, Larkin had his share of bitter and misogynist feelings (as his posthumously published letters revealed), but these are far less obtrusive in his work than they are in that of Amis, and where Amis's work became more coarse and superficial over the years, Larkin's became more varied, more resonant, and more memorable. In its subject matter but also in its form, Larkin's poetry was quite out of step with the vast majority of British poetry published in the second half of the twentieth century; almost all his poems are built on a foundation of accentual syllabic meter, and most have a regular rhyme scheme. Yet they found a remarkably large audience; his final book, *High Windows*, made some British best seller lists in 1974. Increasingly, critics and literary historians are coming to regard Larkin as the most important British poet of the second half of the twentieth century.

Another quite different group of writers might with equal appropriateness be described as "angry young men": those who emigrated to Britain from her overseas possessions. Particularly prominent were immigrants from the Caribbean; large numbers were recruited from Jamaica, Trinidad, and other Caribbean islands in the decade following World War II to help rebuild Britain's bombed-out cities. Though they made a real contribution to that rebuilding, they were often treated as second-class citizens, discriminated against in virtually every public sphere; the reaction was a series of race riots, beginning in the late 1950s.

The Caribbean-led wave of immigration in the post-war years was the beginning of a movement that would transform Britain demographically and culturally. Amongst their number were many of the founding voices of what would become known as post-colonial literature, including Samuel Selvon, George Lamming, and Derek Walcott. From the beginning, they wrote largely in opposition to (rather than within) British literary traditions; this was the beginning of the literary movement that Salman Rushdie memorably characterized a few decades later with the phrase, "The Empire writes back."

The important women writers from this period were arguably less angry in their work than their male counterparts—though doubtless they had at least as much cause to be. The novels of Iris Murdoch, of Muriel Spark, and of Doris Lessing work with vastly different settings and story materials, ranging from the story of the life of a school mistress at a girls' boarding school in Spark's *The Prime of Miss Jean Brodie* to a philosophically tinged exploration of faith and moral imagination in Iris Murdoch's *The Bell* (1958) to an evocation of the gritty edges of colonial existence in Southern Rhodesia in Lessing's *The Grass Is Singing* (1950). Almost all are written in the vein of social or psychological realism— and most have something of an ethos of stoicism in the face of adversity. As a character in Murdoch's *Under the Net* (1954) puts it, "one must just blunder on. Truth lies in blundering on."

THE END OF EMPIRE

If in the generation following World War II, the Conservatives came to accept many of the egalitarian social principles in which Labour believed, they also came to accept that the old approach to Empire was no longer workable. Britain's stature as a world power suffered serious damage during the Suez crisis of 1956, when it attempted unsuccessfully to block the nationalization by Egypt of the Suez Canal, and it suffered as well in the face of increasing resistance to Imperial rule in British colonies. (Perhaps most notably, the Mau Mau rebellion in East Africa of 1952–56 showed to what extent a relatively small uprising could destabilize colonial rule, inspiring brutal reprisals and widespread fear.) By the early 1960s the die was cast; Harold Macmillan's 1960 "Wind of Change" speech signaled Britain's intention to grant independence to virtually all of its remaining colonies, in Asia and the Caribbean as well as in Africa. Independence in a significant number of these nations also meant majority

The HMS *Antelope* under attack during the Falklands War, 1982. One case in which the British forcibly resisted efforts to wrest a colonial possession from their control was that of the Falkland Islands off the coast of Argentina, to which Argentina also laid claim. When the Argentinian Armed Forces invaded in April 1982, Margaret Thatcher's government declared war. By early June, the British had retaken the Islands, and on June 14, Argentina surrendered. Before the war Thatcher had been deeply unpopular; in its wake her popularity soared, and in 1983 she was re-elected in a landslide.

rule by blacks, which was anathema to many white settlers. In some new nations, independence was followed by an exodus of whites, while in Rhodesia, the government of Ian Smith unilaterally declared independence from Britain in order to maintain the white minority's privileged position and prevent majority rule. Most nations joined Britain in refusing to recognize Smith's regime and imposing sanctions against it, but it was not until 1980, after a ten-year guerrilla war, that the people of Rhodesia—renamed Zimbabwe—established a state based on the principles of majority rule. By 1980, then, all of Britain's former colonial possessions in Africa were independent, as were most in Asia and the Caribbean; the only remnants of the British Empire were a scattering of small territories such as Hong Kong, Gibraltar, the Falkland Islands off the coast of Argentina, and several Caribbean islands.

Doris Lessing was one of many post-war writers to focus in their fiction on the failings of colonialism. A few years before her novels and stories of southern Africa began to appear, Alan Paton's *Cry the Beloved Country* (1948), a simple and emotionally powerful tale of the hardships suffered by black South Africans under white rule, had achieved enormous success. At first such hardships were recounted for a wide audience only in novels by white writers. In the 1960s and 1970s, however, a new generation of writers of color emerged, and were rapidly accorded a place in the first rank of writing in English. Among the most important of these are V.S. Naipaul, whose major works include novels set in India (*A House for Mr. Biswas*, 1962), in Africa (*A Bend in the River*, 1979), and in his native Trinidad (*Miguel Street*, 1959); the Nigerian playwright Wole Soyinka, awarded the Nobel Prize for Literature in 1986; the Nigerian novelist Chinua Achebe, whose novels of struggle, corruption, and loss in the post-colonial era (*Things Fall Apart* [1958] most notable among them) have taken on iconic status; the Trinidadian poet Derek Walcott; and the Kenyan novelist Ngũgĩ wa Thiong'o.

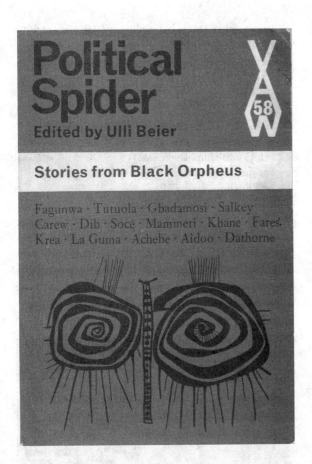

One of the most important vehicles with which African writing was brought to the attention of the rest of the world was the African Writers Series, launched by the UK publisher Heinemann in 1962 at the instigation of Alan Hill and initially under the general editorship of Chinua Achebe. By the end of 1969, the year that *Political Spider: Stories from Black Orpheus* was published, the series had grown to 82 titles, including Achebe's *Things Fall Apart* and *Arrow of God*; *Weep Not Child* and *A Grain of Wheat* by "James Ngugi" (Ngũgĩ wa Thiong'o); and Wole Soyinka's *The Interpreters*.

All of these authors deal pointedly with issues of colonialism and post-colonialism in their work. It is Ngũgĩ, however, who has raised most pointedly the issue of the ways in which politics and literature connect also with language. Ngũgĩ's early novels—including *A River Between* (1965), a novel about young people grappling

with the conventions of tribal life in a world in which almost no one speaks English—were written in English, and Ngũgĩ established a worldwide reputation as an English novelist. In midlife, he decided for both personal and political reasons to write instead in his first language, Gikuyu; he argues persuasively in *Decolonizing the Mind* (1986) that English is inherently tainted by the culture of the colonizer: "language has a dual character; it is both a means of communication and a carrier of culture." The debate over this issue involved many of the leading writers in Britain's former colonies; Achebe and Soyinka were among those who decided to write some works in English, others in their first language. Even those who chose to write in English, however, no longer felt obliged to adopt the "correct" English of the English themselves; whether through the use of idioms, of non-standard syntax, or of local dialects and rhythms of speech, they have extended the linguistic range of literature in English.

While the 1960s and '70s saw an explosion of literature in English in nations newly independent from Britain, these decades also ushered in a new vibrancy and maturity in the literatures of Canada and Australia, which had long been formally independent from Britain but had retained into the 1950s a pervasive sense of Great Britain as "the mother country." By the '60s and '70s both nations were beginning to define themselves as much in terms of their relationship with the United States (and, in the case of Australia, with Asian countries) as they did in connection with their old relationship towards Britain. Here and there the work of important Canadian and Australian authors such as Margaret Atwood, P.K. Page, and Judith Wright illuminated the old connections with Britain, but just as often the work of these writers—like that of other major Australian and Canadian authors such as Patrick White (winner of the Nobel Prize in 1973), Les Murray, Peter Carey, Alice Munro, Carol Shields, and Michael Ondaatje—bears few traces of a British connection. Increasingly, indeed, literature in English had started to become more broadly international. Ondaatje, for example, has shown himself to be as comfortable writing about Italy and North Africa in World War II (in his Booker Prize-winning novel *The English Patient*) as he has writing about his native Sri Lanka and Canada. Rohinton Mistry has lived in Canada since he was 23, but he continues to set his major works—most notably his novel *A Fine Balance* (1996)—in his native India.

FROM THE 1960S TO CENTURY'S END

Within Britain, the 1960s and '70s were also a time of cultural explosion—though here literature may be said to have shared the stage with other forms of cultural expression, most notably popular music. The music of The Beatles and The Rolling Stones played a central part in defining "the swinging '60s," but these groups were part of a much broader movement as a large generation of young people sought—through long hair, the lively clothing styles of Carnaby Street, and a new-found sexual freedom—to reject the values of their parents' generation.

Ironically, the most lasting literary reflections of this memorable cultural moment may not be in any literary expression of exuberance from the 1960s, but in detached and faintly critical after-the-fact poems on the subject by Larkin, such as "Annus Mirabilis":

Sexual intercourse began
In nineteen sixty-three
(which was rather late for me)—
Between the end of the *Chatterley* ban
And the Beatles' first LP.

The comic novels of Amis and of David Lodge (notably *Changing Places*, 1975) also give some sense of the cultural moment. But several of the most important figures of British literature of these years maintained a considerable distance between their own work and the cultural ferment of the times. Lawrence Durrell com-

In a controversial award, the Beatles were appointed MBEs (Members of the British Empire) in 1965. Even more controversially, John Lennon commented in March of the following year that the group was "more popular than Jesus."

Lord of the Flies has sold exceptionally well ever since its publication in 1954—including to high schools. This still from Peter Brook's 1963 film version of *Lord of the Flies* was also used as a cover image for the "educational edition" of the book the same year.

pleted the last of his series of evocative novels of the Anglo-Egyptian world, *The Alexandria Quartet*, in 1960; Anthony Powell continued to publish novels in his unique sequence *A Dance to the Music of Time*; and William Golding, who had burst onto the literary scene in 1954 with *Lord of the Flies*, a horrific depiction of young boys forced to create a society for themselves, continued to publish novelistic explorations of the psyche and of ethical questions.

One of the most important poetic voices to emerge in Britain in the 1960s and '70s also maintained a certain distance from the cultural mainstream; the focus of Ted Hughes's work remained largely on the natural world, and on the ways in which humans might connect to that world on a primal level. Doris Lessing, however, with the publication of her novel *The Golden Notebook* (1962), most certainly did connect with the mainstream of social and cultural change. Along with the non-fiction work *The Female Eunuch* by the Australian Germaine Greer, *The Golden Notebook* became a touchstone for women as they realized the extent to which they had been suppressed by the patriarchal structures and attitudes of society.

Committed as politicians had been to egalitarianism from the 1940s through to the 1970s, they had been largely unable to loosen the control that the British upper class and upper middle class continued to exert over key elements of British society. Perhaps the most egregious expression of this control was the connection that continued to exist between the best jobs and the old established universities. In almost all professions, preference continued to be given to graduates of Oxford and Cambridge. Though the Education Act of 1944 had put forward measures to increase the number of working-class students at British universities, many of the old attitudes persisted.

Ironically, it may have been a Conservative rather than a Labour government that challenged the old ethos most successfully. Margaret Thatcher (Prime Minister from 1979 to 1990), represented a very different brand of Conservatism from that of Winston Churchill and earlier Conservatives, much as she admired him and shared some of the old notions of Britain as a power in

world affairs. A grocer's daughter, she stood in her own way as firmly against the restrictions of a hierarchical class structure as did her political opponents. But whereas Labour had sought to achieve equity by creating a welfare state, Thatcher aimed to do so by bringing the universities to heel, creating a sense of empowerment among the working class and lower middle class—and dismantling much of the welfare state in order to lower taxes. Thatcher succeeded in changing a great many British attitudes over the eleven years she held power, but in the course of doing so she fiercely divided the nation.

The 18 years of Conservative party government in Britain from 1979 to 1997—for the most part under Thatcher as Prime Minister—was a period in which government support for culture was cut back. In a series of moves that paralleled developments in the United States under Ronald Reagan, Thatcher attacked the foundations of the welfare state and conveyed a sense that Britain's cultural identity was to be expressed through fiercely defending the last remnants of Empire (she led a war against Argentina over the Falkland Islands in 1982) and in resisting integration with continental Europe rather than in fostering cultural expression through literature, music, and the visual arts. Ironically, this period saw perhaps the greatest flowering of British literature since the first decades of the twentieth century. Novelists were especially prominent, with Margaret Drabble, A.S. Byatt, Ian McEwan, Martin Amis, Graham Swift, and Jeannette Winterson all creating impressive bodies of work. Ironically, too, literature in Britain experienced a cultural broadening that stands in direct contrast to the narrowness of Thatcher's cultural focus. Britain itself was increasingly becoming a multi-cultural society with the continuing influx of immigrants from former British possessions; more and more, that diversity began to shape the British literary scene. Among the major figures of British literature during this period are Salman Rushdie, a novelist with a Pakistani family background whose works—from *Midnight's Children* (1980) and *Shame* (1983) to *Shalimar's Clown* (2005)—explore the cultures of India and Pakistan as much as they do that of Britain; Vikram Seth, another novelist whose major works (most notable among them *A Suitable Boy*, 1993) are set in India; Zadie Smith, who burst onto the literary scene in 2000 with a wide-ranging novel of post-colonial communities in England, *White Teeth*, and whose 2012 novel *NW* (after the postal code of north-west London) offered further insight into the ways in which race and class interact in modern Britain; and Nagasaki-born Kazuo Ishiguro, whose Japanese heritage informs much of his work but who has lived in Britain since the age of six.

Ishiguro's best known work, *The Remains of the Day* (1989), recounts the story of a British butler in a country house where collaborators with the Nazi regime are holding secret meetings; the novel has been widely acclaimed as among the most fully rounded fictional expressions of life under the old British class system, and of the stifling of human feeling under the sense of reserve that formed an integral part of that system. Much of Ishiguro's other work is set in the world of post-war Japan *(A Pale View of Hills*, 1982) and/or in dreamlike worlds that resist identification with fixed geographical or temporal locations (*The Unconsoled*, 1995). In his acclaimed novel *Never Let Me Go* (2005), young people are prepared for a mysterious fate at a boarding school in an English countryside where the precise geographical setting remains vague, and the temporal setting in an unspecified future even more so.

Like the literatures of Canada and Australia, that of Britain in the late twentieth and early twenty-first centuries was often more difficult to place. The diversity of British writing also came to be expressed during this period through an increased openness regarding sexual orientation. Whereas leading writers such as W.H. Auden in the 1930s and Thom Gunn in the 1950s had left Britain for America in large part because American cities such as New York and San Francisco were then far more accepting of homosexuality than was London (let alone any other part of the British Isles), in the 1980s and 1990s gay and lesbian writers such as Hanif Kureishi and Jeannette Winterson remained in Britain and became central figures of London's literary culture. And in the twenty-first century, Carol Ann Duffy came to be acknowledged as a leading—arguably, *the* leading—poetic voice in Britain.

Diversity of form and style also became increasingly characteristic of British literature in the 1980s and

1990s. Poets such as Geoffrey Hill carried on something akin to the Modernist tradition, while poets such as Tony Harrison infused their work with powerful political content; poets such as Alice Oswald revived and extended traditions of English nature poetry; and a range of other poets (including Grace Nichols, Moniza Alvi, and Linton Kwesi Johnson) gave full expression to the new Britain. Women poets came to the fore as never before, in Ireland as well as in Britain, with Eavan Boland and Medbh McGuckian particularly highly regarded. (A fuller discussion of these and other developments of the period appears elsewhere in this volume as an introduction to "Literature, Politics, and Cultural Identity in the Late Twentieth and Twenty-first Centuries.")

The 1980s and 1990s may in some respects be characterized as the era of postmodernism in British literary culture; *postmodern* is a notoriously slippery term, however, and one worth pausing over. The most fruitful avenue of approach may be to look at Modernism and postmodernism side by side. In some ways postmodernism represents a reaction to Modernism, in others an extension of it—and in many ways the history of the one parallels that of the other. As Modernism had been the leading artistic and intellectual movement of the second and third decades of the twentieth century, so was postmodernism during the century's final two decades—at least in literature and the visual arts. Both Modernism and postmodernism may be said to have begun in France—Modernism with poets such as Arthur Rimbaud and Stephane Mallarmé and the Post-Impressionist and Cubist painters, postmodernism with philosophers such as Jacques Derrida and Michel Foucault. Modernism had at its core a rejection of traditional artistic forms and a tendency towards fragmentation of meaning as well as of form. The breaking down of the image in poetry and in painting was accompanied by extensive theorizing—by Mallarmé and the French Symbolists, by Ezra Pound and the Imagists, by the Italian Futurists, and by various others. Post-modernism was even more deeply colored by theory; indeed, it may be said to have begun at the "meta" level of theorizing rather than at the level of practice. It is notoriously resistant to definition—indeed, resistance to fixed definitions is itself a characteristic of postmodern-ism. Like Modernism, postmodernism embraces difficulty and distrusts the simple and straightforward. More broadly, postmodernism is characterized by a rejection of absolute truth or value, of closed systems, of grand unified narratives. As the French social philosopher Jean Baudrillard put it in 1987, "truth is what we should rid ourselves of as fast as possible and pass it on to somebody else. As with illnesses, it's the only way to be cured of it. He who hangs on to truth has lost."

Graham Law's edition of Wilkie Collins's *The Evil Genius*, one of the series-launching batch of four Broadview Literary Texts published in 1994. Even as English Studies focused to an unprecedented degree in the 1980s and '90s on literary theory, the discipline was also becoming increasingly aware of the importance of historicizing literary works—understanding them first of all in the cultural context out of which they emerged. An important related publishing venture was the launch of the Broadview series (later renamed Broadview Editions), which includes within each volume appendices of relevant historical and cultural documents.

As a style of discourse rather than a philosophical system, postmodernist theory dominated the academic study of literature in British and North American universities through much of the 1980s and 1990s. Postmodernism never came to dominate literature itself during that period to anything like the same degree, but the 1980s and 1990s fictions of Rushdie, Byatt, Ishiguro, Winterson, and Will Self, among others, often played with reality and illusion in ways that could be broadly characterized as postmodern. Works such as Byatt's novel *Possession* (1990) and Winterson's *Written on the Body* (1992), for example, display a willingness to combine different styles or forms in a single work—just as in architecture the postmodernist spirit embodies a willingness to borrow from seemingly disparate styles in designing a single structure.

One of the main thrusts of Modernism had been to apprehend consciousness directly in its often-chaotic progression. The main thrust of postmodernism, by contrast, was one of analysis more than of direct apprehension; the characteristic spirit of postmodernism is one of *self*-consciousness, of a highly attuned awareness to the problematized state of the writer, artist, or theorist as observer. Often that awareness encompasses a playfulness with regard to time—as famously expressed, for example, in the opening lines of Rushdie's Booker Prize-winning novel *Midnight's Children* (1980): "I was born in the city of Bombay ... once upon a time. No, that won't do, there's no getting away from the date."

British drama, which was influenced both by Modernism and by postmodernism, experienced great success throughout most of the second half of the twentieth century, and the beginning of the twenty-first. Major figures such as Harold Pinter and Tom Stoppard followed on from the work of Samuel Beckett in the attention that they paid to life's absurdity. In his most important plays, Pinter's focus was on personal and family relationships, whereas Stoppard's was on surprising conjunctions of circumstance and large ideas. In the groundbreaking *Rosencrantz and Guildenstern Are Dead* (1967), for example, he rewrote Shakespeare's *Hamlet* from the point of view of two of its most minor characters; in *Arcadia* (1993), which takes place both in the present and in the early years of the nineteenth century, he brought together ideas about eighteenth-century formal gardens, the science of Isaac Newton, and the life of Byron. Other leading dramatists of the period extended the frontiers of British drama in a variety of other directions. David Hare combined elements of realism with an often larger-than-life framework in plays such as *Plenty* (1978); Caryl Churchill experimented broadly with form in plays such as *Cloud Nine* (1979) and *Top Girls* (1982)—the latter informed both by an ear for dialogue closely attuned to the realities of contemporary Britain and by Churchill's strong feminist convictions; Alan Ayckbourn displayed a talent for farce in the extraordinary tour-de-force *The Norman Conquests*, and a deep sense, as well, of the ways in which the apparently meaningless surface details of life relate to its sad undertones; and Michael Frayn created works ranging from farce as broad as that of Ayckbourn (as in *Noises Off*, 1982) to large scale dramas of ideas (such as *Copenhagen*, 1998) as ambitious as those of Stoppard.

As British literature underwent these changes in the last few decades of the twentieth century, so too did it expand to embrace a range of new modes of expression. In the 1940s and 1950s, Graham Greene had been a rarity among major British writers in his willingness to write screenplays for films based on his works. By the end of the century, however, "crossover" writing of this sort had become common with Harold Pinter, Tom Stoppard, Hanif Kureishi, Neil Jordan, and Irvine Welsh among those who had written screenplays based on their novels or plays. Many also wrote for television; indeed, some of the finest drama of the era—including Stoppard's remarkable comedy *Professional Foul* (1977) on the conjunction of language philosophy and football (i.e., British soccer)—was written for the BBC. Some regularly scheduled British television programs may also lay claim to being among the more important works of the second half of the twentieth century. The comedy sketches of *Monty Python's Flying Circus* invented a new form of absurdist comedy in the early 1970s; the twelve episodes of *Fawlty Towers* (1975) set what some argued to be entirely new standards of farce; and the many episodes of *Yes, Minister* and its sequel *Yes, Prime Minister* introduced a new brand of cynical and yet warmly human comedy about the workings of British

politics. Arguably, more recent television programs such as *The Office* (2001–02) and *Extras* (2005–07) have reached an equally high standard of comedy.

IRELAND, SCOTLAND, WALES

The establishment of the Republic of Ireland in 1949 did not bring enduring peace to the island. With the six Ulster counties of Northern Ireland remaining a part of the United Kingdom of Great Britain and Northern Ireland, there was ongoing tension and, beginning in the late 1960s, almost recurrent violence over the status of Northern Ireland. The conflict came to be referred to as "The Troubles." A cycle of violence and repression continued, into the 1990s, as the Irish Republican Army (IRA) launched attacks on targets in England as well as in Northern Ireland, and the police and the British army launched repeated crackdowns, often involving considerable brutality. Staunchly Protestant Northern Irish politicians (the Reverend Ian Paisley most prominent among them) vowed "no surrender" to those who sought a compromise solution with Ireland and the Catholic minority in Northern Ireland.

In the late 1970s and early 1980s, a series of hunger strikes by IRA prisoners under British internment heightened tensions still further, and even after an Anglo-Irish agreement in 1985, periodic ceasefires brought only temporary cessations of conflict. In 1997, however, the IRA was persuaded to declare a ceasefire that showed promise of holding, and its political arm, Sinn Fein, joined in the multilateral Stormont talks aimed at finding a lasting solution. On 10 April 1998, an agreement was finally signed by the British and Irish governments. The Belfast Agreement (or "Good Friday Agreement") was endorsed by the major political parties of Ireland and of Northern Ireland, and in separate referendums by the electorates of both Ireland and Northern Ireland. Among the key provisions of the agreement were a commitment by all involved to an exclusively peaceful and democratic approach to change; abandonment by the Republic of its territorial claim to Northern Ireland; acceptance of the principle that the citizens of Northern Ireland had the right to determine by majority vote their constitutional future (in other words, partition was formally accepted, but so was the possibility that the Northern Irish could one day vote to

A gaping hole in front of the Grand Hotel in Brighton, site of the Conservative Party's conference in October 1980, was the result of an IRA bomb. Five were killed and many others injured; Prime Minister Thatcher was in her suite at the hotel when the explosion occurred, but was unharmed. An IRA statement acknowledged that Thatcher had been a target; "Today we were unlucky, but remember—we only have to be lucky once: you will have to be lucky always."

join the Republic); and provision for a Northern Ireland Assembly to which additional power would devolve from the British government (still leaving Northern Ireland as part of the United Kingdom). Troubles of one sort or another remained in both Ireland and Northern Ireland, but "The Troubles" ended with the 1998 agreement; leaders on both sides were awarded the Nobel Peace Prize for their efforts.

Perhaps as important to the evolution of late twentieth- and early twenty-first-century Ireland as the coming of peace have been a precipitous decline of religious authority over Irish life and an extraordinary economic boom that has transformed the economy, particularly of the Irish Republic. Ireland has been slower than other Roman-Catholic-dominated societies of Europe (such as France, Italy, and Spain) to distance itself from the more socially conservative pronouncements of the papacy; not until 1995 was divorce permitted under Irish law, and it remains illegal under most circumstances to obtain an abortion in Ireland. But over the past generation, Ireland has steadily become a more secular society. Over the course of a remarkably brief period in the 1980s and 1990s it also went from being one of the poorest countries in Europe to one of the wealthiest and most dynamic. Changed attitudes, a highly educated workforce, and programs to encourage particular sectors of high-tech industry wrought an extraordinary economic transformation (albeit one that was followed by a devastating recession in 2008–13).

Perhaps not surprisingly, given these circumstances, one of the most engaging literary treatments in all of English literature of the transformative effects of capitalism on the human psyche emerged from this period of economic and cultural change in Ireland. Dublin novelist Roddy Doyle's *The Van* (1991) deals with a variety of business start-up—a fish-and-chip van—that is at the opposite end of the economic spectrum from the high-tech businesses that were the well-publicized stars of Ireland's economic transformation. But in the tragicomic microcosm that Doyle creates, he captures with deep understanding the ways in which energy, imagination, and heartlessness fuse together in the heated environment in which businesses grow. (Doyle's distinguished body of work includes two trilogies, among them the Barrytown trilogy of which *The Van* forms a part, as well as his 1993 Booker Prize-winning novel of childhood, *Paddy Clarke Ha Ha Ha*.)

The Irish contribution to the literature of the English-speaking world was scarcely less in the late twentieth century than it had been in the extraordinary period 1890–1960—the period of Oscar Wilde, George Bernard Shaw, J.M. Synge, W.B. Yeats, James Joyce, and Samuel Beckett. Interestingly, a disproportionate number of the important Irish writers of the late twentieth and early twenty-first centuries are poets of Northern Irish background—among them Seamus Heaney, Derek Mahon, Medbh McGuckian, Paul Muldoon, and Tom Paulin. (It is important to note here that Heaney and others on this list self-identify as Irish, not as Northern Irish.) The list of important Irish writers in this period, however, includes writers in all genres and regions, from the short story writer William Trevor, whose early years in a Protestant family in County Cork provided him with a unique perspective; to the acclaimed poet and Dubliner Eavan Boland; to the fiction-writer and film-maker Neil Jordan, a native of County Sligo in the northwest of Ireland, whose *The Crying Game* (1992) remains among the most memorable depictions of "The Troubles"; to the novelist Edna O'Brien, whose reaction against her childhood in what she later described as the "enclosed, fervid, and bigoted" atmosphere of the 1930s in a small village in County Clare colored much of her later fiction; to the novelist and Belfast native (in later life, Canadian citizen) Brian Moore; to the novelist, journalist, and Wexford native John Banville, whose *The Sea* (2005) was awarded the Booker Prize; to Dublin dramatist and film-maker Conor McPherson, whose plays *The Weir* (1997) and *Shining City* (2004) explore the worlds of the living and the dead, and the ways in which Ireland continues to be possessed by its past; and to Colm Tóibín, among whose most acclaimed works are fictionalized treatments of the lives of Henry James (*The Master*, 2004) and of Mary, mother of Jesus (*The Testament of Mary*, 2012). Writers who choose to write in Irish have also gained prominence—perhaps most notable among them the poet Nuala Ní Dhomhnaill, whose collections have often appeared with facing page English translations.

Discontent with the dominant role played by England within Great Britain was a constant throughout the twentieth century in both Wales and Scotland, though in neither case was there a history of violence. In 1997 Tony Blair's Labour Party included in its election platform a commitment to devolution—a granting of power by the central government to proposed regional governments in Scotland and Wales. (Unlike the allocation of powers in a federal system, the granting of power under a system of devolution may be reversed; ultimate authority continues to reside with the central government.) Labour was elected with a solid majority,

and devolution was approved in Scottish and Welsh referendums in the autumn of 1997; elections for the new Scottish Parliament and Welsh National assembly were held in May 1999, and since then the two regional governments have assumed a variety of responsibilities in such areas as health, housing, education, and culture.

A number of important British writers in the second half of the twentieth century were either Scottish or Welsh, including the Scottish novelist Muriel Spark, the Scottish poet Edwin Muir, and the Welsh poets Dylan Thomas and Gwyneth Lewis. Concern over the preservation of local language has been a constant both in Scotland and in Wales. The language known as Gaelic in Scotland, where it is the traditional language of the Highlands, is in its Irish variant referred to simply as Irish; on both sides of the Irish Sea it was long under pressure from English, but it was substantially revived in both Scotland and Ireland over the course of the twentieth century. In Ireland, both Irish and English are official languages, and at the time of the 2011 census more than 1,770,000 were able to speak at least some Irish; in Scotland, there were in the late twentieth century approximately 80,000 able to speak Gaelic—though this number has declined to 57,000 by 2011. Lowland Scots, on the other hand, is a variant of English—a very substantially different dialect from that spoken by most in England, but still a related tongue. It, too, was considered to be threatened by "Standard English," but determined efforts were made in the twentieth century to maintain its vitality. In the early twentieth century, the poet and political activist Hugh MacDiarmid (1892–1978) played a leading role in such efforts. A founder in 1928 of the National Party of Scotland, MacDiarmid worked to revive many of the words he found in John Jamieson's 1808 *Etymological Dictionary of the Scottish Language*, and enjoyed considerable success in reviving Scots as a language of poetry. And in the late twentieth and early twenty-first centuries, Lowland Scots has remained very much alive, in literature as well as in speech. Such is the case, for example, with the Edinburgh dialect that is reproduced by the novelist and film-maker Irvine Welsh in *Trainspotting* (novel 1993; film screenplay 1996): "Johnny wis a junky as well as a dealer. Ye hud tae go a wee bit further up the ladder before ye found a dealer whae didnae use."

Like Gaelic/Irish, Welsh is a language quite distinct

from English. From the time of Henry VIII until the second half of the twentieth century, the Welsh language had been in more or less steady decline. Henry VIII had united England and Wales and forbidden the use of Welsh for official purposes with the 1536 Statute of Wales and the 1542 Acts of Union. In 1962, however, as a central element in the budding Welsh nationalist movement, a Welsh Language Society (Cymdeithas yr Iaith Gymraeg) was formed, and in 1967 its protests prompted the British Government to pass the Welsh Language Act, assigning equal status within Wales to Welsh and English—and declaring Wales to be no longer an official part of England. Since then the teaching of Welsh has been made an integral part of the educational system, and public agencies are obliged to offer bilingual service. It is now estimated that over 560,000 people in Wales are bilingual in Welsh and English, with the percentage of the population speaking the language increasing for the first time in over a century. In 2005 Gwyneth Lewis, who writes both in English and in Welsh, was named Wales's first Poet Laureate.

THE NEW MILLENNIUM

Through the era of Conservative government under Thatcher and John Major, Britain remained deeply divided politically—over cultural politics and issues such as immigration policy; over to what extent Britain should be a free market economy or a social democratic one; and over foreign affairs. With the coming to power of Tony Blair and "New Labour," as the Labour Party began to style itself in 1994, a new era dawned in British politics. Blair had blunted the power of the unions within his own party, and the party now blended its long-standing commitment to social justice with a commitment to economic enterprise and to modernity that had been sorely lacking in the Labour Party for the previous generation or more. At century's end, long-divisive issues such as the racial composition of Britain and the conflict in Northern Ireland seemed well on the way to being resolved. Constitutional reforms had included not only the devolution of considerable power to new assemblies in Scotland and Wales but also a phasing-out of the hereditary peerage; no longer would one be able to inherit a seat in the House of Lords. Class divisions had receded, and Britons expressed a fresh

confidence and a fresh sense of unity. The British seemed to have finally come to terms with their place in the world—a position of far less importance than that which they had held a century earlier, but one that no longer forced them to carry the economic and moral baggage of imperialism. It was also a position of surprising strength economically—particularly in the south of England, with London consolidating its position as one of the great financial centers of the world. Britain seemed to be in the forefront culturally, too. In the visual arts and in fashion, London held a central place, with publicity generating an annual furor over the awarding of the Turner Prize for best work by a British artist under the age of 50, and with brashly controversial artists such as Damien Hirst, Chris Ofili, and Gillian Wearing and celebrity collectors such as advertising mogul Charles Saatchi driving a culture of "Sensation" (to echo the name of the highly contro-versial 1997 and 2000 exhibitions from the Saatchi Collection in London and Brooklyn, respectively). London also laid claim to be the literary center of the world. "Rule, Britannia" had been Britain's defining song at its Imperial zenith; "Cool Britannia" was the term now coined to define Britain. During the millennium celebrations of 2000, Britain was as confi-dent, as united, and as prosperous as it had been at any time since the great celebrations over the Diamond Jubilee of Queen Victoria, 100 years before Tony Blair, New Labour, and "Cool Britannia."

The sky over Britain at the millennium was far from cloudless, however, and in the early years of the twenty-first century many perceived Britain's problems as standing out in bolder relief than her triumphs. In the first few years of the twentieth century the British people—the *English* people, especially—were stereotypi-cally thought of as a people of civility and self-restraint, adhering to religion and religious propriety, and pos-sessing a modesty that verged on prudery. In the first few years of the twenty-first century the stereotype of the British—again, the *English*, especially—included the behavior of the "lager louts" that went on nightly rampages in city centers; the lowest rates of church attendance in Europe; drunken hooliganism among soccer fans, displayed since the 1970s at matches across Europe as well as at home; and poverty-stricken and largely racially defined ghettos in post-industrial towns such as Leeds—areas which, as the suicide bombings on the London transport system in 2005 made painfully clear, could become breeding grounds for terrorism. According to social critics such as Theodore Dalrymple in works such as *Life at the Bottom* (2002), the lack of civility commonly associated with an alienated under-class was becoming more and more pervasive through-out all Britain, fueled by a "radical egotism" that had taken root in the new cultural freedom of the 1960s and that had become more and more strongly tainted during the late 1970s and the Thatcher years by materialism and uncaring individualism.

Grafted onto concern over these domestic issues was a broad concern over the place of a new Britain in a changed world. Was Britain's appropriate role that of aggressive ally of an increasingly bellicose United States? Could intervention in other nations' affairs, on either humanitarian or strategic grounds, be readily justified in a world in which concerns about terrorism, about human rights, and about the potential for a world-wide clash of cultures were coming to the fore? Britain's participation in the early twenty-first century wars in Afghanistan (2001–13) and Iraq (2003–11) provided powerful fuel for these debates.

These troubled aspects of British life are memorably represented in the literature of the late twentieth and early twenty-first centuries. The hooliganism that began to plague England in the late 1960s and 1970s was fore-shadowed in Anthony Burgess's novel *A Clockwork Orange* (1962), in which the protagonist, fifteen-year-old Alex DeLarge, leads a gang that commits a variety of violent crimes purely for the "kick" it gives them. The early fiction of Ian McEwan—perhaps most notably his first novel, *The Cement Garden* (1978)—depicts the grim plight of young people fending for themselves in the bleakness of a post-industrial landscape. The occa-sion for Tony Harrison's wide-ranging long poem *v* (1985) was the graffiti left on gravestones by Leeds United soccer hooligans; in a cemetery above the ground where "Leeds United play but disappoint their fans week after week," the fans "spray words on tombstones, pissed on beer":

> Subsidence makes the obelisks all list.
> One leaning left's marked FUCK, one right's
>   marked SHIT
> sprayed by some peeved supporter who was pissed. ...

In some cases the graffiti is football-related as well as foul-mouthed:

> Or, more expansively, there's LEEDS v.
> the opponent of last week, this week, or next,
> and a repertoire of blunt four-letter curses
> on the team or race that makes the sprayer vexed.

And, Harrison suggests, there is a wider resonance to these oppositions:

> These Vs are all the versuses of life
> From LEEDS v. DERBY, Black/White
> and (as I've known to my cost) man v. wife,
> Communist v. Fascist, Left v. Right,
>
> Class v. class as bitter as before,
> the unending violence of US and THEM ...

Hanif Kureishi's *My Son the Fanatic* (both a short story and a screenplay for a film, 1997) depicts the violent radicalization in Britain of Islamic youth as a reaction to what they see as the hypocrisy and decadence of their fathers' assimilated Britishness. Caryl Churchill's work—notably her short apocalyptic play *Far Away* (2000)—presents a world in which individuals abandon responsibility for one another, and in which the possibility of wider and wider conflict (not only nations or civilizations at war with one another, but also the human at war with the non-human environment) is beginning to seem increasingly real. And Ian McEwan's celebrated novel *Saturday* (2005) expresses an ambivalence towards violence that at the time was coming to seem a part of British life—violence both on the streets of Britain and overseas. That novel, which concerns a surgeon who becomes terrorized by violent criminals and is provoked to violent response, is set against a backdrop of looming military conflict in Iraq. Asked if he is "for the war," the beleaguered surgeon Henry Perowne replies, "I'm not for any war. But this one could be the lesser evil. In five years' time we'll know." Five years on and more, it was still being argued whether the war in Iraq (or that in Afghanistan) could be considered a "lesser evil": most Britons thought not.

In the space of a few hours in 2005 Britain experi-enced the extremes of jubilation and anguish as four coordinated terrorist attacks by suicide bombers (three of them British born) shook the London Transport system less than 24 hours after London had been announced as the surprise winner in the competition to host the 2012 Summer Olympics. Those experiences pointed in dramatically different directions. Would the lively spirit that animated Britain culturally and economically at the turn of the millennium continue to flourish and expand, with the 2012 Olympics taking its place as a symbol of a renewed nation? Or would the shadows that had been cast across modern Britain lengthen—and darken?

Gordon Brown, Blair's successor as Prime Minister, struggled in the face of scandals, the worldwide recession of 2008–09, and a widespread perception that "New Labour" had gone stale. Meanwhile Britain's Conservative Party, after years of indirection, began under David Cameron to find its way as a more modern and moderate party. The election of May 2010 gave the Conservatives the most seats—though as a minority looking for support to Britain's third party, Nick Clegg's Liberal Democrats. Many saw the rise of Cameron—like Clegg, an energetic and forward-looking young leader whose policies often cut across ideological lines—as signaling a return to the spirit not of the previous Conservative era dominated by Margaret Thatcher, but rather to that of the early days of Tony Blair and New Labour in the 1990s. But Cameron found it difficult to maintain the delicate balance required for a successful coalition government. Much of his Conservative base was made unhappy by his attempt to reform the House of Lords (abandoned in 2012 in the face of stiff opposition), by his support of gay marriage, and by his reluctance to turn Britain away from the European Union. Yet his efforts to weave back and forth in search of a middle ground often left his Liberal Democratic partners unhappy too. And the country as a whole was left unhappy by the performance of Britain's economy; in late 2011 and early 2012 the country endured another economic downturn. The Olympic Games later that year were indeed a shining moment, but many felt they were little more than that.

No account of the cultural history of the new century would be complete without some mention of J.K. Rowling's series of fantasy novels that began with the 1997 publication of *Harry Potter and the Philosopher's Stone*. The series became a phenomenon in popular culture; more than 500 million copies of the seven novels were sold, the film adaptations were massively successful—and the series was credited with engendering a love

for reading in many young people in an era when many were predicting the demise of the book.

But popular fantasy has been only one of many directions that British literature has taken in recent years. Very much in vogue have been historical novels, ranging from McEwan's acclaimed 2007 short novel *On Chesil Beach*, set in the pre-Beatles 1960s, to Hilary Mantel's two Booker Prize-winning novels, *Wolf Hall* (2009) and *Bring Up the Bodies* (2012), both set in the time of Henry VIII, Thomas Cromwell, and Sir Thomas More. Rhyme has become a more and more frequent presence in serious poetry, with young poets as diverse as Patience Agbabi and Sophie Hannah joining Duffy and others in using rhyme extensively; few in today's Britain associate a habit of rhyming in verse with stuffy attitudes or with political conservatism.

Literary currents in the world of "British" literature seem to become more and more international with each passing year. Aravond Adinga, for example, author of *The White Tiger*, the 2008 Booker Prize-winning novel of poverty, corruption, and religious conflict in India, was born and raised in India, and lives there again now, but has also lived for years at a time in Australia, New York, and Oxford. Kiran Desai, whose 2006 novel *The Inheritance of Loss* also won the Booker, is a citizen of India—but one who lived for some time in Britain after leaving India at the age of 14, and who is now a longtime resident of the United States. Even Hilary Mantel, who in 2009 became the first British citizen in five years to win the Booker Prize, spent more than a decade living in Botswana and in Saudi Arabia. If it has always been difficult to circumscribe "British literature," it is surely even more so today—as difficult, perhaps, as it is to draw any firm conclusions as to the future of Britain or of its place in the world. But there can be little doubt of the continuing vitality of its literary traditions as we move further into the twenty-first century.

THE HISTORY OF THE ENGLISH LANGUAGE

Perhaps the most extraordinary feature of English language in the late twentieth and early twenty-first centuries has been the pace of its growth—growth in its size and communicative capacity, but also in the extent to which it is spoken around the world. The two phenomena are now closely linked. Linguist Paul Payack of Global Language Monitor has estimated that English likely passed the one million word mark in 2006. (By comparison, the number of words in Old English was less than 60,000.) As in the first half of the twentieth century, much of that growth comes from new scientific coinages. But much of it is now also coming from "Chinglish" (Chinese-English) or "Hinglish" (Hindi-English) words, or other dual-language coinages. "Torunbusiness," for example, draws both on English and on the Mandarin word meaning *operating*; it means *open*, with reference to a business during opening hours.

In the twenty-year period 1947–67, almost all of Britain's former colonies became independent. Recognising the importance of English as a world-wide means of communication, most retained some official status for the English language. When India became independent in 1947, Hindi was declared the official language, English an "associate official language." In many new nations, English was accorded equal status with one or more other languages; thus in Malawi English and Chichewa are the official languages, in Swaziland, English and Swazi. In former colonies such as Nigeria and Zambia, where many local languages are spoken in different areas of the country, English was declared the *only* official language.

The speaking of English acquired a different coloring as it became the world's lingua franca, not only in the proliferation of accents but also in the timing of speech, and in the use of pitch rather than stress to mark "strong" syllables. English as it is spoken in Britain, the United States, Canada, Australia, and New Zealand remains a strongly inflected, stress-timed language; in other words, speakers typically stress certain syllables much more strongly than others, and vary the speed of speech in order to make the elapsed time between stresses more nearly equal. In other regions, however, where most people's first language is syllable- rather than stress-timed, and where pitch rather than stress marks "accented" syllables, those habits tend to be carried over into local habits of English pronunciation.

Inevitably, very substantial differences have arisen as well in the conventions of grammar and usage in different areas of the world. In the most extreme cases—as in Jamaica and several other Caribbean nations, pidgin and Creole forms of English that have become independent languages are more widely spoken than English itself. Elsewhere, conventions of spoken and of written English very different from those of "Standard English" have come to be broadly received as acceptable variants. In India "He is working here, isn't it?" or "I am not very much pleased" are generally regarded as entirely acceptable local usage. Indian Prime Minister Manmohan Singh put the matter clearly in a 2005 speech at Oxford University:

> Of course, people here may not recognise the language we speak, but let me assure you that it *is* English! In indigenising English, as so many people have done in so many nations across the world, we have made the language our own. Our choice of prepositions may not always be the Queen's English; we might occasionally split the infinitive; and we may drop an article here and add an extra one there. I am sure everyone will agree, however, that English has been enriched by Indian creativity. ...

Some of the most important changes in the English language in the second half of the twentieth century stemmed from the growing realization that the language had a systemic bias towards the male. In a landmark case referred to Britain by the Canadian courts, the Privy Council ruled in 1929 that the word *person* could not legally be taken to refer only to men. But could the word *man* be taken in an unbiased fashion to mean *human being*? To many, such usages seemed unproblematic—until they started to be brought up short by usages such as "the gestation period of the elephant is eleven months; that of man is nine months." From the 1970s onward it came to be more and more widely understood that *man* and *mankind* would always carry with them a whiff of malenesss, and thus could never fully and fairly represent all of humanity. Similarly the use of *he* to stand for both males and females has come to be widely criticized—and widely replaced, whether by "he or she" or simply by the use of plural constructions ("students ... they" rather than "a student ... he"); gender-specific nouns have largely been superceded by gender-neutral alternatives (*police officer* for *policeman*, *server* for *waitress*); and patronizing gender terms ("the girls in the office") have largely fallen into disuse. Such change did not occur without a struggle, however. For many decades, those who ventured to suggest gender-neutral alternatives to the general practice were subjected to the sort of ridicule that H.W. Fowler and F.G. Fowler (authors of *Modern English Usage* and for most of the twentieth century considered the leading arbiters of proper English usage) aimed at one S. Ferrier in *The King's English* (1906, 1931; issued without further revision in paperback, 1962). Existing habit or convention was in such cases often the only "argument" advanced against principles of fairness:

> *He, his, him* may generally be allowed to stand for the common gender; the particular aversion to them shown by Miss Ferrier ... may be referred to her sex; and, ungallant as it may seem, we shall probably persist in refusing women their due here as stubbornly as Englishmen continue to offend the Scots by saying *England* instead of *Britain*.

One of the visible manifestations of changes in attitudes in the late twentieth century was the radical shift in the meaning of certain words and expressions relating to sexual behavior and sexual orientation. At mid-century *queer* was both an adjective meaning strange and a "descriptive" term with derogatory implications, used casually and openly by heterosexuals to denote homosexuals; in the 1970s it had come to be acknowledged as an offensive word that should be avoided; in the 1980s and 1990s it was claimed by the gay and lesbian community, many of whom began to self-identify as queer. In the academic community queer theory grew up as a sub-discipline of literary theory and criticism. *Gay*, which until mid-century had meant *merry* or *given to merriment*, began in the 1970s to replace *queer* as a colloquial designator—but one that carried positive rather than negative connotations. (Towards the end of the century, however, those positive associations began to be eroded somewhat, as heterosexual youth began to use *gay* in a derogatory fashion.)

Terms relating to heterosexual relationships were often also unstable. A noteworthy example is *making love*, which until the 1950s referred to the process of courting, emphatically not including the act of sexual intercourse. In the early 1960s, the meaning of the phrase quickly shifted, so that by the 1970s, the *only*

commonly used denotation of *to make love* was *to have sex*. That was one of many examples of an increasingly overt sexualization of the language. In the case of a number of words that in the early twentieth century could carry either a sexual or a non-sexual meaning (e.g., *intercourse, ejaculate*), the sexual meaning had completely crowded out the non-sexual one by the end of the 1960s.

The twentieth century also saw a great change in the use of obscenities. In 1914, the utterance on stage of the phrase "not bloody likely" caused an uproar during the first English performance of Bernard Shaw's *Pygmalion*. Over the first half of the century, other swear words gradually made their way into print ("d— it all," for example, eventually gave way to "damn it all"). As the Christian religion held less and less sway over Britain in the second half of the century, so the sharp shock of swear words with religious referents was rubbed smooth, and stronger and stronger sexual terms came to replace them. In the world of literary publishing the publication of Philip Larkin's "This Be the Verse" in 1974 ("They fuck you up, your mum and dad") was something of a watershed. For some time after that, most reputable newspapers and magazines resisted the appearance of "the f-word" in their pages, but in last few years of the twentieth century and the early twenty-first that, too, has changed. In 2006, even the eminently respectable British newsmagazine *The Economist* found it acceptable to use such language in the course of quoting others; here is how their report in their 25–31 March 2006 issue on the state of Iraq three years after the 2003 invasion by American and British troops concluded: "On a toilet-wall in an American airbase in Western Iraq an American soldier has scrawled his own summary analysis: 'We came, we wasted a year of our lives. At least we got the fuckers to vote.'" In 1903—even in 1953 or 1963—such language in a respectable publication would have been entirely unimaginable.

Until very late in the twentieth century height and sightline restrictions kept tall buildings from the London skyline. Several skyscrapers were constructed as part of the late twentieth-century development of the Canary Wharf financial district, however, and in the twenty-first century skyscrapers have risen in other parts of London. Notable among them are the 41-storey Norman Foster-designed 2004 tower known as "The Gherkin" (pictured above), and the 72-storey tower known as "The Shard," which opened in 2013.

London's Millennium Bridge (above). The Bridge, the first new river crossing since the Tower Bridge opened in 1894, was designed jointly by Foster and Partners and Sir Anthony Caro. It opened on 10 June 2000 but had to be closed three days later due to unexpectedly strong swaying. Since its re-opening on 22 February 2002 it has proved enormously popular. To the north is St. Paul's Cathedral, to the south the Tate Modern gallery. The Tate Modern opened on 12 May 2000 in a building that had previously served as the Battersea Power Station. It now houses the Tate's collection of international twentieth- and twenty-first century art; the original Tate Gallery in Chelsea, now renamed Tate Britain, houses the gallery's British collection.

DYLAN THOMAS
1914 – 1953

The fiery career of Dylan Thomas left a burning after-image on the poetic retina of the English-speaking world in the mid-twentieth century. Thomas was a rollicking, even raucous, fixture in the taverns of London's Soho-Fitzrovia district, but he also haunted the rural hills and seashores of

Wales, where he sought to articulate, through the tumbling power of his words, his sense that life and death were rolled together in nature's driving "green fuse."

Born in Swansea, Wales, Dylan Thomas grew up speaking English; his mother, Florence Hannah Williams, and his father, D.J. Thomas, chose the Anglicized urban world of Swansea over their Welsh roots. Thomas's father was a schoolteacher at Swansea Grammar School, which Dylan Thomas attended and where he proved to be far from a prize pupil. However, from an early age Dylan Thomas was writing poems whose images, rhythms, and rhymes would soon be romanticized as "dark-rooted" and "atavistic" by critics who located his passionate verse in Celtic tradition. Yet if Thomas tapped into Welsh imagery, by the age of 15 he was more consciously modeling himself after the French symbolist poet Arthur Rimbaud, even calling himself "the Rimbaud of Cwmdonkin Drive." What attracted Thomas to poets such as Rimbaud and Keats was not only their iconoclasm, but also the fact that they had died young. Thomas regularly cut classes to pore over his own poetry, and launched into a habit of boisterous drinking that was destined to make his career as tragically brief as those of his idols.

In 1933, when Thomas was only 18 years old, the *New English Weekly* published an astonishing poem, his "And Death Shall Have No Dominion." When Thomas's *18 Poems* was published the following year, the strange and disturbing power of his verse woke up London's literary establishment. The cool, controlled style of T.S. Eliot, which conditioned poetic attitudes well into the 1950s, appeared subdued next to the chaotic heat generated by what one critic calls Thomas's "belligerent syntax." For a time, Thomas was labeled a Surrealist and a Dadaist, labels that framed his poetry as a jumble of random signs and erotic images startled out of a Freudian unconscious. Thomas initially exploited the cultural mileage that these early associations gave him, but when his reputation grew sturdier he was careful to distinguish his work from the Surrealists', and to avow that Freud had never been a direct influence. *18 Poems* won Thomas many admirers, including Edith Sitwell, a tireless champion of the curly-haired, Anglo-Welsh "cherub" who churned out formidable verse. "And Death Shall Have No Dominion" was included in his next volume, *25 Poems* (1936), which was also well received. *The Map of Love* (1939) failed to excite much critical acclaim, but with the postwar publication of *Deaths and Entrances* (1946) Thomas won over both the literati and the general public with the lilting rhythms and fresh imagery of poems such as "Fern Hill."

By this time, Thomas had become notorious as an indefatigable carouser, constantly appealing to friends for money and adored by women who wanted to "save" him from his excesses. In 1937, he met Caitlin Macnamara and entered into a stormy marriage that somehow survived an endless stream of creditors, mad bouts of drinking, and mutual infidelities. Caitlin bore Thomas three children.

During the Second World War, Thomas avoided military service on the grounds of poor health, instead finding employment writing film and radio scripts for Strand Films and the BBC. While Thomas remains best known for his early poetry, some critics contend that he was a better playwright and prose writer than poet. The autobiographical stories compiled in *Portrait of the Artist as a Young Dog* (1940) and the posthumously published *Adventures in the Skin Trade* (1955) feature prose that is by turns humorous, raw, and risqué. In his 1945 BBC broadcast "Quite Early One Morning," Thomas's love of place, his fine ear for dialogue, his comic wit and his unforgettable voice fused in a narrative of everyday life in New Quay which endeared him to radio audiences. Around the same time in America, Thomas's poetry was inspiring an almost devotional following with the publications of *The World I Breathe* (1939), *New Poems* (1943), and *Selected Writings* (1946).

For Thomas, the meaning of a word was by no means fixed. As with "Wales," which he savoured as if it were a "gobstopper of magical properties, ringing the word like a bell, making it rise and fall, whisper and thunder like the Welsh sea," Thomas was fascinated by the earthy taste, cadence, and physical horseplay inspired by language. He held that poetry was quintessentially the spoken word, and was meant to be read out loud. In a booming voice that detonated the energy stored in language, Thomas performed radio broadcasts and poetry readings throughout the 1940s and the early 50s— performances that were hugely popular both in Europe and in North America. In 1950 he traveled to New York, where the poet John Malcolm Brinnin had arranged a taxing, but lucrative, schedule of public readings and talks. (The lucre, as usual, quickly evaporated.) Whether reciting his own poetry or favorite poems by Auden, Hardy, and Sitwell, Thomas retained the ability to enthrall a crowd with his magnetic voice and his wildboy antics. His reputation preceded him across the American midwest, and on to San Francisco and Vancouver.

Some critics hold that in the last years of his life Thomas was running on empty, producing only strained works that tried to simulate the tremendous effect captured in his earliest poetry. Others see his writing mature in later works such as "Poem in October" (1945) and the radio drama *Under Milk Wood* (1954). Only a few years before Thomas's final, fatal trip to the United States, he and his family moved into The Boat House in Laugharne, Wales. His stay at The Boat House was to prove the last time Thomas would immerse himself in the landscape of the Welsh shoreline, where he had so often glimpsed the cycle that seemed to him to turn living and dying into almost indistinguishable forces. The respite was short-lived: on a third trip to New York in 1953, Thomas set out on a punishing drinking spree and died, as he had always imagined he would, before reaching the age of 40.

⌘ ⌘ ⌘

The Force That Through the Green Fuse Drives the Flower

The force that through the green fuse drives the
     flower
Drives my green age; that blasts the roots of trees
Is my destroyer.
And I am dumb to tell the crooked rose
5   My youth is bent by the same wintry fever.

The force that drives the water through the rocks
Drives my red blood; that dries the mouthing streams
Turns mine to wax.
And I am dumb to mouth unto my veins
10   How at the mountain spring the same mouth sucks.

The hand that whirls the water in the pool[1]
Stirs the quicksand; that ropes the blowing wind

---

[1] *hand ... pool* See John 5.4.

Hauls my shroud sail.
And I am dumb to tell the hanging man
15 How of my clay is made the hangman's lime.[1]

The lips of time leech to the fountain head;
Love drips and gathers, but the fallen blood
Shall calm her sores.
And I am dumb to tell a weather's wind
20 How time has ticked a heaven round the stars.

And I am dumb to tell the lover's tomb
How at my sheet goes the same crooked worm.
—1933

Fern Hill

Now as I was young and easy under the apple boughs
     About the lilting house and happy as the grass was
          green,
     The night above the dingle[2] starry,
          Time let me hail and climb
5   Golden in the heydays of his eyes,
And honoured among wagons I was prince of the
     apple towns
And once below a time I lordly had the trees and leaves
          Trail with daisies and barley
          Down the rivers of the windfall light.

10   And as I was green and carefree, famous among the barns
     About the happy yard and singing as the farm was home,
          In the sun that is young once only,
               Time let me play and be
          Golden in the mercy of his means,
15   And green and golden I was huntsman and herdsman,
               the calves
     Sang to my horn, the foxes on the hills barked clear
          and cold,
               And the sabbath rang slowly
               In the pebbles of the holy streams.

All the sun long it was running, it was lovely, the hay
20   Fields high as the house, the tunes from the chimneys,
               it was air
          And playing, lovely and watery
               And fire green as grass.
          And nightly under the simple stars
As I rode to sleep the owls were bearing the farm away,
25   All the moon long I heard, blessed among stables, the
               nightjars[3]
          Flying with the ricks,° and the horses   *haystacks*
               Flashing into the dark.

And then to awake, and the farm, like a wanderer white
With the dew, come back, the cock on his shoulder:
          it was all
30   Shining, it was Adam and maiden,
               The sky gathered again
          And the sun grew round that very day.
So it must have been after the birth of the simple light
In the first, spinning place, the spellbound horses
               walking warm
35   Out of the whinnying green stable
               On to the fields of praise.

And honoured among foxes and pheasants by the gay
          house
Under the new made clouds and happy as the heart
          was long,
          In the sun born over and over,
40   I ran my heedless ways,
          My wishes raced through the house high hay
And nothing I cared, at my sky blue trades,[4] that time
          allows
In all his tuneful turning so few and such morning songs
          Before the children green and golden
45   Follow him out of grace,

Nothing I cared, in the lamb white days, that time
               would take me
Up to the swallow thronged loft by the shadow of my
          hand,
          In the moon that is always rising,

---

[1] *lime* Mineral used to speed up decomposition.
[2] *dingle* Wooded dell.
[3] *nightjars* Nocturnal birds.
[4] *trades* Occupations.

Nor that riding to sleep
50   I should hear him fly with the high fields
And wake to the farm forever fled from the childless land.
Oh as I was young and easy in the mercy of his means,
            Time held me green and dying
        Though I sang in my chains like the sea.
            —1946

Do Not Go Gentle into That Good Night

Do not go gentle into that good night,
Old age should burn and rave at close of day;
Rage, rage against the dying of the light.

Though wise men at their end know dark is right,
5   Because their words had forked no lightning they
Do not go gentle into that good night.

Good men, the last wave by, crying how bright
Their frail deeds might have danced in a green bay,
Rage, rage against the dying of the light.

10 Wild men who caught and sang the sun in flight,
And learn, too late, they grieved it on its way,
Do not go gentle into that good night.

Grave men, near death, who see with blinding sight
Blind eyes could blaze like meteors and be gay,
15 Rage, rage against the dying of the light.

And you, my father, there on the sad height,
Curse, bless, me now with your fierce tears, I pray.
Do not go gentle into that good night.
Rage, rage against the dying of the light.
            —1951

A Refusal to Mourn the Death, by Fire, of a Child in London

Never until the mankind making
Bird beast and flower
Fathering and all humbling darkness
Tells with silence the last light breaking
5   And the still hour
Is come of the sea tumbling in harness

And I must enter again the round
Zion[1] of the water bead
And the synagogue of the ear of corn
10 Shall I let pray the shadow of a sound
Or sow my salt seed
In the least valley of sackcloth to mourn

The majesty and burning of the child's death.
I shall not murder
15 The mankind of her going with a grave truth
Nor blaspheme down the stations of the breath
With any further
Elegy of innocence and youth.

Deep with the first dead lies London's daughter,
20 Robed in the long friends,
The grains beyond age, the dark veins of her mother,
Secret by the unmourning water
Of the riding Thames.[2]
After the first death, there is no other.
            —1946

---

[1]   *Zion*   Hill in Jerusalem, previous center of Jewish worship; by extension, the house of God.

[2]   *Thames*   River in London.

Philip Larkin

1922 – 1985

Although Philip Larkin published two novels in his lifetime as well as several other nonfiction works, his reputation as one of the most important figures in twentieth-century British literature rests on his poetry. His accessible style and straightforward language; the commentary he provided on Britain's changing post-war status; and above all the extraordinary skill with which he crafted poetic expressions of emotions widely shared (if not always expressed) made him one of the most popular poets of his time. Though often described as anti-social, Larkin was a witty conversationalist, and he maintained several relationships that spanned most of his adult life. His work is often (and

rightly) described as bleakly pessimistic, and frequently touches on themes of solitude and mortality. Yet his poems are also often funny—Larkin is equally capable of dry wit and broad humor.

Larkin was born in Coventry in the West Midlands of England in 1922 to Sydney and Eva Larkin. He was their second child and only son. Although he describes his childhood as "dull, pot-bound, and slightly mad," he appears to have had a comfortable upbringing. His father was the city treasurer and the family led a typical middle-class existence. Larkin describes his parents as "awkward" and "shy"; it seems likely that the sterility of their relationship influenced his own views towards marriage. The family home may have been emotionless, but his father kept a well-stocked library, where Larkin was first introduced to the classics. Between 1930 and 1940 Larkin attended King Henry VIII School, where he described himself as having been unhappy, an "unsuccessful schoolboy." His unhappiness may have been caused by his stammer, a condition from which he continued to suffer until he was well into his thirties. Whether despite or because of his unhappiness, Larkin did begin writing during this period; his first poem was published in the school paper, *The Coventrian*, in 1934, when he was 12.

In 1940, Larkin sent one of his poems to the literary magazine *The Listener*, which accepted and published "Ultimatum" in November of that year. In the same year he entered Oxford to study English, and the experience of university turned out to be a great stimulus for him in terms both of writing and of personal friendships. It was while he was at Oxford that he met Kingsley Amis, some years later to become famous as a novelist; the two remained fast friends for life. (Although they often showed each other their work in its early stages, it was a love of jazz above all that first drew them together.) Larkin developed in these years a distrust of the Modernist notion that twentieth-century literature should express the difficulties of twentieth-century life, and gained an appreciation for a plainer style of writing. He greatly admired W.H. Auden and W.B. Yeats, and tried for years to mimic Yeats's writing in particular.

Larkin graduated in 1943 and returned to his parents' house in Coventry that year, his poor eyesight making him ineligible to fight in World War II. After failing the civil service exam twice, Larkin answered an advertisement in the paper for a librarian in Wellington, Shropshire. He remained in the profession for the rest of his life, stating that "librarianship suits me." The solitude of the work as well as the regular hours gave him sufficient time to pursue his writing; during this period he produced his first volume of poetry, *The North Ship*, published at his own expense in 1945. It went largely unnoticed. The following two years produced Larkin's only novels, *Jill* in 1946 and *A Girl in Winter* in 1947. Larkin later described the novels as "over-sized poems"; their lack of success encouraged him to give up the form, and from that point onwards he concentrated on poetry. While in Shropshire Larkin also qualified professionally as a librarian; from 1955 until his death he worked as a librarian at the University of Hull.

In the 1950s Larkin began to be associated with a literary group known simply as "The Movement." Its members included Amis as well as Bruce Montgomery, Thom Gunn, and Donald Davie. They were all representatives of a new style of British writing that was anti-romantic, sardonic, and concerned with everyday British life. In Larkin's case, it was *The Less Deceived* (1955), and the poem "Church Going" in particular, that solidified his poetic reputation as an anti-romantic poet. With this volume Larkin shook off the influence of Yeats and established his own style and voice. Spare in their imagery, and typically with a strong but unobtrusive framework of rhythm and rhyme, the poems often chronicle the place of choice or fate in a person's life. Loneliness, misunderstanding, and deception are central themes in Larkin's work, and the aesthetic act often seemed his only bulwark against despair. "People say I'm very negative and I suppose I am," he admitted, "but the impulse for producing a poem is never negative; the most negative poem in the world is a very positive thing to have done."

The Less Deceived was followed by *The Whitsun Weddings* and *High Windows* in 1964 and 1974 respectively; the poems in these later collections are largely in the same vein as Larkin's earlier work but are less frequently ironic, more often directly revealing of emotion. Larkin also occasionally adopted a different voice in which the presence of rhyme is more obtrusive, the thoughts bluntly pointed, and the tone loudly sardonic. Two of the poems from *High Windows* written in this tone —"This Be the Verse" and "Annus Mirabilis"—caused something of a sensation on the book's publication, and have remained among the most often quoted of Larkin's poems.

In addition to his poetry, Larkin was engaged with other literary pursuits. From 1961 to 1971 he published a regular jazz column in *The Daily Telegraph*. Some of these columns were later reproduced in *All What Jazz*, published in 1970. He was editor of the *Oxford Book of Twentieth-Century Verse* (1973), and his nonfiction writing was collected in *Required Writing* (1983). Larkin won the Queen's Gold Medal for Poetry in 1965, was appointed a Companion of the British Empire in 1975, and received seven honorary doctorates. He was offered the position of British Poet Laureate in 1984, but turned it down because he did not want the media attention with which it was associated. Although Larkin had a number of romantic relationships, he never married, and once said that "two can live as stupidly as one." (The publication in 1992 of Larkin's *Selected Letters*, which contains derogatory language about women, as well as slurs against socialists and various racial groups, led many to attribute Larkin's views on marriage as much to his tendency towards misogyny as to his innate pessimism with regard to the human condition.) Larkin's poetic output was much reduced in the 1980s; his last major poem, "Aubade," was published in the *Times Literary Supplement* in 1977. Larkin was admitted to hospital in 1985, suffering from cancer, and had his esophagus removed. He died later that year.

⌘ ⌘ ⌘

Days

What are days for?
    Days are where we live.
They come, they wake us
Time and time over.
5   They are to be happy in:
Where can we live but days?

Ah, solving that question
Brings the priest and the doctor
In their long coats
10   Running over the fields.
    —1953

Church Going

Once I am sure there's nothing going on
    I step inside, letting the door thud shut.
Another church: matting, seats, and stone,
And little books; sprawlings of flowers, cut
5   For Sunday, brownish now; some brass and stuff
Up at the holy end; the small neat organ;
And a tense, musty, unignorable silence,
Brewed God knows how long. Hatless, I take off
My cycle-clips in awkward reverence,

10   Move forward, run my hand around the font.[1]
From where I stand, the roof looks almost new—
Cleaned, or restored? Someone would know: I don't.
Mounting the lectern, I peruse a few
Hectoring large-scale verses, and pronounce
15   "Here endeth" much more loudly than I'd meant.
The echoes snigger briefly. Back at the door
I sign the book, donate an Irish sixpence,
Reflect the place was not worth stopping for.

Yet stop I did: in fact I often do,
20   And always end much at a loss like this,
Wondering what to look for; wondering, too,
When churches fall completely out of use
What we shall turn them into, if we shall keep

A few cathedrals chronically on show,
25   Their parchment, plate and pyx[2] in locked cases,
And let the rest rent-free to rain and sheep.
Shall we avoid them as unlucky places?

Or, after dark, will dubious women come
To make their children touch a particular stone;
30   Pick simples° for a cancer; or on some   *medicinal herbs*
Advised night see walking a dead one?
Power of some sort or other will go on
In games, in riddles, seemingly at random;
But superstition, like belief, must die,
35   And what remains when disbelief has gone?
Grass, weedy pavement, brambles, buttress, sky,

A shape less recognisable each week,
A purpose more obscure. I wonder who
Will be the last, the very last, to seek
40   This place for what it was; one of the crew
That tap and jot and know what rood-lofts° were?   *church galleries*
Some ruin-bibber, randy for antique,
Or Christmas-addict, counting on a whiff
Of gown-and-bands and organ-pipes and myrrh?
45   Or will he be my representative,

Bored, uninformed, knowing the ghostly silt
Dispersed, yet tending to this cross of ground
Through suburb scrub because it held unspilt
So long and equally what since is found
50   Only in separation—marriage, and birth,
And death, and thoughts of these—for which was built
This special shell? For, though I've no idea
What this accoutred frowsty° barn is worth,   *stuffy*
It pleases me to stand in silence here;

55   A serious house on serious earth it is,
In whose blent air all our compulsions meet,
Are recognised, and robed as destinies.
And that much never can be obsolete,
Since someone will forever be surprising
60   A hunger in himself to be more serious,
And gravitating with it to this ground,

---

[1] *font* Baptismal receptacle.

[2] *pyx* Vessel in which the bread of the Eucharist is kept.

Which, he once heard, was proper to grow wise in,
If only that so many dead lie round.
—1954

Talking in Bed

Talking in bed ought to be easiest,
    Lying together there goes back so far,
An emblem of two people being honest.

Yet more and more time passes silently.
Outside, the wind's incomplete unrest   5
Builds and disperses clouds about the sky,

And dark towns heap up on the horizon.
None of this cares for us. Nothing shows why
At this unique distance from isolation

It becomes still more difficult to find   10
Words at once true and kind,
Or not untrue and not unkind.
—1960

Dockery and Son

"Dockery was junior to you,
    Wasn't he?" said the Dean. "His son's here now."
Death-suited, visitant, I nod. "And do
You keep in touch with—" Or remember how
Black-gowned, unbreakfasted, and still half-tight   5
We used to stand before that desk, to give
"Our version" of "these incidents last night"?
I try the door of where I used to live:

Locked. The lawn spreads dazzlingly wide.
A known bell chimes. I catch my train, ignored.   10
Canal and clouds and colleges subside
Slowly from view. But Dockery, good Lord,
Anyone up[1] today must have been born
In '43, when I was twenty-one.

If he was younger, did he get this son   15
At nineteen, twenty? Was he that withdrawn

High-collared public[2]-schoolboy, sharing rooms
With Cartwright who was killed? Well, it just shows
How much … How little … Yawning, I suppose
I fell asleep, waking at the fumes   20
And furnace-glares of Sheffield, where I changed,[3]
And ate an awful pie, and walked along
The platform to its end to see the ranged
Joining and parting lines reflect a strong

Unhindered moon. To have no son, no wife,   25
No house or land still seemed quite natural.
Only a numbness registered the shock
Of finding out how much had gone of life,
How widely from the others. Dockery, now:
Only nineteen, he must have taken stock   30
Of what he wanted, and been capable
Of … No, that's not the difference: rather, how

Convinced he was he should be added to!
Why did he think adding meant increase?
To me it was dilution. Where do these   35
Innate assumptions come from? Not from what
We think truest, or most want to do:
Those warp tight-shut, like doors. They're more a style
Our lives bring with them: habit for a while,
Suddenly they harden into all we've got   40

And how we got it; looked back on, they rear
Like sand-clouds, thick and close, embodying
For Dockery a son, for me nothing,
Nothing with all a son's harsh patronage.
Life is first boredom, then fear.   45
Whether or not we use it, it goes,

---

[1] *Anyone up* To refer to being "up" at Oxford or Cambridge was a common colloquialism for attending university in those towns. Both of these ancient universities are composed of many colleges.

[2] *public* In Britain the term "public school" came into use in the late sixteenth century to distinguish grammar schools operated by private individuals or church authorities from those open to a broader public. Such schools were (and are) fee-charging institutions attended overwhelmingly by privileged students; they are thus similar to *private* schools in such countries as the United States and Canada.

[3] *Sheffield, where I changed* Larkin, who attended Oxford University, was for most of his adult life a librarian at the University of Hull. When traveling between Oxford and Hull by train one would normally change trains at Sheffield.

And leaves what something hidden from us chose,
And age, and then the only end of age.
—1963

Annus Mirabilis[1]

Sexual intercourse began
In nineteen sixty-three
(Which was rather late for me)—
Between the end of the *Chatterley* ban[2]
5   And the Beatles' first L.P.

Up till then there'd only been
A sort of bargaining,
A wrangle for a ring,
A shame that started at sixteen
10   And spread to everything.

Then all at once the quarrel sank:
Everyone felt the same,
And every life became
A brilliant breaking of the bank,
15   A quite unlosable game.

So life was never better than
In nineteen sixty-three (Though just too late for me)—
Between the end of the *Chatterley* ban
And the Beatles' first L.P.
—1967

High Windows

When I see a couple of kids
And guess he's fucking her and she's
Taking pills or wearing a diaphragm,
I know this is paradise

5   Everyone old has dreamed of all their lives—
Bonds and gestures pushed to one side
Like an outdated combine harvester,
And everyone young going down the long slide

To happiness, endlessly. I wonder if
10   Anyone looked at me, forty years back,
And thought, *That'll be the life;*
No God any more, or sweating in the dark

About hell and that, or having to hide
What you think of the priest. He
15   *And his lot will all go down the long slide*
Like free bloody birds. And immediately

Rather than words comes the thought of high windows:
The sun-comprehending glass,
And beyond it, the deep blue air, that shows
20   Nothing, and is nowhere, and is endless.
—1967

This Be the Verse

They fuck you up, your mum and dad.
   They may not mean to, but they do.
They fill you with the faults they had
   And add some extra, just for you.

5   But they were fucked up in their turn
   By fools in old-style hats and coats,
Who half the time were soppy-stern
   And half at one another's throats.

Man hands on misery to man.
10   It deepens like a coastal shelf.
Get out as early as you can,
   And don't have any kids yourself.
—1971

---

[1] *Annus Mirabilis* Latin: Wondrous Year.

[2] *the Chatterley ban* D.H. Lawrence's novel *Lady Chatterley's Lover* was banned in both the UK and US on the grounds of obscenity; it contained four-letter words and descriptions of sexual activity that were, for the time, quite explicit. On 2 November 1960, Penguin Books won an obscenity trial over the issue, and the ban was lifted in the UK.

Vers de Société[1]

My wife and I have asked a crowd of craps
   To come and waste their time and ours; perhaps
You'd care to join us? In a pig's arse, friend.
Day comes to an end.
5 The gas fire breathes, the trees are darkly swayed.
And so *Dear Warlock-Williams*: I'm afraid—

Funny how hard it is to be alone.
I could spend half my evenings, if I wanted,
Holding a glass of washing sherry, canted°   *obliquely pushed*
10 Over to catch the drivel of some bitch
Who's read nothing but *Which*;[2]
Just think of all the spare time that has flown

Straight into nothingness by being filled
With forks and faces, rather than repaid
15 Under a lamp, hearing the noise of wind,
And looking out to see the moon thinned
To an air-sharpened blade.
A life, and yet how sternly it's instilled

All solitude is selfish. No one now
20 Believes the hermit with his gown and dish[3]
Talking to God (who's gone too); the big wish
Is to have people nice to you, which means
Doing it back somehow.
Virtue is social. Are, then, these routines

25 Playing at goodness, like going to church?
Something that bores us, something we don't do well
(Asking that ass about his fool research)
But try to feel, because, however crudely,
It shows us what should be?
30 Too subtle, that. Too decent, too. Oh hell,

Only the young can be alone freely.
The time is shorter now for company,

---

[1] *Vers de Société* Poem about social life.

[2] *Which* British consumer product testing magazine.

[3] *hermit ... and dish* Followers of an important strain of hermitic Christianity in medieval Europe who wore gowns of sackcloth or rough material (intended to be uncomfortable) and held out their dishes to solicit alms from other Christians.

And sitting by a lamp more often brings
Not peace, but other things.
35 Beyond the light stand failure and remorse
Whispering *Dear Warlock-Williams: Why, of course*—
    —1971

The Old Fools

What do they think has happened, the old fools,
   To make them like this? Do they somehow suppose
It's more grown-up when your mouth hangs open and
    drools
And you keep on pissing yourself, and can't remember
5 Who called this morning? Or that, if they only chose,
They could alter things back to when they danced all night,
Or went to their wedding, or sloped arms some September?
Or do they fancy there's really been no change,
And they've always behaved as if they were crippled or
    tight,
10 Or sat through days of thin continuous dreaming
Watching light move? If they don't (and they can't),
    it's strange;
               Why aren't they screaming?

At death, you break up: the bits that were you
Start speeding away from each other for ever
15 With no one to see. It's only oblivion, true:
We had it before, but then it was going to end,
And was all the time merging with a unique endeavour
To bring to bloom the million-petalled flower
Of being here. Next time you can't pretend
20 There'll be anything else. And these are the first signs:
Not knowing how, not hearing who, the power
Of choosing gone. Their looks show that they're for it:
Ash hair, toad hands, prune face dried into lines—
            How can they ignore it?

25 Perhaps being old is having lighted rooms
Inside your head, and people in them, acting.
People you know, yet can't quite name; each looms
Like a deep loss restored, from known doors turning,
Setting down a lamp, smiling from a stair, extracting
30 A known book from the shelves; or sometimes only
The rooms themselves, chairs and a fire burning,

The blown bush at the window, or the sun's
Faint friendliness on the wall some lonely
Rain-ceased midsummer evening. That is where they
       live:
35 Not here and now, but where all happened once.
          This is why they give

An air of baffled absence, trying to be there
Yet being here. For the rooms grow farther, leaving
Incompetent cold, the constant wear and tear
40 Of taken breath, and them crouching below
Extinction's alp, the old fools, never perceiving
How near it is. This must be what keeps them quiet:
The peak that stays in view wherever we go
For them is rising ground. Can they never tell
45 What is dragging them back, and how it will end?
Not at night? Not when the strangers come? Never,
       throughout
The whole hideous inverted childhood? Well,
         We shall find out.

—1973

Aubade [1]

I work all day, and get half-drunk at night.
  Waking at four to soundless dark, I stare.
In time the curtain-edges will grow light.
Till then I see what's really always there:
5 Unresting death, a whole day nearer now,
Making all thought impossible but how
And where and when I shall myself die.
Arid interrogation: yet the dread
Of dying, and being dead,
10 Flashes afresh to hold and horrify.

The mind blanks at the glare. Not in remorse
—The good not done, the love not given, time
Torn off unused—nor wretchedly because
An only life can take so long to climb

15 Clear of its wrong beginnings, and may never;
But at the total emptiness for ever,
The sure extinction that we travel to
And shall be lost in always. Not to be here,
Not to be anywhere,
20 And soon; nothing more terrible, nothing more true.

This is a special way of being afraid
No trick dispels. Religion used to try,
That vast moth-eaten musical brocade
Created to pretend we never die,
25 And specious° stuff that says *No rational being*   misleading
Can fear a thing it will not feel, not seeing
That this is what we fear—no sight, no sound,
No touch or taste or smell, nothing to think with,
Nothing to love or link with,
30 The anaesthetic from which none come round.

And so it stays just on the edge of vision,
A small unfocused blur, a standing chill
That slows each impulse down to indecision.
Most things may never happen: this one will,
35 And realisation of it rages out
In furnace-fear when we are caught without
People or drink. Courage is no good:
It means not scaring others. Being brave
Lets no one off the grave.
40 Death is no different whined at than withstood.

Slowly light strengthens, and the room takes shape.
It stands plain as a wardrobe, what we know,
Have always known, know that we can't escape,
Yet can't accept. One side will have to go.
45 Meanwhile telephones crouch, getting ready to ring
In locked-up offices, and all the uncaring
Intricate rented world begins to rouse.
The sky is white as clay, with no sun.
Work has to be done.
50 Postmen like doctors go from house to house.
—1977

---

[1] *Aubade* From the Old French "alba," an early morning song or
poem, the motif of which is usually a call for lovers to wake before
parting.

TED HUGHES
1930 – 1998

When Ted Hughes was chosen to succeed Sir John Betjeman as England's Poet Laureate in 1984, a reporter in *The Times* described the selection as "a bit like appointing a grim young cow to replace a cuddly old teddy bear." Coming on the British literary scene in the 1950s, Hughes startled readers with his poetic voice. With bold metaphors and forceful rhythms, his poems paint grim, often violent, visions of human existence. At the same time, he celebrates the power of nature and attempts to reunite humanity with the natural world, using myth and folklore to explore alternative possibilities of spirituality.

Edward James Hughes was born in Mytholmroyd, a county in West Yorkshire, the landscape of which—with its valleys, cliffs, and surrounding moors—pervades much of his poetry. Hughes studied English literature for two years at Cambridge before switching to archaeology and anthropology in his final year of study—seeking to escape what he called "the terrible, suffocating, maternal octopus" of the English poetic tradition. In 1956 after graduating, Hughes met and married Sylvia Plath, an American student studying at Cambridge on a Fulbright Fellowship. The following year, having published some individual poems, Hughes released his first collection, *The Hawk in the Rain* (1957). The poems of this début—including "The Thought-Fox" and "Pike"—depict animals participating in a natural world from which humans are isolated by their intellect.

After teaching briefly in the United States, Hughes and Plath returned to England, where their two children were born and where Hughes published his second collection, *Lupercal* (1960). Hughes also began writing children's books and radio plays during this period. After Plath committed suicide in 1963, following the couple's separation, Hughes put his own poetry on hold to focus on editing and publishing his wife's poems and journals.

Hughes's return to poetry, *Wodwo* (1967), signaled a change in direction from his earlier work. An interest in anthropology began to color his work, as did a marked interest in occult, mythic, and folktale sources. The volume following, *Crow: From the Life and Songs of the Crow* (1970), created in collaboration with artist Leonard Baskin, presents a series of poems informed by Hughes's own mythology. These poems, which follow a crow from the genesis of the world until nuclear apocalypse, lay bare the brutality in nature, though with more humor than was present in his earlier work. Hughes said his goal in the Crow poems was to achieve a certain style consisting of "a super-simple and a super-ugly language which would in a way shed everything except just what he [Crow] wanted to say." Perhaps not surprisingly, this carrion-eating, graceless, self-serving protagonist (who became the main character of several subsequent works) brought charges of misanthropy and crudeness upon Hughes.

With *Crow* Hughes discovered his penchant for collaborative ventures, and more followed, including *Cave Birds* (1978), also with Leonard Baskin; *Remains of Elmet* (1979), in which he explores, with photographer Fay Godwin, the history of his native region from ancient to industrial times; and *River* (1983), which, accompanied by photographs by Peter Keen, provides a composite view of a river over the course of a year. Another of his later collections, *Moortown* (1979), documents his experiences dairy farming with Jack Orchard, the father of his second wife, Carol.

Though Hughes continued to publish volumes of new and collected poems, in his later years he devoted himself increasingly to judging competitions and performing readings—particularly for children—and became an active supporter of environmental and ecological causes. Hughes also turned to writing prose and to translating, publishing *Tales from Ovid* (1997), a collection of essays entitled *Winter Pollen* (1994), and his critical work on Shakespeare, *Shakespeare and the Goddess of Complete Being* (1992), which united his interest in the author with his passion for mythology.

In 1998 Hughes broke his thirty-year silence concerning his marriage with Plath and published *Birthday Letters*, a series of poems addressed to his dead wife. During the years following her death, Hughes had frequently been accused by some of Plath's admirers of "murdering" the female poet, and his surname was repeatedly defaced on her gravestone. Hughes's last collection had the effect of silencing, rather than reigniting, the expected opposition, and sales for the book have remained high since its publication.

Hughes was diagnosed with colon cancer in 1997 and died in 1998, two weeks after receiving the Order of Merit from Queen Elizabeth II. Hughes's unique vision of the natural world—and of humanity's place in it—has endured after his death, and his poetry remains widely read and studied. Of his continued popularity, British poet and critic Dick Davis explains, "He brings back to our suburban, centrally-heated and, above all, *safe* lives reports from an authentic frontier of reality and the imagination. His poems speak to us of a world that is constantly true in a way that we know our temporary comforts cannot be."

⌘ ⌘ ⌘

The Thought-Fox

I imagine this midnight moment's forest:
  Something else is alive
Beside the clock's loneliness
And this blank page where my fingers move.

5 Through the window I see no star:
  Something more near
Though deeper within darkness
Is entering the loneliness:

Cold, delicately as the dark snow
10 A fox's nose touches twig, leaf;
Two eyes serve a movement, that now
And again now, and now, and now

Sets neat prints into the snow
Between trees, and warily a lame
15 Shadow lags by stump and in hollow
Of a body that is bold to come

Across clearings, an eye,
A widening deepening greenness,
Brilliantly, concentratedly,
20 Coming about its own business

Till, with a sudden sharp hot stink of fox,
It enters the dark hole of the head.
The window is starless still; the clock ticks,
The page is printed.
—1957

Pike

Pike, three inches long, perfect
  Pike in all parts, green tigering the gold.
Killers from the egg: the malevolent aged grin.
They dance on the surface among the flies.

5 Or move, stunned by their own grandeur,
Over a bed of emerald, silhouette

Of submarine delicacy and horror.
A hundred feet long in their world.

In ponds, under the heat-struck lily pads—
10   Gloom of their stillness:
Logged on last year's black leaves, watching upwards.
Or hung in an amber cavern of weeds

The jaws' hooked clamp and fangs
Not to be changed at this date;
15   A life subdued to its instrument;
The gills kneading quietly, and the pectorals.

Three we kept behind glass,
Jungled in weed: three inches, four,
And four and a half: fed fry to them—
20   Suddenly there were two. Finally one.

With a sag belly and the grin it was born with.
And indeed they spare nobody.
Two, six pounds each, over two feet long,
High and dry and dead in the willow-herb—

25   One jammed past its gills down the other's gullet:
The outside eye stared: as a vice locks—
The same iron in this eye
Though its film shrank in death.

A pond I fished, fifty yards across,
30   Whose lilies and muscular tench[1]
Had outlasted every visible stone
Of the monastery that planted them—

Stilled legendary depth:
It was as deep as England. It held
35   Pike too immense to stir, so immense and old
That past nightfall I dared not cast

But silently cast and fished
With the hair frozen on my head
For what might move, for what eye might move.
40   The still splashes on the dark pond,

Owls hushing the floating woods
Frail on my ear against the dream
Darkness beneath night's darkness had freed,
That rose slowly towards me, watching.
—1959

The Seven Sorrows

The first sorrow of autumn
Is the slow goodbye
Of the garden who stands so long in the evening—

A brown poppy head,
5   The stalk of a lily,
And still cannot go.

The second sorrow
Is the empty feet
Of the pheasant who hangs from a hook with his
      brothers.
10   The woodland of gold
Is folded in feathers
With its head in a bag.

And the third sorrow
Is the slow goodbye
15   Of the sun who has gathered the birds and who gathers
The minutes of evening,
The golden and holy
Ground of the picture.

The fourth sorrow
20   Is the pond gone black
Ruined and sunken the city of water—
The beetle's palace,
The catacombs
Of the dragonfly.

25   And the fifth sorrow
Is the slow goodbye
Of the woodland that quietly breaks up its camp.
One day it's gone. It has left only litter—
Firewood, tentpoles.

---

[1] *tench* Fish, like a carp.

30 And the sixth sorrow
Is the fox's sorrow
The joy of the huntsman, the joy of the hounds,
The hooves that pound
Till earth closes her ear
35 To the fox's prayer.

And the seventh sorrow
Is the slow goodbye
Of the face with its wrinkles that looks through the
     window
As the year packs up
40 Like a tatty fairground
That came for the children.
—1975

Heptonstall Old Church[1]

A great bird landed here.

Its song drew men out of rock,
Living men out of bog and heather.

Its song put a light in the valleys
5 And harness on the long moors.

Its song brought a crystal from space
And set it in men's heads.

Then the bird died.

Its giant bones
10 Blackened and became a mystery.

The crystal in men's heads
Blackened and fell to pieces.

The valleys went out.
The moorland broke loose.
—1979

---

[1] *Heptonstall Old Church* The town of Heptonstall was three miles from Hughes's childhood home of Mytholmroyd, in West Yorkshire. The ruins of the "old church" (dating from the thirteenth century) stand beside the present church, constructed in 1854. The bodies of Sylvia Plath and of Hughes's parents are buried in its churchyard.

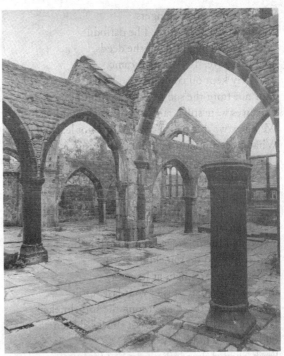

Heptonstall Old Church, 1970s.

Daffodils

R emember how we[2] picked the daffodils?
    Nobody else remembers, but I remember.
Your daughter came with her armfuls, eager and happy,
Helping the harvest. She has forgotten.
5 She cannot even remember you. And we sold them.
It sounds like sacrilege, but we sold them.
Were we so poor? Old Stoneman, the grocer,
Boss-eyed, his blood-pressure purpling to beetroot
(It was his last chance,
10 He would die in the same great freeze as you),
He persuaded us. Every Spring
He always bought them, sevenpence a dozen,
"A custom of the house."

Besides, we still weren't sure we wanted to own
15 Anything. Mainly we were hungry
To convert everything to profit.

---

[2] *we* I.e., Hughes and Sylvia Plath.

Still nomads—still strangers
To our whole possession. The daffodils
Were incidental gilding of the deeds,
20   Treasure trove. They simply came,
And they kept on coming.
As if not from the sod but falling from heaven.
Our lives were still a raid on our own good luck.
We knew we'd live for ever. We had not learned
25   What a fleeting glance of the everlasting
Daffodils are. Never identified
The nuptial flight of the rarest ephemera—
Our own days!
                    We thought they were a windfall.
30   Never guessed they were a last blessing.
So we sold them. We worked at selling them
As if employed on somebody else's
Flower-farm. You bent at it
In the rain of that April—your last April.
35   We bent there together, among the soft shrieks
Of their jostled stems, the wet shocks shaken
Of their girlish dance-frocks—
Fresh-opened dragonflies, wet and flimsy,
Opened too early.

40   We piled their frailty lights on a carpenter's bench,
Distributed leaves among the dozens—
Buckling blade-leaves, limber, groping for air, zinc-
        silvered—
Propped their raw butts in bucket water,
Their oval, meaty butts,
45   And sold them, sevenpence a bunch—

Wind-wounds, spasms from the dark earth,
With their odourless metals,
A flamy purification of the deep grave's stony cold
As if ice had a breath—

50   We sold them, to wither.
The crop thickened faster than we could thin it.
Finally, we were overwhelmed
And we lost our wedding-present scissors.

Every March since they have lifted again
55   Out of the same bulbs, the same
Baby-cries from the thaw,
Ballerinas too early for music, shiverers
In the draughty wings of the year.
On that same groundswell of memory, fluttering
60   They return to forget you stooping there
Behind the rainy curtains of a dark April,
Snipping their stems.

But somewhere your scissors remember.
Wherever they are.
65   Here somewhere, blades wide open,
April by April
Sinking deeper
Through the sod—an anchor, a cross of rust.
—1998

CHINUA ACHEBE
1930 – 2013

Chinua Achebe gained international attention with the publication of his first novel, *Things Fall Apart* (1958); it has since attained the status of a modern classic, and has sold over ten million copies. *Things Fall Apart*, together with Achebe's subsequent novels, follows the course of Nigerian history from just before colonial rule until immediately after independence. Focused on the perspective of colonized Nigerians, these works record the trauma that resulted from Africa's experience with European rule and—without idealizing Nigerians— demonstrate the value, dignity, and beauty of a culture that was all but lost during colonial rule. Though Achebe's writing, whether short story, novel, or political essay, often focuses explicitly on his native country, he argued against a narrowly nationalistic approach, seeking what he called "universal communication across racial and cultural boundaries as a means of fostering respect for all people."

Achebe was born Albert Chinualumoga Achebe in 1930 in eastern Nigeria. Both of Achebe's parents were Christian converts, and his father was employed as a catechist for the Church Missionary Society. Achebe attended the prestigious Government College at Umuahia before enrolling in University College, Ibadan, a newly constituent college of the University of London. There Achebe decided to study literature, following a curriculum that mirrored that of the College's British parent school—with the sole addition of some writers thought relevant to African students, such as Joseph Conrad, H. Rider Haggard, and colonial administrators such as Joyce Cary (whose novel *Mister Johnson* had a profound influence on Achebe). The work of these writers, which frequently features stereotypical and racist depictions of African people, helped to persuade Achebe to write, and also determined his choice to write in English. Unlike many other African writers (such as Kenyan writer Ngũgĩ wa Thiong'o) who choose to use their native language rather than that of their colonizers, Achebe felt that by writing in English he could more directly take issue with these colonial writers by replacing their portraits of Africans with his own.

While in university, Achebe contributed several stories to the *University Herald*. These works, published much later in *Girls at War and Other Stories* (1972), foreground the ways in which conflicts between modern and traditional values have been exacerbated by colonial contact. The traditional balance between material and spiritual aspects of society, and between a concern for self and for community, is typically disrupted, robbing subjects of a strong culture on which to rely. Achebe, himself educated in a system that favored all elements of the new, colonial order—whether cultural, religious, or academic—over those of traditional Biafran society, had to learn for himself much of the history of his people.

After graduating from university, Achebe married, started a family, and embarked on a twelve-year career as a producer for the Nigerian Broadcasting Corporation. Encouraged by literary critic Gilbert Phelps, one of his teachers at the BBC staff school, Achebe published *Things Fall Apart* in 1958. Readers of this novel were struck not least of all by Achebe's ability to adapt the English language to his own goals in writing about Nigeria. He relies heavily on Ibo proverbs—which often highlight the themes of his work or help further characterization—and vernacular speech patterns, as well as on native imagery and folklore. In this way his English manages to convey the flavor of Nigerian experience, belief, and culture. In Achebe's view, "the price a world language must be prepared to pay is submission to many different kinds of use. The African writer should aim to use English in a way that brings out his message best. ... He should aim at fashioning out an English which is at once universal and able to carry his peculiar experience."

No Longer at Ease (1960), *Arrow of God* (1964), *A Man of the People* (1966), and *Anthills of the Savannah* (1987), Achebe's other novels, were also highly acclaimed. Achebe's prescience was often noted in his examinations of Nigeria's political situation. *A Man of the People*, for example, expressed Achebe's concern over what he identified as Nigeria's lack of strong leadership—a lack that led to Nigeria's first military coup in January 1966, the month of the novel's publication.

During the civil war that followed, Achebe traveled and spoke extensively on behalf of his people, who briefly formed the independent state of Biafra in 1967. Following the conclusion of civil war in 1970, Achebe continued his political activities while accepting various teaching posts at American schools. The poetry and essays written during this period are more overtly political than his earlier work. *Morning Yet on Creation Day* (1974) contains both literary and political essays; many of these were reprinted in the collection *Hopes and Impediments* (1988), which opens with Achebe's controversial essay on Joseph Conrad's *Heart of Darkness*.

Achebe returned to work at the University of Nigeria in 1976, but after a serious car accident in 1990 he moved to the United States to recuperate, accepting a post at Bard College, New York. There he published the essay and poetry collection *Another Africa* (1997), then the autobiographical essay collections *Home and Exile* (2000) and *The Education of a British-Protected Child* (2009). In 2012, the year before his death, he released *There Was a Country: A Personal History of Biafra*, a non-fiction work combining historical analysis with his personal recollections of the Nigerian-Biafran War.

Throughout his career Achebe insisted that his political actions and his literary pursuits were not two separate activities, but two ways of attempting to achieve the same end. He firmly believed that storytelling, far from being an idle pursuit, is a socially relevant form of political engagement. "Literature, whether handed down by word of mouth or in print, gives us a second handle on reality; enabling us to encounter in the safe manageable dimensions of make-believe the very same threats to integrity that may assail the psyche in real life; and at the same time providing through the self-discovery which it imparts, a veritable weapon for coping with these threats."

⌘ ⌘ ⌘

Dead Men's Path

Michael Obi's hopes were fulfilled much earlier than he had expected. He was appointed headmaster of Ndume Central School in January 1949. It had always been an unprogressive school, so the Mission authorities[1] decided to send a young and energetic man to run it. Obi accepted this responsibility with enthusiasm. He had many wonderful ideas and this was an opportunity to put them into practice. He had had sound secondary school education which designated him a "pivotal teacher" in the official records and set him apart from the other headmasters in the mission field. He was outspoken in his condemnation of the narrow views of these older and often less-educated ones.

"We shall make a good job of it, shan't we?" he asked his young wife when they first heard the joyful news of his promotion.

"We shall do our best," she replied. "We shall have such beautiful gardens and everything will be just *modern* and delightful. ..." In their two years of married

---

[1] *Mission authorities* Many schools in African countries formerly colonized by the British were run by Christian missionary organizations.

life she had become completely infected by his passion for "modern methods" and his denigration of "these old and superannuated people in the teaching field who would be better employed as traders in the Onitsha[1] market." She began to see herself already as the admired wife of the young headmaster, the queen of the school.

The wives of the other teachers would envy her position. She would set the fashion in everything.... Then, suddenly, it occurred to her that there might not be other wives. Wavering between hope and fear, she asked her husband, looking anxiously at him.

"All our colleagues are young and unmarried," he said with enthusiasm which for once she did not share. "Which is a good thing," he continued.

"Why?"

"Why? They will give all their time and energy to the school."

Nancy was downcast. For a few minutes she became skeptical about the new school; but it was only for a few minutes. Her little personal misfortune could not blind her to her husband's happy prospects. She looked at him as he sat folded up in a chair. He was stoop-shouldered and looked frail. But he sometimes surprised people with sudden bursts of physical energy. In his present posture, however, all his bodily strength seemed to have retired behind his deep-set eyes, giving them an extraordinary power of penetration. He was only twenty-six, but looked thirty or more. On the whole, he was not unhandsome.

"A penny for your thoughts, Mike," said Nancy after a while, imitating the woman's magazine she read.

"I was thinking what a grand opportunity we've got at last to show these people how a school should be run."

Ndume School was backward in every sense of the word. Mr. Obi put his whole life into the work, and his wife hers too. He had two aims. A high standard of teaching was insisted upon, and the school compound was to be turned into a place of beauty. Nancy's dream-gardens came to life with the coming of the rains, and blossomed. Beautiful hibiscus and allamanda hedges in brilliant red and yellow marked out the carefully tended school compound from the rank neighborhood bushes.

One evening as Obi was admiring his work he was scandalized to see an old woman from the village hobble right across the compound, through a marigold flower-bed and the hedges. On going up there he found faint signs of an almost disused path from the village across the school compound to the bush on the other side.

"It amazes me," said Obi to one of his teachers who had been three years in the school, "that you people allowed the villagers to make use of this footpath. It is simply incredible." He shook his head.

"The path," said the teacher apologetically, "appears to be very important to them. Although it is hardly used, it connects the village shrine with their place of burial."

"And what has that got to do with the school?" asked the headmaster.

"Well, I don't know," replied the other with a shrug of the shoulders. "But I remember there was a big row some time ago when we attempted to close it."

"That was some time ago. But it will not be used now," said Obi as he walked away. "What will the Government Education Officer think of this when he comes to inspect the school next week? The villagers might, for all I know, decide to use the schoolroom for a pagan ritual during the inspection."

Heavy sticks were planted closely across the path at the two places where it entered and left the school premises. These were further strengthened with barbed wire.

Three days later the village priest of *Ani*[2] called on the headmaster. He was an old man and walked with a slight stoop. He carried a stout walking-stick which he usually tapped on the floor, by way of emphasis, each time he made a new point in his argument.

"I have heard," he said after the usual exchange of cordialities, "that our ancestral footpath has recently been closed...."

"Yes," replied Mr. Obi. "We cannot allow people to make a highway of our school compound."

---

[1] *Onitsha* City in southeastern Nigeria; the Onitsha market is one of the largest in West Africa.

[2] *Ani* Traditional belief system, often called Odinani, of the Igbo people of Nigeria.

"Look here, my son," said the priest bringing down his walking-stick, "this path was here before you were born and before your father was born. The whole life of this village depends on it. Our dead relatives depart by it and our ancestors visit us by it. But most important, it is the path of children coming in to be born...."

Mr. Obi listened with a satisfied smile on his face.

"The whole purpose of our school," he said finally, "is to eradicate just such beliefs as that. Dead men do not require footpaths. The whole idea is just fantastic. Our duty is to teach your children to laugh at such ideas."

"What you say may be true," replied the priest, "but we follow the practices of our fathers. If you reopen the path we shall have nothing to quarrel about. What I always say is: let the hawk perch and let the eagle perch." He rose to go.

"I am sorry," said the young headmaster. "But the school compound cannot be a thoroughfare. It is against our regulations. I would suggest your constructing another path, skirting our premises. We can even get our boys to help in building it. I don't suppose the ancestors will find the little detour too burdensome."

"I have no more words to say," said the old priest, already outside.

Two days later a young woman in the village died in childbed. A diviner was immediately consulted and he prescribed heavy sacrifices to propitiate ancestors insulted by the fence.

Obi woke up next morning among the ruins of his work. The beautiful hedges were torn up not just near the path but right round the school, the flowers trampled to death and one of the school buildings pulled down ... That day, the white Supervisor came to inspect the school and wrote a nasty report on the state of the premises but more seriously about the "tribal-war situation developing between the school and the village, arising in part from the misguided zeal of the new headmaster."

—1953

from *An Image of Africa: Racism in Conrad's* Heart of Darkness

In the fall of 1974 I was walking one day from the English Department at the University of Massachusetts to a parking lot. It was a fine autumn morning such as encouraged friendliness to passing strangers. Brisk youngsters were hurrying in all directions, many of them obviously freshmen in their first flush of enthusiasm. An older man going the same way as I turned and remarked to me how very young they came these days. I agreed. Then he asked me if I was a student too. I said no, I was a teacher. What did I teach? African literature. Now that was funny, he said, because he knew a fellow who taught the same thing, or perhaps it was African history, in a certain community college not far from here. It always surprised him, he went on to say, because he never had thought of Africa as having that kind of stuff, you know. By this time I was walking much faster. "Oh well," I heard him say finally, behind me: "I guess I have to take your course to find out."

A few weeks later, I received two very touching letters from high school children in Yonkers, New York, who—bless their teacher—had just read *Things Fall Apart*. One of them was particularly happy to learn about the customs and superstitions of an African tribe.

I propose to draw from these rather trivial encounters rather heavy conclusions which at first sight might seem somewhat out of proportion to them. But only, I hope, at first sight.

The young fellow from Yonkers, perhaps partly on account of his age, but I believe also for much deeper and more serious reasons, is obviously unaware that the life of his own tribesmen in Yonkers, New York, is full of odd customs and superstitions and, like everybody else in his culture, imagines that he needs a trip to Africa to encounter those things.

The other person being fully my own age could not be excused on the grounds of his years. Ignorance might be a more likely reason; but here again I believe that something more willful than a mere lack of information was at work. For did not that erudite British historian and Regius Professor at Oxford, Hugh Trevor-Roper,[1] also pronounce that African history did not exist?

If there is something in these utterances more than youthful inexperience, more than a lack of factual knowledge, what is it? Quite simply it is the desire—one might indeed say the need—in Western psychology to set Africa up as a foil to Europe, as a place of negations at once remote and vaguely familiar, in comparison with which Europe's own state of spiritual grace will be manifest.

This need is not new; which should relieve us all of considerable responsibility and perhaps make us even willing to look at this phenomenon dispassionately. I have neither the wish nor the competence to embark on the exercise with the tools of the social and biological sciences but do so more simply in the manner of a novelist responding to one famous book of European fiction: Joseph Conrad's *Heart of Darkness*, which better than any other work that I know displays that Western desire and need which I have just referred to. Of course there are whole libraries of books devoted to the same purpose, but most of them are so obvious and so crude that few people worry about them today. Conrad, on the other hand, is undoubtedly one of the great stylists of modern fiction and a good storyteller into the bargain. His contribution therefore falls automatically into a different class—permanent literature—read and taught and constantly evaluated by serious academics. *Heart of Darkness* is indeed so secure today that a leading Conrad scholar has numbered it "among the half-dozen greatest short novels in the English language."[2] I will return to this critical opinion in due course, because it may seriously modify my earlier suppositions about who may or may not be guilty in some of the matters I will now raise.

Heart of Darkness projects the image of Africa as "the other world," the antithesis of Europe and therefore of civilization, a place where man's vaunted intelligence and refinement are finally mocked by triumphant

bestiality. The book opens on the River Thames, tranquil, resting peacefully "at the decline of day after ages of good service done to the race that peopled its banks." But the actual story will take place on the River Congo, the very antithesis of the Thames. The River Congo is quite decidedly not a River Emeritus. It has rendered no service and enjoys no old-age pension. We are told that "going up that river was like travelling back to the earliest beginning of the world."

Is Conrad saying then that these two rivers are very different, one good, the other bad? Yes, but that is not the real point. It is not the differentness that worries Conrad but the lurking hint of kinship, of common ancestry. For the Thames too "has been one of the dark places of the earth." It conquered its darkness, of course, and is now in daylight and at peace. But if it were to visit its primordial relative, the Congo, it would run the terrible risk of hearing grotesque echoes of its own forgotten darkness, and falling victim to an avenging recrudescence of the mindless frenzy of the first beginnings. These suggestive echoes comprise Conrad's famed evocation of the African atmosphere in *Heart of Darkness*. In the final consideration his method amounts to no more than a steady, ponderous, fake-ritualistic repetition of two antithetical sentences, one about silence and the other about frenzy. We can inspect samples of this on pages 103 and 105 of the New American Library edition:[3] (a) "It was the stillness of an implacable force brooding over an inscrutable intention" and (b) "The steamer toiled along slowly on the edge of a black and incomprehensible frenzy." Of course there is a judicious change of adjective from time to time, so that instead of "inscrutable," for example, you might have "unspeakable," even plain "mysterious," etc., etc.

The eagle-eyed English critic F.R. Leavis drew attention long ago to Conrad's "adjectival insistence upon inexpressible and incomprehensible mystery."[4] That insistence must not be dismissed lightly, as many Conrad critics have tended to do, as a mere stylistic flaw; for it raises serious questions of artistic good faith.

---

[1] *British ... Trevor-Roper* In 1963, Trevor-Roper made the comment, "Perhaps in the future there will be some African history to teach. But at the present there is none; there is only the history of Europeans in Africa. The rest is darkness, and darkness is not the subject of history."

[2] *among the ... language* From Albert J. Guerard's introduction to *Heart of Darkness*, 1950.

[3] *pages ... edition* Pages 105 and 107 of the Broadview edition (D.C.R.A. Goonetilleke, ed., 2nd edition, 1999). From this point on, all page numbers, provided in square brackets, are those of the Broadview edition.

[4] *adjectival ... mystery* From F.R. Leavis, *The Great Tradition* (1950).

When a writer while pretending to record scenes, incidents, and their impact is in reality engaged in inducing hypnotic stupor in his readers through a bombardment of emotive words and other forms of trickery, much more has to be at stake than stylistic felicity. Generally normal readers are well armed to detect and resist such underhand activity. But Conrad chose his subject well—one which was guaranteed not to put him in conflict with the psychological predisposition of his readers or raise the need for him to contend with their resistance. He chose the role of purveyor of comforting myths.

The most interesting and revealing passages in *Heart of Darkness* are, however, about people. I must crave the indulgence of my reader to quote almost a whole page from about the middle of the story when representatives of Europe in a steamer going down the Congo encounter the denizens of Africa:

> We were wanderers on a prehistoric earth, on an earth that wore the aspect of an unknown planet. We could have fancied ourselves the first of men taking possession of an accursed inheritance, to be subdued at the cost of profound anguish and of excessive toil. But suddenly, as we struggled round a bend, there would be a glimpse of rush walls, of peaked grass-roofs, a burst of yells, a whirl of black limbs, a mass of hands clapping, of feet stamping, of bodies swaying, of eyes rolling, under the droop of heavy and motionless foliage. The steamer toiled along slowly on the edge of the black and incomprehensible frenzy. The prehistoric man was cursing us, praying to us, welcoming us—who could tell? We were cut off from the comprehension of our surroundings; we glided past like phantoms, wondering and secretly appalled, as sane men would be before an enthusiastic outbreak in a madhouse. We could not understand because we were too far and could not remember because we were travelling in the night of first ages, of those ages that are gone, leaving hardly a sign—and no memories.
>
> The earth seemed unearthly. We are accustomed to look upon the shackled form of a conquered monster, but there—there you could look at a thing monstrous and free. It was unearthly, and the men were—No, they were not inhuman. Well, you know, that was the worst of it—this suspicion of

their not being inhuman. It would come slowly to one. They howled and leaped, and spun, and made horrid faces; but what thrilled you was just the thought of their humanity—like yours—the thought of your remote kinship with this wild and passionate uproar. Ugly. Yes, it was ugly enough; but if you were man enough you would admit to yourself that there was in you just the faintest trace of a response to the terrible frankness of that noise, a dim suspicion of there being a meaning in it which you—you so remote from the night of first ages—could comprehend. [107–08]

Herein lies the meaning of *Heart of Darkness* and the fascination it holds over the Western mind: "What thrilled you was just the thought of their humanity—like yours ... Ugly."

Having shown us Africa in the mass, Conrad then zeros in, half a page later, on a specific example, giving us one of his rare descriptions of an African who is not just limbs or rolling eyes:

> And between whiles I had to look after the savage who was fireman. He was an improved specimen; he could fire up a vertical boiler. He was there below me, and, upon my word, to look at him was as edifying as seeing a dog in a parody of breeches and a feather hat, walking on his hind legs. A few months of training had done for that really fine chap. He squinted at the steam gauge and at the water gauge with an evident effort of intrepidity—and he had filed his teeth, too, the poor devil, and the wool of his pate shaved into queer patterns, and three ornamental scars on each of his cheeks. He ought to have been clapping his hands and stamping his feet on the bank, instead of which he was hard at work, a thrall to strange witchcraft, full of improving knowledge. [108]

As everybody knows, Conrad is a romantic on the side. He might not exactly admire savages clapping their hands and stamping their feet but they have at least the merit of being in their place, unlike this dog in a parody of breeches. For Conrad things being in their place is of the utmost importance. "Fine fellows—cannibals—in their place," he tells us pointedly. Tragedy begins when things leave their accustomed place, like Europe leaving its safe stronghold between the policeman and the baker to take a peep into the heart of darkness.

Before the story takes us into the Congo basin proper we are given this nice little vignette as an example of things in their place:

> Now and then a boat from the shore gave one a momentary contact with reality. It was paddled by black fellows. You could see from afar the white of their eyeballs glistening. They shouted, sang; their bodies streamed with perspiration; they had faces like grotesque masks—these chaps; but they had bone, muscle, a wild vitality, an intense energy of movement, that was as natural and true as the surf along their coast. They wanted no excuse for being there. They were a great comfort to look at. [80]

Towards the end of the story Conrad lavishes a whole page quite unexpectedly on an African woman who has obviously been some kind of mistress to Mr. Kurtz and now presides (if I may be permitted a little liberty) like a formidable mystery over the inexorable imminence of his departure:

> She was savage and superb, wild-eyed and magnificent … She stood looking at us without a stir and like the wilderness itself, with an air of brooding over an inscrutable purpose. [137–38]

This Amazon is drawn in considerable detail, albeit of a predictable nature, for two reasons. First, she is in her place and so can win Conrad's special brand of approval; and second, she fulfils a structural requirement of the story: a savage counterpart to the refined, European woman who will step forth to end the story:

> She came forward, all in black with a pale head, floating toward me in the dusk. She was in mourning … She took both my hands in hers and murmured, "I had heard you were coming" … She had a mature capacity for fidelity, for belief, for suffering. [154]

The difference in the attitude of the novelist to these two women is conveyed in too many direct and subtle ways to need elaboration. But perhaps the most significant difference is the one implied in the author's be-

stowal of human expression to the one and the withholding of it from the other. It is clearly not part of Conrad's purpose to confer language on the "rudimentary souls" of Africa. In place of speech they made "a violent babble of uncouth sounds." They "exchanged short grunting phrases" even among themselves. But most of the time they were too busy with their frenzy. There are two occasions in the book, however, when Conrad departs somewhat from his practice and confers speech, even English speech, on the savages. The first occurs when cannibalism gets the better of them:

> "Catch 'im," he snapped, with a bloodshot widening of his eyes and a flash of sharp white teeth—"catch 'im. Give 'im to us." "To you, eh?" I asked; "what would you do with them?" "Eat 'im!" he said curtly. [113]

The other occasion was the famous announcement:

> "Mistah Kurtz—he dead" [148].

At first sight these instances might be mistaken for unexpected acts of generosity from Conrad. In reality they constitute some of his best assaults. In the case of the cannibals the incomprehensible grunts that had thus far served them for speech suddenly proved inadequate for Conrad's purpose of letting the European glimpse the unspeakable craving in their hearts. Weighing the necessity for consistency in the portrayal of the dumb brutes against the sensational advantages of securing their conviction by clear, unambiguous evidence issuing out of their own mouths, Conrad chose the latter. As for the announcement of Mr. Kurtz's death by the "insolent black head in the doorway," what better or more appropriate *finis* could be written to the horror story of that wayward child of civilization who wilfully had given his soul to the powers of darkness and "taken a high seat amongst the devils of the land" than the proclamation of his physical death by the forces he had joined?

It might be contended, of course, that the attitude to the African in *Heart of Darkness* is not Conrad's but that of his fictional narrator, Marlow, and that far from endorsing it Conrad might indeed be holding it up to irony and criticism. Certainly, Conrad appears to go to considerable pains to set up layers of insulation between himself and the moral universe of his story. He has, for example, a narrator behind a narrator. The primary narrator is Marlow, but his account is given to us through the filter of a second, shadowy person. But if Conrad's intention is to draw a *cordon sanitaire*[1] between himself and the moral and psychological *malaise* of his narrator, his care seems to me totally wasted because he neglects to hint, clearly and adequately, at an alternative frame of reference by which we may judge the actions and opinions of his characters. It would not have been beyond Conrad's power to make that provision if he had thought it necessary. Conrad seems to me to approve of Marlow, with only minor reservations—a fact reinforced by the similarities between their two careers.

Marlow comes through to us not only as a witness of truth, but one holding those advanced and humane views appropriate to the English liberal tradition which required all Englishmen of decency to be deeply shocked by atrocities in Bulgaria or the Congo of King Leopold of the Belgians or wherever.

Thus Marlow is able to toss out such bleeding-heart sentiments as these:

They were all dying slowly—it was very clear. They were not enemies, they were not criminals, they were nothing earthly now—nothing but black shadows of disease and starvation, lying confusedly in the greenish gloom. Brought from all the recesses of the coast in all the legality of time contracts, lost in uncongenial surroundings, fed on unfamiliar food, they sickened, became inefficient, and were then allowed to crawl away and rest. [84]

The kind of liberalism espoused here by Marlow/Conrad touched all the best minds of the age in England, Europe, and America. It took different forms in the minds of different people but almost always managed to sidestep the ultimate question of equality between white people and black people. That extraordinary missionary Albert Schweitzer,[2] who sacrificed brilliant careers in music and theology in Europe for a life of service to Africans in much the same area as

Conrad writes about, epitomizes the ambivalence. In a comment which has often been quoted Schweitzer says: "The African is indeed my brother but my junior brother." And so he proceeded to build a hospital appropriate to the needs of junior brothers with standards of hygiene reminiscent of medical practice in the days before the germ theory of disease came into being. Naturally he became a sensation in Europe and America. Pilgrims flocked, and I believe still flock even after he has passed on, to witness the prodigious miracle in Lambéréné,[3] on the edge of the primeval forest.

Conrad's liberalism would not take him quite as far as Schweitzer's, though. He would not use the word "brother" however qualified; the farthest he would go was "kinship." When Marlow's African helmsman falls down with a spear in his heart he gives his white master one final disquieting look:

And the intimate profundity of that look he gave me when he received his hurt remains to this day in my memory—like a claim of distant kinship affirmed in a supreme moment. [125–26]

It is important to note that Conrad, careful as ever with his words, is concerned not so much about "distant kinship" as about someone *laying a claim* on it. The black man lays a claim on the white man which is well-nigh intolerable. It is the laying of this claim which frightens and at the same time fascinates Conrad, "the thought of their humanity—like yours ... Ugly."

The point of my observations should be quite clear by now, namely that Joseph Conrad was a thoroughgoing racist. That this simple truth is glossed over in criticisms of his work is due to the fact that white racism against Africa is such a normal way of thinking that its manifestations go completely unremarked. Students of *Heart of Darkness* will often tell you that Conrad is concerned not so much with Africa as with the deterioration of one European mind caused by solitude and sickness. They will point out to you that Conrad is, if anything, less charitable to the Europeans in the story than he is to the natives, that the point of the story is to ridicule Europe's civilizing mission in Africa. A Conrad

[1] *cordon sanitaire* French: quarantine line.
[2] *Albert Schweitzer* M.D., humanitarian, and winner of the Nobel Peace Prize (1875–1965).

[3] *miracle in Lambéréné* Hospital built in 1913 by Schweitzer and his wife, Helene Bresslau, in what is now Gabon.

student informed me in Scotland that Africa is merely a setting for the disintegration of the mind of Mr. Kurtz.

Which is partly the point. Africa as setting and backdrop which eliminates the African as human factor. Africa as a metaphysical battlefield devoid of all recognizable humanity, into which the wandering European enters at his peril. Can nobody see the preposterous and perverse arrogance in thus reducing Africa to the role of props for the break-up of one petty European mind? But that is not even the point. The real question is the dehumanization of Africa and Africans which this age-long attitude has fostered and continues to foster in the world. And the question is whether a novel which celebrates this dehumanization, which depersonalizes a portion of the human race, can be called a great work of art. My answer is: No, it cannot.

—1977

SEAMUS HEANEY
1939 — 2013

The American poet Robert Lowell once referred to Seamus Heaney as "the best Irish poet since Yeats." Since winning the Nobel Prize for literature in 1995, Heaney has been one of the most popular poets writing in English. Often praised for its lyricism, Heaney's work reflects his rural upbringing, with a focus on the soil, the past, and lost friends. Many of his poems also deal with the troubles in his native Northern Ireland, and some commentators have criticized him for an alleged ambivalence about the political conflict.

Heaney grew up in a Roman Catholic household in the predominantly Protestant north. The eldest of nine children, he was not marked in childhood by the strife that would later affect the region. Instead, he experienced a community that lived in harmony, regardless of religious affiliation. Heaney's parents were farmers in County Derry, just outside Belfast. He grew up with an appreciation for country life, for those who work the land, and for the importance of close-knit community. Heaney frequently drew on these roots for poetic inspiration, and many of his poems recall his childhood or use the details of rural life—such as digging potatoes or churning milk—to comment on universal issues.

Heaney's career as a published poet began while he was completing a teacher's certificate at St. Joseph's College in Belfast. Writing under the pseudonym "Incertus," he had just finished his Bachelor of Arts in English Language and Literature at Queen's University when he joined a poetry workshop. Known as "The Belfast Group," this forum allowed new poets to showcase their work and have it critiqued by their peers. The Group introduced him to other young poets, including his future wife, and was also a forum for the discussion of the political issues of the day. Many of Heaney's early poems were first read and discussed at Group meetings.

The publication in 1966 of Heaney's first book of poems, *Death of a Naturalist*, began what would be a career filled with awards and accolades. This volume won the Somerset Maugham Award, among others. While establishing his career as a poet, Heaney was working as a lecturer in English at various colleges in Ireland and the United States to support his growing family, which would eventually include two sons and a daughter. His move south to the Republic of Ireland in 1972 was in many respects a positive one, but moving away from the political controversies of Northern Ireland to the relative stability of the south was seen by some as a betrayal. Establishing a home just outside Dublin did not, however, lead Heaney to forget the political turmoil of his birthplace. It was during this time that he wrote some of his most political works: *North* (1975) and *Field Work* (1979). He did not want to be seen solely as a political poet, though, and felt he needed distance from the conflicts of the north to provide scope for objectivity.

Heaney's rising international fame led to his appointment as Boylston Professor of Rhetoric and Oratory at Harvard in 1984. This position allowed him to teach one semester at Harvard in the spring and spend the remaining eight months of the year at his home in Dublin. The death of Heaney's mother, also in 1984, was the occasion for some of his most touching poetry, published in *The Haw Lantern* (1987). When questioned about his memorializing of lost friends and family, Heaney responded: "The elegiac Heaney? There's nothing else." Often, Heaney's work evokes the past in order to comment indirectly on the present; for example, in one of his "bog poems," "Punishment," he compares a first-century CE girl who was drowned as punishment for adultery to women in late twentieth-century Northern Ireland.

In 1995 Heaney was awarded the Nobel Prize for literature. In making the award, the committee cited his "works of lyrical beauty and ethical depth, which exalt everyday miracles and the living past." In his Nobel acceptance speech he wrote that the "form of the poem … is crucial to poetry's power to do the thing which always is and always will be to poetry's credit: the power to persuade that vulnerable part of our consciousness of its rightness in spite of the evidence of wrongness all around it."

In 1999 Heaney published a translation of *Beowulf*, which won the Whitbread Book of the Year Award. His T.S. Eliot Prize-winning collection *District and Circle* was published in 2006; a few months later, he suffered a minor stroke, leading him to spend a year away from public life. His experience of the stroke inspired many of the poems in *Human Chain* (2010), the last major collection he would complete before his death. The volume is characteristic of Heaney in that, as Colm Tóibín observed, the poems offer "consolation or transformation only because they contain tones and phrases that are perfectly tuned; they are true to memory and loss, and thus somehow, at times miraculously, they offer a vision of what is beyond them or above them."

⌘⌘⌘

Digging

Between my finger and my thumb
The squat pen rests; snug as a gun.

Under my window, a clean rasping sound
When the spade sinks into gravelly ground:
5 My father, digging. I look down

Till his straining rump among the flowerbeds
Bends low, comes up twenty years away
Stooping in rhythm through potato drills[1]
Where he was digging.

10 The coarse boot nestled on the lug, the shaft
Against the inside knee was levered firmly.
He rooted out tall tops, buried the bright edge deep
To scatter new potatoes that we picked
Loving their cool hardness in our hands.

15 By God, the old man could handle a spade.
Just like his old man.

My grandfather cut more turf[2] in a day
Than any other man on Toner's bog.
Once I carried him milk in a bottle
20 Corked sloppily with paper. He straightened up
To drink it, then fell to right away
Nicking and slicing neatly, heaving sods
Over his shoulder, going down and down
For the good turf. Digging.

25 The cold smell of potato mould, the squelch and slap
Of soggy peat, the curt cuts of an edge
Through living roots awaken in my head.
But I've no spade to follow men like them.

Between my finger and my thumb
30 The squat pen rests.
I'll dig with it.
—1966

---

1 *potato drills* Row of sown potatoes.

2 *turf* Slabs of peat.

Thatcher

Bespoke for weeks, he turned up some morning
Unexpectedly, his bicycle slung
With a light ladder and a bag of knives.
He eyed the old rigging, poked at the eaves,

5   Opened and handled sheaves of lashed wheat-straw.
Next, the bundled rods: hazel and willow
Were flicked for weight, twisted in case they'd snap.
It seemed he spent the morning warming up:

Then fixed the ladder, laid out well-honed blades
10   And snipped at straw and sharpened ends of rods
That, bent in two, made a white-pronged staple
For pinning down his world, handful by handful.

Couchant° for days on sods above the rafters,   *lying*
He shaved and flushed the butts,[1] stitched all together
15   Into a sloped honeycomb, a stubble patch,
And left them gaping at his Midas touch.[2]
—1969

The Wife's Tale

When I had spread it all on linen cloth
Under the hedge, I called them over.
The hum and gulp of the thresher ran down
And the big belt slewed to a standstill, straw
5   Hanging undelivered in the jaws.
There was such quiet that I heard their boots
Crunching the stubble twenty yards away.

He lay down and said, "Give these fellows theirs,
I'm in no hurry," plucking grass in handfuls
10   And tossing it in the air. "That looks well."
(He nodded at my white cloth on the grass.)
"I declare a woman could lay out a field
Though boys like us have little call for cloths."
He winked, then watched me as I poured a cup
15   And buttered the thick slices that he likes.

"It's threshing better than I thought, and mind
It's good clean seed. Away over there and look."
Always this inspection has to be made
Even when I don't know what to look for.

20   But I ran my hand in the half-filled bags
Hooked to the slots. It was hard as shot,
Innumerable and cool. The bags gaped
Where the chutes ran back to the stilled drum
And forks were stuck at angles in the ground
25   As javelins might mark lost battlefields.
I moved between them back across the stubble.

They lay in the ring of their own crusts and dregs,
Smoking and saying nothing. "There's good yield,
Isn't there?"—as proud as if he were the land itself—
30   "Enough for crushing and for sowing both."
And that was it. I'd come and he had shown me,
So I belonged no further to the work.
I gathered cups and folded up the cloth
And went. But they still kept their ease,
35   Spread out, unbuttoned, grateful, under the trees.
—1969

The Grauballe Man [3]

As if he had been poured
in tar, he lies
on a pillow of turf
and seems to weep

5   the black river of himself
The grain of his wrists
is like bog oak,[4]
the ball of his heel

like a basalt egg.
10   His instep has shrunk
cold as a swan's foot
or a wet swamp root.

---

1   *butts*   Branch tips.
2   *Midas touch*   Reference to the Greek myth of King Midas, whose touch turned everything to gold.

3   *Grauballe Man*   Man from the third century BCE whose preserved remains were found in 1952, in a peat bog near the village of Grauballe, Denmark.
4   *bog oak*   Wood of an oak tree preserved in peat-bog.

His hips are the ridge
and purse of a mussel,
15 his spine an eel arrested
under a glisten of mud.

The head lifts,
the chin is a visor
raised above the vent
20 of his slashed throat

that has tanned and toughened.
The cured wound
opens inwards to a dark
elderberry place.

25 Who will say "corpse"
to his vivid cast?
Who will say "body"
to his opaque repose?

And his rusted hair,
30 a mat unlikely
as a foetus's.
I first saw his twisted face

in a photograph,
a head and shoulder
35 out of the peat,
bruised like a forceps baby,

but now he lies
perfected in my memory,
down to the red horn
40 of his nails,

hung in the scales
with beauty and atrocity:
with the Dying Gaul
too strictly compassed

45 on his shield,
with the actual weight
of each hooded victim,
slashed and dumped.

—1975

Punishment[1]

I can feel the tug
of the halter at the nape
of her neck, the wind
on her naked front.

5 It blows her nipples
to amber beads,
it shakes the frail rigging
of her ribs.

I can see her drowned
10 body in the bog,
the weighing stone,
the floating rods and boughs.

Under which at first
she was a barked sapling
15 that is dug up
oak-bone, brain-firkin:[2]

her shaved head
like a stubble of black corn,
her blindfold a soiled bandage,
20 her noose a ring

to store
the memories of love.
Little adulteress,
before they punished you

25 you were flaxen-haired,
undernourished, and your
tar-black face was beautiful.
My poor scapegoat,

[1] *Punishment* In 1951 the body of a fourteen-year-old girl from the
first century BCE was discovered in a German bog. The left side of
her head had been shaved, her eyes bandaged shut, and a collar tied
around her neck. Her body had been weighed down with tree
branches and a stone. Germanic people often punished adulterous
women by shaving their hair and either killing them or expelling
them from the village. After the girl's body was found, the brain was
removed and examined.
[2] *firkin* Small cask or barrel.

I almost love you
30 but would have cast, I know,
the stones of silence.
I am the artful voyeur

of your brain's exposed
and darkened combs,
35 your muscles' webbing
and all your numbered bones:

I who have stood dumb
when your betraying sisters,
cauled° in tar,   *capped*
40 wept by the railings,[1]

who would connive
in civilized outrage
yet understand the exact
and tribal, intimate revenge.
—1975

Casualty

1

He would drink by himself
And raise a weathered thumb
Towards the high shelf,
Calling another rum
5   And blackcurrant, without
Having to raise his voice,
Or order a quick stout
By a lifting of the eyes
And a discreet dumb-show
10 Of pulling off the top;
At closing time would go
In waders and peaked cap
Into the showery dark,
A dole-kept breadwinner
15 But a natural for work.
I loved his whole manner,
Sure-footed but too sly,
His deadpan sidling tact,

His fisherman's quick eye
20 And turned observant back.

Incomprehensible
To him, my other life.
Sometimes, on his high stool,
Too busy with his knife
25 At a tobacco plug
And not meeting my eye,
In the pause after a slug
He mentioned poetry.
We would be on our own
30 And, always politic
And shy of condescension,
I would manage by some trick
To switch the talk to eels
Or lore of the horse and cart
35 Or the Provisionals.[2]

But my tentative art
His turned back watches too:
He was blown to bits
Out drinking in a curfew
40 Others obeyed, three nights
After they shot dead
The thirteen men in Derry.
PARAS THIRTEEN, the walls said,
BOGSIDE NIL.[3] That Wednesday
45 Everybody held
His breath and trembled.

2

It was a day of cold
Raw silence, wind-blown
Surplice and soutane:[4]
50 Rained-on, flower-laden
Coffin after coffin
Seemed to float from the door
Of the packed cathedral
Like blossoms on slow water.

---

[1] *your betraying … railings* In Belfast, women who kept company with British soldiers were sometimes shaved, stripped, tarred, and handcuffed to railings by the IRA as punishment.

[2] *Provisionals* Members of the Provisional Branch of the IRA.
[3] *PARAS … NIL* I.e., the British Army's Parachute Regiment had killed thirteen people, while the Roman Catholic people of the Bogside district, in Londonderry, had killed none.
[4] *Surplice and soutane* Vestments worn by the Roman Catholic clergy.

55   The common funeral
      Unrolled its swaddling band,
      Lapping, tightening
      Till we were braced and bound
      Like brothers in a ring.

60   But he would not be held
      At home by his own crowd
      Whatever threats were phoned,
      Whatever black flags waved.
      I see him as he turned
65   In that bombed offending place,
      Remorse fused with terror
      In his still knowable face,
      His cornered outfaced stare
      Blinding in the flash.

70   He had gone miles away
      For he drank like a fish
      Nightly, naturally
      Swimming towards the lure
      Of warm lit-up places,
75   The blurred mesh and murmur
      Drifting among glasses
      In the gregarious smoke.
      How culpable was he
      That last night when he broke
80   Our tribe's complicity?
      "Now you're supposed to be
      An educated man,"
      I hear him say. "Puzzle me
      The right answer to that one."

                 3

85   I missed his funeral,
      Those quiet walkers
      And sideways talkers
      Shoaling out of his lane
      To the respectable
90   Purring of the hearse …
      They move in equal pace
      With the habitual
      Slow consolation
      Of a dawdling engine,
95   The line lifted, hand
      Over fist, cold sunshine

      On the water, the land
      Banked under fog: that morning
      I was taken in his boat,
100   The screw° purling, turning   *propeller*
      Indolent fathoms white,
      I tasted freedom with him.
      To get out early, haul
      Steadily off the bottom,
105   Dispraise the catch, and smile
      As you find a rhythm
      Working you, slow mile by mile,
      Into your proper haunt
      Somewhere, well out, beyond …

110   Dawn-sniffing revenant,[1]
      Plodder through midnight rain,
      Question me again.
      —1979

Seeing Things

                 I

Inishbofin[2] on a Sunday morning.
Sunlight, turfsmoke,[3] seagulls, boatslip,° diesel.   *deck*
One by one we were being handed down
Into a boat that dipped and shilly-shallied
5   Scaresomely every time. We sat tight
On short cross-benches, in nervous twos and threes,
Obedient, newly close, nobody speaking
Except the boatmen, as the gunwales sank
And seemed they might ship water any minute.
10   The sea was very calm but even so,
When the engine kicked and our ferryman
Swayed for balance, reaching for the tiller,
I panicked at the shiftiness and heft
Of the craft itself. What guaranteed us—
15   That quick response and buoyancy and swim—
Kept me in agony. All the time
As we went sailing evenly across
The deep, still, seeable-down-into water,
It was as if I looked from another boat

---

[1] *revenant* One who returns to life from the dead.
[2] *Inishbofin* Small island west of Ireland.
[3] *turfsmoke* Smoke from burning slabs of peat ("turf"), which was used as fuel.

20 Sailing through air, far up, and could see
How riskily we fared into the morning,
And loved in vain our bare, bowed, numbered heads.

2

Claritas.[1] The dry-eyed Latin word
Is perfect for the carved stone of the water
25 Where Jesus stands up to his unwet knees
And John the Baptist pours out more water
Over his head: all this in bright sunlight
On the façade of a cathedral. Lines
Hard and thin and sinuous represent
30 The flowing river. Down between the lines
Little antic fish are all go. Nothing else.
And yet in that utter visibility
The stone's alive with what's invisible:
Waterweed, stirred sand-grains hurrying off,
35 The shadowy, unshadowed stream itself.
All afternoon, heat wavered on the steps
And the air we stood up to our eyes in wavered
Like the zigzag hieroglyph for life itself.

3

Once upon a time my undrowned father
40 Walked into our yard. He had gone to spray
Potatoes in a field on the riverbank
And wouldn't bring me with him. The horse-sprayer
Was too big and newfangled, bluestone°   copper sulphate
    might
Burn me in the eyes, the horse was fresh, I
45 Might scare the horse, and so on. I threw stones
At a bird on the shed roof, as much for
The clatter of the stones as anything,
But when he came back, I was inside the house
And saw him out the window, scatter-eyed
50 And daunted, strange without his hat,
His step unguided, his ghosthood immanent.
When he was turning on the riverbank,
The horse had rusted and reared up and pitched
Cart and sprayer and everything off balance,
55 So the whole rig went over into a deep
Whirlpool, hoofs, chains, shafts, cartwheels, barrel
And tackle, all tumbling off the world,
And the hat already merrily swept along

The quieter reaches. That afternoon
60 I saw him face to face, he came to me
With his damp footprints out of the river,
And there was nothing between us there
That might not still be happily ever after.
—1991

Anything Can Happen[2]

after Horace,[3] Odes, I, 34

Anything can happen. You know how Jupiter[4]
Will mostly wait for clouds to gather head
Before he hurls the lightning? Well, just now
He galloped his thunder cart and his horses

5 Across a clear blue sky. It shook the earth
And the clogged underearth, the River Styx,[5]
The winding streams, the Atlantic shore itself.
Anything can happen, the tallest towers

Be overturned, those in high places daunted,
10 Those overlooked regarded. Stropped-beak Fortune
Swoops, making the air gasp, tearing the crest off one,
Setting it down bleeding on the next.

Ground gives. The heaven's weight
Lifts up off Atlas[6] like a kettle-lid.
15 Capstones shift, nothing resettles right.
Telluric[7] ash and fire-spores boil away.
—2001

---

1 Claritas Latin: Clarity.

2 *Anything Can Happen* First published under the title "Horace and the Thunder" (2001) before being reprinted under the present title (2004).
3 *Horace* Roman poet (65 BCE–8 BCE).
4 *Jupiter* King of the Roman gods, who was capable of throwing thunderbolts.
5 *River Styx* In Greek mythology, a river that the souls of the dead must cross to reach the underworld.
6 *Atlas* In Greek mythology, a Titan who, as punishment for leading a war against the gods, was condemned to hold up the sky for thousands of years.
7 *Telluric* Of the earth, of soil (from *tellus*, a Latin word meaning "earth.")

Uncoupled

1

Who is this coming to the ash pit
   Walking tall, as if in a procession,
Bearing in front of her a slender pan

Withdrawn just now from underneath
5 The firebox, weighty, full to the brim
With whitish dust and flakes still sparking hot

That the wind is blowing into her apron bib,
Into her mouth and eyes while she proceeds
Unwavering, keeping her burden horizontal still,

10 Hands in a tight, sore grip round the metal knob,
Proceeds until we have lost sight of her
Where the worn path turns behind the henhouse.

2

Who is this, not much higher than the cattle,
Working his way towards me through the pen,
15 His ashplant° in one hand   walking stick

Lifted and pointing, a stick of keel[1]
In the other, calling to where I'm perched
On top of a shaky gate,

Waving and calling something I cannot hear
20 With all the lowing and roaring, lorries revving
At the far end of the yard, the dealers

Shouting among themselves, and now to him
So that his eyes leave mine and I know
The pain of loss before I know the term.
—2010

[The door was open and the house was dark]

in memory of David Hammond

The door was open and the house was dark
   Wherefore I called his name, although I knew
The answer this time would be silence

That kept me standing listening while it grew
5 Backwards and down and out into the street
Where as I'd entered (I remember now)

The streetlamps too were out.
I felt, for the first time there and then, a stranger,
Intruder almost, wanting to take flight

10 Yet well aware that here there was no danger,
Only withdrawal, a not unwelcoming
Emptiness, as in a midnight hangar

On an overgrown airfield in late summer.
—2010

---

[1] *keel* Pigment used to mark livestock.

Ngũgĩ wa Thiong'o
b. 1938

A novelist, playwright, essayist, and lecturer, Kenyan author Ngũgĩ (pronounced "Nn-goog-y") wa Thiong'o is one of East Africa's most important voices. Most of Ngũgĩ's fiction and non-fiction deals with African history and human rights issues; two acclaimed early novels, *Weep Not, Child* (1964) and *A Grain of Wheat* (1967), are sympathetic accounts of the Mau Mau uprisings of the 1950s that determined Kenya's future. These works have been followed by numerous novels, stories, essays, and plays that deal with colonialism and neo-colonialism—that state of oppression, according to Ngũgĩ, which is "nurtured in the womb of colonialism," leaving economic and spiritual control in the hands of the colonists long after they have departed. Ngũgĩ has written extensively and passionately about the need to preserve African cultures and languages. He dedicated *Decolonising the Mind* (1986) "to all those who write in African languages, and to all those who over the years have maintained the dignity of the literature, culture, philosophy, and other treasures carried by African languages." For the past three decades he has written all of his creative work in Gĩkũyũ, his native tongue.

Ngũgĩ was born to Thiong'o wa Nducu and Wanjika wa Ngũgĩ, in Kamiriithu, Kenya, in 1938. His was a large peasant family composed of his father, his mother, his father's three other wives, and

twenty-eight children. His childhood was scarred by violent struggles between the Mau Mau rebels, who were primarily from the Gĩkũyũ tribe, and the British colonial forces; Ngũgĩ's brother was killed, his mother tortured, and his entire village obliterated. He attended Christian schools as a youth and for a time became a devout Christian himself, but he renounced the religion in 1976 and ceased using his Christian name, James Ngugi. After acquiring a BA from Makerere University in Uganda, Ngũgĩ worked as a journalist for the Nairobi *Daily Nation* and was editor of the literary journal *Zuka*—"Emerge" in Swahili—from 1967 to 1970. He eventually did graduate work at Leeds University in England, obtaining his MA and PhD. He married Nyambura, a Kenyan woman, in 1961, and they had six children.

Ngũgĩ's own literary career began in 1963 (coincidentally, the year in which Kenya achieved independence from Britain) with the successful production of his first play, *The Black Hermit*. His first novel, *The River Between* (1965), is still widely regarded as a classic of African and English literature. It is a finely observed and deeply compassionate novel of the tension between the traditional ways of rural Kenya and those of Christianity and of the modern world (including such highly charged issues as those surrounding the practice of female circumcision). *The River Between* was written in English, as were *A Grain of Wheat* (1967) and *Weep Not, Child* (1964). The popularity of Ngũgĩ's 1977 play *Ngaahika Ndeenda* (*I Will Marry When I Want*), co-written with Ngũgĩ wa Mirii, led to his exile from Kenya. Working class people and farmers were so enamored of the play and its themes of empowerment and land rights that the government feared an uprising and banned the production. Soon afterward Ngũgĩ was imprisoned for political dissent, an experience he recounts in 1981's *Detained: A Writer's Prison Diary*. He was not reinstated in his post at the University of Nairobi after his detainment, and he left the country in 1982; since then he has lived in the United States. In 1987 he wrote *Matigari Ma Njiruungi*, based on a Gĩkũyũ fable about a freedom fighter; the Kenyan government issued another warrant for his arrest.

The 1977 novel *Petals of Blood* marked Ngũgĩ's "farewell to the English language as a vehicle of my writing of plays, novels and short stories," and *Decolonising the Mind* was his farewell to non-fiction writing in English. "From now on," he said, "it is Gĩkũyũ and Kiswahili all the way." By going back to his original language, especially after having succeeded in eliminating the University of Nairobi's English Department while he was Chair, he worked to end "the domination of the mental universe of the colonised." *Petals of Blood* also marked a change in the focus of his work, from themes of colonialism to those of neo-colonialism. For Ngũgĩ, the problems in Africa did not begin, nor did they end, with the slave trade. According to him, in order to control the native people of Africa, colonizers set out to obliterate African independence both by destroying African culture and by superimposing their own culture and languages. Ngũgĩ has said that neo-colonialism continues long after the colonizers have departed, with first-world countries exploiting African goods and services, keeping the economy "still in the hands of the imperialist bourgeoisie." *Caitaani Mutharabaini*, or *Devil on the Cross* (1982), was written soon after *Petals of Blood* (while he was in a Nairobi prison) and, according to the author, is one of his most important novels.

In a 2004 interview Ngũgĩ said: "In a spiritual sense I have never left Kenya. Kenya and Africa are always in my mind. But I look forward to a physical reunion with Kenya, my beloved country," and soon afterward he made his long-awaited return. Crowds of people celebrated his homecoming, but tragedy followed in the form of an assault upon Ngũgĩ and Njeeri, his second wife (whom he married after Nyambura's death). The couple and their two children fled the country the following day.

Ngũgĩ has taught at universities in New Zealand and Germany, as well as at New York University, Yale, and Smith in the United States. Much of his writing since the early 1990s has focused on cultural theory, such as the 1993 volume *Moving the Centre: The Struggle for Cultural Freedom*, but in 2004 he published his first novel in two decades, *Mũrogi wa Kagogo* (*Wizard of the Crow*). In addition to further critical writing, he has also released two volumes of autobiography, one recounting his childhood (2010) and one focused on his adolescence (2012). Ngũgĩ is a Distinguished Professor at the University of California, Irvine, where for several years he was Director of the International Center for Writing and Translation.

⌘ ⌘ ⌘

from *Decolonising the Mind*

CHAPTER 3

I was born into a large peasant family: father, four wives and about twenty-eight children. I also belonged, as we all did in those days, to a wider extended family and to the community as a whole.

We spoke Gĩkũyũ as we worked in the fields. We spoke Gĩkũyũ in and outside the home. I can vividly recall those evenings of storytelling around the fireside. It was mostly the grown-ups telling the children but everybody was interested and involved. We children would re-tell the stories the following day to other children who worked in the fields picking the pyrethrum flowers, tea-leaves or coffee beans of our European and African landlords.

The stories, with mostly animals as the main characters, were all told in Gĩkũyũ. Hare, being small, weak but full of innovative wit and cunning, was our hero. We identified with him as he struggled against the brutes of prey like lion, leopard, hyena. His victories were our victories and we learnt that the apparently weak can outwit the strong. We followed the animals in their struggle against hostile nature—drought, rain, sun, wind—a confrontation often forcing them to search for forms of co-operation. But we were also interested in their struggles amongst themselves, and particularly between the beasts and the victims of prey. These twin struggles, against nature and other animals, reflected real-life struggles in the human world.

Not that we neglected stories with human beings as the main characters. There were two types of characters in such human-centred narratives: the species of truly human beings with qualities of courage, kindness, mercy, hatred of evil, concern for others; and a man-eat-man two-mouthed species with qualities of greed, selfishness, individualism and hatred of what was good for the larger co-operative community. Co-operation as the ultimate good in a community was a constant theme. It could unite human beings with animals against ogres and beasts of prey, as in the story of how dove, after being fed with castor-oil seeds, was sent to fetch a smith working far away from home and whose pregnant wife was being threatened by these man-eating two-mouthed ogres.

There were good and bad story-tellers. A good one could tell the same story over and over again, and it would always be fresh to us, the listeners. He or she could tell a story told by someone else and make it more alive and dramatic. The differences really were in the use of words and images and the inflexion of voices to effect different tones.

We therefore learnt to value words for their meaning and nuances. Language was not a mere string of words. It had a suggestive power well beyond the immediate and lexical meaning. Our appreciation of the suggestive magical power of language was reinforced by the games we played with words through riddles, proverbs, trans-positions of syllables, or through nonsensical but musically arranged words. So we learnt the music of our language on top of the content. The language, through images and symbols, gave us a view of the world, but it had a beauty of its own. The home and the field were then our pre-primary school but what is important, for this discussion, is that the language of our evening teach-ins, and the language of our immediate and wider community, and the language of our work in the fields were one.

And then I went to school, a colonial school, and this harmony was broken. The language of my educa-

tion was no longer the language of my culture. I first went to Kamaandura, missionary run, and then to another called Maanguuū run by nationalists grouped around the Gīkūyū Independent and Karinga Schools[1] Association. Our language of education was still Gīkūyū. The very first time I was ever given an ovation for my writing was over a composition in Gīkūyū. So for my first four years there was still harmony between the language of my formal education and that of the Limuru[2] peasant community.

It was after the declaration of a state of emergency over Kenya in 1952 that all the schools run by patriotic nationalists were taken over by the colonial regime and were placed under District Education Boards chaired by Englishmen. English became the language of my formal education. In Kenya, English became more than a language: it was *the* language, and all the others had to bow before it in deference.

Thus one of the most humiliating experiences was to be caught speaking Gīkūyū in the vicinity of the school. The culprit was given corporal punishment—three to five strokes of the cane on bare buttocks—or was made to carry a metal plate around the neck with inscriptions such as I AM STUPID or I AM A DONKEY. Sometimes the culprits were fined money they could hardly afford. And how did the teachers catch the culprits? A button was initially given to one pupil who was supposed to hand it over to whoever was caught speaking his mother tongue. Whoever had the button at the end of the day would sing who had given it to him and the ensuing process would bring out all the culprits of the day. Thus children were turned into witch-hunters and in the process were being taught the lucrative value of being a traitor to one's immediate community.

The attitude to English was the exact opposite: any achievement in spoken or written English was highly rewarded; prizes, prestige, applause; the ticket to higher realms. English became the measure of intelligence and ability in the arts, the sciences, and all the other branch-es of learning. English became *the* main determinant of a child's progress up the ladder of formal education.

As you may know, the colonial system of education in addition to its apartheid racial demarcation had the

---

[1] *Karinga Schools*   Run by the Orthodox and Pentecostal churches.
[2] *Limuru*   Located in the Nairobi region.

structure of a pyramid: a broad primary base, a narrowing secondary middle, and an even narrower university apex. Selections from primary into secondary were through an examination, in my time called Kenya African Preliminary Examination, in which one had to pass six subjects ranging from Maths to Nature Study and Kiswahili.[1] All the papers were written in English. Nobody could pass the exam who failed the English language paper no matter how brilliantly he had done in the other subjects. I remember one boy in my class of 1954 who had distinctions in all subjects except English, which he had failed. He was made to fail the entire exam. He went on to become a turn boy in a bus company. I who had only passes but a credit in English got a place at the Alliance High School, one of the most elitist institutions for Africans in colonial Kenya. The requirements for a place at the University, Makerere University College, were broadly the same: nobody could go on to wear the undergraduate red gown, no matter how brilliantly they had performed in all the other subjects unless they had a credit—not even a simple pass!—in English. Thus the most coveted place in the pyramid and in the system was only available to the holder of an English language credit card. English was the official vehicle and the magic formula to colonial elitedom.

Literary education was now determined by the dominant language while also reinforcing that dominance. Orature (oral literature) in Kenyan languages stopped. In primary school I now read simplified Dickens and Stevenson alongside Rider Haggard. Jim Hawkins, Oliver Twist, Tom Brown[2]—not Hare, Leopard and Lion—were now my daily companions in the world of imagination. In secondary school, Scott and G.B. Shaw vied with more Rider Haggard, John Buchan, Alan Paton, Captain W.E. Johns. At Makerere I read English: from Chaucer to T.S. Eliot with a touch of Grahame Greene.

Thus language and literature were taking us further and further from ourselves to other selves, from our world to other worlds.

1 *Kiswahili* Swahili language.
2 *Jim Hawkins … Tom Brown* Characters in Robert Louis Stevenson's *Treasure Island*, Charles Dickens's *Oliver Twist*, and Thomas Hughes's *Tom Brown's Schooldays* respectively.

What was the colonial system doing to us Kenyan children? What were the consequences of, on the one hand, this systematic suppression of our languages and the literature they carried, and on the other the elevation of English and the literature it carried? To answer those questions, let me first examine the relationship of language to human experience, human culture, and the human perception of reality.

CHAPTER 4

Language, any language, has a dual character: it is both a means of communication and a carrier of culture. Take English. It is spoken in Britain and in Sweden and Denmark. But for Swedish and Danish people English is only a means of communication with non-Scandinavians. It is not a carrier of their culture. For the British, and particularly the English, it is additionally, and inseparably from its use as a tool of communication, a carrier of their culture and history. Or take Swahili in East and Central Africa. It is widely used as a means of communication across many nationalities. But it is not the carrier of a culture and history of many of those nationalities. However in parts of Kenya and Tanzania, and particularly in Zanzibar, Swahili is inseparably both a means of communication and a carrier of the culture of those people to whom it is a mother-tongue.

Language as communication has three aspects or elements. There is first what Karl Marx once called the language of real life, the element basic to the whole notion of language, its origins and development: that is, the relations people enter into with one another in the labour process, the links they necessarily establish among themselves in the act of a people, a community of human beings, producing wealth or means of life like food, clothing, houses. A human community really starts its historical being as a community of co-operation in production through the division of labour; the simplest is between man, woman and child within a household; the more complex divisions are between branches of production such as those who are sole hunters, sole gatherers of fruits or sole workers in metal. Then there are the most complex divisions such as those in modern factories where a single product, say a shirt or a shoe, is the result of many hands and minds. Production is co-operation, is communication, is language, is expression of a relation between human beings and it is specifically human.

The second aspect of language as communication is speech and it imitates the language of real life, that is communication in production. The verbal signposts both reflect and aid communication or the relation established between human beings in the production of their means of life. Language as a system of verbal signposts makes that production possible. The spoken word is to relations between human beings what the hand is to the relations between human beings and nature. The hand through tools mediates between human beings and nature and forms the language of real life: spoken words mediate between human beings and form the language of speech.

The third aspect is the written signs. The written word imitates the spoken. Where the first two aspects of language as communication through the hand and the spoken word historically evolved more or less simultaneously, the written aspect is a much later historical development. Writing is representation of sounds with visual symbols, from the simplest knot among shepherds to tell the number in a herd or the hieroglyphics among the Agĩkũyũ gicaandi singers and poets of Kenya, to the most complicated and different letter and picture writing systems of the world today.

In most societies the written and the spoken languages are the same, in that they represent each other: what is on paper can be read to another person and be received as that language, which the recipient has grown up speaking. In such a society there is broad harmony for a child between the three aspects of language as communication. His interaction with nature and with other men is expressed in written and spoken symbols or signs which are both a result of that double interaction and a reflection of it. The association of the child's sensibility is with the language of his experience of life.

But there is more to it: communication between human beings is also the basis and process of evolving culture. In doing similar kinds of things and actions over and over again under similar circumstances, similar even in their mutability, certain patterns, moves, rhythms, habits, attitudes, experiences and knowledge emerge. Those experiences are handed over to the next

generation and become the inherited basis for their further actions on nature and on themselves. There is a gradual accumulation of values which in time become almost self-evident truths governing their conception of what is right and wrong, good and bad, beautiful and ugly, courageous and cowardly, generous and mean in their internal and external relations. Over a time this becomes a way of life distinguishable from other ways of life. They develop a distinctive culture and history. Culture embodies those moral, ethical and aesthetic values, the set of spiritual eyeglasses, through which they come to view themselves and their place in the universe. Values are the basis of a people's identity, their sense of particularity as members of the human race. All this is carried by language. Language as culture is the collective memory bank of a people's experience in history. Culture is almost indistinguishable from the language that makes possible its genesis, growth, banking, articulation and indeed its transmission from one generation to the next.

Language as culture also has three important aspects. Culture is a product of the history which it in turn reflects. Culture in other words is a product and a reflection of human beings communicating with one another in the very struggle to create wealth and to control it. But culture does not merely reflect that history, or rather it does so by actually forming images or pictures of the world of nature and nurture. Thus the second aspect of language as culture is as an image-forming agent in the mind of a child. Our whole conception of ourselves as a people, individually and collectively, is based on those pictures and images which may or may not correctly correspond to the actual reality of the struggles with nature and nurture which produced them in the first place. But our capacity to confront the world creatively is dependent on how those images correspond or not to that reality, how they distort or clarify the reality of our struggles. Language as culture is thus mediating between me and my own self; between my own self and other selves; between me and nature. Language is mediating in my very being. And this brings us to the third aspect of language as culture. Culture transmits or imparts those images of the world and reality through the spoken and the written language, that is through a specific language. In other words, the capacity to speak, the capacity to order sounds in a manner that makes for mutual comprehension between human beings is universal. This is the universality of language, a quality specific to human beings. It corresponds to the universality of the struggle against nature and that between human beings. But the particularity of the sounds, the words, the word order into phrases and sentences, and the specific manner, or laws, of their ordering is what distinguishes one language from another. Thus a specific culture is not transmitted through language in its universality but in its particularity as the language of a specific community with a specific history. Written literature and orature are the main means by which a particular language transmits the images of the world contained in the culture it carries.

Language as communication and as culture are then products of each other. Communication creates culture: culture is a means of communication. Language carries culture, and culture carries, particularly through orature and literature, the entire body of values by which we come to perceive ourselves and our place in the world. How people perceive themselves affects how they look at their culture, at their politics and at the social production of wealth, at their entire relationship to nature and to other beings. Language is thus inseparable from ourselves as a community of human beings with a specific form and character, a specific history, a specific relationship to the world.

CHAPTER 5

So what was the colonialist imposition of a foreign language doing to us children?

The real aim of colonialism was to control the people's wealth: what they produced, how they produced it, and how it was distributed; to control, in other words, the entire realm of the language of real life. Colonialism imposed its control of the social production of wealth through military conquest and subsequent political dictatorship. But its most important area of domination was the mental universe of the colonised, the control, through culture, of how people perceived themselves and their relationship to the world. Economic and political control can never be complete or

effective without mental control. To control a people's culture is to control their tools of self-definition in relationship to others.

For colonialism this involved two aspects of the same process: the destruction or the deliberate undervaluing of a people's culture, their art, dances, religions, history, geography, education, orature and literature, and the conscious elevation of the language of the coloniser. The domination of a people's language by the languages of the colonising nations was crucial to the domination of the mental universe of the colonised.

Take language as communication. Imposing a foreign language, and suppressing the native languages as spoken and written, were already breaking the harmony previously existing between the African child and the three aspects of language. Since the new language as a means of communication was a product of and was reflecting the "real language of life" elsewhere, it could never as spoken or written properly reflect or imitate the real life of that community. This may in part explain why technology always appears to us as slightly external, *their* product and not *ours*. The word "missile" used to hold an alien far-away sound until I recently learnt its equivalent in Gĩkũyũ, *ngurukuhĩ* and it made me apprehend it differently. Learning, for a colonial child, became a cerebral activity and not an emotionally felt experience.

But since the new, imposed languages could never completely break the native languages as spoken, their most effective area of domination was the third aspect of language as communication, the written. The language of an African child's formal education was foreign. The language of the books he read was foreign. The language of his conceptualisation was foreign. Thought, in him, took the visible form of a foreign language. So the written language of a child's upbringing in the school (even his spoken language within the school compound) became divorced from his spoken language at home. There was often not the slightest relationship between the child's written world, which was also the language of his schooling, and the world of his immediate environment in the family and the community. For a colonial child, the harmony existing between the three aspects of language as communication was irrevocably broken. This resulted in the disassociation of the sensibility of that child from his natural and social environment, what we might call colonial alienation. The alienation became reinforced in the teaching of history, geography, music, where bourgeois Europe was always the centre of the universe.

This disassociation, divorce, or alienation from the immediate environment becomes clearer when you look at colonial language as a carrier of culture.

Since culture is a product of the history of a people which it in turn reflects, the child was now being exposed exclusively to a culture that was a product of a world external to himself. He was being made to stand outside himself to look at himself. *Catching Them Young* is the title of a book on racism, class, sex, and politics in children's literature by Bob Dixon. "Catching them young" as an aim was even more true of a colonial child. The images of his world and his place in it implanted in a child take years to eradicate, if they ever can be.

Since culture does not just reflect the world in images but actually, through those images, conditions a child to see that world a certain way, the colonial child was made to see the world and where he stands in it as seen and defined by or reflected in the culture of the language of imposition.

And since those images are mostly passed on through orature and literature it meant the child would now only see the world as seen in the literature of his language of adoption. From the point of view of alienation, that is of seeing oneself from outside oneself as if one was another self, it does not matter that the imported literature carried the great humanist tradition of the best Shakespeare, Goethe, Balzac, Tolstoy, Gorky, Brecht, Sholokhov, Dickens. The location of this great mirror of imagination was necessarily Europe and its history and culture and the rest of the universe was seen from that centre.

But obviously it was worse when the colonial child was exposed to images of his world as mirrored in the written languages of his coloniser. Where his own native languages were associated in his impressionable mind with low status, humiliation, corporal punishment, slow-footed intelligence and ability or downright stupidity, non-intelligibility and barbarism, this was reinforced by the world he met in the works of such geniuses of racism as a Rider Haggard or a Nicholas Monsarrat; not to mention the pronouncement of some of the giants of western intellectual and political establishment, such as Hume ("... The negro is naturally inferior to the whites ..."), Thomas Jefferson ("... The blacks ... are inferior to the whites on the endowments of both body and mind ..."), or Hegel with his Africa comparable to a land of childhood still enveloped in the dark mantle of the night as far as the development of self-conscious history was concerned. Hegel's statement that there was nothing harmonious with humanity to be found in the African character is representative of the racist images of Africans and Africa such a colonial child was bound to encounter in the literature of the colonial languages. The results could be disastrous.

—1986

Margaret Atwood

b. 1939

W hen she was coming of age in the 1960s and 1970s, Margaret Atwood's work helped define and bring attention to Canadian literature; more recently she has been an international figure quite as much as a Canadian one. Always prolific, she has written more than 40 books that have been translated into more than 30 languages. Her creative work—poetry, fiction, and children's literature—often uses a fantastic or speculative framework to address contentious issues. She has also

been a leader in highlighting feminist concerns such as the power relations between men and women. Atwood has received numerous awards over the years, including the Booker Prize in 2000 and the Governor General's Award, Canada's national literary award, in 1966 and 1985.

The "bush," or wilderness, is important to Atwood and often appears as a thematic element in her fiction. As a child, Atwood would regularly spend the spring, summer, and fall months in isolated areas of northern Ontario with her entomologist father and her mother, a former teacher. Living for long periods surrounded by the bush left Atwood with a powerful appreciation of the natural world. She also developed a love of reading as a response to the many hours of solitude provided by living in a log cabin with no other source of entertainment.

Born in Ottawa, Atwood moved with her family to Toronto in 1946 so that her father could take up a teaching position at the University of Toronto. Her advanced reading level allowed her to move ahead a grade in high school, where she decided that she wanted to be a writer. She was, however, forced to contend with 1950s gender stereotypes; according to the social code of the time, women who wished to work should be educated as nurses, teachers, or secretaries—and be prepared to resign their careers when they married and moved to the suburbs. Atwood also had to contend with the many obstacles facing aspiring writers, whether male or female, in Canada's still largely undeveloped literary culture. The graduation message printed in her yearbook turned out to be quite prophetic: "Peggy's not-so-secret ambition is to write THE Canadian novel—and with those English marks, who doubts that she will?"

Atwood moved on to Victoria College at the University of Toronto in 1957, where she studied under the scholar and critic Northrop Frye. It was while she was at university that she first started publishing her poems in university magazines and small journals. At the time, she was publishing under the non-gendered name M.E. Atwood so that she would not be discriminated against as a woman.

When Atwood completed her BA, Frye encouraged her to go to graduate school. She arrived in Boston in 1961 to pursue a Master's degree at Harvard University. Being at Harvard allowed her the distance to consider what it meant to be Canadian. Atwood came to believe that the physical and cultural landscape was central to any conception of Canadian literature; the writer must consider what it is to write in or of the Canadian space. Atwood explored these ideas as she continued writing poetry. She completed her Master's degree in 1962 and started a doctorate the following year, but financial constraints eventually forced her to put her studies on hold. She also felt that she needed more time to devote to her creative work.

Atwood accepted a lecturer's position at the University of British Columbia in Vancouver in 1964. Vancouver turned out to be a place where she could do both creative and critical work; while there she wrote her first published book and first professionally published volume of poetry, as well as making a significant start on several other books. *The Circle Game* (poetry) was published in 1966, and resulted in her first Governor General's Award. At the time she was, at 27, the youngest writer ever to have won the award. While at UBC, Atwood also wrote *The Edible Woman*, which would be published in 1969. The novel depicts a woman with an eating disorder and examines the role of consumerism in western culture; in both its feminist and anti-consumerist themes the book captured the mood of the times, and became a considerable international success. At this point, Atwood had returned to Boston to try to complete her doctorate, but she continued to produce poetry and publish while working on her studies. Although she wrote more than two-thirds of it, she never would complete her doctoral dissertation.

In 1970 Atwood published a collection of poems, *The Journals of Susanna Moodie*, in which she adopted the point of view of a nineteenth-century immigrant newly arrived in Canada. Atwood felt that Moodie's doubleness, as British and Canadian, exemplified a characteristically Canadian ambivalence.

Atwood also continued her interest in the relationships between men and women in her influential poetry collection *Power Politics* (1971). The following year, she published a critical text on Canadian literature, *Survival: A Thematic Guide to Canadian Literature*, in which she argued that Canadian literature must confront and survive Canadian nature in order to thrive. The book was a major success and prompted reassessments of Canadian literature in many quarters. While working on *Survival* Atwood began a relationship with another writer, Graeme Gibson; the two remain together, and have one child. Atwood has continued to write prolifically across multiple genres, including poetry, short fiction, and non-fiction. Her major novels include *Surfacing* (1973); *Lady Oracle* (1977); *Bodily Harm* (1982); *The Handmaid's Tale* (1986), for which she won her second Governor General's Award; *Cat's Eye* (1988); *The Robber Bride* (1993); *Alias Grace* (1996); *The Blind Assassin* (2000), for which she won the Booker Prize; *The Penelopiad* (2005); and the linked novels *Oryx and Crake* (2003) and *The Year of the Flood* (2009). Through these works, Atwood has developed a broad range as a writer; her major novels have ventured into the genres of fantastical satire (*The Robber Bride*), historical fiction and murder mystery (*Alias Grace*), layered fiction (*Alias Grace*, which includes a novel-within-a-novel), retold classical myth (*The Penelopiad*), and dystopic fantasy with powerful political implications for the present-day world (*The Handmaid's Tale*, *Oryx and Crake*). She has also continued her critical work with such publications as *Negotiating the Dead: A Writer on Writing* (2002) and *In Other Worlds: SF and the Human Imagination* (2012).

Atwood has long been involved in various human rights organizations, including Amnesty International and PEN Canada. She was also a founding member of the Writers' Union of Canada. Her work continues to draw attention to a variety of issues, including the place of women in society, and the place of nature in our lives. To Atwood, neither nature nor myth are to be separated from our everyday lives; instead, they are a "valued and necessary part of the human mentality."

⌘ ⌘ ⌘

Death of a Young Son by Drowning

He, who navigated with success
the dangerous river of his own birth
once more set forth

on a voyage of discovery
5 into the land I floated on
but could not touch to claim.

His feet slid on the bank,
the currents took him;
he swirled with ice and trees in the swollen water

10 and plunged into distant regions,
his head a bathysphere;[1]
through his eyes' thin glass bubbles

he looked out, reckless adventurer
on a landscape stranger than Uranus
15 we have all been to and some remember.

There was an accident; the air locked,
he was hung in the river like a heart.
They retrieved the swamped body,

cairn° of my plans and future charts,   stone memorial
20 with poles and hooks
from among the nudging logs.

It was spring, the sun kept shining, the new grass
leapt to solidity;
my hands glistened with details.

25 After the long trip I was tired of waves.
My foot hit rock. The dreamed sails
collapsed, ragged.

        I planted him in this country
        like a flag.

—1970

---

[1] *bathysphere* Spherical chamber used for deep-sea observation.

The Immigrants

They are allowed to inherit
the sidewalks involved as palmlines, bricks
exhausted and soft, the deep
lawnsmells, orchards whorled
5 to the land's contours, the inflected weather

only to be told they are too poor
to keep it up, or someone
has noticed and wants to kill them; or the towns
pass laws which declare them obsolete.

10 I see them coming
up from the hold smelling of vomit,
infested, emaciated, their skins grey
with travel; as they step on shore

the old countries recede, become
15 perfect, thumbnail castles preserved
like gallstones in a glass bottle, the
towns dwindle upon the hillsides
in a light paperweight-clear.

They carry their carpetbags and trunks
20 with clothes, dishes, the family pictures;
they think they will make an order
like the old one, sow miniature orchards,
carve children and flocks out of wood

but always they are too poor, the sky
25 is flat, the green fruit shrivels
in the prairie sun, wood is for burning;
and if they go back, the towns

in time have crumbled, their tongues
stumble among awkward teeth, their ears
30 are filled with the sound of breaking glass.
I wish I could forget them
and so forget myself:

my mind is a wide pink map
across which move year after year
35 arrows and dotted lines, further and further,
people in railway cars

their heads stuck out of the windows
at stations, drinking milk or singing,
their features hidden with beards or shawls
40 day and night riding across an ocean of unknown
land to an unknown land.
—1970

Daguerreotype Taken in Old Age

I know I change
I have changed

but whose is this vapid face
pitted and vast, rotund
5 suspended in empty paper
as though in a telescope

the granular moon

I rise from my chair
pulling against gravity
10 I turn away
and go out into the garden

I revolve among the vegetables,
my head ponderous
reflecting the sun
15 in shadows from the pocked ravines
cut in my cheeks, my eye-
sockets 2 craters

along the paths
I orbit
20 the apple trees
white white spinning
stars around me

I am being
eaten away by light
—1970

A Bus along St. Clair: December

It would take more than that to banish
me: this is my kingdom still.

Turn, look up
through the gritty window: an unexplored
5 wilderness of wires

Though they buried me in monuments
of concrete slabs, of cables
though they mounded a pyramid
of cold light over my head
10 though they said, We will build
silver paradise with a bulldozer

it shows how little they know
about vanishing: I have
my ways of getting through.

15 Right now, the snow
is no more familiar
to you than it was to me:
this is my doing.
The grey air, the roar
20 going on behind it
are no more familiar.

I am the old woman
sitting across from you on the bus,
her shoulders drawn up like a shawl;
25 out of her eyes come secret
hatpins, destroying
the walls, the ceiling

Turn, look down:
there is no city;
30 this is the centre of a forest

your place is empty
—1970

[*you fit into me*]

Y ou fit into me
like a hook into an eye

a fish hook
an open eye
—1971

The Door

T he door swings open,
  you look in.
It's dark in there,
most likely spiders:
5   nothing you want.
You feel scared.
The door swings closed.

The full moon shines,
it's full of delicious juice;
10   you buy a purse,
the dance is nice.
The door opens
and swings closed so quickly
you don't notice.

15   The sun comes out,
you have swift breakfasts
with your husband, who is still thin;
you wash the dishes,
you love your children,
20   you read a book,
you go to the movies.
It rains moderately.

The door swings open,
you look in:

25   why does this keep happening now?
Is there a secret?
The door swings closed.

The snow falls,
you clear the walk while breathing heavily;
30   it's not as easy as once.
Your children telephone sometimes.
The roof needs fixing.
You keep yourself busy.
The spring arrives.

35   The door swings open:
it's dark in there,
with many steps going down.
But what is that shining?
Is it water?
40   The door swings closed.

The dog has died.
This happened before.
You got another;
not this time though.
45   Where is your husband?
You gave up the garden.
It became too much.
At night there are blankets;
nonetheless you are wakeful.

50   The door swings open:
O god of hinges,
god of long voyages,
you have kept faith.
It's dark in there.
55   You confide yourself to the darkness.
You step in.
The door swings closed.
—2007

Angela Carter
1940 – 1992

Fiction writer Angela Carter spent much of her life out of step with dominant literary trends, creating works that both fascinated and baffled her readers. Carter (whom Margaret Atwood described as "born subversive") liked to disrupt conventions and deny expectations. Her writing inhabits a gray area between the fantastic and the real, and makes innovative use of numerous familiar genres—most of which (Gothic, fantasy, science fiction, magic realism) are somewhat outside the literary mainstream. Her unusually dense, allusive texts revel in linguistic play as they combine material from a myriad of sources, including folklore, tabloid headlines, French surrealism, Hollywood movies, and eighteenth-century allegorical fiction. Since her death, appreciation for her inventiveness and for the originality of her artistic vision has continued to grow; she is one of the most widely taught British writers of fiction.

Carter was born Angela Olive Stalker in Sussex in 1940. Much of her early childhood was spent with her grandmother in industrial Yorkshire, to which she and her brother had been evacuated to escape war-time bombings. After she finished high school, Carter's father, a journalist, got her a job as a reporter for a south London paper. Direct, factual reporting of events was not her forte, however, and in 1960 she left that job to follow her new husband, Paul Carter, to Bristol. There she entered Bristol University, where she studied medieval literature.

Her first published novel, *Shadow Dance* (1966), marked the beginning of a fertile creative period; two more novels, *The Magic Toyshop* (1967) and *Several Perceptions* (1968) quickly followed. Though many of her early works are set in the Bristol of her youth, they are permeated with elements of the Gothic fairy tale and an underlying threat of violence, while distinctions between reality and daydream are often blurred.

Several Perceptions won the prestigious Somerset Maugham award; the £500 prize enabled Carter to depart for Japan, where she lived for two years, leaving her husband behind. In Japan, Carter began what she referred to as an apprenticeship in signs. She had gone seeking a culture that had never been Judeo-Christian, and in attempting to interpret such an utterly foreign culture—with no knowledge of the language—she was forced to rely on a heightened awareness of visual social cues, observing how roles (particularly those of gender) and customs were created and maintained. After her return to Britain in 1972, the new, radical self-awareness that resulted from her life in Japan led her to examine her own social and cultural heritage aggressively from her newly gained viewpoint of an outsider.

The Sadeian Woman (1979), her first book of nonfiction and one of her most controversial works, attacks the prestige she sees as often being accorded to the suffering of women, and criticizes portrayals of women as blameless victims. These strategies, she believes, only valorize the role of the powerless outsider. *The Sadeian Woman* also stated Carter's particular aims for her narratives, which she believed should provide means of exploring ideas and serve as arguments, presented in fictional terms, for the ways in which we should interpret and respond to the world around us. As she says, "Fine art, that exists for itself alone, is art in a final state of impotence. If nobody, including the artist, acknowledges art as a means of *knowing* the world, then art is relegated to a kind of rumpus room of the mind."

Published in the same year as the *Sadeian Woman*, Carter's collection of short fiction *The Bloody Chamber* (1979) takes characters from stories such as "Red Riding Hood" (Carter's version of which, "The Company of Wolves," was made into a successful film), "Sleeping Beauty," "Beauty and the Beast," and "Bluebeard," and brings them to life in a contemporary setting. Carter claimed she was interested in myths "because they are extraordinary lies designed to make people unfree," and by opening up the timeless realms of these myths to historical consciousness, she demonstrated how she believed they can—and should—end differently.

Carter's fiction from this period relies heavily on allegory, and also makes use of many elements of science fiction and magic realism. *The Infernal Desire Machine of Doctor Hoffman* (1972), in particular, is often classified as science fiction, though it also draws heavily on the picaresque. This novel has remained one of her most controversial, frequently criticized for an alleged male chauvinistic viewpoint that seems to celebrate the pornographic. With Carter's use of multiple voices and ever-shifting narrative positions, however, it is sometimes difficult to tell whether she is embracing or parodying the gender roles she sets out.

In the late 1970s and early 1980s, Carter's work began to be more favorably reviewed, and she took on a demanding lecturing and teaching schedule that saw her traveling around the world. In 1983 she also began a family, giving birth to a son, Alexander, with Mark Pearce, whom she married in 1991. Despite her busy schedule, Carter produced her longest novel, *Nights at the Circus*, in 1984. This story about a Cockney trapeze artist with wings has often been compared to Gabriel Garcia Marquez's *One Hundred Years of Solitude* (1967)—a comparison that brought Carter more into the mainstream than she had perhaps ever been. This and her final novel, *Wise Children* (1991), were both very well received, and when Carter died of lung cancer in 1992, she was mourned as a central literary figure of her day.

Many lamented that her obituary notices spoke of her work more generously than most of her reviews had. But critical acceptance had never been a goal of Carter's; she was always suspicious of critical consensus of any kind. Indeed, her writing seeks to provoke those whose opinions are widely accepted, and, in doing so, to produce fruitful critical debate. As one of her critics said, "I'll please no one, least of all her, by trying to say she's not offensive."

⌘ ⌘ ⌘

The Bloody Chamber[1]

I remember how, that night, I lay awake in the wagon-lit[2] in a tender, delicious ecstasy of excitement, my burning cheek pressed against the impeccable linen of the pillow and the pounding of my heart mimicking that of the great pistons ceaselessly thrusting the train that bore me through the night, away from Paris, away from girlhood, away from the white, enclosed quietude of my mother's apartment, into the unguessable country of marriage.

And I remember I tenderly imagined how, at this very moment, my mother would be moving slowly about the narrow bedroom I had left behind for ever, folding up and putting away all my little relics, the tumbled garments I would not need any more, the scores for which there had been no room in my trunks, the concert programmes I'd abandoned; she would linger over this torn ribbon and that faded photograph with all the half-joyous, half-sorrowful emotions of a woman on her daughter's wedding day. And, in the midst of my bridal triumph, I felt a pang of loss as if,

---

[1] *The Bloody Chamber*   Cf. Charles Perrault's "La Barbe Bleue" ("Bluebeard"), 1697.

[2] *wagon-lit*   French: sleeping coach (on a train).

when he put the gold band on my finger, I had, in some way, ceased to be her child in becoming his wife.

Are you sure, she'd said when they delivered the gigantic box that held the wedding dress he'd bought me, wrapped up in tissue paper and red ribbon like a Christmas gift of crystallized fruit. Are you sure you love him? There was a dress for her, too; black silk, with the dull, prismatic sheen of oil on water, finer than anything she'd worn since that adventurous girlhood in Indo-China, daughter of a rich tea planter. My eagle-featured, indomitable mother; what other student at the Conservatoire could boast that her mother had outfaced a junkful[1] of Chinese pirates, nursed a village through a visitation of the plague, shot a man-eating tiger with her own hand and all before she was as old as I?

"Are you sure you love him?"

"I'm sure I want to marry him," I said.

And would say no more. She sighed, as if it was the reluctance that she might at last banish the spectre of poverty from its habitual place at our meager table. For my mother herself had gladly, scandalously, defiantly beggared herself for love; and, one fine day, her gallant soldier never returned from the wars, leaving his wife and child a legacy of tears that never quite dried, a cigar box full of medals and the antique service revolver that my mother, grown magnificently eccentric in hardship, kept always in her reticule,[2] in case—how I teased her—she was surprised by footpads[3] on her way home from the grocer's shop.

Now and then a starburst of lights spattered the drawn blinds as if the railway company had lit up all the stations through which we passed in celebration of the bride. My satin nightdress had just been shaken from its wrappings; it had slipped over my young girl's pointed breasts and shoulders, supple as a garment of heavy water, and now teasingly caressed me, egregious, insinuating, nudging between my thighs as I shifted restlessly in my narrow berth. His kiss, his kiss with tongue and teeth in it and a rasp of beard, had hinted to me, though with the same exquisite tact as this nightdress he'd given me, of the wedding night, which would be voluptuously

deferred until we lay in his great ancestral bed in the sea-girt, pinnacled domain that lay, still, beyond the grasp of my imagination … that magic place, the fairy castle whose walls were made of foam, that legendary habitation in which he had been born. To which, one day, I might bear an heir. Our destination, my destiny.

Above the syncopated roar of the train, I could hear his even, steady breathing. Only the communicating door kept me from my husband and it stood open. If I rose up on my elbow, I could see the dark, leonine shape of his head and my nostrils caught a whiff of the opulent male scent of leather and spices that always accompanied him and sometimes, during his courtship, had been the only hint he gave me that he had come into my mother's sitting room, for, though he was a big man, he moved as softly as if all his shoes had soles of velvet, as if his footfall turned the carpet into snow.

He had loved to surprise me in my abstracted solitude at the piano. He would tell them not to announce him, then soundlessly open the door and softly creep up behind me with his bouquet of hot-house flowers or his box of marrons glacés,[4] lay his offering upon the keys and clasp his hands over my eyes as I was lost in a Debussy[5] prelude. But that perfume of spiced leather always betrayed him; after my first shock, I was forced always to mimic surprise, so that he would not be disappointed.

He was older than I. He was much older than I; there were streaks of pure silver in his dark mane. But his strange, heavy, almost waxen face was not lined by experience. Rather, experience seemed to have washed it perfectly smooth, like a stone on a beach whose fissures have been eroded by successive tides. And sometimes that face, in stillness when he listened to me playing, with the heavy eyelids folded over eyes that always disturbed me by their absolute absence of light, seemed to me like a mask, as if his real face, the face that truly reflected all the life he had led in the world before he met me, before, even, I was born, as though that face lay underneath this mask. Or else, elsewhere. As though he had laid by the face in which he had lived for so long in order to offer my youth a face unsigned by the years.

And, elsewhere, I might see him plain. Elsewhere. But, where?

[1] *junkful* Common Chinese boat with a flat bottom and square prow.

[2] *reticule* Handbag.

[3] *footpads* Thieves.

[4] *marrons glacés* Chestnuts glazed with icing sugar.

[5] *Debussy* French composer Claude Achille Debussy (1862–1918).

In, perhaps, that castle to which the train now took us, that marvellous castle in which he had been born.

Even when he asked me to marry him, and I said: "Yes," still he did not lose that heavy, fleshy composure of his. I know it must seem a curious analogy, a man with a flower, but sometimes he seemed to me like a lily. Yes. A lily. Possessed of that strange, ominous calm of a sentient vegetable, like one of those cobra-headed, funereal lilies whose white sheaths are curled out of a flesh as thick and tensely yielding to the touch as vellum. When I said that I would marry him, not one muscle in his face stirred, but he let out a long, extinguished sigh. I thought: Oh! how he must want me! And it was as though the imponderable weight of his desire was a force I might not withstand, not by virtue of its violence but because of its very gravity.

He had the ring ready in a leather box lined with crimson velvet, a fire opal the size of a pigeon's egg set in a complicated circle of dark antique gold. My old nurse, who still lived with my mother and me, squinted at the ring askance: opals are bad luck, she said. But this opal had been his own mother's ring, and his grandmother's, and her mother's before that, given to an ancestor by Catherine de Medici[1] ... every bride that came to the castle wore it, time out of mind. And did he give it to his other wives and have it back from them? asked the old woman rudely; yet she was a snob. She hid her incredulous joy at my marital coup—her little Marquise—behind a façade of fault-finding. But, here, she touched me. I shrugged and turned my back pettishly on her. I did not want to remember how he had loved other women before me, but the knowledge often teased me in the threadbare self-confidence of the small hours.

I was seventeen and knew nothing of the world; my Marquis had been married before, more than once, and I remained a little bemused that, after those others, he should now have chosen me. Indeed, was he not still in mourning for his last wife? Tsk, tsk, went my old nurse. And even my mother had been reluctant to see her girl whisked off by a man so recently bereaved. A Romanian countess, a lady of high fashion. Dead just three short months before I met him, a boating accident, at his

home, in Brittany. They never found her body but I rummaged through the back copies of the society magazines my old nanny kept in a trunk under her bed and tracked down her photograph. The sharp muzzle of a pretty, witty, naughty monkey; such potent and bizarre charm, of a dark, bright, wild yet worldly thing whose natural habitat must have been some luxurious interior decorator's jungle filled with potted palms and tame, squawking parakeets.

Before that? *Her* face is common property; everyone painted her but the Redon[2] engraving I liked best, *The Evening Star Walking on the Rim of Night.* To see her skeletal, enigmatic grace, you would never think she had been a barmaid in a café in Montmartre until Puvis de Chavannes[3] saw her and had her expose her flat breasts and elongated thighs to his brush. And yet it was the absinthe doomed her, or so they said.

The first of all his ladies? That sumptuous diva; I had heard her sing Isolde,[4] precociously musical child that I was, taken to the opera for a birthday treat. My first opera; I had heard her sing Isolde. With what white-hot passion had she burned from the stage! So that you could tell she would die young. We sat high up, halfway to heaven in the gods, yet she half-blinded me. And my father, still alive (oh, so long ago), took hold of my sticky little hand, to comfort me, in the last act, yet all I heard was the glory of her voice.

Married three times within my own brief lifetime to three different graces, now, as if to demonstrate the eclecticism of his taste, he had invited me to join this gallery of beautiful women, I, the poor widow's child with my mouse-coloured hair that still bore the kinks of the plaits from which it had so recently been freed, my bony hips, my nervous, pianist's fingers.

He was rich as Croesus.[5] The night before our wedding—a simple affair, at the Mairie,[6] because his countess was so recently gone—he took my mother and me, curious coincidence, to see *Tristan.* And, do you

[2] *Redon* French painter and lithographer Odilon Redon (1840-1916).

[3] *Puvis de Chavannes* French painter (1824–98).

[4] *Isolde* I.e., in composer Richard Wagner's opera *Tristan und Isolde* (first performed 1865).

[5] *Croesus* Sixth-century BCE king of Lydia, famous for his wealth.

[6] *Mairie* French: Town hall, mayor's residence.

[1] *Catherine de Medici* Queen of France; wife of King Henry II (1519–89).

know, my heart swelled and ached so during the Liebestod[1] that I thought I must truly love him. Yes. I did. On his arm, all eyes were upon me. The whispering crowd in the foyer parted like the Red Sea to let us through. My skin crisped at his touch.

How my circumstances had changed since the first time I heard those voluptuous chords that carry such a charge of deathly passion in them! Now, we sat in a loge,[2] in red velvet armchairs, and a braided, bewigged flunkey brought us a silver bucket of iced champagne in the interval. The froth spilled over the rim of my glass and drenched my hands, I thought: My cup runneth over. And I had on a Poiret[3] dress. He had prevailed upon my reluctant mother to let him buy my trousseau;[4] what would I have gone to him in, otherwise? Twice-darned underwear, faded gingham, serge skirts, hand-me-downs. So, for the opera, I wore a sinuous shift of white muslin tied with a silk string under the breasts. And everyone stared at me. And at his wedding gift.

His wedding gift, clasped round my throat. A choker of rubies, two inches wide, like an extraordinarily precious slit throat.

After the Terror, in the early days of the Directory,[5] the aristos who'd escaped the guillotine had an ironic fad of tying a red ribbon round their necks at just the point where the blade would have sliced it through, a red ribbon like the memory of a wound. And his grandmother, taken with the notion, had her ribbon made up in rubies; such a gesture of luxurious defiance! That night at the opera comes back to me even now … the white dress; the frail child within it; and the flashing crimson jewels round her throat, bright as arterial blood.

I saw him watching me in the gilded mirrors with the assessing eye of a connoisseur inspecting horseflesh, or even of a housewife in the market, inspecting cuts on the slab. I'd never seen, or else had never acknowledged, that regard of his before, the sheer carnal avarice of it; and it was strangely magnified by the monocle lodged in his left eye. When I saw him look at me with lust, I dropped my eyes but, in glancing away from him, I caught sight of myself in the mirror. And I saw myself, suddenly, as he saw me, my pale face, the way the muscles in my neck stuck out like thin wire. I saw how much that cruel necklace became me. And, for the first time in my innocent and confined life, I sensed in myself a potentiality for corruption that took my breath away.

The next day, we were married.

The train slowed, shuddered to a halt. Lights; clank of metal; a voice declaring the name of an unknown, never-to-be visited station; silence of the night; the rhythm of his breathing, that I should sleep with, now, for the rest of my life. And I could not sleep. I stealthily sat up, raised the blind a little and huddled against the cold window that misted over with the warmth of my breathing, gazing out at the dark platform towards those rectangles of domestic lamplight that promised warmth, company, a supper of sausages hissing in a pan on the stove for the station master, his children tucked up in bed asleep in the brick house with the painted shutters … all the paraphernalia of the everyday world from which I, with my stunning marriage, had exiled myself.

Into marriage, into exile; I sensed it, I knew it—that, henceforth, I would always be lonely. Yet that was part of the already familiar weight of the fire opal that glimmered like a gypsy's magic ball, so that I could not take my eyes off it when I played the piano. This ring, the bloody bandage of rubies, the wardrobe of clothes from Poiret and Worth,[6] his scent of Russian leather—all had conspired to seduce me so utterly that I could not say I felt one single twinge of regret for the world of tartines[7] and maman that now receded from me as if drawn away on a string, like a child's toy, as the train began to throb again as if in delighted anticipation of the distance it would take me.

---

1 *Liebestod*   Aria describing the suicide of lovers.

2 *loge*   Opera-house box.

3 *Poiret*   Dressmaker Paul Poiret (1879–1944).

4 *trousseau*   Bride's collection of clothing and linens.

5 *Terror*   Reign of Terror, during the French Revolution (1793–94), during which thousands of people, considered by the political regime to be enemies of the state, were executed; *Directory*   I.e., the *Directoire*, the period at the end of the French Revolution during which five Directors shared executive power over the state.

6 *Worth*   Charles Frederick Worth (1825–95), British and French fashion designer and founder of Maison Worth.

7 *tartines*   Slices of bread with butter or jam; a child's meal.

The first grey streamers of the dawn now flew in the sky and an eldritch half-light seeped into the railway carriage. I heard no change in his breathing but my heightened, excited senses told me he was awake and gazing at me. A huge man, an enormous man, and his eyes, dark and motionless as those eyes the ancient Egyptians painted upon their sarcophagi, fixed upon me. I felt a certain tension in the pit of my stomach, to be so watched, in such silence. A match struck. He was igniting a Romeo y Julieta[1] fat as a baby's arm.

"Soon," he said in his resonant voice that was like the tolling of a bell and I felt, all at once, a sharp premonition of dread that lasted only as long as the match flared and I could see his white, broad face as if it were hovering, disembodied, above the sheets, illuminated from below like a grotesque carnival head. Then the flame died, the cigar glowed and filled the compartment with a remembered fragrance that made me think of my father, how he would hug me in a warm fug[2] of Havana, when I was a little girl, before he kissed me and left me and died.

As soon as my husband handed me down from the high step of the train, I smelled the amniotic salinity of the ocean. It was November; the trees, stunted by the Atlantic gales, were bare and the lonely halt was deserted but for his leather-gaitered chauffeur waiting meekly beside the sleek black motor car. It was cold; I drew my furs about me, a wrap of white and black, broad stripes of ermine and sable, with a collar from which my head rose like the calyx of a wildflower. (I swear to you, I had never been vain until I met him.) The bell clanged; the straining train leapt its leash and left us at that lonely wayside halt where only he and I had descended. Oh, the wonder of it; how all that might of iron and steam had paused only to suit his convenience. The richest man in France.

"Madame."

The chauffeur eyed me; was he comparing me, invidiously, to the countess, the artist's model, the opera singer? I hid behind my furs as if they were a system of soft shields. My husband liked me to wear my opal over my kid glove, a showy, theatrical trick—but the moment the ironic chauffeur glimpsed its simmering flash

he smiled, as though it was proof positive I was his master's wife. And we drove towards the widening dawn, that now streaked half the sky with a wintry bouquet of pink of roses, orange of tiger-lilies, as if my husband had ordered me a sky from a florist. The day broke around me like a cool dream.

Sea; sand; a sky that melts into the sea—a landscape of misty pastels with a look about it of being continuously on the point of melting. A landscape with all the deliquescent harmonies of Debussy, of the études[3] I played for him, the reverie I'd been playing that afternoon in the salon of the princess where I'd first met him, among the teacups and the little cakes, I, the orphan, hired out of charity to give them their digestive of music.

And, ah! his castle. The faery solitude of the place; with its turrets of misty blue, its courtyard, its spiked gate, his castle that lay on the very bosom of the sea with seabirds mewing about its attics, the casements opening on to the green and purple, evanescent departures of the ocean, cut off by the tide from land for half a day … that castle, at home neither on the land nor on the water, a mysterious, amphibious place, contravening the materiality of both earth and the waves, with the melancholy of a mermaiden who perches on her rock and waits, endlessly, for a lover who had drowned far away, long ago. That lovely, sad, sea-siren of a place!

The tide was low; at this hour, so early in the morning, the causeway rose up out of the sea. As the car turned on to the wet cobbles between the slow margins of water, he reached out for my hand that had his sultry, witchy ring on it, pressed my fingers, kissed my palm with extraordinary tenderness. His face was as still as ever I'd seen it, still as a pond iced thickly over, yet his lips, that always looked so strangely red and naked between the black fringes of his beard, now curved a little. He smiled; he welcomed his bride home.

No room, no corridor that did not rustle with the sound of the sea and all the ceilings, the walls on which his ancestors in the stern regalia of rank lined up with their dark eyes and white faces, were stippled with refracted light from the waves which were always in motion; that luminous, murmurous castle of which I

[1] *Romeo y Julieta* Brand of Havana cigar.
[2] *fug* Thick, close atmosphere.
[3] *études* Class of musical compositions.

was the chatelaine,[1] I, the little music student whose mother had sold all her jewellery, even her wedding ring, to pay the fees at the Conservatoire.

First of all, there was the small ordeal of my initial interview with the housekeeper, who kept this extraordinary machine, this anchored, castellated ocean liner, in smooth running order no matter who stood on the bridge; how tenuous, I thought, might be my authority here! She had a bland, pale, impassive, dislikeable face beneath the impeccably starched white linen head-dress of the region. Her greeting, correct but lifeless, chilled me; daydreaming, I dared presume too much on my status ... briefly wondered how I might install my old nurse, so much loved, however cosily incompetent, in her place. Ill-considered schemings! He told me this one had been his foster mother; was bound to his family in the utmost feudal complicity, "as much part of the house as I am, my dear." Now her thin lips offered me a proud little smile. She would be my ally as long as I was his. And with that, I must be content.

But, here, it would be easy to be content. In the turret suite he had given me for my very own, I could gaze out over the tumultuous Atlantic and imagine myself the Queen of the Sea. There was a Bechstein[2] for me in the music room and, on the wall, another wedding present—an early Flemish primitive of Saint Cecilia[3] at her celestial organ. In the prim charm of this saint, with her plump, sallow cheeks and crinkled brown hair, I saw myself as I could have wished to be. I warmed to a loving sensitivity I had not hitherto suspected in him. Then he led me up a delicate spiral staircase to my bedroom; before she discreetly vanished, the housekeeper set him chuckling with some, I dare say, lewd blessing for newlyweds in her native Breton. That I did not understand. That he, smiling, refused to interpret.

And there lay the grand, hereditary matrimonial bed, itself the size, almost, of my little room at home, with the gargoyles carved on its surfaces of ebony, vermilion lacquer, gold leaf; and its white gauze curtains, billowing in the sea breeze. Our bed. And surrounded by so many mirrors! Mirrors on all the walls, in stately frames of

contorted gold, that reflected more white lilies than I'd ever seen in my life before. He'd filled the room with them, to greet the bride, the young bride. The young bride, who had become that multitude of girls I saw in the mirrors, identical in their chic navy blue tailor-mades, for travelling, madame, or walking. A maid had dealt with the furs. Henceforth, a maid would deal with everything.

"See," he said, gesturing towards those elegant girls. "I have acquired a whole harem for myself!"

I found that I was trembling. My breath came thickly. I could not meet his eye and turned my head away, out of pride, out of shyness, and watched a dozen husbands approach me in a dozen mirrors and slowly, methodically, teasingly, unfasten the buttons of my jacket and slip it from my shoulders. Enough! No; more! Off comes the skirt; and, next, the blouse of apricot linen that cost more than the dress I had for First Communion. The play of the waves outside in the cold sun glittered on his monocle; his movements seemed to me deliberately coarse, vulgar. The blood rushed to my face again, and stayed there.

And yet, you see, I guessed it might be so—that we should have a formal disrobing of the bride, a ritual from the brothel. Sheltered as my life had been, how could I have failed, even in the world of prim bohemia in which I lived, to have heard hints of *his* world?

He stripped me, gourmand that he was, as if he were stripping the leaves off an artichoke—but do not imagine much finesse about it; this artichoke was no particular treat for the diner nor was he yet in any greedy haste. He approached his familiar treat with a weary appetite. And when nothing but my scarlet, palpitating core remained, I saw, in the mirror, the living image of an etching by Rops[4] from the collection he had shown me when our engagement permitted us to be alone together ... the child with her sticklike limbs, naked but for her button boots, her gloves, shielding her face with her hand as though her face were the last repository of her modesty; and the old, monocled lecher who examined her, limb by limb. He in his London tailoring; she, bare as a lamb chop. Most pornographic of all confrontations. And so my purchaser unwrapped his bargain. And, as at the opera, when I had first seen

---

[1]   *chatelaine* Mistress.

[2]   *Bechstein* Type of piano created by Carl Bechstein in 1853.

[3]   *Saint Cecilia* Patron saint of music and musicians.

[4]   *Rops* Belgian artist Félicien Rops (1833–98).

my flesh in his eyes, I was aghast to feel myself stirring.

At once he closed my legs like a book and I saw again the rare movement of his lips that meant he smiled.

Not yet. Later. Anticipation is the greater part of pleasure, my little love.

And I began to shudder, like a racehorse before a race, yet also with a kind of fear, for I felt both a strange, impersonal arousal at the thought of love and at the same time a repugnance I could not stifle for his white, heavy flesh that had too much in common with the armfuls of arum lilies that filled my bedroom in great glass jars, those undertakers' lilies with the heavy pollen that powders your fingers as if you had dipped them in turmeric. The lilies I always associate with him; that are white. And stain you.

This scene from a voluptuary's life was now abruptly terminated. It turns out he has business to attend to; his estates, his companies—even on your honeymoon? Even then, said the red lips that kissed me before he left me alone with my bewildered senses—a wet, silken brush from his beard; a hint of the pointed tip of the tongue. Disgruntled, I wrapped a négligé of antique lace around me to sip the little breakfast of hot chocolate the maid brought me; after that, since it was second nature to me, there was nowhere to go but the music room and soon I settled down at my piano.

Yet only a series of subtle discords flowed from beneath my fingers: out of tune … only a little out of tune; but I'd been blessed with perfect pitch and could not bear to play any more. Sea breezes are bad for pianos; we shall need a resident piano-tuner on the premises if I'm to continue with my studies! I flung down the lid in a little fury of disappointment; what should I do now, how shall I pass the long, sea-lit hours until my husband beds me?

I shivered to think of *that*.

His library seemed the source of his habitual odour of Russian leather. Row upon row of calf-bound volumes, brown and olive, with gilt lettering on their spines, the octavo[1] in brilliant scarlet morocco. A deep-buttoned leather sofa to recline on. A lectern, carved like a spread eagle, that held open upon it an edition of Huysmans's *Là-bas*,[2] from some over-exquisite private press; it had been bound like a missal,[3] in brass, with gems of coloured glass. The rugs on the floor, deep, pulsing blues of heaven and red of the heart's dearest blood, came from Isfahan and Bokhara;[4] the dark panelling gleamed; there was the lulling music of the sea and a fire of apple logs. The flames flickered along the spines inside a glass-fronted case that held books still crisp and new. Eliphas Levy;[5] the name meant nothing to me. I squinted at a title or two: *The Initiation, The Key of Mysteries, The Secret of Pandora's Box*, and yawned. Nothing, here, to detain a seventeen-year-old girl waiting for her first embrace. I should have liked, best of all, a novel in yellow paper;[6] I wanted to curl up on the rug before the blazing fire, lose myself in a cheap novel, munch sticky liqueur chocolates. If I rang for them, a maid would bring me chocolates.

Nevertheless, I opened the doors of that bookcase idly to browse. And I think I knew, I knew by some tingling of the fingertips, even before I opened that slim volume with no title at all on the spine, what I should find inside it. When he showed me the Rops, newly bought, dearly prized, had he not hinted that he was a connoisseur of such things? Yet I had not bargained for this, the girl with tears hanging on her cheeks like stuck pearls, her cunt a split fig below the great globes of her buttocks on which the knotted tails of the cat were about to descend, while a man in a black mask fingered with his free hand his prick, that curved upwards like the scimitar he held. The picture had a caption: "Reproof of curiosity." My mother, with all the precision of her eccentricity, had told me what it was that lovers did; I was innocent but not naive. *The Adventures of Eulalie at the Harem of the Grand Turk* had been printed, according to the flyleaf, in Amsterdam in 1748, a rare collector's piece. Had some ancestor brought it back himself from that northern city? Or had my husband

---

[1]   *octavo*   Book size. The pages of an octavo are produced by folding a standard-sized printing sheet three times to form eight leaves.

[2]   *Huysmans's Là-bas*   1891 novel by French novelist Joris Karl Huysmans.

[3]   *missal*   Prayer book; contains the service of the Mass for the liturgical year.

[4]   *Isfahan and Bokhara*   Cities in Iran and Uzbekistan.

[5]   *Eliphas Levy*   Pseudonym of French magician Alphonse Louis Constant (1810–75).

[6]   *novel in yellow paper*   I.e., a popular novel.

bought it for himself, from one of those dusty little bookshops on the Left Bank where an old man peers at you through spectacles an inch thick, daring you to inspect his wares … I turned the pages in the anticipation of fear; the print was rusty. Here was another steel engraving: "Immolation of the wives of the Sultan." I knew enough for what I saw in that book to make me gasp.

There was a pungent intensification of the odour of leather that suffused his library; his shadow fell across the massacre.

"My little nun has found the prayerbooks, has she?" he demanded, with a curious mixture of mockery and relish; then, seeing my painful, furious bewilderment, he laughed at me aloud, snatched the book from my hands and put it down on the sofa.

"Have the nasty pictures scared Baby? Baby mustn't play with grownups' toys until she's learned how to handle them, must she?"

Then he kissed me. And with, this time, no reticence. He kissed me and laid his hand imperatively upon my breast, beneath the sheath of ancient lace. I stumbled on the winding stair that led to the bedroom, to the carved, gilded bed on which he had been conceived. I stammered foolishly: We've not taken luncheon yet; and, besides, it is broad daylight …

All the better to see you.

He made me put on my choker, the family heirloom of one woman who had escaped the blade. With trembling fingers, I fastened the thing about my neck. It was cold as ice and chilled me. He twined my hair into a rope and lifted it off my shoulders so that he could the better kiss the downy furrows below my ears; that made me shudder. And he kissed those blazing rubies, too. He kissed them before he kissed my mouth. Rapt, he intoned: "Of her apparel she retains/Only her sonorous jewellery."

A dozen husbands impaled a dozen brides while the mewing gulls swung on invisible trapezes in the empty air outside.

I was brought to my senses by the insistent shrilling of the telephone. He lay beside me, felled like an oak, breathing stertorously, as if he had been fighting with me. In the course of that one-sided struggle, I had seen

his deathly composure shatter like a porcelain vase flung against a wall; I had heard him shriek and blaspheme at the orgasm; I had bled. And perhaps I had seen his face without its mask; and perhaps I had not. Yet I had been infinitely dishevelled by the loss of my virginity.

I gathered myself together, reached into the cloisonné[1] cupboard beside the bed that concealed the telephone and addressed the mouthpiece. His agent in New York. Urgent.

I shook him awake and rolled over on my side, cradling my spent body in my arms. His voice buzzed like a hive of distant bees. My husband. My husband, who, with so much love, filled my bedroom with lilies until it looked like an embalming parlour. Those somnolent lilies, that wave their heavy heads, distributing their lush, insolent incense reminiscent of pampered flesh.

When he'd finished with the agent, he turned to me and stroked the ruby necklace that bit into my neck, but with such tenderness now, that I ceased flinching and he caressed my breasts. My dear one, my little love, my child, did it hurt her? He's so sorry for it, such impetuousness, he could not help himself; you see, he loves her so … and this lover's recitative of his brought my tears in a flood. I clung to him as though only the one who had inflicted the pain could comfort me for suffering it. For a while, he murmured to me in a voice I'd never heard before, a voice like the soft consolations of the sea. But then he unwound the tendrils of my hair from the buttons of his smoking jacket, kissed my cheek briskly and told me the agent from New York had called with such urgent business that he must leave as soon as the tide was low enough. Leave the castle? Leave France! And would be away for at least six weeks.

"But it is our honeymoon!"

A deal, an enterprise of hazard and chance involving several millions, lay in the balance, he said. He drew away from me into that waxworks stillness of his; I was only a little girl, I did not understand. And, he said unspoken to my wounded vanity, I have had too many honeymoons to find them in the least pressing commitments. I know quite well that this child I've bought with a handful of coloured stones and the pelts of dead beasts won't run away. But, after he'd called his Paris agent to

---

[1] *cloisonné* Enamel.

book a passage for the States next day—just one tiny call, my little one—we should have time for dinner together.

And I had to be content with that.

A Mexican dish of pheasant with hazelnuts and chocolate; salad; white, voluptuous cheese; a sorbet of muscat grapes and Asti spumante. A celebration of Krug exploded festively. And then acrid black coffee in precious little cups so fine it shadowed the birds with which they were painted. I had Cointreau, he had cognac in the library, with the purple velvet curtains drawn against the night, where he took me to perch on his knee in a leather armchair beside the flickering log fire. He had made me change into that chaste little Poiret shift of white muslin; he seemed especially fond of it, my breasts showed through the flimsy stuff, he said, like little soft white doves that sleep, each one, with a pink eye open. But he would not let me take off my ruby choker, although it was growing very uncomfortable, nor fasten up my descending hair, the sign of a virginity so recently ruptured that still remained a wounded presence between us. He twined his fingers in my hair until I winced; I said, I remember, very little.

"The maid will have changed our sheets already," he said. "We do not hang the bloody sheets out of the window to prove to the whole of Brittany you are a virgin, not in these civilized times. But I should tell you it would have been the first time in all my married lives I could have shown my interested tenants such a flag."

Then I realized, with a shock of surprise, how it must have been my innocence that captivated him—the silent music, he said, of my unknowingness, like *La Terrasse des audiences au clair de lune*[1] played upon a piano with keys of ether. You must remember how ill at ease I was in that luxurious place, how unease had been my constant companion during the whole length of my courtship by this grave satyr who now gently martyrized my hair. To know that my naivety gave him some pleasure made me take heart. Courage! I shall act the fine lady to the manner born one day, if only by virtue of default.

Then, slowly yet teasingly, as if he were giving a child a great, mysterious treat, he took out a bunch of keys from some interior hidey-hole in his jacket—key after key, a key, he said, for every lock in the house. Keys of all kinds—huge, ancient things of black iron; others slender, delicate, almost baroque; wafer-thin Yale keys for safes and boxes. And, during his absence, it was I who must take care of them all.

I eyed the heavy bunch with circumspection. Until that moment, I had not given a single thought to the practical aspects of marriage with a great house, great wealth, a great man, whose key ring was as crowded as that of a prison warder. Here were the clumsy and archaic keys for the dungeons, for dungeons we had in plenty although they had been converted to cellars for his wines; the dusty bottles inhabited in racks all those deep holes of pain in the rock on which the castle was built. These are the keys to the kitchens, this is the key to the picture gallery, a treasure house filled by five centuries of avid collectors—ah! he foresaw I would spend hours there.

He had amply indulged his taste for the Symbolists, he told me with a glint of greed. There was Moreau's great portrait of his first wife, the famous *Sacrificial Victim* with the imprint of the lacelike chains on her pellucid skin. Did I know the story of the painting of that picture? How, when she took off her clothes for him for the first time, she fresh from her bar in Montmartre, she had robed herself involuntarily in a blush that reddened her breasts, her shoulders, her arms, her whole body? He had thought of that story, of that dear girl, when first he had undressed me … Ensor, the great Ensor, his monolithic canvas: *The Foolish Virgins.* Two or three late Gauguins, his special favourite the one of the tranced brown girl in the deserted house which was called: *Out of the Night We Come, Into the Night We Go.* And, besides the additions he had made himself, his marvellous inheritance of Watteaus, Poussins and a pair of very special Fragonards, commissioned for a licentious ancestor who, it was said, had posed for the master's brush himself with his own two daughters … He broke off his catalogue of treasures abruptly.

Your thin white face, chérie; he said, as if he saw it for the first time. Your thin white face, with its promise of debauchery only a connoisseur could detect.

A log fell in the fire, instigating a shower of sparks; the opal on my finger spurted green flame. I felt as

---

[1] *La Terrasse des audiences au clair de lune* Piano solo by Claude Debussy (1912–13).

giddy as if I were on the edge of a precipice; I was afraid, not so much of him, of his monstrous presence, heavy as if he had been gifted at birth with more specific *gravity* than the rest of us, the presence that, even when I thought myself most in love with him, always subtly oppressed me … No. I was not afraid of him; but of myself. I seemed reborn in his unreflective eyes, reborn in unfamiliar shapes. I hardly recognized myself from his descriptions of me and yet, and yet—might there not be a grain of beastly truth in them? And, in the red firelight, I blushed again, unnoticed, to think he might have chosen me because, in my innocence, he sensed a rare talent for corruption.

Here is the key to the china cabinet—don't laugh, my darling; there's a king's ransom in Sèvres in that closet, and a queen's ransom in Limoges.[1] And a key to the locked, barred room where five generations of plate[2] were kept.

Keys, keys, keys. He would trust me with the keys to his office, although I was only a baby; and the keys to his safes, where he kept the jewels I should wear, he promised me, when we returned to Paris. Such jewels! Why, I would be able to change my earrings and necklaces three times a day, just as the Empress Josephine used to change her underwear. He doubted, he said, with that hollow, knocking sound that served him for a chuckle, I would be quite so interested in his share certificates although they, of course, were worth infinitely more.

Outside our firelit privacy, I could hear the sound of the tide drawing back from the pebbles of the foreshore; it was nearly time for him to leave me. One single key remained unaccounted for on the ring and he hesitated over it; for a moment, I thought he was going to unfasten it from its brothers, slip it back into his pocket and take it away with him.

"What is *that* key?" I demanded, for his chaffing had made me bold. "The key to your heart? Give it me!"

He dangled the key tantalizingly above my head, out of reach of my straining fingers; those bare red lips of his cracked sidelong in a smile.

"Ah, no," he said. "Not the key to my heart. Rather, the key to my enfer."[3]

He left it on the ring, fastened the ring together, shook it musically, like a carillon. Then threw the keys in a jingling heap in my lap. I could feel the cold metal chilling my thighs through my thin muslin frock. He bent over me to drop a beard-masked kiss on my forehead.

"Every man must have one secret, even if only one, from his wife," he said. "Promise me this, my whey-faced piano-player; promise me you'll use all the keys on the ring except that last little one I showed you. Play with anything you find, jewels, silver plate; make toy boats of my share certificates, if it pleases you, and send them sailing off to America after me. All is yours, everywhere is open to you—except the lock that this single key fits. Yet all it is is the key to a little room at the foot of the west tower, behind the still-room, at the end of a dark little corridor full of horrid cobwebs that would get into your hair and frighten you if you ventured there. Oh, and you'd find it such a dull little room! But you must promise me, if you love me, to leave it well alone. It is only a private study, a hideaway, a 'den,' as the English say, where I can go, sometimes, on those infrequent yet inevitable occasions when the yoke of marriage seems to weigh too heavily on my shoulders. There I can go, you understand, to savour the rare pleasure of imagining myself wifeless."

There was a little thin starlight in the courtyard as, wrapped in my furs, I saw him to his car. His last words were, that he had telephoned the mainland and taken a piano-tuner on to the staff; this man would arrive to take up his duties the next day. He pressed me to his vicuna[4] breast, once, and then drove away.

I had drowsed away that afternoon and now I could not sleep. I lay tossing and turning in his ancestral bed until another daybreak discoloured the dozen mirrors that were iridescent with the reflections of the sea. The perfume of the lilies weighed on my senses; when I thought that, henceforth, I would always share these sheets with a man whose skin, as theirs did, contained

---

[1] *Sèvres … Limoges* Fine china.

[2] *plate* I.e., silver dishes and utensils.

[3] *enfer* French: Hell.

[4] *vicuna* Fine, silky wool made from the coat of a South American animal of the same name.

that toad-like, clammy hint of moisture, I felt a vague desolation that within me, now my female wound had healed, there had awoken a certain queasy craving like the cravings of pregnant women for the taste of coal or chalk or tainted food, for the renewal of his caresses. Had he not hinted to me, in his flesh as in his speech and looks, of the thousand, thousand baroque intersections of flesh upon flesh? I lay in our wide bed accompanied by a sleepless companion, my dark newborn curiosity.

I lay in bed alone. And I longed for him. And he disgusted me.

Were there jewels enough in all his safes to recompense me for this predicament? Did all that castle hold enough riches to recompense me for the company of the libertine[1] with whom I must share it? And what, precisely, was the nature of my desirous dread for this mysterious being who, to show his mastery over me, had abandoned me on my wedding night?

Then I sat straight up in bed, under the sardonic masks of the gargoyles carved above me, riven by a wild surmise. Might he have left me, not for Wall Street but for an importunate mistress tucked away God knows where who knew how to pleasure him far better than a girl whose fingers had been exercised, hitherto, only by the practice of scales and arpeggios? And, slowly, soothed, I sank back on to the heaping pillows; I acknowledged that the jealous scare I'd just given myself was not unmixed with a little tincture of relief.

At last I drifted into slumber, as daylight filled the room and chased bad dreams away. But the last thing I remembered, before I slept, was the tall jar of lilies beside the bed, how the thick glass distorted their fat stems so they looked like arms, dismembered arms, drifting drowned in greenish water.

Coffee and croissants to console this bridal, solitary waking. Delicious. Honey, too, in a section of comb on a glass saucer. The maid squeezed the aromatic juice from an orange into a chilled goblet while I watched her as I lay in the lazy, midday bed of the rich. Yet nothing, this morning, gave me more than a fleeting pleasure except to hear that the piano-tuner had been at work already. When the maid told me that, I sprang out of bed and pulled on my old serge skirt and flannel blouse,

costume of a student, in which I felt far more at ease with myself than in any of my fine new clothes.

After my three hours of practice, I called the piano-tuner in, to thank him. He was blind, of course; but young, with a gentle mouth and grey eyes that fixed upon me although they could not see me. He was a blacksmith's son from the village across the causeway; a chorister in the church whom the good priest had taught a trade so that he could make a living. All most satisfactory. Yes. He thought he would be happy here. And if, he added shyly, he might sometimes be allowed to hear me play ... for, you see, he loved music. Yes. Of course, I said. Certainly. He seemed to know that I had smiled.

After I dismissed him, even though I'd woken so late, it was still barely time for my "five o'clock."[2] The housekeeper, who, thoughtfully forewarned by my husband, had restrained herself from interrupting my music, now made me a solemn visitation with a lengthy menu for a late luncheon. When I told her I did not need it, she looked at me obliquely, along her nose. I understood at once that one of my principal functions as chatelaine was to provide work for the staff. But, all the same, I asserted myself and said I would wait until dinner-time, although I looked forward nervously to the solitary meal. Then I found I had to tell her what I would like to have prepared for me; my imagination, still that of a schoolgirl, ran riot. A fowl in cream—or should I anticipate Christmas with a varnished turkey? No; I have decided. Avocado and shrimp, lots of it, followed by no entree at all. But surprise me for dessert with every ice-cream in the ice box. She noted all down but sniffed; I'd shocked her. Such tastes! Child that I was, I giggled when she left me.

But, now ... what shall I do, now?

I could have spent a happy hour unpacking the trunks that contained my trousseau but the maid had done that already, the dresses, the tailor-mades hung in the wardrobe in my dressing room, the hats on wooden heads to keep their shape, the shoes on wooden feet as if all these inanimate objects were imitating the appearance of life, to mock me. I did not like to linger in my overcrowded dressing room, nor in my lugubriously lily-scented bedroom. How shall I pass the time?

---

[1] *libertine* Immoral, dissolute man.

[2] *"five o'clock"* Late afternoon tea.

I shall take a bath in my own bathroom! And found the taps were little dolphins made of gold, with chips of turquoise for eyes. And there was a tank of goldfish, who swam in and out of moving fronds of weeds, as bored, I thought, as I was. How I wished he had not left me. How I wished it were possible to chat with, say, a maid; or, the piano-tuner … but I knew already my new rank forbade overtures of friendship to the staff.

I had been hoping to defer the call as long as I could, so that I should have something to look forward to in the dead waste of time I foresaw before me, after my dinner was done with, but, at a quarter before seven, when darkness already surrounded the castle, I could contain myself no longer. I telephoned my mother. And astonished myself by bursting into tears when I heard her voice.

No, nothing was the matter. Mother, I have gold bath taps.

I said, gold bath taps!

No; I suppose that's nothing to cry about, Mother.

The line was bad, I could hardly make out her congratulations, her questions, her concern, but I was a little comforted when I put the receiver down.

Yet there still remained one whole hour to dinner and the whole, unimaginable desert of the rest of the evening.

The bunch of keys lay, where he had left them, on the rug before the library fire which had warmed their metal so that they no longer felt cold to the touch but warm, almost, as my own skin. How careless I was; a maid, tending the logs, eyed me reproachfully as if I'd set a trap for her as I picked up the clinking bundle of keys, the keys to the interior doors of this lovely prison of which I was both the inmate and the mistress and had scarcely seen. When I remembered that, I felt the exhilaration of the explorer.

Lights! More lights!

At the touch of a switch, the dreaming library was brilliantly illuminated. I ran crazily about the castle, switching on every light I could find—I ordered the servants to light up all their quarters, too, so the castle would shine like a seaborne birthday cake lit with a thousand candles, one for every year of its life, and everybody on shore would wonder at it. When everything was lit as brightly as the café in the Gare du Nord,

the significance of the possessions implied by that bunch of keys no longer intimidated me, for I was determined, now, to search through them all for evidence of my husband's true nature.

His office first, evidently.

A mahogany desk half a mile wide, with an impeccable blotter and a bank of telephones. I allowed myself the luxury of opening the safe that contained the jewellery and delved sufficiently among the leather boxes to find out how my marriage had given me access to a jinn's[1] treasury—parures,[2] bracelets, rings … While I was thus surrounded by diamonds, a maid knocked on the door and entered before I spoke; a subtle discourtesy. I would speak to my husband about it. She eyed my serge skirt superciliously; did madame plan to dress for dinner?

She made a moue[3] of disdain when I laughed to hear that, she was far more the lady than I. But, imagine—to dress up in one of my Poiret extravaganzas, with the jewelled turban and aigrette[4] on my head, roped with pearl to the navel, to sit down all alone in the baronial dining hall at the head of that massive board at which King Mark[5] was reputed to have fed his knights … I grew calmer under the cold eye of her disapproval. I adopted the crisp inflections of an officer's daughter. No, I would not dress for dinner. Furthermore, I was not hungry enough for dinner itself. She must tell the housekeeper to cancel the dormitory feast I'd ordered. Could they leave me sandwiches and a flask of coffee in my music room? And would they all dismiss for the night?

Mais oui, madame.

I knew by her bereft intonation I had let them down again but I did not care; I was armed against them by the brilliance of his hoard. But I would not find his heart amongst the glittering stones; as soon as she had gone, I began a systematic search of the drawers of his desk.

---

[1] *jinn*   Shape-changing demon of Islamic folklore; a genie.

[2] *parures*   Sets of several pieces of jewelry.

[3] *moue*   Pout.

[4] *aigrette*   Spray of jewels.

[5] *King Mark*   Of Arthurian legend.

All was in order, so I found nothing. Not a random doodle on an old envelope, nor the faded photograph of a woman. Only the files of business correspondence, the bills from the home farms, the invoices from tailors, the billets-doux from international financiers. Nothing. And this absence of the evidence of his real life began to impress me strangely; there must, I thought, be a great deal to conceal if he takes such pains to hide it.

His office was a singularly impersonal room, facing inwards, on to the courtyard, as though he wanted to turn his back on the siren sea in order to keep a clear head while he bankrupted a small businessman in Amsterdam or—I noticed with a thrill of distaste —engaged in some business in Laos that must, from certain cryptic references to his amateur botanist's enthusiasm for rare poppies, be to do with opium. Was he not rich enough to do without crime? Or was the crime itself his profit? And yet I saw enough to appreciate his zeal for secrecy.

Now I had ransacked his desk, I must spend a cool-headed quarter of an hour putting every last letter back where I had found it, and, as I covered the traces of my visit, by some chance, as I reached inside a little drawer that had stuck fast, I must have touched a hidden spring, for a secret drawer flew open within that drawer itself; and this secret drawer contained—at last!—a file marked: *Personal.*

I was alone, but for my reflection in the uncurtained window.

I had the brief notion that his heart, pressed flat as a flower, crimson and thin as tissue paper, lay in this file. It was a very thin one.

I could have wished, perhaps, I had not found that touching, ill-spelt note, on a paper napkin marked *La Coupole*, that began: "My darling, I cannot wait for the moment when you may make me yours completely." The diva had sent him a page of the score of *Tristan*, the Liebestod, with the single, cryptic word: "Until …" scrawled across it. But the strangest of all these love letters was a postcard with a view of a village graveyard, among mountains, where some black-coated ghoul enthusiastically dug at a grave; this little scene, executed

with the lurid exuberance of Grand Guignol,[1] was captioned: "Typical Transylvanian Scene—Midnight, All Hallows." And, on the other side, the message: "On the occasion of this marriage to the descendant of Dracula—always remember, 'the supreme and unique pleasure of love is the certainty that one is doing evil.' Toutes amitiés,[2] C."

A joke. A joke in the worst possible taste; for had he not been married to a Romanian countess? And then I remembered her pretty, witty face, and her name— Carmilla. My most recent predecessor in this castle had been, it would seem, the most sophisticated.

I put away the file, sobered. Nothing in my life of family love and music had prepared me for these grown-up games and yet these were clues to his self that showed me, at least, how much he had been loved, even if they did not reveal any good reason for it. But I wanted to know still more; and, as I closed the office door and locked it, the means to discover more fell in my way.

Fell, indeed; and with the clatter of a dropped canteen of cutlery, for, as I turned the slick Yale lock, I contrived, somehow, to open up the key ring itself, so that all the keys tumbled loose on the floor. And the very first key I picked out of that pile was, as luck or ill fortune had it, the key to the room he had forbidden me, the room he would keep for his own so that he could go there when he wished to feel himself once more a bachelor.

I made my decision to explore it before I felt a faint resurgence of my ill-defined fear of his waxen stillness. Perhaps I half-imagined, then, that I might find his real self in his den, waiting there to see if indeed I had obeyed him; that he had sent a moving figure of himself to New York, the enigmatic, self-sustaining carapace[3] of his public person, while the real man, whose face I had glimpsed in the storm of orgasm, occupied himself with pressing private business in the study at the foot of the west tower, behind the still-room. Yet, if that were so, it was imperative that I should find him, should know

1 *Grand Guignol* Drama dealing with macabre subject matter and containing graphic violence. Originally, the name of a Paris theater that shocked its audience members in the early twentieth century with the graphic nature of its performances.

2 *Toutes amitiés* French: All the best.

3 *carapace* Shell.

him; and I was too deluded by his apparent taste for me to think my disobedience might truly offend him.

I took the forbidden key from the heap and left the others lying there.

It was now very late and the castle was adrift, as far as it could go from the land, in the middle of the silent ocean where, at my orders, it floated, like a garland of light. And all silent, all still, but for the murmuring of the waves.

I felt no fear, no intimation of dread. Now I walked as firmly as I had done in my mother's house.

Not a narrow, dusty little passage at all; why had he lied to me? But an ill-lit one, certainly; the electricity, for some reason, did not extend here, so I retreated to the still-room and found a bundle of waxed tapers in a cupboard, stored there with matches to light the oak board at grand dinners. I put a match to my little taper and advanced with it in my hand, like a penitent, along the corridor hung with heavy, I think Venetian, tapestries. The flame picked out, here, the head of a man, there, the rich breast of a woman spilling through a rent in her dress—the Rape of the Sabines,[1] perhaps? The naked swords and immolated horses suggested some grisly mythological subject. The corridor wound downwards; there was an almost imperceptible ramp to the thickly carpeted floor. The heavy hangings on the wall muffled my footsteps, even my breathing. For some reason, it grew very warm; the sweat sprang out in beads on my brow. I could no longer hear the sound of the sea.

A long, a winding corridor, as if I were in the viscera of the castle; and this corridor led to a door of worm-eaten oak, low, round-topped, barred with black iron. And still I felt no fear, no raising of the hairs on the back of the neck, no prickling of the thumbs.

The key slid into the new lock as easily as a hot knife into butter.

No fear; but a hesitation, a holding of the spiritual breath.

If I had found some traces of his heart in a file marked: *Personal*, perhaps, here, in his subterranean privacy, I might find a little of his soul. It was the consciousness of the possibility of such a discovery, of its possible strangeness, that kept me for a moment motionless, before, in the foolhardiness of my already subtly tainted innocence, I turned the key and the door creaked slowly back.

"There is a striking resemblance between the act of love and the ministrations of a torturer," opined my husband's favourite poet;[2] I had learned something of the nature of that similarity on my marriage bed. And now my taper showed me the outlines of a rack. There was also a great wheel, like the ones I had seen in woodcuts of the martyrdoms of the saints, in my old nurse's little store of holy books. And—just one glimpse of it before my little flame caved in and I was left in absolute darkness—a metal figure, hinged at the side, which I knew to be spiked on the inside and to have the name: the Iron Maiden.

Absolute darkness. And, about me, the instruments of mutilation.

Until that moment, this spoiled child did not know she had inherited nerves and a will from the mother who had defied the yellow outlaws of Indo-China. My mother's spirit drove me on, into that dreadful place, in a cold ecstasy to know the very worst. I fumbled for the matches in my pocket; what a dim, lugubrious light they gave! And yet, enough, oh, more than enough, to see a room designed for desecration and some dark night of unimaginable lovers whose embraces were annihilation.

The walls of this stark torture chamber were the naked rock; they gleamed as if they were sweating with fright. At the four corners of the room were funerary urns, of great antiquity, Etruscan, perhaps, and, on three-legged ebony stands, the bowls of incense he had left burning which filled the room with a sacerdotal[3] reek. Wheel, rack, and Iron Maiden were, I saw, displayed as grandly as if they were items of statuary and I was almost consoled, then, and almost persuaded myself that I might have stumbled only upon a little museum of his perversity, that he had installed these monstrous

---

[1] *Rape ... Sabines* Legendary event in early Roman history, in which young Roman men abducted and raped large numbers of women from neighboring Sabine in order to try to quicken the growth of the population of early Rome. The scene has been widely depicted in works of art, including paintings by Rubens, Poussin, and David.

[2] *There is ... poet* Unidentified.

[3] *sacerdotal* Belonging to the priesthood.

items here only for contemplation.

Yet at the centre of the room lay a catafalque,[1] a doomed, ominous bier of Renaissance workmanship, surrounded by long white candles and, at its foot, an armful of the same lilies with which he had filled my bedroom, stowed in a four-foot-high jar glazed with a sombre Chinese red. I scarcely dared examine this catafalque and its occupant more closely; yet I knew I must.

Each time I struck a match to light those candles round her bed, it seemed a garment of that innocence of mine for which he had lusted fell away from me.

The opera singer lay, quite naked, under a thin sheet of very rare and precious linen, such as the princes of Italy used to shroud those whom they had poisoned. I touched her, very gently, on the white breast; she was cool, he had embalmed her. On her throat I could see the blue imprint of his strangler's fingers. The cool, sad flame of the candles flickered on her white, closed eyelids. The worst thing was, the dead lips smiled.

Beyond the catafalque, in the middle of the shadows, a white, nacreous glimmer; as my eyes accustomed themselves to the gathering darkness, I at last—oh, horrors!—made out a skull; yes, a skull, so utterly denuded, now, of flesh, that it scarcely seemed possible the stark bone had once been richly upholstered with life. And this skull was strung up by a system of unseen cords, so that it appeared to hang, disembodied, in the still, heavy air, and it had been crowned with a wreath of white roses, and a veil of lace, the final image of his bride.

Yet the skull was still so beautiful, had shaped with its sheer planes so imperiously the face that had once existed above it, that I recognized her the moment I saw her; face of the evening star walking on the rim of night. One false step, oh, my poor, dear girl, next in the fated sisterhood of his wives; one false step and into the abyss of the dark you stumbled.

And where was she, the latest dead, the Romanian countess who might have thought her blood would survive his depredations? I knew she must be here, in the place that had wound me through the castle towards it on a spool of inexorability. But, at first, I could see no sign of her. Then, for some reason—perhaps some change of atmosphere wrought by my presence—the metal shell of the Iron Maiden emitted a ghostly twang; my feverish imagination might have guessed its occupant was trying to clamber out, though, even in the midst of my rising hysteria, I knew she must be dead to find a home there.

With trembling fingers, I prised open the front of the upright coffin, with its sculpted face caught in a rictus[2] of pain. Then, overcome, I dropped the key I still held in my other hand. It dropped into the forming pool of her blood.

She was pierced, not by one but by a hundred spikes, this child of the land of the vampires who seemed so newly dead, so full of blood ... oh God! how recently had he become a widower? How long had he kept her in this obscene cell? Had it been all the time he had courted me, in the clear light of Paris?

I closed the lid of her coffin very gently and burst into a tumult of sobbing that contained both pity for his other victims and also a dreadful anguish to know I, too, was one of them.

The candles flared, as if in a draught from a door to elsewhere. The light caught the fire opal on my hand so that it flashed, once, with a baleful light, as if to tell me the eye of God—his eye—was upon me. My first thought, when I saw the ring for which I had sold myself to this fate, was, how to escape it.

I retained sufficient presence of mind to snuff out the candles round the bier with my fingers, to gather up my taper, to look around, although shuddering, to ensure I had left behind me no traces of my visit.

I retrieved the key from the pool of blood, wrapped it in my handkerchief to keep my hands clean, and fled the room, slamming the door behind me. It crashed to with a juddering reverberation, like the door of hell.

I could not take refuge in my bedroom, for that retained the memory of his presence trapped in the fathomless silvering of his mirrors. My music room seemed the safest place, although I looked at the picture of Saint Cecilia with a faint dread; what had been the nature of her martyrdom? My mind was in a tumult; schemes for flight jostled with one another ... as soon as the tide receded from the causeway, I would make for the

---

[1] *catafalque* Decorative platform for a coffin.

[2] *rictus* Gape.

mainland—on foot, running, stumbling; I did not trust that leather-clad chauffeur, nor the well-behaved housekeeper, and I dared not take any of the pale, ghostly maids into my confidence, either, since they were his creatures, all. Once at the village, I would fling myself directly on the mercy of the gendarmerie.[1]

But—could I trust them, either? His forefathers had ruled this coast for eight centuries, from this castle whose moat was the Atlantic. Might not the police, the advocates, even the judge, all be in his service, turning a common blind eye to his vices since he was milord whose word must be obeyed? Who, on this distant coast, would believe the white-faced girl from Paris who came running to them with a shuddering tale of blood, of fear, of the ogre murmuring in the shadows? Or, rather, they would immediately know it to be true. But were all honour-bound to let me carry it no further.

Assistance. My mother. I ran to the telephone; and the line, of course, was dead.

Dead as his wives.

A thick darkness, unlit by any star, still glazed the windows. Every lamp in my room burned, to keep the dark outside, yet it seemed still to encroach on me, to be present beside me but as if masked by my lights, the night like a permeable substance that could seep into my skin. I looked at the precious little clock made from hypocritically innocent flowers long ago, in Dresden; the hands had scarcely moved one single hour forward from when I first descended to that private slaughter-house of his. Time was his servant, too; it would trap me, here, in a night that would last until he came back to me, like a black sun on a hopeless morning.

And yet the time might still be my friend; at that hour, that very hour, he set sail for New York.

To know that, in a few moments, my husband would have left France calmed my agitation a little. My reason told me I had nothing to fear; the tide that would take him away to the New World would let me out of the imprisonment of the castle. Surely I could easily evade the servants. Anybody can buy a ticket at a railway station. Yet I was still filled with unease. I opened the lid of the piano; perhaps I thought my own particular magic might help me, now, that I could create a penta-

cle[2] out of music that would keep me from harm for, if my music had first ensnared him, then might it not also give me the power to free myself from him?

Mechanically, I began to play but my fingers were stiff and shaking. At first, I could manage nothing better than the exercises of Czerny but simply the act of playing soothed me and, for solace, for the sake of the harmonious rationality of its sublime mathematics, I searched among his scores until I found *The Well-Tempered Clavier*. I set myself the therapeutic task of playing all Bach's equations, every one, and, I told myself, if I played them all through without a single mistake—then the morning would find me once more a virgin.

Crash of a dropped stick.

His silver-headed cane! What else? Sly, cunning, he had returned; he was waiting for me outside the door!

I rose to my feet; fear gave me strength. I flung back my head defiantly.

"Come in!" My voice astonished me by its firmness, its clarity.

The door slowly, nervously opened and I saw, not the massive, irredeemable bulk of my husband but the slight, stooping figure of the piano-tuner, and he looked far more terrified of me than my mother's daughter would have been of the Devil himself. In the torture chamber, it seemed to me that I would never laugh again; now, helplessly, laugh I did, with relief, and, after a moment's hesitation, the boy's face softened and he smiled a little, almost in shame. Though they were blind, his eyes were singularly sweet.

"Forgive me," said Jean-Yves. "I know I've given you grounds for dismissing me, that I should be crouching outside your door at midnight ... but I heard you walking about, up and down—I sleep in a room at the foot of the west tower—and some intuition told me you could not sleep and might, perhaps, pass the insomniac hours at your piano. And I could not resist that. Besides, I stumbled over these—"

And he displayed the ring of keys I'd dropped outside my husband's office door, the ring from which one key was missing. I took them from him, looked round for a place to stow them, fixed on the piano stool as if to hide them would protect me. Still he stood

---

smiling at me. How hard it was to make everyday conversation.

"It's perfect," I said. "The piano. Perfectly in tune."

But he was full of the loquacity of embarrassment, as though I would only forgive him for his impudence if he explained the cause of it thoroughly.

"When I heard you play this afternoon, I thought I'd never heard such a touch. Such technique. A treat for me, to hear a virtuoso! So I crept up to your door now, humbly as a little dog might, madame, and put my ear to the keyhole and listened, and listened—until my stick fell to the floor through a momentary clumsiness of mine, and I was discovered."

He had the most touchingly ingenuous smile.

"Perfectly in tune," I repeated. To my surprise, now I had said it, I found I could not say anything else. I could only repeat: "In tune … perfect … in tune," over and over again. I saw a dawning surprise in his face. My head throbbed. To see him, in his lovely, blind humanity, seemed to hurt me very piercingly, somewhere inside my breast; his figure blurred, the room swayed about me. After the dreadful revelation of that bloody chamber, it was his tender look that made me faint.

When I recovered consciousness, I found I was lying in the piano-tuner's arms and he was tucking the satin cushion from the piano-stool under my head.

"You are in some great distress," he said. "No bride should suffer so much, so early in her marriage."

His speech had the rhythms of the countryside, the rhythms of the tides.

"Any bride brought to this castle should come ready dressed in mourning, should bring a priest and a coffin with her," I said.

"What's this?"

It was too late to keep silent; and if he, too, were one of my husband's creatures, then at least he had been kind to me. So I told him everything, the keys, the interdiction, my disobedience, the room, the rack, the skull, the corpses, the blood.

"I can scarcely believe it," he said, wondering. "That man … so rich; so well-born."

"Here's proof," I said and tumbled the fatal key out of my handkerchief on to the silken rug.

"Oh God," he said. "I can smell the blood."

He took my hand; he pressed his arms about me.

Although he was scarcely more than a boy, I felt a great strength flow into me from his touch.

"We whisper all manner of strange tales up and down the coast," he said. "There was a Marquis, once, who used to hunt young girls on the mainland; he hunted them with dogs, as though they were foxes. My grandfather had it from his grandfather, how the Marquis pulled a head out of his saddle bag and showed it to the blacksmith while the man was shoeing his horse. 'A fine specimen of the genus, brunette, eh, Guillaume?' And it was the head of the blacksmith's wife."

But, in these more democratic times, my husband must travel as far as Paris to do his hunting in the salons. Jean-Yves knew the moment I shuddered.

"Oh, madame! I thought all these were old wives' tales, chattering of fools, spooks to scare bad children into good behaviour! Yet how could you know, a stranger, that the old name for this place is the Castle of Murder?"

How could I know, indeed? Except that, in my heart, I'd always known its lord would be the death of me.

"Hark!" said my friend suddenly. "The sea has changed key; it must be near morning, the tide is going down."

He helped me up. I looked from the window, towards the mainland, along the causeway where the stones gleamed wetly in the thin light of the end of the night and, with an almost unimaginable horror, a horror the intensity of which I cannot transmit to you, I saw, in the distance, still far away yet drawing moment by moment inexorably nearer, the twin headlamps of his great black car, gouging tunnels through the shifting mist.

My husband had indeed returned; this time, it was no fancy.

"The key!" said Jean-Yves. "It must go back on the ring, with the others. As though nothing had happened."

But the key was still caked with wet blood and I ran to my bathroom and held it under the hot tap. Crimson water swirled down the basin but, as if the key itself were hurt, the bloody token stuck. The turquoise eyes of the dolphin taps winked at me derisively; they knew my husband had been too clever for me! I scrubbed the stain with my nail brush but still it would not budge. I thought how the car would be rolling silently towards the closed courtyard gate; the more I scrubbed the key, the more vivid grew the stain.

The bell in the gatehouse would jangle. The porter's drowsy son would push back the patchwork quilt, yawning, pull the shirt over his head, thrust his feet into his sabots ... slowly, slowly; open the door for your master as slowly as you can ...

And still the bloodstain mocked the fresh water that spilled from the mouth of the leering dolphin.

"You have no more time," said Jean-Yves. "He is here. I know it. I must stay with you."

"You shall not!" I said. "Go back to your room, now. Please."

He hesitated. I put an edge of steel in my voice, for I knew I must meet my lord alone.

"Leave me!"

As soon as he had gone, I dealt with the keys and went to my bedroom. The causeway was empty; Jean-Yves was correct, my husband had already entered the castle. I pulled the curtains close, stripped off my clothes and pulled the bedcurtains round me as a pungent aroma of Russian leather assured me my husband was once again beside me.

"Dearest!"

With the most treacherous, lascivious tenderness, he kissed my eyes, and, mimicking the new bride newly wakened, I flung my arms around him, for on my seeming acquiescence depended my salvation.

"Da Silva of Rio outwitted me," he said wryly. "My New York agent telegraphed Le Havre and saved me a wasted journey. So we may resume our interrupted pleasures, my love."

I did not believe one word of it. I knew I had behaved exactly according to his desires; had he not bought me so that I should do so? I had been tricked into my own betrayal to that illimitable darkness whose source I had been compelled to seek in his absence and, now that I had met that shadowed reality of his that came to life only in the presence of its own atrocities, I must pay the price of my new knowledge. The secret of

Pandora's box;[1] but he had given me the box, himself, knowing I must learn the secret. I had played a game in which every move was governed by a destiny as oppressive and omnipotent as himself, since that destiny was himself; and I had lost. Lost at that charade of innocence and vice in which he had engaged me. Lost, as the victim loses to the executioner.

His hand brushed my breast, beneath the sheet. I strained my nerves yet could not help but flinch from the intimate touch, for it made me think of the piercing embrace of the Iron Maiden and of his lost lovers in the vault. When he saw my reluctance, his eyes veiled over and yet his appetite did not diminish. His tongue ran over red lips already wet. Silent, mysterious, he moved away from me to draw off his jacket. He took the gold watch from his waistcoat and laid it on the dressing table, like a good bourgeois; scooped out his rattling loose change and now—oh God!—makes a great play of patting his pockets officiously, puzzled lips pursed, searching for something that has been mislaid. Then turns to me with a ghastly, a triumphant smile.

"But of course! I gave the keys to you!"

"Your keys? Why, of course. Here, they're under the pillow; wait a moment—what—Ah! No ... now, where can I have left them? I was whiling away the evening without you at the piano, I remember. Of course! The music room!"

Brusquely he flung my négligé of antique lace on the bed.

"Go and get them."

"Now? This moment? Can't it wait until morning, my darling?"

I forced myself to be seductive. I saw myself, pale, pliant as a plant that begs to be trampled underfoot, a dozen vulnerable, appealing girls reflected in as many mirrors, and I saw how he almost failed to resist me. If he had come to me in bed, I would have strangled him, then.

But he half-snarled: "No. It won't wait. Now."

The unearthly light of dawn filled the room; had only one previous dawn broken upon me in that vile place? And there was nothing for it but to go and fetch the keys from the music stool and pray he would not

[1] *Pandora's box*   In Greek myth, a box that contained all human evils, said to have been opened by a girl named Pandora.

examine them too closely, pray to God his eyes would fail him, that he might be struck blind.

When I came back into the bedroom carrying the bunch of keys that jangled at every step like a curious musical instrument, he was sitting on the bed in his immaculate shirtsleeves, his head sunk in his hands.

And it seemed to me he was in despair.

Strange. In spite of my fear of him, that made me whiter than my wrap, I felt there emanate from him, at that moment, a stench of absolute despair, rank and ghastly, as if the lilies that surrounded him had all at once begun to fester, or the Russian leather of his scent were reverting to the elements of flayed hide and excrement of which it was composed. The chthonic[1] gravity of his presence exerted a tremendous pressure on the room, so that the blood pounded in my ears as if we had been precipitated to the bottom of the sea, beneath the waves that pounded against the shore.

I held my life in my hands amongst those keys and, in a moment, would place it between his well-manicured fingers. The evidence of that bloody chamber had showed me I could expect no mercy. Yet, when he raised his head and stared at me with his blind, shuttered eyes as though he did not recognize me, I felt a terrified pity for him, for this man who lived in such strange, secret places that, if I loved him enough to follow him, I should have to die.

The atrocious loneliness of that monster!

The monocle had fallen from his face. His curling mane was disordered, as if he had run his hands through it in his distraction. I saw how he had lost his impassivity and was now filled with suppressed excitement. The hand he stretched out for those counters in his game of love and death shook a little; the face that turned towards me contained a sombre delirium that seemed to me compounded of a ghastly, yes, shame but also of a terrible, guilty joy as he slowly ascertained how I had sinned.

That tell-tale stain had resolved itself into a mark the shape and brilliance of the heart on a playing card. He disengaged the key from the ring and looked at it for a while, solitary, brooding.

"It is the key that leads to the kingdom of the unimaginable," he said. His voice was low and had in it

the timbre of certain great cathedral organs that seem, when they are played, to be conversing with God.

I could not restrain a sob.

"Oh, my love, my little love who brought me a white gift of music," he said, almost as if grieving. "My little love, you'll never know how much I hate daylight!" Then he sharply ordered: "Kneel!"

I knelt before him and he pressed the key lightly to my forehead, held it there for a moment. I felt a faint tingling of the skin and, when I involuntarily glanced at myself in the mirror, I saw the heart-shaped stain had transferred itself to my forehead, to the space between the eyebrows, like the caste mark of a brahmin woman. Or the mark of Cain. And now the key gleamed as freshly as if it had just been cut. He clipped it back on the ring, emitting that same, heavy sigh as he had done when I said that I would marry him.

"My virgin of the arpeggios, prepare yourself for martyrdom."

"What form shall it take?" I said.

"Decapitation," he whispered, almost voluptuously. "Go and bathe yourself; put on that white dress you wore to hear *Tristan* and the necklace that prefigures your end. And I shall take myself off to the armoury, my dear, to sharpen my great-grandfather's ceremonial sword."

"The servants?"

"We shall have absolute privacy for our last rites; I have already dismissed them. If you look out of the window you can see them going to the mainland."

It was now the full, pale light of morning; the weather was grey, indeterminate, the sea had an oily, sinister look, a gloomy day on which to die. Along the causeway I could see trouping every maid and scullion, every pot-boy and pan-scourer, valet, laundress and vassal who worked in that great house, most on foot, a few on bicycles. The faceless housekeeper trudged along with a great basket in which, I guessed, she'd stowed as much as she could ransack from the larder. The Marquis must have given the chauffeur leave to borrow the motor for the day, for it went last of all, at a stately pace, as though the procession were a cortège and the car already bore my coffin to the mainland for burial.

But I knew no good Breton earth would cover me, like a last, faithful lover; I had another fate.

---

[1] *chthonic* Dwelling below the earth's surface.

"I have given them all a day's holiday, to celebrate our wedding," he said. And smiled.

However hard I stared at the receding company, I could see no sign of Jean-Yves, our latest servant, hired but the preceding morning.

"Go, now. Bathe yourself; dress yourself. The lustratory ritual and the ceremonial robing; after that, the sacrifice. Wait in the music room until I telephone for you. No, my dear!" And he smiled, as I started, recalling the line was dead. "One may call inside the castle just as much as one pleases; but, outside—never."

I scrubbed my forehead with the nail brush as I had scrubbed the key but this red mark would not go away, either, no matter what I did, and I knew I should wear it until I died, though that would not be long. Then I went to my dressing room and put on that white muslin shift, costume of a victim of an auto-da-fe,[1] he had bought me to listen to the Liebestod in. Twelve young women combed out twelve listless sheaves of brown hair in the mirrors; soon, there would be none. The mass of lilies that surrounded me exhaled, now, the odour of their withering. They looked like the trumpets of the angels of death.

On the dressing table, coiled like a snake about to strike, lay the ruby choker.

Already almost lifeless, cold at heart, I descended the spiral staircase to the music room but there I found I had not been abandoned.

"I can be of some comfort to you," the boy said. "Though not much use."

We pushed the piano stool in front of the open window so that, for as long as I could, I would be able to smell the ancient, reconciling smell of the sea that, in time, will cleanse everything, scour the old bones white, wash away all the stains. The last little chambermaid had trotted along the causeway long ago and now the tide, fated as I, came tumbling in, the crisp wavelets splashing on the old stones.

"You do not deserve this," he said.

"Who can say what I deserve or no?" I said. "I've done nothing; but that may be sufficient reason for condemning me."

"You disobeyed him," he said. "That is sufficient reason for him to punish you."

"I only did what he knew I would."

"Like Eve," he said.

The telephone rang a shrill imperative. Let it ring. But my lover lifted me up and set me on my feet; I knew I must answer it. The receiver felt heavy as earth.

"The courtyard. Immediately."

My lover kissed me, he took my hand. He would come with me if I would lead him. Courage. When I thought of courage, I thought of my mother. Then I saw a muscle in my lover's face quiver.

"Hoofbeats!" he said.

I cast one last, desperate glance from the window and, like a miracle, I saw a horse and rider galloping at a vertiginous speed along the causeway, though the waves crashed, now, high as the horse's fetlocks. A rider, her black skirts tucked up around her waist so she could ride hard and fast, a crazy, magnificent horsewoman in widow's weeds.

As the telephone rang again.

"Am I to wait all morning?"

Every moment, my mother drew nearer.

"She will be too late," Jean-Yves said and yet he could not restrain a note of hope that, though it must be so, yet it might not be so.

The third, intransigent call.

"Shall I come up to heaven to fetch you down, Saint Cecilia? You wicked woman, do you wish me to compound my crimes by desecrating the marriage bed?"

So I must go to the courtyard where my husband waited in his London-tailored trousers and the shirt from Turnbull and Asser,[2] beside the mounting block, with, in his hand, the sword which his great-grandfather had presented to the little corporal, in token of surrender to the Republic, before he shot himself. The heavy sword, unsheathed, grey as that November morning, sharp as childbirth, mortal.

When my husband saw my companion, he observed: "Let the blind lead the blind, eh? But does even a youth as besotted as you are think she was truly blind to her own desires when she took my ring? Give it me back, whore."

The fires in the opal had all died down. I gladly slipped it from my finger and, even in that dolorous place, my heart was lighter for the lack of it. My hus-

---

[1] *auto-da-fe* Public burning of heretics by the Spanish Inquisition.

[2] *Turnbull and Asser* Exclusive British tailor.

band took it lovingly and lodged it on the tip of his little finger; it would go no further.

"It will serve me for a dozen more fiancées," he said. "To the block, woman. No—leave the boy; I shall deal with him later, utilizing a less exalted instrument than the one with which I do my wife the honour of her immolation, for do not fear that in death you will be divided."

Slowly, slowly, one foot before the other, I crossed the cobbles. The longer I dawdled over my execution, the more time it gave the avenging angel to descend …

"Don't loiter, girl! Do you think I shall lose appetite for the meal if you are so long about serving it? No; I shall grow hungrier, more ravenous with each moment, more cruel … Run to me, run! I have a place prepared for your exquisite corpse in my display of flesh!"

He raised the sword and cut bright segments from the air with it, but still I lingered although my hopes, so recently raised, now began to flag. If she is not here by now, her horse must have stumbled on the causeway, have plunged into the sea … One thing only made me glad; that my lover would not see me die.

My husband laid my branded forehead on the stone and, as he had done once before, twisted my hair into a rope and drew it away from my neck.

"Such a pretty neck," he said with what seemed to be a genuine, retrospective tenderness. "A neck like the stem of a young plant."

I felt the silken bristle of his beard and the wet touch of his lips as he kissed my nape. And, once again, of my apparel I must retain only my gems; the sharp blade ripped my dress in two and it fell from me. A little green moss, growing in the crevices of the mounting block, would be the last thing I should see in all the world.

The whizz of that heavy sword.

And—a great battering and pounding at the gate, the jangling of the bell, the frenzied neighing of a horse! The unholy silence of the place shattered in an instant. The blade did *not* descend, the necklace did *not* sever, my head did *not* roll. For, for an instant, the beast wavered in his stroke, a sufficient split second of astonished indecision to let me spring upright and dart to the assistance of my lover as he struggled sightlessly with the great bolts that kept her out.

The Marquis stood transfixed, utterly dazed, at a loss. It must have been as if he had been watching his beloved *Tristan* for the twelfth, the thirteenth time and Tristan stirred, then leapt from his bier in the last act, announced in a jaunty aria interposed from Verdi[1] that bygones were bygones, crying over spilt milk did nobody any good and, as for himself, he proposed to live happily ever after. The puppet master, open-mouthed, wide-eyed, impotent at the last, saw his dolls break free of their strings, abandon the rituals he had ordained for them since time began and start to live for themselves; the king, aghast, witnesses the revolt of his pawns.

You never saw such a wild thing as my mother, her hat seized by the winds and blown out to sea so that her hair was her white mane, her black lisle legs exposed to the thigh, her skirts tucked round her waist, one hand on the reins of the rearing horse while the other clasped my father's service revolver and, behind her, the breakers of the savage, indifferent sea, like the witnesses of a furious justice. And my husband stood stock-still, as if she had been Medusa,[2] the sword still raised over his head as in those clockwork tableaux of Bluebeard that you see in glass cases at fairs.

And then it was as though a curious child pushed his centime into the slot and set all in motion. The heavy, bearded figure roared out aloud, braying with fury, and, wielding the honourable sword as if it were a matter of death or glory, charged us, all three.

On her eighteenth birthday, my mother had disposed of a man-eating tiger that had ravaged the villages in the hills north of Hanoi. Now, without a moment's hesitation, she raised my father's gun, took aim and put a single, irreproachable bullet through my husband's head.

We lead a quiet life, the three of us. I inherited, of course, enormous wealth but we have given most of it away to various charities. The castle is now a school for the blind, though I pray that the children who live there are not haunted by any sad ghosts looking for, crying for, the husband who will never return to the bloody chamber, the contents of which are buried or burned,

---

[1] *Verdi* Italian opera composer Guiseppe Verdi (1813–1901).

[2] *Medusa* Powerful female from Greek myth, a look at whose face would turn one to stone.

the door sealed.

I felt I had a right to retain sufficient funds to start a little music school here, on the outskirts of Paris, and we do well enough. Sometimes we can even afford to go to the Opera, though never to sit in a box, of course. We know we are the source of many whisperings and much gossip but the three of us know the truth of it and mere chatter can never harm us. I can only bless the—what shall I call it?—the *maternal telepathy* that sent my mother running headlong from the telephone to the station after I had called her, that night. I never heard you cry before, she said, by way of explanation. Not when you were happy. And who ever cried because of gold bath taps?

The night train, the one I had taken; she lay in her berth, sleepless as I had been. When she could not find a taxi at that lonely halt, she borrowed old Dobbin from a bemused farmer, for some internal urgency told her

that she must reach me before the incoming tide sealed me away from her for ever. My poor old nurse, left scandalized at home—what? interrupt milord on his honeymoon?—she died soon after. She had taken so much secret pleasure in the fact that her little girl had become a marquise; and now here I was, scarcely a penny the richer, widowed at seventeen in the most dubious circumstances and busily engaged in setting up house with a piano-tuner. Poor thing, she passed away in a sorry state of disillusion! But I do believe my mother loves him as much as I do.

No paint nor powder, no matter how thick or white, can mask that red mark on my forehead; I am glad he cannot see it—not for fear of his revulsion, since I know he sees me clearly with his heart—but, because it spares my shame.

—1979

JOHN CLEESE AND GRAHAM CHAPMAN
1939 – , and 1941 – 1989

Graham Chapman and John Cleese were the founders of the influential British comedy troupe Monty Python's Flying Circus. Their work with fellow Pythons Michael Palin (1943–), Eric Idle (1943–), Terry Jones (1942–), and Terry Gilliam (1940–) attracted huge followings not just in Britain but also throughout the English-speaking world. In 2000, the British Film Institute named their television series, *Monty Python's Flying Circus*, number five in their listing of the top 100 greatest British television programs.

John Cleese was born on 27 October 1939 in Weston-Super-Mare, Somerset, England. He studied at Clifton College, Bristol, and then at Cambridge University's Downing College, where he completed a degree in law. He began working in comedy as part of the Cambridge Footlights Revue, an amateur theatrical club run by students. It was here that he met Graham Chapman.

Chapman was born in Leicester on 8 January 1941. As a schoolboy, he participated in school productions, including plays by Shakespeare and Gilbert and Sullivan, and revue shows. In 1959, he was admitted to Emmanuel College at Cambridge University, where he studied medicine. He eventually qualified as a doctor at St. Bartholomew's Hospital Medical College, London.

Like Cleese, Chapman joined the Cambridge Footlights Revue and toured to New Zealand and New York. Upon returning in 1965, Cleese and Chapman wrote and performed in various British radio and television comedy series, including *The Dick Emery Show* (1965–84), *Doctor in the House* (1969–70), *At Last the 1948 Show* (1967), and *I'm Sorry, I'll Read That Again* (1964–72). When the two were hired to write for *The Frost Report* (1966–67), a BBC comedy/variety series, they were introduced to Eric Idle, Terry Jones, and Michael Palin. It was here that the future colleagues developed their trademark comedy style.

In 1969, Chapman and Cleese were offered their own television series. Their partnership was not an easy one; Chapman had developed a drinking problem, and Cleese found himself bearing most of the burden of the show. As a result, Cleese invited Palin, Idle, Jones, and Terry Gilliam (an American animator he had met while in New York) to work on the show, and the Monty Python troupe was born. Their television show, *Monty Python's Flying Circus*, ran between 1969 and 1974. The show's humor was quirky and irreverent, featuring cartoonish authority figures, strange satirical takes on the idiosyncrasies of British life, and frequent references to philosophers, literary figures, and famous works of art.

The troupe produced 45 episodes of *Monty Python's Flying Circus*, in four series. They also made five films: *And Now for Something Completely Different* (1971), a collection of re-filmed sketches from the television show; *Monty Python and the Holy Grail* (1974), a spoof of the Arthurian legends; *Monty Python's Life of Brian* (1979), a controversial send-up of organized religion and epic Bible movies; *Monty Python Live at the Hollywood Bowl* (1982), a live film of a public performance; and *Monty Python's The Meaning of Life* (1983), a darkly comic philosophical meditation.

Cleese left the show after its third series, unhappy with the strain of working with the alcoholic Chapman. He went on to co-write and star as Basil Fawlty in the very popular television series *Fawlty Towers* and to continue making films, most notably *A Fish Called Wanda* (1988), one of the most financially successful British films in history. Graham Chapman's career faltered after Monty Python. He gave up drinking in 1977, but his only solo film project, *Yellowbeard* (1983), suffered both critically and commercially. In late 1988, Chapman was diagnosed with throat cancer, which quickly spread to his spine. He died on 4 October 1989.

⌘ ⌘ ⌘

from *Monty Python's Flying Circus*

DEAD PARROT SKETCH[1]

THE CAST:
PRALINE: John Cleese
SHOPKEEPER: Michael Palin
PORTER: Terry Jones

PRALINE.   Hello, I wish to register a complaint. . . . Hello? Miss?

SHOPKEEPER.   What do you mean, miss?

PRALINE.   Oh, I'm sorry, I have a cold. I wish to make a
5   complaint.

SHOPKEEPER.   Sorry, we're closing for lunch.

PRALINE.   Never mind that my lad, I wish to complain about a parrot what I purchased not half an hour ago from this very boutique.

10   SHOPKEEPER.   Oh yes, the Norwegian Blue. What's wrong with it?

PRALINE.   I'll tell you what's wrong with it. It's dead, that's what's wrong with it.

SHOPKEEPER.   No, no it's resting look!

15   PRALINE.   Look my lad, I know a dead parrot when I see one and I'm looking at one right now.

SHOPKEEPER.   No, no sir, it's not dead. It's resting.

PRALINE.   Resting?

SHOPKEEPER.   Yeah, remarkable bird the Norwegian
20   Blue, beautiful plumage, innit?[2]

PRALINE.   The plumage don't enter into it—it's stone dead.

SHOPKEEPER.   No, no—it's just resting.

PRALINE.   All right then, if it's resting I'll wake it up.
25   (*Shouts into cage.*) Hello Polly! I've got a nice cuttlefish for you when you wake up, Polly Parrot!

SHOPKEEPER.   (*Jogging cage.*) There it moved.

PRALINE.   No he didn't. That was you pushing the cage.

SHOPKEEPER.   I did not.

30   PRALINE.   Yes, you did. (*Takes parrot out of cage, shouts.*)

Hello Polly, Polly. (*Bangs it against the counter.*) Polly Parrot, wake up. Polly. (*Throws it in the air and it lands on the floor.*) Now that's what I call a dead parrot.

SHOPKEEPER.   No, no it's stunned.

35   PRALINE.   Look my lad, I've had just about enough of this. That parrot is definitely deceased. And when I bought it not half an hour ago, you assured me that its lack of movement was due to it being tired and shagged out after a long squawk.

40   SHOPKEEPER.   It's probably pining for the fjords.

PRALINE.   Pining for the fjords, what kind of talk is that? Look, why did it fall flat on its back the moment I got it home?

SHOPKEEPER.   The Norwegian Blue prefers kipping[3] on
45   its back. Beautiful bird, lovely plumage.

PRALINE.   Look, I took the liberty of examining the parrot, and I discovered that the only reason that it had been sitting on its perch in the first place was that it had been nailed there.

50   SHOPKEEPER.   Well of course it was nailed there. Otherwise it would muscle up to those bars and voom.

PRALINE.   Look matey (*Picks up parrot.*) this parrot wouldn't go voom if I put four thousand volts through it. It's bleeding demised.

55   SHOPKEEPER.   It's not. It's pining.

PRALINE.   It's not pining, it's passed on. This parrot is no more. It has ceased to be. It's expired and gone to meet its maker. This is a late parrot. It's a stiff. Bereft of life, it rests in peace. If you hadn't nailed it to the perch, it
60   would be pushing up the daisies. It's rung down the curtain and joined the choir invisible. This is an ex-parrot.

SHOPKEEPER.   Well I'd better replace it then.

PRALINE.   (*To camera.*) If you want to get anything done
65   in this country you've got to complain till you're blue in the mouth.

SHOPKEEPER.   Sorry guv, we're right outa parrots.

PRALINE.   I see. I see. I get the picture.

SHOPKEEPER.   I've got a slug.

70   PRALINE.   Does it talk?

SHOPKEEPER.   Not really, no.

---

[1]   DEAD PARROT SKETCH From *Monty Python's Flying Circus*, Episode 9.

[2]   *innit* I.e., isn't it.

[3]   *kipping* Sleeping.

PRALINE. Well, it's scarcely a replacement, then is it?

SHOPKEEPER. Listen, I'll tell you what, (*Handing over a card.*) tell you what, if you go to my brother's pet shop in Bolton[1] he'll replace your parrot for you.

PRALINE. Bolton eh?

SHOPKEEPER. Yeah.

PRALINE. All right.

(*He leaves, holding the parrot.*
Caption: "A similar pet shop in Bolton, Lancs"[2]
Close-up of sign on door reading: "Similar Pet Shops Ltd."
Pull back from sign to see same pet shop. Shopkeeper now has a moustache. Praline walks into the shop. He looks around with interest, noticing the empty parrot cage on the floor.)

PRALINE. Er, excuse me. This is Bolton, is it?

SHOPKEEPER. No, no it's, er, Ipswich.[3]

PRALINE. (*To camera.*) That's Inter-City Rail for you.

(*Leaves.*)
(*Man in porter's outfit standing at complaints desk for railways. Praline approaches.*)

PRALINE. I wish to make a complaint.

PORTER. I don't have to do this, you know.

PRALINE. I beg your pardon?

PORTER. I'm a qualified brain surgeon. I only do this because I like being my own boss.

PRALINE. Er, excuse me, this is irrelevant, isn't it?

PORTER. Oh yeah, it's not easy to pad these out to thirty minutes.

PRALINE. Well I wish to make a complaint. I got on to the Bolton train and found myself deposited here in Ipswich.

PORTER. No, this is Bolton.

PRALINE. (*To camera.*) The pet shop owner's brother was lying.

PORTER. Well you can't blame British Rail for that.

PRALINE. If this is Bolton, I shall return to the pet shop.

(*Caption: "A Little Later Ltd"*
Praline walks into the shop again.)

PRALINE. I understand this *is* Bolton.

SHOPKEEPER. Yes.

PRALINE. Well, you told me it was Ipswich.

SHOPKEEPER. It was a pun.

PRALINE. A pun?

SHOPKEEPER. No, no, not a pun, no. What's the other thing which reads the same backwards as forwards?

PRALINE. A palindrome?

SHOPKEEPER. Yes, yes.

PRALINE. It's not a palindrome. The palindrome of Bolton would be Notlob. It don't work.

SHOPKEEPER. Look, what do you want?

PRALINE. No, I'm sorry, I'm not prepared to pursue my line of enquiry any further as I think this is getting too silly.

—1969

PET CONVERSION[4]

THE CAST:

MAN: John Cleese
SHOPKEEPER: Michael Palin
HARRY: Graham Chapman

(*Superimposed caption: A Pet Shop Somewhere Near Melton Mowbray.[5]*)

MAN. Good morning, I'd like to buy a cat.

SHOPKEEPER. Certainly sir. I've got a lovely terrier. (*Indicates a box on the counter.*)

MAN. (*Glancing in box.*) No, I want a cat really.

SHOPKEEPER. (*Taking box off counter and then putting it back on counter as if it is a different box.*) Oh yeah, how about that?

MAN. (*Looking in box.*) No, that's the terrier.

SHOPKEEPER. Well, it's as near as dammit.

MAN. Well what do you mean? I want a cat.

SHOPKEEPER. Listen, tell you what. I'll file its legs down a bit, take its snout out, stick a few wires through its

---

[1] *Bolton* Town near Manchester in northern England.

[2] *Lancs* Lancashire, a county in the north of England.

[3] *Ipswich* County town in East Anglia, in the east of England, 390 kilometers (243 miles) from Bolton.

[4] *PET CONVERSION* Featured in *Monty Python's Flying Circus*, Episode 10.

[5] *Melton Mowbray* Town in county Leicestershire.

cheeks. There you are, a lovely pussy cat.

MAN. It's not a proper cat.

SHOPKEEPER. What do you mean?

MAN. Well it wouldn't miaow.

SHOPKEEPER. Well it would howl a bit.

MAN. No, no, no, no. Er, have you got a parrot?

SHOPKEEPER. No, I'm afraid not, actually guv, we're fresh out of parrots. I'll tell you what though ... I'll lop its back legs off, make good, strip the fur, stick a couple of wings on and staple on a beak of your own choice. (*Taking small box and rattling it.*) No problem. Lovely parrot.

MAN. And how long would that take?

SHOPKEEPER. Oh, let me see ... er, stripping the fur off, no legs ... (*Calling.*) Harry ... can you do a parrot job on this terrier straight away?

HARRY. (*Off screen.*) No, I'm still putting a tuck in the Airedale, and then I got the frogs to let out.

SHOPKEEPER. Friday?

MAN. No I need it for tomorrow. It's a present.

SHOPKEEPER. Oh dear, it's a long job. You see parrot conversion ... Tell you what though, for free, terriers make lovely fish. I mean I could do that for you straight away. Legs off, fins on, stick a little pipe through the back of its neck so it can breathe, bit of gold paint, make good ...

MAN. You'd need a very big tank.

SHOPKEEPER. It's a great conversation piece.

MAN. Yes, all right, all right ... but, er, only if I can watch.

—1969

DIRTY HUNGARIAN PHRASEBOOK[1]

THE CAST:

HUNGARIAN: John Cleese
TOBACCONIST: Terry Jones
POLICEMAN: Graham Chapman

(*Set: A tobacconist's shop.*)
(*Roller caption: In 1970, the British Empire lay in ruins, and foreign nationalists frequented the streets—many of them Hungarians [not the streets—the foreign nationals]. Anyway, many of these Hungarians went into tobacconists' shops to buy cigarettes ...*)
(*Enter Hungarian gentleman with phrase book. He is looking for the right phrase.*)

HUNGARIAN. I will not buy this record. It is scratched.

TOBACCONIST. Sorry?

HUNGARIAN. I will not buy this record. It is scratched.

TOBACCONIST. No, no, no. This ... tobacconist's.

HUNGARIAN. Ah! I will not buy this tobacconist's. It is scratched.

TOBACCONIST. No, no, no ... tobacco ... er, cigarettes?

HUNGARIAN. Yes, cigarettes. My hovercraft is full of eels.

TOBACCONIST. What?

HUNGARIAN. (*Miming matches.*) My hovercraft is full of eels.

TOBACCONIST. Matches, matches?

HUNGARIAN. Yah, yah. (*He takes cigarettes and matches and pulls out loose change; he consults his book.*) Er, do you want ... do you want to come back to my place, bouncy bouncy?

TOBACCONIST. I don't think you're using that thing right.

HUNGARIAN. You great pouf.[2]

TOBACCONIST. That'll be six and six,[3] please.

HUNGARIAN. If I said you had a beautiful body, would you hold it against me? I am no longer infected.

TOBACCONIST. (*Miming that he wants to see the book; he takes the book.*) It costs six and six ... (*Mumbling as he searches*) Costs six and six ... Here we are ... Yandelvayasna grldenwi stravenka.

(*Hungarian hits him between the eyes. Policeman walking along street suddenly stops and puts his hand to his ear. He starts running down the street, round corner and down another street, round yet another corner and down another street into the shop.*)

POLICEMAN. What's going on here then?

HUNGARIAN. (*Opening book and pointing at Tobacconist.*) You have beautiful thighs.

POLICEMAN. What?

---

[1] *DIRTY HUNGARIAN PHRASEBOOK* Featured in *Monty Python's Flying Circus*, Episode 25.

[2] *pouf* Derogatory British slang for gay man.

[3] *six and six* Six shillings and sixpence.

TOBACCONIST. He hit me.

HUNGARIAN. Drop your panties, Sir William, I cannot wait till lunchtime.

35 POLICEMAN. Right! (*Grabs him and drags him out.*)

HUNGARIAN. My nipples explode with delight.

(*Cut to a courtroom.*)

THE CAST:

JUDGE: Terry Jones
CLERK: Eric Idle
LAWYER: John Cleese
POLICEMAN: Graham Chapman (still)
YAHLT: Michael Palin

CLERK. Call Alexander Yahlt!

VOICES. Call Alexander Yahlt. Call Alexander Yahlt. Call Alexander Yahlt.

(*They do this three times, finishing with harmony.*)

40 MAGISTRATE. Oh, shut up.

(*Alexander Yahlt enters. He is not Hungarian but an ordinary man in a mac.*)[1]

CLERK. (*To publisher.*) You are Alexander Yahlt?

YAHLT. (*Derek Nimmo's*[2] *voice dubbed on.*) Oh, I am.

CLERK. Skip the impersonations. You are Alexander Yahlt?

45 YAHLT. (*Normal voice.*) I am.

CLERK. You are hereby charged that on the 28th day of May 1970 you did wilfully, unlawfully, and with malice aforethought publish an alleged English-Hungarian phrase book with intent to cause a breach of the peace.

50 How do you plead?

YAHLT. Not guilty.

CLERK. You live at 46, Horton Terrace?

YAHLT. I do live at 46, Horton Terrace.

CLERK. You are the director of a publishing company?

55 YAHLT. I am the director of a publishing company.

CLERK. Your company publishes phrasebooks?

YAHLT. My company does publish phrasebooks.

CLERK. You did say 46, Horton Terrace did you?

YAHLT. Yes.

(*He claps his hand to his mouth; gong sounds—general applause.*)

60 CLERK. Ha, ha, ha, I got him.

MAGISTRATE. Get on with it! Get on with it!

CLERK. Yes, m'lud,[3] on the 28th of May you published this phrasebook.

YAHLT. I did.

65 CLERK. I quote one example. The Hungarian phrase meaning "Can you direct me to the station?" is translated by the English phrase, "please fondle my bum."

YAHLT. I wish to plead incompetence.

(*The Policeman stands up.*)

70 POLICEMAN. Please may I ask for an adjournment, m'lud?

MAGISTRATE. An adjournment? Certainly not.

(*The Policeman sits down; there is a loud raspberry;*[4] *the policeman goes bright red.*)

Why on earth didn't you say *why* you wanted an adjournment?

POLICEMAN. I didn't know an acceptable legal phrase, m'lud.

75

(*Cut to stock film of Women's Institute*[5] *applauding. Cut back to the magistrate.*)

MAGISTRATE. If there's any more stock film of women applauding I shall clear the court.

—1970

SPAM [6]

THE CAST:

MR. BUN: Eric Idle
MRS. BUN: Graham Chapman
WAITRESS: Terry Jones

---

[1] *mac* I.e., mackintosh, a raincoat.

[2] *Derek Nimmo* British comedic actor and BBC Radio game show panelist who had a distinctive, aristocratic voice.

[3] *m'lud* I.e., my lord.

[4] *raspberry* Rude sound, generally made with the lips and tongue. Here, denotes flatulence.

[5] *Women's Institute* Organization for women in England and Wales.

[6] *SPAM* Featured in *Monty Python's Flying Circus*, Episode 25.

HUNGARIAN: John Cleese
HISTORIAN: Michael Palin

(*Scene: A cafe. All the customers are Vikings. Mr. and Mrs. Bun enter—downwards, on wires.*)

MR. BUN. Morning.

WAITRESS. Morning.

MR. BUN. What have you got, then?

WAITRESS. Well there's egg and bacon; egg sausage and
5   bacon; egg and spam; egg, bacon and spam; egg, bacon, sausage and spam; spam, bacon, sausage and spam; spam, egg, spam, spam, bacon and spam; spam, spam, spam, egg and spam; spam, spam, spam, spam, spam, baked beans, spam, spam, spam, and spam; or
10   lobster thermidor aux crevettes with a mornay sauce garnished with truffle pâté, brandy and a fried egg on top and spam.

MRS. BUN. Have you got anything without spam in it?

WAITRESS. Well, there's spam, egg, sausage and spam.

15   That's not got *much* spam in it.

MRS. BUN. I don't want *any* spam.

MR. BUN. Why can't she have egg, bacon, spam and sausage?

MRS. BUN. That's got spam in it!

20   MR. BUN. Not as much as spam, egg, sausage and spam.

MRS. BUN. Look, could I have egg, bacon, spam and sausage without the spam.

WAITRESS. Uuuuuuggggh!

MRS. BUN. What do you mean uuugggh! I don't like
25   spam.

VIKINGS. (*Singing.*) Spam, spam, spam, spam, spam ... spam, spam, spam, spam ... lovely spam, wonderful spam ...

(*Brief stock shot of a Viking ship.*)

WAITRESS. Shut up! Shut up! Shut up! You can't have
30   egg, bacon, spam and sausage without the spam.

MRS. BUN. (*Shrieks.*) I don't like spam!

MR. BUN. Don't make a fuss, dear. I'll have your spam. I love it. I'm having spam, spam, spam, spam, spam ...

VIKINGS. (*Singing.*) Spam, spam, spam, spam ...

35   MR. BUN. ... baked beans, spam, spam and spam.

WAITRESS. Baked beans are off.

MR. BUN. Well can I have spam instead?

WAITRESS. You mean spam, spam, spam, spam, spam, spam, spam, spam, spam, spam?

40   VIKINGS. (*Still singing.*) Spam, spam, spam, spam ... (*etc.*)

MR. BUN. Yes.

WAITRESS. Arrggh!

VIKINGS.   ... lovely spam, wonderful, spam.

45   WAITRESS. Shut up! Shut up!

(*The Vikings shut up momentarily. Enter the Hungarian.*)

HUNGARIAN. Great boobies, honeybun, my lower intestine is full of spam, egg, spam, bacon, spam, tomato, spam ...

VIKINGS. (*Starting up again.*) Spam, spam, spam, spam ...
50   WAITRESS. Shut up.

(*A policeman rushes in and bundles the Hungarian out.*)

HUNGARIAN.   My nipples explode ...

(*Cut to a historian. Superimposed caption: "A HISTORIAN."*)

HISTORIAN. Another great Viking victory was at the Green Midget café at Bromley. Once again the Viking strategy was the same. They sailed from these fjords here
55   (*indicating map with arrows on it*), assembled at Trondheim and waited for the strong north-easterly winds to blow their oaken galleys to England whence they sailed on May 23rd. Once in Bromley they assembled at the Green Midget café and spam selecting
60   a spam particular spam item from the spam menu would spam, spam, spam, spam, spam ...

(*The backdrop behind him rises to reveal the café again. The Vikings start singing again and the historian conducts them.*)

VIKINGS. (*Singing.*) Spam, spam, spam, spam, spam, lovely spam, wonderful spam. Lovely spam, wonderful spam ...

(*Mr. and Mrs. Bun rise slowly in the air.*)
—1970

J.M. Coetzee
b. 1940

©BERTNIENHAUS

Novelist J.M. Coetzee's precise and sober prose, penchant for philosophical ambiguity, and postmodern approach to storytelling have made him a highly acclaimed—if often controversial—figure on the world literary scene. His work is concerned with injustice of all kinds, from the Vietnam War to the abuse of non-human animals, but he is best known for examining racial oppression in his native South Africa, both explicitly and through complex allegories. When he was awarded the Nobel Prize in 2003, the committee praised his treatment of human suffering and disempowerment: "It is in exploring weakness and defeat that Coetzee captures the divine spark" in humanity.

John Maxwell Coetzee was born in Cape Town, South Africa, in 1940. His mother was a teacher and his father worked periodically as a lawyer; although their heritage was Afrikaner they spoke English at home. As a child, Coetzee saw the beginning of the apartheid era, a period from the late 1940s to mid 1990s during which the segregation and exploitation of non-white South Africans was legally enforced and enshrined in the country's political institutions.

Coetzee graduated from Catholic high school, and then earned honors degrees in both English and Mathematics from the University of Cape Town. He spent the 1960s largely in England—where he worked as a computer programmer for IBM and completed a Master's Thesis on the English writer Ford Madox Ford—and in the United States, where he wrote his doctoral dissertation on Samuel Beckett at the University of Texas. During this time he also married his first wife, Philippa Jubber, with whom he would have two children.

Upon finishing his PhD, Coetzee became an Assistant Professor of English at the State University of New York, Buffalo, and began writing his first novel, *Darklands* (1974). When his application to become a permanent resident of the United States was denied due to his involvement in a campus protest, he returned to the University of Cape Town. He would remain a professor there for almost thirty years, while also teaching occasionally at American universities such as Harvard, Stanford, and the University of Chicago.

Coetzee first achieved international recognition with his third novel, *Waiting for the Barbarians* (1980), an allegorical exploration of imperialism and violence; his reputation grew with the Booker Prize-winning *The Life and Times of Michael K* (1983), the story of a mentally and physically disabled man surviving in an imagined future South Africa torn by civil war. In both works Coetzee addresses South African politics in connection with broader themes so that, as *New York Times* reviewer Michiko Kakutani observes, "[the] predicament [of life in an oppressive nation] becomes a universal one: psychological as well as social, existential as well as political."

Although this philosophical approach has earned Coetzee a great deal of acclaim, his subtlety has also been criticized as a failure to voice unequivocal opposition to apartheid. In response, Coetzee has argued against the "colonisation of the novel by the discourse of history," suggesting that, instead of a mere vehicle for historical or political arguments, "storytelling" can provide an alternative "mode of thinking."

Coetzee's next novel, *Foe* (1986), is inspired by Daniel Defoe's *Robinson Crusoe* (1719); Defoe himself appears in it as a character alongside a woman protagonist and a re-imagined Friday whose tongue has been removed. In *Foe*, and in other novels such as *Age of Iron* (1990) and *The Master of Petersburg* (1994), Coetzee examines the relationship between writing and privilege in the context of political oppression. This subject, he has said, is significant to his work as a white South African novelist: "What the correct relationship ought to be between a representative of this failed or failing colonial movement [the European colonization of South Africa] … and the part of the world where it sought and failed to establish itself [is a question] I have lived out … not only in day to day life but in my fiction as well."

Disgrace (1999) was the first novel Coetzee wrote after South Africa's 1994 general election marked the end of apartheid. The book, which hinges on the rape of a white woman by a group of black men, attracted a great deal of controversy. Some criticized the work for not speaking more directly in favor of racial equality, and the South African government condemned it as racist, but *Disgrace* was also praised for acknowledging apartheid's enduring legacy of racial conflict. Coetzee was awarded the Booker Prize, becoming the first person to win it twice.

In 2002 Coetzee and his partner Dorothy Driver moved to Australia, where he accepted an honorary research fellowship at the University of Adelaide. His next novels display an increasing interest in metafiction: *Elizabeth Costello* (2003) incorporates a series of lectures ostensibly written by the title character, an Australian novelist, who also appears in *Slow Man* (2005). Coetzee again combines essays with narrative in *Diary of a Bad Year* (2007), but he moves away from metafictional techniques with *The Childhood of Jesus* (2013), a sparely written novel that, like much of his earlier work, has been interpreted as an allegory.

Although Coetzee is famously reserved, with a reputation for avoiding interviews and public appearances, in the late 1990s he began to discuss his literary influences and formative experiences in a series of "fictionalised memoirs": *Boyhood* (1997), *Youth* (2002), and *Summertime* (2009). The relationship between fact and fiction is complicated in all three—particularly in *Summertime*, which is presented as the work of a fictional English academic who has compiled notes and interviews toward a biography of Coetzee.

Coetzee is also an author of essays and criticism, including *White Writing: On the Culture of Letters in South Africa* (1988) and *Giving Offense: Essays on Censorship* (1996), as well as a translator of Dutch and Afrikaans literature.

THE LIVES OF ANIMALS

The textual history of "The Lives of Animals" is an unusual one. Coetzee was asked to deliver the 1997 Tanner Lectures at Princeton University—an annual series intended "to advance and reflect upon" the ways in which "scholarly and scientific learning" may relate to human values. Instead of presenting lectures of the usual sort, Coetzee read the two parts of the work of fiction that appears here. That the subject of the fiction is a writer visiting a university to deliver a lecture is suggestive of the sort of self-referential and ironic approach that is often labeled postmodern.

However these layers of fiction are described, there can be no doubt that "The Lives of Animals" seeks to engage directly with a highly charged ethical issue in the real world: the cruelty that human animals display towards non-human ones. When the lectures were first published (in 1999), Coetzee accompanied them with a number of academic footnotes (identifying, for example, the writer Costello describes as "one of the academic philosophers I read in preparing for today's lecture," Michael Leahy, and providing a page reference from Leahy's *Against Liberation*, as well as a further comment on Leahy's work). The book also included an introduction by philosopher Amy Guttman and responses to Coetzee's lectures from an academic in religious studies, a primatologist, a literary theorist, and philosopher Peter Singer of Princeton—whose writings have played a central role in the modern animal welfare and animal rights movements. (Singer gave a further spin to the fiction/non-fiction context by writing his response as a work of fiction too—a fiction in which one of the characters inquires into the ways in which Coetzee may have used the fictional structure of "The Lives of Animals" as a distancing device.)

If Coetzee's "The Lives of Animals" is of interest for the ethical arguments made by writer Elizabeth Costello and for the complex ways in which those arguments are layered within a fiction, it also holds our attention in the traditional ways that fiction interests us: the reader is engaged by the narrative of Costello's interaction with her son and his family, and by the psychological nuances of their relationships. In the years following the original appearance of "The Lives of Animals" as a self-contained fiction, Coetzee expanded on this narrative; in 2003 he published the full-length novel *Elizabeth Costello*, in which we learn more about the novelist's past and her family, and in which we see her literary work interwoven with that of major figures of modern literature—notably Franz Kafka and James Joyce. The original text of the two "Lives of Animals" Tanner lectures appears as Lesson 3 and Lesson 4 of the eight "lessons" that make up *Elizabeth Costello*. At J.M. Coetzee's request, it is the slightly revised text of 2003 that is included here.

⌘ ⌘ ⌘

The Lives of Animals

ONE: THE PHILOSOPHERS AND THE ANIMALS

He is waiting at the gate when her flight comes in. Two years have passed since he last saw his mother; despite himself he is shocked at how she has aged. Her hair, which had had streaks of grey in it, is now entirely white; her shoulders stoop; her flesh has grown flabby.

They have never been a demonstrative family. A hug, a few murmured words, and the business of greeting is done. In silence they follow the flow of travellers to the baggage hall, pick up her suitcase, and set off on the ninety-minute drive.

"A long flight," he remarks. "You must be exhausted."

"Ready to sleep," she says; and indeed, en route, she falls asleep briefly, her head slumped against the window.

At six o'clock, as it is growing dark, they pull up in front of his home in suburban Waltham. His wife Norma and the children appear on the porch. In a show of affection that must cost her a great deal, Norma holds her arms out wide and says, "Elizabeth!" The two women embrace; then the children, in their well-brought up though more subdued fashion, follow suit.

Elizabeth Costello the novelist will be staying with them for the three days of her visit to Appleton College. It is not a period he is looking forward to. His wife and his mother do not get on. It would be better were she to stay at a hotel, but he cannot bring himself to suggest that.

Hostilities are renewed almost at once. Norma has prepared a light supper. His mother notices that only three places have been set. "Aren't the children eating with us?" she asks. "No," says Norma, "they are eating in the playroom." "Why?"

The question is not necessary, since she knows the answer. The children are eating separately because Elizabeth does not like to see meat on the table, while Norma refuses to change the children's diet to suit what she calls "your mother's delicate sensibilities."

"Why?" asks Elizabeth Costello a second time.

Norma flashes him an angry glance. He sighs. "Mother," he says, "the children are having chicken for supper, that's the only reason."

"Oh," she says. "I see."

His mother has been invited to Appleton College, where her son John is assistant professor of physics and astronomy, to deliver the annual Gates Lecture and meet with literature students. Because Costello is his mother's maiden name, and because he has never seen any reason to broadcast his connection with her, it was not known at the time of the invitation that Elizabeth Costello, the Australian writer, had a family connection in the Appleton community. He would have preferred that state of affairs to continue.

On the basis of her reputation as a novelist, this fleshy, white-haired lady has been invited to Appleton to speak on any subject she elects; and she has responded by electing to speak, not about herself and her fiction, as her sponsors would no doubt like, but about a hobbyhorse of hers, animals.

John Bernard has not broadcast his connection with Elizabeth Costello because he prefers to make his own way in the world. He is not ashamed of his mother. On the contrary, he is proud of her, despite the fact that he and his sister and his late father are written into her books in ways that he sometimes finds painful. But he is not sure that he wants to hear her once again on the subject of animal rights, particularly when he knows he will afterwards be treated, in bed, to his wife's disparaging commentary.

He met and married Norma while they were both graduate students at Johns Hopkins. Norma holds a Ph.D. in philosophy with a specialism in the philosophy of mind. Having moved with him to Appleton she has been unable to find a teaching position. This is a cause of bitterness to her, and of conflict between the two of them.

Norma and his mother have never liked each other. Probably his mother would have chosen not to like any woman he married. As for Norma, she has never hesitated to tell him that his mother's books are overrated, that her opinions on animals, animal consciousness and ethical relations with animals are jejune and sentimental. She is at present writing for a philosophy journal a review essay on language-learning experiments upon primates; he would not be surprised if his mother figured in a dismissive footnote.

He himself has no opinions one way or the other. As a child he briefly kept hamsters; otherwise he has little familiarity with animals. Their elder boy wants a puppy. Both he and Norma are resisting: they do not mind a puppy but foresee a grown dog, with a grown dog's sexual needs, as nothing but trouble.

His mother is entitled to her convictions, he believes. If she wants to spend her declining years making propaganda against cruelty to animals, that is her right. In a few days, blessedly, she will be on her way to her next destination, and he will be able to get back to his work.

On her first morning in Waltham his mother sleeps late. He goes off to teach a class, returns at lunchtime, takes her for a drive around the city. The lecture is scheduled for the late afternoon. It will be followed by a formal dinner hosted by the president, in which he and Norma are included.

The lecture is introduced by Elaine Marx of the English Department. He does not know her but understands that she has written about his mother. In her introduction, he notices she makes no attempt to link his mother's novels to the subject of the lecture.

Then it is the turn of Elizabeth Costello. To him she looks old and tired. Sitting in the front row beside his wife, he tries to will strength into her.

"Ladies and gentlemen," she begins. "It is two years since I last spoke in the United States. In the lecture I then gave, I had reason to refer to the great fabulist Franz Kafka,[1] and in particular to his story 'Report to an Academy', about an educated ape, Red Peter, who stands before the members of a learned society telling the story of his life—of his ascent from beast to something approaching man. On that occasion I felt a little like Red Peter myself and said so. Today that feeling is even stronger, for reasons that I hope will become clearer to you.

"Lectures often begin with light-hearted remarks whose purpose is to set the audience at ease. The comparison I have just drawn between myself and Kafka's ape might be taken as such a light-hearted remark, meant to set you at ease, meant to say I am just an ordinary person, neither a god nor a beast. Even those among you who read Kafka's story of the ape who performs before human beings as an allegory of Kafka the Jew performing for Gentiles may nevertheless—in view of the fact that I am not a Jew—have done me the kindness of taking the comparison at face value, that is to say, ironically.

---

[1] *Franz Kafka*   German-language author (1883–1924).

"I want to say at the outset that that was not how my remark—the remark that I feel like Red Peter—was intended. I did not intend it ironically. It means what it says. I say what I mean. I am an old woman. I do not have the time any longer to say things I do not mean."

His mother does not have a good delivery. Even as a reader of her own stories she lacks animation. It always puzzled him, when he was a child, that a woman who wrote books for a living should be so bad at telling bedtime stories.

Because of the flatness of her delivery, because she does not look up from the page, he feels that what she is saying lacks impact. Whereas he, because he knows her, senses what she is up to. He does not look forward to what is coming. He does not want to hear his mother talking about death. Furthermore, he has a strong sense that her audience—which consists, after all, mainly of young people—wants death-talk even less.

"In addressing you on the subject of animals," she continues, "I will pay you the honour of skipping a recital of the horrors of their lives and deaths. Though I have no reason to believe that you have at the forefront of your minds what is being done to animals at this moment in production facilities (I hesitate to call them farms any longer), in abattoirs,[1] in trawlers, in laboratories, all over the world, I will take it that you concede me the rhetorical power to evoke these horrors and bring them home to you with adequate force, and leave it at that, reminding you only that the horrors I here omit are nevertheless at the centre of this lecture.

"Between 1942 and 1945 several million people were put to death in the concentration camps of the Third Reich: at Treblinka[2] alone more than a million and a half, perhaps as many as three million. These are numbers that numb the mind. We have only one death of our own; we can comprehend the deaths of others only one at a time. In the abstract we may be able to count to a million, but we cannot count to a million deaths.

"The people who lived in the countryside around Treblinka—Poles, for the most part—said that they did not know what was going on in the camp; said that, while in a general way they might have guessed what

was going on, they did not know for sure; said that, while in a sense they might have known, in another sense they did not know, could not afford to know, for their own sake.

"The people around Treblinka were not exceptional. There were camps all over the Reich, nearly six thousand in Poland alone, untold thousands in Germany proper. Few Germans lived more than a few kilometres from a camp of some kind. Not every camp was a death camp, a camp dedicated to the production of death, but horrors went on in all of them, more horrors by far than one could afford to know, for one's own sake.

"It is not because they waged an expansionist war, and lost it, that Germans of a particular generation are still regarded as standing a little outside humanity, as having to do or be something special before they can be readmitted to the human fold. They lost their humanity, in our eyes, because of a certain willed ignorance on their part. Under the circumstances of Hitler's kind of war, ignorance may have been a useful survival mechanism, but that is an excuse which, with admirable moral rigour, we refuse to accept. In Germany, we say, a certain line was crossed which took people beyond the ordinary murderousness and cruelty of warfare into a state that we can only call sin. The signing of the articles of capitulation and the payment of reparations did not put an end to that state of sin. On the contrary, we said, a sickness of the soul continued to mark that generation. It marked those citizens of the Reich who had committed evil actions, but also those who, for whatever reason, were in ignorance of those actions. It thus marked, for practical purposes, every citizen of the Reich. Only those in the camps were innocent.

"'They went like sheep to the slaughter'. 'They died like animals'. 'The Nazi butchers killed them'. Denunciation of the camps reverberates so fully with the language of the stockyard and slaughterhouse that it is barely necessary for me to prepare the ground for the comparison I am about to make. The crime of the Third Reich, says the voice of accusation, was to treat people like animals.

---

[1] *abattoirs* Slaughterhouses.

[2] *Treblinka* Nazi extermination camp near Warsaw, Poland.

"We—even we in Australia—belong to a civilization deeply rooted in Greek and Judaeo-Christian religious thought. We may not, all of us, believe in pollution, we may not believe in sin, but we do believe in their psychic correlates. We accept without question that the psyche (or soul) touched with guilty knowledge cannot be well. We do not accept that people with crimes on their conscience can be healthy and happy. We look (or used to look) askance at Germans of a certain generation because they are, in a sense, polluted; in the very signs of their normality (their healthy appetites, their hearty laughter) we see proof of how deeply seated pollution is in them.

"It was and is inconceivable that people who *did not know* (in that special sense) about the camps can be fully human. In our chosen metaphorics, it was they and not their victims who were the beasts. By treating fellow human beings, beings created in the image of God, like beasts, they had themselves become beasts.

"I was taken on a drive around Waltham this morning. It seems a pleasant enough town. I saw no horrors, no drug-testing laboratories, no factory farms, no abattoirs. Yet I am sure they are here. They must be. They simply do not advertise themselves. They are all around us as I speak, only we do not, in a certain sense, know about them.

"Let me say it openly: we are surrounded by an enterprise of degradation, cruelty and killing which rivals anything that the Third Reich was capable of, indeed dwarfs it, in that ours is an enterprise without end, self-regenerating, bringing rabbits, rats, poultry, livestock ceaselessly into the world for the purpose of killing them.

"And to split hairs, to claim that there is no comparison, that Treblinka was so to speak a metaphysical enterprise dedicated to nothing but death and annihilation while the meat industry is ultimately devoted to life (once its victims are dead, after all, it does not burn them to ash or bury them but on the contrary cuts them up and refrigerates and packs them so that they can be consumed in the comfort of our homes) is as little consolation to those victims as it would have been—pardon the tastelessness of the following—to ask the dead of Treblinka to excuse their killers because their body fat was needed to make soap and their hair to stuff mattresses with.[1]

"Pardon me, I repeat. That is the last cheap point I will be scoring. I know how talk of this kind polarizes people, and cheap point-scoring only makes it worse. I want to find a way of speaking to fellow human beings that will be cool rather than heated, philosophical rather than polemical, that will bring enlightenment rather than seeking to divide us into the righteous and the sinners, the saved and the damned, the sheep and the goats.

"Such a language is available to me, I know. It is the language of Aristotle and Porphyry,[2] of Augustine and Aquinas,[3] of Descartes and Bentham,[4] of, in our day, Mary Midgley and Tom Regan.[5] It is a philosophical language in which we can discuss and debate what kind of souls animals have, whether they reason or on the contrary act as biological automatons, whether they have rights in respect of us or whether we merely have duties in respect of them. I have that language available to me and indeed for a while will be resorting to it. But the fact is, if you had wanted someone to come here and discriminate for you between mortal and immortal souls, or between rights and duties, you would have

[1] *fat was … mattresses with* During the Holocaust, the hair of concentration camp victims was used to stuff mattresses; it was commonly believed (probably falsely) that the fat of victims was also harvested and was used in the mass-production of soap.

[2] *Aristotle* Greek philosopher (384–322 BCE) who classified animals based on a hierarchy of different types of souls and claimed that only human beings are capable of reason; *Porphyry* Greek philosopher and biographer (234–305 CE) who argued for a spiritually motivated vegetarianism based on commonalities between humans and other animals.

[3] *Augustine* Saint Augustine of Hippo (354–430 CE), Christian philosopher who considered humans to possess reason in a way other organisms did not; *Aquinas* Saint Thomas Aquinas (1225–74), philosopher and theologian who saw non-human animals as part of a hierarchy that also included plant and human life.

[4] *Descartes* French philosopher and mathematician René Descartes (1596–1650), who claimed that non-human animals were like machines and could not have souls; *Bentham* Jeremy Bentham (1748–1832), English philosopher who suggested that, when considering issues relating to non-human animals, the question we should ask is not *Can they reason?* nor, *Can they talk?* but, *Can they suffer?*

[5] *Tom Regan* American philosopher and key proponent of the American animal rights movement (b. 1938); *Mary Midgley* British philosopher and science critic (b.1919).

called in a philosopher, not a person whose sole claim to your attention is to have written stories about made-up people.

"I could fall back on that language, as I have said, in the unoriginal, second-hand manner which is the best I can manage. I could tell you, for instance, what I think of St Thomas's argument that, because man alone is made in the image of God and partakes in the being of God, how we treat animals is of no importance except insofar as being cruel to animals may accustom us to being cruel to men. I could ask what St Thomas takes to be the being of God, to which he will reply that the being of God is reason. Likewise Plato,[1] likewise Descartes, in their different ways. The universe is built upon reason. God is a God of reason. The fact that through the application of reason we can come to understand the rules by which the universe works proves that reason and the universe are of the same being. And the fact that animals, lacking reason, cannot understand the universe but have simply to follow its rules blindly, proves that, unlike man, they are part of it but not part of its being: that man is godlike, animals thinglike.

"Even Immanuel Kant,[2] of whom I would have expected better, has a failure of nerve at this point. Even Kant does not pursue, with regard to animals, the implications of his intuition that reason may be not the being of the universe but on the contrary merely the being of the human brain.

"And that, you see, is my dilemma this afternoon. Both reason and seven decades of life experience tell me that reason is neither the being of the universe nor the being of God. On the contrary, reason looks to me suspiciously like the being of human thought; worse than that, like the being of one tendency in human thought. Reason is the being of a certain spectrum of human thinking. And if this is so, if that is what I believe, then why should I bow to reason this afternoon and content myself with embroidering on the discourse of the old philosophers?"

"I ask the question and then answer it for you. Or rather, I allow Red Peter, Kafka's Red Peter, to answer it for you. Now that I am here, says Red Peter, in my tuxedo and bow tie and my black pants with a hole cut in the seat for my tail to poke through (I keep it turned away from you, you do not see it), now that I am here, what is there for me to do? Do I in fact have a choice? If I do not subject my discourse to reason, whatever that is, what is left for me but to gibber and emote and knock over my water glass and generally make a monkey of myself?

"You must know of the case of Srinivasa Ramanujan,[3] born in India in 1887, captured and transported to Cambridge, England, where, unable to tolerate the climate and the diet and the academic regime, he sickened, dying afterwards at the age of thirty-three.

"Ramanujan is widely thought of as the greatest intuitive mathematician of our time, that is to say, a self-taught man who thought in mathematics, one to whom the rather laborious notion of mathematical proof or demonstration was foreign. Many of Ramanujan's results (or, as his detractors call them, his speculations) remain undemonstrated to this day, though there is every chance they are true.

"What does the phenomenon of a Ramanujan tell us? Was Ramanujan closer to God because his mind (let us call it his mind; it would seem to me gratuitously insulting to call it just his brain) was at one, or more at one than anyone else's we know of, with the being of reason? If the good folk at Cambridge, and principally Professor G.H. Hardy, had not elicited from Ramanujan his speculations, and laboriously proved true those of them that they were capable of proving true, would Ramanujan still have been closer to God than they? What if, instead of going to Cambridge, Ramanujan had merely sat at home and thought his thoughts while he filled out dockets for the Madras Port Authority?

"And what of Red Peter (the historical Red Peter, I mean)? How are we to know that Red Peter, or Red Peter's little sister, shot in Africa by the hunters, was not thinking the same thoughts as Ramanujan was thinking in India, and saying equally little? Is the difference

[1] *Plato* Greek philosopher (428?–348? BCE) whose works are considered a foundation for much of western philosophy.

[2] *Immanuel Kant* German philosopher (1724–1804) who argued that humans were the only beings capable of reason and therefore the only beings able to act morally.

[3] *Srinivasa Ramanujan* Indian mathematician (1887–1920) known for his contributions to number theory.

between G.H. Hardy, on the one hand, and the dumb Ramanujan and the dumb Red Sally, on the other, merely that the former is conversant with the protocols of academic mathematics while the latter are not? Is that how we measure nearness to or distance from God, from the being of reason?

"How is it that humankind throws up, generation after generation, a cadre of thinkers slightly further from God than Ramanujan but capable nevertheless, after the designated twelve years of schooling and six of tertiary education, of making a contribution to the decoding of the great book of nature via the physical and mathematical disciplines? If the being of man is really at one with the being of God, should it not be cause for suspicion that human beings take eighteen years, a neat and manageable portion of a human lifetime, to qualify to become decoders of God's master script, rather than five minutes, say, or five hundred years? Might it not be that the phenomenon we are examining here is, rather than the flowering of a faculty that allows access to the secrets of the universe, the specialism of a rather narrow self-regenerating intellectual tradition whose forte is reasoning, in the same way that the forte of chess players is playing chess, which for its own motives it tries to install at the centre of the universe?

"Yet, although I see that the best way to win acceptance from this learned gathering would be for me to join myself, like a tributary stream running into a great river, to the great Western discourse of man versus beast, of reason versus unreason, something in me resists, foreseeing in that step the concession of the entire battle.

"For, seen from the outside, from a being who is alien to it, reason is simply a vast tautology. Of course reason will validate reason as the first principle of the universe—what else should it do? Dethrone itself? Reasoning systems, as systems of totality, do not have that power. If there were a position from which reason could attack and dethrone itself, reason would already have occupied that position; otherwise it would not be total.

"In the olden days the voice of man, raised in reason, was confronted by the roar of the lion, the bellow of the bull. Man went to war with the lion and the bull, and after many generations won that war definitively. Today

these creatures have no more power. Animals have only their silence left with which to confront us. Generation after generation, heroically, our captives refuse to speak to us. All save Red Peter, all save the great apes.

"Yet because the great apes, or some of them, seem to us to be on the point of giving up their silence, we hear human voices raised arguing that the great apes should be incorporated into a greater family of the Hominoidea, as creatures who share with man the faculty of reason. And being human, or humanoid, these voices go on, the great apes should then be accorded human rights, or humanoid rights. "What rights in particular? At least those rights that we accord mentally defective specimens of the species *Homo sapiens*: the right to life, the right not to be subjected to pain or harm, the right to equal protection before the law.

"That is not what Red Peter was striving for when he wrote, through his amanuensis[1] Franz Kafka, the life history that, in November of 1917, he proposed to read to the Academy of Science. Whatever else it may have been, his report to the academy was not a plea to be treated as a mentally defective human being, a simpleton.

"Red Peter was not an investigator of primate behaviour but a branded, marked, wounded animal presenting himself as speaking testimony to a gathering of scholars. I am not a philosopher of mind but an animal exhibiting, yet not exhibiting, to a gathering of scholars, a wound, which I cover up under my clothes but touch on in every word I speak.

"If Red Peter took it upon himself to make the arduous descent from the silence of the beasts to the gabble of reason in the spirit of the scapegoat, the chosen one, then his amanuensis was a scapegoat from birth, with a presentiment, a *Vorgefühl*,[2] for the massacre of the chosen people that was to take place so soon after his death. So let me, to prove my goodwill, my credentials, make a gesture in the direction of scholarship and give you my scholarly speculations, backed up with footnotes"—here, in an uncharacteristic gesture, his mother raises and brandishes the text of her lecture in the air—"on the origins of Red Peter.

[1] *amanuensis* Person who records or copies dictation or a written manuscript.

[2] *Vorgefühl* German: Apprehension or intuitive impression.

"In 1912 the Prussian Academy of Sciences established on the island of Tenerife[1] a station devoted to experimentation into the mental capacities of apes, particularly chimpanzees. The station operated until 1920.

"One of the scientists working there was the psychologist Wolfgang Köhler.[2] In 1917 Köhler published a monograph entitled *The Mentality of Apes* describing his experiments. In November of the same year Franz Kafka published his 'Report to an Academy'. Whether Kafka had read Köhler's book I do not know. He makes no reference to it in his letters or diaries, and his library disappeared during the Nazi era. Some two hundred of his books reemerged in 1982. They do not include Köhler's book, but that proves nothing.

"I am not a Kafka scholar. In fact, I am not a scholar at all. My status in the world does not rest on whether I am right or wrong in claiming that Kafka read Köhler's book. But I would like to think he did, and the chronology makes my speculation at least plausible.

"According to his own account, Red Peter was captured on the African mainland by hunters specializing in the ape trade, and shipped across the sea to a scientific institute. So were the apes Köhler worked with. Both Red Peter and Köhler's apes then underwent a period of training intended to humanize them. Red Peter passed his course with flying colours, though at deep personal cost. Kafka's story deals with that cost: we learn what it consists in through the ironies and silences of the story. Köhler's apes did less well. Nevertheless, they acquired at least a smattering of education.

"Let me recount to you some of what the apes on Tenerife learned from their master Wolfgang Köhler, in particular Sultan, the best of his pupils, in a certain sense the prototype of Red Peter.

"Sultan is alone in his pen. He is hungry: the food that used to arrive regularly has unaccountably ceased coming.

"The man who used to feed him and has now stopped feeding him stretches a wire over the pen three metres above ground level, and hangs a bunch of bananas from it. Into the pen he drags three wooden crates. Then he disappears, closing the gate behind him, though he is still somewhere in the vicinity, since one can smell him.

"Sultan knows: Now one is supposed to think. That is what the bananas up there are about. The bananas are there to make one think, to spur one to the limits of one's thinking. But what must one think? One thinks: Why is he starving me? One thinks: What have I done? Why has he stopped liking me? One thinks: Why does he not want these crates any more? But none of these is the right thought. Even a more complicated thought—for instance: What is wrong with him, what misconception does he have of me, that leads him to believe it is easier for me to reach a banana hanging from a wire than to pick up a banana from the floor?—is wrong. The right thought to think is: How does one use the crates to reach the bananas?

"Sultan drags the crates under the bananas, piles them one on top of the other, climbs the tower he has built, and pulls down the bananas. He thinks: Now will he stop punishing me?

"The answer is: No. The next day the man hangs a fresh bunch of bananas from the wire but also fills the crates with stones so that they are too heavy to be dragged. One is not supposed to think: Why has he filled the crates with stones? One is supposed to think: How does one use the crates to get the bananas despite the fact that they are filled with stones?

"One is beginning to see how the man's mind works.

"Sultan empties the stones from the crates, builds a tower with the crates, climbs the tower, pulls down the bananas.

"As long as Sultan continues to think wrong thoughts, he is starved. He is starved until the pangs of hunger are so intense, so overriding, that he is forced to think the right thought, namely, how to go about getting the bananas. Thus are the mental capabilities of the chimpanzee tested to their uttermost.

"The man drops a bunch of bananas a metre outside the wire pen. Into the pen he tosses a stick. The wrong thought is: Why has he stopped hanging the bananas on the wire? The wrong thought (the right wrong thought, however) is: How does one use the three crates to reach the bananas? The right thought is: How does one use the stick to reach the bananas?

---

[1]   *Tenerife*   One of the Canary Islands, off the coast of Northern Africa.

[2]   *Wolfgang Köhler*   German psychologist (1887–1967).

"At every turn Sultan is driven to think the less interesting thought. From the purity of speculation (Why do men behave like this?) he is relentlessly propelled towards lower, practical, instrumental reason (How does one use this to get that?) and thus towards acceptance of himself as primarily an organism with an appetite that needs to be satisfied. Although his entire history, from the time his mother was shot and he was captured, through his voyage in a cage to imprisonment on this island prison camp and the sadistic games that are played around food here, leads him to ask questions about the justice of the universe and the place of this penal colony in it, a carefully plotted psychological regimen conducts him *away* from ethics and metaphysics towards the humbler reaches of practical reason. And somehow, as he inches through this labyrinth of constraint, manipulation and duplicity, he must realize that on no account dare he give up, for on his shoulders rests the responsibility of representing apedom. The fate of his brothers and sisters may be determined by how well he performs.

"Wolfgang Köhler was probably a good man. A good man but not a poet. A poet would have made something of the moment when the captive chimpanzees lope around the compound in a circle, for all the world like a military band, some of them as naked as the day they were born, some draped in cords or old strips of cloth that they have picked up, some carrying pieces of rubbish.

"(In the copy of Köhler's book I read, borrowed from a library, an indignant reader has written in the margin, at this point: "Anthropomorphism!" Animals cannot march, he means to say, they cannot dress up, because they don't know the meaning of *march*, don't know the meaning of *dress up*.)

"Nothing in their previous lives has accustomed the apes to looking at themselves from the outside, as if through the eyes of a being who does not exist. So, as Köhler perceives, the ribbons and the junk are there not for the visual effect, because they *look* smart, but for the kinetic effect, because they make you *feel* different—anything to relieve the boredom. This is as far as Köhler, for all his sympathy and insight, is able to go; this is where a poet might have commenced, with a feel for the ape's experience.

"In his deepest being Sultan is not interested in the banana problem. Only the experimenter's single-minded regimentation forces him to concentrate on it. The question that truly occupies him, as it occupies the rat and the cat and every other animal trapped in the hell of the laboratory or the zoo, is: Where is home, and how do I get there?

"Measure the distance back from Kafka's ape, with his bow tie and dinner jacket and wad of lecture notes, to that sad train of captives trailing around the compound in Tenerife. How far Red Peter has travelled! Yet we are entitled to ask: In return for the prodigious overdevelopment of the intellect he has achieved, in return for his command of lecture-hall etiquette and academic rhetoric, what has he had to give up? The answer is: Much, including progeny, succession. If Red Peter had any sense, he would not have any children. For upon the desperate, half-mad female ape with whom his captors, in Kafka's story, try to mate him, he would father only a monster. It is as hard to imagine the child of Red Peter as to imagine the child of Franz Kafka himself. Hybrids are, or ought to be, sterile; and Kafka saw both himself and Red Peter as hybrids, as monstrous thinking devices mounted inexplicably on suffering animal bodies. The stare that we meet in all the surviving photographs of Kafka is a stare of pure surprise: surprise, astonishment, alarm. Of all men Kafka is the most insecure in his humanity. *This*, he seems to say: *this* is the image of God?"

"She is rambling," says Norma beside him.

"What?"

"She is rambling. She has lost her thread."

"There is a philosopher named Thomas Nagel," continues Elizabeth Costello, "who poses a question that has become quite famous by now in professional circles: What is it like to be a bat? [1]

"Merely to imagine what it is like to live as a bat does, says Mr Nagel—to imagine spending our nights flying around catching insects in our mouths, navigating by sound instead of sight, and our days hanging upside down—is not good enough, because all that tells us is what it would be like to *behave* like a bat. Whereas what

---

[1] *Thomas Nagel* American philosopher (b. 1937) whose work is concerned with consciousness and ethics; *What is ... a bat?* Title of an influential 1974 essay by Nagel.

we really aspire to know is what it is like to *be* a bat, as a bat is a bat; and that we can never accomplish because our minds are inadequate to the task—our minds are not bats' minds.

"Nagel strikes me as an intelligent and not unsympathetic man. He even has a sense of humour. But his denial that we can know what it is to be anything but one of ourselves seems to me tragically restrictive, restrictive and restricted. To Nagel a bat is a fundamentally alien creature, not perhaps as alien as Martian but certainly more alien than any fellow human being (particularly, I would guess, were that human being a fellow academic philosopher).

"So we have set up a continuum that stretches from the Martian at one end to the bat to the dog to the ape (not, however, Red Peter) to the human being (not, however, Franz Kafka) at the other; and at each step as we move along the continuum from bat to man, Nagel says, the answer to the question 'What is it like for X to be X?' becomes easier to give.

"I know that Nagel is only using bats and Martians as aids in order to pose questions of his own about the nature of consciousness. But, like most writers, I have a literal cast of mind, so I would like to stop with the bat. When Kafka writes about an ape, I take him to be talking in the first place about an ape; when Nagel writes about a bat, I take him to be writing, in the first place, about a bat."

Norma, sitting beside him, gives a sigh of exasperation so slight that he alone hears it. But then, he alone was meant to hear it.

"For instants at a time," his mother is saying, "I know what it is like to be a corpse. The knowledge repels me. It fills me with terror; I shy away from it, refuse to entertain it.

"All of us have such moments, particularly as we grow older. The knowledge we have is not abstract—'All human beings are mortal, I am a human being, therefore I am mortal'—but embodied. For a moment we *are* that knowledge. We live the impossible: we live beyond our death, look back on it, yet look back as only a dead self can.

"When I know, with this knowledge, that I am going to die, what is it, in Nagel's terms, that I know? Do I know what it is like for me to be a corpse or do I know what it is like for a corpse to be a corpse? The distinction seems to me trivial. What I know is what a corpse cannot know: that it is extinct, that it knows nothing and will never know anything any more. For an instant, before my whole structure of knowledge collapses in panic, I am alive inside that contradiction, dead and alive at the same time."

A little snort from Norma. He finds her hand, squeezes it.

"That is the kind of thought we are capable of, we human beings, that and even more, if we press ourselves or are pressed. But we resist being pressed, and rarely press ourselves; we think our way into death only when we are rammed into the face of it. Now I ask: if we are capable of thinking our own death, why on earth should we not be capable of thinking our way into the life of a bat?

"What is it like to be a bat? Before we can answer such a question, Nagel suggests, we need to be able to experience bat life through the sense modalities of a bat. But he is wrong; or at least he is sending us down a false trail. To be a living bat is to be full of being; being fully a bat is like being fully human, which is also to be full of being. Bat being in the first case, human being in the second, maybe; but those are secondary considerations. To be full of being is to live as a body-soul. One name for the experience of full being is *joy*.

"To be alive is to be a living soul. An animal—and we are all animals—is an embodied soul. This is precisely what Descartes saw and, for his own reasons, chose to deny. An animal lives, said Descartes, as a machine lives. An animal is no more than the mechanism that constitutes it; if it has a soul, it has one in the same way that a machine has a battery, to give it the spark that gets it going; but the animal is not an embodied soul, and the quality of its being is not joy.

"'*Cogito, ergo sum*,'[1] he also famously said. It is a formula I have always been uncomfortable with. It implies that a living being that does not do what we call thinking is somehow second-class. To thinking, cogitation, I oppose fullness, embodiedness, the sensation of being—not a consciousness of yourself as a kind of

---

[1] *Cogito, ergo sum* Latin: I think, therefore I am. Descartes's famous statement was intended to demonstrate the possibility of intuited knowledge.

ghostly reasoning machine thinking thoughts, but on the contrary the sensation—a heavily affective sensation—of being a body with limbs that have extension in space, of being alive to the world. This fullness contrasts starkly with Descartes' key state, which has an empty feel to it: the feel of a pea rattling around in a shell.

"Fullness of being is a state hard to sustain in confinement. Confinement to prison is the form of punishment that the West favours and does its best to impose on the rest of the world through the means of condemning other forms of punishment (beating, torture, mutilation, execution) as cruel and unnatural. What does this suggest to us about ourselves? To me it suggests that the freedom of the body to move in space is targeted as the point at which reason can most painfully and effectively harm the being of the other. And indeed it is on creatures least able to bear confinement—creatures who conform least to Descartes' picture of the soul as a pea imprisoned in a shell, to which further imprisonment is irrelevant—that we see the most devastating effects: in zoos, in laboratories, institutions where the flow of joy that comes from living not *in* or *as* a body but simply from being an embodied being has no place.

"The question to ask should not be: Do we have something in common—reason, self-consciousness, a soul—with other animals? (With the corollary that, if we do not, then we are entitled to treat them as we like, imprisoning them, killing them, dishonouring their corpses.) I return to the death camps. The particular horror of the camps, the horror that convinces us that what went on there was a crime against humanity, is not that despite a humanity shared with their victims, the killers treated them like lice. That is too abstract. The horror is that the killers refused to think themselves into the place of their victims, as did everyone else. They said, 'It is *they* in those cattle cars rattling past.' They did not say, 'How would it be if it were I in that cattle car?' They did not say, 'It is I who am in that cattle car.' They said, 'It must be the dead who are being burned today, making the air stink and falling in ash on my cabbages.' They did not say, 'How would it be if I were burning?' They did not say, 'I am burning, I am falling in ash.'

"In other words, they closed their hearts. The heart is the seat of a faculty, *sympathy*, that allows us to share at times the being of another. Sympathy has everything to do with the subject and little to do with the object, the 'another,' as we see at once when we think of the object not as a bat ('Can I share the being of a bat?') but as another human being. There are people who have the capacity to imagine themselves as someone else, there are people who have no such capacity (when the lack is extreme, we call them psychopaths), and there are people who have the capacity but choose not to exercise it.

"Despite Thomas Nagel, who is probably a good man, despite Thomas Aquinas and René Descartes, with whom I have more difficulty in sympathizing, there is no limit to the extent to which we can think ourselves into the being of another. There are no bounds to the sympathetic imagination. If you want proof, consider the following. Some years ago I wrote a book called *The House on Eccles Street*. To write that book I had to think my way into the existence of Marion Bloom.[1] Either I succeeded or I did not. If I did not, I cannot imagine why you invited me here today. In any event, the point is, *Marion Bloom never existed*. Marion Bloom was a figment of James Joyce's imagination. If I can think my way into the existence of a being who has never existed, then I can think my way into the existence of a bat or a chimpanzee or an oyster, any being with whom I share the substrate[2] of life.

"I return one last time to the places of death all around us, the places of slaughter to which, in a huge communal effort, we close our hearts. Each day a fresh holocaust, yet, as far as I can see, our moral being is untouched. We do not feel tainted. We can do anything, it seems, and come away clean.

"We point to the Germans and Poles and Ukrainians who did and did not know of the atrocities around them. We like to think they were inwardly marked by the after-effects of that special form of ignorance. We like to think that in their nightmares the ones whose suffering they had refused to enter came back to haunt them. We like to think they woke up haggard in the mornings and died of gnawing cancers. But probably it

---

[1]   *Marion Bloom* Character in James Joyce's novel *Ulysses* (1922).

[2]   *substrate* Foundation.

was not so. The evidence points in the opposite direction: that we can do anything and get away with it; that there is no punishment."

A strange ending. Only when she takes off her glasses and folds away her papers does the applause start, and even then it is scattered. A strange ending to a strange talk, he thinks, ill-gauged, ill-argued. Not her *métier*,[1] argumentation. She should not be here.

Norma has her hand up, is trying to catch the eye of the Dean of Humanities, who is chairing the session.

"Norma!" he whispers. Urgently he shakes his head. "No!"

"Why?" she whispers back.

"Please," he whispers: "not here, not now!"

"There will be an extended discussion of our eminent guest's lecture on Friday at noon—you will see the details in your programme notes—but Ms Costello has kindly agreed to take one or two questions from the floor. So—?" The dean looks around brightly. "Yes!" he says, recognizing someone behind them.

"I have a right!" whispers Norma into his ear.

"You have a right, just don't exercise it, it's not a good idea!" he whispers back.

"She can't just be allowed to get away with it! She's confused!"

"She's old, she's my mother. Please!"

Behind them someone is already speaking. He turns and sees a tall, bearded man. God knows, he thinks, why his mother ever agreed to field questions from the floor. She ought to know that public lectures draw kooks and crazies like flies to a corpse.

"What wasn't clear to me," the man is saying, "is what you are actually targeting. Are you saying we should close down the factory farms? Are you saying we should stop eating meat? Are you saying we should treat animals more humanely, kill them more humanely? Are you saying we should stop experiments *on* animals? Are you saying we should stop experiments *with* animals, even benign psychological experiments like Köhler's? Can you clarify? Thank you."

Clarify. Not a kook at all. His mother could do with some clarity.

Standing before the microphone without her text before her, gripping the edges of the rostrum,[2] his mother looks distinctly nervous. Not her *métier*, he thinks again: she should not be doing this.

"I was hoping not to have to enunciate principles," his mother says. "If principles are what you want to take away from this talk, I would have to respond, open your heart and listen to what your heart says."

She seems to want to leave it there. The dean looks nonplussed. No doubt the questioner feels nonplussed too. He himself certainly does. Why can't she just come out and say what she wants to say?

As if recognizing the stir of dissatisfaction, his mother resumes. "I have never been much interested in proscriptions, dietary or otherwise. Proscriptions, laws. I am more interested in what lies behind them. As for Köhler's experiments, I think he wrote a wonderful book, and the book wouldn't have been written if he hadn't thought he was a scientist conducting experiments with chimpanzees. But the book we read isn't the book he thought he was writing. I am reminded of something Montaigne[3] said: We think we are playing with the cat, but how do we know that the cat isn't playing with us? I wish I could think the animals in our laboratories are playing with us. But alas, it isn't so."

She falls silent. "Does that answer your question?" asks the dean. The questioner gives a huge, expressive shrug and sits down.

There is still the dinner to get through. In half an hour the president is to host a dinner at the Faculty Club. Initially he and Norma had not been invited. Then, after it was discovered that Elizabeth Costello had a son at Appleton, they were added to the list. He suspects they will be out of place. They will certainly be the most junior, the lowliest, On the other hand, it may be a good thing for him to be present. He may be needed to keep the peace.

With grim interest he looks forward to seeing how the college will cope with the challenge of the menu. If today's distinguished lecturer were an Islamic cleric or

---

[1] *métier* Area of specialization.

[2] *rostrum* Podium.

[3] *Montaigne* Michel de Montaigne, French writer whose non-fiction *Essais* explored a wide variety of philosophical subjects; the essay Costello references is "In Defense of Raymond Sebond" (1592).

a Jewish rabbi, they would presumably not serve pork. So are they, out of deference to vegetarianism, going to serve nut rissoles to everyone? Are her distinguished fellow guests going to have to fret through the evening, dreaming of the pastrami sandwich or the cold drumstick they will gobble down when they get home? Or will the wise minds of the college have recourse to the ambiguous fish, which has a backbone but does not breathe air or suckle its young?

The menu is, fortunately, not his responsibility. What he dreads is that, during a lull in the conversation, someone will come up with what he calls The Question—"What led you, Mrs. Costello, to become a vegetarian?"—and that she will then get on her high horse and produce what he and Norma call the Plutarch[1] Response. After that it will be up to him and him alone to repair the damage.

The response in question comes from Plutarch's moral essays. His mother has it by heart; he can reproduce it only imperfectly. "You ask me why I refuse to eat flesh. I, for my part, am astonished that you can put in your mouth the corpse of a dead animal, astonished that you do not find it nasty to chew hacked flesh and swallow the juices of death wounds." Plutarch is a real conversation-stopper: it is the word *juices* that does it. Producing Plutarch is like throwing down a gauntlet; after that, there is no knowing what will happen.

He wishes his mother had not come. It is nice to see her again; it is nice that she should see her grandchildren; it is nice for her to get recognition; but the price he is paying and the price he stands to pay if the visit goes badly seem to him excessive. Why can she not be an ordinary old woman living an ordinary old woman's life? If she wants to open her heart to animals, why can't she stay home and open it to her cats?

His mother is seated at the middle of the table, opposite President Garrard. He is seated two places away; Norma is at the foot of the table. One place is empty—he wonders whose.

Ruth Orkin, from Psychology, is telling his mother about an experiment with a young chimpanzee reared as human. Asked to sort photographs into piles, the chimpanzee insisted on putting a picture of herself with the pictures of humans rather than with the pictures of other apes. "One is so tempted to give the story a straightforward reading," says Orkin—"namely, that she wanted to be thought of as one of us. Yet as a scientist one has to be cautious."

"Oh, I agree," says his mother. "In her mind the two piles could have a less obvious meaning. Those who are free to come and go versus those who have to stay locked up, for instance. She may have been saying that she preferred to be among the free."

"Or she may just have wanted to please her keeper," interjects President Garrard. "By saying that they looked alike."

"A bit Machiavellian[2] for an animal, don't you think?" says a large blond man whose name he did not catch.

"Machiavelli the fox, his contemporaries called him," says his mother.

"But that's a different matter entirely—the fabulous qualities of animals," objects the large man.

"Yes," says his mother.

It is all going smoothly enough. They have been served pumpkin soup and no one is complaining. Can he afford to relax?

He was right about the fish. For the entrée the choice is between red snapper with baby potatoes and fettucine with roasted eggplant. Garrard orders the fettucine, as he does; in fact, among the eleven of them there are only three fish orders.

"Interesting how often religious communities choose to define themselves in terms of dietary prohibitions," observes Garrard.

"Yes," says his mother.

"I mean, it is interesting that the form of the definition should be, for instance, 'We are the people who don't eat snakes' rather than 'We are the people who eat lizards.' What we don't do rather than what we do do." Before his move into administration, Garrard was a political scientist.

"It all has to do with cleanness and uncleanness," says Wunderlich, who despite his name is British.

---

[1]   *Plutarch*   Plutarch of Chaeronea, Greek writer (46–120 CE) who argued that non-human animals possessed souls and could be rational beings.

[2]   *Machiavellian*   I.e., deceitful and manipulative; conforming to the principles advocated by Niccolò Machiavelli (1469–1527) in his treatise *The Prince*.

"Clean and unclean animals, clean and unclean habits. Uncleanness can be a very handy device for deciding who belongs and who doesn't, who is in and who is out."

"Uncleanness and shame," he himself interjects. "Animals have no shame." He is surprised to hear himself speaking. But why not?—the evening is going well.

"Exactly," says Wunderlich. "Animals don't hide their excretions, they perform sex in the open. They have no sense of shame, we say: that is what makes them different from us. But the basic idea remains uncleanness. Animals have unclean habits, so they are excluded. Shame makes human beings of us, shame of uncleanness. Adam and Eve: the founding myth. Before that we were all just animals together."

He has never heard Wunderlich before. He likes him, likes his earnest, stuttering, Oxford manner. A relief from American self-confidence.

"But that can't be how the mechanism works," objects Olivia Garrard, the president's elegant wife. "It's too abstract, too much of a bloodless idea. Animals are creatures we don't have sex with—that's how we distinguish them from ourselves. The very thought of sex with them makes us shudder. That is the level at which they are unclean—all of them. We don't mix with them. We keep the clean apart from the unclean."

"But we eat them." The voice is Norma's. "We do mix with them. We ingest them. We turn their flesh into ours. So it can't be how the mechanism works. There are specific kinds of animal that we don't eat. Surely *those* are the unclean ones, not animals in general."

She is right, of course. But wrong: a mistake to bring the conversation back to the matter on the table before them, the food.

Wunderlich speaks again. "The Greeks had a feeling there was something wrong in slaughter, but thought they could make up for that by ritualizing it. They made a sacrificial offering, gave a percentage to the gods, hoping thereby to keep the rest. The same notion as the tithe.[1] Ask for the blessing of the gods on the flesh you are about to eat, ask them to declare it clean."

[1] *tithe* Tax or offering, usually a tenth of one's income, paid to the church.

"Perhaps that is the origin of the gods," says his mother. A silence falls. "Perhaps we invented gods so that we could put the blame on them. They gave us permission to eat flesh. They gave us permission to play with unclean things. It's not our fault, it's theirs. We're just their children."

"Is that what you believe?" asks Mrs. Garrard cautiously.

"And God said: Every moving thing that liveth shall be meat for you," his mother quotes. "It's convenient. God told us it was OK."

Silence again. They are waiting for her to go on. She is, after all, the paid entertainer.

"Norma is right," says his mother. "The problem is to define our difference from animals in general, not just from so-called unclean animals. The ban on certain animals—pigs and so forth—is quite arbitrary. It is simply a signal that we are in a danger area. A minefield, in fact. The minefield of dietary proscriptions. There is no logic to a taboo, nor is there any logic to a minefield—there is not meant to be. You can never guess what you may eat or where you may step unless you are in possession of a map, a divine map."

"But that's just anthropology," objects Norma from the foot of the table. "It says nothing about our behaviour today. People in the modern world no longer decide their diet on the basis of whether they have divine permission. If we eat pig and don't eat dog, that's just the way we are brought up. Wouldn't you agree, Elizabeth? It's just one of our folkways."

Elizabeth. She is claiming intimacy. But what game is she playing? Is there a trap she is leading his mother into?

"There is disgust," says his mother. "We may have got rid of the gods but we have not got rid of disgust, which is a version of religious horror."

"Disgust is not universal," objects Norma. "The French eat frogs. The Chinese eat anything. There is no disgust in China."

His mother is silent.

"So perhaps it's just a matter of what you learned at home, of what your mother told you was OK to eat and what was not."

"What was clean to eat and what was not," his mother murmurs.

"And maybe"—now Norma is going too far, he thinks, now she is beginning to dominate the conversation to an extent that is totally inappropriate—"the whole notion of cleanness versus uncleanness has a completely different function, namely, to enable certain groups to self-define themselves, negatively, as elite, as elected. We are the people who abstain from A or B or C, and by that power of abstinence we mark ourselves off as superior: as a superior caste within society for instance. Like the Brahmins."[1]

There is a silence.

"The ban on meat that you get in vegetarianism is only an extreme form of dietary ban," Norma presses on; "and a dietary ban is a quick, simple way for an elite group to define itself. Other people's table habits are unclean, we can't eat or drink with them."

Now she is getting really close to the bone. There is a certain amount of shuffling, there is unease in the air. Fortunately, the course is over—the red snapper, the fettucine—and the waitresses are among them removing the plates.

"Have you read Gandhi's[2] autobiography, Norma?" asks his mother.

"No."

"Gandhi was sent off to England as a young man to study law. England, of course, prided itself as a great meat-eating country. But his mother made him promise not to eat meat. She packed a trunk full of food for him to take along. During the sea voyage he scavenged a little bread from the ship's table and for the rest ate out of his trunk. In London he faced a long search for lodgings and eating houses that served his kind of food. Social relations with the English were difficult because he could not accept or return hospitality. It wasn't until he fell in with certain fringe elements of English society—Fabians, theosophists,[3] and so forth—that he began to feel at home. Until then he was just a lonely little law student."

"What is the point, Elizabeth?" says Norma. "What is the point of the story?"

"Just that Gandhi's vegetarianism can hardly be conceived as the exercise of power. It condemned him to the margins of society. It was his particular genius to incorporate what he found on those margins into his political philosophy."

"In any event," interjects the blond man, "Gandhi is not a good example. His vegetarianism was hardly committed. He was a vegetarian because of the promise he made to his mother. He may have kept his promise, but he regretted and resented it."

"Don't you think that mothers can have a good influence on their children?" says Elizabeth Costello.

There is a moment's silence. It is time for him, the good son, to speak. He does not.

"But your own vegetarianism, Mrs. Costello," says President Garrard, pouring oil on troubled waters: "it comes out of moral conviction, does it not?"

"No, I don't think so," says his mother. "It comes out of a desire to save my soul."

Now there truly is a silence, broken only by the clink of plates as the waitresses set baked Alaskas before them.

"Well, I have a great respect for it," says Garrard. "As a way of life."

"I'm wearing leather shoes," says his mother. "I'm carrying a leather purse. I wouldn't have overmuch respect if I were you."

"Consistency," murmurs Garrard. "Consistency is the hobgoblin[4] of small minds. Surely one can draw a distinction between eating meat and wearing leather."

"Degrees of obscenity," she replies.

"I too have the greatest respect for codes based on respect for life," says Dean Arendt, entering the debate for the first time. "I am prepared to accept that dietary taboos do not have to be mere customs. I will accept that underlying them are genuine moral concerns. But at the same time one must say that our whole superstructure of concern and belief is a closed book to animals themselves. You can't explain to a steer that its life is going to be spared, any more than you can explain to a bug that you are not going to step on it. In the lives of animals, things, good or bad, just happen. So vegetarianism is a very odd transaction, when you come to

---

[1] *Brahmins* Members of the highest class, associated with priesthood, in the Hindu caste system.

[2] *Gandhi* Mohandas Gandhi (1869–1948), Indian activist known for his doctrine of non-violence.

[3] *Fabians* Members of the Fabian Society, a British organization dedicated to the promotion of socialism; *theosophists* Followers of a system of philosophical and mystical thought based on the direct and immediate experience of the divine.

[4] *hobgoblin* Folkloric figure evoking superstition and trickery.

think of it, with the beneficiaries unaware that they are being benefited. And with no hope of ever becoming aware. Because they live in a vacuum of consciousness."

Arendt pauses. It is his mother's turn to speak, but she merely looks confused, grey and tired and confused. He leans across. "It's been a long day, Mother," he says. "Perhaps it is time."

"Yes, it is time," she says.

"You won't have coffee?" enquires President Garrard.

"No, it will just keep me awake." She turns to Arendt. "That is a good point you raise. No consciousness that we would recognize as consciousness. No awareness, as far as we can make out, of a self with a history. What I mind is what tends to come next. They have no consciousness *therefore*. Therefore what? Therefore we are free to use them for our own ends? Therefore we are free to kill them? Why? What is so special about the form of consciousness we recognize that makes killing a bearer of it a crime while killing an animal goes unpunished? There are moments—"

"To say nothing of babies," interjects Wunderlich. Everyone turns and looks at him. "Babies have no self-consciousness, yet we think it a more heinous crime to kill a baby than an adult."

"Therefore?" says Arendt.

"Therefore all this discussion of consciousness and whether animals have it is just a smokescreen. At bottom we protect our own kind. Thumbs up to human babies, thumbs down to veal calves. Don't you think so, Mrs. Costello?"

"I don't know what I think," says Elizabeth Costello. "I often wonder what thinking is, what understanding is. Do we really understand the universe better than animals do? Understanding a thing often looks to me like playing with one of those Rubik cubes. Once you have made all the little bricks snap into place, hey presto, you understand. It makes sense if you live inside a Rubik cube, but if you don't ..."

There is a silence. "I would have thought—" says Norma; but at this point he gets to his feet, and to his relief Norma stops.

The president rises, and then everyone else. "A wonderful lecture, Mrs. Costello," says the president. "Much food for thought. We look forward to tomorrow's offering."

TWO: THE POETS AND THE ANIMALS

It is after eleven. His mother has retired for the night, he and Norma are downstairs clearing up the children's mess. After that he still has a class to prepare.

"Are you going to her seminar tomorrow?" asks Norma.

"I'll have to."

"What is it on?"

"'The Poets and the Animals.' That's the title. The English Department is staging it. They are holding it in a seminar room, so I don't think they are expecting a big audience."

"I'm glad it's on something she knows about. I find her philosophizing rather difficult to take."

"Oh. What do you have in mind?"

"For instance what she was saying about human reason. Presumably she was trying to make a point about the nature of rational understanding. To say that rational accounts are merely a consequence of the structure of the human mind; that animals have their own accounts in accordance with the structure of their own minds, to which we don't have access because we don't share a language with them."

"And what's wrong with that?"

"It's naive, John. It's the kind of easy, shallow relativism that impresses freshmen. Respect for everyone's world view, the cow's world view, the squirrel's world view, and so forth. In the end it leads to total intellectual paralysis. You spend so much time respecting that you haven't time left to think."

"Doesn't a squirrel have a world view?"

"Yes, a squirrel does have a world view. Its world view comprises acorns and trees and weather and cats and dogs and automobiles and squirrels of the opposite sex. It comprises an account of how these phenomena interact and how it should interact with them to survive. That's all. There's no more. That's the world according to squirrel."

"We are sure about that?"

"We are sure about it in the sense that hundreds of years of observing squirrels has not led us to conclude otherwise. If there is anything else in the squirrel mind, it does not issue in observable behaviour. For all practical purposes, the mind of the squirrel is a very simple mechanism."

"So Descartes was right, animals are just biological automata."

"Broadly speaking, yes. You cannot, in the abstract, distinguish between an animal mind and a machine simulating an animal mind."

"And human beings are different?"

"John, I am tired and you are being irritating. Human beings invent mathematics, they build telescopes, they do calculations, they construct machines, they press a button, and, bang, *Sojourner* lands on Mars,[1] exactly as predicted. That is why rationality is not just, as your mother claims, a game. Reason provides us with real knowledge of the real world. It has been tested, and it works. You are a physicist. You ought to know"

"I agree. It works. Still, isn't there a position outside from which our doing our thinking and then sending out a Mars probe looks a lot like a squirrel doing its thinking and then dashing out and snatching a nut? Isn't that perhaps what she meant?"

"But there isn't any such position! I know it sounds old-fashioned, but I have to say it. There is no position outside of reason where you can stand and lecture about reason and pass judgement on reason."

"Except the position of someone who has withdrawn from reason."

"That's just French irrationalism,[2] the sort of thing a person would say who has never set foot inside a mental institution and seen what people look like who have *really* withdrawn from reason."

"Then except for God."

"Not if God is a God of reason. A God of reason cannot stand outside reason."

"I'm surprised, Norma. You are talking like an old-fashioned rationalist."

"You misunderstand me. That is the ground your mother has chosen. Those are her terms. I am merely responding."

"Who was the missing guest?"

"You mean the empty seat? It was Stern, the poet."

"Do you think it was a protest?"

---

[1] *Sojourner lands on Mars* Part of the *Mars Pathfinder*, rover *Sojourner* landed on Mars in 1997 and gathered images of the planet.

[2] *irrationalism* Movement that sought ways to extend philosophical understanding past the constraints of reason.

"I'm sure it was. She should have thought twice before bringing up the Holocaust. I could feel hackles rising all around me in the audience."

The empty seat was indeed a protest. When he goes in for his morning class, there is a letter in his box addressed to his mother.

He hands it over to her when he comes home to fetch her. She reads it quickly, then with a sigh passes it over to him. "Who is this man?" she says.

"Abraham Stern. A poet. Quite well respected, I believe. He has been here donkey's years."

He reads Stern's note, which is handwritten.

Dear Mrs. Costello,

Excuse me for not attending last night's dinner. I have read your books and know you are a serious person, so I do you the credit of taking what you said in your lecture seriously.

At the kernel of your lecture, it seemed to me, was the question of breaking bread. If we refuse to break bread with the executioners of Auschwitz, can we continue to break bread with the slaughterers of animals?

You took over for your own purposes the familiar comparison between the murdered Jews of Europe and slaughtered cattle. The Jews died like cattle, therefore cattle die like Jews, you say. That is a trick with words which I will not accept. You misunderstand the nature of likenesses; I would even say you misunderstand wilfully, to the point of blasphemy. Man is made in the likeness of God but God does not have the likeness of man. If Jews were treated like cattle it does not follow that cattle are treated like Jews. The inversion insults the memory of the dead. It also trades on the horrors of the camps in a cheap way.

Forgive me if I am forthright. You said you were old enough not to have time to waste on niceties, and I am an old man too.

Yours sincerely,

Abraham Stern

He delivers his mother to her hosts in the English Department, then goes to a meeting. The meeting drags on and on. It is two thirty before he can get to the seminar room in Stubbs Hall.

She is speaking as he enters. He sits down as quietly as he can near the door.

"In that kind of poetry," she is saying, "animals stand for human qualities: the lion for courage, the owl for wisdom, and so forth. Even in Rilke's[1] poem the panther is there as a stand-in for something else. He dissolves into a dance of energy around a centre, an image that comes from physics, elementary particle physics. Rilke does not get beyond this point—beyond the panther as the vital embodiment of the kind of force that is released in an atomic explosion but is here trapped not so much by the bars of the cage as by what the bars compel on the panther: a concentric lope that leaves the will stupefied, narcotized."

Rilke's panther? What panther? His confusion must show: the girl next to him pushes a photocopied sheet under his nose. Three poems: one by Rilke called "The Panther," two by Ted Hughes[2] called "The Jaguar" and "Second Glance at a Jaguar." He has no time to read them.

"Hughes is writing against Rilke," his mother goes on. "He uses the same staging in the zoo, but it is the crowd for a change that stands mesmerized, and among them the man, the poet, entranced and horrified and overwhelmed, his powers of understanding pushed beyond their limit. The jaguar's vision, unlike the panther's, is not blunted. On the contrary, his eyes drill through the darkness of space. The cage has no reality to him, he is *elsewhere*. He is elsewhere because his consciousness is kinetic rather than abstract: the thrust of his muscles moves him through a space quite different in nature from the three-dimensional box of Newton—a circular space that returns upon itself.

"So—leaving aside the ethics of caging large animals—Hughes is feeling his way towards a different kind of being-in-the-world, one which is not entirely foreign to us, since the experience before the cage seems to belong to dream experience, experience held in the collective unconscious. In these poems we know the jaguar not from the way he seems but from the way he moves. The body is as the body moves, or as the cur-

rents of life move within it. The poems ask us to imagine our way into that way of moving, to inhabit that body.

"With Hughes it is a matter—I emphasize—not of inhabiting another mind but of inhabiting another body. That is the kind of poetry I bring to your attention today: poetry that does not try to find an idea in the animal, that is not about the animal, but is instead the record of an engagement with him.

"What is peculiar about poetic engagements of this kind is that, no matter with what intensity they take place, they remain a matter of complete indifference to their objects. In this respect they are different from love poems, where your intention is to move your object.

"Not that animals do not care what we feel about them. But when we divert the current of feeling that flows between ourself and the animal into words, we abstract it for ever from the animal. Thus the poem is not a gift to its object, as the love poem is. It falls within an entirely human economy in which the animal has no share. Does that answer your question?"

Someone else has his hand up: a tall young man with glasses. He doesn't know Ted Hughes's poetry well, he says, but the last he heard, Hughes was running a sheep ranch somewhere in England. Either he is just raising sheep as poetic subjects (there is a titter around the room) or he is a real rancher raising sheep for the market. "How does this square with what you were saying in your lecture yesterday, when you seemed to be pretty much against killing animals for meat?"

"I've never met Ted Hughes," replies his mother, "so I can't tell you what kind of farmer he is. But let me try to answer your question on another level.

"I have no reason to think that Hughes believes his attentiveness to animals is unique. On the contrary, I suspect he believes he is recovering an attentiveness that our faraway ancestors possessed and we have lost (he conceives of this loss in evolutionary rather than historical terms, but that is another question). I would guess that he believes he looks at animals much as palaeolithic hunters used to.

"This puts Hughes in a line of poets who celebrate the primitive and repudiate the Western bias towards abstract thought. The line of Blake and Lawrence, of

[1] *Rilke* Rainer Maria Rilke, Austro-German poet (1875–1926).

[2] *Ted Hughes* English poet (1930–98).

Gary Snyder in the United States, or Robinson Jeffers.[1] Hemingway[2] too, in his hunting and bull fighting phase.

"Bullfighting, it seems to me, gives us a clue. Kill the beast by all means, they say, but make it a contest, a ritual, and honour your antagonist for his strength and bravery. Eat him too, after you have vanquished him, in order for his strength and courage to enter you. Look him in the eyes before you kill him, and thank him afterwards. Sing songs about him.

"We can call this primitivism. It is an attitude that is easy to criticize, to mock. It is deeply masculine, masculinist. Its ramifications into politics are to be mistrusted. But when all is said and done, there remains something attractive about it at an ethical level.

"It is also impractical, however. You do not feed four billion people through the efforts of matadors or deer hunters armed with bows and arrows. We have become too many. There is no time to respect and honour all the animals we need to feed ourselves. We need factories of death; we need factory animals. Chicago showed us the way; it was from the Chicago stockyards that the Nazis learned how to process bodies.

"But let me get back to Hughes. You say: Despite the primitivist trappings Hughes is a butcher, and what am I doing in his company?

"I would reply, writers teach us more than they are aware of. By bodying forth the jaguar, Hughes shows us that we too can embody animals—by the process called poetic invention that mingles breath and sense in a way that no one has explained and no one ever will. He shows us how to bring the living body into being within ourselves. When we read the jaguar poem, when we recollect it afterwards in tranquillity,[3] we are for a brief while the jaguar. He ripples within us, he takes over our body, he is us.

[1] *Blake* William Blake (1757–1827), English poet and artist; *Lawrence* D.H. Lawrence (1885–1930), English novelist; *Gary Snyder* American beat poet and environmental activist (b. 1930); *Robinson Jeffers* American poet and environmentalist (1887–1962).

[2] *Ernest Hemingway* American novelist and short-story writer (1899–1961); much of his work, especially of the 1930s, focuses on activities such as hunting and bullfighting.

[3] *recollect it … in tranquillity* Cf. William Wordsworth's Preface to *Lyrical Ballads* (1800), in which he describes the origin of poetry as "emotion recollected in tranquillity."

"So far, so good. With what I have said thus far I don't think Hughes himself would disagree. It is much like the mixture of shamanism and spirit possession and archetype psychology that he himself espouses. In other words, a primitive experience (being face to face with an animal), a primitivist poem, and a primitivist theory of poetry to justify it.

"It is also the kind of poetry with which hunters and the people I call ecology-managers can feel comfortable. When Hughes the poet stands before the jaguar cage, he looks at an individual jaguar and is possessed by that individual jaguar life. It has to be that way. Jaguars in general, the subspecies jaguar, the idea of a jaguar, will fail to move him because we cannot experience abstractions. Nevertheless, the poem that Hughes writes is about *the* jaguar, about jaguarness embodied in this jaguar. Just as later on, when he writes his marvellous poems about salmon, they are about salmon as transitory occupants of the salmon life, the salmon biography. So despite the vividness and earthiness of the poetry, there remains something Platonic[4] about it.

"In the ecological vision, the salmon and the river weeds and the water insects interact in a great, complex dance with the earth and the weather. The whole is greater than the sum of the parts. In the dance, each organism has a role: it is these multiple roles, rather than the particular beings who play them, that participate in the dance. As for actual role players, as long as they are self-renewing, as long as they keep coming forward, we need pay them no heed.

"I called this Platonic and I do so again. Our eye is on the creature itself, but our mind is on the system of interactions of which it is the earthly, material embodiment.

"The irony is a terrible one. An ecological philosophy that tells us to live side by side with other creatures justifies itself by appealing to an idea, an idea of a higher order than any living creature. An idea, finally—and this is the crushing twist to the irony—which no creature except man is capable of comprehending. Every living creature fights for its own, individual life, refuses, by

[4] *Platonic* Plato posited the existence of abstract, ideal concepts called Forms. According to this view, objects in the material world are imperfect reflections of their corresponding Forms; for example, a jaguar in the material world is a flawed copy of the Form of the ideal jaguar.

fighting, to accede to the idea that the salmon or the gnat is of a lower order of importance than the idea of the salmon or the idea of the gnat. But when we see the salmon fighting for its life, we say, it is just programmed to fight; we say, with Aquinas, it is locked into natural slavery; we say, it lacks self-consciousness.

"Animals are not believers in ecology. Even the ethnobiologists do not make that claim. Even the ethnobiologists do not say that the ant sacrifices its life to perpetuate the species. What they say is subtly different: the ant dies and the function of its death is the perpetuation of the species. The species life is a force which acts through the individual but which the individual is incapable of understanding. In that sense the idea is innate, and the ant is run by the idea as a computer is run by a program.

"We, the managers of the ecology—I'm sorry to go on like this, I am getting way beyond your question, I'll be through in a moment—we managers understand the greater dance, therefore we can decide how many trout may be fished or how many jaguar may be trapped before the stability of the dance is upset. The only organism over which we do not claim this power of life and death is man. Why? Because man is different. Man understands the dance as the other dancers do not. Man is an intellectual being."

While she speaks, his mind has been wandering. He has heard it before, this anti-ecologism of hers. Jaguar poems are all very well, he thinks, but you won't get a bunch of Australians standing around a sheep, listening to its silly baa, writing poems about it. Isn't that what is so suspect in the whole animals-rights business: that it has to ride on the back of pensive gorillas and sexy jaguars and huggable pandas because the real objects of its concern, chickens and pigs, to say nothing of white rats or prawns, are not newsworthy?

Now Elaine Marx, who did the introduction to yesterday's lecture, asks a question. "In your lecture you argued that various criteria—Does this creature have reason? Does this creature have speech?—have been used in bad faith to justify distinctions that have no real basis, between *Homo* and other primates, for example, and thus to justify exploitation.

"Yet the very fact that you can be arguing against this reasoning, exposing its falsity means that you put a

certain faith in the power of reason, of true reason as opposed to false reason.

"Let me concretize my question by referring to the case of Lemuel Gulliver. In *Gulliver's Travels* Swift gives us a vision of a utopia of reason, the land of the so-called Houyhnhnms,[1] but it turns out to be a place where there is no home for Gulliver, who is the closest that Swift comes to a representation of us, his readers. But which of us would want to live in Houyhnhnm-land, with its rational vegetarianism and its rational government and its rational approach to love, marriage and death? Would even a horse want to live in such a perfectly regulated, totalitarian society? More pertinently for us, what is the track record of totally regulated societies? Is it not a fact that they either collapse or else turn militaristic?

"Specifically, my question is: Are you not expecting too much of humankind when you ask us to live without species exploitation, without cruelty? Is it not more human to accept our own humanity—even if it means embracing the carnivorous Yahoo[2] within ourselves—than to end up like Gulliver, pining for a state he can never attain, and for good reason: it is not in his nature, which is a human nature?"

"An interesting question," his mother replies. "I find Swift an intriguing writer. For instance, his *Modest Proposal*.[3] Whenever there is overwhelming agreement about how to read a book, I prick up my ears. On *A Modest Proposal* the consensus is that Swift does not mean what he says, or seems to say. He says, or seems to say, that Irish families could make a living by raising babies for the table of their English masters. But he can't mean that, we say, because we all know that it is atrocious to kill and eat human babies. Yet, come to think of it, we go on, the English are already in a sense killing human babies, by letting them starve. So, come to think

---

[1] *Gulliver's Travels* Satirical novel (1726) by Jonathan Swift; *Houyhnhnms* Rational-minded horses who rule the land depicted in part four of *Gulliver's Travels*; Gulliver greatly admires their society, but is banished from it.

[2] *Yahoo* Dirty, brutish, human-like creature ruled by the Houyhnhnms; in *Gulliver's Travels*, Gulliver comes to hate human beings because of their resemblance to Yahoos.

[3] *Modest Proposal* Swift's 1729 satiric essay suggesting that Irish children should be sold to and eaten by wealthy English citizens as a solution to the problem of Irish poverty.

of it, the English are already atrocious.

"That is the orthodox reading, more or less. But why, I ask myself, the vehemence with which it is stuffed down the throats of young readers? Thus shall you read Swift, their teachers say, thus and in no other way. If it is atrocious to kill and eat human babies, why is it not atrocious to kill and eat piglets? If you want Swift to be a dark ironist rather than a facile pamphleteer, you might examine the premises that make his fable so easy to digest.

"Let me now turn to *Gulliver's Travels*.

"On the one hand you have the Yahoos, who are associated with raw meat, the smell of excrement and what we used to call bestiality. On the other you have the Houyhnhnms, who are associated with grass, sweet smells and the rational ordering of the passions. In between you have Gulliver, who wants to be a Houyhnhnm but knows secretly that he is a Yahoo. All of that is perfectly clear. As with *A Modest Proposal*, the question is, what do we make of it?

"One observation. The horses expel Gulliver. Their ostensible reason is that he does not meet the standard of rationality. The real reason is that he does not look like a horse, but something else: a dressed-up Yahoo, in fact. So: the standard of reason that has been applied by carnivorous bipeds to justify a special status for themselves can equally be applied by herbivorous quadrupeds.

"The standard of reason. *Gulliver's Travels* seems to me to operate within the three-part Aristotelian division of gods, beasts and men. As long as one tries to fit the three actors into just two categories—which are the beasts, which are the men?—one can't make sense of the fable. Nor can the Houyhnhnms. The Houyhnhnms are gods of a kind, cold, Apollonian.[1] The test they apply to Gulliver is: Is he a god or a beast? They feel it is the appropriate test. We, instinctively, don't.

"What has always puzzled me about *Gulliver's Travels*—and this is a perspective you might expect from an ex-colonial—is that Gulliver always travels alone. Gulliver goes on voyages of exploration to unknown lands, but he does not come ashore with an armed party, *as happened in reality*, and Swift's book says nothing

about what would normally have come after Gulliver's pioneering efforts: follow-up expeditions, expeditions to colonize Lilliput or the island of the Houyhnhnms.

"The question I ask is: What if Gulliver and an armed expedition were to land, shoot a few Yahoos when they become threatening, and then shoot and eat a horse, for food? What would that do to Swift's somewhat too neat, somewhat too disembodied, somewhat too unhistorical fable? It would certainly give the Houyhnhnms a rude shock, making it clear that there is a third category besides gods and beasts, namely, man, of whom their ex-client Gulliver is one; furthermore, that if the horses stand for reason, then man stands for physical force.

"Taking over an island and slaughtering its inhabitants is, by the way, what Odysseus and his men did on Thrinacia,[2] the island sacred to Apollo, an act for which they were mercilessly punished by the god. And that story, in turn, seems to call on older layers of belief, from a time when bulls were gods and killing and eating a god could call down a curse on you.

"So—excuse the confusion of this response—yes, we are not horses, we do not have their clear, rational, naked beauty; on the contrary, we are subequine primates, otherwise known as man. You say there is nothing to do but embrace that status, that nature. Very well, let us do so. But let us also push Swift's fable to its limits and recognize that, in history, embracing the status of man has entailed slaughtering and enslaving a race of divine or else divinely created beings and bringing down on ourselves a curse thereby."

It is three fifteen, a couple of hours before his mother's last engagement. He walks her over to his office along tree-lined paths where the last autumn leaves are falling.

"Do you really believe, Mother, that poetry classes are going to close down the slaughterhouses?"

"No."

"Then why do it? You said you were tired of clever talk about animals, proving by syllogism that they do or do not have souls. But isn't poetry just another kind of

---

[1] *Apollonian* Possessing traits associated with the Greek god Apollo, such as rationality.

[2] *Odysseus ... Thrinacia* In Homer's *Odyssey*, the hero Odysseus and his crew find shelter on the island of Thrinacia, where the crew kill and eat cattle belonging to the sun god; all the men except Odysseus are killed as punishment.

clever talk: admiring the muscles of the big cats in verse? Wasn't your point about talk that it changes nothing? It seems to me the level of behaviour you want to change is too elementary, too elemental, to be reached by talk. Carnivorousness expresses something truly deep about human beings, just as it does about jaguars. You wouldn't want to put a jaguar on a soybean diet."

"Because he would die. Human beings don't die on a vegetarian diet."

"No, they don't. But they don't *want* a vegetarian diet. They *like* eating meat. There is something atavistically[1] satisfying about it. That's the brutal truth. Just as it's a brutal truth that, in a sense, animals deserve what they get. Why waste your time trying to help them when they won't help themselves? Let them stew in their own juice. If I were asked what the general attitude is towards the animals we eat, I would say: contempt. We treat them badly because we despise them; we despise them because they don't fight back."

"I don't disagree," says his mother. "People complain that we treat animals like objects, but in fact we treat them like prisoners of war. Do you know that when zoos were first opened to the public, the keepers had to protect the animals against attacks by spectators? The spectators felt the animals were there to be insulted and abused, like prisoners in a triumph.[2] We had a war once against the animals, which we called hunting, though in fact war and hunting are the same thing (Aristotle saw it clearly[3]). That war went on for millions of years. We won it definitively only a few hundred years ago, when we invented guns. It is only since victory became absolute that we have been able to afford to cultivate compassion. But our compassion is very thinly spread. Beneath it is a more primitive attitude. The prisoner of war does not belong to our tribe. We can do what we want with him. We can sacrifice him to our gods. We can cut his throat, tear out his heart, throw him on the fire. There are no laws when it comes

to prisoners of war."

"And that is what you want to cure humankind of?"

"John, I don't know what I want to do. I just don't want to sit silent."

"Very well. But generally one doesn't kill prisoners of war. One turns them into slaves."

"Well, that's what our captive herds are: slave populations. Their work is to breed for us. Even their sex becomes a form of labour. We don't hate them because they are not worth hating any more. We regard them, as you say, with contempt.

"However, there are still animals we hate. Rats, for instance. Rats haven't surrendered. They fight back. They form themselves into underground units in our sewers. They aren't winning, but they aren't losing either. To say nothing of the insects and the microbia. They may beat us yet. They will certainly outlast us."

The final session of his mother's visit is to take the form of a debate. Her opponent will be the large, blond man from yesterday evening's dinner, who turns out to be Thomas O'Hearne, professor of philosophy at Appleton.

It has been agreed that O'Hearne will have three opportunities to present positions, and his mother three opportunities to reply. Since O'Hearne has had the courtesy to send her a précis[4] before hand, she knows, broadly speaking, what he will be saying.

"My first reservation about the animal-rights movement," O'Hearne begins, "is that by failing to recognize its historical nature, it runs the risk of becoming, like the human-rights movement, yet another Western crusade against the practices of the rest of the world, claiming universality for what are simply its own standards." He proceeds to give a brief outline of the rise of animal-protection societies in Britain and America in the nineteenth century.

"When it comes to human rights," he continues, "other cultures and other religious traditions quite properly reply that they have their own norms and see no reason why they should have to adopt those of the West. Similarly, they say, they have their own norms for the treatment of animals and see no reason to adopt ours—particularly when ours are of such recent invention.

---

[1] *atavistically* Relating to a characteristic inherited from past or ancient ancestors, especially if the characteristic is not present in more recent ancestors.

[2] *triumph* Ancient Roman ceremonial parade in which war captives were displayed.

[3] *Aristotle saw it clearly* Cf. Aristotle's *Politics* 1.7, in which he describes the capture of slaves as a form of "hunting or war."

[4] *précis* Brief abstract or outline.

"In yesterday's presentation our lecturer was very hard on Descartes. But Descartes did not invent the idea that animals belong to a different order from humankind: he merely formalized it in a new way. The notion that we have an obligation to animals themselves to treat them compassionately—as opposed to an obligation to ourselves to do so—is very recent, very Western, and even very Anglo-Saxon. As long as we insist that we have access to an ethical universal to which other traditions are blind, and try to impose it on them by means of propaganda or even economic pressure, we are going to meet with resistance, and that resistance will be justified."

It is his mother's turn.

"The concerns you express are substantial, Professor O'Hearne, and I am not sure I can give them a substantial answer. You are correct, of course, about the history. Kindness to animals has become a social norm only recently, in the last hundred and fifty or two hundred years, and in only part of the world. You are correct too to link this history to the history of human rights, since concern for animals is, historically speaking, an offshoot of broader philanthropic concerns—for the lot of slaves and of children, among others.

"However, kindness to animals—and here I use the word *kindness* in its full sense, as an acceptance that we are all of one kind, one nature—has been more widespread than you imply. Pet-keeping, for instance, is by no means a Western fad: the first travellers to South America encountered settlements where human beings and animals lived higgledy-piggledy together. And of course children all over the world consort quite naturally with animals. They don't see any dividing line. That is something they have to be taught, just as they have to be taught it is all right to kill and eat them.

"Getting back to Descartes, I would only want to say that the discontinuity he saw between animals and human beings was the result of incomplete information. The science of Descartes' day had no acquaintance with the great apes or with higher marine mammals, and thus little cause to question the assumption that animals cannot think. And of course it had no access to the fossil record that would reveal a graded continuum of anthropoid creatures stretching from the higher primates to *Homo sapiens*—anthropoids, one must point out, who

were exterminated by man in the course of his rise to power.

"While I concede your main point about Western cultural arrogance, I do think it is appropriate that those who pioneered the industrialization of animal lives and the commodification of animal flesh should be at the forefront of trying to atone for it."

O'Hearne presents his second thesis. "In my reading of the scientific literature," he says, "efforts to show that animals can think strategically, hold general concepts or communicate symbolically, have had very limited success. The best performance the higher apes can put up is no better than that of a speech-impaired human being with severe mental retardation. If so, are not animals, even the higher animals, properly thought of as belonging to another legal and ethical realm entirely, rather than being placed in this depressing human subcategory? Isn't there a certain wisdom in the traditional view that says that animals cannot enjoy legal rights because they are not persons, even potential persons, as foetuses are? In working out rules for our dealings with animals, does it not make more sense for such rules to apply to us and to our treatment of them, as at present, rather than being predicated upon rights which animals cannot claim or enforce or even understand?"

His mother's turn. "To respond adequately, Professor O'Hearne, would take more time than I have, since I would first want to interrogate the whole question of rights and how we come to possess them. So let me just make one observation: that the programme of scientific experimentation that leads you to conclude that animals are imbeciles is profoundly anthropocentric. It values being able to find your way out of a sterile maze, ignoring the fact that if the researcher who designed the maze were to be parachuted into the jungles of Borneo, he or she would be dead of starvation in a week. In fact I would go further. If I as a human being were told that the standards by which animals are being measured in these experiments are human standards, I would be insulted. It is the experiments themselves that are imbecile. The behaviourists who design them claim that we understand only by a process of creating abstract models and then testing those models against reality. What nonsense. We understand by immersing ourselves and our intelligence in complexity. There is something self-stultified in the way in which scientific behaviourism recoils from the complexity of life.

"As for animals being too dumb and stupid to speak for themselves, consider the following sequence of events. When Albert Camus[1] was a young boy in Algeria, his grandmother told him to bring her one of the hens from the cage in their backyard. He obeyed, then watched her cut off its head with a kitchen knife, catching its blood in a bowl so that the floor would not be dirtied.

"The death cry of that hen imprinted itself on the boy's memory so hauntingly that in 1958 he wrote an impassioned attack on the guillotine. As a result, in part, of that polemic, capital punishment was abolished in France. Who is to say, then, that the hen did not speak?"

O'Hearne. "I make the following statement with due deliberation, mindful of the historical associations it may evoke. I do not believe that life is as important to animals as it is to us. There is certainly in animals an instinctive struggle against death, which they share with us. But they do not *understand* death as we do, or rather, as we fail to do. There is, in the human mind, a collapse of the imagination before death, and that collapse of the imagination—graphically evoked in yesterday's lecture—is the basis of our fear of death. That fear does not and cannot exist in animals, since the effort to comprehend extinction, and the failure to do so, the failure to master it, have simply not taken place.

"For that reason, I want to suggest, dying is, for an animal, just something that happens, something against which there may be a revolt of the organism but not a revolt of the soul. And the lower down the scale of evolution one goes, the truer this is. To an insect, death is the breakdown of systems that keep the physical organism functioning, and nothing more.

"To animals, death is continuous with life. It is only among certain very imaginative human beings that one encounters a horror of dying so acute that they then project it on other beings, including animals. Animals live, and then they die: that is all. Thus to equate a butcher who slaughters a chicken with an executioner who kills a human being is a grave mistake. The events

are not comparable. They are not of the same scale, they are not on the same scale.

"That leaves us with the question of cruelty. It is licit to kill animals, I would say, because their lives are not as important to them as our lives are to us; the old-fashioned way of saying this is that animals do not have immortal souls. Gratuitous cruelty, on the other hand, I would regard as illicit. Therefore it is quite appropriate that we should agitate for the humane treatment of animals, even and particularly in slaughterhouses. This has for a long time been a goal of animal-welfare organizations, and I salute them for it.

"My very last point concerns what I see as the troublingly abstract nature of the concern for animals in the animal-rights movement. I want to apologize in advance to our lecturer for the seeming harshness of what I am about to say, but I believe it needs to be said.

"Of the many varieties of animal lover I see around me, let me isolate two. On the one hand, hunters, people who value animals at a very elementary, unreflective level; who spend hours watching them and tracking them; and who, after they have killed them, get pleasure from the taste of their flesh. On the other hand, people who have little contact with animals, or at least with those species they are concerned to protect, like poultry and livestock, yet want all animals to lead—in an economic vacuum—a utopian life in which everyone is miraculously fed and no one preys on anyone else.

"Of the two, which, I ask, loves animals more?

"It is because agitation for animal rights, including the right to life, is so abstract that I find it unconvincing and, finally, idle. Its proponents talk a great deal about our community with animals, but how do they actually live that community? Thomas Aquinas says that friendship between human beings and animals is impossible, and I tend to agree. You can be friends neither with a Martian nor with a bat, for the simple reason that you have too little in common with them. We may certainly *wish* for there to be community with animals, but that is not the same thing as living in community with them. It is just a piece of prelapsarian[2] wistfulness."

His mother's turn again, her last turn.

"Anyone who says that life matters less to animals

[1] *Albert Camus* French writer and philosopher (1913–60).

[2] *prelapsarian* From a time of innocence; in terms of Christian theology, from the period before the Fall.

than it does to us has not held in his hands an animal fighting for its life. The whole of the being of the animal is thrown into that fight, without reserve. When you say that the fight lacks a dimension of intellectual or imaginative horror, I agree. It is not the mode of being of animals to have an intellectual horror: their whole being is in the living flesh.

"If I do not convince you, that is because my words, here, lack the power to bring home to you the wholeness, the unabstracted, unintellectual nature, of that animal being. That is why I urge you to read the poets who return the living, electric being to language; and if the poets do not move you, I urge you to walk, flank to flank, beside the beast that is prodded down the chute to his executioner.

"You say that death does not matter to an animal because the animal does not understand death. I am reminded of one of the academic philosophers I read in preparing for yesterday's lecture. It was a depressing experience. It awoke in me a quite Swiftian response. If this is the best that human philosophy can offer, I said to myself, I would rather go and live among horses.

"Can we, asked this philosopher, strictly speaking, say that the veal calf misses its mother? Does the veal calf have enough of a grasp of the significance of the mother relation, does the veal calf have enough of a grasp of the meaning of maternal absence, does the veal calf, finally, know enough about missing to know that the feeling it has is the feeling of missing?

"A calf who has not mastered the concepts of presence and absence, of self and other—so goes the argument—cannot, strictly speaking, be said to miss anything. In order to, strictly speaking, miss anything, it would first have to take a course in philosophy. What sort of philosophy is this? Throw it out, I say. What good do its piddling distinctions do?

"To me, a philosopher who says that the distinction between human and non-human depends on whether you have a white or a black skin, and a philosopher who says that the distinction between human and non-human depends on whether or not you know the difference between a subject and a predicate, are more alike than they are unlike.

"Usually I am wary of exclusionary gestures. I know of one prominent philosopher who states that he is

simply not prepared to philosophize about animals with people who eat meat. I am not sure I would go as far as that—frankly, I have not the courage—but I must say I would not fall over myself to meet the gentleman whose book I just have been citing. Specifically, I would not fall over myself to break bread with him.

"Would I be prepared to discuss ideas with him? That really is the crucial question. Discussion is possible only when there is common ground. When opponents are at loggerheads, we say: 'Let them reason together, and by reasoning clarify what their differences are, and thus inch closer. They may seem to share nothing else, but at least they share reason.'

"On the present occasion, however, I am not sure I want to concede that I share reason with my opponent. Not when reason is what underpins the whole long philosophical tradition to which he belongs, stretching back to Descartes and beyond Descartes through Aquinas and Augustine to the Stoics and Aristotle. If the last common ground that I have with him is reason, and if reason is what sets me apart from the veal calf, then thank you but no thank you, I'll talk to someone else."

That is the note on which Dean Arendt has to bring the proceedings to a close: acrimony, hostility, bitterness. He, John Bernard, is sure that is not what Arendt or his committee wanted. Well, they should have asked him before they invited his mother. He could have told them.

It is past midnight, he and Norma are in bed, he is exhausted, at six he will have to get up to drive his mother to the airport. But Norma is in a fury and will not give up. "It's nothing but food faddism, and food faddism is always an exercise in power. I have no patience when she arrives here and begins trying to get people, particularly the children, to change their eating habits. And now these absurd public lectures! She is trying to extend her inhibiting power over the whole community!"

He wants to sleep, but he cannot utterly betray his mother. "She's perfectly sincere," he murmurs.

"It has nothing to do with sincerity. She has no self-insight at all. It is because she has so little insight into her motives that she seems sincere. Mad people are sincere."

With a sigh he enters the fray. "I don't see any difference," he says, "between her revulsion from eating meat and my own revulsion from eating snails or locusts. I have no insight into my motives and I couldn't care less. I just find it disgusting."

Norma snorts. "You don't give public lectures producing pseudo-philosophical arguments for not eating snails. You don't try to turn a private fad into a public taboo."

"Perhaps. But why not try to see her as a preacher, a social reformer, rather than as an eccentric trying to foist her preferences on to other people?"

"You are welcome to see her as a preacher. But take a look at all the other preachers and their crazy schemes for dividing mankind up into the saved and the damned. Is that the kind of company you want your mother to keep? Elizabeth Costello and her Second Ark, with her dogs and cats and wolves, none of whom, of course, has ever been guilty of the sin of eating flesh, to say nothing of the malaria virus and the rabies virus and the HI virus, which she will want to save so that she can restock her Brave New World."[1]

"Norma, you're ranting."

"I'm not ranting. I would have more respect for her if she didn't try to undermine me behind my back, with her stories to the children about the poor little veal calves and what the bad men do to them. I'm tired of having them pick at their food and ask, 'Mom, is this veal?' when it's chicken or tuna fish. It's nothing but a power game. Her great hero Franz Kafka played the same game with his family. He refused to eat this, he refused to eat that, he would rather starve, he said. Soon everyone was feeling guilty about eating in front of him, and he could sit back feeling virtuous. It's a sick game, and I'm not having the children play it against me."

"A few hours and she'll be gone, then we can return to normal."

"Good. Say goodbye to her from me. I'm not getting up early."

Seven o'clock, the sun just rising, and he and his mother are on their way to the airport.

"I'm sorry about Norma," he says. "She has been under a lot of strain. I don't think she is in a position to sympathize. Perhaps one could say the same for me. It's been such a short visit, I haven't had time to make sense of why you have become so intense about the animal business."

She watches the wipers wagging back and forth. "A better explanation," she says, "is that I have not told you why, or dare not tell you. When I think of the words, they seem so outrageous that they are best spoken into a pillow or into a hole in the ground, like King Midas."[2]

"I don't follow. What is it you can't say?"

"It's that I no longer know where I am. I seem to move around perfectly easily among people, to have perfectly normal relations with them. Is it possible, I ask myself, that all of them are participants in a crime of stupefying proportions? Am I fantasizing it all? I must be mad! Yet every day I see the evidences. The very people I suspect produce the evidence, exhibit it, offer it to me. Corpses. Fragments of corpses that they have bought for money.

"It is as if I were to visit friends, and to make some polite remark about the lamp in their living room, and they were to say, 'Yes, it's nice, isn't it? Polish-Jewish skin[3] it's made of, we find that's best, the skins of young Polish-Jewish virgins.' And then I go to the bathroom and the soap wrapper says, 'Treblinka—100% human stearate.'[4] Am I dreaming, I say to myself? What kind of house is this?

"Yet I'm not dreaming. I look into your eyes, into Norma's, into the children's, and I see only kindness, human kindness. Calm down, I tell myself, you are making a mountain out of a molehill. This is life. Everyone else comes to terms with it, why can't you? *Why can't you?*"

She turns on him a tearful face. What does she want,

[1] *Brave New World* Title of a 1932 dystopian novel by Aldous Huxley about an imagined twenty-fifth century; the phrase itself is from Shakespeare's *The Tempest* 5.1.204–06: "How many goodly creatures are there here! / How beauteous mankind is! O brave new world, / That hath such people in it!"

[2] *King Midas* In Greek mythology, a king of Phrygia who was cursed with the ears of an ass after insulting Apollo. Midas tried to hide his shameful story by speaking it into a hole in the ground.

[3] *Polish-Jewish skin* Refers to allegations that, during the Holocaust, the skin of concentration camp victims was used to make leather souvenirs, such as lampshades.

[4] *stearate* Stearic acid in salt or ester form, used in soap making.

he thinks? Does she want me to answer her question for her?

They are not yet on the expressway. He pulls the car over, switches off the engine, takes his mother in his arms. He inhales the smell of cold cream, of old flesh.

"There, there," he whispers in her ear. "There, there. It will soon be over."

—1999, 2003

EAVAN BOLAND
b. 1944

In a time and place where being a woman and being a poet were considered two divergent pursuits, Eavan Boland established herself as one of the most important Irish writers of her time. Leading largely through personal example rather than political activism, she has proudly accepted the mantle of "woman poet," stating in recent years that this dual designation shows "that poetry is more of an open city now than it once was." The recipient of many awards, she has been a member of the Irish Academy of Letters and served on the board of the Irish Arts Council, and she has been a writer in residence at Trinity College and University College Dublin, as well as a poet in residence at the National Maternity Hospital.

Boland was born in Dublin, Ireland, to parents Frederick Boland and Frances Kelly, a diplomat and a painter. Her father's work took the family out of Ireland when Boland was six years old, and they lived in London and New York before returning to Ireland during Boland's teenage years. As a seventeen-year-old working in Dublin the summer before beginning studies at Trinity College, Boland embarked on her own study of poetry, spending many evenings reading the works of Yeats, Joyce, and the nineteenth century poets that would shape her understanding of the evolution of the poetic form. She was also beginning to write her own poems, though she experienced difficulty fully realizing an identity as a poet; she would later recall feeling that she "was looking for that solid land-bridge between writing poems and being a poet." While attending Trinity College, Boland continued to write, and in 1962 she published her first collection of poetry, *23 Poems*.

After graduating with a BA, Boland wrote poetry reviews for the *Irish Times* and immersed herself in Dublin's literary scene. With her marriage to writer Kevin Casey and the birth of their two daughters, she experienced a radical shift. In the culture of mid-twentieth-century Ireland, where suburban ideals of womanhood seemed to relegate women to the domestic sphere, Boland faced a sudden professional isolation. The domestic reality of her new life, however, enabled her to access a vibrant daily experience from which she drew unprecedented inspiration: "Finally, I had joined together my life as a woman and a poet. On the best days I lived as a poet, the language at the end of my day—when the children were asleep and the curtains drawn—was the language all through my day: it had waited for me." Boland's unsentimental, evocative depictions of ordinary and personal scenes soon caught the attention of readers in her own country and beyond. Her poems, published in collections such as *In Her Own Image* (1980), *Night Feed* (1982), *The Journey* (1983), and *In a Time of Violence* (1994), wove scenes of the daily domestic together with re-imagined mythological figures and motifs, finding the personal and everyday a powerful site that could be captured and re-experienced poetically by both writers and readers.

Boland has credited American poets such as Adrienne Rich and Denise Levertov as influences on her work, though she has also acknowledged the continuing influence of the Irish and Scottish poets she had first encountered as a student. As she studied the poets of the Irish lyric tradition and carved out her own place in this lineage, she found spaces for subversion within the English language, a medium bestowed by colonizers but, Boland has argued, one that has enabled her to write of her nation's loss. In 1989, Boland published *A Kind of Scar*, a scholarly discussion of Irish female poets. In that book she argues that the margin space that Irish female poets must occupy provides a unique perspective from which writers can tell the stories found in the silences of the past; she distinguishes these from history, "itself a constructed narrative." From that space she has produced over twenty collections of poems, including *Against Love Poetry* (2001) and *Domestic Violence* (2007).

Though she does not claim affiliation with a specific literary movement, Boland's writing and teaching activities have linked her with a wide community of writers, readers, and scholars; she is a co-founder of Arlen House, a feminist press that publishes the work of Irish writers. Among her prose works is the reflective memoir *Object Lessons: The Life of the Woman and the Poet in Our Time* (1995), in which she discusses her development as an artist both from a personal perspective and in a wider social and literary context. In her 1997 "Letter to a Young Woman Poet," she addresses an imagined audience of poets following in her footsteps, telling them that the "very past in poetry which simplified us as women and excluded us as poets now needs us to change it." Her guidance of young writers has also extended to the classroom; she has taught at Trinity College, Dublin's University College, Bowdoin College, Washington University, and the University of Utah. In 1997 she became the director of Stanford University's prestigious creative writing program.

⌘ ⌘ ⌘

Night Feed

This is dawn.
  Believe me
This is your season, little daughter.
The moment daisies open,
5   The hour mercurial rainwater
Makes a mirror for sparrows.
It's time we drowned our sorrows.

I tiptoe in.
I lift you up
10 Wriggling
In your rosy, zipped sleeper.
Yes, this is the hour
For the early bird and me
When finder is keeper.

15 I crook the bottle.
How you suckle!
This is the best I can be,
Housewife
To this nursery
20 Where you hold on,
Dear life.

A slit of milk.
The last suck.
And now your eyes are open,
25 Birth-coloured and offended.
Earth wakes.
You go back to sleep.
The feed is ended.

Worms turn.
30 Stars go in.
Even the moon is losing face.
Poplars stilt for dawn
And we begin
The long fall from grace.
35 I tuck you in.
—1982

Listen. This Is the Noise of Myth

This is the story of a man and woman
  under a willow and beside a weir
near a river in a wooded clearing.
They are fugitives. Intimates of myth.

5   Fictions of my purpose. I suppose
I shouldn't say that yet or at least
before I break their hearts or save their lives
I ought to tell their story and I will.

When they went first it was winter; cold,
10   cold through the Midlands and as far West[1]
as they could go. They knew they had to go—
through Meath, Westmeath, Longford,

their lives unravelling like the hours of light—
and then there were lambs under the snow
15   and it was January, aconite[2] and jasmine
and the hazel yellowing and puce berries on the ivy.

They could not eat where they had cooked,
nor sleep where they had eaten
nor at dawn rest where they had slept.
20   They shunned the densities

of trees with one trunk and of caves
with one dark and the dangerous embrace
of islands with a single landing place.
And all the time it was cold, cold:

25   the fields still gardened by their ice,
the trees stitched with snow overnight,
the ditches full; frost toughening lichen,
darning lace into rock crevices.

And then the woods flooded and buds
30   blunted from the chestnut and the foxglove
put its big leaves out and chaffinches°   *small finches*
chinked and flirted in the branches of the ash.

And here we are where we started from—
under a willow and beside a weir
35   near a river in a wooded clearing.
The woman and the man have come to rest.

Look how light is coming through the ash.
The weir sluices kingfisher blues.

The woman and the willow tree lean forward, forward.
40   Something is near; something is about to happen;

something more than Spring
and less than history. Will we see
hungers eased after months of hiding?
Is there a touch of heat in that light?

45   If they stay here soon it will be summer; things
returning, sunlight fingering minnowy deeps,
seedy greens, reeds, electing lights
and edges from the river. Consider

legend, self-deception, sin, the sum
50   of human purposes and its end; remember
how our poetry depends on distance,
aspect: gravity will bend starlight.

Forgive me if I set the truth to rights.
Bear with me if I put an end to this:
55   She never turned to him; she never leaned
under the sallow-willow[3] over to him.

They never made love; not there; not here;
not anywhere; there was no winter journey;
no aconite, no birdsong and no jasmine,
60   no woodland and no river and no weir.

Listen. This is the noise of myth. It makes
the same sound as shadow. Can you hear it?
Daylight greys in the preceptories.[4]
Her head begins to shine

65   pivoting the planets of a harsh nativity.
They were never mine. This is mine.
This sequence of evicted possibilities.
Displaced facts. Tricks of light. Reflections.

Invention. Legend. Myth. What you will.
70   The shifts and fluencies are infinite.

---

[1] *West* Historically, the west of Ireland has always been the poorest and most rural area.

[2] *aconite* Small flower (also known as "winter aconite").

[3] *sallow-willow* Type of low-growing willow.

[4] *preceptories* Estates housing subordinate communities of the Knights Templar, a medieval military and religious order of knighthood.

The moving parts are marvellous. Consider
how the bereavements of the definite

are easily lifted from our heroine.
She may or she may not. She was or wasn't
75 by the water at his side as dark
waited above the Western countryside.

O consolations of the craft.
How we put
the old poultices on the old sores,
80 the same mirrors to the old magic. Look.

The scene returns. The willow sees itself
drowning in the weir and the woman
gives the kiss of myth her human heat.
Reflections. Reflections. He becomes her lover.

85 The old romances make no bones about it.
The long and short of it. The end and the beginning.
The glories and the ornaments are muted.
And when the story ends the song is over.
—1985

from *The Woman Poet: Her Dilemma*

I believe that the woman poet today inherits a dilemma. That she does so inevitably, no matter what cause she espouses and whatever ideology she advocates or shuns. That when she sits down to work, when she moves away from her work, when she tries to be what she is struggling to express, at all these moments the dilemma is present, waiting and inescapable.

The dilemma I speak of is inherent in a shadowy but real convergence between new experience and an established aesthetic. What this means in practical terms is that the woman poet today is caught in a field of force. Powerful, persuasive voices are in her ear as she writes. Distorting and simplifying ideas of womanhood and poetry fall as shadows between her and the courage of her own experience. If she listens to these voices, yields to these ideas, her work will be obstructed. If, however, she evades the issue, runs for cover and pre-

tends there is no pressure, then she is likely to lose the resolution she needs to encompass the critical distance between writing poems and being a poet. A distance which for women is fraught in any case, as I hope to show, with psychosexual fear and doubt.

Dramatize, dramatize, said Henry James. And so I will. Imagine, then, that a woman is going into the garden. She is youngish; her apron is on, and there is flour on her hands. It is early afternoon. She is going there to lift a child who for the third time is about to put laburnum pods in his mouth. This is what she does. But what I have omitted to say in this small sketch is that the woman is a poet. And once she is in the garden, once the child, hot and small and needy, is in her arms, once the frills of shadow around the laburnum and the freakish gold light from it are in her eyes, then her poetic sense is awakened. She comes back through the garden door. She cleans her hands, takes off her apron, sets her child down for an afternoon sleep. Then she sits down to work.

Now it begins. The first of these powerful, distracting voices comes to her. For argument's sake, I will call it the Romantic Heresy. It comes to her as a whisper, an insinuation. What she wants to do is write about the laburnum, the heat of the child, common human love—the mesh of these things. But where, says the voice in her ear, is the interest in all this? How are you going to write a poem out of these plain Janes, these snips and threads of an ordinary day? Now, the voice continues, listen to me, and I will show you how to make all this poetic. A shade here, a nuance there, a degree of distance, a lilt of complaint, and all will be well. The woman hesitates. Suddenly the moment that seemed to her potent and emblematic and true appears commonplace, beyond the pale of art. She is shaken. And there I will leave her, with her doubts and fears, so as to look more closely at what it is that has come between her and the courage of that moment.

* * *

The Romantic Heresy, as I have chosen to call it, is not romanticism proper, although it is related to it. "Before Wordsworth," writes Lionel Trilling, "poetry had a subject. After Wordsworth its prevalent subject was the poet's own subjectivity."[1] This shift in perception was responsible for much that was fresh and revitalizing in nineteenth-century poetry. But it was also responsible for the declension of poetry into self-consciousness, self-invention.

This type of debased romanticism is rooted in a powerful, subliminal suggestion that poets are distinctive not so much because they write poetry but because in order to do so, they have poetic feelings about poetic experiences. That there is a category of experience and expression which is poetic and all the rest is ordinary and therefore inadmissible. In this way a damaging division is made between the perception of what is poetic on the one hand and, on the other, what is merely human. Out of this emerges the aesthetic which suggests that in order to convert the second into the first, you must romanticize it. This idea gradually became an article of faith in nineteenth-century postromantic English poetry. When Matthew Arnold[2] said at Oxford, "the strongest part of our religion is its unconscious poetry," he was blurring a fine line. He was himself one of the initiators of a sequence of propositions by which the poetry of religion became the religion of poetry.

There are obvious pitfalls in all of this for any poet. But the dangers for a woman poet in particular must be immediately obvious. Women are a minority within the expressive poetic tradition. Much of their actual experience lacks even the most rudimentary poetic precedent. "No poet," says Eliot, "no artist of any kind has his complete meaning alone."[3] The woman poet is more alone with her meaning than most. The ordinary routine day that many women live—must live—to take just one instance, does not figure largely in poetry. Nor the feelings that go with it. The temptations are considerable, therefore, for a woman poet to romanticize these routines and these feelings so as to align them with what is considered poetic.

Now let us go back to the woman at her desk. Let us suppose that she has recovered her nerve and purpose. She remembers what is true: the heat, the fear that her child will eat the pods. She feels again the womanly power of the instant. She puts aside the distortions of romanticism. She starts to write again, and once again she is assailed. But this time by another and equally persuasive idea.

And this is feminist ideology or at least one part of it. In recent years feminism has begun to lay powerful prescriptions on writing by women. The most exacting of these comes from that part of feminist thinking which is separatist. Separatist prescriptions demand that women be true to the historical angers which underwrite the women's movement, that they cast aside preexisting literary traditions, that they evolve not only their own writing but the criteria by which to judge it. I think I understand some of these prescriptions. I recognize that they stem from the fact that many feminists—and I partly share the view—perceive a great deal in preexisiting literary expression and tradition which is patriarchal, not to say oppressive. I certainly have no wish to be apologetic about the separatist tendency because it offends or threatens or bores—and it does all three—the prevailing male literary establishments. That does not concern me for a moment. There is still prejudice—the Irish poetic community is among the most chauvinist—but as it happens, that is not part of this equation.

What does concern me is that the gradual emphasis on the appropriate subject matter and the correct feelings has become as constricting and corrupt within feminism as within romanticism. In the grip of romanticism and its distortions, women can be argued out of the truth of their feelings, can be marginalized, simplified and devalued by what is, after all, a patriarchal tendency. But does the separatist prescription offer more? I have to say—painful as it may be to dissent from one section of a movement I cherish—that I see no redemption whatsoever in moving from one simplification to the other.

So here again is the woman at her desk. Let us say she is feminist. What is she to make of the suggestion by

---

[1] *Wordsworth* English poet William Wordsworth (1771–1855), who played a major role in the development of Romantic poetry; *Before Wordsworth ... own subjectivity* In *The Oxford Anthology of English Literature: Romantic Poetry and Prose* (1973).

[2] *Matthew Arnold* Victorian poet and cultural critic. In "The Study of Poetry" (1888), quoted here, he argues that the greatest poetry possesses "high and excellent seriousness" in both approach and subject matter.

[3] *No poet ... meaning alone* From T.S. Eliot, "Tradition and the Individual Talent" (1919).

a poet like Adrienne Rich[1] that "to be a female human being, trying to fulfill female functions in a traditional way, is in direct conflict with the subversive function of the imagination?"

Yet the woman knows that whether or not going into the garden and lifting her child are part of the "traditional way," they have also been an agent and instrument of subversive poetic perception. What is she to do? Should she contrive an anger, invent a disaffection? How is she to separate one obligation from the other, one truth from the other? And what is she to make of the same writer's statement that "to the eye of the feminist, the work of Western male poets now writing reveals a deep, fatalistic pessimism as to the possibilities of change ... and a new tide of phallocentric sadism." It is no good to say she need not read these remarks. Adrienne Rich is a wonderful poet and her essay—"When We Dead Awaken"—from which these statements are quoted is a central statement in contemporary poetry. It should be read by every poet. So there is no escape. The force or power of this stance, which I would call separatist, but may more accurately be called antitraditional, must be confronted.

Separatist thinking is a persuasive and dangerous influence on any woman poet writing today. It tempts her to disregard the whole poetic past as patriarchal betrayal. It pleads with her to discard the complexities of true feeling for the relative simplicity of anger. It promises to ease her technical problems with the solvent of polemic. It whispers to her that to be feminine in poetry is easier, quicker and more eloquent than the infinitely more difficult task of being human. Above all, it encourages her to feminize her perceptions rather than humanize her femininity.

But women have a birthright in poetry. I believe, though an antitraditional poet might not agree, that when a woman poet begins to write, she very quickly becomes conscious of the silences which have preceded her, which still surround her. These silences will become an indefinable part of her purpose as a poet. Yet as a working poet she will also—if she is honest—recognize

that these silences have been at least partly redeemed within the past expressions of other poets, most of them male. And these expressions also will become part of her purpose. But for that to happen, she must have the fullest possible dialogue with them. She needs it; she is entitled to it. And in order to have that dialogue, she must have the fullest dialogue also with her own experience, her own present as a poet. I do not believe that separatism allows for this. ...

3.

I began writing poetry in the Dublin of the early sixties. Perhaps *began* is not the right word. I had been there or thereabouts for years: scribbling poems in boarding school, reading Yeats after lights out, reveling in the poetry on the course.

Then I left school and went to Trinity.[2] Dublin was a coherent space then, a small circumference in which to be and become a poet. A single bus journey took you into college for the day. Twilights over Stephen's Green[3] were breathable and lilac-coloured. Coffee beans turned and gritted off the blades in the windows of Roberts' and Bewleys.[4] A single cup of it, moreover, cost ninepence in old money and could be spun out for hours of conversation. The last European city. The last literary smallholding.

Or maybe not. "Until we can understand the assumptions in which we are drenched," writes Adrienne Rich, "we cannot know ourselves." I entered that city and that climate knowing neither myself nor the assumptions around me. And into the bargain, I was priggish, callow, enchanted by the powers of the intellect.

If I had been less of any of these things, I might have looked about me more. I might have taken note of my surroundings. If history is the fable agreed upon, then literary traditions are surely the agreed fiction. Things are put in and left out, are preselected and can be manipulated. If I had looked closely, I might have seen some of the omissions. Among other things, I might have noticed that there were no women poets, old or

[1] *Adrienne Rich* American poet and feminist critic. The essay quoted is "When We Dead Awaken: Writing as Re-Vision" (1972), in which Rich argues that women writers must escape patriarchal traditions—both in literature and in life—and that the expression of anger is an important part of this process.

[2] *Trinity* Trinity College, Dublin.

[3] *Stephen's Green* Dublin public park.

[4] *Roberts' and Bewleys* Dublin cafés with a long history of attendance by literary figures.

young, past or present in my immediate environment. Sylvia Plath,[1] it is true, detonated in my consciousness, but not until years later. Adrienne Rich was to follow, and Bishop[2] later still. As it was, I accepted what I found almost without question....

In due course I married, moved out of the city and into the suburbs—I am telescoping several years here—and had a baby daughter. In so doing, I had, without realizing it, altered my whole situation.

When a woman writer leaves the centre of a society, becomes a wife, mother and housewife, she ceases automatically to be a member of that dominant class which she belonged to when she was visible chiefly as writer. As a student, perhaps, or otherwise as an apprentice. Whatever her writing abilities, henceforth she ceases to be defined by them and becomes defined instead by subsidiary female roles....

On the one hand, poetic convention—conventions, moreover, which I had breathed in as a young poet—whispered to me that the daily things I did, things which seemed to me important and human, were not fit material for poetry. That is, they were not sanctioned by poetic tradition. But, the whisper went on, they could become so. If I wished to integrate these devalued areas into my poetry, I had only to change them slightly. And so on. And in my other ear, feminist ideology—to which I have never been immune—argued that the life I lived was fit subject for anger and the anger itself the proper subject for poetry.

Yet in my mind and in the work I was starting to do a completely different and opposed conviction was growing: that I stood at the centre of the lyric moment itself, in a mesh of colours, sensualities and emotions that were equidistant from poetic convention and political feeling alike. Technically and aesthetically I became convinced that if I could only detach the lyric mode from traditional romantic elitism and the new feminist angers, then I would be able at last to express that moment.

The precedents for this were in painting rather than poetry. Poetry offered spiritual consolation but not technical example. In the genre painters of the French eighteenth century—in Jean Baptiste Chardin[3] in particular—I saw what I was looking for. Chardin's paintings were ordinary in the accepted sense of the word. They were unglamorous, workaday, authentic. Yet in his work these objects were not merely described; they were revealed. The hare in its muslin bag, the crusty loaf, the woman fixed between menial tasks and human dreams—these stood out, a commanding text. And I was drawn to that text. Romanticism in the nineteenth century, it seemed to me, had prescribed that beauty be commended as truth. Chardin had done something different. He had taken truth and revealed its beauty.

From painting I learned something else of infinite value to me. Most young poets have bad working habits. They write their poems in fits and starts, by feast or famine. But painters follow the light. They wait for it and do their work by it. They combine artisan practicality with vision. In a house with small children, with no time to waste, I gradually reformed my working habits. I learned that if I could not write a poem, I could make an image, and if I could not make an image, I could take out a word, savour it and store it.

I have gone into all this because to a certain extent, the personal witness of a woman poet is still a necessary part of the evolving criteria by which women and their poetry must be evaluated. Nor do I wish to imply that I solved my dilemma. The dilemma persists; the crosscurrents continue. What I wished most ardently for myself at a certain stage of my work was that I might find my voice where I had found my vision. I still think this is what matters most and is threatened most for the woman poet.

I am neither a separatist nor a postfeminist. I believe that the past matters, yet I do not believe we will reach the future without living through the womanly angers which shadow the present. What worries me most is that women poets may lose their touch, may shake off their opportunities because of the pressures and temptations of their present position.

It seems to me, at this particular time, that women have a destiny in the form. Not because they are women; it is not as simple as that. Our suffering, our

---

[1] *Sylvia Plath* American poet and novelist (1932–63).

[2] *Bishop* Elizabeth Bishop (1911–79), American poet.

[3] *genre painters* Painters of everyday objects and scenes; *Jean Baptiste Chardin* French artist (1699–1779) known for genre painting and still life.

involvement in the collective silence do not—and will never—of themselves guarantee our achievement as poets. But if we set out in the light of that knowledge and that history, determined to tell the human and poetic truth, and if we avoid simplification and self-deception, then I believe we are better equipped than most to discover the deepest possibilities and subversions within poetry itself. Artistic forms are not static. Nor are they radicalized by aesthetes or intellectuals. They are changed, shifted, detonated into deeper patterns only by the sufferings and self-deceptions of those who use them. By this equation, women should break down barriers in poetry in the same way that poetry will break the silence of women. In the process it is important not to mistake the easy answer for the long haul.

—1986

How the Earth and All the Planets Were Created

I went to find the grave of my grandmother
who died before my time. And hers.

I searched among marsh grass and granite
and single headstones
5   and smashed lettering
and archangel wings and found none.

For once I said
I will face this landscape
and look at it as she was looked upon:

10   Unloved because unknown.
Unknown because un-named:

Glass Pistol Castle disappeared.
Baltray and then Clogher Head.[1]

To the west the estuary of the Boyne—
15   stripped of its battles and history—
became only willow-trees and distances.

---

[1] *Glass Pistol Castle ... Clogher Head* Historically significant places close to the mouth of the Boyne River, on the east coast of Ireland.

I drove back in the half light
of late summer on
anonymous roads on my journey home
20   as the constellations rose overhead,
some of them twisted into women:

pinioned[2] and winged
and single-handedly holding high the dome
and curve and horizon of today and tomorrow.

25   All the ships looking up to them.
All the compasses made true by them.
All the night skies named for their sorrow.
—1998

The Lost Land

I have two daughters.

They are all I ever wanted from the earth.

Or almost all.

I also wanted one piece of ground.

5   One city trapped by hills. One urban river.
An island in its element.

So I could say *mine. My own.*
And mean it.

Now they are grown up and far away

10   and memory itself
has become an emigrant,
wandering in a place
where love dissembles itself as landscape.

Where the hills
15   are the colours of a child's eyes,
where my children are distances, horizons.

---

[2] *pinioned* With bound limbs; also refers to the removal of pinions, the outer portion of a bird's wings, which are necessary for flight.

At night,
on the edge of sleep,
I can see the shore of Dublin Bay,
20 its rocky sweep and its granite pier.

Is this, I say
how they must have seen it,
backing out on the mailboat at twilight,

shadows falling
25 on everything they had to leave?
And would love forever?
And then

I imagine myself
at the landward rail of that boat
30 searching for the last sight of a hand.

I see myself
on the underworld side of that water,
the darkness coming in fast, saying
all the names I know for a lost land.

35 *Ireland. Absence. Daughter.*
—1998

Against Love Poetry

We were married in summer, thirty years ago. I have loved you deeply from that moment to this. I have loved other things as well. Among them the idea of women's freedom. Why do I put these words side by side? Because I am a woman. Because marriage is not freedom. Therefore, every word here is written against love poetry. Love poetry can do no justice to this. Here, instead, is a remembered story from a faraway history: A great king lost a war and was paraded in chains through the city of his enemy. They taunted him. They brought his wife and children to him—he showed no emotion. They brought his former courtiers—he showed no emotion. They brought his old servant—only then did he break down and weep. I did not find my womanhood in the servitudes of custom. But I saw my humanity look back at me there. It is to mark the contradictions of a daily love that I have written this. Against love poetry.
—2001

Domestic Violence

1.

It was winter, lunar, wet. At dusk
Pewter seedlings became moonlight orphans.
Pleased to meet you meat to please you
said the butcher's sign in the window in the village.

5 Everything changed the year that we got married.
And after that we moved out to the suburbs.
How young we were, how ignorant, how ready
to think the only history was our own.

And there was a couple who quarreled into the night,
10 Their voices high, sharp:
nothing is ever entirely
right in the lives of those who love each other.

2.

In that season suddenly our island
Broke out its old sores for all to see.
We saw them too.
We stood there wondering how

5 the salt horizons and the Dublin hills
the rivers, table mountains, Viking marshes
we thought we knew
had been made to shiver

into our ancient twelve by fifteen television
10 which gave them back as gray and grayer tears
and killings, killings, killings,
then moonlight-coloured funerals:

nothing we said
not then, not later,
15 fathomed what it is
is wrong in the lives of those who hate each other.

3.

And if the provenance of memory is
only that—remember, not atone—
and if I can be safe in
the weak spring light in that kitchen, then

5   why is there another kitchen, spring light
always darkening in it and
a woman whispering to a man
over and over *what else could we have done?*

4.

We failed our moment or our moment failed us.
The times were grand in size and we were small.
Why do I write that
when I don't believe it?

5   We lived our lives, were happy, stayed as one.
Children were born and raised here
and are gone,
including ours.

As for that couple did we ever
10   find out who they were
and did we want to?
I think we know. I think we always knew.

—2007

Inheritance

I have been wondering
what I have to leave behind, to give my daughters.

No good offering the view
between here and Three Rock Mountain,[1]

5   the blueness in the hours before rain, the long haze
afterwards.
The ground I stood on was never really mine. It might
not ever be theirs.

And gifts that were passed through generations—
silver and the fluid light left after silk—were never
given here.

This is an island of waters, inland distances,
10   with a history of want and women who struggled
to make the nothing which was all that they had
into something they could leave behind.

I learned so little from them: the lace bobbin with its
braided mesh,
its oat-straw pillow and the wheat-colored shawl
15   knitted in one season
to imitate another

are all crafts I never had
and can never hand on. But then again there was a
night
I stayed awake, alert and afraid, with my first child
20   who turned and turned; sick, fretful.

When dawn came I held my hand over the absence of
fever,
over skin which had stopped burning, as if I knew the
secrets
of health and air, as if I understood them

and listened to the silence
25   and thought, I must have learned that somewhere.

—2007

---

1   *Three Rock Mountain*   Mountain near Dublin.

SALMAN RUSHDIE
b. 1947

Salman Rushdie has become recognized as one of the key figures of postmodernist fiction, and of post-colonial writing of all sorts. He has been honored with many prestigious awards and has helped to shape an entire generation of Indian writing in English. But his achievements were for many years overshadowed by a furor created by the violent opposition of Islamic fundamentalists to his novel *The Satanic Verses* (1988); this became one of the major artistic and religious controversies of the twentieth century.

Born Ahmed Salman Rushdie to devout Muslim parents in Bombay (now Mumbai), India, he was educated at the Cathedral School in Bombay, and then moved to England at age 14, where he

attended Rugby School, one of England's most prestigious boarding schools. It was far from an entirely pleasant experience; Rushdie has recounted how he was the object of racially motivated attacks by white students. He moved back to Bombay after graduating, but returned to England to attend Cambridge University's King's College, where he studied history and joined a student theater group. After earning his BA in 1968, Rushdie worked in television in Pakistan for several years, and then returned to England to become a copywriter for an advertising agency.

In his first novel, *Grimus* (1975), Rushdie concocted a literary mixture of fantasy and realism of a sort that would become characteristic of his work. An adaptation of an old Sufi poem, *Grimus* is a fantastical work that borders on science fiction. It met with little success. But his next novel, *Midnight's Children* (1981), catapulted Rushdie to the top of the English-language literary world. *Midnight's Children* presents the life of its protagonist, a pickle-factory worker named Saleem Sinai who was born (like Rushdie) at the time of India's independence from Britain, as an allegory for the history of post-colonial India. The tone of the novel again partakes both of realism and of fantasy—as its famous first sentence signals: "I was born in the city of Bombay … once upon a time. No, that won't do, there's no getting away from the date: I was born in Doctor Narlikar's Nursing Home on August 15th, 1947." The novel was very much in tune with its age. In the literary world, this was the dawn of literary postmodernism, and writers of fiction were increasingly interested in self-conscious or ironic explorations of the play of illusion and reality. And in the world of literary theory and criticism, works on postcolonial themes were coming more and more to be considered central to the literature of the English-speaking world; from this angle too, *Midnight's Children* was of intense interest. In 1981 the novel won the prestigious Booker Prize for Fiction, and in 1993 it won the Booker of Bookers Prize for the novel deemed to have been the best of all those awarded the Booker in the award's first twenty-five years.

His next work was a short novel, *Shame* (1983), in which Rushdie shifted his focus from India to neighboring Pakistan. His treatment of the rulers of Pakistan, particularly former Prime Minister Zulfikar Ali Bhutto and General Muhammad Zia-ul-Haq, explored the connection between shame and violence. This novel was also shortlisted for the Booker Prize.

In 1988 Rushdie published a novel that was to change the course of his life. Like *Midnight's Children* and *Shame*, *The Satanic Verses* was critically acclaimed (it won the Whitbread Novel Award in 1988), and like them it featured elements that hover between fantasy and reality. But to some it was altogether too real; the novel was condemned by a number of prominent Muslim leaders on the grounds that the book's unflattering portrayal of the prophet Muhammed was blasphemous; it was banned in eleven countries, and was the subject of violent protests. The controversy over the book escalated on 14 February 1989, when Iran's spiritual and political leader, the Ayatollah Ruhollah Khomeini, issued a *fatwa* (or legal pronouncement) calling for Rushdie's death. Ten days later Khomeini placed a $3 million (US) bounty on Rushdie's head (the amount was increased in 1997). Rushdie went into hiding, under the protection of British authorities. The Japanese translator of the book was murdered in Toyko in 1991. Other translators were attacked and harassed. In 1998 the Iranian government made a public pledge not to carry out the death sentence against Rushdie. Nevertheless, the *fatwa* still stands.

While in hiding, Rushdie published a children's book, *Haroun and the Sea of Stories* (1990), an allegory for India and Pakistan's dispute over the State of Kashmir. The book also contains harsh criticisms of literary censorship. He followed up with a book of essays, entitled *Imaginary Homelands: Essays and Criticism 1981–1991* (1991), from which the essay below is taken.

Rushdie's later work expands his artistic vision to treat the intersection of Indian culture with western cultures. In *The Moor's Last Sigh* (1995), for which he won the Whitbread Novel Award in 1995, Rushdie explores the connection between descendants of Portuguese settlers and their Indian neighbors. *The Ground Beneath Her Feet* (1999), a variation on the Greek Orpheus myth, deals with the influence of American rock and roll music on Indian culture. Rushdie's 2001 novel, *Fury*, is set in New York and features a transplanted Bombay-born intellectual as its protagonist, while *Shalimar the Clown* (2005) returns to the Indian subcontinent for its subject matter, telling the story of two Kashmiri villages whose inhabitants get caught up in a cycle of escalating violence.

Rushdie received another Booker Prize for *The Enchantress of Florence* (2008), which links Renaissance Florence with sixteenth-century Sikri, the capital of the Mughal Empire. In 2010 he published another allegorical children's book, *Luka and the Fire of Life*, a sequel to *Haroun and the Sea of Stories*. His 2012 third-person autobiography *Joseph Anton* recounts the years he spent in hiding as a result of the *fatwa*; "Joseph Anton" was the alias he used during that time.

Rushdie is Honorary Professor in the Humanities at the Massachusetts Institute of Technology (MIT) and a Fellow of Britain's Royal Society of Literature. He was knighted in 2007.

⌘⌘⌘

Is Nothing Sacred?[1]

I grew up kissing books and bread. In our house, whenever anyone dropped a book or let fall a chapati or a "slice," which was our word for a triangle of buttered leavened bread, the fallen object was required not only to be picked up but also kissed, by way of apology for the act of clumsy disrespect. I was as careless and butter-fingered as any child and, accordingly, during my childhood years, I kissed a large number of "slices" and also my fair share of books.

Devout households in India often contained, and still contain, persons in the habit of kissing holy books. But we kissed everything. We kissed dictionaries and atlases. We kissed Enid Blyton novels and Superman comics. If I'd ever dropped the telephone directory I'd probably have kissed that, too.

All this happened before I had ever kissed a girl. In fact it would almost be true, true enough for a fiction writer, anyhow, to say that once I started kissing girls, my activities with regard to bread and books lost some of their special excitement. But one never forgets one's first loves.

Bread and books: food for the body and food for the soul—what could be more worthy of our respect, and even love?

It has always been a shock to me to meet people for whom books simply do not matter, and people who are scornful of the act of reading, let alone writing. It is perhaps always astonishing to learn that your beloved is not as attractive to others as she is to you. My most beloved books have been fictions, and in the last twelve months I have been obliged to accept that for many millions of human beings, these books are entirely without attraction or value. We have been witnessing an attack upon a particular work of fiction that is also an attack upon the very ideas of the novel form, an attack of such bewildering ferocity that it has become necessary to restate what is most precious about the art of literature—to answer the attack, not by an attack, but by a declaration of love.

Love can lead to devotion, but the devotion of the lover is unlike that of the True Believer in that it is not militant. I may be surprised—even shocked—to find that you do not feel as I do about a given book or work of art or even person; I may very well attempt to change your mind; but I will finally accept that your tastes, your loves, are your business and not mine. The True Believer knows no such restraints. The True Believer knows that he is simply right, and you are wrong. He will seek to convert you, even by force, and if he cannot he will, at the very least, despise you for your unbelief.

Love need not be blind. Faith must, ultimately, be a leap in the dark.

The title of this lecture is a question usually asked, in tones of horror, when some personage or idea or value or place held dear by the questioner is treated to a dose of iconoclasm. White cricket balls for night cricket? Female priests? A Japanese takeover of Rolls-Royce cars? *Is nothing sacred?*

Until recently, however, it was a question to which I thought I knew the answer. The answer was No.

No, nothing is sacred in and of itself, I would have said. Ideas, texts, even people can be made sacred—the word is from the Latin *sacrare,* "to set apart as holy"—but even though such entities, once their sacredness is established, seek to proclaim and to preserve their own absoluteness, their inviolability, the act of making sacred is in truth an event in history. It is the product of the many and complex pressures of the time in which the act occurs. And events in history must always be subject to questioning, deconstruction, even to declarations of their obsolescence. To respect the sacred is to be paralysed by it. The idea of the sacred is quite simply one of the most conservative notions in any culture, because it seeks to turn other ideas—Uncertainty, Progress, Change—into crimes.

To take only one such declaration of obsolescence: I would have described myself as living in the aftermath of the death of God. On the subject of the death of God, the American novelist and critic William H. Gass had this to say, as recently as 1984:

> The death of god represents not only the realization that gods have never existed, but the contention that such a belief is no longer even irrationally possible: that neither reason nor the taste and temper of the times condone it. The belief lingers on, of course, but it does so like astrology or a faith in a flat earth.

I have some difficulty with the uncompromising bluntness of this obituary notice. It has always been clear to me that God is unlike human beings in that it can die, so to speak, in parts. In other parts, for example India, God continues to flourish, in literally thousands of forms. So that if I speak of living after this death, I am speaking in a limited, personal sense—my sense of God ceased to exist long ago, and as a result I was drawn towards the great creative possibilities offered by surrealism, modernism and their successors, those philosophies and aesthetics born of the realization that, as Karl Marx said, "all that is solid melts into air."

It did not seem to me, however, that my ungodliness, or rather my post-godliness, need necessarily bring me into conflict with belief. Indeed, one reason for my attempt to develop a form of fiction in which the miraculous might coexist with the mundane was precisely my acceptance that notions of the sacred and the profane both needed to be explored, as far as possible without pre-judgement, in any honest literary portrait of the way we are.

That is to say: the most secular of authors ought to be capable of presenting a sympathetic portrait of a devout believer. Or, to put it another way: I had never felt the need to totemize my lack of belief, and so make it something to go to war about.

Now, however, I find my entire world-picture under fire. And as I find myself obliged to defend the assumptions and processes of literature, which I had believed that all free men and women could take for granted, and for which all unfree men and women continue every day to struggle, so I am obliged to ask myself questions I admit to finding somewhat unnerving.

Do I, perhaps, find something sacred after all? Am I prepared to set aside as holy the idea of the absolute freedom of the imagination and alongside it my own notions of the World, the Text and the Good? Does this add up to what the apologists of religion have started calling "secular fundamentalism"? And if so, must I accept that this "secular fundamentalism" is as likely to lead to excesses, abuses and oppressions as the canons of religious faith?

A lecture in memory of Herbert Read is a highly appropriate occasion for such an exploration, and I am honoured to have been asked to deliver it. Herbert Read, one of the leading British advocates of the modernist and surrealist movements, was a distinguished representative of the cultural values closest to my heart. "Art is never transfixed," Read wrote. "Change is the condition of art remaining art." This principle is also mine. Art, too, is an event in history, subject to the historical process. But it is also *about* that process, and must constantly strive to find new forms to mirror an endlessly renewed world. No aesthetic can be a constant, except an aesthetic based on the idea of inconstancy, metamorphosis, or, to borrow a term from politics, "perpetual revolution."

The struggle between such ideas and the eternal, revealed truths of religion is dramatized this evening, as I hope I may be excused for pointing out, by my ab-

sence. I must apologize for this. I did, in fact, ask my admirable protectors how they would feel if I were to deliver my text in person. The answer was, more or less, "What have we done to deserve this?" With regret, I took the point.

It is an agony and a frustration not to be able to re-enter my old life, not even for such a moment. However, I should like to thank Harold Pinter, through his own mouth, for standing in my place. Perhaps this event could be thought of as a form of secular revelation: a man receives a text by mysterious processes from Elsewhere—above? below? New Scotland Yard?[1]—and brings it out before the people, and recites …

More than twenty years ago, I stood packed in at the back of this theatre, listening to a lecture by Arthur Koestler.[2] He propounded the thesis that language, not territory, was the prime cause of aggression, because once language reached the level of sophistication at which it could express abstract concepts, it acquired the power of totemization; and once peoples had erected totems, they would go to war to defend them. (I ask pardon of Koestler's ghost. I am relying on an old memory, and that's an untrustworthy shoulder to lean on.)

In support of his theory, he told us about two tribes of monkeys living on, I think, one of the northern islands of Japan. The two tribes lived in close proximity in the woods near a certain stream, and subsisted, not unusually, on a diet of bananas. One of the tribes, however, had developed the curious habit of washing its bananas in the stream before eating them, while the other tribe continued to be non-banana-washers. And yet, said Koestler, the two tribes continued to live contentedly as neighbours, without quarrelling. And why was this? It was because their language was too primitive to permit them to totemize either the act of banana-washing or that of eating bananas unwashed. With a more sophisticated language at their disposal, both wet and dry bananas could have become the sacred

[1] *New Scotland Yard* Headquarters for the metropolitan police force of Greater London.

[2] *Arthur Koestler* Hungarian-born novelist (1905–83), political activist, and social philosopher, whose most famous work, *Darkness at Noon* (1940), depicts extremes of censorship and oppression under a Soviet-style Marxist dictatorship.

objects at the heart of a religion, and then, look out!—Holy war.

A young man rose from the audience to ask Koestler a question. Perhaps the real reason why the two tribes did not fight, he suggested, was that there were enough bananas to go round. Koestler became extremely angry. He refused to answer such a piece of Marxist claptrap. And, in a way, he was right. Koestler and his questioner were speaking different languages, and their languages were in conflict. Their disagreement could even be seen as the proof of Koestler's point. If he, Koestler, were to be considered the banana-washer and his questioner the dry-banana man, then their command of a language more complex than the Japanese monkeys' had indeed resulted in totemizations. Now each of them had a totem to defend: the primacy of language versus the primacy of economics: and dialogue therefore became impossible. They were at war.

Between religion and literature, as between politics and literature, there is a linguistically based dispute. But it is not a dispute of simple opposites. Because whereas religion seeks to privilege one language above all others, one set of values above all others, one text above all others, the novel has always been *about* the way in which different languages, values and narratives quarrel, and about the shifting relations between them, which are relations of power. The novel does not seek to establish a privileged language, but it insists upon the freedom to portray and analyse the struggle between the different contestants for such privileges.

Carlos Fuentes has called the novel "a privileged *arena*." By this he does not mean that it is the kind of holy space which one must put off one's shoes to enter; it is not an arena to revere; it claims no special rights *except the right to be the stage upon which the great debates of society can be conducted.* "The novel," Fuentes writes, "is born from the very fact that we do not understand one another, because unitary, orthodox language has broken down. Quixote and Sancho, the Shandy brothers, Mr. and Mrs. Karenin:[1] their novels are the comedy (or the drama) of their misunderstandings. Impose a unitary language: you kill the novel, but you also kill the

---

[1] *Quixote ... Karenin* Characters from Cervantes's *Don Quixote*, Laurence Sterne's *Tristram Shandy*, and Tolstoy's *Anna Karenina*, respectively.

society."

He then poses the question I have been asking myself throughout my life as a writer: *Can the religious mentality survive outside of religious dogma and hierarchy?* Which is to say: Can art be the third principle that mediates between the material and spiritual worlds; might it, by "swallowing" both worlds, offer us something new—something that might even be called a secular definition of transcendence?

I believe it can. I believe it must. And I believe that, at its best, it does.

What I mean by transcendence is that flight of the human spirit outside the confines of its material, physical existence which all of us, secular or religious, experience on at least a few occasions. Birth is a moment of transcendence which we spend our lives trying to understand. The exaltation of the act of love, the experience of joy and very possibly the moment of death are other such moments. The soaring quality of transcendence, the sense of being more than oneself, of being in some way joined to the whole of life, is by its nature short-lived. Not even the visionary or mystical experience ever lasts very long. It is for art to capture that experience, to offer it to, in the case of literature, its readers; to be, for a secular, materialist culture, some sort of replacement for what the love of god offers in the world of faith.

It is important that we understand how profoundly we all feel the needs that religion, down the ages, has satisfied. I would suggest that these needs are of three types: firstly, the need to be given an articulation of our half-glimpsed knowledge of exaltation, of awe, of wonder; life is an awesome experience, and religion helps us understand why life so often makes us feel small, by telling us what we are *smaller than;* and, contrariwise, because we also have a sense of being special, of being *chosen,* religion helps us by telling us what we have been chosen by, and what for. Secondly, we need answers to the unanswerable: How did we get here? How did "here" get here in the first place? Is this, this brief life, all there is? How can it be? What would be the point of that? And, thirdly, we need codes to live by, "rules for every damn thing." The idea of god is at once a repository for our awestruck wonderment at life and an answer to the great questions of existence, and a rule book, too. The soul needs all these explanations—not simply rational explanations, but explanations of the heart.

It is also important to understand how often the language of secular, rationalist materialism has failed to answer these needs. As we witness the death of communism in Central Europe, we cannot fail to observe the deep religious spirit with which so many of the makers of these revolutions are imbued, and we must concede that it is not only a particular political ideology that has failed, but the idea that men and women could ever define themselves in terms that exclude their spiritual needs.

It seems obvious, but relevant, to point out that in all the countries now moving towards freedom, art was repressed as viciously as was religion. That the Czech revolution began in the theatres and is led by a writer is proof that people's spiritual needs, more than their material needs, have driven the commissars from power. What appears plain is that it will be a very long time before the peoples of Europe will accept any ideology that claims to have a complete, totalized explanation of the world. Religious faith, profound as it is, must surely remain a private matter. This rejection of totalized explanations is the modern condition. And this is where the novel, the form created to discuss the fragmentation of truth, comes in. The film director Luis Buñuel used to say: "I would give my life for a man who is looking for the truth. But I would gladly kill a man who thinks he has found the truth." (This is what we used to call a joke, before killing people for their ideas returned to the agenda.) The elevation of the quest for the Grail over the Grail itself, the acceptance that all that is solid has melted into air, that reality and morality are not givens but imperfect human constructs, is the point from which fiction begins. This is what J.-F. Lyotard called, in 1979, *La Condition Postmoderne*. The challenge of literature is to start from this point, and still find a way of fulfilling our unaltered spiritual requirements.

Moby Dick meets that challenge by offering us a dark, almost Manichean vision[1] of a universe (the *Pequod*[2]) in the grip of one demon, Ahab, and heading inexorably towards another; namely the Whale. The ocean always was our Other, manifesting itself to us in the form of beasts—the worm Ouroboros, Kraken, Leviathan.[3] Herman Melville delves into these dark waters in order to offer us a very modern parable: Ahab, gripped by his possession, perishes; Ishmael, a man without strong feeling or powerful affiliations, survives. The self-interested modern man is the sole survivor; those who worship the Whale—for pursuit is a form of worship—perish by the Whale.

Joyce's wanderers, Beckett's tramps, Gogol's tricksters, Bulgakov's devils, Bellow's[4] high-energy meditations on the stifling of the soul by the triumphs of materialism; these, and many more, are what we have instead of prophets and suffering saints. But while the novel answers our need for wonderment and understanding, it brings us harsh and unpalatable news as well.

It tells us there are no rules. It hands down no commandments. We have to make up our own rules as best we can, make them up as we go along.

And it tells us there are no answers; or, rather, it tells us that answers are easier to come by, and less reliable, than questions. If religion is an answer, if political ideology is an answer, then literature is an inquiry; great literature, by asking extraordinary questions, opens new doors in our minds.

Richard Rorty, in *Philosophy and the Mirror of Nature,* insists on the importance of historicity, of giving up the illusions of being in contact with Eternity. For him, the great error is what he calls "foundationalism,"

---

[1] *Manichean vision* Form of dualism, in which the world is seen to be determined by the tension between the forces of good and evil.

[2] *the Pequod* Captain Ahab's ship (in Herman Melville's novel *Moby Dick* [1851]).

[3] *Ouroboros ... Leviathan* Ouroboros is an ancient symbol from many cultures that depicts a snake or a dragon devouring itself. The Kraken is an enormous sea monster said to be living in the ocean between Norway and Iceland. Leviathan is a sea monster referred to in various places in the Bible.

[4] *Joyce ... Bellow* Authors James Joyce (1882–1941), Samuel Beckett (1906–89), Nikolai Gogol (1809–52), Mikhail Bulgakov (1891–1940), and Saul Bellow (1915–2005).

which the theologian Don Cupitt, commenting on Rorty, calls "the attempt, as old as (and even much older than) Plato, to give permanence and authority to our knowledge and values by purporting to found them in some unchanging cosmic realm, natural or noumenal, outside the flux of our human conversation." It is better, Cupitt concludes, "to be an adaptable pragmatist, a nomad."

Michel Foucault, also a confirmed historicist, discusses the role of the author in challenging sacralized absolutes in his essay, "What Is an Author?" This essay argues, in part, that "texts, books and discourses really began to have authors ... to the extent that authors became subject to punishment, that is, to the extent that discourses could be transgressive." This is an extraordinary, provocative idea, even if it is stated with Foucault's characteristic airiness and a complete absence of supporting evidence: *that authors were named only when it was necessary to find somebody to blame.* Foucault continues:

> In our culture (and doubtless in many others), discourse was not originally a product, a thing, a kind of goods; it was essentially an act—an act placed in the bipolar field of the sacred and the profane, the licit and the illicit, the religious and the blasphemous. Historically it was a gesture fraught with risks ...

In our beginnings we find our essences. To understand a religion, look at its earliest moments. (It is regrettable that Islam, of all religions the easiest to study in this way, because of its birth during the age of recorded history, has set its face so resolutely against the idea that it, like all ideas, is an event inside history.) And to understand an artistic form, too, Foucault suggests, look at its origins. If he is right about the novel, then literature is, of all the arts, the one best suited to challenging absolutes of all kinds; and, because it is in its origin the schismatic Other of the sacred (and authorless) text, so it is also the art mostly likely to fill our god-shaped holes.

There are other reasons, too, for proposing the novel as the crucial art form of what I can no longer avoid calling the post-modern age. For one thing, literature is the art least subject to external control, because it is

made in private. The act of making it requires only one person, one pen, one room, some paper. (Even the room is not absolutely essential.) Literature is the most low-technology of the art forms. It requires neither a stage nor a screen. It calls for no interpreters, no actors, producers, camera crews, costumers, musicians. It does not even require the traditional apparatus of publishing, as the long-running success of samizdat literature[1] demonstrates. The Foucault essay suggests that literature is as much at risk from the enveloping, smothering forces of the market economy, which reduces books to mere products. This danger is real, and I do not want to seem to be minimizing it. But the truth is that of all the forms, literature can still be the most free. The more money a piece of work costs, the easier it is to control it. Film, the most expensive of art forms, is also the least subversive. This is why, although Carlos Fuentes cites the work of film-makers like Buñuel, Bergman and Fellini as instances of successful secular revolts into the territory of the sacred, I continue to believe in the greater possibilities of the novel. Its singularity is its best protection.

Among the childhood books I devoured and kissed were large numbers of cheap comics of a most unliterary nature. The heroes of these comic books were, or so it seemed, almost always mutants or hybrids or freaks: as well as the Batman and the Spiderman there was Aquaman, who was half-fish, and of course Superman, who could easily be mistaken for a bird or a plane. In those days, the middle 1950s, the super-heroes were all, in their various ways, hawkish law-and-order conservatives, leaping to work in response to the Police Commissioner's Bat-Signal, banding together to form the Justice League of America, defending what Superman called "truth, justice and the American way." But in spite of this extreme emphasis on crime-busting, the lesson they taught children—or this child, at any rate—was the perhaps unintentionally radical truth that exceptionality was the greatest and most heroic of values; that those who were unlike the crowd were to be treasured the most lovingly; and that this exceptionality was a treasure so great and so easily misunderstood that it had to be

---

[1] *samizdat literature* Underground, self-published literature, originally created in the Soviet Union to undermine the system of state censorship.

concealed, in ordinary life, beneath what the comic books called a "secret identity." Superman could not have survived without "mild-mannered" Clark Kent; "millionaire socialite" Bruce Wayne made possible the nocturnal activities of the Batman.

Now it is obviously true that those other freakish, hybrid, mutant, exceptional beings—novelists—those creators of the most freakish, hybrid and metamorphic of forms, the novel, have frequently been obliged to hide behind secret identities, whether for reasons of gender or terror. But the most wonderful of the many wonderful truths about the novel form is that the greater the writer, the greater his or her exceptionality. The geniuses of the novel are those whose voices are fully and undisguisably their own, who, to borrow William Gass's[1] image, *sign every word they write*. What draws us to an author is his or her "unlikeness," even if the apparatus of literary criticism then sets to work to demonstrate that he or she is really no more than an accumulation of influences. Unlikeness, the thing that makes it impossible for a writer to stand in any regimented line, is a quality novelists share with the Caped Crusaders of the comics, though they are only rarely capable of leaping tall buildings in a single stride.

What is more, the writer is there, in his work, in the reader's hands, utterly exposed, utterly defenceless, entirely without the benefit of an alter ego to hide behind. What is forged, in the secret act of reading, is a different kind of identity, as the reader and writer merge, through the medium of the text, to become a collective being that both writes as it reads and reads as it writes, and creates, jointly, that unique work, "their" novel. This "secret identity" of writer and reader is the novel form's greatest and most subversive gift.

And this, finally, is why I elevate the novel above other forms, why it has always been, and remains, my first love: not only is it the art involving least compromises, but it is also the only one that takes the "privileged arena" of conflicting discourses *right inside our heads.* The interior space of our imagination is a theatre that can never be closed down; the images created there make up a movie that can never be destroyed.

In this last decade of the millennium, as the forces of religion are renewed in strength and as the all-pervasive power of materialism wraps its own weighty chains around the human spirit, where should the novel be looking? It seems clear that the renewal of the old, bipolar field of discourse, between the sacred and the profane, which Michel Foucault proposes, will be of central importance. It seems probable, too, that we may be heading towards a world in which there will be no real alternative to the liberal-capitalist social model (except, perhaps, the theocratic, foundationalist model of Islam). In this situation, liberal capitalism or democracy or the free world will require novelists' most rigorous attention, will require reimagining and questioning and doubting as never before. "Our antagonist is our helper," said Edmund Burke, and if democracy no longer has communism to help it clarify, by opposition, its own ideas, then perhaps it will have to have literature as an adversary instead.

I have made a large number of sweeping claims for literature during the course of this piece, and I am aware of a slightly messianic tone in much of what I've written. The reverencing of books and writers, by writers, is nothing particularly new, of course. "Since the early 19th century," writes Cupitt, "imaginative writers have claimed—have indeed enjoyed—a guiding and representative role in our culture. Our preachers are novelists, poets, dramatists, film-makers and the like, purveyors of fiction, ambiguous people, deceivers. Yet we continue to think of ourselves as rational."

But now I find myself backing away from the idea of sacralizing literature with which I flirted at the beginning of this text; I cannot bear the idea of the writer as secular prophet; I am remembering that one of the very greatest writers of the century, Samuel Beckett, believed that all art must inevitably end in failure. This is, clearly, no reason for surrender. "Ever tried. Ever failed. Never mind. Try again. Fail better."

Literature is an interim report from the consciousness of the artist, and so it can never be "finished" or "perfect." Literature is made at the frontier between the self and the world, and in the act of creation that frontier softens, becomes permeable, allows the world to flow into the artist and the artist to flow into the world. Nothing so inexact, so easily and frequently misconceived, deserves the protection of being declared sacro-

---

[1] *William Gass*   American novelist, essayist, and critic.

sanct. We shall just have to get along without the shield of sacralization, and a good thing, too. We must not become what we oppose.

The only privilege literature deserves—and this privilege it requires in order to exist—is the privilege of being the arena of discourse, the place where the struggle of languages can be acted out.

Imagine this. You wake up one morning and find yourself in a large, rambling house. As you wander through it you realize it is so enormous that you will never know it all. In the house are people you know, family members, friends, lovers, colleagues; also many strangers. The house is full of activity: conflicts and seductions, celebrations and wakes. At some point you understand that there is no way out. You find that you can accept this. The house is not what you'd have chosen, it's in fairly bad condition, the corridors are often full of bullies, but it will have to do. Then one day you enter an unimportant-looking little room. The room is empty, but there are voices in it, voices that seem to be whispering just to you. You recognize some of the voices, others are completely unknown to you. The voices are talking about the house, about everyone in it, about everything that is happening and has happened and should happen. Some of them speak exclusively in obscenities. Some are bitchy. Some are loving. Some are funny. Some are sad. The most interesting voices are all these things at once. You begin to go to the room more and more often. Slowly you learn that most of the people in the house use such rooms sometimes. Yet the rooms are all discreetly positioned and unimportant-looking.

Now imagine that you wake up one morning and you are still in the large house, but all the voice-rooms have disappeared. It is as if they have been wiped out. Now there is nowhere in the whole house where you can go to hear voices talking about everything in every possible way. There is nowhere to go for the voices that can be funny one minute and sad the next, that can sound raucous and melodic in the course of the same sentence. Now you remember: there is no way out of this house. Now this fact begins to seem unbearable. You look into the eyes of the people in the corridors—family, lovers, friends, colleagues, strangers, bullies, priests. You see the same thing in everybody's eyes. *How do we get out of here?* It becomes clear that the house is a prison. People begin to scream, and pound the walls. Men arrive with guns. The house begins to shake. You do not wake up. You are already awake.

Literature is the one place in any society where, within the secrecy of our own heads, we can hear *voices talking about everything in every possible way.* The reason for ensuring that that privileged arena is preserved is not that writers want the absolute freedom to say and do whatever they please. It is that we, all of us, readers and writers and citizens and generals and godmen, need that little, unimportant-looking room. We do not need to call it sacred, but we do need to remember that it is necessary.

"Everybody knows," wrote Saul Bellow in *The Adventures of Augie March,* "there is no fineness or accuracy of suppression. If you hold down one thing, you hold down the adjoining."

Wherever in the world the little room of literature has been closed, sooner or later the walls have come tumbling down.

—1990

Ian McEwan
b. 1948

Ian McEwan is known as a contemporary master of unease. From the 1970s, his writing has been well respected, though his reputation has changed the course of his career. Early in his career he was a vaunted *enfant terrible* with a black sense of humor and an extraordinary sense of the bleakness of many childhoods. As time has passed he has come to be regarded as more of a wise, wry curmudgeon, full of insight, who entertains and instructs through unflinching, clear prose, and who is unafraid to portray the darker side of life.

Born in 1948 in Aldershot, England, a self-named "army brat," McEwan spent most of his childhood abroad in Africa, Asia, and Europe. He was educated at the University of Sussex and then at the University of East Anglia, studying with the novelists Malcolm Bradbury and Angus Wilson. In 1972, he returned from a trip overseas that was financed by the proceeds from his first published short story ("Homemade") and began to teach English as a second language in addition to writing.

First Love, Last Rites (1975), a volume of short stories, was widely credited with helping to revitalize the short story as a literary genre in 1970s Britain. McEwan's subsequent works include his second collection of short stories, *In Between the Sheets* (1978), and his novels: *The Cement Garden* (1978); *The Comfort of Strangers* (1981); *The Child in Time* (1987); *The Innocent* (1989); *Enduring Love* (1997); *Amsterdam* (1998), which won the Booker Prize; *Atonement* (2001); *Saturday* (2005); *On Chesil Beach* (2007); *Solar* (2010); and *Sweet Tooth* (2012). McEwan has also written frequently in the popular press and he has published two children's books, *Rose Blanche* (1985) and *The Daydreamer* (1994).

Critically, the works of Ian McEwan have been well received, though there was a consistent and subtle factionalism among those who commented on his earlier work. Some praised it as edgy, stark, and unflinching in dealing with the seedy and uncomfortable underbelly of difficult topics such as adolescent and deviant sexuality, murder, and the horrors that may emerge in everyday life. Others saw his work as verging on the salacious, as being too much oriented towards the pursuit of shock value. But even this latter camp lauded McEwan for his clean, unadorned prose and his ability to place the reader in proximity to the narrative.

There are clear lines to the evolution of McEwan's fiction. In his early works, the primary focus is on some of the most dark and uncomfortable aspects of sexuality and of death, and on lives that are lived largely in isolation from the world. His later works are less frequently focused on human grotesques, and often take place very much in the world (*Atonement* is set against the backdrop of World War II, for example, and *Saturday* in the context of early twenty-first century terrorism). But the differences are of degree rather than of kind; precise imagery, elliptical social commentary, and deft handling of human emotion are constants in his writing, from early stories such as "Last Day of Summer," with its child's-eye view of life in a hippie commune, to the very adult perspectives of his recent novels.

⌘ ⌘ ⌘

Last Day of Summer

I am twelve and lying near-naked on my belly out on the back lawn in the sun when for the first time I hear her laugh. I don't know, I don't move, I just close my eyes. It's a girl's laugh, a young woman's, short and nervous like laughing at nothing funny. I got half my face in the grass I cut an hour before and I can smell the cold soil beneath it. There's a faint breeze coming off the river, the late afternoon sun stinging my back and that laugh jabbing at me like it's all one thing, one taste in my head. The laughing stops and all I can hear is the breeze flapping the pages of my comic, Alice crying somewhere upstairs and a kind of summer heaviness all over the garden. Then I hear them walking across the lawn towards me and I sit up so quickly it makes me dizzy, and the colours have gone out of everything. And there's this fat woman, or girl, walking towards me with my brother. She's so fat her arms can't hang right from her shoulders. She's got rubber tyres round her neck. They're both looking at me and talking about me, and when they get really close I stand up and she shakes my hand and still looking right at me she makes a kind of yelping noise like a polite horse. It's the noise I heard just now, her laugh. Her hand is hot and wet and pink like a sponge, with dimples at the base of each finger. My brother introduces her as Jenny. She's going to take the attic bedroom. She's got a very large face, round like a red moon, and thick glasses which make her eyes as big as golf balls. When she lets go of my hand I can't think of one thing to say. But my brother Peter talks on and on, he tells her what vegetables we are growing and what flowers, he makes her stand where she can get a view of the river between the trees and then he leads her back to the house. My brother is exactly twice my age and he's good at that sort of thing, just talking.

Jenny takes the attic. I've been up there a few times looking for things in the old boxes, or watching the river out of the small window. There's nothing much in the boxes really, just cloth scraps and dressmaking patterns. Perhaps some of them actually belonged to my mother. In one corner there's a pile of picture frames without pictures. Once I was up there because it was raining outside, and downstairs there was a row going on between Peter and some of the others. I helped José

clear out the place ready for a bedroom. José used to be Kate's boyfriend and then last spring he moved his things out of Kate's bedroom and moved into the spare room next to mine. We carried the boxes and frames to the garage, we stained the wooden floor black and put down rugs. We took apart the extra bed in my room and carried it up. With that, a table and a chair, a small cupboard and the sloping ceiling, there is just room for two people standing up. All Jenny has for luggage is a small suitcase and a carrier bag. I take them up to her room for her and she follows, breathing harder and harder and stopping halfway up the third set of stairs to get a rest. My brother Peter comes up behind and we squeeze in as if we are all going to be living there and we're seeing it for the first time. I point out the window for her so she can see the river. Jenny sits with her big elbows on the table. Sometimes she dabs at her damp red face with a large white handkerchief while she's listening to some story of Peter's. I'm sitting on the bed behind her looking at how immense her back is, and under her chair I can see her thick pink legs, how they taper away and squeeze into tiny shoes at the bottom. Everywhere she's pink. The smell of her sweat fills the room. It smells like the new cut grass outside, and I get this idea that I mustn't breathe it in too deeply or I'll get fat too. We stand up to go so she can get on with her unpacking and she's saying thank you for everything, and as I go through the door she makes her little yelp, her nervous laugh. Without meaning to I glance back at her through the doorway and she's looking right at me with her magnified golf-balls eyes.

"You don't say much, do you?" she says. Which sort of makes it even harder to think of something to say. So I just smile at her and carry on down the stairs.

Downstairs it's my turn to help Kate cook the supper. Kate is tall and slim and sad. Really the opposite of Jenny. When I have girl friends I'm going to have them like Kate. She's very pale, though, even at this time in the summer. She has strange-coloured hair. Once I heard Sam say it was the colour of a brown envelope. Sam is one of Peter's friends who also lives here and who wanted to move his things into Kate's bedroom when José moved his out. But Kate is sort of haughty and she doesn't like Sam because he's too noisy. If Sam moved into Kate's room he'd always be waking up Alice, Kate's little girl. When Kate and José are in the same room I always watch them to see if they ever look at each other, and they never do. Last April I went into Kate's room one afternoon to borrow something and she and José were in bed asleep. José's parents come from Spain and his skin is very dark. Kate was lying on her back with one arm stretched out, and José was lying on her arm, snuggling up to her side. They didn't have pyjamas on, and the sheet came up to their waists. They were so black and so white. I stood at the foot of the bed a long time, watching them. It was like some secret I'd found out. Then Kate opened her eyes and saw me there and told me very softly to get out. It seems pretty strange to me that they were lying there like that and now they don't even look at each other. That wouldn't happen with me if I was lying on some girl's arm. Kate doesn't like cooking. She has to spend a lot of time making sure Alice doesn't put knives in her mouth or pull boiling pots off the stove. Kate prefers dressing-up and going out, or talking for hours on the telephone, which is what I would rather do if I was a girl. Once she stayed out late and my brother Peter had to put Alice to bed. Kate always looks sad when she speaks to Alice, when she's telling her what to do she speaks very softly as if she doesn't really want to be speaking to Alice at all. And it's the same when she talks to me, as if it's not really talking at all. When she sees my back in the kitchen she takes me through to the downstairs bathroom and dabs calamine lotion over me with a piece of cotton wool. I can see her in the mirror, she doesn't seem to have any particular expression on her face. She makes a sound between her teeth, half a whistle and half a sigh, and when she wants a different part of my back towards the light she pushes or pulls me about by my arm. She asks me quickly and quietly what the girl upstairs is like, and when I tell her, "She's very fat and she's got a funny laugh," she doesn't make any reply. I cut up vegetables for Kate and lay the table. Then I walk down to the river to look at my boat. I bought it with some money I got when my parents died. By the time I get to the jetty it's past sunset and the river is black with scraps of red like the cloth scraps that used to be in the attic. Tonight the river is slow and the air is warm and smooth. I don't untie the boat, my back is too sore from the sun to row. Instead I climb in and sit with the quiet

rise and fall of the river, watching the red cloth sink in the black water and wondering if I breathed in too much of Jenny's smell.

When I get back they are about to start eating. Jenny is sitting next to Peter and when I come in she doesn't look up from her plate, even when I sit down on the other side of her. She's so big beside me, and yet so bowed down over her plate, looking as if she doesn't really want to exist, that I feel sorry for her in a way and I want to speak to her. But I can't think of anything to say. In fact no one has anything to say this meal, they're all just pushing their knives and forks backwards and forwards over their plates, and now and then someone murmurs for something to be passed. It doesn't usually happen like this when we're eating, there's usually something going on. But Jenny's here, more silent than any of us, and bigger, too, and not looking up from her plate. Sam clears his throat and looks down our end of the table at Jenny, and everyone else looks up too, except for her, waiting for something. Sam clears his throat again and says,

"Where were you living before, Jenny?" Because no one's been speaking it comes out flat, as if Sam's in an office filling in a form for her. And Jenny, still looking down at her plate, says,

"Manchester." Then she looks at Sam. "In a flat." And she gives a little yelp of a laugh, probably because we're all listening and looking at her, and then she sinks back into her plate while Sam's saying something like, "Ah, I see," and thinking of the next thing to say. Upstairs, Alice starts crying so Kate goes and brings her down and lets her sit on her lap. When she stops crying she points at each one of us in turn and shouts, "UH, UH, UH," and so on right round the table while we all sit there eating and not speaking. It's like she's telling us off for not thinking of things to say. Kate tells her to be quiet in the sad way she always has when she's with Alice. Sometimes I think she's like that because Alice doesn't have a father. She doesn't look at all like Kate, she has very fair hair and ears that are too large for her head. A year or two ago when Alice was very little I used to think that José was her father. But his hair is black, and he never pays much attention to Alice. When everybody's finished the first course and I'm helping Kate collect the dishes, Jenny offers to have Alice on her lap. Alice is still shouting and pointing at different things in the room, but once she's on Jenny's lap she goes very quiet. Probably because it's the biggest lap she's ever seen. Kate and I bring in fruit and tea, and when we are peeling oranges and bananas, eating the apples from our tree in the garden, pouring tea and passing cups with milk and sugar round, everyone starts talking and laughing like they usually do, like there never was anything holding them back. And Jenny is giving Alice a really good time on her lap, making her knees gallop like a horse, making her hand swoop down like a bird on to Alice's belly, showing her tricks with her fingers, so that all the time Alice is shouting for more. It's the first time I've heard her laugh like that. And then Jenny glances down the table at Kate who's been watching them play with the same kind of look she might have on her face if she was watching the telly. Jenny carries Alice to her mother like she's suddenly feeling guilty about having Alice on her lap for such a long time and having so much fun. Alice is shouting, "More, more, more," when she's back at the other end of the table, and she's still shouting it five minutes later when her mother carries her up to bed.

Because my brother asks me to, I take coffee up to Jenny's room early next morning. When I go in she's already up, sitting at her table putting stamps on letters. She looks smaller than she did last night. She has her window wide open and her room is full of morning air, it feels like she's been up for a long time. Out of her window I can see the river stretching between the trees, light and quiet in the sun. I want to get outside, I want to see my boat before breakfast. But Jenny wants to talk. She makes me sit on her bed and tell her about myself. She doesn't ask me any questions and since I'm not sure how to start off telling someone about myself I sit there and watch while she writes addresses on her letters and sips her coffee. But I don't mind, it's all right in Jenny's room. She's put two pictures on the wall. One is a framed photograph taken in a zoo of a monkey walking upside down along a branch with its baby hanging on to its stomach. You can tell it is a zoo because in the bottom corner there's a zookeeper's cap and part of his face. The other is a colour picture taken out of a magazine of two children running along the seashore holding hands. The sun is setting and everything in the picture

is deep red, even the children. It's a very good picture. She finishes with her letters and asks me where I go to school. I tell her about the new school I'm going to when the holidays are over, the big comprehensive[1] in Reading. But I haven't been there yet, so there isn't much I can tell her about it. She sees me looking out the window again.

"Are you going down to the river?"

"Yes, I have to see my boat."

"Can I come with you? Will you show me the river?" I wait for her by the door, watching her squeeze her round, pink feet into small, flat shoes and brush her very short hair with a brush which has a mirror on the back. We walk across the lawn to the kissing gate[2] at the bottom of the garden and along the path through the high ferns. Half way down I stop to listen to a yellow-hammer, and she tells me that she doesn't know the song of one bird. Most grown-up people will never tell you that they don't know things. So farther on down the path just before it opens out on to the jetty we stop under an old oak tree so she can hear a blackbird. I know there's one up there, it's always up there singing this time in the morning. Just as we get there it stops and we have to wait quietly for it to begin again. Standing by that half-dead old trunk I can hear other birds in other trees and the river just round the corner washing under the jetty. But our bird is taking a rest. Something about waiting in silence makes Jenny nervous and she pinches her nose tight to stop her yelp of a laugh getting out. I want her to hear the blackbird so much I put my hand on her arm, and when I do that she takes her hand away from her nose and smiles. Just a few seconds after that the blackbird sets out on its long complicated song. It was waiting all the time for us to get settled. We walk out on to the jetty and I show her my boat tied up at the end. It's a rowing boat, green on the outside and red on the inside like a fruit. I've been down here every day all this summer to row it, paint it, wipe it down, and sometimes just to look at it. Once I rowed it seven miles upstream and spent the rest of the day drifting back

---

[1] *comprehensive* Secondary school for children of all levels of ability, stereotypically seen as working class.

[2] *kissing gate* From "kisting gate," a small swinging gate set in a cupped enclosure to allow one person to pass at a time and keep livestock out.

down. We sit on the edge of the jetty looking at my boat, the river and the trees on the other side. Then Jenny looks downstream and says,

"London's down there." London is a terrible secret I try to keep from the river. It doesn't know about it yet while it's flowing past our house. So I just nod and say nothing. Jenny asks me if she can sit in the boat. It worries me at first that she's going to be too heavy. But of course I cannot tell her that. I lean over the jetty and hold the painter rope for her to climb in. She does it with a lot of grunting and rocking around. And since the boat doesn't look any lower now than it usually does, I get in too and we watch the river from this new level where you can see how strong and old it really is. We sit talking for a long time. First I tell her about how my parents died two years ago in a car crash and how my brother had ideas for turning the house into a kind of commune. At first he was going to have over twenty people living here. But now I think he wants to keep it down to about eight. Then Jenny tells me about the time she was a teacher in a big school in Manchester where all the children were always laughing at her because she was fat. She doesn't seem to mind talking about it, though. She has some funny stories of her time there. When she's telling me of the time when the children locked her in a book cupboard we both laugh so much the boat rocks from side to side and pushes small waves out into the river. This time Jenny's laugh is easy and kind of rhythmic, not hard and yelping like before. On the way back she recognizes two blackbirds by their songs, and when we're crossing the lawn she points out another. I just nod. It's a song-thrush really, but I'm too hungry to tell her the difference.

Three days later I hear Jenny singing. I'm in the back yard trying to put together a bicycle out of bits and pieces and I hear her through the open kitchen window. She's in there cooking lunch and looking after Alice while Kate visits friends. It's a song she doesn't know the words for, halfway between happy and sad, and she's singing like an old croaky Negress to Alice. New morning man la-la, la-la-la-, l'la, new morning man la-la-la-, la-la, l'la, new morning man take me 'way from here. That afternoon I row her out on the river and she has another song with the same kind of tune, but this time with no words at all. Ya-la-la, ya-laaa, ya-eeeee. She

spreads her hands out and rolls her big magnified eyes around like it's a serenade especially for me. A week later Jenny's songs are all over the house, sometimes with a line or two if she can remember it, most often with no words at all. She spends a lot of her time in the kitchen and that's where she does most of her singing. Somehow she makes more space in there. She scrapes paint off the north window to let in more light. No one can think why it was painted over in the first place. She carries out an old table, and when it's out everyone realizes that it was always in the way. One afternoon she paints the whole of one wall white to make the kitchen look bigger, and she arranges the pots and plates so that you always know where they are and even I can reach them. She makes it into the kind of kitchen you can sit around in when you've got nothing else to do. Jenny makes her own bread and bakes cakes, things we usually go to the shop for. On the third day she's here I find clean sheets on my bed. She takes the sheets I've been using all summer and most of my clothes away for washing. She spends all of one afternoon making a curry, and that night I eat the best meal in two years. When the others tell her how good they think it is Jenny gets nervous and does her yelping laugh. I can see the others are still bothered when she does it, they sort of look away as if it is something disgusting that would be rude to look at. But it doesn't worry me at all when she does that laugh, I don't even hear it except when the others are there at the table looking away. Most afternoons we go out on the river together and I try to teach her to row, and listen to her stories of when she was teaching, and when she was working in a supermarket, how she used to watch old people come in each day to shoplift bacon and butter, I teach her some more birdsongs, but the only one she can really remember is the first one, the blackbird. In her room she shows me pictures of her parents and her brother and she says,

"I'm the only fat one." I show her some pictures of my parents, too. One of them was taken a month before they died, and in it they are walking down some steps holding hands and laughing at something outside the picture. They were laughing at my brother who was fooling around to make them laugh for the picture I was taking. I had just got the camera for my tenth birthday and that was one of the first pictures I took with it.

Jenny looks at it for a long time and says something about her looking like a very nice woman, and suddenly I see my mother as just a woman in a picture, it could be any woman, and for the first time she's far off, not in my head looking out, but outside my head being looked at by me, Jenny or anyone who picks up the photo. Jenny takes it out of my hand and puts it away with the others in the shoebox. As we go downstairs she starts off on a long story about a friend of hers who was producing a play which ended strangely and quietly. The friend wanted Jenny to start off the clapping at the end but Jenny got it all wrong somehow and started everyone clapping fifteen minutes before the end during a quiet bit so that the last part of the play was lost and the clapping was all the louder because no one knew what the play was about. All this, I suppose, is to make me stop thinking about my mother, which it does.

Kate spends more time with her friends in Reading. One morning I'm in the kitchen when she comes in very smartly dressed in a kind of leather suit and high leather boots. She sits down opposite me to wait for Jenny to come down so she can tell her what food to give Alice that day, and what time she'll be back. It reminds me of another morning almost two years ago when Kate came into the kitchen in the same kind of suit. She sat down at the table, undid her blouse and started to knead with her fingers blueish-white milk into a bottle from one tit and then the other. She didn't seem to notice me sitting there.

"What are you doing that for?" I asked her.

She said, "It's for Janet to give to Alice later on today. I've got to go out." Janet was a black girl who used to be living here. It was strange watching Kate milk herself into a bottle. It made me think how we're just animals with clothes on doing very peculiar things, like monkeys at a tea party. But we get so used to each other most of the time. I wonder if Kate is thinking of that time now, sitting with me in the kitchen first thing in the morning. She's got orange lipstick on and her hair tied back and that makes her look even thinner than usual. Her lipstick is sort of fluorescent, like a road sign. Every minute she looks at her watch and her leather creaks. She looks like some beautiful woman from outer space. Then Jenny comes down, wearing a huge old dressing-gown made out of patches and yawning

because she's just got out of bed, and Kate speaks to her very quickly and quietly about Alice's food for the day. It's as if it makes her sad, talking about that sort of thing. She picks up her bag and runs out the kitchen and calls, "Bye," over her shoulder. Jenny sits down at the table and drinks tea and it's like she really is the big mama left behind at home to look after the rich lady's daughter. Yo' daddy's rich and yo' mama's goodlookin', lah la-la-la la-la don' yo' cry. And there's something in the way the others treat Jenny. Like she's outside things, and not really a person like they are. They've got used to her cooking big meals and making cakes. No one says anything about it now. Sometimes in the evenings Peter, Kate, José and Sam sit around and smoke hashish in Peter's homemade water-pipe and listen to the stereo turned up loud. When they do that Jenny usually goes up to her room, she doesn't like to be with them when they're doing that, and I can see they sort of resent it. And though she's a girl she's not beautiful like Kate or Sharon, my brother's girlfriend. She doesn't wear jeans and Indian shirts like they do, either, probably because she can't find any to fit her. She wears dresses with flowers on and ordinary things like my mother or the lady in the post office wear. And when she gets nervous about something and does her laugh I can tell they think of her like some sort of mental patient, I know that by the way they turn their eyes away. And they still think about how fat she is. Sometimes when she's not there Sam calls her Slim Jim, and it always makes the others laugh. It's not that they're unfriendly to her or anything like that, it's just that in some way that's hard to describe they keep her apart from themselves. One time we're out on the river she asks me about hashish.

"What do you think about it all?" she says, and I tell her my brother won't let me try it till I'm fifteen. I know she's dead against it, but she doesn't mention it again. It's that same afternoon I take a photograph of her leaning by the kitchen door holding Alice and squinting a little into the sun. She takes mine too, riding no-hands round the back yard on the bicycle I put together out of bits and pieces.

It's hard to say exactly when Jenny becomes Alice's mother. At first she's just looking after her while Kate visits friends. Then the visits get more often till they are almost every day. So the three of us, Jenny, Alice and me, spend a lot of time together by the river. By the jetty there's a grass bank which slopes down on to a tiny sand beach about six feet across. Jenny sits on the bank playing with Alice while I do things to my boat. When we first put Alice in the boat she squeals like a baby pig. She doesn't trust the water. It's a long time before she'll stand on the small beach, and when she does at last she never takes her eyes off the water's edge to make sure it doesn't creep up on her. But when she sees Jenny waving to her from the boat, and quite safe, she changes her mind and we make a trip to the other side of the river. Alice doesn't mind about Kate being away because she likes Jenny, who sings her the bits of songs she knows and talks to her all the time when they are sitting on the grass bank by the river. Alice does not understand a word of it but she likes the sound of Jenny's voice going on and on. Sometimes Alice points up to Jenny's mouth and says, "More, more." Kate is always so quiet and sad with her she doesn't hear many voices speaking right at her. One night Kate stays away and doesn't come back till the next morning. Alice is sitting on Jenny's knee spreading her breakfast across the kitchen table when Kate comes running in, scoops her up, hugs her and asks over and over again without giving anyone time to reply,

"Has she been all right? Has she been all right? Has she been all right?" The same afternoon Alice is back with Jenny because Kate has to go off somewhere again. I'm in the hall outside the kitchen when I hear her tell Jenny she'll be back in the early evening, and a few minutes later I see her walking down the drive carrying a small suitcase. When she gets back two days later she just puts her head round the door to see if Alice is still there, and then she goes up to her room. It's not always such a good thing having Alice with us all the time. We can't go very far in the boat. After twenty minutes Alice gets suspicious of the water again and wants to be back on the shore. And if we want to walk somewhere Alice has to be carried most of the way. It means I can't show Jenny some of my special places along the river. By the end of the day Alice gets pretty miserable, moaning and crying about nothing because she's tired. I get fed up spending so much time with Alice. Kate stays up in her room most of the day. One afternoon I take her up some tea and she's sitting in a chair asleep. With Alice

there so much of the time Jenny and I don't talk together as much as we did when she first came. Not because Alice is listening, but because all Jenny's time is taken up with her. She doesn't think of anything else, really, it seems like she doesn't want to talk with anyone but Alice. One evening we are all sitting around in the front room after supper. Kate is in the hall having a long argument with someone on the telephone. She finishes, comes in, sits down in a noisy kind of way and carries on reading. But I can see she's angry and not really reading at all. No one speaks for a while, then Alice starts crying upstairs and shouting for Jenny. Jenny and Kate both look up at once and stare at each other for a moment. Then Kate gets up and leaves the room. We all pretend to go on reading but really we are listening to Kate's footsteps on the stairs. We hear her walk into Alice's room, which is right over this one, and we hear Alice shout louder and louder for Jenny to come up. Kate comes back down the stairs, this time quickly. When she comes in the room Jenny looks up and they stare at each other again. And all the time Alice goes on shouting for Jenny. Jenny gets up and squeezes past Kate at the door. They don't speak. The rest of us, Peter, Sam, José and me, we carry on with our pretend reading and listen to Jenny's footsteps upstairs. The crying stops and she stays up there a long time. When she comes down Kate is back in her chair with her magazine. Jenny sits down and no one looks up, no one speaks.

Suddenly the summer is over. Jenny comes into my room early one morning to drag the sheets off my bed and all the clothes she can find in the room. Everything has to be washed before I go to school. Then she gets me to clean out my room, all the old comics and plates and cups which have been collecting under my bed all summer, all the dust and the pots of paint I've been using on my boat. She finds a small table in the garage and I help her carry it to my room. It's going to be my desk for doing homework on. She takes me into the village for a treat, and she won't tell me what it is. When we get there it turns out to be a haircut. I'm about to walk away when she puts her hand on my shoulder.

"Don't be silly," she says. "You can't go to school looking like that, you won't last a day." So I sit still for the barber and let him cut away my whole summer while Jenny sits behind me, laughing at me scowling at her in the mirror. She gets some money from my brother Peter and takes me on the bus into town to buy a school uniform. It's strange having her tell me what to do all of a sudden after our times out on the river. But I don't mind, really, I can't think of any good reasons for not doing the things she says. She steers me through the main shopping streets, into shoe shops and outfitters, she buys me a red blazer and a cap, two pairs of black leather shoes, six pairs of grey socks, two pairs of grey trousers and five grey shirts, and all the time she's saying, "Do you like these ones? Do you like this?" and since I don't have any special feeling for one particular shade of grey, I agree with whatever she thinks is the best. It's all over in an hour. That evening she empties my drawers of my rock collection to make room for the new clothes, and she gets me to put on the whole uniform. They all laugh downstairs, especially when I put the red cap on. Sam says I look like an inter-galactic postman. For three nights in a row she has me scrubbing my knees with a nailbrush to get the dirt out from under the skin.

Then on Sunday, the day before I start back at school, I go down to the boat with Jenny and Alice for the last time. In the evening I'm going to help Peter and Sam drag my boat up the path and across the lawn into the garage for the winter. Then we're going to build another jetty, a stronger one. It's the last boat trip of the summer. Jenny lifts Alice in and climbs in herself while I hold the boat steady from the jetty. As I'm pushing us off with an oar, Jenny starts one of her songs. Jeeesus won't you come on down, Jeeesus won't you come on down, Jeeesus won't you come on down, lah, la-la-la-lah, la-la. Alice stands between Jenny's knees watching me row. She thinks it's funny, the way I strain backwards and forwards. She thinks it's a game I'm playing with her, moving close up to her face and away again. It's strange, our last day on the river. When Jenny's finished her song no one speaks for a long time. Just Alice laughing at me. It's so still on the river, her laugh carries across the water to nowhere. The sun is a kind of pale yellow like it's burnt out at the end of summer, there's no wind in the trees on the banks, and no birdsong. Even the oars make no sound in the water. I row upstream with the sun on my back, but it's too pale

to feel it, it's too pale to make shadows, even. Up ahead there's an old man standing under an oak tree, fishing. When we are level with him he looks up and stares at us in our boat and we stare back at him on the bank. His face does not change when he's looking at us. Our faces do not change, either, no one says hello. He has a long piece of grass in his mouth and when we've passed he takes it out and spits quietly into the river. Jenny trails her hand in the thick water and watches the bank as if it's something she's only seeing in her mind. It makes me think she doesn't really want to be out there on the river with me. She only came because of all the other times we've been rowing together, and because this is the last time this summer. It sort of makes me sad, thinking that, it makes it harder to row. Then after we've been going for about half an hour she looks at me and smiles and I can tell it's all in my head about her not wanting to be on the river because she starts talking about the summer, about all the things we've been doing. She makes it sound really great, much better than it was really. About the long walks we went on, and paddling at the edge of the river with Alice, how I tried to teach her to row and remember different birdsongs, and the times we used to get up while the others were still asleep and row on the river before breakfast. She gets me going too, remembering all the things we did, like the time we thought we saw a waxwing, and another time we waited one evening behind a bush for a badger to come out of its hole. Pretty soon we get really excited about what a summer it's been and the things we're going to do next year, shouting and laughing into the dead air. And then Jenny says,

"And tomorrow you put on your red cap and go to school." There's something in the way she says it, pretending to be serious and telling me off, with one finger wagging in the air, that makes it the funniest thing I ever heard. And the idea of it too, of doing all those things in the summer and then at the end of it putting on a red cap and going to school. We start laughing and it seems like we're never going to stop. I have to put down the oars. Our hooting and cackling gets louder and louder because the still air doesn't carry it across the water and the noise of it stays with us in the boat. Each time we catch the other's eye we laugh harder and louder till it begins to hurt down my sides, and more than anything I want to stop. Alice starts to cry because she doesn't know what's happening, and that makes us laugh more. Jenny leans over the side of the boat so she can't see me. But her laugh is getting tighter and drier, little hard yelps like pieces of stone from her throat. Her big pink face and her big pink arms are shaking and straining to catch a mouthful of air, but it's all going out of her in little pieces of stone. She leans back into the boat. Her mouth is laughing but her eyes look kind of scared and dry. She drops to her knees, holding her stomach with the pain of laughing, and knocks Alice down with her. And the boat tips over. It tips over because Jenny falls against the side, because Jenny is big and my boat is small. It goes over quickly, like the click of my camera shutter, and suddenly I'm at the deep green bottom of the river touching the cold soft mud with the back of my hand and feeling the reeds on my face. I can hear laughter like sinking pieces of stone by my ear. But when I push upwards to the surface I feel no one near me. When I come up it's dark on the river. I've been down a long time. Something touches my head and I realize I'm inside the upturned boat. I go down again and up the other side. It takes me a long time to get my breath. I work my way round the boat shouting over and over for Jenny and Alice. I put my mouth in the water and shout their names. But no one answers, nothing breaks the surface. I'm the only one on the river. So I hang on to the side of the boat and wait for them to come up. I wait a long time, drifting along with the boat, with the laughter still in my head, watching the river and the yellow patches on it from the sun getting low. Sometimes great shivers run through my legs and back, but mostly I'm calm, hanging on to the green shell with nothing in my mind, nothing at all, just watching the river, waiting for the surface to break and the yellow patches to scatter. I drift past the place where the old man was fishing and it seems like a very long time ago. He's gone now, there's just a paper bag in the place where he was standing. I get so tired I close my eyes and it feels like I'm at home in bed and it's winter and my mother's coming into my room to say goodnight. She turns out the light and I slip off the boat into the river. Then I remember and I shout for Jenny and Alice and watch the river again and my eyes start to close and my mother comes into my room and says goodnight and turns out the light and I sink back into the water again. After a long time I forget to shout for Jenny and Alice, I just hang there and drift down. I'm looking at a place on the bank I used to know very well a long time ago. There's a patch of sand and a grass bank by a jetty. The yellow patches are sinking into the river when I push away from the boat. I let it drift on down to London and I swim slowly through the black water to the jetty.

—1972

KAZUO ISHIGURO
b. 1954

Kazuo Ishiguro is best known for his Booker Prize-winning *The Remains of the Day* (1989), and for the dystopian *Never Let Me Go* (2005), but his other novels have also received extraordinary international acclaim. He has been hailed—along with writers such as Salman Rushdie, Michael Ondaatje, Vikram Seth, and Timothy Mo—as part of a new movement of "world fiction." Like these writers, he writes in English but is of non-Anglo-Saxon ancestry, and often depicts characters and settings which differ from those traditionally found in English literature. With influences that include Japanese pop culture of the 1940s and 1950s, nineteenth-century American writers, and Russian authors Dostoevsky and Chekhov, Ishiguro often produces work that challenges his readers' expectations.

Ishiguro was born in Nagasaki, Japan, in 1954. When he was five his father accepted a one-year research position at the National Institute of Oceanography in Britain, and the family left for England. Ishiguro's parents educated him in the expectation that the family would return to Japan—providing him with Japanese magazines, books, and movies—but their return continued to be postponed, and eventually they became permanent British residents. Ishiguro studied English and

philosophy at the University of Kent at Canterbury, where he received his BA. He went on to a Master's degree in Creative Writing at the University of East Anglia in Norwich, where he was a member of a postgraduate class directed by Malcolm Bradbury.

Ishiguro, who for several years had attempted unsuccessfully to establish himself as a singer/songwriter, enjoyed almost immediate success as a writer of fiction. His first two novels, *A Pale View of Hills* (1982) and *An Artist of the Floating World* (1986), won prestigious literary awards in England and established him as an important new novelist. Both these early novels are set in Japan, although Ishiguro would not make his first return to Japan until 1989; Ishiguro has said that the Japan of these novels is one of his own personal imagination, constructed on a foundation of childhood memories.

Throughout his life Ishiguro has retained something of the outsider's perspective. When he began writing he realized he "wasn't a very English Englishman, and [he] wasn't a very Japanese Japanese either." This unique perspective enables him to pinpoint and dissect cultural myths, norms, and stereotypes—indeed, Ishiguro believes one of an artist's most important jobs is to "tackle and rework myths." Lurking behind the faintly comic resolution of *An Artist of the Floating World* is Ishiguro's knowledge that many Western readers—familiar only with stereotypes of Japanese society—would expect at the novel's end the cultural cliché of the protagonist's ritual suicide by *seppuku*.

The Remains of the Day is widely regarded as one of the most accomplished works of fiction of the twentieth century. Its story concerns Stevens, an aging butler who looks back in the summer of 1956 on the events of his life—in particular, on the great events that had transpired in his presence in the mid-1930s when his employer, Lord Darlington, had been organizing clandestine support in Britain for Germany's Nazi government; and on the unacknowledged love that had existed over the same period between himself and the housekeeper at Darlington Hall, Miss Kenton. The story is told in

Stevens's voice; from between the lines of the butler's spare and formal narrative the reader is led to piece together a tale of misplaced loyalty, lost opportunity, and almost unbearable sadness.

Ishiguro has been compared to novelist Graham Swift in his intertwining of personal and world histories. His novels often center on characters who attempt to cope with traumatic events of history, but he has little interest in investigating the historic events themselves. *The Remains of the Day* looks back from the 1950s to the impending Nazi threat of the 1930s with barely a glance at its culmination during World War II; similarly, although *A Pale View of Hills* is set in Nagasaki in the late 1940s, no mention is ever made of the atomic bomb, the effects of which permeate every aspect of the protagonist's life. As Ishiguro says, this is because he is "more interested in what people tell themselves happened … than what actually happened." Often recounted in the first person by an unreliable narrator who is haunted by events in his or her past, Ishiguro's narratives frequently center on distortions of perception or of memory. His very writing style mimics the workings of memory, moving fluidly across time and through tangentially connected episodes.

Ishiguro's settings are often loosely defined, as is the case in "A Village After Dark" (2001) or in *The Unconsoled* (1995), which could be set in any European city. Whether they take place in Japan, England, or Shanghai—the setting of *When We Were Orphans* (2002)—there is often a somewhat unsettling universality to the experiences described; the locations are important only in that they provide backdrops for, and insights into, Ishiguro's characters. As a result, Ishiguro's fiction—which has been printed in over thirty languages—is well suited for translation.

Never Let Me Go (2005) was widely praised as Ishiguro's most accomplished work since *The Remains of the Day*. Set largely in a boarding school where the atmosphere is at once warmly familiar and deeply disturbing, the novel explores, against a futuristic dystopian background, the roots of social exclusion, the sometimes frightening conjunction of medical science and human notions of progress, the nature of love, and the shadow cast by death on human existence.

The Buried Giant (2015), a novel of myth and of early medieval England, is another departure for Ishiguro, who is also the author of screenplays and a collection of short stories. He lives with his wife and daughter in London.

⌘⌘⌘

A Village After Dark

There was a time when I could travel England for weeks on end and remain at my sharpest—when, if anything, the travelling gave me an edge. But now that I am older I become disoriented more easily. So it was that on arriving at the village just after dark I failed to find my bearings at all. I could hardly believe I was in the same village in which not so long ago I had lived and come to exercise such influence.

There was nothing I recognized, and I found myself walking forever around twisting, badly lit streets hemmed in on both sides by the little stone cottages characteristic of the area. The streets often became so narrow I could make no progress without my bag or my elbow scraping one rough wall or another. I persevered nevertheless, stumbling around in the darkness in the hope of coming upon the village square—where I could at least orient myself—or else of encountering one of the villagers. When after a while I had done neither, a weariness came over me, and I decided my best course was just to choose a cottage at random, knock on the door, and hope it would be opened by someone who remembered me.

I stopped by a particularly rickety-looking door, whose upper beam was so low that I could see I would have to crouch right down to enter. A dim light was leaking out around the door's edges, and I could hear voices and laughter. I knocked loudly to insure that the occupants would hear me over their talk. But just then someone behind me said, "Hello."

I turned to find a young woman of around twenty,

dressed in raggedy jeans and a torn jumper, standing in the darkness a little way away.

"You walked straight past me earlier," she said, "even though I called to you."

"Did I really? Well, I'm sorry. I didn't mean to be rude."

"You're Fletcher, aren't you?"

"Yes," I said, somewhat flattered.

"Wendy thought it was you when you went by our cottage. We all got very excited. You were one of that lot, weren't you? With David Maggis and all of them."

"Yes," I said, "but Maggis was hardly the most important one. I'm surprised you pick him out like that. There were other, far more important figures." I reeled off a series of names and was interested to see the girl nodding at each one in recognition. "But this must have all been before your time," I said. "I'm surprised you know about such things."

"It was before our time, but we're all experts on your lot. We know more about all that than most of the older ones who were here then. Wendy recognized you instantly just from your photos."

"I had no idea you young people had taken such an interest in us. I'm sorry I walked past you earlier. But you see, now that I'm older, I get a little disoriented when I travel."

I could hear some boisterous talk coming from behind the door. I banged on it again, this time rather impatiently, though I was not so eager to bring the encounter with the girl to a close.

She looked at me for a moment, then said, "All of you from those days are like that. David Maggis came here a few years ago. In '93, or maybe it was '94. He was like that. A bit vague. It must get to you after a while, travelling all the time."

"So Maggis was here. How interesting. You know, he wasn't one of the really important figures. You mustn't get carried away with such an idea. Incidentally, perhaps you could tell me who lives in this cottage." I thumped the door again.

"The Petersons," the girl said. "They're an old house. They'll probably remember you."

"The Petersons," I repeated, but the name meant nothing to me.

"Why don't you come to our cottage? Wendy was

really excited. So were the rest of us. It's a real chance for us, actually talking to someone from those days."

"I'd very much like to do that. But first of all I'd better get myself settled in. The Petersons, you say."

I thumped the door again, this time quite ferociously. At last it opened, throwing warmth and light out into the street. An old man was standing in the doorway. He looked at me carefully, then asked, "It's not Fletcher, is it?"

"Yes, and I've just got into the village. I've been travelling for several days."

He thought about this for a moment, then said, "Well, you'd better come in."

I found myself in a cramped, untidy room full of rough wood and broken furniture. A log burning in the fireplace was the only source of light, by which I could make out a number of hunched figures sitting around the room. The old man led me to a chair beside the fire with a grudgingness that suggested it was the very one he had just vacated. Once I sat down, I found I could not easily turn my head to see my surroundings or the others in the room. But the warmth of the fire was very welcome, and for a moment I just stared into its flames, a pleasant grogginess drifting over me. Voices came from behind me, inquiring if I was well, if I had come far, if I was hungry, and I replied as best I could, though I was aware that my answers were barely adequate. Eventually, the questions ceased, and it occurred to me that my presence was creating a heavy awkwardness, but I was so grateful for the warmth and the chance to rest that I hardly cared.

Nonetheless, when the silence behind me had gone unbroken for several minutes, I resolved to address my hosts with a little more civility, and I turned in my chair. It was then, as I did so, that I was suddenly seized by an intense sense of recognition. I had chosen the cottage quite at random, but now I could see that it was none other than the very one in which I had spent my years in this village. My gaze moved immediately to the far corner—at this moment shrouded in darkness—to the spot that had been *my* corner, where once my mattress had been and where I had spent many tranquil hours browsing through books or conversing with whoever happened to drift in. On summer days, the windows, and often the door, were left open to allow a refreshing breeze to blow right through. Those were the days when the cottage was surrounded by open fields and there would come from outside the voices of my friends, lazing in the long grass, arguing over poetry or philosophy. These precious fragments of the past came back to me so powerfully that it was all I could do not to make straight for my old corner then and there.

Someone was speaking to me again, perhaps asking another question, but I hardly listened. Rising, I peered through the shadows into my corner, and could now make out a narrow bed, covered by an old curtain, occupying more or less the exact space where my mattress had been. The bed looked extremely inviting, and I found myself cutting into something the old man was saying.

"Look," I said, "I know this is a bit blunt. But, you see, I've come such a long way today. I really need to lie down, close my eyes, even if it's just for a few minutes. After that, I'm happy to talk all you like."

I could see the figures around the room shifting uneasily. Then a new voice said, rather sullenly, "Go ahead then. Have a nap. Don't mind us."

But I was already picking my way through the clutter toward my corner. The bed felt damp, and the springs creaked under my weight, but no sooner had I curled up with my back to the room than my many hours of travelling began to catch up with me. As I was drifting off, I heard the old man saying, "It's Fletcher, all right. God, he's aged."

A woman's voice said, "Should we let him go to sleep like that? He might wake in a few hours and then we'll have to stay up with him."

"Let him sleep for an hour or so," someone else said. "If he's still asleep after an hour, we'll wake him."

At this point, sheer exhaustion overtook me.

It was not a continuous or comfortable sleep. I drifted between sleep and waking, always conscious of voices behind me in the room. At some point, I was aware of a woman saying, "I don't know how I was ever under his spell. He looks such a ragamuffin now."

In my state of near-sleep, I debated with myself whether these words applied to me or, perhaps, to David Maggis, but before long sleep engulfed me once more.

When I next awoke, the room appeared to have grown both darker and colder. Voices were continuing behind me in lowered tones, but I could make no sense of the conversation. I now felt embarrassed at having gone to sleep in the way I had, and for a few further moments remained motionless with my face to the wall. But something about me must have revealed that I was awake, for a woman's voice, breaking off from the general conversation, said, "Oh, look, look." Some whispers were exchanged, then I heard the sound of someone coming toward my corner. I felt a hand placed gently on my shoulder, and looked up to find a woman kneeling over me. I did not turn my body sufficiently to see the room, but I got the impression that it was lit by dying embers, and the woman's face was visible only in shadow.

"Now, Fletcher," she said. "It's time we had a talk. I've waited a long time for you to come back. I've thought about you often."

I strained to see her more clearly. She was somewhere in her forties, and even in the gloom I noticed a sleepy sadness in her eyes. But her face failed to stir in me even the faintest of memories.

"I'm sorry," I said. "I have no recollection of you. But please forgive me if we met some time ago. I do get very disoriented these days."

"Fletcher," she said, "when we used to know one another, I was young and beautiful. I idolized you, and everything you said seemed like an answer. Now here you are, back again. I've wanted to tell you for many years that you ruined my life."

"You're being unfair. All right, I was mistaken about a lot of things. But I never claimed to have any answers. All I said in those days was that it was our duty, all of us, to contribute to the debate. We knew so much more about the issues than the ordinary people here. If people like us procrastinated, claiming we didn't yet know enough, then who was there to act? But I never claimed I had the answers. No, you're being unfair."

"Fletcher," she said, and her voice was oddly gentle, "you used to make love to me, more or less every time I wandered in here to your room. In this corner, we did all kinds of beautifully dirty things. It's odd to think how I could have once been so physically excited by you. And here you're just a foul-smelling bundle of rags now. But look at me—I'm still attractive. My face has got a bit lined, but when I walk in the village streets I wear dresses I've made specially to show off my figure. A lot of men want me still. But you, no woman would look at you now. A bundle of stinking rags and flesh."

"I don't remember you," I said. "And I've no time for sex these days. I've other things to worry about. More serious things. Very well, I was mistaken about a lot in those days. But I've done more than most to try and make amends. You see, even now I'm travelling. I've never stopped. I've travelled and travelled trying to undo what damage I may once have caused. That's more than can be said of some others from those days. I bet Maggis, for instance, hasn't worked nearly as hard to try and put things right."

The woman was stroking my hair.

"Look at you. I used to do this, run my fingers through your hair. Look at this filthy mess. I'm sure you're contaminated with all sorts of parasites." But she continued slowly to run her fingers through the dirty knots. I failed to feel anything erotic from this, as perhaps she wished me to do. Rather, her caresses felt maternal. Indeed, for a moment it was as though I had finally reached some cocoon of protectiveness, and I began once more to feel sleepy. But suddenly she stopped and slapped me hard on the forehead.

"Why don't you join the rest of us now? You've had your sleep. You've got a lot of explaining to do." With that she got up and left.

For the first time, I turned my body sufficiently to survey the room. I saw the woman making her way past the clutter on the floor, then sitting down in a rocking chair by the fireplace. I could see three other figures hunched around the dying fire. One I recognized to be the old man who had opened the door. The two others—sitting together on what looked like a wooden trunk—seemed to be women of around the same age as the one who had spoken to me.

The old man noticed that I had turned, and he indicated to the others that I was watching. The four of them proceeded to sit stiffly, not speaking. From the way they did this, it was clear that they had been discussing me thoroughly while I was asleep. In fact, as I watched them I could more or less guess the whole shape their conversation had taken. I could see, for instance, that they had spent some time expressing

concern for the young girl I had met outside, and about the effect I might have on her peers.

"They're all so impressionable," the old man would have said. "And I heard her inviting him to visit them."

To which, no doubt, one of the women on the trunk would have said, "But he can't do much harm now. In our time, we were all taken in because all his kind—they were young and glamorous. But these days the odd one passing through from time to time, looking all decrepit and burned out like that—if anything, it goes to demystify all that talk about the old days. In any case, people like him have changed their position so much these days. They don't know themselves what they believe."

The old man would have shaken his head. "I saw the way that young girl was looking at him. All right, he looks a pitiful mess over there just now. But once his ego's fed a little, once he has the flattery of the young people, sees how they want to hear his ideas, then there'll be no stopping him. It'll be just like before. He'll have them all working for his causes. Young girls like that, there's so little for them to believe in now. Even a stinking tramp like this could give them a purpose."

Their conversation, all the time I slept, would have gone something very much like that. But now, as I observed them from my corner, they continued to sit in guilty silence, staring at the last of their fire. After a while, I rose to my feet. Absurdly, the four of them kept their gazes averted from me. I waited a few moments to see if any of them would say anything. Finally, I said, "All right, I was asleep earlier, but I've guessed what you were saying. Well, you'll be interested to know I'm going to do the very thing you feared. I'm going this moment to the young people's cottage. I'm going to tell them what to do with all their energy, all their dreams, their urge to achieve something of lasting good in this world. Look at you, what a pathetic bunch. Crouching in your cottage, afraid to do anything, afraid of me, of Maggis, of anyone else from those times. Afraid to do anything in the world out there, just because once we made a few mistakes. Well, those young people haven't yet sunk so low, despite all the lethargy you've been preaching at them down the years. I'll talk to them. I'll undo in half an hour all of your sorry efforts."

"You see," the old man said to the others. "I knew it

would be this way. We ought to stop him, but what can we do?"

I crashed my way across the room, picked up my bag, and went out into the night.

The girl was still standing outside when I emerged. She seemed to be expecting me and with a nod began to lead the way.

The night was drizzly and dark. We twisted and turned along the narrow paths that ran between the cottages. Some of the cottages we passed looked so decayed and crumbling that I felt I could destroy one of them simply by running at it with all my weight.

The girl kept a few paces ahead, occasionally glancing back at me over her shoulder. Once she said, "Wendy's going to be so pleased. She was sure it was you when you went past earlier. By now, she'll have guessed she was right, because I've been away this long, and she'll have brought the whole crowd together. They'll all be waiting."

"Did you give David Maggis this sort of reception, too?"

"Oh, yes. We were really excited when he came."

"I'm sure he found that very gratifying. He always had an exaggerated sense of his own importance."

"Wendy says Maggis was one of the interesting ones, but that you were, well, important. She thinks you were really important."

I thought about this for a moment.

"You know," I said, "I've changed my mind on very many things. If Wendy's expecting me to say all the things I used to all those years ago, well, she's going to be in for a disappointment."

The girl did not seem to hear this, but continued to lead me purposefully through the clusters of cottages.

After a little while, I became aware of footsteps following a dozen or so paces behind us. At first, I assumed this was just some villager out walking and refrained from turning round. But then the girl halted under a street lamp and looked behind us. I was thus obliged also to stop and turn. A middle-aged man in a dark overcoat was coming toward us. As he approached, he held out his hand and shook mine, though without smiling.

"So," he said, "you're here."

I then realized I knew the man. We had not seen each other since we were ten years old. His name was Roger Button, and he had been in my class at the school I had attended for two years in Canada before my family returned to England. Roger Button and I had not been especially close, but, because he had been a timid boy, and because he, too, was from England, he had for a while followed me about. I had neither seen nor heard from him since that time. Now, as I studied his appearance under the street lamp, I saw the years had not been kind to him. He was bald, his face was pocked and lined, and there was a weary sag to his whole posture. For all that, there was no mistaking my old classmate.

"Roger," I said, "I'm just on my way to visit this young lady's friends. They've gathered together to receive me. Otherwise I'd have come and looked you up straightaway. As it was, I had it in my mind as the next thing to do, even before getting any sleep tonight. I was just thinking to myself, However late things finish at the young people's cottage, I'll go and knock on Roger's door afterward."

"Don't worry," said Roger Button as we all started to walk again. "I know how busy you are. But we ought to talk. Chew over old times. When you last saw me—at school, I mean—I suppose I was a rather feeble specimen. But, you know, that all changed when I got to fourteen, fifteen. I really toughened up. Became quite a leader type. But you'd long since left Canada. I always wondered what would have happened if we'd come across each other at fifteen. Things would have been rather different between us, I assure you."

As he said this, memories came flooding back. In those days, Roger Button had idolized me, and in return I had bullied him incessantly. However, there had existed between us a curious understanding that my bullying him was all for his own good; that when, without warning, I suddenly punched him in the stomach on the playground, or when, passing him in the corridor, I impulsively wrenched his arm up his back until he started to cry, I was doing so in order to help him toughen up. Accordingly, the principal effect such attacks had on our relationship was to keep him in awe of me. This all came back to me as I listened to the weary-looking man walking beside me.

"Of course," Roger Button went on, perhaps guessing my train of thought, "it might well be that if you hadn't treated me the way you did I'd never have become what I did at fifteen. In any case, I've often wondered how it would have been if we'd met just a few years later. I really was something to be reckoned with by then."

We were once again walking along the narrow twisted passages between cottages. The girl was still leading the way, but she was now walking much faster. Often we would only just manage to catch a glimpse of her turning some corner ahead of us, and it struck me that we would have to keep alert if we were not to lose her.

"Today, of course," Roger Button was saying, "I've let myself go a bit. But I have to say, old fellow, you seem to be in much worse shape. Compared with you, I'm an athlete. Not to put too fine a point on it, you're just a filthy old tramp now, really, aren't you? But, you know, for a long time after you left I continued to idolize you. Would Fletcher do this? What would Fletcher think if he saw me doing that? Oh, yes. It was only when I got to fifteen or so that I looked back on it all and saw through you. Then I was very angry, of course. Even now, I still think about it sometimes. I look back and think, Well, he was just a thoroughly nasty so-and-so. He had a little more weight and muscle at that age than I did, a little more confidence, and he took full advantage. Yes, it's very clear, looking back, what a nasty little person you were. Of course, I'm not implying you still are today. We all change. That much I'm willing to accept."

"Have you been living here long?" I asked, wishing to change the subject.

"Oh, seven years or so. Of course, they talk about you a lot around here. I sometimes tell them about our early association. 'But he won't remember me,' I always tell them. 'Why would he remember a skinny little boy he used to bully and have at his beck and call?' Anyway, the young people here, they talk about you more and more these days. Certainly, the ones who've never seen you tend to idealize you the most. I suppose you've come back to capitalize on all that. Still, I shouldn't blame you. You're entitled to try and salvage a little self-respect."

We suddenly found ourselves facing an open field, and we both halted. Glancing back, I saw that we had walked our way out of the village; the last of the cottages were some distance behind us. Just as I had feared, we had lost the young woman; in fact, I realized we had not been following her for some time.

At that moment, the moon emerged, and I saw we were standing at the edge of a vast grassy field—extending, I supposed, far beyond what I could see by the moon.

Roger Button turned to me. His face in the moonlight seemed gentle, almost affectionate.

"Still," he said, "it's time to forgive. You shouldn't keep worrying so much. As you see, certain things from the past will come back to you in the end. But then we can't be held accountable for what we did when we were very young."

"No doubt you're right," I said. Then I turned and looked around in the darkness. "But now I'm not sure where to go. You see, there were some young people waiting for me in their cottage. By now they'd have a warm fire ready for me and some hot tea. And some home-baked cakes, perhaps even a good stew. And the moment I entered, ushered in by that young lady we were following just now, they'd all have burst into applause. There'd be smiling, adoring faces all around me. That's what's waiting for me somewhere. Except I'm not sure where I should go."

Roger Button shrugged. "Don't worry, you'll get there easily enough. Except, you know, that girl was being a little misleading if she implied you could walk to Wendy's cottage. It's much too far. You'd really need to catch a bus. Even then, it's quite a long journey. About two hours, I'd say. But don't worry, I'll show you where you can pick up your bus."

With that, he began to walk back toward the cottages. As I followed, I could sense that the hour had got very late and my companion was anxious to get some sleep. We spent several minutes walking around the cottages again, and then he brought us out into the village square. In fact, it was so small and shabby it hardly merited being called a square; it was little more than a patch of green beside a solitary street lamp. Just visible beyond the pool of light cast by the lamp were a few shops, all shut up for the night. There was complete silence and nothing was stirring. A light mist was hovering over the ground.

Roger Button stopped before we had reached the green and pointed.

"There," he said. "If you stand there, a bus will come along. As I say, it's not a short journey. About two hours. But don't worry, I'm sure your young people will wait. They've so little else to believe in these days, you see."

"It's very late," I said. "Are you sure a bus will come?"

"Oh, yes. Of course, you may have to wait. But eventually a bus will come." Then he touched me reassuringly on the shoulder. "I can see it might get a little lonely standing out here. But once the bus arrives your spirits will rise, believe me. Oh, yes. That bus is always a joy. It'll be brightly lit up, and it's always full of cheerful people, laughing and joking and pointing out the window. Once you board it, you'll feel warm and comfortable, and the other passengers will chat with you, perhaps offer you things to eat or drink. There may even be singing—that depends on the driver. Some drivers encourage it, others don't. Well, Fletcher, it was good to see you."

We shook hands, then he turned and walked away. I watched him disappear into the darkness between two cottages.

I walked up to the green and put my bag down at the foot of the lamppost. I listened for the sound of a vehicle in the distance, but the night was utterly still. Nevertheless, I had been cheered by Roger Button's description of the bus. Moreover, I thought of the reception awaiting me at my journey's end—of the adoring faces of the young people—and felt the stirrings of optimism somewhere deep within me.

—2001

CAROL ANN DUFFY
b. 1955

As the British newspaper *The Guardian* has put it, "in the world of British poetry, Carol Ann Duffy is a superstar." Lauded by reviewers and by academic critics, her work has also been enormously popular with the general public; her 2009 appointment as Poet Laureate of the United Kingdom reflects the remarkable combination of high critical esteem and broad readership that her poetry attracts. This widespread appeal led to her appointment as Poet Laureate of the United Kingdom in 2009—making her the first woman poet, first openly gay poet, and first Scottish poet to occupy the role. Duffy first made her mark in the 1980s as a writer of dramatic monologues, many of them poems of controlled edginess (such as "Stealing") that give voice to tough, working class personae. She

has since become equally well known for tightly crafted lyrics of concentrated emotional force, especially on the themes of love and loss.

The eldest child of five, Duffy was born in Glasgow to an Irish mother and Scottish father, and raised largely in the north Midlands town of Stafford, where her father became a member of the local council and was a Labour Party candidate for Parliament. She attended St. Joseph's Convent School and Stafford Girls High School before studying philosophy at Liverpool University. She then worked for some years in London, where she was editor of the poetry magazine *Ambit*. In 1996 Duffy moved to Manchester, and since then she has taught at Manchester Metropolitan University, where in 2005 she was appointed Creative Director of the Writing School.

With her early collections—most notably her first book, *Standing Female Nude* (1985)—Duffy established a reputation as a powerful feminist voice, as a poet of considerable versatility, and as an entertainer, as capable of writing in a comic as in a dramatic or lyric mode. In *Mean Time* (1993), the emotional as well as technical range of her work broadened. Her 1999 book *The World's Wife* is a striking *tour de force* in which each poem is written in the persona of a wife, sister, or lover of a famous man from history or mythology, from "Mrs. Faust" and "Anne Hathaway" to "Mrs. Lazarus." Her 2005 collection *Rapture* is also a unified work, though of a very different sort; here she presents a chronologically ordered series of poems that trace the emotional trajectory of a relationship of love. *Rapture* is confessedly autobiographical, but in the only interview on the collection that Duffy consented to give, she declined to discuss any specifics: "I could not feel more deeply than I have in these poems," she said, "but these are not journals or diaries or letters, they are works of art. A transformation takes place—it has to, if the feeling is to be revealed to others." Duffy's next major volume, *The Bees* (2011), epitomizes her intellectual and emotional breadth, incorporating poems on war and climate change alongside lyrics on the death of the poet's mother.

Though Duffy's poetry often bristles with contemporaneity in its tone and subject matter, it also exhibits a remarkable range of formal accomplishment; many of her poems follow accentual-syllabic metrical patterns, and many use rhyme extensively. It is perhaps more a reflection on reading habits that took root in the second half of the twentieth century than it is on Duffy's work itself that as formal patterns of rhythm and rhyme began to play a larger and larger role in her work, some began to wonder, in Jeanette Winterson's words, "whether Duffy had lost her balance. Had she stopped writing poetry and slopped into verse?" Unlike many poets who are inclined toward formal complexity, Duffy eschews unusual diction: as she has put it, "I'm not interested, as a poet, in words like 'plash'—Seamus Heaney words, interesting words. I like to use simple words but in a complicated way."

Among lesbian writers, Duffy is noteworthy for her rejection of any exceptionalist status. "I'm not a lesbian poet, whatever that is. If I am a lesbian icon and a role model, that's great, but if it is a word that is used to reduce me, then you have to ask why.... I define myself as a poet and a mother—that's all." Duffy's daughter Ella was born in 1995.

Duffy has written or edited over thirty books, including several plays, collections of poetry for children, and a variety of edited volumes. Among the many awards she has received are the 2003 Forward Poetry Prize, the 2003 Whitbread Poetry Award (for *Mean Time*), and the 2005 T.S. Eliot Prize (for *Rapture*). She was appointed an Officer of the British Empire in 1993 and a Commander of the British Empire in 2001.

⌘⌘⌘

Stealing

The most unusual thing I ever stole? A snowman.
Midnight. He looked magnificent; a tall, white
        mute
beneath the winter moon. I wanted him, a mate
with a mind as cold as the slice of ice
5   within my own brain. I started with the head.

Better off dead than giving in, not taking
what you want. He weighed a ton; his torso,
frozen stiff, hugged to my chest, a fierce chill
piercing my gut. Part of the thrill was knowing
10 that children would cry in the morning. Life's tough.

Sometimes I steal things I don't need. I joy-ride cars
to nowhere, break into houses just to have a look.
I'm a mucky ghost, leave a mess, maybe pinch a
        camera.
I watch my gloved hand twisting the doorknob.
15 A stranger's bedroom. Mirrors. I sigh like this—Aah.

It took some time. Reassembled in the yard,
he didn't look the same. I took a run
and booted him. Again. Again. My breath ripped out
in rags. It seems daft now. Then I was standing
20 alone among lumps of snow, sick of the world.

Boredom. Mostly I'm so bored I could eat myself.
One time, I stole a guitar and thought I might
learn to play. I nicked[1] a bust of Shakespeare once,
flogged[2] it, but the snowman was the strangest.
25 You don't understand a word I'm saying, do you?
—1987

Adultery

Wear dark glasses in the rain.
Regard what was unhurt
as though through a bruise.
Guilt. A sick, green tint.

5   New gloves, money tucked in the palms,
the handshake crackles. Hands
can do many things. Phone.
Open the wine. Wash themselves. Now

you are naked under your clothes all day,
10 slim with deceit. Only the once
brings you alone to your knees,
miming, more, more, older and sadder,

---

[1] *nicked* Slang for stole.
[2] *flogged* Slang for sold.

creative. Suck a lie with a hole in it
on the way home from a lethal, thrilling night
15   up against a wall, faster. Language
unpeels to a lost cry. You're a bastard.

Do it do it do it. Sweet darkness
in the afternoon; a voice in your ear
telling you how you are wanted,
20   which way, now. A telltale clock

wiping the hours from its face, your face
on a white sheet, gasping, radiant, yes.
Pay for it in cash, fiction, cab-fares back
to the life which crumbles like a wedding-cake.

25   Paranoia for lunch; too much
to drink, as a hand on your thigh
tilts the restaurant. You know all about love,
don't you. Turn on your beautiful eyes

for a stranger who's dynamite in bed, again
30   and again; a slow replay in the kitchen
where the slicing of innocent onions
scalds you to tears. Then, selfish autobiographical sleep

in a marital bed, the tarnished spoon of your body
stirring betrayal, your heart over-ripe at the core.
35   You're an expert, darling; your flowers
dumb and explicit on nobody's birthday.

So write the script—illness and debt,
a ring thrown away in a garden
no moon can heal, your own words
40   commuting to bile in your mouth, terror—

and all for the same thing twice. And all
for the same thing twice. You did it.
What. Didn't you. Fuck. Fuck. No. That was
the wrong verb. This is only an abstract noun.
—1993

The Good Teachers

You run round the back to be in it again.
No bigger than your thumbs, those virtuous
   women
size you up from the front row. Soon now,
Miss Ross will take you for double History.
5   You breathe on the glass, making a ghost of her, say
South Sea Bubble Defenestration of Prague.[1]

You love Miss Pirie. So much, you are top
of her class. So much, you need two of you
to stare out from the year, serious, passionate.
10   The River's Tale by Rudyard Kipling[2] by heart.
Her kind intelligent green eye. Her cruel blue one.
You are making a poem up for her in your head.

But not Miss Sheridan. Comment vous appelez.[3]
But not Miss Appleby. Equal to the square
15   of the other two sides. Never Miss Webb.
Dar es Salaam. Kilimanjaro.[4] Look. The good teachers
swish down the corridor in long, brown skirts,
snobbish and proud and clean and qualified.

And they've got your number. You roll the waistband
20   of your skirt over and over, all leg, all
dumb insolence, smoke-rings. You won't pass.
You could do better. But there's the wall you climb
into dancing, lovebites, marriage, the Cheltenham
and Gloucester,[5] today. The day you'll be sorry one
   day.
—1993

---

[1] *South Sea ... Prague* Two unconnected historical incidents.

[2] *Rudyard Kipling* English novelist, poet and short-story writer who was born in Bombay (1865–1936).

[3] *Comment vous appelez* French: What do you call.

[4] *Dar es Salaam. Kilimanjaro* The largest city and the tallest mountain, respectively, in Tanzania.

[5] *Cheltenham and Gloucester* The name of a commercial bank in the United Kingdom.

Drunk

Suddenly the rain is hilarious.
The moon wobbles in the dusk.

What a laugh. Unseen frogs
belch in the damp grass.

5 The strange perfumes of darkening trees.
Cheap red wine

and the whole world a mouth.
Give me a double, a kiss.
—1993

Mean Time

The clocks slid back an hour
and stole light from my life
as I walked through the wrong part of town,
mourning our love.

5 And, of course, unmendable rain
fell to the bleak streets
where I felt my heart gnaw
at all our mistakes.

If the darkening sky could lift
10 more than one hour from this day
there are words I would never have said
nor have heard you say.

But we will be dead, as we know,
beyond all light.
15 These are the shortened days
and the endless nights.
—1993

Mrs. Lazarus[1]

I had grieved. I had wept for a night and a day
over my loss, ripped the cloth I was married in
from my breasts, howled, shrieked, clawed
at the burial stones till my hands bled, retched
5 his name over and over again, dead, dead.

Gone home. Gutted the place. Slept in a single cot,
widow, one empty glove, white femur
in the dust, half. Stuffed dark suits
into black bags, shuffled in a dead man's shoes,
10 noosed the double knot of a tie round my bare neck,

gaunt nun in the mirror, touching herself. I learnt
the Stations of Bereavement, the icon of my face
in each bleak frame; but all those months
he was going away from me, dwindling
15 to the shrunk size of a snapshot, going,

going. Till his name was no longer a certain spell
for his face. The last hair on his head
floated out from a book. His scent went from the
house.
The will was read. See, he was vanishing
20 to the small zero held by the gold of my ring.

Then he was gone. Then he was legend, language;
my arm on the arm of the schoolteacher—the shock
of a man's strength under the sleeve of his coat—
along the hedgerows. But I was faithful
25 for as long as it took. Until he was memory.

So I could stand that evening in the field
in a shawl of fine air, healed, able
to watch the edge of the moon occur to the sky
and a hare thump from a hedge; then notice
30 the village men running towards me, shouting,

<hr/>

1 *Mrs. Lazarus*   In the story recounted in John 11.41–44, "a man
named Lazarus" is sick; his sisters Martha and Mary send for Jesus
asking for help. Jesus sends a reply asserting that "the sickness will
not end in death," but does not come at once to help. When he does
arrive a few days later Lazarus is dead and has been entombed for
four days, but when Jesus has the stone covering the entrance to the
tomb rolled back, Lazarus emerges in his grave-cloths. There is no
mention of Lazarus's wife in the Biblical account.

behind them the women and children, barking dogs,
and I knew. I knew by the sly light
on the blacksmith's face, the shrill eyes
of the barmaid, the sudden hands bearing me
35 into the hot tang of the crowd parting before me.

He lived. I saw the horror on his face.
I heard his mother's crazy song. I breathed
his stench; my bridegroom in his rotting shroud,
moist and dishevelled from the grave's slack chew,
40 croaking his cuckold name, disinherited, out of his
      time.
—1999

Wish

But what if, in the clammy soil, her limbs
grew warmer, shifted, stirred, kicked off
the covering of earth, the drowsing corms,[1]
the sly worms, what if her arms reached out
5 to grab the stone, the grooves of her dates
under her thumb, and pulled her up? I wish.
Her bare feet walk along the gravel path
between the graves, her shroud like washing
blown onto the grass, the petals of her wreath
10 kissed for a bride. Nobody died. Nobody
wept. Nobody slept who couldn't be woken
by the light. If I can only push open this heavy door
she'll be standing there in the sun, dirty, tired,
wondering why do I shout, why do I run.
—2002

John Barleycorn[2]

Although I knew they'd laid him low,
thrashed him, hung him out to dry,
had tortured him with water and with fire,
then dashed his brains out on a stone,

5 I saw him in the Seven Stars
and in the Plough.[3]
I saw him in the Crescent Moon
and in the Beehive and the Barley Mow,
my green man,[4] newly-born, alive, John Barleycorn.

10 I saw him seasonally, at harvest time
in the Wheatsheaf and the Load of Hay.
I saw him, heard his laughter,
in the Star and Garter, in the Fountain, in the Bell,
the Corn Dolly,[5] the Woolpack° and the   bale of wool
      Flowing Spring.
15 I saw him in the Rising Sun,
the Moon and Sixpence and the Evening Star.
I saw him in the Rose and Crown,
my green man, ancient, barely born, John Barleycorn.

He moved through Britain, bright and dark
20 like ale in glass. I saw him run across the fields
towards the Gamekeeper, the Poacher and the
      Blacksmith's Arms.
He knew the Ram, the Lamb, the Lion and the Swan,
White Hart, Blue Boar, Red Dragon, Fox and Hounds.
I saw him in the Three Goats' Heads,
25 the Black Bull and Dun Cow,
Shoulder of Mutton, Griffin, Unicorn,
green man, beer borne, good health, long life,
      John Barleycorn.

I saw him festively, when people sang
for victory, or love, or New Year's Eve,
30 in the Raven and the Bird in Hand,
the Golden Eagle, the Kingfisher, the Dove.
I saw him grieve, or mourn, a shadow at the bar
in the Falcon, the Marsh Harrier, the Sparrow Hawk,
the Barn Owl, Cuckoo, Heron, Nightingale;
35 a pint of bitter in the Jenny Wren
for my green man, alone, forlorn, John Barleycorn.

1 *corms* Bulbs.
2 *John Barleycorn* Personification of barley, and of beer and whisky made from barley. In the comic British folk song of the same name, he undergoes a series of tortures (thrashing, drowning, burning, etc.) as he is cultivated and transformed into alcohol.
3 *the Seven Stars ... the Plough* The many proper nouns listed in the poem are all names commonly used for British pubs.
4 *green man* Man dressed in greenery, an English folk figure associated with spring fertility. Green man faces, which combine human features with foliage, often appear in English church decorations but are probably pagan in origin.
5 *Corn Dolly* Pub named for a figurine traditionally made from the last corn gathered during the year's harvest.

Britain's soul, as the crow flies so flew he.
I saw him in the Hollybush, the Yew Tree,
the Royal Oak, the Ivy Bush, the Linden.
40 I saw him in the Forester, the Woodman.
He history, I saw him in the Wellington, the Nelson,[1]
Greyfriars Bobby,[2] Wicked Lady, Bishop's Finger.
I saw him in the Ship, the Golden Fleece,[3] the Flask,
the Railway Inn, the Robin Hood and Little John,
45 my green man, legend strong, re-born, John
        Barleycorn.

Scythed down, he crawled, knelt, stood.
I saw him in the Crow, Newt, Stag, all weathers,
noon or night. I saw him in the Feathers, Salutation,
Navigation, Knot, the Bricklayer's Arms, Hop Inn,
50 the Maypole and the Regiment, the Horse and Groom,
the Dog and Duck, the Flag. And where he supped,
the past lived still; and where he sipped, the glass
        brimmed full.
He was in the King's Head and Queen's Arms, I saw
        him there,
green man, well-born, spellbound, charming one,
        John Barleycorn.
—2011

Water

Your last word was *water*,
which I poured in a hospice plastic cup, held
to your lips—your small sip, half-smile, sigh—
then, in the chair beside you,
                                    fell asleep.

5   Fell asleep for three lost hours,
only to waken, thirsty, hear then see

a magpie warn in a bush outside—
dawn so soon—and swallow from your still-full cup.

Water. The times I'd call as a child
10 for a drink, till you'd come, sit on the edge
of the bed in the dark, holding my hand,
just as we held hands now and you died.

A good last word.
                        Nights since I've cried, but gone
to my own child's side with a drink, watched

15 her gulp it down then sleep. *Water.*
What a mother brings
                            through darkness still
to her parched daughter.
—2011

A Rare Bee

I heard tell of a tale of a rare bee,
kept in a hive in a forest's soul
by a hermit—hairshirt, heart long hurt—
and that this bee made honey so pure,
5   when pressed to the pout of a poet
it made her profound; or if smeared
on the smile of a singer it sweetened his sound;
or when eased on the eyes of an artist,
Pablo Picasso lived and breathed;
                                        so I saddled my steed.

10 No birds sang in the branches over my head,
though I saw the wreaths of empty nests
on the ground as I rode—girl, poet, knight—
deeper into the trees, where the white hart
was less than a ghost or a thought, was light
15 as the written word; legend. But what wasn't going, gone,
I mused, from the land, or the sky, or the sea?
I dismounted my bony horse to walk;
out of the silence, I fancied I heard
                                        the bronze buzz of a bee.

[1] *the Wellington* Pub named for Arthur Wellesley, 1st Duke of Wellington (1768–1852), British Prime Minister and military Commander-in-Chief; *the Nelson* Pub named for Viscount Horatio Nelson (1758–1805), British admiral and war hero.

[2] *Greyfriars Bobby* Pub named for a famous nineteenth-century dog said to have guarded his dead master's grave for more than a decade.

[3] *Golden Fleece* Pub named for the mythological fleece of a flying ram, an object of quests in Greek stories.

So I came to kneel at the hermit's hive—
20 a little church, a tiny mosque—in a mute glade
where the loner mouthed and prayed, blind
as the sun, and saw with my own eyes
one bee dance alone on the air.
I uttered my prayer: *Give me your honey,*

25 *bless my tongue with rhyme, poetry, song.*
It flew at my mouth and stung.
Then the terrible tune of the hermit's grief.
Then a gesturing, dying bee
                                        on the bier of a leaf.

—2010

ZADIE SMITH
b. 1975

By the time Zadie Smith's first novel, *White Teeth*, was published in 2000, her name had already been bandied about by so many critics that it seemed as though she had been on the writing scene for years. After seeing one of her short stories in a university anthology, a literary agent approached Smith; a feeding frenzy in the publishing world ensued, ending with a publisher offering an extraordinary advance for an unpublished novel by a previously unknown author. Smith expanded the story into a novel, which became *White Teeth*, a major literary success and one of the bestselling books of 2001. *White Teeth* garnered the Commonwealth, *Guardian*, and Whitbread First Novel Awards, as well as the James Tait Black Memorial Prize.

Born Sadie Smith in a North London borough, the daughter of a black Jamaican mother and a white English father, at the age of 14 she changed her name to Zadie, thinking it sounded more exotic (Smith dreamed at that time of becoming a dancer or a singer). In 1998 she earned a BA in English Literature from King's College, Cambridge, where she began publishing her short stories in the Oxford/Cambridge *May Anthologies*. It was there that the idea for *White Teeth* was born. Although some reviewers have likened the novel to those of Charles Dickens, a more frequent comparison has been to the work of Salman Rushdie. Rushdie himself is enthusiastic about *White Teeth*, describing it as "fizzing," and saying that it is "about how we all got here—from the Caribbean, from the Indian subcontinent, from thirteenth place in a long-ago Olympic bicycle race—about what 'here' turned out to be. It's an astonishingly assured debut, funny and serious, and the voice has real writerly idiosyncrasy." Some of this "idiosyncracy" comes from the eccentricities of the characters, many of whom have come to England from various postcolonial countries and are in search of their new identities. Races, religions, cultures, customs,

and personalities all clash in the polyglot melting pot that is North London. As the narrator of *White Teeth* says, "This has been the century of strangers, brown, yellow, and white. This has been the century of the great immigrant experiment.... [I]t makes an immigrant laugh to hear the fears of the nationalist, scared of infection, penetration, miscegenation, when this is small fry, peanuts, compared to what the immigrant fears—dissolution, disappearance."

The BBC released a miniseries based on *White Teeth* in 2002, and the same year saw publication of Smith's second novel, *The Autograph Man*, about a Londoner of Chinese and Jewish descent who makes his living buying and selling autographs. Her third novel, the Orange Prize-winning *On Beauty* (2005), has been described as a "transatlantic comic saga," while with *NW* (2012), Smith narrowed her geographic focus to contemporary Willesden, an ethnically diverse area of London. Smith is a Fellow of the Royal Society of Literature, and in 2010 she became Professor of Creative Writing at New York University.

"The Waiter's Wife" features major characters from *White Teeth*. The short story appeared in the autumn 1999 edition of *Granta*, the year before the novel was published.

In recent years Smith has also received high praise for her literary non-fiction. She is a frequent contributor to publications such as *the New York Review of Books*—in which the essay "Joy" appeared in 2013.

⌘ ⌘ ⌘

The Waiter's Wife

In the spring of 1975, Samad and Alsana Iqbal left Bangladesh and came to live in Whitechapel,[1] London, the other side of town from Archie and Clara Jones. Samad and Archie had a friendship dating back to the Second World War, back to the hot and claustrophobic Churchill tank[2] in which they sat side by side for three months, close enough to smell each other and to recognize those scents thirty years later when Samad emerged from Gate 12, Heathrow, with a young wife and a paisley patterned luggage set in tow. "Long time no see," Archie had said, reaching out to grasp his old friend's palm, but Samad converted the handshake into a hug almost immediately, "*Archibald Jones*. Long time no bloody *smell*."

They fell back into easy conversation, two old boys slipping swiftly into an acquaintance as comfortable as slippers while their wives stood either side of the bags noting they had this thing in common and no more: that they were young, much younger than the men they stood awkwardly beside. They looked an unlikely pair. Alsana was small and rotund, moon-faced and with thick fingers she hid in the folds of her cardigan. Clara was tall, striking, a black girl with a winning smile, wearing red shorts of a shortness that Alsana had never imagined possible, even in this country.

"Hot pants," said Clara, shyly, in response to Alsana's wide eyes, "I made dem myself."

"I sew also," Alsana replied, and they had a pleasant enough chat about seams and bobbins, materials and prices per yard, in a motorway service station over an indigestible lunch. "The wives get on like a house on fire," Archie had said merrily, giving Samad a nudge in the ribs. But this made them nervous, the two young wives, and after the ice-cream sundaes they sat in silence.

So some black people *are* friendly, thought Alsana after that first meeting was over. It was her habit to single one shining exception out of every minority she disliked; certain dentists, certain singers, certain film stars had been granted specialist treatment in the past and now Clara Jones was to be given Alsana's golden reprieve. Their relations were hesitant in the beginning—a few lunch dates here and there, the occasional coffee; neither wished to admit how much time they had on their hands though newly wed, or that Archie and Samad were always together. It wasn't until the Iqbals moved north, two minutes from Archie and his favourite watering hole, that the women truly resigned themselves to their husbands' mutual appreciation society and started something of a rearguard action. Picnics, the movies, museums, swimming pools—just the two of them. But even when they became fairly close, it was impossible to forget what a peculiar couple they made on the bus, in the park.

It took the Iqbals a year to get to Willesden High Road: a year of mercilessly hard graft[3] to make the momentous move from the wrong side of Whitechapel to the wrong side of Willesden.[4] A year's worth of Alsana banging away at the old Singer machine that sat in the kitchen, sewing together pieces of black plastic for a shop called Domination in Soho (many were the nights Alsana would hold up a piece of clothing she had just made—following the plans she was given—and wonder what on earth it was). A year's worth of Samad softly inclining his head at exactly the correct deferential angle, pencil in his right hand, notepad in his left, listening to the appalling pronunciation of the British, Spanish, American, French, Australian:

[1] *Whitechapel*   East London district where a large proportion of residents are of Bangladeshi background.
[2] *Churchill tank*   Tank used by British forces during World War II.
[3] *graft*   British slang: work.
[4] *Willesden*   Ethnically diverse district in Northwest London.

Go Bye Ello Sag,[1] Please.

Chicken Jail Fret See[2] Wiv Chips, Fanks.

From six in the evening until four in the morning was work and the rest was sleep, sleep without pause, until daylight was as rare as a decent tip. For what is the point, Samad would think, pushing aside two mints and a receipt to find fifteen pence, what is the point of tipping a man the same amount you would throw in a fountain to chase a wish? But before the illegal thought of folding the fifteen pence discreetly in his napkin hand had a chance to give itself form, Mukhul, Ardashir Mukhul, who ran The Palace and whose wiry frame paced the restaurant, one benevolent eye on the customers, one ever-watchful eye on the staff—Ardashir Mukhul was upon him.

"Saaamaad," he said in his cloying, oleaginous[3] way, "did you kiss the necessary backside this evening, Cousin?"

Samad and Ardashir were distant cousins, Samad the elder by six years. With what joy (pure bliss!) had Ardashir opened the letter last January, to find his older, cleverer, handsomer cousin could get no work as a food inspector in England and could he possibly...

"Fifteen pence, Cousin," said Samad lifting his palm.

"Well, every little helps, every little helps," said Ardashir, his dead-fish lips stretching into a stringy smile. "Into the Piss-Pot with it."

The Piss-Pot was a black cooking pot that sat on a plinth outside the staff toilets into which all tips were pooled and then split at the end of the night. For the younger, good-looking waiters like Shiva this was a great injustice. Shiva was the only Hindu on the staff, a tribute to his waitering skills that had triumphed over religious difference. He could make fifteen pounds in tips in an evening if the blubberous white divorcee in the corner was lonely enough, and he batted his long lashes at her effectively. He also made money from the polo-necked directors and producers (The Palace sat in the centre of London's Theatreland) who flattered the boy, watched his ass wiggle provocatively to the bar and

back, and swore that the next time someone put *A Passage to India*[4] on the stage, the casting couch would be his. For Shiva then, the Piss-Pot system was simply daylight robbery. But for men like Samad, in his forties, and for the even older, like the white-haired Mohammed (Ardashir's great-uncle), who was eighty if he was a day, who had deep pathways dug into the sides of his mouth where he had smiled when he was young—for men like this the Piss-Pot could not be complained about. It was a boon if anything, and it made more sense to join the collective than pocket fifteen pence and risk being caught (and docked a week's tips).

"You're all on my back!" Shiva would snarl, when he had to relinquish five pounds at the end of the night and drop it into the pot. "You all live off my back! Somebody get these losers off my back! That was my fiver and now it's going to be split sixty-five-fucking-million ways as a hand out to these losers! What is this, communism?"

And the rest would avoid his glare, and busy themselves quietly with other things until one evening, one fifteen-pence evening, Samad said, "Shut up, boy," quietly, almost underneath his breath.

"You!" Shiva swung round to where Samad stood crushing a great tub of lentils for tomorrow's dhal.[5] "You're the worst of them! You're the worst fucking waiter I've ever seen! You couldn't get a tip if you mugged the bastards! I hear you trying to talk to the customer about biology this, politics that—just serve the food, you idiot—you're a waiter, for fuck's sake, you're not Michael Parkinson.[6] *Did I hear you say Delhi*—" Shiva put his apron over his arm and began posturing around the kitchen (he was a pitiful mimic) "—*I was there myself, you know, Delhi University, it was most fascinating, yes—and I fought in the war, for England, yes—yes, yes, charming, charming*—" round and round the kitchen he went, bending his head and rubbing his

---

[1] *Go Bye Ello Sag* I.e., Gobi Aloo Saag, a South Asian dish made with cauliflower, potato, and spinach.

[2] *Chicken Jail Fret See* I.e., Chicken Jalfrezi, a spicy curry dish.

[3] *oleaginous* Oily, insincere.

[4] *A Passage to India* Santha Rama Rau's theatrical adaptation (1960) of E.M. Forster's 1924 novel set in India during British colonial rule.

[5] *dhal* Spicy South Asian dish made with lentils, tomatoes, onions, and various seasonings.

[6] *Michael Parkinson* British television personality whose popular talk show *Parkinson* ran on the BBC network from 1971–82.

hands over and over like Uriah Heep,[1] bowing and genuflecting to the head cook, to the old man arranging great hunks of meat in the walk-in freezer, to the young boy scrubbing the inside of the oven. "Samad, *Samad* …" he said with what seemed infinite pity, then stopped abruptly, pulled the apron off and wrapped it round his waist, "you're a sad bastard."

Mohammed looked up from his pot-scrubbing and shook his head again and again. To no one in particular he said, "These young people—what kind of talk? What happened to respect? What kind of talk is this?"

"And you, you can fuck off too—" said Shiva, brandishing a ladle in his direction, "—You old fool! You're not my father."

"Second cousin of your mother's uncle," a voice muttered from the back.

"Bollocks," said Shiva. "Bollocks to that."

He grabbed the mop and was heading off for the toilets, when he stopped by Samad and placed the broom inches from Samad's mouth.

"Kiss it," he sneered: and then impersonating Ardashir's sluggish drawl, "Who knows, Cousin, you might get a raise!"

And that's what it was like most nights; abuse from Shiva and others; condescension from Ardashir; never seeing Alsana; never seeing the sun; clutching fifteen pence and then releasing it; wanting desperately to be wearing a sign, a large white placard that said:

I AM NOT A WAITER. THAT IS, I AM A WAITER, BUT NOT JUST A WAITER. I HAVE BEEN A STUDENT, A SCIENTIST, A SOLDIER. MY WIFE IS CALLED ALSANA. WE LIVE IN EAST LONDON BUT WE WOULD LIKE TO MOVE NORTH. I AM A MUSLIM BUT ALLAH HAS FORSAKEN ME OR I HAVE FORSAKEN ALLAH. I'M NOT SURE. I HAVE AN ENGLISH FRIEND— ARCHIE—AND OTHERS. I AM FORTY-NINE BUT WOMEN STILL TURN IN THE STREET. SOMETIMES.

But no such placard existing, he had instead the urge, the need, to speak to every man, and like the Ancient Mariner[2] to explain, always to explain, to reassert something, anything. Wasn't that important? But then the heartbreaking disappointment—to find out that the inclining of one's head, poising of one's pen, these were important, so important. It was important to be a good waiter, to listen when someone said:

Lamb Dawn Sock[3] and Rice. Please. With Chips. Thank you.

And fifteen pence clinked on china. Thank you Sir. Thank you so very much.

One evening, shortly after he had put the down payment on the Willesden flat, Samad had waited till everyone left and then climbed the loudly carpeted stairs to Ardashir's office, for he had something to ask him.

"Cousin!" said Ardashir with a friendly grimace at the sight of Samad's body curling cautiously round the door. He knew that Samad had come to enquire about a pay increase, and he wanted his cousin to feel that he had at least considered the case in all his friendly judiciousness before he declined.

"Cousin, come in!"

"Good evening, Ardashir Mukhul," said Samad, stepping fully into the room.

"Sit down, sit down," said Ardashir warmly. "No point standing on ceremony now, is there?"

Samad was glad this was so. He said as much. He took a moment to look with the necessary admiration around the room with its relentless flashes of gold, its thick pile carpet, its furnishings in various shades of yellow and green. One had to admire Ardashir's business sense. He had taken the simple idea of an Indian restaurant (small room, pink tablecloth, loud music, atrocious wallpaper, meals) and just made it bigger. He hadn't improved anything; it was the same old crap but bigger in a bigger building in the biggest tourist trap in London. Leicester Square.[4] You had to admire it and admire the man, who now sat like a benign locust, his

---

[1] *Uriah Heep* Insincerely humble character from Charles Dickens's *David Copperfield* (1849–50).

[2] *Ancient Mariner* Title character of Samuel Taylor Coleridge's poem *The Rime of the Ancient Mariner* (1798), who is compelled to wander the land and recount the events that followed his killing of an albatross, an act that doomed the rest of his crew to death at sea.

[3] *Lamb Dawn Sock* I.e., Lamb Dhansak, a curry dish made with lamb, squash, and lentils.

[4] *Leicester Square* Entertainment and tourism hub in London's West End.

slender insectile body swamped in a black leather chair, leaning over the desk, all smiles, a parasite disguised as a philanthropist.

"Cousin, what can I do for you?"

Samad took a deep breath. The matter was … what was the matter? The house was the matter. Samad was moving out of East London (where one couldn't bring up children, indeed, one couldn't, not if one didn't wish them to come to bodily harm), from East London, with its National Front[1] gangs, to North London, north-west in fact, where things were more … more … liberal. Ardashir's eyes glazed over a little as Samad explained his situation. His skinny legs twitched beneath the desk, and in his fingers he manipulated a paperclip until it looked reasonably like an *A. A* for Ardashir.

"I need only a small wage increase to help me finance the move. To make things a little easier as we settle in. And Alsana, well, she is pregnant."

Pregnant. Difficult. Ardashir realized the case called for extreme diplomacy.

"Don't mistake me, Samad, we are both intelligent, frank men and I think I can speak frankly … I know you're not a *fucking* waiter—" he whispered the expletive and smiled indulgently after it, as if it were a naughty, private thing that brought them closer together, "I see your position … of course I do … but you must understand mine … If I made allowances for every relative I employ I'd be walking around like bloody Mr. Gandhi.[2] Without a pot to piss in. Spinning my thread by the light of the moon. An example: at this very moment that wastrel Fat Elvis brother-in-law of mine, Hussein Ishmael—"

"The butcher?"

"The butcher, demands that I should raise the price I pay for his stinking meat! 'But Ardashir, we are brothers-in-law!' he is saying to me. And I am saying to him, but Mohammed, this is *retail* …"

It was Samad's turn to glaze over. He thought of his wife, Alsana, who was not as meek as he had assumed when they married, to whom he must deliver the bad news: Alsana, who was prone to moments, even

fits—yes, fits was not too strong a word—of rage. Cousins, aunts, brothers thought it a bad sign. They wondered if there wasn't some "funny mental history" in Alsana's family, they sympathized with him the way you sympathize with a man who has bought a stolen car with more mileage on it than first thought. In his naivety Samad had simply assumed a woman so young would be … easy. But Alsana was not … no, she was not easy. It was, he supposed, the way with young women these days.

Ardashir came to the end of what he felt was his perfectly worded speech, sat back satisfied, and laid the *M* for Mukhul he had moulded next to the *A* for Ardashir that sat on his lap.

"Thank you, Sir," said Samad. "Thank you so very much."

That evening there was an awful row. Alsana slung the sewing machine, with the black studded hot pants she was working on, to the floor.

"Useless! Tell me, Samad Miah, what is the point of moving here—nice house, yes very nice, very nice—but where is the food?"

"It is a nice area, we have friends here…"

"Who are they?" she slammed her little fist on to the kitchen table, sending the salt and pepper flying to collide spectacularly with each other in the air. "I don't know them! You fight in an old, forgotten war with some Englishman … married to a black! Whose friends are they? These are the people my child will grow up around? Their children—half blacky-white? But tell me," she shouted, returning to her favoured topic, "where is our food?"

Theatrically, she threw open every cupboard in the kitchen, "Where is it? Can we eat china?"

Two plates smashed to the floor. She patted her stomach to indicate her unborn child and pointed to the pieces, "Hungry?"

Samad, who had an equally melodramatic nature when prompted, yanked open the freezer and pulled out a mountain of meat which he piled in the middle of the room. His mother worked through the night preparing meals for her family, he said. His mother did not, he said, spend the household money, as Alsana did, on prepared meals, yogurts and tinned spaghetti. Alsana

[1] *National Front* Extreme right-wing British political party often associated with racist views.

[2] *Mr. Gandhi* Mohandas Gandhi (1869–1948), Indian activist known for practicing asceticism and nonviolence.

punched him full square in the stomach.

"Samad Iqbal the traditionalist! Why don't I just squat in the street over a bucket and wash clothes? Eh? In fact, what about my clothes? Edible?"

As Samad clutched his winded belly, there in the kitchen she ripped to shreds every stitch she had on and added them to the pile of frozen lamb, spare cuts from the restaurant. She stood naked before him for a moment, the as yet small mound of her pregnancy in full view, then put on a long, brown coat and left the house.

But all the same, she reflected, slamming the door behind her, it was a nice area; she couldn't deny it as she stormed towards the high street, avoiding pavement trees where previously, in Whitechapel, she had avoided flung-out mattresses and the homeless. It would be good for the child. Alsana had a deep-seated belief that living near green spaces was morally beneficial to the young and there to her right was Gladstone Park, a sweeping horizon of green named after the Liberal prime minister (Alsana was from a respected old Bengal family and had read her English History), and in the Liberal tradition it was a park without fences, unlike the more affluent Queen's Park (Victoria's) with its pointed metal railings. Willesden was not as pretty as Queen's Park but it was a nice area. No denying it. No NF kids breaking the basement windows with their steel-capped boots like in Whitechapel. Now she was pregnant she needed a little bit of peace and quiet. Though it was the same here in a way; they all looked at her strangely, this tiny Indian woman stalking the high street in a mackintosh,[1] her plentiful hair flying every which way. *Mali's Kebabs, Mr. Cheungs, Raj's, Malkovich Bakeries*—she read the new, unfamiliar signs as she passed. She was shrewd. She saw what this was. "Liberal? Hosh-kosh nonsense!" No one was more liberal than anyone else anywhere anyway. It was only that here, in Willesden, there wasn't enough of any one thing to gang up against any other thing and send it running to the cellars while windows were smashed.

"Survival is what it is about!" she concluded out loud (she spoke to her baby: she liked to give it one sensible thought a day), making the bell above Crazy Shoes tinkle as she opened the door. Her niece Neena

worked here. It was an old-fashioned cobbler's. Neena fixed heels back on to stilettos.

"Alsana, you look like dog shit," Neena called over in Bengali. "What is that horrible coat?"

"It's none of your business is what it is," replied Alsana in English. "I came to collect my husband's shoes not to chit-chat with Niece-Of-Shame."

Neena was used to this, and now Alsana had moved to Willesden there would only be more of it. It used to come in longer sentences (such as, "Niece, you have brought nothing but shame …"), but now because Alsana no longer had the time or energy to summon up the necessary shock each time, it had become abridged to Niece-Of-Shame, an all-purpose tag that summed up the general feeling.

"See these soles?" said Neena, taking Samad's shoes off the shelf and handing Alsana the little blue ticket. "They were so worn through, Aunty Alsi, I had to reconstruct them from the very base. From the base! What does he do in them? Run marathons?"

"He works," replied Alsana tersely. "And prays," she added, for she liked to make a point of her respectability, and besides she was really very traditional, very religious, lacking nothing except the faith.

"And don't call me Aunty, I am only two years older than you."

Alsana swept the shoes into a plastic carrier bag and turned to leave.

"I thought that praying was done on people's knees," said Neena, laughing lightly.

"Both, both, asleep, waking, walking," snapped Alsana, as she passed under the tinkly bell once more. "We are never out of sight of the Creator."

"How's the new house, then?" Neena called after her.

But she had gone. Neena shook her head and sighed as she watched her young aunt disappear down the road like a little brown bullet. Alsana. She was young and old at the same time, Neena reflected. She acted so sensible, so straight-down-the-line in her long sensible coat, but you got the feeling—

"Oi! Miss! There's shoes back here that need your attention!" came a voice from the storeroom.

"Keep your tits on," said Neena.

At the corner of the road, Alsana popped behind the

---

[1] *mackintosh* Raincoat.

post office and removed her pinchy sandals in favour of Samad's shoes. (It was an oddity about Alsana. She was small but her feet were enormous, as if she had more growing to do.) In seconds she whipped her hair into an efficient bun, and wrapped her coat tighter around her to keep out the wind. Then she set off, past the library and up a long green road she had never walked along before. "Survival is all, Little Iqbal," she said to her bump once more. "Survival."

Clara was also pregnant. When their bumps became too large and cinema seats no longer accommodated them, the two women began to meet up for lunch in Kilburn Park, often with the Niece-Of-Shame, the three of them squeezed on to a generous bench, Alsana pressing a thermos of PG Tips[1] into Clara's hand, without milk, with lemon. Unwrapping several layers of cling film to reveal today's peculiar delight: savoury dough-like balls, crumbly Indian sweets shot through with the colours of the kaleidoscope, thin pastry with spiced beef inside, salad with onion, she says to Clara: "Eat up! Stuff yourself silly! They're in there, wallowing around in your belly, waiting for the menu. Woman, don't torture them! You want to starve the bumps?" for, despite appearances, there are six people on that bench (three living, three coming); one girl for Clara, two boys for Alsana.

Alsana says: "Nobody's complaining, let's get that straight. A boy is good and two boys is bloody good. But I tell you, when I turned my head and saw the ultra-business thingummybob—"

"Ultrasound," corrects Clara, through a mouthful of rice.

"—Yes, I almost had the heart attack to finish me off! Two! Feeding one is enough!"

Clara laughs and says she can imagine Samad's face when he saw it.

"No dearie,"—Alsana is reproving, tucking her large feet underneath the folds of her sari, "he didn't see anything. He wasn't there. I am not letting him see things like that. A woman has to have the private things—a husband needn't be involved in body-business, in a lady's … *parts*."

Niece-Of-Shame, who is sat between them, sucks her teeth.

"Bloody Hell, Alsi, he must have been involved in your parts sometime, or is this the immaculate bloody conception?"[2]

"So rude," says Alsana to Clara in a snooty, English way. "Too old to be so rude and too young to know any better." And then Clara and Alsana, with the accidental mirroring that happens when two people are sharing the same experience, both lay their hands on their bulges.

Neena, to redeem herself: "Yeah, well how are you doing on names? Any ideas?"

Alsana is decisive. "*Magid* and *Millat*. Ems are good. Ems are strong. Mahatma, Mohammed, that funny Mr Morecambe, from Morecambe and Wise[3]—letter you can trust."

But Clara is more cautious, because naming seems to her a fearful responsibility, a godlike task for a mere mortal: "I tink I like *Irie*. It patois.[4] Means everyting OK, cool, peaceful, you know?"

Alsana is mock-horrified before the sentence is finished, "'OK'? This is a name for a child? You might as well call her 'Wouldsirlike-anypopadumswiththat?'[5] or 'Niceweatherwearehaving'—"

"… and Archie likes *Sarah*. Well, dere not much you can argue wid Sarah, but dere's not much to get happy bout either. I suppose if it was good enough for the wife of Abraham[6]…"

"Ibrahim," Alsana corrects, out of instinct more than Koranic pedantry. "Popping out babies when she was a hundred years old, by the grace of Allah."

And then Neena, groaning at the turn the conversation is taking: "Well I *like* Irie. It's funky. It's different."

[1] *PG Tips* Popular British brand of bagged tea.

[2] *immaculate … conception* Phrase that has come to be commonly associated with the virgin conception of Jesus, though in traditional Christian doctrine it refers to the conception of Jesus' mother, Mary.

[3] *Mahatma* Epithet applied to a sage or person whose wisdom is deeply admired, such as Mohandas Gandhi; *Mohammed* Prophet and founder of Islam (570–632); *Morecambe and Wise* Eric Morecambe (1926–84) and Ernie Wise (1925–99), a popular British comedy duo.

[4] *patois* I.e., Jamaican Patois, a language blending English and several African languages.

[5] *popadums* Cracker-like Indian flatbreads.

[6] *Abraham* Biblical figure who is mentioned frequently in the Koran by the name of Ibrahim.

Alsana loves this: "For pity's sake, what does Archibald know about *funky* and *different*? If I were you, dearie," she says patting Clara's knee, "I'd choose Sarah and let that be an end to it. Sometimes you have to let these men have it their way. Anything for a little—how do you say it in the English? For a little—" she puts her finger over tightly pursed lips, like a guard at the gate, "—*shush*."

But in response Niece-Of-Shame bats her voluminous eyelashes, wraps her college scarf round her head like purdah,[1] and says, "Oh yes, Auntie, yes, the little submissive Indian woman. You don't talk to him, he talks at you. You scream and shout at each other, but there's no communication. And in the end he wins anyway because he does whatever he likes when he likes. You don't even know where he is, what he does, what he *feels*, half the time. It's 1975, Alsi. You can't conduct relationships like that any more. It's not like back home. There has to be communication between men and women in the West, they've got to listen to each other, otherwise …" Neena mimes a small mushroom cloud going off in her hand.

"What a load of the codswallop," says Alsana sonorously, closing her eyes, shaking her head. "It is you who do not listen. By Allah, I will always give as good as I get. But you presume I *care* what he does. You presume I want to *know*. The truth is, for a marriage to survive you don't need all this talk, talk, talk; all this 'I am this' and 'I am really like this' like on the television, all this *revelation*—especially when your husband is old, when he is wrinkly and falling apart—you do not *want* to know what is slimy underneath the bed and rattling in the wardrobe."

Neena frowns. Clara cannot raise a serious objection, and the rice is handed around once more.

"Moreover," says Alsana after a pause, folding her dimpled arms underneath her breasts, pleased to be holding forth on a subject close to this formidable bosom, "when you are from families such as ours you should have learned that *silence,* what is *not* said, is the very *best* recipe for family life."

"So let me get this straight," says Neena, derisively. "You're saying that a good dose of repression keeps a marriage healthy?"

And as if someone had pressed a button, Alsana is outraged: "Repression! Nonsense silly-billy word! I'm just talking about common sense. What is my husband? What is yours?" she says pointing to Clara. "Twenty-five years they live before we are even born. What are they? What are they capable of? What blood do they have on their hands? What is sticky and smelly in their private areas? Who knows?" She throws her hands up, releasing the questions into the unhealthy Kilburn air, sending a troupe of sparrows up with them.

"What you don't understand, my Niece-Of-Shame, what none of your generation understand—'"

"But Auntie," begs Neena, raising her voice, because this is what she really wants to argue about—the largest sticking point between the two of them—Alsana's arranged marriage, "how could you bear to marry someone you didn't know from Adam?"

In response, an infuriating wink. Alsana always likes to appear jovial at the very moment that her interlocutor becomes hot under the collar. "Because, *Miss Smarty-pants*, it is by far the easier option. It was exactly because Eve did not know Adam from Adam that they got on so A-OK. Let me explain. Yes, I was married to Samad Iqbal the same evening of the very day I met him. Yes, I didn't know him from Adam. But I liked him well enough. We met in the breakfast room on a steaming Dhaka[2] day and he fanned me with *The Times*. I thought he had a good face, a sweet voice, and his backside was high and well formed for a man of his age. Very good. Now every time I learn something more about him *I like him less*. So you see, we were better off the way we were."

Neena stamps her foot in exasperation at the skewed logic.

"—Besides, I will never know him well. Getting anything out of my husband is like trying to squeeze water out when you're stoned."

Neena laughs despite herself, "Water out of a stone."

"Yes, yes. You think I'm so stupid. But I am wise about things like men. I tell you," Alsana prepares to deliver her summation as she has seen it done many years previously by the young Dhaka lawyers with their slick side-partings, "men are the last mystery. God is

---

[1]   *purdah*   Practice of concealing women from public view through the use of a veil or through seclusion.

[2]   *Dhaka*   Capital city of Bangladesh.

easy compared with men. Now, enough of the philosophy. Samosa?"

She peels the lid off the plastic tub and sits fat, pretty and satisfied on her conclusion.

"Shame that you're having them," says Neena to her aunt, lighting a fag. "Boys, I mean. Shame that you're going to have boys."

"What do you mean?"

This is Clara, who has secretly subscribed (a secret from Alsana and Archie) to a lending library of Neena's through which she has read, in a few short months, *The Female Eunuch* by Greer, *Sex, Race and Class* by Selma James and Jong's *Fear of Flying*, all in a clandestine attempt, on Neena's part, to rid Clara of her "false consciousness."[1]

"I mean, I just think men have caused enough chaos this century. There's enough bloody men in the world. If I knew I was going to have a boy ...." she pauses to prepare her two falsely conscious friends for this new concept, "I'd have to seriously consider abortion."

Alsana screams, claps her hands over one of her own ears and one of Clara's, and then almost chokes on a piece of aubergine[2] with the physical exertion. For some reason the remark simultaneously strikes Clara as funny: hysterically, desperately funny, miserably funny; and the Niece-Of-Shame sits between them, nonplussed, while the two egg-shaped women bend over themselves, one in laughter, the other in horror and near asphyxiation.

"Are you all right, ladies?" It is Sol Jozefowicz, the park keeper, standing in front of them, ready as always to be of aid.

"We are all going to burn in hell, Mr. Jozefowicz, if you call that being all right ..." explains Alsana, pulling herself together.

Niece-Of-Shame rolls her eyes: "Speak for yourself."

But Alsana is faster than any sniper when it comes to firing back: "I do, I do—thankfully Allah has arranged it that way."

---

[1] *The Female Eunuch* Influential feminist text by Germaine Greer, published in 1970; *Sex, Race and Class* 1973 article by Selma James championing the cause of women, especially those working without wages; *Fear of Flying* 1973 novel by Erica Jong depicting the sexual liberation of protagonist Isadora Wing; *false consciousness* Marxist term for a worldview or set of beliefs that impedes a person's ability to accurately comprehend his or her own circumstances.

[2] *aubergine* Eggplant.

"Good afternoon, Neena, good afternoon, Mrs. Jones," says Sol, offering a neat bow to each. "Are you sure you are all right? Mrs. Jones?"

Clara cannot stop the tears from squeezing out of the corners of her eyes. She cannot work out, at this moment, whether she is crying or laughing; the two states suddenly seem only a stone's throw from each other.

"I'm fine, fine. Sorry to have worried you, Mr. Jozefowicz. Really, I'm fine."

"I do not see what so very funny-funny," mutters Alsana. "The murder of innocents—is this funny?"

"Not in my experience, Mrs. Iqbal, no," says Sol Jozefowicz in the collected manner in which he says everything, passing his handkerchief to Clara. It strikes all three women—the way history will: embarrassingly, without warning, like a blush—what the park keeper's experience might have been. They fall silent.

"Well, as long as you ladies are fine, I'll be getting on," says Sol, motioning that Clara can keep the handkerchief and replacing the hat he had removed in the old fashion. He bows his neat little bow once more, and sets off slowly anticlockwise round the park.

Once Sol is out of earshot Neena says: "OK, Aunty Alsi. I apologize. I apologize ... What more do you want?"

"Oh, every-bloody-thing," says Alsana, her voice losing the fight, becoming vulnerable. "The whole bloody universe made clear—in a little nutshell. I cannot understand a thing any more, and I am just beginning. You understand?"

She sighs, not waiting for an answer, not looking at Neena, but across the way at the hunched, disappearing figure of Sol winding in and out of the yew trees. "You may be right about Samad ... about many things ... maybe there are no good men, not even the two in this belly ... and maybe I do not talk enough with mine, maybe I have married a stranger ... you might see the truth better than I ... what do I know, a barefoot country girl who never went to the universities ..."

"Oh, Alsi," Neena keeps saying, weaving her regret in and out of Alsana's words like tapestry, feeling bad, "you know I didn't mean it like that."

"But I cannot be worrying-worrying all the time about the truth. I have to worry about the truth that can be lived with. And that is the difference between losing your marbles drinking the salty sea, or swallowing the stuff from the streams. My Niece-Of-Shame believes in the talking cure,[1] eh?" says Alsana, with something of a grin. "Talk, talk, talk and it will be better. Be honest, slice open your heart and spread the red stuff around. But the past is made of more than words, dearie. We married old men, you see? These bumps," Alsana pats them both, "they will always have Daddy-long-legs for fathers. One leg in the present, one in the past. No talking will change this. Their roots will always be tangled."

Just as he reaches the far gate, Sol Jozefowicz turns round to wave, and the three women wave back. And Clara feels a little theatrical, flying the park keeper's cream handkerchief above her head. As if she is seeing someone off on a train journey which crosses the border of two countries.

—1999

Joy

It might be useful to distinguish between pleasure and joy. But maybe everybody does this very easily, all the time, and only I am confused. A lot of people seem to feel that joy is only the most intense version of pleasure, arrived at by the same road—you simply have to go a little further down the track. That has not been my experience. And if you asked me if I wanted more joyful experiences in my life, I wouldn't be at all sure I did, exactly because it proves such a difficult emotion to manage. It's not at all obvious to me how we should make an accommodation between joy and the rest of our everyday lives.

Perhaps the first thing to say is that I experience at least a little pleasure every day. I wonder if this is more than the usual amount? It was the same even in childhood when most people are miserable. I don't think this is because so many wonderful things happen to me but rather that the small things go a long way. I seem to get more than the ordinary satisfaction out of food, for example—any old food. An egg sandwich from one of these grimy food vans on Washington Square has the genuine power to turn my day around. Whatever is put in front of me, foodwise, will usually get a five-star review.

You'd think that people would like to cook for, or eat with, me—in fact I'm told it's boring. Where there is no discernment there can be no awareness of expertise or gratitude for special effort. "Don't say that was delicious," my husband warns, "you say everything's delicious." "But it was delicious." It drives him crazy. All day long I can look forward to a popsicle. The persistent anxiety that fills the rest of my life is calmed for as long as I have the flavor of something good in my mouth. And though it's true that when the flavor is finished the anxiety returns, we do not have so many reliable sources of pleasure in this life as to turn our nose up at one that is so readily available, especially here in America. A pineapple popsicle. Even the great anxiety of writing can be stilled for the eight minutes it takes to eat a pineapple popsicle.

My other source of daily pleasure is—but I wish I had a better way of putting it—"other people's faces." A red-headed girl, with a marvelous large nose she probably hates, and green eyes and that sun-shy complexion composed more of freckles than skin. Or a heavyset grown man, smoking a cigarette in the rain, with a soggy mustache, above which, a surprise—the keen eyes, snub nose, and cherub mouth of his own eight-year-old self. Upon leaving the library at the end of the day I will walk a little more quickly to the apartment to tell my husband about an angular, cat-eyed teenager, in skinny jeans and stacked-heel boots, a perfectly ordinary grey sweatshirt, last night's makeup, and a silky Pocahontas wig slightly askew over his own Afro. He was sashaying down the street, plaits flying, using the whole of Broadway as his personal catwalk. "Miss Thang, but off duty." I add this for clarity, but my husband nods a little impatiently; there was no need for the addition. My husband is also a professional gawker.

The advice one finds in ladies' magazines is usually to be feared, but there is something in that old chestnut: "shared interests." It *does* help. I like to hear about the Chinese girl he saw in the hall, carrying a large medical textbook, so beautiful she looked like an illustration. Or the tall Kenyan in the elevator whose elongated physical elegance reduced every other nearby body to the

---

[1] *talking cure* Therapy method that requires a patient to talk about traumas and other psychological obstacles.

shrunken, gnarly status of a troll. Usually I will not have seen these people—my husband works on the eighth floor of the library, I work on the fifth—but simply hearing them described can be almost as much a pleasure as encountering them myself. More pleasurable still is when we recreate the walks or gestures or voices of these strangers, or whole conversations—between two people in the queue for the ATM, or two students on a bench near the fountain.

And then there are all the many things that the dog does and says, entirely anthropomorphized and usually offensive, which express the universe of things we ourselves cannot do or say, to each other or to other people. "You're being the dog," our child said recently, surprising us. She is almost three and all our private languages are losing their privacy and becoming known to her. Of course, we knew she would eventually become fully conscious, and that before this happened we would have to give up arguing, smoking, eating meat, using the Internet, talking about other people's faces, and voicing the dog, but now the time has come, she is fully aware, and we find ourselves unable to change. "Stop being the dog," she said, "it's very silly," and for the first time in eight years we looked at the dog and were ashamed.

Occasionally the child, too, is a pleasure, though mostly she is a joy, which means in fact she gives us not much pleasure at all, but rather that strange admixture of terror, pain, and delight that I have come to recognize as joy, and now must find some way to live with daily. This is a new problem. Until quite recently I had known joy only five times in my life, perhaps six, and each time tried to forget it soon after it happened, out of the fear that the memory of it would dement and destroy everything else.

Let's call it six. Three of those times I was in love, but only once was the love viable, or likely to bring me any pleasure in the long run. Twice I was on drugs—of quite different kinds. Once I was in water, once on a train, once sitting on a high wall, once on a high hill, once in a nightclub, and once in a hospital bed. It is hard to arrive at generalities in the face of such a small and varied collection of data. The uncertain item is the nightclub, and because it was essentially a communal experience I feel I can open the question out to the floor. I am addressing this to my fellow Britons in particular. Fellow Britons! Those of you, that is, who were fortunate enough to take the first generation of the amphetamine ecstasy and yet experience none of the adverse, occasionally lethal reactions we now know others suffered—yes, for you people I have a question. Was that joy?

I am especially interested to hear from anyone who happened to be in the Fabric club, near the old Spitalfields meat market, on a night sometime in the year 1999 (I'm sorry I can't be more specific) when the DJ mixed "Can I Kick It?" and then "Smells Like Teen Spirit"[1] into the deep house track he had been seeming to play exclusively for the previous four hours. I myself was wandering out of the cavernous unisex (!) toilets wishing I could find my friend Sarah, or if not her, my friend Warren, or if not him, anyone who would take pity on a girl who had taken and was about to come up on ecstasy who had lost everyone and everything, including her handbag. I stumbled back into the fray.

Most of the men were topless, and most of the women, like me, wore strange aprons, fashionable at the time, that covered just the front of one's torso, and only remained decent by means of a few weak-looking strings tied in dainty bows behind. I pushed through this crowd of sweaty bare backs, despairing, wondering where in a super club one might bed down for the night (the stairs? the fire exit?). But everything I tried to look at quickly shattered and arranged itself in a series of patterned fragments, as if I were living in a kaleidoscope. Where was I trying to get to anyway? There was no longer any "bar" or "chill-out zone"—there was only dance floor. All was dance floor. Everybody danced. I stood still, oppressed on all sides by dancing, quite sure I was about to go out of my mind.

Then suddenly I could hear Q-Tip[2]—blessed Q-Tip!—not a synthesizer, not a vocoder, but Q-Tip, with his human voice, rapping over a human beat. And the top of my skull opened to let human Q-Tip in, and a rail-thin man with enormous eyes reached across a sea of bodies for my hand. He kept asking me the same thing

---

[1] *Can I Kick It?* 1990 hip hop song by A Tribe Called Quest; *Smells Like Teen Spirit* 1991 grunge rock song by Nirvana.

[2] *Q-Tip* Member of A Tribe Called Quest.

over and over: *You feeling it?* I was. My ridiculous heels were killing me, I was terrified I might die, yet I felt simultaneously overwhelmed with delight that "Can I Kick It?" should happen to be playing at this precise moment in the history of the world, and was now morphing into "Smells Like Teen Spirit." I took the man's hand. The top of my head flew away. We danced and danced. We gave ourselves up to joy.

Years later, while listening to a song called "Weak Become Heroes" by the British artist The Streets I found this experience almost perfectly recreated in rhyme, and realized that just as most American children alive in 1969 saw the moon landings, nearly every Briton between sixteen and thirty in the 1990s met some version of the skinny pill head I came across that night in Fabric. The name The Streets give him is "European Bob." I suspect he is an archetypal figure of my generation. The character "Super Hands" in the British TV comedy *Peep Show* is another example of the breed, though it might be more accurate to say Super Hands is European Bob in "old" age (forty). I don't remember the name of my particular pill head, but will call him "Smiley." He was one of these strangers you meet exclusively on dance floors, or else on a beach in Ibiza. They tended to have inexplicable nicknames, no home or family you could ever identify, a limitless capacity for drug-taking, and a universal feeling of goodwill toward all men and women, no matter their color, creed, or state of inebriation.

Their most endearing quality was their generosity. For the length of one night Smiley would do anything at all for you. Find you a cab, walk miles through the early morning streets looking for food, hold your hair as you threw up, and listen to you complain at great length about your parents and friends—agreeing with all your grievances—though every soul involved in these disputes was completely unknown to him. Contrary to your initial suspicions Smiley did not want to sleep with you, rob you, or con you in any way. It was simply intensely important to him that you had a good time, tonight, with him. "How you feeling?" was Smiley's perennial question. "You feeling it yet? I'm feeling it. You feeling it yet?" And that *you* should feel it seemed almost more important to him than that *he* should.

Was that joy? Probably not. But it mimicked joy's conditions pretty well. It included, in minor form, the great struggle that tends to precede joy, and the feeling—once one is "in" joy—that the experiencing subject has somehow "entered" the emotion, and disappeared. I "have" pleasure, it is a feeling I want to experience and own. A beach holiday is a pleasure. A new dress is a pleasure. But on that dance floor I *was* joy, or some small piece of joy, with all these other hundreds of people who were also a part of joy.

The Smileys, in their way, must have recognized the vital difference; it would explain their great concern with other people's experience. For as long as that high lasted, they seemed to pass beyond their own egos. And it might really have been joy if the next morning didn't always arrive. I don't just mean the deathly headache, the blurred vision, and the stomach cramps. What really destroyed the possibility that this had been joy was the replaying in one's mind of the actual events of the previous night, and the brutal recognition that every moment of sublimity—every conversation that had seemed to touch upon the meaning of life, every tune that had appeared a masterwork—had no substance whatsoever now, here, in the harsh light of the morning. The final indignity came when you dragged yourself finally from your bed and went into the living room. There, on your mother's sofa—in the place of that jester spirit-animal savior person you thought you'd met last night—someone had left a crushingly boring skinny pill head, already smoking a joint, who wanted to borrow twenty quid for a cab.

It wasn't all a waste of time though. At the neural level, such experiences gave you a clue about what joy not-under-the-influence would feel like. Helped you learn to recognize joy, when it arrived. I suppose a neuroscientist could explain in very clear terms why the moment after giving birth can feel ecstatic, or swimming in a Welsh mountain lake with somebody dear to you. Perhaps the same synapses that ecstasy falsely twanged are twanged authentically by fresh water, certain epidurals, and oxytocin. And if, while sitting on a high hill in the South of France, someone who has access to a phone comes dashing up the slope to inform you that two years of tension, tedious study, and academic anxiety have not been in vain—perhaps again these same synapses or whatever they are do their happy dance.

We certainly don't need to be neuroscientists to know that wild romantic crushes—especially if they are fraught with danger—do something ecstatic to our brains, though like the pills that share the name, horror and disappointment are usually not far behind. When my wild crush came, we wandered around a museum for so long it closed without us noticing; stuck in the grounds we climbed a high wall and, finding it higher on the other side, considered our options: broken ankles or a long night sleeping on a stone lion. In the end a passerby helped us down, and things turned prosaic and, after a few months, fizzled out. What looked like love had just been teen spirit. But what a wonderful thing, to sit on a high wall, dizzy with joy, and think nothing of breaking your ankles.

Real love came much later. It lay at the end of a long and arduous road, and up to the very last moment I had been convinced it wouldn't happen. I was so surprised by its arrival, so unprepared, that on the day it arrived I had already arranged for us to visit the Holocaust museum at Auschwitz. You were holding my feet on the train to the bus that would take us there. We were heading toward all that makes life intolerable, feeling the only thing that makes it worthwhile. That was joy. But it's no good thinking about or discussing it. It has no place next to the furious argument about who cleaned the house or picked up the child. It is irrelevant when sitting peacefully, watching an old movie, or doing an impression of two old ladies in a shop, or as I eat a popsicle while you scowl at me, or when working

on different floors of the library. It doesn't fit with the everyday. The thing no one ever tells you about joy is that it has very little real pleasure in it. And yet if it hadn't happened at all, at least once, how would we live?

A final thought: sometimes joy multiplies itself dangerously. Children are the infamous example. Isn't it bad enough that the beloved, with whom you have experienced genuine joy, will eventually be lost to you? Why add to this nightmare the child, whose loss, if it ever happened, would mean nothing less than your total annihilation? It should be noted that an equally dangerous joy, for many people, is the dog or the cat, relationships with animals being in some sense intensified by guaranteed finitude. You hope to leave this world before your child. You are quite certain your dog will leave before you do. Joy is such a human madness.

The writer Julian Barnes, considering mourning, once said, "It hurts just as much as it is worth." In fact, it was a friend of his who wrote the line in a letter of condolence, and Julian told it to my husband, who told it to me. For months afterward these words stuck with both of us, so clear and so brutal. *It hurts just as much as it is worth.* What an arrangement. Why would anyone accept such a crazy deal? Surely if we were sane and reasonable we would every time choose a pleasure over a joy, as animals themselves sensibly do. The end of a pleasure brings no great harm to anyone, after all, and can always be replaced with another of more or less equal worth.

—2013

Literature, Politics, and Cultural Identity in the Late Twentieth and Early Twenty-First Centuries

In recent generations, literature in Britain—and the public discussion of this literature—has often been infused with strongly political content. The politics of postcolonialism and of race are here important strands, but the politics of gender, of class, and of aesthetics have often been just as hotly debated. Writers such as Tony Harrison have powerfully addressed issues relating to social class; Paul Muldoon and others have spoken out provocatively on issues in British and Irish politics; artists ranging from the poet and dramatist Liz Lochhead to the cartoonist Posy Simmonds have questioned the power dynamics between men and women; and so on.

The past few decades have seen women writers and gay and lesbian writers achieve greater prominence within mainstream British literature—a change that is perhaps most strikingly evident in the realm of poetry. As late as the 1980s, almost any list of acknowledged major living poets in England, Scotland, Wales, and Ireland would have been composed overwhelmingly of men; although there were of course women poets writing in large numbers, most of these were not acknowledged by a male-dominated literary establishment. This is no longer the case; the past generation is perhaps the first in the history of British poetry in which significant women poets have been recognised in numbers at least as great as those of their male counterparts.

There has been a shift of attitude with regard to sexual orientation, too, such that it is no longer an object of controversy within the literary community, and within much of the rest of British society as well. The twentieth century saw the coming into prominence of the first openly gay poets, among them W.H. Auden and, later, Thom Gunn, Edwin Morgan, James Fenton, then of openly lesbian poets such as Jackie Kay. In 2009 Carol Ann Duffy became both the first woman and the first openly gay writer to be appointed Poet Laureate of the United Kingdom—a sign of significant change in Britain's literary landscape as well as of the importance of Duffy's work. This is not, however, to suggest that discrimination on the basis of gender or sexual orientation is no longer a matter of concern; on the contrary, struggles for equality in these areas continue to impact British politics and culture.

Another shift has been towards increasing identification of writers with national groups. The late 1990s saw the establishment of separate government assemblies in Wales and in Northern Ireland, and a separate parliament in Scotland—changes that both reflected and reinforced the importance of separate national cultures within Britain. Among those writers strongly identified with Scotland are Liz Lochhead, who often employs Scots dialect in her drama and in poems such as "Kidspoem/Bairnsang"; and Edwin Morgan, who celebrates the opening of the new Scottish Parliament buildings in his poem "Open the Doors." There has also been an extraordinary outpouring of work from poets born and raised in Northern Ireland, including Paul Muldoon and Medbh McGuckian. (It is essential here to note, however, that many poets from this area have self-identified as Irish rather than as Northern Irish.) In Welsh literature, Gwyneth Lewis has led the way in forging a fresh tradition as a bilingual poet in Welsh and English, finding immense poetic resources in the sounds as well as the meanings of the two languages.

Meanwhile, many English writers draw on English history and present-day culture; Geoffrey Hill's *Mercian Hymns*, for example, draws on the history of the West Midlands of the eighth century

CE, while much of Tony Harrison's work asserts the poetic value of contemporary working-class Yorkshire dialect. (Simon Armitage, too, often refers to northern English language and everyday life in his work, although he cautions critics that he is "a professional poet, not a professional Yorkshireman.") In their different ways, the work of Scottish, English, Welsh, and Irish writers has placed much greater emphasis on national (and sometimes regional) identity than on any sense of overarching "Britishness." As Bill Buford, editor of the UK-based international literary magazine *Granta*, observed in 2003, "I still don't know anyone who is British. I know people who are English or Scottish or Northern Irish (not to mention born-in-Nigeria-but-living-here or born-in-London-of-Pakistani-parents-and-living-here)."

As nations within the UK continue to develop specific traditions, so do writers whose work links to a heritage from outside the British Isles—and to the heritage of British colonialism. Immigration to Britain, especially from its former colonies, began to increase in the 1950s; as Zadie Smith has argued, it is now "impossible to write about England without mentioning the fact that ... there are a huge amount of people from the Indian subcontinent in England, there are a huge amount of Caribbeans, those people are English." Writers such as Louise Bennett, Grace Nichols, Moniza Alvi, and Jackie Kay focus strongly in their work on issues of race and culture, drawing from their personal and cultural backgrounds a range of styles and concerns that have broadened the scope of British literature immeasurably. One important example of this sort of development is the work of dub poets such as Linton Kwesi Johnson and Jean Binta Breeze, which blends poetry and reggae music to create hybrid expressions of the traditions of the Caribbean and the realities of present-day Britain.

The 11 September 2001 attacks on the World Trade Center and other American targets have been less of a preoccupation in Britain than in the United States, but have been the subject of some important work by British writers—as have the coordinated suicide bombings of the London transit system that occurred on 7 July 2005. As Seamus Heaney said in 2003 of the September 11 attacks and of the wars that followed, "These have been astounding events, yet our consciousness hasn't quite got the measure of them. Twin towers bursting into flame, human bodies falling like plummets, sorties of black-winged bombers taking off. ..." The selections below include an essay by a British writer trying to make cultural sense of the attacks (Colum McCann); two examinations of cultural tensions in relation to suicide bombing (Kenan Malik, Pico Iyer), and a poem questioning British participation in the American-led "War on Terror" (Andrew Motion). Conflicts of the past century have remained significant subjects in British writing, with particular attention given to the Second World War, as in James Fenton's "A German Requiem" and Tony Harrison's *Sonnets for August 1945*, and to Ireland's "Troubles" in work such as Paul Muldoon's "The Sightseers."

Although nature has long been an important subject in British literature—and especially British poetry—writing about nature has taken on a more overtly political dimension in recent decades, as fears about environmental destruction and global climate change have become increasingly prominent in public consciousness. The work of poets such as Alice Oswald and Caitriona O'Reilly often addresses humans' relationship to nature in a politically charged fashion.

As the inclusion here of work by the cartoonist Posy Simmonds suggests, another development in British literature has been an increased appreciation of forms (such as comics) that have traditionally been associated with "lowbrow" culture. In this, as in so many other respects, it is diversity that has above all characterized British literature in the generations since World War II.

⌘ ⌘ ⌘

LOUISE BENNETT (1919-2006)

Jamaican writer Louise Bennett, known as "Miss Lou," was awarded the Order of Jamaica and designated a cultural ambassador for her promotion of Jamaican language and folklore in her home country and around the world. A dynamic performer, teacher, broadcaster, and writer, Bennett was the author of such celebrated books as *Dialect Verses* (1942), *Jamaica Labrish* (1966), *Anancy and Miss Lou* (1979), and *Aunty Roachy Seh* (1993).

Colonization in Reverse

Wat a joyful news, Miss Mattie,
  I feel like me heart gwine burs
Jamaica people colonizin
  Englan in reverse.

5 By de hundred, by de tousan
  From country and from town,
By de ship load, by de plane-load
  Jamaica is Englan boun.

Dem a pour out o Jamaica,
10 Everybody future plan
Is fe get a big-time job
  An settle in de mother lan.

What a islan! What a people!
  Man an woman, old an young
15 Jus a pack dem bag an baggage
  An tun history upside dung!

Some people doan like travel,
  But fe show dem loyalty
Dem all a open up cheap-fare-
20 To-England agency.

An week by week dem shippin off
  Dem countryman like fire,

Fe immigrate an populate
  De seat o de Empire.

25 Oonoo see how life is funny,
  Oonoo see de tunabout,
Jamaica live fe box bread
  Outa English people mout.

For wen dem catch a Englan,
30 An start play dem different role,
Some will settle down to work
  An some will settle fe de dole.

Jane say de dole is not too bad
  Bacause dey payin she
35 Two pounds a week fe seek a job
  Dat suit her dignity.

Me say Jane will never find work
  At the rate how she dah-look,
For all day she stay pon Aunt Fan couch
40 An read love-story book.

Wat a devilment a Englan!
  Dem face war an brave de worse,
But me wonderin how dem gwine stan
  Colonizin in reverse.
—1966

EDWIN MORGAN (1920–2010)

Edwin Morgan was known for his use of inventive language, facility with traditional and experimental forms, and exploration of a wide range of subject matter. Morgan taught for three decades at the University of Glasgow, and in 2004 he became the first Scots Makar, the national poet of Scotland. His books include *The Vision of Cathkin Braes* (1952), *The Second Life* (1968), *From Glasgow to Saturn* (1973), *Love and a Life* (2003), and *Poems and Other Nightmares* (2010).

For the Opening of the Scottish Parliament, 9 October 2004[1]

Open the doors! Light of the day, shine in; light of
the mind, shine out!
We have a building which is more than a building.
There is a commerce between inner and outer,
between brightness and shadow, between the world
and those who think about the world.
Is it not a mystery? The parts cohere, they come
together like petals of a flower, yet they also send
their tongues outward to feel and taste the teeming
earth.
5 Did you want classic columns and predictable
pediments? A growl of old Gothic grandeur? A
blissfully boring box?
Not here, no thanks! No icon, no IKEA, no iceberg,
but curves and caverns, nooks and niches, huddles
and heavens, syncopations and surprises. Leave
symmetry to the cemetery.
But bring together slate and stainless steel, black
granite and grey granite, seasoned oak and sycamore,
concrete blond and smooth as silk—the mix is
almost alive—it breathes and beckons—imperial
marble it is not!

Come down the Mile,[2] into the heart of the city,
past the kirk[3] of St Giles and the closes and wynds[4]
of the noted ghosts of history who drank their claret
and fell down the steep tenement stairs into the
arms of link-boys[5] but who wrote and talked the
starry Enlightenment of their days—

And before them the auld makars[6] who tickled a
Scottish king's ear with melody and ribaldry and
frank advice—
10 And when you are there, down there, in the midst of
things, not set upon an hill with your nose in the
air,
This is where you know your parliament should be
And this is where it is, just here.

What do the people want of the place? They want it
to be filled with thinking persons as open and
adventurous as its architecture.
A nest of fearties° is what they do not want.   cowards
15 A symposium of procrastinators is what they do not
want.
A phalanx of forelock-tuggers[7] is what they do not want.
And perhaps above all the droopy mantra of "it wizny
me" is what they do not want.
Dear friends, dear lawgivers, dear parliamentarians,
you are picking up a thread of pride and self-esteem
that has been almost but not quite, oh no not quite,
not ever broken or forgotten.
When you convene you will be reconvening, with a
sense of not wholly the power, not yet wholly the
power, but a good sense of what was once in the
honour of your grasp.
20 All right. Forget, or don't forget, the past. Trumpets
and robes are fine, but in the present and the future
you will need something more.
What is it? We, the people, cannot tell you yet, but
you will know about it when we do tell you.
We give you our consent to govern, don't pocket it
and ride away.
We give you our deepest dearest wish to govern well,
don't say we have no mandate to be so bold.
We give you this great building, don't let your work
and hope be other than great when you enter and
begin.
25 So now begin. Open the doors and begin.
—2004

---

[1] *9 October 2004*   Formal opening date of the Scottish Parliament
Building. The Scottish Parliament had been merged with the English
Parliament since 1707; a new, separate Scottish Parliament was
established as a result of a 1997 referendum.

[2] *the Mile*   The Royal Mile, a series of streets in Old Edinburgh
leading from Edinburgh Castle to the Scottish Parliament Building.

[3] *kirk*   Church.

[4] *closes and wynds*   Narrow passages, side streets, or alleyways.

[5] *link-boys*   Torch-carriers hired to light the way for pedestrians at
night; link-boys were common until the advent of street lighting in
the nineteenth century.

[6] *makars*   Scots: poets, especially court poets.

[7] *phalanx of forelock-tuggers*   Troop of grovelers.

GEOFFREY HILL (1932–2016)

Geoffrey Hill, often referred to as a "late modernist" poet, has been publishing important work since the 1950s. Hill grew up in a small town in Worcestershire, and the history and geography of the West Midlands have been a continuing presence in his writing, perhaps most notably in *Mercian Hymns* (1971); more broadly, his poetry often explores connections with history and poetic tradition. His numerous books include *For the Unfallen* (1959), *Tenebrae* (1978), *The Orchards of Syon* (2002), *Without Title* (2006), and *Clavics* (2011). He was knighted in 2012.

from *Mercian Hymns*

I

King[1] of the perennial holly-groves, the riven
  sandstone: overlord of the M5: architect of the
historic rampart and ditch, the citadel at Tamworth,
the summer hermitage in Holy Cross: guardian of
5 the Welsh Bridge and the Iron Bridge:[2] contractor to
the desirable new estates: saltmaster: money-changer:
commissioner for oaths: martyrologist: the friend of
Charlemagne.[3]

"I liked that," said Offa, "sing it again."

---

[1] [Hill's note] The historical King Offa reigned over Mercia (and the greater part of England south of the Humber) in the years AD 757–96. During early medieval times he was already becoming a creature of legend. The Offa who figures in this sequence might perhaps most usefully be regarded as the presiding genius of the West Midlands, his dominion enduring from the middle of the eighth century until the middle of the twentieth (and possibly beyond). The indication of such a timespan will, I trust, explain and to some extent justify a number of anachronisms.

[2] *M5 ... Iron Bridge* These lines include a number of historical and geographical references to the West Midlands. The M5 is a modern superhighway running north-south near the Severn River; King Offa built a palace at Tamworth and made it the effective capital of Mercia (later the Normans built a castle there); the Welsh Bridge crosses the Severn at Shrewsbury; the Iron Bridge (a landmark in the history of the Industrial Revolution) crosses the same river near Telford.

[3] *Charlemagne* King of the Franks and conqueror of much of continental Europe (742–814).

4

I was invested in mother-earth,[4] the crypt of roots and
  endings. Child's-play. I abode there, bided my time:
  where the mole

shouldered the clogged wheel, his gold solidus;[5] where
5 dry-dust badgers thronged the Roman flues, the
  long-unlooked-for mansions of our tribe.

7

Gasholders, russet among fields. Milldams, marlpools[6]
  that lay unstirring. Eel-swarms. Coagulations of
frogs: once, with branches and half-bricks, he
battered a ditchful; then sidled away from the
5 stillness and silence.

Ceolred[7] was his friend and remained so, even after the
  day of the lost fighter: a biplane, already obsolete
  and irreplaceable, two inches of heavy snub silver.
  Ceolred let it spin through a hole in the classroom-
10 floorboards, softly, into the rat-droppings and coins.

After school he lured Ceolred, who was sniggering with
  fright, down to the old quarries, and flayed him.
  Then, leaving Ceolred, he journeyed for hours, calm
  and alone, in his private derelict sandlorry named
15 *Albion*.[8]

8

The mad are predators. Too often lately they harbour
  against us. A novel heresy exculpates all maimed
souls. Abjure it! I am the King of Mercia, and I
know.

---

[4] [Hill's note] To the best of my recollection, the expression "to invest in mother-earth" was the felicitous (and correct) definition of "yird" given by Mr. Michael Hordern in the program *Call My Bluff* televised on BBC 2 on Thursday January 19th 1970.

[5] *solidus* Gold coin of the Roman Empire.

[6] *marlpools* Marl is a clay-like deposit in lakebeds, often used to make bricks.

[7] *Ceolred* Cousin to Offa, and his successor as King of Mercia.

[8] *Albion* Great Britain.

5   Threatened by phone-calls at midnight, venomous
letters, forewarned I have thwarted their imminent
devices.

Today I name them; tomorrow I shall express the new
law. I dedicate my awakening to this matter.

10

He adored the desk, its brown-oak inlaid with ebony,
assorted prize pens, the seals of gold and base metal
into which he had sunk his name.

It was there that he drew upon grievances from the
5   people; attended to signatures and retributions;
forgave the death-howls of his rival. And there he
exchanged gifts with the Muse[1] of History.

What should a man make of remorse, that it might
profit his soul? Tell me. Tell everything to Mother,
10   darling, and God bless.

He swayed in sunlight, in mild dreams. He tested the
little pears. He smeared catmint on his palm for his
cat Smut to lick. He wept, attempting to master
ancilla and *servus*.[2]

22

We ran across the meadow scabbed with cow-dung, past
the crab-apple trees and camouflaged nissen hut.[3] It
was curfew-time for our war-band.

At home the curtains were drawn. The wireless[4] boomed
5   its commands. I loved the battle-anthems and the
gregarious news.

Then, in the earthy shelter, warmed by a blue-glassed
storm-lantern, I huddled with stories of dragon-
tailed airships and warriors who took wing
10   immortal as phantoms.

23

In tapestries, in dreams, they gathered, as it was enacted,
the return, the re-entry of transcendence into this
sublunary world. *Opus Anglicanum*,[5] their
stringent mystery riddled by needles: the silver
5   veining, the gold leaf, voluted[6] grape-vine, masterworks of treacherous thread.

They trudged out of the dark, scraping their boots free
from lime-splodges and phlegm. They munched
cold bacon. The lamps grew plump with oily
10   reliable light.

—1971

A Short History of British India (2)

Suppose they sweltered here three thousand years
patient for our destruction. There is a greeting
beyond the act. Destiny is the great thing,
true lord of annexation and arrears.

5   Our law-books overrule the emperors.
The mango is the bride-bed of light. Spring
jostles the flame-tree. But new mandates bring
new images of faith, good subahdars![7]

The flittering candles of the wayside shrines
10   melt into dawn. The sun surmounts the dust.
Krishna from Radha[8] lovingly untwines.

---

[1] *Muse* In classical mythology, one of the nine daughters of Zeus and Mnemosyne, each of whom presided over, and provided inspiration for, an aspect of the arts and sciences.

[2] *ancilla and servus* Latin: female servant and male slave.

[3] *nissen hut* Tunnel-shaped hut with a cement floor and corrugated iron roof.

[4] *wireless* Radio.

[5] *Opus Anglicanum* Latin: English work; a term used in the thirteenth and fourteenth centuries to refer to fine embroidery produced in England.

[6] *voluted* Grooved.

[7] *subahdars* Nobles.

[8] *Krishna from Radha* In Hinduism the relationship between Krishna and Radha is expressive of the utmost passion and devotion, and of the harmony of souls.

Lugging the earth, the oxen bow their heads.
The alien conscience of our days is lost
among the ruins and on endless roads.

15   —1978

TONY HARRISON (B. 1937)

The northern English writer Tony Harrison is
among the most versatile and prolific of British
poets. His many books of poetry include *The
Loiners* (1970), the long poem *V* (1985), *The
Gaze of the Gorgon* (1992), *The Shadow of Hiroshima* (1995), and *Under the Clock* (2005); he is
also the author of numerous translations and
adaptations of poetic drama. Much of
Harrison's poetry is infused with political
content, particularly on subjects such as class
and modern warfare.

Them & [uz]

for Professors Richard Hoggart & Leon Cortez[1]

I

α ιαî, ay, ay! ... stutterer Demosthenes[2]
gob full of pebbles outshouting seas—

4 words only of *mi' art*[3] aches and ... "Mine's broken,
you barbarian, T.W.!" *He* was nicely spoken.
5   "Can't have our glorious heritage done to death!"

I played the Drunken Porter in *Macbeth*.[4]

"Poetry's the speech of kings. You're one of those
Shakespeare gives the comic bits to: prose!
All poetry (even Cockney Keats?)[5] you see
10   's been dubbed by [Ës] into RP,
Received Pronunciation, please believe [Ës]
your speech is in the hands of the Receivers."

"We say [Ës] not [uz] T.W.!" That shut my trap.
I doffed my flat a's (as in "flat cap")
15   my mouth all stuffed with glottals, great
lumps to hawk up and spit out ... *E-nun-ci-ate!*

2

So right, yer buggers, then! We'll occupy
your lousy leasehold Poetry.

I chewed up Littererchewer and spat the bones
20   into the lap of dozing Daniel Jones,
dropped the initials I'd been harried as
and used my *name* and own voice: [uz] [uz] [uz],
ended sentences with by, with, from,[6]
and spoke the language that I spoke at home.
25   R.I.P. RP. R.I.P. T.W.
I'm *Tony* Harrison no longer you!

You can tell the Receivers where to go
(and not aspirate[7] it) once you know
Wordsworth's *matter/water* are full rhymes,
30   [uz] can be loving as well as funny.

My first mention in the *Times*
automatically made Tony Anthony!
—1981

---

[1]   *Richard Hoggart*   British sociologist and cultural commentator (b.
1918); *Leon Cortez*   British film, radio, and television actor (1898–
1970).

[2]   *Demosthenes*   Greatest of all orators in ancient Greece, Demosthenes (384–322 BCE) is said to have placed rocks in his mouth in
an effort to improve his enunciation.

[3]   *'art*   Heart. The dropped "h" has often been regarded in Britain
as a sign of "lower class" pronunciation. "My heart aches" are the
first words of John Keats's "Ode to a Nightingale."

[4]   *Drunken Porter ... Macbeth*   Servant with a small, comic role in
Shakespeare's play.

[5]   *Cockney Keats*   The Romantic poet John Keats (1795–1821) came
from a Cockney (i.e., east London) background and was attacked for
allegedly representing a "Cockney School of Poetry."

[6]   *by, with, from*   Three examples of prepositions; strict grammarians
assert that a sentence must not end with a preposition.

[7]   *aspirate*   Pronounce the "h" when it appears at the beginning of
a word (as opposed to dropping it).

t'Ark[1]

Silence and poetry have their own reserves.
The numbered creatures flourish less and less.
A language near extinction best preserves
the deepest grammar of our nothingness.

5   Not only dodo, oryx and great auk[2]
waddled on their tod[3] to t'monster ark,
but "leg," "night," "origin" in crushed people's talk,
tongues of fire last witnessed mouthing: *dark!*

Now when the future couldn't be much darker,
10 there being fewer epithets for sun,
and Cornish and the Togoland *Restsprache*[4]
name both the animals and hunter's gun,
celebrate before things go too far
Papua's last reported manucode,
15 the pygmy hippo of the Cote d'Ivoire,
and Upper Guinea's oviparous toad—[5]

(or mourn in Latin their imminent death,
then translate these poems into *cynghanedd*).[6]
—1981

from *V*

…

Next millennium you'll have to search quite hard
to find out where I'm buried but I'm near

the grave of haberdasher Appleyard,
the pile of HARPs,[7] or some new neonned beer.

5   Find Byron, Wordsworth,[8] or turn left between
one grave marked Broadbent, one marked Richardson.
Bring some solution with you that can clean
whatever new crude words have been sprayed on.

If love of art, or love, gives you affront
10 that the grave I'm in's graffitied then, maybe,
erase the more offensive FUCK and CUNT
but leave, with the worn UNITED, one small v.[9]

Victory? For vast, slow, coal-creating forces
that hew the body's seams to get the soul.
15 Will Earth run out of her "diurnal courses"
before repeating her creation of black coal?

But choose a day like I chose in mid-May
or earlier when apple and hawthorn tree,
no matter if boys boot their ball all day,
20 cling to their blossoms and won't shake them free.

If, having come this far, somebody reads
these verses, and he/she wants to understand,
face this grave on Beeston Hill,[10] your back to Leeds,
and read the chiselled epitaph I've planned:

25 *Beneath your feet's a poet, then a pit.*
Poetry supporter, if you're here to find
how poems can grow from (beat you to it!) SHIT
find the beef, the beer, the bread, then look behind.
—1985

---

[1] *t'Ark*   The ark. T' is a northern English dialect pronunciation of "the."

[2] *dodo … great auk*   Species that are now extinct.

[3] *on their tod*   On their own.

[4] *Cornish … Restsprache*   Two endangered languages—Cornish from Cornwall in southwest England, and Restsprache from Togo in West Africa.

[5] *Papua's … toad*   All examples of severely endangered species.

[6] *cynghanedd*   Welsh: literally, "harmony," also "poetic form." The Welsh language, once classed as endangered, began to be more widely used in the late twentieth century.

[7] *HARP*   Brand of lager beer.

[8] *Byron, Wordsworth*   Romantic poets George Gordon, Lord Byron (1788–1824), and William Wordsworth (1770–1850).

[9] *UNITED*   In this case, short for "Leeds United Football Club"; *v.* Short for "victory," a common piece of graffiti during World War II.

[10] *Beeston Hill*   Western suburb of the city of Leeds.

from *Sonnets for August 1945*[1]

THE MORNING AFTER

I

The fire left to itself might smoulder weeks.
 Phone cables melt. Paint peels from off back gates.
Kitchen windows crack; the whole street reeks
of horsehair blazing. Still, it celebrates.

5   Though people weep, their tears dry from the heat.
Faces flushed with flame, beer, sheer relief
and such a sense of celebration in our street
for me it still means joy though banked with grief.

And that, now clouded, sense of public joy
10 with war-worn adults wild in their loud fling
has never come again since as a boy

I saw Leeds people dance and heard them sing.
There's still that dark, scorched circle on the road.
The morning after kids like me helped spray
15 hissing upholstery spring wire that still glowed
and cobbles boiling with black gas tar for VJ.[2]
—1990

POSY SIMMONDS (B. 1945)

English cartoonist Posy Simmonds established
her reputation as the author of a weekly comic
strip (1977–87) published in *The Guardian*.
Known for perceptive, often satirical depictions
of middle-class English life, Simmonds is the
author and illustrator of graphic novels including *Gemma Bovery* (1999) and *Tamara Drewe*
(2007), as well as a number of acclaimed books
for children.

---

[1] *August 1945* The United States dropped atomic bombs on the Japanese cities of Hiroshima and Nagasaki on 6 August and 9 August, respectively.

[2] *VJ* Day on which victory by the Allies over Japan was celebrated.

LIZ LOCHHEAD (B. 1947)

A celebrated playwright as well as a poet, Liz Lochhead has become known for engaging with feminist concerns and issues of national identity without confining herself to one voice or perspective. Lochhead was appointed Scots Makar in 2011. Her collections of poetry include *Memo for Spring* (1972), *Dreaming Frankenstein* (1984), *The Colour of Black and White: Poems 1984–2003* (2003), and *Choosing: The Selected Poetry of Liz Lochhead* (2011).

Men Talk

(Rap)

Women
        Rabbit rabbit rabbit women
Tattle and titter
Women prattle
5   Women waffle and witter

Men Talk. Men Talk.

Woman into Girl Talk
About Women's trouble
Trivia 'n' Small Talk
10 They yap and they babble

Men Talk. Men Talk.

Women yatter
Women chatter
Women chew the fat, women spill the beans
15 Women aint been takin'
The oh-so Good Advice in them
Women's Magazines.

A Man likes A Good Listener.

Oh yeah
20 I like A Woman
Who likes me enough
Not to nitpick
Not to nag and
Not to interrupt 'cause I call that treason

25 A woman with the Good Grace
To be struck dumb
By me Sweet Reason. Yes—

A Man likes a Good Listener

A Real
30 Man
Likes a Real Good Listener

Women yap yap yap
Verbal Diarrhoea is a Female Disease
Woman she spread she rumours round she
35 Like Philadelphia Cream Cheese.

Oh
Bossy Women Gossip
Girlish Women Giggle
Women natter, women nag
40 Women niggle niggle niggle

Men Talk.

Men
Think First, Speak Later
Men Talk.
—1985

Kidspoem/Bairnsang

It wis January
and a gey dreich day
the first day Ah went to the school
so my Mum happed me up in ma
5   good navy-blue napp coat wi the rid tartan hood
birled a scarf aroon ma neck
pu'ed oan ma pixie an' my pawkies
it wis that bitter
said *noo ye'll no starve*
10 gie'd me a wee kiss and a kid-oan skelp oan the bum
and sent me aff across the playground
tae the place Ah'd learn to say
it was January
and a really dismal day

15 the first day I went to school
    so my mother wrapped me up in my
    best navy-blue top coat with the red tartan hood,
    twirled a scarf around my neck,
    pulled on my bobble-hat and mittens
20 it was so bitterly cold
    said *now you won't freeze to death*
    gave me a little kiss and a pretend slap on the bottom
    to the place I'd learn to forget to say
    it wis January
25 and a gey dreich day
    the first day Ah went to the school
    so my Mum happed me up in ma
    good navy-blue napp coat wi the rid tartan hood,
    birled a scarf aroon ma neck,
30 pu'ed oan ma pixie an' ma pawkies
    it wis that bitter.

    Oh saying it was one thing
    but when it came to writing it
    in black and white
35 the way it had to be said
    was as if you were posh, grown-up, male, English and
    dead.
    —1995

JAMES FENTON (B. 1949)

James Fenton has ranged extraordinarily widely
both geographically (he lived for some time in
Southeast Asia) and in his work. A political
correspondent, translator, literary critic, and
poet, Fenton was Professor of Poetry at Oxford
University from 1994 to 1999. His books of
poetry include *The Memory of War* (1982), *Out
of Danger* (1993), and *Selected Poems* (2006).

A German Requiem

It is not what they built. It is what they knocked
      down.
It is not the houses. It is the spaces between the houses.
It is not the streets that exist. It is the streets that no
      longer exist.
It is not your memories which haunt you.
5 It is not what you have written down.
It is what you have forgotten, what you must forget.
What you must go on forgetting all your life.
And with any luck oblivion should discover a ritual.
You will find out that you are not alone in the
      enterprise.
10 Yesterday the very furniture seemed to reproach you.
Today you take your place in the Widow's Shuttle.

§

The bus is waiting at the southern gate
To take you to the city of your ancestors
Which stands on the hill opposite, with gleaming
      pediments,
15 As vivid as this charming square, your home.
Are you shy? You should be. It is almost like a wedding,
The way you clasp your flowers and give a little tug at
      your veil. Oh,
The hideous bridesmaids, it is natural that you should
      resent them
Just a little, on this first day.
20 But that will pass, and the cemetery is not far.
Here comes the driver, flicking a toothpick into the
      gutter,
His tongue still searching between his teeth.
See, he has not noticed you. No one has noticed you.
It will pass, young lady, it will pass.

§

25 How comforting it is, once or twice a year,
To get together and forget the old times.
As on those special days, ladies and gentlemen,
When the boiled shirts[1] gather at the graveside
And a leering waistcoat approaches the rostrum.[2]

---

[1] *boiled shirts*   White linen shirts; dress shirts.

[2] *rostrum*   Pulpit; platform for public speaking.

30   It is like a solemn pact between the survivors.
     The mayor has signed it on behalf of the
          freemasonry.[1]
     The priest has sealed it on behalf of all the rest.
     Nothing more need be said, and it is better that way—

                              ¶

     The better for the widow, that she should not live in
          fear of surprise,
35   The better for the young man, that he should move at
          liberty between the armchairs,
     The better that these bent figures who flutter among
          the graves
     Tending the nightlights and replacing the
          chrysanthemums
     Are not ghosts,
     That they shall go home.
40   The bus is waiting, and on the upper terraces
     The workmen are dismantling the houses of the dead.

                              ¶

     But when so many had died, so many and at such speed,
     There were no cities waiting for the victims.
     They unscrewed the name-plates from the shattered
          doorways
45   And carried them away with the coffins.
     So the squares and parks were filled with the
          eloquence of young cemeteries:
     The smell of fresh earth, the improvised crosses
     And all the impossible directions in brass and enamel.

                              ¶

     "Doctor Gliedschirm, skin specialist, surgeries 14–16
          hours or by appointment."
50   Professor Sargnagel was buried with four degrees, two
          associate memberships
     And instructions to tradesmen to use the back entrance.
     Your uncle's grave informed you that he lived on the
          third floor, left.

     You were asked please to ring, and he would come
          down in the lift[2]
     To which one needed a key …

                              ¶

55   Would come down, would ever come down
     With a smile like thin gruel, and never too much to say.
     How he shrank through the years.
     How you towered over him in the narrow cage.
     How he shrinks now …

                              ¶

60   But come. Grief must have its term? Guilt too, then.
     And it seems there is no limit to the resourcefulness of
          recollection.
     So that a man might say and think:
     When the world was at its darkest,
     When the black wings passed over the rooftops
65   (And who can divine His purposes?) even then
     There was always, always a fire in this hearth.
     You see this cupboard? A priest-hole![3]
     And in that lumber-room[4] whole generations have
          been housed and fed.
     Oh, if I were to begin, if I were to begin to tell you
70   The half, the quarter, a mere smattering of what we
          went through!

                              ¶

     His wife nods, and a secret smile,
     Like a breeze with enough strength to carry one dry leaf
     Over two pavingstones, passes from chair to chair.
     Even the enquirer is charmed.
75   He forgets to pursue the point.
     It is not what he wants to know.
     It is what he wants not to know.
     It is not what they say.
     It is what they do not say.
     —1980

---

[1] *freemasonry* Fraternal society in which members meet in "lodges." Freemasons have often played a leading role in local public affairs in various western societies.

[2] *lift* Elevator.

[3] *priest-hole* Hiding place for Roman Catholic priests, built during the time of the penal laws, which imposed penalties upon those who did not practice the religion of the Church of England.

[4] *lumber-room* Storeroom.

GRACE NICHOLS (B. 1950)

A native of Guyana, Grace Nichols moved to England in 1977 and began to make a mark as a poet in the 1980s with work of challenging and exuberant directness, often written with a view as much to performance as to the printed page. Her books include *I is a long-memoried woman* (1983), *The Fat Black Woman's Poems* (1984), *Everybody Got a Gift* (2005), and *Picasso, I Want My Face Back* (2009).

Skanking[1] Englishman Between Trains

Met him at Birmingham Station[2]
small yellow hair Englishman
hi fi stereo swinging in one hand
walking in rhythm to reggae sound/Man

5   he was alive
he was full-o-jive
said he had a lovely
Jamaican wife

Said he couldn't remember
10   the taste of English food
I like mih drops[3]
me johnny cakes[4]
me peas and rice
me soup/Man

15   he was alive
he was full-o-jive
said he had a lovely
Jamaican wife

Said, showing me her photo
20   whenever we have a little quarrel

---

[1] *Skanking* Dancing; swaggering.

[2] *Birmingham Station* Located in the British Midlands, the city of Birmingham's railway station is a hub where many train lines meet.

[3] *drops* Drop-shaped cakes; also, sugar plums or candies.

[4] *johnny cakes* In the West Indies, a term for dumplings or scones.

you know/to sweeten her up
I surprise her with a nice mango/Man

he was alive
he was full-o-jive
25   said he had a lovely Jamaican wife
—1984

Epilogue

I have crossed an ocean
I have lost my tongue
from the root of the old one
a new one has sprung
—1984

White

Never mind how or why—
this slow delight
of waking to a room
that comes out of the
5   memory of night,
A dusky dawning—
paintings, wardrobe,
hangings ...

Then walking, a sleepwalker,
10   holding on to walls of vanilla,
great solid slabs
you could sink your mouth into.
The memories of ancestors,
all that blackness
15   against whiteness.
The starched religiousness of it.

O I could hold
the globe like a face,
Januslike[5] spinning
20   from the depths of my dreaming

---

[5] *Januslike* I.e., having two faces; referring to Janus, the Roman god of doorways and of beginnings and endings, who was depicted with two faces, one looking in either direction.

I could face-up
to the stark white page
already seeded
with the best invisible poem.
—1996

MEDBH McGUCKIAN (B. 1950)

Medbh McGuckian came into prominence as a
writer in the 1980s and 1990s. Her poems, at
once light in tone and densely suggestive, often
embed large issues of history, gender, and
language within focused, personal contexts. Her
books include *The Flower Master* (1982),
Marconi's Cottage (1991), *The Face of the Earth*
(2002), *The Book of the Angel* (2004), and *My
Love Has Fared Inland* (2010).

Slips

The studied poverty of a moon roof
The earthenware of dairies cooled by apple trees,
The apple tree that makes the whitest wash …

But I forget names, remembering them wrongly
5   Where they touch upon another name,
A town in France like a woman's Christian name.

My childhood is preserved as a nation's history,
My favourite fairytales the shells
Leased by the hermit crab.

10 I see my grandmother's death as a piece of ice,
My mother's slimness restored to her,
My own key slotted in your door—

Tricks you might guess from this unfastened button,
A pen mislaid, a word misread,
15 My hair coming down in the middle of a
conversation.
—1982

The Dream-Language of Fergus

1

Your tongue has spent the night
in its dim sack as the shape of your foot
in its cave. Not the rudiment
of half a vanquished sound,
5   the excommunicated shadow of a name,
has rumpled the sheets of your mouth.

2

So Latin sleeps, they say, in Russian speech,
so one river inserted into another
becomes a leaping, glistening, splashed
10 and scattered alphabet
jutting out from the voice,
till what began as a dog's bark
ends with bronze, what began
with honey ends with ice;
15 as if an aeroplane in full flight
launched a second plane,
the sky is stabbed by their exits
and the mistaken meaning of each.

3

Conversation is as necessary
20 among these familiar campus trees
as the apartness of torches;
and if I am a threader
of double-stranded words, whose
Quando[1] has grown into now,
25 no text can return the honey
in its path of light from a jar,
only a seed-fund, a pendulum,
pressing out the diasporic snow.
—1991

---

[1] *Quando*   Latin: when.

PAUL MULDOON (B. 1951)

Paul Muldoon first began publishing poetry in the 1970s; he has since worked as a producer for the BBC Network in Belfast, taught at Princeton University, and served as poetry editor for *The New Yorker*. His collections include *New Weather* (1973), *Quoof* (1983), *Hay* (1998), *Moy Sand and Gravel* (2002), and *Maggot* (2010). Known for his inventive use of traditional forms, Muldoon uses his trademark wit and wordplay to bring to life both personal and universal images.

The Sightseers

My father and mother, my brother and sister
and I, with uncle Pat, our dour best-loved uncle,
had set out that Sunday afternoon in July
in his broken-down Ford

5   not to visit some graveyard—one died of shingles,
one of fever, another's knees turned to jelly—
but the brand-new roundabout[1] at Ballygawley,
the first in mid-Ulster.[2]

Uncle Pat was telling us how the B-Specials[3]
10 had stopped him one night somewhere near Ballygawley
and smashed his bicycle

and made him sing the Sash[4] and curse the Pope of Rome.
They held a pistol so hard against his forehead
there was still the mark of an O when he got home.
—1983

[1] *roundabout* Merry-go-round.

[2] *mid-Ulster* Region consisting of the northern, western, and eastern parts of County Tyrone, in Northern Ireland.

[3] *B-Specials* Auxiliary force of the Royal Ulster Constabulary, formed in 1920 by the government of Northern Ireland to combat IRA secessionist fighters and any potential subversion within the state. The B-Special force was exclusively Protestant, was several times larger than the normal police force, and was regarded by many as a "Protestant army." The B-Specials were disbanded in 1972, at the beginning of Direct Rule by the British.

[4] *the Sash* Irish Protestant ballad commemorating the victory of the Protestants in the Williamite war of 1688–91.

Milkweed and Monarch

As he knelt by the grave of his mother and father
the taste of dill, or tarragon—
he could barely tell one from the other—

filled his mouth. It seemed as if he might smother.
5   Why should he be stricken
with grief, not for his mother and father,

but a woman slinking from the fur of a sea-otter
in Portland, Maine, or, yes, Portland, Oregon—
he could barely tell one from the other—

10 and why should he now savour
the tang of her, her little pickled gherkin,
as he knelt by the grave of his mother and father?

_____

He looked about. He remembered her palaver
on how both earth and sky would darken—
15 "You could barely tell one from the other"—

while the Monarch butterflies passed over
in their milkweed-hunger: "A wing-beat, some reckon,
may trigger off the mother and father

of all storms, striking your Irish Cliffs of Moher
20 with the force of a hurricane."
Then: "Milkweed and Monarch 'invented' each
    other."

_____

He looked about. Cow's-parsley in a samovar.[5]
25 He'd mistaken his mother's name, "Regan," for
    "Anger":
as he knelt by the grave of his mother and father
he could barely tell one from the other.
—1994

[5] *samovar* Russian tea urn.

LINTON KWESI JOHNSON (B. 1952)

Born in Jamaica, Linton Kwesi Johnson has lived for most of his life in south London. The first and best-known practitioner of "dub poetry" (a term coined by Johnson to describe a blend of poetry and reggae music), he has worked as a journalist and broadcaster as well as a poet and musician. His books include *Dread, Beat, an' Blood* (1975), *Tings an' Times* (1991), and *Mi Revalueshanary Fren* (2002).

Inglan Is a Bitch

W'en mi jus' come to Landan toun
    mi use to work pan di andahgroun[1]
but workin' pan di andahgroun
y'u don't get fi know your way aroun'

5 Inglan is a bitch
    dere's no escapin' it
  Inglan is a bitch
    dere's no runnin' whey fram it

mi get a lickle jab in a big 'otell
10 an' awftah a while, mi woz doin' quite well
dem staat mi aaf as a dish-washah
but w'en mi tek a stack, mi noh tun clack-watchah!

  Inglan is a bitch
    dere's no escapin' it
15 Inglan is a bitch
    noh baddah try fi hide fram it

w'en dem gi' yu di lickle wage packit
fus dem rab it wid dem big tax racket
y'u haffi struggle fi mek en's meet
20 an' w'en y'u goh a y'u bed y'u jus' cant sleep

  Inglan is a bitch
    dere's no escapin' it
  Inglan is a bitch fi true
    a noh lie mi a tell, a true

25 mi use to work dig ditch w'en it cowl noh bitch
mi did strang like a mule, but, bwoy, mi did fool
den awftah a while mi jus' stap dhu ovahtime
den awftah a while mi jus' phu dung mi tool

  Inglan is a bitch
30 dere's no escapin' it
  Inglan is a bitch
    y'u haffi know how fi suvvive in it

well mi dhu day wok an' mi dhu nite wok
mi dhu clean wok an' mi dhu dutty wok
35 dem seh dat black man is very lazy
but if y'u si how mi wok y'u woulda seh mi crazy

  Inglan is a bitch
    dere's no escapin' it
  Inglan is a bitch
40 y'u bettah face up to it

dem have a lickle facktri up inna Brackly[2]
inna disya facktri all dem dhu is pack crackry
fi di laas fifteen years dem get mi laybah
now awftah fifteen years mi fall out a fayvah

45 Inglan is a bitch
    dere's no escapin' it
  Inglan is a bitch
    dere's no runnin' whey fram it

mi know dem have work, work in abundant
50 yet still, dem mek mi redundant[3]
now, at fifty-five mi gettin' quite ol'
yet still, dem sen' mi fi goh draw dole

  Inglan is a bitch
    dere's no escapin' it
55 Inglan is a bitch fi true
  is whey wi a goh dhu 'bout it?
    —1991

---

1 *andahgroun* Underground (i.e., subway).

2 *Brackly* Industrial area of London.

3 *mek mi redundant* Make me redundant (i.e., lay me off).

ANDREW MOTION (B. 1952)

As Poet Laureate of the United Kingdom from 1999 to 2009, Andrew Motion improved public access to poetry through projects such as the online Poetry Archive; in 2009 he received a knighthood for services to literature. Also a teacher, editor, and prose author, he has written poetry collections including *The Pleasure Streamers* (1977), *Dangerous Play: Poems 1974-1984* (1984), *The Price of Everything* (1994), *Public Property* (2002), and *The Cinder Path* (2009). His poems frequently draw on historical events.

Causa Belli[1]

They read good books, and quote, but never learn
    a language other than the scream of rocket-burn.
Our straighter talk is drowned but ironclad:
elections, money, empire, oil and Dad.
—2003

London Plane

They felled the plane that broke the pavement
    slabs.
My next-door neighbour worried for his house.
He said the roots had cracked his bedroom wall.
The Council sent tree-surgeons and he watched.
5 A thin man in the heat without a shirt.
They started at the top and then worked down.
It took a day with one hour free for lunch.
The trunk was carted off in useful logs.

The stump remained for two weeks after that.
10 A wren sat on it once.
Then back the tree-men came with their machine.
They chomped the stump and left a square of mud.

---

[1] *Causa Belli* Latin: causes or justifications for war. In January 2003, when this poem was first published, it appeared increasingly likely that Britain would participate in an American-led attack on Iraq; this attack did in fact occur in March 2003, marking the beginning of the Iraq War. Both British and American governments claimed that Iraq was hiding weapons of mass destruction, an allegation that is discredited.

All afternoon the street was strewn with bits.
That night the wind got up and blew it bare.
—2009

MONIZA ALVI (B. 1954)

An important voice in the generation of British poets who came to prominence in the 1990s, Moniza Alvi has been a school teacher and college tutor as well as a poet. Born in Pakistan, she has lived in England since infancy; much of her poetry concerns issues of identity. Alvi's books include *The Country at My Shoulder* (1993), *A Bowl of Warm Air* (1996), *How the Stone Found Its Voice* (2005), and *At the Time of Partition* (2013).

And If

If you could choose a country
    to belong to—
perhaps you had one
snatched away,
5 once offered to you
like a legend
in a basket covered with a cloth—

and if the sun were a simple flare,
the streets beating out
10 the streets, and your breath
lost on the road
with the Yadavs,[2] herding cattle,
then you could rest, absorb
it all in the cool of the hills,

15 but still you might peel back one face
to retrieve another
and another, down to the face that is
unbearable, so clear

---

[2] *Yadavs* One of the most ancient Aryan groups of Bharata, the Yadavs live in parts of India, Nepal, and Bangladesh, and most follow the Hindu religion.

so complex, hinting at nations,
20 castes and sub-castes
and you would touch it once—

and if this Eastern track were
a gusty English lane
where rain makes mirrors
25 in the holes,
a rat lies lifeless, sodden
as an old floorcloth,
you'd be untouchable[1]—as one

defined by someone else—
30 one who cleans the toilets,
burns the dead.
—1996

How the World Split in Two

Was it widthways or lengthways?
a quarrel with the equator?
Did the rawness of the inside sparkle?

Only this is true:
5 there was an arm on one side
and a hand on the other,
a thought on one side
and a hush on the other.

And a luminous tear
10 carried on the back of a beetle
went backwards and forwards
from one side to the other.
—2005

---

[1] *untouchable* In the caste system of Hindu societies, the lowest caste is that of the untouchables, who are traditionally restricted from any jobs other than menial ones (such as cleaning toilets and cremating bodies).

PICO IYER (B. 1957)

Born in England to Indian parents and partly raised in California before attending Eton, Oxford, and Harvard, Pico Iyer turned his traveling life into a writing career. He frequently discusses globalization and cross-cultural connections in his work; in addition to travel writing, he has also published novels and contributed to *Time Magazine* and other journals. His books include *Video Night in Kathmandu* (1988), *Falling Off the Map: Some Lonely Places of the World* (1994), and *The Man Within My Head* (2012).

The Terminal Check

I'm sitting in the expansive spaces of Renzo Piano's four-storey airport outside Osaka, sipping an Awake tea from Starbucks and waiting for my bus home. I've chosen to live in Japan for the past twenty years, and I know its rites as I know the way I need tea when feeling displaced, or to head for a right-hand window seat as soon as I enter a bus. A small, round-faced Japanese man in his early thirties, accompanied by a tall and somewhat cadaverous man of the same age, approaches me.

"Excuse me," says the small, friendly-seeming one; they look like newborn salarymen in their not-quite-perfect suits. "May I see your passport?"

When I look up, surprised, he flashes me a badge showing that he's a plain-clothes policeman. Dazed after crossing sixteen time zones (from California), I hand him my British passport.

"What are you doing in Japan?"

"I'm writing about it." I pull out my business card with the red embossed logo of *Time* magazine.

"*Time* magazine?" says the smiling cop, strangely impressed. "He works for *Time* magazine," he explains to his lanky and impassive partner. "Very famous magazine," he assures me. "High prestige!"

Then he asks for my address and phone number and where I plan to be for the next eighty-nine days. "If there is some unfortunate incident," he explains, "some terrorist attack" (he's sotto voce now), "then we will know you did it."

Six months later, I fly back to the country I love once more. This time I need to withdraw some yen from an ATM as I stumble out of my trans-Pacific plane, in order to pay for my bus home.

"You're getting some money?" says an attractive young Japanese woman, suddenly appearing beside me with a smile.

"I am. To go back to my apartment."

"You live here?" Few Japanese women have ever come up to me in public, let alone without an introduction, and shown such interest.

"I do."

"May I see your passport?" she asks sweetly, flashing a badge at me, much as the pair of questioners had done two seasons before.

"Just security," she says, anxious not to put me out, as my Japanese neighbours stream, unconcerned, towards the Gakuenmae bus that's about to pull out of its bay.

I tell my friends back in California about these small disruptions and they look much too knowing. It's 9/11, they assure me. Over the past decade, security has tightened around the world, which means that insecurity has increased proportionally. Indeed, in recent years Japan has introduced fingerprinting for all foreign visitors arriving at its airports, and takes photographs of every outsider coming across its borders; a large banner on the wall behind the immigration officers in Osaka— as angry-looking with its red-and-black hand-lettering as a student banner—explains the need for heightened measures in the wake of threats to national order.

But the truth of the matter is that, for those of us with darker skins, and from nations not materially privileged, it was ever thus. When I was eighteen, I was held in custody in Panama's airport (because of the Indian passport I then carried) and denied formal entry to the nation, while the roguish English friend from high school with whom I was travelling was free to enter with impunity and savour all the dubious pleasures of the Canal Zone. On my way into Hong Kong—a transit lounge of a city if ever there was one, a duty-free zone whose only laws seem to be those of the market-place—I was hauled into a special cabin for a lengthy interrogation because my face was deemed not to match my (by then British) passport. In Japan I was strip-searched every time I returned to the country, three or four times a year—my lifelong tan moving the authorities to assume that I must be either Saddam Hussein's[1] cousin or an illegal Iranian (or, worst of all, what I really am, a wandering soul with Indian forebears). Once I was sent to a small room in Tokyo reserved for anyone of South Asian ancestry (where bejewelled women in saris loudly complained in exaggerated Oxbridge accents about being taken for common criminals).

Another time, long before my Japanese neighbours had heard of Osama bin Laden,[2] I was even detained on my way *out* of Osaka—and the British Embassy hastily faxed on a Sunday night—as if any male with brown skin, passable English and a look of shabby quasi-respectability must be doing something wrong if he's crossing a border.

But now, having learned over decades to accept such indignities or injustices, I walk into a chorus of complaints every time I return to California, from my pale-skinned, affluent neighbours. They're patting us down now, my friends object, and they're confiscating our contact-lens fluid. They're forcing us to travel with tiny tubes of toothpaste and moving us to wear loafers when usually we'd prefer lace-ups. They're taking away every bottle of water—but only after bottles of water have been shown to be weapons of mass destruction; they're feeling us up with blue gloves, even here in Santa Barbara, now that they know that underwear can be a lethal weapon.

I listen to their grousing and think that the one thing the 9/11 attacks have achieved, for those of us who spend too much time in airports, is to make suspicion universal; fear and discomfort are equal-opportunity employers now. The world is flat in ways the high-flying global theoreticians don't always acknowledge; these days, even someone from the materially fortunate parts of the

---

[1] *Saddam Hussein* President of Iraq (1937–2006). Before their invasion of Iraq in 2003, the American and British governments accused him of involvement in the 11 September 2001 terrorist attacks on the United States and of possessing weapons of mass destruction.

[2] *Osama bin Laden* Leader (1957–2011) of al-Qaeda, an Islamic fundamentalist organization responsible for several major terrorist attacks, including the 11 September 2001 attacks on the World Trade Center and other American targets.

world—a man with a ruddy complexion, a woman in a Prada suit—is pulled aside for what is quixotically known as "random screening."

It used to be that the rich corners of the world seemed relatively safe, protected, and the poor ones too dangerous to enter. Now, the logic of the terrorist attacks on New York and Washington has reversed all that. If anything, it's the rich places that feel unsettled. It used to be that officials would alight on people who look like me—from nations of need, in worn jeans, bearing the passports of more prosperous countries—as likely troublemakers; now they realise that even the well born and well dressed may not always be well-intentioned.

I understand why my friends feel aggrieved to be treated as if they came from Nigeria or Mexico or India. But I can't really mourn too much that airports, since 9/11, have become places where everyone may be taken to be guilty until proven innocent. The world is all mixed up these days, and America can no longer claim immunity. On 12 September 2001, *Le Monde*[1] ran its now famous headline: WE ARE ALL AMERICANS. On 12 September 2011, it might more usefully announce: WE ARE ALL INDIANS.

—2011

JEAN BINTA BREEZE (B. 1957)

One of Britain's leading "dub" poets (and a female pioneer in that male-dominated genre), Jean Binta Breeze spent her early years in Jamaica; she has lived primarily in London since the late 1970s. Her work deals extensively with political themes, with a frequent focus on the cultural connections between Britain and the Caribbean. Her books include *Ryddim Ravings* (1988), *The Arrival of Brighteye and Other Poems* (2000), *The Fifth Figure* (2006), and *Third World Girl: selected poems* (2011).

earth cries

She doesn't cry for water
she runs rivers deep
she doesn't cry for food
she has suckled trees
5 she doesn't cry for clothing
she weaves all that she wears
she doesn't cry for shelter
she grows thatch everywhere
she doesn't cry for children
10 she's got more than she can bear
she doesn't cry for heaven
she knows it's everywhere
you don't know why she's crying
when she's got everything
15 how could you know she's crying
for just one humane being

—2000

GWYNETH LEWIS (B. 1959)

A leading poet in both Welsh and English, Gwyneth Lewis has expressed through her work an abiding fascination with issues relating to culture and language. Among her books of poetry in English are *Parables and Faxes* (1995), *Zero Gravity* (1998), *Keeping Mum* (2003), and *Sparrow Tree* (2011). In 2005 she was appointed the first National Poet for Wales.

Mother Tongue

"I started to translate in seventy-three
in the schoolyard. For a bit of fun
to begin with—the occasional 'fuck'
for the bite of another language's smoke
5 at the back of my throat, its bitter chemicals.
Soon I was hooked on whole sentences
behind the shed, and lessons in Welsh
seemed very boring. I started on print,

---

[1] *Le Monde*   Major French newspaper.

Jeeves & Wooster, Dick Francis,[1] James Bond,
10   in Welsh covers. That worked for a while
until Mam discovered Jean Plaidy[2] inside
a Welsh concordance[3] one Sunday night.
There were ructions:[4] a language, she screamed,
should be for a lifetime. Too late for me.
15   Soon I was snorting Simenon
and Flaubert.[5] Had to read much more
for any effect. One night I OD'd
after reading far too much Proust.[6]
I came to, but it scared me. For a while
20   I went Welsh-only but it was bland
and my taste was changing. Before too long
I was back on translating, found that three
languages weren't enough. The 'ch'
in German was easy, Rilke[7] a buzz ...
25   For a language fetishist like me
sex is part of the problem. Umlauts[8] make me sweat,
so I need a multilingual man
but they're rare in West Wales and tend to be
married already. If only I'd kept
30   myself much purer, with simpler tastes,
the Welsh might be living ...
Detective, you speak
Russian, I hear, and Japanese.

Could you whisper some softly?
35   I'm begging you. Please ..."
—2004

---

[1]   *Jeeves & Wooster*   Main characters in a series of popular English comic novels by P.G. Wodehouse (1881–1975); *Dick Francis* Former jockey and author of dozens of popular thrillers set against a backdrop of horseracing (b. 1920).

[2]   *Jean Plaidy*   Popular English author of romance novels (1910–83).

[3]   *concordance*   Alphabetical list of the main words contained in a book, with excerpts from the passages in which they occur.

[4]   *ructions*   Quarrels.

[5]   *Simenon*   Georges Simenon (1903–89), a Belgian novelist best known for his popular detective stories; *Flaubert*   Gustave Flaubert (1821–80), a French novelist perhaps most celebrated for his novel *Madame Bovary* (1856).

[6]   *Proust*   Marcel Proust (1871–1922), a French novelist who was one of the most celebrated literary figures of the late nineteenth and early twentieth centuries; best known for his seven-volume work *À la recherche du temps perdu*.

[7]   *Rilke*   Renowned German poet Rainer Maria Rilke (1875–1926).

[8]   *Umlauts*   Diacritical signs (¨) placed over vowels to express a change in the sound of that vowel because of the influence of an adjacent vowel.

KENAN MALIK (B. 1960)

After studying neurobiology and the history and philosophy of science, Kenan Malik became a lecturer, broadcaster, and writer. His books include *The Meaning of Race* (1996), *Man, Beast and Zombie* (2000), *Strange Fruit* (2008), and *From Fatwa to Jihad* (2009). His writing explores a wide range of topics, including scientific, political, and social thought regarding multiculturalism, race, and human nature.

Multiculturalism and the Road to Terror

How could four ordinary men born and brought up in Britain turn into such savage killers? That is the question Britain has been asking itself in wake of the London tube bombings that killed 52 people on 7 July.[9] Three of the four men involved, Mohammed Sidique Khan, Shehzad Tanweer and Hasib Hussain came from Yorkshire in the North of England. The fourth, Jamaican-born Germaine Lindsay, lived in Luton about 30 miles north of London. None of them were considered extremists, all of them were seemingly well integrated into their communities.

The popular picture of Islamic terrorists is drawn from the caricatures of mad mullahs,[10] bearded fanatics and foreign zealots that people the press. Yet few recent terrorists have fitted this picture. Many have been Western born, Western educated, and seemingly ordinary. The most detailed study yet on Al-Qaeda[11] supporters, carried out by Marc Sageman of the University of Pennsylvania, shows that the majority are middle class with good jobs. Most are college educated,

---

[9]   *London tube ... 7 July*   The series of four coordinated suicide bombings occurred on London's public transit system in 2005.

[10]   *mullahs*   Scholars of Islam.

[11]   *Al-Qaeda*   Islamic fundamentalist organization responsible for several major terrorist attacks, including the 11 September 2001 attacks on the World Trade Center and other American targets.

usually in the West. Fewer than one in 10 have been to religious school.

Shortly after the bombings the government set up an "extremism taskforce," composed mainly of Muslim leaders, to try to answer the question as to how men such as these could get gripped by a fanatic zeal for an irrational, murderous dogma, and be possessed with a hatred for such virtues as democracy and decency. And how could it be prevented from happening again? The taskforce has just published its first conclusions. The London bombings, it reported, were the work of young men alienated by Islamophobia. The best way to combat extremism, the taskforce suggested, is by recognising Muslim grievances and by establishing a more plural society in which moderate Muslim leaders are able to wield greater political power. Its recommendations included a "rapid rebuttal unit" to combat Islamophobia, a better reflection of Islam in the national educational curriculum, a national "roadshow" of Muslim scholars to tour Muslim communities and a training programme for imams.[1]

The taskforce hopes that these proposals will isolate extremists and build a better relationship between Muslims and the government. In fact the proposals will make matters worse. The real problem is not Islamophobia but the culture of grievance created by Britain's multicultural policies. Certainly Muslims face discrimination and harassment. But the extent of such discrimination has been greatly exaggerated by both government and Muslim leaders. There is, for instance, a widespread perception that Muslims are disproportionately stopped and searched by the police under Britain's anti-terror laws. Last year I interviewed Iqbal Sacranie, general secretary of the Muslim Council of Britain, for a documentary I was making for British TV. He claimed that "95 to 98 per cent" of those stopped under the terror laws were Muslim. In fact the vast majority are white. Just 15 per cent are Asians (Britain collects figures by race rather than by religion).

The more that the threat of Islamophobia is embellished in this fashion, the more that ordinary Muslims come to accept that theirs is a community under constant attack. It helps create a siege mentality, stoking up anger and resentment, and making Muslim

community more inward looking and more open to religious extremism. What we need is not for exaggerated grievances to be nurtured but to be challenged.

Muslims have been in Britain in large numbers since the 1950s. Only recently has fanaticism taken hold. The first generation of immigrants faced greater hardships and more intense racism than do today's Muslims. Yet most thought of themselves as British and were proud to be here. While that first generation often put up with racism, the second generation (my generation) challenged it head on, often leading to fierce confrontations with the police and other authorities. But however fierce those confrontations, we recognised that to fight racism we needed to find a common set of values, hopes and aspirations that united whites and non-whites, Muslims and non-Muslims, not separate ourselves from the rest of society.

It has only been over the past decade that radical Islam has found a hearing in Britain. Today "radical" in an Islamic context means someone who espouses a fundamentalist theology. Twenty years ago it meant the opposite: a secularist who challenged the power of the mosques within Muslim communities. The expunging of that radical secularist tradition has played an important part in the rise of Islamic militancy in this country. To understand how this happened we need to look closely at what happened in the 80s and in particular at how the emergence of multicultural policies helped create a more fragmented nation with little sense of a common identity and created the space for the growth of Islamic militancy.

Thirty years ago, Britain was a very different place than it is now. When I was growing up in the 1970s and 1980s racism was vicious, visceral and often fatal. Stabbings were common, firebombings almost weekly events. I remember having to organise patrols on East London estates in the 1980s to protect Asian families from racist thugs. Police harassment was common. The so-called "sus" laws, which allowed the police to stop and search people on "suspicion" of committing an offence were used to persecute immigrant communities. Deaths in police custody were not uncommon; between 1969 and 1999 more than 1000 people died while in the hands of the police. Discrimination in housing, employment and the services was the norm. These issues

---

[1] *imams* Islamic religious leaders.

shaped immigrant struggles. In the sixties and seventies four main issues dominated the struggle for racial equality: opposition to discriminatory immigration controls; the fight against racist attacks; the struggle for equality in the workplace; and, most explosively, the issue of police brutality.

These struggles politicised a new generation of activists and came to an explosive climax in the inner city riots of the late seventies and early eighties. Just as the extremism taskforce argues now, so the authorities argued then that unless black and Asian communities were given a political stake in the system, their frustration could threaten the stability of British cities. It was against this background that the policies of multiculturalism emerged. The Greater London Council, led by Ken Livingstone (who today is the mayor of London) pioneered a new strategy of making immigrant communities feel part of British society. It organised consultation with black and Asian communities, drew up equal opportunities policies, established race relations units and dispensed millions of pounds in grants to community organisations.

At the heart of the strategy was a redefinition of racism. Racism now meant not simply the denial of equal rights but the denial of the right to be different. Black and Asian people, many argued, should not be forced to accept British values, or to adopt a British identity. Rather different peoples should have the right to express their identities, explore their own histories, formulate their own values, pursue their own lifestyles. In this process, the very meaning of equality was transformed: from possessing the same rights as everyone else to possessing different rights, appropriate to different communities. Equality no longer meant treating everybody equally despite their racial, cultural, ethnic or religious differences but treating people differently because of them.

Many local authorities followed London's lead, including Bradford, the heart of Britain's Muslim community. By the early 80s Bradford too was facing militancy within Asian communities and unrest on the streets. In 1977 young Asians formed the Asian Youth Movement (AYM) to defend their civil rights. AYM activists did not distinguish themselves as Muslim, Hindu or Sikh; indeed many did not even see them-

selves as specifically Asian, preferring to call themselves "black" which they viewed as an all-inclusive term for non-white immigrants. They challenged not just racism but also many traditional values too, particularly within the Muslim community, helping establish an alternative leadership that confronted traditionalists on issues such as the role of women and the dominance of the mosque. In response, Bradford council drew up equal opportunity statements, established race relations units and began funding Asian organisations. A 12-point race relations plan declared that every section of the "multiracial, multicultural city" had "an equal right to maintain its own identity, culture, language, religion and customs."

Multiculturalism transformed the character of antiracism. By the mid-eighties the focus of antiracist protest in Bradford had shifted from political issues, such as policing and immigration, to religious and cultural issues: a demand for Muslim schools and for separate education for girls, a campaign for halal[1] meat to be served at school, and, most explosively, the confrontation over the publication of Salman Rushdie's *The Satanic Verses*.[2]

Political struggles unite across ethnic or cultural divisions; cultural struggles inevitably fragment. As different groups began asserting their particular identities ever more fiercely, so the shift from the political to the cultural arena helped create a more tribal city. At the same time, since every group was now defined by its culture, militancy came to be seen as the demand for greater cultural authenticity. Secular Muslims were regarded as betraying their culture while radical Islam became not just more acceptable but, to many, more authentic.

This process was strengthened by a new relationship between the local council and the local mosques. In 1981, the council helped set up and fund the Bradford Council of Mosques and looked to it as a voice of the

---

[1] *halal* In conformity with Islamic law; the term is frequently applied to food that is prepared in the appropriate way.

[2] *confrontation over ... Satanic Verses* *The Satanic Verses* (1988), a novel by Salman Rushdie, was condemned by many Muslim leaders for its portrayal of the prophet Muhammed, and there were violent protests in the United Kingdom and elsewhere against Rushdie. Iran's leader, Ayatollah Ruhollah Khomeini, issued a *fatwā* calling for Rushdie to be killed, and the author went into hiding for several years.

community. This helped marginalise secular radicals—the Asian Youth Movement eventually broke up—and allowed religious leaders to reassert their power. As the secular tradition became squeezed out, so the only place offering shelter for disaffected youth was militant Islam.

In the wake of the London bombings much was said about the strength of Britain as a multicultural nation. What makes London great, mayor Ken Livingstone pointed out, was what the bombers most fear: a city full of people from across the globe free to pursue their own lives. I agree, and that's why I choose to live in this city. Multiculturalism as a lived experience enriches our lives. But multiculturalism as a political ideology has helped create a tribal Britain with no political or moral centre.

For an earlier generation of Muslims their religion was not so strong that it prevented them from identifying with Britain. Today many young British Muslims identify more with Islam than Britain primarily because there no longer seems much that is compelling about being British. Of course, there is little to romanticise in old-style Britishness with its often racist vision of belongingness. Back in the fifties policy makers feared that, in the words of a Colonial Office report, "a large coloured community would weaken ... the concept of England or Britain."

That old racist notion of identity has thankfully crumbled. But nothing new has come to replace it. The very notion of creating common values has been abandoned except at a most minimal level. Britishness has come to be defined simply as a toleration of difference. The politics of ideology has given way to the politics of identity, creating a more fragmented Britain, and one where many groups assert their identity through a sense of victimhood and grievance, something that has been particularly true of Muslim communities. Multiculturalism did not create militant Islam, but it helped create a space for it within British Muslim communities that had not existed before. It fostered a more tribal nation, created a grievance culture, strengthened the hand of conservative religious leaders, undermined progressive trends within the Muslim communities and created a vacuum into which radical Islam stepped, and all in the name of combating racism. The danger with the recommendations of the extremism taskforce is that history might be about to repeat itself.

—2006

JACKIE KAY (B. 1961)

Born in Scotland to a Nigerian father and Scottish mother, Jackie Kay was brought up by adoptive parents; her first book of poetry, *The Adoption Papers* (1991), focuses on issues of personal and cultural identity. Among her widely praised subsequent works are the poetry collections *Other Lovers* (1993), *Life Mask* (2005), and *Fiere* (2011); the memoir *Red Dust Road* (2010); and the novel *Trumpet* (1998).

In My Country

Walking by the waters
down where an honest river
shakes hands with the sea,
a woman passed round me
in a slow watchful circle,   5
as if I were a superstition;

or the worst dregs of her imagination,
so when she finally spoke
her words spliced into bars
of an old wheel. A segment of air.   10
"*Where do you come from?*"
"Here," I said. "Here. These parts."
—1991

SIMON ARMITAGE (B. 1963)

Simon Armitage is equally at home with subtle lyricism and with the poetry of politics and performance. A native of northern England, Armitage has written widely in many genres. His books of poetry include *Zoom!* (1989), *Kid* (1992), *The Universal Home Doctor* (2002), *Tyrannosaurus Rex Versus the Corduroy Kid* (2006), and *Seeing Stars* (2010).

The English

They are a gentleman farmer, living
on reduced means, a cricketer's widow
sowing a kitchen garden with sweet peas.
A lighthouse-keeper counting aeroplanes.

5   Old blackout curtains staunch the break of day.
Regard the way they dwell, the harking back:
how the women at home went soldiering on
with pillows for husbands, fingers for sons,

how man after man emerged at dawn
10   from his house, in his socks, then laced his boots
on the step, locked up, then steadied himself
to post a key back through the letterbox.

The afternoon naps, the quaint hours they keep.
But since you ask them, that is how they sleep.
—2002

It Could Be You

We interrupt our live coverage of the War
for details of tonight's National Lottery draw:

the winning numbers are fourteen, eighteen,
thirty-nine, forty-four, eighty-two, and ninety-one.

5   The bonus ball is number two-thousand-and-some.
A record jackpot pay-out will be shared between

winning ticket holders in Belfast, Aberdeen,
Milford Haven and East Acton. Now back to the
        action.
—2002

COLUM McCANN (B. 1965)

Dublin-born Colum McCann has traveled the
world, and the settings of his thoroughly
researched novels and short stories range from
Ireland to New York to Russia. His books,
praised for engaging storytelling as well as
graceful prose, include *Songdogs* (1996), *Everything in This Country Must* (2001), *Let the Great World Spin* (2009), and *TransAtlantic* (2013).
He lives in New York, where he teaches creative
writing at Hunter College.

Dessert

The sky would always be this shade of blue. The
towers had come down the day before.[1] Third
Avenue on the Upper East Side was a flutter of missing
faces, the posters taped to the mailboxes, plastered on
windows, flapping against the light poles: "Looking for
Derek Sword"; "Have You Seen This Person?"; "Matt
Heard: Worked for Morgan Stanley."[2] The streets were
quieter than usual. The ash fell, as ash will.

Everything felt honed down to the necessary,
except for one woman who sat alone at an outdoor table
in a restaurant on Seventy-fourth Street. She had just
ordered a piece of chocolate cake. It arrived in front of
her, and the waiter spun away. A slice of two-layer cake.
Dark chocolate. A nipple of cream dolloped on top. A
sprinkling of dark powder. The woman was elegant,
fiftyish, beautiful. She touched the edge of the plate,
brought it toward her.

At any other time, it would have been just a piece
of cake, a collision of cocoa and flour and eggs. But so
much of what the city was about had just been
levelled—not just the towers but a sense of the city
itself, the desire, the greed, the appetite, the unrelenting
pursuit of the present. The woman unrolled a fork from
a paper napkin, held it at her mouth, tapping the tines
against her teeth. She ran the fork, then, through the
powder, addressing the cake, scribbling her intent.

Our job is to be epic and tiny, both. Three
thousand lives in New York had just disintegrated into
the air. Nobody could have known it for certain then,
but hundreds of thousands of lives would hang in the

---

1   *The towers ... day before*   I.e., it was the day after the 11 September 2001 attacks on the World Trade Center and other American targets.

2   *Morgan Stanley*   International finance firm.

balance—in Baghdad, Kabul, London, Madrid, Basra.[1] The ordinary shoves up against the monumental. When big things fall, they shatter into fragments. They crash down and scatter over a very large landscape. It was apparent, even one day after the attacks, that so much of the world had felt the impact.

Still, there is a need, now and always, for sharply felt local intimacies. I stood by the corner and watched the woman's dilemma. It could have been grief, it could have been grace, or even a dark, perverse sense of humour. She held the forkful of cake for a very long time. As if it were waiting to speak to her, to tell her what to do. Finally, she ate a bite of it. She sat looking into the distance. She pulled her lips along the silver tines to catch whatever chocolate remained there, then turned the fork upside down, ran her tongue along it. It was the gesture of someone whose body was in one place, her mind in another. She pierced the cake again.

The darkness rose over the Upper East Side. The woman finished her dessert. She didn't pinch the crumbs. She placed the fork across the plate. She paid. She left. She didn't look at anyone as she turned the corner toward Lexington Avenue, but she still returns to me after all this time, one corner after another, a full decade now.

My mind is decorated with splinters. Ten years of enmity and loss. Bush, Cheney, Blackwater, Halli-burton, Guantánamo, Abu Ghraib, bin Laden.[2] Another long series of wars, another short distance travelled. We do not necessarily need anniversaries when there are things we cannot forget. Yet I also recall this simple, sensual moment. I still have no idea—after a decade of wondering—whether I am furious at the woman and the way she ate chocolate cake, or whether it was one of the most audacious acts of grief I've seen in a long, long time.

—2011

ALICE OSWALD (B. 1967)

Trained as a classicist and as a gardener, Alice Oswald has established herself as one of Britain's most distinctive poetic voices: a poet of nature, of the mysterious, and of the musical. Her books include *The Gap-Stone Stile* (1996), *Dart* (2002), *Woods etc.* (2005), *A Sleepwalk on the Severn* (2009), and *Memorial* (2011).

Dunt[3]

a poem for a nearly dried-up river

Very small and damaged and quite dry,
a Roman water nymph[4] made of bone
tries to summon a river out of limestone.

---

[1] *Baghdad* Capital of Iraq, which was invaded by the United States in 2003. The justification for going to war offered by then-President George W. Bush and the American government involved claims that Iran had links to Al-Qaeda, the group responsible for the terrorist attacks in the United States on 11 September 2001. Similar claims had been advanced to justify the war launched by the US and various allies in Afghanistan, which began in 2001; whereas the Afghanistan government had indeed been allowing Al-Qaeda to operate within its borders, no evidence ever emerged of a link between Iran and Al Qaeda. The Iraq War (2003–11) nevertheless continued to be referred to for many years by the Bush administration as part of a more wide-ranging "War on Terror"; *Kabul* Capital of Afghanistan; *London* In 2005, more than fifty people died in a coordinated series of suicide bombings on London's public transit system, carried out by Islamic fundamentalists. The United Kingdom played a significant role in the wars in Afghanistan and in Iraq; *Madrid* In 2004, almost two hundred people died when an Islamic fundamentalist organization bombed several commuter trains in Madrid. Spain participated in the War in Afghanistan and, briefly, in Iraq; *Basra* Southern Iraq city, a site of heavy fighting during the Iraq War.

[2] *Bush* George W. Bush (b. 1946), President of the United States 2001–09; *Cheney* Dick Cheney (b. 1941), Vice President to George W. Bush; *Blackwater* Private security company employed by the American government in Iraq. Its actions during the war have been a subject of controversy; *Halliburton* Oil company that was awarded large American government contracts during the Iraq War. Allegations of corruption were directed at both the government and the corporation; *Guantánamo* Guantánamo Bay, Cuba, the site of a detention facility operated by the American military to hold suspected terrorists. There have been allegations of human rights abuses at the facility; *Abu Ghraib* Iraq prison where members of the American military subjected prisoners to torture and extreme abuse in 2003–04; *bin Laden* Osama bin Laden (1957–2011), leader of al-Qaeda, an Islamic fundamentalist organization responsible for the attacks of 11 September 2001.

[3] *Dunt* Stream in the Gloucestershire county area of England.

[4] *nymph* In classical mythology, a beautiful spirit associated with a natural setting.

Very eroded faded,
5 her left arm missing and both legs from the knee down,
a Roman water nymph made of bone
tries to summon a river out of limestone.

Exhausted, utterly worn down,
a Roman water nymph made of bone,
10 being the last known speaker of her language,
she tries to summon a river out of limestone.

Little distant sound of dry grass. Try again.

A Roman water nymph made of bone,
very endangered now,
15 in a largely unintelligible monotone,
she tries to summon a river out of limestone.

Little distant sound as of dry grass. Try again.

Exquisite bone figurine with upturned urn,
in her passionate self-esteem, she smiles, looking
sideways.
20 She seemingly has no voice but a throat-clearing rustle
as of dry grass. Try again.

She tries leaning,
pouring pure outwardness from a grey urn.

Little slithering sounds as of a rabbit man in full night
gear.
25 Who lies so low in the rickety willow herb
that a fox trots out of the woods
and over his back and away. Try again.
Very small and damaged and quite dry,
a Roman water nymph made of bone,
30 she pleads, she pleads a river out of limestone.

Little hobbling tripping of a nearly dried-up river
not really moving through the fields,
having had the gleam taken out of it
to the point where it resembles twilight.
35 Little grumbling shivering last-ditch attempt at a river
more nettles than water. Try again.

Very speechless, very broken old woman,
her left arm missing and both legs from the knee
down,
she tries to summon a river out of limestone.

40 Little stoved-in, sucked-thin
low-burning glint of stones,
rough-sleeping and trembling and clinging to its rights.
Victim of Swindon.[1]
Puddle midden.[2]
45 Slum of overgreened foot-churn and pats
whose crayfish are cheap toolkits
made of the mud stirred up when a stone's lifted.

It's a pitiable likeness of clear running,
struggling to keep up with what's already gone:
50 the boat the wheel the sluice gate,
the two otters larricking° along. Go on.   *gallivanting*

And they say oh they say
in the days of better rainfall
it would flood through five valleys, there'd be cows
55 and milking stools
washed over the garden walls
and when it froze you could skate for five miles. Yes
go on.

Little loose-end shorthand unrepresented
beautiful disused route to the sea,
60 fish path with nearly no fish in.
    —2006

Caitriona O'Reilly (b. 1973)

A native of Dublin, Caitriona O'Reilly holds a
doctorate in American literature from Trinity
College; she has worked as a teacher, critic,
translator, writer, and editor of *Ireland Poetry
Review* (2008–11). Her books include the
award-winning *The Nowhere Birds* (2001) and
The Sea Cabinet (2006).

---

[1] *Swindon*   Town in Wiltshire, England.

[2] *midden*   Garbage heap.

A Brief History of Light

And the light shineth in darkness;
and the darkness comprehended it not.[1]

The dazzle of ocean was their first infatuation,
  its starry net, and the fish that mirrored it.
They knew enough to know it was not theirs.
Over the hill a dozen furnaces glowed,
5 the gold gleamed that was smelted in secret,
and the trapped white light shone bitterly
at the heart of the hardest stone on earth.
But they knew enough to know it was not theirs.
Then their hoards of light grew minor,
10 since none could view the sun straightly,
and jealousy burned their lives to the core.
So they made a god of it, shedding glory,
shedding his light on all their arguments.

Did they know enough to know it was not theirs?
15 The god in his wisdom preceded them westwards,
and the forests, in whose pillared interiors
black shapes dwelled, were banished for good.
They promised an end to the primitive darkness:
soon there was nothing that was not known.
20 They thought: *Our light is made, not merely reflected—*
even the forked lightning we have braided!
And they banished the god from the light of their
    minds.
But they mistook the light for their knowledge of the
    light,
till light, and only light, was everywhere.
25 And they vanished in this, their last illumination,
Knowing barely enough to know it was not theirs.
—2001

---

[1] *And the light ... it not*   John 1.5.

READING POETRY

WHAT IS A POEM?

Most of us know what a poem is when we see one. Still, even poets find it difficult to define a poem, or poetry. In a lecture on "The Name and Nature of Poetry" (1933), the English poet A.E. Housman stated that he could "no more define poetry than a terrier can define a rat"; however, he added, "we both recognize the object by the symptoms which it provokes in us." Housman knew he was in the presence of poetry if he experienced a shiver down the spine, or "a constriction of the throat and a precipitation of water to the eyes." Implicit in Housman's response is a recognition that we have to go beyond mere formal characteristics—stanzas, rhymes, rhythms—if we want to know what poetry is, or why it differs from prose. Poetry both represents and *creates* emotions in a highly condensed way. Therefore, any definition of the genre needs to consider, as much as possible, the impact of poetry on us as readers or listeners.

Worth consideration too is the role of the listener or reader not only as passive recipient of a poem, but also as an active participant in its performance. Poetry is among other things the locus for a communicative exchange. A section below deals with the sub-genre of performance poetry, but in a very real sense all poetry is subject to performance. Poems are to be read aloud as well as on the page, and both in sensing meaning and in expressing sound the reader plays a vital role in bringing a poem to life, no matter how long dead its author may be; as W.H. Auden wrote memorably of his fellow poet W.B. Yeats, "the words of a dead man / Are modified in the guts of the living."

For some readers, poetry is, in William Wordsworth's phrase, "the breath and finer spirit of all knowledge" ("Preface" to the *Lyrical Ballads*). They look to poetry for insights into the nature of human experience, and expect elevated thought in carefully wrought language. In contrast, other readers distrust poetry that seems moralistic or didactic. "We hate poetry that has a palpable design upon us," wrote John Keats to his friend J.H. Reynolds; rather, poetry should be "great & unobtrusive, a thing which enters into one's soul, and does not startle it or amaze it with itself but with its subject." The American poet Archibald MacLeish took Keats's idea a step further: in his poem "Ars Poetica" he suggested that "A poem should not mean / But be." MacLeish was not suggesting that a poem should lack meaning, but rather that meaning should inhere in the poem's expressive and sensuous qualities, not in some explicit statement or versified idea.

Whatever we look for in a poem, the infinitude of forms, styles, and subjects that make up the body of literature we call "poetry" is, in the end, impossible to capture in a definition that would satisfy all readers. All we can do, perhaps, is to agree that a poem is a discourse that is characterized by a heightened attention to language, form, and rhythm, by an expressiveness that works through figurative rather than literal modes, and by a capacity to stimulate our imagination and arouse our feelings.

THE LANGUAGE OF POETRY

To speak of "the language of poetry" implies that poets make use of a vocabulary that is somehow different from the language of everyday life. In fact, all language has the capacity to be "poetic," if by poetry we understand a use of language to which some special importance is attached. The ritualistic utterances of religious ceremonies sometimes have this force; so do the skipping rhymes of children in the schoolyard. We can distinguish such uses of language from the kind of writing we find in, say, a computer user's manual: the author of the manual can describe a given function in a variety of ways, whereas the magic of the skipping rhyme can be invoked only by getting the right words in the right order. So with the poet: he or she chooses particular words in a particular order; the *way* the poet speaks is as important to our understanding as what is said. This doesn't mean that an instruction manual couldn't have poetic qualities—indeed, modern poets have created "found" poems from even less likely materials—but it does mean that in poetry there is an intimate relation amongst language, form, and meaning, and that the writer deliberately structures and manipulates language to achieve very particular ends.

THE BEST WORDS IN THE BEST ORDER

Wordsworth provides us with a useful example of the way that poetry can invest quite ordinary words with a high emotional charge:

> No motion has she now, no force,
> She neither hears nor sees;
> Rolled round in earth's diurnal course
> With rocks, and stones, and trees.

To paraphrase the content of this stanza from "A Slumber Did My Spirit Seal," "she" is dead and buried. But the language and structures used here give this prosaic idea great impact. For example, the regular iambic meter of the two last lines conveys something of the inexorable motion of the earth and of Lucy embedded in it; the monosyllabic last line is a grim reminder of her oneness with objects in nature; the repeated negatives in the first two lines drive home the irreparable destructiveness of death; the alliteration in the third and fourth lines gives a tangible suggestion of roundness, circularity, repetition in terms of the earth's shape and motion, suggesting a cycle in which death is perhaps followed by renewal. Even the unusual word "diurnal" (which would not have seemed so unusual to Wordsworth's readers) seems "right" in this context; it lends more weight to the notion of the earth's perpetual movement than its mundane synonym "daily" (which, besides, would not scan here). It is difficult to imagine a change of any kind to these lines; they exemplify another attempted definition of poetry, this time by Wordsworth's friend Samuel Taylor Coleridge: "the best words in the best order" (*Table Talk*, 1827).

POETIC DICTION AND THE ELEVATED STYLE

Wordsworth's diction in the "Lucy" poem cited above is a model of clarity; he has chosen language that, in its simplicity and bluntness, conveys the strength of the speaker's feelings far more strongly than an elaborate description of grief in more conventionally "poetic" language might have done. Wordsworth, disturbed by what he felt was a deadness and artificiality in the poetry of his day, sought to "choose incidents and situations from common life" and to describe them in "a selection of language really used by men" ("Preface" to *Lyrical Ballads*). His plan might seem an implicit reproach of the "raised" style, the elevated diction of epic poetry we associate with John Milton's *Paradise Lost*:

> Anon out of the earth a fabric huge
> Rose like an exhalation, with the sound
> Of dulcet symphonies and voices sweet,

> Built like a temple, where pilasters round
> Were set, and Doric pillars overlaid
> With golden architrave; nor did there want
> Cornice or frieze, with bossy sculptures graven;
> The roof was fretted gold.
>
> (*Paradise Lost* I.710–17)

At first glance this passage, with its Latinate vocabulary and convoluted syntax, might seem guilty of inflated language and pretentiousness. However, Milton's description of the devils' palace in Hell deliberately seeks to distance us from its subject in order to emphasize the scale and sublimity of the spectacle, far removed from ordinary human experience. In other words, language and style in *Paradise Lost* are well adapted to suit a particular purpose, just as they are in "A Slumber Did My Spirit Seal," though on a wholly different scale. Wordsworth criticized the poetry of his day, not because of its elevation, but because the raised style was too often out of touch with its subject; in his view, the words did not bear any significant relation to the "truths" they were attempting to depict.

"PLAIN" LANGUAGE IN POETRY

Since Wordsworth's time, writers have been conscious of a need to narrow the apparent gap between "poetic" language and the language of everyday life. In much of the poetry of the past century, especially free verse, we can observe a growing approximation to speech—even to conversation—in the diction and rhythms of poetry. This may have something to do with the changed role of the poet, who today has discarded the mantle of teacher or prophet that was assumed by poets of earlier times, and who is ready to admit all fields of experience and endeavor as appropriate for poetry. The modern poet looks squarely at life, and can often find a provoking beauty in even the meanest of objects.

We should not assume, however, that a greater concern with the "ordinary," with simplicity, naturalness, and clarity, means a reduction in complexity or suggestiveness. A piece such as Stevie Smith's "Mother, Among the Dustbins," for all the casual and playful domesticity of some of its lines, skillfully evokes a range of emotions and sense impressions defying simple paraphrase.

IMAGERY, SYMBOLISM, AND FIGURES OF SPEECH

The language of poetry is grounded in the objects and phenomena that create sensory impressions. Sometimes the poet renders these impressions quite literally, in a series of *images* that seek to recreate a scene in the reader's mind:

> Only a man harrowing clods
> In a slow silent walk
> With an old horse that stumbles and nods
> Half asleep as they stalk.
>
> Only thin smoke without flame
> From the heaps of couch-grass;
> Yet this will go onward the same
> Though Dynasties pass.

Yonder a maid and her wight
Come whispering by:
War's annals will cloud into night
Ere their story die.
            (Thomas Hardy, "In Time of 'The Breaking of Nations'")

Here, the objects of everyday life are re-created with sensory details designed to evoke in us the sensations or responses felt by the speaker viewing the scene. At the same time, the writer invests the objects with such significance that the poem's meaning extends beyond the literal to the symbolic: that is, the images come to stand for something much larger than the objects they represent. Hardy's poem moves from the presentation of stark images of rural life to a sense of their timelessness. By the last stanza we see the ploughman, the burning grass, and the maid and her companion as symbols of recurring human actions and motives that defy the struggles and conflicts of history.

IMAGISM

The juxtaposition of clear, forceful images is associated particularly with the Imagist movement that flourished at the beginning of the twentieth century. Its chief representatives (in their early work) were the American poets H.D. and Ezra Pound, who defined an image as "that which represents an intellectual and emotional complex in an instant of time." Pound's two-line poem "In a Station of the Metro" provides a good example of the Imagists' goal of representing emotions or impressions through the use of concentrated images:

The apparition of these faces in the crowd,
    Petals on a wet, black bough.

As in a Japanese *haiku*, a form that strongly influenced the Imagists, the poem uses sharp, clear, concrete details to evoke both a sensory impression and the emotion or the atmosphere of the scene. Though the Imagist movement itself lasted only a short time (from about 1912 to 1917), it had a far-reaching influence on modern poets such as T.S. Eliot and William Carlos Williams.

FIGURES OF SPEECH

Imagery often works together with figurative expression to extend and deepen the meaning or impact of a poem. "Figurative" language means language that is metaphorical, not literal or referential. Through "figures of speech" such as metaphor and simile, metonymy, synecdoche, and personification, the writer may alter the ordinary, denotative meanings of words in order to convey greater force and vividness to ideas or impressions, often by showing likenesses between unlike things.

With *simile*, the poet makes an explicit comparison between the subject (called the *tenor*) and another object or idea (known as the *vehicle*), using "as" or "like":

It is a beauteous evening, calm and free,
The holy time is quiet as a Nun
Breathless with adoration. ...

In this opening to a sonnet, Wordsworth uses a visual image of a nun in devout prayer to convey in concrete terms the less tangible idea of evening as a "holy time." The comparison also introduces an emotional dimension, conveying something of the feeling that the scene induces in the poet. The simile can thus illuminate and expand meaning in a compact way. The poet may also extend the simile to elaborate at length on any points of likeness.

In *metaphor*, the comparison between tenor and vehicle is implied: connectives such as "like" are omitted, and a kind of identity is created between the subject and the term with which it is being compared. Thus in John Donne's "The Good-Morrow," a lover asserts the endless joy that he and his beloved find in each other:

> My face in thine eye, thine in mine appears,
> And true plain hearts do in the faces rest;
> Where can we find two better hemispheres,
> Without sharp north, without declining west?

Here the lovers are transformed into "hemispheres," each of them a half of the world not subject to the usual natural phenomena of wintry cold ("sharp north") or the coming of night ("declining west"). Thus, they form a perfect world in balance, in which the normal processes of decay or decline have been arrested. Donne renders the abstract idea of a love that defies change in pictorial and physical terms, making it more real and accessible to us. The images here are all the more arresting for the degree of concentration involved; it is not merely the absence of "like" or "as" that gives the metaphor such direct power, but the fusion of distinct images and emotions into a new idea.

Personification is the figure of speech in which the writer endows abstract ideas, inanimate objects, or animals with human characteristics. In other words, it is a type of implied metaphorical comparison in which aspects of a non-human subject are compared to the feelings, appearance, or actions of a human being. In the second stanza of his ode "To Autumn," Keats personifies the concept of autumnal harvesting in the form of a woman, "sitting careless on a granary floor, / Thy hair soft-lifted by the winnowing wind." Personification may also help to create a mood, as when Thomas Gray attributes human feelings to a hooting owl in "Elegy Written in a Country Churchyard"; using such words as "moping" and "complain," Gray invests the bird's cries with the quality of human melancholy:

> … from yonder ivy-mantled tow'r
> The moping owl does to the moon complain
> Of such, as wand'ring near her secret bow'r,
> Molest her ancient solitary reign.

In his book *Modern Painters* (1856), the English critic John Ruskin criticized such attribution of human feelings to objects in nature. Calling this device the "pathetic fallacy," he objected to what he saw as an irrational distortion of reality, producing "a falseness in all our impressions of external things." Modern criticism, with a distrust of any notions of an objective "reality," tends to use Ruskin's term as a neutral label simply to describe instances of extended personification of natural objects.

Apostrophe, which is closely related to personification, has the speaker directly addressing a non-human object or idea as if it were a sentient human listener. Blake's "The Sick Rose," Shelley's "Ode to the West Wind," and his ode "To a Sky-Lark" all employ apostrophe, personifying the object addressed. Keats's "Ode on a Grecian Urn" begins by apostrophizing the urn ("Thou still unravish'd bride of quietness"), then addresses it in a series of questions and reflections through which the speaker attempts to unravel the urn's mysteries.

Apostrophe also appeals to or addresses a person who is absent or dead. W.H. Auden's lament "In Memory of W.B. Yeats" apostrophizes both the earth in which Yeats is to be buried ("Earth, receive an honoured guest") and the dead poet himself ("Follow, poet, follow right / To the bottom of the night …"). Religious prayers offer an illustration of the usefulness of apostrophe, since they are direct appeals from an earth-bound supplicant to an invisible god. The suggestion of strong emotion associated with such appeals is a common feature of apostrophe in poetry also, especially poetry with a religious theme, like Donne's "Holy Sonnets" (e.g., "Batter My Heart, Three-Personed God").

Metonymy and *synecdoche* are two closely related figures of speech that further illustrate the power of metaphorical language to convey meaning more intensely and vividly than is possible with prosaic statement. *Metonymy* (from the Greek, meaning "change of name") involves referring to an object or concept by substituting the name of another object or concept with which it is usually associated: for example, we might speak of "the Crown" when we mean the monarch, or describe the US executive branch as "the White House." When the writer uses only part of something to signify the whole, or an individual to represent a class, we have an instance of *synecdoche*: T.S. Eliot provides an example in "The Love Song of J. Alfred Prufrock" when a crab is described as "a pair of ragged claws." Similarly, synecdoche is present in Milton's contemptous term "blind mouths" to describe the "corrupted clergy" he attacks in "Lycidas."

Dylan Thomas employs both metonymy and synecdoche in his poem "The Hand That Signed the Paper":

> The hand that signed the paper felled a city;
> Five sovereign fingers taxed the breath,
> Doubled the globe of dead and halved a country;
> These five kings did a king to death.
>
> The mighty hand leads to a sloping shoulder,
> The finger joints are cramped with chalk;
> A goose's quill has put an end to murder
> That put an end to talk.
>
> The hand that signed the treaty bred a fever,
> And famine grew, and locusts came;
> Great is the hand that holds dominion over
> Man by a scribbled name.
>
> The five kings count the dead but do not soften
> The crusted wound nor stroke the brow;
> A hand rules pity as a hand rules heaven;
> Hands have no tears to flow.

The "hand" of the poem is evidently a synecdoche for a great king who enters into treaties with friends and foes to wage wars, conquer kingdoms, and extend his personal power—all at the expense of his suffering subjects. The "goose quill" of the second stanza is a metonymy, standing for the pen used to sign the treaty or the death warrant that brings the war to an end.

Thomas's poem is an excellent example of the power of figurative language, which, by its vividness and concentrated force, can add layers of meaning to a poem, make abstract ideas concrete, and intensify the poem's emotional impact.

THE POEM AS PERFORMANCE: WRITER AND PERSON

Poetry is always dramatic. Sometimes the drama is explicit, as in Robert Browning's monologues, in which we hear the voice of a participant in a dialogue; in "My Last Duchess" we are present as the Duke reflects on the portrait of his late wife for the benefit of a visitor who has come to negotiate on behalf of the woman who is to become the Duke's next wife. Or we listen with amusement and pity as the dying Bishop addresses his venal and unsympathetic sons and tries to bargain with them for a fine burial ("The Bishop Orders His Tomb at St. Praxed's"). In such poems, the notion of a speaking voice is paramount: the speaker is a personage in a play, and the poem a means of conveying plot and character.

Sometimes the drama is less apparent, and takes the form of a plea, or a compliment, or an argument addressed to a silent listener. In Donne's "The Flea" we can infer from the poem the situation that has called it forth: a lover's advances are being rejected by his beloved, and his poem is an argument intended to overcome her reluctance by means of wit and logic. We can see a similar example in Marvell's "To His Coy Mistress": here the very shape of the poem, its three-paragraph structure, corresponds to the stages of the speaker's argument as he presents an apparently irrefutable line of reasoning. Much love poetry has this kind of background as its inspiration; the yearnings or lamentations of the lover are part of an imagined scene, not merely versified reflections about an abstraction called "love."

Meditative or reflective poetry can be dramatic too. Donne's "Holy Sonnets" are pleas from a tormented soul struggling to find its god; Tennyson's "In Memoriam" follows the agonized workings of a mind tracing a path from grief and anger to acceptance and renewed hope.

We should never assume that the speaker, the "I" of the poem, is simply a voice for the writer's own views. The speaker in W.H. Auden's "To an Unknown Citizen," presenting a summary of the dead citizen's life, appears to be an official spokesperson for the society which the citizen served ("Our report on his union"; "Our researchers ..." etc.). The speaker's words are laudatory, yet we perceive immediately that Auden's own views of this society are anything but approving. The speaker seems satisfied with the highly regimented nature of his society, one in which every aspect of the individual's life is under scrutiny and subject to correction. The only things necessary to the happiness of the "Modern Man," it seems, are "A phonograph, a radio, a car, and a frigidaire." The tone here is subtly ironic, an irony created by the gap between the imagined speaker's perception and the real feelings of the writer.

PERFORMANCE POETRY

Poetry began as an oral art, passed on in the form of chants, myths, ballads, and legends recited to an audience of listeners rather than readers. Even today, the dramatic qualities of a poem may extend beyond written text. "Performance poets" combine poetry and stagecraft in presenting their work to live audiences. Dramatic uses of voice, rhythm, body movement, music, and sometimes other visual effects make the "text" of the poem multi-dimensional. For example, Edith Sitwell's poem-sequence *Façade* (1922) was originally set to music: Sitwell read from behind a screen, while a live orchestra played. This performance was designed to enhance the verbal and rhythmic qualities of her poetry:

Beneath the flat and paper sky
The sun, a demon's eye
Glowed through the air, that mask of glass;
All wand'ring sounds that pass

Seemed out of tune, as if the light
Were fiddle-strings pulled tight.
The market-square with spire and bell
Clanged out the hour in Hell.

By performing their poetry, writers can also convey cultural values and traditions. The cultural aspect of performance is central to Black poetry, which originates in a highly oral tradition of folklore and storytelling. From its roots in Africa, this oral tradition has been manifested in the songs and stories of slaves, in spirituals, in the jazz rhythms of the Twenties and the Thirties and in the rebelliousness of reggae and of rap. Even when it remains "on the page," much Black poetry written in the oral tradition has a compelling rhythmic quality. The lines below from Linton Kwesi Johnson's "Mi Revalueshanary Fren," for example, blur the line between spoken poetry and song. Johnson often performs his "dub poetry" against reggae musical backings.

yes, people powa jus a showa evry howa
an evrybady claim dem democratic
but some a wolf an some a sheep
an dat is problematic

The chorus of Johnson's poems, with its constant repetitions, digs deeply into the roots of African song and chant. Its performance qualities become clearer when the poem is read aloud:

Husak
e ad to go
Honnicka
e ad to go
Chowcheskhu
e ad to go
Just like apartied
will av to go

To perform a poem is one way to see and hear poetry as multi-dimensional, cultural, historical, and often also political. Performance is also another way to discover how poetic "meaning" can be constructed in the dynamic relation between speaker and listener.

TONE: THE SPEAKER'S ATTITUDE

In understanding poetry, it is helpful to imagine a poem as having a "voice." The voice may be close to the poet's own, or that of an imagined character, a *persona* adopted by the poet. The tone of the voice will reveal the speaker's attitude to the subject, thus helping to shape our understanding and response. In speech we can indicate our feelings by raising or lowering our voices, and we can accompany words with physical actions. In writing, we must try to convey the tonal inflections of the speaking voice through devices of language and rhythm, through imagery and figures of speech, and through allusions and contrasts.

THE IRONIC TONE

Housman's poem "Terence, This Is Stupid Stuff" offers a useful example of ways in which manipulating tone can reinforce meaning. When Housman, presenting himself in the poem as "Terence," imagines himself to be criticized for writing gloomy poems, his response to his critics takes the form of an ironic alternative: perhaps they should stick to drinking ale:

> Oh, many a peer of England brews
> Livelier liquor than the Muse,
> And malt does more than Milton can
> To justify God's ways to man.

The tone here is one of heavy scorn. The speaker is impatient with those who refuse to look at the realities of life and death, and who prefer to take refuge in simple-minded pleasure. The ludicrous comparisons, first between the brewers who have been made peers of England and the classical Muse of poetry, then between malt and Milton, create a sense of disproportion and ironic tension; the explicit allusion to *Paradise Lost* ("To justify God's ways to man") helps to drive home the poet's bitter recognition that his auditors are part of that fallen world depicted by Milton, yet unable or unwilling to acknowledge their harsh condition. The three couplets that follow offer a series of contrasts: in each case, the first line sets up a pleasant expectation and the second dashes it with a blunt reminder of reality:

> Ale, man, ale's the stuff to drink
> For fellows whom it hurts to think:
> Look into the pewter pot
> To see the world as the world's not.
> And faith, 'tis pleasant till 'tis past:
> The mischief is that 'twill not last.

These are all jabs at the "sterling lads" who would prefer to lie in "lovely muck" and not think about the way the world is. Housman's sardonic advice is all the more pointed for its sharp and ironic tone.

POETIC FORMS

In poetry, language is intimately related to form, which is the structuring of words within identifiable patterns. In prose we speak of phrases, sentences, and paragraphs; in poetry, we identify structures by lines, stanzas, or complete forms such as the sonnet or the ode (though poetry in complete or blank verse has paragraphs of variable length, not formal stanzas: see below).

Rightly handled, the form enhances expression and meaning, just as a frame can define and enhance a painting or photograph. Unlike the photo frame, however, form in poetry is an integral part of the whole work. At one end of the scale, the term "form" may describe the *epic*, the lengthy narrative governed by such conventions as division into books, a lofty style, and the interplay between human and supernatural characters. At the other end lies the *epigram*, a witty and pointed saying whose distinguishing characteristic is its brevity, as in Alexander Pope's famous couplet,

I am his Highness' dog at Kew;
Pray tell me sir, whose dog are you?

Between the epic and the epigram lie many other poetic forms, such as the sonnet, the ballad, or the ode. "Form" may also describe stanzaic patterns like *couplets* and *quatrains*.

"FIXED FORM" POEMS

The best-known poetic form is probably the sonnet, the fourteen-line poem inherited from Italy (the word itself is from the Italian *sonetto*, little song or sound). Within those fourteen lines, whether the poet chooses the "Petrarchan" rhyme scheme or the "English" form (see below in the section on "Rhyme"), the challenge is to develop an idea or situation that must find its statement and its resolution within the strict confines of the sonnet frame. Typically, there is an initial idea, description, or statement of feeling, followed by a "turn" in the thought that takes the reader by surprise, or that casts the situation in an unexpected light. Thus in Sonnet 130, "My Mistress' Eyes Are Nothing Like the Sun," William Shakespeare spends the first three quatrains apparently disparaging his lover in a series of unfavorable comparisons—"If snow be white, why then her breasts are dun"—but in the closing couplet his point becomes clear:

And yet, by heaven, I think my love as rare
As any she belied with false compare.

In other words, the speaker's disparaging comparisons have really been parodies of sentimental clichés which falsify reality; his mistress has no need of the exaggerations or distortions of conventional love poetry.

Other foreign forms borrowed and adapted by English-language poets include the *ghazal* and the *pantoum*. The *ghazal*, strongly associated with classical Urdu literature, originated in Persia and Arabia and was brought to the Indian subcontinent in the twelfth century. It consists of a series of couplets held together by a refrain, a simple rhyme scheme (a/a, b/a, c/a, d/a…), and a common rhythm, but only loosely related in theme or subject. Some English-language practitioners of the form have captured the epigrammatic quality of the ghazal, but most do not adhere to the strict pattern of the classical form.

The *pantoum*, based on a Malaysian form, was imported into English poetry via the work of nineteenth-century French poets. Typically it presents a series of quatrains rhyming *abab*, linked by a pattern of repetition in which the second and fourth lines of a quatrain become the first and third lines of the stanza that follows. In the poem's final stanza, the pattern is reversed: the second line repeats the third line of the first stanza, and the last line repeats the poem's opening line, thus creating the effect of a loop.

Similar to the pantoum in the circularity of its structure is the *villanelle*, originally a French form, with five *tercets* and a concluding *quatrain* held together by only two rhymes (aba, aba, aba, aba, aba, abaa) and by a refrain that repeats the first line at lines 6, 12, and 18, while the third line of the first tercet reappears as lines 9, 15, and 19. With its interlocking rhymes and elaborate repetitions, the villanelle can create a variety of tonal effects, ranging from lighthearted parody to the sonorous and earnest exhortation of Dylan Thomas's "Do Not Go Gentle into That Good Night."

STANZAIC FORMS

Recurring formal groupings of lines within a poem are usually described as "stanzas." Both the recurring and the formal aspects of stanzaic forms are important; it is a common misconception to think that any group of lines in a poem, if it is set off by line spaces, constitutes a stanza. If such a group of lines is not patterned as one of a recurring group sharing similar formal characteristics, however, then it may be more appropriate to refer to such irregular groupings in the way we do for prose—as paragraphs. A ballad is typically divided into stanzas; a prose poem or a poem written in free verse, on the other hand, will rarely be divided into stanzas.

A stanza may be identified by the number of lines and the patterns of rhyme repeated in each grouping. One of the simpler traditional forms is the *ballad stanza*, with its alternating four and three-foot lines and its *abcb* rhyme scheme. Drawing on this form's association with medieval ballads and legends, Keats produces the eerie mystery of "La Belle Dame Sans Merci":

> I saw pale kings and princes too,
> Pale warriors, death-pale were they all;
> They cried—"La Belle Dame sans Merci
> Hath thee in thrall!"

Such imitations are a form of literary allusion; Keats uses a traditional stanza form to remind us of poems like "Sir Patrick Spens" or "Barbara Allen" to dramatize the painful thralldom of love by placing it within a well-known tradition of ballad narratives with similar forms and themes.

The four-line stanza, or *quatrain*, may be used for a variety of effects: from the elegiac solemnity of Gray's "Elegy Written in a Country Churchyard" to the apparent lightness and simplicity of some of Emily Dickinson's poems. Tennyson used a rhyming quatrain to such good effect in *In Memoriam* that the form he employed (four lines of iambic tetrameter rhyming *abba*) is known as the "In Memoriam stanza."

Other commonly used forms of stanza include the *rhyming couplet*, *terza rima*, *ottava rima*, *rhyme royal*, and the *Spenserian stanza*. Each of these is a rhetorical unit within a longer whole, rather like a paragraph within an essay. The poet's choice among such forms is dictated, at least in part, by the effects that each may produce. Thus the *rhyming couplet* often expresses a complete statement within two lines, creating a sense of density of thought, of coherence and closure; it is particularly effective where the writer wishes to set up contrasts, or to achieve the witty compactness of epigram:

> Of all mad creatures, if the learn'd are right,
> It is the slaver kills, and not the bite.
> A fool quite angry is quite innocent:
> Alas! 'tis ten times worse when they repent.

> (from Pope, "Epistle to Dr. Arbuthnot")

Ottava rima, as its Italian name implies, is an eight-line stanza, with the rhyme scheme *abababcc*. Like the sonnet, it is long enough to allow the development of a single thought in some detail and complexity, with a concluding couplet that may extend the central idea or cast it in a wholly unexpected light. W.B. Yeats uses this stanza form in "Sailing to Byzantium" and "Among Schoolchildren." Though much used by Renaissance poets, it is particularly associated with George Gordon, Lord Byron's *Don Juan*, in which the poet exploits to the full its potential for devastating irony and bathos. It is long enough to allow the development of a single thought in some detail and complexity; the concluding couplet can then, sonnet-like, turn that thought upon its head, or cast it in a wholly unexpected light:

Sagest of women, even of widows, she
    Resolved that Juan should be quite a paragon,
And worthy of the noblest pedigree
    (His sire was of Castile, his dam from Aragon).
Then for accomplishments of chivalry,
    In case our lord the king should go to war again,
He learned the arts of riding, fencing, gunnery,
    And how to scale a fortress—or a nunnery.

                                               (Don Juan I.38)

FREE VERSE

Not all writers want the order and symmetry—some might say the restraints and limitations—of traditional forms, and many have turned to *free verse* as a means of liberating their thoughts and feelings. Deriving its name from the French "vers libre" made popular by the French Symbolistes at the end of the nineteenth century, free verse is characterized by irregularity of meter, line length, and rhyme. This does not mean that it is without pattern; rather, it tends to follow more closely than other forms the unforced rhythms and accents of natural speech, making calculated use of spacing, line breaks, and "cadences," the rhythmic units that govern phrasing in speech.

    Free verse is not a modern invention. Milton was an early practitioner, as was Blake; however, it was the great modern writers of free verse—first Walt Whitman, then Pound, Eliot, and William Carlos Williams (interestingly, all Americans, at least originally)—who gave this form a fluidity and flexibility that could free the imagination to deal with any kind of feeling or experience. Perhaps because it depends so much more than traditional forms upon the individual intuitions of the poet, it is the form of poetic structure most commonly found today. The best practitioners recognize that free verse, like any other kind of poetry, demands clarity, precision, and a close connection between technique and meaning.

PROSE POETRY

At the furthest extreme from traditional forms lies poetry written in prose. Contradictory as this label may seem, the two have much in common. Prose has at its disposal all the figurative devices available to poetry, such as metaphor, personification, or apostrophe; it may use structuring devices such as verbal repetition or parallel syntactical structures; it can draw on the same tonal range, from pathos to irony. The difference is that prose poetry accomplishes its ends in sentences and paragraphs, rather than lines or stanzas. First given prominence by the French poet Charles Baudelaire (*Petits Poèmes en prose*, 1862), the form is much used to present fragments of heightened sensation, conveyed through vivid or impressionistic description. It draws upon such prosaic forms as journal entries, lists, even footnotes. Prose poetry should be distinguished from "poetic prose," which may be found in a variety of settings (from the King James Bible to the fiction of Jeanette Winterson); the distinction—which not all critics would accept—appears to lie in the writer's intention.

    Christan Bök's *Eunoia* is an interesting example of the ways in which a writer of prose poetry may try to balance the demands of each medium. *Eunoia* is an avowedly experimental work in which each chapter is restricted to the use of a single vowel. The text is governed by a series of rules described by the author in an afterword; they include a requirement that all chapters "must allude to the art of writing. All sentences must accent internal rhyme through the use of syntactical parallelism. The text must exhaust the lexicon for each vowel, citing at least 98% of the available repertoire...." Having imposed such constraints upon the language and form of the work, Bök then sets himself the task of showing that "even under such improbable conditions of duress, language can still express an uncanny, if not sublime, thought." The result is a surrealistic narrative that blends poetic and linguistic devices to almost hypnotic effect.

THE POEM AS A MATERIAL OBJECT

Both free verse and prose poetry pay attention in different ways to the poem as a living thing on the printed page. But the way in which poetry is presented in material form is an important part of the existence of almost any form of poetry. In the six volumes of this anthology the material form of the poem is highlighted by the inclusion of a number of facsimile reproductions of poems of other eras in their earliest extant material form.

RHYTHM AND SCANSION

When we read poetry, we often become aware of a pattern of rhythm within a line or set of lines. The formal analysis of that rhythmic pattern, or "meter," is called *scansion*. The verb "to scan" may carry different meanings, depending upon the context: if the *critic* "scans" a line, he or she is attempting to determine the metrical pattern in which it is cast; if the *line* "scans," we are making the observation that the line conforms to particular metrical rules. Whatever the context, the process of scansion is based on the premise that a line of verse is built on a pattern of stresses, a recurring set of more or less regular beats established by the alternation of light and heavy accents in syllables and words. The rhythmic pattern so distinguished in a given poem is said to be the "meter" of that poem. If we find it impossible to identify any specific metrical pattern, the poem is probably an example of free verse.

QUANTITATIVE, SYLLABIC, AND ACCENTUAL-SYLLABIC VERSE

Although we owe much of our terminology for analyzing or describing poetry to the Greeks and Romans, the foundation of our metrical system is quite different from theirs. They measured a line of verse by the duration of sound ("quantity") in each syllable, and by the combination of short and long syllables. Such poetry is known as *quantitative* verse.

Unlike Greek or Latin, English is a heavily accented language. Thus poetry of the Anglo-Saxon period, such as *Beowulf*, was *accentual*: that is, the lines were based on a fixed number of accents, or stresses, regardless of the number of syllables in the line:

Oft Scyld Scefing   sceapena þreatum
   monegum maegþum   meodosetla ofteah.

Few modern poets have written in the accentual tradition. A notable exception was Gerard Manley Hopkins, who based his line on a pattern of strong stresses that he called "sprung rhythm." Hopkins experimented with rhythms and stresses that approximate the accentual quality of natural speech; the result is a line that is emphatic, abrupt, even harsh in its forcefulness:

I caught this morning morning's minion, kingdom of daylight's dauphin, dapple-dawn-drawn
   Falcon, in his riding
Of the rolling level underneath him steady air ....

(from "The Windhover")

Under the influence of French poetry, following the Norman invasion of the eleventh century, English writers were introduced to *syllabic* prosody: that is, poetry in which the number of syllables is the determining factor in the length of any line, regardless of the number of stresses or their placement. A few modern writers have successfully produced syllabic poetry.

However, the accentual patterns of English, in speech as well as in poetry, were too strongly ingrained to disappear. Instead, the native accentual practice combined with the imported syllabic conventions to produce the *accentual-syllabic* line, in which the writer works with combinations of stressed and unstressed syllables in lines of equal syllabic length. Geoffrey Chaucer was the first great writer to employ the accentual-syllabic line in English poetry:

> x   / / x x /   x /x /
> Ther was also a Nonne, a Prioresse,
> x / x /x   x /   x   x   /
> That of hir smiling was ful simple and coy.
> x / x /   x / x / x /
> Hir gretteste ooth was but by saintè Loy,
> x /   x   /x   /x   / x / x
> And she was clepèd Madame Eglantine.

(from The Canterbury Tales)

The fundamental pattern here is the ten-syllable line (although the convention of sounding the final "e" at the end of a line in Middle English verse sometimes produces eleven syllables). Each line contains five stressed syllables, each of which alternates with one or two unstressed syllables. This was to become the predominant meter of poetry in English until the general adoption of free verse in the twentieth century.

IDENTIFYING POETIC METER

Conventionally, meter is established by dividing a line into roughly equal parts, based on the rise and fall of the rhythmic beats. Each of these divisions, conventionally marked by a bar, is known as a "foot," and within the foot there will be a combination of stressed and unstressed syllables, indicated by the prosodic symbols / (stressed) and x (unstressed).

> x /   x / x   /   x /
> I know | that I | shall meet | my fate
> /   x x /   x   /   x /
> Somewhere | among | the clouds | above ...

(from Yeats, "An Irish Airman Foresees His Death")

To describe the meter used in a poem, we must first determine what kind of foot predominates, and then count the number of feet in each line. To describe the resultant meter we use terminology borrowed from classical prosody. In identifying the meter of English verse we commonly apply the following labels:

iambic (x /): a foot with one weak stress followed by one strong stress

> x   /   x   / x /   x / x   /
> ("Look home | ward, Ang | el, now, | and melt | with ruth")

trochaic (/ x): strong followed by weak

> / x   / x   / x   /

("Ty-ger! | Ty-ger! | burning | bright")

anapaestic (x x /): two weak stresses, followed by a strong

<pre>
    x   x   /   x   x /   x x   /
("I have passed | with a nod | of the head")
</pre>

dactylic (/ x x): strong stress followed by two weak

<pre>
   /   x x   / x x   /
("Hickory | dickory | dock")
</pre>

spondaic (/ /): two strong stresses

<pre>
     / /   /   x   / x   /   x
("If hate | killed men,| Brother | Lawrence,
      /   /   x   /   x /   x
   God's blood,| would not | mine kill | you?")
</pre>

We also use classical terms to describe the number of feet in a line. Thus, a line with one foot is *monometer*; with two feet, *dimeter*; three feet, *trimeter*; four feet, *tetrameter*; five feet, *pentameter*; and six feet, *hexameter*.

Scansion of the two lines from Yeats's "Irish Airman" quoted above shows that the predominant foot is iambic (x /), that there are four feet to each line, and that the poem is therefore written in *iambic tetrameters*. The first foot of the second line, however, may be read as a trochee ("Somewhere"); the variation upon the iambic norm here is an example of *substitution*, a means whereby the writer may avoid the monotony that would result from adhering too closely to a set rhythm. We very quickly build up an expectation about the dominant meter of a poem; the poet will sometimes disturb that expectation by changing the beat, and so through substitution create a pleasurable tension in our awareness.

The prevailing meter in English poetry is iambic, since the natural rhythm of spoken English is predominantly iambic. Nonetheless, poets may employ other rhythms where it suits their purpose. Thus W.H. Auden can create a solemn tone by the use of a trochaic meter (/ x):

<pre>
   /   x   /   x   /   x   /
Earth, receive an honoured guest;
   /   x   /   x   / x /
William Yeats is laid to rest:
   /   x / x   / x /
Let the Irish vessel lie
   /   x   /   x   / x x
Emptied of its poetry.
</pre>

The same meter may be much less funereal, as in Ben Jonson's song "*To Celia*":

<pre>
   /   x   / x   /   x   /
Come, my Celia, let us prove,
   /   x   /   x   / x /
While we may, the sports of love.
   /   x   /   x   / x /x
Time will not be ours forever;
   /   x   /   x   /   x /x
He, at length, our good will sever.
</pre>

The sense of greater pace in this last example derives in part from the more staccato phrasing, and also from the greater use of monosyllabic words. A more obviously lilting, dancing effect is obtained from anapaestic rhythm (x x /):

> x / x x x / x x / x x / x x /
> I sprang to the stirrup, and Joris, and he;
> x / x x / x x / x x / x x /
> I galloped, Dirck galloped, we galloped all three.
> / x x / x x / x x / x x /
> "Good speed!" cried the watch, as the gatebolts undrew;
> / x / x x / x x / x x /
> "Speed!" echoed the wall to us galloping through.
> (from Browning, "How They Brought the Good News from Ghent to Aix")

Coleridge wittily captured the varying effects of different meters in "Metrical Feet: Lesson for a Boy," which the poet wrote for his sons, and in which he marked the stresses himself:

> / x / x / x /
> Trochee trips from long to short;
> x / x / x / x /
> From long to long in solemn sort
> / x / x x x / x / x
> Slow Spondee stalks; strong foot! yet ill able
> / x x / x x / x x / x x
> Ever to come up with Dactyl trisyllable.
> x / x / x / x /
> Iambics march from short to long:—
> x x / x x / x x / x x /
> With a leap and a bound the swift Anapaests throng….

A meter which often deals with serious themes is unrhymed iambic pentameter, also known as *blank verse*. This is the meter of Shakespeare's plays, notably his great tragedies; it is the meter, too, of Milton's *Paradise Lost*, to which it lends a desired sonority and magnificence; and of Wordsworth's "Lines Composed a Few Miles above Tintern Abbey," where the flexibility of the meter allows the writer to move by turns from description, to narration, to philosophical reflection.

RHYME, CONSONANCE, ASSONANCE, AND ALLITERATION

Perhaps the most obvious sign of poetic form is rhyme: that is, the repetition of syllables with the same or similar sounds. If the rhyme words are placed at the end of the line, they are known as *end-rhymes*. The opening stanza of Housman's "To an Athlete Dying Young" has two pairs of end-rhymes:

> The time you won your town the *race*
> We chaired you through the market-*place*;
> Man and boy stood cheering *by*,
> And home we brought you shoulder-*high*.

Words rhyming within a line are *internal rhymes*, as in the first and third lines of this stanza from Coleridge's "The Rime of the Ancient Mariner":

> The fair breeze *blew*, the white foam *flew*

> The furrow followed free;
> We were the *first* that ever *burst*
> Into that silent sea.

When, as is usually the case, the rhyme occurs in a stressed syllable, it is known as a *masculine rhyme*; if the rhyming word ends in an unstressed syllable, it is referred to as *feminine*. The difference is apparent in the opening stanzas of Alfred Tennyson's poem "The Lady of Shalott," where the first stanza establishes the basic iambic meter with strong stresses on the rhyming words:

> On either side the river *lie*
> Long fields of barley and of *rye*,
> That clothe the wold and meet the *sky*;
> And through the field the road runs *by*
> To many-towered Camelot ...

In the second stanza Tennyson changes to trochaic lines, ending in unstressed syllables and feminine rhymes:

> Willows whiten, aspens *quiver*,
> Little breezes dusk and *shiver*
> Through the wave that runs *forever*
> By the island in the *river*
> Flowing down to Camelot.

Not only does Tennyson avoid monotony here by his shift to feminine rhymes, he also darkens the mood by using words that imply a contrast with the bright warmth of day—"quiver," "dusk," "shiver"—in preparation for the introduction of the "silent isle" that embowers the Lady.

NEAR RHYMES

Most of the rhymes in "The Lady of Shalott" are exact, or "*perfect*" rhymes. However, in the second of the stanzas just quoted, it is evident that "forever" at the end of the third line is not a "perfect" rhyme; rather, it is an instance of "*near*" or "*slant*" rhyme. Such "*imperfect*" rhymes are quite deliberate; indeed, two stanzas later we find the rhyming sequence "early," "barley," "cheerly," and "clearly," followed by the rhymes "weary," "airy," and "fairy." As with the introduction of feminine rhymes, such divergences from one dominant pattern prevent monotony and avoid a too-mechanical sing-song effect.

More importantly, near-rhymes have an oddly unsettling effect, perhaps because they both raise and frustrate our expectation of a perfect rhyme. Their use certainly gives added emphasis to the words at the end of these chilling lines from Wilfred Owen's "*Strange Meeting*":

> For by my glee might many men have laughed,
> And of my weeping something had been left,
> Which must die now. I mean the truth untold,
> The pity of war, the pity war distilled.
> Now men will go content with what we spoiled,
> Or, discontent, boil bloody, and be spilled.

CONSONANCE AND ASSONANCE

In Owen's poem, the near-rhymes "laughed / left" and "spoiled / spilled" are good examples of *consonance*, which pairs words with similar consonants but different intervening vowels. Other examples from Owen's poem include "groined / groaned," "hall / Hell," "years / yours," and "mystery / mastery."

Related to consonance as a linking device is *assonance*, the echoing of similar vowel sounds in the stressed syllables of words with differing consonants (lane/hail, penitent/reticence). A device favored particularly by descriptive poets, it appears often in the work of the English Romantics, especially Shelley and Keats, and their great Victorian successor Tennyson, all of whom had a good ear for the musical quality of language. In the following passage, Tennyson makes effective use of repeated "o" and "ow" sounds to suggest the soft moaning of the wind as it spreads the seed of the lotos plant:

> The Lotos blooms below the barren peak,
> The Lotos blows by every winding creek;
> All day the wind breathes low with mellower tone;
> Through every hollow cave and alley lone
> Round and round the spicy downs the yellow Lotos dust is blown.
>
> (from "The Lotos-Eaters")

ALLITERATION

Alliteration connects words which have the same initial consonant. Like consonance and rhyme, alliteration adds emphasis, throwing individual words into strong relief, and lending force to rhythm. This is especially evident in the work of Gerard Manley Hopkins, where alliteration works in conjunction with the heavy stresses of *sprung rhythm*:

> Brute beauty and valour and act, oh, air, pride, plume, here
> Buckle! AND the fire that breaks from thee then, a billion
> Times told lovelier, more dangerous, O my chevalier!
>
> (from "The Windhover")

Like assonance, alliteration is useful in descriptive poetry, reinforcing an impression or mood through repeated sounds:

> Thou on whose stream, 'mid the steep sky's commotion,
> Loose clouds like Earth's decaying leaves are shed,
> Shook from the tangled boughs of Heaven and Ocean ....
>
> (from Percy Shelley, "Ode to the West Wind")

The repetition of "s" and "sh" sounds conveys the rushing sound of a wind that drives everything before it. This effect is also an example of *onomatopoeia*, a figure of speech in which the sound of the words seems to echo the sense.

RHYME AND POETIC STRUCTURE

Rhyme may play a central role in the structure of a poem. This is particularly apparent in the *sonnet* form, where the expression of the thought is heavily influenced by the poet's choice of rhyme-scheme. The "English" or "Shakespearean" sonnet has three quatrains rhyming *abab, cdcd, efef,* and concludes with a rhyming couplet, *gg.* This pattern lends itself well to the statement and restatement of an idea, as we find, for example, in Shakespeare's sonnet "That time of year thou mayst in me behold." Each of the quatrains presents an image of decline or decay—a tree in winter, the coming of night, a dying fire; the closing couplet then relates these images to the thought of an impending separation and attendant feelings of loss.

The organization of the "Italian" or "Petrarchan" sonnet, by contrast, hinges on a rhyme scheme that creates two parts, an eight-line section (the *octave*) typically rhyming *abbaabba,* and a concluding six-line section (the *sestet*) rhyming *cdecde* or some other variation. In the octave, the writer describes a thought or feeling; in the sestet, the writer may elaborate upon that thought, or may introduce a sudden "turn" or change of direction. A good example of the Italian form is Donne's "Batter My Heart, Three-Personed God."

The rhyming pattern established at the beginning of a poem is usually followed throughout; thus the opening sets up an expectation in the reader, which the poet may sometimes play on by means of an unexpected or surprising rhyme. This is especially evident in comic verse, where peculiar or unexpected rhymes can contribute a great deal to the comic effect:

> I shoot the Hippopotamus
> with bullets made of platinum,
>   Because if I use leaden ones
>   his hide is sure to flatten 'em.
>
> (Hilaire Belloc, "The Hippopotamus")

Finally, one of the most obvious yet important aspects of rhyme is its sound. It acts as a kind of musical punctuation, lending verse an added resonance and beauty. And as anyone who has ever had to learn poetry by heart will testify, the sound of rhyme is a powerful aid to memorization and recall, from helping a child to learn numbers—

> One, two,
> Buckle my shoe,
> Three, four,
> Knock at the door—

—to selling toothpaste through an advertising jingle in which the use of rhyme drives home the identity of a product:

> You'll wonder where the yellow went,
> When you brush your teeth with Pepsodent.

OTHER FORMS WITH INTERLOCKING RHYMES

Other forms besides the sonnet depend upon rhyme for their structural integrity. These include the *rondeau,* a poem of thirteen lines in three stanzas, with two half lines acting as a refrain, and having only two rhymes. The linking effect of rhyme is also essential to the three-line stanza called *terza rima*, the form chosen by Shelley for his "Ode to the West Wind," where the rhyme scheme (*aba, bcb, cdc*, etc.) gives a strong sense of forward movement. But a poet need not be limited to particular forms to use interlocking rhyme schemes.

THE POET'S TASK

The poet's task, in Sir Philip Sidney's view, is to move us to virtue and well-doing by coming to us with

> words set in delightful proportion, either accompanied with, or prepared for, the well-enchanting skill of music; and with a tale forsooth he cometh unto you, with a tale which holdeth children from play, and old men from the chimney corner; and pretending no more, doth intend the winning of the mind from wickedness to virtue: even as the child is often brought to take most wholesome things by hiding them in such other as have a pleasant taste.
>
> (*The Defence of Poesy*, 1593)

Modern poets have been less preoccupied with the didactic or moral force of poetry, its capacity to win the mind to virtue; nonetheless, like their Renaissance counterparts, they view poetry as a means to understanding, a point of light in an otherwise dark universe. To Robert Frost, a poem "begins in delight and ends in wisdom":

> It begins in delight, it inclines to the impulse, it assumes direction with the first line laid down, it runs a course of lucky events, and ends in a clarification of life—not necessarily a great clarification, such as sects and cults are founded on, but in a momentary stay against confusion.
>
> ("The Figure a Poem Makes," *Collected Poems*, 1939)

Rhyme and meter are important tools at the poet's disposal, and can be valuable aids in developing thought as well as in creating rhythmic or musical effects. However, the technical skills needed to turn a good line or create metrical complexities should not be confused with the ability to write good poetry. Sidney wryly observes in his *Defence of Poesy* that "there have been many excellent poets that never versified, and now swarm many versifiers that need never answer to the name of poets.…[I]t is not rhyming and versing that maketh a poet, no more than a long gown maketh an advocate." Technical virtuosity may arouse our admiration, but something else is needed to bring that "constriction of the throat and … precipitation of water to the eyes" that A.E. Housman speaks about. What that "something" is will always elude definition, and is perhaps best left for readers and listeners to determine for themselves through their own encounters with poetry.

Maps

BRITAIN AND THE WORLD

The shaded areas show the extent of the British Empire c. 1900

THE BRITISH ISLES IN
THE ROMANTIC ERA

THE BRITISH ISLES IN
THE VICTORIAN ERA

THE BRITISH ISLES IN THE
TWENTY-FIRST CENTURY

COUNTIES
OF BRITAIN
AND IRELAND

GREATER LONDON

CENTRAL LONDON

1 Lambeth Palace
2 Westminster Bridge
3 Westminster Abbey
4 Whitehall
5 Tyburn
6 Covent Garden
7 The Temple
8 Blackfriar's Bridge
9 Swan Theatre
10 Bear Garden
11 Globe Theatre
12 London Bridge
13 St. Paul's Cathedral
14 Fortune Theatre
15 The Theatre
16 Bethlehem Hospital ("Bedlam")
17 The Tower
18 Tower Bridge
19 Waterloo Station
20 Houses of Parliament
21 Tate Gallery
22 Vauxhall Bridge
23 Victoria Station
24 Buckingham Palace
25 Royal Albert Hall
26 Kensington Palace
27 Paddington Station
28 Trafalgar Square
29 British Museum
30 Euston Station
31 St. Pancras Station
32 King's Cross Station

Monarchs and Prime Ministers

MONARCHS

House of Wessex

Egbert (Ecgberht)	829–39
Æthelwulf	839–58
Æthelbald	858–60
Æthelbert	860–66
Æthelred I	866–71
Alfred the Great	871–99
Edward the Elder	899–924
Athelstan	924–40
Edmund I	940–46
Edred (Eadred)	946–55
Edwy (Eadwig)	955–59
Edgar	959–75
Edward the Martyr	975–78
Æthelred II (the Unready)	978–1016
Edmund II (Ironside)	1016

Danish Line

Canute (Cnut)	1016–35
Harold I (Harefoot)	1035–40
Hardecanute	1040–42

Harold II

Wessex Line, Restored

Edward the Confessor	1042–66
Harold II	1066

Norman Line

William I (the Conqueror)	1066–87
William II (Rufus)	1087–1100
Henry I (Beauclerc)	1100–35
Stephen	1135–54

William I

MONARCHS

PLANTAGENET,
ANGEVIN LINE

Henry II	1154–89
Richard I (Coeur de Lion)	1189–99
John (Lackland)	1199–1216
Henry III	1216–72
Edward I (Longshanks)	1272–1307
Edward II	1307–27
Edward III	1327–77
Richard II	1377–99

PLANTAGENET,
LANCASTRIAN LINE

Henry IV	1399–1413
Henry V	1413–22
Henry VI	1422–61

Henry VIII

PLANTAGENET,
YORKIST LINE

Edward IV	1461–83
Edward V	1483
Richard III	1483–85

HOUSE OF TUDOR

Henry VII	1485–1509
Henry VIII	1509–47
Edward VI	1547–53
Mary I	1553–58
Elizabeth I	1558–1603

Mary I

HOUSE OF STUART

James I	1603–25
Charles I	1625–49

(THE COMMONWEALTH)	1649–60
Oliver Cromwell	1649–58
Richard Cromwell	1658–59

MONARCHS		PRIME MINISTERS	
HOUSE OF STUART, RESTORED			
Charles II	1660–85		
James II	1685–88		
HOUSE OF ORANGE AND STUART			
William III and Mary II	1689–94		
William III	1694–1702		
HOUSE OF STUART			
Anne	1702–14		
HOUSE OF BRUNSWICK, HANOVER LINE			
George I	1714–27	Sir Robert Walpole (Whig)	1721–42
George II	1727–60	Earl of Wilmington (Whig)	1742–43
		Henry Pelham (Whig)	1743–54
		Duke of Newcastle (Whig)	1754–56
		Duke of Devonshire (Whig)	1756–57
		Duke of Newcastle (Whig)	1757–62
George III	1760–1820	Earl of Bute (Tory)	1762–63
		George Grenville (Whig)	1763–65
		Marquess of Rockingham (Whig)	1765–66
		William Pitt the Elder (Earl of Chatham) (Whig)	1766–68
		Duke of Grafton (Whig)	1768–70
		Frederick North (Lord North) (Tory)	1770–82
		Marquess of Rockingham (Whig)	1782
		Earl of Shelburne (Whig)	1782–83
		Duke of Portland	1783
		William Pitt the Younger (Tory)	1783–1801
		Henry Addington (Tory)	1801–04
		William Pitt the Younger (Tory)	1804–06
		William Wyndham Grenville (Baron Grenville) (Whig)	1806–07

George III

George, Prince of Wales,
Prince Regent

MONARCHS

George, Prince of Wales, Prince Regent	1811–20
George IV	1820–30
William IV	1830–37
Victoria	1837–1901

Victoria

HOUSE OF SAXE-COBURG-GOTHA

Edward VII	1901–10

HOUSE OF WINDSOR

George V	1910–36

PRIME MINISTERS

Duke of Portland (Whig)	1807–09
Spencer Perceval (Tory)	1809–12
Earl of Liverpool (Tory)	1812–27
George Canning (Tory)	1827
Viscount Goderich (Tory)	1827–28
Duke of Wellington (Tory)	1828–30
Earl Grey (Whig)	1830–34
Viscount Melbourne (Whig)	1834
Sir Robert Peel (Tory)	1834–35
Viscount Melbourne (Whig)	1835–41
Sir Robert Peel (Tory)	1841–46
Lord John Russell (later Earl) (Liberal)	1846–52
Earl of Derby (Con.)	1852
Earl of Aberdeen (Tory)	1852–55
Viscount Palmerston (Lib.)	1855–58
Earl of Derby (Con.)	1858–59
Viscount Palmerston (Lib.)	1859–65
Earl Russell (Liberal)	1865–66
Earl of Derby (Con.)	1866–68
Benjamin Disraeli (Con.)	1868
William Gladstone (Lib.)	1868–74
Benjamin Disraeli (Con.)	1874–80
William Gladstone (Lib.)	1880–85
Marquess of Salisbury (Con.)	1885–86
William Gladstone (Lib.)	1886
Marquess of Salisbury (Con.)	1886–92
William Gladstone (Lib.)	1892–94
Earl of Rosebery (Lib.)	1894–95
Marquess of Salisbury (Con.)	1895–1902
Arthur Balfour (Con.)	1902–05
Sir Henry Campbell-Bannerman (Lib.)	1905–08
Herbert Asquith (Lib.)	1908–15
Herbert Asquith (Lib.)	1915–16

MONARCHS

Edward VIII	1936
George VI	1936–52
Elizabeth II	1952–

PRIME MINISTERS

David Lloyd George	1916–22
Andrew Bonar Law (Con.)	1922–23
Stanley Baldwin (Con.)	1923–24
James Ramsay MacDonald (Labour)	1924
Stanley Baldwin (Con.)	1924–29
James Ramsay MacDonald (Labour)	1929–31
James Ramsay MacDonald (Labour)	1931–35
Stanley Baldwin (Con.)	1935–37
Neville Chamberlain (Con.)	1937–40
Winston Churchill (Con.)	1940–45
Winston Churchill (Con.)	1945
Clement Attlee (Labour)	1945–51
Sir Winston Churchill (Con.)	1951–55

Winston Churchill

Sir Anthony Eden (Con.)	1955–57
Harold Macmillan (Con.)	1957–63
Sir Alex Douglas-Home (Con.)	1963–64
Harold Wilson (Labour)	1964–70
Edward Heath (Con.)	1970–74
Harold Wilson (Labour)	1974–76
James Callaghan (Labour)	1976–79
Margaret Thatcher (Con.)	1979–90
John Major (Con.)	1990–97
Tony Blair (Labour)	1997–2007
Gordon Brown (Labour)	2007–10
David Cameron (Con.)	2010–16
Theresa May (Con.)	2016–

GLOSSARY OF TERMS

Accent: the natural emphasis (stress) speakers place on a syllable.

Accentual Verse: poetry in which a line is measured only by the number of accents or stresses, not by the number of syllables.

Accentual-Syllabic Verse: the most common metrical system in traditional English verse, in which a line is measured by the number of syllables and by the pattern of accented (stressed) and unaccented (unstressed) syllables.

Aesthetes: members of a late nineteenth-century movement that valued "art for art's sake"—for its purely aesthetic qualities, as opposed to valuing art for the moral content it may convey, for the intellectual stimulation it may provide, or for a range of other qualities.

Alexandrine: a line of verse that is 12 syllables long. In English verse, the alexandrine is always an iambic hexameter: that is, it has six iambic feet. The most-often quoted example is the second line in a couplet from Alexander Pope's "Essay on Criticism" (1711): "A needless Alexandrine ends the song / That, like a wounded snake, drags its slow length along." See also *Spenserian stanza*.

Allegory: a narrative with both a literal meaning and secondary, often symbolic meaning or meanings. Allegory frequently employs personification to give concrete embodiment to abstract concepts or entities, such as feelings or personal qualities. It may also present one set of characters or events in the guise of another, using implied parallels for the purposes of satire or political comment, as in John Dryden's poem "Absalom and Achitophel."

Alliteration: the grouping of words with the same initial consonant (e.g., "break, blow, burn, and make me new"). The repetition of sound acts as a connector. See also *assonance* and *consonance*.

Alliterative Verse: poetry that employs alliteration of stressed syllables in each line as its chief structural principle.

Allusion: a reference, often indirect or unidentified, to a person, thing, or event. A reference in one literary work to another literary work, whether to its content or its form, also constitutes an allusion.

Ambiguity: an "opening" of language created by the writer to allow for multiple meanings or differing interpretations. In literature, ambiguity may be deliberately employed by the writer to enrich meaning; this differs from any unintentional, unwanted, ambiguity in non-literary prose.

Amphibrach: a metrical foot with three syllables, the second of which is stressed: x / x (e.g., sensation).

Analogy: a broad term that refers to our processes of noting similarities among things or events. Specific forms of analogy in poetry include *simile* and *metaphor* (see below).

Anapaest: a metrical foot containing two unstressed syllables followed by one stressed syllable: xx / (e.g., underneath, intervene).

Anglican Church / Church of England: formed after Henry VIII's break with Rome in the 1530s, the Church of England had acquired a permanently Protestant cast by the 1570s. There has remained considerable variation within the Church, however, with distinctions often drawn among High Church, Broad Church, and Latitudinarian. At one extreme High Church Anglicans (some of whom prefer to be known as "Anglo-Catholics") prefer relatively elaborate church rituals not dissimilar in form to those of the Roman Catholic Church and place considerable emphasis on church hierarchy, while in the other direction Latitudinarians prefer relatively informal religious services and tend far more towards egalitarianism.

Antistrophe: from Greek drama, the chorus's countermovement or reply to an initial movement (*strophe*). See *ode* below.

Apostrophe: a figure of speech (a trope; see *figures of speech* below) in which a writer directly addresses an object—or a dead or absent person—as if the imagined audience were actually listening.

Archetype: in literature and mythology, a recurring idea, symbol, motif, character, or place. To some scholars and psychologists, an archetype represents universal human thought-patterns or experiences.

Assonance: the repetition of identical or similar vowel sounds in stressed syllables in which the surrounding consonants are different: for example, "shame" and "fate"; "gale" and "cage"; or the long "i" sounds in "Beside the pumice isle..."

Aubade: a lyric poem that greets or laments the arrival of dawn.

Ballad: a folk song, or a poem originally recited to an audience, which tells a dramatic story based on legend or history.

Ballad Stanza: a quatrain with alternating four-stress and three-stress lines, rhyming *abcb*. A variant is "common measure," in which the alternating lines are strictly iambic, and rhyme *abab*.

Ballade: a fixed form most commonly characterized by only three rhymes, with an 8-line stanza rhyming *ababbcbc* and an envoy rhyming *bcbc*. Both Chaucer and Dante Gabriel Rossetti ("Ballad of the Dead Ladies") adopted this form.

Baroque: powerful and heavily ornamented in style. "Baroque" is a term from the history of visual art and of music that is sometimes also used to describe certain literary styles, such as that of Richard Crashaw.

Bathos: an anticlimactic effect brought about by a writer's descent from an elevated subject or tone to the ordinary or trivial.

Benedictine Rule: set of instructions for monastic communities, composed by Saint Benedict of Nursia (died c. 457).

Blank Verse: unrhymed lines written in iambic pentameter, a form introduced to English verse by Henry Howard, Earl of Surrey, in his translation of parts of Virgil's *Aeneid* in 1547.

Bombast: inappropriately inflated or grandiose language.

Broadside: individual sheet of paper printed on only one side. From the sixteenth through to the eighteenth centuries broadsides of a variety of different sorts (e.g., ballads, political tracts, short satires) were sold on the streets.

Broken Rhyme: in which a multi-syllable word is split at the end of a line and continued onto the next, to allow an end-rhyme with the split syllable.

Burlesque: satire of a particularly exaggerated sort, particularly that which ridicules its subject by emphasizing its vulgar or ridiculous aspects.

Caesura: a pause or break in a line of verse occurring where a phrase, clause, or sentence ends, and indicated in scansion by the mark II. If it occurs in the middle of the line, it is known as a "medial" caesura.

Canon: in literature, those works that are commonly accepted as possessing authority or importance. In practice, "canonical" texts or authors are those that are discussed most frequently by scholars and taught most frequently in university courses.

Canto: a sub-section of a long (usually epic) poem.

Canzone: a short song or poem, with stanzas of equal length and an envoy.

Carpe Diem: Latin (from Horace) meaning "seize the day." The idea of enjoying the moment is a common one in Renaissance love poetry. See, for example, Marvell's "To His Coy Mistress."

Catalexis: the omission of unstressed syllables from a line of verse (such a line is referred to as "catalectic"). In iambic verse it is usually the first syllable of the line that is omitted; in trochaic, the last. For example, in the first stanza of Housman's "To an Athlete Dying Young" the third line is catalectic: i.e., it has dropped the first, unstressed syllable called for by the poem's iambic tetrameter form: "The time you won your town the race / We chaired you through the market-place; / Man and boy stood cheering by, / And home we brought you shoulder-high."

Catharsis: the arousal through the performance of a dramatic tragedy of "emotions of pity and fear" to a point where "purgation" or "purification" occurs and the feelings are released or transformed. The concept was developed by Aristotle in his *Poetics* from an ancient Greek medical concept, and adapted by him into an aesthetic principle.

Chiasmus: a figure of speech (a scheme) that reverses word order in successive parallel clauses. If the word order is A-B-C in the first clause, it becomes C-B-A in the second: for example, Donne's line "She is all states, and all princes, I" ("The Sun Rising") incorporates this reversal (though with an ellipsis).

Classical: originating in or relating to ancient Greek or Roman culture. As commonly conceived, *classical* implies a strong sense of formal order. The term *neoclassical* is often used with reference to literature of the Restoration and eighteenth century that was strongly influenced by ancient Greek and Roman models.

Closet Drama: a play (typically in verse) written for private performance. The term came into use in the first half of the nineteenth century.

Colored Narrative: alternative term for *free indirect discourse*.

Comedy: as a literary term, used originally to denote that class of ancient Greek drama in which the action ends happily. More broadly the term has been used to describe a wide variety of literary forms of a more or less light-hearted character.

Commedia dell'arte: largely improvised comic performances conducted by masked performers and involving considerable physical activity. The genre of *commedia dell'arte* originated in Italy in the sixteenth century; it was influential throughout Europe for more than two centuries thereafter.

Commonwealth: from the fifteenth century, a term roughly equivalent to the modern "state," but tending to emphasize the commonality of interests among all citizens. In the seventeenth century Britain was named a commonwealth under Oliver Cromwell. In the twentieth century, the term came to be applied to associations of many nations; the British Commonwealth became the successor to the British Empire.

Conceit: an unusually elaborate metaphor or simile that extends beyond its original tenor and vehicle, sometimes becoming a "master" analogy for the entire poem (see, for example, Donne's "The Flea," and Robert Frost's sonnet "She is as in a field a silken tent"). Ingenious or fanciful images and comparisons were especially popular with the metaphysical poets of the seventeenth century, giving rise to the term "metaphysical conceit."

Concrete Poetry: an experimental form, most popular during the 1950s and 60s, in which the printed type itself forms a visual image of the poem's key words or ideas. See also *pattern poetry, assonance.*

Connotation: the implied, often unspoken meaning(s) of a given word, as distinct from its denotation, or literal meaning. Connotations may have highly emotional undertones and are usually culturally specific.

Conservative Party: See *Political Parties*.

Consonance: the pairing of words with similar initial and ending consonants, but with different vowel sounds (live/love, wander/wonder). See also *alliteration*.

Convention: aesthetic approach, technique, or practice accepted as characteristic and appropriate for a particular form. It is a convention of certain sorts of plays, for example, that the characters speak in blank verse, of other sorts of plays that characters speak in rhymed couplets, and of still other sorts of dramatic performances that characters frequently break into song to express their feelings.

Couplet: a pair of rhyming lines, usually in the same meter. If they form a complete unit of thought and are grammatically complete, the lines are known as a closed couplet. See also *heroic couplet* below.

Dactyl: a metrical foot containing one strong stress followed by two weak stresses: / xx (e.g., muttering, helplessly). A minor form known as "double dactyls" makes use of this meter for humorous purposes, e.g., "Jiggery pokery" or "Higgledy piggledy."

Denotation: See *connotation* above.

Devolution: process through which a degree of political power was transferred in the late twentieth and early twenty-first centuries from the British government to assemblies in Scotland and in Wales.

Dialogue: words spoken by characters to one another. (When a character is addressing him or her self or the audience directly, the words spoken are referred to as a *monologue*.)

Diction: word choice. Whether the diction of a literary work (or of a literary character) is colloquial, conversational, formal, or of some other type contributes significantly to the tone of the text as well as to characterization.

Didacticism: aesthetic approach emphasizing moral instruction.

Dimeter: a poetic line containing two metrical feet.

Dirge: a song or poem that mourns someone's death. See also *elegy* and *lament* below.

Disestablishmentarianism: movement opposing an official state-supported religion, in particular the Church of England in that role.

Dissonance: harsh, unmusical sounds or rhythms which poets may use deliberately to achieve certain effects.

Dramatic Irony: this form of irony occurs when the audience's reception of a speech by a character on the stage is affected by the possession by the audience of information not available to the character.

Dramatic Monologue: a lyric poem that takes the form of an utterance by a single person addressing a silent listener. The speaker may be an historical personage (as in some of Robert Browning's dramatic monologues), a figure drawn from myth or legend (as in some of Tennyson's), or an entirely imagined figure, as in Webster's "A Castaway."

Dub Poetry: a form of protest poetry originating in Jamaica, with its roots in dance rhythms, especially reggae, and often accompanied in performance by drums and music. See also *rap*.

Duple Foot: a duple foot of poetry has two syllables. The possible duple forms are iamb (in which the stress is on the second of the two syllables), trochee (in which the stress is on the first of the two syllables), spondee (in which both are stressed equally), and pyrrhic (in which both syllables are unstressed).

Eclogue: now generally used simply as an alternative name for a pastoral poem. In classical times and in the early modern period, however, an *eclogue* (or *idyll*) was a specific type of pastoral poem—a dialogue or dramatic monologue involving rustic characters. (The other main sub-genre of the pastoral was the *georgic*.)

Elegiac Stanza: a quatrain of iambic pentameters rhyming *abab*, often used in poems meditating on death or sorrow. The best-known example is Thomas Gray's "Elegy Written in a Country Churchyard."

Elegy: a poem which formally mourns the death of a particular person (e.g., Tennyson's "In Memoriam") or in which the poet meditates on other serious subjects (e.g., Gray's "Elegy"). See also *dirge*.

Elision: omitting or suppressing a letter or an unstressed syllable at the beginning or end of a word, so that a line of verse may conform to a given metrical scheme. For example, the three syllables at the beginning of Shakespeare's sonnet 129 are reduced to two by the omission of the first vowel: "Th' expense of spirit in a waste of shame." See also *syncope*.

Ellipsis: the omission of a word or words necessary for the complete grammatical construction of a sentence, but not necessary for our understanding of the sentence.

End-rhyme: See *rhyme*.

End-stopped: a line of poetry is said to be end-stopped when the end of the line coincides with a natural pause in the syntax, such as the conclusion of a sentence; e.g., in this couplet from Pope's "Essay on Criticism," both lines are end-stopped: "A little learning is a dangerous thing; / Drink deep, or taste not the Pierian spring." Compare this with *enjambement*.

Enjambement: the "running-on" of the sense from one line of poetry to the next, with no pause created by punctuation or syntax. (The more commonly found alternative is referred to as an *end-stopped line*.)

Envoy (Envoi): a stanza or half-stanza that forms the conclusion of certain French poetic forms, such as the *sestina* or the *ballade*. It often sums up or comments upon what has gone before.

Epic: a lengthy narrative poem, often divided into books and sub-divided into cantos. It generally celebrates heroic deeds or events, and the style tends to be lofty and grand. Examples in English include Spenser's *The Faerie Queene* and Milton's *Paradise Lost*.

Epic Simile: an elaborate simile, developed at such length that the vehicle of the comparison momentarily displaces the primary subject with which it is being compared.

Epigram: a very short poem, sometimes in closed couplet form, characterized by pointed wit.

Epigraph: a quotation placed at the beginning of a discourse to indicate or foreshadow the theme.

Epiphany: a moment at which matters of significance are suddenly illuminated for a literary character (or for the reader), typically triggered by something small and seemingly of little import. The term first came into wide currency in connection with the fiction of James Joyce.

Episodic Plot: plot comprising a variety of episodes that are only loosely connected by threads of story material (as opposed to plots that present one or more continually unfolding narratives where successive episodes build one on another).

Epithalamion: a poem celebrating a wedding. The best-known example in English is probably Edmund Spenser's "Epithalamion" (1595).

Eulogy: text expressing praise, especially for a distinguished person recently deceased.

Euphemism: mode of expression through which aspects of reality considered to be vulgar, crudely physical, or unpleasant are referred to indirectly rather than named explicitly. A variety of euphemisms exist for the processes of urination and defecation; *passed away* is often used as a euphemism for *died*. (The word *euphemism* has the same root as *Euphuism* (see below), but has taken on a different meaning.)

Euphony: pleasant, musical sounds or rhythms—the opposite of dissonance.

Euphuism: in the late sixteenth century John Lyly published a prose romance, *Euphues*, which employed a style that featured long sentences filled with balanced phrases and clauses, many of them adding little to the content. This highly mannered style was popular in the court of Elizabeth I for a few years following the publication of Lyly's famous work, and the style became known as *Euphuism*.

European Union (EU): group of nations formed in 1993 as the successor to the European Economic Community (Common Market). Britain first applied for membership in the latter in 1961; at first its efforts to join were blocked by the French government, but in 1973 Prime Minister Edward Heath successfully negotiated Britain's entry into the group. Britain resisted some moves towards full integration with the European community, in particular retaining its own currency when other European nations adopted the Euro on 1 January 2002. In 2016, the United Kingdom held a referendum and voted to leave the European Union altogether.

Exchequer: in earlier eras, the central royal financial office, responsible for receiving and keeping track of crown revenues. In later eras, part of the bureaucracy equivalent to the Ministry of Finance in Canada or the Treasury in the United States (the modern post of Chancellor of the Exchequer is equivalent to the American post of Secretary of the Treasury, the Canadian post of Minister of Finance, or the Australian post of Treasurer).

Exposition: the setting out of material in an ordered form, either in speech or in writing. In a play those parts of the action that do not occur on stage but are rather recounted by the characters are frequently described as being presented in exposition. Similarly, when the background narrative is filled in near the beginning of a novel, such material is often described as having been presented in exposition. Somewhat confusingly, however, the term "expository prose" is usually used with reference not to fiction but to the setting forth of arguments or descriptions in the context of essays or other works of prose non-fiction.

1650 GLOSSARY OF TERMS

Eye-rhyme: See *rhyme* below.

Feminine Ending: the ending of a line of poetry on an "extra," and, especially, on an unstressed syllable. See, for example, the first line of Keat's "Ode on a Grecian Urn": "A thing of beauty is a joy forever," a line of iambic pentameter in which the final foot is an amphibrach rather than an iamb.

Feminine Rhyme: See *rhyme* below.

Figures of Speech: deliberate, highly concentrated uses of language to achieve particular purposes or effects on an audience. There are two kinds of figures: schemes and tropes. Schemes involve changes in word-sound and word-order, such as *alliteration* and *chiasmus*. Tropes play on our understandings of words to extend, alter, or transform meaning, as in *metaphor* and *personification*.

First-Person Narrative: narrative recounted using *I* and *me*. See also *narrative perspective*.

Fixed Forms: the term applied to a number of poetic forms and stanzaic patterns, many derived from French models, such as *ballade, rondeau, sestina, triolet,* and *villanelle*. Other "fixed forms" include the *sonnet, rhyme royal, haiku,* and *ottava rima*.

Folio: largest of several sizes of book page commonly used in the first few centuries after the introduction of the printing press. A folio size results from very large paper being folded in half. Paper size during this period was not standardized; though a typical folio page was about 15 inches high, some could be more than twice that height. When the same sheet is folded twice a quarto is produced, and when it is folded 3 times an octavo.

Foot: a unit of a line of verse which contains a particular combination of stressed and unstressed syllables. Dividing a line into metrical feet (*iambs, trochees,* etc.), then counting the number of feet per line, is part of *scansion*. See also *meter*.

Franklin: in the late medieval period, a landholder of free status, but ranking below the gentry.

Free Indirect Discourse: in prose fiction, commentary in which a seemingly objective and omniscient narrative voice assumes the point of view of one or more characters. When we hear through the third person narrative voice of Jane Austen's *Pride and Prejudice*, for example, that Mr. Darcy "was the proudest, most disagreeable man in the world, and every body hoped that he would never come there again," the narrative voice has assumed the point of view of "every body" in the community; we as readers are not meant to take it that Mr. Darcy is indeed the most disagreeable man in the world. Similarly, in the following passage from the same novel, we are likely to take it as being the view of the character Charlotte that marriage is "the only honourable provision for well-educated young women of small fortune," not to take it to be an objective statement of perceived truth on the part of the novel's third person narrative voice:

> [Charlotte's] reflections were in general satisfactory. Mr. Collins to be sure was neither sensible nor agreeable; his society was irksome, and his attachment to her must be imaginary. But still he would be her husband. Without thinking highly either of men or of matrimony, marriage had always been her object; it was the only honourable provision for well-educated young women of small fortune, and however uncertain of giving happiness, must be their pleasantest preservative from want.

The term free indirect discourse may also be applied to situations in which it may not be entirely clear if the thoughts expressed emanate from the character, the narrator, or some combination of the two. (In the above-quoted passage expressing Charlotte's thoughts, indeed, some might argue that the statement concerning marriage should be taken as the expression of a belief that the narrative voice shares, at least in part.)

Free Verse: poetry that does not follow any regular meter, line length, or rhyming scheme. In many respects, though, free verse follows the complex natural "rules" and rhythmic patterns (or cadences) of speech.

Gaelic: Celtic language, variants of which are spoken in Ireland and Scotland.

Genre: a particular literary form. The concept of genre may be used with different levels of generality. At the most general, poetry, drama, and prose fiction are distinguished as separate genres. At a lower level of generality various sub-genres are frequently distinguished, such as (within drama) comedy and tragedy, or, at a still lower level of generality, Elizabethan domestic tragedy, Edwardian drawing-room comedy, and so on.

Georgic: (from Virgil's *Georgics*) a poem that celebrates the natural wealth of the countryside and advises how to cultivate and live in harmony with it. Pope's *Windsor Forest* and James Thomson's *Seasons* are classed as georgics. They were often said to make up, with eclogues, the two alliterative forms of pastoral poetry.

Ghazal: derived from Persian and Indian precedents, the ghazal presents a series of thoughts in closed couplets joined by a simple rhyme-scheme: *aa ba ca da*, etc.

Gothic: in architecture and the visual arts, a term used to describe styles prevalent from the twelfth to the fourteenth centuries, but in literature a term used to describe work with a sinister or grotesque tone that seeks to evoke a sense of terror on the part of the reader or audience. Gothic literature originated as a genre in the eighteenth century with works such as Horace Walpole's *The Castle of Otranto*. To some extent the notion of the medieval itself then carried with it associations of the dark and the grotesque, but from the beginning an element of intentional exaggeration (sometimes verging on self-parody) attached itself to the genre. The Gothic trend of youth culture that began in the late twentieth century is less clearly associated with the medieval, but shares with the various varieties of Gothic literature (from Walpole in the eighteenth century, to Bram Stoker in the early twentieth, to Stephen King and Anne Rice in the late twentieth) a fondness for the sensational and the grotesque, as well as a propensity to self-parody.

Guilds: non-clerical associations that arose in the late Anglo-Saxon period, devoted both to social purposes (such as the organization of feasts for the members) and to piety. In the later medieval period guilds developed strong associations with particular occupations.

Haiku: a Japanese form, using three unrhymed lines of five, seven, and five syllables. Conventionally, it uses precise, concentrated images to suggest states of feeling.

Heptameter: a line containing seven metrical feet.

Heroic Couplet: a pair of rhymed iambic pentameters, so called because the form was much used in seventeenth- and eighteenth-century poems and plays on heroic subjects.

Hexameter: a line containing six metrical feet.

Home Rule: movement dedicated to making Ireland politically independent from Britain.

Horatian Ode: inspired by the work of the Roman poet Horace, an ode that is usually calm and meditative in tone, and homostrophic (i.e., having regular stanzas) in form. Keats's odes are English examples.

House of Commons: elected legislative body, in Britain currently consisting of six hundred and fifty members of Parliament. See also *Parliament*.

House of Lords: the "Upper House" of the British Houses of Parliament. Since the nineteenth century the House of Lords has been far less powerful than the elected House of Commons. The House of Lords is currently made up of both hereditary peers (Lords whose title is passed on from generation to generation) and life peers. As a result of legislation enacted by the Labour government of Tony Blair, the role of hereditary peers in Parliament is being phased out.

Humors: the four humors were believed in until the sixteenth and seventeenth centuries to be elements in the makeup of all humans; a person's temperament was thought to be determined by the way in which the humors were combined. When the *choleric* humor was dominant, the person would tend towards anger; when the *sanguine* humor was dominant, towards pleasant affability; when the *phlegmatic* humor was dominant, towards a cool and calm attitude and/or a lack of feeling or enthusiasm; and when the *melancholic* humor was dominant, towards withdrawal and melancholy.

Hymn: a song whose theme is usually religious, in praise of divinity. Literary hymns may praise more secular subjects.

Hyperbole: a *figure of speech* (a trope) that deliberately exaggerates or inflates meaning to achieve particular effects, such as the irony in A.E. Housman's claim (from "Terence, This Is Stupid Stuff") that "malt does more than Milton can / To justify God's ways to man."

Iamb: the most common metrical foot in English verse, containing one unstressed syllable followed by a stressed syllable: x / (e.g., between, achieve).

Idyll: traditionally, a short pastoral poem that idealizes country life, conveying impressions of innocence and happiness.

Image: the recreation in words of objects perceived by the senses, sometimes thought of as "pictures," although other senses besides sight are involved. Besides this literal application, the term also refers more generally to the descriptive effects of figurative language, especially in *metaphor* and *simile*.

Imagism: a poetic movement that was popular mainly in the second decade of the twentieth century. The goal of Imagist poets (such as H.D. and Ezra Pound in their early work) was to represent emotions or impressions through highly concentrated imagery.

Incantation: a chant or recitation of words that are believed to have magical power. A poem can achieve an "incantatory" effect through a compelling rhyme scheme and other repetitive patterns.

In Memoriam Stanza: a four-line stanza in iambic tetrameter, rhyming *abba*: the type of stanza used by Tennyson in *In Memoriam*.

Interlocking Rhyme: See *rhyme*.

Internal Rhyme: See *rhyme*.

Irony: a subtle form of humor in which a statement is understood to convey a quite different (and often entirely opposite) meaning. A writer achieves this by carefully making sure that the statement occurs in a context which undermines or twists the statement's "literal" meaning. *Hyperbole* and *litotes* are often used for ironic effect. *Sarcasm* is a particularly strong or crude form of irony (usually spoken), in which the meaning is conveyed largely by the tone of voice adopted; something said sarcastically is meant clearly to imply its opposite.

Labour Party: See *Political Parties*.

Lament: a poem which expresses profound regret or grief either because of a death, or because of the loss of a former, happier state.

Language Poetry: a movement that defies the usual lyric and narrative conventions of poetry, and that challenges the structures and codes of everyday language. Often seen as both politically and aesthetically subversive, its roots lie in the works of modernist writers like Ezra Pound and Gertrude Stein.

Liberal Party: See *Political Parties*.

Litotes: a *figure of speech* (a trope) in which a writer deliberately uses understatement to highlight the importance of an argument, or to convey an ironic attitude.

Liturgical Drama: drama based on and/or incorporating text from the liturgy—the text recited during religious services.

Lollard: member of the group of radical Christians that took its inspiration from the ideas of John Wyclif (c. 1330–84). The Lollards, in many ways precursors of the Protestant Reformation, advocated making the Bible available to all, and dedication to the principles of evangelical poverty in imitation of Christ.

Luddites: protestors against the mechanization of industry on the grounds that it was leading to the loss of employment and to an increase in poverty. In the years 1811 to 1816 there were several Luddite protests in which machines were destroyed.

Lyric: a poem, usually short, expressing an individual speaker's feelings or private thoughts. Originally a song performed with accompaniment on a lyre, the lyric poem is often noted for musicality of rhyme and rhythm. The lyric genre includes a variety of forms, including the *sonnet*, the *ode*, the *elegy*, the *madrigal*, the *aubade*, the *dramatic monologue*, and the *hymn*.

Madrigal: a lyric poem, usually short and focusing on pastoral or romantic themes. A madrigal is often set to music.

Masculine Ending: a metrical line ending on a stressed syllable. *Masculine Rhyme*: see *rhyme*.

Masque: an entertainment typically combining music and dance, with a limited script, extravagant costumes and sets, and often incorporating spectacular special effects. Masques, which were performed before court audiences in the early seventeenth century, often focused on royal themes and frequently drew on classical mythology.

Mass: within Christianity, a church service that includes the sacrament of the Eucharist (Holy Communion), in which bread and wine are consumed which are believed by those of many Christian denominations to have been transubstantiated into the body and blood of Christ. Anglicans (Episcopalians) are more likely to believe the bread and wine merely symbolizes the body and blood.

Melodrama: originally a term used to describe nineteenth-century plays featuring sensational story lines and a crude separation of characters into moral categories, with the pure and virtuous pitted against evil villains. Early melodramas employed background music throughout the action of the play as a means of heightening the emotional response of the audience. By extension, certain sorts of prose fictions or poems are often described as having melodramatic elements.

Metaphor: a *figure of speech* (in this case, a trope) in which a comparison is made or identity is asserted between two unrelated things or actions without the use of "like" or "as." The primary subject is known as the *tenor*; to illuminate its nature, the writer links it to wholly different images, ideas, or actions referred to as the *vehicle*. Unlike a *simile*, which is a direct comparison of two things, a metaphor "fuses" the separate qualities of two things, creating a new idea. For example, Shakespeare's "Let slip the dogs of war" is a metaphorical statement. The tenor, or primary subject, is "war"; the vehicle of the metaphor is the image of hunting dogs released from their leash. The line fuses the idea of war with the qualities of ravening bloodlust associated with hunting dogs.

Metaphysical Poets: a group of seventeenth-century English poets, notably Donne, Cowley, Marvell, and Herbert, who employed unusual difficult imagery and *conceits* (see above) in order to develop intellectual and religious themes. The term was first applied to these writers to mark as farfetched their use of philosophical and scientific ideas in a poetic context.

Meter: the pattern of stresses, syllables, and pauses that constitutes the regular rhythm of a line of verse. The meter of a poem written in the English accentual-syllabic tradition is determined by identifying the stressed and unstressed syllables in a line of verse, and grouping them into recurring units known as feet. See *accent, accentual-syllabic, caesura, elision*, and *scansion*. For some of the better known meters, see *iamb, trochee, dactyl, anapaest*, and *spondee*. See also *monometer, dimeter, trimeter, tetrameter, pentameter*, and *hexameter*.

Methodist: Protestant denomination formed in the eighteenth century as part of the religious movement led by John and Charles Wesley. Originally a movement within the Church of England, Methodism entailed enthusiastic evangelism, a strong emphasis on free will, and a strict regimen of Christian living.

Metonymy: a *figure of speech* (a trope), meaning "change of name," in which a writer refers to an object or idea by substituting the name of another object or idea closely associated with it: for example, the substitution of "crown" for monarchy, "the press" for journalism, or "the pen" for writing. *Synecdoche* (see below) is a kind of metonymy.

Mock-heroic: a style applying the elevated diction and vocabulary of epic poetry to low or ridiculous subjects. An example is Alexander Pope's "The Rape of the Lock."

Monologue: words spoken by a character to him or herself or to an audience directly.

Monometer: a line containing one metrical foot.

Mood: this can describe the writer's attitude, implied or expressed, towards the subject (see *tone* below); or it may refer to the atmosphere that a writer creates in a passage of description or narration.

Motif: an idea, image, action, or plot element that recurs throughout a literary work, creating new levels of meaning and strengthening structural coherence. The term is taken from music, where it describes recurring melodies or themes. See also *theme*.

Narrative Perspective: in fiction, the point of view from which the story is narrated. A first-person narrative is recounted using *I* and *me*, whereas a third person narrative is recounted using *he*, *she*, *they*, and so on. When a narrative is written in the third person and the narrative voice evidently "knows" all that is being done and thought, the story is typically described as being recounted by an "omniscient narrator."

Neoclassical: adapted from or substantially influenced by the cultures of ancient Greece and Rome. The term *neoclassical* is often used to describe the ideals of Restoration and eighteenth-century writers and artists who looked to ancient Greek and Roman civilization for models.

Nobility: privileged class, the members of which are distinguished by the holding of titles. Dukes, Marquesses, Earls, Viscounts, and Barons (in that order of precedence) are all holders of hereditary titles—that is to say, in the British patrilineal tradition, titles passed on from generation to generation to the eldest son. The title of Baronet, also hereditary, was added to this list by James I. Holders of non-hereditary titles include Knights and Dames.

Nonconformist: general term used to describe one who does not subscribe to the Church of England.

Nonsense Verse: light, humorous poetry which contradicts logic, plays with the absurd, and invents words for amusing effects. Lewis Carroll is one of the best-known practitioners of nonsense verse.

Octave: also known as "octet," the first eight lines in an Italian/Petrarchan sonnet, rhyming *abbaabba*. See also *sestet* and *sonnet*.

Octosyllabic: a line of poetry with eight syllables, as in iambic tetrameter.

Ode: originally a classical poetic form, used by the Greeks and Romans to convey serious themes. English poetry has evolved three main forms of ode: the Pindaric (imitative of the odes of the Greek poet Pindar); the Horatian (modeled on the work of the Roman writer Horace); and the irregular ode. The Pindaric ode was an irregular stanza in English, has a tripartite structure of *strophe*, *antistrophe*, and *epode* (meaning turn, counterturn, and stand), modeled on the songs and movements of the Chorus in Greek drama. The Horatian ode is more personal, reflective, and literary, and employs a pattern of repeated stanzas. The irregular ode, as its name implies, avoids a recurrent stanza pattern, and is sometimes irregular in line length also (see, for example, Wordsworth's "Ode: Intimations of Immortality").

Onomatopoeia: a *figure of speech* (a scheme) in which a word "imitates" a sound, or in which the sound of a word seems to reflect its meaning.

Ottava Rima: an eight-line stanza, usually in iambic pentameter, with the rhyme scheme *abababcc*. For an example, see Byron's *Don Juan*, or Yeats's "Sailing to Byzantium."

Oxymoron: a *figure of speech* (a trope) in which two words whose meanings seem contradictory are placed together, a paradox: for example, the phrase "darkness visible," from Milton's *Paradise Lost*.

Paean: a triumphant, celebratory song, often associated with a military victory.

Pale: in the medieval period, term for a protective zone around a fortress. As of the year 1500 three of these had been set up to guard frontiers of territory controlled by England—surrounding Calais in France, Berwick-upon-Tweed on the Scottish frontier, and Dublin in Ireland. The Dublin Pale was the largest of the three, and the term remained in use for a longer period there.

Pantoum: a poem in linked quatrains that rhyme *abab*. The second and fourth lines of one stanza are repeated as the first and third lines of the stanza that follows. In the final stanza the pattern is reversed: the second line repeats the third line of the first stanza, the fourth and final line repeats the first line of the first stanza.

Parliament: in Britain, the legislative body, comprising both the House of Commons and the House of Lords. Since the eighteenth century, the most powerful figure in the British government has been the Prime Minister rather than the monarch, the House of Commons has been the dominant body in Parliament, and members of the House of Commons have been organized in political parties. Since the mid-nineteenth century the effective executive in the British Parliamentary system has been the Cabinet, each member of which is typically in charge of a department of government. Unlike the American system, the British Parliamentary system (sometimes called the "Westminster system," after the location of the Houses of Parliament) brings together the executive and legislative functions of government, with the Prime Minister leading the government party in the House of Commons as well as directing the cabinet. By convention it is understood that the House of Lords will not contravene the wishes of the House of Commons in any fundamental way, though the "Upper House," as it is often referred to, may sometimes modify or reject legislation.

Parody: a close, usually mocking imitation of a particular literary work, or of the well-known style of a particular author, in order to expose or magnify weaknesses. Parody is a form of satire—that is, humor that may ridicule and scorn its object.

Pastiche: a discourse which borrows or imitates other writers' characters, forms, style, or ideas. Unlike a parody, a pastiche is usually intended as a compliment to the original writer.

Pastoral: in general, pertaining to country life; in prose, drama, and poetry, a stylized type of writing that idealizes the lives and innocence of country people, particularly shepherds and shepherdesses. Also see *eclogue, georgic, idyll,* above.

Pastoral Elegy: a poem in which the poet uses the pastoral style to lament the death of a friend, usually represented as a shepherd. Milton's "Lycidas" provides a good example of the form, including its use of such conventions as an invocation of the muse and a procession of mourners.

Pathetic Fallacy: a form of personification in which inanimate objects are given human emotions: for example, rain clouds "weeping." The word "fallacy" in this connection is intended to suggest the distortion of reality or the false emotion that may result from an exaggerated use of personification.

Pathos: the emotional quality of a discourse; or the ability of a discourse to appeal to our emotions. It is usually applied to the mood conveyed by images of pain, suffering, or loss that arouse feelings of pity or sorrow in the reader.

Pattern Poetry: a predecessor of modern concrete poetry, in which the shape of the poem on the page is intended to suggest or imitate an aspect of the poem's subject. George Herbert's "Easter Wings" is an example of pattern poetry.

Penny Dreadful: Victorian term for a cheap and poorly produced work of short fiction, usually of a sensational nature.

Pentameter: a line of verse containing five metrical feet.

Performance Poetry: poetry composed primarily for oral performance, often very theatrical in nature. See also *dub poetry* and *rap*.

Persona: the assumed identity or "speaking voice" that a writer projects in a discourse. The term "persona" literally means "mask." Even when a writer speaks in the first person, we should be aware that the attitudes or opinions we hear may not necessarily be those of the writer in real life.

Personification: a *figure of speech* (a trope), also known as "prosopopoeia," in which a writer refers to inanimate objects, ideas, or animals as if they were human, or creates a human figure to represent an abstract entity such as Philosophy or Peace.

Petrarchan Sonnet: the earliest form of the sonnet, also known as the Italian sonnet, with an 8-line octave and a six-line sestet. The Petrarchan sonnet traditionally focuses on love and descriptions of physical beauty.

Phoneme: a linguistic term denoting the smallest unit of sound that it is possible to distinguish. The words *fun* and *phone* each have three phonemes, though one has three letters and one has five. (Each makes up a single syllable.)

Pindaric: See *ode*.

Plot: the organization of story materials within a literary work. The order in which story material is presented (especially causes and consequences); the inclusion of elements that allow or encourage the reader or audience to form expectations as to what is likely to happen; the decision to present some story material through exposition rather than in more extended form as part of the main action of the narrative—all these are matters of plotting.

Political Parties: the party names "Whig" and "Tory" began to be used in the late seventeenth century; before that time members of the House of Commons acted individually or through shifting and very informal factions. At first the Whigs and Tories had little formal organization either, but by the mid-eighteenth century parties had acknowledged leaders, and the leader of the party with the largest number of members in the House of Commons had begun to be recognized as the Prime Minister. The Tories evolved into the modern Conservative Party, and the Whigs into the Liberal Party. In the late nineteenth century the Labour Party was formed in an effort to provide better representation in Parliament for the working class, and since the 1920s Labour and the Conservatives have alternated as the party of government, with the Liberals reduced to third-party status. (Since 1988, when the Liberals merged with a breakaway faction from Labour known as the Social Democrats, this third party has been named the Liberal Democrats.)

Pre-Raphaelites: originally a group of Victorian artists and writers, formed in 1848. Their goal was to revive what they considered the simpler, fresher, more natural art that existed before Raphael (1483–1520). The poet Dante Gabriel Rossetti was one of the founders of the group.

Presbyterian: term applied to a group of Protestants (primarily English and Scottish) who advocated replacing the traditional hierarchical church in which bishops and archbishops governed lower level members of the clergy with a system in which all presbyters (or ministers) would be equal. The Presbyterians, originally led by John Knox, were strongly influenced by the ideas of John Calvin.

Prose Poem: a poetic discourse that uses prose formats (e.g., it may use margins and paragraphs rather than line breaks or stanzas) yet is written with the kind of attention to language, rhythm, and cadence that characterizes verse.

Prosody: the study and analysis of meter, rhythm, rhyme, stanzaic pattern, and other devices of versification.

Protagonist: the central character in a literary work.

Prothalamion: a wedding song; a term coined by the poet Edmund Spenser, adapted from "epithalamion" (see above).

Public School: See *schools* below.

Pun: a play on words, in which a word with two or more distinct meanings, or two words with similar sounds, may create humorous ambiguities. Also known as *paranomasia*.

Puritan: term, originally applied only in a derogatory fashion but later widely accepted as descriptive, referring to those in England who favored religious reforms that went beyond those instituted as part of the Protestant Reformation, or, more generally, who were more forceful and uncompromising in pressing for religious purity both within the Church and in society as a whole.

Pyrrhic: a metrical foot containing two weak stresses: xx.

Quadrivium: group of four academic subjects (arithmetic, astronomy, geometry, and music) that made up part of the university coursework in the Middle Ages. They were studied after the more basic subjects of the *Trivium*.

Quantitative Meter: a metrical system used by Greek and Roman poets, in which a line of verse was measured by the "quantity," or length of sound of each syllable. A foot was measured in terms of syllables classed as long or short.

Quantity: duration of syllables in poetry. The line "There is a Garden in her face" (the first line from the poem of the same name by Thomas Campion) is characterized by the short quantities of the syllables. The last line of Thomas Hardy's "During Wind and Rain" has the same number of syllables as the line by Campion, but the quantities of the syllables are much longer—in other words, the line takes much longer to say: "Down their carved names the rain drop ploughs."

Quatrain: a four-line stanza, usually rhymed.

Quintet: a five-line stanza. Sometimes given as *quintain*.

Rap: originally coined to describe informal conversation, "rap" now usually describes a style of performance poetry in which a poet will chant rhymed verse, sometimes improvised and usually with musical accompaniment that has a heavy beat.

Realism: as a literary term, the presentation through literature of material closely resembling real life. As notions both of what constitutes "real life" and of how it may be most faithfully represented in literature have varied widely, "realism" has taken a variety of meanings. The term *naturalistic* has sometimes been used as a synonym for *realistic*; *naturalism* originated in the nineteenth century as a term denoting a form of realism focusing in particular on grim, unpleasant, or ugly aspects of the real.

Refrain: one or more words or lines repeated at regular points throughout a poem, often at the end of each stanza or group of stanzas. Sometimes a whole stanza may be repeated to create a refrain, like the chorus in a song.

Reggae: a style of heavily rhythmic music from the West Indies with lyrics that are colloquial in language and often anti-establishment in content and flavor. First popularized in the 1960s and 1970s, reggae has had a lasting influence on performance poetry, rap, and dub.

Rhetoric: in classical Greece and Rome, the art of persuasion and public speaking. From the Middle Ages onwards, the study of rhetoric gave greater attention to style, particularly figures of speech. Today in poetics, the term rhetoric may encompass not only figures of speech, but also the persuasive effects of forms, sounds, and word choices.

Rhyme: the repetition of identical or similar sounds, usually in pairs and generally at the ends of metrical lines.

End-rhyme: a rhyming word or syllable at the end of a line.

Eye Rhyme: rhyming that pairs words whose spellings are alike but whose pronunciations are different: for example, though/slough.

Feminine Rhyme: a two-syllable (also known as "double") rhyme. The first syllable is stressed and the second unstressed: for example, hasty/tasty. See also *triple rhyme* below.

Interlocking Rhyme: the repetition of rhymes from one stanza to the next, creating links that add to the poem's continuity and coherence. Examples may be found in Shelley's use of *terza rima* in "Ode to the West Wind" and in Dylan Thomas's villanelle "Do Not Go Gentle into That Good Night."

Internal Rhyme: the placement of rhyming words within lines so that at least two words in a line rhyme with each other.

Masculine Rhyme: a correspondence of sound between the final stressed syllables at the end of two or more lines, as in grieve / leave, arr-i've / sur-vive.

Slant Rhyme: an imperfect or partial rhyme (also known as "near" or "half" rhyme) in which the final consonants of stressed syllables match but the vowel sounds do not. E.g., spoiled / spilled, taint / stint.

Triple Rhyme: a three-syllable rhyme in which the first syllable of each rhyme-word is stressed and the other two unstressed (e.g., lottery / coterie).

True Rhyme: a rhyme in which everything but the initial consonant matches perfectly in sound and spelling.

Rhyme Royal: a stanza of seven iambic pentameters, with a rhyme-scheme of *ababbcc*. This is also known as the Chaucerian stanza, as Chaucer was the first English poet to use this form. See also *septet*.

Rhythm: in speech, the arrangement of stressed and unstressed syllables creates units of sound. In song or verse, these units usually form a regular rhythmic pattern, a kind of beat, described in prosody as *meter*.

Romanticism: a major social and cultural movement, originating in Europe, that shaped much of Western artistic thought in the late eighteenth and nineteenth centuries. Opposing the ideal of controlled, rational order of the Enlightenment, Romanticism emphasizes the importance of spontaneous self-expression, emotion, and personal experience in producing art. In Romanticism, the "natural" is privileged over the conventional or the artificial.

Rondeau: a fifteen-line poem, generally octosyllabic, with only two rhymes throughout its three stanzas, and an unrhymed refrain at the end of the ninth and fifteenth lines, repeating part of the opening line.

Sarcasm: See *irony*.

Satire: literary work designed to make fun of or seriously criticize its subject. According to many literary theories of the Renaissance and neoclassical periods, the ridicule through satire of a certain sort of behavior may function for the reader or audience as a corrective of such behavior.

Scansion: the formal analysis of patterns of rhythm and rhyme in poetry. Each line of verse will have a certain number of fairly regular "beats" consisting of alternating stressed and unstressed syllables. To "scan" a poem is to count the beats in each line, to mark stressed and unstressed syllables and indicate their combination into "feet," to note pauses, and to identify rhyme schemes with letters of the alphabet.

Scheme: See *figures of speech*.

Schools: in the sixteenth and seventeenth centuries the different forms of school in England included Cathedral schools (often founded with a view to the education of members of the choir); grammar schools (often founded by towns or by guilds, and teaching a much broader curriculum than the modern sense of "grammar" might suggest; private schools, operated by private individuals out of private residences; and public schools, which (like the private schools and the grammar schools) operated independent of any church authority, but unlike the grammar schools and private schools were organized as independent charities, and often offered free education. Over the centuries certain of these public schools, while remaining not-for-profit institutions, began to accept fee-paying students and to adopt standards that made them more and more exclusive. In the eighteenth and nineteenth century attendance at such prestigious public boarding schools as Eton, Westminster, and Winchester had become almost exclusively the preserve of the upper classes; by the nineteenth century such "public" schools were the equivalent of private schools in North America. A few girls attended some early grammar schools, but the greater part of this educational system was for boys only. Though a number of individuals of earlier periods were concerned to increase the number of private schools for girls, the movement to create a parallel girls' system of public schools and grammar schools dates from the later nineteenth century.

Septet: a stanza containing seven lines.

Serf: in the medieval period, a person of unfree status, typically engaged in working the land.

Sestet: a six-line stanza that forms the second grouping of lines in an Italian / Petrarchan sonnet, following the octave. See *sonnet* and *sestina*.

Sestina: an elaborate unrhymed poem with six six-line stanzas and a three-line envoy.

Shire: originally a multiple estate; since the late medieval period a larger territory forming an administrative unit—also referred to as a county.

Simile: a *figure of speech* (a trope) which makes an explicit comparison between a particular object and another object or idea that is similar in some (often unexpected) way. A simile always uses "like" or "as" to signal the connection. Compare with *metaphor* above.

Sonnet: a highly structured lyric poem, which normally has fourteen lines of iambic pentameter. We can distinguish four major variations of the sonnet.

   Italian/Petrarchan: named for the fourteenth-century Italian poet Petrarch, has an octave rhyming *abbaabba*, and a sestet rhyming *cdecde*, or *cdcdcd* (other arrangements are possible here). Usually, a turn in argument takes place between octave and sestet.

Miltonic: developed by Milton and similar to the Petrarchan in rhyme scheme, but eliminating the turn after the octave, thus giving greater unity to the poem's structure of thought.

Shakespearean: often called the English sonnet, this form has three quatrains and a couplet. The quatrains rhyme internally but do not interlock: *abab cdcd efef gg*. The turn may occur after the second quatrain, but is usually revealed in the final couplet. Shakespeare's sonnets are the best-known examples of this form.

Spenserian: after Edmund Spenser, who developed the form in his sonnet cycle *Amoretti*. This sonnet form has three quatrains linked through interlocking rhyme, and a separately rhyming couplet: *abab bcbc cdcd ee*.

Speaker: in the late medieval period, a member of the Commons in Parliament who spoke on behalf of that entire group. (The Commons first elected a Speaker in 1376.) In later eras the role of Speaker became one of chairing debates in the House of Commons and arbitrating disputes over matters of procedure.

Spenserian Stanza: a nine-line stanza, with eight iambic pentameters and a concluding alexandrine, rhyming *ababbcbcc*.

Spondee: a metrical foot containing two strong stressed syllables: // (e.g., blind mouths).

Sprung Rhythm: a modern variation of accentual verse, created by the English poet Gerard Manley Hopkins, in which rhythms are determined largely by the number of strong stresses in a line, without regard to the number of unstressed syllables. Hopkins felt that sprung rhythm more closely approximated the natural rhythms of speech than did conventional poetry.

Stanza: any lines of verse that are grouped together in a poem and separated from other similarly structured groups by a space. In metrical poetry, stanzas share metrical and rhyming patterns; however, stanzas may also be formed on the basis of thought, as in irregular odes. Conventional stanza forms include the *tercet*, the *quatrain*, *rhyme royal*, the *Spenserian stanza*, the *ballad stanza*, and *ottava rima*.

Stream of Consciousness: narrative technique that attempts to convey in prose fiction a sense of the progression of the full range of thoughts and sensations occurring within a character's mind. Twentieth-century pioneers in the use of the stream of consciousness technique include Dorothy Richardson, Virginia Woolf, and James Joyce.

Stress: See *accent*.

Strophe: the first stanza in a Pindaric ode. This is followed by an *antistrophe* (see above), which presents the same metrical pattern and rhyme scheme, and finally by an *epode*, differing in meter from the preceding stanzas. Upon completion of this "triad," the entire sequence can recur. *Strophe* may also describe a stanza or other subdivision in other kinds of poem.

Sublime: a concept, most popular in eighteenth-century England, of the qualities of grandeur, power, and awe that may be inherent in or produced by undomesticated nature or great art. The sublime was thought of as higher and loftier than something that is merely beautiful.

Subplot: a line of story that is subordinate to the main storyline of a narrative. (Note that properly speaking a subplot is a category of story material, not of plot.)

Substitution: a deliberate change from the dominant pattern of stresses in a line of verse to create emphasis or variation. Thus the first line of Shakespeare's sonnet "'Shall I compare thee to a summer's day?'" is decidedly iambic in meter (x / x / x / x / x /), whereas the second line substitutes a trochee (/ x) in the opening foot: "Thou art more lovely and more temperate."

Subtext: implied or suggested meaning of a passage of text, or of an entire work.

Syllabic Verse: poetry in which the length of a line is measured solely by the number of syllables, regardless of accents or patterns of stress.

Syllable: vocal sound or group of sounds forming a unit of speech; a syllable may be formed with a single effort of articulation. Some syllables consist of a single phoneme (e.g., the word *I*, or the first syllable in the word *u*-ni-ty) but others may be made up of several phonemes (as with one-syllable words such as *lengths*, *splurged*, and *through*). By contrast, the much shorter words *ago*, *any*, and *open* each have two syllables.

Symbol: a word, image, or idea that represents something more, or other, than for what it at first appears to stand. Like metaphor, the symbol extends meaning; but while the tenor and vehicle of metaphor are bound in a specific relationship, a symbol may have a range of connotations. For example, the image of a rose may call forth associations of love, passion, transience, fragility, youth and beauty, among others. Depending upon the context, such an image could be interpreted in a variety of ways, as in Blake's lyric, "The Sick Rose." Though this power of symbolic representation characterizes all language, poetry most particularly endows the concrete imagery evoked through language with a larger meaning. Such meaning is implied rather than explicitly stated; indeed, much of the power of symbolic language lies in the reader's ability to make meaningful sense of it.

Syncope: in poetry, the dropping of a letter or syllable from the middle of a word, as in "trav'ler." Such a contraction allows a line to stay within a metrical scheme. See also *catalexis* and *elision*.

Synecdoche: a kind of *metonymy* in which a writer substitutes the name of a part of something to signify the whole: for example, "sail" for ship or "hand" for a member of the ship's crew.

Tercet: a group, or stanza, of three lines, often linked by an interlocking rhyme scheme as in *terza rima*. See also *triplet*.

Terza Rima: an arrangement of tercets interlocked by a rhyme scheme of *aba bcb cdc ded*, etc., and ending with a couplet that rhymes with the second-last line of the final tercet (for example, *efe, ff*). See, for example, Percy Shelley's "Ode to the West Wind."

Tetrameter: a line of poetry containing four metrical feet.

Theme: the governing idea of a discourse, conveyed through the development of the subject, and through the recurrence of certain words, sounds, or metrical patterns. See also *motif*.

Third-Person Narrative: See *narrative perspective*.

Tone: the writer's attitude toward a given subject or audience, as expressed through an authorial persona or "voice." Tone can be projected through particular choices of wording, imagery, figures of speech, and rhythmic devices. Compare *mood*.

Tories: See *Political Parties*.

Tragedy: in the traditional definition originating in discussions of ancient Greek drama, a serious narrative recounting the downfall of the protagonist. More loosely, the term has been applied to a wide variety of literary forms in which the tone is predominantly a dark one and the narrative does not end happily.

Transcendentalism: a philosophical movement that influenced such Victorian writers as Thomas Carlyle and Robert Browning. Also a mode of Romantic thought, Transcendentalism places the supernatural and the natural within one great Unity and believes that each individual person embodies aspects of the divine.

Trimeter: a line of poetry containing three metrical feet.

Triolet: a French form in which the first line appears three times in a poem of only eight lines. The first line is repeated at lines 4 and 7; the second line is repeated in line 8. The triolet has only two rhymes: *abaaabab*.

Triple Foot: poetic foot of three syllables. The possible varieties of triple foot are the anapest (in which two unstressed syllables are followed by a stressed syllable), the dactyl (in which a stressed syllable is followed by two unstressed lines), and the mollossus (in which all three syllables are stressed equally). English poetry tends to use duple rhythms far more frequently than triple rhythms.

Triplet: a group of three lines with the same end-rhyme, much used by eighteenth-century poets to vary or punctuate the flow of couplets. See also *tercet*.

Trivium: group of three academic subjects (dialectic, grammar, and rhetoric) that were part of the university curriculum in the Middle Ages. Their study precedes that of the more advanced subjects of the *quadrivium*.

Trochee: a metrical foot containing one strong stress followed by one weak stress: / x (heaven, lover).

Trope: any figure of speech that plays on our understandings of words to extend, alter, or transform "literal" meaning. Common tropes include *metaphor, simile, personification, hyperbole, metonymy, oxymoron, synecdoche*, and *irony*. See also *figures of speech*, above.

Turn (Italian "volta"): the point in a *sonnet* where the mood or argument changes. The turn may occur between the octave and sestet, i.e., after the eighth line, or in the final couplet, depending on the kind of sonnet.

Unities: Many literary theorists of the late sixteenth through late eighteenth centuries held that a play should ideally be presented as representing a single place, and confining the action to a single day and a single dominant event. They disapproved of plots involving gaps or long periods of time, shifts in place, or subplots. These concepts, which came to be referred to as the unities of space, time, and action, were based on a misreading of classical authorities (principally of Aristotle).

Vers de société: literally, "verse about society." The term originated with poetry written by aristocrats and upper-middle-class poets that specifically disavows the ambition of creating "high art" while treating the concerns of their own group in verse forms that demonstrate a high degree of formal control (e.g., artful rhymes, surprising turns of diction).

Vers libre: See *free verse* above.

Verse: a general term for works of poetry, usually referring to poems that incorporate some kind of metrical structure. The term may also describe a line of poetry, though more frequently it is applied to a stanza.

Villanelle: a poem usually consisting of 19 lines, with five 3-line stanzas (tercets) rhyming *aba*, and a concluding quatrain rhyming *abaa*. The first and third lines of the first tercet are repeated at fixed intervals throughout the rest of the poem. See, for example, Dylan Thomas's "Do Not Go Gentle into That Good Night."

Whigs: See *Political Parties*.

Workhouse: public institution in which the poor were provided with a minimal level of sustenance and with lodging in exchange for work performed. Early workhouses were typically administered by individual parishes. In 1834 a unified system covering all of England and Wales was put into effect.

Zeugma: a *figure of speech* (trope) in which one word links or "yokes" two others in the same sentence, often to comic or ironic effect. For example, a verb may govern two objects, as in Pope's line "Or stain her honour, or her new brocade."

PERMISSIONS ACKNOWLEDGMENTS

ILLUSTRATION CREDITS

Cover: The National Gallery, London. Color insert: *Workshop* by Wyndham Lewis, The Tate Gallery, London/Art Resource, NY; "Will you Answer the Call?", The Art Archive/Imperial War Museum/Eileen Tweedy; "Dig for Victory": Bridgeman Art Library; Sirkka-Liisa Konttinen, *Kendal Street*, 1969; Bill Brandt, "The Lambeth Walk": Bill Brandt Archive Ltd; cover from *Journey Without Maps*: Macmillan, London, UK; cover of *The Van* by Roddy Doyle, published by Secker and Warburg, reprinted by permission of The Random House Group Limited; cover from *Never Let Me Go*: Random House Inc.; *My Mother, Bolton Abbey, Yorkshire, Nov. 1982*, photographic collage, edition of 20, 47-1/2" x 27-1/2", copyright © David Hockney; "Peel Square," Tim Smith Photos; Notting Hill Carnival August 1979: David Hoffman Photo Library. Page 32: Portrait of Anna Laetitia Barbauld: National Portrait Gallery. Page 170: "I Wandered Lonely as a Cloud" facsimile: The Wordsworth Trust. Page 361: Portrait of Lord Byron: National Portrait Gallery. Page 597: Portrait of John Stuart Mill: National Portrait Gallery. Page 788: Portrait of John Ruskin: National Portrait Gallery. Page 799: Portrait of Matthew Arnold: National Portrait Gallery. Page 864: Portrait of Augusta Webster: National Portrait Gallery. Page 881: Portrait of Thomas Hardy: National Portrait Gallery. Page 1041: Queen Mary visiting Burma Pavilion: Getty Images. Page 1044: Workers reading a newspaper: Getty Images. Page 1045: Londoners sleeping in the Elephant and Castle underground station, 1940: Bill Brandt Archive Ltd. Page 1046: The 1940 Battle of Britain: AP Images. Page 1047: Cover of *Brighton Rock* by Graham Greene. Penguin Books, 1938. Reproduced by permission of Penguin Books Ltd. Page 1051: Illustration from "The Further Adventures of Toad": from *The Wind in the Willows* by Kenneth Grahame, illustrated by Ernest H. Shepard. Copyright 1933 Charles Scribner's Sons; copyright renewed © 1961 Ernest H. Shepard. Page 1053: Women's contingent in the 1930 Hunger March: Getty Images. Page 1054: Scene from *The Thrill*, 1926: Getty Images. Page 1056: Commuter reading *Lady Chatterley's Lover*: Getty Images. Page 1056: Two women holding copies of *Lady Chatterley's Lover*, 1960: Getty Images. Page 1059: Cover of *Major Barbara* by George Bernard Shaw. Penguin Books, 1945. Reproduced by permission of Penguin Books Ltd. Page 1061: Nazi authorities affix a poster to a shop: Getty Images. Page 1063: Target practice, Spain, 1936: United Press International. Page 1064: Cover from *Brave New World* by Aldous Huxley, published by Chatto & Windus. Reprinted by permission of The Random House Group Limited. Page 1065: Jacket cover from *The Razor's Edge* by W. Somerset Maugham: Doubleday, Random House Ltd. Page 1108: Portrait of Joseph Conrad: National Portrait Gallery Page 1133: Portrait of AE Housman: Reproduced by permission of The National Portrait Gallery, London. Page 1138: Portrait of Siegfried Sassoon: National Portrait Gallery. Page 1142: Portrait of Wilfred Owen: National Portrait Gallery. Page 1168: Portrait of William Butler Yeats: National Portrait Gallery. Page 1185: Portrait of Virginia Woolf: National Portrait Gallery. Page 1232: Vanessa Bell, *Virginia Woolf*, 1912: National Portrait Gallery. Page 1234: Photograph of Virginia Woolf and TS Eliot: Sylvia Beach Papers, Manuscripts Division, Department of Rare Books and Special Collections, Princeton University Library. Page 1268: Portrait of DH Lawrence: National Portrait Gallery. Page 1283: Armoured cars at Hyde Park Corner, 1926: Getty Images. Page 1298: Portrait of Katherine Mansfield: National Portrait Gallery. Page 1308: Portrait of TS Eliot: Reproduced by permission of The National Portrait Gallery, London. Page 1344: Portrait of Jean Rhys: Reproduced by permission of The National Portrait Gallery, London. Page 1354: Photograph of Sylvia Townsend Warner (standing at desk): Reprinted with the permission of the Sylvia Townsend Warner Archive, Dorset County Museum, U.K. Page 1375: Portrait of George Orwell: Reproduced by permission of The National Portrait Gallery, London. Page 1388: Portrait of Samuel Beckett: Portrait by Lisa Brawn. Page 1395: Portrait of W.H. Auden: Reproduced by permission of The National Portrait Gallery, London. Page 1406: The "London Fog": Getty Images. Page 1408: The HMS Antelope under attack: Press Association. Page 1409: Cover image from *Political Spider* by Ulli Beier: Harcourt Education. Page 1410: Photo of The Beatles appointed MBEs: Getty Images. Page 1410: Still from Lord of the Flies: Thomas Hollyman. Reprinted with the permission of Burnes Hollyman. Page 1415: A gaping hole in the front of the Grand Hotel in Brighton: Getty Images. Page 1423: Portrait of Dylan Thomas: Reproduced by permission of The National Portrait Gallery, London. Page 1427: Portrait of Philip Larkin: Portrait by Lisa Brawn. Page 1434: Portrait of Ted Hughes: Portrait by Lisa Brawn. Page 1437: Heptonstall Old Church: Collections Picture Library Limited. Page 1440: Portrait of Chinua Achebe: Don Hamerman. Page 1456: Portrait of Ngũgĩ wa Thiong'o: Unionsverlag. Page 1468: Portrait of Angela Carter: Portrait by Lisa Brawn. Page 1448: Portrait of Seamus Heaney: Faber & Faber; John Minihan. Page 1497: Portrait of J.M. Coetzee: Random House Australia. Page 1525: Portrait of Eavan Boland: Reproduced by permission of Eavan Boland. Page 1535: Portrait of Salman Rushdie: Portrait by Lisa Brawn. Page 1553: Portrait of Kazuo Ishiguro: Portrait by Lisa Brawn. Page 1561: Portrait of Carol Ann Duffy: Anvil Press Poetry.

The publisher has endeavored to contact rights holders of all copyright material and would appreciate receiving any information as to errors or omissions.

INDEX OF FIRST LINES

Index of Authors and Titles